TWENTIETH-CENTURY ROMANCE AND HISTORICAL WRITERS

Twentieth-Century Writers Series

Twentieth-Century Children's Writers

Twentieth-Century Crime and Mystery Writers

Twentieth-Century Science-Fiction Writers

Twentieth-Century Romance and Historical Writers

Twentieth-Century Western Writers

TWENTIETH-CENTURY ROMANCE AND HISTORICAL WRITERS

SECOND EDITION

WITH A PREFACE BY
KAY MUSSELL

EDITOR
LESLEY HENDERSON

CONSULTING EDITOR
D. L. KIRKPATRICK

St J
St James Press

Chicago and London

All rights reserved. For information, write:
ST. JAMES PRESS
233 East Ontario Street
Chicago 60611, U.S.A.
          or
3 Percy Street
London W1P 9FA, England.

British Library Cataloguing in Publication Data
Twentieth-century romance and historical writers.—2nd ed.
  I. Henderson, Lesley, *1963–*
  823′.085′025

ISBN 0–912289–97–X

First edition published 1982;
second edition 1990.

CONTENTS

PREFACE

The roots of both romance and historical fiction lie in the origins of the novel form itself. In the 18th and early 19th centuries the most prominent types of fiction—the seduction story and the gothic tale of terror—were the novelistic predecessors of today's romance and historical fiction; and for two centuries writers on both sides of the Atlantic have written stories of romantic adventure, frequently set in the past, that appealed to a largely middle-class audience.

In their popular manifestations—romance and historical fiction aimed at a mass audience—there is considerable overlap between the two genres. Many novels categorized as romances are set in the past and rely on the conventions of historical fiction. Many novels categorized as historical also employ romance conventions. The works of authors profiled in this volume might best be seen as forming a continuum of novels from straight romances (such as those published by Mills and Boon and Harlequin, with contemporary settings and a clear focus on a single romantic relationship) through historical novels (such as those by Mary Renault, Naomi Mitchison, or Gore Vidal, in which romance is less significant than the fictional reconstruction of historical events). In between lie many varieties of fiction that blend romance and historical elements. Historical fiction as a category is far more diverse than romance.

In the 18th and early 19th centuries many of the most important early novels were either romantic or gothic. The seduction story (Samuel Richardson's *Pamela* or *Clarissa Harlowe*, Susanna Rowson's *Charlotte Temple*) shared the qualities of today's straight romance, a tale that focused almost exclusively on the potential consequences, rewards, and risks of being a woman in love. The gothic novel (Ann Radcliffe's *The Castle of Otranto*) frequently included a romance but derived much of its appeal from exploitation of its setting in the medieval past, much as today's historical novels interpret the past for contemporary readers. But as the novel form matured, the sensational romance and gothic subject matter became the province of popular writers who continued to write such tales while more serious authors examined topics of a more universal character. Critics of early fiction often noted the high percentage of female readers for gothic and romance, in a period when most "serious" novelists were men who assumed they were addressing themselves to an audience that was not sex-specific. Two early exceptions to male dominance of the writing and criticism of serious fiction (Jane Austen and Charlotte Brontë) both wrote novels that derived from romance conventions, and Brontë used gothic conventions as well. Popular romances, however, continued to flourish even in eclipse. Although these novels received little critical attention, publishers and readers kept them alive. The books were written, published, read, and enjoyed whether or not the literary establishment took notice of them and despite the disrepute into which they had fallen.

In the 20th century gothic and romance novels have had a steady popularity, although only a handful of authors before 1960 enjoyed significant public attention, usually through the repeated production of best-sellers or by writing a single blockbuster novel. Mary Roberts Rinehart, for example, who wrote both romantic mysteries and straight romances, was so prolific and so successful that she achieved public prominence over a long period of time. Alternatively, the historical novelists Margaret Mitchell and Ross Lockridge, each the author of one exceptionally popular novel, influenced scores of lesser writers who never achieved an audience as large and devoted as theirs.

For the most part, however, writers of romance and historical novels have worked in relative obscurity. While gothics and romances have been categorized by critics and scholars as "mere" love stories or as unrealistic emotional adventures unworthy of serious consideration, historical novels may be labeled "sensation fiction" or "potboilers." Nevertheless, in the early 1980's two of the five best-selling authors in the world were Janet Dailey—an American author of straight romances—and Barbara Cartland—author of several hundred romantic adventure novels, many with settings in Regency England.

Romance and historical novels are closely related forms of fiction, although within the range of plot conventions there is significant variation in both form and quality. Like other narrative formulas, these books share a common set of interests and take place in predictable fictional worlds. Detective and mystery novels, for example, share a fascination with the mythology of crime. Horror novels and science fiction are always interested in the "what-if," the speculation about alien conditions that might impinge upon the rational world. Westerns are concerned with the grand adventure of settling new territory and building a civilization in the wilderness. Spy stories involve the clash of nations and the dirty business of espionage. Romances and gothics take place in a world in which love and domesticity are central to the protagonist's value system and in which conventional conflicts are often centered around the family, however adventurous a novel's plot may be. Suspense may derive from the exciting historical adventure of living in an age of turmoil; it may come from the titillation of the outrageous and horrifying; or it may result from the exquisite conflict between potential lovers. But whatever the ingredients of the individual plot or formula, all romantic novels share a concern with the details of women's personal lives, of mate selection and family formation, of problems between lovers, and of the impact of events—both public and private—upon domestic affairs. Writers of gothics and romances delineate the effect of extreme situations upon men and women in the realm of their conventional domestic concerns; and these novels often—although not always—portray a woman at the center of the action.

The impact of public and private events upon individuals is also a central concern of historical fiction. Historical novels are unified as a category by only one convention: the novels must be set in a period that is demonstrably different in time from that of the reader. Thus Tolstoy's *War and Peace* is as much an historical novel as Georgette Heyer's *The Grand Sophy* or Belva Plain's *Evergreen*. In an historical novel, history is made accessible to modern readers through dramatizing the impact of public events on individuals, although the historical interpretation need not be "accurate" as historians would judge it. Some historical novels take a position on a historical controversy involving people who actually lived (William Styron's *The Confessions of Nat Turner* or Thomas Keneally's *The Playmaker*). Others are "fictional biographies" of real people (Robert Graves's *I, Claudius*, Gore Vidal's *Burr*, Irving Stone's *Lust for Life* and *The Agony and the Ecstasy*, Anya Seton's *Katherine*). Still others portray fictional characters involved in real historical events (Margaret Mitchell's *Gone with the Wind,* Baroness Orczy's *The Scarlet Pimpernel*, Kathleen Winsor's *Forever Amber*). All historical novels, however, derive at least a measure of their appeal for an audience through purporting to explain or show what life was like in an era far distant from the reader's own.

In general, historical novels are more overtly adventurous than romance novels; but romance authors portray the adventure that can be found within the framework of love relationships. The novels of the softcover romance series focus upon the private, intimate relationships between lovers, charting the course of the couple's developing feelings until they make a lifetime commitment to each other. These romances are usually relatively short and resemble each other to a remarkable degree. Even in series novels, however, there is variation in quality and inventiveness. In the more adventurous gothic romances and some historical romances, characters are threatened less by their personal difficulties than by forces from the world outside. In gothics, potential lovers are kept apart by the machinations of the villain; in historical romances, by the momentous events in the larger world.

Series romances aim at an audience that is almost totally female, and the adventure of such novels rarely transcends the issue of the love story; on the other hand, historical romances and family saga romances paint a picture on a wider canvas, with the family rather than an individual woman at the center. The very essence of romance and gothic, however, remains personal and interior, concerned with motivation and action that brings a story to a kind of domestic stasis. The lovers may be separated or united, the family may be intact or disrupted, but the stories are always told against a domestic value system in which characters are rewarded or punished according to conventional moral norms.

Romance and historical fiction, then, intersect; categorizing some novels as one or the other may depend less on specific characteristics than on the marketing strategy of the publisher. Historical novels, however, are frequently taken more seriously by critics than are romances; they are, for example, reviewed far more often. Compared with many romances, historical novels may seem more substantial; they are usually longer, and they may appeal to a wider audience made up of men as well as women. Both readers and critics consider authors such as Mary Renault, Ford Madox Ford, John Steinbeck, Robert Graves, and John Fowles as mainstream writers who employ historical settings in writing serious fiction. The reputation of historical fiction also benefits from the cultural assumption that history as a subject is more significant than are stories about love.

Despite critical neglect, however, romances have seen a dramatic resurgence in the past three decades. New authors have achieved great success and reprints of older novels have found wide circulation. Romance series have proliferated. In these 30 years, several stages of development in romances have occurred.

In the early 1960's the most popular type of fiction in the gothic/romance genre was the novel of romantic suspense, called conveniently by publishers "gothic romance." British writers were most prominent, but their American colleagues were also active. The modern popularity of the gothic romance can probably be most accurately dated from the publication in 1960 of *Mistress of Mellyn* by Eleanor Burford Hibbert (writing as Victoria Holt). The novel showed its derivation from the Brontës and Daphne du Maurier on almost every page, but it captured the imaginations of readers and writers alike and sparked an upsurge in novels of domestic adventure with sprightly heroines who solved mysteries, protected families and children (not necessarily their own), and won the love of the hero by the final page. For most of that decade, the output of gothic romances remained high, led by Holt, Dorothy Eden, Mary Stewart, and Phyllis A. Whitney, who were imitated by a host of other writers. As the popularity of the gothic romance grew, other romantic formulas also achieved wider distribution. Historical romances also became more prevalent as publishers searched for new authors while also reprinting older works by such writers as Georgette Heyer and Barbara Cartland. In the latter part of the decade and throughout the 1970's Regency romances, inspired by Heyer, achieved great success.

Although the gothic and historical romance formulas were the best known, other related types of women's fiction continued to sell. Various series of romantic love stories were popular in Britain, although their distribution in the United States was only a fraction of its current level. The United States was more an audience for romances than a major producer until the first of the erotic romances (or "bodice-rippers") by such American authors as Kathleen E. Woodiwiss and Rosemary Rogers. The new American romance formula of the 1970's differed from its predecessors in several significant ways. The books were much more sexually explicit, featuring heroines whose sexual encounters (in or out of marriage) were more graphically described than in other romances. Before this change, premarital sex had always been a sign that a character was a "fallen woman," similar to the heroine of Kathleen Winsor's *Forever Amber,* and therefore unworthy of a lasting marriage. The new romances also featured heroines who were more independent and assertive than the women in more traditional romances. Relationships between heroes and heroines, while still deriving substantially from traditional cultural expectations about men and women, also became more egalitarian. At first, these changes were seen primarily in historical romances; but by the middle of the decade, the conventions of the erotic romance were also seen in some romances with contemporary settings. When the publishers of the traditional series romances (including Mills and Boon/Harlequin) recognized the popularity of the new romances, they inaugurated substantial changes in their own formulas.

In the late 1970's and early 1980's, the United States was the scene of intense competition among publishers of series romances. Sales and distribution of series romances increased rapidly as the alliance between Mills and Boon in Britain and Harlequin in Canada moved to dominance in the American market. Both those firms had exceptionally effective marketing strategies, selling books by mail order and subscription as well as in retail outlets. As American publishers recognized the success of Mills and Boon/Harlequin strategy, competition ignited. Simon and Schuster, formerly Harlequin's American distributor, inaugurated the Silhouette Romance series in 1980 to compete for a share of the lucrative market. In the next two years, Silhouette Romances proliferated into four distinct series of romances, including a line for teenagers, a growing segment of the market. Silhouette also lured Mills and Boon authors with some success and began aggressively marketing abroad. After a few years of increasingly destructive competition, however, Harlequin and Silhouette merged.

In the same period other American paperback publishers (Dell, Berkley, Bantam) followed suit. Each of the new series emphasized the company's product through packaging, formula control enforced by author's "tipsheets," and advertising to promote an image of the series' quality and diversity within a narrow range of predictable plots. The formula control of these romance publishers relies upon extensive market research aimed at discovering what women want to read so the editors can tailor the product to particular segments of the market. Such publisher control is relatively new in popular fiction. To be sure, series of novels were published in the 19th century, and certain publishing houses have long been known for issuing particular kinds of genre fiction; but the production and marketing of series romance novels represents a more complex development in popular entertainment, comparable to the way television programs are developed, packaged, and sold. Although some publishers tried to inaugurate series of historical romances, none was entirely successful. Readers of historical fiction seem less interested in series packaging than do romance readers.

Institutional support for romances has also increased. The Romance Writers of America was established to provide services to American authors similar to those offered British writers by the older Romantic Novelists Association. Newsletters for fans of romances proliferated, and conventions for romance readers and authors have been held. Romance is big business today, and the book establishment has had to take notice. The current popularity of romances, however, is probably an aberration, one of those historical moments when the gothic and romance formulas are particularly appealing to a wide audience. Over the past two centuries, these formulas have experienced intermittent waves of prominence that eventually receded, although their production has never entirely disappeared. The novels of especially popular authors remain in print for generations while the more ephemeral works are forgotten.

All kinds of popular fiction experience periods of high popularity followed by periods when sales, although steady, are lower. In the United States, the decade of the 1930's was particularly rich for historical novels, including *Gone with the Wind*, while the 1970's were especially fruitful for romance writers. Some scholars speculate that historical fiction was popular in the 1930's because the widespread social disruption of the era led to the reading public's interest in stories of the past, demonstrating that even under circumstances far more terrible than their own human beings could survive and prosper. Romances may have been especially interesting to women in the 1970's, when the new and sometimes threatening social change fostered by the newly emerging women's movement seemed to call into question the value of traditional female roles.

Only in the past two decades, under the influence of the developing field of popular culture, have scholars begun to look systematically and seriously at many formulas of popular fiction and their readers. Because the area of study is so new, it is hampered by a paucity of bibliographical and critical materials. A reference book like this volume should make basic information on romance and historical writers available for further scholarly consideration.

—KAY MUSSELL

READING LIST

Abartis, Caesarea, "The Ugly-Pretty, Dull-Bright, Weak-Strong Girl in the Gothic Mansion," in *Journal of Popular Culture* (Bowling Green, Ohio), Fall 1979.

Allen, Richard O., "If You Have Tears: Sentimentalism as Soft Romanticism," in *Genre* (Plattsburgh, New York), June 1975.

Anderson, Rachel, *The Purple Heart Throbs: The Sub-Literature of Love*. London, Hodder and Stoughton, 1974.

Bailey, Margaret, "The Women's Magazine Short-Story Heroine in 1957 and 1967," in *Journalism Quarterly* (Minneapolis), 1969.

Bayer-Berenbaum, Linda, *The Gothic Imagination: Expansion in Gothic Literature and Art*. Rutherford, New Jersey, Fairleigh Dickinson University Press, 1982.

Beauman, Nicola, *A Very Great Profession: The Women's Novel 1914–1939*. London, Virago Press, 1983.

Berman, Phyllis, "They Call Us Illegitimate," in *Forbes* (New York), 6 March 1978.

Blacker, Irving R., *The Old West in Fiction*. New York, Obolensky, 1961.

Britton, Anne, and Marion Collin, *Romantic Fiction*. London, Boardman, 1960.

Browne, Ray B., and Marshall W. Fishwick, editors, *The Hero in Transition*. Bowling Green, Ohio, Popular Press, 1983.

Buckley, J. A., and W. T. Williams, *A Guide to British Historical Fiction*. London, Harrap, 1912.

Buhle, Paul, editor, *Popular Culture in America*. Minneapolis, University of Minnesota Press, 1987.

Butterfield, Herbert, *The Historical Novel: An Essay*. Cambridge, Cambridge University Press, and New York, Macmillan, 1924.

Cahalan, James M., *Great Hatred, Little Room: The Irish Historical Novel*. New York, Syracuse University Press, 1983.

Cam, Helen, *Historical Novels*. London, Routledge, 1961.

Cantor, Norman P., and Michael S. Wertham, editors, *The History of Popular Culture*. New York, Macmillan, 1968.

Cawelti, John G., *Adventure, Mystery, and Romance: Formula Stories as Art and Popular Culture*. Chicago, University of Chicago Press, 1976.

Cecil, Mirabel, *Heroines in Love 1750–1974*. London, Joseph, 1974.

Cohn, Jan, *Romance and the Erotics of Property: Mass-Market Fiction for Women*. Durham, North Carolina, Duke University Press, 1988.

Cornillon, Susan Koppelman, editor, *Images of Women in Fiction: Feminist Perspectives*. Bowling Green, Ohio, Popular Press, 1972.

Dataller, Roger, *The Plain Man and the Novel*. London, Nelson, 1940.

Dickinson, A. T., Jr., *American Historical Fiction*. Metuchen, New Jersey, Scarecrow Press, 1958; revised edition, 1971.

Douglas, Ann, "Soft-Porn Culture," in *New Republic* (Washington, D.C.), 30 August 1980.

Drake, Robert Y., Jr., "Tara Twenty Years After," in *Georgia Review* (Athens), Summer 1958.

Duffy, Dennis, *Sounding the Iceberg: An Essay on Canadian Historical Novels*. Toronto, ECW Press, 1986.

Elliot, Thomas R., "Genteel Violence: The Turn-of-the-Century American Historical Novel," in *Journal of Popular Culture* (Bowling Green, Ohio), Spring 1980.

Falk, Kathryn, *Love's Leading Ladies*. New York, Pinnacle, 1983.

Fallon, Eileen, *Words of Love: A Complete Guide to Romantic Fiction*. New York, Garland, 1983.

Fishburn, Katherine, *Women in Popular Culture: A Reference Guide*. Westport, Connecticut, Greenwood Press, 1982.

Fisher, Margery, *The Bright Face of Danger*. London, Hodder and Stoughton, 1986.

Fleenor, Julian E., editor, *The Female Gothic*. Montreal, Eden Press, 1983.

Franzwa, Helen, "Female Roles in Women's Magazine Fiction 1940–1970," in *Woman: Dependent or Independent Vari-*

able?, edited by Rhoda Kesler Unger and Florence L. Denmark. New York, Psychological Dimensions, 1975.

Gaston, Edwin W., Jr., *The Early Novels of the Southwest.* Albuquerque, University of New Mexico Press, 1961.

Greenfeld, Beth, and Julian E. Fleenor, editors, *The Female Gothic.* St. Albans, Vermont, Eden Press, 1982.

Guiley, Rosemary, *Love Lines: The Romance Reader's Guide to Printed Pleasures.* New York, Facts on File, 1983.

Hackett, Alice Payne, and James Henry Burke, *Eighty Years of Best Sellers 1895–1975.* New York, Bowker, 1977.

Harlequin 30th Anniversary 1949–1979: The First 30 Years of the World's Best Romance Fiction. Toronto, Harlequin, 1979.

Harrison, R., "Women and Romantic Fiction: Subordination and Resistance," paper for BSA annual conference (Manchester), April 1982.

Hart, James D., *The Popular Book: A History of America's Literary Taste.* New York, Oxford University Press, 1950.

Harvey, Brett, "Boy Crazy," in *Village Voice* (New York), 10 February 1982.

Hay, Valerie, "The Necessity of Romance," in *Women's Studies Occasional Papers 30* (Canterbury), 1983.

Hazen, Helen, *Endless Rapture: Rape, Romance, and the Female Imagination.* New York, Scribner, 1983.

Higdon, David Leon, *Shadows of the Past in Contemporary British Fiction.* London, Macmillan, and Athens, University of Georgia Press, 1984.

Hoekstra, Ellen, "The Pedestal Myth Reinforced: Women's Magazine Fiction 1900–1920," in *New Dimensions in Popular Culture*, edited by Russel B. Nye. Bowling Green, Ohio, Popular Press, 1972.

Hofstadter, Beatrice, "Popular Culture and the Romantic Heroine," in *American Scholar* (Washington, D.C.), Winter 1960–61.

Honey, Maureen, "New Roles for Women and the Feminine Mystique: Popular Fiction of the 1940's," in *American Studies* (Lawrence, Kansas), Spring 1983.

Inge, M. Thomas, editor, *Handbook of American Popular Culture 1-2* (includes sections on gothic fiction and romantic fiction). Westport, Connecticut, Greenwood Press, 2 vols., 1979–80.

Jensen, Margaret, *Love's $weet Return: The Harlequin Story.* Toronto, Women's Educational Press, 1984.

Karolides, Nicholas J., *The Pioneer in the American Novel 1900–1950.* Norman, University of Oklahoma Press, 1967.

Kay, Mary June, *The Romantic Spirit.* San Antonio, Texas, MJK Enterprises, 4 vols., 1982–88.

Kocmanporá, Jessie, "Novel of Romance: Problems of Genre in Contemporary English Prose Fiction," in *Brno Studies in English* (Czechoslovakia), 1981.

Landrum, Larry N., *American Popular Culture.* Detroit, Gale, 1982.

Lee, Linda, *How to Write and Sell Romance Novels: A Step-by-Step Guide.* Edmonds, Washington, Heartsong Press, 1988.

Leisy, Ernest F., *The American Historical Novel.* Norman, University of Oklahoma Press, 1950.

Levin, David, *In Defense of Historical Literature.* New York, Hill and Wang, 1967.

Light, Alison, "Returning to Manderley—Romance Fiction, Female Sexuality, and Class," in *Feminist Review 16* (London), Summer 1984.

Lively, Robert A., *Fiction Fights the Civil War.* Chapel Hill, University of North Carolina Press, 1957.

Lovell, Terry, *Consuming Fiction.* London, Verso, 1988.

Lytle, Andrew, "The Image as Guide to Meaning in the Historical Novel," in *Sewanee Review* (Tennessee), 1953.

Mann, Peter H., *The Romantic Novel: A Survey of Reading Habits*, and *A New Survey: The Facts about Romantic Fiction.* London, Mills and Boon, 2 vols., 1969–74.

Margolies, David, "Mills and Boon: Guilt Without Sex," in *Red Letters 14* (London), 1982.

Martin, Rhona, *Writing Historical Fiction.* London, A. and C. Black, and New York, St. Martin's Press, 1988.

McGarry, Daniel D., and Sarah Harriman White, *Historical Fiction Guide.* Metuchen, New Jersey, Scarecrow Press, 1963.

Meldrum, Barbara Howard, editor, *Under the Sun: Myth and Realism in Western American Literature.* Troy, New York, Whitston, 1985.

Menendez, Albert J., *Civil War Novels: An Annotated Bibliography.* New York, Garland, 1986.

Miner, Madonne M., *Insatiable Appetites: Twentieth-Century American Women's Bestsellers.* Westport, Connecticut, Greenwood Press, 1984.

Minundri, Regina, "From Jane to Germaine, with Love," in *Library Journal* (New York), 15 February 1973.

Modleski, Tania, "The Disappearing Act: A Study of Harlequin Romances," in *Signs 5* (Stanford, California), Autumn 1980.

Modleski, Tania, *Loving with Vengeance: Mass-Produced Fantasies for Women.* Hamden, Connecticut, Archon, 1982; London, Methuen, 1984.

Moers, Ellen, *Literary Women.* New York, Doubleday, 1976; London, W. H. Allen, 1977.

Montieth, Moira, editor, *Women's Writing: A Challenge to Theory.* Brighton, Harvester Press, 1986.

Mussell, Kay, "Beautiful and Damned: The Sexual Woman in Modern Gothic Fiction," in *Journal of Popular Culture* (Bowling Green, Ohio), Summer 1975.

Mussell, Kay, *Women's Gothic and Romantic Fiction: A Reference Guide.* Westport, Connecticut, Greenwood Press, 1981.

Mussell, Kay, *Fantasy and Reconciliation: Contemporary Formulas of Women's Romance Fiction.* Westport, Connecticut, Greenwood Press, 1984.

Neild, Jonathan, *A Guide to the Best Historical Novels and Tales.* London, Mathews and Marrot, 1902; revised edition, 1902, 1904, 1911, 1929.

Neuburg, Victor, *The Batsford Companion to Popular Literature.* London, Batsford, 1982.

Nye, Russell B., editor, *New Dimensions in Popular Culture.* Bowling Green, Ohio, Popular Press, 1972.

Nye, Russel B., *The Unembarrassed Muse: The Popular Arts in America.* New York, Dial Press, 1970.

O'Toole, Patricia, "Paperback Virgins," in *Human Behavior* (Los Angeles), February 1979.

Pawling, Christopher, editor, *Popular Fiction and Social Change.* London, Macmillan, 1984.

Pilkington, William T., editor, *Critical Essays on the Western American Novel.* Boston, Hall, 1980.

Rabine, Leslie W., "Romance in the Age of Electronics: Harlequin Enterprises," in *Feminist Studies* (College Park, Maryland), 1985.

Rabine, Leslie W., *Reading the Romantic Heroine: Text, History, and Ideology.* Ann Arbor, University of Michigan Press, 1985.

Radcliffe, Elsa J., *Gothic Novels of the Twentieth Century: An Annotated Bibliography.* Metuchen, New Jersey, Scarecrow Press, 1979.

Radford, Jean, editor, *The Progress of Romance: The Politics of Popular Fiction.* London, Routledge, 1987.

Radstone, Susannah, editor, *Sweet Dreams: Sexuality, Gender and Popular Fiction.* London, Lawrence and Wishart, 1988.

Radway, Janice, "The Utopian Impulse in Popular Literature: Gothic Romances and 'Feminist' Protest," in *American Quarterly* (Philadelphia), Summer 1981.

Radway, Janice, *Reading the Romance: Women, Patriarchy, and Popular Fiction*. Chapel Hill, University of North Carolina Press, 1987.

Regan, Nancy, "A Home of One's Own: Women's Bodies in Recent Women's Fiction," in *Journal of Popular Culture* (Bowling Green, Ohio), Spring 1978.

Ritchie, Claire, *Writing the Romantic Novel*. London, Bond Street, 1962.

Robinson, Lillian S., "On Reading Trash," in *Sex, Class, and Culture*. Bloomington, Indiana University Press, 1978.

Roe, Sue, editor, *Women Reading, Women's Writing*. Brighton, Harvester Press, 1987.

"Romance Fiction: A PW Special Report" edited by Daisy Maryles and Robert Dahlin, in *Publishers Weekly* (New York), 13 November 1981.

Rose, Suzanna, "Is Romance Dysfunctional?" in *International Journal of Women's Studies* (Montreal), May–June 1985.

Rose, Willie Lee, *Race and Religion in American Historical Fiction: Four Episodes in Popular Culture*. Oxford, Clarendon Press, 1979.

Ruggiero, Josephine A., and Louise C. Weston, "Pulp Feminists," in *Human Behavior* (Los Angeles), February 1978.

Ruggiero, Josephine A., and Louise C. Weston, "Conflicting Images of Women in Romance Novels, in *International Journal of Women's Studies* (Montreal), January–February 1983.

Russ, Joanna, "Somebody's Trying to Kill Me and I Think It's My Husband: The Modern Gothic," in *Journal of Popular Culture* (Bowling Green, Ohio), 1973.

Saunders, Jean, *The Craft of Writing Romance: A Practical Guide*. London, Allison and Busby, 1986.

Sheppard, Alfred T., *The Art and Practice of Historical Fiction*. London, Toulmin, 1930.

Smith, Herbert F., *The Popular American Novel 1865–1920*. Boston, Twayne, 1980.

Snitow, Ann Barr, "Mass Market Romance: Pornography for Women Is Different" in *Desire: The Politics of Sensuality* edited by Snitow, Christine Stansell, and Sharon Thompson. London, Virago Press, 1984.

Starr, Nathan Comfort, *King Arthur Today: The Arthurian Legend in English and American Literature 1901–1953*. Gainesville, University of Florida Press, 1954.

Strout, Cushing, *The Veracious Imagination: Essays on American History, Literature, and Biography*. Middletown, Connecticut, Wesleyan University Press, 1981.

Sutherland, J. A., *Bestsellers: Popular Fiction of the 1970's*. London, Routledge, 1981.

Taylor, Helen, *Scarlett's Women: Gone with the Wind and Its Female Friends*. London, Virago Press, 1989.

Thurston, Carol, and Barbara Doscher, "Supermarket Erotica: Bodice Busters Put Romantic Myths to Bed," in *Progressive* (New York), April 1982.

Thurston, Carol, "Popular Historical Romances: Agent for Social Change? An Exploration of Methodologies," in *Journal of Popular Culture* (Bowling Green, Ohio), Summer 1985.

Thurston, Carol, *The Romance Revolution: Erotic Novels for Women and the Quest for a New Sexual Identity*. Urbana, University of Illinois Press, 1987.

Turner, Alice K., "The Tempestuous, Turbulent, Torrid, and Terribly Profitable World of Paperback Passion," in *New York*, 1978.

Usborne, Richard, *Clubland Heroes: A Nostalgic Study of Some Recurrent Characters in the Romantic Fiction of Dornford Yates, John Buchan, and Sapper*. London, Constable, 1953; revised edition, London, Barrie and Jenkins, 1975.

Van Auken, Sheldon, "The Southern Historical Novel in the Early Twentieth Century," in *Journal of Southern History* (Baton Rouge, Louisiana), 1948.

Walsh, Mary Roth, "Images of Women Doctors in Popular Fiction," in *Journal of Popular Culture* (Bowling Green, Ohio), Summer 1978.

Wibberly, Mary, *To Writers with Love: On Writing Romantic Novels*. London, Buchan and Enright, 1985.

Wilson, Edmund, *Patriotic Gore: Studies in the Literature of the American Civil War*. New York, Oxford University Press, and London, Deutsch, 1962.

Woodruff, Juliette, "A Spate of Words, Full of Sound and Fury, Signifying Nothing; or, How to Read Harlequin," *Journal of Popular Culture* (Bowling Green, Ohio), 1985.

Zamora, Lois Parkinson, editor, *The Apocalyptic Vision in America*. Bowling Green, Ohio, Popular Press, 1982.

EDITOR'S NOTE

The selection of writers in this book is based on the recommendations of the advisers listed on page xv.

The entry for each writer consists of a biography, a complete list of separately published books, and a signed critical essay. In addition, living entrants were invited to comment on their work.

Original British and United States editions of all books have been listed; other editions are listed only if they are the first editions, though an exception has been made to include publications of Harlequin Books (Toronto). Series characters and locales have been indicated for romance and historical publications. Entries include notations of available bibliographies, manuscript collections, and critical studies. Other critical materials appear in the Reading List of secondary works on the genres.

We would like to thank the entrants and contributors for their patience and cooperation in helping us compile this book.

ADVISERS

Rachel Anderson
Mary Cadogan
Barbara Cartland
Warren French
Rosemary Guiley
David Leon Higdon
Kay Mussell

Victor Neuburg
Elsa J. Radcliffe
Jean Radford
Janice Radway
Jean Saunders
Carol Thurston

CONTRIBUTORS

Patricia Altner
Rachel Anderson
Jane S. Bakerman
Michael Ballin
Earl F. Bargainnier
Melvyn Barnes
Linda S. Bergmann
Susan Quinn Berneis
E. F. Bleiler
Marylaine Block
Wendy Bousfield
Bill Boyle
W. H. Bradley
Susan Branch
Jean Buchanan
Angela Bull
Rose Marie Burwell
Hilary Buswell
Dennis Butts
Mary Cadogan
Margaret Campbell
Jennifer Cargill
Glen Cavaliero
Tessa Rose Chester
Anderson Clark
Pamela Cleaver
Scott Coombs
Peter Desy
Douglas Devaney
Warren French
Marcia G. Fuchs
François Gallix
Judith A. Gifford
Paul Gillen
Thomas S. Gladsky
Pat Gordon-Smith
Jane Gottschalk
Elizabeth Grey
Albert Guerard
Janet V. Haedicke
Marion Hanscom
Barrie Hayne
Joanne Harack Hayne
Michael Held
Allayne C. Heyduk

David Leon Higdon
Joan Hinkemeyer
Ferelith Hordon
Louis James
Margaret Jensen
Heather Iris Jones
Barbara E. Kemp
Larry N. Landrum
Linda Lee
Lornie Leete-Hodge
Frank R. Levstick
Marilyn Lockhart
George C. Longest
Mary C. Lynn
Andrew Macdonald
Gina Macdonald
Joan McGrath
Sally Allen McNall
P. R. Meldrum
Leonard R. Mendelsohn
J. Lawrence Mitchell
Christian H. Moe
Arlene Moore
Thomas J. Morrisey
Marilynn Motteler
Alan Murphy
Kay Mussell
Necia A. Musser
Larry Olpin
Kim Paynter
Joyce Pettis
Kathy Piehl
Nancy H. Pogel
L. M. Quinn
Janice Radway
Simon Raven
Nancy Regan
Judith Rhodes
Bette B. Roberts
Karen Robertson
Lucy Rogers
Josephine A. Ruggiero
Geoffrey Sadler
Anne M. Shields
Alan R. Shucard

Andrea Lee Shuey
Roy Simmonds
Christopher Smith
David Waldron Smithers
Katherine Staples
Sanford Sternlicht
Judith Summers
Jane K. Thompson
Carol Thurston
Thomas R. Tietze
Felicity Trotman
Eleanor Ty

Peter Vansittart
W. M. von Zharen
George Walsh
Catherine S. Wearing
Louise C. Weston
Kerry White
Ray Lewis White
Dorothy Wood
M. Jeanne Yardley
Peggy York
Alan R. Young
Paula M. Zieselman

TWENTIETH-CENTURY ROMANCE AND HISTORICAL WRITERS

Joan Aiken
Patricia Ainsworth
Madame Albanesi
Charlotte Vale Allen
Hervey Allen
Lucilla Andrews
Evelyn Anthony
Jane Arbor
Michael Arlen
Charlotte Armstrong
Harriette Arnow
Elizabeth Ashton
Nan Asquith
Grace Murray Atkin
Jean M. Auel
Ruby M. Ayres

Irving Bacheller
H. C. Bailey
Faith Baldwin
Florence L. Barclay
Countess Barcynska
Pat Barr
Susan Barrie
John Barth
Betty Beaty
Helen Beauclerk
L. Adams Beck
Henry Bellamann
Pamela Belle
Stephen Vincent Benét
Pamela Bennetts
Phyllis Bentley
Evelyn Berckman
Elisabeth Beresford
John Berger
Thomas Berger
Gloria Bevan
Eileen Bigland
Maeve Binchy
Laura Black
Jane Blackmore
Charity Blackstock
Kathryn Blair
Stephanie Blake
Ursula Bloom
Marjorie Bowen
James Boyd
Barbara Taylor Bradford
Marion Zimmer Bradley
Gillian Bradshaw
Rebecca Brandewyne
Madeleine Brent
Ann Bridge
Gwen Bristow
Katrina Britt
Louis Bromfield
Iris Bromige
D. K. Broster
Sandra Brown
Dixie Browning
Bryher
John Buchan
Pearl S. Buck
Nancy Buckingham
Mary Burchell

Lolah Burford
Anthony Burgess
Rose Burghley
G. B. Burgin
Gwendoline Butler
Donn Byrne

James Branch Cabell
Elizabeth Cadell
Hall Caine
Janet Caird
Taylor Caldwell
Sacha Carnegie
Robyn Carr
Angela Carter
Barbara Cartland
David Case
Nancy Cato
Robert W. Chambers
Hester W. Chapman
Mollie Chappell
Judy Chard
Theresa Charles
Elaine Raco Chase
Marion Chesney
Philip Child
Winston Churchill
Brenda Clarke
James Clavell
C. Guy Clayton
Brian Cleeve
Sophia Cleugh
Marian Cockrell
Virginia Coffman
Marion Collin
Catherine Cookson
Jilly Cooper
Lettice Cooper
Barbara Corcoran
Alexander Cordell
Marie Corelli
Bernard Cornwell
Thomas B. Costain
Juanita Coulson
Caroline Courtney
Frances Cowen
Sara Craven
Cecily Crowe

Janet Dailey
Iris Danbury
Clemence Dane
Dorothy Daniels
Clare Darcy
Eleanor Dark
Elizabeth Darrell
Marcia Davenport
Dorothy Salisbury Davis
Celeste de Blasis
Warwick Deeping
E. M. Delafield
Mazo de la Roche
R. F. Delderfield
Barbara Delinsky
Ethel M. Dell
Viña Delmar

August Derleth
Jude Deveraux
Joyce Dingwell
Maud Diver
Jane Donnelly
Lloyd C. Douglas
Arthur Conan Doyle
Anne Duffield
Alfred Duggan
Daphne du Maurier
Dorothy Dunnett
Alice Dwyer-Joyce
Juliet Dymoke

Evelyn Eaton
Suzanne Ebel
Mignon G. Eberhart
Dorothy Eden
Walter D. Edmonds
Anne Edwards
M. Barnard Eldershaw
Mary Elgin
Anne Eliot
Elizabeth
Rosemary Ellerbeck
Julie Ellis
Hebe Elsna
Clare Emsley
John Erskine
Audrey Erskine-Lindop
Susan Ertz

Eleanor Farnes
Jeffery Farnol
J. G. Farrell
Howard Fast
Catherine Fellows
Edna Ferber
Rachel Field
Timothy Findley
Glenna Finley
Julia Fitzgerald
Valerie Fitzgerald
Thomas Flanagan
Inglis Fletcher
Shelby Foote
Esther Forbes
Ford Madox Ford
C. S. Forester
John Fowles
Gilbert Frankau
Rose Franken
George MacDonald Fraser
Ronald Fraser
Cynthia Freeman

Ernest J. Gaines
Patricia Gallagher
Ernest K. Gann
David Garnett
Charles Garvice
Catherine Gaskin
Catherine Gavin
Roberta Gellis
Mary Ann Gibbs
Anna Gilbert

Janice Holt Giles
Judith Glover
Constance Gluyas
Elinor Glyn
Rumer Godden
William Golding
Ethel Edison Gordon
Elizabeth Goudge
Iris Gower
Winston Graham
Joan Grant
Robert Graves
Peter Green
Maysie Greig
Hettie Grimstead
Mabel Barnes Grundy

H. Rider Haggard
Pamela Haines
James Norman Hall
Anne Hampson
Mollie Hardwick
W. G. Hardy
Marilyn Harris
Rosemary Harris
Elizabeth Harrison
Sarah Harrison
Cynthia Harrod-Eagles
Alice Harwood
Brooke Hastings
Phyllis Hastings
Constance Heaven
Maurice Hewlett
Georgette Heyer
Robert Hichens
Grace Livingston Hill
Pamela Hill
Margery Hilton
Naomi A. Hintze
Jane Aiken Hodge
Cecelia Holland
Isabelle Holland
Victoria Holt
Kay Hooper
Anthony Hope
Lance Horner
Linda Howard
Mary Howard
Susan Howatch
Elizabeth Hoy
Susan Hufford
E. M. Hull
Elizabeth Hunter
Fannie Hurst
Baroness von Hutten

Eva Ibbotson
Ion L. Idriess
Susan Inglis
Margaret Irwin

Shirley Jackson
Naomi Jacob
Brenda Jagger
John Jakes
Rosemary Hawley Jarman
Gary Jennings

Iris Johansen
Barbara Ferry Johnson
Susan Johnson
Mary Johnston
Velda Johnston

MacKinlay Kantor
M. M. Kaye
Thomas Keneally
Margaret Kennedy
Barbara Kevern
Frances Parkinson Keyes
Flora Kidd
Katheryn Kimbrough
Russell Kirk
Alanna Knight
Arthur Koestler
Jayne Ann Krentz

Rosalind Laker
Charlotte Lamb
Jane Lane
Roumelia Lane
Jacqueline La Tourrette
Elsie Lee
Doris Leslie
Janet Lewis
Maynah Lewis
Marjorie Lewty
Alice Chetwynd Ley
Laura Jean Libbey
Jack Lindsay
Rachel Lindsay
Johanna Lindsey
Morgan Llywelyn
Ross Lockridge
Nora Lofts
Laura London
Amii Lorin
Emilie Loring
Claire Lorrimer
Elizabeth Lowell
Marie Belloc Lowndes
Margaret Lynn
Andrew Lytle

Dorothy Macardle
Rose Macaulay
Madge Macbeth
Mrs. Patrick MacGill
Colin MacInnes
Leila Mackinlay
Charlotte MacLeod
Jean S. MacLeod
Margaret Maddocks
Eric Malpass
Audrie Manley-Tucker
Alexandra Manners
Jean Marsh
Edison Marshall
Rosamond Marshall
Rhona Martin
John Masefield
A. E. W. Mason
F. Van Wyck Mason
John Masters

Anne Mather
Patricia Matthews
Wynne May
Anne Maybury
Laurie McBain
Colleen McCullough
Philip McCutchan
George Barr McCutcheon
Adeline McElfresh
Marjorie McEvoy
Judith McNaught
Anne Melville
Grace Metalious
Barbara Michaels
Fern Michaels
James A. Michener
Lady Miles
Margaret Millar
Marlys Millhiser
Margaret Mitchell
Naomi Mitchison
L. M. Montgomery
Doris Langley Moore
Alice Morgan
Annette Motley
Edwin Mullins
Neil Munro
D. L. Murray
Frances Murray
Netta Muskett

Betty Neels
Sarah Neilan
Sharan Newman
Christopher Nicole
Frederick Niven
Frederick Nolan
Charles Nordhoff
Kathleen Norris
Kate Norway
Robert Nye

Joyce Carol Oates
Patrick O'Brian
Elisabeth Ogilvie
Rohan O'Grady
Pamela Oldfield
Carola Oman
Oliver Onions
Kyle Onstott
Baroness Orczy

Diana Palmer
Edith Pargeter
Margaret Pargeter
C. Northcote Parkinson
Isabel M. Paterson
Barbara Anne Pauley
Lilian Peake
Margaret Pedler
Sharon K. Penman
Elizabeth O. Peter
Maureen Peters
Natasha Peters
Phyllis Taylor Pianka
Rosamunde Pilcher

Madeleine A. Polland
D. A. Ponsonby
Dudley Pope
Eleanor H. Porter
Gene Stratton Porter
Hal Porter
John Cowper Powys
Heather Graham Pozzessere
H. F. M. Prescott
Fayrene Preston
Ivy Preston
Evadne Price
Nina Pykare

Thomas Head Raddall
Florence Engel Randall
Rona Randall
Claire Rayner
Henrietta Reid
Mary Renault
Elizabeth Renier
Jean Rhys
Barbara Riefe
Mary Roberts Rinehart
Alexandra Ripley
Claire Ritchie
Francine Rivers
Irene Roberts
Janet Louise Roberts
Kenneth Roberts
Nora Roberts
Willo Davis Roberts
Denise Robins
Mary Linn Roby
Rosemary Rogers
Margaret Rome
Berta Ruck

Rafael Sabatini
Mabel St. John
Nicole St. John
Carola Salisbury
Susan Sallis
Laura Goodman Salverson
Helen Hooven Santmyer
Jean Saunders
Elizabeth Savage
Judith Saxton
Evelyn Scott
Sara Seale
Margaret Sebastian
Maura Seger
Kathleen Gilles Seidel
Elizabeth Seifert
Alexandra Sellers
Anya Seton
Virna Sheard
Samuel Shellabarger
Valerie Sherwood
Kathleen Shoesmith
Nevil Shute
Olga Sinclair
Rosemary Anne Sisson
Frank G. Slaughter
Bertrice Small
Doris E. Smith

Lady Eleanor Smith
Joan Smith
Cathy Cash Spellman
LaVyrle Spencer
Elizabeth Sprigge
Sondra Stanford
Danielle Steel
Marguerite Steen
John Steinbeck
G. B. Stern
Anne Stevenson
D. E. Stevenson
Florence Stevenson
Mary Stewart
Jessica Stirling
Irving Stone
Rebecca Stratton
Vivian Stuart
Jean Stubbs
William Styron
Essie Summers
Margaret Summerton
Annie S. Swan
Neil H. Swanson
Madge Swindells

Jill Tattersall
Janelle Taylor
Elswyth Thane
Rosie Thomas
E. V. Thompson
Kay Thorpe
Sylvia Thorpe
Marcella Thum
Nigel Tranter
Betty Trask
Henry Treece
Richard Tresillian
Joanna Trollope

Mrs. George de Horne Vaizey
Karen van der Zee
Peter Vansittart
Helen Van Slyke
Patricia Veryan
Gore Vidal
Donna Vitek

Helen Waddell
Lucy Walker
Margaret Walker
Hugh Walpole
Sheila Walsh
Rex Warner
Sylvia Townsend Warner
Robert Penn Warren
Margaret Way
Anne Weale
Jean Francis Webb
Jean Webster
Jessamyn West
Jan Westcott
Mary Westmacott
Gwen Westwood
Stanley Weyman
Patrick White

T. H. White
Phyllis A. Whitney
Philippa Wiat
Rudy Wiebe
Thornton Wilder
Claudette Williams
C. N. and A. M. Williamson
Kathleen Winsor
Violet Winspear
Daoma Winston
Barbara Wood

Kathleen E. Woodiwiss
Lilian Woodward
Anne Worboys
P. C. Wren
Esther Wyndham
May Wynne

Chelsea Quinn Yarbro
Dornford Yates
Frank Yerby
Stark Young

AIKEN, Joan (Delano). British. Born in Rye, Sussex, 4 September 1924; daughter of the writer Conrad Aiken; sister of Jane Aiken Hodge, *q.v.* Educated at Wychwood School, Oxford, 1936–40. Married 1) Ronald George Brown in 1945 (died 1955), one son and one daughter; 2) Julius Goldstein in 1976. Worked for the BBC, 1942–43; information officer, then librarian, United Nations Information Centre, London, 1943–49; subeditor and features editor, *Argosy*, London, 1955–60; copywriter, J. Walter Thompson, London, 1960–61. Recipient: *Guardian* award, 1969; Mystery Writers of America Edgar Allan Poe award, 1972. Agent: A. M. Heath, 79 St. Martin's Lane, London, WC2N 4AA; or, Brandt and Brandt, 1501 Broadway, New York, New York 10036, U.S.A. Address: The Hermitage, East Street, Petworth, West Sussex GU28 0AB, England.

Romance and Historical Publications

Novels

The Silence of Herondale. New York, Doubleday, 1964; London, Gollancz, 1965.
The Fortune Hunters. New York, Doubleday, 1965.
Trouble with Product X. London, Gollancz, 1966; as *Beware of the Banquet*, New York, Doubleday, 1966.
Hate Begins at Home. London, Gollancz, 1967; as *Dark Interval*, New York, Doubleday, 1967.
The Ribs of Death. London, Gollancz, 1967; as *The Crystal Crow*, New York, Doubleday, 1968.
The Embroidered Sunset. London, Gollancz, and New York, Doubleday, 1970.
Died on a Rainy Sunday. London, Gollancz, and New York, Holt Rinehart, 1972.
The Butterfly Picnic. London, Gollancz, 1972; as *A Cluster of Separate Sparks*, New York, Doubleday, 1972.
Voices in an Empty House. London, Gollancz, and New York, Doubleday, 1975.
Castle Barebane. London, Gollancz, and New York, Viking Press, 1976.
Last Movement. London, Gollancz, and New York, Doubleday, 1977.
The Five-Minute Marriage. London, Gollancz, 1977; New York, Doubleday, 1978.
The Smile of the Stranger. London, Gollancz, and New York, Doubleday, 1978.
The Lightning Tree. London, Gollancz, 1980; as *The Weeping Ash*, New York, Doubleday, 1980.
The Young Lady from Paris. London, Gollancz, 1982; as *The Girl from Paris*, New York, Doubleday, 1982.
Foul Matter. London, Gollancz, and New York, Doubleday, 1983.
Mansfield Revisited. London, Gollancz, 1984; New York, Doubleday, 1985.
Deception. London, Gollancz, 1987; as *If I Were You*, New York, Doubleday, 1987.
Blackground. London, Gollancz, and New York, Doubleday, 1989.

Short Stories

The Windscreen Weepers and Other Tales of Horror and Suspense. London, Gollancz, 1969.

Other Publications (for children)

Fiction

All You've Ever Wanted and Other Stories. London, Cape, 1953.
More Than You Bargained For and Other Stories. London, Cape, 1955; New York, Abelard Schuman, 1957.
The Kingdom and the Cave. London, Abelard Schuman, 1960; New York, Doubleday, 1974.
The Wolves of Willoughby Chase. London, Cape, 1962; New York, Doubleday, 1963.
Black Hearts in Battersea. New York, Doubleday, 1964; London, Cape, 1965.
Nightbirds on Nantucket. London, Cape, and New York, Doubleday, 1966.
The Whispering Mountain. London, Cape, 1968; New York, Doubleday, 1969.
A Necklace of Raindrops and Other Stories. London, Cape, and New York, Doubleday, 1968.
Armitage, Armitage, Fly Away Home. New York, Doubleday, 1968.
A Small Pinch of Weather and Other Stories. London, Cape, 1969.
Night Fall. London, Macmillan, 1969; New York, Holt Rinehart, 1971.
Smoke from Cromwell's Time and Other Stories. New York, Doubleday, 1970.
The Green Flash and Other Tales of Horror, Suspense, and Fantasy. New York, Holt Rinehart, 1971.
The Cuckoo Tree. London, Cape, and New York, Doubleday, 1971.
All and More. London, Cape, 1971.
A Harp of Fishbones and Other Stories. London, Cape, 1972.
Arabel's Raven. London, BBC Publications, 1972; New York, Doubleday, 1974.
The Escaped Black Mamba. London, BBC Publications, 1973.
All But a Few. London, Penguin, 1974.
The Bread Bin. London, BBC Publications, 1974.
Midnight Is a Place. London, Cape, and New York, Viking Press, 1974.
Not What You Expected: A Collection of Short Stories. New York, Doubleday, 1974.
Mortimer's Tie. London, BBC Publications, 1976.
A Bundle of Nerves: Stories of Horror, Suspense, and Fantasy. London, Gollancz, 1976.
The Faithless Lollybird and Other Stories. London, Cape, 1977; New York, Doubleday, 1978.
The Far Forests: Tales of Romance, Fantasy, and Suspense. New York, Viking Press, 1977.
Go Saddle the Sea. New York, Doubleday, 1977; London, Cape, 1978.
Tale of a One-Way Street and Other Stories. London, Cape, 1978; New York, Doubleday, 1979.
Mice and Mendelson, music by John Sebastian Brown. London, Cape, 1978.
Mortimer and the Sword Excalibur. London, BBC Publications, 1979.
The Spiral Stair. London, BBC Publications, 1979.
A Touch of Chill: Stories of Horror, Suspense, and Fantasy. London, Gollancz, 1979; New York, Delacorte Press, 1980.
Arabel and Mortimer (includes *Mortimer's Tie, The Spiral Stair, Mortimer and the Sword Excalibur*). London, Cape, 1980; New York, Doubleday, 1981.
The Shadow Guests. London, Cape, and New York, Delacorte Press, 1980.

Mortimer's Portrait on Glass. London, Hodder and Stoughton, 1981.

The Stolen Lake. London, Cape, and New York, Delacorte Press, 1981.

The Mystery of Mr. Jones's Disappearing Taxi. London, Hodder and Stoughton, 1982.

A Whisper in the Night: Stories of Horror, Suspense, and Fantasy. London, Gollancz, 1982; New York, Delacorte Press, 1984.

Mortimer's Cross. London, Cape, 1983; New York, Harper, 1984.

Bridle the Wind. London, Cape, and New York, Delacorte Press, 1983.

The Kitchen Warriors. London, BBC Publications, 1983.

Up the Chimney Down. London, Cape, and New York, Harper, 1984.

Fog Hounds, Wind Cat, Sea Mice. London, Macmillan, 1984.

Mortimer Says Nothing and Other Stories. London, Cape, 1985; New York, Harper, 1987.

The Last Slice of Rainbow and Other Stories. London, Cape, 1985; New York, Harper, 1988.

Dido and Pa. London, Cape, and New York, Delacorte Press, 1986.

Past Eight O'Clock: Goodnight Stories. London, Cape, 1986.

A Goose on Your Grave. London, Gollancz, 1987.

The Moon's Revenge. London, Cape, and New York, Knopf, 1987.

The Teeth of the Gale. London, Cape, and New York, Harper, 1988.

The Erl King's Daughter. London, Heinemann, 1988.

Voices. London, Hippo, 1988.

Give Yourself a Fright: Thirteen Tales of the Supernatural. New York, Delacorte Press, 1989.

Plays

Winterthing, music by John Sebastian Brown (produced Albany, New York, 1977). New York, Holt Rinehart, 1972; included in *Winterthing, and The Mooncusser's Daughter*, 1973.

Winterthing, and The Mooncusser's Daughter, music by John Sebastian Brown. London, Cape, 1973; *The Mooncusser's Daughter* published separately, New York, Viking Press, 1974.

Street, music by John Sebastian Brown, (produced London, 1977). New York, Viking Press, 1978.

Moon Mill (produced London, 1982).

Television Plays: *The Dark Streets of Kimballs Green*, 1976; *The Apple of Trouble*, 1977; *Midnight Is a Place* (serial), from her own story, 1977; *The Rose of Puddle Fratrum*, 1978; *Armitage, Armitage, Fly Away Home*, from her own story, 1978.

Verse

The Skin Spinners. New York, Viking Press, 1976.

Other

The Kingdom under the Sea and Other Stories (retellings). London, Cape, 1971.

The Way to Write for Children (for adults). London, Elm Tree, 1982; New York, St. Martin's Press, 1983.

Translator, *The Angel Inn*, by Contessa de Ségur. London, Cape, 1976; Owings Mills, Maryland, Stemmer House, 1978.

*

Joan Aiken comments:

I first began reading romantic and gothic fiction professionally in the 1950's when I was working for an English publishing firm, Amalgamated Press, which in its various magazines (*Woman's Journal, Argosy, Suspense, Woman & Home*) used a number of writers such as Charlotte Armstrong, Dorothy Eden, Mary Stewart, Mignon G. Eberhart. I became interested in the gothic/suspense form and, encouraged by my agent, Jean LeRoy (who wrote a useful little manual *Sell Them a Story*, in which, among other things, she urged would-be gothic writers to study *Jane Eyre* as a model), I decided to try my hand at the genre. My first attempt, *House of Shadows*, never got finished (that title has been used several times since, though) but my next, *Hit and Run*, was used serially in *Suspense*, and several others appeared serially in *Everywoman*. At this time a children's book of mine had been sold to the American publishers, Doubleday, whose Crime Club editor, Isabelle Taylor, asked if I had any adult fiction. I showed her my serialised stories and she encouraged me to extend them into full-length novels, which were published as *Hate Begins at Home*, *The Silence of Herondale*, etc. As the gothic market then began to be somewhat saturated I tried my hand at Regency romances, but I still prefer the classic gothic and wish it had not been so over-used. However as this is the case I propose to stick to domestic suspense for my next books.

*   *   *

The very fecundity of her ideas makes Joan Aiken's books difficult to summarize, or indeed to categorize. One of those authors who writes both contemporary gothics and historical romances, Aiken ornaments her conceits with more purely literary skill than many other romance writers. Yet at some point in almost all of her books she seems to skirt, or even fall over, the edge of absurdity. This willingness to take risks, if that is what it is to be called, is one of the most characteristic elements of the Aiken style. For instance, in *Last Movement* Mike Meiklejohn learns the terrible secret about her missing father: following a sex change operation, (s)he is now a prominent Irish soprano. This element of the fantastically improbable, as opposed to the merely unearthly fantastic (forebodings, dreams that foretell the future, haunted houses occur in Aiken's novels), makes Mike laugh when she first hears it; a purely nervous reaction, she claims. But may not the reader, too, laugh? Aiken's fantasies for children are full of this kind of improbability, which is what gives them their air of light-hearted charm. It does not always blend as successfully with the more serious, terrifying, and, sometimes, erotic matter of her adult books.

Aiken's technical virtuosity also shows in her unwillingness to be bound to a simple narrative formula. Several books—*Last Movement*, *The Weeping Ash*—alternate chapters from different viewpoints. An encounter will be described, perhaps, in a third-person narrative focusing on one character's feelings; then a first-person account shows the episode from a different point of view. In *The Weeping Ash* the story goes back and forth between two sets of characters in different continents whose lives are connected as they gradually approach the moment when their paths will converge and the conflicts that exist among them will be settled. In *Voices in an Empty House*, which is possibly more a straight novel than a romance/gothic, this technique is overlaid with multiple flashbacks that explore the relationships between a man, his ex-wife, her dead first husband, and her son, as the man desperately tries to find his step-son to persuade him to undergo crucial heart surgery.

There is nothing unusual in one of Aiken's characters needing surgery: a strong element in her style is her intense interest in physical illness. From Lucy's heart condition in *The Embroidered Sunset* to Mrs. Carteret's frailness and invalidism in *The Five-Minute Marriage*, there is always someone with a serious ailment. This is not mere soap opera. The conditions and consequences of disease play a significant role in the novels. More specifically, many of the ailments involve periods of amnesia. Thomas in *Voices in an Empty House*, Annette in *The Fortune Hunters*, and Caroline in *Hate Begins at Home* are all inconvenienced to some extent and even endangered by their frustrating bouts of amnesia. Scylla in *The Weeping Ash* is semi-conscious for long periods; her brother Cal has epilepsy; their cousin by marriage Fanny has spells that she cannot explain to her domineering and brutal husband.

The Weeping Ash is also an example of Aiken's use of recurrent characters. The benefactor of Fanny's husband is the same Juliana who escaped from the French Revolution by a daring balloon flight in *The Smile of the Stranger*. Juliana herself does not appear in the second book, but some of the other characters from *The Smile of the Stranger* do. Mike Meiklejohn's wooer in *Last Movement* is the ebullient Dr. Adnan who had loved and lost Lucy in *The Embroidered Sunset*.

Children bring out a tenderness in Aiken; even a young infant in *Trouble with Product X* can win hearts. But she can also sacrifice them to the exigencies of her plot; two children die in *Hate Begins at Home*. So the threat to a young child and her infant brother keeps nerves taut in *Died on a Rainy Sunday*. Aside from young children, warm family relationships are almost nonexistent. Only peripheral characters are allowed normal families. The heroines are confined to mothers who are neglectful (*The Ribs of Death*), malignant (*The Smile of the Stranger*), or, at best, dead at an early age (*Died on a Rainy Sunday*). Siblings are usually equally hostile, although the twins Scylla and Cal in *The Weeping Ash* are a rare exception.

Another notable facet of Aiken's style is her sense of place: the isle of Dendros in *Last Movement*, the island of Manhattan in *Voices in an Empty House*, India in *The Weeping Ash* are all actual presences in the stories, seeming at times to come alive as characters in their own right.

Although Aiken has ambitions beyond the gothic, her own wayward imagination keeps the novels at genre level. Her spiky, independent heroines, capable in their careers, nonetheless fall helplessly in love with the wrong person and only free themselves after bizarre struggles, sometimes to find happiness, sometimes just to find the endurance to continue the struggle (*The Ribs of Death*, for example, has an inconclusive ending). Yet her gripping, sensitive style transcends formulas; her well-rounded characters and strong plots carry the reader with her.

—Susan Branch

AINSWORTH, Harriet. See **CADELL, Elizabeth.**

AINSWORTH, Patricia. Pseudonym for Patricia Nina Bigg. Australian. Born in Adelaide, South Australia, 20 March 1932. Educated at Technical High School, Adelaide. Married Robert Bigg in 1955; two sons. Secretary, Commonwealth Trading Bank, 1948–51, and G. R. Wills and Company Ltd., 1952–55, both Adelaide. Address: 3/2 Lorraine Avenue, Mitcham, South Australia 5062, Australia.

ROMANCE AND HISTORICAL PUBLICATIONS

Novels

The Flickering Candle. London, Hale, 1968.
The Candle Rekindled. London, Hale, 1969.
Steady Burns the Candle. London, Hale, 1970.
The Devil's Hole. London, Hale, 1971.
Portrait in Gold. London, Hale, 1971.
A String of Silver Beads. London, Hale, 1972.
The Bridal Lamp. London, Hale, 1975.
The Enchanted Cup. London, Hale, 1980.

*   *   *

The first three novels by Patricia Ainsworth are set in 17th-century England, following the fortunes of the owners of two country estates. In *The Flickering Candle* the main protagonists are Frances Faraday and the Earl of Debenham, and the story describes the growth of their relationship against the background of the outbreak of the Civil War. *The Candle Rekindled* takes up the story 12 years later during the Protectorate, and *Steady Burns the Candle* is set another five years later at the start of the reign of Charles II; some of the characters reappear 15 years on in *The Enchanted Cup*. The novels are light-weight in construction, with no real substance to the characters, and lack a strong story-line. Ainsworth's handling of the historical period involved is also shaky, with details that obtrude rather than blending in. *The Devil's Hole* is more successful, possibly because it is set in the author's native Australia. The background of the early colonial days around 1877 is well described, with feeling for the beauties of the Australian coast, but despite tighter construction, more rounded characters and more realistic dialogue, the pace again is slow and the dramatic sequences not handled quite as well as they could be. *Portrait in Gold* is also set in the Australian colony of Victoria, and the fevered days of the gold-rush are depicted with an authentic period flavour. With *A String of Silver Beads* and *The Bridal Lamp*, the author returns to historical England. The former book is set in the year of the Armada, and tells the story of Crispin Wynwood's reluctance to take up his inheritance, and his troubled romance with Felice Averil: the narrative is better controlled, although the final denouement is a little too far-fetched. In *The Bridal Lamp*, again set in Charles II's reign, drama of a different kind is introduced when Carey suspects her husband of trying to kill her.

Although details of setting and historical period are based on research and create a colourful background, particularly to the later books, Ainsworth cannot quite control her narrative well enough to sustain the dramatic pace and keep up suspense: the development of her characters also suffers from weak handling and many of her protagonists do not mature sufficiently to gain credibility as individuals.

—Tessa Rose Chester

AIRLIE, Catherine. See **MacLEOD, Jean S.**

ALBANESI, Madame (Effie Adelaide Maria Albanesi, née Henderson). Also wrote as Effie Rowlands. British. Born in 1859. Married Le Chevalier Carlo Albanesi (died 1926); one daughter. *Died 16 October 1936.*

ROMANCE AND HISTORICAL PUBLICATIONS

Novels

Margery Daw (published anonymously). London, Stevens, and New York, Munro, 1886.
The Blunder of an Innocent. London, Sands, 1899.
Peter, A Parasite. London, Sands, 1901.
Brave Barbara. New York, Street and Smith, 1901.
Love and Louisa. London, Sands, and Philadelphia, Lippincott, 1902.
Susannah and One Elder. London, Methuen, 1903; as *Susannah and One Other*, Methuen, and New York, McClure, 1904.
Capricious Caroline. London, Methuen, 1904.
Marian Sax. London, Hurst and Blackett, 1905.
The Brown Eyes of Mary. London, Methuen, 1905.
Sweet William. London, Hodder and Stoughton, 1906.
I Know a Maiden. London, Methuen, 1906.
A Little Brown Mouse. London, Hodder and Stoughton, 1906.
A Young Man from the Country. London, Hurst and Blackett, 1906.
Love-in-a-Mist. London, Hodder and Stoughton, 1907.
The Strongest of All Things. London, Hurst and Blackett, 1907.
Simple Simon. London, Newnes, 1907.
Sister Anne. London, Hodder and Stoughton, 1908.
The Rose of Yesterday. London, Hodder and Stoughton, 1908.
Drusilla's Point of View. London, Hurst and Blackett, 1908.
Pretty Polly Pennington. London, Collins, 1908; as *Sweet and Lovely*, 1933.
The Forbidden Road. New York, Cupples and Leon, 1908.
The Laughter of Life. New York, Cupples and Leon, 1908.
The Invincible Amelia; or The Polite Adventuress. London, Methuen, 1909.
A Question of Quality. London, Hurst and Blackett, 1909.
Envious Eliza. London, Nash, 1909.
The Marriage of Margaret. London, Pearson, 1909.
The Glad Heart. London, Methuen, 1910.
For Love of Anne Lambert. London, Pearson, 1910.
Maisie's Romance. London, Pearson, 1910.
A Wonder of Love. London, Stanley Paul, 1911.
Poppies in the Corn. London, Hutchinson, 1911.
Heart of His Heart. London, Stanley Paul, 1911.
Olivia Mary. London, Methuen, 1912.
The Beloved Enemy. London, Methuen, 1913.
One of the Crowd. London, Chapman and Hall, 1913.
Cissy. London, Collins, 1913.
The Cap of Youth. London, Hutchinson, 1914.
The Sunlit Hills. London, Hutchinson, 1914.
Hearts and Sweethearts. London, Hutchinson, 1916.
When Michael Came to Town. London, Hutchinson, 1917.
Truant Happiness. London, Ward Lock, 1918.
Diana Falls in Love. London, Ward Lock, 1919.
Tony's Wife. London, Holden and Hardingham, 1919; as *Punch and Judy*, London, Hardingham, 1919.
Patricia and Life. London, Ward Lock, 1920.
The House That Jane Built. London, Ward Lock, 1921.
Roseanne, London, Collins, 1922.
Truth in a Circle. London, Collins, 1922.
A Bird in a Storm. London, Collins, 1924.
Sally in Her Alley. London, Collins, 1925.

The Shadow Wife. London, Stanley Paul, 1925.
Sally Gets Married. London, Collins, 1927.
The Green Country. London, Ward Lock, 1927.
The Moon Through Glass. London, Collins, 1928.
Claire and Circumstances. London, Collins, 1928; as *In Love with Claire*, 1932.
Gold in the Dust. London, Ward Lock, 1929.
A Heart for Sale. London, Ward Lock, 1929.
The Clear Stream. London, Ward Lock, 1930.
Loyalty. London, Collins, 1930.
The Courage of Love. London, Ward Lock, 1930.
White Flame. London, Ward Lock, 1930.
Coloured Lights. London, Ward Lock, 1931.
All's Well with the World. London, Ward Lock, 1932.
The Moon of Romance. London, Ward Lock, 1932.
Snow in Summer. London, Ward Lock, 1932.
A Star in the Dark. London, Ward Lock, 1933.
White Branches. London, Ward Lock, 1933.
Through the Mist. London, Ward Lock, 1934.
The Half Open Door. London, Ward Lock, 1934.
An Unframed Portrait. London, Nicholson and Watson, 1935.
As a Man Loves. London, Ward Lock, 1936.
The Hidden Gift. London, Nicholson and Watson, 1936.
A Leaf Turned Down. London, Ward Lock, 1936.
The Little Lady. London, Ward Lock, 1937.
The Love That Lives. London, Mellifont Press, 1937.
The One Who Counted. London, Ward Lock, 1937.

Novels as Effie Rowlands

The Spell of Ursula. Philadelphia, Lippincott, 1894.
The Woman Who Came Between. London, Pearson, 1895; New York, Street and Smith, n.d.
At Great Cost. New York, Bonner, 1895.
Little Kit. New York, Bonner, 1895.
A Faithful Traitor. London, Stevens, and Philadelphia, Lippincott, 1896.
The Fault of One. London, Kegan Paul, and Philadelphia, Lippincott, 1897.
The Kingdom of a Heart. London and New York, Routledge, 1899.
They Laugh That Win. London and New York, Routledge, 1899.
A Woman Scorned. New York, Street and Smith, 1899.
A King and a Coward. New York, Street and Smith, 1899; London, Hodder and Stoughton, 1912.
Little Lady Charles. New York, Street and Smith, 1899; London, Stanley Paul, 1910.
The Heart of Hetta. Chicago, Laird and Lee, 1900.
Husband and Foe. New York, Street and Smith, 1900; London, Hutchinson, 1911.
Beneath a Spell. New York, Street and Smith, 1900; London, Stanley Paul, 1910.
A Charity Girl. New York, Street and Smith, 1900; London, Stanley Paul, 1911.
The Man She Loved. New York, Street and Smith, 1900; London, Ward Lock, 1911.
One Man's Evil. New York, Street and Smith, 1900; London, Newnes, 1910.
For Ever True. New York, Street and Smith, 1904; London, Hodder and Stoughton, 1910.
A Love Almost Lost. London, Henderson, 1905.
Angel of Evil. New York, Street and Smith, 1905.
Her Husband and Her Love. New York, Street and Smith, 1905.
So Like a Man. New York, Street and Smith, 1905.

The Splendid Man. New York, Street and Smith, 1905.
The Wiles of a Siren. New York, Street and Smith, 1906.
The End Crowns All. New York, Street and Smith, 1906; London, Hutchinson, 1910.
A Shadowed Happiness. New York, Street and Smith, 1906; London, Newnes, 1910.
For Love of Sigrid. New York, Street and Smith, 1906.
Love's Greatest Gift. New York, Street and Smith, 1906; as *The White in the Black* (as Madame Albanesi), London, Collins, 1926.
My Lady of Dreadwood. New York, Street and Smith, 1906.
A Wife's Triumph. New York, Street and Smith, 1906.
Pretty Penelope. London, Cassell, 1907.
Her Punishment. London, Hurst and Blackett, 1910.
The Man She Married. London, Stanley Paul, 1910.
After Many Days. London, Newnes, 1910.
Contrary Mary. London, Hodder and Stoughton, 1910.
A Dangerous Woman. London, Ward Lock, 1910.
For Love of Speranza. London, Hodder and Stoughton, 1910.
The Game of Life. London, Ward Lock, 1910.
Her Heart's Longing. London, Hurst and Blackett, 1910.
Her Kingdom. London, Amalgamated Press, 1910.
John Galbraith's Wife. London, Hodder and Stoughton, 1910.
Love for Love. London, Hodder and Stoughton, 1910.
A Loyal Man's Love. London, Newnes, 1910.
The Master of Lynch Towers. London, Hodder and Stoughton, 1910.
The Mistress of the Farm. London, Newnes, 1910.
Bitter Sweet. London, Newnes, 1910.
A Splendid Destiny. London, Stanley Paul, 1910.
Barbara's Love Story. London, Hodder and Stoughton, 1911.
Brave Heart. London, Amalgamated Press, 1911.
Carlton's Wife. London, Ward Lock, 1911.
Dare and Do. London, Stanley Paul, 1911.
False Faith. London, Amalgamated Press, 1911.
For Ever and a Day. London, Amalgamated Press, 1911.
A Girl with a Heart. London, Ward Lock, 1911.
Her Mistake. London, Amalgamated Press, 1911.
Leila Vane's Burden. London, Amalgamated Press, 1911.
A Life's Love. London, Hodder and Stoughton, 1911.
Love's Harvest. London, Amalgamated Press, 1911.
The Madness of Love. London, Hodder and Stoughton, 1911.
The Man at the Gate. London, Amalgamated Press, 1911.
The One Woman. London, Hodder and Stoughton, 1911.
The Power of Love. London, Amalgamated Press, 1911.
Splendid Love. London, Amalgamated Press, 1911.
White Abbey. London, Stanley Paul, 1911.
A Wild Rose. London, Amalgamated Press, 1911.
A Woman Worth Winning. London, Amalgamated Press, 1911.
A Woman's Heart. London, Hodder and Stoughton, 1911.
The Young Wife. London, Hodder and Stoughton, 1911.
Love's Fire. London, Hutchinson, 1911.
The Triumph of Love. London, Pearson, 1911.
On the Wings of Fate. New York, Street and Smith, n.d.; London, Newnes, 1916.
Andrew Leicester's Love. New York, Street and Smith, n.d.
Carla. New York, Street and Smith, n.d.
Change of Heart. New York, Street and Smith, n.d.
False and True. New York, Street and Smith, n.d.
For Love and Honor. New York, Street and Smith, n.d.
The Girl's Kingdom. New York, Street and Smith, n.d.
Interloper. Chicago, Donohue, n.d.
Kinsman's Sin. New York, Street and Smith, n.d.
Love's Cruel Whim. New York, Street and Smith, n.d.
Selina's Love Story. New York, Street and Smith, n.d.
Siren's Heart. New York, Street and Smith, n.d.

Spurned Proposal. New York, Street and Smith, n.d.
Temptation of Mary Barr. New York, Street and Smith, n.d.
Tempted by Love. New York, Street and Smith, n.d.
With Heart So True. New York, Street and Smith, n.d.
Woman Against Her. New York, Street and Smith, n.d.
Woman Against Woman. New York, Street and Smith, n.d.
Woman Scorned. New York, Street and Smith, n.d.
A Golden Dawn. London, Hodder and Stoughton, 1912.
A Heart's Triumph. London, Hodder and Stoughton, 1912; New York, Street and Smith, n.d.
Hester Trefusis. London, Hurst and Blackett, 1912.
The House of Sunshine. London, Stanley Paul, 1912.
In Love's Land. London, Ward Lock, 1912.
A Love Match. London, Amalgamated Press, 1912.
The Love of His Life. London, Stanley Paul, 1912.
The Rose of Life. London, Ward Lock, 1912.
Temptation. London, Newnes, 1912.
To Love and to Cherish. London, Everett, 1912.
The Wooing of Rose. London, Stanley Paul, 1912.
His One Love. London, Hurst and Blackett, 1912.
Lavender's Love Story. London, Hurst and Blackett, 1912.
Love Wins. London, Hurst and Blackett, 1912.
A Modern Witch. London, Hurst and Blackett, 1912.
Beth Mason. London, Hodder and Stoughton, 1913.
Elsie Brant's Romance. London, Cassell, 1913.
Hearts at War. London, Hurst and Blackett, 1913.
The Joy of Life. London, Cassell, 1913.
Lady Patricia's Faith. London, Hodder and Stoughton, 1913.
Love's Mask. London, Stanley Paul, 1913.
Margaret Dent. London, Cassell, 1913.
Ruth's Romance. London, Hodder and Stoughton, 1913.
Stranger Than Truth. London, Hodder and Stoughton, 1913.
The Surest Bond. London, Cassell, 1913.
Through Weal and Through Woe. London, Ward Lock, 1913.
In Daffodil Time. London, Pearson, 1913.
The Heart of a Woman. London, Pearson, 1913.
Judged by Fate. London, Hurst and Blackett, 1913.
The Hand of Fate. London, Hodder and Stoughton, 1914.
Her Husband. London, Chatto and Windus, 1914.
An Irish Lover. London, Hodder and Stoughton, 1914.
Money or Wife? London, Ward Lock, 1914.
On the High Road. London, Hurst and Blackett, 1914.
Two Waifs. London, Hodder and Stoughton, 1914.
At Her Mercy. London, Pearson, 1914.
The Price Paid. London, Chatto and Windus, 1914.
Prudence Langford's Ordeal. London, Pearson, 1914.
Love's Young Dream. London, Ward Lock, 1914.
Above All Things. London, Newnes, 1915.
Sunset and Dawn. London, Ward Lock, 1915.
The Woman's Fault. London, Hurst and Blackett, 1915.
The Girl Who Was Brave. London, Pearson, 1916.
The Splendid Friend. London, Hutchinson, 1917.
The Heart of Angela Brent. London, Pearson, 1917.
A Strange Love Story. London, Hurst and Blackett, 1919.
John Helsby's Wife. London, Hurst and Blackett, 1920.
Mary Dunbar's Love. London, Pearson, 1921.
Against the World. London, Pearson, 1923.
The Flame of Love. London, Ward Lock, 1923.
The Garland of Youth. London, Ward Lock, 1923.
Young Hearts. London, Ward Lock, 1924.
The Life Line. London, Hodder and Stoughton, 1924.
Real Gold. London, Hodder and Stoughton, 1924.
Out of a Clear Sky. London, Ward Lock, 1925.
The Way of Youth. London, Hodder and Stoughton, 1925.
Brave Love. London, Ward Lock, 1926.
A Bunch of Blue Ribbons. London, Ward Lock, 1926.

Lady Feo's Daughter. London, Hodder and Stoughton, 1926.
The Gates of Happiness. London, Ward Lock, 1927.
A Man from the West. London, Ward Lock, 1927.
Fateful Promise. New York, Street and Smith, n.d.
Her Golden Secret. New York, Street and Smith, n.d.
Hero for Love's Sake. New York, Street and Smith, n.d.
Unhappy Bargain. New York, Street and Smith, n.d.
Fine Feathers. London, Ward Lock, 1928.
Lights and Shadows. London, Ward Lock, 1928.
Spring in the Heart. London, Ward Lock, 1929.
While Faith Endures. London, Ward Lock, 1929.
Coulton's Wife. London, Ward Lock, 1930.
Dorinda's Lovers. London, Wright and Brown, 1930.
The Fighting Spirit. London, Ward Lock, 1930.
Sunlight Beyond. London, Ward Lock, 1930.
Wings of Chance. London, Ward Lock, 1931.
Princess Charming. London, Wright and Brown, 1931.
Green Valleys. London, Wright and Brown, 1932.
The Laughter of Life. London, Ward Lock, 1932; New York,
  Cupples and Leon, n.d.
A Loyal Defence. London, Ward Lock, 1932.
A Ministering Angel. London, Ward Lock, 1933.
Frances Fights for Herself. London, Ward Lock, 1934.
A School for Hearts. London, Ward Lock, 1934.
A World of Dreams. London, Ward Lock, 1935.
The One Who Paid. London, Ward Lock, 1935.
The Heart Line. London, Ward Lock, 1936.
The Lamp of Friendship. London, Ward Lock, 1936.
Her Father's Wish. London, Ward Lock, 1937.
The Top of the Tree. London, Ward Lock, 1937.

OTHER PUBLICATIONS

Other

Meggie Albanesi. London, Hodder and Stoughton, 1928.

* * *

The upper-class Edwardian's concern for physical comfort and material value is well illustrated by Madame Albanesi's *Temptation* (published under the name Effie Rowlands), in which a young orphaned girl, destitute and starving, is offered a life of ease if she succumbs to the temptation of impersonating a missing heiress, and thus eventually securing for herself marriage to the local squire. The moral, far from suggesting that love brings its own rewards, or that girls who sell their souls risk their lives for material gain will endure a fate worse than death, seems to be the reverse: that ill-gotten gains bring you "all the luxury of appointment that is so necessary and so very ordinary to the very rich."

Albanesi's style is marked by lavish use of the exclamation mark, and the repetition of key words: "Alone in the world! Alone! With only seventeen years of life behind her! She, poor little soul, was alone! Quite-quite alone!" Heroes are sometimes "stained with shame," a blot on their character which can only be lifted by the true love of a good lady (not woman).

During her long career, Albanesi produced over 200 novels, all variations on true-love-with-complications, though none with any marked note of religious, political, or moral quest. There is more than a suggestion that the state of being in love brings in its wake not only mortal happiness but material good fortune too. If a girl's love is true, she will marry the right man, and continue to be rich and happy for the rest of her life. Although many of her titles contain "Love"—*Love's Harvest, Love for*

Love, Brave Love, The Love of His Life, The Flame of Love, The Man She Loved, etc.—there is surprisingly very little kissing. Some of her heroines avoid the kiss by fainting. Others faint anyway: "She gave a low cry, and stretched out her hands. She reeled forward, struggled a little, and then, catching impotently at a chair as she fell, she sank huddled and unconscious."

Albanesi would have shared with a publisher's reader of the time a thorough appreciation of the "eternal importance of love in the financial and popular success of a novel." However, occasionally she branched out from love. *The Clear Stream*, for example, is a family saga, about Marcella Dolamore and her many children; and *An Irish Lover*, although not strictly a hospital romance, contains some details about nurses in the home (circa 1914), and curious notes about home-nursing methods of those days. For instance, that one important item towards helping save the life of Henry is to keep the sound of passing traffic deadened by having straw placed on the street. The ensuing silence, combined with nurse Rachel's miraculous (though unexplained) nursing power, restores his health.

What is most astonishing about Madame Albanesi is how she managed to produce over 200 novels during her career, at a time when the electric tape-recorder had not yet been invented.

—Rachel Anderson

_____

ALEXANDER, Donna. See **VITEK, Donna.**

_____

ALLARDYCE, Paula. See **BLACKSTOCK, Charity.**

_____

ALLEN, Barbara. See **STUART, Vivian.**

_____

ALLEN, Charlotte Vale. Also writes as Claire Vincent. Canadian. Born in Toronto, Ontario, 19 January 1941. Educated at Harbord Collegiate and Northview Heights Collegiate, Toronto. Married 1) Walter Allen in 1970 (divorced 1976), one daughter; 2) Barrie Baldaro in 1980 (divorced 1982). Actress and singer, London, 1961–64, Toronto, 1964–66, and in the United States, 1966–70. Agent: Harold Ober Associates Inc., 40 East 49th Street, New York, New York, 10017; or, David Higham Associates Ltd., 5–8 Lower John Street London W1R 4HA, England. Address: 144 Rowayton Woods Drive, Norwalk, Connecticut 06854, U.S.A.

ROMANCE AND HISTORICAL PUBLICATIONS

Novels

Hidden Meanings. New York, Warner, 1976; London, New English Library, 1983.
Love Life. New York, Delacorte Press, 1976; London, New English Library, 1981.
Sweeter Music. New York, Warner, 1976.
Another Kind of Magic. New York, Warner, 1977.

Becoming. New York, Warner, 1977.

Gentle Stranger. New York, Warner, 1977.

Mixed Emotions. New York, Warner, 1977.

Running Away. New York, New American Library, 1977; London, Magnum, 1979.

Believing in Giants (as Claire Vincent). New York, New American Library, 1978; as Charlotte Vale Allen, London, New English Library, 1983; as *Memories*, New York, Berkley, 1983.

Gifts of Love. New York, New American Library, 1978; London, Magnum, 1980.

Julia's Sister. New York, Warner, 1978; London, New English Library, 1985.

Meet Me in Time. New York, Warner, 1978; London, New English Library, 1980.

Acts of Kindness. New York, New American Library, 1979; London, New English Library, 1982.

Moments of Meaning. New York, New American Library, 1979; London, New English Library, 1982.

Times of Triumph. New York, New American Library, 1979; London, New English Library, 1980.

Promises. New York, Dutton, and London, Hutchinson, 1980.

The Marmalade Man. New York, Dutton, 1981; as *Destinies*, London, Hutchinson, 1981.

Perfect Fools. New York, New American Library, 1981.

Intimate Friends. New York, Dutton, and London, Hutchinson, 1983.

Pieces of Dreams. London, Hutchinson, 1984; Boston, Hall, 1985.

Matters of the Heart. London, Hutchinson, 1985.

Time/Steps. New York, Atheneum, 1986; London, Weidenfeld and Nicolson, 1987.

Illusions. New York, Atheneum, and London, Weidenfeld and Nicolson, 1987.

Dream Train. New York, Atheneum, 1988.

Night Magic. New York, Atheneum, 1989.

OTHER PUBLICATIONS

Other

Daddy's Girl (autobiography). New York, Wyndham, 1980; London, New English Library, 1983.

*   *   *

Charlotte Vale Allen's people seem to live lives of hardly-controlled hysteria, at a higher pitch than normal. Like the nameless little girl of the nursery rhyme, "when they are good, they are very, very good, and when they are bad, they are *horrid*."

It is her "horrid" characters who seem to have got out of control; they are creatures motivated as far as one can tell solely by malice. Frances Holden in *Matters of the Heart* is obsessive; in love almost demonic; chilly to her pathetic daughter Hadleigh, who so patently craves the affection that is never forthcoming, even though her mother will spring like a tigress to protect her if the need arises. Frances is approachable only through her granddaughter Bonita, who by virtue of the role she must play bears an unfortunate resemblance to those problem-solving moppets of television who always know so much more than their elders.

More moving, because so much more believable, is the plight of Caley Burrell, heroine of *Pieces of Dreams*. Hideously deformed in a motor accident, Caley is doing her best against dreadful odds to put her life back into some kind of order. If the partial solution to her tragic, irremediable situation is a little too pat, she at least carries the reader's affectionate sympathy into her new relationship with Martin, a man with crippling emotional problems of his own.

Allen's heroines are often faced with calamitous bolts from the blue, such as Caley's accident, or the traumatically shocking experience of Lynne Craig in *Intimate Friends*, who unsuspectingly enters her home to discover the dead body of her husband, a suicide victim, who has not so much as left a note of explanation or farewell.

Readers of Allen's painful autobiographical work *Daddy's Girl* know that the author was the victim of her father's sexual abuse. Small wonder that so many of her novels include characters whose memories of childhood are, like her own, horrific.

Sarah and Simon are *Perfect Fools*. She, with his help, is slowly overcoming the trauma of a hideous childhood as the rejected "closet" child of a beautiful, cruel mother who kept her daughter's very existence a secret. Her physically flawed daughter is kept locked in her room, and is at last freed only by the mother's sudden death in an air raid. Then an unlikely deliverer, Simon, breezes into her introspective adult life, insists on giving Sarah a new appearance, and encourages her to have the operation that will correct her deformity. Pygmalion and Galatea fall in love in classic style: but this Pygmalion is bisexual. Can a marriage sustain the stresses two fools of love put upon it?

In *Time/Steps* lovely Beatrice Crane has struggled up from a penniless and neglected childhood in the slums all the way to Hollywood stardom, in the heady days when stars *were* stars, and expected to twinkle in the firmament, untouched by human hands. Life is all roses, until Bea becomes pregnant by her life-long love Bobby, another climbing star. Their studio bosses offer her an ugly choice—have an abortion or forget about her career. Shortly thereafter, a jealous and unsuccessful former dancing partner inflicts crippling injuries upon her. It seems that her career is over after all. A marriage, lacking in passion but full of kindness and consideration, proves to be her salvation. Eventually a child is born, but in a vicious twist of fate, her darling daughter proves to be the scourge of Bea's life. *Time/Steps* is the story of the castigation of talent by spiteful mediocrity.

So it goes on, in novel after novel. Allen's people continually behave extravagantly: a "good" sister sacrifices her life to a thankless "bad" sister to honour a promise made to their father; a married woman of enormous wealth and beauty pines after a rotter; a brief trip on the Orient Express becomes a seething cauldron of tangled loves and long-buried resentments; an air-flight inspired fling that has had deep significance to one partner means little more than a one-night stand to the other, precipitating tragic consequences.

Allen's agonized heroines are usually faced with a choice between at least two attractive, sophisticated, dedicated suitors, none of whom ever raises any objection to the continued successful and exciting career of the glamorous loved one. What her women do *not* have to face, ever, are the drab, dreary problems that beset most women's lives—unglamorous and poorly-paid work, aging, and loneliness—which is why those who *do* daily battle with these dragons willingly escape into her highly coloured, hectic world of accident-prone, endlessly romantic love.

—Joan McGrath

ALLEN, (William) Hervey (Jr.). American. Born in Pittsburgh, Pennsylvania, 8 December 1889. Educated at Shady Side

Academy; United States Naval Academy, Annapolis, Maryland, 1910–11; University of Pittsburgh, B.Sc. 1915 (Phi Beta Kappa); Harvard University, Cambridge, Massachusetts, 1920–22. Served in the Pennsylvania National Guard, 1916, and in the United States infantry in France, 1917–18; served with the War Manpower Commission during World War II. Married Ann Hyde Andrew in 1927; two daughters and one son. Worked for Bell Telephone Company, 1915; English teacher, Porter Military Academy, Charleston, South Carolina, 1920–21, and Charleston High School, 1922–24; lecturer, Columbia University, New York, 1924–25, Vassar College, Poughkeepsie, New York, 1926–27, and Bread Loaf School, Vermont, 1930–31. Staff member, *Saturday Review*, New York. Member of the Board of Governors, St. John's College, Annapolis; trustee, University of Miami. Litt.D.: University of Pittsburgh, 1934; Washington and Jefferson College, Washington, Pennsylvania, 1947. Member, American Academy, and Royal Society of Arts. *Died 28 December 1949.*

ROMANCE AND HISTORICAL PUBLICATIONS

Novels

Anthony Adverse. New York, Farrar and Rinehart, 1933; London, Gollancz, 1934.
Action at Aquila. New York, Farrar and Rinehart, and London, Gollancz, 1938.
The City in the Dawn. New York, Rinehart, 1950.
  The Forest and the Fort. New York, Farrar and Rinehart, and London, Heinemann, 1943.
  Bedford Village. New York, Farrar and Rinehart, and London, Heinemann, 1944.
  Toward the Morning. New York, Rinehart, 1948.

Short Stories

It Was Like This: Two Stories of the Great War. New York, Farrar and Rinehart, 1940.

OTHER PUBLICATIONS

Verse

Ballads of the Border. Privately printed, 1916.
Wampum and Old Gold. New Haven, Connecticut, Yale University Press, 1921.
Carolina Chansons: Legends of the Low Country, with DuBose Heyward. New York, Macmillan, 1922.
The Bride of Huitzil: An Aztec Legend. New York, Drake, 1922.
Christmas Epithalamium. Privately printed, 1923.
The Blindman: A Ballad of Nogant L'Aartaud. New Haven, Connecticut, Yale University Press, 1923.
Earth Moods and Other Poems. New York, Harper, 1925.
New Legends. New York, Farrar and Rinehart, 1929.
Sarah Simon, Character Atlantean. New York, Doubleday, 1929.
Songs for Annette. New York, Rudge, 1929.

Other

Israfel: The Life and Times of Edgar Allan Poe. New York, Doran, 1926; London, Gollancz, 1935.

Toward the Flame: A War Diary. New York, Doran, 1926; London, Gollancz, 1934.
DuBose Heyward: A Critical and Biographical Sketch. New York, Doran, 1927.

Editor, with others, *Year Book of the Poetry Society of South Carolina 1921–23.* Privately printed, 3 vols., 1921–23.
Editor, with Thomas Ollive Mabbott, *Poe's Brother: The Poems of William Henry Leonard Poe.* New York, Doran, 1926.
Editor, *The Works of Edgar Allan Poe.* New York, Black 1927.
Editor, *The Best Known Works of Edgar Allan Poe.* New York, Blue Ribbon, 1931.

*

Manuscript Collection: Hillman Library, University of Pittsburgh, Pennsylvania.

*   *   *

Before the sprawling historical novel had become a bestselling commonplace, Hervey Allen's *Anthony Adverse* seemed a revolutionary creation. One huge work, it contained three volumes: each volume made up of three books, and, after all, an epilogue: it was of a breadth unheard of since the palmy days of the Victorian three-decker, and all to tell the story of a single adventurous life.

Allen was a storyteller who assumed the indulgence as well as the interest of a patient audience. He digressed to offer tendentious opinions, to discourse upon the scenery of Europe, Africa, and the New World, to say nothing of the open seas; to wax lyrical, toss in snippets of poems, epitaphs culled from tombstones, proverbs, and trivia of all sorts. The continuity of his story is tenuous at best, and the hero's character does not so much develop as alter with chameleon rapidity from one episode to the next. From the opening chapters in which Anthony's ill-starred parents Maria and Denis have their brief, glorious affair and provoke the undying vengance of Maria's cuckolded husband Don Luis, to the end of the marathon story, Anthony careens from destitution to enormous wealth and back again. He has at least three great loves in his life, as well as numerous passing interludes; he becomes embroiled in several hideous tragedies, in the loathsome slave trade, in the Napoleonic campaigns, in financial dealings with the Rothschilds, in a lazar house-cum-prison, and in this fashion, practically ad infinitum, the story of the romantic foundling plunges and lurches along, from one unlikely coincidence to the next.

Into this one fictional lifetime are crammed enough events and exploits to furnish several novels of ordinary length with plot and to spare. There is a certain fascination in the long-drawn-out odyssey, but throughout the reader is uneasily conscious of prodigious stage management. If ever a novel demanded of its readers "a willing suspension of disbelief," that novel was *Anthony Adverse.* Once committed to this Niagara of improbability, one is swept into a world where no loose ends are ever left to dangle, where parted lovers always meet again, where revenge never falters or fails, and where nemesis stalks the hero as the crocodile stalked Captain Hook. There are a few very affecting scenes, as well as a great deal of material that is totally unnecessary; in that respect, at least, the novel closely resembles life.

Allen went on to write other novels, planning indeed to conjure up a panoramic picture of colonial America, but died before completing the gigantic task. His name was made by and will be remembered for his tremendously successful fictional offspring,

Anthony, the nameless waif born under "adverse conditions" to embody a life of epic adventure.

—Joan McGrath

ALLYSON, Kym. See **KIMBROUGH, Katheryn.**

AMES, Jennifer. See **GREIG, Maysie.**

ANDERSON, Roberta. See **MICHAELS, Fern.**

ANDREWS, Lucilla (Mathew). Also writes as Diana Gordon; Joanna Marcus. British. Born in Suez, Egypt. Trained as a nurse at St. Thomas's Hospital, London, during World War II. Married a doctor in 1947 (died 1954); one daughter. Lives in Edinburgh. Address: c/o Heinemann, 81 Fulham Road, London SW3 6RB, England.

ROMANCE AND HISTORICAL PUBLICATIONS

Novels (series: St. Martha's Hospital)

The Print Petticoat. London, Harrap, 1954.
The Secret Armour. London, Harrap, 1955.
The Quiet Wards. London, Harrap, 1956.
The First Year. London, Harrap, 1957.
A Hospital Summer. London, Harrap, 1958.
My Friend the Professor. London, Harrap, 1960.
Nurse Errant. London, Harrap, 1961.
The Young Doctors Downstairs. London, Harrap, 1963.
Flowers for the Doctor. London, Harrap, 1963.
The New Sister Theatre. London, Harrap, 1964.
The Light in the Ward. London, Harrap, 1965.
A House for Sister Mary. London, Harrap, 1966.
Hospital Circles. London, Harrap, 1967.
A Few Days in Endel (as Diana Gordon). London, Corgi, 1968.
Highland Interlude. London, Harrap, 1968.
The Healing Time. London, Harrap, 1969.
The Edinburgh Excursion. London, Harrap, 1970.
Ring o' Roses. London, Harrap, 1972.
Silent Song. London, Harrap, 1973.
In Storm and in Calm. London, Harrap, 1975.
The Crystal Gull. London, Harrap, 1978.
One Night in London (St. Martha's). London, Heinemann, 1979.
Marsh Blood (as Joanna Marcus). London, Hutchinson, 1980.
A Weekend in the Garden (St. Martha's). London, Heinemann, 1981.
In an Edinburgh Drawing Room (St. Martha's). London, Heinemann, 1983.
After a Famous Victory. London, Heinemann, 1984.
The Lights of London. London, Heinemann, 1985.
The Phoenix Syndrome. London, Heinemann, 1987.

OTHER PUBLICATIONS

Other

No Time for Romance: An Autobiographical Account of a Few Moments in British and Personal History. London, Harrap, 1977.

*   *   *

Lucilla Andrews may, or may not, have "invented" the hospital romance, but she certainly set a pattern which has been followed by innumerable other authors in much the same way as Georgette Heyer begat the Regency novel.

Like most who write this kind of story, she trained as a nurse, in London during World War II, and her grim experiences there have left a lasting impression on the style and content of her novels. She pulls no punches; readers' noses are positively rubbed in medical fact—often gruesome. (A week after she described the results of a motor-bike accident in *Woman's Weekly* the sale of skid-lids soared.) Her war-time experiences, described in her autobiography, ironically titled *No Time for Romance*, make it clear that everything she writes is either based on personal experience, or the result of scrupulous inquiry into the latest medical methods, discoveries, and treatments.

Her stories are not always (though often) set in big teaching hospitals. She likes to introduce remote or unusual backgrounds which, apart from adding colour and excitement to her story, demonstrate the different environments in which nursing (and romance!) occur, and the difficulties under which medical practice must sometimes be undertaken.

A good example of every aspect of her imaginative and ingenious use of her theme, and her topicality, is to be found in *In Storm and in Calm*, which takes its relief-nurse heroine to an isolated Shetland island at the time when the North Sea oil rigs were first coming into use. Charlotte quickly learns that instead of the quiet cottage hospital she expected, Thessa General, though tiny, is ultra modern, staffed and equipped to deal with all kinds of medical and surgical emergencies which come from the islands', and the world's, fishing fleets, and the new oil rigs. Patients arrive by trawler, tanker, lifeboat, helicopter, and ambulance, at all hours, in all seasons. There is, of course, a love story. The author patiently (perhaps a little wearily?) reiterates the fact that nurses and doctors are much given to marrying each other if only because they are too busy to meet anyone else. (She herself married a doctor.)

Anyone who has ever been in hospital, or even visited one, will know that there exists there an enclosed, almost hot-house, atmosphere which heightens the emotions of everyone—be they patient or part of the medical team. This is, perhaps, what makes hospital novels so popular: the romance has an authenticity and an inevitability which give it both credibility and an extra edge, set as it is against the background of emergency. Lucilla Andrews exploits this situation with great skill; but what really sets her apart is the variety she introduces, and her refusal to prettify the reason why her characters are where they are. She isn't afraid to grind axes, either. One of her *bêtes noirs* is the drunken driver. Her descriptions of the aftermath of drinking and driving are enough to put anyone off alcohol for life!

—Elizabeth Grey

ANTHONY, Evelyn. Pseudonym for Evelyn Bridget Patricia Ward-Thomas, née Stephens. British. Born in London, 3 July 1928. Educated at Convent of the Sacred Heart, Roehampton, to 1944, and privately. Married Michael Ward-Thomas in 1955; two daughters and four sons. Recipient: *Yorkshire Post* award, 1973. Freeman, City of London, 1987; Liveryman, Needlemakers' Company, London, 1987. Agent: A. P. Watt Ltd., 20 John Street, London WC1N 2DL. Address: Horham Hall, Thaxted, Essex, England.

ROMANCE AND HISTORICAL PUBLICATIONS

Novels (series: Davina Graham)

Imperial Highness. London, Museum Press, 1953; as *Rebel Princess*, New York Crowell, 1953.
Curse Not the King. London, Museum Press, 1954; as *Royal Intrigue*, New York, Crowell, 1954.
Far Flies the Eagle. New York, Crowell, 1955.
Anne Boleyn. London, Museum Press, and New York, Crowell, 1957.
Victoria and Albert. London, Crowell, 1958; as *Victoria*, London, Museum Press, 1959.
Elizabeth. London, Museum Press, 1960; as *All the Queen's Men*, New York, Crowell, 1960.
Charles the King. London, Museum Press, and New York, Doubleday, 1961.
Clandara. London, Hurst and Blackett, and New York, Doubleday, 1963.
The Heiress. London, Hurst and Blackett, and New York, Doubleday, 1964.
The French Bride. New York, Doubleday, 1964; London, Arrow, 1966.
Valentina. London, Hurst and Blackett, and New York, Doubleday, 1966.
The Rendezvous. London, Hutchinson, 1967; New York, Coward McCann, 1968.
Anne of Austria. London, Hurst and Blackett, 1968; as *The Cardinal and the Queen*, New York, Coward McCann, 1968.
The Legend. London, Hutchinson, and New York, Coward McCann, 1969.
The Assassin. London, Hutchinson, and New York, Coward McCann, 1970.
The Tamarind Seed. London, Hutchinson, and New York, Coward McCann, 1971.
The Poellenberg Inheritance. London, Hutchinson, and New York, Coward McCann, 1972.
The Occupying Power. London, Hutchinson, 1973; as *Stranger at the Gates*, New York, Coward McCann, 1973.
The Malaspiga Exit. London, Hutchinson, 1974; as *Mission to Malaspiga*, New York, Coward McCann, 1974.
The Persian Ransom. London, Hutchinson, 1975; as *The Persian Price*, New York, Coward McCann, 1975.
The Silver Falcon. London, Hutchinson, and New York, Coward McCann, 1977.
The Return. London, Hutchinson, and New York, Coward McCann, 1978.
The Grave of Truth. London, Hutchinson; as *The Janus Imperative*, New York, Coward McCann, 1980.
The Defector (Graham). London, Hutchinson, 1980; New York, Coward McCann, 1981.
The Avenue of the Dead (Graham). London, Hutchinson, 1981; New York, Coward McCann, 1982.
Albatross (Graham). London, Hutchinson, 1982; New York, Putnam, 1983.

The Company of Saints (Graham). London, Hutchinson, 1983; New York, Putnam, 1984.
Voices on the Wind. London, Hutchinson, and New York, Putnam, 1985.
No Enemy But Time. London, Hutchinson, 1987; as *A Place to Hide*, New York, Putnam, 1987.
The House of Vandekar. London, Hutchinson, and New York, Putnam, 1988.

*   *   *

The heroines of Evelyn Anthony's many stories of intrigue and danger are almost interchangeable. They are invariably impeccably ladylike, even if circumstance or inclination has forced them to bend one or another of the commandments. They tend to fragility in appearance, coupled somehow with an almost irresistible sexual attractiveness; they are slight, with long narrow hands and feet, which appear to advantage in the elegant and expensive hand-sewn leather they favour; none of these ladies is obliged to count pennies.

The Anthony lady is often masochistic to a degree which normal persons would find distinctly neurotic; she is capable of astonishing devotion, and she loves only once, forever, although sometimes before she discovers *true* love her heart may have misled her into settling for less, in or out of marriage. But no matter—it cannot last. *Somewhere*, perhaps under an alias, or hiding out in Mexico, or lying in wait for the target he has been engaged to assassinate, is the only man for Louise, or Anna, or Elizabeth, or Judith, or. . . .

Friendly mockery of Anthony's predictable heroines, however, does not mean that her stories are at all laughable. They are taut, gripping, often explosive in their resolutions, such as the holocaust in *The Tamarind Seed* which must be the hero's death pyre; the last-minute, heartbreaking gun battle in *The Legend*, in which their happiness is snatched from the fleeting lovers in the very moment of success; or the shattering passage in *The Occupying Power* in which S.S. reprisal for Allied wartime sabotage threatens the lives of all the children of a tiny French town, and their desperate parents, untrained in the use of arms, struggle to rescue them at the brink of the mass grave dug ready to receive their bodies: these are scenes that can hold their own with the best in suspense fiction.

Though her characters may be almost indistinguishable one from another, her plots are masterful. Once caught up in the skulduggery behind the scenes in the spymaster's hidden headquarters, the slums of Beirut, or the gilded haunts of the Beautiful People, the reader is trapped. These are tales of the sort that once begun must be finished—and readers of Anthony's thrillers know they have little chance of outguessing this ingenious writer.

Oddly enough, considering that her suspense stories revolve around the misadventures of helpless ladies who are pawns in the hands of great powers they do not even try to understand, Anthony also creates romantic fiction often based on the lives of the most powerful and formidable women who ever lived. Elizabeth Tudor, probably the most written-about of all English monarchs, has never been more believably portrayed in all her regal and dangerous unpredictability than by Evelyn Anthony, who convincingly interprets the ways in which the great queen's extraordinary childhood, and the self-seeking men who surrounded her throughout her adult life, shaped a woman whose career still fascinates. More like Anthony's own fictional heroines, the ill-fated Mary Stuart is treated with greater sympathy than most of Elizabeth's biographers accord her. The life of another less glamorous, but equally intriguing English monarch, Victoria, is the subject of a biographical novel dealing with the period between her accession to the throne as an 18-year-old and the fateful day of the Prince Consort's death. Surely Anthony comes as close as anyone can to discovering the character of the incredibly self-willed and stubborn young autocrat who became the Widow of Windsor.

Less familiar to English-speaking readers than the British monarchy are the Russian Tsars, subjects of a fascinating trilogy which deals with the lives of Catherine the Great, her son Paul, whose eccentricities won him the sobriquet of The Death's Head Tsar, and his son Alexander. She casts new light on a blood-soaked dynasty whose exploits do much to explain the revolution that was to come. In these and other costume romances, she brings to life some of history's most brilliant and dramatic personages.

Happily Anthony is a prolific writer, both of suspense and of romantic fiction; happily, because there is an army of devoted readers anxious for the "good read" of which her name on a title page is a certain guarantee.

—Joan McGrath

* * *

ARBOR, Jane. Pseudonym for Eileen Owbridge. British. Widow. Owner of a book shop and circulating library, then free-lance writer until 1984. Address: c/o Mills and Boon Ltd., 18–24 Paradise Road, Richmond, Surrey TW9 1SR, England.

ROMANCE AND HISTORICAL PUBLICATIONS

Novels

This Second Spring. London, Mills and Boon, 1948.
Each Song Twice Over. London, Mills and Boon, 1948.
Ladder of Understanding. London, Mills and Boon, 1949.
Strange Loyalties. London, Mills and Boon, 1949; Toronto, Harlequin, 1962; as *Doctor's Love*, Harlequin, n.d.
By Yet Another Door. London, Mills and Boon, 1950.
No Lease for Love. London, Mills and Boon, 1950; Toronto, Harlequin, 1964; as *My Surgeon Neighbour*, Harlequin, n.d.
The Heart Expects Adventure. London, Mills and Boon, 1951.
Eternal Circle. London, Mills and Boon, 1952; Toronto, Harlequin, 1958; as *Nurse Atholl Returns*, Harlequin, n.d.
Memory Serves My Love. London, Mills and Boon, 1952.
Flower of the Nettle. London, Mills and Boon, 1953.
Such Frail Armour. London, Mills and Boon, 1953; Toronto, Harlequin, 1959.
Jess Mawney, Queen's Nurse. London, Mills and Boon, 1954.
Dear Intruder. London, Mills and Boon, 1955; Toronto, Harlequin, 1965.
Folly of the Heart. London, Mills and Boon, 1955.
Towards the Dawn. London, Mills and Boon, 1956; Toronto, Harlequin, 1959.
City Nurse. London, Mills and Boon, 1956; as *Nurse Greve*, Toronto, Harlequin, n.d.
Yesterday's Magic. London, Mills and Boon, 1957; Toronto, Harlequin, 1967.
Far Sanctuary. London, Mills and Boon, 1958; Toronto, Harlequin, 1960.
Nurse Harlowe. Toronto, Harlequin, 1959.
Sandflower. London, Mills and Boon, 1959; Toronto, Harlequin, 1961.
Consulting Surgeon. Toronto, Harlequin, 1959.

No Silver Spoon. London, Mills and Boon, 1959; Toronto, Harlequin, 1964.
Queen's Nurse. Toronto, Harlequin, 1960.
A Girl Named Smith. London, Mills and Boon, 1960; Toronto, Harlequin, 1966.
Nurse of All Work. London, Mills and Boon, and Toronto, Harlequin, 1962.
Nurse in Waiting. London, Mills and Boon, and Toronto, Harlequin, 1962.
Desert Nurse. London, Mills and Boon, 1963; Toronto, Harlequin, 1964.
Jasmine Harvest. London, Mills and Boon, and Toronto, Harlequin, 1963.
Lake of Shadows. London, Mills and Boon, 1964; Toronto, Harlequin, 1965.
Kingfisher Tide. London, Mills and Boon, and Toronto, Harlequin, 1965.
High Master of Clere. London, Mills and Boon, and Toronto, Harlequin, 1966.
Summer Every Day. London, Mills and Boon, 1966; Toronto, Harlequin, 1967.
Golden Apple Island. London, Mills and Boon, 1967; Toronto, Harlequin, 1968.
Stranger's Trespass. London, Mills and Boon, 1968; Toronto, Harlequin, 1969.
The Cypress Garden. London, Mills and Boon, and Toronto, Harlequin, 1969.
The Feathered Shaft. London, Mills and Boon, and Toronto, Harlequin, 1970.
Walk into the Wind. London, Mills and Boon, and Toronto, Harlequin, 1970.
The Other Miss Donne. London, Mills and Boon, and Toronto, Harlequin, 1971.
The Linden Leaf. London, Mills and Boon, and Toronto, Harlequin, 1971.
The Flower on the Rock. London, Mills and Boon, 1972; Toronto, Harlequin, 1973.
Wildfire Quest. London, Mills and Boon, and Toronto, Harlequin, 1972.
Roman Summer. London, Mills and Boon, and Toronto, Harlequin, 1973.
The Velvet Spur. London, Mills and Boon, and Toronto, Harlequin, 1974.
Meet the Sun Halfway. London, Mills and Boon, and Toronto, Harlequin, 1974.
The Wide Fields of Home. London, Mills and Boon, and Toronto, Harlequin, 1975.
Tree of Paradise. London, Mills and Boon, 1976; Toronto, Harlequin, 1977.
Smoke into Flame. Toronto, Harlequin, 1976.
Flash of Emerald. London, Mills and Boon, 1977.
Two Pins in a Fountain. London, Mills and Boon, and Toronto, Harlequin, 1977.
A Growing Moon. London, Mills and Boon, 1977; Toronto, Harlequin, 1978.
Late Rapture. London, Mills and Boon, 1978; Toronto, Harlequin, 1979.
Return to Silbersee. London, Mills and Boon, 1978; Toronto, Harlequin, 1979.
Pact Without Desire. London, Mills and Boon, 1979.
The Devil Drives. London, Mills and Boon, 1979; Toronto, Harlequin, 1980.
One Brief Sweet Hour. London, Mills and Boon, 1980; Toronto, Harlequin, 1981.
Where the Wolf Leads. London, Mills and Boon, 1980; Toronto, Harlequin, 1981.

Invisible Wife. London, Mills and Boon, 1981.
Handmaid to Midas. London, Mills and Boon, 1982.
The Price of Paradise. London, Mills and Boon, 1982.
House of Discord. London, Mills and Boon, 1983.
Lost Yesterday. London, Mills and Boon, 1984.

*   *   *

Jane Arbor is an English writer who spent her early years owning a book shop and circulating library. This experience proved to be of great value to her, for she gained exceptional knowledge about romance readers. She knows just what they expect and what kinds of romance stories have the greatest appeal.

In a short autobiographical sketch, she used the phrase, "acceptable storyteller." In any discussion of her as a writer, it is a telling phrase, for that is just what she is: a storyteller of great originality and sensitivity; she tangles her skein of characters and background into a many-hued tapestry of love and happiness.

She displays a most enviable discipline for work, for she has published over 60 novels. Her early apprenticeship years produced numerous doctor/nurse stories that still make enjoyable reading, although later she developed the more typical story that is so familiar to her readers. She, herself, admits that character motivation is the element that she prefers to start with when beginning to develop a new novel, although background has been the initial factor in some of her works. In making her observation, she noted the amount of research she carries out in creating the proper setting for a novel. She uses Morocco, Venice, the Greek Islands, Amsterdam, and the Pacific Islands for settings, to mention but a few. She chooses detail carefully and weaves description in so that there is a gradual awareness of the setting. Perhaps this is because of her meticulousness in developing her backgrounds that make them seem so authentic. Arbor avoids the too innocent image in developing her female characters; the girls in her stories are often well-educated and have responsible jobs.

Gillian Harlowe in *Folly of the Heart* is a trained staff nurse in a hospital. Dinah Fleming in *A Growing Moon* travels to Venice to take over a tourist office for her company, while Alice Martin in *Meet the Sun Halfway* has been trained in domestic science so she has the experience and ability to take over a children's convalescent home in Morocco.

For all of their experience and surface sophistication, each makes the mistake of falling in love with a man out of their reach. It is here that Arbor shows particular ability in defining her characters as each girl faces the fact that they can never hope to have their love returned. Gillian succumbs to a brilliant surgeon, Adrian Pilgrim; Dinah befriends the young cousins of Cesare Visdal, an Italian nobleman; while Alice loses her heart to Karim Ibn Charles, a very wealthy and influential Moroccan, who happens to own the home that the children are in.

Generally, action in the story is interwoven with the typical activities the characters are involved with and against the background of the growing awareness and tension between the men and women. In this context Arbor makes use of the triangular plot quite effectively.

Arbor often relies heavily on secondary characters to confound the simplicity of love. There are frequent misunderstandings and an undercurrent of jealousy as each assumes that the other loves someone else. Just as frequently, Arbor includes a potential rival in the form of an old girl-friend or a female colleague who, though not really in love with the hero, is determined to have him anyway. Only at the very end of the story does the heroine begin to realize that she might have won the hero's love after all, although certain incidents throughout the story have left her confused and hopeful, as he seems to offer her faint gestures of encouragement.

Arbor's novels always end on that satisfying note of love's inevitable victory. Her readers have the same satisfying feeling as they reluctantly put down a finished novel.

—Arlene Moore

ARLEN, Leslie. See **NICOLE, Christopher.**

ARLEN, Michael. British. Born Dikran Kouyoumdjian in Rustchuk, Bulgaria, 16 November 1895; emigrated to England, 1901; naturalized as Michael Arlen, 1922. Educated at Malvern College, Worcestershire; studied medicine at the University of Edinburgh, 1913. Served as Civil Defense public relations officer in the West Midlands, 1940–41. Married Atalanta, daughter of Count Mercati, in 1928; one son and one daughter. Staff member, *Ararat: A Searchlight on Armenia*, London, 1916, and columnist, the *Tatler*, London, 1939–40; lived in Cannes, 1928–39, and in New York City after 1945. *Died 23 June 1956.*

ROMANCE AND HISTORICAL PUBLICATIONS

Novels

The London Venture. London, Heinemann, and New York, Dodd Mead, 1920.
Piracy: A Romantic Chronicle of These Days. London, Collins, 1922; New York, Doran, 1923.
The Green Hat: A Romance for a Few People. London, Collins, and New York, Doran, 1924.
Young Men in Love. London, Hutchinson, and New York, Doran, 1927.
Lily Christine. New York, Doubleday, 1928; London, Hutchinson, 1929.
Men Dislike Women: A Romance. London, Heinemann, and New York, Doubleday, 1931.
Man's Mortality. London, Heinemann, and New York, Doubleday, 1933.
Hell! Said the Duchess: A Bed-Time Story. London, Heinemann, and New York, Doubleday, 1934.
Flying Dutchman. London, Heinemann, and New York, Doubleday, 1939.

Short Stories

The Romantic Lady. London, Collins, and New York, Dodd Mead, 1921.
These Charming People. London, Collins, 1923; New York, Doran, 1924; selection, as *The Man with the Broken Nose and Other Stories*, Collins, 1927.
May Fair, in Which Are Told the Last Adventures of These Charming People. London, Collins, and New York, Doran, 1925; selection, as *The Ace of Cads and Other Stories*, Collins, 1927.
Ghost Stories. London, Collins, 1927; New York, Arno Press, 1976.
Babes in the Wood. London, Hutchinson, and New York, Doubleday, 1929.

The Ancient Sin and Other Stories. London, Collins, 1930.
A Young Man Comes to London. Privately printed, 1931.
The Short Stories. London, Collins, 1933.
*The Crooked Coronet and Other Misrepresentations of the Real
    Facts of Life.* London, Heinemann, and New York, Double-
    day, 1937.

OTHER PUBLICATIONS

Plays

Dear Father (produced London, 1924; revised version, as *These
    Charming People*, produced New York, 1925).
Why Shelmerdene Was Late for Dinner, adaptation of his story
    "The Real Reason Why Shelmerdene Was Late for Dinner"
    (produced London, 1924).
The Green Hat, adaptation of his own novel (produced Detroit,
    London, and New York, 1925). New York, Doran, 1925.
The Zoo, with Winchell Smith (produced Southsea and Pitts-
    burgh, 1927). New York and London, French, 1927.
Good Losers, with Walter Hackett (produced London, 1931).
    London, French, 1933.

Screenplay: *The Heavenly Body*, with others, 1943.

*

Critical Study: *Michael Arlen* by Harry Keyishian, Boston,
Twayne, 1975.

*   *   *

"To be as improbable as life will be is as far beyond the honest novelist's courage as it must be against the temper of his
craft. . . . " Michael Arlen said this, but his own story reads
like the most far-fetched romance: unknown young Armenian
with an unpronounceable name offers his first novel to a world-
famous London publisher, and is accepted. Following his publisher's advice, he changes his name to Michael Arlen, goes on
to write *The Green Hat*, and takes the world by storm. (Literally, for his heroine Iris Storm proved the truth of Oscar Wilde's
contention that Nature copies Art. The world did its best to copy
Iris.) The impact of this single novel is now difficult to comprehend. In these television-dominated days, it is impossible to recapture the atmosphere of a time before even radio had taken
firm hold; a time when *everyone* read, not just the few, and not
only read but discussed the latest releases as a matter of some
significance.

World War I had recently rocked the firm foundation of the
universe, and suddenly the unthinkable had become the possible.
The audience of *The Green Hat* had just come through the war
to end all wars, but which instead ended all peace. Old rules and
beliefs were crumbling. The young people fortunate enough to
have escaped the holocaust were disillusioned and jaded. They
were the Bright Young Things; they frightened and disturbed the
older generation who did not, *could* not, understand them.
These were the young people who recognized, or thought they
recognized, themselves as the characters of Michael Arlen's
novels, and they made *The Green Hat* in particular one of the
greatest best sellers of all time.

Today it is a period piece. Even in his lifetime, Arlen was left
behind, while time and fashion remorselessly forged ahead, and
he could not. He was a writer who could do but one thing, and

was fortunate enough to do it at exactly the propitious moment.
Even his quirky brand of idiosyncratic English was forgiven him
then, as it would not have been at another time.

And what, after all, was the furor about? *The Green Hat* is
the muddled story of Iris, a troubled young woman with a
"past" and a dissolute present. She wears two wedding rings—
for two husbands now dead: she carries a smouldering torch for
the one true love of her life, her girlhood sweetheart, from
whom she was parted by his father's interference, and who is but
newly married to a fluttering ingenue named Venice.

Iris does a great deal of restless rushing to and fro in her huge
yellow Hispano-Suiza, which to Arlen seemed to typify the spirit
of the entire era. She is regarded by all her acquaintance as a
depraved character, yet aside from her free-love life-style, she
behaves throughout with self-sacrificing nobility. Much evil is
hinted at, little is explicit, but it becomes plain as the action
lumbers clumsily along that there were dark doings at the time
of Iris's tragic first marriage, and that her husband, idolized by
everyone but his young bride, was not the hero he seemed to be.
The spectre of syphilis, hitherto unmentionable, is raised; it was
a daring stroke for a novelist of the 1920's. For young women,
though not young men, were expected to behave with a certain
decorum and restraint, which Iris did not. The story ends with
the great yellow Hispano-Suiza in flames, and Iris's green hat,
worn "pour le sport," lying in the grass by the roadside. One
last time, the déclassé lady has sacrificed herself for her true
love.

Iris and her set represented for Arlen a distinct race of English
that he believed could not survive the crassness of the 20th century, belonging as they did to a time of different standards and
ideals. "They of the superior nerves had failed, they died that
slow white death which is reserved for privilege in defeat."

—Joan McGrath

———————

ARMSTRONG, Charlotte. Also wrote as Jo Valentine.
American. Born in Vulcan, Michigan, 2 May 1905. Educated
at the University of Wisconsin, Madison 1922–24; Barnard College, New York, B.A. 1925. Married Jack Lewi in 1928; one
daughter and two sons. Worked in the *New York Times* advertising department, as a fashion reporter for *Breath of the Avenue* (a
buyer's guide), and in an accounting firm, 1925–28. Recipient:
Mystery Writers of America Edgar Allan Poe award, 1956. *Died
18 July 1969.*

ROMANCE AND HISTORICAL PUBLICATIONS

Novels (series character: MacDougal Duff)

Lay On, Mac Duff! (Duff). New York, Coward McCann, 1942;
    London, Gifford, 1943.
The Case of the Weird Sisters (Duff). New York, Coward Mc-
    Cann, and London, Gifford, 1943.
The Innocent Flower (Duff). New York, Coward McCann,
    1945; as *Death Filled the Glass*, London, Cherry Tree Books,
    1945.
The Unsuspected. New York, Coward McCann, 1946; London,
    Harrap, 1947.
The Chocolate Cobweb. New York, Coward McCann, 1948;
    London, Davies, 1952.

Mischief. New York, Coward McCann, 1950; London, Davies, 1951.

The Black-Eyed Stranger. New York, Coward McCann, 1951; London, Davies, 1952.

Catch-as-Catch-Can. New York, Coward McCann, 1952; London, Davies, 1953; as *Walk Out on Death*, New York, Pocket Books, 1954.

The Trouble in Thor (as Jo Valentine). New York, Coward Mc-Cann, and London, Davies, 1953; as *And Sometimes Death*, New York, Pocket Books, 1955.

The Better to Eat You. New York, Coward McCann, and London, Davies, 1954; as *Murder's Nest*, New York, Pocket Books, 1955.

The Dream Walker. New York, Coward McCann, and London, Davies, 1955; as *Alibi for Murder*, New York, Pocket Books, 1956.

A Dram of Poison. New York, Coward McCann, and London, Davies, 1956.

The Seventeen Widows of Sans Souci. New York, Coward Mc-Cann, and London, Davies, 1959.

Duo: The Girl with a Secret, Incident at a Corner. New York, Coward McCann, 1959; London, Davies, 1960.

Something Blue. New York, Ace, 1962.

Then Came Two Women. New York, Ace, 1962.

Who's Been Sitting in My Chair? New York, Ace, 1963.

A Little Less Than Kind. New York, Coward McCann, 1963; London, Collins, 1964.

The Mark of the Hand. New York, Ace, 1963.

The One-Faced Girl. New York, Ace, 1963.

The Witch's House. New York, Coward McCann, 1963; London, Collins, 1964.

The Turret Room. New York, Coward McCann, and London, Collins, 1965.

Dream of Fair Woman. New York, Coward McCann, and London, Collins, 1966.

The Gift Shop. New York, Coward McCann, and London, Collins, 1967.

Lemon in the Basket. New York, Coward McCann, 1967; London, Collins, 1968.

The Balloon Man. New York, Coward McCann, and London, Collins, 1968.

Seven Seats to the Moon. New York, Coward McCann, and London, Collins, 1969.

The Protégé. New York, Coward McCann, and London, Collins, 1970.

Short Stories

The Albatross. New York, Coward McCann, 1957; London, Davies, 1958; selection, as *Mask of Evil*, New York, Fawcett, 1958.

I See You. New York, Coward McCann, 1966.

OTHER PUBLICATIONS

Plays

The Happiest Days (produced New York, 1939).

Ring Around Elizabeth (produced New York, 1940). New York, French, 1942.

Screenplays: *The Unsuspected*, 1947; *Don't Bother to Knock*, 1952.

Television Plays: scripts for *Alfred Hitchcock Presents* series, 1955–61.

*

Manuscript Collection: Mugar Memorial Library, Boston University.

*   *   *

"But it's peanut reading," a character in *The Dream Walker* says of his supply of thrillers. "You can't stop till they're all gone." A story by Charlotte Armstrong is peanut reading; you can't put it down until it's finished. And it's wholesome.

MacDougal Duff solved detective puzzles in *Lay On, Mac Duff!*, *The Case of the Weird Sisters*, and *The Innocent Flower*, but in the last he falls in love with Mary Moriarity, and her with seven children. His proposal ended detecting. Thereafter, Armstrong concentrated on suspense. The most marked characteristic of her novels and short stories is a sense of family. Romantic love can be a by-product but is not the main action.

Frequently the evil force is known early on, presented without formula and with great variety in structure, setting, and tone. *The Unsuspected*, the earliest suspense success, features a smooth-talking manipulator, opposed by a cousin and fiancé of his first victim. In *The Dream Walker* the narrator helps her cousin to thwart a revenge plot to discredit their uncle, a statesman of good repute; the plot involves seeming bi-location. *The Witch's House* imprisons a missing college professor whose wife presses the search. A plucky mother's fight for custody of her 4-year-old involves the drug scene (*The Balloon Man*). Good but not best battles against known villains are *The Chocolate Cobweb*, *The Better to Eat You*, and *Something Blue*.

Mental cases? A young psychotic baby-sitter in a New York hotel stars in *Mischief*. *A Little Less Than Kind* offers the added appeal of *Hamlet* parallels and non-parallels, but the son is not putting on the antics of madness. *The Turret Room* hides an ex-husband, discharged from a mental hospital, the victim of the family's protection of another. *Dream of Fair Woman* has a complex identity problem in a young woman who cannot be awakened from sleep.

The hero of *The Black-Eyed Stranger* risks his life to foil the kidnap plan of caricatured criminals—grimly tense. However, when a detective leaves a dying message in a piggy bank (*The Gift Shop*), he begins a fairy-tale spoof of hard-boiled thrillers, and Harry Fairchild leads the chase to find a 7-year-old girl. Equally amusing is *The One-Faced Girl*, about a girl unwittingly involved with criminals.

Lemon in the Basket mixes international intrigue with a family of famous parents, the second son the title character. Caught between rival political factions and family problems, J. Middleton Little celebrates his name in *Seven Seats to the Moon*. It is the most satisfying of the novels that add comment on life to the action. Among the latter, different complications provide different turns and twists of plot in *The Seventeen Widows of Sans Souci* and *The Protégé*.

The Edgar-winning *A Dram of Poison* has compassion and humor. A sister's gross misunderstanding of psychology and his new marriage tempt a 55-year-old professor to suicide, but he loses the bottle of poison. A merry hunt is on, like the tale of the Golden Goose, and eccentrics discuss philosophies as miles and time conclude the cliff hanger.

As Jo Valentine, Armstrong wrote *The Trouble in Thor* about a summer in the 1920's in the fictional shaft-mining town of Thor, in Michigan's Upper Peninsula. After a labored beginning, all narrative threads work toward the attempt to rescue five miners trapped by a collapsed pillar.

The qualities of her best novels are also in her consistently good short stories. Armstrong fans gobble her goobers.

—Jane Gottschalk

ARNOW, Harriette (Louisa, née Simpson). American. Born in Wayne County, Kentucky, 7 July 1908. Educated at St. Helen's Academy; Stanton Academy; Burnside High School, graduated 1924; Berea College, Kentucky, 1924–26; University of Louisville, B.S. 1931. Married Harold B. Arnow in 1939 (died 1985); one daughter and one son. Teacher in Pulaski County, Kentucky, 1926–28, 1931–34, and Louisville, 1934; waitress, Cincinnati, 1934–39. Recipient: Berea College Centennial award, 1955; Friends of American Writers award, 1955; American Association for State and Local History award, 1971; University of Louisville Outstanding Alumni award, 1979. D. Litt.: Albion College, Michigan, 1955; Transylvania University, Lexington, Kentucky, 1979; University of Kentucky, Lexington, 1981. *Died 22 March 1986.*

ROMANCE AND HISTORICAL PUBLICATIONS

Novel

The Kentucky Trace: A Novel of the American Revolution. New York, Knopf, 1974.

OTHER PUBLICATIONS

Novels

Mountain Path. New York, Covici Friede, 1936.
Hunter's Horn. New York, Macmillan, 1949; London, Collins, 1950.
The Dollmaker. New York, Macmillan, 1954; London, Heinemann, 1955.
The Weedkiller's Daughter. New York, Knopf, 1970.

Other

Seedtime on the Cumberland. New York, Macmillan, 1960.
Flowering of the Cumberland. New York, Macmillan, 1963.
Some Musings on the Nature of History (lecture). Ann Arbor, Historical Society of Michigan, 1968.
Old Burnside. Lexington, University Press of Kentucky, 1978.

*

Manuscript Collection: Margaret I. King Library, University of Kentucky, Lexington.

Critical Studies: by Joyce Carol Oates, in *Rediscoveries* edited by David Madden, New York, Crown, 1971; *Harriette Arnow* by Wilton Eckley, New York, Twayne, 1974.

*   *   *

Despite Harriette Arnow's proven skill as a writer, her contributions to American literature have been largely ignored by scholars. The pre-eminence of William Faulkner and the influence of the New Critics have overshadowed many figures who played important roles in the "Southern Literary Renaissance." Arnow's insightful and realistic portrayal of Kentucky rural life, and its ultimate disintegration in the face of industrialism, is a valuable achievement in American letters. Her natural skill at storytelling and rendering memorable characters, combined with a unity of plot and theme to produce novels of high merit. Like that of many fine American novelists Arnow's work has a regional focus which transcends provincialism. Glenda Hobbs wrote that "Arnow alone has rendered Kentucky highlanders fully and fairly, her unique obstinate characters, even in the face of economic ruin and spiritual exhaustion, will endure and prevail."

Arnow's work is in two distinct types. The first is fiction, the bulk of which is contained in a trilogy exploring the mountain people and lifestyle she knew as a girl. It began with *Mountain Path*, which was not commercially successful; but the other two, *Hunter's Horn* and *The Dollmaker*, were both bestsellers. The second group of writing covers social history. Two later books, *Seedtime on the Cumberland* and *Flowering of the Cumberland*, integrate history with reminiscence and commentary further to document the world Arnow describes in her novels. "I was aware that nothing had been written on the Southern migrants," she explained in 1976. Hers was an attempt to show "what was actually happening to them and to their culture."

Mountain Path is the most autobiographical of Arnow's works, concerning a young and naive schoolteacher who goes to a remote village in the Kentucky mountains. The plot itself is contrived, but the real strength of the book lies in the close attention to character and the everyday affairs of the region. This ability rescues her story from the usual melodrama and sentimentality which can plague similar fiction.

Arnow's second novel, *Hunter's Horn*, focuses on the family of Nunnelly Ballew, whose obsession for killing an elusive fox he calls "King Devil" brings his family close to destruction. This novel addresses the individual's struggle to find meaning in a circumscribed environment. In many ways it is a conscious attempt at the heroic stature and epic sweep of Melville or Steinbeck. In one particularly powerful scene the townspeople bury Lureenie Cramer, who has starved while her husband is working in Detroit. Because of a recent religious revival they ignore her suffering, and now they hurry with the ceremony because leaving an open grave after sundown brings bad luck. Superstition increases the callousness initiated by their fundamentalism. In their impatience to get the coffin into the grave, the men tip it too far and there is a dull thud as Lureenie's body strikes the side. Later her husband makes a triumphant return wearing tailored clothes, toting a gilt-edged bible, and claiming he has "seen the light."

Arnow's most well-known work is *The Dollmaker*. It completes her portrait of Kentucky migrants, "rescuing the literary stereotype of the lazy, suspicious, ignorant, maniacally violent hillbilly." It also gives readers Arnow's most resilient and complex character—Gertie Nevels. When her husband is lured to Detroit by tales of wealth and luxury, Gertie sacrifices her own dreams of self-sufficiency to join him. With her she brings a huge block of cherry wood, which she tries to form into a figure of Christ. In the exploitative and vulgar conditions of Detroit slums her family disintegrates, and Gertie feels the corruption of religious intolerance, racism, and self-interest undermine her artistic integrity. The final scene shows Gertie relinquishing her precious, near-completed statue to a scrapwood dealer, where it will be used for cheap, mass-produced dolls.

Arnow's only historical novel, *The Kentucky Trace*, is set in the Kentucky mountains during the Revolutionary War. The novel traces the story of Leslie Collins, a surveyor who had been serving with the rebel colonists. After being captured by bandits and rescued by "overmountain" men, Collins makes his way home only to discover that his farm is deserted and his family gone. In his subsequent search for his family down the Kentucky trace, he comes upon a camp of survivors, each one displaced by the ravages of war. Arnow provides a descriptive document of the daily life and customs of the people of Cumberland during the Revolutionary War. The hero's attempts at healing himself and the land around him of war wounds produces both a namesake and an adoptive son. Although the novel verges on the sentimental, Arnow offers a new and refreshing angle on the revolution focusing on the everyday struggles of families and individuals to stay united and to survive, rather than accounts of battles. Her meticulous research is carefully blended into her fiction giving a precise and detailed description of the time.

Although Arnow wrote only one historical novel, her dark view of history as presented in *The Kentucky Trace* is not untypical of her other work. She held a depressing vision of what history has done to the people who live through it, the people who populate her novels. In Arnow's eyes Americans themselves have ruined their country and must bear this guilt.

—Scott Coombs

ASHFIELD, Helen. See **BENNETTS, Pamela.**

ASHLEY, Ellen. See **SEIFERT, Elizabeth.**

ASHTON, Ann. See **KIMBROUGH, Katheryn.**

ASHTON, Elizabeth. British. Born in 1902. Lives in Halesworth, Suffolk. Address: c/o Mills and Boon Ltd., 18–24 Paradise Road, Richmond, Surrey TW9 1SR, England.

ROMANCE AND HISTORICAL PUBLICATIONS

Novels

The Pied Tulip. London, Mills and Boon, 1969; Toronto, Harlequin, 1970.
The Benevolent Despot. London, Mills and Boon, and Toronto, Harlequin, 1970.
Parisian Adventure. London, Mills and Boon, and Toronto, Harlequin, 1970.
Cousin Mark. London, Mills and Boon, and Toronto, Harlequin, 1971.
The Enchanted Wood. London, Mills and Boon, 1971.
Sweet Simplicity. London, Mills and Boon, 1971.
Flutter of White Wings. London, Mills and Boon, and Toronto, Harlequin, 1972.

A Parade of Peacocks. London, Mills and Boon, 1972; Toronto, Harlequin, 1973.
Scorched Wings. London, Mills and Boon, 1972; Toronto, Harlequin, 1975.
The Rocks of Arachenza. London, Mills and Boon, 1973; Toronto, Harlequin, 1974.
Sigh No More. London, Mills and Boon, 1973; Toronto, Harlequin, 1974.
The Bells of Bruges. London, Mills and Boon, 1973.
Alpine Rhapsody. Toronto, Harlequin, 1973.
Errant Bride. London, Mills and Boon, 1973; Toronto, Harlequin, 1974.
Moorland Magic. London, Mills and Boon, and Toronto, Harlequin, 1973.
Dark Angel. London, Mills and Boon, and Toronto, Harlequin, 1974.
The House of the Eagles. London, Mills and Boon, 1974; Toronto, Harlequin, 1975.
Dangerous to Know. London, Mills and Boon, 1974.
The Road to the Border. London, Mills and Boon, 1974; Toronto, Harlequin, 1975.
The Scent of Sandalwood. London, Mills and Boon, 1974.
Miss Nobody from Nowhere. London, Mills and Boon, and Toronto, Harlequin, 1975.
The Willing Hostage. London, Mills and Boon, 1975.
Crown of Willow. London, Mills and Boon, 1975; Toronto, Harlequin, 1976.
The Player King. London, Mills and Boon, and Toronto, Harlequin, 1975.
Sanctuary in the Desert. London, Mills and Boon, 1976; Toronto, Harlequin, 1977.
My Lady Disdain. London, Mills and Boon, and Toronto, Harlequin, 1976.
Mountain Heritage. London, Mills and Boon, 1976; Toronto, Harlequin, 1977.
Lady in the Limelight. Toronto, Harlequin, 1976.
Aegean Quest. Toronto, Harlequin, 1977.
Voyage of Enchantment. Toronto, Harlequin, 1977.
Green Harvest. Toronto, Harlequin, 1977.
Breeze from the Bosphorus. Toronto, Harlequin, 1978.
The Garden of the Gods. London, Mills and Boon, 1978.
The Golden Girl. London, Mills and Boon, and Toronto, Harlequin, 1978.
The Questing Heart. London, Mills and Boon, and Toronto, Harlequin, 1978.
Rendezvous in Venice. London, Mills and Boon, and Toronto, Harlequin, 1978.
The Joyous Adventure. London, Mills and Boon, 1979.
Moonlight on the Nile. London, Mills and Boon, and Toronto, Harlequin, 1979.
Reluctant Partnership. London, Mills and Boon, 1979; Toronto, Harlequin, 1981.
Borrowed Plumes. London, Mills and Boon, 1980; Toronto, Harlequin, 1981.
The Rekindled Flame. London, Mills and Boon, and Toronto, Harlequin, 1980.
Sicilian Summer. London, Mills and Boon, 1980; Toronto, Harlequin, 1981.
Silver Arrow. London, Mills and Boon, 1980; Toronto, Harlequin, 1981.
Rebel Against Love. London, Mills and Boon, and Toronto, Harlequin, 1981.
Egyptian Honeymoon. London, Mills and Boon, 1981.
White Witch. London, Mills and Boon, 1982.
Bride on Approval. London, Mills and Boon, 1986.

Plays

The Beggarman's Bride. London, Pitman, 1953.
To Serve a King. London, Pitman, 1954.

*   *   *

Elizabeth Ashton has been a published writer since the late 1960's when her first novel *The Pied Tulip* appeared. Since then, she has regularly produced fascinating novels for her many readers. To date, she has written over 40 novels.

Although well within the early guidelines of romance writing, she is one of the "new" romance writers who are becoming increasingly popular. Her style is much more dramatic and forceful. Emotion is heightened in her stories and often the reader is caught in a web of suspense that is nearly over-powering. The fact that the denouement in her novels comes within pages, even paragraphs, of the ending makes her readers' reaction even more intense.

Generally, her heroines are more aware than is usual in romances; that is, they have a surface sophistication and are often exposed to wealthy people and adult situations. Rachel Reed in *The Garden of the Gods* has had an expensive finishing school education. Averil Avon in *Lady in the Limelight*, although from a small village, becomes a leading stage actress, while Renee Thorton in *Parisian Adventure* is an English fashion model.

Although her heroes are experienced men of the world, they tend to display a contempt and cynical attitude towards women in general. However, they are not ones to miss an opportunity in making use of a woman for their own purposes. Leon Sabastian is a well-known couturier who sees Renee and wants to use her as one of his models. Cass Dakers is a famous writer who rescues Rachel as she tries to swim from a yacht off of the island of Corfu. In *Lady in the Limelight* Philip Conway is an important actor and director who is determined to groom Averil to stardom regardless of her own wishes. All are dominating, ruthless, sensual men who fall in love in spite of their determination not to.

Again Elizabeth Ashton is one of those writers who obviously work hard at creating believable backgrounds. Her use of Paris and the world of fashion is fascinating, as are her descriptions of other areas of France, Italy, and Corfu. In using her backgrounds, she skillfully lets the heroines' movement and actions give her impression of her physical surroundings. Since the heroines' reactions are frequently enthusiastic and extremely appreciative, the descriptions are naturally colorful and evocative.

In at least one of her novels, she re-introduces characters from a previous story. Renee and Leon in *Parisian Adventure* become secondary characters in *A Parade of Peacocks*. In this novel, Charmian meets Alex Dimitriou, a wealthy Greek businessman.

In each of her novels, Elizabeth Ashton extends the plot complications and adds a certain element of irresolution in such a way that readers feel the heroine's pathetic situation. Typical of the kinds of complications is that of Francesca in *Dark Angel* who marries Angelo Vittorini. She is going to have his child, but he does not know it when he writes and asks for a permanent separation. She returns to England and eventually has a daughter. He does not learn about it until the end of the story when he visits her to discuss a divorce.

Despondency, heightened passion, and emotional reactions all play dominant parts in Elizabeth Ashton's writing as the heroine faces the failure of her love. Readers may find the heightened suspense overpowering at times, but it does not seem to diminish her audience.

—Arlene Moore

———————

ASHTON, Sharon. See **VAN SLYKE, Helen.**

———————

ASQUITH, Nan. Pseudonym for Nancy Evelyn Pattinson. British. Born in Barnsley, Yorkshire. Educated at St. Winifred's school, Broadstairs, Kent; Winterthorpe, Birkdale, Lancashire. Married to Denis F. C. Pattinson. Has worked as advertising copywriter. Address: c/o Mills and Boon Ltd., 18–24, Paradise Road, Richmond, Surrey TW9 1SR, England.

ROMANCE AND HISTORICAL PUBLICATIONS

Novels

My Dream Is Yours. London, Mills and Boon, 1954; as *Doctor Robert Comes Around*, Toronto, Harlequin, 1965.
With All My Heart. London, Mills and Boon, 1954; Toronto, Harlequin, 1968.
Believe in To-morrow. London, Mills and Boon, 1955; Toronto, Harlequin, 1971.
Only My Heart to Give. London, Mills and Boon, 1955; Toronto, Harlequin, 1969.
The Certain Spring. London, Mills and Boon, 1956; Toronto, Harlequin, 1968.
Honey Island. London, Mills and Boon, 1957.
The House on Brinden Water. London, Mills and Boon, 1958; as *The Doctor Is Engaged*, Toronto, Harlequin, 1962.
The Time for Happiness. London, Mills and Boon, 1959.
Time May Change. London, Mills and Boon, 1961; Toronto, Harlequin, 1974.
The Way the Wind Blows. London, Mills and Boon, 1963.
The Quest. London, Mills and Boon, 1964.
The Summer at San Milo. London, Mills and Boon, 1965.
Dangerous Yesterday. London, Mills and Boon, 1967.
The Garden of Persephone. London, Mills and Boon, 1967; Toronto, Harlequin, 1978.
The Admiral's House. London, Mills and Boon, 1969.
Turn the Page. London, Mills and Boon, and Toronto, Harlequin, 1970.
Beyond the Mountain. London, Mills and Boon, 1970.
Carnival at San Cristobal. London, Mills and Boon, 1971.
Out of the Dark. London, Mills and Boon, 1972.
The Girl from Rome. London, Mills and Boon, and Toronto, Harlequin, 1973.
The Sun in the Morning. London, Mills and Boon, 1974.

*   *   *

Nan Asquith was one of the more traditional romance writers of the 1950's and 1960's. Ten of her novels appeared in the Harlequin Romances beginning in 1962 with the publication of *The House on Brinden Water*. Her charming stories and attractive heroines gained her a wide reading audience during this period. Although some of her novels were written more than 30 years ago, there is a dateless quality in her novels that makes her just as readable today as then.

Despite the fact that they are traditional in formula, there is nothing simplistic about her novels. Complexity of character and well-thought-out plots show Asquith's talent as a romance writer. In her novels she pays close attention to developing her heroines by showing their inner growth. Jane Roper in *The Girl from Rome* falls in love with a young Italian, Gino, only to realize that he has no intention of marrying her. She has just completed the tourist season in Rome as a tour guide and had planned on remaining there, expecting his proposal. Her own moral standards and the realization that she has placed herself in a difficult position eventually force her to leave.

Rowan Langham in *Time May Change* meets Blake Hobart again after several years. She had been engaged to him, but did not have the maturity to make her own decision; consequently, her family influenced her to break the engagement. Since then, Rowan's father has died and she has had to grow up and assume more responsibility. Because of her added maturity, she is able to see Blake and her love in a more adult perspective.

Asquith is able to show the heroines' dilemma in such a way that their actions are well motivated and logical given their background and personality. She provides sufficient depth of character to make them believable by permitting frequent bouts of indecision and "might-have-been" regrets.

Her plots tend to be slower paced and less complicated than those in more recent novels. She makes use of foreign settings and romantic activities such as a Mediterranean cruise, but the focus of her stories remains on her characters.

In developing the personalities of her heroes, Asquith again tends to keep them low key and approachable. They are human with touching lapses of weakness that makes them more realistic. Vance Morley takes Jane with him as his fiancée because he had once been engaged to Anthea, his sister-in-law. He is not sure of his feelings toward her and feels the need of protection, so that his brother will not be upset. Blake Hobart pretends to continue his racing career in order to learn if Rowan really is willing to acknowledge their love regardless of his occupation, for she had originally wanted him to give it up and join her father's company.

Both men show sensitive needs to protect themselves and it adds a further dimension to their characters. They are portrayed as vulnerable people trying to cope with life just as others must. In a sense, it is their masculine outlook and an awareness of their responsibilities that cause them to act as they do. Blake must know that Rowan's sense of love and loyalty will withstand pressures of time and circumstances, a test she had failed once before. Vance, aware of his sister-in-law's tendency to see things only as she wishes to, tries to protect his brother the best way he can.

In a way, Asquith is a subtle writer. On the surface, her novels seem light and frothy. Yet hidden beneath the surface is a delicate blending of love and people. Her readers are constantly exposed to ideals that surround the relationships of men and women. Step by step, she lets her characters realize their own needs and the needs of their loved ones so that the ending is a satisfying blend of suspense and certainty, both for her characters and her readers alike.

—Arlene Moore

ASTLEY, Juliet. See **LOFTS, Nora.**

ATKIN, Grace Murray. Canadian. Born in 1891.

ROMANCE AND HISTORICAL PUBLICATIONS

Novels

The New World. New York, Crowell, 1921.
The Captive Herd. Toronto, McClelland and Stewart, 1922; London, Nash, 1923.
That Which Is Passed. New York, Crowell, 1923.
A Shadow Falls. Toronto, Ryerson Press, and New York, Bouregy, 1954; London, Wright and Brown, 1956.

OTHER PUBLICATIONS

Verse

Flowers of the Wind. New York, Kennerley, 1919.

*   *   *

Grace Murray Atkin is a modernist novelist whose historical sense includes the idea of personal, psychological history. On the dedication page of her novel *The New World* she notes: "I am one of those for whom character exists much more forcibly than action." Unfortunately, characterisation is more frequently defeated than supported by the modernist aspects of her narrative style. Atkin portrays characters moving through events rather than reflecting on the meaning of those events. Often commentary is given to a third-person narrator and the reader loses the illusion of perceiving events from a character's point of view as well as the accompanying sense of understanding the characters that this identificatory illusion gives.

In her two earliest novels, *The New World* and *The Captive Herd*, Atkin explores differing ethnic experiences of the new world. In the former novel, the Italian community in Canada is represented through the young manhood years of the main character, Dante Ricci. The novel is set the period just before, during, and just after World War I and traces Dante's progression from his old world family past to his election to the House of Commons. In the latter novel, the Jewish community in Manhattan provides the context for the events of the story. Both novels are set in time periods contemporaneous with the author's own life. Nevertheless, because of the ethnic point of view, both novels have a strong sense of historical moment. But, even here, the evocation of character psychology is constrained by the problems of narration already noted. The reader does not get a sense of character growth but rather a history of the events the characters have passed through. The conflicting purposes in the text make otherwise well-constructed stories seem trite.

The last novel Atkin wrote for a period of some 30 years, *That Which Is Passed*, is an experiment in an increasingly spare style. The novel is set in Paris shortly after World War I. Atkin develops a complex plot in which youth and age are at once contrasted and reconciled and the opposites of purity and scandal are presented in order to examine the impact of events on personal history. The central character, Peter Magdalen, was a fighter pilot in the war. Magdalen is an Englishman who was raised in Brittany and is fluent in French; he is an outsider who does not feel "outside." The plot unravels the mystery of his parentage skilfully, yet too predictably. While this novel is not strictly historical or a romance, it imaginatively captures a flavour of Paris between the wars from a refreshing perspective, other than that of bohemia and the café scene.

A Shadow Falls is an uneven novel divided into three parts, the first part of which is the least effective in its attempt to develop a "stream-of-consciousness" technique. Parts two and three are closer to conventional realist writing and are more successful. Against a backdrop of the Laurentian mountains and the nearby Canadian capital city, Ottawa, the conflict between Old and New World cultures is enacted. The failure of technique is due to its incompatibility with the treatment of a chronology of the events, rather than a psychological study, of the personal history presented from the narrating character's point of view. However, the tension between realist and modernist technique serves to enhance the dramatic possibilities of the plot.

Atkin's work cannot be identified as historical realist fiction or modernist, stream-of-consciousness psychological writing, but rather a transitional state between realism and the quality of reflexive self-awareness that has become known as metafiction. Her work seems unsatisfying because it does not fit the expectations of readers who may be reading from one of these three points of view. Nevertheless, from a literary historical perspective, her novels are fascinating as they struggle with changing ideas about what writing should or could be.

—Heather Iris Jones

AUEL, Jean M(arie, née Untinen). American. Born in Chicago, Illinois, 18 February 1936. Educated at Portland State University, Oregon; University of Portland, Oregon, M.B.A. 1976. Married Ray Auel in 1954; three daughters and two sons. Clerk, Tektronix Inc., Beaverton, Oregon, 1965–66; circuit board designer, 1966–73; technical writer, 1973–74; credit manager, 1974–76. Agent: Jean V. Naggar Literary Agency, 216 East 75th Street, New York, New York 10021, U.S.A.

ROMANCE AND HISTORICAL PUBLICATIONS

Novels (series: Earth's Children in all books)

The Clan of the Cave Bear. New York, Crown, and London, Hodder and Stoughton, 1980.
The Valley of Horses. New York, Crown, 1982; London, Hodder and Stoughton, 1983.
The Mammoth Hunters. New York, Crown, and London, Hodder and Stoughton, 1985.

*   *   *

The novels in Jean M. Auel's Earth's Children series can perhaps best be described as feminist prehistorical romances. Drawing on feminist theories of matriarchal prehistory and fertility based religion as well as presenting a portrayal of the minutiae of daily cave life drawn from contemporary archaeology, Auel uses the conventions of historical romance to create prehistoric feminist utopias. Throughout the series Auel's sensually and intellectually vibrant characters try to understand and overcome major cultural differences.

The Clan of the Cave Bear, first in the series, is the story of the adoption of the orphaned girl Ayla, who is Homo Sapiens, into a Neanderthal clan. Raised by the clan's shaman and medicine woman, Ayla struggles to adapt to clan ways, but since the differences between her adopted "clan" and the "others" of her birth are based on physiology and rooted in history and culture, her struggles to adjust are doomed. Ayla violates rigid clan con-

ventions, particularly of male dominance and rigid gender separation, by learning to hunt, resisting rape, hiding her mixed-breed child to prevent his being killed as deformed, and by eavesdropping on male rituals. Torn between her needs to belong and to follow her own destiny, Ayla grows into a sensitive and intelligent young woman despite the oppressive clan social order. However, because she is never sufficiently submissive to that order, she is ultimately banished.

The Valley of Horses juxtaposes the story of Ayla's solitary life after leaving the clan with the story of the journey of two brothers of her race, Jondalar and Thonolan of the Zelandonii, who are undertaking a sort of prehistoric Grand Tour. The happy but shallow Thonolan loses interest in life after his wife's death and is ultimately killed by a cave lion. The brooding Jondalar, searching for a deeper meaning to life, attracts many women, but cannot fall in love until he meets Ayla. Because of the dual plot, Auel's second novel offers less sustained emotional involvement than her first. The novel's main interest is in the well-told details of prehistoric life. The brothers' journey introduces a succession of Stone Age cultures—all female-centered, worshipping a divine "Mother" in various guises—and their ingenious ways of providing themselves with the necessary food, shelter, clothing, and entertainment for a satisfying life. Ayla's story has a different focus; in addition to establishing a cave household, the isolated Ayla learns to tame a horse and a cave lion and to produce fire by striking iron pyrite onto flint. Naturally, Ayla's and Jondalar's paths cross, and the final part of the book details their gradual drawing together, surmounting the cultural obstacles to mutual understanding, and their ultimate ecstatic union. Auel's explicit depiction of sexuality, particularly female sexuality, has led to accusations of obscenity; certainly in Jondalar, Auel has provided her heroine with a mate who compensates for the sexual and emotional violation and deprivation of her earlier years.

The Mammoth Hunters sets the romance of Ayla and Jondalar in a social context. Auel recaptures the sexual tension of the previous novel by using the difficulty of communicating across different cultural assumptions to estrange the lovers. A tribe of Mamutoi adopts Ayla, who is considered valuable not only as a female of child-bearing age, but also as the bearer of fire stones and of extraordinary knowledge of medicine and animals. The lovers' relationship barely survives this year, as Jondalar grows jealous of Ayla's position and ashamed of her upbringing by the "flatheads"—Neanderthals—his culture despises. This novel is about race, on two levels. When Ayla is courted by a black Mamutoi, Auel shows how racial differences can be considered "interesting" rather than crucial. However, in this culture differences between Neanderthals and Homo Sapiens *are* crucial, and Jondalar's fears about how first the Mamutoi and then his own people will accept a woman who has borne a mixed son estrange him from Ayla. Only when they face final separation do they gain the courage to risk ignoring the dictates of culture.

Throughout this series Ayla matures as she moves from the repressive, male-dominated society of the clan, to an isolation in which she makes her own meanings, and finally to acceptance and love among the "others," her own kind. Auel has given Ayla heroic attributes, and there is pleasure in seeing a "heroine" who is important in herself, rather than merely a reward for the hero at the end of his quest. If Ayla and Jondalar seem too much the typical WASP romantic leads, and if the correspondence between contemporary feminism and Auel's conception of cave society seems too pat, these excesses are forgivable because of the larger strengths of the novels. For although this series is set in the Stone Age, it raises contemporary feminist concerns about gender roles, and is as much about our own time as about prehistory. Auel uses the Stone Age setting and the conventions of historical romance to suggest that if human equality were institutionalized by a culture and its social structures, then passionate love between men and women would not only exist, but flourish.

—Linda S. Bergmann

———

AYRES, Ruby M(ildred). British. Born in January 1883. Married Reginald William Pocock in 1909. Regular contributor to the *Daily Chronicle* and *Daily Mirror*, both London. *Died 14 November 1955.*

ROMANCE AND HISTORICAL PUBLICATIONS

Novels

Richard Chatterton, V.C. London, Hodder and Stoughton, 1915; New York, Watt, 1919.
The Long Lane to Happiness. London, Hodder and Stoughton, 1915.
The Making of a Man. London, Newnes, 1915.
The Road That Bends. London, Hodder and Stoughton, 1916.
Paper Roses. London, Hodder and Stoughton, 1916.
A Man of His Word. London, Hodder and Stoughton, 1916.
The Year After. London, Newnes, 1916.
The Littl'st Lover. London, Hodder and Stoughton, 1917; New York, Doran, 1925.
The Black Sheep. London, Hodder and Stoughton, 1917.
The Winds of the World. London, Hodder and Stoughton, 1918; New York, Watt, 1921.
The Remembered Kiss. London, Hodder and Stoughton, 1918.
For Love. London, Hodder and Stoughton, 1918.
The Second Honeymoon. London, Hodder and Stoughton, 1918; New York, Watt, 1921.
Invalided Out. London, Hodder and Stoughton, 1918.
The Phantom Lover. London, Hodder and Stoughton, 1919; New York, Watt, 1921.
The Girl Next Door. London, Hodder and Stoughton, 1919.
The One Who Forgot. London, Hodder and Stoughton, 1919.
The Scar. London, Hodder and Stoughton, 1920; New York, Watt, 1921.
A Bachelor Husband. London, Hodder and Stoughton, and New York, Watt, 1920.
The Master Man. London, Hodder and Stoughton, 1920.
The Woman Hater. London, Hodder and Stoughton, 1920.
The Marriage of Barry Wicklow. London, Hodder and Stoughton, 1920; New York, Watt, 1921.
The Beggar Man. London, Hodder and Stoughton, 1920.
The Dancing Master. London, Hodder and Stoughton, 1920.
The Uphill Road. New York, Watt, 1921.
The Waif's Wedding. London, Hodder and Stoughton, 1921.
The Fortune Hunter. London, Hodder and Stoughton, 1921.
Her Way and His. London, Hodder and Stoughton, 1921.
The Highest Bidder. London, Hodder and Stoughton, 1921.
His Word of Honour. London, Hodder and Stoughton, 1921.
The Love of Robert Dennison. London, Hodder and Stoughton, 1921.
Brown Sugar. London, Hodder and Stoughton, 1921.
A Loveless Marriage. London, Hodder and Stoughton, 1921.
The Making of a Lover. London, Hodder and Stoughton, 1921.
The Man's Way. London, Hodder and Stoughton, 1921.
Nobody's Lovers. London, Hodder and Stoughton, 1921.
The One Unwanted. London, Hodder and Stoughton, 1921.

The Street Below. London, Hodder and Stoughton, 1922; New York, Doran, n.d.
A Gamble with Love. London, Hodder and Stoughton, 1922.
The Little Lady in Lodgings. London, Hodder and Stoughton, 1922.
The Lover Who Died. London, Hodder and Stoughton, 1922.
The Matherson Marriage. London, Hodder and Stoughton, 1922; New York, Doran, 1923.
The Romance of a Rogue. London, Hodder and Stoughton, and New York, Doran, 1923.
Love and a Lie. London, Hodder and Stoughton, 1923.
The Man Without a Heart. London, Hodder and Stoughton, 1923; New York, Doran, 1924.
The One Who Stood By. London, Hodder and Stoughton, 1923.
The Eager Search. London, Hodder and Stoughton, 1923.
Candle Light. London, Hodder and Stoughton, and New York, Doran, 1924.
Ribbons and Laces. London, Hodder and Stoughton, 1924.
Paul in Possession. London, Hodder and Stoughton, 1924.
The Man the Women Loved. London, Hodder and Stoughton, 1925; New York, Doran, 1926.
The Marriage Handicap. London, Hodder and Stoughton, 1925.
Overheard. London, Hodder and Stoughton, 1925; New York, Doran, 1926.
Charity's Chosen. London, Hodder and Stoughton, and New York, Doran, 1926.
Spoilt Music. London, Hodder and Stoughton, and New York, Doran, 1926.
The Faint Heart. London, Hodder and Stoughton, 1926.
The Planter and the Tree. London, Hodder and Stoughton, 1926; New York, Doran, 1927.
Wynne of Windwhistle. London, Hodder and Stoughton, 1926.
By the Gate of Pity. New York, Street and Smith, 1927.
The Luckiest Lady. London, Hodder and Stoughton, and New York, Doran, 1927.
Life Steps In. London, Hodder and Stoughton, 1928; New York, Doubleday, 1929.
The Family. London, Hodder and Stoughton, 1928.
Broken. London, Hodder and Stoughton, and New York, Doubleday, 1928.
Lovers. London, Hodder and Stoughton, and New York, Doubleday, 1929.
The Heartbreak Marriage. London, Hodder and Stoughton, 1929.
One Month at Sea, Together with George Who Believed in Allah. London, Hodder and Stoughton, 1929.
In the Day's March. London, Hodder and Stoughton, and New York, Doubleday, 1930.
Giving Him Up. London, Hodder and Stoughton, 1930.
My Old Love Came. London, Hodder and Stoughton, 1930.
One Summer. London, Hodder and Stoughton, and New York, Doubleday, 1930.
The Big Fellah. London, Hodder and Stoughton, and New York, Doubleday, 1931; as *Love Comes to Mary*, New York, Grosset and Dunlap, 1932.
Men Made the Town. London, Hodder and Stoughton, and New York, Doubleday, 1931.
The Little Man. London, Hodder and Stoughton, 1931; as *Winner Take All*, New York, Doubleday, 1937.
The Princess Passes. London, Hodder and Stoughton, 1931.
By the World Forgot. London, Hodder and Stoughton, 1932; New York, Doubleday, 1933.
So Many Miles. New York, Doubleday, 1932; London, Hodder and Stoughton, 1933.

Changing Pilots. London, Hodder and Stoughton, and New York, Doubleday, 1932.

Look to the Spring. London, Hodder and Stoughton, 1932; New York, Doubleday, 1933.

Always Tomorrow. London, Hodder and Stoughton, 1933; New York, Doubleday, 1934.

Come to My Wedding. London, Hodder and Stoughton, and New York, Doubleday, 1933.

Love Is So Blind. London, Hodder and Stoughton, 1933; New York, Doubleday, 1934.

All Over Again. New York, Doubleday, 1934; London, Hodder and Stoughton, 1935.

From This Day Forward. London, Hodder and Stoughton, and New York, Doubleday, 1934.

Much-Loved. London, Hodder and Stoughton, and New York, Doubleday, 1934.

Than This World Dreams Of. London, Hodder and Stoughton, 1934; New York, Doubleday, 1935.

Between You and Me. London, Hodder and Stoughton, 1935.

Feather. New York, Doubleday, 1935; London, Hodder and Stoughton, 1936.

The Man in Her Life. London, Hodder and Stoughton, and New York, Doubleday, 1935.

Some Day. London, Hodder and Stoughton, and New York, Doubleday, 1935.

The Sun and the Sea. London, Hodder and Stoughton, and New York, Doubleday, 1935.

Compromise. London, Hodder and Stoughton, and New York, Doubleday, 1936.

After-Glow. London, Hodder and Stoughton, and New York, Doubleday, 1936.

Follow the Shadow. London, Hodder and Stoughton, 1936; New York, Doubleday, 1937.

High Noon. London, Hodder and Stoughton, 1936; New York, Doubleday, 1937.

Somebody Else. New York, Doubleday, 1936; London, Hodder and Stoughton, 1937.

Too Much Together. London, Hodder and Stoughton, and New York, Doubleday, 1936.

Living Apart. New York, Doubleday, 1937; London, Hodder and Stoughton, 1938.

Owner Gone Abroad. London, Hodder and Stoughton, and New York, Doubleday, 1937.

Silver Wedding. London, Hodder and Stoughton, 1937.

Unofficial Wife. New York, Doubleday, 1937; London, Hodder and Stoughton, 1938.

The Tree Drops a Leaf. London, Hodder and Stoughton, and New York, Doubleday, 1938.

Return Journey. New York, Doubleday, 1938; London, Hodder and Stoughton, 1939.

And Still They Dream. New York, Doubleday, 1938; London, Hodder and Stoughton, 1939.

One to Live With. London, Hodder and Stoughton, and New York, Doubleday, 1938.

There Was Another. London, Hodder and Stoughton, and New York, Doubleday, 1938.

Big Ben. New York, Doubleday, 1939.

The Moon in the Water. New York, Doubleday, 1939.

The Thousandth Man. London, Hodder and Stoughton, and New York, Doubleday, 1939.

Week-End Woman. London, Hodder and Stoughton, and New York, Doubleday, 1939.

Little and Good. London, Hodder and Stoughton, and New York, Doubleday, 1940.

The Little Sinner. London, Hodder and Stoughton, and New York, Doubleday, 1940.

Wallflower. London, Hodder and Stoughton, and New York, Doubleday, 1940.

Sometimes Spring Is Late. London, Hodder and Stoughton, 1941.

Sunrise for Georgie. London, Hodder and Stoughton, 1941.

Still Waters. London, Hodder and Stoughton, and New York, Doubleday, 1941.

The Constant Heart. New York, Doubleday, 1941.

Rosemary—For Forgetting. London, Hodder and Stoughton, 1941.

Young Is My Love. New York, Doubleday, 1941; as *The Young at Heart*, London, Hodder and Stoughton, 1942.

Nothing Lovelier. London, Hodder and Stoughton, 1942.

Lost Property. New York, Doubleday, 1943.

Man Friday. London, Hodder and Stoughton, 1943.

Love Comes Unseen. New York, Doubleday, 1943; as *One Woman Too Many*, London, Hodder and Stoughton, 1952.

Starless Night. London, Hodder and Stoughton, 1943.

The Lady from London. London, Hodder and Stoughton, 1944.

The Dreamer Wakes. London, Hodder and Stoughton, 1945.

April's Day. London, Macdonald, 1945.

Where Are You Going? London, Hodder and Stoughton, 1946.

Salt of the Earth. London, Macdonald, 1946.

Young Shoulders. London, Hodder and Stoughton, 1947.

Missing the Tide. London, Hodder and Stoughton, 1948.

The Story of John Willie. London, Macdonald, 1948.

Steering by a Star. London, Hodder and Stoughton, 1949.

The Day Comes Round. London, Hodder and Stoughton, 1949; New York, Arcadia House, 1950.

The Man from Ceylon. London, Hodder and Stoughton, 1950.

The Man Who Lived Alone. London, Macdonald, 1950.

The Story of Fish and Chips. London, Macdonald, 1951; as *Bright Destiny*, New York, Arcadia House, 1952.

Twice a Boy. London, Hodder and Stoughton, 1951.

The Youngest Aunt. London, Hodder and Stoughton, 1952.

One Sees Stars. London, Hodder and Stoughton, 1952.

Love Without Wings. London, Hodder and Stoughton, 1953; New York, Arcadia House, 1954.

Dark Gentleman. London, Hodder and Stoughton, 1953.

Old-Fashioned Heart. New York, Arcadia House, 1953.

Short Stories

The Shadow Man and Other Stories. London, Hutchinson, 1919.

Our Avenue and Other Stories. London, Pearson, 1922; New York, Arcadia House, 1936.

Happy Endings. London, Jarrolds, 1935.

Autumn Fires: Two Love Stories. London, Hodder and Stoughton, 1951.

OTHER PUBLICATIONS

Other

Castles in Spain: The Chronicles of an April Month. London, Cassell, 1912.

*   *   *

Ruby M. Ayres's first novel (of some 150) was published in the 1910's. Most of them were made of a bland and jokey mixture which proved to be almost timeless. Consequently, many were still selling under the guise of new novels well into the 1960's and 1970's.

Publishers are naturally reluctant to relinquish a steady-selling commercial name. If, by misfortune, a publisher's best-selling author runs out of steam, dies, or cannot keep up with the insatiable appetite of her readers, demand for her works can be fulfilled by re-issuing the novels, just as they are, or as a new novel with an up-to-date dust jacket, or in a modified version. Ayres's novels were eminently suitable for this treatment. *Week-End Woman*, for example, made its first appearance in 1939. Some 30 years later it reappeared with a newly designed jacket, but only minor alterations to the text. In 1939 Slane the shady suitor is, for example, said to be "a man on leave from India." In 1969 he has become "a man on leave from the Middle East oil company in which he had a good job." In 1939 Mariette, "heroine with an angel's face," wears hats when she goes out to lunch. In the less constricting 1960's, she must lunch hatless. In 1939 her rich husband's imperious treatment of restaurant waiters is demanding and aggressive: "Here waiter, keep this stuff hot till I come back," he orders. Then, "Where's my dinner?" and "Come and light the fire some of you fellows—don't just stand there gaping." In the 1969 text the publisher's editor had realised that such treatment of minions is no longer socially acceptable. The stereotype of the ideal man however, remains quite unchanged. In both versions, he has "grey eyes, dark brows, dark hair and a certain ruthlessness about the mouth and chin, good-looking in a manly, rather severe way."

The slightly suggestive title and blurb might lead one to expect some titillation, or at least a hint of illicit sexual activity: "Wealth alone could not compensate for the lack of any real affection. And so she turned to other men. One affair followed another in quick succession as she sought vainly for something real to cling to." This blurb is misleading. Mariette's behaviour may seem plain daft, but is never adulterous, for, as she repeatedly wails to one of her admirers: "I can't—I'm afraid. Yes, of course I love you—but I can't face it—I'm not made that way. I hate scandal—I'm afraid." She has little to be afraid of. We read how the man "ran his hands over her shoulders and slim body" (1939). By 1969, even this innocuous move has been omitted, and he does not lay a finger on her. The book's principal concern, in both versions, is upholding the reputation of the heroine. As society became more permissive, Ayres's stories were re-created to seem more strait-laced.

Rosemary—For Forgetting, similarly, was a successful reissue. It is the tale of a rich girl who falls irrevocably in love with an "unsuitable person." The rich father has him sent away; the engagement is broken off. Rosemary spends the rest of the book trying to forget her childhood sweetheart until, on the penultimate page, her father now being dead, the lovers are reunited. Although first published in 1941, the novel is so totally lacking in topicality that it could be successfully re-issued in 1966 with only minor changes to the text. Indeed, the one careless point is the publishers' choice of illustration. Rosemary is said to live in a large country house a few hours from Paddington Station. She has "fair hair, and her eyes were as blue as forget-me-nots; her tiny hands and feet were perfect, and when she laughed one corner of her mouth lifted itself a little higher than the other corner in an oddly fascinating manner." In the 1966 jacket, although no doubt still oddly fascinating, she is shown as having raven-black hair, coal-dark eyes, and thick symmetrical lips. While being kissed on the ear by a man in a lime-green sports shirt, she is standing in front of what is clearly no wealthy Home Counties residence, but a North American log-chalet. This kind of carelessness in presentation can have done little to raise the prestige of romantic fiction, then at a low ebb.

The cheap re-issues of popular fiction have always been seen as a threat to the more serious novelist. E. H. Lacon Watson, a journalist lecturing in the 1930's, said that they were actually destroying the livelihood of the less well selling writers. "In recent years, every change that has been made in the world of publishing and bookselling has been in favour of the few big sellers and against the author with a small, if select, audience." In fact, the readership of these two types of fiction was different. Ayres herself described, with a touch of self-mockery, the kind of girl who might be reading her own novels. There is "a kind-eyed, sentimental under housemaid," in *The Master Man* "who was young and romantic and devoured every novel she could get hold of."

By "every novel" Ayres clearly does not mean the highbrow heavy weights, but novels such as her own. Hers are fantasy-spinning, harmless escapism, jauntily written, with convoluted plots, and an excess of metaphors piled one on the other. If she had been out to expound some profound message, these many varied metaphors might well have obscured the meaning. But she was not. She was out to entertain. Just occasionally, there is a heroine, such as Marlene (*Where Are You Going?*) who not only starts out confused and upset, but ends up with second best too. "She asked herself the question, 'Where are you going?' and failed to find an answer." Luckily, she ends up with a partner equally unsure where he is going, a tired-looking, discharged soldier "with a slight limp."

She had her craft in perspective, and was quite aware of where *she* was going.

Do you believe really believe in the romance you've written so much about? Do you believe it lasts? I'm frequently asked the question by people who are kind enough to enjoy reading my books and I can imagine it would be very disillusioning if I were to reply—"No, I don't believe in it. I just write love stories because they sell." That wouldn't be true either. I must certainly believe in romance and know that it can and does last providing it is mixed with two most important ingredients—tolerance and a sense of humour. . . . I'm not pretending to be original when I say that more marriages have been ruined by a nagging wife than there can ever be by an atomic bomb. I firmly believe that romance can be lively even when the strawberry season is over and there is only bread and cheese in the larder and no matter whether you agree with me or not, I'll go on writing love stories with happy endings.

—Rachel Anderson

BACHELLER, Irving (Addison). American. Born in Piedmont, New York, 26 September 1859. Educated at St. Lawrence University, Canton, New York, M.S. 1892, M.A. 1901; Middlebury College, Vermont, Ph.D. Married 1) Anna Detmar Schultz in 1883 (died 1924); 2) Mary Elizabeth Sollace (died 1949). Editor, New York *World*, 1898–1900. LL.D.: Rollins College, Winter Park, Florida, 1939. *Died 24 February 1950.*

ROMANCE AND HISTORICAL PUBLICATIONS

Novels (series: Eben Holden)

The Master of Silence. New York, Webster, 1892.
The Still House of O'Darrow. London, Cassell, 1894.
The Story of a Passion. East Aurora, New York, Roycroft, 1899.

Eben Holden. Boston, Lothrop, and London, Richards, 1900.
D'Iri and I. Boston, Lothrop, and London, Richards, 1901.
Darrel of the Blessed Isles. Boston, Lothrop, and London, Watt, 1903.
Vergilius: A Tale of the Coming of Christ. New York, Harper, 1904.
Silas Strong: Emperor of the Woods. New York, Harper, and London, Fisher Unwin, 1906.
Eben Holden's Last Day a-Fishing. New York, Harper, 1907.
The Hand-Made Gentleman. New York, Harper, 1909; as *Cricket Heron,* London, Unwin, 1909.
The Master. New York, Doubleday, 1909.
Keeping Up with Lizzy. New York, Harper, 1911.
Charge It; or, Keeping Up with Harry. New York, Harper, 1912.
The Turning of Griggsby. New York, Harper, 1913.
Marryers. New York, Harper, 1914.
The Light in the Clearing. Indianapolis, Bobbs Merrill, 1917; London, Collins, 1918.
Keeping Up with William. Indianapolis, Bobbs Merrill, 1918.
A Man for the Ages. Indianapolis, Bobbs Merrill, 1919; London, Constable, 1920.
The Prodigal Village: A Christmas Tale. Indianapolis, Bobbs Merrill, 1920.
In the Days of Poor Richard. Indianapolis, Bobbs Merrill, 1922; London, Hutchinson, 1923.
The Scudders: A Story of Today. New York, Macmillan, 1923; London, Mills and Boon, 1924.
Father Abraham. Indianapolis, Bobbs Merrill, and London, Hutchinson, 1925.
Dawn: A Lost Romance of the Time of Christ. New York, Macmillan, 1927; as *The Trumpets of God,* London, Melrose, 1927.
The House of the Three Ganders. Indianapolis, Bobbs Merrill, 1928; London, Hutchinson, 1929.
A Candle in the Wilderness. Indianapolis, Bobbs Merrill, 1930.
Master of Chaos. Indianapolis, Bobbs Merrill, 1932.
Uncle Peel. New York, Grosset and Dunlap, 1933.
The Harvesting. New York, Stokes, 1934.
The Oxen of the Sun. New York, Stokes, 1935.
A Boy for the Ages. New York, Farrar and Rinehart, 1937.

OTHER PUBLICATIONS

Novel

The Winds of God (for children). New York, Farrar and Rinehart, 1941.

Verse

In Various Moods. New York, Harper, 1910.

Other

Opinions of a Cheerful Yankee (autobiography). Indianapolis, Bobbs Merrill, 1926.
Coming Up the Road: Memories of a North Country Boyhood. Indianapolis, Bobbs Merrill, 1928.
Great Moments in the Life of Washington. New York, Grosset and Dunlap, 1932.
From Stores of Memory (memoirs). New York, Farrar and Rinehart, 1938.

Editor, *Best Things from American Literature.* New York, Christian Herald, 1899.

*   *   *

It is difficult to think of Irving Bacheller's literary output without concentrating on the region where he spent his formative years, upstate New York, and the historical romance. Bacheller's most effective creative works are ones which focus on his native state and chronicle the lives and adventures of fictional characters native to that area and nearby states. Written in first-person narrative, Bacheller's work generally is set in the 18th and early 19th centuries; his characters meet major figures in American history such as George Washington, Abraham Lincoln, or Benjamin Franklin.

By far Bacheller's most commercially successful work was *Eben Holden,* which is set in upstate New York and is an account of country life through the eyes of a homespun farmhand. During Bacheller's lifetime this novel sold nearly three-quarters of a million copies. The rural New York connection is pursued with *In the Days of Poor Richard,* which opens in the wilderness of northern New York and closes in Philadelphia. In keeping with Bacheller's dominant chronological emphasis, the reader progresses through the Revolutionary War meeting some of its leading figures and traveling to urban centers intimately associated with that era. Romance is provided as hardy Jack Irons falls in love with Margaret Hare, marries her, and proves himself valiant in peace and war. In *Master of Chaos* Bacheller presents another Revolutionary era romance between Colin Cabot, a Harvard educated supporter of the rebel cause, and Patience Fayerweather, daughter of a strong Loyalist family. Not unlike Irons, Cabot joins the Continental Army serving as a secretary and later recruiting officer under George Washington. *The Light in the Clearing* covers the early portion of the 19th century in upstate New York and revolves around the life of Silas Wright, an early New York governor who befriends a boy named Barton Baynes. Baynes's early years with his Aunt Deel and Uncle Peabody provide a glimpse into the social life of those times.

Bacheller's penchant for characters moving across time and location is further exemplified in *A Man for the Ages,* which concentrates on the early manhood of Abraham Lincoln. The Traylors move from Vermont to New Salem, Illinois in the 1830's and there meet the young Abe Lincoln, become friends, and share in his growth in the frontier community to the point of his entering the United States House of Representatives. Another Lincoln portrait is preserved in *Father Abraham,* where the youthful northerner Randall Hope, inspired by the personality of "Father Abraham" moves south to the home of a relative and engages in a predictable clash of ideas. Hope becomes involved in the Civil War and finds romance and adventure.

Perhaps the most dramatic geographical shift in Bacheller's writing comes in *Dawn: A Lost Romance of the Time of Christ* in which a young Greek woman, Doris of Colossae, falls in love with Apollos, a Christian Jew. Apollos, already married, leaves Doris. Doris converts to Christianity and comes into contact with a number of biblical characters and events. Bacheller's last novel, *Winds of God,* tells the story of an Adirondack guide and timber cutter.

Bacheller wrote more than 30 novels, the majority of which are historical romance. His works emphasize strength of individual character, patriotism, and sturdy American ideals. Critically, the novels met with mixed success; his deification of figures in American history is now unfashionable. The strength of Bacheller's literary work centers on his recreation of the personal character of upstate New Yorkers and his action-filled plots.

—Frank R. Levstick

BAILEY, H(enry) C(hristopher). British. Born in London, 1 February 1878. Educated at the City of London School; Corpus Christi College, Oxford (scholar), B.A. 1901. Married Lydia Haden Janet Guest in 1908; two daughters. Drama critic, war correspondent, and leader writer, *Daily Telegraph*, London, 1901–46. *Died 24 March 1961.*

ROMANCE AND HISTORICAL PUBLICATIONS

Novels

My Lady of Orange. London and New York, Longman, 1901.
Karl of Erbach. New York, Longman, 1902; London, Longman, 1903.
The Master of Gray. London and New York, Longman, 1903.
Beaujeu. London, Murray, 1905.
Under Castle Walls. New York, Appleton, 1906; as *Springtime*, London, Murray, 1907.
Raoul, Gentleman of Fortune. London, Hutchinson, 1907; as *A Gentleman of Fortune*, New York, Appleton, 1907.
The God of Clay. London, Hutchinson, and New York, Brentano's, 1908.
Colonel Stow. London, Hutchinson, 1908; as *Colonel Greatheart*, Indianapolis, Bobbs Merrill, 1908.
Storm and Treasure. London, Methuen, and New York, Brentano's, 1910.
The Lonely Queen. London, Methuen, and New York, Doran, 1911.
The Sea Captain. New York, Doran, 1913; London, Methuen, 1914.
The Gentleman Adventurer. London, Methuen, 1914; New York, Doran, 1915.
The Highwayman. London, Methuen, 1915; New York, Dutton, 1918.
The Gamesters. London, Methuen, 1916; New York, Dutton, 1919.
The Young Lovers. London, Methuen, 1917; New York, Dutton, 1929.
The Pillar of Fire. London, Methuen, 1918.
Barry Leroy. London, Methuen, 1919; New York, Dutton, 1920.
His Serene Highness. London, Methuen, 1920; New York, Dutton, 1922.
The Fool. London, Methuen, 1921.
The Plot. London, Methuen, 1922.
The Rebel. London, Methuen, 1923.
Knight at Arms. London, Methuen, 1924; New York, Dutton, 1925.
The Golden Fleece. London, Methuen, 1925.
The Merchant Prince. London, Methuen, 1926; New York, Dutton, 1929.
Bonaventure. London, Methuen, 1927.
Judy Bovenden. London, Methuen, 1928.
Mr. Cardonnel. London, Ward Lock, 1931.
The Bottle Party. New York, Doubleday, 1940.

OTHER PUBLICATIONS

Novels

Rimingtons. London, Chapman and Hall, 1904.
The Suburban. London, Methuen, 1912.
Garstons. London, Methuen, 1930; as *The Garston Murder Case*, New York, Doubleday, 1930.
The Red Castle. London, Ward Lock, 1932; as *The Red Castle Mystery*, New York, Doubleday, 1932.
The Man in the Cape. London, Benn, 1933.
Shadow on the Wall. London, Gollancz, and New York, Doubleday, 1934.
The Sullen Sky Mystery. London, Gollancz, and New York, Doubleday, 1935.
Black Land, White Land. London, Gollancz, and New York, Doubleday, 1937.
Clunk's Claimant. London, Gollancz, 1937; as *The Twittering Bird Mystery*, New York, Doubleday, 1937.
The Great Game. London, Gollancz, and New York, Doubleday, 1939.
The Veron Mystery. London, Gollancz, 1939; as *Mr. Clunk's Text*, New York, Doubleday, 1939.
The Bishop's Crime. London, Gollancz, 1940; New York, Doubleday, 1941.
The Little Captain. London, Gollancz, 1941; as *Orphan Ann*, New York, Doubleday, 1941.
Dead Man's Shoes. London, Gollancz, 1942; as *Nobody's Vineyard*, New York, Doubleday, 1942.
No Murder. London, Gollancz, 1942; as *The Apprehensive Dog*, New York, Doubleday, 1942.
Mr. Fortune Finds a Pig. London, Gollancz, and New York, Doubleday, 1943.
Slippery Ann. London, Gollancz, 1944; as *The Queen of Spades*, New York, Doubleday, 1944.
The Cat's Whisker. New York, Doubleday, 1944; as *Dead Man's Effects*, London, Macdonald, 1945.
The Wrong Man. New York, Doubleday, 1945; London, Macdonald, 1946.
The Life Sentence. London, Macdonald, and New York, Doubleday, 1946.
Honour among Thieves. London, Macdonald, and New York, Doubleday, 1947.
Saving a Rope. London, Macdonald, 1948; as *Save a Rope*, New York, Doubleday, 1948.
Shrouded Death. London, Macdonald, 1950.

Short Stories

Call Mr. Fortune. London, Methuen, 1920; New York, Dutton, 1921.
Mr. Fortune's Practice. London, Methuen, 1923; New York, Dutton, 1924.
Mr. Fortune's Trials. London, Methuen, 1925; New York, Dutton, 1926.
Mr. Fortune, Please. London, Methuen, and New York, Dutton, 1928.
Mr. Fortune Speaking. London, Ward Lock, 1930; New York, Dutton, 1931.
Mr. Fortune Explains. London, Ward Lock, 1930; New York, Dutton, 1931.
Case for Mr. Fortune. London, Ward Lock, and New York, Doubleday, 1932.
Mr. Fortune Wonders. London, Ward Lock, and New York, Doubleday, 1933.

Mr. Fortune Objects. London, Gollancz, and New York, Doubleday, 1935.

A Clue for Mr. Fortune. London, Gollancz, and New York, Doubleday, 1936.

Mr. Fortune's Case Book (omnibus). London, Methuen, 1936.

This Is Mr. Fortune. London, Gollancz, and New York, Doubleday, 1938.

Mr. Fortune Here. London, Gollancz, and New York, Doubleday, 1940.

Meet Mr. Fortune (selection). New York, Doubleday, 1942.

The Best of Mr. Fortune. New York, Pocket Books, 1943.

Play

The White Hawk, with David Kimball, adaptation of the novel *Beaujeu* by Bailey (produced London, 1909).

Other

Forty Years After: The Story of the Franco-German War, 1870. London, Hodder and Stoughton, 1914.

The Roman Eagles (for children). London, Gill, 1929.

*   *   *

A writer of healthy outdoor swashbucklers that are only passingly concerned with plausibility or characterization, H. C. Bailey does not specialize in time or place, but sets his novels indifferently in an England or Europe with some historical basis (the Peninsular War in *The Young Lovers*, Plantagenet England in *The Fool*) or in a fantasy of Renaissance Italy (*Under Castle Walls*.) Real characters are introduced to some extent, but the emphasis is always on the creatures of Bailey's imagination.

Bailey usually imagined men—and the men who are his heroes are brave, quick-witted, and misunderstood. In some respects, they have the appeal of a jolly English public school boy. The noble Lionardo of *Under Castle Walls* is thought negligible by his court until he is motivated by the cruelties of a neighboring lord to make war. John Newstead, the mercenary soldier who transfers his loyalty from the Duke of Alva to William the Silent in *My Lady of Orange* finds his motives misunderstood by the Dutch and even by his adored Gabrielle, until he proves to them all that he is driven by natural goodness as well as desire for riches. The *Knight at Arms*, Silvain St. Lo, is a kind of Don Quixote, going through 15th-century France and Italy fighting for his honor, confounding again and again those who expect him to seek wealth, love, or political power. His encounters leave him worse off than before, despite his undoubted soldierly skills and his quick mind, because he will not seek advantage for himself or his cynical squire Thibaut. Of course Bran, *The Fool*, who becomes a companion of Henry II makes up for his low social status by his cleverness and instinctive understanding of the English people.

Similarly, Bailey's villains are villainous indeed: Castracane's vicious tortures in *Under Castle Walls* are as well not described since the one that bears description involves feeding his enemies to his wolf pack. We meet the unspeakable betrayals of John Lackland in *The Fool*, although other historical villains, including Roger Mortimer, are treated more gently. Minor henchmen, bullies and rogues, however, are pilloried. The villainous French mercenary Henri Vermeil, who tries to betray Newstead in *My Lady of Orange*, is dyed with darker colors than the Duke of Alva himself. *The Young Lovers*, with a stronger historical basis than most, includes at least one noble French enemy and even a likeable and idealistically motivated French spy.

The Young Lovers is unusual in that circumstances, and the protagonist Jack Lavington himself, are his worst enemies. Showing a weakness in plotting that becomes almost comic, Bailey has Lavington's whole family and some of his friends prone to being kidnapped: cousin David is twice kidnapped for reasons that have nothing to do with Jack, and Jack is twice blamed by David's father and society generally; Jack himself is abducted; Miss Amberly and the Portuguese girl she has befriended are also kidnapped by the French officer who refuses to believe Juana is serious about marrying David Lavington; and Jack's uncle had been kidnapped years ago in Venice. Jack ends up a successful officer under Pakenham, heir to his uncle's large fortune, and engaged to the enchanting Mary Amberly—a happier end than many of Bailey's heroes have. While Bran finally retires to his adoptive daughter's home after Henry II's ignominious death in *The Fool*, Silvain St. Lo, bereft of horses, allies and friends ends *Knight at Arms* as he began, seeking honor on the field of battle.

The women that Bailey creates have much in common, too. They are beautiful, and they may be kind. The three heroines of *Under Castle Walls* are the beautiful Lucrezia, who is more spirited, more fallible—and hence more human—than most; the beautiful and serene Beatrice, who almost loses her husband because of her placidity; and the beautiful and pathetic waif Cecilia, the Marchioness of Frido, a cousin under the skin to the witch child Ia in *The Fool*.

It would be easy to call these figures stereotypes, but they are not similar enough to any real people to be called that. They are more like archetypes, living in a sunny, Britannic Arcady. (None of Bailey's heroes is English, but if Englishmen are available, they are given heroic roles.)

Note should be made of the enticing descriptions of rural scenes with which Bailey enlivens his novels, well-written yet causing no more than a ripple in the smoothly flowing narratives. Although *The Fool* and *Knight at Arms* are both episodic in nature, Bailey contrives to keep the reader interested as event follows event.

While Bailey's novels deal mostly with the upper strata of society, his work is relatively free of the political and racial prejudices that mar other work of his period—largely because he seems to be uninterested in such mundane details. Bran is concerned with peasant and serf in *The Fool*, being himself of the lower orders, and Silvain is kind to the poor—it's the knightly thing to do.

Reading Bailey, one can relax in the conviction that no character the author allows one to become fond of will be killed or even injured (except those whose demise is historically well-established—though Bran tries in vain to save Thomas à Becket) and that all will end well for the right people.

—Susan Branch

————————

BALDWIN, Faith. American. Born in New Rochelle, New York, 1 October 1893. Attended Packer School; Miss Fuller School; Briarcliff School. Married Hugh H. Cuthrell in 1920 (died 1953); two sons and two daughters. Freelance writer: faculty member, Famous Writers School, Westport, Connecticut. *Died 18 March 1978.*

ROMANCE AND HISTORICAL PUBLICATIONS

Novels

Mavis of Green Hill. Boston, Small Maynard, and London, Hodder and Stoughton, 1921.

Laurel of Stonystream. Boston, Small Maynard, 1923; as *The Maid of Stonystream*, London, Sampson Low, 1924.

Magic and Mary Rose. Boston, Small Maynard, 1924.

Thresholds. Boston, Small Maynard, 1925; London, Sampson Low, 1926.

Those Difficult Years. Boston, Small Maynard, 1925; London, Sampson Low, 1926.

Three Women. New York, Dodd Mead, 1926; London, Sampson Low, 1927.

Departing Wings. New York, Dodd Mead, 1927; London, Sampson Low, 1928.

Rosalie's Career. New York, Clode, 1928.

Betty. New York, Clode, and London, Sampson Low, 1928.

Alimony. New York, Dodd Mead, 1928; London, Sampson Low, 1929.

The Incredible Year. New York, Dodd Mead, 1929; London, Sampson Low, 1930.

Garden Oats. New York, Dodd Mead, and London, Sampson Low, 1929.

Broadway Interlude, with Achmed Abdullah. New York, Payson and Clarke, 1929; London, Selwyn and Blount, 1930.

Make-Believe. New York, Dodd Mead, 1930; London, Sampson Low, 1931.

The Office Wife. New York, Dodd Mead, and London, Sampson Low, 1930.

Skyscraper. New York, Cosmopolitan, 1931; London, Sampson Low, 1932; as *Skyscraper Souls*, New York, Grosset and Dunlap, 1932.

Today's Virtue. New York, Dodd Mead, 1931.

Self-Made Woman. New York, Farrar and Rinehart, 1932; London, Sampson Low, 1933.

Week-End Marriage. New York, Farrar and Rinehart, and London, Sampson Low, 1932.

Girl on the Make, with Achmed Abdullah. New York, Long and Smith, and London, Selwyn and Blount, 1932.

District Nurse. New York, Farrar and Rinehart, 1932; London, Sampson Low, 1933.

White-Collar Girl. New York, Farrar and Rinehart, 1933; London, Sampson Low, 1934.

Beauty. New York, Farrar and Rinehart, and London, Sampson Low, 1933.

Love's a Puzzle. New York, Farrar and Rinehart, 1933; London, Sampson Low, 1934.

Innocent Bystander. New York, Farrar and Rinehart, 1934; London, Sampson Low, 1935.

Within a Year. New York, Farrar and Rinehart, and London, Sampson Low, 1934.

Honor Bound. New York, Farrar and Rinehart, 1934; London, Sampson Low, 1936.

American Family. New York, Farrar and Rinehart, 1935; as *Conflict*, London, Sampson Low, 1935.

The Puritan Strain. New York, Farrar and Rinehart, and London, Sampson Low, 1935.

The Moon's Our Home. New York, Farrar and Rinehart, 1936; London, Sampson Low, 1937.

Men Are Such Fools! New York, Farrar and Rinehart, 1936; London, Sampson Low, 1937.

Private Duty. New York, Farrar and Rinehart, 1936; London, Sampson Low, 1938.

That Man Is Mine! London, Sampson Low, 1936; New York, Farrar and Rinehart, 1937.

The Heart Has Wings. New York, Farrar and Rinehart, 1937; London, Sampson Low, 1938.

Twenty-Four Hours a Day. New York, Farrar and Rinehart, 1937; London, Sampson Low, 1939.

Manhattan Nights. New York, Farrar and Rinehart, 1937.

Hotel Hostess. New York, Farrar and Rinehart, 1938; London, Sampson Low, 1940.

Enchanted Oasis. New York, Farrar and Rinehart, 1938; London, Sampson Low, 1940.

Rich Girl, Poor Girl. New York, Farrar and Rinehart, 1938; London, Sampson Low, 1939.

White Magic. New York, Farrar and Rinehart, 1939; London, Sampson Low, 1945.

Station Wagon Set. New York, Farrar and Rinehart, 1939; London, Hale, 1945.

The High Road. New York, Farrar and Rinehart, 1939; London, Sampson Low, 1944.

Career by Proxy. New York, Farrar and Rinehart, 1939; London, Sampson Low, 1943.

Letty and the Law. New York, Farrar and Rinehart, 1940; London, Hale, 1946.

Medical Center. New York, Farrar and Rinehart, 1940; London, Hale, 1946.

Rehearsal for Love. New York, Farrar and Rinehart, 1940; London, Hale, 1946.

Something Special. New York, Farrar and Rinehart, 1940.

Temporary Address: Reno. New York, Farrar and Rinehart, 1941.

And New Stars Burn. New York, Farrar and Rinehart, 1941; London, Hale, 1948.

The Heart Remembers. New York, Farrar and Rinehart, 1941.

Blue Horizons. New York, Farrar and Rinehart, 1942; London, Hale, 1951.

Breath of Life. New York, Farrar and Rinehart, 1942; London, Hale, 1953.

The Rest of My Life with You. New York, Farrar and Rinehart, 1942; London, Hale, 1947.

You Can't Escape. New York, Farrar and Rinehart, 1943; London, Hale, 1952.

Washington, U.S.A. New York, Farrar and Rinehart, 1943.

Change of Heart. New York, Farrar and Rinehart, 1944; London, Hale, 1949.

He Married a Doctor. New York, Farrar and Rinehart, 1944; London, Hale, 1953.

A Job for Jenny. New York, Farrar and Rinehart, 1945; as *Tell Me My Heart*, 1950.

Arizona Star. New York, Farrar and Rinehart, 1945; London, Hale, 1949.

No Private Heaven. New York, Farrar and Rinehart, 1946; London, Hale, 1954.

Woman on Her Own. New York, Rinehart, 1946; London, Hale, 1954.

Give Love the Air. New York, Rinehart, 1947; London, Hale, 1955.

Sleeping Beauty. New York, Rinehart, 1947; London, Hale, 1954.

Marry for Money. New York, Rinehart, 1948; London, Hale, 1955.

The Golden Shoestring. New York, Rinehart, 1949; London, Hale, 1956.

Look Out for Liza. New York, Rinehart, 1950; London, Hale, 1956.

The Whole Armor. New York, Rinehart, 1951; London, Hale, 1956.

The Juniper Tree. New York, Rinehart, 1952; London, Hale, 1957.

Three Faces of Love. New York, Rinehart, 1957; London, Hale, 1958.

Blaze of Sunlight. New York, Rinehart, 1959; London, Hale, 1960.

Testament of Trust. New York, Holt Rinehart, 1960.

Harvest of Hope. New York, Holt Rinehart, 1962.

The West Wind. New York, Holt Rinehart, 1962; London, Hale, 1963.

The Lonely Man. New York, Holt Rinehart, 1964; as *The Lonely Doctor*, London, Hale, 1964; as *Echoes of Another Spring*, New York, Dell, 1965.

There Is a Season. New York, Holt Rinehart, and London, Hale, 1966.

Evening Star. New York, Holt Rinehart, 1966.

The Velvet Hammer. New York, Holt Rinehart, and London, Hale, 1969.

Take What You Want. New York, Holt Rinehart, 1970; London, Hale, 1971.

Any Village. New York, Holt Rinehart, 1971; London, Hale, 1972.

One More Time. New York, Holt Rinehart, 1972; London, Hale, 1974.

No Bed of Roses. New York, Holt Rinehart, 1973; London, Hale, 1975.

Time and the Hour. New York, Holt Rinehart, 1974; London, Hale, 1975.

New Girl in Town. New York, Holt Rinehart, 1975.

Thursday's Child. New York, Holt Rinehart, 1976; London, Hale, 1977.

Hold On to Your Heart. London, Hale, 1976.

Adam's Eden. New York, Holt Rinehart, 1977; London, Hale, 1978.

Short Stories

Wife vs. Secretary. New York, Grosset and Dunlap, 1934.

Five Woman (includes *Star on Her Shoulder, Detour, Let's Do the Town*). New York, Farrar and Rinehart, 1942; London, Hale, 1946.

They Who Love. New York, Rinehart, 1948.

OTHER PUBLICATIONS

Play

Screenplay: *Portia on Trial*, with Samuel Ornitz and E. E. Paramore, Jr., 1937.

Verse

Sign Posts. Boston, Small Maynard, 1924.

Widow's Walk: Variations on a Theme. New York, Rinehart, 1954.

Other

Judy: A Story of Divine Corners (for children). New York, Dodd Mead, 1930.

Babs: A Story of Divine Corners (for children). New York, Dodd Mead, and London, Sampson Low, 1931.

Mary Lou: A Story of Divine Corners (for children). New York, Dodd Mead, 1931.

Myra: A Story of Divine Corners (for children). New York, Dodd Mead, 1932.

Face Toward the Spring. New York, Rinehart, 1956; London, Davies, 1957.

Many Windows: Seasons of the Heart. New York, Rinehart, 1958; London, Davies, 1959.

Living by Faith. New York, Holt Rinehart, 1964.

*   *   *

Unlike most popular romances, Faith Baldwin's novels are neither predatory nor manipulative. In that sense, they are old-fashioned. Most contemporary romances prey on their readers' needs and insecurities, perhaps on their need for insecurity, their mostly unconscious desire to prolong adolescence, that uncertain, indeterminate state where—despite probability—one might indeed turn out to be beautiful, to be wildly loved. Baldwin's books appeal to the obverse of this romantic fantasy, to the need for stability, lifelong sharing, patient familiarity. There is a bit of adolescence to them, particularly to her earlier books, but it is the cozy adolescent fantasy of proximity and protection, as when the young heroines of *The Heart Has Wings* and *Enchanted Oasis* are compelled by "accidents" to spend innocent nights with the men of their dreams. Baldwin's novels are less romances than comedies: ripe, full of sunlight, crowded with people making do with each other. Comedies in the classical sense, her books are pledges of our willingness to live life with others no better than they might be and certainly no better than ourselves.

The folk who populate these novels are usually rich, solid (if sometimes troubled), and almost never dull. They are, fancifully, the burghers of Dutch painting come out of their dark countinghouses into sunlit American suburbs. Ministers, country doctors, district nurses, lawyers (both urban and suburban), booksellers, aviators, real estate agents, and occasionally—earlier in Baldwin's half-century career—a movie star, the idle rich: this is the litany of Baldwin's saints. Remarkably, she makes them come to life, and sometimes brilliantly. Baldwin seems able to do this out of her own generosity of spirit, her willingness to see characters as they are, not (in the unspoken imperative of romance fiction) as they should—but dare not—be. The aptly titled *Blaze of Sunlight*, to my mind Baldwin's richest novel, illustrates her tolerant generosity. Rose Holmes, the widowed heroine, ought to be an exemplar of romance fiction: passionately, almost single-mindedly devoted to her man, during his life and after his death. Yet Baldwin shows that this devotion has enriched Rose by impoverishing her children, and, by inference, the community around her, for it has deprived them of her gifts. This is the lesson Rose must learn. If, unlike classical comedy, *Blaze of Sunlight* does not end with a marriage, it does culminate in Rose's re-attachment: Rose walks out of the dark tunnel of her grief into the sunlit community where actions, even private emotions, have consequence.

Baldwin's tunnel metaphor suits both this character and her work as a whole. For, although her books are love stories, Baldwin is always stretching the radically tight focus of romance fiction and the tunnel-vision it imposes. Children and neighbors are frequent in her books and rarely serve as stage-props: rather they seem about to live busy lives of their own. In a multi-generation novel like *American Family* we get to see those lives intertwine. Moreover, Baldwin's protagonists—almost as often male as female, another departure from standard romance—have careers, again believably, not just as props. Like as not these careers encourage and express human connectedness—lawyers, doctors, teachers, ministers—and, equally likely, Baldwin's characters are immersed in the dailiness of their occupations, not in the moments of high drama each affords.

There are occasional false notes, of course. *Take What You Want*, a late novel, is tonally dissonant, sounding like a standard off-the-rack romance: girl swept off her feet by a rich older man and disapproved of by his family. Or, earlier, the falsely countrified speech of *Make-Believe* where Baldwin's gift for dialogue fails her. Yet Baldwin's is a remarkable 50-year, 60-plus novel career of comfort and progress. Her books are not quite real: there's no landedness to them, no root. Yet they are real as the mind is real, inhabiting problems; living, not without trouble, but with good humor and companionship.

—Nancy Regan

BARCLAY, Ann. See **GREIG, Maysie.**

BARCLAY, Florence L(ouisa, née Charlesworth). Also wrote as Brandon Roy. British. Born in Limpsfield, Surrey, 2 December 1862. Married Charles W. Barclay in 1881; two sons and six daughters. *Died 10 March 1921.*

ROMANCE AND HISTORICAL PUBLICATIONS

Novels

Guy Mervyn (as Brandon Roy). London, Blackett, 3 vols., 1891; edition revised by one of her daughters, New York and London, Putnam, 1932.
A Notable Prisoner. London, Marshall, 1905.
The Wheels of Time. New York, Crowell, 1908; London, Putnam, 1910.
The Rosary. New York and London, Putnam, 1909.
The Mistress of Shenstone. New York and London, Putnam, 1910.
The Following of the Star. New York and London, Putnam, 1911.
Through the Postern Gate. New York and London, Putnam, 1912.
The Upas Tree. London and New York, Putnam, 1912.
The Broken Halo. London and New York, Putnam, 1913.
The Wall of Partition. London and New York, Putnam, 1914.
My Heart's Right There. London and New York, Putnam, 1914.
The White Ladies of Worcester. London and New York, Putnam, 1917.
Returned Empty. London and New York, Putnam, 1920.

OTHER PUBLICATIONS

Other

The Golden Censer. London, Hodder and Stoughton, and New York, Doran, 1914.

In Hoc + Vince: The Story of a Red Cross Flag. London and New York, Putnam, 1915.

*

Critical Study: *The Life of Florence L. Barclay: A Study in Personality* by One of Her Daughters, London and New York, Putnam, 1921.

*   *   *

Florence L. Barclay was not as prolific as most of her contemporaries in the field. She did not need to be. *The Rosary*, published in 1909, roughly halfway through her literary career, secured her an ample readership, for, as the *Publisher's Circular* had already pronounced: "Of all forms of fiction, the semi-religious is the most popular." Within 9 months *The Rosary* sold 150,000 hardback copies; it was still a bestseller 20 years later, and in 1928 was being serialised in *Woman's World*, "the favourite paper of a Million Homes." One admirer of her work assessed that, within two years of publication, *The Rosary* had been "read and wept over by threequarters of the housemaids in Great Britain" (though this generous statistic must be tempered by another popular novelist's judgement that "the tears of the uneducated are proverbially near their eyes").

The predominant theme of all her novels—as befits the work of a parson's wife—concerns the Christian conversion of one or other of the partners in love. Mortal love cannot be wholly real, wholly acceptable, until he, or she, has also found the love of God, this state of grace being described in a succession of metaphors: "Come home to the Father's House," "had his broken halo restored," "until her heart beats in unison with the heart of the Virgin Mother in Bethlehem's starlit stable." The revelation of true earthly love and of true heavenly love is often simultaneous, the one acting as a catalyst on the other.

A recurring subsidiary theme is of the younger man in love with the much older woman, which Barclay first, delicately, touched on in *Guy Mervyn*. This was her first novel, but it made little impact when it originally appeared, chiefly because the publishing firm went bankrupt and only a few copies were distributed. *The Rosary*, too, appeared originally in another form, as a short story or (as she herself preferred it to be known) a *novella*, under the title *Wheels of Fortune*. Unlike some romantic novelists who prided themselves in never changing a line once written, Barclay saw the need for rewriting, reworking, and polishing. No amount of rewriting would diminish her main message:

My aim is: Never to write a line which could introduce the taint of sin or the shadow of shame into any home. Never to draw a character which would tend to lower the ideals of those who, by means of my pen, make intimate acquaintance with a man or a woman of my own creating. There is enough sin in the world without an author's powers of imagination being used in order to add even fictitious sin to the amount. Too many bad, mean, morbid characters already, alas! walk this earth. Why should writers add to their numbers and risk introducing them into beautiful homes, where such people in actual life would never for one moment be tolerated? A great French writer and savant has said: "The only excuse for fiction is that it should be more beautiful than fact."

The result of writing only on subjects which are more beautiful than fact is that there can be no villains in her plots, and the denouements must be brought about by some highly improbable act of fate or natural disaster. *The Rosary* has, probably, the silliest plot of all, its motive force, its suspense, being maintained by the "masquerade device," a technique always popular with romantic novelists in which the heroine poses as maid/titled lady/nurse/secretary in order to be near the one she loves. But only when her true identity is revealed can love flourish.

The religious atmosphere of the books, the tone of spiritual reverence, is conveyed by enthusiastic use of capital letters, both for the personal pronouns of the members of the trinity and for abstractions of anything which sounds remotely mystical—the Unseen, The Great Chance, Love, Life, The Little White Lady. There is a frequent repetition of emotive adverbs and adjectives—thrill, throb, tender, soul, gentle, and strange and sweet, this last one being a compound adjective, like sweet and sour, or his and hers. The religion is chiefly one of nostalgia, for reader as well as the characters. Christmas carols, well-known hymns, and long quotations from the better-known scriptures bring about strange emotional feelings in the players. Searing remembrances of lost childhood result in Christian conversion, and it is in shared emotional-cum-religious experiences that the lovers find their true unity, rather than in any explicit sexual activity. Whenever possible, the desire or opportunity for physical union is postponed, or made impossible by the intricacies of plot. Thus in *The Broken Halo* the elderly wife has a weak heart, and so her youthful husband must keep himself in a separate bedroom and endure an unconsummated marriage. On the night that he finally realizes his true, deep burning love for her, she dies of a heart attack, thus putting off till the Great Forever any possible consummation.

Similarly, in *The Following of the Star* the alliance between rich heiress and poor missionary is entirely a *marriage de convenance*, enabling her to give money for his excellent work in the typhoid-ridden swamps of Central Africa. Immediately after their marriage, he departs forever. Unknown to them, but abundantly clear to the reader, they are desperately in love. An impossible courtship, riddled with crossed letters and misunderstandings, ensues. When at last they are re-united, and a normal relationship for two healthy people would seem feasible, the author's religious imagination prevents them going about it in the normal way. Instead, they enjoy an unusual life-giving intercourse through the arms. The missionary (temporarily indisposed) lies in bed while the heiress kneels at his side in what she admits to be an exceedingly uncomfortable position, clutches his head against her breast and, it being Christmas Eve (note the novel's title), croons "Hark the Herald Angels Sing" to him, knowing that this is the one thing which will save his life. "Every moment of contact with your vital force is vitalizing him," announces a bystander to the scene. "It is like pouring blood into empty veins, only a more subtle and mysterious process, and more wonderful in its result." It was not physiological ignorance which caused Barclay to write so often about marital union in this way. (She herself was happily married, and produced eight children.) As one of her daughters wrote: "She was out to supply her fellow men with joy, refreshment, inspiration. She was not out to make art for art's sake, or to perform a literary tour de force. [Her readers] ask merely to be pleased, rested, interested, amused, inspired to a more living faith in the beauty of human affection and the goodness of God."

The mystical euphoria of her novels gave genuine spiritual comfort to many, for, as the novelist-hero in one of her books explains: "The thing of first importance is to uplift your readers; to raise their ideals; to leave them with a sense of hopefulness, which shall arouse within them a brave optimism such as inspired Browning's oft-quoted noble lines." Even today, there are readers who recall being moved and uplifted by *The Rosary*. A fellow novelist of the time paid Barclay this tribute: "*The Ro-*

sary will probably live, because its power is very uncommon— as uncommon, on its lower plane, as the power of *Wuthering Heights*. . . . Mrs. Barclay . . . was undoubtedly a great writer on her plane—Shakespeare of the servants' hall. Her power is terrific—at any rate in *The Rosary*. I had infinitely rather have written *The Rosary* than *The Forsyte Saga*."

—Rachel Anderson

BARCLAY, Marguerite. See **BARCYNSKA, Countess.**

BARCYNSKA, Countess (Hélène). Pseudonym for Marguerite Florence Jervis; also wrote as Marguerite Barclay; Oliver Sandys. British. Born in Henzada, Burma, in 1894; grew up in India. Educated at schools in Herne Bay, Kent, Crouch End, London, and near Radlett, Hertfordshire; Academy of Dramatic Art, London. Married 1) Armiger Barclay (Count Barcynsky); 2) Caradoc Evans in 1933 (died 1945), one son. Journalist for *Sievier's Monthly*, *World*, and *Answers*, all London; manager, Rogues and Vagabonds Repertory Players in Wales, and a theatre in Broadstairs, Kent. *Died 10 March 1964.*

ROMANCE AND HISTORICAL PUBLICATIONS

Novels (series: Honey Pot)

The Honey Pot: A Story of the Stage. London, Hurst and Blackett, and New York, Dutton, 1916.
If Wishes Were Horses. London, Hurst and Blackett, and New York, Dutton, 1917.
Love Maggy. London, Hurst and Blackett, 1918.
Sanity Jane. London, Hurst and Blackett, 1919.
Love's Last Reward. London, Hurst and Blackett, 1920.
Pretty Dear: A Romance. London, Hurst and Blackett, 1920; as *Rose o' the Sea*, Boston, Houghton Mifflin, 1920.
Jackie. London, Hurst and Blackett, and Boston, Houghton Mifflin, 1921.
Ships Come Home. London, Hurst and Blackett, 1922.
Webs. London, Hurst and Blackett, 1922.
Tesha, A Plaything of Destiny. London, Hurst and Blackett, 1923.
We Women! London, Hurst and Blackett, 1923.
The Russet Jacket: A Story of the Turf. London, Hurst and Blackett, 1924.
Back to the Honey-Pot: A Story of the Stage. London, Hurst and Blackett, 1925.
Hand Painted. London, Hurst and Blackett, 1925.
Decameron Cocktails. London, Hurst and Blackett, 1926.
Mint Walk. London, Hurst and Blackett, 1927.
A Certified Bride. London, Hurst and Blackett, 1928.
Milly Comes to Town. London, Chapman and Hall, 1928.
He Married His Parlourmaid. London, Chapman and Hall, 1929.
Fantoccini. London, Chapman and Hall, 1930.
The Joy Shop. London, Chapman and Hall, 1931.
A Woman of Experience. London, Hurst and Blackett, 1931.
I Loved a Fairy. London, Hurst and Blackett, 1933.
Under the Big Top. London, Hurst and Blackett, 1933.
Exit Renee. London, Hurst and Blackett, 1934.

Publicity Baby. London, Hurst and Blackett, 1935.
Pick Up and Smile. London, Hutchinson, 1936.
God and Mr. Aaronson. London, Hutchinson, 1937.
Keep Cheery. London, Hutchinson, 1937.
Hearts for Gold. London, Hutchinson, 1938.
Sweetbriar Lane. London, Hutchinson, 1938.
Writing Man. London, Hutchinson, 1939.
That Trouble Piece! London, Rich and Cowan, 1939.
Let the Storm Burst. London, Rich and Cowan, 1941.
Black-Out Symphony. London, Rich and Cowan, 1942.
The Wood Is My Pulpit. London, Rich and Cowan, 1942.
Joy Comes After. London, Rich and Cowan, 1943.
Love Never Dies. London, Rich and Cowan, 1943.
Astrologer. London, Rich and Cowan, 1944.
The Tears of Peace. London, Rich and Cowan, 1944.
Love Is a Lady. London, Rich and Cowan, 1945.
We Lost Our Way. London, Rich and Cowan, 1948.
Gorgeous Brute. London, Rich and Cowan, 1949.
Conjuror. London, Rich and Cowan, 1950.
Bubble over Thorn. London, Rich and Cowan, 1951.
Those Dominant Hills. London, Rich and Cowan, 1951.
Beloved Burden. London, Rich and Cowan, 1954.
Miss Venus of Aberdovey. London, Rich and Cowan, 1956.
Angel's Eyes. London, Hurst and Blackett, 1957.
The Jackpot. London, Hurst and Blackett, 1957.
Two Faces of Love. London, Hurst and Blackett, 1958.
Prince's Story. London, Hurst and Blackett, 1959.
Black Harvest. London, Hurst and Blackett, 1960.
These Changing Years. London, Hurst and Blackett, 1961.
I Was Shown Heaven. London, Hurst and Blackett, 1962.
Smile in the Mirror. London, Hurst and Blackett, 1963.

Novels as Oliver Sandys

The Woman in the Firelight. London, Long, 1911.
Chicane. London, Long, 1912.
The Garment of Gold. London, Hurst and Blackett, 1921.
Chappy—That's All. London, Hurst and Blackett, 1922.
The Green Caravan. London, Hurst and Blackett, 1922.
Old Roses. London, Hurst and Blackett, 1923.
The Pleasure Garden. London, Hurst and Blackett, 1923.
Sally Serene. London, Hurst and Blackett, 1924.
Tilly-Make-Haste. London, Hurst and Blackett, 1924.
Blinkeyes. London, Hurst and Blackett, 1925.
Mr. Anthony. London, Hurst and Blackett, 1925.
The Curled Hands. London, Hurst and Blackett, 1926.
The Ginger-Jar. London, Hurst and Blackett, 1926.
The Crimson Ramblers. London, Hurst and Blackett, 1927.
The Sorcerers. London, Hurst and Blackett, 1927.
Mops. London, Hurst and Blackett, 1928.
Vista, The Dancer. London, Hurst and Blackett, 1928.
Cherry. London, Hurst and Blackett, 1929.
The Champagne Kiss. London, Hurst and Blackett, 1929.
Bad Lad. London, Hurst and Blackett, 1930.
Mr. Scribbles. London, Hurst and Blackett, 1930.
Sally of Sloper's. London, Hurst and Blackett, 1930.
Jinks. London, Hurst and Blackett, 1931.
Misty Angel. London, Hurst and Blackett, 1931.
Butterflies. London, Hurst and Blackett, 1932.
Squire. London, Hurst and Blackett, 1932.
Just Lil. London, Hurst and Blackett, 1933.
Sir Boxer. London, Hurst and Blackett, 1933.
Happy Day. London, Hurst and Blackett, 1934.
Spangles. London, Hurst and Blackett, 1934.
Tiptoes. London, Hurst and Blackett, 1935.
The Curtain Will Go Up. London, Hutchinson, 1936.

The Show Must Go On. London, Hutchinson, 1936.
Angel's Kiss. London, Hutchinson, 1937.
The Happy Mummers. London, Hutchinson, 1937.
Prince Charming. London, Hutchinson, 1937.
Crinklenose. London, Hutchinson, 1938.
Love Is a Flower. London, Hurst and Blackett, 1938.
Mud on My Stockings. London, Hurst and Blackett, 1938.
Hollywood Honeymoon. London, Hurst and Blackett, 1939.
Old Hat. London, Hurst and Blackett, 1939.
Whatagirl. London, Hurst and Blackett, 1939.
Calm Waters. London, Hurst and Blackett, 1940.
Singing Uphill. London, Hurst and Blackett, 1940.
Jack Be Nimble. London, Hurst and Blackett, 1941.
Wellington Wendy. London, Hurst and Blackett, 1941.
Lame Daddy. London, Hurst and Blackett, 1942.
Meadowsweet. London, Hurst and Blackett, 1942.
Swell Fellows. London, Hurst and Blackett, 1942.
Merrily All the Way. London, Hurst and Blackett, 1943.
No Faint Heart. London, Hurst and Blackett, 1943.
Miss Paraffin. London, Hurst and Blackett, 1944.
Poppet & Co. London, Hurst and Blackett, 1944.
Deputy Pet. London, Hurst and Blackett, 1945.
Learn to Laugh Again. London, Hurst and Blackett, 1947.
The Constant Rabbit. London, Hurst and Blackett, 1949.
Dot on the Spot. London, Hurst and Blackett, 1949.
Shining Failure. London, Hurst and Blackett, 1950.
Bachelor's Tonic. London, Hurst and Blackett, 1951.
Kiss the Moon. London, Hurst and Blackett, 1951.
Let's All Be Happy. London, Hurst and Blackett, 1952.
Quaint Place. London, Hurst and Blackett, 1952.
Shine My Wings. London, Hurst and Blackett, 1954.
Suffer to Sing. London, Hurst and Blackett, 1955.
The Happiness Stone. London, Hurst and Blackett, 1956.
A New Day. London, Hurst and Blackett, 1957.
Dear Mr. Dean. London, Hurst and Blackett, 1957.
Butterflies in the Rain. London, Hurst and Blackett, 1958.
Cherrystones. London, Hurst and Blackett, 1959.
The Tinsel and the Gold. London, Hurst and Blackett, 1959.
The Wise and the Steadfast. London, Hurst and Blackett, 1961.
The Golden Flame. London, Ward Lock, 1961.
The Poppy and the Rose. London, Hurst and Blackett, 1962.
The Happy Hearts. London, Ward Lock, 1962.
Laughter and Love Remain. London, Ward Lock, 1962.
Madame Adastra. London, Hurst and Blackett, 1964.

Novels as Marguerite Barclay

The Activities of Lavie Jutt, with Armiger Barclay. London, Stanley Paul, 1911.
Letters from Fleet Street, with Armiger Barclay. London, Palmer, 1912.
Where There Are Women, with Armiger Barclay. London, Unwin, 1915; revised edition, as *The Five-Hooded Cobra* (as Oliver Sandys), London, Hurst and Blackett, 1932.
Peter Day-by-Day, with Armiger Barclay. London, Simpkin Marshall, 1916.
Yesterday Is Tomorrow. London, Rich and Cowan, 1950.
Sunset Is Dawn. London, Rich and Cowan, 1953.
The Miracle Stone of Wales. London, Rider, 1957.

Short Stories

Twenty-One. London, Hurst and Blackett, 1924.
The Golden Snail and Other Stories. London, Hurst and Blackett, 1927.

S.O.S. Queenie and Other Stories (as Oliver Sandys). London, Hurst and Blackett, 1928.
Running Free and Other Stories. London, Chapman and Hall, 1929.

OTHER PUBLICATIONS

Other as Oliver Sandys

Full and Frank: The Private Life of a Woman Novelist. London, Hurst and Blackett, 1941.
Caradoc Evans. London, Hurst and Blackett, 1946.
Unbroken Thread: An Intimate Journal. London, Rider, 1948.

Editor, *The Little Mother Who Sits at Home* (as Countess Barcynska). London, Jack, and New York, Dutton, 1915.

*   *   *

Despite a prolific output of novels, published over a span of more than 50 years, Countess Barcynska nevertheless managed to maintain great popularity, beginning with her first full-length novel, *The Honey Pot*, through to her final works in the 1960's. This achievement was due to a high degree of ingenuity in characterization and plot, combined with the consistent ability to produce a gripping story.

The writer's use of two pseudonyms, Countess Barcynska and Oliver Sandys, was due more to the circumstances in which she found herself than to any real dichotomy in style or subject matter of the novels. Fortunately these vicissitudes of her life (described in her autobiography *Full and Frank*) seem to have provided her with a wealth of experience in life and love, enabling her to portray a wide variety of situations and relationships most convincingly.

The experience of running a repertory company herself led to a preoccupation with the theatre in many of her novels, e.g., *The Curtain Will Go Up* and *The Happy Mummers* as Oliver Sandys and *I Was Shown Heaven*, *Smile in the Mirror*, *The Honey Pot*, and *Back to the Honey-Pot*, as Countess Barcynska. In the "honey-pot" novels, for example, the insecurity, frustrations, and glamour of the theatre are clearly witnessed through the story of Maggie Oliver—at first the leading light in her company but later returning under a false name to experience the life of a chorus girl.

Another feature common to many of the novels is the description of various "spiritual experiences" felt by the characters. The schoolboy Peter in *Joy Comes After* "sees" his dead mother in the attic, and Martin Leffley from *If Wishes Were Horses* is "moved" in an unusual way while listening to a simple sermon in a country church to pray for forgiveness for the wrong he did his servant Ada. However, such experiences, where they occur, are not frightening to the characters concerned or to the reader, and indeed the writer took comfort from such experiences in her own life.

To find a weak man such as Martin Leffley in these novels is not unusual, for it was into developing her female characters that Countess Barcynska seems to have channelled most of her energies. When the detail of the plots have long faded, it is the women—the indomitable Aunt Polly in *If Wishes Were Horses*, the gypsy Molly Yetta in *Astrologer*, or the actress Phyllis Clun in *I Was Shown Heaven*—who remain strong in one's memory. Indeed it is in such characterization that the writer's strength lies, for one will look in vain for detailed scenic descriptions or great subtleties of plot. Many of the plots place great reliance on coincidence, as in *Black Harvest* where the two children of the

heroine (one adopted, one not), fall in love and wish to marry, but in fact turn out to be half-brother and sister, an occurrence caused by an extremely unusual set of coincidences!

The "happy-ever-after" ending is also a marked feature of these novels. However many tragedies happen in the course of the books, they always seem to end on a happy note. In *Writing Man*, for example, Dick's wife and baby have both died separately in tragic circumstances but the novel ends with him beginning to write another book, inspired by an awareness of his wife's "presence." Perhaps the authoress Daisy Bell, also in *Writing Man*, expresses Countess Barcynska's own feeling when she says "It's very consoling to make one's characters happy at the end of one's books and it makes people who read them happy too—especially the ones who are sad."

Countess Barcynska took great pains to show, through the fates of various characters, the inevitable consequences of wrong-doing. In her earlier novels the moralistic aphorisms can become rather tiresome. However, in later novels, the morals are less overt and are often centered around the problems of love and human relationships. The penalties of marrying for the wrong reasons came to Evan Evans in *Astrologer*, who married out of chivalry, and to Martin Leffley in *If Wishes Were Horses* for marrying his deceased landlady's daughter almost for convenience.

Despite showing some of the characteristics of an earlier age in her writings, Countess Barcynska was a writer of great ability who, as she said herself, knew how "to make people laugh and smile and weep." In all, her stories have a certain elusive combination which makes for very compelling reading.

—Kim F. Paynter

BARR, Pat(ricia Miriam, née Copping). British. Born in Norwich, Norfolk, 25 April 1934. Educated at Birmingham University, B.A. (honours) in English 1956; University College, London, M.A. 1964. Married John Marshall Barr in 1956 (died). English teacher, Yokohama International School, Japan, 1959–61, and University of Maryland overseas program, Japan, 1961–62; assistant secretary, National Old People's Welfare Council, London, 1965–66. Recipient: Churchill fellowship, for non-fiction, 1971. Agent: Carol Smith Literary Agency, 25 Hornton Court, Kensington High Street, London W8 7RT. Address: 6 Mount Pleasant, Norwich, Norfolk NR2 2DG, England.

ROMANCE AND HISTORICAL PUBLICATIONS

Novels

Jade: A Novel of China. New York, St. Martin's Press, 1982; London, Corgi, 1983.
  Chinese Alice. London, Secker and Warburg, 1981.
  Uncut Jade. London, Secker and Warburg, 1983.
Kenjiro. London, Secker and Warburg, 1985.
Coromandel. London, Hamish Hamilton, 1988.

OTHER PUBLICATIONS

Other

The Coming of the Barbarians. London, Macmillan, and New York, Dutton, 1967.

The Deer Cry Pavillion. London, Macmillan, 1968; New York, Harcourt Brace, 1969.
The Elderly: Handbook on Care and Services. London, National Council of Social Service, 1968.
A Curious Life for a Lady. London, Macmillan, and New York, Doubleday, 1970.
Foreign Devils: Westerners in the Far East. London, Penguin, 1970.
To China with Love. London, Secker and Warburg, 1972; New York, Doubleday, 1973.
The Memsahibs: The Women of Victorian India. London, Secker and Warburg, 1976.
Taming the Jungle. London, Secker and Warburg, 1977.
The Framing of the Female (for children). London, Kestrel, 1978.
Simla: A Hill Station in British India, with Ray Desmond. London, Scolar Press, and New York, Scribner, 1978.
Japan. London, Batsford, 1980.

Editor, *I Remember: An Arrangement for Many Voices*. London, Macmillan, 1970.

*   *   *

Pat Barr's novels are underpinned by personal experience and detailed research, and follow a substantial collection of non-fiction works on China, Japan and the Indian sub-continent. At their best, Barr's novels—like *Chinese Alice* and its sequel *Uncut Jade*—combine her interests and examine the impact and interaction of European and Asian cultures revealed through the eyes of a liberated heroine with definite opinions of her own.

Chinese Alice, the first and possibly the best of Barr's fictional works, introduces the most formidable, and likeable, of her heroines, Alice Greenwood. Daughter of missionary parents killed in anti-Western riots in Tientsin, Alice undergoes capture and concubinage in Hunan, and escapes only to find herself regarded as an outsider by the British family to whom she returns. Caught between two modes of life, British by birth but Chinese by upbringing and predilection, Alice undergoes endless journeyings from one city to another which mirror her own restless search for identity. Through her eyes, Barr shows us the China of the late 19th and early 20th centuries; an ancient civilization overrun by European merchants and missionaries, its traditions increasingly challenged by a growing reformist movement. No attempt is made to romanticize; Barr depicts the filth and squalor, the ignorance and cruelty, while at the same time retaining a genuine love for China and respect for its culture. With the redoubtable Alice the reader encounters the religious bigotry of the Western missionaries, the superficial refinement of Treaty Port society and the internecine warfare of the Chinese conservatives and reformers. A strong, resilient personality with remarkably modern sexual attitudes, Alice meets love and suffering on equal terms, emerging unbroken from rape and widowhood, surviving the Boxer siege of Peking in *Uncut Jade*, to bid a final farewell to the country that has been her home. Her adventures in these first two novels paint an unforgettable picture in the mind, while Alice herself impresses as one of the most notable heroines of recent historical fiction.

Kenjiro is set in 19th-century Japan, and explores the mixed marriage of the samurai hero and an English woman against the background of the country's own struggle between tradition and reform. Interwoven with the central love story of Kenjiro and Elinor are other relationships, in particular the illicit affair of two British expatriates, and the courtship of Kenjiro's sister Ryo. Although this time Barr gives a male character the leading role, the women are far from being subordinates, and for the

most part rebel against the stereotypical behaviour which is expected of them; Elinor condemns her brother's hypocrisy while Ryo takes up the cause of women's rights; as a teacher of young girls. The novel reaches a tragic climax with the death of Kenjiro and Elinor's son at the siege of Port Arthur in 1895. A quieter, more diffuse work than the two previous novels, *Kenjiro* nevertheless holds the interest, and contains thought-provoking depths. As always, the theme of women seeking identity in a man's world is subtly, but strongly, conveyed.

With *Coromandel*, Barr moves further afield, exploring the world of British exiles in Southern India during the 1830's. Her heroine, Amelia, arrives to join her husband—an official employed by the local native ruler—and is quickly drawn into the tangled network of relationships that comprise the uneasy alliance of East and West. Under the surface of a fixed—even tediously routine—universe, lie barely suppressed passions, whether the acquisitive lust of the East India Company for the Raja's land, or the desire of Amelia's husband for his youthful Indian mistress Rukmini. The Afghan War, fought "offstage" and at a distance, serves as an omen of disasters to come. Barr once more provides a superb vision of a country on the verge of colonialism, contrasting the naive conservatism of the Raja with the greed of the Western merchants, and the more subtle prejudices of the anglicising missionaries. A heroine less charismatic and more conventional than Chinese Alice, Amelia has the customary virtues of courage and independence. Barr has her survive the ordeal of her husband's death from cholera to make her own way in the world. Rejecting offers of marriage, Amelia uses her inheritance to establish a school for girls. The novel ends as she visualizes the future: "In her imagination the room was already repeopled with little girls studying at those desks, learning ways to survive."

—Geoffrey Sadler

BARRIE, Susan. Also writes as Anita Charles; Pamela Kent. Address: c/o Mills and Boon Ltd., 18–24 Paradise Road, Richmond, Surrey TW9 1SR, England.

ROMANCE AND HISTORICAL PUBLICATIONS

Novels

Mistress of Brown Furrows. London, Mills and Boon, 1952; Toronto, Harlequin, 1963.
The Gates of Dawn. London, Mills and Boon, 1954; Toronto, Harlequin, 1964.
Marry a Stranger. London, Mills and Boon, 1954; Toronto, Harlequin, 1966.
Carpet of Dreams. London, Mills and Boon, 1955; Toronto, Harlequin, 1967.
Hotel Stardust. London, Mills and Boon, 1955.
Dear Tiberius. London, Mills and Boon, 1956.
The House of the Laird. London, Mills and Boon, 1956; Toronto, Harlequin, 1961.
So Dear to My Heart. London, Mills and Boon, 1956; Toronto, Harlequin, 1961.
Air Ticket. London, Mills and Boon, 1957.
Four Roads to Windrush. London, Mills and Boon, 1957; Toronto, Harlequin, 1962.
Heart Specialist. London, Mills and Boon, 1958; Toronto, Harlequin, 1961.

The Stars of San Cecilio. London, Mills and Boon, 1958; Toronto, Harlequin, 1963.
The Wings of the Morning. London, Mills and Boon, 1960; Toronto, Harlequin, 1965.
Nurse Nolan. Toronto, Harlequin, 1961.
Bride in Waiting. London, Mills and Boon, 1961; Toronto, Harlequin, 1971.
Moon at the Full. London, Mills and Boon, 1961; Toronto, Harlequin, 1965.
Royal Purple. London, Mills and Boon, 1962; Toronto, Harlequin, 1967.
A Case of Heart Trouble. London, Mills and Boon, and Toronto, Harlequin, 1963.
Mountain Magic. London, Mills and Boon, 1964; Toronto, Harlequin, 1965.
Hotel at Treloan. Toronto, Harlequin, 1964.
Castle Thunderbird. London, Mills and Boon, 1965; Toronto, Harlequin, 1966.
No Just Cause. London, Mills and Boon, 1965; Toronto, Harlequin, 1966.
Master of Melincourt. London, Mills and Boon, 1966; Toronto, Harlequin, 1968.
The Quiet Heart. London, Mills and Boon, 1966; Toronto, Harlequin, 1967.
Rose in the Bud. London, Mills and Boon, 1966; Toronto, Harlequin, 1967.
Accidental Bride. London, Mills and Boon, 1967; Toronto, Harlequin, 1968.
Victoria and the Nightingale. London, Mills and Boon, 1967.
The Marriage Wheel. London, Mills and Boon, 1968; Toronto, Harlequin, 1969.
Wild Sonata. London, Mills and Boon, and Toronto, Harlequin, 1968.
Return to Tremarth. Toronto, Harlequin, 1969.
Night of the Singing Birds. London, Mills and Boon, and Toronto, Harlequin, 1970.

Novels as Pamela Kent

Moon over Africa. London, Mills and Boon, 1955; Toronto, Harlequin, 1966.
Desert Doorway. London, Mills and Boon, 1956; Toronto, Harlequin, 1965.
City of Palms. London, Mills and Boon, 1957; Toronto, Harlequin, 1964.
Sweet Barbary. London, Mills and Boon, 1957; Toronto, Harlequin, 1964.
Meet Me in Istanbul. London, Mills and Boon, 1958; Toronto, Harlequin, 1966.
Flight to the Stars. London, Mills and Boon, 1959; Toronto, Harlequin, 1961.
The Chateau of Fire. London, Mills and Boon, 1961.
Dawn on the High Mountain. London, Mills and Boon, 1961.
Journey in the Dark. London, Mills and Boon, 1962.
Bladon's Rock. London, Mills and Boon, 1963; Toronto, Harlequin, 1964.
The Dawning Splendour. London, Mills and Boon, 1963.
Enemy Lover. London, Mills and Boon, 1964; Toronto, Harlequin, 1965.
The Gardenia Tree. London, Mills and Boon, 1965.
Gideon Faber's Choice. London, Mills and Boon, 1965; Toronto, Harlequin, 1966.
Star Creek. London, Mills and Boon, 1965; Toronto, Harlequin, 1966.
Cuckoo in the Night. London, Mills and Boon, 1966; Toronto, Harlequin, 1967.

White Heat. London, Mills and Boon, 1966.
Beloved Enemies. London, Mills and Boon, 1967; Toronto, Harlequin, 1970.
The Man Who Came Back. London, Mills and Boon, and Toronto, Harlequin, 1967.
Desert Gold. London, Mills and Boon, and Toronto, Harlequin, 1968.
Man from the Sea. London, Mills and Boon, 1968; Toronto, Harlequin, 1969.
Nile Dusk. London, Mills and Boon, 1972; Toronto, Harlequin, 1974.
Flight to the Stars. London, Mills and Boon, 1977.

Novels as Anita Charles

The Black Benedicts. London, Wright and Brown, 1956; Toronto, Harlequin, 1966.
My Heart at Your Feet. London, Wright and Brown, 1957.
One Coin in the Fountain. London, Wright and Brown, 1957; Toronto, Harlequin, 1966.
Interlude for Love. Wright and Brown, 1958.
The Moon and Bride's Hill. London, Wright and Brown, 1958.
Autumn Wedding. London, Wright and Brown, 1963.
The King of the Castle. London, Wright and Brown, 1963; Toronto, Harlequin, 1969.
White Rose of Love. London, Wright and Brown, 1963; Toronto, Harlequin, 1968.

*   *   *

Susan Barrie, who also writes as Pamela Kent and Anita Charles, writes the best kind of romances; they are sweet, tender, slightly improbable, and totally loving. She began writing in the mid-1950's and like so many of the writers who wrote then, she took her turn writing doctor/nurse romances and later broadened to the traditional romance that is still popular today.

Her heroines are touchingly innocent and immediately awaken the masculine urge to protect. Their sturdy attempt at independence merely strengthens this urge until marriage is the only weapon to enforce male infallibility. In fact, the typical conclusion of a romance goes like this: "whether you like it or not, I *am* going to marry you!" Such resolution in the face of willing compliance is sufficient for her readers to enjoy her novels over and over again.

Barrie seems to have a special fondness for young innocence as she sets a story moving by having her heroine faced with an immediate problem or new set of circumstances that are very strange to her. Frederica Wells in *The Marriage Wheel* (Susan Barrie) must find a new job, now that her former employer has died. Since she acted as a chauffeur to an elderly lady, Frederica sees no reason why she can't continue in the same occupation; a conclusion that Humphrey Lestrode, her next employer, is quick to dispute. The fact that she has a flighty mother and a helplessly feminine sister merely adds to her worries of being independent and self-sufficient. In *Beloved Enemies* (Pamela Kent) Caprice Vaughan inherits a manor house from a great-uncle. It comes complete with furniture, housekeeper, and an irascible tenant who insists on sharing the house with her.

Surprisingly, the novels that she writes under the name of Anita Charles are quite different. These take on an intensity that has sharp emotional overtones that are far from sweet and tender. In *White Rose of Love* Stephanie Wayne goes to Portugal to visit her brother Tim. He is an artist, while she is a sculptress. Circumstances bring them into contact with Dom Manoel de

Romeirio and his fiancée Madelena Almedia. Love springs up between Stephanie and Dom Manoel, but his sense of honor refuses to let him break his engagement. The torment of unfulfilled love is unbearable for Stephanie until two events occur; a boat wreck, and Madelena's declaration of love for Tim.

Dominating, cynical, ruthless men attempt to deal with Susan Barrie's heorines and it is not surprising that they have unexpected difficulties throughout the stories. They have their own ideas of women and it is not particularly flattering. However, the heroine's inexplicable ability to confound their beliefs defeats them in the end. They find that one can't argue with wide-eyed goodness, sweet honesty, and soft hearts.

Romance readers find Susan Barrie's novels more than delightful nonsense. She has a wonderful sense of story, balanced by charmingly developed characters. She is one of those writers who has that special touch in telling her stories so that it makes her readers return over and over again to a favorite story. Her plots may not be particularly complicated, and the mood of the story may not always be intense or dramatic, but she insures her readers of more than a pleasant hour of reading as she spins her storytelling web about them.

—Arlene Moore

BARRINGTON, E. See **BECK, L. Adams.**

BARTH, John (Simmons). American. Born in Cambridge, Maryland, 27 May 1930. Educated at the Juilliard School of Music, New York; Johns Hopkins University, Baltimore, A.B. 1951, M.A. 1952. Married 1) Anne Strickland in 1950 (divorced 1969), one daughter and two sons; 2) Shelly Rosenberg in 1970. Junior Instructor in English, Johns Hopkins University, 1951–53; Instructor 1953–56, Assistant Professor, 1957–60, and Associate Professor of English, 1960–65, Pennsylvania State University, University Park; Professor of English, 1965–71, and Butler Professor, 1971–73, State University of New York, Buffalo. Since 1973 Centennial Professor of English and Creative Writing, Johns Hopkins University. Recipient: Brandeis University Creative Arts award, 1965; Rockefeller grant, 1965; American Academy grant, 1966; National Book Award, 1973. Litt.D.: University of Maryland, College Park, 1969. Member, American Academy, 1977, and American Academy of Arts and Sciences, 1977. Agent: International Creative Management, 40 West 57th Street, New York, New York 10019. Address: c/o Writing Seminars, Johns Hopkins University, Baltimore, Maryland 21218, U.S.A.

ROMANCE AND HISTORICAL PUBLICATIONS

Novel

The Sot-Weed Factor. New York, Doubleday, 1960; London, Secker and Warburg, 1961; revised edition, Doubleday, 1967.

OTHER PUBLICATIONS

Novels

The Floating Opera. New York, Appleton Century Crofts, 1956; revised edition, New York, Doubleday, 1967; London, Secker and Warburg, 1968.
The End of the Road. New York, Doubleday, 1958; London, Secker and Warburg, 1962; revised edition, Doubleday, 1967.
Giles Goat-Boy; or, The Revised New Syllabus. New York, Doubleday, 1966; London, Secker and Warburg, 1967.
Letters. New York, Putnam, 1979; London, Secker and Warburg, 1980.
Sabbatical: A Romance. New York, Putnam, and London, Secker and Warburg, 1982.
The Tidewater Tales: A Novel. New York, Putnam, 1987; London, Methuen, 1988.

Short Stories

Lost in the Funhouse: Fiction for Print, Tape, Live Voice. New York, Doubleday, 1968; London, Secker and Warburg, 1969.
Chimera. New York, Random House, 1972; London, Deutsch, 1974.
Todd Andrews to the Author. Northridge, California, Lord John Press, 1979.

Other

The Literature of Exhaustion, and The Literature of Replenishment (essays). Northridge, California, Lord John Press, 1982.
The Friday Book: Essays and Other Nonfiction. New York, Putnam, 1984.
Don't Count on It: A Note on the Number of the 1001 Nights. Northridge, California, Lord John Press, 1984.

*

Bibliography: *John Barth: A Descriptive Primary and Annotated Secondary Bibliography* by Joseph Weixlmann, New York, Garland, 1976; *John Barth: An Annotated Bibliography* by Richard Allan Vine, Metuchen, New Jersey, Scarecrow Press, 1977; *John Barth, Jerzy Kosinski, and Thomas Pynchon: A Reference Guide* by Thomas P. Walsh and Cameron Northouse, Boston, Hall, 1977.

Manuscript Collection: Library of Congress, Washington, D.C.

Critical Studies: *John Barth* by Gerhard Joseph, Minneapolis, University of Minnesota Press, 1970; *John Barth: The Comic Sublimity of Paradox* by Jac Tharpe, Carbondale, Southern Illinois University Press, 1974; *The Literature of Exhaustion: Borges, Nabokov, and Barth* by John O. Stark, Durham, North Carolina, Duke University Press, 1974; *John Barth: An Introduction* by David Morrell, University Park, Pennsylvania State University Press, 1976; *Critical Essays on John Barth* edited by Joseph J. Waldmeir, Boston, Hall, 1980; *Passionate Virtuosity: The Fiction of John Barth* by Charles B. Harris, Urbana, University of Illinois Press, 1983; *John Barth* by Heide Ziegler, London, Methuen, 1987.

*   *   *

No 20th-century American novelist has had more influence on the shape and scope of recent fiction than has John Barth, who in practice and in theory has named and exemplified the "literature of exhaustion"—literature written by men and women who have observed the ultimate futility of both living and writing and who must yet somehow write while they choose to live, whether or not their writings happen to be read. Barth, who began his publishing career with two seemingly realistic novels—*The Floating Opera*, a light-hearted debate over suicide; and *The End of the Road*, a satiric study of a triangular love relationship—conceived the idea of writing a third such "nihilistic comedy"; but the happier result, his third novel, was *The Sot-Weed Factor*, a delightful picaresque historical work.

The student of Colonial American literature, after wading through acres of Puritan sermons, political and religious tracts, documentaries of exploration, devotional poetry, and precious little else, comes with delight upon a satiric poem by Ebenezer Cooke (c. 1667–c. 1732)—*The Sot-Weed Factor*; or, *A Voyage to Maryland* (1708). Almost alone in early American literature this short verse satire, in direct imitation of Samuel Butler's Restoration-era *Hudibras*—that well-remembered satire of Puritanism, heroism, and chivalry—brightens with its sharp English wit an otherwise gray American landscape.

The young Barth was struck by his own discovery of Cooke's *Sot-Weed Factor* and its satires of life in the colony of Maryland. Immersing himself in the poem, by Cooke, in the annals of Maryland, and in colonial-era diaries and letters (especially the diaries of William Byrd), Barth in four years wrote and published his own *Sot-Weed Factor*, a very long novel which amazed readers with its wealth of invention as well as its apparent faithfulness to 17th-century American and English history, culture, and language. So well did Barth get right the smallest details of life and speech in his chosen historical era and locale that he could take the greatest liberties in the invention of his fantastic plot, which is expanded far beyond the skeleton story present in Cooke's poetic satire or the few facts actually known about the historical Ebenezer Cooke.

Drawing upon these few facts and upon his own close reading of the satiric picaresque novels by Henry Fielding, Barth presents in *The Sot-Weed Factor* (the title meaning a merchant of tobacco) the same virginal hero who must at the expense of his purse and his happiness protect his virtue in a lusty and materialistic world. Beset by men and women who would gladly take both his innocence and his inheritance, Ebenezer Cooke is bedeviled by all manner of people and events, tossed blithely upon a sea of mischance, mistaken identity, and mischief, so misused in his chosen profession of heroic poet of Maryland that he writes instead of his planned colonial epic, a bitter satire of that colony—the original poem *The Sot-Weed Factor*.

Although the misunderstandings, mistakings, disguises, and revelations in Barth's rich picaresque plot are interesting and exciting to read, his long novel of the innocent (and thus dangerous) tobacco merchant and poet is wonderfully enhanced with fixed debates on such topics as history, innocence, justice, and civility; elaborate literary dreams; bi-lingual swearing contests; catalogues of foods, customs, and proverbs; hitherto unknown diaries, one by Captain John Smith with entries on the epic deflowering of Pocahontas; and revisionist explorations of the sexual preferences of famous English dons, politicians, and scientists.

Yet the pure invention of plot, character, and language is the notable achievement of Barth in *The Sot-Weed Factor*, along with the invention of a would-be poet and his would-be (and, of course, actual) poem about 17th-century England and America. And it is in returning to the source of the English novel that *The Sot-Weed Factor* set the course of Barth's career, for in later novels he recreated and expanded other forms of the early English novel—the universal satire, *Giles Goat-Boy*; the epistolary novel, *Letters*; and the adventure-romance, *Sabbatical*. For an author who believes in and demonstrates the uselessness of the art of writing, Barth has certainly lived well and richly in his imaginative recreation of story-telling in English.

—Ray Lewis White

BATES, Jennie. See **SEGER, Maura**.

BEATY, Betty (Joan Campbell, née Smith). Also writes as Karen Campbell; Catherine Ross. British. Born in Farsley, Yorkshire. Educated at Bradford Girls Grammar School; Leeds University, diploma in social science and public administration. Served in the Women's Auxiliary Air Force. Married the writer David Beaty in 1948; three daughters. Airline hostess, British European Airways, 1946–47; medical social worker, St. Leonard's Hospital, London, 1947–48, and Pembury Hospital, Tunbridge Wells, Kent, 1971–72. Agent: Curtis Brown, 162–168 Regent Street, London W1R 5TB. Address: Manchester House, Church Road, Slindon, Arundel, West Sussex, England.

ROMANCE AND HISTORICAL PUBLICATIONS

Novels

South to the Sun. London, Mills and Boon, 1956; Toronto, Harlequin, 1964.
Maiden Flight. London, Mills and Boon, 1956; Toronto, Harlequin, 1963.
Amber Five. London, Mills and Boon, 1958; Toronto, Harlequin, 1964.
The Butternut Tree. London, Mills and Boon, 1958.
The Top of the Climb. London, Collins, 1962.
The Path of the Moonfish. London, Mills and Boon, 1964; Toronto, Harlequin, 1966.
The Atlantic Sky. London, Mills and Boon, 1967.
Miss Miranda's Walk. London, Mills and Boon, and Toronto, Harlequin, 1967.
The Swallows of San Fedora. London, Mills and Boon, 1970.
Love and the Kentish Maid. London, Mills and Boon, 1971; Toronto, Harlequin, 1976.
Head of Chancery. London, Mills and Boon, 1972; Toronto, Harlequin, 1976.
Master at Arms. London, Mills and Boon, 1973; Toronto, Harlequin, 1977.
Fly Away, Love. London, Mills and Boon, 1975; Toronto, Harlequin, 1977.
Exchange of Hearts. London, Mills and Boon, 1980.
Wings of the Morning, with David Beaty. New York, Coward McCann, and London, Macmillan, 1982.
The Missionary's Daughter. London, Mills and Boon, 1983.
Matchmaker Nurse. London, Mills and Boon, 1984.
Airport Nurse. London, Mills and Boon, 1986.
Wings of Love. London, Mills and Boon, 1988.

Novels as Catherine Ross

From This Day Forward. London, Cape, 1959.
The Colours of the Night. London, Joseph, 1962.

The Trysting Tower. London, Joseph, 1966.
Battle Dress. London, Eyre Methuen, 1979.
The Shadow of the Peak. London, Methuen, 1985.

Novels as Karen Campbell

Suddenly, In the Air. London, Collins, 1969.
Thunder on Sunday. London, Collins, 1972.
Wheel Fortune. London, Collins, 1973.
Death Descending. London, Collins, 1976; New York, Stein and Day, 1977.
The Bells of St. Martin. London, Eyre Methuen, 1979.

*

Betty Beaty comments:

For all my writing I prefer to use a background with which I am familiar. That way, one can explore the characters in greater depth. Most of my present-day novels are set in airlines or hospitals, or occasionally in an embassy. For my historical novels I use the setting of World War II, and for *The Missionary's Daughter* and *The Shadow of the Peak* I drew extensively on the detailed Ceylon diaries of a great Aunt. To achieve greater authenticity I always go and stay in the places I am writing about since there is no substitute for seeing with one's own eyes.

*   *   *

Betty Beaty writes novels under three names. The one thing all have in common is that they are love stories, and the emotional content is convincing because it comes genuinely and directly from the author's own heart. She believes in "real love," and it shows.

As Betty Beaty she has written 19 "straight" Mills and Boon romances, most based on her own experiences as an airline hostess and a medical social worker in a London hospital; or from travelling abroad with her husband, the novelist David Beaty, during a period of seven years he spent as a diplomatic representative of the British Foreign Office—or their joint holidays, often spent big-ship cruising, which provides glamorous settings for shipboard romance. From her flying experience came such books as *Maiden Flight* and *South to the Sun*, which ingeniously combine the love interest with behind-the-scenes glimpses of life as an air-stewardess. Her medical training led to books such as *The Path of the Moonfish*, *Airport Nurse* draws on her experiences from both careers and from a diplomatic visit to South America came *Head of Chancery*.

Beaty's close connection with flying—directly, and indirectly through her husband (who was one of the first post-war commercial transatlantic pilots)—led her to write five slightly tougher novels in the name of Karen Campbell. Outstanding among them is *Suddenly, In the Air*, the story of a sky-jack, in which she slowly and expertly increases the tension until, very near the end of the story, there is an explosion of action and violence which almost lifts the reader off her chair. An added piquancy arises from the story's being told from the standpoint of the only girl-member of the crew: the stewardess.

The Catherine Ross books are longer and more deeply analytical of character and situation. Two are based on war-time experiences in the Women's Royal Air Force, and are the only novels I have encountered which truly capture the spirit and atmosphere of that time from the service-*women's* point of view. *The Colours of the Night* and *Battle Dress* (the first set on an English bomber station, the second on a fighter station in Orkney) are full of domestic detail as well as the excitement and heartache of a moment in history which changed the lives and outlook of

many a hitherto-sheltered middle-class girl, catapulting her into harsh reality, physical danger, and self-reliance; presenting her, often for the first time, with deep emotional challenges at a moment when the man, or men, in her life were at their most vulnerable. These two novels are very much "real-life" love stories, born of the author's immediate experience, at a time in her own life when she too was most exposed to the deepest and most memorable emotional disturbances. (When, in fact, she herself met the man to whom she has been happily married ever since.)

Betty and David Beaty have written their first long, joint, novel: *Wings of the Morning*, a love-story set in the early days of flying.

—Elizabeth Grey

———

BEAUCLERK, Helen (de Vere). Pseudonym for Helen Mary Dorothea Bellingham. British. Born in Cambridge, 20 September 1892. Studied music in Paris. Translator and secretary in London, 1914–18; staff member, London *Evening Standard* and Birmingham *Post. Died in 1969.*

ROMANCE AND HISTORICAL PUBLICATIONS

Novels

The Green Lacquer Pavilion. London, Collins, and New York, Doran, 1926.
The Love of the Foolish Angel. London, Collins, and New York, Cosmopolitan, 1929.
The Mountain and the Tree. London, Collins, 1935; New York, Coward McCann, 1936.
So Frail a Thing: Love Scenes of the Twentieth Century. London, Gollancz, 1940.
Shadows on a Wall. London, Gollancz, 1941.
Where the Treasure Is. London, Gollancz, 1944.
There Were Three Men. London, Gollancz, 1949.

OTHER PUBLICATIONS

Other

Translator, *The Tale of Igor*. London, Beaumont, 1918.
Translator, *War Nursing*, by Charles Richet. London, Heinemann, 1918.
Translator, with Nadia Evrenov, *Thamar Karsavina*, by Valerien Svetlov. London, Beaumont, 1922.
Translator, with Violet Macdonald, *Journey Through Life*, by Amédée Ozenfant. London, Gollancz, 1939.
Translator, *The Beggars*, by L R. des Forêts. London, Dobson, 1949.
Translator, *Philippine*, by Danielle Hunebelle. London, Secker and Warburg, 1955.
Translator, *My Apprenticeships*, by Colette. London, Secker and Warburg, 1957.
Translator, *Honeymoon round the World*, by Dominique Lapierre. London, Secker and Warburg, 1957.
Translator, *Earthly Paradise*, by Colette. London, Secker and Warburg, 1966.

*   *   *

The novels of Helen Beauclerk fall into two groups: those which were produced before World War II and set in much earlier times (*The Green Lacquer Pavilion*, *The Love of the Foolish Angel*, and *The Mountain and the Tree*), and those which appeared during and after the war, had 20th-century settings, and frequently dealt with the war and its effects on men and women (*So Frail a Thing*, *Shadows on a Wall*, *Where the Treasure Is*, and *There Were Three Men*).

The Green Lacquer Pavilion caused quite a stir when it first appeared, and it was well received. Illustrated and decorated by Edmund Dulac, it is a romantic fantasy set in the early 18th century in the country house of Sir John and Lady Taveridge, where the host and hostess and a group of guests suddenly find themselves within the landscape depicted on a green and gold lacquer screen (one of Lady Taveridge's "newly imported Eastern styles") next to a little pavilion the colour of green jade. They have various adventures in this mysterious eastern land and eventually return to their own place and time. Beauclerk conveys splendidly an 18th-century feeling in this novel as regards dialogue, narrative style, details of life and fashion, and the pastiche dedication.

Her next novel, *The Love of the Foolish Angel*, is possibly her most perfect. The *Times Literary Supplement* called it "a creation of an almost flawless loveliness," and it was the first choice of the then newly formed Book Society. Set in Biblical lands in early Christian days, it is the story of Tamael, an angel mistakenly cast out of Heaven along with Lucifer and his crew. Now black and hideous, Tamael proves a very ineffective devil and is sent by his masters to Earth, to tempt the maiden Basilea. To do this he takes the form of a golden haired man (not unlike an angel), falls in love with Basilea, and attempts to protect her from evil, suffering much on her behalf. In the end, the two of them achieve a kind of redemption. The tale is told in a simple, lucid, almost pellucid style, with the strength and directness of a legend.

Legend, mythology, and folk beliefs form the basis of her third book, *The Mountain and the Tree*, which is written in four parts, ambitiously set in a span of times and religions from primitive pagan (nature worship of Mother Earth) to Greek to early Christian. There are four stories, connected by theme as they examine the ancient status of man (Tree) and woman (Mountain) and their relationship against the religion of the time, and there is more than a suggestion that the coming of Christianity removed much of the power and status anciently ascribed to woman. The writing in *The Mountain and the Tree* is very strong and flowing, as though the author is carried along by the power of her sources (*The Golden Bough*, etc., as freely acknowledged in the foreward).

The novels which Beauclerk set in her own time seem rather pale by comparison, although they are written with comparable skill and ease. The effects of the war and people's attitudes and reactions to it loom understandably large: in *Shadows on a Wall* the experiences during the first 12 months of the war of two childhood friends, Jane and Adèle, one in England, one in France, are contrasted; *Where the Treasure Is* is the story of a badly matched husband and wife in wartime. The two remaining novels, *So Frail a Thing* and *There Were Three Men*, deal with the interconnected lives of three people from the century's early years to the beginning of World War II.

—Jean Buchanan

BECK, L(ily) Adams (née Moresby). Also wrote as E. Barrington; Louis Moresby. British. Grew up in Asia; settled in Victoria, British Columbia, after World War I. *Died 3 January 1931.*

ROMANCE AND HISTORICAL PUBLICATIONS

Novels

The Key of Dreams. New York, Dodd Mead, 1922; London, Constable, 1923.
The Treasure of Ho. New York, Dodd Mead, 1924; London, Collins, 1925.
The Way of Stars: A Romance of Reincarnation. New York, Dodd Mead, 1925; London, Collins, 1926.
The House of Fulfilment. New York, Cosmopolitan, and London, Unwin, 1927.
The Garden of Vision. New York, Cosmopolitan, 1929; London, Benn, 1933.
The Joyous Story of Astrid. New York, Cosmopolitan, 1931.

Novels as E. Barrington

The Chaste Diana. New York, Dodd Mead, and London, Lane, 1923.
The Gallants. Boston, Little Brown, 1924; London, Harrap, 1927.
The Divine Lady. New York, Dodd Mead, 1924; London, Harrap, 1925.
Glorious Apollo. New York, Dodd Mead, 1925; London, Harrap, 1926.
The Exquisite Perdita. New York, Dodd Mead, and London, Harrap, 1926.
The Thunderer. New York, Dodd Mead, and London, Harrap, 1927.
The Empress of Hearts. New York, Dodd Mead, and London, Harrap, 1928.
The Laughing Queen: A Romance of Cleopatra. New York, Dodd Mead, and London, Harrap, 1929; as *Cleopatra*, New York, Grosset and Dunlap, 1934.
The Duel of Queens. New York, Doubleday, and London, Cassell, 1930.
The Irish Beauties. New York, Doubleday, and London, Cassell, 1931.
Anne Boleyn. New York, Doubleday, and London, Cassell, 1932.
The Great Romantic. New York, Doubleday, and London, Cassell, 1933.
The Wooing of the Queens. London, Cassell, 1934.
The Graces. London, Cassell, 1934.
The Crowned Lovers. London, Cassell, 1935.

Novels as Louis Moresby

The Glory of Egypt. New York, Doran, and London, Nelson, 1926.
Rubies. New York, Doran, 1927; as Lily Adams Beck, London, Harrap, 1927.
Captain Java. New York, Doubleday, and London, Harrap, 1928.

Short Stories

The Ninth Vibration and Other Stories. New York, Dodd Mead, 1922; London, Unwin, 1929.

The Ladies: A Shining Constellation of Wit and Beauty (as E. Barrington). Boston, Little Brown, and London, Unwin, 1922.
The Perfume of the Rainbow and Other Stories. New York, Dodd Mead, 1923; London, Benn, 1931.
Dreams and Delights. New York, Dodd Mead, 1926; London, Benn, 1932.
The Openers of the Gate: Stories of the Occult. New York, Cosmopolitan, 1930.
Dream Tea. London, Benn, 1934.

OTHER PUBLICATIONS

Other

The Splendour of Asia: The Story and Teaching of the Buddha. New York, Dodd Mead, 1926; London, Collins, 1927; as *The Life of the Buddha*, Collins, 1939.
The Story of Oriental Philosophy. New York, Cosmopolitan, 1928.
The Way of Power: Studies in the Occult. New York, Cosmopolitan, 1928.
The Ghost Plays of Japan. New York, Japan Society, 1933.
A Beginner's Book of Yoga, edited by David Merrill Bramble. New York, Farrar and Rinehart, 1937.

Translator, with S. Yamabe, *Buddhist Psalms.* New York, Dutton, and London, Murray, 1921.

*   *   *

The fiction of L. Adams Beck falls into two main groupings, historical romances published under the pseudonym E. Barrington, and occult and Oriental fiction issued as by L. Adams Beck. A third grouping, adventure novels printed under the name Louis Moresby, is much less important.

E. Barrington's costume romances focus mostly on famous women of history. They embody some sympathy for the woman's role in certain notorious situations, not without a certain amount of sentimentalization and manipulation of history. Typical is *The Divine Lady*, the author's best-known work. This is based on the life of Lady Emma Hamilton, in origin a country girl of great beauty, whose ladder of mistress-ship carried her to Sir William Hamilton, ambassador to the court of Naples, who eventually married her. During the Napoleonic Wars Emma became the mistress of Horatio Nelson in an affair that was notorious in its day and has since been used many times in fiction. Beck expands key moments in Emma's life in an episodic story frequently interrupted by authorial reflections. While opinions of Emma have varied, Beck tries to show her as primarily a simple, devoted, passionate woman, a rather thoughtless pawn of fate, a characterization that does not jell. Nor is the author successful in portraying the complex characters of Hamilton and Nelson. Beck considered historical accuracy important, but managed to overlook the fact that Emma had lost her beauty and was fat and nearly 40 when she met Nelson. In a similar vein of shallow, simplistic sympathy are *Glorious Apollo*, about Lord and Lady Byron; *The Empress of Hearts*, about Marie Antoinette and the Diamond Necklace; and *The Duel of Queens*, about Mary Queen of Scots.

More interesting, perhaps because they are based on a personal commitment, are Beck's occult and Oriental romances. Among these are a short story collection, *The Ninth Vibration*; *The Way of Stars*, a thriller about world peril, war, and romance; *The House of Fulfilment*, a mystical novel; and *The Openers of* the Gate, the cases of a British occult psychologist. Mostly set in the Orient and based on Oriental philosophy and religions, as mediated through Theosophy, these stories deal with such topics as reincarnation and love, karma, hidden teachings, mahatmas, paranormal abilities, and psychic advancement. Sometimes sexuality is important, but at other times sexuality is renounced in favor of a higher call to asceticism. Related to these supernatural fictions is *The Treasure of Ho*, which deals with adventure and romance in China during the reign of the Dowager Empress.

In these occult and Oriental stories the level of craftsmanship is higher than in the sentimental historical novels. The author's knowledge of the Orient and Oriental thought, however, has been characterized as superficial and glib. A nonfiction work in this area, *The Story of Oriental Philosophy*, coordinates the ideas behind much of the author's life and work.

—E. F. Bleiler

———————

BELL, Georgianna. See **MANNERS, Alexandra.**

———————

BELLAMANN, Henry. American. Born Heinrich Hauer in Fulton, Missouri, 28 April 1882. Educated at Westminster College, Missouri; University of Denver; studied in London, Paris, and New York, 1898–1900. Married Katherine Jones in 1907. Dean, School of Fine Arts, Chicora College for Women, Columbia, South Carolina, 1907–24; chairperson of the Examining Board, Juilliard Musical Foundation, 1924–26, and Rockefeller Foundation, 1926–28; lecturer, Vassar College, Poughkeepsie, New York, 1928–29; Dean, Curtis Institute of Music, Philadelphia. Chevalier, Legion of Honour (France), 1931. *Died 16 June 1945.*

ROMANCE AND HISTORICAL PUBLICATIONS

Novels

Petenera's Daughter. New York, Harcourt Brace, 1926; London, Cape, 1927.
Crescendo. New York, Harcourt Brace, 1928.
The Richest Woman in Town. New York, Century, 1932.
Kings Row. New York, Simon and Schuster, 1940; London, Cape, 1941.
Floods of Spring. New York, Simon and Schuster, 1942; London, Cape, 1943.
Victoria Grandolet. New York, Simon and Schuster, 1944; London, Cassell, 1945.
Parris Mitchell of Kings Row, with K. J. Bellamann. New York, Simon and Schuster, 1948; London, Cassell, 1949.

OTHER PUBLICATIONS

Novel

The Gray Man Walks. New York, Doubleday, 1936.

Verse

A Music Teacher's Note Book. New York, Poetry Bookshop, 1920.
Cups of Illusion. Boston, Hougton Mifflin, 1923.
The Upward Pass. Boston, Houghton Mifflin, 1928.

*   *   *

Henry Bellamann was a distinguished musician and music educator who aspired to be a poet. Praise for his novels most often focuses upon his lyrical evocation of pastoral scenes in the 19th-century Mississippi River valley. His early novels, which one reviewer described as "atmosphere saturated," gave little hint of his eventual success and have virtually disappeared. He made his reputation overnight, when he was nearly 60, with *Kings Row*, a revelation of the psychic distresses of a small Missouri community at the turn of the century, which critics compared to Faulkner's work. The *New Yorker*'s taste-making and Faulkner-baiting Clifton Fadiman, in fact, described Bellamann's "operatic concept of character" as less easy to "laugh off" than Faulkner's work, though others found that he lacked the compelling power that distinguished Faulkner. Bellamann is best remembered for the first two-thirds of *Kings Row*, which describes the adolescent sexual awaking of Parris Mitchell, a boy isolated from the rest of the community by his intellectual interests and his love of music, whose first fumbling seduction of a country girl and tactful rejection of the homosexual advances of a classmate were daring subjects for the closeted 1940's. Bellamann provides, however, only fragmentary glimpses of the five years that Parris spends in Vienna studying the then fashionable new Freudian psychiatry; and after Dr. Mitchell returns to Missouri to practice, the focus shifts to the account of the tragic accident that destroys another promising young man (played by Ronald Reagan in the highly successful film version).

Kings Row was originally planned as the first volume of a trilogy that would expose the town's secret life from 1890 to 1940, but Bellamann was diverted from his epic by two grandiose attempts to dip further back into the frontier past. *Floods of Spring*, set in rural Missouri in the middle of the 19th century, followed the career of a figure like Faulkner's Sutpen whose obsessive dedication to building an empire destroyed all his family and personal relationships, but reviewers complained that, although the frontier atmosphere was powerfully evoked, Bellamann never made clear what motivated his character's self-destructive pursuits. The evocation of the sultry atmosphere of plantation Louisiana during the same period in *Victoria Grandolet* was even more highly praised, but again reviewers complained of Bellamann's failure adequately to animate and motivate his stereotyped characters in the conflict between a moody Yankee bride and her hidebound and highly traditional Southern in-laws.

Meanwhile Bellamann during five years of furious activity following his first great success had been making notes for a continuation of *Kings Row*, but he died before beginning to fill in the story outline that he had developed. His wife Katherine, also a poet, undertook to finish *Parris Mitchell of Kings Row*, which she explained was originally intended to have presented a psychoanalysis of the town as viewed and understood by Dr. Mitchell, but which had turned into a personal history of his struggles to drag the backward community, which distrusted his controversial therapies for mental illness, into the 20th century. Ultimately, after being dismissed from his position at the local state hospital for the insane, he regains the respect of the community

with his heroic efforts during the dreadful influenza epidemic after World War I and a happier future is unconvincingly predicted.

Bellamann enjoyed his greatest success for his effusive presentations of the frustrations of alienated adolescents in backward and suspicious communities. Although he exhibited great interest in Freudian psychiatry, he got out of his depth when he tried to imagine and articulate the complex psychological distresses of inhibited adults. Instead of the great gallery of grotesques that—influenced also by Sherwood Anderson's *Winesburg, Ohio*—Faulkner produced, Bellamann populated his lush settings with only conventional shadows.

—Warren French

———————

BELLE, Pamela. British. Born in Ipswich, Suffolk, 16 June 1952. Educated at Ipswich High School, 1964–69; Ipswich School of Art, 1969–70; Ipswich Civic College, 1970–71; University of Sussex, Brighton, 1972–75, B.A. (honours) in history 1975; Coventry College of Education, 1975–76, postgraduate certificate in education 1976. Married Alan Fincher in 1976 (divorced 1983). Library assistant, Hemel Hempstead, Hertfordshire, 1976–77; primary school teacher, Hemel Hempstead, Tring and Berkhamsted, Hertfordshire, 1977–78, and Northchurch St. Mary's School, Berkhamsted, 1978–85. Agent: Vivienne Schuster, John Farquharson Ltd., 162–168 Regent Street, London W1R 5TB. Address: 184 Melksham Lane, Broughton Gifford, Melksham, Wiltshire SN12 8LN, England.

ROMANCE AND HISTORICAL PUBLICATIONS

Novels (series: Heron Family in all books except *Wintercombe*)

The Moon in the Water. London, Pan, 1983; New York, Berkley, 1984.
The Chains of Fate. London, Pan, and New York, Berkley, 1984.
Alathea. London, Pan, and New York, Berkley, 1985.
The Lodestar. London, Bodley Head, 1987.
Wintercombe. London, Bodley Head, and New York, St. Martin's Press, 1988.

*

Pamela Belle comments:
I take a great deal of trouble to make my books as accurate, historically, as possible. My characters seem so real to me that I must make the place and time in which they are set as vivid and convincing as I am able, and try to fit plot and characters into real events, rather than the other way about. All history fascinates me, especially the 17th century, and my particular interests always seem to surface in each book: children, animals (especially dogs, cats, and horses), music, poetry, architecture, warfare, and the minutiae of daily life in a country house, in the garden or on the farm.

*   *   *

While Pamela Belle's novels are a combination of family saga and romance, they are true historical novels because the times in which they are set dictate the course of the character's lives.

She draws characters well and handles large casts with aplomb. She is good at sinister villains like the treacherous, beautiful Meraud Trevelyan in the Goldhayes trilogy, and the Drakelons both in the trilogy and *The Lodestar*.

For the Goldhayes trilogy *The Moon in the Water*, *The Chains of Fate* and *Alathea*, Belle created the Herons, a family with several branches—Drakelons, Trevelyans, Grahams and their friends the Sewells. *The Lodestar* tells of 15th-century Herons and Drakelons. In all her books there are delightful children and endearing animals.

She has a tremendous feeling for place, and describes scenery with feeling but her most loving descriptions are reserved for the houses her characters inhabit—Goldhayes in Suffolk, Ashcott in Oxfordshire, and Wintercombe, the beautiful house in Somerset that gives its name to Belle's finest book.

Her heroines are strong women, survivors all: Thomazine Heron in the Goldhayes trilogy, Thomazine's daughter in *Alathea* and Silence St. Barbe in *Wintercombe*. Christie Heron is the hero of *The Lodestar* but the girl he marries, Julian Bray, who spends most of the book loathing him, is another strong woman. Belle's characters grow and develop, learning lessons from life.

Apart from *The Lodestar* which is set in the reign of Richard III and has an intriguing theory about the fate of the Princes in the Tower, the 17th century is Belle's chosen period. The historical background is well researched and seamlessly woven into her writing. Although the dialogue does not strive for a 17th-century flavour, the thoughts and attitudes of the time ring true. Her knowledge of 17th-century housekeeping and nursing is well used: she never lets us forget that, then, pregnancy or what to us would be a minor illness, could be devastatingly dangerous.

Her plots are exciting and full of action. The Civil War is shown mainly from the royalist point of view in the trilogy but the St. Barbe family of *Wintercombe* are puritans and for parliament.

Alathea is set after the Restoration. We see the fringes of court life and witness the Great Fire through Alathea's eyes. This book is less successful than the others, perhaps because Alathea (a female artist) although she is delightful, behaves untypically for her time; perhaps because her half-brother's incestuous love for her seems unreal and not least because she becomes the mistress of the notorious Earl of Rochester who is portrayed more sympathetically than history paints him.

The love stories at the heart of these historical romances are warm and full of feeling. The complications the lovers suffer are devious and difficult.

Thomazine Heron's love for her cousin Francis threads its way through two books—*The Moon in the Water* and *The Chains of Fate*. They are kept apart by cruel circumstances: Thomazine is betrothed to sinister Dominic Drakelon as a child but falls in love with Francis; their marriage is forbidden by Francis's older brother Simon who is at feud with Francis. Just as they are about to marry, Simon has Francis thrown in prison and when Thomazine hears that Francis is dead she cares so little for her life that she marries Dominic who proves a brutal, unloving husband. Thomazine is pregnant with Dominic's child when she learns that Francis did not die and is in Scotland. After the birth of the child she has to chose between her true love and her son. She travels with immense difficulty and danger to find Francis, only to discover that he no longer trusts her and is tied up with Montrose's campaign. They are reconciled and travelling home separately when Francis is press-ganged into the Roundhead army. Thomazine finds him again after the siege of Colchester and once more they are to be wed but are frustrated by their pernicious cousin Meraud. Marriage and happiness come at last at the end of the second book.

A superb, gentle love story is at the heart of *Wintercombe*. Silence, Lady St. Barbe, holding her manor house for her husband who is in the Roundhead army, surrounded by her children, needled by her dour mother-in-law, has to keep a fine balance between her puritan household and the royalists who take the manor over. Their leader is vile, but his second-in-command is a just man and gradually, Silence falls in love with Nick Hellier and finds herself going against all her beliefs and principles. Wintercombe is besieged by the parliamentary troops and Silence is torn between love and loyalty.

These books can be confidently recommended to all who enjoy a romantic story, a well depicted historical background and a fast-moving plot.

—Pamela Cleaver

BENÉT, Stephen Vincent. American. Born in Bethlehem, Pennsylvania, 22 July 1898; brother of the writer William Rose Benét. Educated at Hitchcock Military Academy, Jacinto, California, 1910–11; Summerville Academy; Yale University, New Haven, Connecticut (chairman, *Yale Literary Magazine*, 1918), 1915–18, 1919–20, A.B. 1919, M.A. 1920; the Sorbonne, Paris, 1920–21. Married Rosemary Carr in 1921; one son and two daughters. Worked for the State Department, Washington, D.C., 1918, and for advertising agency, New York, 1919; lived in Paris, 1926–29; during 1930's and early 1940's was an active lecturer and radio propagandist for the liberal cause. Editor, Yale Younger Poets series. Recipient: Poetry Society of America prize, 1921; Guggenheim fellowship, 1926; Pulitzer Prize, 1929, 1944; O. Henry award, 1932, 1937, 1940; Shelley Memorial award, 1933; American Academy gold medal, 1943. Litt.D.: Yale University, 1937. Member, 1929, and Vice-President, National Institute of Arts and Letters. *Died 13 March 1943.*

ROMANCE AND HISTORICAL PUBLICATIONS

Novels

Jean Huguenot. New York, Holt, 1923; London, Methuen, 1925.
Spanish Bayonet. New York, Doran, and London, Heinemann, 1926.
James Shore's Daughter. New York, Doubleday, and London, Heinemann, 1934.

Short Stories

The Barefoot Saint. New York, Doubleday, 1929.
The Litter of Rose Leaves. New York, Random House, 1930.
Thirteen O'Clock: Stories of Several Worlds. New York, Farrar and Rinehart, 1937; London, Heinemann, 1938.
The Devil and Daniel Webster. New York, Farrar and Rinehart, 1937.
Johnny Pye and the Fool-Killer. New York, Farrar and Rinehart, and London, Heinemann, 1938.
Tales Before Midnight. New York, Farrar and Rinehart, 1939; London, Heinemann, 1940.
Short Stories: A Selection. New York, Farrar and Rinehart, 1942.
O'Halloran's Luck and Other Short Stories. New York, Penguin, 1944.

OTHER PUBLICATIONS

Novels

The Beginning of Wisdom. New York, Holt, 1921; London, Chapman and Dodd, 1922.
Young People's Pride. New York, Holt, 1922.

Plays

Five Men and Pompey: A Series of Dramatic Portraits. Boston, Four Seas, 1915.
Nerves, with John Farrar (produced New York, 1924).
That Awful Mrs. Eaton, with John Farrar (produced New York, 1924).
The Headless Horseman, music by Douglas Moore (broadcast 1937). Boston, Schirmer, 1937.
The Devil and Daniel Webster, music by Douglas Moore, adaptation of the story by Benét (produced New York, 1939). Opera version published New York, Farrar and Rinehart, 1939; play text published New York, Dramatists Play Service, 1939.
Elementals (broadcast 1940–41). Published in *Best Broadcasts of 1940–41,* edited by Max Wylie, New York, McGraw Hill, 1942.
Freedom's Hard Bought Thing, adaptation of his own story (broadcast 1941). Published in *The Free Company Presents,* edited by James Boyd, New York, Dodd Mead, 1941.
Nightmare at Noon, in *The Treasury Star Parade,* edited by William A. Bacher. New York, Farrar and Rinehart, 1942.
A Child Is Born (broadcast 1942). New York, Farrar and Rinehart, 1942.
They Burned the Books (broadcast 1942). New York, Farrar and Rinehart, 1942.
All That Money Can Buy (screenplay), with Dan Totheroh, in *Twenty Best Film Plays,* edited by John Gassner and Dudley Nichols. New York, Crown, 1943.
We Stand United and Other Radio Scripts (includes *A Child Is Born, The Undefended Border, Dear Adolf, Listen to the People, Thanksgiving Day—1941, They Burned the Books, A Time to Reap, Toward the Century of Modern Man, Your Army*). New York, Farrar and Rinehart, 1945.

Screenplays: *Abraham Lincoln,* with Gerrit Lloyd, 1930; *Cheers for Miss Bishop,* with Adelaide Heilbron and Sheridan Gibney, 1941; *All That Money Can Buy,* with Dan Totheroh, 1941.

Radio Plays: *The Headless Horseman,* 1937; *The Undefended Border,* 1940; *We Stand United,* 1940; *Elementals,* 1940–41; *Listen to the People,* 1941; *Thanksgiving Day—1941,* 1941; *Freedom's a Hard Bought Thing,* 1941; *Nightmare at Noon; A Child Is Born,* 1942; *Dear Adolf,* 1942; *They Burned the Books,* 1942; *A Time to Reap,* 1942; *Toward the Century of Modern Man,* 1942; *Your Army,* 1944.

Verse

The Drug-Shop; or, Endymion in Edmonstoun. New Haven, Connecticut, Yale University Press, 1917.
Young Adventure. New Haven, Connecticut, Yale University Press, 1918.
Heavens and Earth. New York, Holt, 1920; London, Heinemann, 1928.
The Ballad of William Sycamore 1790–1880. New York, Hackett, 1923.
King David. New York, Holt, 1923.

Tiger Joy. New York, Doran, 1925.
John Brown's Body. New York, Doubleday, and London, Heinemann, 1928.
Ballads and Poems 1915–1930. New York, Doubleday, 1931; London, Heinemann, 1933.
A Book of Americans, with Rosemary Benét. New York, Farrar and Rinehart, 1933.
Burning City. New York, Farrar and Rinehart, 1936; London, Heinemann, 1937.
The Ballad of the Duke's Mercy. New York, House of Books, 1939.
Nightmare at Noon. New York, Farrar and Rinehart, 1940.
Listen to the People: Independence Day 1941. New York, Council for Democracy, 1941.
Western Star. New York, Farrar and Rinehart, 1943; London, University of London Press, 1944.
The Last Circle: Stories and Poems. New York, Farrar Straus, 1946; London, Heinemann, 1948.

Other

The Magic of Poetry and the Poet's Art. Chicago, Compton, 1936.
A Summons to the Free. New York, Farrar and Rinehart, and London, Oxford University Press, 1941.
Selected Works. New York, Farrar and Rinehart, 2 vols., 1942.
America. New York, Farrar and Rinehart, 1944; London, Heinemann, 1945.
From the Earth to the Moon (letter). Privately printed, 1958.
Selected Poetry and Prose, edited by Basil Davenport. New York, Rinehart, 1960.
Selected Letters, edited by Charles A. Fenton. New Haven, Connecticut, Yale University Press, 1960.
Stephen Vincent Benét on Writing: A Great Writer's Letter of Advice to a Young Beginner, edited by George Abbe. Brattleboro, Vermont, Stephen Greene Press, 1964.

Editor, with others, *The Yale Book of Student Verse 1910–1919.* New Haven, Connecticut, Yale University Press, 1919.
Editor, with Monty Woolley, *Tamburlaine the Great,* by Christopher Marlowe. New Haven, Connecticut, Yale University Press, 1919.

*

Bibliography: by Gladys Louise Maddocks, in *Bulletin of Bibliography 20* (Boston), September 1951 and April 1952.

Manuscript Collection: Beinecke Library, Yale University, New Haven, Connecticut.

Critical Studies: *Stephen Vincent Benét: My Brother Steve* by William Rose Benét, New York, Saturday Review-Farrar and Rinehart, 1943; *Stephen Vincent Benét: The Life and Times of an American Man of Letters* by Charles A. Fenton, New Haven, Connecticut, Yale University Press, 1958; *Stephen Vincent Benét* by Parry Stroud, New York, Twayne, 1962.

*   *   *

Stephen Vincent Benét, a popular writer during his time and a prolific author of verse, short stories, and novels is now and seems destined to be remembered only as a minor writer and the author of two works: *John Brown's Body,* a poetic rendering of the American Civil War that has been called both America's epic poem and a "full-length novel"; and the short story "The

Devil and Daniel Webster'' which skillfully combines an American historical setting and folklore with fantasy. What is vividly remembered in the story is that that greatest orator of American history, old Dan'l himself out-argues the Devil against a packed jury and an evil judge.

Although both of the above works are good and well worth remembering, there are others in a similar vein that are also superior examples of the popular verse and magazine fiction of the time. *Western Star*, an unfinished poem written much in the manner of *John Brown's Body*, is a historical poem that depicts early American Jamestown and Plymouth with a poetic skill that at times equals or surpasses the best poetry of the earlier work. He also wrote a number of stories about the American past similar to ''The Devil and Daniel Webster'' that effectively portray American history, often with a touch of folklore and fantasy. Most notable among these are such stories as ''Jacob and the Indians'' (1938) which deals with a young Jewish scholar, the wilderness, and the somewhat ironic fortunes of young love; ''Freedom's a Hard-Bought Thing'' (1940), a realistic story set in the slave holding south and rendered in a somewhat haunting Negro dialect is a fine story that is only slightly marred by its romantic, unlikely ending; ''The Die Hard'' (1938), set in post Civil War Georgia, deftly combines history and the initiation of a young boy into the evils of adult insanity in the person of an old former Confederate Colonel; and the world of Ireland and an unlikely leprechaun are brought to the New World frontier in ''O'Halloran's Luck'' (1938).

Aside from these and other stories, Benét wrote the short historical novel *Spanish Bayonet* set in Florida before and during the beginning of the American Revolution. Although this novel has been all but forgotten, it is an effective and fast paced story of intrigue and escape laced with a startling initiation of a young boy to a sinister world. Although the novel is too much the traditional adventure story to be the significant achievement Benét hoped it would it be, it is nonetheless a good historical novel that evokes the history and setting of early Florida and does so with fictional characters that have a good deal of life. The publishing history of the novel also says something about the artistic integrity of Benét. At a time when he very much needed the money he turned down $10,000 from a magazine editor who insisted on a ''happy ending.''

Although Benét's historical works focus on the American past, quite often he turned to Europe, usually with good results. ''The Last of the Legions'' (1937) is an excellent story set in Britain at the beginning of the end of the Roman Empire. An even better story with a modern setting, ''Into Egypt'' (1939), depicts the horrors of Nazism as seen through the eyes of a young German lieutenant whose feelings often conflict with the party line he tries to believe in and dutifully carries out. Religious symbolism adds a sharp ironic contrast to the story's action. Benét, writing in 1939, thus exhibited a sure sense of a meaningful moment and its significance in modern Europe as he did at other times with the American scene.

In short, though Benét may well be condemned to be remembered for a single short story and one long poem, his achievement is larger than this. In the realm of historical fiction and poetry alone he wrote one novel, two long poems, and about a dozen short stories that by all rights should continue to find an audience.

—Larry Olpin

BENNETTS, Pamela (neé James). Also wrote as Helen Ashfield; Margaret James. British. Born in Hampstead, London, 23 July 1922. Educated at Emmanuel Church School, Hampstead; St. Marylebone School for Girls, London. Married William George Bennetts in 1942; one daughter. Staff member, London Diocesan Fund, 1938–80: retired as deputy secretary, 1980. *Died 11 December 1986.*

ROMANCE AND HISTORICAL PUBLICATIONS

Novels

The Borgia Prince. London, Hale, 1968; New York, St. Martin's Press, 1975.
The Borgia Bull. London, Hale, 1968.
The Venetian. London, Hale, 1968.
The Suzerain. London, Hale, 1968.
The Adversaries. London, Hale, 1969.
The Black Plantagenet. London, Hale, 1969.
Envoy from Elizabeth. London, Hale, 1970; New York, St. Martin's Press, 1973.
Richard and the Knights of God. London, Hale, 1970; New York, St. Martin's Press, 1973.
The Tudor Ghosts. London, Hale, 1971.
Royal Sword at Agincourt. London, Hale, and New York, St. Martin's Press, 1971.
A Crown for Normandy. London, Hale, 1971.
Bright Son of York. London, Hale, 1971.
The Third Richard. London, Hale, 1972.
The Angevin King. London, Hale, 1972.
The de Montfort Legacy. London, Hale, and New York, St. Martin's Press, 1973.
The Lords of Lancaster. London, Hale, and New York, St. Martin's Press, 1973.
The Barons of Runnymede. London, Hale, and New York, St. Martin's Press, 1974.
A Dragon for Edward. London, Hale, and New York, St. Martin's Press, 1975.
My Dear Lover England. London, Hale, and New York, St. Martin's Press, 1975.
The She-Wolf. London, Hale, 1975; New York, St. Martin's Press, 1976.
Death of the Red King. London, Hale, and New York, St. Martin's Press, 1976.
Stephen and the Sleeping Saints. London, Hale, and New York, St. Martin's Press, 1977.
The House in Candle Square. London, Hale, 1977; as *The Haunting of Sara Lessingham* (as Margaret James), New York, St. Martin's Press, 1978.
Don Pedro's Captain. London, Hale, and New York, St. Martin's Press, 1978.
Ring the Bell Softly. London, Hale, 1978; as Margaret James, New York, St. Martin's Press, 1978.
One Dark Night. London, Hale, 1978.
Footsteps in the Fog. London, Hale, 1979; as Margaret James, New York, St. Martin's Press, 1979.
Marionette. London, Hale, 1979; as Margaret James, New York, St. Martin's Press, 1979.
A Voice in the Darkness. London, Hale, 1979; as Margaret James, New York, St. Martin's Press, 1979.
Amberstone. London, Hale, 1980; as Margaret James, New York, St. Martin's Press, 1980.
The Quick and the Dead. London, Hale, 1980; as Margaret James, New York, St. Martin's Press, 1980.

Lucy's Cottage. London, Hale, 1981; as Margaret James, New York, St. Martin's Press, 1981.

Beau Barron's Lady. London, Hale, 1981.

The Marquis and Miss Jones. London, Hale, 1981; as Helen Ashfield, New York, St. Martin's Press, 1982.

Regency Rogue. London, Hale, 1982.

The Michaelmas Tree. London, Hale, 1982; New York, St. Martin's Press, 1982.

Lady of the Masque. London, Hale, 1982.

The Slave Masters. London, Hale, 1983.

The Loving Highwayman. London, Hale, and New York, St. Martin's Press, 1983.

Emerald. London, Hale, 1983; as Helen Ashfield, New York, St. Martin's Press, 1983.

Midsummer Morning. London, Hale, 1984; as Helen Ashfield, New York, St. Martin's Press, 1984.

Ruby. London, Hale, 1984; as Helen Ashfield, New York, St. Martin's Press, 1984.

Pearl. London, Hale, 1984; as Helen Ashfield, New York, St. Martin's Press, 1985.

Garnet. London, Hale, 1985; as Helen Ashfield, New York, St. Martin's Press, 1985.

Sapphire. London, Hale, 1985; as Helen Ashfield, New York, St. Martin's Press, 1985.

Opal. London, Hale, 1986; as Helen Ashfield, New York, St. Martin's Press, 1986.

Topaz. London, Hale, 1987; as Helen Ashfield, New York, St. Martin's Press, 1987.

Crystal. London, Hale, 1987.

*

Pamela Bennetts commented:

(1982) I had always wanted to write, but kept telling myself that I hadn't got time, having a full-time job, plus a home to run. In 1966 I decided to try: now or never! My intention was, and still is, to entertain my readers. My books, whether historical romances, gothic thrillers, or Georgian romances, are intended as a means of escape from the trials and tribulations of everyday modern life. I want people who are kind enough to read them to enjoy them and forget the H-bomb and the kitchen sink. However, I am always extremely careful to do my research carefully, for I would never knowingly cheat my readers by including inaccurate facts. Being human, I'm sure I fail sometimes, but I do my very best. I hope I can go on writing for many years yet, as I'm only happy when I'm working on a work, and like a lost soul in between novels.

*   *   *

Pamela Bennetts's stories breathe life into characters from the turbulent past. In the Holy Land the Crusader king, Richard the Lionheart, fights the infidel Saladin (*Richard and the Knights of God*). Richard's brother King John reluctantly acknowledges the rights of his nobles in *The Barons of Runnymede*. After initial defeat Henry III and his son, the future Edward I, overcome the enigmatic Simon de Montfort (*The de Montfort Legacy*), and the glory of Edward's own reign is captured in the novel *A Dragon for Edward*. All of the stories are well researched and often contain a bibliography for any reader wishing to pursue the subject.

Although the major historical figures are convincingly portrayed in a Bennetts novel, it is the development of the minor characters that gives substance to the stories. Their private lives and loves thread through the plots and keep the novels from becoming mere fictionalized popular history. There is always a ro-

mance and it often centers on a love/hate relationship which keeps the lovers at odds until almost the very end.

Bennetts is a born storyteller with an appealing way of alternating historical narrative and dramatic scenarios. She conveys a vivid sense of what life was like in those distant times and lightly weaves descriptions of dress, manners, foods, and furnishings into the story.

Bennetts also tells light romantic tales in a 19th-century setting (these appear in the U.S.A. under the pseudonym Helen Ashfield). Among these is the popular Regency Jewel series in which each title is not only the name of a precious stone but the name of the heroine as well. In *Sapphire* the heroine is the daughter of a country parson who shares a childhood friendship with Ashton the son of the Earl of Stonehurst. As adults that friendship turns to love but the difference in their social station as well as the intervention of the wicked Lyndon FitzMaurice prove difficult barriers to surmount. They do surmount these obstacles, of course, as does *Opal*, a music hall singer born in London's worst slums, and the man who loves her, handsome Edward Adare, Earl of Kynston. In these stories and others Bennetts is at her best when describing the difficult life of the poorer classes. This aspect is one often overlooked in romance novels which tend to focus on the upper strata of society.

Another group of novels are stories of frightening events which take over the lives of the innocent (these are published in the U.S.A. under the pseudonym Margaret James). Through vignettes of action, thought, or dialogue, in short mysteries teeming with characters, Bennetts creates a cast of suspicious rogues, any one of whom could be the perpetrator of some horror. As an example, in the novel *Footsteps in the Fog*, terror reigns in Victorian London. An axe-killer is on the loose, but nowhere is the fear more intense than in the house of prostitution where two women have been hideously murdered by decapitation. False clues and innuendo abound in these novels, teasing the reader and keeping her guessing all the way to the end. For the female protagonist there is usually a hint of romance as in *A Voice in the Darkness*. At one point young governess Harriet no longer doubts that her handsome employer (whom she secretly loves) is guilty of the murder and mayhem which beset the village. Of course, he is really innocent. Bennetts has an excellent ear for dialogue and her use of colloquial speech is superb. This British writer's mysteries have proven to be quite popular imports for readers in the United States.

—Patricia Altner

BENTLEY, Jayne. See **KRENTZ, Jayne Ann**.

BENTLEY, Phyllis (Eleanor). British. Born in Halifax, Yorkshire, 19 November 1894. Educated at Cheltenham Ladies' College, Gloucestershire; University of London, B.A. 1914. Fellow, Royal Society of Literature, 1958. D.Litt.: University of Leeds, 1949. O.B.E. (Officer, Order of the British Empire), 1970. *Died 27 June 1977.*

ROMANCE AND HISTORICAL PUBLICATIONS

Novels

Environment. London, Sidgwick and Jackson, 1922; New York, Hillman Curl, 1935.
Cat-in-the-Manger. London, Sidgwick and Jackson, 1923.
The Spinner of the Years. London, Unwin, 1928; New York, Henkle, 1929.
The Partnership. London, Benn, 1928; Boston, Little Brown, 1929.
Carr: The Biography of Philip Joseph Carr. London, Benn, 1929; New York, Macmillan, 1933.
Trio. London, Gollancz, 1930.
Inheritance. London, Gollancz, and New York, Macmillan, 1932.
A Modern Tragedy. London, Gollancz, and New York, Macmillan, 1934.
Freedom, Farewell! London, Gollancz, and New York, Macmillan, 1936.
Sleep in Peace. London, Gollancz, and New York, Macmillan, 1938.
Take Courage. London, Gollancz, 1940; as *The Power and the Glory*, New York, Macmillan, 1940.
Manhold. London, Gollancz, and New York, Macmillan, 1941.
The Rise of Henry Morcar. London, Gollancz, and New York, Macmillan, 1946.
Life Story. London, Gollancz, and New York, Macmillan, 1948.
Quorum. London, Gollancz, 1950; New York, Macmillan, 1951.
The House of Moreys. London, Gollancz, and New York, Macmillan, 1953.
Noble in Reason. London, Gollancz, and New York, Macmillan, 1955.
Crescendo. London, Gollancz, and New York, Macmillan, 1958.
A Man of His Time. London, Gollancz, and New York, Macmillan, 1966.
Oath of Silence. New York, Doubleday, 1967.
Ring in the New. London, Gollancz, 1969.

Short Stories (series: West Riding)

The World's Bane and Other Stories. London, Unwin, 1918.
The Whole of the Short. London, Gollancz, 1935.
Panorama: Tales of the West Riding. London, Gollancz, and New York, Macmillan, 1952.
Love and Money: Seven Tales of the West Riding. London, Gollancz, and New York, Macmillan, 1957.
Kith and Kin: Nine Tales of Family Life. London, Gollancz, and New York, Macmillan, 1960.
More Tales of the West Riding, with John Ogden. London, Gollancz, 1974.

OTHER PUBLICATIONS

Fiction (for children)

The Young Brontës. London, Parrish, 1960; New York, Roy, 1961.
The Adventures of Tom Leigh. London, Macdonald, 1964; New York, Doubleday, 1966.
Ned Carver in Danger. London, Macdonald, 1967.

Gold Pieces. London, Macdonald, 1968; as *Forgery*, New York, Doubleday, 1968.
Sheep May Safely Graze. London, Gollancz, 1972.
The New Venturers. London, Gollancz, 1973.

Play (for children)

The New Apprentice. London, French, 1959.

Other

Pedagomania; or, The Gentle Art of Teaching. London, Unwin, 1918.
Here Is America. London, Gollancz, 1941.
The English Regional Novel. London, Allen and Unwin, 1941.
Some Observations on the Art of the Narrative. London, Home and Van Thal, 1946.
Colne Valley Cloth: From the Earliest Times to the Present Day. Huddersfield, Huddersfield and District Woollen Export Group, 1947.
The Brontës. London, Home and Van Thal, 1947; Denver, Swallow, 1948; revised edition, London, Barker, 1966.
The Brontë Sisters. London, Longman, 1950.
O Dreams, O Destinations (autobiography). London, Gollancz, and New York, Macmillan, 1962.
Committees. London, Collins, 1962.
Public Speaking. London, Collins, 1964.
Enjoy Books: Reading and Collecting. London, Gollancz, 1964.
The Brontës and Their World. London, Thames and Hudson, and New York, Viking Press, 1969.
Haworth of the Brontës. London, Dalton, 1977.

*   *   *

Phyllis Bentley was proud to call herself a regional novelist. Her region was the old West Riding of Yorkshire. Its landscape of rocky hillsides, heathery moors, tumbling streams, and bustling towns, provides a constant backdrop to her stories; her characters—strong-willed, stubborn, passionate, and uncompromising—are seen as the natural products of their setting.

For Bentley, industrial and private life went hand in hand, as her historical sagas demonstrate. The upswings of the Industrial Revolution bring excitement and good fortune to the families in her stories. The downturns cause disaster and tragedy—as they did in Bentley's own life.

Families always fascinated her. Many novels centre on some archetypal Yorkshire mill-owning family, with its money-making and its intellectual branches, and its feuds over marriages, wills, and business affairs. She planted them in the imaginary Ire Valley, with its principal town, Annotsfield; and, as her novels and their sequels proliferated, she constructed whole networks of mingling Oldroyds and Armitages and Bamforths, to be unravelled by diligent readers.

Writing historical romances was not Bentley's first intention. She meant to be a "serious" novelist, depicting life with unsparing realism; hoping that if she showed it "as it really was" (to quote her autobiography), readers might begin to understand their own motives and actions better, and so learn to live more nobly and happily.

Such were the naively idealistic objectives of her early novels. In *The Partnership* her heroine, a plain, earnest girl, finds a vicarious fulfilment in promoting the robustly amorous career of her maid. *The Spinner of the Years* dissects a marriage between a high-minded girl and a down-to-earth millowner, entered upon with good will, but foundering on reefs of total incomprehension. They fit into the feminist novel tradition of the 1920's, without being particularly outstanding.

The novel which brought Bentley fame was *Inheritance*; "my West Riding novel" as she called it, long before she had chosen the name. It is based on the theory that all actions, good or bad, pass as an inheritance from one generation to the next. The story begins with the Luddites of 1812, opposing the introduction of machinery at an Ire Valley mill, and murdering the millowner. It then follows the fortunes of the descendants of all the main characters in this tragedy, for more than a hundred years. The mill-owners prosper, while the heirs of the Luddites turn to other forms of opposition, industrial and intellectual. Finally, through a carefully designed series of marriages, the inheritance of them all is fused in one young man, who, at the genuinely historical point of the 1931 textile slump, draws inspiration from his ancestors to start afresh at the old mill where the murder was committed.

Bentley loved pattern in her novels, but *Inheritance* has more than careful construction. For the first time she really let herself go, in a sweeping saga of passion, aspiration, and tragedy. Bentley found that she could write colourfully about romantic love; and her earlier, earnest heroines change to lively women, matching, and sometimes mastering, their determined, hot-blooded men.

Earnestness was not banished for ever. Bentley felt keenly about the rise of the Fascist tyrannies, using political conflict as the background to a Civil War novel, *Take Courage*, and an ambitious, but not very successful, life of Julius Caesar in *Freedom, Farewell!*, her only non-Yorkshire novel. But she was at her best when she forgot political theorizing, and concentrated on the closely-woven complexities of family life, as in *Carr* and *Life Story*, based respectively on the lives of her father and mother. Even in her best-selling melodrama, *The House of Moreys*, the picture of an early 19th-century household lingers in the mind far longer than the gypsy plots and murders.

Bentley's imagination kindled most, in fact, to middle-class Victorian and Edwardian life, when the distinctions between rich and poor were clear, when women gossiped in their drawing rooms, and men dominated their mills. With a wealth of accurate detail—the legacy of her early passion for "life as it was"—she fitted fiction to fact; and threw a romantic glow over a past when Yorkshire was the proudest county in England, and Yorkshiremen believed themselves to be the most exciting and dynamic people on earth.

—Angela Bull

BERCKMAN, Evelyn (Domenica). American. Born in Philadelphia, Pennsylvania, 18 October 1900. Educated at Columbia University, New York. Concert pianist and composer: compositions include the ballets *From the Odyssey* and *County Fair* and other works. Lived in London after 1960. *Died 18 September 1978.*

ROMANCE AND HISTORICAL PUBLICATIONS

Novels

The Evil of Time. New York, Dodd Mead, 1954; London, Eyre and Spottiswoode, 1955.

The Beckoning Dream. New York, Dodd Mead, 1955; London, Eyre and Spottiswoode, 1956; as *Worse Than Murder*, New York, Dell, 1957.

The Strange Bedfellow. New York, Dodd Mead, 1956; London, Eyre and Spottiswoode, 1957; as *Jewel of Death*, New York, Pyramid, 1968.

The Blind Villain. New York, Dodd Mead, and London, Eyre and Spottiswoode, 1957; as *House of Terror*, New York, Dell, 1960; as *A Hidden Malice*, New York, Belmont, n.d.

The Hovering Darkness. New York, Dodd Mead, 1957; London, Eyre and Spottiswoode, 1958.

No Known Grave. New York, Dodd Mead, 1958; London, Eyre and Spottiswoode, 1959.

Lament for Four Brides. New York, Dodd Mead, 1959; London, Eyre and Spottiswoode, 1960.

Do You Know This Voice? New York, Dodd Mead, 1960; London, Eyre and Spottiswoode, 1961.

Blind-Girl's-Buff. New York, Dodd Mead, and London, Eyre and Spottiswoode, 1962.

A Thing That Happens to You. New York, Dodd Mead, 1964; as *Keys from a Window*, London, Eyre and Spottiswoode, 1965.

A Simple Case of Ill-Will. London, Eyre and Spottiswoode, 1964; New York, Dodd Mead, 1965.

Stalemate. London, Eyre and Spottiswoode, and New York, Doubleday, 1966.

A Case in Nullity. London, Eyre and Spottiswoode, 1967; New York, Doubleday, 1968.

The Heir of Starvelings. New York, Doubleday, 1967; London, Eyre and Spottiswoode, 1968.

The Long Arm of the Prince. London, Hale, 1968.

She Asked for It. New York, Doubleday, 1969; London, Hamish Hamilton, 1970.

The Voice of Air. New York, Doubleday, 1970; London, Hale, 1971.

A Finger to Her Lips. London, Hale, and New York, Doubleday, 1971.

The Stake in the Game. London, Hamish Hamilton, 1971; New York, Doubleday, 1973.

The Fourth Man on the Rope. London, Hamish Hamilton, and New York, Doubleday, 1972.

The Victorian Album. London, Hamish Hamilton, and New York, Doubleday, 1973.

Wait. London, Hamish Hamilton, 1973; as *Wait, Just You Wait*, New York, Doubleday, 1973.

Indecent Exposure. London, Hamish Hamilton, 1975; as *The Nightmare Chase*, New York, Doubleday, 1975.

The Blessed Plot. London, Hamish Hamilton, 1976; as *The Crown Estate*, New York, Doubleday, 1976.

Be All and End All. London, Hamish Hamilton, 1976; as *Journey's End*, New York, Doubleday, 1977.

OTHER PUBLICATIONS

Other

Nelson's Dear Lord: A Portrait of St. Vincent. London, Macmillan, 1962.

The Hidden Navy. London, Hamish Hamilton, 1973.

Creators and Destroyers of the English Navy. London, Hamish Hamilton, 1974.

Victims of Piracy: The Admiralty Court 1575–1678. London, Hamish Hamilton, 1979.

*

Manuscript Collection: Mugar Memorial Library, Boston University.

*   *   *

Although often categorized as a crime writer, Evelyn Berckman produced multi-faceted work and it is virtually impossible to pin a label upon her. Most of her books have the element of mystery, many can be described as psychological thrillers, some have historical settings or make impressive use of long-term flashback techniques, while others are pure gothic; the interesting thing is that she had the ability to fuse several or all of these elements in a single novel, and invariably with commendable attention to detail and literary craftsmanship.

A keen interest in art, history, and archaeology is evident in many of her stories, combining authenticity with an atmosphere of menace in which her women protagonists are more than equal to the occasion. *The Evil of Time*, *The Strange Bedfellow*, and *Lament for Four Brides* are accomplished examples from the early period of her career.

Her forays into history, and particular those stories in which she presents a modern mystery and traces it back to its historical roots, display a masterly technique in a difficult field. *The Victorian Album*, strange and eerie, shows us the innermost thoughts of a latent medium who is impelled by an old album to delve back into a Victorian murder. Berckman's skilled hand shows her heroine's initial curiosity developing into the inexorable pursuit of truth and fulfilment, and a strong line of suspense leads to a disturbing climax. In *The Blessed Plot* she weaves an ingenious connection between events of 1975 and 1214, while *Be All and End All* presents a tantalizing mixture of historical bibliography, complex relationships, a menacing chateau near Paris, and an appalling secret finally revealed. All of these novels embody romance/gothic elements and mystery rather than detection, but she could also produce the highly competent romantic historical novel without complications—as witness *The Long Arm of the Prince*, a most literate and enthralling Elizabethan mystery.

With *The Heir of Starvelings* Berckman made her principal contribution to the truly gothic field. This Victorian tale is replete with foreboding, as genteel Davina Milne occupies her mind following her fiancé's death by taking the post of nursemaid-teacher at a grim old house. "The entire place," she is told, "is a sort of nightmare." With a deft touch, Berckman shows this to be an understatement.

"Miss Berckman," said Violet Grant in the *Daily Telegraph*, "is extremely good at drawing flawed women so perceptively that one cannot but sympathize with them." This is undeniable, and is but one facet of her ability to present credible characters and emotions. We must recognize also her many touches of romance without sentimentality, her superb plotting, her innate sense of history, her excellent use of the English language, and her great versatility; taken together, such qualities should rightfully have placed this remarkable and sadly unsung talent in the front rank of popular novelists.

—Melvyn Barnes

———

BERESFORD, Elisabeth. British. Born in Paris, France. Educated at St. Mary's Hall, Brighton; St. Catherines, Bramley; Ditchling Dame School, Sussex; Brighton and Hove High School. Served as a radio operator in the Women's Royal Naval Service during World War II. Married Max Robertson in 1949; one daughter and one son. Since 1948 freelance journalist. Lives in Alderney, Channel Islands. Agent: David Higham Associates Ltd., 5–8 Lower John Street, London W1R 4HA; or A.M. Heath, 79 St. Martin's Lane, London WC2N 4AA, England.

ROMANCE AND HISTORICAL PUBLICATIONS

Novels

Paradise Island. London, Hale, 1963.
Escape to Happiness. London, Hale, 1964; New York, Nordon, 1980.
Roses round the Door. London, Hale, and New York, Paperback Library, 1965.
Island of Shadows. London, Hale, 1966; New York, Dale, 1980.
Veronica. London, Hale, 1967; New York, Nordon, 1980.
A Tropical Affair. London, Hale, 1967; as *Tropical Affairs*, New York, Dell, 1978.
Saturday's Child. London, Hale, 1968; as *Echoes of Love*, New York, Dell, 1979.
Love Remembered. London, Hale, 1970; New York, Dale, 1978.
Love and the S.S. Beatrice. London, Hale, 1972; as *Thunder of Her Heart*, New York, Dale, 1978.
Pandora. London, Hale, 1974.
The Steadfast Lover. London, Hale, 1980.
The Silver Chain. London, Hale, 1980.
The Restless Heart. New York, Valueback, 1982.
Flight to Happiness. London, Hale, 1983.
A Passionate Adventure. London, Hale, 1983.

OTHER PUBLICATIONS

Fiction (for children)

The Television Mystery. London, Parrish, 1957.
The Flying Doctor Mystery. London, Parrish, 1958.
Trouble at Tullington Castle. London, Parrish, 1958.
Cocky and the Missing Castle. London, Constable, 1959.
Gappy Goes West. London, Parrish, 1959.
The Tullington Film-Makers. London, Parrish, 1960.
Two Gold Dolphins. London, Constable, 1961; Indianapolis, Bobbs Merrill, 1964.
Danger on the Old Pull 'n Push. London, Parrish, 1962.
Strange Hiding Place. London, Parrish, 1962.
Diana in Television. London, Collins, 1963.
The Missing Formula Mystery. London, Parrish, 1963.
The Mulberry Street Team. Penshurst, Kent, Friday Press, 1963.
Awkward Magic. London, Hart Davis, 1964; as *The Magic World*, Indianapolis, Bobbs Merrill, 1965.
The Flying Doctor to the Rescue. London, Parrish, 1964.
Holiday for Slippy. Penshurst, Kent, Friday Press, 1964.
Game, Set, and Match. London, Parrish, 1965.
Knights of the Cardboard Castle. London, Methuen, 1965.
Travelling Magic. London, Hart Davis, 1965; as *The Vanishing Garden*, New York, Funk and Wagnalls, 1967.
The Hidden Mill. London, Benn, 1965; New York, Meredith Press, 1967.
Peter Climbs a Tree. London, Benn, 1966.
Fashion Girl. London, Collins, 1967.
The Black Mountain Mystery. London, Parrish, 1967.
Looking for a Friend. London, Benn, 1967.

The Island Bus. London, Methuen, 1968.
Sea-Green Magic. London, Hart Davis, 1968.
The Wombles. London, Benn, 1968; New York, Meredith Press, 1969.
David Goes Fishing. London, Benn, 1969.
Gordon's Go-Kart. London, Benn, 1970.
Stephen and the Shaggy Dog. London, Methuen, 1970.
Vanishing Magic. London, Hart Davis, 1970.
The Wandering Wombles. London, Benn, 1970.
Dangerous Magic. London, Hart Davis, 1972.
The Invisible Womble and Other Stories. London, Benn, 1973.
The Secret Railway. London, Methuen, 1973.
The Wombles in Danger. London, Benn, 1973.
The Wombles at Work. London, Benn, 1973.
Invisible Magic. London, Hart Davis, 1974.
The Wombles Go to the Seaside. London, World Distributors, 1974.
The Wombles Gift Book. London, Benn, 1975.
The Snow Womble. London, Benn, 1975.
Snuffle to the Rescue. London, Kestrel, 1975.
Tomsk and the Tired Tree. London, Benn, 1975.
Wellington and the Blue Balloon. London, Benn, 1975.
Orinoco Runs Away. London, Benn, 1975.
The Wombles Make a Clean Sweep. London, Benn, 1975.
The Wombles to the Rescue. London, Benn, 1975.
The MacWomble's Pipe Band. London, Benn, 1976.
Madame Cholet's Picnic Party. London, Benn, 1976.
Bungo Knows Best. London, Benn, 1976.
Tobermory's Big Surprise. London, Benn, 1976.
The Wombles Go round the World. London, Benn, 1976.
The World of the Wombles. London, World Distributors, 1976.
Wombling Free. London, Benn, 1978.
Toby's Luck. London, Methuen, 1978.
Secret Magic. London, Hart Davis, 1978.
The Happy Ghost. London, Methuen, 1979.
The Treasure Hunters. London, Methuen, and New York, Elsevier Nelson, 1980.
Curious Magic. London, Granada, and New York, Elsevier Nelson, 1980.
The Four of Us. London, Hutchinson, 1981.
The Animals Nobody Wanted. London, Methuen, 1982.
The Tovers. London, Methuen, 1982.
The Adventures of Poon. London, Hutchinson, 1984.
The Mysterious Island. London, Methuen, 1984.
One of the Family. London, Hutchinson, 1985.
The Ghosts of Lupus Street School. London, Methuen, 1986.
Strange Magic. London, Methuen, 1986.
Emily and the Haunted Castle. London, Hutchinson, 1987.
Once upon a Time Stories. London, Methuen, 1987.
The Secret Room. London, Methuen, 1987.
The Armada Adventure. London, Methuen, 1988.
The Island Railway. London, Hamish Hamilton, 1988.
Rose. London, Hutchinson, 1989.

Plays

The Wombles, adaptation of her own stories (produced London, 1974).
Road to Albutal, with Nick Renton (produced Edinburgh, 1976).
The Best of Friends (produced in the Channel Islands, 1982).

Screenplay: *The Wombles*, 1971.

Television Plays: 60 scripts for *The Wombles* series, from 1973.

Other

The Wombles Annual 1975–1978 (for children). London, World Distributors, 4 vols., 1974–77.
Move On, with Peter Spence. London, BBC Publications, 1978.
Jack and the Magic Stove (for children). London, Hutchinson, 1982.

*

Elisabeth Beresford comments:

In some of my romantic novels, I have based the plot on a mystery including crime and espionage. I try to give all my characters believable personalities, and there's always an occasional touch of humour.

*   *   *

Elisabeth Beresford is an experienced writer whose romances, though on the whole lightweight with little depth to them, are nevertheless fluently written and display a convincing awareness of the transformations love can bring about. All of her work so far has a contemporary background except for *Veronica*, but the surroundings vary from the exotic locations of Trinidad and Greece, to the Australian bush, and back home to London. The characters in her first book, *Paradise Island*, verge on stereotypes, and the plot has a predictable outcome, but in *Escape to Happiness*, the story of an English girl who takes a job on an Australian sheep farm to get away from her emotional problems, the characters have more individuality, and the author gradually suggests the feel of the loneliness of outback life in both description and dialogue, although the narrative still has its implausible aspects. In *Island of Shadows* a more dramatic note is introduced, and the climax is well handled. *Veronica* is altogether a stronger novel, held together by the personality of the main character backed up by a lively and sympathetic view of life in the early 1900's for a young girl on her own in London.

In her later novels, Beresford begins to handle her characters with far more depth and skill, particularly in *A Tropical Affair* and *Saturday's Child*, where the relationships between the main protagonists are touched with wry humour and insight. In *Love Remembered* Beresford again brings in a dramatic hint of danger to the life of luxury led by Achilles Vidal, but the promise of suspense is unfulfilled and the story tails off towards the end. *The Steadfast Lover*, however, is a more sustained and lasting novel, with a touch of the supernatural, and centres round the sad and tragic figure of Emma Smith, escaping to her wild island home from a broken love affair and ruined career. Beresford writes with a verbal facility and an increasing ability to imbue her characters with distinct personalities through smoothly controlled narrative and natural, lively dialogue.

—Tessa Rose Chester

BERGER, John (Peter). British. Born in Stoke Newington, London, 5 November 1926. Attended the Central School of Art and the Chelsea School of Art, London. Served in the Oxford and Buckinghamshire Infantry, 1944–46. Married twice; three children. Painter and drawing teacher, 1948–55; contributor, *Tribune* and *New Statesman*, both London, 1951–60. Narrator, *About Time* television series, 1985. Artist: exhibitions at Wildenstein, Redfern, and Leicester galleries, London. Recipient: Booker prize, 1972; *Guardian* Fiction prize, 1972; James

Tait Black Memorial prize, 1973; New York Critics prize, for screenplay, 1976; George Orwell Memorial prize, 1977. Address: Quincy, Mieussy, 74440 Taninges, France.

ROMANCE AND HISTORICAL PUBLICATIONS

Novel

G. London, Weidenfeld and Nicolson, and New York, Viking Press, 1972.

OTHER PUBLICATIONS

Novels

A Painter of Our Time. London, Secker and Warburg, 1958; New York, Simon and Schuster, 1959.
The Foot of Clive. London, Methuen, 1962.
Corker's Freedom. London, Methuen, 1964.

Short Stories

Pig Earth. London, Writers and Readers, 1979; New York, Pantheon, 1980.
Once in Europa. New York, Simon and Schuster, 1987.

Plays

Jonas qui aura 25 ans en l'an 2000 (screenplay), with Alain Tanner. Lausanne, Cinémathèque Suisse, 1978; translated by Michael Palmer, as *Jonah Who Will Be 25 in the Year 2000*, Berkeley, California, North Atlantic, 1983.
A Question of Geography, with Nella Bielski (produced Marseille, 1984; Stratford-on-Avon, 1987; London, 1988). London, Faber, 1987.
Les Trois Chaleurs (produced Paris, 1985).
Boris, translated into Welsh by Rhiannon Ifans (produced Cardiff, 1985).
Goya's Last Portrait: The Painter Played Today, with Nella Bielski. London Faber, 1989.

Screenplays, with Alain Tanner: *La Salamandre* (*The Salamander*), 1971; *Le Milieu du monde* (*The Middle of the World*), 1974; *Jonas* (*Jonah Who Will Be 25 in the Year 2000*), 1976.

Other

Marcel Frishman, with George Besson. Oxford, Cassirer, 1958.
Permanent Red: Essays in Seeing. London, Methuen, 1960; as *Towards Reality*, New York, Knopf, 1962.
The Success and Failure of Picasso. London, Penguin, 1965; New York, Pantheon, 1980.
A Fortunate Man: The Story of a Country Doctor, photographs by Jean Mohr. London, Allen Lane, and New York, Holt and Rinehart, 1967.
Art and Revolution: Ernst Neizvestny and the Role of the Artist in the U.S.S.R. London, Weidenfeld and Nicolson, and New York, Pantheon, 1969.
The Moment of Cubism and Other Essays. London, Weidenfeld and Nicolson, and New York, Pantheon, 1969.
The Look of Things, edited by Nikos Stangos. London, Penguin, 1972; New York, Viking Press, 1974.

Ways of Seeing, with others. London, BBC-Penguin, 1972; New York, Viking Press, 1973.
A Seventh Man: Migrant Workers in Europe, photographs by Jean Mohr. London, Penguin, and New York, Viking Press, 1975.
About Looking. London, Writers and Readers, and New York, Pantheon, 1980.
Another Way of Telling (on photography), with Jean Mohr. London, Writers and Readers, and New York, Pantheon, 1982.
And Our Faces, My Heart, Brief as Photos. London, Writers and Readers, and New York, Pantheon, 1984.
The White Bird, edited by Lloyd Spencer. London, Chatto and Windus, 1985; as *The Sense of Sight*, New York, Pantheon, 1986.

Translator, with Anya Bostock, *Poems on the Theatre*, by Bertolt Brecht. London, Scorpion Press, 1961; as *The Great Art of Living Together: Poems on the Theatre*, Bingley, Yorkshire, Granville Press, 1972.
Translator, with Anya Bostock, *Helene Weigel, Actress*, by Bertolt Brecht. Leipzig, Veb Edition, 1961.
Translator, with Anya Bostock, *Return to My Native Land*, by Aimé Césaire. London, Penguin, 1969.
Translator, with Lisa Appignanesi, *Oranges for the Son of Asher Levy*, by Nella Bielski. London, Writers and Readers, 1982.

*

Critical Studies: *Seeing Berger: A Revaluation of Ways of Seeing* by Peter Fuller, London, Writers and Readers, 1980, revised edition, as *Seeing Through Berger*, London, Claridge Press, 1988; *Ways of Telling: The Work of John Berger* by Geoff Dyer, London, Pluto, 1986.

*   *   *

John Berger's novel *G* was published in 1972 to a thunderous reception. The controversy was stoked when, receiving the Booker prize that year, the author announced that he would donate the prize money to the Black Panthers. Although, as a Marxist, history and the historical process inform all his work, this is his only piece of fiction that is set in a definite historical past.

His aim in the novel is to perceive and present history as a matrix of conflicting forces, and to concentrate their contradictory patterns into the life of one figure, the eponymous G. G is at once Don Giovanni/Don Juan, bourgeois libertine, and Garibaldi (his nickname at school), revolutionary leader and implacable historical force. The contradictions continue; though resolutely apolitical, he becomes enmeshed in the labyrinthine politics preceding World War I. He is surrounded by the great events of the period: revolution, social upheaval, the advent of new technologies like aviation and new cultural movements like feminism, and finally an apocalyptic war. Yet none of these events seems to concern him directly; his only interest remains the pursuit of women. Berger has said in an interview that he considers the hero a revolutionary nonetheless; his sexual actions are as subversive in his way as the great socialist agitators were in theirs. A climactic scene at the Trieste Red Cross ball toward the end of *G* goes some way to confirming this claim.

It is no accident that the years 1890–1914 (roughly the timespan of *G*) saw the development of both cubist-modernist art and the cinema. The narrative technique of the novel borrows heavily from both forms. Instead of the action following a linear, chronological order, it forms a montage of different perspectives: it ranges through the subjective experience of G himself and the characters around him, through interjected events (synchronous to, but not directly involved in the story) and essays on diverse subjects, to direct addresses from the author concerning his own problems in creating the story. The aim, as avowed in the text, is to ensure that "Never again will a single story be told as though it were the only one." Depending upon the reader's tastes and prejudices, this anti-realistic series of devices may be perceived as exhilarating, or as David Caute characterized their use, "overtaxing." Nevertheless, Berger's aphoristic style lends itself happily to discontinuous and disjointed narrative; and the authorial asides, when not agonisingly precious, are a delight to match the story proper.

These authorial interjections form an extended commentary on absence and the impossibility of communicating experience accurately, perhaps reflecting Picasso's maxim that "Art is the lie which tells the truth." The paradigm Berger chooses for this problem, a fitting one for the Don Juan figure of G, is sex. After G's first sexual experience, Berger turns almost a whole chapter over to the problem of communicating its essence. After a lengthy and closely argued essay on the aesthetics of the event, he admits failure, sketching a crude diagram of male and female genitals. "Perhaps they distort less than the nouns," he decides. Much of the novel is like this, an extended foray into language which exposes what cannot be said. Despite the modernist appearance of this idea, Berger is almost certainly aware that it is one of the oldest tricks in the writer's repertoire; medieval rhetoricians called it *negatio* and recommended its use as a spur to the reader's imagination. Consequently, it is both playful and serious in this novel, implying both real bounds to language and the patent absurdity of the protagonist's situation. For the life of G *is* absurd: in the course of the book he achieves nothing, aspires to only one thing, and says very little. The plot of the novel is flimsy and inconsequential, just as the author intends. Instead it serves as a vehicle for Berger's beautifully detailed observations on the minutiae of social and natural existence. Berger applies a painter's eye to his material; adding for wider scope the historian's panoramic vision of vast human forces. However hard G attempts to reject his time, he is, like all of us, a prisoner of history.

—Alan Murphy

BERGER, Thomas (Louis). American. Born in Cincinnati, Ohio, 20 July 1924. Educated at the University of Cincinnati, B.A. 1948; Columbia University, New York, 1950–51. Served in the United States Army, 1943–46. Married Jeanne Redpath in 1950. Librarian, Rand School of Social Science, New York, 1948–51; staff member, *New York Times Index*, 1951–52; associate editor, *Popular Science Monthly*, New York, 1952–54; film critic, *Esquire*, New York, 1972–73; writer-in-residence, University of Kansas, Lawrence, 1974; Distinguished Visiting Professor, Southampton College, New York, 1975–76; visiting lecturer, Yale University, New Haven, Connecticut, 1981–82; Regents' Lecturer, University of California, Davis, 1982. Recipient: Dial fellowship, 1962; Western Heritage award, 1965; Rosenthal award, 1965. Litt.D.: Long Island University, Greenvale, New York, 1986. Agent: Don Congdon Associates, 156 Fifth Avenue, Suite 625, New York, New York 10010, U.S.A.

ROMANCE AND HISTORICAL PUBLICATIONS

Novels

Little Big Man. New York, Dial Press, 1964; London, Eyre and Spottiswoode, 1965.
Arthur Rex: A Legendary Novel. New York, Delacorte Press, 1978; London, Methuen, 1979.

OTHER PUBLICATIONS

Novels

Crazy in Berlin. New York, Scribner, 1958.
Reinhart in Love. New York, Scribner, 1962; London, Eyre and Spottiswoode, 1963.
Killing Time. New York, Dial Press, 1967; London Eyre and Spottiswoode, 1968.
Vital Parts. New York, Baron, 1970; London, Eyre and Spottiswoode, 1971.
Regiment of Women. New York, Simon and Schuster, 1973; London, Eyre Methuen, 1974.
Sneaky People. New York, Simon and Schuster, 1975; London, Methuen, 1980.
Who Is Teddy Villanova? New York, Delacorte Press, and London, Eyre Methuen, 1977.
Neighbors. New York, Delacorte Press, 1980; London, Methuen, 1981.
Reinhart's Women. New York, Delacorte Press, 1981; London, Methuen, 1982.
The Feud. New York, Delacorte Press, 1983; London, Methuen, 1984.
Nowhere. New York, Delacorte Press, 1985; London, Methuen, 1986.
Being Invisible. Boston, Little Brown, 1987; London, Methuen, 1988.
The Houseguest. Boston, Little Brown, 1988; London, Weidenfeld and Nicolson, 1989.
Changing the Past. Boston, Little Brown, 1989.

Short Story

Granted Wishes. Northridge, California, Lord John Press, 1984.

Play

Other People (produced Stockbridge, Massachusetts, 1970).

*

Bibliography: in "Thomas Berger Issue" of *Studies in American Humor* (San Marcos, Texas), Spring and Fall 1983.

Manuscript Collection: Boston University Library.

*   *   *

Thomas Berger's fictional world is typically bawdy, a Rabelaisian exhibition of the strengths and weaknesses of humankind. *Little Big Man* takes this perspective and applies it to the great American myth of the Wild West. Its hero, the 111-year-old Jack Crabb, narrates his life history from an old folks' home; these reminiscences make up the vast bulk of the voluminous text. His is the tallest story ever told, and the "Editorial Epilogue" admits the possibility that he might be "a liar of insane proportions." He tells of his wild and troubled career as, variously, adopted Cheyenne Indian warrior, trader, gold prospector, card sharp, buffalo hunter, mule driver, army scout, and gunfighter; of his acquaintance with Wild Bill Hickok, General Custer, and other legendary figures; of his being the sole survivor of the Battle of the Little Bighorn. In outline his story seems absurd and incredible, but Berger applies detailed research and a realist's eye to his material, enchanting the reader with the story in the same way Crabb enchants the priggish "editor" of the text.

Jack Crabb is an American Odysseus, the trickster whose very inobstrusiveness and instinct for survival allow him to adapt a new identity at every crisis. First adopted by the Indians at the age of ten, he grows up as a Cheyenne until recaptured by the United States Cavalry; in a typical switch of identity he reveals himself as a white captive when cornered by the troops. From this point on his adventures take him back and forth from white to Indian society, though he never finds himself on the winning side. The character is a triumph for Berger, who has captured the bawdy, laconic style of the American folktale in his presentation of Crabb, who is at once sceptical and sentimental, amoral and compassionate, a storyteller whose wit matches, and masterfully understates his sensational subject.

Jack Crabb's lazy amorality is made all the more appealing by the background against which his story is told. It is the era of "manifest destiny," the ugly ideology which the white man so successfully used to justify the theft of Indian lands and the genocide which accompanied it. During the course of the narrative—which covers only 24 years—the Cheyenne tribe who had adopted Crabb are reduced to a small, beaten group of renegades. At first the story emphasizes the complete otherness of the Indian, being dedicated to the proposition that "Indians are altogether different from anybody you ever knew." The opening scenes are masterpieces of absurd miscommunication, exemplified by the fact that Jack's eccentric father believes the Cheyenne talk Hebrew. But gradually, through the eyes of the growing boy's initiation into the tribe, we begin to see the Indians in the context of their own beliefs and logic. After his recapture, in an episode strongly reminiscent of Huck Finn's rejection of "civilization," the boy is brought back to be fostered by a preacher and his wife. Typically of Berger, both this and the previous adventures are presented with an eye to the ridiculous, though for both the Indian and white cultures the author maintains evident sympathy. Like the boy's Indian foster-father, he respects the fact that both cultures have their patterns and reasons; but the easy tolerance exhibited here is hard to come by in the frontier.

Ultimately the Indians have their sole victory, defeating Custer at Little Bighorn; and the narrative of Jack Crabb ends at this point, the narrator finally succumbing to his incredible old age. The rest, as they say, is history. At several points the novel refers to the mythology of the West, preserved on the rest-home television, only to explode these ballooning myths with their own incredibility.

A similar process is undergone in *Arthur Rex: A Legendary Novel*. This time the target is Arthurian legend. As with the Old West, the Dark Age is presented with its own historical squalor and made to laugh uneasily. The deeds of the court are deflated simply by the shabby details of reality, but the discarded detail of myth is what engages the mind of Berger. T. H. White did something similar with the Arthurian legend in *The Once and Future King*, scaling it down from epic to comic proportions; but Berger's humour is bleaker and less comfortable.

Berger invokes an altogether more indifferent world to that prevalent in our fondest folktales. He moulds a better fiction from their resemblance to our own less excited response to the historical event, the ordinary face of the present. Only after the reader's acceptance of this illusion comes the suspicion, like that of *Little Big Man*'s "editor," that it is all a heroic farce. By this time all that matters is the story.

—Alan Murphy

BETTERIDGE, Anne. See **MELVILLE, Anne.**

BEVAN, Gloria. Pseudonym for Glory Isobel Bevan; has also written as Fiona Murray. New Zealander. Born in Kalgoorlie, Western Australia, 20 July 1911. Married Thomas Henry Bevan in 1937 (died); three daughters. Typist, Watkin and Wallis, Auckland, 1926–36. Address: 1 Hoberia Road, Onehunga, Auckland, New Zealand.

ROMANCE AND HISTORICAL PUBLICATIONS

Novels

The Distant Trap. London, Mills and Boon, 1969; Toronto, Harlequin, 1970.
The Hills of Maketu. London, Mills and Boon, and Toronto, Harlequin, 1969.
Beyond the Ranges. London, Mills and Boon, 1970; Toronto, Harlequin, 1971.
Make Way for Tomorrow. London, Mills and Boon, and Toronto, Harlequin, 1971.
It Began in Te Rangi. London, Mills and Boon, 1971; Toronto, Harlequin, 1972.
Vineyard in a Valley. London, Mills and Boon, and Toronto, Harlequin, 1972.
Flame in Fiji. London, Mills and Boon, and Toronto, Harlequin, 1973.
The Frost and the Fire. London, Mills and Boon, and Toronto, Harlequin, 1973.
Connelly's Castle. London, Mills and Boon, and Toronto, Harlequin, 1974.
High-Country Wife. London, Mills and Boon, 1974; Toronto, Harlequin, 1975.
Always a Rainbow. London, Mills and Boon, and Toronto, Harlequin, 1975.
Dolphin Bay. London, Mills and Boon, and Toronto, Harlequin, 1976.
Bachelor Territory. London, Mills and Boon, and Toronto, Harlequin, 1977.
Plantation Moon. London, Mills and Boon, 1977; Toronto, Harlequin, 1978.
Fringe of Heaven. London, Mills and Boon, and Toronto, Harlequin, 1978.
Kowhai Country. London, Mills and Boon, 1979.
Half a World Away. London, Mills and Boon, 1980; Toronto, Harlequin, 1981.
Master of Mahia. London, Mills and Boon, and Toronto, Harlequin, 1981.
Emerald Cave. London, Mills and Boon, 1981.
Greek Island Magic. London, Mills and Boon, 1983.
The Rouseabout Girl. London, Mills and Boon, 1983.
Southern Sunshine. London, Mills and Boon, 1985.

Golden Bay. London, Mills and Boon, 1987.
Pacific Paradise. London, Mills and Boon, 1989.

OTHER PUBLICATIONS

Novels as Fiona Murray

Invitation to Danger. London, Hale, 1965.
Gold Coast Affair. Sydney, Horowitz, 1967.
A Nice Day for Murder. London, Hale, 1971.

*

Gloria Bevan comments:

I began my writing life as a mystery writer then changed to romance writing, and have been fascinated with it ever since. Writing for Mills and Boon and Harlequin has been a privilege and a pleasure.

Living in far away New Zealand I try to convey to overseas readers the air of freshness, the clarity of atmosphere, and the sparkling seas edged with flawless sandy beaches that I know so well. The climate is sub-tropical, hibiscus flowers bloom in suburban gardens and dense native bush clothes the neighbouring hillsides.

Often I write with a background of wide open spaces where an owner of a sheep station may control thousands of acres of green hills and paddocks.

Exciting holidays spent at the islands of Fiji and Rarotonga have sparked me to write of these beautiful islands that are our neighbours in the South Pacific ocean. I strive to convey the perfume of frangipani, the feeling of warm seas and a relaxed way of life there. I hope I've succeeded.

*   *   *

Although born in Australia, Gloria Bevan considers herself a New Zealander. Her obvious love of her country and her particular talent for weaving interesting background information into her novels makes her one of the more popular romance writers today. Although concentrating on New Zealand background, she does not limit herself to this area.

In *Flame in Fiji* Robyn Carlisle meets David Kinnear who is in the process of re-building and re-decorating a guest house that she and her brother own. As the story unfolds, the heroine experiences events that are unique to the island. She has a sightseeing tour of noted coral reefs early in the story. She also takes part in a "Makiti," an island feast and entertainment. Later in the story she has a chance to see and learn about the "Firewalkers," that is, warriors who walk on white-hot stones. These are but three of the many elements in the story that make it so enjoyable, for Gloria Bevan has included an amazing amount of information in a way that readers find acceptable. Her care for detail, her ability to choose just the right element or incident to develop the story line, gives her an added edge in making her novels so entertaining.

In *Bachelor Territory* Gloria Bevan uses her own country as background, especially the area about Dargaville. Here she depends on two elements in furthering her story, the fact that this part of the country has a large concentration of Yugoslavian settlers and that it was also part of the early Maori area of the country. Again she is able to weave accurate information into her story by having one character engaged in writing a book of original Maori proverbs. Some of these are skillfully used throughout the novel to give an added spark of interest. Because of her fondness of detail and for providing such interesting touches, her novels have an added dimension that her readers enjoy immensely.

At the same time, her characters and plots are particularly effective as she works out her stories. Her heroines are sensitive, caring girls who find themselves with unexpected problems to handle and unexpected decisions to make. In *Flame in Fiji* Robyn clings to memories of an unhappy childhood and the special love she has for her brother. The fact that her brother is reckless and seemingly irresponsible makes it that much harder for her to fall in love with David, for he seems to know only the worse side of her brother, Johnny.

Her heroes are more subtly drawn than usual in romances. They are not the "larger than life" figure, but well balanced and masculine in their actions and beliefs. There is a more realistic portrayal of her men in the sense that they all have some sort of profession or occupation that they really work at. David Kinnear is an architect while Craig Carter in *Bachelor Territory* and Logan Page in *Southern Sunshine* are sheep farmers. Movement in the story makes use of this fact so that day-to-day activities that would be normal for them are carefully used to further the plot.

Gloria Bevan balances character and plot in such a way that her novels are exciting, as she frequently awakens a sense of adventure in her readers. The fact that she makes use of such special backgrounds and adds unusual glimpses of other people and places makes her particularly enjoyable to read. This ability is quite special, for many readers look forward to finding writers who have this particular quality in their writing. The exotic and far-away are brought closer so that the reader has a sense of familiarity with these places and events. In fact, more than one reader has concluded that it is the next best thing to being there, after they have spent a pleasant few hours of reading one of Gloria Bevan's stories.

—Arlene Moore

BIGLAND, Eileen. British. Born in Edinburgh, Scotland.

ROMANCE AND HISTORICAL PUBLICATIONS

Novels

Doctor's Child. London, Barker, 1934.
Gingerbread House. London, Barker, and New York, Appleton Century, 1934.
Alms for Oblivion. London, Hodder and Stoughton, 1937.
Conflict with a God. London, Hodder and Stoughton, 1938.
This Narrow World. London, Hodder and Stoughton, 1938.
You Can Never Look Back. London, Hodder and Stoughton, 1940.
Miranda. London, Jarrolds, 1947.
Clown Without Background. London, Jarrolds, 1950.
Flower Without Root. London, Jarrolds, 1952.

OTHER PUBLICATIONS

Other (for children)

The True Book about Madame Curie. London, Muller, 1955; as *Madame Curie*, New York, Criterion, 1957.
The True Book about Sister Kenny. London, Muller, 1956.

The True Book about Helen Keller. London, Muller, 1957; as
Helen Keller, New York, Phillips, 1967.
The True Book about the Heroines of the Sea. London, Muller,
1958.
Queen Elizabeth I. New York, Criterion, 1965.

Other

Laughing Odyssey. London, Hodder and Stoughton, 1937; New
York, Macmillan, 1938.
The Lake of the Royal Crocodiles. London, Hodder and Stough-
ton, and New York, Macmillan, 1939.
Into China. London, Collins, and New York, Macmillan, 1940.
Pattern in Black and White. London, Drummond, 1940.
The Riddle of the Kremlin. London, Collins, 1940.
Tiger in the Heart. London, Hodder and Stoughton, 1940.
The Key to the Russian Door. London, Putnam, 1942.
Awakening to Danger (autobiography). London, Nicholson and
Watson, 1946.
Britain's Other Army: The Story of the A.T.S. London, Nichol-
son and Watson, 1946.
The Story of the W.R.N.S. London, Nicholson and Watson,
1946.
Journey to Egypt. London, Jarrolds, 1948.
Understanding the Russians. London, People's Universities
Press, 1948.
Ouida: The Passionate Victorian. London, Jarrolds, 1950.
In the Steps of George Borrow. London, Rich and Cowan,
1951.
The Indomitable Mrs. Trollope (biography). London, Barrie,
1953; Philadelphia, Lippincott, 1954.
Marie Corelli: The Woman and the Legend. London, Jarrolds,
1953.
Lord Byron. London, Cassell, 1956; as *Passion for Excitement:
The Life and Personality of the Incredible Lord Byron*, New
York, Coward McCann, 1956.
Mary Shelley (biography). London, Cassell, and New York,
Appleton Century Crofts, 1959.
Russia Has Two Faces. London, Odhams Press, 1960.

Editor, *The Princess Elizabeth Gift Book*, with Cynthia Asquith.
London, Hodder and Stoughton, 1935.
Editor, *Kings and Queens*. London, English Universities Press,
1937.

Translator, *Beauty's Scalpel*, by Jean Boivin. London, Jarrolds,
1958.

*   *   *

The roles of the political analyst, the writer of travel literature, and the biographer intersect in the fiction of Eileen Bigland. Travel literature is filled with distant realms, fascinating,
distinct, and unchanging in the minds of those whose compositions see them as a spectacle, something to be viewed and in-
dulged in as one would a fantasy, which can be withdrawn from
at will. The lands are real, but they are dealt with as the stuff of
dreams. At the level of politics, the area becomes an arena
where the turbulence spills over into the onlookers until they too
become inseparable from the competitors. The biographer's gaze
fixes upon the individual as a distinct manifestation of what the
landscape and the forces have become. All these levels are apparent in Bigland's novels.

Sandra Pym, the central figure in *Gingerbread House*, starts
out as one of those inhabitants whose lives define a place. She
quickly becomes the dreamer as she drives her stubborn donkey

along the arduous trail leading to her unhappy home, reflecting
as she does so upon a gingerbread house, the confectioner's delight, but one that can perhaps be lived in—and the spot would
be idyllic England, the very real home of Bigland. The vision is
of an actual place where residence will be achieved with consequential forces, global as well as personal, endured by the one-
time dreamer.

Actually Sandra's family itself represents a minuscule form of
the family of nations, divided by temperaments to the degree
where understanding is difficult if not impossible. The father,
Sasha, is by blood, character, and outlook a displaced Russian.
Whether in Spain, England, or on his impulsive return to the
Soviet Union, he remains a hard-drinking womanizer of considerable exterior charm (outside the family circle), but with no
discernible ambition. Each of his three children inherits a fragment of his qualities. The son is an insufferable idealist, quick to
adopt causes, even those which are life-threatening. He actually
finds front-line duty in World War I a realization of a dream. He
survives, or at least he is not killed, and the utopian principles
remain intact, but they are of little use. He never manifests the
slightest capacity for forging a lifestyle or a livelihood, choosing
instead the bottle as he sponges off family and anyone else who
chances his way. Sister Brigit is virtually the stereotyped brain-
less beauty with principles as vapid as her capacities. Sandra,
the monkey-faced youngest sibling, shows herself not only astute
and energetically enterprising, but also the only truly compassionate member of an incessantly self-indulgent family circle. She
also turns out to be the most unyielding romantic of them
all—a contradictory condition to be expected from a principle
figure in a Bigland novel.

The pragmatic dreamer, or the inverse, the romantic idealist,
is a familiar fixture in the novels, and, to a lesser extent in Bigland's autobiographies as well. The character is no mere linking of opposites, but an embodied statement that relentless
pursuit of ideals demands something more than bull-headed
determination. Part of what is required is those qualities
manifested in an author whose fictional universe requires coordi-
nating a disciplined methodology with visions of persons and
places whose reality is as yet not fully formed.

Sandra discovers her own exceptional capabilities in what initially appears an unpromising publishing firm, tyrannically run
by a penny-pinching Scot (Bigland enlarges upon but rarely ignores stereotypes). One of her multitude of divergent assignments is to play the role of three different personages (one of
them male) who run columns advising on readers' dilemmas.
The different faces turn out not to be masks, but expansive dimensions of self. In the process of re-arranging the office, Sandra demonstrates a considerable measure of self-reliance, and
also a degree of ruthlessness as she dismisses the entire staff
who preceded her. Compassionate and merciless, the expeditious
dreamer, the woman of several faces—all of them firmly and
permanently attached to her essential self. Sandra (her real
name—Cassandra, the ill-fated paramour of the gods and futile
seer) is the quintessential writer, a traveler, a commentator, a
dreamer, a lover, but also a loner. She is also a feminist in the
fashion of the 1930's.

Another member of Bigland's female pantheon who incorporates such extremes, even to a greater degree, is Nadja of *You
Can Never Look Back*. The tender maiden, then the indelible
lover of the young Danish soldier she nursed back to health,
achieves a well-deserved reputation in Russia as the most inhuman of revolutionaries. Her cruelty is, however, well-founded in
utopian principles. Her rise in the Communist party is not motivated by desire for self-advancement, but upon ideals which find
the state a more deserving recipient of devotion than any human
cause. Sacrifice the individual before you, not with malice, but

in the clarity of vision that a better order for all will eventually arise. Like Sandra, Nadja fires workers but she also fires bullets; the revolutionary idealists of the 1930's and beyond found it expedient to become feared.

Her soldier-lover takes an equally ironic way of displaying the fundamentals of undying devotion. He returns to Denmark, marries, and fathers two children. But he does so with the consciously calculating notion that this is ultimately the surest way to effect a return to Nadja. He is also an idealist of sorts, embracing the causes of Germany and Fascism as a way of improving the quality of life on this planet. His dream landscape is the terrible Russian terrain where he would become reunited with Nadja. They do meet again, and their love proves stronger than their principles. Ideals translated into action are like chemical compounds which produce unexpected results—sometimes tragically violent ones. But such explosions are likely to result when the vision becomes politically alive, and even more so when it is vested in a human form, in this case a fascist-communist love story, which is presented in a believable contest. Devotion has many forms, and the love affair of Nadja and Peter Fransen points up many of the shapes—some not at all appealing—which form the components of the human dream.

Alms for Oblivion takes place almost entirely in England, but it is a Russian who redeems a decadent aristocracy from falling victim to effete sentimentalism and a social elitism no longer viable. A new generation comes of age, but it proves as dishonest in self-assessment as the one which it wishes to replace. The twins, Paul and Patricia, treat their mother as a pre-adolescent, affectionately in need of rearing. Paul eventually finds himself, although only a short time before he is killed in the Spanish Civil War. Serena, his mother, departs the tradition which had reduced her to a lifelong state of infantile idealism, accompanying her Russian fiancé in a return to his motherland. Redemption may not be at hand, but if it is to come, it will be when the individual stops hiding upon landscapes, using ideals to camouflage people from themselves.

Bigland is worth rereading (if for nothing else), for recollection of an era when travel and ideology were principal means of escape from the isolation of self. The futility by no means eclipses the vibrant effort afforded by her visions, not the least of which is the power of self-understanding.

—Leonard R. Mendelsohn

BINCHY, Maeve. Irish. Born in Dublin, 28 May 1940. Educated at Holy Child Convent, Killiney, County Dublin; University College, Dublin, B.A. in education. Married Gordon Snell in 1977. History and French teacher, Pembroke School, Dublin, 1961–68. Since 1968 columnist, *Irish Times*, Dublin. Agent: Christine Green, 18 Albany Mews, Albany Road, London SE5 ODQ. Address: 28 Holland Road, London W14 OLN, England.

ROMANCE AND HISTORICAL PUBLICATIONS

Novels

Light a Penny Candle. London, Century, 1982; New York, Viking, 1983.
Echoes. London, Century, 1985; New York, Viking, 1986.
Firefly Summer. London, Century, 1987; New York, Delacorte Press, 1988.

Short Stories

Central Line. London, Quartet, 1978.
Victoria Line. London, Quartet, 1980.
Dublin 4. Dublin, Ward River Press, 1982; London, Century, 1983.
London Transports (includes *Central Line* and *Victoria Line*). London, Century, 1983.
The Lilac Bus. Dublin, Ward River Press, 1984; London, Century, 1986.
Silver Wedding. London, Century, 1988; New York, Delacorte Press, 1989.

OTHER PUBLICATIONS

Plays

End of Term (produced Dublin, 1976).
Half Promised Land (produced Dublin, 1979).

Radio Play: *Deeply Regretted by—*, 1976.

Television Play: *Echoes*, from her own novel, 1988.

Other

Maeve's Diary. Dublin, Irish Times, 1979.

*

Maeve Binchy comments:
I write novels and stories set within my own experience of time and place, but they are not autobiographical. They mainly touch on the emotions of women and the aspirations and hopes of young Irishwomen growing up in the relatively closed society of Ireland in the 1950's and 1960's.

*   *   *

Maeve Binchy's *The Lilac Bus* is a collection of stories about a group of bus passengers who travel back home from Dublin every weekend. These character sketches, loosely interlinking, join together to form a portrait of provincial Irish life. Binchy, still a columnist for *The Irish Times*, has a journalist's eye for detail and an understanding of the dynamics of power in small towns and villages. Such sociological concerns create an unusual texture and distort the conventional shapes of the romance her novels seem to promise. The romance pattern of love followed by marriage is further complicated by Binchy's decision to pursue her heroines' lives after the altar. In *Echoes*, the heroine's triumphant marriage to the doctor's son is succeeded by a first year of domestic unhappiness, post-partum depression, and despair. In *Light a Penny Candle*, the heroine, safely married, in a quarrel pushes her husband down the stairs and kills him. In both novels, the promise of a safe haven in marriage is complicated by Binchy's clear insight into the terrible restrictions of domesticity.

Binchy's novels are firmly set within the structures of provincial Irish life. Her heroines are constrained by the watchful gossip of the neighbors and the maxims of the Church. Binchy's heroines struggle against, but do not entirely triumph over these circumstances. The satisfactions of romance—in which character determines fate—are not granted fully. Binchy is too aware of particular constraints on Irish women's lives to allow easy rewards. In *Echoes* the conventional bildungsroman features an intelligent heroine Clare, aged 10, who enters an essay competition. We await the triumphant rise of the sweetshop owner's daughter. Yet the necessary boundaries around Clare's triumphs are suggested by the echoing story of the teacher who encourages her. Angela O'Hara was once a successful student. She, like Clare, won a scholarship, yet was inexorably pulled back to Castlebay by the domestic responsibilities for an ailing mother that devolve on an unmarried daughter in an Irish family. Add to that boundary of provincial success for an intellectual woman, the unavailability of contraception, and Binchy has created a life for her heroine more realistically limited than the popular romance usually provides.

Binchy's concern with the depiction of female friendship adds a further complication to the pattern of her work. Her novels describe women whose lives are circumscribed by their connection to men but whose survival is grounded in emotional connection to women. *Light a Penny Candle* traces the story of two women whose friendship began when Elizabeth arrived in a small Irish town as a wartime evacuee. The loyalty of the childhood friendship of Aisling and Elizabeth is deepened through the vicissitudes of feminine experience—an abortion in London, a lover who will never marry, an alcoholic husband, and an unconsummated marriage—yet does not determine where these women chose to live. The pattern of their lives is shaped by the men they marry, until, in a frightening, though not fully confronted moment, the Englishwoman, Elizabeth, pushes her husband down the stairs and kills him accidentally. The silence of her best friend over the manslaughter she has witnessed demonstrates the depth of female bonding, a loyalty far deeper than any temporary ties to men, yet those bonds seem effected only to the detriment of men.

In *Light a Penny Candle*, Binchy suggests that this violent accident may be nurtured by the stifling restraints of bourgeois marriage. Elizabeth's mother dies in an insane asylum after a violent attack on her husband. In *Firefly Summer* the link between character and accident is loosened. Character does not determine the pattern of one's life; it is shaped by coincidence, mishap, a breeze on a smoldering cigarette. The novel records the attempts of Patrick O'Neill—grandson of an immigrant—to resurrect as a luxury hotel, the Georgian house, Fernscourt, that was burned in the Troubles. Binchy clearly delineates the structures of loyalty and caution that bind the people of an Irish midlands village: the wariness of envy, the precautions against feuds, the aggression that flares in petty vandalism. These are the ties that restrict initiative, yet smooth social friction. The novel, like *Echoes*, records the interlocking stories of the villagers and their response to the American and his two children, who hold an irresistible and dangerous glamour for the children of the village. The novel centers on the family of Kate and John Ryan. The Ryans are another of Binchy's complete portraits of a successful marriage that survives the appalling, almost casual, accident that cripples Kate for life. The two eldest children also survive their enchantment with Kerry and Grace O'Neill, though Patrick O'Neill's dream fails. The central characters survive, their lives shadowed by great losses. Binchy's willingness to acknowledge in her novels a sense of a world without purpose—"It was never meant to be like this. Pointless tragedy, and confusion everywhere"—creates a dense picture of Irish life in the 1950's and 1960's.

—Karen Robertson

BLACK, Laura. British. Born in Edinburgh, Scotland. Agent: Curtis Brown, 162–168 Regent Street, London W1R 5TB, England.

ROMANCE AND HISTORICAL PUBLICATIONS

Novels

Glendraco. London, Hamish Hamilton, and New York, St. Martin's Press, 1977.
Castle Raven. London, Hamish Hamilton, 1978; as *Ravenburn*, New York, St. Martin's Press, 1978.
Wild Cat. London, Hamish Hamilton, and New York, St. Martin's Press, 1979.
Strathgallant. London, Hamish Hamilton, and New York, St. Martin's Press, 1981.
Albany. London, Hamish Hamilton, and New York, St. Martin's Press, 1984.
Falls of Gard. London, Hamish Hamilton, and New York, St. Martin's Press, 1986.

*

Laura Black comments:

My novels are set in West Perthshire in the 1860's. The area is one of breathtaking natural beauty, which I know well and in which I have ancient ancestral roots. The period is particularly attractive—remote enough to be a foreign country, near enough to have familiar patterns of speech and attitude. A few minor characters reappear, as also a few imaginary places, but the books do not form a series. The stories take place largely in the castles and palaces of the highest aristocracy, this being the setting of a way of life—for the very last time—of glamour and high excitement without the suffocating opulence and vulgarity of a generation later. My heroines are beautiful and high spirited, and readers have reportedly grown fond of them. The books are much borrowed from public libraries, and my impression is that readers have recommended them to one another. This is extremely gratifying to me.

*   *   *

Laura Black's novels are reminiscent of morality plays, with vice punished and virtue rewarded in the end. What comes before the expected conclusion is more like old-fashioned melodrama. The villain is unredeemably villainous, the heroine utterly pure, and the hero as perfect as the romantic imagination can construct him.

These novels read like pure froth, but they are threaded with a sophisticated good humor that parodies the very style that it copies. There seems to be no middle ground in Black's work. Her heroines are impossibly beautiful, impossibly spirited, and impossibly capable. At the same time, the characters are almost irresistible to the reader, perhaps because there is no common ground between any reader and these literary paragons. The heroes are alluring for much the same reason; they are superhuman creations endowed with every virtue and advantage. The villains are personifications of vice, and yet they manage to show remorse or to die with great style by the end of the books. This is not to say, however, that any of the characters is less than believable. Their greatest charm is their naturalness in the face of such positive and negative perfection.

The plots of Black's novels are difficult to characterize as they contain elements of the pure romance, the gothic, the historical romance, and the novel of romantic suspense. Each style seems to be represented by a subplot in each book. No single style takes constant precedence; all are blended into a surprisingly cohesive whole. What remains constant from book to book are the devices that create the romantic tension. The heroine must choose between suitors, one of whom may mean her harm. Likewise, a personality clash between the heroine and a male character virtually guarantees his eventual success in winning her hand. The books are more frankly sexual than most examples of the genres represented, save the historical romance. While not graphic, the sex goes beyond mere bodice-ripping; incest is a major theme in *Castle Raven*. The resolution of this sexual dilemma is not at all unexpected, for these novels are not meant to shock. Marriage is the goal for these men and women. There may be superbly able women here, but there is no feminism in these pages.

All of Black's work deals with the rather closed society of upper-class Victorian Scotland. The relative smallness of the social circle represented leads to one of the intriguing facets of the novels. The major characters from one book appear in succeeding books, sometimes as relatively important secondary characters and sometimes as figures in the background. This habit of Black's makes her works seem more of a social chronicle rather than individual novels. It is amusing to contemplate a society whose members lead such sequentially romantic and exciting lives. The cleverness and unpredictability of the plots render this milieu real, and at the same time keep each book from reading like a repeat of the previous one.

Black has a genuine ear for both dialogue and dialect. Many of the secondary characters speak Scots dialect, which she makes almost audible to the reader. She also manages to solve the problem of an unfamiliar dialect vocabulary by defining words in context without becoming didactic. The descriptive passages are worthy of note. They are highly detailed yet fluid, so that the reader feels that she knows the smallest facet of the lives and surroundings of the heroines.

Black's work could be called florid, but it is evocative of a florid world that no longer exists—if it ever did. She has created romantic fantasies with a tenuous base in reality, but spun so attractively that the reader can hardly refuse to be drawn within.

—Susan Quinn Berneis

BLACK, Veronica. See **PETERS, Maureen.**

BLACKMORE, Jane. Address: c/o Collins Sons and Company Ltd., 8 Grafton Street, London W1X 3LA, England.

ROMANCE AND HISTORICAL PUBLICATIONS

Novels

Towards Tomorrow. London, Collins, 1941.
They Carry a Torch. London, Collins, 1943.
It Happened to Susan. London, Collins, 1944; New York, Dell, 1973.
Snow in June. London, Collins, 1947.

The Square of Many Colours. London, Collins, 1948; New York, Ace, 1975.
So Dark the Mirror. London, Collins, 1949.
The Nine Commandments. London, Collins, 1950.
The Bridge of Strange Music. London, Collins, 1952; New York, Ace, 1974.
Beloved Stranger. London, Collins, 1953; New York, Dell, 1973.
Perilous Waters. London, Collins, 1954; New York, Dell, 1973.
Three Letters to Pan. London, Collins, 1955; New York, Ace, 1971.
The Closing Door. London, Collins, 1955.
Bitter Love. London, Collins, 1956; New York, Ace, 1973.
Storm in the Family. London, Collins, 1956.
A Woman on Her Own. London, Collins, 1957; New York, Ace, 1971.
The Lonely House. London, Collins, 1957.
Beware the Night. London, Collins, 1958; New York, Ace, 1968.
Dangerous Love. London, Collins, 1958.
Tears in Paradise. London, Collins, 1959; New York, Ace, 1973.
The Missing Hour. London, Collins, 1959; New York, Ace, 1975.
Bitter Honey. London, Collins, 1960.
A Trap for Lovers. London, Collins, 1960.
The Night of the Stranger. London, Collins, 1961; New York, Ace, 1967.
The Dark Between the Stars. London, Collins, 1961; New York, Ace, 1967.
Two in Shadow. London, Collins, 1962.
It Couldn't Happen to Me. London, Collins, 1962; New York, Dell, 1972.
Joanna. London, Collins, 1963; New York, Dell, 1972.
That Night. London, Collins, 1963; New York, Lancer, 1969.
Flight into Love. London, Collins, 1964; New York, Paperback Library, 1966.
Return to Love. London, Collins, 1964; as *Stephanie*, New York, Ace, 1972.
Girl Alone. London, Collins, 1965.
Man of Power. London, Collins, 1966.
Miranda. London, Collins, 1966; New York, Dell, 1973.
Gold for My Girl. London, Collins, 1967; as *Deed of Innocence*, New York, Ace, 1969.
Raw Summer. London, Collins, 1967; New York, Dell, 1972.
The Other Room. London, Collins, 1968; as *A Love Forbidden*, London, Coronet, 1974.
The Velvet Trap. New York, Ace 1969.
The Lilac Is for Sharing. London, Collins, 1969.
Lonely Night. London, Collins, 1969.
Broomstick in the Hall. New York, Ace, 1970; London, Collins, 1971.
Dance on a Hornet's Nest. London, Collins, 1970.
Hunter's Mate. London, Collins, 1971.
The Room in the Tower. London, Collins, 1972; New York, Ace, 1973.
The Deep Pool. London, Collins, and New York, Ace, 1972.
My Sister Erica. London, Collins, 1973; New York, Ace, 1975.
The Cresselly Inheritance. London, Collins, 1973; New York, Ace, 1974.
Angel's Tear. New York, Ace, 1974.
Night of the Bonfire. London, Collins, and New York, Ace, 1974.
And Then There Was Georgia. London, Collins, and New York, Ace, 1975.
Lord of the Manor. London, Collins, 1975.

Ravenden. London, Collins, 1976.
Hawkridge. New York, Ace, 1976.
Silver Unicorn. London, Collins, 1977.
Of Wind and Fire. Loughton, Essex, Piatkus, 1980.
Wildfire Love. Loughton, Essex, Piatkus, 1980.
Flames of Love. Loughton, Essex, Piatkus, 1981.
Tara. London, Severn House, 1985.

*   *   *

The macabre, primitive mystical past, dreams, evil, witches, ghosts, immortality, twilight groves, the occult, telepathy—these are the paraphernalia which Jane Blackmore brings to her writing and which allows her to come tantalizingly close to being a gothic/romance writer. The mysticism, playing with the dim consciousness of the beyond, interweaving forebodings, suspicion, and trepidation with a love triangle and/or an inheritance squabble set a mercurial pace. Because terror and catastrophe are potent ingredients for the reader, Blackmore has the potentiality to write exciting novels.

In *The Deep Pool* the combination is an ancestral estate, a governess, and evil. *The Cresselly Inheritance* formula is similar. Murder is the background for *The Missing Hour*. A variant on these themes is found in *Angel's Tear*. This novel is concerned with the jet-set attempting to find the primal energy through occult worship. A heroine becomes entangled through no fault of her own, finding herself with vague feelings of inferiority and in love with the melancholy, attractive hero who is striving to partake of the elixir of life. Like many of her novels, it has intervals of gloomy expectation, crescendos of emotion amidst wealth and splendor, and conspiratory villains and villainesses, placing the unknowing victim at the mercy of capriciousness. However, in Blackmore's quest to update her gothic romance, allowing spells and enchantments to be produced through LSD, she commits several errors in this and in other novels. Capitulation into ephemeral vocabulary causes the novel to flag, detracting from the pace of the plot's development. In *The Deep Pool* and, to a lesser extent in other novels, the ending fails miserably. There is also a degree of implausibility surrounding too many circumstances; for example, a heroine has just enough wine to be subdued but not enough to prevent her overhearing the discussion of her fate. In *The Cresselly Inheritance* the unity of exposition falters. Often the heroines are improbably desensitized into acquiescence to the terror which is about to befall them.

The gothic romance novel is there in its embryonic stage. It never quite comes to maturation.

—W. M. von Zharen

BLACKSTOCK, Charity. Pseudonym for Ursula Torday; also writes as Paula Allardyce; Lee Blackstock; Charlotte Keppel. British. Born in London. Educated at Kensington High School, London; Lady Margaret Hall, Oxford, B.A. in English; London School of Economics, social science certificate. Worked as a typist at the National Central Library, London. Recipient: Romantic Novelists Association Major award, 1961. Agent: A.P. Watt Ltd., 20 John Street, London WC1N 2DL. Address: 23 Montagu Mansions, London W1H 1LD, England.

ROMANCE AND HISTORICAL PUBLICATIONS

Novels

Dewey Death. London, Heinemann, 1956; with *The Foggy, Foggy Dew*, New York, British Book Centre, 1959.
Miss Fenny. London, Hodder and Stoughton, 1957; as *The Woman in the Woods* (as Lee Blackstock), New York, Doubleday, 1958.
The Foggy, Foggy Dew. London, Hodder and Stoughton, 1958; with *Dewey Death*, New York, British Book Centre, 1959.
All Men Are Murderers (as Lee Blackstock). New York, Doubleday, 1958; as *The Shadow Murder* (as Charity Blackstock), London, Hodder and Stoughton, 1959.
The Bitter Conquest. London, Hodder and Stoughton, 1959; New York, Ballantine, 1964.
The Briar Patch. London, Hodder and Stoughton, 1960; as *Young Lucifer*, Philadelphia, Lippincott, 1960.
The Exorcism. London, Hodder and Stoughton, 1961; as *A House Possessed*, Philadelphia, Lippincott, 1962.
The Gallant. London, Hodder and Stoughton, 1962; New York, Ballantine, 1966.
Mr. Christopoulos. London, Hodder and Stoughton, 1963; New York, British Book Centre, 1964.
The Factor's Wife. London, Hodder and Stoughton, 1964; as *The English Wife*, New York, Coward McCann, 1964.
When the Sun Goes Down. London, Hodder and Stoughton, 1965; as *Monkey on a Chain*, New York, Coward McCann, 1965.
The Knock at Midnight. London, Hodder and Stoughton, 1966; New York, Coward McCann, 1967.
Party in Dolly Creek. London, Hodder and Stoughton, 1967; as *The Widow*, New York, Coward McCann, 1967.
The Melon in the Cornfield. London, Hodder and Stoughton, 1969; as *The Lemmings*, New York, Coward McCann, 1969.
The Daughter. New York, Coward McCann, 1970; London, Hodder and Stoughton, 1971.
The Encounter. New York, Coward McCann, 1971; Loughton, Essex, Piatkus, 1981.
The Jungle. London, Hodder and Stoughton, and New York, Coward McCann, 1972.
The Lonely Strangers. New York, Coward McCann, 1972; London, Hodder and Stoughton, 1973.
People in Glass Houses. London, Hodder and Stoughton, and New York, Coward McCann, 1975.
Ghost Town. London, Hodder and Stoughton, and New York, Coward McCann, 1976.
I Met Murder on the Way. London, Hodder and Stoughton, 1977; as *The Shirt Front*, New York, Coward McCann, 1977.
Miss Charley. London, Hodder and Stoughton, 1979.
With Fondest Thoughts. London, Hodder and Stoughton, 1980.
Dream Towers. London, Hodder and Stoughton, 1981.

Novels as Ursula Torday

The Ballad-Maker of Paris. London, Allan, 1935.
No Peace for the Wicked. London, Nelson, 1937.
The Mirror of the Sun. London, Nelson, 1938.

Novels as Paula Allardyce

After the Lady. London, Ward Lock, 1954.
The Doctor's Daughter. London, Ward Lock, 1955.
A Game of Hazard. London, Ward Lock, 1955.
Adam and Evelina. London, Ward Lock, 1956.
The Man of Wrath. London, Ward Lock, 1956.

The Lady and the Pirate. London, Ward Lock, 1957.

Southarn Folly. London, Ward Lock, 1957.

Beloved Enemy. London, Ward Lock, 1958.

My Dear Miss Emma. London, Ward Lock, 1958; Chicago, Playboy Press, 1980.

Death, My Lover. London, Ward Lock, 1959.

A Marriage Has Been Arranged. London, Ward Lock, 1959.

Johnny Danger. London, Ward Lock, 1960; as *The Rebel Lover*, Chicago, Playboy Press, 1979.

Witches' Sabbath. London, Ward Lock, 1961; New York, Macmillan, 1962.

The Gentle Highwayman. London, Ward Lock, 1961.

Adam's Rib. London, Hodder and Stoughton, 1963; as *Legacy of Pride*, New York, Dell, 1975.

The Respectable Miss Parkington-Smith. London, Hodder and Stoughton, 1964; as *Paradise Row*, New York, Dell, 1976.

Octavia; or, The Trials of a Romantic Novelist. London, Hodder and Stoughton, 1965; New York, Dell, 1977.

The Moonlighters. London, Hodder and Stoughton, 1966; as *Gentleman Rogue*, New York, Dell, 1975.

Six Passengers for the "Sweet Bird." London, Hodder and Stoughton, 1967.

Waiting at the Church. London, Hodder and Stoughton, 1968; as *Emily*, New York, Dell, 1976.

The Ghost of Archie Gilroy. London, Hodder and Stoughton, 1970; as *Shadowed Love*, New York, Dell, 1977.

Miss Jonas's Boy. London, Hodder and Stoughton, 1972; as *Eliza*, New York, Dell, 1975.

The Gentle Sex. London, Hodder and Stoughton, 1974; as *The Carradine Affair*, New York, Pocket Books, 1976.

Miss Philadelphia Smith. London, Hodder and Stoughton, 1977.

Haunting Me. London, Hodder and Stoughton, 1978; New York, St. Martin's Press, 1979.

The Rogue's Lady. Chicago, Playboy Press, 1979.

The Vixen's Revenge. Chicago, Playboy Press, 1980.

Novels as Charlotte Keppel

Madam, You Must Die. London, Hodder and Stoughton, 1975; as *Loving Sands, Deadly Sands*, New York, Delacorte Press, 1975.

My Name Is Clary Brown. New York, Random House, 1976; as *When I Say Goodbye, I'm Clary Brown*, London, Hodder and Stoughton, 1977.

I Could Be Good to You. London, Hutchinson, and New York, St. Martin's Press, 1980.

The Villains. Loughton, Essex, Piatkus, 1980; New York, St. Martin's Press, 1982.

The Ghosts of Fontenoy. Loughton, Essex, Piatkus, 1981.

OTHER PUBLICATIONS

Other

The Children. Boston, Little Brown, 1966; as *Wednesday's Children*, London, Hutchinson, 1967.

*   *   *

A wide-ranging and fertile imagination, tempered by common sense, is a rare quality in a writer of romantic fiction, yet this is a quality that Charity Blackstock possesses. From the beginning of her career her fiction has spanned countries and eras with confident skill.

Two early novels display this diversity and reveal literary techniques that can be observed to develop steadily. *The Bitter Conquest*, a historical novel set in the Scotland of 1750, has as its central character a somewhat reluctant hero, Adams. He is an English soldier bitterly disillusioned by futile bloodletting for a cause in which he has no conviction. The romantic element is introduced early, and develops in careful counterpoint to Adams's exploration of his own and his country's motives. There are gothic elements in the novel as well, including macabre descriptions of the bleak moors around Culloden—and even a severed head. By contrast, *The Briar Patch* is set in Paris four years after World War II, and the protagonists are two teenagers: Deirdre is Irish, attending a finishing school, and Max is a Jewish survivor of Nazi-occupied Poland. Though the portrayal of their developing intimacy is clouded by hopeless pessimism, the novel holds the reader's interest by its sensitive characterisation and a plot packed with exciting incident.

Blackstock returned to a similar period in *The Knock at Midnight*, but switched to modern-day Australia for *Party in Dolly Creek*. This book introduces the theme of soul-searching that pervades many of Blackstock's subsequent novels.

Perhaps the least successful of Blackstock's works is *The Melon in the Cornfield*, mainly because the characters involved in this tale of racial conflict in a West London technical college never come to life. Blackstock, like many other romantic novelists, does not contrive to avoid a patronising tone when dealing with a primarily political subject. *The Lonely Strangers*, however, shows Blackstock at full strength; in it she returns to the mid-18th century and to the people of Scotland, this time a group of exiles in Paris whose spirits are broken by defeat but whose characters are alive with emotion.

The majority of Blackstock's later works have a contemporary setting and rely for their interest and success upon a realistic presentation of modern-day crises. A good example is *Ghost Town* whose main character, Elizabeth Walters, is a former journalist, past middle age, with several unsuccessful relationships behind her. Her mental journey to self-realisation is presented by flashbacks that juxtapose past and present experiences. Mrs. Walters's own views on literature form another aspect of the novel. In *Dream Towers* Barbara Wyatt leaves her unfaithful husband to retreat to their country cottage. The working out of her true feelings toward Ben is linked metaphorically with her curiosity about the occupant of a mysterious mansion—and the laying to the village's "ghost" enables Barbara to lay her own "ghosts" to rest.

Charity Blackstock's consistently realistic characters, whose reactions can be readily related to common experience, have contributed to her success in the field of romantic fiction. Hers is not remote, high-flown romanticism but has at its base "heart and sincerity" without which, as Elizabeth Walters proposed in *Ghost Town*, writing is "no use at all."

—Anne M. Shields

BLACKSTOCK, Lee. See **BLACKSTOCK, Charity.**

BLAIR, Kathryn. Also writes as Rosalind Brett; Celine Conway. Address: c/o Mills and Boon Ltd., 18-24 Paradise Road, Richmond, Surrey TW9 1SR, England.

ROMANCE AND HISTORICAL PUBLICATIONS

Novels

Bewildered Heart. London, Mills and Boon, 1950; Toronto, Harlequin, 1964.
The House at Tegwani. London, Mills and Boon, 1950; Toronto, Harlequin, 1963.
No Other Haven. London, Mills and Boon, 1950; Toronto, Harlequin, 1966.
Dearest Enemy. London, Mills and Boon, 1951; Toronto, Harlequin, 1967.
Flowering Wilderness. London, Mills and Boon, 1951; Toronto, Harlequin, 1967.
Mayenga Farm. London, Mills and Boon, 1951; Toronto, Harlequin, 1965.
The Enchanting Island. London, Mills and Boon, 1952; Toronto, Harlequin, 1963.
The Fair Invader. London, Mills and Boon, 1952; as *Plantation Doctor*, Toronto, Harlequin, 1962.
The White Oleander. London, Mills and Boon, 1953; as *Nurse Laurie*, Toronto Harlequin, 1962.
Dear Adversary. London, Mills and Boon, 1953; Toronto, Harlequin, 1964.
Barbary Moon. London, Mills and Boon, 1954; Toronto, Harlequin, 1965.
Sweet Deceiver. London, Mills and Boon, 1955; Toronto, Harlequin, 1965.
Tamarisk Bay. London, Mills and Boon, 1956; Toronto, Harlequin, 1962.
Wild Crocus. London, Mills and Boon, 1956; Toronto, Harlequin, 1963.
Valley of Flowers. London, Mills and Boon, 1957.
The Tulip Tree. London, Mills and Boon, 1958; Toronto, Harlequin, 1966.
Love This Enemy. London, Mills and Boon, 1958; Toronto, Harlequin, 1964.
The Golden Rose. London, Mills and Boon, 1959; Toronto, Harlequin, 1962.
The Man at Mulera. London, Mills and Boon, 1959; Toronto, Harlequin, 1965.
A Summer at Barbazon. London, Mills and Boon, 1960; as *A Nurse at Barbazon*, Toronto, Harlequin, 1964.
The Primrose Bride. London, Mills and Boon, 1961; Toronto, Harlequin, 1966.
Children's Nurse. Toronto, Harlequin, 1961.
Battle of Love. London, Mills and Boon, 1961; Toronto, Harlequin, 1966.
The Affair in Tangier. London, Mills and Boon, 1962.
They Met in Zanzibar. London, Mills and Boon, 1962; Toronto, Harlequin, 1967.
The Surgeon's Marriage. London, Mills and Boon, 1963; Toronto, Harlequin, 1964.
The Dangerous Kind of Love. London, Mills and Boon, 1964.
This Kind of Love. Toronto, Harlequin, 1964.
Doctor Westland. Toronto, Harlequin, 1965.

Novels as Rosalind Brett

Green Leaves. Hanley, Staffordshire, Locker, 1947.
Pagan Interlude. Hanley, Staffordshire, Locker, 1947.
Secret Marriage. Hanley, Staffordshire, Locker, 1947.
And No Regrets. London, Rich and Cowan, 1948; Toronto, Harlequin, 1974.
Winds of Enchantment. London, Rich and Cowan, 1949; Toronto, Harlequin, 1968.

They Came to Valeira. London, Rich and Cowan, 1950; Toronto, Harlequin, 1974.
Brittle Bondage. London, Rich and Cowan, 1951; Toronto, Harlequin, 1969.
Love This Stranger. London, Rich and Cowan, 1951; Toronto, Harlequin, 1974.
Stormy Haven. London, Mills and Boon, 1952; Toronto, Harlequin, 1962.
Fair Horizon. London, Mills and Boon, 1952; Toronto, Harlequin, 1963.
Towards the Sun. London, Mills and Boon, 1953; Toronto, Harlequin, 1962.
Whispering Palms. London, Mills and Boon, 1954; Toronto, Harlequin, 1963.
Winds in the Wilderness. London, Mills and Boon, 1954; Toronto, Harlequin, 1963.
Sweet Waters. London, Mills and Boon, 1955; Toronto, Harlequin, 1964.
A Cottage in Spain. London, Mills and Boon, 1955; Toronto, Harlequin, 1975.
Portrait of Susan. London, Mills and Boon, 1956; Toronto, Harlequin, 1963.
Quiet Holiday. London, Mills and Boon, 1957; as *Nurse on Holiday*, Toronto, Harlequin, 1963.
Tangle in Sunshine. London, Mills and Boon, 1957; Toronto, Harlequin, 1964.
Young Tracy. London, Mills and Boon, 1958; Toronto, Harlequin, 1964.
Too Young to Marry. London, Mills and Boon, 1958; Toronto, Harlequin, 1964.
The Reluctant Guest. London, Mills and Boon, 1959; Toronto, Harlequin, 1964.
Hotel Mirador. London, Mills and Boon, 1959; Toronto, Harlequin, 1966.
Dangerous Waters. London, Mills and Boon, 1960; Toronto, Harlequin, 1964.
The Bolambo Affair. London, Mills and Boon, 1961; Toronto, Harlequin, 1967.
Spring at the Villa. London, Mills and Boon, 1961; as *Elizabeth Browne, Children's Nurse*, Toronto, Harlequin, 1965.
The Girl at White Drift. London, Mills and Boon, 1962; Toronto, Harlequin, 1967.
For My Sins. London, Mills and Boon, 1966.

Novels as Celine Conway

Return of Simon. London, Mills and Boon, 1953; Toronto, Harlequin, 1965.
The Blue Caribbean. London, Mills and Boon, 1954; Toronto, Harlequin, 1964.
Flowers in the Wind. London, Mills and Boon, 1954; as *Doctor's Assistant*, Toronto, Harlequin, 1964.
Full Tide. London, Mills and Boon, 1954; Toronto, Harlequin, 1964.
Three Women. London, Mills and Boon, 1955; Toronto, Harlequin, 1966.
The Tall Pines. London, Mills and Boon, 1956; Toronto, Harlequin, 1963.
The Rustle of Bamboo. London, Mills and Boon, 1957.
Wide Pastures. London, Mills and Boon, 1957; Toronto, Harlequin, 1962.
At the Villa Massina. London, Mills and Boon, 1958; Toronto, Harlequin, 1965.
My Dear Cousin. London, Mills and Boon, 1959; Toronto, Harlequin, 1965.

Came a Stranger. London, Mills and Boon, 1960; Toronto, Harlequin, 1965.
Flower of the Morning. London, Mills and Boon, 1960; Toronto, Harlequin, 1966.
Perchance to Marry. London, Mills and Boon, 1961; Toronto, Harlequin, 1966.
White Doctor. Toronto, Harlequin, 1961.
The Rancher Needs a Wife. London, Mills and Boon, 1962; Toronto, Harlequin, 1963.
Ship's Surgeon. London, Mills and Boon, 1962; Toronto, Harlequin, 1963.

*   *   *

Kathryn Blair's writing began in the late 1940's and she published numerous novels through the 1960's. She is also a writer who preferred to use a pseudonym, and for years her novels appeared under the names of Rosalind Brett and Celine Conway. In fact, she wrote and published under all three names for some time during the 1950's and 1960's.

Her style of writing is surprising, however, for one does not find the usual limitations in plot or characters that seem to typify romances of those years. In fact, she is quite modern and could easily be mistaken for a contemporary writer. She uses strong characterization, emotional and dramatic involvement, and exotic backgrounds to tell her stories. Many take place in Africa and Europe. Underlying psychological difficulties also seem to play a part in her motivation, as characters fight circumstances and their own hidden fears and desires.

In *Young Tracy* (Rosalind Brett) the heroine, Maggie Tracy, finds herself left in charge of a supply store deep in the wilds of Africa while her parents return on a trip to England. Nick Heward arrives to set up a construction base for a projected bridge in the area. He seeks to establish the store as a base for supplies and encounters Maggie. Another complication in the novel is Don Caldwell and his mother. Don falls in love with Maggie, but she can only think of him as a friend. Gradually Nick and Maggie fall in love, but events constantly set them at odds, until Mrs. Caldwell's growing psychological difficulties bring things to a head. Maggie's youthfulness, her unawareness, and, most of all, her stubborn idealistic need to help her parents all bring out the anger and frustration that Nick feels as he seeks to protect Maggie. The story line centers on several layers of conflict as the heroine and hero finally cut through the many elements of disagreement and confusion.

The Man at Mulera (Kathryn Blair) is no less complex as Lou Prentice arrives in Africa to take charge of her cousin's little boy, Keith. She is disturbed and later horrified to learn that the will making her a guardian of the child also stipulates that she and Ross Gilmore act as joint guardians, even to the extent that neither can marry without the other's permission. Lou finds herself forced to remain in Africa and slowly she becomes involved with Ross on questions of care and discipline for the boy. In this novel Blair makes full use of her creative ability as she draws numerous threads of conflict together in a seemingly impossible situation. Secondary characters such as Greg Allwyn, Ross Gilmore's new manager, and Paula Craddock, the District Commissioner's sister, add their strands to the various sub-plots and conflicts. Greg is a weak, spineless person who plays on Lou's sympathies. Paula is determined to become Ross's wife, regardless of his inclinations. Again Blair's use of psychological overtones raises the suspense and adds tremendously to character motivation.

One may not dismiss Blair as simply another romance writer. She shows unusual talent in developing complex characters and in letting them write their own stories. Her heroines are far from the simple peaches-and-cream caricatures that one thinks of in romances, neither are her heroes so predictable and stereotyped. A timeless quality in her writings makes her one of those rare writers who has something to say to any generation reading her, a fact that modern readers appreciate as they often re-read one of her well-written novels.

—Arlene Moore

———————

BLAKE, Andrea. See **WEALE, Anne.**

———————

BLAKE, Sally. See **SAUNDERS, Jean.**

———————

BLAKE, Stephanie. Pseudonym for Jack Pearl. American. Address: c/o Berkley Publishing Group, 200 Madison Avenue, New York, New York 10016, U.S.A.

ROMANCE AND HISTORICAL PUBLICATIONS

Novels

Victims (as Jack Pearl). New York, Trident Press, 1972; London, Hale, 1976.
Callie Knight (as Jack Pearl). New York, Saturday Review Press, 1974; as Stephanie Blake, London, Hamlyn, 1983.
Flowers of Fire. Chicago, Playboy Press, 1977; London, Hamlyn, 1978.
Daughter of Destiny. Chicago, Playboy Press, 1977; London, Hamlyn, 1978.
Blaze of Passion. Chicago, Playboy Press, 1978; London, Hamlyn, 1979.
So Wicked My Desire. Chicago, Playboy Press, and London, Hamlyn, 1979.
Secret Sins. Chicago, Playboy Press, 1980; London, Hamlyn, 1983.
Wicked Is My Flesh. Chicago, Playboy Press, 1980; London, Hamlyn, 1981.
Scarlet Kisses. Chicago, Playboy Press, 1981; London, Hamlyn, 1982.
Unholy Desires. Chicago, Playboy Press, 1981; London, Hamlyn, 1982.
Fires of the Heart. London, Hamlyn, 1983.
Bride of the Wind. New York, Berkley, 1984.

*   *   *

Sin, passion, and alliteration mark the titles of Stephanie Blake's novels: *Scarlet Kisses, Flowers of Fire, Daughter of Destiny, Blaze of Passion, So Wicked My Desire, Secret Sins, Wicked Is My Flesh, Unholy Desires, Fires of the Heart, Bride of the Wind.* In the most recent novels Blake seems to have—happily—outgrown the incredible coincidences, lifted-from-the-textbook history, and trite literary allusions that characterized her earlier books, but the stereotyped characters, aggressive female sexuality, contemporary faddishness, and spoken vulgarity remain. Still, the fast-moving stories hypnotize like flaming fires, and the passion-filled pages keep the reader's fingers yearning, burning, turning for more. It is easy to understand Blake's blazing popularity.

Flowers of Fire spans the Irish Revolution, the American Civil War, the California Gold Rush, and the early West (with Custer's Last Stand, Chief Crazy Horse, and Butch Cassidy), as it follows Ravena Wilding, a stunningly beautiful woman torn between the twin O'Neil brothers: Roger, "the treacherous, twisted brother who, through lies and deception, takes lovely Ravena for his own," and Brian, "the rogue, who said, 'Hate me or love me, but never forget me,' and captured Ravena's heart for all time." Jefferson Davis and other historical figures appear as characters in the appropriate places, along with characters from other fictions: Scarlett O'Hara ("I tell you," Jefferson Davis tells Ravena, "the last time I set eyes on a beauty such as yours was in Savannah, Georgia. Come to think of it, she was of Irish extraction, too. Scarlett O'Hara is her name. Lovely. Reminds me very much of you, Miss Ravena. Except for the eyes. And to tell the truth, she was a trifle skinny for my tastes"), as does Rhett Butler's new-found brother, Dan, who carries on a love affair with the insatiable Ravena. Ravena is given to quoting John Donne ("No man is an island") and Alfred Lord Tennyson ("Into the valley of death,/Rode the Six Hundred") at critical moments.

In *Daughter of Destiny*, the sweeping continuation of the O'Neil saga, Ravena's daughter, Sabrina, voyages from violent Ireland and England (where her mother has a meeting with Queen Victoria, who "looked like a stouter version of *Whistler's Mother*") to violent India (and the cult of the "Thuggee"), and back to Britain, where she rejects the advances of a rude Winston Churchill. Dan Butler reappears, and Colette, the casual *amour* of Glenn Blake, Sabrina's fiancé (and *not* the French author), sees him at a church wedding and speculates: "Dan Butler . . . Hmmm . . . I'll bet he's good in bed."

Hope Cox is the protagonist of *Bride of the Wind*. "Could any man tame her wild, wanting heart?" teases the novel's paperback cover. It is, in fact, Hope herself who uses sex (or, more accurately, sex teasing) to tame not only the jailer who can free her father Pap, the married minister who can get her the money to buy a small newspaper, indeed the whole Mafia-like Cheyenne Ring. Although Hope does not travel as far, geographically, as do Blake's other heroines—she moves only from the Texas wastelands to the Powder River near Cheyenne—she travels incredibly far politically, from being the 16-year-old daughter of the drunken, lazy Pap to owning her own ranch, being named justice of the peace for the area, and finally being elected Governor of the state of Wyoming. In the meantime, of course, she has fallen in love with the green-eyed Irishman, Timothy O'Callahan, who likewise adores her ("I could forget the Auld Sod sooner than I could forget you"). The novel ends with Tim in jail for his explosive contempt-of-court defense of his adored's purity, and Hope being sworn in as Governor:

"What is the first thing you are going to do in office, Governor Mason?" a reporter asked when the ceremony was over.

"My first action will be to order the Cheyenne Club closed down as a hazard to public health and safety," Hope said. "After that, I'm going to . . ."

Timothy lifted his handcuffed wrist and shook it, a comical expression of pleading on his face.

" . . . And then I'm going to get married to a prisoner in the city jail," Hope finished, slanting her laughing turquoise eyes upward to meet Tim's ardent green gaze.

Blaze of Passion tracks another fiery woman from 19th-century England to a penal colony in Australia. *Secret Sins* details the adventures of three generations of Tate women "from the watery wreckage of the Titanic to the bottomless maelstrom of the Bermuda Triangle." *Wicked Is My Flesh* conglomerates the eruption of Mauna Loa, the San Francisco Fire, and a Swiss avalanche. *Fires of the Heart* follows Dawn Price (who "hides her passionate nature beneath a rough, tomboy exterior") from the backwoods of Michigan to the Far East. It ends with Dawn and her lumberjack husband Jack in their bed in a New York City hotel suite. They decide to return to Michigan. Dawn bends over and kisses Jack, telling him, "I think you are my most favorite feller in the whole world" and asking him for "a little demonstration of the prowess that earned you the sobriquet Bull of the Woods." "Sobriquet? Damn! As many words as I learn, you always come up with another to stump me," protests Jack. "As for the bull part, here's how it goes." He proceeds to take her in his arms and kiss her as "his hands worked the nightgown down over her shoulders, baring her breasts." Dawn "clasped her hands behind his head and pulled his face down into her cleavage," and thinks, as her desire soars, "All this and heaven too."

Before he became "Stephanie Blake," Jack Pearl wrote two novels under his own name—*Victims* and *Callie Knight*—and one can almost detect the bulge of his maleness behind the petticoats of his feisty heroines.

—Marcia G. Fuchs

BLAYNE, Diana. See **PALMER, Diana.**

BLOOM, Ursula (Harvey). Also wrote as Sheila Burns; Mary Essex; Rachel Harvey; Deborah Mann; Lozania Prole; Sara Sloane. British. Born in Chelmsford, Essex, in 1893. Married 1) Arthur Brownlow Denham-Cookes in 1916 (died 1918), one son; 2) Charles Gower Robinson in 1925 (died 1979). Crime reporter, *Empire News* and *Sunday Dispatch*, London; beauty editor, *Woman's Own*; staff member, *Sunday Pictorial*. Fellow, Royal Historical Society. *Died 29 October 1984.*

ROMANCE AND HISTORICAL PUBLICATIONS

Novels

The Great Beginning. London, Hutchinson, 1924.
Vagabond Harvest. London, Hutchinson, 1925.
The Driving of Destiny. London, Hutchinson, 1925.
Our Lady of Marble. London, Hutchinson, 1926.
The Judge of Jerusalem. London, Harrap, 1926.
Spilled Salt: The Story of a Spy. London, Hutchinson, 1927.
Candleshades: The Story of a Soul. London, Hutchinson, 1927; New York, Watt, 1928.
Base Metal: The Story of a Man. London, Hutchinson, 1928; as *Veneer*, New York, Watt, 1929.
An April After. London, Hutchinson, 1928.
To-morrow for Apricots. London, Hutchinson, 1929; as *The Eternal Tomorrow*, New York, Watt, 1929.
Tarnish. London, Hutchinson, 1929

The Secret Lover. London, Hutchinson, 1930; New York, Dutton, 1931.

The Passionate Heart. London, Hutchinson, 1930; Canoga Park, California, Major, 1978.

The Gossamer Dream. London, Hutchinson, 1931.

Pack Mule. London, Hutchinson, 1931; New York, Dutton, 1932.

Trackless Way. London, Hurst and Blackett, 1931.

Fruit on the Bough: The Story of a Brother and Sister. London, Hutchinson, 1931; as *Flood of Passion*, New York, Dutton, 1932.

The Pilgrim Soul. London, Hutchinson, 1932.

Breadwinners. London, Hutchinson, 1932.

The Cypresses Grow Dark. London, Hutchinson, 1932.

Love's Playthings. London, Hutchinson, 1932.

The Log of a Naval Officer's Wife. London, Hurst and Blackett, 1932.

Rose Sweetman. London, Hutchinson, 1933.

Spread Wings. London, Hutchinson, 1933.

Better to Marry. New York, Dutton, 1933.

Wonder Cruise. London, Hutchinson, 1933; New York, Dutton, 1934.

Enchanted Journey. London, Hutchinson, 1933.

Love Is Everything. London, Hutchinson, 1933; as *Love, Old and New*, New York, Dutton, 1933.

Mediterranean Madness. London, Hutchinson, 1934.

The Questing Trout. London, Hutchinson, 1934.

Pastoral. London, Hutchinson, 1934.

Young Parent. London, Hutchinson, 1934.

This Is Marriage. London, Hutchinson, 1935.

Harvest of a House. London, Hutchinson, 1935.

The Gipsy Vans Come Through. London, Hutchinson, 1936.

The Laughing Lady. London, Collins, 1936.

Laughter in Cheyne Walk. London, Collins, 1936; Philadelphia, Lippincott, 1937.

Marriage of Pierrot. London, Cherry Tree, 1936.

Three Cedars. London, Collins, 1937.

Leaves Before the Storm. London, Rich and Cowan, 1937.

The Golden Venture. London, Rich and Cowan, 1938.

Lily-of-the-Valley. London, Rich and Cowan, 1938.

The Brittle Shadow. London, Readers Library, 1938.

Beloved Creditor. London, Cassell, 1939.

These Roots Go Deep. London, Cassell, 1939.

Trailing Glory. London, Hale, 1940.

The Woman Who Was To-morrow. London, Cassell, 1940.

The Flying Swans. London, Cassell, 1940.

Spring in September. London, Hale, 1941.

Silver Orchids. London, Hale, 1941.

The Virgin Thorn. London, Cassell, 1941.

Dinah's Husband. London, Cassell, 1941.

The Golden Flame. London, Hale, 1941.

Age Cannot Wither. London, Cassell, 1942.

Lovely Shadow. London, Cassell, 1942.

No Lady Buys a Cot. London, Chapman and Hall, 1943.

Marriage in Heaven. London, Hale, 1943.

A Robin in a Cage. London, Cassell, 1943.

Nightshade at Morning. London, Mellifont Press, 1944.

No Lady in Bed. London, Chapman and Hall, 1944.

The Fourth Cedar. London, Cassell, 1944.

The Painted Lady. London, Macdonald, 1945.

The Faithless Dove. London, Cassell, 1945.

Three Sons. London, Macdonald, 1946.

A Garden for My Child. London, Gifford, 1946.

No Lady with a Pen. London, Chapman and Hall, 1947.

Adam's Daughters. London, Macdonald, 1947.

Alien Corn. London, Hamish Hamilton, 1947.

Facade. London, Macdonald, 1948.

Next Tuesday. London, Macdonald, 1949.

No Lady in the Cart. London, Convoy, 1949.

Gipsy Flower. London, Hale, 1949.

The King's Wife. London, Hutchinson, 1950; Canoga Park, California, Major, 1979.

Eleanor Jowitt, Antiques. London, Macdonald, 1950.

The Song of Philomel. London, Macdonald, 1950.

How Dark, My Lady! A Novel Concerning the Life of William Shakespeare. London, Hutchinson, 1951.

Pavilion. London, Hutchinson, 1951.

Nine Lives. London, Macdonald, 1951.

Orange Blossom for Sandra. London, Hale, 1951.

The Sentimental Family. London, Macdonald, 1951.

As Bends the Bough. London, Macdonald, 1952.

Twilight of a Tudor. London, Hutchinson, 1952; New York, White Lion, 1976.

Moon Song. London, Hale, 1953.

Sea Fret. London, Hutchinson, 1953.

Marriage of Leonora. London, Hale, 1953.

The First Elizabeth. London, Hutchinson, 1953.

Matthew, Mark, Luke, and John. London, Hutchinson, 1954.

Daughters of the Rectory. London, Hutchinson, 1955.

The Gracious Lady. London, Hutchinson, 1955.

The Girl Who Loved Crippen. London, Hutchinson, 1955.

The Silver Ring. London, Hutchinson, 1955.

The Tides of Spring Flow Fast. London, Hutchinson, 1956.

Brief Springtime. London, Hutchinson, 1957.

The Abiding City. London, Hutchinson, 1958.

Monkey Tree in a Flower Pot. London, Hutchinson, 1958.

Undarkening Green. London, Hutchinson, 1959.

The Romance of Charles Dickens. London, Hale, 1960.

The Thieving Magpie. London, Hutchinson, 1960.

The Cactus Has Courage. London, Hutchinson, 1961.

Prelude to Yesterday. London, Hutchinson, 1961; Los Angeles, Pinnacle, 1978.

Harvest-Home Come Sunday. London, Hutchinson, 1962.

Ship in a Bottle. London, Hutchinson, 1962.

The Gated Road. London, Hutchinson, 1963.

The Ring Tree. London, Hutchinson, 1964.

The House That Died Alone. London, Hutchinson, 1964.

The Quiet Village. London, Hutchinson, 1965.

The Ugly Head. London, Hutchinson, 1965.

The Dandelion Clock. London, Hutchinson, 1966.

The Old Adam. London, Hutchinson, 1967.

Two Pools in a Field. London, Hutchinson, 1967.

Yesterday's Tomorrow. London, Hutchinson, 1968; Canoga Park, California, Major, 1978.

The Dragonfly. London, Hutchinson, 1968.

The Flight of the Falcon. London, Hutchinson, 1969.

The Hunter's Moon. London, Hutchinson, 1969.

The Tune of Time. London, Hutchinson, 1970.

Perchance to Dream. London, Hutchinson, 1971.

The Caravan of Chance. London, Hutchinson, 1971.

Edwardian Day-Dream. London, Hutchinson, 1972.

The Cheval Glass. London, Hutchinson, 1973.

The Old Rectory. London, Hutchinson, 1973.

Mirage on the Horizon. London, Hutchinson, 1974; Canoga Park, California, Major, 1979.

The Old Elm Tree. London, Hutchinson, 1974.

The Twisted Road. London, Hutchinson, 1975.

The Turn of Life's Tide. London, Hutchinson, 1976.

The House on the Hill. London, Hutchinson, 1977.

The Fire and the Rose. Canoga Park, California, Major, 1977.

The Woman Doctor. London, Hutchinson, 1978.

Bittersweet. Canoga Park, California, Major, 1978.

Born for Love. Canoga Park, California, Major, 1978.
Mirage of Love. Canoga Park, California, Major, 1978.
Sunday Love. Canoga Park, California, Major, 1978.
A Change of Heart. Canoga Park, California, Major, 1979.
Forever Autumn. Canoga Park, California, Major, 1979.
Gypsy Flame. Canoga Park, California, Major, 1979.
Honor's Price. Canoga Park, California, Major, 1979.
The Queen's Affair. Canoga Park, California, Major, 1979.
Sweet Spring of April. Canoga Park, California, Major, 1979.

Novels as Sheila Burns

The Passionate Adventure. London, Cassell, 1936.
Dream Awhile. London, Cassell, 1937.
Take a Chance. London, Cassell, 1937.
Honeymoon Island. London, Cassell, 1938.
Lady! This Is Love! London, Cassell, 1938.
Week-end Bride. London, Cassell, 1939.
Wonder Trip. London, Cassell, 1939.
Adventurous Heart. London, Cassell, 1940.
Meet Love on Holiday. London, Cassell, 1940.
Romance Is Mine. London, Cassell, 1941.
The Stronger Passion. London, Cassell, 1941.
Bridal Sweet. London, Cassell, 1942; as *Bride Alone*, New
  York, Arcadia House, 1943.
Thy Bride Am I. London, Cassell, 1942.
Romantic Fugitive. London, Cassell, 1943; New York, Arcadia
  House, 1944.
Romance of Jenny W.R.E.N. London, Cassell, 1944; as *Jenny
  W.R.E.N.*, New York, Arcadia House, 1945.
Vagrant Lover. London, Macdonald, 1945.
Hold Hard, My Heart. London, Macdonald, 1946.
Bride—Maybe. London, Macdonald, 1946.
Desire Is Not Dead. London, Macdonald, 1947.
The Chance Romance. London, Eldon Press, 1948.
Air Liner. London, Eldon Press, 1948.
To-morrow Is Eternal. London, Macdonald, 1948.
Faint with Pursuit. London, Eldon Press, 1949.
No Trespassers in Love. London, Macdonald, 1949.
The Cuckoo Never Weds. London, Eldon Press, 1950.
Primula and Hyacinth. New York, Arcadia House, 1950.
Not Free to Love. London, Eldon Press, 1950; as *Heaven Lies
  Ahead* (as Sara Sloane), New York, Arcadia House, 1951.
Hold Back the Heart. New York, Arcadia House, 1951.
Rosebud and Stardust. London, Eldon Press, 1951.
Live Happily—Love Song. London, Eldon Press, 1952.
Love Me To-morrow. London, Eldon Press, 1952.
Romantic Intruder. London, Hutchinson, 1952.
Tomorrow We Marry. London, Hutchinson, 1953.
Beloved and Unforgettable. London, Hutchinson, 1953.
Please Burn after Reading. London, Hutchinson, 1954.
How Dear Is My Delight! London, Hutchinson, 1955.
Adventure in Romance. London, Hutchinson, 1955.
Romantic Summer Sea. London, Hutchinson, 1956.
The Sweet Impulse. London, Hutchinson, 1956.
How Rich Is Love? London, Hurst and Blackett, 1957.
The Beloved Man. London, Hurst and Blackett, 1957.
This Dragon of Desire. London, Hurst and Blackett, 1958.
The Storm Bird. London, Hurst and Blackett, 1959.
The Lasting Lover. London, Hurst and Blackett, 1959.
Doctor Gregory's Partner. London, Hurst and Blackett, 1960.
Doctor to the Rescue. London, Hurst and Blackett, 1961.
The Disheartened Doctor. London, Hale, 1961.
Dr. Irresistible, M.D. London, Hale, 1962.
The Eyes of Doctor Karl. London, Hale, 1962.
Heartbreak Surgeon. London, Hale, 1963.

Theatre Sister in Love. London, Hale, 1963.
When Doctors Love. London, Hale, 1964.
Doctor's Distress. London, Digit, 1964.
Doctor Delightful. London, Hale, 1964.
Doctor Called David. London, Hale, 1966.
Doctor Divine. London, Hale, 1966.
A Surgeon's Sweetheart. London, Hale, 1966.
The Beauty Surgeon. London, Hale, 1967.
The Flying Nurse. London, Hale, 1967.
Romantic Cottage Hospital. London, Hale, 1967.
The Dark-eyed Sister. London, Hale, 1968.
Casualty Ward. London, Hale, 1968.
Acting Sister. London, Hale, 1968.
Surgeon at Sea. London, Hale, 1969.
The Nurse Who Shocked the Matron. London, Hale, 1970.
Sister Loving Heart. London, Hale, 1971.
Cornish Rhapsody. London, Hale, 1972.
Romance and Nurse Margaret. London, Hale, 1972.
The Bells Still Ring. London, Hale, 1976.

Novels as Mary Essex

Haircut for Samson. London, Chapman and Hall, 1940.
Nesting Cats. London, Chapman and Hall, 1941.
Eve Didn't Care. London, Chapman and Hall, 1941.
Marry to Taste. London, Chapman and Hall, 1942.
Freddy for Fun. London, Chapman and Hall, 1943.
The Amorous Bicycle. London, Chapman and Hall, 1944.
Divorce? Of Course. London, Chapman and Hall, 1945.
Young Kangaroos Prefer Riding. London, Chapman and Hall,
  1947.
Domestic Blister. London, Chapman and Hall, 1948.
Six Fools and a Fairy. London, Jenkins, 1948.
Full Fruit Flavour. London, Jenkins, 1949.
The Herring's Nest. London, Jenkins, 1949.
An Apple for the Doctor. London, Jenkins, 1950.
Tea Is So Intoxicating. London, Jenkins, 1950.
Dark Gentleman, Fair Lady. London, Jenkins, 1951.
A Gentleman Called James. London, Jenkins, 1951.
She Had What It Takes. London, Jenkins, 1952.
Forty Is Beginning. London, Jenkins, 1952.
Danielle, My Darling. London, Dakers, 1954.
The Passionate Springtime. London, Hale, 1956.
Forbidden Fiancé. London, Hale, 1957.
The Dark Lover. London, Hale, 1957.
A Nightingale Once Sang. London, Hale, 1958.
It's Spring, My Heart! London, Hale, 1958.
Romance of Summer. London, Hale, 1959.
This Man Is Not for Marrying. London, Hale, 1959.
The Fugitive Romantic. London, Hale, 1960.
The Love Story of Dr. Duke. London, Hale, 1960.
A Sailor's Love. London, Hale, 1961.
Doctor on Call. London, Hale, 1961.
Date with a Doctor. London, Hale, 1962.
Dr. Guardian of the Gate. London, Hale, 1962.
Nurse from Killarney. London, Hale, 1963.
A Strange Patient for Sister Smith. London, Hale, 1963.
The Sangor Hospital Story. London, Hale, 1963.
The Hard-Hearted Doctor. London, Hale, 1964.
Doctor and Lover. London, Hale, 1964.
Dare-Devil Doctor. London, Hale, 1965.
Romantic Theatre Sister. London, Hale, 1965.
Hospital of the Heart. London, Hale, 1966.
The Little Nurse. London, Hale, 1967.
The Romance of Dr. Dinah. London, Hale, 1967.
Assistant Matron. London, Hale, 1967.

The Adorable Doctor. London, Hale, 1968.
The Ghost of Fiddler's Hill. London, Hale, 1968.
The Sympathetic Surgeon. London, Hale, 1968.
Doctor on Duty Bound. London, Hale, 1969.
When a Woman Doctor Loves. London, Hale, 1969.
The Dangerous Doctor. London, Hale, 1970.
Heart Surgeon. London, Hale, 1971.
The Fascinating Doctor. London, Hale, 1972.
The Nurse Who Fell in Love. London, Hale, 1972.
A Nurse Called Liza. London, Hale, 1973.
The Dark Farm. London, Hale, 1974.
A Doctor's Love. London, Hale, 1974.

Novels as Lozania Prole

Our Dearest Emma. London, Museum Press, 1949; as *The Magnificent Courtesan*, New York, McBride, 1950; as *Emma Hart*, Toronto, Harlequin, 1951.
Pretty, Witty Nell! London, Hale, and New York, McGraw Hill, 1953; as *The Fabulous Nell Gwynne*, Toronto, Harlequin, 1954; as *Sweet Nell*, London, Corgi, 1965.
To-night, Josephine! London, Hale, and New York, McGraw Hill, 1954.
The King's Pleasure. London, Hale, and New York, McGraw Hill, 1954.
The Enchanting Courtesan. London, Hale, 1955; New York, Pocket Books, 1975.
My Wanton Tudor Rose: The Love Story of Lady Katheryn Howard. London, Hale, 1956.
The Little Victoria. London, Hale, 1957.
A Queen for England. London, Hale, 1957.
Harry's Last Love. London, Hale, 1958.
The Stuart Sisters. London, Hale, 1958.
Consort to the Queen. London, Hale, 1959.
The Little Wig-Maker of Bread Street. London, Hale, 1959.
For Love of the King. London, Hale, 1960.
The Tudor Boy. London, Hale, 1960.
The Queen's Midwife. London, Hale, 1961.
My Love! My Little Queen! London, Hale, 1961.
A King's Plaything. London, Hale, 1962.
Queen Guillotine. London, Hale, 1962.
The Ghost That Haunted a King. London, Hale, 1963.
The Wild Daughter. London, Hale, 1963.
Daughter of the Devil. London, Hale, 1963; New York, Pocket Books, 1974.
Henry's Golden Queen. London, Hale, 1964.
The Three Passionate Queens. London, Hale, 1964.
Marlborough's Unfair Lady. London, Hale, 1965.
The Haunted Headsman. London, Hale, 1965.
The Dangerous Husband. London, Hale, 1966.
Nelson's Love. London, Hale, 1966.
The Dark-Eyed Queen. London, Hale, 1967; New York, Pocket Books, 1976.
King Henry's Sweetheart. London, Hale, 1967.
The Queen Who Was a Nun. London, Hale, 1967.
The Greatest Nurse of Them All. London, Hale, 1968.
Prince Philanderer. London, Hale, 1968.
The Loves of a Virgin Princess. London, Hale, 1968.
Sweet Marie-Antoinette. London, Hale, 1969; New York, Pocket Books, 1973.
The Boutique of the Singing Clocks. London, Hale, 1969.
The Enchanting Princess. London, Hale, 1970.
The Last Tsarina. London, Hale, 1970.
Judas Iscariot—Traitor! London, Hale, 1971.
A Queen for the Regent. London, Hale, 1971.

The Two Queen Annes. London, Hale, 1971; New York, Pocket Books, 1973.
The Orange Girl. London, Hale, 1972.
The Ten-Day Queen. London, Hale, 1972.
Taj Mahal, Shrine of Desire. London, Hale, 1972.
The Queen's Daughters. London, Hale, 1973.
Albert the Beloved. London, Hale, 1974.
The Last Love of a King. London, Hale, 1974.
The Lass a King Loved. London, Hale, 1975.
The King's Daughter. London, Hale, 1975.
When Paris Fell. London, Hale, 1976.

Novels as Deborah Mann

The Woman Called Mary. London, Hale, 1960; as *A Woman Called Mary*, London, Corgi, 1966.
Now Barabbas Was a Robber. London, Corgi, 1968.
The Song of Salome. London, Corgi, 1969.
Pilate's Wife. London, Corgi, 1976.

Novels as Rachel Harvey

The Village Nurse. London, Hurst and Blackett, 1967.
Dearest Doctor. London, Hurst and Blackett, 1968.
Weep Not for Dreams. London, Hale, 1968.
The Little Matron of the Cottage Hospital. London, Hale, 1969.
Darling District Nurse. London, Hale, 1970.
Nurse on Bodmin Moor. London, Hale, 1970.
Doctor Called Harry. London, Hale, 1971.
Sister to a Stranger. London, Hale, 1971.
Love Has No Secrets. London, Hale, 1972.
The Gipsy Lover. London, Hale, 1973.
The Doctor Who Fell in Love. London, Hale, 1974.
The Love Story of Nurse Julie. London, Hale, 1975.

Short Stories

Tiger. Privately printed, 1903 (?).
Winifred. Privately printed, 1903.
Girlie. Privately printed, 1904.
The Cherry Hat. Privately printed, 1904.
Crazy Quilt: A Volume of Stories. London, Hutchinson, 1933.
Wartime Beauty. London, Todd, 1943.

OTHER PUBLICATIONS

Plays

A Paymaster in Every Family. London, French, 1943.
One Wedding, Two Brides. London, French, 1943.
What's in a Name? A Nativity Play. London, French, 1947.
Displaced Person. London, French, 1948.

Radio Plays: *Dog Collar* series, 1961, 1963; *Way Through the Wilderness*, 1962; *The Mother*, 1964; *Jean Meadows, Vet* series, 1964; *Green Finger*, 1965; and others.

Other

A Lamp in the Darkness: A Series of Essays on Religion. London, Hutchinson, 1930; Los Angeles, Corwin, 1978.
Mistress of None (autobiography). London, Hutchinson, 1933.
Holiday Mood. London, Hutchinson, 1934.
Without Make-Up. London, Joseph, 1938.

The ABC of Authorship. London, Blackie, 1938; Philadelphia, Westminster, 1973.
A Cad's Guide to Cruising. London, Rich and Cowan, 1938.
Letters to My Son. London, Cassell, 1939.
The Log of No Lady, Being the Story of a London Woman Evacuated Before the Outbreak of War. London, Chapman and Hall, 1940.
The Housewife's Beauty Book. London, Hale, 1941.
Time, Tide and I. London, Chapman and Hall, 1942.
Me—After the War: A Book for Girls Considering the Future. London, Gifford, 1944.
The Changed Village. London, Chapman and Hall, 1945.
The Little Fir Tree (for children). London, Hutchinson, 1945.
Rude Forefathers. London, Macdonald, 1945.
Questions Answered about Knitting [*Beauty*]. London, Jordan, 2 vols., 1945–46.
Ursula's Cook Book for the Woman Who Has No Time to Spare. London, Gifford, 1946.
You and Your Holiday [*Child, Home, Dog, Looks, Life, Fun, Needle*]. London, Gifford, 8 vols., 1946–50.
No Lady Meets No Gentleman. London, Low, 1947.
Pumpkin the Pup (for children). London, Hutchinson, 1947.
Smugglers Cave (for children). London, Riddle, 1947.
Caravan for Three (for children). London, University of London Press, 1947.
Cookery. London, Foyle, 1949.
Three Girls Come to Town (for children). London, Macdonald, 1950.
Mum's Girl Was No Lady. London, Convoy, 1951.
New World round the Corner. London, British Rubber Development Board, 1951.
For the Bride. London, Museum Press, 1952.
Trilogy (autobiography). London, Hutchinson, 1954.
Curtain Call for the Guv'nor: A Biography of George Edwardes. London, Hutchinson, 1954.
The Girls' Book of Popular Hobbies. London, Burke, 1954; New York, Roy, 1956.
Hitler's Eva. London, Hutchinson, 1954.
No Lady Has a Dog's Day: A Casual Book of Reminiscences. London, Hutchinson, 1956.
Victorian Vinaigrette. London, Hutchinson, 1956.
The Elegant Edwardians. London, Hutchinson, 1957.
Down to the Sea in Ships. London, Hutchinson, 1958.
He Lit the Lamp: A Biography of Professor A.M. Low. London, Burke, 1958.
Wanting to Write: A Complete Guide for Would-Be Writers. London, Stanley Paul, 1958.
The Inspired Needle. London, Hurst and Blackett, 1959.
Youth at the Gate. London, Hutchinson, 1959.
Sixty Years of Home. London, Hurst and Blackett, 1960.
War Isn't Wonderful. London, Hutchinson, 1961.
Mrs. Bunthorpe's Respects: A Chronicle of Cooks. London, Hutchinson, 1963.
Parson Extraordinary. London, Hale, 1963.
The Rose of Norfolk. London, Hale, 1964.
Price above Rubies. London, Hutchinson, 1965.
Rosemary for Stratford-on-Avon. London, Hale, 1966.
The Mightier Sword. London, Hale, 1966.
A Roof and Four Walls. London, Hale, 1967.
The House of Kent. London, Hale, 1969.
Rosemary for Frinton. London, Hale, 1970.
The Great Tomorrow. London, Hale, 1971; New York, Zebra, 1978.
Rosemary for Chelsea. London, Hale, 1971.
The Duke of Windsor. London, Hale, 1972.
Requesting the Pleasure. London, Hale, 1973.

Princesses in Love. London, Hale, 1973.
The Royal Baby. London, Hale, 1975.
Life Is No Fairy Tale. London, Hale, 1976.
The Great Queen Consort. London, Hale, 1976.
Edward and Victoria. London, Hale, 1977.

Editor, *Woman's Annual 1951*. London, Elek, 1950.

*   *   *

Ursula Bloom was a woman of rare quality, a great professional, whose writing career spanned many decades. From childhood she wanted to write and began with a children's story, *Tiger*, privately printed when she was seven years old. Marie Corelli helped her, and one of her stories was given to Prince Edward and his sister, Princess Mary. Always keenly interested in people, she was a natural reporter, though women were frowned on in that profession in the years after World War I. She covered the Crippen murder story which was later used as part of one of her books, as was her coverage of the Ruth Ellis case.

One of the most prolific authors in the country, Bloom is listed in the *Guinness Book of Records* credited with 500 full-length titles by 1975. Her first novel, appropriately called *The Great Beginning*, and a best seller, told of a young "slip of a girl who passionately desired motherhood," but whose scheming mother married her to a man whose ancestry, filled with a dread disease, denied her children. But in true romantic fiction style she finds love and there is a happy ending. This success was followed with many romances with a simple boy meets girl theme. Bloom has drawn on her own experience for many of her characters and settings: time spent in hospitals, for instance, was used in her popular hospital tales.

Romantic novels with memorable titles (*An April After*—after what?) soon filled the shelves. She was proud of her family, especially her gypsy forebear (*The Rose of Norfolk*), and this gave her much accurate background when writing about gypsies in stories such as *Gipsy Flower* and *The Caravan of Chance*.

Always an adventurous and energetic writer, Ursula Bloom would tackle any hurdle. She wrote stories, articles, beauty counselling, plays, biographies of her family, autobiographies, and works on the Royal Family. There were books of memory on places such as Stratford-on-Avon where much of her childhood was spent, and she always retained her knowledge and love of the works of Shakespeare. Chelsea took on a new look under her penmanship, and she wrote cookery books and others. Sheila Burns, Mary Essex, Deborah Mann were among the pseudonyms she used for her romances, Burns for the hospital stories, Essex for modern romances, and Mann for historical tales, though at first she used her own name for romances.

In all her books she wrote with a transparent honesty that shines through her lines, setting down life as she experienced it, without varnish. In many ways, her personal life was unusual, tinged with sadness, pain and suffering, grief and pleasure, and she could write with ease about all of those experiences. Maybe her upbringing in a vicarage had an effect, for her heroines were always chaste, though to be fair so were most heroines of the period. She was ever helpful to others—again her "parish" caring background—and was an agony columnist and wrote much on religion, God, and death for a Sunday paper, collecting material from all over the country, indulging herself in reporting. Bloom could write movingly on conditions in the Welsh coal valleys where lack of work created social problems.

Her book *The Secret Lover* was a new departure, a diary telling of an old bachelor hermit who had been an old roué with a secret love in his imagination. The idea of the Editor of the former *Sunday Dispatch* for her to write a historical novel, to be first serialised in the paper, was the forerunner of much success. It was decided that a book on Lady Hamilton would launch the series, and *Our Dearest Emma* was the result. It tells the story of one of the country's most notorious, most forgiven women, and Bloom's simple style of telling that tale without lurid details makes it a historical classic to this day. *Our Dearest Emma* was written under a new pseudonym, Lozania Prole, and began a long series of historical novels. She chose to write many biographical novels of famous women, Nell Gwynn, Florence Nightingale, Mrs. Fitzherbert, Hitler's Eva, Ethel Le Neve; the French Revolution and Regency Brighton formed the background for many of these stirring, robust books.

A resourceful worker, Bloom devoted her life to keeping the wheels of authorship turning with hospital life, light romances, historical novels, and biographies of herself and others. When writing of her own life, her family, her mother (one of her most moving books, *Price above Rubies*), she spared nothing, and the reader joined her when buying a house, living in the country or with the Edwardians. Essentially honest, she never held back from her readers, and they lived again with her the days of poverty, selling possessions, finding a bargain, and the problems of a struggling writer. She had a deep sense of awareness of religion. This is often hid, as with so many children of the vicarage, though she wrote of religious characters, often unusual ones—Judas Iscariot, Barabbas—and a moving story of the Taj Mahal revealing a depth of sensitivity not often revealed in light romances.

—Lornie Leete-Hodge

BOWEN, Marjorie. Pseudonym for Gabrielle Margaret Vere Campbell; also wrote as Robert Paye; George Preedy; Joseph Shearing; John Winch. British. Born on Hayling Island, Hampshire, 29 October 1886. Married 1) Zeffrino Emilio Costanzo in 1912 (died 1916), one son; 2) Arthur L. Long in 1917, two sons. *Died 23 December 1952.*

ROMANCE AND HISTORICAL PUBLICATIONS

Novels (series: Renaissance Trilogy; William III Trilogy)

The Viper of Milan. London, Alston Rivers, and New York, McClure Phillips, 1906.
The Glen o'Weeping. London, Alston Rivers, 1907; as *The Master of Stair*, New York, McClure Phillips, 1907.
The Sword Decides! London, Alston Rivers, and New York, McClure, 1908.
Black Magic: A Tale of the Rise and Fall of Antichrist. London, Alston Rivers, 1909.
The Leopard and the Lily. New York, Doubleday, 1909; London, Methuen, 1920.
William III Trilogy:
  I Will Maintain. London, Methuen, 1910; New York, Dutton, 1911; revised edition, London, Penguin, 1943.
  Defender of the Faith. London, Methuen, and New York, Dutton, 1911.
  God and the King. London, Methuen, 1911; New York, Dutton, 1912.
Lovers' Knots. London, Everett, 1912.
The Quest of Glory. London, Methuen, and New York, Dutton, 1912.

The Rake's Progress. London, Rider, 1912.
The Soldier from Virginia. New York, Appleton, 1912; as *Mister Washington*, London, Methuen, 1915.
The Governor of England. London, Methuen, 1913; New York, Dutton, 1914.
A Knight of Spain. London, Methuen, 1913.
The Two Carnations. London, Cassell, and New York, Reynolds, 1913.
Prince and Heretic. London, Methuen, 1914; New York, Dutton, 1915.
Because of These Things . . . . London, Methuen, 1915.
The Carnival of Florence. London, Methuen, and New York, Dutton, 1915.
William, By the Grace of God—. London, Methuen, 1916; New York, Dutton, 1917; abridged edition, Methuen, 1928.
The Third Estate. London, Methuen, 1917; New York, Dutton, 1918; revised edition, as *Eugénie*, London, Fontana, 1971.
The Burning Glass. London, Collins, 1918; New York, Dutton, 1919.
Kings-at-Arms. London, Methuen, 1918; New York, Dutton, 1919.
Mr. Misfortunate. London, Collins, 1919.
The Cheats. London, Collins, 1920.
The Haunted Vintage. London, Odhams Press, 1921.
Rococo. London, Odhams Press, 1921.
The Jest. London, Odhams Press, 1922.
Affairs of Men (selections from novels). London, Cranton, 1922.
Stinging Nettles. London, Ward Lock, and Boston, Small Maynard, 1923.
The Presence and the Power. London, Ward Lock, 1924.
Five People. London, Ward Lock, 1925.
Boundless Water. London, Ward Lock, 1926.
Nell Gwyn: A Decoration. London, Hodder and Stoughton, 1926; as *Mistress Nell Gwyn*, New York, Appleton, 1926.
Five Winds. London, Hodder and Stoughton, 1927.
The Pagoda: Le Pagode de Chanteloup. London, Hodder and Stoughton, 1927.
The Countess Fanny. London, Hodder and Stoughton, 1928.
Renaissance Trilogy:
  The Golden Roof. London, Hodder and Stoughton, 1928.
  The Triumphant Beast. London, Lane, 1934.
  Trumpets at Rome. London, Hutchinson, 1936.
Dickon. London, Hodder and Stoughton, 1929.
The English Paragon. London, Hodder and Stoughton, 1930.
The Devil's Jig (as Robert Paye). London, Lane, 1930.
Brave Employments. London, Collins, 1931.
Withering Fires. London, Collins, 1931.
The Shadow on Mockways. London, Collins, 1932.
Dark Rosaleen. London, Collins, 1932; Boston, Houghton Mifflin, 1933.
Passion Flower. London, Collins, 1932; as *Beneath the Passion Flower* (as George Preedy), New York, McBride, 1932.
Idlers' Gate (as John Winch). London, Collins, and New York, Morrow, 1932.
Julia Roseingrave (as Robert Paye). London, Benn, 1933.
I Dwelt in High Places. London, Collins, 1933.
Set with Green Herbs. London, Benn, 1933.
The Stolen Bride. London, Lovat Dickson, 1933; abridged edition, London, Mellifont Press, 1946.
The Veil'd Delight. London, Odhams Press, 1933.
A Giant in Chains: Prelude to Revolution—France 1775–1791. London, Hutchinson, 1938.
Trilogy:
  God and the Wedding Dress. London, Hutchinson, 1938.
  Mr. Tyler's Saints. London, Hutchinson, 1939.

The Circle in the Water. London, Hutchinson, 1939.
Exchange Royal. London, Hutchinson, 1940.
Today Is Mine. London, Hutchinson, 1941.
The Man with the Scales. London, Hutchinson, 1954.

Novels as George Preedy

General Crack. London, Lane, and New York, Dodd Mead, 1928.
The Rocklitz. London, Lane, 1930; as *The Prince's Darling*, New York, Dodd Mead, 1930.
Tumult in the North. London, Lane, and New York, Dodd Mead, 1931.
The Pavilion of Honour. London, Lane, 1932.
Violante: Circe and Ermine. London, Cassell, 1932.
The Devil Snar'd. London, Benn, 1932.
Dr. Chaos, and The Devil Snar'd. London, Cassell, 1933.
Double Dallilay. London, Cassell, 1933; as *Queen's Caprice*, New York, King, 1934.
The Autobiography of Cornelius Blake, 1773–1810, of Ditton See, Cambridgeshire. London, Cassell, 1934.
Laurell'd Captains. London, Hutchinson, 1935.
The Poisoners. London, Hutchinson, 1936.
My Tattered Loving. London, Jenkins, 1937; as *The King's Favourite* (as Marjorie Bowen), London, Fontana, 1971.
Painted Angel. London, Jenkins, 1938.
The Fair Young Widow. London, Jenkins, 1939.
Dove in the Mulberry Tree. London, Jenkins, 1939.
Primula. London, Hodder and Stoughton, 1940.
Black Man—White Maiden. London, Hodder and Stoughton, 1941.
Findernes' Flowers. London, Hodder and Stoughton, 1941.
Lyndley Waters. London, Hodder and Stoughton, 1942.
Lady in a Veil. London, Hodder and Stoughton, 1943.
The Fourth Chamber. London, Hodder and Stoughton, 1944.
Nightcap and Plume. London, Hodder and Stoughton, 1945.
No Way Home. London, Hodder and Stoughton, 1947.
The Sacked City. London, Hodder and Stoughton, 1949.
Julia Ballantyne. London, Hodder and Stoughton, 1952.

Novels as Joseph Shearing

Forget-Me-Not. London, Heinemann, 1932; as *Lucile Cléry*, New York, Harper, 1932; as *The Strange Case of Lucile Cléry*, Harper, 1941.
Album Leaf. London, Heinemann, 1933; as *The Spider in the Cup*, New York, Smith and Haas, 1934.
Moss Rose. London, Heinemann, 1934; New York, Smith and Haas, 1935.
The Golden Violet: The Story of a Lady Novelist. London, Heinemann, 1936; New York, Smith and Durrell, 1941; as *Night's Dark Secret* (as Margaret Campbell), New York, New American Library, 1975.
Blanche Fury; or, Fury's Ape. London, Heinemann, and New York, Harrison Hilton, 1939.
Aunt Beardie. London, Hutchinson, and New York, Harrison Hilton, 1940.
Laura Sarelle. London, Hutchinson, 1940; as *The Crime of Laura Sarelle*, New York, Smith and Durrell, 1941.
The Fetch. London, Hutchinson, 1942; as *The Spectral Bride*, New York, Smith and Durrell, 1942.
Airing in a Closed Carriage. London, Hutchinson, and New York, Harper, 1943.
The Abode of Love. London, Hutchinson, 1945.
For Her to See. London, Hutchinson, 1947; as *So Evil My Love*, New York, Harper, 1947.

Mignonette. New York, Harper, 1948; London, Heinemann, 1949.
Within the Bubble. London, Heinemann, 1950; as *The Heiress of Frascati*, New York, Berkley, 1966.
To Bed at Noon. London, Heinemann, 1951.

Short Stories

God's Playthings. London, Smith Elder, 1912; New York, Dutton, 1913.
Shadows of Yesterday: Stories from an Old Catalogue. London, Smith Elder, and New York, Dutton, 1916.
Curious Happenings. London, Mills and Boon, 1917.
Crimes of Old London. London, Odhams Press, 1919.
The Pleasant Husband and Other Stories. London, Hurst and Blackett, 1921.
Seeing Life! and Other Stories. London, Hurst and Blackett, 1923.
The Seven Deadly Sins. London, Hurst and Blackett, 1926.
Dark Ann and Other Stories. London, Lane, 1927.
The Gorgeous Lover and Other Tales. London, Lane, 1929.
Sheep's-Head and Babylon, and Other Stories of Yesterday and Today. London, Lane, 1929.
Old Patch's Medley; or, A London Miscellany. London, Selwyn and Blount, 1930.
Bagatelle and Some Other Diversions (as George Preedy). London, Lane, 1930; New York, Dodd Mead, 1931.
Grace Latouche and the Warringtons: Some Nineteenth-Century Pieces, Mostly Victorian. London, Selwyn and Blount, 1931.
Fond Fancy and Other Stories. London, Selwyn and Blount, 1932.
The Last Bouquet: Some Twilight Tales. London, Lane, 1932.
The Knot Garden: Some Old Fancies Re-Set (as George Preedy). London, Lane, 1933.
Orange Blossoms (as Joseph Shearing). London, Heinemann, 1938.
The Bishop of Hell and Other Stories. London, Lane, 1949.
Kecksies and Other Twilight Tales. Sauk City, Wisconsin, Arkham House, 1976.

OTHER PUBLICATIONS

Plays as George Preedy

Captain Banner (produced London, 1929). London, Lane, 1930.
A Family Comedy, 1840 (as Marjorie Bowen). London, French, 1930.
The Question. London, French, 1931.
The Rocklitz (produced London, 1931).
Rose Giralda (produced London, 1933).
Court Cards (produced London, 1934).
Royal Command (produced Wimbledon, Surrey, 1952).

Screenplay: *The Black Tulip* (as Marjorie Bowen), 1921.

Other

Luctor et Emergo, Being an Historical Essay on the State of England at the Peace of Ryswick. Newcastle upon Tyne, Northumberland Press, 1925.
The Netherlands Display'd; or, The Delights of the Low Countries. London, Lane, 1926; New York, Dodd Mead, 1927.
Holland, Being a General Survey of the Netherlands. London, Harrap, 1928; New York, Doubleday, 1929.

The Winged Trees (for children). Oxford, Blackwell, 1928.
The Story of the Temple and Its Associations. London, Griffin Press, 1928.
Sundry Great Gentlemen: Some Essays in Historical Biography. London, Lane, and New York, Dodd Mead, 1928.
William, Prince of Orange, Afterwards King of England, Being an Account of His Early Life. London, Lane, and New York, Dodd Mead, 1928.
The Lady's Prisoner (for children). Oxford, Blackwell, 1929.
Mademoiselle Maria Gloria (for children). Oxford, Blackwell, 1929.
The Third Mary Stuart, Being a Character Study with Memoirs and Letters of Queen Mary II of England 1662–1694. London, Lane, 1929.
Exits and Farewells, Being Some Account of the Last Days of Certain Historical Characters. London, Selwyn and Blount, 1930.
Mary, Queen of Scots, Daughter of Debate. London, Lane, 1934; New York, Putnam, 1935.
The Scandal of Sophie Dawes. London, Lane, 1934; New York, Appleton Century, 1935.
Patriotic Lady: A Study of Emma, Lady Hamilton, and the Neapolitan Revolution of 1799. London, Lane, 1935; New York, Appleton Century, 1936.
The Angel of Assassination: Marie-Charlotte de Corday d'Armont, Jean-Paul Marat, Jean-Adam Lux: Three Disciples of Rousseau (as Joseph Shearing). London, Heinemann, and New York, Smith and Haas, 1935.
Peter Porcupine: A Study of William Cobbett 1762–1835. London, Longman, 1935; New York, Longman, 1936.
William Hogarth, The Cockney's Mirror. London, Methuen, and New York, Appleton Century, 1936.
Crowns and Sceptres: The Romance and Pageantry of Coronations. London, Long, 1937.
The Lady and the Arsenic: The Life and Death of a Romantic, Marie Capelle, Madame Lafarge (as Joseph Shearing). London, Heinemann, 1937; New York, A. S. Barnes, 1944.
This Shining Woman: Mary Wollstonecraft Godwin 1759–1797 (as George Preedy). London, Collins, and New York, Appleton Century, 1937.
Wrestling Jacob: A Study of the Life of John Wesley and Some Members of His Family. London, Heinemann, 1937; abridged edition, London, Watts, 1948.
World's Wonder and Other Essays. London, Hutchinson, 1938.
The Trumpet and the Swan: An Adventure of the Civil War (for children). London, Pitman, 1938.
The Debate Continues, Being the Autobiography of Marjorie Bowen, by Margaret Campbell. London, Heinemann, 1939.
Ethics in Modern Art (lecture). London, Watts, 1939.
Child of Chequer'd Fortune: The Life, Loves, and Battles of Maurice de Saxe, Maréchal de France (as George Preedy). London, Jenkins, 1939.
Strangers to Freedom (for children). London, Dent, 1940.
The Life of John Knox (as George Preedy). London, Jenkins, 1940.
The Life of Rear-Admiral John Paul Jones 1747–1792 (as George Preedy). London, Jenkins, 1940.
The Courtly Charlatan: The Enigmatic Comte de St. Germain (as George Preedy). London, Jenkins, 1942.
The Church and Social Progress: An Exposition of Rationalism and Reaction. London, Watts, 1945.
In the Steps of Mary, Queen of Scots. London, Rich and Cowan, 1952.

Editor, *Great Tales of Horror.* London, Lane, 1933.
Editor, *More Great Tales of Horror.* London, Lane, 1935.

Editor, *Some Famous Love Letters.* London, Jenkins, 1937.

*   *   *

Most of Margaret Campbell's books, under whichever pseudonym she wrote, are historical novels about real people or romances set in the past. Many of her crime novels either use period settings or are imaginative reconstructions of historical crimes. *My Tattered Loving (The King's Favourite)*, for instance, is a fictionalized account of the celebrated 17th-century Overbury murder.

Her historical novels as Marjorie Bowen are usually fictional biographies, and strongly partisan. She portrays Richard III in *Dickon* as a perfect medieval knight, *sans peur, sans reproche* (but let us not forget he was a contemporary of the Borgias). Her Richard could never have killed his brother Clarence or Henry VI, much less the Princes in the Tower, although the book shys away from this last issue. Her Richard is physically attractive—no mention of a withered arm or humpback here. In *The Governor of England* she portrays Cromwell as a compassionate private man who nevertheless believes that he has a divine mission and so reluctantly concludes that the king's death is necessary. Indeed Bowen seems to have held low opinions of all the Stuarts bar one. She draws a harsh portrait of James I slobbering and fawning in *The King's Favourite*, she refers to Charles II as a man who would but for his birth "have spent his life as a tavern idler buying his indulgences with his quips," and James II she castigates as "a pompous doll bigot—vain, sensuous and arrogant and to a curious degree cruel." Her great hero is William II, one of our dullest kings, little loved by his English subjects and who had little liking for England. Even her partisan writing fails to hide the fact that William only accepted the English crown as a means of vanquishing Louis XIV. Her trilogy on William's life, *I Will Maintain*, *Defender of the Faith*, and *God and the King*, shows this clearly. The first book covers his early years up to the Dutch Revolution of 1672 when he became Stadtholder; the second relates how he reluctantly married his cousin, the English princess Mary, fought Louis, and drew Holland together. The third book is about his time as King of England and shows his frustrations dealing with the English who disliked him. Bowen is above all William's apologist—she even tries to absolve him of any guilt for the Massacre of Glencoe in *The Glen o' Weeping*, but hardly convinces this reader. So fond was she of William and of Holland that, besides several nonfiction books on the subject, she also wrote about William III's ancestor William the Silent in *Prince and Heretic* and *William by the Grace of God* — .

Bowen often featured revolution in her books. *A Giant in Chains* is about the causes of the French revolution of 1789; *Forget-Me-Not* (as Joseph Shearing) concerns France in 1848 in the last days of Louis Philippe. *Dark Rosaleen* tells of the ill-fated Irish uprising of 1798; in it she draws a sympathetic portrait of Edward Fitzgerald, the idealistic younger son of one of Ireland's most important families who, influenced by the French revolution, was anxious to set Ireland free from English oppression. Because he was too noble and selfless to see or expect treachery, he died—not untypically for a Bowen book, for she dearly loved a doom-laden plot—seldom for her the happy ending. In her romances she created unhappy people and loaded the dice against them. *The Viper of Milan*, her first and probably most famous book (written when she was 17), is set in her version of 14th-century Italy. The chief character (one can hardly call one so infamous "hero") is the cruel, ruthless Visconti, ruler of Milan who kills or maims every member of his family, betrays his allies, and even kills his own true love. *Findernes' Flowers* (as George Preedy) and *The Rake's Progress* are typical of her light romances: both are set in the 18th century and tell of doomed families and star-crossed lovers; both have sad endings heavy with wasted lives.

Her historical backgrounds are full of well-researched details with rich descriptions of period clothes, but her style is too florid for today's taste and her dialogue is the most serious stumbling block for the modern reader, being full of "fair sirs" beseeching, t'were, and wert. Immensely popular in her own day, her books are rather neglected nowadays, for modern readers prefer faster moving stories and a lighter touch. Her characterisation lacks depth, and the thoughts and motives attributed to her characters (especially in the romances) are a little superficial, although her historical judgments are usually sound when she is not gripped by bias.

—Pamela Cleaver

BOYD, James. American. Born in Harrisburg, Pennsylvania, 2 July 1888. Educated at Hill School, Pottstown, Pennsylvania, 1901–06; Princeton University, New Jersey 1906–10, B.A. 1910; Trinity College, Cambridge, 1910–12. Served in the New York Infantry, 1916, as a Red Cross volunteer, 1917, and in the United States Army Ambulance Service, in Italy and France, 1917–19: Lieutenant. Married Katharine Lamont in 1917; two sons and one daughter. Staff writer and cartoonist, Harrisburg *Patriot*, 1910; teacher of English and French, Harrisburg Academy, 1912–14; member of the editorial staff, *Country Life in America*, New York, 1916; settled on a farm in Southern Pines, North Carolina, 1919: owner and editor, Southern Pines *Pilot*, 1941–44. Founder and first National Chairman, Free Company of Players, 1941. Honorary degree: University of North Carolina, Chapel Hill, 1938. Member, American Academy, 1937; Society of American Historians, 1939. *Died 25 February 1944*.

ROMANCE AND HISTORICAL PUBLICATIONS

Novels

Drums. New York, Scribner, 1925; London, Unwin, 1928.
Marching On. New York, Scribner, 1927; London, Heinemann, 1928.
Long Hunt. New York, Scribner, 1930; London, Jarrolds, 1931.
Roll River. New York, Scribner, 1935; London, Jarrolds, 1936.
Bitter Creek. New York, Scribner, 1939; London, Heinemann, 1940.

Short Stories

Old Pines and Other Stories. Chapel Hill, University of North Carolina Press, 1952.

OTHER PUBLICATIONS

Play

One More Free Man (broadcast 1941). Published in *The Free Company Presents*, edited by Boyd, New York, Dodd Mead, 1941.

Radio Play: *One More Free Man*, 1941.

Verse

Eighteen Poems. New York, Scribner, 1944.

Other

Mr. Hugh David MacWhirr Looks after His $1.00 Investment in the Pilot Newspaper (sketches). Southern Pines, North Carolina, The Pilot, 1943.

Editor, *The Free Company Presents: A Collection of Plays about the Meaning of America*. New York, Dodd Mead, 1941.

*

Critical Study: *James Boyd* by David E. Whisnant, New York, Twayne, 1972.

* * *

How significant is the central event to the success of a work of historical fiction? The American Civil War has provided the inspiration for several masterpieces, along with a list of books amounting to one a day since its battles ceased. By contrast, the American Revolution, for all its importance in world history, has failed to generate a single memorable work. James Boyd's endeavours with both of these monumental conflagrations provide a perspective not only on his own fiction, but also point up suggestions why a war largely confined to the southern United States shapes a global imagination, while the conflict which to a large effect served to separate Europe from the Americans remains a musty domain inhabited principally by historians and biographers.

Curiously, *Drums*, Boyd's treatment of, what is called by Americans, the War of Independence, is much better known than *Marching On*, which deals with the same family several generations later during the Civil War. *Marching On* still points up issues which were permanently to seize the mind of the young protagonist and which continue as passionate topics to the current day.

> James Fraser was listening now, fascinated and scandalized. These folks mixed up salvation, liquor, parsons and niggers in their talk—made a kind of joke of heaven, anyhow got fun out of talking about heaven—like it was any other place. No good would come of that.

Loosely paraphrased, themes of religion, race, utopia, leaders, and private passions first penetrate the mind through casual eavesdropping, expand into gossip, then take hold as ambition and livelihood, and sometimes embroil the fascinated in destructive conflicts in which the one-time entertained on-lookers become the sacrificial pawns of maniacal designs.

Somehow the often meandering, sometimes unwieldy structures of Boyd's books place the reader in a situation similar to that of the cast of characters. Like the reader, the figures which appear from page to page, seem swept along by circumstance. While it is true they retain a recognizable degree of self-determination, seldom sacrificing principle or surrendering quirks of personality, their principal function turns out to be spectators to grim, if sometime heroic events. Dr. Clapton, who occupies a minor role in *Drums* is a committed scholar and probably a promising author, one whose devotion to art and learning is unshakeable. Yet the war takes as its tithe not only his life, but also destroys the work dedicated to a posterity whose ranks have also been abbreviated by the ravages of sanctioned violence. John Fraser (presumably the great-uncle to James in *Marching On* is ostensibly an active figure. He becomes a student of the classics, studies in England, takes a quiet but dangerous loyalist position in North Carolina, but ends up fighting the British alongside John Paul Jones on the *Bonhomme Richard*. He evades the permanent attachments of love in a way consistent with the sexually unconcerned heroes of American fiction—Ahab, Huck Finn, Natty Bumppo (and their descendants Dick Tracy, Li'l Abner and Dagwood Bumstead), who are primarily walking philosophies rather than flesh and blood figures. John Fraser, for all his travels and involvements, remains that perpetual spectator, a feeling but detached extra on the set of a cinematic spectacular. James Fraser of *Marching On* is also an observer of grand if gory events, but there are signs that he wants to be the center of his own story just as Scarlet O'Hara dominated *Gone with the Wind* and Henry Fleming, in *The Red Badge of Courage*, emerges as perhaps the quintessential character of all Civil War fiction. James is a fiddler, a type of wandering minstrel, even when he remained in one place. He is conscious of ghosts of times past, times he had experienced but was never part of. The girl who occupies his thoughts started out as a voice, not a face or a figure. Eventually, however, the novel concludes with an impending marriage. James is not really a finely drawn character, but there are hints that he could become one. Perhaps it is the ultimate legacy of Civil War figures to seek out the meaning of life in terms of themselves since regional and national ideals proved so devastatingly inhumane. And it is such inward looking self-determination that separates a novel from a treatise. The American Revolution, by contrast, generates the theories which subordinate private lives to epic ideals.

Boyd is more concerned with events and settings than with characters. There is enough in his fiction, however to stimulate the excited status of the onlooker. What he subtracts from his characters he gives in full measure to his readers.

—Leonard R. Mendelsohn

BRADFORD, Barbara Taylor. British. Born in Leeds, Yorkshire, in 1933. Reporter, 1949–51, and women's editor, 1951–53, *Yorkshire Evening Post*, Leeds; fashion editor, *Woman's Own*, London, 1953–54; columnist, London *Evening News*, 1955–57; freelance editor, London, 1959–62; features editor, *Woman*, London, 1962–64; editor, National Design Center, New York, 1964–65; syndicated columnist, *Newsday*, Long Island, New York, 1966. Address: 450 Park Avenue South, New York, New York 10003, U.S.A.

ROMANCE AND HISTORICAL PUBLICATIONS

Novels (series: Harte Family)

A Woman of Substance (Harte). New York, Doubleday, 1979; London, Granada, 1980.
Voice of the Heart. New York, Doubleday, and London, Granada, 1983.
Hold the Dream (Harte). New York, Doubleday, and London, Granada, 1985.
Act of Will. New York, Doubleday, and London, Grafton, 1986.
To Be the Best (Harte). New York, Doubleday, and London, Granada, 1988.

OTHER PUBLICATIONS

Other

How to Be the Perfect Wife: Entertaining to Please Him [*Etiquette to Please Him, Fashions That Please Him*]. New York, Essandess, 3 vols., 1969–70.
Easy Steps to Successful Decorating. New York, Simon and Schuster, 1971.
How to Solve Your Decorating Problems. New York, Simon and Schuster, 1976.
Decorating Ideas for Casual Living. New York, Simon and Schuster, 1977.
Making Space Grow. New York, Simon and Schuster, 1979.
Luxury Designs for Apartment Living. New York, Doubleday, 1981.

Editor, *Children's Stories of the Bible from the Old Testament*. New York, Lion Press, 1966.
Editor, *Children's Stories of Jesus from the New Testament*. New York, Lion Press, 1966.
Editor, *The Dictionary of One Thousand Famous People*, by Samuel Nisenson. New York, Lion Press, 1966.
Editor, *A Garland of Children's Verse*. New York, Lion Press, 1968.
Editor, *The Complete Encyclopedia of Homemaking Ideas*. New York, Meredith Press, 1968.

*   *   *

Barbara Taylor Bradford writes multigenerational sagas, usually about strong women who build fortunes and become important people through their business acumen. There is a rags to riches theme in each of her works, which are full of vivid descriptions of clothing and the interiors and exteriors of buildings—a result of her own background in fashion and decorating.

Although the story outline is familiar, Bradford has added her own touch to the saga of Emma Harte's family and empire. *A Woman of Substance* traces Emma's life from youth into her 80th year. Along the way, she marries twice and maintains a 16-year grand passion with a third lover, having children with each man. Her first daughter, however, is by the son of her employer, a young man who repudiates her when she tells him of her pregnancy. His rejection focuses her attention, and she works hard to make a better life for herself and her children. She builds an empire, becoming one of the richest women in the world, but at the cost of a loving relationship with most of her children. Eventually, they try to betray her, a move she counteracts by bequeathing most of her fortune and businesses to her grandchildren, with whom she has taken the time to build love and trust.

Seven years after the first, Bradford published a sequel, *Hold the Dream*. The events of the earlier book are smoothly woven into this one, making a reprise unnecessary, although the two-page list of characters is helpful. The reader simply picks up the story where it left off. The concentration here is the training of Emma's granddaughter Paula to take over the empire. Along the way, all the grandchildren are assigned responsibilities which match their talents and interests. Emma never stops testing their competence and loyalty.

After Emma's death, betrayal surfaces again in the person of grandson Jonathan. Paula and her brother Alexander oust him from the business and the family. In *To Be the Best*, Jonathan strikes back, causing death and destruction when he can, and at the very least, consternation for Paula. She almost loses everything to him when she tries to prove herself as insightful as her grandmother. She overextends herself dreadfully and has to scramble to save the empire from Jonathan's greedy hands.

The trilogy is like a written soap opera, and that is exactly what Bradford's fans expect. Throughout the three books, life and death, love and hatred vie against each other.

In between each of these books, Bradford wrote other novels not connected with the trilogy. *Voice of the Heart* relates the tale of four people who start life poor and become wealthy through their own creative efforts. Katharine, a major movie star at an early age, is the central figure in the lives of all the other characters, manipulating and using them while justifying her own actions as offering help. She hurts them all deeply and finally returns after a long absence to seek their forgiveness, hoping their great love for her will transcend their anger. This is overly long but quite dramatic.

In *Act of Will*, Audra is forced to abandon her art to support herself and her child. She labors hard to give her daughter the opportunities she did not have and is upset when Christina decides to work in the fashion business instead. Christina, in turn, is perturbed when her daughter rejects fashion to be an artist. *Act of Will* is a light, enjoyable tale, much shorter than Bradford's other titles.

Bradford feels that people should be the emphasis in her writings. She analyzes each character carefully and tries to convey human emotions in such a way that the reader is touched or moved. Consequently, the individuals in her stories seem real. While her books may not become great enduring classics of literature, they are admired and enjoyed by her many fans.

—Andrea Lee Shuey

BRADLEY, Marion Zimmer. Has also written as Lee Chapman; John Dexter; Miriam Gardner; Valerie Graves; Morgan Ives. American. Born in Albany, New York, 3 June 1930. Educated at New York State College for Teachers, 1946–48; Hardin-Simmons University, Abilene, Texas, B.A. 1964; University of California, Berkeley. Married 1) Robert A. Bradley in 1949 (divorced 1963), one son; 2) Walter Henry Breen in 1964, one son and one daughter. Singer and writer. Recipient: *Locus* award, 1984. Agent: Scott Meredith Literary Agency, 845 Third Avenue, New York, New York 10022, U.S.A.

Romance and Historical Publications

Novels

The Mists of Avalon. New York, Knopf, 1982; London, Joseph, 1983.
The Firebrand. New York, Simon and Schuster, 1987; London, Joseph, 1988.

Other Publications

Novels

The Door Through Space. New York, Ace, 1961; London, Arrow, 1979.
Seven from the Stars. New York, Ace, 1962.
The Planet Savers, The Sword of Aldones. New York, Ace, 1962; London, Arrow, 2 vols., 1979.

I Am a Lesbian (as Lee Chapman). Derby, Connecticut, Monarch, 1962.
Spare Her Heaven (as Morgan Ives). Derby, Connecticut, Monarch, 1963; abridged edition, as *Anything Goes*, Sydney, Stag, 1964.
The Bloody Sun. New York, Ace, 1964; London, Arrow, 1978.
Falcons of Narabedla. New York, Ace, 1964; London, Arrow, 1984.
Star of Danger. New York, Ace, 1965; London, Arrow, 1978.
Castle Terror. New York, Lancer, 1965.
Knives of Desire (as Morgan Ives). San Diego, Corinth, 1966.
No Adam for Eve (as John Dexter). San Diego, Corinth, 1966.
Souvenir of Monique. New York, Ace, 1967.
Bluebeard's Daughter. New York, Lancer, 1968.
The Brass Dragon. New York, Ace, 1969; London, Methuen, 1978.
The Winds of Darkover. New York, Ace, 1970; London, Arrow, 1978.
The World Wreckers. New York, Ace, 1971; London, Arrow, 1979.
Darkover Landfall. New York, DAW, 1972; London, Arrow, 1978.
Witch Hill (as Valerie Graves). San Diego, Greenleaf, 1972.
Dark Satanic. New York, Berkley, 1972.
In the Steps of the Master (novelization of television play). New York, Grosset and Dunlap, 1973.
Hunters of the Red Moon. New York, DAW, 1973; London, Arrow, 1979.
The Spell Sword. New York, DAW, 1974; London, Arrow, 1978.
Endless Voyage. New York, Ace, 1975; revised edition, as *Endless Universe*, 1979.
The Heritage of Hastur. New York, DAW, 1975; London, Arrow, 1979.
Can Ellen Be Saved? (novelization of television play). New York, Grosset and Dunlap, 1975.
Drums of Darkness. New York, Ballantine, 1976.
The Shattered Chain. New York, DAW, 1976; London, Arrow, 1978.
The Forbidden Tower. New York, DAW, 1977; London, Prior, 1979.
Stormqueen. New York, DAW, 1978; London, Arrow, 1980.
The Ruins of Isis. Norfolk, Virginia, Donning, 1978; London, Arrow, 1980.
The Survivors, with Paul E. Zimmer. New York, DAW, 1979; London, Arrow, 1985.
The Catch Trap. New York, Ballantine, 1979; London, Sphere, 1986.
The House Between the Worlds. New York, Doubleday, 1980.
Two to Conquer. New York, DAW, 1980; London, Arrow, 1982.
Survey Ship. New York, Ace, 1980.
Sharra's Exile. New York, DAW, 1981; London, Arrow, 1983.
Hawkmistress. New York, DAW, 1982; London, Arrow, 1985.
Web of Light. Norfolk, Virginia, Donning, 1982.
Thendara House. New York, DAW, 1983; London, Arrow, 1985.
Web of Darkness. New York, Pocket Books, 1984; Glasgow, Drew, 1985.
The Inheritor. New York, Tor, 1984.
City of Sorcery. New York, DAW, 1984; London, Arrow, 1986.
Night's Daughter. New York, Ballantine, and London, Inner Circle, 1985.
Warrior Woman. New York, DAW, 1985; London, Arrow, 1987.
Red Sun of Darkover. New York, DAW, 1987.

Novels as Miriam Gardner

The Strange Women. Derby, Connecticut, Monarch, 1962.
My Sister, My Love. Derby, Connecticut, Monarch, 1963.
Twilight Lovers. Derby, Connecticut, Monarch, 1964.

Short Stories

The Dark Intruder and Other Stories. New York, Ace, 1964.
The Jewel of Arwen. Baltimore, T-K Graphics, 1974.
The Parting of Arwen. Baltimore, T-K Graphics, 1974.
Swords of Chaos, with others. New York, DAW, 1982.
Lythande. New York, DAW, 1986.
The Best of Marion Zimmer Bradley, edited by Martin H.
  Greenberg. New York, DAW, 1988.

Other

Songs from Rivendell. Privately printed, 1959.
*A Complete, Cumulative Checklist of Lesbian, Variant, and Ho-
  mosexual Fiction*. Privately printed, 1960.
The Colors of Space (for children). Derby, Connecticut, Monarch, 1963.
Men, Halflings, and Hero-Worship. Baltimore, T-K Graphics,
  1973.
*The Necessity for Beauty: Robert W. Chambers and the Roman-
  tic Tradition*. Baltimore, T-K Graphics, 1974.

Editor, *The Keeper's Price*. New York, DAW, 1980.
Editor, *Greyhaven*. New York, DAW, 1983.
Editor, *Sword and Sorceress 1–2*. New York, DAW, 1984–85;
  vol. 1 published London, Headline, 1988.
Editor, *Free Amazons of Darkover*. New York, DAW, 1985.
Editor, *Four Moons of Darkover*. New York, DAW, 1988.

Translator, *El Villano in su Rincon*, by Lope de Vega. Privately
  printed, 1971.

*

Bibliography: *Leigh Brackett, Marion Zimmer Bradley, Anne
McCaffrey: A Primary and Secondary Bibliography* by Rose-
marie Arbur, Boston, Hall, 1982.

Manuscript Collection: Boston University.

*   *   *

Marion Zimmer Bradley's earlier work was in the field of science fiction, and her imaginary world of Darkover remains immensely popular. It was only with *The Mists of Avalon*, however,
that her name became known to a wider readership; indeed, that
book has if anything gained in popularity since it first became a
bestseller. The book inspires a devoted loyalty almost bordering
upon a cult, especially in the United States where the values it
evokes are shared by a large proportion of "the counterculture."
Its combination of potent feminism, neo-pagan mysticism, and
fantasy were inspired by the student movement of the 1960's.

The plot recounts the Arthurian legend, and in its larger structures adheres to the storyline of Malory's *Le Morte Darthur*; but
it makes a radical departure from the medieval saga by the bold
manner in which the female characters are made to be the principals. The book is narrated entirely from the female perspective, and especially through the figure of Morgaine (Morgan Le
Fay) and her counterpart Gwenhyfar (Queen Guinevere). Thus
transformed, the story's centre of gravity shifts away from the

tales of valour, battle, and questing, to become instead a subtle
web of personal and political intrigue. The women are very often
seen weaving, and it is no coincidence that it is largely through
their agency that the fate of Arthur and his court is woven.

At the centre of the rehabilitated Arthurian legend is the conflict between the pagan powers of Avalon (represented largely
through Morgaine, the high priestess of the cult) and Gwenhyfar,
who converts Arthur and his court to Christianity. One major
flaw in the book is that this dichotomy is in no way presented in
a balanced manner: Morgaine's party, and personality, are dedicated to the pursuit of higher mysteries through a metaphysical
system whose rhythms are natural and sexual; in contrast, Gwenhyfar's Christianity is the result of sexual frustration, ignorance,
and barrenness. In consequence, it ultimately produces nothing
but repression and superstition. In a climactic moment, Morgaine causes the holy Druid relic of the grail to transform into a
magical apparition of great power; Gwenhyfar and the court, receiving the vision, take it to be a Christian omen of the holy
grail. The subsequent quest is divisive and tragically, weakening
to the unity of Arthur's realm. It is easy, as it is in *The Lord of
the Rings*, to read a contemporary political-social allegory into
such episodes, but even without this element the story remains
fascinating for its portrayal of the nexus between personal, political, and religious forces in the detailed characters of its heroines.

The Firebrand does largely the same thing in its retelling of
the legend of Troy. Again, the story comes from the viewpoint
of its women characters; again, the central figure is a priestess
of a cult in which women are respected and powerful. In this
case the protagonist's role is reserved for Kassandra, who in the
Homeric version is little more than pathetic. In this instance she
is invested with the memorable character and tragic stature with
which Morgaine was graced. In many ways the narrative strategies are strictly analogous to those of *The Mists Of Avalon*:
patriarchal society and metaphysics comes to conquer the older,
feminine existence, the strong protagonist is caught in the web of
fate, becoming the victim of changing forces, and finally an
exile. The very existence of the books implies the logical next
process: male society translates the story in its own terms, and
the heroines become the evil enchantresses and witches of legend. This is exemplified from the very first in *The Firebrand*,
when in a prologue the lady Kassandra, years after the events in
the main text, invites a bard to sing. He begins the first few
lines of the *Iliad*, and she cuts him short, warning him not to
misrepresent the events she has witnessed.

These works are not, of course, strictly historical. The legends they recount are only thinly documented at best, and may
in fact be completely fictional. Despite this, they are thoroughly
researched in their respective backgrounds; the rest might be
classified as conjectural fiction. For Bradley, the supernormal
phenomena of clairvoyance and magic may not be entirely fantastic; the introduction to *The Mists Of Avalon* shows that she
takes modern neo-pagan groups very seriously, and may indeed
subscribe to their beliefs. So, while not documentary history,
there is some justification for considering them as historically
inspired. Perhaps, taking our cue from the Arthurian legend, we
could describe them as romances in the oldest sense.

—Alan Murphy

BRADSHAW, Gillian (Marucha). American. Born in Virginia, 14 May 1956. Educated at the University of Michigan,
Ann Arbor (Hopwood award, 1977), B.A. (honors) 1977; Newn-

ham College, Cambridge, M.A. 1979. Married Robin Christopher Ball in 1981. Address: c/o Houghton Mifflin Company, 2 Park Street, Boston, Massachusetts 02108, U.S.A.

ROMANCE AND HISTORICAL PUBLICATIONS

Novels

Down the Long Wind: The Magical Trilogy of Arthurian Britain. London, Methuen, 1984.
   Hawk of May. New York, Simon and Schuster, 1980; London, Eyre Methuen, 1981.
   Kingdom of Summer. New York, Simon and Schuster, and London, Eyre Methuen, 1981.
   In Winter's Shadow. New York, Simon and Schuster, and London, Methuen, 1982.
The Beacon at Alexandria. Boston, Houghton Mifflin, 1986; London, Methuen, 1987.
The Bearkeeper's Daughter. Boston, Houghton Mifflin, 1987; London, Methuen, 1988.
Imperial Purple. Boston, Houghton Mifflin, 1989; as *The Colour of Power*, London, Methuen, 1989.

*   *   *

Gillian Bradshaw takes as her subject the 5th and 6th centuries and the crumbling farthest boundaries of the Roman Empire. Her first three novels are set in Arthurian Britain, the margin of the western empire. She then turns her attention to the borders in the east. To both areas she brings a clear understanding of the consequences of the Roman retreat from the border kingdoms and the ensuing memory of the empire. A vision of the breadth of the empire informs her work: "I closed my eyes and thought of the empire, a ring of cities around the Middle Sea, spreading up the Euxine, up the Nile, up into the inland wildernesses, from remote Britain to the Persian frontier, from the Rhine and the Danube as far south as the deserts of Africa and the lands of the Ethiopians" (*The Beacon at Alexandria*).

The Arthurian trilogy, set in Britain in the century after the departure of the Roman legions, is particularly effective in its evocation of the once luxurious houses of the Romans, the broken hypocaust, the atrium thatched over, and the memory of the imperial system of justice that animates Arthur and his family. Bradshaw centers the trilogy around the story of Gwalchmai, second son of King Lot and Morgawse, in a sequence that grows steadily more powerful. The character, Gwalchmai, is developed from the Gawain stories, but also owes something to Gwalchmei, the Welsh sun god. That element is strongest in the first book, *Hawk of May*, which is narrated by the hero himself as he tells of his youth, his conflict and escape from his sorceress mother, Morgawse. The book manages to make Gwalchmai's transportation to the Otherworld and his acquisition of his magical sword, Caledvwlch, and his horse, Ceincaled, convincing. Despite Arthur's initial reluctance to admit Gwalchmai into the family, for he fears Gwalchmai knows of his incestuous liaison with his half-sister, Morgawse, the novel ends with Gwalchmai's triumphant swearing of the three-fold oath of loyalty to Arthur. The second book, *Kingdom of Summer*, is narrated by Rhys ap Sion, a farmer's son who leaves his clan to serve Gwalchmai, as he seeks out Elidan, the lover who cannot forgive him for his murder of her brother. The third, *In Winter's Shadow*, is narrated by Gwynhwyfar, Arthur's queen and administrator of Camlann.

This final novel weaves together the strands of the story—the familial rivalries of the sons of Morgawse, the adultery of Gwynhwyfar, and the poisonous machinations of Medraut Arthur's son by incest—which destroy Camlann from within. Bradshaw achieves a genuine sense of loss with the destruction of imperial law and the collapse of Britain into warring internecine factions. Though Bradshaw chooses a female narrator for this last book, like Mary Renault, who acclaimed her work, her sympathies are not with the domestic, nor even with love. She presents Gwynhwyfar as an exceptional woman, an administrator of a complex fortress, the executive who buys grain, bargains for wool, and administers justice. Gwynhwyfar's disastrous love for Bedwyr is explained as a result of the strains of rule, not the fires of passionate emotion. The representation of Morgawse as the evil sorceress of darkness, while chilling, remains conventional. Bradshaw's greatest sympathies lie with the courteous and ascetic Gwalchmai and the philosophic and tormented Bedwyr. It is paternal love that is explored most closely in Gwalchmai's joyous discovery of his son, Gwyn.

In *The Beacon at Alexandria*, Bradshaw turns to the eastern empire. The novel begins in Ephesus, with its narrator trapped in the restricted domestic sphere of a 5th-century patrician woman. When Charis cross-dresses to become Chariton, the eunuch, and escapes from home to pursue medical studies in Alexandria, the novel gains energy. The heroine's acquisition of medical knowledge and skill is engaging and celebrates the rich, cosmopolitan intersection of cultures and beliefs in Alexandria. Trapped in sectarian conflict between Arian and Athanasian, Chariton flees to the northern boundaries of Thrace as an army doctor. Bradshaw gives a sympathetic analysis of the repeated betrayals that trapped the Gothic rulers in border kingdoms and precipitated the first disastrous defeat of the Roman legions at Hadrianopolis. She makes clear the provincial rivalries, the ambitions, corruption, and stupidity that eroded the rule of Roman law and encouraged the collapse of empire.

The name of Theodosius the Great, last ruler of the united empire, is evoked throughout Bradshaw's first four novels. *Imperial Purple* centers on Demetrias, a weaver, and her entanglement in a plot for the overthrow of Theodosius II, the weak emperor of the east who had to confront Attila the Hun. Bradshaw has a remarkable ability to animate the intricate political intrigue that preceded the fall of Rome; she gives life to a complex and fascinating period, though she has yet to reach the emotional intensity of her model, Mary Renault.

—Karen Robertson

BRAMWELL, Charlotte. See **KIMBROUGH, Katheryn.**

BRANDEWYNE, Rebecca. American. Born in Knoxville, Tennessee, 4 March 1955. Educated at Wichita State University, Kansas, B.A. (cum laude) in journalism, 1975, M.A. in communications, 1979. Married Gary D. Brock; one son. Worked as a secretary; freelance writer in public relations and advertising. Address: 2203 Winstead Circle, Wichita, Kansas 67226, U.S.A.

ROMANCE AND HISTORICAL PUBLICATIONS

Novels (series: Highclyffe Hall)

No Gentle Love. New York, Warner, 1980.
Forever My Love. New York, Warner, 1982.

Love, Cherish Me. New York, Warner, 1983; London, Panther, 1984.

Rose of Rapture. New York, Warner, and London, Panther, 1984.

And Gold Was Ours. New York, Warner, 1984; London, Grafton, 1986.

The Outlaw Hearts. New York, Warner, 1986; London, Grafton, 1987.

Desire in Disguise. New York, Warner, 1987.

Passion Moon Rising. New York, Pocket Books, 1988.

Upon a Moon-Dark Moor (Highclyffe Hall). New York, Warner, 1988; London, Severn House, 1989.

Across a Starlit Sea (Highclyffe Hall). New York, Warner, 1989.

*   *   *

The historical romances of Rebecca Brandewyne have proven extremely popular since her first novel *No Gentle Love.* In this story and those that follow the hero and heroine experience an immediate desire for each other when they first meet, but misunderstandings, based on their mutual inability to communicate their feelings, create barriers to the love that eventually develops. In *No Gentle Love,* for example, the cousins Morgana and Rian are forced into a marriage plotted by their grandfather. Rian, a notorious womanizer, has trouble acknowledging that there can be only one woman in his life while Morgana consistently misunderstands the actions of her husband when he does reach out to her. Not until almost the very last page do they discover what the reader has known all along, that yes, indeed, they do love one another. In the recent novel, *Upon a Moon-Dark Moor* misunderstandings abound, yet despite these, Maggie and the brooding, half-gypsy hero Draco gradually come to appreciate and care for one another. The characters in this novel are especially well drawn and, unlike many books of this genre, the emphasis here is on plot and character development rather than on how often the heroine and her lover can find sexual fulfillment. That is not to say that elaborate sex scenes are absent. They are essential in stories of this type. But this and other Brandewyne novels seem to have more substance than most books in the romance field.

The historical backgrounds for her novels vary widely. The *Outlaw Hearts* takes place in Missouri where Jenny, a young woman with traumatic memories of the Civil War falls in love with the handsome outlaw Luke Morgan. (Another point worth noting is that the heroine is not beautiful but plain and walks with a noticeable limp; hardly standard fare in a romance novel.) In *Upon a Moon-Dark Moor* Maggie grows up a lonely privileged child, in early 19th-century Cornwall. Lady Isabella Ashley (*Rose of Rapture*) lives under the protection of King Richard III of England; and Mary Carmichael in *Forever My Love* meets her love in the highlands of 15th-century Scotland. When the author researches thoroughly she is quite capable of portraying authentic historical settings; however, the times she does not are painfully obvious. The African scenes of *No Gentle Love* have stereotypical natives marauding through the jungle. There is no pretense of trying to convey the horrifying effects of the slave trade on the African people. Thankfully this lapse seems to be the exception rather than the rule.

Brandewyne has a fascination with "other worldly" events which surfaces from time to time in her works. A ghost haunts the mansion in *No Gentle Love.* Aurora, the heroine of *And Gold Was Ours,* has haunting visions of a lover from a time three centuries before her own. It is therefore not surprising that Brandewyne is one of the few authors successfully to combine two genres—romance and fantasy—which she did with the pu-

lication of *Passion Moon Rising.* The story takes place after a universal, apocalyptic battle between forces of light and darkness. Now the war continues on surviving, isolated planets, here focusing on Tintagel, where the Lady Ileana sin Ariel carries the power of light and the hero Lord Cain holds both light and darkness within him. The florid writing of this novel is the kind often found in other works of fantasy; yet, it contrasts with the usual clear, crisp style found in Brandewyne's other novels. She is especially good at constructing dialog, making the conversation sound natural, even witty at times. The breathless prose usually found in romance novels is saved for scenes of love and passion. Brandewyne brings an intelligence to her fiction often lacking in other works of the genre.

—Patricia Altner

BRANDON, Sheila. See **RAYNER, Claire.**

BRENT, Madeleine. A pseudonym. Recipient: Romantic Novelists Association Major award, 1978. Address: c/o Souvenir Press Ltd., 43 Great Russell Street, London WC1B 3PA, England.

ROMANCE AND HISTORICAL PUBLICATIONS

Novels

Tregaron's Daughter. London, Souvenir Press, and New York, Doubleday, 1971.

Moonraker's Bride. London, Souvenir Press, and New York, Doubleday, 1973.

Kirkby's Changeling. London, Souvenir Press, 1975; as *Stranger at Wildings,* New York, Doubleday, 1976.

Merlin's Keep. London, Souvenir Press, 1977; New York, Doubleday, 1978.

The Capricorn Stone. London, Souvenir Press, 1979; New York, Doubleday, 1980.

The Long Masquerade. London, Souvenir Press, 1981; New York, Doubleday, 1982.

A Heritage of Shadows. London, Souvenir Press, 1983; New York, Doubleday, 1984.

Stormswift. London, Souvenir Press, 1984; New York, Doubleday, 1985.

Golden Urchin. London, Souvenir Press, 1986; New York, Doubleday, 1987.

*   *   *

Madeleine Brent creates heroines who claim to be ordinary but who are really far from average women. While none of them has any pretensions to feminism, each has qualities usually associated in romantic novels with male characters. Their unusual upbringings or early life choices forced upon them make them strong, resourceful, determined, and persistent. As adults, many of them pursue careers. This is an even more interesting detail as the novels are set in Victorian England, a combination of period and location not often associated with women serving in capacities other than menial. None of these delightful women regards her talents as anything but ordinary, whether these talents are the ability to fly on a trapeze (*Merlin's Keep*) or to scent food and water in the Australian outback (*Golden Urchin*). The common thread that connects the heroines in each book is the necessity for each woman to prove herself, first in her early years and then again to create the denouement of the tale. While some of the plots and locations border on the outrageous, involving such melodramatic elements as slavery and concubinage, the writing is uniformly believable and the characters perfectly natural in their interactions.

The locations in Brent's work are as out-of-the-ordinary as the women. England is a sort of home base in each book, but much of the action occurs in places as diverse as Tibet, the Dordogne, China, and Italy. Whether the setting is a fisherman's cottage in Cornwall or a mission in China, however, the descriptions ring true, for Brent has the ability to sketch surroundings with words. In fact, the strength of her descriptions lies in her ability to assume the reader's familiarity with the scene that she portrays. She does not backtrack into an abundance of detail but touches upon salient features as if reminding a friend of a well-known spot.

The men in these novels are more realistically drawn than in many romances. The secondary male characters are quite unusual by being older men; Sembur and Mr. Lambert in *Merlin's Keep* and Sir Robert in *Kirkby's Changeling* are treated sympathetically and at great length. Brent also makes hero look like villain and villain like hero very successfully, as in *Moonraker's Bride*, where the reader is as uncertain as the heroine about which man to trust. The heroes as well as the heroines prove unusual in that they are neither paragons nor prigs, but larger-than-life mortals who live dramatic lives.

Additionally in the ranks of secondary characters, each book contains an older female who assumes the role of mentor to the heroine. Like the central women, these maternal or semi-maternal figures are women out of their times in terms of their wisdom, their free-thinking attitudes and their professional success. It is also interesting to note that Brent is not committed to the idea of exclusively male villains, as she proves in *Stormswift* with the creation of a compelling evil woman.

The plots of these novels are complex, with strong elements of mystery. Each book is bipartite; it almost seems that the works are divided down the middle into compartments in the heroine's life. Neither compartment is complete without the other, but the line of division is strongly marked, often by a geographical shift.

A review of all of Brent's works indicates that the most basic elements of plot and character do not vary from book to book: a strong woman in an extraordinary situation, a choice between hero and villain, the heroine triumphant on the strength of her own character. It might, therefore, be argued that these are formula novels. That description fails to do justice to these fast-moving romances, for it implies a perfunctory style. The skeleton of each book may be the same. The flesh, however, is deft description, naturalistic dialogue, and vivid characterization that give the books their unique personalities and sets them above most romances.

—Susan Quinn Berneis

BRETT, Rosalind. See **BLAIR, Kathryn.**

BRIDGE, Ann. Pseudonym for Lady Mary Dolling O'Malley, née Sanders. British. Born in Shenley, Hertfordshire, 11 September 1889. Educated at the London School of Economics, diploma 1913. Married Sir Owen St. Clair O'Malley in 1913; two daughters and one son. Secretary, Charity Organization Society, London, 1911–13; British Red Cross representative in Hungary, 1940–41; worked with the Polish Red Cross, 1944–45, and relief worker in France after World War II. Fellow, Society of Antiquaries in Scotland. *Died 9 March 1974.*

ROMANCE AND HISTORICAL PUBLICATIONS

Novels (series: Julia Probyn in *The Lighthearted Quest* and all books thereafter)

Peking Picnic. London, Chatto and Windus, and Boston, Little Brown, 1932.
The Ginger Griffin. London, Chatto and Windus, and Boston, Little Brown, 1934.
Illyrian Spring. London, Chatto and Windus, and Boston, Little Brown, 1935.
Enchanter's Nightshade. London, Chatto and Windus, and Boston, Little Brown, 1937.
Four-Part Setting. London, Chatto and Windus, and Boston, Little Brown, 1939.
Frontier Passage. London, Chatto and Windus, and Boston, Little Brown, 1942.
Singing Waters. London, Chatto and Windus, 1945; New York, Macmillan, 1946.
And Then You Came. London, Chatto and Windus, 1948; New York, Macmillan, 1949.
The Dark Moment. London, Chatto and Windus, 1951; New York, Macmillan, 1952.
A Place to Stand. London, Chatto and Windus, and New York, Macmillan, 1953.
The Lighthearted Quest. London, Chatto and Windus, and New York, Macmillan, 1956.
The Portuguese Escape. London, Chatto and Windus, and New York, Macmillan, 1958.
The Numbered Account, with Susan Lowndes. London, Chatto and Windus, and New York, McGraw Hill, 1960.
Julia Involved (omnibus). New York, McGraw Hill, 1962.
The Tightening String. London, Chatto and Windus, and New York, McGraw Hill, 1962.
The Dangerous Islands. New York, McGraw Hill, 1963; London, Chatto and Windus, 1964.
Emergency in the Pyrenees. London, Chatto and Windus, and New York, McGraw Hill, 1965.
The Episode at Toledo. New York, McGraw Hill, 1966; London, Chatto and Windus, 1967.
The Malady in Madeira. New York, McGraw Hill, 1969; London, Chatto and Windus, 1970.
Julia in Ireland. New York, McGraw Hill, 1973.

Short Stories

The Song in the House. London, Chatto and Windus, 1936.

OTHER PUBLICATIONS

Other

The Selective Traveller in Portugal, with Susan Lowndes. London, Evans, 1949; New York, Knopf, 1952; revised edition, London, Chatto and Windus, 1958, 1967; New York, McGraw Hill, 1961.

The House of Kilmartin (for children). London, Evans, 1951.

Portrait of My Mother. London, Chatto and Windus, 1955; as *A Family of Two Worlds*, New York, Macmillan, 1955.

Facts and Fictions: Some Literary Recollections. London, Chatto and Windus, and New York, McGraw Hill, 1968.

Moments of Knowing: Some Personal Experiences Beyond Normal Knowledge. London, Hodder and Stoughton, and New York, McGraw Hill, 1970.

Permission to Resign: Goings-On in the Corridors of Power. London, Sidgwick and Jackson, 1971.

*   *   *

In one of her novels Ann Bridge wrote, "is there any human pleasure much keener than the return after absence to a well-loved place, a place long familiar, full of associations of happiness?" This is the key to her writing, because in each of her books, besides setting in motion believable characters and exploring a human situation, she uses a place as the mainspring of her work. Her experiences as a diplomatic wife in China gave her the background for *Peking Picnic*, *The Ginger Griffin*, *Four-Part Setting* and her best short story "The Buick Saloon." Her experiences and the places she visited while *en poste* with her husband are used in *Frontier Passage*, a novel about the Spanish civil war, and *A Place to Stand* and *The Tightening String*, about Hungary in the 1940's. These three are semi-documentaries, blending historical and imaginary happenings. Another "modern historical novel" is *The Dark Moment*, about the part played by women in Kemal Ataturk's revolution in Turkey. While she was in Turkey she researched it by talking to women who actually took part in the events. *Illyrian Spring*, a story set in Yugoslavia, actually popularised tourism there, a fact she laughs at, caricaturing herself as Susan Glanfield, the authoress who achieved this in *Singing Waters*, a novel about Albania which is otherwise a dull, tiresome read with unsympathetic characters.

Usually her characterisation is good. She mostly writes about well-bred, upper-class people with money and servants—apart from the occasional highland laird who is terribly poor but so well connected that it does not matter (Glasdeir's well-married daughter in *And Then You Came*, for instance, provides new cars and cattle gates with the wave of a fairy godmother's wand). In most of her books there is a charming middle-aged woman in whom the younger heroine can confide—the middle-aged lady is often the nicest character in the book, and is, one feels, probably based on herself. She usually has several aristocratic men about the place—either strong and silent or sensitive and articulate, and always very capable. Her plots centre on happy and unhappy love affairs set against marvellous descriptions of her beloved places. Her characters are not only concerned about marriage but about making the right sort of marriage, and there is a snobbish preoccupation with money and breeding which was probably acceptable in the 1930's and 1940's when she wrote but which jars a little today.

Bridge's writing has a leisurely pace and a certain coolness. If occasionally she runs to a purple passage when her characters' emotions are aroused she soon brings them down to earth by sending them into the village to fetch the fish or down to the market to collect flowers to decorate their charming houses. Nothing really nasty ever happens in a Bridge book, although she often puts an illness into the story to give it tension and does not shy away from death but treats it rather sentimentally. Details of her research are sometimes used too fully with an almost teacherly eagerness, but her plots are well thought out and her characters well rounded.

Bridge's later books are a series of romantic thrillers using a basic cast of the same characters centred on her heroine, Julia Probyn (a cool, beautiful journalist who looks dumb but is not), and Julia's charming middle-aged godmother, Mrs. Hathaway, who do amateur sleuthing in exotic places among delightful, well-connected people—the strain of snobbery is stronger than ever in this series. *The Lighthearted Quest* has Morocco for its setting and smuggling for its plot, *The Episode at Toledo* and *Emergency in the Pyrenees* are set in Spain and Portugal, *The Numbered Account* takes place in Switzerland and contrasts banking and diplomacy, and *The Dangerous Islands* (like her interesting fantasy book *And Then You Came*) uses the West Highlands of Scotland and archaeology.

All Bridge's books (with the exception of *Singing Waters*) have a great deal of charm, many acute observations on life and people, and are very satisfying to read.

—Pamela Cleaver

———————

BRISCO, Patty. See **MATTHEWS, Patricia.**

———————

BRISTOW, Gwen. American. Born in Marion, South Carolina, 16 September 1903. Educated at Anderson College, South Carolina; Judson College, Marion, Alabama, A.B. 1924; Columbia University School of Journalism, New York, 1924–25. Married Bruce Manning in 1929 (died). Journalist, New Orleans *Times-Picayune*, 1925–34. *Died 16 August 1980.*

Romance and Historical Publications

Novels (series: Plantation Trilogy)

Plantation Trilogy. New York, Crowell, 1962.
  Deep Summer. New York, Crowell, and London, Heinemann, 1937.
  The Handsome Road. New York, Crowell, and London, Heinemann, 1938.
  This Side of Glory. New York, Crowell, and London, Heinemann, 1940.
Tomorrow Is Forever. New York, Crowell, 1943; London, Heinemann, 1944.
Jubilee Trail. New York, Crowell, 1950; London, Eyre and Spottiswoode, 1953.
Celia Garth. New York, Crowell, 1959; London, Eyre and Spottiswoode, 1960.
Calico Palace. New York, Crowell, 1970; London, Eyre and Spottiswoode, 1971.

Other Publications

Novels with Bruce Manning

The Invisible Host. New York, Mystery League, 1930; as *The Ninth Guest*, New York Popular Library, 1975.
The Gutenberg Murders. New York, Mystery League, 1931.
Two and Two Make Twenty-Two. New York, Mystery League, 1932.
The Mardi Gras Murders. New York, Mystery League, 1932.

Verse

The Alien and Other Poems. Boston, Badger, 1926.

Other

Gwen Bristow: A Self Portrait. New York, Crowell, 1940.
Golden Dreams. New York, Lippincott and Crowell, 1980.

*   *   *

History takes precedence over romance in the novels of Gwen Bristow. Her plots are detailed and neatly resolved and her characters are sharply drawn, if with broad strokes; but she reserves her greatest skill for the unfolding of American history as displayed around the lives of the people who created it.

For the most part, Bristow's novels follow a central female character through a tumultuous period of America's development. Her *Plantation Trilogy* (which includes *Deep Summer*, *The Handsome Road* and *This Side of Glory*) reads like a single volume with three heroines. They are united by the location of neighboring plantations in Louisiana but separated in time from the 1700's to the 1920's. These three relatively short works form a unified whole about equal in length to the longer single novels like *Jubilee Trail* or *Calico Palace*. Each of the three sections of the trilogy stands alone quite effectively, but only when taken as a whole do they give the author's characteristic overview of history. *Tomorrow Is Forever*, a shorter work published at the height of America's involvement in World War II, is her only contemporary novel. Even so, it flashes back to World War I through the life of Elizabeth, the heroine. There is less emphasis upon the flow of history in this work and more upon the examination of war and its effect on men and nations. The overall effect is more that of propaganda piece than historical novel, and *Tomorrow Is Forever* as a whole seems atypical of Bristow's body of work.

If fault can be found with Bristow's plots it lies in the foreshadowing of pivotal events in the characters' lives, often through undue emphasis on minor details. For example, when Loren in *Calico Palace* warns a child not to sit on a dirty nail the unconscious focus on this minor transaction predicts Loren's death from an injury received from the same nail. At that point in the narrative Loren has served his purpose in the heroine's life and his departure seems ordained. On a larger scale, the true identity of Mr. Kessler in *Tomorrow Is Forever* is predictable, based on the emphasis given to Elizabeth's special relationship with her first husband, Arthur. The tragedies and triumphs experienced by the characters follow relatively obvious patterns with few surprises for the reader. The stories are quite adequate, however, when played out against such exciting times and settings.

Bristow's characters suffer somewhat in comparison to the breadth of her historical knowledge and her skill at developing an era. The heroines of all the novels are nearly identical, being described as attractive rather than beautiful and willful in a style out of keeping with their times. Additionally each is drawn as a loner who craves love and a sense of belonging. The secondary female characters are often "bad girls" and Bristow lavishes more attention on them, sometimes to the detriment of the heroine. In *Calico Palace* she unexpectedly switches the point of view several times from the beleaguered heroine Kendra to the delightfully wicked Marny. The men, the putative makers of history, are divided between charming, weak connivers who appear early in the heroine's life and strong, capable men who form bonds with her after she has proven that she can take care of herself. In some works, these two types are represented by a single hero with both strong and weak traits. The most interesting aspect of the characters in all the novels is how they are changed by history even as they live it. In *Celia Garth* the Tories and the rebels trade social status and power with their fluctuating success in war. In the *Plantation Trilogy* some farmers become aristocrats and some become "poor white trash" depending upon chance and personal choices.

The novelistic portions of these volumes are pleasant, palatable garments for the real focus: American history. While the reader is being entertained, there is also instruction. The periods that Bristow selects are exciting enough in themselves; her eye for just the right detail and her breakneck pace make history a living entity guaranteed to capture her audience.

—Susan Quinn Berneis

———————

BRITT, Katrina. Address: c/o Mills and Boon Ltd., 18–24 Paradise Road, Richmond, Surrey TW9 1SR, England.

ROMANCE AND HISTORICAL PUBLICATIONS

Novels

A Kiss in a Gondola. London, Mills and Boon, 1968; Toronto, Harlequin, 1969.
Healer of Hearts. London, Mills and Boon, 1969; Toronto, Harlequin, 1970.
A Fine Romance. London, Mills and Boon, 1969.
The Fabulous Island. London, Mills and Boon, 1970; Toronto, Harlequin, 1971.
The Masculine Touch. London, Mills and Boon, 1970
The Unknown Quest. London, Mills and Boon, and Toronto, Harlequin, 1971.
The Gentle Flame. London, Mills and Boon, 1971; Toronto, Harlequin, 1973.
A Spray of Edelweiss. London, Mills and Boon, and Toronto, Harlequin, 1972.
Strange Bewilderment. London, Mills and Boon, and Toronto, Harlequin, 1973.
Reluctant Voyager. London, Mills and Boon, and Toronto, Harlequin, 1973.
The Guarded Gates. London, Mills and Boon, 1973; Toronto, Harlequin, 1974.
Famous Island. Toronto, Harlequin, n.d.
The Greater Happiness. London, Mills and Boon, 1974; Toronto, Harlequin, 1975.
The House Called Sakura. London, Mills and Boon, 1974; Toronto, Harlequin, 1975.
The King of Spades. London, Mills and Boon, and Toronto, Harlequin, 1974.
The Cruiser in the Bay. London, Mills and Boon, 1975.
Take Back Your Love. London, Mills and Boon, and Toronto, Harlequin, 1975.
The Spanish Grandee. London, Mills and Boon, 1975; Toronto, Harlequin, 1976.
The Emerald Garden. London, Mills and Boon, and Toronto, Harlequin, 1976.
Girl in Blue. London, Mills and Boon, 1976; Toronto, Harlequin, 1977.
If Today Be Sweet. London, Mills and Boon, 1976; Toronto, Harlequin, 1977.
The Villa Faustina. Toronto, Harlequin, 1977.

The Faithful Heart. London, Mills and Boon, and Toronto, Harlequin, 1977.
The Silver Tree. London, Mills and Boon, 1977; Toronto, Harlequin, 1978.
The Enchanted Woods. London, Mills and Boon, and Toronto, Harlequin, 1978.
The Hills Beyond. London, Mills and Boon, 1978.
Open Not the Door. London, Mills and Boon, and Toronto, Harlequin, 1978.
The Man on the Peak. London, Mills and Boon, 1979.
Flowers for My Love. London, Mills and Boon, 1979; Toronto, Harlequin, 1980.
The Midnight Sun. London, Mills and Boon, 1979.
The Wrong Man. London, Mills and Boon, 1980; Toronto, Harlequin, 1981.
A Girl Called Tegi. London, Mills and Boon, 1980.
Island for Dreams. London, Mills and Boon, and Toronto, Harlequin, 1980.
Hotel Jacarandas. London, Mills and Boon, 1980.
Another Time, Another Place. London, Mills and Boon, 1981.
Conflict of Love. London, Mills and Boon, 1981.
The Man at Key West. London, Mills and Boon, 1982.

*   *   *

Katrina Britt is a Mills and Boon author, reprinted by Harlequin, whose contemporary romances make good reading, partly because she employs a greater variety of plots than the usual romanticist, but mainly because she has a good, clear prose style. While this is formula fiction with heroines "drowning in a pool of bliss," and heroes whose "eyes twinkle devilishly," or whose "lips thin with anger," Britt has the gift of describing romantic feelings well without excessive cloving. Her stories are frequently set in Venice or Spain, but she has also used Nice, Switzerland, the Canary Islands, England, and Tokyo. One theme used frequently is the idea of different worlds or clash of cultures, with her English heroines displaying a cool Saxon strain versus the high-bred passionate Spaniard (*The Guarded Gates* and *The Villa Faustina*). She puts the theme of the villainess sister to good use in *The Spanish Grandee* and *The Emerald Garden*, good stories despite their heroines' long-suffering nobility in refusing to unmask their sisters.

In other novels Britt employs more contemporary themes. The sub-plot in *Take Back Your Love*, set in Tokyo, concerns a hippy pop-singing group, one of whose members dies from drug taking. However, the use of modern themes produces a somewhat spurious effect, since the main plot invariably concerns a dreamy-eyed heroine in love with a masterful, commanding man. The heroine of *The Guarded Gates* even defends her anti-women's rights feelings on several occasions.

In another departure, in *Girl in Blue* Britt seems to attempt to write a story with greater depth and seriousness, but doesn't quite succeed. Felicity marries Curt, a brilliant young lawyer, experiences the death of her mother and brother in an auto accident, believes her husband to be involved with another woman, leaves him, bears his child, of which he knows nothing, and is eventually reunited with him. All this is much too heavy going for a writer who should stay with the lighter romantic story, which she does so well.

—Necia A. Musser

BROMFIELD, Louis. American. Born in Mansfield, Ohio, 27 December 1896. Educated at Cornell University Agricultural College, Ithaca, New York, 1914–15; Columbia University School of Journalism, New York, 1916, honorary war degree 1920. Served in the American Ambulance Corps, with the 34th and 168th divisions of the French Army, 1917–19: Croix de Guerre. Married Mary Appleton Wood in 1921 (died 1952); three daughters. Reporter, City News Service and Associated Press, New York, 1920–22; editor and/or critic, *Musical America*, the *Bookman*, and *Time*, also worked as an assistant to a theatrical producer and as advertising manager of Putnam's, publishers, all New York, 1922–25; lived in Senlis, France, 1925–38; lived on a farm in Richland County, Ohio, 1939–56. President, Emergency Committee for the American Wounded in Spain, 1938; director, United States Chamber of Commerce. Recipient: Pulitzer Prize, 1927. LL.D: Marshall College, Huntington, West Virginia; Parsons College, Fairfield, Iowa; Litt.D.: Ohio Northern University, Ada. Chevalier, Legion of Honor (France), 1939; member, American Academy. *Died 18 March 1956.*

ROMANCE AND HISTORICAL PUBLICATIONS

Novels

The Green Bay Tree. New York, Stokes, and London, Unwin, 1924.
Possession. New York, Stokes, 1925; as *Lilli Barr*, London, Unwin, 1926.
Early Autumn. New York, Stokes, and London, Cape, 1926.
A Good Woman. New York, Stokes and London, Cape, 1927.
The Strange Case of Miss Annie Spragg. New York, Stokes, and London, Cape, 1928.
Twenty-Four Hours. New York, Stokes, and London, Cassell, 1930.
A Modern Hero. New York, Stokes, and London, Cassell, 1932.
The Farm. New York, Harper, and London, Cassell, 1933.
The Man Who Had Everything. New York, Harper, and London, Cassell, 1935.
It Had to Happen. London, Cassell, 1936.
The Rains Came: A Novel of Modern India. New York, Harper, and London, Cassell, 1937.
Night in Bombay. New York, Harper, and London, Cassell, 1940.
Wild Is the River. New York, Harper, 1941; London, Cassell, 1942.
Until the Day Break. New York, Harper, 1942; London, Cassell, 1943.
Mrs. Parkington. New York, Harper, 1943; London, Cassell, 1944.
What Became of Anna Bolton. New York, Harper, 1944; London, Cassell, 1945.
Colorado. New York, Harper, 1947; London, Cassell, 1950.
The Wild Country. New York, Harper, 1948; London, Cassell, 1950.
Mr. Smith. New York, Harper, 1951; London, Cassell, 1952.

Short Stories

Awake and Rehearse. New York, Stokes, and London, Cape, 1929.
Tabloid News. New York, Random House, 1930.
Here Today and Gone Tomorrow: Four Short Novels. New York, Harper, and London, Cassell, 1934.

It Takes All Kinds. New York, Harper, and London, Cassell, 1939; *Bitter Lotus* published separately, Cleveland, World, 1944; selection as *Five Long Short Stories*, New York, Avon, 1945; *McLeod's Folly* published separately, Cleveland, World, 1948; selection as *You Get What You Give*, London, Cassell, 1951.

The World We Live In. New York, Harper, 1944; London, Cassell, 1946.

Kenny. New York, Harper, 1947; London, Cassell, 1949.

OTHER PUBLICATIONS

Plays

The House of Women, adaptation of his novel *The Green Bay Tree* (produced New York, 1927; London, 1928).
De Luxe, with John Gearon (produced New York, 1935).
Times Have Changed, adaptation of a play by Edouard Bourdet (produced New York, 1935).

Screenplays: *One Heavenly Night*, with Sidney Howard, 1930; *Brigham Young—Frontiersman*, with Lamar Trotti, 1940.

Other

The Work of Robert Nathan. Indianapolis, Bobbs Merrill, 1927.
England, A Dying Oligarchy. New York, Harper, 1939.
Pleasant Valley. New York, Harper, 1945; London, Cassell, 1946.
A Few Brass Tacks. New York, Harper, 1946.
Malabar Farm, New York, Harper, 1948; London, Cassell, 1949.
The Works (Malabar Edition). London, Cassell, 15 vols., 1949–54.
Out of the Earth. New York, Harper, 1950; London, Cassell, 1951.
The Wealth of the Soil. Detroit, Ferguson, 1952.
A New Pattern for a Tired World. New York, Harper, and London, Cassell, 1954.
From My Experience: The Pleasures and Miseries of Life on a Farm. New York, Harper, 1955; London, Cassell, 1956.
Animals and Other People. New York, Harper, 1955; London, Cassell, 1956.
Walt Disney's Vanishing Prairie. New York, Simon and Schuster, and London, Harrap, 1956.
Louis Bromfield at Malabar: Writings on Farming and Country Life, edited by Charles E. Little. Baltimore, Johns Hopkins University Press, 1988.

*

Critical Studies: *Louis Bromfield and His Books: An Evaluation* by Morrison Brown, London, Cassell, 1956, Fair Lawn, New Jersey, Essential, 1957; *The Heritage: A Daughter's Memories of Louis Bromfield* by Ellen Geld, New York, Harper, 1962; *Louis Bromfield* by David D. Anderson, New York, Twayne, 1964.

*   *   *

Louis Bromfield is a neglected author who in his own day was very popular and much respected—indeed, he won the Pulitzer Prize for literature with *Early Autumn*, the third book of an inter-related series in which he set out to present a pageant of the changing American scene in the early years of this century while at the same time exploring the idea of escape from con-

vention. The first book of this saga was *The Green Bay Tree*, set in a small town in Ohio at the time when it was changing from a farming community to an industrial town. He shows us different aspects of the community's life by portraying several different families, but the main focus is Lily, a "new woman"—very attractive to men with opportunities to marry, all of which she rejects fearing to be tied down, preferring to have her child outside wedlock. *Possession* is the next book which runs parallel in time and place to the first, but shows us another set of families and glimpses of some of the people from the first book. A new woman is at the centre of this book too: she makes her bid for freedom by rejecting family life for the concert platform. *Early Autumn* is connected with the previous books when the daughter of the family at the centre of this book marries Lily's illegitimate son. This portrait of an old New England family is almost an American Forsyte saga, for it has the same emphasis on money and property and it is the heroine's devotion to duty that triumphs over her longing to escape convention. The fourth book is *A Good Woman*, an ironic title, since the woman arranges her son's life to such a degree that she manoeuvres not only his call to the mission field but also his marriage, and in so doing she ruins three lives while thinking herself good and righteous. The good woman's daughter-in-law can only find escape through death.

Bromfield would have pleased his fans had he gone on with his richly plotted, intricate panoramas but he was ready for another format. *The Strange Case of Miss Annie Spragg* is a loosely connected set of short stories making up a novel. Each chapter tells the tale of one of the several witnesses to a miracle in Italy. The stories are skilfully told, cleverly meshed with superbly drawn characters. *Twenty-Four Hours* was another book of the same type: each of the people attending a dinner one night relates what happens to him or her between dinner and teatime the next day. The whole makes a surprisingly complete book.

The Rains Came is Bromfield's most famous book—perhaps because it became a much-acclaimed film, but also because it was an excellent book. He visited India in 1932 and it took him four years to digest the experience and process it into a novel. Ranchipur, where the story is set, is based on Baroda, one of the most up-to-date Indian states at that time. The destinies of a large number of people are worked out against the tension of the dry season and the bursting of the dam that comes with the monsoon. Bromfield symbolizes the decadence of Europe in the character of Ransome, America through Aunt Phoebe, and contracts it with awakening India symbolized by the Maharajah. *Night in Bombay*, his other Indian novel, was not nearly as successful; nevertheless, the characters are interesting and the descriptions evocative of the sights, sounds, smells, and the feel of India.

Bromfield could write other kinds of books, too. *Wild Is the River* is a romantic historical novel about the American Civil War set against the background of the occupation of New Orleans by the Yankees; *Until the Day Break*, a melodramatic spy story, is set against occupied Paris in the 1940's. *Colorado* is a send-up of the Western, and *The Wild Country* is a strangely beautiful story of a boy growing up in his grandfather's farm observing the people round him.

In all Bromfield's books there is good solid characterization, strong plotting, lush romance, and the exploration of a socially significant theme against beautiful descriptions. It is high time some of his books were brought to the attention of a new generation to whom they would have a great deal to say.

—Pamela Cleaver

BROMIGE, Iris (Amy Edna). British. Born in London in 1910. Educated at the Clapham County Secondary School, London. Married to Alan Frank Bromige. Address: c/o Hodder and Stoughton Ltd., Mill Road, Dunton Green, Sevenoaks, Kent TN13 2YA, England.

ROMANCE AND HISTORICAL PUBLICATIONS

Novels (series: Rainwood family)

The Traceys. London, Longman 1946; New York, Beagle, 1974.

Stay But till Tomorrow. London, Longman, 1946; New York, Ballantine, 1975.

Chequered Pattern. London, Longman, 1947; as *A Chance for Love*, New York, Ballantine, 1975.

Tangled Roots. London, Longman, 1948; New York, Ballantine, 1975.

Marchwood. London, Hodder and Stoughton, 1949; New York, Beagle, 1974.

The Golden Cage. London, Hodder and Stoughton, 1950; New York, Ballantine, 1974.

April Wooing. London, Hodder and Stoughton, 1951; New York, Beagle, 1973.

Laurian Vale. London, Hodder and Stoughton, 1952; New York, Ballantine, 1975.

The House of Conflict. London, Hodder and Stoughton, 1953; as *Shall Love Be Lost?*, New York, Beagle, 1974.

Gay Intruder. London, Hodder and Stoughton, 1954; New York, Ballantine, 1973.

Diana Comes Home. London, Hodder and Stoughton, 1955; New York, Beagle, 1974.

The New Owner. London, Hodder and Stoughton, 1956; New York, Ballantine, 1973.

The Enchanted Garden. London, Hodder and Stoughton, 1956; New York, Beagle, 1972.

A New Life for Joanna. London, Hodder and Stoughton, 1957; New York, Beagle, 1973.

Family Group. London, Hodder and Stoughton, 1958; New York, Ballantine, 1975.

The Conway Touch. London, Hodder and Stoughton, 1958; New York, Ballantine, 1974.

The Flowering Year. London, Hodder and Stoughton, 1959; New York, Beagle, 1973.

The Second Mrs. Rivers. London, Hodder and Stoughton, 1960; New York, Beagle, 1973.

Fair Prisoner. London, Hodder and Stoughton, 1960; New York, Beagle, 1974.

Alex and the Raynhams. London, Hodder and Stoughton, 1961; New York, Pocket Books, 1972.

Come Love, Come Hope. London, Hodder and Stoughton, 1962; New York, Beagle, 1972.

Rosevean. London, Hodder and Stoughton, 1962; Philadelphia, Chilton, 1963.

The Family Web. London, Hodder and Stoughton, 1963; New York, Beagle, 1972.

A House Without Love. London, Hodder and Stoughton, 1964; New York, Beagle, 1973.

The Young Romantic. London, Hodder and Stoughton, 1964; New York, Ballantine, 1975.

The Challenge of Spring. London, Hodder and Stoughton, 1965; New York, Beagle, 1972.

The Lydian Inheritance. London, Hodder and Stoughton, 1966; New York, Beagle, 1972.

The Stepdaughter (Rainwood). London, Hodder and Stoughton, 1966.

The Quiet Hills (Rainwood). London, Hodder and Stoughton, 1967; New York, Beagle, 1974.

An April Girl (Rainwood). London, Hodder and Stoughton, 1967; New York, Beagle, 1971.

Only Our Love. London, Hodder and Stoughton, 1968; New York, Beagle, 1974.

The Master of Heronsbridge. London, Hodder and Stoughton, 1969; New York, Beagle, 1974.

The Tangled Wood (Rainwood). London, Hodder and Stoughton, 1969; New York, Beagle, 1971.

Encounter at Alpenrose. London, Hodder and Stoughton, 1970; New York, Beagle, 1973.

A Sheltering Tree. London, Hodder and Stoughton, 1970; New York, Beagle, 1973.

A Magic Place (Rainwood). London, Hodder and Stoughton, 1971; New York, Beagle, 1973.

Rough Weather. London, Hodder and Stoughton, 1972; New York, Pinnacle, 1981.

Golden Summer. London, Hodder and Stoughton, 1972; New York, Beagle, 1973.

The Broken Bough. London, Hodder and Stoughton, 1973.

The Night of the Party. London, Hodder and Stoughton, 1974.

The Bend in the River (Rainwood). London, Hodder and Stoughton, 1975.

A Haunted Landscape. London, Hodder and Stoughton, 1976.

A Distant Song. London, Hodder and Stoughton, 1977; New York, Pinnacle, 1980.

The Happy Fortress (Rainwood). London, Hodder and Stoughton, 1978.

The Paths of Summer. London, Hodder and Stoughton, 1979.

One Day, My Love (Rainwood). London, Hodder and Stoughton, 1980.

Old Love's Domain. London, Hodder and Stoughton, 1982.

A Slender Thread. London, Hodder and Stoughton, 1985.

Farewell to Winter. London, Hodder and Stoughton, 1986.

The Changing Tide. London, Hodder and Stoughton, 1987.

*   *   *

The quality of Iris Bromige's work has remained remarkably consistent over the past 30 years. Many of her books follow the fortunes of various members of the Rainwood clan presided over by the matriarchal Mirabel, and usually centre on one of her many grandchildren; other members flit in and out as the plot requires, but the Rainwood family as a whole is so scattered and detached that knowledge of previous Rainwood novels does not spoil the reader's appreciation of specific works, and the family as an institution infiltrates most of her work, Rainwood or not.

The plots follow a pattern that seldom varies: the heroine, in her mid-twenties, has reached a turning-point in her life—death of a parent, as in *Only Our Love*, or the sour end to an unsatisfactory relationship, as *Come Love, Come Hope*, necessitating a reappraisal of her position. In *Rosevean*, as an example of a typical situation, Ann joins the Pendine family as secretary-companion to the rich ruling head, facing an unpredictable and challenging future among a cast of differing personalities. The Bromige heroines are resourceful, honest, truthful, and incurable romantics, though they work hard and responsibly at their various jobs. The main male character is usually in his early thirties, the self-possessed and seemingly arrogant type, often determined through past bitter experience not to be drawn into a close relationship. Then follows the gradual breakdown of barriers between the two protagonists, through hostile and gentle encounters, through easy banter and serious discussion, to the heart-searching necessary to all true romance, with misunderstandings brought in just at the thawing stage to heighten the tension. The lovers at last accept their capitulation, and all doubts are resolved in the final obligatory reconciliation scene.

The narrative shape is well handled, despite some early spasmodic weaknesses, as in *Alex and the Raynhams*, which also tends to rely too heavily on dialogue; later novels gain a better balance between dialogue, description, and action. Pauses from the drama are admirably filled by descriptions of the countryside (either the West Country or Northumberland) in its natural beauty, seasonal touches tending to reflect the bitter-sweet pangs of falling in and out of love.

Bromige gives little concession to the loosening of family ties and increased freedom for youth in the last two decades, her books being based on solid middle- and upper-middle-class family values: however old-fashioned and unworldly this seems at times, it gives her work a secure and warm foundation. Her interest in both major and minor characters centres on them not as distinct personalities, but more on the way that the different kinds of relationships experienced by them contrast with the headiness of the passing flirtation and the depth of feeling that goes to make the lasting love necessary for a successful marriage.

—Tessa Rose Chester

BRONTE, Louisa. See **ROBERTS, Janet Louise.**

BROSTER, D(orothy) K(athleen). British. Born in 1877. Educated at Cheltenham Ladies' College; St. Hilda's College, Oxford, M.A. *Died 7 February 1950.*

ROMANCE AND HISTORICAL PUBLICATIONS

Novels (series: Jacobite Trilogy)

Chantemerle, with Gertrude Winifred Taylor. London, Murray, and New York, Brentano's, 1911.
The Vision Splendid, with Gertrude Winifred Taylor. London, Murray, 1913; New York, Brentano's, 1914.
Sir Isumbras at the Ford. London, Murray, 1918.
The Yellow Poppy. London, Duckworth, 1920; New York, McBride, 1922.
The Wounded Name. London, Murray, 1922; New York, Doubleday, 1923.
Mr. Rowl. London, Heinemann, and New York, Doubleday, 1924.
A Jacobite Trilogy. London, Penguin, 1984.
   The Flight of the Heron. London, Heinemann, 1925; New York, Dodd Mead, 1926.
   The Gleam in the North. London, Heinemann, 1927; New York, Coward McCann, 1931.
   The Dark Mile. London, Heinemann, 1929; New York, Coward McCann, 1934.
Ships in the Bay! London, Heinemann, and New York, Coward McCann, 1931.
Almond, Wild Almond. London, Heinemann, 1933.

World under Snow, with G. Forester. London, Heinemann, 1935.
Child Royal. London, Heinemann, 1937.
The Sea Without a Haven. London, Heinemann, 1941.
The Captain's Lady. London, Heinemann, 1947.

Short Stories

A Fire of Driftwood. London, Heinemann, 1932.
Couching at the Door. London, Heinemann, 1942.

OTHER PUBLICATIONS

Verse

The Short Voyage and Other Verses. Privately printed, 1950.

Other

The Happy Warrior. London, Cayme Press, 1926.

*   *   *

D. K. Broster's first two novels, *Chantemerle* and *The Vision Splendid*, were written in collaboration with Miss G. W. Taylor. Although they were not as polished as Broster's later work, they established a writing pattern: carefully constructed historical settings; intelligent presentation, with some consideration of historical ideas behind action; and clear characterizations. Romance per se is central in *Chantemerle*, but in general Broster's work is secondary to period political matters. All in all, the general model for Broster's work would seem to be Robert Louis Stevenson.

The author's most important work is usually considered to be her Jacobite trilogy, *The Flight of the Heron*, *The Gleam in the North*, and *The Dark Mile*. Set in Scotland from 1745 to 1755, they are essentially concerned with the psychological concomitants and aftermaths of the uprising. In *The Flight of the Heron*, when Prince Charles is being hunted by English troops, the focus of the story is on the odd friendship that arises between Ewen Cameron, one of the prince's supporters, and Captain Windham, the leader of the English troops. *The Gleam in the North*, set several years later, centers around the historical capture and execution of Dr. Archibald Cameron, an agent of Prince Charles's. The Scottish feeling that Cameron was being treated harshly in being executed without trial (on the basis of an earlier judgment) is contrasted with the English feeling that Cameron was a dangerous agitator who had done much harm and would do more. The story is told via Ewen Cameron. *The Dark Mile*, set in the Highlands, examines the psychological damage done by the rebellion. Young lovers, one related to Ewen Cameron, discover that family loyalty is stronger than love. Olivia's father had commanded troops that killed Ian's brother in battle, and this can never be forgiven, even though it was only the fortune of war. (The obstacle to love is removed, unfortunately, by a device unworthy of the author.) Moving in the background of the last two books is a fictional version of Pickle the spy. Broster follows Andrew Lang's identification of Pickle. All three volumes are well plotted and carry conviction.

Other historical novels include *Sir Isumbras at the Ford*, set in Scotland and France in the 1790's; *The Wounded Name*, France just before Napoleon's return from Elba; and *Ships in the Bay!*, Wales, 1796, with Irish rebels and French Revolutionaries.

Broster's best-known story is the short story "Couching at the Door," from the collection of the same name. Often anthologized and highly regarded, it is based on the personalities of Oscar Wilde (mingled a little with Aleister Crowley) and Aubrey Beardsley. It describes a unique punishment for having attended a Black Mass.

—E. F. Bleiler

BROWN, Sandra. Also writes as Laura Jordan; Rachel Ryan; Erin St. Claire. American. Born in Waco, Texas, 12 March 1948. Educated at Texas Christian University, Fort Worth; Oklahoma State University, Stillwater; University of Texas, Arlington, 1966–70. Married Michael Brown in 1968; one daughter and one son. Manager, Merle Norman Cosmetics Studio, Tyler, Texas, 1971–73; weather reporter, KLTV-Television, Tyler, 1972–75, and WFAA-Television, Dallas, 1976–79; model, Dallas Apparel Mart, 1976–87. Agent: Maria Carvainis Agency, 235 West End Avenue, New York, New York 10023. Address: 1000 North Bowen, Arlington, Texas 76012, U.S.A.

ROMANCE AND HISTORICAL PUBLICATIONS

Novels (series: Alicia; Coleman and Langston)

Breakfast in Bed (Alicia). New York, Bantam, 1983.
Heaven's Price. New York, Bantam, 1983.
Relentless Desire. New York, Berkley, 1983.
Tempest in Eden. New York, Berkley, 1983.
Temptation's Kiss. New York, Berkley, 1983.
Tomorrow's Promise. Toronto, Harlequin, 1983.
In a Class by Itself. New York, Bantam, 1984.
Send No Flowers (Alicia). New York, Bantam, 1984.
Sunset Embrace (Coleman and Langston). New York, Bantam, 1984.
Riley in the Morning. New York, Bantam, 1985.
Thursday's Child. New York, Bantam, 1985.
Another Dawn (Coleman and Langston). New York, Bantam, 1985.
22 Indigo Place. New York, Bantam, 1986.
The Rana Look. New York, Bantam, 1986.
Demon Rumm. New York, Bantam, 1987.
Fanta C. New York, Bantam, 1987.
Sunny Chandler's Return. New York, Bantam, 1987.
Tidings of Great Joy. New York, Bantam, 1987.
Adam's Fall. New York, Bantam, 1988.
Hawk O'Toole's Hostage. New York, Bantam, 1988.
Slow Heat in Heaven. New York, Warner, 1988.
Long Time Coming. New York, Bantam, 1989.
Temperatures Rising. New York, Bantam, 1989.
Best Kept Secrets. New York, Warner, 1989.

Novels as Rachel Ryan

Love Beyond Reason. New York, Dell, 1981.
Love's Encore. New York, Dell, 1981.
Eloquent Silence. New York, Dell, 1982.
A Treasure Worth Seeking. New York, Dell, 1982.
Prime Time. New York, Dell, 1983.

Novels as Erin St. Claire (series: Jennifer and Cage)

Not Even for Love. New York, Silhouette, 1982.
A Kiss Remembered. New York, Silhouette, 1983.

A Secret Splendor. New York, Silhouette, 1983.
Seduction by Design. New York, Silhouette, 1983.
Bittersweet Rain. New York, Silhouette, 1984.
Words of Silk. New York, Silhouette, 1984.
Led Astray (Jennifer and Cage). New York, Silhouette, 1985.
A Sweet Anger. New York, Silhouette, 1985.
Tiger Prince. New York, Silhouette, 1985.
Above and Beyond. New York, Silhouette, 1986.
Honor Bound. New York, Silhouette, 1986.
The Devil's Own (Jennifer and Cage). New York, Silhouette, 1987.
Two Alone. New York, Silhouette, 1987.
Thrill of Victory. New York, Silhouette, 1989.

Novels as Laura Jordan

Hidden Fires. New York, Pocket Books, 1982.
The Silken Web. New York, Pocket Books, 1982.

*

Sandra Brown comments:
I write love stories about characters I would like to know, incorporating fantasy into realism.

* * *

Writing under her own name and the pseudonyms Rachel Ryan, Erin St. Claire, and Laura Jordan, Sandra Brown has produced a large body of work. She primarily writes contemporary romances but has also tried her hand at historical romances. Within the contemporary categories she writes both short novels and longer, more explicitly sensuous ones. Using a wide variety of settings, Brown focuses on the emotions involved in a romantic relationship. She skillfully brings the reader into a lush romantic world, providing detailed descriptions of the physical environment and sensual descriptions of the emotions and actions of the lovers.

Brown's novels written under the name of Rachel Ryan are probably the least sexually explicit of all her books. As Erin St. Claire she has been much more detailed in her descriptions of sexual situations. Her Sandra Brown novels are a mix. In part, however, the increasingly explicit nature of her books reflects the trend in romance fiction as a whole. Nevertheless, many readers were undoubtedly surprised by the 1988 publication of *Slow Heat in Heaven*. Written outside of the series formulas, it has passionate love, lust, and a great deal of violence. Not only are there unpleasant secrets from the past which surface, but there also are many unsavory characters. There are "sizzling" love scenes along with sexual cruelty, battered women, and even an implication of a homosexual gang rape in prison. This is a significant departure from the sensual nature of Brown's earlier work, but since it is such a recent publication it is too soon yet to tell if it is an anomaly or if it marks a new trend for her.

Two historical novels by Brown also fall outside of the series formula. Set in Brown's native Texas, *Sunset Embrace* and *Another Dawn* are excellent representatives of the sensual historical novel. In *Sunset Embrace*, Lydia Bryant and Ross Coleman flee shadowed pasts to start anew in Texas and find love to sustain them in building their new life together. *Another Dawn* takes up their story 20 years later. This time the focus is their daughter, Banner, and her tempestuous affair with Jake Langston. Brown reverses a fairly common romance novel complication by having Banner believe that Jake loves her mother, Lydia. More unusually, however, Brown radically changes the requisite happy ending. Although Jake and Banner work out their differences and seem destined for happiness, Ross is brutally gunned down. After a touching death scene, Lydia leaves home because her memories make it too painful for her to stay. Such a tragic end to a deep love casts a shadow on the happiness of Jake and Banner.

Brown can be counted on to provide a solid, entertaining romance and escape into a world of feeling almost guaranteed happiness. She lets the reader cry a bit and even laugh, but most importantly she lets the reader enjoy romance.

—Barbara E. Kemp

BROWNING, Dixie (Burrus). Also writes as Zoe Dozier; Bronwyn Williams. American. Born in Elizabeth City, North Carolina, 9 September 1930. Educated at Mary Washington College, Fredericksburg, Virginia, 1946–47; Richmond Professional Institute (now Virginia Commonwealth University), 1947–48; City Memorial School of Nursing, Winston-Salem, North Carolina, 1948–49. Married Leonard Larkin Browning, Jr., in 1950; one daughter and one son. Founder and co-director, Art Gallery Originals, Winston-Salem, 1968-73; co-director, Art V Gallery, Clemmons, North Carolina, 1974–75. Since 1984 president and co-owner, Browning Artworks, Frisco, North Carolina. President, Watercolor Society of North Carolina, 1972–73. Recipient: Romance Writers of America Golden Medallion, 1983. Address: 5316 Robinhood Road, Winston-Salem, North Carolina 27106, U.S.A.

ROMANCE AND HISTORICAL PUBLICATIONS

Novels

Tumbled Wall. New York, Silhouette, 1980.
Unreasonable Summer. New York, Silhouette, 1980.
Chance Tomorrow. New York, Silhouette, 1981.
East of Today. New York, Silhouette, 1981.
Winter Blossom. New York, Silhouette, 1981; London, Hodder and Stoughton, 1982.
Wren of Paradise. New York, Silhouette, 1981.
Finders Keepers. New York, Silhouette, 1982.
Island on the Hill. New York, Silhouette, 1982.
Logic of the Heart. New York, Silhouette, 1982; London, Hodder and Stoughton, 1983.
The Loving Rescue. New York, Silhouette, 1982.
Renegade Player. New York, Silhouette, 1982.
Practical Dreamer. New York, Silhouette, and London, Hodder and Stoughton, 1983.
Reach Out to Cherish. New York, Silhouette, 1983.
A Secret Valentine. New York, Silhouette, 1983.
Shadow of Yesterday. New York, Silhouette, 1983.
First Things Last. New York, Silhouette, 1984.
The Hawk and the Honey. New York, Silhouette, 1984.
Image of Love. New York, Silhouette, 1984.
Journey to Quiet Waters. New York, Silhouette, 1984.
Just Desserts. New York, Silhouette, 1984.
Late Rising Moon. New York, Silhouette, 1984.
The Love Thing. New York, Silhouette, 1984.
Stormwatch. New York, Silhouette, 1984.
Time and Tide. New York, Silhouette, 1984.
Visible Heart. New York, Silhouette, 1984.

A Bird in Hand. New York, Silhouette, 1985.
By Any Other Name. New York, Silhouette, 1985.
Matchmaker's Moon. New York, Silhouette, 1985.
Something for Herself. New York, Silhouette, 1985.
The Tender Barbarian. New York, Silhouette, 1985.
Reluctant Dreamer. New York, Silhouette, 1986.
The Security Man. New York, Silhouette, 1986.
In the Palm of Her Hand. New York, Silhouette, 1986.
A Winter Woman. New York, Silhouette, 1986.
Belonging. New York, Silhouette, 1987.
Henry the Ninth. New York, Silhouette, 1987.
A Matter of Timing. New York, Silhouette, 1987.
There Once Was a Lover. New York, Silhouette, 1987.
Along Came Jones. New York, Silhouette, 1988.
Fate Takes a Holiday. New York, Silhouette, 1988.
White Witch (with Mary Williams, as Bronwyn Williams). Toronto, Harlequin, 1988.
Thin Ice. New York, Silhouette, 1989.

Novels as Zoe Dozier

Home Again My Love. New York, Bouregy, 1977.
Warm Side of the Island. New York, Bouregy, 1977.

*

Manuscript Collection: University of North Carolina Library, Chapel Hill.

Dixie Browning comments:

Just as yesterday's vernacular work is hailed as today's classic, genre literature written today will need the perspective of time to be judged fairly. Romances have always been maligned by those who don't take the time to understand them. Writers of today's romances are merely retelling fables that are as old as language, fables that have enabled women to deal with their often unenviable relationships with men. The basic conflict is the diverse nature of men and women, and, set against a backdrop of today's world with its complex problems, the scope is enormous. Styles change, settings change, but the basic plot structure of the romance novel deals with an underlying truth that will never change. I write about the sort of men and women I know, dealing with problems I can understand. What's ordinary to one person is often exotic to another. Other writers deal with far more glamorous types, with settings I can only dream about, yet the underlying truth in any good romance enables a diverse audience to appreciate and to relate on an emotional level with at least one of the characters. That, I believe, is what ensures the genre a large and varied readership.

*   *   *

Most of Dixie Browning's 40 contemporary romances take place in North Carolina, where she was born. Browning is an artist as well as a writer, and her artist's eye for detail translates well onto the printed page. She uses her settings advantageously, often as backdrops for love scenes, as in *Thin Ice* when Maggie Duncan and Sam Canady make love in a duck blind. Weather phenomena such as thunderstorms, heat lightning, and high temperatures also enhance the encounters of hero and heroine.

Heroines usually are involved in some aspect of the art world; for example, art teacher, painter, gallery worker, wood carver. They vary in physical attributes from thin to voluptuous, from redhead to brunette. Heroes include an environmentalist, a power plant specialist, an engineer, and a college teacher. They have the requisite ultramasculine builds, and most are dark complexioned with silver-tinged hair. "Aggressive chins" and "bench made shoes" are frequent trademarks.

Plots revolve around situations in which the hero and heroine must spend time in each other's company, often in relative isolation. One such pattern has the two residing under the same roof. In *Unreasonable Summer*, art teacher and painter Emily Fairchild rents a cottage for the summer, only to find that the owner also has rented it to art critic George Brandon. *Journey to Quiet Waters* has Ivy de Coursey employed as caretaker of the empty estate that was her family home. Hunter Smith is the new owner. Sometimes the residence is a boat. To escape obnoxious crewmates, Leah Deerfield (*Chance Tomorrow*) stows away on Smith Cairington's yacht. In *The Loving Rescue*, Lacy Davis, stranded in Guatemala, hitches a boat ride with Jordan Stone, on his way to New Orleans. Another pattern has the two main characters living near each other. Frances Harris in *Island on the Hill*, to prove her independence from her family, buys a house near Cabel McCloud. In *Thin Ice*, Sam, who needs to be alone, rents a cabin near Maggie's on the remote Duncan's Neck. Other stories feature similar ploys to allow the lovers to spend nights together. In *Fate Takes a Holiday*, Sophie Pennybaker wins a weekend with Fate Ridgeway. Gale Evanshaw and Saxon (*Belonging*) move into a motel to be near his hospitalized father, and *Winter Blossom*'s Bliss Conner and James Etchison are snowbound in an isolated mountain cabin while looking for a runaway couple.

In the early romances, conflicts revolve around unhappy past relationships and the beautiful "other woman." Heroes are surly, demanding, and condescending. Heroines are meek and anxious to please, and are often relegated to positions of housekeeping and cooking for the males. Accident prone, they are rescued and taken care of by the men. The lovers have little verbal communication but plenty of physical contact, usually while engaged in some pursuit of nature, such as fishing, picnicking, or swimming. Eventually, the heroine realizes she loves the hero, despite the miserable way he treats her. At the end, the hero explains the reasons for his behavior and all is forgiven. In defense of Browning, it must be said that this formula was consistent with the publishers' guidelines of the times. As the guidelines changed, resulting in more sensitive heroes and stronger heroines, so, too, do Brownings' heroes and heroines change. Fate, in *Fate Takes a Holiday*, and Sam, in *Thin Ice*, are good examples of this new breed of romance hero.

However, even though the "other woman" ploy is now cliché, Browning continues to use this device. She has, however, softened the character. For example, in *Belonging*, rival Enid Brachman, although predictably brassy and obnoxious, is willing to admit that Saxon prefers Gale to her. Thus the use of the "other woman" in the later stories seems more a padding device than a legitimate plot element. Browning also uses other minor characters to stretch the story to the required number of pages. In *Island on the Hill*, Frances and Cabel, after a marriage of convenience, travel to a Caribbean island to meet his mother and her latest husband, people not important to the main plot. In *Belonging*, a house party prolongs the story's resolution, and in *Late Rising Moon*, Larraine Ashby and teenage Billie's sailboat ride helps to expand the story.

Browning's strength as a genre writer lies in her ability to build and sustain the romantic relationship, including sexual tension and culminated lovemaking. She knows how to involve the reader in the character's emotions and in their responses to each other, so that one forgets about plot contrivances and clichés. Even though these people are created to fit a formula, in the later books, particularly, they emerge as real people, who suffer emotional pain but who also are capable of knowing the joys of true love.

—Linda Lee

BRYHER. British. Born Annie Winifred Ellerman in Margate, Kent, in 1894. Educated privately and at Queenwood School, Eastbourne, Sussex. Married 1) the writer Robert McAlmon in 1921 (marriage dissolved 1926); 2) Kenneth Macpherson in 1927 (marriage dissolved 1947); one adopted daughter. Began long relationship with the writer Hilda Doolittle ("H. D.") in 1919; joint founder and editor, *Close Up* film journal, Territet, Switzerland, 1927–33. *Died 28 January 1983.*

ROMANCE AND HISTORICAL PUBLICATIONS

Novels

The Fourteenth of October. New York, Pantheon, 1952; London, Collins, 1954.
The Player's Boy. New York, Pantheon, 1953; London, Collins, 1957.
Roman Wall. New York, Pantheon, 1954; London, Collins, 1955.
Gate to the Sea. New York, Pantheon, 1958; London, Collins, 1959.
Ruan. New York, Pantheon, 1960; London, Collins, 1961.
The Coin of Carthage. New York, Harcourt Brace, 1963; London, Collins, 1964.
This January Tale. New York, Harcourt Brace, 1966; London, Secker and Warburg, 1968.
The Colors of Vaud. New York, Harcourt Brace, 1969.

OTHER PUBLICATIONS

Novels

Development. London, Constable, and New York, Macmillan, 1920.
Two Selves. Paris, Contact, 1923(?); New York, Chaucer Head, 1927(?).
Civilians. Territet, Switzerland, Pool, 1927; London, Pool, 1930.
The Light-Hearted Student, with Trude Weiss. Dijon, Pool, 1930.
Beowulf. New York, Pantheon, 1956.
Visa for Avalon. New York, Harcourt Brace, 1965.

Verse

Region of Lutany (as A. W. Ellerman). London, Chapman and Hall, 1914.
Arrow Music, with others. London, Bumpus, 1924.

Other

Amy Lowell: A Critical Appreciation. London, Eyre and Spottiswoode, 1918.
A Picture Geography for Little Children: Asia. London, Cape, 1925.

West (on the USA). London, Cape, 1925.

Film Problems of Soviet Russia. Territet, Switzerland, Pool, 1929.

Cinema Survey, with Robert Herring and Dallas Bower. London, Brendin, 1937.

The Heart to Artemis: A Writer's Memoirs. New York, Harcourt Brace, 1962; London, Collins, 1963.

The Days of Mars: A Memoir 1940–1946. New York, Harcourt Brace, and London, Calder and Boyars, 1972.

Translator, *The Lament for Adonis*, by Bion. London, Humphreys, 1918.

* * *

Bryher's historical novels cover a wide variety of settings, both in time and place, ranging from Paestum in the 4th century B.C. (*Gate to the Sea*) to late 18th-century Switzerland (*The Colors of Vaud*). *The Coin of Carthage* is set on the coasts of southern Italy and North Africa at the time of the Punic Wars, and *Roman Wall* takes place during the 3rd century A.D. in an outpost of the by now crumbling Empire close to the German border. *Ruan* is concerned with the world of Celtic Britain and Ireland in the middle of the 6th century, *The Fourteenth of October* and *This January Tale* with the events surrounding the Norman Conquest and its aftermath and *The Player's Boy* describes the life of a young actor in early 17th-century London. All of these books reveal Bryher's scholarly interest in the past, but if the background events which they describe are historically momentous, their immediate content is largely personal and domestic. The backgrounds themselves are designed to illustrate the particular qualities of certain periods when civilizations were in a state of transition; to this extent Bryher's historical novels are closely related to the period in which she wrote them. They are all by implication concerned with the political, personal, and social issues confronting Europe during the rise of the fascist dictatorships between the two world wars.

Bryher's novels are full of escapes and perilous journeys, and of people who have been ejected from their homes: several of them are poignant with a sense of exile. As she stresses repeatedly in her two books of memoirs, *The Heart to Artemis* and *The Days of Mars*, she clearly foresaw the inevitability of World War II, and her descriptions of the declining Roman Empire and of Anglo-Saxon England are critical portraits of enlightened civilizations which had grown complacent and effete and thus unprepared to defend themselves by fighting their aggressors.

The most well known, if in certain ways the most conventional, of Bryher's historical tales is the first of them, *The Fourteenth of October*. It is the story of a Yorkshire boy who is dispossessed of his family home by Danish raiders and carried overseas as the captive of a Norman baron. He escapes to Cornwall, where he finds love and security. But with the threat of a Norman invasion loyalty compels him to take part in a march across Southern England in support of the beleaguered King Harold, only to witness the aftermath of his defeat at Hastings. He returns to Cornwall, but faced with the prospect of living as a dependent of the hated Normans, he chooses freedom and becomes an exile.

All Bryher's leading themes and concerns are to be found in this novel: her sympathy with those ordinary working people who always have to bear the brunt of the contending ambitions of the powerful and greedy; an affection for the diurnal routines of life, for domesticity and daily work; a response to an atmosphere of mystery, exemplified here in the person of an old Cornish woman who embodies the beliefs and values of a bygone age; a hunger for personal liberty and a delight in the sea as an image of such freedom. This last named theme also features prominently in *Ruan*.

Other novels are more panoramic in technique and less personal in their focus. In *Roman Wall* the Germanic tribes are about to cross the Rhine and assault the slackly guarded borders of the Roman empire in Helvetia. Bryher portrays the onset of catastrophe with obvious reference to events in the Europe of her own day, and does so through a wide range of characters—the decadent Roman governor of the province, his aging mistress and his steward, a Greek trader with an eye to the main chance, soldiers, craftsmen, farmers, a family of loyal Roman settlers. She provides a picture of an entire community; their thoughts and fears and observations build up a mental world that makes the past come most convincingly alive. Bryher employs a similar technique, though on a smaller scale, in her account of life in post-Conquest Exeter, *This January Tale*, in which the plight of refugees is presented with understanding and compassionate restraint.

For all the research that went into their making, her novels are personal statements. This is particularly true of *The Fourteenth of October*, *The Player's Boy* and *Ruan*; in each of them the author impersonates an adolescent boy who grows painfully into manhood. All three are told in the first person; but perhaps because of this one is more aware of inhabiting a bygone environment than one is of inhabiting a bygone consciousness. The language and feelings inevitably products of the 20th century in their literary style and sophisticated awareness. In *The Player's Boy*, which reflects Bryher's love for the work of the Jacobean dramatists, a vein of pessimism obtrudes. This novel stands apart from the others in its relatively static action and its meditative tone. It lacks the delight in travel that inspires the other novels, and which was a strong element in Bryher's character.

Of the books which deal with the Classical world, *Gate to the Sea* is little more than a novella; it describes the escape of a handful of Greek colonists from the conquered city of Paestum, and is a good example of the deft way in which Bryher can evoke suspense. *The Coin of Carthage* is more ambitious, portraying in episodic fashion the separate fortunes of two Greek traders at the time of Rome's wars with Carthage. In both novels the use of third-person narrative ensures a measure of detachment without any loss of physical immediacy, and *The Coin of Carthage* in particular gives one an insight into what life must actually have been like for working people living at the time. The book is also rich in accounts of plants and animals and ancient dwelling places, and conveys a powerful sense of the timelessness of daily life which is an underlying element in all the author's most successful work.

Bryher's novels are distinguished from most historical fiction in dispensing with the intricacies of plot and by their concentration on random happenings. The narrative approach is frequently cinematic; it moves easily from scene to scene, from consciousness to consciousness. A strong sense of fatality pervades the books; Bryher's vision is essentially a tragic one. Very much the products of a particular time, her novels are written in an informal style which in the later books becomes almost offhand, but which gives them at times a parabolic character. Their simplicity makes them readily accessible to younger readers, and indeed one of Bryher's favourite historical novelists was the children's author G. A. Henty. A strong vein of instruction is present in, for instance, *The Colors of Vaud*, which describes the attainment of independence from Bern of the Swiss canton in which Bryher had made her home; in this book characterisation (never a strong point) is sacrificed to the making of historical points. But Bryher is usually more imaginative in her approach than here, and at her finest, as in *The Fourteenth of October*, *The Coin of Carthage*, and *Roman Wall*, her sense of human dignity and the austere and gracious cadence of her prose make these short, deeply felt novels resound with the force and suggestiveness of poetry.

—Glen Cavaliero

BUCHAN, John; 1st Baron Tweedsmuir of Elsfield. British. Born in Broughton Green, Peebles-shire, 26 August 1875. Educated at Hutchison Grammar School, Glasgow; University of Glasgow; Brasenose College, Oxford (scholar, 1895; Stanhope prize, 1897; Newdigate prize, 1898; President of the Union, 1899), B.A. (honours) 1899; Middle Temple, London, called to the Bar, 1901. Served on the Headquarters Staff of the British Army in France, as temporary Lieutenant Colonel, 1916–17; Director of Information under the Prime Minister, 1917–18. Married Susan Charlotte Grosvenor in 1907; three sons and one daughter. Private secretary to the High Commissioner for South Africa, Lord Milner, 1901–03; director, Nelson, publishers, London, from 1903, and Reuters, London, 1919; Conservative Member of Parliament for the Scottish Universities, 1927–35; Lord High Commissioner, Church of Scotland, 1933, 1934; Governor-General of Canada, 1935–40; Privy Councillor, 1937. Curator, Oxford University Chest, 1924–30; President, Scottish History Society, 1929–33; bencher, Middle Temple, 1935; Chancellor, University of Edinburgh, 1937–40; Justice of the Peace, Peebles-shire and Oxfordshire. Recipient: James Tait Black Memorial prize, 1929. D.C.L.: Oxford University; LL.D.: University of Glasgow; University of St. Andrews; University of Edinburgh; McGill University, Montreal; University of Toronto; University of Manitoba, Winnipeg; Harvard University, Cambridge, Massachusetts; Yale University, New Haven, Connecticut; D. Litt.: Columbia University, New York; University of British Columbia, Vancouver; McMaster University, Hamilton, Ontario. Honorary Fellow, Brasenose College, Oxford. Companion of Honour, 1932; created Baron Tweedsmuir, 1935; G.C.M.G. (Knight Grand Cross, Order of St. Michael and St. George), 1935; G.C.V.O. (Knight Grand Cross, Royal Victorian Order), 1939. *Died 11 February 1940.*

ROMANCE AND HISTORICAL PUBLICATIONS

Novels

Sir Quixote of the Moors, Being Some Account of an Episode in the Life of the Sieur de Rohaine. London, Unwin, and New York, Holt, 1895.
John Burnet of Barns. London, Lane, and New York, Dodd Mead, 1898.
A Lost Lady of Old Years. London, Lane, 1899.
Salute to Adventurers. London, Nelson, and Boston, Houghton Mifflin, 1915.
Midwinter: Certain Travellers in Old England. London, Hodder and Stoughton, and New York, Doran, 1923.
Witch Wood. London, Hodder and Stoughton, and Boston, Houghton Mifflin, 1927.
The Blanket of the Dark. London, Hodder and Stoughton, and Boston, Houghton Mifflin, 1931.
The Free Fishers. London, Hodder and Stoughton, and Boston, Houghton Mifflin, 1934.
The Long Traverse. London, Hodder and Stoughton, 1941; as *Lake of Gold*, Boston, Houghton Mifflin, 1941.

Short Stories

The Moon Endureth: Tales and Fancies. Edinburgh, Blackwood, and New York, Sturgis, 1912.
The Path of the King. London, Hodder and Stoughton, and New York, Doran, 1921.

OTHER PUBLICATIONS

Novels

The Half-Hearted. London, Isbister, and Boston, Houghton Mifflin, 1900.
Prester John. London, Nelson, 1910; as *The Great Diamond Pipe*, New York, Dodd Mead, 1911.
The Thirty-Nine Steps. Edinburgh, Blackwood, 1915; New York, Doran, 1916.
The Power-House. Edinburgh, Blackwood, and New York, Doran, 1916.
Greenmantle. London, Hodder and Stoughton, and New York, Doran, 1916.
Mr. Standfast. London, Hodder and Stoughton, and New York, Doran, 1919.
Huntingtower. London, Hodder and Stoughton, and New York, Doran, 1922.
The Three Hostages. London, Hodder and Stoughton, and Boston, Houghton Mifflin, 1924.
John Macnab. London, Hodder and Stoughton, and Boston, Houghton Mifflin, 1925.
The Dancing Floor. London, Hodder and Stoughton, and Boston, Houghton Mifflin, 1926.
The Courts of the Morning. London Hodder and Stoughton, and Boston, Houghton Mifflin, 1929.
Castle Gay. London, Hodder and Stoughton, and Boston, Houghton Mifflin, 1929.
A Prince of the Captivity. London, Hodder and Stoughton, and Boston, Houghton Mifflin, 1933.
The House of the Four Winds. London, Hodder and Stoughton, and Boston, Houghton Mifflin, 1935.
The Island of Sheep. London, Hodder and Stoughton, 1936; as *The Man from the Norlands*, Boston, Houghton Mifflin, 1936.
Sick Heart River. London, Hodder and Stoughton, 1941; as *Mountain Meadow*, Boston, Houghton Mifflin, 1941.

Short Stories

Grey Weather: Moorland Tales of My Own People. London, Lane, 1899.
The Watcher by the Threshold and Other Tales. Edinburgh, Blackwood, 1902; augmented edition, New York, Doran, 1918.
Ordeal by Marriage: An Eclogue. London, R. Clay, 1915.
The Runagates Club. London, Hodder and Stoughton, and Boston, Houghton Mifflin, 1928.
The Gap in the Curtain. London, Hodder and Stoughton, and Boston, Houghton Mifflin, 1932.
The Best Short Stories of John Buchan, edited by David Daniell. London, Joseph, 2 vols., 1980–82.

Play

Screenplay: *The Battles of Coronel and Falkland Islands*, with Harry Engholm and Merritt Crawford, 1927.

Verse

The Pilgrim Fathers. Oxford, Blackwell, 1898.
Poems, Scots and English. London, Jack, 1917; revised edition, London, Nelson, 1936.

Other

Scholar Gipsies. London, Lane, and New York, Macmillan, 1896.
Sir Walter Raleigh. Oxford, Blackwell, 1897.
Brasenose College. London, Robinson, 1898.
The African Colony: Studies in the Reconstruction. Edinburgh, Blackwell, 1903.
The Law Relating to the Taxation of Foreign Income. London, Stevens, 1905.
A Lodge in the Wilderness (published anonymously). Edinburgh, Blackwood, 1906.
Some Eighteenth Century Byways and Other Essays. Edinburgh, Blackwood, 1908.
Sir Walter Raleigh (for children). London, Nelson, and New York, Holt, 1911.
What the Home Rule Bill Means (speech). Peebles, Smythe, 1912.
The Marquis of Montrose. London, Nelson, and New York, Scribner, 1913.
Andrew Jameson, Lord Ardwall. Edinburgh, Blackwood, 1913.
Britain's War by Land. London, Oxford University Press, 1915.
Nelson's History of the War. London, Nelson, 24 vols., 1915–19; as *A History of the Great War*, Nelson, and Boston, Houghton Mifflin, 4 vols., 1921–22.
The Achievement of France. London, Methuen, 1915.
The Future of the War (speech). London, Boyle Son and Watchurst, 1916.
The Purpose of War (speech). London, Dent, 1916.
These for Remembrance. Privately printed, 1919.
The Island of Sheep, with Susan Buchan (as Cadmus and Harmonia). London, Hodder and Stoughton, 1919; Boston, Houghton Mifflin, 1920.
The Battle-Honours of Scotland 1914–1918. Glasgow, Outram, 1919.
The History of the South African Forces in France. London, Nelson, 1920.
Francis and Riversdale Grenfell: A Memoir. London, Nelson, 1920.
A Book of Escapes and Hurried Journeys. London, Nelson, 1922; Boston, Houghton Mifflin, 1923.
The Last Secrets: The Final Mysteries of Exploration. London, Nelson, 1923; Boston, Houghton Mifflin, 1924.
The Memoir of Sir Walter Scott (speech). Privately printed, 1923.
Days to Remember: The British Empire in the Great War, with Henry Newbolt. London, Nelson, 1923.
Some Notes on Sir Walter Scott (speech). London, Oxford University Press, 1924.
Lord Minto: A Memoir. London, Nelson, 1924.
The History of the Royal Scots Fusiliers (1678–1918). London, Nelson, 1925.
The Man and the Book: Sir Walter Raleigh. London, Nelson, 1925.
Two Ordeals of Democracy (lecture). Boston, Houghton Mifflin, 1925.
Homilies and Recreations. London, Nelson, and Boston, Houghton Mifflin, 1926.

To the Electors of the Scottish Universities (speech). Glasgow, Anderson, 1927.
The Fifteenth—Scottish—Division 1914–1919, with John Stewart. Edinburgh, Blackwood, 1926.
Montrose. London, Nelson, and Boston, Houghton Mifflin, 1928.
The Causal and the Casual in History (lecture). Cambridge, University Press, and New York, Macmillan, 1929.
What the Union of the Churches Means to Scotland. Edinburgh, McNivern and Wallace, 1929.
The Kirk in Scotland 1560–1929, with George Adam Smith. London, Hodder and Stoughton, 1930.
Montrose and Leadership (lecture). London, Oxford University Press, 1930.
The Revision of Dogmas (lecture). Ashridge, Wisconsin, Ashridge Journal, 1930.
Lord Rosebery 1847–1930. London, Oxford University Press, 1930.
The Novel and the Fairy Tale. London, Oxford University Press, 1931.
Sir Walter Scott. London, Cassell, and New York, Coward McCann, 1932.
The Magic Walking-Stick (for children). London, Hodder and Stoughton, and Boston, Houghton Mifflin, 1932.
Julius Caesar. London, Davies, and New York, Appleton, 1932.
The Massacre of Glencoe. London, Davies, and New York, Putnam, 1933.
Andrew Lang and the Border (lecture). London, Oxford University Press, 1933.
The Margins of Life (speech). London, Birkbeck College, 1933.
The Principles of Social Service (lecture). Glasgow, Glasgow Society of Social Service, 1934(?).
The Scottish Church and the Empire (speech). Glasgow, Church of Scotland Commission on Colonial Churches, 1934.
Gordon at Khartoum. London, Davies, 1934.
Oliver Cromwell. London, Hodder and Stoughton, and Boston, Houghton Mifflin, 1934.
Men and Deeds. London, Davies, 1935; Freeport, New York, Books for Libraries, 1969.
The King's Grace 1910–35 (on George V). London, Hodder and Stoughton, 1935; as *The People's King*, Boston, Houghton Mifflin, 1935.
An Address [The Western Mind]. Montreal, McGill University, 1935.
Address [A University's Bequest to Youth]. Toronto, Victoria University, 1936.
Augustus. London, Hodder and Stoughton, and Boston, Houghton Mifflin, 1937.
The Interpreter's House (speech). London, Hodder and Stoughton, 1938.
Presbyterianism Yesterday, Today, and Tomorrow. Edinburgh, Church of Scotland, 1938.
Memory Hold-the-Door. London, Hodder and Stoughton, 1940; as *Pilgrim's War: An Essay in Recollection*, Boston, Houghton Mifflin, 1940.
Comments and Characters, edited by W. Forbes Gray. London, Nelson, 1940; Freeport, New York, Books for Libraries, 1970.
Canadian Occasions (lectures). London, Hodder and Stoughton, 1940.
The Clearing House: A Survey of One Man's Mind, edited by Lady Tweedsmuir. London, Hodder and Stoughton, 1946.
Life's Adventure: Extracts from the Works of John Buchan, edited by Lady Tweedsmuir. London, Hodder and Stoughton, 1947.

Editor, *Essays and Apothegms*, by Francis Bacon. London, Scott, 1894.

Editor, *Musa Piscatrix*. London, Lane, and Chicago, McClurg, 1896.

Editor, *The Compleat Angler*, by Izaak Walton. London, Methuen, 1901.

Editor, *The Long Road to Victory*. London, Nelson, 1920.

Editor, *Great Hours in Sport*. London, Nelson, 1921.

Editor, *Miscellanies, Literary and Historical*, by Archibald Primrose, Earl of Rosebery. London, Hodder and Stoughton, 1921.

Editor, *A History of English Literature*. London, Nelson, 1923; New York, Ronald Press, 1938.

Editor, *The Nations of Today; A New History of the World*. London, Hodder and Stoughton, and Boston, Houghton Mifflin, 12 vols., 1923–24.

Editor, *The Northern Muse: An Anthology of Scots Vernacular Poetry*. London, Nelson, 1924.

Editor, *Modern Short Stories*. London, Nelson, 1926.

Editor, *Essays and Studies 12*. Oxford, Clarendon Press, 1926.

Editor, *South Africa*. London, British Empire Educational Press, 1928.

Editor, *The Teaching of History*. London, Nelson, 11 vols., 1928–30.

Editor, *The Poetry of Neil Munro*. Edinburgh, Blackwood, 1931.

*

Bibliography: *John Buchan: A Bibliography* by Archibald Hanna, Jr., Hamden, Connecticut, Shoe String Press, 1953; by J. Randolph Cox, in *English Literature in Transition* (Tempe, Arizona), 1966–67; *The First Editions of John Buchan: A Collector's Bibliography* by Robert G. Blanchard, Hamden, Connecticut, Archon, 1981.

Manuscript Collections: National Library of Scotland, Edinburgh; Edinburgh University Library; Douglas Library, Queen's University, Kingston, Ontario.

Critical Studies: *The Interpreter's House: A Critical Assessment of John Buchan* by David Daniell, London, Nelson, 1975; *John Buchan and His World* by Janet Adam Smith, London, Thames and Hudson, 1979; *John Buchan: A Memoir* by William Buchan, London, Buchan and Enright, 1982.

*   *   *

It is ironic that a writer of such high moral seriousness as John Buchan should be best known because of an inaccurate movie rendition of one of his novels. Yet everyone remembers *The Thirty-Nine Steps*, while his historical novels are left unread. Of course, it is also ironic that this scholar, attorney, soldier, and statesman should have chosen to express so much of his moral passion in the form of historical novels. Yet no matter how breathtaking the action, Buchan's real interest is the demonstration of what he regards as the truths of history and the truths of human psychology.

One of the truths that runs through his books is explicit when Nandy Lammas, that minister of the church and professor of philosophy thinks, "It lay with him to prove that a scholar could also be a man." From Nandy, who is called upon to save his former student from a designing woman and, with *The Free Fishers*, to protect England from Napoleon's spies, to another minister, David Semphill in *Witch Wood*, who must fight the ancient lures of witchcraft in his small parish while the forces

of Montrose and the Covenanters fight for the allegiance and lives of the Scottish people, to—almost unbelievably—Samuel Johnson himself, the middle-aged tutor whose loyalty almost lands him on the bloody battlefield of Culloden in *Midwinter*, Buchan portrays the opposing lures of the life of the mind and the spirit and the physical life. Only Dr. Johnson is ultimately unable to combine both. He must say goodbye to his Scottish friend Alistair McLean, who goes to a losing battle with his Prince, and return to London, to his wife, and to the life of the mind where he will be a victor. Yet even the losses others endure have something good in them. Nandy has served his country well and has had a glimpse of romance, although he knows that the beautiful, wronged Mrs. Cranmer is not for an aging don. He is willing to reenter his scholarly world. But the brotherhood of the free fishers is still open to him, and he has renewed eternally the youth that makes the poet. Similarly, in *Witch Wood*, David exposes the chief of the coven who has made the ancient wood of Caledon heavy and oppressive. But Katrine, the love of his life, lies dead of the plague, and he finds the strictures of the covenant, which he had once gladly accepted, place an intolerable burden on him. He may still serve his God, but he will do it as a soldier of Montrose.

Of all British writers, Buchan may be the one who loves most and writes best about the United States. *Salute to Adventurers* is set in Virginia, and parts of *The Path of the King* in Kentucky, Indiana, and Illinois. *The Path of the King* is a daring experiment for Buchan, perhaps best described as touching and unsuccessful. Starting with the premise that no one knows what noble blood may run in the veins of someone of humble birth who rises to greatness, Buchan traces the fortunes of the descendants of a Viking lordling captured in a raid on the Norman coast. A golden ring passes from parent to child through generations, with the rumor that they are of royal blood. The descendants rise and fall with fortune, although perhaps they rise too much to be quite convincing as humble folk. Creditably for Buchan, the ring passes through the female line on a number of occasions (including a French noblewoman who befriends Joan of Arc). One ring holder is the regicide Lovel, and after the Restoration things go badly for his family, until the remnants move to the American colonies. When the last woman to own the ring learns, on her death bed, that it has been lost, she realizes that the purpose of the ring has been fulfilled; the son she has born to Thomas Linkhorn will be a savior of his people. The description of Lincoln's last days is impressive both in scholarship and in emotion, but the message of the book as a whole is less convincing.

In one of his short stories, Buchan remarks "Every man has a creed, but in his soul he knows that the creed has another side, possibly not less logical, which it does not suit him to produce." This is true of Buchan himself, notably in his attitude toward the House of Stuart. Lovel, the regicide, is perhaps the most balanced, sanest of the portrayals in *The Path of the King*; the aged pretender Charles, Duke of Albany, is shown as a helpless sot in the short story "The Company of Marjorlaine." Yet McLain in *Midwinter* is not the only one devoted to His Majesty's cause, and the Covenanters in *Witch Wood* are clearly drunk with excess of authority. Buchan could compromise on everything except the need for balance. His political views as a whole are less simplistic than it is currently the fashion to believe, and in the historical novels particularly the important things are loyalty and courage, exercised in whatever cause.

The independent, quirky, and stubbornly idiosyncratic have a special place in Buchan's affections, overshadowing his more conventional heroes. *Midwinter*'s eponymous hero is a representative of Old England which Dr. Johnson, another figure wildly out of place in the rigors of an adventure novel, rejects for the hive of London and which McLain also rejects because Scotland is his country, even if it must be a country of exile. John Burnet's serving man Nicol in *John Burnet of Barns* is an honorable eccentric, loyal and reluctant to be bound by routine. Eben Garnock and the other free fishers of that novel counterpoise the English horseman Sir Turnour Wyse as studies of the characteristics of their respective nations.

Buchan's style can be more sophisticated than the impetus of the plots would suggest. The use of music in *Midwinter*, for instance, is an effective unifying theme.

When all that can be said in praise of Buchan has been said—his supple prose, his soldier's grasp of terrain, his naturalist's feeling for the countryside, his depictions of desperate journeys taken against the constraints of time and weather—one must still ask if there is something for the modern reader in his books. The answer must be a qualified yes. Buchan, like his great forebear Scott, often starts his stories slowly and one must wait for the action to begin. There are passages of near-impenetrable dialect (certainly for the American reader). Sadly, one of the worst obstacles between Buchan and the modern reader is his assumption that the reader will recognize minor historical figures and events without undue explanation. Yet for all that, the sweep and magnificence of the history, the flashes of humor, the portrayals of the life of the ordinary Scottish people and the pious warmth of the humble folk, and above all the sheer excitement of the plot will always provide rewards for readers of Buchan.

—Susan Branch

BUCK, Pearl S(ydenstricker). American. Also wrote as John Sedges. Born in Hillsboro, West Virginia, 26 June 1892; daughter of Presbyterian missionaries in China. Educated at boarding school in Shanghai, 1907–09; Randolph-Macon Woman's College, Lynchburg, Virginia, B.A. 1914 (Phi Beta Kappa); Cornell University, Ithaca, New York, M.A. 1926. Married 1) John Lossing Buck in 1917 (divorced 1935), one daughter; 2) Richard J. Walsh in 1935 (died 1960); eight adopted children. Psychology teacher, Randolph-Macon Woman's College, 1914; English teacher, University of Nanking, 1921–31, Southeastern University, Nanking, 1925–27, and Chung Yang University, Nanking, 1928–31; returned to the United States, 1935; co-editor, *Asia* magazine, New York, 1941–46; founder and director, East and West Association, 1941–51; founder, Welcome House, an adoption agency, 1949, and Pearl S. Buck Foundation, 1964; member of the Board of Directors, Weather Engineering Corporation of America, Manchester, New Hampshire, 1966. Recipient: Pulitzer Prize, 1932; American Academy Howells medal, 1935; Nobel Prize for Literature, 1938; National Conference of Christians and Jews Brotherhood award, 1955; President's Commission on Employment of the Physically Handicapped citation, 1958; Women's National Book Association Skinner award, 1960; ELA award, 1969. M.A.: Yale University, New Haven, Connecticut, 1933; D.Litt.: University of West Virginia, Morgantown, 1940; St. Lawrence University, Canton, New York, 1942; Delaware Valley College, Doylestown, Pennsylvania, 1965; LL.D.: Howard University, Washington, D.C., 1942; Muhlenberg College, Allentown, Pennsylvania, 1966; L.H.D.: Lincoln University, Pennsylvania, 1953; Woman's Medical College of Philadelphia, 1954; University of Pittsburgh, 1960; Bethany College, West Virginia, 1963; Hahnemann Medical College, Philadelphia, 1966; Rutgers University, New Brunswick, New Jersey, 1969; D.Mus.: Combs College of Music, Philadelphia, 1962; D.H.: West Virginia State College, Institute, 1963. Member, American Academy. *Died 6 March 1973.*

ROMANCE AND HISTORICAL PUBLICATIONS

Novels

East Wind: West Wind. New York, Day, 1930; London, Methuen, 1931.
House of Earth. New York, Reynal, 1935; London, Methuen, 1936.
  The Good Earth. New York, Day, and London, Methuen, 1931.
  Sons. New York, Day, and London, Methuen, 1932.
  A House Divided. New York, Reynal, and London, Methuen, 1935.
The Mother. New York, Day, and London, Methuen, 1934.
China Sky. Philadelphia, Triangle, 1942.
China Flight. Philadelphia, Triangle, 1945.
The Townsman (as John Sedges). New York, Day, 1945; London, Methuen, 1946.
Portrait of a Marriage. New York, Day, 1945; London, Methuen, 1946.
Pavilion of Women. New York, Day, 1946; London, Methuen, 1947.
The Angry Wife (as John Sedges). New York, Day, 1947; London, Methuen, 1948.
Peony. New York, Day, 1948; as *The Bondmaid*, London, Methuen, 1949.
God's Men. New York, Day, and London, Methuen, 1951.
The Hidden Flower. New York, Day, and London, Methuen, 1952.
Satan Never Sleeps. New York, Pocket Books, 1952.
Come, My Beloved. New York, Day, and London, Methuen, 1953.
Imperial Woman. New York, Day, and London, Methuen, 1956.
Letter from Peking. New York, Day, and London, Methuen, 1957.
The Living Reed. New York, Day, and London, Methuen, 1963.
Death in the Castle. New York, Day, 1965; London, Methuen, 1966.
The Time Is Noon. New York, Day, and London, Methuen, 1967.
The New Year. New York, Day, and London, Methuen, 1968.
The Three Daughters of Madame Liang. New York, Day, and London, Methuen, 1969.
Mandala. New York, Day, 1970; London, Methuen, 1971.
The Goddess Abides. New York, Day, and London, Methuen, 1972.
All under Heaven. New York, Day, and London, Methuen, 1973.
The Rainbow. New York, Day, 1974; London, Eyre Methuen, 1976.

Short Stories

The First Wife and Other Stories. New York, Day, and London, Methuen, 1933.
Today and Forever: Stories of China. New York, Day, and London, Macmillan, 1941.
Far and Near: Stories of Japan, China, and America. New York, Day, 1947; London, Methuen, 1949.
Fourteen Stories. New York, Day, 1961; as *With a Delicate Air and Other Stories*, London, Methuen, 1962.
Hearts Come Home and Other Stories. New York, Pocket Books, 1962.
Stories of China. New York, Day, 1964.
The Good Deed and Other Stories of Asia, Past and Present. New York, Day, 1969; London, Methuen, 1970.

Once upon a Christmas. New York, Day, 1972.
Book of Christmas. New York, Simon and Schuster, 1974.
East and West. New York, Day, 1975; London, Prior, 1976.
Secrets of the Heart. New York, Day, 1976.
The Lovers and Other Stories. New York, Day, 1977; London, Eyre Methuen, 1978.
The Woman Who Was Changed and Other Stories. New York, Crowell, 1979.

OTHER PUBLICATIONS

Novels

This Proud Heart. New York, Reynal and Hitchcock, and London, Methuen, 1938.
The Patriot. New York, Day, 1939; London, Methuen, 1941.
Other Gods: An American Legend. New York, Day, and London, Macmillan, 1940.
Dragon Seed. New York, Day, and London, Macmillan, 1942.
The Promise. New York, Day, 1943; London, Methuen, 1945.
Kinfolk. New York, Day, 1949; London, Methuen, 1950.
Command the Morning. New York, Day, and London, Methuen, 1959.

Novels as John Sedges

The Long Love. New York, Day, 1949; London, Methuen, 1950.
Bright Procession. New York, Day, and London, Methuen, 1952.
Voices in the House. New York, Day, 1953; London, Methuen, 1954.

Plays

Flight into China (produced New York, 1939).
Sun Yat Sen: A Play, Preceded by a Lecture by Dr. Hu-shih. New York, Universal Distributors, and London, China Campaign Committee, 1944(?).
China to America (radio play), in *Free World Theatre*, edited by Arch Oboler and Stephen Longstreet. New York, Random House, 1944.
Will This Earth Hold? (radio play), in *Radio Drama in Action*, edited by Erik Barnouw. New York, Farrar and Rinehart, 1945.
The First Wife (produced New York, 1945).
A Desert Incident (produced New York, 1959).
Christine, with Charles K. Peck, Jr., music by Sammy Fain, lyrics by Paul Francis Webster, adaptation of the novel *My Indian Family* by Hilda Wernher (produced New York, 1960).
The Guide, adaptation of the novel by R. K. Narayan (produced New York, 1965).

Screenplays (with Ted Danielewski): *The Big Wave*, 1962; *The Guide*, 1965.

Verse

Words of Love. New York, Day, 1974.

Other (for children)

The Young Revolutionist. New York, Day, and London, Methuen, 1932.
Stories for Little Children. New York, Day, 1940.

When Fun Begins. London, Methuen, 1941.
The Chinese Children Next Door. New York, Day, 1942; London, Methuen, 1943.
The Water Buffalo Children. New York, Day, 1943; London, Methuen, 1945.
The Dragon Fish. New York, Day, 1944; London, Methuen, 1946.
Yu Lan: Flying Boy of China. New York, Day, 1945; London, Methuen, 1947.
The Big Wave. New York, Day, 1948; London, Methuen, 1956.
One Bright Day. New York, Day, 1950; London, Methuen, 1952.
The Man Who Changed China: The Story of Sun Yat Sen. New York, Random House, 1953; London, Methuen, 1955.
The Beech Tree. New York, Day, 1954.
Johnny Jack and His Beginnings. New York, Day, 1954; London, Methuen, 1955.
Christmas Miniature. New York, Day, 1957; as *The Christmas Mouse*, London, Methuen, 1958.
The Christmas Ghost. New York, Day, 1960; London, Methuen, 1962.
Welcome Child. New York, Day, 1964.
The Big Fight. New York, Day, 1965.
The Little Fox in the Middle. New York, Collier, and London, Macmillan, 1966.
Matthew, Mark, Luke, and John. New York, Day, 1967.
The Chinese Storyteller. New York, Day, 1971.
A Gift for the Children. New York, Day, 1973.
Mrs. Starling's Problem. New York, Day, 1973.

Other

Is There a Case for Foreign Missions? New York, Day, 1932; London, Methuen, 1933.
East and West and the Novel: Sources of the Early Chinese Novel. Peking, College of Chinese Studies, 1932.
The Exile (biography). New York, Reynal, and London, Methuen, 1936.
Fighting Angel: Portrait of a Soul (biography). New York, Reynal, 1936; London, Methuen, 1937.
The Chinese Novel. New York, Day, and London, Macmillan, 1939.
Of Men and Women. New York, Day, 1941; London, Methuen, 1942.
Freedom for All. New York, Post-War World Council, 1942(?).
American Unity and Asia. New York, Day, 1942; as *Asia and Democracy*, London, Methuen, 1943.
What America Means to Me. New York, Day, 1943; London, Methuen, 1944.
Talk about Russia, with Masha Scott. New York, Day, 1945.
Tell the People: Talks with James Yen about the Mass Education Movement. New York, Day, 1945.
How It Happens: Talk about the German People 1914–1933, with Erna von Pustau. New York, Day, 1947.
American Argument, with Eslanda Goode Robeson. New York, Day, 1949; London, Methuen, 1950.
The Child Who Never Grew. New York, Day, 1950; London, Methuen, 1951.
My Several Worlds (autobiography). New York, Day, 1954; London, Methuen, 1955.
Friend to Friend, with Carlos P. Romulo. New York, Day, 1958.
The Delights of Learning. Pittsburgh, University of Pittsburgh Press, 1960.
A Bridge for Passing (autobiography). New York, Day, 1962; London, Methuen, 1963.

The Joy of Children. New York, Day, 1964.
The Gifts They Bring: Our Debts to the Mentally Retarded, with Gweneth T. Zarfoss. New York, Day, 1965.
Children for Adoption. New York, Random House, 1965.
The People of Japan. New York, Simon and Schuster, 1966; London, Hale, 1968.
For Spacious Skies: Journey in Dialogue, with Theodore F. Harris. New York, Day, 1966.
My Mother's House, with others. Richwood, West Virginia, Appalachia Press, 1966.
To My Daughters, With Love. New York, Day, 1967.
The People of China. London, Hale, 1968.
The Kennedy Women: A Personal Appraisal. New York, Cowles-Day, and London, Methuen, 1970.
China as I See It, edited by Theodore F. Harris. New York, Day, 1970; London, Methuen, 1971.
The Story Bible. New York, Bartholomew House, 1971.
Pearl S. Buck's America. New York, Bartholomew House, 1971.
China Past and Present. New York, Day, 1972.
A Community Success Story: The Founding of the Pearl Buck Center. New York, Day, 1972.
Oriental Cookbook. New York, Simon and Schuster, 1972; London, Eyre Methuen, 1974.

Editor, *China in Black and White: An Album of Woodcuts by Contemporary Chinese Artists.* New York, Day, 1945.
Editor, *Fairy Tales of the Orient.* New York, Simon and Schuster, 1965.

Translator, *All Men Are Brothers,* by Shui Hu Chan. New York, Day, and London, Methuen, 1933.

*

Bibliography: by Lucille S. Zinn, in *Bulletin of Bibliography 36* (Boston), 1979.

Critical Studies: *Pearl S. Buck* by Paul A. Doyle, New York, Twayne, 1965, revised edition, 1980; *Pearl S. Buck: A Biography* by Theodore F. Harris, New York, Day, 2 vols., 1969–71, London, Eyre Methuen, 2 vols., 1970–72; *Pearl S. Buck: A Woman in Conflict* by Nora Stirling, Piscataway, New Jersey, New Century, 1983.

* * *

In an astonishingly prolific career, during which she produced more than 70 major works, many of her novels with an American setting under the pseudonym John Sedges, Pearl S. Buck did more to bring the East and West closer together in empathy and understanding than had any previous writer. No Western reader who had come to care, intensely and personally, about the fate of a character in a work of fiction, is likely to pay more than passing attention to the race or creed of that character; what matters is a shared humanity. Through Buck's writings, millions cared, as they had never before been persuaded to do, about the men and women of China, Korea, Japan, and India.

Buck's lasting fame is chiefly that of the writer who made China a real place peopled by three-dimensional human beings; a concept quite revolutionary to readers accustomed to read, if at all, of cardboard figures either quaint, comic, or sinister, moving in a stilted, stylized fashion about an exotic and artificial stage not even intended to convince. *The Good Earth,* Buck's most successful and important novel, changed all that forever.

Buck's Chinese men, and perhaps even moreso her women, were convincingly as real and true to life as were her readers; so too were her Koreans, Indians, Japanese, and Americans. Herself a "missionary kid", Buck well understood the difficulties as well as the benefits of belonging simultaneously to two worlds. She understood too, through personal experience, the unique and fragile bridge between two cultures that can give the deepest joy, and inflict the most bitter pain: that of love between men and women of different races, bestowed in opposition to the hopes, even the demands, of family and community.

Interracial love, almost always star-crossed, rarely allowed to come to rewarding fulfillment, is the recurring theme of Buck's work. Madame Wu, in *Pavilion of Women,* discovers after years of correct and tepid marriage what love can mean, and that even the pain of such a love can be very sweet, through her firmly controlled and suppressed passion for the Italian Brother Andre. What Madame Wu has learned through this forbidden love gives her strength and understanding to help her son when in his turn he loses his heart to an impossible, non-Chinese love.

In *The Hidden Flower,* a traditional Japanese family is overset when the beloved and sheltered daughter, Josui, already betrothed in the correct manner to a worthy young Japanese man, is swept up into a most untraditional, ill-fated love match with Allen Kennedy, an American soldier with the army of occupation. Not even a love story, merely a casual interlude, the coming together of Soonya, a Korean girl, and Chris, an American soldier, has resulted in the birth of a son. In *The New Year,* the forgotten son reaches out to touch the life of his casual American parent, now married to a woman of his own people.

The love of Bettina, a former slave, and Tom, a southerner who fought for the army of the North, tears a proud old family to shreds in *The Angry Wife.* Livy MacArd of *Come My Beloved* is the daughter of a missionary in India, who preached the brotherhood of man, and of equality before God, but who cannot live up to his own professed faith when his daughter falls in love with a young Indian, Jatin.

Peony, a bondmaid in the house of Ezra ben Israel, loves her young master David, but his mother is determined that he shall have a Jewish bride. It is not to be: David does in time marry a Chinese girl, but not faithful Peony, who has helped him to win Kueilan, the rival who supplants her. She knows only too well that a Jewish wife would shut her out of David's life entirely, whereas a Chinese woman would allow their friendship to continue; and her love finds the sacrifice worthwhile.

No matter the setting, the pain is the same, and the outcome over and over again is a slow working-out over generations of the reverberations set astir by patterns broken; the patterns will mend, imperceptibly as a pond mends a shattered reflection; the disruptive rock remains, hidden beneath the calm surface.

Time has passed Buck's work by; in most of the world, the sanctions that caused her people such pain and grief have lost their power, and as the world grows ever smaller, insular attitudes become untenable. It is only fair to remember, however, that "a journey of a thousand miles begins with a single step." Not so very long ago, Buck first invited a great many people to make that all-important step into the future.

—Joan McGrath

———

BUCKINGHAM, Nancy. Pseudonym for John and Nancy Sawyer; also write as Nancy John; Erica Quest. British. **SAWYER, Nancy (Buckingham):** born in Bristol, 10 August

1924. Married John Sawyer in 1949; one son and one daughter. Worked as medical social worker. **SAWYER, John:** born in London, 4 October 1919. Director of a London advertising firm. Both are now full-time writers. Agent: A. M. Heath, 79 St. Martin's Lane, London WC2N 4AA, England; or, Brandt and Brandt, 1501 Broadway, New York, New York 10036, U.S.A.

ROMANCE AND HISTORICAL PUBLICATIONS

Novels

Victim of Love. London, Hale, 1967; as *The Hour Before Moonrise*, New York, Ace, 1967.
Cloud over Malverton. New York, Ace, 1967; London, Hale, 1970.
Heart of Marble. London, Hale, 1967; as *Storm in the Mountains*, New York, Ace, 1967.
Romantic Journey. London, Hale, 1968; as *The Legend of Baverstock Manor,* New York, Ace, 1968.
The Dark Summer. London, Hale, and New York, Ace, 1968.
Call of Glengarron. London, Ace, 1968; New York, Hale, 1969.
Kiss of Hot Sun. London, Hale, 1969.
The Secret of the Ghostly Shroud. New York, Lancer, 1969; as *Shroud of Silence*, London, Hale, 1970.
The House Called Edenhythe. London, Hale, 1970; New York, Hawthorn, 1972.
Return to Vienna. New York, Dell, 1971; London, Hale, 1973.
Quest for Alexis. New York, Hawthorn, 1973; London, Hale, 1974.
Valley of the Ravens. New York, Hawthorn, 1973; London, Hale, 1975.
The Jade Dragon. New York, Hawthorn, 1974; London, Hale, 1976.
The Other Cathy. London, Eyre Methuen, 1978; South Yarmouth, Massachusetts, Curley, 1981.
Vienna Summer. London, Eyre Methuen, and New York, St. Martin's Press, 1979.
Marianna. London, Eyre Methuen, 1981.

Novels as Erica Quest

The Silver Castle. New York, Doubleday, 1978; Long Preston, Yorkshire, Magna Print, 1988.
The October Cabaret. New York, Doubleday, 1979; London, Hale, 1986.
Design for Murder. New York, Doubleday, 1981.
Death Walk. New York, Doubleday, 1988.

Novels as Nancy John

The Spanish House. New York, Pocket Books, and London, Hodder and Stoughton, 1981.
Tormenting Flame. New York, Pocket Books, and London, Hodder and Stoughton, 1981.
To Trust Tomorrow. New York, Pocket Books, and London, Hodder and Stoughton, 1981.
A Man for Always. New York, Pocket Books, 1981; London, Hodder and Stoughton, 1982.
Outback Summer. New York, Pocket Books, and London, Hodder and Stoughton, 1981.
So Many Tomorrows. New York, Pocket Books, and London, Hodder and Stoughton, 1982.

Web of Passion. New York, Pocket Books, 1982; London, Hodder and Stoughton, 1983.
Make-Believe Bride. New York, Pocket Books, and London, Hodder and Stoughton, 1982.
Window to Happiness. New York, Pocket Books, and London, Hodder and Stoughton, 1983.
Summer Rhapsody. New York, Pocket Books, and London, Hodder and Stoughton, 1983.
Never Too Late. New York, Pocket Books, and London, Hodder and Stoughton, 1983.
Dream of Yesterday. New York, Pocket Books, and London, Hodder and Stoughton, 1984.
Champagne Nights. New York, Pocket Books, and London, Hodder and Stoughton, 1984.
Night with a Stranger. New York, Silhouette, 1984.
Rendezvous. New York and London, Silhouette, 1985.
The Moongate Wish. New York and London, Silhouette, 1985.
Lookalike Love. New York and London, Silhouette, 1986.
Secret Love. New York and London, Silhouette, 1986.

*   *   *

The husband and wife team of John Sawyer and Nancy Buckingham is prolific both as to the number of books published as well as to the type of book written. As Nancy Buckingham, they write both gothic and romantic suspense, as Nancy John, "category" romance, and as Erica Quest, romantic suspense and mystery.

Most of Buckingham's early books are more romantic suspense (à la Mary Stewart) than gothic. *Call of Glengarron* has the brooding castle and haunting woods of Scotland as backdrop, but the time is contemporary and the mood is that of a true mystery. In a word, it is pedestrian. *Cloud over Malverton, The Dark Summer*, and *Heart of Marble* are similar, the writing, if anything, more juvenile. *Romantic Journey* is a true modern dress gothic—strange house, weird characters, secret passages, etc. In this book for the first time characters are well drawn and the plot moves well, centered as it is on a double identity. The best of these early works is *Victim of Love*. In this novel of romantic suspense the characterization is full and real. The plot moves quickly and the ending is unusual and far from storybook. *Quest for Alexis* could have been script for a 1950's "B" movie. The muddled love affairs interfere with the plot. With *Valley of the Ravens, The House Called Edenhythe*, and *The Jade Dragon* Buckingham succeeds better. These gothics have Victorian settings with suitable fog, terrain, and characters, though the result is still somewhat lackluster.

As Nancy John and Erica Quest the Sawyers have found their métier. *Tormenting Flame*, and other Nancy John novels are all formula romances written to the specifications of the publishers, but the books are better written than any of their predecessors. Their characters are real and vibrant, and the reader cares what happens to them. Settings are glowingly and accurately described, be they in Australia, Spain, or England. The plots move swiftly; the action is believable. *The Silver Castle*, their first book as Erica Quest, is romantic suspense and could have been written as Nancy Buckingham. It is a "crossover" book. The remaining Quest titles have emerged as pure mystery story.

The Sawyers display amazing versatility. Nancy Buckingham, while not the greatest of the gothic/romantic suspense authors, is far from the worst. Erica Quest could become one of the top

flight mystery writers. Nancy John is one of the best of the for-
mula/category romance writers. They are a formidable combination.

—Paula M. Zieselman

———————

BURCHELL, Mary. Pseudonym for Ida Cook. British. Born
in Sunderland, County Durham. Educated at the Duchess'
School, Alnwick, Northumberland. Former President, Romantic
Novelists Association. *Died 22 December 1986.*

ROMANCE AND HISTORICAL PUBLICATIONS

Novels

Wife to Christopher. London, Mills and Boon, 1936.
Nobody Asked Me. London, Mills and Boon, 1937; Toronto,
Harlequin, 1976.
Except My Love. London, Mills and Boon, 1937; Toronto, Har-
lequin, 1973.
Call—And I'll Come. London, Mills and Boon, 1937; Toronto,
Harlequin, 1973.
But Not for Me. London, Mills and Boon, 1938; Toronto, Har-
lequin, 1971.
Other Lips Have Loved You. London, Mills and Boon, 1938; as
Two Loves Have I, 1976.
With All My Worldly Goods. London, Mills and Boon, 1938;
Toronto, Harlequin, 1961.
Yet Love Remains. London, Mills and Boon, 1938; Toronto,
Harlequin, 1975.
After Office Hours. London, Mills and Boon, 1939.
Little Sister. London, Mills and Boon, 1939; New York, Arca-
dia House, 1947.
One of the Family. London, Mills and Boon, 1939.
Such Is Love. London, Mills and Boon, 1939; Toronto, Harle-
quin, 1975.
Yours with Love. London, Mills and Boon, 1940.
Pay Me Tomorrow. London, Mills and Boon, 1940; Toronto,
Harlequin, 1974.
One Man's Heart. London, Mills and Boon, 1940; Toronto,
Harlequin, 1972.
I'll Go With You. London, Mills and Boon, 1940.
Accompanied by His Wife. London, Mills and Boon, 1941; Tor-
onto, Harlequin, 1974.
Always Yours. London, Mills and Boon, 1941.
Just a Nice Girl. London, Mills and Boon, 1941; Toronto, Har-
lequin, 1975.
Strangers May Marry. London, Mills and Boon, 1941; Toronto,
Harlequin, 1974.
Where Shall I Wander? London, Mills and Boon, 1942.
Thine Is My Heart. London, Mills and Boon, 1942.
Love Made the Choice. London, Mills and Boon, 1942; Tor-
onto, Harlequin, 1975.
Dare I Be Happy? London, Mills and Boon, 1943; Toronto,
Harlequin, 1975.
My Old Love Came. London, Mills and Boon, 1943.
Thanks to Elizabeth. London, Mills and Boon, 1944.
Take Me with You. London, Mills and Boon, 1944; Toronto,
Harlequin, 1965.
Dearly Beloved. London, Mills and Boon, 1944; Toronto, Har-
lequin, 1967.

Away Went Love. London, Mills and Boon, 1945; Toronto, Har-
lequin, 1964.
Cinderella after Midnight. London, Mills and Boon, 1945; Tor-
onto, Harlequin, 1967.
Meant for Each Other. London, Mills and Boon, 1945; Tor-
onto, Harlequin, 1966.
Wife by Arrangement. London, Mills and Boon, 1946; Toronto,
Harlequin, 1960.
It's Rumoured in the Village. London, Mills and Boon, 1946;
Toronto, Harlequin, 1973.
First Love—Last Love. London, Mills and Boon, 1946.
Find Out the Way. London, Mills and Boon, 1946.
Not Without You. London, Mills and Boon, 1947.
Under Joint Management. London, Mills and Boon, 1947.
Ward of Lucifer. London, Mills and Boon, 1947; Toronto, Har-
lequin, 1967.
The Brave in Heart. London, Mills and Boon, 1948; Toronto,
Harlequin, 1975.
If You Care. London, Mills and Boon, 1948.
Then Come Kiss Me. London, Mills and Boon, 1948; Toronto,
Harlequin, 1958.
Wish on the Moon. London, Mills and Boon, 1949.
If This Were All. London, Mills and Boon, 1949.
I Will Love You Still. London, Mills and Boon, 1949.
Choose Which You Will. London, Mills and Boon, 1949; Tor-
onto, Harlequin, 1966.
At First Sight. London, Mills and Boon, 1950.
A Letter for Don. London, Mills and Boon, 1950.
Love Him or Leave Him. London, Mills and Boon, 1950; Tor-
onto, Harlequin, 1961.
Tell Me My Fortune. London, Mills and Boon, 1951; Toronto,
Harlequin, 1975.
Mine for a Day. London, Mills and Boon, 1951.
Here I Belong. London, Mills and Boon, 1951.
Over the Blue Mountains. London, Mills and Boon, 1952; Tor-
onto, Harlequin, 1960.
Stolen Heart. London, Mills and Boon, 1952; Toronto, Harle-
quin, 1962.
Sweet Adventure. London, Mills and Boon, 1952; Toronto, Har-
lequin, 1968.
A Ring on Her Finger. London, Mills and Boon, 1953.
No Real Relation. London, Mills and Boon, 1953.
The Heart Must Choose. London, Mills and Boon, 1953.
The Heart Cannot Forget. London, Mills and Boon, 1953; Tor-
onto, Harlequin, 1966.
Meet Me Again. London, Mills and Boon, 1954; as *Nurse Al-
ison's Trust,* Toronto, Harlequin, 1964.
When Love's Beginning. London, Mills and Boon, 1954; Tor-
onto, Harlequin, 1969.
Under the Stars of Paris. London, Mills and Boon, 1954; Tor-
onto, Harlequin, 1976.
Yours to Command. London, Mills and Boon, 1955; Toronto,
Harlequin, 1964.
The Prettiest Girl. London, Mills and Boon, 1955.
Hospital Corridors. London, Mills and Boon, 1955; Toronto,
Harlequin, 1958.
For Ever and Ever. London, Mills and Boon, 1956; Toronto,
Harlequin, 1959.
Loving Is Giving. London, Mills and Boon, 1956; Toronto, Har-
lequin, 1967.
On the Air. London, Mills and Boon, 1956; Toronto, Harle-
quin, 1960.
To Journey Together. London, Mills and Boon, 1956; Toronto,
Harlequin, 1970.
Loyal in All. London, Mills and Boon, 1957; as *Nurse Marika,
Loyal in All,* Toronto, Harlequin, 1963.

Love Is My Reason. London, Mills and Boon, 1957; Toronto, Harlequin, 1959.

Joanna at the Grange. London, Mills and Boon, 1957.

And Falsely Pledge My Love. London, Mills and Boon, 1957; Toronto, Harlequin, 1965.

Dear Sir. London, Mills and Boon, 1958; Toronto, Harlequin, 1961.

Dear Trustee. London, Mills and Boon, 1958; Toronto, Harlequin, 1959.

The Girl in the Blue Dress. London, Mills and Boon, 1958; Toronto, Harlequin, 1976.

Star Quality. London, Mills and Boon, 1959; as *Surgeon of Distinction*, Toronto, Harlequin, 1959.

Honey. London, Mills and Boon, 1959; Toronto, Harlequin, 1977.

Corner House. London, Mills and Boon, 1959.

Across the Counter. London, Mills and Boon, 1960; Toronto, Harlequin, 1961.

Choose the One You'll Marry. London, Mills and Boon, and Toronto, Harlequin, 1960.

Paris—And My Love. London, Mills and Boon, 1960; Toronto, Harlequin, 1961.

My Sister Celia. London, Mills and Boon, 1961; Toronto, Harlequin, 1971.

Reluctant Relation. London, Mills and Boon, 1961; Toronto, Harlequin, 1962.

The Wedding Dress. London, Mills and Boon, 1962; Toronto, Harlequin, 1964.

House of Conflict. London, Mills and Boon, 1962; Toronto, Harlequin, 1963.

Inherit My Heart. London, Mills and Boon, 1962; Toronto, Harlequin, 1963.

Dangerous Loving. London, Mills and Boon, 1963.

Sweet Meadows. London, Mills and Boon, 1963.

Do Not Go, My Love. London, Mills and Boon, 1964; Toronto, Harlequin, 1972.

The Strange Quest of Anne Weston. London, Mills and Boon, 1964; as *The Strange Quest of Nurse Anne*, Toronto, Harlequin, 1965.

Girl with a Challenge. London, Mills and Boon, 1965; Toronto, Harlequin, 1970.

Her Sister's Children. London, Mills and Boon, 1965.

A Song Begins. London, Mills and Boon, 1965; Toronto, Harlequin, 1966.

The Other Linding Girl. London, Mills and Boon, 1966; Toronto, Harlequin, 1970.

The Broken Wing. London, Mills and Boon, 1966; Toronto, Harlequin, 1967; as *Damaged Angel*, Mills and Boon, 1967.

When Love Is Blind. London, Mills and Boon, 1967; Toronto, Harlequin, 1968.

Though Worlds Apart. London, Mills and Boon, 1967; Toronto, Harlequin, 1969.

The Marshall Family. London, Mills and Boon, 1967; Toronto, Harlequin, 1968.

A Home for Joy. London, Mills and Boon, 1968; Toronto, Harlequin, 1969.

Missing from Home. London, Mills and Boon, 1968; Toronto, Harlequin, 1969.

The Curtain Rises. London, Mills and Boon, 1969; Toronto, Harlequin, 1970.

The Rosewood Box. London, Mills and Boon, 1970.

Child of Music. London, Mills and Boon, 1970; Toronto, Harlequin, 1971.

Second Marriage. London, Mills and Boon, 1971.

Music of the Heart. London, Mills and Boon, and Toronto, Harlequin, 1972.

Design for Loving. London, Mills and Boon, 1972.

Unbidden Melody. London, Mills and Boon, 1973; Toronto, Harlequin, 1974.

Song Cycle. London, Mills and Boon, and Toronto, Harlequin, 1974.

Remembered Serenade. London, Mills and Boon, and Toronto, Harlequin, 1975.

Elusive Harmony. London, Mills and Boon, 1976; Toronto, Harlequin, 1977.

Nightingales. London, Mills and Boon, and Toronto, Harlequin, 1980.

Masquerade with Music. London, Mills and Boon, 1982.

On Wings of Song. London, Mills and Boon, 1985.

OTHER PUBLICATIONS

Other as Ida Cook

We Followed Our Stars (on opera singers). London, Hamish Hamilton, and New York, Morrow, 1950.

My Life, with Tito Gobbi. London, Macdonald and Jane's, 1979.

*   *   *

Mary Burchell's favorite setting for her contemporary romances is the world of opera. An avid fan herself, Burchell realistically describes the hard work and discipline required from opera singers who must fiercely compete for prize roles at the same time that she lovingly portrays the excitement and glamour that result from the creation of beautiful music by talented, temperamental stars. Burchell's world of opera is a proverbial "small world," for these romances either revolve around or at least mention the same cast of characters. In fact, a number of the romances have been grouped together as "The Warrender Saga" after one of the main characters, Sir Oscar Warrender, a conductor. His romance with and marriage to a young girl whom he trains to be a singer are told in *A Song Begins*. He and his wife play an essential but supporting role in the other romances. Other musical characters who reappear include Conrad Schreiner, another teacher and conductor, and his mistress, Manora Venescu, a singer. Florian, a fashion designer, is also alluded to in several novels. Thus, once Burchell develops a character she is fond of, she carried him or her over into other novels. This is an interesting, effective technique for involving readers.

Burchell experiments in other ways as well. For example, in one novel *Call—And I'll Come*, the first three chapters and the last chapter are written from the perspective of the hero while the middle of the novel is written from the heroine's perspective, an unusual arrangement for a formula romance. In other Burchell romances the reader is aware that she is being told a story by a narrator who occasionally draws back to make editorial comments on the characters and their behaviour, although the narrator is usually telling the story from the heroine's perspective.

Burchell is not a dramatic writer with a taste for flamboyant, impossible characters and fast-paced, violent action. Most of the characters in her romances, even the rival suitors, are nice but flawed human beings. There are very few arch villains. The heroines are quiet, serious, maternal young women who have sufficient flashes of humor and temper to make them intriguing to the heroes who are basically unromantic but loyal and thoughtful, vitally alive men who are dedicated to their work. Most of the "action" consists of the heroes and heroines maturing. The heroines develop their occupational and social skills and become increasingly self-confident while the heroes are shaken from their rather oblivious confidence that they will get their way in all things. This growth takes place over weeks or even months, and much of that time is spent apart from each other. In the end, of course, they are united, both wiser than before.

Burchell was a romance writer whose approach to romance changed very little over the last 20 years. She did not dwell on passion; nor did she describe fiery love-making between the hero and heroine. These traits may make her romances seem rather tame for modern tastes but what they lack in passion they make up for in sincerity and a certain charm, particularly the novels that deal with opera.

—Margaret Jensen

BURFORD, Eleanor. See **HOLT, Victoria.**

BURFORD, Lolah. American. Born in 1931. Educated at Bryn Mawr College, Pennsylvania. Address: c/o Macmillan Inc., 866 Third Avenue, New York, New York, 10022, U.S.A.

ROMANCE AND HISTORICAL PUBLICATIONS

Novels

Vice Avenged: A Moral Tale. New York, Macmillan, and London, Macmillan, 1971.
The Vision of Stephen: An Elegy. New York, Macmillan, 1972; London, Cassell, 1973.
Edward, Edward. New York, Macmillan, 1973; London, Cassell, 1974.
MacLyon. New York, Macmillan, 1974; London, Weidenfeld and Nicolson, 1975.
Alyx. New York, Macmillan, 1977.
Seacage. New York, Macmillan, 1979.

*   *   *

Lolah Burford's novels are neither for the meek nor the militant, the little old lady or the strident feminist. Raw sex is the major element of each novel—sex of every variety, from rape to incest, sadism, and homosexuality. Though cloaked in velvet prose, Burford's "polite pornography" is explicit and pervasive.

The typical Burford novel begins with an act of sexual violence. *Vice Avenged: A Moral Tale,* Burford's first novel, set in 18th-century London, opens with a round of cards; the winner must "ravish" a "virgin of good family" and return with the bloody proof of his deed. Young Marquis Bysshe Gore is the rakish victor in this cruel and dangerous game. Cressida, daughter of the Duke of Salisbury, is the innocent victim whom the players have chosen by lot. The rape occurs: Gore is violent and merciless; Cressida frightened and submissive, but (according to Burford) she gradually enjoys being taken and falls in love with Gore. *Alyx,* a more recent Burford effusion, set on an 18th-century Caribbean sugar plantation, begins with Smith, the "plantation stud," taking by force an inexperienced young slave girl. Alyx, too, falls in love with the rapacious villain. But villain turns out to be hero when "Smith" turns out to be Simon,

the kidnapped Sixth Earl of Halford. As if to justify these fictional reactions, Burford quotes Alexander Pope: "Ev'ry woman is at heart a rake."

Diverging from her standard plot devices, Burford, in *The Vision of Stephen*, combines the 7th century with the 19th. Young Margery discovers behind her piano a grate through which 7th-century Stephen enters her world—the England of 1822—and magically disappears and re-appears to live out a 1200-year time-shuttle. To establish validity for her deft contraposition of time sequences, Burford studied Bede's *Ecclesiastical History of the English Nation.* Rather pretentiously, Burford concludes her novel with Alfred's preface to the translation of *The Pastoral Care* (AD 894), in Old English—a bit difficult for those who are not medievalists.

Burford's plots are fast-paced, full of action and intrigue. The well-researched, historically correct settings are various: 18th-century London (*Vice Avenged*); the 7th-century Anglo-Saxon kingdom of Northumbria (*The Vision of Stephen*); the 19th-century pre-Regency unrest in England, Napoleonic Wars, and flowering of Vienna (*Edward, Edward*); the 18th-century Protestant Rebellion in Scotland (*MacLyon*); the 18th-century Caribbean sugar plantation (*Alyx*); and "Another Time" in an unnamed land (*Seacage*). Burford's prose style is sophisticated, and consists mostly of dialogue, spoken with the formality and grandiloquence of times past, and few descriptive passages.

—Marcia G. Fuchs

BURGESS, Anthony. Pseudonym for John Anthony Burgess Wilson; also writes as Joseph Kell. British. Born in Manchester, Lancashire, 25 February 1917. Educated at Xaverian College, Manchester; Manchester University, B.A. (honours) in English 1940. Served in the British Army Education Corps, 1940–46: Sergeant-Major. Married 1) Llewela Isherwood Jones in 1942 (died 1968); 2) Liliana Macellari in 1968, one son. Lecturer, Extra-Mural Department, Birmingham University, 1946–48; education officer and lecturer, Central Advisory Council for Adult Education in the Forces, 1946–48; Lecturer in Phonetics, Ministry of Education, 1948–50; English master, Banbury Grammar School, Oxfordshire, 1950–54; Senior Lecturer in English, Malayan Teachers Training College, Khata Baru, 1954–57; English language specialist, Department of Education, Brunei, Borneo, 1958–59. Writer-in-residence, University of North Carolina, Chapel Hill, 1969–70; Professor, Columbia University, New York, 1970–71; Visiting Fellow, Princeton University, New Jersey, 1970–71; Distinguished Professor, City University of New York, 1972–73; literary adviser, Guthrie Theatre, Minneapolis, 1972–75. Also composer. Recipient: National Arts Club award, 1973; Foreign Book prize (France), 1981; *Sunday Times* Mort Blanc award, 1987. D.Litt.: Manchester University, 1982. Fellow, Royal Society of Literature, 1969; Commandeur de Mérite Culturel (Monaco), 1986; Commandeur des Arts et des Lettres (France), 1986. Address: 44 rue Grimaldi, MC 98000, Monaco.

ROMANCE AND HISTORICAL PUBLICATIONS

Novels

Time for a Tiger. London, Heinemann, 1956.
The Enemy in the Blanket. London, Heinemann, 1958.
Beds in the East. London, Heinemann, 1959.

Devil of a State. London, Heinemann, 1961; New York, Norton, 1962.
Nothing Like the Sun: A Story of Shakespeare's Love-Life. London, Heinemann, and New York, Norton, 1964.
MF. London, Cape, and New York, Knopf, 1971.
Napoleon Symphony. London, Cape, and New York, Knopf, 1974.
Abba Abba. London, Faber, and Boston, Little Brown, 1977.
Man of Nazareth. New York, McGraw Hill, 1979; London, Magnum, 1980.
The End of the World News. London, Hutchinson, 1982; New York, McGraw Hill, 1983.
The Kingdom of the Wicked. London, Hutchinson, and New York, Arbor House, 1985.
Any Old Iron. London, Hutchinson, and New York, Random House, 1989.

OTHER PUBLICATIONS

Novels

The Right to an Answer. London, Heinemann, 1960; New York, Norton, 1961.
The Doctor Is Sick. London, Heinemann, and New York, Norton, 1960.
The Worm and the Ring. London, Heinemann, 1961; revised edition, 1970.
One Hand Clapping (as Joseph Kell). London, Davies, 1961; as Anthony Burgess, New York, Knopf, 1972.
A Clockwork Orange. London, Heinemann, 1962; New York, Norton, 1963.
The Wanting Seed. London, Heinemann, 1962; New York, Norton, 1963.
Honey for the Bears. London, Heinemann, 1963; New York, Norton, 1964.
Inside Mr. Enderby (as Joseph Kell). London, Heinemann, 1963.
The Eve of Saint Venus. London, Sidgwick and Jackson, 1964; New York, Norton, 1967.
The Malayan Trilogy (includes *Time for a Tiger*, *The Enemy in the Blanket*, *Beds in the East*). London, Heinemann, 1964; as *The Long Day Wanes*, New York, Norton, 1965.
A Vision of Battlements. London, Sidgwick and Jackson, 1965; New York, Norton, 1966.
Tremor of Intent. London, Heinemann, and New York, Norton, 1966.
Enderby Outside. London, Heinemann, 1968.
Enderby (includes *Inside Mr. Enderby* and *Enderby Outside*). New York, Norton, 1968.
The Clockwork Testament; or, Enderby's End. London, Hart Davis MacGibbon, 1974; New York, Knopf, 1975.
Beard's Roman Women. New York, McGraw Hill, 1976; London, Hutchinson, 1977.
1985. London, Hutchinson, and New York, Simon and Schuster, 1980.
Earthly Powers. London, Hutchinson, and New York, Simon and Schuster, 1980.
Enderby (includes *Inside Mr. Enderby*, *Enderby Outside*, *The Clockwork Testament*). London, Penguin, 1982.
Enderby's Dark Lady; or, No End to Enderby. London, Hutchinson, and New York, McGraw Hill, 1984.
The Pianoplayers. London, Hutchinson, and New York, Arbor House, 1986.

Short Story

Will and Testament: A Fragment of Biography. Verona, Italy, Plain Wrapper Press, 1977.

Plays

Cyrano de Bergerac, adaptation of the play by Rostand (produced Minneapolis, 1971). New York, Knopf, 1971; musical version, as *Cyrano*, music by Michael Lewis, lyrics by Burgess (produced New York, 1972).
Oedipus the King, adaptation of a play by Sophocles (produced Minneapolis, 1972; Southampton, Hampshire, 1979). Minneapolis, University of Minnesota Press, 1972; London, Oxford University Press, 1973.
The Cavalier of the Rose (story adaptation), in *Der Rosenkavalier*, libretto by Hofmannsthal, music by Richard Strauss. Boston, Little Brown, 1982; London, Joseph, 1983.
Cyrano de Bergerac (not same as 1971 version), adaptation of the play by Rostand (produced London, 1983). London, Hutchinson, 1985.
Blooms of Dublin, music by Burgess, adaptation of the novel *Ulysses* by Joyce (broadcast 1983). London, Hutchinson, 1986.
Oberon Old and New (includes original libretto by James Robinson Planché), music by Carl Maria von Weber. London, Hutchinson, 1985.
Carmen, adaptation of the libretto by Henri Meilhac and Ludovic Halévy, music by Georges Bizet (produced London, 1986). London, Hutchinson, 1986.
A Clockwork Orange, music by Burgess, adaptation of his own novel. London, Hutchinson, 1987.

Screenplay: special languages for *Quest for Fire*, 1981.

Radio Play: *Blooms of Dublin*, music by Burgess, 1983.

Television Plays: *Moses—The Lawgiver*, with others, 1975; *Jesus of Nazareth*, with others, 1977; *A Kind of Failure* (documentary; *Writers and Places* series), 1981; *The Childhood of Christ*, music by Berlioz, 1985; *A.D.*, 1985.

Verse

Moses: A Narrative. London, Dempsey and Squires, and New York, Stonehill, 1976.
A Christmas Recipe. Verona, Italy, Plain Wrapper Press, 1977.

Other

English Literature: A Survey for Students (as John Burgess Wilson). London, Longman, 1958.
The Novel Today. London, Longman, 1963.
Language Made Plain (as John Burgess Wilson). London, English Universities Press, 1964; New York, Crowell, 1965; revised edition, London, Fontana, 1975.
Here Comes Everybody: An Introduction to James Joyce for the Ordinary Reader. London, Faber, 1965; revised edition, London, Hamlyn, 1982; as *Re Joyce*, New York, Norton, 1965.
The Novel Now: A Student's Guide to Contemporary Fiction. London, Faber, and New York, Norton, 1967; revised edition, Faber, 1971.
Urgent Copy: Literary Studies. London, Cape, and New York, Norton, 1968.
Shakespeare. London, Cape, and New York, Knopf, 1970.

Joysprick: An Introduction to the Language of James Joyce.
London, Deutsch, 1973; New York, Harcourt Brace, 1975.

Obscenity and the Arts (lecture). Valletta, Malta Library Association, 1973.

A Long Trip to Teatime (for children). London, Dempsey and Squires, and New York, Stonehill, 1976.

New York, with the editors of Time-Life books. New York, Time-Life, 1976.

Ernest Hemingway and His World. London, Thames and Hudson, and New York, Scribner, 1978.

The Land Where Ice Cream Grows (for children). London, Benn, and New York, Doubleday, 1979.

On Going to Bed. London, Deutsch, and New York, Abbeville, 1982.

This Man and Music. London, Hutchinson, 1982; New York, McGraw Hill, 1983.

Ninety-Nine Novels: The Best in English since 1939: A Personal Choice. London, Allison and Busby, and New York, Summit, 1984.

Flame into Being: The Life and Work of D. H. Lawrence. London, Heinemann, and New York, Arbor House, 1985.

Homage to QWERT YUIOP: Selected Journalism 1978–1985. London, Hutchinson, 1986; as *But Do Blondes Prefer Gentlemen?*, New York, McGraw Hill, 1986.

Little Wilson and Big God, Being the First Part of the Confessions of Anthony Burgess. New York, Weidenfeld and Nicolson, 1986; London, Heinemann, 1987.

They Wrote in English. London, Hutchinson, 1988.

Editor, *The Coaching Days of England 1750–1850.* London, Elek, and New York, Time-Life, 1966.

Editor, *A Journal of the Plague Year*, by Daniel Defoe. London, Penguin, 1966.

Editor, *A Shorter Finnegans Wake*, by James Joyce. London, Faber, and New York, Viking Press, 1966.

Editor, with Francis Haskell, *The Age of the Grand Tour.* London, Elek, and New York, Crown, 1967.

Editor, *Malaysian Stories*, by W. Somerset Maugham. Singapore, Heinemann, 1969.

Translator, with Llewela Burgess, *The New Aristocrats*, by Michel de Saint-Pierre. London, Gollancz, 1962; Boston, Houghton Mifflin, 1963.

Translator, with Llewela Burgess, *The Olive Trees of Justice*, by Jean Pelegri. London, Sidgwick and Jackson, 1962.

Translator, *The Man Who Robbed Poor Boxes*, by Jean Servin. London, Gollancz, 1965.

*

Bibliography: *Anthony Burgess: A Bibliography* by Jeutonne Brewer, Metuchen, New Jersey, Scarecrow Press, 1980; *Anthony Burgess: An Annotated Bibliography and Reference Guide* by Paul Boytinck, New York, Garland, 1985.

Manuscript Collection: Mills Memorial Library, Hamilton, Ontario.

Critical Studies: in *The Red Hot Vacuum* by Theodore Solotaroff, New York, Atheneum, 1970; *Shakespeare's Lives* by Samuel Schoenbaum, Oxford, Clarendon Press, 1970; *Anthony Burgess* by Carol M. Dix, London, Longman, 1971; *The Consolations of Ambiguity: An Essay on the Novels of Anthony Burgess* by Robert K. Morris, Columbia, University of Missouri Press, 1971; *Anthony Burgess* by A. A. DeVitis, New York, Twayne, 1972; *The Clockwork Universe of Anthony Burgess* by Richard Mathews, San Bernardino, California, Borgo Press, 1978; *Anthony Burgess: The Artist as Novelist* by Geoffrey Aggeler, University, University of Alabama Press, 1979, and *Critical Essays on Anthony Burgess* edited by Aggeler, Boston, Hall 1986; *Anthony Burgess* by Samuel Coale, New York, Ungar, 1981; *Anthony Burgess: A Study in Character* by Martina Ghosh-Schellhorn, Frankfurt, Germany, Lang, 1986.

*   *   *

Anthony Burgess would seem at first glance a less focused, less committed, more sentimental George Orwell: a teacher and critic with socialist interests mixed with a dislike of colonialism and a cynicism about government hierarchies. Yet an inescapable Roman Catholic heritage affects his vision and produces its moral and philosophical ambiguities. He takes an almost exhibitionist delight in metaphoric and linguistic by-play and almost always incorporates in his oeuvre rag-tags from various languages, both modern and classical. His style is to debunk, demythologize, and mock while at the same time to sympathize and revere; in other words, he tries to have it both ways: comic and serious, liberal and conservative, believer and skeptic, humanist and scientist, historian and fantasy writer.

Burgess's historical fiction suggests there is no real factual record and that all is subject to interpretation, but he also postulates a need for values. It is scatological and melodramatic, with images of mindless violence, sexual ambiguity, double think, and evil with a capital "E". It usually denounces materialism and opts for the life of the mind, while at the same time demonstrating the hatred, divisiveness, and fanaticism of mankind, particularly man en masse, and the powerful sway of the physical, and most particularly the sexual, over the intellectual. It combines philosophic despair with slapstick, and suggests a cyclical view of history which Burgess sees as alternating between two negative extremes, the "Pelagian" and the "Augustinian": socialistic and liberal humanism and idealism, and brutal, unregenerate tyranny. Its central characters are bumbling antiheroes, at odds with authority, weak, well-meaning, powerless, and out-of-touch with themselves and with reality; rather than actively participate in life, they tend merely to look on as "human beings squeaked and gibbered, and their passions and convictions buzzed like gnats." Burgess is preoccupied with fate, with the role of the artist, with the decay of society paralleled in the decay of love, and with a quest for meaning amid alien cultures. In exploring these themes, he sacrifices verisimilitude and exactness for his personal reinterpretations of the past as indicative of the present and the future, all a mythological mix of truth and lie.

Burgess's literary works grow out of his personal experiences and build on central characters that incorporate much of himself. A number of these figures are teachers, searching for knowledge and understanding, expecting the best, but somehow too often finding the worst, hence the vaguely cynical stance that dominates his canon. *Malayan Trilogy*, with its realistic portraits of British Colonials in Malaya and events from the 1950s, reflects Burgess's lifetime interest in language, weaving in numerous words and phrases from Malay, Urdu, Arabic, Tamil, and Chinese, with a glossary at the end (as he would later do with his innovative experimentation with a futuristic language in *A Clockwork Orange*). It depicts the dark side of Eastern civilization, the internecine strife, the bigotry, the corruption that would continue to plague Malaya as it moved toward self-rule. *Devil of a State*, possibly based on Burgess's experiences in Borneo, also treats of the transition from British colony to independent state.

Burgess's treatments of Shelley and Byron in Switzerland, James Joyce, Shakespeare, Keats, Moses, Jesus, and Napoleon mingle fact with fiction to project personal interpretations of great literary and historical figures. His novel, *Nothing Like the Sun*, gives a sense of the violent, lively, but unsanitary nature of Elizabethan England, while at the same time it reconstructs the unknowable, Shakespeare's love-life, to argue a totally personal thesis: that satyriasis was responsible for Shakespeare's literary productivity. In fact, Burgess has "WS" scornfully dismiss spiritual pretensions by saying, "There is the flesh and the flesh makes all. Literature is an epiphenomenon of the action of the flesh." The novel purports to be Burgess's final lecture to his Malaysian students, and, as such, attempts to transport them into 16th-century England, imitating its diction and peeking in on a young Shakespeare dreaming of his "dark golden lady" who inspires his verse and his sexual exploits. Nevertheless, it suggests that pederasty forced him into an acting career, that the earl of Southampton won his homosexual attentions, and that an East Indian was the dark lady who sexually enslaved him until her personal ambitions led to her affair with the bisexual Southampton. Burgess has Shakespeare end as a syphilitic, a disease he finds responsible for the flowering of genius in a number of individuals.

The Burgess pattern throughout his canon is to focus on the physical to try bring the historical myth to the human level and to fuse his own concerns and identity with that of his historical figure so that Moses and Jesus, Saul and the martyred Stephen, Shakespeare and Napoleon all at some point voice the Burgess view. Overall, Burgess's women inspire, tease and damage, while his men are often frail posturers, seeking a tenuous salvation.

Napoleon Symphony builds most precisely on Beethoven's *Eroica* Symphony in four movements to trace the life of Napoleon Bonaparte from an overture to Josephine to his immortalization in the final coda. Burgess's Napoleon is the erotic lover, the farcical cuckold, the domineering and capable soldier with his ups and downs, the tyrant Colossus straddling a continent, the doomed Prometheus, bringer of the fire of a new order, and finally the mythical legend who remakes fact to create his own self-image, posthumously crowned for, to some degree, unifying Europe. He slides down the Alps, eats a new chicken dish on the battlefield, and faces Russian wastelands and Waterloo with equal gusto. The point of view shifts from Napoleon's own self-rationalizations to the more cynical perspectives of less romantic observers (Josephine, his foot soldiers, political observers), and the work itself is more about the creative process than about Napoleon *per se*.

Abba Abba, mainly a series of translated sonnets, introduces a literary mystery, the hypothetical meeting of John Keats and the Italian sonneteer Guiseppe Belli (noted for his blasphemous street diction) in Rome of the 1820's, just before Keats's death, and raises questions about hypothetical potential influences, each on each. It was followed by a series of television specials on historical figures: Moses, Shakespeare, Michelangelo, Jesus of Nazareth, "Vinegar Joe" Stillwell, and Cyrus the Great. (The Jesus production was based on *Man of Nazareth*, the story of Christ from the perspective of an accountant for a wine merchant.) *The End of the World News* provides a fictional biography of Sigmund Freud (the intellectual giant vs. the failed husband and father), a musical based on Leon Trotsky's 1917 visit to New York (rhetorical spouting delivered with song and dance), and a projected cosmic disaster in 2000, with each in its own way bringing an end to history. *The Kingdom of the Wicked*, in turn, builds on *I, Claudius* and the movie *Caligula* to interpret the early years of Christianity set against the decline of a decadent, sadistic, ineffectual Rome. Burgess's Jesus is a burly

hulk, a con man colossus who survived crucifixion and merely used the idea of resurrection to promote himself. The book proceeds in this vein with miracles explained away and the raising of Dorcas from the dead, for example, transformed into slapstick. His two-dimensional characters and trivial substance transform a complex historical situation into a superficial mockery, but one replete with convincing debates between disagreeing factions.

Burgess always incorporates long Greek and Latinate terms (phrases like "an octopudium of hoofs"), and often depends on a mock epic format and on metaphor and allusion to lend a greater sense of depth to his perceptions, for example, calling Nabby Adams (*Malaya Trilogy*) "a Prometheus with the eagles of drink and debt pecking at his liver," or reducing Aeneas to the bumbling sergeant of *A Vision of Battlements* and his Mediterranean wanderings to exploring Gibraltar. His histories involve a form of gamesmanship, with puns and neologisms, acronyms and deflations, with lavatorial and masturbatory humor, with chaos and ambiguity mixed with old-fashioned values and with repetitive cycles that switch from despair to hope and back again.

—Gina Macdonald

BURGHLEY, Rose. Address: c/o Mills and Boon Ltd., 18–24 Paradise Road, Richmond, Surrey TW9 1SR, England.

ROMANCE AND HISTORICAL PUBLICATIONS

Novels

And Be Thy Love. London, Mills and Boon, 1958; Toronto, Harlequin, 1961.
Love in the Afternoon. London, Mills and Boon, 1959.
The Sweet Surrender. London, Mills and Boon, 1959; Toronto, Harlequin, 1966.
Bride by Arrangement. London, Mills and Boon, 1960.
A Moment in Paris. London, Mills and Boon, 1961.
Highland Mist. London, Mills and Boon, 1962; Toronto, Harlequin, 1967.
The Garden of Don José. London, Mills and Boon, 1964; Toronto, Harlequin, 1965.
Man of Destiny. London, Mills and Boon, and Toronto, Harlequin, 1965.
A Quality of Magic. London, Mills and Boon, 1966; Toronto, Harlequin, 1967.
The Afterglow. London, Mills and Boon, 1966; as *Alpine Doctor*, Toronto, Harlequin, 1970.
Bride of Alaine. London, Mills and Boon, and Toronto, Harlequin, 1966.
Folly of the Heart. London, Mills and Boon, 1967.
The Bay of Moonlight. London, Mills and Boon, and Toronto, Harlequin, 1968.
Return to Tremarth. London, Mills and Boon, 1969.

*   *   *

Between 1958 and 1969, Rose Burghley wrote 14 novels, yet her romances remain as some of the most charming and well-written novels of those years. She, as other romance writers of that period, seemed to have delighted in telling tender stories of love and happiness. Her novels followed a standard pattern and her characters had typical characteristics. However, these facts do not detract from the overall effect of her stories. For that matter, it may have been one of the elements that helped to make her a popular writer. Her readers were familiar with the kind of novel she wrote and they knew that each new novel would be just as entertaining. Generally, her novels centered on sweet, young girls who suddenly find themselves in unusual circumstances which eventually led to them falling in love. Actually, Burghley's novels could be modern adaptions of the "Beggar Maid Story," for in each example of her writings one finds the heroine completely out of her depth and struggling to cope with new and unexpected situations and emotions.

Her story of Lois Tarrant, in the novel *The Garden of Don José,* is perhaps her most delightful, for it satisfies every romantic dream imaginable. Lois has been sent by a London fashion house to deliver a trousseau to a young girl in Spain. Just as Lois is about to return home, she learns that Doña Inez's intended husband has been critically injured in a car accident. Ruthlessly, her guardian, Don José, insists that Lois stay to support Doña Inez during those terrifying hours. Her sympathy and compassion are instantly played upon through the rest of the novel as she is skillfully manipulated by Don José. Her efforts to remember "her place," to avoid falling in love with Don José, come to nothing as he forces her to admit her love.

In another novel Burghley uses a different approach. In *Bride of Alaine* Amanda Wells and her wealthy friend, Judy Macrae, are stranded on a Scottish island after Judy insists on viewing the large tower dwelling that dominates the island. When Amanda has to go for help because Judy has hurt her ankle, she is greeted by a servant with the words, "I'll tell the master the Bride of Alaine is here!" Later, Amanda understands that he referred to a local superstition where a young heiress would come to the island to restore wealth to the family. Complications develop as Judy becomes fascinated by Alaine Urquhart, the owner of the island. Amanda feels she must stay in the background and watch Judy's seemingly successful pursuit of Alaine, not realizing that local legend can not be disregarded.

The typical elements of romance in these stories should have made them trite. Burghley's sympathetic handling of her heroines' dilemmas, her truly outstanding ability to convey the tentative dawning of love, make her novels unexpectedly touching. Her creative use of plot complication and skillful character development all help her to tell tender, endearing stories that can not be dismissed so lightly. In fact, this is the basis for her well-earned reputation as a romance writer.

—Arlene Moore

BURGIN, G(eorge) B(rown). British. Born in Croydon, Surrey, 15 January 1856. Educated at Totteridge Park Public School. Married Georgina Benington in 1893 (died 1940). Private secretary to Baker Pasha and accompanied him to Asia Minor in the 1880's; sub-editor, the *Idler,* to 1899; general editor, New Vagabond Library, 1896–97. Secretary, Authors' Club, 1905–08. Fellow, Institute of Journalists. *Died 20 June 1944.*

ROMANCE AND HISTORICAL PUBLICATIONS

Novels

The Dance at the Four Corners. Bristol, Arrowsmith, 1894.

Tuxter's Little Maid. London, Cassell, 1895; as *At Tuxter's,* New York, Putnam, 1895.
Gascoigne's Ghost. London, Beeman, and New York, Harper, 1896.
The Judge of the Four Corners. London, Innes, 1896.
Tomalyn's Quest. London, Innes, and New York, Harper, 1896.
Fortune's Footballs. London, Pearson, and New York, Appleton, 1897.
"Old Man's" Marriage. London, Richards, 1897.
The Cattle Man. London, Richards, 1898.
Settled Out of Court. London, Pearson, 1898.
The Bread of Tears. London, Long, 1899.
The Hermits of Gray's Inn. London, Pearson, 1899.
The Tiger's Claw. London, Pearson, 1900.
The Person in the House. London, Hurst and Blackett, 1900.
The Way Out. London, Long, 1900.
A Goddess of Gray's Inn. London, Pearson, 1901.
A Son of Mammon. London, Long, 1901.
A Wilful Woman. London, Long, 1902.
The Man Who Died. London, Everett, 1903.
The Ladies of the Manor. London, Richards, 1903; New York, Smart Set, 1904.
The Hermit of Bonneville. London, Richards, 1904.
The Land of Silence. London, Nash, 1904.
The Devil's Due. London, Hutchinson, 1905.
The Marble City. London, Hutchinson, 1905.
The Belles of Vaudroy. London, Hutchinson, 1906.
The Only World. London, Richards, 1906.
Peggy the Pilgrim. London, Richards, 1907.
Which Woman? London, Nash, 1907.
Fanuela. London, Hutchinson, 1907.
Flowers of Fire. London, Nash, 1908.
Galahad's Garden. London, Nash, 1908.
A Woman's Way. London, Hutchinson, 1908.
Simple Savage. London, Hutchinson, 1909.
The Slaves of Allah. London, Hutchinson, 1909.
The Trickster. London, Stanley Paul, 1909.
Diana of Dreams. London, Hutchinson, 1910.
The King of Four Corners. London, Hutchinson, 1910.
This Son of Adam. London, Hutchinson, 1910.
The Belle of Santiago. London, Hutchinson, 1911.
A Lady of Spain. London, Hutchinson, 1911.
The Vision of Balmaine. London, Hutchinson, 1911.
Dickie Dilver. London, Hutchinson, 1912.
Varick's Legacy. London, Hutchinson, 1912.
The Love That Lasts. London, Hodder and Stoughton, 1913.
The "Second-Sighter's" Daughter. London, Hutchinson, 1913.
The Duke's Twins. London, Hutchinson, 1914.
Within the Gates. London, Hutchinson, 1914.
A Game of Hearts. London, Hutchinson, 1915.
The Herb of Healing. London, Hutchinson, 1915.
The Girl Who Got Out. London, Hutchinson, 1916.
The Hut by the River. London, Hutchinson, 1916.
The Greater Gain. London, Hutchinson, 1917.
The Puller of Strings: An Ottawa Valley Romance. London, Hutchinson, 1917.
Lady Mary's Money. London, Hutchinson, 1918.
The Throw-Back. London, Hutchinson, 1918.
A Gentle Despot. London, Hutchinson, 1919.
A Rubber Princess. London, Hutchinson, 1919.
Pilgrims of Circumstance. London, Hutchinson, 1920.
Uncle Jeremy. London, Hutchinson, 1920.
The Faithful Fool. London, Books, 1921.
The Man from Turkey. London, Hutchinson, 1921.
Cyrilla Seeks Herself. London, Hutchinson, 1922.
Love and the Locusts. London, Hutchinson, 1922.

Manetta's Marriage. London, Hutchinson, 1922.
The Man Behind. London, Hutchinson, 1923.
Sally's Sweetheart. London, Hutchinson, 1923.
The Kiss. London, Hutchinson, 1924.
The Lord of Little Langton. London, Hutchinson, 1924.
The Spending of the Pile. London, Hutchinson, 1924.
The Young Labelle. London, Hutchinson, 1924.
Fleurette of Four Corners. London, Hutchinson, 1925.
The Hate That Lasts. London, Hutchinson, 1925.
Mariette's Lovers. London, Hutchinson, 1925.
The Forest Lure. London, Hutchinson, 1926.
Young Deloraine. London, Hutchinson, 1926.
The Dale of Dreams. London, Hutchinson, 1927.
The Hundredth Man. London, Hutchinson, 1927.
The House of Fiske. London, Hutchinson, 1927.
Allandale's Daughters. London, Hutchinson, 1928.
The Final Test. London, Hutchinson, 1928.
Nitana. London, Hutchinson, 1928.
All Things Come Round. London, Hutchinson, 1929.
Out of the Swim. London, Wright and Brown, 1930.
The Woman Without a Heart. London, Alexander Ouseley, 1930.
The Duke's Stratagem. London, Wright and Brown, 1931.
One Traveller Returns. London, Wright and Brown, 1931.
Eternal Justice. London, Wright and Brown, 1932.
When Dreams Come True. London, Wright and Brown, 1932.
The Wrong Woman. London, Wright and Brown, 1932.
The Wheels of Fate. London, Wright and Brown, 1933.
A Poor Millionaire. London, Wright and Brown, 1933.
A Fateful Fraud. London, Wright and Brown, 1934.
The Honour of Four Corners. London, Wright and Brown, 1934.
Pierrepont's Daughters. London, Wright and Brown, 1935.
Who Loses Pays. London, Wright and Brown, 1935.
Slaves of the Ring. London, Hutchinson, 1936.
Uncle Patterley's Money. London, Wright and Brown, 1936.
The Golden Penny. London, Wright and Brown, 1937.
The Ills Men Do. London, Wright and Brown, 1937.
A Pious Fraud. London, Wright and Brown, 1938.
The Man in the Corner. London, Wright and Brown, 1939.

Short Stories

His Lordship, and Others. London, Henry, 1893.

OTHER PUBLICATIONS

Other

Memoirs of a Clubman. London, Hutchinson, 1921; New York, Dutton, 1922.
More Memoirs (and Some Travels). London, Hutchinson, and New York, Dutton, 1922.
Many Memories. London, Hutchinson, 1922; New York, Dutton, 1923.
Some More Memoirs. London, Hutchinson, 1924.

Editor, *The Vagabond's Annual*. Bristol, Arrowsmith, 1893.

*   *   *

Behind the initials of G. B. Burgin lurks that rarity among romantic novelists—the male writer. Working from the mid-

1890's until the late 1930's, Burgin produced 100 novels. Other male novelists of the period, such as P. C. Wren and Rafael Sabatini, mixed up the love element with a fair amount of adventure, escapism, travel, and excitement, rather than concentrating only on matters of the heart. G. B. Burgin is openly sentimental about love, and keeps his heroines firmly on their pedestals. Suitors declare their love with vigorous, straightforward ardour: "Cyrilla, you are divinely, most exquisitely beautiful. You are so beautiful that I am afraid of you. You hurt me. . . . Don't you see, Cyrilla, don't you know, that you are the embodiment of all that is sweetest and dearest in the world to me? You're heaven's explanation on earth. You know what I mean?" The heroine wanted to be swept off her feet, held tightly in strong arms, and perhaps even to be very slightly maltreated. "Frankly, she liked men and their society. There was . . . an unconscious brutality with most of them, which gave a girl something to think about."

The sentimental nonsense of tales like *The Kiss* or *Cyrilla Seeks Herself* is harmless daydreaming; however the dissemination of the belief that some girls actually *like* being brutalised is more questionable.

—Rachel Anderson

———————

BURNS, Sheila. See **BLOOM, Ursula.**

———————

BUTLER, Gwendoline (née Williams). Also writes as Jennie Melville. British. Born in London, 19 August 1922. Educated at Haberdashers' Aske's Hatcham Girls' School, London, 1939–42; Lady Margaret Hall, Oxford, 1944–49, B.A. in modern history 1949. Married Lionel Butler in 1949 (died 1981); one daughter. Taught at two Oxford colleges for a short time. Recipient: Crime Writers Association Silver Dagger, 1973; Romantic Novelists Association Major award, 1981. Agent: John Farquharson Ltd., 162–168 Regent Street, London W1R 5TB. Address: 32 Harvest Road, Englefield Green, Surrey TW20 0QS England.

ROMANCE AND HISTORICAL PUBLICATIONS

Novels (series: Inspector John Coffin; Inspector/Superintendent William Winter)

Receipt for Murder. London, Bles, 1956.
Dead in a Row (Coffin; Winter). London, Bles, 1957.
The Dull Dead (Coffin; Winter). London, Bles, 1958; New York, Walker, 1962.
The Murdering Kind (Coffin; Winter). London, Bles, 1958; New York, Roy, 1964.
The Interloper. London, Bles, 1959.
Death Lives Next Door (Coffin). London, Bles, 1960; as *Dine and Be Dead*, New York, Macmillan, 1960.

Make Me a Murderer (Coffin). London, Bles, 1961.
Coffin in Oxford. London, Bles, 1962.
Coffin for Baby. London, Bles, and New York, Walker, 1963.
Coffin Waiting. London, Bles, 1963; New York, Walker, 1965.
Coffin in Malta. London, Bles, 1964; New York, Walker, 1965.
A Nameless Coffin. London, Bles, 1966; New York, Walker, 1967.
Coffin Following. London, Bles, 1968.
Coffin's Dark Number. London, Bles, 1969.
A Coffin from the Past. London, Bles, 1970.
A Coffin for Pandora. London, Macmillan, 1973; as *Olivia*, New York, Coward McCann, 1974.
A Coffin for the Canary. London, Macmillan, 1974; as *Sarsen Place*, New York, Coward McCann, 1974.
The Vesey Inheritance. New York, Coward McCann, 1975; London, Macmillan, 1976.
The Brides of Friedberg. London, Macmillan, 1977; as *Meadowstreet*, New York, Coward McCann, 1977.
The Red Staircase. New York, Coward McCann, 1979; London, Collins, 1980.
Albion Walk. New York, Coward McCann, 1982; London, Collins, 1983; as *Cavalcade*, London, Fontana, 1984.
Coffin on the Water. London, Collins, 1986; New York, St. Martin's Press, 1989.
Coffin in Fashion. London, Collins, 1987.
Coffin Underground. London, Collins, 1988.
Coffin in the Black Museum. London, Collins, 1989.

Novels as Jennie Melville (series: Charmian Daniels)

Come Home and Be Killed (Daniels). London, Joseph, 1962; New York, British Book Centre, 1964.
Burning Is a Substitute for Loving (Daniels). London, Joseph, 1963; New York, British Book Centre, 1964.
Murderers' Houses (Daniels). London, Joseph, 1964.
There Lies Your Love (Daniels). London, Joseph, 1965.
Nell Alone (Daniels). London, Joseph, 1966.
A Different Kind of Summer (Daniels). London, Joseph, 1967.
The Hunter in the Shadows. London, Hodder and Stoughton, 1969; New York, McKay, 1970.
A New Kind of Killer, An Old Kind of Death (Daniels). London, Hodder and Stoughton, 1970; as *A New Kind of Killer*, New York, McKay, 1971.
The Summer Assassin. London, Hodder and Stoughton, 1971.
Ironwood. London, Hodder and Stoughton, and New York, McKay, 1972.
Nun's Castle. New York, McKay, 1973; London, Hodder and Stoughton, 1974.
Raven's Forge. London, Macmillan, and New York, McKay, 1975.
Dragon's Eye. New York, Simon and Schuster, 1976; London, Macmillan, 1977.
Axwater. London, Macmillan, 1978; as *Tarot's Tower*, New York, Simon and Schuster, 1978.
Murder Has a Pretty Face (Daniels). London, Macmillan, 1981.
The Painted Castle. London, Macmillan, 1982.
The Hand of Glass. London, Macmillan, 1983.
Listen to the Children. London, Macmillan, 1986.
Death in the Garden. London, Macmillan, 1987.
Windsor Red. London, Macmillan, and New York, St. Martin's Press, 1988.
A Cure for Dying. London, Macmillan, 1989.

OTHER PUBLICATIONS

Play

Radio Play: *Nell Alone*, from her own novel, 1968.

*   *   *

Edmund Crispin once wrote in the *Sunday Times*: "Miss Melville is as satisfying as Miss Gwendoline Butler, whom in some important respects she resembles." It could have been tongue-in-cheek on the part of that witty reviewer, but the fact remains that for some time the crime novels of Gwendoline Butler and Jennie Melville enjoyed separate identities; later they became more obviously products of the one deft hand, particularly when they developed into the romantic/gothic field.

The high point for Gwendoline Butler occurred with *A Coffin for Pandora*, a feast of suspense in 19th-century Oxford. A tale of kidnapping and mysterious death, with a rather independent young governess in danger, it is not only superbly plotted but marvellously evocative of the period with its upstairs and downstairs contrasts between rich and poor. This skill in conveying an atmosphere of haunting menace against an authentic social background is also evident in later books. *The Vesey Inheritance* is a substantial novel set in Victorian London, involving an innocent 19-year-old heroine up from the country who senses something mysterious in her family history and fears that her half-brother means to harm her. *The Brides of Friedberg* stays in period, but switches location to Germany and follows the fortunes of two girls from an English upper-class family; it is a tale of poison, again portraying the social scene from the rich in their palaces to the poor and exploited to complement the main storyline.

Gwendoline Butler was praised by Patrick Cosgrave in the *Spectator* for her writing, characterisation, and touch; indeed, he called her "the Jane Austen of the crime story." If this is applied specifically to her beguiling mysteries in the gothic tradition, it must be noted that her work in this field has been mainly under the Melville pseudonym. As Melville she is one of the foremost exponents of stories featuring young women caught up in lonely buildings permeated with an air of evil and corruption.

Melville's settings are diverse—a remote mansion, an old observatory, a redundant iron foundry—and yet they share the common aura of "something wicked this way comes." The narrator-heroine is confused about the source of her mortal danger, and on the brink of fatally misguided choices between apparent friends and enemies. Romance plays a key part, but handsome and charming men are not always what they seem and the ruthless and masterful male is not easily identifiable by the heroine as lover or villain and may well be both. In spite of these common features, however, Melville's novels are by no means formulistic. While such books as *Ironwood*, *Raven's Forge*, *Dragon's Eye*, and *Axwater* are uniform in displaying gripping readability, an intimate style, blended perceptiveness and ironic humor, and, above all, an ability to squeeze every sinister nuance from a character or situation, they also show her versatility as a superlative plotter.

—Melvyn Barnes

———

BUTTERWORTH, Michael. See **SALISBURY, Carola.**

———

BYRNE, Donn. Irish. Born Brian Oswald Donn-Byrne in New York City, 20 November 1889; brought up in Ireland. Educated at the Royal University of Ireland, 1907–10, B.A. 1910; University College, Dublin; studied at the Sorbonne, Paris, and in Leipzig, Germany. Married Dorothea Cadogan in 1911. Lived in New York after 1911. *Died 18 June 1928*.

ROMANCE AND HISTORICAL PUBLICATIONS

Novels

Messer Marco Polo. New York, Century, 1921; London, Sampson Low, 1922.
The Wind Bloweth. New York, Century, and London, Sampson Low, 1922.
Blind Raftery and His Wife Hilaria. New York, Century, 1924; London, Sampson Low, 1925.
O'Malley of Shanganagh. New York, Century, 1925; as *An Untitled Story*, London, Sampson Low, 1925.
Hangman's House. New York, Century, and London, Sampson Low, 1926.
Brother Saul. New York, Century, and London, Sampson Low, 1927.
Crusade. Boston, Little Brown, and London, Sampson Low, 1928.
Field of Honor. New York, Century, 1929; as *The Power of the Dog*, London, Sampson Low, 1929.
A Party of Baccarat. New York, Century, 1930; as *The Golden Goat*, London, Sampson Low, 1930.

Short Stories

Stories Without Women. New York, Hearst, 1915; London, Sampson Low, 1931.
Changeling and Other Stories. New York, Century, 1924; London, Sampson Low, 1925.
Destiny Bay. Boston, Little Brown, and London, Sampson Low, 1928.
Rivers of Damascus and Other Stories. London, Sampson Low, and New York, Century, 1931.
The Island of Youth and Other Stories. London, Sampson Low, 1932; New York, Century, 1933.
Sargasso Sea and Other Stories. London, Sampson Low, 1932; as *A Woman of the Shee and Other Stories*, New York, Century, 1932.
An Alley of Flashing Spears and Other Stories. London, Sampson Low, 1933; New York, Appleton Century, 1934.
A Daughter of the Medici and Other Stories. London, Sampson Low, 1933; New York, Appleton Century, 1935.
The Hound of Ireland and Other Stories. London, Sampson Low, 1934; New York, Appleton Century, 1935.

OTHER PUBLICATIONS

Novels

The Stranger's Banquet. New York, Harper, 1919.
The Foolish Matrons. New York, Harper, 1920; London, Sampson Low, 1923.

Verse

Poems. London, Sampson Low, 1934.

Other

Ireland: The Rock Whence I Was Hewn (memoirs). Boston, Little Brown, and London, Sampson Low, 1929

*

Manuscript Collection: New York Public Library.

Bibliography: *Donn Byrne: A Descriptive Bibliography 1912–1935* by Henry S. Bannister, New York, Garland, 1982.

Critical Studies: *Donn Byrne: His Place in Literature* by Paul Mellon, New York, Century, 1927; *Donn Byrne: Bard of Armagh* by Thurston Macauley, New York, Century, 1929; London, Sampson Low, 1931.

*   *   *

Don Byrne follows a tradition of Irish novelists. His characters are at their happiest in Ireland however much they boast of knowing and enjoying other countries. As he claims in his foreword to *Hangman's House*, "The proper subject of conversation for an Irishman is Ireland. I have written a book of Ireland for Irishmen."

The myths and ancient tales of the country pervade Byrne's stories; his characters discuss and refer to them as if they are contemporary, thus conveying a particular way of thinking and feeling. Byrne's descriptions of the countryside, in all weathers, and this background of myth and folklore convey another way of life, the Ireland of yesterday. Byrne's works came as relevations to many English readers when they were first published.

Hangman's House is set in Dublin in the last days of the Victorian era. In his dying moments, a famous hanging judge persuades Connaught, his only child, to marry John D'Arcy, a man with a great future in politics. The story is full of excellent accounts of hunts, races, steeplechases, and coursing in which a motley collection of characters come alive. These scenes are interspersed with detailed views of the countryside, from the distant mountains to the small creatures who creep through the grass. John proves a weak villain who is finally ostracized for shooting his wife's famous racehorse, "Had he killed a man or a woman even, it would not have mattered, but to kill a horse . . . " A disguised fenian comes and goes, adding drama; the house is burnt down in a grand finale and virtue in the shape of the good neighbour Dermot triumphs.

The atmosphere rather takes over in *The Wind Bloweth* as Shane Campbell, who of course loves his native Ireland, sails round the world in the days when sail was giving way to steam. The plot is somewhat weak, but by the end of the book Shane has found happiness in love.

Destiny Bay is full of good talk, endless storytelling, and original characters ranging from blind Aunt Jenepher who knows everything that goes on, to hectoring Uncle Valentine. The plot is rather far-fetched: an elderly Spanish nobleman arrives in Ulster in search of gold hidden at the time of the Armada. He is accompanied by his young grandson who eventually turns out to be his granddaughter. There are telling phrases such as, "You will be thinking of the beauty of some women, or better still the beauty of a horse." The stories include the tale of the golfer Gilligan, with its dramatic ending, "as he flung his severed right hand on the papers before us."

Sadness pervades *An Untitled Story*, as an elderly Irishman haunts various Dublin pubs recalling a time in his youth when

Joan, an Anglican nun, left her convent to be with him. Together they found only unhappiness and Joan finally returned to her religious life.

When Byrne leaves his native land and his Gaelic he plunges into other countries and other centuries with enthusiasm. *The Golden Goat* follows the adventures of two American women gambling in the South of France. *Messer Marco Polo* brings the medieval explorer to life in Italy and China, while *Brother Saul* gives a full and convincing account of the early days of Christianity.

Violence from the men of all nations fills *Crusade*. Irish Sir Miles O'Neill rides to Jerusalem, is taken prisoner but later released by the Saracens, the only well-behaved people in the 12th century. Byrne was fascinated by the different cultures in Ireland and claimed in *Blind Raftery* that "In no country of the world has there been such mixture of races as Ireland has seen." This love story of the blind poet who is persuaded by the oily Welshman to marry his cast-off Spanish woman Hilaria, is full of rich chivalry although set in the time of the South Sea Bubble. Throughout the novel poor Raftery is honoured wherever he goes, in the streets, in the country inns, in the Irish House of Commons, the Irish House of Lords, and the Dublin Theatre.

Byrne was successful in creating a picture of Ireland at the turn of the century before the Troubles. His many successors draw a different picture. J. G. Farrell and Brian Moore have lost this background of ancient stories and are more concerned with the present grievances. In a real sense Byrne wrote period pieces, but his novels still convey the feeling that he knew the Irish people.

—Margaret Campbell

CABELL, James Branch. American. Born in Richmond, Virginia, 14 April 1879. Educated at the College of William and Mary, Williamsburg, Virginia, 1894–98, A.B. 1898. Married 1) Priscilla Bradley Shepherd in 1913 (died 1949), one son; 2) Margaret Waller Freeman in 1950. Instructor in Greek and French at the College of William and Mary while an undergraduate, 1896–97; staff member, Richmond *Times*, 1898, New York *Herald*, 1899–1901, and Richmond *News*, 1901; genealogical researcher in America and Europe, 1901–11; office worker at coal mine in West Virginia, 1911–13; genealogist, Virginia Society of Colonial Wars, 1916–28, and Virginia Sons of the American Revolution, 1917–24; editor, Virginia War History Commission, 1919–26; silent editor, *Reviewer*, Richmond, 1921; an editor, *American Spectator*, 1932–35. President, Virginia Writers Association, 1918–21. Member American Academy. *Died 5 May 1958*.

ROMANCE AND HISTORICAL PUBLICATIONS

Novels

The Eagle's Shadow. New York, Doubleday, and London, Heinemann, 1904; revised edition, New York, McBride, 1923.
The Cords of Vanity. New York, Doubleday, and London, Hutchinson, 1909; revised edition, New York, McBride, 1920; London, Lane, 1925.
The Soul of Melicent. New York, Stokes; 1913, revised edition, as *Domnei*, New York, McBride, 1920; London, Lane, 1927.
The Rivet in Grandfather's Neck. New York, McBride, and London, McBride Nast, 1915.

The Cream of the Jest. New York, McBride, 1917; London, Lane, 1923.
Beyond Life. New York, McBride, 1919; London, Lane, 1925.
Jurgen. New York, McBride, 1919; London, Lane, 1921.
Figures of Earth. New York, McBride, 1921; London, Lane, 1922.
The High Place. New York, McBride, and London, Lane, 1923.
The Silver Stallion. New York, McBride, and London, Lane, 1926.
Something about Eve. New York, McBride, and London, Lane, 1927.
The Works (Storisende Edition; includes "The Biography of the Life of Manuel": revised editions of earlier works, plus new material). New York, McBride, 18 vols., 1927–30.
The Way of Ecben. New York, McBride, and London, Lane, 1929.
Smirt: An Urbane Nightmare. New York, McBride, 1934.
Smith: A Sylvan Interlude. New York, McBride, 1935.
Smire: An Acceptance in the Third Person. New York, Doubleday, 1937.
The King Was in His Counting House. New York, Farrar and Rinehart, 1938; London, Lane, 1939.
Hamlet Had an Uncle. New York, Farrar and Rinehart, and London, Lane, 1940.
The First Gentleman of America. New York, Farrar and Rinehart, 1942; as *The First American Gentleman*, London, Lane, 1942.
There Were Two Pirates. New York, Farrar Straus, 1946; London, Lane, 1947.
The Devil's Own Dear Son. New York, Farrar Straus, 1949; London, Lane, 1950.

Short Stories

The Line of Love. New York, Harper, 1905; revised edition, New York, McBride, 1921; London, Lane, 1929.
Gallantry. New York, Harper, 1907; revised edition, New York, McBride, 1922; London, Lane, 1928.
Chivalry. New York, Harper, 1909; revised edition, New York, McBride, 1921; London, Lane, 1928.
The Certain Hour. New York, McBride, 1916; London, McBride Nast, 1917.
The Music from Behind the Moon. New York, Day, 1926.
The White Robe. New York, McBride, and London, Lane, 1928.
The Witch-Woman (includes revised editions of *The Music from Behind the Moon*, *The Way of Ecben*, *The White Robe*). New York, Farrar Straus, 1948.

OTHER PUBLICATIONS

Play

The Jewel Merchants (produced Richmond, 1921). New York, McBride, 1921.

Verse

From the Hidden Way. New York, McBride, 1916; revised edition, 1924.
Ballades from the Hidden Way. New York, Crosby Gaige, 1928.
Sonnets from Antan. New York, Fountain Press, 1929.

Other

Branchiana (genealogy). Privately printed, 1907.
Branch of Abingdon. Privately printed, 1911.
The Majors and Their Marriages. Richmond, Hill, 1915.
The Judging of Jurgen. Chicago, Bookfellows, 1920.
Jurgen and the Censor. Privately printed, 1920.
Taboo: A Legend Retold from the Dirghic of Saevius Nicanor. New York, McBride, 1921.
Joseph Hergesheimer. Chicago, Bookfellows, 1921.
The Lineage of Lichfield: An Essay in Eugenics. New York, McBride, 1922.
Straws and Prayer-Books. New York, McBride, 1924; London, Lane, 1926.
Some of Us: An Essay in Epitaphs. New York, McBride, and London, Lane, 1930.
Townsend of Lichfield. New York, McBride, 1930.
Between Dawn and Sunrise: Selections, edited by John Macy. New York, McBride, and London, Lane, 1930.
These Restless Heads: A Trilogy of Romantics. New York, McBride, 1932.
Special Delivery: A Packet of Replies. New York, McBride, 1933; London, Philip Allan, 1934.
Ladies and Gentlemen: A Parcel of Reconsiderations. New York, McBride, 1934.
Preface to the Past. New York, McBride, 1936.
The Nightmare Has Triplets: An Author's Note on Smire. New York, Doubleday, 1937.
Of Ellen Glasgow: An Inscribed Portrait. New York, Maverick Press, 1938.
The St. John's: A Parade of Diversities, with A. J. Hanna. New York, Farrar and Rinehart, 1943.
Let Me Lie. New York, Farrar Straus, 1947.
Quiet, Please. Gainesville, University of Florida Press, 1952.
As I Remember It: Some Epilogues in Recollection. New York, McBride, 1955.
Between Friends: Letters of James Branch Cabell and Others, edited by Padraic Colum and Margaret Freeman Cabell. New York, Harcourt Brace, 1962.
The Letters of James Branch Cabell, edited by Edward Wagenknecht. Norman, University of Oklahoma Press, 1975.

*

Bibliography: *James Branch Cabell: A Complete Bibliography* by James N. Hall, New York, Revisionist Press, 1974; *James Branch Cabell: A Reference Guide* by Maurice Duke, Boston, Hall, and London, Prior, 1979.

Manuscript Collection: University of Virginia Library, Charlottesville.

Critical Studies: *No Place on Earth: Ellen Glasgow, James Branch Cabell, and Richmond-in-Virginia* by Louis D. Rubin, Jr., Austin, University of Texas Press, 1959; *James Branch Cabell* by Joe Lee Davis, New York, Twayne, 1962; *Jesting Moses: A Study in Cabellian Comedy* by Arvin R. Wells, Gainesville, University of Florida Press, 1962; *Cabell: The Dream and the Reality* by Desmond Tarrant, Norman, University of Oklahoma Press, 1967; *James Branch Cabell: Three Essays* by Carl Van Doren, H. L. Mencken, and Hugh Walpole, Port Washington, New York, Kennikat Press, 1967; *Cabell under Fire: Four Essays* by Geoffrey Morley-Mower, New York, Revisionist Press, 1975; *James Branch Cabell: The Richmond Iconoclast* by Dorothy B. Schlegel, New York, Revisionist Press, 1975; *In Quest of Cabell: Five Exploratory Essays* by William Leigh Godshalk,

New York, Revisionist Press, 1976; *James Branch Cabell: Centennial Essays* edited by M. Thomas Inge and Edgar E. MacDonald, Baton Rouge, Louisiana State University Press, 1983.

* * *

James Branch Cabell's historical fiction demands of a reader something more than conventional dedication and commitment. It requires a spontaneously flexible sensibility and a total engagement of the intellect over a period of time which must be gauged in years not hours, months, or days. The demands are similar to those dictated by James Joyce. But unlike the labyrinthine and often obscure passages in *Finnegans Wake,* Cabell's plots are, ostensibly at least, clear to the reader. It is almost always possible to provide a statement of what is going on. This seeming clarity, however, soon signals its own elusive and illusive qualities. More is happening than is immediately apparent, so much so that the ever expansive creativity of the author often spills over into the domain of the readers, becoming their burden and responsibility. Cabell makes it explicit that the 18 substantial volumes of the Storisende edition of his works must be regarded as a single book. He was by no means unaware of the enormity of the task imposed on what must be considered a quite uncommon reader. "To demand of your readers that they labor through no modest *Iliad*-length of some 16,000 hexameters, but through 18 extensive volumes, in order to find out just what the writer may be driving at, is to ignore a great deal more widely than did Homer's blindness the firm limits of human nature" (*Some of Us: An Essay in Epitaphs*).

The Herculean labors laid upon the presumed devotee readership are sweetened considerably by an engaging narrative line, almost always presented in chapters of digestible length. A prose style which borders upon the poetic seldom if ever belabors itself. Though the sagas of Manuel may in word-count far exceed what was expended upon Aeneas, Ulysses, Hector, and Achilles, it is always apparent that there is a story in progress.

Cabell's complexity lies largely in the design of his technique which might be described as a literary grid with lines of parallel perspectives of the author and the principal characters, and intersected by three distinct impulses which he terms the chivalrous, the gallant, and the poetic. Cabell defines each of these impulses in the preface to *Beyond Life,* the first of the monumental 18 volumes of fictions, the totality of which he calls "Biography of the Life of Manuel." This overtitle of the 18 books contains no redundancy. "Life" is not the equivalency of "biography," but refers to the complex of vital forces which are manifest in and through Manuel, but are ultimately independent of him and endure after he passes from the scene. The same is true of Jurgen, another imposing "life," which is developed in volume six, the most widely read of all the fictions. "Biography" is a term Cabell employs in the conventional sense of a literary ordering of events and details. In other words, collectively the set of 18 reveals not only the landmarks, legends, and interpretations of Manuel's story, fascinating episodes in and of themselves, but goes beyond the raconteur's art to uncover those consuming and creative forces which work through and upon the main character. Through a comprehensive grasp of these interwoven perspectives and impulses (the biography), a reader is to become eventually equipped to deal with the larger concept, the "life."

It would seem that even a failed enterprise would not be written off as a loss, but as an engaging endeavour. Manuel, who often speaks for himself, breaks out of the impulse of chivalry and its desire to seek that which is admirable and suddenly effects an abrupt transition into the impulse of gallantry, the objective of which is to preserve life. When it becomes apparent that either Manuel or Niafer must mount the black horse which will bear the rider to his death, Manuel starts his determination in the chivalric and quickly transfers to the gallant. "At all events," he declares, "I love Niafer better than I love any other person, but I do not value Niafer's life more highly than I value my own, and it would be nonsense to say so" (*Figures of Earth*). The sudden shift of sentiment should not be unexpected since the grid of values allows for a variety of perspectives for a character, none of whom is held responsible for sustaining a consistency of attitudes. Manuel appears at times to have secured successful Freudian counselling in those misty eras of pre-antiquity from which he learned to merge primitive urges and ideals.

Some might question whether Cabell's gargantuan undertaking is in fact historical fiction. The setting is partially legendary, part historical, part the making of the bard Cabell, and in part the Virginia in which the author lived. Poictesme is Cabell's own invention, a mythical place which bears distinct resemblances to Virginia, itself a melange with vestiges of the Old South and its Hellenic heritage, and its painful throes of reconstruction. Whether a culture or an environment is real, mythic, or fictional depends not upon facts but upon the impulses which throb within the grid. Among the lesser attainments of those who undertake the entire excursion through a landscape at once romantic, epic, and contemporary, should be a better defined notion of the problems and the possibilities explored in historical fiction.

—Leonard R. Mendelsohn

CADE, Robin. See **NICOLE, Christopher.**

CADELL, (Violet) Elizabeth (née Vandyke). Also writes as Harriet Ainsworth. British. Born in Calcutta, India, 10 November 1903. Married H. D. R. M. Cadell in 1928 (died); one son and one daughter. Address: c/o Hodder and Stoughton, Mill Road, Dunton Green, Sevenoaks, Kent TN13 2YA, England.

ROMANCE AND HISTORICAL PUBLICATIONS

Novels

My Dear Aunt Flora. London, Hale, 1946.
Last Straw for Harriet. New York, Morrow, 1947; as *Fishy, Said the Admiral*, London, Hale, 1948.
River Lodge. London, Hale, 1948.
Gay Pursuit. New York, Morrow, 1948; London, Hale, 1950; as *Family Gathering*, Hale, 1979.
Iris in Winter. New York, Morrow, 1949; London, Hale, 1951.
Brimstone in the Garden. New York, Morrow, 1950.
The Greenwood Shady. London, Hodder and Stoughton, 1951.
Enter Mrs. Belchamber. New York, Morrow, 1951; as *The Frenchman and the Lady*, London, Hodder and Stoughton, 1952.
Men and Angels. London, Hodder and Stoughton, 1952.
Crystal Clear. New York, Morrow, 1953; as *Journey's Eve*, London, Hodder and Stoughton, 1953.
Spring Green. London, Hodder and Stoughton, 1953.
The Cuckoo in Spring. New York, Morrow, and London, Hodder and Stoughton, 1954.

Around the Rugged Rock. New York, Morrow, 1954; as *The Gentlemen Go By*, London, Hodder and Stoughton, 1954.
The Lark Shall Sing. New York, Morrow, and London, Hodder and Stoughton, 1955; as *The Singing Heart*, New York, Berkley, 1959.
The Blue Sky of Spring. London, Hodder and Stoughton, 1956.
I Love a Lass. New York, Morrow, 1956.
Bridal Array. London, Hodder and Stoughton, 1957; Toronto, Harlequin, 1959.
The Green Empress. London, Hodder and Stoughton, 1958.
Sugar Candy Cottage. London, Hodder and Stoughton, 1958.
Alice, Where Art Thou? London, Hodder and Stoughton, 1959.
The Yellow Brick Road. London, Hodder and Stoughton, and New York, Morrow, 1960.
Honey for Tea. London, Hodder and Stoughton, 1961; New York, Morrow, 1962.
Six Impossible Things. London, Hodder and Stoughton, and New York, Morrow, 1961.
Language of the Heart. London, Hodder and Stoughton, 1962; as *The Toy Sword*, New York, Morrow, 1962.
Letter to My Love. London, Hodder and Stoughton, 1963.
Mixed Marriage: The Diary of a Portuguese Bride. London, Hodder and Stoughton, 1963.
Be My Guest. London, Hodder and Stoughton, 1964; as *Come Be My Guest*, New York, Morrow, 1964.
Canary Yellow. London, Hodder and Stoughton, and New York, Morrow, 1965.
The Fox from His Lair. London, Hodder and Stoughton, 1965; New York, Morrow, 1966.
The Corner Shop. London, Hodder and Stoughton, 1966; New York, Morrow, 1967.
The Stratton Story. London, Hodder and Stoughton, 1967.
Mrs. Westerby Changes Course. New York, Morrow, 1968.
The Golden Collar. London, Hodder and Stoughton, and New York, Morrow, 1969.
The Friendly Air. London, Hodder and Stoughton, 1970; New York, Morrow, 1971.
The Past Tense of Love. London, Hodder and Stoughton, and New York, Morrow, 1970.
Home for the Wedding. London, Hodder and Stoughton, 1971; New York, Morrow, 1972.
The Haymaker. London, Hodder and Stoughton, 1972.
Royal Summons. New York, Morrow, 1973.
Deck with Flowers. London, Hodder and Stoughton, 1973; New York, Morrow, 1974.
The Fledgling. London, Hodder and Stoughton, and New York, Morrow, 1975.
Game in Diamonds. London, Hodder and Stoughton, and New York, Morrow, 1976.
Parson's House. London, Hodder and Stoughton, and New York, Morrow, 1977.
Round Dozen. London, Hodder and Stoughton, and New York, Morrow, 1978.
Return Match. London, Hodder and Stoughton, and New York, Morrow, 1979.
The Marrying Kind. London, Hodder and Stoughton, and New York, Morrow, 1980.
Any Two Can Play. New York, Morrow, 1981.
A Lion in the Way. London, Hodder and Stoughton, and New York, Morrow, 1982.
Remains to Be Seen. London, Hodder and Stoughton, and New York, Morrow, 1983.
The Waiting Game. London, Hodder and Stoughton, and New York, Morrow, 1985.
The Empty Nest. London, Hodder and Stoughton, and New York, Morrow, 1986.

Out of the Nest. London, Hodder and Stoughton, and New York, Morrow, 1987.

Novels as Harriet Ainsworth

Consider the Lilies. London, Hodder and Stoughton, 1956.
Shadows on the Water. London, Hodder and Stoughton, 1958; as Elizabeth Cadell, New York, Morrow, 1958.
Death among Friends. London, Hodder and Stoughton, 1964.

OTHER PUBLICATIONS

Other

Sun in the Morning (for children). New York, Morrow, 1950; London, Hodder and Stoughton, 1951.

* * *

Normality is the essence of Elizabeth Cadell's popular novels. Her heroines are usually intelligent, practical, efficient, their faults the result of impulsiveness and warm-heartedness. Sometimes their suitors will chafe as this impulsiveness brings in its wake a stream of young nephews, eccentric old ladies, and lovable animals to interfere with their courtship. But even imperious suitors accept this, ultimately, or are replaced by more understanding young men.

Beyond this, the novels are substantially middle class. There are few Cinderellas swept away by titled millionaires. Alexandra (*The Cuckoo in Spring*) is one of Cadell's most humbly circumstanced heroines, yet she is self-supporting, a secretary with a firm of solicitors. On some level, the Cadell hero and heroine must meet as equals, since her basic plot shows two people of the same class finding each other and overcoming obstacles that are mildly amusing, to the reader if not to the protagonists.

Often giving her books a Spanish or Portuguese setting, Cadell provides a good read, a piece of escapism where the crucial phone call does not go unanswered and even the rejected suitor is not too crushed by his rejection. Like another prolific writer of romances, D. E. Stevenson, Cadell has a limpid charm of writing that, with the many bizarre subsidiary characters, turns the best of her romances, like *Honey for Tea*, into comedies of manners. And this comic tone allows Cadell to be more realistic than similar authors in areas where her characters are less than perfect. Lucille in *The Lark Shall Sing* is frankly bossy; her beautiful sister tends to ineffectual tears. Kerry's long-lost mother has spent 20 years as mistress to a series of successful men in *The Past Tense of Love*.

Another example of Cadell's realistic streak in the midst of romantic fantasy is her clear-eyed portrayal of children. The three youngest Waynes in *The Lark Shall Sing* are individualized, charming to read about, but possibly less than charming to have to live with. The epitome of the objective portrayal of the child is Tory Brooke in *The Fledgling*. Eponymous heroine though she may be, Tory's determination to recast her circumstances to suit herself shows her as too deliberate and calculating to be altogether attractive. As she waits for her widowed father and the woman of his, and her, choice to announce the happy ending she has contrived for them all, she can be seen, whether or not Cadell intends it, as too cold-blooded for comfort.

At the other end of the scale, particularly in some of her earlier books, Cadell shows an attractive middle-aged woman involved in romantic or family problems. In *Last Straw for Harriet* it is Harriet who holds stage center, not the romantic young peo-

ple. The eye that Cadell turns on the aged, like the eye she turns on the young, is sympathetic but not sentimental.

Mrs. Westerby Changes Course and *Canary Yellow* may veer in the direction of the suspense story; *Brimstone in the Garden* has a supernatural slant; but Cadell's real genre is clearly romance in perhaps its safest, most wholesome form. If "life isn't like that," it is clearly life's fault, not Cadell's.

—Susan Branch

———

CAINE, (Thomas Henry) Hall. British. Born in Runcorn, Cheshire, 14 May 1858. Educated at schools on the Isle of Man and in Liverpool. Married Mary Chandler in 1882; two sons. Worked as an architect's clerk, schoolmaster, then a journalist, Liverpool *Mercury*; companion-secretary to D. G. Rossetti, in London until Rossetti's death, 1882, then lived on the Isle of Man. Lecturer, Royal Institution, London, 1892; Justice of the Peace, and member of the House of Keys, Isle of Man. Freeman of Douglas, Isle of Man, 1928. Officer of the Order of Leopold, Belgium; Companion of Honour, 1922. Knighted, 1918. *Died 31 August 1931.*

ROMANCE AND HISTORICAL PUBLICATIONS

Novels

The Shadow of a Crime. London, Chatto and Windus, 3 vols., and New York, Harper, 3 vols., 1885.
She's All the World to Me. New York, Harper, 1885.
The Deemster. London, Chatto and Windus, 3 vols., 1887; New York, Appleton, 1 vol., 1888.
A Son of Hagar. London, Chatto and Windus, 1887; New York, Fenno, 1895.
The Bondman: A New Saga. New York, Lovell, 1889; London, Heinemann, 3 vols., 1890.
The Scapegoat. London, Heinemann, 2 vols., 1891; New York, Lovell, 1 vol., 1891.
The Manxman. London, Heinemann, and New York, Appleton, 1894.
The Mahdi; or, Love and Race. New York, Appleton, and London, Clarke, 1894.
The Christian. London, Heinemann, and New York, Appleton, 1897.
The Eternal City. London, Heinemann, and New York, Appleton, 1901.
The Prodigal Son. London, Heinemann, and New York, Appleton, 1904.
Drink: A Love Story on a Great Question. London, Newnes, 1906; New York, Appleton, 1907.
The White Prophet. London, Heinemann, 2 vols., 1909; New York, Appleton, 1 vol., 1909; revised edition, Heinemann, 1 vol., 1911.
The Woman Thou Gavest Me. London, Heinemann, and Philadelphia, Lippincott, 1913.
The Master of Man. London, Heinemann, and Philadelphia, Lippincott, 1921.
The Woman of Knockaloe: A Parable. London, Cassell, and New York, Dodd Mead, 1923.

Short Stories

Capt'n Davy's Honeymoon, The Last Confession, The Blind Mother. London, Heinemann, 1892; *Capt'n Davy's Honeymoon* published New York, Appleton, 1892; *The Last Confession, The Blind Mother* published New York, Tait, 1892.

OTHER PUBLICATIONS

Plays

The Ben-my-Chree, with Wilson Barrett (produced London, 1888).
The Good Old Times, with Wilson Barrett (produced London, 1889).
The Bondman, (produced Bolton, Lancashire, 1892; London, 1906). London, Daily Mail, 1906.
The Christian, adaptation of his own novel (produced Liverpool and London, 1899; revised version, produced London, 1907). London, Collier, 1907.
Yan, The Icelander; or, Home Sweet Home (produced Hartlepool, 1900; as *The Quality of Mercy*, produced Manchester, 1911). Privately printed, 1896.
The Eternal City, adaptation of his own novel (produced London and New York, 1902). Privately printed, 1902.
The Prodigal Son, adaptation of his own novel (produced London and New York, 1905). Privately printed, 1905.
Pete, with Louis N. Parker, adaptation of the novel *The Manxman* by Caine (produced London, 1908). London, Collier, 1908.
The Fatal Error (produced London, 1908).
The Bishop's Son, adaptation of his novel *The Deemster* (produced London, 1910). Privately printed, 1910.
The Eternal Question, adaptation of his novel *The Eternal City* (produced London, 1910). Privately printed, 1910.
The Prime Minister (produced Atlantic City, 1916; as *Margaret Schiller*, produced New York, 1916; as *The Prime Minister*, produced London, 1918). Privately printed, 1918.
The Iron Hand (produced London, 1916).
The Woman Thou Gavest Me, adaptation of his own novel (produced Boston, 1917).

Screenplays: *Victory and Peace*, 1918; *Darby and Joan*, 1919.

Other

Richard III and Macbeth . . . : A Dramatic Study. London, Simpkin Marshall, 1877.
Recollections of Dante Gabriel Rossetti. London, Stock, 1882; Boston, Roberts, 1883; revised edition, London, Cassell, 1928.
Cobwebs of Criticism. London, Stock, 1883; New York, Dutton, 1908.
Life of Samuel Taylor Coleridge. London, Scott, 1887; New York, Scribner, n.d.
The Prophet: A Parable. London, Heinemann, 1890.
The Little Manx Nation. London, Heinemann, and New York, United States Book Company, 1891.
Mary Magdalene: The New Apocrypha. Privately printed, 1891.
The Little Man Island: Scenes and Specimen Days in the Isle-of-Man. Douglas, Steam Packet Company, 1894.
My Story. London, Heinemann, 1908; New York, Appleton, 1909.
Why I Wrote ''The White Prophet.'' Privately printed, 1909.

King Edward: A Prince and a Great Man. London, Collier, 1910.
The Drama of Three Hundred Sixty Five Days: Scenes in the Great War. London, Heinemann, and Philadelphia, Lippincott, 1915.
Our Girls: Their Work for the War. London, Hutchinson, 1916.
Life of Christ, edited by Sir Derwent Hall Caine. London, Collins, and New York, Doubleday, 1938.

Editor, *Sonnets of Three Centuries*. London, Stock, 1882; Boston, Clarke, 1883.
Editor, *King Albert's Book: A Tribute to the Belgian King and People*. London, Daily Telegraph, 1914.

*   *   *

Hall Caine was one of the great names of popular fiction at the turn of the century and continued to be so for three decades afterwards. He mingled with the great, was championed by other writers and poets of the time, fought vociferously for the cause of the one-volume (as against the cumbersome three-volume) novel in order that cheaper and more manageable fiction, including his own, could reach a wider public. Thus, his enthusiastic readership included not only the highly literate, but the great uneducated masses. He wrote with moral passion on great and noble subjects and saw himself as ''the Shakespeare of the novel.'' With the decline of religious authority, it seemed necessary for writers such as he to take on themselves the mammoth task of maintaining among the reading masses the moral standards which he felt to be lacking. Today his name is almost forgotten. What is astonishing is that a writer who was so pretentious, so self-important, and whose skill was so inadequate for the task he set himself should have ever been taken seriously in the first place.

The most popular of his 20th-century novels was *The Woman of Knockaloe*, set, like many, on the Isle of Man. He was a pacifist for most of his life, and this romance, written shortly after the end of World War I telling of the forbidden and unacceptable love between a Manxwoman and a German prisoner-of-war, is an impassioned anti-war cry. As Claud Cockburn pointed out in *Best Seller*, the Great War, for all its horror, provided excellent literary food for the popular writers. It was ''a gift, a natural, manna from heaven. It furnished him with a range of fictional and dramatic equipment such as had been ready to hand in the workshops of the Greek classical dramatists.''

The noble intentions of the author of *The Woman of Knockaloe*, the fine motives of his driving force, the proper care to try to end all future war by the power of his pen, contrast strongly with the banality of treatment. The love between Mona and Oskar is necessarily furtive, but utterly pure. Their affair is hopelessly doomed from the start, for the rest of the world is against them. They are driven to a mutual suicide pact. At dawn, they climb a heather-clad mountain to make their love leap from the top, to the ''heaving and singing'' sea below. They agree that their leap must be simultaneous, so, as in some ludicrous charade, they solemnly strap themselves together with Oskar's long coat belt. ''They are now eye to eye, breast to breast, heart to heart.''

Hall Caine's lifelong enemy was the equally popular romantic novelist, Marie Corelli, whose own first novel he had turned down for publication. She, too, believed herself to be a Shakespeare of the prose form. They had much in common. Q. D. Leavis, in *Fiction and the Reading Public*, said that their novels ''make play with the key words of the emotional vocabulary which provoke the vague warm surges of feeling associated with religion and religion substitutes—e.g., life, death, love, good, evil, sin, home, mother, noble, gallant, purity, honour. These responses can be touched off with a dangerous ease.''

—Rachel Anderson

CAIRD, Janet (Hinshaw, née Kirkwood). British. Born in Livingstonia, Malawi, 24 April 1913. Educated at Dollar Academy, Clackmannan; Edinburgh University, 1931–35, M.A. (honours) in English literature 1935; University of Grenoble and the Sorbonne, Paris (Stevenson exchange scholar), 1935–36; St. George's Training College, Edinburgh, 1936–37. Married James Bowman Caird in 1938; two daughters. English, Latin, and French teacher, Park School for Girls, Glasgow, 1937–38, Royal High School, Edinburgh, 1940–41, and Dollar Academy, 1941–43. Agent: A. M. Heath, 79 St. Martin's Lane, London WC2N 4AA, England. Address: 1 Drummond Crescent, Inverness IV2 4QW, Scotland.

ROMANCE AND HISTORICAL PUBLICATIONS

Novels

Murder Reflected. London, Bles, 1965; as *In a Glass Darkly*, New York, Morrow, 1966.
Perturbing Spirit. London, Bles, and New York, Doubleday, 1966.
Murder Scholastic. London, Bles, 1967; New York, Doubleday, 1968.
The Loch. London, Bles, 1968; New York, Doubleday, 1969.
Murder Remote. New York, Doubleday, 1973; as *The Shrouded Way*, New York, New American Library, 1973.
The Umbrella-Maker's Daughter. London, Macmillan, and New York, St. Martin's Press, 1980.

OTHER PUBLICATIONS

Verse

Some Walk a Narrow Path. Edinburgh, Ramsay Head Press, 1977.
A Distant Urn. Edinburgh, Ramsay Head Press, 1983.
John Donne You Were Wrong. Edinburgh, Ramsay Head Press, 1988.

Other

Angus the Tartan Partan (for children). London, Nelson, 1961.

*

Manuscript Collections: Mugar Memorial Library, Boston University; National Library of Scotland, Edinburgh.

*   *   *

Janet Caird's particular gift is for creating an atmosphere of menace. Her stories are set in small towns in Scotland, and the intense, inbred relationships of village life are minutely observed.

In her first mystery, *Murder Reflected*, the heroine, looking through the town's camera obscura, observes murder being done. As she is unable to keep this fact secret, several other murders follow, and her own life is endangered. The heroine is unnecessarily silly, but the other characters are both interesting and well-developed. *Murder Scholastic* involves blackmail and murder at a Scottish academy. There's an especially brilliant, nightmarish scene in which weird masked figures skate in flickering firelight, the villain and heroine among them in a cat-and-mouse chase. In *Perturbing Spirit* Caird's gift for the eerie and theatrical shows itself again as a village festival is taken over by a mysterious stranger who invests it with the trappings of ancient, sacrificial religions while he attempts to use it for his own sinister purposes. In *The Loch* the lake itself has always been an object of superstitious awe for the villagers of Lochie, an awe which increases when the loch floods the town and then recedes into nothing, exposing caves tenanted by a pre-Celtic people. Tragedy is inevitable from the moment rumors circulate of treasure hidden in the cave. In *Murder Remote* unscrupulous men in search of treasure commit murder and hold an entire isolated village hostage. *The Umbrella-Maker's Daughter* is by far her best book, and is in fact genuine literature. The umbrella-maker's daughter is an outsider in a community normally suspicious of outsiders. But when disaster hits the town, normal standards of behavior lapse, and unfocused feelings of rage and despair find a vicious outlet.

Romance is present in all these novels, but it is the least satisfactory element because Caird's heroes and heroines fail to involve the reader; subsidiary characters are often fascinating, but her heroines are boring. One reads Caird less for the romance than for the gothic atmosphere she draws so well.

—Marylaine Block

CALDWELL, (Janet Miriam) Taylor (Holland). Also wrote as Max Reiner. American. Born in Prestwich, Manchester, England, 7 September 1900. Educated at the University of Buffalo, now State University of New York, A.B. 1931. Served in the United States Naval Reserve, 1918–19. Married 1) William Fairfax Combs in 1919 (divorced 1931), one daughter; 2) Marcus Reback in 1931 (died 1970), one daughter; 3) William E. Stancell in 1972 (divorced 1973); 4) William Robert Prestie in 1978. Court reporter, New York State Department of Labor, Buffalo, 1923–24; member of the Board of Special Inquiry, Department of Justice, Buffalo, 1924–31. Recipient: National League of American Pen Women gold medal, 1948; Buffalo *Evening News* award, 1949; Grand Prix Chatrain, 1956. D.Litt.: D'Youville College, Buffalo, 1964; St. Bonaventure College, New York, 1977. *Died 30 August 1985.*

ROMANCE AND HISTORICAL PUBLICATIONS

Novels (series: Barbours and Bouchards)

Dynasty of Death (Barbours and Bouchards). New York, Scribner, 1938; London, Collins, 1939.
The Eagles Gather (Barbours and Bouchards). New York, Scribner, and London, Collins, 1940.
Time No Longer (as Max Reiner). New York, Scribner, 1941.
The Earth Is the Lord's. New York, Scribner, and London, Collins, 1941.

The Strong City. New York, Scribner, and London, Collins, 1942.

The Arm and the Darkness. New York, Scribner, and London, Collins, 1943.

The Turnbulls. New York, Scribner, 1943; London, Collins, 1944.

The Final Hour (Barbours and Bouchards). New York, Scribner, 1944; London, Collins, 1945.

The Wide House. New York, Scribner, 1945; London, Collins, 1946.

This Side of Innocence. New York, Scribner, 1946; London, Collins, 1947.

There Was a Time. New York, Scribner, 1947; London, Collins, 1948.

Melissa. New York, Scribner, 1948; London, Collins, 1949.

Let Love Come Last. New York, Scribner, 1948; London, Collins, 1950.

The Balance Wheel. New York, Scribner, 1951; as *The Beautiful Is Vanished*, London, Collins, 1951.

The Devil's Advocate. New York, Crown, 1952.

Maggie, Her Marriage. New York, Fawcett, 1953; London, Muller, 1954.

Never Victorious, Never Defeated. New York, McGraw Hill, and London, Collins, 1954.

Your Sins and Mine. New York, Fawcett, 1955; London, Muller, 1956.

Tender Victory. New York, McGraw Hill, and London, Collins, 1956.

The Sound of Thunder. New York, Doubleday, 1957; London, Collins, 1958.

Dear and Glorious Physician. New York, Doubleday, and London, Collins, 1959.

The Listener. New York, Doubleday, 1960; as *The Man Who Listens*, London, Collins, 1961.

A Prologue to Love. New York, Doubleday, 1961; London, Collins, 1962.

Grandmother and the Priests. New York, Doubleday, 1963; as *To See the Glory*, London, Collins, 1963.

The Late Clare Beame. New York, Doubleday, 1963; London, Collins, 1964.

A Pillar of Iron. New York, Doubleday, 1965; London, Collins, 1966.

Wicked Angel. New York, Fawcett, 1965; London, Coronet, 1966.

No One Hears But Him. New York, Doubleday, and London, Collins, 1966.

Testimony of Two Men. New York, Doubleday, 1968; London, Collins, 1969.

Great Lion of God. New York, Doubleday, and London, Collins, 1970.

Captains and the Kings. New York, Doubleday, 1972; London, Collins, 1973.

Glory and the Lightning. New York, Doubleday, 1974; London, Collins, 1975.

To Look and Pass. London, White Lion, 1974.

The Romance of Atlantis, with Jess Stearn. New York, Morrow, 1975; London, Fontana, 1976.

Ceremony of the Innocent. New York, Doubleday, 1976; London, Collins, 1977.

I, Judas, with Jess Stearn. New York, Atheneum, 1977; London, New English Library, 1978.

Bright Flows the River. New York, Doubleday, 1978; London, Collins, 1979.

Answer As a Man. New York, Putnam, and London, Collins, 1981.

OTHER PUBLICATIONS

Other

Dialogues with the Devil. New York, Doubleday, 1967; London, Collins, 1968.

On Growing Up Tough. Old Greenwich, Connecticut, Devin Adair, 1971; as *Growing Up Tough*, London, Stacey, 1971.

*

Critical Study: *In Search of Taylor Caldwell* by Jess Stearn, New York, Stein and Day, 1981.

*   *   *

Taylor Caldwell's long list of successes as a popular author began only in 1938 with the wide acceptance of her first published novel. However, she had a life-long interest in writing having completed her first novel at 12. Caldwell's published works reflect her views and wide-ranging interests. They include historical novels in settings as disparate as ancient Greece and Rome and Richelieu's France; Biblical novels interpreting the events and figures of the Gospels; one detective tale; and novels which discuss the author's religious views. However, Caldwell's most characteristic works, best selling and critically acclaimed, are her epic novels about the growth and influence of American political and industrial dynasties and the lives and loves of the families that comprise them. The continuing appeal of these long, complex, and often didactic works lie in their evaluation of the American Dream in terms of domestic and moral values. In over 20 novels of monumental scope and length, Caldwell demonstrates that the glamor, prestige, and beauty of the social elite must be governed by the moral values of the home if it is to be a meaningful or happy world for the people who inhabit it. In Caldwell's fiction, women's love as wives and mothers provides the basis for the moral continuity her industrialist heroes too often ignore or reject.

Caldwell's first novel, *Dynasty of Death*, and its two sequels, *The Eagles Gather* and *The Final Hour*, develop the saga of two French-American families, the Barbours and the Bouchards, whose power in the armaments industry can shape world policy and economics, elect and defeat presidents, and begin and end world wars in the interests of family wealth and influence. The marriages between the 52 members of the Barbour and Bouchard clan become political alliances, often loveless, often betrayed, and producing an increasingly refined line of American aristocrats, absorbed in their own superiority and power. The absolute power of the Barbour/Bouchard dynasty ends as the last scion admits, however grudgingly, the merits of democracy, forces the members of his clan to support the American effort against Nazi Germany, and marries for love, amid plots, counterplots, adultery, heartbreak, and scandal.

Caldwell's powerful industrialists are typically self-made men of pronounced ethnic background; the heroes of *The Strong City* and *The Balance Wheel*, for example, are German immigrants. In addition, Caldwell's novels tend to trace the fortunes of the families they discuss through more than one generation, like the Irish political dynasty of *Captains and the Kings*. Favorite Caldwell themes are ethnic, religious, and personal intolerance (*The Wide House*), the failure of parental discipline (*Let Love Come Last*), and the conflict between the desire for power and money and the humane values of love, marital love, parental love, and Christian *caritas* (*Melissa, A Prologue to Love, Bright Flows the River, Answer As a Man*). The victories Caldwell grants love and virtue over greed, self-indulgence, and decadence are few and reserved. She parallels the conflict between power and action to love and contemplation in ancient times to the same conflict in the 19th and 20th centuries: the Post-Industrial Age is inevitably the moral loser. Caldwell's good and generous women suffer; her self-made men are consumed morally and spiritually by selfish delusions, blighting the larger world they themselves consume.

Despite her gloomy themes, wordy and often platitudinous prose, and stylised characterisation, Caldwell is an expert story-teller who plays on themes popular with readers, especially with women readers, since the popularity of the domestic novel of the 19th century. In Caldwell's fiction, women represent the good, even if they must suffer for it; sexuality and sexual purity represent personal power; money, the root of all evil, is a masculine addition; harmonious relations between the generations are the duty and the reward of mothers; and powerful dynasties must be based on convoluted conspiracies and moral seduction. Caldwell adapted her formula to a variety of painstakingly researched American settings and periods, and her novels, despite their slow development, carefully evoke time and place. Most important, and most fascinating to Caldwell's mass audience, she presents the equally glamorous and repellent world of the American Dream, a world in which women are, although not politically powerful without men, at least moral victors in their own right.

—Katherine Staples

CAMPBELL, Karen. See **BEATY, Betty.**

CARLEON, A. See **O'GRADY, Rohan.**

CARNEGIE, Sacha (Raymond Alexander Carnegie). British. Born in Edinburgh, Scotland, 9 July 1920. Educated at Eton College, 1933–37. Married 1) Patricia Dawson in 1943, two daughters; 2) the Countess of Erroll in 1964 (died 1978), one child. Served in the Scots Guards, 1940–52: Major. Agent: John Johnson, 45–47 Clerkenwell Green, London EC1R 0HT, England. Address: Crimonmogate, Lonmay, Aberdeenshire, Scotland.

ROMANCE AND HISTORICAL PUBLICATIONS

Novels (series: Destiny of Eagles in all "Banners" books)

Noble Purpose. London, Davies, 1954.
Sunset in the East. London, Davies, 1955.
The Devil and the Deep. London, Davies, and New York, Appleton Century Crofts, 1957.
The Lion and Francis Conway. London, Davies, 1958.
The Dark Night. London, Davies, 1960.
The Deerslayers. London, Davies, 1961.
The Guardian. London, Davies, and New York, Dodd Mead, 1966; as *The Colonel*, London, Magnum, 1979.
The Banners of Love. London, Davies, 1968; as *Scarlet Banners of Love*, New York, Dodd Mead, 1968.

Banners of War. London, Davies, and New York, Dodd Mead, 1970.
Banners of Power. London, Davies, 1972; as *Kasia and the Empress*, New York, Dodd Mead, 1973.
Banners of Courage. London, Davies, 1976.
Banners of Revolt. London, Davies, 1977.

OTHER PUBLICATIONS

Other

Holiday from Life. London, Davies, 1957.
Pigs I Have Known. London, Davies, 1958.
Red Dust of Africa. London, Davies, 1959.
The Golden Years (memoirs). London, Davies, 1962.
A Dash of Russia (travel). London, Davies, 1966.

*   *   *

An ex-professional soldier, Sacha Carnegie has written a number of both fiction and non-fiction books, and in the Major Gair Mainwaring novels uses his own military experience to good effect. But it is for the series of novels set in 18th-century Poland that he is best known.

Collectively (and perhaps rather grandiosely) entitled Destiny of Eagles the five linked books describe the lives of Henryk Barinski and Kasia Radienska, whose love affair is inextricably linked with the fortunes of Poland in the 18th century. Henryk is engaged in the struggle for Polish independence from Russia, a struggle made more difficult by the incursions of other warring factions. This was an extremely complex period in the history of Poland and her neighbouring countries, and we are presented with a bewildering array of Cossacks, Turks, Tatars, Poles, and Russians. An impressive amount of research has obviously gone into these novels, and the historical period and geographical setting form a combination which is not often found in fiction.

In fact, these historical events form the only reference point for the novels, as it is impossible to tell from the language used or from the social settings that they are indeed placed in the 18th century. One cannot help speculating that if the novels had been written within the last five years the structure of the sequence would have been rather different. There is in them the raw material for a saga comprising two or three volumes of 500–600 pages each, and then the opportunity would have existed to explore the fascinating and unusual setting and to delve more deeply into the motivations of even the minor characters. In fact, it is only in *The Banners of Love* (the first of the sequence) that Carnegie comes anywhere near exploiting the potential of his subject matter. This book is far longer and more detailed than any of the others, and it is here that we gain an insight not only into the characters of Henryk and Kasia, but through Kasia's experiences (and they are many and varied) into environments ranging from a Cossack village to the Russian court.

This depth is not sustained in the other four novels. They are at once slighter and more superficial, and although each book can supposedly stand independently of the rest, in fact without the background and character analysis given in *The Banners of Love*, the later novels make somewhat poor reading. Each of the first four books ends inconclusively (the hallmark of a multi-volume sequence) and it is only in *The Banners of Revolt*, the final volume, that events are structured in such a way as to bring the individual novel to a satisfying conclusion.

The twin threads running through the sequence of novels are the fortunes of the country, and those of Henryk and Kasia; as Poland's fate hangs in the balance, so does the very existence of their romantic partnership, for both are seriously affected by the vicissitudes of war and politics. Although the two lovers have grown up as neighbours, and share childhood experiences, yet the relationship between Kasia and Henryk assumes an importance beyond that of their individual personalities. Another childhood friend is "Figgy," who through an extremely advantageous marriage becomes Grand Duchess, and ultimately Empress, Catherine the Great of Russia; it is not hard to see how this relationship can be exploited in terms of the novelistic device of linking the fortunes of characters directly to political or national developments. This is not to say that these novels exist solely in a semi-allegorical framework; they also contain much which can be described as pure adventure. In *The Banners of War*, Henryk has been condemned to imprisonment by the Russian Secret Chancellery; he escapes and makes his way to England but is press-ganged into service in the English navy. This is the time of the Seven Years' War, and the naval actions in which Henryk takes part are described in tense and exciting prose. Meanwhile, back in Poland, Kasia's life too is far from easy, and even after she is reunited with Henryk (between the end of *The Banners of War* and the beginning of the following volume, *The Banners of Power*) this unusually strong and independent 18th-century heroine has much to cope with before she and her husband can embrace anything approaching a settled married life.

—Judith Rhodes

CARR, Philippa. See **HOLT, Victoria.**

CARR, Roberta. See **ROBERTS, Irene.**

CARR, Robyn. American. Born in St. Paul, Minnesota, 25 July 1951. Educated at Arthur B. Anker School of Nursing, St. Paul, 1969–71. Married James R. Carr; two sons. Address: c/o St. Martin's Press, 175 Fifth Avenue, New York, New York 10010, U.S.A.

ROMANCE AND HISTORICAL PUBLICATIONS

Novels

Chelynne. Boston, Little Brown, 1980.
The Blue Falcon. Boston, Little Brown, 1981.
The Bellerose Bargain. Boston, Little Brown, 1982.
The Braeswood Tapestry. Boston, Little Brown, 1984.
The Troubadour's Romance. Boston, Little Brown, 1985.
By Right of Arms. Boston, Little Brown, 1986.
The Everlasting Covenant. Boston, Little Brown, 1987.
Informed Risk. New York, Silhouette, 1989.

*   *   *

Since her promising debut with *Chelynne* in 1980, Robyn Carr has published almost a book a year, and, in doing so, has established a solid reputation as a leading author of historical ro-

mances. Set primarily in England and France in medieval times or the Restoration, Carr's novels feature strong heroines, whose pride and independence are sources of that inner strength they must exhibit to overcome the obstacles thrown against them.

In most of the novels, the heroine is matched to her lord by unusual circumstances, and only after respect and trust develop does love grow. Both Chelynne and Felise Scelfton in *The Troubadour's Romance* enter into arranged marriages, while Jocelyn Cutler (*The Braeswood Tapestry*) is Sir Trent Westcott's mistress before marrying him, Alicia (*The Bellerose Bargain*) is hired to impersonate another, and Lady Aurelie (*By Right of Arms*) is a prize of war won by Sir Hyatt Laidley. In spite of rocky beginnings, however, these strong individuals, tempered by trials, become true partners, equal to the task of founding and holding dynasties.

In general, Carr's novels have intricate and often suspenseful plots, a strong sense of time and place, and well-developed, likeable characters. Only in *The Blue Falcon* does she fail to develop fully her characters and intertwine their stories. These characters are stiff and their dialogue is stilted, as if Carr is not truly at home in the England of King Richard and the Crusaders. The narrative is not smooth and overall the pace is slow. Even the inclusion of a hint of the occult in the person of the clairvoyant Giselle does not succeed. Carr cannot seem to make up her mind to believe in her own creation here and fails fully to exploit the possibilities. *The Everlasting Covenant*, set during the Wars of the Roses, also is slow-paced but succeeds in holding the reader's interest more fully. Anne Gifford and Dylan deFrayne are lovers torn apart by a family feud and civil war. Their starcrossed love changes but endures over a quarter of a century as they themselves mature and change.

More successful, however, are the novels which are more focused and faster-paced. Here, one can appreciate a feeling of a woman's power of self identity and determination in spite of the contemporary mores which limit her life. Even a village girl like Jocelyn Cutler can better herself. The same seems true for Alicia, who is willing to support Geoffrey, Lord Seavers, in fraud, but the effect is weakened when too coincidentally, she is discovered to be the long-lost daughter of another noble family. *Chelynne*, *The Troubadour's Romance*, and *By Right of Arms* remain Carr's most complete novels, with a satisfactory mix of romance and historical detail and characters guided by a strong sense of honor and duty.

With a solid body of work behind her now, Carr clearly has developed the potential shown by her early work.

—Barbara E. Kemp

CARTER, Angela (Olive, née Stalker). British. Born in Eastbourne, Sussex, 7 May 1940. Educated at the University of Bristol, 1962–65, B.A. in English 1965. Married Paul Carter in 1960 (divorced 1972). Journalist, Croydon, Surrey, 1958–61. Arts Council Fellow in Creative Writing, University of Sheffield, 1976–78; Visiting Professor of Creative Writing, Brown University, Providence, Rhode Island, 1980–81; writer-in-residence, University of Adelaide, Australia, 1984. Recipient: Rhys Memorial prize, 1968; Maugham award, 1969; Cheltenham Festival prize, 1979; Maschler award, for children's book, 1982; James Tait Black Memorial prize, 1985. Agent: Deborah Rogers Ltd., 20 Powis Mews, London W11 1JN. Address: c/o Virago Press, 20–23 Mandela Street, London NW1 0HQ, England.

ROMANCE AND HISTORICAL PUBLICATIONS

Novel

Nights at the Circus. London, Chatto and Windus, 1984; New York, Viking, 1985.

Short Stories

Black Venus's Tale. London, Faber-Next, 1980.
Black Venus. London, Chatto and Windus, 1985; as *Saints and Strangers*, New York, Viking, 1986.

OTHER PUBLICATIONS

Novels

Shadow Dance. London, Heinemann, 1966; as *Honeybuzzard*, New York, Simon and Schuster, 1967.
The Magic Toyshop. London, Heinemann, 1967; New York, Simon and Schuster, 1968.
Several Perceptions. London, Heinemann, 1968; New York, Simon and Schuster, 1969.
Heroes and Villains. London, Heinemann, 1969; New York, Simon and Schuster, 1970.
Love. London, Hart Davis, 1971.
The Infernal Desire Machines of Dr. Hoffman. London, Hart Davis, 1972; as *The War of Dreams*, New York, Harcourt Brace, 1974.
The Passion of New Eve. London, Gollancz, and New York, Harcourt Brace, 1977.

Short Stories

Fireworks: Nine Profane Pieces. London, Quartet, 1974; New York, Harper, 1981.
The Bloody Chamber and Other Stories. London, Gollancz, 1979; New York, Harper, 1980.

Plays

Vampirella (broadcast 1976; produced London, 1986). Included in *Come unto These Yellow Sands*, 1984.
Come unto These Yellow Sands (radio plays; includes *The Company of Wolves*, *Vampirella*, *Puss in Boots*). Newcastle-upon-Tyne, Bloodaxe, 1984.

Screenplays: *The Company of Wolves*, with Neil Jordan, 1984; *The Magic Toyshop*, 1987.

Radio Plays: *Vampirella*, 1976; *Come unto These Yellow Sands*, 1979; *The Company of Wolves*, from her own story, 1980; *Puss in Boots*, 1982; *A Self-Made Man* (on Ronald Firbank), 1984.

Verse

Unicorn. Leeds, Location Press, 1966.

Other

Miss Z, The Dark Young Lady (for children). London, Heinemann, and New York, Simon and Schuster, 1970.
The Donkey Prince (for children). New York, Simon and Schuster, 1970.

Comic and Curious Cats, illustrated by Martin Leman. London, Gollancz, and New York, Crown, 1979.
The Sadeian Woman: An Exercise in Cultural History. London, Virago Press, 1979; as *The Sadeian Woman and the Ideology of Pornography*, New York, Pantheon, 1979.
Nothing Sacred: Selected Writings. London, Virago Press, 1982.
Moonshadow (for children). London, Gollancz, 1982.
Sleeping Beauty and Other Favourite Fairy Tales. London, Gollancz, 1982; New York, Schocken, 1984.

Editor, *Wayward Girls and Wicked Women*. London, Virago Press, 1986.

Translator, *The Fairy Tales of Charles Perrault*. London, Gollancz, 1977; New York, Avon, 1978.

*   *   *

Yet, even then, even in these remote regions, in those days, those last, bewildering days before history, that is, history as we know it, that is white history, that is, European history, that is, Yanqui history—in that final little breathing space before history as such extended its tentacles to grasp the entire globe. . . . it still seemed possible their flexible and resilient mythology would be able to incorporate the future into itself and so prevent its believers from disappearing into the past.

Angela Carter's novel *Nights at the Circus* and her collection of short stories, *Black Venus*, both involve a complex and specific attitude toward the animal we term "history." There is a strong, though understated, sense in both works that behind the words lives a historical context and backdrop of knowledge, but it is not the focus of concern in either book. Thus it is not until the final pages of *Nights at the Circus* that the reader needs to have confirmed the political realities of Lizzie's and Fevvers lives, central though they are.

Rather, the writer is exploring the problematic and invisible boundaries that separate the provinces of imagination and verifiable fact. As the narrator of the novel declares, this narrative does not belong to "the violence of authentic history"; yet that "authentic" or "Yanqui history" is seminal as a point of reaction and departure. While the novel has been very deliberately placed at the turn of this century, "the cusp of the modern age," and the stories all inhabit specific and various historical locations and times—from 18th-century Paris to 19th-century Massachusetts, authenticity is not the chief concern.

This leads to writing of an elusively but profoundly political kind. For, before our very eyes, the author is subtly rewriting history in the shape of original fiction. This is achieved in two clear ways. One approach lies in giving language to voices previously obscured and silenced by historical orthodoxy; the abandoned and those relegated to the margins of mainstream society. Thus Jeanne Duval, the black mistress of Baudelaire, springs to life in the title story of *Black Venus*, and Fevvers, the heroine of the novel, feathered women, fact or fiction, symbol or person, but certainly circus freak and performer. Life and utterance are once more restored to these forgotten actors, suggesting that what can inform our sense of the past and present are not our beloved, heralded heroes but the outcasts and the lost.

Yet Carter also knows that the stories we tell ourselves, however bizarrely archetypal, grow out of, and into, particular realities and political weapons. They are too important to be left untouched. From this emerges the second line of approach: these tales make magic in order to break the spell of the past. So, the stories in *Black Venus*, are about everyday life among the mythic classes. Real people live alongside entirely imaginary beings.

Given Carter's acute fascination with the light gender differences throw on our sense of ourselves, what inevitably emerges is a collection of newly discovered female personages and perspectives. She is not a writer by any means confined to valorising "the woman's point of view"—precisely the opposite in fact. Here is a writer who flits disarmingly and with seeming ease from voice to voice, male and female alike. Her male characters, credible though they are, move from being patriarchal monsters like Andrew Borden in "The Fall River Axe Murders," a story in the collection, to those whose sexuality and sexual identity are more ambiguous and problematic, as exemplified in "The Cabinet of Edgar Allan Poe."

This sense that there are no sexual truths, no stipulations about what constitutes masculine and feminine is a recurring theme. Rather, we witness women who behave "like men," men like women, but all of whom are trying to negotiate life under the shadow of society's shoulds and oughts. This sexual ambiguity reaches a powerful climactic statement in "Overture and Incidental Music for a Midsummer Night's Dream," told to us by "the Golden Herm."

Carter has language at her fingertips, her work is dense and tightly packed. Indeed, she has been hailed as "the poet of the short story." She constantly shifts her semantic ground so that tired metaphor or familiar phrase simply do not appear. By turns colloquial, surrealist, bawdy and hilarious, each observation is tilted to shed a clearer, brighter light. Words glow from this pen, with a Shakespearian sense of linguistic innovation.

In *Nights at the Circus* we are taken back to a rich, turn of the 19th-century world, which reeks of human and animal variety. It has all the baroque splendour, fairytale horror and vision of the alienated wreckage of a future world evident in her non-historical fiction, but here we are most definitely in Victorian England. The first part is the autobiography of our heroine, Fevvers, with her rich, raucous, Cockney voice. The novel then extends to embrace the life of the circus, that animal that "could absorb madness and slaughter into itself with the enthusiasm of a boa constrictor, and so continue," and through its travels and travails across a Siberian wasteland. Multi-layered though the novel's ending is, one leaves the book breathless with the kaleidoscope of life here presented.

The stories in *Black Venus* inhabit the steamy world of the seven deadly sins, each one a compact world, "a story in simple, geometric shapes and the bold colours of a child's box of crayons." Shocking yet humane, innovative in form and structure, this writing makes demanding reading and constitutes a unique contribution to this century's historical fiction.

—Catherine S. Wearing

CARTER, Elizabeth Eliot. See **HOLLAND, Cecelia.**

CARTLAND, Barbara (Hamilton). Has also written as Barbara McCorquodale. British. Educated at Malvern Girls' College; Abbey House, Netley Abbey, Hampshire. Married 1) Alexander George McCorquodale in 1927 (divorced 1933), one daughter; 2) Hugh McCorquodale in 1936 (died 1963), two sons. Freelance writer since 1925. Honorary junior commander, Aux-iliary Territorial Service, and Bedfordshire welfare officer and librarian, 1941–49; Bedfordshire cadet officer, St. John Ambulance Brigade, 1943–47, and County vice-president cadets, 1948–50; Hertfordshire vice-president, nursing cadets, 1951; Hertfordshire Chairman, St. John Council; county councillor, Hertfordshire, 1955–64; President, Hertfordshire branch of Royal College of Midwives, 1957. Editor, Library of Love series. Vice-President, Romantic Novelists Association and Oxfam; President, National Association of Health, 1966. Certificate of Merit, Eastern Command, 1946; Dame of Grace, St. John of Jerusalem; Fellow Royal Society of Arts, 1984. Address: Camfield Place, Hatfield, Hertfordshire, England.

ROMANCE AND HISTORICAL PUBLICATIONS

Novels

Jig-Saw. London, Duckworth, 1925.
Sawdust. London, Duckworth, 1926.
If the Tree Is Saved. London, Duckworth, 1929.
For What? London, Hutchinson, 1930.
Sweet Punishment. London, Hutchinson, 1931; New York Pyramid, 1973.
A Virgin in Mayfair. London, Hutchinson, 1932.
Just Off Piccadilly. London, Hutchinson, 1933; as *Dance on My Heart*, London, Arrow, 1977.
Not Love Alone. London, Hutchinson, 1933.
A Beggar Wished . . . . London, Hutchinson, 1934; as *Rainbow to Heaven*, London, Arrow, 1976.
Passionate Attainment. London, Hutchinson, 1935.
First Class, Lady? London, Hutchinson, 1935; as *Love and Linda*, London, Arrow, 1976.
Dangerous Experiment. London, Hutchinson, 1936; as *Search for Love*, New York, Greenberg, 1937.
Desperate Defiance. London, Hutchinson, 1936.
The Forgotten City. London, Hutchinson, 1936.
Saga at Forty. London, Hutchinson, 1937; as *Love at Forty*, London, Arrow, 1977.
But Never Free. London, Hutchinson, 1937; as *The Adventurer*, London, Arrow, 1977.
Broken Barriers. London, Hutchinson, 1938.
Bitter Winds. London, Hutchinson, 1938; as *Bitter Winds of Love*, London, Arrow, 1976; New York, Berkley, 1978.
The Gods Forget. London, Hutchinson, 1939; as *Love in Pity*, London, Arrow, 1977.
The Black Panther. London, Rich and Cowan, 1939; as *Lost Love*, New York, Pyramid, 1970.
Stolen Halo. London, Rich and Cowan, 1940; New York, Pyramid, 1973.
Now Rough—Now Smooth. London, Hutchinson, 1941.
Open Wings. London, Hutchinson, 1942.
The Leaping Flame. London, Hale, 1942.
The Dark Stream. London, Hutchinson, 1944; as *This Time It's Love*, London, Arrow, 1977; New York, Berkley, 1979.
After the Night. London, Hutchinson, 1944; as *Towards the Stars*, London, Arrow, 1971.
Yet She Follows. London, Hale, 1944; as *A Heart Is Broken*, 1972.
Escape from Passion. London, Hale, 1945.
Armour Against Love. London, Hutchinson, 1945; New York, Pyramid, 1974.
Out of Reach. London, Hutchinson, 1945.
The Hidden Heart. London, Hutchinson, 1946; New York, Pyramid, 1970.
Against the Stream. London, Hutchinson, 1946.

The Dream Within. London, Hutchinson, 1947.
If We Will. London, Hutchinson, 1947; as *Where Is Love?*, London, Arrow, 1971.
Again This Rapture. London, Hutchinson, 1947.
No Heart Is Free. London, Rich and Cowan, 1948.
A Hazard of Hearts. London, Rich and Cowan, 1949; New York, Pyramid, 1969.
The Enchanted Moment. London, Rich and Cowan, 1949.
A Duel of Hearts. London, Rich and Cowan, 1949; New York, Pyramid, 1970.
The Knave of Hearts. London, Rich and Cowan, 1950; New York, Pyramid, 1971.
The Little Pretender. London, Rich and Cowan, 1951; New York, Pyramid, 1971.
Love Is an Eagle. London, Rich and Cowan, 1951.
A Ghost in Monte Carlo. London, Rich and Cowan, 1951.
Love Is the Enemy. London, Rich and Cowan, 1952; New York, Pyramid, 1970.
Cupid Rides Pillion. London, Hutchinson, 1952.
Elizabethan Lover. London, Hutchinson, 1953; New York, Pyramid, 1971.
Love Me for Ever. London, Hutchinson, 1953; as *Love Me Forever*, New York, Pyramid, 1970.
Desire of the Heart. London, Hutchinson, 1954; New York, Pyramid, 1969.
The Enchanted Waltz. London, Hutchinson, 1955; New York, Pyramid, 1971.
The Kiss of the Devil. London, Hutchinson, 1955.
The Captive Heart. London, Hutchinson, 1956; New York, Pyramid, 1970.
The Coin of Love. London, Hutchinson, 1956; New York, Pyramid, 1969.
Sweet Adventure. London, Hutchinson, 1957; New York, Pyramid, 1970.
Stars in My Heart. London, Hutchinson, 1957; New York, Pyramid, 1971.
The Golden Gondola. London, Hutchinson, 1958; New York, Pyramid, 1971.
Love in Hiding. London, Hutchinson, 1959; New York, Pyramid, 1969.
The Smuggled Heart. London, Hutchinson, 1959.
Love under Fire. London, Hutchinson, 1960.
Messenger of Love. London, Hutchinson, 1961; New York, Pyramid, 1971.
The Wings of Love. London, Hutchinson, 1962; New York, Pyramid, 1971.
The Hidden Evil. London, Hutchinson, 1963; New York, Pyramid, 1971.
The Fire of Love. London, Hutchinson, 1964; New York, Avon, 1970.
The Unpredictable Bride. London, Hutchinson, 1964; New York, Pyramid, 1969.
Love Holds the Cards. London, Hutchinson, 1965; New York, Pyramid, 1970.
A Virgin in Paris. London, Hutchinson, 1966; New York, Pyramid, 1971.
Love to the Rescue. London, Hutchinson, 1967; New York, Pyramid, 1970.
Love Is Contraband. London, Hutchinson, 1968; New York, Pyramid, 1970.
The Enchanting Evil. London, Hutchinson, 1968; New York, Pyramid, 1969.
The Unknown Heart. London, Hutchinson, 1969; New York, Pyramid, 1971.
Debt of Honor. New York, Pyramid, 1970.
Innocent Heiress. New York, Pyramid, 1970.

The Reluctant Bride. London, Hutchinson, 1970.
The Royal Pledge. New York, Pyramid, 1970.
The Secret Fear. London, Hutchinson, 1970; New York, Pyramid, 1971.
The Secret Heart. New York, Pyramid, 1970.
The Pretty Horse-Breakers. London, Hutchinson, 1971.
The Queen's Messenger. New York, Pyramid, 1971.
Stars in Her Eyes. New York, Pyramid, 1971.
Innocent in Paris. New York, Pyramid, 1971.
The Audacious Adventuress. London, Hutchinson, 1971; New York, Pyramid, 1972.
A Halo for the Devil. London, Arrow, 1972.
The Irresistible Buck. London, Arrow, 1972.
The Complacent Wife. London, Hutchinson, 1972.
Lost Enchantment. London, Hutchinson, 1972; New York, Pyramid, 1973.
The Odious Duke. London, Arrow, 1973.
The Little Adventure. London, Hutchinson, 1973; New York, Bantam, 1974.
The Daring Deception. London, Arrow, 1973.
The Wicked Marquis. London, Hutchinson, 1973; New York, Bantam, 1974.
No Darkness for Love. London, Hutchinson, and New York, Bantam, 1974.
The Ruthless Rake. London, Pan, and New York, Bantam, 1974.
The Glittering Lights. New York, Bantam, 1974; London, Corgi, 1975.
A Sword to the Heart. New York, Bantam, 1974; London, Corgi, 1975.
The Penniless Peer. London, Pan, and New York, Bantam, 1974.
The Magnificent Marriage. London, Corgi, 1974; New York, Bantam, 1975.
Lessons in Love. London, Arrow, and New York, Bantam, 1974.
The Karma of Love. London, Corgi, 1974; New York, Bantam, 1975.
The Bored Bridegroom. London, Pan, and New York, Bantam, 1974.
The Castle of Fear. London, Pan, and New York, Bantam, 1974.
The Cruel Count. London, Pan, 1974; New York, Bantam, 1975.
The Dangerous Dandy. London, Pan, and New York, Bantam, 1974.
Journey to Paradise. London, Arrow, and New York, Bantam, 1974.
Call of the Heart. London, Pan, and New York, Bantam, 1975.
Love Is Innocent. London, Hutchinson, and New York, Bantam, 1975.
Shadow of Sin. London, Corgi, 1975.
Bewitched. London, Corgi, and New York, Bantam, 1975.
The Devil in Love. London, Corgi, and New York, Bantam, 1975.
Fire on the Snow. London, Hutchinson, 1975; New York, Bantam, 1976.
The Flame Is Love. London, Pan, 1975.
The Frightened Bride. London, Pan, and New York, Bantam, 1975.
The Impetuous Duchess. London, Corgi, and New York, Bantam, 1975.
The Mask of Love. London, Corgi, and New York, Bantam, 1975.
The Tears of Love. London, Corgi, and New York, Bantam, 1975.

A Very Naughty Angel. London, Pan, and New York, Bantam, 1975.

An Arrow of Love. London, Pan, 1975; New York, Bantam, 1976.

As Eagles Fly. London, Pan, and New York, Bantam, 1975.

A Frame of Dreams. London, Pan, 1975; New York, Bantam, 1976.

A Gamble with Hearts. London, Pan, 1975; New York, Bantam, 1976.

A Kiss for the King. London, Pan, 1975; New York, Bantam, 1976.

Say Yes, Samantha. London, Pan, and New York, Bantam, 1975.

The Elusive Earl. London, Hutchinson, and New York, Bantam, 1976.

The Blue-Eyed Witch. London, Hutchinson, 1976.

An Angel in Hell. London, Pan, 1976.

A Dream from the Night. London, Corgi, and New York, Bantam, 1976.

Fragrant Flower. London, Pan, and New York, Bantam, 1976.

The Golden Illusion. London, Pan, and New York, Bantam, 1976.

The Heart Triumphant. London, Corgi, 1976.

Hungry for Love. London, Corgi, 1976.

The Husband Hunters. London, Pan, and New York, Bantam, 1976.

The Incredible Honeymoon. London, Pan, and New York, Bantam, 1976.

Moon over Eden. London, Pan, and New York, Bantam, 1976.

Never Laugh at Love. London, Corgi, 1976.

No Time for Love. London, Pan, and New York, Bantam, 1976.

Passions in the Sand. London, Pan, and New York, Bantam, 1976.

The Proud Princess. London, Corgi, 1976.

The Secret of the Glen. London, Corgi, 1976.

The Slaves of Love. London, Pan, 1976.

The Wild Cry of Love. London, Pan, and New York, Bantam, 1976.

The Disgraceful Duke. London, Corgi, 1976.

The Mysterious Maid-Servant. London, Hutchinson, 1977.

The Dragon and the Pearl. London, Hutchinson, and Williamsport, Pennsylvania, Duron, 1977.

Conquered by Love. London, Pan, 1977.

The Curse of the Clan. London, Pan, and Williamsport, Pennsylvania, Duron, 1977.

The Dream and the Glory. London, Pan, 1977.

A Duel with Destiny. London, Corgi, 1977.

Kiss the Moonlight. London, Pan, 1977.

Look, Listen, and Love. London, Pan, and Williamsport, Pennsylvania, Duron, 1977.

Love Locked In. London, Pan, and New York, Dutton, 1977.

The Magic of Love. London, Pan, 1977.

The Marquis Who Hated Women. London, Pan, and Williamsport, Pennsylvania, Duron, 1977.

The Outrageous Lady. London, Pan, and Williamsport, Pennsylvania, Duron, 1977.

The Sign of Love. Williamsport, Pennsylvania, Duron, 1977; London, Pan, 1978.

A Rhapsody of Love. London, Pan, 1977.

The Taming of Lady Lorinda. London, Pan, 1977.

Vote for Love. London, Corgi, 1977.

The Wild, Unwilling Wife. London, Pan, and New York, Dutton, 1977.

The Love Pirate. Williamsport, Pennsylvania, Duron, 1977; London, Corgi, 1978.

Punishment of a Vixen. Williamsport, Pennsylvania, Duron, and London, Corgi, 1977.

A Touch of Love. Williamsport, Pennsylvania, Duron, 1977; London, Corgi, 1978.

The Temptation of Torilla. Williamsport, Pennsylvania, Duron, 1977; London, Corgi, 1978.

Love and the Loathsome Leopard. Williamsport, Pennsylvania, Duron, 1977; London, Corgi, 1978.

The Hell-Cat and the King. Williamsport, Pennsylvania, Duron, 1977; London, Pan, 1978.

No Escape from Love. Williamsport, Pennsylvania, Duron, 1977; London, Corgi, 1978.

The Saint and the Sinner. Williamsport, Pennsylvania, Duron, 1977; London, Corgi, 1978.

The Naked Battle. Williamsport, Pennsylvania, Duron, 1977; London, Hutchinson, 1978.

Love Leaves at Midnight. London, Hutchinson, and Williamsport, Pennsylvania, Duron, 1978.

The Passion and the Flower. London, Pan, and New York, Dutton, 1978.

Love, Lords, and Lady-Birds. London, Pan, and New York, Dutton, 1978.

A Fugitive from Love. London, Pan, and Williamsport, Pennsylvania, Duron, 1978.

The Problems of Love. London, Corgi, and Williamsport, Pennsylvania, Duron, 1978.

The Twists and Turns of Love. London, Arrow, and Williamsport, Pennsylvania, Duron, 1978.

Magic or Mirage? London, Corgi, and Williamsport, Pennsylvania, Duron, 1978.

The Castle Made for Love. London, Pan, and Williamsport, Pennsylvania, Duron, 1978.

The Ghost Who Fell in Love. London, Pan, and New York, Dutton, 1978.

The Chieftain Without a Heart. London, Corgi, and New York, Dutton, 1978.

Lord Ravenscar's Revenge. London, Corgi, and Williamsport, Pennsylvania, Duron, 1978.

A Runaway Star. London, Pan, and Williamsport, Pennsylvania, Duron, 1978.

A Princess in Distress. London, Pan, and Williamsport, Pennsylvania, Duron, 1978.

The Judgement of Love. Williamsport, Pennsylvania, Duron, 1978; London, Hutchinson, 1979.

Lovers in Paradise. Williamsport, Pennsylvania, Duron, 1978; London, Pan, 1979.

The Race for Love. Williamsport, Pennsylvania, Duron, 1978; London, Corgi, 1979.

Flowers for the God of Love. London, Pan, 1978; New York, Dutton, 1979.

The Irresistible Force. London, Arrow, and Williamsport, Pennsylvania, Duron, 1978.

Alone in Paris. London, Arrow, 1978; Williamsport, Pennsylvania, Duron, 1979.

Love in the Dark. London, Hutchinson, and Williamsport, Pennsylvania, Duron, 1979.

The Duke and the Preacher's Daughter. London, Corgi, and Williamsport, Pennsylvania, Duron, 1979.

The Drums of Love. London, Pan, and Williamsport, Pennsylvania, Duron, 1979.

The Prince and the Pekingese. London, Pan, and Williamsport, Pennsylvania, Duron, 1979.

A Serpent of Satan. London, Pan, and Williamsport, Pennsylvania, Duron, 1979.

Love in the Clouds. London, Corgi, and New York, Dutton, 1979.

The Treasure Is Love. London, Arrow, and Williamsport, Pennsylvania, Duron, 1979.

Imperial Splendour. London, Pan, and New York, Dutton, 1979.

Light of the Moon. London, Pan, and Williamsport, Pennsylvania, Duron, 1979.

The Prisoner of Love. London, Arrow, and Williamsport, Pennsylvania, Duron, 1979.

The Duchess Disappeared. London, Pan, and Williamsport, Pennsylvania, Duron, 1979.

Love Climbs In. London, Corgi, and Williamsport, Pennsylvania, Duron, 1979.

A Nightingale Sang. London, Corgi, and Williamsport, Pennsylvania, Duron, 1979.

Terror in the Sun. London, Pan, and New York, Bantam, 1979.

Who Can Deny Love? London, Corgi, and Williamsport, Pennsylvania, Duron, 1979.

Bride to the King. London, Corgi, 1979; New York, Dutton, 1980.

Only Love. London, Arrow, 1979; New York, Bantam, 1980.

The Dawn of Love. London, Corgi, 1979; New York, Dutton, 1980.

Love Has His Way. London, Corgi, 1979; New York, Dutton, 1980.

A Gentleman in Love. London, Pan, 1979.

Women Have Hearts. London, Pan, 1979; New York, Bantam, 1980.

The Explosion of Love. London, Hutchinson, 1980.

A Heart Is Stolen. London, Corgi, 1980.

The Power and the Prince. London, Pan, 1980.

Free From Fear. London, Pan, and New York, Bantam, 1980.

A Song of Love. London, Pan, and New York, Berkley, 1980.

Love for Sale. London, Corgi, and New York, Dutton, 1980.

Little White Doves of Love. London, Pan, and New York, Bantam, 1980.

The Perfection of Love. London, Corgi, and New York, Bantam, 1980.

Lost Laughter. London, Pan, and New York, Dutton, 1980.

Punished with Love. London, Pan, and New York, Bantam, 1980.

Lucifer and the Angel. London, Hutchinson, 1980.

Ola and the Sea Wolf. London, Arrow, and New York, Bantam, 1980.

The Prude and the Prodigal. London, Pan, and New York, Bantam, 1980.

The Goddess and the Gaiety Girl. London, Pan, and New York, Bantam, 1980.

Signpost to Love. London, Corgi, 1980; New York, Bantam, 1981.

Money, Magic, and Marriage. London, Arrow, 1980.

Love in the Moon. London, New English Library, 1980.

The Horizons of Love. London, Pan, 1980.

Pride and the Poor Princess. London, Corgi, 1980.

The Waltz of Hearts. London, Pan, 1980.

From Hell to Heaven. London, Corgi, and New York, Bantam, 1981.

The Kiss of Life. London, Hutchinson, 1981.

Afraid. London, Arrow, 1981.

Dreams Do Come True. London, Pan, 1981.

In the Arms of Love. London, Hutchinson, 1981.

For All Eternity. New York, Berkley, 1981; London, Corgi, 1982.

Pure and Untouched. London, Arrow, and New York, Everest House, 1981.

Count the Stars. London, New English Library, 1981.

The Wings of Ecstasy. London, Pan, 1981.

A Night of Gaiety. London, Pan, 1981.

The River of Love. London, Pan, 1981.

Gift of the Gods. London, Pan, 1981.

The Heart of the Clan. London, Arrow, 1981.

Love Wins. London, Pan, 1981.

The Light of Love. New York, Dell, 1981.

An Innocent in Russia. London, Pan, 1981.

Winged Magic. London, Corgi, 1981.

Dollars for the Duke. London, Corgi, 1981.

The Lioness and the Lily. London, Corgi, and New York, Bantam, 1981.

A Miracle in Music. New York, Berkley, 1982; London, Corgi, 1983.

A King in Love. New York, Everest House, 1982.

A Portrait of Love. London, Corgi, 1982.

A Shaft of Sunlight. London, Corgi, 1982.

Caught by Love. London, Arrow, 1982.

Kneel for Mercy. London, New English Library, 1982.

Looking for Love. London, Hutchinson, 1982.

Love and the Marquis. London, Pan, 1982.

Love Rules. London, New English Library, 1982.

Lucky in Love. London, Pan, 1982.

Moments of Love. London, Pan, 1982.

Music from the Heart. London, Pan, 1982.

Riding to the Moon. New York, Everest House, 1982; London, Arrow, 1983.

Secret Harbour. London, Corgi, 1982.

The Call of the Highlands. London, Hutchinson, 1982.

The Poor Governess. New York, Berkley, 1982; London, Corgi, 1983.

Touch a Star. London, Corgi, 1982.

Vibration of Love. London, Corgi, 1982.

Winged Victory. London, Pan, and New York, Berkley, 1982.

A Duke in Danger. London, Pan, 1983.

A Marriage Made in Heaven. London, Corgi, 1983.

Diona and a Dalmation. London, Hutchinson, 1983.

Fire in the Blood. London, Pan, 1983.

Gypsy Magic. London, Pan, 1983.

From Hate to Love. London, New English Library, 1983.

Lies for Love. London, Corgi, 1983.

Lights, Laughter and a Lady. London, New English Library, 1983.

Love and Lucia. London, Pan, 1983.

Love on the Wind. London, Pan, 1983; New York, Severn House, 1986.

Mission to Monte Carlo. London, Corgi, 1983.

Tempted to Love. London, Pan, 1983.

Wish for Love. London, Corgi, 1983.

The Scots Never Forget. London, Corgi, 1984.

Theresa and a Tiger. London, New English Library, 1984.

The Unbreakable Spell. London, Corgi, 1984.

The Unwanted Wedding. London, Corgi, 1984.

The Island of Love. London, Pan, 1984.

Journey to a Star. London, Corgi, 1984.

The Peril and the Princess. London, New English Library, 1984.

Moonlight on the Sphinx. London, Hutchinson, 1984.

Bride to a Brigand. London, New English Library, and New York, Berkley, 1984.

Love Comes West. London, Pan, and New York, Berkley, 1984.

A Witch's Spell. London, Corgi, and New York, Berkley, 1984.

White Lilac. London, Pan, and New York, Berkley, 1984.

Miracle for a Madonna. London, Hutchinson, 1984.

Royal Punishment. London, Severn House, 1984.

Revenge of the Heart. London, Pan, 1984.
A Very Unusual Wife. London, Pan, 1984.
The Duke Comes Home. London, Corgi, 1984.
Help from the Heart. London, Arrow, 1984.
Light of the Gods. London, Corgi, 1984.
Love Is Heaven. London, Pan, 1984.
Love Is a Gamble. London, Pan, 1985.
A Rebel Princess. London, Corgi, 1985.
Safe at Last. London, Pan, 1985.
The Devilish Deception. London, New English Library, 1985.
Escape. London, Severn House, 1985.
The Storms of Love. London, Corgi, 1985.
Temptation for a Teacher. London, Pan, 1985.
Look with Love. London, Pan, 1985.
A Victory for Love. London, Pan, 1985.
Alone and Afraid. London, Pan, 1985.
Crowned with Love. London, Eaglemoss, 1985.
The Devil Defeated. London, Eaglemoss, 1985.
Secrets. London, Corgi, 1985.
The Secret of the Mosque. London, Pan, 1986.
Haunted. London, Pan, 1986.
The Love Trap. London, Pan, 1986.
Paradise Found. London, Arrow, 1986.
Never Forget Love. London, New English Library, 1986.
Love Casts out Fears. London, Severn House, 1986.
An Angel Runs Away. London, Pan, 1986; New York, Berkley, 1987.
Helga in Hiding. London, Arrow, 1986.
A Dream in Spain. London, Pan, 1986.
Love Joins the Clan. London, Pan, 1986.
The Perfume of the Gods. London, New English Library, 1987.
The Goddess of Love. London, Pan, 1987.
A Herb for Happiness. London, Pan, 1987.
Lovers in Lisbon. London, Pan, 1987.
Sapphires in Siam. London, Pan, 1987.
Saved by Love. London, Pan, 1987.
A Circus for Love. London, Pan, 1987.
A Revolution of Love. London, Pan, 1987.
The Temple of Love. London, Pan, 1988.

Novels as Barbara McCorquodale

Sleeping Swords. London, Hale, 1942.
Love Is Mine. London, Rich and Cowan, 1952; as Barbara Cartland, New York, Pyramid, 1972.
The Passionate Pilgrim. London, Rich and Cowan, 1952.
Blue Heather. London, Rich and Cowan, 1953.
Wings on My Heart. London, Rich and Cowan, 1954.
The Kiss of Paris. London, Rich and Cowan, 1956.
The Thief of Love. London, Jenkins, 1957.
Love Forbidden. London, Rich and Cowan, 1957.
Lights of Love. London, Jenkins, 1958; as Barbara Cartland, New York, Pyramid, 1973.
Sweet Enchantress. London, Jenkins, 1958.
A Kiss of Silk. London, Jenkins, 1959.
The Price Is Love. London, Jenkins, 1960.
The Runaway Heart. London, Jenkins, 1961.
A Light to the Heart. London, Ward Lock, 1962.
Love Is Dangerous. London, Ward Lock, 1963.
Danger by the Nile. London, Ward Lock, 1964.
Love on the Run. London, Ward Lock, 1965; as Barbara Cartland, New York, Pyramid, 1973.
Theft of the Heart. London, Ward Lock, 1966.

OTHER PUBLICATIONS

Plays

Blood Money (produced London, 1925).
French Dressing, with Bruce Woodhouse (produced London, 1943).

Radio Plays: *The Rose and the Violet*, music by Mark Lubbock, 1942; *The Caged Bird*, 1957.

Verse

Lines on Life and Love. London, Hutchinson, 1972.

Other

Touch the Stars: A Clue to Happiness. London, Rider, 1935.
Ronald Cartland. London, Collins, 1942; as *My Brother, Ronald*, London, Sheldon Press, 1980.
The Isthmus Years 1919–1939 (autobiography). London, Hutchinson, 1943.
You—in the Home. London, Standard Art, 1946.
The Years of Opportunity 1939–1945 (autobiography). London, Hutchinson, 1948.
The Fascinating Forties: A Book for the Over-Forties. London, Jenkins, 1954; revised edition, London, Corgi, 1973.
Marriage for Moderns. London, Jenkins, 1955.
Bewitching Women. London, Muller, 1955.
The Outrageous Queen: A Biography of Christina of Sweden. London, Muller, 1956.
Polly—My Wonderful Mother. London, Jenkins, 1956.
Be Vivid, Be Vital. London, Jenkins, 1956.
Love, Life and Sex. London, Jenkins, 1957; revised edition, London, Corgi, 1973.
The Scandalous Life of King Carol. London, Muller, 1957.
The Private Life of Charles II: The Women He Loved. London, Muller, 1958.
Look Lovely, Be Lovely. London, Jenkins, 1958.
Vitamins for Vitality. London, Foyle, 1959.
The Private Life of Elizabeth, Empress of Austria. London, Muller, 1959; New York, Pyramid, 1974.
Husbands and Wives. London, Barker, 1961; revised edition, as *Love and Marriage*, London, Thorsons, 1971.
Josephine, Empress of France. London, Hutchinson, 1961; New York, Pyramid, 1974.
Diane de Poitiers. London, Hutchinson, 1962.
Etiquette Handbook. London, Hamlyn, 1963; revised edition, as *Book of Etiquette*, London, Hutchinson, 1972.
The Many Facets of Love. London, W. H. Allen, 1963.
Metternich, The Passionate Diplomat. London, Hutchinson, 1964.
Sex and the Teenager. London, Muller, 1964.
Living Together. London, Muller, 1965.
The Pan Book of Charm. London, Pan, 1965.
Woman: The Enigma. London, Frewin, 1965; New York, Pyramid, 1974.
I Search for Rainbows 1946–1966 (autobiography). London, Hutchinson, 1967; New York, Bantam, 1977.
The Youth Secret. London, Corgi, 1968.
The Magic of Honey. London, Corgi, 1970; revised edition, 1976.
We Danced All Night 1919–1929 (autobiography). London, Hutchinson, 1970; New York, Pyramid, 1972.
Health Food Cookery Book. London, Hodder and Stoughton, 1971.

Book of Beauty and Health. London, Hodder and Stoughton, 1972.

Men Are Wonderful. London, Corgi, 1973.

Food for Love. London, Corgi, 1975.

The Magic of Honey Cookbook. London, Corgi, 1976.

Recipes for Lovers, with Nigel Gordon. London, Corgi, 1977.

Book of Useless Information. London, Corgi, 1977.

I Seek the Miraculous (autobiography) London, Sheldon Press, and New York, Dutton, 1978.

Book of Love and Lovers. London, Joseph, and New York, Ballantine, 1978.

Love at the Helm (Mountbatten Memorial Trust volume). London, Weidenfeld and Nicolson, 1980; New York, Everest House, 1981.

Romantic Royal Marriages. New York, Beaufort, 1981.

Keep Young and Beautiful (selections), with Elinor Glyn. London, Duckworth, 1982.

The Romance of Food. London, Hamlyn, and New York, Doubleday, 1984.

Getting Older, Growing Younger. London, Sidgwick and Jackson, and New York, Dodd Mead, 1984.

Etiquette for Love and Romance. New York, Pocket Books, 1984; Bath, Firecrest, 1985.

Princess to the Rescue (for children). London, Hamlyn, and New York, Watts, 1984.

Book of Health (for children). Poole, Dorset, Blandford Press, 1985.

Year of Royal Days. Luton, Bedfordshire, Lennard, 1988.

Editor, *The Common Problem*, by Ronald Cartland. London, Hutchinson, 1943.

Editor, *The Light of Love: A Thought for Every Day.* London, Sheldon Press, and New York, Elsevier Nelson, 1979.

Editor, *Written with Love* (letters). London, Hutchinson, 1982.

*

Critical Studies: *Barbara Cartland, Crusader in Pink* by Henry Cloud, London, Weidenfeld and Nicolson, 1979; *Barbara Cartland: An Authorised Biography* by Gwen Robyns, London, Sidgwick and Jackson, 1984, New York, Doubleday, 1985.

*   *   *

It is a daunting task to assess the work of Barbara Cartland, whose prodigious output of more than 400 books, vast sales of over 100 million copies, and reputation as the Queen of the Genre are overwhelming. Each branch of 20th-century English light fiction has its phenomenon—and the achievements of Cartland are to romantic fiction what those of Charles Hamilton (''Frank Richards'') are to the school story, or those of Agatha Christie are to detective fiction.

Her reputation as an unsurpassed contributor to the genre became established by the end of the 1960's; since then she has gone from strength to strength and there seems no slackening in the pace of her production of romantic stories. Still the innocent but exotically named heroines—the Deloras, Magnolias, Darcias, and Udelas—flare into vivid and passionate life, fresh from the Cartland typewriter or dictating-machine, and still they are avidly received by millions of readers all over the world. The books, though one might have thought them a peculiarly English caprice, have been translated into many languages. They are flagrantly escapist and unconcerned with social issues; they are class-ridden and anti-feminist—the apotheosis, in fact, of attitudes that are today condemned by trendy critics—but their success speaks for itself. Cartland provides for her millions of loyal

readers the confirmation that romance is alive and well, even in our materialistic society, and that the individual is still important, in this age of group-causes and group-lobbying and group-consciousness. Her confidence in her beliefs is magnificent; her passion for the quintessential English gentleman or aristocrat is idealistic but engaging; and her feelings for innocence, for the feminine aspects of life, and for simple decency are deep-rooted and sincere.

In literary terms, of course, one can find flaws in the Cartland canon. Inevitably, in a writing career that has spanned over half a century, she has established a formula on which she falls back with increasing dependence. The more recent books have a facile quality, a carelessness, which is not evident in her early works. The novels now are slim, and often issued immediately in paperback. They are unlikely to be preserved for posterity in the collections of public or university libraries, although these institutions will almost certainly retain many of her earlier, more substantial hard-backed novels. Her heroines, despite their distinctive and gloriously feminine, romantic names, are, in fact, interchangeable and without individualization. Similarly, her heroes are now symbolic embodiments of masculine strength, magnetism, and charisma rather than real human beings.

It is an intriguing exercise, however, to look back at Cartland's early novels, and to savour their freshness, incisive and occasionally acerbic comments, and sheer storytelling skill. One hopes that the author might one day pause in the production line of 20-plus novels every year to read once again her own early books, and to create, from the vitality of these and the light of her later expertise and experience of life one or two romances that will become Cartland classics for posterity.

Her first novel, *Jig-Saw*, has charm and conviction as well as an appropriate freshness. It starts on a spring day, with ''excitements, sensations—all palpitating to be discovered,'' with ''a poignancy in the atmosphere as a catch of breath before a tremendously thrilling experience. . . . '' *And* it is Paris which abounds in the *gaîté de coeur* for which the city is celebrated. Mona Vivien, as English as they come despite her ''strikingly beautiful'' resemblance to the ''type beloved of Botticelli,'' is packing up after her last day as a pupil at a St. Cloud convent-school to return to London. She is on the tremulous threshold of young womanhood, which Cartland conveys so well. Back in Belgrave Square, life is ''a fairy cinematograph . . . of hectic sensations,'' a cultural and social round which thrills Mona, and, of course, produces for her the young Marquis who turns out to be her true and upright love—despite the rival claims of his mysterious, fascinating and worldly half-brother, who one day whisks her off unchaperoned ''to see the sunrise in a fairyland of silver birches.'' This turns out, rather prosaically perhaps to those who know its much-trodden picnic-littered paths, to be Wimbledon Common at dawn. But Cartland acknowledges the elusive quality of such magically romantic excursions when Mona reflects, on her return to Belgrave Square and disillusioning daytime brightness, that ''Romance, criticised with the hideous sanity of breakfast-time, droops its wings and slinks away.''

Nevertheless this, like the other early novels, has a reflective and lyrical quality that has sadly disappeared from the recent books. In *Jig-Saw*, for example, Mona's love of London, of poetry, and her joy and eagerness in new experiences come across with sensitivity and conviction. Innocence in the stories of the 1920's and 1930's was filled out and made persuasive by passionate questioning of the darker areas of life. Her heroines then were distinctive personalities who were, in a sympathetic and believable way, awakened to broader and deeper areas of experience, passion, and wonder by the heroes.

A look at the recent books shows that although this awakening through romance still continues for the leading Cartland ladies, it has settled firmly into a pattern. The dialogue at the end of each book is, one feels, interchangeable with that of any of the others. When Seldon, the handsome, aristocratic and arrogant Duke of Otterburn, and the American heiress Magnolia Vandevilt acknowledge their love, after a lot of time and languishing looks, at the end of *Dollars for the Duke*, their final clinch predictably carries them "on waves of ecstasy into the starlit sky." At the end of *Love for Sale* another worldly-wise Duke and his innocent teenage beloved share a kiss which, she felt, "carried her up towards the stars that were now shining in the sky outside." And the heroines share the same tremulous, breathless, and ecstatic manner of speech: "I have . . . always wanted to . . . have your . . . children," says Darcia in a whisper at the end of *The Perfection of Love*, while Udela husks in *Love for Sale*, " . . . when I have been awake in the darkness I have . . . pretended that you were . . . kissing me"; Magnolia caps it all in *Dollars for the Duke* by her whispered and wondering affirmation of passion: "I love . . . you and everything you do . . . will be perfect and . . . also . . . Divine."

Really, perhaps, it is greedy to ask more from Barbara Cartland than this superb romanticism—but one feels that she is capable of something very much more searching, sympathetic "and . . . also . . . " real.

—Mary Cadogan

CASE, David. American. Born in Gloversville, New York, 22 December 1937. Educated at the State University of New York, Albany, 1956; Endicott College, Beverly, Massachusetts, 1959. Married Valerie Priest; three children. Full-time writer: has published some 300 works under pseudonyms; has lived in England since 1960. Agent: Richard Curtis Associates Inc., 164 East 64th Street, Suite 1, New York, New York 10021, U.S.A.

ROMANCE AND HISTORICAL PUBLICATIONS

Novels

Fengriffen: A Chilling Tale. New York, Hill and Wang, 1970.
The Third Grave. Sauk City, Wisconsin, Arkham House, 1981.

Short Stories

The Cell: Three Tales of Horror. New York, Hill and Wang, 1969; as *The Cell and Other Tales of Horror*, London, Macdonald, 1969.
Fengriffin and Other Stories. London, Macdonald, 1971; as *And Now the Screaming Starts*, London, Pan, 1973.
Among the Wolves and Other Tales. Sauk City, Wisconsin, Arkham House, 1982.

OTHER PUBLICATIONS

Novels

Plumb Drillin'. New York, Stein and Day, 1975; London, W. H. Allen, 1976; as *Gold Fever*, New York, Belmont, 1982.
The Fighting Breed. New York, Zebra, 1980.
Wolf Tracks. New York, Belmont, 1980.
Guns of Valentine. New York, Ace, 1982.

*   *   *

My first impression of Fengriffen House was skeletal. I saw it from the carriage, rising against a stormy sundown like the blackened bones of some monstrous beast—not the fragile, bleached bones of decaying man, but the massive, arched columns of a primordial saurian who had wandered to this desolate moor and there lay down and died, perhaps of loneliness, long ages before. The spires and towers loomed up in sharp silhouette and the structure squatted beneath, sunken but not cowed, crouched ready to spring, so that the house seemed to exist on two planes at the same time—massive and slender, bulky and light, gross and fragile. It was a building that had aged through a series of architectural blunders, and it was awesome. . . . as I gazed upon this remarkable construction, I sensed a pervading evil, an adumbration of unholy darkness. . . . The wind was in the trees, playing a leitmotif behind the horses' clattering hooves. Perhaps it was the chill in the air that caused me to shiver. . . .

The mood of David Case's *Fengriffen: A Chilling Tale* is set in this opening scene. Loneliness pervades. Leitmotives hover. Adumbrations loom. Readers shiver, caught up in such drama as one might expect from an experienced writer. Readers must be impressed also with the rococo overlay of profuse prose squatting on the classic Gothic plot.

Fengriffen (marsh-monster?) tells the story of a beautiful young woman, Catherine Fengriffen. Her husband, Charles Fengriffen, has called in Doctor Pope, a young psychologist (psychology is the new field of scientific inquiry) to talk to Catherine and to determine the cause of her recent strange behavior. A man of science and hence a skeptic, Doctor Pope—who tells the tale—uncovers the Fengriffen Curse, a horrible superstition—or terrible truth?—that, like some "primordial saurian" holds Catherine—as it does all Fengriffen brides—in its chelate death grip. When her baby is born with the mark of the beast, Catherine leaps with the child from one of Fengriffen Manor's prisonous towers to the rocks below.

The "Three Tales of Horror" that comprise *The Cell*, Case's first work of Gothic fiction, are similarly adorned and equally chilling. "The Hunter," lurking in the dark moor of Dartmoor, is a monstrous creature who preys on solitary travelers and takes off—and takes off with—their heads. The title story, "The Cell," is another chiller, this time of lycanthropy (according to the *Oxford English Dictionary*, a kind of insanity in which the patient, imagining himself a wolf, exhibits all a wolf's instincts and propensities). The sombre theme of the final story, "The Dead End," is, as one may surmise, the end of the world.

Fengriffen, written in 1970, seems to mark the end of Case's Gothic world. Five years later, with *Plumb Drillin'*, and then in *The Fighting Breed* and *Wolf Tracks*, Case turns to the Wild West for inspiration and, possibly, relief. The settings change, as does the dialogue (" 'Kee-rist!' Dalton snorted."), but the winds over the desert—as Case so skillfully evokes them—are as chilling as the winds over his moors and fens.

—Marcia G. Fuchs

CASTLE, Jayne. See **KRENTZ, Jayne Ann.**

CATO, Nancy (Fotheringham). Australian. Born in Adelaide, South Australia, 11 March 1917. Educated at Presbyterian Girls'

College, Adelaide, 1923–34; Adelaide University, 1938–39; South Australian School of Arts, 1954–55. Married Eldred de Bracton Norman in 1941 (died 1971); one daughter and two sons. Journalist, 1936–41, and art critic, 1957–58, Adelaide *News*. Assistant editor, *Poetry Australia*, Sydney, 1947–48; advisory editor, *Overland*, Melbourne, 1960–62. Vice president, South Australian Fellowship of Writers; member, Australian Society of Authors. Recipient: Poetry Society award, 1963; Commonwealth Literature Fund fellowship, 1968. Member, Order of Australia, 1984. Address: P.O. Box 47, Noosa Heads, Queensland 4567, Australia.

ROMANCE AND HISTORICAL PUBLICATIONS

Novels (series: Murray River Trilogy)

All the Rivers Run (Murray River). New York, St. Martin's Press, 1978; London, New English Library, 1981.
  All the Rivers Run. London, Heinemann, 1958.
  Time, Flow Softly. London, Heinemann, 1960.
  But Still the Stream. London, Heinemann, 1962.
Green Grows the Vine. London, Heinemann, 1960.
North-West by South. London, Heinemann, 1965.
Brown Sugar. London, Heinemann, 1974; New York, St. Martin's Press, 1975.
Queen Truganini: Queen or Traitor?, with Vivienne Rae Ellis. London, Heinemann, 1976.
Forefathers. New York, St. Martin's Press, 1982; London, New English Library, 1983.
The Lady Lost in Time. Sydney, Collins, 1985.
A Distant Island. London, New English Library, 1988.
The Heart of the Continent. London, New English Library, and New York, St. Martin's Press, 1989.

Short Stories

The Sea Ants and Other Stories. London, Heinemann, 1964.

OTHER PUBLICATIONS

Play

Travellers Through the Night (produced Noosa Heads, Queensland, 1979).

Verse

The Darkened Window. Sydney, Lyre Bird Writers, 1950.
The Dancing Bough. Sydney, Angus and Robertson, 1957; London, Heinemann, 1988.

Other

Nin and the Scribblies (for children). Milton, Queensland, Jacaranda Press, 1976.
Mister Malogo; Daniel Matthews and His Mission. St. Lucia, Queensland, University of Queensland Press, 1976.
The Noosa Story: A Study in Unplanned Development. Milton, Queensland, Jacaranda Press, 1979.

Editor, *Jindyworobak Anthology*. St. Lucia, Queensland, University of Queensland Press, 1950.

*

Manuscript Collections: National Library of Australia, Canberra; Oxley Library, Brisbane.

*

Nancy Cato comments:
   I write mainly historical fiction based on Australian history and historical characters. One of my novels is set in 17th-century London. *All the Rivers Run* originally a trilogy has been made into a television series and is a world bestseller. I enjoy researching and strive for absolute accuracy. *Brown Sugar,* the story of kanaka (slave) labour in Queensland, is also to be filmed. I have also written short stories, verse and non-fiction historical works and biography.

*   *   *

   Nancy Cato's novels are all set in her native Australia, and the vast majority take place in the past; they are thoroughly researched and imbued with Cato's obvious fascination with the history of her country.
   This shows most clearly in *All the Rivers Run*, a novel set at the end of the last century and the beginning of this. It describes the life of Philadelphia Gordon from her emergence from the sea, the sole survivor of a shipwreck which has killed her parents, to an enigmatic ending, again in the sea, at the end of a long and fulfilling life. The story takes place around the Murray and Darling Rivers and describes in detail the communities which have grown up on their banks. A constant theme is the flowing of the river and the parallel currents in the lives of the characters, the people inhabiting these communities. Philadelphia, an artist by temperament and training, is fascinated by the river and, untypically for a woman at that time, buys part ownership of a riverboat. This forms the vehicle not only for her own wanderings but also for the plot, and it enables the author to incorporate vivid descriptions of the surrounding countryside. The many relationships which the heroine forms are as fluid as the river, and throughout the novel we are led to draw parallels between the progression of the river and Philadelphia's character as it develops. She grows in stature and independence and eventually, after an accident which deprives her husband of the use of his legs, she successfully becomes the first woman master of a river steamboat. Cato originally wrote this story as three shorter novels but there is no doubt that the continuity provided by their republication in one volume lends strength to the metaphor used to develop the plot and characterisations.
   The same potential exists in the subject matter of *North-West by South*, a novel set in Tasmania in the first half of the 19th century. The main characters are Sir John Franklin (governor of Van Diemen's Land, as Tasmania was then known) and his second wife Jane, another emancipated and intelligent woman. Extensively researched, the novel explores the lives and relationships of the English men and women sent to govern and administer the island; the style is terse, even journalistic, and unfortunately this detracts from the undoubtedly fertile material. An immense amount of information is packed into a novel of only average length and even the descriptions of the beautiful countryside have a certain breathlessness. The occasional flashes of humour (when Lady Franklin has been attacked in the press her husband suspects that she has been "wounded by the slings and arrows of outrageous journalism") are buried in the concise recital of events.
   In *A Distant Island* Cato tells the story of Tasmania's famous botanist Ronald Gunn, who is a minor character in *North-West*

by *South*; there is indeed a certain amount of overlap with the earlier novel, and thus Lady Franklin and various other familiar personages reappear.

Another novel describing some of these characters and events is *Queen Truganini*, written jointly with Vivienne Rae Ellis and published some 11 years after *North-West by South*. This expands one of the themes of the earlier novel, the shameful and degrading extermination of the natives of Tasmania (the Trucanini of the title was the last surviving member of her tribe). Here again the style is intense; though not entirely satisfactory in a work of fiction it does indicate something of the crusading spirit in which this book was obviously written. The contrast between this and *North-West by South*, although they are somewhat similar in scope, lies in their emphasis. The latter might have benefited from a stylistic expansion, as the relationships (often unsatisfactorily described) form an important part of the whole. To give this treatment to *Queen Trucanini* would have resulted no doubt in a powerful novel, but would probably have diminished the portrayal of the outrageous events and attitudes which form the basis of the story.

The award winning *Forefathers* and its companion volume *Brown Sugar* are set a few years later and, like *All the Rivers Run*, are completely fictional. Also like *All the Rivers Run*, they are more successful stylistically, and describe in detail an interesting facet of Australia's economic and social development.

A complete contrast to all these books is *Green Grows the Vine*. This is a short novel covering a brief period of time (barely two months) and the characters hardly have time to be introduced to us, let alone to develop. Here again is the raw material for a stronger novel; instead this tale of three girls grape picking in South Australia is superficial and disappointing. The most satisfying reading is provided by the verses from the Rubaiyat of Omar Khayyam which head every chapter; that Cato herself is a poet is demonstrated in all her books by the strength of her descriptive prose when she allows herself to elaborate upon the landscape and scenery.

—Judith Rhodes

CHACE, Isobel. See **HUNTER, Elizabeth.**

CHAMBERS, Robert W(illiam). American. Born in Brooklyn, New York, 26 May 1865. Educated at the Art Students' League, New York; École des Beaux Arts and Académie Julien, Paris. Married Elsa Vaughn Moller in 1898; one son. Illustrator for *Life*, *Truth*, and *Vogue*, New York. Member, National Institute of Arts and Letters. *Died 16 December 1933.*

ROMANCE AND HISTORICAL PUBLICATIONS

Novels (series: Franco-Prussian War; Johnson Family)

In the Quarter. New York, Neely, 1894; London, Chatto and Windus, 1895.
The Red Republic: A Romance of the Commune (Franco-Prussian War). New York, Putnam, 1895; London, Nash, 1903.
The King and a Few Dukes. New York, Putnam, 1896; London, Greening, 1906.
Lorraine (Franco-Prussian War). New York, Harper, 1897.

Ashes of Empire (Franco-Prussian War). New York, Stokes, and London, Macmillan, 1898.
The Conspirators. New York, Harper, 1899.
Cardigan (Johnson). New York, Harper, and London, Constable, 1901.
The Shining Band. London, Ward Lock, 1901.
The Maids of Paradise (Franco-Prussian War). New York, Harper, 1902; London, Constable, 1903.
The Maid-at-Arms (Johnson). New York, Harper, and London, Constable, 1902.
The Reckoning. New York, Appleton, and London, Constable, 1905.
Special Messenger. New York, Appleton, 1909; London, Laurie, 1910.
Ailsa Page. New York, Appleton, and London, Newnes, 1910.
Barbarians. New York, Appleton, 1917.
The Little Red Foot. New York, Doran, and London, Hodder and Stoughton, 1921.
America; or, The Sacrifice: A Romance of the American Revolution. New York, Grosset and Dunlap, 1924.
The Men They Hanged. New York, Appleton, 1926.
The Drums of Aulone. New York, Appleton, 1927.
The Sun Hawk. New York, Appleton, and London, Cassell, 1929.
The Rake and the Hussy. New York, Appleton, 1930.
The Painted Minx. New York, Appleton, 1930.
Gitana. New York, Appleton, 1931.
War Paint and Rouge. New York, Appleton, 1931.
Whistling Cat. New York, Appleton, 1932.
Secret-Service Operator. New York, Appleton Century, 1934; as *Spy Number 13*, London, Philip Allan, 1935.

Short Stories

The King in Yellow. New York, Neely, and London, Chatto and Windus, 1895.
The Maker of Moons. New York, Putnam, 1896.
The Mystery of Choice. New York, Appleton, 1897.
The Haunts of Men. New York, Stokes, and London, Bowden, 1899.
A Young Man in a Hurry and Other Short Stories. New York, Harper, 1904; London, Constable, 1905.
The Tree of Heaven. New York, Appleton, 1907; London, Constable, 1908.
The Better Man. New York, Appleton, 1916.
The Mask and Other Stories. Racine, Wisconsin, Whitman, 1929.

OTHER PUBLICATIONS

Novels

The Cambric Mask. New York, Stokes, 1899; London, Macmillan, 1900.
Outsiders: An Outline. New York, Stokes, 1899; London, Richards, 1900.
In Search of the Unknown. New York, Harper, 1904; London, Constable, 1905.
Iole. New York, Appleton, 1905; London, Constable, 1906.
The Fighting Chance. New York, Appleton, 1906; London, Constable, 1907.
The Tracer of Lost Persons. New York, Appleton, 1906; London, Murray, 1907.
The Firing Line. New York, Appleton, 1908.

Some Ladies in Haste. New York, Appleton, and London, Constable, 1908.

The Danger Mark. New York, Appleton, 1909.

The Adventures of a Modest Man. New York, Appleton, and London, Newnes, 1911.

The Common Law. New York, Appleton, 1911.

The Streets of Ascalon: Episodes in the Unfinished Career of Richard Quarren Esq. New York, Appleton, 1912; London, Newnes, 1915.

The Business of Life. New York, Appleton, 1913; London, Newnes, 1915.

The Gay Rebellion. New York, Appleton, 1913.

Between Friends. New York, Appleton, 1914.

Athalie. New York, Appleton, 1915; London, Pearson, 1927.

The Girl Philippa. New York, Appleton, 1916.

The Dark Star. New York, Appleton, 1917.

The Restless Sex. New York, Appleton, 1918; London, Pearson, 1928.

In Secret. New York, Doran, and London, Hodder and Stoughton, 1919.

The Moonlit Way. New York, Appleton, 1919.

The Crimson Tide. New York, Appleton, 1919.

The Slayer of Souls. New York, Doran, and London, Hodder and Stoughton, 1920.

The Flaming Jewel. New York, Doran, 1922.

Eris. New York, Doran, and London, Hodder and Stoughton, 1923.

The Talkers. New York, Doran, 1923; London, Unwin, 1925.

The Mystery Lady. New York, Grossett and Dunlap, 1925; London, Cassell, 1926.

Beating Wings. London, Cassell, 1928; New York, Appleton Century, 1930.

The Rogue's Moon. New York, Appleton, 1928; London, Cassell, 1929.

Whatever Love Is. New York, Appleton Century, 1933.

The Young Man's Girl. New York, Appleton Century, 1934.

The Gold Chase. New York, Appleton Century, 1935.

Love and the Lieutenant. New York, Appleton Century, 1935.

The Girl in Golden Rags. New York, Appleton Century, 1936.

The Fifth Horseman. New York, Appleton Century, 1937.

Marie Halket. London, Unwin, 1926; New York, Appleton Century, 1937.

Smoke of Battle. New York, Appleton Century, 1938.

Fiction (for children)

Outdoorland. New York, Harper, 1902.

Orchard-land. New York, Harper, 1903.

River-land. New York, Harper, 1904.

Forest-land. New York, Appleton, 1905; as *Hide and Seek in Forest Land*, Appleton, 1909.

Mountain-land. New York, Appleton, 1906.

The Younger Set. New York, Appleton, and London, Constable, 1907.

Garden-land. New York, Appleton, 1907.

The Green Mouse. New York, Appleton, 1910.

Blue-bird Weather. New York, Appleton, 1912.

Japonette. New York, Appleton, 1912.

The Hidden Children. New York, Appleton, 1914.

Quick Action. New York, Appleton, 1914.

Anne's Bridge. New York, Appleton, 1914.

Police!! New York, Appleton, 1915.

Who Goes There. New York, Appleton, 1915.

The Laughing Girl. New York, Appleton, 1918.

The Happy Parrot. New York, Appleton, and London, Cassell, 1929.

Verse

With the Band. New York, Stone and Kimball, 1896.

*   *   *

A best-selling writer for more than 40 years, Robert W. Chambers produced fantasies, historical romances, and novels of society and domestic life. Before turning to fiction, Chambers had been a successful illustrator, his work appearing in *Vogue*, *Life*, and other magazines. Drawing on experiences during seven years as an art student in Paris, Chambers wrote *In the Quarter*, concerning a romance between an American art student and a Parisian model. This and *The King in Yellow*, a collection of stories published the following year, were so popular that Chambers turned to fiction full time. Deploring his improbable plots and wooden characters, critics maintained that Chambers's early commercial success had convinced the young writer that painstaking attention to literary craftsmanship was superfluous.

Praised by H. P. Lovecraft in *Supernatural Horror in Literature*, four related stories in *The King in Yellow* are Chambers's most lasting work. Linked by references to an imaginary play, *The King in Yellow*, "The Mask," "In the Court of the Dragon," "The Repairer of Reputations," and "The Yellow Sign" all illustrate the deadly effect of reading "words in which the essence of purest poison lurked." Drawn in part from Ambrose Bierce's story, "An Inhabitant of Carcosa," mock allusions to the play including striking images: the "Pallid Mask"; the city of Carcosa, "where black stars hang in the heavens"; and Hali, a lake where "cloud waves roll and break on the shores." In "The Mask," a sculptor invents a solution that turns living things to marble. Hopelessly in love with her husband's best friend, the sculptor's beautiful young wife immerses herself in a fountain filled with the liquid and becomes a statue. After the sculptor's suicide, she becomes flesh again and is united with the man she truly loves. Reading *The King in Yellow*, the narrator of "In the Court of the Dragon" is driven insane. In a wonderfully eerie scene, he sits in church, horrified by the blasphemous sermon and demonic organ music, both of which the congregation accepts as perfectly ordinary. "The Repairer of Reputations" is set in a future United States (1920) that, having repealed suicide laws, has installed the first "government lethal chamber" in New York's Washington Square. Nearby, a hideously deformed "repairer of reputations" makes a fortune by somehow obliterating the consequences of seductions, gambling debts, and other disgraces. His friend, a deranged reader of *The King in Yellow*, attempts murder so that he may be next in succession to the "Imperial Dynasty of America." The story is haunting because the mind struggles to find a pattern in the three plot strands, juxtaposed with a dreamlike inconsequence. In "The Yellow Sign" two lovers decline physically and mentally after poring together over a copy of the forbidden play. They have identical nightmares about a dead coachman, who carries away the man, still living, in a coffin. The blatant improbabilities of plot and disregard for human psychology that characterize all of Chambers's work are, paradoxically, what gives these stores their dreamlike power. A later collection of fantasy stories, *The Maker of Moons* also demonstrates Chambers's talent for arresting names and images.

Chambers specialized in historical romances, many, like his fantasies, with New York settings. His grossly stereotyped characters and insensitive humor at the expense of ethnic types make this body of work offputting to readers of the late 20th century. Because Chambers found it necessary to include love affairs between caddish heroes and interchangeable, sexually willing women, critics of his day charged him with immorality. Chambers's trivializing of human relationships is regrettable, since his recreation of period details of dress and daily life is vivid and historically accurate.

Between 1895 and 1903, Chambers wrote four novels dealing with the Franco-Prussian War: *Lorraine*, *Ashes of Empire*, *The Red Republic*, and *Maids of Paradise*. *Special Messenger*, *Ailsa Page*, and *Whistling Cat* are set during the American Civil War. Chambers's most highly praised historical novel, *Cardigan*, takes place at the outset of the American Revolution. Written for young readers, *Cardigan* is the coming-of-age story of a teenager, sent by Sir William Johnson on a peace mission to Indians of the Six Nations, whom unscrupulous British authorities have incited to attack the colonists. Loyal to the British crown at the outset, this idealistic young man is forced by British duplicity to shift his allegiance to the "Patriots."

Despite Chambers's painterly eye for striking imagery and undeniable ability to recreate historic events, his fiction is unknown and, except for *The King in Yellow* and *Cardigan*, exceedingly difficult to obtain. Because Chambers's work lacks convincing human relationships, it is unlikely to come back into fashion.

—Wendy Bousfield

CHANDOS, Fay. See **CHARLES, Theresa.**

CHAPMAN, Hester W(olferstan, née Pellatt). British. Born in London, 26 November 1899. Educated privately. Worked for the American Red Cross during World War II. Married 1) N. K. Chapman in 1926 (died); 2) R. L. Griffin in 1938 (died). Worked as a model in Paris and a telephone operator, secretary, governess, and schoolmistress in London. *Died 6 April 1976.*

ROMANCE AND HISTORICAL PUBLICATIONS

Novels

She Saw Them Go By. London, Gollancz, and Boston, Houghton Mifflin, 1933.
To Be a King: A Tale of Adventure. London, Gollancz, 1934.
Long Division. London, Secker and Warburg, 1943.
I Will Be Good. London, Secker and Warburg, 1945; Boston, Houghton Mifflin, 1946.
Worlds Apart. London, Secker and Warburg, 1946.
Ivor Novello's King's Rhapsody (novelization of stage play). London, Harrap, 1950; Boston, Houghton Mifflin, 1951.
Ever Thine. London, Cape, 1951.
Falling Stream. London, Cape, 1954.
The Stone Lily. London, Cape, 1957.
Eugenie. London, Cape, and Boston, Little Brown, 1961.
Lucy. London, Cape, 1965; New York, Reynal, 1966.
Fear No More. London, Cape, and New York, Reynal, 1968.
Limmerston Hall. London, Cape, 1972; New York, Coward McCann, 1973.

OTHER PUBLICATIONS

Other

Great Villiers: A Study of George Villiers, Second Duke of Buckingham. London, Secker and Warburg, 1949.
Mary II, Queen of England. London, Cape, 1953; Westport, Connecticut, Greenwood Press, 1976.
Queen Anne's Son: A Memoir of William Henry, Duke of Gloucester. London, Deutsch, 1954.
The Last Tudor King: A Study of Edward VI. London, Cape, 1958; New York, Macmillan, 1959.
Two Tudor Portraits: Henry Howard, Earl of Surrey, and Lady Katherine Grey. London, Cape, 1960; Boston, Little Brown, 1963.
Lady Jane Grey. London, Cape, 1962; Boston, Little Brown, 1963.
The Tragedy of Charles II in the Years 1630–1660. London, Cape, and Boston, Little Brown, 1964.
Privileged Persons: Four Seventeenth-Century Studies. London, Cape, and New York, Reynal, 1966.
The Sisters of Henry VIII: Margaret Tudor, Queen of Scotland . . . Mary Tudor, Queen of France and Duchess of Suffolk. London, Cape, 1969; as *The Thistle and the Rose*, New York, Coward McCann, 1971.
Caroline Matilda, Queen of Denmark. London, Cape, 1971; New York, Coward McCann, 1972.
Anne Boleyn. London, Cape, 1974; as *The Challenge of Anne Boleyn*, New York, Coward McCann, 1974.
Four Fine Gentlemen. London, Constable, and Lincoln, University of Nebraska Press, 1977.

Editor, with Princess Romanovsky-Pavlovsky, *Diversion*. London, Collins, 1946.

*   *   *

Although at first sight Hester W. Chapman's books are very different from each other (historical novels, costume romances, old-fashioned gothic, modern comedies of manners), they are in fact a homogeneous whole because each of them explores in a different way the effect of a strong, overpowering woman on the people round her. To my mind her best books are her historical novels, and the best of all is *Fear No More*. This is a book of quite extraordinary power which stays in the mind long after it is finished. It is the story of the downfall of the French monarchy and all the events that led up to the revolution, but it is seen entirely through the eyes of the little Dauphin. Everything is described in the strange half-comprehending way that things appear to a child with little things magnified and big things trivialised. The total picture that emerges thus amazes. The strong woman of this book is, of course, Marie Antoinette who is always seen obliquely.

Another historical novel *Lucy*, is set in 17th-century London. It is primarily about the effect of Lucy's devastating personality on the people around her, but because these people are all actors and courtiers it is also the story of the Restoration theatre. *The Stone Lily* is about the revolution in Sicily in 1848, a subject which appealed to Chapman for she wrote two more books about revolution—*To Be a King* and *She Saw Them Go By*—but she created imaginary countries and situations for these books and used characters with an English point-of-view to enable her to comment on the decadence and pretension of old ruling families. She also wrote a novelised version of Ivor Novello's romantic musical *King's Rhapsody*.

All these books feature strange, strong women, but her strangest female characters are reserved for her gothic novels. In *Ever Thine*, set in a boy's prep school, there is Victoire, a woman who ruins the lives of two men and two children through her willfulness. The heroine of *Limmerston Hall*, a Victorian gothic piece, behaves with almost decorous impropriety in her unrequited passion for the man who she believes may have killed her sister and may, even as she tries to attract him, be attempting to kill her nephew and niece. But although this book promises much with its hints and foreshadowing, it delivers little. *I Will Be Good* is a book of almost stupefying dullness even though its murder plot is potentially gripping. *Falling Stream* is a surprising modern novel, lightly written, but featuring a strong willful woman masquerading as a weak invalid and spoiling the lives of everyone with whom she comes into contact—a delightful light read.

An air of sadness hangs over all Chapman's books; "how splendid things might have been," they seem to say, but the strongly drawn, overpowering women are there to put a stop to that. Her style changes to fit the period portrayed. Her pace is perhaps a little leisurely for today's taste, except for the exquisite *Fear No More*—that has an air of timelessness and the power to haunt.

—Pamela Cleaver

CHAPPELL, Mollie. British. Born in Rhymney, Wales, 16 August 1913. Educated at Hengood County School for Girls; Cardiff University, B.A. Married R. G. Chappell in 1939 (died); one daughter. Lived in Southern Rhodesia (now Zimbabwe), 1946–61. Agent: Curtis Brown, 162–168 Regent Street, London W1R 5TB, England.

ROMANCE AND HISTORICAL PUBLICATIONS

Novels

The Widow Jones. London, Collins, 1956.
Endearing Young Charms. London, Collins, 1957.
Bachelor Heaven. London, Collins, 1958.
A Wreath of Holly. London, Collins, 1959.
One Little Room. London, Collins, 1960.
A Lesson in Loving. London, Collins, 1961; New York, Fawcett, 1975.
The Measure of Love. London, Collins, 1961.
Caroline. London, Collins, 1962; New York, Fawcett, 1975.
Come by Chance. London, Collins, 1963.
The Garden Room. London, Collins, 1964.
The Ladies of Lark. London, Collins, 1965.
Bright Promise. London, Collins, 1966.
Bid Me Live. London, Collins, 1967.
Since Summer. London, Collins, 1967.
The Wind in the Green Trees. London, Collins, 1969.
The Hasting Day. London, Collins, 1970.
Summer Story. London, Collins, 1972.
Valley of Lilacs. London, Collins, 1972.
Family Portrait. London, Collins, 1973.
Cressy. London, Collins, 1973.
Five Farthings. London, Collins, 1974.
A Letter from Lydia. London, Collins, 1974.
Seton's Wife. London, Collins, 1975.
In Search of Mr. Rochester. London, Collins, 1976.

The Loving Heart. London, Collins, 1977; New York, Fawcett, 1979.
Country Air. London, Collins, 1977.
The Romantic Widow. London, Collins, 1978; New York, Fawcett, 1979.
Wintersweet. London, Collins, 1978.
Serena. London, Hale, 1980.
Dearest Neighbour. London, Hale, 1981.
Cousin Amelia. London, Hale, 1982.
Springtime for Sophie. London, Hale, 1983.
The Yellow Straw Hat. London, Hale, 1983.
Stepping Stones. London, Hale, 1985.
The Family at Redburn. London, Severn House, 1985.

OTHER PUBLICATIONS

Other (for children)

Little Tom Sparrow. Leeds, E. J. Arnold, 1950.
Tusker Tales. Leeds, E. J. Arnold, 1950.
Rhodesian Adventure. London, Collins, 1950.
The Gentle Giant. Leeds, E. J. Arnold, 1951.
The House on the Kopje. London, Collins, 1951.
The Sugar and Spice. London, Collins, 1952.
St. Simon Square. London, Nelson, 1952.
The Fortunes of Frisk. London, Collins, 1953.
Cat with No Fiddle. London, Collins, 1954.
The Mystery of the Silver Circle. London, Collins, 1955.
Kit and the Mystery Man. London, Collins, 1955.

*   *   *

Mollie Chappell has evolved from being a writer of short stories for children, as in *Tusker Tales*, and for young girls, as in *Rhodesian Adventure* (both with African settings) via the light comedy of *Bachelor Heaven* to being a writer of romantic novels suitable for mature women.

Chappell's novels form a distinct species in the romantic class and, in their rather whimsical way, go against the general run. Romance in her novels is very controlled and chaste, and is seen vicariously rather than experienced in the first person. The world of her books is the world of comfortably off middle-aged womanhood in Southern England in the present, though some of the novels are set in mid-19th-century England. Her stories do not contain much action and plots are modest. The stories are, however, overburdened with characters, many dead or unmet, but ranging from the occasional odd and seedy type, such as Jacko in *The Hasting Day*, to the more common cool and crisp young woman, such as Lucy in *Summer Story*. Most characters are somewhat ordinary and there is often little opportunity for them to be developed.

In *Country Air* one sees the variations between brothers in their life achievements with careful gradation. This book contains many of the elements to be found in Chappell's other works: a setting in the English country towns of Clout and Carvel, careful assessment of strangers and relatives, including their clothes. On a rather deeper level is the presence of orphans who have lost both parents, as also occurs in *In Search of Mr. Rochester*, *Serena*, and *Dearest Neighbour*.

Settings are predictable, being either a rather vague and wearisome London and pretty villages such as Wintersweet (*Wintersweet*) as well as the frequently occurring Clout and Carvel. Family relationships are often complex and difficult to work out exactly, and involve distantly related members of the same family. Other relationships often include not-so-close friends and also those with a special closeness such as secretaries and housekeepers.

Chappell has also written historical romances, such as *Serena* and *Dearest Neighbour*, and the well-established themes of orphaned children are dealt with at length. The setting of a genteel mid-Victorian England helps to add to the pathos and sentimentality of the treatment. While in *Dearest Neighbour* there is a setting of rectories and solid country houses, there is nevertheless a controlled amount of melodrama and tragedy. It is largely a feminine world of daughters "coming out," and ends in a chaste pledging of love between hero and heroine. True to the Chappell style there is an approving eye cast on these proceedings by the girl's former governess. In *Serena* a stronger moral attitude (similar to that in *Seton's Wife*) is developed when the courage of the heroine is combined with love to defeat despair when the girl achieves the serenity befitting her name.

A serenity does, in fact, pervade most of Chappell's work through the detached posture of the narrators. The essence of the main characters is that they look out on life from on observing viewpoint rather than from actual experience. Many of the minor characters are very shallow indeed; gossip rather than passion rules. The style of writing is often flat and simple. While it is almost naive, at times it also has the effect of producing a "stream of consciousness" type of prose fitting the very internalised thoughts and action.

—P. R. Meldrum

CHARD, Judy (née Gordon). Also writes as Lyndon Chase. British. Born in Tuffley, Gloucestershire, 8 May 1916. Educated at Kippington House Junior School, Sevenoaks, Kent; Elstree Junior School and St. Winifred's Senior School, both Eastbourne, Sussex. Married Maurice Noel Chard in 1942. Assistant secretary, Guy Motors, Wolverhampton, West Midlands, 1939–42; editor, *Devon Life*, Exeter, 1979–82. Since 1989 director of studies, David and Charles Writing College, Newton Abbot, Devon. Address: Morley Farm, Morley Road, Highweek, Newton Abbot, Devon TQ12 6NA, England.

ROMANCE AND HISTORICAL PUBLICATIONS

Novels

Through the Green Woods. London, Hale, 1974.
The Weeping and the Laughter. London, Hale, 1975.
Encounter in Berlin. London, Hale, 1976.
The Uncertain Heart. London, Hale, 1976.
The Other Side of Sorrow. London, Hale, 1977.
In the Heart of Love. London, Hale, 1978.
Out of the Shadows. London, Hale, 1978.
All Passion Spent. London, Hale, 1979.
Seven Lonely Years. London, Hale, 1980.
The Darkening Skies. London, Hale, 1981.
When the Journey's Over. London, Hale, 1981.
Haunted by the Past. London, Hale, 1982.
Sweet Love Remembered. London, Hale, 1982.
Where the Dream Begins. London, Hale, 1982.
Rendezvous with Love. London, Hale, 1983.
Hold Me in Your Heart. London, Hale, 1983.
Tormentil (as Lyndon Chase). London, Hale, 1984.
To Live with Fear. London, Hale, 1985.

Wings of the Morning. London, Hale, 1985.
A Time to Love. London, Hale, 1987.
Wild Justice. London, Hale, 1987.
For Love's Sake Only. London, Hale, 1988.
Person Unknown. London, Hale, 1988.
To Be So Loved. London, Hale, 1988.
Enchantment. London, Hale, 1989.

OTHER PUBLICATIONS

Other

Along the Lemon. Bodmin, Cornwall, Bossiney, 1978.
Along the Dart. Bodmin, Cornwall, Bossiney, 1979.
About Widecombe. Bodmin, Cornwall, Bossiney, 1979.
Devon Mysteries. Bodmin, Cornwall, Bossiney, 1979.
The South Hams. Bodmin, Cornwall, Bossiney, 1980.
Along the Teign. Bodmin, Cornwall, Bossiney, 1981.
Devon County Companion. London, Cadogan, 1984.
Tales of the Unexplained in Devon. Exeter, Obelisk, 1986.
Haunted Happenings. Exeter, Obelisk, 1987.
Burgh Island and Bigbury Bay. Exeter, Obelisk, 1988.

Editor, *Traditional Devonshire Recipes*. Exeter, Obelisk, 1985.

*

Judy Chard comments:

My romantic novels always include some suspense and mystery as well as the romantic angle. I find it impossible to write what I would describe as a straight romance; there must be some suspense whether it be smuggling, kidnapping or even murder.

I enjoyed writing my one historical novel, *Tormentil* (under the name of Lyndon Chase), about Victorian Devon and Exeter including Dartmoor, and would have liked to continue in this genre. I would also like to write more straight crime.

I like to use a wide range of backgrounds, from my own native Devon to East Berlin and Bolivia, all of which takes a great deal of research as I am very careful to make these as authentic as possible. I do considerable preliminary work on my characters for they are the basis of my novels, the raw material. The plot comes later.

*   *   *

Judy Chard writes contemporary romance novels with more than a dash of adventure or political intrigue thrown in for good measure. Many of Chard's books involve murders, kidnappings, drug smuggling, and a variety of other crimes, and the hero and heroine are often trapped together in difficult situations. The novels often have exotic locations, and Chard's research of backgrounds is always thorough. The novels, however, remain traditional in approach, and the reader is safe in the knowledge that once inside Chard's romantic world love will conquer all.

To Be So Loved is set in Bolivia. This is instantly apparent because the background is sketched once and for all in a single line: "a volcanic explosive country, and yet diverse, holding a charm all of its own." What more could be necessary? What need of scene setting is there anyway, when the real "meat" of the story is but a plane seat away? "She noticed his eyes were rimmed with darker blue round the iris—incredibly compelling eyes—they smiled, but the muscles of his mouth did not move in confirmation." This is of course, the first male romantic lead. He is a top international writer, preparing a series of features which will expose the Bolivian drug trade. One would assume that such a topical and intensely complicated subject would require some detailed development and exposition, but instead the urgent need is to introduce the second romantic male lead. He is, it transpires, the heroine's childhood companion, now matured into the leader of the Bolivian People's Protection Army. Coincidence?

Well, ". . her mouth was dry, her tongue stuck to the roof of her mouth," but apart from that, "it was one of the most miserable moments of her life." There are more than 150 pages like this, as the heroine "is torn between her love for the two, with their widely differing ideals and morals." At least, the reader assumes they have ideals, because the story unfortunately doesn't allow any of the characters to develop a complete identity, never mind any political philosophy.

Wings of the Morning is a poignant tale of country love, with a dash of kidnapping and a second place finish in the Grand National thrown in. Wings of the Morning, as an enticement for followers of the turf, is a horse. Joss, the hero, is unlucky in love but rich in Grand National place money; he thinks the horse is the "hub of his life, his raison d'être." Sally, originally in love with Joss, but soon to opt for Simon, is the focal point of the romantic interest throughout the story. She is ultimately swayed in her choice of mate by Simon's capacity for decision making, demonstrated as early as their first date. "They went to a wine bar and ate a huge curry, washed down with rosé wine." She queried the aesthetics of the combination "from the purist point of view." "I like to make my own rules," is Simon's masterful comment.

For Love's Sake Only traces the progression of Helen and Hugh Kendall's idyllic rural marriage through the business and personal pressures that result in the couple drifting apart. Helen is awash with nostalgia for the original status quo to be reestablished with Hugh, "so tall, handsome and attentive." However, when she follows Hugh's example with the artistic Maureen, and falls for someone else, he can't just be anyone. "She caught her breath . . he was so like Paul Newman, the film star. The intensely blue eyes, crinkled at the corners, regarded her." Unfortunately the sexual stereotyping, flatly painted characters, and lack of any depth of background to make actions believable continually pull the rug from under the author's own feet.

Wild Justice takes as its starting point the gunning down of a policeman, witnessed by Christopher Roberts. His testimony results in the life imprisonment of the murderer. Subsequent developments, with the murderer's father attempting revenge on Christopher, are told through Christopher's eyes. This male viewpoint gives the story a different slant from most of Chard's novels. There are still under-developed characters such as Fiona, who is packaged and presented in a couple of lines, "with her red hair and freckles, her tip-tilted nose and green eyes; lively, bubbling and full of fun, not much more than a child herself, although she was twenty-one." The reversal of the "hero" role unfortunately doesn't do much to ameliorate the patronising attitude that pervades the treatment of the female characters. "He reached the block of flats where Fiona lived. The firm paid her a good salary. She was worth it."

While Chard's work certainly doesn't set out to challenge the stereotypes so often found in romance novels she does provide original plots and the safe haven of a world where her characters do live "happily ever after."

—Bill Boyle

CHARLES, Anita. See BARRIE, Susan.

CHARLES, Theresa. Pseudonym for Irene Maude Swatridge, née Mossop; also writes as Fay Chandos; Leslie Lance; Virginia Storm; Jan Tempest. British. Born in Woking, Surrey. Educated privately. Married Charles John Swatridge in 1934. Agent: Curtis Brown, 162–168 Regent Street, London W1R 5TB, England.

ROMANCE AND HISTORICAL PUBLICATIONS

Novels (with Charles Swatridge)

The Distant Drum. London, Longman, 1940.
My Enemy and I. London, Longman, 1941.
To Save My Life. London, Longman, 1946.
Happy Now I Go. London, Longman, 1947; as *Dark Legacy*, New York, Dell, 1968.
Man-Made Miracle. London, Longman, 1949.
The Ugly Prince (as Virginia Storm). New York, Arcadia House, 1950.
At a Touch I Yield. London, Cassell, 1952.
Fairer Than She. London, Cassell, 1953; New York, Dell, 1968.
My Only Love. London, Cassell, 1954.
The Kinder Love. London, Cassell, 1955.
The Burning Beacon. London, Cassell, 1956; New York, Lancer, 1966.
The Ultimate Surrender. London, Cassell, 1958.
A Girl Called Evelyn. London, Hale, 1959.
No Through Road. London, Hale, 1960.
House on the Rocks. London, Hale, 1962; New York, Paperback Library, 1966.
Ring for Nurse Raine. London, Hale, 1962.
Widower's Wife. London, Hale, 1963; as *Return to Terror*, New York, Paperback Library, 1966.
Patient in Love. London, Hale, 1963.
Nurse Alice in Love. London, Hale, 1964; as *Lady in the Mist*, New York, Ace, 1966.
The Man for Me. London, Hale, 1965; as *The Shrouded Tower*, New York, Ace, 1966.
How Much You Mean to Me. London, Hale, 1966.
Proud Citadel. London, Hale, and New York, Dell, 1967.
The Way Men Love. London, Hale, 1967.
The Shadowy Third. London, Hale, 1968.
From Fairest Flowers. London, Hale, 1969.
Wayward as the Swallow. London, Hale, 1970.
Second Honeymoon. London, Hale, 1970.
My True Love. London, Hale, 1971.
Therefore Must Be Loved. London, Hale, 1972.
Castle Kelpiesloch. London, Hale, 1973.
Nurse by Accident. London, Hale, 1974.
The Flower and the Nettle. London, Hale, 1975.
Trust Me, My Love. London, Hale, 1975.
One Who Remembers. London, Hale, 1976.
Rainbow after Rain. London, Hale, 1977.
Crisis at St. Chad's. London, Hale, 1977.
Just for One Weekend. London, Hale, 1978.
Surgeon's Reputation. London, Hale, 1979.
With Somebody Else. London, Hale, 1981.
Surgeon's Sweetheart. London, Hale, 1981.

No Easier Road to Love. London, Hale, 1983.
Always in My Heart. London, Severn House, 1985.

Novels as Jan Tempest

Stepmother of Five. London, Mills and Boon, 1936.
Someone New to Love. London, Mills and Boon, 1936.
Be Still, My Heart! London, Mills and Boon, 1936.
Kiss—and Forget. London, Mills and Boon, 1936.
Believe Me, Beloved—. London, Mills and Boon, 1936.
All This I Gave. London, Mills and Boon, 1937.
If I Love Again. London, Mills and Boon, 1937.
No Other Man—. London, Mills and Boon, 1937.
Grow Up, Little Lady! London, Mills and Boon, 1937.
Carey, Come Back! London, Mills and Boon, 1937.
Face the Music—for Love. London, Mills and Boon, 1938.
Man—and Waif. London, Mills and Boon, 1938.
Because My Love Is Come. London, Mills and Boon, 1938; as
    Because My Love Is Coming, 1958.
When First I Loved. . . . London, Mills and Boon, 1938.
Hilary in His Heart. London, Mills and Boon, 1938.
Say You're Sorry. London, Mills and Boon, 1939.
My Only Love. London, Mills and Boon, 1939.
Uninvited Guest. London, Mills and Boon, 1939.
I'll Try Anything Once. London, Mills and Boon, 1939.
Top of the Beanstalk. London, Mills and Boon, 1940.
The Broken Gate. London, Mills and Boon, 1940.
Why Wouldn't He Wait? London, Mills and Boon, 1940.
Little Brown Girl. London, Mills and Boon, 1940.
Always Another Man. London, Mills and Boon, 1941.
The Moment I Saw You. London, Mills and Boon, 1941.
The Unknown Joy. London, Mills and Boon, 1941.
Ghost of June. London, Mills and Boon, 1941.
No Time for a Man. London, Mills and Boon, 1942.
Romance on Ice. London, Mills and Boon, 1942.
If You'll Marry Me. London, Mills and Boon, 1942.
A Prince for Portia. London, Mills and Boon, 1943.
Wife after Work. London, Mills and Boon, 1943.
The Long Way Home. London, Mills and Boon, 1943.
''Never Again!'' Said Nicola. London, Mills and Boon, 1944.
The One Thing I Wanted. London, Mills and Boon, 1944.
Utility Husband. London, Mills and Boon, 1944.
Westward to My Love. London, Mills and Boon, 1944.
Love While You Wait. London, Mills and Boon, 1944.
Not for This Alone. London, Mills and Boon, 1945.
To Be a Bride. London, Mills and Boon, 1945.
The Orange Blossom Shop. London, Mills and Boon, 1946.
Happy with Either. London, Mills and Boon, 1946.
House of the Pines. London, Mills and Boon, 1946; New York,
    Ace, 1967; as *House of Pines*, Ace, 1975.
Bachelor's Bride. London, Mills and Boon, 1946.
Lovely, Though Late. London, Mills and Boon, 1946.
Close Your Eyes. London, Mills and Boon, 1947.
Teach Me to Love. London, Mills and Boon, 1947.
How Can I Forget? London, Mills and Boon, 1948; as *First I
    Must Forget* (as Virginia Storm), New York, Arcadia House,
    1951.
Cinderella Had Two Sisters. London, Mills and Boon, 1948; as
    Virginia Storm, New York, Arcadia House, 1950.
Short-Cut to the Stars. London, Mills and Boon, 1949.
Never Another Love. London, Mills and Boon, 1949; New
    York, Arcadia House, 1950.
Promise of Paradise. New York, Gramercy, 1949.
Nobody Else—Ever. London, Mills and Boon, 1950.
A Match Is Made. London, Mills and Boon, 1950.
Now and Always. New York, Arcadia House, 1950.

Until I Find Her. New York, Arcadia House, 1950; London,
    Mills and Boon, 1951.
Two Loves for Tamara. London, Mills and Boon, 1951.
Open the Door to Love. London, Mills and Boon, 1952.
Without a Honeymoon. London, Mills and Boon, 1952.
Happy Is the Wooing. London, Mills and Boon, 1952.
Meet Me by Moonlight. London, Mills and Boon, 1953.
Give Her Gardenias. London, Mills and Boon, 1953.
Enchanted Valley. London, Mills and Boon, 1954.
First-Time of Asking. London, Mills and Boon, 1954.
Ask Me Again. London, Mills and Boon, 1955.
Where the Heart Is. London, Mills and Boon, 1955.
For Those in Love. London, Mills and Boon, 1956.
Wedding Bells for Willow. London, Mills and Boon, 1956.
Craddock's Kingdom. London, Mills and Boon, 1957.
. . . Will Not Now Take Place. London, Mills and Boon, 1957.
The Youngest Sister. London, Mills and Boon, 1958.
Because There Is Hope. London, Mills and Boon, 1958.
Romance for Rose. London, Mills and Boon, 1959.
Stranger to Love. London, Mills and Boon, 1960.
Mistress of Castlemount. London, Mills and Boon, 1961.
The Turning Point. London, Mills and Boon, 1961.
That Nice Nurse Nevin. London, Mills and Boon, and Toronto,
    Harlequin, 1963.
The Madderleys Married. London, Mills and Boon, 1963.
The Flower and the Fruit. London, Mills and Boon, 1964.
Nurse Willow's Ward. Toronto, Harlequin, 1965.
The Way We Used to Be. London, Mills and Boon, 1965.
Jubilee Hospital. Toronto, Harlequin, 1966.
The Lonesome Road. London, Mills and Boon, 1966.
Meant to Meet. London, Mills and Boon, 1967.
Lyra, My Love. Chicago, Moody Press, 1969.

Novels as Fay Chandos

No Limit to Love. London, Mills and Boon, 1937.
No Escape from Love. London, Mills and Boon, 1937.
Man of My Dreams. London, Mills and Boon, 1937.
Before I Make You Mine. London, Mills and Boon, 1938.
Wife for a Wager. London, Mills and Boon, 1938.
Gay Knight I Love. London, Mills and Boon, 1938.
All I Ask. London, Mills and Boon, 1939.
Another Woman's Shoes. London, Mills and Boon, 1939.
When Three Walk Together. London, Mills and Boon, 1939.
The Man Who Wasn't Mac. London, Mills and Boon, 1939.
Husband for Hire. London, Mills and Boon, 1940.
You Should Have Warned Me. London, Mills and Boon, 1940.
When We Two Parted. London, Mills and Boon, 1940.
Substitute for Sherry. London, Mills and Boon, 1940.
Women Are So Simple. London, Mills and Boon, 1941.
Only a Touch. London, Mills and Boon, 1941.
Awake, My Love! London, Mills and Boon, 1942.
A Letter to My Love. London, Mills and Boon, 1942.
Eve and I. London, Mills and Boon, 1943.
A Man to Follow. London, Mills and Boon, 1943.
Away from Each Other. London, Mills and Boon, 1944.
Made to Marry. London, Mills and Boon, 1944.
Just a Little Longer. London, Mills and Boon, 1944.
Last Year's Roses. London, Mills and Boon, 1945.
A Man for Margaret. London, Mills and Boon, 1945.
Three Roads to Romance. London, Mills and Boon, 1945.
When Time Stands Still. London, Mills and Boon, 1946.
Home Is the Hero. London, Mills and Boon, 1946.
Because I Wear Your Ring. London, Mills and Boon, 1947.
Cousins May Kiss. London, Mills and Boon, 1947.
Lost Summer. London, Mills and Boon, 1948.

Since First We Met. London, Mills and Boon, 1948.
June in Her Eyes. London, Mills and Boon, 1949.
For a Dream's Sake. London, Mills and Boon, 1949.
Fugitive from Love. London, Mills and Boon, 1950.
There Is a Tide. . . . London, Mills and Boon, 1950.
This Time It's Love. London, Mills and Boon, 1951.
First and Favourite Wife. London, Mills and Boon, 1952.
Families Are Such Fun. London, Mills and Boon, 1952.
Leave It to Nancy. London, Mills and Boon, 1953.
The Other One. London, Mills and Boon, 1953.
Find Another Eden. London, Mills and Boon, 1953.
Just Before the Wedding. London, Mills and Boon, 1954.
Doctors Are Different. London, Mills and Boon, 1954.
Husbands at Home. London, Mills and Boon, 1955.
Hibiscus House. London, Mills and Boon, 1955; as *Nurse Incognito*, Toronto, Harlequin, 1964.
So Nearly Married. London, Mills and Boon, 1956.
The Romantic Touch. London, Mills and Boon, 1957.
Partners Are a Problem. London, Mills and Boon, 1957.
Model Girl's Farm. London, Mills and Boon, 1958.
Nan—and the New Owner. London, Mills and Boon, 1959.
Wild Violets. London, Mills and Boon, 1959.
When Four Ways Meet. London, Mills and Boon, 1961.
Sister Sylvan. London, Mills and Boon, 1962.
Two Other People. London, Mills and Boon, 1964.
Don't Give Your Heart Away. London, Mills and Boon, 1966.
Stranger in Love. London, Mills and Boon, 1966.
Farm by the Sea. London, Mills and Boon, 1967.
The Three of Us. London, Mills and Boon, 1970.
Sweet Rosemary. London, Mills and Boon, 1972.

Novels as Leslie Lance

Alice, Where Are You? London, Hodder and Stoughton, 1940.
Take a Chance. London, Hodder and Stoughton, 1940.
The Dark Stranger. London, Sampson Low, 1946.
Man of the Family. London, Hurst and Blackett, 1952.
Spun by the Moon. London, Ward Lock, 1960.
Sisters in Love. London, Ward Lock, 1960.
A Summer's Grace. London, Ward Lock, 1961.
Springtime for Sally. London, Ward Lock, 1962.
Spreading Sails. London, Ward Lock, 1963.
The Young Curmudgeon. London, Ward Lock, 1964.
I'll Ride Beside You. London, Ward Lock, 1965.
Bright Winter. London, Ward Lock, 1965.
No Summer Beauty. London, Ward Lock, 1967.
Return to King's Mere. London, Hale, 1967.
Bride of Emersham. New York, Pyramid, 1967.
Nurse in the Woods. London, Hale, 1969.
The Summer People. London, Hale, 1969.
Nurse Verena in Weirwater. London, Hale, 1970.
No Laggard in Love. London, Hale, 1971.
The New Lord Whinbridge. London, Hale, 1973.
Now I Can Forget. London, Hale, 1973.
The Love That Lasts. London, Hale, 1974.
The Maverton Heiress. London, Hale, 1975.
The Return of the Cuckoo. London, Hale, 1976.
Romance at Wrecker's End. London, Hale, 1976.
Island House. London, Hale, 1976.
Cousins by Courtesy. London, Hale, 1977.
The Family at the Farm. London, Hale, 1978.
Orchid Girl. London, Hale, 1978.
The Girl in the Mauve Mini. London, Hale, 1979.
The Rose Princess. London, Hale, 1979.
Doctor in the Snow. London, Hale, 1980.
The House in the Woods. New York, Ace, 1980.

Hawk's Head. London, Hale, 1981.
Someone Who Cares. London, Hale, 1982.
Dear Patience. London, Hale, 1983.
Heiress to the Isle. London, Hale, 1987.

OTHER PUBLICATIONS (for children) as Irene Mossop

Other

Well Played, Juliana! London, Sampson Low, 1928.
Prunella Plays the Game. London, Sampson Low, 1929.
Freesia's Feud. London, Warne, 1930.
The Luck of the Oakleighs. London, Warne, 1930.
Chris in Command. London, Sampson Low, 1930.
Sylvia Sways the School. London, Sampson Low, 1930.
Theresa's First Term. London, Nisbet, 1930.
Vivien of St. Val's. London, Shaw, 1931.
Charm's Last Chance. London, Nisbet, 1931.
Nicky—New Girl. London, Sampson Low, 1931.
Rona's Rival. London, Warne, 1931.
A Rebel at "Rowans." London, Sampson Low, 1932.
Barbara Black-Sheep. London, Warne, 1932.
Una Wins Through. London, Warne, 1932.
Feud in the Fifth. London, Sampson Low, 1933.
Hilary Leads the Way. London, Warne, 1933.
The Taming of Pickles. London, Shaw, 1933.
The Fifth at Cliff House. London, Warne, 1934.
The Four V's. London, Warne, 1934.
The Fourth at St. Faith's. London, Shaw, 1934.
Play Up, Pine House! London, Sampson Low, 1934.
Theresa on Trial. London, Warne, 1935.
Theda Marsh. London, Shaw, 1935.
The Gay Adventure. London, Warne, 1937.

*   *   *

Irene Mossop began writing at the end of the 1920's and has produced some 240 novels. However, her books, mostly romantic stories, have managed to retain their sense of crisp inventiveness. Her pen names—particularly Virginia Storm and Jan Tempest—are well chosen and appropriate for the exciting and atmospheric moods of many of her romantic adventures. The titles also endorse the flavour of the books—*No Limit to Love, Husband for Hire, Meant to Meet,* etc.

Several of the author's heroines start out in a rather calculating way, going to the lengths of participating in forced or fake marriages in order to improve their circumstances, or those of someone dear to them. But, by the final pages of each novel, these phoney marriages have generally focussed satisfyingly into liaisons of true love.

There are also accounts of steady and happy marriages that begin to misfire because the heroine becomes insensitive to her spouse's psychological needs. In *The Way We Used to Be,* for instance, Leonie's parents suddenly make a lot of money, and Leonie fails to recognize that the resultant parental subsidy is damaging her hard-working veterinary-surgeon husband's masculine pride—and, of course, their marriage. But happily she comes to her senses, and a realistic appraisal of the illogical qualities of married interdependence just in time to salvage her romantic relationship with her husband.

Variations on these married and romantic themes are deftly handled in the flow of novels by this writer. She is also skilled at manipulating the romantic thriller story, as in *The Girl in the Mauve Mini,* for example. (Her children's stories, written as Irene Mossop, are also rich in excitement and suspense.)

She writes as Theresa Charles in collaboration with her husband, Charles John Swatridge, and as co-authors in the romantic genre they have the briskness and colour that remind one of the flavour of stories by the earlier husband and wife partnership of C. N. and A. M. Williamson. *Nurse by Accident* introduces an intriguing new angle on romance—that of the accident-prone heroine whose love life, as well as her career, is threatened by her habit of unintentionally making things go cockeyed. Nurse Nicola Warren falls in love in this accident-prone way—always with the wrong man, of course—until she meets an almost-too-charming-to-be-true solicitor, who knows that the solution to her problem is for him to gather her into his arms with the unoriginal but, in this case, extremely apt comment: "You need a husband to keep an eye on you. . . . "

—Mary Cadogan

CHASE, Elaine Raco. American. Born in Schenectady, New York, 31 August 1949. Educated at Mohonasen High School, Rotterdam, New York, graduated 1967; Albany Business College, New York, 1967–68, A.A. in computing; State University of New York, Albany, 1977. Married Gary D. Chase in 1969; one daughter and one son. Secretary, Narcotic Addiction Control Commission, Albany, 1967–68; audio visual librarian, WGY–WRGB Television, Schenectady, 1968–70; copywriter, Beckman Advertising, Albany, 1970–71. Agent: Denise Marcil Agency, 316 West 82nd Street, New York, New York 10024. Address: 4451 Majestic Lane, Fairfax, Virginia 22030 U.S.A.

ROMANCE AND HISTORICAL PUBLICATIONS

Novels (series Roman Cantrell and Nikki Holden)

Rules of the Game. New York, Dell, 1980.
Tender Yearnings. New York, Dell, 1981; London, Corgi, 1983.
A Dream Come True. New York, Dell, 1982.
Double Occupancy. New York, Dell, 1982.
Designing Woman. New York, Dell, 1982.
Calculated Risk. New York, Silhouette, 1983.
No Easy Way Out. New York, Dell, 1983.
Video Vixen. New York, Dell, 1983.
Best Laid Plans. New York, Avon, 1984.
Lady Be Bad. New York, Silhouette, 1984.
Special Delivery. New York, Dell, 1984.
Dare the Devil. New York, Dell, 1987.
Dangerous Places (Cantrell and Holden). New York, Bantam, 1987.
Dark Corners (Cantrell and Holden). New York, Bantam, 1988.

*

Elaine Raco Chase comments:
When I first started writing contemporary romance novels I felt three things were missing: 1) strong intelligent heroines, 2) male point of view for heroes, and 3) humor. I was delighted to see the readers thought so as well. I've also enjoyed doing role reversals; using humor to highlight important topics such as dyslexia, drunken drivers, and orthopedic injury recovery. In my current romantic suspense series, my heroine was an abused and sexually battered child who proves a strong survivor.

*　　　*　　　*

Elaine Raco Chase has her feet firmly planted in the 20th century. The heroines of her contemporary romances are bright, capable, and talented. Most have active careers which are satisfying in themselves. They work in fields such as business (*Tender Yearnings*, *Special Delivery*, *Calculated Risk*), entertainment or media (*Video Vixen*, *Dare the Devil*, *Double Occupancy*), and science (*No Easy Way Out*, *Designing Woman*). They do not *need* a man to be complete, although a loving relationship is not to be denied if it develops.

One distinguishing characteristic of Chase's novels is a sense of humor, often displayed in the situations in which the main characters are first induced. When Thor Devlin finds a cavewoman accompanied by a saber-toothed tiger and a woolly mammoth on his ranch in *Dare the Devil* he is understandably startled. He does manage to recover rapidly and coolly states, "You, the hairy elephant, and the cat with the overbite are not the norm in Montana." Things become even more comic when the tiger, whose name is Pumpkin, loses his teeth and the mammoth is introduced as Ramon. It all is explained when the cavewoman admits she is movie stuntwoman, Cam Stirling. In *No Easy Way Out*, brilliant physicist Dr. Virginia Farrell attends a Halloween party as a very sexy bunny and loses her inhibitions. Roxanne Murdoch, in *Special Delivery*, delivers a "belly-gram" to the vice-president of a bank and ends up stranded with him in the bank during a blizzard. Abigail Wetherby, heroine of *Tender Yearnings*, creates havoc with Nick Maxwell's company computer when she tries to cancel her store's acceptance of credit cards.

Chase also often uses the device of disguises and illusions distorting and altering reality. In addition to the Halloween party in *No Easy Way Out*, there are several instances of masquerades. Brandy Abbott (*Designing Woman*) is an architect but masquerades as a nighttime *femme fatale*. Nick Maxwell hides his true identity from Abigail and Cam Stirling deals in the illusions of the film world. Vikki Kirkland, in *Video Vixen*, plays two roles: one as a soap opera siren and another in her personal life. Kit Forrester of *A Dream Come True* also lives in a world of illusions. A rare romance heroine, she is very insecure and vulnerable. Lacking self-esteem, she fantasizes about a different life, yet views herself as a liar. Fantasy and reality join when she begins to play the role of Rafe Morgan's fiancée.

Recently Chase has branched out of the category romance field into detective fiction. Although there still is an important element of romance, the mystery and action components are more prominent. *Dangerous Places* introduces Nikki Holden and Roman Cantrell. She is a journalist and he is a private investigator. Both have scarred pasts, but Nikki's is particularly dark. An abused child and former juvenile delinquent, she is extremely distrustful of any relationship. Starting as rivals on a murder case, they eventually join forces to solve it and in the process fall in love. Nikki and Roman return in *Dark Corners*. They start with different assignments, but their cases converge. Again the mystery and action take center stage, but one also can see the relationship between the lovers deepening.

Chase's contemporary romances are good fun and enjoyable reading with enough humor to make them livelier than the average formula romance. However, her move to the detective/romance fiction field holds great promise for the future. She shows real talent in plotting complicated, suspenseful stories an her development of Nikki's and Roman's characters and their relationship truly involves the reader.

—Barbara E. Kemp

CHASE, Lyndon. See **CHARD, Judy.**

CHESNEY, Marion. Also writes as Helen Crampton; Ann Fairfax; Jennie Tremaine. British. Born in Glasgow, Scotland, 10 June 1936. Address: c/o St. Martin's Press, 175 Fifth Avenue, New York, New York 10010, U.S.A.

ROMANCE AND HISTORICAL PUBLICATIONS

Novels (series: A House for the Season; Six Sisters; Westerbury)

Lady Margery's Intrigues. New York, Fawcett, and London, Macdonald, 1980.
Regency Gold. New York, Fawcett, and London, Macdonald, 1980.
The Constant Companion. New York, Fawcett, 1980; London, Macdonald, 1982.
My Lords, Ladies, and Marjorie. New York, Fawcett, 1981.
Quadrille. New York, Fawcett, 1981; London, Macdonald, 1982.
Love and Lady Lovelace. New York, Fawcett, 1982.
Minerva (Six Sisters). New York, St. Martin's Press, 1982; London, Macdonald, 1983.
The Marquis Takes a Bride (as Helen Crampton). London, Macdonald, 1982.
The Westerbury Inheritance. New York, Pinnacle, 1982.
Deirdre and Desire (Six Sisters). New York, St. Martin's Press, 1983; London, Macdonald, 1984.
Duke's Diamonds. New York, Fawcett, 1983.
The Highland Countess. London, Macdonald, 1983.
The Taming of Annabelle (Six Sisters). New York, St. Martin's Press, and London, Macdonald, 1983.
The Viscount's Revenge. New York, New American Library, 1983.
The Westerbury Sisters. New York, Pinnacle, 1983.
Daphne (Six Sisters). New York, St. Martin's Press, and London, Macdonald, 1984.
The French Affair. New York, Fawcett, and London, Macdonald, 1984.
The Poor Relation. New York, New American Library, 1984.
Rake's Progress (House for the Season). New York, St. Martin's Press, 1984.
Sweet Masquerade. New York, Fawcett, 1984.
Diana the Huntress (Six Sisters). New York, St. Martin's Press, and London, Macdonald, 1985.
Frederica in Fashion (Six Sisters). New York, St. Martin's Press, and London, Macdonald, 1985.
The Education of Miss Paterson. New York, New American Library, 1985.
The Flirt. New York, Fawcett, 1985.
The Original Miss Honeyford. New York, New American Library, 1985.
The Miser of Mayfair (House for the Season). New York, St. Martin's Press, 1986; Bath, Firecrest, 1987.
Plain Jane (House for the Season). New York, St. Martin's Press, 1986; Bath, Firecrest, 1987.
Those Endearing Young Charms. New York, Fawcett, 1986; London, Hale, 1987.
To Dream of Love. New York, Fawcett, 1986.
The Adventuress (House for the Season). New York, St. Martin's Press, 1987.
Lessons in Love. New York, Fawcett, 1987.

Milady in Love (House for the Season). New York, Ballantine, 1987.
Miss Fiona's Fancy. New York, New American Library, 1987.
At the Sign of the Golden Pineapple. New York, Fawcett, 1987.
The Wicked Grandmother (House for the Season). New York, St. Martin's Press, 1987; Bath, Firecrest, 1988.
Rainbird's Revenge (House for the Season). New York, St. Martin's Press, 1988.
The Perfect Gentleman. New York, Ballantine, 1988.
The Savage Marquess. New York, New American Library, 1988.
Refining Felicity. New York, St. Martin's Press, 1988.

Novels as Ann Fairfax

My Dear Duchess. New York, Berkley, and London, Macdonald, 1979.
Henrietta. New York, Berkley, 1979; London, Macdonald, 1980.
Annabelle. New York, Berkley, 1980; London, Macdonald, 1981.
Penelope. New York, Berkley, 1982; London, Macdonald, 1983.

Novels as Jennie Tremaine

Ginny. New York, Dell, 1980.
Kitty. New York, Dell, 1980.
Molly. New York, Dell, 1980.
Lucy. New York, Dell, 1980.
Polly. New York, Dell, 1980.
Susie. New York, Dell, 1981.
Tilly. New York, Dell, 1981.
Poppy. New York, Dell, 1982.
Sally. New York, Dell, 1982.
Maggie. New York, Dell, 1984.
Lady Anne's Deception. New York, Fawcett, 1986.

* * *

Marion Chesney has become one of the most noted "Regency" writers of today. Actually, Chesney did not become a success overnight for we have been reading her novels since the late 1970's, when they began to be published under various pseudonyms.

One of Chesney's strongest points as a writer is her ability to look at the world from the other side of the fence, that is, she shows the Regency and Victorian world through the eyes of servants or middle-class people. By using members of different social classes as central characters, Chesney takes the genre out of the flat, single dimensional form that writers frequently depict in Regency novels and creates a world with depth and understanding. She humanizes both the gentry and the lower classes by illustrating that all people, regardless of social status, have the same problems, the same fears, and the same need for love and dreams.

Susie, written as Jennie Tremaine, is a typical example of Chesney's use of social class and social position. Susie is from the solid middle class. Her father is a doctor, her mother a toadying, social climber willing to do anything for social recognition. This includes manipulating 17-year-old Susie into marriage with a man in his late fifties.

Susie dreams of a "kind but homely young man" in love with her. She is hopelessly naive, caught in daydreams more vivid than real life and, given her marriage to the Earl of Blackhall, far more preferable. Fortunately, the Earl dies on his wedding night by falling out of a window. Susie returns to her dreams but this time as the Dowager Countess of Blackhall.

The Earl's nephew, Giles Warden, is both fascinated and repelled by Susie. She is beautiful, innocent, and in his eyes hopelessly stupid. She has no social graces, no smart chatter and apparently will never learn to take her place in society, yet despite this he marries her. The major thrust of the story is Susie's love for Giles, their eventual marriage, and how they manage to make it "forever and ever."

Most of the Tremaine novels could be characterized as "shop girl" tales where the heroine is raised far beyond her social level and must use her own resources to win the love of the hero and take her place by his side. In some ways they are frothy, melodramatic tales but readers find them relaxing and good escapist reading. Surprisingly, these novels closely parallel the romances churned out in the story newspapers of the late Victorian period. They had the same characterizations, plot devices, and calamitous events that Chesney delights in.

The novels written under her own name fall into two categories. The single romance such as *The Constant Companion* or *Regency Gold* are standard "Regency" fare. Appealing heroines, manly heroes, and nasty villains combine to provide hours of entertaining reading. They are charming well-rounded stories that readers look forward to. Warning! They should not be dismissed as just another Regency.

Her most noted works are those that are written as series novels. Her first series centers on the six Armitage sisters. Character development is more detailed, conflict more critical, and the fun and games of winning a matrimonial prize more subtle.

The more recent series, A House for the Season covers six volumes. It is a unique series that surpasses her other works in this genre. The plot is far from simple for it operates on two levels. A house is rented for the London season by various ladies who hope to find a husband for themselves or a relative. Part of each novel is their story, with all of the usual difficulties normally encountered in such a hunt. It provides a pleasant counterpoint to the second element of the plot. This centers on the servants in the house. The staff consists of the butler, Mr. Rainbird; the housekeeper, Mrs. Middleton; the cook, Angus Macgregor; the housemaids, Alice, Jenny, and Lizzie; and Joseph the footman. Each had lost a position and could not produce references for another good job. Mr. Palmer, the Duke of Pelham's agent gives them all jobs, but then cheats them of most of their wages. Slowly, they begin to look to Mr. Rainbird as their leader and eventually a "family" unit emerges. All decide to pool their money so they can become independent. Their goal is to purchase an inn on the outskirts of the city and each novel in the series brings them closer to their goal. As usual, the ending is not quite what one expects.

In reality this series is about the servants. For the first time we are allowed to peek behind the rigid masks, the bobbing curtsies, and the silent stares. With this series, one can see that Chesney has well earned her recognition as an outstanding "Regency" writer.

—Arlene Moore

———————

CHESTERTON, Denise. See **ROBINS, Denise.**

———————

CHILD, Philip. Canadian. Born in Hamilton, Ontario, 9 January 1898. Educated at Trinity College, University of Toronto, B.A. 1921; Cambridge University, 1921–22; Harvard University, Cambridge, Massachusetts, A.M. 1923, Ph.D. 1929. Served in the Canadian Royal Garrison Artillery during World War I: Lieutenant. Married Gertrude Helen Potts in 1924; one son and one daughter. Lecturer, 1923–26 and 1941–42, and Professor of English from 1942, Trinity College, University of Toronto; Assistant Professor of English, University of British Columbia, Vancouver, 1928–29; tutor, Harvard University, 1929–36. Member of the Editorial Board, *University of Toronto Quarterly*, 1940–49. Recipient: Ryerson fiction award, 1945, 1949; Governor-General's award, 1950. *Died in 1978.*

ROMANCE AND HISTORICAL PUBLICATIONS

Novel

The Village of Souls. London, Butterworth, 1933.

OTHER PUBLICATIONS

Novels

God's Sparrows. London, Butterworth, 1937.
Blow Wind Come Wrack. London, Jarrolds, 1945.
Day of Wrath. Toronto, Ryerson Press, 1945.
Mr. Ames Against Time. Toronto, Ryerson Press, 1949.

Verse

The Victorian House and Other Poems. Toronto, Ryerson Press, 1951.
The Wood of the Nightingale. Toronto, Ryerson Press, 1965.

Other

Dynamic Democracy with John W. Holmes. Toronto, Canadian Association for Adult Education and Canadian Institute of International Affairs, 1941.

*   *   *

History is of keen importance in the writing of Philip Child. He has confirmed this not only by writing historical non-fiction but also by producing a number of imaginative works that are historically-specific in their settings. His book-length narrative poem *The Wood of the Nightingale* is set during World War I, as is much of the novel *God's Sparrows*, and *Day of Wrath* takes place in Nazi Germany. His first novel, *The Village of Souls*, however, is the only piece of fiction set in a historical period before his own lifetime.

The Village of Souls portrays several months of life in the 17th-century colony of New France and includes commentary on Indian ways of life and differences between Indians and Europeans. While the overwhelming wilderness is perhaps the most powerful presence in the novel, primarily the narrative is focused on the polarized contrasts between individuals. Jornay, the male protagonist, is a well-born but poor young immigrant from France—with a marked tendency towards introspection and a conscious search for self-knowledge—who has become a *coureur de bois*. Lys, his wife of only a few weeks, has, although she is also aristocratic, come to New France as a *fille du roi* (as were known the single women imported to ease the shortage of potential wives) and is fearful of sharing what is to her a terrible secret. Titange is a violent and unreliable *métis* or halfbreed, a brutal figure with only the crudest of consciences. Anne is a young Indian runaway, initially a primitive following the message of a dream but gradually becoming indoctrinated into Christianity and the white man's ways. And Father Bernard is a devout Jesuit missionary, committed to the saving of souls and lured by the prospect of discovering a river to the west.

In this presentation of human spirits and their torments, *The Village of Souls* is typical of all of Child's work. Certainly, it is emblematic of his common concerns and themes in its demonstration of modernist humanism. Jornay and the two women are engaged in the pursuit of inner peace and happiness, and all come eventually to adopt a faith founded in human relations in the face of a cosmically ironic universe. Interestingly, Lys, the white woman, both explains her understanding of this modernist "truth" and parallels the narrative itself by telling Jornay an Indian story in which a man must choose between a charm from his past that commits him to "the village of souls" and a female guide who cannot live in this land of the dead. As the narrator's final appraisal makes clear, "only in the consummation of love can a man share his loneliness with another and make for himself a dust-speck world within the infinite wilderness, forgetting for a little its pressure which never entirely ceases upon a man's spirit." Even so, the future holds no guarantees; Jornay knows only that "life would go on."

As historical realist fiction, the novel is deliberately situated in a specific setting and time. Quotations from contemporary documents, such as *The Jesuit Relation*, as chapter epigrams contribute to its sense of authenticity, and generally the narrative strives to reproduce a genuine flavour of the time. Although the narrator's 20th-century philosophical concerns at times seem imposed upon characters to whom mere physical survival is so clearly paramount, the novel accords well with other Canadian works describing this historical period. In addition, the author protects himself in a prefacing "note" admitting some variations in historical fact and claiming a story-teller's license to "treat imaginatively the character and passions of individuals."

The Village of Souls is considered by many readers to be Child's most finely developed novel. It is perhaps flawed by an uneven portrayal of its female characters and a tendency to define Indians as a race of subhuman savages. (Notably, Anne, who is permitted to rise above this evaluation, is also suspected of being at least part white.) Notwithstanding these problems, however, the novel is carefully crafted and presents an interesting example of the modernist rewriting of early Canadian history.

—M. Jeanne Yardley.

CHOLMONDELEY, Alice. See **Elizabeth.**

CHRISTIE, Agatha. See **WESTMACOTT, Mary.**

CHURCHILL, Winston. American. Born in St. Louis, Missouri, 10 November 1871. Educated at Smith Academy, St. Louis, 1879–88; United States Naval Academy, Annapolis, Maryland, 1890–94; naval cadet on the cruiser *San Francisco*, New York Navy Yard, 1894. Married Mabel Harlakenden Hall in 1895 (died 1945); one daughter and two sons. Editor, *Army and Navy Journal*, New York, 1894; managing editor, *Cosmopolitan*, New York, 1895; full-time writer from 1895; Republican member for Cornish, New Hampshire Legislature, 1903–05; delegate for New Hampshire, Republican National Convention, Chicago, 1904; Progressive Party candidate for the New Hampshire governorship, 1912; toured European battle fronts, and wrote for *Scribner's*, New York, 1917–18. President, Authors League of America, 1913. *Died 12 March 1947.*

ROMANCE AND HISTORICAL PUBLICATIONS

Novels

Richard Carvel. New York and London, Macmillan, 1899.
The Crisis. New York and London, Macmillan, 1901.
The Crossing. New York and London, Macmillan, 1904.

OTHER PUBLICATIONS

Novels

The Celebrity: An Episode. New York and London, Macmillan, 1898.
Coniston. New York and London, Macmillan, 1906.
Mr. Crewe's Career. New York and London, Macmillan, 1908.
A Modern Chronicle. New York and London, Macmillan, 1910.
The Inside of the Cup. New York and London, Macmillan, 1913.
A Far Country. New York and London, Macmillan, 1915.
The Dwelling-Place of Light. New York and London, Macmillan, 1917.

Short Stories

Mr. Keegan's Elopement. New York and London, Macmillan, 1903.

Plays

The Crisis, adaptation of his own novel (produced New York, 1902). New York, French, 1927.
The Title-Mart (produced London, 1905; New York, 1906). New York, Macmillan, 1905.
The Crossing, with Louis Evan Shipman, adaptation of the novel by Churchill (produced New York, 1906).
Dr. Jonathan. New York, Macmillan, 1919.

Other

A Traveller in War-Time, With an Essay on the American Contribution and the Democratic Idea. New York, Macmillan, 1918.
The Green Bay Tree. New York, Macmillan, 1920.
The Uncharted Way: The Psychology of the Gospel Doctrine. Philadelphia, Dorrance, 1940.

*

Bibliography: *Winston Churchill: A Reference Guide* by Eric Steinbaugh, Boston, Hall, 1985.

Critical Studies: *The Romantic Compromise in the Novels of Winston Churchill* by Charles C. Walcutt, Ann Arbor, University of Michigan, 1951; *Winston Churchill* by Warren I. Titus, New

York, Twayne, 1963; *Novelist to a Generation: The Life and Thought of Winston Churchill* by Robert W. Schneider, Bowling Green, Ohio, Popular Press, 1976.

*   *   *

Winston Churchill (no relation to the British statesman) has apparently always seemed a little old-fashioned. In 1911 a contemporary labeled him a mid-Victorian who had not recognized an advance or change in the art of fiction since the work of William Makepeace Thackeray. If he seemed old-fashioned in his own day he must seem doubly so today. Indeed he rather smells of Victorian houses and mothballs, and he makes one think of reading triple-decker novels aloud on the porch or in the sitting room in the evening.

This old-fashionedness is especially apparent in Churchill's three historical romances written early in his career. The first, *Richard Carvel*, is set in pre-Revolutionary War Maryland with a long episode in London and a short but adventurous episode on the high seas. The second, *The Crisis*, is set mostly in Civil War St. Louis. The third, *The Crossing*, deals with westward expansion and has the broadest scope of all, ranging from South Carolina to the Kentucky wilderness, and from the old Northwest to New Orleans.

Churchill took particular care to be historically accurate in his novels. He always did his homework, reading the historical material available to him and carefully checking historical facts. He paid special attention to biographies and used them to benefit his fiction. Famous people are liberally sprinkled throughout his novels in both minor and major roles. In *Richard Carvel* such notables as George Washington, John Paul Jones, Horace Walpole, and Charles Fox play roles of varying importance. In *The Crisis* Lincoln is an important character and Generals Grant and Sherman make brief appearances. In *The Crossing* with its theme of exploration of the wilderness and battles for the territories such predictable historical figures as Daniel Boone, Andrew Jackson, and George Rogers Clark play significant roles.

In general Churchill's skill in portraying historical figures is better when the figures are minor characters rather than major ones, something that is also true of his fictive characters. For example, in *The Crisis* his picture of Lincoln, a major character much praised by the critics, is not entirely satisfactory. He is too much the grand figure of legend, too much the genial but tragic jokester to emerge as fully realized. In fact *The Crisis* is brought to a symbolic and highly predictable end by Lincoln serving as a go-between for the marriage of the hero, a Union officer, and a pro-Confederate Southern belle as a symbolic healing gesture. Although this surely has pleased many readers it is more cliché than literary art.

Churchill's historical novels all have the strong mark of their author, and thus the reader will receive a good introduction to his work by reading any of the three. They certainly have the same strengths and weaknesses. Churchill is almost always good at evoking atmosphere and scene. His portrayal of history seems accurate, and he is able to capture the essence of a minor character whether from history or totally from his imagination quickly and effectively. In contrast, his weaknesses are all too glaring to the modern reader. His plotting is loose and episodic and he relies too heavily on coincidence. His handling of romance is sentimental and awkward. He also has difficulty drawing major characters who are almost always entirely virtuous and noble or villainous and ignoble, and what is worse he cannot refrain from making this point repeatedly. Finally, Churchill tries to do too much in each novel. His novels are too long and too broad in their scope given his constant repetitions and his penchant for seeing everything through the restricted sense of absolute right and wrong.

Although it is easy to find fault with Churchill's novels, in each of them there are moments rendered with considerable skill. In *Richard Carvel* both 18th-century Maryland and London are effectively portrayed in detail. *The Crisis* is an outstanding depiction of Civil War St. Louis with its conflict between the pro-Union mostly Dutch-German population and the pro-Confederate aristocrats of the city. *The Crossing* has effective wilderness scenes and battles and creates a memorable picture of New Orleans during a particularly volatile time.

Although Churchill originally planned to follow *The Crossing* with other historical romances, other interests intervened, and he shifted to other genres never to return to the historical novel. However, between 1899 and 1904 he wrote three of the most popular historical novels ever produced in America, and in doing so he created two avenues into the American past. First, his novels as highly successful bestsellers are important barometers of public taste in reading at the turn of the century, and second and more importantly in their historical accuracy and skillful evocation of important events and scenes from American history, these novels do what all good historical fiction does, that is create a strong sense of the atmosphere of the past.

—Larry Olpin

CLARE, Ellen. See **SINCLAIR, Olga.**

CLARKE, Brenda (Margaret Lilian, née Honeyman). British. Born in Bristol, 30 July 1926. Educated at Red Maids' School, Westbury-on-Trym, Bristol. Married Ronald John Clarke in 1955; one son and one daughter. Civil Service clerical officer, Bristol, 1943–55. Agent: David Grossman Literary Agency, 110–114 Clerkenwell Road, London EC1M 5SA. Address: 25 Torridge Road, Keynsham, Bristol, Avon BS18 1QQ, England.

ROMANCE AND HISTORICAL PUBLICATIONS

Novels

The Glass Island. London, Collins, 1978.
The Lofty Banners. New York, Fawcett, 1979; London, Hamlyn, 1980.
The Far Morning. London, Hamlyn, and New York, Fawcett, 1982.
All Through the Day. London, Hamlyn, 1983.
A Rose in May. London, Hutchinson, 1984.
Three Women. London, Hutchinson, 1985.
Winter Landscape. London, Century Hutchinson, 1986.
Under Heaven. London, Bantam, 1988.
An Equal Chance. London, Bantam, 1989.

Novels as Brenda Honeyman

Richard by Grace of God. London, Hale, 1968.
The Kingmaker. London, Hale, 1969.
Richmond and Elizabeth. London, Hale, 1970; New York, Pinnacle, 1973.

Harry the King. London, Hale, 1971; as *The Warrior King*, New York, Pinnacle, 1972.
Brother Bedford. London, Hale, 1972.
Good Duke Humphrey. London, Hale, 1973.
The King's Minions. London, Hale, 1974.
The Queen and Mortimer. London, Hale, 1974.
Edward the Warrior. London, Hale, 1975.
All the King's Sons. London, Hale, 1976.
The Golden Griffin. London, Hale, 1976.
At the King's Court. London, Hale, 1977.
The King's Tale. London, Hale, 1977.
Macbeth, King of Scots. London, Hale, 1977.
Emma the Queen. London, Hale, 1978.
Harold of the English. London, Hale, 1979.

*   *   *

As Brenda Honeyman, Brenda Clarke wrote about a dozen historical novels, set mostly in the 14th to 16th centuries. Stylistically, these works are well-crafted and readable, but contain little to distinguish them from the many others written within this framework. In her attempts to encompass a complex period of history, and to portray as many of the characters and events as possible (within the restrictions of the brief formulaic novel), Clarke achieves only a superficial treatment of her subject. A review of *Harry the King* says that "Brenda Honeyman leaves no royal relation unmentioned nor any royal relationship unexplained"; this may have been intended as a compliment, but in fact can be seen as a disadvantage in the context of a relatively brief novel.

Edward the Warrior deals with the reign of Edward III, a period attractive to chroniclers of medieval history; the events are described in a straightforward fashion, and the dialogue is mercifully unembellished with prithees or sithees. However, in introducing the full range of major personages of the period, and in describing numerous events in a fairly brief narrative, Honeyman does not give her characters a chance to develop and does not give the reader any real understanding of those characters or of the situations. The rare introduction of non-essential description (e.g., "Her hands beat together on her lap, two white birds, hovering frustratedly in a silken cage") strikes the reader as incongruous and a trifle extravagant.

In turning to a different type of fiction, written under her married name, Brenda Clarke did both herself and her readers a great service, and turned to advantage her predilection for broad canvasses and large casts of characters. All her novels have strong central female characters but these do vary markedly—there are those who were born independent, and those who achieve independence (and even one who has independence thrust upon her!).

The first type is exemplified by Elizabeth Evans in *Three Women*, who even at the age of 14 acts independently of her parents to defy her older sister's employer. She goes on to query the role of women and takes a job which has traditionally always been performed by men, eventually starting her own money lending business, flying in the face of her staunch Methodist background. Integral to the plot is a veritable waltz of romantic partners: Lizzie is loved by Jack but she herself loves Ben, who becomes the second husband of Lizzie's cousin Helen. Lizzie eventually marries Jack, but only after both she and he have been widowed (he by Lizzie's sister Mary, she by her sister Mary's stepson). Confused? Who wouldn't be! The whole delicate counterpoint is marred only by the too-convenient deaths of the two unpleasant and redundant (to the plot) male characters.

These deaths, while admittedly very useful, strike a contrived note in a novel in which nothing else has come easily, and it is Lizzie's own fierce independence which has contributed to the complications in her own and other people's romantic relationships.

In a similar vein, *The Far Morning*, while being a novel built round a vast complexity of characters and relationships, also tackles all the issues traditional to novels written about the first half of this century—the effect of World War I, the role of women, and changes in society and the class system. This scenario is now very common in romantic fiction and for a sound reason, as all the components listed above provide an ideal background against which to portray a thoughtful and intelligent heroine.

Winter Landscape and *All Through the Day* both have heroines who at the beginning of their respective stories are subordinate characters, and who by the end are independent, even dominant. Sally in *Winter Landscape* has our sympathy from the very beginning when, aged 16, she is dominated and overshadowed by her extremely bitchy and totally selfish mother. Sally loves two men: the German prisoner of war Werner and the older married Charles. As in many romantic novels Sally has what seems to be the best of both worlds, and marries the two men in turn, but both she and her two respective husbands go through much unhappiness and self denial.

In contrast, Emily in *All Through the Day* is initially selfish and weak, but becomes a strong, independent, and even manipulative businesswoman, although the reader's credulity is somewhat strained when she quotes Nietzsche. In both this novel and *Three Women* the heroine's strength contrasts with the weakness of virtually all the other female characters, and the two novels also have in common an immensely complicated web of relationships.

It is obvious from the name of the heroine of *An Equal Chance* (Harriet Chance-Canossa-Contarini-Cavendish-Georgiadis-Wingfield) that this lady has had more married partners than the average person has had hot dinners. Taken to the United States as a pregnant G.I. bride, Harriet is abandoned by her husband and is forced to become self-reliant, and this she achieves despite, rather than because of, her succession of husbands and other partners. Although in most of Clarke's novels the complexities of the relationships defy belief, the books nevertheless remain interesting and readable. Only when her heroine starts as a comparative nonentity and does not develop in the course of the novel, (Katherine in *Under Heaven*), does the narrative ever lack pace and fail to capture the reader's interest.

—Judith Rhodes

———————

CLAVELL, James (du Maresq). American. Born in England, 10 October 1942; moved to the United States in 1953; became citizen, 1963. Educated at Portsmouth Grammar School; University of Birmingham, 1946–47. Served with the Royal Artillery, 1940–46; prisoner of war in the Far East, 1941–45. Married April Stride in 1953; two daughters. Carpenter, 1953–54. Since 1954 screenwriter, director, and producer. Recipient: Writers Guild award, for screenplay, 1964. Ph.D.: University of Maryland, College Park, 1980; D. Litt.: University of Bradford, 1986. Address: c/o Foreign Rights Inc., 200 West 57th Street, Suite 1007, New York, New York 10019, U.S.A.

ROMANCE AND HISTORICAL PUBLICATIONS

Novels

Tai-Pan: A Novel of Hong Kong. New York, Atheneum, 1966;
London, Joseph, 1967.
Shōgun. New York, Atheneum, and London, Hodder and
Stoughton, 1975.
Noble House. New York, Delacorte Press, and London, Hodder
and Stoughton, 1981.
Whirlwind. New York, Morrow, and London, Hodder and
Stoughton, 1986.

OTHER PUBLICATIONS

Novel

King Rat. Boston, Little Brown, 1962; London, Joseph, 1963.

Plays

Screenplays: *The Fly*, 1958; *Watusi*, 1959; *Five Gates to Hell*,
1959; *Walk Like a Dragon*, with Daniel Mainwaring, 1960; *The
Great Escape*, with W. R. Burnett, 1963; *633 Squadron*, with
Howard Koch, 1964; *The Satan Bug*, with Edward Anhalt, 1965;
To Sir, With Love, 1967; *The Last Valley*, 1970; *Children's
Story . . . But Not for Children*, 1982.

Other

Children's Story, with Michaela Clavell Crisman. New York,
Delacorte Press, 1981; London, Hodder and Stoughton, 1982.
Thrump-o-moto, with G. Sharp and Ken Wilson. New York,
Delacorte Press, and London, Hodder and Stoughton, 1986.

Editor, *The Art of War*, by Sun Tzu. London, Hodder and
Stoughton, 1981; New York, Delacorte Press, 1983.

*

Theatrical Activities:
Director: **Films**—*Five Gates to Hell*, 1959; *Walk Like a
Dragon*,1960; *To Sir, With Love*, 1967; *Where's Jack?*, 1969;
The Last Valley, 1970; *Children's Story . . . But Not for Chil-
dren*, 1982.

*   *   *

English-born American novelist James Clavell is most famous
for his action-packed Far and Mid-Eastern historical adventures.
Notable for their energy and scope, they combine treachery, intrigue, sex, and violence, with local color, studies of Oriental
minds, and analyses of money and power in action.

These works depend on a clash of cultures, with Elizabethan
Englishmen encountering Japanese Warlords (*Shōgun*); 19th-
century British learning to deal with Hong Kong Chinese (*Tai-
Pan*), and passing on the clash of cultures and ideologies to their
20th-century descendants (*Noble House*); World War II American and British prisoners of war facing the horrors and alienation of a Japanese prison camp (*King Rat*); and Westerners
getting caught up in the Islamic reforms of post-Shah Iran
(*Whirlwind*). They provide interesting studies in culture. *Tai-Pan*
and *Noble House*, for example, give a good sense of the manners, mores, business attitudes and methods, and politics of both
the British and the Chinese as they bring to life the Hong Kong
motto, "moh ching, moh meng," "No money, no life." *Shōgun*,
in turn, captures the flavor of samurai intrigue as the Japanese
warlord Toranaga (based on a real warlord) and his associates
draw the shipwrecked Englishman Blackthorne into their plots
and counterplots and cleverly exploit him, all the while deluding
him into thinking he is in control of his fate. It depicts the very
different attitudes of Japanese and Europeans toward baths, sex,
food, and drink, and the very different perspectives that allow
each to learn from each.

These novels all deal with questions of survival: what must
prisoners endure to survive? how does the process of survival
change an individual? what special effort does it take to found
and preserve a dynasty? how can one protect a company or a
territory from take-overs by rival businessmen, rival politicians,
rival leaders? how can one deal with fanatics or with those who
break all the rules of civilized conflict? *King Rat*, Clavell's first
novel, based on the repugnant and terrifying three years he himself spent in a Japanese prisoner of war camp, studies human
nature under survival stress: the grim physical suffering, the
moral deterioration, the chicanery, the callousness, the black humor situations, the fundamental confusion of men cut off from
the familiar and safe, the Darwinian struggle for food and dominance. Within the Changi compound thousands face the evil
depersonalization of torture and abuse, of subhuman living conditions, of rats, cholera, lice, and filth, some to escape into insanity, others to turn informant, scavenger, or bully, and a very
few to rise to the heroic. Therein a frighteningly adaptable
American corporal, "the King," a man determined to survive no
matter the cost to his compatriots, and an aristocratic British
flight lieutenant, Peter Marlowe, who becomes the "King's"
best friend, are played off against the provost marshal, lieutenant
Grey, who values rank, honor, integrity, and sharing and who
passionately hates both the corporal and the flight lieutenant for
compromising these values. When peace returns, the skeletal
survivors find the insanity of their animal existence more secure
than the horrified stares of their appalled rescuers. In *Shōgun*
Blackthorne, a seaman shipwrecked in Japan, must not only
adapt to an alien culture but learn to work within its intricate
systems of courtesy and obligation. In *Tai-Pan* and *Noble House*
those businessmen who survive learn to play by the very taxing
"Hong Kong" rules.

Often in a Clavell novel survival is inexorably linked to finances, with men gambling on life by gambling on business
odds and with a lust for money and for power determining motive and act. In *Tai-Pan* an Englishman, Dirk Struan, and a Chinese of the Chen clan join forces to secure English rights to
Hong Kong. In the process the Scottish Struan becomes "Tai-
Pan" ("big-shot"), borrows $5 million in silver from an Orien-
tal tycoon, invents binoculars, corners the world supply of
cinchona bark, sets up a plan to smash the Triads, and founds a
dynasty, but one that depends on its Chinese associates to help it
deal with cutthroat business operations, tea and opium dealers,
pirates, betrayals, treacheries, and intrigues. The novel explores
the Chinese concept of "face" and "joss" and the Oriental
sense of long-term familial obligations passed on from generation to generation, but mainly in relationship to the rise and fall
of great houses. *Noble House* continues the saga, focusing on
Ian Dunross, the new heir-apparent to the banking house and
international shipping firm established by Dirk Struan. As he
juggles international concerns and struggles to protect free enterprise and to undercut the Soviet threat to Hong Kong, he, at
the same time, protects women and children, maintains a lucrative base to support his friends and relatives, and worries about
fulfilling obligations assumed a century before. The plot centers
around an economic war for control of the Noble house, a war

involving shifting alliances, sexual liaisons, lush parties, attacks on banks and airlines, kidnapping, murder, swindles, and espionage. The rival houses of Dunross and Gornt use bank runs and the stock market to battle each other, while the KGB, MI.6, the CIA, the People's Republic of China, the Mafia, and the Macao gold traders join in this power play behind the scenes, with each vying for the most advantageous alliance or compromise. Both heroes and villains are ruthless entrepreneurs, with the only real difference the fact that the villains will sacrifice anyone to attain their goals while the hero will perhaps use the same tactics or tools, but to take care of those dependent on him. Each stands alone, battling to the end. *Whirlwind* continues the sagas begun in the earlier books, bringing together representatives of the Noble House who are struggling to control helicopter concessions in war-torn Iran, and the descendants of the house of Toranaga, representing the Toda shipping company, struggling to gain oil and gas concessions for Japan in the Persian Gulf.

Whenever Clavell depicts male rivalry for position, power, and wealth, he also includes a rivalry for love. Often Clavell's central characters fall madly in love with an alien woman, young, beautiful, and fascinating because of her totally different perspective, manners, and values. Sometimes she is a plant by a business rival, intended to distract and to spy; at other times she is what she seems; but always male and female prove as different as the different cultures portrayed in the works, as if they were races apart, intriguing, possessable, but forever alien.

In all Clavell's works there are arbitrary shifts in point of view, lots of interior monologue, and a gigantic cast of sometimes interchangeable characters (30 to 40 in *Noble House*). The plots are at times unwieldy, and, where there is no one central character, diffuse. Nevertheless, the background is always carefully and intelligently established to make another world come alive for readers. One is left with the flavor of Hong Kong, her people and their values, or of 16th-century Japan, with its high culture and its barbarism. It is this sensitivity to worlds apart that raises Clavell's work above the average historical adventure-romance.

—Andrew and Gina Macdonald

CLAYTON, C(olin) Guy. British. Born in Horsham, Sussex, 5 November 1936. Educated at Collyer's Grammar School, Horsham, 1947–55; Hertford College, Oxford, 1958–61, M.A. in English 1961. Served in the Royal Army Education Corps, 1956–58. Married Linda-Jane Pashley in 1970; two sons. Teacher at a boys grammar school, Ashby de la Zouch, Leicestershire, 1961–63, and at Devonport High School for Boys, Plymouth, 1963–76. Since 1976 teacher, St. Ninians High School, Douglas, Isle of Man. Agent: London Management, 235 Regent Street, London W1A 2JT. Address: Davian, Main Road, Foxdale, Isle of Man, United Kingdom.

ROMANCE AND HISTORICAL PUBLICATIONS

Novels (series: Blakeney Papers in all books)

Daughters of the Revolution. London, Macdonald, 1984.
Such a Mighty Race. London, Macdonald, 1985.
Bordeaux Red. London, Macdonald, 1986.

*

C. Guy Clayton comments:

The initial idea for the Blakeney papers came in a single moment. I happened to glance through a copy of *The Scarlet Pimpernel* I came upon while sorting out a school stock cupboard and two separate compartments of my mind came together with a click. Why, I asked myself was all fiction of the French Revolution ignorant of any development in historical knowledge since Lamartine and Carlyle? What was needed was an energetic series of novels showing at least some sympathy with the revolutionary point of view. Baroness Orczy's heroine was a potential gem, provided of course one stripped away the sentimental façade and exposed the woman she really was; an actress in the Comédie Française who knew real people and lived through the most extraordinary political event of the past thousand years. So that was my purpose; to write living stories of the revolutionary period, while at the same time remaining true to the real events as the 20th century sees them rather than a 19th-century myth.

*   *   *

There are as many versions of history as there are authors. Historians rewrite truths—certain occurrences cannot be denied, but their significance is open to interpretation, after which the events themselves sink into comparative oblivion. C. Guy Clayton adapts this process, presenting the already invented world of the Scarlet Pimpernel as historical fact, based on a contemporary manuscript complete with editorial notes. It becomes impossible to distinguish the fiction, and his resulting trilogy is richer than the original Baroness Orczy story and more realistic than a bare listing of the highlights of the French Revolution.

The narrator and central character is Marie Callot, daughter of a small-town lawyer who changes her identity and sex at the drop of a powdered wig. En route she writes the history of France, England, and the rest of Europe too. She first makes her mark when, as a teenager, she composes a poem on behalf of Robespierre enabling him to join the Societé des Rosati and thus further his career, becomes a member of the Jacobin Club agitating for a new France, and eventually even marries Percy Blakeney to spy for her country. What she fails to do is create herself with similar gusto.

Marie is intelligent, but never considers the academic reasons or future effects of her actions. Theory and speechifying have always precipitated the most crucial events in her life and consequently she has no great faith in the books she reads. Living for the moment means she can never be a full person with a developed philosophy of how she got there, why, and where to now, but her strength is this simplicity. Immediate reality is all that matters and without this lack of self-awareness she would become tangled in doubt and end up guillotined with the people she hates.

Altering appearance and personality leads occasionally to inconsistency. It seems hard to reconcile the honoured figure who was present at the storming of the Bastille with the coquette who later devotes herself to redecorating her new husband's stately home and complains about the ineptitude of English plasterers, but, thanks to the narrator's skills, this reconciliation happens. Marie exemplifies the flightiness of the stereo-typical irrational female (albeit with a more developed instinct for self-preservation then most) but is accepted by us because of her style.

She tells her story in lively ingenuous language, with enough self-deprecation to hover this side of false modesty. She claims that everyone is equal and later scorns her husband's common touch with inn-keepers and ostlers, but we remain charmed. Marie's disgust with the two tramps scavenging the smouldering remains of a convent is our disgust because we see the scene through her eyes, and like her we dismiss it because we too realise that the Revolution has solved few problems. She expresses her cynicism with a witty remark, and consequently we remain on her side and at one with her perceptions.

Marie is bullied, raped, insulted, beaten, pursued, imprisoned, and virtually drowned. She betrays, commits sacrilege, murders, steals, fights, and impersonates her way through life. It's gory, but we are reminded of this only occasionally when she interrupts her pacy tale with a chilling phrase or sentence. At the height of her success at the Comédie Française for example, she announces in a new, hollow tone that "one night after the performance I had a caller at the theatre" thus heralding a change for the worse. Despite her enthusiastic descriptions, danger is never very far away, but her humour generally protects us from it.

In addition, the bloodiness of the Revolution itself is kept in perspective by high comedy. The account of her wedding night, the coach-trip she shares with her lover, former paramour, and husband crammed into a confined space getting along famously and the constant bumbling of the francophobic Dewhurst are some of many moments of pure farce which belie the violence of the times. Marie is not only the prima donna of the French theatre, she is very much Clayton's leading lady, playing a part worthy of Racine on the stage of one of the most important events of the 18th century.

Marie's view of history is that it only justifies the Revolution. The author is equally dismissive. He uses history to achieve objectivity (which is the legitimate stance of the genuine historian) and then treats events and chronology with the manipulation of the novelist and the disdain of the farceur. What happens when is less important than what it signifies—a means of distancing themes. Issues such as the role of women in a society where their only access to power is through deceit or seduction and the nature of violence as a revolutionary tool appear frequently, but no solutions are offered.

England's answer is rule by the vapid and fatuous Prinny, and a parliamentary process which depends on the appearance of Whig or Tory on ball invitation lists for its effectiveness—an unacceptable compromise of democracy. France fares no better, because the successors to the aristocratic order prove that mastery still belongs to human imperfection. Robespierre is paranoid and every provincial civil servant is bureaucratic, corrupt, or just plain stupid. This is what Marie should oppose, but tragically she lacks the analytical skills to see it, and the position to do anything about it. But our disappointment never lasts for long because of Clayton's skill in blending so many disparate elements—history, fiction, myth, drama, and adventure with very stylish wit.

—L. M. Quinn

CLEEVE, Brian (Brendan Talbot). Irish. Born in Thorpe Bay, Essex, England, 22 November 1921. Educated at Selwyn House, Broadstairs, Kent, 1930–35; St. Edward's School, Oxford, 1935–38; University of South Africa, Johannesburg, 1951–53, B.A. 1953; National University of Ireland, Dublin, 1954–56, Ph.D. 1956. Served in the British Merchant Navy, 1939–45. Married Veronica McAdie in 1945; two daughters. Freelance journalist in South Africa, 1948–54, and in Ireland since 1954.

Broadcaster, Radio Telefis Eireann, Dublin, 1962–72. Address: 60 Heytesbury Lane, Ballsbridge, Dublin 4, Ireland.

ROMANCE AND HISTORICAL PUBLICATIONS

Novels

Cry of Morning. London, Joseph, 1971; as *The Triumph of O'Rourke*, New York, Doubleday, 1972.
Sara. London, Cassell, and New York, Coward McCann, 1976.
Kate. London, Cassell, and New York, Coward McCann, 1977.
Judith. London, Cassell, and New York, Coward McCann, 1978.
Hester. London, Cassell, 1979; New York, Coward McCann, 1980.
The House on the Rock. London, Watkins, 1980.
The Seven Mansions. London, Watkins, 1980.
The Fourth Mary. Dublin, Co-op, 1982.

OTHER PUBLICATIONS

Novels

The Far Hills. London, Jarrolds, 1952.
Portrait of My City. London, Jarrolds, 1952.
Birth of a Dark Soul. London, Jarrolds, 1953; as *The Night Winds*, Boston, Houghton Mifflin, 1954.
Assignment to Vengeance. London, Hammond, 1961.
Death of a Painted Lady. London, Hammond, 1962; New York, Random House, 1963.
Death of a Wicked Servant. London, Hammond, 1963; New York, Random House, 1964.
Vote X for Treason. London, Collins, 1964; New York, Random House, 1965; as *Counterspy*, London, Lancer, 1966.
Dark Blood, Dark Terror. New York, Random House, 1965; London, Hammond, 1966.
The Judas Goat. London, Hammond, 1966; as *Vice Isn't Private*, New York, Random House, 1966.
Violent Death of a Bitter Englishman. New York, Random House, 1967; London, Corgi, 1969.
You Must Never Go Back. New York, Random House, 1968.
Exit from Prague. London, Corgi, 1970; as *Escape from Prague*, New York, Pinnacle, 1973.
Tread Softly in This Place. London, Cassell, and New York, Day, 1972.
The Dark Side of the Sun. London, Cassell, 1973.
A Question of Inheritance. London, Cassell, 1974; as *For Love of Crannagh Castle*, New York, Dutton, 1975.

Short Stories

The Horse Thieves of Ballysaggert and Other Stories. Cork, Mercier Press, 1966.

Other

Colonial Policies in Africa. Johannesburg, St. Benedict's House, 1954.
Dictionary of Irish Writers. Cork, Mercier Press, 3 vols., 1967–71; revised edition, with Anne M. Brady, as *A Biographical Dictionary of Irish Writers*, Mullingar, Westmeath, Lilliput Press, and New York, St. Martin's Press, 1 vol., 1985.
1938: A World Vanishing. London, Buchan and Enright, 1982.
A View of the Irish. London, Buchan and Enright, 1983.

Editor, *W. B. Yeats and the Designing of Ireland's Coinage*. Dublin, Dolmen Press, 1972.

*

Manuscript Collection: Mugar Memorial Library, Boston University.

*

Brian Cleeve comments:

I began writing romantic fiction by mistake. I meant to write a historical family saga covering the 19th century, beginning with a Spanish gypsy orphan in the Peninsular War. She took over the book and the whole novel became her story, as *Sara*. People liked the book, and I wrote three more, with vaguely similar themes, and young heroines in extravagant, romantic, yet historically accurate (I hope) situations. I thought of them as historical novels rather than as romances. I wanted to explore the idea of young women striving for personal liberation at a period when this was becoming even more difficult to achieve than it had been a hundred years earlier.

*   *   *

Irish writer Brian Cleeve has achieved international attention for his hard-hitting, sometimes brutal analyses of national and international conflicts in his spy and murder novels, and some of these same qualities and concerns are also reflected in his romances. Therein he has been particularly concerned with man, government, and religion's cruelty to women. His hard-boiled crime novels begin the pattern of rape and sadism, hypocrisy, racism, class conflicts, and "machismo" that his romances continue to explore from a historical perspective.

Cleeve's Regency romances continue past concerns, but with a new twist, following Dickensian patterns to expose the horrors of 19th-century life (the wars and revolutions, the poverty and crime, the prisons and insane asylums) and to provide a vivid picture of the daily life of young people trapped and initially defenseless amid the follies of their day. There are vivid descriptions of the snares and seductions of Regency London: gaming houses and gentlemen's clubs, sparring rings and cockpits, country-house weekends and an underworld of pickpockets and assassins. These works are also Dickensian in their sentimentality and their emphasis on class differences as a major source of evil. Their villains are ruthless and powerful, their heroines initially naive and vulnerable.

In *Judith*, a young lady, pressured by her father's illness and the resultant financial necessity, consorts with smugglers and suffers the consequences—choosing the brutal horrors of Bedlam and the unforgiving poverty of London streets over a loveless, shameful marriage to a rich pervert. The description of Bedlam is particularly grim and terrible. The heroine of *Sara*, a gypsy girl trained in rural witchcraft, works in a disreputable gambling house, while that of *Kate*, an actress by trade and a rebel by heart, consorts with the London "Upright Men" to promote smuggling operations. Sara has witnessed her parents' slaughter by Bonaparte's soldiers in Spain, while Kate is the sole survivor of a political massacre; both barely escape the London white slave market. *Hester*'s women, caught up in the monstrosities and injustices of the French Revolution, its glories and insanities, act on principles, not necessity; Hester herself learns to ride, fight and kill like a man, to accept discomfort and daily knowledge of possible death, and yet to retain her feminine allure and self-respect.

Each of these works focuses on women from the past who are swept along by history, trapped by sexual roles, and forced into choices that can destroy them; they must learn to deal with human cruelty, prejudice, hypocrisy, and greed. Their histories are a tangled web of love and intrigue, class conflicts, and sexual battles, as they seek to liberate themselves from the strictures of a hypocritical society and learn to trust instinct, to reassess old values, and finally to seize their destiny like a man. Writing in a feminist tradition, Cleeve depicts women who are as passionate, proud, resourceful, and daring as men, tossed by fate, bound by social manacles, oppressed by brutal males, but capable of rising above their psychological, economic, and sometimes physical chains to find meaning, purpose, and strength. It is as if he sees in the abuse of women the same mentality at work that he depicts so vividly in his treatment of racism in South Africa.

Cleeve captures the nuances of street slang and dialect, and includes highly sensory, detailed descriptions of place. His historical details are accurate and credible, and vividly reflect an interplay of culture and values and opposing philosophies. His main characters are alienated from each other and their world; absurdist figures, out of place and out of step in a sinister universe, a world gone mad, one that sweeps them blindly and helplessly toward the unknown, sometimes disastrously, sometimes successfully. Ultimately what makes life endurable are the human touchstones; his heroines' sense of personal responsibility for the weak, the injured, the vulnerable lends them strength and helps them survive and thrive. Through his romances Cleeve provides graphic and realistic images of man's inhumanity to man, to take a moral stance against political and social oppression and against inhumanity in its varied forms. He faces pain and human misery head on, vividly evoking the shivers of a malaria attack or the pangs of chronic dysentery. His heroine, Sara, is a shining model of goodness set against the wickedness and degradation of most of Cleeve's characters; an orphan herself, she burdens her life with caring for orphans, and finds it a joy, as she argues, "When you see a child cold and hungry and naked and afraid, it is quite a natural thing to wish to take care of it."

Cleeve's Irish works at their best are novels of manners, capturing shifting Irish scenes, interweaving sub-themes and subplots, interspersing social commentary, and drawing a variety of vivid character portraits: fanatical communist, radical priest, itinerant tinker, posing artist, real estate tycoon, television commentator, small-town girl made good. *Cry of Morning*, in particular, has been called "one of the best recent novels in modern Ireland," partly because of its rendering of Ireland's metamorphosis from a 19th-century hold-over to a 20th-century economically important nation and its questioning of values that place country above citizens. Ultimately, Cleeve's vision of Ireland and its people is one of paradox—a charming mix of good and bad.

Cleeve's most recent efforts, controversial religious studies that have become bestsellers in Ireland, are the stories of people who lived in Jerusalem at the time of the Crucifixion. Written to convey an unorthodox, though Catholic, spiritual view, they defy classification. *The Fourth Mary* in particular has a striking point of view: that of a servant girl attached to the High Priestess of a sado-masochistic cult, Judas' lover; in other words, it is the Crucifixion story told from the viewpoint of Christ's enemies, enemies who planned it and consider it a triumph. The other two books, *The House on the Rock* and *The Seven Mansions*, provide the historical background preparatory to the Crucifixion. Despite its religious focus, this trilogy graphically portrays the hatred, sadism, and sexuality of characters caught up in events of historical moment.

Cleeve brings to history and romance a social conscience and raises questions of social justice, national character, and personal responsibility. Even his religious histories powerfully dramatize the excuses that ordinary men and women invent to avoid involvement and to deny the realities of suffering and oppression. In sum, they key lesson of Cleeve's canon is that any violation of human dignity and freedom, whether race against race, class against class, or man against woman, is a reversion to the animal savagery of man's Darwinian origins, and must be fought tooth and claw if civilization and mankind are to endure.

—Gina Macdonald

CLEUGH, Sophia. Married Dennis Cleugh.

ROMANCE AND HISTORICAL PUBLICATIONS

Novels

Matilda, Governess of the English. New York, Macmillan, 1924; London, Butterworth, 1925.
Ernestine Sophie. New York, Macmillan, 1925; London, Butterworth, 1926.
Jeanne Margot. New York, Macmillan, and London, Butterworth, 1927.
A Common Cheat. New York, Macmillan, and London, Butterworth, 1928.
Spring. New York, Macmillan, and London, Hodder and Stoughton, 1929.
Song Bird. Boston, Houghton Mifflin, and London, Hodder and Stoughton, 1930.
Enchanting Clementina. London, Hodder and Stoughton, 1930; Boston, Houghton Mifflin, 1931.
The Daisy Boy. London, Hodder and Stoughton, 1931; as *Young Jonathan*, Boston, Houghton Mifflin, 1932.
Loyal Lady. London, Hodder and Stoughton, 1932; as *Anne Marguerite*, Boston, Houghton Mifflin, 1932.
The Hazards of Belinda. London, Hodder and Stoughton, and Boston, Houghton Mifflin, 1933.
Lindy Lou. London, Hodder and Stoughton, 1934.
The Angel Who Couldn't Sing. London, Hodder and Stoughton, and New York, Doubleday, 1935.
Wind Which Moved a Ship. London, Newnes, and New York, Doubleday, 1936.

*   *   *

Sophia Cleugh, a romance writer of the 1920's and 1930's plunges the modern reader into another world. Few things can reveal the changes that have occurred in gothic romances as vividly as actually reading material written over half a century ago. Two aspects disturb the modern reader. Cleugh's persistent habit of alternating lengthy involved and often convoluted sentences with sentence fragments is particularly jarring. Frequent rereading for sentence sense is essential for the reader unfamiliar with this style. Also disturbing to most modern readers are the lengthy descriptive passages as well as detailed discussions of the most minute details of daily life accompanied by thorough relating of all accompanying emotional responses.

In *The Daisy Boy* numerous pages are devoted to desultory descriptions and idle chatter during an afternoon tea while Jonathan is assiduously digging daisies from the lawn. An even greater impasse to the plot is apparent in *Matilda, Governess of the English* during numerous exchanges between the Duchess and her maid, Mrs. Kincaid. In *Spring* the initial descriptions and the languorous pace of the novel recall another more leisurely time and place when the reader could luxuriate in a novel that was much ado about little.

Yet, while Cleugh's plots move at the same pace as do those of Henry James, her fine wit more than compensates for the absence of fast-paced action or heady romance, or even great mystery. A multitude of aphorisms and clichés only serve to add a special charm and authenticity to these early works ("But, as we have heard time and again, tread on the veriest worm too often, and the creature will turn").

Romantic names such as Sweet William, Gilliflower, Larkspur, Nina, and various titles of nobility abound in Cleugh's novels. She also shows a rather 19th-century interest in children. Children of various ages figure prominently in all of her books, and they are not just property and appendages of their parents but complete personages in their own rights and often described with great wit and clarity.

Although reading aloud is no longer in vogue, were it a habit to which we might someday return, Cleugh, with her often clever turning of a phrase, should be read aloud. While the plot lines—of young maidens seeking a romance not guided by their Mamas or poor young people making good—are not original, a novel which treats language as if it were a treasure has lasting value. In addition, Sophia Cleugh's novels remain as representative novels of manners of another time and place.

—Joan Hinkemeyer

COATES, Sheila. See **LAMB, Charlotte.**

COCKRELL, Marian (née Brown). American. Born in Birmingham, Alabama, 15 March 1909. Educated at Sophie Newcomb College, New Orleans, 1926–29; Metropolitan Art School, New York, 1929–30. Married Francis Marion Cockrell in 1931; one daughter. Agent: Oliver G. Swan, Collier Associates, 280 Madison Avenue, New York, New York 10016. Address: 6118 Circle Creek Drive, Boones Mill, Virginia 24065, U.S.A.

ROMANCE AND HISTORICAL PUBLICATIONS

Novels

Yesterday's Madness. New York, Harper, 1943.
Lillian Harley. New York, Harper, 1943.
Dark Waters, with Frank Cockrell. Cleveland, World, 1944.
Something Between. New York, Harper, 1946.
The Revolt of Sarah Perkins. New York, McKay, 1965; London, Hurst and Blackett, 1966.
Mixed Blessings. New York, Times Books, 1978.
The Misadventures of Bethany Price. New York, Times Books, 1979.
Mixed Company. New York, Popular Library, 1979.

Other Publications

Plays

Screenplay: *Dark Waters*, with Joan Harrison, 1945.

Television Plays: for *Alfred Hitchcock* series.

Other

Shadow Castle (for children). New York, McGraw Hill, 1945.

*

Manuscript Collection: Mugar Memorial Library, Boston University.

Marian Cockrell comments:

I enjoy writing. I write to interest and entertain, with life-like characters and amusing conversation. The protagonists are all women, and tend to develop a sense of independence in trying to solve their own problems in their particular time and circumstances. I now prefer to write about the past—early 1900's or 1870's. There is always a love story, but the books are not *about* the love story, but about the difficulties of the heroine, of which the love story is a part.

*　　*　　*

The chief flaw, for me, in much romantic fiction, is the emotional vacuum in which the heroines live. They have few, if any, friends and relatives, and are totally dependent on the men they love for emotional warmth. This is why I find Marian Cockrell's books unusually appealing. Her characters are all part of a small community; her people know everything about each other, gossip about each other, and care about each other. Her characters are richly varied and entirely believable, ranging from normal and kindly characters, through mild eccentrics, full-blown lunatics, and self-righteous, malicious gossips.

Her novels written in the 1940's have contemporary settings, and they now seem dated, though likable. *Something Between*, which brings three pleasant romances to fruition, is nevertheless primarily about a confused adolescent boy trying to prevent his mother's remarriage. Her historical romances work much better. *The Revolt of Sarah Perkins* tells of a small Colorado town during the 1860's which sets out to find a schoolteacher too plain to get married and too beaten-down to give them any trouble. What they get instead is a woman of intelligence, spirit, and humor, who shakes up the town by demanding not only decent facilities, but also that those facilities be shared with all children, including the daughter of a prostitute, and a child who is half-Indian. Cockrell herself says that her book is about the women of the west, "their strengths and weaknesses, gentleness and compassion, bigotry and intolerance." *Mixed Blessings*, set in a small Southern town in the early 1900's, tells of the tribulations of a young woman trying to support herself and her brother by running a boarding house inhabited by a certifiable looney, two warring women, and their offspring. The heroine is warm and loving, and cheerfully accepts the burdens of those she loves. It takes a while for her to find a man who can live up to her. *The Misadventures of Bethany Price* has a 16-year-old heroine who, faced with a middle-aged husband she dislikes and a stepson who rapes her, runs away. She finds friends in a small pioneer community, but she also arouses public hostility by her unconventional behavior and uncompromising honesty and fairness.

The world Cockrell creates is not only believable; it is also entertaining. Her perceptions of the world are acute and amusing. While her chief strength lies in the reality of her characters, her plots are briskly paced and funny.

—Marylaine Block

———

COFFMAN, Virginia (Edith). Also writes as Victor Cross; Jeanne Duval; Virginia C. DuVaul; Diana Saunders; Anne Stanfield. American. Born in San Francisco, California, 30 July 1914. Educated at schools in San Francisco and Long Beach, California; University of California, Berkeley, 1933–38, A.B. 1938. Secretary in fan mail and publicity departments, David O. Selznick Studios, Culver City, California, 1944. Monogram Studios, Hollywood, 1945–50, RKO-Howard Hughes Studios, Hollywood, 1951–52, Columbia Studios, Hollywood, 1952–53, and Hal Roach Television, Culver City, 1953–56; secretary, H. F. Bennett, realtors, Reno, Nevada, 1965–66. Agent: Jay Garon-Brooke Associates, 415 Central Park West, New York, New York 10025. Address: Arlington Towers, 100 North Arlington, Apartment 9-F, Reno, Nevada 89501, U.S.A.

Romance and Historical Publications

Novels (series: Cavalcade; Lucifer Cove; Moura; Napoleon I and III)

Moura. New York, Crown, 1959.
The Affair of Alkali. New York, Arcadia House, 1960; as *Nevada Gunslinger*, London, Gresham, 1962.
The Beckoning. New York, Ace, 1965; as *The Beckoning from Moura*, 1977.
Curse of the Island Pool. New York, Lancer, 1965.
Castle Barra. New York, Paperback Library, 1966.
The Secret of Shower Tree. New York, Lancer, 1966; as *Strange Secrets*, New York, New American Library, 1976; London, Piatkus, 1984.
Black Heather. New York, Lancer, 1966.
The High Terrace. New York, Lancer, 1966; as *To Love a Dark Stranger*, London, Hale, 1969.
Castle at Witches' Coven. New York, Lancer, 1966.
A Haunted Place. New York, Lancer, 1966; Aylesbury, Buckinghamshire, Milton House, 1975.
The Demon Tower. New York, New American Library, 1966; London, Piatkus, 1986.
The Devil Vicar. New York, Ace, 1966; revised edition, as *Vicar of Moura*, 1972.
The Shadow Box. New York, Lancer, 1966.
Blood Sport (as Victor Cross). New York, Award, 1966; London, Tandem, 1967.
The Small Tawny Cat. New York, Lancer, 1967; as *The Stalking Terror*, New York, New American Library, 1977; London, Piatkus, 1983.
Richest Girl in the World. New York, Lancer, 1967; London, Severn House, 1988.
The Chinese Door. New York, Lancer, 1967; London, Hale, 1971.
The Rest Is Silence. New York, Lancer, 1967; London, Piatkus, 1985.
A Few Fiends to Tea. New York, Belmont, 1967.

The Hounds of Hell. New York, Belmont, 1967.

One Man Too Many. New York, Lancer, 1968; London, Severn House, 1988.

The Villa Fountains. New York, Belmont, 1968.

The Mist at Darkness. New York, New American Library, 1968.

Call of the Flesh. New York, Lancer, 1968.

The Candidate's Wife. New York, Lancer, 1968.

The Dark Gondola. New York, Ace, 1968; as *The Dark Beyond Moura*, 1977.

Of Love and Intrigue. New York, New American Library, 1969.

Lucifer Cove:

1. *The Devil's Mistress.* New York, Lancer, 1969; London, Piatkus, 1987.
2. *Priestess of the Damned.* New York, Lancer, 1970; Loughton, Essex, Piatkus, 1982.
3. *The Devil's Virgin.* New York, Lancer, 1970.
4. *Masque of Satan.* New York, Lancer, 1971; London, Piatkus, 1987.
5. *Chalet Diabolique.* New York, Lancer, 1971; as *Chalet of the Devil*, London, Piatkus, 1988.
6. *From Satan, With Love.* New York, Lancer, 1972; London, Piatkus, 1983.

Isle of the Undead. New York, Lancer, 1969; as *Voodoo Widow*, London, Hale, 1970.

The Beach House. New York, New American Library, 1970; Loughton, Essex, Piatkus, 1982.

Masque by Gaslight. New York, Ace, 1970; (as Virginia C. Du Vaul) London, Hale, 1971.

The Vampyre of Moura. New York, Ace, 1970.

The Master of Blue Mire. New York, Dell, 1971; Aylesbury, Buckinghamshire, Milton House, 1975.

Night at Sea Abbey. New York, Lancer, 1972; Loughton, Essex, Piatkus, 1981.

The House on the Moat. New York, Lancer, 1972.

Mistress Devon. New York, Arbor House, 1972; London, Souvenir Press, 1982.

The Cliffs of Dread. New York, Lancer, 1972; Loughton, Essex, Piatkus, 1981.

The Dark Palazzo. New York, Arbor House, 1973; Loughton, Essex, Piatkus, 1980.

Garden of Shadows. New York, Lancer, 1973.

A Fear of Heights. New York, Lancer, 1973; as *Legacy of Fear*, New York, New American Library, 1979; London, Piatkus, 1983.

The Evil at Queens Priory. New York, Lancer, 1973; Loughton, Essex, Piatkus, 1980.

Survivor of Darkness. New York, Lancer, 1973.

The House at Sandalwood. New York, Arbor House, 1974; Aylesbury, Buckinghamshire, Milton House, 1975.

Hyde Place. New York, Arbor House, 1974.

The Ice Forest. New York, Dell, 1975.

Veronique (Napoleon). New York, Arbor House, 1975; London, Souvenir Press, 1978.

Marsanne (Napoleon). New York, Arbor House, 1976; London, Souvenir Press, 1979.

The Alpine Coach (Napoleon). New York, Dell, 1976; London, Souvenir Press, 1980.

Careen. New York, Dell, 1977.

Enemy of Love. New York, Dell, 1977; London, Piatkus, 1989.

Fire Dawn. New York, Arbor House, 1977; Loughton, Essex, Piatkus, 1979.

The Gaynor Women. New York, Arbor House, 1978; London, Souvenir Press, 1981.

Looking-Glass. New York, Dell, 1979; London, Piatkus, 1984.

Dinah Faire. New York, Arbor House, 1979; London, Souvenir Press, 1982.

The Lady Serena (as Jeanne Duval). New York, New American Library, 1979.

Ravishers (as Jeanne Duval). New York, New American Library, 1980.

Pacific Cavalcade. New York, Arbor House, 1981; London, Severn House, 1986.

The Golden Marguerite (as Anne Stanfield). New York, Fawcett, 1981.

The Lombard Cavalcade. New York, Arbor House, 1982; London, Severn House, 1986.

The Lombard Heiress (Cavalcade). New York, Arbor House, 1983; London, Severn House, 1986.

The Orchid Tree. New York, Arbor House, 1984; London, Severn House, 1985.

Dark Winds (Napoleon). New York, Arbor House, 1985; London, Souvenir Press, 1986.

Royal Summer (as Anne Stanfield). New York, Fawcett, 1986.

Doxy Masque (as Anne Stanfield). New York, Fawcett, 1986.

Tana Maguire (as Diana Saunders). New York, Fine, 1986; as Virginia Coffman, London, Severn House, 1987.

Dark Desire (Napoleon). New York, Popular Library, 1987.

Passion of Letty Fox (as Diana Saunders). New York, Fine, 1987.

The Jewelled Darkness. London, Severn House, 1989.

*

Virginia Coffman comments:

At the age of 6 I was telling some pretty scary stories to other classmates on the steps of our school. I made the stories up and acted them out, the spookier the better, because, like a lot of plain little girls, I wanted to live the romantic, exciting life of a beautiful heroine. I was more actress than writer, obviously. A childhood of one tiresome illness after another only made me more passionate to live on paper. And I loved spooky Saturday serials.

Time marched on. I felt much the same at 26 as I did at 6, and finally got down to a smidgeon of reality (my heroines) surrounded by historical events of romance, terror and danger, after 12 years in the gothic world of the Hollywood studios. My most popular books still have this mixture (*Moura*, *Dark Winds*). When I write realistically about a world I lived through, two World Wars, a Great Depression, Korea and Vietnam, my popularity falls off. The truth is, I don't really live in that world. I never did! When I visit Paris I walk those magic streets and become my French ancestors living the Revolution and the dazzling Napoleonic Era (both Napoleons!). I go to Yorkshire or Rye, Sussex, and revert to 1810–50. Today doesn't exist.

So be very careful in applying that sage advice: "Write about what you know." You just might know some exotic country or period better than your own. I certainly do!

*   *   *

Virginia Coffman, who has some 70 novels to her credit, combines elements of several genres in her works: the apparently supernatural threat of the gothic novel, the crime-solving of detective fiction, and the period atmosphere of the historical romance. Writing in the first person or using an omniscient narrative voice, she typically focuses upon suspenseful action and intrigue rather than psychological and philosophical exploration. She resolves her plots at the end by defeating the corrupt forces and by elaborately explaining their mysteries.

Although she does use the gothic convention of the innocent heroine pursued by evil, as in the case with 18-year-old Climene Beauhan who purchases on her own an estate in *Castle at Witches' Coven*, Coffman also presents more individualized female protagonists who depart from the romantic stereotype and complete their fates without happy marriages: Kay Aronson, a thrice-married widow of 35 who seeks the answers to her husband's death in *Chalet Diabolique* (No. 5 of the *Lucifer Cove* series); Judith Cameron, a 33-year-old parolee from a prison, whose attraction for Stephen Giles remains unfulfilled in *The House at Sandalwood*; Veronique, from the novel of the same name, who must go through life to raise her daughter without her dead love, Gilles Marsan. Two examples whose outcomes in love are conventionally fortunate are still unique as gothic heroines: Anne Killian of *The Mist at Darkness* is a widow; Lady Leslie Fisher is unhappily married and then widowed in *Isle of the Undead*. These women tend to have an experience and an understated realism atypical of their counterparts in other romances, along with a modern sensual quality and desire unsuitable for the traditional innocent heroine.

Romantic interest is thus secondary to gothic effects of terror and suspense in Coffman's fiction, with her protagonists confronting a variety of seemingly supernatural powers, such as witches, voodoo artists, zombies, tribal curses, and ghosts, in dark, forbidding places. We gradually learn that these threats are created by human corruption—greedy relatives, smugglers, or opportunists, jilted lovers, mad aristocrats—but for a time they are described in convincing atmospheres that bewilder and scare the reader, as well as the heroine. In her Radcliffean *The Mist at Darkness*, for instance, "The creature loomed in the darkness as an enormous, evil bird. Its wrappings, like wings, threatened to engulf the very walls in its pursuit of me." Whether in 19th-century European countrysides or contemporary California, Hawaii, and Caribbean landscapes, the settings of her novels convey the obscurity and remoteness appropriate for supernatural terror.

Appealing especially to female readers of gothic romances, Coffman's books offer light entertainment with occasionally substantial heroines.

—Bette B. Roberts

COGHLAN, Peggie. See **STIRLING, Jessica.**

COLLIN, Marion (née Cripps). British. Born in Aylesbury, Buckinghamshire, 12 May 1928. Married to John W. H. Collin; two children. Student nurse, Isle of Wight, 1945–48; medical secretary, London, 1948–52; secretary, 10th International Congress of Dermatologists, London; fiction editor, *Woman's Own*, London, 1952–56; Lecturer in Business and Commerce, West Kent College of Further Education, Tonbridge, Kent, 1973–88. Agent: Elaine Greene Ltd., 31 Newington Green, London N16 9PU. Address: 20 Eridge Road, Tunbridge Wells, Kent TN4 8HJ, England.

ROMANCE AND HISTORICAL PUBLICATIONS

Novels

Nurse Maria. London, Mills and Boon, 1963.
Nurse at the Top. London, Mills and Boon, and Toronto, Harlequin, 1964.
Doctors Three. London, Mills and Boon, 1964; Toronto, Harlequin, 1965.
Nurse in the Dark. London, Mills and Boon, 1965.
The Doctor's Delusion. London, Mills and Boon, 1967; Toronto, Harlequin, 1968.
The Shadow of the Court. London, Mills and Boon, 1967.
The Man on the Island. London, Mills and Boon, 1968.
Sun on the Mountain. London, Mills and Boon, 1969.
Nurse on an Island. London, Mills and Boon, 1970.
Calling Dr. Savage. London, Mills and Boon, 1970.
House of Dreams. London, Mills and Boon, 1971.
Sawdust and Spangles. London, Mills and Boon, 1972.
Nurses in the House. London, Mills and Boon, 1989.

OTHER PUBLICATIONS

Other

Romantic Fiction, with Anne Britton. London, Boardman, 1960.
Hospital Office Practice. London, Ballière Tindall, 1981; 5th edition, with Michael Drury, as *The Medical Secretary's and Receptionist's Handbook*, 1986.

*

Marion Collin comments:
As most of my titles indicate, I have a predilection for medical romances, but I also enjoy the research entailed in historical and foreign settings. While the former is the basis for future work, I do not rule out the occasional foray into a more exotic field.

*　　*　　*

In *Romantic Fiction* (1960) Marion Collin and Anne Britton presented their formula for the successful love story: *girl meets boy, girl gets boy, girl loses boy, girl gets boy*. Having arrived at her formula, Collin used it for her first novel, *Nurse Maria*, and thereafter rang the changes upon it. Her principal medium is the doctor/nurse romance (recognisable by title), with the splendid variant of the doctor/doctor romance in which the heroine is also a doctor (*Doctors Three* and *The Doctor's Delusion*). The atmosphere of the hospital, even of the operating theatre, pervades these books. The descriptions of disease, treatments, and surgery are convincing, and are frequently not for the faint-hearted ("The rotting appendix reared us easily, and . . . she severed it from the bowel"—*The Doctor's Delusion*). The smaller details of hospital life are there too—nurses chatting in the sluice, the eternal bedpan, etc. There is a certain incongruity, no doubt occurring in real life, about love and the hospital ("She could never rid herself of guilt when he kissed her in uniform." "She had created love out of a dream. The real thing had been under her nose up on Men's Surgical"—*Nurse at the Top*). We have to assume that as hospitals can produce medically dramatic situations endlessly they can also produce romantically dramatic situations in considerable profusion (while still functioning perfectly).

All of Collin's novels except one are set in modern times (*The Shadow of the Court* is set in the Crimean War). Locations range from an industrial English city (notably St. Luke's Infirmary, later General Hospital, in Manchester), to exotic islands in the Caribbean, to tea-plantations in Ceylon. Some later novels have non-medical settings and non-medical heroines: Jo in *House of Dreams* is a model, Kate in *Sawdust and Spangles* is Girl Friday in a circus, and Jan in *Sun on the Mountain* is P.A. in her father's tea company. But the lure of the stethoscope is strong and the characters in these novels are never too far from medicine: Jo suffers from a burst appendix, accidents happen in the circus, and in Ceylon Jan meets a glamorous woman doctor and her widowed father takes up with a lapsed nurse.

The heroines of Collin's novels are capable, honest, serious young women who are conscious of their responsibilities. Her medical heroines are dedicated, competent professionals, sometimes almost cases of Lamp Fever; they always put their patients first, even when their private lives are turmoils of emotion (which they are most of the time, until a happy conclusion is reached). If Collin's heroines do have a fault, it is their naivety which, helped along by their dedication to medicine and other responsibilities, makes them unaware of their physical attractiveness. The heroine is frequently contrasted with some predatory pussycattish *femme fatale* who wreaks havock in her romantic life. But this is all part of the growing-up process which accompanies each heroine's progress towards true love as she resists or sees through the attractions of some spurious (or merely less earnest) charmer who temporarily impedes her path to the worthier man. Collin is particularly good at providing male red herrings, so that the reader is as much in two minds about possible husbands as the heroine.

—Jean Buchanan

COLT, Zandra. See STEVENSON, Florence.

CONWAY, Celine. See BLAIR, Kathryn.

CONWAY, Laura. See ELSNA, Hebe.

COOKSON, Catherine (Ann née McMullen). Has also written as Catherine Marchant. British. Born in Tyne Dock, County Durham, 20 June 1906. Married Thomas H. Cookson in 1940. Recipient: Royal Society of Literature Winifred Holtby prize, 1968. M.A.: University of Newcastle upon Tyne, 1983. O.B.E. (Officer, Order of the British Empire), 1985. Agent: Anthony Sheil Associates Ltd., 43 Doughty Street, London WC1N 2LF. Address: Bristol Lodge, Langley on Tyne, Hexham, Northumberland NE47 5LA, England.

ROMANCE AND HISTORICAL PUBLICATIONS

Novel (series: Bill Bailey; Hamilton; Mallen; Mary Ann; Tilly Trotter)

Kate Hannigan. London, Macdonald, 1950; New York, Bantam, 1972.
The Fifteen Streets. London, Macdonald, 1952; New York, Bantam, 1973.
Colour Blind. London, Macdonald, 1953; New York, New American Library, 1977.
A Grand Man. London, Macdonald, 1954; New York, Macmillan, 1955.
Maggie Rowan. London, Macdonald, 1954; New York, New American Library, 1975.
The Lord and Mary Ann. London, Macdonald, 1956; New York, Morrow, 1975.
Rooney. London, Macdonald, 1957; New York, Bantam, 1976.
The Devil and Mary Ann. London, Macdonald, 1958; New York, Morrow, 1976.
The Menagerie. London, Macdonald, 1958; New York, Bantam, 1975.
Slinky Jane. London, Macdonald, 1959; New York, New American Library, 1976.
Fanny McBride. London, Macdonald, 1959; New York, Bantam, 1976.
Fenwick Houses. London Macdonald, 1960; New York, Bantam, 1973.
Love and Mary Ann. London, Macdonald, 1961; New York, Morrow, 1976.
The Garment. London, Macdonald, 1962; New York, New American Library, 1974.
Life and Mary Ann. London, Macdonald, 1962; New York, Morrow, 1977.
The Blind Miller. London, Macdonald, 1963; New York, New American Library, 1974.
Marriage and Mary Ann. London, Macdonald, 1964; New York, Morrow, 1978.
Hannah Massey. London, Macdonald, 1964; New York, New American Library, 1973.
Mary Ann's Angels. London, Macdonald, 1965; New York, Morrow, 1978.
The Long Corridor. London, Macdonald, 1965; New York, New American Library, 1976.
The Unbaited Trap. London, Macdonald, 1966; New York, New American Library, 1974.
Mary Ann and Bill. London, Macdonald, 1967; New York, Morrow, 1979.
Katie Mulholland. London, Macdonald, and Indianapolis, Bobbs Merrill, 1967.
The Round Tower. London, Macdonald, 1968; New York, New American Library, 1975.
The Glass Virgin. Indianapolis, Bobbs Merrill, 1969; London, Macdonald, 1970.
The Nice Bloke. London, Macdonald, 1969; as *The Husband*, New York, New American Library, 1976.
The Invitation. London, Macdonald, 1970; New York, New American Library, 1974.
The Dwelling Place. London, Macdonald, and Indianapolis, Bobbs Merrill, 1971.
Feathers in the Fire. London, Macdonald, 1971; Indianapolis, Bobbs Merrill, 1972.
Pure as the Lily. London, Macdonald, 1972; Indianapolis, Bobbs Merrill, 1973.

The Mallen Novels. London, Heinemann, 1979.
   The Mallen Girl. New York, Dutton, 1973; London, Heinemann, 1974.
   The Mallen Streak. London, Heinemann, and New York, Dutton, 1973.
   The Mallen Lot. New York, Dutton, 1974; as *The Mallen Litter*, London, Heinemann, 1974.
The Invisible Cord. London, Heinemann, and New York, Dutton, 1975.
The Gambling Man. London, Heinemann, and New York, Morrow, 1975.
The Tide of Life. London, Heinemann, and New York, Morrow, 1976.
The Girl. London, Heinemann, and New York, Morrow, 1977.
The Cinder Path. London, Heinemann, and New York, Morrow, 1978.
The Man Who Cried. London, Heinemann, and New York, Morrow, 1979.
Tilly Trotter. London, Heinemann, 1980; as *Tilly*, New York, Morrow, 1980.
Tilly Trotter Wed. London, Heinemann, 1981; as *Tilly Wed*, New York, Morrow, 1981.
Tilly Trotter Widowed. London Heinemann, 1982; as *Tilly Alone*, New York, Morrow, 1982.
The Whip. London, Heinemann, and New York, Summit, 1983.
Hamilton. London, Heinemann, 1983.
The Black Velvet Gown. London, Heinemann, and New York, Summit, 1984.
Goodbye Hamilton. London, Heinemann, 1984.
A Dinner of Herbs. London, Heinemann, 1985; as *The Bannaman Legacy*, New York, Summit, 1985.
Harold (Hamilton). London, Heinemann, 1985.
The Moth. London, Heinemann, and New York, Summit, 1986.
Bill Bailey. London, Heinemann, 1986.
The Parson's Daughter. London, Heinemann, and New York, Summit, 1987.
Bill Bailey's Lot. London, Bantam, 1987.
The Cultured Handmaiden. London, Heinemann, 1988.
Bill Bailey's Daughter. London, Bantam, 1988.
The Harrogate Secret. New York, Summit, 1988; London, Bantam, 1989.
The Bailey Chronicles. New York, Summit, 1989.

Novels as Catherine Marchant

Heritage of Folly. London, Macdonald, 1962; New York, Lancer, 1965.
The Fen Tiger. London, Macdonald, 1963; as *The House on the Fens*, New York, Lancer, 1965.
House of Men. London, Macdonald, 1963; New York, Lancer, 1965.
The Mists of Memory. New York, Lancer, 1965.
Evil at Roger's Cross. New York, Lancer, 1966; as *The Iron Facade*, London, Heinemann, 1976.
Miss Martha Mary Crawford. London, Heinemann, 1975; New York, Morrow, 1976.
The Slow Awakening. London, Heinemann, 1976; New York, Morrow, 1977.

OTHER PUBLICATIONS

Play

Screenplay: *Jacqueline*, with others, 1956.

Other

Matty Doolin (for children). London, Macdonald, 1965; New York, New American Library, 1976.
Joe and the Gladiator (for children). London, Macdonald, 1968; New York, New American Library, 1977.
Our Kate: An Autobiography. London, Macdonald, 1969; Indianapolis, Bobbs Merrill, 1971; revised edition, Macdonald, 1982.
The Nipper (for children). London, Macdonald, and Indianapolis, Bobbs Merrill, 1970.
Blue Baccy (for children). London, Macdonald, 1972; Indianapolis, Bobbs Merrill, 1973.
Our John Willy (for children). London, Macdonald, and Indianapolis, Bobbs Merrill, 1974.
Mrs. Flannagan's Trumpet (for children). London, Macdonald and Jane's, 1976; New York, Lothrop, 1980.
Go Tell It to Mrs. Golightly (for children). London, Macdonald and Jane's, 1977; New York, Lothrop, 1980.
Lanky Jones (for children). London, Macdonald, and New York, Lothrop, 1981.
Nancy Nutall and the Mongrel (for children). London, Macdonald, 1982.
Catherine Cookson Country. London, Heinemann, 1986.
Let Me Make Myself Plain. London, Bantam, 1988.

*

Manuscript Collection: Boston University.

*   *   *

Jarrow, Shields, Tyneside, towns of northern industrialized England, make up Catherine Cookson country, alive with the evil of exploitation: by the middle class of the workers in the mills, by a decadent upper class free to work its will on the helpless without fear of retribution, by religion so harsh, narrow, and dogmatic that its presence means fear rather than refuge. Cookson villains create darkness which is lit only by the common people as they struggle to rise above their present economic, moral, or religious strife. From *Pure as the Lily*, Cookson speaks:

> I view you not, Jarrow, through
> the misty, nostalgic glow of love:
> They whom the new generation
> would forget,
> they are my Jarrow.

Secure in her knowledge of the times and people, Cookson has based her prolific career in romantic literature on casting real people as heroes and heroines dwelling in the darkness but hoping and working for a better day.

From Katie (1967), through Mary, Tillie, Cissie, Edward, Abel, and many others up to Freddie (1988), these protagonists represent solid, hardworking, good people. Theirs are the goodness and charity of which the Bible speaks. Symbolically, Cookson heroines and heroes continually share their pitiful bits with family or with loved ones, shouldering responsibilities which seem far beyond their ages or ability to bear. It is not unknown for Cookson protagonists to sell themselves into economic or marital slavery in order to support those they love. They desire to be clean (how identified cleanliness is with a desire to better one's circumstances!), to be honest, to love and be loved, and to be allowed to work honestly for a decent wage. However, they usually face an array of people in the middle/upper class just as determined to harm them, who, in fact, consider it not only their right but also their duty to do so. This focus and Cookson's talent combine to create some ingenious scenes of violence, which occur more in the books up to 1980, than after.

The key turning point in the Cookson canon is the Tilly Trotter series (1980–82) where Tilly not only rises from the lowest of farms to be the master's mistress, but also moves away from northern England to Texas in an attempt to escape her origins. Typically of these early plots, which twist almost incestuously, Tilly is mistress to one man and then marries the man's oldest son by his wife. In the end a widowed Tilly comes home, with not only the heir to the manor but also a small Indian child whom she believes is her husband's (*Tilly Wed*). Texas as a location is not a success; its landscape and people lack the richness of character a reader expects from Cookson and never attain the emotional realism of Cookson's northern England landscapes and people.

This attempt at new horizons symbolizes Cookson's plots moving away from the mines and the mills. The novels since 1982 have their origins there so that the people are recognizable, but the focus changes. Set farther away from the rawness of the earlier tales in content and violence, and outside Jarrow, Shields, and Tyneside, these stories focus more on the struggle to break out of poverty, ignorance, and violence, and the problems associated with breaking the class system, and less on the poverty, ignorance, and violence themselves which characterized early Cookson novels.

The final volume in Tilly's saga, *Tilly Alone*, explores a new social issue. Is it possible really to "become" upper class? Tilly is now indistinguishable from the gentry as far as gentility, speech, and manners go—even better; however, she is more at home with the servants she grew up with and the man from the farm whom she had earlier scorned than most of the gentry. The story asks the question: what is home? A crucial question for any upwardly mobile generation.

This mobility is traced again in *The Black Velvet Gown*, a rather odd story. Begun in tragedy, as most Cookson plots are, this story has two heroines, Riah Millican, who dominates the first half, and her daughter, Biddy, who finishes the tale. It also begins in the mines. Riah's husband dies from being able to read and write: not literally of course, but as the catalyst for the entire plot. The first line reads, "The pit shaft would have been in their backyard. . . . ," but with Riah's eviction, the reader is taken out of the mine area to the farm owned by an eccentric upper-middle class teacher. Riah tears up the gown offered by the teacher because she misunderstands why he offers it.

Her daughter Biddy would have understood that he was not offering corruption as Riah thinks, but genuine esteem. Biddy, courtesy of her father and teacher, not only knows how to read and write, but also has studied the classics and can speak French. For these accomplishments she is temporarily punished while the reader is treated to how the laundry was done in a very large establishment in the 19th century. Here occurs the typical, but in the case of this story, only, scene of violence which Cookson fans have come to expect. Biddy is rescued by her future husband, a nephew of the house, and taken into service by the Grandmamma (one of several notable Cookson Grandmammas) where she had worked before as third laundry girl. This elderly aristocrat is more original and tolerant than the later generations, but she is still unable to accept the lower class Biddy, whom she likes, into the family. The newlyweds plan to start a school where they will admit equal numbers of men and women to study the same subjects—rather revolutionary for 1828.

The best of the latest Cookson offerings, *A Dinner of Herbs*, set in the early 19th century, and spanning three generations, proves that Cookson's powers have not diminished as so often happens with prolific authors. The twists of plot beginning with the murder of Roddy Greenbank's father, through Hal and Mary Ellen's rise to prosperous landowners who in their rise adopt some questionable attitudes associated with the middle class through the last line, "Moreover she would teach it [her child] not to hate" make one of Cookson's finest and most powerful novels.

Cookson is an amazing author. For someone who styles herself "simply a teller of tales," she has managed to maintain her quality of setting, character, plot, and rich, historically accurate detail for more than 20 years. The locale may have moved out of the mines but the mines remain a real presence. True to her promise, Cookson continues to remember "They whom the new generation would forget." She has the enviable ability to create protagonists complex enough to be interesting whom the reader genuinely cares about: real people in real places. Her villains are usually the fanatically religious or the very rich middle class or the decadent aristocracy, but these categories are neither rigidly nor shallowly structured. Just as the reader is tempted to think she must run out of good plots she surprises us with a book the quality of *A Dinner of Herbs* which is as good a tale as any of her best. Mix passion, violence, courage, and responsibility; characters in search of education, love, and economic stability; set these against a landscape peopled with dark villains as violent as any in romance/gothic literature—and we have the reasons why Cookson continues to enjoy such a superb and well-deserved reputation.

—Marilynn Motteler

COOMBS, Ann. See **PYKARE, Nina.**

COOMBS, Nina. See **PYKARE, Nina.**

COOPER, Henry St. John. See **ST. JOHN, Mabel.**

COOPER, Jilly (née Sallitt). British. Born in Hornchurch, Essex, 21 February 1937. Educated at Godolphin School, Salisbury. Married Leo Cooper in 1961; one son and one daughter. Reporter, *Middlesex Independent*, Brentford, 1957–59; worked as account executive, copywriter, publishers reader, receptionist, model, and typist; columnist, *Sunday Times*, London, 1969–82. Since 1982 columnist, *Mail on Sunday*, London. Agent: Desmond Elliot, 15–17 King Street, London S.W.1. Address: c/o Mail on Sunday, Carmelite House, Carmelite Street, London EC4Y 0JA, England.

<small>ROMANCE AND HISTORICAL PUBLICATIONS</small>

Novels

Emily. London, Arlington, 1975.
Bella. London, Arlington, 1976.

Harriet. London, Arlington, 1976.
Octavia. London, Arlington, 1977.
Imogen. London, Arlington, 1978.
Prudence. London, Arlington, 1978.
Riders. London, Arlington, 1985; New York, Ballantine, 1986.
Rivals. London, Bantam, 1988; as *Players*, New York, Ballantine, 1989.

OTHER PUBLICATIONS

Other

How to Stay Married. London, Methuen, 1969; New York, Taplinger, 1970.
How to Survive from Nine to Five. London, Methuen, 1970.
Jolly Super. London, Methuen, 1971.
Men and Super Men. London, Eyre Methuen, 1972.
Jolly Super Too. London, Eyre Methuen, 1973.
Women and Super Women. London, Eyre Methuen, 1974.
Jolly Superlative. London, Eyre Methuen, 1975.
Super Men and Super Women (omnibus). London, Eyre Methuen, 1976.
Work and Wedlock (omnibus). London, Magnum, 1977.
Superjilly. London, Eyre Methuen, 1977.
Class: A View from Middle England. London, Eyre Methuen, 1979.
Supercooper. London, Eyre Methuen, 1980.
Little Mabel (for children). London, Granada, 1980.
Little Mabel's Great Escape (for children). London, Granada, 1981.
Love and Other Heartaches. London, Arlington, 1981.
Intelligent and Loyal: A Celebration of the Mongrel, photographs by Graham Wood. London, Methuen, 1981.
Jolly Marsupial. London, Methuen, 1982.
Little Mabel Wins the Day (for children). London, Granada, 1982.
Animals in War. London, Heinemann, 1983.
The Common Years: The Country Diary of an Urban Lady. London, Methuen, 1984.
On Rugby, with Leo Cooper. London, Bell and Hyman, 1984.
On Cricket, with Leo Cooper. London, Bell and Hyman, 1985.
Little Mabel Saves the Day (for children). London, Granada, 1985.
Hotfoot to Zabriskie Point, photographs by Patrick Lichfield. London, Constable, 1985.
Horse Mania, with Leo Cooper. London, Bell and Hyman, 1986.
How to Survive Christmas. London, Methuen, 1986.
Turn Right at the Spotted Dog and Other Diversions. London, Methuen, 1987.

Editor, with Tom Hartman, *Violets and Vinegar: An Anthology of Women's Writings and Sayings*. London, Allen and Unwin, 1980.
Editor, *The British in Love*. London, Arlington, 1980.

*   *   *

The discernment and observation that have sharpened many of the love stories of the last decade have reached an apex in Jilly Cooper's accounts of heroines who are romantically inclined but also wry, gutsy, earthy, and at times anarchic. Her stories are at the far end of the spectrum from, say, those of Barbara Cartland which are in the classic and sentimental mould. Jilly Cooper (like Mabel St. John in 1908) gives the romantic novel a fresh,

invigorating, and frequently funny slant. With her stories, one feels that the genre is on the brink of a breakthrough into an exciting and still uncharted new lease of life.

She has her own highly individual style and method of packaging her novels, of course. The title of each book is the name of its heroine, and possibly every heroine reflects certain aspects of her author. (It is the representation of Cooper's own face—in many moods—that provides cover illustrations for the stories and no other picture would seem more relevant to the different plots.) Sometimes rueful, sometimes racy, but always romantically persuasive, the narratives are at their most stylish when in the first person (*Emily*, *Prudence*, and *Octavia*, for example). Her novels are extremely inventive and occasionally outrageous. They present a glittering mosaic of misunderstandings and changing partners, idealism and disillusionment, glamour and good nature, in settings as varied as colleges, canal barges, and haunted Highland castles.

With *Riders* there is a considerable enlargement of Cooper's canvas, although romance remains a strong ingredient. *Riders* has as its setting the tensely glittering world of show jumping. When the book first appeared, a reviewer wrote "Sex and horses: who could ask for more?" Certainly in the hands of Cooper these two themes are handled invigoratingly enough to make entertaining reading even for those who might normally have little feeling for the mystique of equestrian endeavours. Ambition and the fear of failure spill over from field events into romantic relationships, and bitter rivalries between the hard-up, half-gypsy Jake and the promiscuous upper-class cad Rupert Campbell-Black are played out in a riot of horsey happenings from home-counties gymkhanas to the Los Angeles Olympics.

Rivals is another romantic block-buster in which the now divorced and still dissolute Rupert pursues a political career. The book's vital atmosphere is provided by the conflict between warring groups and individuals who seek the franchise of a Cotswolds television company. Here, as in *Riders*, cut-throat ambition crosses the divide between business and personal affairs. Cooper is at her most deliciously barbed in these bed-to-boardroom exploits, and, despite the general frothiness of the story there are some moments of serious social challenge.

—Mary Cadogan

———————

COOPER, Lettice (Ulpha). British. Born in Eccles, Lancashire, 3 September 1897. Educated at St. Cuthbert's School, Southbourne; Lady Margaret Hall, Oxford, 1916–18, B.A. Editorial assistant and drama critic, *Time and Tide*, London, 1939–40. Public relations officer, Ministry of Food, London, 1940–45. President, Robert Louis Stevenson Club, 1958–74; Vice Chairman, 1975–78, and President, 1979–81, English PEN Club. Recipient: Arts Council bursary, 1968, 1979; Eric Gregory traveling scholarship, 1977. O.B.E. (Officer, Order of the British Empire), 1980. Agent: A. P. Watt Ltd., 20 John Street, London WC1N 2DL. Address: 95 Canfield Gardens, London NW6 3DY, England.

ROMANCE AND HISTORICAL PUBLICATONS

Novels

The Lighted Room. London, Hodder and Stoughton, 1925.
The Old Fox. London, Hodder and Stoughton, 1927.
Good Venture. London, Hodder and Stoughton, 1928.

Likewise the Lyon. London, Hodder and Stoughton, 1928.
The Ship of Truth. London, Hodder and Stoughton, and Boston, Little Brown, 1930.
Private Enterprise. London, Hodder and Stoughton, 1931.
Hark to Rover! London, Hodder and Stoughton, 1933.
We Have Come to a Country. London, Gollancz, 1935.
The New House. London, Gollancz, and New York, Macmillan, 1936.
National Provincial. London, Gollancz, and New York, Macmillan, 1938.
Black Bethlehem. London, Gollancz, and New York, Macmillan, 1947.
Fenny. London, Gollancz, 1953.
Three Lives. London, Gollancz, 1957.
A Certain Compass. London, Gollancz, 1960.
The Double Heart. London, Gollancz, 1962.
Late in the Afternoon. London, Gollancz, 1971.
Tea on Sunday. London, Gollancz, 1973.
Snow and Roses. London, Gollancz, 1976.
Desirable Residence. London, Gollancz, 1980.
Unusual Behaviour. London, Gollancz, 1986.

OTHER PUBLICATIONS

Fiction (for children)

Blackberry's Kitten. Leicester, Brockhampton Press, 1961; New York, Vanguard Press, 1963.
The Bear Who Was Too Big. London, Parrish, 1963; Chicago, Follett, 1966.
Bob-a-Job. Leicester, Brockhampton Press, 1963.
Contadino. London, Cape, 1964.
The Twig of Cypress. London, Deutsch, 1965; New York, Washburn, 1966.
We Shall Have Snow. Leicester, Brockhampton Press, 1966.
Robert the Spy Hunter. London, Kaye and Ward, 1973.
Parkin. London, Harrap, 1977.

Other (for children)

Great Men of Yorkshire (West Riding). London, Lane, 1955.
The Young Florence Nightingale. London, Lane, 1960; New York, Roy, 1961.
The Young Victoria. London, Parrish, 1961; New York, Roy, 1962.
James Watt. London, A. and C. Black, 1963.
Garibaldi. London, Methuen, 1964; New York, Roy, 1966.
The Young Edgar Allan Poe. London, Parrish, 1964; New York, Roy, 1965.
The Fugitive King. London, Parrish, 1965.
A Hand upon the Time: A Life of Charles Dickens. New York, Pantheon, 1968; London, Gollancz, 1971.
Robert Louis Stevenson. London, Burns and Oates, 1969.
Gunpowder: Treason and Plot. London, Abelard Schuman, 1970.

Other

Robert Louis Stevenson. London, Home and Van Thal, 1947; Denver, Alan Swallow, 1948.
Yorkshire: West Riding. London, Hale, 1950.
George Eliot. London, Longman, 1951; revised edition, 1960, 1964.

*

Manuscript Collection: Eccles Public Library, Lancashire.

*   *   *

Mary Welburn in *National Provincial* is just what Lettice Cooper herself must have been like at a similar age—a clever girl who went to university, moved away from her northern roots and became involved in a new life and the new ideas that surrounded her, held down an involving and exciting job, was tolerant, broadminded, fascinated by other people, and open to every new experience. She is a brilliant and born writer. Her books read so effortlessly that it is easy to overlook the superb writing that makes the reading such a pleasure.

Cooper has a clarity of mind, a breadth of learning, and a depth of understanding that enable her to describe other people's lives with immense sympathy and appreciation. She understands what makes people tick: their worries, fears, and indecisions; the little things that concern them, and their bewilderment and feelings of inadequacy when faced with big issues and problems they don't really understand. Cooper makes one feel for the unhappy nouveau riche Ward children in *National Provincial,* and sympathize as Stephen Harding wrestles with his awakening political consciousness, which sets him apart from his wife and family, and everything he was brought up to think right. And you know from the beginning that there is no future for them. The character of Fenny (in the book of the same name), also stays in the mind; she loses the first man she loves because she is too inexperienced and nice, and cannot see, until it is too late, what is happening. And the reader hopes that Rhoda, in *The New House,* will find the courage to break away from the gentle but vice-like clutches of her mother and at last live her own life; that the new house will, in fact, mean a new beginning for them all; and that she will not become a mirror image of her Aunt Ellen. She deserves better.

What is striking about Cooper's novels is that despite the fact that they were written 50 years ago, the issues they confront and the way in which they are written are as relevant today as they were then. And her places are as alive as her characters: for example the Florence she so lovingly portrays in *Fenny.*

Cooper, in her new introduction to the reissue of *National Provincial,* published in honour of her 90th birthday, describes the book as ''a piece of Yorkshire tapestry.'' But all her novels weave together the strands of politics and philosophy, love and friendship, hatred and jealousy. She says of Mary Welburn that ''it was impossible for her to go on a railway journey without feeling that at the other end of it there was likely to be something interesting.'' Her readers feel the same about beginning a Lettice Cooper novel.

—Dorothy Wood

CORCORAN, Barbara. Also writes as Paige Dixon; Gail Hamilton. American. Born in Hamilton, Massachusetts, 12 April 1911. Educated at Wellesley College, Massachusetts, 1929–33, B.A. in English 1933; University of Montana, Missoula, 1954–55, M.A. in English 1955. Served as an electronics inspector in the United States Navy and a code clerk in the United States Army Signal Corps during World War II. Researcher, Celebrity Service, Hollywood, 1945–53; copywriter, Station KGVO, Missoula, 1953–54; Instructor in English, University of Kentucky, Covington, 1956–57; researcher, CBS Television story department, Hollywood, 1957–59; English teacher, Marlboro School, Los Angeles, 1959–60; Instructor in English, University of Colorado, Boulder, 1960–65, and Palomar College, San Marcos, California, 1965–69. Recipient: National Science Teachers' award, 1975; National Endowment for the Arts grant, 1978. Agent: McIntosh and Otis, 310 Madison Avenue, New York, New York 10017. Address: P.O. Box 4394, Missoula, Montana 59806, U.S.A.

ROMANCE AND HISTORICAL PUBLICATIONS

Novels

Abbie in Love. New York, Ballantine, 1981.
Abigail. New York, Ballantine, 1981.
Beloved Enemy. New York, Ballantine, 1981.
By the Silvery Moon. New York, Ballantine, 1981.
Call of the Heart. New York, Ballantine, 1981.
A Husband for Gail. New York, Ballantine, 1981.
Love Is Not Enough. New York, Ballantine, 1981.
Song for Two Voices. New York, Ballantine, 1981.

OTHER PUBLICATIONS (for children)

Fiction

Sam. New York, Atheneum, 1967.
A Row of Tigers. New York, Atheneum, 1969.
Sasha, My Friend. New York, Atheneum, 1969.
The Long Journey, with Bradford Angier. New York, Atheneum, 1970.
A Star to the North, with Bradford Angier. New York, Nelson, 1970.
The Lifestyle of Robie Tuckerman. New York, Nelson, 1971.
This Is a Recording. New York, Atheneum, 1971.
Don't Slam the Door When You Go. New York, Atheneum, 1972.
A Trick of Light. New York, Atheneum, 1972.
All the Summer Voices. New York, Atheneum, 1973.
A Dance to Still Music. New York, Atheneum, 1974.
The Winds of Time. New York, Atheneum, 1974.
The Clown. New York, Atheneum, 1975; as *A Time to Love, A Time to Mourn*, New York, Scholastic, 1975; as *I Wish You Love*, Scholastic, 1977.
Meet Me at Tamerlane's Tomb. New York, Atheneum, 1975.
Axe-Time, Sword-Time. New York, Atheneum, 1976.
Cabin in the Sky. New York, Atheneum, 1976.
Faraway Island. New York, Atheneum, 1977.
Make No Sound. New York, Atheneum, 1977.
Ask for Love, and They Give You Rice Pudding, with Bradford Angier. Boston, Houghton Mifflin, 1977.
Hey, That's My Soul You're Stomping On. New York, Atheneum, 1978.
Me and You and a Dog Named Blue. New York, Atheneum, 1979.
The Person in the Potting Shed. New York, Atheneum, 1980.
Rising Damp. New York, Atheneum, 1980.
Making It. Boston, Little Brown, 1981.
You're Allegro Dead. New York, Atheneum, 1981.
Child of the Morning. New York, Atheneum, 1982.
A Watery Grave. New York, Atheneum, 1982.
Strike! New York, Atheneum, 1983.
Which Witch Is Which? New York, Atheneum, 1983.
August, Die She Must. New York, Atheneum, 1984.

The Woman in Your Life. New York, Atheneum, 1984.
Face the Music. New York, Atheneum, 1985.
Mystery on Ice. New York, Atheneum, 1985.
The Shadowed Path. New York, Archway, 1985.
When Darkness Falls. New York, Archway, 1985.
A Horse Named Sky. New York, Archway, 1986.
I Am the Universe. New York, Atheneum, 1986.
The Hideaway. New York, Atheneum, 1987.
The Sky Is Falling. New York, Atheneum, 1988.
The Private Wars of Lillian Adams. New York, Atheneum, 1989.

Fiction as Paige Dixon

Lion on the Mountain. New York, Atheneum, 1972.
Silver Wolf. New York, Atheneum, 1973.
Promises to Keep. New York, Atheneum, 1974.
The Young Grizzly. New York, Atheneum, 1974.
May I Cross Your Golden River? New York, Atheneum, 1975.
Pimm's Cup for Everybody. New York, Atheneum, 1976.
The Search for Charlie. New York, Atheneum, 1976.
Summer of the White Goat. New York, Atheneum, 1977.
The Loner: A Story of the Wolverine. New York, Atheneum, 1978.
The Mustang and Other Stories. New York, Atheneum, 1978.
Skipper. New York, Atheneum, 1979.
Walk My Way. New York, Atheneum, 1980.

Fiction as Gail Hamilton

A Candle to the Devil. New York, Atheneum, 1975.
Titania's Lodestone. New York, Atheneum, 1975.
Love Comes to Eunice K. O'Herlihy. New York, Atheneum, 1977.

*

Manuscript Collection: de Grummond Collection, University of Southern Mississippi, Hattiesburg; Central Missouri State University, Warrensburg.

*   *   *

Perhaps Barbara Corcoran's experience in writing novels for young adults influences her historical and romance fiction more than one might expect. As a novelist, for whatever age group, she seems most interested in the process by which a young person breaks free of family ties and gains some independence. In that newly independent state, her protagonist may love family members more than before, but it is a love based on understanding rather than on duty.

Also perhaps a reminder of her young adult novels is her tendency to focus on one central character. Even though the subsidiary characters are important to the plot, they tend to be insubstantial when regarded closely. In *Call of the Heart*, one of her most conventionally romantic historic novels, even the hero, Tom Weatherby, a self-made industrialist, is presented in a fragmented way: his character does not develop organically. Doty Connor-Jones, the heroine, is a young governess for a wealthy family as America enters World War I. Her Irish charm wins the hearts of Weatherby and also of young Sam Winchester, her employer's brother. Doty's engagement to Sam and her care for his elderly parents when he is killed as a Canadian pilot make a poignant story, although the novel also clearly shows Corcoran's major failing as a writer of historical novels—her inability to give a true period feeling to her stories. The historical characters always seem like modern people in period costume. The aristocratic episcopalean Winchesters make no complaint about Sam's sudden engagement to an Irish catholic girl who attends Mass with some regularity.

Similarly, Abigail, the eponymous heroine of Corcoran's novel about Civil War New England, goes as a school teacher to a small village. Even her stodgy, proper mother accepts the need for Abigail to make a living working outside the home. Abigail is seduced by the school board president, a rich man whose wife is addicted to opium. She goes home, pregnant and in disgrace. But her mother calmly accepts her condition, and her brother writes "As for your child, I shall love it like my own." Apparently no one in her home community, among her relatives or even among the local church congregation, audibly disapproves of her illegitimate baby. While details like the brief meeting with Henry Cabot Lodge in the Old Corner Book Store may be true to period, the attitudes and opinions of the characters are atypical of their eras. Perhaps this provides some reassurance to readers who would be dismayed by changing standards of tolerance between our day and earlier times.

Some of Corcoran's work straddles the line between adult novels and those written for young adults. *Skipper* has a protagonist who goes to an ancestral estate to find a long-lost father, meeting enemies and unexpected friends. But Skipper is not a typical gothic heroine, but a high school student looking for his roots in the wake of his beloved brother's death. Instead of love, he finds the understanding that he must live his own life while continuing to cherish his brother's memory.

It is, in fact, not unusual for romance to be secondary. In *Axe-Time, Sword-Time*, a girl with learning disabilities finds a way to help the United States war effort in the early 1940's, while defining her independence from her conventional mother. Elinor is in love with a neighbor but their relationship is a stable background to her life, rather than an exciting novelty. In *Abigail*, the heroine takes her baby west to make a new life in Colorado, leaving behind a young man who cares for her, after one last bitter encounter with her wealthy seducer, who is still trying to convince her he is serious about getting a divorce someday. Abigail and her baby will be, one is to assume, sufficient unto themselves. Abigail has finally defined herself in such a way that she is a woman who may not need a lover—not as a romantic heroine after all.

—Susan Branch

CORDELL, Alexander. Pseudonym for George Alexander Graber. British. Born in Colombo, Ceylon (now Sri Lanka), 9 September 1914. Educated privately, and at Marist Brothers' College, 1921–30. Served in the British Army, 1932–36; Royal Engineers, 1939–45: Major. Married 1) Rosina Wells in 1937 (died 1972), one daughter; 2) Elsie May Donovan. Quantity surveyor in Wales, 1936–68. Since 1968 full-time writer. Address: The Conifers, Railway Road, Rhosddu, Wrexham, Clwyd, Wales.

ROMANCE AND HISTORICAL PUBLICATIONS

Novels

A Thought of Honour. London, Museum Press, 1954; as *The Enemy Within*, London, Coronet, 1974.

Rape of the Fair Country. London, Gollancz, and New York, Doubleday, 1959.
The Hosts of Rebecca. London, Gollancz, 1960; as *Robe of Honor*, New York, Doubleday, 1960.
Race of the Tiger. London, Gollancz, 1963.
The Sinews of Love. London, Gollancz, 1965; New York, Doubleday, 1966.
The Bright Cantonese. London, Gollancz, 1967; as *The Deadly Eurasian*, New York, Weybright and Talley, 1968.
Song of the Earth. London, Gollancz, 1969; New York, Simon and Schuster, 1970.
The Fire People. London, Hodder and Stoughton, 1972.
If You Believe the Soldiers. London, Hodder and Stoughton, 1973; New York, Doubleday, 1974.
The Dream and the Destiny. London, Hodder and Stoughton, and New York, Doubleday, 1975.
This Sweet and Bitter Earth. London, Hodder and Stoughton, 1977; New York, St. Martin's Press, 1978.
To Slay the Dreamer. London, Hodder and Stoughton, and New York, St. Martin's Press, 1980.
Rogue's March. London, Hodder and Stoughton, 1981.
Land of My Fathers. London, Hodder and Stoughton, 1983.
Peerless Jim. London, Hodder and Stoughton, 1984.
Tunnel Tigers. London, Weidenfeld and Nicolson, 1986.
This Proud and Savage Land. London, Weidenfeld and Nicolson, 1987.
Requiem for a Patriot. London, Weidenfeld and Nicolson, 1988.
Moll Walbee. London, Weidenfeld and Nicolson, 1989.

Short Stories

Tales from Tiger Bay. Abergavenny, Monmouth, Blorenge Press, 1986.

OTHER PUBLICATIONS (for children)

Fiction

The White Cockade. Leicester, Brockhampton Press, and New York, Viking Press, 1970.
Witches' Sabbath. Leicester, Brockhampton Press, and New York, Viking Press, 1970.
The Healing Blade. Leicester, Brockhampton Press, and New York, Viking Press, 1971.
The Traitor Within. Leicester, Brockhampton Press, 1971; Nashville, Nelson, 1973.
Sea-Urchin. London, Collins, 1979.

*

Manuscript Collection: Boston University.

*   *   *

You have to appreciate Wales and the Welsh to enjoy fully Alexander Cordell's stirring novels, because his writing is so deeply steeped in Welsh idiom and the lilting speech of the valleys. Probably best known for his famous trilogy, *Rape of the Fair Country, The Hosts of Rebecca*, and *Song of the Earth*, he likes a big canvas on which he can paint large, and industrial Wales in the 19th century provides him with a wonderful backcloth for his history of the industrial revolution, and the rise of the trades union and Chartist movements. His sweeping lyrical novels are a wonderful way to learn history.

It was Benjamin Disraeli who first described Britain as a nation divided (at this time between the rich and the poor) and the division has never been shown more clearly than in Wales at this time. The thriving Welsh industrial towns were a magnet for a rich stew of people: they came from the North of England, Ireland, and Scotland to earn a pitiful living in the mills and mines of Wales, while the mine owners and iron masters grew rich and prosperous. Cordell has based many of his stories on the folk memories of the people he has met, and he pulls no punches. The conditions the ordinary people lived and worked in were appalling: cholera was rampant, two out of every three children died by the age of five, and those who survived were employed down the pits, put there by their desperate parents so that they could feed them. The employers thought nothing of cutting wages, or laying off workers when times were hard. But what comes through Cordell's novels is the amazing resilience and humour of the ordinary working people, and their charity and compassion to one another.

Some of Cordell's most memorable characters are the martyrs of the Chartist movement—Dic Penderyn in *The Fire People*; the legendary martyr of the Welsh working class who was wrongfully hanged and in *Requiem for a Patriot*, John Frost—the idealistic Mayor of Newport and the acknowledged leader of the Chartist rebellion, who survived deportation to Van Dieman's Land, and who was greeted by a crowd of 20 thousand people when he finally returned to England in 1857 still preaching against parliament and the economic and social prejudices still so widespread.

There is also a less-Welsh side to Cordell; it comes through in two of his most readable novels. *Peerless Jim* is the fictionalized account of the life of Jim Driscoll—British and European featherweight boxing champion, and unofficial champion of the world, known as "Peerless" for his incomparable left hand—a generous man and a great fighter, probably one of the greatest the British Isles has ever produced, Irish by birth, but Welsh by adoption.

Jim McAndrew in *Rouge's March*, is one of Cordell's most engaging characters—a bawdy, brilliant, drunken, womanizing artist. Jim is cashiered from the army for breaking into the regimental museum and dressing up as an officer, striking a superior, and persistent desertion. He lives in Paris and befriends Toulouse-Lautrec, marries a woman who doesn't even like him very much but thinks he will be good for her business, and paints day and night. It is refreshing to read a novel of Cordell's that is so different, though still with its roots in the period he knows so well.

Cordell, like Peerless Jim, is Welsh by adoption, but if you want to immerse yourself in 19th-century Wales, you will find no finer guide than this writer.

—Dorothy Wood

CORELLI, Marie. Psuedonym for Mary Mackay. British. Born in Bayswater, London, 1 May 1855. Educated privately; studied music and made debut as a pianist, London, 1884. Writer from 1885; settled in Stratford-on-Avon, 1901. *Died 21 April 1924.*

ROMANCE AND HISTORICAL PUBLICATIONS

Novels

A Romance of Two Worlds. London, Bentley, 2 vols., 1886; New York, Ivers, 1 vol., n.d.

Vendetta; or, The Story of One Forgotten. London, Bentley, 3 vols., 1886; New York, Ivers, 1 vol., n.d.

Thelma: A Society Novel. London, Bentley, 3 vols., 1887; New York, Ivers, 1 vol., n.d.

Ardath: The Story of a Dead Self. London, Bentley, 3 vols., 1889; New York, Ivers, 1 vol., n.d.

My Wonderful Wife: A Study in Smoke. London, White, 1889; New York, Ivers, 1890.

Wormwood: A Drama of Paris. London, Bentley, 3 vols., 1890; New York, Munro, 1 vol., 1890.

The Soul of Lilith. London, Bentley, 3 vols., 1892; New York, Lovell, 1 vol., 1892.

Barabbas: A Dream of the World's Tragedy. London, Methuen, 3 vols., 1893; Philadelphia, Lippincott, 1 vol., 1893.

The Sorrows of Satan; or, The Strange Experiences of One Geoffrey Tempest, Millionaire: A Romance. London, Methuen, 3 vols., 1895; Philadelphia, Lippincott, 1 vol., 1896.

Silence of the Maharajah. New York, Merriam, 1895.

The Distant Voices, A Fact or Fancy. Phladelphia, Lippincott, 1896.

The Murder of Delicia. London, Skeffington, and Philadelphia, Lippincott, 1896; as *Delicia,* London, Constable, 1917.

The Mighty Atom. London, Hutchinson, and Philadelphia, Lippincott, 1896.

Ziska. Bristol, Arrowsmith, and Chicago, Stone and Kimball, 1897.

Jane: A Social Incident. London, Huchinson, and Philadelphia, Lippincott, 1897.

Boy. London, Hutchinson, and Philadelphia, Lippincott, 1900.

The Master-Christian. London, Methuen, and New York, Dodd Mead, 1900.

Angel's Wickedness: A True Story. New York, Beers, 1900.

Temporal Power: A Study in Supremacy. London, Methuen, and New York, Dodd Mead, 1902.

God's Good Man: A Simple Love Story. London, Methuen, and New York, Dodd Mead, 1904.

The Strange Visitation of Josiah McNason: A Christmas Ghost Story. London, Newnes, 1904; as *The Strange Visitation,* London, Hodder and Stoughton, 1912.

The Treasure of Heaven: A Romance of Riches. London, Constable, and New York, Dodd Mead, 1906.

Holy Orders. London, Methuen, and New York, Stokes, 1908.

The Devil's Motor. London, Hodder and Stoughton, and New York, Doran, 1910.

The Life Everlasting: A Reality of Romance. London, Methuen, and New York, Doran, 1911.

The Philosopher and the Sentimentalist. New York, Paget, 1911.

Innocent: Her Fancy and His Fact. London, Hodder and Stoughton, and New York, Doran, 1914.

The Young Diana: An Experience of the Future. London, Hutchinson, and New York, Doran, 1918.

My "Little Bit." London, Collins, and New York, Doran, 1919.

The Secret Power. London, Methuen, and New York, Doubleday, 1921.

Love—and the Philosopher: A Study in Sentiment. London, Methuen, and New York, Doran, 1923.

Short Stories

The Hired Baby and Other Stories and Social Sketches. Leipzig, Tauchnitz, 1891; New York, Optimus, 1894.
Three Wise Men of Gotham. Philadelphia, Lippincott, 1896.
Cameos. London, Hutchinson, and Philadelphia, Lippincott, 1896.
The Song of Miriam and Other Stories. New York, Munro, 1898.
The Love of Long Ago and Other Stories. London, Methuen, 1920; New York, Doubleday, 1921.

Other Publications

Verse

Poems, edited by Bertha Vyver. London, Hutchinson, 1925; New York, Doran, 1926.

Other

The Silver Domino; or, Side-Whispers, Social and Literary. London, Lamley, 1892.
Patriotism or Self-Advertisement? A Social Note on the War. London, Greening, and Philadelphia, Lippincott, 1900.
The Greatest Queen in the World: A Tribute to the Majesty of England 1837–1900. London, Skeffington, 1900.
An Open Letter to His Eminence Cardinal Vaughan. London, Lamley, 1900.
A Christmas Greeting of Various Thoughts, Verses, and Fancies. London, Methuen, 1901; New York, Dodd Mead, 1902.
The Passing of the Great Queen. London, Methuen, and New York, Dodd Mead, 1901.
The Vanishing Gift: An Address on the Decay of the Imagination. Edinburgh, Philosophical Institution, 1902.
The Plain Truth of the Stratford-upon-Avon Controversy. London, Methuen, 1903.
Free Opinions Freely Expressed on Certain Phases of Modern Social Life and Conduct. London, Constable, and New York, Dodd Mead, 1905.
Faith Versus Flunkeyism: A Word on the Spanish Royal Marriage. London, Rapid Review, 1906.
Woman or Suffragette? A Question of National Choice. London, Pearson, 1907.
America's Possession in Shakespeare's Town. Edinburgh, Morrison and Gibb, 1909.
Is All Well with England? London, Jarrolds, 1917.
Eyes of the Sea (on the Grand Fleet). London, Marshall, 1917.
Mistaken Both Ways. New York, Paget, 1922.
Praise and Prayer: A Simple Home Service. London, Methuen, 1923.
Open Confession to a Man from a Woman. London, Hutchinson, 1924; New York, Doran, 1925.
Harvard House Guide Book, with Percy S. Brentnall and Bertha Vyver. Privately printed, 1931.

*

Bibliography: by Richard L. Kowdczyk, in *Bulletin of Bibliography* (Boston), 1973.

Critical Studies: *Marie Corelli: The Life and Death of a Best-Seller* by George Bullock, London, Constable, 1940; *Marie Corelli: The Woman and the Legend* by Eileen Bigland, London, Jarrolds, 1953; *Marie Corelli: The Story of a Friendship* by William Stuart Scott, London, Hutchinson, 1955; *Now Barabbas Was a Rotter: The Extraordinary Life of Marie Corelli* by Brian Masters, London, Hamish Hamilton, 1978.

*   *   *

Marie Corelli has been claimed as the first modern "bestseller" author for the reading public expanded by Forster's 1870 Education Act. At the time of her death *The Sorrows of Satan* and *Thelma* had gone through 60 and 56 editions respectively. In the face of mainly hostile reception from the literary establishment, she refused after 1893 to send out review copies, but this did nothing to lessen her popularity: Richard Hoggart has noted that his aunts in working-class Leeds considered *The Sorrows of Satan* "a classic"; it was also praised by Queen Victoria. The huge popularity of her novels makes her of social interest, but her writing itself has the fascination of an intense, emotive imagination almost totally uninhibited by considerations of style, taste, or factual reality.

Her life itself was an elaborately cultivated fantasy. Born in London, May 1, 1855, the illegitimate daughter of Charles Mackay, songwriter, and Ellen Mills, she claimed to be born in 1854 of aristocratic Italian blood. In 1884 she made a well-received debut as an *improvatrice* pianist in London—a character to emerge, thinly disguised, as the heroine of her first novel, *A Romance of Two Worlds*, who, on the verge of a nervous breakdown, was released through the help of a Paris scientist Heliobas to discover her "personal electricity" and so explore the spiritual realm. This curious blend of mysticism and pseudo-science was to become one hallmark of her writing. It gave comforting assurance to those disturbed by the impact of science—in particular Darwinism—on the thought and life of the period. Wireless telegraphy and light-rays, she informed readers of *The Life Everlasting*, were known to Egyptian priests and the Hermetic Brethren "ages before the coming of Christ," and the mystic Heliobas, who appears in several of her works, was a Chaldean descended from the Wise Men from the East.

The Soul of Lilith combines the myths of Frankenstein and Pygmalion. El-Râmi, an Egyptian sage, uses a chemical elixir to bring to life a child who grows up as Lilith. Controlling her body, he wishes to possess her soul, considering a female soul a minor entity. Although warned of his error by Heliobas, he professes to Lilith his love for her, and she dissolves to dust. The horror of a scientific view of life was even more sensationally attacked in *The Mighty Atom*, which owes a possible debt to J. S. Mill's *Autobiography* (1873). The 11-year-old Lionel Valliscourt is told by his materialist teacher, Professor Cadman-Gore, that the basis of all existence is the atom. Lionel pertly out-argues his mentor; nevertheless when his child love Jessamine, daughter of the local sexton, dies, he determines to find out whether there is life after death and hangs himself. (Combe-Martin, the setting for the story, became a minor place of pilgrimage due to the popularity of the novel.)

In *Barabbas* she pioneered the Biblical epic. Spiced with a subplot showing Judas Escariot to have betrayed Christ under the prompting of his sister Judith Escariot, who is a lover of Caiaphas, and with accounts of the Crucifixion that in emotionalism border on the pornographic, the book could be attacked but not ignored. *The Master-Christian* is a more subdued work. It tells how Christ returned to earth as Manuel, a street urchin discovered outside the Cathedral in Rouen. Rejected by the Roman Catholic Church, Manuel is taken in by Cardinal Felix Bonport who, in a sensational scene, is received up into heaven.

Throughout her work she savagely attacked both the established churches and the society of the day whose attentions she in private life courted with paranoiac intensity. *Thelma* concerns a pure and mystic Norwegian girl discovered on a visit to that country by Sir Philip Bruce-Errington, and brought back to England to be his wife. She is more than a match in debate for the sensual, hypocritical Anglican clergyman Charles Dyceworthy, but when the evil Lady Winsleigh has her husband suspect her of unchastity, she retires to Norway, finally to be recovered by the penitent Sir Philip. Apart from the account of corrupt London society life, the novel is remarkable for its evocation of the wild Norse landscape and religion that is set against it. Although Marie Corelli had never been to Norway, guides were soon showing visitors Thelma's rock.

Corelli is, however, most likely to be remembered by *The Sorrows of Satan*. The hero, Geoffrey Tempest, is mysteriously left five million pounds by an uncle, and is befriended by Prince Lucio Ramañez. It is soon clear that the Prince is Satan, after Tempest's soul. The contest is complicated by the two women in his life, the wicked Lady Sibyl Elton and the brilliant, spiritual Mavis Clare, author, who as critics were quick to point out, had the same initials as her creator. The originality of this Faust story is that Prince Lucio himself hopes for Tempest's salvation—forced to expiate his fall from heaven, when man ceases to worship him, he will be free to return to grace. A strong story line and the melodramatic life of the main characters made it deservedly her most popular work.

Corelli saw herself as fulfilling a mission to assert "the underlying spiritual quality of life as it really is," and her work was widely quoted by both fashionable and popular preachers. Her success points to an undoubted thirst for religious literature. She also made it comfortable: the only evil was that willed by man, and every reader had the power for spiritual growth towards total goodness. She embodied this message in fiction that is vulgar in the fullest sense, clichéd, melodramatic, uninformed; yet with an imaginative flair, theatricality, and self-conviction that ultimately defies criticism by literary conventions.

—Louis James

CORNWELL, Bernard. British. Born in London, 23 February 1944. Educated at the University of London, B.A. 1967. Married Judy Acker in 1980. Producer, London, 1969-76, and head of current affairs, Belfast, 1976-79, BBC Television; news editor, Thames Television, London, 1979-80. Agent: Toby Eady, Toby Eady Associates Ltd., 7 Gledhow Gardens, London SW5 0BL, England.

ROMANCE AND HISTORICAL PUBLICATIONS

Novels (series: Richard Sharpe)

Sharpe's Eagle. London, Collins, and New York, Viking Press, 1981.
Sharpe's Gold. London, Collins, 1981; New York, Viking Press, 1982.
Sharpe's Company. London, Collins, and New York, Viking Press, 1982.
Sharpe's Sword. London, Collins, and New York, Viking Press, 1983.
Sharpe's Enemy. London, Collins, and New York, Viking, 1984.
Sharpe's Honour. London, Collins, and New York, Viking, 1985.

Sharpe's Regiment. London, Collins, and New York, Viking, 1986.
Sharpe's Siege. London, Collins, and New York, Viking, 1987.
Redcoat. London, Joseph, 1987; New York, Viking, 1988.
Sharpe's Rifles. London, Collins, and New York, Viking, 1988.
Sharpe's Revenge. London, Collins, and New York, Viking, 1989.

OTHER PUBLICATIONS

Novels

Wildtrack. London, Joseph, 1988.
Sea Lord. London, Joseph, and New York, Putnam, 1989.
Killer's Wake. New York, Putnam, 1989.

*   *   *

By now, the sequence of Sharpe novels is almost complete. With only the year of Waterloo undocumented, Bernard Cornwell's monolithic task—of tracing the course of the Peninsular War through the eyes of his rifleman hero—is virtually accomplished, and only the final defeat of Napoleon remains to be told. It is an altogether impressive achievement, a memorable portrayal of Wellington's army worthy of comparison with the Hornblower novels of C. S. Forester, from whom its author drew his original inspiration. Cornwell's painstaking research, his sure grasp of authentic period detail, enable him to bring home to the reader the scent and feeling of those vanished times, forcing him to witness afresh the savage butchery of the battles, the squalor and corruption that marks life in the early 19th century.

In the character of Richard Sharpe, the grim, scarred rifle officer commissioned from the ranks, Cornwell has created a fitting hero for his canon. Low-born and illegitimate, a ruthless professional soldier, Sharpe is convincingly presented as a man of strong and complex desires, his unremitting hatred for the enemy counter-balanced by his fierce attachment to the men under his command, his physical lusts matched by an austere code of honour from which he never deviates. While it is possible to cite the figure of Hornblower, and perhaps the rifleman Matthew Dodd in Forester's *Death to the French* as his spiritual precursors, Sharpe impresses as a powerful individual creation in his own right.

It is with Sharpe, and his giant Irish comrade Patrick Harper, that Cornwell follows the fortunes of the Peninsular Army from Moore's retreat at Corunna to Wellington's final expulsion of the French from Spain. Each novel has a particular campaign as its background, over which is superimposed Sharpe's personal mission. Cornwell excels in scenes of action, with individual duels merged into the engulfing carnage of the Napoleonic battles. The strength of his narrative impels the reader along with Sharpe and Harper and the men of the South Essex Regiment through the murderous storm of Badajoz, or the vicious close-quarter fighting at the capture of the French Eagle standard at Talavera in *Sharpe's Eagle*. Cornwell recreates the fearful destruction of the citadel at Almeida (*Sharpe's Gold*), the struggle for Salamanca (*Sharpe's Sword*), and the incredible riches of Napoleon's plundered baggage train after the battle of Vitoria (*Sharpe's Honour*). Each is perfectly complemented by Sharpe's own encounters—his duel with the French swordsman Leroux, his fight to the death with the crazed bandit El Catolico outside Almeida, his love-hate relationship with the beautiful but faithless Marquesa. In every case, the work is enhanced by the wealth of minor characters, briefly but expertly drawn, whose presence helps to bring Cornwell's Napoleonic universe to life.

So high is the standard of the writing, it seems invidious to single out any one novel from the rest. Suffice it to say that, for all the excellence of the earlier books, the later novels display a greater imagination and maturity. Particularly striking is *Sharpe's Regiment*, where Sharpe and Harper return to England in search of a regiment appropriated by military speculators. Cornwell's presentation of the corruption and privilege of the army administration at this period is both salutary and utterly believable. *Sharpe's Rifles*, which chronologically predates the other novels, and *Sharpe's Siege*, which describes an ill-advised invasion of France in 1814, are almost equally good.

With *Redcoat*, Cornwell ventures beyond the confines of the Napoleonic age to depict an episode from the American Revolution. Set in and around Philadelphia in the years 1777 and 1778, the novel describes the bitter conflict between the British and their erstwhile colonists, from the viewpoint of a disillusioned British soldier. Cornwell's knowledge of 18th-century warfare is thorough and accomplished, and brings home the brutality of this savage family dispute. Sam Gilpin's struggle with his divided loyalties, and his final choice, are rendered more poignant and credible by the author's masterly evocation of a forgotten place and time. *Redcoat* is an excellent historical novel, and gives further evidence of Cornwell's versatile talent.

This said, it is the Sharpe stories which provide a basis for Bernard Cornwell's reputation, and which serve to establish him as a leading historical novelist. Sharpe is one of the best fictional creations of recent years, and his adventures yield fresh insights into the Napoleonic period. With him the reader re-lives a vanished age, learning the techniques of skirmish and ambush, the handling of the deadly Baker rifle and its fearsome sword-bayonet. Cornwell brings the time alive in a manner unrivaled since Forester. On the evidence of what he has already written, he is deserving of such exalted company.

—Geoffrey Sadler

COSTAIN, Thomas B(ertram). American. Born in Brantford, Ontario, Canada, 8 May 1885. Educated at schools in Brantford. Married Ida Randolph Spragge in 1910; two daughters. Reporter, Brantford *Courier*; editor, Guelph *Daily Mercury*, Ontario, 1908–10, and *Maclean's*, Toronto, 1914–20; chief associate editor, *Saturday Evening Post*, Philadelphia, 1920–34; story editor, Twentieth Century-Fox, 1934–36; advisory editor, Doubleday, publishers, New York, 1939–46. Founding editor, *American Cavalcade* magazine, Chicago, 1937. D. Litt.: University of Western Ontario, London. *Died 8 October 1965.*

ROMANCE AND HISTORICAL PUBLICATIONS

Novels

For My Great Folly. New York, Putnam, 1942.
Ride with Me. New York, Doubleday, 1944.
The Black Rose. New York, Doubleday, 1945; London, Staples Press, 1947.
The Moneyman. New York, Doubleday, 1947; London, Staples Press, 1948.
High Towers. New York, Doubleday, and London, Staples Press, 1949.
Son of a Hundred Kings. New York, Doubleday, 1950.
The Silver Chalice. New York, Doubleday, 1952; London, Hodder and Stoughton, 1953.

The Tontine. New York, Doubleday, 2 vols., 1955; London, Collins, 1956.
Below the Salt. New York, Doubleday, 1957; London, Collins, 1958.
The Darkness and the Dawn. New York, Doubleday, 1959; London, Collins, 1960.
The Last Love. New York, Doubleday, 1963; London, W. H. Allen, 1964.

OTHER PUBLICATIONS

Other

Joshua, Leader of a United People, with Rogers MacVeagh. New York, MacVeagh, 1943.
A History of the Plantagenets:
  The Conquerors. New York, Doubleday, 1949; as *The Conquering Family*, 1962.
  The Magnificent Century. New York, Doubleday, 1951.
  The Three Edwards. New York, Doubleday, 1958.
  The Last Plantagenets. New York, Doubleday, 1962.
The White and the Gold: The French Regime in Canada. New York, Doubleday, 1954; London, Collins, 1957.
The Mississippi (for children). New York, Random House, 1955.
William the Conqueror (for children). New York, Random House, 1959; as *All about William the Conqueror*, London, W. H. Allen, 1961.
The Chord of Steel: The Story of the Invention of the Telephone. New York, Doubleday, 1960.

Editor, with John Beecroft, *Stories [More Stories, 30 Stories] to Remember*. New York, Doubleday, 5 vols., 1956-61.
Editor, *Twelve Short Novels*. New York, Doubleday, 1961.
Editor, *Read with Me*. New York, Doubleday, 1965.

*

Manuscript Collections: University of California, San Diego; University of Pennsylvania, Philadelphia; University of Texas, Austin.

*   *   *

Thomas B. Costain's historical romances combine a fascination with historical minutiae with a deep-seated desire to expose tyranny in all its facets and to promote democracy as the only truly humanistic form of government. At their best (*The Black Rose, Below the Salt, For My Great Folly*) his novels integrate historical events of great moment with the romantic frustrations of a young couple, usually separated by rank and family. The historical events range from Attila the Hun's final assault on Rome to Genghis Khan's invasion of China, from the Norman Conquest to the Magna Carta, from the founding of New Orleans to the final days of Napoleon. At their weakest, history is superimposed on romance to produce digressions and references inexplicable in terms of plot and character (*Son of a Hundred Kings, The Last Love, High Towers*). Costain's favorite digressions trace linguistic origins of words like "rubbernecking," relate the personal history of obscure associates of famous personalities, or expostulate on democratic theories. Costain's historical evaluations are always in terms of modern American democratic values and perspectives rather than historical necessities, expectations, and sensibilities. The result is, despite the wealth of fact, ancients who talk like moderns, adolescents who could be your neighbors, and past cultures and conflicts that seem to foreshadow present democratic concepts.

His Plantagenet tetralogy is vital to understanding the virtues and vices of his historical romances. A moving pageant of history, rich in humanizing details and anecdotes ordinary histories so often ignore, it is marred by disrupted chronology necessitating repetition and by an all too modern interpretation of historical actions and relationships; Costain tries to right the record and show how even the best of kings is but a tyrant, his good acts undercut by cruelty and indifference, and how, even in medieval times, the democratic spirit was at work as peasants rebelled for more rights, freedom, and privilege. Such a stance leads to his justifying even their destructive acts, deploring the nobility that punished them, eulogizing the Wat Tylers and John Balls of the past. In a way this historical account verges on romance, for it pays special tribute to Richard II's love for Isabel, Henry V's for Katherine, Richard III's for Anne. Its panoramic sweep and plethora of characters and events, its attempts to reinterpret the past from a modern perspective are typical of Costain's fictive technique.

Often his heroes are men out of time who have come to view their culture—its customs, politics, and values—with disdain or disgust. Frequently they meet a visionary who looks forward to an age of democracy, fairness, and scientific advancement (Roger Bacon, Galileo, St. Peter). Occasionally there are anachronisms: an awe-struck 17th-century youth musing over "the elevated conversations, the universal truths," propounded by Shakespeare, Jonson, Dekker, and Sly in the Mermaid Tavern, or the first Christians talking like 20th-century protestants. These heroes take pride in the competitive skills of their culture, and eventually match them against experts, proving they can make the longest shot, produce the fastest horse, or make a chalice worthy of Christ's last cup. They break bad laws in the name of justice and suffer long journeys and separation as self-made outcasts.

The scene frequently moves back and forth from the steppes to Rome, from Jerusalem to Antioch, from London to Peking, from Montreal to New Orleans. Ultimately these men find their destiny in a noble woman, sometimes met on journeys (*The Black Rose, Ride with Me, The Silver Chalice*), but more often a rich neighbor, loved since childhood (*Son of a Hundred Kings, For My Great Folly, High Towers, The Darkness and the Dawn, Below the Salt*). Romance thrives despite differences of race, culture, loyalty, or creed: Christian loves pagan; Norman, Saxon; orphaned factory worker, wealthy heiress. The man, always lower ranked, achieves position through courage, industry, and initiative; the factory worker turns star reporter, the lowly Saxon gains knighthood and wealth, the waif turns architectural genius.

Costain strives to integrate historical pageant with the trials and tribulations of his lovers. *The Darkness and the Dawn* traces the last years of Attila the Hun, particularly his final unsuccessful assault on Rome, to contrast the effete decadence of Roman culture with the hearty practicality of Mongolian hordes, to emphasize the dehumanizing effects of both extremes, and to eulogize the rebelliousness of spirited plainsmen who must toy with tyranny ultimately to be free—play Rome against Hun for their own advantage. To win his Norman lady's hand in *The Black Rose*, a Saxon noble, his fortune lost to Norman invaders, seeks fame and fortune in a daring trip to China where he meets, rescues, and falls in love with the captive daughter of a Saxon crusader. To save her, he must outwit slave traders and Mongols alike, and put his trust in a Chinese legend about pale visitors who foretell the will of gods. In *Below the Salt*, a novel mix of modern and medieval, an American Senator employs a young writer to help him write his biography, trace the Plantagenet line in Ireland, uncover a Saxon document that inspired the Magna

Carta, and confirm his Saxon past and 20th-century present. The story moves from the sadistic tortures, dank cells, and limited horizons that Costain always associates with tyrannies to a modern romance involving descendants of the ghost who walks their hills. *For My Great Folly* is a convincing portrait of the Free Rovers, brave and lusty English sea captains like John Ward, who, despite James I's opposition, modelled their seamanship on Sir Walter Raleigh and fought to keep the lanes open for English ships—attacking Spanish vessels, freeing slaves, and taking rich booty. The tale sweeps through the Mediterranean and captures the grim horrors of sea life (rickets, scurvy, death-in-a-basket, becalmed seas) as well as the pride in seamanship and craftsmanship that made English sailors great. Its central character spurns court posturing for the romance and patriotism of the high seas, and acts with courage to force a foolish king to act for England's honor and safety. *Ride with Me* follows the romantic adventures of a lame newspaper man, who uses his paper to goad the government into decisive action against Napoleon; who initiates use of carrier pigeons, war correspondents, "special" editions, and the power press to improve news service; and who pursues his vivacious French mistress, a Royalist turned Bonapartist, through the major steps in the Napoleonic saga: Spain, Russia, escape from Elba, defeat at Waterloo, and bloody reprisal thereafter. Doubtful of his prowess and ability, the hero discovers his strengths as, separated by distance, by scandal, by political conviction, he seeks his beloved. As is clear from each of these books, it is the amalgam of beautiful women, idealistic men, and tyrannical threats that most interests Costain. Too often, however, in an attempt to make a political point, Costain makes his heroes and heroines sacrificial idealists, his villains self-centered sadists.

Several of Costain's books involve the history of important merchant families. *The Moneyman* focuses on the influence of wealthy merchant Jacques Coeur and his family on trade and politics during the reign of Charles VII; *The Tontine* involves two families entangled in an annuity-lottery-insurance scheme; *High Towers* traces the LeMoyne family's willing sacrifice of individual members for a greater cause—conquering the wilderness and building an empire for France; their success in driving out hostile Indians, frustrating greedy countrymen, and manipulating a hesitant king to found New Orleans and control the Mississippi seems to justify this stance. *Son of a Hundred Kings* deals with one of Costain's many orphans who seek their heritage, but its main thrust is the conflicts, competitions, and hatreds of a wealthy, turn-of-the-century Canadian family that rose to fame and wealth through investments in journalism and motorcars.

When Costain is content to focus on plot and character and to discuss historical events only as they relate to his central focus, his books have a compelling force that commands interest, but when he lets his fascination with detail lead him to wander from the plot, his novels degenerate into a disconnected patchwork of anecdotes. *The Last Love* is typical of his attempts to do too much, for it tries to recreate Napoleon's drive, power, triumph, and genius; humanize him; characterize those important figures around him, including past loves; summarize his significant acts and battles; and follow the metamorphosis of his final, would-be mistress from childhood to womanhood. Thus Costain must be evaluated in terms of how well he reconciles his different but ambitious goals, the extremes of depicting detailed history, creating exciting plot, indulging in sentimental romance, and defending democratic idealism.

—Gina Macdonald

COULSON, Juanita (Ruth, née Wellons). American. Born in Anderson, Indiana, 12 February 1933. Educated at Ball State University, Muncie, Indiana, B.S. 1954, M.A. 1961. Married the writer Robert Coulson in 1954; one son. Elementary school teacher, Huntington, Indiana, 1954–55; collator, Heckman Book Bindery, North Manchester, Indiana, 1955–57; publisher, *SFWA Forum*, two years. Since 1953 editor, with Robert Coulson, *Yandro* fan magazine; since 1963 freelance writer. Recipient: Hugo award, for editing, 1965. Guest of Honor, World Science Fiction Convention, 1972. Agent: Virginia Kidd, 538 East Harford Street, Milford, Pennsylvania 18337. Address: 2677W 500N, Hartford City, Indiana 47348, U.S.A.

ROMANCE AND HISTORICAL PUBLICATIONS

Novels

The Secret of Seven Oaks. New York, Berkley, 1972.
Door into Terror. New York, Berkley, 1972.
Stone of Blood. New York, Ballantine, 1975.
Fear Stalks the Bayou. New York, Ballantine, and Skirden, Lancashire, Magna, 1976.
Dark Priestess. New York, Ballantine, 1977.
Fire of the Andes. New York, Ballantine, 1979.

OTHER PUBLICATIONS

Novels

Crisis on Cheiron. New York, Ace, 1967.
The Singing Stones. New York, Ace, 1968.
Unto the Last Generation. Toronto, Laser, 1975.
Space Trap. Toronto, Laser, 1976.
The Web of Wizardry. New York, Ballantine, 1978.
The Death God's Citadel. New York, Ballantine, 1980.
Children of the Stars:
    1. *Tomorrow's Heritage.* New York, Ballantine, 1981.
    2. *Outward Bound.* New York, Ballantine, 1982.
    3. *Legacy of Earth.* New York, Ballantine, 1989.

*

Juanita Coulson comments:

In my romance and gothic novels I always try to include an element of fantasy, sometimes partially explained at the conclusion—offering an alternate, "rational" reason for some of the mysterious events of the story. But in the instance of *Dark Priestess* the form and time-set of the novel allowed me to dispense with all modern rationalizations. A romance, by its very nature, calls for suspension of disbelief. And if the protagonist—heroine—genuinely believes in the supernatural element affecting her life and the lives of others within the story, I feel the characters should respond accordingly. In modern times, perhaps not *all* events are explainable by hard, cold logic. The most outrageous things may someday be proved true. For a very long time, science disdained the theory of the German meteorologist Wegener, who suggested that certain peculiarities of the globe could be explained by means of drifting continents. It took a very long time for the experts to realize he was right after all. So it may not be wise to dismiss intuition, hunches, and other paraphysical phenomena—such as I've employed in telling my romances and gothics. Maybe it's all nonsense. And maybe some

if it contains a kernel of truth. Time may tell. And thus I provide, in most cases, a choice: solid reason and the heroine's inner feelings.

*   *   *

Juanita Coulson's books try to fit modern liberated career women into the traditional gothic style without offending anyone's sensibilities. In other words, the women must not be too capable, too sexually free, in the last analysis, too modern. Some authors have successfully done this—Barbara Mertz, especially in her books under the name Elizabeth Peters, is one example. But when Coulson tries to force her characters into the gothic mold, their independence will not fit. When danger threatens, the feisty heroine turns around and starts looking for a man to get her out of her predicament. This not only undercuts Coulson's thrust, but also makes the heroines rather less interesting than they might otherwise be. The male characters also exemplify stereotypes all too familiar in gothics: for instance, the wild brother who is really reliable; the solid brother who is really a villain.

Coulson's failure in characterization is especially surprising when one compares her gothics to her science-fiction books, where she does portray a fairly wide array of independent women characters (the two sisters in *The Death God's Citadel*, for instance, are different in many ways, but even the timorous Ilissa has her own strength). Eileen, in *Fear Stalks the Bayou*, on the other hand, is little more than a woman who bites off more than she can chew and wants help as soon as she realizes it.

Fear Stalks the Bayou is one of a series of "Zodiac Gothics": the characters' astrological signs are given and after the denouement a "note" explains how an astrological analysis made everyone's actions and motives apparent, if not inevitable, from the first. This format is perhaps responsible for some of the woodenness in the plotting in the book, as well as the strain on Coulson's writing, never more than workmanlike, as she tries to insert birthdates inconspicuously in the text.

The contemporary real-estate development motive and the heroines' interest in modern art contrast with the more old-fashioned mildly exotic background of a clannish family in Creole New Orleans. So even in the incidentals of this story can be seen the conflict that plagues Coulson—a conflict between the traditional elements of the gothic romance and the more current type of romantic suspense story.

—Susan Branch

COURTNEY, Caroline. Address: c/o Arlington Books, 15–17 King Street, London S.W.1, England.

ROMANCE AND HISTORICAL PUBLICATIONS

Novels

Duchess in Disguise. New York, Warner, and London, Arlington, 1979.

A Wager for Love. New York, Warner, and London, Arlington, 1979.

Love Unmasked. New York, Warner, and London, Arlington, 1979.

Guardian of the Heart. New York, Warner, 1979; London, Arlington, 1980.

Dangerous Engagement. New York, Warner, 1979; London, Arlington, 1980.

The Fortunes of Love. New York, Warner, and London, Arlington, 1980.

Forbidden Love. New York, Warner, 1980; London, Arlington, 1982.

Love Triumphant. New York, Warner, 1980.

Heart of Honour. London, Arlington, 1980.

The Romantic Rivals. New York, Warner, and Arlington, 1980.

Love's Masquerade. London, Arlington, 1981.

Love of My Life. New York, Warner, 1981; London, Arlington, 1983.

Libertine in Love. London, Arlington, 1982.

Abandoned for Love. Boston, G. K. Hall, 1982; London, Arlington, 1983.

Destiny's Duchess. London, Arlington, 1983.

The Tempestuous Affair. London, Arlington, 1983; Boston, G. K. Hall, 1985.

The Daring Heart. Boston, G. K. Hall, 1983; London, Arlington, 1985.

The Masquerading Heart. London, Arlington, 1984.

A Lover's Victory. London, Arlington, 1984.

Love in Waiting. London, Arlington, 1984.

The Courier of Love. London, Arlington, 1984; Boston, G. K. Hall, 1986.

Hearts or Diamonds. London, Arlington, 1985.

Prisoner of Passion. London, Arlington, 1985.

Dual Enchantment. London, Arlington, 1985.

Conspiracy of Kisses. London, Arlington, 1986.

*   *   *

Of all the contemporary romance novelists, Caroline Courtney is the most likely to succeed, Barbara Cartland as the grande dame of the formula romance. Her characters and style recall the early Cartland at her best, before her heroines became too breathless or incoherent to speak in complete sentences. The plots are simplistic and focus on the heroine and her emotions. The innocent heroines and stalwart heroes are likable people who display all the requisite virtues, such as sensitivity, fidelity, tenderness, and self-sacrifice. Even the names are right: Clorinda, Davinia, Candida, Serenity, Valeria; Julian, Gilles, Justin, Greville, Auberon. Whatever the names, however, the hero and heroine are clearly meant for each other from the moment they meet, although there are always problems to overcome before they can be united and love triumph over all.

One of her earliest novels, *Duchess in Disguise*, exhibits the general characteristics and themes found in her other books. Clorinda, a pure, young country miss, weds a notorious rake, the Duke of Westhampton. Dismissed to one of his country estates, she resolves to seek revenge. She disguises herself and poses as yet another virginal innocent, and in this guise she wins his love. He learns the value of true love and is ready to sacrifice his reputation to pursue this ideal. Mutual love is revealed and everyone lives happily ever after.

The idea of the masquerade or disguise appears in about half of Courtney's novels, and is directly reflected in several titles. Similarly the theme of the disillusioned rake redeemed by pure love occurs frequently (*A Wager for Love, Guardian of the Heart, Forbidden Love, Libertine in Love*). Obviously none of

this is particularly original. Fans of Barbara Cartland and Georgette Heyer will undoubtedly recognize many of the elements in Courtney's plots. However, Caroline Courtney has polished the romance formula to a fine sheen. For sheer escapist, romantic fantasy, she is hard to beat.

—Barbara E. Kemp

———————

COWEN, Frances. Also writes as Eleanor Hyde. British. Born in Oxford, 27 December 1915. Educated at Ursuline Convent, Oxford, 1920–28; Milham Ford School, Oxford, 1928–35. Married George Heinrich Munthe in 1938 (died 1941); one daughter. Worked for Blackwell, publishers, Oxford 1938–39; member of Air Raid Precautions staff, Dartmouth, Devon, 1940–44; assistant secretary, Royal Literary Fund, London, 1955–66. Address: c/o Robert Hale Ltd., 45–47 Clerkenwell Green, London EC1R 0HT, England.

ROMANCE AND HISTORICAL PUBLICATIONS

Novels

The Little Heiress. London, Gresham, 1961.

The Balcony. London, Gresham, 1962.

A Step in the Dark. London, Gresham, 1962.

The Desperate Holiday. London, Gresham, 1962.

The Elusive Quest. London, Gresham, 1965.

The Bitter Reason. London, Gresham, 1966.

Scented Danger. London, Gresham, 1966.

The One Between. London, Hale, 1967.

The Gentle Obsession. London, Hale, 1968.

The Fractured Silence. London, Hale, 1969.

The Daylight Fear. London, Hale, 1969; New York, Ace, 1973.

The Shadow of Polperro. London, Hale, 1969; New York, Ace, 1973.

Edge of Terror. London, Hale, 1970.

The Hounds of Carvello. London, Hale, 1970; New York, Ace, 1973.

The Nightmare Ends. London, Hale, 1970; New York, Ace, 1972.

The Lake of Darkness. London, Hale, 1971; New York, Ace, 1974.

The Unforgiving Moment. London, Hale, 1971.

The Curse of the Clodaghs. London, Hale, 1973; New York, Ace, 1974.

Shadow of Theale. London, Hale, and New York, Ace, 1974.

The Village of Fear. New York, Ace, 1974; London, Hale, 1975.

The Secret of Weir House. London, Hale, 1975.

The Dangerous Child. London, Hale, 1975.

The Haunting of Helen Farley. London, Hale, 1976.

The Medusa Connection. London, Hale, 1976.

Sinister Melody. London, Hale, 1976.

The Silent Pool. London, Hale, 1977.

The Lost One. London, Hale, 1977.

Gateway to Nowhere. London, Hale, 1978.

The House Without a Heart. London, Hale, 1978.

House of Larne. London, Hale, 1980.

Wait for Night. London, Hale, 1980.

The Elusive Lover. London, Hale, 1981.

Sunrise at Even. London, Hale, 1982.

Novels as Eleanor Hyde (series: Tudor)

Tudor Maid. London, Hale, 1972.
Tudor Masquerade. London, Hale, 1972.
Tudor Mayhem. London, Hale, 1973.
Tudor Mystery. London, Hale, 1974.
Tudor Myth. London, Hale, 1976.
Tudor Mausoleum. London, Hale, 1977.
Tudor Murder. London, Hale, 1977.
Tudor Mansion. London, Hale, 1978.
Tudor Malice. London, Hale, 1979.
The Princess Passes. London, Hale, 1979.

OTHER PUBLICATIONS

Other (for children)

In the Clutch of the Green Hand. London, Nelson, 1929.
The Wings That Failed. London, Collins, 1931; abridged, as
    The Plot That Failed, 1933.
The Milhurst Mystery. London, Blackie, 1933.
The Conspiracy of Silence. London, Sheldon Press, 1935.
The Perilous Adventure. London, Queensway Press, 1936.
Children's Book of Pantomimes. London, Cassell, 1936.
Laddie's Way: The Adventures of a Fox Terrier. London, Lut-
    terworth Press, 1939.
The Girl Who Knew Too Much. London, Lutterworth Press,
    1940.
Mystery Tower. London, Lutterworth Press, 1945.
Honor Bound. London, Lutterworth Press, 1946.
Castle in Wales. Huddersfield, Schofield and Sims, 1947.
The Secret of Arrival. Huddersfield, Schofield and Sims, 1947.
Mystery at the Walled House. London, Lutterworth Press,
    1951.
The Little Countess. London, Thames, 1954.
The Riddle of the Rocks. London, Lutterworth Press, 1956.
Clover Cottage. London, Blackie, 1958.
The Secret of Grange Farm. London, Children's Press, 1961.
The Secret of the Loch. London, Children's Press, 1963.

*   *   *

Frances Cowen is adept at producing emotional suspense stories—for children in full-length books and tales published in the
Girl's Own Paper and in adult detective fiction and thriller romances. She has been writing for more than five decades but her
feeling for the romantic gothic mood is as intense as ever. *The
Secret of Weir House* combines the flavours of Edwardian and
modern life with English and American interest. Gisele—from
the USA—inherits a Thames-side Victorian house from a remote
English relative, but when she arrives to claim her property, it is
not only occupied by squatters but overhung with a ghostly mystery that is linked to the death by drowning of a great aunt just
before World War I. Stephen, a London social worker, however,
not only helps Gisele to unravel the mystery but, of course, to
find love.

Cowen is most strongly associated with romance when she
writes historical novels as Eleanor Hyde. There are nine of these
books in the "Tudor" series, with vivid conveyance of the period by discerning use of historical trappings, ritual pageantry
and splendours. There are the sights and sounds of viol, lute,
and recorder playing in the musicians' gallery of great houses;
the herb garden of a country manor; the "chaotic medley" of
men-at-arms, ladies-in-waiting, and courtiers attending "Glori-
ana" on one of her journeys—and so on. Events in the first of

these novels (*Tudor Maid*) clearly illustrate the dramatic and romantic nature of the series. Ann de Chaubriez, the illegitimate
daughter of a French marquis and an English mother, is brought
up in France. Eventually, orphaned abruptly by her father's murder, and unprovided for, she is taken to England to work ostensibly as a governess in the home of an unscrupulous plotter
against the Queen: he tries to use Ann's auburn-haired, pale-
faced resemblance to the Queen in a scheme to overthrow her.

Ann undergoes some hair-raising adventures before being rescued from these intrigues by Richard Davenant—a young Englishman who not only clears her reputation but marries her.
Similar themes recur in the books. In the last novel of the series,
Tudor Malice, there is another orphaned heroine, Isobelle, who
finds herself exposed to black magic as well as court intrigues.
In her case too, romantic love—in the shape of a miller's son,
Matthew Holborn—lifts her out of the hazards of association
with magic and majesty.

—Mary Cadogan

_____

CRAIG, Alisa. See **MacLEOD, Charlotte**.

_____

CRAMPTON, Helen. See **CHESNEY, Marion**.

_____

CRAVEN, Sara. Pseudonym for Ann Thomas. Address: c/o
Mills and Boon Ltd., 18–24 Paradise Road, Richmond, Surrey
TW9 1SR, England.

ROMANCE AND HISTORICAL PUBLICATIONS

Novels

The Garden of Dreams. London, Mills and Boon, 1975.
A Gift for a Lion. London, Mills and Boon, 1977.
A Place of Storms. London, Mills and Boon, 1977.
Strange Adventure. London, Mills and Boon, 1977.
Temple of the Moon. London, Mills and Boon, 1977.
Wild Melody. London, Mills and Boon, 1977.
Dragon's Lair. London, Mills and Boon, 1978.
High Tide at Midnight. London, Mills and Boon, 1978.
Past All Forgetting. London, Mills and Boon, 1978 .
The Devil at Archangel. London, Mills and Boon, 1978.
Flame of Diablo. London, Mills and Boon, 1979.
Moth to the Flame. London, Mills and Boon, 1979.
Solitaire. London, Mills and Boon, 1979.
Fugitive Wife. London, Mills and Boon, 1980.
Moon of Aphrodite. London, Mills and Boon, 1980.
Shadow of Desire. London, Mills and Boon, 1980.
Dark Summer Dawn. London, Mills and Boon, 1981.
Summer of the Raven. London, Mills and Boon, 1981.
Witching Hour. London, Mills and Boon, 1981.
Counterfeit Bride. London, Mills and Boon, 1982.
Unguarded Moment. London, Mills and Boon, 1982.
A Bad Enemy. London, Mills and Boon, 1983.
Pagan Adversary. London, Mills and Boon, 1983.
Sup with the Devil. London, Mills and Boon, 1983.

Dark Paradise. London, Mills and Boon, 1984.
Alien Vengeance. London, Mills and Boon, 1985.
Act of Betrayal. London, Mills and Boon, 1985.
Escape Me Never. London, Mills and Boon, 1985.
Promise of the Unicorn. London, Mills and Boon, 1985.
A High Price to Pay. London, Mills and Boon, 1986.
The Marriage Deal. London, Mills and Boon, 1986.
Night of the Condor. London, Mills and Boon, 1987.
Outsider. London, Mills and Boon, 1987.
Witch's Harvest. London, Mills and Boon, 1987.
Flawless. London, Mills and Boon, 1989.

*   *   *

Fortunately for romance readers, editors are careful to select only the best and most talented writers to join the ranks of the original favorites in the Mills and Boon or Harlequin series. Sara Craven, in real life Ann Thomas, is one of those special writers who have achieved such enviable status. In fact, her name on the cover is sufficient reason for many readers to buy a novel.

How did Craven manage to make the change from merely being a romance writer to being a Mills and Boon or Harlequin writer? In the first place, she concentrated on developing well defined characters. Contrary to popular opinion, the romance genre is not simplistic. Character development with true depth is essential to the novels, as is believable motivation and conflict. It is in these areas that Craven is particularly talented and creative. Perhaps one of the reasons for her success is the fact that she has decided to concentrate on a specific type of romance, rather than attempting to hit several different types of markets. American readers find her novels in the Harlequin ''Presents'' series and this seems to be the audience that she feels most comfortable in writing for. These novels are more than the ''sweet'' romance, but less explicit than novels in some of the other series.

Generally, her heroines are innocent, although some have suffered an ''ill-fated'' romance earlier in their lives. They are usually in their early twenties. They also have some sort of job skills and thus are capable women who are able to face life on their own terms. Except fate, circumstances, and events conspire to place them in a vulnerable position. Perhaps it is this combination of capability and vulnerability that make her heroines so believable and empathetic. It might be that her readers see a bit of themselves in her heroines as they cope with their own needs and demands.

The heroes are usually arrogant, sophisticated, macho males who can't stand to see the woman struggling through her own problems, even if they are self-created. It is not her innocence that is always the primary factor in creating interest between the main characters, although it certainly helps. Rather, it is the heroine's character and beliefs that attract him, often unwillingly.

In *Shadow of Desire*, Ginevra Clayton, or Ginny as she is usually called, faces a daunting future. Her parents were recently killed in an accident, leaving Ginny with an 11-year-old brother and a great-aunt in her mid-seventies to care for, without help from her older sister, Barbara. Compounding her problems is the fact that their house must be sold to meet debts. Ginny manages to get a position as a resident housekeeper with an apartment as part of her salary. She also had secretarial training and hopes to do part time typing.

The new tenant of the house arrives and Ginny is terrified that she will lose her position, and thus her home. Naturally, her first encounter with the hero is less than successful. The hero is Max Hendrick, an extremely successful playwright who sees Ginny as just another woman chasing after his cousin, Toby. Plot compli-

cations include the owner of the house, Vivien Lanyon, who is fascinated by Max and sees Ginny as a definite problem. Ginny's sister, Barbara, adds more difficulty for she is an actress determined to get a part in Max's new play. It seems the harder Ginny tries, the worse things get. To cap it all off, Ginny falls in love with Max, bad temper and all. As one can see, this story is a complex tangle of hidden motives and hidden needs.

Counterfeit Bride is just as complicated as Craven weaves a story of cultural differences, an autocratic Grandee, and an independent English secretary into an emotional novel of misunderstandings, unrequited love, and mistaken pride.

Nicola Tarrent is just finishing a job in Mexico and plans to take a vacation there. Before she can leave, she becomes involved with a plan to help a girlfriend avoid an arranged marriage. Nicola sets out to impersonate her and neatly falls into a trap set by Luis Alvarado de Montalba, the intended bridegroom. Both fall in love with each other, but go to any extreme to deny it. Besides the conflict between the two, his aunt and cousin create all sorts of difficulties for Nicola. The ending is more than romantic as both Nicola and Luis toss pride aside and admit their love.

Again, Craven creates believable characters that readers can care about. She shows their complexity, their needs, and their growth towards each other as they face the uncertainties of unacknowledged and unreturned love. Perhaps one of Craven's strongest talents is her ability to create the tension of physical love without opening the bedroom door too far, or too often. When she does, such scenes are used to further the story, to show conflict or love. The scenes grow out of the story—they do not interrupt it. For some of her readers, this is a decided plus.

—Arlene Moore

CROMWELL, Elsie. See **LEE, Elsie.**

CROSS, Victor. See **COFFMAN, Virginia.**

CROWE, Cecily (née Teague). American. Born in New York City. Educated at St. Agatha School, New York; Columbia University, New York. Married 1) Richard H. Crowe (died), one daughter; 2) James A. Bentley in 1975. Agent: Harold Ober Associates, 40 East 49th Street, New York, New York 10017. Address: Brick House, Mirror Lake, New Hampshire 03853, U.S.A.

ROMANCE AND HISTORICAL PUBLICATIONS

Novels

Miss Spring. New York, Random House, 1953.
The Tower of Kilraven. New York, Holt Rinehart, 1965.
Northwater. New York, Holt Rinehart, 1968.
The Twice-Born. New York, Random House, 1972.
Abbeygate. New York, Coward McCann, 1977.
The Talisman. New York, St. Martin's Press, 1979.

Bloodrose House. New York, St. Martin's Press, 1985.

*

Manuscript Collection: Boston University Library.

*　　*　　*

It is obvious that Cecily Crowe honed her novelistic skills by writing short stories. Her prose style is exquisitely crafted and tight as befits the short story which must reveal much in a confined space. Crowe's novels burst with highly detailed, almost practiced descriptive passages. One feels that she knows every secret of the lives of even her minor characters.

While these novels fall into the category of romantic suspense their true emphasis is on romance, in the sense that both the characters and the reader are transported to a world remote from ordinary life. The heroines are as a rule rather unglamorous women, often older than the average romantic heroine. For the most part they are widows or in some manner losers at love. When these women are transplanted into exotic environments like castles and brought into contact with traditionally brooding Gothic heroes their adventures are escapist entertainment of the highest order. Crowe's sense of humor saves her work from being merely frothy. There is a tongue-in-cheek feeling about much of her work that seems lovingly to parody the style that she has chosen. Her humor is evident in *The Tower of Kilraven* when she first describes the frankly sexual allure of one of the heroes and then describes him as mounted upon a "tall, self-centered-looking horse." Flashes of such humor and mockery as this run through most of her work.

The characters in Cecily Crowe's writing are so painstakingly delineated that they stand out against the rich backgrounds like beautifully detailed miniatures. Even children, who often get very short shrift in romances, are treated as full characters rather than plot devices. Thomas, Maggie, and Anne in *Abbeygate* are memorable for their complete naturalness. They are neither perfect creatures nor monsters, but believably troubled children. The secondary characters in all the novels are drawn with somewhat broader stokes, like Dottie in *The Talisman*, whose passion for costumes like a Hawaiian print skirt, shocking pink sweater, and Tartan shawl is a metaphor for her personality. The heroes are perhaps the least realistic of all the characters since they are made in the Heathcliff-Mr. Rochester mold. Nevertheless, they are human and attractive in their flaws so that the reader can hardly fail to respond to their charms.

Crowe's training in the short story emerges again in the endings of her books. She avoids the over-writing and the sensation of winding down that is often found in romances. In *The Tower of Kilraven* the love story is left hanging as the heroine leaves the castle without having made a choice between two prospective lovers. A less confident author might have written this ending to death. The crispness and finality of these denouements leave the reader satisfied rather than sated.

—Susan Quinn Berneis

———

CURRIE, Katy. See **PALMER, Diana.**

———

CURTIN, Philip. See **LOWNDES, Marie Belloc.**

———

CURTIS, Peter. See **LOFTS, Nora.**

———

CURTIS, Sharon. See **LONDON, Laura.**

———

CURTIS, Thomas. See **LONDON, Laura.**

———

CURZON, Lucia. See **STEVENSON, Florence.**

———

DAILEY, Janet. American. Born in Storm Lake, Iowa, 21 May 1944. Educated at Independence High School, Iowa, graduated 1962. Married William Dailey; two stepchildren. Secretary, Omaha, Nebraska, 1963–74. Recipient: Romance Writers of America Golden Heart award, 1981. Agent: Janbill Ltd., Star Route 4, Box 2197, Branson, Missouri 65616, U.S.A.

ROMANCE AND HISTORICAL PUBLICATIONS

Novels (series: Calder)

No Quarter Asked. London, Mills and Boon, 1974; Toronto, Harlequin, 1976.
Savage Land. London, Mills and Boon, 1974; Toronto, Harlequin, 1976.
Something Extra. London, Mills and Boon, 1975; Toronto, Harlequin, 1978.
Fire and Ice. London, Mills and Boon, 1975; Toronto, Harlequin, 1976.
Boss Man from Ogallala. London, Mills and Boon, 1975; Toronto, Harlequin, 1976.
After the Storm. London, Mills and Boon, 1975; Toronto, Harlequin, 1976.
Land of Enchantment. London, Mills and Boon, 1975; Toronto, Harlequin, 1976.
Sweet Promise. London, Mills and Boon, 1976; Toronto, Harlequin, 1979.
The Homeplace. London, Mills and Boon, and Toronto, Harlequin, 1976.
Dangerous Masquerade. London, Mills and Boon, 1976; Toronto, Harlequin, 1977.
Show Me. London, Mills and Boon, 1976; Toronto, Harlequin, 1977.
Valley of the Vapours. London, Mills and Boon, 1976; Toronto, Harlequin, 1977.
The Night of the Cotillion. London, Mills and Boon, 1976; Toronto, Harlequin, 1977.
Fiesta San Antonio. London, Mills and Boon, and Toronto, Harlequin, 1977.

Bluegrass King. London, Mills and Boon, and Toronto, Harlequin, 1977.

A Lyon's Share. London, Mills and Boon, and Toronto, Harlequin, 1977.

The Widow and the Wastrel. London, Mills and Boon, and Toronto, Harlequin, 1977.

The Ivory Cane. London, Mills and Boon, 1977; Toronto, Harlequin, 1978.

Six White Horses. London, Mills and Boon, 1977; Toronto, Harlequin, 1979.

To Tell the Truth. London, Mills and Boon, 1977; Toronto, Harlequin, 1978.

The Master Fiddler. London, Mills and Boon, 1977; Toronto, Harlequin, 1978.

Giant of Medabi. London, Mills and Boon, and Toronto, Harlequin, 1978.

Beware of the Stranger. London, Mills and Boon, and Toronto, Harlequin, 1978.

Darling Jenny. London, Mills and Boon, and Toronto, Harlequin, 1978.

The Indy Man. London, Mills and Boon, and Toronto, Harlequin, 1978.

Reilly's Woman. London, Mills and Boon, and Toronto, Harlequin, 1978.

For Bitter or Worse. London, Mills and Boon, 1978; Toronto, Harlequin, 1979.

Tidewater Lover. London, Mills and Boon, 1978; Toronto, Harlequin, 1979.

The Bride of the Delta Queen. London, Mills and Boon, 1978; Toronto, Harlequin, 1979.

Green Mountain Man. London, Mills and Boon, 1978; Toronto, Harlequin, 1979.

Sonora Sundown. London, Mills and Boon, and Toronto, Harlequin, 1978.

Summer Mahogany. London, Mills and Boon, 1978; Toronto, Harlequin, 1979.

The Matchmakers. London, Mills and Boon, and Toronto, Harlequin, 1978.

Big Sky Country. London, Mills and Boon, and Toronto, Harlequin, 1978.

Low Country Liar. London, Mills and Boon, and Toronto, Harlequin, 1979.

Strange Bedfellow. London, Mills and Boon, and Toronto, Harlequin, 1979.

For Mike's Sake. London, Mills and Boon, and Toronto, Harlequin, 1979.

Sentimental Journey. London, Mills and Boon, and Toronto, Harlequin, 1979.

Sweet Promise. London, Mills and Boon, and Toronto, Harlequin, 1979.

Bed of Grass. London, Mills and Boon, 1979; Toronto, Harlequin, 1980.

That Boston Man. London, Mills and Boon, 1979; Toronto, Harlequin, 1980.

Kona Winds. London, Mills and Boon, 1979; Toronto, Harlequin, 1980.

A Land Called Deseret. London, Mills and Boon, and Torrance, Harlequin, 1979.

Touch the Wind. New York, Pocket Books, 1979; London, Fontana, 1980.

Difficult Decision. London, Mills and Boon, and Toronto, Harlequin, 1980.

Enemy in Camp. London, Mills and Boon, and Toronto, Harlequin, 1980.

Heart of Stone. London, Mills and Boon, and Toronto, Harlequin, 1980.

Lord of the High Lonesome. London, Mills and Boon, and Toronto, Harlequin, 1980.

The Mating Season. London, Mills and Boon, and Toronto, Harlequin, 1980.

Southern Nights. London, Mills and Boon, and Toronto, Harlequin, 1980.

The Thawing of Mara. London, Mills and Boon, and Toronto, Harlequin, 1980.

One of the Boys. London, Mills and Boon, and Toronto, Harlequin, 1980.

The Rogue. New York, Pocket Books, and London, Fontana, 1980.

Wild and Wonderful. London, Mills and Boon, 1980; Toronto, Harlequin, 1981.

Ride the Thunder. New York, Pocket Books, and London, Fontana, 1981.

The Travelling Kind. London, Mills and Boon, and Toronto, Harlequin, 1981.

Dakota Dreamin'. London, Mills and Boon, and Toronto, Harlequin, 1981.

The Hostage Bride. New York, Silhouette, 1981.

With a Little Luck. London, Mills and Boon, and Toronto, Harlequin, 1981.

That Carolina Summer. London, Mills and Boon, and Toronto, Harlequin, 1981.

Night Way. New York, Pocket Books, and London, Futura, 1981.

The Lancaster Men. New York, Silhouette, 1981; London, Hodder and Stoughton, 1982.

This Calder Sky. New York, Pocket Books, 1981; London, Futura, 1982.

For the Love of God. New York, Silhouette, 1981; London, Hodder and Stoughton, 1982.

A Tradition of Pride. London, Mills and Boon, and Toronto, Harlequin, 1982.

Northern Magic. London, Mills and Boon, and Toronto, Harlequin, 1982.

Terms of Surrender. New York, Silhouette, and London, Hodder and Stoughton, 1982.

Wildcatter's Woman. New York, Silhouette, and London, Hodder and Stoughton, 1982.

This Calder Range. New York, Pocket Books, 1982; London, Hodder and Stoughton, 1983.

Stands a Calder Man. New York, Pocket Books, 1982; London, Hodder and Stoughton, 1983.

Foxfire Light. New York, Silhouette, 1982; Bath, Firecrest, 1985.

The Second Time. New York, Silhouette, 1982; London, Hodder and Stoughton, 1983.

Mistletoe and Holly. New York, Silhouette, 1982; London, Hodder and Stoughton, 1983.

Separate Cabins. New York, Silhouette, 1983; Bath, Chivers, 1984.

Western Man. New York, Silhouette, and London, Hodder and Stoughton, 1983.

The Best Way to Lose. New York, Silhouette, 1983; London, Hodder and Stoughton, 1984.

Calder Born, Calder Bred. New York, Pocket Books, 1983; London, Hodder and Stoughton, 1984.

Leftover Love. New York, Silhouette, and London, Hodder and Stoughton, 1984.

Silver Wings, Santiago Blue. New York, Poseidon Press, 1984.

The Pride of Hannah Wade. New York, Pocket Books, and London, Hodder and Stoughton, 1985.

The Glory Game. New York, Poseidon Press, 1985; London, Joseph, 1986.

The Great Alone. New York, Poseidon Press, and London, Joseph, 1986.
Heiress. Boston, Little Brown, and London, Joseph, 1987.
Rivals. Boston, Little Brown, and London, Joseph, 1989.

*

Janet Dailey comments:

I consider myself to be a teller of stories about the inter-relationships of people whether it be in the multi-character form of my major novels or the one-on-one, man/woman relationships of my romance stories. To me, it is extremely important that each story be uniquely different, even if they retain common elements such as conflicts that are resolved to "happy endings." I write my stories to entertain. That is their purpose for being. It's very rewarding for an author artistically to learn of the hours of enjoyment people have derived from reading his or her works. I know it's been true for me.

*   *   *

Every afternoon American television dramatizes in soap opera after soap opera the story of a passionate, successful man desperately in love with a beautiful, partially rejecting woman. Because soap operas, like other folklore, weave their spells through stretching and repetition, these heroically devoted men conceive affections that last literally for years, through marriages, divorces, remarriages, even through casting changes. What they can never outlast, it seems, is their audience's patient attention to a tale of diligent pursuit, or rather, of what it is like to be diligently pursued. These are women's stories, after all; a permanently smitten man is necessary, but women's stories still tell the tale of the pursued. From such a point of view, a strong man is not diminished by his hopelessly undying passion, even if he is made to whimper occasionally. Rather, he increases in importance and attractiveness because he manifests emotional vulnerability. Whatever else they give their audiences, American soap operas provide women with embodiment of this fantasy. You are beautiful, they insinuate; you are hesitatingly passionate, you are desperately loved.

The novels of Janet Dailey tell this insistent story, too, though in fore-shortened versions. Hers are not leisurely tales like the incrementally repeated afternoon soaps. Rather, Dailey writes urgent novels of rapid, briefly thwarted pursuit, often in hurried prose, especially in those done to the ten-chapter tune of her trademark romances, Harlequin and Silhouette. These brief romances are indeed "silhouettes"—one-dimensional portraits of single-minded characters; they are bare-bones books, which pay little attention to secondary characters, personal histories, temporal settings (other than a vague "now"), or even to place. In fact, though the back covers of Dailey's Harlequins reiterate her intention to set a romance in each of the 50 states, place has little resonance in her novels. Janet Dailey's shorter novels are Rest-Stop Romances, replete with a fleeting mention of each state's highlights, but lacking the leisure and warmth of long acquaintance with any.

When we enter Dailey's fictional world we trade "leisure," "warmth," and "long acquaintance" for haste, ardent fires, and instant recognition. The "ardent fires" and "instant recognition" take place, of course, between the two principals, whose often denied but utterly undeniable attraction for each other sparks each book. Dailey is a canny writer and varies the circumstances of each fateful attraction without ever altering the supra-rational impetus behind it. "Physical chemistry" is the way the heroine of *Touch the Wind* "rationalizes" this passion—

in her case a puzzling ardor for the Mexican outlaw who has kidnapped her. Other heroines explain in different but equally fatal terms the myth that underlies Dailey's world: "It was always you," Kit pronounces at the end of *Lord of the High Lonesome*, "There was never anyone else but you." For Dailey's women this is inevitably true. Even if they have had previous lovers or husbands, they have not been really *touched* before. In *Dakota Dreamin'* Edie's late husband has never moved her the way her truculent new neighbor has; in *Green Mountain Men* the dead husband is fictitious; in *Show Me* even the heroine's prior sexual encounter with the hero has been fabricated to protect a child. In this sense, each Dailey heroine is chaste; even if experienced she is essentially untouched until the grand passion depicted in each book awakens her.

This awakening, of course, is disturbing, because in true romance fashion Dailey's heroines find themselves devastatingly aroused by men they initially dislike and don't entirely trust. The fearsomeness of this arousal leaves the heroine in a prolonged state of semi-surrender, as Dailey treats hero and reader alike to continual, teasing *romantus interruptus*, punctuated by the heroine's frantic, belated cries of "No!" Given the radically tight focus of romance fiction, I am surprised to find that Dailey's love and sex scenes are often the most poorly written parts of her books. Stock phrases show up in novel after novel: each hero has "muscular thighs," impresses upon each heroine his "hard male shape" (as genitally explicit as Dailey gets), and "forays upon the slopes" of her breasts. The woman, meanwhile, is responsible but resistant until the man's insistent kiss has "parted her lips"; she then finds "flames leaping within her" at the "searing fire in his kiss," or, alternatively, finds herself "drowning in his kisses" and seeks "the lifeline of his mouth." This writing about the heart is itself without heart, cliché-ridden, hasty and dispirited. It may be typical of romance, but it is not indicative of what Dailey is able to do, for elsewhere she shows herself capable of better, more compelling prose. Generally, her longer books are superior pieces of workmanship, not simply padded Harlequins. In *Touch The Wind, The Rogue, Ride the Thunder*, and *Night Way* Dailey tackles more ambitious subjects and her writing perks up. It is as if in writing about outlaws and Indians, ranching and riding she comes much closer to her own emotional center of gravity, either because these are activities she knows or because they spring from her personal fantasy life. *Night Way*, to my mind her best book, shows what Dailey can do when she is controlling her romance formula rather than letting it take over her books. In this novel she develops several characters, historically and emotionally, shifts point of view and setting, lovingly details place and local culture, and sustains the narrative with greater skill. In no way does Dailey sacrifice her strong-man-loves-somewhat-unwilling-woman formula in *Night Way* and the other longer books; she simply fleshes out her silhouettes.

The contrast between Dailey's improbably urgent short romances and her longer, better written romantic novels suggests in some ways that there are two Janet Dailey's available to romance readers. The trademark romances have won Dailey her audience and made her fortune, but they have not elicited her best work. Her four-volume Calder saga, as well as her recent promotion of Silhouette's "longer editions" suggest that Dailey herself is aware of this and has chosen to move on. Though her trailer may continue around the Interstates, Dailey is ready to add to her formulaic strong-man-in-pursuit novels that other staple of romance fiction, devotion to place.

—Nancy Regan

DAKERS, Elaine. See **LANE, Jane.**

DANBURY, Iris. British. Married. Worked as typist and secretary; owner of a typing business; then full-time writer. Address: c/o Mills and Boon Ltd., 18–24 Paradise Road, Richmond, Surrey TW9 1SR, England.

ROMANCE AND HISTORICAL PUBLICATIONS

Novels

The Gentle Invader. London, Mills and Boon, 1957.
My Heart a Traitor. London, Mills and Boon, 1958.
One Enchanted Summer. London, Mills and Boon, 1958.
Feather in the Wind. London, Mills and Boon, 1959.
The Rose-Walled Castle. London, Mills and Boon, 1959.
The Rainbow Shell. London, Mills and Boon, 1960.
The Silent Nightingale. London, Mills and Boon, 1961.
Hotel Belvedere. London, Mills and Boon, 1961; Toronto, Harlequin, 1969.
Bride of Kylsaig. London, Mills and Boon, 1963; Toronto, Harlequin, 1968.
Story de Luxe. London, Mills and Boon, 1963.
Home from the Sky. London, Mills and Boon, 1964.
The Marble Mountain. London, Mills and Boon, 1964.
Bonfire in the Dusk. London, Mills and Boon, 1965.
Illyrian Summer. London, Mills and Boon, 1965.
Doctor at Drumlochan. London, Mills and Boon, 1966; Toronto, Harlequin, 1967.
The Eagle of Segarra. London, Mills and Boon, 1966.
Doctor at Villa Ronda. London, Mills and Boon, 1967; Toronto, Harlequin, 1968.
Rendezvous in Lisbon. London, Mills and Boon, 1967; Toronto, Harlequin, 1968.
Feast of the Candles. London, Mills and Boon, 1968; Toronto, Harlequin, 1970.
Hotel by the Loch. London, Mills and Boon, 1968; Toronto, Harlequin, 1969.
Chateau of Pines. London, Mills and Boon, and New York, Golden Press, 1969.
Isle of Pomegranates. London, Mills and Boon, 1969; Toronto, Harlequin, 1970.
Island of Mermaids. London, Mills and Boon, 1970; Toronto, Harlequin, 1971.
Serenade at Santa Rosa. London, Mills and Boon, and Toronto, Harlequin, 1970.
The Legend of Roscano. London, Mills and Boon, 1971; Toronto, Harlequin, 1972.
Summer Comes to Albarosa. London, Mills and Boon, and Toronto, Harlequin, 1971.
Jacaranda Island. London, Mills and Boon, and Toronto, Harlequin, 1972.
Mandolins of Mantori. London, Mills and Boon, and Toronto, Harlequin, 1973.
The Silver Stallion. London, Mills and Boon, 1973; Toronto, Harlequin, 1974.
The Fires of Torretta. London, Mills and Boon, and Toronto, Harlequin, 1974.
The Amethyst Meadows. London, Mills and Boon, and Toronto, Harlequin, 1974.
A Pavement of Pearl. Toronto, Harlequin, 1975.

The Scented Island. London, Mills and Boon, 1976; Toronto, Harlequin, 1977.
The Windmill of Kalakos. London, Mills and Boon, and Toronto, Harlequin, 1976.
The Painted Palace. Toronto, Harlequin, 1977.

*   *   *

Iris Danbury, a Mills and Boon author reprinted by Harlequin Books, writes contemporary romances. She has a particular affinity for island locales as well as other foreign settings. After a few shaky earlier novels, such as *Hotel Belvedere*, Danbury hit her stride in *Isle of Pomegranates* and *Island of Mermaids*. The formula she evolves here and follows in her later novels includes first, the heroine who travels to some Mediterranean area; second, the hero, and intriguing man seemingly indifferent to the heroine; third, various alternative men who are romantic possibilities; fourth, various women who serve to arouse the heroine's jealousy; and last, a resolution when hero and heroine finally break through the misconceptions that have kept them apart. Her men and women are types, used over again in novel after novel. The heroines are spunky, resourceful, independent, and determined not to be duped or to reveal their love. The heroes are usually engineers or geologists, with occupations appropriate to their being stationed in the foreign locale and to their being reluctant to form permanent attachments. They may appear brusque, arrogant, and overbearing, but underneath it all they are true-blue English types, with all the proper feelings. Their rivals are often local Spanish dons or Italian signors, who fascinate but do not win the heroine.

Since Danbury's plots are so similar, much of the interest in her stories is provided by the background, which ranges from the Lamini Islands of Italy to Capri, the Canary Islands, Sicily, Rhodes, Corsica, Portugal, and Spain. The author is obviously familiar with these locales, and describes the local scenery and tourist spots. Local foods, festivals (as in *The Fires of Torretta*), and living conditions liven her plots. However, the setting remains a backdrop for the romance, and there is no real involvement with the people. The matter of finding a poor family a home in *Summer Comes to Albarosa*, one of Danbury's better books, is about as serious as her stories ever get. The author's chief limitation is a repetitious and prolix style which rather quickly induces boredom, However, her novels are cheerful and pleasant, and certainly in the middle rank within the genre.

—Necia A. Musser

DANE, Clemence. Pseudonym for Winifred Ashton. British. Born in Blackheath, London, in 1887. Educated at private schools, and at the Slade School of Art, London, 1904–06; studied art in Dresden, 1906–07. French teacher in Geneva, 1903, and in Ireland, 1907–13; teacher at a girls' school during World War I; actress, as Diana Portis, 1913–18. General editor, Novels of Tomorrow series, Michael Joseph, publishers, London, from 1955. President, Society of Women Journalists, 1941. Recipient: Oscar, for screenplay, 1947. C.B.E. (Commander, Order of the British Empire), 1953. *Died 28 March 1965.*

ROMANCE AND HISTORICAL PUBLICATIONS

Novels

Regiment of Women. London, Heinemann, and New York, Macmillan, 1917.
First the Blade: A Comedy of Growth. London, Heinemann, and New York, Macmillan, 1918.
Legend. London, Heinemann, 1919; New York, Macmillan, 1920.
Wandering Stars, Together with The Lover. London, Heinemann, and New York, Macmillan, 1924.
The Dearly Beloved of Benjamin Cobb. London, Benn, 1927.
The Babyons: A Family Chronicle. London, Heinemann, and New York, Doubleday, 1928.
Broome Stages. London, Heinemann, and New York, Doubleday, 1931.
The Moon Is Feminine. London, Heinemann, and New York, Doubleday, 1938.
He Brings Great News. London, Heinemann, 1944; New York, Random House, 1945.
The Flower Girls. London, Joseph, 1954; New York, Norton, 1955.
The Godson: A Fantasy. London, Joseph, and New York, Norton, 1964.

Short Stories

The King Waits. London, Heinemann, 1929.
Fate Cries Out: Nine Tales. London, Heinemann, and New York, Doubleday, 1935.

OTHER PUBLICATIONS

Novels

Enter Sir John, with Helen Simpson. London, Hodder and Stoughton, and New York, Cosmopolitan, 1928.
Printer's Devil, with Helen Simpson. London, Hodder and Stoughton, 1930; as *Author Unknown*, New York, Cosmopolitan, 1930.
The Floating Admiral, with others. London, Hodder and Stoughton, 1931; New York, Doubleday, 1932.
Re-Enter Sir John, with Helen Simpson. London, Hodder and Stoughton, and New York, Farrar and Rinehart, 1932.
The Arrogant History of White Ben. London, Heinemann, and New York, Doubleday, 1939.

Plays

A Bill of Divorcement (produced London and New York, 1921). London, Heinemann, and New York, Macmillan, 1921.
The Terror (produced Liverpool, 1921).
Will Shakespeare: An Invention (produced London, 1921; New York, 1923). London, Heinemann, 1921; New York, Macmillan, 1922.
The Way Things Happen: A Story, adaptation of her novel *Legend* (produced Newark, New Jersey, 1923; New York and London, 1924). London, Heinemann, and New York, Macmillan, 1924.
Shivering Shocks; or, The Hiding Place: A Play for Boys. London, French, 1923.
Naboth's Vineyard. London, Heinemann, 1925; New York, Macmillan, 1926.

Granite (produced London, 1926; New York, 1927). London, Heinemann, and New York, Macmillan, 1926.
Mariners (produced New York, 1927; London, 1929). London, Heinemann, and New York, Macmillan, 1927.
Mr. Fox: A Play for Boys. London, French, 1927.
A Traveller Returns. London, French, 1927.
Adam's Opera, music by Richard Addinsell (produced London, 1928). London, Heinemann, 1928; New York, Doubleday, 1929.
Gooseberry Fool, with Helen Simpson (produced London, 1929).
Wild Decembers (produced London, 1933). London, Heinemann, 1932; New York, Doubleday, 1933.
Come of Age, music by Richard Addinsell (produced New York, 1934). New York, Doubleday, 1934; London, Heinemann, 1938.
L'Aiglon, music by Richard Addinsell, adaptation of the play by Rostand (produced New York, 1934; London, 1936). New York, Doubleday, 1934.
Moonlight Is Silver (also director: produced London, 1934). London, Heinemann, 1934.
Richard of Bordeaux (produced New York, 1934).
The Laughing Woman (produced New York, 1936).
The Happy Hypocrite, adaptation of the story by Max Beerbohm (produced London, 1936).
Herod and Mariamne, adaptation of the play by Friedrich Hebbel (produced Pittsburgh, 1938). New York, Doubleday, 1938; London, Heinemann, 1939.
England's Darling, music by Richard Addinsell. London, Heinemann, 1940.
Cousin Muriel (produced London, 1940). London, Heinemann, 1940.
The Saviours: Seven Plays on One Theme (includes *Merlin, The Hope of Britain, England's Darling, The May King, The Light of Britain, Remember Nelson, The Unknown Soldier*), music by Richard Addinsell (broadcast 1940–41). London, Heinemann, and New York, Doubleday, 1942.
The Golden Reign of Queen Elizabeth (produced York, 1941). London, French, 1941.
Cathedral Steps (produced London, 1942).
Alice's Adventures in Wonderland and Through the Looking-Glass, music by Richard Addinsell, adaptation of the novels by Lewis Carroll (produced London, 1943). London, French, 1948.
The Lion and the Unicorn (produced Thame, Oxfordshire, 1959). London, Heinemann, 1943.
Call Home the Heart (produced London, 1947). London, Heinemann, 1947.
Scandal at Coventry (broadcast 1958). Included in *The Collected Plays*, 1961.
Eighty in the Shade (produced Newcastle, 1958; London, 1959). London, Heinemann, 1959.
Till Time Shall End (televised 1958). Included in *The Collected Plays*, 1961.
The Collected Plays of Clemence Dane (includes *Scandal at Coventry, Granite, A Bill of Divorcement, Till Time Shall End*). London, Heinemann, 1961.

Screenplays: *The Lame Duck*, 1921; *The Tunnel* (*Transatlantic Tunnel*), with Curt Siodmak and L. DuGarde Peach, 1935; *Anna Karenina*, with Salka Viertel, 1935; *The Amateur Gentleman*, with Edward Knoblock, 1936; *Farewell Again* (*Troopship*), with Patrick Kirwan, 1937; *Fire over England*, with Sergei Nolbandov, 1937; *St. Martin's Lane* (*Sidewalks of London*), 1938; *Salute John Citizen*, with Elizabeth Baron, 1942; *Perfect Strangers* (*Vacation from Marriage*), with Anthony Pelissier, 1945; *Bonnie*

Prince Charlie, 1948; *Bride of Vengeance*, with Cyril Hume and Michael Hogan, 1949; *The Angel with the Trumpet*, with Karl Hartl and Franz Tassie, 1950.

Radio Plays: *The Scoop* (serial), with others, 1931; *The Saviours* (7 plays), 1940–41; *Henry VIII*, from the play by Shakespeare, 1954; *Don Carlos*, from the play by Schiller, 1955; *Scandal at Coventry*, 1958.

Television Play: *Till Time Shall End*, 1958.

Verse

Trafalgar Day 1940. London, Heinemann, 1940; New York, Doubleday, 1941.
Christmas in War-Time. New York, Doubleday, 1941.

Other

The Woman's Side. London, Jenkins, 1926; New York, Doran, 1927.
Tradition and Hugh Walpole. New York, Doubleday, 1929; London, Heinemann, 1930.
Recapture: A Clemence Dane Omnibus. London, Heinemann, 1932.
Claude Houghton: Appreciations, with Hugh Walpole. London, Heinemann, 1935.
Mozart's Così fan Tutte: Essays, with Edward J. Dent and Eric Blom. London, Lane, 1945.
Approaches to Drama (address). London, English Association, 1961.
London Has a Garden (on Covent Garden). London, Joseph, and New York, Norton, 1964.

Editor, *A Hundred Enchanted Tales*. London, Joseph, 1937.
Editor, *The Shelter Book: A Gathering of Tales, Poems, Essays, Notes and Notions for Use in Shelters, Tubes, Basements and Cellars in War-Time*. London, Longman, 1940.
Editor, *The Nelson Touch: An Anthology of Lord Nelson's Letters*. London, Heinemann, 1942.

*

Theatrical Activities:
Director: **Play**—*Moonlight Is Silver*, London, 1934.
Actress (as Diana Portis): **Plays**—Vera Lawrence, in *Eliza Comes to Stay* by H. V. Esmond, London, 1913; Baroness des Herbettes, in *This Way* by Sydney Blow and Douglas Hoare, London, 1913; Sidonie in *Oh, I Say!* by Sydney Blow and Douglas Hoare, toured 1914.

*   *   *

Clemence Dane is best remembered for her play *A Bill of Divorcement* in which Meggie Albanesi made a great success on the London stage and Katharine Hepburn obtained her first film part in Hollywood. She also wrote several historical works mostly set in the Elizabethan period.

Her first novel, *Regiment of Women* has a delicately handled lesbian theme. Clare Hartill, a gifted teacher, enslaves a pretty junior mistress aged 19 and is loved by a talented girl of 13 whom she coaches. The girl kills herself falling from a window because she feels rejected and the junior mistress marries leaving Clare angry and lonely with a partnership in the school and her teaching to console her. This well written, sensitive study

was presented at a time when discussion of such relationships was rare. It was bold, controversial, and perceptive, dealing with "a lot of women at close quarters all enthusiasm and fussing and importance."

Legend, is one of Dane's most successful works. It covers one evening meeting of a literary circle to which news arrives of the death in childbirth of one of their number, Madala Grey, a successful novelist they all admired, were jealous of, used to their own advantage, but never really knew. They quarrel, make sharp remarks, and discuss their work while the reader learns about Madala Grey. The reader also comes to understand each member of the circle just by listening to their conversation and observing their behaviour. It is a minor triumph.

First the Blade is a sad little "comedy" about a neglected young woman devoted to her fiancé, a self-centred, humourless, spoiled young man ruled by a passion for collecting birds' eggs. In desperation she smashes his collection trying to divert his attention without success. It has similarities to Somerset Maugham's story "The Kite," in which Herbert Sunbury's wife breaks up his much loved kite which has become an obsession, with a similar lack of success. *The Babyons* is a four-part family chronicle with hauntings, suicide, murder, and baleful family influences. The best section is "Creeping Jenny" in which Robert Thistledallow's daughter by a gypsy girl, slighted by his relations for her illegitimacy, triumps over the family, inherits her father's fortune and becomes Lady Babyon.

Wandering Stars, *Broome Stages*, and *The Flower Girls* are three theatrical novels. *Broome Stages*, Dane's most famous novel, is still popular today. It starts with the foundation of the Broome family's theatrical ventures in 1715 and continues with their domination of the English theatre for 200 years. In a curious arrangement the family parallels the names and characteristics of the Plantagenet Kings of England. The Broomes are great actor-managers whose family loyalty is permeated by a ruthless pursuit of fame and a jealousy of the success of their own children as they challenge for dominance and authority. One kills himself in his theatre when his son triumphs as Shylock after tricking him out of his leading position in management and depriving him of leading roles. His son also dies in the theatre of a heart attack at his own son's debut. There are some well drawn, effective female members of the clan. It is a big book and a tour de force. *The Flower Girls*, written 23 years later, follows another theatrical family, less dramatically but with charm, humour, and many fine characters, some in the minor parts, and some clearly drawn from the great stage performers of the day.

The Moon Is Feminine begins as a pleasant fantasy with Henry Cope who believes in his green ancestors from St. Martin's Land, based on William of Newburgh's story of the green children who arrived in East Anglia in 1150, and a beguiling, mysterious, dangerous boy who has a second life as a seal. It is well told and keenly observed but has a totally unexpected, violent, and horrifying ending for which the reader has not been adequately prepared.

The Arrogant History of White Ben is an allegory "about a Hitleresque personage" who starts and ends as a scarecrow, and a combination of power, stupidity, hatred, and the use of rhetoric to inflame and dominate a crowd. *The Godson* tells of Sir William Davenant, Shakespeare's godson, who wrote an opera, became a Lieutenant General and the Poet Laureate. On Shakespeare's birthday in Stratford, Will Davenant, as a boy, presents his own production of *A Midsummer Night's Dream* in which he plays Puck. His mother almost admits that he is really Shakespeare's son in one of Dane's fancifully suggested versions of Elizabethan history. *He Brings Great News* is a novel about the arrival of the news of the victory of Trafalgar, dealing with Nelson, one of Dane's particular heroes.

Dane's work is always well written and an easy pleasure to read. The best is quite outstanding, inventive, and richly deserving of a revival in interest.

—David Waldron Smithers

DANE, Eva. See **DARRELL, Elizabeth**.

DANIELS, Dorothy (née Smith). Also writes as Danielle Dorsett; Angela Gray; Cynthia Kavanaugh; Helaine Ross; Suzanne Somers; Geraldine Thayer; Helen Gray Weston. American. Born in Waterbury, Connecticut, 1 July 1915. Educated at Central Connecticut State College, New Britain. Married to Norman A. Daniels. Formerly actress and school teacher. Agent: Richard Curtis Associates, 164 East 64th Street, New York, New York 10021. Address: 6107 Village 6, Camarillo, California 93010, U.S.A.

ROMANCE AND HISTORICAL PUBLICATIONS

Novels (series: Valcour)

The Dark Rider (as Geraldine Thayer). New York, Avalon, 1961.
Jennifer James, R.N. New York, Fawcett, 1962.
No Tears Tomorrow (as Helaine Ross). New York, Avalon, 1962.
Eve Originals. New York, Lancer, 1962.
Cruise Ship Nurse. New York, Paperback Library, 1963.
Country Nurse. New York, Berkley, 1963.
World's Fair Nurse. New York, Paperback Library, 1964.
Island Nurse. New York, Paperback Library, 1964.
The Tower Room. New York, Lancer, 1965.
The Leland Legacy. New York, Pyramid, 1965.
Shadow Glen. New York, Paperback Library, 1965.
Marriott Hall. New York, Paperback Library, 1965.
Darkhaven. New York, Paperback Library, 1965.
The Unguarded. New York, Lancer, 1965.
The Mistress of Falcon Hill. New York, Pyramid, 1965.
Dance in Darkness. New York, Lancer, 1965.
Cliffside Castle. New York, Lancer, 1965.
The Lily Pond. New York, Paperback Library, 1965.
Marble Leaf. New York, Lancer, 1966; as *The Marble Angel*, 1970.
Midday Moon. New York, Lancer, 1966.
Knight in Red Armor. New York, Lancer, 1966.
Nurse at Danger Mansion. New York, Lancer, 1966; as *Danger Mansion*, n.d.
Dark Villa. New York, Lancer, 1966.
Bride of Lenore (as Cynthia Kavanaugh). New York, Pyramid, 1966.
The Deception (as Cynthia Kavanaugh). New York, Pyramid, 1966.
Mystic Manor (as Helen Gray Weston). New York, Paperback Library, 1966.
The Templeton Memoirs. New York, Lancer, 1966.
This Ancient Evil. New York, Lancer, 1966.
The Last of the Mansions. New York, Lancer, 1966; as *Survivors of Darkness*, 1969.
House of False Faces (as Helen Gray Weston). New York, Paperback Library, 1967.

House of Stolen Memories. New York, Lancer, 1967; as *Mansion of Lost Memories*, 1969.
The Sevier Secrets. New York, Lancer, 1967.
Screen Test for Laurel. New York, Avon, 1967.
Traitor's Road. New York, Lancer, 1967.
House of Seven Courts. New York, Lancer, 1967.
The Eagle's Nest. New York, Lancer, 1967.
Mostly by Moonlight. New York, Lancer, 1968.
Blue Devil Suite. New York, Belmont, 1968.
Affair at Marrakesh. New York, Pyramid, 1968.
Candle in the Sun. New York, Lancer, 1968.
Lady of the Shadows. New York, Paperback Library, 1968.
Duet. New York, Lancer, 1968.
Strange Paradise. New York, Paperback Library, 1969.
Affair in Hong Kong. New York, Pyramid, 1969.
Voice on the Wind. New York, Paperback Library, 1969.
The Carson Inheritance. New York, Paperback Library, 1969.
The Tormented. New York, Paperback Library, 1969.
The Curse of Mallory Hall. New York, Fawcett, 1970; London, Coronet, 1972.
The Man from Yesterday. New York, Paperback Library, 1970.
The Dark Stage. New York, Paperback Library, 1970.
Emerald Hill. New York, Paperback Library, 1970.
Willow Weep. New York, Pyramid, 1970.
Island of Evil (novelization of TV series). New York, Paperback Library, 1970.
Raxl, Voodoo Princess (novelization of TV series). New York, Paperback Library, 1970.
The Raging Waters. New York, Pyramid, 1970.
The Attic Rope. New York, Lancer, 1970.
The Unearthly. New York, Lancer, 1970.
Journey into Terror. New York, Pyramid, 1971.
Key Diablo. New York, Paperback Library, 1971.
The House of Many Doors. New York, Paperback Library, 1971.
The Bell. New York, Paperback Library, 1971.
Diablo Manor. New York, Paperback Library, 1971; London, Star, 1977.
Witch's Castle. New York, Paperback Library, 1971.
The Beaumont Tradition. New York, Paperback Library, 1971.
The Lattimer Legend. New York, Lancer, 1971.
Shadows of Tomorrow. New York, Paperback Library, 1971.
Dueling Oaks (as Danielle Dorsett). New York, Pinnacle, 1972.
The Spanish Chapel. New York, Belmont, 1972.
Conover's Folly. New York, Paperback Library, 1972.
The House of Broken Dolls. New York, Paperback Library, 1972.
The Lanier Riddle. New York, Paperback Library, 1972.
Castle Morvant. New York, Paperback Library, 1972.
Maya Temple. New York, Paperback Library, 1972.
The Larrabee Heiress. New York, Paperback Library, 1972.
Shadows from the Past. New York, Paperback Library, 1972.
The House on Circus Hill. New York, Paperback Library, 1972.
Dark Island. New York, Paperback Library, 1972.
Witch's Island. New York, Paperback Library, 1972.
The Stone House. New York, Paperback Library, 1973.
The Duncan Dynasty. New York, Paperback Library, 1973.
The Silent Halls of Ashenden. New York, Paperback Library, 1973.
The Possession of Tracy Corbin. New York, Paperback Library, 1973.
Hills of Fire. New York, Paperback Library, 1973.
The Prisoner of Malville Hall. New York, Paperback Library, 1973.
Jade Green. New York, Paperback Library, 1973.
The Caldwell Shadow. New York, Paperback Library, 1973.

Image of a Ghost. New York, Paperback Library, 1973.
The Apollo Fountain. New York, Warner, 1974.
Island of Bitter Memories. New York, Warner, 1974.
Child of Darkness. New York, Pocket Books, 1974.
Ghost Song. New York, Pocket Books, 1974.
The Two Worlds of Peggy Scott. New York, Pocket Books, 1974; Bolton-by-Bowland, Lancashire, Magna, 1977.
The Exorcism of Jenny Slade. New York, Pocket Books, 1974.
A Web of Peril. New York, Pyramid, 1974.
Illusion at Haven's Edge. New York, Pocket Books, 1975; Bolton-by-Bowland, Lancashire, Magna, 1977.
The Possessed. New York, Pocket Books, 1975.
The Guardian of Willow House. New York, Pocket Books, 1975; Bolton-by-Bowland, Lancashire, Magna, 1977.
The Unlamented. New York, Pocket Books, 1975.
The Tide Mill. New York, Popular Library, 1975.
Shadow of a Man. New York, Popular Library, 1975.
Marble Hills. New York, Warner, 1975.
Blackthorn. New York, Pocket Books, 1975.
Whistle in the Wind. New York, Pocket Books, 1976.
Night Shade. New York, Pocket Books, 1976.
The Vineyard Chapel. New York, Pocket Books, 1976.
Circle of Guilt. New York, Pocket Books, 1976.
Juniper Hill. New York, Pocket Books, 1976.
Portrait of a Witch. New York, Pocket Books, 1976.
The Summer House. New York, Warner, 1976.
Terror of the Twin. New York, Berkley, 1976.
Dark Heritage. New York, New American Library, 1976.
Twilight of the Elms. New York, New American Library, 1976.
Poison Flower. New York, Pocket Books, 1977.
Nightfall. New York, Pocket Books, 1977.
Wines of Cyprien. New York, Pyramid, 1977.
A Woman in Silk and Shadows. New York, New American Library, 1977.
In the Shadows. New York, New American Library, 1978.
The Lonely Place. New York, New American Library, 1978.
Hermitage Hill. New York, New American Library, 1978.
Perrine. New York, Warner, 1978.
The Magic Ring. New York, Warner, 1978.
Meg. New York, New American Library, 1979.
The Cormac Legend. New York, New American Library, 1979.
Yesterday's Evil. New York, New American Library, 1979.
Veil of Treachery. New York, New American Library, 1979.
The Purple and the Gold. New York, New American Library, 1980.
Legend of Death. New York, New American Library, 1980.
Valley of the Shadows. New York, New American Library, 1980.
Bridal Black. New York, New American Library, 1980.
House of Silence. New York, New American Library, 1980.
Nicola. New York, Belmont, 1980.
Sisters of Valcour. New York, Warner, 1981.
Saratoga. New York, Belmont, 1981.
Monte Carlo. New York, Belmont, 1981.
For Love and Valcour. New York, Warner, 1983.
Crisis at Valcour. New York, Warner, 1985.

Novels as Suzanne Somers

The Caduceus Tree. New York, Avalon, 1961; as *A Nurse for Doctor Keith* (as Dorothy Daniels), New York, Paperback Library, 1962.
House of Eve. New York, Avalon, 1962.
Image of Truth. New York, Avalon, 1963.
The Mists of Mourning. New York, Belmont, 1966.

The Romany Curse. New York, Belmont, 1971.
The House on Thunder Hill. New York, Curtis, 1973.
Touch Me. Los Angeles, Nash, 1973.
Until Death. New York, Curtis, 1973.

Novels as Angela Gray

The Ghost Dancers. New York, Lancer, 1971.
The Golden Packet. New York, Lancer, 1971.
The Lattimore Arch. New York, Lancer, 1971.
Blackwell's Ghost. New York, Lancer, 1972.
Ashes of Falconwyck. New York, Lancer, 1973.
The Watcher in the Dark. New York, Ballantine, 1973.
Nightmare at Riverview. New York, Lancer, 1973.
Ravenswood Hall. New York, Lancer, 1973.
The Warlock's Daughter. New York, Lancer, 1973.
The Love of the Lion. New York, Pocket Books, 1980.

*

Manuscript Collection: Bowling Green State University, Ohio.

*   *   *

Dorothy Daniels's publications include some 150 novels written since the early 1940's. Offering gothic fare, her works typically present an innocent and unprotected heroine pursued by a murderous villain in a remote setting. This bewildered yet courageous protagonist, who moves from one life-threatening incident to the next, finally triumphs over her trials to marry a suitable young man at the end of the novel, when all mysteries and motives are elaborately explained. Avoiding the actual supernatural and the psychological complexity of evil, the author mingles elements of romantic and detective fiction in her works, as falling in love and finding the right clues lighten scenes of terror.

As the titles of her novels indicate, Daniels relies heavily upon setting to create gothic effects. Although she makes no serious effort to develop her historical or geographical material, her scenes are as vivid as they are varied in evoking fear. All manner of ominous mansions, estates, castles, and chapels with mysterious rooms are described: a chamber of horrors in the secluded mansion on the jungle of a Florida Key; a secret room for restraining insane family members in the Beaudin estate on Long Island; a labyrinthine Virginian forest hiding a killer at Mallory Hall; a remote chapel with a secret entry at Mystic Manor near the Hudson River. Though seemingly the abodes of witches, voodoo artists, and ghosts, these settings house human villainy. In *The Eagle's Nest* members of a new Nazi movement rather than Nazi ghosts walk the castle grounds; in *Castle Morvant* the writer of the ballet rather than a supernatural counterpart sabotages the performance. Moving away from the gothic in *Saratoga* and *Monte Carlo*, Daniels discards the apparent supernatural for portraits of ruthless, moneyed criminals.

To endure and outwit these evil forces, the female protagonist must be courageous and determined, as well as young and beautiful. Despite the variety of careers Daniels assigns to her heroines—companion, governess, social secretary, hotel manager, nurse, reporter, scientist, ballet dancer—the ultimate goals are survival and a successful marriage. Daniels's books attract the female reader interested in the entertainment provided by a combination of gothic terror, mystery, and love story in fiction.

—Bette B. Roberts

DANIELS, Norman. See LEE, Elsie.

DANIELS, Olga. See SINCLAIR, Olga.

DANTON, Rebecca. See ROBERTS, Janet Louise.

DARBY, Catherine. See PETERS, Maureen.

DARCY, Clare. American. Address: c/o Walker, 720 Fifth Avenue, New York, New York 10019, U.S.A.

ROMANCE AND HISTORICAL PUBLICATIONS

Novels

Georgina. New York, Walker, 1971; London, Wingate, 1974.
Cecily; or, A Young Lady of Quality. New York, Walker, 1972; London, Wingate, 1975.
Lydia; or, Love in Town. New York, Walker, 1973; London, Wingate, 1976.
Victoire. New York, Walker, 1974; London, Wingate, 1976.
Allegra. New York, Walker, 1975; London, Wingate, 1976.
Lady Pamela. New York, Walker, 1975; London, Wingate, 1977.
Regina. New York, Walker, 1976; London, Raven, 1977.
Elyza. New York, Walker, 1976; London, Raven-Macdonald and Jane's, 1977.
Cressida. New York, Walker, 1977; London, Raven, 1978.
Eugenia. New York, Walker, 1977; London, Raven, 1978.
Gwendolen. New York, Walker, 1978; London, Raven, 1979.
Rolande. New York, Walker, 1978; London, Raven, 1979.
Letty. New York, Walker, and London, Futura, 1980.
Caroline and Julia. New York, Walker, and London, Macdonald, 1982.

*   *   *

Clare Darcy's lively and entertaining tales are set in the Regency period described so well in the novels of Georgette Heyer. Like Heyer, Darcy writes comedies of manners with the obligatory happy endings. Unlike many others who have followed in Heyer's footsteps, Darcy takes some pains over her historical accuracy. The manners and customs of high society, the elegant dress of both men and women, the geography of the fashionable world from Brighton to London to Vienna, even the vocabulary

of her characters are all portrayed with careful attention to detail and authenticity. The historical characters who appear amid the fictional creations are also depicted convincingly, from Wellington to Lady Jersey. Thus the novels, each of which bears the name of its spirited heroine, have a depth and a substance unusual in the genre. This is particularly true of Darcy's early efforts; in recent years the pressures of success seem to have taken their toll and her work adheres much more closely to established formulae.

Darcy's heroines are invariably orphans, adrift in the world, and they make their way towards their happy endings aided by their own wits and their sense of adventure. Most, although of good family, are penniless, unprotected by family or friends; some (as in *Elyza* and *Letty*) are runaways. A few (*Lady Pamela*, *Cressida*) are wealthy, and past their girlhood, but they too lack love and a sense of belonging. While clearly virtuous and innocent, Darcy heroines are decidedly unconventional and a bit reckless. The threats of social scandal and financial disaster dismay them only temporarily, for they are unquenchingly optimistic about their futures, with good reason. Each one ends up in the arms of an older and more experienced hero, wealthy, and titled, who has until that moment thought himself immune to love. Sometimes, the hero and heroine have been involved in an earlier, blighted, romance (*Allegra* and *Cressida*); they always quarrel before true love conquers all. To each other they are at once infuriating and irresistible. Although her characters follow a set pattern, they are not cardboard figures; Darcy endows them with flaws as well as virtues, and most have a believable vitality.

The plots of Darcy's novels are simple and predictable. The fatherless heroine sets out in the world fleeing grasping guardians or trying to solve another's problems (frequently a brother or friend, rarely her own). She meets the hero, a notorious rake, and is drawn to him, but does not admit her attraction, as they immediately quarrel. Rather comical villains threaten to thwart the heroine's plans, but she, ever valiant, perseveres in her journey through the perils of the fashionable world. In the end, all misunderstandings and coincidences are cleared up, and the hero and heroine admit their love for each other. The heroine's future is assured, and clearly a happy one.

Darcy's vignettes of Regency London are entertaining fare. Her strong-willed heroines appeal to 20th-century readers, while her darkly attractive heroes are tamed by love in a thoroughly satisfying, albeit anachronistic way. Darcy's reviewers have designated her as Georgette Heyer's successor with some justice, for she describes the same imaginary world with the same light touch.

—Mary C. Lynn

D'ARCY, Pamela. See ROBY, Mary Linn.

DARK, Eleanor (née O'Reilly). Australian. Born in Sydney, New South Wales, 26 August 1901. Educated at Redlands, Neutral Bay, Sydney. Married Eric Dark in 1922; one son. Recipient: Australian Literature Society Gold Medal, 1934, 1936, Officer, Order of Australia, 1977.

ROMANCE AND HISTORICAL PUBLICATIONS

Novels

The Timeless Land. London, Collins, and New York, Macmillan, 1941.
Storm of Time. London, Collins, 1945; New York, McGraw Hill, 1950.
No Barrier. London, Collins, 1953.

OTHER PUBLICATIONS

Novels

Slow Dawning. London, Lane, 1932.
Prelude to Christopher. Sydney, Stephenson, 1934; London, Collins, 1936.
Return to Coolami. London, Collins, and New York, Macmillan, 1936.
Sun Across the Sky. London, Collins, and New York, Macmillan, 1937.
Waterway. London, Collins, and New York, Macmillan, 1938.
The Little Company. London, Collins, and New York, Macmillan, 1945.
Latana Lane. London, Collins, 1959.

*

Bibliography: "Eleanor Dark: A Handlist of Her Books and Critical References" by Hugh Anderson, in *Biblio News* (Sydney), 1954.

Critical Study: *Eleanor Dark* by A. Grove Day, Boston, Twayne, 1976.

*   *   *

The most noticeable characteristic of Eleanor Dark's writing is a stream-of-consciousness technique, through which the reader is drawn into the most intimate thoughts of the protagonists. Although this suggests a concentration on individuals in later books Dark writes about the actions and attitudes of her characters in a social and political context. She is a novelist of ideas, who writes about women and men, families and love as an interrogator seeking out patterns and connections between individual lives and the wider society.

Dark is best known for *The Timeless Land*, the first novel in an historical trilogy set in the earliest years of white settlement in Australia from 1788 to 1814. This trilogy is her only historical work, all other novels having contemporary settings, although links between the style and subject of the trilogy and novels such as *Prelude to Christopher*, *Sun Across the Sky*, *Waterway*, and *The Little Company* are strong. In the tradition of convict novels, a central theme in *The Timeless Land* is freedom, and Dark sets liberty as the principal component of human happiness. In this overtly political novel, black and white society are contrasted in order to argue that all the Europeans, jailers and convicts alike, are shackled by their supposed rationality and dependence on possessions. Dark suggests that a society which elevates men of wealth over those in inner resources and strength will inevitably weaken. It is obvious that in choosing to look at the beginnings of her own society, Dark was exploring the deficiencies of the present—that is the 1930's world depression and looming world war—although what she has to say about Western society seems no less relevant today. The protagonists, the

Aboriginal songmaker Bennilong and the British Governor Arthur Phillip, are depicted as strong but flawed men who hold to a high personal code while around them the precarious white settlement and the original inhabitants are threatened by disease, starvation, and moral degradation. Dark quotes the authentic diaries and letters of her historical characters and goes behind these records to create characters who are believable and varied in their reactions to the "timeless land!" She also takes up the challenge of writing from the inside of the black society, and although some of her interpretations of Aboriginal philosophy might be debatable, the result is artistically satisfying. There is little action in the novel and for most readers, particularly for Australians, part of the drama comes from knowing the outcome of the story and the fate of the Aboriginals who so generously help the Europeans, thinking that the white people, like a dream, will soon go away.

The sequels, *Storm of Time* and *No Barrier*, take up the stories of two families from *The Timeless Land*, the wealthy Mannions and the convict Prentices. Both these families have links to the native community through Johnny Prentice, who as a boy ran away from home and lives a tribal life, and through Dilboong, daughter of Bennilong, who is a servant in the Mannion household. All of these characters are fictional although their lives are certainly no more extraordinary than the historical figures in these two novels such as the Governors William Bligh and Hunter, or the sheep baron Macarthur. After the wise government of Phillip, the colony is now functioning at the whim of the greedy large landholders. Governor Hunter, in a moment of what he considers near insanity, reflects that perhaps chains are on the wrong people. It is a point that Dark returns to often. The greatest crime, these two novels suggests, is the loss of an opportunity to build a better society, that the men in power are guilty of a deficiency of imagination and compassion. Generally women characters play a minor role although the majority are depicted as having considerably more insight into the nature of their society than their menfolk and, most particularly, an awareness of the special characteristics of the land itself. Strong characterization, a feel for the landscape, drama based on historical fact together with political insight make all three novels compelling reading.

—Kerry White

DARRELL, Elizabeth. Pseudonym for Edna Dawes; also writes as Eva Dane; Eleanor Drew; Emma Drummond. British. Address: c/o Gollancz Ltd., 14 Henrietta Street, London WC2E 8QJ, England.

ROMANCE AND HISTORICAL PUBLICATIONS

Novels (series: Sheridan Family)

Burn All Your Bridges (as Eleanor Drew). London, Macdonald and Jane's, 1976.
The Jade Alliance. New York, Putnam, 1979; London, Hodder and Stoughton, 1980.
The Gathering Wolves. New York, Coward McCann, 1980; London, Hodder and Stoughton, 1981.
At the Going Down of the Sun (Sheridan). London, Century, 1984; New York, St. Martin's Press, 1985.
And in the Morning (Sheridan). London, Century, 1986; New York, St. Martin's Press, 1987.

The Flight of the Flamingo. London, Century, 1989.

Novels as Emma Drummond

Scarlet Shadows. London, Troubadour, and New York, Dell, 1978.
The Burning Land. London, Macdonald and Jane's, and New York, Dell, 1979.
The Rice Dragon. London, Macdonald, 1980; New York, Dell, 1982.
Beyond All Frontiers. London, Gollancz, and New York, St. Martin's Press, 1983.
Forget the Glory. London, Gollancz, and New York, St. Martin's Press, 1985.
The Bridge of a Hundred Dragons. London, Gollancz, and New York, St. Martin's Press, 1986.
A Captive Freedom. London, Gollancz, and New York, St. Martin's Press, 1987.
Some Far Elusive Dawn. London, Gollancz, 1988.

Novels as Eva Dane

A Lion by the Mane. London, Macdonald and Jane's, 1975.
Shadows in the Fire. London, Macdonald and Jane's, 1975.
The Vaaldorp Diamond. London, Macdonald and Jane's, 1978.

Novels as Edna Dawes

Dearest Tiger. London, Hale, 1975.
Pink Snow. London, Hale, 1975.
A Hidden Heart of Fire. London, Hale, 1976.
Fly with My Love. London, Hale, 1978.

*   *   *

Elizabeth Darrell chronicles the lives of individuals and societies wracked by the horrors of war. Employing settings familiar to her from her foreign travel and periods of residence abroad, she often examines tensions that occur when men and women from different cultures fall in love.

In *The Jade Alliance*, the Brusilovs, an aristocratic family, flee from their native Russia after the head of the family is murdered by revolutionaries in 1905. Settling in Hong Kong, they build up a thriving jade business. To Ivan Brusilov, the family heir who intends to return to Russia as soon as he reaches his 21st birthday, such activity in the world of trade is abhorrent. He maintains his aristocratic outlook and entirely misreads the rules of the unfamiliar culture around him. This myopia brings disastrous results after he seduces the daughter of a powerful Hong Kong comprador.

Ivan's twin sister Nadia does not share his desire to return to Russia, particularly as she comes to love Andrew Stanton, a British agent. Andrew had been posted to Hong Kong to quiet scandal after his actress wife dies when he drove their carriage into a wall while he was drunk. Andrew's growing attraction to Nadia threatens to cost him not only his position in society but his career because of British distrust of anything Russian. The budding romance is further endangered by the unexpected arrival of Anna Brusilov, whose family had believed her dead. When a devastating typhoon strikes the colony, Andrew is forced to choose between the two women.

The Gathering Wolves also concerns the relationship between the British and Russians. Set slightly later in time, the novel deals with the turmoil immediately following the Bolshevik Revolution. British soldiers, including engineer Paul Anderson, have been sent to aid the White Russians. Paul's task is to help keep the railway line open between Murmansk and Petrograd. To do so, Paul and a handful of British soldiers must construct a bridge.

To assist in the project is a contingent of White Russians under the command of Alexander (Sasha) Swarovsky, a member of the aristocracy. He is accompanied by his sister Olga and his wife Irina, who serves as a nurse. Tension runs high between Paul and Sasha about who is in command, as one incident of sabotage after another delays construction. The feud is further exacerbated when Paul and Irina fall in love. The arrival of Sasha's former mistress along with his brother Vladimir, who has been forced to join the Red Army, further complicates the lives of those thrown together in the remote forest. Finally Paul completes the bridge only to receive orders to escape north and destroy his work to prevent the advance of the Red Army.

After portraying conflicts on foreign soil, Darrell turned to her native England for her companion volumes *At the Going Down of the Sun* and *And in the Morning*, set during World Wars I and II respectively.

Of all her novels *At the Going Down of the Sun* is the most moving because of an overpowering sense of loss of an innocent and carefree life that could never be recaptured. Darrell concentrates on three brothers, Roland, Rex, and Christopher Sheridan, who have lived their short lives in aristocratic comfort. However, their father's massive gambling debts and suicide ruin them financially at the same moment Europe plunges into war.

Too poor to finish medical school, Roland, the eldest, stays home to run the estate and raise crops to support the war effort. However, as casualties mount, the community turns against him until he is forced to enlist. Choosing the medical corps, he gallantly saves others' lives in the netherworld of the trenches until his own life is ended by a land mine.

Rex becomes a flying ace, downing dozens of German fighter planes. As he sees scores of young men fly to their death, his disillusionment with war increases, especially when he realizes that many have enlisted to emulate his exploits. Only his passion for a radiant London actress sustains him, and their fairy-tale romance, marriage, and deaths provide fodder for the tabloids.

Christopher, the youngest, survives the conflict but bears deep mental and emotional scars. A brilliant scholar, Chris is forced to give up his chance to enroll at Cambridge after he impregnates the daughter of the local doctor. Roland forces Chris to marry Marion to legitimate the child's birth, but 18-year-old Chris cannot face the prospect of suffering a loveless life to pay for the consequences of one afternoon of passion. Fleeing his wife and son, he enlists in the army, where his talent for languages leads him to intelligence work. At Gallipolli he endures so much horror that his mind snaps, and he spends several years struggling to remember and deal with his past. At the end of the war he and Marion agree to try to sustain their marriage for their son's sake.

20 years later Europe again enters war. In *And in the Morning*, Christopher and Marion have led separate lives, Marion devoting herself to her son, David. He hates his father for having deserted him but idolizes his uncle Rex, a legend in the Royal Air Force, of which David is a member. His sister Vesta, an artist, has been much closer to her father although Christopher has spent long periods away from home on secret missions to governments throughout Europe.

This war draws many more women, including Vesta, into active service. Both she and David encounter random death and senseless destruction. His torture by the Japanese scars him for life but also leads him to reassignment in the same secret service to which Christopher has devoted his energy. Father and son find reconciliation, and before Christopher's death he even manages to experience romantic love for the first time. A brilliant artist brings beauty and passion to the man whose marriage had been a sham from its forced beginning.

Although Darrell's descriptions and plot are as strong in the second half of the Sheridan saga as in the first, *And in the Morning* lacks the poignancy of *At the Going Down of the Sun*. Those who entered World War I had an eagerness and innocence that could never be recaptured, and Darrell's evocation of the loss of that world view is powerful.

Darrell's historical novels written under the pseudonym of Emma Drummond have themes and settings similar to those of her other books. For example, *A Captive Freedom* and *The Burning Land* both center on British soldiers who fight in the Boer War as Andrew Stanton from *The Jade Alliance* had done. *The Bridge of a Hundred Dragons*, set during the Shanghai emergency of 1927, focuses on Mark Rawlings, a member of the British Royal Engineers, who had rescued an aristocractic Russian family during the civil war described in *The Gathering of Wolves*.

—Kathy Piehl

DAVENPORT, Marcia (née Gluck). American. Born in New York City, 9 June 1903; daughter of the singer Alma Gluck. Educated at Shipley School, Philadelphia; Wellesley College, Massachusetts, 1921–22; University of Grenoble, Summer 1922. Married Russell Davenport in 1929 (divorced), one daughter; also one daughter from first marriage. Copywriter in Philadelphia, 1924–27; staff member, *New Yorker*, 1927–30; music critic for Theatre Guild newsletter, later called *Stage*, 1930–38; commentator for Salzburg and Metropolitan opera broadcasts, 1936–37. Agent: Brandt and Brandt, 1501 Broadway, New York, New York 10036, U.S.A.

ROMANCE AND HISTORICAL PUBLICATIONS

Novels

Of Lena Geyer. New York, Scribner, and London, Heinemann, 1936; as *Lena Geyer*, London, Collins, 1949.
The Valley of Decision. New York, Scribner, 1942; London, Collins, 1944.
East Side, West Side. New York, Scribner, 1947; London, Collins, 1948.
My Brother's Keeper. New York, Scribner, and London, Collins, 1954.
The Constant Image. New York, Scribner, and London, Collins, 1960.

OTHER PUBLICATIONS

Other

Mozart. New York, Scribner, 1932; London, Heinemann, 1933; revised edition, Scribner, 1956.
Garibaldi, Father of Modern Italy (for children). New York, Random House, 1957.
Too Strong for Fantasy (autobiography). New York, Scribner, 1967; London, Collins, 1968.

*

Manuscript Collection: Library of Congress, Washington, D.C.

*   *   *

Marcia Davenport seems obsessed with the theme of unhealthy self-denial. In *Of Lena Geyer* the diva of the title resolutely denies herself the consolation of love, starving a naturally passionate nature, because she is convinced that any satisfaction of carnal desire will be detrimental to the music to which she has devoted her life. Not until her voice seems irretrievably lost, at the end of her long career, does she behave like a normal human being and her eccentricities infect those who surround her and dance attendance upon her. Another Davenport heroine, Jessie Bourne of *East Side, West Side*, wilfully imprisons herself in a sterile charade of marriage, preferring a life of empty elegance over any attempt to escape into real life. Even more perverse is the behaviour of Mary Rafferty in *The Valley of Decision*. Having refused to marry the man she loves with all her heart, for what seem insufficient and unconvincing reasons, she then proceeds to egg him into a disastrous marriage, while she becomes housekeeper in his home, presiding over the desolation she has created. Generations of her unlucky lover's descendants puzzle over the curious relationship—and small wonder. It *is* a puzzle.

Most bizarre, yet strangely the most likeable of all the Davenport menagerie of odd characters, are Seymour and Randall Holt, of *My Brother's Keeper*. Warped in their formative years by the tyranny of an evil, power-mad grandmother, the brothers become in time caricatures of the very person they so hated; miserly, reclusive, life-denying, they live and die miserably in the crumbling, rubbish-choked brownstone that has become their mausoleum even during their dismal lifetimes.

Least attractive, on the other hand, are the romantic pair whose story is the subject of *The Constant Image*. Having embarked in a completely cold-blooded fashion upon an adulterous affair—apparently simply because that is what the "beautiful people" are doing this season—Harriet Piers is dismayed to discover that the amusing interlude has taken on an unexpected dimension. She has unintentionally fallen desparately in love with Carlo, and he with her. Everyone in their cosmopolitan circle sees this as an excellent opportunity for Carlo's long-suffering wife to behave nobly yet again; and when this time she fails to do so, her false friend and faithless husband magically become the injured parties, in both their own and the author's estimation. The self-denial in this particular story happens along a little after the fact, but happen it does. There is peculiar taint about *The Constant Image*, as of a moral code spoiled and left rotting.

Davenport's people are unpleasant creatures, concerned with appearance and the conventions more than with reality. For all their misadventures, most of them are well-cushioned against the rudeness of a crude world: only the well-to-do play significant roles upon her state. Popular in their day, Davenport's novels now seem shallow and unrealistic. Seekers after sensation ensnared by paperback editions with torrid jacket illustrations will suffer one more disappointment: no hot blood flows through these flaccid veins.

—Joan McGrath

DAVIS, Dorothy Salisbury. American. Born in Chicago, Illinois, 26 April 1916. Educated at Holy Child High School, Waukegan, Illinois; Barat College, Lake Forest, Illinois, A.B. 1938. Married Harry Davis in 1946. Writer, Swift and Com-

7pany, Chicago; research librarian, and editor, the *Merchandiser*, New York, 1940–46. Past President, Mystery Writers of America. Recipient: Mystery Writers of America Grand Master award, 1985. Agent: McIntosh and Otis Inc., 310 Madison Avenue, New York, New York 10017. Address: Snedens Landing, Palisades, New York 10964, U.S.A.

ROMANCE AND HISTORICAL PUBLICATIONS

Novels (series: Julie Hayes; Mrs. Norris and Jasper Tully)

The Judas Cat. New York, Scribner, 1949; London, Corgi, 1952.
The Clay Hand. New York, Scribner, 1950; London, Corgi, 1952.
A Gentle Murderer. New York, Scribner, 1951; London, Corgi, 1953.
A Town of Masks. New York, Scribner, 1952.
Death of an Old Sinner (Norris and Tully). New York, Scribner, 1957; London, Secker and Warburg, 1958.
A Gentleman Called (Norris and Tully). New York, Scribner, and London, Secker and Warburg, 1958.
Old Sinners Never Die (Norris). New York, Scribner, 1959; London, Secker and Warburg, 1960.
Black Sheep, White Lamb. New York, Scribner, 1963; London, Boardman, 1964.
The Pale Betrayer. New York, Scribner, 1965; London, Hodder and Stoughton, 1967.
Enemy and Brother. New York, Scribner, 1966; London, Hodder and Stoughton, 1967.
God Speed the Night, with Jerome Ross. New York, Scribner, 1968; London, Hodder and Stoughton, 1969.
Where the Dark Streets Go. New York, Scribner, 1969; London, Hodder and Stoughton, 1970.
Shock Wave. New York, Scribner, 1972; London, Hodder and Stoughton, 1974.
The Little Brothers. New York, Scribner, 1973; London, Barker, 1974.
A Death in the Life (Hayes). New York, Scribner, 1976; London, Gollancz, 1977.
Scarlet Night (Hayes). New York, Scribner, 1980; London, Gollancz, 1981.
Lullaby of Murder (Hayes). New York, Scribner, and London, Gollancz, 1984.
The Habit of Fear. New York, Scribner, 1987.

Short Stories

Tales for a Stormy Night: The Collected Crime Stories. Woodstock, Vermont, Countryman Press, 1984.

OTHER PUBLICATIONS

Novels

Men of No Property. New York, Scribner, 1956.
The Evening of the Good Samaritan. New York, Scribner, 1961.

Other

Editor, *A Choice of Murders*. New York, Scribner, 1958; London, Macdonald, 1960.
Editor, *Crime Without Murder*. New York, Scribner, 1970.

*

Manuscript Collection: Brooklyn College Library, City University, New York.

*   *   *

The work of Dorothy Salisbury Davis indicates her keen perception as a student of human nature. A distinguishing feature of her writings—ironic, perhaps, in one so opposed to physical violence—is the preoccupation with crime and criminal psychology. Following the early success of *The Clay Hand* and *The Judas Cat*, this interest became apparent in such works as *A Gentle Murderer*, with its sympathetic portrayal of a killer who must be found in order to avert further tragedy. Davis's explorations of the criminal mind are far from morbid. Rather she seeks for the minor flaws of character, the unforeseen shifts of circumstance, that lead certain human beings to break the confines of the law, and the often disastrous consequences of their actions. The theme is central to one of her most celebrated books, *Death of an Old Sinner*, where a retired general finds himself drawn into blackmail and eventually pays with his life. So intrigued was the author by the character she had created that the lovable rogue is revisited in a "prequel," *Old Sinners Never Die*. Much of the interest of the Davis novel stems from the battle of wits between hunter and hunted, with close parallels often being drawn between the detective and his prey. *The Pale Betrayer* is a good example, its "criminal" a college lecturer who finds himself involved in an act of espionage which gets out of hand and results in the death of a friend. In the ensuing course of the detection, where Mather at last atones by the sacrifice of his own life, he and the detective Marks come to a close understanding of each other's innermost nature. Similar themes pervade the excellent *Enemy and Brother* and *Where the Dark Streets Go*. *God Speed the Night*, written with Jerome Ross, is set in occupied France. A Jewish refugee is helped by a nun who disguises herself as his wife after the latter dies in the local convent. The two are pursued in a dual of wits by the dissolute, hen-pecked Vichy police chief, whose power as a hunter of criminals is his only claim to self-respect. As always, the subtle workings of the human mind are set down in the clean unadorned style which is Davis's hallmark.

An excellent writer of short stories, Davis's skill and psychological penetration serve her well in the shorter forms of fiction. Some of her later works might be described as "straightforward" detective stories, with the difference that her probing intelligence gives them a depth denied to most. Marks, the detective, returns in *The Little Brothers*, a fast-paced thriller involving a teenage gang, murder, and drug trafficking. *Shock Wave* investigates a similar crime against a backcloth of racial unrest in the Deep South. Recently, she has produced three fine novels starring the female sleuth Julie Hayes. *A Death in the Life* has her tracking down a murderer in the red light district, art theft is the theme of *Scarlet Night* and in *Lullaby of Murder* she become involved in solving a murder while reporting on a dance marathon. Julie Hayes is a lively and credible—if unorthodox—detective, and a tribute to the subtle skills of her creator.

—Geoffrey Sadler

DAVIS, Julia. See **WOODWARD, Lilian**.

DAWES, Edna. See **DARRELL, Elizabeth**.

DEAN, Shelley. See **WALKER, Lucy**.

DE BLASIS, Celeste (Ninette). American. Born in Santa Monica, California, 8 May 1946. Educated at Wellesley College, Massachusetts, 1964–65; Oregon State University, Corvallis, 1965–66; Pomona College, Claremont, California, B.A. (cum laude) in English 1968. Lives in California. Agent: Jane Rotrosen Agency, 318 East 51st Street, New York, New York 10022, U.S.A.

ROMANCE AND HISTORICAL PUBLICATIONS

Novels (series: Swan)

The Night Child. New York, Coward McCann, and London, Millington, 1975.
Suffer a Sea Change. New York, Coward McCann, 1976.
The Proud Breed. New York, Coward McCann, 1978; London, Arrow, 1979.
The Tiger's Woman. New York, Delacorte Press, 1981; London, Granada, 1982.
Wild Swan. New York, Bantam, 1984.
Swan's Chance. New York, Bantam, 1985; London, Bantam, 1987.
A Season of Swans. New York, Bantam, 1989.

*

Celeste De Blasis comments:

My name is unfortunate. It sounds wildly romantic to Anglo-Saxon ears, but it is no more than the result of having an Italian father. I write historical novels based on solid research from hundreds, often thousands of primary and secondary sources. The books are not ''bodice rippers,'' though they contain romance in the old sense of the heroic, the adventurous, the emotional lives of human beings depicted on a broad canvas. There is love in the books—love between men and women, between generations, love for friends, for ideas, for a particular piece of earth or a particular way of life. There are also hatred, prejudice, envy, greed—all the counterweights of love. Surely, good fiction explores the light and dark of the human spirit, and good historical novels should expand that exploration to include the light and dark of the collective heart people form to govern themselves and others. In the best combination, readers are both informed and entertained, and I hope that is what my novels do.

*   *   *

Three themes run through Celeste De Blasis' works: love of the sea; love of animals, especially horses; and the intense love of two human beings which overpowers everything else.

The Night Child is her only book which does not express the author's love of the sea, but horses and dogs are there. The setting is the interior of Maine in 1869. This is an old-fashioned gothic romance with a heroine who has plenty of backbone, though De Blasis tries to mislead the reader by making Brandy

appear more timorous than she is. Brandy is hired by Grey King to care for his daughter Missy, who has exhibited autistic behavior since her mother's death. As the child begins to respond to Brandy's experiments, strange and sometimes dangerous things begin to happen to Brandy. The knowledge that Missy's mother died in a stable fire two years earlier makes Brandy wonder who is trying to kill her. Clues to the miscreant are placed throughout until, by the finale, all the loose ends are tied up, and love vanquishes evil.

Suffer a Sea Change owes more than a little to Shakespeare's *The Tempest*. Jess is Miranda, Winston St. James her Caliban, etc. Although animals are not of great import here, the sea is. Jess accepts a trip to Bermuda from an avuncular gentleman she does not really know very well. He not only insists she join the tour group, he directs her to wear an ornate emerald ring while she is there. No sooner does the plane land than Jess is compelled to assist an obviously terrified native man whom she sees again at the resort. She is drawn toward the American, Kyre Tarkington, even as she is frightened by the Englishman, St. James. Despite the danger, Jess is pulled deeper into the mystery. She almost loses her life to ocean-going drug smugglers before the criminal activities are resolved, and she accepts the love of the right man. This is a page-turner even if the opening premise is unrealistic.

In *The Proud Breed* the animals take center stage in the form of palomino horses. Tessa's family raises them in the 1840's. Of mixed Spanish and American heritage, Tessa marries Yankee Gavin Ramsey after almost killing him. Disaster follows disaster (flood, drought, rape, Indian raids, war, and attempted abortion among others) as the history of California is related through three generations of the Ramsey family. Lots of violence and sex underscore the deep love between the characters in this long, satisfying read.

Tiger's Woman brings all of the author's loves into full flower. Jason Drake owns ships, logging camps, property in San Fransisco, and several businesses. The one thing he is not interested in is a woman to replace his dead wife. Mary Smith is only interested in his protection and feels safe only on his island off the coast of Seattle. Neither Jason nor the reader becomes privy to her horrible secret until much further in their relationship. In fact, Mary withholds information from Jason until it is almost too late. But the love they finally recognize as binding them together keeps them alive when survival seems impossible. Again, violence and sex are major parts of the plot.

Wild Swan and *Swan's Chance* span 50 years and detail the lives of Alexandria Thaine and Rane Falconer. Beginning in 1813 in Devon, England, Rane falls in love with Alex while she is still a child. Unaware of his feelings, or even her own, she returns home and weds her dead sister's husband, moving to Maryland to legitimize the marriage. The couple establish a tavern and a breeding farm for race horses, both named Wild Swan. St. John is killed in a fall from a horse, and some years later Alex and Rane marry. In the sequel, Rane has founded a Baltimore shipyard and builds clipper ships, while Alex breeds and races her horses. Their love is strong but tempestuous, and their children and grandchildren have their own adventures, following the examples of their elders. The underground railroad, women's rights, the relocation of the Cherokee Indians, the Civil War, and improvements in medical care all become important issues in a dramatic and interesting tale.

De Blasis keeps meticulous notes on each of her characters, even the animals. She records physical descriptions, psychological profiles, and genealogical charts for each. She believes in happy endings, too, so love always wins in the end, regardless of the amount of sex and violence which precede the victory.

Her work shows growth from one book to the next, and this bodes well for future novels.

—Andrea Lee Shuey

———

de CRESPIGNY, Charles. See **WILLIAMSON, C. N. and A. M.**

———

DEEPING, (George) Warwick. British. Born in Southend, Essex, 28 May 1877. Educated at Merchant Taylors' School, London; Trinity College, Cambridge, B.A., M.A., M.B.; studied medicine at Middlesex Hospital, London, and practiced as a doctor for one year. Served in the Royal Army Medical Corps, 1915–18. Married Maude Phyllis Merrill. *Died 20 April 1950.*

Romance and Historical Publications

Novels

Uther and Igraine. London, Richards, and New York, Outlook, 1903.
Love among the Ruins. London, Richards, and New York, Macmillan, 1904.
The Seven Streams. London, Nash, 1905; New York, Fenno, 1909.
The Slanderers. New York, Harper, 1905; London, Cassell, 1907.
Bess of the Woods. London and New York, Harper, 1906.
A Woman's War. London and New York, Harper, 1907.
Bertrand of Brittany. London and New York, Harper, 1908.
Mad Barbara. London, Cassell, 1908; New York, Harper, 1909.
The Red Saint. London, Cassell, 1909; New York, McBride, 1940.
The Return of the Petticoat. London and New York, Harper, 1909; revised edition, London, Cassell, 1913.
The Lame Englishman. London, Cassell, 1910.
The Rust of Rome. London, Cassell, 1910.
Fox Farm. London, Cassell, 1911; as *The Eyes of Love*, New York, McBride, 1933.
Joan of the Tower. London, Cassell, 1911; New York, McBride, 1941.
Sincerity. London, Cassell, 1912; as *The Strong Hand*, 1912; as *The Challenge of Love*, New York, McBride, 1932.
The House of Spies. London and New York, Cassell, 1913.
The White Gate. London, Cassell, 1913; New York, McBride, 1914.
The King Behind the King. London, Cassell, and New York, McBride, 1914.
The Pride of Eve. London, Cassell, 1914.
Marriage by Conquest. London, Cassell, and New York, McBride, 1915.
Unrest. London, Cassell, 1916; as *Bridge of Desire*, New York, McBride, 1916.
Martin Valliant. London, Cassell, and New York, McBride, 1917.
Valour. London, Cassell, 1918; New York, McBride, 1934.
Second Youth. London, Cassell, 1919; New York, Grosset and Dunlap, 1932.

The Prophetic Marriage. London, Cassell, 1920; New York, Grosset and Dunlap, 1932.
The House of Adventure. London, Cassell, 1921; New York, Macmillan, 1922.
Lantern Lane. London, Cassell, 1921.
Orchards. London, Cassell, 1922; as *The Captive Wife*, New York, Grosset and Dunlap, 1933.
Apples of Gold. London, Cassell, 1923.
The Secret Sanctuary; or, The Saving of John Stretton. London, Cassell, 1923.
Suvla John. London, Cassell, 1924.
Three Rooms. London, Cassell, 1924.
Sorrell and Son. London, Cassell, 1925; New York, Knopf, 1926.
Doomsday. London, Cassell, and New York, Knopf, 1927.
Kitty. London, Cassell, and New York, Knopf, 1927.
Old Pybus. London, Cassell, and New York, Knopf, 1928.
Roper's Row. London, Cassell, and New York, Knopf, 1929.
Exiles. London, Cassell, 1930; as *Exile*, New York, Knopf, 1930.
The Road. London, Cassell, 1931; as *The Ten Commandments*, New York, Knopf, 1931.
Old Wine and New. London, Cassell, and New York, Knopf, 1932.
Smith. London, Cassell, and New York, Knopf, 1932.
Two Black Sheep. London, Cassell, and New York, Knopf, 1933.
The Man on the White Horse. London, Cassell, and New York, Knopf, 1934.
Seven Men Came Back. London, Cassell, and New York, Knopf, 1934.
Sackcloth into Silk. London, Cassell, 1935; as *The Golden Cord*, New York, Knopf, 1935.
No Hero—This. London, Cassell, and New York, Knopf, 1936.
Blind Man's Year. London, Cassell, and New York, Knopf, 1937.
These White Hands. New York, McBride, 1937.
The Woman at the Door. London, Cassell, and New York, Knopf, 1937.
The Malice of Men. London, Cassell, and New York, Knopf, 1938.
Fantasia. London, Cassell, 1939; as *Bluewater*, New York, Knopf, 1939.
Shabby Summer. London, Cassell, 1939; as *Folly Island*, New York, Knopf, 1939.
The Man Who Went Back. London, Cassell, and New York, Knopf, 1940.
The Shield of Love. London, Cassell, and New York, McBride, 1940.
Corn in Egypt. London, Cassell, 1941; New York, Knopf, 1942.
The Dark House. London, Cassell, and New York, Knopf, 1941.
I Live Again. London, Cassell, and New York, Knopf, 1942.
Slade. London, Cassell, and New York, Dial Press, 1943.
Mr. Gurney and Mr. Slade. London, Cassell, 1944; as *The Cleric's Secret*, New York, Dial Press, 1944.
Reprieve. London, Cassell, and New York, Dial Press, 1945.
The Impudence of Youth. London, Cassell, and New York, Dial Press, 1946.
Laughing House. London, Cassell, 1946; New York, Dial Press, 1947.
Portrait of a Playboy. London, Cassell, 1947; as *The Playboy*, New York, Dial Press, 1948.
Paradise Place. London, Cassell, 1949.
Old Mischief. London, Cassell, 1950.

Time to Heal. London, Cassell, 1952.
Man in Chains. London, Cassell, 1953.
The Old World Dies. London, Cassell, 1954.
Caroline Terrace. London, Cassell, 1955.
The Serpent's Tooth. London, Cassell, 1956.
The Sword and the Cross. London, Cassell, 1957.

Short Stories

Countess Glika and Other Stories. London, Cassell, 1919.
Martyrdom, with *The House Behind the Judas Tree* by Gilbert Frankau and *Forbidden Music* by Ethel Mannin. London, Readers Library, 1929; as *Three Stories of Romance*, 1936.
The Short Stories of Warwick Deeping. London, Cassell, 1930.
Stories of Love, Courage, and Compassion. New York, Knopf, 1930.
Two in a Train and Other Stories. London, Cassell, 1935.

*   *   *

Traditionalist Warwick Deeping turned out 70 novels in an effort to keep alive the pastoral vision of Edwardian England in the years after World War I; but only his early *Sorrell and Son* (1925) became a mass audience favorite in the United States as well as the British Empire. This harrowing tale of an aristocratic World War I veteran's returning to find himself destitute and deserted by his wife recounts Stephen Sorrell's successful struggle to emerge from a demeaning position to regain dignity and wealth, while continuing to command the loyalty of his son. Throughout his travails, Sorrell's obsession is to remain a gentleman and have his son educated as befits a gentleman. The reviewer for *The New Statesman* complained that "it is difficult to understand how a man so wisely determined when he reaches bottom could have fallen so low" (31 October 1925); but the criticism misses the source of the novel's enduring popularity. *Sorrell and Son* is no Samuel Smiles success story, but rather a secularized allegory in the tradition of *Pilgrim's Progress.* The author arbitrarily reduces Sorrell to a Job-like state so that he can describe the sort of person who can rehabilitate himself in a fictional reincarnation of the "stiff upper lip" tradition that kept Britons going through demoralizing times. His son, Christopher, even becomes a doctor, not just because the position is properly genteel, but so that in a heart-rending conclusion he can administer an overdose of morphine that ends his father's physical sufferings after this man has triumphed over moral defeats the world has administered to him. *Sorrell and Son* appeared the same year as *The Great Gatsby*; and it can be read as an unintended reply to Fitzgerald's cynical, ironic tale of father-son relationships destroyed in a squalid world. Deeping's tribute to the triumph of the old verities was enormously more popular than Fitzgerald's novel at the time of their publication; but Deeping never again found the formula to shape his nostalgic vision into a popular myth.

—Warren French

DELAFIELD, E. M. Pseudonym for Edmée Elizabeth Monica De la Pasture. British. Born in Aldrinton, Sussex, 9 June 1890; daughter of the writer Mrs. Henry De la Pasture. Educated at convent schools; postulant with religious order in Belgium, 1911–12. Served in the Voluntary Aid Detachment, 1914–17, then with the Ministry of National Service, Bristol, 1917–18.

Married Arthur Paul Dashwood in 1919; one son and one daughter. Journalist: regular contributor to *Time and Tide* and *Punch.* Justice of the Peace, Cullompton, Devon. *Died 2 December 1943.*

ROMANCE AND HISTORICAL PUBLICATIONS

Novels (series: Provincial Lady)

Zella Sees Herself. London, Heinemann, and New York, Knopf, 1917.
The War-Workers. London, Heinemann, and New York, Knopf, 1918.
The Pelicans. London, Heinemann, 1918; New York, Knopf, 1919.
Consequences. London, Hodder and Stoughton, and New York, Knopf, 1919.
Tension. London, Hutchinson, and New York, Macmillan, 1920.
The Heel of Achilles. London, Hutchinson, and New York, Macmillan, 1921.
Humbug. London, Hutchinson, 1921; New York, Macmillan, 1922.
The Optimist. London, Hutchinson, and New York, Macmillan, 1922.
A Reversion to Type. London, Hutchinson, and New York, Macmillan, 1923.
Mrs. Harter. London, Hutchinson, 1924; New York, Harper, 1925.
Messalina of the Suburbs (includes story and play). London, Hutchinson, 1924.
The Chip and the Block. London, Hutchinson, 1925; New York, Harper, 1926.
Jill. London, Hutchinson, 1926; New York, Harper, 1927.
The Way Things Are. London, Hutchinson, 1927; New York, Harper, 1928.
The Suburban Young Man. London, Hutchinson, 1928.
What Is Love? London, Macmillan, 1928; as *First Love*, New York, Harper, 1929.
Turn Back the Leaves. London, Macmillan, and New York, Harper, 1930.
Diary of a Provincial Lady. London, Macmillan, 1930; New York, Harper, 1931.
Challenge to Clarissa. London, Macmillan, 1931; as *House Party*, New York, Harper, 1931.
Thank Heaven Fasting. London, Macmillan, 1932; as *A Good Man's Love*, New York, Harper, 1932.
The Provincial Lady Goes Further. London, Macmillan, 1932; as *The Provincial Lady in London*, New York, Harper, 1933.
Gay Life. London, Macmillan, and New York, Harper, 1933.
The Provincial Lady in America. London, Macmillan, and New York, Harper, 1934.
The Bazalgettes: A Tale (published anonymously). London, Hamish Hamilton, 1935.
Faster! Faster! London, Macmillan, and New York, Harper, 1936.
Nothing Is Safe. London, Macmillan, and New York, Harper, 1937.
The Provincial Lady in War-Time. London, Macmillan, and New York, Harper, 1940.
No One Now Will Know. London, Macmillan, and New York, Harper, 1941.
Late and Soon. London, Macmillan, and New York, Harper, 1943.

Short Stories

The Entertainment. London, Hutchinson, and New York, Harper, 1927.
Women Are Like That: Short Stories. London, Macmillan, 1929; New York, Harper, 1930.
When Women Love. New York, Harper, 1938; as *Three Marriages*, London, Macmillan, 1939.
Love Has No Resurrection and Other Stories. London, Macmillan, 1939.

OTHER PUBLICATIONS

Plays

To See Ourselves: A Domestic Comedy (produced London, 1930; New York, 1935). London and New York, French, 1932.
The Glass Wall (produced London, 1933). London, Gollancz, 1933.

Screenplays: *Crime on the Hill*, with others 1933; *Moonlight Sonata* (*The Charmer*), with Edward Knoblock and Hans Rameau, 1937.

Radio Plays: *The Little Boy*, 1934; *Case for the Defense*; *Vice Versa*, from the novel by F. Anstey; *Home Life Relayed* (sketches); *Home Is Like That* (sketches), 1938.

Other

General Impressions. London, Macmillan, 1933.
Ladies and Gentlemen in Victorian Fiction. London, Hogarth Press, and New York, Harper, 1937.
As Others Hear Us: A Miscellany. London, Macmillan, 1937.
Straw Without Bricks: I Visit Soviet Russia. London, Macmillan, 1937; as *I Visit the Soviets: The Provincial Lady Looks at Russia*, New York, Harper, 1937.
People You Love. London, Collins, 1940.
This War We Wage. New York, Emerson, 1941.

Editor, *The Time and Tide Album.* London, Hamish Hamilton, 1932.
Editor, *The Brontës: Their Lives Recorded by Their Contemporaries.* London, Hogarth Press, 1935; Westport, Connecticut, Meckler, 1980.

*

Bibliography: in *Ten Contemporaries*, 2nd series by John Gawsworth, London, Benn, 1933.

Critical Study: *The Life of a Provincial Lady: A Study of E. M. Delafield* by Violet Powell, London, Heinemann, 1988.

*   *   *

A prolific writer whose work spans three decades, E. M. Delafield explores the human capacity for self-deception and self-love, often revealed in affairs of the heart. These aspects are present in her first novel—appropriately titled *Zella Sees Herself*—and recur constantly in later books. Nowadays Delafield is best known for her superb comic masterpiece *Diary of a Provincial Lady*, a work justly famous for its sardonic wit and shrewd insights into human nature. Its popularity led to a number of sequels, all of which are amusing without matching the excellence of their original. Unfortunately the fame of the "Provincial Lady" has tended to detract from other novels of a different kind, where the humor is muted, and the author approaches various facets of life and love in a witty but serious manner.

Delafield's best novel in this style is generally thought to be *Thank Heaven Fasting*, where the heroine experiences and rejects romantic passion for the staid affections of a reliable middle-aged suitor. The pressures of upper-class society, where marriage is regarded as all-important and spinsterhood a fate worse than death, is admirably portrayed. So, too, is the heroine's ability to think herself in love at each encounter. This, though, is to give too cynical an interpretation of Delafield's motives. Though gothic elements are occasional and slight—her study of a female criminal in *Messalina of the Suburbs*, and parts of *When Women Love* (*Three Marriages*) are exceptions—romance figures largely in her work. Delafield is no stranger to passion, though her recounting of it is often dispassionate. The early novel *The Heel of Achilles* concentrates on the possessive self-love of Lydia Raymond, who throughout her life ruthlessly claims the centre of the stage for herself under the guise of caring for others. Lydia, who marries without love, is brought to her downfall by her daughter Jennie, the one person for whom she cares. Her selfishness and hypocrisy are laid bare at last in her vain struggle to usurp the life experience of Jennie for herself. Though the ending has rather too much of the sermon about it, its character studies go deeper than those of *Thank Heaven Fasting*. Like many of Delafield's novels, it is unjustly neglected.

Turn Back the Leaves centres on the growth to womanhood of Stella, child of an illicit liaison, who is brought up as a "cousin" in the household of the wronged husband. Delafield describes her impact on the family, and its eventual break-up. The story is interesting, but an uneasy shift of focus from Stella to her "cousins" near the end weakens the book as a whole. More effective is *When Women Love* which views three different relationships in 1857, 1897, and 1937 respectively. The first, "The Wedding of Rose Barlow," deals with the young bride in a marriage of convenience who falls in love with her French cousin, and is finally reunited with him after surviving the horrors of the Cawnpore massacre, where her husband dies. "A Girl of the Period" looks satirically at a "modern" girl of 1897, who is engaged without being in love, and openly scorns sentiment. When her fiancé falls for someone else she strikes a noble pose in "releasing" him, but when she herself becomes infatuated by the rakish Courtenay, promised to her friend, Violet fights viciously with her rival rather than give him up. "We Meant to Be Happy" describes an ill-fated extra-marital affair where disillusion sets in, and the husband's illness serves to blackmail the erring wife into submission. The three stories are skilfully related, the tone varied in each case.

In *No One Now Will Know* the author explores Rosalie Meredith's love for the Creole Lucian Lempriere, her illicit passion for his brother Fred, and her violent death. This central theme—described in retrospect over three generations—is paralleled by Rosalie's friend Kate, and her unrequited love for Lucian. There is an ironic echo a generation later, when Rosalie's daughter Callie loses her own lover to her best friend, Elisabeth. The tangle of relationships is adroitly presented, the author refraining from comment to let the reader draw his own conclusions.

Late and Soon is Delafield's last novel, and ranks among her best. The story takes place over a winter weekend in 1942, at the country home of Valentine, Lady Arbell. A group of soldiers are billeted there, and Valentine recognizes their Colonel—Rory Lonergan—as the young Irish artist with whom she fell in love as a girl, but was prevented from marrying. Now he re-enters her life as the lover of her worldly daughter, Primrose. The re-awakening of their love and its traumatic resolution are brilliantly depicted by Delafield, who eyes her characters with a wry affection. *Late and Soon* is a worthy conclusion to her career, marred as it was by her premature death.

Delafield's work extends beyond the novel. She produced three collections of short stories, which display all her familiar talents. *Love Has No Resurrection* is typical, with tales ranging from the tragic to the comic and mundane, often touching on the deluding power of passion and its consequences. Other works include plays, socio-political commentaries, and literary criticism. Her articles for *Punch* and *Time and Tide*, many of them masterly examples of humorous dialogue, are collected in *As Others Hear Us*. Delafield's vision is broad as it is deep, her analyses of human character at once sharp and sympathetic. Her writing reveals a natural warmth, a wary fondness for the human heart, no matter how often it deceives.

—Geoffrey Sadler

---

de la ROCHE, Mazo (Louise). Canadian. Born in Newmarket, Ontario, 15 January 1879. Educated at schools in Galt, Ontario, and Toronto; Parkdale Collegiate Institute, Toronto; University of Toronto. Had two adopted daughters. Full-time writer from childhood; lived in Windsor, England, 1929–39; thereafter lived in Toronto. Recipient: Lorne Pierce medal, 1938; University of Alberta National Award, 1951. Litt.D.: University of Toronto, 1954. *Died 12 July 1961.*

ROMANCE AND HISTORICAL PUBLICATIONS

Novels (series: Jalna)

Possession. New York and London, Macmillan, 1923.
Delight. New York and London, Macmillan, 1926.
Jalna. Boston, Little Brown, and London, Hodder and Stoughton, 1927.
Whiteoaks of Jalna. Boston, Little Brown, 1929; as *Whiteoaks*, London, Macmillan, 1929.
Finch's Fortune (Jalna). Boston, Little Brown, and London, Macmillan, 1931.
Lark Ascending. Boston, Little Brown, and London, Macmillan, 1932.
The Thunder of New Wings, in *Chatelaine* (Toronto), June-December 1932.
The Master of Jalna. Boston, Little Brown, and London, Macmillan, 1933.
Beside a Norman Tower. Boston, Little Brown, and London, Macmillan, 1934.
Young Renny (Jalna). Boston, Little Brown, and London, Macmillan, 1935.
Whiteoak Harvest (Jalna). Boston, Little Brown, and London, Macmillan, 1936.
The Very House. Boston, Little Brown, and London, Macmillan, 1937.
Growth of a Man. Boston, Little Brown, and London, Macmillan, 1938.
Whiteoak Heritage (Jalna). Boston, Little Brown, and London, Macmillan, 1940.
Wakefield's Course (Jalna). Boston, Little Brown, 1941; London, Macmillan, 1942.
The Two Saplings. London, Macmillan, 1942.

The Building of Jalna. Boston, Little Brown, 1944; London, Macmillan, 1945.
Return to Jalna. Boston, Little Brown, 1946; London, Macmillan, 1948.
Mary Wakefield (Jalna). Boston, Little Brown, and London, Macmillan, 1949.
Renny's Daughter (Jalna). Boston, Little Brown, and London, Macmillan, 1951.
The Whiteoak Brothers (Jalna). Boston, Little Brown, and London, Macmillan, 1953.
Variable Winds at Jalna. Boston, Little Brown, and London, Macmillan, 1955.
Centenary at Jalna. Boston, Little Brown, and London, Macmillan, 1958.
Morning at Jalna. Boston, Little Brown, and London, Macmillan, 1960.

Short Stories

Explorers of the Dawn. New York, Knopf, and London, Cassell, 1922.
The Sacred Bullock and Other Stories of Animals. Boston, Little Brown, and London, Macmillan, 1939.
A Boy in the House and Other Stories. Boston, Little Brown, and London, Macmillan, 1952.
Selected Stories, edited by Douglas Daymond. Ottawa, University of Ottawa Press, 1979.

OTHER PUBLICATIONS

Plays

Low Life (produced Montreal, 1925). Toronto, Macmillan, 1925; in *Low Life and Other Plays*, 1929.
Come True (produced Toronto, 1927). Toronto, Macmillan, 1927; in *Low Life and Other Plays*, 1929.
The Return of the Emigrant (produced Toronto, 1928). Included in *Low Life and Other Plays*, 1929.
Low Life and Other Plays (includes *Come True* and *The Return of the Emigrant*). Toronto, Macmillan, and Boston, Little Brown, 1929.
Whiteoaks, adaptation of her own novel (produced London, 1936; New York, 1938). Boston, Little Brown, and London, Macmillan, 1936.
The Mistress of Jalna (produced London, 1952).

Other

Portrait of a Dog. Boston, Little Brown, and London, Macmillan, 1930.
Quebec, Historic Seaport. New York, Doubleday, 1944; London, Macmillan, 1946.
The Song of Lambert (for children). Boston, Little Brown, and London, Macmillan, 1955.
Ringing the Changes: An Autobiography. Boston, Little Brown, and New York, Macmillan, 1957.
Bill and Coo (for children). Boston, Little Brown, and London, Macmillan, 1958.

*

Critical Studies: *Mazo de la Roche of Jalna* by Ronald Hambleton, New York, Hawthorn, 1966; *Mazo de la Roche* by George Hendrick, New York, Twayne, 1970.

*   *   *

The Whiteoaks of Jalna are among the most famous families in the popular fiction of the 20th century; they have been favourably compared with Galsworthy's Forsytes for their enduring ability to fascinate. Through some 15 titles the Whiteoaks held their course; neither wealthy nor particularly distinguished, having no social pretensions, indeed, completely self-absorbed. They lived in fairy-tale British Colonial style in and around the rambling Southern Ontario mansion from which the series takes its title. Old Adelaide, the family autocrat whose 100th birthday celebrations provided one of the highpoints of the saga, is the most powerful figure in this matriarchal society. For years she keeps her family in line by holding the secret of her mysterious will over their heads like a liontamer's whip, for she owns all the family fortune. Even after she has finally left the scene her influence pervades the action, and she is apparently reincarnated in the person of her great granddaughter Adelaide in the later stories.

The Whiteoaks are no average family. Several generations live under the roof of Jalna, and seldom amicably. Passions flare in an extraordinary fashion—the Jalna countryside is dotted, figuratively speaking, with illegitimate Whiteoak offspring. Elopements, jiltings, and various forms of interfamilial chicanery and double dealing are practically a matter of routine; incest by mistake is but narrowly avoided. Renny, the master of Jalna, eschews subtlety, and darkly suspects the artistic talent of his half-brothers as a sign of fundamental weakness and undependability, but he is a father figure to all, except when occupied by falling in or out of love with their womenfolk. The brothers seduce or run off with their sisters-in-law or the au pair; bicker and squabble viciously among themselves; enter or leave a monastery with complete sang-froid; and present a united front to the world, no matter what may be happening behind the family facade.

Obviously, any attempt to summarize a Jalna plot will suggest sensationalism comparable with that of a soap opera; but this does less than justice to Mazo de la Roche's magical ability to create larger-than-life characters in whom wild eccentricities seem only what might be expected. Her stories sweep along at such a pace that the reader is caught up and carried away, unprotesting. Jalna was a never-never land that became more real than reality to generations of de la Roche's devoted readers all over the world, who could scarcely believe that with her death the Whiteoak saga came, unresolved, to its ending. A long, well-filled shelf of *Jalna* stories was not enough for the devotees who now will never know for certain whether Renny's wilful daughter, young Adelaide, could have filled the place of the formidable Gran she so closely resembled.

De la Roche wrote of other subjects through the years, and with some success, but only the Jalna series lives on. It was not, and never claimed to be, great literature; but it was no small achievement to create, as de la Roche created, a fictional empire so full of life, vigour, and personality, that it has survived its author and her times to become a minor tradition.

—Joan McGrath

DELDERFIELD, R(onald) F(rederick). British. Born in Greenwich, London, 12 February 1912. Attended West Buckland School, Devon. Served in the Royal Air Force, 1940–45: public relations officer, 1944–45. Married May Evans in 1936; one son and one daughter. Reporter, sub-editor, and editor, *Exmouth Chronicle*, Devon, 1929–39 and 1945–47, then freelance writer. *Died 24 June 1972.*

ROMANCE AND HISTORICAL PUBLICATIONS

Novels

All over the Town. London, Bles, 1947; New York, Simon and Schuster, 1977.
Seven Men of Gascony. London, Laurie, and Indianapolis, Bobbs Merrill, 1949.
Farewell the Tranquil Mind. London, Laurie, 1950; as *Farewell the Tranquil*, New York, Dutton, 1950.
The Avenue Story. London, Hodder and Stoughton, 1964; as *The Avenue*, New York, Simon and Schuster, 1969.
  The Dreaming Suburb. London, Hodder and Stoughton, 1958.
  The Avenue Goes to War. London, Hodder and Stoughton, 1958.
The Was a Fair Maid Dwelling. London, Hodder and Stoughton, 1960; as *Diana*, New York, Putnam, 1960.
Stop at a Winner. London, Hodder and Stoughton, 1961; New York, Simon and Schuster, 1978.
The Unjust Skies. London, Hodder and Stoughton, 1962.
The Spring Madness of Mr. Sermon. London, Hodder and Stoughton, 1963; as *Mr. Sermon*, New York, Simon and Schuster, 1970.
Too Few for Drums. London, Hodder and Stoughton, 1964; New York, Simon and Schuster, 1971.
A Horseman Riding By. London, Hodder and Stoughton, 1966; New York, Simon and Schuster, 1967.
Cheap Day Return. London, Hodder and Stoughton, 1967; as *Return Journey*, New York, Simon and Schuster, 1974.
The Green Gauntlet. London, Hodder and Stoughton, and New York, Simon and Schuster, 1968.
Come Home Charlie and Face Them. London, Hodder and Stoughton, 1969; as *Charlie Come Home*, New York, Simon and Schuster, 1976.
God Is an Englishman. London, Hodder and Stoughton, and New York, Simon and Schuster, 1970.
Their Was the Kingdom. London, Hodder and Stoughton, and New York, Simon and Schuster, 1971.
To Serve Them All My Days. London, Hodder and Stoughton, and New York, Simon and Schuster, 1972.
Give Us This Day. London, Hodder and Stoughton, and New York, Simon and Schuster, 1973.
Post of Honor. New York, Ballantine, 1974.
Long Summer Days. New York, Pocket Books, 1974.

OTHER PUBLICATIONS

Plays

Spark in Judaea (produced London, 1937). Boston, Baker, 1951; London, de Wolfe and Stone, 1953.
Twilight Call (produced Birmingham, 1939).
Printer's Devil (produced London, 1939).
This Is My Life, with Basil Thomas (as *Matron*, produced Wolverhampton, 1942). London, Fox, 1944.
Worm's Eye View (produced London, 1945). Published in *Embassy Successes 1*, London, Sampson Low, 1946; New York, French, 1948.
The Spinster of South Street (produced London, 1945).
Peace Comes to Peckham (produced London, 1946). London, French, 1948.
All over the Town, adaptation of his own novel (produced London, 1947). London, French, 1948.
The Queen Came By (produced London, 1948). London, Deane, and Boston, Baker, 1949.

Sailors Beware: An Elizabethan Improbability. London, Deane, 1950.

The Elephant's Graveyard (produced Chesterfield, 1951).

Waggonload o'Monkeys: Further Adventures of Porter and Taffy (produced London, 1951). London, Deane, 1952.

Golden Rain (produced Windsor, 1952). London, French, 1953.

Miaow! Miaow! London, French, 1952.

The Old Lady of Cheadle. London, Deane, 1952.

Made to Measure (broadcast 1953). London, French, 1952.

The Bride Wore an Opal Ring (broadcast 1954). London, French, 1952.

Follow the Plough (produced Leatherhead, Surrey, and London, 1953).

The Testimonial (broadcast 1953). London, French, 1953.

Glad Tidings (produced 1953).

The Offending Hand (produced Northampton, 1953). London, Deane, 1955.

The Orchard Walls (produced Aldershot, Hampshire, and London, 1953). London, French, 1954.

Absent Lover: A Plantagenet Improbability. London, French, 1953.

Smoke in the Valley (broadcast 1954). London, French, 1953.

The Guinea-Pigs. London, Deane, 1954.

Home Is the Hunted. London, French, 1954.

Musical Switch. London, de Wolfe and Stone, 1954.

The Rounderlay Tradition. London, Deane, 1954.

Ten till Five. London, de Wolfe and Stone, 1954.

Where There's a Will. London, French, 1954.

And Then There Were None (broadcast 1955). London, French, 1954.

Uncle's Little Lapse. London, de Wolfe and Stone, 1955.

The Mayerling Affair (produced Pitlochry, 1957). London, French, 1958.

Duty and the Beast, adaptation of a work by Hans Keuls (produced Worthing, Sussex, 1957).

Flashpoint. London, French, 1958.

Once Aboard a Lugger. London, French, 1962.

Wild Mink. London, French, 1962.

My Dearest Angel (produced Pitlochry, 1963).

Screenplays: *All over Town*, with others, 1949; *Worm's Eye View*, with Jack Marks, 1951; *Value for Money*, with William Fairchild, 1955; *Where There's a Will*, 1955; *Now and Forever*, with Michael Pertwee, 1956; *Keep It Clean*, with Carl Nystrom, 1956; *Home and Away*, with Vernon Sewell, 1956; *On the Fiddle*, with Harold Buchman, 1961.

Radio Plays: *The Cocklemouth Comet*, 1938; *The Comet Covers a Wedding*, 1939; *Made to Measure*, 1953; *The Testimonial*, 1953; *The Bride Wore an Opal Ring*, 1954; *Smoke in the Valley*, 1954; *And Then There Were None*, 1955; *This Happy Brood*, 1956; *Midal Beach*, 1960; *Napoleon in Love*, 1960; *The Avenue Goes to War*, from his own novel, 1961; *The Dreaming Suburb*, from his own novel, 1962; *A Horseman Riding By*, from his own novel, 1967.

Television Plays: *The Day of the Sputnik*, 1963; *Jezebel*, 1963 (USA).

Other

These Clicks Made History: The Stories of Stanley ("Glorious") Devon, Fleet Street Photographer. Exmouth, Devon, Raleigh Press, 1946.

Nobody Shouted Author (autobiography). London, Laurie, 1951.

Bird's Eye View: An Autobiography. London, Constable, 1954.

The Adventures of Ben Gunn (for children). London, Hodder and Stoughton, 1956; Indianapolis, Bobbs Merrill, 1957.

Napoleon in Love. London, Hodder and Stoughton, 1959; Boston, Little Brown, 1960.

The March of the Twenty-Six: The Story of Napoleon's Marshals. London, Hodder and Stoughton, 1962; as *Napoleon's Marshals*, Philadelphia, Chilton, 1966.

Under an English Sky. London, Hodder and Stoughton, 1964.

The Golden Millstones: Napoleon's Brothers and Sisters. London, Weidenfeld and Nicolson, 1964; New York, Harper, 1965.

The Retreat from Moscow. London, Hodder and Stoughton, and New York, Atheneum, 1967.

Imperial Sunset: The Fall of Napoleon 1813–1814. Philadelphia, Chilton, 1968; London, Hodder and Stoughton, 1969.

For My Own Amusement (autobiography). London, Hodder and Stoughton, 1968; New York, Simon and Schuster, 1972.

Overture for Beginners (autobiography). London, Hodder and Stoughton, 1970.

Editor, *Tales Out of School: An Anthology of West Buckland Reminiscences 1895–1963*. St. Austell, Cornwall, H. E. Warne, 1963.

*

Critical Study: *R. F. Delderfield* by Sanford Sternlicht, Boston, Twayne, 1988.

*   *   *

R. F. Delderfield's novels are not so much classic love stories as family sagas punctuated by strong romantic impulses. In *The Avenue Goes to War*, for instance, the hard-bitten, self-seeking Elaine abandons affluence and security with a rich lover to live with the impoverished and disgraced Archie. In *God Is an Englishman* Adam Swan makes a sudden and surprising decision to marry the fiercely independent but terribly vulnerable 18-year-old Henrietta. Broader canvasses of the English country or suburban scene, and astute socio-political comment adds realism and drama to Delderfield's romantic relationships, which are basically straightforward and described strictly from a masculine stance—something that is unusual in the general run of romantic novels. There is none of the tremulous, long-winded lead up and final-scene-only clinch that forms the love story pattern when the narrative viewpoint is that of the traditional heroine of the genre. Delderfield's emphasis is on married love and mutuality, not only of passion but of various levels of experience. In *God Is an Englishman* Adam's and Henrietta's relationship only really begins to flower when, after seven years of marriage, Henrietta is forced to become actively involved in her husband's work commitments. David Powlett-Jones, the boarding-school headmaster hero of *To Serve Them All My Days*, far from wanting a merely ornamental or domesticated wife, encourages Chris in her career ambitions. She is his second wife, as David marries once in his youth and again in middle-age.

Romantic relationships in Delderfield's books are in fact often of the second-time-around, middle-aged, or even elderly variety. In *The Dreaming Suburb* Jim Carver loses his first wife almost as soon as he returns home from the trenches at the end of World War I. He does not marry his second wife, Edith—a spinster neighbour he has known for over 25 years—until the end of World War II (in the closing pages of *The Avenue Goes to War*, the sequel to *The Dreaming Suburb*). Edith and Jim are in their sixties; they have suffered bombing and bereavement, and each is sustained by the friendship of the other and by the helpfulness of neighbours. (There is always a strong community feeling in Delderfield's novels, even when his heroes and heroines go against the tide of popular opinion.) Their marriage is a satisfying one. Even though love is often expressed by the brewing of pots of tea and the filling of hot water bottles for each other rather than by acts of passion, theirs is nevertheless a romantic story.

Second or late marriages, of course, add variety to any novel, and particularly to those of the family saga type which the author handled so well. (At least three of the leading male characters in *The Avenue Goes to War* marry twice.) Although Delderfield's emphasis is on very much-married love, there is, however, always a place in his novels for the realistic extramarital affair. In *The Dreaming Suburb* Archie Carver, as a teenage errand boy during World War I, engages in grocery blackmarketeering which brings him, as well as a great deal of extra cash, a satisfying sexual initiation with the lovely and fullblooded wife of an officer who is away at the front. Archie is a go-getter, and so—in the sequel—is Elaine Frith. Delderfield is at his best when writing of non-conformist characters of a complex disposition, and particularly about their romantic involvements. Elaine quickly discards the claustrophobic morality of her narrow-minded upbringing, and as a very young girl begins to exploit her sexual power over men. Later on, she purposefully harnesses this to further her clearly defined material ambitions, and she is untroubled by the strictures of neighbours on her activities: "Marvellous what some women'll do nowadays for a pound of granulated and a tin of pineapple chunks, isn't it?" (The provider of wartime black market goodies is once again Archie Carver.)

Generally speaking, however, in Delderfield's novels the brief affair or sexual encounter, whatever its intensity, is prevented by its tucked away nature from having deep significance in the hero's life. He cannot achieve with a mistress the mutuality at all levels of experience that he might (hopefully) know with a wife.

Love and war are inextricably intertwined in these severalgenerational sagas in a way that is inevitable when the influence of the two world wars plays such an important part in the author's assessment of life. Delderfield's most poignant vignette of a romantic encounter in a war setting occurs in *A Horseman Riding By*. Paul Craddock, an Army Officer at the Western Front in 1915, has a chance meeting on the road to Messines with his ex-wife, Grace, who is serving as an ambulance driver. They meet again by mutual consent, and amid the mud and carnage and disillusionment they communicate with a completeness that they never managed to achieve in their once comfortable life in England. The residual bitterness of his breakup with Grace is wiped away for Paul—and the encounter helps him to understand aspects of his present marriage to Claire, a much younger woman. But his new found and comradely closeness to Grace is soon shattered. She is killed by the blast of an enemy bomb on one of her ambulance runs. In the hands of a less skilful storyteller, this encounter could have been embarrassing or banal—but it works, in the unsentimental and robust manner in which all Delderfield's fictional romantic situations do.

—Mary Cadogan

DELINSKY, Barbara (Ruth, née Greenberg). Has also written as Billie Douglass; Bonnie Drake. American. Born in Boston, Massachusetts, 9 August 1945. Educated at Tufts University, Medford, Massachusetts, B.A. in psychology 1967; Boston College, M.A. in sociology 1969. Married Stephen R. Delinsky in 1967; three sons. Researcher, Children's Protective Services, Boston, 1968–69; photographer and reporter, Belmont *Herald*, Massachusetts. Recipient: Romance Writers of America Golden Medallion, 1988. Lives in Needham, Massachusetts. Address: c/o Harlequin Enterprises Ltd., 225 Duncan Mill Road, Don Mills, Ontario M3B 3K9, Canada.

ROMANCE AND HISTORICAL PUBLICATIONS

Novels

A Special Something. Toronto, Harlequin, 1984.
Bronze Mystique. Toronto, Harlequin, 1984.
Finger Prints. Toronto, Worldwide, 1984.
The Forever Instinct. Toronto, Harlequin, 1985.
Secret of the Stone. Toronto, Harlequin, 1985.
Chances Are. Toronto, Harlequin, 1985.
First Things First. Toronto, Harlequin, 1985.
Threats and Promises. Toronto, Harlequin, 1986.
Straight from the Heart. Toronto, Harlequin, 1986.
Within Reach. Toronto, Worldwide, 1986.
First, Best and Only. Toronto, Harlequin, 1986.
Jasmine Sorcery. Toronto, Harlequin, 1986.
The Real Thing. Toronto, Harlequin, 1987.
Twelve Across. Toronto, Harlequin, 1987.
A Single Rose. Toronto, Harlequin, 1987.
Twilight Whispers. New York, Warner, 1987.
Cardinal Rules. Toronto, Harlequin, 1987.
Heatwave. Toronto, Harlequin, 1987.
Commitments. New York, Warner, 1988.
TLC. Toronto, Harlequin, 1988.
Fulfillment. Toronto, Harlequin, 1988.
Through My Eyes. Toronto, Harlequin, 1989.

Novels as Bonnie Drake

The Passionate Touch. New York, Dell, 1981.
Surrender by Moonlight. New York, Dell, 1981.
Sweet Ember. New York, Dell, 1981.
Sensuous Burgundy. New York, Dell, 1981.
The Ardent Protector. New York, Dell, 1982.
Whispered Promise. New York, Dell, 1982.
Lilac Awakening. New York, Dell, 1982.
Amber Enchantment. New York, Dell, 1982.
Lover from the Sea. New York, Dell, 1983.
The Silver Fox. New York, Dell, 1983.
Passion and Illusion. New York, Dell, 1983.
Gemstone. New York, Dell, 1983.
Moment to Moment. New York, Dell, 1984.

Novels as Billie Douglass

Search for a New Dawn. New York, Silhouette, 1982.
A Time to Love. New York, Silhouette, 1982.
Knightly Love. New York, Silhouette, 1982.
Sweet Serenity. New York, Silhouette, 1983.
Fast Courting. New York, Silhouette, 1983.
Flip Side of Yesterday. New York, Silhouette, 1983.
Beyond Fantasy. New York, Silhouette, 1983.
An Irresistible Impulse. New York, Silhouette, 1983.
The Carpenter's Lady. New York, Silhouette, 1983.
Variation on a Theme. New York, Silhouette, 1985.

*   *   *

Bonnie Drake and Billie Douglass are familiar names to readers of the earlier Silhouette Ecstasy series and the Intimate Moment novels. More recently, readers met her under her real name, Barbara Delinsky. Delinsky is another of those romance writers who moved toward more sensual writing with very successful results. Perhaps she felt that contemporary women wanted more realism and more honesty in their novels. Certainly it must have seemed ridiculous and somehow contradictory to be writing "sweet" romances for women caught in the sexual revolution of the 1960's and 1970's. The decade of the 1980's saw women move out of the homes and kitchens and into businesses, offices, and professional positions and, at the same time, saw them come of age in the contemporary world. It would not be an exaggeration to say that Delinsky's novels helped many women see their own potential and, in some cases, set their feet on the road toward growth and achievement.

Having sharpened her skills in the early 1980's, she has emerged as one of the leading contemporary romance writers. Since 1985 Delinsky has been writing for the Harlequin Temptation series. Readers can expect to find themselves fascinated, intrigued, and thoroughly beguiled by the heroes and heroines in her novels.

While Delinsky's earlier novels were straight "romances," her later ones are very much more sophisticated and complex. Plotting is intricate and in depth with subplots and different narrative threads woven throughout. Character development is multi-faceted, with strong individualizing detail. There is such a subtlety of characterization, in some instances, that it tends to be hidden within the plot development. In *TLC*, a recent Harlequin Temptation romance, the main characters are Karen Drew and Bruce Carlin. The basic plot centers on the fact that both people are psychological "loners" due to childhood experiences. Karen is now a struggling "older" college student. Bruce is a pediatrician. He rescues her during a snow storm, takes her home, and treats the pneumonia she's contracted by overwork and lack of care. Delinsky brought out nuances of character by using indirect illustration. They both notice things about each other and they store these bits and pieces in their minds. This slow evolution of each character also builds a picture in the reader's mind. On the surface, the novel almost seems to be without a plot, certainly not the clear cut "conflict" sort that definitely pits adversaries against each other. The slowly unfolding relationship, the willingness of each character to open themselves to someone else is a well executed effort in writing and creativity.

Delinsky is equally adept in writing suspense novels. In these, plotting is more traditional, emphasis is on conflict that is usually outside of the heroine's control. The heroine faces threats, attacks on her life, and the tension of danger, all against the backdrop of growing love with its uncertainties and insecurities.

In *Threats and Promises*, Laurel Stevenson is recovering from recent plastic surgery. She is mistaken for a mobster's girlfriend who had disappeared with money and furs. Matt Kruger, her brother's friend meets her, falls in love with her, and eventually sets out with Laurel to find the "real" girlfriend. It takes several accidents, a dog attacking Laurel, and her house being broken into before they admit that they must do this. Good plotting, believable reactions by the characters, and a clever use of foreshadowing make this novel a good candidate for re-reading.

Finally, one of her best known suspense novels, *Finger Prints*, offers more than enough menace and mayhem. Carly Quinn is a witness who has been relocated under the Federal witness protection program. In the past, Carly had been a newspaper reporter who had broken an arson story that resulted in the conviction of some powerful men. She is now a teacher at a private school in Cambridge, Massachusetts, and lives in an ex-clusive apartment building. Suddenly she meets a new tenant, Ryan Cornell, a lawyer who has sub-leased an apartment on another floor. Slowly, they become friends, and eventually lovers, although Carly does not tell him about her former life since she is still under the protection of the United States Marshal service.

Conflict in the novel centers on Carly's inability to accept the changes in her life. She is very afraid of being found and killed. Naturally, conflict develops between her and Ryan as they quickly fall in love. The fact that Carly is not open and confiding bothers Ryan. Threats of a new trial for the criminals and evidence that she has been identified as Robyn Hart by them adds even further tension. The ending contains the usual twist of events and clashing characters. What makes the novel enjoyable is the fact that the reader's awareness of the events does not minimize the suspense. The conclusion holds as much action and conflict as the rest of the story, and, naturally, the ending has an unexpected twist that neatly ties everything together.

Given Delinsky's well earned success, and her obvious talent as a truly creative writer, readers can look forward to her future novels with more than a touch of enthusiasm and impatience.

—Arlene Moore

DELL, Ethel M(ary). British. Born in Streatham, London, 2 August 1881. Educated at Streatham College for Girls, 1893–98. Married Gerald Tahourdin Savage in 1922. *Died 19 September 1939.*

ROMANCE AND HISTORICAL PUBLICATIONS

Novels

The Way of an Eagle. New York, Putnam, 1911; London, Unwin, 1912.
The Knave of Diamonds. London, Unwin, and New York, Putnam, 1913.
The Rocks of Valpré. New York, Putnam, 1913; London, Unwin, 1914.
The Desire of His Life (includes "Her Compensation"). London, Holden and Hardingham, 1914; New York, Burt, 1927.
The Keeper of the Door. London, Unwin, and New York, Putnam, 1915.
The Bars of Iron. London, Hutchinson, and New York, Putnam, 1916.
The Hundredth Chance. London, Hutchinson, and New York, Putnam, 1917.
The Rose of Dawn. New York, Putnam, 1917.
Greatheart. London, Unwin, and New York, Putnam, 1918.
The Lamp in the Desert. London, Hutchinson, and New York, Putnam, 1919.
The Top of the World. London, Cassell, and New York, Putnam, 1920.
The Princess's Game. London, Hardingham, 1920.
The Lucky Number. New York, Putnam, 1920.
The Obstacle Race. London, Cassell, and New York, Putnam, 1921.
Charles Rex. London, Hutchinson, and New York, Putnam, 1922.
Tetherstones. London, Hutchinson, and New York, Putnam, 1923.

The Unknown Quantity. London, Hutchinson, and New York, Putnam, 1924.

A Man under Authority. London, Cassell, 1925; New York, Putnam, 1926.

The Black Knight. London, Cassell, and New York, Putnam, 1926.

By Request. London, Unwin, 1927; as *Peggy by Request*, New York, Putnam, 1928.

The Gate Marked "Private." London, Cassell, and New York, Putnam, 1928.

The Altar of Honour. London, Hutchinson, 1929; New York, Putnam, 1930.

Storm Drift. London, Hutchinson, 1930; New York, Putnam, 1931.

Pullman (omnibus). London, Benn, 1930.

The Silver Wedding. London, Hutchinson, 1932; as *The Silver Bride*, New York, Putnam, 1932.

The Prison Wall. London, Cassell, 1932; New York, Putnam, 1933.

Dona Celestis. London, Benn, and New York, Putnam, 1933.

The Electric Torch. London, Cassell, and New York, Putnam, 1934.

Where Three Roads Meet. London, Cassell 1935; New York, Putnam, 1936.

Honeyball Farm. London, Hutchinson, and New York, Putnam, 1937.

The Juice of the Pomegranate. London, Cassell, and New York, Doubleday, 1938.

The Serpent in the Garden. London, Cassell, and New York, Doubleday, 1938.

Sown among Thorns. London, Cassell, and New York, Doubleday, 1939.

Short Stories

The Swindler and Other Stories. London, Unwin, and New York, Putnam, 1914.

The Safety-Curtain and Other Stories. London, Unwin, and New York, Putnam, 1917.

The Tidal Wave and Other Stories. London, Cassell, 1919; New York Putnam, 1920.

Rosa Mundi and Other Stories. London, Cassell, and New York, Putnam, 1921.

The Odds and Other Stories. London, Cassell, and New York, Putnam, 1922.

The Passerby and Other Stories. London, Hutchinson, and New York, Putnam, 1925.

The House of Happiness and Other Stories. London, Cassell, and New York, Putnam, 1927.

The Live Bait and Other Stories. London, Benn, and New York, Putnam, 1932.

OTHER PUBLICATIONS

Verse

Verses. London, Hutchinson, and New York, Putnam, 1923.

*

Critical Study: *Nettie and Sissie: The Biography of Ethel M. Dell and Her Sister Ella* by Penelope Dell, London, Hamish Hamilton, 1977.

*　　*　　*

Absurd though they may at first seem, the novels of Ethel M. Dell have nonetheless a boisterous power, an irresistible quality about them, defined by Queenie Leavis as sheer luxuriant vitality: "Even the most critical reader who brings only an ironical appreciation to their work cannot avoid noticing a certain power, the secret of their success with the majority. Bad writing, false sentiment, sheer silliness, and a preposterous narrative are all carried along by the magnificent vitality of the author, as they are in *Jane Eyre*."

Such gripping tales as *The Way of an Eagle, The Lamp in the Desert, The Hundredth Chance, The Black Knight,* and *The Knave of Diamonds* are a highly readable mixture which combines quasi-religious themes with drama, action, and full-blooded adventure. Dashing officer heroes with murky pasts, exercising gallantry and bravery, are reminiscent of some of the 19th-century heroes of a Ouida or a Rhoda Broughton novel. The heroines, sensitive and virginal, strong but innocent, are no longer tormented by urgent doctrinal doubt, misgivings about the 39 Articles or the meaning of the original sin. For, as interest in orthodox Christianity gradually waned, it was replaced, in popular romantic fiction, by a new, less clearly defined spiritual quest. The heroines are driven by passions which are simultaneously of an earthly and a heavenly nature. Their vague, mystical uncertainty runs a parallel course to their difficulties and sufferings of mortal love. Thus, for example, Ann Carfax is tormented by the need for a prayerful life, but, in her darkest hour finds total inability to pray: "Powerless, she sank upon her knees by the open window, striving painfully, piteously, vainly, to pray. But no words came to her, no prayer rose from her wrung heart. It was as though she knelt in outer darkness before a locked door." (This is from *The Knave of Diamonds*, the title referring to the ambiguous, but probably sinful, nature of the hero.) Stella, similarly, in *The Way of an Eagle*, is beset by intense inner doubts and fears, not specifically religious, but rather, spiritually worthy "feelings": "And again, very deep down in her soul there stirred that blind, unconscious entity, of the existence of which she herself had so vague a knowledge, feeling upwards, groping outwards, to the light."

Ill-defined though such feelings may be, the implication is that they have a worth, a value, which is as good, if not better, than orthodox religion. Heroines (less often heroes) grapple with their doubt for a couple of hundred pages, before the ultimate discovery of some symbol in their lives which represents for them a renewal and refreshment of the spirit. In *The Lamp in the Desert* that symbol is clear. Christ is the lamp, which lights up the Desert of the World: "Her halting feet were now guided by God's Lamp. She had come to realise that the wanderers in the wilderness are ever His especial care, and that she would come at last into the Presence of God Himself." Her acceptance of her Creator; after such a prolonged period of confusion, occurs at the same time as her rediscovery of her love for her long-lost husband.

In *The Way of an Eagle* that symbolic bird refers less to our Lord, more to the primeval, bird-like nature of the fierce husband whom she both fears, and dreams of longingly. He is the eagle who will gather her up, and bear her swiftly through wide spaces to his eyrie in the mountains. The eagle-hero is not without his acknowledgement of one greater than he. When hero and heroine, thwarted pair, uncover their mutual passion while communing with nature at the top of the mountain, it is the man who decides that prayer would be appropriate: "Do you know what we are going to do as soon as we are married, sweetheart? We are going to climb the highest mountain in the world, to see the sun rise, and to thank God."

The searing, or burning, or scorching, kiss became one of the hallmarks of romance; and Dell was an early perfectionist at hot literary embraces. "His quick breath scorched her face, and in a moment almost before she knew what was happening, his lips were on her own. He kissed her as she had never been kissed before—a single fiery kiss that sent all the blood in tumult to her heart." Or "There was sheer unshackled savagery in the holding of his arms, and dismay thrilled her through and through." And "Again his lips pressed hers, and again from head to foot she felt as if a flame had scorched her." Today, Barbara Cartland may declare that what readers want is innocence and chastity. In the 1930's what they wanted was hot kissing and unbridled passion. Ray Smith's Twopenny Library reported in 1933 that the three women authors most in demand were Ethel M. Dell, Elinor Glyn, and Marie Corelli, in that order.

Despite the "religious" content, the novels are full of blood, guts, and thunder. Dell included tempests, infant deaths, runaway horses, wife-beating, men going violently mad, fine young lovers crippled for life, an electric storm, falling meteors, and a mutiny at the Northwest frontier. During times of chaos, men are aware of the importance of risking life to protect the honour of the heroine. This bravery results in a number of hand-to-hand fights to the death: "So long as his heart should beat he would defend that one precious possession that yet remained—the honour of the woman who loved him and whom he loved as only the few knew how to love."

Dell did not have the pretensions of some other popular novelists of her era. She was not seeking literary glory; nor did she continually complain, as did Marie Corelli or Elinor Glyn, that her work was misunderstood by the critics. She did not hold herself out as some female latter-day Shakespeare like Ouida or Hall Caine. The loyalty of her readers was the reward she sought and enjoyed. She repaid them by dedicating to them one of her novels, *By Request*, a gesture which signals the importance, for popular writers, of a close reader/writer relationship. Those who do not have it, aspire to it; those who do, rightly nurture it.

Rachel Anderson

DELMAR, Viña (née Croter). American. Born in New York City, 29 January 1905. Educated at public schools in New York. Married Eugene Delmar in 1921; one child. Worked as typist, switchboard operator, usher, actress, and theatre manager, then free-lance writer. Address: c/o Harcourt Brace Jovanovich, 1250 Sixth Avenue, San Diego, California 92101, U.S.A.

ROMANCE AND HISTORICAL PUBLICATIONS

Novels

Bad Girl. New York, Harcourt Brace, 1928; London, Allan, 1929.
Kept Woman. New York, Harcourt Brace, 1929; as *The Other Woman*, London, Allan, 1930.
Women Live Too Long. New York, Harcourt Brace, and London, Allan, 1932; as *The Restless Passion,* New York, Avon, 1947.
The Marriage Racket. New York, Harcourt Brace, and London, Allan, 1933.
Mystery at Little Heaven. Los Angeles, Times Mirror Press, 1933.
The End of the World. New York, International Magazine Company, 1934.

The Love Trap. New York, Avon, 1949.
New Orleans Lady. New York, Avon, 1949.
About Mrs. Leslie. New York, Harcourt Brace, 1950; London, Hale, 1952.
Strangers in Love. New York, Dell, 1951.
The Marcaboth Women. New York, Harcourt Brace, 1951; London, Hale, 1953.
The Laughing Stranger. New York, Harcourt Brace, 1953; London, Hale, 1954.
Ruby. New York, Pocket Books, 1953.
Beloved. New York, Harcourt Brace, 1956; London, Hale, 1957.
The Breeze from Camelot. New York, Harcourt Brace, 1959; London, Davies, 1960.
The Big Family. New York, Harcourt Brace, 1961.
The Enchanted. New York, Harcourt Brace, 1965.
Grandmère. New York, Harcourt Brace, 1967.
The Freeways. New York, Harcourt Brace, 1971.
A Time for Titans. New York, Harcourt Brace, 1974.
McKeever. New York, Harcourt Brace, 1976.

Short Stories

Loose Ladies. New York, Harcourt Brace, 1929; as *Women Who Pass By*, London, Allan, 1929.

OTHER PUBLICATIONS

Plays

Bad Girl, with Brian Marlowe, adaptation of the novel by Delmar (produced New York, 1930).
The Rich, Full Life (produced New York, 1945). New York, French, 1945.
Mid-Summer (produced New York, 1953). New York, French, 1954.
Warm Wednesday. New York, French, 1959.
The Rest Is Silence, adaptation of her screenplay *Make Way for Tomorrow* (produced Moscow, 1970).

Screenplays: *A Soldier's Plaything*, with Perry Vikroff, 1930; *The Awful Truth*, with Dwight Taylor, 1937; *Make Way for Tomorrow*, 1937.

Other

The Becker Scandal: A Time Remembered (autobiography). New York, Harcourt Brace, 1968.

*   *   *

Viña Delmar is essentially a formulator of character studies. Her early novels recount the experiences of lower-middle-class women typical of their times. In later creations she describes persons of a higher social and educational milieu. Her works range from light fiction to deeper historical novels. Most involve romance to some degree, but love is not the prevailing theme in all her stories.

Delmar's entertaining first novel, *Bad Girl*, tells the story of the meeting and hasty wedding of a very young couple and the birth of their child. They have never learned the principles of communication, and each hopes the other will automatically know his wants and feelings. A major misunderstanding occurs when each thinks the other does not truly want the baby which, in reality, both are excited about. After the birth, they shyly reveal their pleasure to each other, but there is little hope for increased communication despite this experience. Both characters are clearly delineated and alive.

Ruby's birthday is the signal in *The Marcaboth Women* for the women to review their own lives and accomplishments. Each of the Marcaboth wives has a problem to deal with when her husband insists she drop everything to buy and deliver a birthday gift to the new wife of the oldest brother. Ruby is 20 years old, selfish, and, by her existence, capable of changing the lives of the other family members. Even the clan matriarch recognizes the impending alteration of her family dominance. The characters are deftly drawn with a few strokes of the pen and neatly interwoven with each other. This skillfully painted family portrait entices the reader to the end.

With *Beloved* Delmar delves into historical biography. Her subject is Judah Benjamin, Governor of Louisiana and Confederate Secretary of State and an attorney of great accomplishment. Benjamin marries a beautiful Creole incapable of remaining faithful to one man and, by his understanding of her character, earns her love and the appellation "Beloved" in her letters to him. It is a tale of tenderness surrounded by doubt, prejudice, and war. The story is carefully developed and the characters seem to mature naturally. Some of the novelist's assumptions about the Civil War could cause debate among historical purists, but the book is recommended for lovers of the genre.

The John Slidell family is the subject of *The Big Family*, members of whom were important in early American history. Delmar has faithfully adhered to historical fact. There is an amplitude of romantic detail and exciting events, but since the novel covers three generations there is little depth. The reader gets a more complete picture of the New Orleanean Slidell in *Beloved* than is available in this work. It is, nevertheless, an interesting and masterful example of Delmar's abilities as an historical novelist.

Delmar is an author of distinction, and her works have been popular and widely reviewed. Her skill in character development and dialogue has increased over the years and hers is an important name in romantic and historical fiction.

—Andrea Lee Shuey

DERLETH, August (William). Also wrote as Stephen Grendon; Tally Mason. American. Born in Sauk City, Wisconsin, 24 February 1909. Educated at St. Aloysius School; Sauk City High School; University of Wisconsin, Madison, B.A. 1930. Married Sandra Winters in 1953 (divorced 1959); one daughter and one son. Editor, Fawcett Publications, Minneapolis, 1930–31; editor, the *Midwesterner*, Madison, 1931; Lecturer in American Regional Literature, University of Wisconsin, 1939–43. Owner and co-founder (with Donald Wandrei, 1939–42), Arkham House Publishers (including the imprints Mycroft and Moran, and Stanton and Lee), Sauk City, 1939–71. Editor, *Mind Magic*, 1931; literary editor and columnist, Madison *Capital Times*, 1941–71; editor, *The Arkham Sampler*, 1948–49, *Hawk and Whippoorwill*, 1960–63, and *The Arkham Collector*, 1967–71, all Sauk City. Recipient: Guggenheim fellowship, 1938; *Scholastic* award, 1958; Ann Radcliffe award, 1967. *Died 4 July 1971.*

ROMANCE AND HISTORICAL PUBLICATIONS

Novels (series: Sac Prairie; Wisconsin)

Still Is the Summer Night (Sac Prairie). New York, Scribner, 1937.
Wind over Wisconsin (Sac Prairie). New York, Scribner, 1938.
Restless Is the River (Sac Prairie). New York, Scribner, 1939.
Bright Journey (Wisconsin). New York, Scribner, 1940.
Evening in Spring (Sac Prairie). New York, Scribner, 1941.
Sweet Genevieve (Sac Prairie). New York, Scribner, 1942.
Shadow of Night (Sac Prairie). New York, Scribner, 1943.
The House on the Mound (Wisconsin). New York, Duell, 1958.
The Hills Stand Watch (Wisconsin). New York, Duell, 1960.
The Shadow in the Glass (Wisconsin). New York, Duell, 1963.
The Wind Leans West (Wisconsin). New York, Candlelight Press, 1969.

OTHER PUBLICATIONS

Novels

Murder Stalks the Wakely Family. New York, Loring and Mussey, 1934; as *Death Stalks the Wakely Family*, London, Newnes, 1937.
The Man on All Fours. New York, Loring and Mussey, 1934; London, Newnes, 1936.
Three Who Died. New York, Loring and Mussey, 1935.
Sign of Fear. New York, Loring and Mussey, 1935; London, Newnes, 1936.
Sentence Deferred. New York, Scribner, 1939; London, Heinemann, 1940.
The Narracong Riddle. New York, Scribner, 1940.
The Seven Who Waited. New York, Scribner, 1943; London, Muller, 1945.
Mischief in the Lane. New York, Scribner, 1944; London, Muller, 1948.
No Future for Luana. New York, Scribner, 1945; London, Muller, 1948.
The Shield of the Valiant. New York, Scribner, 1945.
The Lurker at the Threshold, with H. P. Lovecraft. Sauk City, Wisconsin, Arkham House, 1945; London, Gollancz, 1948.
Fell Purpose. New York, Arcadia House, 1953.
Death by Design. New York, Arcadia House, 1953.
The Trail of Cthulhu. Sauk City, Wisconsin, Arkham House, 1962; London, Spearman, 1974.
Mr. Fairlie's Final Journey. Sauk City, Wisconsin, Mycroft and Moran, 1968.

Short Stories

Place of Hawks. New York, Loring and Mussey, 1935.
Any Day Now. Chicago, Normandie House, 1938.
Country Growth. New York, Scribner, 1940.
Someone in the Dark. Sauk City, Wisconsin, Arkham House, 1941.
Something Near. Sauk City, Wisconsin, Arkham House, 1945.
"In Re: Sherlock Holmes"—The Adventures of Solar Pons. Sauk City, Wisconsin, Mycroft and Moran, 1945; as *Regarding Sherlock Holmes*, New York, Pinnacle, 1974; as *The Adventures of Solar Pons*, London, Robson, 1975.
Sac Prairie People. Sauk City, Wisconsin, Stanton and Lee, 1948.

Not Long for This World. Sauk City, Wisconsin, Arkham House, 1948.

The Memoirs of Solar Pons. Sauk City, Wisconsin, Mycroft and Moran, 1951.

Three Problems for Solar Pons. Sauk City, Wisconsin, Mycroft and Moran, 1952.

The House of Moonlight. Iowa City, Prairie Press, 1953.

The Survivor and Others, with H. P. Lovecraft. Sauk City, Wisconsin, Arkham House, 1957.

The Return of Solar Pons. Sauk City, Wisconsin, Mycroft and Moran, 1958.

The Mask of Cthulhu. Sauk City, Wisconsin, Arkham House, 1958; London, Consul, 1961.

The Reminiscences of Solar Pons. Sauk City, Wisconsin, Mycroft and Moran, 1961.

Wisconsin in Their Bones. New York, Duell, 1961.

Lonesome Places. Sauk City, Wisconsin, Arkham House, 1962.

Mr. George and Other Odd Persons (as Stephen Grendon). Sauk City, Wisconsin, Arkham House, 1963; as *When Graveyards Yawn*, London, Tandem, 1965.

The Casebook of Solar Pons. Sauk City, Wisconsin, Mycroft and Moran, 1965.

Praed Street Papers. New York, Candlelight Press, 1965.

The Adventure of the Orient Express. New York, Candlelight Press, 1965; London, Panther, 1975.

Colonel Markesan and Less Pleasant People, with Mark Schorer. Sauk City, Wisconsin, Arkham House, 1966.

The Adventure of the Unique Dickensians. Sauk City, Wisconsin, Mycroft and Moran, 1968.

A Praed Street Dossier. Sauk City, Wisconsin, Mycroft and Moran, 1968.

The Shadow Out of Time and Other Tales of Horror, with H. P. Lovecraft. London, Gollancz, 1968; abridged edition, as *The Shuttered Room and Other Tales of Horror*, London, Panther, 1970.

A House above Cuzco. New York, Candlelight Press, 1969.

The Shuttered Room and Other Tales of Terror, with H. P. Lovecraft. New York, Beagle, 1971.

The Chronicles of Solar Pons. Sauk City, Wisconsin, Mycroft and Moran, 1973; London, Robson, 1975.

The Watchers Out of Time and Others, with H. P. Lovecraft. Sauk City, Wisconsin, Arkham House, 1974.

Harrigan's File. Sauk City, Wisconsin, Arkham House, 1975.

Dwellers in Darkness. Sauk City, Wisconsin, Arkham House, 1976.

The Solar Pons Omnibus. Sauk City, Wisconsin, Arkham House, 1982.

Verse

To Remember, with *Salute Before Dawn*, by Albert Edward Clements. Hartland Four Corners, Vermont, Windsor, 1931.

Hawk on the Wind. Philadelphia, Ritten House, 1938.

Elegy: On a Flake of Snow. Muscatine, Iowa, Prairie Press, 1939.

Man Track Here. Philadelphia, Ritten House, 1939.

Here on a Darkling Plain. Philadelphia, Ritten House, 1941.

Wind in the Elms. Philadelphia, Ritten House, 1941.

Rind of Earth. Prairie City, Illinois, Decker Press, 1942.

Selected Poems. Prairie City, Illinois, Decker Press, 1944.

And You, Thoreau! New York, New Directions, 1944.

The Edge of Night. Prairie City, Illinois, Decker Press, 1945.

Habitant of Dusk: A Garland for Cassandra. Boston, Walden Press, 1946.

Rendezvous in a Landscape. New York, Fine Editions Press, 1952.

Psyche. Iowa City, Prairie Press, 1953.

Country Poems. Iowa City, Prairie Press, 1956.

Elegy: On the Umbral Moon. Forest Park, Illinois, Acorn Press, 1957.

West of Morning. Francestown, New Hampshire, Golden Quill Press, 1960.

This Wound. Iowa City, Prairie Press, 1962.

Country Places. Iowa City, Prairie Press, 1965.

The Only Place We Live. Iowa City, Prairie Press, 1966.

By Owl Light. Iowa City, Prairie Press, 1967.

Collected Poems, 1937–1967. New York, Candlelight Press, 1967.

Caitlin. Iowa City, Prairie Press, 1969.

The Landscape of the Heart. Iowa City, Prairie Press, 1970.

Listening to the Wind. New York, Candlelight Press, 1971.

Last Light. New York, Candlelight Press, 1971.

Recordings: *Psyche: A Sequence of Love Lyrics*, Cuca, 1960; *Sugar Bush by Moonlight and Other Poems of Man and Nature*, Cuca, 1962; *Caitlin*, Cuca, 1971.

Other

The Heritage of Sauk City. Sauk City, Wisconsin, Pioneer Press, 1931.

Consider Your Verdict: Ten Coroner's Cases for You To Solve (as Tally Mason). New York, Stackpole, 1937.

Atmosphere of Houses. Muscatine, Iowa, Prairie Press, 1939.

Still Small Voice: The Biography of Zona Gale. New York, Appleton Century, 1940.

Village Year: A Sac Prairie Journal. New York, Coward McCann, 1941.

Wisconsin Regional Literature. Privately printed, 1941; revised edition, 1942.

The Wisconsin: River of a Thousand Isles. New York, Farrar and Rinehart, 1942.

H. P. L.: A Memoir (on H. P. Lovecraft). New York, Abramson, 1945.

Oliver, The Wayward Owl (for children). Sauk City, Wisconsin, Stanton and Lee, 1945.

Writing Fiction. Boston, The Writer, 1946.

Village Daybook: A Sac Prairie Journal. Chicago, Pellegrini and Cudahy, 1947.

A Boy's Way: Poems (for children). Sauk City, Wisconsin, Stanton and Lee, 1947.

Sauk County: A Centennial History. Baraboo, Wisconsin, Sauk County Centennial Committee, 1948.

It's a Boy's World: Poems (for children). Sauk City, Wisconsin, Stanton and Lee, 1948.

Wisconsin Earth: A Sac Prairie Sampler (selection). Sauk City, Wisconsin, Stanton and Lee, 1948.

The Milwaukee Road: Its First 100 Years. New York, Creative Age Press, 1948.

The Country of the Hawk (for children). New York, Aladdin, 1952.

The Captive Island (for children). New York, Duell, 1952.

Empire of Fur: Trading in the Lake Superior Region (for children). New York, Aladdin, 1953.

Land of Gray Gold: Lead Mining in Wisconsin (for children). New York, Aladdin, 1954.

Father Marquette and the Great Rivers (for children). New York, Farrar Straus, 1955; London, Burns and Oates, 1956.

Land of Sky-Blue Waters (for children). New York, Aladdin, 1955.

St. Ignatius and the Company of Jesus (for children). New York, Farrar Straus, and London, Burns and Oates, 1956.

Columbus and the New World (for children). New York, Farrar Straus, and London, Burns and Oates, 1957.

The Moon Tenders (for children). New York, Duell, 1958.

The Mill Creek Irregulars (for children). New York, Duell, 1959.

Wilbur, The Trusting Whippoorwill (for children). Sauk City, Wisconsin, Stanton and Lee, 1959.

Arkham House: The First Twenty Years 1939–1959. Sauk City, Wisconsin, Arkham House, 1959.

Some Notes on H. P. Lovecraft. Sauk City, Wisconsin, Arkham House, 1959.

The Pinkertons Ride Again (for children). New York, Duell, 1960.

The Ghost of Black Hawk Island (for children). New York, Duell, 1961.

Walden West (autobiography). New York, Duell, 1961.

Sweet Land of Michigan (for children). New York, Duell, 1962.

Concord Rebel: A Life of Henry D. Thoreau. Philadelphia, Chilton, 1962.

Countryman's Journal. New York, Duell, 1963.

The Tent Show Summer (for children). New York, Duell, 1963.

Three Literary Men: A Memoir of Sinclair Lewis, Sherwood Anderson, Edgar Lee Masters. New York, Candlelight Press, 1963.

The Irregulars Strike Again (for children). New York, Duell, 1964.

Forest Orphans (for children). New York, Ernest, 1964; as *Mr. Conservation*, Park Falls, Wisconsin, MacGregor, 1971.

Wisconsin Country: A Sac Prairie Journal. New York, Candlelight Press, 1965.

The House by the River (for children). New York, Duell, 1965.

The Watcher on the Heights (for children). New York, Duell, 1966.

Wisconsin (for children). New York, Coward McCann, 1967.

The Beast in Holger's Woods (for children). New York, Crowell, 1968.

The Prince Goes West (for children). New York, Meredith Press, 1968.

Vincennes: Portal to the West. Englewood Cliffs, New Jersey, Prentice Hall, 1968.

Walden Pond: Homage to Thoreau. Iowa City, Prairie Press, 1968.

Wisconsin Murders. Sauk City, Wisconsin, Mycroft and Moran, 1968.

The Wisconsin Valley. New York, Teachers College Press, 1969.

Thirty Years of Arkham House 1939–1969: A History and a Bibliography. Sauk City, Wisconsin, Arkham House, 1970.

The Three Straw Men (for children). New York, Candlelight Press, 1970.

Return to Walden West. New York, Candlelight Press, 1970.

Love Letters to Caitlin. New York, Candlelight Press, 1971.

Emerson, Our Contemporary. New York, Crowell Collier, 1971.

Editor, with R. E. Larsson, *Poetry Out of Wisconsin.* New York, Harrison, 1937.

Editor, with Donald Wandrei, *The Outsider and Others*, by H. P. Lovecraft. Sauk City, Wisconsin, Arkham House, 1939.

Editor, with Donald Wandrei, *Beyond the Wall of Sleep*, by H. P. Lovecraft. Sauk City, Wisconsin, Arkham House, 1943.

Editor, with Donald Wandrei, *Marginalia*, by H. P. Lovecraft. Sauk City, Wisconsin, Arkham House, 1944.

Editor, *Sleep No More: Twenty Masterpieces of Horror for the Connoisseur.* New York, Farrar and Rinehart, 1944; abridged edition, London, Panther, 1964.

Editor, *The Best Supernatural Stories of H. P. Lovecraft.* Cleveland, World, 1945; revised edition, as *The Dunwich Horror and Others*, Sauk City, Wisconsin, Arkham House, 1963.

Editor, *Who Knocks? Twenty Masterpieces of the Spectral for the Connoisseur.* New York, Rinehart, 1946; abridged edition, London, Panther, 1964.

Editor, *The Night Side: Masterpieces of the Strange and Terrible.* New York, Rinehart, 1947; abridged edition, London, New English Library, 1966.

Editor, *The Sleeping and the Dead.* Chicago, Pellegrini and Cudahy, 1947; as *The Sleeping and the Dead* and *The Unquiet Grave*, London, New English Library, 2 vols., 1963–64.

Editor, *Dark of the Moon: Poems of Fantasy and the Macabre.* Sauk City, Wisconsin, Arkham House, 1947.

Editor, *Strange Ports of Call.* New York, Pellegrini and Cudahy, 1948.

Editor, *The Other Side of the Moon.* New York, Pellegrini and Cudahy, 1949; abridged edition, London, Grayson, 1956.

Editor, *Something about Cats and Other Pieces*, by H. P. Lovecraft. Sauk City, Wisconsin, Arkham House, 1949.

Editor, *Beyond Time and Space.* New York, Pellegrini and Cudahy, 1950.

Editor, *Far Boundaries: 20 Science-Fiction Stories.* New York, Pellegrini and Cudahy, 1951; London, Consul, 1965.

Editor, *The Outer Reaches: Favorite Science-Fiction Tales Chosen by Their Authors.* New York, Pellegrini and Cudahy, 1951; as *The Outer Reaches* and *The Time of Infinity*, London, Consul, 2 vols., 1963.

Editor, *Beachheads in Space.* New York, Pellegrini and Cudahy, 1952; abridged edition, London, Weidenfeld and Nicolson, 1954; as *From Other Worlds*, London, New English Library, 1964.

Editor, *Night's Yawning Peal: A Ghostly Company.* Sauk City, Wisconsin, Arkham House, 1952; London, Consul, 1965.

Editor, *Worlds of Tomorrow: Science Fiction with a Difference.* New York, Pellegrini and Cudahy, 1953; abridged edition, London, Weidenfeld and Nicolson, 1954; as *New Worlds for Old*, London, New English Library, 1963.

Editor, *Time to Come: Science-Fiction Stories of Tomorrow.* New York, Farrar Straus, 1954; London, Consul, 1963.

Editor, *Portals of Tomorrow: The Best Tales of Science Fiction and Other Fantasy.* New York, Rinehart, 1954; London, Cassell, 1956.

Editor, *The Shuttered Room and Other Pieces by H. P. Lovecraft and Divers Hands.* Sauk City, Wisconsin, Arkham House, 1959.

Editor, *Fire and Sleet and Candlelight: New Poems of the Macabre.* Sauk City, Wisconsin, Arkham House, 1961.

Editor, *Dark Mind, Dark Heart.* Sauk City, Wisconsin, Arkham House 1962; London, Mayflower, 1963.

Editor, *When Evil Wakes: A New Anthology of the Macabre.* London, Souvenir Press, 1963.

Editor, *Over the Edge.* Sauk City, Wisconsin, Arkham House, 1964; London, Gollancz, 1967.

Editor, *At the Mountains of Madness and Other Novels*, by H. P. Lovecraft. Sauk City, Wisconsin, Arkham House, 1964; London, Gollancz, 1966.

Editor, *Dagon and Other Macabre Tales*, by H. P. Lovecraft. Sauk City, Wisconsin, Arkham House, 1965; London, Gollancz, 1967.

Editor, with Donald Wandrei (3 vols.) and James Turner (2 vols), *Selected Letters*, by H. P. Lovecraft. Sauk City, Wisconsin Arkham House, 5 vols., 1965–76.

Editor, *The Dark Brotherhood and Other Pieces*, by H. P. Lovecraft and others. Sauk City, Wisconsin, Arkham House, 1966.
Editor, *A Wisconsin Harvest*. Sauk City, Wisconsin, Stanton and Lee, 1966.
Editor, *Travellers by Night*. Sauk City, Wisconsin, Arkham House, 1967; London, Gollancz, 1968.
Editor, *New Poetry Out of Wisconsin*. Sauk City, Wisconsin, Stanton and Lee, 1969.
Editor, *Tales of the Cthulhu Mythos*, by H. P. Lovecraft and others. Sauk City, Wisconsin, Arkham House, 1969.
Editor, *The Horror in the Museum and Other Revisions*, by H. P. Lovecraft. Sauk City, Wisconsin, Arkham House, 1970; abridged edition, London, Panther, 1975.
Editor, *Dark Things*. Sauk City, Wisconsin, Arkham House, 1971.

*

Bibliography: *100 Books by August Derleth*, Sauk City, Wisconsin, Arkham House, 1962; *August Derleth: A Bibliography* by Alison M. Wilson, Metuchen, New Jersey, Scarecrow Press, 1983.

Manuscript Collection: State Historical Society of Wisconsin Library, Madison.

*   *   *

Few authors can match August Derleth in the sheer quantity of their literary output and the breadth of their interests. He was not only one of the 20th century's premier American regional writers, he was also a publisher, poet, and collector of horror and science fiction stories.

Derleth is inseparable from his portion of the United States, namely the midwest and specifically his native state, Wisconsin. His love for Wisconsin's heritage is best exemplified by the Sac Prairie saga, which sought to chronicle Wisconsin life from the early 1800's to the 1950's. To many, the magnitude of the Sac Prairie saga, can find few rivals in the entire history of world literature. While it is a work of fiction, the inspirational sources of the saga came from Derleth's experiences and deep reverence for his own and his region's historical roots.

Although lesser known as a writer of history, Derleth also created the Wisconsin saga, focusing on historical events. The history and characters in this series are well researched and described. Though the saga novels are fictionalized versions of authentic individuals' lives, they are largely biographical profiles of early Wisconsin leaders. Beginning with *Bright Journey*, which focuses on the youth of Hercules Dousman, the midwest's first millionaire, they contine through *The House on the Mound*, which centers on Dousman's latter years. Others include *The Hills Stand Watch*, about Welsh coal miners, *The Shadow in the Glass*, on the life of Governor Nelson Dewey, and *The Wind Leans West* with its focus on Alexander Mitchell and early Wisconsin banking.

Besides his historical fiction, Derleth's prodigious literary output includes biographies of Thoreau, Emerson, and his fellow Wisconsin writer Zona Gale. Derleth's earliest attempt at conventional history came with the publication of *The Wisconsin: River of a Thousand Isles*. Based on historical source material, this book portrays the river as the most important passage between the Great Lakes and the Mississippi with critical movements in American history taking place along its banks. It was followed by *The Milwaukee Road: Its First 100 Years*, a narrative history of the first century of the Chicago, Milwaukee, St.

Paul and Pacific Railroad. Later came biographical works for younger readers, *Father Marquette and the Great Rivers* and *St. Ignatius and the Company of Jesus* which deal with the region so close to Derleth's heart, Wisconsin and the midwest. His last historical study, *Vincennes: Portal to the West*, centers on the American Revolution in the west with a particular focus on George Rogers Clark's exploits and his successes against the British. Sources for this book included contemporary records left by participants in the western campaigns of the American Revolution.

Derleth is a writer who knew his historical subjects and their setting completely. His tales unfold the saga of American history with a focus on the land and its common people rarely seen before or since his time.

—Frank R. Levstick

de SALVALLO, Donna Teresa. See WILLIAMSON, C. N. and A. M.

DEVERAUX, Jude. Pseudonym for Jude White, née Gilliam. American. Born in Louisville, Kentucky, 20 September 1947. Educated at Murray State University, Murray, Kentucky, B.S. 1970; College of Santa Fe, New Mexico, teaching certificate 1973; University of New Mexico, Albuquerque, 1976. Married 1) Richard Sides in 1967 (divorced 1969); 2) Claude White in 1970. Elementary school teacher, Santa Fe, 1973–77. Address: Route 9, Box 53JW, Santa Fe, New Mexico 87505, U.S.A.

ROMANCE AND HISTORICAL PUBLICATIONS

Novels (series: James River; Montgomery; Twin).

The Enchanted Land. New York, Avon, 1978; London, Hamlyn, 1979.
The Black Lyon. New York, Avon, 1980.
The Temptress. New York, Pocket Books, 1980; London, Century, 1988.
The Velvet Promise (Montgomery). New York, Pocket Books, 1981; London, Arrow, 1984.
Casa Grande. New York, Avon, 1982.
Highland Velvet (Montgomery). New York, Pocket Books, 1982; London, Arrow, 1984.
Song of Promise. New York, Pocket Books, 1983.
Sweetbriar. New York, Pocket Books, and London, Hodder and Stoughton, 1983.
Velvet Angel (Montgomery). New York, Pocket Books, 1983; London, Arrow, 1984.
Velvet Song (Montgomery). New York, Pocket Books, 1983; London, Arrow, 1984.
Counterfeit Lady (James River). New York, Pocket Books, 1984; Bath, Firecrest, 1985.
Lost Lady (James River). New York, Pocket Books, 1985; Bath, Firecrest, 1986.
Twin of Fire. New York, Pocket Books, 1985.
Twin of Ice. New York, Pocket Books, 1985.
River Lady (James River). New York, Pocket Books, 1985; Bath, Firecrest, 1986.

The Awakening. New York, Pocket Books, 1987; London, Century, 1989.
The Raider. New York, Pocket Books, 1987.
The Princess. New York, Pocket Books, and London, Century, 1988.
The Maiden. New York, Pocket Books, 1988.
The Taming. New York, Pocket Books, 1989.
A Knight in Shining Armor. New York, Pocket Books, 1989.

*   *   *

After publishing her less than successful modern novel *Casa Grande*, Jude Deveraux stated "God gave me the ability to write. He didn't extend it very far. All I want to do is write the very best historical romances that I possibly can—and historicals seem to be all I'm capable of. I don't want to write family sagas or occult books, and I have no intention of again trying to ruin the contemporary market."

Having outlined this ambition, albeit in a very limited field, Deveraux sets out with verve, gusto and every plot device known to woman to create a very large number of light but nevertheless entertaining historical romances, often known more colloquially as "bodice rippers."

The plots do tend to contain similar elements—man, woman, other woman, kidnapping, class barriers, abduction (there's a lot of this), forced marriages, mistaken identities—the list is almost, but not quite, endless. However, a definite redeeming feature of her work is the glint of humour that appears here and there; enough, at times, to make the reader wonder whether the whole novel is written tongue-in-cheek.

A common theme in such romantic fiction (we have only to think of the Scarlet Pimpernel) is that of the bold crusading hero cunningly concealed inside the persona of the least likely (and usually most effeminate) male character. In *The Raider*, Deveraux takes this device to extremes (and even beyond) as she endows Alexander Montgomery not only with effeminate mannerisms, but also with a badly fitting wig and vast amounts of padding—the prime use of the latter is to make him appear mundane and unheroic but it is also extremely useful for concealing his gun, his mask, and the other tools of his trade. This character is of course the raider, and when not actively engaged in raiding he conducts a passionate although intermittent relationship with the heroine; unfortunately for this lady (and also for the story's credibility) she does not detect any similarity between her secret lover and the overweight and balding gentleman whom she is forced to marry.

This is only one of many novels dealing with the Montgomery clan in its many manifestations. These range from the Velvet series, all set in correctly romantic periods of history, to *The Princess* which brings us almost up to date. In *Velvet Song* the current member of the Montgomery clan is a Robin Hood-type figure (many of the male Montgomerys seem to model themselves on heroes of romantic fiction!) into whose convenient arms the heroine, Alyx, flees, hotly pursued by an evil squire. Our hero, of course, falls instantly in love with her and only later pauses to consider the wisdom of this reaction, as Alyx is disguised as a boy. Her lot is actually fairly reasonable compared with that of the female Montgomerys, who in this and other books regularly suffer pursuit, kidnap, and humiliation, not to mention the inevitable fate worse than death.

Having discovered most of the plot devices in popular use, Deveraux obviously aimed to assemble as many as she could in *The Princess*. This is set during World War II at a time when America's shortage of vanadium deposits was seriously endangering the war effort. By an amazing coincidence one small desert island becomes temporary accommodation for an American naval officer (handsome, heroic, rich—and a Montgomery) and a princess (beautiful, strong-willed—and whose native Lanconia just happens to be rich in vanadium). The following events happen in fairly quick succession—a kidnap, a rescue, a romantic interlude, a forced marriage, an unromantic interlude, mistaken identities, a happy ending—and while all this has been going on the vanadium is helping America to win the war.

The James River trilogy (*River Lady, Counterfeit Lady* and *Lost Lady*) is relatively, but alas not totally, free of Montgomerys; but each novel does contain a forced marriage followed by an estrangement, during which time the respective heroines have time to develop hitherto unsuspected talents. One manages a grain mill, one becomes a weaver, and the third enterprising lady runs a tavern—while using all the clichés under the sun, Deveraux is certainly not short of a fresh idea or two!

These three books do not run consecutively, but are interlocking, a device which the author also utilises in *Twin of Ice* and *Twin of Fire*. These two books tell the simultaneous stories of twins Houston (ice) and Blair (fire) Chandler, and their respective husbands Kane Taggert (uncouth hunk) and Leander Westfield (relative wimp). Apart from the by now expected kidnapping, forced marriage, estrangement, misunderstandings, and mistaken identity (don't forget we have twins in this novel!), there are also several added ingredients. One heroine is a newly qualified doctor, the other is involved in undercover activities bringing aid to the families of oppressed miners; and both attend secret meetings of The Sisterhood, whose social and political gathering develops into a hen party which is enlivened by the presence of a male stripper—all pretty strong stuff for the 1890's!

Deveraux's novels are probably taken totally seriously by many of her millions of readers, but one cannot help feeling that they miss a lot of enjoyment. The novels have a drive and gusto which lift them out of the normal run of such works; one can only admire Deveraux for her ability to incorporate some rather sly digs at the genre while exploiting it to the full.

—Judith Rhodes

———————

de VERE, Jane. See **FITZGERALD, Julia.**

———————

DEVINE, Raynard. See **TRESSILIAN, Richard.**

———————

DINGWELL, Joyce. Has also written as Kate Starr. Australian. Born in Sydney, New South Wales, in 1912. Educated at Fort Street High School, Sydney. Married Leonard Dingwall in 1939. Address: 10/2 Stanhill Drive, Surfers Paradise, Queensland 4217, Australia.

ROMANCE AND HISTORICAL PUBLICATIONS

Novels

Australian Hospital. London, Mills and Boon, 1955; Toronto, Harlequin, 1960.
Greenfingers Farm. London, Mills and Boon, 1955; Toronto, Harlequin, 1966.
Second Chance. London, Mills and Boon, 1956.
Wednesday's Children. London, Mills and Boon, 1957; as *Nurse Trent's Children*, Toronto, Harlequin, 1961.
Will You Surrender? London, Mills and Boon, 1957; Toronto, Harlequin, 1968.
The Coral Tree. London, Mills and Boon, 1958; Toronto, Harlequin, 1961.
If Love You Hold. London, Mills and Boon, 1958; as *Doctor Benedict*, Toronto, Harlequin, 1962; as *Love and Doctor Benedict*, Toronto, Harlequin, 1978.
The Girl at Snowy River. London, Mills and Boon, 1959; Toronto, Harlequin, 1964.
The House in the Timberwoods. London, Mills and Boon, 1959; Toronto, Harlequin, 1963.
Nurse Jess. London, Mills and Boon, and Toronto, Harlequin, 1959.
Tender Conquest. London, Mills and Boon, 1960; Toronto, Harlequin, 1964.
The Third in the House. London, Mills and Boon, 1961; Toronto, Harlequin, 1965.
The Wind and the Spray. London, Mills and Boon, 1961; Toronto, Harlequin, 1969.
The Boomerang Girl. London, Mills and Boon, 1962; Toronto, Harlequin, 1967.
River Nurse. London, Mills and Boon, 1962; Toronto, Harlequin, 1963.
The New Zealander. London, Mills and Boon, 1963; Toronto, Harlequin, 1967.
The Timber Man. London, Mills and Boon, 1964; Toronto, Harlequin, 1965.
The English Boss. London, Mills and Boon, 1964.
The Kindly Giant. London, Mills and Boon, 1964.
The Man from the Valley. London, Mills and Boon, and Toronto, Harlequin, 1966.
The Feel of Silk. London, Mills and Boon, 1967; Toronto, Harlequin, 1969.
I and My Heart. London, Mills and Boon, 1967; Toronto, Harlequin, 1970.
Clove Orange. London, Mills and Boon, 1967; Toronto, Harlequin, 1971.
A Taste for Love. London, Mills and Boon, 1967; Toronto, Harlequin, 1968.
Hotel Southerly. London, Mills and Boon, 1968; Toronto, Harlequin, 1970.
Venice Affair. London, Mills and Boon, and Toronto, Harlequin, 1968.
Nurse Smith, Cook. London, Mills and Boon, 1968; as *No Females Wanted*, Toronto, Harlequin, 1970.
The Drummer and the Song. London, Mills and Boon, and New York, Golden Press, 1969.
One String for Nurse Bow. London, Mills and Boon, 1969; as *One String for Her Bow*, Toronto, Harlequin, 1970.
Spanish Lace. London, Mills and Boon, and Toronto, Harlequin, 1969.
Crown of Flowers. London, Mills and Boon, 1969; Toronto, Harlequin, 1971.
Demi-Semi Nurse. London, Mills and Boon, 1969.

September Street. London, Mills and Boon, 1969; Toronto, Harlequin, 1972.
West of the River. London, Mills and Boon, 1970; as *Guardian Nurse*, Toronto, Harlequin, 1970.
Pool of Pink Lilies. London, Mills and Boon, 1970; Toronto, Harlequin, 1973.
Mr. Victoria. London, Mills and Boon, 1970.
Nickel Wife. London, Mills and Boon, 1970; Toronto, Harlequin, 1972.
Sister Pussycat. London, Mills and Boon, 1971; Toronto, Harlequin, 1974.
A Thousand Candles. London, Mills and Boon, 1971; Toronto, Harlequin, 1972.
Red Ginger Blossom. London, Mills and Boon, and Toronto, Harlequin, 1972.
Wife to Sim. London, Mills and Boon, 1972; Toronto, Harlequin, 1973.
Friday's Laughter. London, Mills and Boon, 1972.
There Were Three Princes. London, Mills and Boon, 1972; Toronto, Harlequin, 1974.
The Mutual Look. London, Mills and Boon, and Toronto, Harlequin, 1973.
The Cattleman. London, Mills and Boon, 1974; Toronto, Harlequin, 1975.
The New Broom. London, Mills and Boon, 1974; Toronto, Harlequin, 1976.
Flamingo Flying South. London, Mills and Boon, 1974; Toronto, Harlequin, 1975.
The Habit of Love. London, Mills and Boon, and Toronto, Harlequin, 1974.
The Kissing Gate. Toronto, Harlequin, 1975.
Cane Music. London, Mills and Boon, and Toronto, Harlequin, 1975.
Love and Lucy Brown. Toronto, Harlequin, 1975.
Corporation Boss. London, Mills and Boon, 1975; Toronto, Harlequin, 1976.
Inland Paradise. London, Mills and Boon, 1976; Toronto, Harlequin, 1977.
Deep in the Forest. Toronto, Harlequin, 1976.
The Road Boss. Toronto, Harlequin, 1976.
A Drift of Jasmine. Toronto, Harlequin, 1977.
The Truth Game. London, Mills and Boon, 1978.
All the Days of Summer. Toronto, Harlequin, 1978.
Remember September. Toronto, Harlequin, 1978.
The Tender Winds of Spring. London, Mills and Boon, 1978.
The Boss's Daughter. London, Mills and Boon, 1978.
Year of the Dragon. Toronto, Harlequin, 1978.
The Angry Man. London, Mills and Boon, 1979.
The All-the-Way Man. London, Mills and Boon, 1980; Toronto, Harlequin, 1981.
Come Back to Love. London, Mills and Boon, 1980; Toronto, Harlequin, 1981.
A Man Like Brady. London, Mills and Boon, 1981.
Brother Wolf. London, Mills and Boon, 1983.
The Arousing Touch. London, Mills and Boon, 1983.
Indian Silk. London, Mills and Boon, 1986.
A Thousand Ways of Loving. London, Mills and Boon, 1986.

Novels as Kate Starr

The Nurse Most Likely. London, Mills and Boon, 1962.
Ship's Doctor. London, Mills and Boon, 1964.
The Enchanted Trap. London, Mills and Boon, 1965.
Bells in the Wind. London, Mills and Boon, 1967.
Wrong Doctor John. London, Mills and Boon, 1967.
Dalton's Daughter. London, Mills and Boon, 1967.

Dolan of Sugar Hills. London, Mills and Boon, 1967.
Satin for the Bride. London, Mills and Boon, 1968.

*

Joyce Dingwell comments:

My romance writing began with an avid romance-reading mother who devoured so many romances each week that I decided to save library trips by supplementing the supply myself.

*   *   *

Joyce Dingwell, an Australian writer, is an author who has adapted herself to the changing demands of the reading public. In the late 1950's and early 1960's, she wrote traditional nurse-doctor romances. However, as the popularity of this type of romance waned, she switched her approach. Her major characters are now in various occupations and the interaction between the hero and heroine is "spicier" or "racier" than before, although her basic plot has remained the same. In fact, in at least one instance she has published the same book twice with only minor revisions. The romance formula and individual patterns of style do not allow for a wide range of variation within romantic fiction as a whole or within the work of a specific author. Nevertheless, one is surprised and disappointed to discover Dingwell repeating herself.

The Angry Man, published in 1979, is an almost identical version of *Greenfingers Farm*, published in 1955. Characters, general plot, concrete situations like an argument about appropriate nightwear on a safari, and even line-for-line dialogue are carried over from the earlier work to the later. This duplication with its slight alterations does serve the purpose of illustrating the changes in Dingwell. A meaningful glance between the hero and the heroine in *Greenfingers Farm* becomes a passionate embrace which includes the hero unbuttoning the heroine's blouse and touching her breast in *The Angry Man*. The hero's cousin in the earlier work is transformed into an illegitimate brother in the later book, and so on.

Dingwell's main appeal and most distinctive feature is her use of Australian settings, although she occasionally moves her stories to other locales, usually in the South Pacific. In addition, she develops a story line with a fairly large cast of characters. As a result, there are frequently several romances occurring in any one book which may end in multiple marriages. The story line may also typically include elements of danger or sadness. Dingwell's romances are not "stress-free." Heroines, in particular, experience painful losses such as the death of a beloved father. One of the hero's tasks, then, is to break through the heroine's emotional barriers to alleviate her pain with his love. Dingwell's strength, however, lies in her creation of secondary characters and plots rather than in the development of a complex relationship between the hero and heroine.

—Margaret Jensen

* * *

DIVER, (Katherine Helen) Maud (née Marshall). British. Born in Murree, India, in 1867 (?). Educated in England, but spent early years in India and Ceylon. Married T. Diver in 1896 (died 1941); one son. Lived in England after 1896: journalist. *Died 14 October 1945.*

ROMANCE AND HISTORICAL PUBLICATIONS

Novels

The Men of the Frontier Force. London, Newnes, 1930.
   Capt. Desmond, V.C. Edinburgh, Blackwood, 1907; New York, Lane, 1908; revised edition, New York, Putnam, 1914; Blackwood, 1915.
   The Great Amulet. Edinburgh, Blackwood, and New York, Lane, 1908.
   Desmond's Daughter. Edinburgh, Blackwood, and New York, Putnam, 1916.
Candles in the Wind. Edinburgh, Blackwood, and New York, Lane, 1909.
Lilamani. London, Hutchinson, 1911; as *Awakening*, New York, Lane, 1911.
The Hero of Herat. London, Constable, 1912; New York, Putnam, 1913.
The Judgement of the Sword. London, Constable, 1913; New York, Putnam, 1914.
Unconquered. London, Murray, and New York, Putnam, 1917.
Strange Roads. London, Constable, 1918.
The Strong Hours. London, Constable, and Boston, Houghton Mifflin, 1919.
Far to Seek. Edinburgh, Blackwood, and Boston, Houghton Mifflin, 1921.
Lonely Furrow. London, Murray, and Boston, Houghton Mifflin, 1923.
Coombe St. Mary's. Edinburgh, Blackwood, and Boston, Houghton Mifflin, 1925.
But Yesterday—. London, Murray, and New York, Dodd Mead, 1927.
Together. London, Newnes, 1928.
A Wild Bird. London, Murray, and Boston, Houghton Mifflin, 1929.
Ships of Youth. Edinburgh, Blackwood, and Boston, Houghton Mifflin, 1931.
The Singer Passes. Edinburgh, Blackwood, and New York, Dodd Mead, 1934.
The Dream Prevails. London, Murray, and Boston, Houghton Mifflin, 1938.
Sylvia Lyndon. Edinburgh, Blackwood, and Boston, Houghton Mifflin, 1940.

Short Stories

Sunia and Other Stories. Edinburgh, Blackwood, and New York, Putnam, 1913.
Siege Perilous and Other Stories. London, Murray, and Boston, Houghton Mifflin, 1924.

OTHER PUBLICATIONS

Other

The Englishwoman in India. Edinburgh, Blackwood, 1909.
Kabul to Kandahar. London, Davies, 1935.
Honoria Lawrence: A Fragment of Indian History. London, Murray, and Boston, Houghton Mifflin, 1936.
Royal India: A Descriptive and Historical Study of India's Fifteen Principal States and Their Rulers. London, Hodder and Stoughton, and New York, Appleton Century, 1942.

The Unsung: A Record of British Services in India. Edinburgh, Blackwood, 1945.

*   *   *

Maud Diver's early life in India and Ceylon provided her with the background for many of her tales. "I don't know how or why I am so successful in getting the Indian quality of my characters so true. I have really known very few Indians: One didn't know them in my day. It is some sort of sympathetic insight that guides me—and guides me right."

Her first novel, *Capt. Desmond, V.C.*, is set in and around the Punjab cavalry regiment, and at the frontier station of Kohat. With its alluring mixture of exotica, passion, and reassuring confirmation of all the clichés about life, men, love, marriage, and sex, it established her reputation as a popular writer. Diver specialised in marvelously voluptuous overwriting. Even minor descriptive passages which have no bearing on plot, characters, or theme are given full rein, the same weight. Thus, a sunrise: "By now the moon's last rim formed a golden sickle behind a blunt shoulder of rock; while over the eastward levels the topaz-yellow of an Indian dawn rushed at one stride to the zenith of heaven." This is what her readers wanted—that soothing mixture of accepted generalisations, and with a daring, foreign feel. However, lest the background material prove too exotic for her less well-travelled readers, the text is lightly spattered with footnotes explaining the meaning of some less familiar Indian terms (*chuprassee*, a government servant; *chota hazri*, a small breakfast) which add still more to the eastern flavour without confusing. Any obscurity in her novels is caused, less by the foreign setting, more by the luxuriant enthusiasm of her over-written style.

The Hero of Herat was another "frontier biography," and *The Judgement of the Sword* is set in Kabul. At the end of the Great War, she attempted two companion novels, *Strange Roads* and *The Strong Hours*, an ambitious attempt at the family saga story, which tries to show the effects of war on the lives and loves of the Blounts of Avonleigh, "an ancient family dating back to the days of Coeur de Lion." To give the prose more importance, she was partial to the conceit of attaching a literary (and sometimes not so literary) heading or quotation to the start of each brief chapter. These appear to have been selected almost at random, some so trite as to be more like cracker mottos, some popular philosophical tags, others from Emerson, E. M. Forster, Shakespeare, and St. Luke's gospel.

The lack of any sense of proportion is the biggest limitation to many romantic novelists. Most writers get to a point where they realise that there is something that they cannot do in their work. Second-rate novelists such as Maud Diver never reach this point. Nothing is beyond her sublime confidence. She did not relinquish the attempt to ask important moral questions, to tackle impossibly large themes.

—Rachel Anderson

DONNELLY, Jane. British. Married twice; one daughter. Reporter, Birmingham *Gazette* group; then television critic, feature writer, and women's page editor. Lives in Warwickshire. Address: c/o Mills and Boon Ltd., 18–24 Paradise Road, Richmond, Surrey TW9 1SR, England.

ROMANCE AND HISTORICAL PUBLICATIONS

Novels

A Man Apart. London, Mills and Boon, 1968.
Don't Walk Alone. London, Mills and Boon, 1969.
Shadows from the Sea. London, Mills and Boon, 1970.
Take the Far Dream. London, Mills and Boon, 1970.
Halfway to the Stars. London, Mills and Boon, 1971.
Never Turn Back. London, Mills and Boon, 1971.
The Man in the Next Room. London, Mills and Boon, 1971.
The Mill in the Meadow. London, Mills and Boon, 1972.
A Stranger Came. London, Mills and Boon, 1972.
The Long Shadow. London, Mills and Boon, 1973.
Rocks under Shining Water. London, Mills and Boon, 1973.
A Man Called Mallory. London, Mills and Boon, 1974.
Collision Course. London, Mills and Boon, 1975.
The Man Outside. London, Mills and Boon, 1975.
Ride Out the Storm. London, Mills and Boon, 1975.
Dark Pursuer. London, Mills and Boon, 1976.
The Silver Cage. London, Mills and Boon, 1976.
Dear Caliban. London, Mills and Boon, 1977.
Four Weeks in Winter. London, Mills and Boon, 1977.
The Intruder. London, Mills and Boon, 1977.
Forest of the Night. London, Mills and Boon, 1978.
Love for a Stranger. London, Mills and Boon, 1978.
Spell of the Seven Stones. London, Mills and Boon, 1978.
The Black Hunter. London, Mills and Boon, 1978.
Touched by Fire. London, Mills and Boon, 1978.
A Man to Watch. London, Mills and Boon, 1979.
A Savage Sanctuary. London, Mills and Boon, 1979.
Behind a Closed Door. London, Mills and Boon, 1979.
No Way Out. London, Mills and Boon, 1980.
When Lightning Strikes. London, Mills and Boon, 1980.
Flash Point. London, Mills and Boon, 1981.
So Long a Winter. London, Mills and Boon, 1981.
The Frozen Jungle. London, Mills and Boon, 1981.
Diamond Cut Diamond. London, Mills and Boon, 1982.
A Fierce Encounter. London, Mills and Boon, 1983.
Call Up the Storm. London, Mills and Boon, 1983.
Face the Tiger. London, Mills and Boon, 1983.
Moon Lady. London, Mills and Boon, 1984.
Ring of Crystal. London, Mills and Boon, 1985.
To Cage a Whirlwind. London, Mills and Boon, 1985.
Force Field. London, Mills and Boon, 1987.
Run a Wild Horse. Toronto, Harlequin, 1987.
The Frozen Heart. Toronto, Harlequin, 1988.
No Place to Run. Toronto, Harlequin, 1988.
Fetters of Gold. Toronto, Harlequin, 1988.
When We're Alone. London, Mills and Boon, 1989.

*

Jane Donnelly comments:

My novels as with all Mills and Boon books, are happy escapist reading. My heroines are smart girls, with minds of their own and nobody's fool. Although part of the fun of the book is in the awful things that happen to them on the way, I try to leave the reader feeling that the future is bright, and really fancying the hero!

*   *   *

Jane Donnelly has a solid following of readers who look forward to each new novel. While she seems to write the classical "sweet" romance exclusively, this does not mean that her novels lack the depth of characterization or the complexity of plot that readers expect.

In fact, she uses a unique method in developing her characters, especially her heroes. Impressions of the man, his reactions and his attitudes are all shown through the heroine's eyes or through dialogue with other people. Internal dialogue on the heroine's part is also used to develop the reader's knowledge. Her reactions and perceptions, her failings and beliefs are crystallized into one central need. To know this man! To become the kind of woman that he needs, to become so indispensable to him that he cannot live without her.

Inherent in this need is the concept of growth. Donnelly's heroines do mature, graciously and eagerly. The heroines aren't so mature that they won't try their feminine wiles in attempts to see their loved one, to be near him. They are both drawn to him, yet are afraid to come too close. In the end, forces stronger than themselves resolve the conflict and help them to take the final step of commitment.

Nowhere is this method of characterization more clearly evident than in *Halfway to the Stars*, one of Donnelly's early novels. Shena Douglas works on a women's magazine as a writer. She becomes engaged to Rob Howard, a television producer. In time, he takes her home to meet his mother and brother. Cal Howard is a world famous mountain climber, sportsman, and writer. From the moment of meeting, Shena finds herself drawn to Cal. In spite of efforts to fight this attraction, she continually does things that will help her learn more about him. Shena is afraid of heights, but she climbs up the mountainside to his cabin. She listens to comments by Rob, his mother, and Cal's ex-girlfriend. Slowly Shena realizes that Cal has been ruthlessly used by all of them in the past. She also realizes that his strength is coupled with sensitivity, humor, and a great capacity for love. Cal appears in only a few scenes with Shena, yet, the reader knows him. The vividness of the writing, the little details of characterization brought out in conversation and the compelling personality of the hero made this one of Donnelly's best novels, an extremely enjoyable story with a hero her readers cannot forget.

In *Ring of Crystal*, Donnelly's readers are again caught in her spell of forceful heroes. Annie Bennett, a newspaper writer, is suddenly confronted by Adam Corbett, the new editor of the paper she works on. Annie has two other problems besides coping with a new boss. Her parents want her married and she somehow seems to change boyfriends with frightening regularity. Adam's arrival acts as a catalyst. He is a world famous journalist who is recovering from injuries received on a recent assignment. Annie is confused by him, fascinated and finally caught in his spell of strength, integrity, honor, and love.

Again Donnelly uses the viewpoint of the heroine to characterize Adam. To a degree, Annie is obsessed by him. She has always had her choice of boyfriends, but she is aware of the fact that she cannot make Adam see her as anything but a flighty girl.

In this novel, there is more than enough of Donnelly's touch of characterization to lend suspense and interest as well as elements of the classical romance plotting to add to the conflict. Jealous ex-boyfriends, the "other woman" and elderly parents all contribute to an entertaining story.

A more recent novel, *Fetters of Gold*, shows that Donnelly has not lost any of her skill in keeping the interest of her readers. In this novel Dinah Marsden, a freelance photographer, falls in love with Nicholas Christophi, a well known jewelry designer and younger brother of Marcus Christophi, a wealthy businessman. No sooner has Nic proposed than he has an accident. This results in a loss of memory, just when he had asked Dinah to marry him. Dinah had not responded to the proposal and later

conflict with Marcus makes her determined never to tell Marcus her answer. Marcus in turn, thinks she has lied about the proposal. To keep her under his eye, he asks her to go with Nic to their home on Styros, a Greek island. Misunderstandings, another woman, and an unexpected attraction between Dinah and Marcus provide the drama and conflict throughout the novel.

Considering the number of romances that Donnelly has written, one would think that plotting and characterization would become more difficult over the years. Not true! *Fetters of Gold* tends to be more rounded and more balanced between characterization, plot, and setting. It results in a delightful story that is typical of the Mills and Boon or Harlequin romance series and shows a good writer going on to become a better one.

—Arlene Moore

DORSETT, Danielle. See **DANIELS, Dorothy.**

DOUGLAS, Barbara. See **LAKER, Rosalind.**

DOUGLAS, Lloyd C(assell). American. Born in Columbia City, Indiana, 27 August 1877. Educated at Wittenberg College, Springfield, Ohio, A.B. Married Bessie Porch in 1904. Lutheran minister. LL.D.: Gettysburg College, Pennsylvania, 1935; D. Litt.: Northeastern University, Boston, 1936. *Died 13 February 1951.*

ROMANCE AND HISTORICAL PUBLICATIONS

Novels

Magnificent Obsession. Boston, Houghton Mifflin, 1929; London, Allen and Unwin, 1932.
Forgive Us Our Trespasses. Boston, Houghton Mifflin, 1932; London, Lovat Dickson, 1937.
Precious Jeopardy: A Christmas Story. Boston, Houghton Mifflin, 1933; London, Davies, 1949.
Green Light. Boston, Houghton Mifflin, and London, Dickson and Thompson, 1935.
White Banners. Boston, Houghton Mifflin, and London, Lovat Dickson, 1936.
Home for Christmas. Boston, Houghton Mifflin, and London, Lovat Dickson, 1937.
Disputed Passage. Boston, Houghton Mifflin, and London, Lovat Dickson, 1939.
Dr. Hudson's Secret Journal. Boston, Houghton Mifflin, 1939; London, Davies, 1940.
Invitation to Live. Boston, Houghton Mifflin, 1940; London, Davies, 1941.
The Robe. Boston, Houghton Mifflin, 1942; London, Davies, 1943.
The Big Fisherman. Boston, Houghton Mifflin, 1948; London, Davies, 1949.

OTHER PUBLICATIONS

Other

The Fate of the Limited. New York, Associated Press, 1919.
Wanted: A Congregation. Chicago, Christian Century Press, 1920.
An Affair of the Heart. Akron, Ohio, Summit, 1922.
The Minister's Everyday Life. New York, Scribner, 1924.
These Sayings of Mine: An Interpretation of the Teachings of Jesus. New York, Scribner, 1926.
Those Disturbing Miracles. New York, Harper, 1927.
The College Student Facing a Muddled World. Sackville, New Brunswick, Mount Allison University, 1933.
A Time to Remember (autobiography). Boston, Houghton Mifflin, 1951; London, Davies, 1952.
The Living Faith: Selected Sermons. Boston, Houghton Mifflin, and London, Davies, 1955.

*

Critical Study: *The Shape of Sunday: An Intimate Biography of Lloyd C. Douglas* by Virginia Douglas Dawson and Betty Douglas Wilson, Boston, Houghton Mifflin, 1952.

*   *   *

If Lloyd C. Douglas is still read it will be for his two historical novels, *The Robe* and *The Big Fisherman*. Both share the same background, the New Testament world of Palestine and Rome and both are concerned with the events surrounding the founding of the early Christian Church including the last days of Christ. It may be that their survival owes at least as much to their appearance on the lists of the subscription book clubs of the day and to the fact that they were both made into films, as to their literary merit. The interest aroused by the subject of the books and the use of the gospel narratives must also have contributed.

Naturally the two books overlap in the events they describe and they have many characters in common. *The Robe* is the story of how the robe of Christ, won in a dice game at the foot of the cross by Marcellus, changes his life; *The Big Fisherman* follows the ministry of Christ and the life of Peter. However, despite many similarities, the two novels are quite different. In the first place, *The Robe*, the earlier of the two, is the more readable. The hero, Marcellus, is an attractive, talented young man whose outspoken behaviour in Rome causes him to be sent to Palestine to command the notorious Gaza fort. Visiting Jerusalem during the Passover and in his capacity as Commander of Gaza, he is assigned the task of crucifying Christ. The event is traumatic and under the influence of the strange robe Marcellus finds himself searching for the truth about Jesus and for peace of mind. This he will find only in the arena of the Colosseum in Rome. By focusing on one character Douglas maintains interest and it is easy for the reader to feel sympathy for Marcellus, both in his quest and in his love for the beautiful Diana.

The Big Fisherman is a more diffuse novel pursuing several stories—the story of Esther, daughter of an Arabian princess and Antipas, son of Herod; the romance between Esther and Voldi; the ministry of Christ and the story of Peter, the big fisherman. The crowded plot makes it difficult for the reader to feel particularly involved with any one character, although the portrayal of Peter is human and far from saintly.

The two novels achieved popularity when first published, although today, their style both stilted and tendentious, severely limits their attraction. Although not lacking historical accuracy—the Roman world of the early Christian Church is carefully drawn—a sense of period is curiously absent from the books. Rather Douglas maintains an unrelievedly modern style in both dialogue and description. One can hear his characters speaking with American accents. Despite this approach his characters fail to achieve a sense of vitality. While Douglas's attempt to clothe the shadowy figures familiar to us from the gospels, is interesting, these characters do not become memorable. The young lovers Marcellus and Diana, Esther and Voldi, fare no better. They are sympathetically portrayed but little more than stereotypes of romantic fiction–handsome, exquisitely beautiful, brave, and true. In fact Douglas's main purpose is to present a Christian thesis in the form of a novel by expanding the rather austere gospel narratives to include the human interest of a romance. The form allows him to introduce a wide range of characters, various viewpoints, and to indulge in speculative dialogue. However, the reader cannot help but feel that these novels succeed better translated to the movement and colour of the cinema screen.

The serious purpose of both *The Robe* and *The Big Fisherman* is the presentation of Christ and the Christian faith. This preoccupation underlies all Douglas's other novels—though in these it is the author's own particular thesis which is put forward. They are mostly romances and, though dated, are enjoyable, however their didactic approach, lacking the warmth and humanity present in Elizabeth Goudge's books, must have helped to prevent them from surviving.

Douglas's first novel, *Magnificent Obsession*, is very readable and introduces themes that reappear in later books—a medical setting (appropriate to Douglas's view that religion can be seen as a science); the wealthy background; the conversion of the atheist hero to a practising Christian, all within the framework of the traditional romantic novel. Several of the books share characters—*Green Light* introduces Dean Harcourt who appears in subsequent novels in the role of father confessor and inspiration, but even he remains a shadowy figure, as do the other characters who in the final analysis are still very much stereotypes of the genre.

—Ferelith Hordon

DOUGLASS, Billie. See **DELINSKY, Barbara.**

DOYLE, (Sir) Arthur Conan. British. Born in Edinburgh, Scotland, 22 May 1859. Educated at the Hodder School, Lancashire, 1868–70, Stonyhurst College, Lancashire, 1870–75, and the Jesuit School, Feldkirch, Austria (editor, *Feldkirchian Gazette*), 1875–76; studied medicine at the University of Edinburgh, 1876–81, M.B. 1881, M.D. 1885. Served as senior physician at a field hospital in South Africa during the Boer War, 1899–1902: knighted, 1902. Married 1) Louise Hawkins in 1885 (died 1906), one daughter and one son; 2) Jean Leckie in 1907, two sons and one daughter. Practised medicine in Southsea, Hampshire, 1882–90; full-time writer from 1891; stood for Parliament as Unionist candidate for Central Edinburgh, 1900, and tariff reform candidate for the Hawick Burghs, 1906. Member, Society for Psychical Research, 1893–1930 (resigned). LL.D.: University of Edinburgh, 1905. Knight of Grace of the Order of St. John of Jerusalem. *Died 7 July 1930.*

ROMANCE AND HISTORICAL PUBLICATIONS

Novels (series: Sir Nigel Loring)

Micah Clarke. London, Longman, and New York, Harper, 1889.
The White Company (Sir Nigel). London, Smith Elder, 3 vols., 1891; New York, Lovell, 1 vol., 1891.
The Great Shadow. New York, Harper, 1892.
The Great Shadow, and Beyond the City. Bristol, Arrowsmith, 1893; New York, Ogilvie, 1894.
The Refugees. London, Longman, 3 vols., 1893; New York, Harper, 1 vol., 1893.
Rodney Stone. London, Smith Elder, and New York, Appleton, 1896.
Uncle Bernac: A Memory of the Empire. London, Smith Elder, and New York, Appleton, 1897.
Sir Nigel. London, Smith Elder, and New York, McClure, 1906.

Short Stories (series: Brigadier Gerard)

The Exploits of Brigadier Gerard. London, Newnes, and New York, Appleton, 1896.
Adventures of Gerard. London, Newnes, and New York, McClure, 1903.
The Last Galley: Impressions and Tales. London, Smith Elder, and New York, Doubleday, 1911.
Tales of Pirates and Blue Water. London, Murray, 1922; as *The Dealings of Captain Sharkey and Other Tales of Pirates*, New York, Doran, 1925.
Tales of Long Ago. London, Murray, 1922; as *The Last of the Legions and Other Tales of Long Ago*, New York, Doran, 1925.
The Conan Doyle Historical Romances. London, Murray, 2 vols., 1931–32.

OTHER PUBLICATIONS

Novels

A Study in Scarlet. London, Ward Lock, 1888; Philadelphia, Lippincott, 1890.
The Mystery of Cloomber. London, Ward and Downey, 1888; New York, Fenno, 1896(?).
The Firm of Girdlestone. London, Chatto and Windus, and New York, Lovell, 1890.
The Sign of Four. London, Blackett, 1890; New York, Collier, 1891.
The Doings of Raffles Haw. London, Cassell, and New York, Lovell, 1892.
The Parasite. London, Constable, and New York, Harper, 1894.
The Stark Munro Letters. London, Longman, and New York, Appleton, 1895.
The Tragedy of Korosko. London, Smith Elder, 1898; as *A Desert Drama*, Philadelphia, Lippincott, 1898.
A Duet, with an Occasional Chorus. London, Grant Richards, and New York, Appleton, 1899; revised edition, London, Smith Elder, 1910.
The Hound of the Baskervilles. London, Newnes, and New York, McClure, 1902.
The Lost World. London, Hodder and Stoughton, 1912; New York, Doran, 1915.
The Poison Belt. London, Hodder and Stoughton, and New York, Doran, 1913.

The Valley of Fear. New York, Doran, and London, Smith Elder, 1915.
The Land of Mist. London, Hutchinson, 1925; New York, Doran, 1926.

Short Stories

Mysteries and Adventures. London, Scott, 1889; as *The Gully of Bluemansdyke and Other Stories*, 1892.
The Captain of the Polestar and Other Tales. London, Longman, 1890; New York, Munro, 1894.
The Adventures of Sherlock Holmes. London, Newnes, and New York, Harper, 1892.
My Friend the Murderer and Other Mysteries and Adventures. New York, Lovell, 1893.
The Memoirs of Sherlock Holmes. London, Newnes, 1893; New York, Harper, 1894.
The Great Keinplatz Experiment and Other Stories. Chicago, Rand McNally, 1894.
Round the Red Lamp, Being Facts and Fancies of Medical Life. London, Methuen, and New York, Appleton, 1894.
The Man from Archangel and Other Stories. New York, Street and Smith, 1898.
Hilda Wade (completion of work by Grant Allen). London, Richards, and New York, Putnam, 1900.
The Green Flag and Other Stories of War and Sport. London, Smith Elder, and New York, McClure, 1900.
The Return of Sherlock Holmes. London, Newnes, and New York, McClure, 1905.
Round the Fire Stories. London, Smith Elder, and New York, McClure, 1908.
His Last Bow: Some Reminiscences of Sherlock Holmes. London, Murray, and New York, Doran, 1917.
Danger! and Other Stories. London, Murray, 1918; New York, Doran, 1919.
Tales of the Ring and Camp. London, Murray, 1922; as *The Croxley Master and Other Tales of the Ring and Camp*, New York, Doran, 1925.
Tales of Terror and Mystery. London, Murray, 1922; as *The Black Doctor and Other Tales of Terror and Mystery*, New York, Doran, 1925.
Tales of Twilight and the Unseen. London, Murray, 1922; as *The Great Keinplatz Experiment and Other Tales of Twilight and the Unseen*, New York, Doran, 1925.
Tales of Adventure and Medical Life. London, Murray, 1922; as *The Man from Archangel and Other Tales of Adventure*, New York, Doran, 1925.
The Case-Book of Sherlock Holmes. London, Murray, and New York, Doran, 1927.
The Maracot Deep and Other Stories. London, Murray, and New York, Doubleday, 1929.
The Field Bazaar. Privately printed, 1934; Summit, New Jersey, Pamphlet House, 1947.
The Professor Challenger Stories. London, Murray, 1952.
Great Stories, edited by John Dickson Carr. London, Murray, and New York, London House and Maxwell, 1959.
The Annotated Sherlock Holmes, edited by William S. Baring-Gould. New York, Potter, 2 vols., 1967; London, Murray, 2 vols., 1968.
The Adventures of Sherlock Holmes (facsimile of magazine stories). New York, Schocken, 1976; as *The Sherlock Holmes Illustrated Omnibus*, London, Murray-Cape, 1978.
The Best Supernatural Tales of Arthur Conan Doyle, edited by E. F. Bleiler. New York, Dover, 1979.
Sherlock Holmes: The Published Apocrypha, with others, edited by Jack Tracy. Boston, Houghton Mifflin, 1980.

The Final Adventures of Sherlock Holmes, edited by Peter Haining. London, W. H. Allen, 1981.

The Edinburgh Stories. Edinburgh, Polygon, 1981.

The Best Science Fiction of Arthur Conan Doyle, edited by Charles G. Waugh and Martin H. Greenberg. Carbondale, Southern Illinois University Press, 1981.

Uncollected Stories, edited by John Michael Gibson and Richard Lancelyn Green. London, Secker and Warburg, and New York, Doubleday, 1982.

The Best Horror Stories of Arthur Conan Doyle, edited by Martin H. Greenberg and Charles G. Waugh. Chicago, Academy, 1988.

The Supernatural Tales of Sir Arthur Conan Doyle, edited by Peter Haining. Slough, Berkshire, Foulsham, 1988.

Plays

Jane Annie; or, The Good Conduct Prize, with J. M. Barrie, music by Ernest Ford (produced London, 1893). London, Chappell, and New York, Novello Ewer, 1893.

Foreign Policy, adaptation of his own story "A Question of Diplomacy" (produced London, 1893).

Waterloo, adaptation of his story "A Straggler of 15" (as *A Story of Waterloo,* produced Bristol, 1894; London, 1895; as *Waterloo,* produced New York, 1899). London, French, 1907; in *One-Act Plays of To-day,* 2nd series, edited by J. W. Marriott, Boston, Small Maynard, 1926.

Halves, adaptation of the story by James Payn (produced Aberdeen and London, 1899).

Sherlock Holmes, with William Gillette, adaptation of works by Doyle (produced Buffalo and New York, 1899; Liverpool and London, 1901).

A Duet (A Duologue) (produced London, 1902). London, French, 1903.

Brigadier Gerard, adaptation of his own stories (produced London and New York, 1906).

The Fires of Fate: A Modern Morality, adaptation of his novel *The Tragedy of Korosko* (produced Liverpool, London, and New York, 1909).

The House of Temperley, adaptation of his novel *Rodney Stone* (produced London, 1910).

The Pot of Caviare, adaptation of his own story (produced London, 1910).

The Speckled Band: An Adventure of Sherlock Holmes (produced London and New York, 1910). London, French, 1912.

The Crown Diamond (produced Bristol and London, 1921). Privately printed, 1958.

It's Time Something Happened. New York, Appleton, 1925.

Verse

Songs of Action. London, Smith Elder, and New York, Doubleday, 1898.

Songs of the Road. London, Smith Elder, and New York, Doubleday, 1911.

The Guards Came Through and Other Poems. London, Murray, 1919; New York, Doran, 1920.

The Poems of Arthur Conan Doyle: Collected Edition (includes play *The Journey*). London, Murray, 1922.

Other

The Great Boer War. London, Smith Elder, and New York, McClure, 1900.

The War in South Africa: Its Cause and Conduct. London, Smith Elder, and New York, McClure, 1902.

Works (Author's Edition). London, Smith Elder, 12 vols., and New York, Appleton, 13 vols., 1903.

The Fiscal Question. Hawick, Roxburgh, Henderson, 1905.

An Incursion into Diplomacy. London, Smith Elder, 1906.

The Story of Mr. George Edalji. London, Daily Telegraph, 1907.

Through the Magic Door (essays). London, Smith Elder, 1907; New York, McClure, 1908.

The Crime of the Congo. London, Hutchinson, and New York, Doubleday, 1909.

Divorce Law Reform: An Essay. London, Divorce Law Reform Union, 1909.

Sir Arthur Conan Doyle: Why He Is Now in Favour of Home Rule. London, Liberal Publication Department, 1911.

The Case of Oscar Slater. London, Hodder and Stoughton, 1912; New York, Doran, 1913.

Divorce and the Church, with Lord Hugh Cecil. London, Divorce Law Reform Union, 1913.

Great Britain and the Next War. Boston, Small Maynard, 1914.

In Quest of Truth, Being a Correspondence Between Sir Arthur Conan Doyle and Captain H. Stansbury. London, Watts, 1914.

To Arms! London, Hodder and Stoughton, 1914.

The German War. London, Hodder and Stoughton, 1914; New York, Doran, 1915.

Western Wanderings (travel in Canada). New York, Doran, 1915.

The Outlook on the War. London, Daily Chronicle, 1915.

An Appreciation of Sir John French. London, Daily Chronicle, 1916.

A Petition to the Prime Minister on Behalf of Sir Roger Casement. Privately printed, 1916.

A Visit to Three Fronts: Glimpses of British, Italian, and French Lines. London, Hodder and Stoughton, and New York, Doran 1916.

The British Campaign in France and Flanders. London, Hodder and Stoughton, 6 vols., 1916–20; New York, Doran, 6 vols., 1916–20; revised edition, as *The British Campaigns in Europe 1914–1918,* London, Bles, 1 vol., 1928.

The New Revelation. London, Hodder and Stoughton, and New York, Doran, 1918.

The Vital Message (on spiritualism). London, Hodder and Stoughton, and New York, Doran, 1919.

Our Reply to the Cleric. London, Spiritualists' National Union, 1920.

A Public Debate on the Truth of Spiritualism, with Joseph McCabe. London, Watts, 1920; as *Debate on Spiritualism,* Girard, Kansas, Haldeman Julius, 1922.

Spiritualism and Rationalism. London, Hodder and Stoughton, 1920.

The Wanderings of a Spiritualist. London, Hodder and Stoughton, and New York, Doran, 1921.

Spiritualism: Some Straight Questions and Direct Answers. Manchester, Two Worlds, 1922.

The Case for Spirit Photography, with others. London, Hutchinson, 1922; New York, Doran, 1923.

The Coming of the Fairies. London, Hodder and Stoughton, and New York, Doran, 1922.

Three of Them: A Reminiscence. London, Murray, 1923.

Our American Adventure. London, Hodder and Stoughton, and New York, Doran, 1923.

Our Second American Adventure. London, Hodder and Stoughton, and Boston, Little Brown, 1924.

Memories and Adventures. London, Hodder and Stoughton, and Boston, Little Brown, 1924.

Psychic Experiences. London and New York, Putnam, 1925.

The Early Christian Church and Modern Spiritualism. London, Psychic Bookshop, 1925.

The History of Spiritualism. London, Cassell, 2 vols., and New York, Doran, 2 vols., 1926.

Pheneas Speaks: Direct Spirit Communications. London, Psychic Press, and New York, Doran, 1927.

What Does Spiritualism Actually Teach and Stand For? London, Psychic Bookshop, 1928.

A Word of Warning. London, Psychic Press, 1928.

An Open Letter to Those of My Generation. London, Psychic Press, 1929.

Our African Winter. London, Murray, 1929.

The Roman Catholic Church: A Rejoinder. London, Psychic Press, 1929.

The Edge of the Unknown. London, Murray, and New York, Putnam, 1930.

Works (Crowborough Edition). New York, Doubleday, 24 vols., 1930.

Strange Studies from Life, edited by Peter Ruber. New York, Candlelight Press, 1963.

Arthur Conan Doyle on Sherlock Holmes. London, Favil, 1981.

Essays on Photography, edited by John Michael Gibson and Richard Lancelyn Green. London, Secker and Warburg, 1982.

Letters to the Press, edited by John Michael Gibson and Richard Lancelyn Green. London Secker and Warburg, and Iowa City, University of Iowa Press, 1986.

Editor, *D. D. Home: His Life and Mission,* by Mrs. Dunglas Home. London, Kegan Paul Trench Trubner, 1921.

Editor, *The Spiritualists' Reader.* Manchester, Two Worlds, 1924.

Translator, *The Mystery of Joan of Arc,* by Léon Denis. London, Murray, 1924; New York, Dutton, 1925.

*

Bibliography: *The World Bibliography of Sherlock Holmes and Dr. Watson* by Ronald Burt De Waal, Boston, New York Graphic Society, 1975; *A Bibliography of A. Conan Doyle* by Richard Lancelyn Green and John Michael Gibson, Oxford, Clarendon Press, 1983.

Manuscript Collection: Humanities Research Center, University of Texas, Austin.

Critical Studies (selection): *The Private Life of Sherlock Holmes* by Vincent Starrett, New York, Macmillan, 1933, London, Nicholson and Watson, 1934, revised edition, Chicago, University of Chicago Press, 1960, London, Allen and Unwin, 1961; *Conan Doyle: His Life and Art* by Hesketh Pearson, London, Methuen, 1943, New York, Walker, 1961; *The Life of Sir Arthur Conan Doyle* by John Dickson Carr, London, Murray, and New York, Harper, 1949; *Conan Doyle: A Biography* by Pierre Nordon, London, Murray, 1966, New York, Holt Rinehart, 1967; *Conan Doyle: A Biography of the Creator of Sherlock Holmes* by Ivor Brown, London, Hamish Hamilton, 1972; *The Adventures of Conan Doyle: The Life of the Creator of Sherlock Holmes* by Charles Higham, London, Hamish Hamilton, and New York, Norton, 1976; *The Encyclopedia Sherlockiana* by Jack Tracy, New York, Doubleday, 1977, London, New English Library, 1978; *Conan Doyle: A Biographical Solution* by Ronald Pearsall, London, Weidenfeld and Nicolson, 1977; *Sherlock Holmes and His Creator* by Trevor H. Hall, London, Duckworth, 1978, New York, St. Martin's Press, 1983; *Conan Doyle:*

Portrait of an Artist by Julian Symons, London, G. Whizzard, 1979; *Sherlock Holmes: The Man and His World* by H. R. F. Keating, London, Thames and Hudson, and New York, Scribner, 1979; *The Quest for Sherlock Holmes: A Biographical Study of the Early Life of Sir Arthur Conan Doyle* by Owen Dudley Edwards, Edinburgh, Mainstream, and Totowa, New Jersey, Barnes and Noble, 1983; *Arthur Conan Doyle* by Don Richard Cox, New York, Ungar, 1985; *The Unrevealed Life of Doctor Arthur Conan Doyle: A Study in Southsea* by Geoffrey Stavert, Horndean, Hampshire, Milestone, 1987; *Arthur Conan Doyle* by Jacqueline A. Jaffe, Boston, Twayne, 1987; *The Quest for Sir Arthur Conan Doyle: Thirteen Biographers in Search of a Life* edited by Jon L. Lellenberg, Carbondale, Southern Illinois University Press, 1987.

*   *   *

Arthur Conan Doyle was a successful doctor, a war correspondent, a military historian, a champion of prisoners doubtfully convicted or too severely punished and twice stood for Parliament. His fame rests on his creation of Sherlock Holmes but there are many people, including Winston Churchill and Doyle himself, who preferred his historical romances.

Doyle sought a greater literary standing than he thought the Holmes stories provided. His love of adventure resulted in the first, longest, and best of his romances, *Micah Clark.* This was a gratifying and immediate success, fully repaying the two years of research Doyle put into it. The book was praised by Oscar Wilde and went to four editions in the first year. Micah Clark, the hero, passes from childhood to participation in Monmouth's rebellion, to capture, trial by Judge Jeffreys and escape secured by the great character of the tale, the soldier of fortune Decimus Saxon. The account of the battle of Sedgemoor and the portrait of Jeffrys are the high points. It is a fine cloak and dagger adventure story for any age, even if best met for the first time as a child.

Other stories of history, chivalry, and romance followed: *The White Company, The Refugees, The Exploits of Brigadier Gerard, Rodney Stone, Uncle Bernac,* and *Sir Nigel,* all steeped in action and adventure and located in a variety of times and places.

The White Company, set in the Middle Ages, is one of the best, though you may weary of "By Saint Paul!," "My fair lord," "By my hilt!," "Pest take him!," "In sooth," and the like. Three companions, Alleyne Edricson, a clerk fresh from the Abbey at Beaulieu, Hordle John, a vast, red-headed forester, and Samkin Aylward a war-hardened archer, join Sir Nigel to march into Spain. There are so many adventures along the way that it is nearly the end of the book before the company arrives. An engagement with a pirate ship, a jousting at which an unidentified French knight arrives at its close to challenge five Knights to meet him each with the weapon of his own choice and beats them all except Sir Nigel, an escape from a burning castle taken by a mob, desperate fighting, slaughter, chivalry, and love enliven Sir Nigel's journey.

The White Company is a sequel to *Sir Nigel* although the earlier story was written 15 years later. In *Sir Nigel,* our hero serves in France for Edward III as squire to Sir John Chandos and vows to perform three great and noble deeds before claiming the Lady Mary as his bride. The mixture of ruthless slaughter and generous chivalry is a fair reflection of the times, indeed much of the tale is taken from life and confirmed by contemporary sources. The reality of those times required little embellishment.

The Refugees is told in two halves, the first is placed in France with the Court of Louis XIV and persecution of the Huguenots, the second, set in America, is concerned with the Huguenots' flight and their struggles both with a harsh new environment and with the Indians. *Uncle Bernac* takes Louis de Laval from Kent to intrigue and danger in France where his Uncle Bernac has acquired his family estates. It contains a fine study of Napoleon. *The Exploits of Brigadier Gerard*, presents that dashing, swashbuckling character, who was one of the most popular of Doyle's creations.

Rodney Stone is a story of prize-fighters, Bucks, Corinthians, wagers, and perfection in cravats. It is a grand tale in which, as in *The White Company*, an unknown challenger, Boy Jim, appears at a supper party given for the fancy and offers to take on anyone they may choose from among all the great fighters present. It also contains a grand account of a great match between Crab Wilson and the representative of Sir Charles Tregellis; the old Champion Harrison throws his hat into the ring with one minute to spare when Boy Jim, brought up by him to work in his forge, is called away on finding that he is really the heir to Lord Avon.

Doyle's historical novels certainly varied in quality but *Micah Clarke*, *The White Company*, and *Rodney Stone* stand high in any list of such romances; in their own field they equal and indeed outshine some of the works of Rider Haggard and Anthony Hope.

—David Waldron Smithers

DOZIER, Zoe. See **BROWNING, Dixie.**

DRAKE, Bonnie. See **DELINSKY, Barbara.**

DRAKE, Shannon. See **POZZESSERE, Heather Graham.**

DREW, Eleanor. See **DARRELL, Elizabeth.**

DRUMMOND, Emma. See **DARRELL, Elizabeth.**

DRYDEN, Lennox. See **STEEN, Marguerite.**

DUFFIELD, Anne (née Tate). American. Born in Orange, New Jersey, 20 November 1893. Educated at a private school in Toronto; the Sorbonne, Paris. Married Edgar Duffield in 1922.

ROMANCE AND HISTORICAL PUBLICATIONS

Novels

Miss Mayhew and Ming Yun: A Story of East and West. New York, Stokes, 1928.
The Lacquer Couch. London, Murray, 1928.
Predestined. London, Murray, 1929.
Passionate Interlude. London, Murray, 1931.
Phantasy. London, Cassell, 1932.
Lantern-Light. London, Cassell, 1933; New York, Arcadia House, 1943.
Fleeing Shadows. London, Cassell, 1934; as *Stamboul Love*, New York, Knopf, 1934.
Flaming Felicia. London, Cassell, 1934; New York, Arcadia House, 1941.
Golden Horizons. London, Cassell, 1935; New York, Arcadia House, 1942.
Silver Peaks. London, Cassell, 1935; New York, Arcadia House, 1941.
Wild Memory. London, Cassell, 1935; as *Love's Memory*, New York, Arcadia House, 1936.
Glittering Heights. London, Cassell, 1936.
Moon over Stamboul. London, Cassell, 1936; New York, Arcadia House, 1937.
Paradise. London, Cassell, 1936; as *Brief Rapture*, New York, Arcadia House, 1938.
Bitter Rapture. London, Cassell, 1937.
Enchantment. New York, Curl, 1937.
The House on the Nile. London, Cassell, 1937; as *Gossip*, New York, Curl, 1938.
Gay Fiesta. New York, Arcadia House, 1938; as *The Dragon's Tail*, London, Cassell, 1939.
Grecian Rhapsody. London, Cassell, 1938; as *High Heaven*, 1939.
Desert Moon. London, Cassell, 1939; New York, Arcadia House, 1940.
False Star. New York, Arcadia House, 1939.
Karen's Memory. London, Cassell, and New York, Arcadia House, 1939.
Bubbling Springs. London, Cassell, and New York, Arcadia House, 1940.
The Sweeping Tide. London, Cassell, and New York, Arcadia House, 1940.
The Shadow of the Pines. London, Cassell, 1940; New York, Arcadia House, 1941.
A Bevy of Maids. London, Cassell, 1941; as *Volunteer Nurse*, New York, Arcadia House, 1942.
Old Glory. London, Cassell, 1942; New York, Arcadia House, 1943.
The Inscrutable Nymph. London, Cassell, 1942; as *This Alien Heart*, New York, Arcadia House, 1942.
Sunrise. London, Cassell, 1943; New York, Arcadia House, 1944.
Out of the Shadows. London, Cassell, 1944; as *Turn to the Sun*, New York, Arcadia House, 1944.
Taffy Came to Cairo. London, Cassell, 1944; New York, Arcadia House, 1945.
Repent at Leisure. London, Cassell, 1945; New York, Arcadia House, 1946.
Forever To-morrow. London, Cassell, 1946; New York, Arcadia House, 1951.
Song of the Mocking Bird. London, Cassell, 1946; as *The Lonely Bride*, New York, Arcadia House, 1947.
Wise Is the Heart. New York, Arcadia House, 1947.
Arkady. London, Cassell, 1948.

Dusty Dawn. London, Cassell, 1949; New York, Arcadia House, 1953.
Lovable Stranger. Philadelphia, Macrae Smith, 1949.
Beloved Enemy. London, Cassell, 1950.
Love Deferred. Philadelphia, Macrae Smith, 1951; as *Tomorrow Is Theirs*, London, Cassell, 1952.
Sugar Island. London, Cassell, 1951.
Harbour Lights. London, Cassell, 1953; New York, Arcadia House, 1954.
The Golden Summer. London, Cassell, 1954; New York, Arcadia House, 1955.
The Grand Duchess. London, Cassell, and New York, Arcadia House, 1954.
Come Back, Miranda. London, Cassell, 1955; New York, Berkley, 1974.
Fiametta. London, Cassell, 1956; New York, Arcadia House, 1958.
Castle in Spain. London, Cassell, 1958.
Violetta. London, Cassell, 1960.

*   *   *

Anne Duffield wrote from the 1920's until 1960. The appeal of her books lies in the settings which invariably involve foreign travel on ships. The romance of this world is pretty dated by modern standards and the consistency of the formula which Duffield applies means that her books will have less and less appeal. Duffield belongs to the ocean liner age, and features of that age have disappeared completely, such as the Anglo-Egyptian Community, plantation colonies, and plentiful servants. The romance of being abroad and being in love abroad, however, is a very enduring theme in Duffield's books. Whereas in *Flaming Felicia* (1934) the setting is Egypt, in the novels from the 1950's the settings move closer to home. The mystery of the orient as in *Moon over Stamboul* (1936) gives way to a more conventional holiday setting of Spain in *Castle in Spain* (1958). The traditional mystery settings of romantic novels give way to summer-holiday settings agreeable to conventional young girls. The very foreignness of the men the girls fall in love with, such as Don Eduardo in *Castle in Spain*, makes them that much more attractive. Mixed in with the excitement of foreign settings is an element of danger and mystery, such as the unexpected encounter with snakes in *Bitter Rapture* and *Bubbling Springs*. Voodoo appears in *Sugar Island*.

The girls in Duffield's books are charmingly flirtatious, attractive, and lively. Yet they are coy about revealing their true feelings for the man they love until they are ready to fall into his arms. Indeed the progression from initial repulsion from a man (for various reasons) to eventual falling in love with him forms the main interest of these novels. Other matters, such as the second man who is also in love with the heroine and the eventual outcome of his relationship with her, are inevitably incidental. The plots are drawn out and slight. They also include rather contrived incidents, such as the use of a car crash or falls from cliffs. Duffield is good at drawing the minutiae of the social relationships of various groups in the middle ranges of society, such as West Indies planter types and the expatriate British. She is very skilful with description of the clothes her heroines and other female characters wear.

Duffield's best attribute is her ability to depict local colour in foreign lands. There is, however, something dated about this as well as the clothes. Even though her 1950's novels were re-printed as late as the 1970's, to the young reader Paris and Spain are no longer romantic in themselves.

—P. R. Meldrum

DUGGAN, Alfred (Leo). British. Born in Buenos Aires, Argentina, in 1903. Educated at Balliol College, Oxford. Served in the Territorial Army in Norway, 1938–41. Married Laura Hill in 1953; one son. *Died in 1964.*

ROMANCE AND HISTORICAL PUBLICATIONS

Novels

Knight with Armour. London, Faber, and New York, Coward McCann, 1950.
Conscience of the King. London, Faber, and New York, Coward McCann, 1951.
The Little Emperors. London, Faber, 1951; New York, Coward McCann, 1953.
The Lady for Ransom. London, Faber, and New York, Coward McCann, 1953.
Leopards and Lilies. London, Faber, and New York, Coward McCann, 1954.
God and My Right. London, Faber, 1955; as *My Life for My Sheep*, New York, Coward McCann, 1955.
Winter Quarters. London, Faber, and New York, Coward McCann, 1956.
Three's Company. London, Faber, and New York, Coward McCann, 1958.
Founding Fathers. London, Faber, 1959; as *Children of the Wolf*, New York, Coward McCann, 1959.
The Cunning of the Dove. London, Faber, and New York, Pantheon, 1960.
The King of Athelrey. London, Faber, 1961; as *The Right Line of Cedric*, New York, Pantheon, 1961.
Lord Geoffrey's Fancy. London, Faber, and New York, Pantheon, 1962.
Elephants and Castles. London, Faber, 1963; as *Besieger of Cities*, New York, Pantheon, 1963.
Count Bohemond. London, Faber, 1964; New York, Pantheon, 1965.

Short Stories

Family Favourites. London, Faber, 1960; New York, Pantheon, 1961.

OTHER PUBLICATIONS

Other

Thomas Becket of Canterbury. London, Faber, 1952; as *The Falcon and the Dove: A Life of Thomas Becket of Canterbury*, New York, Pantheon, 1966.
Julius Caesar: A Great Life in Brief (biography). London, Hutchinson, and New York, Knopf, 1955.
Devil's Brood: The Angevin Family. London, Faber, and New York, Coward McCann, 1957.

He Died Old: Mithradates Eupator, King of Pontus. London, Faber, 1958; as *King of Pontus: The Life of Mithradates Eupator*, New York, Coward McCann, 1959.
The Story of the Crusades 1097–1291. London, Faber, 1963; New York, Pantheon, 1964.

Other (for children)

Look at Castles. London, Hamish Hamilton, 1960; as *The Castle Book*, New York, Pantheon, 1960.
Look at Churches. London, Hamish Hamilton, 1961; as *Arches and Spires: A Short History of English Churches from Anglo-Saxon Times*, New York, Pantheon, 1962.
Growing Up in the Thirteenth Century. London, Faber, 1962; as *Growing Up in Thirteenth-Century England*, New York, Pantheon, 1962.
The Romans. Cleveland, World, 1964.
Growing Up with the Norman Conquest. London, Faber, 1965; New York, Pantheon, 1966.

*   *   *

Alfred Duggan's historical novels stand roughly midway between those, the majority, in which our ancestors are very much like ourselves, though in bizarre costume, and those in which they are an almost alien species, haunted, indeed obsessed, by the unseen world of gods and the dead. He was particularly at home in the Roman era, the Dark Ages, Plantagenet England, and crusading Europe, liking to illuminate periods and figures hitherto only dimly seen by most readers: Romulus, Elagabalus, Cerdic, Alfred, Bohemond of Antioch. With women characters he was less sure; few of them convey the profounder sensations of an individual woman, within the hazards of worlds predominantly masculine. From the outside, however, his information is copious and suggestive.

Some women had ugly or repulsive husbands, as some women had birthdays during the Twelve Days of Christmas, never enjoying a proper celebration for themselves; it was a piece of bad luck which could not be altered. But a wife, even the wife of a nasty little boy, had a very much better time than the most beautiful or sought-after maiden. Above all, a married lady could experiment with the dangerous inclinations of love. A maiden was supposed to be as cold as ice; any gentleman of ordinary politeness who sat by her at table, or chatted with her in hall, was expected to fill his conversation with extravagant expressions of adoration; but if he met with the slightest return of his conventional affection he would be dismayed, and the bystanders would be shocked, that a woman should be so ignorant of the rules of polite society. A wife was different. By common consent she could not be in love with her husband, since he took by right what all women desired to yield as a favour; but she had been awakened to the possibilities of love, and public opinion would be pleased if she took some knight as her official cavalier to serve her in public and wear her colours in battle. Whether his extremely public devotion was ever rewarded in private hardly mattered except to her husband: possibly the cavalier himself enjoyed the ardours of the chase without any desire to capture his quarry; but a formal attachment was one of the recognised diversions permitted to a lady of a great castle.

This passage (from *Leopards and Lilies*) is typical: precise, cool, dryly amused at human behaviour.

All the novels are excellent stories enclosing serious themes. Moral principles clash with urgent political expediencies: wars, particularly religious wars, expose markedly ambiguous motives: power and faith can be mere appetite, can be responsibility. Evelyn Waugh wrote: "His religious faith is latent in all he wrote. Never a propagandist or an apologist, he accepted the Church as the only proper milieu of man, and man as being naturally prone to fall below Christian principle." Perhaps one of his finest passages is the ironical conclusion of *Conscience of the King*, in which Cerdic, the remote ancestor of our own royal house, reflects that he has survived the barbarian invaders, made his peace with them, defected from the Church, become a ruler among people with gross habits. He has seen a civilisation dissolve but all is as well as could be hoped. And then the doubt: "Suppose all that nonsense (Christianity) that my brother used to preach is really true after all?"

Duggan's first novel was published when he was 47. Thereafter he never very obviously developed, certainly never lapsed, but continued imperturbably grappling with far-off passions and illusions, battles and intrigues, adventures and betrayals, without deviating into glib romanticism or eloquent sentimentality. History without operatics. Indeed, his dialogue may jar on those used to the Prithee-Tush school.

"Ah, there you are, Edgar," she began with a charming smile, "Can you spare me a moment? There's something I want from the King, something very absurd, I'm afraid. If I ask him at the wrong time he may tell me not to be silly. Yet I really want it, to please a great friend of mine. Do you know Godiva, the wife of Wulf? (*The Cunning of the Dove*). Detractors may giggle, then complain that Duggan offers animated chronicles rather than novels, compromising between fact and fiction, without fully realising either. Admirers can retort that art is a useful access to history, and that, in his economical way, Duggan is not exploiting history for jocose vulgarity or a fireworks display of "atmosphere." His "Dove" is Edward the Confessor, portrayed not as a conventional pious nonentity but as a practical ruler of exceptional courage and moral stamina, whose values and resources baffle, irritate, finally outface most of his violent peers. It is the strength of the reed in the wind. A sight of an intellectual engaged in brutal realities is always absorbing, as are the problems of authority. Edward never masters the direct management of men, but also never falters in his patient insistence on civilised values. His sainthood is neither smug nor archaic, but convincing, necessary and, however obliquely, powerful. Beneath a manner often casual, even chatty, Duggan's achievement here and in his other novels, biographies and children's histories deserves attention and should certainly give pleasure.

—Peter Vansittart

---

du MAURIER, Daphne. British. Born in London, 13 May 1907; daughter of the actor/manager Sir Gerald du Maurier; granddaughter of the writer George du Maurier. Educated privately and in Paris. Married Lieutenant-General Sir Frederick Browning in 1932 (died 1965); two daughters and one son. Recipient: Mystery Writers of America Grand Master award, 1977. Fellow, Royal Society of Literature, 1952. D.B.E. (Dame Commander, Order of the British Empire), 1969. *Died 19 April 1989.*

ROMANCE AND HISTORICAL PUBLICATIONS

Novels

The Loving Spirit. London, Heinemann, and New York, Doubleday, 1931.
I'll Never Be Young Again. London, Heinemann, and New York, Doubleday, 1932.
The Progress of Julius. London, Heinemann, and New York, Doubleday, 1933.
Jamaica Inn. London, Gollancz, and New York, Doubleday, 1936.
Rebecca. London, Gollancz, and New York, Doubleday, 1938.
Frenchman's Creek. London, Gollancz, 1941; New York, Doubleday, 1942.
Hungry Hill. London, Gollancz, and New York, Doubleday, 1943.
The King's General. London, Gollancz, and New York, Doubleday, 1946.
The Parasites. London, Gollancz, 1949; New York, Doubleday, 1950.
My Cousin Rachel. London, Gollancz, 1951; New York, Doubleday, 1952.
Mary Anne. London, Gollancz, and New York, Doubleday, 1954.
The Scapegoat. London, Gollancz, and New York, Doubleday, 1957.
Castle Dor, by Arthur Quiller-Couch, completed by du Maurier. London, Dent, and New York, Doubleday, 1962.
The Glass-Blowers. London, Gollancz, and New York, Doubleday, 1963.
The Flight of the Falcon. London, Gollancz, and New York, Doubleday, 1965.
The House on the Strand. London, Gollancz, and New York, Doubleday, 1969.
Rule Britannia. London, Gollancz, 1972; New York, Doubleday, 1973.

Short Stories

Happy Christmas (story). New York, Doubleday 1940; London, Todd, 1943.
Come Wind, Come Weather. London, Heinemann, 1940; New York, Doubleday, 1941.
Nothing Hurts for Long, and Escort. London, Todd, 1943.
Consider the Lilies (story). London, Todd, 1943.
Spring Picture (story). London, Todd, 1944.
Leading Lady (story). London, Vallancey Press, 1945.
London and Paris (two stories). London, Vallancey Press, 1945.
The Apple Tree: A Short Novel, and Some Stories. London, Gollancz, 1952; as *Kiss Me Again, Stranger: A Collection of Eight Stories, Long and Short*, New York, Doubleday, 1953; as *The Birds and Other Stories*, London, Penguin, 1968.
Early Stories. London, Todd, 1954.
The Breaking Point: Eight Stories. London, Gollancz, and New York, Doubleday, 1959; as *The Blue Lenses and Other Stories*, London, Penguin, 1970.
The Treasury of du Maurier Short Stories. London, Gollancz, 1960.
The Lover and Other Stories. London, Ace, 1961.
Not after Midnight and Other Stories. London, Gollancz, 1971; as *Don't Look Now*, New York, Doubleday, 1971.
Echoes from the Macabre: Selected Stories. London, Gollancz, 1976; New York, Doubleday, 1977.
The Rendezvous and Other Stories. London, Gollancz, 1980.

Classics of the Macabre. London, Gollancz, and New York, Doubleday, 1987.

OTHER PUBLICATIONS

Plays

Rebecca, adaptation of her own novel (produced Manchester and London, 1940; New York, 1945). London, Gollancz, 1940; New York, Dramatists Play Service, 1943.
The Years Between (produced Manchester, 1944; London, 1945). London, Gollancz, 1945; New York, Doubleday, 1946.
September Tide (produced Oxford and London, 1948). London, Gollancz, 1949; New York, Doubleday, 1950.

Screenplay: *Hungry Hill*, with Terence Young and Francis Crowdry, 1947.

Television Play: *The Breakthrough*, 1976.

Other

Gerald: A Portrait (on Gerald du Maurier). London, Gollancz, 1934; New York, Doubleday, 1935.
The du Mauriers. London, Gollancz, and New York, Doubleday, 1937.
The Infernal World of Branwell Brontë. London, Gollancz, 1960; New York, Doubleday, 1961.
Vanishing Cornwall, photographs of Christian Browning. London, Gollancz, and New York, Doubleday, 1967.
Golden Lads: Sir Francis Bacon, Anthony Bacon and Their Friends. London, Gollancz, and New York, Doubleday, 1975.
The Winding Stair: Francis Bacon, His Rise and Fall. London, Gollancz, 1976; New York, Doubleday, 1977.
Growing Pains: The Shaping of a Writer (autobiography). London, Gollancz, 1977; as *Myself When Young*, New York, Doubleday, 1977.
The Rebecca Notebook and Other Memories (includes short stories). New York, Doubleday, 1980; London, Gollancz, 1981.

Editor, *The Young George du Maurier: A Selection of His Letters 1860–1867*. London, Davies, 1951; New York, Doubleday, 1952.
Editor, *Best Stories*, by Phyllis Bottome. London, Faber, 1963.

*   *   *

A prolific and inventive writer, Daphne du Maurier never hesitated to experiment with genres, and she has been widely praised for her short stories, plays, biographies, and autobiographies. It is her novels, however, which won her the widest fame and a vast following among readers, many of whom consider her to be primarily a consummate writer of love stories.

Certainly a love story is an important facet of almost every du Maurier novel; moreover, there are several other recurring devices—the settings often celebrate her chosen home county, Cornwall, and frequently she depicts some exciting historical period. Furthermore, du Maurier's most successful, most famous novels fall into three general categories: gothics, romances, and family sagas.

Nevertheless, each book is fresh and different from the others because of the ingenuity and variety with which she combined these elements. *The House on the Strand*, for example, is perhaps her most daring blend, a combination of historical novel, science fiction, and crime tale. Here, two very difficult love affairs, one in the 14th century, one in the 20th, parallel and complicate each other through the time travels of the protagonist, Richard Young. In *The Scapegoat*, featuring one of du Maurier's most improbable but remarkably persuasive plots (one man's forced impersonation of another), a courtship long since destroyed by ambition and greed remains the source of familial hatred and disruption. The introduction of John, the contemporary hero, to sexual fulfillment parallels and illuminates the older story.

The family sagas *The Loving Spirit* and *Hungry Hill* focus upon history, locale, and personality. The novels depict several members of their central families—the Cornish, seafaring Coombes (*Spirit*) and the Irish, copper-mining Brodricks (*Hill*)—comparing and contrasting the dominant personality in various generations. In these novels the love stories serve primarily to reveal character or to motivate subplot. In *The Flight of the Falcon* and *Rule Britannia*, also family histories though much less panoramic, the love interest is again subordinated, employed as but one of several traditional devices which stimulate the maturations of the protagonists who must confront political oppression, the novels' themes. All four books concern themselves with heritage, with relatives' use of similar and contrasting abilities and traits.

In her gothic novels, however, du Maurier moves the maturation story to center stage, and the love motif becomes the major motivating force. *Jamaica Inn* recounts the adventures of orphaned Mary Yellan who comes to live with her aunt and her uncle, a criminal. Smuggler Joss Merlyn; his outlaw brother, Jem; and Francis Davey, a local vicar, are all attracted to and attract Mary, and she struggles with head, heart, and honor to balance passion, family loyalty, and regard for human life, ultimately opting to follow her heart despite the high cost. Dona St. Columb, the protagonist of *Frenchman's Creek*, a bored, beautiful noblewoman, plays at crime and flirts with infidelity until she takes a daring French pirate as her lover. From him she learns the meaning of responsibility, maturing at last into the woman she was meant to be. Ironically, his lessons in love and duty force her back into the roles of wife and mother, largely in order to free her lover to meet his own destiny. Prisoners of their sex, Mary Yellan accepts and Dona St. Columb renounces a lover because passion leaves them no choice; maturation means surrender.

For Philip Ashley, protagonist of *My Cousin Rachel*, maturity means torment, for he falls in love with the widow of Ambrose, his cousin and foster father, only to come to suspect Rachel of having poisoned Ambrose. An indecisive youth, Philip finally takes independent, irreversible action (symbol of his delayed maturation), resigning himself to constant future doubt over Rachel's true guilt. In a clever twist, the gothic protagonist here is a young man rather than a girl, and ultimately, Philip opts for kin and heritage rather than for passionate love.

Rebecca, du Maurier's finest and best-known novel, is considered a prototype for the modern gothic. It is the story of a penniless, unnamed girl, a Cinderella figure, who makes an apparently ideal marriage to wealthy Maxim de Winter, a widower. But the heroine's dream of marital happiness and of self-confidence, identity, and maturity as mistress of Manderley, one of Britain's great houses, is quickly banished by the haunting memory of the seemingly perfect, glamorous, beautiful Rebecca, Maxim's first wife. Not until grim secrets about Rebecca are revealed and Maxim's life is consequently threatened can the protagonist take her place as his genuine helpmeet, as a grown woman. Her delayed maturation and happiness are dimmed, however, yielding only subdued, if steadfast, love. This "fairy tale" has a realistic, ironic ending.

Du Maurier's romances are also well laced with irony, a quality which combines with deft characterization to set them above many similar novels. *The King's General* is the story of crippled Honor Harris's lifelong love for Sir Richard Grenvile, the title character. Their fortunes are linked to the history of Menabilly (also partial inspiration for the Manderley of *Rebecca*), and the house stands for the endurance of the leading families amid the conflict between the Royalists and the Parliamentary Armies.

Also bittersweet is the love affair central to *Castle Dor* (begun by Arthur Quiller-Couch and completed by du Maurier), a treatment of the Tristan and Iseult legend set in the 19th century. The doomed romance between Richard, a *Bildungsroman* hero, and Hesta, his first love, is the most memorable section of *I'll Never Be Young Again*, and it is this relationship more than any other which forms Richard's character.

Readers' praise of du Maurier's ability as a teller of love tales is clearly an appropriate response to her fiction; it should not, however, overshadow appreciation of her equally great skill as an innovator with plot, character, and setting.

—Jane S. Bakerman

DUNNETT, Dorothy (née Halliday). Also writes as Dorothy Halliday. British. Born in Dunfermline, Fife, 25 August 1923. Educated at James Gillespie's High School, Edinburgh; Edinburgh College of Art; Glasgow School of Art. Married Alastair M. Dunnett in 1946; two sons. Assistant press officer, Scottish government departments, Edinburgh, 1940–46; member of the Board of Trade Scottish Economic Research Department, Glasgow, 1946–55. Since 1950 professional portrait painter: exhibitions at the Royal Scottish Academy, Edinburgh; since 1979 director, Scottish Television plc, Edinburgh. Since 1986 trustee, National Library of Scotland. Recipient: Scottish Arts Council award, 1976. Fellow, Royal Society of Arts, 1986. Agent: Curtis Brown, 162–168 Regent Street, London W1R 5TB, England. Address: 87 Colinton Road, Edinburgh EH10 5DF, Scotland.

ROMANCE AND HISTORICAL PUBLICATIONS

Novels (series: Dolly; House of Niccolò; Lymond; Dolly books prior to *Bird of Paradise* published as Dorothy Halliday in UK)

The Game of Kings (Lymond). New York, Putnam, 1961; London, Cassell, 1962.
Queens' Play (Lymond). London, Cassell, and New York, Putnam, 1964.
The Disorderly Knights (Lymond). London, Cassell, and New York, Putnam, 1966.
Dolly and the Singing Bird. London, Cassell, 1968; as *The Photogenic Soprano*, Boston, Houghton Mifflin, 1968.
Pawn in Frankincense (Lymond). London, Cassell, and New York, Putnam, 1969.
Dolly and the Cookie Bird. London, Cassell, 1970; as *Murder in the Round*, Boston, Houghton Mifflin, 1970.
The Ringed Castle (Lymond). London, Cassell, 1971; New York, Putnam, 1972.
Dolly and the Doctor Bird. London, Cassell, 1971; as *Match for a Murderer*, Boston, Houghton Mifflin, 1971.
Dolly and the Starry Bird. London, Cassell, 1973; as *Murder in Focus*, Boston, Houghton Mifflin, 1973.

Checkmate (Lymond). London, Cassell, and New York, Putnam, 1975.
Dolly and the Nanny Bird. London, Joseph, 1976; New York, Knopf, 1982.
King Hereafter. London, Joseph, and New York, Knopf, 1982.
Dolly and the Bird of Paradise. London, Joseph, 1983; New York, Knopf, 1984.
Niccolò Rising. London, Joseph, and New York, Knopf, 1986.
The Spring of the Ram (Niccolò). London, Joseph 1987; New York, Knopf, 1988.

OTHER PUBLICATIONS

Other

The Scottish Highlands, with Alastair M. Dunnett, photographs by David Paterson. Edinburgh, Mainstream, 1988.

*

Bibliography: in *Book and Magazine Collector 53* (London), August 1988.

* * *

Dorothy Dunnett's historical novels were once described by a reviewer as "a stylish blend of high romance and high camp." This is true, but they are more than this. They are long, complex books, full of action and violence, wit and surprises. The research is thorough, not only for the everyday life of the times but for esoteric details. Above all her characters are fully realised, their dialogue sophisticated and allusive.

King Hereafter is more serious than her series books, starker and more saga-like as befits the tale of Thorfinn, Earl of Orkney who, we learn almost in an aside, was also known as Macbeth. He and his wife are totally unlike their counterparts in Shakespeare's play, but probably closer to the realities of the 11th century. Thorfinn is a difficult man, courageous and skillful, a wonderful lover, a Viking sea-rover as well as a prince who, in the end, sacrifices himself for his people. But this is a less appealing book than her others. The dialogue is occasionally obscure and the sheer number of characters is sometimes confusing, but novelized historical biography tends to be less shapely than historical romance.

The Lymond stories chart 10 years in the life of a younger son of an aristocratic Scottish family in the 16th century who travels the known world of his time, even uncharted Russia in *The Ringed Castle.* Each one of the six books is fascinating and makes one want to read the next in the series. Francis Crawford of Lymond has a talent for getting into scrapes and out again, he is a leader of men and a charmer of women. He is one of the most attractive heroes in Dunnett's historical romance—"a man of wit and crooked felicities, born to luxury and heir to a fortune." There is a mystery about his birth which is pursued throughout the series and is finally uncovered by Philippa Somerville. She is an unlikely heroine, starting off as a stolid 10-year-old who hates him. After a country upbringing in Northumberland, because of her concern for Lymond's bastard child, she travels to the Middle East and has the harem of Suleiman the Magnificent as a finishing school. She is married to Lymond for convention's sake and she determines to solve the riddle of his origins. Lymond finally falls in love with her just when she can't bear him to touch her because of a hideous experience during her search. When all seems lost, it all ends happily.

The The House of Niccolò books are set in the 15th century. Claes, the hero (also known as Nicholas and Niccolò) is a 17-year-old apprentice of the House of Charretty of Bruges—dyers, merchants and suppliers of mercenaries. We are told he is "good natured, randy and innocent." He is also an accomplished mimic and clown, clever with his fingers, brilliant at figures, and loyal to his employer, Marian de Charretty. She took him in at 10, the bastard of a distant relative.

In *Niccolò Rising* Claes falls foul of an arrogant Scottish nobleman and a feud begins. It is soon apparent that Claes is not the fool he pretends to be, nor is he as innocent. Like Lymond's, there is something mysterious about his parentage which we assume will be unravelled as the series progresses. Adventures and complications abound. Claes goes to Italy where his many gifts bring him into contact and familiarity with important merchants, bankers, and princes. Secrets about alum, so important to dyers, are confided to him. He returns to Bruges having set up a courier and intelligence service. There he has to deal with malice, jealousy, and danger. He ends the book married to Marian de Charretty which gives him power and status.

The Spring of the Ram takes Nicholas to Trebizond as a merchant adventurer and charts his adventures among the Byzantine Greeks. Besides his enemies from the first book, he aquires new ones, including his young step daughter and her malicious husband. He acquires friends and colleagues too and begins to learn painful lessons about himself and his relationships with others.

Although Nicholas and Lymond come from very different backgrounds, there are similarities. Both of them have an arrogance and stubbornness which make them vulnerable; both change and develop as the books progress through meeting brutal challenges and having to make difficult choices. Both are wonderful lovers. Both are pitted against suave villains who are cruel, ruthless and have venomous tongues. Several times both heroes are brought close to death, Lymond even by his own hand.

It all makes for wonderful reading for Dunnett excels in portraying spectacular set pieces which are at once heart-stopping and witty, set against richly textured backgrounds. In *Queens' Play* there is a reckless, moonlit treasure hunt across the roofs of Blois undertaken by the young bloods of Henri II's dissolute court; *Pawn in Frankincense* features a game of chess with live chess pieces who are killed as they are forfeited; in *Niccolò Rising* the hero has to escape from a barrel on a fire-ship in the midst of a firework display.

There are wonderful moments of farce, too, like the fight in the Turkish bath caused by spies disguised as nuns in *Pawn in Frankincense* and the three young men lolling in the Duke of Burgundy's gold bath aboard a lighter which inadvertently sinks the gun the Duke was sending to the King of Scots in *Niccolò Rising*, a book which ends with Nicholas having a wild ride on a plucked ostrich.

These elegantly crafted books are a joy to read and so intricately plotted that they can be read and reread with undiminished pleasure.

—Pamela Cleaver

————

DUVAL, Jeanne. See **COFFMAN, Virginia.**

————

DWYER-JOYCE, Alice (Louise, née Myles). British. Born in Birr, Offaly, Ireland, 7 September 1913. Educated at Birr Model School; Alexandra College, Dublin; Royal College of Surgeons, Dublin, medical degree 1936; Richmond Hospital, Dublin. Married Robert Dwyer-Joyce in 1936; one son. In general medical practice with her husband, 1936–78, Histon, Cambridgeshire; medical officer, Midfield Children's Home, Oakington, Cambridgeshire, for 20 years. *Died 9 February 1986.*

ROMANCE AND HISTORICAL PUBLICATIONS

Novels (series: Dr. Esmond Ross)

Price of Inheritance. London, Hale, 1963.
The Silent Lady. London, Hale, 1964.
Dr. Ross of Harton. London, Hale, 1966.
The Story of Doctor Esmond Ross. London, Hale, 1967.
Verdict on Doctor Esmond Ross. London, Hale, 1968.
Dial Emergency for Dr. Ross. London, Hale, 1969.
Don't Cage Me Wild. London, Hale, 1970.
For I Have Lived Today. London, Hale, 1971.
Message for Doctor Ross. London, Hale, 1971.
Cry the Soft Rain. London, Hale, 1972; New York, St. Martin's Press, 1974.
Reach for the Shadows. London, Hale, 1972; New York, St. Martin's Press, 1973.
The Rainbow Glass. London, Hale, and New York, St. Martin's Press, 1973.
The Brass Islands. London, Hale, 1974.
Prescription for Melissa. London, Hale, 1974.
The Moonlit Way. London, Hale, and New York, St. Martin's Press, 1974.
The Strolling Players. London, Hale, and New York, St. Martin's Press, 1975.
The Diamond Cage. London, Hale, and New York, St. Martin's Press, 1976.
The Master of Jethart. London, Hale, and New York, St. Martin's Press, 1976.
The Gingerbread House. London, Hale, and New York, St. Martin's Press, 1977.
The Banshee Tide. London, Hale, 1977.
The Storm of Wrath. London, Hale, 1977; New York, St. Martin's Press, 1978.
The Glitter-Dust. London, Hale, and New York, St. Martin's Press, 1978.
Lachlan's Woman. London, Hale, and New York, St. Martin's Press, 1979.
Danny Boy. London, Hale, 1979.
The Swiftest Eagle. London, Hale, and New York, St. Martin's Press, 1979.
The House of Jackdaws. London, Hale, and New York, St. Martin's Press, 1980.
The Chieftain. London, Hale, 1980.
The Penny Box. London, Hale, and New York, St. Martin's Press, 1980.
The Glass Heiress. London, Hale, 1981; New York, St. Martin's Press, 1982.
The Cornelian Strand. London, Hale, 1982.
The Unwinding Corner. London, Hale, and New York, St. Martin's Press, 1983.
Gibbet Fen. London, Hale, and New York, St. Martin's Press, 1984.

*

Alice Dwyer-Joyce commented:

(1982) I started to write in about 1960, in the midst of a life full of activity, and I was glad of it in 1978 when I got severe arthritis. The authorship has been my escape from the ferocity of disablement.

*   *   *

Alice Dwyer-Joyce brings the stuff of dreams to an everyday world. A touch of magic gilds the remote island communities of her novels, with their ruined castles and half-remembered ancestral ghosts. Elements of folklore and fairytale seem always present—whether the wicked stepmother of *The Gingerbread House*, or the hero of princely lineage who appears in so many of her works. The line between good and evil is sharply drawn—heroes are perfect and unflawed, villains irredeemably wicked. The morality, as in most fairy tales, is Old Testament, with such crimes as adultery and deception punished by death and the wrongdoers irrevocably damned. The shadow of old wrongs remains to haunt later generations, and her books abound with talismans to ward off the unappeased spirits—''The Penny Box,'' the waterfall in *The Rainbow Glass*, the woolly monkey in *The Master of Jethart*.

A natural prose poet, Dwyer-Joyce is also a qualified doctor, and in many of her works the roles of artist and healer are given an equal emphasis. The early ''Dr. Ross'' novels which helped to establish her popularity made effective use of her medical knowledge, and the hospital environment serves as background for the novels featuring Dr. Catriona Chisholm—*For I Have Lived Today* and *Prescription for Melissa*. The missionary figure of the doctor martyred in Third World revolution is also a recurrent theme, notably in *Lachlan's Woman*, whose story includes a princely hero betrayed by a faithless wife. There are other works with exotic locations, for example *The Swiftest Eagle*, where action moves from Malaya to Cambodia and its exodus of refugees. Always, though, the author returns to those bleak coastal settings—Ireland or the West Isles—where her atmosphere is strongest, and her Celtic gifts as a storyteller are allowed their fullest expression. Such works as *The Banshee Tide*, with its picture of rural Ireland, or *The Brass Islands* are typical, the highly poeticised speech of the characters in keeping with the landscape they inhabit. *The Chieftain* follows an Irish-American tycoon in search of his roots, evoked by the diary of an ancestor in the 1850's, and *The Glass Heiress* explores the theme of a ghostly past. Essentially her message remains the same: the determined heroine struggling against evil or circumstance, fulfilled at last by the love of the noble prince-hero come out of the West, who will help her rebuild the fallen castle and bring back the greatness to their house.

—Geoffrey Sadler

DYMOKE, Juliet. Pseudonym for Juliet Dymoke de Schanschieff. British. Born in Enfield, Middlesex, 28 June 1919. Educated at Chantry Mount School. Married Hugo de Schanschieff in 1942; one daughter. Worked for the Bank of England, London, 1937–42, and for the Canadian Army Medical Records department, London, 1942–44; script reader, Ealing Film Studios, Paramount Films, and Samuel Bronston Productions, 1950–63. Address: c/o Severn House Publishers, 35 Manor Road, Wellington, Surrey SM6 0BW, England.

ROMANCE AND HISTORICAL PUBLICATIONS

Novels (series: Plantagenets)

The Orange Sash. London, Jarrolds, 1958.
Born for Victory. London, Jarrolds, 1960.
Treason in November. London, Jarrolds, 1961.
Bend Sinister. London, Jarrolds, 1962.
The Cloisterman. London, Dobson, 1969.
Of the Ring of Earls. London, Dobson, 1970.
Henry of the High Rock. London, Dobson, 1971.
Serpent in Eden. London, Wingate, 1973.
The Lion's Legacy. London, Dobson, 1974.
Shadows on a Throne. London, Wingate, 1976.
A Pride of Kings (Plantagenets). London, Dobson, 1978.
The Royal Griffin (Plantagenets). London, Dobson, 1978; New York, Ace, 1980.
The White Cockade. London, Dobson, 1979.
Lady of the Garter (Plantagenets). London, Dobson, 1979; New York, Ace, 1980.
The Lion of Mortimer (Plantagenets). London, Dobson, 1979; New York, Ace, 1980.
The Lord of Greenwich (Plantagenets). London, Dobson, 1980.
The Sun in Splendour (Plantagenets). London, Dobson, 1980.
A Kind of Warfare. London, Dobson, 1981.
The Queen's Diamond. London, Severn House, 1983.
March to Corunna. London, Severn House, 1985.
Two Flags for France. London, Severn House, 1986.
A Border Knight. London, Severn House, 1987.

OTHER PUBLICATIONS

Other (for children)

The Sons of the Tribune: An Adventure on the Roman Wall. London, Arnold, 1956.
London in the 18th Century. London, Longman, 1958.
Prisoner of Rome. London, Dobson, 1975.
Aboard the Mary Rose. London, Severn House, 1985.
The Spanish Boy. London, Severn House, 1987.

*

Juliet Dymoke comments:

My work as an historical novelist naturally includes a great deal of research, and this perhaps is the most exacting as well as a very pleasurable part of my work. I write mainly about England as I know and love England, and I try not to start on a description of a place I do not know without making every effort to see it—it is so easy to be caught out! I am passionately interested in history, European as well as English, but it is the past of these islands that interests me most, and I am fascinated by the lives of our forebears, and how they are similar to and dissimilar from our own. I can trace my own ancestry back to the Norman Conquest and perhaps this was the spur, or the inheritance, that set me on my career. I hope through my work to reach a large number of people, to interest them in the history that has made this country, perhaps in some way to influence them for good— as I myself was influenced by the historical writers I once read.

*   *   *

Juliet Dymoke restricts herself neither to one historical era nor to one set mode of novel construction: these facts give some idea of her ambitiousness. Realism and simplicity rather than gothic

sensationalism or high drama are hallmarks of her style. Romance, too, is a central feature, often driving forward the historical action.

Dymoke mingles fact and fiction in all her works. In her early novel *Treason in November* she recounts actual events with the focus on a central, fictitious character. Piers Mallory becomes implicated in the Gunpowder Plot of 1605 through a chance acquaintance with one of its instigators, Robert Catesby. Romance is something of a sideline, the central theme being Piers's journey of self-discovery and the restoring of his good name. Similarly, *The Cloisterman* shows Dymoke's own creations coexisting and interacting with historical figures. However, *The Cloisterman* is less reliant upon fact: it is the tale of a fictitious individual in the historical milieu of the early reign of Henry VIII. The opening depicts Sir Thomas More, awaiting execution, writing a farewell note to Julian, the central character. The origin and development of their friendship, in flashback, forms the story.

Shadows on a Throne, though dealing with similar material, could not hope to match the horror and depth of Shakespeare's *Macbeth*. Dymoke's approach better suits her brand of historical fact than legend, with all its irrationality and mysticism. Her series on the Plantagenet dynasty, a daunting enterprise, illustrates this well.

The first in the series, *A Pride of Kings*, covers much ground: the action moves swiftly, sometimes from one country to another, without loss of continuity. William Marshall is seen to serve the successive monarchs Henry III, Richard the Lionheart, and John. Meanwhile, his marriage at middle-age to a 16-year-old girl is sensitively portrayed, as is its development into a satisfying companionship. In *The Royal Griffin* King John's daughter Eleanor marries her first husband for security and her second, Simon de Montfort, for excitement; alongside the comparison of these two marriages, de Montfort's career from commoner to duke is followed to its tragic end. *The Lion of Mortimer* explores the relationship between Edward II and Piers Gaveston. *The Lord of Greenwich* shows the extremes of scholasticism and sensuousness in the personality of Humfrey of Gloucester, while the reader is also taken through the campaigns against France, including an account of the Battle of Agincourt.

The Queen's Diamond, set mainly in France during the latter stages of the revolution, involves some of the descendants of characters in Dymoke's 18th-century Scottish novel *The White Cockade* and depends for much of its theme on the tension between political and personal allegiances. This issue is taken up again in *Two Flags for France*, set some 20 years later, though in the latter novel the relationship between Louis de la Rouelle and his ward, Julie, throws these dilemmas into much sharper focus. The political situation and Napoleon's attempt to reassert power serve not merely as a backdrop, but come to be inextricably linked to the course of Louis and Julie's relationship.

Dymoke's most recent work, *A Border Knight*, returns to the era of the Plantagenets, focusing this time upon the career of Harry "Hotspur" Percy.

—Anne M. Shields

EAGLES, Cynthia Harrod. See HARROD-EAGLES, Cynthia.

EATON, Evelyn (Sybil Mary). American. Born in Montreux, Switzerland, 22 December 1902; became United States citizen, 1944. Educated at the Sorbonne, Paris, 1920–21. Married Ernst Paul Richard Viedt in 1928 (divorced 1934); one daughter. Lecturer, Columbia University, New York, 1949–51, for the arts program of the Association of American Colleges, 1950–60, at Sweet Briar College, Virginia, 1951–60, Adult Education Centers, Virginia, 1955–60, Mary Washington College, Fredericksburg, Virginia, 1957–59, Montalvo Association, 1960 and 1963, Hartford Foundation, 1960 and 1962, Deep Springs College, 1961, Ohio University, Athens, 1962, and Pershing College, 1967. Member, Board of Directors, Draco Foundation of Virginia, 1958; founder, Draco Foundation of California Inc., 1965, and Deepest Valley Theater, Owens Valley, California, 1965. Vice-president, Canadian Authors Association, 1940–41. Recipient: John Masefield award, 1923.

ROMANCE AND HISTORICAL PUBLICATIONS

Novels (series: Arcadian trilogy)

The Hours of Iris. London, Baskerville, 1928.
Summer Dust. London, Bles, 1936.
Pray to the Earth. Boston, Houghton Mifflin, 1938; London, Cassell, 1946.
Canadian Circus. London, Nelson, 1939.
Arcadian trilogy:
    Quietly My Captain Waits. New York, Harper, and London, Cassell, 1940.
    Restless Are the Sails. New York, Harper, 1941; London, Cassell, 1942.
    The Sea Is So Wide. New York, Harper, 1943; London, Cassell, 1944.
In What Torn Ship. New York, Harper, 1944; London, Cassell, 1946.
Heart in Pilgrimage, with E. R. Moore. New York, Harper, 1948.
Give Me Your Golden Hand. New York, Farrar Straus, 1951.
Flight. Indianapolis, Bobbs Merrill, and London, Gollancz, 1954.
I Saw My Mortal Sight. New York, Random House, 1959; London, Cassell, 1960.
The King Is a Witch. London, Cassell, 1965; New York, St. Martin's Press, 1974.
Go Ask the River. New York, Harcourt Brace, and London, Cassell, 1969.

OTHER PUBLICATIONS

Novels

Desire—Spanish Version. London, Chapman and Hall, 1932; New York, Morrow, 1933.
Canadian Circus. London, Nelson, 1939.
By Just Exchange. London, Cassell, 1952.

Verse

Stolen Hours. London, Selwyn and Blount, 1923.
The Interpreter. London, Selwyn and Blount, 1925.
The Encircling Mist (includes prose). London, Selwyn and Blount, 1935.
Birds Before Dawn. Toronto, Ryerson, 1943.

The Small Hour. Francis Town, New Hampshire, Golden Quill Press, 1955.
Love Is Recognition. Georgetown, California, Dragon's Teeth Press, 1971.

Other

Every Month Was May (autobiography), with Edward Roberts Moore. New York, Harper, 1947; London, Gollancz, 1949.
The North Star Is Nearer (autobiography). New York, Farrar Straus, and London, Gollancz, 1949.

*   *   *

In her historical writings Evelyn Eaton specialized in the European and Canadian scene during the first three-quarters of the 18th century. *Every Month Was May* and *The North Star Is Nearer*, Eaton's two autobiographical volumes, indicate that she used historical settings with which she was personally familiar in their present day character: Nova Scotia, New England, England, Paris, southern France, and Corsica. Indeed, her life story seems to have provided the background material for most of her fiction.

Two novels, *Canadian Circus*, a kidnapping mystery located in Nova Scotia, and *Desire—Spanish Version*, based on Eaton's experiences at the Paramount studios near Paris, are not historical, strictly speaking, but provide documentation of events that are of interest to the reader who sees the text as historical in itself. The latter novel provides a wealth of detail for anyone interested in film production in the early 1930's.

Pray to the Earth and *In What Torn Ship* derive their sense of immediacy from Eaton's knowledge of the Callian-in-the-Var region of southern France and of Corsica, respectively. *Pray to the Earth*, apart from describing the rural conditions at the time of the Spanish Civil War, also concerns itself with scenes from the life of the main character, Louis-Jean Jacquier, variously a herdsman and farm hand, a member of the Carpathian Knights Templar, and a reluctant fighter with the Spanish leftists. Covering the period 1755 to 1769, *In What Torn Ship* follows the generalship of Pascal Paoli who attempted to unite Corsica against the Genoese, losing the island in the end to France. Again, Eaton's knowledge of the land allows her to draw the landscape with a fine hand.

Two very different novels characterize her later work in the 1950's and 1960's. The main character in *Give Me Your Golden Hand* is Axford Daigle, eldest son of George III of England and a Quaker girl whom he married when he was underage, who emigrates and settles in the American colonies at the outbreak of the American revolution. *Go Ask the River*, Eaton's last historical novel, reflects the interest in China she developed during a visit there as a news correspondent shortly after becoming an American citizen. The main character is a Tang dynasty courtesan, Hsueh T'ao, and the novel presents her life from A.D. 760 to 824. This novel is rich in philosophical and cultural detail and is Eaton's most densely and skilfully written book.

But ultimately Eaton's reputation as a writer of fine historical fiction rests on three novels written in the middle of her career. *Quietly My Captain Waits* is set mainly in Fort Port Royal, New France, between the years 1691 and 1710, and focuses on the life of Madame Freneuse and her love for Pierre de Bonaventure. *Restless Are the Sails* covers 1744 to 1746 and deals with the siege and fall of Louisbourg from France to England. *The Sea Is So Wide* forcefully presents the expulsion of the Acadians by the English in 1755. Close attention to historical detail is present in each of these novels in the form of maps, transcriptions, and translations by the author of evidence ranging from official dispatches to personal letters. Such documentation, skilfully worked into the narrative, rather than set aside in a preface or notes, adds to the sense of period and locale given in detailed descriptions of buildings, persons, costumes, manners, conveyances, and landscape. However, historical verisimilitude in these novels serves to heighten the sense of the atrocities around which the plots are built rather than to distance them through nostalgia or romance.

Apart from the Acadian trilogy, Eaton's most successful historical novel is *Heart in Pilgrimage*, which presents the life of Elizabeth Ann Seton, who founded the Sisters of Charity and became Mother Superior of the Convent of the Sisters of St. Joseph in New York City, from her marriage in 1794 to her death in 1821. The novel is filled with the details of both the prosperous household of her husband's shipping family and the austere conditions of Elizabeth's life after her conversion to Catholicism. The novel successfully persuades us to accept this abrupt change as Elizabeth's response to the poverty into which she was thrown upon the death of her husband; the most significant alteration to her circumstances was her move to a house that faced the wharves where the poorest immigrants landed and were temporarily housed. Eaton's compelling fictionalisation of Elizabeth's history approaches the best work in her Acadian novels.

Eaton's touch is not a delicate one in that she graphically depicts violent actions with an eye to a very human sort of cruelty and pathetic scenes of the filth of bodily processes, natural and diseased, with unsettlingly memorable images. But her emphasis on the strength of the spirit in her characters balances the picture and lends a poignancy to the fleeting romantic element in her work frequently missing from less thorough historical realist fiction.

—Heather Iris Jones

EBEL, Suzanne. Also writes as Suzanne Goodwin; Cecily Shelbourne. British. Born in London. Educated at Roman Catholic schools in England and Belgium. Married John Goodwin in 1948; one daughter and two sons. Journalist, *The Times*, London; public relations director, Young and Rubicam, advertising agency, London, 1950–72. Recipient: Romantic Novelists Association Major award, 1964; British Travel Association award, 1986. Agent: Curtis Brown, 162–168 Regent Street, London W1R 5TB. Address 52-A Digby Mansions, Hammersmith Bridge Road, London W6 9DF, England.

ROMANCE AND HISTORICAL PUBLICATIONS

Novels

Love, The Magician. London, Muller, 1956.
Journey from Yesterday. London, Collins, 1963.
The Half-Enchanted. London, Collins, 1964.
The Love Campaign. London, Collins, 1965.
The Dangerous Winter. London, Collins, 1965.
A Perfect Stranger. London, Collins, 1966.
A Name in Lights. London, Collins, 1968; New York, Fawcett, 1975.
A Most Auspicious Star. London, Collins, 1968.
Somersault. London, Collins, 1971.
Portrait of Jill. London, Collins, 1972.
Dear Kate. London, Collins, 1972; New York, Fawcett, 1974.

To Seek a Star. London, Collins, 1973; New York, Fawcett, 1975.
The Family Feeling. London, Collins, 1973; New York, Fawcett, 1975.
Girl by the Sea. London, Collins, 1974; New York, Fawcett, 1976.
Music in Winter. London, Collins, 1975.
A Grove of Olives. London, Collins, 1976.
River Voices. London, Collins, 1976.
The Double Rainbow. London, Collins, 1977.
A Rose in Heather. London, Collins, 1978.
Julia's Sister. London, Severn House, 1982.
The House of Nightingales. London, Severn House, 1985.
The Clover Field. London, Severn House, 1987.
Reflections in a Lake. Bath, Firecrest, 1988.

Novels as Suzanne Goodwin

The Winter Spring. London, Bodley Head, 1978; as *Stage of Love* (as Cecily Shelbourne), New York, Putnam, 1978.
The Winter Sisters. London, Bodley Head, 1980.
Emerald. London, Magnum, 1980.
Floodtide. London, Severn House, and New York, St. Martin's Press, 1983.
Sisters. London, Severn House, 1984; New York, St. Martin's Press, 1985.
Cousins. New York, St. Martin's Press, 1985; London, Severn House, 1986.
Daughters. New York, St. Martin's Press, and London, Joseph, 1987.
Lovers. London, Joseph, 1988.

OTHER PUBLICATIONS

Play

Radio Play: *Chords and Discords*, 1975.

Other

Explore the Cotswolds by Bicycle, with Doreen Impey. London, Ward Lock, 1973.
London's Riverside, From Hampton Court in the West to Greenwich Palace in the East, with Doreen Impey. London, Luscombe, 1975; New York, Ballantine, 1976; revised edition, as *A Guide to London's Riverside: Hampton Court to Greenwich*, London, Constable, 1985.
Godfrey: A Special Time Remembered (on Godfrey Seymour Tearle; as Suzanne Goodwin), with Jill Bennett. London, Hodder and Stoughton, 1983.

*   *   *

Although the backgrounds to Suzanne Ebel's novels, and many of her characters, have for most of us an aura of glamour, she imbues them with an authenticity which springs partly from personal experience, partly from verbal dexterity: from time to time she produces flashing phrases which throw a shaft of dazzling light on to a character or setting which makes the reader see it anew, with startling clarity.

Many of the "glamorous" backgrounds are her own everyday ones. At one time she had three homes: a flat in Hammersmith close to the Thames where she still does her writing; a second, now abandoned, in Stratford-on-Avon (until he moved to the National Theatre, her husband, John Goodwin, was publicity director to the Royal Shakespeare Company); and another flat, converted from a granary at the top of an 18th-century house, in the hills above Cannes. She makes good, observant, use of all these settings, and the ambience of the theatre in which her husband moves. For example, *River Voices* is set on a houseboat on the Thames; *A Grove of Olives* has a Provençal background; and *The Double Rainbow* obviously evolved out of her contacts with the theatre world.

The heroine of *The Double Rainbow* is one of her most fully realised heroines, a girl who "grows" convincingly throughout the story from a shy, diffident Oxford undergraduate playing Perdita in *The Tempest* in a scruffy church hall, to an actress of some stature, able to take her place in a company of distinguished players. She is not the only fully realised character. Each member of the Two Rivers Company has been completely conceived. Even the minor ones are real people. Faith's Oxford tutor, Dr. Barrington, is no cut-out-and-stuck-on don: he has his individual quirks which bring him sharply into focus. Mrs. Gratowski, her Polish landlady, could easily have been just a "comic character" but instead she, too, is real person—funny, but with dignity, warmth, and pathos. Even the director's housekeeper, though only lightly etched in, has mysterious depths. The reader senses much in her that the author does not specifically state. Good character-drawing, again, is at the heart of *A Grove of Olives*, which hinges on the relationship between a mother and daughter. Elizabeth, the mother (a sculptor), is especially alive and enchanting. But the setting—a comfortable, rather ramshackle farmhouse in southern France, used by Elizabeth as her studio—is also memorably evoked.

The longer novels, as Suzanne Goodwin, *The Winter Spring* and *The Winter Sisters*, break new ground. While retaining the theatrical theme they are set in the early 19th century, and give an interesting insight into what it was like to act in the wake of Kean and the shadow of Kemble. The Winters are a theatrical family, father Thomas an actor-manager, his wife Ellen the company's costume designer and general dogsbody, daughters Isabella and Lettice actresses. Of the two only Lettice is dedicated to her career. Isabella, a social climber, soon escapes from theatrical "drudgery" into a desirable marriage. There is a slightly deeper and more serious note to these novels than to the average Regency romp. The girls make mistakes, and learn from them painfully. These first (for Suzanne Goodwin) "period" stories catch the atmosphere of the time with precision, without being archly or aggressively "period" in tone. And, as always, the characters are well-rounded people with whom the reader can relate.

—Elizabeth Grey

EBERHART, Mignon G(ood). American. Born in University Place, Nebraska, 6 July 1899. Educated in local schools; Nebraska Wesleyan University, Lincoln, 1917–20. Married 1) Alanson C. Eberhart in 1923 (divorced); remarried in 1948 (died); 2) John P. Hazen Perry in 1946 (died). Since 1930 full-time writer. Past president, Mystery Writers of America. Recipient: Scotland Yard prize, 1931; Mystery Writers of America Grand Master award, 1970. D.Litt: Nebraska Wesleyan University, 1935. Agent: Brandt and Brandt, 1501 Broadway, New York, New York 10036. Address: c/o Random House, 201 East 50th Street, New York, New York 10022, U.S.A.

ROMANCE AND HISTORICAL PUBLICATIONS

Novels (series: Sarah Keate and Lance O'Leary)

The Patient in Room 18 (Keate and O'Leary). New York, Doubleday, and London, Heinemann, 1929.
The Mystery of Hunting's End (Keate and O'Leary). New York, Doubleday, 1930; London, Heinemann, 1931.
While the Patient Slept (Keate and O'Leary). New York, Doubleday, and London, Heinemann, 1930.
From This Dark Stairway (Keate and O'Leary). New York, Doubleday, 1931; London, Heinemann, 1932.
Murder by an Aristocrat (Keate and O'Leary). New York, Doubleday, 1932; as *Murder of My Patient*, London, Lane, 1934.
The Dark Garden (Keate and O'Leary). New York, Doubleday, 1933; as *Death in the Fog*, London, Lane, 1934.
The White Cockatoo. New York, Doubleday, and London, Falcon Books, 1933.
The House on the Roof. New York, Doubleday, and London, Collins, 1935.
Fair Warning. New York, Doubleday, and London, Collins, 1936.
Danger in the Dark.. New York, Doubleday, 1937; as *Hand in Glove*, London, Collins, 1937.
The Pattern. New York, Doubleday, and London, Collins, 1937; as *Pattern of Murder*, New York, Popular Library, 1948.
The Glass Slipper. New York, Doubleday, and London, Collins, 1938.
Hasty Wedding. New York, Doubleday, 1938; London, Collins, 1939.
Brief Return. London, Collins, 1939.
The Chiffon Scarf. New York, Doubleday, 1939; London, Collins, 1940.
The Hangman's Whip. New York, Doubleday, 1940; London, Collins, 1941.
Strangers in Flight. Los Angeles, Bantam, 1941; revised edition, as *Speak No Evil*, New York, Random House, and London, Collins, 1941.
With This Ring. New York, Random House, 1941; London, Collins, 1942.
Wolf in Man's Clothing (Keate). New York, Random House, 1942; London, Collins, 1943.
The Man Next Door. New York, Random House, 1943; London, Collins, 1944.
Unidentified Woman. New York, Random House, 1943; London, Collins, 1944.
Escape the Night. New York, Random House, 1944; London, Collins, 1945.
Wings of Fear. New York, Random House, 1945; London, Collins, 1946.
Five Passengers from Lisbon. New York, Random House, and London, Collins, 1946.
The White Dress. New York, Random House, 1946; London, Collins, 1947.
Another Woman's House. New York, Random House, 1947; London, Collins, 1948.
House of Storm. New York, Random House, and London, Collins, 1949.
Hunt with the Hounds. New York, Random House, 1950; London, Collins, 1951.
Never Look Back. New York, Random House, and London, Collins, 1951.
Dead Men's Plans. New York, Random House, 1952; London, Collins, 1953.
The Unknown Quantity. New York, Random House, and London, Collins, 1953.

Man Missing (Keate). New York, Random House, and London, Collins, 1954.

Postmark Murder. New York, Random House, and London, Collins, 1956.

Another Man's Murder. New York, Random House, 1957; London, Collins, 1958.

Melora. New York, Random House, 1959; London, Collins, 1960; as *The Promise of Murder*, New York, Dell, 1961.

Jury of One. New York, Random House, 1960; London, Collins, 1961.

The Cup, The Blade, or the Gun. New York, Random House, 1961; as *The Crime at Honotassa*, London, Collins, 1962.

Enemy in the House. New York, Random House, 1962; London, Collins, 1963.

Run Scared. New York, Random House, 1963; London, Collins, 1964.

Call after Midnight. New York, Random House, 1964; London, Collins, 1965.

R.S.V.P. Murder. New York, Random House, 1965; London, Collins, 1966.

Witness at Large. New York, Random House, 1966; London, Collins, 1967.

Woman on the Roof. New York, Random House, and London, Collins, 1968.

Message from Hong Kong. New York, Random House, and London, Collins, 1969.

El Rancho Rio. New York, Random House, 1970; London, Collins, 1971.

Two Little Rich Girls. New York, Random House, and London, Collins, 1972.

The House by the Sea. New York, Pocket Books, 1972.

Murder in Waiting. New York, Random House, 1973; London, Collins, 1974.

Danger Money. New York, Random House, and London, Collins, 1975.

Family Fortune. New York, Random House, 1976; London, Collins, 1977.

Nine O'Clock Tide. New York, Random House, and London, Collins, 1978.

The Bayou Road. New York, Random House, and London, Collins, 1979.

Casa Madrone. New York, Random House, and London, Collins, 1980.

Family Affair. New York, Random House, and London, Collins, 1981.

Next of Kin. New York, Random House, 1982; London, Collins, 1983.

The Patient in Cabin C. New York, Random House, 1983; London, Collins, 1984.

Alpine Condo Cross Fire. New York, Random House, 1984; London, Collins, 1985.

A Fighting Chance. New York, Random House, 1986; London, Collins, 1987.

Three Days for Emeralds. New York, Random House, and London, Collins, 1988.

Short Stories

The Cases of Susan Dare. New York, Doubleday, 1934; London, Lane, 1935.

Five of My Best: Deadly Is the Diamond, Bermuda Grapevine, Murder Goes to Market, Strangers in Flight, Express to Danger. London, Hammond, 1949.

Deadly Is the Diamond. New York, Dell, 1951.

Deadly Is the Diamond and Three Other Novelettes of Murder: Bermuda Grapevine, The Crimson Paw, Murder in Waltz Time. New York, Random House, 1958; Hornchurch, Essex, Henry, 1981.

The Crimson Paw. London, Hammond, 1959.

OTHER PUBLICATIONS

Plays

320 College Avenue, with Fred Ballard. New York, French, 1938.

Eight O'Clock Tuesday, with Robert Wallsten, adaptation of a novel by Eberhart (produced New York, 1941). New York, French, 1941.

*

Manuscript Collection: Mugar Memorial Library, Boston University.

*   *   *

Mignon G. Eberhart is the pre-eminent American woman in the mystery field, but her claim is even wider. In short, she has consistently produced the hybrid mystery-romance-gothic novel with a skill very few writers have been able to emulate successfully. With Mignon Eberhart, said the *New Yorker*, "the ingredients are tested and the cook's hand is remarkably sure."

Her early books gave little indication of the heights she was to reach. In the tradition of Mary Roberts Rinehart, they featured the middle-aged Nurse Sarah Keate in a succession of melodramatic situations; the menacing atmosphere of darkened hospital wards or old mansions was there in plenty, with Nurse Keate threatened by shadowy villains and rescued from mortal danger at the last minute by the masterful male. There were gothic and romantic touches, the air was suitably eerie, and impending perils were well conveyed, but the heroine left much to be desired. Later Keate novels, *Wolf in Man's Clothing* and *Man Missing*, deserve honourable mention nonetheless. Her other series detective, attractive Susan Dare, appeared in a collection of short stories which are good examples of neat puzzles spiced with romance.

As her career developed, the mystery-romance-gothic combination became more evenly balanced. Her heroines are not only involved in perilous situations, like the young secretary's flirtation with espionage in *The Man Next Door*, but are frequently the principal suspects with the web of circumstances enmeshing them more securely as they struggle. An air of helplessness prevails, sometimes engendered by inability to distinguish between the upright males and the villain who would do her ill. Good examples are *The White Cockatoo*, *Speak No Evil*, and *With This Ring*; while for sheer psychological suspense, competently blending mystery with terror, among her best are *Fair Warning*, *Another Man's Murder*, and *Run Scared*.

She is a master of locale. Much travelled herself, she manages invariably to convey the feel and colour of her settings. Sometimes, but not always, these are exotic; she has the perfect gift for putting a plot against just the right background, then skilfully exploiting that background to project mystery and deception and menace. The best gothic romances can extract as much tension and atmosphere from a rambling house or lonely island or street festival, for example, as from a darkly mysterious stranger, and Eberhart is a superb exponent.

A critic once stated that an Eberhart novel, without need of a mystery plot, would stand on its own as a mirror of the modes and manners of the 20th century. That may well be so, but is perhaps a trifle clinical. The fact that she is literate, plausible, entertaining, and intelligent, and devises stories of compelling readability, is the more likely basis of her considerable popularity with countless readers throughout the world.

—Melvyn Barnes

EDEN, Dorothy (Enid). Also writes as Mary Paradise. British. Born in Canterbury Plains, near Christchurch, New Zealand, 3 April 1912. Educated at a village school and a secretarial college. Secretary, 1929–39; lived in London from the 1950's. *Died 4 March 1982.*

ROMANCE AND HISTORICAL PUBLICATIONS

Novels

Singing Shadows. London, Stanley Paul, 1940.
The Laughing Ghost. London, Macdonald, 1943; New York, Ace, 1968.
We Are for the Dark. London, Macdonald, 1944.
Summer Sunday. London, Macdonald, 1946.
Walk into My Parlour. London, Macdonald, 1947.
The Schoolmaster's Daughters. London, Macdonald, 1948; as *The Daughters of Ardmore Hall*, New York, Ace, 1968.
Crow Hollow. London, Macdonald, 1950; New York, Ace, 1967.
The Voice of the Dolls. London, Macdonald, 1950; New York, Ace, 1971.
Cat's Prey. London, Macdonald, 1952; New York, Ace, 1967.
Lamb to the Slaughter. London, Macdonald, 1953; as *The Brooding Lake*, New York, Ace, 1966.
Bride by Candlelight. London, Macdonald, 1954; New York, Ace, 1972.
Darling Clementine. London, Macdonald, 1955; as *The Night of the Letter*, New York, Ace, 1967.
Death Is a Red Rose. London, Macdonald, 1956; New York, Ace, 1970.
The Pretty Ones. London, Macdonald, 1957; New York, Ace, 1966.
Listen to Danger. London, Macdonald, 1958; New York, Ace, 1967.
The Deadly Travellers. London, Macdonald, 1959; New York, Ace, 1966.
The Sleeping Bride. London, Macdonald, 1959; New York, Ace, 1969.
Samantha. London, Hodder and Stoughton, 1960; as *Lady of Mallow*, New York, Coward McCann, 1962.
Sleep in the Woods. London, Hodder and Stoughton, 1960; New York, Coward McCann, 1961.
Face of an Angel (as Mary Paradise). London, Hale, 1961; New York, Ace, 1966.
Shadow of a Witch (as Mary Paradise). London, Hale, 1962; New York, Ace, 1966.
Whistle for the Crows. London, Hodder and Stoughton, 1962; New York, Ace, 1964.
Afternoon for Lizards. London, Hodder and Stoughton, 1962; as *The Bridge of Fear*, New York, Ace, 1966.

The Bird in the Chimney. London, Hodder and Stoughton, 1963; as *Darkwater*, New York, Coward McCann, 1964.
Bella. London, Hodder and Stoughton, 1964; as *Ravenscroft*, New York, Coward McCann, 1965.
The Marriage Chest. London, Hodder and Stoughton, 1965; as Mary Paradise, New York, Coward McCann, 1966.
Never Call It Loving. London, Hodder and Stoughton, and New York, Coward McCann, 1966.
Siege in the Sun. London, Hodder and Stoughton, and New York, Coward McCann, 1967.
Winterwood. London, Hodder and Stoughton, and New York, Coward McCann, 1967.
The Shadow Wife. London, Hodder and Stoughton, and New York, Coward McCann, 1968.
The Vines of Yarrabee. London, Hodder and Stoughton, and New York, Coward McCann, 1969.
Melbury Square. London, Hodder and Stoughton, 1970; New York, Coward McCann, 1971.
Waiting for Willa. London, Hodder and Stoughton, and New York, Coward McCann, 1970.
Afternoon Walk. London, Hodder and Stoughton, and New York, Coward McCann, 1971.
A Linnet Singing. New York, Pocket Books, 1972.
Speak to Me of Love. London, Hodder and Stoughton, and New York, Coward McCann, 1972.
The Millionaire's Daughter. London, Hodder and Stoughton, and New York, Coward McCann, 1974.
The Time of the Dragon. London, Hodder and Stoughton, and New York, Coward McCann, 1975.
The Salamanca Drum. London, Hodder and Stoughton, and New York, Coward McCann, 1977.
The Storrington Papers. New York, Coward McCann, 1978; London, Hodder and Stoughton, 1979.
Depart in Peace. London, Hodder and Stoughton, 1979.
The American Heiress. London, Hodder and Stoughton, and New York, Coward McCann, 1980.
An Important Family. New York, Morrow, and London, Hodder and Stoughton, 1982.

Short Stories

Yellow Is for Fear and Other Stories. New York, Ace, 1968; London, Coronet, 1976.
The House on Hay Hill and Other Stories. London, Coronet, and New York, Fawcett, 1976.

*

Manuscript Collection: Mugar Memorial Library, Boston University.

*   *   *

Dorothy Eden published steadily from the 1940's until the early 1980's. Since 1970 more than five million copies of her books have been sold and she now numbers more than 30 books in print. These figures alone place her as one of the *grande dames* of romance/gothic.

Her plots are traditional in that the heroines must meet the challenge of 1) finding the right mate, 2) being poor and becoming rich or the reverse, and 3) coping with a frontier land. Her typical heroine is content to find and secure her true mate and run his house, mansion, or castle correctly and well. She must be prepared to repel or charm the threatening natives, survive disasters, and protect other women, children, and dependents.

Eden's heroines are usually without family and poor, or they have lost the wealth they once had. Briar in *Sleep in the Woods* was found in a ditch as a baby, clasped in her dead presumed mother's arms. Raised and educated beyond her station by a poor schoolmaster, she goes out as a ladies' maid to New Zealand, facing the untamed frontier and capturing the most eligible bachelor in Wellington. After moving to the bush, she must wrestle with a recalcitrant husband, the man-eating Maori, and her own lies about her non-existent family in England. Briar has a sister in Harriet "Hetty" Brown in *The American Heiress*, published twenty years later in 1980.

Also born on the wrong side of the blanket, Hetty is left on her natural father's doorstep by her poor and dying mother. Her father takes her in but then dies; so the wicked stepmother trains Hetty as her daughter's maid. The trick here is that Hetty is a look-alike for Clemency, her half-sister, so much so that she substitutes for Clemency on dates with her more dull suitors. Therein lies the tale. Hetty, Clemency, and mother sail for England and Clemency's elegant marriage on the *Lusitania*. Briar lies about her non-existent family; Hetty, the lone survivor of this trio, takes Clemency's place, marrying the dashing Major Hugo, Lord Hazzard, heir to one of England's most venerable titles. She, like Briar, must continually struggle with her conscience and wonder when and if she will be found out. For both of them the motivation is, at first, possession of a house/castle and social position. They eventually come to love their husbands, however, but only after trials which reveal their mates' worthiness. Both Hetty and Briar suffer for their lies and both are discovered, though in Hetty's case it takes the next generation to reveal her impersonation. Both characters are saved from triviality by their likeableness and independent spirit. Eden handles the Cinderella story with controlled realism in the areas of sexual implication and setting.

The famous *The Vines of Yarrabee*, perhaps Eden's most widely read novel, tells of the Australian outback, convict labor, and violence mixed with the background of grape-growing and wine-making. In this case, a genteel Eugenia marries Gilbert Massingham and goes to Australia, a most ungenteel place. She, unlike Briar and Hetty, is legitimately of fine English breeding and possesses impeccable social sense, for which quality Gilbert has married her. Eugenia's struggles are concerned with finding her true mate and coping with the frontier. She must adjust to the Australian outback without the prior toughening experiences of Briar and Hetty. Rough times develop character whether rich or poor. Shady financial schemes and love triangles complicate Eugenia's search for her happy ending.

In the Eden canon, *Melbury Square* and *Never Call It Loving* should be singled out as exceptional. In the former, a fashionable portrait artist rules his Kensington Square house, crippling the emotional lives of both his wife and daughter. Maud Lucie, the daughter and protagonist, is a beautiful Edwardian debutante afflicted with a father fixation. Maud carelessly drifts through her youth being her father's favorite model and finds any search on her part for love and happiness thwarted by her dominating father. A selfish and obtuse Maud represents a reality not usually found in gothic/romance heroines. Maud's moment of truth comes only in her crotchety old age when, her father dead, herself tricked, swindled, and poor, she finally finds her independence: "The one left might be old and ugly, but at least she was entirely herself."

Never Call It Loving fictionalizes the real love affair between Charles Stewart Parnell and Katherine O'Shea. In reality their affair ruined Parnell's reputation, which indirectly destroyed the chances for Irish Home Rule and ultimately drove Parnell to an early death. A historical novel *par excellence*, this sensitive recounting proves Eden's ability to write successfully outside the romance/gothic formula.

Eden has been universally praised for her well-researched backgrounds—Australia, Peking, Denmark, New Zealand, Ireland. No country or time period was too remote if it interested the author. There has been some faint carping about unoriginal and artificial plots but for a prolific and successful writer such problems are bound to occur. On the whole, an Eden story is a reliable source of entertainment, well-told and well-researched.

—Marilynn Motteler

EDGAR, Josephine. See **HOWARD, Mary.**

EDMONDS, Walter D(umaux). American. Born in Boonville, New York, 15 July 1903. Educated at Cutler School, New York, 1914–16; St. Paul's School, Concord, New Hampshire, 1916–19; Choate School, Wallingford, Connecticut, 1919–21; Harvard University, Cambridge, Massachusetts (staff member from 1922, secretary, 1924–25, and president, 1925–26, *Harvard Advocate*), 1921–26, A.B. 1926 (Phi Beta Kappa). Married 1) Eleanor Livingston Stetson in 1930 (died 1956), one son and two daughters; 2) Katharine Howe Baker-Carr in 1956. Member of the Board of Overseers, Harvard College, 1945–50; director, 1955–72, and president and publisher, 1957–66, *Harvard Alumni Bulletin*. Recipient (for children's books): American Library Association Newbery Medal, 1942; National Book award, 1976; Christopher award, 1976. Litt.D.: Union College, Schenectady, New York, 1936; Rutgers University, New Brunswick, New Jersey, 1940; Colgate University, Hamilton, New York, 1947; Harvard University, 1952. Member, American Academy of Arts and Sciences. Agent: Harold Ober Associates, 40 East 49th Street, New York, New York 10017. Address: 27 River Street, Concord, Massachusetts 01742, U.S.A.

ROMANCE AND HISTORICAL PUBLICATIONS

Novels

Rome Haul. Boston, Little Brown, and London, Sampson Low, 1929.
The Big Barn. Boston, Little Brown, 1930; London, Sampson Low, 1931.
Erie Water. Boston, Little Brown, 1933; London, Hurst and Blackett, 1934.
Drums along the Mohawk. Boston, Little Brown, and London, Jarrolds, 1936.
Chad Hanna. Boston, Little Brown, and London, Collins, 1940.
Young Ames. Boston, Little Brown, and London, Collins, 1942.
In the Hands of the Senecas. Boston, Little Brown, and London, Collins, 1947; as *The Captive Woman*, New York, Bantam, 1962.
The Wedding Journey. Boston, Little Brown, 1947.
The Boyds of Black River. New York, Dodd Mead, and London, Collins, 1953.
The South African Quirt. Boston, Little Brown, 1985.

Short Stories

Mostly Canallers: Collected Stories. Boston, Little Brown, 1934.

*

Critical Study: *Walter D. Edmonds, Storyteller* by Lionel D. Wyld, Syracuse, New York, Syracuse University Press, 1982.

*   *   *

Walter D. Edmonds is known, among readers of historical novels, almost exclusively for his *Drums along the Mohawk* (made into a film in 1939). He is also known for his children's books, for which he has won several awards. His strengths as a novelist are abundantly and clearly displayed in his first novel, *Rome Haul* (1929). *Drums along the Mohawk* and *Rome Haul* reveal his natural abilities to recreate specific historical periods with teeming, well-rendered detail; to delineate character through external action; and to blend history and fiction with an authority so finely managed as to blur the distinction between the two. Edmonds's latest novel, *The South African Quirt*, is quite different from his other fiction.

Rome Haul reveals at once Edmonds's ability to create with fidelity and Dickensian realism the life on the Erie Canal during its halcyon days in the 1850's, before railroads made them nearly obsolete. Edmonds convinces the reader that these brief years were as uniquely American and as important as the old New England whaling days or the frontier years following the Civil War; it was a distinct culture, and Edmonds makes it resonate with vibrant detail: the sweaty horses and mules, the barge ropes, the bawdy language, the shapes and noises of freight-laden boats, the itinerant peddlers and the bullies. The life among the "canawlers" is suffused with a thick and satisfying atmospheric reality. The story is told against a richly textured background.

While the novel is fully peopled, at times the narrative is loose. The two main narrative threads—the chase of Gentleman Joe Calash by the Justice Department, and the love story of Dan Harrow and Mollie Larkin (the main characters of the novel)—do not always intertwine or relate tightly enough. Mollie is the most fully realized character, perhaps because she is the most thoroughly and realistically treated; she is both cook and near-roustabout with the men, and also their lover. Her amorality is the most believable characteristic in the entire novel. The story sometimes rambles, but is always alive and convincing.

Drums along the Mohawk, though more panoramic, hardly advances the talent so evident in *Rome Haul*, and that is more than acceptable because Edmonds's abilities are immense. Like *Rome Haul*, the setting is specific—northern New York State in 1782. The historical occasion is the "war" during the American Revolution when the farmers of the Mohawk Valley were separated from the Continental forces and had to fight both the British and the Indians. But the fighting, often dramatically rendered, is not the real focus or intent of the novel.

Edmonds tries to subordinate action to character. Though he does not probe the "inner" realities of his men and women, he does define their lives in terms of their dailiness and their rough virtues, especially the courage they display in clearing the land and making it serve their purposes. The principal characters—Gilbert Martin, a poor backwoods farmer and a member of the militia from Deerfield settlement, and his wife Lana with whom he makes a life out of the wilderness—are strong presences in the novel, but their conflicts remain unexplored, though never sentimentalized. The problem is one of omission; he also fails to register horror at the increasing brutality of the Indian attacks.

Again, as in *Rome Haul*, Edmonds makes his characters eminently real, but he does not provide them with enough force to make them fully realized. Perhaps this is partly due to Edmonds introducing too many episodic elements into this longish tale. But it should be reiterated that his characters, given the kind of novel *Drums along the Mohawk* is, are utterly believable, as evidenced by the equally realistic treatment given historic and fictional characters—they are indistinguishable throughout the novel. Edmonds deals here with the frontier men and women whose enduring strengths made America possible. He teaches us about the national character, almost to the point of illustrating an American philosophy.

Edmonds's most recent novel, *The South American Quirt*, has little in common with his earlier novels, perhaps because it is autobiographical and deals with childhood rites-of-passage, a common enough theme in American literature, but not for Edmonds (although some might want to place his *Chad Hanna* in the same category). The book seems to be more concerned with personal purgation than with exploration of character or the influence of locale, although the setting is specific, the Mohawk Valley region of New York in the 1830's.

The story centers on a 12-year-old boy, Natty Dunston, and his cruel father who is given to blinding, uncontrollable rages. Mr. Dunstan receives a gift of a South African quirt (a riding crop made of rhinoceros hide); the reader immediately feels there is, inevitably, going to be violence, perhaps inflicted on Natty's mongrel dog Bingo, perhaps on Natty himself. The father is a terrifying presence throughout the novel, but in the absence of any attributal motivation for Mr. Dunston's behavior, the novel has nowhere to go and lacks substance. Here the flaw is almost fatal because there is no rich background, interesting characters, or action to divert the reader, who merely want to see Mr. Dunstan die or suffer. The novel is somewhat redeemed by the boy's revenge against his father, but the ending is inconclusive and murky, though arresting and surprising.

Edmonds's abilities are considerable, and his talent is unquestionable. He might have been even more notable had he not been so strict an heir of the local colorists and the early American realists.

—Peter Desy

EDWARDS, Anne (née Josephson). American. Born in New York City, 20 August 1927. Educated at the University of California, Los Angeles, 1944–46; Southern Methodist University, Dallas, 1947–48. Married Stephen Citron; one son and one daughter. President, Authors Guild. Agent: Mitch Douglas, International Creative Management, 40 West 57th Street, New York, New York 10019, U.S.A.; or, A. P. Watt Ltd., 20 John Street, London WC1N 2DL, England.

ROMANCE AND HISTORICAL PUBLICATIONS

Novels

The Survivors. New York, Holt Rinehart, and London, W. H. Allen, 1968.
Miklos Alexandrovitch Is Missing. New York, Coward McCann, 1970; as *Alexandrovitch is Missing!*, London, Hodder and Stoughton, 1970.
Shadow of a Lion. New York, Coward McCann, and London, Hodder and Stoughton, 1971.
Haunted Summer. New York, Coward McCann, 1972; London, Hodder and Stoughton, 1973.
The Hesitant Heart. New York, Random House, and London Cassell, 1974.
Child of Night. New York, Random House, 1975.
Raven Wings. London, Millington, 1977.

OTHER PUBLICATIONS

Plays

Screenplays: *Quantez*, with Robert Wright Campbell, 1957; *A Question of Adultery*, 1959.

Other

A Child's Bible. London, Penguin, 1967; New York, Golden Books, 1970.
Judy Garland: A Biography. New York, Simon and Schuster, and London, Constable, 1975.
The Inn and Us, with Stephen Citron. New York, Random House, 1976.
Vivien Leigh: A Biography. New York, Simon and Schuster, and London, W. H. Allen, 1977.

The Great Houdini (for children). New York, Putnam, 1977.
P. T. Barnum (for children). New York, Putnam, 1977.
Sonya: The Life of Countess Tolstoy. New York, Simon and Schuster, and London, Hodder and Stoughton, 1981.
The Road to Tara: The Life of Margaret Mitchell. New Haven, Connecticut, Ticknor and Fields, and London, Hodder and Stoughton, 1983.
Matriarch: Queen Mary and the House of Windsor. New York, Morrow, and London, Hodder and Stoughton, 1984.
A Remarkable Woman: A Biography of Katharine Hepburn. New York, Morrow, 1985; as *Katharine Hepburn: A Biography*, London, Hodder and Stoughton, 1986.
Early Reagan: The Rise of an American Hero. New York, Morrow, and London, Hodder and Stoughton, 1987.
Shirley Temple: American Princess. New York, Morrow, and London, Collins, 1988.
The De Milles: An American Family. New York, Abrams, 1988; London, Collins, 1989.

*

Manuscript Collection: University of California, Los Angeles.

*   *   *

One rarely finds an author so gifted and so versatile as to be capable of writing all things well, yet Anne Edwards possesses just such a talent. Not only does the subject matter for her novels vary considerably, but her style is so flexible that it is appropriate to the subject matter and character of each novel. In addition, her characters often transcend the cardboard figures of most novels of this genre.

In *The Survivors*, a novel of modern times, the heroine departs slightly from the formula gothic strong-willed beautiful non-traditional female. Luanne's psyche is a fragile thread as she leaves the refuge of Laurel Groves, the rest home where she retreated after the mass murder of her entire family. Yet in true gothic style Luanne has a handsome male protector. Hans not only enables Luanne to dispel the ghosts of her past, but his unwavering love for her transforms the frightened unworldly girl into an assured confident woman able to confront her ghosts and a murderess all in less than a fortnight. However, the suspense builds so rapidly in this novel that the reader accepts the character incongruities.

Emily Dickinson is the unlikely heroine of *The Hesitant Heart*. Edwards's flexibility shows strongly in this romantic work about the enigmatic recluse of Amherst. Sentence patterns and style blend smoothly with excerpts of poetry and letters of the poet. While the true scholar of Emily Dickinson may shudder at the Emily portrayed here, so many myths surround her that it is fun to suspend our disbelief and play "What if" with Edwards.

Again drawing from history for her characters, Edwards uses some of history's greatest romantics for *Haunted Summer*. Who are better suited to haunt the pages of a gothic romance than Shelley, Lord Byron, and Mary Shelley? Here Edwards creates an aura of horror as she explores the complex relationships between these young people during the summer they spent near the haunted castle of Chillon. The horror mounts through the development of volatile interpersonal relationships and descriptions of the castle until the reader is finally prepared for the ultimate emergence of the monster Frankenstein.

Although previously mentioned novels would lead one to believe that Edwards has her feet firmly planted in some murky past and that she is a writer of only romantic gothic novels, *Shadow of a Lion* reveals her to be equally competent in the modern world when she uses tinselly Hollywood for her setting. This work, which tells the story of film industry personages who were caught in the McCarthy witch hunts of the 1950's, lies realms apart from such books as *The Hesitant Heart*. Yet the same skilled craft of a superb storyteller and analyst of the human character exists here.

With Edwards's interest in the past and with her finely honed writing skills, it's not surprising that *Sonya: The Life of Countess Tolstoy*, a very solid competent biography, reads as smoothly as her lighter novels.

—Joan Hinkemeyer

———————

ELDERSHAW, M. Barnard. Pseudonym for Marjorie Barnard and Flora Eldershaw. Australians. **BARNARD, Marjorie (Faith):** Born in Ashfield, New South Wales, 16 August 1897. Educated at Cambridge School, Hunters' Hill; Sydney Girls' High School; University of Sydney (exhibitioner; University medal, 1920), 1916–20, B.A. (honours) in history 1920; Sydney Teachers College, 1920. Librarian, Sydney Public Library and Sydney Technical College Library, 1920–35; free-lance writer, 1935–42; librarian, Sydney Public Library, 1942, and Commonwealth Scientific and Industrial Research Organization Library, Sydney, 1942–50. Recipient: *Bulletin* prize, 1928; Patrick White award, 1983. Member, Order of Australia, 1979. Agent: Curtis Brown (Australia) Pty. Ltd., 27 Union Street, Paddington, New South Wales 2021. Address: 29 Sunshine Drive, Point Clare, New South Wales 2250, Australia. **ELDERSHAW, Flora (Sydney Patricia):** Born in Darlinghurst, New South Wales, 16 March 1897. Educated at school in Wagga Wagga, New South Wales; University of Sydney, B.A. 1918. Secretary, University Women's Union, 1917–21; teacher, Cremorne Grammar School, 1921–22, and Presbyterian Ladies College, Croydon, 1923–40, both New South Wales; worked in the Department of Reconstruction, Canberra, 1941–42, and the Welfare Division, Department of Labour and National Service, Melbourne, 1943–47; from 1948 industrial consultant in private practice. President, Fellowship of Australian Writers, 1935, 1943; member of the Advisory Board, Commonwealth Literary Fund, 1939–53. Recipient: *Bulletin* prize, 1928. Fellow, Australian Institute of Management, 1950. *Died 20 September 1956.*

ROMANCE AND HISTORICAL PUBLICATIONS

Novels

A House Is Built. London, Harrap, and New York, Harcourt Brace, 1929.
Green Memory. London, Harrap, and New York, Harcourt Brace, 1931.

OTHER PUBLICATIONS

Novels

The Glasshouse. London, Harrap, 1936.
Plaque with Laurel. London, Harrap, 1937.

Short Stories by Marjorie Barnard

The Persimmon Tree and Other Stories. Sydney, Clarendon, 1943; revised edition, London, Virago Press, 1985.

Play

The Watch on the Headland, in *Australian Radio Plays*, edited by Leslie Rees. Sydney, Angus and Robertson, 1946.

Other

Phillip of Australia: An Account of the Settlement at Sydney Cove 1788–1792. London, Harrap, 1938.
Essays in Australian Fiction. Melbourne, Melbourne University Press, 1938; Freeport, New York, Books for Libraries, 1970.
The Life and Times of Captain John Piper. Sydney, Australian Limited Editions Society, 1939.
My Australia. London, Jarrolds, 1939; revised edition, 1951.

Editor, *Coast to Coast 1946*. Sydney, Angus and Robertson, 1947.

OTHER PUBLICATIONS by Marjorie Barnard

Novel

Tomorrow and Tomorrow. Melbourne, Georgian House, 1947; London, Phoenix House, 1949; complete text, as *Tomorrow and Tomorrow and Tomorrow*, London, Virago Press, 1983; New York, Doubleday, 1984.

Other

The Ivory Gate (for children). Privately printed, 1920.
Macquarie's World. Sydney, Australian Limited Editions Society, 1941.
Australian Outline. Sydney, Ure Smith, 1943; revised edition, 1949.
The Sydney Book. Sydney, Ure Smith, 1947.
Sydney: The Story of a City. Melbourne, Melbourne University Press, 1956.
Australia's First Architect: Francis Greenway. London, Longman, 1961.
A History of Australia. Sydney, Angus and Robertson, 1962; revised edition, 1963; New York, Praeger, 1963.
Georgian Architecture in Australia, with others. Sydney, Ure Smith, 1963.
Lachlan Macquarie. Melbourne, Oxford University Press, 1964.
Miles Franklin. New York, Twayne, 1967; revised edition, Melbourne, Hill of Content, 1967.

OTHER PUBLICATIONS by Flora Eldershaw

Other

Contemporary Australian Women Writers. Sydney, Australian English Association, 1931.
Australian Literature Society Medallists. Sydney, Australian English Association, 1935.

Editor, *Australian Writers' Annual*. Sydney, Fellowship of Australian Writers, 1936.

Editor, *The Peaceful Army: A Memorial to the Pioneer Women of Australia 1788–1938*. Sydney, Women's Executive Committee and Advisory Council of Australia's 150th Anniversary Celebrations, 1938.

*

Critical Study: *Marjorie Barnard and M. Barnard Eldershaw* by Louise E. Rorabacher, New York, Twayne, 1973.

*   *   *

A House Is Built, the first novel produced from the collaboration of Marjorie Barnard and Flora Eldershaw is their best. The robust and positive character of the central figure, the quartermaster, brings a vitality to the narrative that is lacking in their next historical work, *Green Memory*. These two novels are the extent of their fictional histories although their knowledge and love for Australian history is apparent in later historical studies such as *Phillip of Australia*.

In *A House Is Built*, James Hyde, at the age of 50, decides it is time to retire from his career as a quartermaster in the Royal Navy and make a fresh beginning. He is stimulated by the possibilities of a new country and the youthfulness of the colony of New South Wales in the 1830's speaks to his own exuberant nature. He brings his two daughters Fanny and Maud, as well as his more reluctant son William, to his new supply business on Sydney's waterfront. Through hard work and an eye for the main chance his wealth and social standing grows, the House of Hyde is built and in time he comes to live in a mansion at Hunter's Hill. None of his children has all his qualities. Maud, outgoing and beautiful, marries well and happily. William is a prig, who works in the business capably but lacks his father's energy and good nature. His unyielding and mean-spirited ways are most apparent in his relationship with his wife Adela. Fanny is the quartermaster's natural successor, but is denied a proper role due to her sex. During the labour crisis brought about by the Gold Rush, Fanny gets a chance to work in the office, but eventually is brought home by Adela's illness and William uses this as an excuse to replace her in the business.

Together, the fortunes of the quartermaster and Fanny express the ironies of the new colony where, early on, it was possible to overcome some of the barriers of class, but where the lines of gender are still rigidly defined. Fanny rejects marriage as her only future, but the realities of the time leave her no option for her abundant energy and intelligence except genteel charity work. As well, the parallels Eldershaw draws between the fortunes of James Hyde's house and the nature of the newly settled continent, suggest old certainties of wealth and inheritance might not be secure. William's son James, once a "lusty baby" and a confirmation for his father and grandfather that their actions are somehow sanctioned and part of a "pattern," betrays his family and then dies in a boating accident. The novel ends with Lionel, the younger brother regarded as effeminate by his father, taking on an inheritance he feels duty bound to uphold. The title of the novel begs the question, on what foundation is the house or nation built?

The historical setting is important in *A House Is Built*, but *Green Memory*, minus a few crinolines and hansom cabs, could be set at any time. Whereas the former novel begins with hope, *Green Memory* opens with a suicide in the late 1850's. The concentration on the tensions within one family, fallen from high position, gives the novel an air of hysterical morbidity. The protagonist Lucy Haven is, like Fanny Hyde, an intelligent woman, frustrated by the accident of her sex. Unfortunately where Fanny seemed proud and tragic, Lucy seems priggish and mean, al-though she does stand out among an unsympathetic group of characters. Also missing is the humour evident in *A House Is Built*, particularly the debunking of romantic set pieces and the mocking of William's empire-building vanities.

—Kerry White

ELGIN, Mary. Pseudonym for Dorothy Mary Stewart, née Okell. British. Born in Douglas, Isle of Man, 7 October 1917. Educated at St. Felix School, Southwold, Suffolk, 1928–34; London University, 1934–35; Mrs. Hoster's Secretarial School, 1938. Married Walter Stewart in 1947; one son and one daughter. Secretary, Short Brothers; manager in an aircraft repair organization, Cambridge, 1940–45; secretary to the director, Wellcome Foundation Laboratories, London, 1945–47. Recipient: Romantic Novelists Association award, 1964. *Died 23 March 1965*.

ROMANCE AND HISTORICAL PUBLICATIONS

Novels

Visibility Nil. London, Hodder and Stoughton, 1963; as *A Man from the Mist*, New York, Mill, 1965.
Return to Glenshael. London, Hodder and Stoughton, 1965; as *Highland Masquerade*, New York, Mill, 1966.
The Wood and the Trees. London, Hodder and Stoughton, and New York, Mill, 1967.

*

Manuscript Collection: Boston University Libraries.

*   *   *

Mary Elgin's gothic romances displayed her unique ability to create and use a setting to inform a story. For *Visibility Nil* and *Return to Glenshael* she created a mythical region in the Highlands of northwest Scotland. The country around Anacher and Glenshael is wild and mysterious, but inevitable signs of modernization create tension. Old mansions have been bought by rich newcomers. A massive hydroelectric scheme changes the landscape and creates jobs. A river is dammed, but salmon runs preserve the native fish. One character in both books is clan chief to the neighbors but also a hard-working engineer.

The novels are domestic gothic, relying upon family history, impostures, feuds, and the exoticism of the Highlands for their suspense rather than upon genuine villains or violence. There are mysteries to solve, but they are neither life-threatening nor complex. More important is the heroines' emerging sense of self as they learn to live in the changing environment and come to love the heroes.

Elgin's ability to evoke the language of the Highlands was unusually fine; in one novel she describes the regional speech as a derivation of Scots Gaelic rather than a literal translation from it. Her heroines in these first-person novels are lively and strong, speaking in a charming but astringently honest voice.

Because the hero and heroine of one book recur as secondary characters in another, Elgin's works contain a rare picture of a romantic hero and heroine after marriage. The characters have changed and matured, and their relationship is stable; but they are still interesting, acerbic, and witty. Her output may have been meager; but the quality of Elgin's work is consistently high.

—Kay Mussell

* * *

ELIOT, Anne. Pseudonym for Lois Dwight Taylor, née Cole; also wrote as Caroline Arnett; Lynn Avery; Nancy Dudley; Allan Dwight; Anne Lattin. American. Born in New York City in 1903. Educated at Smith College, Northampton, Massachusetts, B.A. 1924. Married Turney Allan Taylor (died 1968); one son and one daughter. Associate editor, Macmillan, New York; editor, Whittlesey House and Putnam's Sons, New York; senior editor, William Morrow and Walker and Company, New York. *Died 20 July 1979.*

ROMANCE AND HISTORICAL PUBLICATIONS

Novels

Return to Aylforth. New York, Meredith Press, 1967.
Shadows Waiting. New York, Meredith Press, 1969.
Stranger at Pembroke. New York, Hawthorn, 1971.
Incident at Villa Rahmana. New York, Hawthorn, 1972; London, Hale, 1975.
The Dark Beneath the Pines. New York, Hawthorn, 1974; London, Hale, 1976.

Novels as Caroline Arnett

Melinda. New York, Fawcett, 1975.
Clarissa. New York, Fawcett, 1976.
Theodora. New York, Fawcett, 1977.
Claudia. New York, Fawcett, 1978.
Stephanie. New York, Fawcett, 1979.
Christina. New York, Fawcett, 1980.

OTHER PUBLICATIONS (for children)

Novels as Allan Dwight, with Turney Allan Taylor

Spaniards' Mark. New York, Macmillan, 1933.
Linn Dickson, Confederate. New York, Macmillan, 1934.
The First Virginians. New York, Nelson, 1936; London, Nelson, 1938.
Drums in the Forest. New York, Macmillan, 1936.
Kentucky Cargo. New York, Macmillan, 1939.
The Silver Dagger. New York, Macmillan, 1959; London, Collier Macmillan, 1963.
Guns at Quebec. New York, Macmillan, 1962; London, Collier Macmillan, 1963.
To the Walls of Cartegena. Williamsburg, Virginia, Colonial Williamsburg, 1967.

Novels as Nancy Dudley

Linda Goes to the Hospital [*Travels Alone, Goes to a TV Studio, Goes on a Cruise*]. New York, Coward McCann, 4 vols., 1953–58.
Linda's First Flight. New York, Coward McCann, 1956.
Cappy and the River (as Lynn Avery). New York, Duell, 1960.

Jorie of Dogtown Common (as Anne Eliot). New York, Abingdon Press, 1962.
The Mystery of the Vanishing Horses (as Lynn Avery). New York, Duell, 1963.

Novels as Anne Lattin

Peter Liked to Draw. Chicago, Wilcox and Follett, 1953.
Peter's Policeman. Chicago, Follett, 1958.
Sparky's Fireman. Chicago, Follett, 1968.

Other

Soldier and Patriot: The Life of General Israel Putnam (as Allan Dwight, with Turney Allan Taylor). New York, Washburn, 1965.

Editor (i.e., adaptor), *Timothy's Shoes and Two Other Stories*, by Mrs. Ewing. New York, Macmillan, 1932.

* * *

Lois Dwight Cole began her early writing career with children's novels published under the pseudonyms Allan Dwight, Nancy Dudley, and Lynn Avery. She then entered the field of adult romances, turning out titles in two of its most popular genres—gothic romance and regency romance.

As Anne Eliot, she wrote several quite competent and enjoyable novels set in exotic locations and filled with the appropriate gothic atmosphere. Because the last novel was published in 1974, some of the material is dated, and, when compared to some of today's sexy fare, these can be considered quite tame. Still, it's not easy to find a well-paced gothic with a plot that isn't obviously predictable—so these novels can be savored for that alone. For example, *Stranger at Pembroke* is a swift-paced gothic tale about a young woman, Tory Ballard, who inherits an old house in Natchez, Mississippi—but only if she can locate the papers of her ancestor Timothy Ballard in three weeks. Two handsome men are eager to aid her in her search, one of them Tory's distant cousin who will become the next heir if her quest fails. The story is skillfully done and the characterizations believable, but the best thing about this novel is the atmosphere of the old South with its Spanish moss and decaying aristocratic mansions.

Incident at Villa Rahmana has a picturesque exotic setting in modern Morocco where Kate Haskell is plunged headlong into a web of intrigue when she comes to help transform the Villa Rahmana into a luxury hotel. Some of the material in the story is now dated, what with the enormous changes in the Arab world in the last 15 years, but the book is still an enjoyable read. *The Dark Beneath the Pines* has Andrea Wilmot returning to Five Pines, a camp in the Adirondack Mountains where she had spent her childhood summers. Her uncle, who had run the camp, has mysteriously disappeared along with a large sum of money. Her grandmother has decided to sell the camp to strangers, leaving Andrea no choice but to try to find her uncle and the missing money. Her life is in danger as she tries to discover just who of the several guests and family is behind the entire scheme. The plot is neat and tight, the atmosphere romantically evocative of the slower paced bygone days of private railroad cars and servants.

Cole's later efforts constituted a switch from her earlier gothics to the extremely popular regency era romance. Not unexpectedly, as Caroline Arnett, she combines all the ingredients in the right proportions in novels that enchant and delight. These works bring to mind one of the most popular authors in this subgenre, Clare Darcy. Both novelists use the Regency period to tell the story of the heroine, after whom the book is always named, and her quest for happiness.

One example is *Melinda*, a regency novel that boasts a strong intelligent heroine. There is a plan afoot to marry her off to a cruel and dishonest man who will surely steal her inheritance and probably rough her up in the bargain. The research has been done well, and the reader is treated to an enchanting tour of rural and urban England. The characters are shaded in with a fine eye to personality and human foibles, the atmosphere is excellent, and the story is top notch. This is a very pleasant read and guaranteed to satisfy even the most discerning critic of the genre.

Another well-written story is *Clarissa*. This is a from-rags-to-riches and ugly-duckling-to-beautiful-swan tale about a paid companion who is literally plucked from the dinner table to be married to one of society's most eligible bachelors. After she is walked down the aisle and taken to London, she blossoms into a beauty, to the great astonishment of the entire town. As if that weren't enough, she ends by saving her husband's life from Napoleon's spies, winning his love and gaining herself a happy everafter. The reader roots for the heroine the entire way.

—Marilyn Lockhart

ELIZABETH. Pseudonym for Mary Annette, Countess von Arnim, later Countess Russell, née Beauchamp. Also wrote as Alice Cholmondeley. British. Born in Sydney, New South Wales, Australia, 31 August 1866; grew up in Lausanne and London. Educated privately; Blythwood House, London; Miss Summerhayes's School, Ealing, London, 1881–84; Royal College of Music, London. Married 1) Count Henning August von Arnim-Schlagenthin in 1891 (died 1910), four daughters and one son; 2) Francis Russell, Earl Russell in 1916 (separated 1919; died 1931). Lived in Germany, 1891–1908, then in England. *Died 9 February 1941.*

ROMANCE AND HISTORICAL PUBLICATIONS

Novels

The Benefactress. London and New York, Macmillan, 1901.
The Ordeal of Elizabeth. New York, Taylor, 1901.
The Princess Priscilla's Fortnight. London, Smith Elder, and New York, Scribner, 1905.
Fräulein Schmidt and Mr. Anstruther, Being the Letters of an Independent Woman. London, Smith Elder, and New York, Scribner, 1907.
The Caravaners. London, Smith Elder, and New York, Doubleday, 1909.
The Pastor's Wife. London, Smith Elder, and New York, Doubleday, 1914.
Christine (as Alice Cholmondeley). London and New York, Macmillan, 1917.
Christopher and Columbus. London, Macmillan, and New York, Doubleday, 1919.
In the Mountains (published anonymously). London, Macmillan, and New York, Doubleday, 1920.
Vera. London, Macmillan, and New York, Doubleday, 1921.
The Enchanted April. London, Macmillan, 1922; New York, Doubleday, 1923.
Love. London, Macmillan, and New York, Doubleday, 1925.

Introduction to Sally. London, Macmillan, and New York, Doubleday, 1926.
Expiation. London, Macmillan, and New York, Doubleday, 1929.
Father. London, Macmillan, and New York, Doubleday, 1931.
Jasmine Farm. London, Heinemann, and New York, Doubleday, 1934.
Mr. Skeffington. London, Heinemann, and New York, Doubleday, 1940.

Short Stories

The Pious Pilgrimage. Boston, Badger, 1901.

OTHER PUBLICATIONS

Play

Priscilla Runs Away, adaptation of her novel *The Princess Priscilla's Fortnight* (produced London, 1910).

Other

Elizabeth and Her German Garden. London and New York, Macmillan, 1898; revised edition, 1900.
The Solitary Summer. London and New York, Macmillan, 1899.
The April Baby's Book of Tunes, with the Story of How They Came to Be Written (for children). London and New York, Macmillan, 1900.
The Adventures of Elizabeth in Rügen. London and New York, Macmillan, 1904.
All the Dogs of My Life. London, Heinemann, and New York, Doubleday, 1936.
One Thing in Common (omnibus). New York, Doubleday, 1941.

*

Manuscript Collection: Huntington Library, San Marino, California.

Critical Studies: *Elizabeth of the German Garden: A Biography* by Leslie de Charms, London, Heinemann, 1958; *Elizabeth: The Author of "Elizabeth and Her German Garden"* by Karen Usborne, London, Bodley Head, 1986.

*   *   *

After reading Virginia Woolf's *To the Lighthouse*, Elizabeth wrote to a friend: "it beats everything anyone else has done hollow. How strident, how vulgar, how coarse *my* stuff for instance seems (and is) after reading that" (quoted in Leslie de Charms's biography). Yet Elizabeth does herself an injustice. She was generally praised by serious critics throughout her long writing career (John Middleton Murry, the husband of her cousin Katherine Mansfield, referred to her novel *Vera* as "a *Wuthering Heights* written by Jane Austen"), and her intelligence and wit are as admirable now as they were when Elizabeth was an internationally known author.

Her first book—*Elizabeth and Her German Garden*, a huge success—was a short autobiographical account of the first year (spring to spring) spent in the country house near Stetten in north Germany of her husband, Count von Arnim. The charm and verbal facility on the surface of the account—of her April, May, and June babies, of the servants who don't know how to account for a (foreign) mistress who won't take regular meals and who prefers roses and hollyhocks to domestic routine, of her husband, the Man of Wrath, who doesn't understand her interest in the seemingly boring landscape, of the friends who fear her husband has exiled her away from the pleasures of Berlin—are undeniable, but we aren't surprised when the dark side of all the charm is revealed in her later books, after her first marriage (to von Arnim), and indeed her second (to Earl Russell), had broken down.

Many of the novels are light and charming, though almost all have a touch of irony about them. *The Benefactress* is an elaborate "opening out" of several motifs of *Elizabeth and Her German Garden*. The socially sophisticated but emotionally naive Anna Estcourt, on inheriting a large estate in north Germany, decides to open the house to women of good family with no means of support. The society friends—both English and German—are given space to reveal themselves ("Trudi's new friends always did think her delightful; and she never has any old ones"); the local middle class is ineffably snobbish and blinkered (the parson "puffing Christianity as though it were a quack medicine"). The Man of Wrath motif is transferred to almost all the men in the book (except her brother, who has become a philosopher and spends his time fishing): even the 20-year-old assistant vicar condescends to Anna, since she is a woman. The English-German theme is solidly used as the basis of the general misunderstandings that run through the book. The actual plot—a rather thin one—centers on her landowning neighbor who aids but disapproves of her charity: when she is finally able to comfort *him* (he is falsely imprisoned), she realizes she loves him. *The Princess Priscilla's Fortnight* and *The Caravaners* reverse the English-Lady-in-Germany theme by bringing a runaway German princess to a small Somerset village in the first, and a pompous German Baron and his party of holiday-makers to Kent in the second. (The German theme is more negatively presented in *Christine*, published during World War I under a pseudonym: what had been a subject of irony and fun in previous works becomes the basis of tragedy in this book.) Sally (*Introduction to Sally*) is a luscious grocer's daughter who marries a Cambridge undergraduate; his snobbish mother drives her away, but Sally's charm is such that a duke and his daughter rescue her, and facilitate a reconciliation. Snobbery figures again in *Jasmine Farm*, where Lady Terence has an affair with her mother's married secretary, Andrew. Since her mother had a rake for a husband, she is very moral; since Andrew's wife's mother is an ex-actress and a social climber, she is willing to compromise—so the two older ladies are able to resolve the dilemma.

Other novels deal with groups of women in differing relationships to each other. *The Enchanted April* shows the effect of the Mediterranean on four women, all of whom are troubled and react to the beauty of the setting in positive ways. *In the Mountains*, set in Switzerland, has a similar theme, though here the three ladies have a more complicated relationship. The narrator (the book is in diary form) is getting away from an intolerable personal situation (never explained), licking her wounds, and the other two are strangers, one ultra conventional, the other a charming, mindless beauty, Dolly, who had kept marrying Germans. The arrival of the narrator's uncle, a Dean ("relieved to find his niece . . . securely, as it were, embedded in widows") solves all problems, since he promptly falls in love with Dolly. *Expiation* centers on a widow, Millie Bott, forced to live out her widowhood in "correct" form surrounded by female Botts; her old lover of 10 years standing can't help her, though her mother-in-law, the only charming Bott, can.

If *Expiation* is a rather bleak look at love and marriage, several of Elizabeth's other novels are even more revealing. *Love,*

which according to Elizabeth's biographer had an autobiographical basis, concerns a 47-year old widow courted by and possibly in love with a 25-year-old man. The climax comes when her priggish son-in-law forces her to marry the young man because they had been forced to stay overnight together. (The theme of the aging beauty is neatly and touchingly told in *Mr. Skeffington*, possibly her best-known work, at least indirectly, since it was made into a movie starring Bette Davis.) But *Fräulein Schmidt and Mr. Anstruther* and *Vera* are probably her bleakest books. The first consists of letters from Fräulein Rose-Marie Schmidt to Roger Anstruther, who had stayed for a year in the Schmidt's house in Jena where he was coached in German by Rose-Marie's father, Professor Schmidt. Reversing the usual progress from coolness to passion, the book begins with Rose-Marie utterly in love with Roger, based on a last-minute avowal before Roger returned to England, and moves haltingly through their break-up, his engagement to an English girl, that engagement's break-up in turn, and Roger's slowly revived interest in Rose-Marie, who by this time regards him only as a friend. Rose-Marie's sensitivity and charm, and her cooling passion, are beautifully revealed (we never read the other side of the correspondence). *Vera* is even more chilling—a convincing portrait of a pure egotist, Everard Wemyss, and a charming woman, Lucy Entwhistle, who becomes involved with him. Wemyss's egotism is revealed to the reader only as Lucy becomes aware of it—she marries him, finds out the ambiguous nature of his previous wife's suicide, and at the end of the book is caught in a position that can lead only to her complete submission to her husband or to an end like his first wife's.

Despite her sometimes bleak views (possibly reflecting her own marriages), what is remembered of Elizabeth's books is their wit and charm. We are often given the chance to see the bully bullied, the egotist defeated, the worm turning—and almost always with a lightness of touch and a verbal felicity that remind us of the numerous comparisons her contemporaries made to Jane Austen.

—George Walsh

ELLERBECK, Rosemary (Anne L'Estrange). Also writes as Anna L'Estrange; Nicola Thorne; Katherine Yorke. British. Born in Cape Town, South Africa. Educated at the London School of Economics, B.Sc. in sociology. Publishers reader and editor until 1975, then full-time writer. Agent: Richard Scott Simon, 32 College Cross, London N1 1PR, England.

ROMANCE AND HISTORICAL PUBLICATIONS

Novels

Inclination to Murder. London, Hodder and Stoughton, 1965.
Hammersleigh. New York, McKay, and London, Hale, 1976.
Return to Wuthering Heights (as Anna L'Estrange). New York, Pinnacle, 1977; London, Corgi, 1978.
Rose, Rose, Where Are You? London, Hale, and New York, Coward McCann, 1978.

Novels as Katherine Yorke (series: Enchantress Saga)

Enchantess Saga (revised edition; as Nicola Thorne). London, Granada, 1985.
  The Enchantress. London, Futura, and New York, Pocket Books, 1979.
  Falcon Gold. London, Futura, 1980; New York, Pinnacle, 1981.
  Lady of the Lakes. London, Futura, 1981.
A Woman's Place. London, Macdonald, 1983.
The Pair Bond. London, Macdonald, 1984.
Swift Flows the River. London, Macdonald, 1988.

Novels as Nicola Thorne (series: Askham Quartet)

The Girls. London, Heinemann, and New York, Random House, 1967.
Bridie Climbing. London, Mayflower, 1969.
In Love. London, Quartet, 1974.
A Woman Like Us. London, Heinemann, and New York, St. Martin's Press, 1979.
The Perfect Wife and Mother. London, Heinemann, 1980; New York, St. Martin's Press, 1981.
The Daughters of the House. London, Granada, and New York, Doubleday, 1981.
Where the Rivers Meet. London, Granada, 1982; as *Cashmere*, New York, Doubleday, 1982.
Affairs of Love. London, Granada, 1983; New York, Doubleday, 1984.
Askham Quartet:
  Never Such Innocence. London, Granada, 1985.
  Yesterday's Promises. London, Grafton, 1986.
  Bright Morning. London, Grafton, 1986.
  A Place in the Sun. London, Grafton, 1987.
Champagne. London, Bantam, 1989.
Pride of Place. London, Grafton, 1989.

*   *   *

Rosemary Ellerbeck's novels entertain the reader with a good old fashioned yarn often involving history or a real historical character. Ghosts and the English and French settings provide the ingredients for an interesting, dual story—with the present often repeating or paralleling the past.

Hammersleigh is a good example. Set in the Yorkshire countryside, the gothic story revolves around a legend that tells of the forbidden love between a monk and a nun, Agatha, the beautiful Prioress of Hammersleigh Priory over five hundred years ago. Karen Blackwood returns to Hammersleigh village, her childhood home, after the death of her husband. After she meets the reckless and handsome master of the great Hammersleigh Hall, she begins to wonder if her decision to return was her own or somehow involved with the tragic events of the past. This is a good tale of suspense and the world of psychic forces.

Rose, Rose, Where Are You? concerns the past in a different way. Clare Trafford goes to the charming coastal town of Port St. Pierre in order to work on a biography of Joan of Arc. She meets the DeFrigecourts who live in the Chateau de Moulin which is built over the site where Joan was once imprisoned. According to legend, she left a curse on the family, and strange accidents have occurred since then. The Rose of the title is the governess who disappears. At the root of it all is a stolen medieval treasure. This book has mystery in the forefront; romance is secondary, for Clare returns to her estranged husband after his timely appearance near the denouement.

As Nicola Thorne, Ellerbeck writes general category fiction pertaining mostly to a female audience with stories of everyday life and its small trials and tribulations. But Ellerbeck's interest in the past again crops up in *Return to Wuthering Heights*, written as Anna L'Estrange. This is a surprisingly good, quite compelling sequel to Emily Brontë's classic masterpiece, and continues the story of Catherine's daughter, Cathy, after she marries Hareton. Into their lives comes Jack, Heathcliff's natural son, and the hostilities and passions of the past threaten to break loose once again.

—Marilyn Lockhart

ELLIS, Julie. Also writes as Alison Lord; Jeffrey Lord; Susan Marino; Julie Marvin; Susan Marvin; Susan Richard. American. Born in Columbus, Georgia, 21 February 1933. Married (husband deceased); two children. Lives in New York City. Agent: Jane Gelfman, John Farquharson Ltd., 250 West 57th Street, New York, New York 10107. Address: c/o William Morrow Inc., 105 Madison Avenue, New York, New York 10016, U.S.A.

ROMANCE AND HISTORICAL PUBLICATIONS

Novels (series: Hampton)

Deedee (as Alison Lord). New York, Pyramid, 1969; as *The Strip*, London, Sphere, 1970.
Jeb (as Jeffrey Lord). New York, Pyramid, and London, New English Library, 1970.
Evil at Hillcrest. New York, Avon, 1971.
Vendetta Castle (as Susan Marino). New York, Avon, 1971.
The Jeweled Dagger. New York, Dell, 1973.
Walk into Darkness. New York, Dell, 1973.
Kara. New York, Dell, 1974.
Eden. New York, Simon and Schuster, 1975.
Walk a Tightrope. New York, Dell, 1975.
Eulalie. New York, Avon, 1976.
The Magnolias. New York, Simon and Schuster, 1976.
The Girl in White. New York, Pocket Books, 1976.
Rendezvous in Vienna. New York, Dell, 1976.
Wexford. New York, Pocket Books, 1976.
Savage Oaks. New York, Simon and Schuster, 1977.
Long Dark Night of the Soul. New York, Pocket Books, 1978.
The Hampton Heritage. New York, Simon and Schuster, 1978.
The Hampton Women. New York, Simon and Schuster, 1980.
Glorious Morning. New York, Arbor House, 1982; London, Grafton, 1989.
East Wind. New York, Arbor House, 1983; London, Grafton, 1988.
Maison Jennie. New York, Arbor House, 1984.
Rich Is Best. New York, Arbor House, 1985; London, Sidgwick and Jackson, 1989.
The Only Sin. New York, Arbor House, and London, Sidgwick and Jackson, 1986.
The Velvet Jungle. New York, Arbor House, 1987; London, Sidgwick and Jackson, 1988.
The Daughter's Promise. New York, Arbor House, and London, Sidgwick and Jackson, 1988.

Novels as Susan Marvin

The Secret of the Villa Como. New York, Lancer, 1966.
Chateau in the Shadows. New York, Dell, 1969.
Summer of Fear. New York, Dell, 1971.
The Secret of Chateau Laval. New York, Avon, 1973; as Susan Richard, 1975.
Where Is Holly Carleton? New York, Beagle, 1974.
Chateau Bougy-Villars. New York, Zebra, 1975.

Novels as Susan Richard

Ashley Hall. New York, Paperback Library, 1967.
Intruder at Maison Benedict. New York, Paperback Library, 1967.
The Secret of Chateau Kendall. New York, Paperback Library, 1967.
Chateau Saxony. New York, Paperback Library, 1970.
Terror at Nelson Woods. New York, Paperback Library, 1973.

OTHER PUBLICATIONS

Other

The Women Around R.F.K. New York, Lancer, 1967.
Revolt of the Second Sex (as Julie Marvin). New York, Lancer, 1970.

*   *   *

Julie Ellis summarizes her fictional viewpoint in one of her most recent titles—*Rich Is Best.* Her novels treat the lives of the rich and sometimes famous, dealing primarily with the super-rich. It is hard to believe that her beleaguered heroines have the time to establish successful careers and to accumulate wealth beyond dreams of avarice, but they certainly manage to do so in these fast-paced tales.

Ellis's heroines are determined women who, while they are devoted to the idea of establishing themselves in the material world, feel that they are incomplete without a man. While suffragism appears repeatedly in these works, feminist principles apply only to the workplace and not to the realm of male–female relationships. Unfortunately, the most consistent theme, next to the desirability of wealth, is the undependability of men. Some heroines, like Caroline Hampton in *The Hampton Heritage* and *The Hampton Women,* cleave to a single man who betrays her but finally returns, after much suffering on her part. Others, like Diane in *Rich Is Best,* run through man after man, being betrayed again and again by men who look perfect until marriage vows have been exchanged. Even the best of men in Ellis's books, can be counted upon to display the most caddish behavior before settling down to being the perfect husband and father.

Children as well often appear in a dual role; at first, they are gifts from God, but as they grow up they become rebellious and unloving drains on the heroine's existence. It often seems that Ellis follows the life of her leading female character until she has lost the freshness of her youth, and then switches the focus of the entire novel to one or more daughters, as in *The Only Sin.* Secondary characters come and go with great rapidity, often disappearing for many chapters and popping up unannounced later. Even major characters are dealt with ruthlessly when they have served their purposes. Divorce and death are frequent visitors.

The novels take place over some of the most fascinating eras of history. Ellis does her research well, fleshing out the stories with plenty of historical details. If this research often gives the impression of historical name-dropping, it certainly helps to speed the plots along. One constant element in the novels is the emphasis on anti-semitism and racism. Ellis handles this quite well, often incorporating strands of history to tell the tale of prejudice. For instance, in *The Hampton Women,* she blends the true story of Leo Frank's lynching with the lives of her fictional characters. Sometimes the lead characters are Jewish and sometimes they are non-Jewish fighters against intolerance. In either case, Ellis's intense concern about the issues of prejudice shines through.

The lives of the characters in an Ellis novel cannot run smoothly, in fact, a happy period in the heroine's life almost seems a signal that disaster is about to strike. Not a single trendy trauma is missed, from adultery through incest to autism. Outdated husbands do not merely move away; they go down on the *Titanic* or the *Lusitania.* In fact, these characters are far more involved with the events of history than are most ordinary people; they miss no major event. There are not a lot of surprises in these stories. It is easy to identify the good and bad characters and to predict which situations are destined to go wrong. What makes the books splendid entertainments is the express-train pace and the sheer variety of disasters and rescues. The characters might even be called paper dolls, but they are glamorous two-dimensional creatures living action-packed lives. What keeps the reader moving is the certainty that the heroine will come to a happy ending and the sheer volume of distress that she must experience to achieve such a completion. The trappings of wealth and power that illustrate each book add to the allure of the stories.

These are not deep works; they are entertainments, pure and simple. Romance is far more important than history, and melodrama more important than realism. But they are very successful because they never strive to be anything other than what they are.

—Susan Quinn Berneis

———

ELSNA, Hebe. Pseudonym for Dorothy Phoebe Ansle; also writes as Laura Conway; Vicky Lancaster; Lyndon Snow. Agent: Curtis Brown, 162–168 Regent Street, London W1R 5TB, England.

ROMANCE AND HISTORICAL PUBLICATIONS

Novels

Child of Passion. London, Hurst and Blackett, 1928.
The Third Wife. London, Hurst and Blackett, 1928.
Sweeter Unpossessed. London, Hurst and Blackett, 1929.
Strait-Jacket. London, Hurst and Blackett, 1930.
Study of Sara. London, Hurst and Blackett, 1930.
We Are the Pilgrims. London, Hurst and Blackett, 1931; as *I Know Not Whither* (as Laura Conway), London, Hale, 1979.
Other People's Fires. London, Hurst and Blackett, 1931.
All Swans. London, Hurst and Blackett, 1932.
Upturned Palms. London, Hurst and Blackett, 1933.
You Never Knew. London, Hurst and Blackett, 1933.
Women Always Forgive. London, Hurst and Blackett, 1934.
Half Sisters. London, Hurst and Blackett, 1934.
Receipt for Hardness. London, Rich and Cowan, 1935.
Uncertain Lover. London, Rich and Cowan, 1935.
Crista Moon. London, Rich and Cowan, 1936.

Brief Heroine. London, Jarrolds, 1937.
People Are So Respectable. London, Jarrolds, 1937.
The Price of Pleasure. London, Amalgamated Press, 1937.
All Visitors Ashore. London, Collins, 1938; revised edition (as Laura Conway), 1979.
Like Summer Brave. London, Jarrolds, 1938.
This Clay Suburb. London, Jarrolds, 1938; revised edition, as *Bid Time Return*, London, Hale, 1979.
The Wedding Took Place. London, Jarrolds, 1939.
The First Week in September. London, Hutchinson, 1940.
Lady Misjudged. London, Hutchinson, 1941.
Everyone Loves Lorraine. London, Collins, 1941; as *Portrait of Lorraine* (as Laura Conway), 1971.
Our Little Life. London, Collins, 1942; as *Yesterday and Tomorrow* (as Lyndon Snow), 1971.
None Can Return. London, Collins, 1942.
See My Shining Palace. London, Collins, 1942.
Young and Broke. London, Collins, 1943.
No Fields of Amaranth. London, Collins, 1943; revised edition, as Lyndon Snow, 1971.
The Happiest Year. London, Collins, 1944.
I Have Lived Today. London, Collins, 1944; as *The Songless Wood* (as Lyndon Snow), London, Hale, 1979.
Echo from Afar. London, Collins, 1945; revised edition (as Laura Conway), 1976.
The Gilded Ladder. London, Collins, 1945.
Cafeteria. London, Collins, 1946.
Clemency Page. London, Collins, 1947.
The Dream and the World. London, Collins, 1947; as *A Link in the Chain*, 1975.
Midnight Matinée. London, Collins, 1949.
The Soul of Mary Olivane. London, Collins, 1949; revised edition, as *Mary Olivane*, 1973.
The Door Between. London, Collins, 1950; revised edition, 1971.
No Shallow Stream. London, Collins, 1950; as *The World of Christy Pembroke* (as Lyndon Snow), 1978.
Happy Birthday to You. London, Collins, 1951; as *The Conjurer's Daughter* (as Lyndon Snow), 1979.
The Convert. London, Hale, 1952.
A Day of Grace. London, Hale, 1952.
A Girl Disappears. London, Hale, 1953.
Gail Talbot. London, Hale, 1953; as *If This Be Sin* (as Laura Conway), London, Collins, 1975.
Consider These Women. London, Hale, 1954.
A Shade of Darkness. London, Hale, 1954.
The Season's Greetings. London, Hale, 1954.
The Sweet Lost Years. London, Hale, 1955.
I Bequeath. London, Hale, 1955; revised edition (as Laura Conway), London, Collins, 1976.
Strange Visitor. London, Hale, 1956; revised edition (as Laura Conway), London, Collins 1973; New York, Saturday Review Press, 1975.
The Love Match. London, Hale, 1956.
My Dear Lady. London, Hale, 1957.
The Marrying Kind. London, Collins, 1957.
Mrs. Melbourne. London, Hale, 1958; revised edition, 1972.
The Gay Unfortunate. London, Hale, 1958.
The Younger Miss Nightingale. London, Hale, 1959.
Marks upon the Snow. London, Hale, 1960.
Time Is—Time Was. London, Hale, 1960.
The Little Goddess. London, Hale, 1961.
The Lonely Dreamer. London, Hale, 1961; revised edition (as Laura Conway), 1972.
Vicky. London, Hale, 1961; revised edition, as *The Eldest Daughter*, 1974.

Beyond Reasonable Doubt. London, Hale, 1962.
Take Pity upon Youth. London, Hale, 1962.
Minstrel's Court. London, Hale, 1963; revised edition (as Lyndon Snow), London, Collins, 1974.
Lady on the Coin, with Margaret Barnes. London, Macdonald, and Philadelphia, Macrae Smith, 1963.
A House Called Pleasance. London, Hale, 1963; as Laura Conway, New York, Dutton, 1979.
The Undying Past. London, Hale, 1964; as Laura Conway, New York, Dutton, 1980.
Too Well Beloved. London, Hale, 1964; revised edition (as Laura Conway), London, Collins, 1978, New York, Dutton, 1979.
The Brimming Cup. London, Collins, 1965.
The China Princess. London, Collins, 1965.
Saxon's Folly. London, Collins, 1966.
The Queen's Ward. London, Collins, 1967.
The Heir of Garlands. London, Collins, 1968.
The Pursuit of Pleasure. London, Collins, 1969.
The Abbot's House. London, Collins, 1969; as Laura Conway, New York, Saturday Review Press, 1974.
Take Heed of Loving Me. London, Collins, 1970; as Laura Conway, New York, Saturday Review Press, 1976.
Sing for Your Supper. London, Collins, 1970.
The Mask of Comedy. London, Collins, 1970.
The King's Bastard. London, Collins, 1971.
Prelude for Two Queens. London, Collins, 1972.
The Elusive Crown. London, Collins, 1973.
The Cherished Ones. London, Collins, 1974; as Laura Conway, Long Preston, Yorkshire, Magna Print, 1983.
Distant Landscape. London, Collins, 1975; as Laura Conway, Long Preston, Yorkshire, Magna Print, 1982.
Cast a Long Shadow. London, Collins, 1976; as Laura Conway, New York, Dutton, 1978.
Heiress Presumptive. London, Hale, 1981.
Red-Headed Bastard. London, Hale, 1981.

Novels as Vicky Lancaster

Gypsy Virtue. London, Mills and Boon, 1936.
Dawn Through the Shutters. London, Mills and Boon, 1937.
Men Are So Strange. London, Mills and Boon, 1937.
Heartbreaker. London, Mills and Boon, 1938.
Masquerade for Love. London, Mills and Boon, 1938.
This Wild Enchantment. London, Mills and Boon, 1938.
Daughter at Home. London, Hurst and Blackett, 1939.
Three Roads to Heaven. London, Mills and Boon, 1939.
Farewell to Veronica. London, Hurst and Blackett, 1940.
Sometimes Spring Returns. London, Hurst and Blackett, 1940.
Must the Dream End. London, Hurst and Blackett, 1941.
Sweet Shipwreck. London, Hale, 1942.
Beggar Girl's Gift. London, Hale, 1943.
The Happy Cinderella. London, Hale, 1943.
Lady—Look Ahead. London, Hale, 1944.
They Loved in Donegal. London, Hale, 1944.
The Sunset Hour. London, Hale, 1946.
Fixed as the Stars. London, Hale, 1946.
So Many Worlds. London, Hale, 1948; revised edition, as *The Sisters* (as Laura Conway), London, Collins, 1971.
All Past Years. London, Hale, 1949.
Perfect Marriage. London, Hale, 1949.
Draw Back the Curtain. London, Hale, 1950.
Short Lease. London, Hale, 1950.
Homecoming. London, Hale, 1951; as *Journey Home* (as Laura Conway), London, Collins, 1978.

They Were Not Divided. London, Hale, 1952; revised edition, as Laura Conway, London, Collins, 1972.
The Career of Stella Merlin. London, Hale, 1953.
Passing Sweet. London, Hale, 1953.
Lover's Staff. London, Hale, 1954.
Many a Human Heart. London, Hale, 1954.
Lovers in Darkness. London, Hale, 1955.
In Search of Love. London, Hale, 1955.
Suspicion. London, Hale, 1955.
The Way of a Man. London, Hale, 1956.
Women in Love. London, Hale, 1957.
Princess in Love. London, Hale, 1957.
Royal Deputy. London, Hale, 1957.
All Our Tomorrows. London, Hale, 1958.
The Amazing Marriage. London, Hale, 1958.
The Unbroken Link. London, Hale, 1959.
The Past Must Die. London, Hale, 1959.
Secret Lives. London, Hale, 1960.
Sweet Wine of Youth. London, Hale, 1960.
The Cobweb Mist. London, Hale, 1961.
Snake in the Grass. London, Hale, 1961.
Doctor in Suspense. London, Hale, 1962.
Love's Second Chance. London, Hale, 1962.
No Good as a Nurse. London, Hale, 1962.

Novels as Lyndon Snow

Young Love Wakes. London, Collins, 1940.
Follow Your Star. London, Collins, 1941.
Second Thoughts. London, Collins, 1941.
But Joy Kissed Me. London, Collins, 1942.
Three Latch Keys. London, Collins, 1943; as *Latchkeys*, 1978.
Dream Daughter. London, Collins, 1944.
Christening Party. London, Collins, 1945.
Dear Yesterday. London, Collins, 1946.
Early Blossom. London, Collins, 1946.
Two Walk Apart. London, Collins, 1948.
The Gift of My Heart. London, Collins, 1948.
Come to My Wedding. London, Collins, 1949.
Golden Future. London, Collins, 1950.
All in the Day's Work. London, Collins, 1950.
A Year of Her Life. London, Collins, 1951.
Poor Butterfly. London, Collins, 1951.
Honoured Guest. London, Collins, 1952.
Made in Heaven. London, Collins, 1952.
Dearest Enemy. London, Collins, 1953; as *The Case Is Closed* (as Laura Conway), London, Hale, 1980.
Wayward Love. London, Collins, 1953.
Always Remember. London, Collins, 1954.
Do Not Forget Me. London, Collins, 1954.
Love Me for Ever. London, Collins, 1955.
Alone with You. London, Collins, 1955.
So Fair My Love. London, Collins, 1956.
To-morrow's Promise. London, Collins, 1956.
For Love Alone. London, Collins, 1957.
Romance Is Always Young. London, Collins, 1957; revised edition, 1975.
Silence Is Golden. London, Collins, 1958.
A Heart to Be Won. London, Collins, 1958.
Moonlight Witchery. London, Collins, 1959.
Stealer of Hearts. London, Collins, 1959.
Happy Event. London, Collins, 1960.
Some Day You'll Love Me. London, Collins, 1960.
The Fabulous Marriage. London, Collins, 1961.

After All. London, Collins, 1961.
Anything Can Happen. London, Collins, 1962.
My Dream Fulfilled. London, Collins, 1962.
Prima Donna. London, Collins, 1963.
Difficult to Love. London, Collins, 1963.
My Brother's Wife. London, Collins, 1964.
The One Who Looked On. London, Collins, 1965.
Bright Face of Honour. London, Collins, 1965.
His Shadow on the Wall. London, Collins, 1965.
My Cousin Lola. London, Collins, 1966.
Spinster of This Parish. London, Collins, 1966.
The Head of the House. London, Collins, 1967.
Poor Relation. London, Collins, 1968.
Moment of Truth. London, Collins, 1968; as Laura Conway, New York, Saturday Review Press, 1975.
Francesca. London, Collins, 1970; as Laura Conway, New York, Saturday Review Press, 1973.
An Arrow in My Heart. London, Collins, 1972.
Trial and Error. London, Collins, 1973.
Don't Shut Me Out. London, Collins, 1974.
Best Loved Person. London, Collins, 1976.

Novels as Laura Conway

Love Calls Me Home. London, Collins, 1952.
Loving You Always. London, Collins, 1953.
Innocent Enchantress. London, Collins, 1953.
Love's Prisoner. London, Collins, 1954.
So New to Love. London, Collins, 1955.
Enchantment. London, Collins, 1956.
Hard to Win. London, Collins, 1956.
Be True to Me. London, Collins, 1957.
When Next We Meet. London, Collins, 1957.
Wish upon a Dream. London, Collins, 1958; as *Dark Dream*, New York, Dutton, 1976.
No Regrets. London, Collins, 1958.
The Sun Still Shines. London, Collins, 1959.
By Love Transformed. London, Collins, 1959.
Bargain in Love. London, Collins, 1960.
The Turn of the Road. London, Collins, 1960.
Teach Me to Forget. London, Collins, 1961.
Shadow Marriage. London, Collins, 1961.
It's Lonely Without You. London, Collins, 1962.
Lovers in Waiting. London, Collins, 1962.
A Way Through the Maze. London, Collins, 1963.
Safety for My Love. London, Collins, 1963.
Loving Is Different. London, Collins, 1964.
A Butterfly's Hour. London, Collins, 1964; New York, Saturday Review Press, 1973.
Two Fair Daughters. London, Collins, 1965.
Gifted Friend. London, Collins, 1965.
Heiress Apparent. London, Collins, 1966; New York, McCall, 1970.
Five Mrs. Lorrimers. London, Collins, 1966.
For a Dream's Sake. London, Collins, 1967.
The Unforgotten. London, Collins, 1967; New York, Saturday Review Press, 1972.
Dearest Mamma. London, Collins, 1969.
The Night of the Party. London, Collins, 1969; New York, McCall, 1971.
Living with Paula. London, Collins, 1972.
Dark Symmetry. New York, Saturday Review Press, 1973.
Acquittal. London, Collins, 1973.
A Link in the Chain. New York, Dutton, 1975.

Short Stories

The Silver Boy and Other Stories. London, Rich and Cowan, 1936.

OTHER PUBLICATIONS

Plays

The Season's Greetings (produced London, 1953). London, Deane, and Boston, Baker, 1954.
A Shade of Difference, adaptation of her own novel (produced Ventnor, Isle of Wight, 1954).
I Bequeath (produced London, 1954).

Other

Unwanted Wife: A Defence of Mrs. Charles Dickens. London, Jarrolds, 1963.
Catherine of Braganza, Charles II's Queen. London, Hale, 1967.

* * *

A prolific author who writes under several pseudonyms. Dorothy Ansle skirts the edge of the gothic tradition. Mysterious forces, reincarnation, occult happenings, and time travel are some of the common, recurring elements which appear in her works. However, the thrills and suspense which can be created by these components are often dulled in Ansle's novels by a heavy emphasis on conversation and the lack of physical action. Although the romantic entanglements end happily enough, the love stories are generally weak. Her interest in her characters seems to be primarily psychological. Consequently there is little emotional involvement for the reader.

In common with many gothic writers. Ansle often uses a house as an actual character in her stories. In *A House Called Pleasance* excessive love for a house creates the motivating force for the actions of the Grenton women. The houses in *The Dream and the World* and *Take Heed of Loving Me* play more sinister roles, in each case acting as a medium through which occult forces are channeled. Houses or estates also figure prominently in *Heiress Apparent*, *The Night of the Party*, and *The Abbot's House*. Despite its potential, this device is not as fully exploited as it is in the works of some of the topflight gothic authors like Barbara Mertz.

Ansle seems more at home in developing themes of reincarnation and what, for lack of a better term, might be called time travel. In *The Dream and the World* (reprinted as *A Link in the Chain*) the supernatural ties which bind the characters to the past and set them on the path to relive an old tragedy are only gradually revealed. It is this forging of the "chain" which leads to a growing tension for the reader. Parallel worlds in time exist in *Take Heed of Loving Me* and *The Unforgotten*. Characters in these novels have the ability to live in different times and, to a certain extent, to influence events in other eras.

In spite of these modest successes Ansle remains in the shadow of the better gothic novelists. Lack of true suspense and too little emphasis on the development of characters prevent her from joining the ranks of the leaders of the genre.

—Barbara E. Kemp

EMSLEY, Clare. Pseudonym for Clare (Emsley) Plummer. British. Born in Coventry, Warwickshire, 23 September 1912. Educated privately. Worked for a group of women's magazines; full-time writer from 1955. *Died 12 April 1980.*

ROMANCE AND HISTORICAL PUBLICATIONS

Novels

Painted Clay. London, Stanley Paul, 1947.
Keep Thy Heart. London, Stanley Paul, 1949.
The Broken Arcs. London, Stanley Paul, 1951.
The Fatal Gift. London, Stanley Paul, 1951.
Lonely Pinnacle. London, Stanley Paul, 1952.
Unjust Recompense. London, Stanley Paul, 1953.
The True Physician. London, Stanley Paul, 1954.
Flame of Youth. London, Stanley Paul, 1957.
Call Back Yesterday. London, Hurst and Blackett, 1958.
The Long Journey. London, Hurst and Blackett, 1959.
Doctor Michael's Bondage. London, Hurst and Blackett, 1962.
A Nurse's Sacrifice. London, Hurst and Blackett, 1962.
A Surgeon's Folly. London, Hurst and Blackett, 1963.
Doctor at the Crossroads. London, Hurst and Blackett, 1966.
Nurse Catherine's Marriage. London, Hurst and Blackett, 1967.
Sister Rachel's Vigil. London, Hurst and Blackett, 1968.
Doctor Rowland's Daughters. London, Hurst and Blackett, 1970.
A Time to Heal. London, Hurst and Blackett, 1972.
Highway to Fate. London, Hurst and Blackett, 1973.
A Heart's Captivity. London, Hurst and Blackett, 1976.

Novels as Clare Plummer

Unknown Heritage. London, Hale, 1963.
Doctor Adam's Past. London, Hale, 1965.
The Awakening of Nurse Grant. London, Hale, 1967.
An Island for Doctor Phillipa. London, Hale, 1969.
Chris Baynton, S.R.N. London, Hale, 1971.

* * *

Clare Plummer, who also writes as Clare Emsley, has produced a large number of romances, many set in a medical context which seems to encourage her imagination to produce varied and convincing stories. However, for Plummer the course of romance is seen very much as a series of choices. Indeed, the basic plot of many of her novels is the choice which has to be made by the protagonist between two prospective partners, who often have markedly different qualities of character. In *Lonely Pinnacle* Richard Flemming's ambition to become a surgeon is hindered by his hesitation between two girls: Jess Oakley, the lovable companion of his childhood, and the rich and beautiful Julie Graham. Although circumstances permit him to marry each in turn he finds that their different qualities give rise to very different experiences within the relationship.

The reverse situation, where a woman has to make the choice between two men, is found in *A Heart's Captivity*. Here Sister Caroline Grange has a hard time choosing between her star patient, David Armitage, and her former (now "reformed") husband. The story unfolds around the intriguing of a dominant mother who uses Caroline's daughter Jenny as a pawn in her power game.

Very forceful mothers are a common feature of Plummer's novels, and the course of a career or a romance is often dictated by the loyalty or obligation a character feels towards his or her mother. So too, the "price that children pay for broken marriages" (*A Heart's Captivity*) is an oft-made point. The fate of Piero in *Unjust Recompense* is a typical example.

Again and again the same "recipe" of one person and two possible partners (e.g., in *Chris Baynton S.R.N.*, *Unjust Recompense*, and *The Broken Arcs*) is used to produce an interesting and very human story. Although such a pattern could easily lead to a series of predictable plots, the writer has used her creative skills to the full. There is no inevitable choice of "goodie" over "baddie," no trite moral judgements, and few obvious happy endings. For example, in *A Heart's Captivity*, the desire of Elsa Franelli to break free of what she sees as the restrictions caused by a husband and son, is shown to be the only route she can take to find true happiness. Even Julie Graham, the arch villain throughout *Lonely Pinnacle*, finally has a change of heart and returns to her husband, quite contrary to the reader's expectations.

While basically convincing, the plots of these novels are often let down by stilted use of language. Conversation alternates between easy use of natural language and some rather false phraseology. "There was no-one to whom he could explain the feeling of power which was beginning to flow through him in the dissecting room" is one such "gem" which does not ring true, even when encountered in context (in *Lonely Pinnacle*), and Piero's accent and his use of the English language (*Unjust Recompense*) also seem rather unusual for a young boy who has hitherto spent all his life in Italy.

Despite these reservations, Plummer displays a consistent ability to write an enjoyable romance. The medical setting is a successful medium for her characters and plots, and the very human dilemmas she describes are imbued with that touch of reality which is the hallmark of a good story.

—Kim Paynter

ERSKINE, John. American. Born in New York City, 5 October 1879. Educated at Columbia University, New York, B.A. 1900, M.A. 1901, Ph.D. 1903. Married 1) Pauline Ives in 1915 (divorced 1945); 2) Helen Worden, two children. Lecturer, Amherst College, Massachusetts, 1903–09; Columbia University, 1909–23; pianist, New York Symphony Orchestra; president, Juilliard School of Music, New York, 1928–37. *Died 2 June 1951.*

ROMANCE AND HISTORICAL PUBLICATIONS

Novels

The Private Life of Helen of Troy. Indianapolis, Bobbs Merrill, 1925; London, Nash and Grayson, 1926.
Galahad: Enough of His Life to Explain His Reputation. Indianapolis, Bobbs Merrill, and London, Nash and Grayson, 1926.
Adam and Eve: Though He Knew Better. Indianapolis, Bobbs Merrill, 1927; London, Nash and Grayson, 1928.
Penelope's Man: The Homing Instinct. Indianapolis, Bobbs Merrill, 1928; London, Nash and Grayson, 1929.
Tristan and Isolde: Restoring Palamede. Indianapolis, Bobbs Merrill, 1932; London, Lane, 1933.
Solomon, My Son! Indianapolis, Bobbs Merrill, 1935; London, Joseph, 1936.

The Brief Hour of François Villon. Indianapolis, Bobbs Merrill, 1937; London, Joseph, 1938.
Give Me Liberty. New York, Stokes, 1940.
Casanova's Women: Eleven Months of a Year. New York, Stokes, 1941.
The Voyage of Captain Bart. Philadelphia, Lippincott, 1943.
Venus, The Lonely Goddess. New York, Morrow, 1949; London, Wingate, 1950.

OTHER PUBLICATIONS

Novels

Sincerity: A Story of Our Time. Indianapolis, Bobbs Merrill, 1929; as *Experiment in Sincerity*, London, Putnam, 1930.
Uncle Sam in the Eyes of His Family. Indianapolis, Bobbs Merrill, 1930.
Unfinished Business. Indianapolis, Bobbs Merrill, 1931.
Bachelor-of-Arts. Indianapolis, Bobbs Merrill, 1934.
Forget If You Can. Indianapolis, Bobbs Merrill, 1935.
The Start of the Road. New York, Stokes, 1938.
Mrs. Doratt. New York, Stokes, 1941.

Short Stories

Cinderella's Daughter and Other Sequels and Consequences. Indianapolis, Bobbs Merrill, 1930.
Peter Kills the Bear. London, Mathews and Marrot, 1930.
Young Love: Variations on a Theme. Indianapolis, Bobbs Merrill, 1936.
The Memory of Certain Persons. Philadelphia, Lippincott, 1947.

Plays

A Pageant of the Thirteenth Century for the Seven Hundreth Anniversary of Roger Bacon. New York, Columbia University, 1914.
Hearts Enduring: A Play in One Scene. New York, Duffield, 1920.
Jack and the Beanstalk, music by Louis Gruenberg (produced New York, 1931). Indianapolis, Bobbs Merrill, 1931.
Helen Retires (opera libretto). Indianapolis, Bobbs Merrill, 1934.

Verse

Actaeon and Other Poems. New York, Lane, 1907.
The Shadowed Hour. New York, Lyric, 1917.
Collected Poems 1907–22. New York, Duffield, 1922.
Sonata and Other Poems. New York, Duffield, 1925.

Other

The Elizabethan Lyric. New York, Macmillan, 1903.
Leading American Novelists. New York, Holt, 1910.
Written English: A Guide to the Rules of Composition, with Helen Erskine. New York, Century, 1910; revised edition, 1913, 1917.
The Moral Obligation to Be Intelligent and Other Essays. New York, Duffield, 1915; revised edition, London, Davies, 1921.
Democracy and Ideals. New York, Doran, 1920.
The Kinds of Poetry and Other Essays. New York, Duffield, 1920; London, Nash and Grayson, 1927.

The Literary Discipline. New York, Duffield, 1923; London, Nash and Grayson, 1927.

American Character and Other Essays. New York, Chautauqua Press, 1927.

Prohibition and Christianity, and Other Paradoxes of the American Spirit. Indianapolis, Bobbs Merrill, and London, Nash and Grayson, 1927.

The Delight of Great Books. Indianapolis, Bobbs Merrill, and London, Nash and Grayson, 1928.

The Influence of Women and Its Cure. Indianapolis, Bobbs Merrill, 1936.

Song Without Words: The Story of Felix Mendelssohn (biography). New York, Messner, 1941.

The Complete Life. New York, Messner, 1943; London, Melrose, 1945.

The Philharmonic Symphony Society of New York: Its First Hundred Years. New York, Macmillan, 1943.

What Is Music? Philadelphia, Lippincott, 1944.

The Human Life of Jesus (biography). New York, Morrow, 1945.

My Life as a Teacher. Philadelphia, Lippincott, 1948.

My Life in Music. New York, Morrow, 1950.

Editor, *Selections from Spenser's The Faerie Queen.* New York, Longman, 1905.

Editor, *Selections from Tennyson's Idylls of the King.* New York, Holt, 1912.

Editor, with W. P. Trent, *Great Writers of America.* New York, Holt, and London, Williams and Norgate, 1912.

Editor, *Interpretations of Literature*, by Lafcadio Hearn. New York, Dodd Mead, 1915.

Editor, *Appreciations of Poetry*, by Lafcadio Hearn. New York, Dodd Mead, 1916; London, Heinemann, 1919.

Editor, *Life and Literature*, by Lafcadio Hearn. New York, Dodd Mead, 1917.

Editor, with others, *The Cambridge History of American Literature.* New York, Putnam, 4 vols., 1917–21; as *A History of American Literature*, Cambridge, Cambridge University Press, 4 vols., 1918–21.

Editor, *Talks with Writers*, by Lafcadio Hearn. New York, Dodd Mead, 1920.

Editor, *Books and Habits*, by Lafcadio Hearn. New York, Dodd Mead, 1921; London, Heinemann, 1922.

Editor, *Pre-Raphaelite and Other Poets*, by Lafcadio Hearn. New York, Dodd Mead, 1922; London, Heinemann, 1923.

Editor, *A Musical Companion: A Guide to the Understanding and Enjoyment of Music.* New York, Knopf, 1935.

*

Critical Studies: "John Erskine: Enough of His Mind to Explain His Art" by William S. Knickerbocker, in *Sewanee Review 35* (Tennessee), 1927; "John Erskine" by Annie R. Marble, in *A Study of the Modern Novel: British and American Since 1900*, New York, Appleton, 1928.

*   *   *

We shall tell the story as it happened in our world, to people like ourselves, or only a little better—the story . . . before poets lifted it out of its origin and used it as a language for remote and mystical things. In its humble form it had its own meaning . . . we confine our report to . . . life on its way to be poetry. (*Galahad*)

Whether it be Greek myth, English medieval legend or biblical folklore, the works of John Erskine display a consistent attempt to demythologise, to bring back to the here and now some of the most poignant myths of our civilisation: Helen of Troy; Adam, Eve and Lilith; Tristan and Isolde. By stripping these tales bare and lifting them from their historical location and specificity, Erskine places upon them the values and prejudices of a 19th-century middle class English mind. There is the boon of increased access to and popularisation of these classic stories, but concomitant with that, the burdened machinations of Greek myth often lie uneasily within an English, domestic environment.

Erskine's body of work develops steadily; moving from the raw narrative structure of *The Private Life of Helen of Troy*, entirely dependent on dialogue and lacking in authorial voice and control, towards the narrative complexity of *Tristan and Isolde* and *The Brief Hour of François Villon*.

The Private Life of Helen of Troy begins with her problematic return to husband Menaleus and daughter Hermione after the protracted Trojan war. The aftermath of the battle, in particular the tale of Clytemnestra's revenge of Agamemnon and death at the hands of her son, Orestes, provides the novel's landscape, while Erskine focuses on the domestic family trio. Helen is portrayed as a modern thinker, the paragon and purveyor of romantic truths and wordly wisdom: while her husband and daughter are bound still by the older ideals of duty and reverence. In a telling note prefacing the text we learn; "After Troy, Helen reestablished herself in the home. It will be seen that apart from her divine beauty and entire frankness she was a conventional woman." While gesturing towards her mystery, Helen is finally tamed.

Erskine returns to classical mythology in *Penelope's Man: The Homing Instinct.* Exploring the "attractive ideal of a victorious hero homeward bound," the novel traces Odysseus's 10 year long journey home from Troy. His adventuring takes him through various romantic liaisons with various women—Daphne, Circe, the Sirens, Calypso—but finally the "homing instinct" wins out and he returns to his wife, Penelope, and immediate marital dispute. His nurse Eurycleia charges him to set forth again or tell the full story of his sexual adventures: she dies in the attempt to persuade him no middle ground is possible.

Erskine's treatment of medieval legend in *Galahad* and *Tristan and Isolde* witnesses a further exploration of romantic love, its codes and social influence. He shows, too, an abiding interest in the people history has seemingly ignored: alongside the love story Tristan and Isolde, a second narrative runs, that of Palmede, his introduction to Christianity and love for Isolde. In *Galahad* the fatal menage of Arthur, Guinevere, and Lancelot, is carefully interlaced with Arthur's illicit affair with Elaine and his bastard son Galahad's future career.

Perhaps the two most original works are *François Villon* and *Adam and Eve.* Set in France at the time of Joan of Arc, *François Villon* is the story of "a poet by nature, sinner by impulse, and fugitive by necessity." *Adam and Eve* is an unusual rendering of the Genesis story: Lilith is introduced as a principle actor—"the woman who liked him to be free," while Eve is cast as the civilising agent. Dichotomies of sensuality versus duty, nature as against nurture are revealed, "although Adam knew better."

—Catherine S. Wearing

ERSKINE-LINDOP, Audrey (Beatrice Noël). British. Born in London, 26 December 1920. Educated at the Convent of Our Lady of Lourdes, Hatch End, Middlesex; Blackdown School, Wellington, Somerset. Married Dudley Gordon Leslie in 1945. Actress with Worthing Repertory Company; then screenwriter in England and Hollywood. Recipient: Prix Roman Policier, 1968. *Died 7 November 1986.*

ROMANCE AND HISTORICAL PUBLICATIONS

Novels

Fortune My Foe. New York, Harper, 1947; as *In Me My Enemy*, London, Harrap, 1948.
Soldiers' Daughters Never Cry. New York, Simon and Schuster, 1948; London, Heinemann, 1949.
The Tall Headlines. London, Heinemann, and New York, Macmillan, 1950.
Out of the Whirlwind. London, Heinemann, 1951; New York, Appleton Century Crofts, 1952.
The Singer Not the Song. London, Heinemann, and New York, Appleton Century Crofts, 1953; as *The Bandit and the Priest*, New York, Pocket Books, 1953.
Details of Jeremy. London, Heinemann, 1955; as *The Outer Ring*, New York, Appleton Century Crofts, 1955.
The Judas Figures. London, Heinemann, and New York, Appleton Century Crofts, 1956.
Mist over Talla. New York, Doubleday, 1957; as *I Thank a Fool*, London, Collins, 1958.
Nicola. New York, Doubleday, 1959; London, Collins, 1964.
The Way to the Lantern. London, Collins, and New York, Doubleday, 1961.
I Start Counting. London, Collins, and New York, Doubleday, 1966.
Sight Unseen. London, Collins, and New York, Doubleday, 1969.
Journey into Stone. New York, Doubleday, 1972; London, Macmillan, 1973.
The Self-Appointed Saint. London, Macmillan, and New York, Doubleday, 1975.

OTHER PUBLICATIONS

Plays

Let's Talk Turkey, with Dudley Leslie (produced Windsor, 1954).
Beware of Angels, with Dudley Leslie (produced London, 1959).

Screenplays: *Blanche Fury*, with Hugh Mills and Cecil McGivern, 1948; *Tall Headlines (The Frightened Bride)*, with Dudley Leslie, 1952; *The Rough and the Smooth (Portrait of a Sinner)*, with Dudley Leslie, 1959.

Other

The Adventures of the Wuffle (for children). London, Methuen, 1966; New York, McGraw Hill, 1968.

*   *   *

"It is the people behind their beliefs that fascinate me far more than what they believe in. . . . " Thus Audrey Erskine-Lindop describes her reasons for writing *The Singer Not the Song*. This statement holds true for her other works as well. In a variety of genres—romantic, historical, sociological—characterization is all important.

The Singer Not the Song is the most obvious example. Father Keogh depicts pure good, and his evil counterpart is Malo. The people of the small Mexican village are pulled first one way and then another between the two men. The battle is to the death over a period of years, and Malo stops at nothing to have his way. The love between the young priest and a romantic child is touching and dangerous for the whole village. The novel is overlong and improbable but tastefully written and intriguing.

Age differences also are important in *I Start Counting*. Wynne at 14 loves George despite the 21 years that separate them. Her love drives her to protect him when she suspects him to be the strangler terrorizing the village. She destroys evidence, withholds information, and tries to make a suicide look like murder to mislead the police. She is partly responsible for her best friend's death and nearly gets herself killed through subterfuge. The killer remains an indistinct person, but Wynne and her family become very real people. The story, finally, is merely diverting.

In *Mist over Talla* an unusual advertisement in the London paper takes Harriet to Shropshire and Ireland as companion to a woman whose husband wants her accompanied every minute. The reasons for this are not explained at first, and Harriet finds understanding her charge very difficult. It is even harder to hide her feelings for Lead Stewart from his wife's eyes. That love would lead to death and the poor prospect for happiness. While not as masterful as her other works, the novel weaves a haunting spell.

The Way to the Lantern is the story of the French Revolution told from the perspective of an English actor who wants to make his fortune but cannot stay away from women. He uses different identities for several woman and finds himself in trouble with each of them as well as with the motley French authorities. This entertaining novel is an unusual and original view of history.

Other novels treat various social problems: irresponsible selfishness in *Out of the Whirlwind*, the effect of a murderer's crime on his own family in *The Tall Headlines*, boredom in *Fortune My Foe*, and homosexuality in *Details of Jeremy*. *Soldiers' Daughters Never Cry* deals with the Nazi takeover of Austria. Some are well done, but others are melodramatic and implausible.

Erskine-Lindop seldom ends her novels happily ever after, but she leaves hope for a brighter future. Each of them is a study of personality and the events that lead to its development. She is a writer of talent, though the quality of her work is uneven.

—Andrea Lee Shuey

ERTZ, Susan. British. Born of American parents in Walton-on-Thames, Surrey, in 1894; taken to the United States as an infant. Educated privately in England, 1901–06, and in California, 1906–12. Did war work in England and France during World War I. Married John Ronald McCrindle in 1932 (died 1977). Fellow, Royal Society of Literature. *Died 11 April 1985.*

ROMANCE AND HISTORICAL PUBLICATIONS

Novels

Madam Claire. London, Unwin, and New York, Appleton, 1923.

Nina. London, Unwin, and New York, Appleton, 1924.

After Noon. London, Unwin, and New York, Appleton, 1926.

Now East, Now West. London, Benn, and New York, Appleton, 1927.

The Galaxy. London, Hodder and Stoughton, and New York, Appleton, 1929.

Julian Probert. London, Hodder and Stoughton, 1931; as *The Story of Julian*, New York, Appleton, 1931.

The Proselyte. London, Hodder and Stoughton, and New York, Appleton Century, 1933.

Now We Set Out. London, Hodder and Stoughton, 1934; New York, Appleton Century, 1935.

Woman Alive. London, Hodder and Stoughton, 1935; New York, Appleton Century, 1936.

No Hearts to Break. London, Hodder and Stoughton, and New York, Appleton Century, 1937.

One Fight More. New York, Appleton Century, 1939; London, Hodder and Stoughton, 1940.

Anger in the Sky. London, Hodder and Stoughton, and New York, Harper, 1943.

Two Names under the Shore. London, Hodder and Stoughton, 1947; as *Mary Hallam*, New York, Harper, 1947.

The Prodigal Heart. London, Hodder and Stoughton, and New York, Harper, 1950.

The Undefended Gate. London, Hodder and Stoughton, 1953; as *Invitation to Folly*, New York, Harper, 1953.

Charmed Circle. London, Collins, and New York, Harper, 1956.

In the Cool of the Day. New York, Harper, 1960; London, Collins, 1961.

Devices and Desires. London, Collins, 1972; as *Summer's Lease*, New York, Harper, 1972.

The Philosopher's Daughter. London, Collins, and New York, Harper, 1976.

Short Stories

And Then Face to Face and Other Stories. London, Unwin, 1927; as *The Wind of Complication*, New York, Appleton, 1927.

Big Frogs and Little Frogs. London, Hodder and Stoughton, 1938; New York, Harper, 1939.

OTHER PUBLICATIONS

Other

Black, White and Caroline (for children). London, Hodder and Stoughton, and New York, Appleton Century, 1938.

*   *   *

Susan Ertz enjoyed a long and cosmopolitan career as a writer of fiction. Although her novels may be said to fall into the general category of "romance," this description does not really do justice to her range and originality. Her books rarely follow an established formula, though they may contain formulaic elements; the central interest lies not in plot, but rather in the psychology of individual characters. In this respect, her works often strike one as essentially gothic in tone, and, occasionally, as excessively ingenious.

Nina, the story of a woman's hopeless infatuation for an unfaithful husband, exemplifies the author's approach to romantic love. Her novels are filled with examples of romances which end unhappily, or which contain elements of selfishness, manipula-

tion, or cruelty. A recurring theme is the unhealthy influence of families upon their members, and the difficulty experienced by individuals in escaping from what the title of one novel refers to, ironically, as a *Charmed Circle*. The effectiveness of this theme is sometimes blurred, however, by a tendency to present secondary characters as caricatures: *Charmed Circle* is narrated by one son who manages to escape the clutches of his family, who appear to have no redeeming qualities whatever. There is often an element of mystery in the novels, usually associated with an event which occurred in the past. However, as she is essentially unconcerned with plot, this element results in some rather unconvincing convolutions. In *The Philosopher's Daughter*, for example, a girl falls in love with the man she assumes to be her long-lost half-brother. Although generally free from the fascination with exotic locale which characterizes the work of many romance writers, the novels frequently present some version of what might be called the "international theme." *Now East, Now West* presents a contrast between the societies of England and America; *In the Cool of the Day* provides a combination of high romance and travelogue; and *Devices and Desires* is the story of an English woman, unhappily married to a faithless American husband, who is loved by a Frenchman and an American professor, and who, sacrificing herself to her son, loses the love of both. This plot illustrates both the weaknesses and the strengths of the author, who once declared that she preferred "a new idea . . . to a diamond watch."

—Joanne Harack Hayne

———————

ESSEX, Mary. See **BLOOM, Ursula**.

———————

ESTEVEN, John. See **SHELLABARGER, Samuel**.

———————

EYRE, Annette. See **WORBOYS, Anne**.

———————

FAIRE, Zabrina. See **STEVENSON, Florence**.

———————

FAIRFAX, Ann. See **CHESNEY, Marion**.

———————

FARNES, Eleanor. British. Married; two sons. Address: c/o Mills and Boon Ltd., 18–24 Paradise Road, Richmond, Surrey TW9 1SR, England.

ROMANCE AND HISTORICAL PUBLICATIONS

Novels

Merry Goes the Time. London, Mills and Boon, 1935.
Tangled Harmonies. London, Mills and Boon, 1936.
Three Happy Pilgrims. London, Mills and Boon, 1937.
Romantic Melody. London, Mills and Boon, 1938.
Hesitation Waltz. London, Mills and Boon, 1939.
The Crystal Spring. London, Mills and Boon, 1940.
I Walk the Mountain Tops. London, Mills and Boon, 1940.
Bloom on the Gorse. London, Mills and Boon, 1941.
Reckless Adventure. London, Mills and Boon, 1942.
Fruits of the Year. London, Mills and Boon, 1942.
The Doctor's Wife. London, Mills and Boon, 1943.
Summer Motley. London, Mills and Boon, 1943.
Brief Excursion. London, Mills and Boon, 1944.
The Quiet Valley. London, Mills and Boon, 1944.
Stormcloud and Sunrise. London, Mills and Boon, 1945.
Journey for Two Travellers. London, Mills and Boon, 1946.
Mistress of the House. London, Mills and Boon, 1946; Toronto, Harlequin, 1966.
The Deep, Wide River. London, Mills and Boon, 1947.
The Opening Flower. London, Mills and Boon, 1948.
The Wayward Stream. London, Mills and Boon, 1949.
The Faithless Friend. London, Mills and Boon, 1949.
Captive Daughter. London, Mills and Boon, 1950.
The Dream and the Dancer. London, Mills and Boon, 1951; Toronto, Harlequin, 1965.
The Golden Peaks. London, Mills and Boon, 1951; Toronto, Harlequin, 1964.
The House by the Lake. London, Mills and Boon, 1952.
Magic Symphony. London, Mills and Boon, 1952; Toronto, Harlequin, 1966.
The Wings of Memory. London, Mills and Boon, 1953; Toronto, Harlequin, 1968.
The Young Intruder. London, Mills and Boon, 1953; Toronto, Harlequin, 1968.
A Home for Jocelyn. London, Mills and Boon, 1953; Toronto, Harlequin, 1967.
Song of Summer. London, Mills and Boon, 1954; as *Doctor's Orders*, Toronto, Harlequin, 1963.
Sister of the Housemaster. London, Mills and Boon, 1954; Toronto, Harlequin, 1965.
The Fortunes of Springfield. London, Mills and Boon, 1955; Toronto, Harlequin, 1967.
The Mist of Morning. London, Mills and Boon, 1955.
Secret Heiress. London, Mills and Boon, 1956; Toronto, Harlequin, 1967.
The Constant Heart. London, Mills and Boon, 1956; Toronto, Harlequin, 1968.
A Season of Enchantment. London, Mills and Boon, 1956.
The Way Through the Forest. London, Mills and Boon, 1957.
The Persistent Lover. London, Mills and Boon, 1957.
The Blessing in Disguise. London, Mills and Boon, 1958.
The Happy Enterprise. London, Mills and Boon, 1958; Toronto, Harlequin, 1959.
The Flight of the Swan. London, Mills and Boon, 1959; Toronto, Harlequin, 1969.
A Stronger Spell. London, Mills and Boon, 1959.
The Painted Ceiling. London, Mills and Boon, 1960.
The Red Cliffs. London, Mills and Boon, 1961; Toronto, Harlequin, 1969.
Lovers' Meeting. London, Mills and Boon, 1962.
A Change of Heart. London, Mills and Boon, 1963; as *Doctor Max*, Toronto, Harlequin, 1963.

The Tangled Web. London, Mills and Boon, 1963.
The Daring Deception. London, Mills and Boon, 1965.
The Pursuit and the Capture. London, Mills and Boon, 1966.
Loving and Giving. London, Mills and Boon, 1968.
The Rose and the Thorn. London, Mills and Boon, 1968.
Rubies for My Love. London, Mills and Boon, 1969.
The Doctor's Circle. London, Mills and Boon, 1970; Toronto, Harlequin, 1971.
The Enchanted Island. London, Mills and Boon, 1970; Toronto, Harlequin, 1971.
A Castle in Spain. London, Mills and Boon, 1971; Toronto, Harlequin, 1972.
A Serpent in Eden. London, Mills and Boon, 1971; Toronto, Harlequin, 1973.
The Valley of the Eagles. London, Mills and Boon, and Toronto, Harlequin, 1972.
The Shadow of Suspicion. London, Mills and Boon, 1972.
The Splendid Legacy. London, Mills and Boon, 1973; Toronto, Harlequin, 1974.
The Runaway Visitors. London, Mills and Boon, 1973; Toronto, Harlequin, 1974.
Homeward Bound. London, Mills and Boon, 1975.
This Golden Estate. London, Mills and Boon, 1975.
The Amaranth Flower. London, Mills and Boon, 1979.

*   *   *

Eleanor Farnes has been writing romance novels since the 1930's and has had more than 60 published. Although she is an English writer, she has traveled widely in Europe, South Africa, and North America. She also spends part of each year in Spain where her family has a home.

Her novels reflect her intimate knowledge of the countries she writes about, and she is able to select just the right detail to make that country familiar to her readers. She is another writer who developed her writing skills by beginning with doctor/nurse novels. It was a productive apprenticeship, for she has a sensitive way of developing her characters and telling their stories.

One of her most effective novels is *A Castle in Spain*. Evocative as the title is, it sets the mood of the novel for it is one of her most tender love stories. Venetia Hamilton takes a motoring tour through Spain. She encounters car problems and is aided by Don Andres de Arevado. He arranges for her car to be repaired and also offers her the hospitality of his home. His cousin and her three daughters live there as well, so propriety is maintained.

From this somewhat ordinary start, Eleanor Farnes builds a lovely novel of misunderstood love as conflicting cultures hit head on. Venetia is an independent young woman, who revels in using her mind and abilities. She is not a forward person, but one who was taught from childhood to think for herself and to hold to her own beliefs. Her breezy freshness and strong streak of independence are not qualities that Don Andres wants his cousins exposed to. Almost from her first introduction to the family, she finds herself held up as a bad example, even when she is asked to stay and teach them English.

Farnes develops the story from this point by letting Venetia and Don Andres react to each other as each tries to cling to their individual beliefs. Subtly Venetia is allowed to show Don Andres that far from being a disruptive influence, she is actually a warm, capable person with strong depths of feeling and love. Gradually they fall in love despite their cultural differences, and, step by step, Farnes shows the changes in attitude of Don Andres as he realizes that he truly loves Venetia. He also realizes that her independence and initiative are qualities he can't help but acknowledge for they have made her into the kind of woman he can love.

In writing this particular story, Farnes displays a sensitive understanding of today's young girls as they try to balance their own inner resources against the traditional limits of other people. At the same time, she makes it obvious that love is the strongest force in drawing two people together. The early antagonism between Venetia and Don Andres can only end in love as each grows to understand and respect the other.

In *The Runaway Visitors* Victoria Fenn must take her younger brother and sister to spend the summer with a family friend in Italy. She is a responsive girl who feels the awkwardness of the arrangement for her parents have made it a habit of "dumping" the family on unsuspecting friends and relatives for the summer, while they carry on research activities abroad. Charles Duncan's frequent mention of foundlings being dropped on other people's doorsteps merely adds to her embarrassment and makes her sensitive to other instances of slight.

In developing her heroines, Farnes holds to more traditional characterization by having them young, innocent, and often unsure of themselves in an emotional situation. Even Venetia is unawakened to love for all of her abilities and independence. She is still naive in this situation but she does hold true to character by acknowledging the difficulties she must face if she gives into her love for Don Andres.

Farnes's heroes are maturer and again traditional in the sense that they are more sophisticated than the heroine and more experienced in love and love affairs. Yet they have a certain degree of sensitivity to people that is not a standard characteristic in romance novels.

In assessing Farnes as a romance writer, one might cite several popular clichés; for instance, she makes her characters live, or she tells a wonderful story. But she does far more than that: her readers not only enjoy her novels the first time around, they can not resist the urge to go back time and time again to re-read them. She is one of those romance writers who remain fresh, exciting and romantic no matter how often one reads her novels.

—Arlene Moore

* * *

FARNOL, (John) Jeffery. British. Born in Warwickshire, 10 February 1878. Educated privately; apprenticed briefly to a brass foundry in Birmingham; studied at Westminster School of Art, London. Married 1) Blanche V. W. Hawley in 1900 (divorced 1938), one daughter; 2) Phyllis Clarke in 1938, one adopted daughter. Worked in his father's business; lived in the U.S., 1902–10: scene painter, Astor Theatre, New York, for two years; lived in England after 1910. *Died 9 August 1952.*

ROMANCE AND HISTORICAL PUBLICATIONS

Novels

My Lady Caprice. London, Stevens and Brown, and New York, Dodd Mead, 1907; as *The Chronicles of the Imp*, London, Sampson Low, 1915.

The Broad Highway. London, Sampson Low, 1910; Boston, Little Brown, 1911.

The Money Moon. London, Sampson Low, and Boston, Little Brown, 1911.

The Oubliette. London, Watt, 1912.

The Amateur Gentleman. London, Sampson Low, and Boston, Little Brown, 1913.

The Honourable Mr. Tawnish. London, Sampson Low, and Boston, Little Brown, 1913.

Beltane the Smith. London, Sampson Low, and Boston, Little Brown, 1915.

The Definite Object. London, Sampson Low, and Boston, Little Brown, 1917.

Our Admirable Betty. London, Sampson Low, and Boston, Little Brown, 1918.

The Geste of Duke Jocelyn. London, Sampson Low, 1919; Boston, Little Brown, 1920.

Black Bartlemy's Treasure. London, Sampson Low, and Boston, Little Brown, 1920.

Martin Conisby's Vengeance. London, Sampson Low, and Boston, Little Brown, 1921.

Peregrine's Progress. London, Sampson Low, and Boston, Little Brown, 1922.

Sir John Dering. London, Sampson Low, and Boston, Little Brown, 1923.

The Loring Mystery. London, Sampson Low, and Boston, Little Brown, 1925.

The High Adventure. London, Sampson Low, and Boston, Little Brown, 1926.

The Quest of Youth. London, Sampson Low, and Boston, Little Brown, 1927.

Gyfford of Weare. London, Sampson Low, 1928; as *Guyfford of Weare*, Boston, Little Brown, 1928.

Over the Hills. London, Sampson Low, and Boston, Little Brown, 1930.

The Jade of Destiny. London, Sampson Low, 1931; as *A Jade of Destiny*, Boston, Little Brown, 1931.

Charmian, Lady Vibart. London, Sampson Low, and Boston, Little Brown, 1932.

The Way Beyond. London, Sampson Low, and Boston, Little Brown, 1933.

Winds of Fortune. London, Sampson Low, 1934; as *Winds of Chance*, Boston, Little Brown, 1934.

A Portrait of a Gentleman in Colours: The Romance of Mr. Lewis Berger. London, Sampson Low, 1935.

John o' the Green. London, Sampson Low, and Boston, Little Brown, 1935.

A Pageant of Victory. London, Sampson Low, and Boston, Little Brown, 1936.

The Crooked Furrow. London, Sampson Low, 1937; New York, Doubleday, 1938.

The Lonely Road. London, Sampson Low, and New York, Doubleday, 1938.

The Happy Harvest. London, Sampson Low, 1939; New York, Doubleday, 1940.

Adam Penfeather, Buccaneer. London, Sampson Low, 1940; New York, Doubleday, 1941.

Murder by Nail. London, Sampson Low, 1942; as *Valley of Night*, New York, Doubleday, 1942.

The King Liveth. London, Sampson Low, 1943; New York, Doubleday, 1944.

The "Piping Times." London, Sampson Low, 1945.

Heritage Perilous. London, Sampson Low, 1946; New York, McBride, 1947.

My Lord of Wrybourne. London, Sampson Low, 1948; as *Most Sacred of All*, New York, McBride, 1948.

The Fool Beloved. London, Sampson Low, 1949.

The Ninth Earl. London, Sampson Low, 1950.

The Glad Summer. London, Sampson Low, 1951.

Waif of the River. London, Sampson Low, 1952.

Justice by Midnight, completed by Phyllis Farnol. London, Sampson Low, 1956.

Short Stories

The Shadow and Other Stories. London, Sampson Low, and
Boston, Little Brown, 1929.
Voices from the Dust, Being Romances of Old London. London,
Macmillan, and Boston, Little Brown, 1932.
A Matter of Business and Other Stories. London, Sampson
Low, and Boston, Little Brown, 1940.

OTHER PUBLICATIONS

Play

The Honourable Mr. Tawnish, adaptation of his own novel (produced Manchester, 1920; London, 1924).

Other

Some War Impressions. London, Sampson Low, 1918; as *Great
Britain at War*, Boston, Little Brown, 1918.
Epics of the Fancy. London, Sampson Low, 1928; as *Famous
Prize Fights; or, Epics of "The Fancy,"* Boston, Little Brown,
1928.
Hove. Privately printed, 1937.
A Book [New Book] for Jane (for children). London, Sampson
Low, 2 vols., 1937–39.

*

Critical Studies: *Jeffery Farnol*, Beaminster, Cox, 1964, and
More Memories of My Brother Jack: Jeffery Farnol, Beaminster,
Cox, 1966, both by E. E. Farnol.

*   *   *

Jeffery Farnol provides a link between the major writers of the
19th century and the popular romancers of the present. While no
one could call him a serious writer like Scott or Dickens, one
can easily note traces of both these writers in his works. The
quaint lower-class characters, the concern for social evils speak
of Dickens; the heroes who were "out with the Jacobites" look
back to Scott. Yet the moral purpose of the earlier writers is
lacking; the whole cumbersome plot mechanism merely provides
the opportunity to get two young people together and let them
get on with their own business.

Even the formulas that Farnol uses are not really formulas;
they are more like convention in which he felt comfortable letting his imagination work. For instance, the hero and heroine
are often disguised when they meet. Either he does not know
who she is, so he can unwittingly disparage her public persona
(as in *John o' the Green*, where John tells the girl "Lia" that
the Duchess Ippolita's name " 'tis neigh of horse, 'tis sneeze,
'tis hiccough"); or she fails to recognize that he is a member of
the family of her hereditary enemies (Lady Joan Brandon in
Black Bartlemy's Treasure). She is usually quicker than he to
realize the truth, however. Farnol's women are slow only to realize that they are falling in love; other than that, they are independent, intelligent, and only too likely to try to take control
from the heroes when those gentlemen are moving too slowly. In
The Money Moon, however, a modern dress version of Farnol's
favorite tale, the hero recognizes what is happening sooner than
Anthea; he is also the one in disguise, and it is not until the end
that she discovers he is really at once Prince Charming and millionaire deus ex machina come to pay off the mortgage.

What makes all this foolishness pleasant is Farnol's innocent
enthusiasm. The whole-heartedness with which his characters
fall into and out of their scrapes and their insistence on doing
what they perceive of as the right thing are curiously endearing.
Even the villainous Mr. Dartry (in *The Lonely Road*) can have a
change of heart when Jason reminds him of his mother. It's sentimental, of course; but it is still reassuring, on some level. Even
conventional romances today do not guarantee quite this level of
escapism.

Farnol's prose may be too rich for the modern reader, but his
crazy vehicles of plots do carry the reader along willy-nilly, dialogues full of ellipses and dashes, fevered but chaste passions,
poetic descriptions of scenery, broadly rendered accents and all.
At his best—in *The Crooked Furrow* and *The Happy Harvest*—
Farnol presents genuinely attractive characters in a model of
what a picaresque novel should be. That descendent of the
Roundheads, Oliver, and his cousin, the impulsive "cavalier"
Roland, go off at the behest of their stern guardian uncle to find
out how well they can live on a guinea a week in an Arcadian
Georgian England, where friendly gypsies, honorable highwaymen, and faithful servants abound. Oliver, a complete romantic
at heart, adopts an abused child and helps his uncle find the wife
he had mistakenly cast off years before. But the beautiful heroine prefers Roland. Despite his broken heart, Oliver finds comfort in the fact that he and Roland are finally reconciled, the
friends their mothers hoped they would become. And in the sequel Oliver's virtues find their reward. The little foundling,
grown to be a bewitching young woman, overcomes her fears
about her unknown parentage and Oliver's fears about the difference in their ages and her informal engagement to his other
ward, Robin. Clia redeems her promise at the end of *The
Crooked Furrow* to marry Oliver when she is old enough. Clia is
not really one of Farnol's happiest female creations; she is as
cloying as a child, and as full of imperious wiles as an adult.
Yet she's what Oliver wants and for Oliver, through the third
person narration of *The Crooked Furrow* and the rather stuffy
first person narration of *The Happy Harvest*, one develops a
fondness. Oliver's ward Robin, incidentally, decides that, despite
his own love for Clia, the passion that she and Oliver share is so
perfect that he cannot sully it with jealousy. Thus Farnol provides an all-around happy ending without the necessity of
sketching a second female lead, always a chore for him (the tear-
ful Angela in *Gyfford of Weare* is one example.)

Oliver and Roland find adventures, in both books, in the
midst of the crime and poverty of London, which is relieved in
part by the work of the ladies of "The Jolly Young Waterman,"
running the equivalent of a settlement house in a pub in the
roughest part of the vast city. London is not present in all Farnol's books, except as an implicit contrast to the idyllic scenes
of the southern English countryside. Urban criminals may be
misguided louts; rural gypsies, complete with Romany vocabu-
laries, are noble and charming, and cant-spouting highwaymen
are helpful to the causes of right.

Farnol's ventures away from his favorite, though vaguely delineated, Regency period are not always happy; that adult fairy-
tale without magic, *John o' the Green*, is set mistily "in King
Tristan's day"; we are always aware of the disparity between
modern life as we know it and the picture presented to us in *The
Money Moon*. The linked short stories of *Voices from the Dust*
follow the reincarnation of two lovers through English history;
they vary from the entertaining ("White Friars") to the absurd
("The White Tower").

Ultimately, what Farnol brings to his chosen genre is the unusual viewpoint of a man writing for women. In Farnol's world
women are beautiful but mysterious creatures, the repository of
exalted ideals about family and sanctity. But his men never

really understand them very well. Women can read his books with bemused condescension at how like children the men in his books are. Men can read his books with fellow feeling, and because there is always a share of fighting and swordplay. Contemporary romances are usually written either by a woman or from a woman's point of view; and they are read almost exclusively by women. Reading Farnol reminds us that this is not the way things have to be, and makes us wonder if something has been lost to us that we used to have.

—Susan Branch

FARRELL, J(ames) G(ordon). British. Born in Liverpool, Lancashire, 23 January 1935. Educated at Rossall School, Fleetwood, Lancashire, 1947–53; Brasenose College, Oxford, 1956, 1957–60, B.A. in French and Spanish 1960. Teacher in Dublin, 1954–55; labourer, fireman, and clerk for Early Warning Defence System, Baffin Island, Northwest Territories, Canada, 1955–56; language teacher in France, 1961–63; teacher of English as a foreign language and publisher's reader, London, 1964–66; lived in New York, 1966–68, London, 1969–78, and County Cork, Ireland, 1979. Contracted polio, 1956. Recipient: Harkness fellowship, 1966; Arts Council award, 1970; Faber Memorial prize, 1971; Booker prize, 1973. *Died 12 August 1979.*

ROMANCE AND HISTORICAL PUBLICATIONS

Novels

Troubles. London, Cape, 1970; New York, Knopf, 1971.
The Siege of Krishnapur. London, Weidenfeld and Nicolson, 1973; New York, Harcourt Brace, 1974.
The Singapore Grip. London, Weidenfeld and Nicolson, 1978; New York, Knopf, 1979.

OTHER PUBLICATIONS

Novels

A Man from Elsewhere. London, Hutchinson, 1963.
The Lung. London, Hutchinson, 1965.
A Girl in the Head. London, Cape, 1967; New York, Harper, 1969.
The Hill Station: An Unfinished Novel, and An Indian Diary, edited by John Spurling. London, Weidenfeld and Nicolson, 1981.

*

Manuscript Collection: Trinity College, Dublin.

Critical Study: *J. G. Farrell* by Ronald Binns, London, Methuen, 1986.

* * *

The works of J. G. Farrell—notably *Troubles* and *The Siege of Krishnapur*—provide a brave contribution to this century's historical fiction. His is a distinctive and courageous voice.

Farrell was fascinated by historical problems and problematic historical periods; times when the issues appear black and white, when people are called on to "take sides," but where the reality is inevitably more complex. This fascination is evident in Farrell's most accomplished book, *Troubles,* which is set in a post-1916 Ireland, as the sectarian struggle between Protestants and Catholics is beginning to emerge in its modern form. The situation is further complicated by the looming "threat" of partition, and the nervous British presence, as personified by the novel's protagonist Major Brendan.

In *The Siege of Krishnapur* Farrell explores the 19th-century Indian Mutiny in Krishnapur, presenting it as the inevitable expression of native outrage against a colonial and exploitative power. As Farrell states in his Afterword: "The reality of the Indian Mutiny constantly defies imagination," and so his "fiction" is based on: "Actual events, taken from the mass of diaries, letters and memoirs written by eye witnesses."

Civilisation versus a native culture, high art and primitivism, materialism, and spiritualism, these are some of the dichotomies the novel explores and eventually explodes, arguing for an integrated notion of humanity, one that defies the crippling logic of oppositions.

It is a tribute to Farrell's skill that throughout all his works the narrative voice is controlled yet passionate, refusing to take sides. His is not a partisan voice. Another courageous feature of the writing lies in its innovative structures and eclectic style.

The Siege is a relatively straightforward narrative that maps out the experience of a British community administering British justice, culture, and religion to the Indian town of Krishnapur. Fleury and his sister Miriam arrive from England as the first signs of revolt break out. While the Maharaja and his son vainly try to mimic the British way of life the native uprising gains momentum until the town is placed under self-imposed siege. Starvation and cholera ravage the community: "India itself was now a different place, the fiction of happy natives being led forward along the road to civilisation could no longer be sustained." Episodes of savage realism chart the community's fall from "respectable" behaviour in its fight for survival. At points Farrell is graphic and disturbing. Relief finally arrives, but the novel closes with ironic portraits of the major characters many years on: people who have chosen to forget their experiences.

Troubles is a more daring narrative which moves in and out of domestic realism, like surreal humour reminiscent of Flann O'Brien, and journalistic news coverage of both the Irish and Indian struggles for self-determination in the post-colonial, modern world.

Major Brendan is a British soldier, shattered by his experience of World War I. He arrives at the Majestic Hotel in Ireland to find out if his rash engagement to Angela made years previously still holds true. Gradually this nervous, eager-to-please man is drawn into the family's various obsessions and intrigues and the situation in Ireland. Angela dies, but Sarah, a wild and independent woman, emerges as his doomed lover. The struggles and troubles bubble away in the background until the novel finally reaches its powerful climax: the Major nearly loses his life at the hands of the Sinn Feiners, the Hotel lies ransacked and abandoned, the family disrupted and the country partitioned.

The title is intriguing: the novel suggests the modern "troubles" need to be understood in the light of their earlier history in the 1920's. The language of the media is under close scrutiny: as the story line is continually interrupted by press flashes from around the world, we see the human consequences of these historical movements enacted by a small cast of individuals.

—Catherine S. Wearing

FAST, Howard (Melvin). American. Born in New York City, 11 November 1914. Educated at George Washington High School, New York, graduated 1931; National Academy of Design, New York. Served with the Office of War Information, 1942–43, and the Army Film Project, 1944. Married Bette Cohen in 1937; one daughter and one son, the writer Jonathan Fast. War correspondent in the Far East for *Esquire* and *Coronet* magazines, 1945. Teacher at Indiana University, Bloomington, Summer 1947; imprisoned for contempt of Congress, 1947; owner, Blue Heron Press, New York, 1952–57. Founder, World Peace Movement and member, World Peace Council, 1950–55; currently, member of the Fellowship for Reconciliation. American-Labor Party candidate for Congress for 23rd District of New York, 1952. Recipient: Bread Loaf Writers Conference award, 1933; Schomburg Race Relations award, 1944; Newspaper Guild award, 1947; Jewish Book Council of America award, 1948; Stalin International Peace prize (now Soviet International Peace prize), 1954; Screenwriters award, 1960; National Association of Independent Schools award, 1962; Emmy Award, for television play, 1976. Agent: Sterling Lord Literistic Inc., 1 Madison Avenue, New York, New York 10010. Address: 31 East 79th Street, New York, New York 10021, U.S.A.

ROMANCE AND HISTORICAL PUBLICATIONS

Novels (series: The Immigrants)

Two Valleys. New York, Dial Press, 1933; London, Dickson, 1934.
Strange Yesterday. New York, Dodd Mead, 1934.
Conceived in Liberty: A Novel of Valley Forge. New York, Simon and Schuster, and London, Joseph, 1939.
The Last Frontier. New York, Duell, 1941; London, Lane, 1948.
The Unvanquished. New York, Duell, 1942; London, Lane, 1947.
The Tall Hunter. New York, Harper, 1942.
Citizen Tom Paine. New York, Duell, 1943; London, Lane, 1945.
Freedom Road. New York, Duell, 1944; London, Lane, 1946.
The American: A Middle Western Legend. New York, Duell, 1946; London, Lane, 1949.
Clarkton. New York, Duell, 1947.
My Glorious Brothers. Boston, Little Brown, 1948; London, Lane, 1950.
The Proud and the Free. Boston, Little Brown, 1950; London, Lane, 1952.
Spartacus. Privately printed, 1951; London, Lane, 1952.
Moses, Prince of Egypt. New York, Crown, 1958; London, Methuen, 1959.
April Morning. New York, Crown, and London, Methuen, 1961.
Agrippa's Daughter. New York, Doubleday, 1964; London, Methuen, 1965.
Torquemada. New York, Doubleday, 1966; London, Methuen, 1967.
The Crossing. New York, Morrow, 1971; London, Eyre Methuen, 1972.
The Hessian. New York, Morrow, 1972; London, Hodder and Stoughton, 1973.
The Immigrants:
   The Immigrants. Boston, Houghton Mifflin, 1977; London, Hodder and Stoughton, 1978.
   Second Generation. Boston, Houghton Mifflin, and London, Hodder and Stoughton, 1978.

The Establishment. Boston, Houghton Mifflin, 1979; London, Hodder and Stoughton, 1980.
The Call of Fife and Drum: Three Novels of the Revolution (includes *The Unvanquished, Conceived in Liberty, The Proud and the Free*). Secaucus, New Jersey, Citadel Press, 1987.

Short Stories

Patrick Henry and the Frigate's Keel and Other Stories of a Young Nation. New York, Duell, 1945.
Departures and Other Stories. Boston, Little Brown, 1949.
The Last Supper and Other Stories. New York, Blue Heron Press, 1955; London, Lane, 1956.

OTHER PUBLICATIONS

Novels

Place in the City. New York, Harcourt Brace, 1937.
The Children. New York, Duell, 1947.
Fallen Angel (as Walter Ericson). Boston, Little Brown, 1952; as *The Darkness Within*, New York, Ace, 1953; as *Mirage* (as Howard Fast), New York, Fawcett, 1965.
Silas Timberman. New York, Blue Heron Press, 1954; London, Lane, 1955.
The Story of Lola Gregg. New York, Blue Heron Press, 1956; London, Lane, 1957.
The Winston Affair. New York, Crown, 1959; London, Methuen, 1960.
The Golden River, in *The Howard Fast Reader.* New York, Crown, 1960.
Power. New York, Doubleday, 1962; London, Methuen, 1963.
The Hunter and the Trap. New York, Dial Press, 1967.
The Legacy. Boston, Houghton Mifflin, and London, Hodder and Stoughton, 1981.
Max. Boston, Houghton Mifflin, 1982; London, Hodder and Stoughton, 1983.
The Outsider. Boston, Houghton Mifflin, 1984; London, Hodder and Stoughton, 1985.
The Immigrant's Daughter. Boston, Houghton Mifflin, 1985; London, Hodder and Stoughton, 1986.
The Dinner Party. Boston, Houghton Mifflin, and London, Hodder and Stoughton, 1987.
The Pledge. Boston, Houghton Mifflin, 1988; London, Hodder and Stoughton, 1989.
The Confession of Joe Cullen. Boston, Houghton Mifflin, 1989.

Novels as E. V. Cunningham

Sylvia. New York, Doubleday, 1960; London, Deutsch, 1962.
Phyllis. New York, Doubleday, and London, Deutsch, 1962.
Alice. New York, Doubleday, 1963; London, Deutsch, 1965.
Lydia. New York, Doubleday, 1964; London, Deutsch, 1965.
Shirley. New York, Doubleday, and London, Deutsch, 1964.
Penelope. New York, Doubleday, 1965; London, Deutsch, 1966.
Helen. New York, Doubleday, 1966; London, Deutsch, 1967.
Margie. New York, Morrow, 1966; London, Deutsch, 1968.
Sally. New York, Morrow, and London, Deutsch, 1967.
Samantha. New York, Morrow, 1967; London, Deutsch, 1968; as *The Case of the Angry Actress*, New York, Dell, 1984.
Cynthia. New York, Morrow, 1968; London, Deutsch, 1969.
The Assassin Who Gave Up His Gun. New York, Morrow, 1969; London, Deutsch, 1970.
Millie. New York, Morrow, 1973; London, Deutsch, 1975.

The Case of the One-Penny Orange. New York, Holt Rinehart, 1977; London, Deutsch, 1978.
The Case of the Russian Diplomat. New York, Holt Rinehart, 1978; London, Deutsch, 1979.
The Case of the Poisoned Eclairs. New York, Holt Rinehart, 1979; London, Deutsch, 1980.
The Case of the Sliding Pool. New York, Delacorte Press, 1981; London, Gollancz, 1982.
The Case of the Kidnapped Angel. New York, Delacorte Press, 1982; London, Gollancz, 1983.
The Case of the Murdered Mackenzie. New York, Delacorte Press, 1984; London, Gollancz, 1985.
The Wabash Factor. New York, Delacorte Press, 1986; London, Gollancz, 1987.

Short Stories

The Edge of Tomorrow. New York, Bantam, 1961; London, Corgi, 1962.
The General Zapped an Angel. New York, Morrow, 1970.
A Touch of Infinity. New York, Morrow, 1973; London, Hodder and Stoughton, 1975.
Time and the Riddle: Thirty-One Zen Stories. Pasadena, California, Ward Ritchie Press, 1975.

Plays

The Hammer (produced New York, 1950).
Thirty Pieces of Silver (produced Melbourne, 1951; London, 1984). New York, Blue Heron Press, and London, Lane, 1954.
General Washington and the Water Witch. London, Lane, 1956.
The Crossing (produced Dallas, 1962).
The Hill (screenplay). New York, Doubleday, 1964.
David and Paula (produced New York, 1982).
Citizen Tom Paine, adaptation of his own novel (produced Williamstown, Massachusetts, 1985). Boston, Houghton Mifflin, 1986.

Screenplay: *The Hessian,* 1971.

Television Plays: *What's a Nice Girl Like You . . . ?,* 1971; *The Ambassador* (*Benjamin Franklin* series), 1974; *21 Hours at Munich,* with Edward Hume, 1976.

Verse

Never to Forget the Battle of the Warsaw Ghetto, with William Gropper. New York, Jewish Peoples Fraternal Order, 1946.

Other

The Romance of a People (for children). New York, Hebrew Publishing Company, 1941.
Lord Baden-Powell of the Boy Scouts. New York, Messner, 1941.
Haym Salomon, Son of Liberty. New York, Messner, 1941.
The Picture-Book History of the Jews, with Bette Fast. New York, Hebrew Publishing Company, 1942.
Goethals and the Panama Canal. New York, Messner, 1942.
The Incredible Tito. New York, Magazine House, 1944.
Intellectuals in the Fight for Peace. New York, Masses and Mainstream, 1949.
Tito and His People. Winnipeg, Manitoba, Contemporary Publishers, 1950.

Literature and Reality. New York, International Publishers, 1950.
Peekskill, U.S.A.: A Personal Experience. New York, Civil Rights Congress, and London, International Publishing Company, 1951.
Korean Lullaby. New York, American Peace Crusade, n.d.
Tony and the Wonderful Door (for children). New York, Blue Heron Press, 1952; as *The Magic Door,* Culver City, California, Peace Press, 1979.
Spain and Peace. New York, Joint Anti-Fascist Refugee Committee, 1952.
The Passion of Sacco and Vanzetti: A New England Legend. New York, Blue Heron Press, 1953; London, Lane, 1954.
The Naked God: The Writer and the Communist Party. New York, Praeger, 1957; London, Bodley Head, 1958.
The Howard Fast Reader. New York, Crown, 1960.
The Jews: Story of a People. New York, Dial Press, 1968; London, Cassell, 1970.
The Art of Zen Meditation. Culver City, California, Peace Press, 1977.

Editor, *The Selected Work of Tom Paine.* New York, Modern Library, 1946; London, Lane, 1948.
Editor, *Best Short Stories of Theodore Dreiser.* Cleveland, World, 1947.

*

Manuscript Collections: University of Pennsylvania Library, Philadelphia; University of Wisconsin, Madison.

*   *   *

Howard Fast is a prolific writer (two or more books a year) whose works, with their quickly sketched characterization, their clear, simple dialogue, their straightforward plots, their sequence of dramatic scenes embodying conflicts of ideals, their sentimentality, and their sometimes heavy-handed, black-and-white treatment of morality, transfer easily to the movie screen. Fast's works vary in quality from the highly effective and gripping to the melodramatic and propagandistic, but they are almost always interesting. Fast has always believed, since he began writing at age 18, that his works should both teach and please, that behind every romance should be a lesson and that every treatment of historical events should reduce the monumental to the personal, the understandable, the human. He is a master at trivializing the great and in turn at showing the great in the commonplace; his most common historical theme is how men of seemingly little note can be transformed by circumstances into men of great accomplishments and great ideals. Fast brings a social conscience to his historical fiction, with works that expose the pitfalls of power and wealth and the virtues of the simple life, of family, and of personal human concern. He has been praised for his life-like characters and action-packed narratives, but it is his commitment to liberal and humanitarian values that marks his canon as special. His works sympathetically treat women as courageous, witty, intuitive, and reasonable; they project an empathy with cultural outcasts, an understanding of the pressures that sometimes force decent men to conform, and a disdain for prejudice, hypocrisy, and abuse of power. In sum, Fast combines political statement with enjoyable entertainment.

As a liberal committed to a heritage of freedom, Fast, in his early novels, focuses primarily on the American Revolutionary War, exploring how harassed human beings paid the price for liberty. His first book, *Two Valleys,* captures the terrors and the potentials of life on the edge of civilization. Among his most compelling treatments of the American Revolution and its heroes are *Conceived in Liberty*, a grimly realistic study of Valley Forge, *The Unvanquished*, an analysis of how a "confused, humble, indecisive foxhunter" (George Washington) slowly developed into "a leader of men," and *Citizen Tom Paine*, a complex portrait of Paine as a foolish, weak, incompetent politician, and yet a committed visionary and a great radical. These provocative works try to humanize history and historical figures, admitting their weaknesses, reversing conventional perspectives, and demonstrating the processes that led such men to greatness. They vividly evoke the stormy background of the times. Of a similar quality and concern is *The Last Frontier*, a work which has received particular praise as a taut and moving story of the abuse and extermination of 300 Cheyenne, an incident indicative of how any violation of principle paves the way for abuse.

In the 1940's Fast's anti-fascist feeling led him to communism and to one-dimensional, doctrinaire works with capitalist villains and proletarian heroes. He continued to write historical fiction, but more and more with a marxist focus. *Freedom Road*, for example, portrays virtuous blacks struggling against Simon Legree whites during the traumas of post-Civil War Reconstruction, and in particular one slave's rise to statesman and martyr; *Clarkton* provides a socialist view of a Massachusetts mill town; *The American* explores why a midwestern politician pardoned three anarchists convicted of the Haymarket bombings (1886); and *Silas Timberman* and *The Story of Lola Gregg* depict the good (communists or fellow travelers) battling the bad (strikebreakers or FBI agents). *Spartacus*, written while Fast was serving a prison term for contempt of Congress, is a controversial treatment of the great slave revolt of 71 B.C., one Anthony Manousos calls a metaphor for all oppressed people's struggle to throw off the shackles of their inhuman oppressors. Its slaves are proletariat heroes; its Romans capitalist villains; its arena a symbol of the life-and-death struggles between oppressors and oppressed. A bestseller and a movie, it brought Fast the Stalin International Peace prize in 1954 and the Screenwriters award in 1960. *My Glorious Brothers* is a similar treatment of the Maccabean uprising against Greek tyrants. Most of the works of this period gloss over historical realities and rewrite events to suit Fast's message, but, ironically, only *The Passion of Sacco and Vanzetti* comes close to expressing any coherent communist dream. By 1957, tired of communist pressures to change his works to please party functionaries and disenchanted overall with the Party, Fast wrote *The Naked God* to recant clearly and completely.

Since then he has turned out a book a year of historical fiction (mainly about the American Revolution and Civil War days, immigrants, and biblical figures), science fiction, and thrillers. These vary greatly in quality, teaching less about politics than in the past and more about the personal and the religious; in other words the doctrinal has given way to the compassionate and the humanistic. Fast always includes people tinged with prejudice but convinced they have none: prejudice against blacks, Jews, Catholics, Nisei, and outsiders of all sorts. He is particularly disturbed by anti-Jewish sentiments, having early in his career written a semi-fictional life of a Polish-Jewish broker/financier who helped the American Revolutionary cause as well as a picture-book history of the Jews. *Torquemada* predictably addresses what motivates men to do evil in the name of good. His biblical stories, like *Moses, Prince of Egypt* and *Agrippa's Daughter*, trace the development of Jewish heroes from spoiled youth to rebel to compassionate and competent leader. Among his most popular works in this later period is his trilogy: *The Immigrants*, *Second Generation*, and *The Establishment*. Criticized for "milking emotions" and for reading like "soap history," they trace the changes wrought in four immigrant families

(Protestant, Catholic, Jewish, and Chinese) as they fight to become established members of a new San Francisco society. The novels focus, in particular, on a poor Italian-French immigrant, who ambitiously builds a corporate empire in the first novel, only to lose it more quickly than he gained it. The last two in the series concern the hardships of reestablishment and of dual identities. The novels play off the legitimate but selfish Nob Hill family of the founder against his kinder, more humane illegitimate Chinese offspring. Also notable are *April Morning* (a teenager's coming of age at the Battle of Lexington), *The Hessian* (Quakers struggling with conscience over a Hessian youth sought by irate and vengeful townsmen and later tried in a kangaroo court), and *The Crossing* (Washington's famous 1776 Christmas crossing of the Delaware). Always an idealist, Fast believes that books "open a thousand doors, they shape lives and answer questions, they widen horizons, they offer hope for the heart and food for the soul."

Though the politics change slightly over the years, with some of his later novels celebrating precisely those capitalist and intellectual types whom he identified with the oppressing class in earlier works, throughout Fast's canon there is a consistent thread of moralism and of strongly anti-fascist sentiments. Fast's method throughout his works is to suggest the world's weaknesses and wrongs through a selected individual crisis. Ultimately for Fast awareness is not enough; action, even self-destructive action, must result from feeling if man is to be free in heart and mind.

In the main Fast's writing is straightforward, simple, and unadorned. What often gives it its greatest strength is his handling of point of view. Fast describes the retreat from New York in 1776 through the eyes of Washington himself in order to, as Malcolm Cowley points out, bring alive the meaning of a phrase like "the soul of the Revolution." Fast's description of the defiant journey of the Cheyenne from their reservations to the Montana Territory that had been their home depends totally on biased white points of view, perspectives that end up lending the Indians more dignity and suggesting more of a sense of their right than would the same story told through the Indians' own eyes.

Basically, Fast's canon reflects his concern with man's historical and present struggles for liberty and for a government that recognizes the rights and needs of the individual. Fast disapproves of all that reduces man to a catchphrase, a class, an ideology, a nonentity. For him struggle, self-awareness, love and affection, family, privacy, and humanitarian values give life meaning. He disapproves of any group, no matter what the governmental system, that tries to force the human into mechanical categories or that denies genuine emotion. For him the message outweighs all else; as Fast himself says, "His [an artist's] only obligation is to truth."

—Gina Macdonald

FECHER, Constance. See HEAVEN, Constance.

FELLOWS, Catherine. Recipient: Romantic Novelists Association Netta Muskett award, 1970. Address: c/o Hodder and Stoughton, Mill Road, Dunton Green, Sevenoaks, Kent TN13 2YA, England.

ROMANCE AND HISTORICAL PUBLICATIONS

Novels

Leonora. London, Hurst and Blackett, 1972; New York, Fawcett, 1974.
The Marriage Masque. London, Hodder and Stoughton, and New York, Dell, 1974.
The Heywood Inheritance. London, Hodder and Stoughton, 1975; as *The Love Match*, New York, Dell, 1977.
Vanessa. New York, Dell, 1978.
Entanglement. London, Hodder and Stoughton, and New York, Fawcett, 1979.

*   *   *

Catherine Fellows is one of the better imitators of Georgette Heyer. Most of these imitators have no problem creating the farcical elements, frenetic activity, and period trappings Heyer was known for. Fellows and Joan Smith, however, are able to accomplish the more difficult task of creating memorable characters while using stylish, witty, and precisely chosen language.

In Fellows' first novel *Leonora*, the heroine knows a deep dark secret about the hero and spends a fair amount of time thinking he wants to marry her only to shut her up. The believability is marred by the heroine's unquestioning acceptance of the crime the hero committed. *The Marriage Masque* is excellent romantic adventure: a managing woman reconciles the hero to the daughter he despises, successfully steers her through her youthful romantic follies to a suitable marriage, and then arranges a marriage for herself. It is carried off with great style and humor. In *Vanessa* two sisters end up with desirable husbands after a farcical series of deceptions prompted by the hero's determination to find a woman who wants to marry him, not his wealth and position. *Entanglement* brings off two romances, both exceedingly unlikely, while incidentally thwarting a murderous plot against one of the heroes.

—Marylaine Block

FERBER, Edna. American. Born in Kalamazoo, Michigan, 15 August 1885. Educated at Ryan High School, Appleton, Wisconsin, graduated 1902. Reporter, Appleton *Daily Crescent*, 1902–04, Milwaukee *Journal*, 1905–08, and Chicago *Tribune*; full-time writer from 1910; lived in New York after 1912; served with the Writers War Board and as a war correspondent with the United States Army Air Force during World War II. Recipient: Pulitzer prize, 1924. Litt.D.: Columbia University, New York; Adelphi College, Garden City, New York. Member, American Academy. *Died 16 April 1968.*

ROMANCE AND HISTORICAL PUBLICATIONS

Novels

Dawn O'Hara, The Girl Who Laughed. New York, Stokes, 1911; London, Methuen, 1925.
Fanny Herself. New York, Stokes, 1917; London, Methuen, 1923.
The Girls. New York, Doubleday, 1921; London, Heinemann, 1922.
So Big. New York, Doubleday, and London, Heinemann, 1924.
Show Boat. New York, Doubleday, and London, Heinemann, 1926.
Cimarron. New York, Doubleday, and London, Heinemann, 1930.
American Beauty. New York, Doubleday, and London, Heinemann, 1931.
Come and Get It. New York, Doubleday, and London, Heinemann, 1935.
Nobody's in Town (includes *Trees Die at the Top*). New York, Doubleday, and London, Heinemann, 1938.
Saratoga Trunk. New York, Doubleday, 1941; London, Heinemann, 1942.
Great Son. New York, Doubleday, and London, Heinemann, 1945.
Giant. New York, Doubleday, and London, Gollancz, 1952.
Ice Palace. New York, Doubleday, and London, Gollancz, 1958.

Short Stories

Buttered Side Down. New York, Stokes, 1912; London, Methuen, 1926.
Roast Beef, Medium: The Business Adventures of Emma McChesney and Her Son, Jock. New York, Stokes, 1913; London, Methuen, 1920.
Personality Plus: Some Experiences of Emma McChesney and Her Son, Jock. New York, Stokes, 1914.
Emma McChesney & Co. New York, Stokes, 1915.
Cheerful, By Request. New York, Doubleday, 1918; London, Methuen, 1919.
Half Portions. New York, Doubleday, 1920.
Gigolo. New York, Doubleday, 1922; as *Among Those Present*, London, Nash and Grayson, 1923.
Mother Knows Best. New York, Doubleday, and London, Heinemann, 1927.
They Brought Their Women. New York, Doubleday, and London, Heinemann, 1933.
No Room at the Inn. New York, Doubleday, 1941.
One Basket: Thirty-One Stories. New York, Simon and Schuster, 1947.

OTHER PUBLICATIONS

Plays

Our Mrs. McChesney, with George V. Hobart (produced New York, 1915).
$1200 a Year, with Newman Levy. New York, Doubleday, 1920.
Minick, with George S. Kaufman, adaptation of the story "Old Man Minick" by Ferber (produced New York, 1924). Published as *Old Man Minick: A Short Story . . . Minick: A Play*, New York, Doubleday, 1924; London, Heinemann, 1925.
The Eldest: A Drama of American Life. New York, Appleton, 1925.
The Royal Family, with George S. Kaufman (produced New York, 1927). New York, Doubleday, 1928; as *Theatre Royal* (produced London, 1935), London, French, 1936.
Dinner at Eight, with George S. Kaufman (produced New York, 1932; London, 1933). New York, Doubleday, 1932; London, Heinemann, 1933.
Stage Door, with George S. Kaufman (produced New York, 1936; London, 1946). New York, Doubleday, 1936; London, Heinemann, 1937.

The Land Is Bright, with George S. Kaufman (produced New York, 1941). New York, Doubleday, 1941.
Bravo!, with George S. Kaufman (produced New York, 1948). New York, Dramatists Play Service, 1949.

Screenplay: *A Gay Old Dog*, 1919.

Other (autobiography)

A Peculiar Treasure. New York, Doubleday, and London, Heinemann, 1939.
A Kind of Magic. New York, Doubleday, and London, Gollancz, 1963.

*

Manuscript Collection: State Historical Society of Wisconsin, Madison.

Critical Studies: *Women and Success in American Society in the Works of Edna Ferber* by Mary Rose Shaughnessy, New York, Gordon Press, 1977; *Edna Ferber: A Biography* by Julie Goldsmith Gilbert, New York, Doubleday, 1978.

*   *   *

Though she was also a successful short story writer and playwright, Edna Ferber's greatest literary works are her novels in which she variously combines four major elements: intense and often difficult love affairs; strong, able female protagonists; dramatic portraits of intriguing American locales; and serious, if not always profound, examinations of American values. The American Dream she dissects theoretically includes not only professional success and economic security but also genuine personal fulfillment within a successful marriage and applies to women as well as to men.

In *Saratoga Trunk* Ferber creates tolerance for her tough, angry heroine, Clio Dulaine, a stunning beauty of mixed blood, not only through Clio's decision to marry impecunious gambler Clint Maroon for love but also by distancing Clio's story amid the garish "elegance" of the racing set of the 1880's. Thus Clio and Clint become acceptable prototypes of Americans who overcome class bias by exploiting their cleverness and guile, for they achieve the Dream.

But within the Ferber canon, Dream usually differs sharply from the gritty reality which she depicts and which takes into account racial prejudice, class snobbery, and sexism. Few of her heroines make happy, lasting marriages; professional success tends to be more attainable largely because they can achieve it by themselves, by means of personal determination.

At times, Ferber hangs her crowded plots upon exciting historical books; *Cimarron* sweeps from the Land Rush of 1899 into the 1920's attempting to encapsulate Oklahoma history. Against this background, the marriage of Sabra and Yancey Cravat is both enlarged (they symbolize divergent responses to frontier life) and diminished (place sometimes briefly over-shadows character). *Ice Palace*, a family saga set in Alaska, capitalizes on characters' memories of such early events as the Gold Rush as well as on the territory's thrust toward statehood, using heroine Chris Storm's choice of a mate—dashing Outsider or stalwart Alaskan—to reflect conflicting political and economic impulses. In *Giant* the love between cultured Leslie Benedict and her brash husband, Bick, is threatened by tension between her more traditional values and his pragmatic ones. Their personal conflict parallels the struggle between cattle and oil interests in

Texas. These stories are vigorous, brisk, and exciting, though the symbolism is a bit obvious.

Show Boat, Ferber's most famous novel, contrasts the pain in the lives of two pairs of lovers—Julie and Steve, victims of miscegenation legislation, and Magnolia and Gaylord Ravenal, victims of conflicting standards—to the glittering, romantic facade of river life. Similarly, *So Big*, a Pulitzer Prize winner, undercuts the myth of idyllic farm life through the account of Selina Peake's struggle to earn a living. Both novels touch upon the problems of single motherhood.

While Ferber clearly depicts the tremendous power of passionate love, she generally demonstrates that romance alone is an inadequate basis for marriage; this theme united with her examination of the American Dream results in worthy, vivid, compelling fiction.

—Jane S. Bakerman

FIELD, Rachel (Lyman). American. Born in New York City, 19 September 1894. Educated at Springfield High School, Massachusetts; Radcliffe College, Cambridge, Massachusetts, 1914–18. Married Arthur Siegfried Pederson in 1935; one adopted daughter. Member of the editorial department, Famous Players-Lasky film company, Hollywood, 1918–23. Recipient: Drama League of America prize, 1918; American Library Association Newbery Medal, for children's book, 1930. *Died 15 March 1942.*

ROMANCE AND HISTORICAL PUBLICATIONS

Novels

Time Out of Mind. New York, Macmillan, 1935; London, Macmillan, 1937.
To See Ourselves, with Arthur Pederson. New York, Macmillan, 1937; London, Collins, 1939.
All This and Heaven Too. New York, Macmillan, 1938; London, Collins, 1939.
And Now Tomorrow. New York, Macmillan, 1942; London, Collins, 1943.

Short Story

Christmas in London. Privately printed, 1946.

OTHER PUBLICATIONS

Fiction (for children)

Eliza and the Elves. New York, Macmillan, 1926.
The Magic Pawnshop: A New Year's Eve Fantasy. New York, Dutton, 1927; London, Dent, 1928.
Little Dog Toby. New York, Macmillan, 1928.
Polly Patchwork. New York, Doubleday, 1928.
Hitty, Her First Hundred Years. New York, Macmillan, 1929; as *Hitty: The Life and Adventures of a Wooden Doll*, London, Routledge, 1932.
Pocket-Handkerchief Park. New York, Doubleday, 1929.
Calico Bush. New York, Macmillan, 1931; London, Collier Macmillan, 1966.
The Yellow Shop. New York, Doubleday, 1931.

The Bird Began to Sing. New York, Morrow, 1932.
Hepatica Hawkes. New York, Macmillan, 1932.
Just Across the Street. New York, Macmillan, 1933.
Susanna B. and William C. New York, Morrow, 1934.
The Rachel Field Story Book (includes *The Yellow Shop, Pocket-Handkerchief Park, Polly Patchwork*). New York, Doubleday, 1958; Kingswood, Surrey, World's Work, 1960.

Plays (for children)

Everygirl, in *St. Nicholas* (New York), October 1913.
Three Pills in a Bottle (produced Cambridge, Massachusetts, 1917; New York, 1923). Included in *Six Plays*, 1924.
Rise Up, Jennie Smith (produced Cambridge, Massachusetts, 1918). New York, French, 1918.
Time Will Tell (produced Cambridge, Massachusetts, 1920).
The Fifteenth Candle. New York, French, 1921.
Six Plays (includes *Cinderella Married, Three Pills in a Bottle, Columbine in Business, The Patchwork Quilt, Wisdom Teeth, Theories and Thumbs*). New York, Scribner, 1924; *The Patchwork Quilt* published in *One-Act Plays of Today*, edited by J. W. Marriott, London, Gollancz, 1928.
The Cross-Stitch Heart and Other Plays (includes *Greasy Luck, The Nine Days' Queen, The Londonderry Air, At the Junction, Bargains in Cathay*). New York, Scribner, 1927.
Patchwork Plays (includes *Polly Patchwork; Little Square-Toes; Miss Ant, Miss Grasshopper, and Mr. Cricket; Chimney Sweeps' Holiday; The Sentimental Scarecrow*). New York, Doubleday, 1930.
First Class Matter. New York, French, 1936.
The Bad Penny. New York, French, 1938.

Verse

The Pointed People: Verses and Silhouettes (for children). New Haven, Connecticut, Yale University Press, and London, Oxford University Press, 1924.
An Alphabet for Boys and Girls (for children). New York, Doubleday, and London, Heinemann, 1926.
Taxis and Toadstools: Verses and Decorations (for children). New York, Doubleday, and London, Heinemann, 1926.
A Little Book of Days (for children). New York, Doubleday, and London, Heinemann, 1927.
Points East: Narratives of New England. New York, Brewer and Warren, 1930.
A Circus Garland. Washington, D.C., Winter Wheat Press, 1930.
Branches Green. New York, Macmillan, 1934.
Fear Is the Thorn. New York, Macmillan, 1936.
Christmas Time (for children). New York, Macmillan, 1941.
Poems (for children). New York, Macmillan, 1957.
Poems for Children. Kingswood, Surrey, World's Work, 1978.

Other

Fortune's Caravan (for children), from translation by Marion Saunders of a work by Lily Jean-Javal. New York, Morrow, 1933; London, Oxford University Press, 1935.
God's Pocket: The Story of Captain Samuel Hadlock, Junior, of the Cranberry Isles, Maine. New York, Macmillan, 1934; London, Macmillan, 1937.
Ave Maria: An Interpretation from Walt Disney's "Fantasia" Inspired by the Music of Franz Schubert. New York, Random House, 1940.
All Through the Night (for children). New York, Macmillan, 1940; London, Collins, 1954.

Prayer for a Child (for children). New York, Macmillan, 1944.

Editor, *The White Cat and Other Old French Fairy Tales*, by Marie Catherine d'Aulnoy. New York, Macmillan, 1928.
Editor, *American Folk and Fairy Tales.* New York and London, Scribner, 1929.
Editor, *People from Dickens: A Presentation of Leading Characters from the Books of Charles Dickens.* New York and London, Scribner, 1935.

*   *   *

In August, 1847, Paris rocked with scandal: the brutal murder of the Duchesse de Praslin was in every headline, on every lip. It was a *cause célèbre* of the juiciest kind, involving as it did a ducal household, a handsome, mysterious governess, identified only as Mlle D., nine orphaned children, and all the titillation, bloodied handprints and the Duc's botched suicide by arsenic could provide. Obviously, it was a scandalmonger's delight.

Nearly a century later, the great-niece by marriage of that scarlet lady, Mlle D., told her version of the famous affair in *All This and Heaven Too*, her most successful novel. The almost forgotten players in the 19th-century tragedy are warmed to life by the author's possibly partisan interest in the ancestress on whose tombstone she cracked nuts in her childhood. To Rachel Field, Henriette Deluzy-Desportes was a figure of family legend, not of suggestive headlines. She tells the story of a young governess unfortunate enough to find herself trapped between the unpredictable passions of the half-mad, vindictive Duchesse, and her estranged husband, the blondely Byronic Duc. The truth of the sad story will never now be known, and scarcely matters; but in its day the Praslin murder had an unexpected effect upon the fate of an entire nation, for the scandal helped to topple a shakey monarchy.

Henriette's life took a turn for the better when, hoping to leave notoriety behind, she left Europe to make a new life in America as a schoolmistress. Here she forged her link with the future when she married the novelist's great uncle the Rev. Henry M. Field, and became for her remaining, happier years, a respected if mildly quirky matron. The closing chapters of her life, and her relations with her husband's famous family (brother Cyrus laid the first Trans-Atlantic cable) are not as fascinating as the earlier, unhappy years—but such is life. In this novel, as in none of her others, Field created a fully rounded, flawed, but sympathetic character in Mlle D. Perhaps she and her great-aunt are each in the other's debt, one for her inspiration, the other for an impassioned defender.

—Joan McGrath

───────────

FINLAY, Fiona. See **STUART, Vivian.**

───────────

FINDLEY, Timothy. Canadian. Born in Toronto, Ontario, 30 October 1930. Educated at Rosedale Public School, Toronto; St. Andrews College, Aurora, Ontario; Jarvis Collegiate, Toronto; Royal Conservatory of Music, Toronto, 1950–53; Central School of Speech and Drama, London. Stage, television, and radio actor, 1951–62: charter member, Stratford Shakespearean Festival, Ontario, 1953; contract player with H. M. Tennent, London, 1953–56; toured U.S. in *The Matchmaker*, 1956–57; studio writer, CBS, Hollywood, 1957–58; copywriter, CFGM Radio, Richmond Hill, Ontario. Playwright-in-residence, National Arts Centre, Ottawa, 1974–75; writer-in-residence, University of Toronto, 1979–80, Trent University, Peterborough, Ontario, 1984, and University of Winnipeg, 1985. Chairman, Writers Union of Canada, 1977–78. Recipient: Canada Council award, 1968, 1978; Armstrong award, for radio writing, 1971; ACTRA award, for television documentary, 1975; Toronto Book award, 1977; Governor General's award, 1977; Anik award, for television writing, 1980; Canadian Authors Association prize, 1985. D.Litt.: Trent University, 1982; University of Guelph, Ontario, 1984. Officer, Order of Canada, 1986. Agent: Colbert Agency, 303 Davenport Road, Toronto, Ontario M5R 1K5. Address: Box 419, Cannington, Ontario L0E 1EO, Canada.

ROMANCE AND HISTORICAL PUBLICATIONS

Novels

The Butterfly Plague. New York, Viking Press, 1969; London, Deutsch, 1970.
The Wars. Toronto, Clarke Irwin, 1977; New York, Delacorte Press, and London, Macmillan, 1978.
Famous Last Words. Toronto, Clarke Irwin, and New York, Delacorte Press, 1981; London, Macmillan, 1987.
Not Wanted on the Voyage. Toronto, Viking, 1984; New York, Delacorte Press, and London, Macmillan, 1985.

Short Stories

Dinner Along the Amazon. Toronto and London, Penguin, 1984; New York, Penguin, 1985.

OTHER PUBLICATIONS

Novels

The Last of the Crazy People. New York, Meredith Press, and London, Macdonald, 1967.
The Telling of Lies. Toronto, Penguin, 1986; London, Macmillan, and New York, Dell, 1988.

Plays

The Paper People (televised 1968). Published in *Canadian Drama* (Toronto), vol. 9, no. 1, 1983.
The Journey (broadcast 1971). Published in *Canadian Drama* (Toronto), vol. 10, no. 1, 1984.
Can You See Me Yet? (produced Ottawa, 1976). Vancouver, Talonbooks, 1977.
John A., Himself music by Berthold Carriere (produced London, Ontario, 1979).
Strangers at the Door (radio script), in *Quarry* (Kingston, Ontario), 1982.
Daybreak at Pisa: 1945, in *Tamarack Review* (Toronto), Winter 1982.

Screenplays: *Don't Let the Angels Fall*, 1970; *The Wars*, 1983.

Radio Plays and Documentaries: *The Learning Stage* and *Ideas* series, 1963–73; *Adrift*, 1968; *Matinee* series, 1970–71; *The Journey*, 1971; *Missionaries*, 1973.

Television Plays and Documentaries: *Umbrella* series, 1964–66; *Who Crucified Christ?*, 1966; *The Paper People*, 1968; *The Whiteoaks of Jalna* (7 episodes), from books by Mazo de la Roche, 1971–72; *The National Dream* series (8 episodes), with William Whitehead, 1974; *The Garden and the Cage*, with William Whitehead, 1977; *1832* and *1911* (*The Newcomers* series), 1978–79; *Dieppe 1942*, with William Whitehead, 1979; *Other People's Children*, 1981; *Islands in the Sun* and *Turn the World Around* (*Belafonte Sings* series), with William Whitehead, 1983.

Other

Imaginings, with Janis Rapaport, illustrated by Heather Cooper. Toronto, Ethos, 1982.

*

Critical Studies: "Timothy Findley Issue" of *Canadian Literature* (Vancouver), Winter 1981; *Timothy Findley* by Wilfred Cude, Toronto, Dundurn Press, 1982.

*   *   *

Though Timothy Findley has now established his reputation as one of Canada's most successful contemporary novelists, he was not always a writer of fiction. In his twenties he was an actor, performing with such stars as Alec Guinness and Ruth Gordon on stage. In the next few years he played parts on television; wrote television scripts and ads for a country and western radio station; and reported on the arts for a CBC radio program.

By 1962 he began to write full-time, working on a number of short stories. Some of these pieces were collected in *Dinner Along the Amazon.* His first novel, *The Last of the Crazy People,* is set in southern Ontario, and, like his early stories, is strongly autobiographical. It concerns a lonely child's struggle for survival in a mad and strange world. The demise and disintegration of one eccentric family is told with terrifying horror. Findley's second novel, *The Butterfly Plague,* was praised by Rex Reed as "the best book about Hollywood" he had ever read, but did not gain the author critical acclaim. Illustrating Findley's fascination with decadence and corruption, the book is set in early decades of the 20th century and deals with the movie industry, film directors, and superstars. It shows the brutality of the real world in comparison to cinematic ideals and illusions. As one critic pointed out, the North American dreamer's "dreams of immortality, . . . of dynasties, . . . of peace, and . . . beauty" are analogous to "Monarch butterflies: beautiful and ostensibly fragile creatures whose annual migration" in thousands are like a "plague of dreams."

In the early 1970's Findley received critical recognition for his work on radio and on television documentaries. As playwright-in-residence at the National Arts Centre, Ottawa, he wrote *Can You See Me Yet?*, produced in March 1976. This play is set in an insane asylum in southern Ontario, late in the summer of 1938. The question, posed in the title of the psychodrama, is the central theme of the work. Is there anyone there to see the life of the inmate Cassandra Wakelin? Does anyone care enough to know and accept her as she is?

The need to pay attention to another human being is an issue that Findley brings out again and again. In his most important literary achievements to date, the two historical novels about wars, *The Wars* and *Famous Last Words*, Findley asserts the validity of an individual's experience in the midst of chaos, senseless violence, and confusion. In both of these novels the reader is made to see how history and factual or newspaper accounts of events do not necessarily tell the "truth" about any incident. Both these novels have been labelled by critics as examples of postmodernist fiction; *Famous Last Words* specifically as "historiographic metafiction."

The Wars describes the emotional and psychological breakdown of a soldier in World War I. John Moss remarks that "other novelists have conveyed the terrors of the battlefield with more authority, but none has so vividly portrayed the sheer carnage and waste, the desolation and depravity of corpse piled upon corpse upon corpse, the mutilations and putrefaction of flesh, and always the mud, and the shifting earth, the flames, the gas." The climax of the novel, with Robert Ross trapped in a burning barn with about fifty horses, the "black mare and the dog," conjures up images of the fiery apocalypse and is a fitting, culmination of the hellish experience. In addition, there are several other powerfully emotional scenes—one where a well-meaning, innocent German soldier is erroneously shot as he reaches for his binoculars, and another where Ross is raped and sodomized in a public bath by his fellow soldiers.

Findley's artistry is revealed in the restraint of the narrative. The use of the second-person point of view avoids excessive sentimentality and overt authorial commentary on the events. As in much postmodernist fiction, the reader is made aware of the act of creation. The author deliberately lets us see how the fiction is put together, by showing us photographs, newspaper clippings, transcripts of interviews, and archival records. As readers, we become co-researchers, and by implication, co-creators of the story as we piece together the bits and pieces of information before us in order to understand what really happened.

In a similar fashion we have to construct the events surrounding the Duke and the Duchess of Windsor between 1910 to 1945 in *Famous Last Words*. This panoramic historical novel includes characters from both literature and real life. The hero, Hugh Selwyn Mauberley, is a fictionalization of a character found in Ezra Pound's 13-part poem of the same name published in 1920. Nonfictional personages, such as Rudolf Hess, Ezra Pound, Joachim von Ribbentrop, and Sir Harry Oakes seem indistinguishable from Findley's own fictional characters. Mauberley, a minor writer, becomes involved in a complicated and dangerous plot composed of high-ranking figures from both the Allied and Axis causes. He becomes the key witness and the reporter of a secret cabal which aimed at restoring the Windsors to the throne as puppet rulers after the destruction of the two world forces. Flirting with and attracted to the splendour of wealth, power, and elitist fascism, Mauberley, "out of key with his time," slowly becomes entangled in the web of corruptions, betrayals, and failures of the power-hungry glittery people with whom he associates. A brilliant and paradoxical line that sums up both Mauberley's and Findley's view of their writing is found scrawled on the walls of the Grand Elysium Hotel: "All I have written here, is true; except the lies."

—Eleanor Ty

* * *

FINLEY, Glenna. American. Born in Puyallup, Washington, 12 June 1925. Educated at Stanford University, California, B.A. (cum laude) 1945; graduate study at University of Washington, Seattle, and Seattle Pacific University, 1957–60. Married Donald MacLeod Witte in 1951; one son. Announcer, KEVR Radio, Seattle, 1941–42; producer, NBC International Division, New York, 1945–47; film librarian, *March of Time* newsreel series, New York, 1947–48; member of the news bureau staff, Time Inc., New York, 1948–49; publicity and copywriter, Seattle,

1950–51. Since 1957 freelance writer. Agent: Ann Elmo Agency, 60 East 42nd Street, New York, New York 10165. Address: P.O. Box 866182, Plano, Texas 75086, U.S.A.

ROMANCE AND HISTORICAL PUBLICATIONS

Novels

Death Strikes Out. New York, Arcadia House, 1957.
Career Wife. New York, Arcadia House, 1964.
Nurse Pro Tem. New York, Arcadia House, 1967.
A Tycoon for Ann. New York, Lancer, 1968.
Journey to Love. New York, New American Library, 1970; London, New English Library, 1977.
Love's Hidden Fire. New York, New American Library, 1971.
Treasure of the Heart. New York, New American Library, 1971.
Love Lies North. New York, New American Library, 1972.
Bridal Affair. New York, New American Library, 1972; London, New English Library, 1975.
Kiss a Stranger. New York, New American Library, 1972.
Love in Danger. New York, New American Library, 1973.
When Love Speaks. New York, New American Library, 1973.
The Romantic Spirit. New York, New American Library, 1973.
Surrender, My Love. New York, New American Library, 1974.
A Promising Affair. New York, New American Library, 1974.
Love's Magic Spell. New York, New American Library, 1974.
The Reluctant Maiden. New York, New American Library, 1975.
The Captured Heart. New York, New American Library, 1975.
Holiday for Love. New York, New American Library, 1976.
Love for a Rogue. New York, New American Library, 1976.
Storm of Desire. New York, New American Library, 1977.
Dare to Love. New York, New American Library, 1977.
To Catch a Bride. New York, New American Library, 1977.
Master of Love. New York, New American Library, 1978.
Beware My Heart. New York, New American Library, 1978.
The Marriage Merger. New York, New American Library, 1978.
Wildfire of Love. New York, New American Library, 1979.
Timed for Love. New York, New American Library, 1979.
Love's Temptation. New York, New American Library, 1979.
Stateroom for Two. New York, New American Library, 1980.
Affairs of Love. New York, New American Library, 1980.
Midnight Encounter. New York, New American Library, 1981.
Return Engagement. New York, New American Library, 1981.
One Way to Love. New York, New American Library, 1982.
Taken by Storm. New York, New American Library, 1982.
A Business Affair. New York, New American Library, 1983.
Wanted for Love. New York, New American Library, 1983.
A Weekend for Love. New York, New American Library, 1984.
A Touch of Love. New York, New American Library, 1985.
Love's Waiting Game. New York, New American Library, 1985.
Diamonds for My Love. New York, New American Library, 1986.
Secret of Love. New York, New American Library, 1987.

*

Glenna Finley comments:

A good romance novel should contain attractive characters, have a carefully researched locale, and offer a plausible plot—

but most of all I think it must be fun to read. In other words, after the reader has paid for the book—all suffering should cease!

*   *   *

Glenna Finley wants to be a romantic writer. Her continual implausible chance incidents, superficial characterizations, and mid-stream alteration of style prevent her from reaching her goal. Infrequently, the reader notices a striving for sustenance with attempts at historical references and psychological descriptions, too minor to be credible amidst the loosely constructed events. Complications stem from obvious improbabilities, aleatory circumstances. Excitement is secondary to the attire of the heroine and hero.

Even though Finley has worked in business, she displays sparse knowledge of the business woman mentality, covering this inadequacy by depicting the women as mere flesh for a wearing-apparel exhibition. For example, in *Beware My Heart* she attempts to create an energetic, intelligent business woman through the responsiveness of Cristina Kelly, assistant hotel manager and, at least in the opening pages, introduces her with a margin of verve. But this limited formidability is quick-lived and she soon succumbs to the Finley female portraiture, wholly manipulable. The action is halted with exasperating longeurs devoted to detailed descriptions of "camel-colored slacks and matching open-throated silk shirts cut low at the neckline" to complement her figure.

Minor characters are bovine; major ones belong to a world of affluence and power (for who else could purchase the Diors?). Although typically Finley attempts to present characters of contrast, what is illuminated instead is assuredness and haughty egoism versus even more assuredness and haughtier egoism. The point of view, with only a few exceptions, is that of the heroine. In the majority of Finley's novels, the heroine is wealthy or potentially wealthy due to an inheritance; she is matched with a too-good-to-be-true hero. These characters, however, are tedious; they lack depth; their dialogue is mechanical and easily anticipated by the reader. She attempts to inject humor into the monologues of the heroines but it is always ill-placed, a phrase tacked on here and there. Indeed her settings lack individuality: the chalet in one novel has the same decor as the chalet in another novel. Physical descriptions of characters are often too reminiscent of characters from her other books.

The detractions are too numerous to give stylistic integrity and cohesiveness to her work. Even at her best, Finley never achieves the writing of a solid romance novel for which she strives.

—W. M. von Zharen

FISKE, Sharon. See **HILL, Pamela.**

FITZGERALD, Ellen. See **STEVENSON, Florence.**

FITZGERALD, Julia. Pseudonym for Julia Watson; also writes as Jane de Vere; Julia Hamilton. British. Born in Bangor, North Wales, 18 September 1943. Educated at Elland Grammar School, and Huddersfield College of Art, both Yorkshire. Married and divorced twice; one daughter and one son. Has worked as an artist, jewelry designer, model, and historical adviser to Sphere Books. Lives in High Wycombe, Buckinghamshire. Agent: c/o June Hall, 5th Floor, The Chambers, Chelsea Harbour, Lots Road, London SW10 0XF, England.

ROMANCE AND HISTORICAL PUBLICATIONS

Novels (series: Astromance)

The Scarlet Women (as Jane de Vere). London, Corgi, 1969.
Royal Slave. London, Futura, and New York, Ballantine, 1978.
Scarlet Woman. London, Futura, 1979; New York, Nordon, 1981.
Slave Lady. London, Futura, 1980.
Salamander. London, Futura, 1981.
Fallen Woman. London, Futura, 1981.
Venus Rising. London, Futura, 1982.
The Princess and the Pagan. London, Futura, 1983; as *Silken Captive*, New York, Pinnacle, 1986.
Firebird. London, Century, 1983; n.p., Leisure Circle, 1988.
The Jewelled Serpent. London, Century, 1984; as *Beyond Ecstasy*, New York, Pinnacle, 1985.
Taboo. London, Century, 1985; New York, Bart, 1988.
Desert Queen. London, Century, 1986; New York, Bart, 1988.
Astromance:
   1. *Flame of the East.* London, Macdonald, 1986; New York, Bart, 1988.
   2. *Daughter of the Gods.* London, Macdonald, 1986; New York, Bart, 1988.
   3. *Pasadoble.* London, Futura, 1986; New York, Bart, 1988.
   4. *A Kiss from Aphrodite.* London, Futura, 1987; New York, Bart, 1988.
   5. *Castle of the Enchantress.* London, Futura, 1987; New York, Bart, 1988.
   6. *Jade Moon.* New York, Bart, 1988.
   7. *Devil in My Arms.* New York, Bart, 1989.
   8. *Temple of Butterflies.* New York, Bart, 1989.
   9. *Glade of Jewels.* New York, Bart, 1989.
   10. *Bridge of Rainbows.* New York, Bart, 1989.
   11. *Pagan Blossoms.* New York, Bart, 1989.
Beauty of the Devil. London, Century, 1988.
Earth Queen, Sky King. London, Century, 1989.

Novels as Julia Watson (series: Gentian)

The Lovechild. London, Hale, 1967; New York, Bantam, 1968.
Medici Mistress. London, Corgi, 1968.
The Gentian Trilogy:
   A Mistress for the Valois. London, Hale, 1969.
   The King's Mistress. London, Corgi, 1970.
   The Wolf and the Unicorn. London, Corgi, 1971.
Winter of the Witch. London, Corgi, 1971; New York, Bantam, 1972.
The Tudor Rose. London, Hale, 1972.
Saffron. London, Corgi, 1972.
Love Song. London, Futura, 1981.

Novels as Julia Hamilton (series: Habsburg)

The Last of the Tudors. London, Hale, 1971.

Katherine of Aragon. London, Sphere, and New York, Beagle, 1972; as *Katherine the Tragic Tudor*, London, Hale, 1974.
Anne of Cleves. London, Sphere, and New York, Beagle, 1972.
Son of York. London, Sphere, 1973.
Habsburg series:
    The Changeling Queen. London, Hale, 1977.
    The Emperor's Daughter. London, Hale, 1978.
    The Pearl of the Habsburgs. London, Hale, 1978.
    The Snow Queen. London, Hale, 1978.
    The Habsburg Inheritance. London, Hale, 1980.

OTHER PUBLICATIONS

Other

Healthy Signs. London, Arrow, 1989; Wallingford, Pennsylvania, Middle Atlantic Press, 1989.

*

Julia Fitzgerald comments:

"Live dangerously in print" is my motto for today's women readers who are so often tied down by both jobs and families. The passionate, epic love stories that I create are a feast which won't make my readers overweight and which won't have any unpleasant repercussions (unless the dinner's allowed to burn while they're being read). I believe implicitly in love, that it is everything, that it can conquer all, that life would be empty and meaningless without it; and this is also the opinion of my strong-minded, spirited, and undaunted heroines—although my heroes take a little longer to be persuaded! Despite trials and adversities, my heroes and heroines find they can't live without one another, which is exactly the point of love, in my opinion. They are also sensual characters with strong appetites for each other, whose love story is played out against an authentic deeply researched background. Turkey, Venice, London, Arabia, Egypt, India, Dublin and Tipperary, Algiers, Yorkshire, Liverpool, and Greece are just some of the settings featured in my books. Pirates, sultans, pashas, renegades, princes, dukes, kings and queens, magicians, astrologers, and royal intriguers feature among my characters, as do ladies of fashion, princesses, courtesans, gypsies, daughters of dukes, and wilful heiresses.

*   *   *

It is the sad lot of the romance novelist not to be taken seriously as a writer. To many people, the genre is "like a drug," which presents readers with "a dewy-eyed vision of romantic love . . . that bears little relation to real life experience." So claims Greek businessman Loukas Lyssarides, the anti-hero of Julia Fitzgerald's novel *A Kiss from Aphrodite.* The object of his confused affections, a romance novelist called Melody de Blase, sees her work in a rather different light: "I write uplifting stories of men and women and love, and how the strength of love can overcome all problems if it is true love." She later adds the more serious claim that "if men read love stories, there'd be no need for wars and political divisions and all that heartache that men cause with their ruthless ambitions and their steely aptitude for riding roughshod over women."

Melody is perhaps taking romance fiction, and herself, a little too seriously. But, like her creator, she is a self-confessed incurable romantic who firmly believes that her novels can "elevate the spirit and reassure the reader." Despite this, she is a success-

ful and thoroughly modern woman who has no intention of playing second fiddle to any man—certainly not to one who has scant respect for her work. In effect, she epitomises Fitzgerald's feisty and independent heroines.

A Kiss from Aphrodite was written as part of Fitzgerald's Astromance series, which, as the name implies, intended to unite the author's interests in astrology and love. Each novel in this series is preceded by short descriptions of the astrological traits of the male and female protagonists. In *Castle of the Enchantress*, Taurean Nicolette ("slow to anger, but terrifying when roused") goes to work as an antique restorer in a French chateau belonging to an avant-garde French aristocrat, Alain, Comte de Mariac, who is an Aquarian ("elusive and infuriatingly detached"). Similarly, every chapter is preceded by a short horoscope outlining the planetary influences that will affect the fate of the characters that day: for example, "Those headstrong ways of yours are having the inevitable result, Miss Taurus, and you aren't going to like it at all" and "sometimes the freedom you revere backfires on you, Mr. Aquarius, and you wish you'd never had it. Being footloose isn't always so wonderful."

Neat and fail-safe as this formula sounds, the horoscopes are an irrelevance. Take them away and one is left with a straight and rather predictable romance which somehow lacks the verve, passion, and authenticity of the more popular historical romances with which Fitzgerald made her name.

If true love can overcome all problems, as Fitzgerald's alter ego in *A Kiss from Aphrodite* claims, throwing problems in the path of true love is surely the raw meat of writers in the romance genre, and in her Troubadour historical romance series, which Fitzgerald began in 1978 with the bestselling *Royal Slave*, troubles relentlessly bombard the heroines. Forced to undergo adventure, sexual degradation—often at the hands of the man they love—and dangers which range from shipwreck on a desert island to gang rape, Fitzgerald's heroines never succumb to despair, but emerge physically unscathed and emotionally stronger for their experiences. They are high-spirited women without any trace of prudery who will eagerly abandon themselves to sexual passion when in love, yet who are determined to preserve their identity when it is under threat. Men can crush their stays, but never their integrity. And crush their stays men do: mutual sexual desire, and sometimes brutish male lust, dominate Fitzgerald's novels, allowing her to place her heroines in graphically described situations of overwhelming, almost spiritual passion (Kitty McDonagh's lovemaking with Carrick in *Venus Rising*) or utter humiliation (Cassia Morbilly's experiences in the slave markets of Constantinople in *Royal Slave*.)

The need of men to conquer women, be it by love or by force, is a central theme of Fitzgerald's work. Time and again her heroines fall prey to selfish and violent men who are intent on satisfying their lust at women's expense. *Royal Slave*, set in the 17th century, has its heroine, Cassia, captured by slave pirates at the very moment she is being raped by her villainous fiancé. Rescued from being raped again, this time by pirates, Cassia proceeds to fall in love with her saviour/captor, the slave-ship's captain, Vincent de Sauvage, and he with her. Vincent, typifying Fitzgerald's male anti-heroes, has been deeply wounded by previous unhappy emotional involvements, and denying his love for Cassia, he decides to go ahead and sell her to a Sultan's harem. Before he can do so, she is kidnapped by his scaley-skinned sexually perverted rival, and she eventually ends up in a harem as the Sultan's favorite concubine. After a passionate night spent with Vincent, who has broken into the harem to see her, Cassia is tied in a sack and thrown into the Bosphorus. Just as she is on the point of drowning she is rescued by an English earl who imprisons her in his island villa, planning to use her for his own diabolical sexual ends. Given the unscrupulousness of these male characters, it is surprising that Fitzgerald's heroines manage to maintain their utter belief in the power of love.

Highly dramatic, somewhat titilating plots such as *Royal Slave* and the more recent *The Jewelled Serpent*, in which an Elizabethan heroine accompanies her swashbuckling future brother-in-law into the alien Muslim world of North Africa in order to rescue her kidnapped sister, are offset against detailed historical backgrounds which encompass both the decadence of the rich and the hardships of the destitute. One might accuse Fitzgerald of over-romanticising her characters (her women are all young and beautiful, her heroes fiery, handsome God-like beings) but the worlds they inhabit are exceptionally grim. The reader is first introduced to 10-year-old heroine of *Scarlet Woman*, Meggie Blunt, as she crouches in a curtained-off corner of a rat-infested slum where her violent drunken father is raping her sick mother. After her mother's death, Meggie tries hard to make a "respectable" living, but soon discovers that prostitution is her only means of survival. Similarly Kitty, in *Venus Rising*, witnesses the death by famine of her entire family, and is forced to beg before finding a rich protector.

Fitzgerald is at her strongest when describing scenes of poverty, hunger, and the invidious position of women who are forced to sell their bodies in order to survive. Yet, despite the realism of their settings, her books have moments when the reader is hard-pushed to believe the heroine's luck—when, for example, four men attempt to gang-rape Allegra, in *The Jewelled Serpent*, not one of them actually succeeds.

Fitzgerald's epic novels, however, are interesting and well-crafted. Her heroines share a sense of female solidarity. Feminism creeps in, if slowly: "She had begun this venture for two reasons," comments the author on Allegra's adventure in *The Jewelled Serpent*, "to find her sister, and to show the world that women could succeed in such matters as well as men; if not better." Yet it is the men who step in to the plot at the last minute and perform the miraculous acts of rescue. One suspects it will be some time before a Fitzgerald heroine manages to save herself.

—Judith Summers

* * *

FITZGERALD, Valerie. Canadian. Born in India in 1927. Educated in India and England. Married E. P. Fitzgerald; one daughter and one son. Left India in 1947; has lived in England, Switzerland, Ireland, Kenya and Italy; now lives in Ottawa. Recipient: Georgette Heyer award, 1981; Romantic Novelists Association Major award, 1982; Elizabeth Goudge Historical trophy, 1982. Address: c/o Bodley Head Ltd., 32 Bedford Square, London WC1B 3EL, England.

ROMANCE AND HISTORICAL PUBLICATIONS

Novels

Zemindar. London, Bodley Head, 1981.

* * *

Valerie Fitzgerald's sprawling but adroitly executed novel, *Zemindar*, deservedly won the 1981 Georgette Heyer award for an historical novel. It is a romantic story of unusual discernment, set against the dramatic background of India during the 1857 Mutiny. The plot is a traditional one, with the heroine Laura, becoming involved in hazardous exploits and, in the process, discovering truths about herself and her feelings for the hero Oliver.

The novel's strong strand of romance is enhanced by the vivid realism in which this is rooted, and from which it flowers. *Zemindar*'s refulgent descriptions of the Indian natural scene and its conveyance of life in the villages and bazaars are authoritative and compelling. They arise from the author's personal memories of growing up in India on a zemindari estate similar to that which is featured in the book, and there is throughout a feeling for the "real India" which so deeply appeals to both Laura and Oliver. As the zemindar (landowner) of a vast estate, Oliver has a passionate sense of responsibility for his land and his people. He is a believable and fleshed-out character, although it is amusing to trace in his contradictory moods of glinting appeal and brooding arrogance a combination of certain characteristics of Heathcliff and Darcy. Fitzgerald, as an "enthusiastic Austenite," acknowledges the possible influence of Jane Austen in her work, if not that of Emily Brontë. Her own heroine is able to demolish social hypocrisies with something of Elizabeth Bennet's wit and economy of style. Laura is both reflective and robust: she reads Marcus Aurelius for pleasure, studies Urdu as part of her effort to understand the real nature of India, but also learns how to handle a revolver to protect herself against the possible "ultimate outrage."

Despite its length of almost 800 pages, *Zemindar* sustains its romantic interest and suspence until the end. In the convention of romantic fiction, the author manages to keep the couple at arm's length until the book's later stages. She does this convincingly by making the first frightening eruptions of the Mutiny curtail Laura's stay at the zemindari estate. It is only after a series of terrifying happenings that Laura, caught up in the five-month siege of Lucknow, discovers the true quality of her feelings for Oliver.

In this satisfying novel Fitzgerald illustrates her capacity to present the panoramic as well as an intimate view of events; she knows, too, exactly when to use succinctness in the expression of human emotions, and—most of all—when and how to harness the lusher images of romance.

—Mary Cadogan

* * *

FLANAGAN, Thomas (James Bonner). American. Born in Greenwich, Connecticut, 5 November 1923. Educated at Amherst College, Massachusetts, B.A. 1945; Columbia University, New York, M.A. 1948, Ph.D. in English 1958. Served in the United States Naval Reserve, 1942–44. Married Jean Parker in 1949; two daughters. Instructor, 1949–52, and Assistant Professor, 1952–59, Columbia University; Assistant Professor, 1960–67, Associate Professor, 1967–73, Professor, 1973–78, and Chairman of the Department of English, 1973–76, University of California, Los Angeles. Since 1978 Professor of English, State University of New York, Stony Brook. Recipient: American Council of Learned Societies grant, 1962; Guggenheim fellowship, 1962; National Book Critics Circle award, 1979. Address: Department of English, State University of New York, Stony Brook, New York 11794, U.S.A.

ROMANCE AND HISTORICAL PUBLICATIONS

Novels

The Year of the French. New York, Holt Rinehart, and London, Macmillan, 1979.
The Tenants of Time. New York, Dutton, and London, Bantam, 1988.

OTHER PUBLICATIONS

Other

The Irish Novelists 1800–1850. New York, Columbia University Press, 1959.

*   *   *

Thomas Flanagan's novels *The Year of the French* and *The Tenants of Time* span three centuries of Irish history, from the invasion of Cromwell to 1908. Each book focusses on a specific act of rebellion, each relies on a dizzying array of narrative voices, each blends historical and fictional characters, and each ultimately views the study of history as a romance but the living of it as a perplexing and often tragic burden. To some extent his characters make history, but most are unmade by it, caught in the dangerous vortex of cross-currents that is the sad, often merciless, history of Ireland.

The central event in *The Year of the French* is the brief series of battles in 1798 between Irish-speaking peasants of County Mayo, led by an army from republican France, and a huge English force commanded by Lord Cornwallis. The skeletal history is simple: the English were victorious, the French were deported, the Irish were massacred or hanged, and the Act of Union was forced upon the farcical Irish Parliament. It is, however, the flesh and blood history that Flanagan seeks, the story of the internal and external forces that led men to lift pikes in rebellion or to hang rebels for king and country.

Flanagan explores his characters' motives by allowing them to narrate most of the book (there is also a nameless general narrator that provides a matrix for their stories). The most important voices are those of Owen McCarthy and Rev. Mr. Broome, Anglican vicar of Killala, County Mayo.

McCarthy speaks Irish and English and, in a sense, straddles two worlds. He is an itinerant schoolmaster, teaching English, Latin, and other subjects. He is also an accomplished Gaelic poet, drunkard, and seducer. He sees himself as carrying on the ancient bardic tradition, and, indeed, he recites his verses throughout the west and south, where Irish was the dominant tongue until the Great Famine. Hearing about his countrymen in Munster rising up to fight the English at "Tara of the Kings," and seeing the gradual decline of the Gaelic language and culture that give meaning to his work and life, he joins in the Mayo revolt and is hanged.

Rev. Mr. Broome is a loyal English subject who spends years trying to reconcile his distaste for what he deems to be a barbarous Irish culture with the shame he feels for the unchristian treatment of the Irish by absentee landlords and their agents. Broome attempts to write what he calls an "Impartial Narrative" of the rebellion, and he succeeds up to a point. He sets aside racial and religious prejudice, but he does not and cannot learn of the inner lives of the peasants for whom he has sympathy; he does not speak their language, either literally or figuratively.

McCarthy and Broome are assisted by other narrators. Together, they help recreate and juxtapose a collection of images that for a time give the reader the illusion of knowing what 1798 was like.

The Tenants of Time is a darker book, a kaleidoscopic remembrance of the dismal Fenian rebellion of 1867, the subsequent rise of the Land League, and the rise and fall of Parnell. In Kilpeder, County Cork, the principal setting for the novel, a small band of rebels attack a police barracks, skirmish in Clonbrony Wood, and surrender in the face of a cavalry onslaught. The surviving rebels are jailed and mistreated, and spend the rest of their lives trying to understand and give meaning to their one moment of youthful bravado.

Once again, Flanagan relies on a variety of narrators, among them Hugh McMahon, a gentle schoolmaster and former Fenian; Patrick Prentiss, son of a Catholic barrister and self-styled historian; and Lionel Forrester, cousin to the Earl of Ardmor, "owner" of Kilpeder. Through them and a nameless narrative voice, we hear others—Ned Nolan, Fenian rebel and I.R.A. assassin; Lord and Lady Ardmor, the latter the lover of Robert Delaney, former rebel and M.P. for Cork; the great Parnell himself; and many others.

Although there are light moments, the interrelated stories of the demise of the Fenians and those close to them, the ruthless in-fighting among the Irish politicians, and the duplicity of the English government are somber reading. The underlying message, that we are all time's tenants, here on a lease of unknown length or dubious purpose, haunts the self-conscious characters and the reader as well.

Flanagan's books are pro-Irish, but the clouded definition of exactly who is Irish makes this an uncertain pronouncement. He lavishes sympathy and scorn on Catholics, Anglo-Irish Protestants, and Englishmen alike. Ireland is both a place and a state of mind. Flanagan attempts with great success to give us history as experienced by the diverse religious, economic, political, and social groupings that have for centuries had a stake in Ireland.

—Thomas J. Morrisey

FLEMING, Caroline. See **MATHER, Anne.**

FLETCHER, Inglis (née Clark). American. Born in Alton, Illinois, in 1888. Educated at St. Louis School of Fine Arts; Washington University, St. Louis; University of California, Berkeley. Married John George Fletcher; one son. Recipient: Sir Walter Raleigh award, 1953; North Carolina Governor's Gold Metal. Litt.D.: Greensboro College, North Carolina.

ROMANCE AND HISTORICAL PUBLICATIONS

Novels (series: Carolina)

Carolina series:
Raleigh's Eden. Indianapolis, Bobbs Merrill, 1940; London, Hutchinson, 1941.
Men of Albemarle. Indianapolis, Bobbs Merrill, 1942; London, Hutchinson, 1943.
Lusty Wind for Carolina. Indianapolis, Bobbs Merrill, 1944; London, Hutchinson, 1947.

Toil of the Brave. Indianapolis, Bobbs Merrill, 1946; London, Hutchinson, 1948.

Roanoke Hundred. Indianapolis, Bobbs Merrill, 1948; London, Hutchinson, 1949.

Bennett's Welcome. Indianapolis, Bobbs Merrill, 1950; London, Hutchinson, 1952.

Queen's Gift. Indianapolis, Bobbs Merrill, 1952; London, Hutchinson, 1953.

The Young Commissioner. London, Hutchinson, 1951.

The Scotswoman. Indianapolis, Bobbs Merrill, 1955; London, Hutchinson, 1956.

The Wind in the Forest. Indianapolis, Bobbs Merrill, 1957; London, Hutchinson, 1958.

Cormorant's Breed. Philadelphia, Lippincott, 1959.

Wicked Lady. Indianapolis, Bobbs Merrill, 1962.

Rogue's Harbor. Indianapolis, Bobbs Merrill, 1964.

OTHER PUBLICATIONS

Novels

The White Leopard. Indianapolis, Bobbs Merrill, and London, Hodder and Stoughton, 1931.

Red Jasmine. Indianapolis, Bobbs Merrill, 1932; London, Hutchinson, 1933.

Other

Pay, Pack, and Follow (autobiography). New York, Holt, 1959.

*   *   *

Although Inglis Fletcher began her writing career with two novels about Africa (*The White Leopard* and *Red Jasmine*), her reputation as an historical romance writer rests upon her numerous works about the Carolinas. Her Carolina series comprises seven novels detailing the development of the Albemarle region of North Carolina from its earliest settlement through the days immediately following the American Revolution. Additionally, Fletcher wrote several more Carolina novels not officially included in the Carolina series.

Fletcher's interest in the turbulent birth of the Carolinas stems from her family history; her genealogical researches were the springboard for the intensive historical studies that produced her books. In her novels she combines actual historical personages with fictional characters, some of them bearing the names of her own ancestors. Her talent as a writer meshes perfectly with her talent as an historical researcher, for her plots weave believably in and out of the events of her chosen period with both fact and fiction ringing equally true. It is the case that on occasion, to speed the development of a plot, she rearranges the dates of some historical occurrences; but, as in *Lusty Wind for Carolina*, she takes care to admit a compression of period so that the reader might be well-informed as well as entertained.

The characters in Fletcher's work are three-dimensional; she does not allow history to do her work in developing her more famous characters, but takes the trouble to show them as personalities. It would be incorrect to say that her books have heroes and heroines as do many historical-romantic novels. Rather, the realistic nature of the stories dictates that the characters be real people with human problems stemming on the one hand from their personal relationships and on the other from their participation in the creation of a new country. The heroes and heroines of these volumes are the human focus of the times. This is not to deny the romance in the Carolina novels, for there are multiple

romantic entanglements in each book. The love affairs are true to life rather than larger than life, even when dealing with such near-mythic figures as Flora MacDonald (*The Scotswoman*) or Anne Bonney. It is interesting to note that much of the romance involved in the books is between married partners; while courtship is not neglected, Fletcher paints a charming but real picture of married love again and again. The characters that she creates (and recreates) are thinking people who set more store by reason than by pure emotion.

In each book the history is vividly detailed. Fletcher has a great facility for providing historical background necessary to the plot without becoming bogged down in lengthy exposition. Instead, she uses the devices of letters or conversations to provide information while advancing the plot at a crisp, steady pace. The reader who prefers the romantic side to the historical is not forgotten, however, for the books have plenty of adventure, from pirate attacks to thwarted love. The dialogue has a "period" feel without being stilted or static. Likewise, the dialect of the slaves is understandable and not overdone. Fletcher treats all social classes, from aristocrats to slaves, as individuals. Her view of the place of each social class in daily life has the feel of truth.

For the reader of all Fletcher's books there is a sense of continuity. In the Carolina series, the families of her fictional characters are followed through several generations, and, of course, the contemporary historical personalities appear from one book to the next. It is a bit unnerving for the reader who completes *Queen's Gift*, the last volume of the Carolina series, and then reads *Wicked Lady*, a non-series title published a few years later. The two books read like different treatments of the same plot, with variances in some characters and dates. In view of Fletcher's inventiveness, this duplication is inexplicable. Both books are quite readable, with the earlier volume being much more detailed, and consequently the superior tale. Aside from this anomaly, Fletcher's novels provide a chronicle of life in early America as it probably was lived.

—Susan Quinn Berneis

_____

FOOTE, Shelby. American. Born in Greenville, Mississippi, 17 November 1916. Educated at the University of North Carolina, Chapel Hill, 1935–37. Served in the United States Army, 1940–44: Captain; and Marine Corps, 1944–45. Married Gwyn Rainer in 1956 (second marriage); two children. Novelist-in-residence, University of Virginia, Charlottesville, November 1963; playwright-in-residence, Arena Stage, Washington, D.C., 1963–64; writer-in-residence, Hollins College, Virginia, 1968. Recipient: Guggenheim fellowship, 1955, 1956, 1957; Ford fellowship, for drama, 1963; Fletcher Pratt award, for non-fiction, 1964, 1974; University of North Carolina award, 1975. D.Litt.: University of the South, Sewanee, Tennessee, 1981; Southwestern University, Memphis, Tennessee, 1982. Address: 542 East Parkway South, Memphis, Tennessee 38104, U.S.A.

ROMANCE AND HISTORICAL PUBLICATIONS

Novels

Tournament. New York, Dial Press, 1949.

Follow Me Down. New York, Dial Press, 1950; London, Hamish Hamilton, 1951.

Love in a Dry Season. New York, Dial Press, 1951.

Shiloh. New York, Dial Press, 1952.
Jordan County: A Landscape in Narrative (includes stories). New York, Dial Press, 1954.
September September. New York, Random House, 1978.

OTHER PUBLICATIONS

Play

Jordan County: A Landscape in the Round (produced Washington, D.C., 1964).

Other

The Civil War: A Narrative:
  1. *Fort Sumter to Perryville*. New York, Random House, 1958.
  2. *Fredericksburg to Meridian*. New York, Random House, 1963.
  3. *Red River to Appomattox*. New York, Random House, 1974.
The Novelist's View of History. Winston-Salem, North Carolina, Palaemon Press, 1981.
Conversations with Shelby Foote, edited by William C. Carter. Jackson, University Press of Mississippi, 1989.

*

Manuscript Collection: Southern Historical Collection, Chapel Hill, North Carolina.

Critical Studies: "Shelby Foote Issue" (includes bibliography) of *Mississippi Quarterly* (State College), October 1971, and *Delta* (Montpellier, France), 1977; *Shelby Foote* by Helen White and Reading Sugg, Boston, Twayne, 1982.

*   *   *

Shelby Foote appears to succeed as a historian, not as a novelist; his multi-volume history *The Civil War: A Narrative* shows his ability to best advantage. However, one should remember that his entree into the literary world came as a promising novelist. His novels show a serious craftsman at work.

Foote experimented with technique. *Tournament* is a character study—approaching biography—with an objective omniscient point of view. *Follow Me Down* takes a single plot but incorporates a multiple point of view. This method is interesting because it allows eight characters—including protagonist and minor characters—to comment in a limited first-person viewpoint on their reactions to a violent murder. *Love in a Dry Season* is a *tour de force* in which the author links two separate stories centered on the subject of money by a character who tries and fails to obtain a place in the financial elite of a small delta town. *Shiloh* enters the domain of historical fiction as the author recreates that Civil War battle through the eyes of six soldiers from both camps. Unlike the viewers in *Follow Me Down*, these narrators describe different aspects of the three-day confrontation, and only by adroit maneuvering does the author bring the respective narratives into contact. The battle, therefore, becomes the hero of the novel. *Jordan County* is a collection of seven tales or episodes ranging from 1950 backwards to 1797. In each case the locale is Bristol, Jordan County, Mississippi. As his previous novel focused on a single battle, so this chronicles hu-

man drama of a fictional area, which becomes the only constant in a world of flux.

With the exception of his historical novel, all of Foote's novels are located in his microcosm, the delta country around Lake Jordan. This fictive locale includes two counties, Issawamba and Jordan, Solitaire Plantation, and the town of Bristol on the Mississippi River. Through a habit of cross reference, Foote links episodes from one novel to another. For instance, the novella "Pillar of Fire" (*Jordan County*) relates the story of Isaac Jameson, founder of Solitaire Plantation and a patriarch of the delta, while *Tournament* supplies information about the man, Hugh Bart, who brought Solitaire back from devastation by war and reconstruction.

Foote's use of setting, as well as style, subject matter, themes, and characterization, invites comparison with his geographical neighbor, Faulkner, but Foote's accomplishments suffer thereby. Foote is competent, not great. Normally his style is simple, lean, and direct; it seldom takes on richly suggestive qualities. Most of his themes move in the negative, anti-social direction: violence instead of peace; lust rather than love; avarice, power, and pride instead of self-sacrifice; and loneliness rather than participation in community. At his best Foote deals effectively with dramatic situations and characterizations, for example, the concatenation of episodes in the life of Hugh Bart or Luther Eustis's murder (*Follow Me Down*); however, Harley Drew's career (*Love in a Dry Season*) of lust and avarice seems an exploitation of violence rather than art. Foote chronicles events in the realistic tradition without conveying a larger insight than the particular—an insight necessary for him to achieve a significant place in southern literature.

—Anderson Clark

———

FORBES, Esther. American. Born in Westborough, Massachusetts, 28 June 1891. Educated at Bradford Junior College, graduated 1912; University of Wisconsin, Madison, 1916–18. Married Albert Learned Hoskins in 1926 (divorced 1933). Staff member, Houghton Mifflin Company, publishers, Boston, 1920–26, 1942–46. Recipient: Pulitzer prize, for history, 1943; American Library Association Newbery Medal, for children's book, 1944. Litt.D.: Clark University, Worcester, Massachusetts, 1943; University of Maine, Orono, 1943; University of Wisconsin, 1949; Northeastern University, Boston, 1949; Wellesley College, Massachusetts, 1959; LL.D.: Tufts University, Medford, Massachusetts. Member, American Academy of Arts and Sciences. *Died 12 August 1967.*

ROMANCE AND HISTORICAL PUBLICATIONS

Novels

O Genteel Lady! Boston, Houghton Mifflin, 1926; London, Heinemann, 1927.
Miss Marvel. Boston, Houghton Mifflin, 1935.
Paradise. New York, Harcourt Brace, and London, Chatto and Windus, 1937.
The General's Lady. New York, Harcourt Brace, 1938; London, Chatto and Windus, 1939.
The Running of the Tide. Boston, Houghton Mifflin, 1948; London, Chatto and Windus, 1949.
Rainbow on the Road. Boston, Houghton Mifflin, 1954; London, Chatto and Windus, 1955.

OTHER PUBLICATIONS

Fiction (for children)

Johnny Tremain. Boston, Houghton Mifflin, 1943; London, Chatto and Windus, 1944.

Other

Ann Douglas Sedgwick: An Interview. Boston, Houghton Mifflin, 1928.
A Mirror for Witches, in Which Is Reflected the Life, Machinations, and Death of Famous Doll Bilby, Who, with a More Than Feminine Perversity, Preferred a Demon to a Mortal Lover. Boston, Houghton Mifflin, and London, Heinemann, 1928.
Paul Revere and the World He Lived In. Boston, Houghton Mifflin, 1942.
America's Paul Revere (for children). Boston, Houghton Mifflin, 1946.
The Boston Book. Boston, Houghton Mifflin, 1947.

*

Manuscript Collections: American Antiquarian Society, Worcester, Massachusetts; Clark University Library, Worcester, Massachusetts.

Critical Study: *Esther Forbes* by Margaret Erskine, Worcester, Massachusetts, Worcester Bicentennial Committee, 1976.

*   *   *

It is difficult to reflect on Esther Forbes and her writing without focusing on her native state and region, Massachusetts and New England. Few authors are so identified with their heritage. Forbes's range of literary skills brought her critical acclaim for both her adult and children's historical fiction, and a Pulitzer prize in history for her first non-fiction book.

This book, *Paul Revere and the World He Lived In*, was more than a biography. It also provided an insight into 18th-century Boston and the leading figures behind the American struggle for independence. Forbes was able to turn her extensive research into primary sources to good use in two later publications.

She is best known for her Newbery Medal-winning book for children, *Johnny Tremain*. This book relates the story of a young apprentice silversmith on the eve of the American Revolution, who after receiving an injury re-evaluates his life, and becomes affiliated with the colonists' cause. Written in the days following the Japanese bombing of Pearl Harbor when it was difficult for any American to remain neutral on the subject of his country, *Johnny Tremain* suffers from being entirely from the perspective of the rebels with little sympathy for the Tory position. The book is written from a pre-Vietnam perspective on war when there still seemed to be clear-cut issues of right and wrong.

Forbes's other books, while not as critically or commercially successful as the two prize-winners, are also based on New England history. The early *A Mirror for Witches* conveys the hysteria leading up to the hanging of the Salem witches and is unique for being told from the accused witches' point of view. While the narrative voice is that of a clergyman, the story is that of Doll Bilby, a young girl who in the course of the witch hunt convinces herself that she is a witch. *Miss Marvel*, a psychological study, focuses on the life of a New England spinster during the last three decades of the 19th century and the years prior to

World War I. *Paradise* concentrates on the construction and settlement of a 17th-century Massachusetts community. In keeping with Forbes's regional emphasis, *The General's Lady* portrays the story of a woman sympathetic to the Tory cause, whose life ends on the gallows.

The Running of the Tide, one of Forbes's last books, traces the rise and decline of Salem, Massachusetts, as a seaport and through it the loves and adventures of Captain Dash Inman and Polly Mompeson. Forbes's last major publication, *America's Paul Revere*, returned to a familiar subject. Written for children, this biography focuses on not only Revere but also the lives and times of New Englanders in the revolutionary era.

Forbes does try to present a real picture of the times and communities in which her characters lived, but her viewpoint, despite her sympathies and diligence as a researcher, remains limited. Her perspective was that of the mainstream American historians of her time. Fifty years later her work appears well out of the mainstream, primarily because she lacked any critical perspective on her materials.

—Frank R. Levstik

FORD, Elbur. See HOLT, Victoria.

FORD, Elizabeth. See GIBBS, Mary Ann.

FORD, Ford Madox. Also wrote as Daniel Chaucer; Fenil Haig. British. Born Ford Hermann Hueffer in Merton, Surrey, 17 December 1873; grandson of the artist Ford Madox Brown; changed name to Ford Madox Ford, 1919 (work published under this name from 1923). Educated privately in Folkestone, Kent; at University College School, London. Served in France as an officer in the Welch Regiment during World War I. Married Elsie Martindale in 1894 (separated 1909); two daughters. Writer from 1892; collaborated with Joseph Conrad, 1898–1906; founding editor, *English Review*, London 1908–10; moved to Paris after World War I: founding editor, *Transatlantic Review*, Paris, 1924; in later years lived in the south of France and in New York City. D.Litt.: Olivet College, Michigan, 1938. *Died 26 June 1939.*

ROMANCE AND HISTORICAL PUBLICATIONS

Novels (series: Fifth Queen)

Romance, with Joseph Conrad. London, Smith Elder, 1903; New York, McClure, 1904.
The Fifth Queen:
    The Fifth Queen and How She Came to Court. London, Rivers, 1906.
    Privy Seal: His Last Venture. London, Rivers, 1907.
    The Fifth Queen Crowned: A Romance. London, Nash, 1908.
The Half Moon: A Romance of the Old World and the New. London, Nash, and New York, Doubleday, 1909.
The Portrait. London, Methuen, 1910.

Ladies Whose Bright Eyes: A Romance. London, Constable, 1911; New York, Doubleday, 1912; revised edition, Philadelphia, Lippincott, 1935.
The Young Lovell: A Romance. London, Chatto and Windus, 1913.
A Little Less Than Gods: A Romance. London, Duckworth, and New York, Viking Press, 1928.

OTHER PUBLICATIONS

Novels

The Shifting of the Fire. London, Unwin, and New York, Putnam, 1892.
The Inheritors: An Extravagant Story, with Joseph Conrad. New York, McClure Philips, and London, Heinemann, 1901.
The Benefactor: A Tale of a Small Circle. London, Brown Langham, 1905.
An English Girl: A Romance. London, Methuen, 1907.
Mr. Apollo: A Just Possible Story. London, Methuen, 1908.
A Call: The Tale of Two Passions. London, Chatto and Windus, 1910.
The Simple Life Limited (as Daniel Chaucer). London and New York, Lane, 1911.
The Panel: A Sheer Comedy. London, Constable, 1912; revised edition, as *Ring for Nancy*, Constable, and Indianapolis, Bobbs Merrill, 1913.
The New Humpty-Dumpty (as Daniel Chaucer). London and New York, Lane, 1912.
Mr. Fleight. London, Latimer, 1913.
The Good Soldier: A Tale of Passion. London and New York, Lane, 1915.
The Marsden Case: A Romance. London, Duckworth, 1923.
Parade's End (The Tietjens Tetralogy). New York, Knopf, 1950.
  Some Do Not. London, Duckworth, and New York, Seltzer, 1924.
  No More Parades. London, Duckworth, and New York, Boni, 1925.
  A Man Could Stand Up. London, Duckworth, and New York, Boni, 1926.
  The Last Post. New York, Boni, 1928; as *Last Post*, London, Duckworth, 1928.
The Nature of a Crime, with Joseph Conrad. London, Duckworth, and New York, Doubleday, 1924.
When the Wicked Man. New York, Liveright, 1931; London, Cape, 1932.
The Rash Act. New York, Long and Smith, and London, Cape, 1933.
Henry for Hugh. Philadelphia, Lippincott, 1934.
Vive le Roy. Philadelphia, Lippincott, 1936; London, Allen and Unwin, 1937.

Plays

The Fifth Queen Crowned, with F. N. Connell, adaptation of the novel by Ford (produced London, 1909).
Mister Bosphorus and the Muses; or, A Short History of Poetry in Britain. London, Duckworth, 1923.

Verse

The Questions at the Well, with Sundry Other Verses for Notes of Music (as Fenil Haig). London, Digby Long, 1893.

Poems for Pictures and for Notes of Music. London, MacQueen, 1900.
The Face of the Night: A Second Series of Poems for Pictures. London, MacQueen, 1904.
From Inland and Other Poems. London, Rivers, 1907.
Songs from London. London, Mathews, 1910.
High Germany: Eleven Sets of Verse. London, Duckworth, 1912.
Collected Poems. London, Goschen, 1913.
Antwerp. London, Poetry Bookshop, 1915.
On Heaven, and Poems Written on Active Service. London, Lane, 1918.
A House. London, Poetry Bookshop, 1921.
New Poems. New York, Rudge, 1927.
Collected Poems. New York, Oxford University Press, 1936.
Buckshee. Cambridge, Massachusetts, Pym Randall Press, 1966.

Other

The Brown Owl: A Fairy Story (for children). London, Unwin, and New York, Stokes, 1892.
The Feather (for children). London, Unwin, and New York, Cassell, 1892.
The Queen Who Flew: A Fairy Story (for children). London, Bliss Sands and Foster, 1894.
Ford Madox Brown: A Record of His Life and Work. London, Longman, 1896.
The Cinque Ports: A Historical and Descriptive Record. Edinburgh, Blackwood, 1900.
Rossetti: A Critical Essay on His Art. London, Duckworth, and New York, Dutton, 1902.
Hans Holbein the Younger: A Critical Monograph. London, Duckworth, and New York, Dutton, 1905.
England and the English: An Interpretation. New York, McClure, 1907.
  The Soul of London: A Survey of a Modern City. London, Rivers, 1905.
  The Heart of the Country: A Survey of a Modern Land. London, Rivers, 1906.
  The Spirit of the People: An Analysis of the English Mind. London, Rivers, 1907.
Christina's Fairy Book (for children). London, Rivers, 1906.
The Pre-Raphaelite Brotherhood: A Critical Monograph. London, Duckworth, and New York, Dutton, 1907.
Ancient Lights and Certain New Reflections. London, Chapman and Hall, 1911; as *Memories and Impressions: A Study in Atmospheres*, New York, Harper, 1911.
The Critical Attitude. London, Duckworth, 1911.
This Monstrous Regiment of Women. London, Minerva, 1913.
The Desirable Alien: At Home in Germany, with Violet Hunt. London, Chatto and Windus, 1913.
Henry James: A Critical Study. London, Secker, 1914; New York, Boni, 1915.
When Blood Is Their Argument: An Analysis of Prussian Culture. London, Hodder and Stoughton, 1915.
Between St. Dennis and St. George: A Sketch of Three Civilizations. London, Hodder and Stoughton, 1915.
Zeppelin Nights: A London Entertainment, with Violet Hunt. London, Lane, 1915.
Thus to Revisit: Some Reminiscences. London, Chapman and Hall, and New York, Dutton, 1921.
Women and Men. Paris, Three Mountain Press, 1923.
Joseph Conrad: A Personal Remembrance. London, Duckworth, and Boston, Little Brown, 1924.

A Mirror to France. London, Duckworth, and New York, Boni, 1926.

New York Is Not America. London, Duckworth, and New York, Boni, 1927.

New York Essays. New York, Rudge, 1927.

No Enemy: A Tale of Reconstruction. New York, Macaulay, 1929.

The English Novel from the Earliest Days to the Death of Conrad. Philadelphia, Lippincott, 1929; London, Constable, 1930.

Return to Yesterday (Reminiscences 1894–1914). London, Gollancz, 1931; New York, Liveright, 1932.

It Was the Nightingale (reminiscences). Philadelphia, Lippincott, 1933; London, Heinemann, 1934.

Provence: From Minstrels to the Machine. Philadelphia, Lippincott, 1935; London, Allen and Unwin, 1938.

Great Trade Route. New York, Oxford University Press, and London, Allen and Unwin, 1937.

Portraits from Life: Memories and Criticisms. Boston, Houghton Mifflin, 1937; as *Mightier Than the Sword*, London, Allen and Unwin, 1938.

The March of Literature from Confucius' Day to Our Own. New York, Dial Press, 1938; as *The March of Literature from Confucius to Modern Times*, London, Allen and Unwin, 1939.

The Bodley Head Ford Madox Ford, edited by Graham Greene. London, Bodley Head, 4 vols., 1962–63.

Critical Writings, edited by Frank MacShane. Lincoln, University of Nebraska Press, 1964.

Letters of Ford Madox Ford, edited by Richard M. Ludwig. Princeton, New Jersey, Princeton University Press, 1965.

Your Mirror to My Times (reminiscences), edited by Michael Killigrew. New York, Holt Rinehart, 1971; as *Memories and Impressions* (not same as 1911 book), London, Penguin, 1979.

Pound/Ford: The Story of a Literary Friendship (correspondence with Ezra Pound), edited by Brita Lindberg-Seyersted. London, Faber, and New York, New Directions, 1982.

The Ford Madox Ford Reader, edited by Sondra J. Stang. Manchester, Carcanet, 1986.

A History of Our Own Times, edited by Solon Beinfeld and Sondra J. Stang. Bloomington, Indiana University Press, 1988.

Translator, *The Trail of the Barbarians*, by Pierre Loti. London, Longman, 1917.

*

Bibliography: *Ford Madox Ford 1873–1939: A Bibliography of Works and Criticism* by D. D. Harvey, Princeton, New Jersey, Princeton University Press, 1962; by P. Armato, in *English Literature in Transition 10* (Greensboro, North Carolina), 1967.

Manuscript Collections: Princeton University Library, New Jersey; Yale University Library, New Haven, Connecticut; University of Virginia Library, Charlottesville.

Critical Studies: *Ford Madox Ford: A Study of His Novels* by Richard A. Cassell, Baltimore, Johns Hopkins University Press, 1961, and *Ford: Modern Judgements* edited by Cassell, London, Macmillan, 1972; *Ford Madox Ford's Novels: A Critical Study* by John A. Meixner, Minneapolis, University of Minnesota Press, 1962; *Novelist of Three Worlds: Ford Madox Ford* by Paul L. Wiley, Syracuse, New York, Syracuse University Press, 1962; *Ford Madox Ford: The Essence of His Art* by R. W. Lid, Berkeley, University of California Press, 1964; *Ford Madox Ford: From Apprentice to Craftsman* by Carol Burke Ohmann, Middletown, Connecticut, Wesleyan University Press, 1964; *The Life and Work of Ford Madox Ford* by Frank MacShane, New York, Horizon Press, and London, Routledge, 1965, and *Ford: The Critical Heritage* edited by MacShane, Routledge, 1972; *The Limited Hero in the Novels of Ford* by Norman Leer, East Lansing, Michigan State University Press, 1966; *Ford Madox Ford* by Charles G. Hoffmann, New York, Twayne, 1967; *The Alien Protagonist of Ford Madox Ford* by H. Robert Huntley, Chapel Hill, University of North Carolina Press, 1970; *The Saddest Story: A Biography of Ford Madox Ford* by Arthur Mizener, New York, World, 1971, London, Bodley Head, 1972; *Ford Madox Ford* by Sondra J. Stang, New York, Ungar, 1977, and *The Presence of Ford Madox Ford* edited by Stang, Philadelphia, University of Pennsylvania Press, 1981; *The Life in the Fiction of Ford Madox Ford* by Thomas C. Moser, Princeton, New Jersey, Princeton University Press, 1980; *Ford Madox Ford: Prose and Politics* by Robert Green, London, Cambridge University Press, 1981; *Ford Madox Ford and the Voice of Uncertainty* by Ann Barr Snitow, Baton Rouge, Louisiana State University Press, 1984; *Fairy Tale and Romance in Works of Ford Madox Ford* by Timothy Weiss, Lanham, Maryland, University Press of America, 1984; "Ford Madox Ford Issue" of *Antaeus* (New York), Spring 1986.

*   *   *

Ford Madox Ford wrote more than 70 books, including several volumes of outstanding poetry. He is better known for his work in genres other than historical fiction, for example his personal favourite *The Good Soldier* and the Tietjens books (*Some Do Not*, *No More Parades*, *A Man Could Stand Up*, and *The Last Post*).

However, a significant proportion of the oeuvre do come under Ford's own title of "romance" and *The Fifth Queen* trilogy is a vast and important, work of historical fiction. Together, they make up a significant part of his corpus and cast an intriguing light on the better known work.

In the trilogy Ford experiments with his historical knowledge, bringing a psychological realism and human motive to the material. This was commented on when the trilogy first appeared. A reviewer for the *Daily News* wrote: "There is a power and thought in the characterization, and the whole work has an astonishing effect in revealing to us the flesh and blood side of history." These qualities are still evident and remain the chief sources of the trilogy's abiding interest for readers.

The tale of Katharine Howard's career at court, culminating in her becoming Henry's fifth Queen and eventual fifth victim in the tower, surrounded as it is by Machiavellian intrigue and religious reformations, in the hands of a less skilful writer could so easily have become merely a series of factional plots and counter plotting, of little interest to contemporary readers. But Ford, while placing his cast of thousands within a huge historical setting, actually keeps the narrative focus small, preferring rather to explore in detail the lives of a few principal characters. Ford produced what amounts to an historical whodunnit, where suspense and danger are the key. The works exploit an obvious fascination with a crisis moment in English history: the "Old Faith" is set against the "New Learning," religion against heresy, the ideas of the infamous Machiavelli are evident in the culture, "the walls have ears" and: "God hath withdrawn himself . . . and all mankind goeth a-mumming" (*Privy Seal*).

The Fifth Queen begins with Henry's unhappy marriage to Anne of Cleves and the burgeoning Protestant movement that is sweeping the land. Into this world arrives the poor, yet learned Catholic, Katharine Howard, who steadily gains influence at court and with the King. This narrative line is the link between the three volumes, around which several other narratives are interwoven—Thomas Cromwell's rise and demise, the schism between Church and State, the tragic tale of Sir Thomas Culpepper who loves Katharine yet unwittingly becomes the source of her downfall.

Privy Seal sees the blossoming of Katharine's career, Henry's proposal and her gaining permission from Anne of Cleves to annul the previous marriage. The ageing King and young Queen weave a powerful love story surrounded by the intrigue of Cromwell's world: "He played upon people's fear, troubled them with apprehensions. It was part of the tradition that Cromwell had given all his men. He ruled England by such fears."

In the final volume the focus is a familial one: a tender peace has returned as Kat tries to heal the wounds within Henry's warring brood. Yet her integrity proves her downfall, a tragic end for a powerful woman: "I must be the same make of Queen that I am as a woman."

The trilogy remains the most compelling of Ford's works. His other "romances" tend to be sketchy and less interesting. In *The Young Lovell* he returns to Tudor times; *Ladies Whose Bright Eyes* is a dream narrative in which the publisher Mr. Sorrell travels back to 1326 and falls in love with a woman "600 years dead." The most interesting of these novels is *An English Girl* with its Citizen Kane-like tale of corruption and insightful investigation of the culture clash when a young English heroine falls in love with the all-American boy.

—Catherine S. Wearing

FORESTER, C(ecil) S(cott). British. Born in Cairo, Egypt, 27 August 1899; grew up in the London suburbs. Educated at Alleyne's School, London, and Dulwich College, London, 1910–17; studied medicine at Guy's Hospital, London, but left without qualifying. Married 1) Kathleen Belcher in 1926 (divorced 1944), two sons; 2) Dorothy Ellen Foster in 1947. Writer from 1917; screenwriter in Hollywood, 1932; war correspondent for *The Times*, London, in Spain, 1936–37, and subsequently in Czechoslovakia during the Nazi occupation; in later life lived in Berkeley, California. Recipient: James Tait Black Memorial prize, 1940. *Died 2 April 1966.*

ROMANCE AND HISTORICAL PUBLICATIONS

Novels (series: Horatio Hornblower)

The Shadow of the Hawk. London, Lane, 1928; as *The Daughter of the Hawk*, Indianapolis, Bobbs Merrill, 1928.
Death to the French. London, Lane, 1932; as *Rifleman Dodd*, with *The Gun*, Boston, Little Brown, 1943.
The Gun. London, Lane, and Boston, Little Brown, 1933.
The Happy Return (Hornblower). London, Joseph, 1937; as *Beat to Quarters*, Boston, Little Brown, 1937.
Flying Colours (Hornblower). London, Joseph, 1938; Boston, Little Brown, 1939.
A Ship of the Line (Hornblower). London, Joseph, 1938; as *Ship of the Line*, Boston, Little Brown, 1938.
The Captain from Connecticut. London, Joseph, and Boston, Little Brown, 1941.
The Commodore. London, Joseph, 1945; as *Commodore Hornblower*, Boston, Little Brown, 1945.
Lord Hornblower. London, Joseph, and Boston, Little Brown, 1946.
Mr. Midshipman Hornblower. London, Joseph, and Boston, Little Brown, 1950.

Lieutenant Hornblower. London, Joseph, and Boston, Little Brown, 1952.
Hornblower and the Atropos. London, Joseph, and Boston, Little Brown, 1953.
Hornblower in the West Indies. London, Joseph, 1958; as *Admiral Hornblower in the West Indies*, Boston, Little Brown, 1958.
Hornblower and the Hotspur. London, Joseph, and Boston, Little Brown, 1962.
Hornblower and the Crisis: An Unfinished Novel (includes story "The Last Encounter"). London, Joseph, 1967.

Short Stories

Two-and-Twenty. London Lane, and New York, Appleton, 1931.
The Nightmare. London, Joseph, and Boston, Little Brown, 1954.
The Man in the Yellow Raft. London, Joseph, and Boston, Little Brown, 1969.
Gold from Crete. Boston, Little Brown, 1970; London, Joseph, 1971.

OTHER PUBLICATIONS

Novels

A Pawn among Kings. London, Methuen, 1924.
Payment Deferred. London, Lane, 1926; Boston, Little Brown, 1942.
Love Lies Dreaming. London, Lane, and Indianapolis, Bobbs Merrill, 1927.
The Wonderful Week. London, Lane, 1927; as *One Wonderful Week*, Indianapolis, Bobbs Merrill, 1927.
Brown on Resolution. London, Lane, 1929; as *Single-Handed*, New York, Putnam, 1929.
Plain Murder. London, Lane, 1930; New York, Dell, 1954.
The Peacemaker. London, Heinemann, and Boston, Little Brown, 1934.
The African Queen. London, Heinemann, and Boston, Little Brown, 1935.
The General. London, Joseph, and Boston, Little Brown, 1936.
The Ship. London, Joseph, and Boston, Little Brown, 1943.
The Sky and the Forest. London, Joseph, and Boston, Little Brown, 1948.
Randall and the River of Time. Boston, Little Brown, 1950; London, Joseph, 1951.
The Good Shepherd. London, Joseph, and Boston, Little Brown, 1955.
Hunting the Bismarck. London, Joseph, 1959; as *The Last Nine Days of the Bismarck*, Boston, Little Brown, 1959; as *Sink the Bismarck!*, New York, Bantam, 1959.

Short Stories

The Paid Piper. London, Methuen, 1924.

Plays

U 97. London, Lane, 1931.
Nurse Cavell, with C. E. Bechhofer Roberts (produced London, 1934). London, Lane, 1933.

Screenplays: *Forever and a Day*, with others, 1944; *Captain Horatio Hornblower*, with others, 1951.

Other

Napoleon and His Court. London, Methuen, and New York, Dodd Mead, 1924.

Josephine, Napoleon's Empress. London, Methuen, and New York, Dodd Mead, 1925.

Victor Emmanuel II and the Union of Italy. London, Methuen, and New York, Dodd Mead, 1927.

Louis XIV, King of France and Navarre. London, Methuen, and New York, Dodd Mead, 1928.

Nelson (biography). London, Lane, 1929; as *Lord Nelson*, Indianapolis, Bobbs Merrill, 1929.

The Voyage of the Annie Marble. London, Lane, 1929.

The Annie Marble in Germany. London, Lane, 1930.

Marionettes at Home. London, Joseph, 1936.

The Earthly Paradise. London, Joseph, 1940; as *To the Indies*, Boston, Little Brown, 1940.

Poo-Poo and the Dragons (for children). London, Joseph, and Boston, Little Brown, 1942.

The Barbary Pirates (for children). New York, Random House, 1953; London, Macdonald, 1956.

The Age of Fighting Sail: The Story of the Naval War of 1812. New York, Doubleday, 1956; as *The Naval War of 1812*, London, Joseph, 1957.

The Hornblower Companion. London, Joseph, and Boston, Little Brown, 1964.

Long Before Forty (autobiography). London, Joseph, 1967; Boston, Little Brown, 1968.

Editor, *The Adventures of John Wetherell*. New York, Doubleday, 1953; London, Joseph, 1954.

*

Critical Study: *C.S. Forester* by Sanford Sternlicht, Boston, Twayne, 1981.

*   *   *

He never won a Nobel prize or a Pulitzer or any major literary award, but when Cecil Scott Forester died in 1966 his obituary commenced on the front page of the *New York Times*, eight million copies of his books had been sold, and the name of his great creation, the 20th-century superhero of historical fiction was a household word: Captain Horatio Hornblower. Paperback editions, the film *Captain Horatio Hornblower*, and serialization in the *Saturday Evening Post* ensured that Hornblower was in the public eye for more than 30 years. Not until Ian Fleming's James Bond smashed his way into the collective consciousness of the Anglo-American reading public in the 1950's was Hornblower's primacy in escapist fiction challenged. That a 19th-century British naval officer was ultimately replaced by a contemporary British undercover agent as the nonpareil fantasy hero of the general reading public indicated a shift in values during the last half of the 20th century. Hornblower was a hero of and for the World War II generation, and Bond was the darling of the Cold War generation.

Forester was a genuinely great storyteller who loved the creative, imaginative process that turned words into the illusion of a past reality. Forester's strengths are sharp, swift, sometimes Dickensian characterization, carefully thought-out plots, and, most of all, absolutely accurate historical details. Forester was an avid reader of naval history. He studied all aspects of life at sea in the age of sail, and masterfully integrated accurate technical information into a fascinating narrative. Particularly, he based the character of Hornblower on his deep knowledge of the

life and times of Admiral Horatio Nelson, and of another real-life British naval hero of the Napoleonic Wars, Captain Thomas, Lord Cochrane. Furthermore, he created an historical naval milieu by studying the once popular nautical novels of Captain Frederick Marryat, like *Mr. Midshipman Easy* (1836).

The 11-novel Hornblower saga is best read and enjoyed in historical order, not in the order of writing. In *Mr. Midshipman Hornblower* the 17-year-old Hornblower reports aboard HMS *Justinian*, becomes seasick (a weakness he never shakes in 30 years at sea), is involved in a duel, but fortunately is transferred to the frigate *Indefatigable*, under the command of the dashing Captain Sir Edward Pellew, his mentor and model. Hornblower gets his first taste of command when he brings a prize to port. Along the way he is captured by the Spanish but released after an heroic act.

Four years pass and in *Lieutenant Hornblower* Horatio serves under the Queeg-like Captain Sawyer and his pusillanimous successor. He saves the day for England by planning and executing a courageous action against a Spanish fort. He returns to England with a prize, but is then a lieutenant without a billet, waiting for war with France to break out again. In this work the reader meets two major architectonic characters in the saga: Hornblower's life-long friend and shipmate, Lieutenant William Bush, and Maria Mason, "dumpy and not quite young," the daughter of his landlady, to whom he proposes as war erupts and he receives a command.

In *Hornblower and the Hotspur*, Horatio is in command of the sloop *Hotspur*. He marries Maria and Bush is his first lieutenant. Hornblower attacks French shore installations and then defeats a much larger French warship. Maria has a son and then becomes pregnant again when her husband returns to Portsmouth. As the novel ends Hornblower is promoted to captain.

In *Hornblower and the Crisis*, unfinished at Forester's death, Hornblower is preparing for the French invasion of Britain. He captures some documents that help him to force the French to sea where Nelson can get at them. Voilà: Trafalgar!

Hornblower and the Atropos is post-Trafalgar. Maria is pregnant again, and Horatio, a junior captain, gets the *Atropos*. A daughter is born as Hornblower finishes directing Nelson's funeral. After cruising successfully with the *Atropos* in the Mediterranean, Hornblower loses the ship, for it is given to the King of the Two Sicilies. Disgusted, Hornblower returns home to seek command of a new frigate. In Portsmouth he learns that his children are ill with smallpox.

Six months later he is at sea again, captain of the frigate *Lydia*, in *The Happy Return* (*Beat to Quarters*). Again Bush is his first lieutenant, and we meet Lady Barbara Wellesley, who will be Hornblower's second wife. Meanwhile, his children have died of smallpox. Hornblower must help an odious rebel band capture a Spanish ship of the line, which he turns over to the dictator El Supremo. Learning that Spain has quit Napoleon and joined the Allies, he must recapture the *Natividad* even though Lady Barbara is aboard the *Lydia*. The battle is vicious and the victorious *Lydia* is badly battered. Lady Barbara succors the wounded while Hornblower repairs his ship. He falls in love with the beautiful aristocrat but cannot bring himself, a married man, to make love to her. She angrily, if temporarily, sweeps out of his life, and Horatio returns home to Maria, seemingly relieved at having escaped commitment and scandal.

A Ship of the Line finds Hornblower in command of the "battleship" *Sutherland*. Bush is still his first lieutenant. Lady Barbara has married an admiral, Hornblower's superior. Horatio saves a fleet of East Indiamen from French privateers through brilliant shiphandling. Then he attacks the Spanish coast and routs with his batteries a French army marching down a road.

Not surprisingly, he does not get on well with Barbara's husband, who orders him to attack a French fort, an effort doomed to failure. The *Sutherland* winds up fighting four French ships of the line. Hornblower is taken prisoner and faces years of captivity.

Flying Colours, however, finds Hornblower escaping in France, building a small boat, having an affair with a French girl, and rowing down the Loire to Nantes, where disguised as Dutch officers loyal to the French, he and the maimed Bush recapture a British cutter and sail her to the British Channel fleet. He soon learns that Lady Barbara's husband is dead and Maria too has died, giving birth to a son who survived. Hornblower the hero is honoured by the Prince Regent. Now affluent and famous, Hornblower takes his infant son to Lady Barbara and the yarn ends with Hornblower knowing "she was his for the asking" and the clear indication that he would ask.

The Commodore (*Commodore Hornblower*) opens with Horatio and Barbara married. Hornblower is promoted to commodore and sent to the Baltic to harass French shipping and exert diplomatic pressure on the Swedes and the Russians. He is now a major player on the stage of world events. After victorious sea fights directed from his flagship, the *Nonsuch*, Hornblower the diplomat sails to Russia where he stiffens Czar Alexander's resolve to defy Napoleon. He prevents an assassination of the Czar, gets drunk for the first time, and has sex with the countess Caterine, who gives him fleas. At the siege of Riga, Hornblower on horseback saves the Russian defenders by leading a counterattack. The Russian army and the British fleet check the French while Napoleon meets his destiny at Moscow. Hornblower gets the Prussians to desert Napoleon, and thus he is instrumental in the overthrow of the despot, but then the hero falls ill with typhus (the fleas!). He recovers at home in Barbara's arms.

Lord Hornblower finds the hero suppressing a mutiny and accepting the surrender of Le Havre. He becomes provisional governor (like MacArthur in Japan). His friend Bush is killed in action while Hornblower is elevated to a peerage. He returns to England, but soon goes back to France to rescue his former mistress, who dies in the attempt. Hornblower is captured and sentenced to death, but is saved by Waterloo.

Hornblower in the West Indies (*Admiral Hornblower in the West Indies*) has the hero a rear admiral, commanding the British West Indies squadron long after the end of the Napoleonic War. He thwarts an attempt to rescue his old nemesis from St. Helena. On the way home from his last command Hornblower saves his wife and the other passengers of the ship they are embarked in, through superior seamanship in a storm. Lady Barbara tells her husband that she has never loved anyone but him, and Hornblower has been made happy forever.

The short story, "The Last Encounter." published with *Hornblower and the Crisis*, concludes the saga. In 1848 the 72-year-old Hornblower, now Admiral of the Fleet and retired, is visited by a "madman" who turns out to be the future Napoleon III. Thus the saga ends on a humorous note.

The theme of the Hornblower saga is "the man alone." Forester discourses on the problems of independent command and its stresses on character, honour, integrity, and courage. For Forester the ultimate source of virtue is a well-developed conscience.

The key to the success of Forester's historical novels lies in his training as a film writer. The works are episodic, vivid, and easily visualized. Characterization is unambiguous and emphasis is decidedly on entertainment.

Forester's historical novels about the Penninsular War, *Death to the French* (*Rifleman Dodd*) and *The Gun*, are well worth the read. In *The Captain from Connecticut* Forester tried to intro-duce an American Hornblower, Capt. Joshua Peabody, USN, but failed. It is Hornblower who sails on.

—Sanford Sternlicht

FOWLES, John (Robert). British. Born in Leigh-on-Sea, Essex, 31 March 1926. Educated at Bedford School, 1940–44; Edinburgh University, 1944; New College, Oxford, B.A. (honours) in French 1950. Served in the Royal Marines, 1945–46. Married Elizabeth Whitton in 1956. Lecturer in English, University of Poitiers, 1950–51; teacher at Anargyrios College, Spetsai, Greece, 1951–52, and in London, 1953–63. Recipient: Silver Pen award, 1969; W. H. Smith award, 1970; Christopher award, 1981. Agent: Anthony Sheil Associates, 43 Doughty Street, London WC1N 2LF, England.

ROMANCE AND HISTORICAL PUBLICATIONS

Novels

The French Lieutenant's Woman. London, Cape, and Boston, Little Brown, 1969.
A Maggot. London, Cape, and Boston, Little Brown, 1985.

OTHER PUBLICATIONS

Novels

The Collector. London, Cape, and Boston, Little Brown, 1963.
The Magus. Boston, Little Brown, 1965; London, Cape, 1966; revised edition, Cape, 1977; Little Brown, 1978.
Daniel Martin. Boston, Little Brown, and London, Cape, 1977.
Mantissa. London, Cape, and Boston, Little Brown, 1982.

Short Stories

The Ebony Tower: Collected Novellas. London, Cape, and Boston, Little Brown, 1974.

Plays

Don Juan, adaptation of the play by Molière (produced London, 1981).
Lorenzaccio, adaptation of the play by Alfred de Musset (produced London, 1983).
Martine, adaptation of a play by Jean Jacques Bernard (produced London, 1985).

Screenplay: *The Magus*, 1968.

Verse

Poems. New York, Ecco Press, 1973.
Conditional. Northridge, California, Lord John Press, 1979.

Other

The Aristos: A Self-Portrait in Ideas. Boston, Little Brown, 1964; London, Cape, 1965; revised edition, London, Pan, 1968; Little Brown, 1970.

Shipwreck, photographs by the Gibsons of Scilly. London, Cape, 1974; Boston, Little Brown, 1975.

Islands, photographs by Fay Godwin. London, Cape, 1978; Boston, Little Brown, 1979.

The Tree, photographs by Frank Horvat. London, Aurum Press, 1979; Boston, Little Brown, 1980.

The Enigma of Stonehenge, photographs by Barry Brukoff. London, Cape, and New York, Summit, 1980.

A Brief History of Lyme. Lyme Regis, Dorset, Friends of the Lyme Regis Museum, 1981.

A Short History of Lyme Regis. Wimborne, Dorset, Dovecote Press, 1982; Boston, Little Brown, 1983.

Of Memoirs and Magpies. Austin, Texas, Taylor, 1983.

Land, photographs by Fay Godwin. London, Heinemann, and Boston, Little Brown, 1985.

Editor, *Steep Holm: A Case History in the Study of Evolution*. Sherborne, Dorset, Allsop Memorial Trust, 1978.

Editor, with Rodney Legg, *Monumenta Britannica*, by John Aubrey. Sherborne, Dorset Publishing Company, 2 vols., 1980–82; vol. 1, Boston, Little Brown, 1981.

Editor, *Thomas Hardy's England*, by Jo Draper. London, Cape, and Boston, Little Brown, 1984.

Translator, *Cinderella*, by Perrault. London, Cape, 1974; Boston, Little Brown, 1975.

Translator, *Ourika*, by Claire de Durfort. Austin, Texas, Taylor, 1977.

*

Bibliography: "John Fowles: An Annotated Bibliography 1963–76" by Karen Magee Myers, in *Bulletin of Bibliography* (Boston), vol. 33, no. 4, 1976; *John Fowles: A Reference Guide* by Barry N. Olshen and Toni A. Olshen, Boston, Hall, 1980; "John Fowles: A Bibliographical Checklist" by Ray A. Roberts, in *American Book Collector* (New York), September–October, 1980; "Criticism of John Fowles: A Selected Checklist" by Ronald C. Dixon, in *Modern Fiction Studies* (Lafayette, Indiana), Spring 1985.

Manuscript Collection: University of Tulsa, Oklahoma.

Critical Studies: *The Fiction of John Fowles: Tradition, Art, and the Loneliness of Selfhood* by William J. Palmer, Columbia, University of Missouri Press, 1974; *John Fowles, Magus and Moralist* by Peter Wolfe, Lewisburg, Pennsylvania, Bucknell University Press, 1976, revised edition, 1979; *Etudes sur "The French Lieutenant's Woman" de John Fowles* edited by Jean Chevalier, Caen, University of Caen, 1977; *John Fowles* by Barry N. Olshen, New York, Ungar, 1978; *John Fowles* by Robert Huffaker, New York, Twayne, 1980; "John Fowles Issue" of *Journal of Modern Literature* (Philadelphia), vol. 8, no. 2, 1981; *John Fowles* by Peter J. Conradi, London, Methuen, 1982; *The Timescapes of John Fowles* by H. W. Fawkner, Rutherford, New Jersey, Fairleigh Dickinson University Press, 1983; *Male Mythologies: John Fowles and Masculinity* by Bruce Woodcock, Brighton, Harvester Press, 1984; *The Romances of John Fowles* by Simon Loveday, London, Macmillan, 1985; "John Fowles Issue" of *Modern Fiction Studies* (Lafayette, Indiana), Spring 1985.

*   *   *

Despite the fact that two of his six novels are clearly grounded in English history, John Fowles does not wish to be considered an historical novelist. Of *The French Lieutenant's Woman*, he wrote: "I don't think of it as a historical novel, a genre in which I have very little interest," and the epilogue to *A Maggot* informs the reader that those "who know something of what that Manchester baby was to become will not need telling how little this is a historical novel." Given the meticulous recreation of Victorian England of 1867 to 1869 in the former and the similar concern for historical details in portraying Devonshire in 1736 in the latter, Fowles's novels, whatever the author's disclaimers, have a rich sense of historical period, created by careful research, even though their first allegiance is to fiction. His own interest in history outside fiction is even more firmly established by his several landscape and monument books, including *A Short History of Lyme Regis*.

The French Lieutenant's Woman, Fowles's best-known and certainly his most successful novel, carefully examines certain aspects of the Victorian period at a crucial moment in time, 1867, when a new age begins to emerge. The novel is a stunningly successful pastiche of Victorian fiction, in particular a homage to Thomas Hardy. Virtually every major convention of the fiction of Dickens, Thackeray, Eliot, Meredith, Hardy, and other Victorian novelists is replicated, but then refracted through a 20th-century perspective. Like Lawrence, Fowles is particularly drawn to the English landscape, and his descriptions of the landscape of Dorset and the architecture of the houses are no less detailed than his exploration of the relationship of masters and mistresses and servants, between the powerful mercantile and the aristocratic classes, and of their language, ideas, medicines, amusements, and dress than are the probing comments about the thoughts of Karl Marx and Charles Darwin, the two major voices in the period for gradual evolution. The story focuses on Charles Smithson's love for Ernestina Freeman and Sarah Woodruff, a typical Victorian triangle, but with Ernestina's conformity to Victorian society reducing her to the status of an object and with Sarah's rebellion ultimately casting her out of society. Charles's relationships with the two women free him, but leave him at a point where the prospect of a free, authentic, new life almost paralyzes him. The novel's most notorious feature, its three endings, allows the reader to measure himself or herself in order to determine if he or she is a Victorian, an Edwardian, or a modern existentialist. Throughout the novel, Fowles establishes a dialogue between the Victorian and the modern periods, using each as a critique of the other.

A Maggot, idiosyncratically titled and considerably less popular than Fowles's earlier novels, tells a mystery story about the disappearance of a Duke's son and the finding of the hanged body of his devoted servant, with violets growing from his mouth. The son had hired two actors and a prostitute from London to impersonate his uncle and companions on a ride from London to Bideford on the Devon coast, without telling them the exact purposes of the journey. The novel consists of Henry Ayscough's interrogations of eight individuals knowing something of the trip, six letters from Ayscough to the Duke, several letters from individuals contributing information about the Duke's son, six sections of third-person narrative, reproductions from the *Historical Register* from April 1736 to October 1736, and an epilogue by Fowles informing the reader that the pregnancy of Rebecca Lee, the reformed prostitute, resulted in the birth of Ann Lee (1736–84), also known as Mother Ann, the leader of the Shakers and "the female principle in Christ." After being imprisoned in England several times for crimes against established religion, Ann Lee migrated to Watervliet, New York, and spent the rest of her life preaching and faith-healing among the Shakers.

Fowles's novel is a "maggot," that is, a "whim or quirk" borne "out of obsession with a theme." The theme concerns Fowles's interest throughout his career with the freedom of the individual, the eruptions of the irrational, even the supernatural, into human life, and the human response to these eruptions. In its opening section, the novel quite accurately describes the clothing of rural England in 1736, the conditions of the roads, the riding equipment, the breeds of animals popular at the time, and the inns, all the while reproducing Devon dialect. The rest of the novel, however, consists of static interrogation scenes, which, depending on the reader's interest in solving the mystery of what actually happened in the Devon cavern from which the missing lord seems never to have emerged, will be intellectually challenging or needlessly evasive.

—David Leon Higdon

FRANKAU, Gilbert. British. Born in London, 21 April 1884; son of the writer Julia Davis Frankau (i.e., Frank Danby). Educated at Eton College. Served in the 9th East Surrey Regiment, 1914; transferred to the Royal Field Artillery; Adjutant to the 107th Brigade; invalided out, 1918: Captain; recommissioned in 1939; invalided out, 1941: Squadron Leader. Married 1) Dorothea Frances Black in 1905 (divorced), two daughters, including the writer Pamela Frankau; 2) Aimée de Burgh in 1922 (divorced); 3) Susan Lorna Harris in 1932. Joined his father's wholesale cigar business in 1904: managing director; full-time writer after World War I: editor, *Britannia*, 1928. *Died 4 November 1952.*

ROMANCE AND HISTORICAL PUBLICATIONS

Novels

The Woman of the Horizon: A Romance of Nineteen-Thirteen. London, Chatto and Windus, 1917; New York, Century, 1923.
Peter Jackson, Cigar Merchant: A Romance of Married Life. London, Hutchinson, 1920; as *Peter Jameson: A Modern Romance*, New York, Knopf, 1920.
The Seeds of Enchantment. London, Hutchinson, and New York, Doubleday, 1921.
The Love-Story of Aliette Brunton. London, Hutchinson, and New York, Century, 1922.
Gerald Cranston's Lady: A Romance. London, Hutchinson, and New York, Century, 1924.
Life—and Erica: A Romance. New York, Century, 1924; London, Hutchinson, 1925.
Masterson: A Study of an English Gentleman. London, Hutchinson, and New York, Harper, 1926.
So Much Good. London, Hutchinson, and New York, Harper, 1928.
Dance, Little Gentleman! London, Hutchinson 1929; New York, Harper, 1930.
Martin Make-Believe: A Romance. London, Hutchinson 1930; New York, Harper, 1931.
Christopher Strong: A Romance. London, Hutchinson, and New York, Dutton, 1932.
The Lonely Man: A Romance of Love and the Secret Service. London, Hutchinson, 1932; New York, Dutton, 1933.
Everywoman. New York, Dutton, 1933; London, Hutchinson, 1934.

Three Englishmen: A Romance of Married Lives. London, Hutchinson, and New York, Dutton, 1935.
Farewell Romance. London, Hutchinson, and New York, Dutton, 1936.
The Dangerous Years: A Trilogy. London, Hutchinson 1937; New York, Dutton, 1938.
Royal Regiment: A Drama of Contemporary Behaviours. London, Hutchinson 1938; New York, Dutton, 1939.
Winter of Discontent. London, Hutchinson 1941; as *Air Ministry, Room 28*, New York, Dutton, 1942.
World Without End. London, Hutchinson, and New York, Dutton, 1943.
Michael's Wife. London, Macdonald, and New York, Dutton, 1948.
Son of the Morning. London, Macdonald, 1949.
Oliver Trenton, K.C. London, Macdonald, 1951.
Unborn Tomorrow: A Last Story. London, Macdonald, 1953.

Short Stories

Men, Maids, and Mustard-Pot: A Collection of Tales. London, Hutchinson, 1923; New York, Century, 1924.
Twelve Tales. London, Hutchinson, 1927.
The House Behind the Judas Tree, with *Martyrdom* by Warwick Deeping and *Forbidden Music* by Ethel Mannin. London, Readers Library, 1929; as *Three Stories of Romance*, 1936.
Concerning Peter Jackson and Others. London, Hutchinson, 1931.
Wine, Women, and Waiters. London, Hutchinson, 1932.
Secret Services. London, Hutchinson, 1934.
Experiments in Crime and Other Stories. London, Hutchinson, and New York, Dutton, 1937.
Escape to Yesterday: A Miscellany of Tales. London, Hutchinson, 1942.

OTHER PUBLICATIONS

Verse

Eton Echoes: A Volume of Humorous Verse. Eton, G. New, 1901.
The XYZ of Bridge. London, King, 1906.
One of Us: A Novel in Verse. London, Chatto and Windus, 1912; as *Jack—One of Us*, New York, Doran, 1912.
"Tid' apa" (What Does It Matter?). New York, Huebsch, 1914; London, Chatto and Windus, 1915.
The Guns. London, Chatto and Windus, 1916; as *A Song of the Guns*, Boston, Houghton Mifflin, 1916; as *A Song of the Guns in Flanders*, New York, Federal, 1916.
How Rifleman Brown Came to Valhalla. New York, Federal, 1916.
The City of Fear and Other Poems. London, Chatto and Windus, 1917.
One of Them: A Novelette in Verse. London, Hutchinson, 1918.
The Judgement of Valhalla. London, Chatto and Windus, and New York, Federal, 1918.
The Other Side and Other Poems. New York, Knopf, 1918.
The Poetical Works of Gilbert Frankau. London, Chatto and Windus, 2 vols., 1923.
More of Us, Being the Present-Day Adventures of "One of Us": A Novel in Verse. London, Hutchinson, and New York, Dutton, 1937.
Selected Verses. London, Macdonald, 1943.

Other

The Dominant Type of Man. London, Dorland Agency, 1925.
My Unsentimental Journey. London, Hutchinson, 1926.
Gilbert Frankau's Self-Portrait: A Novel of His Own Life. London, Hutchinson, and New York, Dutton, 1940.

Editor, *A Century of Love Stories.* London, Hutchinson, 1935.

*   *   *

The novels of Gilbert Frankau are almost unreadable outside the context of his times. He was deeply concerned with the place in society, still far from being determined, of "the Modern Woman" of the 1920's and 1930's. The reader must constantly readjust contemporary assumptions to the confinements of a day, not so very distant in time, but incredibly so in flavour, in which even persons in circumstances far from affluent had *such* problems with their servants' upstart independent ideas; when for a woman, as now in an odd reversal for a man, cutting or not cutting one's hair was a "statement" of sorts; when it was a daring step for any young woman to attempt to earn a living outside the home or to live apart from her family; and above all, at a time when iron divorce laws could still crush the lives of those unhappy enough to fall afoul of them, as Frankau himself did.

His bright young things, with their snappy conversations, affectations, and nicknames, are all so impossibly dated now that it will require at least another generation before their true charm will begin to reveal itself to the literary researcher's penetratingly anthropological eye. For the present, they are simply too tediously outdated to be readable, not yet antique enough to have attained the period charm of, for example, Regency chit-chat, which was equally as slangy and colloquial.

Above all, Frankau was a product of an age in which the double standard of sexual morality was in fullest flower, and he spends a good deal of time and thought on the exploration of this theme. He appears to accept the premise without question, while deploring the damaging results upon mere fallible human beings unable to uphold unrealistic standards of conduct. Mildly daring in their day, his are the works of a man strictly of his time and milieu—and both have passed.

—Joan McGrath

FRANKEN, Rose (Dorothy, née Lewin). Also writes as Margaret Grant; Franken Meloney. American. Born in Gainesville, Texas, 28 December 1895. Educated at Ethical Culture School, New York. Married 1) S. W. A. Franken in 1914 (died 1932), three sons; 2) William Brown Meloney in 1937 (died 1970). *Died 22 June 1988.*

ROMANCE AND HISTORICAL PUBLICATIONS

Novels (series: Claudia)

Pattern. New York, Scribner, 1925.
Twice Born. New York, Scribner, 1935; London, W. H. Allen, 1969.
Call Back Love (as Margaret Grant, with W. B. Meloney). New York, Farrar and Rinehart, 1937.

Of Great Riches. New York, Longman, 1937; as *Gold Pennies*, London, Constable, 1938.
Claudia: The Story of a Marriage. New York, Farrar and Rinehart, 1939; London, W. H. Allen, 1946.
Claudia and David. New York, Farrar and Rinehart, 1940; London, W. H. Allen, 1946.
Another Claudia. New York, Farrar and Rinehart, 1943; London, W. H. Allen, 1946.
Young Claudia. New York, Rinehart, 1946; London, W. H. Allen, 1947.
The Marriage of Claudia. New York, Rinehart, and London, W. H. Allen, 1948.
From Claudia to David. London, W. H. Allen, 1949; New York, Harper, 1950.
The Fragile Years. New York, Doubleday, 1952; as *Those Fragile Years*, London, W. H. Allen, 1952; as *The Return of Claudia*, London, W. H. Allen, 1957.
Rendezvous. New York, Doubleday, 1954; as *The Quiet Heart*, London, W. H. Allen, 1954.
Intimate Story. New York, Doubleday, and London, W. H. Allen, 1955.
The Antic Years. New York, Doubleday, 1958.

Novels as Franken Meloney (with W. B. Meloney)

Strange Victory. New York, Farrar and Rinehart, 1939.
When Doctors Disagree. New York, Farrar and Rinehart, 1940.
American Bred. New York, Farrar and Rinehart, 1941.

OTHER PUBLICATIONS

Plays

Another Language (produced New York and London, 1932). New York, French, 1932; London, Rich and Cowan, 1933.
Mr. Dooley, Jr. (for children), with Jane Lewin. New York, French, 1932.
Claudia, adaptation of her own novel (produced New York, 1941; London, 1942). New York, Farrar and Rinehart, 1941.
Outrageous Fortune (produced New York, 1943). New York, French, 1944.
Doctors Disagree, adaptation of her own novel *When Doctors Disagree* (produced New York, 1943).
Soldier's Wife (produced New York, 1944; London, 1946). New York, French, 1945.
The Hallams (produced New York, 1948). New York, French, 1948.

Screenplays: *Alias Mary Dow*, 1935; *Beloved Enemy*, with John Balderston and William Brown Meloney, 1936; *Made for Each Other*, with Jo Swerling, 1939; *Claudia and David*, with William Brown Meloney and Vera Caspary, 1946; *The Secret Heart*, with others, 1946.

Other

When All Is Said and Done (autobiography). London, W. H. Allen, 1962; New York, Doubleday, 1963.
You're Well Out of Hospital. London, W. H. Allen, and New York, Doubleday, 1966.

*   *   *

Once upon a time—not all that long ago—a story of young, innocent love won the hearts of a nation. Within the charmed circle of Claudia's wedding ring, it seemed, were contained all warmth and love, the ideals, hopes, and virtues, of a country in the flower of its youth and promise. Claudia and her David embodied innocence. It was one of Claudia's greatest charms in her husband's eyes, as well as her mother's and (all too obviously) her creator's, that she *was* such an innocent. Married practically out of the schoolroom, to a young man she regarded as being mature and worldly, but who was in fact only 25, the child-bride was launched upon a career of wedded bliss that was to last for nine volumes, in magazine serials, on stage and screen, on radio and television, and in translations all over the world. Plainly the world adored Claudia, through episode after episode. Franken believed that it was a woman's perception of a love story that carried the emotional wallop, and wrote accordingly, on and on and on; apparently the world agreed with her.

Sadly, to return to Claudia's world decades later is to find it a tarnished paradise. The youth of the central characters excuses much, but not all of their smugness, their comfortable wealth that sees itself as straitened circumstances, and their self-consciously "special" carryings-on. It was only to be expected, in Claudia's world, for example, that everyone would adore the young bride, and that domestic servants would gladly set aside their own lives to provide a comfortable background for hers and David's. It is quite impossible now to take seriously this sweetly two-dimensional creation once glowingly described as "one of the classical characters of American literature."

Franken wrote in a style that belonged to the golden era of serialization for magazines with enormous mass circulation—most of them now dead and gone. She wrote prolifically, at great speed, without reading, let alone rewriting, and it shows. Times and tastes have changed. Even her more "hard-hitting" works, daring in their day (*Twice Born* dared to hint at the existence and problems of homosexuality) have long been overtaken and forgotten. Franken was an author who spoke clearly and compellingly to a particular, specific audience; the lonely service wives of World War II, who waited anxiously for their men to return. Their gallantly held ideals of home and fireside, their special war-born reverence for a threatened way of life, lent Franken's work an enormous popularity; but today, *Claudia*, the once so dearly beloved, has faded to a footnote in the history of American popular literature.

—Joan McGrath

FRASER, George MacDonald. British. Born in Carlisle, Cumberland, 2 April 1925. Educated at Carlisle Grammar School, 1932–38; Glasgow Academy, 1938–43. Served in the British Army, 1943–47: Lieutenant. Married Kathleen Margarette Hetherington in 1949; two sons and one daughter. Reporter, Carlisle *Journal*, 1947–49, and Regina *Leader-Post*, Saskatchewan, 1949–50; reporter and sub-editor, Cumberland *News*, Carlisle, 1950–53; deputy editor, Glasgow *Herald*, 1953–69. Recipient: Arts Council award, 1972; Screenwriters Guild award, 1973; *Playboy* award, 1974, 1975; Krug award, 1980. Lives on the Isle of Man. Agent: John Farquharson Ltd., 162–168 Regent Street, London W1R 5TB, England.

ROMANCE AND HISTORICAL PUBLICATIONS

Novels (series: Flashman)

Flashman. London, Jenkins, and New York, World, 1969.

Royal Flash (Flashman). London, Barrie and Jenkins, and New York, Knopf, 1970.
Flash for Freedom! (Flashman). London, Barrie and Jenkins, 1971; New York, Knopf, 1972.
Flashman at the Charge. London, Barrie and Jenkins, and New York, Knopf, 1973.
Flashman in the Great Game. London, Barrie and Jenkins, and New York, Knopf, 1975.
Flashman's Lady. London, Barrie and Jenkins, 1977; New York, Knopf, 1978.
Mr. American. London, Collins, and New York, Simon and Schuster, 1980.
Flashman and the Redskins. London, Collins, and New York, Knopf, 1982.
The Pyrates. London, Collins, 1983; New York, Knopf, 1984.
Flashman and the Dragon. London, Collins, and New York, Knopf, 1986.

Short Stories

The General Danced at Dawn. London, Barrie and Jenkins, 1970; New York, Knopf, 1973.
McAuslan in the Rough. London, Barrie and Jenkins, and New York, Knopf, 1974.
The Sheikh and the Dustbin. London, Collins, 1988.

OTHER PUBLICATIONS

Plays

Screenplays: *The Three Musketeers*, 1973; *The Four Musketeers*, 1974; *Royal Flash*, 1975; *The Prince and the Pauper* (*Crossed Swords*), 1977; *Octopussy*, with Richard Maibaum and Michael G. Wilson, 1983; *Red Sonja*, with Clive Exton, 1984; *Return of the Musketeers*, 1989.

Television Play: *Casanova*, 1987.

Other

The Steel Bonnets: The Story of the Anglo-Scottish Border Reivers. London, Barrie and Jenkins, 1971; New York, Knopf, 1972.
The Hollywood History of the World. London, Joseph, and New York, Morrow, 1988.

*

George MacDonald Fraser comments:

The Flashman novels purport to be the adult memoirs of the school bully of *Tom Brown's School Days*, and describe his adventures in various campaigns and episodes of Victorian history. The three volumes of short stories are based on my experience as a subaltern in a Highland regiment. *The Pyrates* is a historical fantasy, and *Mr. American* is a conventional novel set in England before World War I.

*　　　*　　　*

Like his fellow-novelists Angus Wilson, Andrew Sinclair, and Graham Swift, George MacDonald Fraser is an historian, quite comfortable with writing a book such as *The Steel Bonnets*, his study of Anglo-Scottish border counties, which garnered praise from the distinguished historian, Hugh Trevor-Roper, for being "a splendid book, both scholarly and readable, accurate and alive." His contributions to historical fiction, however, have come in the form of eight novels, equally grounded in history, known collectively as The Flashman Papers, so called because this vast personal memoir is identified as the papers of the late Harry Paget Flashman, discovered "during a sale of household furniture at Ashby, Leicestershire in 1965" and given to Fraser to "edit." The eight volumes which have appeared so far have hewed so closely to actual historical events and persons and have maintained such an authentic tone, that the first volume duped more than one reviewer into treating it as an actual memoir, an eyewitness account of many of the 19th-century's significant historical events, an impression Fraser's publisher hurried to correct.

The volumes easily fall into two grouping. In *Flashman*, *Royal Flash*, *Flash for Freedom!*, and, to a certain extent, *Flashman at the Charge*, Fraser has turned literary history upside-down because he has invaded *Tom Brown's Schooldays*, *The Prisoner of Zenda*, *Uncle Tom's Cabin*, and much *Charge* literature, has appropriated their characters, actions, and occasionally themes, making them totally his own and has presented the "real historical truth" glibly muddled or deliberately obscured by Thomas Hughes, Anthony Hope, and Harriet Beecher Stowe. The novels are more than parodies; they so skillfully replicate and are so adroitly interwoven into the interstices of history that a reader can quickly find himself or herself believing that Flashman was actually a Victorian gentleman, that the Schleswig-Holstein affair, Otto von Bismarck, and Lola Montez are the true life figures behind the characters in *The Prisoner of Zenda*, and that Flashman was actually sold into slavery in the American South. In these novels, Fraser is doing more than guying Victorian novels and debunking Victorian beliefs; he is participating in one of the most obvious activities of postmodernism: that of impeaching an earlier book's authority and creating a counter-book such as William Golding, Brian Aldiss, Jean Rhys, and John Fowles have done in *Lord of the Flies*, *Frankenstein Unbound*, *Wide Sargasso Sea*, and *The French Lieutenant's Woman*.

The volumes since *Flashman at the Charge* have not always had specific targets and, as a result, have somewhat looser, more picaresque structures; they do maintain and at times refine the enormous energy and comic vitality of the earlier books, but do not always enjoy the same narrative drive. Only *Flashman's Lady* may actually be said to disappoint, and it signals a slightly darker turn in the novels which followed it. All in all, the later novels have unrolled a panorama of 19th-century Asian, African, and North American history, presenting Flashman during the Indian Mutiny (1857–58), in James Brooke's Borneo and Queen Ranavalona I's Madagascar (1842–45), the American gold rush and the infamous Battle of Little Bighorn (1849–50, 1875–76), and, most recently, the Taiping Rebellion in China and the burning of the Summer Palace in 1860. Yet to come are promised volumes on Flashman's exploits in the American Union Army, with Emperor Maximilian of Mexico, and in the South African Zulu Wars, incidents mentioned in *Flashman's Who's Who* entry.

The novels surely attract readers because of their clear philosophy of history and their irrepressible anti-hero. Both Fraser and Flashman believe that the romantic school of history which glamorizes and the historical specialist school which documents lack perspective and have forgotten the force of human personality. For Flashman, history is more often made by "some aristocratic harlot waggling her backside," some sailor getting drunk, or some forgetful encounter which ultimately "perhaps shaped the destiny of British India." Fraser's agenda involves revealing the "truth" hidden behind the Victorian masks called honour,

duty, bravery, and patriotism, the values lauded in Thomas Hughes's *Tom Brown's Schooldays*, an author and a book which Flashman attacks throughout the papers. He sees human beings as governed by two main forces: the desire to survive at all costs no matter what values must be compromised or sacrificed—the first principle to Flashman whether facing a pit full of serpents in Afghanistan, a Dahomey cannibal, Sioux warriors, or Chinese torture—and the desire to get what one can, sexually, financially and socially.

Harry Paget Flashman is truly one of the "other" Victorians. Fraser has taken the notorious bully of *Tom Brown's Schooldays* and allowed him to admit to being "a scoundrel, a liar, a cheat, a thief, a coward—and, oh yes, a toady." Flashman is all these and more as he strives to escape whatever danger confronts him, but his sexual energies, his audacious impostures, his unbelievable luck, his disarming frankness, his candid criticism of the heroes of the age, his unvarnished look at the corruption of man's actions, and his sheer vitality transform him into an ultimate anti-hero. Best of all, the reader is constantly in on the joke. As each of the volumes has depicted Flashman in yet more swashbuckling adventures, his complexity has increased and so has the awareness of the effect his father's rejection has had on his life. The father-son tensions culminate in a moving confrontation between Flashman and his own illegitimate Indian son during the Battle of Little Bighorn.

—David Leon Higdon

FRASER, Jane. See **PILCHER, Rosamunde.**

FRASER, (Sir Arthur) Ronald. British. Born 3 November 1888. Educated at St. Paul's School, London. Served in World War I. Married Sylvia Blanche Powell in 1915; two sons. Civil servant: general secretary during Anglo-American negotiations, 1933; Board of Trade representative to the British Ambassador, Buenos Aires, 1933; commercial minister, British Embassy, Paris, 1944–49; resident government director, Suez Canal company. President, Caledonian Society of France, 1946–53. M.B.E. (Member, Order of the British Empire), 1930; C.M.G. (Companion, Order of St. Michael and St. George), 1934; K.B.E. (Knight Commander, Order of the British Empire), 1949; Companion, Order of Orange (Nassau). *Died 12 September 1974.*

ROMANCE AND HISTORICAL PUBLICATIONS

Novels

The Flying Draper. London, Unwin, 1924.
Landscape with Figures. London, Unwin, 1925; New York, Boni and Liveright, 1926.
Flower Phantoms. London, Cape, and, New York, Boni and Liveright, 1926.
The Vista. London, Cape, 1928.
Rose Anstey. London, Cape, 1930.
Marriage in Heaven. London, Cape, 1932; New York, Scribner, 1933.
Tropical Waters. London, Cape, 1933.
The Ninth of July. London, Cape, 1934.

Surprising Results. London, Cape, 1935.
A House in the Park. London, Cape, 1937.
Bird under Glass. London, Cape, 1938.
Miss Lucifer. London, Cape, 1939.
Financial Times. London, Cape, 1942.
The Fiery Gate. London, Cape, 1943.
Circular Tour. London, Cape, 1946.
Maia. London, Cape, 1948.
Sun in Scorpio. London, Cape, 1949.
Beetle's Career. London, Cape, 1951.
Glimpses of the Sun. London, Cape, 1952.
Bell from a Distant Temple. London, Cape, 1954.
Flight of Wild Geese. London, Cape, 1955.
Lord of the East. London, Cape, 1956.
The Wine of Illusion. London, Cape, 1957.
Jupiter in the Chair. London, Cape, 1958.
A Visit from Venus. London, Cape, 1958.
Trout's Testament. London, Cape, 1960.
City of the Sun. London, Cape, 1961.

OTHER PUBLICATIONS

Other

Latin America: A Personal Survey. London, Hutchinson, 1953.
A Work of the Imagination: The Pen, the Brush, the Well.
  Gerrards Cross, Buckinghamshire, Smythe, 1973.

Translator, *Her-Bak, Egyptian Initiate*, by Schwaller de Lubicz.
  London, Hodder and Stoughton, 1967.
Translator, *The Mysteries of Chartres Cathedral*, by Louis Charpentier. London, Research into Lost Knowledge Organisation, 1972.

*   *   *

Taken together, the works of Ronald Fraser constitute a ceaseless epic of humanity's encounters with its own nature. In this expansive venture Fraser positions himself neither as raconteur nor psychologist. He offers a discernible plot line, to be sure, as well as a number of intriguingly drawn personalities. But his narrators prove only incidentally concerned with what has happened, and the text is gratifyingly free of extended analytic perceptions of people and events. Even when circumstance and idiosyncrasy are exceptional, such oddities cannot obscure the principal objective of the author—an enhanced understanding of the inevitable and an accompanying awareness of the still substantial options accessible to those who remain spiritually alert.

The capacity to recognize an essential is, of course, a difficult acquisition. The necessary search and the attendant exercises extend to the reader and the narrator as well as to individual characters—all of whom must find it difficult to isolate the crucial from a heap of glittering trivialities. The very title of Fraser's first book, *The Flying Draper*, dangles a non-issue before the reader. It is soon apparent that flight is probably one of Coddling's lesser achievements, at best another manifestation of his insight into the necessary mastery of one's self. Several times Fraser's narrators tender a kind of uneasy apology for interposing a scene which the common reader might deem improbable. In *Bell from a Distant Temple* an ousted Chinese emperor beset by guilt and misfortune craves forgiveness from a peerless concubine, whom in a futile effort to retain his throne, he had allowed his enemies to strangle. The woman returns, seemingly in the flesh. She sits at tea, graciously assuring her former lover that she had already tendered her pardon. Nothing at all touches

upon unreality in the scene as Fraser wisely declines to argue the basics of plausibility. The reality of the occurrence is not at issue. The scene having made its point, that forgiveness is forever possible, the narrative turns quickly from the easy process of attaining pardon to the difficult task of using what has been acquired. Miracles are neither possible nor improbable. They are irrelevant. How to handle the present is a far greater challenge than interpreting the past or arguing the existence of life after death. The former emperor, having been granted what seemed unlikely, fails miserably in applying what he has gained. Communication with the departed and a generous measure of absolution cannot redeem a self-pitying soul from guilt and preoccupation with loss. He soon meets his end, slain ignobly by assassins.

Fraser deals with commonalities, but in a direct and unusual way. Frequently his theme is marriage, or more precisely, the relationships between the sexes, identifying in the process what it is that makes potentially ideal and caring partners distant from one another. Solutions are never facile, often not even forthcoming. But diagnosis is a necessary step if there is to be any recovery from a deadly lethargy. *Flower Phantoms*, a work as engagingly lovely as its title, finds a young woman shortly before her marriage communicating more freely with plants than with her fiancé. In Fraser's presentation, her preoccupation is far from grotesque, certainly far less so than her husband-to-be's presumably affectionate reference to her as "my golden lily." Such seemingly innocent metaphors reflect a chronic by-pass of any meaningful discourse. It matters not whether one speaks to plants, fish (as Fraser's characters are apt to do), or people, but whether the speaker views the other party as a distinct and comprehensible entity, and desires an interchange. Judy (*Flower Phantoms*) laments to Roland, "no doubt, I am not living to you, but only a character, a figment, an assemblage of images."

Usually Fraser's couples are ostensibly ideally matched in terms of intellect, interest, sensibility, and station in life. Sometimes they are drawn to each other as well by that irrational passion which underlies most liaisons. Fraser is concerned not with defining characteristics but with charting the vectors in the relationships and the uncertain destinations they point toward. Marlene (*Tropical Waters*) retains her irrational passion for Pino, her husband, alongside the apparently matched sensibilities she shares with the man whom everyone calls Hog. Hog soon emerges as that predictable but ever compelling figure who inevitably appears in a Fraser novel, the person forever committed to direct and honest discourse first of all with himself and then with all creation. These characters do not intend to become gurus, although they inevitably end up in this guise. It is expected that they attract others into a form of romantic love, but marriage or similar romantic involvements is not the destination, a recognition shared not only by the parties themselves, but by the mates of the female characters, who generally end up with a similar devotion of their own, followed by a profound sadness when the master-of-living departs from the scene. This masterful figure can range from the wizened eccentric draper to the debonair Geoffrey of *Maia*. The triangles, true to their geometric model, turn out to be strikingly stable structures. Fraser drops any notion of platonic relationships, replacing them with an expanded insight afforded by the participating parties. "I look forward," Geoffrey says, "to watching this scene recorded. We shall see the same object as it is received in . . . different psyches. Henry will reveal the lineaments of a vital entity that is hidden from the rest of us. Maia will discover subtleties of line, contour and arrangements that lie in her own delicate soul." And, had it not been for Geoffrey, a relationship of great potential would have led to something worse than dissolution—to the soul-sapping strangeness of those who for all their desires and capacities had so far failed at communion.

Those looking for answers are not likely to find them. But the serious business of reading Fraser is certain to uncover many a vulgar error in the science and saga of human affairs. While reading is not necessarily a self-help opportunity, the joyful seriousness of the Fraser canon is surely to evoke something of Lydia's sentiment "All I know for certain is that there are more women in me than one" (*The Flying Draper*). The quicker anyone realizes the multiplicity within the self, the sooner is the recognition of the complexity of all creation. It seems strange that Fraser's works are not invoked more often in this necessary search to connect and to comprehend.

—Leonard R. Mendelsohn

FREEMAN, Cynthia. Pseudonym for Bea Feinberg. American. Born in New York City in 1915. Educated at the University of California, Berkeley. Married Herman Feinberg in 1933; one son and one daughter. Worked as an interior designer. *Died 22 October 1988.*

ROMANCE AND HISTORICAL PUBLICATIONS

Novels

A World Full of Strangers. New York, Arbor House, 1975; London, Corgi, 1976.
Fairytales. New York, Arbor House, 1977; London, Bantam, 1978.
The Days of Winter. New York, Arbor House, 1978; London, Corgi, 1979.
Portraits. New York, Arbor House, 1979; Loughton, Essex, Piatkus, 1980.
Come Pour the Wine. New York, Bantam, and Loughton, Essex, Piatkus, 1981.
No Time for Tears. New York, Arbor House, and Loughton, Essex, Piatkus, 1981.
Catch the Gentle Dawn. New York, Arbor House, 1983.
Illusions of Love. New York, Putnam, and London, Collins, 1984.
Seasons of the Heart. New York, Putnam, and London, Collins, 1986.
The Last Princess. New York, Putnam, and London, Collins, 1988.

*   *   *

Romance is always a strong element in Cynthia Freeman's novels, though these fall into the category of the family saga as well as the love story, and their main concerns are with root-seeking and power.

Freeman's books tend to have the flavour of travelogues through place and time with action ranging through diversely colourful settings (from Polish ghetto to Californian expansiveness in *Portraits*), as well as through several generations. The author occasionally over-indulges her vivid feeling for place, though often she skilfully harnesses it to accentuate the moods of her characters and the impact of events.

Several of the novels have backgrounds of displacement and disorientation (*A World Full of Strangers, Fairytales, Portraits*), and immigrant characters who are engaged in seeking social identity and racial roots. Their approach to this is romantic rather than realistic, but nevertheless compelling. It is *Portraits*,

her four-generational chronicle of a Jewish immigrant family, that most clearly illustrates Freeman's storytelling skill, through its intense and well-realized relationships, and her characters' convincing struggles to cling to their spiritual heritage in an alien environment.

Perversely, this passionate identification with a specific racial group that gives *Portraits* its vitality produces a serious flaw in her more conventional love story, *Come Pour the Wine*. Allan, a middle-aged Jewish hero, is rather artificially introduced during the book's later stages in order to give heroine Janet the deep and sensitive love that her gentile husband, Bill, lacks the maturity to provide. Bill's inadequacies are carefully rehearsed but—though this is almost certainly not the author's intention—despite his shortcomings he still emerges as a more appealing character than Allan. Janet, however, eventually settles for the duller but more determined of the two men. (Her pairing off with Allan is a literary let-down similar to that produced by Louisa Alcott in *Little Women*, when she made Jo reject lively handsome Laurie for the protective but prosaic Professor Bhaer.)

Apart from this weakness of plot, *Come Pour the Wine* represents the romantic story at its most persuasive. The action unfolds believably from the viewpoint of the intelligent heroine; the "will-he, won't he" themes, although repetitive and lengthy, are enlivened by Freeman's capacity to get beneath the skin of her characters, and to enlist her readers' sympathy for their inadequacies and approbation of their strengths.

—Mary Cadogan

FRENCH, Ashley. See ROBINS, Denise.

GAINES, Ernest J(ames). American. Born in Oscar, Louisiana, 15 January 1933. Educated at Vallejo Junior College; San Francisco State College, 1955–57, B.A. 1957; Stanford University, California (Stegner fellow, 1958), 1958–59. Served in the United States Army, 1953–55. Writer-in-residence, Denison University, Granville, Ohio, 1971, Stanford University, Spring 1981, and Whittier College, California, 1982. Since 1983 Professor of English and writer-in-residence, University of Southwestern Louisiana, Lafayette. Recipient: San Francisco Foundation Joseph Henry Jackson award, 1959; National Endowment for the Arts grant, 1966; Rockefeller grant, 1970; Guggenheim grant, 1970; Black Academy of Arts and Letters award, 1972; San Francisco Art Commission award, 1983. D.Litt.: Denison University, 1980; Brown University, Providence, Rhode Island, 1985; Bard College, Annandale-on-Hudson, New York, 1985; D.H.L.: Whittier College, 1986. Agent: Dorothea Oppenheimer, 435 East 79th Street, Apartment 4-M, New York, New York 10021. Address: 932 Division Street, San Francisco, California 94115, U.S.A.

ROMANCE AND HISTORICAL PUBLICATIONS

Novel

The Autobiography of Miss Jane Pittman. New York, Dial Press, 1971; London, Joseph, 1973.

OTHER PUBLICATIONS

Novels

Catherine Carmier. New York, Atheneum, 1964; London, Secker and Warburg, 1966.
Of Love and Dust. New York, Dial Press, 1967; London, Secker and Warburg, 1968.
In My Father's House. New York, Knopf, and London, Prior, 1978.
A Gathering of Old Men. New York, Knopf, 1983; London, Heinemann, 1984.

Short Stories

Bloodline. New York, Dial Press, 1968.

Other

A Long Day in November (for children). New York, Dial Press, 1971.

*

Manuscript Collection: Dupree Library, University of Southwestern Louisiana, Lafayette.

*   *   *

Some of the prominence of *The Autobiography of Miss Jane Pittman* among Ernest J. Gaines's fiction is traceable to its adaptation for television film, where Cecily Tyson's depiction of Miss Jane Pittman incorporated all the nuances of character and voice that Gaines had indicated in the novel. *The Autobiography* is the only Gaines novel that meets the general definition of historical fiction, that is, set in an identifiable period of the past. Two earlier novels and a short fiction collection, however, seem dress rehearsals for *The Autobiography*, for an unmistakably strong consciousness of the southern past, of its hold on the present, marks Gaines's work. The historical novel therefore seems a logical outcome of his preoccupation with the past as theme.

The settings of Gaines's novels have been restricted to Louisiana, as William Faulkner's were to Mississippi, to its bayous, rivers, living quarters, plantations, and parishes. Gaines writes about an environment that was once home to him, one that he seems either unable or unwilling to separate himself from, although he left Louisiana when he was 15 years old.

The Autobiography may be called a folk autobiography, preceded in structure and content by its literary forerunner, the slave narrative. Although the text begins with the invasion of the Union army and the subsequent freeing of the slaves, general characteristics between the novel and slave narratives are apparent. Jane, for example, takes on a new name, symbolic of casting off the slave identity. She begins travelling to the north, a feature of slave narratives; and the novel, narrated in the first person, constitutes the story of her life. Whereas the slave narrative emphasizes the experiences of the enslaved against the system as institution, the narrative of Jane Pittman emphasizes her growth and durability against the backdrop of southern history in rural Louisiana. She lives in rapport with time and change, flowing with their movement instead of struggling against their currents. Thus she remains psychically whole.

Jane Pittman is fashioned in high relief against the general history of her years. At age 110 she tells the events of her life to a young history teacher who records them because her life history can help him explain things to his students. The chronological narrative follows the cycle of her life from a child approximately seven years old to a young woman who marries, is widowed, matures, and faces old age. Jane's experiences encompass many other lives and stories and these, additionally, become inseparable parts of her narrative. They include the experiences of Ned, the young boy to whom Jane becomes surrogate mother; Joe Pittman, the only man whom Jane marries; and the stories of others on the Samson plantation, where she lives for such long periods of her life. These include Tee Bob and Timmy as well as Tee Bob and Agnes, where the racial mixtures specific to New Orleans and attitudes concerning them create conflict and death.

The history teacher and recorder of Jane's memories imposes the chronological order on her narrative by dividing the memories into four books—the war years, Reconstruction, the plantation, and the quarters. The 110 years of Jane's life span the most repressive years for southern black people. Historical time advances subtly in the narrative, moving just beneath the surface, shaping and influencing Jane's experiences which include the early work of black politicians, the birth of the night-riding groups, the absolutism of southern white rule, and the desperate migration of black people to the north.

The creation of Jane's voice is a major accomplishment in this text. It evokes the timbre and cadence of the spoken word in the mouths of the elderly black characters. The texture of the spoken voice, which communicates the strength of Jane's character, sustains the entire narrative. Miss Jane's direct and forceful language reflects the speech patterns and nuances of the black southern spoken word. Gaines reflects both southern and African cultural traditions through the incorporation of Jane's voice and speech, and through the emphasis on oral tradition.

The narrative concludes with the onset of the Civil Rights movement of the 1960's signalled by the sit-ins and demonstrations. Jane Pittman, whose life has been marked by so many journeys, both literal and metaphorical, concludes the narrative embarking on still another journey. Recognizing her chance to replace fear and uncertainty with leadership, confirming her rapport with time and change, she begins the march into Bayonne to defy and protest the separatist policies of segregation. The population of the plantation follows.

The appropriateness of the ending is confirmed by the original conception and form of the novel—the odyssey of African-Americans through United States history, symbolized in the experience of one woman, Jane Pittman.

—Joyce Pettis

GALLAGHER, Patricia (née Bienek). American. Born in Lockhart, Texas. Educated at Trinity University, San Antonio, Texas, 1951. Married James D. Gallagher (died 1966); one son. Staff member, KTSA Radio, San Antonio, 1950–51. Agent: Scott Meredith Literary Agency, 845 Third Avenue, New York, New York, 10022, U.S.A. Address: c/o Berkley, 200 Madison Avenue, New York, New York 10016, U.S.A.

ROMANCE AND HISTORICAL PUBLICATIONS

Novels

The Sons and the Daughters. New York, Messner, and London, Muller, 1961.

Answer to Heaven. London, Muller, 1962; New York, Avon, 1964.

The Fires of Brimstone. New York, Avon, 1966.

Shannon. New York, Avon, 1967.

Shadows of Passion. New York, Avon, 1971.

Summer of Sighs. New York, Avon, 1971.

The Thicket. New York, Avon, 1973.

Castles in the Air. New York, Avon, 1976; London, Corgi, 1984.

Mystic Rose. New York, Avon, 1977; London, Hamlyn, 1978.

No Greater Love. New York, Avon, 1979; London, Corgi, 1984.

All for Love. New York, Avon, 1981.

Echoes and Embers. New York, Avon, 1983; London, Corgi, 1986.

Love Springs Eternal. New York, Berkley, 1985.

On Wings of Dreams. New York, Berkley, 1985.

A Perfect Love. New York, Berkley, 1987.

*   *   *

Patricia Gallagher is a romance novelist who employs the conventions of the genre for unusual goals. This generalization is appropriate to any of her novels (compared to many of her contemporaries she has not written a great deal); it is particularly apt of *Castles in the Air*, her most famous, most popular, work.

Suspend expectation. Devon Marshall, the heroine, does not pursue the hero; he pursues her—and "gets her" within the first 20 pages, in less than exalted circumstances. Devon is a penniless refugee from post-Civil War Virginia, trying to make her way north; she has worked for her father, a newspaper proprietor, before his death; she hopes to get work as a journalist in New York City. Keith, a wealthy Wall Street banker, allows her to stow away in his private railway car, then demands recompense: he rapes her. Gallagher doesn't mince her scenes. That this one seems credible is a compliment to her powers in conveying the desperation of the times; that she causes both Devon and the reader to subsequently care for, then admire, Keith is a credit to the breadth of her sympathies, her cunning in conveying his own desperation, and her view of the contrariness of human life. Keith loves at first sight, but he is trapped in a hopeless and in some ways despicable marriage by society, his position, and his own conscience. After her initial resistance, Devon and Keith become lovers—passionate, selfless, honorable adulterers; they produce a son, live in the second home that Keith provides for them, then, in the end, after five years, part when it becomes apparent that Keith's now half-crazed wife will never release him or conveniently die. They part at Devon's instigation: she agrees to marry a man she does not love, gives up the man and child she does love, and prepares to go live with her new husband half a continent away. A story that begins with a violent passion, then deals with its refinement, ends with its defeat. And lest the reader console himself that Devon may "find happiness" after the last page—that expectation is firmly squelched, as the novel ends, in Devon's dreams, fevered, horrible dreams of the world to which she has exiled herself.

The novel provokes respect. Not only for this vision of the destruction of happy and fulfilling love by society but also for its undoubted expertise as a novel—in its construction, in its handling of time, and in its characterizations. Gallagher's talent is immediately obvious: the first chapter introduces the main characters, vividly renders Devon's situation in post-war Richmond, establishes the themes that will be developed throughout the book—and does so not in laborious exposition but in a very few seemingly random conversations. Her setting of scene is also admirable: New York City, though its elegance is finely conveyed, is for much of the novel not a world of romance but of seedy rooming houses, dirt, and human greed, poverty and squalor. Most impressive, the love story is not the only story or perhaps even the main one. For "castles in the air" are the dreams of women; and if love, children and family are some of those dreams, so too, and just as important, is the dream of achieving self-hood, of being an entity—as a man may be. Devon's goal is a simple-sounding one: she wishes to be a good journalist; and the main plot of *Castles in the Air* is really of the struggle and hardships such a goal involves—if one is a woman. This quest also ends in defeat.

Devon asks herself early on, trying to make her own way without Keith, whether it is possible for any woman to survive on her own terms "without dissembling and mendacity and guile." Thwarted in her main ambition, she takes a series of servile jobs in order to stay alive, does all of them well, then discovers that she's been given chances because she's physically desirable. Finally, she succumbs to Keith, to the kind of help and comfort his money can provide, and also becomes a protégée of one of Boss Tweed's men, whose influence gains her access to a newspaper. She's successful: she becomes a society reporter (appropriate journalistic work for a woman), excels at her work, eventually becomes known to the best New York society, and earns the right to move from coverage of that society to that of the presidential party in Washington. Still, in any real sense, she never wins. Keith, loving in all other ways, never conceives her work or her aspirations to another kind of reportage as anything other than exercise for exasperatingly attractive high spirits. Her benefactor waits for her to weary. The world—even other women engaged in the same kind of work—fail to take her or (it is implied) each other very seriously.

Early in the story Devon befriends Mally, a poor Irish girl at the rooming house where they both live in less than genteel poverty. Considering Devon's ambitions, Mally says to her: "But you can't marry a dream. . . . And what else is there for a girl? Marriage and children. That's all there is for us." Devon asks: "But why, Mally? *Why* must it be all there is for us." Mally replies: "Because we're female." Devon sets out to prove Mandy wrong—but in fact proves something else. What separates Mandy from her is not the difference in their ambitions or even in their capacity for vision; the difference is in how well each can survive in a marketplace in which the currency is physical attractiveness. Devon is beautiful; Mally is not; Devon is loved by a rich man and desired by a politically powerful one, they provide her with her opportunities; Mally, conversely, is plain, she has nothing to barter: she never moves from poverty and hopelessness, she falls for the wrong man, her life ends tragically. Mally is not "regarded;" but then neither is Devon, except as an object of love and passion who, in return for inspiring lust, is allowed to "play." The world to which Devon finally gains entrance is described as beautiful because it *is* beautiful—but not for a woman. For if she aspires to being something more than one of the beautiful things, she will be defeated—in the definition of self, in any kind of moral or intellectual fulfillment.

Gallagher is too good a writer to labor any of these points (indeed, within so obviously feminist a novel, she is scrupulously fair to men: some are rats, some are decent). She presents situation, leaves moral reflection to her readers. And this interest in something beyond a conventional romantic plot, this use of romantic devices to convey her own themes, is common to many of her novels. Yet one puts down any of them with a mild but gnawing dissatisfaction. The problem is language.

Castles in the Air—any of the novels—provides rich examples. The very names of her main characters are risible. And they stare into a "dense opacity." They feel like mice "on a treadmill to oblivion." In conveying information, women sound like a teacher who has presented the same lecture too many times. In being masculine, men reach for the diction and cadences of the King James Bible. If her plots are the antithesis of cliché, her language falls into all the traps.

And yet. The criticism, once made, seems wrong. For every three scenes of bad dialogue, there is one good one. Some of her descriptions are downright embarrassing; some are masterful. She allows some of her "physical" scenes to become mawkish—but, in any of her books, there is sex which is stylishly described, pleasantly torrid. Often—too often—she conveys the emotional relations between people in ways that are, frankly, corny; other times, she invokes feeling with such exactness as to be genuinely affecting and profound. It is as if she is not so much unskillful as lazy with language—or, perhaps, that she devotes such time and effort to "getting it right" in plot, setting, scene, that she has little energy left for words themselves. The result is hit or miss. If she can now refine language as she has perfected the other aspects of her craft, Gallagher can almost certainly set a standard against which other romance novelists will be measured.

—George Walsh

GANN, Ernest K(ellogg). American. Born in Lincoln, Nebraska, 13 October 1910. Educated at Culver Military Academy; Yale University, New Haven, Connecticut, 1930–32. Served in the United States Air Force Air Transport Command, 1942–46: Captain. Married 1) Eleanor Michaud in 1933 (divorced), two sons (one deceased) and one daughter; 2) Dodie Post in 1966. Agent: Scott Meredith Literary Agency, 845 Third Avenue, New York, New York 10022, U.S.A.

ROMANCE AND HISTORICAL PUBLICATIONS

Novels

The Antagonists. New York, Simon and Schuster, 1970; London, Hodder and Stoughton, 1971.
The Triumph. New York, Simon and Schuster, and London, Hodder and Stoughton, 1986.

OTHER PUBLICATIONS

Novels

Island in the Sky. New York, Viking Press, 1944; London, Joseph, 1945.
Blaze at Noon. New York, Holt, 1946; London, Aldor, 1947.
Benjamin Lawless. New York, Sloane, 1948.
Fiddler's Green. New York, Sloane, 1950; London, Hodder and Stoughton, 1954.
Twilight for the Gods. New York, Sloane, 1950; London, Hodder and Stoughton, 1956.
The High and the Mighty. New York, Sloane, and London, Hodder and Stoughton, 1953.
Soldier of Fortune. New York, Sloane, 1954; London, Hodder and Stoughton, 1955.
Trouble with Lazy Ethel. New York, Sloane, 1958; London, Hodder and Stoughton, 1959.
Of Good and Evil. New York, Simon and Schuster, and London, Hodder and Stoughton, 1963.

In the Company of Eagles. New York, Simon and Schuster, 1966; London, Hodder and Stoughton, 1967.
The Song of the Siren. New York, Simon and Schuster, 1968; London, Hodder and Stoughton, 1969.
Band of Brothers. New York, Simon and Schuster, 1973; London, Hodder and Stoughton, 1974.
Brain 2000. New York, Doubleday, and London, Hodder and Stoughton, 1980.
The Aviator. New York, Arbor House, and London, Hodder and Stoughton, 1981.
The Magistrate. New York, Arbor House, 1982; London, Hodder and Stoughton, 1983.
Gentlemen of Adventure. New York, Arbor House, 1983; London, Hodder and Stoughton, 1984.
The Bad Angel. New York, Arbor House, 1987; London, Hodder and Stoughton, 1988.

Plays

Screenplays: *The Raging Tide*, 1951; *Island in the Sky*, 1953; *The High and the Mighty*, 1954; *Soldier of Fortune*, 1955; *Twilight for the Gods*, 1958.

Other

Sky Roads. New York, Crowell, 1940.
All American Aircraft. New York, Crowell, 1941.
Getting Them into the Blue. New York, Crowell, 1942.
Fate Is the Hunter (memoirs). New York, Simon and Schuster, and London, Hodder and Stoughton, 1961.
Flying Circus. New York, Macmillan, 1974; London, Hodder and Stoughton, 1976.
A Hostage to Fortune (autobiography). New York, Knopf, 1978; London, Hodder and Stoughton, 1979.
The Black Watch: America's Spy Pilots and Their Planes. New York, Random House, 1989.

*   *   *

To think of Ernest K. Gann is to conjure up the John Waynes and Clark Gables of Hollywood flying high and mighty in the clouds, for Gann's novels, nearly all bestsellers, have been primarily about airplanes and pilots and have succeeded on screen as well as in bookstores. Until 1970 his historical fiction took place in the 20th century. As a pilot himself, it is little wonder that his first book *Island in the Sky*, and many subsequent ones dealt with flying. How then can we explain *The Antagonists* after some 12 books and many years later? In his autobiography, *A Hostage to Fortune* Gann explains how this came about. While taking a vacation from writing he came across Israel's Yigael Yadin's archeological report on Masada, the mountain fortress in the Judean desert where the last battle between the Romans and Jews was waged in the first century A.D. He became fascinated by the lore of the Judean desert and the siege that took place there 1900 years before. With research a joyous prelude to writing, Gann threw himself into the exploration of the siege that precious little had been written about in this century before Yadin. His Jewish friends had heard about Masada, but knew very little about it. Though Gann had studied the "hearsay" account of Josephus, the Jewish general turned Roman who was a contemporary of the antagonists General Flavius Silva and Eleazar ben Yair, he based his fictional tale more closely on the Yadin archeological findings. Josephus was not present at Masada—but the ruins of Herod's once impregnable stronghold still are.

The Antagonists is a marvelous novel. The situation itself is very dramatic—a three-year siege by Silva's famed Roman 10th legion attempting to capture the Jewish stronghold and the 960 zealots led by Eleazar; the ancient machines of war—catapults and attack towers moving up the giant ramp built with slave labor, all described as if Gann could actually see it. We can't truly know what Silva and Eleazar were like, but it is easy enough to accept Gann's portrayal of the two men as they hurl sardonic insults at each other from far above and far below. The natural acoustics of the place make this believable. The final scene is both exhilarating and tragic—as the Romans scale the mountain fortress only to discover the mass suicide of the zealots who preferred death to captivity.

Though Gann believed in 1970 that Silva had disappeared from history after Masada (according to his preface to *The Antagonists*) he obviously continued his research, fascinated perhaps by both the historical Silva and the Silva of his own creation, for that same patrician general appears 16 years later as the main character in his second historical novel, *The Triumph*. This is indeed a sequel to *The Antagonists* as it begins just where the Masada tale left off—with Silva weary and sick at heart at his hollow victory. But time heals, and so does the love of a woman, Domitillia, daughter of the aging Emperor Vespasian and childhood friend to Silva. *The Triumph* is very different from its predecessor save that the same detail of archeological research is evident, but spread over a much wider area, primarily the city of Rome. This is a story of love, intrigue, and adventure from 74 to 79 A.D., when Vespasian's sons, Titus and Domitian, vied to succeed him. Gann has chosen Titus as his favorite (as did the historical Silva who reappeared in history for a few years more) while treating Domitian much less kindly than many historians have done. Gann does not pretend to recreate the facts accurately in this novel, but he vividly pictures the street scenes of teeming slums and magnificent palaces, glimpses of the Christians praying to their unseen God, the building of the Colosseum and the horror of the bloodletting that went on in it and in other arenas. Most colorful of all is the description of the "triumph," the magnificent parade planned to honor the aging Emperor which instead became his funeral procession. But it was glorious: 200 pipers led the way, followed by trumpeters, mourning women (who were forbidden by law to tear out their hair), flute players, actors, mimes, and buffoons, machines of war, gladiators, beasts in cages, and the surviving family, wending their way through the narrow streets to the forum to set fire to the funeral pyre. A fitting end to Vespasian and to Gann's second historical novel.

—Marion Hanscom

GARNETT, David. Also wrote as Leda Burke. British. Born in Brighton, Sussex, 9 March 1892; son of the writer Edward Garnett and the translator Constance Garnett. Educated at University College School, London, 1906–08; Imperial College of Science and Technology, London, 1910–15, A.R.C.S. 1913, D.I.C. 1915. Conscientious objector in World War I; served in the Royal Air Force Volunteer Reserve, 1939–40: Flight Lieutenant; planning officer and historian, Political Warfare Executive, 1941–46. Married 1) Rachel Alice Marshall in 1921 (died 1940), two sons; 2) Angelica Bell in 1942, four daughters. Partner, Birrell and Garnett, booksellers, London, 1920–24; partner, Nonesuch Press, London, 1923–35; literary editor, *New Statesman and Nation*, London, 1932–34; director, Rupert Hart-Davis Ltd., publishers, London, 1946–52. Recipient: Hawthornden prize, 1923; James Tait Black Memorial prize, 1923. Fellow, Imperial College of Science and Technology, 1956; fellow, and

Companion of Literature, 1977, Royal Society of Literature. D.Litt.: University of Birmingham, 1977. C.B.E. (Commander, Order of the British Empire), 1952. *Died 17 February 1981.*

ROMANCE AND HISTORICAL PUBLICATIONS

Novels

Lady into Fox. London, Chatto and Windus, 1922; New York, Knopf, 1923.
A Man in the Zoo. London, Chatto and Windus, and New York, Knopf, 1924.
The Sailor's Return. London, Chatto and Windus, and New York, Knopf, 1925.
Pocahontas; or, The Nonparell of Virginia. London, Chatto and Windus, and New York, Harcourt Brace, 1933.
Two by Two: A Story of Survival. London, Longman, 1963; New York, Atheneum, 1964.
The Sons of the Falcon. London, Macmillan, 1972.
Up She Rises. London, Macmillan, 1977; New York, St. Martin's Press, 1978.

OTHER PUBLICATIONS

Novels

Dope-Darling (as Leda Burke). London, Laurie, 1919.
Go She Must! London, Chatto and Windus, and New York, Knopf, 1927.
No Love. London, Chatto and Windus, and New York, Knopf, 1929.
The Grasshoppers Come. London, Chatto and Windus, and New York, Brewer Warren and Putnam, 1931.
Beany-Eye. London, Chatto and Windus, and New York, Harcourt Brace, 1935.
Aspects of Love. London, Chatto and Windus, 1955; New York, Harcourt Brace, 1956.
A Shot in the Dark. London, Longman, 1958; Boston, Little Brown, 1959.
A Net for Venus. London, Longman, 1959.
Ulterior Motives. London, Longman, 1966; New York, Harcourt Brace, 1967.
A Clean Slate. London, Hamish Hamilton, 1971.
Plough over the Bones. London, Macmillan, 1973.

Short Stories

The Old Dovecote and Other Stories. London, Mathews and Marrot, 1928.
A Terrible Day. London, Joiner and Steele, 1932.
An Old Master and Other Stories. Tokyo, Yamaguchi Shoten, 1967.
Purl and Plain and Other Stories. London, Macmillan, 1973.

Other

Never Be a Bookseller. London, Chatto and Windus, and New York, Knopf, 1929.
A Rabbit in the Air: Notes from a Diary Kept While Learning to Handle an Aeroplane. London, Chatto and Windus, and New York, Brewer Warren and Putnam, 1932.
War in the Air September 1939–May 1941. London, Chatto and Windus, and New York, Doubleday, 1941.

The Campaign in Greece and Crete. London, His Majesty's Stationery Office, 1942.

The Golden Echo (autobiography):
  The Golden Echo. London, Chatto and Windus, 1953; New York, Harcourt Brace, 1954.
  The Flowers of the Forest. London, Chatto and Windus, 1955; New York, Harcourt Brace, 1956.
  The Familiar Faces. London, Chatto and Windus, 1962; New York, Harcourt Brace, 1963.

The White-Garnett Letters (correspondence with T. H. White), edited by Garnett. London, Cape, and New York, Viking Press, 1968.

First "Hippy" Revolution. Cerrillos, New Mexico, San Marcos Press, 1970.

The Master Cat: The True and Unexpurgated Story of Puss in Boots (for children). London, Macmillan, 1974.

Sir Geoffrey Keynes: A Tribute. Privately printed, 1978.

Great Friends: Portraits of Seventeen Writers. London, Macmillan, 1979; New York, Atheneum, 1980.

Editor, with others, *The Week-End Book*. London, Nonesuch Press, and New York, Dial Press, 1924.

Editor, *The Letters of T. E. Lawrence*. London, Cape, 1938; New York, Doubleday, 1939.

Editor, *The Battle of Britain*, by H. A. St. George Saunders. London, Air Ministry, 1941.

Editor, *Fourteen Stories*, by Henry James. London, Hart Davis, 1946.

Editor, *The Novels of Thomas Love Peacock*. London, Hart Davis, 1948.

Editor, *The Essential T. E. Lawrence*. London, Cape, and New York, Dutton, 1951.

Editor, *The Selected Letters of T. E. Lawrence*. London, Cape, 1952; Westport, Connecticut, Hyperion Press, 1979.

Editor, *Carrington: Letters and Extracts from Her Diaries*. London, Cape, 1970; New York, Holt Rinehart, 1971.

Translator, *The Kitchen Garden and Its Management*, by V. A. Gressent. London, Selwyn and Blount, 1919.

Translator, *A Voyage to the Island of the Articoles*, by André Maurois. London, Cape, 1928; New York, Appleton, 1929.

Translator, *338171 T. E. (Lawrence of Arabia)*, by Victoria Ocampo. London, Gollancz, and New York, Dutton, 1963.

*

Manuscript Collection: University of Texas, Austin.

*   *   *

One does not at first think of David Garnett as a historical novelist; but, in fact, from the first, there was a strong historical vein in his work, a tendency to look backwards rather than forwards. Two of his first three novels—*Lady into Fox* and *The Sailor's Return*—are set in the 19th century, and, in *Lady into Fox*, the stylistic influence of Defoe is readily apparent. However, not until *Pocahontas* did he essay a work unequivocally historical. For this work, he and Frances Partridge (to whom the book is dedicated under her maiden name, Frances Marshall) did a good deal of research. But, from the first, Garnett recognized the dangers that beset the historical novelist. As he put it succinctly in his preface: "Facts begin by inspiring the imagination: they end by imprisoning it in a strait-waistcoat, and the following work was written in their fetters."

Pocahontas (1595–1617)—whose story is as much part of American mythology as history—was the daughter of Powhatan, an Indian chief of Virginia, whose destiny it was to marry John Rolfe, and to die in England. Her title of "la belle sauvage" became the name of a London pub on Ludgate Hill, where legend has it she once stayed, and the name was subsequently adopted as the logo of Cassell Publishing when they took over the premises. Garnett appropriately sets her up in this establishment, upon her arrival in London. Of the "real" Pocahontas there remains only a contemporary engraving by Simon van de Passe, the basis for the later oil-painting reproduced as the frontispiece in Garnett's novel. There is also a set of earrings in the Rolfe family which are said to have belonged to Pocahontas; in the novel they are presented by the Earl of Northumberland, imprisoned in the Tower, in the presence of Sir Walter Raleigh.

In Garnett's story, Pocahontas appears at first as little more than a youthful and apparently unaffected observer of Indian society. But from the moment when the 11-year-old Pocahontas flings herself across the body of John Smith to save him from imprisonment or worse, she becomes the central figure. Some have suggested that this incident was itself a figment of John Smith's imagination, inserted in his account simply as a way of drawing attention to himself. It seems unlikely that he understood enough Algonquian to follow the events he observed—which may, in fact, have been intended as a ritual of adoption. Whatever its historical status, Garnett represents the dramatic moment as an impulsive gesture which soon turns to love (not without sexual overtones); the ritual of adoption is portrayed as an entirely separate, and subsequent, ceremony. And it is hard not to interpret the intervention of Pocahontas as the first fateful step towards repudiation of her own culture and adoption of what she took to be a superior way of life.

Throughout the book, Garnett tries to play the "objective" historian, and resolutely withholds condemnation even of the most brutal acts. The early scene in which women of Pocahontas's tribe torture a Monacan warrior by stripping the flesh from him and cutting off his fingers, toes, and ears, is horrifying, the more so since there seems no evidence that it occurred. But it is balanced by the comparable cruelty of the colonists to their own. When Sir Thomas Dale arrived in Jamestown, for example, in the spring of 1611, he is shown enforcing discipline upon the unruly settlers in direct military fashion: "there were continual floggings and many bloody executions . . . he hanged some, broke others on the wheel, and tied three men to trees . . . and set an armed guard over them until they had starved to death." Moreover, for Pocahontas, the ritual associated with the hanging of Francis Lymbry, a Spanish spy, on the journey to England and civilization, is an abomination "more horrible than an Indian torture." Particularly ironic is the way in which John Rolfe, her husband, "rushed down to fetch his Bible from the cabin, thus adding the decorum of religion to the scene." This is about as close as Garnett ever comes to explicit criticism. Is the point of it all that, in fact, Indian and settler are the same—capable of the same disturbing vacillations between compassion and violence, between love and hate? The similarity of the two races, red and white, is certainly emphasized in the narrator's comment after Chief Japazaws and Captain Argall finish explaining their respective beliefs:

They had revealed to each other that they were essentially alike; they had come to understand one another, respect one another, and respect themselves anew. . . . To both of them God was the great anodyne, the conscience-comforting balm which enabled them to forget their ugliness and to commit the vilest treacheries, and the pettiest bits of cheating, with the knowledge that they were superior to all happy, gay, trustful and beautiful creatures on the earth.

In this passage we can isolate one of those rare moments in which the omniscient narrator speaks as the detached observer of humankind; yet it is through such statements that the book transcends the limits of historical romance to which some contemporary reviewers—focusing on the incomprehensible love of Pocahontas for the roguish John Smith and for the sober John Rolfe—were ready to consign it.

For Pocahontas, the country of her dreams inevitably proves to be illusory—the journey is a nightmare of sickness and squalor, London is dirty and noisy, and the Court of James I does not stand comparison with the regal simplicity of Powhatan's. Ben Jonson appears as a drunkard who shouts at her husband; and even her beloved "Bear," John Smith, is a shadow of the man who won her heart with his smile. Though she longs for the simple virtues of the Virginian forest, she cannot go back, and dies of consumption at Gravesend. In her dying dream, Jesus and the tortured Indian rise from her childhood memories to become one with her own pain until she passes "limply into death."

In this novel, Garnett reveals his continuing interest in the theme of metamorphosis—Pocahontas, la belle sauvage, is tamed and transformed by her contact with and love for white society. But, the author implies, she is betrayed by that society; and, out of her natural environment, she is bound to die. Here, then, we have the mirror image of the story in *Lady into Fox* in which a civilized woman is transformed into a creature of the wild, only to die at the hands of the civilization from which she retreated—represented by the huntsmen whose dogs tear her to pieces. *Pocahontas* can also be seen as a variant of the story of *The Sailor's Return* in which a princess, H.R.H. Princess Gundemey of Dahomey, is brought to an alien land and culture in 1858 by her English husband, a retired sea-captain, William Targett, who has become the new proprietor of The Sailor's Return pub (a real pub, incidentally, in East Chaldon, Dorset). The villagers resent the couple, and she is treated cruelly by these supposedly civilized and Christian natives. When her husband is killed in a fight with a prize-fighter, Tulip, as she has come to be known, is reduced to the status of a drudge or slave in her own former home. The message is clear enough—Dorset, and by implication, English, society is far more savage, not to mention hypocritical, than the primitive and heathen land she left so willingly and with such faith.

Garnett did not really return to historical fiction until his old age. Only brief mention need be made of *Two by Two*, which Garnett himself called "a frivolous gloss upon the most charming story in the Bible"—the story of Noah and the Flood. More substantial is *The Sons of the Falcon*, which is set in the mountains of Transcaucasia in the 1860's, and which attempts to recreate a strange and distant world of feud, violence, and superstition, home to fierce mountain tribes and nomadic horsemen who milk their mares. The novel recounts the struggle of Prince Valeri to free himself from his tribal past and to seek a rational future within the orbit of encroaching Russian culture. It is a well-written and highly readable narrative; but its world is somehow too remote to engage more than our passing attention.

More than forty years separate *Up She Rises*, Garnett's last novel, from *Pocahontas*, his first full-scale excursion into historical fiction. Yet the years seem to have left undiminished the sheer energy with which he is able to tell a tale. The book is jam-packed with incident, and is all the more intriguing for its association with the Garnett family itself. Indeed, it is, among other things, a fictionalized history of some of Garnett's Scottish forebears—hardy crofters and fisherfolk on the east coast of Scotland. It is dedicated to Garnett's redoubtable mother, Constance, the translator of Russian, and the heroine is his great-grandmother, on his mother's side, here identified as Clementina

Lamond (née Carey). At first, it seems unlikely that the novel will ever take us out of Scotland; but before she dies, Clementina and her mariner husband, Peter, have lived in France, Germany, and Russia, as well as in London. However, her longest journey (symbolically as well as literally), and her first real venture abroad, takes her on foot from her own humble home in Forfarshire to Portsmouth to catch a glimpse of her husband, pressed into service years before and now returning as a wounded hero, "who had fought beside Lord Nelson on the *Victory*" at the battle of Trafalgar. Her adventures on the road lend a picaresque quality to this portion of the novel; within a few pages, for example, she accidentally burns a hay-barn, is treated with kindness by a shepherd woman, threatened by an itinerant gypsy (until she reveals her knowledge of Romany), befriended by a stray greyhound, attacked by soldiers, and entertained by gypsy friends of her father. It is only a tenacity borne of love that allows her to overcome all adversity on this arduous journey; and once again the hypocrisy of society is revealed. One old friend, now married, refuses to give Clementina shelter for a night on the orders of her husband, "a good man . . . who will have no hand in wrong-doing." His objections are to the fact that her father, David Carey, has been transported to Australia for smuggling, and that she has consorted with gypsies and can speak their language. Mistress Reekie, a neighbour who takes Clementina in, articulates the irony of this position in her caustic remark: "I'm not such a good Christian that I have to turn a tired woman from my door." However, Clementina is also rebuffed by a Church of England Canon outside Oxford who exclaims indignantly: "it is a piece of gross impertinence for you, a Calvinist, to expect assistance, when you do not belong to the Established Church."

The title of the novel is from an old sea-shanty, and draws attention to the dramatic rise in Clementina's fortune—from illiterate crofter's daughter to the wife of the naval architect to the Tsar of Russia. Indeed, so great is the transformation that one former acquaintance fails to recognize her at all, and another knows her only from her voice. Yet the stout Scottish matron with the pock-marked visage (evidence of her triumph over smallpox) still harbours a secret yearning for the simple life of her youth. And her encounter with Sarah, a childhood gypsy friend, whose beauty has *not* been lost, makes clear the price she has paid for advancement. Her mind is drawn back to the world she has lost, and she conjures up: "the dew on the grass, the smell of the wood-fire, the hobbled ponies, woodpigeons cooing." This "secret part of her" is, of course, something she shares with other Garnett heroines—Tulip and Pocahontas in particular—but, unlike them, Clementina never herself becomes a victim. She suffers, she changes, she overcomes. So, although she leaves her husband buried in Russia, she is able to retire to Brighton with her family. And, as her life draws to its end, it is Romany culture that comforts her—the charms, proverbs, and songs of childhood—not the grandeur of the Imperial Court of Russia.

—J. Lawrence Mitchell

GARVICE, Charles. Also wrote as Charles Gibson; Caroline Hart. British. Born in 1833. Journalist; county councillor, Northam, Devon. President, Institute of Lecturers, and Farmers and Landowners Association. Fellow, Royal Society of Literature. *Died 1 March 1920.*

ROMANCE AND HISTORICAL PUBLICATIONS

Novels

Maurice Durant. London, Smith, 3 vols., 1875; New York, Ogilvie, n.d.; as *Eyes of Love*, New York, Street and Smith, n.d.

On Love's Altar. New York, Munro, 1892; London, King, 1908; as *A Wasted Love* (as Caroline Hart), Cleveland, Westbrook, n.d.

Paid For! New York, Munro, 1892; London, Hutchinson, 1909.

Married at Sight. New York, Munro, 1894.

The Price of Honour (as Charles Gibson). Cleveland, Westbrook, n.d.

His Love So True. New York, Munro, 1896.

The Marquis. New York, Munro, 1896.

Just a Girl. London, Bowden, 1898; as *An Innocent Girl*, New York, Munro, 1898.

She Loved Him. New York, Street and Smith, 1899; London, Hutchinson, 1909.

Claire. New York, Street and Smith, 1899.

Lorrie. New York, Street and Smith, 1899; London, Hodder and Stoughton, 1910.

Modern Juliet. New York, Street and Smith, 1900; London, Pearson, 1910.

Nell of Shorne Mills. New York, Street and Smith, 1900; London, Hutchinson, 1908.

Nance. London, Sands, 1900.

Her Heart's Desire. London, Sands, 1900; New York, Hurst, 1903.

An Outcast of the Family. London, Sands, 1900.

A Coronet of Shame. London, Sands, 1900; New York, Ogilvie, n.d.

Leola Dale's Fortune. New York, Street and Smith, 1901; London, Hutchinson, 1910.

Maida. New York, Street and Smith, 1901.

Only a Girl's Love. New York, Street and Smith, 1901; London, Hodder and Stoughton, 1911.

For Her Only. New York, Street and Smith, 1902; London, Hodder and Stoughton, 1911.

The Lady of Darracourt. New York, Street and Smith, 1902; London, Hodder and Stoughton, 1911.

Jeanne. New York, Street and Smith, 1902.

Heir of Vering. New York, Street and Smith, 1902; London, Hutchinson, 1910.

Woman's Soul. New York, Street and Smith, 1902.

So Nearly Lost. New York, Street and Smith, 1902; as *The Spring-Time of Love*, London, Hodder and Stoughton, 1910.

So Fair, So False. New York, Street and Smith, 1902.

Love's Dilemma. New York, Street and Smith, 1902; London, Hodder and Stoughton, 1917; as *For an Earldom*, New York, Ogilvie, n.d.

Martyred Love. New York, Street and Smith, 1902.

My Lady Pride. New York, Street and Smith, 1902.

Olivia. New York, Street and Smith, 1902.

In Cupid's Chains. London, Sands, 1902.

Woven on Fate's Loom, and The Snowdrift. New York, Street and Smith, 1903.

Staunch of the Heart. New York, Street and Smith, 1903; as *Adrien Leroy*, London, Newnes, 1912.

Her Ransom. New York, Hurst, 1903.

Led by Love. New York, Street and Smith, 1903.

Staunch as a Woman. New York, Street and Smith, 1903; London, Hodder and Stoughton, 1910.

A Jest of Fate. New York, Munro, 1904; London, Newnes, 1909.

Her Humble Lover. Cleveland, Westbrook, 1904; as *The Usurper*, Chicago, Donohue, n.d.

Love Decides. London, Hutchinson, 1904.

Linked by Fate. London, Hutchinson, 1905.

Love, The Tyrant. London, Hutchinson, 1905.

Edna's Secret Marriage. New York, Street and Smith, 1905.

The Other Woman. New York, Street and Smith, 1905.

When Love Meets Love. New York, Street and Smith, 1906.

A Girl of Spirit. London, Hutchinson, 1906; New York, Street and Smith, n.d.

Diana and Destiny. London, Hodder and Stoughton, 1906; as *Diana's Destiny*, New York, Burt, n.d.

Where Love Leads. London, Hutchinson, 1907.

The Gold in the Gutter. London, Hutchinson, 1907.

Sacrifice to Art. Chicago, Stein, 1908.

Sample of Prejudice. Chicago, Stein, 1908.

Slave of the Lake. Chicago, Stein, 1908.

Taming of Princess Olga. Chicago, Stein, 1908.

Woman Decides. Chicago, Stein, 1908.

My Lady of Snow. Chicago, Stein, 1908.

Linnie. Chicago, Stein, 1908.

Olivia and Others. London, Hutchinson, 1908.

A Love Comedy. Chicago, Stein, 1908; London, Hodder and Stoughton, 1912.

Marcia Drayton. London, Newnes, 1908.

Female Editor. Chicago, Stein, 1908.

Leave Love to Itself. Chicago, Stein, 1908.

First and Last. Chicago, Stein, 1908.

In the Matter of a Letter. Chicago, Stein, 1908.

Farmer Holt's Daughter. Chicago, Stein, 1908.

Story of a Passion. London, Hutchinson, 1908; New York, Burt, n.d.

Kyra's Fate. London, Hutchinson, 1908; New York, Burt, n.d.

The Rugged Path. London, Hodder and Stoughton, 1908.

In Wolf's Clothing. London, Hodder and Stoughton, 1908.

Queen Kate. London, Hodder and Stoughton, 1909.

The Scribblers' Club. London, Hodder and Stoughton, 1909.

The Fatal Ruby. London, Hodder and Stoughton, and New York, Doran, 1909.

By Dangerous Ways. London, Amalgamated Press, 1909; New York, Burt, n.d.

A Fair Imposter. London, Newnes, 1909.

A Heritage of Hate. London, Amalgamated Press, 1909.

The Mistress of Court Regina. London, Hutchinson, 1909; Philadelphia, Royal, n.d.

At Love's Cost. London, Hutchinson, 1909; New York, Burt, n.d.

Ashes of Love. New York, Ogilvie, 1910.

Barriers Between. London, Hodder and Stoughton, 1910.

The Beauty of the Season. London, Hodder and Stoughton, 1910.

Better Than Life. London, Hodder and Stoughton, 1910.

Dulcie. London, Hodder and Stoughton, 1910.

The Earl's Daughter. London, Hodder and Stoughton, 1910; as *The Earl's Heir*, Chicago, Donohue, n.d.

A Girl from the South. London, Cassell, 1910.

The Heart of a Maid. London, Hodder and Stoughton, 1910.

Once in a Life. London, Hodder and Stoughton, 1910.

Only One Love. London, Hodder and Stoughton, 1910; New York, Street and Smith, n.d.

A Passion Flower. London, Hodder and Stoughton, 1910; New York, Street and Smith, n.d.

With All Her Heart. London, Newnes, 1910.

Floris. London, Hutchinson, 1910.

Signa's Sweetheart. London, Hutchinson, 1910.

Sweet as a Rose. London, Hutchinson, 1910.

Leslie's Loyalty. London, Hodder and Stoughton, 1911; New York, Street and Smith, n.d.; as *Her Love So True*, Philadelphia, Royal, n.d.
Miss Estcourt. London, Hutchinson, 1911.
My Love Kitty. London, Hutchinson, 1911.
That Strange Girl. London, Hutchinson, 1911.
Violet. London, Hutchinson, 1911.
Doris. London, Newnes, 1911.
Elaine. London, Newnes, 1911; New York, Street and Smith, n.d.
He Loves Me, He Loves Me Not. London, Hodder and Stoughton, 1911; New York, Street and Smith, n.d.
His Guardian Angel. London, Newnes, 1911; New York, Street and Smith, n.d.
Lord of Himself. London, Hodder and Stoughton, 1911.
The Other Girl. London, Hodder and Stoughton, 1911.
Sweet Cymbeline. London, Newnes, 1911; New York, Street and Smith, n.d.
A Wilful Maid. London, Newnes, 1911; New York, Street and Smith, n.d.; as *Phillippa*, Chicago, Donohue, n.d.
The Woman in It. London, Hodder and Stoughton, 1911.
Wounded Heart. New York, Ogilvie, 1911.
Breta's Double. New York, Street and Smith, n.d.
His Perfect Trust. Philadelphia, Royal, n.d.
Imogene. New York, Street and Smith, n.d.
Love of a Life Time. Philadelphia, Royal, n.d.
Lucille. Chicago, Donohue, n.d.
Out of the Past. New York, Street and Smith, n.d.
Price of Honor. Philadelphia, Royal, n.d.
Pride of Her Life. New York, Street and Smith, n.d.
Royal Signet. Philadelphia, Royal, n.d.
The Spider and the Fly. New York, Street and Smith, n.d.
Sydney. New York, Street and Smith, n.d.
'Twix Smile and Tear. New York, Street and Smith, n.d.
Wasted Love. New York, Street and Smith, n.d.
Love in a Snare. London, Hodder and Stoughton, 1912.
Fate. London, Newnes, 1912; New York, Ogilvie, 1913.
Fickle Fortune. London, Newnes, 1912.
In Fine Feathers. London, Hodder and Stoughton, 1912.
Stella's Fortune. London, Hodder and Stoughton, 1912; New York, Street and Smith, n.d.; as *Sculptor's Wooing*, New York, Ogilvie, n.d.
Two Maids and a Man. London, Hodder and Stoughton, 1912; as *Two Girls and a Man*, London, Wright and Brown, 1937.
The Verdict of the Heart. London, Newnes, 1912.
Country Love. London, Hutchinson, 1912.
Reuben. London, Hutchinson, 1912.
Nellie. London, Hutchinson, 1913; as Caroline Hart, Cleveland, Westbrook, n.d.
The Loom of Fate. London, Newnes, 1913.
The Woman's Way. London, Hodder and Stoughton, 1914.
Iris. London, Newnes, 1914.
The Call of the Heart. London, Hodder and Stoughton, 1914.
In Exchange for Love. London, Hodder and Stoughton, 1914.
The One Girl in the World. London, Hodder and Stoughton, 1915.
Love, The Adventurous. London, Hodder and Stoughton, 1917.
Creatures of Destiny. New York, Burt, n.d.
Heart for Heart. New York, Burt, n.d.
Love and a Lie. New York, Burt, n.d.
Shadow of Her Life. New York, Burt, n.d.
'Twas Love's Fault. New York, Burt, n.d.
When Love Is Young. New York, Burt, n.d.
The Waster. London, Lloyds, 1918.
The Girl in Love. London, Skeffington, 1919.
Wicked Sir Dare. London, Hutchinson, 1938.

Novels as Caroline Hart

A Hidden Terror. Cleveland, Westbrook, 1910.
Angela's Lover. Cleveland, Westbrook, n.d.
For Love or Honor. Cleveland, Westbrook, n.d.
From Want to Wealth. Cleveland, Westbrook, n.d.
From Worse Than Death. Cleveland, Westbrook, n.d.
Game of Love. Cleveland, Westbrook, n.d.
Haunted Life. Cleveland, Westbrook, n.d.
Hearts of Fire. Cleveland, Westbrook, n.d.
Her Right to Love. Cleveland, Westbrook, n.d.
Lil, The Dancing Girl. Cleveland, Westbrook, n.d.
Lillian's Vow. Cleveland, Westbrook, n.d.
Little Princess. Cleveland, Westbrook, n.d.
Love's Rugged Path. Cleveland, Westbrook, n.d.
Madness of Love. Cleveland, Westbrook, n.d.
Nameless Bess. Cleveland, Westbrook, n.d.
Nobody's Wife. Cleveland, Westbrook, n.d.
Redeemed by Love. Cleveland, Westbrook, n.d.
Rival Heiresses. Cleveland, Westbrook, n.d.
She Loved Not Wisely. Cleveland, Westbrook, n.d.
Strange Marriage. Cleveland, Westbrook, n.d.
That Awful Scar. Cleveland, Westbrook, n.d.
Vengeance of Love. Cleveland, Westbrook, n.d.
Women Who Came Between. Cleveland, Westbrook, n.d.
Woman Wronged. Cleveland, Westbrook, n.d.
Working Girl's Honor. Cleveland, Westbrook, n.d.

Short Stories

The Girl Without a Heart and Other Stories. London, Newnes, 1912.
A Relenting Fate and Other Stories. London, Newnes, 1912.
All Is Not Fair in Love and Other Stories. London, Newnes, 1913.
The Tessacott Tragedy and Other Stories. London, Newnes, 1913.
The Girl in the 'bacca Shop. London, Skeffington, 1920.
Miss Smith's Fortune and Other Stories. London, Skeffington, 1920.

OTHER PUBLICATIONS

Plays

The Fisherman's Daughter (produced London, 1881).
A Life's Mistake. London, Hutchinson, 1910.
Marigold, with Allan F. Abbott (produced Glasgow, 1914).

Verse

Eve and Other Verses. Privately printed, 1873.

Other

A Farm in Creamland: A Book of the Devon Countryside. London, Hodder and Stoughton, 1911; New York, Doran, 1912.

Editor, *The Red Budget of Stories*. London, Hodder and Stoughton, 1912.

*   *   *

Charles Garvice was an English writer of the early 1900's. His novels actually became popular in the mid-1890's and were so well received by American readers that many of his works were printed by American publishers in pirated editions even after the 1891 international copyright agreement.

Garvice's style and his frequent diversions into social commentary would tend to put modern readers off from fully enjoying his works today. Often his stories begin by drawing comparisons between his developing characters and the common people of the poorer sections of London. Frequently his characters display a deep and unusual social consciousness that make them aware of economic and labor changes of the day that worked to the detriment of the working classes. In fact, this theme of helping the working classes or of accepting people as people remains a solid underlying force throughout many of his novels. On another level it is his consistent emphasis on natural, instinctive qualities within the lower classes that make these people just as socially acceptable as those from the upper ranks. Often the reader finds phrases such as ''He had the instincts of a gentleman'' or ''She moved and spoke in the manner born'' applied to characters from the working classes. The fact that these qualities could be found in the lower classes made that person even more exceptional and valued. From this element in his novels alone, one can understand why they appealed so greatly to American readers.

That is not, however, the major cause of his popularity. For Garvice had an unusual ability to weave fast-paced and intricate and believable plots that do not need to rely on coincidence to succeed. Missing jewels or treasures are combined with missing or lost heiresses. His plots usually center on the hero of the story, and the action is told from his viewpoint. He is often from a titled family and he usually succeeds to the title or is reinstated into his father's good graces. In *The Gold in the Gutter* Clive Harvey is the third son of a family of notable rakes and spendthrifts who becomes a radical thinker and wins a seat in the House of Commons. Basically, the development of Garvice's stories rests on the hero's ability to overcome obstacles and in the process, of course, to win the girl who has captured his heart. If any major flaw emerges in Garvice's writing, it is his tendency to draw his characters larger than life; even the hero's faults assume a virtuous glow so that one does not come to grips with the real person Garvice is attempting to characterize. He is too good, too virtuous, too everything to be readily acceptable to today's readers. In spite of this drawback, one must conclude that his writings fall very definitely into the romance genre. Actually Garvice is within the traditional guidelines of the misunderstood hero who faces all sorts of trials before he succeeds in achieving his goal.

Dialogue is often cleverly used to round out a character. It is sharp, and frequently colorful and rich, adding to the speaker's overall character. Description is not always kept as short as one would like, but from the period in which he was writing, that cannot be considered a fault. Certainly he mastered the technique of telling a good, moving story that kept readers waiting for the next chapter.

His writing apparently appealed to men as well as women, for some of his works actually could be classified as adventure stories rather than straight romances. For example, in *The Rugged Path* Jack, the son of Sir William Morton, leaves home after disagreeing with his father. He is literally cut off from his father and any money his father would leave him. The prospect certainly does not upset him, for he sails to Australia and undertakes a whole new life for himself. The Australian scenes are quite well presented by Garvice, indicating careful research to lend accuracy to his works. The scene shifts back to England, with the death of his father and the arrival of the villain in the

person of his cousin, Hesketh Carton. Contested wills, fetching girls of the new breed, and the hero's own queer sense of honor add to an intriguing story and eventual happiness.

It is difficult to summarize Garvice as a romance writer. Barring stylistic elements that certainly date his work, he still can be enjoyably read by anyone. In fact, careful editing and the presentation of his works as historical novels might make them appealing even now. Yet, he was not an outstanding writer. He may not have had that special spark that would allow for such liberties to be taken. Perhaps it would make no difference, for romance writers tend to want to tell a good story and to make people experience, just for a moment, someone else's life and happiness. The fact that Garvice wrote well over 150 novels indicates that he may have achieved his purpose and did not particularly care for lasting fame.

—Arlene Moore

GASCOIGNE, Marguerite. See **GILBERT, Anna.**

GASKIN, Catherine. Irish. Born in Dundalk, County Louth, 2 April 1929. Educated at Holy Cross College, Sydney, Australia. Married Sol Cornberg in 1955. Lived in London, 1948–55, New York, 1955–65, the Virgin Islands 1965–67, and Ireland 1967–81. Address: White Rigg, East Ballaterson, Maughold, Isle of Man, United Kingdom.

ROMANCE AND HISTORICAL PUBLICATIONS

Novels

This Other Eden. London, Collins, 1947.
With Every Year. London, Collins, 1949.
Dust in the Sunlight. London, Collins, 1950.
All Else Is Folly. London, Collins, and New York, Harper, 1951.
Daughter of the House. London, Collins, 1952; New York, Harper, 1953.
Sara Dane. London, Collins, and Philadelphia, Lippincott, 1955.
Blake's Reach. London, Collins, and Philadelphia, Lippincott, 1958.
Corporation Wife. London, Collins, and New York, Doubleday, 1960.
I Know My Love. London, Collins, and New York, Doubleday, 1962.
The Tilsit Inheritance. London, Collins, and New York, Doubleday, 1963.
The File on Devlin. London, Collins, and New York, Doubleday, 1965.
Edge of Glass. London, Collins, and New York, Doubleday, 1967.
Fiona. London, Collins, and New York, Doubleday, 1970.
A Falcon for a Queen. London, Collins, and New York, Doubleday, 1972.
The Property of a Gentleman. London, Collins, and New York, Doubleday, 1974.

The Lynmara Legacy. London, Collins, 1975; New York, Doubleday, 1976.
The Summer of the Spanish Woman. London, Collins, and New York, Doubleday, 1977.
Family Affairs. London, Collins, and New York, Doubleday, 1980.
Promises. London, Collins, and New York, Doubleday, 1982.
The Ambassador's Women. London, Collins, 1985; New York, Scribner, 1986.
The Charmed Circle. London, Collins, 1988; New York, Scribner, 1989.

*

Catherine Gaskin comments:
I write to entertain and I expend enormous effort on my writing so that the end product will appear effortless.

* * *

Catherine Gaskin has created her own niche in the world of the romance novel. Her works contain the familiar gothic elements—disputed inheritance, forbidden love, mysterious strangers, ancestral homes and their hidden skeletons, and the culminating act of violence. What sets her apart is her ability to integrate these elements into the fabric of a modern world so convincingly drawn as to anchor the fantastic firmly to earth. *This Other Eden*, the first novel she later rewrote as *The Lynmara Legacy*, reveals the talent as already fully formed. Its theme, of an American girl's succession to an English inheritance, is basically the same in both versions, and displays Gaskin's skill in blending realism and romance.

Since then, Gaskin's writing is roughly divisible into two main streams: modern stories with gothic ingredients, and historical romances. The latter tend to be longer, and sometimes more ambitious; viewed critically, they are often less satisfying. Though immensely popular, *Sara Dane* lacks the sense of solid reality that marks even the earliest of Gaskin's contemporary novels. Without the social background so ably provided in the modern works, its events seem unnecessarily theatrical and shorn of conviction. The story—of a transported servant girl who rises to wealth and power in colonial Australia—moves uncertainly from one crisis to another, with the arrivals and departures of Sara's prospective lovers rendered improbably convenient. Comparison with Susan Taite, the sophisticated and sensual fashion editor of *All Else Is Folly*, reveals Sara's deficiencies; she is merely a character in a book, while Susan impresses as a living woman evoked by words. *Blake's Reach*, a story of smuggling adventure off the Romney marshes in the 18th century, and *I Know My Love* with its historical Australian setting, both suffer from the same defects. Although they are exciting period tales, they do not possess the depth of penetration found in other works. Measured beside Gaskin's finest creations, the romances are costume dramas rather than portrayals of life. Later attempts in the genre, notably *A Falcon for a Queen*, achieve a greater degree of success, but serve as exceptions that prove the rule.

Corporation Wife, one of Gaskin's most satisfying books, explores the lives of four women in a small town taken over by an industrial company. Gaskin studies the women—two executive wives and two "natives"—in terms of their loves and ambitions, and the differing ways in which each adapts to the pressures of the corporation in her life. Her touch is sure, romance and tragedy made part of a convincing social scene, the characters perfectly and subtly realized. Equally skilled are *The Tilsit Inheritance*, where a pottery business provides the background

for a disputed legacy and love for a dark stranger, and the imaginative spy mystery *The File on Devlin*. Gaskin shows a keen awareness of various crafts and their commercial applications, and this knowledge is effectively used in most of her works. Examples include the mechanics of glass production in *Edge of Glass*, fashion in *All Else Is Folly*, and viticulture in *The Summer of the Spanish Woman*. Presentation of her characters at work is a major factor in the authenticity of Gaskin's best novels.

The Property of a Gentleman displays the aspects of the Gaskin novel in perfect balance. Against a background of art auctioneering, the heroine falls in love with the heir to a Lakeland mansion. Action revolves around the discovery of a skeleton and related art treasures, and the book has a violent denouement. This novel shares another factor with many of Gaskin's works, the emphasis on the family and the ancestral home. This last theme forms the core of *The Lynmara Legacy*, whose self-reliant, determined heroine is typical of the "Gaskin woman" in other novels. This theme is a significant aspect of more recent books, longer contemporary family chronicles reminiscent of the historical romances, into which the violent, gothic items are more fitfully inserted. Such works present a larger world-view, and usually depict an elite, privileged group of people, whether financial (*The Ambassador's Women*), political (*Family Affairs*), artistic (*The Charmed Circle*), or industrial (*Promises*). Each contains the recurrent theme of the outsider, adapted by the powerful head of the family, coming into her inheritance, usually after rivalry and death. Gaskin's storytelling gift is undiminished, but the later sagas lack the coherence and balance of previous works, the gothic elements somehow more intrusive and less integral than before. Gaskin has produced an impressive body of work, unique of its kind. More than most, she has brought a modern dimension to the gothic romance.

—Geoffrey Sadler

GAVIN, Catherine (Irvine). British. Born in Aberdeen, Scotland, in 1907. Educated at the University of Aberdeen, M.A. (honours) 1928, Ph.D. 1931. Married John Ashcraft in 1948. Lecturer in History, University of Aberdeen, 1932–34, 1941–43, and University of Glasgow, 1934–36; editorial writer, European bureau chief, and war correspondent, Kemsley Newspapers, 1943–45; correspondent in the Middle East and Ethiopia, *Daily Express*, London, 1945–47; staff member, *Time*, New York, 1950–52; public lecturer in the U.S., 1952–60. Active in Scottish politics in the 1930's: Conservative candidate for Parliament twice. D.Litt.: University of Aberdeen, 1986. Address: 1201 California Street, San Francisco, California 94109, U.S.A.

Romance and Historical Publications

Novels (series: Second Empire; Second World War)

Clyde Valley. London, Barker, 1938.
The Hostile Shore. London, Methuen, 1940.
The Black Milestone. London, Methuen, 1941.
The Mountain of Light. London, Methuen, 1944.
Second Empire Quartet:
  Madeleine. New York, St. Martin's Press, 1957; London, Macmillan, 1958.
  The Cactus and the Crown. London, Hodder and Stoughton, and New York, Doubleday, 1962.

The Fortress. London, Hodder and Stoughton, and New York, Doubleday, 1964.

The Moon into Blood. London, Hodder and Stoughton, 1966.

The Devil in Harbour. London, Hodder and Stoughton, and New York, Morrow, 1968.

The House of War. London, Hodder and Stoughton, and New York, Morrow, 1970.

Give Me the Daggers. London, Hodder and Stoughton, and New York, Morrow, 1972.

The Snow Mountain. London, Hodder and Stoughton, 1973; New York, Pantheon, 1974.

Second World War trilogy:

Traitors' Gate. London, Hodder and Stoughton, and New York, St. Martin's Press, 1976.

None Dare Call It Treason. London, Hodder and Stoughton, and New York, St. Martin's Press, 1978.

How Sleep the Brave. London, Hodder and Stoughton, and New York, St. Martin's Press, 1980.

The Sunset Dream. London, Hodder and Stoughton, 1983; New York, St. Martin's Press, 1984.

A Light Woman. London, Grafton, 1986.

The Glory Road. London, Grafton, 1987.

A Dawn of Splendour. London, Grafton, 1989.

OTHER PUBLICATIONS

Other

Louis Philippe, King of the French. London, Methuen, 1933.

Britain and France: A Study of Twentieth Century Relations, The Entente Cordiale. London, Cape, 1941.

Edward the Seventh: A Biography. London, Cape, 1941.

Liberated France. London, Cape, and New York, St. Martin's Press, 1955.

*   *   *

The closer a historical novelist sets her books to the present day, the more she puts her scholarship on the line and invites criticism, for many readers will remember the events and will be quick enough to say "this did not happen" or "this did happen but not for that reason" if she is wrong. Catherine Gavin passes this test with flying colours in what she calls her "war novels"—four about World War I and a trilogy about World War II—all of which will have readers who lived through the events portrayed. They will agree that not only does she get her history right but that she has a masterly way of evoking the atmosphere of a given place at a precise moment in time. Thus having found her accounts of times we are competent to judge trustworthy, we feel she must be right, too, when she tells us about earlier periods of history.

Her Second Empire Quartet is a series of books set in the 19th century and loosely connected by their theme: they set out to explore various revolutionary struggles, mixing fictional characters with historical personalities. *The Fortress* tells of the naval campaign in the Baltic in 1885 through the eyes of an American in the Royal Navy and adumbrates Finland's struggles through his Finnish wife; *The Moon into Blood* is about the Risorgimento in Italy with a fictional American hero who works with Cavour and Garibaldi; *Madeleine* is about the Second Empire in France, and *The Cactus and the Crown* the ill-fated Hapsburg intervention in Mexico. The Mexican countryside is the real star of this book and the American characters are more royalist than revolutionary, although Gavin lets her heroine have her cake and eat it too.

The World War I novels are concerned with the pressures of war, the way such pressures distort behaviour, and the way change may grow out of it. *The Devil in Harbour* is about spying and divided loyalties and the battle of Jutland. *The Snow Mountain*, about the fall of the Romanovs, is a poignant recreation of that sad story; Gavin's interpretations of the Czar and Czarina's motives are excellent, and the fictitious American consul, the Russian officer, and the revolutionary girl who share the story are extremely believable. *Give Me the Daggers* is about General Mannerheim's fight for Finnish independence in 1918, but also about a young man coming to terms with a disfiguring wound and a spoiled young girl learning unselfishness. *The House of War* is about Kemal Ataturk's struggle for Turkish freedom in 1922 but also about the break up of a marriage. The history in all these books is accurate and well integrated into the fiction, the descriptions of places is excellent and the characterization of factual and fictional people is so good you cannot "see the join." A felicitous touch which adds verity is the way a character who plays a major part in one novel gets a walk-on part in another—descendants of people in *The Fortress* turn up in *Give Me the Daggers* and Joe Calvert the consul in *The Snow Mountain* appears as godfather to the heroine of *None Dare Call It Treason*, one of the World War II novels.

This remarkable trilogy is about France's struggle. *Traitors' Gate*, set in London and Brazil, evokes the atmosphere and emotions of 1940 quite amazingly; *None Dare Call It Treason* takes place in the unoccupied zone of France, mainly in Nice and Menton, and explores different kinds of loyalty and betrayal. *How Sleep the Brave* takes the story through the liberation to the end of the war, and includes an understated yet unforgettably horrific description of the massacre at Oradour-sur-Glane. Throughout the trilogy hardly anyone has a good word to say for de Gaulle, and the reader will probably never be able to think of him in quite the same way again.

Gavin is extremely skilful at blending fact and fiction, and if occasionally readers feel she is giving us too big a chunk of history it is because the romance is so entertaining that we are impatient to know what will happen next.

—Pamela Cleaver

GELLIS, Roberta (Leah, née Jacobs). Also writes as Max Daniels; Priscilla Hamilton; Leah Jacobs. American. Born in New York City, 27 September 1927. Educated at Hunter College, New York, 1943–47, B.A. 1947; Brooklyn Polytechnic Institute, 1949–52, M.A. 1952; New York University, 1953–58, M.A. Married Charles Gellis in 1947; one son. Chemist, Foster D. Snell Inc., New York, 1947–53; editor, McGraw-Hill Book Company, New York, 1953–56; then freelance editor, for Macmillan Company, New York, 1956–58 and since 1971, and for Academic Press, New York, 1956–70. Address: P.O. Box 483, Roslyn Heights, New York 11577, U.S.A.

ROMANCE AND HISTORICAL PUBLICATIONS

Novels (series: Heiress; Roselynde; Royal Dynasty)

Knight's Honor. New York, Doubleday, 1964; London, Mayflower, 1979.

Bond of Blood. New York, Doubleday, 1965; London, Mayflower, 1979.

The Psychiatrist's Wife (as Leah Jacobs). New York, New American Library, 1966.

Sing Witch, Sing Death. New York, Bantam, 1975.

The Sword and the Swan. Chicago, Playboy Press, 1977; London, Mayflower, 1979.

The Dragon and the Rose. Chicago, Playboy Press, 1977; London, Mayflower, 1979.

The Roselynde Chronicles:

1. *Roselynde.* Chicago, Playboy Press, 1978; London, Hamlyn, 1979.
2. *Alinor.* Chicago, Playboy Press, 1978; London, Hamlyn, 1979.
3. *Joanna.* Chicago, Playboy Press, 1978; London, Hamlyn, 1979.
4. *Gilliane.* Chicago, Playboy Press, and London, Hamlyn, 1979.
5. *Rhiannon.* Chicago, Playboy Press, 1982; Bath, Chivers, 1985.
6. *Sybelle.* New York, Berkley, 1983; Bath, Chivers, 1985.

Love Token (as Priscilla Hamilton). Chicago, Playboy Press, 1979.

Heiress series:

The English Heiress. New York, Dell, 1980.
The Cornish Heiress. New York, Dell, 1981.
The Kent Heiress. New York, Dell, 1982.
Fortune's Bride. New York, Dell, 1983.
A Woman's Estate. New York, Dell, 1984.

Royal Dynasty series:

Siren Song. Chicago, Playboy Press, 1981.
Winter Song. New York, Playboy Press, 1982.
Fire Song. New York, Berkley, 1984.
A Silver Mirror. New York, Berkley, 1989.

A Tapestry of Dreams. New York, Berkley, 1985.

The Rope Dancer. New York, Berkley, 1986.

Fires of Winter. New York, Berkley, 1987.

Masques of Gold. New York, Berkley, 1988.

*

Roberta Gellis comments:

Perhaps in reaction against the cynical attitudes and impersonal horrors perpetrated by humankind on humankind, I have always been fascinated by the past. In medieval times, there was a passionate belief in honor, truth, courage, and loyalty. This is not to say that I think men and women at that time were different or better; they were not. However, when they diverged from the path, when they were dishonorable or cowardly, they knew they had done wrong; they did not tell themselves that "everybody does it." And, although cruelty and slaughter were as rife then as now, one at least had to face one's victim; there were no bombs that killed faceless thousands impersonally.

The combination of these high standards and my awareness that people are people in any place or time has led me to attempt to present the social and political history of the medieval period, especially medieval England, in human terms. In any time the two great desires of human beings are for love and power. Thus, I try to weave together a strong love story and the political events, showing the latter through the eyes of the people affected. Most of my books are in continuing series, which permits me to give a chronological history not only of the nation but also of a family.

The Roselynde Chronicles, for example, begin with the young heiress, Alinor of Roselynde, and detail, through her two marriages, the reign of Richard the Lionhearted and the early years of King John. In *Joanna* I deal with the marriage of Alinor's daughter and the last four years of John's reign, showing how Joanna's marriage increased both the power and the responsibilities of the family. The spread of influence of the Roselynde clan is increased still further in Volume 4 of the Chronicles, when Alinor's eldest son marries another heiress, twice widowed. Through all the books I attempt to show the conditions, both physical and social, in which these people lived. Moreover, I try to present events as *these* people saw and felt them by the use of chronicles written at the time rather than by the use of modern history books, although I also consult modern texts. Historical events and historical personages are presented as accurately as possible, although the central characters of my books are almost always fictional.

However, I do not want any reader to believe that I am writing historical texts. To my characters, as to any human being, their own personal affairs are of essential importance, of far greater importance than any political event—unless that political event affects them directly. It is, thus, the love story in each book that is the central theme, not political and social history. To each man and woman personal need and desire are not only of overriding importance, but these emotions color all other events. So I emphasize the personal element, for in real life that is how we frail humans perceive our world, and that is how my characters perceived theirs.

*   *   *

When one reads a Roberta Gellis novel, one should be prepared to enter an historical world of great vitality. Her stories are carefully researched and are loaded with details of life and manners of the period. Historical figures wander easily into the narrative or may even take center stage, as does Henry VII, the central figure in *The Dragon and the Rose*. In some of her more recent novels Gellis has extended her writings from the world of the nobility to that of traveling players in *The Rope Dancer* and the guilds of *Masques of Gold*. No matter the status of the protagonists, however, there is a wealth of detail that immerses the reader in another time and place. Although that same detail might seem overwhelming, Gellis creates such real characters that they bring all the facts into focus and make history a living thing rather than a collection of dry dates and events. The underlying love stories serve to point out how historical events affect individuals.

Most of Gellis's prolific output has been devoted to the medieval period. *A Tapestry of Dreams* and *Fires of Winter* are set during the struggles of Stephen and Matilda for the throne of England. The popular Roselynde series takes the reader through one of the most tumultuous eras of English history. Action in the first two volumes, *Roselynde* and *Alinor*, moves to the Crusades and into the rebellion against King John. Later volumes involve the characters in events leading to the Magna Carta, war with France, and later rebellions against Henry III. No less historically accurate than Roselynde series, *The English Heiress*, *The Cornish Heiress*, and *The Kent Heiress* are set in the more familiar 18th and 19th centuries.

Perhaps the most striking thing about Gellis's creations is the courage, strength, and integrity shown by her female characters. Alinor, first of the exceptional Roselynde women, is not only beautiful and intelligent, but has the almost mystical bond to the land that is usually reserved for males. She may be caught up in great events, but her love for and protection of her land and family remain paramount. Indeed, it is a measure of the importance of women in these stories that the great estate of Roselynde is passed on through the female line. Alinor's daughter and granddaughter, Joanna and Sybelle, are worthy successors to the dynasty. Even Alinor's sons, Adam and Simon, search for and find strong, independent women in *Gilliane* and *Rhiannon*. It is to

Gellis's credit that she is able to portray such strong women so believably. It would be a mistake, however, to think that these women dominate their male companions. The women may be the central focus, but the men are their equals. They too are fiercely independent, passionate, and devoted to duty and honor. Secure in themselves, they are not threatened by the Roselynde women.

Although the focus may shift somewhat to the male characters, as it does in the Heiress books, or to the lower classes, the same strength and independence of the men and women come through. It is this view of men and women as individuals who are equal, who are able to maintain their individuality and equality in their male-female relationships, that sets a different tone in the historical romance genre.

—Barbara E. Kemp

* * *

GIBBS, Mary Ann. Pseudonym for Marjory Elizabeth Sarah Bidwell, née Lambe; also wrote as Elizabeth Ford. British. Born in Seaford, Sussex. Attended secondary schools in Seaford. Married Thomas Edward Palmer Bidwell (died 1965); one son. *Died in January 1985.*

ROMANCE AND HISTORICAL PUBLICATIONS

Novels

A Young Man with Ideas. London, Davies, 1950.
Enchantment: A Pastoral. London, Davies, 1952.
A Bit of a Bounder: An Edwardian Trifle. London, Davies, 1952.
The Guardian. London, Hurst and Blackett, 1958; New York, Beagle, 1974.
Young Lady with Red Hair. London, Hurst and Blackett, 1959; New York, Beagle, 1974; as *The Penniless Heiress*, London, Coronet, 1975.
Horatia. London, Hurst and Blackett, 1961; New York, Beagle, 1973.
The Apothecary's Daughter. London, Hurst and Blackett, 1962; New York, Beagle, 1974.
Polly Kettle. London, Hurst and Blackett, 1963; New York, Beagle, 1973; as *The Nursery Maid*, London, Coronet, 1975.
The Amateur Governess. London, Hurst and Blackett, 1964; as *The House of Ravensbourne*, New York, Pyramid, 1965.
The Sugar Mouse. London, Hurst and Blackett, 1965; New York, Beagle, 1974.
The Romantic Frenchman. London, Hurst and Blackett, 1967; New York, Beagle, 1973.
The Sea Urchins. London, Hurst and Blackett, 1968; New York, Beagle, 1973.
A Parcel of Land. London, Hurst and Blackett, 1969; New York, Beagle, 1973.
A Lady in Berkshire. London, Hurst and Blackett, 1970; New York, Beagle, 1973.
The Year of the Pageant. London, Hurst and Blackett, 1971; New York, Beagle, 1973.
The Moon in a Bucket. London, Hurst and Blackett, 1972; New York, Beagle, 1973.
The Glass Palace. London, Hurst and Blackett, 1973; New York, Mason Charter, 1975.
A Wife for the Admiral. London, Hurst and Blackett, 1974; as *The Admiral's Lady*, New York, Mason Charter, 1975.

A Most Romantic City. London, Hurst and Blackett, and New York, Mason Charter, 1976.
The Tempestuous Petticoat. London, Hurst and Blackett, and New York, Mason Charter, 1977.
A Young Lady of Fashion. London, Hurst and Blackett, 1978; New York, Fawcett, 1979.
The Tulip Tree. London, Hurst and Blackett, and New York, Fawcett, 1979.
Dinah. Loughton, Essex, Piatkus, and New York, Fawcett, 1981.
The Milliner's Shop. Loughton, Essex, Piatkus, 1981; as *Renegade Girl*, New York, Fawcett, 1981.
The Marquess. Loughton, Essex, Piatkus, 1982.

Novels as Elizabeth Ford (series: Maplechester)

Fog. London, Chapman and Hall, 1933.
The House with the Myrtle Trees. London, Lutterworth Press, 1942.
The Blue Cockade: A Romantic Novel of 1780. London, Lutterworth Press, 1943.
Queen's Harbour. London, Hurst and Blackett, 1944.
The Young Ladies' Room. London, Hurst and Blackett, 1945.
The Irresponsibles. London, Hurst and Blackett, 1946.
Mountford Show. London, Hurst and Blackett, 1948.
Spring Comes to the Crescent. London, Hurst and Blackett, 1949.
So Deep Suspicion. London, Hurst and Blackett, 1950.
Four Days in June. London, Hurst and Blackett, 1951.
Just Around the Corner. London, Hurst and Blackett, 1952.
English Rose. London, Hurst and Blackett, 1953.
One Fine Day. London, Hurst and Blackett, 1954.
Meeting in the Spring. London, Hurst and Blackett, 1954.
Outrageous Fortune. London, Hurst and Blackett, 1955.
That Summer at Bacclesea. London, Hurst and Blackett, 1956.
The Empty Heart. London, Hurst and Blackett, 1957.
The Cottage at Drimble. London, Hurst and Blackett, 1957.
Butter Market House. London, Hurst and Blackett, 1958.
Heron's Nest. London, Hurst and Blackett, 1960.
A Week by the Sea. London, Hurst and Blackett, 1962.
A Holiday Engagement (Maplechester). London, Hurst and Blackett, 1963.
No Room for Joanna (Maplechester). London, Hurst and Blackett, 1964.
A Country Holiday. London, Hurst and Blackett, 1966; as *Dangerous Holiday*, New York, Ace, 1967.
The Turbulent Messiters. London, Hurst and Blackett, 1967.
Limelight for Jane. London, Hurst and Blackett, 1970.
The Day of the Storm. London, Hurst and Blackett, 1971.
The Green Beetle. London, Hurst and Blackett, 1972.
The Belvedere. London, Hurst and Blackett, 1973.
Young Ann. London, Hurst and Blackett, 1973.
A Charming Couple. London, Hurst and Blackett, 1975.
The Amber Cat. London, Hurst and Blackett, 1976.
Open Day at the Manor. London, Hurst and Blackett, 1977.

OTHER PUBLICATIONS

Other

The Years of the Nannies. London, Hutchinson, 1960.

*

Mary Ann Gibbs commented:

(1982) I am meticulous as to research and always do my own. I find that only by reading journals, diaries, letters, guides, and fiction of the era in which my books are set, and by studying minutely dress, jewellery, maps, transport, etc., can I recreate the atmosphere of the time. I never use what I call "gadsookery" in dialogue, as I have often found that many of the expressions used today were used as a matter of course at the beginning of the last century, and a word here and there will be enough to bring the reader back to the years in which the books are set. I never dictate my books. I do not think I could even use a dictaphone. I type them out as a first draft, which is then scribbled over and re-typed several times before I embark on the final typing, and even then I change phrases and sometimes characters, as I go. In other words I live in and with the book while I am writing.

*   *   *

A plucky girl with a zest for life and a refusal to let its adversities overwhelm her characterize the type of heroine always present in a Mary Ann Gibbs romance. The fact that the girl is usually not a stunning beauty and might even be considered plain does not prevent her from winning one of society's more desirable bachelors. She lives in a place and time (19th-century England) where morals and manners are applied rigidly. A Gibbs heroine often finds it necessary to abandon conventional manners in order to survive catastrophe while still remaining a lady and keeping a sense of self-worth. In *The Apothecary's Daughter* Susanna becomes the recipient of expensive gifts from Lord Vigilant, a much older man with a rakish past. That she is his long lost illegitimate daughter is kept secret at the insistence of her foster father, the apothecary. The scandal threatens to ruin Susanna's good name forever, but in the end the truth comes out. Meanwhile a man of position, Hugo Vigilant, the Lord's cousin and heir, has come to love her and finally wins her hand.

Often the young ladies of Gibb's romances are left destitute by a negligent father and must give up the dream of marrying an eligible man of society, their impoverishment making them no longer acceptable. In *The Amateur Governess* Catherine finds herself penniless after the sudden death of a father from whom she inherits nothing but debts. Taking the job of governess to the young daughter of a wealthy tradesman, Catherine solves the mystery of the child's mistreatment by a cruel aunt and wins the love of the little girl's father. Similarly, Vicky Langford of *The Milliner's Shop* must make her own way when her father leaves the country, the charge of fraud following in his wake. She provides for herself and her brother by taking a job as a clerk in a milliner's shop; she does not feel sorry for herself when all of her proper society friends cross her permanently off their lists. All, that is, except for a very few, one of whom is Sebastian, whose love for this young lady knows no bounds.

A novel by Gibbs tells of old-fashioned romance in which love has a special tenderness. There often exists an element of mystery—in fact Gibbs writes suspense novels as Elizabeth Ford—but the stories mainly center on the many obstacles the lovers must overcome in order to live happily ever after.

—Patricia Altner

—————

GIBSON, Charles. See **GARVICE, Charles.**

GILBERT, Anna. Pseudonym for Marguerite Lazarus; also writes as Marguerite Gascoigne. British. Born in Durham, 1 May 1916. Educated at Durham University, B.A. (honours) 1937, M.A. 1945. Married Jack Lazarus in 1956. Grammar school English teacher, 1941–73. Recipient: Romantic Novelists Association Major award, 1976. Agent: Watson Little Ltd., Suite 8, 26 Charing Cross Road, London WC2H 0DG. Address: Oakley Cottage, Swainsea Lane, Pickering, North Yorkshire, England.

ROMANCE AND HISTORICAL PUBLICATIONS

Novels

Images of Rose. London, Hodder and Stoughton, and New York, Delacorte Press, 1974.
The Look of Innocence. London, Hodder and Stoughton, and New York, St. Martin's Press, 1975.
A Family Likeness. London, Hodder and Stoughton, 1977; New York, St. Martin's Press, 1978.
Remembering Louise. London, Hodder and Stoughton, and New York, St. Martin's Press, 1978.
The Leavetaking. London, Hodder and Stoughton, 1979; New York, St. Martin's Press, 1980.
Flowers for Lilian. London, Hodder and Stoughton, 1980; New York, St. Martin's Press, 1981.
Miss Bede Is Staying. Loughton, Essex, Piatkus, 1982; New York, St. Martin's Press, 1983.
The Long Shadow. Loughton, Essex, Piatkus, 1983; New York, St. Martin's Press, 1985.
A Walk in the Wood. New York, St. Martin's Press, 1989.

OTHER PUBLICATIONS

Fiction (for children)

The Song of the Gipsy (as Marguerite Gascoigne). London, Warne, 1953.

*

Anna Gilbert comments:

My books are romantic in atmosphere in so far as romanticism implies a selection of the pleasing and picturesque aspects of reality, rather than the squalid. My aim is to charm and intrigue the reader, and to create tension by other means than the use of sensational material. I hope to appeal to women who want the reassurance of traditional values in stories which involve convincing characters in experiences of universal interest: love, loss, sadness, fear, forgiveness resolving into happiness, though the ultimate happiness is not always unalloyed.

The stories depend upon a strong plot and are set in Victorian England: a society near enough in time to be well documented but far enough away to offer escape from the complications of contemporary life; or the first half of the 20th century. I choose close-knit, claustrophobic situations and relationships. Tension arises from some element of mystery and the gradual accumulation of significant detail leading to its disclosure: secrecy, deception, illusion—created and dispelled. I am particularly interested in the way innocence and generosity are exploited by selfishness and greed.

My favourite setting is the English countryside: remote hamlets and villages, woods and moors, small market towns: a country in itself mysterious, beautiful, and menacing, and for me constantly interfused with haunting glimpses of the ideal.

*   *   *

Anna Gilbert's first book, *Images of Rose*, was shortlisted for the 1974 Romantic Novelists Association Major award. In 1976 she won the award with her second book, *The Look of Innocence*. She writes Victorian stories with a strong element of mystery—classics of their kind. Gilbert's plots are intricate and subtle. Her favourite theme is the quiet but relentless manipulation of people by each other, and the helplessness of the good and innocent in the face of ruthless egotism and jealousy. The manner, as much as the matter, is important. Her work is stylish and elegant. She writes with fastidious care, making every word count (not for nothing has she taught English to a high level), and she is past mistress at the art of heightening tension by placing a gentle finger on the reader's nerves.

In *Remembering Louise*, for example, the story begins in a deceptively low key, carefully setting the scene and filling in the heroine's background with loving detail, with little more than a hint of underlying unease. Character, place, and small, apparently trivial, incidents dominate the early pages and absorb the attention. Even when Hesther, the narrator, becomes involved in a shockingly violent incident, it at first seems peripheral to the story. Hesther is the daughter of a jeweller and watchmaker in the small north-country town of Wickborough. She is overjoyed when her pretty sister who has lived for many years in Scotland comes home unexpectedly. But from the moment she arrives Louise, sweet, docile, and housewifely though she is, has a disrupting influence. Without lifting a finger, or her eyes, she manages, apparently unwittingly, to destroy not only Hesther's present contentment, but her lovingly planned future too. However, Hesther continues to love her, and as her world crumbles around her she worries about the mysterious stranger in black whose life she might have saved, but didn't.

Gilbert returns again and again (notably in *Flowers for Lilian*) to this theme of a relationship in which one person, usually a woman, remorselessly dominates and takes advantage of another in order to get her own way. The plots differ and the stories are far from repetitious, but Gilbert's pre-occupation with the subject is a continuing thread throughout her work.

Her understanding of the period about which she writes, and the countryside in which her stories are set, the northeast of England, are inherent in everything she writes. She brings the landscape of life graphically and memorably. Her insight into rural life in that part of the world in the 19th century is in some measure explained by her deep interest in the literature, history, diaries, memoirs, letters, and biographies of the time, which results in minute, almost "eyewitness" descriptions of everyday dress and household objects, as well as the daily routine of those who lived in small, often remote, communities in those days. The vividness with which Gilbert conveys their lives and surroundings draws the reader inexorably into the atmosphere of her novels.

—Elizabeth Grey

GILES, Janice Holt. American. Born in Altus, Arkansas, 28 March 1909. Educated at the University of Arkansas, Fayetteville; Transylvania University, Lexington, Kentucky. Married 1) Otto Moore in 1927 (divorced 1939), one daughter; 2) Henry Giles in 1945. Assistant to the Dean, Presbyterian Seminary,

Louisville, 1941–50; director of religious education, Pulaski Heights Community Church, and director of children's work for Arkansas Board of Missions, both Little Rock. *Died 1 June 1979.*

ROMANCE AND HISTORICAL PUBLICATIONS

Novels

The Enduring Hills. Philadelphia, Westminster Press, 1950.
Miss Willie. Philadelphia, Westminster Press, 1951.
Tara's Healing. Philadelphia, Westminster Press, 1951.
Harbin's Ridge, with Henry Giles. Boston, Houghton Mifflin, 1951.
40 Acres and No Mule. Philadelphia, Westminster Press, 1952.
The Kentuckians. Boston, Houghton Mifflin, 1953.
The Plum Thicket. Boston, Houghton Mifflin, 1954.
Hannah Fowler. Boston, Houghton Mifflin, 1956.
The Believers. Boston, Houghton Mifflin, 1957.
The Land Beyond the Mountains. Boston, Houghton Mifflin, 1958.
Johnny Osage. Boston, Houghton Mifflin, 1960.
Savanna. Boston, Houghton Mifflin, 1961.
Voyage to Santa Fe. Boston, Houghton Mifflin, 1962.
Find Me a River. Boston, Houghton Mifflin, 1964.
Time of Glory. Boston, Houghton Mifflin, 1966.
Special Breed. Boston, Houghton Mifflin, 1966.
The Great Adventure. Boston, Houghton Mifflin, 1966.
Shady Grove. Boston, Houghton Mifflin, 1968.
Six-Horse Hitch. Boston, Houghton Mifflin, 1969.

Short Stories

Wellspring. Boston, Houghton Mifflin, 1975.

OTHER PUBLICATIONS

Other

A Little Better Than Plumb: The Biography of a House, with Henry Giles. Boston, Houghton Mifflin, 1963.
The Damned Engineers. Boston, Houghton Mifflin, 1970.
Around Our House, with Henry Giles. Boston, Houghton Mifflin, 1971.
The Kinta Years (autobiography). Boston, Houghton Mifflin, 1973.

Editor, *The G.I. Journal of Sergeant Giles*, by Henry Giles. Boston, Houghton Mifflin, 1965.

*   *   *

It is impossible to think of Janice Holt Giles's work without envisioning her own particular part of the world. A regional writer in the best sense, her novels project the spirit of the pioneers who first tamed the rugged forest country of Kentucky and the westward wilderness. Her best tales unfold the continuing saga of a pioneering family, the Fowlers, through several generations, beginning with her most truly memorable fictional heroine, Hannah Fowler. Hannah is a true child of the new world. Born and raised among the hills by a restlessly wandering father, she dimly remembers a town-bred mother who tried out but could not learn to love the new life Hannah needs if she is to thrive. Where her mother pined for company of her own kind,

Hannah shies from it like any forest creature; her ideal home is a cabin in a clearing, out of sight of the nearest neighbour folk, for she holds with the old frontier saying that "If you can see their smoke, they're too close." Alone in the world after her father's death, which is as hard and lonely as the life he has chosen to lead, Hannah is forced to marry, against her independent inclinations. Women are scarce and sought-after, here at the back of the beyond, and men need strong and capable wives who will give them the children the country life requires. Hannah can have her pick of the single men of the fort, for all come courting in the abrupt and unromantic fashion of the time and place—but Hannah has chosen her own mate, Tice, and the matter is soon settled.

In Giles's hands this oddly arranged marriage of convenience becomes one of the deepest and most touching, if most understated, love stories of the frontier. Two less articulate people would be hard to find, but speech is scarcely necessary to Hannah and Tice; they completely understand one another. Through the vicissitudes of a very hard life, they become steadily more devoted, and from their strength and understanding grow new generations of the Fowler family, the subjects of further adventures as the country continues to open westward.

Giles is a writer who knows her subject and her setting absolutely. The day-to-day detail of her peoples' lives is as fascinating as their encounters with marauding Indians, ferocious weather, and the incredible privations that were a part of life at the outermost edge of civilization. It is humbling for a city-bred 20th-century reader to realize the proud self-sufficiency of these people of the not-so-long-ago, who could survive in the trackless forest equipped only with a knife and a flintlock gun; make a home and raise a family, and see the accomplishment as nothing remarkable. They had an independence that their remote descendants have long since exchanged for comforts and luxuries undreamt of by Hannah. How heartily she would have despised so poor an example of horse trading: a birthright frittered away for a mess of inferior pottage.

—Joan McGrath

GILLEN, Lucy. See **STRATTON, Rebecca.**

GLADSTONE, Arthur. See **SEBASTIAN, Margaret.**

GLADSTONE, Maggie. See **SEBASTIAN, Margaret.**

GLASS, Amanda. See **KRENTZ, Jayne Ann.**

GLOVER, Judith. British. Born in Wolverhampton, West Midlands, 31 March 1943. Educated at Wolverhampton High School for Girls, 1954–59; Aston Polytechnic, Birmingham, 1960. Married 1) Anthony Rowley in 1961 (marriage annulled);

2) Stanley Martin in 1985 (died), two daughters. Journalist, Wolverhampton *Express and Star*, 1960–61; freelance features writer, 1962–74. Agent: Artellus Ltd., 30 Dorset House, Gloucester Place, London NW1 5AD. Address: 9 Barclay Close, Albrighton, near Wolverhampton, West Midlands WV7 3PX, England.

ROMANCE AND HISTORICAL PUBLICATIONS

Novels (series: Sussex Quartet)

The Sussex Quartet
The Stallion Man. London, Hodder and Stoughton, 1982; New York, St. Martin's Press, 1983.
Sisters and Brothers. London, Hodder and Stoughton, and New York, St. Martin's Press, 1984.
To Everything a Season. London, Hodder and Stoughton, 1986.
Birds in a Gilded Cage. London, Hodder and Stoughton, 1988.
The Imagination of the Heart. London, Hodder and Stoughton, 1989.

OTHER PUBLICATIONS

Other

The Place Names of Sussex. London, Batsford, 1974.
The Batsford Colour Book of Sussex. London, Batsford, 1975.
The Batsford Colour Book of Kent. London, Batsford, 1976.
Sussex in Photographs, photographs by Anthony Kersting. London, Batsford, 1976.
The Place Names of Kent. London, Batsford, 1976.
Drink Your Own Garden (on wine making). London, Batsford, 1979.

*

Judith Glover comments:
History is people—all the drama of their individual lives creates the tapestry of the past. By writing historical romantic fiction, it is ever my intention to recreate the colours of that tapestry, weaving stories which come vividly alive through the everyday events of Victorian and Edwardian England, in the lives of those men and women who are my characters.

*   *   *

Although each of Judith Glover's four historical romances can be read independently, they form a continuing saga of the intertwined lives of several families in Sussex. The series spans the time from the 1850's, when Frank Morgan in *The Stallion Man*, indiscriminately sires children during his travels through the countryside, to 1912, when Europe is poised on the brink of war.

For the most part Frank Morgan's sexual liaisons are as casual as those of his stallion, which he mates with mares for a living. His pursuit of women, married and unmarried, reveals his arrogance and his lack of morality. *The Stallion Man* centers on his attempts to seduce Rachel Bates, the wife of a curate unable to consummate his marriage because of psychological problems. Esmond Bates had been denied a normal childhood because of the rigid fundamentalism of his father, who delighted in flogging his servants, pupils, wife, and son for any impropriety.

Mistakenly convinced that Rachel has welcomed Frank's advances, Esmond attacks Morgan in a fight that results in both men's deaths under the hoofs of Morgan's stallion. Released from her husband's insane domination, Rachel eventually marries widower George Bashford, a well-to-do farmer.

Morgan's descendants populate the pages of the three sequels. Two of his children, Frank and Isabelle Flynn, are one of the pairs of *Sisters and Brothers* in the first. Like his father, Frank lets his violence and sexual appetites cause his downfall. Although he marries wealthy Rosannah Weldrake after she tricks him into fathering a child, he continues an affair with Lizzie Newbrook despite the fact that Lizzie is already married. Tom Newbrook's attempt to defend his honor ends in his death at Frank's hands. The murder trial brings even more horror when Frank and Lizzie learn that they are both children of Frank Morgan.

Isabelle's involvement with unscrupulous Harry Weldrake ends in her imprisonment in a brothel, from which she is rescued by Alec Bethway, a parson who eventually marries her. Their children continue the family tradition of unhappy love affairs. For example, daughter Dinah loses her husband of a few months when he dies in the Boer War in *To Everything a Season* and is duped into marrying a bigamist before recognizing the steadfast love of Stephen Moore (*Birds in a Gilded Cage*). Francis Bethway inherits his grandfather's penchant for promiscuity, eventually adopting the name Frank Morgan as he and his mistress undertake a doomed voyage to the United States on the *Titanic*.

The first two books of the series contain a good deal of violence, including harsh sexual relationships. Esmond finally consummates his marriage to Rachel only when his enraged jealousy drives him to rape her. Rosannah Weldrake is attracted to Frank Flynn because of his violent nature. She tells her brother, " 'I need the kind of man who'll abuse me, hurt me, exact my submission by violence . . . oh, how I love it when he mistreats me.' " Their mother had been beaten to death in a sado-masochistic encounter. Although Glover's later characters remain duplicitous in their sexual relationships, the violence in her books decreases.

For the most part, the women in Glover's books have little control over their own lives. An independent income provides some leverage, as Adelaide Winter discovers when she successfully uses threats of withdrawing her family's support if her errant husband Harry Weldrake continues to gamble in *Sisters and Brothers*. But Dinah Garland finds no legal remedy to stop her gambler husband Warwick Enderby from depleting her resources in *Birds in a Gilded Cage*.

Again and again characters are misled by displays of wealth and respectability. In *To Everything a Season* Ellis Bates hides behind his respectable position as inspector of schools to shield his involvement with a married woman. Even though some truly honorable men and women inhabit Glover's society, for the most part she casts the motives and actions of her characters in a negative light.

—Kathy Piehl

GLUYAS, Constance. Born in England, in 1920. Served in the British Women's Auxiliary Air Force during World War II. Married Donald Gluyas in 1944. Lives in California. Address: c/o Robert Hale Ltd., 45–47 Clerkenwell Green, London EC1R 0HT, England.

ROMANCE AND HISTORICAL PUBLICATIONS

Novels

The King's Brat. Englewood Cliffs, New Jersey, Prentice Hall, 1972; London, Hale, 1974.
Born to Be King. Englewood Cliffs, New Jersey, Prentice Hall, 1974; London, Hale, 1976.
My Lady Benbrook. Englewood Cliffs, New Jersey, Prentice Hall, 1975.
Brief Is the Glory. New York, McKay, 1975.
The House on Twyford Street. New York, McKay, 1976; London, Magnum, 1978.
My Lord Foxe. New York, McKay, 1976; London, Magnum, 1980.
Savage Eden. New York, New American Library, 1976; London, Sphere, 1978.
Rogue's Mistress. New York, New American Library, 1977; London, Sphere, 1978.
Woman of Fury. New York, New American Library, 1978; London, Hale, 1980.
Flame of the South. New York, New American Library, 1979; London, Sphere, 1981.
Madame Tudor. New York, New American Library, 1979.
Lord Sin. New York, New American Library, 1980; London, Sphere, 1985.
The Passionate Savage. New York, New American Library, 1980; London, Sphere, 1982.
The Bridge to Yesterday. New York, New American Library, 1981; London, Sphere, 1983.
Brandy Kane. London, Hale, 1985.

*   *   *

Constance Gluyas depicts a universe of romantic violence. Her novels have historical settings, and are notable for the turbulent passions of their heroines and the torture and humiliation to which they are subjected. Whether struggling for a crust in the gutters of Restoration London, or slaving on a tobacco plantation, Gluyas's ladies undergo brutal punishment, and display a breath-taking sexual vigour. Strong in endurance, they challenge all that a cruel world flings at them. It follows that the man of their choice must be even stronger and more masterful.

The King's Brat is typical, its urchin heroine imprisoned in Newgate for theft. Freed by Charles II, the intrepid Angel quickly works her way into society. Sought after by the King, she herself chooses the artist Nicholas Tavington. Though the course of their love is marred, they survive the horrors of the Great Plague to find wedded bliss. *The King's Brat* is a touch long-winded (verbosity is a familiar Gluyas failing), but the story is lively and the action full-blooded, the author dwelling equally on the delights of love and the squalor of poverty and prison in the 1660's.

Born to Be King is set during the 1745 Jacobite rebellion, with Elizabeth Drummond disguising herself as a man to join the rebels. The novel centres on her love-affair with the Englishman Moncrieff, who intends to betray the Prince but is later won over to his cause. The fortunes of the Jacobites are followed to Culloden, and final exile. Faster-moving than *The King's Brat, Born to Be King*, contains the usual ingredients—wilful heroine, dark satanic hero, and their fierce love-hate relationship—that recur constantly in Gluyas's work.

Woman of Fury, with its witch-finder villain, is closer to fantasy than most. The perverted lustful Matthew Lorne, who covets his adopted daughter and kills wife and son with casual brutality, is so incredibly evil he teeters on the edge of absurdity.

Some of the coincidences, too, are scarcely to be believed. But Gluyas's creations do not inhabit the real world. Theirs is the fevered kingdom of the imagination, where subtleties of character and plot give way to the garish visions of nightmare and dream. This accepted, the fast and furious action helps to suspend disbelief.

Among the most famous Gluyas novels are *Savage Eden* and *Rogue's Mistress*, with their central characters of Justin "Rogue" Lawrence and Caroline Fane. The works follow Lawrence and Caroline in their adventures as robbers in England, and later as convict settlers in the United States. The ferocity of love and hate is continually present. Like other Gluyas heroes and heroines, Justin and Caroline quarrel frequently, and their very lovemaking partakes of violence. *Flame of the South* deals with similar leading characters who combine passion with their efforts to free black slaves from the Southern plantations. The action is swift and savage as ever, the appetites as unquenchable.

Gluyas's creations, with their fiery heroines and formidable heroes, are of a world other than our own. Though a far from satisfactory stylist—sometimes prolix, at other times cramming the action into too short a compass—her writing drives home the one unvarying theme: the clash of strong woman with stronger man, and their physical union. The battle of the sexes becomes tedious, but on its own gothic grounds it remains valid. Gluyas writes with animal vigour, and shows herself fully aware of the beast beneath the skin.

—Geoffrey Sadler

GLYN, Elinor (née Sutherland). British. Born in Jersey, Channel Islands, 17 October 1864, of Canadian parents; grew up in Ontario and Jersey. Educated privately. Married Clayton Glyn in 1892 (died 1915); two daughters. Canteen worker and war correspondent during World War I. Lived in the U.S., 1920–29: film producer, writer, and director. *Died 23 September 1943.*

ROMANCE AND HISTORICAL PUBLICATIONS

Novels (series: Elizabeth)

The Visits of Elizabeth. London, Duckworth, 1900; New York, Lane, 1901.
The Reflections of Ambrosine. London, Duckworth, and New York, Harper, 1902; as *The Seventh Commandment*, New York, Macaulay, n.d.
The Damsel and the Sage. London, Duckworth, and New York, Harper, 1903.
The Vicissitudes of Evangeline. London, Duckworth, and New York, Harper, 1905; as *Red Hair*, New York, Macaulay, n.d.
Beyond the Rocks. London, Duckworth, and New York, Harper, 1906.
Three Weeks. London, Duckworth, and New York, Business Press, 1907.
Elizabeth Visits America. London, Duckworth, and New York, Duffield, 1909.
His Hour. London, Duckworth, and New York, Appleton, 1910; as *When His Hour Came*, London, Newnes, 1915.
The Reason Why. London, Duckworth, and New York, Appleton, 1911.

Halcyone. London, Duckworth, and New York, Appleton, 1912; as *Love Itself*, Auburn, New York, Author's Press, 1924 (?).
The Sequence 1905–1912. London, Duckworth, 1913; as *Guinevere's Lover*, New York, Appleton, 1913.
The Man and the Moment. New York, Appleton, 1914; London, Duckworth, 1915.
The Career of Katherine Bush. New York, Appleton, 1916; London, Duckworth, 1917.
The Price of Things. London, Duckworth, 1919; as *Family*, New York, Appleton, 1919.
Man and Maid—Renaissance. London, Duckworth, 1922; as *Man and Maid*, Philadelphia, Lippincott, 1922.
The Great Moment. London, Duckworth, and Philadelphia, Lippincott, 1923.
Six Days. London, Duckworth, and Philadelphia, Lippincott, 1924.
This Passion Called Love. London, Duckworth, and Auburn, New York, Author's Press, 1925.
Love's Blindness. London, Duckworth, and Auburn, New York, Author's Press, 1926.
The Flirt and the Flapper. London, Duckworth, 1930.
Love's Hour. London, Duckworth, and New York, Macaulay, 1932.
Glorious Flames (novelization of screenplay). London, Benn, 1932; New York, Macaulay, 1933.
Sooner or Later. London, Rich and Cowan, 1933; New York, Macaulay, 1935.
Did She? London, Rich and Cowan, 1934.
The Third Eye. London, Long, 1940.

Short Stories

The Contract and Other Stories. London, Duckworth, 1913; *The Point of View* published separately, New York, Appleton, 1913.
It and Other Stories. London, Duckworth, and New York, Macaulay, 1927.
Saint or Satyr? and Other Stories. London, Duckworth, 1933; as *Such Men Are Dangerous*, New York, Macaulay, 1933.

OTHER PUBLICATIONS

Plays

Three Weeks, adaptation of her own novel (produced London, 1908).

Screenplays: *The Great Moment*, with Monte M. Katterjohn, 1921; *The World's a Stage*, with Colin Campbell and George Bertholon, 1922; *His Hour*, with King Vidor and Maude Fulton, 1924; *Three Weeks (The Romance of a Queen)*, with Carey Wilson, 1924; *How to Educate a Wife*, with Douglas Z. Doty and Grant Carpenter, 1924; *Man and Maid*, 1925; *The Only Thing*, 1925; *Love's Blindness*, 1926; *Ritzy*, with others, 1927; *It*, with others, 1927; *Three Week-Ends*, with others, 1928; *The Man and the Moment*, with Agnes Christine Johnston and Paul Perez, 1929; *Such Men Are Dangerous*, with Ernst Vajda, 1930; *Knowing Men*, with Edward Knoblock, 1930.

Other

The Sayings of Grandmama and Others. London, Duckworth, and New York, Duffield, 1908.

Letters to Caroline. London, Duckworth, 1914; as *Your Affectionate Godmother*, New York, Appleton, 1914.
Three Things. London, Duckworth, and New York, Hearst, 1915.
Destruction. London, Duckworth, 1918.
Points of View. London, Duckworth, 1920.
The Philosophy of Love. London, Duckworth, 1920.
The Elinor Glyn System of Writing. Auburn, New York, Author's Press, 4 vols., 1922.
The Philosophy of Love (different from 1920 book). Auburn, New York, Author's Press, 1923; as *Love—What I Think of It*, London, Readers Library, 1928.
Letters from Spain. London, Duckworth, 1924.
The Wrinkle Book; or, How to Keep Looking Young. London, Duckworth, 1927; as *Eternal Youth*, New York, Macmillan, 1928.
Romantic Adventure (autobiography). London, Nicholson and Watson, 1936; New York, Dutton, 1937.
Keep Young and Beautiful (selections), with Barbara Cartland. London, Duckworth, 1982.

*

Critical Studies: *Elinor Glyn: A Biography* by Anthony Glyn, London, Hutchinson, 1955, revised edition, 1968; *The "It" Girls: Lucy, Lady Duff Gordon, the Couturière "Lucile" and Elinor Glyn, Romantic Novelist* by Meredith Etherington-Smith and Jeremy Pilcher, London, Hamish Hamilton, 1986, New York, Harcourt Brace, 1987.

Theatrical Activities:
Director: **Films**—*Knowing Men*, 1930; *The Price of Things*, 1930.
Actress: **Play**—The Queen in *Three Weeks*, London, 1908.

*   *   *

Elinor Glyn always felt that writing should stress feeling rather than ideas. Perhaps this explains why, when she addressed the 1931 International P.E.N. Congress as a best-selling author of 30 years' standing, she described herself as "A society person of no particular brains or talents." She added, "I can't think why my books sell and make so much money." Glyn's loyal readers found both intelligence and appeal in her romances, and the fantasy world of rank, beauty, breeding, passion, and heroic self-restraint these works created.

Glyn's first novel, *The Visits of Elizabeth*, is a naughty epistolary romance featuring a pert, charming ingenue narrator who observes the eccentricities and extra-martial adventures of French and English nobility at a series of house-parties she attends. The novel created a great stir among Glyn's society acquaintances, on whom it was based. The tone, form, and malicious good humor appeared in two other novels, *Elizabeth Visits America*, and "Elizabeth's Daughter." The three Elizabeth novels all reflect Glyn's views, travels, and preoccupation with good breeding and physical beauty.

A second romance formula appears in a series of novels based on mismatches, marriages between sensitive, beautiful aristocrats and unfeeling, unmannered newly rich. *The Reflections of Ambrosine, The Vicissitudes of Evangeline*, and *Beyond the Rocks* are representative. The titled half of the pair finds a true soulmate in a handsome and titled suitor. However, sorely tempted by adulterous passion, the heroines of these tales resist until their moneyed louts die and they are free to marry again. These novels reflect a mistrust of money and a snobbish insistence on rank difficult for the modern reader to accept.

Glyn's greatest success, the one work which best displays her style, her characters, and her favorite themes of elegant snobbery and spiritual/sexual attraction is *Three Weeks*—a purple prose hymn to aristocratic soul passion. Roughly inspired by the assassination of Queen Draga of Serbia, *Three Weeks* describes the spiritual and sensual awakening of a handsome young English nobel, Paul, by an unnamed, dark, wilful Slavic beauty of nobel rank—the Lady. After their meeting in Switzerland, Paul presents the Lady with a gift that he feels reflects her untamed and splendid spirit: a tigerskin. When he next calls on the Lady, he sees:

a bright fire burnt in the grate, and some palest mauve curtains were drawn. . . . And loveliest sight of all, in front of the fire, stretched at full length, was his tiger—and on him—also at full length—reclined his lady, garbed in some strange clinging garment of heavy purple crepe, one white arm resting on the beast's head, her back supported by a pile of velvet cusions and a heap of rarely bound books at her side, while between her lips was a rose not redder than they—an almost scarlet rose.

The relationship between Paul and the Lady soon blossoms into a short but intense affair that takes them to Venice, where they part, never to meet again. The Lady, however, has conceived a son who will some day inherit the throne of Russia.

Despite its heady mixture of eroticism and exoticism, *Three Weeks* remains remarkably moral in tone. The adulterous love of Paul and the Lady is based on a mutually lofty recognition of beauty and nobility; their physical union represents a small portion of their spiritual experience. Denied each other by fate, the lovers are punished for their adultery by the Lady's brutal murder at the hands of her degenerate husband. Critical response to *Three Weeks* was favorable but guarded; popular response was spectacular. Glyn became a household word and all of her works best-sellers. Moral objection was voiced largely in America, where the novel was banned in several states. However, readers on both sides of the Atlantic were drawn by the image of passion blazing beyond sexuality in *Three Weeks*; "It," sexuality and attraction, was delineated, but never so vividly, in Glyn's later films and fiction.

Glyn's travels in the United States and her work in the developing American film industry modified her rigid early views on noble blood and gentle breeding. Her later works, notably *The Career of Katherine Bush*, show that independent, handsome, disciplined men and women can train themselves for social standing. This theme demonstrates that character can triumph over circumstances to allow a hero or heroine to find ennobling love.

The shortcomings of Glyn's 25 romances—the defense of snobbery, the equation of character with physical beauty, the remarkable combination of bourgeois prudishness and aristocratic passion—are the very elements that made her romances so appealing to her readers. Glyn herself described romance as "spiritual disguise created by the imagination with which to envelop material happenings with desires and thus bring them into greater harmony with the soul." Glyn's novels created a romance world which her readers could otherwise never know. With her and through her work, generations of readers lived this fantasy of romance.

—Katherine Staples

GODDEN, (Margaret) Rumer. British. Born in Sussex, 10 December 1907. Educated privately and at Moira House, Eastbourne, Sussex. Married 1) Laurence Sinclair Foster in 1934 (died), two daughters; 2) James Lesley Haynes Dixon in 1949 (died 1973). Director of a children's ballet school, Calcutta, 1930's. Recipient: Whitbread award, for children's book, 1973. Agent: Curtis Brown, 162–168 Regent Street, London W1R 5TA, England; or, 10 Astor Place, New York, New York 10003, U.S.A. Address: Ardnacloich, Moniaive, Thornhill, Dumfries and Galloway DG3 4HZ, Scotland.

ROMANCE AND HISTORICAL PUBLICATIONS

Novels

Chinese Puzzle. London, Davies, 1936.
The Lady and the Unicorn. London, Davies, 1937.
Black Narcissus. London, Davies, and Boston, Little Brown, 1939.
Gypsy, Gypsy. London, Davies, and Boston, Little Brown, 1940.
Breakfast with the Nikolides. London, Davies, and Boston, Little Brown, 1942.
A Fugue in Time. London, Joseph, 1945; as *Take Three Tenses: A Fugue in Time*, Boston, Little Brown, 1945.
The River. London, Joseph, and Boston, Little Brown, 1946.
A Candle for St. Jude. London, Joseph, and New York, Viking Press, 1948.
A Breath of Air. London, Joseph, 1950; New York, Viking Press, 1951.
Kingfishers Catch Fire. London, Macmillan, and New York, Viking Press, 1953.
An Episode of Sparrows. New York, Viking Press, 1955; London, Macmillan, 1956.
The Greengage Summer. London, Macmillan, and New York, Viking Press, 1958.
China Court: The Hours of a Country House. London, Macmillan, and New York, Viking Press, 1961.
The Battle of the Villa Fiorita. London, Macmillan, and New York, Viking Press, 1963.
In This House of Brede. London, Macmillan, and New York, Viking Press, 1969.
The Peacock Spring. London, Macmillan, 1975; New York, Viking Press, 1976.
Five for Sorrow, Ten for Joy. London, Macmillan, and New York, Viking Press, 1979.
The Dark Horse. London, Macmillan, 1981; New York, Viking Press, 1982.
Thursday's Children. London, Macmillan, and New York, Viking, 1984.

Short Stories

Mooltiki and Other Stories and Poems of India. London, Macmillan, and New York, Viking Press, 1957.
Swans and Turtles: Stories. London, Macmillan, 1968; as *Gone: A Thread of Stories*, New York, Viking Press, 1968.

OTHER PUBLICATIONS

Fiction (for children)

The Doll's House. London, Joseph, 1947; New York, Viking Press, 1948; as *Tottie*, London, Penguin, 1983.

The Mousewife. London, Macmillan, and New York, Viking Press, 1951.
Four Dolls. London, Macmillan, 1983; New York, Greenwillow, 1984.
Impunity Jane: The Story of a Pocket Doll. New York, Viking Press, 1954; London, Macmillan, 1955.
The Fairy Doll. London, Macmillan, and New York, Viking Press, 1956.
The Story of Holly and Ivy. London, Macmillan, and New York, Viking Press, 1958.
Candy Floss. London, Macmillan, and New York, Viking Press, 1960.
Mouse House. New York, Viking Press, 1957; London, Macmillan, 1958.
Miss Happiness and Miss Flower. London, Macmillan, and New York, Viking Press, 1961.
Little Plum. London, Macmillan, and New York, Viking Press, 1963.
Home Is the Sailor. London, Macmillan, and New York, Viking Press, 1964.
The Kitchen Madonna. London, Macmillan, and New York, Viking Press, 1967.
Operation Sippacik. London, Macmillan, and New York, Viking Press, 1969.
The Old Woman Who Lived in a Vinegar Bottle. London, Macmillan, and New York, Viking Press, 1972.
The Diddakoi. London, Macmillan, and New York, Viking Press, 1972.
Mr. McFadden's Hallowe'en. London, Macmillan, and New York, Viking Press, 1975.
The Rocking Horse Secret. London, Macmillan, 1977; New York, Viking Press, 1978.
A Kindle of Kittens. London, Macmillan, 1978; New York, Viking Press, 1979.
The Dragon of Og. London, Macmillan, and New York, Viking Press, 1981.
The Valiant Chatti-Maker. London, Macmillan, and New York, Viking Press, 1983.
Fu-Dog. London, MacRae, 1989.

Plays

Screenplays: *The River*, with Jean Renoir, 1951; *Innocent Sinners*, with Neil Patterson, 1958.

Verse (for children)

In Noah's Ark. London, Joseph, and New York, Viking Press, 1949.
St. Jerome and the Lion. London, Macmillan, and New York, Viking Press, 1961.

Other

Rungli-Rungliot (Thus Far and No Further). London, Davies, 1943; as *Rungli-Rungliot Means in Paharia, Thus Far and No Further*, Boston, Little Brown, 1946; as *Thus Far and No Further*, London, Macmillan, 1961.
Bengal Journey: A Story of the Part Played by Women in the Province 1939–1945. London, Longman, 1945.
Hans Christian Andersen: A Great Life in Brief. London, Hutchinson, and New York, Knopf, 1955.
Two Under the Indian Sun (autobiography), with Jon Godden. London, Macmillan, and New York, Knopf, 1966.
The Tale of Tales: The Beatrix Potter Ballet. London, Warne, 1971.

Shiva's Pigeons: An Experience of India, with Jon Godden. London, Chatto and Windus, and New York, Viking Press, 1972.

The Butterfly Lions: The Story of the Pekingese in History, Legend, and Art. London, Macmillan, 1977; New York, Viking Press, 1978.

Gulbadan: Portrait of a Rose Princess at the Mughal Court. London, Macmillan, 1980; New York, Viking Press, 1981.

A Time to Dance, No Time to Weep (autobiography). London, Macmillan, and New York, Morrow, 1987.

A House With Four Rooms (autobiography). London, Macmillan, 1989.

Editor, *Round the Day, Round the Year, The World Around: Poetry Programmes for Classroom or Library.* London, Macmillan, 6 vols., 1966–67.

Editor, *A Letter to the World: Poems for Young Readers*, by Emily Dickinson. London, Bodley Head, 1968; New York, Macmillan, 1969.

Editor, *Mrs. Manders' Cookbook*, by Olga Manders. London, Macmillan, and New York, Viking Press, 1968.

Editor, *The Raphael Bible.* London, Macmillan, and New York, Viking Press, 1970.

Translator, *Prayers from the Ark* (verse), by Carmen de Gasztold. New York, Viking Press, 1962; London, Macmillan, 1963.

Translator, *The Creatures' Choir* (verse), by Carmen de Gasztold. New York, Viking Press, 1965; as *The Beasts' Choir*, London, Macmillan, 1967.

*

Manuscript Collection: Mugar Memorial Library, Boston University.

Critical Study: *Rumer Godden* by Hassell A. Simpson, New York, Twayne, 1973.

*   *   *

Although many of Rumer Godden's novels might fit into the broad category of romance, they rarely concentrate on an individual's solitary search for love and happiness. Instead, her characters always exist as part of larger entities from which they cannot escape.

First, a person is part of his culture. This fact is most clear in the novels set in India. Europeans can never change or become part of the Indian world. The nuns in *Black Narcissus* discover this in the Himalayas. Instead of changing the local people by bringing them modern education and medicine, the sisters' own discipline breaks down as rules are bent to accommodate the foreign life. After one sister goes mad, the nuns are forced to leave, realizing that their stay will have made no impact and will be quickly forgotten. Just as the Indians will not change to conform to European ways, neither can an English person become an Indian. Despite Sophie Ward's desire to live like the peasants in Kashmir in *Kingfishers Catch Fire*, she cannot understand village ways. Her blindness to local customs puts her children in danger. After her daughter is badly beaten, Sophie must leave.

Secondly, people are bound by their religion. The submission of the individual to religion is most apparent in *Black Narcissus*, *In This House of Brede*, and *Five for Sorrow, Ten for Joy*, which concern women in religious communities. But the presence of the Divine is felt in other works as well. For example, in *A Candle for St. Jude* Miss Ilse is convinced that disaster at her sister-in-law's ballet school is averted because of her prayers to St. Jude, patron of impossible causes.

Above all, an individual is part of a family. As young Harriet discovers in *The River*, within a family one learns fundamental lessons about life, love, birth, and death during the passage from childhood to adulthood. Fanny Clavering (*The Battle of the Villa Fiorita*) discovers that family ties cannot be broken. When she runs away to Italy with her lover, her children follow, and a saddened and subdued Fanny returns with them to England. The continuity of family is most apparent in *A Fugue in Time* and *China Court*, both of which are set in houses that have been part of a family for generations. In *China Court* Mrs. Quin wills the estate to her granddaughter on the condition that she marry a man she has never met but whom Mrs. Quin admires because he has restored her farm. This arranged marriage is the antithesis of the modern idea of romance, but Peter and Tracy agree. These two books employ one of Godden's most successful devices, the parallel inclusion of past, present, and future time. Layers on layers of family sayings fill *China Court*, and their meanings become clear only as the history of the house is revealed.

The juxtaposition of past, present, and future events enriches some of her best books, *In This House of Brede* and *Five for Sorrow, Ten for Joy*. Godden maintains reader interest in details of the nuns' present life, and the characters gradually assume more depth as their former lives are revealed through flashbacks.

Godden's fine handling of time shifts is one of the techniques that enrich her writing. Another is her evocation of place. Her descriptive skill is especially apparent in her Indian novels, notably *The River*.

Although her books do not demand rereading or in-depth study to be understood, they reveal Godden's careful attention to the craft of writing. As Virgilia Peterson said, "If it can be objected that Miss Godden's reach never exceeds her grasp, it can also be argued that perfection, on any scale, does not need to be justified."

—Kathy Piehl

GOLDING, (Sir) William (Gerald). British. Born in St. Columb Minor, Cornwall, 19 September 1911. Educated at Marlborough Grammar School; Brasenose College, Oxford, B.A. 1935. Served in the Royal Navy, 1940–45. Married Ann Brookfield in 1939; one son and one daughter. Writer, actor, and producer in small theatre companies, 1934–40; schoolmaster, Bishop Wordsworth's School, Salisbury, Wiltshire, 1945–61; Visiting Professor, Hollins College, Virginia, 1961–62. Recipient: James Tait Black Memorial prize, 1980; Booker prize, 1980; Nobel Prize for Literature, 1983. M.A.: Oxford University, 1961; D.Litt.: University of Sussex, Brighton, 1970; University of Kent, Canterbury, 1974; University of Warwick, Coventry, 1981; the Sorbonne, Paris, 1983; Oxford University, 1983; LL.D.: University of Bristol, 1984. Honorary Fellow, Brasenose College, 1966. Fellow, 1955, and Companion of Literature, 1984, Royal Society of Literature. C.B.E. (Commander, Order of the British Empire), 1966. Knighted, 1988. Address: c/o Faber and Faber Ltd., 3 Queen Square, London WC1N 3AU, England.

ROMANCE AND HISTORICAL PUBLICATIONS

Novels (series: Sea trilogy)

The Inheritors. London, Faber, 1955; New York, Coward Mc-
Cann, 1956.
The Spire. London, Faber, and New York, Harcourt Brace,
1964.
Rites of Passage (Sea). London, Faber, and New York, Farrar
Straus, 1980.
Close Quarters (Sea). London, Faber, and New York, Farrar
Straus, 1987.
Fire Down Below (Sea). London, Faber, and New York, Farrar
Straus, 1989.

Short Stories

The Scorpion God. London, Faber, 1971; New York, Harcourt
Brace, 1972.

OTHER PUBLICATIONS

Novels

Lord of the Flies. London, Faber, 1954; New York, Coward,
McCann, 1955.
Pincher Martin. London, Faber, 1956; as The Two Deaths of
Christopher Martin, New York, Harcourt Brace, 1957.
Free Fall. London, Faber, 1959; New York, Harcourt Brace,
1960.
The Pyramid. London, Faber, and New York, Harcourt Brace,
1967.
Darkness Visible. London, Faber, and New York, Farrar Straus,
1979.
The Paper Men. London, Faber, and New York, Farrar Straus,
1984.

Plays

The Brass Butterfly, adaptation of his story "Envoy Extraordinary" (produced London, 1958; New York, 1970). London,
Faber, 1958; Chicago, Dramatic Publishing Company, n.d.

Radio Plays: Miss Pulkinhorn, 1960; Break My Heart, 1962.

Verse

Poems. London, Macmillan, 1934; New York, Macmillan,
1935.

Other

The Hot Gates and Other Occasional Pieces. London, Faber,
1965; New York, Harcourt Brace, 1966.
Talk: Conversations with William Golding, with Jack I. Biles.
New York, Harcourt Brace, 1970.
A Moving Target (essays). London, Faber, and New York,
Farrar Straus, 1982.
An Egyptian Journal. London, Faber, 1985.

*

Critical Studies: (selection): William Golding by Samuel Hynes,
New York, Columbia University Press, 1964; William Golding:
A Critical Study by James R. Baker, New York, St. Martin's
Press, 1965, and Critical Essays on William Golding edited by
Baker, Boston, Hall, 1988; The Art of William Golding by Ber-
nard S. Oldsey and Stanley Weintraub, New York, Harcourt
Brace, 1965; William Golding by Bernard F. Dick, New York,
Twayne, 1967; William Golding: A Critical Study by Mark
Kinkead-Weekes and Ian Gregor, London, Faber, 1967, New
York, Harcourt Brace, 1968, revised edition, Faber, 1984;
William Golding by Leighton Hodson, Edinburgh, Oliver and
Boyd, 1969, New York, Putnam, 1971; The Novels of William
Golding by Howard S. Babb, Columbus, Ohio State University
Press, 1970; William Golding: The Dark Fields of Discovery by
Virginia Tiger, London, Calder and Boyars, and Atlantic High-
lands, New Jersey, Humanities Press, 1974; William Golding by
Stephen Medcalf, London, Longman, 1975; William Golding:
Some Critical Considerations edited by Jack I. Biles and Robert
O. Evans, Lexington, University Press of Kentucky, 1978; Of
Earth and Darkness: The Novels of William Golding by Arnold
Johnston, Columbia, University of Missouri Press, 1980; A View
from the Spire: William Golding's Later Novels by Don Cromp-
ton, Oxford, Blackwell, 1985; William Golding: The Man and
His Books: A Tribute on His 75th Birthday edited by John Carey,
London, Faber, 1986, New York, Farrar Straus, 1987; William
Golding: A Structural Reading of His Fiction by Philip Redpath,
London, Vision Press, 1986; The Novels of William Golding by
Stephen Boyd, Brighton, Sussex, Harvester Press, and New
York, St. Martin's Press, 1988; William Golding by James Gin-
din, London, Macmillan, and New York, St. Martin's Press,
1988.

*   *   *

William Golding's fiction embraces a time-span that ranges
from the world of Neanderthal man (The Inheritors) to the
present day (The Paper Men), including three novels (Free Fall,
The Pyramid, and The Darkness Visible) which are specifically
concerned with the periods immediately before and after World
War II. But whatever the period in which they are set, all his
novels are explorations of certain basic Christian themes, in particular the Fall of Man, the vain quest to recover lost innocence,
and the possibilities of supernatural redemption; allied to these
is a repeated insistence on the limitations of human knowledge,
which expresses itself in a literary technique designed to keep
the reader guessing. The novels are, to a greater or lesser extent,
puzzles that seem to call for a solution; but in each case the
puzzle turns out to be a mystery in which the "solution" only
serves to open up new perspectives upon the experiences described. The author is not concerned simply with the world of
time and, either in their wholes or in their parts, his novels contain moments which enshrine a vision of an eternal, transcendent
order of being.

To this extent, therefore, it is misleading to label any of Golding's fiction "historical" as the term is generally understood.
Even in those novels set in verifiable past times (The Spire,
Rites of Passage, Close Quarters, Fire Down Below) it is not
historical accuracy as such which is the author's main concern.
Nevertheless, these four novels do exhibit an intuitive understanding of past ways of life. Rites of Passage, Close Quarters,
and Fire Down Below constitute Golding's Sea trilogy; the
former, however, a work of great humanity and verve, exists as a
satisfying entity on its own. The Sea trilogy, an account of a
voyage to the Antipodes in an early 19th century sailing vessel,
is heavily laced with contemporary nautical terms and is transmitted through the journal of an ambitious, self-sufficient young
man of the period, whose thought processes and instinctive responses are convincingly of their time. The inner, hidden significance of the story, however, is conveyed to the reader in a

characteristically indirect and elliptical manner, and is not an intrinsic aspect of the period the books describe.

In *The Spire* subject matter, theme, and style are more closely approximated. The novel is a thinly disguised account of the building of the 14th-century spire of Salisbury Cathedral, at 404 feet the highest in England. The action is seen through the eyes of Jocelyn, Dean of the cathedral and originator of the spire, whose dreams and ambitions are bound up with its construction. As in all Golding's work, one has to be alert for clues as to what is actually going on, and to interpret the inner meaning of events: Jocelyn's own point of view is in question and not necessarily to be trusted. But the enigmatic nature of the story does not prevent the author from giving a brilliant account of the spire's construction, a gripping descriptive feat that shows an understanding of the mechanical problems involved and a knowledge of medieval building methods. The erection of the spire is both convincingly authentic at the material level and also symbolically appropriate, for its rise coincides with the physical and nervous breakdown of its instigator, Jocelyn, as his motives in insisting on its completion are sifted and variously assessed.

The book provides a graphic picture not only of the workings of the cathedral clergy but also of the lives and superstitious beliefs of the semi-pagan workmen who actually build the spire. The historical details are recorded unobtrusively as things which Jocelyn himself sees and takes for granted; one is not so much being shown past time by an instructive author as being imaginatively transported into it. Golding demonstrates how the supernaturalising of natural events was a characteristic process of the medieval mind, and, as in *The Inheritors*, he is thus able to comment on the assumptions of his own age from the point of view of another one. Indeed, *The Spire* is as much fable as a piece of realistic historical fiction; but this in no way detracts from its impression of historical accuracy.

In *The Inheritors* and in the novella "The Scorpion God" (a remarkable evocation of an Egyptian community 3000 years ago) Golding is relying still more on imaginative intuition; he refers engagingly to this faculty in "Digging for Pictures," an essay on his archaeological interests which he reprinted in the collection *The Hot Gates*. *The Inheritors* is certainly a *tour de force* in its presentation of the pre-rational mind, and calls for the kind of attentive reading that not everyone finds it easy to give. It is a historical novel by implication, attempting to capture the innocence of a community whose endowments and experience preclude any sense of history in a rational sense. Another tale to throw an ironic light upon notions of historical progress is the relatively light-hearted "Envoy Extraordinary." Easily the most amusing of Golding's stories, this was adapted to make his only publicly performed play, *The Brass Butterfly*. In it he portrays the premature invention of printing, steam navigation, and explosives in a Roman world unwilling to adopt them, the only thing that interests the world-weary Emperor being a pressure-cooker. The tale appears in *The Scorpion God* collection, as does "Cronk Cronk," an almost mimetic description of a prehistoric African tribe.

Golding's interest in anthropology gives a clue to the nature of his historical concerns, and in this respect he is a writer who has extended the boundaries of the historical novel and helped to incorporate it into the mainstream of 20th-century English fiction.

—Glen Cavaliero

GOODWIN, Suzanne. See **EBEL, Suzanne.**

GORDON, Diana. See **ANDREWS, Lucilla.**

GORDON, Ethel Edison. American. Born in New York City, 5 May 1915. Educated at Washington Square College, New York University, B.A. (cum laude) 1936 (Phi Beta Kappa). Married Herman Gordon in 1936; one son. Agent: John Schaffner Associates, 264 Fifth Avenue, New York, New York 10001. Address: 105 Lake Drive, Hewlett Harbor, New York 11557, U.S.A.

ROMANCE AND HISTORICAL PUBLICATIONS

Novels

Freer's Cove. New York, Coward McCann, 1972.
The Chaperone. New York, Coward McCann, 1973; London, Barker, 1974.
The Birdwatcher. New York, McKay, 1974; London, Barker, 1975.
The Freebody Heiress. New York, McKay, and London, Barker, 1974.
The French Husband. New York, Crowell, 1977.
The Venetian Lover. New York, Dell, 1982.

OTHER PUBLICATIONS

Fiction (for children)

Where Does the Summer Go. New York, Crowell, 1967.
So Far From Home. New York, Crowell, 1968.

*

Ethel Edison Gordon comments:
I have always enjoyed using an interesting foreign locale—foreign to me in America, that is—as a background for my fiction. Usually an American girl finds herself in a suspenseful situation in an environment that is different from her own. She moves from one continent to the other, to unravel the romantic but hostile predicament. This gives me a chance to re-visit the places I've enjoyed through fiction—from the Shetland Isles to the mountains of France to the lagoons of Venice.

*   *   *

In the 1970's, Ethel Edison Gordon turned to writing gothic romance after having published two novels for young people and numerous romantic short stories. All of her work has a modern and relevant theme.

In her first novel, *Where Does the Summer Go*, 15-year-old Freddie learns to accept adult imperfections and loses much of her idealism as she forges new relationships with her boyfriend and family. The book is written with perception and realism and is satisfying for young adult readers, but the next novel, *So Far From Home*, suffers from awkward time changes. Orphaned at 13, Miranda clings to an idealized past, and, at 18, recognizes that people and events probably were not as she remembers them.

Freer's Cove is Gordon's only gothic novel set entirely in the United States. Pregnant, Daisy becomes a companion to the expectant wife of Amos Freer. She snoops into family affairs and attempts to solve the mystery of the death of Ernest Freer's wife. She finds herself in grave danger after her son is born. To dip into this book is to be committed to the end.

In *The Chaperone* Carrie Belding, a teacher, accompanies a student on a trip to France and must assess the love between Maria and an American hotelier. When death threatens and then occurs, Carrie wonders if the killer is the man with whom she has reluctantly fallen in love. The story is entertaining and easy to read.

The Birdwatcher involves some missing top-secret research notes. A visit to the Shetland Isles is designed to help Lisette forget the missing papers and her dead fiancé, but it offers attempts on her life instead. She cannot understand her cousin's demented behavior or her husband's apparently callous reactions. The novel is packed with red herrings which keep the reader turning pages steadily.

The Freebody Heiress begins in New England when a young college professor rents an unused gatehouse from an overprotected and extremely shy heiress. Iris falls in love with Sexton as he teaches her independence, but she cannot trust him and flees to France where Sexton finds and marries her. Honeymooning in Switzerland, Iris's life is threatened. The twists and turns are expected, but the writing is professional and well done.

In *The French Husband* Luc has been disinherited from his family's vineyards and is obsessed with getting reinstated. Emily follows him to France and becomes involved in the family history as well as with her husband's brother. Hatred and revenge almost get her killed as Luc loses grip on reality. An obvious plot has some interesting turns, and the setting is lovely and vividly described.

Readers can relate to Gordon's writings and to her main characters because they are contemporary and real. What she began in her short stories, she expanded in her novels, often using the same themes and character types. Short stories and novels alike reveal a talented and professional writer who offers her readers well-thought-out entertainment.

—Andrea Lee Shuey

GORDON, Jane. See **LEE, Elsie.**

GOUDGE, Elizabeth (de Beauchamp). British. Born in Wells, Somerset, 24 April 1900. Educated at Grassendale School, Southbourne, Hampshire; Reading University School of Art. Teacher of design and applied art, Ely and Oxford, 1922–32. Recipient: Library Association Carnegie Medal, for children's book, 1947. Fellow, Royal Society of Literature, 1945. *Died 1 April 1984.*

ROMANCE AND HISTORICAL PUBLICATIONS

Novels

Island Magic. London, Duckworth, and New York, Coward McCann, 1934.

The Middle Window. London, Duckworth, 1935; New York, Coward McCann, 1939.
A City of Bells. London, Duckworth, and New York, Coward McCann, 1936.
Towers in the Mist. London, Duckworth, and New York, Coward McCann, 1938.
The Bird in the Tree. London, Duckworth, and New York, Coward McCann, 1940.
The Castle on the Hill. London, Duckworth, and New York, Coward McCann, 1941.
Green Dolphin Country. London, Hodder and Stoughton, 1944; as *Green Dolphin Street*, New York, Coward McCann, 1944.
The Herb of Grace. London, Hodder and Stoughton, 1948; as *Pilgrim's Inn*, New York, Coward McCann, 1948.
Gentian Hill. London, Hodder and Stoughton, and New York, Coward McCann, 1949.
The Heart of the Family. London, Hodder and Stoughton, and New York, Coward McCann, 1953.
The Rosemary Tree. London, Hodder and Stoughton, and New York, Coward McCann, 1956.
The White Witch. London, Hodder and Stoughton, and New York, Coward McCann, 1958.
The Dean's Watch. London, Hodder and Stoughton, and New York, Coward McCann, 1960.
The Scent of Water. London, Hodder and Stoughton, and New York, Coward McCann, 1963.
The Child from the Sea. London, Hodder and Stoughton, and New York, Coward McCann, 1970.

Short Stories

The Fairies' Baby and Other Stories. London, Foyle, 1919.
A Pedlar's Pack and Other Stories. London, Duckworth, and New York, Coward McCann, 1937.
The Golden Skylark and Other Stories. London, Duckworth, and New York, Coward McCann, 1941.
The Ikon on the Wall and Other Stories. London, Duckworth, 1943.
The Reward of Faith and Other Stories. London, Duckworth, 1950; New York, Coward McCann, 1951.
White Wings: Collected Short Stories. London, Duckworth, 1952.
The Lost Angel. London, Hodder and Stoughton, and New York, Coward McCann, 1971.

OTHER PUBLICATIONS

Fiction (for children)

Sister of the Angels: A Christmas Story. London, Duckworth, and New York, Coward McCann, 1939.
Smoky-House. London, Duckworth, and New York, Coward McCann, 1940.
The Well of the Star. New York, Coward McCann, 1941.
Henrietta's House. London, University of London Press-Hodder and Stoughton, 1942; as *The Blue Hills*, New York, Coward McCann, 1942.
The Little White Horse. London, University of London Press, 1946; New York, Coward McCann, 1947.
Make-Believe. London, Duckworth, 1949; Boston, Bentley, 1953.
The Valley of Song. London, University of London Press, 1951; New York, Coward McCann, 1952.
Linnets and Valerians. Leicester, Brockhampton Press, and New York, Coward McCann, 1964.

I Saw Three Ships. Leicester, Brockhampton Press, and New York, Coward McCann, 1969.

Plays

The Brontës of Haworth (produced London, 1932). Included in *Three Plays*, 1939.
Joy Will Come Back (produced London, 1937).
Suomi (produced London, 1938). Included in *Three Plays*, 1939.
Fanny Burney (produced Oldham, Lancashire, 1949). Included in *Three Plays*, 1939.
Three Plays: Suomi, The Brontës of Haworth, and Fanny Burney. London, Duckworth, 1939.

Verse

Songs and Verses. London, Duckworth, 1947; New York, Coward McCann, 1948.

Other

The Elizabeth Goudge Reader, edited by Rose Dobbs. New York, Coward McCann, 1946; as *At the Sign of the Dolphin: An Elizabeth Goudge Anthology*, London, Hodder and Stoughton, 1947.
God So Loved the World: A Life of Christ (for children). London, Hodder and Stoughton, and New York, Coward McCann, 1951.
Saint Francis of Assisi. London, Duckworth, 1959; as *My God and My All: The Life of St. Francis of Assisi*, New York, Coward McCann, 1959.
The Chapel of the Blessed Virgin Mary, Buckler's Hard, Beaulieu. Privately printed, 1966.
A Christmas Book (anthology). London, Hodder and Stoughton, and New York, Coward McCann, 1967.
The Ten Gifts (anthology), edited by Mary Baldwin. London, Hodder and Stoughton, and New York, Coward McCann, 1969.
The Joy of the Snow: An Autobiography. London, Hodder and Stoughton, and New York, Coward McCann, 1974.
Pattern of People: An Elizabeth Goudge Anthology, edited by Muriel Grainger. London, Hodder and Stoughton, 1978; New York, Coward McCann, 1979.

Editor, *A Book of Comfort: An Anthology*. London, Joseph, and New York, Coward McCann, 1964.
Editor, *A Diary of Prayer*. London, Hodder and Stoughton, and New York, Coward McCann, 1966.
Editor, *A Book of Peace: An Anthology*. London, Joseph, 1967; New York, Coward McCann, 1968.
Editor, *A Book of Faith*. London, Hodder and Stoughton, and New York, Coward McCann, 1976.

*   *   *

Elizabeth Goudge's sun-warmed world is not one of unruffled serenity—but it is one of deep underlying peace and certainty. Troubles and grief will certainly come to her people, but they are made bearable by the faith that they will in time, like the grain of sand that chafes the oyster, be transmuted into pearls.

Her own religious convictions provide a bedrock for the roster of stories which have for so many years charmed and enchanted huge audiences. Charmed, for they are charming as Dresden figurines or filigree music boxes are charming: not the hard gritty stuff of real life, nor ever pretending to be so; prettier and finer

textured than the world they scarcely resemble. Enchanted, as well, for these stories are magical in the fairy tale sense. Goudge's stories for young readers, like the notably successful *The Little White Horse*, are indeed fairy tales of unicorns and enchanted castles, and the magical aura remains in her stories for adult readers, those loyal souls who boldly keep faith with the creed of "happily ever after."

Goudge's romances seem especially concerned with two categories of lovers who seldom play prominent roles in such tales, the very young, too young even to become engaged, and the very old, still devoted after long years of marriage, or reunited after a lifetime of separation. Her best-loved work, which triumphantly combined both of these perspectives, is *Green Dolphin Country* (*Green Dolphin Street*). In this long tale of three interwoven life stories, the trio of young lovers, Marianne, Marguerite, and William, meet as children, far too young, it would seem, for them to form any lasting attachments, too young indeed to think of any such matters. But these are not ordinary children, they are *Goudge* children, and they meet on a day of enchantment. They do learn to love—forever.

But there are three of them, and alas, one man can marry only one sister, not two. When the trio are grown, and William has made his way to the other side of the world and won his fortune, he, the beloved of both sisters, must choose one to be his bride. Marguerite has always been his true love, although he has a sharp admiration for the spirited elder sister, Marianne. In the letter proposing marriage to the one woman he longs for, William's hand betrays his heart—he addresses the letter to the wrong sister, and is accepted. A true gentleman, William resolves to live and die with his mistake locked in his memory, never to hurt the woman he has married so reluctantly. No one shall ever know . . . and indeed, William and Marianne make a life for themselves, though not the life either had dreamed of, while Marguerite becomes a nun, and fills an empty life with prayer and eventual peace. Suddenly, long years later, in a fit of anger with his wife, William lets slip the truth that their life together has been based upon a lie and a sham; that he married Marianne out of pity, not for love. Marianne is shocked, both by what has been hidden from her, and that William has made this lifelong gallant gesture to save her pride. Bravely she tells Marguerite of William's old mistake. It is all a tale of long ago, but Marguerite's life is illuminated with joy that she had not been mistaken in William's devotion, and that it remains true. And Marianne has her reward; by telling her sister the secret, as William would not have done out of loyalty to her, she wins his admiring love after all. This story, with its panoramic sweep of action from the Channel Islands to New Zealand, and its strongly contrasted characterization, captured the fancy of an admiring public, and is as readable today as ever.

It has worn better, perhaps, than others of her stories, most of them set in the peaceful English cathedral towns she loves so well. Placid exteriors may sometimes conceal highly coloured drama, but Goudge's quiet, sunny cities of church towers and bells provide settings for gentle, wistful romances in which true love never goes unrequited, and hearts, though broken, always mend in time.

Roly-poly loveable vicars are endlessly understanding; deans may appear formidable, but are melted butter beneath the stern façade; young men desert families or sweethearts, have returned broken and aimless from the wars, or have fled the brutal life of midshipmen: they must inevitably meet growing young women who will make all well. A young actress, for instance, who longs to lay aside her laurels for a life of placid domesticity, adores to work in an unlikely little book store and longs to live in a cottage—or, more unlikely still, who contrives to combine this life with one of amazing success on the West End stage.

Goudge's children are not like those who burden and glorify the lives of ordinary folk. There is in her work a fairly definite division between youngsters of two sorts, typified by the children of *A City of Bells* (and other titles), Hugh Anthony and Henrietta. The boy is a thoughtless, healthily selfish freckled ball of endless energy, who will almost always do the right thing if it is only explained to him in a tactful way: the girl is a sensitive wisp, prey to storms of emotion, given to moments of transcendent joy of the world, who forgives her feckless father for his neglect, and adores her bumptious step-brother.

In varied guises—for occasionally it is the boy who is introspective and super-sensitive—these children appear and reappear, and are recognizable still in most of her adult characters. It is easy to trace the source of the angel child who sees the world's beauty with thankful joy: she must closely resemble her literary mother, who describes scenes of beauty so vividly that they are spread before the readers' eyes in colours that live.

Goudge is a writer for a clearly defined audience; for readers who know what they like, and who happily read it over and over again, preferring only minor variations on the theme; who deplore horrid surprises or harsh truths, and who like nice people living in nice places to have stories that end nicely. There is little here of passion, but a great deal of enduring love. For those who prefer the steadily burning candle to the fitful blaze, Goudge's books are quiet, dependable beacons across the stormy seas of ordinary life.

—Joan McGrath

GOWER, Iris. Pseudonym for Iris Davies. British. Born inSwansea, West Glamorgan, Wales, 4 February 1939. Educated at Swansea Technical College; Swansea College of Art. Married W. T. Davies in 1957; two daughters and two sons. Agent: June Hall, 5th Floor, The Chambers, Chelsea Harbour, Lots Road, London SW10 0XF, England. Address: 16 Major Street, Manselton, Swansea, West Glamorgan SA5 9NN, Wales.

ROMANCE AND HISTORICAL PUBLICATIONS

Novels (series: Sweyn's Eye)

The Copper Cloud. London, Hale, 1976.
Return to Tip Row. London, Hale, 1977.
Beloved Captive. London, Macdonald, 1981.
Beloved Traitor. London, Macdonald, 1981.
Copper Kingdom (Sweyn). London, Century, and New York, St. Martin's Press, 1983.
Proud Mary (Sweyn). London, Century, 1984; New York, St. Martin's Press, 1985.
Spinner's Wharf (Sweyn). London, Century, and New York, St. Martin's Press, 1985.
Morgan's Woman (Sweyn). London, Century, 1986.
Fiddler's Ferry (Sweyn). London, Century, 1987; New York, St. Martin's Press, 1988.
Black Gold (Sweyn). London, Century, 1988.

* * *

Because Iris Gower's series of novels set in Wales is narrowly focused both in time and place, they form a rich tapestry of stories that examine different aspects of a society. The six books span approximately 15 years before, during, and after World War I. Although some of the characters travel to England, Europe, and the United States, Gower's focus remains on Sweyn's Eye (old Swansea).

In the first book of the series, *Copper Kingdom*, Gower introduces three women whose lives weave in and out of the pages of the subsequent novels. Mali Llewelyn, the daughter of a widowed copper worker, leads a meager life in a cottage along Copperman's Row. Next door lives Katie Murphy and her family, who run a fresh fish shop. Both Mali and Katie work at the Canal Street laundry, under the supervision of Mary Jenkins.

After her mother's death, Mali attracts the attention of Sterling Richardson, the young heir of the copper works. Their romance provides the main narrative line of *Copper Kingdom*, but, as in all the books in the series, numerous subplots contribute to the novel's complexity. Katie is used and abandoned by William Owen, a young copperman unworthy of the love she lavishes upon him. Sterling has an affair with Bea Cardigan, a woman from his own class, who turns out to be his half-sister. Sterling's unscrupulous younger brother Rickie plots against him to gain control of the family fortune. Rickie, Will Owen, and others rig an explosion they hope will devastate Sterling's fortunes and possibly kill him. However, Will dies in the attempt while Sterling survives and marries Mali.

Mali's and Sterling's marriage remains strong throughout the series despite the class differences that divided them at first. Mali never forgets her life of poverty and remains kind to her old friends. She works with unwed mothers in *Fiddler's Ferry* and serves nourishing meals at a soup kitchen during the coal strike in *Black Gold*. Although Mali has times of worry, as when Sterling is away at war in *Spinner's Wharf*, for the most part, her life and marriage contain undiminished joy. As Mary tells her in *Black Gold*, "Yours is one marriage that has never faltered—not for you and Sterling doubts and infidelities."

Mary's years are not as calm. *Proud Mary* concentrates on her rise as a successful businesswoman in the city, and her business acumen is apparent in other novels as well. Although she eventually amasses a fortune, wealth cannot buy her family happiness. The first years of her marriage to Brandon Sutton bring increasing unhappiness as she remains childless. When she hears that Brandon is missing in action and presumed dead shortly after leaving for war, she seeks comfort in the arms of Dr. Paul Soames (*Spinner's Wharf*). Shortly thereafter, she discovers she is pregnant but cannot be certain of the child's father.

When Brandon returns, Mary confesses her infidelity. He leaves her and refuses to acknowledge the boy, even though Stephan resembles Brandon more and more as he grows up. A car accident with Mary at the wheel results in Stephan's blindness. Mary and Brandon reunite and travel to the United States, Brandon's home. After his lingering illness and death, Mary returns to Sweyn's Eye, where she marries Paul Soames, who still loves her (*Black Gold*).

Katie Murphy is less fortunate in love than either Mali or Mary. Will Owen's death in *Copper Kingdom* is followed by more tragedy. Her husband of a few months, Mark, drowns at sea as the pair return from France (*Morgan's Woman*). Katie miscarries as a result of that same accident. She rejects the love of Ceri Llewelyn, Mali's cousin in (*Fiddler's Ferry*), only to fall in love with a married man, Luke Proud, in *Black Gold*. Luke, who insists on keeping his coal mine operating is stoned by strikers and dies in Katie's arms.

The last scene of *Black Gold* closely resembles that of *Copper Kingdom*. In each, an unmarried pregnant women rushes to a mine to learn her lover's fate. Mali finds Sterling and achieves a happy marriage; Katie receives yet another disappointment.

Friends and families of the three women inhabit the pages of all the books. Each volume examines one family in some detail while drawing strands from many other lives. For example, *Fiddler's Ferry* considers the family of Siona Llewelyn, Mali's uncle. In the course of the novel he meets and marries Nerys Beynon, who had cared for Stephan Sutton.

The book most removed from others in the series is *Morgan's Woman*, in part because it is set in the countryside, not the city. Although each book can stand alone, they are best read as a set. In fact, in the later volumes Gower sometimes gets bogged down in explaining the complex histories she has created. But she needs to provide such information for those unfamiliar with earlier books.

One of Gower's strengths is the lilting speech of her characters that gives even everyday conversations a pleasant rhythm. Another is her ability to incorporate history into a story without turning a novel into a textbook.

In contrast, her far-fetched romance *Beloved Captive* is filled with contrived situations and shopworn language. Among other tribulations, the heroine is shipwrecked, captured by a primitive Russian tribe, then rescued only to be drugged and forced to be the Tsar's mistress. Gower is on much firmer authorial ground when she writes of her native Wales.

—Kathy Piehl

GRAHAM, Heather. See **POZZESSERE, Heather Graham.**

GRAHAM, Winston (Mawdsley). British. Born in Victoria Park, Manchester, Lancashire, in 1909(?). Married Jean Mary Williamson in 1939; one son and one daughter. Chairman, Society of Authors, London, 1967–69. Recipient: Crime Writers Association prize, 1956. Fellow, Royal Society of Literature, 1968. O.B.E. (Officer, Order of the British Empire), 1983. Agent: A. M. Heath, 79 St. Martin's Lane, London WC2N 4AA. Address: Abbotswood House, Buxted, East Sussex, England.

ROMANCE AND HISTORICAL PUBLICATIONS

Novels (series: Ross Poldark in all Cornwall novels)

The Forgotten Story. London, Ward Lock, 1945; as *The Wreck of the Grey Cat*, New York, Doubleday, 1958.
Ross Poldark: A Novel of Cornwall 1783–1787. London, Ward Lock, 1945; as *The Renegade*, New York, Doubleday, 1951.
Demelza: A Novel of Cornwall 1788–1790. London, Ward Lock, 1946; New York, Doubleday, 1953.
Cordelia. London, Ward Lock, 1949; New York, Doubleday, 1950.
Jeremy Poldark: A Novel of Cornwall 1790–1791. London, Ward Lock, 1950; as *Venture Once More*, New York, Doubleday, 1954.
Warleggan: A Novel of Cornwall 1792–1793. London, Ward Lock, 1953; as *The Last Gamble*, New York, Doubleday, 1955.
The Grove of Eagles. London, Hodder and Stoughton, 1963; New York, Doubleday, 1964.
The Black Moon: A Novel of Cornwall 1794–1795. London, Collins, 1973; New York, Doubleday, 1974.

The Four Swans: A Novel of Cornwall 1795–1797. London, Collins, 1976; New York, Doubleday, 1977.
The Angry Tide: A Novel of Cornwall 1798–1799. London, Collins, 1977; New York, Doubleday, 1978.
The Stranger from the Sea: A Novel of Cornwall 1810–1811. London, Collins, 1981; New York, Doubleday, 1982.
The Miller's Dance: A Novel of Cornwall 1812–1813. London, Collins, 1982; New York, Doubleday, 1983.
The Loving Cup: A Novel of Cornwall 1813–1815. London, Collins, 1984; New York, Doubleday, 1985.

Short Stories

The Japanese Girl and Other Stories. London, Collins, 1971; New York, Doubleday, 1972.
The Cornish Farm. Bath, Chivers, 1982.

OTHER PUBLICATIONS

Novels

The House with the Stained-Glass Windows. London, Ward Lock, 1934.
Into the Fog. London, Ward Lock, 1935.
The Riddle of John Rowe. London, Ward Lock, 1935.
Without Motive. London, Ward Lock, 1936.
The Dangerous Pawn. London, Ward Lock, 1937.
The Giant's Chair. London, Ward Lock, 1938.
Strangers Meeting. London, Ward Lock, 1939.
Keys of Chance. London, Ward Lock, 1939.
No Exit: An Adventure. London, Ward Lock, 1940.
Night Journey. London, Ward Lock, 1941; New York, Doubleday, 1968.
My Turn Next. London, Ward Lock, 1942.
The Merciless Ladies. London, Ward Lock, 1944; revised edition, London, Bodley Head, 1979; New York, Doubleday, 1980.
Take My Life. London, Ward Lock, 1947; New York, Doubleday, 1967.
Night Without Stars. London, Hodder and Stoughton, and New York, Doubleday, 1950.
Fortune Is a Woman. London, Hodder and Stoughton, and New York, Doubleday, 1953.
The Little Walls. London, Hodder and Stoughton, and New York, Doubleday, 1955; abridged edition, as *Bridge to Vengeance*, New York, Spivak, 1957.
The Sleeping Partner. London, Hodder and Stoughton, and New York, Doubleday, 1956.
Greek Fire. London, Hodder and Stoughton, and New York, Doubleday, 1958.
The Tumbled House. London, Hodder and Stoughton, 1959; New York, Doubleday, 1960.
Marnie. London, Hodder and Stoughton, and New York, Doubleday, 1961.
After the Act. London, Hodder and Stoughton, 1965; New York, Doubleday, 1966.
The Walking Stick. London, Collins, and New York, Doubleday, 1967.
Angell, Pearl and Little God. London, Collins, and New York, Doubleday, 1970.
Woman in the Mirror. London, Bodley Head, and New York, Doubleday, 1975.
The Green Flash. London, Collins, 1986; New York, Random House, 1987.
Cameo. London, Collins, 1988.

Plays

Shadow Play (produced Salisbury, 1978).
Circumstantial Evidence (produced Guildford, Surrey, 1979).

Screenplays: *Take My Life*, with Valerie Taylor and Margaret Kennedy, 1948; *Night Without Stars*, 1951.

Television Play: *Sleeping Partner*, 1967.

Other

The Spanish Armadas. London, Collins, and New York, Doubleday, 1972.
Poldark's Cornwall, photographs by Simon McBride. London, Bodley Head, 1983.

*   *   *

Winston Graham brings to the history and romance genres a versatility and variety that breaks formulas, that mixes history, romance, adventure, politics, murder, and intrigue, and that explores the deeply-rooted motives and deeds of the past that have produced the conflicts, doubts, hesitations, and peculiarities of the present. Graham enjoys exposing seething passions beneath cold exteriors. Critics praise Graham's works for their "tense, dramatic realism," "their crisp narrative style," their "understatement which . . . gives . . . sensitivity and depth." It is his good solid writing, interesting characterization, clever and sensitive psychoanalysis, and vivid images of Cornish life that have won the most critical praise.

Graham has made the coast of Cornwall, with its cliffs and caves, sea and sky, his hallmark. Though he never includes travelogues or lengthy descriptions for their own sake, Graham has an eye for those particulars that bring a scene to life. His method is to focus on quality of detail, with setting illuminating character and conflict. Memorable are scenes of drudgery and terrors of 18th-century life, the conspiracies and illegal trafficking, the wary fellowship of local taverns where a wrong word breeds ill-will but the right gesture can elicit acceptance and camaraderie. *The Forgotten Story* captures the dangers of the Cornish coast as it tells of a shipwreck, a rescue attempt, and an old love rekindled, while the Poldark series in particular focuses on the people of Cornwall, their struggles against an unforgiving land, their economic troubles, their social conflicts, their patriotism, treachery, loves, and lies.

The Poldark series, starring Robin Ellis in the BBC production, reflects the concern with social, economic, and political relationships that lies behind all Graham's works. It traces the adventures of Captain Ross Poldark, a man who "lives on a knife edge," as he returns to his rundown estate in Cornwall at the end of the American Revolution, finds his beloved engaged to his cousin, and, making the best of it, plunges wholeheartedly into restoring his estate and championing the cause of the lower classes of the area. It is a story of secret love, warring families and social conflicts. Captain Ross Poldark partakes of the dour strength of his land; he plays a lone hand and does not suffer fools. One act misunderstood by all involves transforming Demelza, the mistreated daughter of a miner, from scullerymaid to lady of the manor in a pattern perhaps more Victorian than 18th century. Demelza embodies the strength of Cornwall: its tenacious hold on life despite the bitter struggles ordained by nature. The novel *Delmelza* continues the story begun in *Ross Poldark* as the Poldarks struggle to cope with social disdain, class consciousness, and the ever-present economic conflicts of the grim Cornish coast as it shares in the trouble and tensions of

the French Revolution. A *New York Times* reviewer rightly praised its "realistic and somber descriptions of Cornish farmers, fishermen and miners pushed to the verge of revolution by unjust laws" and in particular the scene of "an illegal raid on a prison in which innocent and guilty are left to die of disease and starvation, and another of the looting of two wrecked ships by the starving population." *Jeremy Poldark* finds Poldark preparing for the birth of his son, dealing with an attempted take-over of the local copper mines, and facing charges of instigating locals to plunder and riot. *Warleggan*, in turn, manages four plots, bound together by rich images of seacoast life and characters, as Poldark flees revenue agents and deals with possible bankruptcy and marital strife. *The Black Moon* and *The Four Swans* continue the saga, with old relationships and old feuds motivating present behavior and present passions. The past impinges on the present as the smoldering rivalry between Poldark and Warleggan is passed on to their children in *The Stranger from the Sea*, a story centered on the relationship between young Jeremy, his sister Clowance, and a seeming stranger rescued from a shipwreck. Hatred begets hatred and rivalry works itself out in fiery competitions for land and power and love. These books are almost novels of manner as they trace family and relationships through a period of social change and provide insights into the expectations and social behavior of the period. Poldark is, as Richard Match describes him, "a kind of Heathcliffian Mr. Rochester." The story of his life and loves, his fiery defiance of convention, and his sympathy for the working classes is one of growth and transformation.

Graham's other historical works include *The Grove of Eagles*, a fictionalized history of the Elizabethan years, packed with local lore and the minutiae of daily life, but all from a safe perspective of an outsider, and *The Spanish Armadas*, popular historiography focused on the Elizabethan war with Spain, particularly Grenville's fight with a *flota*, the Lisbon and Cadiz raids, and the five true *armadas*. The first novel is told from the point of view of a Cornish man, Maugham Killigrew, a man who survived the Spanish Inquisition, fought with Raleigh at the capture of Cadiz and the defeat of the second Armada, and was tried before the Queen's Privy Council. The second covers some of the same territory in a more scholarly way, but avoiding technicalities to focus on a fluent narrative and a clear record.

Graham's romances, though not purely so, are interesting psychological studies. *The Walking Stick* makes credible a young polio victim's transformation from wallflower to dancer, skater, and robber through skilfully interweaving her past and present experiences with life and love. In turn, the seemingly cold, unreachable Marnie, in the novel of the same title, must discover and face the secrets of her childhood if she is ever to cope normally with life and love. Throughout his canon Graham explores the way experience transforms and shapes a person and the way individuals act as catalysts molding and changing human relationships.

In sum, Graham's novels derive their success in part from the psychological, the conflicts of classes, and from the deep-seated spirit of rebellion they portray—rebellion against demeaning social conditions, unjust rulers, and a fickle fate. They derive it in part too from a strong sense of place and atmosphere, but most of all from the moral dilemmas, the images of men and women caught up in circumstances beyond their control, not knowing how to act nor to whom to turn, acting impetuously according to the moment and finding themselves thereby trapped in patterns that separate them farther and farther from what they want most. At their best his characters discover that they must look within, find their hidden reservoirs of strength, and face their deepest fears about themselves and their relationships before they can turn outward and deal with the ever more pressing problems around them. Graham provides poignant images of failures of humanity, indifference to others, betrayals of trust or of need, obsessions with the past, with the land, with social position, with one's heritage, set against images of love and passion and human obligation.

—Gina Macdonald

GRANGE, Peter. See **NICOLE, Christopher.**

GRANT, Joan (née Marshall). British. Born in London, 12 April 1907. Educated privately. Married 1) Leslie Grant in 1927, one daughter; 2) Charles Beatty in 1940; 3) Denys Kelsey in 1960.

ROMANCE AND HISTORICAL PUBLICATIONS

Novels

Winged Pharaoh. London, Barker, 1937; New York, Harper, 1938.
Life as Carola. London, Methuen, 1939; New York, Harper, 1940.
Eyes of Horus. London, Methuen, 1942.
Lord of the Horizon. London, Methuen, 1943.
Scarlet Feather. London, Methuen, 1945.
Return to Elysium. London, Methuen, 1947.
The Laird and the Lady. London, Methuen, 1949.
So Moses Was Born. London, Methuen, 1952.

Short Stories

The Scarlet Fish and Other Stories. London, Methuen, 1942.
Redskin Morning and Other Stories. London, Methuen, 1944.

OTHER PUBLICATIONS

Other

Vague Vacation (travel). London, Barker, 1947.
Time out of Mind (autobiography). London, Barker, 1956; as *Far Memory*, New York, Harper, 1956.
A Lot to Remember, with Denys Kelsey. London, Hale, 1962.
Many Lifetimes, with Denys Kelsey. New York, Doubleday, 1967; London, Gollancz, 1969.
The Complete Works of Joan Grant. New York, Arno Press, 12 vols., 1980.

*   *   *

Joan Grant is probably unique among historical novelists for instead of beginning a book by plotting and research, she begins by going into a trance. A believer in reincarnation and a psychotherapist, she learned how to explore and relive the lives led by the immortal part of her inner self and to dictate her experiences and then assemble them into books.

Her first historical novel, *Winged Pharaoh*, tells the story of Seeketa, an Egyptian princess of the 1st Dynasty. Destined to rule over Egypt, Seeketa was trained in the temple to use her far-memory. The book describes in great detail her initiation and the ordeals she had to undergo to become an initiate and then tells of her life as co-ruler of Egypt.

Life as Carola is Grant's recollection of her life in 16th-century Italy as the bastard daughter of a Perugian nobleman and a sewing woman. Music is her love and solace. Her life follows the wheel of fortune as it turns from luxury to poverty and degradation, and the cruelties and superstitions of the time are vividly depicted.

Another Egyptian life, this time during the 11th Dynasty (approximately 3,500 B.C.) is that of a military commander, a Nomarch or provincial ruler. Grant claims that she has been a man in her past lives as well as a woman. Ra-ab's story is told in *Eyes of Horus* and its sequel *Lord of the Horizon*. Egypt at that time had become decadent; the Eyes of Horus was the name of a resistance movement dedicated to overthrowing the venal authorities.

Scarlet Feather is the story of a female North American Indian warrior, entitled to wear the red feather of the Brave because she had undergone all the trials and ordeals of initiation for a male warrior. She is concerned to try to break down the conventional attitudes to male and female roles, not as a feminist but because the immortal soul is androgynous—male in some lives, female in others. The tribe's beliefs are summed up in the question they believed they would be asked by the Great Hunter before entering heaven: "How many people are happier because you were born?"

Return to Elysium is the story of a Greek girl, Lucina, in the 2nd century B.C. who is the ward and pupil of a philosopher. Because of Lucina's understanding of her own far-memories, she disagrees with her guardian's denial of immortality and sets out to prove him wrong.

Whether you believe in reincarnation and regression or not, these books are interesting to read as stories in their own right. The style is a rather mannered first-person narrative and the books are slow-moving. Many details of the way people lived in the various times are portrayed, but even more thoroughly investigated are the ideas of the time, as Grant perceived them. The motivation for Grant's books might be summed up in this quotation from *Winged Pharaoh*: "It matters little what people wear, what houses they live in or what things they use. It is their thoughts which should endure through time; the span of their knowledge, their burnishing to Light."

—Pamela Cleaver

GRANT, Margaret. See **FRANKEN, Rose.**

GRAVES, Robert (von Ranke). Also wrote as John Doyle. British. Born in Wimbledon, London, 24 July 1895. Educated at King's College School and Rokeby School, Wimbledon; Copthorne School, Sussex; Charterhouse School, Surrey, 1907–14; St. John's College, Oxford (exhibitioner; editor, the *Owl*, from 1919, and *Winter Owl*, 1923), 1919–25, B.Litt. 1925. Served in the Royal Welch Fusiliers, 1914–19: Captain; was refused admittance into the armed forces in World War II. Married 1) Nancy Nicholson in 1918 (divorced 1949), two daughters and two sons;

2) Beryl Pritchard in 1950 (lived with her from 1939), three sons and one daughter. Professor of English, Egyptian University, Cairo, 1926; with Laura Riding established the Seizin Press, 1928, and *Epilogue* magazine, 1935. Lived in Deyá, Mallorca, 1929–36, the U.S., 1936, England, 1937–46, and Deyá after 1946. Clark Lecturer, Trinity College, Cambridge, 1954–55; Professor of Poetry, Oxford University, 1961–66; Arthur Dehon Little Memorial Lecturer, Massachusetts Institute of Technology, Cambridge, 1963. Recipient: Bronze Medal for Poetry, Olympic Games, Paris, 1924; Hawthornden prize, for fiction, 1935; James Tait Black Memorial prize, for fiction, 1935; Femina Vie Heureuse prize, for fiction, 1939; Loines award, for poetry, 1958; National Poetry Society of America Gold Medal, 1960; Foyle Poetry prize, 1960; Arts Council award, 1962; Italia prize, for radio play, 1965; Gold Medal for Poetry, Cultural Olympics, Mexico City, 1968; Queen's Gold Medal for Poetry, 1969. M.A.: Oxford University, 1961. Honorary Member, American Academy of Arts and Sciences, 1970; Honorary Fellow, St. John's College, 1971. *Died 7 December 1985.*

ROMANCE AND HISTORICAL PUBLICATIONS

Novels (series: Claudius; Sergeant Lamb)

My Head! My Head! London, Secker, and New York, Knopf, 1925.

The Real David Copperfield. London, Barker, 1933; as *David Copperfield by Charles Dickens, Condensed by Robert Graves*, edited by Merrill P. Paine, New York, Harcourt Brace, 1934.

I, Claudius. . . . London, Barker, and New York, Smith and Haas, 1934.

Claudius the God and His Wife Messalina. . . . London, Barker, 1934; New York, Smith and Haas, 1935.

Count Belisarius. London, Cassell, and New York, Random House, 1938.

Sergeant Lamb of the Ninth. London, Methuen, 1940; as *Sergeant Lamb's America*, New York, Random House, 1940.

Proceed, Sergeant Lamb. London, Methuen, and New York, Random House, 1941.

The Story of Marie Powell: Wife to Mr. Milton. London, Cassell, 1943; as *Wife to Mr. Milton*, New York, Creative Age Press, 1944.

The Golden Fleece. London, Cassell, 1944; as *Hercules, My Shipmate*, New York, Creative Age Press, 1945.

King Jesus. New York, Creative Age Press, and London, Cassell, 1946.

Watch the North Wind Rise. New York, Creative Age Press, 1949; as *Seven Days in New Crete*, London, Cassell, 1949.

The Islands of Unwisdom. New York, Doubleday, 1949; as *The Isles of Unwisdom*, London, Cassell, 1950.

Homer's Daughter. London, Cassell, and New York, Doubleday, 1955.

They Hanged My Saintly Billy. London, Cassell, and New York, Doubleday, 1957.

Short Stories

¡Catacrok! Mostly Stories, Mostly Funny. London, Cassell, 1956.

Collected Short Stories. New York, Doubleday, 1964; London, Cassell, 1965; as *The Shout and Other Stories*, London, Penguin, 1978.

OTHER PUBLICATIONS

Novel

Antigua, Penny, Puce. Deyá, Mallorca, Seizin Press, and London, Constable, 1936; as *The Antigua Stamp*, New York, Random House, 1937.

Short Story

The Shout. London, Mathews and Marrot, 1929.

Plays

John Kemp's Wager: A Ballad Opera. Oxford, Blackwell, and New York, Edwards, 1925.

Nausicaa (opera libretto), adaptation of his novel *Homer's Daughter*, music by Peggy Glanville-Hicks (produced Athens, 1961).

Television Documentary: *Greece: The Inner World*, 1964 (USA).

Verse

Over the Brazier. London, Poetry Bookshop, 1916; New York, St. Martin's Press, 1975.

Goliath and David. London, Chiswick Press, 1916.

Fairies and Fusiliers. London, Heinemann, 1917; New York, Knopf, 1918.

The Treasure Box. London, Chiswick Press, 1919.

Country Sentiment. London, Secker, and New York, Knopf, 1920.

The Pier-Glass. London, Secker, and New York, Knopf, 1921.

Whipperginny. London, Heinemann, and New York, Knopf, 1923.

The Feather Bed. Richmond, Surrey, Hogarth Press, 1923.

Mock Beggar Hall. London, Hogarth Press, 1924.

Welchman's Hose. London, The Fleuron, 1925.

(Poems). London, Benn, 1925.

The Marmosite's Miscellany (as John Doyle). London, Hogarth Press, 1925.

Poems (1914–1926). London, Heinemann, 1927; New York, Doubleday, 1929.

Poems (1914–1927). London, Heinemann, 1927.

Poems 1929. London, Seizin Press, 1929.

Ten Poems More. Paris, Hours Press, 1930.

Poems 1926–1930. London, Heinemann, 1931.

To Whom Else? Deyá, Mallorca, Seizin Press, 1931.

Poems 1930–1933. London, Barker, 1933.

Collected Poems. London, Cassell, and New York, Random House, 1938.

No More Ghosts: Selected Poems. London, Faber, 1940.

Work in Hand, with Alan Hodge and Norman Cameron. London, Hogarth Press, 1942.

(Poems). London, Eyre and Spottiswoode, 1943.

Poems 1938–1945. London, Cassell, 1945; New York, Creative Age Press, 1946.

Collected Poems (1914–1947). London, Cassell, 1948.

Poems and Satires 1951. London, Cassell, 1951.

Poems 1953. London, Cassell, 1953.

Collected Poems 1955. New York, Doubleday, 1955.

Poems Selected by Himself. London, Penguin, 1957; revised edition, 1961, 1966, 1972.

The Poems of Robert Graves. New York, Doubleday, 1958.

Collected Poems 1959. London, Cassell, 1959.

More Poems 1961. London, Cassell, 1961

Collected Poems. New York, Doubleday, 1961.

New Poems 1962. London, Cassell, 1962; as *New Poems*, New York, Doubleday, 1963.

The More Deserving Cases: Eighteen Old Poems for Reconsideration. Marlborough, Wiltshire, Marlborough College Press, 1962.

Man Does, Woman Is 1964. London, Cassell, and New York, Doubleday, 1964.

Love Respelt. London, Cassell, 1965.

Collected Poems 1965. London, Cassell, 1965.

Seventeen Poems Missing from "Love Respelt." Privately printed, 1966.

Collected Poems 1966. New York, Doubleday, 1966.

Colophon to "Love Respelt." Privately printed, 1967.

(Poems), with D. H. Lawrence, edited by Leonard Clark. London, Longman, 1967.

Poems 1965–1968. London, Cassell, 1968; New York, Doubleday, 1969.

Poems about Love. London, Cassell, and New York, Doubleday, 1969.

Love Respelt Again. New York, Doubleday, 1969.

Beyond Giving. Privately printed, 1969.

Poems 1968–1970. London, Cassell, 1970.

Advice from a Mother. London, Poem-of-the-Month Club, 1970.

The Green-Sailed Vessel. Privately printed, 1971.

Corgi Modern Poets in Focus 3, with others, edited by Dannie Abse. London, Corgi, 1971.

Poems 1970–1972. London, Cassell, 1972; New York, Doubleday, 1973.

Deyá. London, Motif Editions, 1973.

Timeless Meeting. London, Rota, 1973.

At the Gate. London, Rota, 1974.

Collected Poems 1975. London, Cassell, 1975; New York, Oxford University Press, 1988.

New Collected Poems. New York, Doubleday, 1977.

Eleven Songs. Deyá, Mallorca, Seizin Press, 1983.

Selected Poems, edited by Paul O'Prey. London, Penguin, 1986.

Poems about War. London, Cassell, 1988.

Recordings: *Robert Graves Reading His Own Poems*, Argo and Listen, 1960; *Robert Graves Reading His Own Poetry and The White Goddess*, Caedmon; *The Rubaiyat of Omar Khayyam*, Spoken Arts.

Other

On English Poetry. New York, Knopf, and London, Heinemann, 1922.

The Meaning of Dreams. London, Cecil Palmer, 1924; New York, Greenberg, 1925.

Poetic Unreason and Other Studies. London, Cecil Palmer, 1925.

Contemporary Techniques of Poetry: A Political Analogy. London, Hogarth Press, 1925.

Another Future of Poetry. London, Hogarth Press, 1926.

Impenetrability; or, The Proper Habit of English. London, Hogarth Press, 1926.

The English Ballad: A Short Critical Survey. London, Benn, 1927; revised edition, as *English and Scottish Ballads*, London, Heinemann, and New York, Macmillan, 1957.

Lars Porsena; or, The Future of Swearing and Improper Language. London, Kegan Paul Trench Trubner, and New York, Dutton, 1927; revised edition, as *The Future of Swearing and Improper Language*, Kegan Paul Trench Trubner, 1936.

A Survey of Modernist Poetry, with Laura Riding. London, Heinemann, 1927; New York, Doubleday, 1928.

Lawrence and the Arabs. London, Cape, 1927; as *Lawrence and the Arabian Adventure*, New York, Doubleday, 1928.

A Pamphlet Against Anthologies, with Laura Riding. London, Cape, 1928; as *Against Anthologies*, New York, Doubleday, 1928.

Mrs. Fisher; or, The Future of Humour. London, Kegan Paul Trench Trubner, 1928.

Goodbye to All That: An Autobiography. London, Cape, 1929; New York, Cape and Smith, 1930; revised edition, New York, Doubleday, and London, Cassell, 1957; London, Penguin, 1960.

But It Still Goes On: A Miscellany. London, Cape, and New York, Cape and Smith, 1930.

T. E. Lawrence to His Biographer Robert Graves. New York, Doubleday, 1938; London, Faber, 1939.

The Long Week-end: A Social History of Great Britain 1918–1939, with Alan Hodge. London, Faber, 1940; New York, Macmillan, 1941.

The Reader over Your Shoulder: A Handbook for Writers of English Prose, with Alan Hodge. London, Cape, 1943; New York, Macmillan, 1944.

The White Goddess: A Historical Grammar of Poetic Myth. London, Faber, and New York, Creative Age Press, 1948; revised edition, Faber, 1952, 1966; New York, Knopf, 1958.

The Common Asphodel: Collected Essays on Poetry 1922–1949. London, Hamish Hamilton, 1949.

Occupation: Writer (includes the play *Horses*). New York, Creative Age Press, 1950; London, Cassell, 1951.

The Nazarene Gospel Restored, with Joshua Podro. London, Cassell, 1953; New York, Doubleday, 1954.

The Crowning Privilege: The Clark Lectures 1954–1955; Also Various Essays on Poetry and Sixteen New Poems. London, Cassell, 1955; as *The Crowning Privilege: Collected Essays on Poetry*, New York, Doubleday, 1956.

Adam's Rib and Other Anomalous Elements in the Hebrew Creation Myth: A New View. London, Trianon Press, 1955; New York, Yoseloff, 1958.

The Greek Myths. London, Penguin, 2 vols., 1955; Mount Kisco, New York, Moyer Bell, 1 vol., 1988.

Jesus in Rome: A Historical Conjecture, with Joshua Podro. London, Cassell, 1957.

5 Pens in Hand. New York, Doubleday, 1958.

Steps: Stories, Talks, Essays, Poems, Studies in History. London, Cassell, 1958.

Food for Centaurs: Stories, Talks, Critical Studies, Poems. New York, Doubleday, 1960.

The Penny Fiddle: Poems for Children. London, Cassell, 1960; New York, Doubleday, 1961.

Greek Gods and Heroes (for children). New York, Doubleday, 1960; as *Myths of Ancient Greece*, London, Cassell, 1961.

Selected Poetry and Prose, edited by James Reeves. London, Hutchinson, 1961.

The Siege and Fall of Troy (for children). London, Cassell, 1962; New York, Doubleday, 1963.

The Big Green Book. New York, Crowell Collier, 1962; London, Penguin, 1978.

Oxford Addresses on Poetry. London, Cassell, and New York, Doubleday, 1962.

Nine Hundred Iron Chariots: The Twelfth Arthur Dehon Little Memorial Lecture. Cambridge, Massachusetts Institute of Technology, 1963.

The Hebrew Myths: The Book of Genesis, with Raphael Patai. New York, Doubleday, and London, Cassell, 1964.

Ann at Highwood Hall: Poems for Children. London, Cassell, 1964.

Majorca Observed. London, Cassell, and New York, Doubleday, 1965.

Mammon and the Black Goddess. London, Cassell, and New York, Doubleday, 1965.

Two Wise Children (for children). New York, Harlin Quist, 1966; London, W. H. Allen, 1967.

Poetic Craft and Principle. London, Cassell, 1967.

The Poor Boy Who Followed His Star (for children). London, Cassell, 1968; New York, Doubleday, 1969.

The Crane Bag and Other Disputed Subjects. London, Cassell, 1969.

On Poetry: Collected Talks and Essays. New York, Doubleday, 1969.

Poems: Abridged for Dolls and Princes (for children). London, Cassell, and New York, Doubleday, 1971.

Difficult Questions, Easy Answers. London, Cassell, 1972; New York, Doubleday, 1973.

An Ancient Castle (for children), edited by W. D. Thomas. London, Owen, 1980; New York, Kesend, 1981.

Selected Letters of Robert Graves, edited by Paul O'Prey:
1. *In Broken Images: 1914–1946.* London, Hutchinson, 1982; Mount Kisco, New York, Moyer Bell, 1988.
2. *Between Moon and Moon: 1946–1972.* London, Hutchinson, 1984.

Editor, with Alan Porter and Richard Hughes, *Oxford Poetry 1921.* Oxford, Blackwell, 1921.

Editor, *John Skelton (Laureate), 1460(?)–1529.* London, Benn, 1927.

Editor, *The Less Familiar Nursery Rhymes.* London, Benn, 1927.

Editor, *The Comedies of Terence.* New York, Doubleday, 1962; London, Cassell, 1963.

Translator, with Laura Riding, *Almost Forgotten Germany*, by Georg Schwarz. Deyá, Mallorca, Seizin Press, London, Constable, and New York, Random House, 1936.

Translator, *The Transformation of Lucius, Otherwise Known as The Golden Ass*, by Apuleius. London, Penguin, 1950; New York, Farrar Straus, 1951.

Translator, *The Cross and the Sword*, by Manuel de Jésus Galván. Bloomington, Indiana University Press, 1955; London, Gollancz, 1956.

Translator, *The Infant with the Globe*, by Pedro Antonio de Alarcón. London, Trianon Press, 1955; New York, Yoseloff, 1958.

Translator, *Winter in Majorca*, by George Sand. London, Cassell, 1956.

Translator, *Pharsalia: Dramatic Episodes of the Civil Wars*, by Lucan. London, Penguin, 1956.

Translator, *The Twelve Caesars*, by Suetonius. London, Penguin, 1957.

Translator, *The Anger of Achilles: Homer's Iliad.* New York, Doubleday, 1959; London, Cassell, 1960.

Translator, with Omar Ali-Shah, *Rubaiyat of Omar Khayyam.* London, Cassell, 1967; New York, Doubleday, 1968.

Translator, *The Song of Songs.* New York, Potter, and London, Collins, 1973.

*

Bibliography: *A Bibliography of the Works of Robert Graves* by Fred H. Higginson, London, Vane, 1966, revised edition, as *Robert Graves: A Bibliography*, by W. P. Williams, Winchester, St. Paul's, and Charlottesville, University Press of Virginia, 1987; *Robert Graves: An Annotated Bibliography* by Hallman Bell Bryant, New York, Garland, 1986.

Manuscript Collections: Lockwood Memorial Library, State University of New York at Buffalo; University of Victoria, British Columbia; New York City Public Library; University of Texas Library, Austin.

Critical Studies (selection): *Robert Graves*, London, Longman, 1956, revised edition, 1965, 1970, and *Robert Graves: His Life and Work*, London, Hutchinson, 1982, New York, Holt Rinehart, 1983, both by Martin Seymour-Smith; *Robert Graves* by J. M. Cohen, Edinburgh, Oliver and Boyd, 1960, New York, Barnes and Noble, 1965; *Robert Graves* by George Stade, New York, Columbia University Press, 1967; *Robert Graves, Peace-Weaver* by James S. Mehoke, The Hague, Mouton, 1975; *Robert Graves* by Katherine Snipes, New York, Ungar, 1979; *Robert Graves* by Robert H. Canary, Boston, Twayne, 1980; *Robert Graves: The Assault Heroic 1895–1926* by Richard Perceval Graves, London, Weidenfeld and Nicolson, 1986.

*   *   *

Although Robert Graves denigrated his own historical fiction, saying that "all I really care about is poetry," it is an ironic fact that his novels are now more widely read and acclaimed both by critics and the general public than are his many collections of poems. Graves was an accomplished, and invariably contentious, historian; the backgrounds of his novels are researched so exhaustively that, no matter how unlikely the incidents related, they are always plausible. When applying his research to fiction, he practised what he described as the "analeptic method: the intuitive recovery of forgotten events by a deliberate suspension of time." He immersed himself totally in his subject, becoming so deeply entranced at times that he imagined his protagonists to be physically present in the room with him. The result of this fusion of painstaking research and imaginative projection is a series of historical fiction in which the reader is engaged in the beliefs, thoughts, and realities of a previous time. No other historical writer this century has been as successful in bringing the past to a contemporary audience.

I, Claudius and *Claudius the God* combine as a diptych portrait of one of the most enigmatic figures in history. Claudius was an outsider in his own Imperial family, reckoned a fool and a coward by each successive ruler. The first book describes his tenuous survival through the reigns of Augustus, Tiberius, and Caligula, each more tyrannical, suspicious, and dangerous than his predecessor. It comes to a climax during the last days of Caligula's power, as the insane Emperor creates a nightmarish environment of terror and surreal cruelty. Claudius has survived, almost the sole member of the Augustan dynasty left alive, by becoming Caligula's court jester. As the novel ends, with a desperate assassination removing the monstrous Caligula, Claudius is declared Emperor almost by accident. The subsequent book relates his reign as Emperor, an honourable though pragmatic man in harsh and ambitious times. As his power wanes even he succumbs to the Imperial disease and becomes a tyrant; masterfully, Graves has the reader come to perceive this though the narrative never makes this tyranny explicit.

As exciting as the story is in itself, as fascinating as the detail becomes in the developing narrative, the greatest achievement of these books is the portrayal of the protagonist and narrator, Claudius. It is he who is telling the tale, to be sealed in a lead casket and "found again some nineteen hundred years hence."

His official autobiography, he tells us, has been made deliberately dull; this is "myself writing as I feel . . . a confidential history." To this central premiss the books remain faithful, and the result is a narrative that remains as convincing as it is speculative. Claudius becomes the reader's confidant, describing the events of his amoral world with calm irony; only he can afford to do so, being a survivor of the political intrigue. In the second book he becomes triumphant, winning the last frontier conquest of the Empire of Britain. The latter half of *Claudius the God*, however, is much darker in tone, as he prepares his children for his inevitable demise. From the epic black farce of the first volume, and the first half of the second, develops a more sombre and tragic story. All through his reign he plans to restore the Republic; finally he abandons this ambition and accepts the inevitability of his own death, and with it the last hopes of republicanism.

Count Belisarius takes up the story of the Empire from its last days in the 6th century. Belisarius is the commander of the army of Emperor Justinian, who comes to hate his general for the heroic reputation he gains in his defence of the Empire. Although the story is provided with the customary amount of period detail and incident, it remains rather lacklustre in comparison to the Claudius novels, if only because these show a greater development in the central character. Here Belisarius, noble forerunner of the medieval knight, is flat; by contrast the literally Byzantine workings of the court politics are almost incomprehensible in their subtlety.

Following his explorations of Roman history, though pressed to write a novel based on the life of Nero, Graves ranged closer to home in search of subjects. Two adventure yarns relate the life of Sergeant Lamb during the American War of Independence: *Sergeant Lamb of the Ninth* and *Proceed, Sergeant Lamb*. The research into even these rather simple tales is thorough and detailed; but the novelistic imagination seems rarely to have been engaged. Only with *The Story of Marie Powell: Wife to Mr. Milton* did Graves recapture the immediacy of his earlier novels. This is the story of a young countrywoman who, because of her father's debt, was made to marry John Milton. The exact details of the marriage, apart from its disastrous unsuitability, remain unknown today; but Graves reconstructs the life of Marie through her memoirs, presenting a less than flattering portrait of Milton. As their marriage falls apart, the country falls prey to Civil War. Milton's fortune is in the ascendant with that of parliament, but Marie's family declines as their royalist faction loses the day. Graves's contentious statement that Milton suffered from "trichomania," a morbid obsession with hair, is not the least of the charges that Diana Trilling and other critics objected to. Milton is made out to be an opportunist, prepared to use the chaos of war to further his ambition. In contrast to their awkward, hostile marriage, Marie maintains a protracted and platonic affair with a royalist officer, Sir Edmund ("Mun") Verney. Their love, free from the gruesome realities of the time, continues on an etheric plane as the Milton marriage becomes harsher. This dichotomy, as with the larger narrative, is presented entirely in 17th-century idiom, which prevents the more fantastic conceits of the relationships from lapsing entirely into absurdity. Graves confessed that he made use of this device so that the assumptions of 20th-century psychology did not interfere with the vivid air of authenticity. Marie Powell stands out as one of his greatest characters, a convincing voice who speaks for the obscure and vulnerable in a cataclysmic time.

The subject matter of his next novels was influenced radically by the research undertaken for his great work of comparative theology, *The White Goddess*. The thesis of this work is that the original religions of mankind were matriarchal in nature, and that traces of this goddess-worship still survive in existing scrip-

tures, mythology, and archaeology. *The Golden Fleece* recounts the Argonaut legend, borrowing heavily from the version by Apollonius of Rhodes. In it the Orphic myth becomes a potent symbol of death and rebirth, an offering to the goddess on whom society depended for fertility. *King Jesus* was a bolder recasting of myth, a re-examination of the legend at the heart of our culture. Graves takes the view that Jesus was a secret grandson of Herod, equipped both spiritually and temporally for the Messiahship to which Herod also aspired. The narrative follows broadly the accounts given in the canonical gospels, but the result is a version of Christ that proved unacceptable to Christian orthodoxy. To take just one example, the book explains the term Christos (the anointed one) as Chrestos (the fool); the early church embraces this gladly and become the sect of fools. Jesus attempts to remove all traces of the archaic and ecstatic goddess religions from Judaism, allying himself with the Pharisees. In his attempt he plans to become the Messiah Son of David, a political and spiritual leader; but his attempt fails and he becomes instead the lowly shepherd, groom and sacrifice to the vestigial goddess. The gentler nature of the religion that results is, ironically, the means whereby it takes over the Roman empire: the outcast and lowly of civilisation come to claim this aristocratic Messiah as their own. The combination of historical event and prophetic symbol becomes inexorably powerful, and his deification is assured. *King Jesus* is a fascinating exposition of the problematic identity of the most significant figure in history, though the complexity of detail is sometimes allowed to overwhelm the narrative; at times the story becomes lost in Graves's passionate concern to prove his case.

The last three novels of the author's career are altogether less momentous, more worthy of the "potboiler" disclaimer that Graves applied to the Claudius novels. *The Islands of Unwisdom* describes the sea adventures of Isabelle de Baretto, privateer and explorer in the age of discovery and piracy. *Homer's Daughter* is set in Sicily around 750 B.C. and relates the exploits of a conjectural Nausicca. *They Hanged My Saintly Billy* examines the evidence in the celebrated case of Dr. William Palmer of Rugely, convicted for poisoning and hanged in 1857; characteristically, Graves ignores the accepted guilt of his subject and finds him not guilty. Though widely diverse in content, the books share a view of humanity we might associate with Claudius: tolerant, non-judgemental, and disputatious. William Palmer, for instance, might be a cheat, liar, and thief, but Graves (or his anonymous narrator) evinces an affection for him, and considers him incapable of murder. The same robust and elastic sensibility informs all of Graves's work.

For all their varied milieux, Graves's novels all take place in times of radical transformation, underscoring the dangerous nature of human existence by reference to exceptional circumstances. If they are adventure stories, it is not only because they portray sensational incidents, but because the author is adventuring in the human personality. Graves himself appeared to believe he was in some way travelling to the past; his great achievement is that he convincingly performed the same magic on the reader, the supreme illusion of bringing the dead to life.

—Alan Murphy

GRAY, Angela. See **DANIELS, Dorothy.**

GRAY, Caroline. See **NICOLE, Christopher.**

GRAY, Ellington. See **JACOB, Naomi.**

GRAY, Harriet. See **ROBINS, Denise.**

GREAVES, Richard. See **McCUTCHEON, George Barr.**

GREEN, Peter (Morris). Also writes as Denis Delaney. British. Born in London, 22 December 1924. Educated at Charterhouse School, Surrey; Trinity College, Cambridge (Craven scholar and student, 1950), 1947–52, B.A. (honours) in classics 1950; M.A. and Ph.D. 1954. Served in the Royal Air Force Volunteer Reserve, 1943–47: with Burma Command, 1944–46. Married 1) Lalage Isobel Pulvertaft in 1951 (marriage dissolved), two sons and one daughter; 2) Carin Margreta Christensen in 1975. Editor, *Cambridge Review*, 1950–51; Director of Studies in Classics, Selwyn College, Cambridge, 1951–52; fiction critic, *Daily Telegraph*, London, 1953–63; literary adviser, Bodley Head Ltd., publishers, London, 1957–58; consultant editor, Hodder and Stoughton Ltd., publishers, London, 1960–63; television critic, the *Listener*, London, 1961–63; film critic, *John o' London's*, 1961–63; full-time writer in Greece, 1963–71: teacher of Greek history and literature, College Year in Athens, 1966–71. Visiting Professor, 1971–72, since 1973 Professor of Classics, and since 1982 James R. Dougherty Jr. Centennial Professor of Classics, University of Texas, Austin. Visiting Professor of Classics, University of California, Los Angeles, 1976; Mellon Professor of Humanities, Tulane University, New Orleans, 1986. Recipient: Royal Society of Literature Heinemann award, 1958; National Endowment for the Humanities fellowship, 1983. Fellow, 1956, and member of the Council, 1958–63, Royal Society of Literature. Address: Department of Classics, University of Texas, 123 Waggener Hall, Austin, Texas 78712, U.S.A.

ROMANCE AND HISTORICAL PUBLICATIONS

Novels

Achilles His Armour. London, Murray, 1955; New York, Doubleday, 1967.
The Sword of Pleasure. London, Murray, 1957; Cleveland, World, 1958.
The Laughter of Aphrodite. London, Murray, 1965; New York, Doubleday, 1966.

OTHER PUBLICATIONS

Novel

Cat in Gloves (as Denis Delaney). London, Gryphon, 1956.

Short Stories

Habeas Corpus and Other Stories. London, Hamish Hamilton, 1962; Cleveland, World, 1963.

Other

The Expanding Eye: A First Journey to the Mediterranean. London, Dobson, 1953; New York, Abelard Schuman, 1957.
Sir Thomas Browne. London, Longman, 1959.
Kenneth Grahame 1859–1932: A Study of His Life, Work and Times. London, Murray, 1959; as *Kenneth Grahame: A Biography*, Cleveland, World, 1959; abridged edition, as *Beyond the Wild Wood: The World of Kenneth Grahame*, Exeter, Devon, Webb and Bower, 1982; New York, Facts on File, 1983.
Essays in Antiquity. London, Murray, and Cleveland, World, 1960.
John Skelton. London, Longman, 1960.
Look at the Romans (for children). London, Hamish Hamilton, 1963.
Alexander the Great: A Biography. London, Weidenfeld and Nicolson, and New York, Praeger, 1970.
Armada from Athens. New York, Doubleday, 1970; London, Hodder and Stoughton, 1971.
The Year of Salamis 480–479 B.C.. London, Weidenfeld and Nicolson, 1970; as *Xerxes at Salamis*, New York, Praeger, 1970.
The Shadow of the Parthenon: Studies in Ancient History and Literature. London, Temple Smith, and Berkeley, University of California Press, 1972.
A Concise History of Ancient Greece to the Close of the Classical Era. London, Thames and Hudson, 1973; as *Ancient Greece: An Illustrated History*, New York, Viking Press, 1973.
The Parthenon, with the Editors of Newsweek. New York, Newsweek, and London, Readers Digest, 1973.
Alexander of Macedon 356–323 B.C.: A Historical Biography. London, Penguin, 1974.

Editor, *Poetry from Cambridge, 1947–1950*. London, Fortune Press, 1951.
Editor, *Appreciations: Essays*, by Clifton Fadiman. London, Hodder and Stoughton, 1962.

Translator, *The Fountain at Marlieux*, by Claude Aveline. London, Dobson, and New York, Roy, 1954.
Translator, *Tanguy: The Story of a Child of Our Time*, by Michel del Castillo. London, Muller, 1958; as *A Child of Our Time*, New York, Knopf, 1958.
Translator, *The Lottery*, by Paul Guimard. London, Faber, 1958; as *House of Happiness*, Boston, Houghton Mifflin, 1960.
Translator, *The Lion*, by Joseph Kessel. London, Hart Davis, and New York, Knopf, 1959.
Translator, *Antoine*, by Marie Gisèle Landes. London, Muller, 1959.
Translator, *The Children of Lilith*, by Guy Piazzini. London, Hodder and Stoughton, and New York, Dutton, 1960.
Translator, *Journey into the Blue*, by Gusztáv Rab. London, Sidgwick and Jackson, and New York, Pantheon, 1960.
Translator, *A Room in Budapest*, by Gusztáv Rab. London, Sidgwick and Jackson, 1961.
Translator, *Destiny of Fire*, by Zoe Oldenbourg. London, Gollancz, and New York, Pantheon, 1961.
Translator, *Massacre of Montségur: A History of the Albigensian Crusade*, by Zoe Oldenbourg. London, Weidenfeld and Nicolson, 1961; New York, Pantheon, 1962.

Translator, *The Novice*, by Giovanni Arpino. London, Hodder and Stoughton, 1961; New York, Braziller, 1962.

Translator, *The Prime of Life*, by Simone de Beauvoir. London, Deutsch-Weidenfeld and Nicolson, and Cleveland, World, 1962.

Translator, *The Black Dove*, by Enrico Emanuelli. London, Macdonald, 1962.

Translator, *Innocence*, by Diane Giguère. London, Gollancz, 1962.

Translator, *Douchka: The Story of a Dog*, by Colette Andry. London, Souvenir Press, 1963; as *Behind the Bathtub: The Story of a French Dog*, Boston, Little Brown, 1963.

Translator, *Diamond River*, by Sadio Garavini de Turno. London, Hamish Hamilton, and New York, Harcourt Brace, 1963.

Translator, *Love Without Grace*, by Luciana d' Arad. London, Muller, 1963.

Translator, *Calvary Street*, by Miklós Bátori. London, Constable, 1963.

Translator, *Okapi Fever*, by Philippe Diolé. London, Souvenir Press, and New York, Viking Press, 1965.

Translator, *Cordelia and Other Stories*, by Françoise Mallet-Joris. New York, Farrar Straus, and London, W. H. Allen, 1965.

Translator, *The Novel Computer*, by Robert Escarpit. London, Secker and Warburg, 1966.

Translator, *The Flood*, by J.-M. G. Le Clézio. London, Hamish Hamilton, 1966; New York, Atheneum, 1968.

Translator, *The Sixteen Satires of Juvenal*. London, Penguin, 1967.

Translator, *The Sardinian Smile*, by Petru Dumitriu. London, Collins, and New York, Holt Rinehart, 1968.

Translator, *Ovid: The Erotic Poems*. London, Penguin, 1982; New York, Penguin, 1983.

Translator of other historical and biographical works.

*   *   *

Peter Green is one of the few contemporary "men of letters." Although copious and various both in his functions and his publications, he is probably at his best when working in the fields of ancient history and classical literature; and of his four works of fiction three are novels set in antiquity.

Achilles His Armour is based on the life of the Athenian hero and traitor, Alcibiades. The writing is self-indulgent, prolix and full of clichés; it is also vigorous, fluent and clear. The treatment is "modern," in the sense that motive and action, whether political or personal, are rendered in terms which would be immediately comprehensible by "the man on the Bakerloo line;" but there is no attempt to draw vulgar or pretentious comparisons between Alcibiades's era and our own. The historical background, as known to scholars, is described with loving skill; and where speculation is required, Green speculates with the same zestful abandon as his hero exhibits (rather too repeatedly) in his romps through battlefield and brothel.

The Sword of Pleasure is altogether a more mature performance. Purporting to be the lost memoirs of the Roman dictator, Lucius Cornelius Sulla, it is not quite so alarmingly hectic as the previous novel and far more concise. Green introduces a new element of articulate melancholy, which at its best embodies much pithy moral comment, and certainly helps to maintain the illusion that we are reading the testament of a worldy and worn out aristocrat. There is some sharp and memorable events both historical and fictitious; and Green's characters have now begun to talk to each other instead of reciprocating lectures.

The Laughter of Aphrodite is about the poet Sappho, a far more difficult subject than either Alcibiades or Sulla, if only because next to nothing is known of her. Green fabricates his own Sappho with the aid of a poetic but perhaps overheated fancy, which he deploys with a canny sense of literary tactics learnt (by this stage of his career) from the long experience of reviewing other writers' novels. The result is sometimes sentimental, sometimes lurid, but always fascinating, and convincing. This is the first of Green's novels which one closes quite definitely wishing it were longer.

Green's paramount gift as a novelist is for presenting blow-by-blow accounts of what happens and why with the immediacy of a brilliant if often tasteless on-the-spot reporter. He is also a man for making, and then insisting upon, unpopular but irrefutable common sense judgments about men and affairs: he dearly loves to coin and "unacceptable" or unfashionable truth. The short stories in *Habeas Corpus* contain several such, as applied to sexual activities.

The one thing Green has not learnt over the years is to disguise his relish at the annoyance which he knows these truths will cause. Inside the weighty and respected *Littérateur* there is always the jeering fourth-former cocking two-handed snooks.

—Simon Raven

GREIG, Maysie. Pseudonym for Jennifer Greig-Smith; also wrote as Jennifer Ames; Ann Barclay; Mary Douglas Warre; Mary Douglas Warren. Australian. Born in Sydney, New South Wales, in 1902. Educated at Presbyterian Ladies' College, Pymble, New South Wales. Married 1) Delano Ames; 2) the writer Maxwell Murray in 1937 (died 1956); 3) Jan Sopoushek in 1959. Journalist, Sydney *Sun*, 1919–20, before coming to London: contributor to *Westminster Gazette*, *Daily Sketch*, and *Mirror*; also worked in New York and Boston. Vice-President, New South Wales PEN. *Died 10 June 1971.*

ROMANCE AND HISTORICAL PUBLICATIONS

Novels

Peggy of Beacon Hill. Boston, Small Maynard, 1924; London, Jenkins, 1926.
The Luxury Husband. London, Long, and New York, Dial Press, 1928.
Ragamuffin. London, Long, 1929.
Satin Straps. London, Long, and New York, Dial Press, 1929.
Jasmine—Take Care! or, A Girl Must Marry. London, Benn, 1930; as *A Girl Must Marry*, New York, Dial Press, 1931.
Lovely Clay. London, Benn, 1930; New York, Doubleday, 1933.
A Nice Girl Comes to Town. London, Long, and New York, Dial Press, 1930.
The Man She Bought. New York, Dial Press, 1930.
This Way to Happiness. London, Long, 1931; New York, Dial Press, 1932; as *Janice*, Cleveland, World, 1947.
One-Man Girl. London, Benn, and New York, Dial Press, 1931.
The Women Money Buys. New York, Dial Press, 1931.
Faint Heart, Fair Lady. London, Long, 1932.
Laughing Cavalier. London, Long, 1932.
Little Sisters Don't Count. London, Benn, 1932; New York, Doubleday, 1934.

Cake Without Icing. London, Benn, and New York, Dial Press, 1932; revised edition, as *Marriage Without a Ring*, London, Collins, 1972.

Professional Lover. London, Benn, and New York, Doubleday, 1933; as *Screen Lover*, London, Collins, 1969.

Parents Are a Problem. London, Hodder and Stoughton, 1933; as *Love, Honour, and Obey*, New York, Doubleday, 1933.

A Bad Girl Leaves Town. New York, Doubleday, 1933.

Men Act That Way. New York, Doubleday, 1933.

Heart Appeal. London, Hodder and Stoughton, 1934; New York, Doubleday, 1935.

She Walked into His Parlour. London, Hodder and Stoughton, 1934.

Ten Cent Love. New York, Doubleday, 1934.

I Lost My Heart. London, Hodder and Stoughton, 1935; New York, Doubleday, 1936; as *The Sinister Island* (as Jennifer Ames), London, Collins, 1968.

Love and Let Me Go. New York, Doubleday, 1935; London, Hodder and Stoughton, 1936; as *Love Me*, London, Collins, 1971.

Marry in Haste. London, Hodder and Stoughton, and New York, Doubleday, 1935.

Rich Man, Poor Girl. London, Hodder and Stoughton, and New York, Doubleday, 1935.

Challenge to Happiness. London, Hodder and Stoughton, 1936; New York, Doubleday, 1937.

The Girl from Nowhere. Hanley, Staffordshire, Locker, 1936; New York, Doubleday, 1942; as *The Girl Who Wasn't Welcome*, London, Collins, 1969.

Odds on Love. London, Hodder and Stoughton, and New York, Doubleday, 1936.

Workaday Lady. London, Hodder and Stoughton, and New York, Doubleday, 1936.

Touching the Clouds. New York, Doubleday, 1936.

New Moon Through a Window. London, Hodder and Stoughton, and New York, Doubleday, 1937.

Retreat from Love. London, Hodder and Stoughton, 1937; as Jennifer Ames, New York, Doubleday, 1937.

The Pretty One. London, Hodder and Stoughton, 1937; as Jennifer Ames, New York, Doubleday, 1937.

The Girl Men Talked About. London, Hodder and Stoughton, 1938; as *Stopover in Paradise*, New York, Doubleday, 1938; as *The Golden Garden*, London, Collins, 1968.

Young Man Without Money. London, Hodder and Stoughton, 1938; as *Debutante in Uniform*, New York, Doubleday, 1938.

Stepping under Ladders. London, Hodder and Stoughton, 1938; New York, Doubleday, 1939; as *Girl in Jeopardy*, London, Collins, 1967.

Other Women's Beauty. London, Hodder and Stoughton, 1938.

Strange Beauty. New York, Doubleday, 1938.

Ask the Parlourmaid. London, Hodder and Stoughton, 1939; as *Unmarried Couple*, New York, Doubleday, 1940.

Girl on His Hands. London, Hodder and Stoughton, and New York, Doubleday, 1939.

A Man to Protect You. London, Hodder and Stoughton, and New York, Doubleday, 1939.

Grand Relations. London, Hodder and Stoughton, 1940; as *A Fortune in Romance*, New York, Doubleday, 1940; as *A Girl and Her Money*, London, Collins, 1971.

The Man Is Always Right. London, Hodder and Stoughton, and New York, Doubleday, 1940.

Rich Twin, Poor Twin. London, Hodder and Stoughton, and New York, Doubleday, 1940.

Girl Without Credit. New York, Doubleday, 1941; London, Hodder and Stoughton, 1942.

This Desirable Bachelor. London, Hodder and Stoughton, and New York, Doubleday, 1941.

Heaven Isn't Here. New York, Doubleday, 1941.

No Retreat from Love. New York, Doubleday, 1942; Hanley, Staffordshire, Locker, 1947.

Salute Me Darling. London, Hodder and Stoughton, 1942; as *Heartbreak for Two*, New York, Doubleday, 1942.

The Wishing Star. New York, Doubleday, 1942; as Mary Douglas Warre, London, Hutchinson, 1943.

Pathway to Paradise. New York, Doubleday, 1942; London, Collins, 1943.

Professional Hero. London, Collins, and New York, Doubleday, 1943.

I've Always Loved You. New York, Doubleday, 1943.

Reluctant Millionaire. London, Collins, 1944; New York, Random House, 1945.

One Room for His Highness. London, Collins, 1944.

Girl with a Million. London, Collins, 1945.

I Loved Her Yesterday. London, Collins, 1945.

Darling Clementine. London, Collins, 1946; as *Candidate for Love*, New York, Random House, 1947.

Table for Two. London, Collins, and New York, Random House, 1946.

Castle in the Air. London, Collins, 1947.

The Thirteenth Girl. Hanley, Staffordshire, Locker, 1947.

Take This Man. London, Collins, 1947.

I Met Him Again. London, Collins, 1948.

Yours Forever. London, Collins, and New York, Random House, 1948.

Whispers in the Sun. London, Collins, and New York, Random House, 1949; as *The Reluctant Cinderella* (as Jennifer Ames), New York, Avalon, and Collins, 1952.

Dark Carnival. New York, Random House, 1950; as Jennifer Ames, London, Collins, 1951.

My Heart's Down Under. London, Collins, 1951; as Jennifer Ames, New York, Avalon, 1951.

It Happened One Flight. London, Collins, 1951; New York, Macfadden, 1966.

London, Here I Come. London, Collins, 1951; as *Assignment to Love* (as Jennifer Ames), New York, Avalon, 1953.

Wagon to a Star. London, Collins, 1952; as Jennifer Ames, New York, Avalon, 1953.

Lovers under the Sun. London, Collins, 1954; as *Passport to Happiness*, New York, Avalon, 1955; as *Ship's Doctor*, Collins, 1966.

That Girl in Nice. London, Collins, 1954; as *Love Is a Gamble* (as Jennifer Ames), New York, Avalon, 1954.

Cloak and Dagger Lover. London, Collins, 1955; as *Moon over the Water* (as Mary Douglas Warren), New York, Arcadia House, 1956.

Kiss in Sunlight. London, Collins, 1956; New York, Avalon, 1957.

Girl Without Money. London, Collins, 1957.

No Dowry for Jennifer. New York, Avalon, 1957.

Love Is a Gambler. London, Collins, 1958.

Love Is a Thief. London, Collins, 1959; New York, Macfadden, 1966.

Send for Miss Marshall. London, Collins, 1959.

Follow Your Love. New York, Avalon, 1959.

Doctor in Exile. London, Collins, 1960; New York, Avalon, 1961.

Catch Up to Love. New York, Avalon, 1960.

Kiss of Promise. New York, Avalon, 1960.

Cherry Blossom Love. London, Collins, 1961; New York, Macfadden, 1967.

Every Woman's Man. London, Collins, 1961; New York, Macfadden, 1966.

The Doctor Is a Lady. London, Collins, 1962.

Nurse at St. Catherine's. London, Collins, 1963.

French Girl in Love. London, Collins, 1963.

Every Woman's Doctor. London, Collins, 1964.

Married Quarters. London, Collins, 1964; New York, Macfadden, 1966.

Nurse in Danger. London, Collins, 1964.

The Doctor and the Dancer. London, Collins, 1965.

Doctor on Wings. London, Collins, 1966.

Never the Same. London, Collins, 1970.

Novels as Jennifer Ames

Pandora Lifts the Veil. New York, Dial Press, 1932; London, Hodder and Stoughton, 1933.

Anything But Love. London, Hodder and Stoughton, 1933.

Cruise. London, Hodder and Stoughton, 1934; as *Romance on a Cruise* (as Maysie Greig), New York, Doubleday, 1935.

Good Sport. London, Hodder and Stoughton, 1934; as Maysie Greig, New York, Doubleday, 1934; as *Love Will Win*, London, Fontana, 1969.

Romance for Sale. London, Hodder and Stoughton, 1934; as Maysie Greig, New York, Doubleday, 1934.

I'll Get over It. London, Hodder and Stoughton, 1935; as Maysie Greig, New York, Doubleday, 1936; as *Jilted* (as Jennifer Ames), London, Collins, 1968.

Sweet Peril. London, Hodder and Stoughton, 1935; as *Sweet Danger* (as Maysie Greig), New York, Doubleday, 1935.

I Seek My Love. London, Hodder and Stoughton, 1936; as *Dreams Get You Nowhere* (as Maysie Greig), New York, Doubleday, 1937.

Tinted Dream. London, Hodder and Stoughton, 1936; as *Doctor's Wife* (as Maysie Greig), New York, Doubleday, 1937; as *Doctor Brad's Nurse*, London, Collins, 1966.

Her World of Men. London, Hodder and Stoughton, 1937; as Maysie Greig, New York, Doubleday, 1938.

Elder Sister. London, Hodder and Stoughton, 1938; New York, Doubleday, 1939.

Stranger Sweetheart. London, Hodder and Stoughton, 1938; as *Honeymoons Arranged* (as Maysie Greig), New York, Doubleday, 1938.

Bury the Past. London, Hodder and Stoughton, 1939; as Maysie Greig, New York, Doubleday, 1939.

Dangerous Holiday. London, Hodder and Stoughton, 1939; as *Dangerous Cruise* (as Maysie Greig), New York, Doubleday, 1940.

Not One of Us. London, Hodder and Stoughton, 1939; as Maysie Greig, New York, Doubleday, 1939.

Make the Man Notice You. London, Hodder and Stoughton, 1940; as Maysie Greig, New York, Doubleday, 1940.

Honeymoon Alone. London, Hodder and Stoughton, 1940; as Maysie Greig, New York, Doubleday, 1941; as *Honeymoon for One*, London, Collins, 1971.

Ring Without Romance. London, Hodder and Stoughton, 1940; as Maysie Greig, New York, Doubleday, 1941.

Too Many Women. London, Hodder and Stoughton, 1941; as Maysie Greig, New York, Doubleday, 1941.

Diplomatic Honeymoon. London, Collins, 1942; as Maysie Greig, New York, Doubleday, 1942.

Dark Sunlight. London, Collins, 1943.

The Impossible Marriage. London, Collins, 1943.

At the Same Time Tomorrow. London, Collins, 1944; as Maysie Greig, New York, Doubleday, 1944.

Restless Beauty. London, Collins, 1944.

I Married Mr. Richardson. London, Collins, 1945.

Journey in the Dark. London, Collins, 1945.

Lovers in the Dark. London, Collins, 1946.

Take Your Choice, Lady. London, Collins, 1946.

Fear Kissed My Lips. London, Collins, 1947.

Heart in Darkness. New York, Arcadia House, 1947.

Shadow Across My Heart. London, Collins, 1948; as Mary Douglas Warren, New York, Arcadia House, 1952.

She'll Take the High Road. London, Collins, 1948.

Danger Wakes My Heart. London, Collins, 1949; as *Danger in Eden*, New York, Avalon, 1950.

Lips for a Stranger. London, Collins, 1949.

Too Much Alone. London, Collins, 1950.

Flight to Happiness. New York, Avalon, 1950.

After Tomorrow. New York, Avalon, 1951; as *Overseas Nurse*, New York, Ace, 1961.

The Frightened Heart. London, Collins, 1952; as *Date with Danger* (as Maysie Greig), New York, Random House, 1952.

The Fearful Paradise. London, Collins, 1953; as *This Fearful Paradise* (as Maysie Greig), New York, Random House, 1953.

Flight into Fear. London, Collins, and New York, Avalon, 1954.

Shadows Across the Sun. London, Collins, 1955; as *Shadow over the Island* (as Mary Douglas Warren), New York, Arcadia House, 1955.

Rough Seas to Sunrise. London, Collins, 1956; as *Winds of Fear* (as Maysie Greig), New York, Avalon, 1956.

Night of Carnival. London, Collins, 1956.

Love on Dark Wings. London, Collins, 1957.

Follow Your Dream. New York, Avalon, 1957.

Beloved Knight. London, Collins, 1958; New York, Avalon, 1959.

Doctor's Nurse. London, Collins, 1959.

Love in a Far Country. London, Collins, 1960; New York, Avalon, 1965.

Love in the East. London, Collins, 1960.

Perilous Quest. New York, Avalon, 1960.

Her Heart's Desire. New York, Avalon, 1961.

Diana Goes to Tokyo. London, Collins, 1961.

It Started in Hongkong. London, Collins, 1961.

The Timid Cleopatra. London, Collins, 1962.

Honeymoon in Manila. London, Collins, 1962.

Geisha in the House. London, Collins, 1963.

Sinners in Paradise. London, Collins, 1963.

The Two of Us. London, Collins, 1964.

Happy Island. London, Collins, 1964.

Nurse's Holiday. London, Collins, 1965.

Nurse's Story. London, Collins, 1965.

Doctor Ted's Clinic. London, Collins, 1967.

The Doctor Takes a Holiday. London, Collins, 1969.

Write from the Heart. London, Hale, 1972.

Novels as Ann Barclay

Other Men's Arms. London, Collins, 1936.

Swing High, Swing Low. London, Collins, 1936.

Men as Her Stepping Stones. London, Collins, 1937; as Maysie Greig, New York, Doubleday, 1938.

Novels as Mary Douglas Warren

Reunion in Reno. New York, Carlton House, 1941.

The Rich Are Not Proud. New York, Carlton House, 1942.

Southern Star. New York, Arcadia House, 1950.

The Manor Farm. New York, Arcadia House, 1951.

The Sunny Island. New York, Arcadia House, 1952.
Salt Harbor. New York, Arcadia House, 1953.
The High Road. New York, Arcadia House, 1954.
The Doctor Decides. London, Collins, 1963.

*   *   *

Maysie Greig, writing prolifically under several names, favoured a heroine who was pert and petite rather than philosophical and introspective. Unlike the romantic heroines of only a very few years earlier, Greig's do not believe in a personal God, nor are they stirred by Christian doubt or reflection, although some of the activities usually associated with belief in a deity are practised by hero and heroine, particularly at times of great stress or sexual tension. Thus, for example, in *Love and Let Me Go* we see Sally and Red, an unreliable wandering artist, rush into a marriage against the wishes of Sally's beastly family who believe in "duty above love." Sally's dad won't let them sleep together even after marriage. Having originally met on a camping holiday (hiking, cycling, walking, and the great outdoors were much in vogue in the mid-1930's), Sally and Red finally manage to consummate that marriage while camping in the Lake District. As Red carries his girlish bride into their honeymoon tent, he is moved to pray to an un-named deity. " 'I'm not a religious man but I feel like going down on my knees right now and praying that our love will always be as glorious as it is now.' She nodded slowly." This camping scene is not typical. On the whole, Greig liked her heroines to be sophisticated, elegant, languid, fascinated by good clothes and firm men. While it used to be a girl's soul that counted for so much, now it is her clothes and make-up. Greig's girls spend a great deal of time getting ready to go out, wondering what to wear to suit the surroundings: "I'll wear it tonight when he takes me out to dinner somewhere swish." While being courted, a girl liked to be taken out to dine in Soho or Knightsbridge, followed by a show or a visit to a nightclub. Occasionally, beneath her desire for would-be glamorous outings with urban lustre, a girl showed a wide-eyed, breathless spirit, questing for adventure, which could be absorbed by a variation on background. Greig tried out various settings—the hospital romance, travel, a forest fire, a romance set in "Jamaica's fashionable Montego Bay," and even a political romance, *Rich Twin, Poor Twin*.

Although some of the girls hold down jobs—Jennifer Prudence in *Anything But Love* is a successful magazine illustrator, Annette in *Kiss in Sunlight* a restless nurse, while the occupation of the heroine of *The Doctor Is a Lady* is self-explanatory—the chief occupation of these girls is to preserve reputation and to find a man, preferably as described in the title *A Man to Protect You*. Such chaps are lean and hard: "Jason, lean, dark-skinned, was very distinctive in full dress kit. Jenny felt all the other women in the dining room must be envying her. Or if they weren't they should be!" Nigel, we read, looked very attractive in his well-cut dark blue suit. And on another occasion, we see how the cut accentuated his height and powerful shoulders. But despite many jutting jaws and powerful shoulders, the heroes conform to an ideal of middle-class gentility and prim pleasantness. The ideal man is a soft-centred savage in city clothes.

In the 1920's and 1930's new ideas on sexual freedom, on allowing the biological urge to follow its natural course, were being advocated by more serious writers and philosophers, while practical advice was being offered by Marie Stopes. Despite alluringly daring titles like *Too Many Women*, *Anything But Love*, *Professional Lover*, or *Fear Kissed My Lips*, sexual freedom (either before or after marriage) was not sought by a Greig girl. There was still one man for one woman. Chastity was a much prized virtue, and virginity, although not openly named as such, was "something very precious." It was, as a heroine who has narrowly avoided seduction, observes: "Something which she had kept locked inside her for years. Something which, once broken, could never be repaired. Something he probably didn't know about, couldn't even guess at."

Any critique of Greig's approach to her craft, is best summed up in her own resumé of her philosophy.

I write happy love stories because I believe happiness is the greatest virtue in the world and misery the greatest sin. You can so infect people with your own misery that you can make them miserable when they were quite happy and contented before. To be happy is as though you opened every window in your mind and let in strong, clean sunlight. That is why I think everyone should try to be happy, and read stories that make one happy, rather than those that increase one's sense of futility and despair. If I tried to write a really miserable story I think I should end up by committing suicide!

This happiness was only to be found in the discovery of a true and lasting love. That love, once established, carried a sanctity. One must revere happy love. Her own beliefs were echoed by her characters.

"Happiness is the most important thing," he said quietly, "and love. Not only love of a woman, but love of the whole world you are living in. Why waste time scrambling for wordly goods when but to live happily and simply gives one such an intense pleasure? . . . Do you think that God intended any of us to lead a life of miserable self-sacrifice for the sake of others? Do you think He would have given us the power of love if He meant us to deny that love when it came to us? No, your first duty lies to our love, because that's the most important thing in the world."

Medieval courtly love may have held that true love was only possible through a passion created by suffering, continual partings and re-unions, and ultimate separation. Greig, however, held that true love could, and should, be happy love, and that this happiness was a beginning and an end in itself. This was not only what she believed, but what her reading public wanted. She gave it to them, and "won the affection of a great and admiring public," who shared her view that "Love is the most fascinating, inspiring, complete emotion in the world. Happiness is the greatest virtue, and misery the greatest sin in the world." Shallow, vacuous statements to some, but indisputable and convincing dogma to her and her readership.

—Rachel Anderson

———

GREY, Belinda. See **PETERS, Maureen.**

———

GREY, Brenda. See **MACKINLAY, Leila.**

———

GREY, Georgina. See **ROBY, Mary Linn.**

GRIMSTEAD, Hettie. Also writes as Marsha Manning. British. Born in Manchester, Lancashire. Educated privately. Overseas press officer, ENSA, during World War II. Journalist, United Press International, for 25 years. Agent: Curtis Brown, 162–168 Regent Street, London W1R 5TB. Address: c/o Robert Hale Ltd., 45–47 Clerkenwell Green, London EC1R 0HT, England.

ROMANCE AND HISTORICAL PUBLICATIONS

Novels

Painted Virgin. London, Daniel, 1931.
The Journey Home. London, Mills and Boon, 1950.
Navy Blue Lady. London, Mills and Boon, 1951.
The Twisted Road. London, Mills and Boon, 1951.
The Captured Heart. London, Mills and Boon, 1952.
Strangers May Kiss. London, Mills and Boon, 1952.
The Passionate Summer. London, Mills and Boon, 1953.
Song of Surrender. London, Mills and Boon, 1953.
Candles for Love. London, Mills and Boon, 1954.
Winds of Desire. London, Mills and Boon, 1954.
Enchanted August. London, Mills and Boon, 1955.
The Tender Pilgrim. London, Mills and Boon, 1955.
The Burning Flame. London, Mills and Boon, 1956.
Escape to Paradise. London, Mills and Boon, 1956.
The Reluctant Bride. London, Mills and Boon, 1957.
Scales of Love. London, Mills and Boon, 1957.
The Unknown Heart. London, Mills and Boon, 1958.
Tinsel Kisses. London, Mills and Boon, 1958.
Dream Street. London, Mills and Boon, 1959.
A Kiss in the Sun. London, Mills and Boon, 1959; New York, Paperback Library, 1966.
The Path to Love. London, Mills and Boon, 1960.
Sweet Prisoner. London, Mills and Boon, 1961.
The Golden Moment. London, Mills and Boon, 1962.
Love Has Two Faces. London, Mills and Boon, 1962.
Wedding for Three. London, Mills and Boon, 1963.
Whisper to the Stars. London, Mills and Boon, 1963; Toronto, Harlequin, 1970.
When April Sings. London, Mills and Boon, 1964.
The Door of the Heart. London, Mills and Boon, 1965.
Once upon a Kiss. London, Mills and Boon, 1965.
Shake Down the Moon. London, Mills and Boon, 1966.
The Sweetheart Tree. London, Mills and Boon, 1966.
Orchids for the Bride. London, Mills and Boon, 1967.
The Tender Chord. London, Mills and Boon, 1967.
Chase a Rainbow. London, Mills and Boon, 1968.
Portrait of Paula. London, Mills and Boon, 1968; New York, Fawcett, 1975.
September's Girl. London, Mills and Boon, 1969; New York, Fawcett, 1975.
The Lovely Day. London, Mills and Boon, 1970.
Roses for Breakfast. London, Mills and Boon, 1970; New York, Fawcett, 1975.
Island Affair. London, Mills and Boon, 1971; New York, Fawcett, 1975.
The Winter Rose. London, Mills and Boon, 1972; New York, Fawcett, 1975.
Fires of Spring. London, Mills and Boon, 1973; New York, Fawcett, 1975.
Tuesday's Child. London, Mills and Boon, 1973; New York, Fawcett, 1975.
The Tender Vine. London, Mills and Boon, 1974; New York, Fawcett, 1976.

Sister Rose's Holiday. London, Mills and Boon, 1975.

Novels as Marsha Manning

Kisses for Three. London, Ward Lock, 1958; New York, Paperback Library, 1966.
Passport to Love. London, Ward Lock, 1958.
The Heart Alone. London, Ward Lock, 1959.
Skyscraper Hotel. London, Ward Lock, 1959.
Because You're Mine. London, Ward Lock, 1960.
Magic of the Moon. London, Ward Lock, 1961.
Star of Desire. London, Ward Lock, 1961.
Circle of Dreams. London, Ward Lock, 1962.
Roses for the Bride. London, Ward Lock, 1962.
Flower of the Heart. London, Ward Lock, 1963.
Lucy in London. London, Ward Lock, 1964.
Our Miss Penny. London, Ward Lock, 1964.
Sister Marion's Summer. London, Ward Lock, 1965.
Lover Come Lonely. London, Ward Lock, 1965; New York, Arcadia House, 1967.
Full Summer's Kiss. London, Ward Lock, 1966.
The Proud Lover. London, Ward Lock, 1966; New York, Fawcett, 1975.
Four of Hearts. London, Ward Lock, and New York, Arcadia House, 1967.
Dreams in the Sun. London, Ward Lock, 1967; New York, Bantam, 1971.
Friend of the Bride. London, Ward Lock, 1968.
Some Day My Love. London, Ward Lock, 1968.
Yesterday's Lover. London, Mills and Boon, 1969.
Holiday Affair. London, Mills and Boon, 1969.
To Catch a Dream. London, Mills and Boon, 1970; New York, Fawcett, 1974.
Summer Song. London, Mills and Boon, 1971; New York, Fawcett, 1975.
The Smiling Moon. London, Mills and Boon, 1972; New York, Fawcett, 1974.
Sweet Friday. London, Mills and Boon, 1972; New York, Fawcett, 1974.
The Magic City. London, Mills and Boon, 1973; New York, Fawcett, 1976.
Dance of Summer. London, Mills and Boon, 1974; New York, Fawcett, 1976.
Wedding of the Year. London, Mills and Boon, 1974; New York, Fawcett, 1976.
Chance Encounter. London, Mills and Boon, 1975.
Day of Roses. London, Mills and Boon, 1976.
The Passionate Rivals. London, Hale, 1978.

*   *   *

Hettie Grimstead has had a long career as a romance novelist beginning with *Painted Virgin* (1931), a classic story of the girl going from rags to riches via the stage and giving it up for love. There are period colour and social observations in the book.

After something of a gap, Grimstead returned to a successful romance writing formula which involves classic romantic situations, such as the shipboard romance of *The Captured Heart*. There the romantic situations are seen through the eyes of a young heroine, and are predictable and kept fairly simple. There is often glamour added by a foreign setting. The emotions displayed are healthy and conventional and do not transgress safe bounds. Romantic attraction often occurs as a disturbing but unspecified effect.

The plots of Grimstead's novels revolve about the theme of unusually sensible, attractive, but colourless young women who, on entering a new career, are confronted with the dilemma of choosing between two young men, one of whom is a steady reliable suitor, the other a dashing Don Juan. The different novels present variations upon that basically triangular theme: thus in *Roses for Breakfast* the dashing male really does love her, and, in the dramatic turn, where she only discovers his love at the very end of the novel, she gives up her steady fiancé who loves her to go off and marry the other. In *Chase a Rainbow* there are two Don Juan types, one perfidious and the other awakening too late to his true feeling for her, but the heroine chooses steady love over both of these. In *The Lovely Day* the Don Juan is unmasked as a gold digger and the heroine is then able to appreciate the steady one who loves her.

There is not much character or emotional development in Grimstead's novels. Love is based on proven immediate physical attraction by the first kiss the hero and heroine share: thus the heroine in *Chase a Rainbow* could say, "when you kissed me, that was the proof I needed. Now I am sure of your love." The heroines are uncomplicated and trusting, believing in a happy ever after love and marriage.

Another way in which Grimstead achieves variety in her many novels is by changing the career of the heroine and her environment. She chooses careers such as office girl, student au-pair, and actress which have wide and varying degrees of appeal to the young reading public. Within this apparently realistic context her heroines unrealistically find themselves pursued by rich, handsome, eligible bachelors who are head over heels in love with them. Usually the heroine doesn't seem worthy of such devotion. This type of romance would appeal to previous generations of young inexperienced women, but the love displayed is almost too chaste by modern standards.

This style of writing, even though it dates from the 1950's to the 1970's, is fixed in an earlier tradition, and, with its rather simple titles, naive attitudes, and brittle glamour, would be considered very dated to a much more cynical generation.

—P. R. Meldrum

GRUNDY, (Mrs.) Mabel (Sarah) Barnes.

Romance and Historical Publications

Novels

A Thames Camp. Bristol, Arrowsmith, 1902; as *Two in a Tent—and Jane*, 1913.
The Vacillations of Hazel. Bristol, Arrowsmith, 1905.
Marguerite's Wonderful Year. Bristol, Arrowsmith, 1906.
Hazel of Heatherland. New York, Baker and Taylor, 1906.
Dimbie and I—and Amelia. New York, Baker and Taylor, 1907.
Hilary on Her Own. New York, Baker and Taylor, and London, Hutchinson, 1908.
Gwenda. New York, Baker and Taylor, 1910; as *Two Men and Gwenda*, 1910.
The Third Miss Wenderby. New York, Baker and Taylor, and London, Hutchinson, 1911.
Patricia Plays a Part. London, Hutchinson, 1913; New York, Dodd Mead, 1914.
Candytuft—I Mean Veronica. London, Hutchinson, 1914.
An Undressed Heroine. London, Hutchinson, 1916.

Her Mad Month. London, Hutchinson, 1917.
A Girl for Sale. London, Hutchinson, 1920.
The Great Husband Hunt. London, Hutchinson, 1922.
The Mating of Marcus. London, Hutchinson, 1923.
Sleeping Dogs. London, Hodder and Stoughton, 1924; New York, Stokes, 1926.
Three People. London, Hodder and Stoughton, 1926.
The Strategy of Suzanne. London, Hutchinson, 1929.
Pippa. London, Hutchinson, 1932.
Sally in a Service Flat. London, Hutchinson, 1934.
Private Hotel—Anywhere. London, Hutchinson, 1937.
Paying Pests. London, Hutchinson, 1941.
Mary Ann and Jane. London, Hutchinson, 1944.
The Two Miss Speckles. London, Hutchinson, 1946.

*   *   *

A novel by Mabel Barnes Grundy reads like a breath of fresh air. This author, whose 24 books were published between 1902 and 1946, writes with verve, enthusiasm, and energy in a distinctive style which is characterised by its ease and wit. Grundy's novels are mostly of the "roads to matrimony" type. They move along at a brisk pace with plenty of action and ingenious plots. Their atmosphere is gently romantic rather than loaded with emotion. Their heroines are charming, enterprising, high-spirited, independent-minded, witty, modern enough to smoke and drink cocktails (in the 1920's and 1930's), but ultimately traditionalist in that they marry solid, reliable, *nice* men whom they will allow to take care of them. The personality of the heroine is strongly established, particularly in those novels in which the heroine is narrator, as Peronelle, the heroine/narrator of *The Great Husband Hunt*, and Sally of *Sally in a Service Flat*, who describes one morning's post thus: "*July 7* Another repulsive Income Tax paper has arrived and of the same sticky hue. I suppose those who perpetuate these abominable documents imagine that we will be reminded of sunshine when we catch sight of their yellow envelopes, but nothing of the sort, jaundice or yellow-fever is nearer the mark."

Grundy's characters are endearing, good-humoured people, sometimes benignly eccentric (and consequently good at helping the plot along) as, for instance, the uncle in *The Great Husband Hunt* who offers £1,000 and a substantial dowry to the first of his four dependent nieces to get engaged. The dialogue is consistently light-hearted and amusing, as this exchange between Hazel and her pompous, over-aesthetic fiancé, Eustace: "There is a little book on monistic and genetic philosophy I want to read to you," he said. "I think it will help you to feel happier." "Is it about monasteries?" I inquired (*The Vacillations of Hazel*; Eustace later asks to be released from their engagement, and Hazel marries nice, comfortable Mr. Ickworth, her devoted admirer for many years).

The wit with which Grundy habitually treats her plots, characters, and dialogue extends also to the titles of her novels, which are alliterative, eyecatching, and intriguing. Sometimes they may even appear rather risqué, though of course they prove to be entirely respectable. The *Undressed Heroine* is simply a dowdily dressed young woman whose romantic prospects improve no end when she is provided with artistic and beautiful clothes by Mrs. Clinton Tomkins, an eccentric well-wisher. *Her Mad Month* is the time spent in Harrogate by an independent-minded heroine who runs away in her stern grandmother's absence and incidentally "meets her fate." The heroine of *A Girl for Sale* is the enterprising and modern Whiff Woffran who finds herself without a job after the Armistice and in desperation advertises in the newspaper for a new employer (whom she marries).

Grundy's delightful novels brought her many admirers, including *Times Literary Supplement* reviewers, and although they would today be regarded as period pieces it is a shame that they are so difficult to come by.

—Jean Buchanan

HAGGARD, (Sir) H(enry) Rider. British. Born in Bradenham, Norfolk, 22 June 1856. Educated at Ipswich Grammar School, Suffolk; Lincoln's Inn, London, 1881–85: called to the Bar 1885. Married Louisa Mariana Margitson in 1880; one son and three daughters. Lived in South Africa, as secretary to Sir Henry Bulwer, Lieutenant-Governor of Natal, 1875–77, member of the staff of Sir Theophilus Shepstone, Special Commissioner in the Transvaal, 1877, and master and registrar of the High Court of the Transvaal, 1877–79; returned to England, 1879; managed his wife's estate in Norfolk, from 1880; worked in chambers of Henry Bargave Deane, 1885–87; Unionist and Agricultural candidate for East Norfolk, 1895; co-editor, *African Review*, 1898; travelled throughout England investigating condition of agriculture and the rural population, 1901–02; British Government special commissioner to report on Salvation Army settlements in the U.S., 1905; chairman, Reclamation and Unemployed Labour Committee, Royal Commission on Coast Erosion and Afforestation, 1906–11; travelled around the world as a member of the Dominions Royal Commission, 1912–17. Chairman of the Committee, Society of Authors, 1896–98; Vice-president, Royal Colonial Institute, 1917. Knighted, 1912; K.B.E. (Knight Commander, Order of the British Empire), 1919. *Died 14 May 1925.*

ROMANCE AND HISTORICAL PUBLICATIONS

Novels (series: Allan Quatermain; She)

Dawn. London, Hurst and Blackett, 3 vols., 1884; New York, Appleton, 1 vol., 1887.
The Witch's Head. London, Hurst and Blackett, 3 vols., 1884; New York, Appleton, 1 vol., 1885.
King Solomon's Mines (Quatermain). London and New York, Cassell, 1885.
She: A History of Adventure. New York, Harper, 1886; London, Longman, 1887.
Allan Quatermain. London, Longman, and New York, Harper, 1887.
Jess. London, Smith Elder, and New York, Harper, 1887.
A Tale of Three Lions, and On Going Back. New York, Munro, 1887.
Mr. Meeson's Will. New York, Harper, and London, Spencer Blackett, 1888.
Maiwa's Revenge. New York, Harper, and London, Longman, 1888.
My Fellow Laborer (includes "The Wreck of the Copeland"). New York, Munro, 1888.
Colonel Quaritch, V. C. New York, Lovell, 1888; London, Longman, 3 vols., 1888.
Cleopatra. London, Longman, and New York, Harper, 1889.
Beatrice. London, Longman, and New York, Harper, 1890.
The World's Desire, with Andrew Lang. London, Longman, and New York, Harper, 1890.
Eric Brighteyes. London, Longman, and New York, United States Book Company, 1891.

Nada the Lily. New York and London, Longman, 1892.
Montezuma's Daughter. New York and London, Longman, 1893.
The People of the Mist. London and New York, Longman, 1894.
Heart of the World. New York, Longman, 1895; London, Longman, 1896.
Joan Haste. London and New York, Longman, 1895.
The Wizard. Bristol, Arrowsmith, and New York, Longman, 1896.
Doctor Therne. London and New York, Longman, 1898.
Swallow. New York and London, Longman, 1899.
The Spring of a Lion. New York, Neeley, 1899.
Lysbeth. New York and London, Longman, 1901.
Pearl-Maiden. London and New York, Longman, 1903.
The Brethren. London, Cassell, and New York, Doubleday, 1904.
Stella Fregelius: A Tale of Three Destinies. London and New York, Longman, 1904.
Ayesha: The Return of She. London, Ward Lock, and New York, Doubleday, 1905.
Benita: An African Romance. London, Cassell, 1906; as *The Spirit of Bambatse,* New York, Longman, 1906.
The Way of the Spirit. London, Hutchinson, 1906.
Fair Margaret. London, Hutchinson, 1907; as *Margaret,* New York, Longman, 1907.
The Lady of the Heavens. New York, Authors and Newspapers Association, 1908; as *The Ghost Kings,* London, Cassell, 1908.
The Yellow God. New York, Cupples and Leon, 1908; London, Cassell, 1909.
The Lady of Blossholme. London, Hodder and Stoughton, 1909.
Morning Star. London, Cassell, and New York, Longman, 1910.
Queen Sheba's Ring. London, Nash, and New York, Doubleday, 1910.
The Mahatma and the Hare: A Dream Story. London, Longman, and New York, Holt, 1911.
Red Eve. London, Hodder and Stoughton, and New York, Doubleday, 1911.
Marie. London, Cassell, and New York, Longman, 1912.
Child of Storm. London, Cassell, and New York, Longman, 1913.
The Wanderer's Necklace. London, Cassell, and New York, Longman, 1914.
The Holy Flower. London, Ward Lock, 1915; as *Allan and the Holy Flower,* New York, Longman, 1915.
The Ivory Child. London, Cassell, and New York, Longman, 1916.
Finished. London, Ward Lock, and New York, Longman, 1917.
Moon of Israel. London, Murray, and New York, Longman, 1918.
Love Eternal. London, Cassell, and New York, Longman, 1918.
When the World Shook. London, Cassell, and New York, Longman, 1919.
The Ancient Allan. London, Cassell, and New York, Longman, 1920.
She and Allan. New York, Longman, and London, Hutchinson, 1921.
The Virgin of the Sun. London, Cassell, and New York, Doubleday, 1922.
Wisdom's Daughter. London, Hutchinson, and New York, Doubleday, 1923.
Heu-Heu; or, The Monster (Quatermain). London, Hutchinson, and New York, Doubleday, 1924.

Queen of the Dawn. New York, Doubleday, and London, Hutchinson, 1925.

The Treasure of the Lake. New York, Doubleday, and London, Hutchinson, 1926.

Allan and the Ice-Gods. London, Hutchinson, and New York, Doubleday, 1927.

Mary of Marion Isle. London, Hutchinson, and New York, Doubleday, 1929.

Belshazzar. London, Paul, and New York, Doubleday, 1930.

Short Stories

Allan's Wife and Other Tales. London, Blackett, and New York, Harper, 1889.

Black Heart and White Heart, and Other Stories. London, Longman, 1900; as *Elissa, and Black Heart and White Heart*, New York, Longman, 1900.

Smith and the Pharaohs and Other Tales. Bristol, Arrowsmith, 1920; New York, Longman, 1921.

The Best Short Stories of Rider Haggard, edited by Peter Haining. London, Joseph, 1981.

OTHER PUBLICATIONS

Other

Cetywayo and His White Neighbours; or, Remarks on Recent Events in Zululand, Natal, and the Transvaal. London, Trübner, 1882; revised edition, 1888; reprinted in part, as *The Last Boer War*, London, Kegan Paul, 1899; as *A History of the Transvaal*, New York, New Amsterdam, 1899.

Church and the State: An Appeal to the Laity. Privately printed, 1895.

A Farmer's Year, Being His Commonplace Book for 1898. London and New York, Longman, 1899.

The New South Africa. London, Pearson, 1900.

A Winter Pilgrimage: . . . Travels Through Palestine, Italy, and the Island of Cyprus. London and New York, Longman, 1901.

Rural England. London and New York, Longman, 2 vols., 1902.

A Gardener's Year. London and New York, Longman, 1905.

Report on the Salvation Army Colonies. London, His Majesty's Stationery Office, 1905; as *The Poor and the Land*, London and New York, Longman, 1905.

Regeneration, Being an Account of the Social Work of the Salvation Army in Great Britain. London, Longman, 1910; New York, Longman, 1911.

Rural Denmark and Its Lessons. London and New York, Longman, 1911.

A Call to Arms to the Men of East Anglia. Privately printed, 1914.

The After-War Settlement and the Employment of Ex-Service Men in the Oversea Dominions. London, Saint Catherine Press, 1916.

The Days of My Life: An Autobiography, edited by C. J. Longman. London and New York, Longman, 2 vols., 1926.

The Private Diaries of Sir H. Rider Haggard 1914–1925, edited by D. S. Higgins. London, Cassell, and New York, Stein and Day, 1980.

*

Bibliography: *A Bibliography of the Writings of Sir Henry Rider Haggard* by J. E. Scott, London, Elkin Mathews, 1947.

Critical Studies: *The Cloak That I Left* (biography) by Lilias Rider Haggard, London, Hodder and Stoughton, 1951; *Rider Haggard: His Life and Works* by Morton N. Cohen, London, Hutchinson, 1960, New York, Walker, 1961, revised edition, London, Macmillan, 1968; *H. Rider Haggard: A Voice from the Infinite* by Peter Berresford Ellis, London, Routledge, 1978; *Rider Haggard, The Great Storyteller* by D. S. Higgins, London, Cassell, 1981, New York, Stein and Day, 1983; *Rider Haggard and the Fiction of Empire: A Critical Study of British Imperial Fiction* by Wendy R. Katz, Cambridge, Cambridge University Press, 1988.

*   *   *

H. Rider Haggard was above all a spinner of yarns, a teller of tales. That most of them were tall tales does not matter in the least, for in his books, through the power of his writing, the wildly impossible is made to seem not only possible but convincingly true. He is probably best known for his books set in Africa which he knew well, and he had a great fondness for and sympathy with its native peoples. The Zulu nation in particular appealed to him, and in *Nada the Lily* (which was his own favourite among his many books) he told the story of the Zulu king Chaka through the eyes of Mopo, Chaka's witch doctor. In the romances *Marie*, *Child of Storm* and *Finished* he completed the history of the Zulus down to his own time.

From time to time Haggard has been criticized because his attitude to war and his descriptions of battles make him seem to relish bloodshed. This is not necessarily his own attitude but his interpretation of the Zulu philosophy which can be summed up in the words he puts in the mouth of Umslopogas in *Allan Quatermain*—"man is born to kill. He who kills not when his blood is hot is a woman and no man." Nor must we forget the very different atmosphere of his jingoistic era.

Besides historical novels, Haggard wrote romances pure and simple often with an African background. The best known are *King Solomon's Mines* with its classic treasure motif and *She* and its sequel *Ayesha*, two books that are wonderfully erotic without the sex being in any way explicit, and also to some degree feminist without any sacrifice of the traditional "Boys' Own" adventure motif. Also set in Africa is *Swallow* which charts the great trek of the Boers; in *The People of the Mist* he gives us his version of Africa's pre-history.

Haggard was master of description; he had the ability to bring a vivid picture of the countryside he was describing immediately before the reader's eyes. His characterization varied—he was especially good at Africans like the unforgettable Umslopogas, the Zulu prince who often accompanied Allan Quatermain on his adventures; Allan, the archetypal great white hunter, was also a well-drawn character, being based partly on himself and partly on a friend. But in some of his historical novels his characters are rather two-dimensional—perhaps because the stories run on at such a pace and action is all. For instance, in *Red Eve*, a stirring tale set at the time of Crécy dealing with the eternal triangle and the battle between the powers of good and evil, the hero, heroine, and villain are all stock characters. The incidents, however—battles, narrow escapes, brushes with the Plague, appearance at the court of the Doge of Venice—keep one reading until the end. *Eric Brighteyes*, set in ancient Iceland, is more satisfying because the characters are better drawn; and there is a wonderful atmosphere with saga overtones in this doom laden tale. Haggard's fertile imagination roamed far and wide in many different periods of history. *Pearl-Maiden* is about early Christian martyrs, *The Brethren* is about the Crusades, and *Lysbeth* is set in the days of William the Silent.

Haggard was immensely successful in his own lifetime; his books were best sellers, and much admired by fellow writers like Rudyard Kipling and Andrew Lang. Many of his books are little known today (although *King Solomon's Mines* and *She* are undying classics), but Haggard never wrote a dull book and many of his other stories repay attention and can still be enjoyed by lovers of the imaginative romance and the ripping yarn.

—Pamela Cleaver

HAINES, Pamela (Mary). British. Born in Harrogate, Yorkshire, 4 November 1929. Educated at St. Joseph's Convent, Tamworth, Staffordshire, 1938; Newnham College, Cambridge, 1949–52, M.A. in English. Married Tony Haines in 1955; three daughters and two sons. Recipient: *Spectator* New Writing prize, 1971; Yorkshire Art award, 1975. Agent: A. D. Peters, 5th Floor, Chelsea Harbour, Lots Road, London SW10 0XF. Address: c/o Collins, 8 Grafton Street, London W1X 3LA, England.

ROMANCE AND HISTORICAL PUBLICATIONS

Novels

Tea at Gunter's. London, Heinemann, 1974.
A Kind of War. London, Heinemann, 1976.
Men on White Horses. London, Collins, 1978.
The Kissing Gate. London, Collins, and New York, Doubleday, 1981.
The Diamond Waterfall. London, Collins, and New York, Doubleday, 1984.
The Golden Lion. London, Collins, and New York, Scribner, 1986.
Daughter of the Northern Fields. London, Collins, 1987.

*   *   *

The novels of Pamela Haines share a nucleus of common themes. All portray the growth of a young girl to womanhood, the fight for independence from the smothering shadow of the past, the idealized love for the flawed love object. All are pervaded by a strong tragic sense and the lurking threat of violence. From the first there are indications that the early balanced precision will be foresaken in favour of a greater breadth of vision, a wider compass. It seems inevitable that their author should eventually come to the full-scale family saga of *The Kissing Gate*.

Tea at Gunter's focuses on the heroine's attempts at self-realization, which are threatened by the pervasive dream-world of her mother, still living in a romanticized past of love for her effete step-brother Gervase. When Lucy herself falls in love, her freedom is achieved only at a terrible cost. A poised, subtle work, *Tea at Gunter's* is the most perfect of Haines's creations, the author displaying a mastery of tone and considerable psychological penetration. *A Kind of War* explores the minds of three women, each of a different generation, whose lives lack a fulfilling relationship. Skilfully the novel traces each through past and present, moving towards the concluding tragedy in a clean underplayed style which reveals the nature of the differing characters, the grief tinged with welcome touches of humour. Already in *A Kind of War* one senses a movement outward from the confines of the work, a yearning for larger forms.

Men on White Horses describes Edwina's growth from childhood to maturity in Edwardian Yorkshire. Beginning with a brilliant portrayal of her early years, the author reveals the threat to her selfhood posed by her mother, and later by a domineering school friend. Physically and spiritually scarred by life, her one secret love tragically killed, Edwina finds fulfillment in her music and its related symbol, the sea. When at last she feels life return in waves in her pianist's hands, the reader knows that her spirit remains unconquered by its suffering. Some of the later chapters are less satisfying, but the novel as a whole is a remarkable achievement.

The Kissing Gate, which combines gothic romance with the psychological subtlety of the previous novels, is the most ambitious of Haines's works, and follows the Rawson family through three generations of the last century. The kissing gate of the title—symbol of love and death—is central to the book. Here Sarah Rawson rescues the squire's son, and begins the involvement between the Rawsons and the aristocratic Inghams which spans the course of the novel. The story is continued through Sarah's children, and ends with her granddaughter, another Sarah, leaving the kissing gate for a new life. Most of the action, though, is dominated by two Catherines—both outsiders brought to Downham by Sarah's son John. Catriona Drummond, who marries him, and Kate the Irish girl he saves from starvation in the Great Famine. Their personalities overshadow the plot, and give the work its direction. Violence flares throughout, and the railway runs a dark thread through the story, instrument of disgrace and death. A huge epic novel, *The Kissing Gate* lacks the perfect balance of Haines's earlier works. There are flaws in the fabric—too many unhappy marriages, unfortunate accidents, fortuitous deaths—but interest is sustained to such an extent that they are scarcely noticed. In its vast scale and the sureness of its insights, this is the most impressive of Haines's novels.

The subsequent novels are similar in form to *The Kissing Gate*, and cover several generations. In *The Diamond Waterfall* the reader follows three heroines from Edwardian times to 1945, exploring their luckless marriages and joyful, forbidden loves. *The Golden Lion* examines the relationship between a Sicilian girl raised by a Yorkshire family, and her own adopted daughter. These works, too, plunge deep into the darker side of pre-war life, uncovering the repressed violence and sexuality seething beneath the respectable facade. Such an interest sometimes appears obsessive, but there is no doubting the author's assured control, or her mastery of detail. *Daughter of the Northern Fields* pursues a new direction, telling the story of Christabel, natural daughter of Branwell Brontë. Its theme—the destructive force of illicit love—and the device of the internal narrative recall the Brontë novels, but it impresses as a strong, intriguing story in its own right.

Haines's writings show an excellent period sense. Whether contemporary or historical, the feel of the time is splendidly caught. Her grasp of character is sure, her dialogue superb. Her books present the essence of life, its tragedy leavened by sharp flashes of humour. With a clear but sympathetic eye she depicts the transient joys, the harrowing griefs, the slow poignant awakening of love.

—Geoffrey Sadler

HALL, James Norman. See **NORDHOFF, Charles** and **HALL, James Norman.**

HALLIDAY, Dorothy. See **DUNNETT, Dorothy.**

HAMILL, Ethel. See **WEBB, Jean Francis.**

HAMILTON, Hervey. See **ROBINS, Denise.**

HAMILTON, Julia. See **FITZGERALD, Julia.**

HAMILTON, Mollie. See **KAYE, M. M.**

HAMILTON, Priscilla. See **GELLIS, Roberta.**

HAMPSON, Anne. British. Left school at age 14; later attended Manchester College of Education, teaching certificate. Married for 14 years; one son. Cafe owner, sewing factory worker, and operated a milk route; teacher for four years, then full-time writer. Address: c/o Hodder and Stoughton Ltd., Mill Road, Dunton Green, Sevenoaks, Kent TN13 2YA, England.

ROMANCE AND HISTORICAL PUBLICATIONS

Novels

Eternal Summer. London, Mills and Boon, 1969; Toronto, Harlequin, 1970.
Precious Waif. London, Mills and Boon, 1969; Toronto, Harlequin, 1970.
Unwary Heart. London, Mills and Boon, 1969; Toronto, Harlequin, 1970.
The Autocrat of Melhurst. London, Mills and Boon, 1969; Toronto, Harlequin, 1970.
Gates of Steel. London, Mills and Boon, 1970; Toronto, Harlequin, 1973.
By Fountains Wild. London, Mills and Boon, 1970; Toronto, Harlequin, 1973.
Heaven Is High. London, Mills and Boon, 1970; Toronto, Harlequin, 1972.
Love Hath an Island. London, Mills and Boon, 1970; Toronto, Harlequin, 1971.
The Hawk and the Dove. London, Mills and Boon, 1970; Toronto, Harlequin, 1973.
Beyond the Sweet Waters. London, Mills and Boon, 1970; Toronto, Harlequin, 1971.

When the Bough Breaks. London, Mills and Boon, 1970; Toronto, Harlequin, 1971.
An Eagle Swooped. London, Mills and Boon, 1970; Toronto, Harlequin, 1974.
Isle of the Rainbows. London, Mills and Boon, 1970; Toronto, Harlequin, 1972.
Dark Hills Rising. London, Mills and Boon, 1971; Toronto, Harlequin, 1975.
The Rebel Bride. London, Mills and Boon, 1971; Toronto, Harlequin, 1973.
Stars of Spring. London, Mills and Boon, and Toronto, Harlequin, 1971.
Wings of the Night. London, Mills and Boon, 1971; Toronto, Harlequin, 1973.
Follow a Shadow. London, Mills and Boon, 1971; Toronto, Harlequin, 1977.
Gold Is the Sunrise. London, Mills and Boon, 1971; Toronto, Harlequin, 1972.
Petals Drifting. London, Mills and Boon, 1971; Toronto, Harlequin, 1974.
South of Mandraki. London, Mills and Boon, 1971; Toronto, Harlequin, 1973.
Waves of Fire. London, Mills and Boon, 1971; Toronto, Harlequin, 1973.
The Fair Island. London, Mills and Boon, 1972; Toronto, Harlequin, 1975.
Enchanted Dawn. London, Mills and Boon, 1972; Toronto, Harlequin, 1976.
Beloved Rake. London, Mills and Boon, 1972; Toronto, Harlequin, 1974.
The Plantation Boss. London, Mills and Boon, 1972; Toronto, Harlequin, 1973.
There Came a Tyrant. London, Mills and Boon, and Toronto, Harlequin, 1972.
Dark Avenger. London, Mills and Boon, 1972; Toronto, Harlequin, 1973.
Wife for a Penny. London, Mills and Boon, 1972; Toronto, Harlequin, 1974.
Hunter of the East. London, Mills and Boon, 1973; Toronto, Harlequin, 1974.
Boss of Bali Creek. London, Mills and Boon, 1973; Toronto, Harlequin, 1977.
Blue Hills of Sintra. London, Mills and Boon, 1973; Toronto, Harlequin, 1974.
Dear Stranger. London, Mills and Boon, and Toronto, Harlequin, 1973.
Stormy the Way. London, Mills and Boon, 1973; Toronto, Harlequin, 1974.
When Clouds Part. London, Mills and Boon, 1973; Toronto, Harlequin, 1974.
Master of Moonrock. Toronto, Harlequin, 1973.
Windward Crest. London, Mills and Boon, 1973.
A Kiss from Satan. Toronto, Harlequin, 1973.
The Black Eagle. London, Mills and Boon, 1973; Toronto, Harlequin, 1975.
Dear Plutocrat. London, Mills and Boon, 1973; Toronto, Harlequin, 1976.
After Sundown. Toronto, Harlequin, 1974.
Stars over Sarawak. London, Mills and Boon, and Toronto, Harlequin, 1974.
Fetters of Hate. London, Mills and Boon, 1974; Toronto, Harlequin, 1975.
Pride and Power. London, Mills and Boon, 1974; Toronto, Harlequin, 1975.
The Way of a Tyrant. London, Mills and Boon, and Toronto, Harlequin, 1974.

Moon Without Stars. London, Mills and Boon, 1974; Toronto, Harlequin, 1977.

Not Far from Heaven. London, Mills and Boon, 1974.

Two of a Kind. London, Mills and Boon, 1974.

Autumn Twilight. London, Mills and Boon, 1975; Toronto, Harlequin, 1976.

Flame of Fate. London, Mills and Boon, 1975.

Jonty in Love. London, Mills and Boon, 1975.

Reap the Whirlwind. London, Mills and Boon, 1975.

South of Capricorn. London, Mills and Boon, 1975.

Sunset Cloud. London, Mills and Boon, 1976; New York, Oxford University Press, 1979.

Song of the Waves. London, Mills and Boon, 1976; Toronto, Harlequin, 1977.

Dangerous Friendship. Toronto, Harlequin, 1976.

Satan and the Nymph. London, Mills and Boon, 1976.

A Man to Be Feared. London, Mills and Boon, and Toronto, Harlequin, 1976.

Isle at the Rainbow's End. London, Mills and Boon, 1976; Toronto, Harlequin, 1977.

Hills of Kalamata. London, Mills and Boon, 1976; Toronto, Harlequin, 1977.

Fire Meets Fire. London, Mills and Boon, 1976.

Dear Benefactor. London, Mills and Boon, 1976.

Call of the Outback. London, Mills and Boon, 1976; Toronto, Harlequin, 1977.

Call of the Veld. London, Mills and Boon, 1977; Toronto, Harlequin, 1978.

Harbour of Love. London, Mills and Boon, 1977; Toronto, Harlequin, 1979.

The Shadow Between. London, Mills and Boon, 1977; Toronto, Harlequin, 1978.

Sweet Is the Web. London, Mills and Boon, 1977; Toronto, Harlequin, 1978.

Moon Dragon. London, Mills and Boon, 1978.

To Tame a Vixen. London, Mills and Boon, 1978.

Master of Forrestmead. London, Mills and Boon, 1978.

Under Moonglow. London, Mills and Boon, and Toronto, Harlequin, 1978.

For Love of a Pagan. London, Mills and Boon, 1978.

Leaf in the Storm. London, Mills and Boon, and Toronto, Harlequin, 1978.

Above Rubies. Toronto, Harlequin, 1978.

Fly Beyond the Sunset. Toronto, Harlequin, 1978.

Isle of Desire. Toronto, Harlequin, 1978.

South of the Moon. Toronto, Harlequin, 1979.

Bride for a Night. London, Mills and Boon, 1979; Toronto, Harlequin, 1981.

Chateau in the Palms. London, Mills and Boon, 1979.

Coolibah Creek. London, Mills and Boon, 1979.

A Rose from Lucifer. London, Mills and Boon, 1979.

Temple of Dawn. London, Mills and Boon, 1979.

Call of the Heathen. London, Mills and Boon, 1980.

The Laird of Locharrun. London, Mills and Boon, 1980.

Pagan Lover. London, Mills and Boon, 1980.

The Dawn Steals Softly. New York and London, Silhouette, 1980.

Stormy Masquerade. New York and London, Silhouette, 1980.

Second Tomorrow. London, Silhouette, 1980.

Man of the Outback. New York, Silhouette, 1980; London, Silhouette, 1981.

Where Eagles Nest. New York, Silhouette, 1980; London, Silhouette, 1981.

Payment in Full. New York and London, Silhouette, 1980.

Beloved Vagabond. Toronto, Harlequin, 1981.

Man Without a Heart. New York, Silhouette, 1981.

Shadow of Apollo. New York, Silhouette, 1981.

Fascination. New York, Silhouette, 1981.

Desire. New York, Silhouette, 1981; London, Hodder and Stoughton, 1982.

Bitter Harvest. Toronto, Harlequin, 1982.

Unwanted Bride. Toronto, Harlequin, 1982.

Enchantment. London, Hodder and Stoughton, and New York, Silhouette, 1982.

Too Hot to Handle. Toronto, Harlequin, 1982.

A Kiss and a Promise. London, Hodder and Stoughton, 1982.

Man Without Honour. London, Hodder and Stoughton, 1982.

Realm of the Pagans. London, Hodder and Stoughton, 1982.

Stardust. London, Hodder and Stoughton, and New York, Silhouette, 1982.

Strangers May Marry. London, Hodder and Stoughton, 1982; New York, Silhouette, 1983.

Another Eden. New York, Silhouette, 1982; London, Hodder and Stoughton, 1983.

The Tender Years. New York, Silhouette, 1982; London, Hodder and Stoughton, 1983.

Devotion. London, Hodder and Stoughton, 1983.

The Dawn Is Golden. London, Hodder and Stoughton, 1983; New York, Silhouette, 1984.

Love So Rare. New York, Silhouette, 1983.

Dreamtime. London, Hodder and Stoughton, 1983.

Spell of the Island. New York, Silhouette, 1983; London, Hodder and Stoughton, 1984.

Soft Velvet Night. New York, Silhouette, 1983.

To Buy a Memory. London, Hodder and Stoughton, 1983.

When Love Comes. London, Hodder and Stoughton, and New York, Silhouette, 1983.

There Must Be Showers. New York, Silhouette, 1983; London, Hodder and Stoughton, 1984.

Sweet Second Love. New York, Silhouette, 1984.

*   *   *

Anne Hampson's version of the romantic formula focuses primarily upon intense, frequently physically violent interaction between an unfathomable hero and a transparent heroine. This emphasis is well chosen because it articulates in pleasant fantasy some of the personal concerns and experiences of women in reality. The story is told from the heroine's perspective so the reader identifies with her and her feelings of vulnerability. The heroine feels dangerously exposed to the dominant male hero: "The black eyes, marble-hard, were fixed upon her in a searching scrutiny which seemed to be absorbing every single thing about her . . . even what went on in the secret places of her mind" (*Leaf in the Storm*). In contrast, the hero is impenetrable, seemingly invulnerable. The same novel describes the heroine's struggles to understand him: "His eyes held the most odd expression; nothing she could read was there, yet she felt that if she could have read the expression it would have been revealing in a way that was totally unexpected." This portrayal is appealing since, traditionally, men have been socialized to repress their feelings, particularly loving ones. Compared to women, they disclose little of themselves. Women, therefore, are often left feeling exposed in a one-sided exchange of emotions while men remain enigmas. Hampson incorporates this emotionally charged state of affairs in her romances.

The heroine's distance from the hero is further stressed by Hampson's frequent use of forced marriages or marriages of convenience, or "pretend" engagements and marriages as a plot device. In these situations, the hero and heroine are bound by the most intimate of ties yet they are strangers. The heroine of

For Love of a Pagan agonizes over her lack of knowledge about men in general and her husband specifically: "The doubts hurt, since she would rather feel she had full trust in her husband. Mingling with the doubts was a return of her fear of him, of the uncertainty as to how he would eventually turn out. She knew so little about him, about his inner nature. . . . "

The relationship is not only baffling to her but also frightening. Encounters are often violent, ranging from spankings and shakings to rapes (within the bonds of marriage). Many critics have condemned writers like Hampson for glamorizing sexual violence but I think that, in this case, they have underestimated the intent of the writer and the sophistication of the readers. In these violent episodes, the heroine is usually sexually responsive so the "rape" is not entirely against her will. In fact, she would not be resisting at all but she does not want him to make love to her if he does not love her. It is at this point that the reader and the heroine temporarily part company for the astute reader knows the hero would not be attempting to overcome her resistance if he did not love her already. The violence is an expression of the emotion that the heroine is afraid the hero does not feel and that he has hidden so successfully. Hampson gives the readers clues to guide their interpretation in this direction: "This was a side of him she had suspected but never expected to see, for usually he was so calm and self-possessed, more than able to control his passions. But not now . . . " (*Temple of Dawn*). This emotional breakthrough is a relief because the hero is no longer so remote. Savagery eventually gives way to tenderness. The message is clear to the reader who knows that the happy ending means that the violence between the hero and heroine is over because now they can express their love directly. Hampson is explicit about getting this point across: " 'I will never frighten you again, my darling,' he promised and she knew without any doubt at all that he spoke the truth" (*For Love of a Pagan*).

Hampson also devotes attention to the settings of her stories. Two of her favorite settings seem to be South Africa and Greece and the Greek Islands. Her affectionate descriptions of the flora, fauna, topography, and customs of these places also add to the appeal of her romances.

—Margaret Jensen

HARDWICK, Mollie (née Greenhalgh). Also writes as Mary Atkinson; John Drinkrow. British. Born in Manchester. Educated at Manchester High School for Girls. Married the writer Michael Hardwick in 1961; one son. Announcer, Manchester, 1940–45, and drama script editor and producer, London, 1946–62, BBC Radio; then freelance writer. Recipient: Romantic Novelists Association Major award, 1977. Fellow, Royal Society of Arts. Agent: London Management Ltd., 235 Regent Street, London, W1A 2JT. Address: c/o Century Hutchinson Ltd., 62–65 Chandos Place, London WC2N 4NW, England.

ROMANCE AND HISTORICAL PUBLICATIONS

Novels (series: Atkinson Heritage; Duchess of Duke Street; Upstairs, Downstairs)

Upstairs, Downstairs (novelization of television series):
  Sarah's Story. London, Sphere, 1973; New York, Pocket Books, 1975.
  The Years of Change. London, Sphere, and New York, Dell, 1974.
  Mrs. Bridges' Story. London, Sphere, 1975.

The War to End Wars. London, Sphere, and New York, Dell, 1975.
Thomas and Sarah. London, Sphere, 1978.
The Duchess of Duke Street (novelization of television series). New York, Holt Rinehart, 1977.
  The Way Up. London, Futura, 1976.
  The Golden Years. London, Futura, 1976.
  The World Keeps Turning. London, Futura, 1977.
Beauty's Daughter: The Story of Lady Hamilton's "Lost" Daughter. London, Eyre Methuen, 1976; New York, Coward McCann, 1977.
Charlie Is My Darling. London, Eyre Methuen, and New York, Coward McCann, 1977.
The Atkinson Heritage:
  The Atkinson Heritage. London, Futura, 1978.
  Sisters in Love. London, Futura, 1979.
  Dove's Nest. London, Futura, 1980; as *The Atkinson Century*, London, Severn House, 1980.
Lovers Meeting. London, Eyre Methuen, and New York, St. Martin's Press, 1979.
Willowwood. London, Eyre Methuen, and New York, St. Martin's Press, 1980.
Monday's Child. London, Macdonald, 1981; New York, St. Martin's Press, 1982.
I Remember Love. London, Macdonald, 1982; New York, St. Martin's Press, 1983.
The Shakespeare Girl. London, Methuen, and New York, St. Martin's Press, 1983.
By the Sword Divided (novelization of television series). London, Century, 1983; New York, Penguin, 1986.
The Merry Maid. London, Methuen, 1984; New York, St. Martin's Press, 1985.
The Girl with the Crystal Dove. London, Methuen, and New York, St. Martin's Press, 1985.
Malice Domestic. London, Century, and New York, St. Martin's Press, 1986.
Parson's Pleasure. London, Century, and New York, St. Martin's Press, 1987.
Uneaseful Death. London, Century, and New York, St. Martin's Press, 1988.
Blood Royal. London, Methuen, 1988; New York, St. Martin's Press, 1989.
The Bandersnatch. London, Century, 1989.

OTHER PUBLICATIONS

Novels (novelizations)

The Private Life of Sherlock Holmes, with Michael Hardwick. London, Mayflower, 1970; New York, Bantam, 1971.
The Gaslight Boy, with Michael Hardwick. London, Weidenfeld and Nicolson, 1976.
Juliet Bravo. London, Pan, 2 vols., 1980.
Calling Juliet Bravo. London, BBC Publications, 1981.
Juliet Bravo 2. London, Severn House, 1981.

Plays

Four [and *Four More*] *Sherlock Holmes Plays*, with Michael Hardwick. London, Murray, 2 vols., 1964–73; New York, French, 2 vols., 1964–74.
The Game's Afoot: Sherlock Holmes Plays, with Michael Hardwick. London, Murray, 1969; New York, French, 1970.
Plays from Dickens, with Michael Hardwick. London, Murray, and New York, French, 1970.

Alice in Wonderland, adaptation of the story by Lewis Carroll. London, Davis Poynter, 1974.
A Christmas Carol, adaptation of the story by Dickens. London, Davis Poynter, 1974.
The Hound of the Baskervilles and Other Sherlock Holmes Plays, with Michael Hardwick. London, Murray, 1982.

Radio Plays: *The Corpse in the Case*, 1962; *Going Concern*, 1963; *The Prisoner's Friend*, from a work by Andrew Garve, 1964; *A Shadow of Doubt*, 1964; *Mrs. Thompson*, 1965; *Sarah Churchill*, 1966; *Dear Miss Prior*, from a story by Thackeray, 1970; *The French Lieutenant's Woman*, from the novel by John Fowles, 1974; and others.

Television Plays: *A Question of Values*, with Michael Hardwick, 1976; *The Cedar Tree*; *The Dickens of a Christmas*; *Charles Dickens, Storyteller Extraordinary*; and others.

Other with Michael Hardwick

The Jolly Toper. London, Jenkins, 1961; New York, State Mutual, 1978.
The Sherlock Holmes Companion. London, Murray, 1962; New York, Doubleday, 1963.
Sherlock Holmes Investigates. New York, Lothrop, 1963.
The Man Who Was Sherlock Holmes. London, Murray, and New York, Doubleday, 1964.
The Charles Dickens Companion. London, Murray, 1965; New York, Holt Rinehart, 1966.
The Plague and the Fire of London. London, Parrish, 1966.
Writers' Houses: A Literary Journey in England. London, Phoenix House, 1968; as *A Literary Journey*, South Brunswick, New Jersey, A. S. Barnes, 1970.
Alfred Deller: A Singularity of Voice. London, Cassell, 1968; New York, Praeger, 1969.
Dickens's England. London, Dent, and South Brunswick, New Jersey, A. S. Barnes, 1970.
Charles Dickens . . . As They Saw Him. London, Harrap, 1970.
The Vintage Operetta Book (as John Drinkrow). London, Osprey, 1972.
The Charles Dickens Encyclopedia. London, Osprey, and New York, Scribner, 1973.
The Bernard Shaw Companion. London, Murray, 1973; New York, St. Martin's Press, 1974.
The Vintage Musical Comedy Book (as John Drinkrow). London, Osprey, 1974.
The Charles Dickens Quiz Book. London, Luscombe, and New York, Larousse, 1974.

Editor, *The World's Greatest Sea Mysteries*. London, Odhams Press, 1967.

Other

Emma, Lady Hamilton. London, Cassell, 1969; New York, Holt Rinehart, 1970.
Mrs. Dizzy: The Life of Mary Ann Disraeli. London, Cassell, and New York, St. Martin's Press, 1972.
The Thames-Side Book (as Mary Atkinson). London, Osprey, 1973.
The World of Upstairs, Downstairs. Newton Abbot, David and Charles, and New York, Holt Rinehart, 1976.

Editor, *Stories from Dickens*. London, Arnold, 1968.

*

Mollie Hardwick comments:
I would describe myself as an historical, rather than a romantic/gothic novelist. My novels grew out of my non-fiction works (i.e., *Emma, Lady Hamilton*), by way of a request from Sphere Books to write an original novel based on the character of Sarah the housemaid from *Upstairs, Downstairs*. I write, in general, out of my personal enthusiasms (the age of Nelson, the Jacobite Rising of 1745, the Regency theatre, cricket, etc.). In general I stick to the 18th century and the early 19th, disliking Victoriana as such; though *Monday's Child* is set in the 1880's. My next novel is set much farther back in time, beginning during the Wars of the Roses. I might one day write a gothic novel, with a strong supernormal element—who knows? My motivation in writing fiction is to tell a story that will entertain my readers (and incidentally myself) and perhaps provide them with a temporary escape from everyday life.

*   *   *

Mollie Hardwick is one of the most prolific and versatile writers in the field of light fiction. Her work ranges from bestselling novels to standard literary studies, biographies, and anthologies (especially of Dickens and Conan Doyle), from television, stage, and radio plays to features in women's magazines.

Writing for television and writing a novel require totally different techniques. Television drama emphasizes dialogue and clarity of plot, while the structure is dictated by the length of time allotted to each episode by the network in consideration of commercial breaks, and the atmosphere can be created by technical expertise and sensitive camerawork. An author of fiction can rely only on his or her facility with words to create plot and atmosphere. Uniting these two forms into a successful spin-off novel calls for a particular skill which Hardwick possesses.

Hardwick has written a number of novelizations of successful television series including *By the Sword Divided*. Unfortunately the result of many novelizations is literally a pale reflection of what the original series was, or more frustratingly, what it might have been, but Hardwick avoids the pitfalls by reproducing the panoramic impact of television as well as the basic storyline which combine to produce absorbing novels. In the opening passages of *By the Sword Divided* for example, where the reader is gradually drawn into the scene, Hardwick has captured the cinematic process and retained it for effect, evoking an atmosphere and a feeling by verbally recreating the langorous sweep of the camera as it slowly absorbs the surrounding environment and then homes in on the characters. There are, however, moments where she could benefit from the judicious scissors of a V.T.R. editor. The battle for Arnscote Castle made for excellent television, but is less successful on paper.

Ingenuity is always called for in presenting bloodshed—trying to achieve a balance between widescale violence and the individual suffering it causes in order to trigger the reader's moral disgust and at the same time maintain his or her sympathy.

Unfortunately Hardwick achieves neither whenever she attempts to imitate the technique of television too closely instead of allowing her natural novelist's instinct to guide her. In Hardwick's original fiction her feeling for a good story well narrated is given complete freedom and she explores different periods in history from a very idiosyncratic angle. Regardless of the century in which the story is set, she treats her characters with warmth and compassion, heedless of their moral state. The scheming Gideon Baldwin in *The Merry Maid* is just as gently drawn an invention as the much set upon heroine herself, although his actions are despicable, particularly his manipulation of the religious corruption and civic xenophobia of the 16th century.

Such contradictions are a feature of Hardwick's work. Jacquette is almost raped by the local yokels at one point, but the sinister tone is played down and the episode is even made risible since they initially mistake her for a mermaid. Nell in *The Girl with the Crystal Dove* is another child abroad who initially manages to survive various assaults on her virtue in Victorian London, even with a liability in the form of a younger brother in tow. He himself was sexually abused at boarding school, but has emerged relatively unscathed. This is, after all, fiction.

Hardwick's novels portray an imaginary world, despite being set in a real historical context, because they compromise the truth about human nature. In this book, Pym, the mad satanist, involves the virginal Nell in a necromantic plot to dispose of his pregnant wife, leaving him free to marry his mistress. Thanks to his bumbling spell-making and untidy cauldron habits in the garden shed (recounted by Hardwick with dry wit) he gets his come-uppance and everyone lives happily ever after. What is in effect a tale of infidelity, witchcraft, and attempted murder becomes part of a fairytale where innocence ultimately triumphs.

There is always an underlying melodrama in Hardwick's novels, full as they are of orphans, insanity, elopements, relations whose names are never spoken, and other taboo subjects, but her treatment plays down the darker side of humanity and of society as a whole. In *Sisters in Love*, for example, there is, besides the familiar features of divided families, illicit love, and betrayal, a realistic depiction of life in the Blackburn mills during the Industrial Revolution. It is a depressing picture, but since Hardwick is not a social writer in the mould of Dickens, we feel no outrage and our attention is swept back to the steamy affair between the young Benjamin Disraeli and Eleanor, the black sheep of the family.

This is a simplistic, rosy treatment of the past, and is as valid as any other since, in Hardwick's work, history is nothing more than incidental to her creations and their doings. As a result these novels are more romantic than historical, evolving at a measured methodical pace, conscious always that characters are more important than plot, and people are more important than events. The environment can alter dramatically, but the individual sets his or her own response to change, if he or she decides to change at all.

Possibly Hardwick's best known associations are with *Upstairs*, *Downstairs* and *The Duchess of Duke Street*. They are perfect examples of the person-centered approach so indicative of her work. There is a place somewhere for the hapless whining scullery maid and the glittering head of the house, and everyone within the system acknowledges that this is so. The two can never touch, although they interact on a daily basis, and this is much to the satisfaction of both and the maintenance of social order. Their way of life is not the issue, but how they cope with their private tribulations in the midst of social norms and upheavals is. Hardwick's eclectic sympathy in presenting her characters allows us to see the common humanity which Hudson and Lady Bellamy share with each other, with the rest of the household, and with the audience in equal proportion.

—L.M. Quinn

HARDY, Laura. See **LAMB, Charlotte.**

HARDY, W(illiam) G(eorge). Canadian. Born in Oakwood, Ontario, 3 February 1895. Educated at the University of Toronto, B.A. 1917, M.A. 1920; University of Chicago, Ph.D. 1922. Married Llewella May Sonley in 1919 (died), two daughters and one son. Lecturer in Classics, University of Toronto, 1918–20; Lecturer, 1920–22, Assistant Professor, 1922–28, Associate Professor, 1928–33, and Professor of Classics, 1933–65, University of Alberta, Edmonton. President, 1930, and play producer, Edmonton Little Theatre. President, Canadian Authors Association, 1950–52; member of the Council, Classical Association of Canada. Recipient: University of Alberta National award, 1962. *Died in 1979.*

ROMANCE AND HISTORICAL PUBLICATIONS

Novels (series: Roman trilogy)

Abraham, Prince of Ur. New York, Dodd Mead, 1935; as *Father Abraham*, London, Lovat Dickson, 1935.
Turn Back the River. New York, Dodd Mead, and London, Lovat Dickson, 1938.
All the Trumpets Sounded. New York, Coward McCann, 1942; London, Macdonald, 1946.
The Unfulfilled. Toronto, McClelland and Stewart, 1951; New York, Appleton Century Crofts, 1952.
Roman trilogy:
    The City of Libertines. Toronto, McClelland and Stewart, and New York, Appleton Century Crofts, 1957; London, Heinemann, 1959.
    The Scarlet Mantle: A Novel of Julius Caesar. Toronto, Macmillan, 1978.
    The Bloodied Toga: A Novel of Julius Caesar. Toronto, Macmillan, 1979.

OTHER PUBLICATIONS

Other

Education in Alberta. Calgary, Calgary Herald, 1946.
From Sea unto Sea: Canada 1850–1920: The Road to Nationhood. New York, Doubleday, 1960.
The Greek and Roman World: Ten Radio Talks. Toronto, Canadian Broadcasting Corporation, 1960; revised edition, Cambridge, Massachusetts, Schenkman, 1962, 1970.
Our Heritage from the Past. Toronto, McClelland and Stewart, 1964.
Journey into the Past, with J. W. R. Gwyne-Timothy. Toronto, McClelland and Stewart, 1965.
Origins and Ordeals of the Western World. Cambridge, Massachusetts, Schenkman, 1968.

Editor, *The Alberta Golden Jubilee Anthology.* Toronto, McClelland and Stewart, 1955.
Editor, *Alberta: A Natural History.* Edmonton, Hurtig, 1967.

*   *   *

The early works of W. G. Hardy were based upon social commentary on the Canada of the day: *The Unfulfilled* examined Canadian/British Canadian/American relations. These novels were flavoured by what was for the day a surprising emphasis on explictly sexual carryings-on; but even so, Hardy's first few books made relatively little stir. His fame rests in large part upon his Roman trilogy, three massive volumes which are not precisely a series, since they are readable as self-sufficient works, but sharing certain elements, most notably the presence of Julius Caesar.

City of Libertines examines the politics and decadence of Roman life in the latter days of the Republic. The plot hinges upon the destructive adoration of the poet Catullus for his faithless "Lesbia." She was in real life Clodia Pulcher, sister of that Clodius Pulcher who created the scandal of a scandalous era by profaning the sacred rites of the Good Goddess, a religious ceremony forbidden to men. The uproar caused by his blasphemous act, and the subsequent manipulation of the Roman population by the self-seeking libertines of the title, provide a jolting comparison with the political manipulation of peoples of the 20th century. Although not the central figure in this novel, Caesar plays a significant role as a presence on the periphery, watchfully prepared to seize any opportunity the fates may afford him.

The Scarlet Mantle covers the mid-period of the life of Julius Caesar. Here is the warrior, the renegade who led his troops, more loyal to himself than to Rome, across the Rubicon, thus casting his personal challenge in the teeth of the Republic. Parallel with Caesar's story runs another thread, that of the life of a humble soldier, Fadius, a fictional character whose changing life and perceptions reflect the effects of Caesar's career upon his times and countrymen.

The Roman trilogy concludes with *The Bloodied Toga*, telling of the climax of Caesar's life and reign, and of his relations with the voluptuous Egyptian queen Cleopatra.

Hardy certainly was comfortably familiar with the historic accounts that provide a basis for his Roman stories, and included the facts as a comprehensible and coherent chain of events in a convincing fashion, but the baldly contemporary language of his Romans is obtrusive and tends to undercut the effect of his ease and familiarity with the intricacies of ancient history.

Apparently jealous of the commercial success of the "slick" novels of the era, some of which his writer persona scornfully lists in *The Unfulfilled*, Hardy seems to have resolved to conquer cheap fiction from within. His obsessive emphasis on sexual relations, in particular sex as a manipulative weapon especially though not exclusively of women, becomes tiresomely repetitive and predictable. Let any man and woman occupy adjacent space in any of his Roman titles, and inevitably their clothing will shortly slither to the floor to the accompaniment of a good deal of embarrassingly adolescent bedroom badinage. Though his work would have benefitted by the attentions of a ruthless editor, Hardy's later novels won for him an extensive public who may, at intervals, have learned something about ancient Rome backstage.

—Joan McGrath

HARLE, Elizabeth. See **ROBERTS, Irene.**

HARLEY, John. See **WOODWARD, Lilian.**

HARRIS, Marilyn. American. Born in Oklahoma City, Oklahoma, 4 June 1931. Educated at Cottey College, Nevada, Missouri, 1949–51; University of Oklahoma, Norman, B.A. 1953, M.A. 1955. Married Edgar V. Springer, Jr., in 1953; one son and one daughter. Address: 1846 Rolling Hills, Norman, Oklahoma 73069, U.S.A.

ROMANCE AND HISTORICAL PUBLICATIONS

Novels (series: Eden)

Bledding Sorrow. New York, Putnam, 1976.
This Other Eden. New York, Putnam, 1977; London, Futura, 1980.
The Prince of Eden. New York, Putnam, 1978; London, Futura, 1980.
The Eden Passion. New York, Putnam, 1979; London, Macdonald, 1981.
The Women of Eden. New York, Putnam, 1980.
The Portent. New York, Putnam, 1980.
The Last Great Love. New York, Putnam, 1981.
Eden Rising. New York, Putnam, 1982.
The Diviner. New York, Putnam, 1983.
Warrick. New York, Doubleday, 1985.
Night Games. New York, Doubleday, 1987.
American Eden. New York, Doubleday, 1987.

OTHER PUBLICATIONS

Novels

In the Midst of Earth. New York, Doubleday, 1969.
Hatter Fox. New York, Random House, 1973; London, Gollancz, 1974.
The Conjurers. New York, Random House, 1974; London, Panther, 1977.

Short Stories

King's Ex. New York, Doubleday, and London, Gollancz, 1967.

Other (for children)

The Peppersalt Land. New York, Four Winds Press, 1970.
The Runaway's Diary. New York, Four Winds Press, 1971.

*   *   *

In Marilyn Harris's first gothic romance, *Bledding Sorrow*, a three-century-old drama of imprisonment, madness, adultery, mutilation, and murder slowly and plausibly repeats itself in the present. In her masterpiece of historical romance, the Eden novels, Harris also sounds, believably, the rest of the painful notes in the scale of passion: abandonment, exile, bastardy, betrayal, incest, rape, and sado-masochism. *This Other Eden*, set in the 1790's, beings when Thomas Eden has his servant girl, Marianne, stripped and flogged for insubordination. The book chronicles his attacks of remorse and his attempts to possess her, which include persuading her sister to abet a kidnapping, and also a sham marriage. They finally plunge together into "the whole ecstatic process of domination and submission." But when a child, Edward, is born, Thomas suffers another personality change and rejects them both. In order to get Marianne back this time, he has *himself* flogged. She nurses him back to health, they marry, and a legitimate son, James, is born. Harris turns history to good account with frequent and bizarre appearances by Beckford (author and builder, of an early gothic novel and castle) and by Lord Nelson's mistress Emma Hamilton, who gains social acceptance for Marianne.

The Prince of Eden, however, is less love story than tragedy of circumstance. The "Prince," Edward, as a result of his parents' marriage settlement, owns Eden. He is selling it off piecemeal to finance various rescue operations among the poor and criminal classes of London in the 1830's. Opium addiction (learned from De Quincey, practised with Branwell Brontë) and a grand passion for his brother's intended bride, Harriet, drive Edward farther outside the bounds of bourgeois respectability. Harriet refuses to run off with Edward. Unfortunately, she is pregnant and must feign a long illness before her wedding; fortunately, Edward learns of this in time to rescue his son, John.

Edward's revulsion from the charade of respectability is further underlined by his involvement with the radical causes of the day. When he proposes to use half the Eden estate on a friend's system of Ragged Schools, James sues for the right to the property. He loses, but Edward, in a typical act of self-immolation, gives it up. He is subsequently killed in an industrial accident, leaving John with nothing but the dream of Eden.

In *The Eden Passion* John realizes this dream, but ironically at the cost of rejecting all his father's beliefs. With this novel, in fact, Harris begins to undermine the conventions of her genre: she creates no more romantic heroes. John, bastard of a bastard, returns to Eden and has for the first and only love of his life his own mother, Harriet, and the rest of the Eden novels chart the pathology of his exile from this love. Although this is gothic romance at its source, Harris's increased attention to themes of social injustice and crimes of imperialism ultimately debunks the myth of the Great Family Estate. When the doomed lovers learn the truth, Harriet blinds and imprisons herself, while John flees to commerce in the City, in the Crimea (where his war wounds are tended by Florence Nightingale), and to India, in search of fortune. He returns to England with an Indian woman who has had her tongue cut out while rescuing him during the 1857 mutiny in Delhi. With Dhari's and Harriet's mutilation, Harris says more than "Passion is dangerous." While John, in his pain, amasses a great fortune, marries, and acquires Eden at last, his women have no consolation but that of being among his valued acquisitions.

In *The Women of Eden* Harris develops this theme. The title is that of a painting of John's wife Lila, Dhari, Harriett's daughter Mary, and Elizabeth, the former prostitute who raised him. An observer says they look sick to their stomachs. Certainly John's behavior becomes increasingly sickening. His wife is repeatedly subjected to marital rape and dies in grotesque agony of a neglected uterine cancer. Dhari is brutalized. Mary is at first a wretched prisoner of his idea of her as a pure maiden; when he sees her in her American lover's embrace, he arranges to have her raped by a gang of thugs. John hates women (especially suffragettes—Elizabeth, by the way, is one), radicals, the poor, Americans, and those he terms Sodomites, whom he also plots to victimize. John's frustrated desire for social acceptance is, he thinks, blocked by a newspaper columnist's attack: "Eden present[s] a contradiction of material splendor and moral bankruptcy, though unwittingly he serve[s] as the most polished mirror ever held to English society in recent times." Eden is denied revenge upon the writer, who is Mary's lover. They escape to America, Dhari and John's lawyer marry and leave for Canada, and Elizabeth joins the French feminists. So much for the Women of Eden and for English society in 1870. Harris has

ended the Eden series by accusing a society of providing gothic materials.

—Sally Allen McNall

HARRIS, Rosemary (Jeanne).** British. Born in London, 20 February 1923. Educated at Thorneloe School, Weymouth; St. Martin's, Central, and Chelsea schools of art, London; Department of Technology, Courtauld Institute, London, 1950. Served in the Red Cross Nursing Auxiliary, Westminster Division, London, 1941–45. Picture restorer, 1949; reader, Metro-Goldwyn-Mayer, 1951–52; children's book reviewer, the *Times*, London, 1970–73. Recipient: Library Association Carnegie Medal, for children's book, 1969; Arts Council grant, 1971. Lives in London. Agent: A. P. Watt Ltd., 20 John Street, London WC1N 2DR, England.

ROMANCE AND HISTORICAL PUBLICATIONS

Novels

The Summer-House. London, Hamish Hamilton, 1956.
Voyage to Cythera. London, Bodley Head, 1958.
Venus with Sparrows. London, Faber, 1961.
All My Enemies. London, Faber, 1967; New York, Simon and Schuster, 1973.
The Nice Girl's Story. London, Faber, 1968; as *Nor Evil Dreams*, New York, Simon and Schuster, 1974.
A Wicked Pack of Cards. London, Faber, 1969; New York, Walker, 1970.
The Double Snare. London, Faber, 1974; New York, Simon and Schuster, 1975.
Three Candles for the Dark. London, Faber, 1976.

OTHER PUBLICATIONS (for children)

Fiction

The Moon in the Cloud. London, Faber, 1968; New York, Macmillan, 1969.
The Shadow on the Sun. London, Faber, and New York, Macmillan, 1970.
The Seal-Singing. London, Faber, and New York, Macmillan, 1971.
The Bright and Morning Star. London, Faber, and New York, Macmillan, 1972.
The King's White Elephant. London, Faber, 1973.
The Flying Ship. London, Faber, 1975.
I Want to Be a Fish. London, Kestrel, 1977.
A Quest for Orion. London, Faber, 1978.
Green Finger House. London, Eel Pie, 1980; New York, Kampmann, 1982.
Tower of the Stars. London, Faber, 1980.
The Enchanted Horse. London, Kestrel, 1981.
Janni's Stork. London, Blackie, and New York, Harper, 1982.
Zed. London, Faber, 1982.
Summers of the Wild Rose. London, Faber, 1987.
Colm of the Islands. London, Walker Books, 1989.

Plays

Television Plays: *Peronik*, 1976; *The Unknown Enchantment*, 1982.

Other

The Child in the Bamboo Grove (legend). London, Faber, 1971; New York, Phillips, 1972.
The Lotus and the Grail: Legends from East to West. London, Faber, 1974; abridged edition, as *Sea Magic and Other Stories of Enchantment*, New York, Macmillan, 1974.
The Little Dog of Fo (legend). London, Faber, 1976.
Beauty and the Beast. London, Faber, 1979; New York, Doubleday, 1980.
Heidi. London, Benn, 1983.

Editor, *Love and the Merry-Go-Round*. London, Hamish Hamilton, 1988.

*

Rosemary Harris comments:

My fiction for adults greq primarily out of a thwarted desire to produce plays for the theatre—and I hope some of what I learned about drama, dialogue, and character in action was a help when it came to a novel-writing. I still believe that a strong plot combined with character development is the truly important basis on which most fiction or dramatic writers need to lean. Look, for instance, at Shaffer's play *Amadeus* which has all the traditional elements, combined with a truly modern approach of his own. If I could do something half as good as that in a novel or play, I should be more than delighted.

*   *   *

Rosemary Harris's first novel, *The Summer-House*, is different from her later books although it has some of the ingredients of the later Harrises—the smooth urbane style with a sophisticated sparkle, a heroine who has two chaps to choose between (lucky girl), and close-knit, tangled family relationships and friendships. But the main difference between this book and its successors is that it is a straightforward tale without terror whereas all the other books are modern gothics—intensely feminine stories of fear and romance. What makes them all the more frightening and claustrophobic is that the menace usually comes from someone who is beloved and should be above suspicion. *All My Enemies* tells of a twin sister who murders the heroine's husband and tries to pretend that her sister is mad as well as bad; *A Wicked Pack of Cards* throws suspicion on both of the heroine's suitors and is laden with red herrings as well as literary allusions. In *The Nice Girl's Story* the villain has to be either the heroine's step-son or her husband—but which? *The Double Snare* has an amnesiac heroine who does not know whom she should love or whom she should fear, and who suspects everyone, even her own previous persona. In *Three Candles for the Dark*, however, Harris has gone over the top with her gothic ingredients which include a scarred heroine, a lonely house, a mad woman, incest, a pyromaniac, killer dogs, a helpless child to hamper the heroine and tug at her heart strings, a sadist, and a double-cross. How's that for Grand Guignol?

Harris is excellent at character drawing; she is a distinguished children's writer and, as one would expect, she produces lively, believable child characters too. *A Wicked Pack of Cards* (my favourite of her gothics) features a whole family of well-drawn and sharply differentiated children, especially Culbertson (so-

called because she was taken out to bridge-parties while in her carry cot), the ten-year-old balletomane who is the lynch-pin of the plot. Joss, the imprisoned boy in *Three Candles for the Dark*, is the most believable character in the book. All her thillers are written in the first person from the heroine's point-of-view, and Harris finds a different style and tone for each one in keeping with her profession (teacher, actress, journalist, and novelist) and, what is much more difficult, manages to convey her heroine's faults within this framework. The other thing that Harris does well is convey a sense of place. It is more than giving us evocative descriptions, it is dozens of well-chosen little details which make you feel as if you are actually there: Paris in *The Summer-House*, Italy in *The Double Snare*, a suburban comprehensive school with all its inwardness in *The Nice Girl's Story*, London and Alexandria in *All My Enemies*, an English seaside town in *A Wicked Pack of Cards* and the Vermont countryside in *Three Candles for the Dark*.

Harris's books are always a pleasure to read and deserve to be better known.

—Pamela Cleaver

HARRISON, Elizabeth (Francourt). Address: c/o Mills and Boon Ltd., 18–24 Paradise Road, Richmond, Surrey TW9 1SR, England.

ROMANCE AND HISTORICAL PUBLICATIONS

Novels

Coffee at Dobree's. London, Ward Lock, 1965.
The Physicians. London, Ward Lock, 1966.
The Ravelston Affair. London, Ward Lock, 1967.
Emergency Call. London, Hurst and Blackett, 1970.
Accident Call. London, Hurst and Blackett, 1971.
Ambulance Call. London, Hurst and Blackett, 1972.
Surgeon's Call. London, Hurst and Blackett, 1973.
On Call. London, Hurst and Blackett, 1974.
Hospital Call. London, Hurst and Blackett, 1975.
Dangerous Call. London, Hurst and Blackett, 1976.
To Mend a Heart. London, Hurst and Blackett, 1977.
Young Doctor Goddard. London, Hurst and Blackett, 1978.
A Doctor Called Caroline. London, Hurst and Blackett, 1979.
A Surgeon Called Amanda. London, Hale, 1982.
A Surgeon's Life. London, Hale, 1983.
Marrying a Doctor. London, Hale, 1984.
A Surgeon's Affair. London, Mills and Boon, 1985.
A Surgeon at St. Mark's. London, Mills and Boon, 1986.
The Surgeon She Married. London, Mills and Boon, 1988.

*   *   *

Unlike most "hospital" novelists, Elizabeth Harrison has never nursed, though for most of her working life she has been closely connected with the medical profession, mainly in an administrative and research capacity. This, I think, has been to her (and the reader's) advantage. Hers are not the conventional doctor-nurse romances. She rarely writes about nurses. Her central characters are usually doctors, and it is from their point of view that we see life. She sees doctors not as little tin gods, though, but as all-too-human, often arrogant on the upper slopes, prone to human frailty at every level.

Her novels are almost all set in the fictional Central London Hospital. This gives her scope to develop character from story to story, which she does. Sons and daughters follow eminent fathers into the profession through "their" hospital. The reader comes to know them, and their foibles.

One of her most interesting and complex characters is Leo Rosenstein, an outstanding young surgeon, over-conscious of his lowly (East End) origins compared to his colleagues, all of whom have the "right" accent, clothes, school, and family backgrounds—a fact which drives Leo to hide his sensitivity and sharp intelligence behind an exaggerated lack of "couth."

The exploration of personality, as much as the medical detail and the love-interest, obviously fascinates Harrison. The high-and-mighty Ravelstons, for example: "No heart—all brain, the lot of them; supercilious too, and moneyed," is how one embittered colleague sums them up. But one of them is riding for a fall in *The Ravelston Affair*, which leads to his being "struck off," the worst, and most humiliating, punishment a doctor can suffer. Here, too, is one romantic hospital writer who acknowledges the fact that not all doctors these days are WASPS. There is a touch of racial tension in *The Ravelston Affair*.

In at least two books young doctors get a taste of what it is like to be a patient. *Emergency Call* shows especial insight into the devastating psychological effects on a young man—dominant partner in a happy marriage—of paralysis following a railway accident in which he attempts to rescue a passenger. His young wife's inability to help him back to full life bewilders and frightens her, especially when the pretty nurse assigned to him has more success. The reasons are not the obvious ones. Harrison's subtle and delicate handling of this tricky theme sets the seal, for me, on her shrewd understanding of human nature, in addition to her ability to write dramatic stories and credible dialogue.

Like Lucilla Andrews she keeps up to date in medical matters and the way hospitals are run—and also in contemporary morals. In *Young Doctor Goddard*, for example, the heroine's close friend, another nurse, cheerfully shacks up with one of the doctors (of course they are engaged, and fully intend to marry . . .). And, to my personal regret, the hospital "politics" which spice the earlier novels are played down in the later ones because, the author explains, that is how it now is in real life.

—Elizabeth Grey

HARRISON, Sarah (née Martyn). British. Born in Exeter, Devon, 7 August 1946. Educated at the University of London, B.A. (honours) 1967. Married Jeremy Harrison in 1969; one son and two daughters. Journalist, International Publishing Corporation, London, 1967–70. Agent: Carol Smith, 25 Hornton Court, Kensington High Street, London W8 7RT, England.

ROMANCE AND HISTORICAL PUBLICATIONS

Novels

The Flowers of the Field. London, Futura, and New York, Coward McCann, 1980.
A Flower That's Free. London, Futura, and New York, Simon and Schuster, 1984.
Hot Breath. London, Futura, 1985.

An Imperfect Lady. London, Futura, 1988; New York, Warner, 1989.

OTHER PUBLICATIONS (for children)

Other

In Granny's Garden. London, Cape, and New York, Holt Rinehart, 1980.
Laura and Edmund [*Old Lumber, the Lady, the Squire*]. London, Hutchinson, 4 vols., 1986.

*   *   *

In her first two novels, *The Flowers of the Field* and *A Flower That's Free*, Sarah Harrison treats us to a total of almost 1400 pages of a family saga, spanning the obligatory 50 years and three generations. Although this format is something of a cliché, and the period covered (1890's–1940's) one of the most frequently written about, Harrison handles her subject in a deft and professional manner.

With settings as diverse as the Kentish Weald, Paris, Berlin, Malta, and Kenya, and a period including both world wars, these novels could truly be described as panoramic, and one has the feeling that Harrison has indeed had this adjective in mind. It is hard to think of any character type or any aspect of social life which does not make an appearance in one or the other of these two novels. Had this been Harrison's brief she could not have succeeded better. This in no way detracts from a compelling story fluently and interestingly told.

The heroine of the first book, Thea Tennant, is very much a 20th-century woman, becoming involved in the suffragette movement and later serving as an ambulance driver in France. As a young girl she falls in love with Jack Kingsley, but their burgeoning romance encounters a slight setback when he is successfully seduced by her younger sister Dulcie. The two girls travel to Vienna where Thea meets a new love, Josef von Crieff; Dulcie again disrupts her sister's life, this time by eloping to Paris with the tutor of Josef's younger brother. (Dulcie does at least put her experiences to good use when she becomes the "whore with a heart of gold," offering hospitality to British soldiers in Paris during World War I). By the very long arm of coincidence so beloved of romance writers, Jack and Josef meet in the trenches without knowing of their mutual acquaintances and exchange tokens. Josef is later killed and Thea does eventually marry Jack. More briefly, but in fact far more movingly portrayed is the unrequited love between Thea's cousin Maurice, a conscientious objector during the war, and Primmy, the maidservant. These and other characters seen against the turbulence not only of the war, but also of social conditions prevailing at home, give depth to a fulfilling and stirring tale.

The second book, *A Flower That's Free*, has as its main character Thea's adopted (and Dulcie's actual) daughter Kate. Brought up by Jack and Thea in Kenya, Kate knows that she is adopted, but has no idea who her mother is, and in fact does not find out until after Dulcie's death. Here again we have a heroine who is very much her own woman, and who ultimately has to make the choice between her loving and fairly unexceptional husband, and an older man who (just to complicate matters a little) has in fact been her mother's (i.e., Dulcie's) lover. And once more the backdrop of a world war provides opportunities for the novelist to introduce the extra tensions of brief relationships, contributing to a fast moving plot.

One receives the impression that Harrison was perhaps thankful to turn away from the conventionalities of a family saga to her far from conventional third novel *Hot Breath*. Harrison assures us that she is not portraying herself in the person of Harriet Dare, historical novelist and heroine of *Hot Breath*—does the lady perhaps protest too much? Whatever the truth of the matter she provides us with an outrageously funny and immensely original romance novel, in which the heroine has an extramarital affair with Kostaki Ghikas, a good looking, oversexed and unfortunately not quite credible Greek doctor. Meanwhile Harriet's husband George is in his turn having an affair with Ghikas' mother, who is "a marine archaeologist with a man in every port." Not really believable is it? But great fun, and so enjoyable that one readily forgives the basic improbability.

With *An Imperfect Lady* Harrison returns to the family saga, giving us this time an even wider sweep in both time (more than 70 years) and space (the West Country to the Caribbean, taking in France and Ireland on the way). Again we are offered a very independent-minded heroine, Adeline Gundry, who certainly needs her immense strength of character in order to overcome the constant emotional obstacles and challenges which life throws at her.

Her first marriage (at the age of 18, to a boyhood friend of her brother) ends after only a couple of years when her husband commits suicide. She later finds out that the wounds he had received in World War I were self-inflicted, and that he was beset by doubts and uncertainties. Following a happy four years at the Slade School of Art, Adeline embarks upon a lesbian relationship; she later marries, has a child and then is divorced. After a third marriage Adeline has a stillborn baby; this marriage deteriorates as her husband's gambling problems become insurmountable. This would daunt many a lesser woman, but Adeline (by now a much sought-after portrait painter) also manages to cope with the scandal when her lesbian relationship becomes public knowledge many years after the event, and with the ultimate demise of her husband, who dies as they are about to become reconciled.

This latest novel does not succeed as well as her first two in this genre, and yet there is no doubt that Harrison is a major talent in the field of romance writing.

—Judith Rhodes

HARROD-EAGLES, Cynthia. Also writes as Elizabeth Bennett; Emma Woodhouse. British. Born in London, 13 August 1948. Educated at Burlington Grammar School, London, 1959–66; Edinburgh University 1966–67; University College, London, 1969–72, B.A. (honours) 1972. Address: c/o Macdonald and Company Ltd., 66–73 Shoe Lane, London EC4P 4AP, England.

ROMANCE AND HISTORICAL PUBLICATIONS

Novels (series: Dynasty)

The Waiting Game. London, New English Library, 1972.
Shadows on the Mountain. London, New English Library, 1973.
Hollow Night. London, Magnum, 1980.
Dynasty:
  1. *The Founding*. London, Macdonald, and New York, Dell, 1980.
  2. *The Dark Rose*. London, Macdonald, and New York, Dell, 1981.
  3. *The Princeling*. London, Macdonald, 1981; as *The Distant Wood*, New York, Dell, 1981.
  4. *The Oak Apple*. London, Macdonald, 1982; as *The Crystal Crown*, New York, Dell, 1982.
  5. *The Black Pearl*. London, Macdonald, and New York, Dell, 1982.
  6. *The Long Shadow*. London, Macdonald, and New York, Dell, 1983.
  7. *The Chevalier*. London, Macdonald, 1984.
  8. *The Maiden*. London, Macdonald, 1985.
  9. *The Flood-Tide*. London, Macdonald, 1986.
  10. *The Tangled Thread*. London, Macdonald, 1987.
  11. *The Emperor*. London, Macdonald, 1988.
  12. *The Victory*. London, Macdonald, 1989.
Deadfall. London, Methuen, 1982.

Novels as Emma Woodhouse

A Rainbow Summer. London, Mayflower, 1976.
A Well-Painted Passion. London, Mayflower, 1976.
Romany Magic. London, Mayflower, 1977.
Love's Perilous Passage. London, Sphere, 1978.
On Wings of Love. London, Sphere, 1978.
Never Love a Stranger. London, Sphere, 1978.

Novels as Elizabeth Bennett

Title Role. London, New English Library, 1980.
The Unfinished. London, New English Library, 1983.
Even Chance. London, New English Library, 1984.
Last Run. London, New English Library, 1984.

*

Cynthia Harrod-Eagles comments:
  The Dynasty series was conceived as a kind of history without tears, a saga following the fortunes of the late Middle Ages to the present day. While the Morland family is purely fictional, the background to their lives is the real history of England, carefully researched and accurately recorded, so that the reader should emerge with a good overview of the flow of social development during the last 500 years: how people lived, what they ate, what they wore, how they viewed the world they lived in. Originally commissioned as a 12-book series, it now has been extended to at least 17.

*   *   *

With the exception of her first novel, *The Waiting Game*, and three other books, Cynthia Harrod-Eagles has concentrated on a long series of historical novels—12 to date—tracing the history of the fictional Morland family. Aptly entitled the Dynasty series, the novels carry the reader from the Wars of the Roses to the Napoleonic era (and, it is claimed, eventually to World War II).

The first of the Morland novels, *The Founding*, introduces the family established through the marriage of Eleanor Courtney to Robert Morland the younger son of a Yorkshire sheep farmer. Spanning the years 1434 to 1486 and crowded with characters, it sets the formula for the subsequent books. For though Harrod-Eagles manages to avoid writing quite the same novel throughout the series, thus maintaining interest in the fortunes of the Morlands, nevertheless her readers can enjoy the security engendered by recurring themes and situations and characters. The changes are adroitly rung; different historical periods, varying viewpoints, each book with a different time span—some of them encompass several generations of the family (*The Founding*, *The Princeling*), others—*The Emperor* for example—a mere decade, sometimes more than one volume will follow the careers of one generation.

As a historian Harrod-Eagles includes a short list of source material with each title thus ensuring her work can be seen in a more serious light than mere historical romance. Further weight is added to this creation of a dynastic family by a family tree relevant to the particular generation in each volume. The final touch is a plan of Morland Place of that period. For it is Morland Place built under the aegis of the first Eleanor Morland that provides the link between the increasingly farflung elements of the family, a central point to return to, reflecting as it grows in grandeur their rise in fortune and at the same time providing the key to their status. For it the status of the Morlands as landed gentry that ensures the dynastic marriages that are a central and repeated feature of the saga—marriages that ensure their progress upwards. And it is their status that allows Harrod-Eagles to introduce the great events and prominent historical figures of each period into the action, while the marriages also ensure that her characters move further afield than Yorkshire. Thus the alliance of Lettice Morland to the Scottish Lord, Robert Hamilton (*The Princeling*), introduces the court of Mary, Queen of Scots, and the murders of Rizio and Darnley; while *The Flood-Tide* transports the reader to pre-revolutionary France and also to America on the eve of the War of Independence. Nor is it just the action which is wide ranging. The whole gamut of political opinion and allegiance is represented—Lancastrian and Yorkist, Cavalier and Roundhead, Catholic and Protestant, British and American patriot.

Harrod-Eagles does not rely on major events alone to set the historical background to each title. Details of dress, food, architecture, the occasional nuance of speech—all of these touches allow each period to be differentiated though without the exuberant immediacy of a Georgette Heyer. By and large the narrative and dialogue are modern in tone. Period excesses may be avoided but much is made of such social details as the position of women, the frequency of pregnancies, and the high rate of infant mortality. For though attention is paid to the many male characters (frequently sharing the same first name to the confusion of the inattentive reader), it is the women who emerge as the more memorable and most distinctive. Though Morland Place is handed down from father to son in the traditional manner, in the end it is the ladies of Morland Place who emerge as the dominant and enduring characters—the first Eleanor, Nanette, Annunciata, Jemima. The Morland dynasty is, in the final analysis, a matriarchy, and history is seen from the woman's point of view.

The Dynasty saga may be designed to unfold the panorama of English history—the Morland family fortunes in their rise from sheep farmer to the aristocracy, mirroring the ascendancy of the country through trading superiority to military success and the acquisition of an empire. But they are also romances and it is the interest generated by the relations between the characters, their progress in love and hate, their interraction as members of an increasingly complex family that holds the reader's attention. Harrod-Eagles's technique is to present the action from a multiplicity of viewpoints thus ensuring the widest variety of characteristics and the inclusion of many aspects of the social scene from the court to the world of the strolling players. However though none of her characters is outstanding and they are frequently stereotypes of the romance genre, when she allows them enough space in the action to develop, Harrod-Eagles can create enjoyable and distinctive people who enlist sympathy and add depth to the relentless progress of the Morland saga.

—Ferelith Hordon

HART, Caroline. See **GARVICE, Charles.**

———————

HARTE, Marjorie. See **McEVOY, Marjorie.**

———————

HARVEY, Caroline. See **TROLLOPE, Joanna.**

———————

HARVEY, Kathryn. See **WOOD, Barbara.**

———————

HARVEY, Rachel. See **BLOOM, Ursula.**

———————

HARWOOD, Alice. British. Born in West Bromwich, Staffordshire. Educated at King Edward VI School and Edgbaston College, both Birmingham; Bedford College, University of London, B.A. 1932. Assistant editor, *New Chronicle of Christian Education*, London, 1933–35; staff member, British Red Cross Education Department, Oxford, 1943–45. *Died 19 December 1985.*

ROMANCE AND HISTORICAL PUBLICATIONS

Novels

Caedmon: A Lyrical Drama. London, S.P.C.K., 1937.
So Merciful a Queen, So Cruel a Woman. New York, Hutchinson, 1939; as *The Star of the Greys*, London, Hutchinson, 1939.
She Had to Be Queen, London, Bodley Head, 1948; as *The Lily and the Leopards*. Indianapolis, Bobbs Merrill, 1949.
Merchant of the Ruby. London, Bodley Head, and Indianapolis, Bobbs Merrill, 1951.
The Strangeling. London, Bodley Head, and Indianapolis, Bobbs Merrill, 1954.
Seats of the Mighty. Indianapolis, Bobbs Merrill, 1956; as *At Heart a King*, London, Bodley Head, 1957.
No Smoke Without Fire. Indianapolis, Bobbs Merrill, 1964.
The Living Phantom. London, Hale, 1973.
The Clandestine Queen. London, Hale, 1979.
The Uncrowned Queen. London, Hale, 1983.

*   *   *

In Alice Harwood's *The Strangeling* Michal, the main protagonist, comments at one point "those who write books live others' lives." If this is so then Harwood herself is inconsistent with such an avowed principle because the last thing her work concerns is anyone's life. She writes instead about the various actual political and social situations which occurred in the past to which the people were simply adjuncts. Consequently her books are one-dimensional and totally factual narratives. Harwood is thereby more true to the concept of an historical novel than many writers who claim to belong to the same school but who in fact write novels in an historical setting.

The difference is subtle but nevertheless exists, and Harwood has purity of purpose and a cast iron integrity in handling her data. Her stories are well researched and extremely detailed, and the readers' familiarity with the central events and figures from history lends a certain security to reading the novels. We already know the outcome, and Harwood never contradicts us, but she does encourage speculation on the what-might-have-beens had the circumstances been different.

Harwood raises many historical questions which she doesn't really go on to answer. They are, however, purely rhetorical, and suggest new perceptions which we might not have thought about before, but at the same time she promotes many other preconceptions. Darnley, in *No Smoke Without Fire*, is the archetypal insecure wimp of popular myth, so that our picture of him, built up from common sources already is ratified instead of being queried.

Although Harwood does occasionally try to explore and develop her characters through frequent soliloquies or stream of consciousness passages, they fail to come across as real, believable, and fully fleshed out figures. Our pre-knowledge of the characters can prevent our acceptance of a new interpretation, and Harwood is more concerned with making us contemplate other possible historical scenarios than with making us understand the people responsible for them. Even centering on one small group like the Grey family, as she does frequently (providing a loose link between the books) fails to convey any intimate knowledge of their individuality. They are simply playing their part in history and relating themselves into the greater social order.

In *So Merciful a Queen, So Cruel a Woman*, for example, Harwood concentrates on comparatively minor figures like Kathryn, Lady Jane Grey's younger sister. Kathryn is a relatively unknown historical figure so one would expect there to be more scope for creative development than with the major well-known kings, queens, and politicians. Kathryn is not, however, the angst-ridden 13-year-old adolescent one would expect considering her life so far, and she therefore rings false, untrue to her experiences and unable to provoke our sympathy. There are exceptions of course: Michal is a more believable character because she is not immediately identifiable as an historical personage and the author is therefore free to expand her creation in any chosen direction.

For Harwood, then, history provides boundaries to the fictional elements of plot and characterisation. However, it also supplies her with the opportunity to exploit her strong sense of place and contemporary atmosphere. Kinross village in *Seats of the Mighty (At Heart a King)* and the London of *So Merciful a Queen, So Cruel a Woman* are equally evocative of the 16th century and there are also some brilliant passages of archaic dialect in *Merchant of the Ruby*. Features like these lighten the otherwise pondorous style crammed as it is with the occasional touches of tongue-in-cheek cynicism—in *She Had to Be Queen* we meet the bored and worldly-wise Winchester receiving Elizabeth "hardened by this time to the spectacle of princesses in trouble."

Harwood also exhibits a keen eye for human failings. Mary in *The Strangeling* is more than a little uneasy at her first ever train journey, although she has survived for years abroad in much less civilized places than Lime Street railway station. There are occasional strokes of drama where the unexpected can happen—well-known literary figures—the Brontës, Erasmus, Thomas More—wander in and out of the pages, purely for effect.

The net result is a very ideosyncratic approach to the historical novel, which Harwood justifies as fact being stranger than fiction. This is her excuse for poking into obscure corners of the past, but not into the human psyches of the inhabitants. She brushes the dust off forgotten but important figures like Elizabeth Woodville and places them in our already existing historical knowledge. We reassess accepted truths as a consequence, and this is a refreshingly original treatment of a well established genre.

—L.M. Quinn

HASTINGS Brooke. Pseudonym for Deborah Hannes Gordon. American. Born in New York City, 31 May 1946. Educated at Yorktown High School, Yorktown Heights, New York, graduated 1964; Brandeis University, Waltham, Massachusetts, B.A. in political science, 1968 (Phi Beta Kappa). Married David W. Gordon in 1967; one daughter and one son. Research assistant, Columbia University, New York, 1968–70; secretary, Huron Institute and *Working Papers* magazine, Cambridge, Massachusetts, 1971–73; researcher and writer, CARD Consultants, Sacramento, California, 1979. Recipient: Romantic Writers of America golden medallion, 1982. Address: 1240 Noonan Drive, Sacramento, California 95822, U.S.A.

ROMANCE AND HISTORICAL PUBLICATIONS

Novels

Desert Fire. New York, Silhouette, 1980.
Innocent Fire. New York, Silhouette, 1980.
Playing for Keeps. New York, Silhouette, 1980.
Island Conquest. New York, Silhouette, 1981.
Winner Take All. New York, Silhouette, 1981; London, Hodder and Stoughton, 1982.
A Matter of Time. New York, Silhouette, 1982.
Intimate Strangers. New York, Silhouette, 1982.
Rough Diamond. New York, Silhouette, 1982.
An Act of Love. New York, Silhouette, 1983.
Interested Parties. New York, Silhouette, 1984.
Reasonable Doubts. New York, Silhouette, 1984.
Tell Me No Lies. New York, Silhouette, 1984.
Hard to Handle. New York, Silhouette, 1985.
As Time Goes By. New York, Silhouette, 1986.
Double Jeopardy. New York, Silhouette, 1986.
Forward Pass. New York, Silhouette, 1986.
Too Close for Comfort. New York, Silhouette, 1987.
Forbidden Fruit. New York, Silhouette, 1987.
Both Sides Now. New York, Silhouette, 1988.
Catch a Falling Star. New York, Silhouette, 1988.
So Sweet a Sin. New York, Silhouette, 1989.

*

Brooke Hastings comments:

I see my typical reader as a woman who's probably juggling two or three or four very demanding roles—homemaker, student, wife, mother, paid employee and/or volunteer, for example. She probably has more stress in her life than she can handle. I hope my books will entertain her . . . that they'll provide a few hours of escape from the daily grind, an evening or two of emotion, adventure, and mystery. I want to leave her with a warm feeling in her heart, a smile on her face, and even a few joyful tears in her eyes. And if in the process, I can say a few things about subjects such as the importance of a woman being able to stand up for herself and take care of herself financially if she has to . . . of men and women caring for each other, trusting each other and bringing out what's best in each other . . . of love, family, and charity being far more meaningful and fulfilling than fancy cars, clothing, and condos . . . well, then, so much the better.

*　　*　　*

Brooke Hastings has written more than 20 contemporary romance novels for Silhouette's Romance, Special Edition, and Intimate Moments lines. Her Romance *Winner Take All* won the Romance Writers of America's golden medallion.

Hastings uses a variety of settings for her stories, from the United States to Hong Kong to the fictitious Jammipur. Her characters' livelihoods are diverse, too. *A Matter of Time* features thoroughbred racing and whiskey distilling; *Intimate Strangers*, gourmet cooking; and *Rough Diamond*, baseball.

Hastings's heroes and heroines usually come from wealthy backgrounds. Their families are very much a part of the story. Sometimes there are so many characters that one wishes for a cast list to help keep track. Often, one of these relatives creates a situation that initially throws the two lovers together. For example, in *Intimate Strangers*, Rachel Grant is hired by Olivia Bennett to cook for her writer son Jason Wilder. Rachel does not know that Jason is the man who wrote a controversial book about her own past. In *Rough Diamond*, Dani Ronsard inherits millions from her father, but only if she agrees to manage his baseball team, of which Ty Morgan is the star. Julia Harcourt's father (*Innocent Fire*) threatens to withdraw his financial support from a college unless she is allowed to take an art course from professor Derek Veblen. In *Desert Fire*, Jenny Ross's father contrives to have her employed as Nick Butler's housekeeper. Ken Gunnison (*Catch a Falling Star*) is told by his father-in-law that he must help Kristie Clarke solve an industrial counterfeiting mystery or risk losing an inheritance.

These manipulative relatives then drop conveniently into the background while the hero and heroine fall in love and struggle with their conflicts. They may surface when needed to keep the plot moving, though; for example, in *Innocent Fire*, *Desert Fire*, and *Both Sides Now*, father steps in and demands marriage when he thinks his daughter has been compromised.

Relatives also provide subplots which contribute to the conflict between hero and heroine. *Hard to Handle* has Doug Hunter disapproving of Melanie, the woman his best friend Edward has chosen to marry. This complicates Doug's falling in love with Melanie's sister, Cassie Valdenberg. In *An Act of Love*, Luke Griffin is angry because heroine Miranda Dunne's sister is having an affair with his brother-in-law. *Both Sides Now* shows Bradley Fraser's favorite aunt involved with the rakish father of heroine Sabrina Lang.

The plethora of characters and subplots results in variety but also in confusion and lack of unity. For example, in *Both Sides Now*, the first part of the story focuses on the conflict over Brad's aunt's relationship with Sabrina's father, while the second part features the rescue of Sabrina's friend, a prisoner in Jammipur. In *Reasonable Doubts*, Laura Silver initially is repelled by Gregory Steiger because she feels he is indirectly responsible for her father's death. As the story progresses, however, this issue is lost as new subplots develop.

Other conflicts between the lovers revolve around the obligatory unhappy past relationship, usually marriage to the wrong person. Sylvie Kruger's attorney husband was unfaithful (*A Matter of Time*). Sabrina Lang was married to the domineering king of Jammipur in *Both Sides Now*. *Intimate Stranger*'s Rachel Grant's former spouse was a corrupt South American dictator.

During the story the heroine and hero engage in much self analysis as they attempt to work through their pain. This preoccupation creates a rather depressing atmosphere. Even when the lovers make love it is with a joyless desperation. On the plus side, their self-absorbtion does result in a remarkable honesty that paves the way for the harmonious ending.

In the early stories, true to genre demands, the heroine suffers at the hands of the arrogant, mercurial hero. However, she has fallen in love with him and thus endures. At some point during the story, usually near the crisis, she is reduced to tears and utterly humiliated. She then flees to find solace with one of the sympathetic relatives or friends. At the end, the man explains the reason for his behavior (i.e., an unhappy past relationship), and all is forgiven. These early heroes do have some decency and sensitivity, but because these positive traits are told rather than shown the effectiveness is diminished.

Some of the women have careers, but these are not as important as their romantic relationships. Sylvie Kruger (*A Matter of Time*) gives up her career as a dress designer to join Jordan Rutledge at his new winery. Jenny Ross in *Desert Fire* spends more time trying to cope with Nick Butler than pursuing her trade as a silversmith.

In the later stories, in keeping with genre changes, heroes are more sensitive and heroines are stronger. For example, in *Both Sides Now*, Brad is the one who wants to marry Sabrina, now that she is pregnant with his child, but she wants to maintain her freedom.

Too Close for Comfort has a lighter tone than most of Hastings's novels. To keep her safe from manipulative relatives, Jessica Lawrence's fiancé has her spirited away by private detective Griff Marshall. The humor is clever and the characters display a refreshing frivolity. Also, hero Griff is mellower and more likeable than earlier heroes.

Hastings is skilled at developing the sexual aspect of the romantic relationship and her love scenes are rich in sensuality. That some of her characters suffer from sexual dysfunction as a result of their past experiences allows for a variety of sexual expression and eroticism.

Intense love scenes, characters who attempt to understand themselves, and interesting settings have made Hastings a popular contemporary series romance writer.

—Linda Lee

HASTINGS, Phyllis (Dora, née Hodge). Also writes as John Bedford; Julia Mayfield. British. Born in Bristol. Educated at Edgebaston Church of England College for Girls. Married Philip Norman Hastings in 1938; one child. Ballet dancer as a child; later operator of a dairy farm and an antique business. Recipient: Romantic Novelists Association Historical award, 1973. Address: c/o Robert Hale Ltd., 45–47 Clerkenwell Green, London EC1R 0HT, England.

ROMANCE AND HISTORICAL PUBLICATIONS

Novels (series: Sussex)

As Long as You Live. London, Jenkins, 1951.
Far from Jupiter. London, Jenkins, 1952.
Crowning Glory. London, Jenkins, 1952.
Rapture in My Rags. London, Dent, and New York, Dutton, 1954; as *Scarecrow Lover*, London, Pan, 1960; as *Rapture*, London, Consul, and New York, Popular Library, 1966.
Dust Is My Pillow. London, Dent, and New York, Dutton, 1955.
The Field of Roses. London, Dent, 1955; as *Her French Husband*, New York, Dutton, 1956.
The Black Virgin of the Gold Mountain. London, Dent, 1956.
The Innocent and the Wicked. New York, Popular Library, 1956.
The Signpost Has Four Arms. London, Dent, 1957.
The Forest of Stone (as Julia Mayfield). London, Hale, 1957.
A Time for Pleasure. New York, Popular Library, 1957.
The Happy Man. London, Hutchinson, 1958.
Golden Apollo. London, Hutchinson, 1958.
The Fountain of Youth. London, Hutchinson, 1959.
Sandals for My Feet. London, Hutchinson, 1960.
Long Barnaby. London, Hodder and Stoughton, 1961; as *Hot Day in High Summer*, London, May Fair, 1962.
The Night the Roof Blew Off. London, Hodder and Stoughton, 1962.
Their Flowers Were Always Black. London, Hale, 1967; as *The Harlot's Daughter*, London, New English Library, 1967.
The Swan River Story. London, Hale, 1968.
The Sussex Saga:
    All Earth to Love. London, Corgi, 1968.
    Day of the Dancing Sun. London, Corgi, 1971.
An Act of Darkness. London, Hale, 1969; as *The House on Malador Street*, New York, Putnam, 1970.
The Stars Are My Children. London, Hale, 1970.
The Temporary Boy. London, Hale, 1971.
When the Gallows Is High. London, Hale, 1971.
The Conservatory. London, Hale, 1973; New York, Pocket Books, 1974.
The Gates of Morning. London, Corgi, 1973.
Bartholomew Fair. London, Hale, 1974.
House of the Twelve Caesars. London, Hale, 1975; New York, Berkley, 1976.
The Image-Maker. London, Hale, 1976.
The Candles of the Night. London, Cassell, 1977.
The Death-Scented Flower. London, Hale, 1977.
Field of the Forty Footsteps. London, Cassell, 1978; New York, St. Martin's Press, 1979.
The Stratford Affair. London, Hale, 1978.
The Feast of the Peacock. London, Cassell, 1978.
Running Thursday. London, Hale, 1980.
Buttercup Joe. London, Hale, 1980.
Tiger's Heaven. London, Hale, 1981.
A Delight of Angels. London, Hale, 1981.
The Overlooker. London, Hale, 1982.
Blackberry Summer. London, Hale, 1982.
The Lion at the Door. London, Hale, 1983.
The Free Traders. London, Hale, 1984.
My Four Uncles. London, Hale, 1984.
The Women Barbers of Drury Lane. London, Hale, 1985.

The Julian Maze. London, Hale, 1986.
The Naked Runner. London, Hale, 1987.

OTHER PUBLICATIONS

Other as John Bedford

Looking [and *More Looking*] *in Junk Shops*. London, Parrish, 2 vols., 1961–62.
Talking about Teapots. London, Parrish, 1964.
Collector's Pieces 1–12. London, Cassell, 12 vols., 1964–67.
London's Burning. London, Abelard Schuman, 1966.
Delftware. London, Cassell, 1966.
Still Looking for Junk. London, Macdonald, 1969.

*   *   *

One of Phyllis Hastings's earlier novels, *Rapture in My Rags*, was described in the *New York Times Book Review* (18 July 1954) as ''A touching story of a girl's search for affection, her achieving a kind of protective maturity, and her revolt to preserve her new found identity.'' Many of the author's female characters fit this very description although their personalities and their predicaments vary widely. Endeavoring to overcome loneliness in the midst of coping with peculiar situations is a hallmark of Hastings's heroines. From the confused Anna in *Dust Is My Pillow*, gullible Rose in *The Field of Roses* (US title *Her French Husband*), and responsible Ellie in *The Conservatory* to stalwart Melita in *The Swan River Story*, warped Victoria in *An Act of Darkness* (US title *The House on Malador Street*), and even the indomitable Caroline Dyke in *The Gates of Morning*, the author relentlessly examines the problems and powers of being female in largely male-dominated situations.

While the trials of women dealing with men in their lives is the primary focus of romance and gothic fiction, Hastings's style is distinctly her own. She can dispose of years in a sentence or two and describe wide-ranging adventures in understated terms as she does in *The Stars Are My Children*. One delights in the bright bits of humor that crop up sometimes in the most unlikely situations. She distinctively crafts her stories around characters or circumstances that are slightly offbeat, a shade removed from the normal. Hastings has a flair for portraying the neurotic character, such as the obsessed patriarch Isaac Shipton in *Dust Is My Pillow* and religious fanatic Stand Fast Dyke in *The Gates of Morning* as well as the evil sister Margaret in *The Conservatory*. She is also a master at portraying the growing sexual awareness of her heroines. Repressed sexuality accounts for the tension in many of her novels, and she also explores the touchy area of relationships between older women and younger men with humor in *The Stars Are My Children* and sensitivity in *The Gates of Morning*.

Hastings is an insightful student of human nature, always in control of her narrative, often lyrical in her descriptions of country life, but it is her original characters and her taste for the unusual that make her repertoire of stories truly entertaining. A minor character in *The Stars Are My Children* expresses what might well be the author's own philosophy. After Arthur Balmer relates the fantastic tale of his rescue from slavery by a woman who gave him her infant daughter before perishing in a shipwreck and his later 15-year separation from the girl after his impressment, the listener, an old sailor, proclaims, '''Tis a mighty strange story though I have heard stranger. The earth teems with strange stories, it being the dwelling place of such odd creatures as human beings.''

—Allayne C. Heyduk

HAYGOOD, Arnold G. See **SLAUGHTER, Frank G.**

HEATH, Sharon. See **RITCHIE, Claire.**

HEAVEN, Constance (née Fecher). Also writes as Constance Fecher; Christina Merlin. British. Born in Enfield, Middlesex, 6 August 1911. Educated at The Convent, Woodford Green, Essex, 1921–28; King's College, London, 1928–31, B.A. (honours) 1931; London College of Music, Licentiate 1931. Married William Heaven in 1939 (died 1958). Actress, 1939–66; operated theatre companies at Henley-on-Thames with her husband; tutor in English literature, history and creative writing, City Literary Institute, London, 1967–79. Chairwoman, Romantic Novelists Association, 1981. Recipient: Romantic Novelists Association Major award, 1973. Address: 37 Teddington Park Road, Teddington, Middlesex TW11 8NB, England.

ROMANCE AND HISTORICAL PUBLICATIONS

Novels (series: Kuragin; Ravensley)

The House of Kuragin. London, Heinemann, and New York, Coward McCann, 1972.
The Astrov Inheritance (Kuragin). London, Heinemann, 1973; as *The Astrov Legacy*, New York, Coward McCann, 1973.
Castle of Eagles. London, Heinemann, and New York, Coward McCann, 1974.
The Place of Stones. London, Heinemann, and New York, Coward McCann, 1975.
The Fires of Glenlochy. London, Heinemann, and New York, Coward McCann, 1976.
The Queen and the Gypsy. London, Heinemann, and New York, Coward McCann, 1977.
Lord of Ravensley. London, Heinemann, and New York, Coward McCann, 1978.
Heir to Kuragin. London, Heinemann, 1978; New York, Coward McCann, 1979.
The Spy Concerto (as Christina Merlin). London, Hale, and New York, St. Martin's Press, 1980.
The Wildcliffe Bird. London, Heinemann, 1981; New York, Coward McCann, 1983.
The Ravensley Touch. London, Heinemann, and New York, Coward McCann, 1982.
Sword of Mithras (as Christina Merlin). London, Hale, 1982.
Daughter of Marignac. London, Heinemann, 1983; New York, Putnam, 1984.
Castle of Doves. London, Heinemann, 1984; New York, Putnam, 1985.

Larksghyll. London, Heinemann, 1986.
The Craven Legacy. New York, Putnam, 1986.
The Raging Fire. London, Heinemann, 1987; New York, Putnam, 1988.
The Fire Still Burns. London, Heinemann, 1989.

Novels as Constance Fecher (series: Tudor trilogy)

Tudor trilogy:
    Queen's Delight. London, Hale, 1966; as *Queen's Favorite*, New York, Dell, 1974.
    Traitor's Son. London, Hale, 1967; New York, Dell, 1976.
    King's Legacy. London, Hale, 1967; New York, Dell, 1976.
Player Queen. London, Hale, 1968; as *The Lovely Wanton*, New York, Dell, 1977.
Lion of Trevarrock. London, Hale, 1969.
The Night of the Wolf. London, Hale, 1972; New York, Delacorte Press, 1974.
By the Light of the Moon. London, Hale, 1985.

OTHER PUBLICATIONS

Other (for children)

Venture for a Crown. New York, Farrar Straus, 1968.
Heir to Pendarrow. New York, Farrar Straus, 1969.
Bright Star: A Portrait of Ellen Terry. New York, Farrar Straus, 1970; London, Gollancz, 1971.
The Link Boys (as Constance Fecher). New York, Farrar Straus, 1971.
The Last Elizabethan: A Portrait of Sir Walter Raleigh. New York, Farrar Straus, 1972.
The Leopard Dagger (as Constance Fecher). New York, Farrar Straus, 1973.

*

Constance Heaven comments:

I came to writing late after some 25 years in the theatre with my husband and then alone after his early death. A lifelong interest in history gave me my first inspiration—a biographical novel about Sir Walter Ralegh which turned into a trilogy covering his son and grandson. From choosing real historical characters I turned to fictional heroes and heroines, and my first true romance was *The House of Kuragin* set in pre-revolutionary Russia. Quite small incidents often spark off a story: a holiday in the Highlands rich in family feuds, a fascination with the Camargue in southern France, an abiding interest in the Fen country—and before I know where I am I'm deep in research and inventing a plot to fit the scene. I cannot write to any formula. Plot and people have to come out of the circumstances and often develop in their own way, sometimes against my will. I am of a practical turn of mind so my characters tend to follow suit and I'm not given to the wilder flights of romance. My two recent modern tales (as Christina Merlin) are a relief and contrast to my usual work. Basically I think I write to please myself. It's what I enjoy reading and I hope that others will find the same interest.

*   *   *

The writing of Constance Heaven has strong links with the Brontës. For the most part it inhabits the same 19th century, and uncovers the same dark passions, violence simmering beneath Victorian respectability. Her heroes are formidable and proud, with a definite streak of ruthlessness. Her governess heroines are spirited, often artistic, their quiet natures masking their inner strength. To this world Heaven brings her own individual voice.

As Constance Fecher she wrote the Tudor trilogy—*Queen's Delight*, *Traitor's Son*, *King's Legacy*—where historical characters and events are given a fictional treatment. *Queen's Delight* follows the life of Sir Walter Ralegh from his youth to final execution in the reign of James I. The work is perfectly achieved, the understated style honed to essentials. The author presents the complex nature of Ralegh, his varying fortunes, the triumph and tragedy of his life, without glamour or false dramatics. *Queen's Delight* is a remarkable novel, its restrained skill typical of the trilogy as a whole. *Lion of Trevarrock* and *The Night of the Wolf* are more conventionally gothic stories, well-written though lacking the depth of the Tudor novels. The latter, with its Russian setting, indicates the future course of her work.

The House of Kuragin marks her debut as Constance Heaven, and describes her governess heroine's adventures with the Kuragin family in Tsarist Russia. Her love for the proud Andrei provides the central thread of the story. Quarrels over an inheritance, the sensual Natasha with her murky past, the steward who proves to be the old count's bastard son—all are skillfully interwoven, and the Russian setting beautifully evoked. *The Astrov Inheritance* is an effective sequel.

Castle of Eagles and *The Place of Stones* retain heroes and heroines of the gothic type, the settings respectively Vienna and Napoleonic France. Both are ably written, though they somehow lack the spark of the Kuragin novels. Better is *The Fires of Glenlochy*, set in the Scottish Highlands. The atmosphere is excellently caught, the plot exciting with secret passages and sudden discoveries, the brooding violence erupting in a climax of destruction.

The Queen and the Gypsy is outstanding. A return to Elizabethan history, it presents the tragic figure of Robert Earl of Leicester, torn between ambition and love, for his wife and his queen. Tracking through time, Heaven focuses on the sequence of events that leads to final tragedy. All the old skills are displayed, the characters brought brilliantly to life.

Later writings display considerable period research, with precise historical dates and authentic—predominantly 19th-century—backgrounds. There is, too, a continual and intriguing contrast between the down-to-earth and the exotic in Heaven's locations. The Fen country provides a landscape for *Lord of Ravensley* and its sequel *The Ravensley Touch*, while *The Wildcliffe Bird*, one of her most impressive novels, is imaginatively set in Victorian Staffordshire. *Larksghyll* has a Yorkshire setting, its impoverished heroine working as a teacher in a mill town of the 1840's. Like *Wildcliffe Bird*, *Larksghyll* and its successor *The Craven Legacy* compel belief, the characters and the world they inhabit drawn with strength and conviction. The same is true of the more obviously "romantic" stories like *Heir to Kuragin*, where the second Kuragin generation is followed to the Caucasus, and where the standard of authentic background and existing plot is maintained. More recently, *Castle of Doves* and *Daughter of Marignac* explore 19th-century Continental locations, the former set in Spain during the Carlist rebellion, the latter following its aristocratic heroine and her American lover through the Franco-Prussian war to the siege of Paris. With few exceptions these later novels succeed totally, the atmosphere capably evoked, the period detail captured without strain. The novels are often set against backgrounds of warfare and civil strife; the horrors are touched upon, but not unduly laboured. Through-

out, the constant theme recurs, of hero and heroine locked in a battle of the sexes, their conflict eventually resolved by love.

—Geoffrey Sadler

HEWLETT, Maurice (Henry). British. Born in Addington, Kent, 22 January 1861. Educated at the London International College; studied law, 1879–91. Married Hilda Beatrice Herbert in 1888. Lecturer in Medieval Art, South Kensington University, London; keeper of the Land Revenue Records and Enrollments for the Record Office, London, 1898–1900. *Died 16 June 1923.*

ROMANCE AND HISTORICAL PUBLICATIONS

Novels (series: John Maxwell Senhouse)

The Forest Lovers. London, Macmillan, and New York, Scribner, 1898.
The Life and Death of Richard Yea-and-Nay. London, Macmillan, 1900.
The Queen's Quair. London, Macmillan, 1904.
The Fool Errant. London, Heinemann, and New York, Macmillan, 1905.
The Stooping Lady. London, Macmillan, and New York, Dodd Mead, 1907.
The Spanish Jade. London, Cassell, and New York, Doubleday, 1908.
Halfway House: A Comedy of Degrees (Senhouse). London, Chapman and Hall, and New York, Scribner, 1908.
Letters to Sanchia. Privately printed, 1908.
Open Country: A Comedy with a Sting (Senhouse). London, Macmillan, and New York, Scribner, 1909.
Rest Harrow: A Comedy of Resolution (Senhouse). London, Macmillan, and New York, Scribner, 1910.
Brazenhead the Great. London, Smith Elder, and New York, Scribner, 1911.
The Song of Renny. London, Macmillan, and New York, Scribner, 1911.
Mrs. Lancelot: A Comedy of Assumptions. London, Macmillan, and New York, Century, 1912.
Bendish: A Study of Prodigality. London, Macmillan, and New York, Scribner, 1913.
The Little Iliad. London, Heinemann, and Philadelphia, Lippincott, 1915.
A Lovers' Tale. London, Ward Lock, 1915; New York, Scribner, 1916.
Frey and His Wife. London, Ward Lock, and New York, McBride, 1916.
Love and Lucy. London, Macmillan, and New York, Dodd Mead, 1916.
Thorgils of Treadholt. London, Ward Lock, 1917; as *Thorgils*, New York, Dodd Mead, 1917.
Gudrid the Fair. London, Constable, and New York, Dodd Mead, 1918.
The Outlaw. London, Constable, 1919; New York, Dodd Mead, 1920.
Flowers in the Grass: Wiltshire Plainsong. London, Constable, 1920.
The Light Heart. London, Chapman and Hall, and New York, Holt, 1920.
Mainwaring. New York, Dodd Mead, 1920; London, Collins, 1921.

Short Stories

Little Novels of Italy. London, Chapman and Hall, and New York, Macmillan, 1899.
New Canterbury Tales. London, Constable, and New York, Macmillan, 1901.
Fond Adventures. London, Macmillan, and New York, Harper, 1905.
The Ruinous Face. New York, Harper, 1909.
The Birth of Roland. Chicago, Seymour, 1911.

OTHER PUBLICATIONS

Verse

A Masque of Dead Florentines. London, Dent, 1895; Portland, Maine, Mosher, 1911.
Songs and Meditations. London, Constable, 1896.
Pan and the Young Shepherd. London, Lane, 1898; New York, Macmillan, 1906.
Artemision: Idylls and Songs. London, Mathews, and New York, Scribner, 1909.
The Agonists: A Trilogy of God and Man. London, Macmillan, and New York, Scribner, 1911.
Songs of Loss (published anonymously). Privately printed, 1911.
Helen Redeemed and Other Poems. London, Macmillan, and New York, Scribner, 1913.
Sing-Songs of the War. London, Poetry Bookshop, 1914.
The Wreath. Privately printed, 1914.
A Ballad of The Gloster and The Goeben. London, Poetry Bookshop, 1914.
Gai Saber: Tales and Songs. London, Mathews, and New York, Putnam, 1916.
The Song of the Plow. London, Heinemann, and New York, Macmillan, 1916.
The Loving History of Peridore and Paravail. London, Collins, 1917.
The Village Wife's Lament. London, Secker, and New York, Putnam, 1918.
Selected Poems. London, Benn, 1926.

Other

Earthwork Out of Tuscany. London, Dent, 1895; revised edition, 1899, 1901; New York, Putnam, 1899; revised edition, 1900.
The Road in Tuscany (travel). London, Macmillan, 2 vols., 1904.
Lore of Proserpine (essays and stories). London, Macmillan, and New York, Scribner, 1913.
In a Green Shade: A Country Commentary. London, Bell, 1920.
Wiltshire Essays. London, Oxford University Press, 1921.
Extemporary Essays. London, Oxford University Press, 1922.
Last Essays. London, Heinemann, and New York, Scribner, 1924.
The Letters of Maurice Hewlett: To Which Is Added a Diary in Greece, edited by Lawrence Binyon. London, Methuen, 1926.

Translator, *The Iliad: The First Twelve Stanzas.* London, Cresset Press, 1928.

*　　*　　*

Maurice Hewlett was a deservedly popular historical novelist who was scrupulous about the factual background to his books and who took pride in his precise use of evocative language. His ambition was to win recognition as a poet, and rather perversely he claimed to have been disappointed that the public kept on demanding prose romances from him. Certainly the diversity of his work is some indication of his unwillingness to continue ploughing the same furrow time and again.

The Forest Lovers is a remarkable achievement in the creation of atmosphere and tone. Hewlett drew on his deep knowledge and instinctive sympathy with Malory's *Le Morte Darthur* to devise a romance of his own. The story is basically simple, and Hewlett wrote in one of his letters that his aim was always to invent plots in which everything, however disparate the elements might seem as they occurred, would knit together into a seemingly inevitable unity. Prosper Le Gai rides out on his horse into a great forest which may, another of Hewlett's letters states, be best identified with the New Forest in Hampshire. The young man discovers a mysterious damsel in distress. He is kindly, she is smitten, but the two part, and it is only after many complications, which seem to be reflected in the long journeys through the shady ways of the forest, that the pair come together at the end. Menace is ever-present, made all the worse because it is connected with the church, which has spiritual and secular power and few hesitations about the way it uses it. Origins in particular are always doubtful and pose endless threats to the present and the future. Permeating all this, as in so much gothic fiction, is powerful sensuality, and Hewlett conveys a strong sense of the sexuality which is always just below the surface of this superficially chaste romance.

In *The Life and Death of Richard Yea-and-Nay* there are equally strong passions. But the scene changes: Hewlett offers here an account of the life of Richard Coeur de Lion which is set in Anjou and the Levant. Possibly smarting from the accusation that in that book he had twisted historical accuracy a little too much to make it serve his theme of the conflict between human passions and religious obligations, Hewlett took special care to ensure that the facts were accurate in his next novel, *The Queen's Quair.* The queen referred to is Mary, Queen of Scots, whose inner nature had in Hewlett's view never been properly understood before, and "quair" is a word meaning "book" (a sense which is preserved in the stationer's term "a quire of paper"). First appearing in serial form in the *Pall Mall*, *The Queen's Quair* was a great commercial success, but failed to gain Hewlett the critical appreciation he craved. He was similarly disappointed by the reception of *The Fool Errant*, which is set in 18th-century Italy.

Towards the end of his life Hewlett turned to the Vikings as a final source of inspiration. Once again he informed himself fully about stirring times, and *Gudrid the Fair*, for instance, focuses on the great adventure of the Viking discovery of the shores of North America. In these novels Hewlett seems short of details of everyday life to give substance to his characters and fails to offer much psychological insight into them. The style lacks the distinction of his earlier works, which, though perhaps somewhat dated and mannered, can still give a lot of pleasure to readers who are prepared to accept a fairly leisurely style of narration.

—Christopher Smith

HEYER, Georgette. Also wrote as Stella Martin. British. Born in Wimbledon, Surrey, 16 August 1902. Educated at seminary schools and Westminster College, London. Married George Ronald Rougier in 1925; one son. Lived in Tanganyika (now Tanzania), 1927–28, Yugoslavia, 1928–29, Sussex 1930–42, and London after 1942. *Died 5 July 1974.*

ROMANCE AND HISTORICAL PUBLICATIONS

Novels (series: Superintendent Hannasyde; Inspector Hemingway)

The Black Moth. London, Constable, and Boston, Houghton Mifflin, 1921.
The Great Roxhythe. London, Hutchinson, 1922; Boston, Small Maynard, 1923.
The Transformation of Philip Jettan (as Stella Martin). London, Mills and Boon, 1923; as *Powder and Patch* (as Georgette Heyer), London, Heinemann, 1930; New York, Dutton, 1968.
Instead of the Thorn. London, Hutchinson, 1923; Boston, Small Maynard, 1924.
Simon the Coldheart. London, Heinemann, and Boston, Small Maynard, 1925.
These Old Shades. London, Heinemann, and Boston, Small Maynard, 1926.
Helen. London and New York, Longman, 1928.
The Masqueraders. London, Heinemann, 1928; New York, Longman, 1929.
Beauvallet. London, Heinemann, 1929; New York, Longman, 1930.
Pastel. London and New York, Longman, 1929.
Barren Corn. London and New York, Longman, 1930.
The Conqueror. London, Heinemann, 1931; New York, Dutton, 1966.
Footsteps in the Dark. London, Longman, 1932.
Why Shoot a Butler? London, Longman, 1933; New York, Doubleday, 1936.
The Unfinished Clue. London, Longman, 1934; New York, Doubleday, 1937.
The Convenient Marriage. London, Heinemann, 1934; New York, Dutton, 1966.
Devil's Cub. London, Heinemann, 1934; New York, Dutton, 1966.
Regency Buck. London, Heinemann, 1935; New York, Dutton, 1966.
Death in the Stocks (Hannasyde). London, Longman, 1935; as *Merely Murder*, New York, Doubleday, 1935.
Behold, Here's Poison! (Hannasyde). London, Hodder and Stoughton, and New York, Doubleday, 1936.
The Talisman Ring. London, Heinemann, 1936; New York, Doubleday, 1937.
An Infamous Army. London, Heinemann, 1937; New York, Doubleday, 1938.
They Found Him Dead (Hannasyde). London, Hodder and Stoughton, and New York, Doubleday, 1937.
A Blunt Instrument (Hannasyde). London, Hodder and Stoughton, and New York, Doubleday, 1938.
Royal Escape. London, Heinemann, 1938; New York, Doubleday, 1939.
No Wind of Blame (Hemingway). London, Hodder and Stoughton, and New York, Doubleday, 1939.
The Spanish Bride. London, Heinemann, and New York, Doubleday, 1940.
The Corinthian. London, Heinemann, 1940; as *Beau Wyndham*, New York, Doubleday, 1941.

Faro's Daughter. London, Heinemann, 1941; New York, Doubleday, 1942.
Envious Casca (Hemingway). London, Hodder and Stoughton, and New York, Doubleday, 1941.
Penhallow. London, Heinemann, 1942; New York, Doubleday, 1943.
Friday's Child. London, Heinemann, 1944; New York, Putnam, 1946.
The Reluctant Widow. London, Heinemann, and New York, Putnam, 1946.
The Foundling. London, Heinemann, and New York, Putnam, 1948.
Arabella. London, Heinemann, and New York, Putnam, 1949.
The Grand Sophy. London, Heinemann, and New York, Putnam, 1950.
The Quiet Gentleman. London, Heinemann, 1951; New York, Putnam, 1952.
Duplicate Death (Hemingway). London, Heinemann, 1951; New York, Dutton, 1969.
Detection Unlimited (Hemingway). London, Heinemann, 1953; New York, Dutton, 1969.
Cotillion. London, Heinemann, and New York, Putnam, 1953.
The Toll-Gate. London, Heinemann, and New York, Putnam, 1954.
Bath Tangle. London, Heinemann, and New York, Putnam, 1955.
Sprig Muslin. London, Heinemann, and New York, Putnam, 1956.
April Lady. London, Heinemann, and New York, Putnam, 1957.
Sylvester; or, The Wicked Uncle. London, Heinemann, and New York, Putnam, 1957.
Venetia. London, Heinemann, 1958; New York, Putnam, 1959.
The Unknown Ajax. London, Heinemann, 1959; New York, Putnam, 1960.
A Civil Contract. London, Heinemann, 1961; New York, Putnam, 1962.
The Nonesuch. London, Heinemann, 1962; New York, Dutton, 1963.
False Colours. London, Bodley Head, 1963; New York, Dutton, 1964.
Frederica. London, Bodley Head, and New York, Dutton, 1965.
Black Sheep. London, Bodley Head, 1966; New York, Dutton, 1967.
Cousin Kate. London, Bodley Head, 1968; New York, Dutton, 1969.
Charity Girl. London, Bodley Head, and New York, Dutton, 1970.
Lady of Quality. London, Bodley Head, and New York, Dutton, 1972.
My Lord John. London, Bodley Head, and New York, Dutton, 1975.

Short Stories

Pistols for Two and Other Stories. London, Heinemann, 1960; New York, Dutton, 1964.

*

Critical Study: *The Private World of Georgette Heyer* by Jane Aiken Hodge, London, Bodley Head, 1984.

*   *   *

Everyone knows—and almost no one enjoys—the kind of historic fiction that has aptly been described as "writing forsoothly," in which modern sentiments are thinly concealed in a contrived form of contemporary speech peppered with "thee" and "thou." That, plus a swirling cape and jack-boots, or, for a female, a fan and red-heeled shoes, is apparently all the author feels is required to establish "period." On the other end of the scale of historic fiction, we find the works of Georgette Heyer. Surely, if by magic she had been transported into the midst of faddish, slangy Regency society, she would have been perfectly in her element, and would never have missed a word or a phrase. Few writers in any field have ever so thoroughly and convincingly immersed themselves in the trivia of their chosen era, until it became as natural to her writing as daily speech. She captured in meticulous detail the ephemeral, so-soon-forgotten catch-phrases and slang that above all give to any time, place, or society its special, inimitable flavour.

Heyer's people are butterflies—the bubbles on the champagne of a favoured way of life lived at the expense of the forgotten ones below: but her books are not tracts, and the dark side of Regency life seldom obtrudes. Her gilded ones toil not, neither do they spin, and they often neglect to pay the bills of those who do the toiling and spinning for them—but never their gambling debts! Their peculiar convictions on the subject of honour are an odd aspect of the times which Heyer fully understands (which is not to say that she approves).

Her menfolk are by modern standards incredibly concerned with their clothing. They spend untold hours with their tailor or bootmaker; hours tying a cravat *just so*. They inflict upon themselves collars so high and stiff that the wearer cannot turn his head, and have their leathers cleaned with champagne in emulation of Mr. Brummell. When at last they are fit to be seen by an admiring public, they wander off for a bare-knuckled boxing match with a professional pug at Jackson's Saloon, risk their own and all bystanders' lives by driving precarious high-perch phaetons "to an inch," with scarcely controllable teams of powerful horses on bad, ill-lit roads, and become involved in duels at the drop of a hat or an eyelash.

Her women lead lives of decorative uselessness, fussing endlessly with the matching of ribbons and reticules, finding the latest novel in the lending library, sending and receiving invitations to this and that, or—horrors!—*not* receiving them, and, always and above all, marrying to advantage. There was, after all, nothing else for a lady to do, except in desperation to accept a post as governess or companion, a fate scarcely better than death.

These, roughly, were the ground rules of a peculiarly individualistic form of society, at once super-refined and heartlessly brutal, and, above all, decorative. It is all so distant now that only a few charming fragments like the Brighton Pavilion remain—except in the pages of the Regency romance. Others have tried, but no one else has succeeded in capturing that mayfly society to the life as Heyer did. She essayed other periods and settings with mixed success—Tudor, late Mediaeval, even the modern mystery in its heyday of the 1920's—but only in the brief golden time of the disreputable Prinny, the Prince Regent, does she excel all others.

Her plots are slight and their outcome predictable. Two nice people, usually well connected and "possessed of a competency" (although the young lady may have fallen upon difficult times through no fault of her own, victimized perhaps by a profligate brother or wastrel father) meet, fall in love, have difficulties either before or directly after marriage, sort it all out, and the story ends with a certain gleam in the hero's eye, and the heroine murmuring wistfully about the joys of "setting up her nurseries." If plot were all, the popularity of Heyer's work

would be totally inexplicable, but her countless fans could explain that plot has very little to do with it. It is the bubbling good humour, the endlessly complicated social situations, the inspired silliness of the lovely creatures who perform these fantastic courtship rituals, that brings them back time and again for another of her stories.

Her dialogue is extraordinary. Page after page will go by, and the action, such as it is, is not one whit advanced; perhaps one numbskull is trying to enlighten another on a point of philosophy; a pretty young wife is spinning a complicated story to conceal a harmless peccadillo from her apparently stern but generally indulgent husband; a dandy pretends to be a tollgate keeper and exchanges insults with a passing carter; and one reads on and on in fascination. The badinage occupying these pages—and they are her very best pages—might seem to the novice to call for the use of a dictionary of Regency slang, and more than a little background reading in that period: but never mind. As the aficionados say patronizingly "You'll soon catch on," and it's true. You find yourself chuckling as one character "makes a perfect cake of himself" or another asks if "you take me for a flat?" You quite see how important it is for a young lady to have vouchers for Almack's, and that it would never do for her to be seen on St. James's St., under the eyes of the gentlemen's clubs.

Heyer's work is intended to amuse rather than to enlighten, and if there ever was a writer who could brighten a grey day, it was she. She has been criticized for slight historical inaccuracies, for using too much difficult period slang, for slightness and silliness. There may be some truth in the criticism—but no other writer has yet been able to wear her fallen mantle, though many have tried. As Noël Coward once remarked of his own work, he had "a talent to amuse"; Heyer had that precious talent, and, like the good servant in the parable, she never buried it. She left an astonishing number of gay, happy books, and her grateful readers are indeed amused.

—Joan McGrath

HICHENS, Robert (Smythe). British. Born in Speldhurst, Kent, 14 November 1864. Educated at Clifton College, Bristol; Royal College of Music, London; London School of Journalism. Music critic, *The World*. Fellow, Royal Society of Literature, 1926. *Died 20 July 1950.*

ROMANCE AND HISTORICAL PUBLICATIONS

Novels

The Green Carnation (published anonymously). London, Heinemann, and New York, Appleton, 1894.
After Tomorrow, and The New Love. New York, Merriam, 1895.
An Imaginative Man. London, Heinemann, and New York, Appleton, 1895.
Flames: A London Phantasy. London, Heinemann, and Chicago, Stone, 1897.
The Londoners: An Absurdity. London, Heinemann, and Chicago, Stone, 1898.
The Daughters of Babylon, with Wilson Barrett. London, Macqueen, and Philadelphia, Lippincott, 1899.

The Slave. London, Heinemann, and Chicago, Stone, 1899.

The Prophet of Berkeley Square: A Tragic Extravaganza. London, Methuen, and New York, Dodd Mead, 1901.

Felix: Three Years of a Life. London, Methuen, 1902; New York, Stokes, 1903.

The Garden of Allah. London, Methuen, and New York, Stokes, 1904.

The Women with the Fan. London, Methuen, and New York, Stokes, 1904.

The Call of the Blood. London, Methuen, and New York, Harper, 1906.

Barbary Sheep. New York, Harper, 1907; London, Methuen, 1909.

A Spirit in Prison. London, Hutchinson, and New York, Harper, 1908.

Bella Donna. London, Heinemann, and Philadelphia, Lippincott, 1909.

The Knock on the Door. London, Heinemann, and Philadelphia, Lippincott, 1909.

The Dweller on the Threshold. London, Methuen, and New York, Century, 1911.

The Fruitful Vine. London, Unwin, and New York, Stokes, 1911.

The Way of Ambition. London, Methuen, and New York, Stokes, 1913.

In the Wilderness. London, Methuen, and New York, Stokes, 1917.

Mrs. Marden. London, Cassell, and New York, Doran, 1919.

The Spirit of the Time. London, Cassell, and New York, Doubleday, 1921.

December Love. London, Cassell, and New York, Doran, 1922.

After the Verdict. London, Methuen, and New York, Doran, 1924.

The God Within Him. London, Methuen, 1926; as *The Unearthly*, New York, Cosmopolitan, 1926.

The Bacchante and the Nun. London, Methuen, 1927; as *The Bacchante*, New York, Cosmopolitan, 1927.

Dr. Artz. London, Hutchinson, and New York, Cosmopolitan, 1929.

On the Screen. London, Cassell, 1929.

The Bracelet. London, Cassell, and New York, Cosmopolitan, 1930.

The First Lady Brendon. London, Cassell, and New York, Doubleday, 1931.

Mortimer Brice: A Bit of His Life. London, Cassell, and New York, Doubleday, 1932.

The Paradine Case. London, Benn, and New York, Doubleday, 1933.

The Power to Kill. London, Benn, and New York, Doubleday, 1934.

"Susie's" Career. London, Cassell, 1935; as *The Pyramid*, New York, Doubleday, 1936.

The Sixth of October. London, Cassell, and New York, Doubleday, 1936.

Daniel Airlie. London, Cassell, and New York, Doubleday, 1937.

The Journey Up. London, Cassell, and New York, Doubleday, 1938.

Secret Information. London, Hurst and Blackett, and New York, Doubleday, 1938.

That Which Is Hidden. London, Cassell, 1939; New York, Doubleday, 1940.

The Million: An Entertainment. London, Cassell, 1940; New York, Doubleday, 1941.

Married or Unmarried. London, Cassell, 1941.

A New Way of Life. London, Hutchinson, and New York, Doubleday, 1942.

Veils. London, Hutchinson, 1943; as *Young Mrs. Brand*, Philadelphia, Macrae Smith, 1944.

Harps in the Wind. London, Cassell, 1945; as *The Woman in the House*, Philadelphia, Macrae Smith, 1945.

Incognito. London, Hutchinson, 1947; New York, McBride, 1948.

Too Much Love of Living. Philadelphia, Macrae Smith, 1947; London, Cassell, 1948.

Beneath the Magic. London, Hutchinson, 1950; as *Strange Lady*, Philadelphia, Macrae Smith, 1950.

The Mask. London, Hutchinson, 1951.

Nightbound. London, Cassell, 1951.

Short Stories

The Folly of Eustace and Other Stories. London, Heinemann, and New York, Appleton, 1896.

Byeways. London, Methuen, and New York, Dodd Mead, 1897.

Tongues of Conscience. London, Methuen, and New York, Stokes, 1900.

The Black Spaniel and Other Stories. London, Methuen, and New York, Stokes, 1905.

The Hindu. New York, Ainslee, 1917.

Snake-Bite and Other Stories. London, Cassell, and New York, Doran, 1919.

The Last Time and Other Stories. London, Hutchinson, 1923; New York, Doran, 1924.

The Streets and Other Stories. London, Hutchinson, 1928.

The Gate of Paradise and Other Stories. London, Cassell, 1930.

My Desert Friend and Other Stories. London, Cassell, 1931.

The Gardenia and Other Stories. London, Hutchinson, 1934.

The Afterglow and Other Stories. London, Cassell, 1935.

The Man in the Mirror and Other Stories. London, Cassell, 1950.

OTHER PUBLICATIONS

Plays

The Medicine Man, with H. D. Traill (produced London, 1898). New York, De Vinne Press, 1898.

Becky Sharp, with Cosmo Gordon-Lennox, adaptation of the novel *Vanity Fair* by Thackeray (produced London, 1901; as *Vanity Fair*, produced New York, 1911).

The Real Woman (produced London, 1909).

The Garden of Allah, with Mary Anderson, adaptation of his own novel (produced New York, 1911; London, 1920).

The Law of the Sands (produced London, 1916).

Black Magic (produced London, 1917).

Press the Button! (produced London, 1918).

The Voice from the Minaret (produced London 1919; New York, 1922).

Screenplay: *Bella Donna*, with Ouida Bergère, 1923.

Other

The Coastguard's Secret (for children). London, Sonnenschein, 1886.

Homes of the Passing Show, with others. London, Savoy Press, 1900.

Egypt and Its Monuments. London, Hodder and Stoughton, and New York, Century, 1908; as *The Spell of Egypt*, Hodder and Stoughton, 1910; Century, 1911.
The Holy Land. London, Hodder and Stoughton, and New York, Century, 1910.
The Near East. London, Hodder and Stoughton, and New York, Century, 1913.
Yesterday: The Autobiography of Robert Hichens. London, Cassell, 1947.

*   *   *

Although Robert Hichens had written earlier material, he first achieved fame with *The Green Carnation*, a very amusing take-off on Oscar Wilde and the Aesthetic Movement, filled with bon mots, strokes of wit, and comic touches. Its intrinsic merit can be seen from the fact that it retained its popularity after the Wilde scandals and is still in print.

A more commercial phenomenon was *The Garden of Allah*, Hichens's best-known work. It sold close to a million copies, was staged, and was filmed at least three times. Although superficially it is a sentimental romance, in substructure (like much of Hichens's other work) it is antisexual, anticipating the earlier versions of *Lady Chatterley's Lover* in its concept of the loathly bridegroom. It is the story of Domini Enfilden, a lonely masculine British spinster who comes to a minor tourist town in North Africa and forces herself upon the only other tourist, the gauche Androvsky. Under the influence of the desert (the garden of Allah) they experience passion and marry. But Androvsky is a runaway monk from a Trappist monastery. He and Domini agree that he must return to his vows, and Domini, after bearing his child, settles in the area without him. The narrative, however, is less significant than the background. Hichens went all out to create North African local color, with the result that for the close reader a remarkable picture emerges of landscape, Arab personality types, and Franco-Arabic social life, all much more interesting than the narrative.

Hichens's next two important works also deal with impermissible love, in this case, adultery. In *The Call of the Blood*, set in Sicily, when Maurice Delarey becomes irritated because his wife has returned to England for a visit, he has an affair with Maddalena, a peasant girl. He is murdered by the girl's father, but his wife never learns what had happened. A sequel, *A Spirit in Prison*, set 16 years later, is concerned with Ruffino, the by-blow of Delarey's affair. In both novels Italian local color is applied almost obsessively.

Most of Hichens's other work is romantic fiction of this sort, usually based on a theme of sex gone astray. His stories usually deal with a formalized upper society group, and his treatment of potentially sensational matter always remained restrained and polite. While he outgrew the tendency to fill pages with painterly detail of exotic landscapes and authorial reflections, he substituted for these highly detailed descriptions of events, and his fiction was often overdeveloped and word-choked.

In the 1920's and 1930's Hichens applied himself occasionally to crime situations. Although such fiction was undoubtedly intended to meet the market demand for detective stories, there is little mystery or detection in such stories, but much about the psychological surroundings of crime. *After the Verdict* describes a society man who has been tried and found innocent of murdering his mistress. But, like Androvsky in *The Garden of Allah*, he cannot tolerate his role in marriage and confesses to his wife that he had been an accomplice to suicide. The most important of these crime-romances is *The Paradine Case*, based on a triangle of psychologies: vicious intellect (Justice Horfield), foolish sentiment and emotion (Keane, a barrister), and selfish, ruthless sensuality (Mrs. Paradine). Keane, who is defending Mrs. Paradine in her trial for the murder of her husband, has the misfortune to fall in love with her. His case and his ego both collapse when his thoughtlessness and passion cause him to take the wrong line during the trial. The characters in this novel are better drawn than is usual with Hichens, but it must be admitted that a reader who has seen the motion picture made from it may see Horfield as enlarged by Charles Laughton.

Hichens also wrote a fair amount of supernatural and occult fiction. The most important works are: "The Return of the Soul" (*The Folly of Eustace*), dealing with the reincarnation of an abused cat as a vengeful woman; *Flames*, a very long novel about black magic, personality interchange, and redemption by love; *Tongues of Conscience*, short stories in which obsessions are portrayed in terms of fantasy; and *The Dweller on the Threshold*, a novel concerned with psychic research and spiritual vampirism of a sort.

Since little is known about Hichens as a man, it is not possible to say why he failed to realize his early promise. His technical virtuosity, his facility, his remarkable eye for picturesque detail, his originality of thought should have produced better work than overblown society romances. Only a little of the large corpus of his work is still vital: *The Green Carnation*, for its exuberant wit and Roman à clef elements; *The Garden of Allah*, for its rich evocation of Africa; and perhaps the motion picture version of *The Paradine Case*.

—E. F. Bleiler

HILL, Grace Livingston. Also wrote as Marcia Macdonald; some of her works were signed Grace Livingston and Grace Livingston Hill-Lutz. American. Born in Wellsville, New York, 16 April 1865. Educated privately; Cincinnati Art School; Elmira College, New York. Married 1) Thomas Franklin Hill in 1892 (died 1899), two daughters; 2) Flavius J. Lutz. Syndicated columnist for religious newspapers. *Died 23 February 1947.*

ROMANCE AND HISTORICAL PUBLICATIONS

Novels

A Chautauqua Idyl. Boston, Lothrop, 1887.
The Parkerstown Delegate. Boston, Lothrop, 1892.
In the Way. Philadelphia, American Baptist Publication Society, 1897.
Lone Point: A Summer Outing. Philadelphia, American Baptist Publication Society, and London, Baptist Tract and Book Society, 1898.
A Daily Rate. Philadelphia, Union Press, 1900.
An Unwilling Guest. Philadelphia, American Baptist Publication Society, 1902.
The Angel of His Presence. Philadelphia, American Baptist Publication Society, 1902.
The Story of a Whim. Boston, Golden Rule, 1903.
According to the Pattern. Philadelphia, Griffith and Rowland, 1903.
Because of Stephen. Boston, Golden Rule, 1904.
The Girl from Montana. Boston, Golden Rule, 1908.
Marcia Schuyler. Philadelphia, Lippincott, 1908; as *Marcia*, London, Hodder and Stoughton, 1921.
Phoebe Dean. Philadelphia, Lippincott, 1909; London, Hodder and Stoughton, 1921.

Aunt Crete's Emancipation. Boston, Golden Rule, 1911.
Dawn of the Morning. Philadelphia, Lippincott, 1911.
The Mystery of Mary. Philadelphia, Lippincott, 1912.
Lo, Michael! Philadelphia, Lippincott, 1913; London, Hodder and Stoughton, 1923.
The Man of the Desert. New York, Revell, 1914.
The Best Man. Philadelphia, Lippincott, 1914; London, Newnes, 1919.
Miranda. Philadelphia, Lippincott, 1914; London, Hodder and Stoughton, 1922.
The Obsession of Victoria Gracen. Philadelphia, Lippincott, 1915.
The Finding of Jasper Holt. Philadelphia, Lippincott, 1916.
A Voice in the Wilderness. New York, Harper, 1916.
The Witness. New York, Harper, 1917.
The Enchanted Barn. Philadelphia, Lippincott, 1918.
The Search. Philadelphia, Lippincott, 1919.
The Red Signal. Philadelphia, Lippincott, 1919.
Cloudy Jewel. Philadelphia, Lippincott, 1920.
Exit Betty. Philadelphia, Lippincott, 1920.
The Tryst. Philadelphia, Lippincott, 1921.
The City of Fire. Philadelphia, Lippincott, 1922.
Tomorrow about This Time. Philadelphia, Lippincott, 1923.
The Big Blue Soldier. Philadelphia, Lippincott, 1923.
Re-Creations. Philadelphia, Lippincott, 1924.
Ariel Custer. Philadelphia, Lippincott, 1925.
Not under the Law. Philadelphia, Lippincott, 1925.
A New Name. Philadelphia, Lippincott, 1926.
Coming Through the Rye. Philadelphia, Lippincott, 1926.
Job's Niece. Philadelphia, Lippincott, 1927.
The White Flower. Philadelphia, Lippincott, 1927.
Crimson Roses. Philadelphia, Lippincott, 1928.
Blue Ruin. Philadelphia, Lippincott, 1928.
Duskin. Philadelphia, Lippincott, 1929.
The Prodigal Girl. Philadelphia, Lippincott, 1929.
Ladybird. Philadelphia, Lippincott, 1930.
The Gold Shoe. Philadelphia, Lippincott, 1930.
Silver Wings. Philadelphia, Lippincott, 1931.
The Chance of a Lifetime. Philadelphia, Lippincott, 1931.
Kerry. Philadelphia, Lippincott, 1931.
The Challengers. Philadelphia, Lippincott, 1932.
Happiness Hill. Philadelphia, Lippincott, 1932.
The Story of the Lost Star. Philadelphia, Lippincott, 1932.
The Patch of Blue. Philadelphia, Lippincott, 1932.
The Ransom. Philadelphia, Lippincott, 1933.
Matched Pearls. Philadelphia, Lippincott, 1933.
The Beloved Stranger. Philadelphia, Lippincott, 1933.
Rainbow Cottage. Philadelphia, Lippincott, 1934.
Amorelle. Philadelphia, Lippincott, 1934.
The Christmas Bride. Philadelphia, Lippincott, 1934.
Beauty for Ashes. Philadelphia, Lippincott, 1935; London, Lane, 1936.
White Orchids. Philadelphia, Lippincott, 1935.
The Strange Proposal. Philadelphia, Lippincott, 1935.
April Gold. Philadelphia, Lippincott, 1936.
Mystery Flowers. Philadelphia, Lippincott, 1936.
The Substitute Guest. Philadelphia, Lippincott, 1936.
Sunrise. Philadelphia, Lippincott, 1937.
Daphne Deane. Philadelphia, Lippincott, 1937.
Brentwood. Philadelphia, Lippincott, 1937.
Marigold. Philadelphia, Lippincott, 1938.
The Minister's Son. Philadelphia, Lippincott, 1938.
The Divided Battle. Philadelphia, Lippincott, 1938.
Dwelling. Philadelphia, Lippincott, 1938.
The Lost Message. Philadelphia, Lippincott, 1938.
Maris. Philadelphia, Lippincott, 1938.

Homing. Philadelphia, Lippincott, 1938.
The Seventh Hour. Philadelphia, Lippincott, 1939.
Patricia. Philadelphia, Lippincott, 1939.
Stranger Within the Gates. Philadelphia, Lippincott, 1939.
Head of the House. Philadelphia, Lippincott, 1940.
Rose Galbraith. Philadelphia, Lippincott, 1940.
Partners. Philadelphia, Lippincott, 1940.
By Way of the Silverthorns. Philadelphia, Lippincott, 1941.
In Tune with Wedding Bells. Philadelphia, Lippincott, 1941.
Astra. Philadelphia, Lippincott, 1941.
The Girl of the Woods. Philadelphia, Lippincott, 1942.
Crimson Mountain. Philadelphia, Lippincott, 1942.
The Street of the City. Philadelphia, Lippincott, 1942.
Spice Box. Philadelphia, Lippincott, 1943.
The Sound of the Trumpet. Philadelphia, Lippincott, 1943.
Through These Fires. Philadelphia, Lippincott, 1943.
More Than Conqueror. Philadelphia, Lippincott, 1944.
Time of the Singing of Birds. Philadelphia, Lippincott, 1944.
All Through the Night. Philadelphia, Lippincott, 1945.
A Girl to Come Home To. Philadelphia, Lippincott, 1945.
Bright Arrows. Philadelphia, Lippincott, 1946.
Where Two Ways Met. Philadelphia, Lippincott, 1947.
Mary Arden, completed by Ruth Livingston Hill. Philadelphia, Lippincott, 1948.

Novels as Marcia Macdonald

The Honor Girl. Philadelphia, Lippincott, 1927.
Found Treasure. Philadelphia, Lippincott, 1928.
Out of the Storm. Philadelphia, Lippincott, 1929.
The White Lady. Philadelphia, Lippincott, 1930.

Short Stories

Katharine's Yesterday and Other Christian Endeavor Stories. Boston, Lothrop, 1895.
Beggarman. Philadelphia, Lippincott, 1932.
Her Wedding Garment. Philadelphia, Lippincott, 1932.
The House Across the Hedge. Philadelphia, Lippincott, 1932.
Miss Lavinia's Call and Other Stories. Philadelphia, Lippincott, 1949.
The Short Stories of Grace Livingston Hill, edited by J. E. Clauss. New York, American Reprint Company, 1976.

OTHER PUBLICATIONS

Plays

A Colonial Girl, with Abbey Sage Richardson (produced New York, 1898).
The Best Birthday: A Christmas Entertainment for Children. Philadelphia, Lippincott, 1938.

Other

Christian Endeavor Hour, with R. G. F. Hill. New York, Revell, 2 vols., 1895–96.
The War Romance of the Salvation Army, with Evangeline Booth. Philadelphia, Lippincott, 1919.

Editor, *Memories of Yesterdays*, by Isabella Alden. Philadelphia, Lippincott, 1931.

*

Critical Study: *Grace Livingston Hill* by Robert Munce, Wheaton, Illinois, Tyndale House, 1986.

* * *

"The truth is I never did consciously prepare for my literary career, and furthermore, I have no method at all. Coming from a family of authors, it never came into my mind that preparation was necessary." Grace Livingston Hill remained true to that statement throughout her fecund literary career, preparing little, if any, for the writing of her novels. Although she was surrounded by strong religious background and atmosphere, one finds in her work a myriad of religious contradictions which readily detract from the plot. Hill attempts to simplify complex issues and events by thumbing through the Bible, always with a banal love affair looming around the edges of her evangelical message. This evangelicalism permeates, no, suffocates the reader. Although humility is supposedly the focal point, Hill never fails to allow her characters (whose awareness of the world is characterized by lamentable ignorance) ultimately to luxuriate in affluence; money is the reward for being humble. With frequently prolonged Biblical quotes, expostulations, and interpretations, the pace stagnates.

Hill's works contain no gothic attributes and only a hint at romance. A variant on the typical theme is found in *Head of the House*: A college-age girl (Hill refers to the heroines as "girl" and the heroes as "men") valiantly escapes with her six brothers and sisters and hides away for three months to avoid being separated after the death of their parents. This novel is the exception. Other works such as *Happiness Hill* and *Rainbow Cottage* are so sugary, the characters so far removed from even homespun decency, the plot so trite, that the writing is more of an endurance test for the reader; one is almost forced to laugh at the naivety of pitting the "bad, bad guy" against the purity squad. In *Happiness Hill* the characters literally fall all over each other trying to outdo the other in meekness. In *Rainbow Cottage* a slap administered by the heroine is enough to provoke a suicide. *All Through the Night* again presents the contradictions of Christianity, allowing the heroine to espouse the virtues of kindness, tolerance, and gentility while the hero, also a "Christian," is "responsible for definitely wiping out as many of the enemy as possible . . . , setting the world free for peace and quietness." The gratuitous insults and vituperation that the heroine allows from her parsimonious relative exemplifies her "if-I-were-hanging-by-my-fingers-from-a-cliff, I'd-call-it-climbing-a-mountain" attitude, all adding up to obvious implausibility. The heroine is reduced to a prig.

In addition many references throughout her works are made to the unflappable and supported WASP dominance. There are careless lines of racial slurs and indictments of white superiority in this Christian atmosphere.

Hill is out of date and out of touch; rather than edifying, her "afflation" forces the reader to succumb to intolerable tedium. She should be classified under religious writers and poor ones, at that, failing piteously as a gothic romance novelist.

—W. M. von Zharen

HILL, Pamela. Also writes as Sharon Fiske. British. Born in Nairobi, Kenya, 26 November 1920. Educated at Hutchesons' Grammar School, Glasgow; Glasgow School of Art, D.A. 1943; Glasgow University. Has worked as a pottery and biology teacher, and as a mink farmer. Address: 89-A Winchester Street, London SW1V 4NU, England.

ROMANCE AND HISTORICAL PUBLICATIONS

Novels

Flaming Janet: A Lady of Galloway. London, Chatto and Windus, 1954; as *The King's Vixen*, New York, Putnam, 1954.
Shadow of Palaces: The Story of Françoise d'Aubigné, Marquise de Maintenon. London, Chatto and Windus, 1955; as *The Crown and the Shadow*, New York, Putnam, 1955.
Marjorie of Scotland. London, Chatto and Windus, and New York, Putnam, 1956.
Here Lies Margot. London, Chatto and Windus, 1957; New York, Putnam, 1958.
Maddalena. London, Cassell, 1963.
Forget Not Ariadne. London, Cassell, 1965; South Brunswick, New Jersey, A. S. Barnes, 1967.
Julia. London, Cassell, 1967.
The Devil of Aske. London, Hodder and Stoughton, 1972; New York, St. Martin's Press, 1973.
The Malvie Inheritance. London, Hodder and Stoughton, 1973; New York, St. Martin's Press, 1974.
The Incumbent. London, Hodder and Stoughton, 1974; as *The Heatherton Heritage*, New York, St. Martin's Press, 1976.
Whitton's Folly. London, Hodder and Stoughton, and New York, St. Martin's Press, 1975.
Norah Stroyan. London, Hodder and Stoughton, 1976; as *Norah*, New York, St. Martin's Press, 1976.
The Green Salamander. London, Hodder and Stoughton, and New York, St. Martin's Press, 1977.
Tsar's Woman. London, Hale, 1977; New York, St. Martin's Press, 1985.
Strangers' Forest. London, Hale, and New York, St. Martin's Press, 1978.
Daneclere. London, Hale, 1978; New York, St. Martin's Press, 1979.
Homage to a Rose. London, Hale, 1979.
Daughter of Midnight. London, Hale, 1979.
Fire Opal. London, Hale, and New York, St. Martin's Press, 1980.
A Place of Ravens. London, Hale, 1980; New York, St. Martin's Press, 1981.
Summer Cypress (as Sharon Fiske). London, Hale, 1981.
Knock at a Star. London, Hale, 1981.
House of Cray. London, Hale, and New York, St. Martin's Press, 1982.
The Fairest of All. London, Hale, 1982.
Duchess Caine. London, Hale, 1983.
Bride of Ae. London, Hale, and New York, St. Martin's Press, 1983.
The Copper-Haired Marshal. London, Hale, 1983.
Still Blooms the Rose. London, Hale, 1984.
Children of Lucifer. London, Hale, 1984.
The Governess. London, Hale, 1985.
Sable for the Count. London, Hale, 1985.
My Lady Glamis. London, Hale, 1985; New York, St. Martin's Press, 1987.
Venables. London, Hale, 1986.
The Sisters. London, Hale, 1986; Boston, Hall, 1988.
Digby. London, Hale, 1987.
Fenfallow. London, Hale, 1987.

The Sutburys. London, Hale, and New York, St. Martin's Press, 1988.
Jeannie Urquhart. London, Hale, 1988.
The Woman in the Cloak. London, Hale, 1988.
Artemia. London, Hale, 1989.
Trevithick. London, Hale, 1989.

*   *   *

Pamela Hill says that she got the idea for her first story—"The One Night," written in 1951—on a bus travelling between Glasgow and Edinburgh. Her imagination—and her pen—have been in the fast lane ever since, speeding through more than 40 historical romance/gothic novels since then.

Hill endows the heroines of her romances with equal stamina. In fact, many of them are practically Amazonian—true daughters of Queen Boadicea, the 1st-century British ruler who led the revolt against the Romans—in their courage, strength, and physical abilities (in Hill's world, the *heroes* play the supportive roles): *Flaming Janet: A Lady of Galloway* (U.S. title *The King's Vixen*); Françoise d'Aubigné, Marquis of Maintenon (in *Shadow of Palaces*; U.S. title *The Crown and the Shadow*); *Marjorie of Scotland*; the ruthless and iron-willed Madame of Aske (*The Devil of Aske*); Livia (*The Malvie Inheritance*), who survives a house of correction to become a guiding force at the Doon estate; the headstrong Primrose Tebb, who at the age of 12 marries Andrew Farquhar (*Strangers' Forest*); the courageous and ambitious Margaret Douglas, mother of Lord Darnley, who in turn was to become the husband of Mary, Queen of Scots in *The Green Salamander*; Fiona/Fiametta in *Fire Opal*, whose extraordinarily powerful swimming ability saves her from the Turks and helps the Knights of Malta in their defense of Christianity; Marfa Skavronsky, the orphaned Russian peasant girl who escapes from poverty by marrying a soldier, goes on to marry the Tsar (and indeed shaves her head, dons a helmet, and is at his side on the front lines of battle), and upon Peter's death becomes Catherine I, empress of the Russian people ("Marfa Skavronskaya. . . there is nothing you cannot do if you set your mind to it" she was told as a girl); Sara Ryder (*Bride of Ae*), who, in order to escape the dreary milliner's shop where she is apprenticed makes a marriage of convenience with the ill-tempered Francis Atherstone, squire of Ae ("one of the oldest—though not the largest—properties in England [whose] particulars go back to the Domesday Book"); and the beautiful Jonet Douglas (*My Lady Glamis*), who bravely rejects the advances of a captive (and very determined) King James V of Scotland. Several of Hill's heroines—Marjorie of Scotland; Margaret Douglas and her sister Jonet; Françoise d'Aubigné, Marquise of Maintenon; Catherine I of Russia—are actual historical (though highly dramatized) figures.

In a recent novel, *The Sutburys*, Hill's characters are more believable, perhaps, but their lives and predicaments are just as fantastic. A feud between the two Sutbury brothers results in a family curse, bringing with it the birth of a grossly handicapped child, the birth of a black child (to a seemingly white couple), deathbed confessions vital to the plot, and, as we have by now proceeded into the age of the railroad, several tragically relevant train accidents.

As though she were still looking out the window of that bus, Hill sets her gothic adventures primarily in her native Scotland, crossing the border into England from time to time, now and then dreaming of more exotic realms, her inner eye seeing the people and places of centuries past (most often, the 17th and 18th). Her pen is swift, her characters vividly drawn, and her adventures highly suspenseful.

—Marcia G. Fuchs

HILTON, Margery. British. Married. Address: c/o Mills and Boon Ltd., 18–24 Paradise Road, Richmond, Surrey TW9 1SR, England.

ROMANCE AND HISTORICAL PUBLICATIONS

Novels

The Dutch Uncle. London, Mills and Boon, 1966.
Young Ellis. London, Mills and Boon, 1966.
Darling Radamanthas! London, Mills and Boon, 1966.
The Grotto of Jade. London, Mills and Boon, 1967.
Girl Crusoe. London, Mills and Boon, 1969.
Interlude in Arcady. London, Mills and Boon, 1969.
The Flower of Eternity. London, Mills and Boon, 1970.
Bitter Masquerade. London, Mills and Boon, 1970.
The House of the Amulet. London, Mills and Boon, 1970.
Frail Sanctuary. London, Mills and Boon, 1970.
The Inshine Girl. London, Mills and Boon, 1970.
Miss Columbine and Harley Quinn. London, Mills and Boon, 1970.
A Man Without Mercy. London, Mills and Boon, 1971.
The Whispering Grove. London, Mills and Boon, 1971.
Trust in Tomorrow. London, Mills and Boon, 1971.
Dear Conquistador. London, Mills and Boon, 1972.
The Spell of the Enchanter. London, Mills and Boon, 1972.
Miranda's Marriage. London, Mills and Boon, 1973.
The Beach of Sweet Returns. London, Mills and Boon, 1975.
Time of Curtain Fall. London, Mills and Boon, 1976.
The House of Strange Music. London, Mills and Boon, 1976.
The Dark Side of Marriage. London, Mills and Boon, 1978.
Snow Bride. London, Mills and Boon, 1979.
The Velvet Touch. London, Mills and Boon, 1979.
Way of a Man. London, Mills and Boon, 1981.

*   *   *

Margery Hilton has written a string of successful romances, some of which are considered classics of the genre. Although adept at creating strongly male and fervently feminine stereotypes, she manages to inject these with shafts of subtlety and sharpness which lift her books from conventional ordinary-girl-meets-glamorous-Mr.-Right romances into interesting complexes of challenge and response.

One of her most powerful stories is *A Man Without Mercy*. In this her heroine, Gerda, has to face some fearful situations. Her marriage to a very sick man is a tragic business: then, widowed and grappling with career problems, she finds that her romantic aspirations become terribly tangled with misunderstandings, intrigues, and an obsessive desire for vengeance on the part of the man to whom she gives her at first unrequited passion. Hatred from the past threatens to overwhelm the present, but Gerda's responses show that, as befits her robust business-girl image, she is far more than a mere shuttlecock in the winds of fate.

The leading character in *Girl Crusoe* is similarly resilient. Jan, a skilled commercial photographer, gets stranded on an uninhabited Pacific island with Nick Redfern the irritatingly superior pilot of the small airplane in which she has been travelling. Of course it is inevitable that enforced proximity and the struggle for survival will eventually throw each into the other's arms, but, true to the traditions of the genre Hilton contrives, by means of some compelling psychological sparring between girl and boy, to defer the truly passionate clinches until the end of the book (when rescue provides the possibility of respectable matrimony).

Girl Crusoe embodies some of Hilton's most atmospheric description of locations, as the delights and difficulties of the island terrain are uncovered. Strong local colour is an enlivening feature of many of her stories, whether it embraces "the romantic island of Salamander in the Indian Ocean'' (to which Toni retreats after an accident has ended her ballet-dancing career in *The Whispering Grove*), the steamy Peruvian jungle in *The Flower of Eternity* (which lures Gail into the search for a lost valley *and* a lover among "those strong, silent explorer types"), or simply the London of flat-sharing working girls in *Miss Columbine and Harley Quinn*. Whatever the setting, Hilton can be relied upon to provide engaging characters and lively plots as well as the expected dollops of romance.

—Mary Cadogan

HINTZE, Naomi A(gans). American. Born in Camden, Illinois, 8 July 1909. Educated at Maryville College, Tennessee, 1927–29; Ball State Teachers College (now University), Muncie, Indiana, 1929–30. Married Harold Sanborn Hintze in 1930; two sons and one daughter. Member of the Advisory Board, Virginia Center for the Creative Arts. Recipient: Mystery Writers of America Edgar Allan Poe award, 1970. Agent: McIntosh and Otis Inc., 310 Madison Avenue, New York, New York 10017, U.S.A.

ROMANCE AND HISTORICAL PUBLICATIONS

Novels

You'll Like My Mother. New York, Putnam, 1969; as *The House with the Watching Eyes*, London, Hale, 1970.
The Stone Carnation. New York, Random House, 1971; London, Hale, 1973.
Aloha Means Goodbye. New York, Random House, 1972; as *Hawaii for Danger*, London, Hale, 1973.
Listen, Please Listen. New York, Random House, 1974; London, Hale, 1975.
Cry Witch. New York, Random House, 1975; London, Collins, 1976.
The Ghost Child. New York, Fawcett, 1983.

OTHER PUBLICATIONS

Other

Buried Treasure Waits for You. Indianapolis, Bobbs Merrill, 1962.
The Psychic Realm: What Can You Believe?, with J. Gaither Pratt. New York, Random House, 1975.
Time Bomb, with Peter van der Linde. New York, Doubleday, 1978.

*   *   *

One could describe the novels of Naomi A. Hintze as short and sweet, but for the sting that hides in each one. Her novels are short works of romantic suspense with straightforward and uncomplicated plots. But each novel has a bitter touch to the expected happy ending. Generally the counterpoint to the romance is the death of a character for whom the reader has come to care. In addition, in *The Stone Carnation* and *You'll Like My Mother* the heroines must rebuild ruined lives through new romantic relationships.

Before turning to novels of romantic suspense, Hintze wrote for children. The experience seems to color her style in that a number of her works have plots and characters that would hold strong appeal for the late adolescent reader. It is a measure of her skill as a storyteller that this slant does not prevent the books from reaching a broader readership. Her prose is rather simple and the books often contain moments of literary hesitation. The heroines always seem to apply makeup as a means of transition from one scene to another. The dialogue is smooth and natural, however, and makes up for any lack of fluidity in the descriptive passages.

The flawed characters in Hintze's work—the retarded girl in *You'll Like My Mother*, the terminally ill boy in *Aloha Means Goodbye*, the child molester in *Listen, Please Listen*, the old madwoman in *The Stone Carnation*—are drawn with special care. Often they seem more real, more sympathetic than the main characters. This is the means that the author uses to "sting" the reader, for she avoids the flaws in characterization often found in this genre. Her villains are never wholly evil, just as her heroes are heroines are never wholly perfect. Nor is any character too insignificant to escape her notice. The Ginter family in *The Stone Carnation* almost begs to be drawn out into caricatures, but Hintze treats them with a kind of affectionate respect.

The suspense element of these novels carries more weight than the romance, but the two parts would not be as likely to stand alone. The resolution of the mystery in each novel is not totally unexpected, but at the same time is not obvious to the reader far in advance. If there are no surprises, there are also no jarring elements or missing clues to confuse the reader. Despite the bittersweet tone of the endings the novels are satisfying in that all has been said that needs to be said. Perhaps Hintze's novels do not demand very much from the reader, but they consistently deliver tightly plotted and conclusive stories.

—Susan Quinn Berneis

HODGE, Jane Aiken. British. Born in Watertown, Massachusetts, United States, 4 December 1917; daughter of the writer Conrad Aiken; sister of Joan Aiken, *q.v.* Educated at Hayes Court, Kent, 1929–34; Somerville College, Oxford (Lefevre fellow), 1935–38, B.A. (honours) 1938; Harvard University, Cambridge, Massachusetts, 1938–39, A.M. 1939. Married the writer Alan Hodge in 1948 (died 1979); two daughters. Worked for the British Board of Trade, Washington, D.C., 1941–44, and the British Supply Council of North America, 1944–45; researcher, Time Inc., New York, 1945–47, and for *Life* magazine, in London, 1947–48; reader for film companies and publishers, and freelance reviewer, 1950's and 1960's. Agent: David Higham Associates, 5–8 Lower John Street, London W1R 4HA. Address: 23 Eastport Lane, Lewes, East Sussex BN7 1TL, England.

ROMANCE AND HISTORICAL PUBLICATIONS

Novels

Maulever Hall. London, Hale, and New York, Doubleday, 1964.
The Adventurers. New York, Doubleday, 1965; London, Hodder and Stoughton, 1966.
Watch the Wall, My Darling. New York, Doubleday, 1966; London, Hodder and Stoughton, 1967.
Here Comes a Candle. London, Hodder and Stoughton, and New York, Doubleday, 1967; as *The Master of Penrose*, New York, Dell, 1968.
The Winding Stair. London, Hodder and Stoughton, 1968; New York, Doubleday, 1969.
Marry in Haste. London, Hodder and Stoughton, 1969; New York, Doubleday, 1970.
Greek Wedding. London, Hodder and Stoughton, and New York, Doubleday, 1970.
Savannah Purchase. London, Hodder and Stoughton, and New York, Doubleday, 1971.
Strangers in Company. London, Hodder and Stoughton, and New York, Coward McCann, 1973.
Shadow of a Lady. New York, Coward McCann, 1973; London, Hodder and Stoughton, 1974.
One Way to Venice. London, Hodder and Stoughton, 1974; New York, Coward McCann, 1975.
Rebel Heiress. London, Hodder and Stoughton, and New York, Coward McCann, 1975.
Runaway Bride. New York, Fawcett, 1975; London, Coronet, 1976.
Judas Flowering. London, Hodder and Stoughton, and New York, Coward McCann, 1976.
Red Sky at Night: Lovers' Delight? New York, Coward McCann, 1977; London, Hodder and Stoughton, 1979.
Last Act. London, Hodder and Stoughton, and New York, Coward McCann, 1979.
Wide Is the Water. London, Hodder and Stoughton, and New York, Coward McCann, 1981.
The Lost Garden. London, Hodder and Stoughton, and New York, Coward McCann, 1982.
Secret Island. London, Hodder and Stoughton, and New York, Putnam, 1985.
Polonaise. London, Hodder and Stoughton, and New York, Putnam, 1987.
First Night. London, Hodder and Stoughton, and New York, Putnam, 1989.

OTHER PUBLICATIONS

Other

The Double Life of Jane Austen. London, Hodder and Stoughton, 1972; as *Only a Novel: The Double Life of Jane Austen*, New York, Coward McCann, 1972.
The Private World of Georgette Heyer. London, Bodley Head, 1984.

*

Jane Aiken Hodge comments:

I would rather be called a writer of romance than of gothic. The term gothic now seems to imply a kind of violent horror that I think out of place in books written as entertainment. There is too much violence and horror in real life, and they should be written about seriously, not to titillate. Besides, I prefer the tension of feeling to the spurious kind provided by violence. I hope to keep my reader happily hooked without ever making her (or him) shocked, or sick. This is one reason why I write mainly historical romance, in which it is easier to indulge in moral standards, and a happy ending. A reviewer once said of one of my early books that it was a blend of Jane Austen and the Brontës, and I think this is the comment that has pleased me most in my writing career. I also owe a vast debt to Georgette Heyer, whose impeccable historical accuracy I have always tried to emulate. The background research is part of the pleasure, and so is the tension between historical fact and the vagaries of one's characters. I have, however, also written three novels of modern romantic suspense, enjoyed them very much, and hope to do more. In them, too, I aim for excitement without excessive violence. There seems to be a terrible dearth, just now, of the kind of civilised light reading provided by writers like Dorothy Sayers, Georgette Heyer, or Mary Stewart. It is my immodest ambition to be classed with them.

*   *   *

Jane Aiken Hodge writes some of the best historical fiction now being published. She is prolific and popular without being imprisoned by formula or falling back on predictable, stereotyped characters. Her romances are historical, imbued with a past that has clearly become as real to her as the present is to a writer of contemporary fiction. Hodge's skillful use of historical settings is the key to her success and to the literary quality of her work.

Unlike other practitioners of the genre, Hodge doesn't overwhelm her reader with a mass of historical detail. She masters the history of her period so well that her settings never seem artificial or contrived. Dialogue is often used to set the scene and establish a sense of place, and this is a far more effective technique than the lengthy descriptions of historical settings on which less able writers fall back. Hodge's characters seldom speak in dialect or use period expressions, but they don't use anachronistic metaphors, either. Artifacts, houses, cities, and costume are described only as they are relevant to her plot.

Hodge uses history to add depth to her romantic adventures. Although most of her work is set in the early 19th century (with the exception of two books set in the 1770's), she provides variety by placing the action in several different countries: America, England, Greece, Portugal, France, and Germany. Historical events add both realism and pace to the stories, which occur in and around the Napoleonic Wars, the Greek struggle for independence, the War of 1812, and the American Revolution. Because we know these conflicts did in fact take place, we are able to see Hodge's stories as more than romantic fantasies, and we can empathize with and experience the conflicts of the hero, heroine, and assorted villains.

In contrast to her historical novels, Hodge's three works of contemporary romance (*Strangers in Company*, *One Way to Venice*, and *Last Act*) are much less effective. While each plot involves suspense as well as romance, the action is slow-moving, the characters rather sketchily described, and their predicaments unbelievable. The three heroines are unfortunately passive: one wrongly believes she is terminally ill, another is a tranquilized and deserted wife and mother, a third is the target of a truly bizarre (and ultimately unconvincing) plot. While all three of these romances entertain, the reader feels pity rather an empathy for the unhappy heroines.

Most of Hodge's women are much more interesting. While her heroines follow the typical pattern of the genre in being orphaned or alone in the world, they are never the passive victims of events beyond their control for long. They confront their villains bravely, and reach out to take the necessary risks. Hodge's heroes are also typical of the genre in being older, capable, usually established in society (but unlucky in love), but the world her heroes move in is the world of affairs, not simply the world of fashion. The typical Hodge hero may be a politician (Mark Maulever in *Maulever Hall*), a secret agent (Lord Leominster in *Marry in Haste*, Charles Vincent in *The Adventurers*, and Gair Varlow in *The Winding Stair*), a businessman (Jonathan Penrose in *Here Comes a Candle*), or a successful planter (Hart Purchis in *Judas Flowering* and *Wide Is the Water*, his grandson Hyde Purchis in *Savannah Purchase*). Hodge's heroines must face not mad monks or jealous rivals, but enemy troops, revolutionary mobs, Barbary pirates, and Greek brigands. Their most impressive asset is their courage, and their independence is firmly asserted. Hodge allows her heroines to enjoy their adventures, and in doing so effectively demolishes the traditional stereotypes about the repressed and delicate ladies of the pre-Victorian era. Mercy Philips (of *Judas Flowering* and *Wide Is the Water*) works as the "Rebel Printer" in British-occupied Savannah; Juana Brett penetrates a Portuguese secret society for a British agent (*The Winding Stair*) and Phyllida Vannick escapes from a Turkish harem (which she prosaically describes as a rather dull all-female society—these books are not melodramas) in *Greek Wedding*. Hodge rarely uses actual historical characters in any but minor and supporting roles, with the successful exception of Emma Hamilton, Lord Nelson's inamorata, who plays a crucial role in *Shadow of a Lady*. Each character has a past, and each is developed well enough so that the reader rather expects them to live on beyond the events of Hodge's story. While the heroes and heroines do follow a common pattern, they are also individuals, with their own characters, occupations (only four of the heroines, for example, are governesses!), and experiences.

Each of Hodge's historical novels has two plots. One is the romance of the hero and heroine, while the other revolves around the suspenseful adventure in which they both participate. Christina Tretton and her cousin Ross Tretteign are involved with smugglers and spies (*Watch the Wall, My Darling*), Kate Croston must rescue Jonathan Penrose's daughter from a kidnapper (*Here Comes a Candle*), Henrietta Marchmont must convince Simon Rivers that she is not a Yankee spy (*Rebel Heiress*), and Kate Warrender, disguised as a man, must expose a radical plot to overthrow the British crown (*Red Sky at Night: Lovers' Delight?*). The course of true love is carefully intertwined with the progress of the mystery, while the diverse historical settings provide authenticity. In two of the novels (*The Adventurers* and *Red Sky at Night: Lovers' Delight?*) there are two heroines, one maturely beautiful, the other young and innocent (and temporarily passing as a boy). Both pairs of heroines eventually find suitable pairs of heroes.

Without Hodge's skillful use of history, her books would be quite ordinary, with very familiar characters following well-worn plots. Instead, history makes these novels work. Hodge catches her readers up in the past, and we willingly suspend our disbelief to enjoy the suspenseful story. The books are very readable, and the characters interesting enough to sustain our interest until the conclusion. Hodge doesn't lay her history on with a heavy hand, and has described historical novels as "icebergs," for "there is more to them than meets the eye" (in *The Writer*, June 1972). Her own grasp of the period she describes is so sure that the historical details she does provide have the convincing ring of authenticity. We are sure that the rest of the iceberg is there, below the visible surface of the story. Hodge provides just enough of the less romantic and more realistic detail of history (the pain of slavery, the suffering in the lower decks of a British man of war, the hungry citizens of a besieged city) to show us

that the past she portrays is the real past, and not a sanitized, museum-pretty version. Her work is believable, entertaining, well-crafted, and very much worth reading.

—Mary C. Lynn

HOHL, Joan M. See **LORIN, Amii.**

HOLLAND, Cecelia (Anastasia). Also writes as Elizabeth Eliot Carter. American. Born in Henderson, Nevada, 31 December 1943. Educated at Pennsylvania State University, University Park, 1961–62; Connecticut College, New London, B.A. 1965. Visiting Professor of English, Connecticut College, 1979. Recipient: Guggenheim fellowship, 1981. Address: c/o Houghton Mifflin Company, 2 Park Street, Boston, Massachusetts 02108, U.S.A.

ROMANCE AND HISTORICAL PUBLICATIONS

Novels

The Firedrake. New York, Atheneum, 1966; London, Hodder and Stoughton, 1967.
Rakóssy. New York, Atheneum, and London, Hodder and Stoughton, 1967.
The Kings in Winter. New York, Atheneum, and London, Hodder and Stoughton, 1968.
Until the Sun Falls. New York, Atheneum, and London, Hodder and Stoughton, 1969.
Antichrist. New York, Atheneum, 1970; as *The Wonder of the World*, London, Hodder and Stoughton, 1970.
The Earl. New York, Knopf, 1971; as *Hammer for Princes*, London, Hodder and Stoughton, 1972.
The Death of Attila. New York, Knopf, 1973; London, Hodder and Stoughton, 1974.
Great Maria. New York, Knopf, 1974; London, Hodder and Stoughton, 1975.
Two Ravens. New York, Knopf, and London, Gollancz, 1977.
Valley of the Kings (as Elizabeth Eliot Carter). New York, Dutton, 1977; as Cecelia Holland, London, Gollancz, 1978.
City of God. New York, Knopf, and London, Gollancz, 1979.
The Sea Beggars. New York, Knopf, and London, Gollancz, 1982.
The Belt of Gold. New York, Knopf, and London, Gollancz, 1984.
Pillar of the Sky. New York, Knopf, and London, Gollancz, 1985.
The Lords of Vaumartin. Boston, Houghton Mifflin, 1988.

OTHER PUBLICATIONS

Novels

Floating Worlds. New York, Knopf, and London, Gollancz, 1976.
Home Ground. New York, Knopf, and London, Gollancz, 1981.

Other (for children)

Ghost on the Steppe. New York, Atheneum, 1969.
The King's Road. New York, Atheneum, 1970.

*   *   *

Cecelia Holland had been out of college only a year when her first novel, *The Firedrake* was published in 1966. Since then, hardly a year has gone by without a Holland novel offered to hungry historical fiction buffs. Her time and place settings range from pre-history with *Pillar of the Sky*, set at Stonehenge on England's Salisbury plain, to 16th-century Hungary with *Rakóssy*, a rough, uncultured Magyar nobleman, and *The Sea Beggars*, the story of Dutch Calvinists fighting the heretic-hunting Spanish for their religious freedom—with one unsuccessful foray into science fiction (*Floating Worlds*) and one contemporary novel (*Home Ground*).

Holland's historical novels have received mixed reviews, but weighted heavily on the positive side. Her first novel was criticized for the use of very short, plain, often abrupt language and simple sentence structure, but praised for the sound research about England just before the Norman conquest. Those early reviews clearly did not disturb Holland unduly, for 20 years later, her style has not changed and in fact her disdain for the ornate language often found in historical novels has become a hallmark of her work, which is now frequently praised for the immediacy her prose brings to her stories. Some reviewers have taken a different tack in their criticism by challenging her facts while praising her imagination. Though she is obviously intrigued by primitive cultures and remote historical periods, these only set the stage for her tales. Holland is above all a storyteller who has a wonderful way of transporting herself back in time and taking us along with her. One can feel the eerie and terrifying atmosphere in a scene from *City of God* (a story of the Borgias in early 16th-century Rome), which takes place at the Vatican where Pope Alexander sports with his mistress on his lap while his illegitimate son, Valentino, also know as Cesare Borgia, turns his pet leopard loose on drunken palace revelers. Or the reader can experience the joy and frivolity of a May Day celebration in Norman England with the young men and girls singing and dancing and leading "a creature made of leaves, strutting from side to side. Green boughs covered it from its pointed head to the ground." This description of the King of the Green is a bright spot in the rather grim story *Two Ravens* about the wanderings of an 11th-century Icelander estranged from his cruel father who returns home to wreak his revenge.

Another Holland signature is the frequent use and description of animals, especially horses who play roles in most of her novels, including the contemporary *Home Ground*. As for characterizations, she is at her best and most believable when free to create imaginary characters. Frequently the protagonists in her novels are colleagues, companions, or servants to the more wooden historical folk whose actions and personalities have been documented. Read history books to learn the facts about a given age, but read Holland to soak up the atmosphere.

—Marion Hanscom

HOLLAND, Isabelle. Has also written as Francesca Hunt. American. Born in Basel, Switzerland, 16 June 1920. Educated at private schools in England; University of Liverpool, 1938–40; Tulane University, New Orleans, B.A. in English 1942. Publicity

director, Crown Publishers, New York, 1956–60, and Lippincott, publishers, Philadelphia, 1960–66; assistant to the publisher, *Harper's* magazine, New York, 1967–68; publicity director, Putnam, publishers, New York, 1968–69. Recipient: Church and Synagogue Library Association Ott award, for children's book, 1983 (twice). Lives in New York City. Agent: Elaine Markson Literary Agency, 44 Greenwich Avenue, New York, New York 10011, U.S.A.

ROMANCE AND HISTORICAL PUBLICATIONS

Novels

Kilgaren. New York, Weybright and Talley, 1974; London, Collins, 1975.
Trelawny. New York, Weybright and Talley, 1974; as *Trelawny's Fell*, London, Collins, 1976.
Moncrieff. New York, Weybright and Talley, 1975; as *The Standish Place*, London, Collins, 1976.
Darcourt. New York, Weybright and Talley, 1976; London, Collins, 1977.
Grenelle. New York, Rawson, 1976; London, Collins, 1978.
The deMaury Papers. New York, Rawson, 1977; London, Collins, 1978.
Tower Abbey. New York, Rawson, 1978; London, Collins, 1979.
The Marchington Inheritance. New York, Rawson, 1979; London, Collins, 1980.
Counterpoint. New York, Rawson, 1980; London, Collins, 1981.
The Lost Madonna. New York, Rawson, 1981; London, Collins, 1982.
A Death at St. Anselm's. New York, Doubleday, 1984; London, Severn House, 1985.
Flight of the Archangel. New York, Doubleday, 1985; London, Severn House, 1986.
A Lover Scorned. New York, Doubleday, 1986; London, Severn House, 1987.
Bump in the Night. New York, Doubleday, 1988; London, Severn House, 1989.

OTHER PUBLICATIONS (for children)

Fiction

Cecily. Philadelphia, Lippincott, 1967; London, Severn House, 1985.
Amanda's Choice. Philadelphia, Lippincott, 1970.
The Man Without a Face. Philadelphia, Lippincott, 1972.
The Mystery of Castle Renaldi (as Francesca Hunt). Middletown, Connecticut, Xerox, 1972.
Heads You Win, Tails I Lose. Philadelphia, Lippincott, 1973.
Journey for Three. Middletown, Connecticut, Xerox, 1974; London, Macdonald and Jane's, 1978.
Of Love and Death and Other Journeys. Philadelphia, Lippincott, 1975; as *Ask No Questions*, London, Macdonald and Jane's, 1978.
Alan and the Animal Kingdom. Philadelphia, Lippincott, 1977; London, Macdonald and Jane's, 1979.
Hitchhike. Philadelphia, Lippincott, 1977.
Dinah and the Green Fat Kingdom. Philadelphia, Lippincott, 1978.
Now Is Not Too Late. New York, Lothrop, 1980.

Summer of My First Love. New York, Fawcett, 1981; London, Severn House, 1987.
A Horse Named Peaceable. New York, Lothrop, 1982.
Abbie's God Book. Philadelphia, Westminster Press, 1982.
After the First Love. New York, Fawcett, 1983; London, Severn House, 1988.
Perdita. Boston, Little Brown, 1983; London, Severn House, 1987.
God, Mrs. Muskrat, and Aunt Dot. Philadelphia, Westminster Press, 1983.
The Empty House. New York, Lippincott, 1983; London, Severn House, 1985.
Kevin's Hat. New York, Lothrop, 1984.
Green Andrew Green. Philadelphia, Westminster Press, 1984.
The Island. Boston, Little Brown, 1985; London, Severn House, 1986.
Jenny Kiss'd Me. New York, Fawcett, 1985; London, Severn House, 1986.
Henry and Grudge. New York, Walker, 1986.
Love and the Genetic Factor. New York, Fawcett, 1987.
The Christmas Cat. New York, Golden, 1987.
Toby the Splendid. New York, Walker, 1987.
Thief. New York, Fawcett, 1989.
The Easter Donkey. New York, Golden, 1989.

*

Manuscript Collections (children's books): Kerlan Collection, University of Minnesota, Minneapolis; de Grummond Collection, University of Southern Mississippi, Hattiesburg.

*   *   *

Individually, Isabelle Holland's psychological gothics appear complex, with complicated relationships to be explained as the key to dangers that threaten the heroine. Viewed collectively, however, the books are similar, and the reader will quickly determine the essential ingredients of the basic Holland plot.

Because the story is told by a young woman, and the other characters are seen from her perspective, the reader can never be sure about their motives and is often led astray by the heroine's misconceptions. The Holland devotee soon realizes, though, that the man the heroine dislikes most is the one whom she will eventually love and marry while the man she trusts for most of the book is no good. The heroine usually harbors deep-seated prejudices against her husband-to-be for some real or imagined wrong he has done to her or her family. For example, years ago, Antonia Moncrieff had a one-night fling with a professor who was too drunk to remember the incident (*Moncrieff*). Now she is reluctant to help him edit a book for her publishing company, partly because she never told him about their son.

Usually at least part of the story is set in an old mansion with mysterious passageways, sudden drafts, or strange sounds. The locales range from England (*The deMaury Papers*) to Italy (*The Lost Madonna*) to the West Indies (*Kilgaren*), but the terror of wandering through unfamiliar settings is about the same. One reason the heroines undertake nocturnal ramblings is their search for straying pets. All Holland's gothics include at least one animal, and her heroines are generally devoted to their furry companions. Although the animals sometimes lead their owners into trouble, they also help them make important discoveries or warn them of danger.

Children also have a central role in many of the books. In *A Death at St. Anselm's*, a boy's quick thinking saves his mother from a murderer. In *Grenelle* one child is murdered and another

kidnapped by members of a drug ring. In *The Marchington Inheritance* a terrorist group uses a pre-school as a front.

As these incidents indicate, Holland often incorporates topics of current interest in her plots. Exorcism (*Tower Abbey*), Vietnam veterans (*Trelawny*), wife abuse (*Flight of the Archangel*), and political corruption (*The deMaury Papers*) are only some of the subjects she uses.

Underlying these topics is one recurring theme: the gulf between classes. Sometimes the heroine dislikes someone rich and powerful and mouths anti-Establishment clichés, but she invariably discovers that the rich are misunderstood. In *Darcourt* the heroine suspects Tristram Darcourt of negotiating deals with the Arabs to control the oil market. In reality, he is cooperating with the government to stop others from doing just that. Tristram asks a properly humbled heroine, "After all . . . don't the IRA and most other revolutionaries wish to become the Establishment, after, of course, they've unseated the present one?" In other books, such as *Grenelle* and *Trelawny*, the jealousy of a man from the lower class drives him to do anything, even murder, for wealth and power he doesn't deserve.

Holland's more recent romances include numerous psychic experiences that help unravel some sort of mystery, usually involving the heroine. The most extensive use of psychic phenomena occurs in *The Lost Madonna*, in which Julia Winthrop experiences dreams and visions of her murdered step-grandmother until the murderer is caught. Letty Dalrymple, a psychic, helps police solve mysteries in both *Flight of the Archangel* and *A Lover Scorned*.

These two novels plus *A Death at St. Anselm's* feature many of the same characters, including the Rev. Claire Aldington, assistant rector of a wealthy New York City parish, and Lieutenant O'Neill, a police detective. Claire's romance with wealthy parishoner, Brett Cunningham, develops during *A Death at St. Anselm's* and continues in *A Lover Scorned*. Like heroines in Holland's earlier novels, Claire must abandon her liberal anti-Establishment biases to appreciate Brett's hard-headed approach to charity and to life.

The long-suffering upper class is but one recurring motif in Holland's novels. Although locales and situations seem exotic for a while, the path through her settings has been well worn.

—Kathy Piehl

———

HOLLAND, Sheila. See **LAMB, Charlotte.**

———

HOLT, Victoria. Pseudonym for Eleanor Alice Hibbert, née Burford; also writes as Philippa Carr; Jean Plaidy; has also written as Eleanor Burford; Elbur Ford; Kathleen Kellow; Ellalice Tate. British. Born in London in 1906. Educated privately. Married G. P. Hibbert. Agent: A. M. Heath, 79 St. Martin's Lane, London WC2N 4AA, England.

<small>ROMANCE AND HISTORICAL PUBLICATIONS</small>

Novels

Mistress of Mellyn. New York, Doubleday, 1960; London, Collins, 1961.

Kirkland Revels. London, Collins, and New York, Doubleday, 1962.

Bride of Pendorric. London, Collins, and New York, Doubleday, 1963.

The Legend of the Seventh Virgin. London, Collins, and New York, Doubleday, 1965.

Menfreya. London, Collins, 1966; as *Menfreya in the Morning*, New York, Doubleday, 1966.

The King of the Castle. London, Collins, and New York, Doubleday, 1967.

The Queen's Confession. London, Collins, and New York, Doubleday, 1968.

The Shivering Sands. London, Collins, and New York, Doubleday, 1969.

The Secret Woman. New York, Doubleday, 1970; London, Collins, 1971.

The Shadow of the Lynx. New York, Doubleday, 1971; London, Collins, 1972.

On the Night of the Seventh Moon. New York, Doubleday, 1972; London, Collins, 1973.

The Curse of the Kings. London, Collins, and New York, Doubleday, 1973.

The House of a Thousand Lanterns. London, Collins, and New York, Doubleday, 1974.

Lord of the Far Island. London, Collins, and New York, Doubleday, 1975.

The Pride of the Peacock. London, Collins, and New York, Doubleday, 1976.

The Devil on Horseback. London, Collins, and New York, Doubleday, 1977.

My Enemy the Queen. London, Collins, and New York, Doubleday, 1978.

The Spring of the Tiger. London, Collins, and New York, Doubleday, 1979.

The Mask of the Enchantress. London, Collins, and New York, Doubleday, 1980.

The Judas Kiss. London, Collins, and New York, Doubleday, 1981.

The Demon Lover. London, Collins, and New York, Doubleday, 1982.

The Time of the Hunter's Moon. London, Collins, and New York, Doubleday, 1983.

The Landower Legacy. London, Collins, and New York, Doubleday, 1984.

The Road to Paradise Island. London, Collins, and New York, Doubleday, 1985.

Secret for a Nightingale. London, Collins, and New York, Doubleday, 1986.

The Silk Vendetta. London, Collins, and New York, Doubleday, 1987.

The India Fan. London, Collins, and New York, Doubleday, 1988.

The Captive. New York, Doubleday, 1989.

Novels as Eleanor Burford

Daughter of Anna. London, Jenkins, 1941.

Passionate Witness. London, Jenkins, 1941.

The Married Lover. London, Jenkins, 1942.

When All the World Is Young. London, Jenkins, 1943.

So the Dreams Depart. London, Jenkins, 1944.

Not in Our Stars. London, Jenkins, 1945.

Dear Chance. London, Jenkins, 1947.

Alexa. London, Jenkins, 1948.

The House at Cupid's Cross. London, Jenkins, 1949.

Believe the Heart. London, Jenkins, 1950.

The Love Child. London, Jenkins, 1950.

Saint or Sinner? London, Jenkins, 1951.

Dear Delusion. London, Jenkins, 1952.

Bright Tomorrow. London, Jenkins, 1952.

Leave Me My Love. London, Jenkins, 1953.

When We Are Married. London, Jenkins, 1953.

Castles in Spain. London, Jenkins, 1954.

Heart's Afire. London, Jenkins, 1954.

When Other Hearts. London, Jenkins, 1955.

Two Loves in Her Life. London, Jenkins, 1955.

Begin to Live. London, Mills and Boon, 1956.

Married in Haste. London, Mills and Boon, 1956.

To Meet a Stranger. London, Mills and Boon, 1957.

Pride of the Morning. London, Mills and Boon, 1958.

Blaze of Noon. London, Mills and Boon, 1958.

The Dawn Chorus. London, Mills and Boon, 1959.

Red Sky at Night. London, Mills and Boon, 1959.

Night of Stars. London, Mills and Boon, 1960.

Now That April's Gone. London, Mills and Boon, 1961.

Who's Calling. London, Mills and Boon, 1962.

Novels as Jean Plaidy (series: Catherine de'Medici; Charles II; Georgian; Isabella and Ferdinand; Katharine of Aragon; Lucrezia Borgia; Norman; Plantagenet; Queens of England; Stuarts; Victorian)

Together They Ride. London, Swan, 1945.

Beyond the Blue Mountains. New York, Appleton Century, 1947; London, Hale, 1948.

Murder Most Royal. London, Hale, 1949; New York, Putnam, 1972; as *The King's Pleasure*, New York, Appleton Century Crofts, 1949.

The Goldsmith's Wife. London, Hale, and New York, Appleton Century Crofts, 1950; as *The King's Mistress*, New York, Pyramid, 1952.

Catherine de'Medici. London, Hale, 1969.

    Madame Serpent. London, Hale, and New York, Appleton Century Crofts, 1951.

    The Italian Woman. London, Hale, 1952; New York, Putnam, 1975.

    Queen Jezebel. London, Hale, and New York, Appleton Century Crofts, 1953.

Daughter of Satan. London, Hale, 1952; New York, Putnam, 1973; as *The Unholy Woman*, Toronto, Harlequin, 1954.

The Sixth Wife. London, Hale, 1953; New York, Putnam, 1969.

The Spanish Bridegroom. London, Hale, 1954; Philadelphia, Macrae Smith, 1956.

St. Thomas's Eve. London, Hale, 1954; New York, Putnam, 1970.

Gay Lord Robert. London, Hale, 1955; New York, Putnam, 1972.

Royal Road to Fotheringay. London, Hale, 1955; New York, Putnam, 1968.

Charles II. London, Hale, 1972.

    The Wandering Prince. London, Hale, 1956; New York, Putnam, 1971.

    A Health unto His Majesty. London, Hale, 1956; New York, Putnam, 1972.

    Here Lies Our Sovereign Lord. London, Hale, 1957; New York, Putnam, 1973.

Flaunting Extravagant Queen (Marie Antionette). London, Hale, 1957.

Lucrezia Borgia. London, Hale, 1976.

    Madonna of the Seven Hills. London, Hale, 1958; New York, Putnam, 1974.

Light on Lucrezia. London, Hale, 1958; New York, Putnam, 1976.
Louis, The Well-Beloved. London, Hale, 1959.
The Road to Compiègne. London, Hale, 1959.
Isabella and Ferdinand. London, Hale, 1970.
  Castile for Isabella. London, Hale, 1960.
  Spain for the Sovereigns. London, Hale, 1960.
  Daughters of Spain. London, Hale, 1961.
Katharine of Aragon. London, Hale, 1968.
  Katharine, The Virgin Widow. London, Hale, 1961.
  The Shadow of the Pomegranate. London, Hale, 1962.
  The King's Secret Matter. London, Hale, 1962.
The Captive Queen of Scots. London, Hale, 1963; New York, Putnam, 1970.
The Thistle and the Rose. London, Hale, 1963; New York, Putnam, 1973.
Mary, Queen of France. London, Hale, 1964.
The Murder in the Tower. London, Hale, 1964; New York, Putnam, 1974.
Evergreen Gallant. London, Hale, 1965; New York, Putnam, 1973.
The Last of the Stuarts. London, Hale, 1977.
  The Three Crowns. London, Hale, 1965; New York, Putnam, 1977.
  The Haunted Sisters. London, Hale, 1966; New York, Putnam, 1977.
  The Queen's Favourites. London, Hale, 1966; New York, Putnam, 1978.
Georgian Saga:
  1. *The Princess of Celle*. London, Hale, 1967; New York, Putnam, 1985.
  2. *Queen in Waiting*. London, Hale, 1967; New York, Putnam, 1985.
  3. *The Prince and the Quakeress*. London, Hale, 1968; New York, Putnam, 1986.
  4. *Caroline, The Queen*. London, Hale, 1968; New York, Putnam, 1986.
  5. *The Third George*. London, Hale, 1969; New York, Putnam, 1987.
  6. *Perdita's Prince*. London, Hale, 1969; New York, Putnam, 1987.
  7. *Sweet Lass of Richmond Hill*. London, Hale, 1970; New York, Putnam, 1988.
  8. *Indiscretions of the Queen*. London, Hale, 1970; New York, Putnam, 1988.
  9. *The Regent's Daughter*. London, Hale, 1971; New York, Putnam, 1989.
  10. *Goddess of the Green Room*. London, Hale, 1971.
Victorian Saga:
  1. *The Captive of Kensington Palace*. London, Hale, 1972; New York, Putnam, 1976.
  2. *Victoria in the Wings*. London, Hale, 1972.
  3. *The Queen and Lord M*. London, Hale, 1973; New York, Putnam, 1977.
  4. *The Queen's Husband*. London, Hale, 1973; New York, Putnam, 1978.
  5. *The Widow of Windsor*. London, Hale, 1974; New York, Putnam, 1978.
Norman Trilogy:
  1. *The Bastard King*. London, Hale, 1974; New York, Putnam, 1979.
  2. *The Lion of Justice*. London, Hale, 1975; New York, Putnam, 1979.
  3. *The Passionate Enemies*. London, Hale, 1976; New York, Putnam, 1979.

Plantagenet Saga:
  1. *The Plantagenet Prelude*. London, Hale, 1976; New York, Putnam, 1980.
  2. *The Revolt of the Eaglets*. London, Hale, 1977; New York, Putnam, 1980.
  3. *The Heart of the Lion*. London, Hale, 1977; New York, Putnam, 1980.
  4. *The Prince of Darkness*. London, Hale, 1978; New York, Putnam, 1980.
  5. *The Battle of the Queens*. London, Hale, 1978; New York, Putnam, 1981.
  6. *The Queen from Provence*. London, Hale, 1979; New York, Putnam, 1981.
  7. *Edward Longshanks*. London, Hale, 1979; as *Hammer of the Scots*, New York, Putnam, 1981.
  8. *The Follies of the King*. London, Hale, 1980; New York, Putnam, 1982.
  9. *The Vow on the Heron*. London, Hale, 1980; New York, Putnam, 1982.
  10. *Passage to Pontefract*. London, Hale, 1981; New York, Putnam, 1982.
  11. *The Star of Lancaster*. London, Hale, 1981; New York, Putnam, 1982.
  12. *Epitaph for Three Women*. London, Hale, 1981; New York, Putnam, 1983.
  13. *Red Rose of Anjou*. London, Hale, 1982; New York, Putnam, 1983.
  14. *The Sun in Splendour*. London, Hale, 1982; New York, Putnam, 1983.
  15. *Uneasy Lies the Head*. London, Hale, 1982; New York, Putnam, 1984.
Queens of England Series:
  1. *My Self, My Enemy*. London, Hale, 1983; New York, Putnam, 1984.
  2. *Queen of This Realm: The Story of Queen Elizabeth I*. London, Hale, 1984; New York, Putnam, 1985.
  3. *Victoria Victorious*. London, Hale, 1985; New York, Putnam, 1986.
  4. *The Lady in the Tower*. London, Hale, and New York, Putnam, 1986.
  5. *The Courts of Love*. London, Hale, 1987; New York, Putnam, 1988.
  6. *In the Shadow of the Crown*. London, Hale, 1988; New York, Putnam, 1989.

Novels as Elbur Ford

Poison in Pimlico. London, Laurie, 1950.
Flesh and the Devil. London, Laurie, 1950.
The Bed Disturbed. London, Laurie, 1952.
Such Bitter Business. London, Heinemann, 1953; as *Evil in the House*, New York, Morrow, 1954.

Novels as Kathleen Kellow

Danse Macabre. London, Hale, 1952.
Rooms at Mrs. Oliver's. London, Hale, 1953.
Lilith. London, Hale, 1954.
It Began in Vauxhall Gardens. London, Hale, 1955.
Call of the Blood. London, Hale, 1956.
Rochester, The Mad Earl. London, Hale, 1957.
Milady Charlotte. London, Hale, 1959.
The World's a Stage. London, Hale, 1960.

Novels as Ellalice Tate

Defenders of the Faith. London, Hodder and Stoughton, 1956.
The Scarlet Cloak. London, Hodder and Stoughton, 1957.
The Queen of Diamonds. London, Hodder and Stoughton, 1958.
Madame du Barry. London, Hodder and Stoughton, 1959.
This Was a Man. London, Hodder and Stoughton, 1961.

Novels as Philippa Carr (series: Daughters of England)

Daughters of England series:
1. *The Miracle at St. Bruno's*. London, Collins, and New York, Putnam, 1972.
2. *The Lion Triumphant*. London, Collins, and New York, Putnam, 1974.
3. *The Witch from the Sea*. London, Collins, and New York, Putnam, 1975.
4. *Saraband for Two Sisters*. London, Collins, and New York, Putnam, 1976.
5. *Lament for a Lost Lover*. London, Collins, and New York, Putnam, 1977.
6. *The Love-Child*. London, Collins, and New York, Putnam, 1978.
7. *The Song of the Siren*. London, Collins, and New York, Putnam, 1980.
8. *The Drop of the Dice*. London, Collins, and New York, Putnam, 1981.
9. *The Adultress*. London, Collins, and New York, Putnam, 1982.
10. *Zipporah's Daughter*. London, Collins, 1983; as *Knave of Hearts*, New York, Putnam, 1983.
11. *Voices in a Haunted Room*. London, Collins, and New York, Putnam, 1984.
12. *The Return of the Gypsy*. London, Collins, and New York, Putnam, 1985.
13. *Midsummer's Eve*. London, Collins, and New York, Putnam, 1986.
14. *The Pool of St. Branok*. London, Collins, and New York, Putnam, 1987.
The Changeling. London, Collins, and New York, Putnam, 1989.

OTHER PUBLICATIONS

Other as Jean Plaidy

The Triptych of Poisoners. London, Hale, 1958.
The Rise [Growth, End] of the Spanish Inquisition. London, Hale, 3 vols., 1959–61; as *The Spanish Inquisition: Its Rise, Growth, and End*, New York, Citadel Press, 1 vol., 1967.
The Young Elizabeth (for children). London, Parrish, and New York, Roy, 1961.
Meg Roper, Daughter of Sir Thomas More (for children). London, Constable, 1961; New York, Roy, 1964.
The Young Mary Queen of Scots (for children). London, Parrish, 1962; New York, Roy, 1963.
Mary, Queen of Scots, The Fair Devil of Scotland. London, Hale, and New York, Putnam, 1975.

*   *   *

Writing under various pseudonyms, Eleanor Burford Hibbert has been one of the most prolific and popular romance writers of the past several decades. Most of her Jean Plaidy historical romances are based upon the lives of actual women in history; her Victoria Holt romances sparked a renewed interest in women's gothic; and her Philippa Carr "historical gothics" made her prominent as a writer of family saga romances.

As Jean Plaidy, Hibbert seems to have attempted to describe the lives of prominent European women since the Renaissance. Although they are not uniform in quality, her books all follow a similar pattern. She selects a woman in history—usually connected by birth, marriage, or illicit liaison to a Royal family—whose story she can place at the center of a tale written as though virtually all of the events of the period had had a direct effect on the heroine. Many of the Plaidy books come in sets or series about families: the Plantagenets, the Medicis, the Tudors, the Stuarts, the Georgians, the Victorians, the French Royal Family, the Queens of England. The books are popularized history, employing a relatively unsophisticated level of historical analysis, although her knowledge of detail is encyclopedic. She avoids historical controversy by relying upon standard interpretations of character and event and by defining history as it might have appeared to the woman at the center of the story. Some characters who recur in more than one story may seem sympathetic when at the center of the action and unsympathetic when peripheral.

Hibbert's Victoria Holt gothics usually divide into one of three plot types: the "suspicious husband" plot in which the heroine thinks her husband is trying to kill her, "the governess gothic" in which a heroine becomes an employee in a mansion where she discovers terror and danger, and the "adventuress" plot featuring women who engage in impostures and frauds. Holt's villains are crazed members of the mansion's family who use the ancient milieu as a weapon against innocent characters. All her Holt novels are set between the French Revolution and the Edwardian Age and she sometimes uses the Pacific Islands or Australia as backgrounds along with her more traditional background of landed estates in England. She is particularly adept at creating terror in a confined space and in imagining interesting motives for her villains. In her gothics, the past always holds the key to the mystery and the heroine must find out the truth before it is too late.

Hibbert's most fully realized gothics include *Mistress of Mellyn* and *Bride of Pendorric*, both set in Cornwall, one of her favorite locales. *Mistress of Mellyn* (1960), the novel that set off the wide popularity of gothic romances in the ensuing decade and a half, has close narrative and thematic similarities to both *Jane Eyre* and *Rebecca*. The governess of the tale solves the mystery of the past, nurtures the hero's troubled daughter, and earns the hero's love by redeeming him from his disillusion about women. Two of her Victoria Holt novels, *My Enemy the Queen* and *The Queen's Confession*, are about actual women in history but the stories are told from the first person as are her other Holt books.

Hibbert's Philippa Carr novels, which she calls "historical gothics," follow the fortunes of a particular family through several generations. The series began with *The Miracle at St. Bruno's*, a novel of the English Reformation. Subsequent books pose two women of a later generation against a background of historical controversy, often involving the religious wars of the period. These books have not been as popular as her Plaidy and Holt novels.

Hibbert is prolific, probably too much so for her own good. Over the past decade, there has been a significant decrease in the complexity and believability of her plots in all three types. Her best work is probably her first five or six Victoria Holt novels when she was setting standards for a host of authors who imitated her formula, although few could match her in the evocation of terror. In recent years, her writing has become tired and dull; her plots, diffuse.

Mistress of Mellyn, however, deserves a place among the most important gothic romances of the century, placing Hibbert (as Holt) near the top of her field as an heiress of Daphne du Maurier, whose *Rebecca* remains the premier gothic romance of our time.

—Kay Mussell

HONEYMAN, Brenda. See **CLARKE, Brenda.**

HOOPER, Kay. Also writes as Kay Robbins. American. Address: c/o Dell Publishing, 666 Fifth Avenue, New York, New York 10103, U.S.A.

ROMANCE AND HISTORICAL PUBLICATIONS

Novels (series: Delaneys; Hagen; Shamrock)

Lady Thief. New York, Dell, 1981.
Breathless Surrender. New York, Dell, 1982.
Mask of Passion. New York, Dell, 1982.
Breathless Summer. New York, Dell, 1982.
On the Wings of Magic. New York, Dell, 1983.
C. J.'s Fate. New York, Bantam, 1984.
If There Be Dragons. New York, Bantam, 1984.
Pepper's Way. New York, Bantam, 1984.
Something Different. New York, Bantam, 1984.
Illegal Possession. New York, Bantam, 1985.
Rafe the Maverick (Shamrock). New York, Bantam, 1986.
Rebel Waltz. New York, Bantam, 1986.
Time after Time. New York, Bantam, 1986.
Larger than Life. New York, Bantam, 1986.
Adelaide the Enchantress (Delaneys). New York, Bantam, 1987.
In Serena's Web (Hagen). New York, Bantam, 1987.
Raven on the Wing (Hagen). New York, Bantam, 1987.
Rafferty's Wife (Hagen). New York, Bantam, 1987.
Zach's Law (Hagen). New York, Bantam, 1987.
Summer of the Unicorn. New York, Bantam, 1988.
The Fall of Lucas Kendrick (Hagen). New York, Bantam, 1988.
Unmasking Kelsey (Hagen). New York, Bantam, 1988.
Outlaw Derek (Hagen). New York, Bantam, 1988.
Shades of Gray (Hagen). New York, Bantam, 1988.
Captain's Paradise (Hagen). New York, Bantam, 1988.
Golden Flames (Delaneys). New York, Bantam, 1988.
Velvet Lightning (Delaneys). New York, Bantam, 1988.
It Takes a Thief (Hagen). New York, Bantam, 1989.
Aces High (Hagen). New York, Bantam, 1989.

Novels as Kay Robbins

Return Engagement. New York, Berkley, 1982.
Elusive Dawn. New York, Berkley, 1983.
Kissed by Magic. New York, Berkley, 1983.
Taken by Storm. New York, Berkley, 1983.
Moonlight Rhapsody. New York, Berkley, 1984.
Eye of the Beholder. New York, Berkley, 1985.

Belonging to Taylor. New York, Berkley, 1986.
On Her Doorstep. New York, Berkley, 1986.

*   *   *

Another of the Loveswept series' prolific authors, Kay Hooper is one of the best of the contemporary romance writers now at work. Hooper has created memorable characters and placed them in intriguing circumstances. She also has shown a willingness to expand the limits of romance fiction and succeeded in her attempt.

Hooper's creation of a series of books connected by the machinations of the wiley government agent, Hagen, has been a delight, and each installment has been eagerly awaited. Many readers will be disappointed that the recently published *Aces High* is to be the last in the series.

While *In Serena's Web* is not really in the Hagen series, it does introduce the first of Hagen's "victims." It is Serena's brother, Josh Long, who is the hero of *Raven on the Wing*. He falls in love with a woman who seems to be a criminal but is in reality one of Hagen's undercover agents. Josh is a wealthy, powerful man himself, but his carefully selected cadre of top aides are, one by one, drawn into Hagen's net. While each takes center stage in turn, the others always return to help in the newest assignment. One standing joke among the closely knit circle of friends is that Hagen is an inadvertent matchmaker. Each adventure leads to the development of romance for one of his agents so that he runs the risk of losing all of them to love. Counting *In Serena's Web*, there are eleven Hagen books. The others are *Raven on the Wing*, *Rafferty's Wife*, *Zach's Law*, *The Fall of Lucas Kendrick*, *Unmasking Kelsey*, *Outlaw Derek*, *Shades of Gray*, *Captain's Paradise*, *It Takes a Thief*, and *Aces High*. Hagen himself remains very much in the background throughout, although he gradually emerges as a character, as opposed to being simply a name. He is manipulative and secretive, often sending agents into the field without all the available information. This understandably upsets the agents and makes them reluctant to work for him. Hooper gets a measure of revenge in *Aces High* by pairing Hagen off with another agent.

Along with Iris Johansen and Fayrene Preston, Kay Hooper has collaborated on several trilogies centering on the Delaney family. She wrote *Rafe the Maverick* for the Shamrock Trinity, the story of the Delaney brothers. For the Delaneys of Killaroo, the story of three sisters in the Australian branch of the family, she wrote *Adelaide the Enchantress*. Based on the success of these trilogies, the three authors developed two Delaney "prequel" trilogies: The Untamed Years and The Untamed Years II. Both *Golden Flames* and *Velvet Lightning* tell the story of Falcon Delaney and Victoria Fontaine, but the latter book branches out to an intriguing story about the fate of Abraham Lincoln as seen through the eyes of Marcus Tyrone and Catherine Waltrip.

In 1988, Hooper also experimented with a longer fantasy/science fiction romance, *Summer of the Unicorn*. Set in some indefinite future, beginning on another planet, it is a story of a quest for a myth and dreams, as personified by the unicorn. The hero, Hunter Morgan, is on a quest to find the mythical beast in order to win a throne. The heroine, Siri, is daughter of a mermaid and guardian of the unicorns and other mythical or extinct animals. Together they fight Hunter's evil brother who would destroy the last unicorns. They also must find a way in which they will be able to exist together, since according to legend, Siri cannot live outside the Valley of the Unicorns.

Hooper is one of the best romance novelists writing today. She writes with humor and passion, develops her characters well and is adept at creating intriguing plots. Her willingness to experiment also is promising for the future development of the genre.

—Barbara E. Kemp

———————

HOPE, Anthony. Pseudonym for Sir Anthony Hope Hawkins. British. Born in London, 9 February 1863. Educated at St. John's Foundation School, London and subsequently in Leatherhead, Surrey; Marlborough School, 1876–81; Balliol College, Oxford (exhibitioner, then scholar), 1881–85, graduated with honours; Middle Temple, London, called to the Bar 1887. Served the government in the Editorial and Public Branch Department, 1914–18. Married Elizabeth Somerville Sheldon in 1903; two sons and one daughter. Practiced law in London, 1887–94, then full-time writer. Liberal Parliamentary candidate for South Buckinghamshire, 1892. Chairman of the Committee, 1900–03, 1907, and founder of the pension scheme, Authors' Society. Knighted, 1918. *Died 8 July 1933.*

ROMANCE AND HISTORICAL PUBLICATIONS

Novels

A Man of Mark. London, Remington, 1890; New York, Holt, 1895.
Father Stafford. London and New York, Cassell, 1891.
Mr. Witt's Widow. London, Innes, and New York, United States Book Company, 1892.
A Change of Air. London, Methuen, 1893; New York, Holt, 1894.
Half a Hero. London, Innes, 2 vols., 1893; New York, Harper, 1 vol., 1893.
The Dolly Dialogues. London, Westminster Gazette, and New York, Holt, 1894.
The God in the Car. London, Methuen, 2 vols., 1894; New York, Appleton, 1 vol., 1894.
The Indiscretion of the Duchess. Bristol, Arrowsmith, and New York, Holt, 1894.
The Prisoner of Zenda. Bristol, Arrowsmith, and New York, Holt, 1894.
The Lady of the Pool. New York, Appleton, 1894.
The Chronicles of Count Antonio. London, Methuen, and New York, Appleton, 1895.
Phroso. London, Methuen, and New York, Stokes, 1897.
Rupert of Hentzau. Bristol, Arrowsmith, and New York, Holt, 1898.
Simon Dale. London, Methuen, and New York, Stokes, 1898.
The King's Mirror. London, Methuen, and New York, Appleton, 1899.
Quisanté. London, Methuen, and New York, Stokes, 1900.
Captain Dieppe. New York, Doubleday, 1900; London, Skeffington, 1918.
Tristam of Blent. London, Murray, and New York, McClure, 1901.
The Intrusions of Peggy. London, Smith Elder, and New York, Harper, 1902.
Double Harness. London, Hutchinson, and New York, McClure, 1904.
A Servant of the Public. London, Methuen, and New York, Stokes, 1905.
Sophy of Kravonia. Bristol, Arrowsmith, and New York, Harper, 1906.
Tales of Two People. London, Methuen, 1907.

Helena's Path. New York, McClure, 1907.
The Great Miss Driver. London, Methuen, and New York, McClure, 1908.
Second String. London, Nelson, and New York, Doubleday, 1910.
Mrs. Maxon Protests. London, Methuen, and New York, Harper, 1911.
A Young Man's Year. London, Methuen, and New York, Appleton, 1915.
Beaumaroy Home from the Wars. London, Methuen, 1919; as *The Secret of the Tower*, New York, Appleton, 1919.
Lucinda. London, Hutchinson, and New York, Appleton, 1920.
Little Tiger. London, Hutchinson, and New York, Doran, 1925.

Short Stories

Sport Royal and Other Stories. London, Innes, 1893; New York, Holt, 1895.
Lover's Fate, and A Friend's Counsel. Chicago, Neely, 1894.
Frivolous Cupid. New York, Platt Bruce, 1895.
Comedies of Courtship. London, Innes, and New York, Scribner, 1896.
The Heart of Princess Osra and Other Stories. London, Longman, and New York, Stokes, 1896.
A Man and His Model (includes "An Embassy"). New York, Merriam, n.d.
A Cut and a Kiss. Boston, Brown, 1899.
Love's Logic and Other Stories. New York, McClure, 1908.

OTHER PUBLICATIONS

Plays

The Adventure of Lady Ursula (produced New York and London, 1898). New York, Russell, and London, French, 1898.
When a Man's in Love, with Edward Rose (produced London, 1898).
Rupert of Hentzau, adaptation of his own novel (produced Glasgow, 1899; London, 1900).
English Nell, with Edward Rose, adaptation of the novel *Simon Dale* by Hope (produced London, 1900).
Pilkerton's Peerage (produced London, 1902). London, French, 1909.
Captain Dieppe, with Harrison Rhodes (produced New York, 1903; London, 1904).
Helena's Path, with Cosmo Gordon-Lennox (produced London, 1910).
In Account with Mr. Peters, in *Windsor Magazine* (London), December 1914.
Love's Song (produced London, 1916).
The Philosopher in the Apple Orchard: A Pastoral. New York, French, 1936.

Other

Dialogue (address). Privately printed, 1909.
The New—German—Testament: Some Texts and a Commentary. London, Methuen, 1914; New York, Appleton, 1915.
Militarism, German and British. London, Darling, 1915.
Why Italy Is with the Allies. London, Clay, 1917.
Selected Works. London, Harrap, 10 vols., 1925.
Memories and Notes. London, Hutchinson, 1927; New York, Doubleday, 1928.

*

Critical Studies: *Anthony Hope and His Books* by Charles Mallet, London, Hutchinson, 1935; "The Prisoner of the Prisoner of Zenda: Hope and the Novel of Society" by S. Gorley Putt, in *Essays in Criticism 6* (Brill, Buckinghamshire), 1956.

*   *   *

Anthony Hope is best known for *The Prisoner of Zenda*, yet he was a man of several parts, both in his career and as a writer. The son of a clergyman, he became a Balliol College Scholar, was elected President of the Oxford Union, and took a First Class degree. He was called to the Bar in 1887, and faced a brilliant legal career. Interested in politics, he made a respectable stand as a Liberal against the incumbent Conservative member in 1892. Although he was to become a prolific novelist with over 30 works of fiction to his credit, he remained ambivalent to this profession. He called his popular romance *Phroso* "tosh," while taking most pains over a serious novel such as *Quinsanté* which he did not expect the public to notice. In 1918 he was knighted for his war work.

He began his published writing with social satire and political fiction. *The Dolly Dialogues*, first published in *The Westminster Review*, received wide attention as a witty and pointed dramatisation of fashionable foibles. *The God in the Car*, which still has interest as a sensitive study of political life, achieved some notoriety for its parallel with the career of Cecil Rhodes. Willy Rushton, chief founder of the Great Omofaga Company, rides roughshod over his colleagues and suppresses his own humanity in his quest for power. Maggie Dennison, who loves him, finally refuses to interpose in his life, recognising this will compromise his real desires. In *Quinsanté* Hope was to portray another odious but brilliant politician who is himself exploited for his popularity, and dies of heart failure after making a speech.

But in 1890, in *A Man of Mark*, a privately printed collection of short stories, he had experimented with adventure set in an imaginary world—in this case the South American state of Aurentland. At the end of 1893, exuberant with winning a legal case, he imagined a tale set in a middle European country, Ruritania, and wrote *The Prisoner of Zenda* in spare moments during four weeks. When it appeared the following year its immediate and overwhelming success made him abandon the law for a full-time writing career—perhaps to the detriment of his fiction, for he never recaptured the fresh immediacy of this early work.

The appeal of *The Prisoner of Zenda* lies both in its high spirits and in the way in which its world of Ruritania is at once contemporary and antique. A world of feudal ceremony, it can be reached by train (although once there Rassendyll tends to ride on horseback). The castle is half modern residence and half gothic pile with fearful mysteries. In the world of firearms, honour can still be defended in a duel, and political struggles are fought out in romantic adventure. Uniting the two worlds is Rudolph Rassendyll, himself a genetic throwback to a romantic *alliance*, in 1733, of the redheaded Rudolph the Third of Ruritania. He is a modern Cavalier, brave, excellent horseman and swordsman, yet with a hint of self-mockery in his heroism. His narrative voice seduces the reader into willing complicity with the absurd story. The plot itself has some archetypal patterns—double identity, the conflict between Black Michael and Red Ephberg, the love for an unreachable Princess. But any submerged symbolism is contained within the rapidly moving narrative.

Rupert of Hentzau returns to Ruritania some years later. Black Michael is dead, and Rudolph's red hair shows streaks of grey. The danger is now from Rupert, who captures a compromising letter from Queen (earlier Princess) Flavia. Rudolph destroys the

letter and saves the Queen's honour—at the cost of his life. The theme of chivalry present in the earlier work here becomes overworked; the basis for the plot is thin, and the narrator is the old retainer Fritz von Tarlehein, who is no substitute for Rudolph. But the narrative pace is still fast, the swashbuckling is exhilarating. Hope wrote other tales of Ruritania, none of them wholly successful. *The Heart of Princess Osra*, for instance, is a series of tales from the country in olden times, in which Osra is educated through five loves—from Stephen the silversmith to the Grand Duke of Mittenheim—into the meanings of the passion. But what the first readers found charming the modern audience is likely to consider heavy-handed and sentimental.

Hope had a weak historical imagination. In *Simon Dale*, for example, he explores his theme of chivalry in 17th-century England. Dale, a country boy, goes to London and enters the employ of Charles I. He offers his pure love to Nell Gwyn against that of the dissolute monarch. Later he leaves the King, respectfully telling him that he pays too high a price for his power. He lives to bring up his own children honorably. By comparison *Sophy of Kravonia* also has an incredible plot. Sophy, an Essex kitchen maid, rises to become for a few days Queen of Kravonic, a Balkan state split into warring parties, and to revenge her dead royal husband. Yet, although Hope had not been to the Balkans, the novel gives a convincing sense of present-day eastern Europe, and it remains one of his most readable novels. It was one of the books that turned Graham Greene to a life of travel.

Hope was one of the group of adventure story writers that included Robert Louis Stevenson, Rider Haggard and Conan Doyle. But he never achieved a consistent narrative style, and he remains notable for *The Prisoner of Zenda* alone. This introduced "Ruritania" into the English language; it was directly reflected in prose imitations, dramatisations, and film: more remarkably, it entered into the popular consciousness. It established the romantic image of middle Europe for England and America.

—Louis James

———

HOPE, Margaret. See **KNIGHT, Alanna.**

———

HORNER, Lance, and Kyle ONSTOTT. Americans. **HORNER, Lance**: born Kenric Lancaster Horner in Stateville, New York, 5 August 1902. Educated at Boston University. Worked as a commercial art director, advertising copywriter, antique dealer. *Died in 1973.* **ONSTOTT, Kyle**: born in DuQuoin, Illinois, 12 January 1887. Had one son. Licensed by the American Kennel Club as an all-breeds judge. *Died in 1966.*

ROMANCE AND HISTORICAL PUBLICATIONS

Novels by Lance Horner (series: Falconhurst)

The Street of the Sun. New York, Abelard Schuman, 1956.
Falconhurst series:
  Mandingo, with Kyle Onstott. Richmond, Virginia, Denlinger, 1957; London, Longman, 1959.

Drum. New York, Dial Press, 1962; London, W. H. Allen, 1963.

Master of Falconhurst. New York, Dial Press, 1964; London, W. H. Allen, 1965.

Falconhurst Fancy. New York, Fawcett, 1966; London, W. H. Allen, 1967.

The Mustee. New York, Fawcett, 1967; London, W. H. Allen, 1968.

Heir to Falconhurst. New York, Fawcett, 1968; London, W. H. Allen, 1969.

Flight to Falconhurst. New York, Fawcett, 1971; London, W. H. Allen, 1972.

Mistress of Falconhurst. New York, Fawcett, and London, W. H. Allen, 1973.

The Tattooed Road. Middleburg, Virginia, Denlinger, 1960; London, Souvenir Press, 1962; as *Santiago Road*, London, Pan, 1967.

Rogue Roman. New York, Pyramid, 1965; London, W. H. Allen, 1969.

Child of the Sun. London, W. H. Allen, 1966.

The Black Sun. New York, Fawcett, 1967; London, W. H. Allen, 1968.

The Mahound. New York, Fawcett, 1969.

Golden Stud. New York, Fawcett, 1975; as *Six-Fingered Stud*, London, W. H. Allen, 1975.

OTHER PUBLICATIONS by Kyle Onstott

Other

Your Dog as a Hobby, with Irving C. Ackerman. New York, Harper, 1940.

Beekeeping as a Hobby. New York, Harper, 1941.

The Art of Breeding Better Dogs. Washington, D.C., Denlinger, 1946.

*   *   *

As the above biography indicates, Lance Horner and Kyle Onstott have to be considered together, for though Onstott wrote only *Mandingo*, his name appears alone on two others and with Horner's on four more in most bibliographies; these six, along with the other eight, are solely by Horner.

Selling in the millions, but dismissed by critics as "trashy," "slimy," or even "regurgitory," Horner and Onstott's novels are formulaic in plot, theme, and character. The plot structure of all the novels is centered upon the system of slavery, whether in the anti-bellum South, the Caribbean, north Africa, or ancient Rome. The effect of slavery upon both masters and slaves is their one theme, and that theme can be summarized in a single phrase: sex, sadism, and miscegenation. Life is presented as being sex-obsessed and filled with violent cruelty resulting from that obsessive sex. The combination of sex and slavery creates a feverish tension among and between blacks and whites, and this tension provides the impetus for the action, which is often lurid. Not only is almost every imaginable form of sex included, but also such extremes of violence as crucifixion, biting through jugular veins, and boiling of human beings. Altogether, sex and violence are pervasive; indeed, they are the essence of Horner and Onstott's fiction.

The eight novels forming the "Falconhurst series" have been the most popular. They present, in discontinuous fashion, the lives of the Maxwell family, their acquaintances, and their slaves at Falconhurst plantation in southwestern Alabama from 1797 to 1887, and they fully illustrate the theme of sex, sadism, and miscegenation. Among the 25 major characters and 50 secondary ones of the eight novels, central is Ham(mond) Maxwell, who appears in all but *Heir to Falconhurst*. He grows up at Falconhurst, which is a slave-breeding plantation, considers it paradise, continually beds the female blacks while believing himself utterly superior to their race, finds sex with white women difficult, and is, whether intended so by the authors, a warped, pathetic bigot. His self-satisfaction is matched by the other white males, who revel in their crude, backward world, exalted by their faith in their superiority to all blacks. The white women, even the capable Dovie Verder of *Falconhurst Fancy* and *Flight to Falconhurst*, seem principally interested in bedding the black male slaves, the result of which is always more violence. Horner and Onstott's presentation of blacks is confused. Sympathy is shown to all. A few are given exceptional qualities, but most have a fear of responsibility and surrender completely to their sexual drives. Slavery is given most of the blame for their weaknesses, but at times they are also presented as being essentially children, savages, or animals. The authors seem uncertain in creating a focused image of blacks; however, sex and callous degradation emerge as the two prime elements of that image and contribute significantly to the total image of the novels. For many readers, novels such as the Falconhurst series provide their only knowledge of the ante-bellum South, just as did earlier romances of "moonlight and magnolias," but whereas those works sentimentalized plantation life, the Falconhurst novels present it as a violent world of inter-racial sex and sadism.

The heroes of the non-Falconhurst novels are similar to Ham Maxwell in their virility, but they are more often slaves, at least for a time, than slaveowners. (However, the heroes of *The Mahound* and *The Black Sun* are respectively a slave trader and a Haitian plantation owner.) *The Tattooed Road*, *The Street of the Sun*, and *Rogue Roman* follow the changes of fortune for their heroes from freeman to slave and back to freedom. This formula is not greatly varied in *Golden Stud*, as well as *Master of Falconhurst*, *The Mustee*, and *Falconhurst Fancy*, by having a black male of light skin pretend to be white, with the ever-present threat of discovery providing suspense and plot twists. All of the non-Falconhurst heroes are in the picaresque tradition, young men attempting to survive, to gain freedom and wealth, and to make love as often as possible by their wit, courage, and looks. Since the novels are so male-dominated, women—black or white, high or low, Southern or Roman—are sex objects. The hero generally has two or three "loves," aside from casual sexual encounters, in the course of a novel before finally winning an idealized woman, previously unattainable because of social differences.

It is easy to ridicule the novels of these two men. There are errors in chronology and anachronisms; the plots are episodic, particularly in the non-Falconhurst novels, and contain massive amounts of coincidence; the characters, both black and white, are stereotypes which are repeated again and again; and sex and violence are so overdone as to become almost parodic. Nevertheless, the novels still sell; the millions in print increase, and since the death of Horner, Harry Whittington (as Ashley Carter) has carried on the line with *Sword of the Golden Stud* (1977) and *Taproots of Falconhurst* (1979). It seems likely that, whatever critics may think of the image the novels present of slavery, that image of sex, sadism, and miscegenation will continue to have popular appeal. *Why* is another question.

—Earl F. Bargainnier

HOWARD, Linda. Pseudonym for Linda S. Howington. American. Born in Gadsden, Alabama, 3 August 1950. Married Gary F. Howington. Secretary, Bowman Transportation, Gadsden, 1969–86. Agent: Robin Rue, Anita Diamant Agency, 310 Madison Avenue, New York, New York 10017. Address: 116 Louise Avenue, Gadsden, Alabama 35903, U.S.A.

ROMANCE AND HISTORICAL PUBLICATIONS

Novels (series: Midnight Rainbow; Sarah's Child)

All That Glitters. New York, Silhouette, 1982.
An Independent Wife. New York, Silhouette, 1982.
Against the Rules. New York, Silhouette, 1983.
Come Lie with Me. New York, Silhouette, 1984.
Tears of the Renegade. New York, Silhouette, 1985.
Sarah's Child. New York, Silhouette, 1985.
The Cutting Edge. New York, Silhouette, 1985.
Midnight Rainbow. New York, Silhouette, 1986.
Almost Forever (Sarah's Child). New York, Silhouette, 1986.
Diamond Bay (Midnight Rainbow). New York, Silhouette, 1987.
Bluebird Winter (Sarah's Child). New York, Silhouette, 1987.
Heartbreaker (Midnight Rainbow). New York, Silhouette, 1987.
White Lies (Midnight Rainbow). New York, Silhouette, 1988.
MacKenzie's Mountain. New York, Silhouette, 1989.

*

Linda Howard comments:
I work with two aims in mind. One is to write for myself, period. The other is to entertain the reader. That's what writers are for.

*   *   *

Although the body of Linda Howard's work is still relatively small, her popularity is indicated by the reissuing of at least one of her novels in a ''classics'' series, only five years after its original publication. Her work is distinguished by strong character development and fast-paced, well-developed action.

Howard's heroines are determined, independent, modern women and her heroes are powerful, often dangerous men. While such portrayals can easily degenerate into romance stereotypes, Howard's skill as a writer breathes real life into the characters and saves them from becoming mere clichés. Writing somewhat longer novels, she has the time fully to develop her characters, providing them with context and meaning.

The high pressure world of business is a favorite setting for Howard. The heroes in these stories wield a great deal of power and tend to be both ruthless and possessive. Their attempts to manipulate and even dominate their women lead to deep rifts in their relationships that are difficult to heal. Nikolas Constantinos is willing to take Jessica Stanton as his mistress in *All That Glitters*, as long as he gets some shares of stock he wants from her. Wrongly assuming she had ''sold'' herself to an older, wealthy husband for security, he punishes her with cruelty, in part because he despises himself for wanting her. In *Sarah's Child*, widowed Rome Matthews, also a strong businessman, marries Sarah but refuses to have children. When she does become pregnant, he puts her in an almost untenable position by refusing to have anything to do with the child. Rome's right-hand man, Max Conroy, uses his charm to insinuate himself into the good graces of Claire Westbook (*Almost Forever*) before taking over the com-

pany for which she works. In *The Cutting Edge*, Brett Rutland puts Tessa Conway through hell when he mistakenly believes she is guilty of embezzlement. Like Nikolas, he despises himself for still loving her even though he believes she is a criminal.

Howard has also created several heroes who are even more hard-edged and dangerous. Government agents, they move in situations presenting physical danger as well as the emotional turmoil between men and women. In *Midnight Rainbow*, retired agent Grant Sullivan must rescue Jane Greer from Central American rebels. In *Diamond Bay*, Grant's boss, Kell Sabin, is rescued and cared for by Rachel Jones. She, in turn, is critically wounded in a shoot-out with Kell's pursuers. Another of Sabin's agents, Lucas Stone, involves Jay Granger in a deadly charade to trap a dangerous criminal (*White Lies*). These men, living in the shadows, find it difficult to admit their need of anyone, which makes their developing relationships even more tenuous.

Facing Howard's strong heroes, who make their own rules and laws, her heroines often endure hurt and humiliation. Yet the men discover that in hurting someone they love they hurt themselves too. They are torn by their very possessiveness and protectiveness. Howard's women have much to forgive, but the men they win are worthy of their pain.

—Barbara E. Kemp

HOWARD, Linden. See MANLEY-TUCKER, Audrie.

HOWARD, Mary. Pseudonym for Mary Mussi, née Edgar; also writes as Josephine Edgar. British. Born in London, 27 December 1907. Educated privately. Married Rudolph F. Mussi in 1934; one son and one daughter. Past chairwoman, Society of Women Writers and Journalists. Recipient: Romantic Novelists Association Major award, 1960, 1979, 1980, and Elinor Glyn award, 1961. Agent: David Higham Associates, 5–8 Lower John Street, London W1R 3PE. Address: 30 Oxford Court, Oxford Road, London SW15 2LQ, England.

ROMANCE AND HISTORICAL PUBLICATIONS

Novels

Windier Skies. London, Long, 1930.
Dark Morality. London, Lane, 1932.
Partners for Playtime. London, Collins, 1938.
Stranger in Love. London, Collins, 1939; New York, Doubleday, 1941.
It Was Romance. London, Collins, 1939.
The Untamed Heart. London, Collins, 1940.
Far Blue Horizons. London, Collins, 1940; New York, Doubleday, 1942.
Uncharted Romance. New York, Doubleday, 1941.
Devil in My Heart. London, Collins, and New York, Doubleday, 1941.
To-morrow's Hero. London, Collins, 1941; New York, Doubleday, 1942.
Reef of Dreams. London, Collins, 1942.
Gay Is Life. London, Collins, and New York, Doubleday, 1943.
Have Courage, My Heart. London, Collins, 1943.

Anna Heritage. London, Collins, 1944; New York, Arcadia House, 1945.

The Wise Forget. London, Collins, 1944; New York, Arcadia House, 1945.

Family Orchestra. London, Collins, and New York, Arcadia House, 1945.

The Man from Singapore. London, Collins, 1946.

Return to Love. New York, Arcadia House, 1946.

Weave Me Some Wings. London, Collins, 1947.

The Clouded Moon. New York, Arcadia House, 1948.

Strange Paths. London, Collins, 1948.

Star-Crossed. London, Collins, 1949.

There Will I Follow. London, Collins, and New York, Arcadia House, 1949.

Two Loves Have I. London, Collins, 1950; as *Mist on the Hills*, New York, Arcadia House, 1950.

Bow to the Storm. London, Collins, 1950; as *The Young Lady*, New York, Arcadia House, 1950.

Sixpence in Her Shoe. London, Collins, 1950; New York, Arcadia House, 1954.

Promise of Delight. London, Collins, and New York, Arcadia House, 1952.

The Gate Leads Nowhere. London, Collins, 1953.

Fool's Haven. London, Collins, 1954; New York, Arcadia House, 1955 (?).

Sew a Fine Seam. London, Hale, 1954.

Before I Kissed. London, Collins, 1955.

The Grafton Girls. London, Collins, 1956.

A Lady Fell in Love. London, Hale, 1956.

Shadows in the Sun. London, Collins, 1957.

Man of Stone. London, Collins, 1958.

The Intruder. London, Collins, 1959.

The House of Lies. London, Collins, 1960; as *The Crystal Villa*, New York, Lenox Hill Press, 1970.

More Than Friendship. London, Collins, 1960.

Surgeon's Dilemma. London, Collins, 1961.

The Pretenders. London, Collins, 1962.

The Big Man. London, Collins, 1965.

The Interloper. London, Collins, 1967.

The Repeating Pattern. London, Collins, 1968.

The Bachelor Girls. London, Collins, 1968.

The Pleasure Seekers. London, Collins, 1970.

Home to My Country. London, Collins, 1971.

A Right Grand Girl. London, Collins, 1972.

The Cottager's Daughter. New York, Dell, 1972.

Soldiers and Lovers. London, Collins, 1973.

Who Knows Sammy Halliday? London, Collins, 1974.

The Young Ones. London, Collins, 1975.

The Spanish Summer. London, Collins, 1977.

Mr. Rodriguez. London, Collins, 1979.

Success Story. London, Piatkus, 1984.

Novels as Josephine Edgar

My Sister Sophie. London, Collins, 1964; New York, Pocket Books, 1974.

The Dark Tower. London, Collins, 1966; New York, Dell, 1969.

The Dancer's Daughter. London, Collins, 1968; New York, Dell, 1970.

Time of Dreaming. London, Collins, 1968; New York, Pocket Books, 1974.

The Devil's Innocents. London, Collins, 1972; New York, Dell, 1975.

The Stranger at the Gate. London, Collins, 1973; New York, Pocket Books, 1975.

The Lady of Wildersley. London, Macdonald and Jane's, 1975; New York, Pocket Books, 1977.

Duchess. London, Macdonald and Jane's, and New York, St. Martin's Press, 1976.

Countess. London, Macdonald and Jane's, and New York, St. Martin's Press, 1978.

Margaret Normanby. Loughton, Essex, Piatkus, 1982; New York, St. Martin's Press, 1983.

Bright Young Things. London, Piatkus, and New York, St. Martin's Press, 1986.

*

Mary Howard comments:

Until 1961 I wrote in the conventional light, popular romantic Style, but with *The Big Man* I began my series of more realistic romantic stories under the Mary Howard name, trying to combine a "good read" with a feeling of contemporary life, and avoiding the clichés of boy meets girl, boy is separated from girl, boy finds girl again/is reconciled after explanations/happy ending. This series culminated with *The Spanish Summer* and *Mr. Rodriguez*.

I also began the Josephine Edgar books, set in the 19th century, and developed the family saga in *Duchess* and *Countess*, which begin in 1900 and end in the early 1920's.

*   *   *

Mary Howard published her first romantic novels as long ago as the 1930's, but her work has never dated. In 1960 she won the very first Romantic Novelists Association Major award for the best romantic novel of the year with *More Than Friendship*.

Her most recent novels show all the freshness of a new talent, happily combined with the experience of a mature one. She keeps well in tune with the times, both in theme and outlook. *Soldiers and Lovers*, set in World War II, accurately reflected the feelings and difficulties of that era from the point of view of three women, each different in age, class, and background, brought together in a small country village to battle with ration-cards, blackouts, children, the constant anxiety of the death-dealing enemy in the sky—and other, more personal, agonies: of love, tenderness, passion, and parting which only war can bring, and only those who have lived through it can fully understand.

Today she accepts the more liberal attitude towards sexual morals with easy grace, but with due regard for delicate sensibilities. *Mr. Rodriguez*, which won the 1980 Major award, is a model of its kind. The setting is mildly exotic (Spain), the topic very much up-to-date (a happy extra-marital affair which hurts no one but the participants), the ending sad, but satisfying, and totally lacking in sentimentality. The characters, too, are recognisably of their decade, the 1970's.

Many of her recent novels have been set on the Spanish coast for the very good reason that Howard's artist daughter Susan married a Spanish surgeon and now lives in Barcelona. Howard visits her Spanish family every summer and this gives her plenty of opportunity to absorb the atmosphere of Spain's holiday coast (a useful background for romantic novels) and observe both the Spanish people and English people on holiday. Among other memorable novels with this setting are *A Right Grand Girl* and *The Pleasure Seekers*.

Howard's alter ego, Josephine Edgar, writes period novels set mainly in the 19th century (e.g., the gothic *The Lady of Wildersley*). Outstanding among these are *Duchess*, and its sequel *Countess*—a rags-to-riches story about Viola Corbett, a Victorian working-class girl, the illegitimate offspring of a solid Yorkshire mother and an itinerant Italian acrobat. A girl of instinctive poise, driving ambition, and great natural beauty, she engineers her own transfer from Leeds to London and a job in a fashionable store as a springboard to better things. Needless to say not all the "things" are better, Viola is a tough and resilient, as well as an enchanting heroine and in the end she gets her deserts.

These two are among the best of the "blockbusters" of the 1970's, coming as they do from the pen of an experienced and accomplished author who knows—and respects—her audience. It was with *Countess* that Josephine Edgar won her third Major award.

—Elizabeth Grey

HOWATCH, Susan (Elizabeth, née Sturt). British. Born in Leatherhead, Surrey, 14 July 1940. Educated at King's College, London, LL.B. 1961. Married Joseph Howatch in 1964; one daughter. Law clerk, Masons of London, 1961–62; secretary, R.C.A. Victor Record Corporation, 1964–65. Lives in London. Agent: Harold Ober Associates, 40 East 49th Street, New York, New York 10017, U.S.A.; or, Aitken and Stone, 29 Fernshaw Road, London SW10 0TG, England

ROMANCE AND HISTORICAL PUBLICATIONS

Novels

The Dark Shore. New York, Ace, 1965; London, Hamish Hamilton, 1972.
The Waiting Sands. New York, Ace, 1966; London, Hamish Hamilton, 1972.
Call in the Night. New York, Ace, 1967; London, Hamish Hamilton, 1972.
The Shrouded Walls. New York, Ace, 1968; London, Hamish Hamilton, 1972.
April's Grave. New York, Ace, 1969; London, Hamish Hamilton, 1973.
The Devil on Lammas Night. New York, Ace, 1970; London, Hamish Hamilton, 1973.
Penmarric. New York, Simon and Schuster, and London, Hamish Hamilton, 1971.
Cashelmara. New York, Simon and Schuster, and London, Hamish Hamilton, 1974.
The Rich Are Different. New York, Simon and Schuster, and London, Hamish Hamilton, 1977.
Sins of the Fathers. New York, Simon and Schuster, and London, Hamish Hamilton, 1980.
The Wheel of Fortune. New York, Simon and Schuster, and London, Hamish Hamilton, 1984.
Glittering Images. New York, Knopf, and London, Collins, 1987.
Glamorous Powers. New York, Knopf, and London, Collins, 1988.
Ultimate Prizes. New York, Knopf, and London, Collins, 1989.

*   *   *

Susan Howatch began writing as a child and started submitting her work for publication as a teenager. Her first novel, *The Dark Shore*, was published when she was in her 20's. Despite her surprise at critics' classification of it as a "modern gothic," *The Dark Shore* launched her career as a writer in this genre.

She then produced, in rapid succession, five more modern gothics and two gothic epics or sagas.

Although she's been a resident in the United States since 1964, Howatch's love of Scotland and England, especially Cornwall, is reflected in the British settings of many of her novels. Howatch believes (*The Writer*, May 1974) that settings should provide more than just "scenic glamour"; location should be integral to the story both in terms of plot and atmosphere. So *April's Grave* is set in a remote part of Scotland reachable only by boat; in this novel, and in *The Waiting Sands*, the remoteness itself becomes psychologically unnerving and suspenseful.

Howatch's interest in realism and mystery is also seen in her plots and her characterizations. She shows a fondness for such plot devices as anonymous phone calls, missing characters, shallow graves, surprise murderers, and touches of the occult. Her characters are as three-dimensional as possible, given the constraints of this genre. Howatch says she pays more attention than other gothic writers to her heroes' characterizations, trying to show them as more than just a "splendid facade." Howatch's heroines are spunky, sensible, and risk-taking, as the genre demands, but also can be vulnerable when the occasion arises. Her realistic characters are portrayed with a range of traits—both positive and negative—and interests, including sexual interests and desires. But, they also fit the gothic "formula" enough to move the plot along and provide mystery and suspense as well as romance.

Howatch's six gothics contain all of the above elements, in various mixes and with varying degrees of success. She perceived *The Dark Shore* originally as the story of the hero, for example. Jon was "burdened with loneliness" and his problems were triggered, to some extent, by an anonymous phone call about his dead wife. Howatch tells us, however, that her editor saw this first book as a romantic mystery about a girl in distress at a sinister house by the sea and—"instant gothic."

April's Grave, *Call in the Night*, and *The Waiting Sands* all offer the reader sexual entanglements along with missing characters and shallow graves to advance the plot. Karen, the heroine of *April's Grave*, is introduced to the hero, an English professor, and turned, " . . . expecting to see a white-haired, stooping scholar, and had come face to face with all six foot of the charm and grace and frank sexual interest which emanated from Neville Bennett." To get the mystery started, however, is not quite so easy. Not only is April's grave missing but, as one reviewer notes, "April herself has been missing for three years without causing the slightest ripple of concern" (*Best Seller*, 1 March 1974). Eventually, though, April's buried suitcases are accidentally discovered and the web of mystery grows, culminating in another killing and a surprise murderer.

Just as Karen, April's twin, initiated the search for April, so Claire sets off to Europe to find her missing sister, in *Call in the Night*. Here again are shallow graves, broken engagements, and entangled relationships! Claire persists in searching for Gina despite her growing fascination with Garth (the hero) and despite her qualms that he may be not only a murderer, but also a womanizer.

Sexual entanglements also dominate *The Waiting Sands*. Decima invites her oldest friend, Rachel (the heroine), to her 21st birthday party at remote Roshven off the coast of Scotland. But the invitation carries with it a plea for protection from a suspected murder plot by her husband Charles. Decima is due to inherit Roshven on her birthday—if she lives that long! Unusual plot twists involve Charles's sexual liasion with a house guest, gossip and innuendo, suspense, quicksand, and a double murder.

In *The Shrouded Walls* Howatch builds suspense with a surprise heir, a marriage of convenience, murder, and a touch of the occult—a local witch who supplies potions and poisons. She also uses the heroine's persistent curiosity to trigger the plot resolution. This novel, however, is not regarded as one of Howatch's better gothics. One reviewer terms it "strictly a ho-hum affair" (*Best Seller*, 1 December 1971), and a second reviewer credits Howatch with producing interesting characters propelled by believable motives but criticizes her for "sometimes melodramatic prose" (*Library Journal*, 15 January 1972).

Black magic, only a secondary theme in *The Shrouded Walls*, becomes central in *The Devil on Lammas Night*. Howatch's skillful interweaving of realistic characters and complex situations makes a bizarre theme plausible and frightening. The plot involves Nicola and Evan (former lovers) and their possible reconciliation. The action focuses primarily around the sinister Tristan Poole who has leased Colwyn Court (Evan's ancestral home). Poole's Society for the Propagation of Nature Foods is in actuality a witches' coven—and Poole, a warlock. Howatch provides supernatural occurrences, convenient "accidental" deaths, and a celebration of Lammas Night featuring a plot to use the heroine in a Satanic wedding.

Despite considerable success with these modern gothics, Howatch's reputation as a writer of note was not firmly established until the publication of her best-selling gothic epic or saga *Penmarric* in 1971. It was followed by another highly acclaimed saga, *Cashelmara*. In *Penmarric*, set in Cornwall, and *Cashelmara*, set in Ireland, England, and America, the sprawling and complex tale of several generations of a family is told in turn by each of the characters from their own moral and emotional perspective. These two novels set the style for her family sagas (but not gothics), *The Rich Are Different*, *Sins of the Fathers*, and *The Wheel of Fortune*. It may be that the sagas offer Howatch a more flexible vehicle for pursuing her love of realism. Certainly they allow her more exploration of sexual themes and more complex character development, especially of the male characters who tend to dominate her sagas.

Howatch's career entered a new phase in the late 1980's with the publication of *Glittering Images* and *Glamorous Powers* (the first two books of a planned trilogy about the Church of England in the 20th century, with the third in progress, *Ultimate Prizes*). Each novel is narrated by an Anglican clergyman and continues Howatch's exploration of both sexual themes and male character development. Her particular focus in this series is on the nature of reality, the conflict between illusions and reality, and the often large disparity between public image and private self. At the core is the issue of father/son relationships and the misunderstandings which arise, resulting from and causing the images both fathers and sons project and protect. The female characters are not terribly well developed in these novels. They are somewhat sexually stereotyped, possibly because the reader sees the women's images only through the viewpoint of the male narrators.

Most critics view this trilogy as the start of a whole new era in Howatch's writing. However, it may be that *The Wheel of Fortune* provides a bridge between Howatch's epics or sagas and these recent, more philosophical novels. While *The Wheel of Fortune* is somewhat more gothic in its tone, focusing on a family's obsession with the manor, Oxmoon, it also explores the far-reaching impact of uncontrollable forces such as fortune or chance on human behavior. As a result, this novel starts to raise some of the philosophical issues explored in much greater depth in this current trilogy.

—Josephine A. Ruggiero and Louise C. Weston

HOY, Elizabeth. Pseudonym for (Alice) Nina Conarain. Irish. Born in Dublin. Married. Worked as a nurse and secretary-receptionist; staff member, *Daily News*, London, Address: c/o Mills and Boon Ltd., 18–24 Paradise Road, Richmond, Surrey TW9 1SR, England.

ROMANCE AND HISTORICAL PUBLICATIONS

Novels

Love in Apron Strings. London, Hodder and Stoughton, 1933.
Roses in the Snow. London, Mills and Boon, 1936.
Crown for a Lady. London, Mills and Boon, 1937.
Sally in the Sunshine. London, Mills and Boon, 1937.
Shadow of the Hills. London, Mills and Boon, 1938.
Stars over Egypt. London, Mills and Boon, 1938.
You Belong to Me. London, Mills and Boon, 1938.
Mirage for Love. London, Mills and Boon, 1939.
Runaway Bride. London, Mills and Boon, 1939.
You Took My Heart. London, Mills and Boon, 1939; Toronto, Harlequin, 1959.
Enchanted Wilderness. London, Mills and Boon, 1940.
Heart, Take Care! London, Mills and Boon, 1940.
It Had to Be You. London, Mills and Boon, 1940.
You Can't Lose Yesterday. London, Mills and Boon, 1940.
I'll Find You Again. London, Mills and Boon, 1941.
Take Love Easy. London, Mills and Boon, 1941.
Come Back My Dream. London, Mills and Boon, 1942; Toronto, Harlequin, 1959.
Hearts at Random. London, Mills and Boon, 1942.
Proud Citadel. London, Mills and Boon, 1942; Toronto, Harlequin, 1975.
Ask Only Love. London, Mills and Boon, 1943.
One Step from Heaven. London, Mills and Boon, 1943.
You Can't Live Alone. London, Mills and Boon, 1944.
Give Me New Wings. London, Mills and Boon, 1944; New York, Arcadia House, 1945.
Sylvia Sorelle. London, Mills and Boon, 1944.
Heart's Haven. London, Mills and Boon, 1945; as *The Heart Remembers*, New York, Arcadia House, 1946.
It's Wise to Forget. London, Mills and Boon, 1945; as *Shatter the Rainbow*, New York, Arcadia House, 1946.
Dear Stranger. London, Mills and Boon, 1946; New York, Arcadia House, 1947.
Sword in the Sun. London, Mills and Boon, 1946.
To Win a Paradise. London, Mills and Boon, 1947; Toronto, Harlequin, 1960.
The Dark Loch. London, Mills and Boon, 1948.
Though I Bid Farewell. London, Mills and Boon, 1948.
Background to Hyacinthe. London, Mills and Boon, 1949.
Immortal Morning. London, Mills and Boon, 1949.
June for Enchantment. London, Mills and Boon, 1949.
The Vanquished Heart. London, Mills and Boon, 1949.
For Love's Sake Only. New York, Arcadia House, 1951.
Silver Maiden. London, Mills and Boon, 1951.
When You Have Found Me. London, Mills and Boon, and New York, Arcadia House, 1951.
White Hunter. London, Mills and Boon, 1951; Toronto, Harlequin, 1961.
The Enchanted. London, Mills and Boon, 1952.
The Web of Love. London, Mills and Boon, 1952.
Fanfare for Lovers. London, Mills and Boon, 1953.
If Love Were Wise. London, Mills and Boon, 1954; Toronto, Harlequin, 1970.

So Loved and So Far. London, Mills and Boon, 1954; Toronto, Harlequin, 1965.

Snare the Wild Heart. London, Mills and Boon, 1955; Toronto, Harlequin, 1966.

Who Loves Believes. London, Mills and Boon, 1955; Toronto, Harlequin, 1965.

Young Doctor Kirkdene. London, Mills and Boon, 1955; Toronto, Harlequin, 1959.

Because of Doctor Danville. London, Mills and Boon, 1956; Toronto, Harlequin, 1958.

My Heart Has Wings. London, Mills and Boon, 1957; Toronto, Harlequin, 1959.

Do Something Dangerous. London, Mills and Boon, 1958; Toronto, Harlequin, 1959.

City of Dreams. London, Mills and Boon, 1959; Toronto, Harlequin, 1960.

Dark Horse, Dark Rider. London, Mills and Boon, 1960; Toronto, Harlequin, 1967.

Dear Fugitive. London, Mills and Boon, and Toronto, Harlequin, 1960.

The Door into the Rose Garden. London, Mills and Boon, 1961.

Heart, Have You No Wisdom? London, Mills and Boon, 1962.

Her Wild Voice Singing. London, Mills and Boon, 1963.

Homeward the Heart. London, Mills and Boon, 1964; Toronto, Harlequin, 1965.

Flowering Desert. London, Mills and Boon, 1965; Toronto, Harlequin, 1966.

The Faithless One. London, Mills and Boon, 1966; Toronto, Harlequin, 1967.

My Secret Love. London, Mills and Boon, 1967.

Honeymoon Holiday. London, Mills and Boon, 1967; Toronto, Harlequin, 1968.

Be More Than Dreams. London, Mills and Boon, 1968; Toronto, Harlequin, 1969.

Music I Hear with You. London, Mills and Boon, 1969; Toronto, Harlequin, 1970.

It Happened in Paris. London, Mills and Boon, 1970; Toronto, Harlequin, 1971.

African Dream. London, Mills and Boon, 1971.

Into a Golden Land. London, Mills and Boon, and Toronto, Harlequin, 1971.

Immortal Flower. London, Mills and Boon, and Toronto, Harlequin, 1972.

That Island Summer. London, Mills and Boon, and Toronto, Harlequin, 1973.

The Girl in the Green Valley. London, Mills and Boon, 1973; Toronto, Harlequin, 1974.

Shadows on the Sand. London, Mills and Boon, and Toronto, Harlequin, 1974.

The Blue Jacaranda. London, Mills and Boon, and Toronto, Harlequin, 1975.

When the Dream Fades. London, Mills and Boon, 1980.

OTHER PUBLICATIONS

Other as Nina Conarain

Editor, with Kay Boyle and Laurence Vail, *365 Days*. New York, Harcourt Brace, and London, Cape, 1936.

*   *   *

Elizabeth Hoy's novels reflect her Irish childhood and her early fondness for writing which later evolved into a journalistic career with the London *Daily News*. From this, it was a short step to writing romance novels which she began publishing in the 1930's. She is one of those writers who feels that she can only write about things she has experienced herself, and that her characters, although imaginary, must have some "foundation in reality." Consequently, her novels often reflect experiences with incidents, background, and people in her life. She spent some time in nurse's training before she had to leave it, but the experiences remained with her, lending a greater degree of authenticity to her early doctor/nurse novels.

A holiday trip to Australia provided her with sufficient material for her to use in her writing and she describes the people and the country with comfortable familiarity. Besides Australia, Hoy uses Ireland, England, and Africa as settings for her other novels.

Because of her own inclination and, perhaps, because of the period she wrote in, Hoy's romances have a more traditional outlook as she describes her heroines and heroes. She also has a touch of the true romantic's ability to make her readers believe the unbelievable. Not, however, without some very genuine soul-searching by the heroine.

The Blue Jacaranda illustrates this and offers a good example of her writing ability. In this novel, Lena Shannon travels from England to Queensland, Australia, to stay with her Uncle Tom. Before her arrival, he dies, leaving a will that thoroughly insures impossible complications. She is to live on his estate for six months with the other inheritor, Rod Carron, and his daughter. By the end of six months, he expects them to marry each other or both lose any inheritance. The fact that Rod has a daughter is an added difficulty, although Lena and she become friends immediately. Both Lena and Rod resent the conditions and are extremely suspicious of each other for they can't feel that such a marriage would work. The estate stands between them as each wonders about the other's willingness to marry for money. Personality clashes and instinctive efforts at self-defense continue to complicate matters until a devastating cyclone strikes the estate. The cyclone is the final touch and shows them the way to resolve their differences.

Shadows on the Sand has an entirely different mood. Alison Gray is sent by a research institution to Cairo to substitute for an elderly secretary. Her arrival instantly brings Scott Crane, her temporary boss, storming down on her as he refuses to let her stay. He is forced to wait for a replacement and he does let her work. Alison's fresh sweetness is not so ingrained that she cannot stand up for herself and frequent clashes occur between her and Scott. The novel takes place against the background of scientific research, primitive desert country, and the excitement of new archaeological findings. Secondary characters such as other members of the team and an old girl friend play their roles in furthering the plot complications, as do sand storms, antagonistic natives, and unexpected dangers such as falling rocks near the excavation.

Romance readers find Hoy's novels satisfyingly filled with the right mixture of romance, danger, and suspense. Her heroines are well drawn, and not the conventional naive or helpless romance heroine. Her heroes are also a complex assortment; they keep their feet firmly on the ground, their hands and minds in control of every tiniest detail but their hearts, which unaccountably refuse to behave. It is this constant source of amusement which keeps her readers so involved as they wonder just how the "mighty will fall" under Hoy's adept connivance.

—Arlene Moore

HUFFORD, Susan. American. Born in Cincinnati, Ohio, 15 December 1940. Educated at DePauw University, Greencastle, Indiana, B.A. 1960; Temple University, Philadelphia, M.A. 1961. Actress and singer. Agent: Jane Jordan Browne, 410 South Michigan Avenue, Room 828, Chicago, Illinois 60615, U.S.A.

ROMANCE AND HISTORICAL PUBLICATIONS

Novels

Midnight Sailing. New York, Popular Library, 1975.
The Devil's Sonata. New York, Popular Library, 1976.
A Delicate Deceit. New York, Popular Library, 1976.
Cove's End. New York, Popular Library, 1977.
Satan's Sunset. New York, Popular Library, 1977.
Skin Deep. New York, Popular Library, 1978.
Trial of Innocence. New York, Popular Library, 1978.
Melody of Malice. New York, Popular Library, 1979.
Going All the Way. New York, New American Library, 1980.
Reflections. New York, Seaview, 1981; London, Methuen, 1982.

*   *   *

Susan Hufford tells fast-paced stories of beautiful women plunged into frightening situations and familiar, seemingly tranquil surroundings; surface peace is disrupted by evil and death, and even friends and lovers cannot escape suspicion, as heroines seek to come to terms with their family, their past, and their tenuous future.

Her tetralogy, *Midnight Sailing*, *The Devil's Sonata*, *A Delicate Deceit*, and *Satan's Sunset*, traces the changing adventures of 25-year-old Hilda Hughes, a petite yet beautiful university professor from Ann Arbor, Michigan, as she deals with terror on romantic cruiseships, amid tropical paradises, and in stunning mansions. Old friends and new acquaintances always seem involved in strange conspiracies that seek to use and abuse her wealth and her psychic sensitivity; handsome psychotic males play power games that end in sadism and death; and her newly discovered sister, Ursula, proves a neurotic, murderous tool of diabolical schemers, both male and female. Her father's sins are visited upon his daughters, who are pursued by vengeful madmen and cultists. The father's adultery endangers both sisters as a psychotic returns from the grave to bring more madness and death in *The Devil's Sonata*. Hilda's love for a crippled but forceful pianist draws her into greater danger in *Satan's Sunset*, wherein a mad artist and a rejected lover plot her demise. Sensitive to threatening atmospheres, but unsure of whom to trust, Hilda usually makes bad judgments, believing the smooth tales of villains and fearing the contradictions and hesitations of friends.

In *Cove's End* New York's top model, a popular jet-setter, escapes to her grandparents' home in Maine, seeking peace and quiet and a new sense of self, only to find a childhood friend murdered, her inheritance a mystery, and her own life threatened. Her lover's acts make him a suspect, despite the absence of motive, and her only relative proves no relative at all.

Hufford's most compelling work, *Trial of Innocence*, set in the 19th century, records the nightmarish experiences of a young girl who leaves a beloved aunt to follow a desperate but cryptic call for aid from her dead sister's husband; but the invitation proves a hoax, and she is left a penniless stranger in a strange land where in-laws believe her a scheming fortune hunter and where, amid Victorian elegance in a rambling Tudor home, an intricate web of lies threatens sanity and life. The naive and in-nocent heroine must learn to cope with her own unexpected fascination with a cyncial, worldly man who both frightens and allures; to compete with a beautiful, catty adventuress whose feminine wiles seem to have already ensnared both love and wealth; and to deal with amoral children whose feigned innocence and make-believe fantasies hide a murderous reality. Here, and throughout Hufford's canon, the secret compulsions of the seeming innocent endanger the truly innocent.

—Gina Macdonald

———

HUGHES, Matilda. See **MacLEOD, Charlotte.**

———

HULL, E(dith) M(aude). British. Married. Lived in Derbyshire.

ROMANCE AND HISTORICAL PUBLICATIONS

Novels

The Sheik. London, Nash, 1919; Boston, Small Maynard, 1921.
The Shadow of the East. London, Nash, and Boston, Small Maynard, 1921.
The Desert Healer. London, Nash, and Boston, Small Maynard, 1923.
The Sons of the Sheik. Boston, Small Maynard, 1925; London, Nash, 1926.
The Lion-Tamer. London, Nash, and New York, Dodd Mead, 1928.
The Captive of Sahara. London, Methuen, and New York, Dodd Mead, 1931.
The Forest of Terrible Things. London, Hutchinson, 1939; as *Jungle Captive*, New York, Dodd Mead, 1939.

OTHER PUBLICATIONS

Other

Camping in the Sahara. London, Nash, 1926; New York, Dodd Mead, 1927.

*   *   *

Robert Hichens, writing a decade earlier, first made a romantic speciality out of deserts. So, too, Elinor Glyn sent a heroine to consult with a sphinx in the desert (in *His Hour*, 1909). Katharine Rhodes, popular in the 1910's, wrote tales of "the fire and passion of the relentless desert." But it was E. M. Hull who, with *The Sheik* in 1919, first put the desert on the map as a fine place for sexual encounter. The heroine, beautiful but haughty Diana Mayo, pale-skinned but spirited English aristocrat, is the first romantic heroine to be physically assaulted, to learn in the course of 300 pages to enjoy it, and to marry the man who kept on doing it. The morality of whether a man guilty of rape should be ultimately rewarded is highly questionable. Diana's adventures with the Sheik were, possibly, a compensation for E. M. Hull's own lack of amorous excitement, for she was married to a dull pig-breeder called Percy, and, though her real name was Edith Maude, preferred to be called Diana like her ravished heroine.

At the time of writing *The Sheik*, Hull had never set foot in a desert. But this was no disadvantage, for her imagination filled in the background of sunsets, dust, and thirst. The excitement of nightly struggles in the sheik's barbarous yet luxurious tent in the oasis are interspersed with other ''eastern'' thrills—attacks by rebel Arabs, horse-taming, horse-shooting, servant beating, escapes on horseback into the cruel and inhospitable wastes, the threat of death by vulture or by sandstorm, attempted suicide by the heroine, attempted rape by a rival sheik which proves to be far worse than submission to Diana's own regular assaulter, murder, and many violent deaths of the expendable natives. Erotic passion is linked with fear and pain, and there is a streak of sado-masochism running through the book. The rival rapist is seized by the sheik and throttled to death before Diana's eyes: ''With the terrible smile always on his lips, he choked him slowly to death, till the dying man's body arched and writhed in his last agony, till blood burst from his nose and mouth, pouring over the hands that held him like a vice.''

The initial rape is distanced, and thus made more discreet, by being reported in the past historic: ''She *had* fought until the unequal struggle *had* left her exhausted and helpless in his arms, until her whole body was one agonised ache from the brutal hands that forced her to compliance, until her courageous spirit was crushed by the realization of her own powerlessness.'' And subsequent struggles are conveyed by constant repetition of crush, kiss, hot, fierce, fire, lips, thrill. In one dialogue between Diana and the sheik, the author finds no less than 11 different variations on ''he said'' and ''she said.'' Thus, on a single page of text, Diana burst out passionately, and she choked furiously. Then she began desperately. He replied drily. She gasped. He went on evenly. She whispered with dry lips. His reply was given carelessly. She whispered again, but this time jerkily. He continued sarcastically. She murmured faintly.

When she has given up gasping and learned to obey and love, he expresses himself more tenderly. The pinnacle of his passion is a kiss on the upturned palm of her hands. This act of devotion had already been performed in previous romances (e.g., by the blind hero of Florence Barclay's *The Rosary*) but it was in *The Sheik* that it became an established convention, and a gesture which Rudolph Valentino, star of the film version of *The Sheik*, borrowed from the script and used as his trade-mark of passion in other roles.

Diana's relationship with the desert echoes her relationship with the man. The desert both repels and lures her, it tames and brutalises her. ''It was the desert at last, the desert that she felt she had been longing for all her life. It was welcoming her softly with the faint rustle of the whispering sand, the mysterious charm of its billowy, shifting surface that seemed beckoning her to penetrate further and further into its unknown obscurities.''

Hull followed her highly successful first novel with *The Sons of the Sheik*, but the sons lacked their father's strength and brutality, and the work is sentimental rather than passionate or violent. Hull visited Algeria to produce the non-fiction *Camping in the Sahara* and a small handful of other eastern/desert romance novels, but none had the same impact as her first, which was responsible for sparking off a whole series of sandy romances from other writers, and established the convention of desert passion whose basic elements have remained almost unchanged to the present day. Time and again, never seeming to learn from the experience of others, a spirited girl goes off into the desert and is captured by a mysterious and cruel Arab who tames her. Love blossoms, whereupon it transpires that, for all his foreign ways, he is no arab, but as white-skinned and safely European as herself.

A contemporary, but rival, novelist, Philip Gibbs, wished to make quite clear the distinction between Hull's books, and his own novels, which, while selling well, never reached the peak of *The Sheik*: ''My own view is that such freak sales as those of *The Sheik* are not representative of the general reading public of average intelligence—a public which is steadily growing larger and more critical.''

—Rachel Anderson

HUNTER, Elizabeth (Mary Theresa). Also writes as Isobel Chace. Born in 1934. Address: c/o Mills and Boon Ltd., 18–24 Paradise Road, Richmond, Surrey TW9 1SR, England.

ROMANCE AND HISTORICAL PUBLICATIONS

Novels

Cherry-Blossom Clinic. London, Mills and Boon, 1961; Toronto, Harlequin, 1962.
Spiced with Cloves. London, Mills and Boon, 1962; Toronto, Harlequin, 1966.
Watch the Wall My Darling. London, Mills and Boon, 1963.
No Sooner Met. London, Mills and Boon, 1965.
There Were Nine Castles. London, Mills and Boon, 1967.
The Crescent Moon. London, Mills and Boon, 1973; Toronto, Harlequin, 1974.
The Tree of Idleness. London, Mills and Boon, 1973; Toronto, Harlequin, 1974.
The Tower of the Winds. London, Mills and Boon, 1973; Toronto, Harlequin, 1974.
The Beads of Nemesis. London, Mills and Boon, 1974; Toronto, Harlequin, 1975.
The Bride Price. London, Mills and Boon, 1974; Toronto, Harlequin, 1976.
The Bonds of Matrimony. London, Mills and Boon, and Toronto, Harlequin, 1975.
The Spanish Inheritance. London, Mills and Boon, and Toronto, Harlequin, 1975.
The Voice in the Thunder. London, Mills and Boon, and Toronto, Harlequin, 1975.
The Sycamore Song. London, Mills and Boon, 1975; Toronto, Harlequin, 1976.
The Realms of Gold. London, Mills and Boon, 1976; Toronto, Harlequin, 1977.
Pride of Madeira. Toronto, Harlequin, 1977.
Bride of the Sun. New York, Silhouette, 1980.
The Lion's Shadow. New York, Silhouette, 1980.
A Touch of Magic. New York, Silhouette, 1981.
One More Time. London, Hodder and Stoughton, 1982.
Written in the Stars. London, Hodder and Stoughton, 1982.
A Silver Nutmeg. New York, Silhouette, 1982.
A Tower of Strength. New York, Silhouette, 1983; London, Hodder and Stoughton, 1984.
Fountains of Paradise. New York, Silhouette, 1983.
London Pride. New York, Silhouette, and London, Hodder and Stoughton, 1983.
A Time to Wed. New York, Silhouette, 1984.
Rain on the Wind. New York, Silhouette, 1984.
Shared Destiny. London, Hodder and Stoughton, 1984.
The Tides of Love. New York, Silhouette, 1988.

Novels as Isobel Chace

The African Mountain. London, Mills and Boon, 1960.

The Japanese Lantern. London, Mills and Boon, 1960; Toronto, Harlequin, 1966.

Flamingoes on the Lake. London, Mills and Boon, 1961; Toronto, Harlequin, 1965.

The Song and the Sea. London, Mills and Boon, 1962; Toronto, Harlequin, 1963.

The Hospital of Fatima. London, Mills and Boon, 1963; Toronto, Harlequin, 1975.

The Wild Land. London, Mills and Boon, 1963; Toronto, Harlequin, 1964.

A House for Sharing. London, Mills and Boon, 1964; Toronto, Harlequin, 1965.

The Rhythm of Flamenco. London, Mills and Boon, and Toronto, Harlequin, 1966.

The Spider's Web. London, Mills and Boon, 1966; as *The Secret Marriage*, 1966.

The Land of the Lotus-Eaters. London, Mills and Boon, 1966; Toronto, Harlequin, 1971.

A Garland of Marigolds. London, Mills and Boon, and Toronto, Harlequin, 1967.

Brittany Blue. London, Mills and Boon, 1967.

Oranges and Lemons. London, Mills and Boon, 1967; Toronto, Harlequin, 1968.

The Saffron Sky. London, Mills and Boon, and Toronto, Harlequin, 1968.

The Damask Rose. London, Mills and Boon, 1968; Toronto, Harlequin, 1969.

A Handful of Silver. London, Mills and Boon, 1968; Toronto, Harlequin, 1969.

The Legend of Katmandu. London, Mills and Boon, 1969.

Flower of Ethiopia. London, Mills and Boon, 1969.

Sugar in the Morning. London, Mills and Boon, 1969; Toronto, Harlequin, 1970.

The Day That the Rain Came Down. London, Mills and Boon, and Toronto, Harlequin, 1970.

The Flowering Cactus. London, Mills and Boon, 1970; Toronto, Harlequin, 1971.

To Marry a Tiger. London, Mills and Boon, 1971; Toronto, Harlequin, 1972.

The Wealth of the Islands. London, Mills and Boon, 1971; Toronto, Harlequin, 1972.

Home Is Goodbye. London, Mills and Boon, 1971; Toronto, Harlequin, 1972.

The Flamboyant Tree. London, Mills and Boon, 1972; Toronto, Harlequin, 1973.

The English Daughter. London, Mills and Boon, 1972.

Cadence of Portugal. London, Mills and Boon, 1972; Toronto, Harlequin, 1973.

A Pride of Lions. London, Mills and Boon, 1972; Toronto, Harlequin, 1973.

The Tartan Touch. London, Mills and Boon, 1972; Toronto, Harlequin, 1973.

The House of Scissors. London, Mills and Boon, 1972; Toronto, Harlequin, 1974.

The Dragon's Cave. London, Mills and Boon, 1972; Toronto, Harlequin, 1974.

The Edge of Beyond. London, Mills and Boon, 1973; Toronto, Harlequin, 1974.

A Man of Kent. London, Mills and Boon, 1973; Toronto, Harlequin, 1974.

The Cornish Hearth. London, Mills and Boon, and Toronto, Harlequin, 1975.

A Canopy of Rose Leaves. London, Mills and Boon, 1976; Toronto, Harlequin, 1977.

The Clouded Veil. London, Mills and Boon, and Toronto, Harlequin, 1976.

The Desert Castle. Toronto, Harlequin, 1976.

Singing in the Wilderness. London, Mills and Boon, and Toronto, Harlequin, 1976.

The Whistling Thorn. Toronto, Harlequin, 1977.

The Mouth of Truth. Toronto, Harlequin, 1977.

Second Best Wife. Toronto, Harlequin, 1978.

*　　　*　　　*

Elizabeth Hunter has long been a popular romance writer with a particularly individual style of writing that is quite distinctive, although she also writes under the name of Isobel Chace.

She enjoys taking an improbable situation and making her readers believe it. She must—for she is a past master at "once upon a time" beginnings and "they lived happily ever after" endings. Her novels are "happy novels" regardless of the trials and suspense the heroine must encounter before she finds that strongest of havens, her loved one's arms.

In *The Bonds of Matrimony* Hero Kaufman needs to gain British nationality in order to migrate to Britain. To achieve it, she offers her farm in the drought-struck part of Kenya to Benedict Carmichael in exchange for a wedding ring. Morag Grant meets Pericles Holmes and his two children in *The Beads of Nemesis* while she is on a walking holiday in Greece. He takes her in charge so that she can mind the children, but, with true Greek thoroughness, he marries her out of hand before she really knows what is going on. These are typical of the stories that she writes as Elizabeth Hunter.

Writing under the name of Isobel Chace, she devises plots equally daring. *To Marry a Tiger* finds Ruth Arnold trying to protect her flighty sister and ending by being forced into marriage by Mario Verdecchio, a Sicilian. Although the encounter was innocent enough, she still had stayed the night in his home without a chaperon. Finally, Kirsty MacTaggart in *The Tartan Touch* finds herself married to Andrew Fraser, a stranger, within days of her father's death. He has come to Scotland from Australia to research family records, and, once he finds what he is looking for, he seems to sweep Kirsty along with him.

In each of these novels, the writer develops strong motivation, believable characters, and an added touch of romance. She has a special knack of describing the backgrounds that she portrays in her novels as she uses Scotland, the Mediterranean countries, and Australia as locales. She also includes special scenes and descriptions of each country in such a way that the reader has a sense of authenticity in the things she mentions. Certainly she depends heavily on various customs in these countries to help her make the story work. For instance, Ruth in *To Marry a Tiger* is unaware of the Sicilian concept of honor so that, when the marriage takes place, she believes it is solely because of the antiquated beliefs of the people and not because Mario is attracted to her.

Improbable as some of her plots seem, it is impossible for the reader not to become absorbed in the story almost immediately. Her characters emerge quite naturally as they move and speak against the background of the unfolding plot. Perhaps it is this element of characterization that makes her novels work, for she has a delicacy of touch in this facet of writing that few romance writers can match. She is able to make her heroines come alive in the nicest way as they meet and fall in love with the man in the story. Depth of character is woven lightly but effectively through her novels as both the girl and man react to the situation they find themselves in.

Hunter has recently stepped out of the standard romance formula. This departure has resulted in glowing reviews of her latest novel in the Silhouette line.

In *The Tides of Love*, Ruth Gaynor, an-up-and-coming actress is accused of murder! The murder happens in a crowded pub. During the confusion, Ruth receives a slash on her arm because she had been standing very close to the victim. She is held in custody temporarily and is finally released through the efforts of Aidan Wakefield, a barrister who represents her. Charges are eventually dropped for lack of evidence and Ruth retreats to Lindisfarne Island where she has inherited a cottage. A notorious "resting" actress is not quite in demand for new work, especially if she might yet be charged with the crime.

Aidan traces her there for he is anxious to help clear her of the charge. Predictably, he falls in love with her. Mysterious events about the cottage, a hidden art collection, and a not so subtle attempt on her life lend more than enough conflict and confusion to the story line.

What is enjoyable about this novel is the fact that Hunter has been able to maintain the sense of a typical romance, but has also added this new dimension to it. The combination of romance and mystery/murder, in this instance, does not take the novel out of Hunter's usual series. It can't be mistaken for a Harlequin Intrigue for instance. There are enough pending trouble, missing keys, and unknown phone callers to give it heightened suspense and excitement but the emphasis is on romance. General opinion is that Hunter has a winning combination going for her.

—Arlene Moore

HUNTER, Hall. See **MARSHALL, Edison.**

HURST, Fannie. American. Born in Hamilton, Ohio, 18 October 1887. Educated at Washington University, St. Louis, B.A. 1909; Columbia University, New York, 1910. Married Jacques S. Danielson in 1915 (died 1952). Actress in New York before becoming full-time writer. Chairwoman, Woman's National Housing Commission, 1936–37; member of the National Advisory Committee to the WPA, 1940–41; U.S. delegate to the U.N. World Health Assembly, Geneva. President, 1936–37, and vice-president, 1944–46, 1947, Authors League; trustee, Heckscher Foundation, 1940–60. D.Litt.: Washington University, 1953; Fairleigh Dickinson University, Rutherford, New Jersey. *Died 23 February 1968.*

ROMANCE AND HISTORICAL PUBLICATIONS

Novels

Star-Dust: The Story of an American Girl. New York, Harper, 1921.
Lummox. New York, Harper, 1923; London, Cape, 1924.
Appassionata. New York, Knopf, and London, Cape, 1926.
Mannequin. New York, Knopf, 1926.
A President Is Born. New York, Harper, and London, Cape, 1928.
Five and Ten. New York, Harper, and London, Cape, 1929.

Back Street. New York, Cosmopolitan, and London, Cape, 1931.
Imitation of Life. New York, Harper, 1933.
Anitra's Dance. New York, Harper, and London, Cape, 1934.
Great Laughter. New York, Harper, 1936; London, Cape, 1937.
Lonely Parade. New York, Harper, and London, Cape, 1942.
White Christmas. New York, Doubleday, 1942.
Hallelujah. New York, Harper, 1944.
The Hands of Veronica. New York, Harper, and London, Lane, 1947.
Anywoman. New York, Harper, and London, Cape, 1950.
The Name Is Mary. New York, Dell, 1951.
The Man with One Hand. London, Cape, 1953.
Family! New York, Doubleday, 1960.
God Must Be Sad. New York, Doubleday, 1961.
Fool—Be Still. New York, Doubleday, 1964; London, Hale, 1966.

Short Stories

Just Around the Corner: Romance en Casserole. New York, Harper, 1914.
Every Soul Hath Its Song. New York, Harper, 1916.
Gaslight Sonatas. New York, Harper, and London, Hodder and Stoughton, 1918.
Humoresque: A Laugh on Life with a Tear Behind It. New York, Harper, 1919.
The Vertical City. New York, Harper, 1922.
Song of Life. New York, Knopf, and London, Cape, 1927.
Procession. New York, Harper, and London, Cape, 1929.
We Are Ten. New York, Harper, 1937.

OTHER PUBLICATIONS

Plays

The Land of the Free, with Harriet Ford (produced New York, 1917).
Back Pay (produced New York, 1921).
Humoresque (produced New York, 1923).
It Is to Laugh (produced New York, 1927).

Screenplays: *The Younger Generation*, with Sonya Levien and Howard J. Green, 1929; *Lummox*, with Elizabeth Meehan, 1930.

Other

No Food with My Meals. New York, Harper, 1935.
Today Is Ladies' Day. New York, Home Institute, 1939.
Anatomy of Me: A Wonderer in Search of Herself. New York, Doubleday, 1958; London, Cape, 1959.

*

Manuscript Collections: Olin Library, Washington University, St. Louis; Goldfarb Library, Brandeis University, Waltham, Massachusetts; University of Texas, Austin.

Critical Study: *Myths about Love and Women: The Fiction of Fannie Hurst* by Mary Rose Shaughnessy, New York, Gordon Press, 1980.

*   *   *

Fannie Hurst may be the worst writer ever to have become an internationally famous best seller. In her heyday, she earned the more-or-less affectionate sobriquet "Queen of the Sob Sisters," but the only aspect of her work likely to inspire tears today would be its truly abysmal style and grammar.

Hurst's stock in trade was the ill-advised golden-hearted woman who gives her all to some unworthy man, and is not thereafter rewarded, in this world at any rate. Of all her many short stories and novels, probably the quintessential Hurst title was *Back Street*, a real tear jerker, later translated into a "three-hankie" moving picture. It is the long-drawn-out, painful story of Ray Schmidt, a flashily attractive young working girl of the turn of the century. Courted and admired by many men, Ray chooses to waste her young womanhood as the guilty secret of an ostensibly respectable married man's life. Her lover, Walter Saxel, is a pillar of the community, blessed with a lovely wife and three adored children. In the "back street" of his life, content to live on stolen bits and scraps of his affection and time, Ray lives a life of seclusion and degradation redeemed only by her lifelong devotion to the man she loves.

Walter loves too, in a selfish and possessive way—but he fails to make any provision for the woman he has kept hidden in a stuffy "love-nest," isolated from the world; and after his untimely death, Ray's declining years are a decrescendo of misery and privation. The moral lesson couldn't be plainer—and could scarcely be wordier, lasting as it does for hundreds of tear-soaked pages.

Hurst was a product of an age in which the double standards of conduct for men and women remained for the most part unchallenged; and she well understood the effects upon high spirited youth of censoriousness, continual, critical surveillance, and lack of guidance. If present day readers can still find a lesson worth learning in her writings, it must surely be that of gratitude that they live in a less puritanical era, one in which both men and women have greater freedom to shape their own lives than Hurst or her creation, Ray Schmidt, ever dreamed of.

—Joan McGrath

HUTTEN, Baroness von. American. Born Betsey Riddle in Erie, Pennsylvania, 14 February 1874. Educated in New York. Married Freiherr von Hutten zum Stolzenberg in 1897 (divorced 1909; regained American nationality, 1938); two sons and two daughters. *Died 26 January 1957.*

ROMANCE AND HISTORICAL PUBLICATIONS

Novels (series: Pam)

Miss Carmichael's Conscience: A Study in Fluctuations. Philadelphia, Lippincott, 1900; London, Pearson, 1902.
Marr'd in Making. Philadelphia, Lippincott, and London, Constable, 1901.
Our Lady of the Beeches. Boston, Houghton Mifflin, 1902; London, Heinemann, 1907.
Violett: A Chronicle. Boston, Houghton Mifflin, 1904.
Pam. London, Heinemann, 1904; New York, Dodd Mead, 1905.
Araby. New York, Smart Set, 1904.

He and Hecuba. New York, Appleton, 1905.
What Became of Pam. London, Heinemann, 1906; as *Pam Decides*, New York, Dodd Mead, 1906.
The One Way Out. New York, Dodd Mead, 1906.
The Halo. New York, Dodd Mead, and London, Methuen, 1907.
Beechy; or, The Lordship of Love. New York, Stokes, 1909; as *The Lordship of Love*, London, Hutchinson, 1909.
Kingsmead. London, Hutchinson, and New York, Dodd Mead, 1909.
The Green Patch. London, Hutchinson, and New York, Stokes, 1910.
Sharrow. London, Hutchinson, and New York, Appleton, 1910.
Mrs. Drummond's Vocation. London, Heinemann, 1913.
Maria. London, Hutchinson, and New York, Appleton, 1914.
Birds' Fountain. London, Hutchinson, and New York, Appleton, 1915.
Mag Pye. London, Hutchinson, and New York, Appleton, 1917.
The Bag of Saffron. London, Hutchinson, 1917; New York, Appleton, 1918.
Happy House. London, Hutchinson, 1919; New York, Doran, 1920.
Mothers-in-Law. London, Cassell, and New York, Doran, 1922.
Pam at Fifty. London, Cassell, and New York, Doran, 1924.
Julia. London, Hutchinson, and New York, Doran, 1924.
Eddy and Edouard. London, Hutchinson, 1928; New York, Doubleday, 1929.
The Loves of an Actress. London, Readers Library, 1929.
Pam's Own Story. London, Hutchinson, 1930; Philadelphia, Lippincott, 1931.
Swan House. London, Hutchinson, 1930.
Monkey-Puzzle. London, Long, 1932.
Mice for Amusement. London, Hutchinson, 1933; New York, Dutton, 1934.
The Mem. London, Hutchinson, 1934; as *Lives of a Woman*, New York, Dutton, 1935.
Die She Must. London, Hutchinson, 1934; New York, Dutton, 1936.
Cowardly Custard. London, Hutchinson, 1936; as *Gentlemen's Agreement*, New York, Dutton, 1936.
The Elgin Marble. London, Hutchinson, 1937; as *Youth Without Glory*, New York, Dutton, 1938.
What Happened Is This. London, Hutchinson, 1938; New York, Dutton, 1939.

Short Stories

Helping Hersey. New York, Doran, 1914; London, Skeffington, 1918.
Candy and Other Stories. London, Mills and Boon, 1925.
Flies. London, Mills and Boon, 1927.
The Curate's Egg: A Volume of Stories. London, Mills and Boon, 1930; Freeport, New York, Books for Libraries, 1961.
In the Portico and Others. London, Mills and Boon, 1931.
The Notorious Mrs. Gatacre and Other Stories. London, Hutchinson, 1933.

OTHER PUBLICATIONS

Other

The Courtesan: The Life of Cora Pearl. London, Davies, 1933.

Translator, *The Rocket to the Moon*, by Thea von Harbou. New York, World Wide, and London, Readers Library, 1930.

*   *   *

Baroness von Hutten produced some 40 novels and collections of short stories, published on both sides of the Atlantic in the first four decades of the century. Her first novel, *Miss Carmichael's Conscience*, was a conventional high-society romance. It was with *Pam* a few years later that resounding success came. *Pam* was immensely popular—it is the story of a society scandal, of the romantic elopement of a beautiful aristocratic English lady and a handsome Italian tenor, who settle in Italy (where people understand about these things and the landscape is romantic); Pam is their illegitimate child, and her story so enthralled readers that Baroness von Hutten produced several sequels, *What Became of Pam*, *Pam at Fifty*, and *Pam's Own Story*. After *Pam*, Baroness von Hutten's next great success was *Kingsmead* whose charming, wistful young hero, Tommy, Earl of Kingsmead, was much admired.

Hutten appeared never to be at a loss for a plot. Her cosmopolitan background allowed her to set her books in Britain, America, and Europe, and her characters came from all levels of society from the highest to the lowest. Some of her settings are very sleazy indeed: Margaret Pye (*Mag Pye*) the daughter of a gentleman fallen on reduced circumstances, is brought up in the Chelsea Workmen's Dwellings, and the central character of *Monkey-Puzzle* is the transparently named Jess Lightfoot, a prostitute who attempts to maintain a respectable front for the sake of her son, the son of a lord. (About the same time as *Monkey-Puzzle*, Hutten also produced a biography of Cora Pearl, *The Courtesan*.)

Hutten wrote at a great rate, and her writing was frequently praised for its crispness, facility and assurance. Her range as a writer was considerable. Although she made her name as a writer of romance novels and "family novels" of a fairly melodramatic nature, she also included some psychological portraiture, particularly in *Mothers-in-Law* in which are contrasted the characters of two mothers-in-law (one American, one Italian) of very different upbringing and outlook who meet with the marriage of their children, and in *Eddy and Edouard* in which the hero, the son of a French aristocrat and her American husband, finds himself torn between two countries and two identities.

With an astute eye to changing tastes in fiction, Hutten included in her repertoire from the late 1920's onwards elements of the murder story and the detective story. Most of the short stories in *Flies* are about murders or murderers, whereas the previous volume of short stories, *Candy* was "a collection of pretty and sentimental tales" (*Times Literary Supplement*). *Die She Must* and *What Happened Is This* included elements of the thriller/detective story, though it is characteristic of Hutten's capacity to manoeuvre plot and character that neither of these is a straightforward example of its kind.

—Jean Buchanan

HYDE, Eleanor. See **COWEN, Frances.**

IBBOTSON, Eva (Maria Charlotte Michele, née Wiesner). British. Born in Vienna, Austria, 21 January 1925. Educated at private schools in Vienna; Dartington Hall School, Devon, 1934–41; Bedford College, University of London, 1941–45, B.Sc. (honours) in physiology; University of Durham, diploma in education 1965. Married Alan Ibbotson in 1948; one daughter and three sons. Lecturer, University of London, 1946–48; teacher, Department of Education, Newcastle upon Tyne. Recipient: Romantic Novelists Association Major award, 1983. Agent: Curtis Brown, 162–168 Regent Street, London W1R 5TB. Address: 2 Collingwood Terrace, Jesmond, Newcastle upon Tyne NE2 2JP, England.

ROMANCE AND HISTORICAL PUBLICATIONS

Novels

A Countess Below Stairs. London, Macdonald, 1981.
Magic Flutes. London, Century, and New York, St. Martin's Press, 1982.
A Company of Swans. London, Century, and New York, St. Martin's Press, 1985.
Madensky Square. London, Century, and New York, St. Martin's Press, 1988.

Short Stories

A Glove Shop in Vienna. London, Century, 1984.

OTHER PUBLICATIONS

Fiction (for children)

The Great Ghost Rescue. London, Macmillan, and New York, Walck, 1975.
Which Witch. London, Macmillan, 1979.
The Worm and the Toffee Nosed Princess. London, Macmillan, 1983.
The Haunting of Hiram C. Hopgood. London, Macmillan, 1987.

Play

Television Play: *Linda Came Today*, 1965.

*

Eva Ibbotson comments:
As the child of a broken home, growing up in a country (Austria before the war) soon to be destroyed; I found myself pursuing security in love and "happy endings", with a particular assiduity, both as a writer and a person. My long and fulfilling marriage has convinced me that there is nothing false or absurd in the belief that two people can give each other abiding love. This doesn't mean that I have found writing romantic novels easy: the simpler the story, the more difficult (for me) the technique.

*   *   *

With her first novel for adults, *A Countess Below Stairs*, Eva Ibbotson made a successful transition from the field of children's fiction (one of her novels was runner-up for the British Library Association's prestigious Carnegie Medal) to that of adult fiction, where she won the Romantic Novelists award.

A Countess Below Stairs is promoted as a "magical novel with the taste of pure champagne"—but do not let this deter you: Ibbotson manages to interweave an admittedly rather lush romanticism with wit and freshness, in a combination that is unique. This and her next two full-length novels, *Magic Flutes* and *A Company of Swans*, have much in common, each featuring a young heroine who is forced suddenly into an unaccustomed role. Tessa works as junior wardrobe mistress, assistant lighting engineer, deputy wig maker, assistant stage manager, prompter, and errand girl for an opera company in *Magic Flutes*; she is in reality the poverty-stricken Princess Theresa-Maria of Pfaffenstein, Princess of Breganzer, Duchess of Unterthur, Countess of Malk, of Zeeburg, and of Freischule. Given this scenario it is inevitable that a combination of a rich dark brooding hero, a case of mistaken identity, and a romantic setting will lead to a satisfying conclusion. Coincidentally, virtually the same set of circumstances crop up in *A Company of Swans*. This story, set in 1912, concerns Harriet, "Professor Morton's clever daughter, Miss Morton's quiet niece," who flees her repressive Cambridge upbringing to dance with a classical ballet troupe in a legendary opera house set in the South American jungle. In both of these novels a host of affectionately drawn minor characters give life and variety to what might appear to be a run of the mill plot.

In a way both these novels constitute "the mixture as before," as all these ingredients also appear in *A Countess Below Stairs*, the story of Countess Anna Grazinsky who, orphaned in the Russian Revolution, explodes upon the scene determined to earn her living as a housemaid. Armed with *The Domestic Servant's Compendium* by Serena Strickland (2003 pages of invaluable and ultimately tiresome advice), she melts the hearts of an entire household—which happens to include a rich dark brooding hero!

Madensky Square is something of a departure from this formula as our heroine Susanna is mature, comfortably off, totally besotted with a middle-aged, pessimistic, married Field Marshal, and the mother of an illegitimate child. In this novel the minor characters (Herr Egger with his nasty little habit, Frau Schultzer who on her honeymoon reads Goethe's *Trilogy of Passion* while her new husband waits downstairs) assume far greater importance and it is their interaction with Susanna which forms the structure for the story.

In *Madensky Square*, *Magic Flutes* and some of the short stories in *A Glove Shop in Vienna*, Ibbotson shares with the reader her familiarity with and obvious love of her native Vienna. The beauty and atmosphere of the city in the early years of this century provide the ideal setting for her lighthearted yet rather moving romances. Several of the short stories feature children as their main characters, from the excitable little nieces in the "Great Carp Ferdinand" to the anxious Jeremy in "Osmandine," and here Ibbotson demonstrates another facet of her skill as a storyteller.

—Judith Rhodes

IDRIESS, Ion L(lewellyn). Australian. Born in Sydney, New South Wales, in 1890. Had a variety of jobs including miner and drover. *Died in 1979.*

ROMANCE AND HISTORICAL PUBLICATIONS

Novels

Lasseter's Last Ride: An Epic of Central Australian Gold Discovery. Sydney, Angus and Robertson, 1931; London, Cape, 1936.
Flynn of the Inland. Sydney, Angus and Robertson, 1932.
Drums of Mer. Sydney, Angus and Robertson, 1933.
The Great Boomerang. Sydney, Angus and Robertson, 1941.
Headhunters of the Coral Sea. Sydney, Angus and Robertson, 1941.
Isles of Despair. Sydney, Angus and Robertson, 1947.
The Red Chief. Sydney, Angus and Robertson, 1953.
Our Living Stone Age. Sydney, Angus and Robertson, 1963.

Short Stories

The Yellow Joss and Other Tales. Sydney, Angus and Robertson, 1934.

OTHER PUBLICATIONS

Other

Madman's Island. Sydney, Cornstalk, 1927.
Prospecting for Gold. Sydney, Angus and Robertson, 1931.
The Desert Column: Leaves from the Diary of an Australian Trooper in Gallipoli, Sinai, and Palestine. Sydney, Angus and Robertson, 1932.
Men of the Jungle (memoirs). Sydney, Angus and Robertson, 1932.
Gold-Dust and Ashes: The Romantic Story of the New Guinea Goldfields. Sydney, Angus and Robertson, 1933.
Man Tracks. Sydney, Angus and Robertson, 1933; London, Cape, 1937.
The Cattle King: The Story of Sir Sidney Kidman. Sydney, Angus and Robertson, 1936.
Forty Fathoms Deep. Sydney, Angus and Robertson, 1937.
Over the Range. Sydney, Angus and Robertson, 1937.
Must Australia Fight? Sydney, Angus and Robertson, 1939.
Cyaniding for Gold. Sydney, Angus and Robertson, 1939.
Lightning Ridge, The Land of Black Opals (autobiography). Sydney, Angus and Robertson, 1940.
Nemarluk, King of the Wilds. Sydney, Angus and Robertson, 1941.
Australian Guerilla series (military handbooks)
    Shoot to Kill. Sydney, Angus and Robertson, 1942.
    Sniping. Sydney, Angus and Robertson, 1942.
    Guerilla Tactics. Sydney, Angus and Robertson, 1942.
    Trapping the Jap. Sydney, Angus and Robertson, 1942.
    The Scout. Sydney, Angus and Robertson, 1943.
Onward Australia: Developing a Continent. Sydney, Angus and Robertson, 1944.
The Silent Service: Action Stories of the Anzac Navy, with T. M. Jones. Sydney, Angus and Robertson, 1944.
Horrie the Wog-Dog. Sydney, Angus and Robertson, 1945; as *Dog of the Desert*, Indianapolis, Bobbs Merrill, 1945.
In Crocodile Land: Wandering in Northern Australia. Sydney, Angus and Robertson, 1946.
Stone of Destiny. Sydney, Angus and Robertson, 1948; as *The Diamond: Stone of Destiny*, 1969.
The Opium Smugglers. Sydney, Angus and Robertson, 1948.
One Wet Season. Sydney, Angus and Robertson, 1949.

The Wild White Man of Badu: A Story of the Coral Sea. Sydney, Angus and Robertson, 1950.
Across the Nullarbor: A Modern Argosy. Sydney, Angus and Robertson, 1951.
Outlaws of the Leopolds. Sydney, Angus and Robertson, 1952.
The Nor-Westers (memoirs). Sydney, Angus and Robertson, 1954.
The Vanished People. Sydney, Angus and Robertson, 1955.
The Silver City (memoirs). Sydney, Angus and Robertson, 1956.
Coral Sea Calling. Sydney, Angus and Robertson, 1957.
Back O'Cairns. Sydney, Angus and Robertson, 1959.
The Tin Scratchers. Sydney, Angus and Robertson, 1960.
The Wild North. Sydney, Angus and Robertson, 1960.
Tracks of Destiny. Sydney, Angus and Robertson, 1961.
My Mate Dick. Sydney, Angus and Robertson, 1962.
Our Stone Age Mystery. Sydney, Angus and Robertson, 1964.
Opals and Sapphires: How to Work, Mine, Class, Cut, Polish and Sell Them. Sydney, Angus and Robertson, 1967; Palo Alto, California, Pacific, 1970.
Challenge of the North: Wealth from Australia's Northern Shores. Sydney, Angus and Robertson, 1969.

* * *

Are the books of Ion L. Idriess fact or fiction? He himself claimed that all of them were "true." Even the highly imaginative romance *Drums of Mer* is announced as "in all essentials historical fact," and many of his works are expressly biographical or autobiographical.

It must be conceded that for Idriess plot and character development count for less than the authentic evocation of a time, place, culture, or event. Yet regardless of how libraries choose to catalogue them, even his most "factual" books, like *The Cattle King*, a biography of Sid Kidman, and *The Silver City*, a history of Broken Hill, read like novels. Idriess may base his writing on documentary evidence—even quote it at length to give the flavour of authenticity—but around the framework of the bare facts he invariably weaves a thick fabric of invented conversation, interior monologue, and dramatic—often melodramatic—incident.

Though born in Sydney, Idriess spent most of the first 30 years of his life as a wanderer and casual worker in remote areas of Australia and New Guinea. His experience of these, together with his war service in the Middle East, supplied most of the raw material for his subsequent career as a prolific and popular writer.

His favourite settings, Torres Strait and Central Australia, were among the last areas to be conquered by Europeans, and Idriess is therefore fairly characterised as a writer of the final phase of colonial advance in the Pacific. He writes from the point of view of the colonist, but because his knowledge is intimate and his sympathies wide, his view is complicated. Possibly the clearest sign of the colonial mentality in his writing is the prominence of the "dreamer," the individual who struggles to achieve a great goal against the odds. Sometimes, like the prospector in *Lasseter's Last Ride*, the dreamer is doomed to failure, but just as often he (it is always *he*) succeeds gloriously, like Sid Kidman, or the founder of the outback Flying Doctor Service, *Flynn of the Inland*. Idriess himself had a dream: the rerouting of coastal rivers to make fertile pasture of the dry outback, which he advocated passionately in *The Great Boomerang*.

Idriess is most interesting for his treatment of the other side of colonialism. He is fascinated by indigenous peoples and their clash with "civilisation," and his books provide some of the most vivid descriptions of tribal life in popular literature. It is true that these are seriously marred by the author's pervasive racism. Not only does he depict native peoples as emotionally and intellectually immature: to be fair, his characterisation of Europeans is also simplistic. Indigenous peoples—especially Australians—are made the butt of crude jokes and slurs. But for all that, he is capable at times of forcefully conveying the moral strains of colonialism. And it is also true that by the 1950's the earlier derision had been replaced by a benign paternalism and even romanticised admiration (*The Red Chief*, *Our Living Stone Age*).

The aspect of tribal life most intriguing to him is its "savage" religion—the dark world of magic, witchcraft, and sorcery. The priest C'Zarcke (*sic!*) in *Drums of Mer* is the most complete rendition of the "Witch Doctor," a figure who recurs almost obsessively. (Probably such a person had profoundly impressed Idriess's imagination when he was "a lad in a strange new world sailing the Coral Sea in a cockroach infested cutter.") Idriess depicts the Witch Doctor as the bearer of the deepest values of tribal culture. He is thus the natural enemy of Europeans and, being closer to the source of an uncorrupted spirituality, in a sense superior to them. At the same time he, the wild spirituality he embodies, and the people he represents, are doomed.

The complement to the Witch Doctor is the lone white man or woman stranded in the midst of tribal culture. This situation dramatically reverses the terms of colonialism. Here it is the European who is in an inferior and dependent position. This is another theme which Idriess returned to many times. At one extreme there is Lasseter, eventually left to die by the group which had rescued him from starvation, at the other Wongai, the "wild white man of Badu," who becomes a feared chieftain. In between are those who adapt but later return to their own society: Jakara in *Drums of Mer*, the two boys in *Headhunters of the Coral Sea*, Barbara Thomson in *Isles of Despair*.

The authorial personality which Idriess's work conveys conforms to the Australian "type" which continues to live in popular prejudice and the mass media, though Australian literature has long since shunned it. He displays both its strengths and its weaknesses: a friendly but complacent egalitarianism—at least towards fellow whites; a warm curiosity about people and their doings which can be insensitive; a zest for action which easily becomes jingoistic; a wry humour which can turn nasty. For as long as this cultural type lives, people will read him with pleasure. *Drums of Mer*, his most enduringly popular book, may also be his best. Besides evoking memorably a (no doubt overdone) atmosphere of "superstition and savage power," it is a suspenseful and fast-moving adventure, written with considerable dash.

—Paul Gillen

———

INGLIS, Susan. Pseudonym for Doris Mackie.

ROMANCE AND HISTORICAL PUBLICATIONS

Novels

Married Man's Girl. London, Mills and Boon, 1934.
The Marriage of Mary Chard. London, Mills and Boon, 1935.
She Acted on Impulse. London, Mills and Boon, 1936.
Uncertain Flame. London, Mills and Boon, 1937.
Ice Girl. London, Mills and Boon, 1938.
Tender Only to One. London, Mills and Boon, 1938.

To Wear Your Ring. London, Mills and Boon, 1938.
Put Love Aside. London, Mills and Boon, 1939.
Too Many Men. London, Mills and Boon, 1939.
Because I Love You. London, Mills and Boon, 1940.
This Foolish Heart. London, Mills and Boon, 1940.
Sara Steps In. London, Hurst and Blackett, 1947.
Dick Heriot's Wife. London, Hurst and Blackett, 1947.
Jill Takes a Chance. London, Hurst and Blackett, 1949.
Deb and Destiny. London, Hurst and Blackett, 1950.
Happiness Can't Wait. London, Hurst and Blackett, 1950.
Three Men in Her Life. London, Hurst and Blackett, 1951.
Highland Holiday. London, Hurst and Blackett, 1952.
Sister Christine. London, Hurst and Blackett, 1953.
The Loving Heart. London, Hurst and Blackett, 1954.
Steven's Wife. London, Hurst and Blackett, 1958.
The Secret Heart. London, Hurst and Blackett, 1959.
The Old Hunting Lodge. London, Hurst and Blackett, 1961.

*   *   *

Susan Inglis is a writer of light contemporary romances set in vague surroundings and peopled by shadowy figures. Most of her books centre round the eternal triangle: the heroine has to choose between a charming but weak and shallow adventurer and a strong, patient, and resourceful hero, to whom she turns in the end, as in *Uncertain Flame*, *Ice Girl*, and *Deb and Destiny*. Both *The Marriage of Mary Chard* and *Sister Christine* concern marriage for business purposes, in the former, so that Mary can control the wayward daughter of a famous explorer, and in the latter, to satisfy an Indian Rajah that no unmarried woman is nursing his sick son. In both cases the couple's feelings for each other eventually ripen into real love. Other plots deal with. the problems of falling for married men (for example, *Married Man's Girl*), or being married to the wrong man (as in *Because I Love You*). *Dick Heriot's Wife* is a slightly stronger story in which a nurse marries a dying man to make him happy, only to find he has left her his estate, which she turns down. Forced to take a job for financial reasons she finds herself nursing the sister of her late husband's cousin, who now owns the estate. Here the characters are more sympathetically realized, and the setting more fully drawn, although the ending, in common with other of her works, is rather too convenient to be credible. *Highland Holiday* also has a more interesting plot, with a varied cast of eight who re-meet each other after a gap of 10 years at Allt-na-Culan in the Scottish Highlands.

The majority of Inglis's novels, however, lack variety: her characters are stereotyped, with little depth or individuality, and although the narrative is brisk and set at a determined pace, the themes are slight and insubstantial, set against pale backgrounds that could be anywhere, and written with little involvement and no real suspense. Both style and theme seem to fit the rather conventional ''romance'' mood of the 1930's and the postwar period.

—Tessa Rose Chester

INNES, Jean. See **SAUNDERS, Jean.**

IRWIN, Margaret (Emma Faith). British. Born in London in 1889. Educated at Clifton School, Bristol; Oxford University.

Married the artist John Robert Monsell in 1929. *Died 11 December 1967.*

ROMANCE AND HISTORICAL PUBLICATIONS

Novels

How Many Miles to Babylon? London, Constable, 1913.
Come Out to Play. London, Constable, 1914; New York, Doran, 1915.
Out of the House. London, Constable, and New York, Doran, 1916.
Still She Wished for Company. London, Heinemann, 1924.
Who Will Remember? New York, Seltzer, 1924.
These Mortals. London, Heinemann, 1925.
Knock Four Times. London, Heinemann, and New York, Harcourt Brace, 1927.
Fire Down Below. London, Heinemann, and New York, Harcourt Brace, 1928.
None So Pretty. London, Chatto and Windus, and New York, Harcourt Brace, 1930.
Royal Flush: The Story of Minette. London, Chatto and Windus, and New York, Harcourt Brace, 1932.
The Proud Servant: The Story of Montrose. London, Chatto and Windus, and New York, Harcourt Brace, 1934.
The Stranger Prince: The Story of Rupert of the Rhine. London, Chatto and Windus, and New York, Harcourt Brace, 1937.
The Bride: The Story of Louise and Montrose. London, Chatto and Windus, and New York, Harcourt Brace, 1939.
The Gay Galliard: The Love Story of Mary Queen of Scots. London, Chatto and Windus, 1941; New York, Harcourt Brace, 1942.
Young Bess. London, Chatto and Windus, 1944; New York, Harcourt Brace, 1945.
Elizabeth, Captive Princess. London, Chatto and Windus, and New York, Harcourt Brace, 1948.
Elizabeth and the Prince of Spain. London, Chatto and Windus, and New York, Harcourt Brace, 1953.

Short Stories

Madame Fears the Dark: Seven Stories and a Play. London, Chatto and Windus, 1935.
Mrs. Oliver Cromwell and Other Stories. London, Chatto and Windus, 1940.
Bloodstock and Other Stories. London, Chatto and Windus, 1953; New York, Harcourt Brace, 1954.

OTHER PUBLICATIONS

Plays

The Happy Man: A Sketch for Acting. London, Oxford University Press, 1921; Boston, Baker, 1938.
Check to the King of France (for children). London, French, 1933.
Minette (for children). London and New York, French, 1933.
Save the Children (for children). London, French, 1933.
The King's Son, in *Nash's* (London), February 1934.
Madame Fears the Dark (produced London, 1936). London, Chatto and Windus, 1936.

Other

South Molton Street. London, Mate, 1927.
The Great Lucifer: A Portrait of Sir Walter Raleigh. London, Chatto and Windus, 1936; New York, Harcourt Brace, 1960.

* * *

The historical novel can be a paraphrase of history with puppet-like characters moving stiffly, it can be a costume drama interspersed with sexual encounters, or it can be an account of what happened illuminated by imaginatively interpreted characters. Margaret Irwin's historical novels are the last kind, and the best known of these is the series about the Stuarts. She began with *Royal Flush* in which the English royal family and the French court are vividly portrayed. Her heroine, Minette, is Charles II's sister who married the horrid Monsieur, perverted brother of Louis XIV. Next came *The Proud Servant* about Montrose the charming Scottish hero, both poet and soldier, who was so badly treated by Charles I of whom she draws a singularly unsympathetic portrait; this is further amplified in *The Stranger Prince*, the story of Rupert of the Rhine, the son of one of England's most popular princesses, Elizabeth Queen of Bohemia. In it Irwin draws lively, fascinating portraits of this branch of the Stuart family and although she is not sympathetic to Charles I she is equally critical of Cromwell, neither of whom did justice to her hero Rupert. One of Rupert's sisters, the tomboy Louise marries Montrose and is the heroine of *The Bride*. These books move at a leisurely pace and are full of accurate historical details and delightful revealing touches.

She went back to earlier Stuart history in *The Gay Galliard* which shows us a Mary, Queen of Scots probably more sensible and sensitive than she was in real life and makes Bothwell (surely a rogue in reality?) a charming hero. But if her picture of Mary as a romantic, ill-used lady was hard on Elizabeth, Irwin balanced it with a trilogy about the rival queen. *Young Bess*, *Elizabeth*, *Captive Princess*, and *Elizabeth and the Prince of Spain* give a vivid, full-length portrait of Elizabeth and are probably her best books. Irwin's interpretation of Elizabeth's thoughts and motives is plausible, and her gift for visualising people brings to life Elizabeth's family, servants, friends, and courtiers.

But Irwin did not only write historical novels; she had a light hand with fantasy too. *These Mortals*, for instance, is a full-blown fairy tale for adults about an enchanter's daughter who can make herself invisible and uses this gift for clandestine meetings with her imprisoned lover-prince. After a traditional change of the substance for the shadow, the story leads one to draw two equally traditional morals—that looks are not everything and that love conquers all. *Still She Wished for Company* is a ghost story that, Janus-like, faces both ways: a girl in the present is dissatisfied with her life and is looking for her ideal man whose 18th-century portrait she has cherished since she was a schoolgirl. This story is interwoven with that of a young girl in the 18th century whose ex-Hellfire club brother is using her to find his ideal woman, a girl he has glimpsed in dreams since boyhood. The girl in the present sees ghosts of the past and the girl in the past sees into the future with near fatal results.

All these books are written in elegant, lucid prose and although they have an air of sadness, they are a pleasure to read.

—Pamela Cleaver

JACKSON, Shirley (Hardie). American. Born in San Francisco, California, 14 December 1919. Educated at Burlingame High School, California; Brighton High School, Rochester, New York; University of Rochester, 1934–36; Syracuse University, New York, 1937–40, B.A. 1940. Married the writer Stanley Edgar Hyman in 1940; two daughters and two sons. Recipient: Mystery Writers of America Edgar Allan Poe award, 1961; Syracuse University Arents Medal, 1965. *Died 8 August 1965.*

ROMANCE AND HISTORICAL PUBLICATIONS

Novels

The Road Through the Wall. New York, Farrar Straus, 1948; as *The Other Side of the Street*, New York, Pyramid, 1956.
Hangsaman. New York, Farrar Straus, and London, Gollancz, 1951.
The Bird's Nest. New York, Farrar Straus, 1954; London, Joseph, 1955; as *Lizzie*, New York, New American Library, 1957.
The Sundial. New York, Farrar Straus, and London, Joseph, 1958.
The Haunting of Hill House. New York, Viking Press, 1959; London, Joseph, 1960.
We Have Always Lived in the Castle. New York, Viking Press, 1962; London, Joseph, 1963.

Short Stories

The Lottery; or, The Adventures of James Harris. New York, Farrar Straus, 1949; London, Gollancz, 1950.

OTHER PUBLICATIONS

Plays

The Lottery, adaptation of her own short story, in *Best Television Plays 1950–1951*, edited by William I. Kauffman. New York, Merlin Press, 1952.
The Bad Children: A Play in One Act for Bad Children. Chicago, Dramatic Publishing Company, 1959.

Other

Life among the Savages. New York, Farrar Straus, 1953; London, Joseph, 1954.
The Witchcraft of Salem Village (for children). New York, Random House, 1956.
Raising Demons. New York, Farrar Straus, and London, Joseph, 1957.
Special Delivery: A Useful Book for Brand-New Mothers . . . . Boston, Little Brown, 1960; as *And Baby Makes Three . . .*, New York, Grosset and Dunlap, 1960.
9 Magic Wishes (for children). New York, Crowell Collier, 1963.
Famous Sally (for children). New York, Harlin Quist, 1966.
The Magic of Shirley Jackson, edited by Stanley Edgar Hyman. New York, Farrar Straus, 1966.
Come Along with Me: Part of a Novel, Sixteen Stories, and Three Lectures, edited by Stanley Edgar Hyman. New York, Viking Press, 1968.

*

Critical Studies: *Shirley Jackson* by Lenemaja Friedman, Boston, Twayne, 1975; *Private Demons: The Life of Shirley Jackson* by Judy Oppenheimer, New York, Putnam, 1988.

*   *   *

Shirley Jackson's gothic fiction substitutes decaying mansions for castle ruins; presences, stirrings, and psychotic imaginings for straightforward ghostly sightings; neurotic spinsters, turned inward in despair, for traditional romantic heroines; and evil that grows out of the internal fears and anxieties of individuals and communities for external forces. Yet hers is still a gothic world of dreams and shadows, of sinister threats and nameless fears, of the familiar grown unfamiliar. Reality and nightmare merge in tales of terror, frustration, loneliness, and isolation: a frightening return to childhood in "The Bus," phantom lovers in "The Beautiful Stranger" and "The Daemon Lover," modern daytime ghosts in "The Visit," murderous ghostly hitchikers in "Home," psychic voices in *Come Along with Me,* oldsters who prove witches at heart in "The Little House," "Trial by Combat," "Whistler's Grandmother," and "The Possibility of Evil," and horrifying human cruelty in "The Renegade," "All She Said Was Yes," and "The Lottery."

Hangsaman, The Bird's Nest, and *We Have Always Lived in the Castle* are more psychological than gothic, given their central focus on the disintegration and fragmentation of personality, but partake of gothic elements, sensibilities, and themes. *Hangsaman* unveils the private world of an ill-adjusted 17-year-old who retreats into Tarot cards, a secret diary, and friendship with an imaginary friend to compensate for being an unpopular outsider. She finally perceives her schizoid condition as dangerous in a late night foray in a dark, wooded area where her friend becomes elusive and unreal, a ghostly, threatening wraith that glides eerily through trees. *The Bird's Nest,* with its shifting points of view, exposes the terror within: conflicting and antagonistic parts of a single self, wherein good and evil are so separated that one persecutes and seeks to discredit the other in unnerving ways, from destruction of property to mud sandwiches to attempted murder. *We Have Always Lived in the Castle* focuses on a lively, likeable young psychotic, Merricat, who poisoned four family members with arsenic and left a fifth crippled. Preoccupied with death and the supernatural, with signs, omens, and hexes to ward off evil, her only friend a cat, she dreams of murder and mayhem, and resorts to pyrotechnics when a greedy, intruding cousin threatens to tempt away her sister. Later the two sisters withdraw into their vine-covered manor, a burned, smashed castle-like ruin, where they live a secret life, nourished by private dreams and the irregular offerings of guilty townspeople.

Like *We Have Always Lived in the Castle*, Jackson's two clearly gothic works, *The Sundial* and *The Haunting of Hill House,* center on a large dark mansion where mysterious and inexplicable events occur. In *The Sundial* it is a 40-room New England mansion, complete with symmetrical architecture, cryptic maxims carved in frontispieces, and formal gardens with maze and lake; but it is marred by a damp grotto, vicious swans, and a misaligned sundial. The story begins with a funeral and hints of foul play, followed by warnings from the dead, voodoo dolls, seances, the mysterious death of a queen figure, and a storm that batters the house and cuts its occupants off from the outside world. Symbolic warnings abound: a snake glides menacingly across the carpet; a glass picture window shatters; statues prove warm; a non-existent gardener appears and disappears; mist shrouds the gardens; a young virgin distinguishes fortune's

sign in a hazy mirror. In *The Haunting of Hill House* four intelligent, receptive people meet by prearrangement to record psychic phenomena in Hill House: "a house without kindness," an isolated structure of concentric circles and odd angles, with dangerous towers, dark musty rooms, unfriendly spirits, and a history of "accidental" deaths. The spirits which stir when the gates are locked and night falls take the form of a sub-zero cold spot; hollow knockings, small squeaking sounds, giggles and quiet laughter; turning doorknobs, moving furniture, swaying walls; an unidentified hand in the dark and a small creature darting through the house, writing summons on walls in chalk and blood. The most vulnerable researcher, subject to a stone-throwing poltergeist in her youth and a loveless, frustrated adulthood, tries to identify with her fellow researchers, but, when repelled, begins to hear voices, identify with the house, and seek to become one of its spirits; she claims to obey its summons, for "no one else could satisfy it."

Thus, Jackson's main contribution to the genre is not her use of updated gothic trappings, but her focus on the "gothic" mind, the psychology of the outsider, the loner, who begins to construct her own reality. For Jackson the real horror is being shut out of the group, being alienated for whatever cause, and, as a result, losing a grasp of what is real and what is not. By carefully controlling point of view, Jackson causes the reader to share in this ambiguity of perception and to vacillate in understanding what is imagination, what reality. Thus she goes beyond the one-dimensional, imposed gothic to deal with the irregular and the imbalanced that arise out of genuine human fears, fears of rejection, of hate, of singularity, of isolation.

—Gina Macdonald

JACOB, Naomi (Ellington). Also wrote as Ellington Gray. British. Born in Ripon, Yorkshire, 1 July 1884. Educated at Middlesbrough High School. Teacher in a Middlesbrough school; secretary and companion to Marguerite Broadfoot and Eva Moore, music hall entertainers; actress; supervisor in munitions factory during World War I; welfare officer in Overseas Service during World War II. After 1930 lived in Sirmione, Italy. *Died 26 August 1964.*

ROMANCE AND HISTORICAL PUBLICATIONS

Novels (series: Broad Acres; Gollantz)

Jacob Ussher. London, Butterworth, 1925.
Rock and Sand. London, Butterworth, 1926.
Power. London, Butterworth, 1927.
The Plough. London, Butterworth, 1928.
Saffroned Bridesails (as Ellington Gray). London, Butterworth, 1928.
The Man Who Found Himself. London, Butterworth, 1929; revised edition, London, Pan, 1952.
The Beloved Physician. London, Butterworth, 1930.
Gollantz Saga:
  1. *The Founder of the House.* London, Hutchinson, 1935; New York, Macmillan, 1956.
  2. *That Wild Lie—.* London, Hutchinson, 1930.
  3. *Young Emmanuel.* London, Hutchinson, 1932; New York, New American Library, 1973.
  4. *Four Generations.* London, Hutchinson, and New York, Macmillan, 1934.

5. *Private Gollantz*. London, Hutchinson, 1943.
6. *Gollantz: London, Paris, Milan*. London, Hutchinson, 1948.
7. *Gollantz and Partners*. London, Hutchinson, 1958.
Tales of the Broad Acres. London, Hutchinson, 1955.
Roots. London, Hutchinson, 1931.
The Loaded Stick. London, Hutchinson, 1934; New York, Macmillan, 1935.
Sally Scarth. London, Hutchinson, 1940.
Seen Unknown . . . . London, Hutchinson, 1931.
Props. London, Hutchinson, 1932.
Groping. London, Hutchinson, 1933.
Poor Straws! London, Hutchinson, 1933.
Honour Comes Back—. London, Hutchinson, and New York, Macmillan, 1935.
Time Piece. London, Hutchinson, 1936; New York, Macmillan, 1937.
Barren Metal. London, Hutchinson, and New York, Macmillan, 1936.
Fade Out. London, Hutchinson, and New York, Macmillan, 1937.
The Lenient God. London, Hutchinson, 1937; New York, Macmillan, 1938.
Straws in Amber. London, Hutchinson, 1938; New York, Macmillan, 1939.
No Easy Way. London, Hutchinson, 1938.
Full Meridian. London, Hutchinson, 1939; New York, Macmillan, 1940.
This Porcelain Clay. London, Hutchinson, and New York, Macmillan, 1939.
They Left the Land. London, Hutchinson, and New York, Macmillan, 1940.
Under New Management. London, Hutchinson, 1941.
The Cap of Youth. London, Hutchinson, and New York, Macmillan, 1941.
Leopards and Spots. London, Hutchinson, 1942.
White Wool. London, Hutchinson, 1944.
Susan Crowther. London, Hutchinson, 1945.
Honour's a Mistress. London, Hutchinson, 1947.
A Passage Perilous. London, Hutchinson, 1948.
Mary of Delight. London, Hutchinson, 1949.
Every Other Gift. London, Hutchinson, 1950.
The Heart of the House. London, Hutchinson, 1951.
A Late Lark Singing. London, Hutchinson, 1952.
The Morning Will Come. London, Hutchinson, 1953.
Antonia. London, Hutchinson, 1954.
Second Harvest. London, Hutchinson, 1954.
The Irish Boy: A Romantic Biography. London, Hutchinson, 1955.
Wind on the Heath. London, Hutchinson, 1956.
What's to Come. London, Hutchinson, 1958.
Search for a Background. London, Hutchinson, 1960.
Three Men and Jennie. London, Hutchinson, 1960.
Strange Beginning. London, Hale, 1961.
Great Black Oxen. London, Hale, 1962.
Yolanda. London, Hale, 1963.
Long Shadows. London, Hale, 1964.
Flavia. London, Hale 1965.

OTHER PUBLICATIONS

Play

The Dawn (produced Glasgow, 1923).

Other

Me: A Chronicle about Other People. London, Hutchinson, 1933.
Me—in the Kitchen. London, Hutchinson, 1935.
Our Marie: Marie Lloyd: A Biography. London, Hutchinson, 1936.
Me—Again. London, Hutchinson, 1937.
More about Me. London, Hutchinson, 1939.
Shadow Drama, by Nina Abbott, completed by Jacob. London, Duckworth, 1940.
Me—In War-Time. London, Hutchinson, 1940.
Balance Suspended, by Nina Abbott, completed by Jacob. London, Duckworth, 1942.
Me and the Mediterranean. London, Hutchinson, 1945.
Me—Over There. London, Hutchinson, 1947.
Opera in Italy, with James C. Robertson. London, Hutchinson, 1948; Freeport, New York, Books for Libraries, 1970.
Me and Mine, You and Yours. London, Hutchinson, 1949.
Me—Looking Back. London, Hutchinson, 1950.
Impressions from Italy. London, Hutchinson, 1952.
Robert, Nana, and—Me. London, Hutchinson, 1952.
Just about Us. London, Hutchinson, 1953.
Me—Likes and Dislikes. London, Hutchinson, 1954.
Prince China. London, Hutchinson, 1955.
Me—Yesterday and To-day. London, Kimber, 1957.
Me—and the Stags. London, Kimber, 1962.
Me—and the Swans. London, Kimber, 1963.
Me—Thinking Things Over. London, Kimber, 1964.

Theatrical Activities:

Actress: **Plays**—Julia Cragworthy in *The Young Idea* by Noël Coward, London, 1923; Mrs. Hackitt in *The Ringer* by Edgar Wallace, London, 1926; Ma Gennochio in *The Nutmeg Tree* by Margery Sharp, London, 1941; Nurse in *Love for Love* by Congreve, London, 1943.

*

Critical Study: *Naomi Jacob: The Seven Ages of "Me"* by James Norbury, London, Kimber, 1965.

*   *   *

The full list of Naomi Jacob's output over the years is staggering. How could any writer have had so much to say? She accomplished her impressive feat by recording the ordinary, but by doing so in a generously florid style that ran to untold pages. She tended to become infatuated with the characters of her own invention—the "good" ones, at any rate. Grudgingly she would sometimes allow some tiny defect or character flaw to one of her pets, such as Emmanuel Gollantz, patriarch of her popular multi-generational family saga, but would hasten to better than redeem it with heaped-up evidence of her dear one's excellence. Her villains, by contrast, are of deepest dye. Julian Gollantz, one of the black sheep, is a near approach to the mustachio-twirling "bad guys" of the early cinema: relentlessly evil, unmotivated in his Iago-like malice, and a foil for the many virtuous Gollantz characters.

For all her broad and sweeping strokes, Jacob was somehow unable, though infinitely willing, to create a convincingly *important* character. Good or bad (and some of them are indeed quite interesting and/or likeable; one wants to learn their eventual fates), her people do not live up to her own obviously high opinion of them. They remain—ordinary. Like the rest of us, they are earthbound with family concerns of enormous complication and difficulty; though usually quite comfortably fixed, the occasional one must pinch and scrape a little; all are deeply concerned with the mechanics of making a living, with their feet solidly planted on the commercial ground. This does indeed set them apart from the creations of a great many other authors of the romance novel, whose characters appear to exist like the lilies of the field, neither toiling nor spinning, living only for love.

As well as working, Jacob's people do love, however. Intensely, burningly, with enormous fervor, self-sacrifice, and dedication: each of them adores—some other ordinary creation. Jacob has a habit of overburdening little characters with giant, heroic emotions that they cannot gracefully sustain. Although this inevitably flattens the sought-after effect of romantic magnificence, it may be that this very quality of "commonplaceness" served to endear her undeniably popular novels to a large, faithful, and "ordinary" public, after all.

—Joan McGrath

JACOBS, Leah. See **GELLIS, Roberta.**

JAGGER, Brenda. British. Born in Yorkshire in 1936. Married; three daughters. Worked in Paris and as a probation officer in the north of England. Recipient: Romantic Novelists Association Major award, 1986. *Died in 1986.*

ROMANCE AND HISTORICAL PUBLICATIONS

Novels (series: Barforth)

Antonia. London, Hodder and Stoughton, 1978.
The Clouded Hills (Barforth). London, Macdonald, 1980.
Verity. New York, Doubleday, 1980.
Daughter of Aphrodite. London, Constable, 1981.
Flints and Roses (Barforth). London, Macdonald, 1981.
The Sleeping Sword (Barforth). London, Macdonald, 1982.
The Barforth Women. New York, Doubleday, 1982.
An Independent Woman. New York, New American Library, 1983.
Days of Grace. London, Collins, 1983; New York, Morrow, 1984.
A Winter's Child. London, Collins, and New York, Morrow, 1984.
A Song Twice Over. London, Collins, and New York, Morrow, 1985.
Distant Choices. London, Collins, and New York, Morrow, 1986.

*   *   *

Brenda Jagger's two early novels *Antonia* and *Daughter of Aphrodite* are set in Ancient Rome. The characters, and the atmosphere of the courts of Tiberius and Galba, form a fascinating setting for the stories, both of which centre around young girls whose lives and loves develop against a time-honoured background of power, treachery, murder, and money. The heroines differ in their positions in society: Antonia is an heiress whose

wealth makes her a political pawn in the intrigue following Nero's death, Danae a rich courtesan who has fought her way up from the slums of Subura. Each bears the hallmarks of a Jagger heroine; tenacity, a strong sense of survival, and a capacity to develop and to learn from all the experiences that life and the author throw at them. This description would encompass a typical heroine of most traditional historical and romantic novels, but what is unusual about Jagger's work is the interesting way in which she describes in some detail the socio-political structures of the period about which she writes.

However, it is not until her first trilogy—*The Clouded Hills*, *Flints and Roses* and *The Sleeping Sword*—that her real strength in this area emerges. These three books, set in the 19th century, chart the uneven progress of a mill-owning family as it faces industrialisation, riots, and subsequently the implementation of the Reform Act. Many novels have been written about this period, but few offer such a compelling blend of love and politics, or deal so convincingly with the development of the role of women. None of the heroines, who become increasingly militant as the books progress, is outrageous or unbelievable; rather, each is developed in a sympathetic and moving way. The restrictions of the conventions of Victorian England are skilfully drawn, and in each novel the tension gradually builds as the individuality of the strong-minded female character develops to a point where rebellion in some form becomes inevitable. Verity, in *The Clouded Hills*, accepts a marriage of convenience which she uses to give her a freedom to find love elsewhere; Grace Agbrigg in *The Sleeping Sword* resists her natural emotions and marries as expected, but she breaks free and defies convention to become the only divorcee in Cullingford.

Throughout the trilogy, the plight of the homeless and working conditions in the cities are described graphically, and form not a mere adjunct to the plot but an integral part of the action. For example, in *The Clouded Hills* Hannah is involved in improving social conditions in the worst working areas, while in *Flints and Roses* Dr. Giles Ashburn, the heroine's first husband, dies fighting a cholera epidemic in the slums. Contrasting starkly with the grim realities of these authentically drawn situations are Jagger's vivid descriptions of the Yorkshire countryside.

In *Days of Grace* Jagger extends her geographical range to Paris and London but returns once again to her native Yorkshire for the denouement of the story. She uses the atmosphere of the moors and the emotions and ambitions of the strong-willed women (and men) who people them, to depict the tensions of those turbulent times.

Several of the themes only touched upon in her trilogy are developed in her later novels. In *A Winter's Child*, set in the years following World War I, Clare, having experienced the freedom ironically offered to many women during those years, is now forced to return from nursing in France to the closed society of a Yorkshire town. She is unable to accept the position that society offers her, and chooses to use the money left to her by her husband (killed in the trenches) to set up a house of her own, living a "bohemian" lifestyle. She is allowed to follow this course of action only as a result of the somewhat unexpected acquiescence of Benedict (the trustee of her father-in-law's estate and thus the holder of the purse-strings). Less unexpected is the development of their relationship despite the constraints still in force at the time.

The overall theme of a woman's freedom to choose her destiny is also present in Jagger's later novels *A Song Twice Over* and *Distant Choices*. The barriers are still there—the expectations of society, social background, and convention—as are the strengths to overcome these barriers. Jagger's powerful writing brings to life the often agonizing and painful choices inflicted upon Victorian women from all social backgrounds, and offers a picture of their emotional plight no less vivid than in her earlier works.

—Judith Rhodes

JAKES, John (William). Also writes as William Ard; Alan Payne; Rachel Ann Payne; Jay Scotland. American. Born in Chicago, Illinois, 31 March 1932. Educated at DePauw University, Greencastle, Indiana, A.B. 1953; Ohio State University, Columbus, M.A. in American literature 1954. Married Rachel Ann Payne in 1951; three daughters and one son. Copywriter, then promotion manager, Abbott Laboratories, North Chicago, 1954–60; copywriter, Rumrill Company, Rochester, New York, 1960–61; free-lance writer, 1961–65; copywriter, Kircher Helton and Collett, Dayton, Ohio, 1965–68; copy chief, then Vice-President, Oppenheim Herminghausen and Clarke, Dayton, 1968–70; creative director, Dancer Fitzgerald Sample, Dayton, 1970–71. Since 1971 freelance writer. Writer-in-residence, DePauw University, Fall 1979. LL.D.: Wright State University, Dayton, Ohio, 1976; Litt.D.: DePauw University, 1977. Address: c/o Rembar and Curtis, Attorneys, 19 West 44th Street, New York, New York 10036, U.S.A.

ROMANCE AND HISTORICAL PUBLICATIONS

Novels (series: North and South; Kent Family)

Kent Family Chronicles:
   The Bastard. New York, Pyramid, 1974; as *Fortune's Whirlwind* and *To an Unknown Shore*, London, Corgi, 2 vols., 1975.
   The Rebels. New York, Pyramid, 1975; London, Corgi, 1979.
   The Seekers. New York, Pyramid, 1975; London, Corgi, 1979.
   The Furies. New York, Pyramid, 1976; London, Corgi, 1979.
   The Titans. New York, Pyramid, 1976; London, Corgi, 1979.
   The Warriors. New York, Pyramid, 1977; London, Corgi, 1979.
   The Lawless. New York, Berkley, 1978; London, Corgi, 1979.
   The Americans. New York, Berkley, 1980.
North and South Trilogy:
   North and South. New York, Harcourt Brace, and London, Collins, 1982.
   Love and War. New York, Harcourt Brace, 1984; London, Collins, 1985.
   Heaven and Hell. San Diego, Harcourt Brace, and London, Collins, 1987.
California Gold. New York, Random House, 1989.

Novels as Jay Scotland

Strike the Black Flag. New York, Ace, 1961.
Sir Scoundrel. New York, Ace, 1962; revised edition, as *King's Crusader*, New York, Pinnacle 1977.
Veils of Salome. New York, Avon, 1962.
Arena. New York, Ace, 1963.

Traitors' Legion. New York, Ace, 1963; revised edition, as *The Man from Cannae*, New York, Pinnacle, 1977.

OTHER PUBLICATIONS

Novels

Gonzaga's Woman. New York, Universal, 1953.
Wear a Fast Gun. New York, Arcadia House, 1956; London, Ward Lock, 1957.
A Night for Treason. New York, Bouregy, 1956.
The Devil Has Four Faces. New York, Bouregy, 1958.
This'll Slay You (as Alan Payne). New York, Ace, 1958.
The Seventh Man (as Jay Scotland). New York, Bouregy, 1958.
I, Barbarian (as Jay Scotland). New York, Avon, 1959; revised edition, as John Jakes, New York, Pinnacle, 1976.
The Imposter. New York, Bouregy, 1959.
Johnny Havoc. New York, Belmont, 1960.
Johnny Havoc Meets Zelda. New York, Belmont, 1962.
Johnny Havoc and the Doll Who Had "It." New York, Belmont, 1963.
G.I. Girls. Derby, Connecticut, Monarch, 1963.
Ghostwind (as Rachel Ann Payne). New York, Paperback Library, 1966.
When the Star Kings Die. New York, Ace, 1967.
Making It Big. New York, Belmont, 1968.
The Asylum World. New York, Paperback Library, 1969; London, New English Library, 1978.
Brak Versus the Mark of the Demons. New York, Paperback Library, 1969; as *Brak the Barbarian—The Mark of the Demons*, London, Tandem, 1970.
Brak the Barbarian Versus the Sorceress. New York, Paperback Library, 1969; as *Brak the Barbarian—The Sorceress*, London, Tandem, 1969.
The Hybrid. New York, Paperback Library, 1969.
The Last Magicians. New York, New American Library, 1969.
The Planet Wizard. New York, Ace, 1969.
Tonight We Steal the Stars. New York, Ace, 1969.
Black in Time. New York, Paperback Library, 1970.
Mask of Chaos. New York, Ace, 1970.
Master of the Dark Gate. New York, Lancer, 1970.
Monte Cristo 99. New York, Curtis, 1970.
Six-Gun Planet. New York, Paperback Library, 1970; London, New English Library, 1978.
Mention My Name in Atlantis. New York, DAW, 1972.
Witch of the Dark Gate. New York, Lancer, 1972.
Conquest of the Planet of the Apes (novelization of screenplay). New York, Award, 1972.
On Wheels. New York, Paperback Library, 1973.
Brak: When the Idols Walked. New York, Pocket Books, 1978.
Excalibur!, with Gil Kane. New York, Dell, 1980.

Novels as William Ard

Make Mine Mavis. Derby, Connecticut, Monarch, 1961.
And So to Bed. Derby, Connecticut, Monarch, 1962.
Give Me This Woman. Derby, Connecticut, Monarch, 1962.

Short Stories

Brak the Barbarian. New York, Avon, 1968; London, Tandem, 1970.
The Best of John Jakes, edited by Martin H. Greenberg and Joseph D. Olander. New York, DAW, 1977.
Fortunes of Brak. New York, Dell, 1980.

Plays

Dracula, Baby (lyrics only). Chicago, Dramatic Publishing Company, 1970.
Wind in the Willows. Elgin, Illinois, Performance, 1972.
A Spell of Evil. Chicago, Dramatic Publishing Company, 1972.
Violence. Elgin, Illinois, Performance, 1972.
Stranger with Roses, adaptation of his own story. Chicago, Dramatic Publishing Company, 1972.
For I Am a Jealous People, adaptation of the story by Lester del Rey. Elgin, Illinois, Performance, 1972.
Gaslight Girl. Chicago, Dramatic Publishing Company, 1973.
Pardon Me, Is This Planet Taken? Chicago, Dramatic Publishing Company, 1973.
Doctor, Doctor!, music by Gilbert M. Martin, adaptation of a play by Molière. New York, McAfee Music, 1973.
Shepherd Song. New York, McAfee Music, 1974.

Other

The Texans Ride North (for children). Philadelphia, Winston, 1952.
Tiros: Weather Eye in Space. New York, Messner, 1966.
Famous Firsts in Sports. New York, Putnam, 1967.
Great War Correspondents. New York, Putnam, 1968.
Great Women Reporters. New York, Putnam, 1969.
Secrets of Stardeep (for children). Philadelphia, Westminster Press, 1969.
Time Gate (for children). Philadelphia, Westminster Press, 1972.
The Bastard Photostory. New York, Berkley, 1980.
Susanna at the Alamo: A True Story (for children). San Diego, Harcourt Brace, 1986.

*

Manuscript Collection: University of Wyoming, Laramie.

Critical Study: *The Kent Family Chronicles Encyclopedia* edited by Robert Hawkins, New York, Bantam, 1979.

John Jakes comments:

An early interest in historical novels and films, as well as the study of history, led to a series of paperback historical novels in the 1960's. These in turn perhaps presaged the enormous success of the eight-volume Kent Family Chronicles and then the North and South Trilogy. In historical fiction I found, at last, my strength and my real audience. I was gratified when the Los Angeles *Times* referred to me as the "godfather of historical novelists."

*   *   *

Anyone who got caught up in the excitement of the American bicentennial and celebrated by reading the Kent Family Chronicles knows that John Jakes is a prolific writer. After all, he wrote eight long novels detailing this family saga from 1770 to 1890, and he did it in only six years. Since then he was written three more novels about the Civil War—before, during, and after. What most readers probably don't realize is that Jakes was a prolific writer before he burst on the popular scene with *The Bastard*, the first Kent Family book in 1974. He had written short stories, science fiction, plays, song lyrics, and advertising copy long before even thinking about the Kents. His first book, *The Texans Ride North*, was published in 1952 while he was still in college at DePauw University.

The beginning of the Kent Family Chronicles was quiet and inauspicious—partly because *The Bastard* and its successor were issued in paperback and partly because the title was offputting to some. But the red, white, and blue volumes were eyecatching, and with so many Americans thinking about their roots as the country neared its 200th birthday, it didn't take long for historical fiction buffs to clear the bookshelves and spread the good news.

The American Kents began with Phillipe Charboneau, born in France in 1753, the illegitimate son of a French actress and the English Duke of Kentland. Young Phillipe travels to England to claim his birthright but the machinations of the ailing Duke's family shut him out. Stranded in London, his first lucky break is his apprenticeship to a printer—a fortunate occurrence that has a great bearing on all the Kent generations that follow for by the time we get to the eighth volume, the Kent family has made a fortune in the publishing business. One of the side pleasures in reading these novels is meeting well-known historical characters. This is especially true of Benjamin Franklin, patriot and printer, whom Phillipe calls on in London. To his surprise and ours, Franklin is seated totally nude, except for his spectacles, in front of three wide open windows in the dead of winter—a glass of madeira in his hand. When Phillipe decides to travel to the colonies, he changes his name to Philip Kent.

The Rebels takes place from 1775 to 1781 and covers Philip's adventures in the American Revolution and introduces us to his sons Abraham and Gilbert. Volumes three and four, *The Seekers* and *The Furies* follow Philip Kent's heirs from 1794 to 1852 as they travel west, to Kansas, to Texas, to the Northwest Territory, and fight the British again in the War of 1812. By now, the Kents are fast approaching the Civil War, the "chronicles" are bestsellers, and new hardcover editions of the first four volumes have been issued. As in any family, there are the good and the bad, the passionate and the cool, the strong and the weak, the successful and the failures, and so it is with the Kents. Jared, son of Abraham, has married an Indian woman and produced Jephtha, a one-time, now disillusioned preacher who is estranged from his pro-slavery wife and sons. Philip's son Gilbert, physically weak, is the father of one of the strongest Kent women—Amanda, who in turn bore Louis—a most unworthy Kent who is only concerned about the war as long as he can profit from it. Julia Sedgwick divorced one Kent, Louis, only to marry another in the next generation, Gideon, son of Jephtha and brother of Jeremiah, gunfighter and outlaw. The Kent story ends in 1890 having followed the family through the Civil War and Reconstruction, the westward expansion and the building of railroads, the rise of the labor unions, the Chicago fire, the powerful industrialists, the Johnstown flood, the slums of New York, and thousands of other happenings in the growth of the United States. The characters move the story along, but the facts are all there.

Jakes's narrative pattern is the same with his Civil War trilogy—*North and South*, *Love and War*, *Heaven and Hell*; but this time he followed two families—the Mains from South Carolina and the Hazards from Pennsylvania. Orry Main and George Hazard meet as plebes at West Point in 1842, become best friends, and remain so, throughout the following 20 years even though one is the son of a plantation owner, and the other the son of an industrialist. The story is entertaining, the characters endearing, the history authentic, and no sides are taken. Jakes has made history students of readers who would never think of opening a textbook. On the negative side, there are so many characters and subplots, and so many historical facts to absorb that a sense of atmosphere and immediacy is missing.

One of the unique features of Jakes's work is the "afterword" that accompanies many of his novels. It is as if he were having a personal conversation with the reader—revealing the happenings in his life that occurred while writing, the family deaths, his own illness, giving up cigarettes, even what he thinks about his own work. In the afterword to *Heaven and Hell* he regrets that he concentrated so much on the continuing struggles of the blacks, while ignoring the plight of the American Indians, and hints that an Indian family saga may be in the works.

—Marion Hanscom

JAMES, Margaret. See **BENNETTS, Pamela.**

JAMES, Robin. See **LONDON, Laura.**

JAMES, Stephanie. See **KRENTZ, Jayne Ann.**

JARMAN, Rosemary (Josephine) Hawley (née Smith). British. Born in Worcester, 27 April 1935. Educated at the Alice Ottley School, Worcester, 1946–52; studied opera in London, 1952–55. Married David C. Jarman in 1958 (divorced 1970). Local government officer, Worcester, 1962–68; receptionist, Midlands Electricity, Worcester, 1969; secretary, Rural District Council, Lipton on Severn, Worcestershire, 1970. Recipient: Silver Quill award, 1971. Agent: A. M. Heath, 79 St. Martin's Lane, London, WC2N 4AA, England. Address: Llanungar Cottage, Whitchurch, Solva, Haverfordwest, Dyfed SA62 6UD, Wales.

ROMANCE AND HISTORICAL PUBLICATIONS

Novels

We Speak No Treason. London, Collins, and Boston, Little Brown, 1971.
The King's Grey Mare. London, Collins, and Boston, Little Brown, 1973; as *Crown of Glory*, New York, Berkley, 1987.
Crown in Candlelight. London, Collins, and Boston, Little Brown, 1978.
The Courts of Illusion. London, Collins, and Boston, Little Brown, 1983.

OTHER PUBLICATIONS

Other

Crispin's Day. London, Collins, and Boston, Little Brown, 1979.

*

Rosemary Hawley Jarman comments:
25 years ago I discovered my literary métier—history as it was lived—when I fell totally and irrevocably in love with King Richard III.

Now history became real, the characters fully fleshed, the climate of the times oddly familiar as if I drew upon past experience. To me the 15th century, in which all my work to date is set, was a time for flowers and blood, swords and viols, when courtly manners rode in tandem with dreadful punishments. This was a world which, although light years away in morals and manners, seemed somehow keyed to modern living. Good men went unrewarded even then, and corruption flourished, yet candles bloomed in dusky abbeys, lovers met, and music was made in heaven.

I have always been totally convinced that Richard Plantagenet's historical reputation was the result of a careful propaganda exercise begun by the Tudors and perpetuated by the world's greatest playwright. Academic rehabilitation of this monarch is slowly taking place, by my obsession, when writing *We Speak No Treason*, was to state his case in the best way I could. Research was profound, and intuition flourished as I sought to inform through entertainment; the cause was paramount.

The King's Grey Mare dealt with the Wars of the Roses—seen from the sinister side. The chief protagonist, Elizabeth Woodville, Queen of Edward IV, was responsible in many ways for the machinations which caused Richard's downfall. I gained enough insights to find understanding of, if not sympathy for this "Witch Queen," and later, summoned enough impartiality to write *Crown in Candlelight*. This novel describes the extraordinary career of Owen ap Tydier, a Welsh esquire who, by his seduction of Henry V's widow, was destined to found the powerful dynasty of Tudor.

The Courts of Illusion rounds off the quartet and is in a way a sequel to the first book. Some of the old characters reappear and the tale is told by the son of the Man of Keen Sight, one of the three principal narrators in *We Speak No Treason*. The novel is crueller, more abrasive than its predecessors, which to me is aptly significant, since its action takes place during the reign of Henry VII, when the golden age of Platagenet was over. It is also the summation of my defence of Richard, as it shows that Perkin Warbeck (whose character forms the hub of the plot) was indeed no pretender to the English throne but one of the allegedly murdered Princes in the Tower—alive and well.

*   *   *

Rosemary Hawley Jarman's works all deal with the Middle Ages in England. The three fictional characters of the first book appear, with varying degrees of importance, in at least one of the other stories.

We Speak No Treason uses these three people to tell of the reign of Richard III. Each serves the king in a different capacity: mistress, fool, and keen-sighted messenger. Each loves Richard of York dearly and, consequently, speaks of him favorably as noble and courageous. (Shakespeare worked for a Tudor monarch and reflected the enmity of the Tudors for the Yorks.) Jarman offers a plausible explanation for the deaths of the two princes in the Tower in a well-told, richly colorful story with lots of excitement.

The King's Grey Mare is the medieval people's epithet for Elizabeth Woodville. Widow of Sir John Grey, Elizabeth refuses Edward IV's suit until he marries her. She and her mother are suspected of using witchcraft to entrap the king. Once crowned, she finds positions at court for all of her relatives until the government is overrun by Woodvilles. The mistress who later becomes a nun, the fool, and the keen-sighted messenger all play a role. There is less action in this story as Elizabeth is the focal character, and women do not go to war. Still another version of the deaths of the two princes in the Tower is put forth. Lots of plotting and counterplotting could completely confuse the reader, but Jarman keeps the threads straight.

Crown in Candlelight takes up the life of Henry V and is told from the point of view of his Queen, Katherine of Valois. A lot of unfamiliar history is covered, especially when Jarman tells of Katherine's childhood. Younger daughter of Charles VI of France, known as The Mad, Katherine is unloved, hungry, and terrified of both parents. She is used as a pawn to unite England with one of the French political factions and is pleasantly surprised to find herself married to a man she can love. She bears him a son who becomes Henry VI and who inherits his grandfather's malady. After the king's death in France, Katherine returns to England. There, several years later, she falls in love with Owen Tydier, Henry's favorite minstrel. She bears him three sons before they are forcibly separated by the new king and his advisers. One of the little boys will be the father of the first Tudor king, Henry VII. Witchcraft and visions in smoke are commonplace experiences, providing an unreal element to the story. The sheer number of characters is overwhelming, and even the genealogical listings at the front and back of the book do not answer all the questions. The love story is warmly delineated, however, and the characterizations are incisive. The reader can see the faint traces of the madness which manifests itself later in the life of Henry VI beginning to show themselves in the child. The mistress, fool, and messenger do not appear, as this book takes place earlier than any of the others.

The Courts of Illusion is the tragedy of Nicholas Archer, illegitimate son of the keen-sighted messenger. After his brother Edmund's death, for which he holds himself responsible, Nicholas, in atonement, takes Edmund's place in the service of the man who claims to be Richard IV, son of Edward IV and one of the two young princes from the Tower. Henry VII and history call him Perkin Warbeck, imposter. Nicholas comes to love him and serves him well. But as with everyone he cares about, from his father to his best friend to his precious bride-to-be, Nicholas loses him tragically. The story evokes sympathy for Nicholas, who is buffeted by ill fortune whichever way he turns. Most novels deal with the Perkin Warbeck affair from Henry's point of view. This book is unique in taking the other side and using a servitor as the focal character. It offers the reader a chance to decide whether Warbeck is really the prince or an imposter. The nun and fool also appear.

Jarman has a tendency to list things interminably. She describes an army by numbering the representatives from each country, counting the types of soldiers, and adding up the cannons, horses, and war machines. Or she details the many steps in getting the king awake and dressed. The impetus comes to a complete halt until the end of the list. The research is good, however, and the stories are well told and entertaining. The four books are history made easy to swallow.

—Andrea Lee Shuey

JASON, Veronica. See **JOHNSTON, Velda.**

JENNINGS, Gary. Also writes as Gabriel Quyth. American. Born in Buena Vista, Virginia, 20 September 1928. Educated at the Art Students' League, New York, 1949–51. Served in the United States Army Infantry, 1952–54: Bronze Star. Has one son. Advertising copywriter and account executive, New York, 1947–52, 1954–58; newspaper reporter, California and Virginia, 1958–61; managing editor, *Duke* and *Gent* magazines, New York, 1962–63. Agent: McIntosh and Otis Inc., 310 Madison Avenue, New York, New York 10017. Address: P.O. Box 1371, Lexington, Virginia 24450, U.S.A.

ROMANCE AND HISTORICAL PUBLICATIONS

Novels

Sow the Seeds of Hemp. New York, Norton, 1976.
Aztec. New York, Atheneum, 1980; London, Macdonald, 1981.
The Journeyer. New York, Atheneum, and London, Hutchinson, 1984.
Spangle. New York, Atheneum, 1987; London, Muller, 1988.

OTHER PUBLICATIONS

Novels

The Terrible Teague Bunch. New York, Norton, 1975.
The Lively Lives of Quentin Mobey (as Gabriel Quyth). New York, Atheneum, 1988.

Other (for children)

March of the Robots. New York, Dial Press, 1962.
The Movie Book. New York, Dial Press, 1963.
Black Magic, White Magic. New York, Dial Press, 1964; London, Hart Davis, 1967.
Parades! Philadelphia, Lippincott, 1966.
The Killer Storms. Philadelphia, Lippincott, 1970.
The Teenager's Realistic Guide to Astrology. New York, Association Press, 1971.
The Shrinking Outdoors. Philadelphia, Lippincott, 1972.
The Earth Book. Philadelphia, Lippincott, 1974.
March of the Heroes. New York, Association Press, 1975.
The Rope in the Jungle. Philadelphia, Lippincott, 1976.
March of the Gods. New York, Association Press, 1976.
March of the Demons. New York, Association Press, 1977.

Other

Personalities of Language. New York, Crowell, 1965; London, Gollancz, 1967; as *World of Words*, New York, Atheneum, 1984.
The Treasure of the Superstition Mountains. New York, Norton, 1973.

*

Manuscript Collection: Boston University, Massachusetts.

Gary Jennings comments:

I choose for my novels a subject, an historical incident, or an era that has never before been treated in fiction—or that I believe has not been *adequately* treated. Each of my novels involves a journey of both extent and duration, and (I hope) illustrates and celebrates the perdurability of human beings. That theme appears to have a fairly universal appeal.

*   *   *

There can be little doubt that Gary Jennings's historical fiction is among the most meticulously researched in the genre. He devotes painstaking time and effort into his background work, travelling through the territory described in his novels and interviewing countless experts. His evident enthusiasm for travel is reflected in the common theme of journeying in his novels, in which the picaresque tradition of bawdy irreverence is used to some effect.

Jennings's first historical novel, *Aztec*, rests on the conceit that the Spanish emperor Charles I has commissioned the memoirs of Mixtli, an "elderly male Indian" as research into the society of the newly-conquered territory of Mexico. Born 50 years before the invasion of the conquistadores, Mixtli undertakes a series of journeys and adventures in the Aztec empire, becoming in turn scholar, trader, soldier, and minister before Cortés descends upon his civilisation. His somewhat pedestrian style and lack of emotional engagement with the characters does not prevent the panoply of exotic detail from almost overwhelming the reader with a stunning sense of how different this central American society was before the advent of the white man. Threaded through the narrative are circumstantial data about the religion (drug use and human sacrifice), art, and technology, all of which combine to present a clear and powerful picture of a lost world. Some of the detail is genuinely shocking: torture, rape, and inhuman executions form the cruel background from which the civilisation seeks to reach the gods, and Mixtli's exhaustive series of sexual encounters are not to everybody's taste. Yet all this seems almost insignificant when the Spaniards arrive, bent on exploitation and apparent genocide. No Aztec ever came to write an entire life history, the real Charles I not being as curious as his fictional counterpart, but Jennings does a craftsmanlike job of recreating an entire society, from top to bottom, through the mosaic of scavenged historical fact that remains of the imperial plunder.

The Journeyer purports to be another true-life confession, this time of a figure who has definitely not vanished from history. The first-person account of Marco Polo reads as an unexpurgated version of his travels; the published version was, after all, intended as a report to his fellow Venetian merchants and therefore did not have to include such exotic scenes as appear here. Jennings's fascination with bizarre and vicarious perversity re-emerges in this novel, and students of exquisite torture or the seemingly limitless sexual potential of the mysterious East will be well satisfied. The Marco Polo of this tale is not the business-like merchant we might expect, but a reckless adventurer in search of "the beauty of danger and the danger of beauty." Again, Jennings has incorporated endless amounts of circumstantial detail, building a cumulative picture of the lands and peoples whom he meets in his voyages through the middle eastern empires, through to China and Kublai Khan himself, the most powerful and richest man in the world.

Jennings's most recent novel, *Spangle*, gives a clue to the method by which Jennings hopes to create a comprehensive and believable illusion. In an extended metaphor toward the beginning of this novel of circus life, a character reflects on the fact that the small, almost tawdry, sequins and "spangles" on the troupers' costumes are transmuted into a starry spectacle in the ring. Likewise, the petty rivalries and hatred of the troupe are subsumed into the needs of the show, which evolves from a raggle-taggle group of refugees into one of the most prominent circuses in the world. No doubt Jennings sees his diligent research, his piling of fact upon fact, in a similar way, trusting that (as it often does) there will be a total effect which sweeps the reader into his chosen milieu. *Spangle* relates the story of Florian's Flourishing Florilegium from the end of the American Civil War in 1865 to the end of the Franco-Prussian War in 1871. Colonel Zachary Edge, late of the defeated Confederate Army, joins the troupe as they flee the debilitating debacle of postwar Reconstruction. Sergeant Obie Yount, Sancho Panza to Edge's Quixote, tags along as strongman. As they travel from America to Europe, taking the great Empires of Austria-Hungary, Russia, and France, they become embroiled in the complexities of European politics and at the same time attain unrivalled eminence in the circus world. By now the reader is primed to expect both a rich complexity of background detail and a wealth of diverse characters, and Jennings does not disappoint: the circus becomes a pretext for a gathering of bizarre personnel, each from a different culture and each with a different sexual inclination. The resulting tangle of events is hugely enjoyable, and the nostalgia for the grand heyday of circus infectious. The sweep of international affairs, and the catastrophic siege of Paris which makes up the climactic conclusion, are handled resourcefully.

Jennings's novels are at once bawdy ventures into the picaresque realm of the low and scandalous, and detailed documentary reconstructions. His strengths as a researcher and a storyteller conceal, for the most part, his sometimes inelegant use of language and paucity of characterisation. Yet there is no doubt of his immense popular appeal: his novels are all bestsellers, the readers undoubtedly obtaining the satisfying sense of having been both entertained and edified. His work does not attain the status of high art, and there is no reason to suppose he intends it to do so. But it creates imaginative journeys into past (often forgotten) worlds, accessible at last to the general reader.

—Alan Murphy

JENNINGS, Sara. See **SEGER, Maura.**

JOHANSEN, Iris. Address: c/o Bantam Publishing, 666 Fifth Avenue, New York, New York 10103, U.S.A.

ROMANCE AND HISTORICAL PUBLICATIONS

Novels (series: Delaneys; Shamrock)

Stormy Vows. New York, Bantam, 1983.
Tempest at Sea. New York, Bantam, 1983.
The Reluctant Lark. New York, Bantam, 1983.
The Bronzed Hawk. New York, Bantam, 1983.
The Lady and the Unicorn. New York, Bantam, 1984.
The Golden Valkyrie. New York, Bantam, 1984.
The Trustworthy Redhead. New York, Bantam, 1984.
Return to Santa Flores. New York, Bantam, 1984.
No Red Roses. New York, Bantam, 1984.
Capture the Rainbow. New York, Bantam, 1984.
Touch the Horizon. New York, Bantam, 1984.
The Forever Dream. New York, Bantam, 1985.
White Satin. New York, Bantam, 1985.
Blue Velvet. New York, Bantam, 1985.
A Summer Smile. New York, Bantam, 1985.
And the Desert Blooms. New York, Bantam, 1986.

Always. New York, Bantam, 1986.
Everlasting. New York, Bantam, 1986.
York the Renegade (Shamrock). New York, Bantam, 1986.
'Til the End of Time. New York, Bantam, 1987.
Matilda the Adventuress (Delaneys). New York, Bantam, 1987.
Last Bridge Home. New York, Bantam, 1987.
Across the River of Yesterday. New York, Bantam, 1987.
The Spellbinder. New York, Bantam, 1987.
Magnificent Folly. New York, Bantam, 1987.
Wild Silver (Delaneys). New York, Bantam, 1988.
Satin Ice (Delaneys). New York, Bantam, 1988.
One Touch of Topaz. New York, Bantam, 1988.
Star Light, Star Bright. New York, Bantam, 1988.
This Fierce Splendor. New York, Bantam, 1988.
Man from Half Moon Bay. New York, Bantam, 1988.
Blue Skies and Shining Promises. New York, Bantam, 1988.
Strong, Hot Winds. New York, Bantam, 1988.

*   *   *

Iris Johansen has rapidly become one of the most prolific and innovative writers of romance fiction. Working mostly in the series romance field, she has stretched the boundaries of the standard formulas.

Beginning with her first Loveswept novel in 1983, *Stormy Vows,* Johansen has linked many of her novels by recurring characters. *The Golden Valkyrie* introduced the first in a long line of interconnected stories about the inhabitants of two imaginary present-day countries. The Middle Eastern kingdom of Sedikhan is featured most prominently, but the Balkan Kingdom of Tamrovia is occasionally used as a locale. They are linked through the royal families, the Ben Raschids and the Rubinoffs. Even some of the characters from the first novels make brief appearances or are mentioned in these subsequent books. Although other novels intervene, Johansen returns time and again to Sedikhan and Tamrovia. Some of these stories are especially poignant. David Bradford, a recovering drug addict introduced in *The Trustworthy Redhead,* is shown to have found peace and finds love in *Touch the Horizon.* His love is Billie Callahan, a generous waif, who played a major role in *Capture the Rainbow.* Later, in *A Summer Smile,* Johansen tells the story of Zilah, a young girl who had been sold into prostitution but was rescued by David. She finds her peace and happiness with Daniel Seifert, who himself appeared earlier in *Blue Velvet.* Gradually Johansen has created a far-flung, but related world. Sedikhan also figures in two novels in which Johansen crosses over into fantasy. Both *Last Bridge Home* and *Star Light, Star Bright* use Sedikhan as a refuge for the Clanad, people with very special powers who are persecuted by a shadowy government agency.

Johansen has collaborated with two other romance writers, Kay Hooper and Fayrene Preston, on a series of novels. Each author wrote one book in the Shamrock trilogy, which tells the story of the Delaney brothers. Johansen's contribution is *York the Renegade.* The family series was continued when the three authors created the Delaneys of Killaroo series. This time the focus was on three sisters in the Australian branch of the family, with Johansen contributing *Matilda the Adventuress.* Obviously having developed a real winner in the romance field, the three writers have continued with two Delaney "prequel" trilogies: The Untamed Years and The Untamed Years II. Johansen's contributions in these series are, respectively, *Wild Silver* and *Satin Ice.* Both follow the story of Silver Delaney and the Russian Prince Nicholas Savron. Johansen also wrote *This Fierce Splendor,* which is the story of Dominic Delaney and Elspeth Mac-

Gregor and seems to be, at least so far, the first story of the Delaney clan.

Johansen's skill as a romance writer and her willingness to experiment with new storylines and formats has firmly established her as one of the leading authors of romance fiction writing today.

—Barbara E. Kemp

JOHN, Nancy. See **BUCKINGHAM, Nancy.**

JOHNSON, Barbara Ferry. American. Born in Grosse Pointe, Michigan, 7 July 1923. Educated at Northwestern University, Evanston, Illinois, B.S. 1945; Clemson University, South Carolina, M.A. 1964. Married William David Johnson in 1947; one son and two daughters. Associate editor, *American Lumberman* magazine, Chicago, 1945–48; high school English teacher, Myrtle Beach, South Carolina, 1960–62. Since 1964 member of the English Department, Columbia College, South Carolina. Agent: Writers House Inc., 21 West 26th Street, New York, New York 10010. Address: Route 1, Box 214, Shallotte, North Carolina 28459, U.S.A.

ROMANCE AND HISTORICAL PUBLICATIONS

Novels

Lionors. New York, Avon, 1975; London, Sphere, 1977.
Delta Blood. New York, Avon, 1977; London, Sphere, 1978.
Tara's Song. New York, Avon, 1978; London, Sphere, 1980.
Homeward Winds the River. New York, Avon, 1979; London, Sphere, 1980.
The Heirs of Love. New York, Avon, 1980.
Echoes from the Hills. New York, Warner, 1983; London, Sphere, 1984.

*   *   *

Barbara Ferry Johnson is most interested in the confrontation of men and women from alien cultures and alien backgrounds; she depicts the way love helps them transcend personal prejudices and personal limitations to come to terms with another's values and to learn to see and think with new eyes. In *Tara's Song* an English earl's daughter, taken from a convent in a Viking raid, learns to love a Viking prince and his family, appreciate their values, and fight for their causes. In *Lionors* King Arthur's first love must learn from Merlin and Arthur to see with Nature's eyes and to sacrifice personal need for a nation's vision as her lover is transformed from an orphan of little significance to King of England. In *Delta Blood* and *Homeward Winds the River* a New Orleanean octoroon, Leah, attempts to escape the restrictions imposed by her black blood, but love and war transform her perceptions and lead her to defend southern values and southern traditions against Union barbarism and hypocrisy, to work uncomplainingly as a nurse comforting wounded Confederate soldiers and to help save from death and destruction both them and a plantation (the symbol of the slave tradition which has constricted and limited her life). In *Homeward* she moves north to fulfill her life-long dream—to pass for white, only to learn that each person is trapped in some way, if not by skin color, then by differences in values and ways of life, and that her heritage, though black, is also southern. The final book in this trilogy, *The Heirs of Love*, traces her children's attempts to come to terms with their white/black heritage and to discover who and what they are and where they truly belong. In *Echoes from the Hills* a young Belgian girl, Alys Prevou, in love with a resistance fighter killed by the Germans, must first come to terms with her rape by arrogant, vengeful German officers and then with the child that it produces. Later she chances loss of family and execution to save, protect, and nurture a comatose, then aphasic and amnesiac American soldier, knowing all the while that his recovery of memory will mean his loss of all knowledge of her and her love and aid. In each of these books Johnson's heroines must adapt to changing conditions of war and conflict, death, disease, and drudgery, and somehow maintain their spirit and inspire their men to endure seemingly impossible difficulties. Johnson's women are strong and enduring. Despite their emotional conflicts, they learn to cope, to survive, and to lend strength and courage to those around them. Where others would yield, they determinedly and selflessly persist.

Mystic elements play important roles in these sagas: magic runes embodying ancient secrets in *Tara's Song*, seers and magicians in *Lionors*, voodoo rites and voodoo princesses in the New Orleans trilogy, and deep-seated, sub-conscious psychological responses in *Echoes from the Hills*. Yet each is down-to-earth in its specific detailing of the difficult day-to-day skills women in different ages have had to master, particularly skills vital to the continuation of life and comfort, work born of necessity in hard times—learning to cultivate the land, organize help, preserve and store food, sew, redecorate, rear children, nurse, and even fight. Typical is the heroine of *Echoes from the Hills*, who, her world a no-man's land dominated by Americans and Germans in turn, nonetheless manages to produce and raise two children, support her aging parents, teach and tend the children of her war-torn neighborhood, and nurse the wounded of both sides. Intrigued by the genetic complexities that reproduce, modify and mold each generation, Johnson examines child-parent conflicts, advocates different approaches to child-rearing for different psychologies, and suggests the difficulty of ever predicting the final results of environment and genes.

But the focus of her books is the psychology of women's love—Lionors who must hide her love despite her deep romantic yearnings; Tara who fears love's betrayal and learns its selflessness only after suffering slavery, imprisonment and culture shock in Turkey; Leah whose emotional and physical needs lead her to become a rich plantation owner's mistress when her deeper longing is to be a wife and mother; and Alys, whose husband has totally forgotten not only their love but her very existence, but who keeps silent to protect his privacy and to free him to choose with a whole mind. Each of Johnson's heroines is threatened by or endures brutal attack by libidinous males; each finds strength and comfort in a deeply romantic and sexually satisfying love that demands sacrifice and understanding. Each must deal with rivals in love; and each must help her beloved regain his sense of vitality and manhood which injury and humiliation threaten.

Though Johnson makes occasional minor slips in locale and custom, in the main her books conjure up past times with delightful detail, clearly and carefully evoking the hardships and pleasures of by-gone ages to make the alien familiar. Although they vividly depict the psychology of men in war and conflict, they focus most particularly on the psychology of women, abandoned, maltreated, loved, or disdained, and are a tribute to the strengths that have made men and women and love endure, despite the insanities that beset them.

—Gina Macdonald

JOHNSON, Susan. American. Born in Hibbing, Minnesota, 7 June 1939. Educated at the University of Minnesota, Minneapolis, B.A. in studio art 1960, M.A. in art history 1969. Married 1) Pat MacKay in 1957, two children; 2) Craig Johnson in 1966, one child. Librarian, University of Minnesota, 1966–79. Agent: Oscar Collier, 2000 Flat Run Road, Seaman, Ohio 45679. Address: Route 2, Box 85, North Branch, Minnesota 55056, U.S.A.

ROMANCE AND HISTORICAL PUBLICATIONS

Novels (series: Braddock-Black; Kuzan)

Seized by Love (Kuzan). New York, Playboy Press, 1979.
Love Storm (Kuzan). New York, Playboy Press, 1981.
Sweet Love, Survive (Kuzan). New York, Berkley, 1985.
Blaze (Braddock-Black). New York, Berkley, 1986.
The Play. New York, Fawcett, 1987.
Silver Flame (Braddock-Black). New York, Berkley, 1988.

*

Susan Johnson comments:

It does not take great maestri, Danilo Kiš noted, to describe life as hell. I agree. What I hope to do instead is entertain, but also inform, seduce, perhaps even astonish and disturb, all with a painter's eye for atmospheric reality and lyrical detail. Within this reality I strive to make my characters come alive—so you can hear them breathe.

*   *   *

In Susan Johnson's historical romance *Silver Flame* the heroine, Empress Jordan, accuses the hero, Trey Braddock-Black, of being scandalous. "But entertaining," he adds with a grin. One might say the same of Johnson.

She began her writing career with Playboy Press which placed no editorial restrictions on her erotic imagination. Consequently, her first three novels, a Russian trilogy set from 1874 to 1920, featuring the sexual and military exploits of three generations of the Kuzan family men, are spicy well beyond the limits of most historical romances. The second in the Russian series, *Love Storm*, is a masterpiece of erotica. A particularly lavish scene set in a Turkish encampment, complete with hypnotic music, hashish, richly woven Persian carpets, aphrodisiacs, sexual teasing, and purple plums earned Johnson the nickname "Plum Lady" in some romance reading circles. Sex, in Johnson's novels, is pure delight for both men and women, an intensely pleasurable physical experience devoid of guilt or cloying sentimentality.

Johnson's next two historical novels, set predominantly in the American west from 1861 to 1890, are less daring in sexual content, although sexuality is still an essential part of their focus and appeal. *Blaze* is about the love affair between Jon Hazard Black, an Absarokee Indian chief, and Blaze Braddock, a beautiful, spoiled Bostonian debutante; *Silver Flame* is the story of their son, Trey. A third novel featuring Jon Hazard Black's natural daughter, Daisy, is in the works.

Although a reader may initially focus only on the sexuality in Johnson's novels, her work has other qualities that recommend it. One of the major challenges facing writers of popular historical fiction is finding a balance between "history" and "the story." Johnson never lets historical detail overwhelm her story; yet, she clearly loves history. Trained in art history, she is a frequent speaker at regional and national romance conferences on historical research. Each of her novels is a blend of fictional and real historical characters and events which she smoothly incorporates in the text or describes in endnotes which provide fascinating information on a wide range of subjects from frontier political corruption and Indian customs to the sleeping and drinking habits of Alexander II and Erik Satie.

Besides the vividly portrayed sex and history, Johnson's novels are notable for their wry wit. For example, in *Silver Flame*, she makes the following simple but damning observation about a rather sleazy villain: "Duncan's intrigues occasionally outstripped his intelligence." Her humor also enlivens the sex scenes, as in this description of a "hot and steamy" glance exchanged by the hero and heroine: "The look he gave her could have boiled every coffee pot in Montana for a month."

Her fictional style, which has steadily developed since her first novel, *Seized by Love* is an interesting combination of regency romance, erotica, and "glitz and glamour." The fantasy she constructs is reinforced by her use of multiple points of view—the hero, heroine, or even a minor character, an onlooker—which draw the reader into the story.

Johnson favors "larger than life" characters rather than realistic "boy/girl-next door" characters. Her heroes, the real focus of her stories, are invariably rich aristocrats—charming and arrogant men who make love, ride horses, hunt wild game, play politics, plan military strategy, gamble, and drink with graceful expertise. The heroines are not quite the match of the heroes although the heroes think they are. Certainly the heroines are not mere simpering misses or delicate flowers. They put up a good fight and manage to cure the hero of a little of his arrogance by the story's end.

In addition to her five historical novels, Johnson has published a romance for teenagers *The Play*, and has another Russian historical novel and a contemporary spy thriller in press. Although she is known exclusively as a romance writer thus far, the spy thriller may mark her transition into more mainstream popular fiction. One welcomes the expansion of her scope and talent.

—Margaret Jensen

———————

JOHNSTON, Mary. American. Born in Buchanan, Virginia, 21 November 1870. Educated at home. *Died 9 May 1936.*

ROMANCE AND HISTORICAL PUBLICATIONS

Novels

The Prisoners of Hope: A Tale of Colonial Virginia. Boston, Houghton Mifflin, 1898; as *The Old Dominion*, London, Constable, 1899.
To Have and to Hold. Boston, Houghton Mifflin, 1900; as *By Order of the Company*, London, Constable, 1900.
Audrey. Boston, Houghton Mifflin, and London, Constable, 1902.

Sir Mortimer. New York, Harper, and London, Constable, 1904.
Lewis Rand. Boston, Houghton Mifflin, and London, Constable, 1908.
The Long Roll. Boston, Houghton Mifflin, 1911.
Cease Firing. Boston, Houghton Mifflin, and London, Constable, 1912.
Hagar. Boston, Houghton Mifflin, and London, Constable, 1913.
The Witch. Boston, Houghton Mifflin, and London, Constable, 1914.
The Fortunes of Garin. Boston, Houghton Mifflin, and London, Constable, 1915.
Foes. New York, Harper, 1918; as *The Laird of Glenfernie*, London, Constable, 1919.
Michael Forth. New York, Harper, 1919; London, Constable, 1920.
Sweet Rocket. New York, Harper, and London, Constable, 1920.
Silver Cross. Boston, Little Brown, and London, Butterworth, 1922.
1492. Boston, Little Brown, 1922; as *Admiral of the Ocean-Sea*, London, Butterworth, 1923.
Croatan. Boston, Little Brown, 1923; London, Butterworth, 1924.
The Slave Ship. Boston, Little Brown, 1924; London, Butterworth, 1925.
The Great Valley. Boston, Little Brown, and London, Butterworth, 1926.
The Exile. Boston, Little Brown, and London, Butterworth, 1927.
Hunting Shirt. Boston, Little Brown, 1931; London, Butterworth, 1932.
Miss Delicia Allen. Boston, Little Brown, and London, Butterworth, 1933.
Drury Randall. Boston, Little Brown, 1934; London, Butterworth, 1935.

Short Stories

The Wanderers. Boston, Houghton Mifflin, and London, Constable, 1917.
Collected Short Stories, edited by Annie and Hensley C. Woodbridge. Troy, New York, Whitston, 1982.

OTHER PUBLICATIONS

Play

The Goddess of Reason (produced New York, 1909). Boston, Houghton Mifflin, and London, Constable, 1907.

Other

An Address Read at Vicksburg. . . . Privately printed, 1907.
The Status of Women. Richmond, Virginia, Equal Suffrage League of Virginia, 1909.
The Reason Why. Privately printed, 1910 (?).
To the House of Governors (address). New York, National American Women Suffrage Association, 1912.
Pioneers of the Old South: A Chronicle of English Colonial Beginnings. New Haven, Connecticut, Yale University Press, 1918.

*

Bibliography: in *Three Virginia Writers: A Reference Guide* by George C. Longest, Boston, Hall, 1978.

Manuscript Collection: Alderman Library, University of Virginia, Charlottesville.

Critical Study: *Mary Johnston* by C. Ronald Cella, Boston, Twayne, 1981.

*   *   *

For all practical purposes, Mary Johnston's career began in 1898 with publication of *The Prisoners of Hope*, a romance of colonial Virginia. That initial historical romance acts as a paradigm of her work in the genre: superior story-telling and romantic sensitivity to landscape are wedded to an acute interest in colonial Virginia history. Although frequently compared by early reviewers to Thackeray, Johnston lacked Thackeray's insight into human nature. In the first romance, her portrait of Sir William Berkeley, for example, is wooden, her dialogue artificial. Emphasis in her romances clearly falls on action born of quest. Character, at best, is the by-product of quest, or the by-product of a Victorian ideal.

The most successful of her historical romances, however, was *To Have and to Hold*, a considerably more refined romance than *The Prisoners of Hope*, and the number one best-seller for 1900. Grounded in Virginia history, the romance involves the 1622 Indian massacre of Jamestown. It owes its appeal, however, as Ronald Cella has observed, to the love story of Captain Ralph Percy and Lady Jocelyn Smith and the triangle created by her former suitor, the villainous Lord Carnal. The romance, melodramatic though it may be, remains her best-known work.

Audrey, a romance set in colonial Virginia, capitalizes on the vogue created by *To Have and to Hold*. Emphasizing manners, customs, and history, the romance, as *The Independent* observed on 20 November 1902, made a "romantic rainbow of colonial civilization in Virginia." Replacing the traditional forest scene with a colorful town scene, the setting of *Audrey* becomes "illustrative of character" (*New York Times*, 22 February 1902).

Sir Mortimer, set in late 16th-century England; *The Fortunes of Garin*, set in 11th-century France, *Foes*, set in Jacobite Scotland during the 1745 uprising; and *Silver Cross*, set in Tudor England, suggest Johnston's continued exploitation of the genre and her diminishing talent for it. In the European romances the history is superficial and the characterization too frequently "ideal." *Silver Cross*, however, is the most important work in the European corpus. Johnston's mixture of superstition and mysticism in *Silver Cross* creates, as William Rose Benét early perceived, a "telegraphic" style bordering on pointillism (*New York Evening Post*, 18 March 1922). The style, although inappropriate to the romance, does, however, document Johnston's conflicting interests in romance and novel genres.

Croatan, *The Great Valley*, and *Hunting Shirt* mark Johnston's return to her best mode. In all three romances, setting is of major importance, historical event is motivation, character is ideal, and quest suggests the coherence and definition of the plot. *Croatan* achieves a James Fenimore Cooper suspense in its rendering of pursuit and escape. As *The Athenaeum* reviewer observed (17 July 1926), *The Great Valley* owes its success to its depiction of the effect of wilderness on "natures marked out by a poetic mysticism of Celtic birth." Somewhat similarly, *Hunting Shirt* creates a highly successful view of the link between

American Indians and Scottish settlers. All these romances are considerably strengthened by the author's familiarity with Virginia setting.

—George C. Longest

JOHNSTON, Velda. Also writes as Veronica Jason. American. Educated at schools in California. Address: c/o Dodd Mead, 79 Madison Avenue, New York, New York, 10016, U.S.A.

ROMANCE AND HISTORICAL PUBLICATIONS

Novels

Along a Dark Path. New York, Dodd Mead, 1967; Aylesbury, Buckinghamshire, Milton House, 1974.
House above Hollywood. New York, Dodd Mead, 1968; Aylesbury, Buckinghamshire, Milton House, 1974.
A Howling in the Woods. New York, Dodd Mead, 1968; London, Hale, 1969.
I Came to the Castle. New York, Dodd Mead, 1969; as *Castle Perilous*, London, Hale, 1971.
The Light in the Swamp. New York, Dodd Mead, 1970; London, Hale, 1972.
The Phantom Cottage. New York, Dodd Mead, 1970; London, Hale, 1971.
The Face in the Shadows. New York, Dodd Mead, 1971; London, Hale, 1973.
The People on the Hill. New York, Dodd Mead, 1971; as *Circle of Evil*, London, Hale, 1972.
The Mourning Trees. New York, Dodd Mead, 1972; Aylesbury, Buckinghamshire, Milton House, 1974.
The Late Mrs. Fonsell. New York, Dodd Mead, 1972; Aylesbury, Buckinghamshire, Milton House, 1974.
The White Pavilion. New York, Dodd Mead, 1973; Aylesbury, Buckinghamshire, Milton House, 1974.
Masquerade in Venice. New York, Dodd Mead, 1973; Aylesbury, Buckinghamshire, Milton House, 1974.
I Came to the Highlands. New York, Dodd Mead, 1974; Aylesbury, Buckinghamshire, Milton House, 1975.
The House on the Left Bank. New York, Dodd Mead, 1975.
A Room with Dark Mirrors. New York, Dodd Mead, 1975; London, Prior, 1976.
Deveron Hall. New York, Dodd Mead, 1976; London, Prior, 1977.
The Frenchman. New York, Dodd Mead, and London, Prior, 1976.
The Etruscan Smile. New York, Dodd Mead, 1977; London, W. H. Allen, 1980.
The Hour Before Midnight. New York, Dodd Mead, 1978; London, W. H. Allen, 1981.
The Silver Dolphin. New York, Dodd Mead, 1979; London, Prior, 1981.
The People from the Sea. New York, Dodd Mead, 1979.
A Presence in an Empty Room. New York, Dodd Mead, 1980; London, W. H. Allen, 1982.
The Stone Maiden. New York, Dodd Mead, 1980; Bath, Chivers, 1983.
The Fateful Summer. New York, Dodd Mead, 1981; Bath, Chivers, 1983.

So Wild a Heart (as Veronica Jason). New York, New American Library, 1981.

The Other Karen. New York, Dodd Mead, 1983.

Voice in the Night. New York, Dodd Mead, 1984; Bath, Chivers, 1985.

Shadow Behind the Curtain. New York, Dodd Mead, 1985; London, Severn House, 1986.

The Crystal Cat. New York, Dodd Mead, 1985; London, Severn House, 1987.

Fatal Affair. New York, Dodd Mead, 1986; Bath, Firecrest, 1988.

The House on Bostwick Square. New York, Dodd Mead, 1987.

The Girl on the Beach. New York, Dodd Mead, 1987.

The Man at Windmere. New York, Dodd Mead, 1988.

*   *   *

From the prolific pen of Velda Johnston come historical and contemporary romance mysteries in which young, vulnerable women find their lives plunged into perilous circumstances. Usually an unsolved murder has occurred and the heroine, sometimes innocently but often because of her own curious nature, becomes the killer's next target.

In the historical novel *The Late Mrs. Fonsell* Irene is forced into a marriage with the dark, brooding Jason Fonsell. Many years before, Jason's stepmother had been mysteriously and brutally murdered. Irene, intrigued by this mystery, brings the killer's unwelcome attentions upon herself. Meanwhile, the marriage of convenience to Jason eventually becomes one of love. In the end it is Jason who comes to Irene's rescue as she is stalked by the killer. The novel, *A Presence in an Empty Room*, has an added touch of the supernatural. The evil antagonist whom the newly married Susan Summerslee must overcome is the spirit of her husband's first wife who had plotted the death of her husband by paying someone to sabotage his private plane. Instead it was she who dies in the fiery crash. Aspiring actress Kathy Mayhew (*The Other Karen*) is hired to impersonate a young woman who disappeared years ago. This "acting assignment" almost leads to her death.

What makes Johnston's characters so appealing is their believability. Most of the women are attractive without being overwhelmingly beautiful, and the men, while virile, do not necessarily carry a heavy macho image. Her contemporary heroines are firmly rooted in their middle-class origins and usually have a career, while those of the historical periods belong to the genteel class but with families often skirting the edges of poverty. Many of these women have suffered some recent tragedy or mishap. In *The House on Bostwick Square*, the recently widowed Laura Harmon, an American with a six-year-old daughter, must turn to her wealthy English in-laws when she finds herself without resources. There is little welcome for her or her daughter in this grim household. Diana (*The People from the Sea*) must take a leave of absence from her job as a children's book editor to recover from a breakdown following divorce. In the historical novel *I Came to the Highlands* Elizabeth, thinking she has lost the love of John, allows herself to succumb to the charms of Charles Stuart, pretender to the English throne, and gives birth to his illegitimate son.

Another attraction of Johnston's novels is the richness of her settings, which come from her obviously intimate knowledge of the locations of her stories. Often the mystery unfolds in an isolated area of wild beauty along eastern Long Island. But her descriptions of other exotic locales are equally well done. In the contemporary novel *The Frenchman* and the historical novel *Masquerade in Venice* the reader feels the enchantment of this age-old city of canals.

For all the romance and mystery that are the hallmarks of a Johnston story there is little emphasis on sex (much taking place by innuendo), and there is minimal description of violence. However this emphasis changes when she writes historical romances as Veronica Jason. These novels have a theme of male/female antagonism as their basis, but unlike so many of this genre the characters are well developed, the plots believable, and the sexual tension of the hero and heroine is handled in good taste. Her first book under this pen name is an excellent example. Here the heroine Elizabeth Montlow finds herself pregnant by the Anglo-Irish Lord Patrick Stanford who, in an uncharacteristic moment of savagery, raped this woman whom he blamed for allowing his young ward's killer to go free. After their hasty marriage Elizabeth's finds herself living first as a lady of some social standing and later as a fugitive fleeing Britain with her husband, for Patrick has been denounced as a secret organizer in Ireland's fight for independence.

Whether writing as Johnston or Jason, this author is an excellent story teller. All of her novels are well plotted with neat twists and turns that give an element of drama and excitement all the way through.

—Patricia Altner

JORDAN, Laura. See BROWN, Sandra.

KANE, Julia. See ROBINS, Denise.

KANTOR, MacKinlay. American. Born in Webster City, Iowa, 4 February 1904. Educated at Webster City High School. Married Florence Irene Layne in 1926; two sons. Reporter, Webster City *Daily News*, 1921–24; advertiser in Chicago, 1925–26; reporter, Cedar Rapids *Republican*, Iowa, 1927; columnist, Des Moines *Tribune*, Iowa, 1930–31; scenario writer for Hollywood studios; war correspondent for United States and British air forces, 1943, 1950, and technical consultant to the United States Air Force, 1951–53; member of the uniformed division, New York City Police, 1948–50. Member of the National Council, Boy Scouts of America; trustee, Lincoln College, Illinois, 1960–68. Recipient: Pulitzer prize, 1956; National Association of Independent Schools award, 1956. D.Litt.: Grinnell College, Iowa, 1957; Drake University, Des Moines, 1958; Lincoln College, 1959; Ripon College, Wisconsin, 1961; LL.D.: Iowa Wesleyan College, Mount Pleasant, 1961. Fellow, Society of American Historians. *Died 11 October 1977.*

ROMANCE AND HISTORICAL PUBLICATIONS

Novels (series: Civil War trilogy)

Long Remember. New York, Coward McCann, and London, Selwyn and Blount, 1934.

The Voice of Bugle Ann (Civil War). New York, Coward McCann, and London, Selwyn and Blount, 1935.

Arouse and Beware (Civil War). New York, Coward McCann, 1936; London, Gollancz, 1937.

The Romance of Rosy Ridge (Civil War). New York, Coward McCann, 1937.

Cuba Libre. New York, Coward McCann, 1940.

Gentle Annie: A Western Novel. New York, Coward McCann, 1942; London, Hale, 1951; as *The Goss Boys*, London, Corgi, 1958.

Wicked Water: An American Primitive. New York, Random House, 1949; London, Falcon Press, 1950.

Warwhoop: Two Short Novels of the Frontier (includes *Behold the Brown-Faced Man* and *Missouri Moon*). New York, Random House, 1952.

The Daughter of Bugle Ann. New York, Random House, 1953.

Andersonville. Cleveland, World, 1955; London, W. H. Allen, 1956.

Spirit Lake. Cleveland, World, 1961; London, W. H. Allen, 1962.

If the South Had Won the Civil War. New York, Bantam, 1961.

Beauty Beast. New York, Putnam, 1968.

Valley Forge. New York, Evans, 1975.

Short Stories

Author's Choice: 40 Stories. New York, Coward McCann, 1944.

Silent Grow the Guns and Other Tales of the American Civil War. New York, New American Library, 1958.

Again the Bugle. New York, American Weekly, 1958.

Frontier: Tales of the American Adventure. New York, New American Library, 1959.

The Gun-Toter and Other Stories of the Missouri Hills. New York, New American Library, 1963.

Story Teller. New York, Doubleday, 1967.

OTHER PUBLICATIONS

Novels

Diversey. New York, Coward McCann, 1928.

El Goes South. New York, Coward McCann, 1930.

The Jaybird. New York, Coward McCann, 1932.

The Noise of Their Wings. New York, Coward McCann, 1938; London, Hale, 1939.

Valedictory. New York, Coward McCann, 1939.

Happy Land. New York, Coward McCann, 1943.

Glory for Me (in verse). New York, Coward McCann, 1945.

Midnight Lace. New York, Random House, 1948; London, Falcon Press, 1949.

The Good Family. New York, Coward McCann, 1949.

One Wild Oat. New York, Fawcett, 1950; London, W. H. Allen, 1952.

Signal Thirty-Two. New York, Random House, 1950.

Don't Touch Me. New York, Random House, 1951; London, W. H. Allen, 1952.

God and My Country. Cleveland, World, 1954.

The Work of St. Francis. Cleveland, World, 1958; as *The Unseen Witness*, London, W. H. Allen, 1959.

I Love You, Irene. New York, Doubleday, 1972; London, W. H. Allen, 1973.

The Children Sing. New York, Hawthorn, 1973; London, Hale, 1974.

Short Stories

The Boy in the Dark. Webster Groves, Missouri, International Mark Twain Society, 1937.

It's about Crime. New York, New American Library, 1960.

Plays

Screenplays: *Gun Crazy* (*Deadly Is the Female*), with Millard Kaufman, 1950; *Hannah Lee*, with Rip Von Ronkel, 1953.

Verse

Turkey in the Straw: A Book of American Ballads and Primitive Verse. New York, Coward McCann, 1935.

Other

Angleworms on Toast (for children). New York, Coward McCann, 1942.

But Look, the Morn: The Story of a Childhood (reminiscences). New York, Coward McCann, 1947; London, Falcon Press, 1951.

Lee and Grant at Appomattox (for children). New York, Random House, 1950.

Gettysburg (for children). New York, Random House, 1952.

Three Views of the Novel, with John O'Hara and Irving Stone. Washington, D.C., Library of Congress, 1957.

Lobo (reminiscences). Cleveland, World, 1957; London, W. H. Allen, 1958.

Mission with LeMay: My Story, with General Curtis LeMay. New York, Doubleday, 1965.

The Historical Novelist's Obligation to History (lecture). Macon, Georgia, Wesley College, 1967.

The Day I Met a Lion. New York, Doubleday, 1968.

Missouri Bittersweet (reminiscences). New York, Doubleday, 1969; London, Hale, 1970.

Hamilton County, photographs by Tim Kantor. New York, Macmillan, 1970.

*

Manuscript Collections: Library of Congress, Washington, D.C.; University of Iowa Library, Iowa City.

Critical Study: *My Father's Voice: MacKinlay Kantor Long Remembered* by Tim Kantor, New York, McGraw Hill, 1988.

*   *   *

A prolific, versatile author whose novel *Glory for Me* was made into the award-winning film *The Best Years of Our Lives*, Mackinlay Kantor has nevertheless come to be regarded primarily as a historical writer, and as such ranks high among the chroniclers of the American past. The bitter, divisive War between the States is the event which dominates most of his fiction in this genre—Kantor was the descendant of a Civil War veteran—and to this recurring scenario he applies a strongly individual style which breaks down the narrative to a fragmented sequence of incident and reflection, combining humour, reportage and interior monologue. It is a style already discernible in Kantor's first important novel, *Long Remember*, and one which is developed in later works.

In *Long Remember*, which depicts the carnage of the Gettysburg campaign, Kantor eschews the illusory glamour of warfare to present a grimmer reality where the humdrum and the horrific maintain an uneasy co-existence. Subsequent writings, especially the trilogy *The Voice of Bugle Ann*, *Arouse and Beware*, and *The Romance of Rosy Ridge*, show a continuing exploration of the Civil War theme in the context of human relationships and desires, and a further stylistic development. As in *Long Remember*, conventional heroics are ignored, sometimes to the extent of sidestepping the battles.

Arouse and Beware, for instance, focuses on two escaped Union prisoners and their hazardous trek to freedom through a hostile Virginia landscape. Narrated by one of the main characters, the novel incorporates interior monologue and flashback with descriptions of the terrain and dramatic action passages. The result is an impressive work, whose central image of the starving, half-crazed men, wandering in a malevolent wilderness with their mysterious female companion, lingers powerfully in the mind. The trilogy is a milestone in Kantor's growth as a writer, and is excelled only by his masterpiece, *Andersonville*.

This monolithic novel, which occupied its author for several years, and for which he was awarded a Pulitzer prize, recounts the history of the infamous Georgia prison camp from its initial surveying to its demolition at the end of the Civil War. Kantor builds up each scene gradually to attain a relentless momentum, switching his vision from one set of characters to another to present a convincing microcosm of the life inside the prison. Captives, guards, and onlookers are shown as individuals, their lives and deaths described soberly and almost without comment, in a manner which renders the endless catalogue of starvation and disease all the more appalling. Kantor lays bare the mind of the camp commandant, whose inadequacies express themselves in severity and neglect of the prisoners, and counters him with the dedicated prison surgeon, whose love for a local planter's daughter is an important strand of the novel. The fragmented, incident-based style enables Kantor to construct his prison-universe in a memorable, and often shocking, narrative. A novel of compelling realism, and deep psychological insights, *Andersonville* is justifiably recognized as Kantor's greatest achievement.

With *Spirit Lake* and *Beauty Beast*, Kantor delves further back into American history, exploring pioneer and plantation life in the 1850's. While neither novel equals the power and scope of *Andersonville*, each has definite merits. In *Spirit Lake* particularly Kantor approaches his earlier masterpiece, using the same broken, multi-faceted style to describe the massacre of Iowa settlers by the renegade Inkpaduta and his band. As with *Andersonville*, he follows his characters through their past lives to the final nemesis. The writing shows comparable skill, and individuals are strikingly realized, but *Spirit Lake* does not have the coherence of *Andersonville*, and lacks any obvious unifying theme. A flawed major work, it fails to achieve its considerable promise. *Beauty Beast*, which examines racism, slavery, and sexual desire in the ante-bellum south, is less ambitious but possibly more successful. The story centres on the unrequited love of a female plantation owner for her cultured black house servant, and its eventual tragic outcome. Kantor investigates the many subtle varieties of enslavement—the white mistress in thrall to her uncontrollable passion, the black servant's vision of the great composers as slaves of their patrons—and although the ending is predictable, many of the novel's conclusions are original and unexpected. *Beauty Beast*, like *Spirit Lake*, is less satisfying than some of Kantor's earlier works. All the same, both are worthy of mention as part of an impressive body of fiction by one of America's foremost historical writers.

—Geoffrey Sadler

KAVANAUGH, Cynthia. See **DANIELS, Dorothy.**

KAYE, M(ary) M(argaret). Also writes as Mollie Hamilton; Mollie Kaye. British. Born in Simla, India, 21 August 1908. Educated at the Lawn School, Clevedon, Somerset. Married Geoffrey John Hamilton in 1942 (died 1985); two daughters. Writer and painter. Fellow, Royal Society of Literature. Agent: David Higham Associates, 5–8 Lower John Street, London W1R 4HA, England.

ROMANCE AND HISTORICAL PUBLICATIONS

Novels

Shadow of the Moon. London, Longman, and New York, Messner, 1957.
Trade Wind. London, Longman, 1963; New York, Coward McCann, 1964.
The Far Pavilions. London, Allen Lane, and New York, St. Martin's Press, 1978.

OTHER PUBLICATIONS

Novels

Strange Island. Calcutta, Thacker Spink, n.d.
Six Bars at Seven. London, Hutchinson, 1940.
Death Walked in Kashmir. London, Staples Press, 1953; as *Death in Kashmir*, New York, St. Martin's Press, 1984.
Death Walked in Berlin. London, Staples Press, 1955; as *Death in Berlin*, New York, St. Martin's Press, 1983.
Death Walked in Cypress. London, Staples Press, 1956; as *Death in Cypress*, New York, St. Martin's Press, 1984.
Later than You Think. London, Longman, 1958; as Mollie Hamilton, New York, Coward McCann, 1959; as *It's Later than You Think*, Manchester, World Distributors, 1960; as *Death in Kenya*. London, Allen Lane, 1983.
The House of Shade. London, Longman, and New York, Coward McCann, 1959; as *Death in Zanzibar*, London, Allen Lane, 1983.
Night on the Island. London, Longman, 1960; as *Death in the Andamans*, New York, Viking, 1985.

OTHER PUBLICATIONS

Fiction (for children) as Mollie Kaye

Potter Pinner series (*Potter Pinner Meadow*, *Black Bramble Wood*, *Willow Witches Brook*, *Gold Gorse Common*). London, Collins, 4 vols., 1937–45.
The Ordinary Princess. London, Kestrel, 1980; New York, 1984.
Thistledown. London, Quartet, 1981.

Play

Radio Play: *England Wakes*, 1941.

Other

Editor, *The Golden Calm: An English Lady's Life in Moghul Delhi*, by Emily Bayley and Thomas Metcalfe. New York, Viking Press, and Exeter, Devon, Webb and Bower, 1980.
Editor, *Moon and Other Days: M. M. Kaye's Kipling: Favourite Verses*. London, Hodder and Stoughton, 1988.

*   *   *

There are few who would deny or even challenge M. M. Kaye's position as an authority on India and its past. Her family served the Raj for three generations, as did her husband's. She spent most of her childhood and early married life there. Thus, when she relates the details of the Indian Mutiny and the second Afghan Rising, one can be sure that her account is not only judicious but accurate.

However, this wealth of knowledge proves to be a literary bain as well as a blessing; so taken is she with relating historical events and their significance that she allows them to become the central focus of attention. It almost appears as though Kaye is demanding recognition of their import simply because they are facts, thus relegating the narrative of her fiction to the status of a melodramatic diversion.

The word "melodramatic" need not be pejorative and is used here in its purest sense. Kaye relates tales of forbidden love—Englishman for Hindu in *The Far Pavilions*; army officer for superior's wife in *Shadow of the Moon*—that are punctuated by incidents where death or disaster are always imminent, and where characters are linked by astounding coincidences and twists of fate. It is a style as popular today in the form of the soap opera as it was in its supposed Victorian heyday.

The style and scope of her novels draw further comparisons with those of a bygone age, calling to mind such Victorian epics as Dickens's *Great Expectations*, especially in the case of *The Far Pavilions*, telling as it does of the birth, early life, and growth to maturity of Ashton Pelham-Martyn, or Ash. Ash is an orphan raised as a Hindu after the death of his parents in India just prior to the fabled Mutiny; his childhood is one beset with self-deception and palace intrigue, with his "expectations" as an Englishman only presenting themselves when death seems closest at hand. The Victorian flavour of the story emerges in the obvious echoes of Kipling's *Jungle Book* stories and in Kaye's fondness for authorial moralising.

Kaye writes with the traditionalist intentions of "education, entertainment, and information." How is one to assess her realisation of them? It is undeniable that the mass of information provided by Kaye is educational. Her summary of the causes of the Indian Mutiny, glossary of Indian words, and provision of various historical notes indicate a scholarly approach of educational validity equal to that of any textbook. While this factual data has a tendency to overwhelm the plot, there is little denying that, when the fiction does resurface, as with all melodramas, it is enjoyable. One can hardly help but be caught up in the romance, no matter how farfetched it may seem. However, it is when we come to analyse Kaye's work for its value as information that a different conclusion must be reached.

For all of her authority, Kaye is hardly the first person to write of the days of Empire and the Raj. There is a veritable treasure trove of material on the subject, the source for cultural assumptions concerning the place and period. Clearly, these assumptions are bound to colour the reader's perceptions of the events that Kaye relates in *The Far Pavilions* and *Shadow of the Moon*. Yet not only does she bring nothing new to these assumptions, she relies upon them herself. As with her historical facts, the geographical setting and its subconscious implications are supposed to speak for themselves. Thus her Indian characters not only punctuate their conversations with distracting colloquialisms, but speak in the stilted syntax that we have come to know as Indian via Hollywood. Likewise, the Indians themselves are almost caricatures: unless in sympathy with the British, in which case they are granted a dignified bearing, they remain little more than the barbaric and childish archetypes so beloved of imperial propagandists. Despite her familiarity with and love of the country, Kaye's view of India, unsurprising given her heritage, is that of a member of the old Raj. Instead of informing, she chooses to reinforce those myths of empire and military daring that give us a decidedly warped view of our past, and it is for this reason—more than any other that Kaye ultimately fails from her own traditionalist standpoint.

—Douglas Devaney

KELLOW, Kathleen. See **HOLT, Victoria.**

KENEALLY, Thomas (Michael). Australian. Born in Sydney, New South Wales, 7 October 1935. Educated at St. Patrick's College, Strathfield, New South Wales; studied for the priesthood and studied law. Served in the Australian Citizens Military Forces. Married Judith Mary Martin in 1965; two daughters. High school teacher in Sydney, 1960–64; Lecturer in Drama, University of New England, Armidale, New South Wales, 1968–69. Visiting Professor of English, University of California, Irvine, 1985; Berg Professor of English, New York University, 1988. Since 1985 President, National Book Council of Australia; since 1987 chairman, Australian Society of Authors. Recipient: Commonwealth Literary Fund fellowship, 1966, 1968, 1972; Miles Franklin award, 1968, 1969; Captain Cook Bi-Centenary prize, 1970; Royal Society of Literature Heinemann award, 1973; Booker prize, 1982; *Los Angeles Times* award, 1983. Fellow, Royal Society of Literature, 1973; Officer, Order of Australia, 1983. Agent: Tessa Sayle Agency, 11 Jubilee Place, London SW3 3TE, England.

ROMANCE AND HISTORICAL PUBLICATIONS

Novels

Bring Larks and Heroes. Melbourne, Cassell, 1967; London, Cassell, and New York, Viking Press, 1968.
The Chant of Jimmie Blacksmith. Sydney and London, Angus and Robertson, and New York, Viking Press, 1972.
Blood Red, Sister Rose. London, Collins, and New York, Viking Press, 1974.
Moses the Lawgiver (novelization of television play). London, Collins-ATV, and New York, Harper, 1975.
Gossip from the Forest. London, Collins, 1975; New York, Harcourt Brace, 1976.
A Victim of the Aurora. London, Collins, 1977; New York, Harcourt Brace, 1978.
Confederates. London, Collins, 1979; New York, Harper, 1980.
The Playmaker. London, Hodder and Stoughton, and New York, Simon and Schuster, 1987.

OTHER PUBLICATIONS

Novels

The Place at Whitton. Melbourne and London, Cassell, 1964;
  New York, Walker, 1965.
The Fear. Melbourne and London, Cassell, 1965.
Three Cheers for the Paraclete. Sydney, Angus and Robertson,
  1968; London, Angus and Robertson, and New York, Viking
  Press, 1969.
The Survivor. Sydney, Angus and Robertson, 1969; London,
  Angus and Robertson, and New York, Viking Press, 1970.
A Dutiful Daughter. Sydney and London, Angus and Robert-
  son, and New York, Viking Press, 1971.
Season in Purgatory. London, Collins, 1976; New York, Har-
  court Brace, 1977.
Passenger. London, Collins, and New York, Harcourt Brace,
  1979.
The Cut-Rate Kingdom. Sydney, Wildcat Press, 1980; London,
  Allen Lane, 1984.
Schindler's Ark. London, Hodder and Stoughton, 1982; as
  Schindler's List, New York, Simon and Schuster, 1982.
A Family Madness. London, Hodder and Stoughton, 1985; New
  York, Simon and Schuster, 1986.
Towards Asmara. London, Hodder and Stoughton, 1989.

Plays

Halloran's Little Boat, adaptation of his novel *Bring Larks and
  Heroes* (produced Sydney, 1966). Published in *Penguin Aus-
  tralian Drama 2*, Melbourne, Penguin, 1975.
Childermass (produced Sydney, 1968).
An Awful Rose (produced Sydney, 1972).
Bullie's House (produced Sydney 1980; New Haven, Connecti-
  cut, 1985). Sydney, Currency Press, 1981.

Screenplay: *The Priest* (episode in *Libido*), 1973.

Television Writing (UK): *Essington*, 1974; *The World's Wrong
End* (documentary; *Writers and Places* series), 1981; *Australia*
series, 1987.

Other

Ned Kelly and the City of Bees (for children). London, Cape,
  1978; Boston, Godine, 1981.
Outback, photographs by Gary Hansen and Mark Lang. Sydney
  and London, Hodder and Stoughton, 1983.
Australia: Beyond the Dreamtime, with Patsy Adam-Smith and
  Robyn Davidson. London, BBC Publications, 1987; New
  York, Facts on File, 1989.

*

Manuscript Collections: Mitchell Library, Sydney; Australian
National Library, Canberra.

Theatrical Activities:
Actor: **Films**—*The Devil's Playground*, 1976; *The Chant of Jimmie Blacksmith*, 1978.

*   *   *

Thomas Keneally trained as a Catholic priest, abandoning the
vocation just before ordination, and his work demonstrates a
sensibility profoundly coloured by religious ideas: drama and
magic, ritual and redemption are recurrent themes. Although
events in his fictional world move in a wild chaotic flux, his
characters invest all of their energy into interpreting patterns of
significance. Faced with alien and surreal experience they apply
an astonishing range of belief and ritualistic behaviour, as if
sympathetic magic could offer fixed points in a vertiginous
world of horror and bewilderment. Despite this, his books are
by no means morose or morbid; his pessimism is relieved by a
sharp, often bleak, humour.

The history of Keneally's native Australia is a model for this
process: from a haggard and undifferentiated mass of convicts
emerges a vital, though often brutal culture. Australia's convict
past was by no means fully acknowledged when Keneally began
his writing career, though by the time of *The Playmaker* there
were more open historical accounts available. This novel focuses
on the actual, but almost surreal, event of the new nation's first
drama: a production of George Farquhar's *The Recruiting Officer*
in the desperate famine year of 1789, within the first few months
of the penal colony's existence. The event reflects other beginnings in the nascent colony's history: the first executions, the
first murders, the first native massacres. Lieutenant Ralph Clark,
the idealistic young marine appointed to produce the play with a
convict cast, strives to bring together an artistic creation in the
face of complete social breakdown. As the play's elegant comedy parodies the corrupt English society from which they have
been exiled, so too does Sydney Cove itself come to resemble a
ghastly travesty of civilisation at the boundaries of the known
world. More than an examination of colonialism and repression,
and the complete otherness of the new world is emphasized to
make the novel almost a dream narrative. The convicts take on
the roles of fops and gentlemen, while the real fops and gentlemen take the chance to enact their most perverse fantasies. At
times the scene resembles Kafka's penal settlement, and the macabre motifs of violent death, putrescence, decay, and predatory
sexuality are characteristic Keneally themes.

A more comprehensive survey of his historical fiction could
show both the primacy of Australia in his imagination, and the
variety of his sources and interests beyond. His reputation was
first established in 1967 with *Bring Larks and Heroes*, based on
the Vinegar Hill uprising of Irish convicts in 1804. The carniv-
orous nature of the early Australian colony is shown with brutal
clarity, and the story is dense with action. The accelerated pace
continues in *The Chant of Jimmie Blacksmith* which was inspired by the Jimmy Governor murders in 1900. Jimmie is a
thwarted conformist, and aborigine brought up by white missionaries to wish for permanence and respectability. Neither the
white settlers nor his own people sympathize with this aspiration, and when he marries a white girl he commits the ultimate
act of hubris. Society conspires to ruin him step by step, demanding from him that he concede to each small humiliation.
He takes revenge in an unexpected atrocity, an act that puts him
instantly beyond the pale of either white or black humanity.
Meanwhile, in the larger historical scale, Australia prepares for
federation; the book constantly refers to the ironic conjunction of
events, as if the nation is being baptised in blood. The novel
remains Keneally's best known and most widely read; it also inspired a film adaptation.

With *Blood Red, Sister Rose* and *Gossip from the Forest* Keneally demonstrated historical interests beyond his own country.
The former is an authentically researched and vividly realised
account of the life of Joan of Arc; the latter depicts the tortuous
wranglings for armistice at the close of World War I. Keneally's
Joan is a fragile figure. In his world even a prophetess remains
bemused and vulnerable, prey to uncertainties. This is proved
especially true in the face of the gross obscenity of war. Joan is

a revolutionary: she behaves as if war is real, while her chivalric companions continue to play their knightly games. The novel bears close comparison with Umberto Eco's *The Name of the Rose* which also brings medieval society to detailed and terrifying life. In *Gossip from the Forest* similar courtly punctiliousness threatens the halting process of peace; while the generals and politicians play out a fantasy of civilised values, the slaughter continues in the trenches. War is also the theme of *Confederates*, another closely researched fictionalisation. It describes the American Civil War campaigns of General Stonewall Jackson. Taken together, the three books form a body of writing on war which matches the best of any fiction on the subject. Only *A Victim of the Aurora* is a completely fictional story. Set in Antarctica, during a polar expedition by a group of Edwardian explorers, it is both adventure yarn and murder mystery. But even here, the atmosphere is completely alien, the period detail emphasising how out of place these English gentlemen are at the very end of the earth. A potent air of menace pervades the inhuman landscape.

Keneally's history is not a scholarly matter of getting names, dates, and costumes right. He aims to draw the lives of these dead individuals into an immediate contact with the reader. Many historical novelists set that as a goal; Keneally succeeds better than most. *The Chant of Jimmie Blacksmith* raised an outcry on publication because its relevance to the racism of the contemporary Australian state was plain to everyone who read it. Likewise *The Playmaker* was published at the height of the Australian bicentennial celebrations. It reflected a harsher light on the establishment of white settlement than was being promulgated by the official commemorations. Keneally stands as a master sceptic, who challenges the mythic status we tend to place on historical events. His heroes are heroic because of their open-eyed recognition they give to reality, their endeavours to create (however perversely) history, rather than have history create them.

—Alan Murphy

KENNEDY, Margaret (Moore). British. Born in London, 23 April 1896. Educated at Cheltenham Ladies College, Gloucestershire, 1912–15; Somerville College, Oxford, B.A. in history. Married David (later Sir David) Davies in 1925 (died 1964); one son and two daughters. Recipient: James Tait Black Memorial prize, 1954. Fellow, Royal Society of Literature. *Died 31 July 1967.*

ROMANCE AND HISTORICAL PUBLICATIONS

Novels

The Ladies of Lyndon. London, Heinemann, 1923; New York, Doubleday, 1925.
The Constant Nymph. London, Heinemann, 1924; New York, Doubleday, 1925.
Red Sky at Morning. London, Heinemann, and New York, Doubleday, 1927.
The Fool of the Family. London, Heinemann, and New York, Doubleday, 1930.
Return I Dare Not. London, Heinemann, and New York, Doubleday, 1931.
A Long Time Ago. London, Heinemann, and New York, Doubleday, 1932.

Together and Apart. London, Cassell, 1936; New York, Random House, 1937.
The Midas Touch. London, Cassell, 1938; New York, Random House, 1939.
The Feast. London, Cassell, and New York, Rinehart, 1950.
Lucy Carmichael. New York, Rinehart, and London, Macmillan, 1951.
Troy Chimneys. New York, Rinehart, 1952; London, Macmillan, 1953.
The Oracles. London, Macmillan, 1955; as *Act of God*, New York, Rinehart, 1955.
The Heroes of Clone. London, Macmillan, 1957; as *The Wild Swan*, New York, Rinehart, 1957.
A Night in Cold Harbour. London, Macmillan, and New York, St. Martin's Press, 1960.
The Forgotten Smile. London, Macmillan, 1961; New York, Macmillan, 1962.
Not in the Calendar. London, Macmillan, and New York, Macmillan, 1964.

Short Stories

A Long Week-End. London, Heinemann, and New York, Doubleday, 1927.
Dewdrops. London, Heinemann, 1928.
The Game and the Candle. London, Heinemann, 1928.
Women at Work. London, Macmillan, 1966.

OTHER PUBLICATIONS

Plays

The Constant Nymph, with Basil Dean, adaptation of her novel (produced London and New York, 1926). London, Heinemann, and New York, Doubleday, 1926.
Come with Me, with Basil Dean (produced London, 1928; New York, 1935). London, Heinemann, 1928.
Jordan (produced London, 1928).
Escape Me Never!, adaptation of her novel *The Fool of the Family* (produced Manchester and London, 1933). London, Heinemann, 1934; New York, Doubleday, 1935.
Autumn, with Gregory Ratoff, adaptation of a play by Ilya Surguchev (produced Manchester and London, 1937). London, Nelson, 1940.
Who Will Remember? Chicago, Dramatic Publishing Company, 1946.
Happy with Either (produced London, 1948).

Screenplays: *The Constant Nymph*, with Basil Dean and Dorothy Farnum, 1933; *The Old Curiosity Shop*, with Ralph Neale, 1934; *Little Friend*, with Christopher Isherwood and Berthold Viertel, 1934; *Whom the Gods Love* (Mozart), 1936; *Dreaming Lips*, with Carl Mayer and Cynthia Asquith, 1937; *Prison Without Bars*, with Hans Wilhelm and Arthur Wimperis, 1938; *Stolen Life*, with George Barraud, 1939; *Return to Yesterday*, with others, 1940; *Rhythm Serenade*, with others, 1943; *The Man in Grey*, with Doreen Montgomery and Leslie Arliss, 1943; *One Exciting Night* (*You Can't Do Without Love*), with others, 1944; *Take My Life*, with Winston Graham and Valerie Taylor, 1947.

Other

A Century of Revolution 1789–1920. London, Methuen, 1922.
Where Stands a Wingèd Sentry. New Haven, Connecticut, Yale University Press, 1941.

The Mechanized Muse (on film). London, Allen and Unwin, 1942.
Jane Austen. London, Barker, 1950; Denver, Swallow, 1952; revised edition, Barker, 1957.
The Outlaws on Parnassus (on the novel). London, Cresset Press, 1958; New York, Viking Press, 1960.

*

Critical Study: *The Constant Novelist: A Study of Margaret Kennedy 1896–1967* by Violet Powell, London, Heinemann, 1983.

*   *   *

The Constant Nymph was the literary sensation of an era. *Everyone* read it; everyone was bowled over. The compulsively readable tale of a sprawling family of genius left its mark indelibly upon a generation of young writers—but no one ever matched its triumph, not even Margaret Kennedy herself.

In this famous story, the ill-disciplined brood of an expatriate British composer is notorious among its victims as "Sanger's Circus." Here and there across Europe, at home everywhere and nowhere, they lead a straggling, unpredictable life: they were wild, amoral, and dishonest in all ways but one; to each of them music alone is sacred and apart, not to be treated as lightly as mere matters of life, love, or death. Suddenly Albert Sanger, the father whose larger-than-life personality has been the sun around which the wild family circles in orbit, collapses and dies. What is to become of his uncouth children?

Into their gypsy life, on a mission of mercy, comes respectability in the person of a determined female cousin with conventional ideas. The rest of the novel, and its sequel, *The Fool of the Family*, explores the inevitable clash between self-willed artistic temperament and law-abiding society. Little Tessa, the nymph whose constancy causes her death, is the pathetic and unforgettable victim crushed between the irresistible force of her love, and the immovable object that is her respectable cousin's determination that she shall conform to a code she can never understand.

The fame of this one stunningly successful book has somewhat obscured the fact that Kennedy was the author of other novels, one of the most notable being the prize-winning *Troy Chimneys*. The haunting tale of a dual personality, half sensitive, penniless charmer, half self-seeking, conscienceless political climber, is told in a series of brief flashes, as his correspondence is discovered and interpreted years after his untimely death. Miles Lufton, the hero, is a complex creation, slave to the conventions of his age and the ugly necessities of his poverty, but always conscious within himself that he is capable of better things. This tragi-comedy of a man who gained *almost* everything he ever wanted, but found that the price had been too high, and his soul lost in the endeavour, is a beautifully crafted and memorable example of Kennedy's artistry.

—Joan McGrath

KENT, Pamela. See **BARRIE, Susan.**

KEPPEL, Charlotte. See **BLACKSTOCK, Charity.**

KEVERN, Barbara. Pseudonym for Donald Lee Shepherd. American. Born in Jackson, Michigan, 26 May 1932. Educated at Los Angeles Harbor College, A.A. 1960; California Polytechnic University, Pomona, B.A. 1966. Served in the United States Army, 1952–56. Married Barbara Kevern in 1954; two daughters and one son. Magazine and book editor. Since 1969 owner, Don Shepherd Agency. Address: Don Shepherd Agency, 1680 Vine Street, Suite 1105, Hollywood, California 90028, U.S.A.

ROMANCE AND HISTORICAL PUBLICATIONS

Novels

Dark Eden. New York, Pocket Books, 1973.
Darkness Falling. New York, Pinnacle, 1974.
The Key. New York, Ballantine, 1974.
The Devil's Vineyard. New York, Pinnacle, 1975.

*   *   *

In Barbara Kevern's tales of gothic horror, seemingly competent young career women find themselves beset by incomprehensible horrors that only they seem to experience and believe: usually knife-wielding ghosts that appear from behind seemingly solid walls. As a result they must face an even greater horror—the question of whether they are drifting into madness or are the victims of some insidious game of psychological torture. The friends or relatives who should support them claim ignorance of murderous sights and sounds, and react with scepticism and statements about nervous breakdowns. Ultimately, however, secret wills, secret passageways, and secret sins make all clear; the heroine is vindicated; and whatever handsome young man is involved understands her suffering and becomes her protector.

Necessary to such plots are monumental, isolated mansions, set amid mist and woods and stone, with winding staircases, precarious balconies, a labyrinth of rooms, ancient crypts, and secret passages to terror. In *The Key* the castle is much like Mont St. Michel, embedded in the cliffs of a rugged island, while the manor in *The Devil's Vineyard* combines old world elegance with a modern California estate to produce hidden corridors for spying on guests, aquariums filled with man-eating sharks, elaborate light shows, and torture chambers for drugged sadists. Occasionally the heroine must balance along slippery ledges to escape the murderous clutches of villainous madmen. Mixed in amid the fake ghosts that haunt such dwellings are the luminescent spirits of the truly dead, spirits that use their energies to guide the heroines from danger and to the secrets that will unlock the motives of their persecutors.

In *Dark Eden* the young heiress suffers the psychological trauma of locks removed by night and replaced by day, tappings from the walls, and a friendly ghost that possesses her body to save her soul. In *The Devil's Vineyard* an old schoolmate lures the heroine to a decadent cultist scene where drug pushers exploit users, and sex and sadism distort reality. *Darkness Falling* focuses on a young woman who leaves the city to escape the guilty memories of a friend's tragic suicide only to find herself dealing with a weird goat woman and her retarded son, fighting off a redneck lynch mob, and protecting a supposed invalid whose goal is murder. As nurse-companion to an eccentric old sea captain in *The Key* the heroine must cope with her sanity being questioned, her employer murdered, and his handsome son suspect. Thus, although Kevern adheres to the same pattern of knife and ghost and will, she lends enough variety of character and scene to make each book unique.

—Gina Macdonald

* * *

KEYES, Frances Parkinson (née Wheeler). American. Born in Charlottesville, Virginia, 21 June 1885. Educated privately; Miss Carroll's School and Winsor School, Boston; Mlle. Dardelle's School, Switzerland. Married Henry Wilder Keyes (Governor of New Hampshire, 1917–19, and United States Senator, 1919–31) in 1904 (died 1938); three sons. Associate editor, *Good Housekeeping*, New York, 1923–35; editor, *National Historical Magazine*, 1937–39. Recipient: Siena Medal, 1946; Christopher Medal, 1953. Litt.D.: George Washington University, Washington, D.C., 1921; Bates College, Lewiston, Maine, 1934; L.H.D.: University of New Hampshire, Durham, 1951. Legion of Honor, 1962. *Died 3 July 1970.*

ROMANCE AND HISTORICAL PUBLICATIONS

Novels

The Old Gray Homestead. Boston, Houghton Mifflin, and London, Hodder and Stoughton, 1919; as *Sylvia Cary*, New York, Paperback Library, 1962.
The Career of David Noble. New York, Stokes, 1921; London, Nash, 1923.
Queen Anne's Lace. New York, Liveright, 1930; London, Eyre and Spottiswoode, 1940.
Lady Blanche Farm: A Romance of the Commonplace. New York, Liveright, 1931; London, Eyre and Spottiswoode, 1940.
Senator Marlowe's Daughter. New York, Messner, 1933; as *Christian Marlowe's Daughter*, London, Eyre and Spottiswoode, 1934.
The Safe Bridge. New York, Messner, 1934; London, Eyre and Spottiswoode, 1935.
Honor Bright. New York, Messner, and London, Eyre and Spottiswoode, 1936.
Parts Unknown. New York, Messner, 1938; as *The Ambassadress*, London, Eyre and Spottiswoode, 1938.
The Great Tradition. New York, Messner, and London, Eyre and Spottiswoode, 1939.
Fielding's Folly. New York, Messner, and London, Eyre and Spottiswoode, 1940.
All That Glitters. New York, Messner, and London, Eyre and Spottiswoode, 1941.
Crescent Carnival. New York, Messner, 1942; as *If Ever I Cease to Love*, London, Eyre and Spottiswoode, 1943.
Also the Hills. New York, Messner, 1943; London, Eyre and Spottiswoode, 1944.
The River Road. New York, Messner, 1945; as *The River Road* and *Vail d'Alvery*, London, Eyre and Spottiswoode, 2 vols., 1946–47.
Came a Cavalier. New York, Messner, 1947; London, Eyre and Spottiswoode, 1948.
Dinner at Antoine's. New York, Messner, 1948; London, Eyre and Spottiswoode, 1949.
Joy Street. New York, Messner, 1950; London, Eyre and Spottiswoode, 1951.
Steamboat Gothic. New York, Messner, 1952; as *Steamboat Gothic* and *Larry Vincent*, London, Eyre and Spottiswoode, 2 vols., 1952–53.

The Royal Box. New York, Messner, and London, Eyre and Spottiswoode, 1954.
Blue Camellia. New York, Messner, and London, Eyre and Spottiswoode, 1957.
Victorine. New York, Messner, 1958; as *The Gold Slippers*, London, Eyre and Spottiswoode, 1958.
Station Wagon in Spain. New York, Farrar Straus, 1959; as *The Letter from Spain*, London, Eyre and Spottiswoode, 1959.
The Chess Players. New York, Farrar Straus, 1960; London, Eyre and Spottiswoode, 1961.
Madame Castel's Lodger. New York, Farrar Straus, 1962; London, Eyre and Spottiswoode, 1963.
The Explorer. New York, McGraw Hill, 1964; London, Eyre and Spottiswoode, 1965.
I, The King. New York, McGraw Hill, and London, Eyre and Spottiswoode, 1966.
The Heritage. New York, McGraw Hill, and London, Eyre and Spottiswoode, 1968.

Short Stories

The Restless Lady and Other Stories. New York, Liveright, 1963; London, Eyre and Spottiswoode, 1964.

OTHER PUBLICATIONS

Verse

The Happy Wanderer. New York, Messner, 1935.

Other

Letters from a Senator's Wife. New York, Appleton, 1924.
Silver Seas and Golden Cities: A Joyous Journey Through Latin Lands. New York, Liveright, 1931.
Capital Kaleidoscope: The Story of a Washington Hostess. New York, Harper, 1937.
Written in Heaven: The Life on Earth of the Little Flower of Lisieux. New York, Messner, and London, Eyre and Spottiswoode, 1937; as *Therese, Saint of a Little Way*, Messner, 1950; as *St. Teresa of Lisieux*, Eyre and Spottiswoode, 1950.
Pioneering People in Northern New England: A Series of Early Sketches. Washington, D.C., Judd and Detweiler, 1937.
Along a Little Way. New York, Kenedy, and London, Burns Oates, 1940; revised edition, New York, Hawthorn, 1962.
Bernadette, Maid of Lourdes. New York, Messner, 1940; revised edition, as *The Sublime Shepherdess*, Messner, and London, Burns Oates, 1940; revised edition, as *Bernadette of Lourdes: Shepherdess, Sister, and Saint*, Messner, 1953; London, Hollis and Carter, 1954.
The Grace of Guadalupe. New York, Messner, 1941; London, Burns Oates, 1951.
Once an Esplanade: A Cycle of Two Creole Weddings (for children). New York, Dodd Mead, 1947; London, Hollis and Carter, 1949.
All This Is Louisiana. New York, Harper, 1950.
The Cost of a Best Seller (memoirs). New York, Messner, 1950; London, Eyre and Spottiswoode, 1953.
The Frances Parkinson Keyes Cookbook. New York, Doubleday, 1955; London, Muller, 1956.
St. Anne: Grandmother of Our Saviour. New York, Messner, 1955; London, Wingate, 1956; revised edition, New York, Hawthorn, 1962.
Guadalupe to Lourdes (omnibus). St. Paul, Catechetical Guild Educational Society, 1957.

The Land of Stones and Saints (on Spain). New York, Double-
day, 1957; London, Davies, 1958.
Christmas Gift. New York, Hawthorn, 1959; London, Davies,
1960.
Mother Cabrini, Missionary to the World. New York, Farrar
Straus, and London, Burns Oates, 1959.
Roses in December (autobiography). New York, Doubleday, and
London, Davies, 1960; revised edition, New York, Liveright,
1966.
*The Rose and the Lily: The Lives and Times of Two South Amer-
ican Saints*. New York, Hawthorn, 1961; London, Davies,
1962.
Three Ways of Love. New York, Hawthorn, 1963; London,
Davies, 1964.
Tongues of Fire. New York, Coward McCann, 1966.
All Flags Flying: Reminiscences. New York, McGraw Hill,
1972.

Editor, *A Treasury of Favorite Poems*. New York, Hawthorn,
1963.

Translator, *The Third Mystic: The Self Revelation of María Vela
of Avila*. New York, Farrar Straus, and London, Davies,
1960.

*   *   *

Frances Parkinson Keyes, the favorite novelist of many American readers during the middle third of this century, received
only a few sympathetic and understanding criticisms during her
lifetime. In the most notable of these, "The Queens of Fiction"
(*Life*, 6 April 1959), Robert Warnick compared her with Taylor
Caldwell and Edna Ferber, noting that then all the fiction of all
three was in print. By 1980, the situation had changed; nearly
all of Caldwell and Ferber's epics remained available, but almost
all of Keyes's had disappeared from print. How could a popular
favorite so soon lose her place in readers' affections? The mystery of this "generation gap" poses an important problem in
changing tastes, much like the elusive problems that often provide the leisurely momentum for this lady's tales.

One of Warnick's distinctions between these three practitioners of the "big, old-fashioned novel" suggests an answer; he
sharply contrasts the "strident world" of Edna Ferber's tales
and "the nightmare world" of Taylor Caldwell's with the "gentle and aristocratic world" of Keyes's. As television epics like
Dallas and *Dynasty* that are the descendants of the work of these
novelists show, the Ferber/Caldwell tradition of violence and
nightmare has appropriated an audience that increasingly con-
fuses aristocracy with just being rich.

Although Keyes wrote popular novels about rural New England, Boston, Washington, D.C., and London, among the many
places to which her extensive travels had taken her, she discovered the ambiance that best suited her talents and led to her
greatest successes when friends lured her to New Orleans in the
late 1930's. She lived in a fine old house in the restored French
Quarter and elsewhere about Louisiana off and on for the rest of
her life, absorbing the unique atmosphere that provided the
groundwork for the intricately designed tapestries of her eight
tales of traditional Creole society from *Crescent Carnival* to *The
Chess Players*. Whether she was creating a tale that spanned
three generations (*Crescent Carnival*, *Steamboat Gothic*) or only
a few days that brought to a head years of frustration (*Dinner at
Antoine's*, *Victorine*), whether she was writing nostalgically for
children (*Once an Esplanade*) or with more chic for her contemporaries (*The River Road*), whether she moved out of the magic
city to the back country (*Blue Camellia*) or to other exotic ports

of call around the world (*The Chess Players*), Keyes's legends,
to the delight of her lending-library readers and the despair of
fashionable reviewers, were richly decorated with the fruits of
long and careful research into the culture—in both the artistic
and anthropological senses—of the regions that intrigued her.

Reviewers who faulted her indifferent plotting, rambling narratives, flabby style, overindulgence in background material,
and long, confidential prefaces sharing her struggles in creating
the books and acknowledging the help of those who befriended
her missed altogether the source of her appeal. Reading a novel
by Keyes was not a way to pass the time restlessly on idle days,
it was rather like a chatty visit from an old and welcome friend
who had just returned from fabulous places, brimming over with
their quaint lore and exciting gossip.

Since the pattern of all her works—too imprecise to be labeled a formula—is similar, one provides a model for all these
local color tales. *Dinner at Antoine's* remains of possibly most
interest because of the ever increasing fame of the titular restaurant the characters frequent. Although built around a mysterious
murder, it is no detective story, as fans of that genre complained.
Too little of the tale concerns the improbable crime and its solution; the event serves simply to hold together a knowing account of the resorts and activities of the glamorous characters as
they either adjust to the increasingly commercial society that is
destroying their elegant world or simply fade out of the changing
picture. The weakness of the novel, like others of the same
weave, is that Keyes never quite finds the skill to blend the con-
ventionalized foreground figures into the overpowering background; but this lack of sophisticated technique didn't bother
readers who liked to enjoy each page for itself and regretted
reaching the drawn-out endings of the meandering tales.

Length and detail alone do not distinguish Keyes's novels
from Ferber's and Caldwell's. The reason for the comparative
impermanence of Keyes's fabrications is most likely that the societies she portrayed have faded with the passing years. Although neither Keyes nor her readers would probably have
thought of themselves as decadent, they were profoundly so; and
this fascination with decadence suggests the reason that Creole
Louisiana and its hothouse culture provided the ideal vehicle for
rewarding their tastes. Keyes has since failed to attract readers
that still revel in the lusty works of Ferber and Caldwell; but she
would not have cared for such vulgarians or their affection. She
had the joy of writing for a fastidious class that loved her and
whose fantasy world can now only be recaptured through her
works.

—Warren French

––––––––––

KIDD, Flora. Canadian. Born in England. Educated at the
University of Liverpool, 1944–49, B.A. Married Robert Kidd;
four children. Taught in London. Address: Sandy Point Road,
Saint John, New Brunswick, Canada.

ROMANCE AND HISTORICAL PUBLICATIONS

Novels

Visit to Rowanbank. London, Mills and Boon, 1966.
Whistle and I'll Come. London, Mills and Boon, 1966; Toronto, Harlequin, 1967.
Nurse at Rowanbank. Toronto, Harlequin, 1966; London, Mills
and Boon, 1967.

Love Alters Not. London, Mills and Boon, 1967; Toronto, Harlequin, 1968.

Wind So Gay. London, Mills and Boon, 1968.

Strange as a Dream. London, Mills and Boon, 1968; Toronto, Harlequin, 1969.

When Birds Do Sing. London, Mills and Boon, 1970; Toronto, Harlequin, 1971.

Love Is Fire. London, Mills and Boon, 1971; Toronto, Harlequin, 1972.

My Heart Remembers. London, Mills and Boon, and Toronto, Harlequin, 1971.

The Dazzle on the Sea. London, Mills and Boon, and Toronto, Harlequin, 1971.

If Love Be Love. London, Mills and Boon, and Toronto, Harlequin, 1972.

Remedy for Love. London, Mills and Boon, and Toronto, Harlequin, 1972.

The Taming of Lisa. London, Mills and Boon, 1972; Toronto, Harlequin, 1973.

The Cave of the White Rose. London, Mills and Boon, 1972; Toronto, Harlequin, 1973.

Beyond the Sunset. London, Mills and Boon, and Toronto, Harlequin, 1973.

Night on the Mountain. London, Mills and Boon, 1973.

The Legend of the Swans. London, Mills and Boon, 1973; Toronto, Harlequin, 1974.

Gallant's Fancy. London, Mills and Boon, and Toronto, Harlequin, 1974.

The Paper Marriage. London, Mills and Boon, and Toronto, Harlequin, 1974.

Stranger in the Glen. London, Mills and Boon, and Toronto, Harlequin, 1975.

Enchantment in Blue. London, Mills and Boon, and Toronto, Harlequin, 1975.

The Bargain Bride. London, Mills and Boon, 1976; Toronto, Harlequin, 1979.

The Black Knight. London, Mills and Boon, 1976; Toronto, Harlequin, 1977.

The Dance of Courtship. London, Mills and Boon, and Toronto, Harlequin, 1976.

The Summer Wife. London, Mills and Boon, and Toronto, Harlequin, 1976.

Dangerous Pretence. London, Mills and Boon, and Toronto, Harlequin, 1977.

Night of the Yellow Moon. London, Mills and Boon, 1977; Toronto, Harlequin, 1978.

To Play with Fire. London, Mills and Boon, 1977; Toronto, Harlequin, 1978.

Jungle of Desire. London, Mills and Boon, and Toronto, Harlequin, 1977.

Marriage in Mexico. London, Mills and Boon, and Toronto, Harlequin, 1978.

Castle of Temptation. London, Mills and Boon, and Toronto, Harlequin, 1978.

Sweet Torment. London, Mills and Boon, and Toronto, Harlequin, 1978.

Canadian Affair. London, Mills and Boon, 1979.

Passionate Encounter. London, Mills and Boon, and Toronto, Harlequin, 1979.

Stay Through the Night. London, Mills and Boon, and Toronto, Harlequin, 1979.

Tangled Shadows. London, Mills and Boon, 1979; Toronto, Harlequin, 1980.

Together Again. London, Mills and Boon, and Toronto, Harlequin, 1979.

The Arranged Marriage. London, Mills and Boon, and Toronto, Harlequin, 1980.

The Silken Bond. London, Mills and Boon, and Toronto, Harlequin, 1980.

Wife by Contract. London, Mills and Boon, and Toronto, Harlequin, 1980.

Beyond Control. London, Mills and Boon, and Toronto, Harlequin, 1981.

Passionate Stranger. London, Mills and Boon, and Toronto, Harlequin, 1981.

Personal Affair. London, Mills and Boon, and Toronto, Harlequin, 1981.

Meeting at Midnight. London, Mills and Boon, 1981; Toronto, Harlequin, 1982.

Bride for a Captain. London, Mills and Boon, and Toronto, Harlequin, 1981.

Makebelieve Marriage. London, Mills and Boon, and Toronto, Harlequin, 1982.

Between Pride and Passion. London, Mills and Boon, and Toronto, Harlequin, 1982.

Tempted to Love. London, Mills and Boon, 1982; Toronto, Harlequin, 1983.

Dangerous Encounter. London, Mills and Boon, 1983; Toronto, Harlequin, 1984.

Dark Seduction. London, Mills and Boon, 1983; Toronto, Harlequin, 1984.

Tropical Tempest. London, Mills and Boon, 1983; Toronto, Harlequin, 1984.

Desperate Desire. London, Mills and Boon, 1984; Toronto, Harlequin, 1985.

The Open Marriage. London, Mills and Boon, 1984; Toronto, Harlequin, 1985.

Passionate Pursuit. London, Mills and Boon, 1984; Toronto, Harlequin, 1985.

A Secret Pleasure. London, Mills and Boon, 1985; Toronto, Harlequin, 1986.

Passionate Choice. London, Mills and Boon, 1986; Toronto, Harlequin, 1987.

The Arrogant Lover. London, Mills and Boon, 1986; Toronto, Harlequin, 1987.

Beloved Deceiver. London, Mills and Boon, 1987; Toronto, Harlequin, 1988.

The Married Lovers. London, Mills and Boon, 1987; Toronto, Harlequin, 1988.

Masquerade Marriage. London, Mills and Boon, 1987; Toronto, Harlequin, 1988.

When Lovers Meet. London, Mills and Boon, 1987; Toronto, Harlequin, 1988.

The Loving Gamble. London, Mills and Boon, 1988.

*   *   *

Flora Kidd is an English writer who now lives in Canada. The change in country did not occur immediately for she first spent several years living in Scotland. She has also visited several South American countries and later used them as backgrounds for her novels. *Sweet Torment* takes place in Colombia, while *Enchantment in Blue* takes place in the Caribbean. For the most part, however, Kidd is most known for her novels with Scottish settings. Here she excels in bringing the country and people to life for her readers.

Sandy Phillips in *The Black Knight* journeys to Scotland to help a cousin. Her trip takes her through many historic places such as Carlisle, Gretna Green, and on into the Galloway part of Scotland. Juliet Grey in *The Cave of the White Rose* is able to travel on into the Highlands and the story is developed against the backgrounds of the moors and mists of Scotland.

Kidd provides a subtle blending that lessens the impact of the physical surroundings and concentrates on the development of character and plot instead. Her heroines tend to be rather young, with a fresh, engaging manner to them. Sandy has just completed a university degree in history and is considering going on for an advanced degree. Juliet, on the other hand, is virtually alone except for relatives who do not care for her. Both have been sheltered, though, and both are unaware of themselves as women. It is this aspect of Kidd's heroines that makes her stories so readable. Slowly and quite cleverly, she lets her heroines grow up and become aware of their capacity to love.

In developing her male characters, she gives them just the right level of experience to help them eventually win their loved ones. They are naturally older and have more experience, but one does not feel that they are too sophisticated and completely out of reach of the heroines.

In a way, it is difficult to categorize Kidd as a romance writer, for she balances everything so well that glaring differences are not found in her novels. Background stays that way, while character and plot support each other easily. She is intensely creative in developing her characters so that each emerges as a rounded figure.

Her later novels, however, are more dramatic and have an added touch of sophistication and maturity in them that her earlier romances lack. Although her heroines are yet naive and unsure of themselves, they face more emotional turmoil throughout the story, and the endings are more suspenseful than in her earlier novels. In these books the heroine is faced with a hopeless love for a man who is far beyond her reach, and it is not until the very end of the novel that she learns that her love is returned.

The hero is often cynical and hardened. His treatment of the heroine at times borders on cruelty and contempt. The emotional overtones in these novels is heightened and the "despairing" sort of reaction leaves the reader in a turmoil at the end of the novel, for the change of pace is often abrupt.

Kidd is one of the more prolific novelists who publishes in the Harlequin Presents Series. It is this type of novel that dominates this series. It is of particular note that Kidd is able to adapt her style of writing to both kinds of novels, that is, the familiar "sweet" romance and the more modern "sophisticated" ones. Certainly she has developed an avid readership for both types over the last few years.

—Arlene Moore

KIMBRO, Jean. See **KIMBROUGH, Katheryn.**

KIMBROUGH, Katheryn. Pseudonym for John M. Kimbro; also writes as Kym Allyson; Ann Ashton; Charlotte Bramwell; Jean Kimbro. American. Born 12 July 1929. Educated at Pasadena City College, California, 1947–49; California State College (now University), Los Angeles, 1949–51; Institute of Religious Science, 1969–71. Stage director, composer, teacher, masseur, actor. Agent: Oscar Collier, 280 Madison Avenue, New York, New York 10016. Address: c/o Doubleday, 666 Fifth Avenue, New York, New York 10103, U.S.A.

ROMANCE AND HISTORICAL PUBLICATIONS

Novels (series: Phenwick Women)

The House on Windswept Ridge. New York, Popular Library, 1971; London, Sphere, 1973.
The Twisted Cameo. New York, Popular Library, 1971; London, Sphere, 1973.
The Children of Houndstooth. New York, Popular Library, 1972.
Thanesworth House. New York, Popular Library, 1972.
The Broken Sphinx. New York, Popular Library, 1972.
Heiress to Wolfskill. New York, Popular Library, 1973.
The Phantom Flame of Wind House. New York, Popular Library, 1973.
The Three Sisters of Briarwick. New York, Popular Library, 1973.
The Specter of Dolphin Cove. New York, Popular Library, 1973.
Unseen Torment. New York, Popular Library, 1974.
The Shadow over Pheasant Heath. New York, Popular Library, 1974.

Phenwick Women:
1. *Augusta, The First.* New York, Popular Library, 1975.
2. *Jane, The Courageous.* New York, Popular Library, 1975.
3. *Margaret, The Faithful.* New York, Popular Library, 1975.
4. *Patricia, The Beautiful.* New York, Popular Library, 1975.
5. *Rachel, The Possessed.* New York, Popular Library, 1975.
6. *Susannah, The Righteous.* New York, Popular Library, 1975.
7. *Rebecca, The Mysterious.* New York, Popular Library, 1975.
8. *Joanne, The Unpredictable.* New York, Popular Library, 1976.
9. *Olivia, The Tormented.* New York, Popular Library, 1976.
10. *Harriet, The Haunted.* New York, Popular Library, 1976.
11. *Nancy, The Daring.* New York, Popular Library, 1976.
12. *Marcia, The Innocent.* New York, Popular Library, 1976.
13. *Kate, The Curious.* New York, Popular Library, 1976.
14. *Ilene, The Superstitious.* New York, Popular Library, 1977.
15. *Millijoy, The Determined.* New York, Popular Library, 1977.
16. *Barbara, The Valiant.* New York, Popular Library, 1977.
17. *Ruth, The Unsuspecting.* New York, Popular Library, 1977.
18. *Ophelia, The Anxious.* New York, Popular Library, 1977.
19. *Dorothy, The Terrified.* New York, Popular Library, 1977.
20. *Ann, The Gentle.* New York, Popular Library, 1978.
21. *Nellie, The Obvious.* New York, Popular Library, 1978.
22. *Isabelle, The Frantic.* New York, Popular Library, 1978.
23. *Evelyn, The Ambitious.* New York, Popular Library, 1978.
24. *Louise, The Restless.* New York, Popular Library, 1978.
25. *Polly, The Worried.* New York, Popular Library, 1978.
26. *Yvonne, The Confident.* New York, Popular Library, 1979.
27. *Joyce, The Beloved.* New York, Popular Library, 1979.
28. *Augusta, The Second.* New York, Popular Library, 1979.
29. *Carol, The Pursued.* New York, Popular Library, 1979.

30. *Katherine, The Returned.* New York, Popular Library, 1980.
31. *Peggy, The Concerned.* New York, Popular Library, 1981.
32. *Alexandra, The Ambivalent.* New York, Popular Library, 1981.
33. *Laura, The Emperiled.* New York, Popular Library, 1981.
34. *Letitia, The Dreamer.* New York, Popular Library, 1981.
35. *Romula, The Dedicated.* New York, Popular Library, 1981.
36. *Iris, The Bewitched.* New York, Popular Library, 1982.

A Shriek in the Midnight Tower. New York, Popular Library, 1975.
The Moon Shadow (as Kym Allyson). New York, Berkley, 1976.
Twilight Return: An Astrological Gothic Novel: Cancer (as Jean Kimbro). New York, Ballantine, 1976.
Night of Tears (as John M. Kimbro). New York, Ballantine, 1976.
The Lovely and the Lonely. New York, Doubleday, 1984.

Novels as Charlotte Bramwell

Cousin to Terror. New York, Beagle, 1972.
Stepmother's House. New York, Beagle, 1972.
Brother Sinister. New York, Beagle, 1973.

Novels as Ann Ashton

The Haunted Portrait. New York, Doubleday, 1976.
The Phantom Reflection. New York, Doubleday, 1978; as *Reflection*, New York, Dell, 1979.
Three Cries of Terror. New York, Doubleday, 1980.
Concession. New York, Doubleday, 1981.
Star Eyes. New York, Doubleday, and London, Hale, 1983.
The Right Time to Love. New York, Doubleday, 1986.
If Love Comes. New York, Doubleday, 1987.

OTHER PUBLICATIONS

Plays as Kym Allyson

The Wounded Dove, music by Allyson (produced Hollywood, 1958).
Three Ladies Named Grace (produced Los Angeles, 1958).
Scrooge, music by Allyson, adaptation of the story *A Christmas Carol* by Dickens (produced Monterey Park, California, 1965).
Clown World (produced Monterey Park, California, 1966).

*   *   *

John Kimbro, under the pseudonym of Katheryn Kimbrough, has written many gothic romances. He is essentially a hack writer, who even manages to joke about it. In *A Shriek in the Midnight Tower*, for instance, a character states, "I met a person once whose initials are K.K. who has been writing the things [gothic romances] for years and making a nice living out of it." And in *The Phantom Flame of Wind House* one of the minor characters is a mystery writer named Charlotte Bramwell, also a Kimbro pseudonym.

Kimbro's stories tend to prove that the gothic genre is a difficult one for a man to master. In place of mood and atmosphere, he gives the reader disorganized action and complicated plots, which in some cases even verge on the ridiculous. The perpetrator of a series of murders in *A Shriek in the Midnight Tower* turns out to be a middle-aged midget who through plastic surgery is pretending to be her own 12-year-old niece. Kimbro's characters have absolutely no validity for the reader, and his books give the general impression of being somewhat comic pastiches of the gothic novel.

In 1975 Kimbro began a series of historical novels called the Saga of the Phenwick Women. The series is chiefly remarkable for his having written so many so quickly. The stories are an odd mixture of the historical novel and rambling family saga, laced with violent happenings, and mixed with touches of the supernatural. *Augusta, The First*, set in 1742 in New England, is the first of the series; later volumes carry the Phenwick family through the Revolution and the Civil War. Augusta's spirit, which continues on after her death, appears to the later Phenwick women, and provides one unifying theme throughout the stories. The Phenwick fortune, founded on pirate treasure, provides another, as various caches hidden by Augusta are discovered by later Phenwicks. While the emphasis in the series is on the family saga, the supernatural element sometimes dominates, as in *Rachel, The Possessed*, in which the spirits of two Salem witches fight to possess the heroine. In *Nellie, The Obvious* the idea of reincarnation is introduced. Nellie, living in 1869, believes herself to be the reincarnation of Edward Phenwick, Augusta's son. The series has come full cycle. Intricate as it is, the poor quality of the writing and the artificiality of the characters and plots give the reader to conclude that the whole saga is much ado about nothing.

—Necia A. Musser

KIRK, Russell (Amos). American. Born in Plymouth, Michigan, 19 October 1918. Educated at Plymouth High School, graduated 1936; Michigan State University, East Lansing, B.A. 1940; Duke University, Durham, North Carolina, M.A. 1941; St. Andrews University, Scotland, D.Litt. 1952. Served in the United States Army, 1942–46: Staff Sergeant. Married Annette Yvonne Cecile Courtemanche in 1964; four daughters. Assistant Professor of History, Michigan State University, 1946–53; Daly Lecturer, University of Detroit, 1954; Research Professor of Politics, C. W. Post College, Long Island University, Greenvale, New York, 1957–61; member of the Politics Faculty, New School for Social Research, New York, 1959–61; also visiting professor at several universities. Columnist ("From the Academy"), *National Review*, New York, 1955–80, and for *Los Angeles Times* Syndicate, 1962–75. Since 1960 editor, *University Bookman*. President, since 1960, Educational Reviewer, and since 1979, Marguerite Eyer Wilbur Foundation; director, Educational Research Council of America Social Science Program, 1979–83. Recipient: American Council of Learned Societies Senior fellowship, 1950; Guggenheim Fellowship, 1956; Ann Radcliffe award, 1966; Christopher award, for non-fiction, 1972; World Fantasy award, 1977; Ingersoll award, 1985. Honorary doctorates: Boston College; St. John's University; Park College, Kansas City; Loyola College, Baltimore; LeMoyne College, Syracuse, New York; Gannon College, Erie, Pennsylvania; Niagara University, New York; Olivet College, Michigan; Albion College, Michigan; Central Michigan University, Mount Pleasant. Agent: Kirby McCauley, 432 Park Avenue South, Suite 1509, New York, New York 10016. Address: Piety Hill, Mecosta, Michigan 49332, U.S.A.

ROMANCE AND HISTORICAL PUBLICATIONS

Novels

Old House of Fear. New York, Fleet, 1961; London, Gollancz, 1962.
A Creature of the Twilight: His Memorials. New York, Fleet, 1966.
Lord of the Hollow Dark. New York, St. Martin's Press, 1979.

Short Stories

The Surly Sullen Bell: Ten Stories and Sketches, Uncanny or Uncomfortable, with a Note on the Ghostly Tale. New York, Fleet, 1962; as *Lost Lake*, New York, Paperback Library, 1966.
The Princess of All Lands. Sauk City, Wisconsin, Arkham House, 1979.
Watchers at the Strait Gate. Sauk City, Wisconsin, Arkham House, 1984.

OTHER PUBLICATIONS

Other

Randolph of Roanoke: A Study in Conservative Thought. Chicago, University of Chicago Press, 1951; as *John Randolph of Roanoke*, Chicago, Regnery, 1964.
The Conservative Mind from Burke to Santayana. Chicago, Regnery, 1953; London, Faber, 1954; revised edition, Regnery, 1964; revised edition, as *The Conservative Mind from Burke to Eliot*, Regnery, 1972.
St. Andrews. London, Batsford, 1954.
A Program for Conservatives. Chicago, Regnery, 1954; revised edition, 1962; abridged edition, as *Prospects for Conservatives*, 1956.
Academic Freedom: An Essay in Definition. Chicago Regnery, 1955.
Beyond the Dreams of Avarice: Essays of a Social Critic. Chicago, Regnery, 1956.
The Intelligent Woman's Guide to Conservatism. New York, Devin Adair, 1957.
The American Cause. Chicago, Regnery, 1957.
Confessions of a Bohemian Tory: Episodes and Reflections of a Vagrant Career. New York, Fleet, 1963.
The Intemperate Professor and Other Cultural Splenetics. Baton Rouge, Louisiana State University Press, 1965; revised edition, Peru, Illinois, Sugden, 1988.
Edmund Burke: A Genius Reconsidered. New Rochelle, New York, Arlington, House, 1967; revised edition, Peru, Illinois, Sugden, 1988.
The Political Principles of Robert A. Taft, with James McClellan. New York, Fleet, 1967.
Enemies of the Permanent Things: Observations of Abnormality in Literature and Politics. New Rochelle, New York, Arlington House, 1969; revised edition, Peru, Illinois, Sugden, 1988.
Eliot and His Age: T. S. Eliot's Moral Imagination in the Twentieth Century. New York, Random House, 1971; revised edition, Peru, Illinois, Sugden, 1988.
The Roots of American Order. La Salle, Illinois, Open Court, 1974.
Decadence and Renewal in the Higher Learning: An Episodic History of American University and College since 1953. South Bend, Indiana, Regnery, 1978.

Reclaiming a Patrimony (lectures). Washington, D.C., Heritage Foundation, 1982.
Irving Babbitt 1865–1933: Literature and the American College (lecture). Washington, D.C., National Humanity Institute, 1986.
The Wise Men Know What Wicked Things Are Written on the Sky (essays). Chicago, Regnery, 1987.
The Conservative Cause (lecture). Washington, D.C., Heritage Foundation, 1987.

Editor, *The Scallion Stone*, by Basil A. Smith. Chapel Hill, North Carolina, Whispers Press, 1980.
Editor, *The Portable Conservative Reader*. New York, Viking Press, and London, Penguin, 1982.
Editor, *The Assault on Religion*. Lanham, Maryland, University Press of America, 1986.

*

Bibliography: *Russell Kirk: A Bibliography* by Charles Brown, Mount Pleasant, Michigan, Clarke Historical Library, 1981.

Manuscript Collection: Clarke Historical Library, Central Michigan University, Mount Pleasant.

Russell Kirk comments:

My uncanny tales are intended to wake the moral imagination. As Gerald Heard remarked to me once, good tales of the supernatural must be founded upon theological postulates. (An admirable example of this is Heard's story "The Chapel of Ease.") According to Heard's principle, my fiction is concerned with the mysteries of time and circumstance, with evil and regeneration, mystically delineated. Like W. B. Yeats, I was reared in a family that never questioned the reality of ghosts and such phenomena—spending my summers, indeed, in an ancestral house long haunted. Some considerable grains of true narration lie at the core of all my stories—drawn from my own experiences in Britain or America, or from friends' mischances. Can Grande della Scala inquired of Dante whether *The Divine Comedy* was to be taken literally or figuratively. Dante replied that his poem might be applied in either sense. So it is, in their small way, with my uncanny tales. The characters in them, incidentally, ordinarily are taken from the life. "Frank Sarsfield," in my tale "A Long, Long Trail a-Windin'," lived in my house for the last six years of his life—and died in a snowdrift, as I had predicted he would.

*   *   *

Best known for his advocacy of conservative philosophy, Russell Kirk writes what he has called "unabashedly Gothic" stories and novels. In present-day settings, Kirk employs such gothic devices as prophetic dreams, ghosts, and ancient houses saturated with the evils of previous inhabitants. Kirk's treatment of the traditionally gothic struggle between agents of good and evil is profoundly religious. Some of Kirk's villains are social reformers, determined to reduce mankind to dreary conformity (Jackman in *Old House of Fear*, Mr. S. G. W. Barner in "Ex Tenebris"); others are evil spirits who have gained control of human bodies (Mr. Apollinax in *Lord of the Hollow Dark*, Gerontion in "The Peculiar Demesne"). Two characters reappearing in a number of works, Ralph Bain and Manfred Arcane, are powerful guardians of the weak and innocent. In "A Cautionary Note on the Ghostly Tale," Kirk calls for "a return to the ghostly and the Gothic" because "it can touch keenly upon the old reality of evil—and upon injustice and retribution."

One of the pleasures of Kirk's fiction is its allusiveness, lines from Shakespeare, Longfellow, and other poets appearing in surprising contexts. T. S. Eliot is a potent influence. Kirk's characters may find themselves in a "timeless moment," what Eliot calls "the still point of the turning world," in which dead and living interact freely. The damned, like the dead Indian in "The Princess of All Lands," are fixed in time, perpetually acting out some hideous depravity and seeking others to share their suffering. To the saved, timeless moments constitute heaven. As the Canon explains in "Saviourgate," "all the good moments or hours or days that you ever experience are forever present to you, whenever you want them. . . . " For those in a state of sin or despair, timeless moments provide opportunities for redemption. In Kirk's best story, winner of a World Fantasy award, "There's a Long, Long Trail a-Windin'," a tramp redeems a life of petty thievery by journeying into the past to save children from murderous escaped convicts. Touching upon what Kirk calls "the darkness or the light in souls," his fiction concerns hell, the purgatory of spiritual progress, and salvation—conditions that individuals may experience both before and after they have crossed the border between life and death.

—Wendy Bousfield

KNIGHT, Alanna (née Cleet). Also writes as Margaret Hope. British. Born in County Durham. Educated privately. Married Alexander Harrow Knight in 1951; two sons. Secretary, 1949–51. Fellow, Society of Antiquaries. Recipient: Romantic Novelists Association Netta Muskett award, 1968. Agent: Anthony Sheil Associates, 43 Doughty Street, London WC1N 2LF, England. Address: 24 March Hall Crescent, Edinburgh EH16 5HL, Scotland.

ROMANCE AND HISTORICAL PUBLICATIONS

Novels (series: Inspector Faro)

Legend of the Loch. London, Hurst and Blackett, 1969; New York, Lancer, 1970.
The October Witch. London, Hurst and Blackett, and New York, Lancer, 1971.
This Outward Angel. New York, Lancer, 1972.
Castle Clodha. London, Hurst and Blackett, and New York, Avon, 1972.
Lament for Lost Lovers. London, Hurst and Blackett, 1972; New York, Avon, 1973.
The White Rose. London, Hurst and Blackett, 1973; New York, Avon, 1974.
A Stranger Came By. London, Hurst and Blackett, 1974; New York, Avon, 1975.
The Passionate Kindness. Aylesbury, Buckinghamshire, Milton House, 1974.
A Drink for the Bridge. London, Macmillan, 1976.
The Wicked Wynsleys. New York, Nordon, 1977.
The "Black Duchess." London, Futura, and New York, Doubleday, 1980.
Castle of Foxes. New York, Doubleday, 1981.
Colla's Children. London, Macdonald, 1982.
The Clan. London, Macdonald, 1985.
Estella. London, Macdonald, and New York, St. Martin's Press, 1986.

Enter Second Murderer (Faro). London, Macmillan, 1988; New York, St. Martin's Press, 1989.
Blood Line (Faro). London, Macmillan, 1989.

Novels as Margaret Hope

The Queen's Captain. New York, Masquerade, 1978.
Hostage Most Royal. New York, Masquerade, 1979; London, Mills and Boon, 1980.
The Shadow Queen. New York, Masquerade, 1979; London, Mills and Boon, 1980.
Perilous Voyage. London, Mills and Boon, 1983.

OTHER PUBLICATIONS

Plays

The Private Life of Robert Louis Stevenson, with John Cairney (produced Edinburgh, 1975).
Girl on an Empty Swing (produced Cambridge, 1981). Macclesfield, New Playwrights Network, 1978.

Radio Writing: *Don Roberto: Life of R. B. Cunninghame Graham*, 1975; *Across the Plains*, from a work by Robert Louis Stevenson, 1981; *Someday I'll Find You*, 1987.

Other

Editor, *The Robert Louis Stevenson Treasury.* London, Shepheard Walwyn, 1982; New York, St. Martin's Press, 1985.
Editor, *RLS in the South Seas: An Intimate Photographic Record* (on Robert Louis Stevenson). Edinburgh, Mainstream, 1986; New York, Paragon, 1987.

*   *   *

Scenes of wild beauty that dot the landscape of Scotland become the background of Alanna Knight's eerie gothic tales. A land of tempestuous weather, looming mountains, enchanting lochs, and castles rich with turbulent histories, Scotland is the ideal setting for danger and romance. The female protagonists in Knight's stories are not young ingenues but rather mature women who have either been bitterly disappointed in love or who still wait, wondering if love will ever come. All lead rather dreary lives. Then, suddenly, events turn as each heroine unexpectedly finds herself hurled into a mystery with psychic elements in which their own death looms as a frightening possibility. This new twist in their lives also brings the romance each has sought; the men involved are often cast in the heroic image of Robert the Bruce.

Lucy MacAeden (*This Outward Angel*) has a recurring nightmare of being chased through a strange red desert by some unseen horror. Rescue comes in the guise of the Protector who carries her away from the swiftly pursuing danger. His is a face she recognizes only in dreams, but the pendant of a Thunderbird which he wears has a counterpoint in the real world. Summoned to the side of her former husband's dying uncle, she meets an intriguing young man whom she calls the Barbaric Stranger for his Aztec Indian features. He also wears the Thunderbird. Another novel with a dream motif is *The White Rose*. While the guest of Fraser, the young bachelor laird of Deveron, Candida sees visions of a white rose. In a vivid dream she relives the last moments of this courageous girl who had sacrificed her life in order to help Bonnie Prince Charlie escape from the British soldiers.

The castles that populate the novels of Knight always have a sinister legend or curse, along with lots of empty wings or turrets to inspire ghostly doings. The turret room of *Castle Clodha* was once the prison of the beautiful witch Rowan, starved to death by an avaricious laird who wanted to marry not this lovely girl carrying his child, but a rich heiress who could bring him much-needed wealth. It takes the modern-day love of May Lachlan and Laird Roderick Malcom MacMhor to dispel the curse of Rowan.

Castle of Foxes has less of a supernatural flavor although ghostly, gothic trappings abound. It is set in the Scottish Highlands during the time of Queen Victoria and Prince Albert. The reader glimpses not only the narrator Tanya's frightening escapades at Devenick Castle but also enchanting scenes of court life at nearby Balmoral.

All of Knight's stories combine melodic prose and powerful allusion to produce quality gothic adventure with a dash of Scottish nationalism.

—Patricia Altner

KNOX, Gilbert. See **MACBETH, Madge.**

KOESTLER, Arthur. Also wrote as Alfrède Costler. British. Born in Budapest, Hungary, 5 September 1905; became British citizen, 1948. Educated at the Polytechnic High School, Vienna; University of Vienna, 1922–26. Married 1) Dorothy Asher in 1935 (divorced 1950); 2) Mamaine Paget in 1950 (divorced 1953); 3) Cynthia Jefferies in 1965 (died with Koestler, in suicide pact, 1983); one daughter. Private secretary to Vladimir Jabolinsky, a Zionist leader, c. 1925; worked as laborer in a Jezreel Valley collective settlement, lemonade vendor in Haifa, assistant to an Arabian architect, and editor of a Cairo weekly, 1926–29; Middle East correspondent, 1927–29, Paris correspondent, 1929–30, and member of Editorial Board, 1930–32, Ullstein Newspapers, Berlin; also science editor, *Vossische Zeitung*, and foreign editor, *B.Z. am Mittag*, 1930; sole journalist aboard Graf Zeppelin Arctic expedition, summer 1931; member of the Communist Party, 1932–38; travelled through Soviet Central Asia, 1932–33; freelance journalist in Paris, London, and Zurich, 1933–36; Spanish Civil War correspondent, London *News Chronicle*, 1936–37; imprisoned by Franco's Nationalists in Malaga and Seville, sentenced to death, then released after 3 months, 1937; editor, *Zukunft*, Paris, 1938; arrested by French as anti-fascist refugee, imprisoned at Le Vernet, October 1939 to January 1940; member of French Foreign Legion under assumed name Albert Dubert, 1940–41; escaped France to Britain; jailed for having false papers, 1941; member of British Pioneer Corps, 1941–42; worked for Ministry of Information, for the BBC, and as a night ambulance driver until 1944; Palestine correspondent, *The Times*, London, 1945–47; Palestine war correspondent, Manchester *Guardian* and New York *Herald Tribune*, 1948; full-time writer from 1950. Chubb Fellow, Yale University, New Haven, Connecticut, 1950; travelled in India and Japan, 1957–59; fellow, Center for Advanced Study in the Behavioral Sciences, Stanford University, California, 1964–65. Vice-President, Exit, voluntary euthanasia society, 1981–83. Recipient: University of Copenhagen Sonning prize, 1968. Fellow, 1958, and Companion of Literature, 1974, Royal Society of Literature; Fellow, Royal Astronomical Society, 1976; Honorary Member, American Academy of Arts and Sciences, 1977. LL.D.: Queen's University, Kingston, Ontario, 1968; D.Litt.: Leeds University, 1977; D.Sc.: University of Manchester, 1981. C.B.E. (Commander, Order of the British Empire), 1972. *Died (suicide) 3 March 1983.*

ROMANCE AND HISTORICAL PUBLICATIONS

Novel

The Gladiators, translated by Edith Simon. London, Cape, and New York, Macmillan, 1939.

OTHER PUBLICATIONS

Novels

Darkness at Noon, translated by Daphne Hardy. London, Cape, 1940; New York, Macmillan, 1941.
Arrival and Departure. London, Cape, and New York, Macmillan, 1943.
Thieves in the Night: Chronicle of an Experiment. London, Macmillan, and New York, Macmillan, 1946.
The Age of Longing. London, Collins, and New York, Macmillan, 1951.
The Call-Girls: A Tragi-Comedy with Prologue and Epilogue. London, Hutchinson, 1972; New York, Random House, 1973.

Plays

Twilight Bar: An Escapade in Four Acts (produced Paris and Baltimore, 1946). London, Cape, and New York, Macmillan, 1945.

Screenplay: *Lift Your Head, Comrade* (documentary), 1944.

Other

Von Weissen Nächten und Roten Tagen. Kharkov, Ukrainian State Publishers for National Minorities, 1933.
Encyclopédie de la vie sexuelle (as Alfrède Costler), with Ludwig Léry-Lenz and A. Willey. Paris, Aldor, 1934; as *Encyclopedia of Sexual Knowledge*, edited by Norman Haire, New York, Eugenics Publishing, 1936.
Menschenopfer Unerhört. Paris, Carrefour, 1937.
Spanish Testament (autobiography). London, Gollancz, 1937; excerpt, as *Dialogue with Death*, translated by Phyllis and Trevor Blewitt, London, Macmillan, 1938; New York, Macmillan, 1942.
Scum of the Earth (autobiography). London, Cape, and New York, Macmillan, 1941.
The Yogi and the Commissar and Other Essays. London, Cape, and New York, Macmillan, 1945.
Sexual Anomalies and Perversions: A Summary of the Works of Magnus Hirschfeld. London, Torch, 1946; revised edition, edited by Norman Haire, London, Encyclopaedic Press, 1952.
L'Encyclopédie de la Famille, with Manes Sperber. Paris, n.d.
Insight and Outlook: An Inquiry into the Common Foundations of Science, Art, and Social Ethics. London, Macmillan, and New York, Macmillan, 1949.
Promise and Fulfillment: Palestine 1917–1949. London, Macmillan, and New York, Macmillan, 1949.
The God That Failed: Six Studies in Communism, with others, edited by Richard Crossman. London, Hamish Hamilton, and New York, Harper, 1950.

Arrow in the Blue (autobiography). London, Collins-Hamish Hamilton, and New York, Macmillan, 1952.

The Invisible Writing (autobiography). London, Collins-Hamish Hamilton, 1954; Boston, Beacon Press, 1955.

The Trail of the Dinosaur and Other Essays. London, Collins, and New York, Macmillan, 1955.

Reflections on Hanging. London, Gollancz, 1956; New York, Macmillan, 1957.

Reflexions sur la peine capitale, with Albert Camus. Paris, Calmann Levy, 1957.

The Sleepwalkers: A History of Man's Changing Vision of the Universe. London, Hutchinson, and New York, Macmillan, 1959; section published as *The Watershed: A Biography of Johannes Kepler*, New York, Doubleday, 1960; London, Heinemann, 1961.

The Lotus and the Robot. London, Hutchinson, 1960; New York, Macmillan, 1961.

Hanged by the Neck: An Exposure of Capital Punishment in England, with C. H. Rolph. London, Penguin, 1961.

The Act of Creation. London, Hutchinson, and New York, Macmillan, 1964.

The Ghost in the Machine. London, Hutchinson, 1967; New York, Macmillan, 1968.

Drinkers of Infinity: Essays 1955–1967. London, Hutchinson, 1968; New York, Macmillan, 1969.

The Case of the Midwife Toad. London, Hutchinson, 1971; New York, Random House, 1972.

The Roots of Coincidence. London, Hutchinson, and New York, Random House, 1972.

The Lion and the Ostrich (lecture). London, Oxford University Press, 1973.

The Challenge of Chance: Experiments and Speculations, with Alister Hardy and Robert Harvie. London, Hutchinson, 1973; New York, Random House, 1974.

The Heel of Achilles: Essays 1968–1973. London, Hutchinson, 1974; New York, Random House, 1975.

The Thirteenth Tribe: The Khazar Empire and Its Heritage. London, Hutchinson, and New York, Random House, 1976.

Janus: A Summing Up. London, Hutchinson, and New York, Random House, 1978.

Bricks to Babel: Selected Writings with Comments. London, Hutchinson, 1980; New York, Random House, 1981.

Kaleidoscope (essays). London, Hutchinson, 1981.

Stranger on the Square, with Cynthia Koestler, edited by Harold Harris. London, Hutchinson, 1983; New York, Random House, 1984.

Editor, *Suicide of a Nation? An Enquiry into the State of Britain Today.* London, Hutchinson, 1963; New York, Macmillan, 1964.

Editor, with J. R. Smythies, *Beyond Reductionism: New Perspectives in the Life Sciences.* London, Hutchinson, 1969; New York, Macmillan, 1970.

*

Bibliography: *Arthur Koestler: An International Bibliography* by Reed B. Merrill and Thomas Frazier, Ann Arbor, Michigan, Ardis, 1979.

Critical Studies (selection): *Arthur Koestler* by J. Nedava, London, Anscombe, 1948; *Arthur Koestler* by John Atkins, London, Spearman, and New York, Roy, 1956; *Arthur Koestler: Das Literarische Werk* by Peter Alfred Zuber, Zurich, Fretz und Wasmuth, 1962; *Chronicles of Conscience: A Study of George Orwell and Arthur Koestler* by Jenni Calder, London, Secker and Warburg, 1968, Pittsburgh, University of Pittsburgh Press, 1969; *Arthur Koestler* by Wolfe Mays, Guildford, Surrey, Lutterworth Press, and Valley Forge, Pennsylvania, Judson Press, 1973; *Astride the Two Cultures: Arthur Koestler at 70* edited by Harold Harris, London, Hutchinson, 1975, New York, Random House, 1976; *Arthur Koestler: A Collection of Critical Essays* edited by Murray A. Sperber, Englewood Cliffs, New Jersey, Prentice Hall, 1977; *Arthur Koestler* by Sidney A. Pearson Jr., Boston, Twayne, 1978; *Koestler: A Biography* by Iain Hamilton, London, Secker and Warburg, and New York, Macmillan, 1982; *Arthur Koestler: The Story of a Friendship* by George Mikes, London, Deutsch, 1983; *Arthur Koestler* by Mark Levene, New York, Ungar, 1984, London, Wolff, 1985.

*   *   *

Filled with vivid descriptions, learned allusions, and intriguing anecdotes and metaphors, Arthur Koestler's novels wrestle with the problems of political idealism and power that led Koestler to reject Nazi racism and later Soviet communism. They explore the difficulties of translating ideals into action and of avoiding the mistakes of one's political opposites. Although ideologically drawn, their characters are usually credible, complicated people, torn between emotion and reason, between a longing for commitment and a sense of the flaws and limitations of political and philosophical stances. All these works have an ironic wit and an analytical clarity that make them readily readable and often chilling, and a concern for the complexity of ultimate issues that lends them weight and credibility. Koestler writes with deliberate detachment to provide insights into the minds of the extreme left and of the extreme right, minds that created crucifixion, the gladiatorial games, the concentration camp, mass asphyxiation, the purge, and other abuses in the name of social and moral justice, class superiority, reform, or "purity." Whether exploring the politics of 73 B.C. or of the 1930's and 1940's, his concern is with political man and the inner wells from which his theories spring. Ultimately Koestler's vision is existential in its view of man's alienation from his fellow man and from his universe, his loneliness, his despair, his lack of any final significance except what he himself creates.

Koestler's one historical novel, *The Gladiators*, demonstrates destructive historical patterns, while drawing an authentic portrait of the pre-Christian world, based on Livy, Plutarch, Appian, Florus, and Sallust, as well as on background material on the social conditions and intrigues of the time. Like *Darkness at Noon* and *Arrival and Departure*, the other two works in Koestler's trilogy, it concerns historical inevitability, revolutionary and political ethics, the motives which spur man to political actions, and the question of whether evil can indeed produce good. Koestler's characters must repeatedly face dilemmas out of which there is no right way. Koestler brings to life what he sees as a representative historic moment, a time when, against a century of social unrest, revolution and mass-upheaval, a band of 70 Roman circus fighters grew within a few months into a people's army that, allied with pirates and barbarians, captured the hearts of a discontented and rebellious populace and for two years controlled half of Italy. Koestler, speaking in part through the chronicler Fulvius, investigates the multiple causes that produced so successful a rebellion, speculates about possible Judaic-Essene inspiration (a philosophical base that he sees as the cornerstone of humanistic ideals), expands on the socialistic utopian community that history only hints at, and ultimately argues that the slave revolt which Spartacus led against ancient Rome was doomed to failure because of factional disputes brought on by Spartacus's refusal to punish the more undisciplined of his followers and because of the "law of detours" which compelled him to immediate ruthlessness for the sake of long term goals. Through the eyes of Fulvius he captures the initial fascination of the movement, the inevitable contradictions and disillusionment, and the indestructible dream, despite seeming failure.

Koestler's Spartacus is a man in the right place at the right time to express the sense of injustice and outrage of the ordinary man. He and his fellow gladiators at first think only of themselves and of their personal cause as they sweep the opposition before them, using the martial skills so carefully honed in the Roman circus. However, as more and more of the simple, the poor, the downtrodden, and the hopeful turn to them for guidance and beg to join their cause against the imperialism of Rome and the injustices perpetuated by its local representatives, Spartacus develops a vision of the Utopian future that might be: a workers' paradise of communal living, shared labor, and shared rewards, a communist ideal of a classless society that embodies the principle of from each according to his abilities and to each according to his needs. Nonetheless, the sordid details of day-to-day reality, the social and racial differences, the petty squabbles, and the limitations of frail humanity lead to division, to fragmentation, and ultimately to the self-destruction of a high ideal dreamed in the hearts of common people throughout the Empire. Spartacus becomes as dictatorial and as cruel as those he opposes, an iron man meting out cold punishments in the name of long-term goals, and only in defeat recaptures the idealistic and self-sacrificing spirit of his earlier days. Koestler makes real the struggles of these distant people, even in the final days of despair as Spartacus leads his starving troops against impossible odds and then as the Roman conquerors line the road to Rome with the crucified bodies of the crushed rebels.

In *Darkness at Noon*, a tragically ironic fictionalized account of the 1938 Moscow Trials which denigrates Stalinism as antihumanistic absolutism and which explores the consequences of revolutionary faith, Koestler looks at another side of the coin. The prosecutor uses brutal methods to win his case and the condemned man, Rubashov, unlike Spartacus, follows "the law of detours" to the end and modifies logic with human sensitivity. For Koestler both the way of Rubashov and of Spartacus are doomed to tragedy. *Arrival and Departure*, in turn, explores a young Trotskyite's dilemma: whether to sacrifice himself for a cause which his newly acquired insights have made him doubt or to give up politics and concern himself merely with his own life. His finds his personal answer after a debate with a Nazi purist who argues with cold scientific logic for a biological revolution, one that rejects intuition and ethical beliefs, and that justifies concentration camps, gas chambers, mass executions, and biological experimentation on human subjects.

Thieves in the Night, based on Koestler's personal experiences, provides a close-up look at the idealism, the conflicts, and the dedication that produced the early Israeli kibbutz. The story begins with the founding of a kibbutz as a socialist dream of European Jewish Communists, and traces the changes wrought in the original founders as they come to terms with the harsh land, the poverty and asceticism of their new way of life, the charming but reactionary Arabs, and the British, for whom dealing with "non-natives" in a colonial situation is unknown territory. The British restriction of Jewish immigration of landpurchases in Palestine, hand-in-hand with news of Nazi atrocities, forces people like Joseph, a pioneer on a collective farm, to face the built-in contradictions of their new situation. Despite the multiple perspectives (Arab, British, American, socialist), the recognition of the Arab Palestinian cause, and the negative portraits of Jewish fanaticism, ultimately Koestler argues the justice of the Jewish cause and places it within a modern world view of social struggle, violence, betrayal, and despair: what he calls "a political ice age." Koestler attacks British imperialism,

and praises the Jewish communes as socialist experiments in democracy and equality, models of man trying to master his fate rather than submit to it. While Koestler usually argues that governments must not act on the principle that the ends justify the means, in the case of the Jewish cause he finds a world conspiracy to terrorize a desperate, oppressed people an exception to his rule; he concludes that a fight for genetic survival is a just fight.

The Age of Longing tells of an American girl in Paris in the mid 1950's who comes to detest so strongly her Russian lover's commitment to a philosophy of historical inevitability that she tries to shoot him as a political statement, only to have her act interpreted as jealous pique. On one level it is a story of romantic disillusionment; on another level it is a study of European ideologies in conflict, of the horrors of autocratic governments, of the inertia and spiritual emptiness of the West, of the private motivations of public acts, and of the ideological base that produces private acts.

Koestler draws on historical situations to demonstrate the irrational sources of political conviction, the betrayal of ideals, the ambiguous morality of political acts, and the pitfalls awaiting any who would translate ideology into act and would attempt to create justice, harmony, and progress. His overall conclusion is that man is imperfect and that freedom is ultimately unrealizable; commitment means giving up freedom, and giving up one's own freedom is the first step toward giving up someone else's. His commitment to humanitarian values and to a revitalized socialism form a solid base on which his novels function. Their value rests in their authenticity; Koestler writes in detail of what he knows well: the individual's struggle to find a political faith that will have personal meaning in an impersonal world.

—Gina Macdonald

KRENTZ, Jayne Ann. Also writes as Jayne Bentley; Jayne Castle; Amanda Glass; Stephanie James; Jayne Taylor. American. Born in San Diego, California, 28 March 1948. Educated at the University of California, Santa Cruz, B.A. (honors) in history; San Jose State University, California, M.A. in librarianship, 1971. Married. Worked as a librarian. Lives in Seattle. Agent: Joan Schulhafer, Jesco Associates, 17 James Street, Bloomfield, New Jersey 07003, U.S.A.

ROMANCE AND HISTORICAL PUBLICATIONS

Novels (series: Verity Ames and Jonas Quarrel)

Whirlwind Courtship (as Jayne Taylor). New York, Tiara, 1979.
Uneasy Alliance. Toronto, Harlequin, 1984; London, Mills and Boon, 1985.
Call It Destiny. Toronto, Harlequin, 1984.
Ghost of a Chance. Toronto, Harlequin, 1984; London, Mills and Boon, 1985.
Man with a Past. Toronto, Harlequin, 1985.
Witchcraft. Toronto, Harlequin, 1985; London, Mills and Boon, 1986.
Legacy. Toronto, Harlequin, 1985.
The Waiting Game. Toronto, Harlequin, 1985.
True Colors. Toronto, Harlequin, and London, Mills and Boon, 1986.
Ties That Bind. Toronto, Harlequin, 1986; London, Mills and Boon, 1987.

Between the Lines. Toronto, Harlequin, 1986; London, Mills and Boon, 1987.
Sweet Starfire. New York, Popular Library, 1986.
Crystal Flame. New York, Popular Library, 1986.
Twist of Fate. Toronto, Worldwide, 1986.
The Family Way. Toronto, Harlequin, 1987.
The Main Attraction. Toronto, Harlequin, 1987.
A Coral Kiss. New York, Popular Library, 1987.
Chance of a Lifetime. Toronto, Harlequin, 1987.
Midnight Jewels. New York, Popular Library, 1987.
Test of Time. Toronto, Harlequin, 1987.
Full Bloom. Toronto, Harlequin, 1988.
Joy. Toronto, Harlequin, 1988.
Gift of Gold (Ames and Quarrel). New York, Popular Library, 1988.
Dreams 1–2. Toronto, Harlequin, 2 vols., 1988.
Gift of Fire (Ames and Quarrel). New York, Popular Library, 1989.
A Woman's Touch. Toronto, Harlequin, 1989.
Lady's Choice. Toronto, Harlequin, 1989.
Shield's Lady (as Amanda Glass). New York, Popular Library, 1989.

Novels as Jayne Bentley

A Moment Past Midnight. New York, Macfadden, 1979.
Turning Towards Home. New York, Macfadden, 1979.
Maiden of the Morning. New York, Macfadden, 1979.

Novels as Jayne Castle (series: Guinevere Jones)

Vintage of Surrender. New York, Macfadden, 1979.
Queen of Hearts. New York, Macfadden, 1979.
The Gentle Pirates. New York, Dell, 1980.
Bargain with the Devil. New York, Dell, 1981; London, Corgi, 1983.
Right of Possession. New York, Dell, 1981; London, Corgi, 1983.
Wagered Weekend. New York, Dell, 1981; London, Corgi, 1983.
A Man's Protection. New York, Dell, 1982.
A Negotiated Surrender. New York, Dell, 1982.
Affair of Risk. New York, Dell, 1982.
Power Play. New York, Dell, 1982.
Relentless Adversary. New York, Dell, 1982.
Spellbound. New York, Dell, 1982.
Conflict of Interest. New York, Dell, 1983.
Double Dealing. New York, Dell, 1984.
Trading Secrets. New York, Dell, 1985.
The Desperate Game (Jones). New York, Dell, 1986.
The Chilling Deception (Jones). New York, Dell, 1986.
The Sinister Touch (Jones). New York, Dell, 1986.
The Fatal Fortune (Jones). New York, Dell, 1986.

Novels as Stephanie James

A Passionate Business. New York, Silhouette, 1981.
The Dangerous Magic. New York, Silhouette, 1982.
Stormy Challenge. New York, Silhouette, 1982.
Corporate Affair. New York, Silhouette, 1982.
Velvet Touch. New York, Silhouette, 1982.
Lover in Pursuit. New York, Silhouette, 1982.
Renaissance Man. New York, Silhouette, 1982.
A Reckless Passion. New York, Silhouette, 1982.
The Price of Surrender. New York, Silhouette, 1983.
To Tame the Hunter. New York, Silhouette, 1983.

Affair of Honor. New York, Silhouette, 1983.
Gamesmaster. New York, Silhouette, 1983.
The Silver Snare. New York, Silhouette, 1983.
Battle Prize. New York, Silhouette, 1983.
Bodyguard. New York, Silhouette, 1983.
Serpent in Paradise. New York, Silhouette, 1983.
Gambler's Woman. New York, Silhouette, 1984.
Fabulous Beast. New York, Silhouette, 1984.
Devil to Pay. New York, Silhouette, 1984.
Night of the Magician. New York, Silhouette, 1984.
Nightwalker. New York, Silhouette, 1984.
Raven's Prey. New York, Silhouette, 1984.
Golden Goddess. New York, Silhouette, 1985.
Wizard. New York, Silhouette, 1985.
Cautious Lover. New York, Silhouette, 1985.
Green Fire. New York, Silhouette, 1986.
Second Wife. New York, Silhouette, 1986.
Challoner Bride. New York, Silhouette, 1987.
Saxon's Lady. New York, Silhouette, 1987.

*   *   *

Jayne Ann Krentz is a well-known and very prolific writer who has created some of the very best romance fiction. Writing under a number of pseudonyms, she ranges from the Candlelight Ecstasy series, through the standard romance lines and is now becoming known as a truly creative writer of mid-list novels.

Back in the early 1980's when the Candlelight Ecstasy series first appeared on bookshelves, the name Jayne Castle was synonymous with "bedroom scenes" and "spicy" plots. Castle was one of the first romance writers to let her readers peek into the bedroom to see and feel the sensual and the sexual. In many ways, she set the standards for aspiring romance writers. However, just when her readers had come to expect silk teddies and masculine hands removing them, she would surprise them with a new Jayne Castle.

Writing as Stephanie James, she published in the Desire Line and Silhouette special editions. More recently she has written for the Harlequin Temptation series. Besides moving away from the series novels, she has written several futuristic romances such as *Sweet Starfire* and *Crystal Flame*. Futuristic romances may be classed as science fiction, but in this case, the emphasis is on the romance element.

Perhaps one of the most exciting changes that Krentz has made in her writing, has been the shift toward romantic suspense. Two of her latest in this category are *Double Dealing* and *Trading Secrets*. She has also created her own female private detective series with Guinevere Jones as the heroine.

In general, her heroines are strong, assertive; independent women and more than a match for the hero. On the other hand, they are not dominating, calculating, or manipulative. They meet the hero toe to toe and lips to lips as total equals. This is seen as a refreshing change by some of the male characters. For others it is a maddening, frustrating experience until they are able to realize that their own attitudes and biases are creating problems and not the women they love.

Krentz has written so many enjoyable and outstanding novels that finding one or two to illustrate her techniques is frustrating. However, *Trading Secrets* and *Gift of Fire* are among her latest novels and, perhaps, are most representative of her current work.

In *Trading Secrets* she starts with a tender scene of seduction. In other words, Sabrina Chase, businesswoman on her first romantic vacation in Acapulco, is about to pick up a man in a bar. Her choice is Matt August, an ex-major trained in Central American operations. Currently, Matt, who is no longer in the military, is the owner and manager of a book store in Acapulco. He generally lets the world go by with little regret—until Sabrina arrives. After a shaky beginning when she literally tosses him and his knife out of her hotel room, events return to normal as both try to understand what had happened. In reality, Sabrina wanted romance with a capital "R." He wanted to teach her a lesson about picking up strange men in a strange bar. With that start, things could only get better.

Sabrina finally returns to Dallas where she owns a "tacky" tourist shop filled with unbelievably hideous souvenirs. Matt follows her, hoping to get to know her better and also because his ex-wife refuses to cope any longer with their teenage son, Brad. Suddenly Sabrina and Matt are mixed up with crooked intelligence agents, threats are made to her and Brad, and Matt disappears on a "mission." How it ends should not be given away. It is sufficient to know that love and a slight touch of larceny give a delightful ending.

In *Gift of Fire*, Krentz makes another switch from her usual straight romance. This is the second novel with Verity Ames and Jonas Quarrel as lead characters. They first met in *Gift of Gold*, when Jonas saves Verity from being attacked. Later, Verity meets him in California, where he is applying for a job as a dishwasher in her own restaurant. Jonas is really a recognized renaissance scholar who is strongly psychic. Unfortunately, Jonas does not know how to control his power until he meets Verity. She is able to help him develop safe control and a very close psychic bond is forged between them.

In the *Gift of Fire*, Jonas is hired to find a lost medieval treasure. What they find is a murder, an attempted murder, and the treasure. Time tunnels, crystal power, and psychic phenomena are intertwined in this complexly plotted novel.

In all, Krentz's novels are fast paced, intriguing, wildly adventurous stories that leave nothing for the reader to wish for. They are a blend of romance, sensual delight, and appealing perfect lovers.

—Arlene Moore

KUCZKIR, Mary. See **MICHAELS, Fern.**

KYLE, Susan. See **PALMER, Diana.**

LAKE, Rozella. See **LINDSAY, Rachel.**

LAKER, Rosalind. Pseudonym for Barbara Øvstedal; has also written as Barbara Douglas; Barbara Paul. Recipient: Elizabeth Goudge Historical award, 1986. Agent: Laurence Pollinger Ltd., 18 Maddox Street, London W1R 0EU, England. Address: c/o Doubleday, 666 Fifth Avenue, New York, New York 10103, U.S.A.

ROMANCE AND HISTORICAL PUBLICATIONS

Novels (series: Warwyck)

Sovereign's Key. London, Hale, 1969.
Far Seeks the Heart. London, Hale, 1970.
Sail a Jeweled Ship. London, Hale, 1971.
The Shripney Lady. London, Hale, 1972.
Fair Wind of Love. London, Hale, 1974; as Barbara Douglas, New York, Doubleday, 1980.
The Smuggler's Bride. New York, Doubleday, 1975; London, Hale, 1976.
Ride the Blue Riband. New York, Doubleday, 1977; London, Hale, 1978.
Warwyck's Woman. New York, Doubleday, 1978; as *Warwyck's Wife*, London, Eyre Methuen, 1979.
Claudine's Daughter. New York, Doubleday, and London, Eyre Methuen, 1979.
Warwyck's Choice. New York, Doubleday, 1980; as *The Warwycks of Easthampton*, London, Eyre Methuen, 1980.
Banners of Silk. New York, Doubleday, 1981; London, Methuen, 1982.
Gilded Splendour. New York, Doubleday, and London, Methuen, 1982.
Jewelled Path. London, Methuen, and New York, Doubleday, 1983.
What the Heart Keeps. London, Methuen, and New York, Doubleday, 1984.
This Shining Land. London, Methuen, and New York, Doubleday, 1985.
Tree of Gold. London, Methuen, and New York, Doubleday, 1986.
The Silver Touch. London, Methuen, and New York, Doubleday, 1987.
To Dance with Kings. London, Methuen, 1988; New York, Doubleday, 1989.

Novels as Barbara Øvstedal

Red Cherry Summer. London, Hale, 1973.
Valley of the Reindeer. London, Hale, 1973.
Souvenir from Sweden. London, Hale, 1974.

Novels as Barbara Paul

The Seventeenth Stair. London, Macdonald and Jane's, and New York, St. Martin's Press, 1975.
The Curse of Halewood. London, Macdonald and Jane's, 1976; as *Devil's Fire, Love's Revenge*, New York, St. Martin's Press, 1976.
The Frenchwoman. London, Macdonald and Jane's, and New York, St. Martin's Press, 1977.
A Wild Cry of Love. London, Macdonald and Jane's, 1978; as *To Love a Stranger*, New York, St. Martin's Press, 1978.

OTHER PUBLICATIONS

Other

Norway (as Barbara Øvstedal). London, Batsford, and New York, Hastings House, 1973.

*   *   *

Since the appearance of her very first novel, Rosalind Laker has presented her readers with a broad range of offerings from period gothics to fictionalized biography. As might be expected with such a variety of periods and settings, she achieves varying degrees of success while on the whole providing well-written, tightly woven books.

The Smuggler's Bride begins with the typical premise of an orphan turned governess for the spoiled daughters of a snobbish wealthy family whose grown son considers the attractive new employee fair game. The first of a number of unusual twists occurs when the young woman begins to see and hear strange goings-on from the adjoining home of a reclusive neighbor. In an attempt to dispel the children's claim that the house is haunted, the governess explores it and, finding the occupant alone and injured, agrees to stay on as his nurse and housekeeper. When sufficiently recovered the man offers marriage as a means of salvaging her reputation and upon his death she finds herself well-provided for from the proceeds of her husband's unsavory former occupation.

Set in mid-19th-century England, *Claudine's Daughter* deals with events in the life of Lucy di Castelloni, orphaned at a young age, raised in an Italian convent, and married off to a wealthy elderly landowner. Now widowed, Lucy travels to Easthampton seeking freedom and a home, but unprepared for love or the revival of a scandal from past decades which involved another beautiful woman and holds the key to Lucy's past and future.

Warwyck's Choice continues recounting the relationship of love, hate, rivalry, jealousy, and loyalty of three generations of the wealthy Radcliffe and Warwycke families whose saga began in the earlier *Warwyck's Woman*.

Yet another portrayal of the spectacular European playgrounds and pastimes of the rich and famous at the turn of the century unfolds in *Jewelled Path*. The daugher of an eminent London jeweller seeks to make her own mark in the world of jewelry design despite her father's preferring to see her safely married and his opposition to her exciting new designs being promoted by Tiffany and Fabergé.

Abandoning the glitz and glamour of such period pieces, *What the Heart Keeps* follows Lisa Shaw, a "home" child sent from an English orphanage to the freedom of an adoptive home in North America—a freedom which is, in fact, the equivalent of indentured servitude. With determination and strength of character, she overcomes all obstacles finally to fulfill her destiny in life and love.

In what is perhaps Laker's strongest effort, *This Shining Land* is set in Norway during the German occupation and provides the reader with a genuine sense of the horrors and degradation facing the ordinary citizen in such extraordinary circumstances, and the quiet courage and determination with which they strove to survive as individuals and as a nation. She offers a grim portrait of the experiences of the concentration camps without excessively gruesome detail nor gratuitous violence or presenting her protagonists as superhuman heroes.

All of Laker's novels are carefully researched and meticulously crafted, but it is in the more recent settings, rather than those of centuries past, that her characters most successfully rise above the tendency interchangeable stock types and take on life as real individuals.

—Judith A. Gifford

LAMB, Charlotte. Pseudonym for Sheila Holland, née Coates; also writes as Sheila Coates; Laura Hardy; Sheila Lancaster; Victoria Woolf. British. Born in London, 22 December 1937. Educated at Ursuline Convent, Ilford, Essex. Married Richard Holland in 1959; two sons and three daughters. Secretary, Bank of England, London, 1954–56, and BBC, London, 1956–58. Agent: Jacqueline Korn, David Higham Associates, 5–8 Lower John Street, London W1R 4HA, England. Address: Crogga, Santon, Isle of Man, United Kingdom.

ROMANCE AND HISTORICAL PUBLICATIONS

Novels

Follow a Stranger. London, Mills and Boon, and Toronto, Harlequin, 1973.
Carnival Coast. London, Mills and Boon, 1973; Toronto, Harlequin, 1974.
A Family Affair. London, Mills and Boon, and Toronto, Harlequin, 1974.
Star-Crossed. London, Mills and Boon, 1976; New York, Oxford University Press, 1978.
Sweet Sanctuary. London, Mills and Boon, and Toronto, Harlequin, 1976.
Festival Summer. London, Mills and Boon, and Toronto, Harlequin, 1977.
Florentine Spring. London, Mills and Boon, and Toronto, Harlequin, 1977.
Hawk in a Blue Sky. London, Mills and Boon, 1977; Toronto, Harlequin, 1978.
Kingfisher Morning. London, Mills and Boon, 1977.
Master of Comus. London, Mills and Boon, 1977; Toronto, Harlequin, 1978.
Call Back Yesterday. London, Mills and Boon, and Toronto, Harlequin, 1978.
Desert Barbarian. London, Mills and Boon, and Toronto, Harlequin, 1978.
Disturbing Stranger. London, Mills and Boon, 1978; Toronto, Harlequin, 1979.
Autumn Conquest. London, Mills and Boon, 1978.
The Long Surrender. London, Mills and Boon, 1978.
The Cruel Flame. London, Mills and Boon, 1978; Toronto, Harlequin, 1980.
Duel of Desire. London, Mills and Boon, 1978.
The Devil's Arms. London, Mills and Boon, 1978; Toronto, Harlequin, 1979.
Pagan Encounter. London, Mills and Boon, 1978; Toronto, Harlequin, 1979.
Sweet Compulsion (as Victoria Woolf). London, Mills and Boon, and Toronto, Harlequin, 1979.
Forbidden Fire. London, Mills and Boon, 1979.
The Silken Trap. London, Mills and Boon, 1979; Toronto, Harlequin, 1980.
Dark Dominion. London, Mills and Boon, 1979.
Fever. London, Mills and Boon, 1979; Toronto, Harlequin, 1980.
Dark Master. London, Mills and Boon, 1979.
Temptation. London, Mills and Boon, and Toronto, Harlequin, 1979.
Twist of Fate. London, Mills and Boon, 1979; Toronto, Harlequin, 1980.
Possession. London, Mills and Boon, 1979.
Love Is a Frenzy. London, Mills and Boon, 1979; Toronto, Harlequin, 1980.
Frustration. London, Mills and Boon, 1979.

Sensation. London, Mills and Boon, 1979; Toronto, Harlequin, 1980.
Compulsion. London, Mills and Boon, 1980; Toronto, Harlequin, 1981.
Crescendo. London, Mills and Boon, 1980; Toronto, Harlequin, 1981.
Stranger in the Night. London, Mills and Boon, 1980; Toronto, Harlequin, 1981.
Storm Centre. London, Mills and Boon, and Toronto, Harlequin, 1980.
Seduction. London, Mills and Boon, 1980; Toronto, Harlequin, 1981.
Savage Surrender. London, Mills and Boon, and Toronto, Harlequin, 1980.
A Frozen Fire. London, Mills and Boon, and Toronto, Harlequin, 1980.
Man's World. London, Mills and Boon, 1980; Toronto, Harlequin, 1981.
Night Music. London, Mills and Boon, 1980; Toronto, Harlequin, 1981.
Obsession. London, Mills and Boon, 1980.
Retribution. London, Mills and Boon, and Toronto, Harlequin, 1981.
Illusion. London, Mills and Boon, and Toronto, Harlequin, 1981.
Heartbreaker. London, Mills and Boon, and Toronto, Harlequin, 1981.
Desire. London, Mills and Boon, and Toronto, Harlequin, 1981.
Dangerous. London, Mills and Boon, and Toronto, Harlequin, 1981.
Abduction. London, Mills and Boon, and Toronto, Harlequin, 1981.
The Girl from Nowhere. London, Mills and Boon, 1981.
Midnight Lover. London, Mills and Boon, 1982.
A Wild Affair. London, Mills and Boon, 1982.
Betrayal. London, Mills and Boon, 1983.
The Sex War. London, Mills and Boon, 1983.
Haunted. London, Mills and Boon, 1983.
Darkness of the Heart. London, Mills and Boon, 1983.
A Secret Intimacy. London, Mills and Boon, 1983.
A Violation. London, Fontana, and Toronto, Harlequin, 1983.
Infatuation. London, Mills and Boon, 1984.
Scandalous. London, Mills and Boon, 1984.
For Adults Only. London, Mills and Boon, 1984.
Love Games. London, Mills and Boon, 1984.
A Naked Flame. London, Mills and Boon, 1984.
Man Hunt. London, Mills and Boon, 1985.
Who's Been Sleeping in My Bed? London, Mills and Boon, 1985.
Sleeping Desire. London, Mills and Boon, 1985.
The Bride Said No. London, Mills and Boon, 1985.
Explosive Meeting. London, Mills and Boon, 1985.
Heat of the Night. London, Mills and Boon, 1986; Toronto, Harlequin, 1987.
Love in the Dark. London, Mills and Boon, 1986; Toronto, Harlequin, 1987.
Hide and Seek. London, Mills and Boon, and Toronto, Harlequin, 1987.
Circle of Fate. London, Mills and Boon, and Toronto, Harlequin, 1987.
Kiss of Fire. London, Mills and Boon, 1987; Toronto, Harlequin, 1988.
Whirlwind. London, Mills and Boon, 1987; Toronto, Harlequin, 1988.
You Can Love a Stranger. London, Mills and Boon, 1988.

Echo of Passion. London, Mills and Boon, 1988.
Out of Control. London, Mills and Boon, 1988.
No More Lonely Nights. London, Mills and Boon, 1988.
Seductive Stranger. London, Mills and Boon, 1989.

Novels as Sheila Holland

Love in a Mist. London, Hale, 1971.
Prisoner of the Heart. London, Hale, 1972.
A Lantern in the Night. London, Hale, 1973.
Falcon on the Hill. London, Hale, 1974.
Shadows at Dawn. London, Hale, 1975; Chicago, Playboy Press, 1979.
The Growing Season. London, Hale, 1975.
The Gold of Apollo. London, Hale, 1976.
The Caring Kind. London, Hale, 1976.
The Devil and Miss Hay. London, Hale, 1977.
Eleanor of Aquitaine. London, Hale, 1978.
Maiden Castle. Chicago, Playboy Press, 1978.
Love's Bright Flame. Chicago, Playboy Press, 1978.
Dancing Hill. Chicago, Playboy Press, 1978.
Folly by Candlelight. London, Hale, 1978; Chicago, Playboy Press, 1979; as *The Notorious Gentleman*, Playboy Press, 1980.
Sophia. Chicago, Playboy Press, 1979.
The Masque. New York, Zebra, 1979.
The Merchant's Daughter. Chicago, Playboy Press, 1980.
Miss Charlotte's Fancy. Chicago, Playboy Press, 1980.
Secrets to Keep. Chicago, Playboy Press, 1980.
Secrets. London, Fontana, 1983; Toronto, Harlequin, 1984.
A Woman of Iron. London, Collins, 1985.

Novels as Sheila Coates

A Crown Usurped. London, Hale, 1972.
The Queen's Letter. London, Hale, 1973.
The Flight of the Swan. London, Hale, 1973.
The Bells of the City. London, Hale, 1975.

Novels as Sheila Lancaster

Dark Sweet Wanton. London, Hodder and Stoughton, 1979; New York, Berkley, 1980.
The Tilthammer. London, Hodder and Stoughton, 1980.
Mistress of Fortune. London, Hodder and Stoughton, 1982.

Novels as Laura Hardy

Burning Memories. London, Silhouette, 1981.
Playing with Fire. London, Silhouette, 1981.
Dream Master. London, Silhouette, 1982.
Tears and Red Roses. London, Silhouette, 1982.
Dark Fantasy. London, Silhouette, 1983.
Men Are Dangerous. London, Silhouette, 1984.

*

Charlotte Lamb comments:

I try to write romantic novels which have very real characters and situations, but which never lose sight of the basic truth about romantic fiction—that we are creating dreams for our readers, dreams which must be rooted in real life if they are to be intensely powerful. The more closely a reader can identify with the book, the more she can respond to it and enjoy it. Women are both highly practical and deeply emotional, and what they want in their fiction is a mixture of warmly observed life and powerful emotion. All fiction is invented; the best fiction is close to reality yet with that added dimension of an escape into dreams.

*   *   *

Charlotte Lamb's series romances are characterized by energy and sensation despite their large number. For a considerable period of time, Lamb published one novel per month. Often identified by highly charged one-word titles (*Obsession*, *Desire*, *Frustration*, *Infatuation*, *Scandalous*), her novels detail the romantic entanglements of characters with deep-seated problems, often related to sexuality.

Although Lamb's heroines are occasionally country girls, their most typical milieu is London. Some are secretaries to playboy businessmen; others are actresses, singers, or artists. They are usually young, occasionally naive, and always more inhibited than other women in the books. Her heroes are older, highly successful, and domineering without being excessively brutal. She knows how to suggest an appealing vulnerability in traditionally "macho" men.

Lamb often writes about heroines who have been victims of sexual trauma. In *Stranger in the Night* and *Seduction* her women are unwillingly seduced and are marked by the experience. She writes about troubled marriages in *Sensation* and *A Frozen Fire*. In *Dark Dominion* the hero is almost pathologically jealous. In *Frustration* the heroine is debilitated by the death of her husband. Most heroines need to be shown how to express sexuality; most heroes need to be taught fidelity. Although Lamb's topics are often more potentially sensational than those of other series writers, she handles the material with circumspection. Any author as prolific as Lamb will produce uneven work, but despite her productivity she is unusually inventive within the restricted range of series romance formulas.

—Kay Mussell

LAMONT, Marianne. See **MANNERS, Alexandra.**

LANCASTER, Sheila. See **LAMB, Charlotte.**

LANCASTER, Vicky. See **ELSNA, Hebe.**

LANCE, Leslie. See **CHARLES, Theresa.**

LANE, Jane. Pseudonym for Elaine Dakers, née Kidner. British. Born in Ruislip, Middlesex, in 1905. Attended schools in Middlesex. Married the publisher Andrew Dakers in 1937; one son. *Died 6 January 1978.*

ROMANCE AND HISTORICAL PUBLICATIONS

Novels

Undaunted. London, Heath Cranton, 1934.
Be Valiant Still. London, Rich and Cowan, 1935.
King's Critic. London, Rich and Cowan, 1936.
Prelude to Kingship. London, Rich and Cowan, 1936.
Come to the March. London, Rich and Cowan, 1937.
Sir Devil-May-Care. London, Methuen, 1937.
You Can't Run Away. London, Methuen, 1940.
He Stooped to Conquer. London, Dakers, 1943.
England for Sale. London, Dakers, 1943.
Gin and Bitters. London, Dakers, 1945; as *Madame Geneva*, New York, Rinehart, 1946.
His Fight Is Ours. London, Dakers, 1946.
London Goes to Heaven. London, Dakers, 1947.
Parcel of Rogues. London, Dakers, and New York, Rinehart, 1948.
Fortress in the Forth. London, Dakers, 1950.
Dark Conspiracy. London, Hale, 1952.
The Sealed Knot. London, Hale, 1952.
The Lady of the House. London, Hale, 1953; as *Countess at War*, London, Davies, 1974.
The Phoenix and the Laurel. London, Hale, 1954.
Thunder on St. Paul's Day. London, Hale, and Westminster, Maryland, Newman Press, 1954.
Conies in the Hay. London, Hale, 1957; as *Rabbits in the Hay*, Westminster, Maryland, Newman Press, 1958.
Command Performance. London, Hale, 1957.
Queen of the Castle. London, Hale, 1958.
Cat among the Pigeons. London, Hale, 1959.
Sow the Tempest. London, Muller, 1960.
Ember in the Ashes. London, Muller, 1960.
Farewell to the White Cockade. London, Muller, 1961.
The Crown for a Lie. London, Muller, 1962.
A State of Mind. London, Muller, 1964.
A Wind Through the Heather: A Novel of the Highland Clearances. London, Muller, 1965.
From the Snare of the Hunter. London, Muller, 1968.
The Young and Lonely King. London, Muller, 1969.
The Questing Beast. London, Muller, 1970.
A Call of Trumpets. London, Muller, 1971.
The Severed Crown. London, Davies, 1972; New York, Simon and Schuster, 1973.
Bridge of Sighs. London, Davies, 1973; New York, Day, 1975.
Heirs of Squire Harry. London, Davies, 1974.
A Summer Storm. London, Davies, 1976.
A Secret Chronicle. London, Davies, 1977.

OTHER PUBLICATIONS

Fiction (for children)

The Escape of the King. London, Evans, 1950.
The Escape of the Prince. London, Evans, 1951.
Desperate Battle. London, Evans, 1953.
The Escape of the Queen. London, Evans, 1957.
The Escape of the Duke. London, Evans, 1960.
The Escape of the Princess. London, Evans, 1962.
The Trial of the King. London, Evans, 1963.
The Return of the King. London, Evans, 1964.
The March of the Prince. London, Evans, 1965.
The Champion of the King. London, Evans, 1966.

Other

The Last of the Hales; For Church and King (articles). London, Manresa Press, 1931.
King James the Last. London, Dakers, 1942.
Titus Oates: A Biography. London, Dakers, 1949; Westport, Connecticut, Greenwood Press, 1971.
Puritan, Rake and Squire. London, Evans, 1950.
The Reign of King Convenant (on Scotland 1633–61). London, Hale, 1956.

*   *   *

The output of historical novels by Elaine Dakers, who wrote as Jane Lane, was prolific. She enjoyed great popularity and most of her books were reprinted many times. She wrote three different kinds of book—straight historical novels, social histories of a short period of time when a way of life was changing, and a third kind in which an historical story is told in the form of extracts from diaries, memoirs, and letters.

All her books were exhaustively researched and every tiny detail of the life of the time is crammed in to show how people lived. If, as one critic has said, there are two kinds of historical novels—those that show our ancestors as very like us and those that show what strange lives they led—Lane was definitely of the second school of thought.

She set many of her books in the 17th and 18th centuries and was very pro-Stuart. Typical of her straight historical novels are her Scottish stories. *He Stooped to Conquer* tells the shameful story of the Massacre of Glencoe when William III tried to have the Glencoe sept of the Macdonalds treacherously wiped out. In *His Fight Is Ours* the story of the years between the 1715 and 1745 uprisings is told by the chief of the Macdonalds from his poverty-stricken exile in Paris. These books are beautifully written and read as if they are translated from the Gaelic and are full of details of Highland life.

The Questing Beast tells of the run up to the Civil War, concentrating on Pym, the Parliamentarian leader. *A Call of Trumpets* shows the Royalist cause in the Civil War doomed by the feud between Queen Henrietta Maria and Prince Rupert, with King Charles sitting on the fence between them. Lane also wrote novels set in the 16th century: *Parcel of Rogues* is about Mary Queen of Scots and *Heirs of Squire Harry* about Henry VIII's children.

Another straight historical novel but with a very different subject is *From the Snare of the Hunter*, a moving, detailed account of Jesus's last days from the entry to Jerusalem to the finding of the empty tomb.

Her "social history" novels are typified by *London Goes to Heaven* and *Gin and Bitters*. In the first we see the Interregnum from the day of Charles I's beheading to the day of Charles II's restoration through the bewildered eyes of Samuel Guffin, a London inn-keeper. He cannot come to terms with the times and we see many shades of opinion and behaviour through his family. His daughter runs after every religious sect, Levellers, Ranters, Friends, and Diggers and his son is a hell-fire bigot in the Roundhead army.

A similar formula is used in *Gin and Bitters* covering the years from 1688 to 1720. Nathaniel Vance can no more accept the new ideas of his time than can Guffin. He does not understand his son who wins money in a lottery and becomes a banker only to lose everything in the South Sea Bubble. He doesn't understand the fever for oblivion from cheap gin that seduces his wife and many others from his good ale nor the Jacobite plotting of his bookkeeper and his apprentice. In these books the story is

slight, merely a vehicle to show off the minutiae of the life and thought of the times, but absorbing nonetheless.

Lane's third type of books tells stories through what purport to be documents of the time. Although these are all good stories, they are harder to read for they are written "forsoothly," as Josephine Tey used to refer to language supposed to be contemporary with the time portrayed. *A Secret Chronicle* is the story of Edward II's miserable death as discovered for his daughter, the Queen of Scots, by her chronicler. It has testimony from people who knew him—his old nurse, his Queen's Lady-in-Waiting and a Welsh Bard whose "Look you, boyo" contribution is hard to take. *Fortress in the Forth* uses letters and diaries to tell the story of Jacobite prisoners immured there. *The Severed Crown* uses letters, memoirs, and diaries to tell of Charles I's last days from the time he ran away from Oxford to join the Scottish army who basely sold him to the Parliamentarians, to his imprisonment and his execution.

All of Lane's books are filled with accurate historical detail. All are fiercely partisan towards the characters she favours but they are so well-written and so powerfully told that, even knowing the outcome, one is still gripped by them and still one hopes as one reads that *this* time history will turn out differently and that this time the story will end happily.

—Pamela Cleaver

LANE, Roumelia. Pseudonym for Kay Green. British. Born in Bradford, Yorkshire, 31 December 1927. Educated at Bolling High School for Girls, Yorkshire. Married Gavin Green in 1949; one son and one daughter. Journalist, Bournemouth *Echo*. Address: Casa Mimosa, Santa Eugenia, Mallorca 07142, Spain.

ROMANCE AND HISTORICAL PUBLICATIONS

Novels

Rose of the Desert. London, Mills and Boon, 1967; Toronto, Harlequin, 1968.
Hideaway Heart. London, Mills and Boon, 1967; Toronto, Harlequin, 1968.
House of the Winds. London, Mills and Boon, and Toronto, Harlequin, 1968.
A Summer to Love. London, Mills and Boon, 1968; Toronto, Harlequin, 1969.
Terminus Tehran. London, Mills and Boon, 1969; Toronto, Harlequin, 1970.
Sea of Zanj. London, Mills and Boon, and Toronto, Harlequin, 1969.
The Scented Hills. London, Mills and Boon, 1970; Toronto, Harlequin, 1971.
Café Mimosa. London, Mills and Boon, and Toronto, Harlequin, 1971.
In the Shade of the Palms. London, Mills and Boon, 1972; Toronto, Harlequin, 1973.
Nurse at Noongwalla. London, Mills and Boon, 1973; Toronto, Harlequin, 1974.
Across the Lagoon. London, Mills and Boon, and Toronto, Harlequin, 1974.
Stormy Encounter. London, Mills and Boon, 1974; Toronto, Harlequin, 1975.
Where the Moonflower Weaves. London, Mills and Boon, 1974.

Harbour of Deceit. London, Mills and Boon, and Toronto, Harlequin, 1975.
The Tenant of San Mateo. London, Mills and Boon, and Toronto, Harlequin, 1976.
Himalayan Moonlight. London, Mills and Boon, 1977.
Bamboo Wedding. Toronto, Harlequin, 1977.
The Brightest Star. London, Mills and Boon, 1978.
Hidden Rapture. London, Mills and Boon, 1978; Toronto, Harlequin, 1979.
Second Spring. London, Mills and Boon, 1980.
Dream Island. London, Mills and Boon, 1981.
Desert Haven. London, Mills and Boon, 1981.
Lupin Valley. London, Mills and Boon, 1982.
The Fires of Heaven. London, Mills and Boon, 1983.
Summer of Conflict. London, Mills and Boon, 1984.
Dear Brute. London, Mills and Boon, 1984.
Night of the Beguine. London, Mills and Boon, 1985.
Master of Her Fate. London, Mills and Boon, 1986.
Tempest in the Tropics. London, Mills and Boon, 1986.

*

Roumelia Lane comments:

I like to think that my novels are truly representative of traditional romance fiction. The romance novel is going through a great change. Carnal desire is so often substituted for heartfelt emotions, and this I think is a pity. Some of the finest love stories ever told have survived because of their spiritual appeal. One wonders how many of today's "romances" will stand the test of time.

*   *   *

Roumelia Lane was first published in the Harlequin Romance series in 1968 and since then has easily established herself as one of the better romance writers. She has exceptional ability for combining exotic backgrounds with fresh, vivid characters that her readers thoroughly enjoy. The jungle forests of Ceylon, romantic, sunny Italy, and primitive Tanzania all become the stage for her novels, for she is one of the romance writers who deliberately draws her readers to far away places and unknown experiences.

Because of her penchant for unusual settings, Lane takes particular care in researching the material for her backgrounds. This is quite evident in novels such as *Where the Moonflower Weaves.* After her father's death, Jodi Lawrence tries to earn passage money back to England by caring for an older woman who is also returning to England. Blake Morrison is to take them by truck to the seaport to catch their ship, but during the trip a bridge collapses and they are left stranded deep in the Ceylon jungle. It takes them three weeks to reach civilization, and during this time they undergo terrifying experiences as they look for food, water, and shelter during their long march. The vivid detail and graphic descriptions of scenery and people make this novel one of her most fascinating.

Surprisingly, the background does not overpower the characters. Jodi Lawrence's quiet courage and sense of integrity help her withstand the animosity of Blake Morrison as he misunderstands her relationship with a neighboring planter just before they leave. The trek itself is a ruthless test of character and will which she stubbornly sets out to overcome. Blake Morrison exhibits the same sort of courage and resourcefulness in spite of overwhelming odds. Actually the entire story may be used as a classic example of plotting, for it shows man against man, man against self, and man against nature. The use of one such element makes a novel strong, but to combine all three elements of plotting successfully makes an exciting and unusually moving novel to read.

In *House of the Winds* Lane resorts to a similar plotting technique, as Laurie Weldon sets out to convince Ryan Holt to take her on safari in Tanzania. She is determined to gain recognition as a photographer, and she feels that the photographs from the safari will achieve this purpose. The constant interplay of conflicting emotions against the dangerous background of wild animals and vast areas of wilderness offers Lane endless choice of motivation and plotting intricacies. Laurie is young, ambitious, and vulnerable, while Ryan is a hardened hunter and safari master.

A Summer to Love is an unexpected change of pace. Stacey Roberts takes a job as a tourist guide in Sorrento for the summer. It should have been fun, especially as she looked forward to working with Jeremy again, but she finds herself under the domination of the ruthless hotel manager, Mark Lawford, who sees to it she does a full day's job of keeping other people happy.

Nowhere is balance so evident as in the writing of Lane. Her novels are exceptionally complicated in detail and characterization. Most of all, they are the sort of novels her readers avidly anticipate. Although she has evidently mastered the more gripping sort of novel, she yet manages to produce the occasional simple romance that her readers enjoy.

—Arlene Moore

LA TOURRETTE, Jacqueline. American. Born in Denver, Colorado, 5 May 1926. Educated at San Jose State University, California, 1948–51; trained as a nurse at St. Margaret's Hospital, Epping, Essex, 1958. Married David Gibeson in 1948; three children. Teletype operator, Alaska Communications System, 1954–55; medical secretary, Massachusetts Institute of Technology, Cambridge, 1961–69. Since 1969 medical secretary, Kaiser-Permanente Medical Center, Santa Clara, California. Agent: Raines and Raines, 71 Park Avenue, New York, New York 10016, U.S.A.

ROMANCE AND HISTORICAL PUBLICATIONS

Novels

The Joseph Stone. New York, Nordon, 1971.
A Matter of Sixpence. New York, Dell, 1972.
The Madonna Creek Witch. New York, Dell, 1973.
The Previous Lady. New York, Dell, 1974.
The Pompeii Scroll. New York, Delacorte Press, 1975.
Shadows in Umbria. New York, Putnam, 1979.
The Wild Harp. New York, Fawcett, 1981.
Patarran. New York, Fawcett, 1983.
The House on Octavia Street. New York, Beaufort, 1984.
The Incense Tree. New York, Fawcett, 1986.

*   *   *

Jacqueline La Tourrette's earlier novels are mostly horror stories in the style of Thomas Tryon. *The Madonna Creek Witch,* for example, is set in the Arizona Territory in the late 19th century, where a large, strange family is haunted by a witch. It was favorably received, some reviewers comparing it favorably with Tom Tryon's *The Other.*

The Previous Lady, also a horror novel involving little real action, concerns Amanda, a young woman who rents a secluded old English house from a lawyer. He is reluctant to let her have it, since the place has not been lived in since a former tenant went mad and died there. Amanda discovers a manuscript written by the insane tenant which tells about Christoper Lance who occupied the premises during the Victorian era. Naturally, Amanda becomes obsessed with the long-dead Lance and slowly begins losing her own sanity.

From these earlier novels, La Tourrette makes a sudden switch in style in *The Pompeii Scroll*, an adventurous and fun-filled story about collectors of illegal antiquities. The heroine, Joyce Lacey, digs up a smiling Etruscan statue in Greece which mysteriously disappears. She is framed for the theft and expelled from Greece in disgrace. Her pride in tatters, she retreats to Pompeii where she meets Antonio, a handsome Italian guide of archaeological sites. Together they begin a casual search for a legendary scroll stolen from Pompeii more than a century before, only to discover there is a connection between the missing scroll and the stolen statue. From this point the plot moves swiftly, providing sheer entertainment all the way. The dialogue is sophisticated and clever, and moves the plotline forward rather than just supplying filler. Inspector Vizzini is an excellently drawn character. Add to all this a love story with class, and you have a real treat.

Shadows in Umbria follows suit. This romantic suspense tale again takes place in Italy and involves a woman archaeologist, Christina Matthews, and a bullying Italian male archaeologist. They are digging up an Etruscan site on the land of an attractive Italian count whom the villagers consider in league with the devil. When the Count showers Christina with unwanted attention, she escapes him only to land herself in the arms of a grave robber. The story is rather implausible, and so many complications are often hard to make sense of. However, if the reader is willing to suspend disbelief, the novel is an interesting light read.

Embodying another change in style and content, *The Wild Harp* is a three-generational family saga about Irish immigrants who settle in Boston in the 1850's. The emphasis is on the women, who are the pillars of the family. The fate of the Noonans, after early years of squalor in Boston's Irish ghetto, takes a turn for the better when Mary is hired as a wet nurse by the wealthy Maddigan household. Mary's gifted daughter, Rosaleen, is allowed to attend tutored classes with the four Maddigan sons, one of whom she eventually marries. This is a well-told tale, well-paced and with fleshed-out characterizations.

All in all, La Tourrette is a talented author who seems to be trying out many different genres of fiction, achieving success in each of them. Any of her books can be recommended with confidence.

—Marilyn Lockhart

LAW, Elizabeth. See **PETERS, Maureen.**

LAWRENCE, Irene. See **WOODWARD, Lilian.**

LEE, Elsie (née Williams). Also wrote as Elsie Cromwell; Norman Daniels; Jane Gordon; Lee Sheridan. American. Born in Brooklyn, New York, 24 January 1912. Educated at Swarthmore College, Pennsylvania, 1929–32; Pratt Institute, New York, 1932–33. Married Marton Lee in 1941 (died). Librarian, Waterhouse and Company, New York, 1937–42; office manager, Reeves Laboratories, New York, 1942–45; librarian, Gulf Oil Company, New York, 1947–51; executive secretary, Andrews Clark and Buckley, New York, 1951–53. *Died 8 February 1987.*

ROMANCE AND HISTORICAL PUBLICATIONS

Novels

The Blood Red Oscar. New York, Lancer, 1962.
Sam Benedict: Cast the First Stone (novelization of TV series; as Norman Daniels). New York, Lancer, 1963.
A Comedy of Terrors (novelization of screenplay). New York, Lancer, 1964.
The Masque of the Red Death (novelization of screenplay). New York, Lancer, 1964.
Muscle Beach (novelization of screenplay). New York, Lancer, 1964.
Season of Evil. New York, Lancer, 1965; as *Two Hearts Apart* (as Jane Gordon), London, Hale, 1973.
Dark Moon, Lost Lady. New York, Lancer, 1965; London, Hale, 1973.
Clouds over Vellanti. New York, Lancer, 1965; London, Hale, 1972.
The Curse of Carranca. New York, Lancer, 1966; as *The Second Romance*, London, Hale, 1974.
Mansion of the Golden Windows. New York, Lancer, 1966.
The Drifting Sands. New York, Lancer, 1966.
Sinister Abbey. New York, Lancer, 1967; as *Romance on the Rhine*, London, Hale, 1974.
The Spy at the Villa Miranda. New York, Lancer, 1967; as *The Unhappy Parting*, London, Hale, 1973.
Doctor's Office. New York, Lancer, 1968.
The Governess (as Elsie Cromwell). New York, Paperback Library, 1969; as *Guardian of Love*, London, Hale, 1972.
Satan's Coast. New York, Lancer, 1969; as *Mystery Castle*, London, Hale, 1973.
Fulfillment. New York, Lancer, 1969.
Barrow Sinister. New York, Dell, 1969; as *Romantic Assignment*, London, Hale, 1974.
Ivorstone Manor (as Elsie Cromwell). New York, Pocket Books, 1970; London, Hale, 1973.
Silence Is Golden. New York, Dell, 1971.
Wingarden. New York, Arbor House, 1971.
The Diplomatic Lover. New York, Dell, 1971.
Star of Danger. New York, Dell, 1971.
The Passions of Medora Graeme. New York, Arbor House, 1972.
A Prior Betrothal. New York, Arbor House, 1973; London, Hale, 1976.
The Wicked Guardian. New York, Dell, 1973; London, Sphere, 1979.
Second Season. New York, Dell, 1973; London, Sphere, 1981.
An Eligible Connection. Bath, Chivers, 1974; New York, Dell, 1975.
Roomates. New York, Dell, 1976.
The Nabob's Widow. New York, Delacorte Press, 1976; London, Sphere, 1982.
Mistress of Mount Fair. New York, Dell, 1977.

OTHER PUBLICATIONS

Other as Lee Sheridan (with Michael Sheridan)

How to Get the Most Out of Your Tape Recording. Flushing, New York, Robins, 1958.
More Fun with Your Tape Recorders and Stereo. Los Angeles, Trend, 1958.
The Bachelor's Cookbook. New York, Collier, 1962.

Other

The Exciting World of Rocks and Gems. Los Angeles, Trend, 1959.
Easy Gourmet Cooking. New York, Lancer, 1962.
At Home with Plants: A Guide to Successful Indoor Gardening. New York, Macmillan, and London, Collier Macmillan, 1966.
Second Easy Gourmet Cookbook. New York, Lancer, 1968.
Book of Simple Gourmet Cookery. New York, Arbor House, 1971.
Party Cookbook. New York, Arbor House, 1974.

*   *   *

Elsie Lee, who also wrote as Elsie Cromwell and Jane Gordon, was a versatile author whose works include "modern gothics," Regency romances, and gourmet cookbooks. She began writing in the 1940's and sold her first stories to *Ladies Home Journal.* Those novels classified as modern gothics did not appear in print until the early 1960's. The period since then was a prolific and successful one for Lee, resulting in the publication of more than 20 romantic novels.

Although others consider her a modern gothic writer, Lee said (in *The Writer,* May 1973), " . . . despite fifteen of my novels so advertised, I do not write gothics. . . . The novels I write are better described as fairy tales for grownups—primarily women. . . . " She also pointed out how her novels differ from "true" gothics like *The Castle of Otranto.* Lee's novels are contemporary; built around possible (although not probable) situations; contain little violence and terror; focus on characters who, although imaginary, are portrayed realistically—a young, usually American heroine who is intelligent, well-educated, and quick-witted plus a solid dependable, older hero who tends to underestimate the heroine at first and who always works at some career. Lee's novels also do not fit the gothic formula which requires, in addition to the hero and heroine, at least one minor male and female character. For Lee, there is the hero, heroine, and villain—and the secret or puzzle around which the plot revolves. Lee's novels are also more "spicy" than the gothics written by many others which typically gloss over the sexual aspects of the male-female relationship.

Two of Lee's most popular modern gothics—*The Passions of Medora Graeme* and *Wingarden*—illustrate the style and approach that form the core of her appeal to readers. *The Passions of Medora Graeme,* for example, has been called a "lovely little romance" but "spicier" than many others in that genre because of love affairs past and present and because of the "earthy" Greek setting. One reviewer (*Library Journal,* 15 October 1972) notes that the Greek island—where "Dolly-Medora-Medarling-Graeme" and Simeon Vladow meet— " . . . is a great healer, and their affair doesn't do them a bit of harm either." Dolly and Simeon, like most of Lee's leading characters, work in interesting fields. Dolly is a successful fabric and dress designer; Simeon is a promising London surgeon. What gets the plot going is their need for long vacations to recover from emotional upsets: Dolly's discovery that her business partner/lover wants to marry another woman and Simeon's loss of two patients, one of them his girlfriend. Lee also adds some social and economic reality to the story as Dolly and Simeon help the islanders to buy a new generator to power the looms critical to their economic livelihood.

In *Wingarden* Lee paints Chloe as an intelligent heroine who has very strong opinions and isn't afraid to voice them and who has a healthy streak of skepticism along with the requisite sense of responsibility to family and tradition. One critic commented about *Wingarden's* female lead, "For a gothic heroine, Chloe is unusually intelligent, forthright, and determined." The sole heir to the estate of a grandmother she never knew, Chloe successfully solves the "puzzle" by finding the missing letter of instruction her grandmother Amelia wrote before her death and by discovering what is really going on at the supposedly "haunted" Wingarden. True to the contemporary setting and realistic characterization of her actors, Lee also does something that writers of modern gothics typically do not do. She incorporates into the plot an awareness of social issues (more fully realized than in *Medora Graeme* or other novels). *Wingarden* is set in Virginia, in a rigidly segregationist part of the South, and the interaction between Chloe's grandmother and her black servants reflects these long-standing patterns. On the surface, Amelia treated her black help no differently than the cultural definitions of the town prescribed. In actuality, however, she was concerned about their welfare and provided them with the opportunity to become self-sufficient through a bequest of property in her will. Lee thus portrays Amelia as a woman who is shrewd enough to avoid antagonizing the townspeople and unnecessarily risking outbreaks of racial violence.

Lee's ability to create realistic characters is evident in the portrait of Amelia that emerges via Chloe. Even though Amelia is dead as the novel begins, Lee makes her come alive through Chloe's insights into how her grandmother might have felt and acted towards the family and towards the blacks. There is almost a mystical sense of connection between Amelia and Chloe who never met but who look remarkably alike and have some of the same strong will and spirit.

Whether we describe her novels as "liberated modern gothics" or as "fairy tales for grownups," it is clear that Lee is a writer of skill and social awareness. Women readers in particular would find much to admire in her heroines. Previous research that we conducted on modern gothic novels suggested that the strong sex-role characterization of the heroines is a large part of the appeal of these novels. Most of the heroines in the gothics we analyzed were portrayed as toward the non-traditional end of the scale in terms of personality traits (i.e., not submissive or passive) and attitudes toward careers and marriage (i.e., likely to work and to have other goals besides finding a husband) (*Pacific Sociological Review,* April 1977). Clearly Lee's heroines would be of the same type and they are probably a major reason for the continuing appeal of her gothic romances.

—Josephine A. Ruggiero and Louise C. Weston

————

LEIGH, Roberta. See **LINDSAY, Rachel.**

————

LENANTON, C. See **OMAN, Carola.**

LESLIE, Doris (née Oppenheim). British. Born in London, c. 1902. Educated privately in London, and in Brussels; studied art in Florence. Married 1) John Leslie (died); 2) Sir Walter Fergusson Hannay in 1936 (died 1961). Served in Civil Defence, 1941–45. *Died 31 May 1982.*

ROMANCE AND HISTORICAL PUBLICATIONS

Novels

The Starling. London, Hurst and Blackett, and New York, Century, 1927.
Fools in Mortar. London, Hurst and Blackett, and New York, Century, 1928.
The Echoing Green. London, Hurst and Blackett, 1929.
Terminus. London, Hurst and Blackett, 1931.
Puppets Parade. London, Lane, 1932.
Full Flavour. London, Lane, and New York, Macmillan, 1934.
Fair Company. London, Lane, and New York, Macmillan, 1936.
Concord in Jeopardy. London, Hutchinson, and New York, Macmillan, 1938.
Another Cynthia: The Adventures of Cynthia, Lady Ffulkes 1780–1850. London, Hutchinson, and New York, Macmillan, 1939.
Royal William: The Story of a Democrat. London, Hutchinson, 1940; New York, Macmillan, 1941.
House in the Dust. London, Hutchinson, and New York, Macmillan, 1942.
Polonaise. London, Hutchinson, 1943.
Folly's End. London, Hutchinson, 1944.
The Peverills. London, Hutchinson, 1946.
Wreath for Arabella. London, Hutchinson, 1948; New York, Popular Library, 1973.
That Enchantress. London, Hutchinson, 1950; New York, Popular Library, 1973.
A Toast to Lady Mary. London, Hutchinson, 1954; New York, Popular Library, 1973.
Peridot Flight. London, Hutchinson, 1956.
Tales of Grace and Favour (omnibus). London, Hutchinson, 1956.
As the Tree Falls. London, Hodder and Stoughton, 1958; as *The King's Traitor*, New York, Popular Library, 1973.
The Perfect Wife. London, Hodder and Stoughton, 1960; as *The Prime Minister's Wife*, New York, Doubleday, 1961.
I Return. London, Hodder and Stoughton, 1962; as *Vagabond's Way*, New York, Doubleday, 1962.
This for Caroline. London, Heinemann, 1964; New York, Popular Library, 1973.
Paragon Street. London, Heinemann, 1965.
The Sceptre and the Rose. London, Heinemann, 1967.
The Marriage of Martha Todd. London, Heinemann, 1968.
The Rebel Princess. London, Heinemann, 1970; New York, Popular Library, 1973.
A Young Wives' Tale. London, Heinemann, 1971.
The Desert Queen. London, Heinemann, 1972.
The Dragon's Head. London, Heinemann, 1973.
The Incredible Duchess. London, Heinemann, 1974.
Call Back Yesterday. London, Heinemann, 1975.
Notorious Lady. London, Heinemann, 1976.

The Warrior King. London, Heinemann, 1977.
Crown of Thorns. London, Heinemann, 1979.

OTHER PUBLICATIONS

Other

The Great Corinthian: A Portrait of the Prince Regent. London, Eyre and Spottiswoode, 1952; New York, Oxford University Press, 1953.

*   *   *

Doris Leslie has an impressive list of titles to her credit, both novels and "biographical studies." Her period research was intensive; seldom if ever can she be faulted in any detail, and she projects a real sense of history. She wrote of people important to her who, through her, become so to the reader. It is the day-to-dayness of ordinary life that animates her novels, rather than engrossing plot or suspense. Events do occur, but in an apparently formless, accidental way as in most lives, only forming recognizable patterns in retrospect. Her characters, though convincing and well-rounded, seem all to speak in the same voice, however their circumstances may differ; and while it is a voice worth hearing, it provides little variety.

She is best known for her biographical studies, in part perhaps because she ventured into territories heretofore the province of the scholar only. Readers of the romantic-historical genre have at their command literally dozens of titles based upon the familiar story of Elizabeth Tudor, her tragic mother and monstrous golden father; similarly, there are scores of works based on the lives of Queen Victoria, Empress Josephine, Louis XIV, and others of that category of historical personage whose own vividly dramatic lives attract the romance novelist as a lightning rod draws the thunderbolt. But what other author has seen the possibilities inherent in the relatively unfamiliar stories of Lady Blessington, bluff and foolish William IV, or Queen Anne's beloved Lady Masham? Though Leslie has traversed more popularly familiar terrain with her stories of the Prince Regent, Caro Lamb, and Chopin, it is the lesser historical personages in her pageant of fortune's fools and favourites that best hold the reader's interest.

A failing in her work is the recurring tendency to suggest the workings of incomprehensible providence at work in a tiresomely portentous manner; as in making reference, quite out of context to the story in hand, to the fact that even as the action takes place, across the dark city, that selfsame night, a young girl is untimely called from her bed in Kensington Palace . . . Victoria! (She is also in the habit of referring to her own other novels in asterisked footnotes.)

In spite of a few such annoying mannerisms, as well as a propensity for documenting the facts of a life in essay form, interpolating patches of very readable dialogue, and renaming it a study, Leslie has earned her popularity, if for no other reason than as the author of a painless mini-course in history. She proves that history is peopled with characters any one of whom, if singled out by a sympathetic, period-conscious writer, provides a fresh perspective on familiar, often-worked literary and historical ground.

—Joan McGrath

L'ESTRANGE, Anna. See **ELLERBECK, Rosemary.**

LEWIS, Janet. American. Born in Chicago, Illinois, 17 August 1899. Educated at the Lewis Institute, Chicago, A.A. 1918; University of Chicago, Ph.B. 1920. Married the writer Yvor Winters in 1926 (died 1968); one daughter and one son. Passport Bureau clerk, American Consulate, Paris, 1920; proof reader, *Redbook* magazine, Chicago, 1921; English teacher, Lewis Institute, 1921–22; editor, with Howard Baker and Yvor Winters, *Gyroscope*, Palo Alto, California, 1929–30. Lecturer, Writers Workshop, University of Missouri, Columbia, 1952, and University of Denver, 1956; Visiting Lecturer, then Lecturer in English, Stanford University, California, 1960, 1966, 1969, 1970. Recipient: Friends of American Literature award, 1932; Shelley Memorial award, for poetry, 1948; Guggenheim fellowship, 1950; Los Angeles *Times* Kirsch award, 1985. Address: 143 West Portola Avenue, Los Altos, California 94022, U.S.A.

ROMANCE AND HISTORICAL PUBLICATIONS

Novels

The Invasion: A Narrative of Events Concerning the Johnston Family of St. Mary's. New York, Harcourt Brace, 1932.
The Wife of Martin Guerre. San Francisco, Colt Press, 1941; London, Rapp and Carroll, 1967.
The Trial of Sören Qvist. New York, Doubleday, 1947; London, Gollancz, 1967.
The Ghost of Monsieur Scarron. New York, Doubleday, and London, Gollancz, 1959.

OTHER PUBLICATIONS

Novel

Against a Darkening Sky. New York, Doubleday, 1943.

Short Stories

Goodbye, Son, and Other Stories. New York, Doubleday, 1946.

Plays (opera libretti)

The Wife of Martin Guerre, music by William Bergsma, adaptation of the novel by Lewis (produced New York, 1956). Denver, Swallow, 1958.
The Last of the Mohicans, adaptation of the novel by Cooper, music by Alva Henderson (produced Wilmington, Delaware, 1976).
A Birthday of the Infanta, adaptation of the story by Wilde, music by Malcolm Seagrave (produced Carmel, California, 1977). Los Angeles, Symposium Press, 1979.
Mulberry Street, music by Alva Henderson. Onset, Massachusetts, Dermont, 1981.
The Swans. Santa Barbara, California, Daniel, 1986.

Verse

The Indians in the Woods. Bonn, Germany, Monroe Wheeler, 1922; Palo Alto, California, Matrix Press, 1980.
The Wheel in Midsummer. Lynn, Massachusetts, Lone Gull Press, 1927.
The Earth-Bound 1924–1944. Aurora, New York, Wells College, 1946.
The Hangar at Sunnyvale 1937. San Francisco, Book Club of California, 1947.

Poems 1924–1944. Denver, Swallow, 1950.
The Ancient Ones. Portola Valley, California, No Dead Lines, 1979.
Poems Old and New 1918–1978. Athens, Ohio University Press-Swallow Press, 1981.

Other

The Friendly Adventure of Ollie Ostrich (for children). New York, Doubleday, 1923.
Keiko's Bubble (for children). New York, Doubleday, 1961; Kingswood, Surrey, World's Work, 1963.
The U.S. and Canada, with others. Green Bay, University of Wisconsin Press, 1970.

*

Manuscript Collection: Stanford University Library, California.

Critical Study: "The Historical Novels of Janet Lewis" by Donald Davie, in *Southern Review* (Baton Rouge, Louisiana), January 1966.

*   *   *

Janet Lewis is admired as one of the purest stylists in contemporary fiction, and as a novelist who continued to write quietly probing dramas of psycho-moral ambiguity with almost total disregard for the changing fashions of American fiction. She is to be compared, in the quiet integrity of her art, with Willa Cather, Caroline Gordon, and her friend Elizabeth Madox Roberts. Only her modest volume of short stories (*Goodbye, Son*) and the slow-paced, intelligent, at times dreary *Against a Darkening Sky* are contemporary in scene. Her reputation rests instead on her four historical novels, one related to her own part-Indian background, the others set in remote European times.

The Invasion occupies a surprisingly satisfying border region between fiction and history, and contains some of the loveliest prose in modern American literature. Its singular achievement is to present without pretentiousness or strain an Indian culture from within (the Ojibway of the Lake Superior area), and its gradual change and slow obliteration over a century and a half. The family chronicle extends from 1791, when we meet the 14-year-old Woman of the Glade, who married the trader John Johnston, to the death in 1944 of Anna Maria Johnston, the Red Leaf. The novel is the work of a poet recording delicate nuances of landscape and mood, and of a scrupulous historian contemplating with equanimity the inevitable outrages of human passion and eroding time. It combines with remarkable success an intimate immersion in scene (a succession of lived moments) and a flow of time that is calm as well as swift. The chronicle's exceptional authenticity is strengthened by the fact that the famous ethnologist, linguist, and Indian agent Henry Rowe Schoolcraft is a central figure in the family history.

Three very different historical novels are based on incidents recorded in Phillips's *Famous Cases of Circumstantial Evidence*, an early 19th-century work. *The Trial of Sören Qvist*, set in 17th-century Denmark, is the story of a saintly pastor executed for a crime he did not commit. This is a spare and dramatic novel, but meditative too, like everything Lewis has written. *The Ghost of Monsieur Scarron* is the product of years of research, some of it in a part of Paris that has not greatly changed since 1694. It is the minutely realistic story of a bookbinder falsely accused of authoring a libelous pamphlet directed against Louis XIV and Madame de Maintenon. The evocation of the Paris of that time is remarkable.

The best of these novels, one of the greatest short novels in American literature, is *The Wife of Martin Guerre*, a quietly authentic, immaculately written story of a man whose physical "double" (but far more considerate and more loving than the original) returns to claim the wife of a soldier supposed dead in the wars of 16th-century France. Here as in her other two novels of ambiguous crime and punishment Lewis dramatizes, always calmly, situations exerting extreme pressure on her characters. The marriage of Martin Guerre and Bertrande de Rols, at 11, is of its time, and so too the execution 21 years later. A sentence from Lewis's Foreword suggests the human understanding underlying all her work: "The rules of evidence vary from century to century, and the morality which compels many of the actions of men and women varies also, but the capacities of the human soul for suffering and for joy remain very much the same."

—Albert Guerard

LEWIS, Maynah (née McIntire). British. Born in Liverpool, Lancashire, 14 April 1919. Educated at schools in Scotland. Married Victor Lewis in 1936; one son. Professional musician and teacher; full-time writer from 1958. Recipient: Romantic Novelists Association Ayres award, 1962, and Major award, 1967, 1972. *Died 16 July 1988.*

ROMANCE AND HISTORICAL PUBLICATIONS

Novels

No Place for Love. London, Hurst and Blackett, 1963.
Give Me This Day. London, Hurst and Blackett, 1964.
See the Bright Morning. London, Hurst and Blackett, 1965.
Make Way for Tomorrow. London, Hurst and Blackett, 1966;
  New York, Beagle, 1973.
The Long, Hot Days. London, Hurst and Blackett, 1966.
The Future Is Forever. London, Hurst and Blackett, 1967.
Till Then, My Love. London, Hurst and Blackett, 1968.
Of No Fixed Abode. London, Hurst and Blackett, 1968.
Symphony for Two Players. London, Hurst and Blackett, 1969.
A Corner of Eden. London, Hurst and Blackett, 1970.
A Pride of Innocence. London, Hurst and Blackett, 1971; New
  York, Beagle, 1973.
Too Late for Tears. London, Hurst and Blackett, 1972.
The Town That Nearly Died. London, Collins, 1973.
The Miracle of Lac Blanche. London, Collins, 1973.
The Unforgiven. London, Collins, 1974; New York, Ace, 1976.
The Other Side of Paradise. London, Collins, 1975.
Yesterday Came Suddenly. London, Collins, 1975.
A Woman of Property. London, Collins, 1976.
These My Children. London, Collins, 1977.
Love Has Two Faces. London, Hamlyn, 1981.
Barren Harvest. London, Hale, 1981.
Hour of the Siesta. London, Hale, 1982.
Whisper Who Dares. London, Hale, 1983.

*   *   *

Maynah Lewis, a professional musician turned prolific novelist, no doubt had little time to be idle, and this is reflected in the activity and diversity of her novels. Her heroes and heroines are all working (though not necessarily "working-class") people, deeply involved in their jobs or careers, be they in the legal or

medical professions, or running a corner store. Each novel is set in different and definite surroundings: a Caribbean island (*The Other Side of Paradise*), a small industrial Northern town (*A Woman of Property*), a home for handicapped children (*Love Has Two Faces*). The characters are not on the whole seekers of experience. Often they are settled, rather staid people forced into action by tangible problems: the loss of memory, the forces of big business, the difficulties of dealing with a delinquent child. Neither do they long for romance: love creeps up on them accidentally after an acquaintanceship, or reappears from a long-distant past.

Nowhere is this better illustrated than in *Yesterday Came Suddenly*, where the hero, Edward, a 38-year-old right-wing lawyer who has taken a public stand against declining moral standards, is approached out of the blue by the girlfriend of his university days, the mysterious, dark-eyed, apparently widowed Eleanor. Eleanor begs him to defend her delinquent son David, who, while driving a stolen car with a gang of friends, has run over and badly injured an elderly man. When Edward discovers that Eleanor has never been married and that David is indeed his own illegitimate son, he is thrown into confusion. Suddenly on the other side of the moral fence he flounders between his desire to protect his son, his renewed passion for Eleanor, and his unwillingness to be seen as a hypocrite in the eyes of his colleagues, his clinging mother, and his beautiful, clever, undemanding too-good-to-be-true doctor fiancée. But in typical Lewis style, his problems are sorted out as neatly as they happened: his colleagues rally round him, David is given a suspended sentence, his fiancée, retaining her pride, goes off to South Africa, sparing him even the ordeal of making a clean break with her, and Edward is reunited with his one real love, with the approval of her mother if not his own. Although Edward's dilemma is a real one, and well set up, he remains a dislikable character throughout the book, shirking responsibility wherever he can. One at times feels that this learned lawyer should, at his age, be a bit more grown-up.

Also guilty of shirking parental responsibility is Robert, the lawyer hero of *These My Children* who, until the death of his forceful wife prompts him into action, has taken no interest in the upbringing of his children. Now alone and lonely, Robert sets out to reestablish contact with his grown-up daughters and son. The theme of child/parent conflict re-emerges often in Lewis's books. More often than not the young are striking out by themselves in the face of parental opposition, either to pursue an "unsuitable" partner (Hilary and Carol in *These My Children*) or to take a stand against something they believe to be morally wrong (Veronica and Stuart in *A Woman of Property*). Any guilty feelings they may have about hurting or leaving an aged relative are, in the end, exonerated: Lewis's predilection for happy endings for all ensures a reunion in the end, by which time the parent is well on the way to forming a lasting relationship with someone of his or her own generation.

It is difficult to sum up work of such diversity as Lewis's. She is at her best in devising interesting plots and settings for her characters though one might wish, at times, that the tensions inherent in these situations could have been more fully explored. However, the richness of her novels has ensured her continuing popularity, and is the reason, no doubt, why she has twice been winner of the Romantic Novelists Association Major award.

—Judith Summers

LEWTY, Marjorie (née Lobb). British. Born in Wallasey, Cheshire, 8 April 1906. Educated at Queen Mary High School, Liverpool. Married Richard Arthur Lewty in 1933; one son and one daughter. Secretary, District Bank Ltd., Liverpool, 1923–33. Address: c/o Mills and Boon Ltd., 18–24 Paradise Road, Richmond, Surrey TW9 1SR, England.

ROMANCE AND HISTORICAL PUBLICATIONS

Novels

Never Call It Loving. London, Mills and Boon, 1958; Toronto, Harlequin, 1968.
The Million Stars. London, Mills and Boon, 1959.
The Imperfect Secretary. London, Mills and Boon, 1959; Toronto, Harlequin, 1967.
The Lucky One. London, Mills and Boon, 1961; Toronto, Harlequin, 1968.
This Must Be for Ever. London, Mills and Boon, 1962.
Alex Rayner, Dental Nurse. London, Mills and Boon, and Toronto, Harlequin, 1965.
Dental Nurse at Denley's. London, Mills and Boon, 1968; Toronto, Harlequin, 1969.
Town Nurse—Country Nurse. London, Mills and Boon, 1970; Toronto, Harlequin, 1971.
The Extraordinary Engagement. London, Mills and Boon, 1972; Toronto, Harlequin, 1973.
The Rest Is Magic. London, Mills and Boon, 1973; Toronto, Harlequin, 1974.
All Made of Wishes. London, Mills and Boon, and Toronto, Harlequin, 1974.
Flowers in Stony Places. London, Mills and Boon, and Toronto, Harlequin, 1975.
The Fire in the Diamond. London, Mills and Boon, and Toronto, Harlequin, 1976.
To Catch a Butterfly. London, Mills and Boon, and Toronto, Harlequin, 1977.
The Time and the Loving. London, Mills and Boon, 1977; Toronto, Harlequin, 1978.
The Short Engagement. London, Mills and Boon, and Toronto, Harlequin, 1978.
A Very Special Man. London, Mills and Boon, 1979.
A Certain Smile. London, Mills and Boon, 1979; Toronto, Harlequin, 1980.
Prisoner in Paradise. London, Mills and Boon, 1980.
Love Is a Dangerous Game. London, Mills and Boon, 1980.
Beyond the Lagoon. London, Mills and Boon, 1981.
A Girl Bewitched. London, Mills and Boon, 1981.
Makeshift Marriage. London, Mills and Boon, 1982.
One Who Kisses. London, Mills and Boon, 1983.
Dangerous Male. London, Mills and Boon, 1983.
Riviera Romance. London, Mills and Boon, 1984.
A Lake in Kyoto. London, Mills and Boon, 1985.
Acapulco Moonlight. London, Mills and Boon, 1985.
Villa in the Sun. London, Mills and Boon, 1986.
In Love with the Man. London, Mills and Boon, 1986.
Honeymoon Island. London, Mills and Boon, 1987.
Falling in Love Again. London, Mills and Boon, 1988.

*

Marjorie Lewty comments:

All I can say about my work is that I write to please the reader, as well as myself. I believe the purpose of fiction is to tell a story, and that a story is what most people enjoy. I write romantic novels because I was born and brought up in a romantic age, the age of the 1920's, when there was still optimism in the world. I don't think romantic stories are necessarily "escapist," using the word in its pejorative sense, any more than a trip into the countryside is "escapist." I think the "romantic" formula corresponds to the basic myth of all time: the descent into despair, followed by the rise again to happiness—the happy ending. This myth is built into our culture, which would account for the popularity of the romantic novel through the ages.

* * *

Marjorie Lewty is a British writer who has developed her own individual style of writing romance novels. Usually her novels are written against a background to English towns and the countryside, so that much of the story development rests with the day in, day out activities of her characters as they meet and eventually fall in love. The strongest element in her writing is her characterization. Here she draws on her own interest in psychology to portray not only believable characters, but complex ones.

For instance, in *Flowers in Stony Places* she develops the character of Lisa, the sister of Samantha, her heroine in the novel. Lisa is a light, frivolous person who is shallow and self-centered to an unbelievable degree. She plays an indirect role in creating tension between the leading characters and appears at particularly crucial times in the story. Lewty's use of Lisa in the story to establish Samantha's character and to provide motivation for Adam Royle's attitude toward Samantha is particularly well done, and illustrates her ability to portray well-rounded characters. Besides Lisa and Samantha, Lewty adds the character of Estelle Norton, the new matron for the school where Samantha and Adam Royle work. She is a cold, calculating person with little empathy for the boys in her care. Lewty's ability to balance the motivation of the three women in a single novel is quite remarkable and shows her command of characterization.

One of her most enjoyable novels is *The Imperfect Secretary*. In this story, Lewty develops the character of Carol Waring, described as an attractive girl who is warm-hearted, generous, and lively. But she is also young and impulsive, and frequently displays those qualities that are not considered "professional" in a good secretary. Her employer is determined to change her into his idea of a good secretary and much of the story revolves around his attempts to make her so. The hero, Clive Benedict, is the head of a large construction company and sees the task as a challenge. It is Carol's warm-heartedness that helps to solve a particularly nasty problem when a very old lady refuses to move from her cottage into a newer housing area. Officialdom sees her as cantankerous and obstinate, while Carol learns that she really fears losing touch with her grandson if he can not find her once she has left her old home. Carol constantly acts from instinctive qualities of goodness and kindness, rather than business-like efficiency. In the end, naturally, Clive Benedict finds that these qualities are far more important to him than an efficient secretary.

Carol Waring is typical of her heroines, and perhaps in a way Clive Benedict is just as typical of her heroes. They are often businessmen who have to make hard decisions and who have to maintain a wall of defense in order to be as successful as they are. It is not until the heroine learns more about him and is able to get beyond the outer wall that she realizes just what kind of difficulties the hero must constantly deal with. Frequently he is a sensitive person who is able to understand and empathize with the dreamers of the world.

Throughout her writing, Lewty is able to maintain the suspense of the story and is able to inter-weave plot, motivation, and character in such a way that her readers are unaware of just how skillfully they are being led in a particular direction. There are no towering heights to be climbed, nor extraordinary depths to be plumbed; yet, her novels hold her readers and take them away from their own cares for a while, a fact that is extremely important to them and perhaps accounts for her popularity as a writer.

—Arlene Moore

LEY, Alice Chetwynd (née Humphrey). British. Born in Halifax, Yorkshire, 12 October 1913. Educated at King Edward VI Grammar School, Birmingham; London University, diploma in sociology 1962. Married Kenneth James Ley in 1945; two sons. Tutor in Creative Writing, Harrow College of Further Education, Middlesex 1963–84. Past chairwoman, Romantic Novelists Association. Agent: Curtis Brown, 162–168 Regent Street, London WIR 5TB. Address: 42 Cannonbury Avenue, Pinner, Middlesex HA5 1TS, England.

ROMANCE AND HISTORICAL PUBLICATIONS

Novels (series: Justin Rutherford and Anthea)

The Jewelled Snuff Box. London, Hale, 1959; New York, Beagle, 1974.
The Georgian Rake. London, Hale, 1960; New York, Beagle 1974.
The Guinea Stamp. London, Hale, 1961; as *The Courting of Joanna*, New York, Ballantine, 1976.
Master of Liversedge. London, Hale, 1966; as *The Master and the Maiden*, New York, Ballantine, 1977.
The Clandestine Betrothal. London, Hale, 1967; New York, Ballantine, 1976.
The Toast of the Town. London, Hale, 1969; New York, Ballantine, 1976.
Letters for a Spy. London, Hale, 1970; as *The Sentimental Spy*, New York, Ballantine, 1977.
A Season at Brighton. London, Hale, 1971; New York, Ballantine, 1976.
Tenant of Chesdene Manor. London, Hale, 1974; as *Beloved Diana*, New York, Ballantine, 1977.
The Beau and the Bluestocking. London, Hale, 1975; New York, Ballantine, 1977.
At Dark of the Moon. London, Hale, 1977; New York, Ballantine, 1978.
An Advantageous Marriage. London, Hale, 1977; New York, Ballantine, 1978.
A Regency Scandal. New York, Ballantine, and London, Futura, 1979.
A Conformable Wife. New York, Ballantine, 1981; London, Severn House, 1988.
The Intrepid Miss Hayden. New York, Fawcett, 1983; London, Severn House, 1987.
A Reputation Dies (Rutherford and Anthea). London, Methuen, 1984; New York, St. Martin's Press, 1985.
A Fatal Assignation (Rutherford and Anthea). London, Severn House, and New York, St. Martin's Press, 1987.
Masquerade of Vengeance (Rutherford and Anthea). London, Severn House, 1989.

*

Alice Chetwynd Ley comments:

My novels are set in the late Georgian period, i.e., 1760–1816. Several are in the Regency period. I made a study of the period when working on the social history section of my diploma course, and have always been a devotee of Jane Austen. This gives an authentic background to my work, but my novels are essentially romantic.

*   *   *

In a career spanning more than two decades, Alice Chetwynd Ley has proven herself to be one of the finest, most consistent authors of historical romances. In tone, style, and qualities her work is reminiscent of that of Georgette Heyer, yet she remains much less widely known.

Most of Ley's books are Regency romances, with a few taking place in the Georgian period. Like Heyer, she concentrates on developing her characters and giving them life. The care she takes in portraying even minor characters brings a depth to her stories not often found in formula romances, which frequently feature one- or two-dimensional figures.

Under Ley's pen, the aristocratic worlds of Georgian and Regency fashionable society comes to life. Enough movement to keep a story briskly paced is supplied, but the real focus is on the characters and their relationships. Feverish action is not necessary to interest the reader in the lovers of *The Clandestine Betrothal* or *The Beau and the Bluestocking*. Even in the more eventful novels, such as *Tenant of Chesdene Manor* or *The Jewelled Snuff Box*, the people are more important than specific events. The most action-filled of Ley's novels are those set against the background of the war with France. *The Guinea Stamp, At Dark of the Moon*, and *Letters for a Spy* all draw on the English fears of a French invasion and Napoleonic spies, yet most of the problems remain on a personal level for the protagonists. The heroes of these books are double agents or counter spies, and confusion of identities and mistaken motives lead to much of the action. Ley does manage to slip a few slightly unexpected twists into these plots when Elizabeth is the one suspected of being a spy in *Letters for a Spy* and the double agent, Captain Jackson, in *The Guinea Stamp* is revealed as also leading a double life in England.

The 1981 Ballantine edition of *A Conformable Wife* proclaims Alice Chetwynd Ley "the new queen of Regency romance." While in the main such a statement is accurate, it is somewhat misleading. It is true that she has authored many quality romances, yet her long career hardly qualifies her for a title as a *new* leader of the genre. Instead, real devotees of historical romances will recognize her as one of their best kept secrets.

—Barbara E. Kemp

LEYTON, Sophie. See **WALSH, Sheila.**

LIBBEY, Laura Jean. American. Born in New York City in 1862. Educated privately. Married Von Mater Sitwell in 1898. Editor, *Fashion Bazaar*, New York, 1881–94; correspondent, New York *Evening World*, 1899–1901. *Died 25 October 1924.*

ROMANCE AND HISTORICAL PUBLICATIONS

Novels

Madolin Rivers; or, The Little Beauty of Red Oak Seminary. New York, Munro, 1885.

Junie's Love Test. New York, Ogilvie, 1886.

Miss Middleton's Lover; or, They Parted on Their Bridal Tour. New York, American News, 1888.

A Forbidden Marriage; or, In Love with a Handsome Spend-thrift. New York, American News, 1888.

A Fatal Wooing. New York, Lovell, 1888.

Little Rosebud's Lovers; or, A Cruel Revenge. New York, Munro, 1888.

That Pretty Young Girl. New York, American News, 1889; London, Milner, 1902.

Daisy Brooks; or, A Perilous Love. New York, Munro, 1889; as *A Bride for a Day,* Cleveland, Westbrook, n.d.

The Heiress of Cameron Hall. New York, Munro, 1889.

All for the Love of a Fair Face; or, Broken Betrothal. New York, Munro, 1889.

A Struggle for a Heart; or, Crystabel's Fatal Love. New York, Munro, 1889.

Leonie Locke; or, The Romance of a Beautiful New York Working-Girl. New York, Munro, 1889.

Pretty Freda's Lovers; or, Married by Mistake. New York, Munro, 1889.

The Flirtations of a Beauty; or, A Summer's Romance at Newport. New York, Munro, 1890.

Ione: A Broken Love Dream. New York, Bonner, 1890.

A Mad Betrothal; or, Nadine's Vow. New York, Bonner, 1890.

Parted by Fate. New York, Bonner, 1890.

Willful Gaynel; or, The Little Beauty of the Passaic Cotton Mills. New York, Munro, 1890.

My Sweetheart Idabell; or, The Romance of a Pretty Coquette. Cleveland, Westbrook, 1890.

He Loved but Was Lured Away. New York, Ogilvie, 1891.

Little Leafy, The Cloakmaker's Beautiful Daughter. New York, Munro, 1891.

The Crime of Hallo-e'en; or, The Heiress of Graystone Hall. New York, Ogilvie, 1891.

We Parted at the Altar. New York, Bonner, 1892.

Florabel's Lover; or, Rival Belles. New York, Bonner, 1892; London, Milner, n.d.

Beautiful Ione's Lover. New York, Munro, 1892.

Lyndall's Temptation; or, Blinded by Love. New York, Munro, 1892.

A Master Workman's Oath; or, Coralie, The Unfortunate. New York, Ogilvie, 1892.

Only a Mechanic's Daughter. New York, Munro, 1892.

Olive's Courtship. New York, American News, 1892.

The Alphabet of Love. New York, Munro, 1892.

The Beautiful Coquette; or, The Love That Won Her. New York, Munro, 1892.

Daisy Gordon's Folly; or, The World Lost for Love's Sake. New York, Munro, 1892.

Dora Miller; or, A Young Girl's Love and Pride. New York, Munro, 1892.

The Romance of Enola. Cleveland, Westbrook, 1893.

When His Love Grew Cold. New York, Ogilvie, 1895.

When Lovely Maiden Stoops to Folly. New York, American News, 1896.

Garnetta, The Silver King's Daughter; or, The Startling Secret of the Old Mine. Cleveland, Westbrook, 1897.

Sweet Kitty Clover. New York, Street and Smith, 1898.

Sweetheart Will You Be True? or, Lovely Corine, The Queen of the Golf-Links. New York, Street and Smith, 1901.

True Love's Reward. New York, Weekly Budget Novels, 1904.

Shadows and Sunshine. New York, Weekly Budget Novels, 1904.

Only Love's Cross for Her; or, Shadow of the Cross. Brooklyn, Eagle Press, 1908.

The Clutch of the Marriage Tie; or, Jilbett, The Story of the Second Class. Brooklyn, Eagle Press, 1920.

Wooden Wives. New York, Publisher's Printing, 1923.

Cora, The Pet of the Regiment. Cleveland, Westbrook, n.d.

A Dangerous Flirtation; or, Did Ida May Sin? Cleveland, Westbrook, n.d.

Della's Handsome Lover; or, A Hasty Ballroom Betrothal. Cleveland, Westbrook, n.d.

A Fatal Elopement; or, A Too Hasty Love Match. Cleveland, Westbrook, n.d.

Flora Garland's Courtship; or, The Race for a Young Girl's Heart. Cleveland, Westbrook, n.d.

Flora Temple; or, All for Love's Sake. Cleveland, Westbrook, n.d.

Aleta's Terrible Secret; or, The Strange Mystery of a Wedding Eve. Cleveland, Westbrook, n.d.

The Girl He Forsook; or, The Young Doctor's Secret. Cleveland, Westbrook, n.d.

Gladiola's Two Lovers. Cleveland, Westbrook, n.d.

A Handsome Engineer's Flirtation; or, How He Won the Hearts of Girls. Cleveland, Westbrook, n.d.

Happy-Go-Lucky Lotty. New York, Ogilvie, n.d.

Jolly Sally Pendleton; or, The Wife Who Was Not a Wife. Cleveland, Westbrook, n.d.

Little Romp Edda. New York, Ogilvie, n.d.

The Loan of a Lover; or, Vera's Flirtation. Cleveland, Westbrook, n.d.

Pretty Madcap Dorothy; or, How She Won a Lover. Cleveland, Westbrook, n.d.

Was She Sweetheart or Wife? or, Pretty Gualda's Love. Cleveland, Westbrook, n.d.

*   *   *

Few modern readers will recognize the name Laura Jean Libbey. However, 90 years ago, most readers of story newspapers would have eagerly reached for their weekly issue of the *Family Story Paper* or the *Fireside Companion* to read the latest installment of Libbey's current novel.

She was an extremely popular novelist who was avidly read by female audiences from the late 1880's through to the early 1920's. Because she wrote for the story newspapers, her novels enjoyed enormous reprinting runs due to publishing practices of that period. Her income was reported to have been over $50,000 a year during much of her writing career. At least one novel, *Kidnapped at the Altar*, netted her $10,000 when it appeared in the *Fireside Companion* during 1892.

Libbey specialized in romance stories that appealed to young working girls as well as to women of the middle classes. Her plots were extremely predictable and very melodramatic. The heroine was always a young, working girl or a girl suddenly left penniless and homeless. The course of the novel followed the heroine through countless adversities and misunderstandings. These adversities were compounded by villainous machinations or were temporarily relieved by the quick intervention of the hero.

The narratives are a succession of calamities, each foreshadowing the next dire threat and barely accounting for the previous difficulty in her heroine's life. Phrases such as "I am only a poor working girl . . . '' and ''God can take care of unprotected working girls'' are typical expressions uttered by her heroines.

The last few years have seen a reevaluation of Libbey's place in early 20th-century fiction. Her novels are being studied as examples of feminist literature or as examples of reform movement advocacy. However, neither position can be supported by historical data or by the contents of her stories. This conclusion is based on two facts. First, editorial control of the novels effectively limited an author's ability to take definite stands on specific social problems. It was the willingness of editors to recognize the problems of social conditions and to encourage the writers to use them in their novels that prompted stories similar to Libbey's.

The second factor is Libbey's own strongly conservative attitudes. Her heroines did not necessarily seek to change working conditions, they merely wanted to escape such conditions by the only socially accepted way—marriage. To this end, the heroines did attempt to show initiative, especially when getting themselves out of grave difficulties. For instance, in *Leonie Locke* the heroine is kidnapped and held by a ruthless man determined to marry her. Leonie thinks nothing of climbing out of a window and descending a narrow fire ladder fastened to the wall. In most other situations, the heroines were content to wait for rescue with an attitude of appealing helplessness, or they tried to improve their situation by doing something that was so unrealistic that it was sure to fail.

In depicting working girls Libbey lets her heroine's reactions speak for her. Generally, the working companions of the heroine do not emerge very well. There is the occasional ''friend,'' but for the most part, they are most definitely ''working class.'' Their interests and standards are sharply if briefly illustrated and the contrast between them and the heroine is quite distinct. The reader is aware that the heroine is different from the other girls. There is always that illusive ''something'' about her.

Modern readers will find her novels difficult to believe, given the improbability of many of the incidents in her stories. In *Kidnapped at the Altar*, Girelda Northrup goes to the house of her former fiancé, Hubert Varrick. He believed her to be dead and had fallen in love with Jessie Bain. Girelda is only slightly disguised, yet she works as a seamstress in the house for several weeks without being recognized. Frequently Hubert makes hurried journeys that should take many hours or even several days. He makes them in two or three hours at the most. In another incident, Jessie has a letter mailed for her by a nurse just before lunch and it is delivered to Hubert by mid-afternoon. Coincidence plays a major role in keeping Libbey's conflicts going, which, especially for modern readers, reduces the believability of her novels. In *Pretty Madcap Dorothy* the heroine is accidentally lost overboard from an excursion boat to Staten Island. She is rescued and pulled back aboard. Suddenly, an elderly man notices a birth mark on her chest and identifies her as the daughter of his ward who had died years ago.

It is unfortunate that the deficiencies of Libbey's style and her improbable plots are so evident, as these serve to relegate her novels to curiosities. Their value is mainly to students of publishing history and popular culture. One must be cautious in reading too much of social or cultural significance into them.

—Arlene Moore

LINDOP, Audrey Erskine. See **ERSKINE-LINDOP, Audrey.**

LINDSAY, Jack. Also writes as Richard Preston. Australian. Born in Melbourne, Victoria, 20 October 1900; son of the writer and artist Norman Lindsay. Educated at Brisbane Grammar School; University of Queensland, Brisbane, 1918–21, B.A. (honours) in classics 1921. Served in the British Army, 1941–45, in the Royal Corps of Signals, 1941–43, and as a scriptwriter in the War Office, 1943–45. Married 1) Janet Beaton; 2) Ann Davies (died 1954); 3) Meta Waterdrinker in 1958, one son and one daughter. Editor, with Kenneth Slessor and F. Johnson, *Vision*, Sydney, 1923–24; moved to England, 1926; proprietor and director, Fanfrolico Press, London, 1927–30; editor, with P. R. Stephensen, *London Aphrodite*, 1928–29; editor, *Poetry and the People*, London, 1938–39; editor, *Anvil*, London, 1947; editor, with John Davenport and Randall Swingler, *Arena*, London, 1949–51. Recipient: Australian Literature Society Couch Gold Medal, 1960; Order of Merit (USSR), 1968. D.Litt.: University of Queensland, 1973. Fellow, Royal Society of Literature, 1945, Ancient Monuments Society, 1961 and, Australian Academy of Humanities; Member, Order of Australia, 1981. Agent: Murray Pollinger, 4 Garrick Street, London WC2E 9BH. Address: 56 Maids Causeway, Cambridge, England.

ROMANCE AND HISTORICAL PUBLICATIONS

Novels

Cressida's First Lover: A Tale of Ancient Greece. London, Lane, 1931; New York, Long and Smith, 1932.
Rome for Sale. London, Mathews and Marrot, and New York, Harper, 1934.
Caesar Is Dead. London, Nicholson and Watson, 1934.
Last Days with Cleopatra. London, Nicholson and Watson, 1935.
Despoiling Venus. London, Nicholson and Watson, 1935.
Storm at Sea. London, Golden Cockerel Press, 1935.
The Wanderings of Wenamen: 1115–1114 B.C. London, Nicholson and Watson, 1936.
Shadow and Flame (as Richard Preston). London, Chapman and Hall, 1936.
Adam of a New World. London, Nicholson and Watson, 1936.
Sue Verney. London, Nicholson and Watson, 1937.
End of Cornwall (as Richard Preston). London, Cape, 1937.
1649: A Novel of a Year. London, Methuen, 1938.
Brief Light: A Novel of Catullus. London, Methuen, 1939.
Lost Birthright. London, Methuen, 1939.
Giuliano the Magnificent, adapted from a work by Dorothy Johnson. London, Dakers, 1940.
Light in Italy. London, Gollancz, 1941.
Hannibal Takes a Hand. London, Dakers, 1941.
Men of Forty-Eight. London, Methuen, 1948.
Fires in Smithfield. London, Lane, 1950.
The Passionate Pastoral. London, Lane, 1951.
The Great Oak: A Story of 1549. London, Bodley Head, 1957.
Thunder Underground: A Story of Nero's Rome. London, Muller, 1965.

Short Stories

Come Home at Last and Other Stories. London, Nicholson and Watson, 1936.
Death of a Spartan King and Two Other Stories of the Ancient World. London, Inca, 1974.

Other Publications

Novels

The Stormy Violence. London, Dakers, 1941.
We Shall Return: A Novel of Dunkirk and the French Campaign. London, Dakers, 1942.
Beyond Terror: A Novel of the Battle of Crete. London, Dakers, 1943.
The Barriers Are Down: A Tale of the Collapse of a Civilisation. London, Gollancz, 1945.
Hullo Stranger. London, Dakers, 1945.
Time to Live. London, Dakers, 1946.
The Subtle Knot. London, Dakers, 1947.
Betrayed Spring: A Novel of the British Way. London, Lane, 1953.
Rising Tide. London, Lane, 1953.
The Moment of Choice. London, Lane, 1955.
A Local Habitation: A Novel of the British Way. London, Bodley Head, 1957.
The Revolt of the Sons. London, Muller, 1960.
All on the Never-Never: A Novel of the British Way of Life. London, Muller, 1961.
The Way the Ball Bounces. London, Muller, 1962.
Masks and Faces. London, Muller, 1963.
Choice of Times. London, Muller, 1964.
The Blood-Vote. St. Lucia, University of Queensland Press, 1985; New York, University of Queensland Press, 1986.

Plays

Marino Faliero: A Verse-Play. London, Fanfrolico Press, 1927.
Helen Comes of Age: Three Original Plays in Verse (includes *Ragnhild* and *Bussy d'Amboise*). London, Fanfrolico Press, 1927.
Hereward: A Verse Drama, music by J. Gough. London, Fanfrolico Press, 1930.
The Whole Armour of God (produced London, 1944).
Robin of England (produced London, 1945).
The Face of Coal, with B. L. Coombes (produced London, 1946).
Iphigeneia in Aulis, adaptation of a play by Euripides (produced London, 1967).
Hecuba, adaptation of a play by Euripides (produced London, 1967).
Electra, adaptation of a play by Euripides (produced London, 1967).
Orestes, adaptation of a play by Euripides (produced London, 1967).
Nathan the Wise, adaptation of a play by Lessing (produced London, 1967).

Verse

Fauns and Ladies. Sydney, Kirtley, 1923.
The Pleasante Conceited Narrative of Panurge's Fantastic Ally Brocaded Codpiece. Sydney, Panurgean Society, 1924.
The Spanish Main and Tavern. Sydney, Panurgean Society, 1924.
The Passionate Neatherd. London, Fanfrolico Press, 1926.
Into Action: The Battle of Dieppe. London, Dakers, 1942.
Second Front. London, Dakers, 1944.
Clue of Darkness. London, Dakers, 1949.
Peace Is Our Answer. London, Collet, 1950.
Three Letters to Nikolai Tikhonov. London, Fore, 1951.
Three Elegies. Sudbury, Suffolk, Myriad Press, 1957.
Faces and Places. Toronto, Basilike, 1974.
Collected Poems. Lake Forest, Illinois, Cheiron, 1981.

Other

William Blake: Creative Will and the Poetic Image. London, Fanfrolico Press, 1927; revised edition, 1929; New York, Haskell House, 1971.
Dionysos; or, Nietzsche contra Nietzsche: An Essay in Lyrical Philosophy. London, Fanfrolico Press, 1928.
The Romans. London, Black, 1935.
Runaway (for children). London, Oxford University Press, 1935.
Rebels of the Goldfields (for children). London, Lawrence and Wishart, 1936.
Marc Antony: His World and His Contemporaries. London, Routledge, 1936; New York, Dutton, 1937.
John Bunyan: Maker of Myths. London, Methuen, 1937; New York, Kelley, 1969.
The Anatomy of Spirit: An Enquiry into the Origins of Religious Emotions. London, Methuen, 1937.
To Arms! A Story of Ancient Gaul (for children). London, Oxford University Press, 1938.
England, My England. London, Fore, 1939.
A Short History of Culture. London, Gollancz, 1939; revised edition, London, Studio, 1962; New York, Citadel Press, 1964.
The Dons Sight Devon: A Story of the Defeat of the Invincible Armada (for children). London, Oxford University Press, 1942.
Perspective for Poetry. London, Fore, 1944.
British Achievement in Art and Music. London, Pilot Press, 1945.
Mulk Raj Anand: A Critical Essay. Bombay, Hind Kitabs, 1948; revised edition, as *The Elephant and the Lotus*, Bombay, Kutub Popular, 1954.
Song of a Falling World: Culture During the Break-up of the Roman Empire (A.D. 350–600). London, Dakers, 1948; Westport, Connecticut, Hyperion Press, 1979.
Marxism and Contemporary Science; or, The Fulness of Life. London, Dobson, 1949.
A World Ahead: Journal of a Soviet Journey. London, Fore, 1950.
Charles Dickens: A Biographical and Critical Study. London, Dakers, and New York, Philosophical Library, 1950.
Byzantium into Europe: The Story of Byzantium as the First Europe (362–1204 A.D.) and Its Further Contribution till 1453 A.D. London, Lane, 1952.
Rumanian Summer, with M. Cornforth. London, Lawrence and Wishart, 1953.
Civil War in England: The Cromwellian Revolution. London, Muller, 1954; New York, Barnes and Noble, 1967.
George Meredith: His Life and Work. London, Lane, 1956; New York, Kraus, 1973.
The Romans Were Here: The Roman Period in Britain and Its Place in Our History. London, Muller, 1956; New York, Barnes and Noble, 1969.
After the Thirties: The Novel in Britain and Its Future. London, Lawrence and Wishart, 1956.
Life Rarely Tells (autobiography). Ringwood, Victoria, Penguin, 1982.
  Life Rarely Tells: An Autobiographical Account Ending in the Year 1921 and Situated Mostly in Brisbane, Queensland. London, Bodley Head, 1958.
  The Roaring Twenties: Literary Life in Sydney, New South Wales, in the Years 1921–26. London, Bodley Head, 1960.
Fanfrolico and After. London, Bodley Head, 1962.

Arthur and His Times: Britain in the Dark Ages. London, Muller, 1958; New York, Barnes and Noble, 1966.

The Discovery of Britain: A Guide to Archaeology. London, Merlin Press, 1958.

1764: The Hurly-Burly of Daily Life Exemplified in One Year of the 18th Century. London, Muller, 1959.

The Writing on the Wall: An Account of Pompeii in Its Last Days. London, Muller, 1960.

Death of the Hero: French Painting from David to Delacroix. London, Studio, 1960.

William Morris: Writer. London, William Morris Society, 1961.

Our Celtic Heritage. London, Weidenfeld and Nicolson, 1962.

Daily Life in Roman Egypt. London, Muller, 1963; New York, Barnes and Noble, 1964.

Nine Days' Hero: Wat Tyler. London, Dobson, 1964.

The Clashing Rocks: A Study of Early Greek Religion and Culture, and the Origins of Drama. London, Chapman and Hall, 1965.

Leisure and Pleasure in Roman Egypt. London, Muller, 1965; New York, Barnes and Noble, 1966.

Our Anglo-Saxon Heritage. London, Weidenfeld and Nicolson, 1965.

J. M. W. Turner: His Life and Work: A Critical Biography. London, Adams and MacKay, and Greenwich, Connecticut, New York Graphic Society, 1966.

Our Roman Heritage. London, Weidenfeld and Nicolson, 1967.

Meetings with Poets: Memories of Dylan Thomas, Edith Sitwell, Louis Aragon, Paul Eluard, Tristan Tzara. London, Muller, 1968; New York, Ungar, 1969.

Men and Gods on the Roman Nile. London, Muller, and New York, Barnes and Noble, 1968.

The Ancient World: Manners and Morals. London, Weidenfeld and Nicolson, and New York, Putnam, 1968.

Cézanne: His Life and Art. London, Adams and MacKay, and Greenwich, Connecticut, New York Graphic Society, 1969.

The Origins of Alchemy in Graeco-Roman Egypt. London, Muller, and New York, Barnes and Noble, 1970.

Cleopatra. London, Constable, and New York, Coward McCann, 1971.

Origins of Astrology. London, Muller, and New York, Barnes and Noble, 1971.

Gustave Courbet: His Life and Work. Bath, Adams and Dart, 1973; New York, Harper, 1974.

Helen of Troy: Woman and Goddess. London, Constable, and Totowa, New Jersey, Rowman and Littlefield, 1974.

Blast-Power and Ballistics: Concepts of Force and Energy in the Ancient World. London, Muller, and New York, Barnes and Noble, 1974.

The Normans and Their World. London, Hart Davis MacGibbon, 1974; New York, St. Martin's Press, 1975.

William Morris: His Life and Work. London, Constable, 1975; New York, Taplinger, 1979.

Decay and Renewal: Critical Essays on Twentieth Century Writing. Sydney, Wild and Woolley, 1976; London, Lawrence and Wishart, 1977.

The Troubadours and Their World of the Twelfth and Thirteenth Centuries. London, Muller, 1976.

Hogarth: His Art and World. London, Hart Davis MacGibbon, 1977; New York, Taplinger, 1979.

William Blake: His Life and Work. London, Constable, 1978; New York, Braziller, 1979.

The Monster City: Defoe's London 1688–1730. London, Hart Davis MacGibbon, and New York, St. Martin's Press, 1978.

Thomas Gainsborough: His Life and Art. London, Granada, and New York, Universe, 1981.

The Crisis in Marxism. Bradford on Avon, Wiltshire, Moonraker Press, and New York, Barnes and Noble, 1981.

Turner: The Man and His Art. London, Granada, and New York, Watts, 1985.

Editor, with Kenneth Slessor, *Poetry in Australia.* Sydney, Vision Press, 1923.

Editor, with P. Warlock, *Loving Mad Tom: Bedlamite Verses of the XVI and XVII Centuries.* London, Fanfrolico Press, 1927; New York, Kelley, 1970.

Editor, *The Metamorphosis of Aiax,* by Sir John Harington. New York, McKee, 1928.

Editor, *The Parlement of Pratlers.* London, Fanfrolico Press, 1928.

Editor (as Peter Meadows), *Delighted Earth,* by Robert Herrick. London, Fanfrolico Press, 1928.

Editor, *Inspiration.* London, Fanfrolico Press, 1928.

Editor, *Letters of Philip Stanhope, Second Earl of Chesterfield.* London, Fanfrolico Press, 1930.

Editor, with Edgell Rickword, *A Handbook of Freedom: A Record of English Democracy Through Twelve Centuries.* London, Lawrence and Wishart, and New York, International Publishers, 1939.

Editor, with Maurice Carpenter and Honor Arundel, *New Lyrical Ballads.* London, Editions Poetry, 1945.

Editor, *Anvil: Life and the Arts: A Miscellany.* London, Meridian, and New York, Universal Distributors, 1947.

Editor, *New Development Series.* London, Lane, 1947–48.

Editor, *Herrick: A Selection.* London, Grey Walls Press, 1948.

Editor, *William Morris: A Selection.* London, Grey Walls Press, 1948.

Editor, with Randall Swingler, *Key Poets.* London, Fore, 1950.

Editor, *Barefoot,* by Z. Stancu. London, Fore 1950.

Editor, *Paintings and Drawings of Leslie Hurry.* London, Grey Walls Press, 1952.

Editor, *The Sunset Ship: Poems of J. M. W. Turner.* Lowestoft, Suffolk, Scorpion Press, 1966.

Editor, *The Autiobiography of Joseph Priestley.* Bath, Adams and Dart, 1970; Teaneck, New Jersey, Fairleigh Dickinson University Press, 1971.

Translator, *Lysistrata,* by Aristophanes. Sydney, Kirtley, 1925; London, Fanfrolico Press, 1926.

Translator, *Propertius in Love.* London, Fanfrolico Press, 1927.

Translator, *Satyricon and Poems,* by Petronius. London, Fanfrolico Press, 1927; revised edition, London, Elek, 1960.

Translator, *Homage to Sappho.* London, Fanfrolico Press, 1928.

Translator, *Complete Poems of Theocritus.* London, Fanfrolico Press, 1929.

Translator, *Hymns to Aphrodite,* by Homer. London, Fanfrolico Press, 1929.

Translator, *Women in Parliament,* by Aristophanes. London, Fanfrolico Press, 1929.

Translator, *The Mimiambs of Herondas.* London, Fanfrolico Press, 1929.

Translator, *The Complete Poetry of Gaius Catullus.* London, Fanfrolico Press, 1930; revised edition, London, Sylvan Press, 1948.

Translator, *Sulpicia's Garland: Roman Poems.* New York, McKee, 1930.

Translator, *Patchwork Quilt: Poems by Ausonius.* London, Fanfrolico Press, 1930.

Translator, *The Golden Ass,* by Apuleius. New York, Limited Editions Club, 1931; revised edition, London, Elek, and Bloomington, Indiana University Press, 1960.

Translator, *I Am a Roman*. London, Mathews and Marrot, 1934.

Translator, *Medieval Latin Poets*. London, Mathews and Marrot, 1934.

Translator, *Daphnis and Chloe*, by Longus. London, Daimon Press, 1948.

Translator, with S. Jolly, *Song of Peace*, by V. Nezval. London, Fore, 1951.

Translator, *Poems of Adam Mickiewicz*. London, Sylvan Press, and New York, Transatlantic Arts, 1957.

Translator, *Russian Poetry 1917–1955*. London, Lane, 1957; Chester Springs, Pennsylvania, Dufour, 1961.

Translator, *Asklepiades in Love*. Twinstead, Essex, Myriad Press, 1960.

Translator, *Modern Russian Poetry*. London, Vista, 1960.

Translator, *Cause, Principle, and Unity: 5 Dialogues*, by Giordano Bruno. London, Daimon Press, 1962; New York, International Publishers, 1964.

Translator, *Ribaldry of Ancient Greece*. London, Elek, and New York, Ungar, 1965.

Translator, *Ribaldry of Ancient Rome*. London, Elek, and New York, Ungar, 1965.

Translator, *The Elegy of Haido*, by Tefcros Anthias. London, Anthias Publications, 1966.

Translator, *The Age of Akhenaten*, by Eleonore Bille-de-Mot. London, Adams and MacKay, 1967; New York, McGraw Hill, 1968.

Translator, *Greece, I Keep My Vigil for You*, by Tefcros Anthias. London, Anthias Publications, 1968.

Translator, *The Twelve, and The Scythians*, by Alexander Blok. London, Journeyman Press, 1982.

*

Bibliography: *Jack Lindsay: A Catalogue of First Editions* by Harry F. Chaplin, Sydney, Wentworth Press, 1983.

Manuscript Collection: University of Queensland, St. Lucia.

Critical Studies: *Mountain in the Sunlight* by Alick West, London, Lawrence and Wishart, 1958; *A Garland for Jack Lindsay* edited by Edgell Rickword, London, Piccolo Press, 1980; *Jack Lindsay: The Thirties and Forties* edited by Robert Mackie, London, Institute of Commonwealth Studies, 1984; *Culture and History: Essays Presented in Honour of Jack Lindsay* edited by Bernard Smith, Sydney, Hale and Iremonger, 1984.

*   *   *

Before the 1930's Jack Lindsay's abundant energies were concentrated on poetry, translation, cultural criticism, editing, and publishing, In Sydney he and his father, the artist Norman Lindsay, created the shortlived but influential magazine *Vision*, and later in London he and P. R. Stephensen, another Australian expatriate, founded the literary periodical *London Aphrodite* and the upmarket Fanfrolico Press.

Lindsay's historical fiction belongs mainly to the middle period of his long literary career. He wrote 16 examples before 1941 and five thereafter. His later output shifted to contemporary fiction and biographical and historical studies, which he continued to write into the 1980's. Between 1934 and 1941 Lindsay produced seven other prose works, six volumes of verse and verse translation, and a large quantity of short stories and criti-

cal essays. The historical novels thus belong to a phase of phenomenal literary output, possibly surpassed only by Lindsay's own postwar production.

Lindsay's writing is shaped by an idiosyncratic philosophy—a Romanticism influenced by Blake and Nietzsche, blended with Marxist historicism. He himself characterised his work as being concerned primarily with "alienation . . . and the struggle against alienation." But these abstract concerns seldom detract from the readability of his novels, which are vividly descriptive and dramatic. At one level the struggle for and against alienation means Tyranny versus Liberty. But it also refers to the efforts of individuals to achieve awareness, freedom, and fulfilment in their private lives. This passage from confinement to freedom recurs throughout Lindsay's novels, with many different resolutions: mystical ecstasy; self-destructive despair; joyous acceptance of life and work; death.

His stories are usually set in periods of fundamental crisis. They convey an intense feeling for history as an organic force which drives people to act in ways they scarcely understand, with consequences they cannot fathom. Often the cycle of a year is used as a narrative frame to stress the interconnection of natural, ritual, and social elements. Connected with this is a focus on the "irrational"—poetry, sex, religion, dancing, and drunkenness. And while he takes great pains to ensure historical authenticity (to reproduce, in his own words, "the particular intonation of an age, its coloration and resonance") he is also driven to uncover deep universals in human experience: "the effect should be simultaneously: how like ourselves, how unlike." This makes for a characteristic tension which is often dark and disturbing.

Lindsay has his weaknesses. Although well-crafted, the great speed with which his novels were written is betrayed by an occasional slackness of style, while their sheer quantity exposes a certain repetitiveness of theme and technique. At times, especially in the novels of the late 1930's and 1940's he is prone to tendentious rhetoric and simplistic analysis, though this hardly amounts to the "crude propaganda" he has been accused of. On the whole, these works do not deserve the relative obscurity into which they have fallen, and it is to be hoped that critical interest will help spark a revival.

Lindsay's career as a classicist gave him an easy familiarity with Graeco-Roman antiquity, and it was to this period that he turned when he began writing novels. *Rome for Sale* announces the major preoccupations of his maturity. Concerned with the abortive rebellion of Catalina in the dying days of the Roman Republic, it evokes a delirious atmosphere of sophisticated corruption, religious fanaticism, perverse sexuality, poetry, violence, honour, and futility. It was followed quickly by *Caesar Is Dead*, a particularly successful recreation of the explosive political situation following the dictator's assassination. The more conventional *Last Days with Cleopatra* completed a trilogy on the Caesarian revolution.

Lindsay soon began to write novels with an English setting. In 1939 he completed a trilogy on English revolutionary periods, using the techniques he had developed in the Roman novels— the yearly cycle, the interweaving of multiple viewpoints, the use of contemporary writings, and the linking of political change with religious ideology and personal life.

1649 is set in the year following the execution of Charles I, memorably depicting the relations between the fervently religious Puritans, the idealistic radicalism of the Levellers and the individualism and commercialism of the rising middle class. According to a normally unsympathetic critic (David Smith), this novel "gave to Marxist ideology a life and conviction that few British novelists had so far been able to do." *Lost Birthright* deals with the Wilkesite disturbances of 1769, contrasting the lives of two brothers cheated of their inheritance; *Men of Forty-Eight* is concerned with the Chartist movement.

The English novels met with a cooler critical reception than the Roman novels. Conservatives considered them provokingly radical, while most of the left felt they were too concerned with culture and personality at the expense of political and economic issues. The width of critical opinion about Lindsay can be judged by the contrast between Edith Sitwell's verdict on *Men of Forty-Eight* as "profoundly impressive and as moving as it is impressive," and David Smith's comment on the same novel: "too much like a Left Wing history textbook."

During the war Lindsay worked as a scriptwriter for the army Theatre Unit and afterwards began the "British Way" series of contemporary novels. Only in 1950 did *Fires in Smithfield* appear. Concerned with the political and religious disturbances of 1558, it is one of his best and most characteristic works. Of the many remaining historical novels, the most important is *Adam of a New World*, an account of the trial and execution of Giordano Bruno, who was for Lindsay a symbol of the yearning for human freedom and unity. Widely read as a parable of fascism—which was part of its author's intention—it remains both a fierce condemnation of institutionalised repression and a troubled reflection on the nature of power and freedom, ideology, and truth.

By the mid 1950's the exposure of Stalin's crimes and the Russian invasion of Hungary produced unresolvable stresses in Lindsay's never smooth relationship with the Communist movement. The simplifications and enthusiasms which tempted him in earlier decades were no longer possible. Significantly, in his last historical novel, *Thunder Underground*, there is a conspicuous return to the period and atmosphere of his early novels. Rebellion against Nero and the Empire smoulders undirected in the social depths, surfacing in the religious cults of the populace and the artisic fashions of the intelligentsia. Throughout his writings Lindsay adverted to cycles—of decay and renewal, becoming and return. This masterly conclusion to his career as a novelist also closes a cycle, coming back to a symbolic point of origin in the history of culture and in Lindsay's own work: the turmoil of Ancient Rome at the height of its power.

—Paul Gillen

LINDSAY, Rachel. Also writes as Rozella Lake; Roberta Leigh; Janey Scott. Address: c/o Mills and Boon Ltd., 18–24 Paradise Road, Richmond, Surrey TW9 1SR, England.

ROMANCE AND HISTORICAL PUBLICATIONS

Novels

The Widening Stream. London, Hutchinson, 1952.
Alien Corn. London, Hutchinson, 1954; Toronto, Harlequin, 1973.
Healing Hands. London, Hutchinson, 1955.
Mask of Gold. London, Hutchinson, 1956; Toronto, Harlequin, 1974.
Castle in the Trees. London, Hurst and Blackett, 1958; Toronto, Harlequin, 1974.
House of Lorraine. London, Mills and Boon, 1959; Toronto, Harlequin, 1966.

The Taming of Laura. London, Mills and Boon, 1959; Toronto, Harlequin, 1966.
Business Affair. London, Mills and Boon, 1960; Toronto, Harlequin, 1974.
Heart of a Rose. London, Mills and Boon, 1961; Toronto, Harlequin, 1965.
Song in My Heart. London, Mills and Boon, 1961.
Lesley Forrest, M.D. New York, Berkley, 1962.
Moonlight and Magic. London, Mills and Boon, 1962; Toronto, Harlequin, 1972.
Design for Murder. London, Mills and Boon, 1964.
No Business to Love. London, Mills and Boon, 1966.
Love and Lucy Granger. London, Mills and Boon, 1967; Toronto, Harlequin, 1972.
Price of Love. London, Mills and Boon, 1967; Toronto, Harlequin, 1974.
Love and Dr. Forrest. London, Mills and Boon, 1971; Toronto, Harlequin, 1978.
The Latitude of Love. London, Mills and Boon, 1971.
A Question of Marriage. London, Mills and Boon, 1972; Toronto, Harlequin, 1973.
Cage of Gold. London, Mills and Boon, 1973; Toronto, Harlequin, 1974.
Chateau in Provence. London, Mills and Boon, 1973.
Food for Love. Toronto, Harlequin, 1974; London, Mills and Boon, 1975.
Affair in Venice. London, Mills and Boon, and Toronto, Harlequin, 1975.
Love in Disguise. London, Mills and Boon, and Toronto, Harlequin, 1975.
Innocent Deception. London, Mills and Boon, and Toronto, Harlequin, 1975.
Prince for Sale. London, Mills and Boon, and Toronto, Harlequin, 1975.
The Marquis Takes a Wife. London, Mills and Boon, 1976; Toronto, Harlequin, 1977.
Roman Affair. London, Mills and Boon, 1976; Toronto, Harlequin, 1977.
Secretary Wife. London, Mills and Boon, and Toronto, Harlequin, 1976.
Tinsel Star. London, Mills and Boon, 1976; Toronto, Harlequin, 1977.
A Man to Tame. London, Mills and Boon, 1976; Toronto, Harlequin, 1977.
Forbidden Love. London, Mills and Boon, and Toronto, Harlequin, 1977.
Prescription for Love. London, Mills and Boon, and Toronto, Harlequin, 1977.
Rough Diamond Lover. Toronto, Harlequin, 1978; London, Mills and Boon, 1979.
An Affair to Forget. London, Mills and Boon, and Toronto, Harlequin, 1978.
Forgotten Marriage. Toronto, Harlequin, 1978; as Roberta Leigh, London, Mills and Boon, 1978.
Brazilian Affair. Toronto, Harlequin, 1978.
My Sister's Keeper. London, Mills and Boon, 1979.
Man of Ice. London, Mills and Boon, and Toronto, Harlequin, 1980.
Untouched Wife. Toronto, Harlequin, 1981.

Novels as Roberta Leigh

In Name Only. London, Falcon Press, 1951; Toronto, Harlequin, 1973.
Dark Inheritance. London, Hutchinson, 1952; Toronto, Harlequin, 1968.

The Vengeful Heart. London, Hutchinson, 1952; Toronto, Harlequin, 1970.
Beloved Ballerina. London, Hutchinson, 1953; Toronto, Harlequin, 1974.
And Then Came Love. London, Hutchinson, 1954; Toronto, Harlequin, 1974.
Pretence. London, Hutchinson, 1956; Toronto, Harlequin, 1969.
Stacy. London, Heinemann, 1958.
My Heart's a Dancer. London, Mills and Boon, 1970; Toronto, Harlequin, 1973.
Cinderella in Mink. London, Mills and Boon, 1973; Toronto, Harlequin, 1974.
If Dreams Came True. London, Mills and Boon, 1974; as Rozella Lake, Toronto, Harlequin, 1975.
Shade of the Palms. London, Mills and Boon, and Toronto, Harlequin, 1974.
Heart of the Lion. London, Mills and Boon, and Toronto, Harlequin, 1975.
Chateau in Provence (as Rozella Lake). Toronto, Harlequin, 1975.
Man in a Million. London, Mills and Boon, 1975; Toronto, Harlequin, 1976.
Temporary Wife. London, Mills and Boon, and Toronto, Harlequin, 1975.
Cupboard Love. London, Mills and Boon, and Toronto, Harlequin, 1976.
To Buy a Bride. London, Mills and Boon, and Toronto, Harlequin, 1976.
The Unwilling Bridegroom. London, Mills and Boon, 1976; Toronto, Harlequin, 1977.
Man Without a Heart. London, Mills and Boon, 1976; Toronto, Harlequin, 1977.
Girl for a Millionaire. London, Mills and Boon, and Toronto, Harlequin, 1977.
Too Young for Love. Toronto, Harlequin, 1977.
Facts of Love. London, Mills and Boon, 1978.
Night of Love. London, Mills and Boon, 1978; New York, Fawcett, 1979.
The Savage Aristocrat. London, Mills and Boon, 1978; New York, Fawcett, 1979.
Not a Marrying Man. Toronto, Harlequin, 1978.
Love in Store. New York, Fawcett, 1978.
Flower of the Desert. New York, Fawcett, 1979; London, Mills and Boon, 1983.
Love and No Marriage. London, Mills and Boon, 1980.
Rent a Wife. London, Mills and Boon, 1980; as Rachel Lindsay, Toronto, Harlequin, 1980.
Wife for a Year. London, Mills and Boon, 1980; as Rachel Lindsay, Toronto, Harlequin, 1981.
Love Match. New York, Fawcett, 1980.
Confirmed Bachelor. London, Mills and Boon, and Toronto, Harlequin, 1981.
No Time for Marriage. London, Mills and Boon, 1985.
An Impossible Man to Love. London, Mills and Boon, 1987.
Too Bad to Be True. London, Mills and Boon, 1987.
Not Without Love. London, Mills and Boon, 1989.
No Man's Mistress. London, Mills and Boon, 1989.

Novels as Janey Scott

Memory of Love. London, Mills and Boon, 1959.
Melody of Love. London, Mills and Boon, 1960.
A Time to Love. London, Mills and Boon, 1960; revised edition, as *Unwanted Wife* (as Rachel Lindsay) Mills and Boon, 1976; Toronto, Harlequin, 1978.

Sara Gay—Model Girl [*in Mayfair, in New York, in Monte Carlo*]. London, World, 4 vols., 1961.

*   *   *

Rachel Lindsay's primary theme is how much easier it is to love than it is to trust. Her stories show passionate physical attraction between people from vastly different backgrounds, holding vastly different beliefs and values. Usually the girl is innocent and ordinary, while the man is rich, arrogant, and sexually experienced. Another standard motif is the patient Griselda story: an arrogant man assumes the innocent heroine to be devious and scheming and therefore treats her brutally and insultingly. She naturally falls in love with him and patiently puts up with his abuse until he realizes her innocence and abases himself before her. There is more sex in her novels than in most Harlequins, though heavy petting always stops short of consummation.

In *The Widening Stream* two people who love each other without knowing each other very well are pushed apart by the lies of a scheming woman. *The Taming of Laura* is a Cinderella story. Eric Berne suggested that after Cinderella married the prince she would still spend her time sweeping up the cinders. In this novel and in *Affair in Venice* and *Secretary Wife*, Lindsay's Cinderellas have this problem of adjusting to their new position and wealth. *Forgotten Marriage* is the patient Griselda story par excellence. The heroine has the double disadvantage of being accused of vile actions, and having amnesia and therefore being unable to disprove the accusations. While her falling in love with her accuser is incomprehensible, his subsequent groveling is satisfying to heroine and reader alike. In *Unwanted Wife* a refugee from an iron curtain country seeks her English husband only to find he is under the impression she has divorced him, and is planning to marry again. Since the heroine is blonde and beautiful, one can tell the difference between her and the doormat, though with some difficulty. Other patient Griselda stories include *Roman Affair* and *Man of Ice*. *An Affair to Forget* concerns a rock singer and a sweet country girl whose values are so different that only total surrender by one of them (guess who?) will make this relationship possible. *Song in My Heart* deals with a pop singer who falls in love with a married man. When his wife conveniently dies, the story becomes a murder mystery. *Price of Love* reverses the normal situation; an arrogant woman doctor loves a man she regards as hopelessly frivolous and unreliable, and she is the one who has to change. *Design for Murder* is a murder mystery and love story set in the world of high fashion. In *A Man to Tame* a woman doctor overcomes sex discrimination, demonstrates her courage, and wins the heart of an arrogant man. In *Prescription for Love* neither hero nor heroine is sufficiently self-confident to admit their love. Were there no intermediary to resolve this romance, no doubt they would have pined genteely for each other for the rest of their lives. In *My Sister's Keeper* the heroine deeply distrusts the man she loves because of her preconceptions of his values. In *Love and No Marriage* a successful dress designer allows the hero to continue to believe she is a professional housekeeper, albeit a not very good one. *Wife for a Year* is another one of those books where only an intermediary can make the romance happen at all.

Bizarre and unlikely things happen in Lindsay's world: heroines rescue people from burning buildings and emerge with nary an unsightly scar; 22-year-old women own their own fabulously successful businesses; opera singers become rock singers; worst of all, her heroines live in a peculiarly friendless vacuum. Nevertheless, between her heroes and heroines, there is great emotional realism. Though some of her heroines do silly, irrational things, and several of her men are brutal and insensitive, most of her characters are reasonable people, trying to reconcile their differences and to develop trust and understanding as well as love.

—Marylaine Block

LINDSEY, Johanna. American. Born in Frankfurt, Germany, 10 March 1952. Educated at high schools in Kailua and Hawaii. Married Ralph B. Lindsey in 1970; three sons. Lives in Kaneohe, Hawaii. Address: c/o Avon Books, 105 Madison Avenue, New York, New York 10016, U.S.A.

ROMANCE AND HISTORICAL PUBLICATIONS

Novels

Captive Bride. New York, Avon, 1977; London, Hamlyn, 1978.
A Pirate's Love. New York, Avon, 1978; London, Hamlyn, 1979.
Fires of Winter. New York, Avon, 1980; London, Hamlyn, 1981.
Paradise Wild. New York, Avon, 1981; London, Hamlyn, 1982.
Glorious Angel. New York, Avon, 1982; London, Corgi, 1985.
So Speaks the Heart. New York, Avon, and London, Corgi, 1983.
Heart of Thunder. New York, Avon, 1983; London, Corgi, 1984.
A Gentle Feuding. New York, Avon, and London, Corgi, 1984.
Brave the Wild Wind. New York, Avon, 1984; London, Corgi, 1985.
Love Only Once. New York, Avon, 1985; London, Corgi, 1986.
Tender Is the Storm. New York, Avon, and London, Corgi, 1985.
A Heart So Wild. New York, Avon, 1986; London, Corgi, 1987.
When Love Awaits. New York, Avon, and London, Corgi, 1986.
Hearts Aflame. New York, Avon, and London, Corgi, 1987.
Secret Fire. New York, Avon, 1987.
Tender Rebel. New York, Avon, 1988.
Silver Angel. New York, Avon, 1988.
Defy Not the Heart. New York, Avon, 1989.

*

Johanna Lindsey comments:

My writing career began in 1977 when my first historical romance was published. My success as a writer wouldn't have been possible without the loyalty and support of my many readers, who have enjoyed my characters' adventures in love and folly, and my many different settings, from pirate ships and Viking strongholds to medieval castles and the American west. Each time I learn that I have made someone laugh, or cry a little, or just feel good for a while, I am deeply gratified and hopeful that in the years ahead, I will continue to touch others lives with my stories.

*   *   *

Johanna Lindsey's novels feature a wide variety of locations and historical periods. Although England, Scotland, and the American west in the 19th century are among her favorite settings (*Glorious Angel*, *Heart of Thunder*, *Brave the Wild Wind*, *Tender Is the Storm*, *Love Only Once*, *A Heart So Wild*, and *Tender Rebel*), Lindsey also has written several stories set in medieval times or in exotic locations. *Captive Bride* and *Silver Angel* are set in the Middle East, *Fires of Winter* and *Hearts Aflame* treat the Viking raids of England, while *Secret Fire* takes place primarily in Russia. No matter the time or place, however, Lindsey's books provide a real sense of accurate environment.

There are common plot devices and themes to be seen throughout Lindsey's work. Abduction of the heroine, usually by the hero, is a familiar ploy used to throw the leading characters together in a situation destined to spark with hostility. Often the abduction involves some mistaken identity such as the belief that the young noblewoman is of lower class or is a boy. Some variation of the heroine-held-prisoner figures prominently in many of the works, including *Captive Bride*, *Fires of Winter*, *A Gentle Feuding*, *Love Only Once*, *Secret Fire*, and *Silver Angel*.

A basic violence, both in external events and the male-female relationships is found throughout, as is a strong aura of sensuality. Love, as seen by Lindsey, has a dark side which shows itself in distrust, misunderstandings, and violent physical love. The latter even extends to the rape of the heroine, although a passionate love affair develops in which the woman usually is a demanding partner. This sexual violence and cruelty creates a deep tension and lets the relationship teeter on a point between destruction and total fulfillment. Of course, a romance will veer towards the latter, but the heroine endures humiliation before attaining happiness. Many may view this portrayal of women accepting physical violence as perpetuating a harmful myth of rape, but it seems clear that Lindsey's readers expect such scenes.

In general, the characters in these novels are well-developed and believable. At times, however, credibility is strained. This is particularly true in *Silver Angel*, in which the hero, Derek Sinclair, the Earl of Mulbury, also is the twin brother of Jamil, a Barbary Coast Dey. The relationship is explained but is more than usually difficult to accept. Nevertheless, Derek is an appropriately brooding and masterful hero.

Like many other romance authors, Lindsey also writes linked books with related or continuing characters. Kristen, the young Viking woman of *Hearts Aflame* is the daughter of Brenna and Garrick (*Fires of Winter*). Both Kristen's parents and her brother, Selig, return to help her in the later story. Hank Chavez, the enigmatic bandit of *Glorious Angel*, returns as the hero of *Heart of Thunder*, and Anthony Mallory, one of Regina's four uncles in *Love Only Once*, gets his own story in *Tender Rebel*.

Although the explicit sensuality and occasional abusiveness found in Lindsey's works may disturb some readers, her well thought out, fast moving stories appeal to many more. Anchored by authentic descriptions and historical detail and focusing on the turbulent passions in the battle of the sexes, her books are among the best of the sensuous historical novels.

—Barbara E. Kemp

LLOYD, Levanah. See **PETERS, Maureen.**

LLYWELYN, Morgan. Irish. Born in the United States, 3 December 1937. Married Charles Llywelyn (died); one son. Has worked as a horse trainer, model, dance teacher, and legal secretary. Agent: Abner Stein, 10 Roland Gardens, London SW7 3PH, England.

ROMANCE AND HISTORICAL PUBLICATIONS

Novels

The Wind from Hastings. Boston, Houghton Mifflin, 1978; London, Hale, 1980.
Lion of Ireland: The Legend of Brian Boru. Boston, Houghton Mifflin, 1979; London, Bodley Head, 1980.
The Horse Goddess. Boston, Houghton Mifflin, 1982; London, Macdonald, 1983.
Bard: The Odyssey of the Irish. Boston, Houghton Mifflin, 1984; London, Sphere, 1985.
Grania: She-King of the Irish Seas. Boston, Houghton Mifflin, 1986; London, Sphere, 1987.
Red Branch. New York, Morrow, 1989.
The Isles of the Blest. New York, Ace, 1989.

OTHER PUBLICATIONS

Other

Xerxes. New York, Chelsea House, 1988.

*

Manuscript Collection: University of Maryland, College Park.

Morgan Llywelyn comments:
    The entire body of my work comprises a look at the Celtic culture of Western Europe, from its emergence through its decline, with special emphasis on Ireland. The Celts were the foundation stock of Europe, exerting a powerful influence on subsequent Western civilization that even their conquest by the Romans could not destroy. Celtic literature, music, concepts of individual freedom and acting in harmony with nature, are all relevant in today's world. Through my novels, I hope to reacquaint the modern descendants of this ancient people with the high level of their civilization. They have become the stuff of legend and fairy tale, spawning 10,000 fantasies from King Arthur to Druids in Outer Space, yet they were real people whose contribution to our own culture has never been sufficiently recognized or appreciated. Because they were so vigorous, so colourful, so passionate, their historical deeds are more exciting than fiction and will continue to inspire me, I hope, for many years to come.

*   *   *

    Drawing on the history and lore that are part of her own heritage, the works of Morgan Llywelyn concern themselves with Celtic heroes and heroines, both real and mythical, bringing them and the times they inhabited to life with stunning clarity. She recounts historical events and expands upon traditional tales, maintaining the integrity of their factual basis and offering feasible projections consistent with the core of their legends while presenting her characters as realistic human beings.
    The Wind from Hastings deals with the events leading up to the famous battle in 1066. It is told not, as one might expect, from the viewpoint of one of the leading participants, nor even that of a common footsoldier. Llywelyn has chosen instead to

describe events from the perspective of the wife of the Prince of Wales who, when her husband has been dispatched by Harold, becomes his prisoner and property and then, as he seeks to unite Welsh and Saxon in the face of the coming Norman invasion, his wife and mother of his unborn child. The tale concludes on the field at Hastings with the woman preparing to flee the Norman troops and save her own life and that of her Welsh children together with the future of Saxon England as personified by Harold's unborn baby. She discovers in this moment of terrifying uncertainty that her one-time enemy has proven to be a man of principle and courage whom she has come to respect and grudgingly admire and Llywelyn leaves open to speculation the fact that some direct descendant of the Saxon king may have in fact survived the Norman conquest.
    The saga of Brian Boru, a 10th-century king who stood against the Norse invaders and led his people to the heights of a golden age, unfolds in *Lion of Ireland*. A giant of a man, Boru epitomizes the warrior-poet of Celtic tradition, fighting and loving with equal passion as he strives to realize his dreams of glory for himself and his country.
    The Horse Goddess transports the reader back to an earlier age, eight centuries before Christ. Llywelyn proposes a possible scenario to form the basis of the evolution of Epona, an independent headstrong daughter of a mountain chieftain who had been selected by the Druid priest to serve his ritualistic needs and personal desires, to her position in Celtic mythology as goddess and protector of Ireland's beloved horses.
    Llywelyn's efforts to penetrate the mists enshrouding Ireland's early history continue with *Bard* which follows the odyssey of the Gaelic bard Amergin, whose poetic vision leads his people from Spain to the fabled Erin and brought about the birth of the Irish nation, complete with its love of the mystic and mythical, of music and poetry, of romance and bloodcurdling battles. Another famous and fabled headstrong Irish heroine springs to life in the pages of *Grania* with the adventures of Grace O'Malley, pirate queen of Connaught who dared what many a man only dreamed of, a gallant confrontation with the forces of Queen Elizabeth I in their efforts to crush the proud and independent spirit of the Irish people.
    So powerfully written are these tales of Celtic history and heroism that they stir the blood of those who share this heritage and offer to those who do not an exciting, entertaining, and realistic portrayal of the history of a proud and ancient people.

—Judith A. Gifford

_____

LOCKRIDGE, Ross. American. Born in Bloomington, Indiana, 25 April 1914. Educated at Indiana University, Bloomington, 1931–35, B.A. (summa cum laude) in English 1935 (Phi Beta Kappa); post-graduate study, Harvard University, Cambridge, Massachusetts, 1940–41. Married Vernice Baker in 1937; four children. Instructor in English, Indiana University, 1936–40, and Simmons College, Boston, 1941–45. *Died (suicide) 6 March 1948.*

ROMANCE AND HISTORICAL PUBLICATIONS

Novel

Raintree County. Boston, Houghton Mifflin, 1948; London, Macdonald, 1949.

*

Critical Study: *Ross and Tom: Two American Tragedies* (on Lockridge and Thomas Heggen) by John Leggett, New York, Simon and Schuster, 1974.

*   *   *

Ross Lockridge is known for only one book, *Raintree County*, published in 1948 to acclaim and financial success. The novel, 1066 pages long and dense with history, event, and personality, is a conscious attempt to create and profit from creating "the Great American Novel"—the novel at last deep and wide enough to encompass the entire U.S.A. in its development and nature.

Warning the reader in the front matter of *Raintree County* that the county "is not the country of perishable fact. It is the country of the enduring fiction," Lockridge nevertheless built his novel upon knowledge of Indiana, that central state of the U.S.A. which might be thought the most typical of the nation's people and history. Son of a talented amateur historian and a Christian Science mother obsessed with having one of her children become an outstanding American, Lockridge, after university and while teaching at college, tried to meet the challenge of his parents by becoming what would most please them: a historical novelist with national acclaim and great prosperity.

Deciding that he would in *Raintree County* narrate the history of his main character and his nation at once, Lockridge chose one day in his hero's life—4 July 1892, the nation's Independence Day—for detailed narration of the present, this one day's events to be expanded into historical and national scope by the addition of 52 flashbacks to describe critical experiences in his hero's life and his nation's life. These flashbacks cover the life of the major character, John Wickliff Shawnessy, from 1844, when he was very young, to the recent past, when his wife and daughter reflect their pride in their husband and father. They round out the life of a typical young American from his boyhood in Indiana, near the National Road leading westward, into the maturity of the character at 53, rich in experience and exemplary of the best qualities of his countrymen.

Lockridge, being trained by his historian father for the writing and interpreting of history, worked into his novel the story of his nation, giving, for example, the first settlement of the area of Raintree County by Indians, their replacement by whites, the frontier nature of the area, the crisis over slavery, the involvement of the citizens in the Civil War over that slavery, the assassination of President Lincoln, the corruption of the government in the gilded age after that war, and the optimism of the citizens as the new century approached, with its hint and promise of even greater success, individual and national.

In the *Bildungsroman* aspects of *Raintree County* Shawnessy is made by idealistic parents into a reflective youth, soon tempted and educated toward maturity through love of an unattainable local blonde goddess, then a fire-scarred, dark-haired southern slave holder, then a worldly, beautiful, and confident New York City actress, and finally a youthful and fine average Indiana girl. At every stage of his life Shawnessy is contrasted with his contemporaries in Raintree County: Cassius P. Carney, who goes eastward to become a financial mogul; Garwood B. Jones, who goes eastward to become a leading senator in the federal government; and—most important of all—Jerusalem Webster Stiles, who becomes an educator, a journalist, a war reporter, and always an alter ego to John Wickliff Shawnessy (note the identical initials of the two names). Stiles is the cynical, worldly, realistic, deterministic counterforce to the romantic philosophising hero, who all his life seeks for the mythical "raintree" that would reign in the ideal garden of human life and that represents the unknowable secret of that human life.

Epic in concept and achievement, *Raintree County* was chosen immediately at publication for the members of the Book-of-the-Month Club subscription company, excerpted in *Life* magazine, and won for its author $150,000 from the M.G.M. film company for rights to make the novel into a movie. Despite this success, Lockridge, diagnosed as clinically depressed amid success, having pleased his ambitious parents, committed suicide weeks after his one novel was published.

—Ray Lewis White

LOFTS, Norah (née Robinson). Also wrote as Juliet Astley; Peter Curtis. British. Born in Shipdham, Norfolk, 27 August 1904. Educated at West Suffolk County School; Norwich Training College, teaching diploma 1925. Married 1) Geoffrey Lofts in 1933 (died 1948), one son; 2) Robert Jorisch in 1949. Taught English and history at Guildhall Feoffment Girl's School, 1925–36. Recipient: Georgette Heyer prize, for historical novel, 1978. *Died 10 September 1983.*

ROMANCE AND HISTORICAL PUBLICATIONS

Novels (series: Suffolk Trilogy)

Here Was a Man: A Romantic History of Sir Walter Raleigh. London, Methuen, and New York, Knopf, 1936.
White Hell of Pity. London, Methuen, and New York, Knopf, 1937.
Requiem for Idols. London, Methuen, and New York, Knopf, 1938.
Out of This Nettle. London, Gollancz, 1938; as *Colin Lowrie*, New York, Knopf, 1939.
Blossom Like the Rose. London, Gollancz, and New York, Knopf, 1939.
Hester Roon. London, Davies, and New York, Knopf, 1940.
The Road to Revelation. London, Davies, 1941.
The Brittle Glass. London, Joseph, 1942; New York, Knopf, 1943.
Michael and All the Angels. London, Joseph, 1943; as *The Golden Fleece*, New York, Knopf, 1944.
Jassy. London, Joseph, and New York, Knopf, 1944.
To See a Fine Lady. London, Joseph, and New York, Knopf, 1946.
Silver Nutmeg. London, Joseph, and New York, Doubleday, 1947.
A Calf for Venus. London, Joseph, and New York, Doubleday, 1949; as *Letty*, New York, Pyramid, 1968.
Esther. New York, Macmillan, 1950; London, Joseph, 1951.
The Lute Player. London, Joseph, and New York, Doubleday, 1951.
Bless This House. London, Joseph, and New York, Doubleday, 1954.
Winter Harvest. New York, Doubleday, 1955.
Queen in Waiting. London, Joseph, 1955; as *Eleanor the Queen*, New York, Doubleday, 1955; as *Queen in Waiting*, Doubleday, 1958.
Afternoon of an Autocrat. London, Joseph, and New York, Doubleday, 1956; as *The Devil in Clevely*, Leeds, Morley Barker, 1968.

Scent of Cloves. New York, Doubleday, 1957; London, Hutchinson, 1958.

Suffolk Trilogy:
> *The Town House*. London, Hutchinson, and New York, Doubleday, 1959.
> *The House at Old Vine*. London, Hutchinson, and New York, Doubleday, 1961.
> *The House at Sunset*. New York, Doubleday, 1962; London, Hutchinson, 1963.

The Concubine: A Novel Based upon the Life of Anne Boleyn. New York, Doubleday, 1963; London, Hutchinson, 1964; as *Concubine*, London, Arrow, 1965.

How Far to Bethlehem? London, Hutchinson, and New York, Doubleday, 1965.

The Lost Ones. London, Hutchinson, 1969; as *The Lost Queen*, New York, Doubleday, 1969; London, Corgi, 1970.

Madselin. London, Corgi, 1969; New York, Bantam, 1970.

The King's Pleasure. New York, Doubleday, 1969; London, Hodder and Stoughton, 1970.

Lovers All Untrue. London, Hodder and Stoughton, and New York, Doubleday, 1970.

A Rose for Virtue. London, Hodder and Stoughton, and New York, Doubleday, 1971.

Charlotte. London, Hodder and Stoughton, 1972; as *Out of the Dark*, New York, Doubleday, 1972.

Nethergate. London, Hodder and Stoughton, and New York, Doubleday, 1973.

Crown of Aloes. London, Hodder and Stoughton, and New York, Doubleday, 1974.

Walk into My Parlour. London, Corgi, 1975.

Knight's Acre. London, Hodder and Stoughton, and New York, Doubleday, 1975.

The Homecoming. London, Hodder and Stoughton, 1975; New York, Doubleday, 1976.

Checkmate. London, Corgi, 1975; New York, Fawcett, 1978.

The Fall of Midas (as Juliet Astley). New York, Coward McCann, 1975; London, Joseph, 1976.

The Lonely Furrow. London, Hodder and Stoughton, 1976; New York, Doubleday, 1977.

Gad's Hall. London, Hodder and Stoughton, 1977; New York, Doubleday, 1978.

Copsi Castle (as Juliet Astley). London, Joseph, and New York, Coward McCann, 1978.

Haunted House. London, Hodder and Stoughton, 1978; as *The Haunting of Gad's Hall*, New York, Doubleday, 1979.

The Day of the Butterfly. London, Bodley Head, 1979; New York, Doubleday, 1980.

A Wayside Tavern. London, Hodder and Stoughton, and New York, Doubleday, 1980.

The Old Priory. London, Bodley Head, 1981; New York, Doubleday, 1982.

The Claw. London, Hodder and Stoughton, 1981; New York, Doubleday, 1982.

Pargeters. London, Hodder and Stoughton, 1984; New York, Doubleday, 1986.

Novels as Peter Curtis

Dead March in Three Keys. London, Davies, 1940; as *No Question of Murder*, New York, Doubleday, 1959; as *The Bride of Moat House*, New York, Dell, 1969.

You're Best Alone. London, Macdonald, 1943; with *Requiem for Idols*, in *Two by Norah Lofts*, New York, Doubleday, 1981.

Lady Living Alone. London, Macdonald, 1945.

The Devil's Own. London, Macdonald, and New York, Doubleday, 1960; as *The Witches*, London, Pan, 1966; as *The Little Wax Doll*, London, Hodder and Stoughton, and New York, Doubleday, 1970.

Short Stories

I Met a Gypsy. London, Methuen, and New York, Knopf, 1935.

Heaven in Your Hand and Other Stories. New York, Doubleday, 1958; London, Joseph, 1959.

Is Anybody There? London, Corgi, 1974; as *Hauntings: Is Anybody There?*, New York, Doubleday, 1975.

Saving Face and Other Stories. London, Hodder and Stoughton, 1983; New York, Doubleday, 1984.

OTHER PUBLICATIONS

Other

Women in the Old Testament: Twenty Psychological Portraits. London, Sampson Low, and New York, Macmillan, 1949.

Eternal France: A History of France 1789–1944, with Margery Weiner. New York, Doubleday, 1968; London, Hodder and Stoughton, 1969.

The Story of Maude Reed (for children). London, Transworld, 1971; as *The Maude Reed Tale*, New York, Nelson, 1972.

Rupert Hatton's Story (for children). London, Carousel, 1972.

Domestic Life in England. London, Weidenfeld and Nicolson, and New York, Doubleday, 1976.

Queens of Britain. London, Hodder and Stoughton, 1977; as *The Queens of England*, New York, Doubleday, 1977.

Emma Hamilton. London, Joseph, and New York, Coward McCann, 1978.

Anne Boleyn. New York, Coward McCann, and London, Orbis, 1979.

*

Norah Lofts commented:

(1982) Strictly speaking I don't think I belong in the romance or gothic class. I write books about ordinary people some of whom happen to live in the past. The love story is never dominant; most of my people are concerned with earning a living, achieving an ambition, holding their own in a harsh world. And gothic I never understood—I thought it was a form of architecture. I do tend to write about old houses because they fascinate me. Some of my houses are haunted—but never with spectres—mainly by emotions that have made impact on the atmosphere. Some of my houses are said to be cursed; but it is the people themselves who bring the bad luck into operation.

*   *   *

Norah Lofts wrote historical romances for 50 years and has innumerable admirers. Above all, Lofts can tell a story: her inventive power, her very real gift of narrative, and her instinct for a story have been much praised. Her vigorous style of storytelling, whether in the first or the third person, carries the reader along as a multiplicity of events unfolds. Often in one historical romance the stories of several lives are told, sometimes down along the generations, and we see how these lives, socially or geographically remote from each other though they may be, touch and intertwine so as to affect each other irretrievably, for good or ill. Sometimes the stories span continents and oceans, as *Blossom Like the Rose* and *The Road to Revelation*, both set in England and the American colonies in the 17th century, and *Silver Nutmeg* and *Scent of Cloves*, both set in Europe and in the

Dutch East Indies in the 17th century and involving "glove marriages" of girls sent out from Europe to marry unseen Dutch traders. Lofts's wide historical knowledge, which includes small social details as well as the details of great events, enables her to place her stories at home and abroad from the Anglo-Saxon period onwards. Her sense of history and her capacity to transmit the fascination of the past are remarkable, though it must be said that the first-person narrators in her historical romances have their narrative styles firmly rooted in the 20th century, regardless of the times in which they operate.

Lofts's first book was *I Met a Gypsy*, a collection of short stories which are linked by the gypsy blood which flows in the veins of a dominant character in each story. The stories range in time and location from the dissolution of the monasteries in England to a British mission in China in the 1930's. There is much in this book which is found again and again in Lofts's work: the fascination with gypsies and their association with the supernatural; the dynastic or sequential ideas implicit in the arrangement of the stories which show a connection through history and through the generations; and the refusal to gloss over the brutality, nastiness, and squalor of previous ages. Stylistically, the inter-linking of several first-person narratives into one book is a technique which Lofts uses very successfully in many novels.

Lofts has a strong sense of time and a strong sense of place. Many of her historical novels are set in Suffolk, and many of them are set around houses. Both landscape and houses have a permanency which their occupants lack, although the occupants may leave impressions. The "Suffolk Trilogy" (*The Town House*, *The House at Old Vine*, and *The House at Sunset*) spans six hundred years in the history of a house, from its beginnings as the home of a medieval wool-merchant to the present day, and *Bless This House* tells the story of the fortunes of a beautiful Elizabethan house in Suffolk in eight episodes, each narrated by a different character who plays a part in its history.

Lofts portrays with skill and sympathy the economic and social positions of women from highest to lowest. Indeed, her women characters are her most interesting. We see their reactions to chance and opportunities; we see what they make of their successes and failures, whether they make the best of their lot or become indifferent or embittered. There is an idea of "what you get and what you're prepared to pay for it" in the stories of many of Lofts's heroines, from Walter Raleigh's wife, Beth (in *Here Was a Man*), who has to share her husband with the ageing, coquettish Queen and with his own political and seafaring ambitions, to Hester (in *Hester Roon*) and the heroine of *Day of the Butterfly* who rise from the most abject and squalid poverty by their own efforts. Such women as these last two who are prepared to take their destinies into their own hands contrast sharply with, for instance, poor little Emmie in *White Hell of Pity*, who refuses the opportunity of further schooling out of an over-nice conscience and ends her days prematurely as an exhausted skivvy.

—Jean Buchanan

—————

LOGAN, Mark. See **NICOLE, Christopher.**

—————

LONDON, Laura. Pseudonym for Thomas Dale Curtis and Sharon Curtis; also write as Robin James. Americans. **CURTIS, Thomas Dale**: born in Antigo, Wisconsin, 11 No-

vember 1952. Educated at the University of Wisconsin, Madison. Married Sharon Curtis in 1970; one son and one daughter. Has worked as a professional musician, newswriter, television reporter, actor, and truck driver. **CURTIS, Sharon**: born in Dahran, Saudi Arabia, 6 March 1951. Educated at schools in Turkey, Pakistan, and Iran; Marymount School for Girls, Kingston-on-Thames, Surrey; University of Wisconsin, Madison. Address: c/o Berkley, 200 Madison Avenue, New York, New York 10016, U.S.A.

ROMANCE AND HISTORICAL PUBLICATIONS

Novels

A Heart Too Proud. New York, Dell, 1978.
The Bad Baron's Daughter. New York, Dell, 1978.
Moonlight Mist. New York, Dell, 1979.
Love's a Stage. New York, Dell, 1980.
The Gypsy Heiress. New York, Dell, 1981.
The Golden Touch (as Robin James). New York, Berkley, 1982.
The Windflower. New York, Dell, 1984.

*

Laura London comments:
We've always wanted to be writers, and for us our career has been like a pleasant drift into a dream. Our finished works can be described as long conversations between the co-authors from which the interruptions have been edited. We believe in the romantic point of view and try to give our readers the quality craftsmanship they deserve.

We enjoy the research end of our work, and feel best when we can share some obscure fact with our readers in an original way. We read as many as 30 books to gain the background for one Regency romance.

*   *   *

The hallmark of books by Sharon and Tom Curtis, who write most often as Laura London and Robin James, is the humor displayed in the exchanges between the hero and heroine. Certainly the basic plots used in the regency-style novels of Laura London conform to the formula of the genre: a lively virginal heroine and a strong, handsome hero confront perilous situations. Yet when the verbal sparring begins, it is difficult not to smile or even laugh out loud at the dialogue, which has a very modern quality that verges on the sarcastic.

In *The Bad Baron's Daughter*, Katie (who has been found in a low tavern called The Merry Maidenhead) rebels against Lord Linden's plans and tells him that she would rather "lose my maidenhead fifty times first." His cool response is to tell her that that is "an anatomical impossibility" and that her reputation cannot get any worse anyway. Frances, in *Love's a Stage*, protests David's lovemaking, "Because I intend to marry a virgin." David laughingly confesses that he, unfortunately, can no longer meet that requirement. In a longer novel, *The Windflower*, the heroine, Merry Wilding, is kidnapped in error and taken aboard a pirate ship, appropriately named *Black Joke*. When in an argument she bites Devon, her pirate captor, he inquires, "Do you want to speak . . . or gnaw?" This mocking style carries over to the embellishments given to the standard romance plots. How else to explain an experienced nobleman (who also happens to be "The Bard of the Lakeland") who lets his bride bring her twin sister on their honeymoon (*Moonlight Mist*), a mysterious highwayman whose claim to a title is supported by the strange physical characteristic of one blue eye and one brown (also in *Moonlight Mist*), or a villain who keeps a wolf on a leash and lets it loose to attack his enemies once every four years (*The Gypsy Heiress*).

This deft comic touch also is apparent in the modern novels written under the name Robin James, like *The Golden Touch* and *The Testimony* and those issued under the Curtis's own name (*Lightning That Lingers, Sunshine and Shadow*). *Lightning That Lingers* is very much a modern regency, with its shy, virginal heroine, Jennifer, who is a children's librarian. She falls in love with Philip, a wildlife biologist who moonlights as a male dancer in the Cougar Club in order to earn money to support his wildlife preserve. In *The Golden Touch*, Kathy Carter is a widow, but in relation to rock star Neil Stratton's experience, she is very much a beginner. She is a fast learner, however, and even manages to pursue Neil after a break-up by bribing his fans to throw her on stage at one of his concerts. The underlying theme of *The Testimony* is more somber in that it deals with the adjustments and problems facing a couple after the husband, a reporter, spends six months in jail. In spite of the seriousness, there is a thread of humor in the sharp dialogue of the characters. *Sunshine and Shadow*, a longer contemporary romance features another unusual pair of lovers: Susan Peachey, a young Amish widow and Alan Wilde, a cynical Hollywood director.

The contemporary romances, along with *The Windflower*, all feature more explicit lovemaking, but there is laughter as well as passion. After the diet of saccharin prose and seduction scenes verging on rape which are found in so many "romance" novels, it is refreshing to find characters who enjoy themselves and one another, even as they work through their problems.

—Barbara E. Kemp

LONG, William Stuart. See **STUART, Vivian.**

LORD, Alison. See **ELLIS, Julie.**

LORD, Jeffrey. See **ELLIS, Julie.**

LORIN, Amii. Pseudonym for Joan M. Hohl; also writes as Paula Roberts. American. Address: c/o Silhouette Books, 300 East 42nd Street, New York, New York 10017, U.S.A.

ROMANCE AND HISTORICAL PUBLICATIONS

Novels

Morning Rose, Evening Savage. New York, Dell, 1980; as *Morning Rose*, London, Mills and Boon, 1982.
The Tawny Gold Man. New York, Dell, 1980.
Breeze off the Ocean. New York, Dell, 1980; London, Corgi, 1983.

Come Home To Love (as Paula Roberts). New York, Tower, 1980.
Morgan Wade's Woman. New York, Dell, 1981.
The Game Is Played. New York, Dell, 1981.
Snowbound Weekend. New York, Dell, 1982.
Gambler's Love. New York, Dell, 1982.
Candleglow. London, Mills and Boon, 1983.
While the Fire Rages. New York, Dell, 1984.
Night Striker. New York, Dell, 1985.
Power and Seduction. New York, Dell, 1985.

Novels as Joan Hohl (series: Sharp Family; Vanzant Family; Window)

Thorne's Way. New York, Silhouette, 1982.
Moments Harsh, Moments Gentle. New York, Silhouette, 1984.
A Taste for Rich Things. New York, Silhouette, 1984.
A Much Needed Holiday. New York, Silhouette, 1986.
Someone Waiting. New York, Silhouette, 1986.
The Scent of Lilacs. New York, Silhouette, 1986.
Texas Gold (Sharp). New York, Silhouette, 1986.
California Copper (Sharp). New York, Silhouette, 1986.
Nevada Silver (Sharp). New York, Silhouette, 1987.
Lady Ice (Vanzant). New York, Silhouette, 1987.
One Tough Hombre (Vanzant). New York, Silhouette, 1987.
Falcon's Flight. New York, Silhouette, 1987.
Forever Spring (Vanzant). New York, Silhouette, 1988.
Window on Yesterday. New York, Berkley, 1988.
Window on Today. New York, Berkley, 1989.
Window on Tomorrow. New York, Berkley, 1989.
The Gentleman Insists. New York, Silhouette, 1989.

*   *   *

Amii Lorin, who also writes under her real name, Joan M. Hohl, is a prolific, bestselling author under both names. A Lorin title, *The Tawny Gold Man*, was chosen to start Dell's "Candlelight Ecstasy Romance" series, which signaled the arrival of an important new author of romantic fiction.

Lorin's novels feature arrogant, commanding men who frequently try to dominate the heroine. Their success in getting their way depends largely on the strength and independence of the heroines. Often they clash over a serious misunderstanding. In *The Tawny Gold Man*, Jud Cammeron suspects his stepsister of a liaison with his own father and of conspiring to have him banished from his family, yet he still loves her. He marries her but remains cold and distant since he still does not fully trust her. Samantha and Morgan (*Morgan Wade's Woman*) hurt one another badly because they cannot seem to communicate. Both are proud and arrogant and see yielding as losing. Samantha's cousin, Courtney, has similar problems with the enigmatic Rio McCord, an ex-agent and mercenary in *Night Striker*. One of the silliest problems caused by lack of communication occurs in *Breeze off the Ocean*. Micki Durrant is forced into marriage with Wolf Renniger because, believing she had a voluntary abortion, he feels she "owes" him a child. In actual fact she miscarried early in her pregnancy. The situation could be easily explained, but Micki does not explain until after marrying Wolf and suffering a cruel rejection. Lorin manages to treat such foolish behavior so realistically that it does not seem outrageous or unconvincing.

Many of the novels written as Joan Hohl are linked by related characters. *Texas Gold* and *California Copper* feature twin brothers, Thackery and Zackery Sharp, who were separated as children, each being raised by one of his parents. *Nevada Silver* tells the story of their half sister, Kit Aimsley, and Flint Falcon of

Falcon's Flight was also introduced in *Nevada Silver*. Another character from *Texas Gold*, Peter Vanzant, began another related series with *Lady Ice*. His sister's story is continued in *One Tough Hombre*. The Vanzants' father, Paul, is the hero of *Forever Spring*. These novels are entertaining but not outstanding. Nevertheless, the linking of novels provides a continuity which satisfies the reader's desire to know what happens beyond a single story and, very practically, encourages continued sales.

In a recent trilogy, Hohl experiments a bit with the traditional romance formula. Tracing stories of three older college roommates, she adds a touch of the unexplained. In *Window on Yesterday*, a history student seems to travel back in time and becomes her own ancestor and meets the ancestor of her contemporary love. The love affair in *Window on Today* seems to follow standard lines, but in *Window on Tomorrow*, Hohl hints at an extraterrestrial connection. She strongly implies that the perfect hero of the story is really from outer space, and that the heroine leaves with him in the end.

Whether writing as Joan Hohl or Amii Lorin, Hohl has not been, until recently, an innovator in romance fiction. However, she has developed a solid reputation for providing light, but satisfying, stories.

—Barbara E. Kemp

LORING, Emilie (née Baker). Also wrote as Josephine Story. American. Born in Boston, Massachusetts. Educated privately. Married Victor J. Loring; two sons. *Died 14 March 1951.*

ROMANCE AND HISTORICAL PUBLICATIONS

Novels

The Trail of Conflict. Philadelphia, Penn, 1922; London, Unwin, 1923.
Here Comes the Sun! Philadelphia, Penn, 1924.
The Dragon-Slayer. London, Unwin, 1924.
A Certain Crossroad. Philadelphia, Penn, 1925.
The Solitary Horseman. Philadelphia, Penn, 1927.
Gay Courage. Philadelphia, Penn, 1928; London, Long, 1929.
Swift Water. Philadelphia, Penn, 1929.
Lighted Windows. Philadelphia, Penn, 1930; London, Hale, 1974.
Fair Tomorrow. Philadelphia, Penn, 1931; London, Stanley Paul, 1932.
Uncharted Seas. Philadelphia, Penn, 1932; London, Hale, 1975.
Hilltops Clear. Philadelphia, Penn, 1933; London, Stanley Paul, 1934.
Come On, Fortune! London, Stanley Paul, 1933.
We Ride the Gale! Philadelphia, Penn, 1934; London, Stanley Paul, 1935.
With Banners. Philadelphia, Penn, 1934; London, Stanley Paul, 1935.
It's a Great World! Philadelphia, Penn, 1935.
Give Me One Summer. Philadelphia, Penn, 1936.
As Long as I Live. Philadelphia, Penn, 1937; London, Hale, 1972.
Today Is Yours. Boston, Little Brown, 1938.
High of Heart. Boston, Little Brown, 1938.
Across the Years. Boston, Little Brown, 1939.

There Is Always Love. Boston, Little Brown, 1940; London, Foulsham, 1951.
Stars in Your Eyes. Boston, Little Brown, 1941; London, Nicholson and Watson, 1943.
Where Beauty Dwells. Boston, Little Brown, 1941.
Rainbow at Dusk. Boston, Little Brown, 1942; London, Hale, 1976.
When Hearts Are Light Again. Boston, Little Brown, 1943; London, Foulsham, 1953.
Keepers of the Faith. Boston, Little Brown, 1944; London, Hale, 1975.
Beyond the Sound of Guns. Boston, Little Brown, 1945.
Bright Skies. Boston, Little Brown, 1946; London, Hale, 1984.
Beckoning Trails. Boston, Little Brown, 1947; London, Foulsham, 1952.
I Hear Adventure Calling. Boston, Little Brown, 1948; London, Hale, 1976.
Love Came Laughing. Boston, Little Brown, 1949; London, Foulsham, 1951.
To Love and to Honor. Boston, Little Brown, 1950; London, Foulsham, 1951.
For All Your Life. Boston, Little Brown, 1952; London, Hale, 1970.
I Take This Man. Boston, Little Brown, 1954; London, Foulsham, 1955.
My Dearest Love. Boston, Little Brown, 1954; London, Hale, 1972; as *My Love*, London, Foulsham, 1955.
The Shadow of Suspicion. Boston, Little Brown, 1955; London, Hale, 1965.
What Then Is Love. Boston, Little Brown, 1956; London, Hale, 1965.
Look to the Stars. Boston, Little Brown, 1957; London, Hale, 1966; as *Scott Pelham's Princess*, London, Foulsham, 1958.
Behind the Cloud. Boston, Little Brown, 1958; London, Hale, 1967.
With This Ring. Boston, Little Brown, 1959; London, Hale, 1966.
How Can the Heart Forget. Boston, Little Brown, 1960; London, Hale, 1966.
Throw Wide the Door. Boston, Little Brown, 1962.
Follow Your Heart. Boston, Little Brown, 1963; London, Hale, 1964.
A Candle in Her Heart. Boston, Little Brown, 1964; London, Hale, 1969.
Forever and a Day. Boston, Little Brown, 1965.
Spring Always Comes. Boston, Little Brown, 1966; London, Hale, 1968.
A Key to Many Doors. Boston, Little Brown, 1967; London, Hale, 1969.
In Times Like These. Boston, Little Brown, 1968; London, Hale, 1976.
Love with Honor. Boston, Little Brown, 1969; London, Hale, 1970.
No Time for Love. Boston, Little Brown, 1970; London, Hale, 1971.
Forsaking All Others. Boston, Little Brown, 1971; London, Hale, 1973.
The Shining Years. Boston, Little Brown, 1972; London, Hale, 1974.

OTHER PUBLICATIONS

Play

Where's Peter? Philadelphia, Penn, 1928.

Other as Josephine Story

For the Comfort of the Family: A Vacation Experiment. New York, Doran, 1914.
The Mother in the House. Boston, Pilgrim Press, 1917.

* * *

Emilie Loring was an American writer of patriotic, moralistic romances that comment upon some of the major socio-political events occurring in the United States during the period in which they were published. Loring's version of the romance formula has had an enduring appeal, for, although her books were written in the first half of the century, their multiple printings up to the present day attest to their continued popularity.

Strong pro-Americanism is the most striking feature of Loring's fiction. Her books constitute a resounding defense of democratic capitalism. The heroines declare themselves to be fierce patriots ("my country, right or wrong"), and the heroes are either benevolent industrialists, war heroes, lawyers and politicians fighting for the "American Way," or "trouble-shooters for Uncle Sam." Whenever the American system of business or government is under attack, as is usually the case in Loring's plots, the main characters respond with impassioned speeches and may even burst into the Pledge of Allegiance to the Flag. Anyone who disagrees with this creed is considered to be a weak, inadequate person who blames society for his personal failures.

The moral tone of Loring's romances is consistent with her patriotic conservativeness. She bemoans the loosening of morals of the modern world, particularly the increase of divorce, and wishes for a return to stricter ethics. She continually attacks idleness, cheapness, spinelessness, selfishness, and pessimism, and admires integrity, modesty, graciousness, loyalty, sweetness, self-discipline, and a sense of humor.

Loring philosophizes most about marriage. Characters are apt to quote from the marriage service and discuss the components of a good marriage, as in *Swift Water*:

> . . . marriage fundamentally is a matter of sympathetic companionship shot through and through with gleams of passion, love. It should be productive of fidelity, loyalty, responsibility, of the stamina to see a difficult situation through if necessary. It is not just the business of two persons. A marriage which breaks down threatens the institution.

When marriage breaks down, Loring adds elsewhere, society breaks down. Many romance writers portray love and courtship but stop short of portraying real marriages. Loring does not shirk this task. In fact, she frequently portrays even very unhappy marriages. These she uses to convey moral lessons. Loring advocates a "bite the bullet" approach to marriage. Once married, partners are irrevocably committed to each other, no matter what. Faithful spouses are always ultimately rewarded in Loring's novels. If one lives by a code of honor, "Things have a marvelous, unbelievable way of coming right." Thus, Loring's romances are optimistic and "up-lifting."

Loring differs from many writers of romances in another way as well. She describes and comments on crucial, contemporary social events such as World Wars I and II, the Korean conflict, Red scares, unionization, racketeer crime, wide-scale immigration, urbanization, and the Great Depression. Once again, her political conservatism is noticeably evident. For example, all union organizing is attributed to outside agitators, parasites, and ungrateful aliens. One hero (in *The Shadow of Suspicion*) tells a group of striking workers: "You've been getting a dose of propaganda. And do you know who paid for it? The Reds!" He proceeds to outline the evils of Russian communism. Loring's novels are full of traitors, spies, and subversives against whom one must be ever vigilant. Throughout her romances, Loring openly supports McCarthy-era tactics, the Cold War hostility, and the armaments race.

In addition to the romance and political intrigue, Loring's novels blend a number of stylistic and plot devices like humor, dialects, colloquialisms, and details of local color to make them distinctive. Every novel features amusing incidents which usually involve innocent but embarrassingly outspoken children or servants, or cute pets. Gay repartee also provides a sense of high spirits. Loring also has fun with characters' names which often reveal the nature of the character. Thus, a detective is called Tom Search; a formal butler is named Propper; a religious fanatic is Luther Calvin. These are rather heavy-handed and obvious, of course, but Loring apparently delights in them as they are a consistent pattern. Loring's minor characters (servants, farmers, and foreigners) speak in pronounced dialect with stereotypical mannerisms. For example, in *Across the Years* Loring describes a typical plump "Southern mammy" who talks like this: "Ah sure is glad to see yo', Mistuh Duke. . . . Let me tak' dat coat, honey-girl." While this technique adds "color" to Loring's writing style and is probably not intended to be racist, it is simplistic and condescending.

Loring has a fine eye for detail and she can skillfully create vivid scenes. However, she frequently relies too heavily on naming colors to evoke a mood. In addition, she sometimes gets trapped in a repetitive series of descriptive phrases that end up being irritating like in the following: "She darted in and out of a drove of bleating blackfaced sheep; did a running high jump over a squealing pig; ducked under the nose of a pawing colt; skirted a dog fight and shooed away a flock of cackling geese . . . " (*High of Heart*).

One final criticism of Loring's style stems from her moral lessons and patriotic lectures which result in some very stilted dialogue. One does not usually break into the Pledge of Allegiance in a casual, social conversation. Loring's flair for the dramatic leads her astray in these cases.

—Margaret Jensen

LORING, Peter. See **SHELLABARGER, Samuel.**

LORRIMER, Claire. Pseudonym for Patricia Denise Clark, née Robins; has also written as Patricia Robins. British. Born in Hove, Sussex, 1 February 1921; daughter of Denise Robins, *q.v.* Educated at Parents' National Educational Union, Burgess Hill, Sussex, 1927–30; Effingham House, Bexhill-on-Sea, Sussex, 1930–35; Institut Prealpina, Switzerland, 1935–37; and in Munich, 1937–38. Served in the radar filter room, Women's Auxiliary Air Force, 1940–45: Flight Officer. Married D. C. Clark in 1948 (divorced); two sons and one daughter. Sub-editor, *Woman's Illustrated*, London, 1938–40. Agent: Anthea Morton Saner, Curtis Brown, 162–168 Regent Street, London W1R 5TB. Address: Chiswell Barn, Christmas Mill Lane, Marsh Green, Edenbridge, Kent TN8 5AP, England.

ROMANCE AND HISTORICAL PUBLICATIONS

Novels (series: Rochford)

A Voice in the Dark. London, Souvenir Press, 1967; New York, Avon, 1968.
The Shadow Falls. New York, Avon, 1974.
Relentless Storm. New York, Avon, 1975; London, Arlington, 1979.
The Secret of Quarry House. New York, Avon, 1976; London, Century, 1988.
Mavreen. London, Arlington, 1976; New York, Bantam, 1977.
Tamarisk. London, Arlington, 1978; New York, Bantam, 1979.
Chantal. London, Arlington, 1980; New York, Bantam, 1981.
The Chatelaine (Rochford). London, Arlington, 1981; New York, Ballantine, 1982.
The Wilderling (Rochford). London, Arlington, 1982; New York, Ballantine, 1983.
Last Year's Nightingale. London, Century, 1984.
Frost in the Sun. London, Century, 1986.

Novels as Patricia Robins

To the Stars. London, Hutchinson, 1944.
See No Evil. London, Hutchinson, 1945.
Statues of Snow. London, Hutchinson, 1947.
Three Loves. London, Hutchinson, 1949.
Awake My Heart. London, Hutchinson, 1950.
Beneath the Moon. London, Hutchinson, 1951.
Leave My Heart Alone. London, Hutchinson, 1951.
The Fair Deal. London, Hutchinson, 1952.
Heart's Desire. London, Hutchinson, 1953.
So This Is Love. London, Hutchinson, 1953.
Heaven in Our Hearts. London, Hutchinson, 1954.
One Who Cares. London, Hutchinson, 1954.
Love Cannot Die. London, Hutchinson, 1955.
The Foolish Heart. London, Hutchinson, 1956.
Give All to Love. London, Hutchinson, 1956.
Where Duty Lies. London, Hutchinson, 1957.
He Is Mine. London, Hurst and Blackett, 1957.
Love Must Wait. London, Hurst and Blackett, 1958.
Lonely Quest. London, Hurst and Blackett, 1959.
Lady Chatterley's Daughter. London, Consul, and New York, Ace, 1961.
The Last Chance. London, Hurst and Blackett, 1961.
The Long Wait. London, Hurst and Blackett, 1962.
The Runaways. London, Hurst and Blackett, 1962.
Seven Loves. London, Consul, 1962.
With All My Love. London, Hurst and Blackett, 1963.
The Constant Heart. London, Hurst and Blackett, 1964.
Second Love. London, Hurst and Blackett, 1964.
The Night Is Thine. London, Consul, 1964.
There Is But One. London, Hurst and Blackett, 1965.
No More Loving. London, Consul, 1965.
Topaz Island. London, Hurst and Blackett, 1965.
Love Me Tomorrow. London, Hurst and Blackett, 1966.
The Uncertain Joy. London, Hurst and Blackett, 1966.
Forbidden. London, Mayflower, 1967.
The Man Behind the Mask. London, Sphere, 1967.
Sapphire in the Sand. London, Arrow, 1968.
Return to Love. London, Hurst and Blackett, 1968.
Laugh on Friday. London, Hurst and Blackett, 1969.
No Stone Unturned. London, Hurst and Blackett, 1969.
Cinnabar House. London, Hurst and Blackett, 1970.
Under the Sky. London, Hurst and Blackett, 1970; New York, Atlantic Monthly Press, 1988.

The Crimson Tapestry. London, Hurst and Blackett, 1971; New York, Atlantic Monthly Press, 1988.
Play Fair with Love. London, Hurst and Blackett, 1972; New York, Atlantic Monthly Press, 1988.
None But He. London, Hurst and Blackett, 1973.

OTHER PUBLICATIONS

Verse as Patricia Robins

Seven Days Leave. London, Hutchinson, 1943.

Other (for children) as Patricia Robins

The Adventures of the Three Baby Bunnies. London, Nicholson and Watson, 1934.
Tree Fairies. London, Hutchinson, 1945.
Sea Magic. London, Hutchinson, 1946.
The Heart of a Rose. London, Hutchinson, 1947.
The £100 Reward. Exeter, Wheaton, 1966.

Other

The Garden. London, Arlington, 1980.
House of Tomorrow. London, Century, 1987.

*

Claire Lorrimer comments:

When I decided to become a freelance writer after World War II, it seemed natural to continue writing the kind of light romantic fiction I had been associated with as a junior sub-editor on a magazine before the war. It did not occur to me to change to anything else until the 1970's when my agent, Desmond Elliott, suggested I could improve the standard of my work. I wrote *Mavreen* in 1975 and when it went immediately into the bestseller list in the USA, I decided to make a permanent change and virtually begin a new career. I like to think the standard of my work is improving with each book and the critical reviews I have been receiving suggest this is so. I prefer the relative realism of my Clair Lorrimers in which I try to make certain that no one says or does anything that in real life they might not have done or said, and although the stories are full of action and adventure I hope to convince my reader that these characters really could have existed and have led the lives I have given them. I often end up believing them real myself. Of all my reviews, I am most satisfied by George Thaw's (*Daily Mirror*) in which he concludes the *Chatelaine* review with the words: "A slice of life." I am never satisfied with the finished product. Of everything I have written in my life, my favourite is *The Garden*.

*   *   *

Claire Lorrimer's approach to her work is primarily instinctive. In her opinion, a story writes itself. The method has virtues, but the drawbacks are also evident at times. Many of her novels seem too long for the thematic material they support. There is a tendency towards verbosity, which often draws out the thread of a story to breaking point. This is particularly true of *Relentless Storm*, whose characters with their forbidden passions are the very stuff of gothic dream, but whose presentation fails to save a short story stretched to novel length. Characters lack depth, and the plot and its climaxes are predictable. It is melodramatic, but it fails to convince. *A Voice in the Dark* is more satisfying. The story is again conventional gothic romance, a young girl on holiday in Florence becoming involved with Italian aristocrats at their ancestral home. The long arm of coincidence is virtually dislocated in the opening pages, but the story moves more rapidly than *Relentless Storm*. The characters do not linger over their speeches, climaxes are reached without delay, and a happy ending secured at last. The least ambitious of her books, it is among the most successful.

It is the heorines of *Mavreen*, *Tamarisk*, and *Chantal* who have established Lorrimer's reputation. Mavreen sets the pace, and is the dominating presence of the trilogy. Natural daughter of an English nobleman, raised as a child by Sussex farmers, she enters into passionate love affairs with the French aristocrat Gerard de Valle and the titled highwayman Sir Perry Waite, taking part in the latter's robberies. She, together with Tamarisk and Chantal, tastes triumph and disaster in the aristocratic world of the Regency and enjoys the friendship of the great. The three heroines overshadow their men, although Gerard and Sir Perry are ably drawn. The novels are stories of individuals rather than a picture of the times—the Regency atmosphere is less strong than in the "Haggard" novels of Nicole—but this is unimportant. The characters compel and convince.

The Chatelaine is set in the early part of this century. Willow, daughter of an American millionaire, marries Rowell Rochford, not knowing the impoverished English nobleman is after her money. The Rochford mansion with its dominant matriarch, the dark secret of hereditary illness, and the imprisonment of Rowell's crippled sister all bring back gothic echoes of *A Voice in the Dark*. *The Chatelaine* is the most impressive of Lorrimer's novels to date, compact and well crafted. Willow, in her gradual assertion of independence from Rowell and his dragon of a mother, is at once interesting and credible. Her presence throws her male counterparts into the shade, but secondary characters are more fully realized in this work. Lorrimer continues the story of the Rochfords in the *The Wilderling*. Covering the period 1911 to 1918, the novel deals with the trials and tribulations of the younger generation of Rochfords during World War I. With her latest work, Lorrimer has moved onto another successful family saga. *Frost in the Sun* is set in Spain and concentrates on two rival families, the Costains and the Monteros, during the first half of this century. Lorrimer seems to have found a comfortable genre in the family saga, which allows her the scope in which to develop fully her characters.

—Geoffrey Sadler

LOWELL, Elizabeth. Pseudonym for Ann Elizabeth Maxwell; also writes as A. E. Maxwell. American. Born in Milwaukee, Wisconsin, 5 April 1944. Educated at the University of California, Davis, 1962–63, and Riverside, 1963–66, B.A. in English. Married Evan Lowell Maxwell in 1966; one son and one daughter. Agent: Jim and Elizabeth Trupin, JET Literary Associates, 124 East 84th Street, New York, New York 10028. Address: P.O. Box 7857, Laguna Niguel, California 92677, U.S.A.

ROMANCE AND HISTORICAL PUBLICATIONS

Novels

Golden Empire (as A. E. Maxwell). New York, Fawcett, 1979.
Summer Thunder. New York, Silhouette, 1983.
The Danvers Touch. New York, Silhouette, 1983.
Forget Me Not. New York, Silhouette, 1984.

Lover in the Rough. New York, Silhouette, 1984.
Summer Games. New York, Silhouette, 1984.
A Woman Without Lies. New York, Silhouette, 1985.
The Valley of the Sun. New York, Silhouette, 1985.
Traveling Man. New York, Silhouette, 1985.
Fires of Eden. New York, Silhouette, 1986.
Sequel. New York, Silhouette, 1986.
The Fire of Spring. New York, Silhouette, 1986.
Too Hot to Handle. New York, Silhouette, 1986.
Tell Me No Lies. Toronto, Worldwide, 1986.
Love Song for a Raven. New York, Silhouette, 1987.
Sweet Wind, Wild Wind. New York, Silhouette, 1987.
Redwood Empire (as A. E. Maxwell). Toronto, Worldwide, 1987.
Fever. New York, Silhouette, 1988.
Chain Lightning. New York, Silhouette, 1988.
Dark Fire. New York, Silhouette, 1988.
Reckless Love. Toronto, Worldwide, 1989.

OTHER PUBLICATIONS

Novels as Ann Maxwell

Change. New York, Popular Library, 1975.
The Singer Enigma. New York, Popular Library, 1976.
A Dead God Dancing. New York, Avon, 1979.
Name of a Shadow. New York, Avon, 1980.
The Jaws of Menx. New York, New American Library, 1981.
Fire Dancer. New York, New American Library, and London, Orbit, 1982.
Dancer's Luck. New York, New American Library, and London, Orbit, 1983.
Dancer's Illusion. New York, New American Library, and London, Orbit, 1983.
Timeshadow Rider. New York, Tor, 1986.

Novels (as A. E. Maxwell, with Evan Maxwell)

Steal the Sun. New York, Marek, 1981.
Just Another Day in Paradise. New York, Doubleday, 1985.
The Frog and the Scorpion. New York, Doubleday, 1986.
Gatsby's Vineyard. New York, Doubleday, 1987.
Just Enough Light to Kill. New York, Doubleday, 1988.
The Art of Survival. New York, Doubleday, 1989.

Other (as A. E. Maxwell, with Evan Maxwell)

The Year-Long Day, with Ivar Ruud. Philadelphia, Lippincott, 1976; London, Gollancz, 1977.

*

Elizabeth Lowell comments:
I enjoy writing romance fiction because it is the only area of modern fiction in which an author is permitted to celebrate the beauty that a man and a woman can bring to each other. To me, romance fiction is an extension of a mythic tradition that began long before our present dour Existential age and will endure long after Existentialism is little more than a footnote in the history of humanity.

*   *   *

The majority of Elizabeth Lowell's romances have been published in two series, but the quality of her writing is much higher than the average formula romance. Her novels are distinguished by strong, well-developed characters and a use of language that frequently borders on the poetic.

In most of the books the hero is an emotionally scarred, cynical man, who does not believe in love or dreams. The heroine is strong and intelligent. Often she has been hurt in some way but finds the strength to go on and love again. Losing her fiancé in a car crash just before their wedding, Angel manages to create a new life for herself in *A Woman Without Lies*. Although it is painful for her, she comes to love Hawk but is brutally rejected by him. However, her softness, strength, and courage reach beneath his protective shell to find the gentleness he has hidden. Rio, the drifter and water witcher in *The Valley of the Sun*, finds his dreams and peace in Hope Gardener's determination to create her own dream. Cat Cochran (*The Danvers Touch*) almost loses everything before the embittered Travis Danvers accepts the reality of her love. Doubting herself after a disastrous marriage, Janna Moran can still find the strength to love Carlson Raven (*Love Song for a Raven*) and convince him of her love.

In contrast to Lowell's heroines, her heroes have difficulty in offering or accepting love. Loving another is taking a risk which opens the giver to pain. Frequently, the man rejects the woman's love because in his ignorance he cannot recognize it for what it is. His rejection may be gentle or cruel, but it nearly always strips the woman's feelings to her soul.

Lowell also writes widely in other genres, especially science fiction and mysteries, under her own name, Ann Maxwell, and another pseudonym, A. E. Maxwell. Her experience in developing action plots is apparent in the romance thriller of international intrigue, *Tell Me No Lies*. A shadowy, shifting world of dangerous conspiracies and smuggling of Chinese artifacts is an effective setting for a more complex contemporary romance. In fact, the action is the primary focus, but Lowell develops a solid romance for the main characters, Lindsay Danner and Jacob Catlin.

Lowell's novels focus on the power and beauty of love and love that is worthy of trust. Her characters find that although loving is taking a risk, loving another brings a new kind of freedom. As she writes in the last line of *A Woman Without Lies*, it is "pain transformed into peace by the surpassing beauty of love."

—Barbara E. Kemp

LOWNDES, Marie (Adelaide) Belloc. Also wrote as Philip Curtin. British. Born in 1868; sister of the writer Hilaire Belloc. Married the writer Frederic Sawrey Lowndes (died 1940); one son and two daughters. *Died 14 November 1947.*

ROMANCE AND HISTORICAL PUBLICATIONS

Novels (series: Duchess Laura)

The Heart of Penelope. London, Heinemann, 1904; New York, Dutton, 1915.
Barbara Rebell. London, Heinemann, 1905; New York, Dodge, 1907.
The Pulse of Life. London, Heinemann, 1908; New York, Dodd Mead, 1909.
The Uttermost Farthing. London, Heinemann, 1908; New York, Kennerley, 1909.

When No Man Pursueth. London, Heinemann, 1910; New York, Kennerley, 1911.
Jane Oglander. London, Heinemann, and New York, Scribner, 1911.
The Chink in the Armour. London, Methuen, and New York, Scribner, 1912; as *The House of Peril*, London, Readers Library, 1935.
Mary Pechell. London, Methuen, and New York, Scribner, 1912.
The Lodger. London, Methuen, and New York, Scribner, 1913.
The End of Her Honeymoon. New York, Scribner, 1913; London, Methuen, 1914.
Good Old Anna. London, Hutchinson, 1915; New York, Doran, 1916.
The Red Cross Barge. London, Smith Elder, 1916; New York, Doran, 1918.
Lilla: A Part of Her Life. London, Hutchinson, 1916; New York, Doran, 1917.
Love and Hatred. London, Chapman and Hall, and New York, Doran, 1917.
Out of the War? London, Chapman and Hall, 1918; as *Gentleman Anonymous*, London, Philip Allan, 1934.
From the Vasty Deep. London, Hutchinson, 1920; as *From Out the Vasty Deep*, New York, Doran, 1921.
The Lonely House. London, Hutchinson, and New York, Doran, 1920.
What Timmy Did. London, Hutchinson, 1921; New York, Doran, 1922.
The Terriford Mystery. London, Hutchinson, and New York, Doubleday, 1924.
What Really Happened. London, Hutchinson, and New York, Doubleday, 1926.
The Story of Ivy. London, Heinemann, 1927; New York, Doubleday, 1928.
Thou Shalt Not Kill. London, Hutchinson, 1927.
Cressida: No Mystery. London, Heinemann, 1928; New York, Knopf, 1930.
Duchess Laura: Certain Days of Her Life. London, Ward Lock, 1929; as *The Duchess Intervenes*, New York, Putnam, 1933.
Love's Revenge. London, Readers Library, 1929.
One of Those Ways. London, Heinemann, and New York, Knopf, 1929.
Letty Lynton. London, Heinemann, and New York, Cape and Smith, 1931.
Vanderlyn's Adventure. New York, Cape and Smith, 1931; as *The House by the Sea*, London, Heinemann, 1937.
Jenny Newstead. London, Heinemann, and New York, Putnam, 1932.
Love Is a Flame. London, Benn, 1932.
The Reason Why. London, Benn, 1932.
Duchess Laura: Further Days from Her Life. New York, Longman, 1933.
Another Man's Wife. London, Heinemann, and New York, Longman, 1934.
The Chianti Flask. New York, Longman, 1934; London, Heinemann, 1935.
Who Rides on a Tiger. New York, Longman, 1935; London, Heinemann, 1936.
And Call It Accident. New York, Longman, 1936; London, Hutchinson, 1939.
The Second Key. New York, Longman, 1936; as *The Injured Lover*, London, Hutchinson, 1939.
The Marriage-Broker. London, Heinemann, 1937; as *The Fortune of Bridget Malone*, New York, Longman, 1937.
Motive. London, Heinemann, 1938; as *Why It Happened*, New York, Longman, 1938.

Lizzie Borden: A Study in Conjecture. New York, Longman, 1939; London, Hutchinson, 1940.
Reckless Angel. New York, Longman, 1939.
The Christine Diamond. London, Hutchinson, and New York, Longman, 1940.
Before the Storm. New York, Longman, 1941.
She Dwelt with Beauty. London, Macmillan, 1949.

Short Stories

Studies in Wives. London, Heinemann, 1909; New York, Kennerley, 1910.
Studies in Love and Terror. London, Methuen, and New York, Scribner, 1913.
Why They Married. London, Heinemann, 1923.
Bread of Deceit. London, Hutchinson, 1925; as *Afterwards*, New York, Doubleday, 1925.
Some Men and Women. London, Hutchinson, 1925; New York, Doubleday, 1928.
What of the Night? New York, Dodd Mead, 1943.
A Labour of Hercules. London, Todd, 1943.

OTHER PUBLICATIONS

Plays

The Lonely House, with Charles Randolph, adaptation of the novel by Lowndes (produced Eastbourne, Sussex, 1924).
The Key: A Love Drama (as *The Second Key*, produced London, 1935). London, Benn, 1930.
With All John's Love. London, Benn, 1930.
Why Be Lonely?, with F. S. A. Lowndes. London, Benn, 1931.
What Really Happened, adaptation of her own novel (produced London, 1936). London, Benn, 1932.
Her Last Adventure (produced London, 1936).
The Empress Eugenie. New York, Longman, 1938.

Other

H.R.H. the Prince of Wales: An Account of His Career (published anonymously). London, Richards, and New York, Appleton, 1898; revised edition, as *His Most Gracious Majesty King Edward VII* (as Mrs. Belloc Lowndes), Richards, 1901.
The Philosophy of the Marquise (sketches and dialogues). London, Richards, 1899.
T.R.H. the Prince and Princess of Wales (published anonymously). London, Newnes, 1902.
Noted Murder Mysteries (as Philip Curtin). London, Simpkin Marshall, 1914.
Told in Gallant Deeds: A Child's History of the War. London, Nisbet, 1914.
I, Too, Have Lived in Arcadia: A Record of Love and of Childhood. London, Macmillan, 1941; New York, Dodd Mead, 1942.
Where Love and Friendship Dwelt (autobiography). London, Macmillan, and New York, Dodd Mead, 1943.
The Merry Wives of Westminster (autobiography). London, Macmillan, 1946.
A Passing World (autobiography). London, Macmillan, 1948.
The Young Hilaire Belloc. New York, Kenedy, 1956.

Editor and Translator, with M. Shedlock, *Edmund and Jules de Goncourt, with Letters and Leaves from Their Journals*.

London, Heinemann, and New York, Dodd Mead, 2 vols., 1895.

*   *   *

Marie Belloc Lowndes's romances capture changing moral values from Victorian elders to Edwardian youth, from pre-war idealists to post-war cynics, the sence of propriety, respectability, and practicality in love of the one, the more liberal, convention-breaking affairs of the other. Frequently her love stories involve elements of the supernatural, with seances, forewarnings, and apparitions, or criminal activities that involve the reputations of young innocents caught in a web of treachery. Staid and proper members of society find themselves unexpectedly seized by alien feelings of jealousy and shameless desire; young men and women sacrifice their reputations and virtue for love or money, find themselves manipulated and abused, their honesty questioned, their beloved driven into the arms of devious rivals. Occasionally the situation is an adulterous one, pregnant with mixed feelings of love and remorse. Always Lowndes portrays the joys and horrors of the everyday. Her forte is a compassionate understanding of the diversity and complexity of human motives, the shades of gray, the unspoken and the hidden. Her novels are replete with sad adventuresses, rich but eccentric relatives, gossipy neighbors, potential scandals, driving hatreds, and surprising human generosity. Her historical romance *She Dwelt with Beauty* is typical of her domestic interests, focusing on the courtship and marriage of Eugenie de Montijo and Louis Napoleon, not for the historical repercussions, but for the human conflicts that grow out of the failure of the sexes to understand their differing natures and needs: Napoleon's sexually rampant nature; Eugenie's naivety, her shock at his infidelities, her mixture of love and abhorrence.

Occasionally Lowndes's tales seem conventionally Victorian: a cold-hearted, rich, young man, rejected by a kind-hearted beauty, seeks revenge on his rival, a generous and much-admired new arrival with a dark past, only to find his own aunt aiding the young lovers' escape. Such novels usually feature a decaying manor, family scandal, and scheming relatives. But more frequently Lowndes depends on psychological portraits and ironic twists: an unexpected call announcing death traps a philanderer who has seduced his best friend's wife; another philanderer, dependent on the security of a bedridden wife to protect him from his various conquests' demands for marriage, finds one lover who takes his toying all too seriously, murders his wife, and leaves him to face the consequences; a betrayed wife realizes her own responsibility for her divorced husband's acts and, upon the death of his second wife, hesitantly returns to his arms; a wealthy widow, upon learning her ex-lover has seduced her daughter into a secret engagement, executes their mutual lover—for her daughter's sake; a greedy woman, obsessed by money, starves herself to death; thereafter, her bereaved husband squanders the hard-earned wealth on a poor, young, neighboring beauty (*Some Men and Women*). Often they verge on the gothic: a spoiled, self-righteous prude seeking revenge for her husband's infidelity in an illicit affair is warned from the act by the ghost of a woman whose illicit love she had once condemned; her insane husband having decapitated his rival in love, a terrified wife must return the head to the scene of horror to hide her shame and protect her family; a submarine captain and his mistress share a final farewell as the ship sinks, and the proud and loveless husband must use his wits to hide the scandal and preserve his honor (*Studies in Love and Terror*). The last focuses on the husband's guilt in the affair, and the cold self-possession that clearly alienated his gentle wife and allowed him to take the horror of her death so calmly. Always secret sins have public repercussions, and reputation is almost as important as survival.

Duchess Laura and *Duchess Laura: Further Days from Her Life*, sum up the contrast in generations, the first focusing on the very proper romance and marriage of a Victorian lady, the second, portraying episodically her forced readjustment to a changing world as she saves her son from a loveless marriage, helps an adventuress afford her true love, rescues a cynical young girl from the loathsome advances of a rich lecher, brings together an overprotected blind girl and a bitter, horribly scarred heir, prevents a repressed neice from poisoning her cantankerous old aunt, and faces the shock of her son wedding a poor, unattractive, roadhouse worker for her kindness and intelligence rather than family or beauty. Her difficulties in adjusting to the new morality and the breakdown of class differences among the younger generation are typical of the conflicts facing many of Lowndes's characters. *The Christine Diamond*, like many of her crime romances, deals with love beyond class bounds and the social patterns and taboos of upstairs/downstairs, as a rich young playboy takes pity on, then falls in love with, his aunt's secretary, to find he can win her love only by finding a stolen diamond and a clever thief. In *Reckless Angel* a spoiled debutante, moving in a rich, fast crowd, develops a reputation for carefree, thoughtless acts, yet becomes enamoured of a steady, puritanical naval officer whose only flaw is moral bondage to a grasping older woman; only involvement in murder and theft, and the near loss of love and reputation finally teach her to be more careful of her loyalties. In *Love Is a Flame*, an unusual mixture of the highly cynical and highly romantic, a hard-working young woman's honesty sends her lover into the arms of a spoiled and petulant acquaintance who marries him on a whim, then sends him to possible death; only after blackmail, murder, suicide, and a blinding, crippling war injury does true love win out.

Thus, Lowndes portrays sympathetically domestic conflicts between generations, classes, and sexes; the misunderstandings and rationale of love; the attraction of opposites; the disillusionment of the naive; and the rewards of the faithful. With its commonplace horrors and its focus on the contradictory impulses of individuals, her canon reflects the war-induced breakdown of moral codes and the consequent confusion of decent characters caught in a morass of dimly understood shifting values. As a result, her work speaks to our time as well as her own.

—Gina Macdonald

LURGAN, Lester. See **WYNNE, May.**

LUTYENS, Mary. See **WYNDHAM, Esther.**

LYALL, David. See **SWAN, Annie S.**

LYNN, Margaret. Pseudonym for Gladys Starkey Battye. British. Born in Halifax, Yorkshire, in 1915. Worked as a textile designer and hotelier. *Died.*

ROMANCE AND HISTORICAL PUBLICATIONS

Novels

To See a Stranger. London, Hodder and Stoughton, 1961; New York, Doubleday, 1962.
Stranger by Night. London, Hodder and Stoughton, 1963; as *Mrs. Maitland's Affair*, New York, Doubleday, 1963.
Whisper of Darkness. London, Hodder and Stoughton, 1965; New York, Paperback Library, 1966.
A Light in the Window. London, Hodder and Stoughton, 1967; New York, Doubleday, 1968.
Sunday Evening. London, Hodder and Stoughton, 1969; New York, Doubleday, 1971.
Sweet Epitaph. London, Hodder and Stoughton, 1971; New York, Doubleday, 1972.

*   *   *

Margaret Lynn's novels of suspense appeal to all our latent paranoia. Her typical heroine is an isolated woman, surrounded by people she cannot trust, who suspect her of things she is certain she did not do, although the pressure of their suspicions sometimes forces her to question her own sanity. Lynn involves us totally with her heroine, and the reader believes in her despite her invidious position (for often enough we find the heroine is concealing something); because of this identification with the heroine, the level of suspense is high.

Her first novel, *To See a Stranger*, is her best. In it, a woman wakes up thinking she is a 20-year-old girl about to be married, and discovers she is instead a 40-year-old matron married to a man she dislikes; worse, she finds she does not like the person she apparently is. There is a claustrophobic feeling here, as we enter the mind of a woman convinced she must be going mad. In *Whisper of Darkness* a woman who all her life has been despised and bullied marries to achieve freedom and finds she is still tied by the terms of a will both to the house she hates and to her husband; to make things worse, everyone around her believes her responsible for a series of increasingly malicious tricks culminating in murder attempts on her husband. *A Light in the Window* deals with the wife of an Englishman accused of being a communist spy. Her life is threatened by a communist organization, while the police do not believe in her innocence. In *Sunday Evening* a woman recovering from a nervous breakdown is suspected of the kidnap-murder of a child; her mind still clouded by her emotional breakdown, she not only cannot prove her innocence, but is not at all certain she *is* innocent. *Sweet Epitaph* is the least successful of her suspense novels, and much more akin to the conventional murder mystery. A woman is held captive for 42 days by unknown persons, apparently to keep her from seeing a dying relative who might alter his will in her favor. As in all Lynn's novels, truth is elusive and constantly shifting, and no one is to be trusted.

Few writers of Gothics have managed to create as much suspense and emotional involvement as Lynn has.

—Marylaine Block

LYTLE, Andrew (Nelson). American. Born in Murfreesboro, Tennessee, 26 December 1902. Educated at Sewanee Military Academy, Tennessee; Exeter College, Oxford, 1920; Vanderbilt University, Nashville, B.A. 1925 (Phi Beta Kappa); Yale University School of Drama, New Haven, Connecticut, 1927–29. Married Edna Langdon Barker in 1938 (died 1963); three daughters. Professor of History, Southwestern College, Memphis, Tennessee, 1936; Professor of History, University of the South, Sewanee, Tennessee, and managing editor, *Sewanee Review*, 1942–43; Lecturer, 1946–48, and Acting Head, 1947–48, University of Iowa School of Writing, Iowa City; Lecturer in Creative Writing, University of Florida, Gainesville, 1948–61; Lecturer in English, 1961–67, and Professor of English, 1968–73, University of the South, and editor, *Sewanee Review*, 1961–73. Recipient: Guggenheim fellowship, 1940, 1941, 1960; National Endowment for the Arts grant, 1966; University of the South Brown fellowship, 1978, 1981; Lyndhurst Foundation prize, 1985; Ingersoll Foundation prize, 1986. Litt.D.: Kenyon College, Gambier, Ohio, 1965; University of Florida, 1970; University of the South, 1973; D.H.L.: Hillsdale College, Michigan, 1985. Address: Department of English, University of the South, Sewanee, Tennessee 37375; or, Log Cabin, Monteagle, Tennessee 37356, U.S.A.

ROMANCE AND HISTORICAL PUBLICATIONS

Novels

The Long Night. Indianapolis, Bobbs Merrill, 1936; London, Eyre and Spottiswoode, 1937.
At the Moon's Inn. Indianapolis, Bobbs Merrill, 1941; London, Eyre and Spottiswoode, 1943.
A Name for Evil. Indianapolis, Bobbs Merrill, 1947.
The Velvet Horn. New York, McDowell Obolensky, 1957.

Short Stories

A Novel, A Novella and Four Stories. New York, McDowell Obolensky, 1958.
Alchemy. Winston-Salem, North Carolina, Palaemon Press, 1979.
Stories: Alchemy and Others. Sewanee, Tennessee, University of the South, 1984.

OTHER PUBLICATIONS

Other

Bedford Forrest and His Critter Company (biography). New York, Minton Balch, 1931; London, Eyre and Spottiswoode, 1939; revised edition, New York, McDowell Obolensky, 1960.
The Hero with the Private Parts: Essays (literary criticism). Baton Rouge, Louisiana State University Press, 1966.
A Wake for the Living: A Family Chronicle. New York, Crown, 1975.
The Lytle/Tate Letters, with Allen Tate, edited by Thomas Daniel Young and Elizabeth Sarcone. Jackson, University Press of Mississippi, 1987.
Southerners and Europeans: Essays in a Time of Disorder. Baton Rouge, Louisiana State University Press, 1988.

Editor, *Craft and Vision: The Best Fiction from The Sewanee Review*. New York, Delacorte Press, 1971.

*

Bibliography: *An Andrew Lytle Checklist* by Jack De Bellis, Charlottesville, Bibliographical Society of the University of Virginia, 1960; *Andrew Nelson Lytle: A Bibliography 1920–1982* by Stuart Wright, Sewanee, Tennessee, University of the South, 1982; *Andrew Lytle, Walker Percy, Peter Taylor: A Reference Guide* by Victor A. Kramer, Boston, Hall, 1983.

Manuscript Collections: Joint University Libraries (Vanderbilt University), Nashville, Tennessee; University of Florida Library, Gainesville.

Critical Studies: "Andrew Lytle Issue" of *Mississippi Quarterly* (State College), Fall 1970; *The Form Discovered: Essays on the Achievement of Andrew Lytle* edited by M. E. Bradford, Jackson, University and College Press of Mississippi, 1973; "Novels as History: The Art of Andrew Lytle" by Gregory Wolfe, in *Continuity* (Bryn Mawr, Pennsylvania), Fall 1984.

*   *   *

Influenced by both the Fugitive and Agrarian movements of the early 20th century in America, Andrew Lytle was intensely southern, his works often speaking for the nature and quality of the southern way of life, past and present, antebellum and modern. In the largest sense his historical novels constitute direct or subliminal defenses of the southern identity in the presence of a threatening but blandly homogenous American one.

The Long Night, which suggests the novelist's familiarity with Senecan drama, is a revenge tragedy set during the Civil War. Unified by the narrator Pleasant McIvor, the novel, with particularly moving Civil War battle scenes, is the history of family duty, including revenge for a murdered father. The plot for the novel was suggested by Lytle's friend, historian Frank Owsley.

The novel, however, transcends the limitations of Senecan convention in its theme of moral responsibility which is brought sharply to focus in Pleasant McIvor's conflict between a family duty of personal revenge and his larger responsibility in the war . . . symbolic of the war's destruction of the code-sanctioned values of the Old South.

At the Moon's Inn which chronicles the quest of DeSoto in 16th-century Florida, speaks in a theme consistent with southern thought. In 1938 Lytle, for example, wrote to his editor D. L. Chambers that "the new world will be seen as the old world's sin, even its destruction." The relationship of past to present, though subliminal in the novel, may be viewed as the clash between the Agrarians of the south and contemporary American industrialization and commerce. In his materialistic quest DeSoto violates all the Agrarian sentiments, destroying much that was beautiful in the native tradition of the Seminoles.

A Name for Evil, may well be the least effective novel Lytle wrote. It is, nonetheless, as one critic noted, an "unflinching look at the ambiguities of a Southern allegiance that craves the past" as well as a criticism of betrayal of land and family. When the troubled narrator buys and restores a country house, he becomes obsessed with the past (the psychological ghost of the house) and order. Obsession with the past results in the narrator's wife's death, a psychology reminiscent, as critics further note, of James's "A Turn of the Screw."

The Velvet Horn is Lytle's masterpiece. Set in rural, late 19th-century Tennessee, the novel follows Lucius Cree's maturation into the attainment of harmony and a recognition of how to live with others. The novel, however, is not limited to maturation alone, since it epitomizes yearning for paradise, for innocence and wholeness. The hero's real growth is consequently dependent upon his acceptance of man's fallen condition and redemption in Christ.

With its rich symbolism and myth, clearly developed character, and acute historical awareness, *The Velvet Horn* remains Lytle's greatest achievement in historical writing. Its adroit intermingling of past and present and subtle and direct references to incest—literal and symbolic—make it a classic in the southern canon.

—George C. Longest

MACARDLE, Dorothy (Margaret Callan). Irish. Born in 1899. Educated at University College, Dublin. Active in the Irish nationalist movement: jailed; taught at Alexandra College; became a journalist: correspondent at the League of Nations, Geneva; after World War II worked with displaced and refugee children. *Died 23 December 1958.*

ROMANCE AND HISTORICAL PUBLICATIONS

Novels

Uneasy Freehold. London, Davies, 1941; as *The Uninvited,* New York, Doubleday, 1942.
The Seed Was Kind. London, Davies, 1944.
Fantastic Summer. London, Davies, 1946; as *The Unforeseen,* New York, Doubleday, 1946.
Dark Enchantment. London, Davies, and New York, Doubleday, 1953.

Short Stories

Earth-Bound: Nine Stories of Ireland. Worcester, Massachusetts, Harrigan Press, 1924.

OTHER PUBLICATIONS

Plays

Atonement (produced Dublin, 1918).
Asthara (produced Dublin, 1918).
Ann Kavanagh (produced Dublin, 1922). New York, French, 1937.
The Old Man (produced Dublin, 1925).
Witch's Brew. London, Deane, 1931.
The Children's Guest (for children). London, Oxford University Press, 1940.
The Loving-Cup (for children). London, Nelson, 1943.

Other

Tragedies of Kerry 1922–1923. Dublin, Emton Press, 1924.
The Irish Republic: A Documented Chronicle of the Anglo-Irish Conflict and the Partitioning of Ireland, with a Detailed Account of the Period 1916–1923. London, Gollancz, 1937; New York, Farrar Straus, 1965.
Without Fanfares: Some Reflections on the Republic of Eire. Dublin, Gill, 1946.
Children of Europe: A Study of the Children of Liberated Countries . . . . London, Gollancz, 1949; Boston, Beacon Press, 1951.
Shakespeare, Man and Boy, edited by George Bott. London, Faber, 1961.

*   *   *

Although Dorothy Macardle has written a long history of the Irish state and has been a performed playwright, she is best-remembered as the author of the supernatural romance *Uneasy Freehold* which was made into a successful motion picture. Essentially a story of the persistence of emotions (expressed in fantastic terms), it describes the blighting effect of a haunting on what would otherwise have been a smooth, happy romance and marriage. For years Stella has been kept away from her dead father's closed house. When she enters, she awakens a haunting and her life is threatened. A mystery emerges, the solution to which is not likely to astonish the reader familiar with gothic devices. Instead, the reader is more likely to be impatient at the author's inability to characterize a male narrator. All in all, the motion picture *The Uninvited* (1944) is superior to the book.

A second supernatural novel, *Fantastic Summer* set in Ireland, is based on complications caused by the sudden emergence of the second sight. Virgilia Wilde is afflicted by premonitory visions that at first are only annoying, but become nightmarish when she foresees her daughter being strangled by her fiancé. (The situation is reminiscent of Hector Bolitho's "The House on Half-Moon Street.") The daughter's romance is interwoven with episodes of Virgilia's uncomfortable gift. Technically, the book is weaker than *Uneasy Freehold*, what with a feeble story line, flaccid characterizations, and excessive sentimentality. A foreword states that the story is based on fact, but it is not known whether this statement is meant seriously or is a literary device.

A third novel, *Dark Enchantment*, is set in the Maritime Alps of France. It has two themes, the maturation of a young Englishwoman tourist who stays in the area to become a helper in an inn, and the presence of ambivalent evil in the person of a gypsy witch. The witch's activities arouse the latent fears and brutalities of the natives. Treatment of both themes is superficial and confused, while the peasants are pallid if compared with similar types in the work of Ramuz.

—E. F. Bleiler

MACAULAY, (Emilie) Rose. British. Born in Rugby, Warwickshire, 1 August 1881; lived with her family in Varazze, Italy, 1887–94. Educated at Oxford High School for Girls, 1894–99; Somerville College, Oxford, 1900–03. Full-time writer from 1903; lived in Wales, 1903–05, Cambridgeshire, 1905–16, Beaconsfield, 1916–25, and London from 1925; worked in a hospital, as a land girl, in the War Office, and in the Ministry of Information, during World War I; publisher's reader for Constable, London, 1919; special reporter, London *Daily Chronicle*, in Geneva, 1925; columnist ("Marginal Comments"), *Spectator*, London, 1935–36. Recipient: Femina-Vie Heureuse prize, 1922; James Tait Black Memorial prize, 1957. D.Litt.: Cambridge University, 1951. D.B.E. (Dame Commander, Order of the British Empire), 1958. *Died 30 October 1958.*

ROMANCE AND HISTORICAL PUBLICATIONS

Novel

They Were Defeated. London, Collins, 1932; as *The Shadow Flies*, New York, Harper, 1932.

OTHER PUBLICATIONS

Novels

Abbots Verney. London, Murray, 1906.
The Furnace. London, Murray, 1907.
The Secret River. London, Murray, 1909.
The Valley Captives. London, Murray, and New York, Holt, 1911.
Views and Vagabonds. London, Murray, and New York, Holt, 1912.
The Lee Shore. London, Hodder and Stoughton, and New York, Doran, 1912.
The Making of a Bigot. London, Hodder and Stoughton, 1914.
What Not: A Prophetic Comedy. London, Constable, 1918.
Potterism: A Tragi-Farcical Tract. London, Collins, and New York, Boni and Liveright, 1920.
Dangerous Ages. London, Collins, and New York, Boni and Liveright, 1921.
Mystery at Geneva. London, Collins, 1922; New York, Boni and Liveright, 1923.
Told by an Idiot. London, Collins, and New York, Boni and Liveright, 1923.
Orphan Island. London, Collins, 1924; New York, Boni and Liveright, 1925.
Crewe Train. London, Collins, and New York, Boni and Liveright, 1926.
Keeping Up Appearances. London, Collins, 1928; as *Daisy and Daphne*, New York, Boni and Liveright, 1928.
Staying with Relations. London, Collins, and New York, Liveright, 1930.
Going Abroad. London, Collins, and New York, Harper, 1934.
I Would Be Private. London, Collins, and New York, Harper, 1937.
And No Man's Wit. London, Collins, and Boston, Little Brown, 1940.
The World My Wilderness. London, Collins, and Boston, Little Brown, 1950.
The Towers of Trebizond. London, Collins, 1956; New York, Farrar Straus, 1957.

Short Stories

Non-Combatants and Others. London, Hodder and Stoughton, 1916.

Verse

The Two Blind Countries. London, Sidgwick and Jackson, 1914.
Three Days. London, Constable, 1919.
(Poems). London, Benn, 1927.

Other

A Casual Commentary (essays). London, Methuen, 1925; New York, Boni and Liveright, 1926.
Catchwords and Claptrap (essays). London, Hogarth Press, 1926.
Some Religious Elements in English Literature. London, Hogarth Press, and New York, Harcourt Brace, 1931.
Milton. London, Duckworth, 1934; New York, Harper, 1935; revised edition, Duckworth, and New York, Macmillan, 1957.
Personal Pleasures. London, Gollancz, 1935; New York, Macmillan, 1936.

An Open Letter to a Non-Pacifist. London, Peace Pledge Union, 1937.
The Writings of E. M. Forster. London, Hogarth Press, and New York, Harcourt Brace, 1938.
Life among the English. London, Collins, 1942.
They Went to Portugal. London, Cape, 1946.
Fabled Shore: From the Pyrenees to Portugal. London, Hamish Hamilton, 1949; New York, Farrar Straus, 1951.
Pleasure of Ruins. London, Weidenfeld and Nicolson, 1953; New York, Walker, 1966; edited by Constance Babington Smith, London, Thames and Hudson, and New York, Holt Rinehart, 1977.
Letters to a Friend 1950–1952 and *Last Letters to a Friend 1952–1958* (to J. H. C. Johnson), edited by Constance Babington Smith. London, Collins, 2 vols., 1961–62; New York, Atheneum, 2 vols., 1962–63.
Letters to a Sister (to Jean Macaulay), edited by Constance Babington Smith. London, Collins, and New York, Atheneum, 1964.

Editor, *The Minor Pleasures of Life*. London, Gollancz, 1934; New York, Harper, 1935.
Editor, with Daniel George, *All in a Maze: A Collection of Prose and Verse*. London, Collins, 1938.

*

Critical Studies: *Rose Macaulay* by Alice R. Bensen, New York, Twayne, 1969; *Rose Macaulay* (biography) by Constance Babington Smith, London, Collins, 1972; *Eros and Androgyny: The Legacy of Rose Macaulay* by Jeanette N. Passty, Rutherford, New Jersey, Fairleigh Dickinson University Press, 1988.

*   *   *

Rose Macaulay's one historical novel, *They Were Defeated*, was her own favourite among her works, and testifies to her love for and knowledge of the early 17th century, a knowledge equally apparent in her anthology, *The Minor Pleasures of Life*, published two years later. The story of *They Were Defeated* takes place during the period immediately prior to the outbreak of the English Civil War, and centres on the fortunes and aspirations of Julian Conybeare, the 15-year-old daughter of a country doctor, who comes to Cambridge from Devonshire to visit her undergraduate brother, only to fall in love with his tutor, the cynical and worldly poet, John Cleveland. The novel contrasts the backward life of the rural West Country with the intellectual tumult of a university divided in its political and religious allegiances. The central section of the book is dense with discussion and debate, the historian rather than the novelist being most in evidence; and the narrative emphasises the continuing relevance of the issues which move and divide the characters. The latter include such well-known individuals as John Milton, Andrew Marvell, Richard Crashaw, John Suckling, Abraham Cowley, Kenelm Digby, and Henry More, and at times the text becomes implausibly burdened with celebrities. But there is a feeling of genuine authenticity where physical settings and domestic details are concerned, and Macauley claimed that she had not given her characters any words to speak that would not have been in use at the time.

The Devonshire scenes are equally persuasive. Here the central character is Robert Herrick, vicar of Dean Prior; he is presented as very much a man of his time in his conservatism, yet full of commonsense, wary of the superstition of his parishioners, and attempting to succour the victim of a witch-hunt while remaining resistant to the open scepticism of Julian's father.

Julian's brother, on the other hand, becomes a Roman Catholic; and the activities of the Jesuits in Cambridge form a significant thread in a narrative that also takes into account the happenings in London, such as the calling of the Long Parliament, the attainder of Strafford, and the arrest of Land, which determine directly or indirectly the fates of all the characters.

Julian's father, the doctor, is a humanitarian sceptic, whose easy-going attitude to belief brings disaster on those he loves; the origins of this subtly drawn portrait may be found in the social and religious radicalism of the time of Macaulay's youth. Her own sympathies with the Anglican ideals of liberal catholicism, of moderation and intellectual integrity, are in evidence throughout. In the character of Julian, Macaulay provides a portrait of a girl whose intellectual and artistic gifts are thwarted and tragically frustrated by the age in which she lives; in this respect *They Were Defeated* could be described as a feminist historical novel. Cleveland's refusal to take Julian's poems and treatise seriously makes familiarly painful reading. Another feminist aspect is seen in the character of Julian's tomboy friend, the squire's granddaughter, chafing against the relentless social customs which entrap her. One of the merits of the novel is the way in which the relationships between the characters are themselves seen as aspects of the time: Macaulay's people are not so much perennial types as such as modifications of those types in 17th century terms.

Macaulay makes telling use of the conflict in Herrick's own character, as evident in his two collections of poems, the secular *Hesperides* and the sacred *Noble Numbers*; she quotes from them in the text and even ascribes the "Elegy on Strafford" (one of Cleveland's doubtfully authentic poems) to her fictional heroine. Accounts of clothing, furnishing, food, and household work are slipped in at every turn in the story, rather in the style of the 19th-century historical novelist Anne Manning, whose *The Household of Sir Thomas More* (1852) and *Mary Powell* (1849) appeared in Everyman's Library in 1906 and 1908 respectively, and which Macaulay would probably have known. A similar blend of sympathy and unpedantic learning characterizes her own work in the field.

—Glen Cavaliero

MACBETH, Madge (Hamilton). Also wrote as W. S. Dill; Gilbert Knox. Canadian. Born in Philadelphia, Pennsylvania, United States, in 1878. Educated privately; at Helmuth College, London, Ontario. Married Charles Macbeth; two sons. Past president of the Canadian Authors Association.

ROMANCE AND HISTORICAL PUBLICATIONS

Novels

The Winning Game. New York, Broadway, 1910.
Kleath. Boston, Small Maynard, 1917.
The Patterson Limit. Toronto, Hodder and Stoughton, 1923.
The Land of Afternoon (as Gilbert Knox). Ottawa, Graphic, 1925.
Shackles. Ottawa, Graphic, 1926; New York, Waterson, 1927.
The Great Fright; Onesiphore, Our Neighbor, with A. B. Conway. Montreal, Carrier, 1929; *Onesiphore, Our Neighbor* published as *Your Neighbour*, London, Stanley Paul, 1929.
The Kinder Bees (as Gilbert Knox). London, Dickson and Thompson, 1935.

Wings in the West. London, John Hamilton, 1937.
Shreds of Circumstance. London, W. H. Allen, 1947.
Lost: A Cavalier. London, W. H. Allen, 1948.

OTHER PUBLICATIONS

Play

Curiosity Rewarded (as Gilbert Knox). Ottawa, Graphic, 1926.
The Goose's Sauce. Toronto, French, 1935.

Other

The Long Day (reminiscences of the Yukon; as W. S. Dill). Ottawa, Graphic, 1926.
Over the Gangplank to Spain. Ottawa, Graphic, 1931.
Over My Shoulder (autobiography). Toronto, Ryerson Press, 1953.
Boulevard Career. Toronto, Kingswood House, 1957.

*   *   *

Madge Macbeth stretched the idea of the "historical" novel to include the history of the idea of femininity and its impact on women's lives in the first half of the 20th century. Although documenting her own times, an historical perspective forms the core of all her novels. Macbeth uses plot twists and fine psychological detail to construct and then to question the conventions which determine the reader's expectations. She does this by denying the comic ending, the anticipated happy marriage of the central female character. Romance conventions are undermined further by frank references to women's sexual desire and experience and to the hypocritical social and cultural mores which repress women's natural physicality. *The Great Fright* and *Wings in the West* excepted, her novels develop a plot and psychological framework in which a female character is central.

Kleath and *Wings in the West* are adventure novels of the Canadian Klondike and of northern Ontario, respectively. *Wings in the West*, an action-oriented novel is not particularly effective. In concrete description of winter in a northern Canadian forest and in reference to the newly discovered potential of the uranium deposits, however, the novel does succeed in giving the reader a sense of the still unexplored north of this period. *Wings in the West* and *The Great Fright*, episodic and written in French-Canadian dialect, are Macbeth's least satisfying novels. *Kleath*, a very enjoyable novel of gold rush days, is based on the mystery surrounding Kleath's past. Conflict develops between Clare and Goldie. While these latter two characters are represented mainly within a conventional angel/monster dualism, the narrator's commentary does not allow complacent acceptance of this contrast. A third female character, Kleath's wife recently released from prison, disrupts our expectations and gives the marriage of Goldie and Kleath, reported on the last page, a sense of closure that is technically, but not emotionally, achieved.

The Kinder Bees and *The Land of Afternoon* are bitingly witty satires of politics and culture in Canada's capital city, Ottawa. In using a masculine pseudonym, Gilbert Knox, perhaps Macbeth had in mind Sara Jeannette Duncan's *The Imperialist* (1904), which was ridiculed from the position that, as a woman, the author could not understand political issues and, therefore, should not have attempted to represent them. A permanent resident of Ottawa, Macbeth was able to pack these two well-crafted novels with local detail and a sense of moment that are fundamental to the historical novel form. In both novels, Macbeth's critique of the government, the sphere of men, is balanced by an equally acerbic view of the social hierarchy, the sphere of women.

The Patterson Limit and *The Winning Game* explore the boundaries of women's sphere. In both novels the main characters are given sexually indeterminate names, Ray Lane and Leslie Loring, respectively. *The Winning Game*, Macbeth's first novel, presents a woman's life as determined by her relationship to men; *The Patterson Limit* presents a woman determining her life in terms of her own ideas and desires. Both novels are skillfully constructed and powerfully evoke contrasting and specific historical moments in women's thinking about themselves.

Shreds of Circumstance stretches the conventions of romance writing insofar as the central female character, Dagmar Kalany, has several sexual encounters, enjoys them all, and remains unmarried and happy at the end. Dagmar, her mother Nena, and friend Ellen, each represent different ideas of femininity. For all three characters, social and cultural expectations of women conflict with each woman's sense of personal happiness. Through Dagmar's cosmopolitanism, Macbeth avoids promoting any one national cultural or social model and suggests, therefore, the shared frustrations facing women in Europe and North America at the time between the two world wars.

Lost: A Cavalier and *Shackles*, Macbeth's best work, deal with women writers. Both novels are finely-wrought and develop excruciating tension. Both present female characters, Stephanie Barstow and Naomi Lennox, respectively, trapped by a man in an intolerable relationship that is both a perfection and perversion of accepted social and cultural conventions, including those of realist fiction. Prefacing *Shackles*, Macbeth notes that "Woman is passing though a cultural transition. Instinctively, she is bound to the old order of things; intellectually, she clamours for the new. And vacillating, she stands between them." Thus her female characters are estranged psychologically from the femininity they must enact. Macbeth not only achieves the idea of objective distance required to give the reader a sense of history revisited necessary to the historical novel form but also makes us aware that, in her own work, this distance is both because of and made problematic by a woman's point of view.

—Heather Iris Jones

MACDONALD, Marcia. See **HILL, Grace Livingston.**

MacGILL, Mrs. Patrick (Margaret MacGill, née Gibbons).

ROMANCE AND HISTORICAL PUBLICATIONS

Novels

The Rose of Glenconnel. London, Thomson, 1916.
An Anzac's Bride. London, Jenkins, 1917.
Whom Love Hath Chosen. London, Jenkins, 1919.
The Bartered Bride. London, Jenkins, 1920.
Each Hour a Peril. London, Thomson, 1921.
The Flame of Life. London, Jenkins, 1921.
Hidden Fires. London, Jenkins, 1921.
The Highest Bidder. London, Thomson, 1921.
His Dupe. London, Thomson, 1922.

Molly of the Lone Pine. London, Thomson, 1922.
Shifting Sands. London, Jenkins, 1922.
A Lover on Loan. London, Jenkins, 1923.
Her Undying Past. London, Jenkins, 1924.
Love—and Carol. London, Jenkins, 1925.
Her Dancing Partner. London, Jenkins, 1926.
Love's Defiance. London, Thomson, 1926.
The Ukelele Girl. London, Jenkins, 1927; as *His Ukelele Girl*, London, Thomson, 1927.
Dancers in the Dark. London, Jenkins, 1929.
Painted Butterflies. London, Jenkins, 1931.
Hollywood Madness. London, Jenkins, 1936; as *Hollywood Star Dust*, New York, Chelsea House, 1936.

OTHER PUBLICATIONS

Other

The "Good-Night" Stories (for children; as Margaret Gibbons). London, Year Book Press, 1912.

*　　*　　*

Mrs. Patrick MacGill's first book, *The "Good-Night" Stories*, was a collection of stories for children. It has a stories-within-a-story framework, and is set in the Vane household whose numerous children are told bedtime stories by their mother before the Golden Dustman comes to throw magic dust on their eyes and send them to the enchanted realm of Slumberland. The stories are chiefly about fairies—"The bluebells tinkle merrily, and the fairies and elves form a ring round the Queen, who always sailed down in the moon to these gatherings (*sc.* on Hampstead Heath)."

MacGill went from writing fairy stories for children to writing fairy stories for adults. Her romantic novels, which appeared between 1916 and 1936, are highly melodramatic, as their titles suggest. The plots are packed with incident—the result of genteel poverty, gambling fathers, spendthrift siblings, rascally employers, false accusations, bankruptcy, intrigue, treachery, deceit, gangsters—so that the hero and heroine are kept well apart until the final chapters.

The heroines of the earlier novels tend to be either unprotected orphan girls (such as the Rose of Glenconnel, born Rosalie Moran, who was brought up on a mining and lumber camp in the Yukon and turns out to be the grand-daughter of a baronet) or young wives having trouble with their husbands (through shell-shock or a forced marriage). The heroines of the later novels (with an eye to changing social conditions) are in paid employment, doing jobs which are quite advanced for the time, glamorous, or even daring—"girl clerk," assistant in a Bond Street hat shop, society dress designer, Exhibition Dancer in a night club, film actress. Though the heroines do not vary much in type, their settings do, from the Canadian backwoods, to titled circles in London, to Hollywood. MacGill seems to have been particularly smitten by "the Tinsel Kingdom, Filmdom's capital," and much of the action in her last two novels takes place in Hollywood, where (of course) two of her earlier works, *The Flame of Life* and *Hidden Fires*, are being turned into films. A *Times Literary Supplement* reviewer had already accused her of having an eye to "another mode of presentation than that of print" (1924 review of *Her Undying Past*).

Her literary style was as melodramatic as her plots, and did not change much over 20 novels: "She was shy now, this fragrant, beautiful little bride, and a burning, blushing face was pressed close to Ronald's breast. But the young trapper, with eyes and heart aflame, bent down and raised his wife's face to his own . . . (*The Rose of Glenconnel*, 1916); or " 'Let me look after you, sweetheart.' The low, deep voice was vibrant with passion, but very kindly and tender . . . as, stemming the tide of his own desire to press wild ecstatic kisses on the soft red mouth, he said, 'You are afraid of love, Peggy . . . ' " (*Hollywood Madness*, 1936).

—Jean Buchanan

MacINNES, Colin. British. Born Colin McInnes in London, 20 August 1914; son of the writer Angela Thirkell and the singer James Campbell McInnes; moved to Australia, 1920. Educated at Grimwade House and Scotch College, both Melbourne. Served in the British Army, 1939–40, and the Intelligence Corps, 1941–46: Sergeant. Returned to England, 1930; staff member, Imperial Continental Gas Association, Antwerp and Brussels, 1931–36; studied painting, Chelsea Polytechnic and Euston Road School of Painting and Drawing, both London, 1936–38; free-lance journalist and broadcaster in London, 1946–69, and in Folkestone, Kent, from 1970. *Died 23 April 1976.*

ROMANCE AND HISTORICAL PUBLICATIONS

Novels

Westward to Laughter. London, MacGibbon and Kee, 1969; New York, Farrar Straus, 1970.
Three Years to Play. London, MacGibbon and Kee, and New York, Farrar Straus, 1970.

OTHER PUBLICATIONS

Novels

To the Victors the Spoils. London, MacGibbon and Kee, 1950.
June in Her Spring. London, MacGibbon and Kee, 1952.
City of Spades. London, MacGibbon and Kee, 1957; New York, Macmillan, 1958.
Absolute Beginners. London, MacGibbon and Kee, 1959; New York, Macmillan, 1960.
Mr. Love and Justice. London, MacGibbon and Kee, 1960; New York, Dutton, 1961.
All Day Saturday. London, MacGibbon and Kee, 1966.
Visions of London (includes *City of Spades, Absolute Beginners, Mr. Love and Justice*). London, MacGibbon and Kee, 1969; as *The London Novels*, New York, Farrar Straus, 1969.
Out of the Garden. London, Hart Davis MacGibbon, 1974.

Other

England, Half English (essays). London, MacGibbon and Kee, 1961; New York, Random House, 1962.
London: City of Any Dream, photographs by Erwin Fieger. London, Thames and Hudson, 1962.
Australia and New Zealand, with the editors of *Life*. New York, Time, 1964.
Sweet Saturday Night. London, MacGibbon and Kee, 1967.
Loving Them Both: A Study of Bisexuality and Bisexuals. London, Martin Brian and O'Keeffe, 1974.
No Novel Reader. London, Martin Brian and O'Keeffe, 1975.

Out of the Way: Later Essays. London, Martin Brian and O'Keeffe, 1979.
Absolute MacInnes: The Best of Colin MacInnes, edited by Tony Gould. London, Allison and Busby, 1985.

*

Critical Study: *Inside Outsider: The Life and Times of Colin MacInnes* by Tony Gould, London, Chatto and Windus, 1983.

*   *   *

It is likely that Colin MacInnes will always be best remembered for his novels of swinging London of the 1950's, especially for *Absolute Beginners*, which was made into a film, and *June in Her Spring*, a more or less autobiographical romance set in Australia where the author spent a formative part of his youth.

The historical fiction of MacInnes has not been so well received, but it has a distinct quality and flavour of its own. *Westward to Laughter* is an intriguing work, in part a parody of children's adventure fiction and in part a philosophical fable. Alexander Nairn is a Scottish 16-year-old who is left an orphan after the Jacobite Rebellion of 1745 and turns to his rascally uncle for help. In no time at all he is embarked on a slave ship which crosses the Atlantic, making for the British West Indian Island of St. Laughter (hence travelling "westwards to Laughter"). The irony and the humour in the name are typical of the novel as a whole. A naive and seemingly irrepressibly optimistic observer of a world whose horrors are all too apparent to the reader, Alexander owes, as the author admits, much to Candide, the youthful hero of Voltaire's philosophical tale which is a devastating critique of 18th-century society. The first-person narration conveys a strange lack of awareness of horrors on every side, and so it is artfully left to the reader to respond in a more appropriate way. The language is not by any means a full-scale recreation of authentic period style, but words are used sparingly, in a manner which is often thought to be characteristic of the tight-lipped Scots, and the odd touch of historical colour—just spelling the adjective "pathetick" with that extra letter at the end, for instance—goes a long way to convey a sense of the past. The object is not so much to give an impression that this is indeed an 18th-century narration as to make it clear that this essentially tragic tale is in fact a comment on the predicaments of modern man. Alexander's faith in humanity and justice is assailed at every turn as he finds himself betrayed again and again, and his fate is to be hanged at the age of 19. There seems no escaping the conclusion that the world is in the grip of evil, and Alexander's faith in providence is shown to be quite vain. The juxtaposition of surface cheerfulness and deep-seated despair about the human condition is a very powerful device.

A young man is also the hero of MacInnes's second—and distinctly longer—historical novel, *Three Years to Play*, which appeared a year after *Westward to Laughter*, in 1970. The setting is England towards the end of the Elizabethan era, and MacInnes is, not unexpectedly, especially successful in recreating the atmosphere of the London underworld. The "Three Years to Play" of the title refer to the period of time during which the young Aubrey has to learn his skills as a boy-actor in the Shakesperean theatre and gain his fame. As well as some reflection of political conditions, the novel offers a portrayal of Shakespeare himself who finds in Aubrey's adventures the situations he was to develop in *As You Like It*, and this is the starting point for some consideration of the mechanisms of artistic production. MacInnes, who found much to admire in the freer moral attitudes of England in the late Renaissance, also takes the opportunity of exploring aspects of bisexuality. As in *Westward to Laughter* there is some control of language and style, if not to imitate the idiom of the day exactly, then at least to convey a pervading sense of the era in which the novel is set.

—Christopher Smith

MACKINLAY, Leila (Antoinette Sterling). Also writes as Brenda Grey. British. Born in London, 5 September 1910. Educated at Camden House School, London; trained as a singer and actress. Music critic, *Dancing Times*, 1935–39, and from 1946 for *Amateur Stage*; publishers reader, and drama and verse adjudicator. Recipient: Romantic Novelists Association President's prize, 1966. Address: 4-N Portman Mansions, Chiltern Street, London W1M 1LF, England.

ROMANCE AND HISTORICAL PUBLICATIONS

Novels

Little Mountebank. London, Mills and Boon, 1930.
Fame's Fetters. London, Mills and Boon, 1931.
Madame Juno. London, Mills and Boon, 1931.
An Exotic Young Lady. London, Mills and Boon, 1932.
Willed to Wed. London, Mills and Boon, 1933.
The Pro's Daughter. London, Ward Lock, 1934.
Shadow Lawn. London, Ward Lock, 1934.
Love Goes South. London, Ward Lock, 1935.
Into the Net. London, Ward Lock, 1935.
Night Bell. London, Ward Lock, 1936.
Young Man's Slave. London, Ward Lock, 1936.
Doubting Heart. London, Ward Lock, 1937.
Apron-Strings. London, Ward Lock, 1937.
Caretaker Within. London, Ward Lock, 1938.
Theme Song. London, Ward Lock, 1938.
Only Her Husband. London, Ward Lock, 1939.
The Reluctant Bride. London, Ward Lock, 1939.
Man Always Pays. London, Ward Lock, 1940.
Woman at the Wheel. London, Ward Lock, 1940.
Ridin' High. London, Ward Lock, 1941.
None Better Loved. London, Ward Lock, 1941.
Time on Her Hands. London, Ward Lock, 1942.
The Brave Live On. London, Ward Lock, 1942.
Green Limelight. London, Ward Lock, 1943.
Lady of the Torch. London, Ward Lock, 1944.
Two Walk Together. London, Ward Lock, 1945.
Piper's Pool. London, Ward Lock, 1946.
Piccadilly Inn. London, Ward Lock, 1946.
Blue Shutters. London, Ward Lock, 1947.
Echo of Applause. London, Ward Lock, 1948.
Peacock Hill. London, Ward Lock, 1948.
Restless Dream. London, Ward Lock, 1949.
Pilot's Point. London, Ward Lock, 1949.
Six Wax Candles. London, Ward Lock, 1950.
Spider Dance. London, Ward Lock, 1950.
Guilt's Pavilions. London, Ward Lock, 1951.
Five Houses. London, Ward Lock, 1952.
Unwise Wanderer. London, Ward Lock, 1952.
Cuckoo Cottage. London, Ward Lock, 1953.
She Married Another. London, Ward Lock, 1953.
Midnight Is Mine. London, Ward Lock, 1954.
Fiddler's Green. London, Ward Lock, 1954.

Vagabond Daughter. London, Ward Lock, 1955.
Riddle of a Lady. London, Ward Lock, 1955.
Man of the Moment. London, Ward Lock, 1956.
She Moved to Music. London, Ward Lock, 1956.
Divided Duty. London, Ward Lock, 1957.
Mantle of Innocence. London, Ward Lock, 1957.
Love on a Shoestring. London, Ward Lock, 1958.
The Secret in Her Life. London, Ward Lock, 1958.
Seven Red Roses. London, Ward Lock, 1959.
Uneasy Conquest. London, Ward Lock, 1959.
Food of Love. London, Ward Lock, 1960.
Spotlight on Susan. London, Ward Lock, 1960.
Beauty's Tears. London, Ward Lock, 1961.
Spring Rainbow. London, Ward Lock, 1961.
Vain Delights. London, Ward Lock, 1962.
Broken Armour. London, Ward Lock, 1963.
False Relations. London, Ward Lock, 1963.
Fool of Virtue. London, Ward Lock, 1964.
Practice for Sale. London, Ward Lock, 1964.
Ring of Hope. London, Ward Lock, 1965.
No Room for Loneliness. London, Ward Lock, 1965.
An Outside Chance. London, Ward Lock, 1966.
The Third Boat. London, Ward Lock, 1967.
Mists of the Moor. London, Ward Lock, 1967.
Frost at Dawn. London, Ward Lock, 1968.
Homesick for a Dream. London, Ward Lock, 1968.
Wanted—Girl Friday. London, Ward Lock, 1968.
Farewell to Sadness. London, Hale, 1970.
The Silken Purse. London, Hale, 1970.
Bridal Wreath. London, Hale, 1971.
Strange Involvement. London, Hale, 1972.
Birds of Silence. London, Hale, 1974.
Fortune's Slave. London, Hale, 1975.
Twilight Moment. London, Hale, 1976.
The Uphill Path. London, Hale, 1979.

Novels as Brenda Grey

Modern Micawbers. London, Eldon Press, 1933.
Stardust in Her Eyes. London, Gresham, 1964.
Girl of His Choice. London, Gresham, 1965.
How High the Moon. London, Gresham, 1966.
Throw Your Bouquet. London, Gresham, 1967.
A Very Special Person. London, Gresham, 1967.
Shadow of a Smile. London, Gresham, 1968.
Tread Softly on Dreams. London, Gresham, 1970.
Son of Summer. London, Gresham, 1970.
Mixed Singles. London, Gresham, 1971.
Husband in Name. London, Hale, 1972.

OTHER PUBLICATIONS

Other

Musical Productions. London, Jenkins, 1955.

*   *   *

Leila Mackinlay has had one of the longest careers of living romantic fiction writers. Her first novel, *Little Mountebank*, came out in 1930, and she continued writing until the late 1970's. She has also written fiction under the name of Brenda Grey and drama criticism. She received the Romantic Novelists Association President's prize in 1966.

Most of Mackinlay's novels concern the world of the theatre or singing, and her own training and involvement in the stage have served as a source of inspiration. Many of her books concern pupils or young entertainers. *An Exotic Young Lady*, for instance, is set in a popular environment of an Italian singing school in London and contains a very convincing description of this milieu.

The promotion of young and obscure theatrical talent has become a familiar theme, but there is a wide variety of plots, and love invariably is involved. In *Food of Love* the singer is a young miner and he has to be helped to overcome the disadvantages of his background and the jealous opposition of his small town fiancée. After the breaking off of the hero's engagement, a love triangle results between the hero's lady agent and her younger friend. The book is saved from being clichéd by a very sympathetic drawing of character, especially of the older woman whose attraction stirs in her long dormant feelings. A classic British theme of the time, the conflict between a rising hero and his working-class background is convincingly handled.

The world of the professional theatre can be inward looking but Mackinlay is able to give the reader a perspective on the life of a stage family in *An Outside Chance*. The position of second-team actors and actresses is convincingly summarized. The principal character, a young actress, is well drawn and shows us that she is quite normal and stable, somewhat against our expectations. True to a tradition in romance writing, glamour is pointed up by the grotesque: the heroine is the object of romantic advances from her fiancé's hideously crippled brother. The men are weak but the women are strong, and the heroine is able to cope with difficult situations and becomes the lynch pin of her own family.

True to the theatrical tradition, careers have their ups and downs. In *The Uphill Path* the heroine is able to turn round her fortunes and rebuild her career; although painful memories are recalled, she rediscovers and renews her original love affair.

As well as a very accurate background setting of the theatre, Mackinlay gives a considerable credibility in her novels to her characters. Unexpected depths are found in people and she shows the hard work necessary for success. Ordinary people outside show business come across very well, too, and display a mature and steady attitude to emotional relationships despite being, in some cases, just out of their teens. Some minor characters, for instance in *Fool of Virtue*, are glaring exceptions to this rule.

Dialogue does not overburden her books and is neither trite nor silly. The plots are interesting and credible. The narrative is well written although occasionally slow.

The great achievement of Mackinlay is to be able to keep her books up to date for each decade. The heroine in *An Exotic Young Lady* of 1932 is an orthodox girl of the decade. *None Better Loved* of 1941 has an appropriate setting of air raid shelters. In *The Uphill Path* (1979) the modern post-1960's pop scene, its mores and attendant problems for a girl, is very well drawn as is the character of the girl herself.

As befits the tradition of romantic novels, Mackinlay's have a moral but it is palatable and does not spoil a good story.

—P. R. Meldrum

MacLEOD, Charlotte (Matilda). Also writes as Alisa Craig; Matilda Hughes. American. Born in Bath, New Brunswick, Canada, 12 November 1922. Educated at public schools in Weymouth, Massachusetts; Art Institute of Boston. Staff member, later Vice-President, N.H. Miller, advertising agency, Boston, 1952–82. Lives in Sudbury, Massachusetts. Agent: Jed Mattes, International Creative Management, 40 West 57th Street, New York, New York 10019, U.S.A.

ROMANCE AND HISTORICAL PUBLICATIONS

Novels (series: Sarah Kelling; Peter Shandy)

Mystery of the White Knight. New York, Avalon, 1964.
The Food of Love (as Matilda Hughes). New York, Avalon, 1965.
Next Door to Danger. New York, Avalon, 1965.
Headlines for Caroline (as Matilda Hughes). New York, Avalon, 1967.
The Fat Lady's Ghost. New York, Weybright and Talley, 1968.
Ask Me No Questions. Philadelphia, Macrae Smith, 1971.
King Devil. New York, Atheneum, 1978.
Rest You Merry (Shandy). New York, Doubleday, 1978; London, Collins, 1979.
The Family Vault (Kelling). New York, Doubleday, 1979; London, Collins, 1980.
The Luck Runs Out (Shandy). New York, Doubleday, 1979; London, Collins, 1981.
We Dare Not Go a-Hunting. New York, Atheneum, 1980.
The Withdrawing Room (Kelling). New York, Doubleday, 1980; London, Collins, 1981.
The Palace Guard (Kelling). New York, Doubleday, 1981; London, Collins, 1982.
Wrack and Rune (Shandy). New York, Doubleday, and London, Collins, 1982.
The Bilbao Looking Glass (Kelling). New York, Doubleday, and London, Collins, 1983.
Something the Cat Dragged In (Shandy). New York, Doubleday, 1983; London, Collins, 1984.
The Convivial Codfish (Kelling). New York, Doubleday, and London, Collins, 1984.
The Curse of the Giant Hogweed (Shandy). New York, Doubleday, 1985.
The Plain Old Man (Kelling). New York, Doubleday, and London, Collins, 1985.
The Corpse in Oozak's Pond (Shandy). London, Collins, 1986; New York, Mysterious Press, 1987.
The Recycled Citizen (Kelling). London, Collins, 1987; New York, Mysterious Press, 1988.
The Silver Ghost (Kelling). London, Collins, 1987; New York, Mysterious Press, 1988.
Vane Pursuit (Shandy). New York, Mysterious Press, and London, Collins, 1989.

Novels as Alisa Craig (series: Lobelia Falls; Madoc Rhys)

A Pint of Murder (Rhys). New York, Doubleday, 1980.
The Grub-and-Stakers Move a Mountain (Lobelia Falls). New York, Doubleday, 1981.
Murder Goes Mumming (Rhys). New York, Doubleday, 1981.
The Terrible Tide. New York, Doubleday, 1983; London, Hale, 1985.
The Grub-and-Stakers Quilt a Bee (Lobelia Falls). New York, Doubleday, 1985.
A Dismal Thing to Do. New York, Doubleday, 1986.
The Grub-and-Stakers Pinch a Poke (Lobelia Falls). New York, Doubleday, 1988.

OTHER PUBLICATIONS

Other

Mouse's Vineyard (for children). New York, Weybright and Talley, 1968.
Brass Pounder (for children). Boston, Little Brown, 1971.
Astrology for Sceptics. New York, Macmillan, 1972; London, Turnstone, 1973.
Cirak's Daughter (for children). New York, Atheneum, 1982.
Maid of Honor (for children). New York, Atheneum, 1984.

*

Manuscript Collection: Mugar Memorial Library, Boston University.

*   *   *

Charlotte MacLeod, who becomes Alisa Craig when she writes about her native Canada, is unfailingly entertaining in whatever genre she chooses to write. It is hard to say what one most appreciates in her books: her witty dialogue, her characters, or her cheerfully cynical view of the world.

That some of her novels are classed as young adult fiction has more to do with the publishers' marketing strategy than substance; they are perfectly satisfactory to adult readers of romantic suspense. The Fat Lady's Ghost is the least successful of these; in it, a snobbish and egotistical heroine turns into a likable human being, while solving a mystery involving a jewel thief and a haunted kitchen. King Devil is both a pleasing romance and a study in the banality of evil; characters who at first appear only to be foolish and mildly malicious turn out to be murderously egocentric. We Dare Not Go a-Hunting offers romance, kidnapping, and conflict between the full-time residents and rich summer visitors on an island community.

MacLeod has written several mysteries involving Peter Shandy, professor of agrology at Balaclava College. In the first, Rest You Merry, Shandy goes maliciously overboard with his house decorations for the campus Grand Illuminations at Christmas. When he returns, he finds the campus busybody dead in his home, apparently fallen in the act of removing the offending decor. Peter correctly suspects murder, and aided by a charming librarian, investigates. The plot is funny, the characters interesting, and the romance delightful. The Luck Runs Out is even better, featuring a kidnapped sow, a murdered farrier, vigilant vegetarians, and three separate romances. It begins to challenge probability for so many murders to happen at Balaclava College, so in subsequent adventures (Wrack and Rune, Something the Cat Dragged In, and The Corpse in Oozak's Pond), Peter and his librarian branch out into neighboring towns. In Curse of the Giant Hogweed, the entire medieval adventure is a bizarre fantasy stemming from something Peter drank while traveling in England. It does feature a charming story of a hapless (and stupid) swain and his enchanted love.

As Alisa Craig, MacLeod has written two series. The first involves Mountie Madoc Rhys, introduced in A Pint of Murder. He falls in love with one of the less likely suspects in two murders committed in a small town. He marries her, and they subsequently reappear in Murder Goes Mumming (an Agatha Christie-style murder at a country estate) and in A Dismal Thing To Do. These are both competent mysteries, with the love interest, if anything, a bit excessive; MacLeod's heroes tend to dote on their ladies.

The other series takes place in the town of Lobelia Falls, where, in the initial novel, The Grub-and Stakers Move a Moun-

tain, the heroine discovers murder and civic corruption involving a plot to turn the "Enchanted Mountain," which is public property, into private property. While helping to solve the murder, she and her friends hastily put together a campaign to elect a candidate of their own choice. Action is frenetic and funny, as the bad guys resort to skullduggery, and the ladies retaliate. Virtue triumphs, and the heroine finds an unlikely hero. She and her new husband return in The Grub-and-Stakers Quilt a Bee and The Grub-and-Stakers Pinch a Poke. Neither are as funny as the first, but they are still enjoyable.

MacLeod's Sarah Kelling novels, beginning with The Family Vault, are equally witty, though more subdued. The heroine is a member of an infinite (and infinitely stuffy) Bostonian family who keep stumbling into murders which she and her eventual husband, a Jewish expert in art fraud, help solve. Sarah's romance flowers very gradually, over six novels, but by the time of The Silver Ghost, the most recent in the series, she has married him and had a baby. This series relies heavily on MacLeod's gift for creating eccentrics, as the hero and heroine do not appear to know anyone "normal."

—Marylaine Block

MacLEOD, Jean S. Also writes as Catherine Airlie. British. Born in Glasgow, Scotland, 20 January 1908. Educated at Bearsden Academy, near Glasgow; High School for Girls, Swansea, Wales. Married Lionel Walton in 1935; one son. Secretary, British Ministry of Labour, Newcastle-upon-Tyne, 1930–35. Recipient: Cartland Historical Novel award, 1962. Address: c/o Mills and Boon Ltd., 18–24 Paradise Road, Richmond, Surrey TW9 1SR, England.

ROMANCE AND HISTORICAL PUBLICATIONS

Novels

Life for Two. London, Mills and Boon, 1936.
Human Symphony. London, Mills and Boon, 1937.
Summer Rain. London, Mills and Boon, 1938.
Sequel to Youth. London, Mills and Boon, 1938.
Mist Across the Hills. London, Mills and Boon, 1938; Toronto, Harlequin, 1967.
Dangerous Obsession. London, Mills and Boon, 1938; Toronto, Harlequin, 1962.
Run Away from Love. London, Mills and Boon, 1939; Toronto, Harlequin, 1961.
Return to Spring. London, Mills and Boon, 1939; Toronto, Harlequin, 1971.
The Rainbow Isle. London, Mills and Boon, 1939.
The Whim of Fate. London, Mills and Boon, 1940.
Silent Bondage. London, Mills and Boon, 1940; Toronto, Harlequin, 1961.
The Lonely Farrow. London, Mills and Boon, 1940.
Heatherbloom. London, Mills and Boon, 1940.
The Reckless Pilgrim. London, Mills and Boon, 1941.
The Shadow of a Vow. London, Mills and Boon, 1941.
One Way Out. London, Mills and Boon, 1941.
Forbidden Rapture. London, Mills and Boon, 1941.
Penalty for Living. London, Mills and Boon, 1942.
Blind Journey. London, Mills and Boon, 1942.
Bleak Heritage. London, Mills and Boon, 1942; Toronto, Harlequin, 1970.

Reluctant Folly. London, Mills and Boon, 1942.
Unseen To-morrow. London, Mills and Boon, 1943.
The Rowan Tree. London, Mills and Boon, 1943.
Flower o' the Broom. London, Mills and Boon, 1943.
The Circle of Doubt. London, Mills and Boon, 1943.
Lamont of Ardgoyne. London, Mills and Boon, 1944.
Two Paths. London, Mills and Boon, 1944; Toronto, Harlequin, 1966.
Brief Fulfillment. London, Mills and Boon, 1945.
The Bridge of Years. London, Mills and Boon, 1945.
This Much to Give. London, Mills and Boon, 1945; Toronto, Harlequin, 1961.
One Love. London, Mills and Boon, 1945; Toronto, Harlequin, 1970.
The Tranquil Haven. London, Mills and Boon, 1946.
Sown in the Wind. London, Mills and Boon, 1946; Toronto, Harlequin, 1970.
The House of Oliver. London, Mills and Boon, 1947; Toronto, Harlequin, 1968.
And We in Dreams. London, Mills and Boon, 1947.
The Chalet in the Sun. London, Mills and Boon, 1948.
Ravenscrag. London, Mills and Boon, 1948.
Above the Lattice. London, Mills and Boon, 1949.
To-morrow's Bargain. London, Mills and Boon, 1949.
Katherine. London, Mills and Boon, 1950.
The Valley of Palms. London, Mills and Boon, 1950; Toronto, Harlequin, 1963.
Roadway to the Past. London, Mills and Boon, 1951.
Once to Every Heart. London, Mills and Boon, 1951.
Cameron of Gare. London, Mills and Boon, 1952; Toronto, Harlequin, 1961.
Music at Midnight. London, Mills and Boon, 1952.
The Silent Valley. London, Mills and Boon, 1953; Toronto, Harlequin, 1958.
The Stranger in Their Midst. London, Mills and Boon, 1953; Toronto, Harlequin, 1961.
Dear Doctor Everett. London, Mills and Boon, 1954; Toronto, Harlequin, 1958.
The Man in Authority. London, Mills and Boon, 1954.
After Long Journeying. London, Mills and Boon, 1955.
Master of Glenkeith. London, Mills and Boon, 1955; Toronto, Harlequin, 1969.
The Way in the Dark. London, Mills and Boon, 1956; Toronto, Harlequin, 1960.
My Heart's in the Highlands. London, Mills and Boon, 1956; Toronto, Harlequin, 1963.
Journey in the Sun. London, Mills and Boon, 1957; Toronto, Harlequin, 1960.
The Prisoner of Love. London, Mills and Boon, 1958; Toronto, Harlequin, 1960.
The Gated Road. London, Mills and Boon, 1959; Toronto, Harlequin, 1960.
Air Ambulance. London, Mills and Boon, and Toronto, Harlequin, 1959.
The Little Doctor. London, Mills and Boon, and Toronto, Harlequin, 1960.
Nurse Lang. Toronto, Harlequin, 1960.
The White Cockade. London, Mills and Boon, 1960.
The Silver Dragon. London, Mills and Boon, 1961; Toronto, Harlequin, 1962.
Slave of the Wind. London, Mills and Boon, 1962; Toronto, Harlequin, 1969.
The Dark Fortune. London, Mills and Boon, 1962.
Mountain Clinic. Toronto, Harlequin, 1962.
Sugar Island. London, Mills and Boon, and Toronto, Harlequin, 1964.

The Black Cameron. London, Mills and Boon, and Toronto, Harlequin, 1964.
Crane Castle. London, Mills and Boon, and Toronto, Harlequin, 1965.
The Wolf of Heimra. London, Mills and Boon, 1965; Toronto, Harlequin, 1966.
Doctor's Daughter. Toronto, Harlequin, 1965.
The Tender Glory. London, Mills and Boon, 1965; Toronto, Harlequin, 1967.
The Drummer of Corrae. London, Mills and Boon, and Toronto, Harlequin, 1966.
Lament for a Lover. London, Mills and Boon, and Toronto, Harlequin, 1967.
The Master of Keills. London, Mills and Boon, 1967; Toronto, Harlequin, 1968.
The Bride of Mingalay. London, Mills and Boon, and Toronto, Harlequin, 1967.
The Moonflower. London, Mills and Boon, 1967; Toronto, Harlequin, 1968.
Summer Island. London, Mills and Boon, 1968; Toronto, Harlequin, 1969.
The Joshua Tree. London, Mills and Boon, 1970.
The Fortress. London, Mills and Boon, 1970.
The Way Through the Valley. London, Mills and Boon, and Toronto, Harlequin, 1971.
The Scent of Juniper. London, Mills and Boon, 1971.
Light in the Tower. London, Mills and Boon, and Toronto, Harlequin, 1971.
Moment of Decision. London, Mills and Boon, and Toronto, Harlequin, 1972.
Adam's Wife. London, Mills and Boon, 1972; Toronto, Harlequin, 1973.
The Rainbow Days. London, Mills and Boon, and Toronto, Harlequin, 1973.
Over the Castle Wall. London, Mills and Boon, 1974.
Time Suspended. London, Mills and Boon, 1974; Toronto, Harlequin, 1975.
The Phantom Pipes. London, Mills and Boon, 1975.
Journey into Spring. London, Mills and Boon, and Toronto, Harlequin, 1976.
Island Stranger. London, Mills and Boon, 1977; Toronto, Harlequin, 1978.
Viking Song. London, Mills and Boon, 1977.
The Ruaig Inheritance. London, Mills and Boon, 1978.
Search for Yesterday. London, Mills and Boon, and Toronto, Harlequin, 1978.
Meeting in Madrid. London, Mills and Boon, 1979.
Brief Enchantment. London, Mills and Boon, 1979.
Black Sand, White Sand. London, Mills and Boon, 1981.
Moreton's Kingdom. London, Mills and Boon, and Toronto, Harlequin, 1981.
Cruel Deception. London, Mills and Boon, and Toronto, Harlequin, 1981.
Zamora. London, Mills and Boon, and Toronto, Harlequin, 1983.
A Distant Paradise. London, Mills and Boon, and Toronto, Harlequin, 1984.
Beyond the Reef. London, Mills and Boon, and Toronto, Harlequin, 1984.
Valley of the Snows. London, Mills and Boon, and Toronto, Harlequin, 1985.
The Apollo Man. London, Mills and Boon, 1986.
The Olive Grove. London, Mills and Boon, 1986.
After the Hurricane. London, Mills and Boon, and Toronto, Harlequin, 1987.

Call Back the Past. London, Mills and Boon, and Toronto, Harlequin, 1988.
Legacy of Doubt. London, Mills and Boon, and Toronto, Harlequin, 1989.
Shadow on the Hills. London, Mills and Boon, and Toronto, Harlequin, 1989.

Novels as Catherine Airlie

The Wild Macraes. London, Mills and Boon, 1948.
From Such a Seed. London, Mills and Boon, 1949.
The Restless Years. London, Mills and Boon, 1950.
Fabric of Dreams. London, Mills and Boon, 1951.
Strange Recompense. London, Mills and Boon, 1952; Toronto, Harlequin, 1960.
The Green Rushes. London, Mills and Boon, 1953; Toronto, Harlequin, 1968.
Hidden in the Wind. London, Mills and Boon, 1953.
A Wind Sighing. London, Mills and Boon, 1954; Toronto, Harlequin, 1969.
Nobody's Child. London, Mills and Boon, 1954; Toronto, Harlequin, 1968.
The Valley of Desire. London, Mills and Boon, 1955; Toronto, Harlequin, 1967.
The Ways of Love. London, Mills and Boon, 1955; Toronto, Harlequin, 1970.
The Mountain of Stars. London, Mills and Boon, 1956; Toronto, Harlequin, 1969.
The Unguarded Hour. London, Mills and Boon, 1956.
Land of Heart's Desire. London, Mills and Boon, 1957; Toronto, Harlequin, 1968.
Red Lotus. London, Mills and Boon, 1958; Toronto, Harlequin, 1968.
The Last of the Kintyres. London, Mills and Boon, 1959; Toronto, Harlequin, 1969.
Shadow on the Sun. London, Mills and Boon, 1960.
One Summer's Day. London, Mills and Boon, 1961; Toronto, Harlequin, 1966.
The Country of the Heart. London, Mills and Boon, 1961; Toronto, Harlequin, 1964.
The Unlived Year. London, Mills and Boon, 1962; Toronto, Harlequin, 1971.
Passing Strangers. London, Mills and Boon, 1963.
The Wheels of Chance. London, Mills and Boon, 1964.
The Sea Change. London, Mills and Boon, 1965.
Doctor Overboard. Toronto, Harlequin, 1966.
Nurse Jane in Teneriffe. Toronto, Harlequin, 1967.

*

Jean S. MacLeod comments:
   After writing romantic and historical fiction for over 50 years I have come to the conclusion that I am happily employed in my chosen career which, even now, I would not like to be without. I have been most fortunate in my connection with Mills and Boon Ltd. and all the women's magazine editors with whom I have worked in that time.

*   *   *

   Jean S. MacLeod is a writer who captivates the reader with unusual stories in exotic settings. It is obvious that she has thoroughly researched the background to her novels. Her characters seem to be equally at home in the mountains of Norway and the warmth of the Canary Islands as in her own native Scotland. More than mere settings, her milieux form an intrinsic part of the action, with unobtrusive descriptions of customs and natural phenomena providing an air of authenticity.

   The majority of the novels are set in some part of Scotland: amid the cliffs and seas (*The Prisoner of Love*), in the Hebrides (*The Bride of Mingalay*), or in the Western Highlands (*Above the Lattice*). And in these books it is clear that the writer is in her element. However, there is an equal feeling of affinity in the novels which deal with less familiar places. The description of the Norwegian mountains in *The Mountain of Stars* (Catherine Airlie), for example, include many references to real places. The characters' observance of customs, such as that of the "bridal veil," whether real or not, also give an air of authenticity. This feeling of reality is also conveyed by the dialogues and interaction between the characters, such as that between Felicity and Philip in *Red Lotus*, whose relationship is moving and very plausible.

   The force of the elements is strongly felt in all MacLeod's works, and one may even say that natural forces seem to influence events at times or at least to be in sympathy with them. In *Music at Midnight* Kay goes to Norway to take her dead sister's son to his grandparents. The writer manages to portray very convincingly the weighty fear of an avalanche, and in *Red Lotus* the volcanic eruption that traps Felicity and Philip on the mountain plays a frightening part in the action. *The Man in Authority* also contains a strong feeling of the power of places and the elements. Here, as in a number of these novels, the main character comes to possess a feeling of "belonging" to a location which was alien when the story began. Perhaps significantly, many of the novels (e.g., *After Long Journeying*) begin with someone standing on a quayside or waving from the deck of a ship at the commencement of a journey.

   This travel element is often combined with a medical setting, a tried and tested favourite for romances of this kind. The formula is obviously well chosen in this case. The romances which MacLeod invents are often characterized by misunderstanding or lack of communication between the parties concerned. Margaret and Thor marry (in *The Mountain of Stars*) although each is under the illusion that the other does not love him. In *Time Suspended* Ruth at first thinks Logan could be either "a gentleman or a pirate," but they finally settle happily together in Antigua. So, too, in *The Bride of Mingalay* Rowena ends up marrying Andrew Fenwick despite her initial detestation.

   In conclusion, it may be said that MacLeod, whether writing under this name or her pseudonym of Catherine Airlie, has written carefully researched romances with some depth. The well-chosen settings combine effectively with the events of the plot to give an unusual and entertaining final product.

—Kim Paynter

MacNEIL, Duncan. See **McCUTCHAN, Philip.**

MacNEILL, Anne. See **SEGER, Maura.**

MADDOCKS, Margaret (Kathleen Avern). British. Born in Caversham, Berkshire, 10 August 1906. Educated at St. Helen's School, Northwood, Middlesex, and in Dresden. Married Richard Maddocks in 1937 (died 1970). Recipient: Romantic Novelists Association Major award, 1962, 1965, 1970, 1976. Address: 40 Heathfield Green, Midhurst, West Sussex GU29 9QA, England.

ROMANCE AND HISTORICAL PUBLICATIONS

Novels

Come Lasses and Lads. London, Hurst and Blackett, 1944.
The Quiet House. London, Hurst and Blackett, 1947.
Remembered Spring. London, Hurst and Blackett, 1949.
Fair Shines the Day. London, Hurst and Blackett, 1952; as *The Open Door*, London, Hamlyn, 1980.
Piper's Tune. London, Hurst and Blackett, 1954.
A Summer Gone. London, Hurst and Blackett, 1957.
The Frozen Fountain. London, Hurst and Blackett, 1959.
Larksbrook. London, Hurst and Blackett, 1962.
The Green Grass. London, Hurst and Blackett, 1963.
November Tree. London, Hurst and Blackett, 1964.
The Silver Answer. London, Hurst and Blackett, 1965.
Dance Barefoot. London, Hurst and Blackett, 1966.
Fool's Enchantment. London, Hurst and Blackett, 1968.
Thea. London, Hurst and Blackett, 1969; New York, Ace, 1973.
The Weathercock. London, Hurst and Blackett, 1971; New York, Ace, 1973.
A View of the Sea. London, Hurst and Blackett, 1973.
The Moon Is Square. London, Hurst and Blackett, 1975.

OTHER PUBLICATIONS

Other

An Unlessoned Girl (autobiography). London, Hutchinson, 1977.

*

Margaret Maddocks comments:

Any writer must find it difficult to assess her own work honestly and objectively, so I can only say that I hope my books may be considered as well-written. They appear to be popular among all age groups in the nine countries where they have been published. This is probably because the reader can believe in the characters and the plot holds the interest to the end. They tend to cheer rather than depress.

* * *

The heroines of Margaret Maddocks's novels are less concerned with finding true love than with finding themselves. The last thing on their minds is falling in love; rather they are concerned with rebuilding their lives after a time of great unhappiness, for example, the death of a spouse. Going it alone, after having depended on someone else to deal with the practicalities of life, may be tough, but Maddocks's heroines cope admirably. In fact they flourish, growing in spirit and personality as they meet and surmount the obstacles in their way. It is almost as if, in a brief but passionate marriage or a too-close relationship with a child, they have suppressed part of themselves. The constraints of adapting their temperaments to suit that of someone else are lifted, and the women are free to be, in fact they are forced to be, themselves. Such freedom brings its own difficul-

ties, emotional and physical isolation being the most pressing. The characters yearn not for passion and romance, which they have experienced in the past, but for companionship and understanding, and someone to laugh with them at the problems that come their way. In short, the ability to make love seems a less important quality to look for in a lover than the ability to make a good joke.

Despite strong elements of realism in some novels, elements of clichéd romanticism are still to be found. Jane, the attractive young heroine of *The Silver Answer* (winner of the Romantic Novelists Association Major award—one of four such awards that Maddocks has received), has been widowed after a brief passionate year of marriage. We meet her two years on, having recovered from the nervous breakdown and miscarriage that followed Alan's death, setting out over one summer to write a book about the mountaineering expedition in which he was tragically killed. Before long she has won the hearts of not one, not two, but three men! Two of these, the artistic, humorous Mike Harling and the sensible, understanding Lawrence Stafford, were friends of Alan's, and companions on the fatal expedition. The third is an untruthful actor, the hairy, "bear-like" egoistic Aubrey Charles. Though Jane declares that she could never fall in love again, and that she holds Mike and Lawrence responsible for Alan's death and thus "hates" them, her actual behaviour shows little evidence of this, and she spends the entire summer vacillating between the three men. After having a brief affair with the attractive/repulsive Aubrey, she ends up, rather predictably, with the man we knew she would end up with on page one. Still, elements of realism creep into the rather thin plot: the book that Jane writes over the summer turns out to be a rather self-indulgent failure, and is even rejected by her friends and former employers, who run a literary agency; and Jane's relationship with her aging, tight-lipped parents casts a gloomy shadow over the summer months.

The theme of child/parent relationships is one that obviously concerns Maddocks, and she deals with it admirably. The heroine of *Thea*, one of her most moving works, has recently been widowed after a long, superficially happy marriage to a man more than 20 years her senior. Not only must she now build a new life for herself but she must also cope with the problems of her two daughters, the rather remote and volatile Harriet whose stormy marriage is going through a crucial phase, and the endearing warm-hearted 18-year-old Lizzy, Thea's "other-self." When Harriet walks out on her husband and arrives back on her mother's doorstep with her three-year-old son, and Lizzy falls in love with Jonah, a man Thea's age, Thea is forced to re-examine her marriage, which she finds to have had many faults, and is torn between concern for her children's futures and the need to explore and assert her own new-found independence. When she expresses her fears that Lizzy will, by marrying a man in a different generation, miss out on much of her youth, as she herself did, a rift forms for the first time between mother and daughter. Things are further complicated when Lizzy accuses Thea of wanting Jonah herself. *Thea* is a rich novel, realistic in plot and execution. The characters are all the more believable for having their imperfections (bad temper, insensitivity, Thea's obsession with feeding extra mouths), and the central portrait of a woman struggling for the first time in her life to put herself before her children is a convincing one.

The relationship between child and parent, or rather the lack of it, forms the basis of *The Moon Is Square*. In this case the "child" in question, teenage Stephen, far from needing his widowed mother Judith, disappears from home on the brink of the university career for which she has such high hopes. Left with no information of his whereabouts other than the fact that he is "walking to India," Judith, who had in the past turned down a proposal of marriage in order to devote herself to her son (or so she tells herself), is shocked, worried, and confused. Suddenly she realizes that she had not really known Stephen as a person, so involved has she been in the world of romantic fiction, which she has been writing for financial reasons during her long widowhood. As in many of Maddocks's novels, the feeling of isolation predominates: the heroine has few friends, lives in an isolated country cottage, and has no one to turn to who understands her mixed reactions to Stephen's departure. The reappearance of her rejected suitor, Paul, and the rewarding if uneasy friendship she forms with one of Stephen's "drop-out" friends, Jan, through whom she begins to understand her son, lead her to reject the idea of forming a relationship with the attractive Paul, who treats her as "an unreasonable child," and towards a union of compassionate understanding with Jan's father, Ross.

Maddocks's novels are not so much about women falling in love as about women discovering themselves through adversity. Though, as in most romantic fiction, the hero and heroine get together in time for a happy, or at least hopeful, ending, what draws them together is companionship rather than passion, and far more important, and best explored, is what happens to them on the way.

—Judith Summers

MALPASS, Eric. British. Born in Derby, 14 November 1910. Educated at King Henry VIII School, Coventry. Served in the Royal Air Force Volunteer Reserve, 1941–46. Married Muriel Gladys Barnett in 1936; one son. Cashier, Barclays Bank, Nottingham, 1926–66. Agent: Campbell Thomson and McLaughlin Ltd., 31 Newington Green, London N16 9PU. Address: 216 Breedon Street, Long Eaton, Nottingham NG10 4FD, England.

ROMANCE AND HISTORICAL PUBLICATIONS

Novels (series: Shakespeare trilogy)

Sweet Will (Shakespeare). London, Macmillan, 1973; New York, St. Martin's Press, 1974.
The Cleopatra Boy (Shakespeare). London, Macmillan, 1974; New York, St. Martin's Press, 1975.
A House of Women (Shakespeare). London, Macmillan, and New York, St. Martin's Press, 1975.
The Wind Brings Up the Rain. London, Heinemann, and New York, St. Martin's Press, 1978.
The Lamplight and the Stars. London, Hamlyn, 1985.
Of Human Frailty. London, Hale, 1987.

OTHER PUBLICATIONS

Novels

Beefy Jones. London, Longman, 1957.
Morning's at Seven. London, Heinemann, 1965; New York, Viking Press, 1966.
At the Height of the Moon. London, Heinemann, 1967.
Fortinbras Has Escaped. London, Pan, and New York, Transworld, 1970.
Oh My Darling Daughter. London, Eyre and Spottiswoode, 1970.

Summer Awakening. London, Corgi, 1978.
The Long Long Dances. London, Corgi, 1978.

*

Eric Malpass comments:
My subjects present the attractive side of life: good humoured family unity, traditional values, appreciation of nature and the English countryside.

*   *   *

Eric Malpass had his first novel published in Germany, and—in spite of a growing recognition of his achievement by British readers—remains far more celebrated a writer on the Continent than in his native land. Never a "fashionable" author, his work displays those virtues of the storyteller's art which, in an age where innovation and experiment are often lauded, have tended to be undervalued. The early success of *Morning's at Seven* and his other humorous novels featuring the Pentecost family has been followed by an altogether more lasting and substantial reputation as one of today's leading writers of historical fiction. It is a reputation which he has more than earned in the last decade.

Foremost of his works in the genre, and arguably the peak of his achievement as a novelist, is the Shakespeare trilogy—*Sweet Will*, *The Cleopatra Boy*, and *A House of Women*—in which Malpass provides an inspired fictional treatment of the Bard's life from early boyhood to death. The first volume concentrates on the Elizabethan period, detailing Will's courtship and marriage to Anne Hathaway, and his rise to fame as an actor and playwright in London. It also presents a convincing account of Shakespeare's dangerous involvement with Essex and Southampton, and his narrow escape from punishment after their failed rebellion against Elizabeth I. *The Cleopatra Boy* follows the mature writer through his creation of *Hamlet* and *Antony and Cleopatra* during the uneasy days of James I's accession, and his friendship with the catholic Peyre family, which almost implicates him in the Gunpowder Plot of Guy Fawkes and his associates. *A House of Women* describes Shakespeare's last years in Stratford, and the writing of his final plays against a background of his daughters' enmities, loves, and marriages. Using a strong, often almost poetic prose style, Malpass captures the atmosphere of the Elizabethan and Jacobean ages, contrasting in memorable fashion the robust life of the common people and its precarious nature, continually menaced by filth and plague, and the chilling cruelty of the state.

The intensity of a knife-edge existence is brilliantly conveyed throughout the trilogy, and from this superbly evoked background Malpass moves in closer to enter the mind of Shakespeare himself. Each novel explores the complexities of this quiet, affable man possessed by the overwhelming need to write, the respectable Stratford burgher and social climber who at the same time contains within himself the soul of a far-sighted, supremely gifted artist. Shakespeare's conflicting "halves" are effectively mirrored by the shifting of focus between rural Stratford and the anthill universe of the capital, each of which exerts its spell on the Bard at different periods of his life. A magnificent achievement, the Shakespeare trilogy places Malpass unmistakably in the front rank of historical novelists.

With *The Lamplight and the Stars* Malpass leaves the Elizabethan age to describe the fortunes of a Midland family at the turn of this century. Action centres on Nathan Cranswick's move from an industrial town to a rural village on the estate of a local landowner, Robert Heron. The nonconformist preacher's country idyll is threatened by his sister's illicit love for a clergyman who later commits suicide, and is then caught in the upheaval of the

Boer War, in which Robert Heron dies. The novel ends with the Cranswick's chastened return to the town, choosing domesticity rather than an illusory retreat from the world. Characters are ably presented, and the 1890's Midland landscape caught to perfection, but with all its merits *The Lamplight and the Stars* fails to achieve the heights of the Shakespeare novels. Somehow it veers rather too closely to family saga-land for total conviction, and falls short of Malpass's finest work.

Far more impressive, and worthy of comparison with the trilogy, is *Of Human Frailty*, Malpass's "biographical novel" of Thomas Cranmer, where the author returns to the Tudor period for fictional treatment of another eminent personality of the age. Once more, Malpass investigates the complex nature of a Renaissance man, the shy, unambitious scholar who by a chance meeting rises to power at the court of Henry VIII, and eventually becomes Archbishop of Canterbury. Malpass explores the flawed, yet heroic figure of Cranmer, and through him the palace intrigues and dynastic plots that interweave with England's emergence from domination by Rome. His final, tragic fall, another victim of the merciless Tudor state machine, is quietly but sympathetically rendered. *Of Human Frailty* is a worthy addition to an already excellent body of work, and gives further proof of Malpass's mature skill as a writer of historical fiction.

—Geoffrey Sadler

MANLEY-TUCKER, Audrie. Also wrote as Linden Howard. British. Born in 1924. *Died in 1983.*

ROMANCE AND HISTORICAL PUBLICATIONS

Novels (series: Julie Barden)

Leonie. London, Mills and Boon, 1958.
Lost Melody. London, Mills and Boon, 1959.
A Love Song in Springtime. London, Mills and Boon, 1960.
Piper's Gate. London, Mills and Boon, 1960.
Dark Bondage. London, Mills and Boon, 1961.
A Memory of Summer. London, Mills and Boon, 1961; New York, Paperback Library, 1966.
The Promise of Morning. London, Mills and Boon, 1962.
Candlemas Street. London, Mills and Boon, 1963.
The Loved and the Cherished. London, Mills and Boon, 1964.
A Rainbow in My Hand. London, Mills and Boon, 1965.
Shadow of Yesterday. London, Mills and Boon, 1965.
Champagne Girl. London, Mills and Boon, 1967.
Love, Spread Your Wings. London, Mills and Boon, 1967; Toronto, Harlequin, 1973.
Door Without a Key. London, Mills and Boon, 1967; Toronto, Harlequin, 1973.
Julie Barden, District Nurse. London, Mills and Boon, 1968.
Return to Sender. London, Mills and Boon, 1968.
Julie Barden, Doctor's Wife. London, Mills and Boon, 1969.
A Room Without a Door. London, Mills and Boon, 1970.
Assistance Unlimited. London, Mills and Boon, 1971.
Every Goose a Swan. London, Mills and Boon, 1972.
Shetland Summer. London, Mills and Boon, 1973; New York, Pinnacle, 1980.
The Piper in the Hills. London, Mills and Boon, 1974.
Life Begins Tomorrow. London, Mills and Boon, 1975.
Two for Joy. London, Mills and Boon, 1979.
Tamberlyn. London, Mills and Boon, 1981.
The Lonely Road. London, Mills and Boon, 1983.

Novels as Linden Howard

Foxglove Country. New York, St. Martin's Press, 1977; London, Millington, 1978.
The Devil's Lady. London, Millington, and New York, St. Martin's Press, 1980.

*   *   *

Audrie Manley-Tucker's romantic novels fulfil their function—to give enjoyment. It is one of her attributes that she makes really nice people interesting. The heroines are bright modern girls who tackle their problems with spirit and pluck. The reader identifies with them straightaway because they have to deal with difficulties that face every girl. Serena in *Shetland Summer*, for instance, is in love with a married man but is realistic enough to see there is no (happy) future in that. With characteristic courage she decides to make a clean break and goes off to Shetland.

Another bonus of Manley-Tucker's novels is her excellent description: "That hat in the milliner's window looked like an upturned rush basket spilling artificial daises and had two long streamers of pale green ribbon hanging down the back." An unusual little shop, a village garden, or the Scottish Highlands become vivid verbal paintings. The descriptions are so deftly inserted that they never hold up the narrative but enhance it.

As topical as today's news is the problem of the adopted child. Should she try to find her "real" mother and risk hurting her adoptive parents or stifle her curiosity and be content with her present environment? Sandy Drummond in *Every Goose a Swan* is determined to seek out her "mother," and she carries the reader along in her search.

With very few exceptions none of Manley-Tucker's heroines has glamorous jobs or goes to exotic places. They have ordinary jobs and mostly live at home with their parents. The same could be said of the men, the majority of whom are likable and worthy of the heroines. The few children appearing are life-like and not at all angelic.

Gothic novels by Manley-Tucker are written under the name of Linden Howard. These conform to the usual gothic tradition of a young girl facing a new life in an ancient mansion set in the country, and also facing, although she does not know it, hostility and danger. Manley-Tucker shows her adaptability in being able to tackle convincingly novels with so many restricted plot conventions. *Foxglove Country* and *The Devil's Lady* are excellent examples of this genre. The former novel has a powerful character (the grandfather) and a charming heroine in Sara Pryce. The background of the desolate Welsh Beacons adds to the tension and menace. There are accidents, death, and love stories woven into this fast-moving and convincing book. Manley-Tucker's descriptive gifts and perceptive insight into character makes this gothic compelling reading.

—Lucy Rogers and Peggy York

MANN, Deborah. See **BLOOM, Ursula.**

MANNERS, Alexandra. Pseudonym for Anne Rundle, née Lamb; also writes as Georgianna Bell; Marianne Lamont; Joanne Marshall; Jeanne Saunders. British. Born in Berwick-on-Tweed, Northumberland. Educated at army schools, and Berwick High School for Girls. Married Edwin Charles Rundle in 1949; one daughter and two sons. Civil servant, Berwick, Newcastle-upon-Tyne, and London, to 1951. Recipient: Romantic Novelists Association Netta Muskett award, 1967, and Major award, 1970, 1971. Agent: John McLaughlin, Campbell Thomson and McLaughlin, 31 Newington Green, London N16 9PU, England.

ROMANCE AND HISTORICAL PUBLICATIONS

Novels (series: Island)

Passionate Jade (as Georgianna Bell). London, Fontana, 1969; New York, Pocket Books, 1981.
The Stone Maiden. New York, Putnam, 1973; London Millington, 1974.
Spindrift (as Jeanne Saunders). London, Hale, 1974.
Candles in the Wood. New York, Putnam, 1974; London, Millington, 1975.
The Singing Swans. New York, Putnam, 1975; London, Millington, 1976.
Sable Hunter. New York, Putnam, 1977; London, Collins, 1978; as *Cardigan Square*, New York, Berkley, 1977.
Wildford's Daughter. New York, Putnam, 1978; as *The White Moths*, London, Collins, 1979.
Echoing Yesterday (Island). London, Corgi, 1981.
Karran Kinrade (Island). London, Corgi, 1982.
The Red Bird (Island). London, Corgi, 1984.
The Gaming House (Island). London, Corgi, 1984.

Novels as Anne Rundle

The Moon Marriage. London, Hurst and Blackett, 1967.
Swordlight. London, Hurst and Blackett, 1968.
Forest of Fear. London, Hurst and Blackett, 1969.
Rakehell. London, Hurst and Blackett, 1970.
Lost Lotus. London, Hale, 1972.
Amberwood. London, Hale, 1972; New York, Bantam, 1974.
Heronbrook. New York, Bantam, 1974; London, Hale, 1975.
Judith Lammeter. London, Hale, 1976.
Grey Ghyll. London, Hale, 1978; New York, St. Martin's Press, 1979.
Moonbranches. New York, Macmillan, 1986.

Novels as Joanne Marshall

Cuckoo at Candlemas. London, Jenkins, 1968.
Cat on a Broomstick. London, Jenkins, 1969.
The Dreaming Tower. London, Jenkins, 1969.
Flower of Silence. London, Mills and Boon, 1970; New York, Avon, 1974.
Babylon Was Dust. London, Mills and Boon, 1971.
Wild Boar Wood. London, Mills and Boon, 1972; New York, Avon, 1973.
The Trellised Walk. London, Mills and Boon, 1973.
Sea-Song. London, Mills and Boon, 1973.
Follow a Shadow. London, Collins, and New York, Putnam, 1974.
Valley of Tall Chimneys. London, Collins, 1975.
The Peacock Bed. London, Collins, and New York, St. Martin's Press, 1978.

Novels as Marianne Lamont

Dark Changeling. London, Hurst and Blackett, 1970; New York, Avon, 1973.
Green Glass Moon. London, Hurst and Blackett, 1970.
Bitter Bride-Bed. London, Hurst and Blackett, 1971.
Nine Moons Wasted. London, Constable, and New York, Putnam, 1977.
Horns of the Moon. London, Constable, 1979.
A Serpent's Tooth. London, Constable, 1983.

OTHER PUBLICATIONS

Other (for children)

Dragonscale. London, Hutchinson, 1969.
Tamlane. London, Hutchinson, 1970.
Last Act (as Joanne Marshall). London, Collins, and New York, Putnam, 1976.

*   *   *

The early books by Alexandra Manners are gothic romances but, after three novels, she ceased to use as many gothic elements and began to write historical romance. History plays a major role in each of her works, and she portrays the times and places realistically. She also shows an ability to depict children well, a theme appearing in most of her books.

The Stone Maiden is a Victorian gothic set near Stirling in Scotland. The title comes from an island rock formation which broods over the area. Now orphaned, Maggie comes to live with her father's relatives. She is pulled by undercurrents of the past as well as the present and is simultaneously welcomed and rejected by her new family. The neighbor's son Buck provides the romantic interest and is compared to Heathcliff throughout the novel. Aside from his brooding good looks, there seems little resemblance. The reader knows early on who really wants to harm Maggie. There are many overheard conversations, a device exploited in most of Manners's works. The story is somewhat overwritten, and at times the plot appears too contrived to convince fully.

Candles in the Wood opens with the seven-year-old daughter of a servant to the Scottish Grants of Gallowmerry as the narrator. One night, Helen's mother runs away with a valet, her father is transported for illegal whisky smuggling, and Helen is traumatized by the discovery of a fake body in a medieval torture device in the dungeon of the castle. Years later, having been educated with the money her father made in Australia, Helen returns incognito. She is accepted into the Grant's house as a friend, proving herself worthy of their sanction before her real identity is revealed. The child Manners features in this novel is the ghost of a girl allegedly buried in the foundations of the castle centuries earlier and who, using Helen, acts as a catalyst affecting all the characters' lives. The youngest son provides the romantic element. The complicated plot holds the reader's interest, and the evil-doer is too obvious to be immediately suspected.

In *The Singing Swans*, 10-year-old Meraud's prostitute mother is murdered in Paris. Her Scottish father, who may or may not be the killer, takes Meraud to his home on the Island of Skye, where she tries to win his love. She absorbs the superstitious customs and legends of the villagers and attempts to discover who is trustworthy, other than the neighboring 13-year-old boy who rescues her after one of two attempts are made on her life.

This eerie story is permeated with evil but is not wholly convincing or enjoyable.

As a child Sable Martin (in *Sable Hunter*), a young servant girl in late 18th-century England, watches the Hunter family through their mansion windows and falls in love with the younger son Morgan. She becomes a companion to an elderly woman and quickly learns a cultured manner and speech. Sable is eventually driven away by an insidious plot and rescued by Adam Hunter, a member of parliament. Proving herself intelligent, she becomes his assistant and works to eliminate the injustice of kidnapping young children for whoredom. Morgan's reappearance results in a duel, pregnancy, and Sable's marriage to Adam. Sable's increasing love for her unresponsive husband fails to impress him until danger threatens them both. This political romance teaches as well as entertains.

Wildford's Daughter is Emma, the spoiled only child of banker Luke Wildford. His frigid wife flees her womanizing husband, who thinks he can buy whatever he desires, and Emma elects to stay with her father. By the time she is 18 Emma has acquired some of her father's worst traits: arrogance, stubbornness, and jealousy. But she has a tender heart too. She helps the quaker Elizabeth Fry alleviate some of the suffering of the female inmates of Newgate prison. Even there, her naivety gets her into trouble when a blackmailer promises to remain silent about a murder Emma has tried to cover up. Her youth and inexperience also cause problems in her love life; she falls for a ruthless, ambitious man, but refuses to accept the truth about him. Her father's overseer rescues her from one dangerous escapade after another. Interesting, complex characters enhance a well told tale.

The Island series charts the trials and tribulations of Karran Kinrade. *Echoing Yesterday*, the first in the series, sets the scene and depicts the passionate courtship between Clemence and Luke, Karran's parents. *Karran Kinrade*, *The Red Bird*, and *The Gaming House* follow Karran through a turbulent childhood to adulthood, with all the problems of growing up in a small community where suspicion is rife and "outsiders" are barely tolerated. Manners's gripping saga is full of romance, excitement, and tragedy.

Manners seems entranced with the underside of life and her works have an air of melancholy. She shows both the dark and the good sides of her characters, and contrasts the elegance and poverty of the times. Her works are uneven in quality but are often interesting particularly for their depiction of local customs and settings.

—Andrea Lee Shuey

MANNING, Marsha. See **GRIMSTEAD, Hettie.**

MARCHANT, Catherine. See **COOKSON, Catherine.**

MARCUS, Joanna. See **ANDREWS, Lucilla.**

MARINO, Susan. See **ELLIS, Julie.**

MARSH, Jean. Pseudonym for Evelyn Marshall; has also written as Lesley Bourne. British. Born in Pershore, Worcestershire, 2 December 1897. Educated at Bournville High School; Halesowen Grammar School, Worcestershire; Oxford Senior Certificate for teaching. Married Gerald Eric Marshall in 1917 (died 1964); one son (deceased) and one daughter. Teacher in Halesowen until 1919, then journalist for Thomson and Leng groups until late 1920's; contract writer for Amalgamated Press group until 1939; broadcaster during World War II; writer for *Children's Hour* until 1956. Lives in Bewdley, Worcestershire. Agent: Shirley Russell, Rupert Crew Ltd., King's Mews, London WC1N 2JA, England.

ROMANCE AND HISTORICAL PUBLICATIONS

Novels

Sand Against the Wind. London, Hale, 1973.
Loving Partnership. London, Hale, 1978; Rolling Meadows, Illinois, Aston Hall, 1979.
The Family at Castle Trevissa. London, Hale, 1979.
Sawdust and Dreams. London, Hale, 1980.
Mistress of Tanglewood. London, Hale, 1981.
Unbidden Dream. London, Hale, 1981.
The Rekindled Flame. London, Hale, 1982.
This Foolish Love. London, Hale, 1982.
The Divided Heart. London, Hale, 1983.
Sanctuary for Louise. London, Hale, 1983.
Quest for Love. London, Hale, 1984.
Destiny at Castle Rock. London, Hale, 1985.
Pride of Vallon. London, Hale, 1985.
The Golden Parakeet. London, Hale, 1986.
Loving Heritage. London, Hale, 1987.
Island of Dreams. London, Hale, 1987.
Mission to Argana. London, Hale, 1988.
Love in Hazard. London, Hale, 1989.
The Wayward Heart. London, Hale, 1989.

OTHER PUBLICATIONS

Novels

The Shore House Mystery. London, Hamilton, 1931.
Murder Next Door. London, Long, 1933.
Death Stalks the Bride. London, Long, 1943.
Identity Unwanted. London, Long, 1951.
Death Visits the Circus. London, Long, 1953.
The Pattern Is Murder. London, Long, 1954.
Death among the Stars. London, Long, 1955.
Death at Peak Hour. London, Long, 1957.

Plays

Radio Serials: *Mystery of Castle Rock Zoo*, 1945; *On the Trail of the Albatross*, 1949; *Judith and the Dolls*, 1950; *Secret of the Pygmy Herd*, 1951; *Adventure with a Boffin*, 1952; *Death Visits the Circus*, 1952; *Ghost Ship*, 1952; *Helen Had a Daughter*,

1953; *Johnny Pilgrim Again*, 1953; *The Small Beginning*, 1954; *Valley of Silent Sound*, 1956; *The White Sapphire*, 1956; *Pocahontas*.

Other (for children)

On the Trail of the Albatross (adaptation of radio serial). London, Burke, 1950.
Secret of the Pygmy Herd (adaptation of radio serial). London, Burke, 1951.
Trouble for Tembo (as Lesley Bourne). London, University of London Press, 1958.
Adventure with a Boffin (adaptation of radio serial). London, University of London Press, 1962.
The Valley of Silent Sound (adaptation of radio serial). London, University of London Press, 1962.

Other

Bewdley, XV Century Sanctuary Town. Kinver, Staffordshire, Halmar, 1979.
All Saints' Centenary. Kinver, Staffordshire, Halmar, 1980.

*

Jean Marsh comments:

I began my writing career at the end of World War I with the object, of necessity, of making a living at it. Being fortunate enough to have a contract with the multi-magazine publishers Amalgamated Press, this was possible. Short stories and serials were turned out as required by the group editor. With the advent of the 1939 war, most writings and broadcast talks were geared to the war effort both on home and overseas programmes. But at this time I discovered the delight of writing the kind of detective novels I had always wanted to write. These paved the way to writing adventure serials for BBC *Children's Hour* when the war ended. This was also the period when I wrote a number of adult radio plays and documentaries. After *Children's Hour* closed, I returned to the romantic novels written earlier as magazine serials. But now they have a country background, many of them featuring animals as well as human characters. These have proved popular first as series in *Woman's Story Magazine*, later in book form. I am still doing them. Fortunately even in one's eighties the creative urge is as strong as ever. It's the fingers that become a little stiff on the typewriter keys.

* * *

Jean Marsh's novels are a blend of the magazine fiction she cut her teeth on in the early part of her lengthy career, and the detective fiction which she took to writing during World War II. They are set in small, inward-looking and closely-knit communities crowded with a multitude of characters whose lives and problems form the core of her plots. Romance takes second place to outside events, such as business problems, and to friendship. Her heroes and heroines are drawn together less by an immediate passion than by a particular situation in which they find themselves allied. As the situation unfolds, so their alliance develops into a stronger tie to which there is no real opposition.

Her heroines are usually professional women: veterinary surgeons (*Unbidden Dream*), nurses (*Island of Dreams*, *The Golden Parakeet*), or accountants (*The Rekindled Flame*). If they are seeking fulfilment, it is not necessarily through romance. For example, nurse Amanda Hicks in *The Golden Parakeet*, who

takes a job with a large construction company's hospital in the Andes, is in reality setting out on a private pilgrimage to revisit the country where she was brought up and where her father died in a tragic earthquake accident. This immediately unites her with Dr. Mark Donnelly, whose own brother has apparently died in a more recent earthquake. However, while handling her notoriously difficult boss, Dr. Ettrick, with aplomb, Amanda hangs back from any involvement with Mark, almost as if she does not feel herself worthy of him. Believing him to be involved with the beautiful Della Marchant, she selflessly helps him unravel the mystery of his brother's disappearance, showing her worth through her skills as a nurse and an interpreter.

Amanda is typical of Marsh's heroines in being more confident in her professional role than in her "role" as a woman. For in relationship to men, Marsh's heroines are passive, content for the men in their lives to do the running and, later, to decide their fate. This old-fashioned attitude is echoed by her careful heroes, who will not make a move towards the women they secretly love until any complicated emotional or financial situations of their own have been fully sorted out. Matt Erskine, the hero of *Island of Dreams*, is involved in an uncomfortable business deal with his widowed sister-in-law Anthea, who, unknown to him, is scheming to trick him out of a fair share of the Corfu estate he owned jointly with his late brother. He is attracted to Claire, a private nurse who comes to Corfu to care for his invalid aunt Flora, but makes no move towards her. It is only when Flora and Claire, through their own detective work, uncover Anthea's duplicity, thus freeing Matt from his financial burdens, that he feels free to declare his love for Claire.

Pride of Vallon illustrates another important Marsh trait: the synonymity of relationship and marriage, particularly in the hero's eyes. Melita Kane accompanies her famous film-star aunt, Lorna, to the Camargue in southern France, where Lorna hopes to persuade her ex-lover, composer Maurice Delorme, to let her film at Vallon, his ranching estate. But Maurice's adopted son, Antoine, heir to Vallon, is against such a venture, and Melita finds herself torn between agreeing with him and supporting her aunt, who is also her employer. Eventually Melita earns Antoine's love by helping him uncover a ring of horse thieves. Still she is uncertain if they have a future, and she tells him openly that it is up to him to decide their fate. Given this go-ahead, he immediately announces their engagement at a large party—without giving Melita the chance to say yes or no.

Melita is more at home nursing a new-born foal in a stable than in the glamorous world of show business, and in her ability to relate to animals she is similar to many Marsh heroines. Marsh's settings are predominantly rural: farms (*Loving Heritage*), wild-life parks (*Unbidden Dream*), and riding schools (*Mistress of Tanglewood*); her characters often work in professions which bring them in close contact with a wide variety of animals. In *Sawdust and Dreams* the story of Melissa, the teen-age daughter of a circus-owning family who is suddenly called upon to take over her sister-in-law's elephant act, we encounter the joys and difficulties of dealing with animals which are, though apparently tame, still wild at heart. In *Unbidden Dream* the heroine, Sue, a veterinary surgeon, has to cope with anything from a wounded lion to a baby giraffe. *The Family at Castle Trevissa* features, among other animals, a sick dolphin and a shoal of stranded seals. Though she tends at time towards a sentimental attitude to her animals (piglets are being fattened up for market on the farm in *The Rekindled Flame*, but there's not so much as a whisper of the word abattoir), one feels at times that it is only in their relationship to animals that the characters dare reveal their true warmth. Marsh deals with the problems of caring for animals with compassion and authority, and this lends a great deal of weight to her work.

Marsh's description of people and settings can, at times, be sketchy. What is important for her are the twists and turns of plot. For many years Marsh was a writer of detective fiction; it seems that she is even now, in her nineties, unable to stop herself placing her characters under some kind of threat. Yet the denouements of these mysteries are sometimes disappointingly handled, and might benefit from some further twist at the end.

—Judith Summers

MARSH, Joan. See **WOODWARD, Lilian.**

MARSH, John. See **WOODWARD, Lilian.**

MARSHALL, Edison (Tesla). Also wrote as Hall Hunter. American. Born in Rensselaer, Indiana, 28 August 1894. Educated at the University of Oregon, Eugene, 1913–16. Served in the United States Army Ordnance Field Services, 1918: Lieutenant; educational film writer for Department of Defense during World War II. Married Agnes Sharp Flythe in 1920; one son and one daughter. Hunter and explorer, then freelance writer. Recipient: O. Henry award, for short story, 1921. M.A.: University of Oregon, 1941. *Died 29 October 1967.*

ROMANCE AND HISTORICAL PUBLICATIONS

Novels

Benjamin Blake. New York, Farrar and Rinehart, 1941.
Great Smith. New York, Farrar and Rinehart, 1943; London, Aldor, 1947.
The Upstart. New York, Farrar Straus 1945; London, World Distributors, 1959.
Yankee Pasha: The Adventures of Jason Starbuck. New York, Farrar Straus 1948; London, Redman, 1950.
Castle in the Swamp: A Tale of Old Carolina. New York, Farrar Straus 1948; London, Muller, 1949.
Gypsy Sixpence. New York, Farrar Straus 1949; London, Muller, 1950.
The Infinite Woman. New York, Farrar Straus 1950; London, Muller, 1951.
The Viking. New York, Farrar Straus 1951; London, Muller, 1952.
The Bengal Tiger: A Tale of India (as Hall Hunter). New York, Doubleday, 1952; as *Rogue Gentleman*, as Edison Marshall, New York, Popular Library, 1963.
American Captain. New York, Farrar Straus, 1954; as *Captain's Saga*, London, Muller, 1955.
Caravan to Xanadu: A Novel of Marco Polo. New York, Farrar Straus, 1954; London, Muller, 1955.
The Gentleman. New York, Farrar Straus, and London, Muller, 1956.
The Inevitable Hour: A Novel of Martinique. New York, Putnam, 1957; London, Muller, 1958.

Princess Sophia. New York, Doubleday, 1958; London, Muller, 1959.
The Pagan King. New York, Doubleday, 1959; London, Muller, 1960.
Earth Giant. New York, Doubleday, 1960; London, Muller, 1961.
West with the Vikings. New York, Doubleday, 1961.
The Conqueror. New York, Doubleday, 1962.
Cortez and Marina. New York, Doubleday, 1963.
The Lost Colony. New York, Doubleday, 1964.

Short Stories

The Heart of Little Shikara and Other Stories. Boston, Little Brown, 1922; London, Hodder and Stoughton, 1924.
Love Stories of India. New York, Farrar Straus, 1950.

OTHER PUBLICATIONS

Novels

The Voice of the Pack. Boston, Little Brown, and London, Hodder and Stoughton, 1920.
The Strength of the Pines. Boston, Little Brown, and London, Hodder and Stoughton, 1921.
The Snowshoe Trail. Boston, Little Brown, and London, Hodder and Stoughton, 1921.
Shepherds of the Wild. Boston, Little Brown, and London, Hodder and Stoughton, 1922.
The Sky Line of Spruce. Boston, Little Brown, 1922; as *The Sky-Line*, London, Hodder and Stoughton, 1922.
The Land of Forgotten Men. Boston, Little Brown, 1923; London, Hodder and Stoughton, 1924.
The Isle of Retribution. Boston, Little Brown, and London, Hodder and Stoughton, 1923.
The Death Bell. New York, Garden City Publishing Company, 1924.
Seward's Folly. Boston, Little Brown, and London, Hodder and Stoughton, 1924.
The Sleeper of the Moonlit Ranges. New York, Cosmopolitan, and London, Hodder and Stoughton, 1925.
Child of the Wild: A Story of Alaska. New York, Cosmopolitan, and London, Hodder and Stoughton, 1926.
The Deadfall. New York, Cosmopolitan, and London, Hodder and Stoughton, 1927.
The Far Call. New York, Cosmopolitan, and London, Hodder and Stoughton, 1928.
The Fish Hawk. New York, Cosmopolitan, and London, Hodder and Stoughton, 1929.
Singing Arrows. London, Hodder and Stoughton, 1929.
The Missionary. New York, Cosmopolitan, and London, Hodder and Stoughton, 1930.
The Doctor of Lonesome River. New York, Cosmopolitan, and London, Hodder and Stoughton, 1931.
The Deputy at Snow Mountain. New York, Kinsey, and London, Hodder and Stoughton, 1932.
Forlorn Island. New York, Kinsey, and London, Hodder and Stoughton, 1932.
The Light in the Jungle. New York, Kinsey, 1933; as *Victory in the Jungle*, London, Hodder and Stoughton, 1933.
The Splendid Quest. New York, Kinsey, 1934.
Ogden's Strange Story. New York, Kinsey, 1934.
Dian of the Lost Land. New York, Kinsey, 1935; as *The Lost Land*, New York, Curtis, 1966.

Sam Campbell, Gentleman. New York, Kinsey, 1935; London, Hodder and Stoughton, 1936.
The Stolen God. New York, Kinsey, 1936; London, Hodder and Stoughton, 1937.
The White Brigand. New York, Kinsey, 1937; London, Hodder and Stoughton, 1938.
Darzee, Girl of India. New York, Kinsey, 1937; as *The Flower Dancer*, London, Hodder and Stoughton, 1937.
The Jewel of Malabar. New York, Kinsey, and London, Hodder and Stoughton, 1938.

Other

Ocean Gold (for children). New York, Harper, 1925.
Campfire Courage: The Woodsmoke Boys in the Canadian Rockies (for children). New York, Harper, 1926.
Shikar and Safari: Reminiscences of Jungle Hunting. New York, Farrar Straus, 1947; London, Museum Press, 1950.
The Heart of the Hunter (autobiography). New York, McGraw Hill, 1956; London, Muller, 1957.

* * *

Edison Marshall's long career was a sweeping curve upward to the position of the foremost historical novelist of the 1940's and 1950's, but since his death the reputation of his fiction has not so much declined as that fiction has simply been ignored. In spite of his success, including 10 films based upon his works, he perhaps expected his fate when he said, "I am an anachronism, and my career is *contre tempes*."

His work falls neatly into two groups on the basis of both chronology and subject matter. Until the late 1930's, most of his writing consisted of short stories and magazine serials in the adventure-thriller genre. Many were based upon his own hunting expeditions around the world, especially in southern Asia and Alaska. "The Heart of Little Shikara," winner of the O. Henry prize in 1921, *The Light in the Jungle*, and *The Jewel of Malabar* are examples of the Asian stories. Even more prevalent are those set in Alaska or the American northwest; there are more than a dozen. Marshall stated that he was "Obsessed by nature to a degree of passion that would floor Freud," and these works are filled with close and accurate descriptions of nature, often to emphasize its redeeming power of various city types who find themselves suddenly amidst its wonders, as in *The Voice of the Pack, Shepherds of the Wild*, and *The Isle of Retribution*. Though the plots are often repetitive, these works can still have appeal for lovers of adventure and admirers of nature.

Even more successful with readers than these adventure stories were the historical novels beginning with *Benjamin Blake*. Ranging throughout history and varied in locale, they were novels of action and romance. Some centered on actual persons, as *Great Smith* (Captain John Smith) and *The Infinite Woman* (based on Lola Montez), while the central characters of others were imaginary: *Yankee Pasha* and *Gypsy Sixpence*. A major success was *The Viking*, with the legendary Ogier the Dane as its hero. Whether set in early America, India, the Caribbean, or Norseland, and whatever the time period, Marshall's novels were well-researched, fast-paced, and colorful in the presentation of customs and sights. The heroes and heroines were generally noble in deed, if not in title, and the sexual element was treated conservatively. With Marshall's many excellent qualities as a historical novelist, it may be that the lack of explicit sex is the reason for his being replaced by other novelists of lesser talent who provide titillation in historical guise for their readers. If so, that says more about the readers about than Marshall's ability as novelist.

—Earl F. Bargainnier

———

MARSHALL, Joanne. See **MANNERS, Alexandra.**

———

MARSHALL, Rosamond (Van der Zee). American. Born in New York City, 17 October 1902. Educated at Miss Eaton's School, Pasadena, California; Lycée des Jeunes Filles, Dijon; Real Gymnasium, Vienna; University of Munich. Married Albert Earl Marshall (second marriage); one daughter. Amateur mountaineer. *Died 13 November 1957.*

ROMANCE AND HISTORICAL PUBLICATIONS

Novels

Kitty. New York, Duell, 1943; London, Redman, 1956.
Duchess Hotspur. New York, Prentice Hall, 1946; London, Redman, 1958.
Celeste. New York, Prentice Hall, 1949.
Laird's Choice. New York, Prentice Hall, 1951; London, Redman, 1952.
Bond of the Flesh. New York, Doubleday, 1952; London, Redman, 1953.
Jane Hadden. New York, Prentice Hall, 1952; London, Redman, 1953.
The Temptress. New York, New American Library, 1952.
The General's Wench. New York, Prentice Hall, 1953; London, Redman, 1954.
The Dollmaster. New York, Prentice Hall, 1954; London, Redman, 1955; as *Mistress of Rogues*, New York, Popular Library, 1956.
The Loving Meddler. New York, Doubleday, 1954; London, Redman, 1955.
Rogue Cavalier. New York, Doubleday, 1955; London, Redman, 1956.
The Rib of the Hawk. New York, Appleton Century Crofts, 1956; London, Redman, 1957.
Captain Ironhand. New York, Appleton Century Crofts, and London, Redman, 1957.
The Bixby Girls. New York, Doubleday, 1957; London, Redman, 1958.

Other novels (in French): *L'Enfant du Cirque*, 1930; *La Main d'Acier*, 1931; *Plaisirs d'Amour*, 1932; *Le Vaisseau Fantôme*, 1933; *Vengeance du Sheik*, 1934; *Mystères de Chinatown*, 1934; *Mystères de Londres*, 1935.

OTHER PUBLICATIONS

Other (for children)

None But the Brave: A Story of Holland. Boston, Houghton Mifflin, 1942; London, Hutchinson, 1946.
The Treasure of Shafto. New York, Messner, 1946.

* * *

The traditional Horatio Alger "rags to riches" success story based upon hard work and righteous living has long been a favourite in the world of adult fairy tales, but Rosamond Marshall gave the old theme a surprising new twist with her best-selling period romance *Kitty*. This quite different success story tells of a nameless child of the 18th-century London gutters, her virginity sold for a few pence to a lecherous sexton when she was but eight years old by the heartless bawd who holds her bond. Kitty lives by petty theft and prostitution, until one day her gamin charm catches the eye of a great painter in want of a model. Thomas Gainsborough recognizes great beauty disguised by dirt, and the bath and arbitrary surname he provides for the lovely waif are her keys to a new life. Working her way up from man to man, finally attaining a peak of success as a duchess, Kitty has something the "Moll Flanders" version of fictional harlot lacked—a heart. She never forgets her own miserable beginnings, nor ceases to pity the plight of other child victims. At the height of her triumph, Kitty risks her own safety and happiness for the benefit of the wretched mill-children on her inherited estate.

As though to prove that a rake can progress in either direction, Marshall followed the success of *Kitty* with another light-hearted romp, *Duchess Hotspur*, the tale of a high-born lady with an eclectic taste in lusty men, who falls in love at last with a penniless journalist. Duchess Percy thinks at first that it will be a simple matter to bring her scruffy lover up to a standard of appearances acceptable to her privileged circle by means of a few judicious gifts, but not so. He is a proud fellow, who regards such treatment as an insult to his manhood. A compromise must be reached between the wanton, lovely duchess and the stiff-necked quill-pusher, and it makes for a rousing tale.

Marshall's books, considered daring in their day, are unlikely now to raise any eyebrows. Good humoured pre-Regency fun and games, they make cheerfully diverting bedtime stories.

—Joan McGrath

* * *

MARTIN, Rhona. British. Born in London, 3 June 1922. Educated at private schools; Redland High School, Bristol; West of England College of Art, 1937–39. Married 1) Peter Wilfrid Alcock in 1941 (divorced 1957), two daughters; 2) Thomas Neighbour in 1959 (divorced). Fashion artist, Willsons Ltd., Bristol, 1940–41; clerk, Fire Guard Office, Weston-super-Mare, 1942–45; freelance theatrical designer, 1946–48; catering manager, Club Labamba, Tunbridge Wells, 1963–68; assistant manager, Odeon, Sevenoaks, 1968–72; accounts secretary and office manager, Crown Chemical Company, Lamberhurst, Kent, 1972–79; then full-time writer. Recipient: Georgette Heyer prize, for historical novel, 1978. Agent: John McLaughlin, Campbell Thomson and McLaughlin Ltd., 31 Newington Green, London N16 9PU. Address: c/o The Bodley Head Ltd., 32 Bedford Square, London WC1B 3EL, England.

ROMANCE AND HISTORICAL PUBLICATIONS

Novels

Gallows Wedding. London, Bodley Head, 1978; New York, Coward McCann, 1979.

Mango Walk. London, Bodley Head, 1981; New York, Bantam, 1982.
The Unicorn Summer. London, Bodley Head, 1984.

OTHER PUBLICATIONS

Novel

Goodbye, Sally. London, Bodley Head, 1987.

Other

Writing Historical Fiction. London, A. and C. Black, and New York, St. Martin's Press, 1988.

*

Rhona Martin comments:

I am not sure that I would classify my writing as either romance or gothic—but then classification is in any case best left to the reader. With me, a novel comes from first one idea and then two, usually a character and a situation, which interact and grow in darkness until they are gnawing a hole in me and have to be got out of my system. I am blessed or cursed with a fertile imagination to which these tiny seeds of thought cling and germinate like mushroom spores, sometimes with little awareness on my part. Suddenly there they are, refusing to be suppressed or ignored, thrusting upwards towards the light and pushing up pavingstones if need be to get there. I prefer not to be tied to a category, modern, historical or whatever; it is people who interest me, their reactions to each other and to the situations in which they find themselves, and to explore these fascinating avenues one must be free. *Gallows Wedding* happened as a result of wondering how a girl would feel who is reduced to buying a stranger from the gallows for the sake of his protection . . . and how would the couple fare afterwards? As I could find no book to tell me, I had to write it myself in order to find out. *Mango Walk* sprang from a dream I was unable to shake off; the figures in it remained to haunt me until I gave in and put their story down on paper. From here my work could go in any direction. I have to write what fires me, and to quote from one of my own verses, "joy's a nymph, not captured one way twice."

* * *

Rhona Martin's comparatively late start as a novelist, at the age of 56, was almost immediately rewarded. The award of the Georgette Heyer Historical Novel prize for her first book, *Gallows Wedding*, in 1978, heralded the arrival of Martin into the world of romance writers.

However, even that elastically generalised classification is stretched to its parameters to encompass *Gallows Wedding*. The book's theme, soon discovered to be heavyweight, the depth of its treatment, the obvious social conscience of the writer, defy its inclusion within the lightweight cloak of the Georgette Heyer-inspired romance genre. For example, the dialogue, indeed all the language throughout, is without compromise. Martin conceals nothing to save the blushes of the squeamish, who have wandered unwittingly to its pages.

Announcing her intentions with an introduction as raw as the realities of the childbirth that she is describing, she pulls no linguistic punches. Proceeding formidably from the "blood soaked ruin of a bed," which heralds the struggling birth of the "changeling," the "witchmarked baby," she embarks on an investigative exposé of superstition riddled 16th-century England. An England where the very sniff of witchcraft (proven or not), or the malicious tongue of neighbourhood gossip could lead to a brutal death.

Although the tale is set in the reign of Henry VIII, Martin ignores the "romance" of those corridors of power, to concentrate on the lives of the unfashionable, the common people, the lowest of the low, scratching for existence as best they could.

The love story of Hazel, the "witchmarked baby" and Black John, the outlaw, is told without saccharine. Their marriage in a "Gallows Wedding" is placed firmly in the context of that violent period, when anarchy was set at the pinnacle of power. For, just as Henry defied convention to achieve his feudal and carnal ambitions, so the boundaries of decency and compassion were similarly distorted and compressed by his loyal subjects. Martin's lovers are as doomed as the godless edifice which Henry was wantonly constructing in celebration of mammon. The book's conclusion is certainly not for the faint-hearted, but is valid both in its inevitability and in reflecting the cruelty of the period.

Martin's second book, *Mango Walk*, is another unconventional love story. Set in the 1940's and 1950's it is a poignant tale of two people from totally different cultural backgrounds. An even further social taboo, curiously currently topical, is the wide age gap separating the lovers. The animosity and blatantly open hostility which their decision to share their lives attracts, is the core of the story.

The Unicorn Summer continues the story begun in *Gallows Wedding*. The novel tells the tale of Joanna and Angel, both reminders of the legend of Black John and Hazel the witch. Joanna and Angel are bound together by an old story of love, magic, and violence. They prove to be the catalysts, the weapon that will destroy Lord Eustace Pengerran, and restore the great lands of Buxford and Pengerron to the bloodline of Black John. Martin's meticulous research is apparent and she handles this powerful tale with great skill.

Martin's novels are original, well-written, and distinctive. She has something to contribute as a social observer, a true social historian using the novel as her vehicle, with her books making valid comments on the mores of her chosen periods.

—Bill Boyle

MARTIN, Stella. See **HEYER, Georgette.**

MARVIN, Susan. See **ELLIS, Julie.**

MASEFIELD, John (Edward). British. Born in Ledbury, Herefordshire, 1 June 1878. Educated at Warwick School, 1888–90; cadet on merchant training ship *Conway*, Liverpool, 1891–93. Served in the British Red Cross in France and Gallipoli, 1915; commissioned by British government to observe and write on Battle of the Somme, 1916–17. Married Constance de la Cherois Crommelin in 1903 (died 1960); one daughter and one son. Apprentice on White Star barque *Gilcruix* on trip to Chile, 1894; sixth officer, White Star mail ship *Adriatic*, 1895; bartender, Columbian Hotel, New York, 1895; worked at Alexander

Smith carpet factory, Yonkers, New York, 1895–97; worked in City of London, 1897; clerk, Capital and Counties Bank, London, 1898–1901; art exhibition secretary, Wolverhampton, 1902; sub-editor, *Speaker* magazine, London, 1903; staff member, Manchester *Guardian*, 1904–05, and feature writer from 1907. Lectured in the United States, 1916 and 1918, and for the British Council in many European countries. President, Society of Authors, 1937–67; First President, National Book League; member, British Council Books and Periodicals Committee. Recipient (for poetry): Royal Society of Literature Polignac prize, 1912; Shakespeare Prize (Hamburg), 1938; William Foyle prize, 1961; National Book League prize, 1964. D.Litt.: Yale University, New Haven, Connecticut, 1918; Harvard University, Cambridge, Massachusetts, 1918; Oxford University, 1922; Cambridge University, 1931; LL.D.: University of Aberdeen, 1922; Honorary degrees: universities of Glasgow, 1923, Manchester, 1923, Liverpool, 1930, St. Andrews, 1930, and Wales, 1932. Honorary member, American Academy, 1930; named Poet Laureate, 1930; Order of Merit, 1935; Royal Society of Literature Companion of Literature, 1961. *Died 12 May 1967.*

ROMANCE AND HISTORICAL PUBLICATIONS

Novels (series: Edward "Ned" Mansell; Santa Barbara)

Captain Margaret: A Romance. London, Grant Richards, and Philadelphia, Lippincott, 1908.
Sard Harker (Santa Barbara). London, Heinemann, and New York, Macmillan, 1924.
Odtaa (Santa Barbara). London, Heinemann, and New York, Macmillan, 1926.
The Bird of Dawning; or, The Fortune of the Sea. London, Heinemann, and New York, Macmillan, 1933.
The Taking of the Gry (Santa Barbara). London, Heinemann, and New York, Macmillan, 1934.
Dead Ned: The Autobiography of a Corpse (Mansell). London, Heinemann, and New York, Macmillan, 1938.
Live and Kicking Ned (Mansell). London, Heinemann, and New York, Macmillan, 1939.
Basilissa: A Tale of the Empress Theodora. London, Heinemann, and New York, Macmillan, 1940.
Conquer: A Tale of the Nika Rebellion in Byzantium. London, Heinemann, and New York, Macmillan, 1941.
Badon Parchments. London, Heinemann, 1947.

OTHER PUBLICATIONS

Novels

Multitude and Solitude. London, Grant Richards, 1909; New York, Kennerley, 1910.
The Street of To-Day. London, Dent, and New York, Dutton, 1911.
The Hawbucks. London, Heinemann, and New York, Macmillan, 1929.
Victorious Troy!; or, The Hurrying Angel. London, Heinemann, and New York, Macmillan, 1935.
Eggs and Baker; or, The Days of Trial. London, Heinemann, and New York, Macmillan, 1936.
The Square Peg; or, The Gun Fella. London, Heinemann, and New York, Macmillan, 1937.

Short Stories

A Mainsail Haul. London, Elkin Mathews, 1905; revised edition, 1913; New York, Macmillan, 1913.

A Tarpaulin Muster. London, Grant Richards, 1907; New York, Dodge, 1908.

The Taking of Helen. London, Heinemann, and New York, Macmillan, 1923.

Fiction (for children)

A Book of Discoveries. London, Wells Gardner, and New York, Stokes, 1910.

Lost Endeavour. London, Nelson, 1910; New York, Macmillan, 1917.

Martin Hyde, The Duke's Messenger. London, Wells Gardner, and Boston, Little Brown, 1910.

Jim Davis; or, The Captive of the Smugglers. London, Wells Gardner, 1911; New York, Stokes, 1912.

The Midnight Folk. London, Heinemann, and New York, Macmillan, 1927.

The Box of Delights; or, When the Wolves Were Running. London, Heinemann, and New York, Macmillan, 1935.

Plays

The Campden Wonder (produced London, 1907). Included in *The Tragedy of Nan and Other Plays*, 1909.

The Tragedy of Nan (produced London, 1908). Included in *The Tragedy of Nan and Other Plays*, 1909.

The Tragedy of Nan and Other Plays (includes *The Campden Wonder* and *Mrs. Harrison*). London, Grant Richards, and New York, Kennerley, 1909.

The Tragedy of Pompey the Great (produced London, 1910). London, Sidgwick and Jackson, and Boston, Little Brown, 1910; revised version (produced Manchester, 1914), Sidgwick and Jackson, and New York, Macmillan, 1914.

The Witch, adaptation of a play by Hans Wiers-Jenssen (produced Glasgow, 1910; London, 1911). New York, Brentano's, 1926; as *Anne Pedersdotter*, Boston, Little Brown, 1917.

Philip the King (produced Bristol and London, 1914). Included in *Philip the King and Other Poems*, 1914.

The Faithful (produced Birmingham, 1915; London and New York, 1919). London, Heinemann, and New York, Macmillan, 1915.

Good Friday: A Dramatic Poem (produced London, 1917). New York, Macmillan, 1915; as *Good Friday: A Play in Verse*, Letchworth, Hertfordshire, Garden City Press, 1916.

The Sweeps of Ninety-Eight (produced Birmingham, 1916). With *The Locked Chest*, Letchworth, Hertfordshire, Garden City Press, and New York, Macmillan, 1916.

The Locked Chest (produced London, 1920). With *The Sweeps of Ninety-Eight*, Letchworth, Hertfordshire, Garden City Press, and New York, Macmillan, 1916.

Esther, adaptation of the play by Racine (produced Wootton, Berkshire, 1921). London, Heinemann, and New York, Macmillan, 1922.

Berenice, adaptation of the play by Racine (produced Oxford, 1921). London, Heinemann, and New York, Macmillan, 1922.

Melloney Holtspur (produced London, 1923). London, Heinemann, and New York, Macmillan, 1922.

A King's Daughter: A Tragedy in Verse (produced Oxford, 1923; London, 1928). London, Heinemann, and New York, Macmillan, 1923.

Tristan and Isolt: A Play in Verse (produced Oxford, 1923; London, 1927). London, Heinemann, and New York, Macmillan, 1927.

The Trial of Jesus (produced London, 1926). London, Heinemann, and New York, Macmillan, 1925.

Verse and *Prose Plays.* New York, Macmillan, 2 vols., 1925.

The Coming of Christ (produced Oxford, 1928). London, Heinemann, and New York, Macmillan, 1928.

Easter: A Play for Singers. London, Heinemann, and New York, Macmillan, 1929.

End and Beginning. London, Heinemann, and New York, Macmillan, 1933.

A Play of Saint George. London, Heinemann, and New York, Macmillan, 1948.

Verse

Salt-Water Ballads. London, Grant Richards, 1902; New York, Macmillan, 1913.

Ballads. London, Elkin Mathews, 1903; revised edition, as *Ballads and Poems*, 1910.

The Everlasting Mercy. London, Sidgwick and Jackson, and Portland, Maine, Smith and Sale, 1911.

The Story of a Round-House and Other Poems. New York, Macmillan, 1912; revised edition, 1913.

The Widow in the Bye Street. London, Sidgwick and Jackson, 1912; with *The Everlasting Mercy*, New York, Macmillan, 1912.

Dauber. London, Heinemann, 1913; with *The Daffodil Fields*, New York, Macmillan, 1923.

The Daffodil Fields. London, Heinemann, and New York, Macmillan, 1913.

Philip the King and Other Poems. London, Heinemann, and New York, Macmillan, 1914.

Good Friday and Other Poems. New York, Macmillan, 1916.

Sonnets. New York, Macmillan, 1916.

Salt-Water Poems and Ballads. New York, Macmillan, 1916; revised edition, as *Poems*, 1929, 1935, 1953.

Sonnets and Poems. Letchworth, Hertfordshire, Garden City Press, 1916.

The Cold Cotswolds. Privately printed, 1917.

Poems of John Masefield, edited by Henry Seidel Canby and others. New York, Macmillan, 1917.

Lollingdon Downs and Other Poems. New York, Macmillan, and London, Heinemann, 1917.

Rosas. New York, Macmillan, 1918.

Reynard the Fox; or, The Ghost Heath Run. New York, Macmillan, and London, Heinemann, 1919.

Animula. London, Chiswick Press, 1920.

Enslaved. New York, Macmillan, 1920.

Enslaved and Other Poems. London, Heinemann, and New York, Macmillan, 1920.

Right Royal. New York, Macmillan, and London, Heinemann, 1920.

King Cole. London, Heinemann, and New York, Macmillan, 1921.

The Dream. London, Heinemann, and New York, Macmillan, 1922.

Selected Poems. London, Heinemann, 1922; New York, Macmillan, 1923; revised edition, 1938.

King Cole and Other Poems. London, Heinemann, 1923; as *King Cole, The Dream, and Other Poems*, New York, Macmillan, 1923.

The Dream and Other Poems. New York, Macmillan, 1923.

The Collected Poems of John Masefield. London, Heinemann, 1923; revised edition, 1932, 1938; as *Poems*, 1946.

Poems. New York, Macmillan, 2 vols., 1925.

Sonnets of Good Cheer to the Lena Ashwell Players. . . . London, Mendip Press, 1926.

Midsummer Night and Other Tales in Verse. London, Heinemann, and New York, Macmillan, 1928.

South and East. London, Medici Society, and New York, Macmillan, 1929.

The Wanderer of Liverpool (verse and prose). London, Heinemann, and New York, Macmillan, 1930.

Poems of the Wanderer: The Ending. Privately printed, 1930.

Minnie Maylow's Story and Other Tales and Scenes. London, Heinemann, and New York, Macmillan, 1931.

A Tale of Troy. London, Heinemann, and New York, Macmillan, 1932.

A Letter from Pontus and Other Verse. London, Heinemann, and New York, Macmillan, 1936.

Lines on the Tercentenary of Harvard University. New York, Macmillan, 1936; London, Heinemann, 1937.

The Country Scene in Poems and Pictures, illustrated by Edward Seago. London, Collins, 1936; New York, Collins, 1938.

Tribute to Ballet in Poems and Pictures, illustrated by Edward Seago. London, Collins, and New York, Macmillan, 1938.

Some Verses to Some Germans. London, Heinemann, and New York, Macmillan, 1939.

Shopping in Oxford. London, Heinemann, 1941.

Gautama the Enlightened and Other Verse. London, Heinemann, and New York, Macmillan, 1941.

Natalie Maisie and Pavilastukay: Two Tales in Verse. London, Heinemann, and New York, Macmillan, 1942.

A Generation Risen. London, Collins, 1942; New York, Macmillan, 1943.

Land Workers. London, Heinemann, 1942; New York, Macmillan, 1943.

Wonderings: Between One and Six Years. London, Heinemann, and New York, Macmillan, 1943.

Reynard the Fox . . . with Selected Sonnets and Lyrics. London, Heinemann, 1946.

On the Hill. London, Heinemann, and New York, Macmillan, 1949.

Selected Poems (new selection). London, Heinemann, and New York, Macmillan, 1950.

In Praise of Nurses. London, Heinemann, 1950.

Bluebells and Other Verse. London, Heinemann, and New York, Macmillan, 1961.

Old Raiger and Other Verse. London, Heinemann, 1964; New York, Macmillan, 1965.

In Glad Thanksgiving. London, Heinemann, and New York, Macmillan, 1967.

The Sea Poems. London, Heinemann, 1978.

Selected Poems, edited by John Betjeman. London, Heinemann, and New York, Macmillan, 1978.

Selected Poems, edited by Donald E. Stanford. Manchester, Carcanet, 1984.

Other

Sea Life in Nelson's Time. London, Methuen, 1905; New York, Macmillan, 1925.

On the Spanish Main; or, Some English Forays on the Isthmus of Darien. . . . London, Methuen, and New York, Macmillan, 1906.

Chronicles of the Pilgrim Fathers. London, Dent, and New York, Dutton, 1910.

My Faith in Woman Suffrage. London, Woman's Press, 1910.

William Shakespeare. London, Williams and Norgate, and New York, Holt, 1911; revised edition, London, Heinemann, and New York, Macmillan, 1954.

John M. Synge: A Few Personal Recollections. . . . Churchtown, Ireland, Cuala Press, and New York, Macmillan, 1915.

Gallipoli. London, Heinemann, and New York, Macmillan, 1916.

The Old Front Line; or, The Beginning of the Battle of the Somme. London, Heinemann, and New York, Macmillan, 1917.

The War and the Future. New York, Macmillan, 1918; as *St. George and the Dragon*, London, Heinemann, 1919.

The Poems and Plays of John Masefield. New York, Macmillan, 2 vols., 1918.

The Battle of the Somme. London, Heinemann, 1919.

John Ruskin. Privately printed, 1920.

The Taking of Helen and Other Prose Selections. New York, Macmillan, 1924; as *Recent Prose*, London, Heinemann, 1924; revised edition, Heinemann, 1932; Macmillan, 1933.

Shakespeare and Spiritual Life (lecture). London and New York, Oxford University Press, 1924.

With the Living Voice (lecture). London, Heinemann, and New York, Macmillan, 1925.

Oxford Recitations. New York, Macmillan, 1928.

Chaucer (lecture). Cambridge, University Press, and New York, Macmillan, 1931.

Poetry (lecture). London, Heinemann, 1931; New York, Macmillan, 1932.

The Conway: From Her Foundation to the Present Day. London, Heinemann, and New York, Macmillan, 1933; revised edition, Heinemann, 1953; Macmillan, 1954.

Collected Works (Wanderer Edition). London, Heinemann, 5 vols., 1935–37.

Some Memories of W. B. Yeats (includes verse). Dublin, Cuala Press, and New York, Macmillan, 1940.

In the Mill (autobiography). London, Heinemann, and New York, Macmillan, 1941.

The Nine Days Wonder: The Operation Dynamo. London, Heinemann, and New York, Macmillan, 1941.

The Twenty Five Days. London, Heinemann, 1941.

I Want! I Want! London, National Book Council, 1944; New York, Macmillan, 1945.

New Chum (autobiography). London, Heinemann, 1944; New York, Macmillan, 1945.

A Macbeth Production. London, Heinemann, 1945; New York, Macmillan, 1946.

Thanks Before Going. . . . London, Heinemann, 1946; New York, Macmillan, 1947; revised edition, Heinemann, 1947.

A Book of Both Sorts: Selections from the Verse and Prose of John Masefield. London, Heinemann, 1947.

A Book of Prose Selections. London, Heinemann, and New York, Macmillan, 1950.

St. Katherine of Ledbury and Other Ledbury Papers. London, Heinemann, 1951.

So Long to Learn: Chapters of an Autobiography. London, Heinemann, and New York, Macmillan, 1952.

An Elizabethan Theatre in London. Privately printed, 1954.

The Story of Ossian. London, Heinemann, and New York, Macmillan, 1959.

Grace Before Ploughing: Fragments of Autobiography. London, Heinemann, and New York, Macmillan, 1966.

The Letters of John Masefield to Florence Lamont, edited by Corliss and Lansing Lamont. London, Macmillan, and New York, Columbia University Press, 1979.

Letters to Reyna, edited by William Buchan. London, Buchan and Enright, 1983.

Letters to Margaret Bridge, 1915–1919, edited by Donald E. Stanford. Manchester, Carcanet, 1984.

Letters from the Front 1915–17, edited by Peter Vansittart. London, Constable, 1984; New York, Watts, 1985.

Brangwen: The Poet and the Dancer (letters), edited by John Gregory. Lewes, Sussex, Book Guild, 1988.

Editor, with Constance Masefield, *Lyrists of the Restoration.* . . . London, Grant Richards, 1905; New York, Stokes, n.d.

Editor, *The Poems of Robert Herrick.* London, Grant Richards, 1906.

Editor, *Dampier's Voyages.* . . . London, Grant Richards, 2 vols., 1906; New York, Dutton, 1907.

Editor, *A Sailor's Garland.* London, Methuen, and New York, Macmillan, 1906.

Editor, *The Lyrics of Ben Jonson, Beaumont, and Fletcher.* London, Grant Richards, 1906.

Editor, with Constance Masefield, *Essays, Moral and Polite 1660–1714.* London, Grant Richards, 1906; Freeport, New York, Books for Libraries Press, 1971.

Editor, *An English Prose Miscellany.* London, Methuen, 1907.

Editor, *Defoe* (selections). London, Bell, and New York, Macmillan, 1909.

Editor, *The Loyal Subject*, in *The Works of Beaumont and Fletcher*, edited by A. H. Bullen. London, Bell, 1910.

Editor, *My Favourite English Poems.* London, Heinemann, and New York, Macmillan, 1950.

Translator, *Polyxena's Speech from the Hecuba of Euripides.* New York, Macmillan, 1928.

*

Bibliography: *Bibliography of John Masefield* by C. H. Simmons, New York, Columbia University Press, 1930; London, Oxford University Press, 1931.

Critical Studies: *John Masefield* by L. A. G. Strong, London, Longman, 1952; *John Masefield* by Muriel Spark, London, Peter Nevill, 1953; *John Masefield* by Margery Fisher, London, Bodley Head, and New York, Walck, 1963; *Remembering John Masefield* by Corliss Lamont, Rutherford, New Jersey, Fairleigh Dickinson University Press, 1971, London, Kaye and Ward, 1972; *John Masefield* by Sanford Sternlicht, Boston, Twayne, 1977; *John Masefield: A Life* by Constance Babington Smith, London, Oxford University Press, and New York, Macmillan, 1978.

*   *   *

John Masefield, Poet Laureate from 1930 to his death in 1967 at the age of 89, is best remembered as a poet of the sea, whose finest work reflected his early life as a junior merchant marine officer, shipping in windjammers; and whose next best work consisted of long narrative poems that realistically depicted aspects of English society, like the life of agricultural workers, village crime and tragedy, and fox-hunting.

However, Masefield was a novelist too, with 10 historical novels to his credit. They range in quality from stirring and competent to embarrassingly bad. Exquisitely wrought passages can be followed by surprising lapses of imagination. Plots are frequently obfuscated and prose sometimes platitudinous. The historical novels have various settings and themes but can be divided into three categories: sea adventures, novels of the third world, and novels of the ancient world. As a whole these works are leisurely paced, contain rich description, tend to a morality where good always triumphs, avoid sexual reference or activity, present women as cardboard figures if included at all, are emotionally restrained and shallow, use stereotypical characterization, and offer quirky lectures that inculcate tautologically that the meaning of life is that life has meaning.

When Masefield wrote about what he knew well—life at sea—he worked skillfully, but when he was over his head in waters he had not fathomed, such as in writing about Africa, he was absurdly bad.

Masefield's values as a novelist are courage, honour, and the acceptance of responsibility. The stories are wholesome if humourless, and although they seldom connect with common experience, they do offer the reader an introduction to a principled man and a generous mind.

Captain Margaret: A Romance and *The Bird of Dawning* are sea adventures. The former is an apprentice work and the latter is Masefield's best novel. *Captain Margaret* is also a love story but Masefield primarily is imitating Robert Louis Stevenson. Charles Margaret, a handsome, chivalric, 18th-century English gentleman, owns the sloop *Broken Heart*, so christened because of his disappointment in his love for the beautiful Olivia, now married to the criminal Stukely whose nature she is oblivious to. They all sail together on a privateering expedition to the Spanish Main, where Captain Margaret captures a town, Stukely dies, and Olivia and Margaret set out for England to marry and live happily ever after.

The Bird of Dawning, written 25 years later, is set in the late 19th century, and shows Masefield at the height of his power as a novelist. Plot and characterization are strong in this novel, and there is no attempt at a love story. The uncomplicated yarn tells of a sailing-ship race between clippers in the China tea trade, in which the 24-year-old Cyril (Cruiser) Trewsbury, a true English leader, overcomes great vicissitudes to win the race.

Sard Harker, Odtaa ("One Damn Thing After Another"), and *The Taking of the Gry* are located in the imaginary Central American Republic of Santa Barbara, which Masefield created for allegorical purposes just as Joseph Conrad created Costaguana in *Nostromo* (1904). Masefield draws maps of the area he calls the Sugar States and gives it a political and economic history. The events of the trilogy cover 25 years of revolution, war, repression, dictatorship, and benign British intervention. Of the three, *The Taking of the Gry*, a womanless naval saga, is the most successful.

The African novels, *Dead Ned* and *Live and Kicking Ned*, do not work well, for Masefield is never convincing in his secondhand evocation of the "Dark Continent." The two novels tell one story, the adventures of Edward (Ned) Mansell, a young 18th-century Londoner who has just finished medical training when he is unjustly accused of murder, found guilty, and "hanged," but revived in secret by a physician friend. He escapes to Africa where he finds a lost civilization of whites (!), descendent from ancient Greece. A black army threatens to destroy these "Kranois" but Ned's leadership saves them. He then returns to England where he is exonerated.

Masefield's ancient tales, *Basilissa* and *Conquer*, which take place in the Byzantium of Justinian, and *Badon Parchments*, an addition to the Arthuriad, are the author's last works of fiction. They are unsuccessful in that they never achieve believable characterization or transcend the narration of historical events.

Masefield was not a great historical novelist. Though sometimes entertaining, the stories when they are not at sea, are mainly lifeless and humourless. The Santa Barbara novels are a noble failure. *The Bird of Dawning* and the contemporary sea novel *Victorious Troy!; or, The Hurrying Angel*, are the two Masefield novels most worth reading.

—Sanford Sternlicht

MASON, A(lfred) E(dward) W(oodley). British. Born in Camberwell, London, 7 May 1865. Educated at Dulwich College, London, 1878–84; Trinity College, Oxford (exhibitioner in classics, 1887), 1884–87, degrees in classics 1886, 1888. Served in the Royal Marine Light Infantry in World War I, and involved in Naval Intelligence Division secret service missions in Spain, Gibraltar, Morocco, and Mexico. Actor in provincial touring companies, 1888–94 (appeared in first performance of *Arms and the Man*, 1894); Liberal Member of Parliament for Coventry, 1906–10. Honorary Fellow, Trinity College, 1943. *Died 22 November 1948.*

ROMANCE AND HISTORICAL PUBLICATIONS

Novels

The Courtship of Morrice Buckler. London, Macmillan, 1896; New York, Macmillan, 1903.
Lawrence Clavering. London, Innes, and New York, Dodd Mead, 1897.
Parson Kelly. London and New York, Longman, 1900.
Clementina. London, Methuen, and New York, Stokes, 1901.
Fire over England. London, Hodder and Stoughton, and New York, Doubleday, 1936.
Königsmark. London, Hodder and Stoughton, 1938; New York, Doubleday, 1939.
Musk and Amber. London, Hodder and Stoughton, and New York, Doubleday, 1942.

OTHER PUBLICATIONS

Novels

A Romance of Wastdale. London, Mathews, and New York, Stokes, 1895.
The Philanderers. London and New York, Macmillan, 1897.
Miranda of the Balcony. London and New York, Macmillan, 1899.
The Watchers. Bristol, Arrowsmith, and New York, Stokes, 1899.
The Four Feathers. London, Smith Elder, and New York, Macmillan, 1902.
The Truants. London, Smith Elder, and New York, Harper, 1904.
The Broken Road. London, Smith Elder, and New York, Scribner, 1907.
Running Water. London, Hodder and Stoughton, and New York, Century, 1907.
At the Villa Rose. London, Hodder and Stoughton, and New York, Scribner, 1910.
The Turnstile. London, Hodder and Stoughton, and New York, Scribner, 1912.
The Witness for the Defence. London, Hodder and Stoughton, 1913; New York, Scribner, 1914.
The Summons. London, Hodder and Stoughton, and New York, Doran, 1920.

The Winding Stair. London, Hodder and Stoughton, and New York, Doran, 1923.
The House of the Arrow. London, Hodder and Stoughton, and New York, Doran, 1924.
No Other Tiger. London, Hodder and Stoughton, and New York, Doran, 1927.
The Prisoner in the Opal. London, Hodder and Stoughton, and New York, Doubleday, 1928.
The Dean's Elbow. London, Hodder and Stoughton, 1930; New York, Doubleday, 1931.
The Three Gentlemen. London, Hodder and Stoughton, and New York, Doubleday, 1932.
The Sapphire. London, Hodder and Stoughton, and New York, Doubleday, 1933.
They Wouldn't Be Chessmen. London, Hodder and Stoughton, and New York, Doubleday, 1935.
The Drum. London, Hodder and Stoughton, and New York, Doubleday, 1937.
The House in Lordship Lane. London, Hodder and Stoughton, and New York, Dodd Mead, 1946.

Short Stories

Ensign Knightley and Other Stories. London, Constable, and New York, Stokes, 1901.
The Clock. New York, Paget, 1910.
Making Good. New York, Paget, 1910.
The Four Corners of the World. London, Hodder and Stoughton, and New York, Scribner, 1917.
The Episode of the Thermometer. New York, Paget, 1918.
Dilemmas. London, Hodder and Stoughton, 1934; New York, Doubleday, 1935.
The Secret Fear. New York, Doubleday, 1940.

Plays

Blanche de Malètroit, adaptation of the story "The Sire de Malètroit's Door" by Robert Louis Stevenson (produced London, 1894). London, Capper and Newton, 1894.
The Courtship of Morrice Buckler, with Isabel Bateman, adaptation of the novel by Mason (produced London, 1897).
Marjory Strode (produced London, 1908).
Colonel Smith (produced London, 1909). London, privately printed, 1909; revised version, as *Green Stockings* (produced New York, 1911), New York and London, French, 1914.
The Princess Clementina, with George Pleydell Bancroft, adaptation of the novel *Clementina* by Mason (produced Cardiff and London, 1910).
The Witness for the Defence, adaptation of his own novel (produced London and New York, 1911). Privately printed, 1911.
Open Windows (produced London, 1913).
At the Villa Rose, adaptation of his own novel (produced London, 1920). London, Hodder and Stoughton, 1928.
Running Water (produced London, 1922).
The House of the Arrow, adaptation of his own novel (produced London, 1928).
No Other Tiger, adaptation of his own novel (produced Leicester and London, 1928).
A Present from Margate, with Ian Hay (produced London, 1933). London, French, 1934.

Other

The Royal Exchange. London, Royal Exchange, 1920.
Sir George Alexander and the St. James' Theatre. London, Macmillan, 1935.

The Life of Francis Drake. London, Hodder and Stoughton, 1941; New York, Doubleday, 1942.

*

Critical Study: *A. E. W. Mason: The Adventures of a Story Teller* by Roger Lancelyn Green, London, Parrish, 1952.

* * *

Though A. E. W. Mason is perhaps primarily known today for his near-contemporary adventure story *The Four Feathers*, and his detective stories about Inspector Hanaud, such as *At the Villa Rose*, his reputation as one of the best and most popular storytellers in the first half of the 20th century also derived to a great extent from his skill as a writer of historical romances, which he produced at the beginning and end of his career.

Through the work of Scott and Dumas, and their followers, the popularity of the historical tale was in full flood at the end of the 19th century when Mason began to write. Stevenson's masterpieces *Treasure Island* and *Kidnapped* were still on everyone's lips, and a host of successors—Quiller-Couch, Conan Doyle, Stanley Weyman, Samuel Rutherford Crockett—sought to emulate him.

Mason, who turned to writing in his late twenties after appearing on the stage for several years, worked in this established tradition of the tale of adventure set in the historical past, which was sometimes called the costume novel. His novels are usually set somewhere between the Elizabethan age and the middle of the 18th century, where Mason's acting experience gave him considerable facility in period dialogue as well as an understanding of costume and manners, and his plots usually deal with intrigues and romances among kings and princesses, aristocrats and statesmen. This is the world of Handel and Walsingham—not Hogarth and Mother Courage.

A characteristic plot involves a handsome young hero setting out on a difficult mission—to work for the Jacobite rising or to spy on the Spanish Armada. He is then caught up in political intrigues and personal feuds, and manipulated by older and unscrupulous figures. There is plenty of action with the hero having to defend himself with swashbuckling sword-play as Charles Wogan does in *Clementina*, or destroying with gunpowder a Spanish galleon as Robin Aubrey does in *Fire over England*. Duels are not uncommon, and there is many a desperate gallop by night. There is nearly always a love-element in Mason's romances, but the hero is not always fortunate, for though Robin does win his sweetheart, both Wogan and Philip von Königsmark fall passionately in love with women forbidden to them, and end unhappily.

There is indeed a curious awareness of betrayal and failure present in all the novels. Lawrence feels that he has accidentally betrayed Herbert and must atone for it with his life, if necessary, in *Lawrence Clavering*. Wogan and his princess feel guilty about their love in *Clementina*; Robin's father accidentally betrays his own son and commits suicide in *Fire over England*; and Philip is brought down by the envy of his friend Anthony in *Königsmark*.

In the end, in fact, a mood of romantic sadness pervades most of the tales. Though Lawrence outwits his villainous cousin and escapes to France at the conclusion of the very Stevensonian *Lawrence Clavering*, the treachery of his cousin and the failure of the Jacobite cause create a sombre tone. Similarly, although *Clementina* achieves a rattling pace after a clumsy expository beginning, and the hero outwits his Hanoverian enemies enabling Clementina to marry James III, a sense of doom is created, not only by the unhappy failure of that marriage but by the hero's forebodings of disaster.

Fire over England is the one exception to this melancholy pattern, for although the young hero fails to rescue his father, he does help to defeat the Spanish Armada and is happily re-united with Cynthia. But the atmosphere of *Königsmark* is overcast from the beginning when young Philip is imprisoned and humiliated by a political enemy, and though he grows up to become a dashing military hero, he is haunted by memories of his shameful past, so that, when he does find true love, it is too late.

Finally, in *Musk and Amber*, which Roger Lancelyn Green has described as Mason's "highest point . . . on the very snow-line of great literature," the hero is doomed from the beginning. Young Julian, Earl of Linchcombe, and heir to the beautiful 18th-century estate of Grest, is kidnapped by relations, and passed to Italian peasants who have him castrated and then trained as an opera singer. Though Julian achieves great success and uses his power and wealth to return to England and take his revenge, the novel ends with him renouncing his title and returning to live in obscurity in Italy.

There is an individual flavour about Mason's best work, and, though his historical romances come very close to "tushery" at times, his craftsmanship and zest usually enable him to avoid the worst excesses. In *Fire over England* and *Musk and Amber* there are moments of pain and sadness unusual in the genre for the period.

—Dennis Butts

———

MASON, F(rancis) Van Wyck. Also wrote as Geoffrey Coffin (with Helen Brawner); Frank W. Mason; Ward Weaver. American. Born in Boston, Massachusetts, 11 November 1901. Educated at Berkshire School, 1919–20; Harvard University, Cambridge, Massachusetts, B.S. 1924. Served in the Allied Expeditionary Forces in France, 1918–19: Second Lieutenant; New York National Guard Cavalry, 1924–29: Sergeant; Maryland National Guard Field Artillery, 1930–33: First Lieutenant; General Staff Corps Officer and Chief Historian, Civil and Military Government Section, 1942–45; Supreme Headquarters, Allied Expeditionary Force, 1943–45: Colonel; Medaille de Sauvetage, Croix de Guerre with two palms, French Legion of Honor. Married 1) Dorothy Louise Macready in 1927 (died 1958), two children; 2) Jeanne-Louise Hand in 1958. Importer and after 1928 self-employed writer; lived in Bermuda, 1956–78. Recipient: Valley Forge Foundation Medal, 1953; Society of Colonial Wars Citation of Honour, 1960. *Died 29 August 1978.*

ROMANCE AND HISTORICAL PUBLICATIONS

Novels

Captain Nemesis. New York, Putnam, 1931; London, Hale, 1959.
Three Harbours. Philadelphia, Lippincott, 1938; London, Jarrolds, 1939.
Stars on the Sea. Philadelphia, Lippincott, and London, Jarrolds, 1940.
Hang My Wreath (as Ward Weaver). New York, Funk and Wagnalls, 1941; London, Jarrolds, 1942.
Rivers of Glory. Philadelphia, Lippincott, 1942; London, Jarrolds, 1944.
End of Track (as Ward Weaver). New York, Reynal, 1943.
Eagle in the Sky. Philadelphia, Lippincott, 1948; London, Jarrolds, 1949.

Cutlass Empire. New York, Doubleday, 1949; London, Jarrolds, 1950.

Valley Forge: 24 December 1777. New York, Doubleday, 1950.

Proud New Flags. Philadelphia, Lippincott, 1951; London, Jarrolds, 1952.

Golden Admiral: A Novel of Sir Francis Drake and the Armada. New York, Doubleday, 1953; London, Jarrolds, 1954.

Wild Drums Beat. New York, Pocket Books, 1954.

The Barbarians. New York, Pocket Books, 1954; London, Hale, 1956.

Blue Hurricane. Philadelphia, Lippincott, 1954; London, Jarrolds, 1955.

Silver Leopard. New York, Doubleday, 1955; London, Jarrolds, 1956.

Captain Judas. New York, Pocket Books, 1955; London, Hale, 1957.

Our Valiant Few. Boston, Little Brown, 1956; as *To Whom Be Glory*, London, Jarrolds, 1957.

Lysander. New York, Pocket Books, 1956; London, Hale, 1958.

The Young Titan. New York, Doubleday, 1959; London, Hutchinson, 1960.

Return of the Eagles. New York, Pocket Books, 1959.

Manila Galleon. Boston, Little Brown, and London, Hutchinson, 1961.

The Sea 'venture. New York, Doubleday, 1961; London, Hutchinson, 1962.

Rascals' Heaven. New York, Doubleday, and London, Hutchinson, 1965.

Wild Horizon. Boston, Little Brown, 1966.

Harpoon in Eden. New York, Doubleday, 1969.

Brimstone Club. Boston, Little Brown, 1971; London, Hutchinson, 1972.

Roads to Liberty (includes *Three Harbours, Stars on the Sea, Eagle in the Sky*). Boston, Little Brown, 1972.

Guns for Rebellion. New York, Doubleday, 1977; London, Hutchinson, 1978.

Armored Giants. Boston, Little Brown, 1980; London, Hutchinson, 1981.

OTHER PUBLICATIONS

Novels

Seeds of Murder. New York, Doubleday, 1930; London, Eldon Press, 1937.

The Vesper Service Murders. New York, Doubleday, 1931; London, Eldon Press, 1935.

The Fort Terror Murders. New York, Doubleday, 1931; London, Eldon Press, 1936.

The Yellow Arrow Murders. New York, Doubleday, 1932; London, Eldon Press, 1935.

The Branded Spy Murders. New York, Doubleday, 1932; London, Eldon Press, 1936.

Spider House. New York, Mystery League, 1932; London, Hale, 1959.

The Shanghai Bund Murders. New York, Doubleday, 1933; London, Eldon Press, 1934; revised edition, as *The China Sea Murders*, New York, Pocket Books, 1959; London, Consul, 1961.

The Sulu Sea Murders. New York, Doubleday, 1933; London, Eldon Press, 1936.

Oriental Division G-2 (omnibus). New York, Reynal, n.d.

The Budapest Parade Murders. New York, Doubleday, and London, Eldon Press, 1935.

Murder in the Senate (as Geoffrey Coffin, with Helen Brawner). New York, Dodge, 1935; London, Hurst and Blackett, 1936.

The Washington Legation Murders. New York, Doubleday, 1935; London, Eldon Press, 1937.

The Forgotten Fleet Mystery (as Geoffrey Coffin, with Helen Brawner). New York, Dodge, 1936; London, Jarrolds, 1943.

The Seven Seas Murders (novelets). New York, Doubleday, 1936; London, Eldon Press, 1937.

The Castle Island Case. New York, Reynal, 1937; London, Jarrolds, 1938; revised edition, as *The Multi-Million Dollar Murders*, New York, Pocket Books, 1960; London, Hale, 1961.

The Hong Kong Airbase Murders. New York, Doubleday, 1937; London, Jarrolds, 1940.

The Cairo Garter Murders. New York, Doubleday, and London, Jarrolds, 1938.

The Singapore Exile Murders. New York, Doubleday, and London, Jarrolds, 1939.

The Bucharest Ballerina Murders. New York, Stokes, 1940; London, Jarrolds, 1941.

Military Intelligence—8 (omnibus). New York, Stokes, 1941.

The Rio Casino Intrigue. New York, Reynal, 1941; London, Jarrolds, 1942.

The Man from G-2 (omnibus). New York, Reynal, n.d.

Saigon Singer. New York, Doubleday, 1946; London, Barker, 1948.

Dardanelles Derelict. New York, Doubleday, 1949; London, Barker, 1950.

Himalayan Assignment. New York, Doubleday, 1952; London, Hale, 1953.

Two Tickets to Tangier. New York, Doubleday, 1955; London, Hale, 1956.

The Gracious Lily Affair. New York, Doubleday, 1957; London, Hale, 1958.

Secret Mission to Bangkok. New York, Doubleday, 1960; London, Hale, 1961.

Trouble in Burma. New York, Doubleday, 1962; London, Hale, 1963.

Zanzibar Intrigue. New York, Doubleday, 1963; London, Hale, 1964.

Maracaibo Mission. New York, Doubleday, 1965; London, Hale, 1966.

The Deadly Orbit Mission. New York, Doubleday, and London, Hale, 1968.

Novels as Frank W. Mason

Q-Boat. Philadelphia, Lippincott, 1943.

Pilots, Man Your Planes! Philadelphia, Lippincott, 1944.

Flight into Danger. Philadelphia, Lippincott, 1946.

Other

The Winter at Valley Forge (for children). New York, Random House, 1953; as *Washington at Valley Forge*, Eau Claire, Wisconsin, E. M. Hale, 1953.

The Battle of Lake Erie (for children). Boston, Houghton Mifflin, 1960.

The Battle for New Orleans (for children). Boston, Houghton Mifflin, 1962.

The Battle for Quebec (for children). Boston, Houghton Mifflin, 1965.

The Maryland Colony (for children). New York, Macmillan, 1969.

Editor, *The Fighting American*. New York, Reynal, 1943; London, Jarrolds, 1945.

Editor, *American Men at Arms*. Boston, Little Brown, 1964.

*   *   *

F. Van Wyck Mason retired from a successful business career in the 1920's, a dedicated advocate of the American free enterprise system and American military superiority, to write a series of detective stories featuring a U.S. Army intelligence officer named North, which he continued to produce at intervals throughout his career. These mystery stories never achieved the reputation, or sales, of those of S. S. Van Dine, Ellery Queen, or Erle Stanley Gardner; but Mason found the metier in which he would triumph in the historical romance. A first venture into this field—*Captain Nemesis*, about Caribbean pirates—attracted few reviews or sales in the depression year of 1931, when the book business was generally bad; but in 1938, as improved economic conditions resulted in improved book sales and the hoopla attendant upon the celebration of the sesquicentennial of the American Constitution led to an unprecedented demand for romances of national glory, Mason hit the bestseller lists with *Three Harbours*. This rousing tale of Norfolk, Boston, and Bermuda (as well as Salem and Philadelphia), is the first of a tetralogy on the founding of the American Navy in 1774–75 as the Revolution was brewing. *Stars on the Sea*, *Rivers of Glory*, and *Eagle in the Sky* carried readers forward to the defeat of Cornwallis in 1781.

In a foreword Mason set forth his concept of the historical novel that set the pattern for more than a dozen volumes to follow:

> . . . the main facts, dates, and figures are as nearly correct as a painstaking and selective research can make them. The same also applies to such details as uniforms, military movements, legal proceedings, customs, currency, and documents. The writer of a novel which employs a historical setting is, I believe, to the careful historian somewhat as a landscape painter to an architect. . . . Therefore, in the selection of incidents used in this tale I have necessarily omitted or glossed over some historical events of great importance which unfortunately did not bear on the story.

Contemporary reviewers were not much impressed, however, observing that Mason was not in a league with such respected historical novelists as Kenneth Roberts and Esther Forbes. Holmes Alexander in the *Saturday Review of Literature* labeled productions like Mason's "costume novels," noteworthy for their excitement and color. Readers were intrigued, however, by Mason's vivid rendition of incidents designed to further his "underlying purpose" of telling how "the early merchants of America's Eastern Coast lived, to show what they did and, on occasion, what they suffered" in order to "be reasonably free in the conduct of a business." "They met a crisis and defeated it without the aid of a paternalistic regime," Mason concludes, expressing the hope that should contemporary merchants meet such a challenge, they would act "as courageously as did their forbears."

At a time when highbrow intellectuals were attacking bourgeois American traditions and trying to proselytize readers with "proletarian" novels, Mason was offering patriotic audiences the comfortable message that though their ancestors wore funny clothes, they spoke the same language and dreamed the same dream as their descendants. Although the trappings of his tales are 18th-century, the sentiments and even the language are straight from the "go-getter" stories of Clarence Buddington Kelland in the *Saturday Evening Post*: as Mason's hero exclaims, for example, at a crucial point in the action, "Well, it stands to reason that without merchants to do her business, America can never amount to anything. . . . Fortunes will be made by those who get started early, but they'll have to run risks no assurance underwriter would cover."

Not all Mason's romances were bestsellers, but the tales that he spun from his formula at his Bermuda retreat continued to entertain readers enjoying historical sanction for their booster philosophy. Since Mason's novels remained remarkably consistent in quality, one's preferences among them may depend upon their historical backgrounds ranging from modern Europeans' first quest for colonial empire to the little-known struggle to keep the Mississippi River open for trade during the Civil War. Since his titles are not self-explanatory, a listing of the order for reading his major works chronologically by setting is useful: *Silver Leopard* (the First Crusade), *Golden Admiral* (Sir Francis Drake and Spanish Armada), *Cutlass Empire* (Sir Henry Morgan, Caribbean pirate), *The Sea 'venture* (British colonies in Jamestown and Bermuda), *The Young Titan* (New England during the French and Indian Wars), *Manila Galleon* (the British in the Pacific in the 1840's), *Proud New Flags*, *Blue Hurricane*, and *Our Valiant Few* (the navy in the Civil War). Mason also reworked some of his old material with new in books intended to interest teenagers in history, especially that of America's mercantile princes.

—Warren French

MASTERS, John. American. Born with British nationality in Calcutta, India, 26 October 1914; became U.S. citizen, 1954. Educated at Wellington School, Somerset; Royal Military College, Sandhurst, Surrey. Married Barbara Allcard; one son and two daughters. Served in the British Army, 1934 until his retirement as Lieutenant Colonel in 1948: commissioned 2nd Lieutenant, Indian Army, 1934; served in the 2nd Battalion, 4th Prince of Wales's Own Gurkha Rifles, 1935; served on the North West Frontier, 1936–37; Adjutant, 1939; served in Iraq, Syria, and Persia, 1941; Brigade Major, 114th Indian Infantry Brigade, 1942, and 111th Indian Infantry Brigade, 1943; Commandant, 3rd Battalion, 1944; served in Burma, 1944–45; General Staff Officer-1, 19th Indian Division, 1945; General Staff Officer-2, Staff College, Camberley, Surrey, 1947: D.S.O. (Companion, Distinguished Service Order), 1944; O.B.E. (Officer, Order of the British Empire), 1945. Lived many years in Santa Fe, New Mexico. *Died 7 May 1983.*

ROMANCE AND HISTORICAL PUBLICATIONS

Novels (series: Loss of Eden; Savage Family)

An Indian Trilogy (Savage). London, Joseph, 1978.
  Nightrunners of Bengal. London, Joseph, and New York, Viking Press, 1951.
  The Deceivers. London, Joseph, and New York, Viking Press, 1952.
  Bhowani Junction. London, Joseph, and New York, Viking Press, 1954.
The Lotus and the Wind. London, Joseph, and New York, Viking Press, 1953.
Coromandel! London, Joseph, and New York, Viking Press, 1955.
Far, Far the Mountain Peak. London, Joseph, and New York, Viking Press, 1957.

The Venus of Konpara. London, Joseph, and New York, Harper, 1960.
The Rock. London, Joseph, and New York, Putnam, 1970.
Loss of Eden trilogy:
  Now, God Be Thanked. London, Joseph, and New York, McGraw Hill, 1979.
  Heart of War. London, Joseph, and New York, McGraw Hill, 1980.
  By the Green of the Spring. London, Joseph, and New York, McGraw Hill, 1981.

OTHER PUBLICATIONS

Novels

Fandango Rock. London, Joseph, and New York, Harper, 1959.
To the Coral Strand. London, Joseph, and New York, Harper, 1962.
Trial at Monomoy. London, Joseph, and New York, Harper, 1964.
Fourteen Eighteen. London, Joseph, 1965.
The Breaking Strain. London, Joseph, and New York, Delacorte Press, 1967.
The Ravi Lancers. London, Joseph, and New York, Doubleday, 1972.
Thunder at Sunset. London, Joseph, and New York, Doubleday, 1974.
The Field-Marshal's Memoirs. London, Joseph, and New York, Doubleday, 1975.
The Himalaya Concerto. London, Joseph, and New York, Doubleday, 1976.
Man of War. London, Joseph, 1983; as *High Command*, New York, Morrow, 1984.

Other

The Compleat Indian Angler. London, Country Life, 1938.
Bugles and a Tiger: A Personal Adventure. London, Joseph, and New York, Viking Press, 1956.
The Road Past Mandalay (autobiography). London, Joseph, and New York, Viking Press, 1961.
Casanova. London, Joseph, and New York, Geis, 1969.
Pilgrim Son: A Personal Odyssey. London, Joseph, and New York, Putnam, 1971.

*   *   *

John Masters's India is a place where the constraints of European civilisation can be shrugged off, where (in the words of Joseph Conrad's narrator in *Heart of Darkness*) the white man is liberated "by the awakening of forgotten and brutal instincts, by the memory of gratified and monstrous passions." In his first novel, a character complains that the English occupy only "the surface of India"; in the course of his tales the protagonist ventures beneath this surface and encounters himself, transmogrified into the savage.

Ironically, it is the Savage family whose adventures Masters intended to chronicle in his projected series of 30 or more novels. The scope of his ambition can be gauged by the fact that the series would encompass all of the years of the English presence in India, from around 1600 to Independence in 1947. In the end, he completed only a few of these, and collected three of them as *An Indian Trilogy: Nightrunners of Bengal, The Deceivers,* and *Bhowani Junction.* Of these, the latter falls outside the scope of this essay as it deals with the events immediately prior to Independence.

Nightrunners of Bengal is in many ways Masters's most accomplished novel; despite the overindulgences of gothic melodrama, it displays most eloquently his fascination with the exotic and horrific essence of the subcontinent. The novel is set in 1857, the year of the Great Mutiny of the sepoys and the centenary of British rule in India. Rodney Savage, the protagonist, is a workhorse of Anglo-Indian administration, an officer of the East India Company. He is in charge of a company of sepoys whom he devotedly trusts, but whose minds and imaginations he is forced to recognize are closed to him. The devastating tedium of garrison life is portrayed with bitter accuracy; Masters himself was an officer in charge of native troops, and describes the petty rivalries, intrigues, and snobberies in astonishing detail. Savage sees his life as a colonial functionary stretch into infinity: promotion by slow degrees, retirement to England, death. But two events, linked in a byzantine plot, disrupt the humdrum stability. The first is a conspiracy to murder the prince of a neighbouring "independent" state. Savage, sent to police the subsequent disturbance, becomes involved in a passionate affair with its new ruler. The proud, cruel, beautiful harlot-queen Sumitra is an index to the author's notion of one aspect of India, as a repository of an exotic sensuality to which the civilised man is barred. Savage is tempted by her offer to become lord both of her and her state, but finds himself unable to cross over into "the other room" as a dominant metaphor describes it.

He returns to the bloodless, enervated Anglo-India to which he belongs, the incident apparently finished. But the second event occurs, abruptly, but foreshadowed by signals to which the English have been oblivious. The sepoys rise up and in one bloody night manage to murder, rape, and destroy all trace of British rule in Savage's garrison. This scene is rendered in all the brutal detail the author can muster; interestingly, it breaks with the straightforward linear course of the narrative so far and becomes a dizzying montage of horrific chaos. The experience turns Savage's mind, and when he escapes with his badly injured son and another survivor, he retreats into murderous paranoid fantasies of revenge and apocalypse. The remainder of the novel relates their escape to safe territory, and the climactic battle with the mutinous sepoys. It is a fast-paced, exhilarating, and sometimes brutal tale, flavoured with the melodramatic passion of a story narrated at a high pitch of emotion. It addresses the problem of independence through the device of Savage's love affair with Sumitra, whose ardent nationalism is revealed to have engineered the uprising. Confronted, after the gruesome death of his wife, with the choice between her and the other English survivor, Caroline Langford, he chooses the latter; by this decision, through the workings of the labyrinthine plot, he is revealed to have saved all India from revolt. This far-reaching (or far-fetched) consequence is characteristic of Masters's novels, where the plot is tightly bound and few actions are without effects.

The Deceivers, though published a year later, relates the events of a previous generation. Rodney Savage's father William infiltrates and destroys the *thugee* organisation, who are the deceivers of the title. The thugs, who are estimated to have killed over a million people, were a religious sect who devoted themselves to robbery and murder in the service of the destroyer-goddess Kali. Masters freely admits to using the novelist's freedom to create a new situation, and there is no doubt that he employs this licence to glamourise the historical facts behind the suppression of *thugee.* William Savage, on learning of a series of unexplained murders in his district, adopts the identity of a thug, travelling with a band and participating in their murders until he gains enough evidence to present to the administration.

So good is he at impersonating the devoted killer, he actually takes command of the band; more dangerously, he begins to lose his previous identity and finds his true vocation as a thug. Only a massive act of will enables him to return to Anglo-Indian life and expose the corruption below the apparent surface of the country. For he has been a poor "paper administrator," clumsy, inarticulate, and inept when dealing with administrative routine; his only skill has been a profound empathy with the land and native population. Once again, the foray into Indian life, crossing over into "the other room," has provided the protagonist with the kind of existential freedom to confront terrible aspects of his own self. Masters has been accused of subtle racism in his portrayal of the squalid aspects of Indian life and culture; but in fact he suggests that at his centre "civilised" man harbours the same horror-driven impulses toward unlimited destruction and sexual fulfilment. Moreover, the situations he portrays in these books are, to say the least, extreme. Despite his claim that he understands the Indians "better than Kipling," Masters feels under no obligation to present ordinary Indian life.

Other historical works include *The Lotus and the Wind*, set in the troubled times of tension with Russia in the 1880's; *Far, Far the Mountain Peak*, which relates the adventure of a group of mountaineers in a Himalayan expedition; and *The Venus of Konpara*, in which a young prince discovers his exotic love and her exact double graven in rock thousands of years beforehand. This latter book cleverly exploits the dichotomy hinted at in earlier works, in which Indian comes to stand for erotic gratification and English for sexual inhibitions. The remarkable heroine of this book becomes the focus of a multiple sexual rivalry between the young prince, educated in Eton and Sandhurst, his mentor Mr. Kendrick (revealed to be impotent), his wife, and others. Although the book aims at a grand tragic conclusion, Masters succumbs to the demands of an excessively romanticised plot and schematic symbolism.

It would be absurd to claim that Masters has created works of subliminal beauty; to make comparisons with D. H. Lawrence (as some have done) would be fatuous at best. But his novels are adventure stories in the classic mould, laden with excitement, historical detail, and melodramatic sensibility, vastly enjoyable and compelling. At his fantastic best, he presents lurid images of the self which reflect, as do all gothic fantasies, a bizarre truth about the self. He aims, with his India, to offer an alternative realm of the unlimited for his European reader.

—Alan Murphy

MATHER, Anne. Also writes as Caroline Fleming. Address: c/o Mills and Boon Ltd., 18–24 Paradise Road, Richmond, Surrey TW9 1SR, England.

ROMANCE AND HISTORICAL PUBLICATIONS

Novels

Caroline. London, Hale, 1965.
Beloved Stranger. London, Hale, 1966; as *Legacy of the Past*, London, Mills and Boon, 1975; Toronto, Harlequin, 1974.
Design for Loving. London, Hale, 1966.
Masquerade. London, Hale, 1966; Toronto, Harlequin, 1972.
The Arrogance of Love. London, Hale, 1968; Toronto, Harlequin, 1976.

Dark Venetian (as Caroline Fleming). London, Hale, 1969; as Anne Mather, Toronto, Harlequin, 1976.
The Enchanted Island. London, Hale, 1969.
Dangerous Rhapsody. London, Hale, 1969; Toronto, Harlequin, 1977.
Legend of Lexandros. London, Mills and Boon, 1969; Toronto, Harlequin, 1973.
Dangerous Enchantment. London, Mills and Boon, 1969; Toronto, Harlequin, 1974.
Tangled Tapestry. London, Mills and Boon, 1969.
The Arrogant Duke. London, Mills and Boon, and Toronto, Harlequin, 1970.
Charlotte's Hurricane. London, Mills and Boon, 1970; Toronto, Harlequin, 1971.
Lord of Zaracus. London, Mills and Boon, 1970; Toronto, Harlequin, 1972.
Sweet Revenge. London, Mills and Boon, 1970; Toronto, Harlequin, 1973.
Who Rides the Tiger. London, Mills and Boon, 1970; Toronto, Harlequin, 1973.
Moon Witch. London, Mills and Boon, 1970; Toronto, Harlequin, 1974.
Master of Falcon's Head. London, Mills and Boon, 1970; Toronto, Harlequin, 1974.
The Reluctant Governess. London, Mills and Boon, 1971; Toronto, Harlequin, 1972.
The Pleasure and the Pain. London, Mills and Boon, 1971; Toronto, Harlequin, 1973.
The Sanchez Tradition. London, Mills and Boon, 1971; Toronto, Harlequin, 1973.
Storm in a Rain Barrel. London, Mills and Boon, 1971; Toronto, Harlequin, 1973.
Dark Enemy. London, Mills and Boon, 1971; Toronto, Harlequin, 1973.
All the Fire. London, Mills and Boon, 1971; Toronto, Harlequin, 1976.
The High Valley. London, Mills and Boon, 1971; Toronto, Harlequin, 1976.
The Autumn of the Witch. London, Mills and Boon, 1972; Toronto, Harlequin, 1973.
Living with Adam. London, Mills and Boon, 1972; Toronto, Harlequin, 1973.
A Distant Sound of Thunder. London, Mills and Boon, 1972; Toronto, Harlequin, 1973.
Monkshood. London, Mills and Boon, 1972; Toronto, Harlequin, 1973.
Prelude to Enchantment. London, Mills and Boon, 1972; Toronto, Harlequin, 1974.
The Night of the Bulls. London, Mills and Boon, 1972; Toronto, Harlequin, 1974.
Jake Howard's Wife. London, Mills and Boon, 1973; Toronto, Harlequin, 1974.
A Savage Beauty. London, Mills and Boon, 1973; Toronto, Harlequin, 1974.
Chase a Green Shadow. London, Mills and Boon, 1973; Toronto, Harlequin, 1974.
White Rose of Winter. London, Mills and Boon, 1973; Toronto, Harlequin, 1974.
Mask of Scars. London, Mills and Boon, 1973; Toronto, Harlequin, 1975.
The Waterfalls of the Moon. London, Mills and Boon, 1973; Toronto, Harlequin, 1975.
The Shrouded Web. London, Mills and Boon, 1973; Toronto, Harlequin, 1976.
Seen by Candlelight. Toronto, Harlequin, 1974.

Leopard in the Snow. London, Mills and Boon, and Toronto, Harlequin, 1974.

The Japanese Screen. London, Mills and Boon, 1974; Toronto, Harlequin, 1975.

Rachel Trevellyan. London, Mills and Boon, 1974; Toronto, Harlequin, 1975.

Silver Fruit upon Silver Trees. London, Mills and Boon, 1974; Toronto, Harlequin, 1975.

Dark Moonless Night. London, Mills and Boon, 1974; Toronto, Harlequin, 1975.

Witchstone. London, Mills and Boon, 1974; Toronto, Harlequin, 1975.

No Gentle Possession. Toronto, Harlequin, 1975.

Pale Dawn, Dark Sunset. London, Mills and Boon, and Toronto, Harlequin, 1975.

Take What You Want. London, Mills and Boon, 1975; Toronto, Harlequin, 1976.

Come the Vintage. London, Mills and Boon, 1975; Toronto, Harlequin, 1976.

Dark Castle. London, Mills and Boon, 1975; Toronto, Harlequin, 1976.

Country of the Falcon. London, Mills and Boon, 1975; Toronto, Harlequin, 1976.

For the Love of Sara. London, Mills and Boon, 1975; Toronto, Harlequin, 1976.

Valley Deep, Mountain High. London, Mills and Boon, 1976; Toronto, Harlequin, 1977.

The Smouldering Flame. London, Mills and Boon, 1976; Toronto, Harlequin, 1977.

Wild Enchantress. London, Mills and Boon, 1976; Toronto, Harlequin, 1977.

Beware the Beast. London, Mills and Boon, 1976; Toronto, Harlequin, 1977.

Devil's Mount. London, Mills and Boon, 1976; Toronto, Harlequin, 1977.

Forbidden. London, Mills and Boon, 1976; Toronto, Harlequin, 1978.

Come Running. London, Mills and Boon, 1976; Toronto, Harlequin, 1978.

Alien Wife. London, Mills and Boon, and Toronto, Harlequin, 1977.

The Medici Lover. London, Mills and Boon, and Toronto, Harlequin, 1977.

Born Out of Love. London, Mills and Boon, and Toronto, Harlequin, 1977.

A Trial Marriage. London, Mills and Boon, and Toronto, Harlequin, 1977.

Devil in Velvet. London, Mills and Boon, 1977; Toronto, Harlequin, 1978.

Loren's Baby. London, Mills and Boon, and Toronto, Harlequin, 1978.

Rooted in Dishonour. London, Mills and Boon, and Toronto, Harlequin, 1978.

Proud Harvest. London, Mills and Boon, and Toronto, Harlequin, 1978.

Scorpions' Dance. London, Mills and Boon, and Toronto, Harlequin, 1978.

Captive Destiny. London, Mills and Boon, 1978; Toronto, Harlequin, 1981.

Fallen Angel. London, Mills and Boon, 1978; Toronto, Harlequin, 1979.

Apollo's Seed. London, Mills and Boon, 1979; Toronto, Harlequin, 1980.

Hell or High Water. London, Mills and Boon, 1979.

The Judas Trap. London, Mills and Boon, 1979.

Lure of Eagles. London, Mills and Boon, and Toronto, Harlequin, 1979.

Melting Fire. London, Mills and Boon, 1979.

Images of Love. London, Mills and Boon, and Toronto, Harlequin, 1980.

Sandstorm. London, Mills and Boon, and Toronto, Harlequin, 1980.

Spirit of Atlantis. London, Mills and Boon, and Toronto, Harlequin, 1980.

Whisper of Darkness. London, Mills and Boon, and Toronto, Harlequin, 1980.

Castles of Sand. London, Mills and Boon, 1981.

Forbidden Flame. London, Mills and Boon, and Toronto, Harlequin, 1981.

A Haunting Compulsion. London, Mills and Boon, and Toronto, Harlequin, 1981.

Innocent Obsession. London, Mills and Boon, and Toronto, Harlequin, 1981.

Duelling Fire. London, Mills and Boon, 1981.

Edge of Temptation. London, Mills and Boon, and Toronto, Harlequin, 1982.

Stormspell. London, Mills and Boon, and Toronto, Harlequin, 1982.

Impetuous Masquerade. London, Mills and Boon, 1982.

A Passionate Affair. London, Mills and Boon, 1982.

Smokescreen. London, Mills and Boon, 1982.

Season of Mist. London, Mills and Boon, 1982.

Cage of Shadows. London, Mills and Boon, 1983.

Green Lightning. London, Mills and Boon, 1983.

An Elusive Desire. London, Mills and Boon, 1983.

Sirocco. London, Mills and Boon, 1983.

Wild Concerto. London, Mills and Boon, and Toronto, Harlequin, 1983.

Moondrift. London, Mills and Boon, 1984.

Pale Orchid. London, Mills and Boon, 1985.

Act of Possession. London, Mills and Boon, 1985.

An All Consuming Passion. London, Mills and Boon, 1985.

Stolen Summer. London, Mills and Boon, 1985.

Hidden in the Flame. London, Mills and Boon, and Toronto, Worldwide, 1985.

The Longest Pleasure. Toronto, Harlequin, 1986.

Burning Inheritance. London, Mills and Boon, 1987.

Night Heat. London, Mills and Boon, and Toronto, Harlequin, 1987.

Dark Mosaic. London, Mills and Boon, 1989.

A Fever in the Blood. London, Mills and Boon, 1989.

OTHER PUBLICATIONS

Play

Screenplay: *Leopard in the Snow,* with Jill Hyem, 1978.

*   *   *

Among the most prolific of the series romance writers, Anne Mather often writes novels that are more complex than those of her contemporaries. Her books have more subplots and she employs more texture and mood in her stories. Occasionally, her books have subtle gothic overtones with brooding heroes who live in inaccessible and mysterious places with secret problems for the heroine to solve. In *Whisper of Darkness* the hero is maimed and convinced no one could love him. The heroine liberates him from his self-imposed exile and helps his troubled daughter, much as the heroines in "governess gothics" do although she has no mystery to solve. In *Edge of Temptation* and *Come Running* the hero is a married man whose wife must be disposed of before the characters can come together. Mather's heroines often seem less passive than those of other series romance writers. Although most of her novels are set in England, Mather also employs exotic locations abroad to provide romantic suspense. Because of her richer plots, her characters are occasionally kept apart by outside forces rather than by the internal conflicts and misunderstandings of most series romances.

Mather was one of the first series writers to use premarital sex in her novels and one of the few whose heroines fell in love with married men. But despite her innovations that move beyond the usual situations of series romances, Mather always handles potentially scandalous material with care and taste.

—Kay Mussell

MATTHEWS, Patricia (Anne, née Ernst). Also writes as P. A. Brisco; Patty Brisco; Laura Wylie. American. Born in San Fernando, California, 1 July 1927. Educated at Pasadena Junior College, California; Mt. San Antonio Junior College, California; California State University, Los Angeles. Married 1) Marvin Owen Brisco in 1946 (divorced 1961), two sons; 2) Clayton Hartley Matthews in 1971. Secretary and administrator, California State University, 1959–77. Recipient: *West Coast Review of Books* award, 1979, 1983. Address: P.O. Box 277, Bonsall, California 92003, U.S.A.

Romance and Historical Publications

Novels

Love's Avenging Heart. New York, Pinnacle, and London, Corgi, 1977.
Love's Wildest Promise. New York, Pinnacle, 1977; London, Corgi, 1978.
Love, Forever More. New York, Pinnacle, 1977; London, Corgi, 1978.
Love's Daring Dream. New York, Pinnacle, 1978; London, Corgi, 1979.
Love's Pagan Heart. New York, Pinnacle, 1978; London, Corgi, 1979.
Love's Magic Moment. New York, Pinnacle, and London, Corgi, 1979.
Love's Golden Destiny. New York, Pinnacle, 1979; London, Corgi, 1980.
The Night Visitor (as Laura Wylie). New York, Bantam, 1979; as Patricia Matthews, London, Severn House, 1987.
Love's Raging Tide. New York, Pinnacle, and London, Corgi, 1980.
Love's Bold Journey. New York, Pinnacle, 1980; London, Corgi, 1981.
Love's Sweet Agony. New York, Pinnacle, 1980; London, Corgi, 1981.
Tides of Love. New York, Bantam, and London, Corgi, 1981.
Midnight Whispers, with Clayton Matthews. New York, Bantam, 1981; London, Corgi, 1982.
Embers of Dawn. New York, Bantam, and London, Corgi, 1982.
Empire, with Clayton Matthews. New York, Bantam, 1982; London, Corgi, 1983.

Flames of Glory. New York, Bantam, and London, Corgi, 1983.
Dancer of Dreams. New York, Bantam, and London, Century, 1984.
Gambler in Love. New York, Bantam, and London, Corgi, 1985.
Midnight Lavender, with Clayton Matthews. New York, Bantam, 1985; London, Corgi, 1986.
Tame the Restless Heart. New York, Bantam, 1986.
Enchanted. Toronto, Worldwide, 1987.
Thursday and the Lady. Toronto, Worldwide, 1987.
Mirrors. Toronto, Worldwide, 1988.
Oasis. Toronto, Worldwide, 1988; London, Severn House, 1989.
The Dreaming Tree. Toronto, Worldwide, and London, Severn House, 1989.

Novels as Patty Brisco, with Clayton Matthews

Horror at Gull House. New York, Belmont, 1970.
House of Candles. New York, Manor, 1973.
The Crystal Window. New York, Avon, 1973.
Mist of Evil. New York, Manor, 1976.

Other Publications

Novel as P. A. Brisco

The Other People. Reseda, California, Powell, 1979.

Verse

Love's Many Faces. New York, Bantam, 1979.

Other (for children)

Destruction at Dawn. Belmont, California, Lake, 1986.
Twister. Belmont, California, Lake, 1986.

Other (for children) as Patty Brisco

Merry's Treasure. New York, Avalon, 1970.
The Carnival Mystery. New York, Scholastic, 1974.
The Campus Mystery. New York, Scholastic, 1977.
Raging Rapids. Minneapolis, Creative Education, 1979.
Too Much in Love. New York, Scholastic, 1979.

*

Manuscript Collection: California State College, Fullerton.

Patricia Matthews comments:
    To me there are a magic and mystery in the past. During my more than 30 years of writing I have written, and enjoyed writing, many different types of fiction; however, the historical novel has the firmest grip upon my imagination. The past is like a huge jigsaw puzzle, with millions of fascinating pieces. Through anthropology, archeology, and historical research, we find some of those pieces, and in putting them together, begin to understand our world and the sort of people we once were. I have written 20 historical novels so far, but I never grow tired of them. Each book I research teaches me more, and gives me more pieces of that marvelous puzzle; the nature of mankind.

*   *   *

With a powerful blending of passion, violence, and intrigue, Patricia Matthews has perfected her distinctive formula for the historical romance. Her heroines are sensual and wildly spirited, which is fortunate as they are usually subjected to a physical and psychological assault that would destroy less resilient characters. Unlike the leading ladies of traditional romance novels, Matthews's heroines rarely retain their virginity beyond the opening chapters. There is none of the conventional slow build-up to physical contact, and the girls have to endure sadistic beatings and rapes, enforced prostitution and slavery.

Male characters from different backgrounds and occupations have astounding depths of brutality—even missionaries turn out to be lecherous! It is surprising, after suffering so much degradation at the hands of men, that Matthews's heroines are always able, eventually, to attain not only romantic but rapturous fulfil-

umiliations that
victims of cir-
mple, a half-
resilience; the
eart is not only
ading character
:w Yorker with

arries not only
d lusty books,
colonial adven-
f" who refuses
her novels cer-
al backgrounds
she has written

Mary Cadogan

MAY, Wynne (Winifred Jean May). South African. Born in North Rand, Transvaal. Educated at Rand College, Johannesburg; studied journalism at technical college, Durban. Married Douglas Claude May in 1944; two sons. Secretary, African Explosives and Chemical Industries Ltd., North Rand, and African Consolidated Films, Ltd. and South African Broadcasting Corporation, both Johannesburg. Address: 43 Cotham Road, Moseley, Natal 4093, South Africa.

ROMANCE AND HISTORICAL PUBLICATIONS

Novels

A Cluster of Palms. London, Mills and Boon, 1967.
The Highest Peak. London, Mills and Boon, 1967.
The Valley of Aloes. London, Mills and Boon, and Toronto, Harlequin, 1967.
Tawny Are the Leaves. London, Mills and Boon, 1968; Toronto, Harlequin, 1969.
Tamboti Moon. London, Mills and Boon, and New York, Golden Press, 1969.
Where Breezes Falter. London, Mills and Boon, 1970.
Sun, Sea and Sand. London, Mills and Boon, 1970.
The Tide at Full. London, Mills and Boon, 1971.
A Grain of Gold. London, Mills and Boon, 1971.
A Slither of Silk. London, Mills and Boon, 1972.
A Bowl of Stars. London, Mills and Boon, and Toronto, Harlequin, 1973.
Pink Sands. London, Mills and Boon, and Toronto, Harlequin, 1974.
A Plume of Dust. London, Mills and Boon, and Toronto, Harlequin, 1975.
A Plantation of Vines. London, Mills and Boon, and Toronto, Harlequin, 1977.
Island of Cyclones. London, Mills and Boon, 1979.
A Scarf of Flame. London, Mills and Boon, 1979.
Peacock in the Jungle. London, Mills and Boon, 1982; Toronto, Harlequin, 1983.
Wayside Flower. London, Mills and Boon, 1982; Toronto, Harlequin, 1983.
Iceberg in the Tropics. London, Mills and Boon, 1983.
Fire in the Ash. London, Mills and Boon, 1984.
The Leopard's Lair. London, Mills and Boon, 1984.
A Boma in the Bush. London, Mills and Boon, 1985.
A Flaunting Cactus. London, Mills and Boon, 1986.
Peak of the Furnace. London, Mills and Boon, 1986.
Tomorrow's Sun. London, Mills and Boon, 1989.
Diamonds and Daisies. London, Mills and Boon, 1989.

*

Wynne May comments:

I knew from the day I started school that I wanted to write. Marriage and the problems which this state of affairs often brings about—in my case the tragic loss of our first two children—left me feeling "stranded" and, although I became active in other spheres, I did not write. That had to come later, when I was ready for it. My aim, at this stage, was to write for women. I only wish I had started earlier—but, at least I started. I realise that to "escape" in the form of romance fiction is important to many women. Who wants to be confronted with stark reality all the time?

*   *   *

Wynne May is one of the few romance writers who uses Africa and the Indian Ocean as backgrounds. With her, it is natural, however, for she has lived much of her life in South Africa. Her use of settings with which she is familiar makes her stories individual and instantly successful with her readers. In developing her backgrounds, she also tends to select the most fascinating elements to include in her stories.

Island of Cyclones describes the island of Mauritius in the Indian Ocean, with action set against the backgrounds of sugar cane plantations, expensive hotels, and an exclusive beauty clinic in one of these hotels. *A Plantation of Vines* uses the South African wine country as setting, while *A Scarf of Flame* tells about an African art gallery that is not far from a wild game reserve. Her unusual settings and the choice of detail she includes gives her readers a sense of modern South Africa. In fact, it plays a dominating role in her novels, but not to the point that her plots and characters are overshadowed.

Her heroes are often domineering men who are wealthy, successful, and extremely attractive. Philip de Berg in *A Plantation of Vines* owns a family home, one of the very old "Cape Houses" which he has turned into a hotel. He meets Nikki de Mist who returns to the country to take a job as a public relations specialist for the La Provence vineyard. Rey Stark in *A Scarf of Flame* combines a wild game reserve and a hotel that caters to very wealthy people. Although he has a constant attraction for women, Mistelle Hudson fights becoming just another woman to him as she helps her step-mother in her art gallery. Laurent Sevigny owns one of the fashionable hotels on Mauritius and it is here that Jade Lawford gets a job as a beauty consultant. She has arrived with the intention of marrying Marlow Lewis, a sugar cane planter.

While May uses considerable talent in depicting her characters and often creates sympathetic ones, her strongest creative ability centers on plot development. A wide range of secondary characters and conflicting needs frequently produces all sorts of plot complications. Usually the heroine and hero are, or seem to be, committed to other people and they seem on the verge of marriage to them. In *Island of Cyclones* Jade is planning to marry Marlow Lewis, but she falls in love with Laurent Sevigny. She believes him to be in love with Nicole de Speville or another woman. Actually Nicole and Marlow are in love and only the ending finds everyone sorted out with the right person. This somewhat complicated series of relationships naturally adds unusual and often conflicting clues to the plot line and offers a wide range of possible sub-plots and events.

May's readers have come to expect this kind of complexity and she does not disappoint them. Neither does she attempt to show her heroines as being too naive or dewy-eyed, although they are virtuous as all good heroines should be. In a way, they are feminine women who are on the edge of wanting and needing a permanent relationship which can only be marriage. There is an adult feeling about her heroines and less of the "girl" image to them. Overall, May offers well-balanced but complex novels that appeal to today's romance readers. Her unusual settings, sharply drawn characters, and intricate plots are just what they want.

—Arlene Moore

MAYBURY, Anne. Pseudonym for Anne Buxton, née Arundel; also writes as Katherine Troy. British. Married Charles Burdon Buxton. Vice-president, Society of Women Journalists, and Romantic Novelists Association. Agent: A.M. Heath, 79 St. Martin's Lane, London WC2N 4AA, England.

ROMANCE AND HISTORICAL PUBLICATIONS

Novels

The Best Love of All. London, Mills and Boon, 1932.
The Enchanted Kingdom. London, Mills and Boon, 1932.
The Love That Is Stronger Than Life. London, Mills and Boon, 1932.
Love Triumphant. London, Mills and Boon, 1932.
The Way of Compassion. London, Mills and Boon, 1933.
The Second Winning. London, Mills and Boon, 1933.
Farewell to Dreams. London, Mills and Boon, 1934.

Harness the Winds. London, Mills and Boon, 1934.
Catch at a Rainbow. London, Mills and Boon, 1935.
Come Autumn—Come Winter. London, Mills and Boon, 1935.
The Garden of Wishes. London, Mills and Boon, 1935.
The Starry Wood. London, Mills and Boon, 1935.
The Wondrous To-Morrow. London, Mills and Boon, 1936.
Give Me Back My Dreams. London, Mills and Boon, 1936.
Lovely Destiny. London, Mills and Boon, 1936.
The Stars Grow Pale. London, Mills and Boon, 1936.
This Errant Heart. London, Mills and Boon, 1937.
This Lovely Hour. London, Mills and Boon, 1937.
I Dare Not Dream. London, Mills and Boon, 1937.
Oh, Darling Joy! London, Mills and Boon, 1937.
Lady, It Is Spring! London, Mills and Boon, 1938.
The Shadow of My Loving. London, Mills and Boon, 1938.
They Dreamed Too Much. London, Mills and Boon, 1938.
Chained Eagle. London, Mills and Boon, 1939.
Gather Up the Years. London, Mills and Boon, 1939.
Return to Love. London, Mills and Boon, 1939.
The Barrier Between Us. London, Mills and Boon, 1940.
Dare to Marry. London, Mills and Boon, 1940.
I'll Walk with My Love. London, Mills and Boon, 1940.
Dangerous Living. London, Mills and Boon, 1941.
The Secret of the Rose. London, Collins, 1941.
All Enchantments Die. London, Collins, 1941.
To-Day We Live. London, Collins, 1942.
Arise, Oh Sun! London, Collins, 1942.
A Lady Fell in Love. London, Collins, 1943.
Journey into Morning. London, Collins, 1944; New York, Arcadia House, 1945.
Can I Forget You? London, Collins, 1944.
The Valley of Roses. London, Collins, 1945.
The Young Invader. London, Collins, 1947.
The Winds of Spring. London, Collins, 1948.
Storm Heaven. London, Collins, 1949.
The Sharon Women. London, Collins, 1950.
First, The Dream. London, Collins, 1951.
Goodbye, My Love. London, Collins, 1952.
The Music of Our House. London, Cherry Tree, 1952.
Her Name Was Eve. London, Collins, 1953.
The Heart Is Never Fair. London, Collins, 1954.
Prelude to Louise. London, Collins, 1954.
Follow Your Hearts. London, Collins, 1955.
The Other Juliet. London, Collins, 1955.
Forbidden. London, Collins, 1956.
Dear Lost Love. London, Collins, 1957.
Beloved Enemy. London, Collins, 1957.
The Stars Cannot Tell. London, Collins, 1958.
My Love Has a Secret. London, Collins, 1958.
The Gay of Heart. London, Collins, 1959.
The Rebel Heart. London, Collins, 1959.
Shadow of a Stranger. London, Collins, 1960; New York, Ace, 1966.
Bridge to the Moon. London, Collins, 1960.
Stay Until Tomorrow. London, Collins, 1961; New York, Ace, 1967.
The Night My Enemy. London, Collins, 1962; New York, Ace, 1967.
I Am Gabriella! London, Collins, 1962; New York, Ace, 1966; as *Gabriella*, London, Fontana, 1979.
Green Fire. London, Collins, 1963; New York, Ace, 1965.
My Dearest Elizabeth. London, Collins, 1964; as *The Brides of Bellenmore*, New York, Ace, 1964.
Pavilion at Monkshood. New York, Ace, 1965; London, Fontana, 1966.
Jessica. London, Collins, 1965.

The Moonlit Door. London, Hodder and Stoughton, and New York, Holt Rinehart, 1967.
The Minerva Stone. London, Hodder and Stoughton, and New York, Holt Rinehart, 1968.
Ride a White Dolphin. London, Hodder and Stoughton, and New York, Random House, 1971.
The Terracotta Palace. London, Hodder and Stoughton, and New York, Random House, 1971.
Walk in the Paradise Garden. New York, Random House, 1972; London, Collins, 1973.
The Midnight Dancers. New York, Random House, 1973; London, Collins, 1974.
Jessamy Court. New York, Random House, 1974; London, Collins, 1975.
The Jewelled Daughter. London, Collins, and New York, Random House, 1976.
Dark Star. New York, Random House, 1977; London, Collins, 1978.
Radiance. New York, Random House, 1979.
Invitation to Alannah. Loughton, Essex, Piatkus, 1983.

Novels as Katherine Troy

Someone Waiting. London, Collins, 1961; as Anne Maybury, New York, Ace, 1966.
Whisper in the Dark. London, Collins, 1961; as Anne Maybury, New York, Ace, 1966.
Enchanter's Nightshade. London, Collins, 1963; as *The Winds of Night* (as Anne Maybury), New York, Ace, 1967.
Falcon's Shadow. London, Collins, 1964; as Anne Maybury, New York, Ace, 1967.
The House of Fand. London, Collins, 1966; as Anne Maybury, New York, Ace, 1966.
The Night of the Enchantress. London, Hodder and Stoughton, 1967.
Farramonde. New York, McKay, 1968.
Storm over Roseheath. London, Hodder and Stoughton, 1969; as *Roseheath*, New York, McKay, 1969.

* * *

Anne Maybury has attracted a steady number of fans with her gothic novels, though she had earlier written many romances. Since about 1968 she has published approximately a book a year, and has never failed her audience in their expectations of a good gothic/romance, sensuously and delicately well-told. Maybury rises above the strait jacket of formula with well-conceived plots, sympathetic characters, and lushly described settings.

In Maybury's stories, the person under the most suspicion is the husband or the fiancé of the heroine, whom she both loves and suspects of foul deeds at the same time. The situation is complicated by the presence of a dependent, usually a child of nine or ten, or a friend for whom the heroine feels responsible. These relationships are complicated and tenuous, involving excruciating decisions for the heroine, often *for* the dependent and *against* the loved male. For example, Cathy Mountavon in *The Midnight Dancers* is responsible for Pippa, aged nine, her husband's child by his first wife. Pippa worships her father while innuendos abound that he is responsible for her mother's death. These tangled relationships are always complicated by the heroine's doubt about her prospective/actual mate. The true male mate for the heroine usually emerges only at the conclusion as misunderstood and gallantly heroic, a Galahad who has been searching for the truth all along and trying to defend the heroine, all unknown to her or the reader. But these are not the males' stories; they belong to the woman as she independently explores

both dangerous situations and her own emotions. The plots center on her ability not only to endure a threatening environment, but also to rise above situations bordering on the tragic.

Setting is always significant, varied, and expertly invoked. Maybury specializes in atmosphere, with the result that whether the setting is a castle in England or Rome, a pavilion in Hong Kong, or a house on a Greek island, the beauty of each serves as a contrast to the threatening atmosphere of the unknown—the unknown culture and the unfamiliar place. A fine balance is maintained between the heightened emotions of love and fear in a suffocating atmosphere of suspicion and the delicious beauty of each setting.

Maybury's heroines have come a long way from the fainting innocents of the first gothic fiction. Most are at the least able to support themselves; moreover, in *The Jewelled Daughter* Sarah Brendt is a trained gemologist and in *The Midnight Dancers* Cathy Mountavon is an artist trained in stained glass. That these heroines have professions introduces a new thread to the formulaic plot of new gothic, exploring the complications and rewards of further female independence. The villains are brilliant, but power mad. Insanity is the result of their being thwarted in whatever Machiavellian plans they have secretly laid throughout the novel. Of course, the twist is that they may be either male or female, the loved male of the female friend.

Maybury's stories represent the best and newest of the genre and can be counted on for vivid characters, basically sound plots, and carefully researched and lusciously described settings.

—Marilynn Motteler

MAYFIELD, Julia. See **HASTINGS, Phyllis.**

McBAIN, Laurie (Lee). American. Born in Riverside, California, 15 October 1949. Educated at San Bernardino Valley College, California, and California State University, San Bernardino, 1967–72. Address: c/o Avon, 105 Madison Avenue, New York, New York 10016, U.S.A.

ROMANCE AND HISTORICAL PUBLICATIONS

Novels

Devil's Desire. New York, Avon, 1975.
Moonstruck Madness. New York, Avon, 1977; London, Futura, 1978.
Tears of Gold. New York, Avon, and London, Futura, 1979.
Chance the Winds of Fortune. New York, Avon, 1980.
Dark Before the Rising Sun. New York, Avon, 1982.
Wild Bells to the Wild Sky. New York, Avon, 1983; London, Piatkus, 1984.
When the Splendor Falls. New York, Avon, 1985; London, Inner Circle, 1986.

* * *

Laurie McBain's novels are the type that often are described as "sweeping sagas," in which the heroine moves from adventure to adventure, usually in dire peril and in conflict with the hero. The action may take place in England, but often moves to other, more exotic locations. Mara O'Flynn (*Tears of Gold*) travels from England to California in Gold Rush days, and finally to Louisiana before embarking again for England. Sabrina Verrick (*Moonstruck Madness*) supports her family as a Robin Hood-style highwayman. Later she appears as Rhea Dominick's mother in *Chance the Winds of Fortune*, a less than staid duchess, who agonizes over her daughter's adventures. Rhea is sold as an indentured servant in the colonies and roams about the lush Caribbean before returning home. Lily Christian (*Wild Bells to the Wild Sky*), daughter of an English privateer and his willing Spanish conquest, is involved in intrigue in England and the West Indies. Leigh Travers (*When the Splendor Falls*) survives the American Civil War and travels to the New Mexico Territory before winning through to happiness.

Description of period dress and mannerisms fill the books, while much of the dialogue in the earlier works is laced with colloquialisms. It is all meant to help the reader "experience" the period, but at times the obsolete terms and phrases get in the way. In her more recent works, especially *Wild Bells to the Wild Sky* and *When the Splendor Falls*, McBain has gone a long way in correcting the occasional stiltedness which marred the early novels.

In spite of the locations and historical details, the main interest in McBain's novels remains the romance and its attendant problems. The course of true love is never allowed to run smoothly since there is hostility or tension between the hero and heroine. The hero is strong, older, more experienced, usually cynical, and preferably titled (or the American equivalent, wealthy). The heroine is young, relatively innocent, and something of a spitfire. The conflict between them allows for many twists and turns of the plot before she is tamed (but not broken) and he surrenders and confesses his love for her. The characters and plots are pretty standard fare, but McBain succeeds in developing her characters within the limitations of the genre and inventing some interesting stories and subplots. Another plus for McBain is that she allows her heroines to mature. The original "spitfire" often seems to be little more than a spoiled brat rather than a woman fighting for independence, but McBain manages to alter the strident overtones as the romantic conflict is resolved.

Although her body of work remains relatively small, McBain has developed a solid reputation for delivering a satisfying romance.

—Barbara E. Kemp

McCORQUODALE, Barbara. See CARTLAND, Barbara.

McCULLOUGH, Colleen. Australian. Born in Wellington, New South Wales, in 1937. Educated at the University of Sydney. Married Ric Robinson in 1984. Researcher, School of International Medicine, Yale University, New Haven, Connecticut, 1967–76. Since 1976 full-time writer. Address: c/o Harper and Row, 10 East 53rd Street, New York, New York 10022, U.S.A.

ROMANCE AND HISTORICAL PUBLICATIONS

Novels

The Thornbirds. New York, Harper, and London, Raven, 1977.
An Indecent Obsession. New York, Harper, and London, Macdonald, 1981.
The Ladies of Missalonghi. New York, Harper, and London, Hutchinson, 1987.

OTHER PUBLICATIONS

Novels

Tim. New York, Harper, 1974; London, Angus and Robertson, 1975.
A Creed for the Third Millennium. New York, Harper, and London, Macdonald, 1987.

Other

Cooking with Colleen McCullough and Jean Easthope. New York, Harper, and London, Macdonald, 1982.

*   *   *

Colleen McCullough is best known for her racy second novel, *The Thornbirds*, set in outback Australia, although all her other books have had considerable success by any standards. *The Thornbirds*, *An Indecent Obsession*, and *The Ladies of Missalonghi* are historical novels, and *Tim* is a modern romance. *A Creed for the Third Millennium*, an unconvincing exploration of the basis of faith, is set in the future, as the title might suggest. Leaving aside *A Creed for the Third Millennium*, which is written in the style of an historical romance but does not fit that definition, all of McCullough's books feature an Australian woman who, at some point in her life, has to make a decision to pursue a course of conduct at odds with received opinion. In *Tim* a middle-aged spinster decides to marry a young mentally-retarded man who loves her. The beautiful heroine Meggie in *The Thornbirds* has a child by a priest. Nurse Langtry in *An Indecent Obsession* chooses between career and marriage, and in *The Ladies of Missalonghi* the heroine Missy tricks a man into marrying her. Frequently plots turn on taboo subjects such as the sexual needs of priests, older women, and the mentally retarded. A motif is the transformation of a dull or insignificant woman into someone spirited and outgoing. Money, particularly the freedom it can bring a single woman, is a central concern and often there is a progression from poverty to riches.

Although plot summaries might suggest otherwise, McCullough's books are not feminist in tone. Relationships between men and women are depicted in a cliché-ridden manner. Despite heroines achieving a degree of autonomy, the status quo is maintained and they are more or less dependent on relationships with men. Even Nurse Langtry's choice suggests the cloister rather than liberty. McCullough's chief talent is in her description of landscape and in depicting vivid scenes such as the deathbed of Mary Carson in *The Thornbirds* which is both gruesome and memorable. In the same novel, the author casts a wide net and convincingly covers subjects as diverse as Vatican politics to sugar cane cutting in Queensland.

McCullough uses well-worn plots in all her novels but has the ability to make even hackneyed situations fresh and appealing. She was a voracious reader as a child, and it is apparent that many situations from childhood reading have stayed with her.

The Ladies of Missalonghi attracted comment on publication when it was alleged the novel was a rewrite of Canadian novelist's L. M. Montgomery's *The Blue Castle*. Despite numerous similarities between the two books, the actions of McCullough's heroine alter the entire tone of the tale. Montgomery's heroine is a victim of circumstance whereas Missy, once off the leash, takes an active part in determining her future. However, in this and other novels McCullough's characters are one-dimensional and she cannot create convincing dialogue. A reader's faith is sorely tested by the sudden changes in the various heroines, and by such unlikely lines as "Sweet suffering rock oysters" and "Holy man-eating toads!" only two examples from a repertoire of expressions given to Mary's boss (a professional man) in *Tim*. Also often commented on by critics is the author's addition to florid metaphors drawn out to absurd lengths. It is perhaps a tribute to McCullough's storytelling ability that her novels are still immensely readable despite very apparent flaws in technique.

—Kerry White

McCUTCHAN, Philip (Donald). Also writes as Robert Conington Galway; Duncan MacNeil; T. I. G. Wigg. British. Born in Cambridge, 13 October 1920. Educated at St. Helens' College, Southsea, Hampshire, 1926–34; studied for H.M. Forces entry examination, 1934–38; Royal Military College, Sandhurst, Surrey, 1938. Served in the Royal Naval Volunteer Reserve, 1939–46: Lieutenant. Married Elizabeth May Ryan in 1951; one son and one daughter. Assistant purser, Orient Steam Navigation Company, London, 1946–49; accounts assistant, Anglo-Iranian Oil Company, London, 1949–52; teacher in preparatory schools, 1952–54; owner of a teashop, 1953–60. Full-time writer since 1960. Chairman, Crime Writers Association, 1965–66. Address: 107 Portland Road, Worthing, West Sussex BN11 1QA, England.

ROMANCE AND HISTORICAL PUBLICATIONS

Novels (series: Lieutenant St. Vincent Halfhyde in all books)

Beware, Beware the Bight of Benin. London, Barker, 1974; as *Beware the Bight of Benin*, New York, St. Martin's Press, 1975.
Halfhyde's Island. London, Weidenfeld and Nicolson, 1975; New York, St. Martin's Press, 1976.
The Guns of Arrest. London, Weidenfeld and Nicolson, and New York, St. Martin's Press, 1976.
Halfhyde to the Narrows. London, Weidenfeld and Nicolson, and New York, St. Martin's Press, 1977.
Halfhyde for the Queen. London, Weidenfeld and Nicolson, and New York, St. Martin's Press, 1978.
Halfhyde Ordered South. London, Weidenfeld and Nicolson, 1979; New York, St. Martin's Press, 1980.
Halfhyde and the Flag Captain. London, Weidenfeld and Nicolson, 1980; New York, St. Martin's Press, 1981.
Halfhyde on the Yangtze. London, Weidenfeld and Nicolson, 1981.
Halfhyde on Zanatu. London, Weidenfeld and Nicolson, and New York, St. Martin's Press, 1982.

Halfhyde Outward Bound. London, Weidenfeld and Nicolson, 1983; New York, St. Martin's Press, 1984.
The Halfhyde Line. London, Weidenfeld and Nicolson, 1984; New York, St. Martin's Press, 1985.
Halfhyde and the Chain Gangs. London, Weidenfeld and Nicolson, 1985; New York, St. Martin's Press, 1986.
Halfhyde Goes to War. London, Weidenfeld and Nicolson, 1986; New York, St. Martin's Press, 1987.
Halfhyde on the Amazon. London, Weidenfeld and Nicolson, and New York, St. Martin's Press, 1988.
Halfhyde All at Sea. London, Weidenfeld and Nicolson, 1989.

Novels as Duncan MacNeil (series: James Ogilvie in all books)

Drums along the Khyber. London, Hodder and Stoughton, 1969; New York, St. Martin's Press, 1973.
Lieutenant of the Line. London, Hodder and Stoughton, 1970; New York, St. Martin's Press, 1973.
Sadhu on the Mountain Peak. London, Hodder and Stoughton, 1971; New York, St. Martin's Press, 1974.
The Gates of Kunarja. London, Hodder and Stoughton, 1972; New York, St. Martin's Press, 1974.
The Red Daniel. London, Hodder and Stoughton, 1973; New York, St. Martin's Press, 1974.
Subaltern's Choice. London, Hodder and Stoughton, and New York, St. Martin's Press, 1974.
By Command of the Viceroy. London, Hodder and Stoughton, and New York, St. Martin's Press, 1975.
The Mullah from Kashmir. London, Hodder and Stoughton, 1976; New York, St. Martin's Press, 1977.
Wolf in the Fold. London, Hodder and Stoughton, and New York, St. Martin's Press, 1977.
Charge of Cowardice. London, Hodder and Stoughton, and New York, St. Martin's Press, 1978.
The Restless Frontier. London, Hodder and Stoughton, 1979; New York, St. Martin's Press, 1980.
Cunningham's Revenge. London, Hodder and Stoughton, 1980; New York, Walker, 1985.
The Train at Bundarbar. London, Hodder and Stoughton, 1981; New York, Walker, 1986.
A Matter for the Regiment. London, Hodder and Stoughton, 1982.

OTHER PUBLICATIONS

Novels

Whistle and I'll Come. London, Harrap, 1957.
The Kid. London, Harrap, 1958.
Storm South. London, Harrap, 1959.
Gibraltar Road. London, Harrap, 1960; New York, Berkley, 1965.
Redcap. London, Harrap, 1961; New York, Berkley, 1965.
Hopkinson and the Devil of Hate. London, Harrap, 1961.
Bluebolt One. London, Harrap, 1962; New York, Berkley, 1965.
Leave the Dead Behind Us. London, Harrap, 1962.
Marley's Empire. London, Harrap, 1963.
The Man from Moscow. London, Harrap, 1963; New York, Day, 1965.
Warmaster. London, Harrap, 1963; New York, Day, 1964.
Moscow Coach. London, Harrap, 1964; New York, Day, 1966.
Bowering's Breakwater. London, Harrap, 1964.
Sladd's Evil. London, Harrap, 1965; New York, Day, 1967.
A Time for Survival. London, Harrap, 1966.

The Dead Line. London, Harrap, and New York, Berkley, 1966.
Skyprobe. London, Harrap, 1966; New York, Day, 1967.
Poulter's Passage. London, Harrap, 1967.
The Day of the Coastwatch. London, Harrap, 1968.
The Screaming Dead Balloons. London, Harrap, and New York, Day, 1968.
The Bright Red Businessmen. London, Harrap, and New York, Day, 1969.
The All-Purpose Bodies. London, Harrap, 1969; New York, Day, 1970.
Hartinger's Mouse. London, Harrap, 1970.
Man, Let's Go On. London, Harrap, 1970.
Half a Bag of Stringer. London, Harrap, 1971.
This Drakotny. London, Harrap, 1971.
The German Helmet. London, Harrap, 1972.
The Oil Bastards. London, Harrap, 1972.
Pull My String. London, Harrap, 1973.
Coach North. London, Harrap, 1974; New York, Walker, 1975.
Call for Simon Shard. London, Harrap, 1974.
A Very Big Bang. London, Hodder and Stoughton, 1975.
Blood Run East. London, Hodder and Stoughton, 1976.
The Eros Affair. London, Hodder and Stoughton, 1977.
Blackmail North. London, Hodder and Stoughton, 1978.
Sunstrike. London, Hodder and Stoughton, 1979.
Corpse. London, Hodder and Stoughton, 1980.
Cameron, Ordinary Seaman. London, Barker, 1980.
Cameron Comes Through. London, Barker, 1980; New York, St. Martin's Press, 1986.
Cameron of the Castle Bay. London, Barker, 1981.
Lieutenant Cameron RNVR. London, Barker, 1981; New York, St. Martin's Press, 1985.
Shard Calls the Tune. London, Hodder and Stoughton, 1981.
Werewolf. London, Hodder and Stoughton, 1982.
Cameron's Convoy. London, Barker, 1982.
Cameron in the Gap. London, Barker, 1982; New York, St. Martin's Press, 1983.
Orders for Cameron. London, Barker, and New York, St. Martin's Press, 1983.
Cameron in Command. London, Barker, 1983; New York, St. Martin's Press, 1984.
The Hoof. London, Hodder and Stoughton, 1983.
Rollerball. London, Hodder and Stoughton, 1984.
Cameron and the Kaiserhof. London, Barker, and New York, St. Martin's Press, 1984.
Cameron's Raid. London, Weidenfeld and Nicolson, and New York, St. Martin's Press, 1985.
Shard at Bay. London, Hodder and Stoughton, 1985.
The Executioners. London, Hodder and Stoughton, 1986.
Cameron's Chase. London, Weidenfeld and Nicolson, and New York, St. Martin's Press, 1986.
The Convoy Commodore. London, Weidenfeld and Nicolson, 1986; New York, St. Martin's Press, 1987.
Greenfly. London, Hodder and Stoughton, 1987.
Cameron's Troop Lift. London, Weidenfeld and Nicolson, and New York, St. Martin's Press, 1987.
Convoy North. London, Weidenfeld and Nicolson, 1987; New York, St. Martin's Press, 1988.
Overnight Express. London, Hodder and Stoughton, 1988.
Convoy South. London, Weidenfeld and Nicolson, and New York, St. Martin's Press, 1988.
The Boy Who Liked Monsters. London, Hodder and Stoughton, 1989.
Cameron's Commitment. London, Weidenfeld and Nicolson, and New York, St. Martin's Press, 1989.
Convoy East. London, Weidenfeld and Nicolson, 1989.

Novels as T. I. G. Wigg

A Job with the Boys. London, Dobson, 1958.
For the Sons of Gentlemen. London, Dobson, 1960.
A Rum for the Captain. London, Dobson, 1961.

Novels as Robert Conington Galway

The Timeless Sleep. London, Hale, 1963.
Assignment New York. London, Hale, 1963.
Assignment London. London, Hale, 1963.
Assignment Andalusia. London, Hale, 1965.
Assignment Malta. London, Hale, 1966.
Assignment Gaolbreak. London, Hale, 1968.
Assignment Argentina. London, Hale, 1969.
Assignment Fenland. London, Hale, 1969.
Assignment Seabed. London, Hale, 1969.
Assignment Sydney. London, Hale, 1970.
Assignment Death Squad. London, Hale, 1970.
The Negative Man. London, Hale, 1971.

Plays

Radio Plays and Features: *The Proper Service Manner,* 1954; *Unlawful Occasions,* 1954; *First Command,* 1954; *The Feast of Lanterns,* 1955; *Thirty-Four for Tea,* 1955; *A Run Ashore,* 1956; *Flash Point,* 1956; *The Great Siege,* 1956; *In Partnership,* 1958; *O'Flynn of UB1* (for children), 1963.

Other

On Course for Danger (for children). London, Macmillan, and New York, St. Martin's Press, 1959.
Tall Ships: The Golden Age of Sail. London, Weidenfeld and Nicolson, and New York, Crown, 1976.
Great Yachts. London, Weidenfeld and Nicolson, and New York, Crown, 1979.

*

Philip McCutchan comments:
My main work falls into six series. Two of these series are historical: under the pseudonym Duncan MacNeil I write an army series based on a fictitious Highland Regiment fighting on the North-West Frontier of India in the 1890's, and I write a naval series featuring Lieutenant St. Vincent Halfhyde, also set in the 1890's. Four series are set in more modern times. One features Commander Esmonde Shaw, ex-Naval Intelligence; one features Detective Chief Superintendent Simon Shard, attached to a special-special branch in the Foreign Office; and two are naval series set in World War II, featuring Donald Cameron and Commodore John Mason Kemp. I have also written a number of non-series adventure thrillers. I am tending more and more to concentrate on naval fiction.

*   *   *

Variety, as opposed to versatility, is the mark of Philip McCutchan's novels. From a Pitlochry industrial estate to Australia's Barrier Reef to the Kola Penninsula of Russia, various heroes, differentiated only in name, battle evil. Shaw, Shard, Cameron, and Mason Kemp become involved in fascism, terrorism, blackmail (nuclear and otherwise), theft, treason, and espionage, travelling anywhere from Yorkshire to Valparaiso in under 200 pages. The female side-kick is an optional, but always the villains are of the classic school and work for abbreviated agencies like WUSWIPP. Although the picture is as simple as an early Hollywood gangster film, the elements are rooted in the late 1980's.

The destruction of the ozone layer, brain-washing in a Libyan gaol, a Belfast bomber's threat to blow up a chemical defence establishment—these are likely scenarios but perhaps not appropriate material for a writer like McCutchan. He trivialises these issues which are close to the hearts of many, and unless they are handled with thoughtfulness and sensitivity it would be better not to exploit such topics at all. Writers like Ian Fleming do succeed with similar concepts because they move completely into fantasy with tongue firmly in cheek, but McCutchan lacks this redeeming characteristic. In trying to mix the headlines of the daily newspaper with the requirement of a gripping thriller, he flounders.

McCutchan comes home when he writes about the past, when the pressure to be "relevent" lessens. His element is the sea, with sailing ships a way of life and every sailor a hero. The best of these is the Halfhyde series. Set in the late 1800's and early 20th century, it tells of the adventures of St. Vincent Halfhyde, first in the Royal Navy and later as commander of a merchant vessel. The detail reflects the author's knowledge of seamanship and military matters, but not to the extent that it overshadows the basic story line. Some jargon creates an atmosphere of authenticity so that his narrative rings true and renders what he has to say more plausible. What he has to say is a severe indictment of the times.

Although the 14 books are chronological, Halfhyde's persona remains constant from volume to volume. Even his failed marriage to Mildred and his subsequent passionate affair with Victoria Penn leave him spiritually unchanged and he gains nothing more than memories from his scrapes. He reminds the reader of Horatio Hornblower, but without Hornblower's increasing maturity as he advances in rank. Halfhyde's immutability is not necessarily a bad thing in this context, however. McCutchan has pitted him against the British Empire and all that was wrong with it, represented by his commanding officers and their land-bound puppeteers. Because Halfhyde's foe is his own side he cannot afford the luxury of developing his own self-awareness. He must be left inviolate to stand firm against this pervasive, close, and domineering force, and if stability means stasis then that is the sacrifice McCutchan makes. Otherwise the focus would be split between Halfhyde's growing consciousness and his role as righter of imperial wrong—a juggling act which is wisely avoided.

McCutchan is not anti-imperialist as such, but he does object to a society which places small-minded, well-connected men in positions of power for which they are ill-qualified. In *Halfhyde and the Flag Captain*, Watkiss, Halfhyde's senior officer, exacerbates an already volatile situation with an act of aggression without considering the possible consequences. The diplomatic corps has the opposite blind-spot, making well-planned decisions in London which prove impractical on the high seas.

The ordinary seaman is held responsible for any resulting errors of command judgment, despite the fact that they simply carry out orders. Halfhyde for one refuses to be a pawn in this type of power game, and he constantly challenges his superiors' decisions, forcing them either to modify their original demands or at least momentarily to question their own convictions. Later, when he himself is in a position of authority, he consults his men (most notably his first lieutenant) and considers all options before acting. The result is invariably a success, having been brought about through his natural leadership abilities.

Halfhyde's chief function is to confront the moguls who try to manipulate his destiny. McCutchan uses the ensuing conflict to expose the status of a power which relies on tradition for its potency, not on the intrinsic value of its individuals. This conflict disappears and takes with it much of the thematic content once Halfhyde quits the Royal Navy as he does in *Halfhyde Outward Bound*. Suspended on half-pay, he joins the crew of a merchant ship bound for Sydney. The conditions are disgusting, and the first mate, appropriately named Bullock, turns out to be a tyrannical bully with the obligatory sadistic tendencies. Halfhyde's enemy from previous books appears again, this time with a personal vendetta to capture Halfhyde and present him as a prisoner to the Kaiser. Luckily he fails.

The elements are there as previously—chases, battles, skullduggery, and general excitement, but it rings hollow because the context is different. Halfhyde, having left the navy behind him, is now not fighting against his own side to preserve his integrity, nor is he even defending queen and country except in a very general way. He has lost all his thematic purpose as a figure once that framework was taken away, and what is left, random grappling with random evil, is far from satisfactory. The British government and naval command continue to make cameo appearances, in *The Halfhyde Line* for example, where a large arms cache is smuggled into Ireland through the ineptitude of officialdom. Bureaucracy is here an object which precipitates events rather than the subject of commentary as it would have been earlier in the series. It certainly contributes to the plot, but is no longer McCutchan's main concern.

This is characteristic of a less than successful historical novel. The background of history—its institutions and events—is the ideal vehicle to explore the past and what has gone into making the present. However when history becomes just another aspect of the story-line, its potency is wasted and the reader is left with just another cheap adventure yarn. Swashbuckling stories have many merits and are great fun to read, but in the case of the Halfhyde books the reader is left cheated out of the thoughtfulness the early work promised.

—L. M. Quinn

McCUTCHEON, George Barr. Also wrote as Richard Greaves. American. Born near Lafayette, Indiana, 26 July 1866. Educated at Purdue University, Lafayette, two years. Married Marie Fay in 1904; one stepson. Reporter, *Journal*, 1889, columnist, *Sunday Journal*, 1890, and city editor, 1893 and part-time staff member until 1905, *Courier*, all in Lafayette. President, Authors League, 1924–26. *Died 23 October 1928.*

ROMANCE AND HISTORICAL PUBLICATIONS

Novels (series: Graustark)

Graustark: The Story of a Love Behind a Throne. Chicago, Stone, 1901; London, Richards, 1902.
Castle Craneycrow. Chicago, Stone, 1902; London, Richards, 1903.
Brewster's Millions (as Richard Greaves). Chicago, Stone, 1903; London, Collier, 1907.
The Sherrods. New York, Dodd Mead, 1903; London, Ward Lock, 1905.
Beverly of Graustark. New York, Dodd Mead, and London, Stevens and Brown, 1904.
The Day of the Dog. New York, Dodd Mead, 1904; revised edition, 1916.

Nedra. New York, Dodd Mead, and London, Stevens and Brown, 1905.

The Purple Parasol. New York, Dodd Mead, 1905.

Cowardice Court. New York, Dodd Mead, 1906.

Jane Cable. New York, Dodd Mead, and London, Hodder and Stoughton, 1906.

The Flyers. New York, Dodd Mead, and London, Stevens and Brown, 1907.

The Husbands of Edith. New York, Dodd Mead, 1908; London, Holden and Hardingham, 1912.

The Man from Brodney's. New York, Dodd Mead, and London, Hodder and Stoughton, 1908.

The Alternative. New York, Dodd Mead, 1909.

Truxton King: A Story of Graustark. New York, Dodd Mead, and London, Stevens and Brown, 1909.

The Butterfly Man. New York, Dodd Mead, 1910.

The Rose in the Ring. New York, Dodd Mead, and London, Everett, 1910.

Mary Midthorne. New York, Dodd Mead, and London, Stevens and Brown, 1911.

What's-His-Name. New York, Dodd Mead, and London, Stevens and Brown, 1911.

The Hollow of Her Hand. New York, Dodd Mead, and London, Stevens and Brown, 1912.

A Fool and His Money. New York, Dodd Mead, and London, Stevens and Brown, 1913.

Black Is White. New York, Dodd Mead, 1914; London, Everett, 1915.

The Prince of Graustark. New York, Dodd Mead, and London, Stevens and Brown, 1914.

Mr. Bingle. New York, Dodd Mead, and London, Stevens and Brown, 1915.

From the Housetops. New York, Dodd Mead, and London, Stevens and Brown, 1916.

The Light That Lies. New York, Dodd Mead, 1916; London, Jenkins, 1917.

Green Fancy. New York, Dodd Mead, 1917; London, Hodder and Stoughton, 1918.

The City of Masks. New York, Dodd Mead, 1918; as *The Court of New York*, London, Melrose, 1919.

Shot with Crimson. New York, Dodd Mead, 1918; London, Jenkins, 1920.

Sherry. New York, Dodd Mead, 1919.

West Wind Drift. New York, Dodd Mead, 1920; London, Nash, 1921.

Quill's Window. New York, Dodd Mead, 1921; London, Nash, 1922.

Yollop. New York, Dodd Mead, 1922.

Viola Gwyn. New York, Dodd Mead, and London, Nash, 1922.

Oliver October. New York, Dodd Mead, 1923; London, Harrap, 1924.

East of the Setting Sun: A Story of Graustark. New York, Dodd Mead, 1924; London, Harrap, 1925.

Romeo in Moon Village. New York, Dodd Mead, 1925; London, Nash, 1926.

The Inn of the Hawk and Raven: A Tale of Old Graustark. New York, Dodd Mead, 1926; London, Lane, 1927.

Kindling and Ashes; or, The Heart of Barbara Wayne. New York, Dodd Mead, 1926; London, Lane, 1927.

Blades. New York, Dodd Mead, and London, Lane, 1928.

The Merivales. New York, Dodd Mead, 1929.

Short Stories

Her Weight in Gold. Privately printed, 1911; revised edition, New York, Dodd Mead, 1912.

OTHER PUBLICATIONS

Novel

The Daughter of Anderson Crow. New York, Dodd Mead, and London, Hodder and Stoughton, 1907.

Short Stories

Anderson Crow, Detective. New York, Dodd Mead, 1920.
Anderson, The Joker, in *Three Yarns*, with Booth Tarkington and G. K. Chesterton. Chicago, Blue Ribbon, 1924.

Plays

Brood House. Privately printed, 1910.
One Score and Ten. Privately printed, 1919.
Daddy Dumplings, with Earl Carroll (produced New York, 1920).

Other

Books Once Were Men: An Essay for Booklovers. New York, Dodd Mead, 1931.
The Young Mathematician Series. Skokie, Illinois, National Textbook, 6 vols., 1968–70.

*

Critical Study: *Beyond Graustark: George Barr McCutcheon: Playwright Discovered*, by A. L. Lazarus and Victor H. Jones, Port Washington, New York, Kennikat Press, 1981.

*   *   *

George Barr McCutcheon wrote more than 40 novels, a number of plays and novelettes, and several essays, but he is best remembered for six popular romances, the Graustark stories.

A product of the turn-of-the-century midwestern American imagination, McCutcheon reflected both America's attraction to European culture and its self-conscious pride in her own youth and independence during years when she was becoming a world power. McCutcheon's work attempts to resolve this tension, yet gives America the edge in the argument. A faith in the wholesomeness, ingenuity, and democracy of the optimistic American hero characterizes McCutcheon's most important work.

Related to adventure-romances like Anthony Hope's *Prisoner of Zenda*, and influenced by his early reading in 19th-century dime novels, McCutcheon's Graustark books were predominantly departures from the domestic, female-protagonist romances of the 19th century and excursions into a world of male action and resourcefulness. The Graustark novels are all set in a mythical Balkan state and in and around Edelweiss, its central city. Most of the six novels are male versions of the familiar Cinderella formula, but the commoner hero's reward for valor is not money or Christian salvation, but acceptance by the aristocratic community. Sometimes charmingly innocent before formal European ways, McCutcheon's heroes are over-simplified Jamesian Americans abroad. Unlike Henry James's realistic characters, however, McCutcheon's heroes overcome countless obstacles and manage to save beautiful aristocratic women from European villains and to bring them home to New York or Washington, D.C.

The Graustark novels tend to begin slowly with background to the hero's search for love and adventure, then pick up with his sudden, undermotivated attraction for a beautiful, mysterious woman who leads him into a labyrinth of improbable intrigues and through a lengthy catalogue of obstructions that increase in difficulty until the plot reaches a culminating action and the hero's triumph. With his victory comes the defeat of evil forces and less worthy suitors for his lover's hand, the stability of marriage, and the respect of the aristocrats who doubted his abilities.

In the best-selling *Graustark*, the first of the series, Count Halfont finds it difficult to accept commoner hero Grenville Lorry's proposal of marriage to Graustark's Princess Yetive, even though Halfont finds Lorry to be ''the soul of honor, of courage, of manliness.'' Lorry's reply summarizes the democratic American bias throughout McCutcheon's books.

> . . . every born American may become ruler of the greatest nation in the world—the United States. His home is his kingdom; his wife, his mother, his sisters are his queens and princesses; his fellow citizens are his admiring subjects if he is wise and good. In my land you will find the poor man climbing to the highest pinnacle side by side with the rich man. . . . We recognize little as impossible. Until death destroys this power to love and to hope I must say to you that I shall not consider Princess Yetive beyond my reach.

Love triumphs: Lorry married the Princess, and with that marriage begins the saga that includes the continuing story of Yetive and Lorry in *Beverly of Graustark*, the tale of Prince Robin, the Lorry's son and his protectors in *Truxton King*, Robin's courtship and marriage to an American woman in *The Prince of Graustark*, and the postwar adventures of an American writer in Graustark in *East of the Setting Sun*. The final Graustark novel, *The Inn of the Hawk and Raven*, returns to the years before Yetive's marriage to Lorry.

Although McCutcheon made his name on the Graustark books, he wrote 40 additional novels; many were similar formula romances with robust American heroes, but most were set in the United States. The best known of these, *Brewster's Millions*, published under the pseudonym Richard Greaves, became a popular film. In the American romances McCutcheon experimented more with realistic techniques, paying greater attention to local color settings, regional dialects, and humor.

McCutcheon's style and most of his characterizations are flat and pedestrian, his plot construction competent, but slow moving. His achievement comes in his clever conceptions for stories and most importantly in his creation of likeable, democratic American heroes of near-mythical proportions.

—Nancy Pogel

McELFRESH, (Elizabeth) Adeline. Also writes as John Cleveland; Jane Scott; Elizabeth Wesley. American. Born in Knox County, Indiana, 28 May 1918. Educated at a high school in Bruceville, Indiana. Proofreader, 1936–42, and feature editor, 1943–56, Vincennes *Sun-Commercial*, Indiana; reporter, Troy *Daily News*, Ohio, 1942–43. Since 1966, director of public relations, Good Samaritan Hospital, Vincennes. Address: R.R.3, Vincennes, Indiana, U.S.A.

ROMANCE AND HISTORICAL PUBLICATIONS

Novels (series: Dr. Jane; Jill Nolan)

Charlotte Wade. New York, Arcadia House, 1952.
Homecoming. New York, Arcadia House, 1953.
The Old Baxter Place. New York, Arcadia House, 1954.
Doctor Jane. New York, Avalon, 1954; London, Corgi, 1958.
Ann and the Hoosier Doctor. New York, Avalon, 1955; as *Hill Country Nurse*, New York, Bantam, 1959.
Young Doctor Randall. New York, Avalon, 1957.
Nurse Kathy. New York, Avalon, 1957.
Calling Doctor Jane. New York, Avalon, 1957; London, Corgi, 1959.
Dr. Jane's Mission. New York, Avalon, 1958.
Dr. Jane Comes Home. New York, Avalon, 1959; London, Corgi, 1961.
Kay Manion, M.D. New York, Dell, 1959; as *Kay Mannion, M.D.*, London, Corgi, 1960.
Team-Up for Ann. London, Ward Lock, 1959.
Wings for Nurse Bennett. New York, Dell, 1960.
Ann Kenyon, Surgeon. New York, Dell, 1960.
Dr. Jane's Choice. New York, Avalon, 1961.
To Each Her Dream. Indianapolis, Bobbs Merrill, 1961.
Night Call. New York, Dell, 1961.
Hospital Hill. New York, Dell, 1961.
Romantic Assignment. London, Ward Lock, 1961.
Jeff Benton, M.D. New York, Dell, 1962; London, Mayflower, 1964.
Jill Nolan, Surgical Nurse. New York, Dell, 1962.
Jill Nolan, R.N. New York, Dell, 1962.
Challenge for Dr. Jane. New York, Avalon, 1963.
Jill Nolan's Choice. New York, Dell, 1963.
The Magic Scalpel of Dr. Farrer. New York, Avalon, 1965.
Nurse Nolan's Private Duty. New York, Dell, 1966.
Dr. Jane, Interne. New York, Bantam, 1966.
Nurse for Mercy's Mission. New York, Belmont, 1976.

Novels as Elizabeth Wesley (series: Dr. Dee)

Nora Meade, M.D. New York, Avalon, 1955; London, Corgi, 1958.
Ann Foster, Lab Technician. New York, Avalon, 1956.
Sharon James, Free-lance Photographer. New York, Avalon, 1956.
Polly's Summer Stock. New York, Avalon, 1957; as *Summer Stock Romance*, New York, Berkley, 1961.
Doctor Barbara. New York, Avalon, 1958.
Nurse Judy. New York, Avalon, 1958.
Jane Ryan, Dietician. New York, Avalon, 1959.
Doctor Dee. New York, Avalon, 1960.
Dr. Dee's Choice. New York, Avalon, 1962.
Dr. Dorothy's Choice. New York, Paperback Library, 1963.

Novels as Jane Scott

Barbara Owen, Girl Reporter. New York, Avalon, 1956.
Kay Rogers, Copy Writer. New York, Avalon, 1956.
A New Love for Cynthia. New York, Avalon, 1958.
Nurse Nancy. New York, Avalon, 1959.
A Nurse for Rebels' Run. New York, Avalon, 1960.

OTHER PUBLICATIONS

Novels

My Heart Went Dead. New York, Phoenix Press, 1949.
Murder with Roses. New York, Phoenix Press, 1950; London, Foulsham, 1953.
Keep Back the Dark. New York, Phoenix Press, 1951.
Minus One Corpse (as John Cleveland). New York, Arcadia House, 1954.
Shattered Halo. New York, Avalon, 1956; London, Ward Lock, 1960.

Other (for children)

Career for Jenny. New York, Avalon, 1958.
Summer Change. Indianapolis, Bobbs Merrill, 1960.

*   *   *

After writing a few early mystery novels, Adeline McElfresh found her niche in the medical-romance novel, and generally remained with it in the books published under her own name and under pseudonyms. Along with a number of individual novels, she wrote two longer series, the Dr. Jane stories and the Jill Nolan stories. However, similar situations, themes, and backgrounds run through both her series and separates, as she stays with her basic pattern. The novels are generally set in small towns in southern Indiana, with nurses and doctors at the local hospital as the chief characters. There are very detailed descriptions of operations and medical procedures; crises in the form of traffic accidents, fires, mine cave-ins, and natural disasters for the medics to cope with. The stories have a nice home-spun rural midwestern America feel to them. There is occasionally the more serious theme of the need for social reform, as in *Dr. Jane Comes Home*, in which a greedy industrialist provides substandard housing for his workers; and in *Jill Nolan, R.N.*, in which the nurse heroine leaves a doctor's wealthy society practice for a clinic in a small Kentucky town to work with poor coal-miners' families.

Romance plays a distinctly secondary role in these novels. While the heroines always have a romantic interest, usually a fellow medic, but often a local journalist, the love interest can shift from book to book in the series. The usual long descriptions of infatuations found in most romances take a back seat to long, and very good, descriptions of skull-fracture operations and deliveries of babies. In *Hospital Hill* the chief character, in a switch, is Chris Roman, a male doctor, in love with a woman journalist. But the themes remain the same. Chris must work to restore the hospital to the charitable clinic it had been in the past, before a new director put the emphasis on medicine for the well-to-do only. Another typical story, and one of the best is *Kay Manion, M.D.* Kay, stranded in a flood in the small town of Woodbine, helps flood victims, stays on through a typhoid outbreak, and ultimately decides to leave her big-city hospital for life in Woodbine. While this is formula fiction, it is pleasantly written. The characters may be stock, and the plots may be predictable, but the feel for rural American life is good, and the medicine is above reproach.

—Necia A. Musser

McEVOY, Marjorie (née Harte). Also writes as Marjorie Harte. British. Born in York. Educated at a private girls school. Married William Noel McEvoy (died); one son and one daughter. Journalist; has also worked as a matron in a girls school and an auxiliary nurse. Address: 54 Miriam Avenue, Chesterfield, Derbyshire S40 3NF, England.

ROMANCE AND HISTORICAL PUBLICATIONS

Novels

No Castle of Dreams. London, Jenkins, 1960; New York, Lenox Hill Press, 1971.
A Red, Red Rose. London, Jenkins, 1960.
The Meaning of a Kiss. London, Jenkins, 1961.
Forever Faithful. London, Jenkins, 1962.
Softly Treads Danger. London, Jenkins, 1963; New York, Lenox Hill Press, 1967.
Calling Nurse Stewart. London, Jenkins, 1963.
Moon over the Danube. London, Jenkins, 1966.
Who Walks by Moonlight? London, Jenkins, 1966; New York, Lenox Hill Press, 1973.
Brazilian Stardust. New York, Arcadia House, 1967.
Dusky Cactus. London, Jenkins, 1968.
The Grenfell Legacy. London, Jenkins, 1968; New York, Pyramid, 1971.
The White Castello. London, Jenkins, 1969; as *Castle Doom*, New York, Lenox Hill Press, 1970.
The Hermitage Bell. New York, Lenox Hill Press, 1971.
My Love Johnny. London, Hale, 1971; as *Eaglescliffe*, New York, Lenox Hill Press, 1971.
Peril at Polvellyn. New York, Beagle, 1973.
The Chinese Box. New York, Lenox Hill Press, 1973.
Ravensmount. New York, Beagle, 1974.
The Wych Stone. New York, Beagle, 1974.
The Queen of Spades. New York, Ballantine, 1975.
Echoes from the Past. New York, Doubleday, 1979.
Calabrian Summer. New York, Doubleday, 1980.
The Sleeping Tiger. New York, Doubleday, 1983.
Star of Rendevi. New York, Doubleday, and London, Hale, 1984.
Temple Bells. New York, Doubleday, 1985.
Camelot Country. New York, Doubleday, 1986.
The Black Pearl. New York, Doubleday, 1988.

Novels as Marjorie Harte

A Call for the Doctor. London, Hale, 1961.
Goodbye, Doctor Garland. London, Hale, 1962.
Nurse in the Orient. London, Hale, 1962.
Doctors in Conflict. London, Hale, 1963.
Masquerade for a Nurse. London, Hale, 1964.
No Orchids for a Nurse. London, Hale, 1964; as *Strange Journey*, New York, Prestige, n.d.
Doctor Mysterious. London, Hale, 1965.
Cover Girl. London, Hale, 1968; as *The Closing Web*, New York, Lenox Hill Press, 1973.
No Eden for a Nurse. London, Hale, 1971.

*

Marjorie McEvoy comments:

I am primarily an entertainer, but take care that details and locations are accurate. I travel abroad extensively to gain personal knowledge of my background, as well as researching. I have made two extended tours of India for my novel of the Indian mutiny, *The Sleeping Tiger*.

*   *   *

Marjorie McEvoy writes gothic novels with all the proper accoutrements that are the substance of this genre. In a characteristic story a lovely heroine becomes innocently involved with a family possessed of an evil secret. The hero is quite handsome and the heroine is almost always attracted to him from the beginning, instinctively knowing that he is trustworthy. It is equally obvious whom she must beware, since early on the odious character shows the darkness of his personality. A typical example is *The Hermitage Bell*. The time is the mid-19th century and the setting a centuries-old manor located in an isolated region of Wales. Desperately poor but ravishingly beautiful Victoria takes the position of companion to aged Lady Samantha, the strong-willed matriarch of the Tallyfont family. Very shortly Victoria realizes that this family's haunted past may spell danger for herself. The villain is David, Lady Samantha's adopted son, who wants the entire estate for himself. The hero is Huw, another adopted son with a brooding Celtic handsomeness that causes Victoria to fall in love immediately. Huw, quite naturally, reciprocates these feeling. David is responsible for some murder and mayhem, but, when he seeks to do away with Victoria, Huw comes to the rescue proclaiming his everlasting love.

Recently, McEvoy has used modern day Tunisia for the setting of her novel *The Black Pearl*. Lynne Redesdale leaves England to join her fiancé Andrew only to find when she arrives that he has been injured in an automobile accident. She also discovers, to her dismay, that Andrew is not the wonderful man she thought. Not only was he involved in an affair with his employer's wife, he has also stolen a precious black pearl (which carries a curse) and tries to involve Lynne in his evil scheme. It is Victor Crawford, the employer deceived by Andrew that comes to love Lynne and rescue her from danger.

Under the pseudonym of Marjorie Harte, the author spins stories of romance, usually in a contemporary setting, and often involving a nurse as the heroine. Although an element of danger is frequently present, the main theme centers on how the heroine will overcome seemingly insurmountable obstacles to marry the man she loves. In *Strange Journey* nurse Sally Bloom takes a job in North Borneo to search for a husband missing for six years. She eventually finds him, only to discover that he suffers from amnesia and doesn't recognize her. Meanwhile she has fallen in love with the very married Dr. Dirk Greaves. When Dirk's wife leaves him for another man and Sally's husband conveniently dies of lung cancer the two protagonists are free to marry.

All of McEvoy/Harte's stories have standard plots with little intricacy, but they are fast-paced and there is enough action to keep the attention of avid romance readers.

—Patricia Altner

McKAY, Simon. See **NICOLE, Christopher.**

McNAUGHT, Judith. American. Born in California, 10 May 1944. Educated at Northwestern University, Evanston, Illinois, 1962–66, B.S. in business administration. Married Michael McNaught (died 1983); one daughter and one son from earlier marriage. Stewardess and personnel interviewer, United Airlines, Chicago, 1966–67; executive producer, KMOX-CBS Radio, St. Louis, 1970–73; assistant director and motion picture director, Moritz Inc., St. Louis, 1973–76; legal administrator, Sommers Schwartz Inc., Detroit, 1976–78; controller, U.S. Transportation Company, Detroit, 1978; president, Pro-Temps Inc., St. Louis, 1979–85. Agent: Perry Knowlton, Curtis Brown, 10 Astor Place, New York, New York 10003. Address: 5237 West Plano Parkway, Plano, Texas 75093, U.S.A.

ROMANCE AND HISTORICAL PUBLICATIONS

Novels

Tender Triumph. Toronto, Harlequin, 1983; New York, Pocket Books, 1986.
Double Standards. Toronto, Harlequin, 1984; New York, Pocket Books, 1986.
Whitney, My Love. New York, Pocket Books, 1985; London, Corgi, 1986.
Once and Always. New York, Pocket Books, 1987; London, Corgi, 1988.
Something Wonderful. New York, Pocket Books, 1988; London, Corgi, 1989.
A Kingdom of Dreams. New York, Pocket Books, 1989.

*

Judith McNaught comments:

I believe the success of my novels lies in the fact that each of them seems to be able to make readers laugh and cry—and then leave them smiling. I try to appeal to reader's emotions; to make readers really *feel* the joy, the sorrow, the tension experienced by all my characters.

*   *   *

Although the number of Judith McNaught's published novels is still relatively small, she has developed a strong following among romance readers. Moving easily between historical and contemporary romances, she delivers a solid story and sympathetic, believable characters.

McNaught's heroines are intelligent, proud, and independent. When faced with a difficult situation, they take action, often in the face of anticipated pain or retribution. Alexandra, in *Something Wonderful*, protects her husband physically in spite of his distrust of her. Jennifer Merrick (*A Kingdom of Dreams*) plans and executes a daring escape from her captors, showing all the finesse of a born soldier. The heroes of McNaught's novels are strong, determined men, who are distinguished by an innate sensitivity. Although they might appear hard and even ruthless to others, they are capable of deep emotion. In many ways, then, the protagonists of each sex demonstrate the most admirable virtues of the other.

While there are tensions between the lovers and problems to be solved, McNaught does not rely heavily on the common ploy of a simple clash of personalities. Often there are serious issues which divide the lovers so resolution is not so much a question of taming or yielding, as it is of understanding and compromise.

In her first novel, *Tender Triumph*, set in contemporary times, McNaught tackles the basic question of a woman's role. Katie is very much a modern woman with a good job and a bad marriage in her past. Falling in love with Ramon, she is unprepared to accept his traditional, "old world" view of their relationship. She expects to be his equal, sharing his problems and victories, while he believes that she should be shielded and protected by him at all costs. This basic philosophical difference is exacerbated by a clash of cultures, when Katie and Ramon return to his home in Puerto Rico to be married. Similar conflicts in culture occur in the historical romances *Once and Always* and *A Kingdom of Dreams*. In the former, American Victoria comes to England to live, while in the latter, Jennifer, a fiery Scot, must marry her English enemy and, eventually, choose between him and her beloved clan. McNaught makes it clear that these women face difficult choices, but their situations are made a little easier by their husbands'/lovers' ability to make concessions in their own beliefs.

With her most recent novel, *A Kingdom of Dreams*, McNaught also joins many other romance authors in linking stories through related characters. In what is now popularly known as a "prequel," readers are introduced to Royce Westmoreland, the first Duke of Claymore. It is his descendant, Clayton Westmoreland, the ninth Duke, who is the hero of *Whitney, My Love*.

In view of her current popularity and the quality of the work she has already produced, it is clear that McNaught is one of the rising stars of romance fiction. She has the versatility and breadth of vision necessary for the foundation of a long career.

—Barbara E. Kemp

MEADMORE, Susan. See **SALLIS, Susan.**

MELONEY, Franken. See **FRANKEN, Rose.**

MELVILLE, Anne. Pseudonym for Margaret Edith Potter, née Newman; also writes as Anne Betteridge; Margaret Newman; Margaret Potter. British. Born in Harrow, Middlesex, 21 June 1926. Educated at Harrow County School for Girls, 1937–44; St. Hugh's College, Oxford (Major scholar), 1944–47, B.A. 1947, M.A. 1952. Married Jeremy Potter in 1950; two children. Teacher in Egypt and England, 1947–50; editor, *King's Messenger* children's magazine, London, 1950–55; adviser, Citizen's Advice Bureau, Twickenham, Middlesex, 1962–70. Recipient: Romantic Novelists Association Major award, 1966. Agent: Peters Fraser and Dunlop, 5th Floor, The Chambers, Chelsea Harbour, Lots Road, London SW10 0XF, England.

ROMANCE AND HISTORICAL PUBLICATIONS

Novels (series: Hardie; Lorimer)

The Lorimer Line. London, Heinemann, and New York, Doubleday, 1977.
The Lorimer Legacy. London, Heinemann, 1979; as *Alexa*, New York, Doubleday, 1979.
Lorimers at War. London, Heinemann, 1980.
Lorimers in Love. London, Heinemann, 1981.
Blaize (includes *Lorimers at War* and *Lorimers in Love*). New York, Doubleday, 1981.

The Last of the Lorimers. London, Heinemann, 1983.
Lorimer Loyalties. London, Heinemann, 1984.
Family Fortunes. New York, Doubleday, 1984.
The House of Hardie. London, Grafton, 1987.
Grace Hardie. London, Grafton, 1988.

Novels as Anne Betteridge

The Foreign Girl. London, Hurst and Blackett, 1960.
The Young Widow. London, Hurst and Blackett, 1961.
Spring in Morocco. London, Hurst and Blackett, 1962; New York, Beagle, 1973.
The Long Dance of Love. London, Hurst and Blackett, 1963.
The Younger Sister. London, Hurst and Blackett, 1964.
Return to Delphi. London, Hurst and Blackett, 1964.
Single to New York. London, Hurst and Blackett, 1965; New York, Beagle, 1973.
The Chains of Love. London, Hurst and Blackett, 1965; New York, Beagle, 1973.
The Truth Game. London, Hurst and Blackett, 1966; New York, Beagle, 1973.
A Portuguese Affair. London, Hurst and Blackett, 1966; New York, Beagle, 1973.
A Little Bit of Luck. London, Hurst and Blackett, 1967; New York, Beagle, 1973.
Shooting Star. London, Hurst and Blackett, 1968.
Love in a Rainy Country. London, Hurst and Blackett, 1969.
Sirocco. London, Hurst and Blackett, 1970; New York, Beagle, 1973.
The Girl Outside. London, Hurst and Blackett, 1971; New York, Beagle, 1973.
Journey from a Foreign Land. London, Hurst and Blackett, 1972.
The Sacrifice. London, Hurst and Blackett, 1973.
The Stranger on the Beach. London, Hurst and Blackett, 1974.
The Temp. London, Hurst and Blackett, 1976.
The Tiger and the Goat. London, Hurst and Blackett, 1978.

Short Stories

A Time of Their Lives. London, Hurst and Blackett, 1974.
A Place for Everyone. London, Hurst and Blackett, 1977.

OTHER PUBLICATIONS

Novels

Murder to Music (as Margaret Newman). London, Long, 1959.
Unto the Fourth Generation (as Margaret Potter). London, W. H. Allen, 1986.
Lochandar (as Margaret Potter). London, W. H. Allen, 1988.

Other (for children) as Margaret Potter

The Touch-and-Go Year. London, Dobson, 1968; New York, Meredith Press, 1969.
The Blow-and-Grow Year. London, Dobson, 1969.
Sandy's Safari. London, Dobson, 1971.
The Story of the Stolen Necklace. London, Dobson, 1974.
Trouble on Sunday. London, Methuen, 1974.
Smoke over Shap. London, BBC Publications, 1975.
The Motorway Mob. London, Methuen, 1976.
Tony's Special Place. London, Bodley Head, 1977.

The Boys Who Disappeared. London, Hodder and Stoughton, 1985.
Tilly and the Princess. London, Methuen, 1987.

*　　*　　*

To write a saga spanning generations is an ambitious aim, and in the Lorimer series Anne Melville attempts to do just that. In order to control such a vast corpus of material she divides the books rigidly by place or more frequently by date, giving a diary effect with the respective events slotted into their appropriate position. The result is a highly organized account of a family's changing fortunes with references to the concurrent major upheavals in society.

By presenting world history and its effects in this way Melville loses the human touch essential to any work which claims to be ultimately a fiction. There is no sense of authorial voice, of a writer who cares about her inventions and wishes to communicate this feeling to the reader, or even of a zealous historian determined to educate. Instead we are given a textbook where we refer to page 97 to discover what happened in 1916 for example, and where the most useful item is the family tree preceding each volume. We need this because continuity between scenes is uncomfortable, illogical, or simply non-existent.

Her detachment is sometimes distracting. Robert Scott's letter in *Lorimers at War* is one point where the exactitudes of date, time, and place could readily have been dispensed with and the situation allowed to speak for itself—a 21-year-old consigning to paper what may be his last words to his worshipped mother. Rare moments like this, where self-conscious control is relaxed, for example at Brindsley's death or Kate's reunion with Sergei in the following book are moving in their simplicity. We have an overall impression of a disciplined writer who is only on occasion saved from heartlessness.

Melville is in a potentially no-win situation. She either mislays the reader among the factual details which are necessary because of the scope of the work, or else uses these factual details to impose a pattern. She rightly opts for the latter because it has benefits besides providing a reference point for her audience. A diarist's style is double edged, especially when under such taut direction. As a result, although she does not consistently capture her characters' feelings, she captures the attitudes of the age time and time again.

Melville's refusal to become personally involved through her use of this rigid structure is mirrored in the world she depicts. In *The Lorimer Legacy* we observe, but hardly empathise with, the dilemma of Alexa, who cannot become a singer because of her need to guard her reputation (later overcome) and the snobbery of Baden-Baden, where "most of its visitors suffer from nothing more than greed." Convention is stifling, and the formalised boundary within which Melville treats the subject conveys it better than any amount of impassioned railing against the system ever could.

Both social and sexual sacred cows are equally indicted, but Melville reserved her greatest criticism for specifically British traditions. Her central characters inhabit a world of position, power, and money, where the task of turning boy into a man is left to Eton and where a bohemian artist still feels obliged to do the right thing by the woman he seduces. An upper-lip, sometimes extra-stiffened by grief, is the strength of the Lorimers, but English prejudice also means insensitivity to anything foreign or otherwise suspect.

Individual outsiders are accepted only because of the protestant duty ethic and not from any real spirit of tolerance. Generosity to one's fellow man is an act of charity, but nobody ever seriously addresses the reasons why charity should be necessary in the first place. Melville particularly explores the imperialist attitude, the patronising "them and us" mentality as evidenced by, for example observations on the Russians: as a race they are said to have an aptitude for suffering and a fatalism which has evolved over centuries. She never needs to criticise England directly at any point—it is perfectly capable of damning itself through its benevolent oppression of everything else.

The Hardie books continue many of these themes, but especially that of the position of women. Although Kate in the Lorimer series exerts her right to self-determination, building on her predecessor's success in forging a medical career in a male dominated world, she eventually marries a prince but (true to history as opposed to fairy story) they do not live happily ever after. Aunt Midge in *Grace Hardie* marries too, after blissful years of spinsterhood, but a continually single woman, like Beatrice, grows in unpopularity as her husbandless years increase and she devotes herself to the women's movement. It seems a shame that Melville's female characters are compromised into either renouncing their independence or femininity in order to be fulfilled.

It will be interesting to see if Grace herself, "A sort of farmer . . . spinster and carver of shapes," in future books succumbs to one of the roles which society still dictates—the perfectly acceptable smooth-handed romantic heroine of the pitiable indignity of spinsterhood. Either way Melville will hopefully maintain her position as a moralist without preaching to her audience. She emerges as a very socially aware historical author and maintains her deeply committed liberal viewpoint throughout.

—L. M. Quinn

─────────

MELVILLE, Jennie. See **BUTLER, Gwendoline.**

─────────

MERLIN, Christina. See **HEAVEN, Constance.**

─────────

METALIOUS, Grace (née Repentigny). British. Born in Manchester, Lancashire, 8 September 1924. Married George Metalious in 1942; two daughters and one son. *Died 25 February 1964.*

ROMANCE AND HISTORICAL PUBLICATIONS

Novels (series: Peyton Place)

Peyton Place. New York, Messner, 1956; London, Muller, 1957.
Return to Peyton Place. New York, Messner, 1959; London, Muller, 1960.
The Tight White Collar. New York, Messner, and London, Muller, 1960.
No Adam in Eden. New York, Trident, 1963; London, Muller, 1964.

*

Critical Studies: *The Girl from Peyton Place* (biography) by George Metalious and June O'Shea, New York, Dell, 1965.

*   *   *

At the height of its prestige as America's showcase community, Peyton Place—its townscape drawn from Gilmanton, New Hampshire; its name evoked by nearby but otherwise uninvolved Potter Place—was the setting and subject of the second bestselling novel in the United States to that time, of a hit film that was nominated for several Academy awards, and of the first prime time television soap opera, beamed three nights a week into millions of homes after kiddies' bedtimes. Today the book is out of print, the soap opera a fading memory, the movie and a sequel occasionally revived for nostalgic old-timers.

The meteoric rise and rapid fizzling-out of the trio were the result of Grace Metalious's having both the fortune and misfortune to produce her masterpiece at just the time that its titillating genre was at the peak of its appeal before being replaced by an offspring that made the parent look pale indeed. *Peyton Place* was the culmination of the fictional exposures of small-town American life whose authors inched their way along in efforts to see how far they could go in chronicling the cycle of the seasons in towns "rampant with murder, incest, adultery, and general disagreeableness," as an anonymous reviewer for *Library Journal* put it, before censors suppressed the works and the authors were punished for libel and obscenity.

The genre originated late in the 19th century with Joseph Kirkland's and E. M. Howe's vindictive but veiled accounts of the meanness and frustration of life in midwestern small towns. It flourished especially in the iconoclastic 1920's in the avidly read and bitterly denounced *Winesburg, Ohio* by Sherwood Anderson and *Main Street* by Sinclair Lewis and climaxed in Henry Bellaman's probe of *King's Row*, to which *Peyton Place* is often compared. William Faulkner and Erskine Caldwell instituted a southern subgenre, but the Currier-and-Ives villages of New England had remained off-limits, despite some grim glimpses in Edith Wharton's *Ethan Frome* and some of Robert Frost's poems. Metalious's penetration of the heavily draped and shuttered windows of the staid communities where those like laconic President Calvin Coolidge kept any secrets inviolate outraged this last stronghold of national propriety and elated scandal-mongers everywhere.

Metalious's daring proved, however, her downfall. Although her first novel perilously walked the narrow line that bordered permissible tale-telling, it went just far enough to help tumble down the crumbling barriers of legal pre-restraint on fiction and film in the United States.

Metalious was never able to repeat her early success. Reviewers complained that *Return to Peyton Place* was a labored tale that added nothing to the original except self-pitying details of an author's attempt to write and publish a book like *Peyton Place* in the face of community hostility. Having apparently exhausted her personal experiences, Metalious tried to draw upon limited powers of invention for *The Tight White Collar*, another tale of small town life, and *No Adam in Eden*, an episodic history of three generations of French Canadian women's search for love. Reviewers complained that these were "pallid stuff," lacking any central theme or direction.

The most cogent summary of the reasons for Metalious's fleeting celebrity comes, as often such judgments do, from a distant source that could view her real and fictional worlds objectively. A London *Times* reviewer observed that she was "expert at evoking sex-ridden adolescence—the permanent condition of most of her characters," but that she was "addicted to a strident and ultimately risible vulgarity that infects much of what she writes."

—Warren French

* * *

MICHAELS, Barbara. Pseudonym for Barbara (Louise) G(ross) Mertz; also writes as Elizabeth Peters. American. Born in Canton, Illinois, 29 September 1927. Educated at the University of Chicago Oriental Institute, Ph.B 1947, M.A. 1950, Ph.D. 1952. Married Richard R. Mertz in 1950 (divorced 1968); one daughter and one son. Agent: Dominick Abel, 498 West End Avenue, New York, New York 10026. Address: c/o Congdon and Weed, 298 Fifth Avenue, New York, New York 10001, U.S.A.

ROMANCE AND HISTORICAL PUBLICATIONS

Novels

The Master of Blacktower. New York, Appleton Century Crofts, 1966; London, Jenkins, 1967.
Sons of the Wolf. New York, Meredith, 1967; London, Jenkins, 1968; as *Mystery on the Moors*, New York, Paperback Library, 1968.
Ammie, Come Home. New York, Meredith, 1968; London, Jenkins, 1969.
Prince of Darkness. New York, Meredith, 1969; London, Hodder and Stoughton, 1971.
The Dark on the Other Side. New York, Dodd Mead, 1970; London, Souvenir Press, 1973.
Greygallows. New York, Dodd Mead, 1972; London, Souvenir Press, 1974.
The Crying Child. New York, Dodd Mead, and London, Souvenir Press, 1973.
Witch. New York, Dodd Mead, 1973; London, Souvenir Press, 1975.
House of Many Shadows. New York, Dodd Mead, 1974; London, Souvenir Press, 1976.
The Sea King's Daughter. New York, Dodd Mead, 1975; London, Souvenir Press, 1977.
Patriot's Dream. New York, Dodd Mead, 1976; London, Souvenir Press, 1978.
Wings of the Falcon. New York, Dodd Mead, 1977; London, Souvenir Press, 1979.
Wait for What Will Come. New York, Dodd Mead, 1978; London, Souvenir Press, 1980.
The Walker in Shadows. New York, Dodd Mead, 1979; London, Souvenir Press, 1981.
The Wizard's Daughter. New York, Dodd Mead, 1980; London, Souvenir Press, 1982.
Someone in the House. New York, Dodd Mead, 1981; London, Souvenir Press, 1983.
Black Rainbow. New York, Congdon and Weed, 1982; London, Souvenir Press, 1983.
Here I Stay. New York, Congdon and Weed, 1983; London, Souvenir Press, 1985.
Dark Duet (includes *Ammie, Come Home* and *Prince of Darkness*). New York, Congdon and Weed, 1983.
The Grey Beginning. New York, Congdon and Weed, 1984; London, Souvenir Press, 1986.
Be Buried in the Rain. New York, Atheneum, 1985; London Piatkus, 1986.

Shattered Silk. New York, Atheneum, 1986; London, Piatkus, 1987.
Search for the Shadows. New York, Atheneum, 1987; as *Search the Shadows*, London Piatkus, 1988.
Smoke and Mirrors. New York, Simon and Schuster, and London, Piatkus, 1989.

Novels as Elizabeth Peters (series: Vicky Bliss; Jacqueline Kirby; Amelia Peabody)

The Jackal's Head. New York, Meredith, 1968; London, Jenkins, 1969.
The Camelot Caper. New York, Meredith, 1969; London, Cassell, 1976.
The Dead Sea Cipher. New York, Dodd Mead, 1970; London, Cassell, 1975.
The Night of Four Hundred Rabbits. New York, Dodd Mead, 1971; as *Shadows in the Moonlight*, London, Coronet, 1975.
The Seventh Sinner (Kirby). New York, Dodd Mead, 1972; London, Coronet, 1975.
Borrower of the Night (Bliss). New York, Dodd Mead, 1973; London, Cassell, 1974.
The Murders of Richard III (Kirby). New York, Dodd Mead, 1974; London, Piatkus, 1989.
Crocodile on the Sandbank (Peabody). New York, Dodd Mead, 1975; London, Cassell, 1976.
Legend in Green Velvet. New York, Dodd Mead, 1976; as *Ghost in Green Velvet*, London, Cassell, 1977.
Devil-May-Care. New York, Dodd Mead, 1977; London, Cassell, 1978.
Street of the Five Moons (Bliss). New York, Dodd Mead, 1978; London, Piatkus, 1988.
Summer of the Dragon. New York, Dodd Mead, 1979; London, Souvenir Press, 1980.
The Love Talker. New York, Dodd Mead, 1980; London, Souvenir Press, 1981.
The Curse of the Pharaohs (Peabody). New York, Dodd Mead, 1981; London, Souvenir Press, 1982.
The Copenhagen Connection. New York, Congdon and Lattès, 1982; London, Souvenir Press, 1983.
Silhouette in Scarlet (Bliss). New York, Congdon and Weed, 1983; London, Souvenir Press, 1984.
Die for Love (Kirby). New York, Congdon and Weed, 1984; London, Souvenir Press, 1985.
The Mummy Case (Peabody). New York, Congdon and Weed, 1985; London, Souvenir Press, 1986.
Lion in the Valley (Peabody). New York, Atheneum, 1986; London, Piatkus, 1987.
Trojan Gold (Bliss). New York, Atheneum, and London, Piatkus, 1987.
The Deeds of the Disturber (Peabody). New York, Atheneum, and London, Piatkus, 1988.
Naked Once More (Kirby). New York, Warner, 1989.

OTHER PUBLICATIONS

Other as Barbara G. Mertz

Temples, Tombs, and Hieroglyphs: The Story of Egyptology. New York, Coward McCann, and London, Gollancz, 1964; revised edition, New York, Dodd Mead, 1978.
Red Land, Black Land: The World of the Ancient Egyptians. New York, Coward McCann, 1966; London, Hodder and Stoughton, 1967; revised edition, New York, Dodd Mead, 1978.

Two Thousand Years in Rome, with Richard Mertz. New York, Coward McCann, 1968; London, Dent, 1969.

*

Manuscript Collections: Mugar Memorial Library, Boston University; University of Wyoming, Laramie.

Barbara Michaels comments:
I do not consider myself a writer of romances and I abhor the word gothic as applied to anything except the novels of Mrs. Radcliffe and "Monk" Lewis. The Elizabeth Peters books are mysteries; so are the Barbara Michaels novels. Both are written from the point of view of a female protagonist and both incorporate romantic plot elements; in my opinion, this does not make them romance novels any more than the presence of a romance between Richard Hannay and Mary makes *Mr. Steadfast* by John Buchan a romance novel.

"Romantic Suspense" is another term which has been applied to my books and those of other women writers. It is marginally more acceptable than gothic, but the question remains—why is it applied only to suspense novels by *women*? Most mystery and suspense novels include a love story—even tough private eyes maintain a romantic or sexual relationship with one or more women, so why make this distinction contingent upon the gender of the author? As Peters, I write straight mysteries; as Michaels I write suspense novels. I like and use a strong romantic element, but I don't believe that word should label my books.

*   *   *

Barbara Michaels is a pseudonym of Egyptologist Barbara G. Mertz, who also writes fiction under the name Elizabeth Peters. The Peters books are mystery/romances with strong detective elements; frequently, they have a background or archaeological interest, and are either set in the modern period or comment upon an historical period from a modern perspective. Indeed, the best of these novels provide a kind of pastiche of the genre, with the heroine exhibiting more interest in her research than in snaring the hero. These books are lucidly written, and are infused with an irrestible combination of scholarly plausibility and good humour. The author's erudition is never conveyed as solemnity, and various academic details essential to the plots are presented with a notable lack of self-consciousness.

As Michaels, Mertz writes novels of historical romance, as well as books which explore facets of the supernatural. Imbued with the author's characteristic intelligence, these are, on the whole, rather less satisfying works, perhaps because the element of pastiche is missing. The best of the Michaels novels are those with a historical setting (*Wings of the Falcon*), or those in which a historical background figures prominently (*Wait for What Will Come*). Those which take place in the present, but in which supernatural events are rooted in history to legend (*Ammie, Come Home*), are more convincing than those in which the supernatural is a literal element in the plot (*The Dark on the Other Side*).

In fact, one has the sense that Mertz herself is uncomfortable with the supernatural as a theme, and her discomfort is revealed in occasional confusion of tone. Having saved the heroine from a husband who was a practicing warlock, the hero jokes about silver bullets; the psychiatrist who diagnosed a "delusion of lycanthropy" remarks: "You're her hero, aren't you? Fighting the powers of darkness for her soul. . . . What are lions compared to that?" And the warlock must be destroyed not merely because he is deluded/evil, but because he is thinking of running for political office, and the (Jewish) analyst recognizes certain Hitlerian tendencies.

On the other hand, the historical romances contain writing which rivals the best of Elizabeth Peters, which is to say that, while not precisely tongue-in-cheek, they have a lightheartedness of tone which derives from the transparently contrived genre to which they belong. Accuracy of detail, combined with an intelligent presentation of female characters, sets these books apart from the mundane.

—Joanne Harack Hayne

MICHAELS, Fern. Pseudonym for Roberta Anderson and Mary Kuczkir. Americans. **ANDERSON, Roberta:** Born in New Jersey, 22 August 1942. Married Alfred P. Anderson; one daughter and one son. Worked as a supervisor and freelance jobber in market research. **KUCZKIR, Mary:** Born in Hastings, Pennsylvania, 9 April 1933. Married Michael Kuczkir in 1952; three daughters and two sons. Address: c/o Ballantine, 201 East 50th Street, New York, New York 10022, U.S.A.

ROMANCE AND HISTORICAL PUBLICATIONS

Novels (series: Captive; Texas)

Pride and Passion. New York, Ballantine, 1975.
Vixen in Velvet. New York, Ballantine, 1976.
Captive Passions. New York, Ballantine, 1977.
Valentina. New York, Ballantine, 1978.
Captive Embraces. New York, Ballantine, 1979.
Captive Splendors. New York, Ballantine, 1980.
The Delta Ladies. New York, Pocket Books, 1980.
Golden Lasso. New York, Silhouette, 1980.
Sea Gypsy. Boston, Hall, 1980; London, Silhouette, 1981.
Beyond Tomorrow. London, Hodder and Stoughton, 1981; Boston, Hall, 1985.
Captive Innocence. New York, Ballantine, 1981.
Whisper My Name. New York, Silhouette, 1981.
Without Warning. New York, Pocket Books, 1981.
Nightstar. Boston, Hall, 1982.
Paint Me Rainbows. Boston, Hall, and London, Hodder and Stoughton, 1982.
Wild Honey. New York, Pocket Books, 1982; London, Arrow, 1984.
All She Can Be. New York, Ballantine, 1983.
Free Spirit. New York, Ballantine, 1983.
Tender Warrior. New York, Ballantine, 1983.
Cinders to Satin. New York, Ballantine, and London, Futura, 1984.
Texas Rich. New York, Ballantine, 1985; London, Severn House, 1989.
Texas Heat. New York, Ballantine, 1986.
To Taste the Wine. New York, Ballantine, 1987.
Texas Fury. New York, Ballantine, 1989.

OTHER PUBLICATIONS

Novels

Without Warning. New York, Pocket Books, 1981.
Panda Bear Is Critical. London, Macmillan, 1982; New York, Pocket Books, 1984.

Other by Mary Kuczkir

My Dish Towel Flies at Half Mast. New York, Ballantine, 1979.

*   *   *

The team of Roberta Anderson and Mary Kuczkir are commercial writers first and foremost, since they change direction depending on which way the market winds happen to be blowing at any given time. During the 1970's they wrote erotic historical romance novels typical of the "bodice rippers" of the period (e.g., *Vixen in Velvet*, *Captive Passions*, which were re-issued in the late 1980's in response to the renewed popularity of historical romances). These early stories are filled with piracy, passion, and possession, with the occasional rape thrown in to season a brew already boiling with adventure and rebellious heroines. Then, in the early 1980's, when the romance market began to focus on the concerns of contemporary women, Anderson and Kuczkir produced two short novels—*Free Spirit* and *All She Can Be*—which were issued as titles in a unique series published by Ballantine, called Love and Life: Women's Stories for Today, in which the heroines all develop a strong sense of self. Certainly *All She Can Be* is a landmark in the evolution of the genre, because it so closely reflects the personal experiences and fantasies of so many women (including, one suspects, its creators) who came of age *as women* during the 1960's and 1970's, one of the most turbulent periods of social change in this century.

Free Spirit is the story of a successful magazine editor who decides to go all out for domesticity, giving in to the pull of society's traditional socialization of females because she is unsure of the validity of her own newfound values and goals in life. It is a decision that turns disastrous, and in the end she realizes she not only misread but distrusted both herself and the man she loves. Most of all, it was a betrayal of her true self. *All She Can Be* is a more incisively developed story (no mean achievement in this novelette form) about a middle-aged woman's attempt to redefine herself as an individual and a woman rather than as wife and mother, after her husband leaves her for another woman. In the process, she must deal with her feelings about her former husband (who is starting a second family with a younger woman) and also change the "rules" for her relationships with her three adult children, while continuing to work at a career that is denigrated by just about everyone—writing romance novels!—even though it has brought her financial independence. After a new man appears in her life, who is ten years her junior, she eventually comes to realize that he is the only kind of man possible for the woman she has become. He is, in fact, the "new hero"—strong, supportive, and sexually secure enough to be a partner rather than the boss—demanded by the "new heroine," who at last has emerged as a whole woman, possessing intellectual and professional talents as well as emotions, and capable of being both mother and a sexual being.

By the mid-1980's, Anderson and Kuczkir had moved on to glitz, glamour, and dynasty novels such as *Texas Rich* (which is strongly reminiscent of Edna Ferber's *Giant*), continuing to follow the fads and fancies of commercial fiction—where they are again just one of the crowd—which is disappointing to say the least, in part because they have left us with a sense of promise unfulfilled and talent squandered. In 1989 Kuczkir obtained full legal right to use the Fern Michaels name, bringing this collaboration to an end.

—Carol Thurston

MICHENER, James A(lbert). American. Born in 1907(?); brought up by foster parents. Educated at Doylestown High School, Pennsylvania; Swarthmore College, Pennsylvania, A.B. (summa cum laude) 1929 (Phi Beta Kappa); University of Northern Colorado, Greeley, A.M. 1935; University of St. Andrews, Scotland. Served in the United States Navy, 1944–45: Lieutenant Commander. Married 1) Patti Koon in 1935 (divorced 1948); 2) Vange Nord in 1948 (divorced 1955); 3) Mari Yoriko Sabusawa in 1955. Master, Hill School, Pottstown, Pennsylvania, 1929–31, and George School, Newtown, Pennsylvania, 1934–36; Professor, University of Northern Colorado, 1936–40; Visiting Professor, Harvard University, Cambridge, Massachusetts, 1940–41; associate editor, Macmillan Company, New York, 1941–49. Since 1949 free-lance writer. Member, Advisory Committee on the Arts, United States Department of State, 1957; Chairman, President Kennedy's Food for Peace Program, 1961; secretary, Pennsylvania Constitution Convention, 1967–68; member of the Advisory Committee, United States Information Agency, 1970–76, and NASA, 1980–83. Since 1983 member of the Board, International Broadcasting. Recipient: Pultizer prize, 1948; National Association of Independent Schools award, 1954, 1958; Einstein award, 1967; National Medal of Freedom, 1971. D.H.L.: Rider College, Lawrenceville, New Jersey, 1950; Swarthmore College, 1954; LL.D.: Temple University, Philadelphia, 1957; Litt.D.: Washington University, St. Louis, 1967; Yeshiva University, New York, 1974; D.Sc.: Jefferson Medical College, Philadelphia, 1979. Address: c/o Random House Inc., 201 East 50th Street, New York, New York 10022, U.S.A.

ROMANCE AND HISTORICAL PUBLICATIONS

Novels

Hawaii. New York, Random House, 1959; London, Secker and Warburg, 1960.
The Source. New York, Random House, and London, Secker and Warburg, 1965.
Centennial. New York, Random House, and London, Secker and Warburg, 1974.
Chesapeake. New York, Random House, and London, Secker and Warburg, 1978; selections published as *The Watermen*, Random House, 1979.
The Covenant. New York, Random House, and London, Secker and Warburg, 1980.
Poland. New York, Random House, and London, Secker and Warburg, 1983.
Texas. New York, Random House, and London, Secker and Warburg, 1985.
Legacy. New York, Random House, and London, Secker and Warburg, 1987.
Alaska. New York, Random House, and London, Secker and Warburg, 1988.
Journey. New York, Random House, and London, Secker and Warburg, 1989.
Caribbean. New York, Random House, 1989.

OTHER PUBLICATIONS

Novels

The Fires of Spring. New York, Random House, 1949; London, Corgi, 1960.

The Bridges at Toko-Ri. New York, Random House, and London, Secker and Warburg, 1953.
Sayonara. New York, Random House, and London, Secker and Warburg, 1954.
The Bridge at Andau. New York, Random House, and London, Secker and Warburg, 1957.
Caravans. New York, Random House, 1963; London, Secker and Warburg, 1964.
The Drifters. New York, Random House, and London, Secker and Warburg, 1971.
Space. New York, Random House, and London, Secker and Warburg, 1982.

Short Stories

Tales of the South Pacific. New York, Macmillan, 1947; London, Collins, 1951.
Return to Paradise. New York, Random House, and London, Secker and Warburg, 1951.

Other

The Unit in the Social Studies, with Harold M. Long. Cambridge, Massachusetts, Harvard University Graduate School of Education, 1940.
The Voice of Asia. New York, Random House, 1951; as *Voices of Asia*, London, Secker and Warburg, 1952.
The Floating World (on Japanese art). New York, Random House, 1954; London, Secker and Warburg, 1955.
Rascals in Paradise, with A. Grove Day. New York, Random House, and London, Secker and Warburg, 1957.
Selected Writings. New York, Modern Library, 1957.
Japanese Prints from the Early Masters to the Modern. Rutland, Vermont, Tuttle, and London, Paterson, 1959.
Report of the County Chairman. New York, Random House, and London, Secker and Warburg, 1961.
The Modern Japanese Print: An Introduction. Rutland, Vermont, Tuttle, 1962.
Iberia: Spanish Travels and Reflections. New York, Random House, and London, Secker and Warburg, 1968.
The Subject Is Israel: A Conversation Between James A. Michener and Dore Schary. New York, Anti-Defamation League of B'nai B'rith, 1968.
Presidential Lottery: The Reckless Gamble in Our Electoral System. New York, Random House, and London, Secker and Warburg, 1969.
The Quality of Life. Philadelphia, Lippincott, 1970; London, Secker and Warburg, 1971.
Facing East: A Study of the Art of Jack Levine. New York, Random House, 1970.
Kent State: What Happened and Why. New York, Random House, and London, Secker and Warburg, 1971.
A Michener Miscellany 1950–1970, edited by Ben Hibbs. New York, Random House, 1973; London, Corgi, 1975.
About "Centennial": Some Notes on the Novel. New York, Random House, 1974.
Sports in America. New York, Random House, 1976; as *Michener on Sport*, London, Secker and Warburg, 1976.
Testimony. Honolulu, White Knight, 1983.
Collectors, Forgers—and a Writer: A Memoir. New York, Targ, 1983.

Editor, *The Future of the Social Studies: Proposals for an Experimental Social-Studies Curriculum.* New York, National Council for the Social Studies, 1939.

Editor, *The Hokusai Sketch Books: Selections from the Manga*. Rutland, Vermont, Tuttle, 1958.

Editor, *Firstfruits: A Harvest of 25 Years of Israeli Writing*. Philadelphia, Jewish Publication Society of America, 1973.

*

Manuscript Collection: Library of Congress, Washington, D.C.

Critical Studies: *James Michener* by A. Grove Day, New York, Twayne, 1964, revised edition, 1977; *James Michener* by George J. Becker, New York, Ungar, 1983; *James A. Michener: A Biography* by John P. Hayes, Indianapolis, Bobbs Merrill, 1984.

* * *

James A. Michener has the Yankee gift, like Walt Whitman before him, of managing to include a vast array of experience and action in his work. His novels are swollen with tales inspired by this or that item of apparent trivia; a footnote in some historical survey becomes in his hands the tale of a generation. In his historical novel *Chesapeake* his commitment to the ecological processes of life becomes the pattern of narrative; this interleaving of lives within the historical stream has always been his aim, but in this novel the links are clearly made between the workings of nature and history. It was his stated aim as early as *Hawaii* (1959) to be a "kind of novelistic social historian," and in this aim we can see both his strengths and his weaknesses.

Michener's historical novels are voluminous in size and compendious in content; often he leaves the reader wishing that they were less of an educational experience and more like the adventures they portray. Yet there is no doubting the integrity of his edifying principle, which leads him to take risks unprecedented in the world of the bestseller: *Hawaii*, for example, commences with a long (80 or so pages) exposition covering the geological ages of the islands' formation. His individual characters run the gamut of human life, ranging from culture to culture in a display of eclecticism rarely seen in American literature; the novels can also include non-human "characters" such as the goose Onkor—in *Chesapeake*.

No character comes without a heavy burden of social and personal history, and often it can be to their detriment as individuals who can come alive for the reader. They are often dimly distinguished from their ancestors over many generations. A passage in *Chesapeake* displays his genetic determinism: "No family among the Choptank had a more vigorous life force than the Turlocks . . . all members of the family possessed an animal cunning that protected them. With their genetic gifts they should have owned the river." Naturally, with this as the basis for his conception of character, many of the individuals revert to stereotypes; one swamp-living backwoodsman like the founder of the Turlock clan gives rise to centuries of identical progeny.

Like the solid Quakers of his American novels (and it may be noted that he is himself a Quaker), Michener respects the value of a simple, sturdy structure. As the shipwright Paxmores refuse to build a vessel without an integral keel, so the author bases his book on a strong central narrative. The unit of his novels is the story, self-contained in each historical section, but making its own impression on events following, in the same way genetic characteristics are retained.

Despite his profound attachment to North America, other cultures and landscapes exert their fascination. *Hawaii* describes the waxing of the Polynesian civilization on those islands, its colonization and domination by the British and American empires, and the subsequent influx of other races: English, American, Chinese, and Japanese; it ends on the eve of Hawaii "growing up" and achieving statehood and equality within the United States. During the course of the novel, the tensions between cultures give rise to conflict, slavery, and finally a kind of forced accommodation. Michener boldly gives equal weight to each of the various communities, though ultimately (and historically) the races can only achieve independence within the context of English-speaking America. In *Centennial* and *Chesapeake*, too, the indigenous culture is shown dwindling away, pathetically inadequate to the armed challenge of the white man.

After the success of *Hawaii*, which established him as a bestselling author, Michener went on to publish a range of books both historical and contemporary in subject matter. Apart from *The Source*, which combines an archaeological exploration in the present with a series of historical flashbacks to the history of Palestine and the Jews, his historical books tend to be inspired by the United States. *Centennial* covers the history of a small village in Colorado, again taking its story from geological prehistory to the present day. But his strongest and most representative novel is *Chesapeake* which springs from a deep respect for the eastern bay he knew as a youth; in it the creation of the democratic experiment of America is charted by means of a tiny area of land and its few inhabitants. In this book, Michener's stereotyped characters are no longer such a flaw; he uses their generalized qualities to stand for a whole nation, creating a broad tapestry of intricate design.

—Alan Murphy

MILES, Lady (Favell Mary Miles, née Hill). British. Born in Bath, Somerset. Married Sir Charles Miles in 1912 (died 1966); two sons. *Died 3 January 1969.*

ROMANCE AND HISTORICAL PUBLICATIONS

Novels

The Red Flame. London, Hutchinson, 1921.
Red, White, and Grey. London, Hutchinson, 1921.
Ralph Carey. London, Hutchinson, 1922.
Stony Ground. London, Hutchinson, 1923.
The Fanatic. London, Hutchinson, 1924.
Tread Softly. London, Hutchinson, 1926.
Love's Cousin. London, Hutchinson, 1927.
Dark Dream. London, Hutchinson, 1929.
Lorna Neale. London, Hutchinson, 1932.
This Flower. London, Hutchinson, 1933.
The Second Lesson. London, Hutchinson, 1936.

* * *

Lady Miles's first novel, *The Red Flame*, appeared in 1921. Her heroine is a red-haired *femme fatale* with a strange childhood in India behind her. She is "a lovely scrap of a disreputable thing, who'd look well à la mode on a tiger skin," and she goes through life (and her marriage) bringing unhappiness. The novel presents a picture of an unlovely character and her effect on others. The *Times Literary Supplement* reviewer pointed out that this novel "does not succeed in absorbing the attention of the reader," and this criticism continued to be made of subsequent novels, although reviewers acknowledged the care with which Miles wrote.

The people in Miles's novels tend to be unsympathetic characters and to live unhappy lives, frequently as the result of dismal and unloving childhoods. Consequently the stories of their lives abound in frustrated or misplaced affections, unfortunate marriages (of which they may or may not attempt to make the best), and cycles of failure in the capacity to love. Various ways of ensuring unhappiness are examined—obsession with religion (*The Fanatic*), obsession with spiritual forces communicating mysteriously à la Joan of Arc (*Dark Dream*), obsession with introspective questionings after an unhappy childhood (*Ralph Carey*), and vast over-sensitiveness and over-imagination (*Lorna Neale*).

Emotions and motives are examined and analysed at considerable length both by the author (as narrator) and by the characters who think and talk a great deal about their relationships with one another ("What must Michael be thinking of her? Granted the courage of a mouse, she would not have deserted him, but she hadn't a mouse's courage. She always deserted those she loved . . . Glen? Glen had trusted her. She had led him to believe that she could save them both. The spirit is willing but the flesh is weak. The flesh is weak because the spirit is not willing enough; because, beneath a show of strength, the spirit is fatally weak, too. She had thrust Glen away . . . He, not Michael, needed her." *Lorna Neale*).

Plot, consequently, tends to arise from character, or to be a demonstration of character, and in some of the novels nothing much happens. The novels variously end unhappily, when the heroine falls down a quarry (*Dark Dream*) or walks into the sea in a religious ecstasy (*The Fanatic*), or with qualified happiness, when the hero and heroine decide to make the best of their lot or when (as the *TLS* said of *The Second Lesson*) disaster is averted but not very convincingly.

—Jean Buchanan

MILLAR, Margaret (Ellis, née Sturm). American. Born in Kitchener, Ontario, Canada, 5 February 1915. Educated at Kitchener Collegiate Institute, 1929–33; University of Toronto, 1933–36. Married the writer Kenneth Millar, i.e., Ross Macdonald, in 1938 (died 1983); one daughter (deceased). Screenwriter, Warner Brothers, Hollywood, 1945–46. President, Mystery Writers of America, 1957–58. Recipient: Mystery Writers of America Edgar Allan Poe award, 1956, and Grand Master award, 1983; Los Angeles *Times* Woman of the Year award, 1965. Agent: Harold Ober Associates Inc., 40 East 49th Street, New York, New York 10017, U.S.A.

ROMANCE AND HISTORICAL PUBLICATIONS

Novels (series: Tom Aragon; Dr. Paul Prye; Inspector Sands)

The Invisible Worm (Prye). New York, Doubleday, 1941; London, Long, 1943.
The Weak-Eyed Bat (Prye). New York, Doubleday, 1942.
The Devil Loves Me (Prye; Sands). New York, Doubleday, 1942.

Wall of Eyes (Sands). New York, Random House, 1943; London, Lancer, 1966.
Fire Will Freeze. New York, Random House, 1944.
The Iron Gates (Sands). New York, Random House, 1945; as *Taste of Fears*, London, Hale, 1950.
Experiment in Springtime. New York, Random House, 1947.
It's All in the Family. New York, Random House, 1948.
The Cannibal Heart. New York, Random House, 1949; London, Hamish Hamilton, 1950.
Do Evil in Return. New York, Random House, 1950; London, Museum Press, 1952.
Rose's Last Summer. New York, Random House, 1952; London, Museum Press, 1954; as *The Lively Corpse*, New York, Dell, 1956.
Vanish in an Instant. New York, Random House, 1952; London, Museum Press, 1953.
Wives and Lovers. New York, Random House, 1954.
Beast in View. New York, Random House, and London, Gollancz, 1955.
An Air That Kills. New York, Random House, 1957; as *The Soft Talkers*, London, Gollancz, 1957.
The Listening Walls. New York, Random House, and London, Gollancz, 1959.
A Stranger in My Grave. New York, Random House, and London, Gollancz, 1960.
How Like an Angel. New York, Random House, and London, Gollancz, 1962.
The Fiend. New York, Random House, and London, Gollancz, 1964.
Beyond This Point Are Monsters. New York, Random House, 1970; London, Gollancz, 1971.
Ask for Me Tomorrow (Aragon). New York, Random House, 1976; London, Gollancz, 1977.
The Murder of Miranda (Aragon). New York, Random House, 1979; London, Gollancz, 1980.
Mermaid (Aragon). New York, Morrow, and London, Gollancz, 1982.
Banshee. New York, Morrow, and London, Gollancz, 1983.
Spider Webs. New York, Morrow, 1986; London, Gollancz, 1987.

OTHER PUBLICATIONS

Other

The Birds and the Beasts Were There (autobiography). New York, Random House, 1968.

*   *   *

The works of Margaret Millar have justly won recognition as mysteries: they develop tight plots, parallel subplots, gripping suspense, and plausible characters. However, Millar's evocation of evil as a force psychologically motivated, resolved only psychologically, makes her works interesting treatments of gothic themes as well as detective ones.

A Stranger in My Grave, Millar's finest novel, illustrates the ways in which the author combines themes and genres. Childless and overprotected housewife Daisy Harker is haunted by nightmares of her own grave. To her horror, and that of her husband, she realizes that she has in fact seen the grave before; she determines to discover why she is dreaming about it. With the help of Steve Pinata, a detective in search of his own identity, she discovers the truth: the stranger in her grave is her real father, a Mexican-American whom her mother had denied and whom her presumptive father had murdered in a jealous rage. Her identity discovered, her nightmare purged, Daisy is able to leave her barren and dishonest marriage to begin a new life with Pinata.

While Steve Pinata acts as the detective of *A Stranger in My Grave*, he also acts as therapist, helping Daisy to remember and accept people and events she has repressed. Pinata's motivation lies both in his sympathy for Daisy's search for identity and in his growing respect and love for her. In gothic terms, Daisy is both the victim and the pursuer of the hidden evil which imprisons her, the truth hidden in her own subconscious. The real resolution of *A Stranger in My Grave* is the union between Daisy and Pinata, a marriage whose children will have the identity and family love denied to their parents.

Millar's mystery/gothics tend to deal with poor marital or sexual adjustment and to revolve around central women characters. *The Cannibal Heart*, *Do Evil in Return*, and *Beast in View* discuss the frightening consequences of the unhealthy repression that can drive women to act out their fantasies on the lives of others. *Experiment in Springtime*, *Beyond This Point Are Monsters*, and *Ask for Me Tomorrow* demonstrate the sick and sometimes violent consequences of flawed marriage: jealousy, obsession, guilt, revenge. A favorite Millar theme, sexual competition between women, appears in *Wall of Eyes*, *The Listening Walls*, and *The Murder of Miranda*.

Millar's most gothic tale, *The Fiend*, parallels the struggles of a convicted child abuser to overcome his obsession for a little girl to the child's own painful struggle to accept the flaws in her parents' marriage and to understand the sexual attractions between grownup men and women. The themes of *The Fiend* reappear interestingly in *Banshee*, in which a mourning father tries obsessively but vainly to assign the guilt for his young daughter's death to a variety of plausible suspects. Millar also plays interestingly on the gothic theme of the innocent pursued victim who is in fact the real source of evil. In *Beast in View*, a quiet, retiring heiress is persecuted by her own outgoing, sexual, and aggressive alter ego. In *Mermaid*, the childlike, innocent young retarded woman who asks for a detective's help becomes the amoral, vicious, and violent evil who harms others. *Spider Webs* is Millar's most deft, ambitious, and successful treatment of guilt and hidden evil, tracing the devious psychological motivations of all of the characters involved in the defense of a handsome young black man accused of murdering a frivolous, rich white woman.

Millar combines domestic themes and situations, convincing characterization, and plots which trace and reveal psychological horror. She analyzes gothic evil as psychological illness, tracing its roots both in individuals and in the society which forms them. Millar's ability as a writer makes her fictional analyses vivid and meaningful.

—Katherine Staples

MILLHISER, Marlys (Joy, née Enabnit). American. Born in Charles City, Iowa, 27 May 1938. Educated at the University of Iowa, Iowa City, 1956–60, B.A. in history, 1960; University of Colorado, Boulder, 1961–63, M.A. in history 1963. Married David Millhiser in 1960; one son and one daughter. History teacher, Boulder Valley schools, Lafayette, Colorado, 1963–65. Address: c/o Putnam, 200 Madison Avenue, New York, New York 10016, U.S.A.

ROMANCE AND HISTORICAL PUBLICATIONS

Novels

Michael's Wife. New York, Putnam, 1972.
Nella Waits. New York, Putnam, 1974.
Willing Hostage. New York, Putnam, 1976.
The Mirror. New York, Putnam, 1978.
Nightmare Country. New York, Putnam, 1981.
The Threshold. New York, Putnam, 1984.

*

Manuscript Collection: University of Wyoming, Laramie.

Marlys Millhiser comments:

I don't consider my work necessarily in a romance/gothic genre. I do not write to formula. But because I am female I tend to view life that way and I have no desire to imitate the other sex. So I do naturally include much of the human and especially female/male relationship in my stories. They've been billed as everything from romantic to supernatural to horror. My only hope is that they are not boring.

*   *   *

Marlys Millhiser can hardly be said to write escapist fiction. In fact, the settings, characters, and situations in her novels are often so grim that the reader must wonder why the *heroines* do not escape. Millhiser's command of descriptive language is excellent; so good, in fact, that it is difficult for a reader to become involved in her earliest works because of the unrelieved bleakness that she conveys. Her first novel, *Michael's Wife*, presents us with an amnesic young woman who returns to the husband that she abandoned and the child of whose existence she has been unaware. The husband seems to have murder in mind; his family makes no secret of their hatred for the prodigal wife. Even the secretary-babysitter seems determined to engineer Laurel's downfall or death. Further to complicate the situation all of these characters are isolated in a house in the desert. Laurel's stated reason for remaining in an environment so dangerous and unpleasant—that the child needs his mother—is unconvincing since the character of the boy remains two-dimensional and Laurel's relationship to him is somewhat undeveloped. The same sort of entrapment of the heroine occurs in each novel, yet only in *The Mirror* is one convinced that the young woman cannot free herself without physical or emotional trauma.

It is a measure of Millhiser's skill in plotting that her novels rise above such unpromising opening chapters to capture the reader's attention and interest. One can see an improvement in style from book to book, if not in the gloominess of setting and character. These novels are unusual for their genre in that, with the exception of *Willing Hostage*, they take place over very long spans of time. *The Mirror*, in fact, spans the lifetimes of a woman and her granddaughter. This time factor is one area in which Millhiser's increased skill is demonstrated in successive novels. *Michael's Wife* proceeds so slowly at times that the action seems almost to stop, while the later books are paced much more smoothly. It should also be noted that *Michael's Wife* with its detailed descriptions of hippies and their costumes is so typical that it now seems very dated. The later books have a more timeless, contemporary feeling about them.

The area in which this writer shines is in her handling of the supernatural. Both *Nella Waits* and *The Mirror* are supernatural tales. Both are exceptionally complex and yet vastly different from each other. The malevolent haunting and equivocal ending of *Nella Waits* is breathlessly believable. The transfer of souls in *The Mirror*, while not a new concept, is handled with a freshness and consistency that easily permit the reader's suspension of disbelief.

Millhiser's world is not easy to enter and not always entertaining in the lighest sense; but once the reader has entered, settings, characters, and style are secondary to the irresistible flow of these intricate plots.

—Susan Quinn Berneis

———

MITCHELL, Margaret (Munnerlyn). American. Born in Atlanta, Georgia, 8 November 1900. Educated at Washington Seminary, Atlanta, 1914–18; Smith College, Northampton, Massachusetts, 1918–19. Married 1) Berrien Kinnard Upshaw in 1922 (divorced); 2) John R. Marsh in 1925. Feature writer and reporter, Atlanta *Journal and Constitution* and *Sunday Journal Magazine*, 1922–26. Recipient: Pulitzer prize, 1937; Bohmenberger Memorial award, 1938. M.A.: Smith College, 1939. *Died 16 August 1949.*

ROMANCE AND HISTORICAL PUBLICATIONS

Novel

Gone with the Wind. New York and London, Macmillan, 1936.

OTHER PUBLICATIONS

Other

Margaret Mitchell's Gone with the Wind Letters 1936–1949, edited by Richard Harwell. New York, Macmillan, and London, Collier Macmillan, 1976.
Margaret Mitchell, A Dynamo Going to Waste: Letters to Allen Edee 1919–1921, edited by Jane Peacock. Atlanta, Peachtree, 1985.

*

Manuscript Collections: University of Georgia, Athens; Atlanta Public Library.

Critical Studies: *Margaret Mitchell of Atlanta* by Finis Farr, New York, Morrow, 1965; *The Road to Tara: The Life of Margaret Mitchell* by Anne Edwards, New Haven, Connecticut, Ticknor and Fields, and London, Hodder and Stoughton, 1983; *Gone with the Wind as Book and Film* edited by Richard Harwell, Columbia, University of South Carolina Press, 1983.

*   *   *

In the more than 50 years since their first appearance, the characters in Margaret Mitchell's *Gone with the Wind* have stepped out of its pages and taken up permanent residence in our imaginations. They are a curious group, at once reductive romantic stereotypes, recognizably distinct individuals, and expansive mythic figures. Their author, for one, neither doubted nor denied that headstrong, thoughtless Scarlett O'Hara and cynical villainous Rhett Butler were stereotypes. But, she maintained, they were stock characters of a generation, not a genre. Rhett

had to be a cynical rogue because the South of his day was populated by them, even as Scarlett was gritty and determined and mostly unscrupulous because that was the type of woman who survived and prospered in post-war Atlanta, of which she is a symbol. A histrionic plot was needed less to satisfy the demands of romance readers than to fulfill the exigencies of retelling events in Georgia during the 1860's. Yet these historical limitations work to Mitchell's advantage, for it is just this rootedness in time and place which allows her characters to become legendary. Scarlett, Rhett, Melanie, and Ashley can step out of Mitchell's pages and into myth because they have first been allowed to stand upon firm ground, in this case the red Georgia clay. For all their typicality, they are realistic, idiosyncratic characters whose choices are genuinely limited by their imagined existence in a real past.

The historically limited choices which Mitchell's characters make are well enough known: Scarlett's marriages, her killing of an intruding Yankee soldier, her manipulation of the postwar lumber business by hiring convicts, and, broadly, her decision to shoulder the responsibility for the O'Hara household after its ruin; Melanie's constantly repeated decision to stand by Scarlett, and—if one can be said to choose a compulsion—her decision to remain ignorant of people's motives and acts; Ashley's decision to die spiritually with the old South (a culture into which, ironically, he hardly fits, as Gerald O'Hara testifies early in the novel), his willful indecision about his feelings for Scarlett; Rhett's scandalous profiteering, his belated decision to enlist in the South's lost cause, his will to protect his child from the shame of Scarlett's bad reputation, his final, irrevocable decision to leave. The pulling and pushing of emotions, which so many of these catalogued decisions achieve, is nothing new to romance fiction. What is different is that so many of these decisions are wrong, unwise, lead to unhappy outcomes for the principals, and do so permanently. Many a romance heroine has hastily married the wrong man like Scarlett, but few so knowingly. Many also have married the right man mistakenly, but few have finally declared their love only to have him leave permanently. Few romances, that is, take place in a world in which one can indeed be fatefully wrong.

Few, moreover, proceed at life's own pace, as does *Gone with the Wind*. The typically first-person narration of romance fiction is customarily urgent: whatever is going to happen is going to happen fast. Mitchell's novel, on the other hand, is leisurely. Although it builds to many climaxes, it does so always within the course of large events, sprawling beyond the confines of romance time (usually days or weeks) to cover 10 years. Even the most conventionally romantic element of the book, the Rhett-Scarlett-Ashley triangle, upends expectation. Not only does it not turn out as we might have hoped, it doesn't even begin as it should. Scarlett's is a fatal, dogged desire for Ashley, but it does not start, as do most romances with an attraction/repulsion or as love-at-first-sight, but rather is an adolescent outgrowth in Scarlett of a long childhood friendship. Similarly, her belatedly recognized love for Rhett arises from their long living together in mutual dependence, not out of sudden, puzzling attraction. In *Gone with the Wind*, as in its readers' lives, people grow into affections, even as they sometimes outgrow them, and they do both within the context of larger, sometimes overwhelming, historical events.

Mitchell's pacing, her use of a solidly limiting past, and her characters' consequential choices set *Gone with the Wind* apart from other historical romances, making it more like *War and Peace* than like genre fiction. Is it excessive to compare a popular romance to a literary classic? Of course. Yet the extravagant comparison serves; for unlike other historical romances—and especially unlike most plantation novels—*Gone with the Wind* is set in the past not for its vagueness but for its specificity. If Mitchell's tortuous account of Scarlett and Ashley and Rhett is what keeps romance readers turning pages, what they are likely to find on the overleaf is not a passionate encounter, but instead an analysis of the role of profiteers in Georgia's wartime economy, or General Johnston's strategy in defending Atlanta, or the advantages of owning lumber in post-war, burnt-out Atlanta. Happily, Mitchell grinds her historical axes more quietly than her distant counterpart Tolstoy; economic and political details fit into the book as gracefully as Pittypat's swoons. What results is a neat dovetail joining of the historical and the individual, a book whose broad characters lead intensely personal lives and make consequential choices, the limits of which are determined far more by historical circumstances and inner compulsion than by the conventions of romance.

—Nancy Regan

MITCHISON, Naomi (Margaret, née Haldane). British. Born in Edinburgh, Scotland, 1 November 1897; daughter of the scientist John Scott Haldane; sister of the writer J. B. S. Haldane. Educated at Lynam's School, Oxford; St. Anne's College, Oxford. Served as a volunteer nurse, 1915. Married G. R. Mitchison (who became Lord Mitchison, 1964) in 1916 (died 1970); three sons and two daughters. Labour candidate for Parliament, Scottish Universities constituency, 1935; member, Argyll County Council, 1945–66; member, Highland Panel, 1947–64, and Highlands and Islands Development Council, 1966–76. Tribal adviser, and Mmarona (Mother), to the Bakgatla of Botswana, 1963–89. D.Univ.: University of Stirling, Scotland, 1976; University of Dundee, Scotland, 1985; D.Litt.: University of Strathclyde, Glasgow, 1983. Honorary Fellow, St. Anne's College, 1980, and Wolfson College, 1983, both Oxford. Officer, French Academy, 1924. C.B.E. (Commander, Order of the British Empire), 1985. Address: Carradale House, Campbeltown, Argyll, Scotland.

ROMANCE AND HISTORICAL PUBLICATIONS

Novels

The Conquered. London, Cape, and New York, Harcourt Brace, 1923.
Cloud Cuckoo Land. London, Cape, 1925; New York, Harcourt Brace, 1926.
The Corn King and the Spring Queen. London, Cape, and New York, Harcourt Brace, 1931; as *The Barbarian*, New York, Cameron, 1961.
The Blood of the Martyrs. London, Constable, 1939; New York, McGraw Hill, 1948.
Behold Your King. London, Muller, 1957.

Short Stories

When the Bough Breaks and Other Stories. London, Cape, and New York, Harcourt Brace, 1924.
Black Sparta: Greek Stories. London, Cape, and New York, Harcourt Brace, 1928.
Barbarian Stories. London, Cape, and New York, Harcourt Brace, 1929.

Beyond This Limit: Selected Shorter Fiction of Naomi Mitchison, edited by Isobel Murray. Edinburgh, Scottish Academic Press, 1986.

OTHER PUBLICATIONS

Novels

The Powers of Light. London, Cape, and New York, Peter Smith, 1932.
Beyond This Limit. London, Cape, 1935.
We Have Been Warned. London, Constable, 1935; New York, Vanguard Press, 1936.
The Bull Calves. London, Cape, 1947.
Lobsters on the Agenda. London, Gollancz, 1952.
Travel Light. London, Faber, 1952.
To the Chapel Perilous. London, Allen and Unwin, 1955.
Memoirs of a Spacewoman. London, Gollancz, 1962.
When We Become Men. London, Collins, 1965.
Cleopatra's People. London, Heinemann, 1972.
Solution Three. London, Dobson, and New York, Warner, 1975.
Not by Bread Alone. London, Boyars, 1983.
Early in Orcadia. Glasgow, Drew, 1987.

Short Stories

The Delicate Fire: Short Stories and Poems. London, Cape, and New York, Harcourt Brace, 1933.
The Fourth Pig: Stories and Verses. London, Constable, 1936.
Five Men and a Swan: Short Stories and Poems. London, Allen and Unwin, 1958.
Images of Africa. Edinburgh, Canongate, 1980.
What Do You Think Yourself? Scottish Short Stories. Edinburgh, Harris, 1982.

Plays

Nix-Nought-Nothing: Four Plays for Children (includes *My Ain Sel'*, *Hobyah! Hobyah!*, *Elfen Hill*). London, Cape, 1928; New York, Harcourt Brace, 1929.
Kate Crackernuts: A Fairy Play. Oxford, Alden Press, 1931.
The Price of Freedom, with L. E. Gielgud (produced Cheltenham, 1949). London, Cape, 1931.
Full Fathom Five, with L. E. Gielgud (produced London, 1932).
An End and a Beginning and Other Plays (includes *The City and the Citizens*, *For This Man Is a Roman*, *In the Time of Constantine*, *Wild Men Invade the Roman Empire*, *Charlemagne and His Court*, *The Thing That Is Plain*, *Cortez in Mexico*, *Akbar*, *But Still It Moves*, *The New Calendar*, *American Britons*). London, Constable, 1937; as *Historical Plays for Schools*, 2 vols., 1939.
As It Was in the Beginning, with L. E. Gielgud. London, Cape, 1939.
The Corn King, music by Brian Easdale, adaptation of the novel by Mitchison (produced Glasgow, 1951). London, French, 1951.
Spindrift, with Denis Macintosh (produced Glasgow, 1951). London, French, 1951.

Verse

The Laburnum Branch. London, Cape, 1926.
The Alban Goes Out. Harrow, Middlesex, Raven Press, 1939.

The Cleansing of the Knife and Other Poems. Edinburgh, Canongate, 1978.

Other (for children)

The Hostages and Other Stories for Boys and Girls. London, Cape, 1930; New York, Harcourt Brace, 1931.
Boys and Girls and Gods. London, Watts, 1931.
The Big House. London, Faber, 1950.
Graeme and the Dragon. London, Faber, 1954.
The Swan's Road. London, Naldrett Press, 1954.
The Land the Ravens Found. London, Collins, 1955.
Little Boxes. London, Faber, 1956.
The Far Harbour. London, Collins, 1957.
Judy and Lakshmi. London, Collins, 1959.
The Rib of the Green Umbrella. London, Collins, 1960.
The Young Alexander the Great. London, Parrish, 1960; New York, Roy, 1961.
Karensgaard: The Story of a Danish Farm. London, Collins, 1961.
The Young Alfred the Great. London, Parrish, 1962; New York, Roy, 1963.
The Fairy Who Couldn't Tell a Lie. London, Collins, 1963.
Alexander the Great. London, Longman, 1964.
Henny and Crispies. Wellington, New Zealand, Department of Education, 1964.
Ketse and the Chief. London, Nelson, 1965; New York, Nelson, 1967.
A Mochudi Family. Wellington, New Zealand, Department of Education, 1965.
Friends and Enemies. London, Collins, 1966; New York, Day, 1968.
The Big Surprise. London, Kaye and Ward, 1967.
Highland Holiday. Wellington, New Zealand, Department of Education, 1967.
African Heroes. London, Bodley Head, 1968; New York, Farrar Straus, 1969.
Don't Look Back. London, Kaye and Ward, 1969.
The Family at Ditlabeng. London, Collins, 1969; New York, Farrar Straus, 1970.
Sun and Moon. London, Bodley Head, 1970; Nashville, Nelson, 1973.
Sunrise Tomorrow. London, Collins, and New York, Farrar Straus, 1973.
The Danish Teapot. London, Kaye and Ward, 1973.
Snake! London, Collins, 1976.
The Little Sister, with works by Ian Kirby and Keetla Masogo. Cape Town, Oxford University Press, 1976.
The Wild Dogs, with works by Megan Biesele. Cape Town, Oxford University Press, 1977.
The Brave Nurse and Other Stories. Cape Town, Oxford University Press, 1977.
The Two Magicians, with Dick Mitchison. London, Dobson, 1978.
The Vegetable War. London, Hamish Hamilton, 1980.

Other

Anna Comnena. London, Howe, 1928.
Comments on Birth Control. London, Faber, 1930.
The Home and a Changing Civilisation. London, Lane, 1934.
Vienna Diary. London, Gollancz, and New York, Smith and Haas, 1934.
Socrates, with Richard Crossman. London, Hogarth Press, 1937; Harrisburg, Pennsylvania, Stackpole, 1938.

The Moral Basis of Politics. London, Constable, 1938; Port Washington, New York, Kennikat Press, 1971.
The Kingdom of Heaven. London, Heinemann, 1939.
Men and Herring: A Documentary, with Denis Macintosh. Edinburgh, Serif, 1949.
Other People's Worlds (travel). London, Secker and Warburg, 1958.
A Fishing Village on the Clyde, with G. W. L. Paterson. London, Oxford University Press, 1960.
Presenting Other People's Children. London, Hamlyn, 1961.
Return to the Fairy Hill (autobiography and sociology). London, Heinemann, and New York, Day, 1966.
The Africans: A History. London, Blond, 1970.
Small Talk: Memories of an Edwardian Childhood. London, Bodley Head, 1973.
A Life for Africa: The Story of Bram Fischer. London, Merlin Press, and Boston, Carrier Pigeon, 1973.
Oil for the Highlands? London, Fabian Society, 1974.
All Change Here: Girlhood and Marriage (autobiography). London, Bodley Head, 1975.
Sittlichkeit (lecture). London, Birkbeck College, 1975.
You May Well Ask: A Memoir 1920–1940. London, Gollancz, 1979.
Mucking Around: Five Continents over Fifty Years. London, Gollancz, 1981.
Margaret Cole 1893–1980. London, Fabian Society, 1982.
Among You, Taking Notes: The Wartime Diary of Naomi Mitchison 1939–1945, edited by Dorothy Sheridan. London, Gollancz, 1985.
Naomi Mitchison (autobiographical sketch). Edinburgh, Saltire Society, 1986.

Editor, *An Outline for Boys and Girls and Their Parents.* London, Gollancz, 1932.
Editor, with Robert Britton and George Kilgour, *Re-Educating Scotland.* Glasgow, Scoop, 1944.
Editor, *What the Human Race Is Up To.* London, Gollancz, 1962.

*

Manuscript Collections: National Library of Scotland, Edinburgh; University of Texas, Austin.

*   *   *

"Friendships were such lovely, brittle things, they broke unless one was very, very careful." This sentence from *Cloud Cuckoo Land* holds the key to much of Naomi Mitchison's historical fiction. The complex fragility of human relationships is continually emphasized in her writing, and underlies all the other major themes—flight and exile, culture clash, the search for fulfilment and its tragic failure—inherent in her work. Beneath them all, one feels the unifying thread of shared lives, of communal and individual love and loss. The significance of such relationships, their frailty and abuse, pervades the early stories in *Black Sparta,* where on several occasions an unrequited love is used by the beloved for personal advantage, and the lover promptly abandoned. Already, in these stories, one senses the attraction of ancient Greece for Mitchison, and her ability to enter a vanished age at will.

Mitchison's fame was established with the historical novels and stories she produced during the 1920's, and which remain among the finest of her creations. In them she depicts the interaction of opposing cultures, observing from the viewpoint of the vanquished underdog the disintegration and painful adjustment that follow in the wake of conquest. Her narrators are invariably victims, decent but unheroic individuals obliged to compromise in order to fit the changed circumstances of their lives. Robbed of stability and self-respect, their only recourse is to adapt, or to flee to exile. Through their eyes, Mitchison chronicles the fall of civilisations, the wrecking of families, the undermining of communal tribal faiths by newer, secular systems which lead to questioning and discontent. Her exploration of the inner lives of her characters shows her art at its subtlest, capturing the human sensibilities of another time. To each of these historical works, Mitchison brings a contemporary voice, employing a modern, colloquial style with current patterns of speech and thought. By these apparently anachronistic means, she succeeds totally in evoking the remote past in all its multilayered complexity and emotional depth.

Mitchison's first novel, *The Conquered*, is set in Gaul at the time of Caesar's campaigns, where Meromic, son of a local chieftain, witnesses the tribe's defeat and the death of his family. Taken prisoner by the Romans, he subsequently fights with them against the Gallic army of Vercingetorix. Meromic's conflicting loyalties—to his former people, and to his Roman master—are adroitly displayed by Mitchison, who presents each scene clearly and without undue comment, leaving readers to judge for themselves. Her understated, contemporary style conveys to perfection the world of the volatile, feuding Celts, where fact and magic mingle indissolubly together. Such a world cannot endure the impact of the practical, ordered universe of the Romans, whose methodical skill in battle proves too much for the foolhardy heroism of the Gauls. Vercingetorix dies, and the hopelessly torn Meromic finds his own solution by retreating into tribalism and mystery, metamorphosing into the wolf totem of the Veneti. Mitchison traces the decline, the reduction of a proud people to vassal status, with a vision at once sympathetic and pared of sentiment. Her ability to get inside the mind of Meromic, seeing the tragedy through his eyes, renders that vision all the more moving. *The Conquered* is a powerful story, whose exploration of the psychology of its main characters is a foretaste of things to come. Its insights are surpassed in *Cloud Cuckoo Land*, where the author examines an ancient Greece fallen from its previous greatness.

Cloud Cuckoo Land follows the fortunes of the central character, Alxenor, who with his sweetheart Moiro flees his native island after a Spartan coup. Forced into a life of exile, the ill-fated lovers spend time in the three dominant states of the period, with tragic consequences. Moiro is seduced into a love affair with a Spartan warrior, and dies in childbirth. Alxenor returns to help liberate his own island, but finds the place still beset with factions and intrigue. He ends the book an exile, serving as a mercenary in the wards of the Persian king. Mitchison charts the progress of her hounded, amiable "hero" through an intricate weave of political manoeuvre, violence, and domestic turmoil. The familiar style accommodates some beautiful descriptive passages, but its main strength is its presentation of the varying states of mind of Mitchison's creations. The seemingly casual brutality, heartlessness even, of some scenes—Moiro's taking of a lover, her exposure of an unwanted child, her eventual death—is counterbalanced by extreme sensitivity in the treatment of relationships, and of the complex mass of contradictions that constitute a human personality. It is this network of individual lives and feelings that provides the core of the book, and against which the fall of nations strikes a more cosmic resonance. *Cloud Cuckoo Land* marks an advance on *The Conquered*, its insights more skilfully developed, its psychology more subtle. It brings, too, a fuller evocation of the Greece of *Black Sparta*, a landscape of the mind to which Mitchison was to return in an even more memorable work of fiction.

The Corn King and the Spring Queen is Mitchison's masterpiece, the crown of her achievement as a historical novelist. Set in Marob, a farming kingdom ruled by the fertility ritual of Corn King and Spring Queen, characters and action move to Sparta and Ptolemaic Egypt before a return to Marob brings final resolution. Once again the novel is centred on individual relationships, from which the author works outward to examine other, universal themes. Action focuses on Tarrik and Erif Der—the King and Queen of the title—and the effect of outside pressures on their lives. Their personalities, and the world of tribal magic and religion which they represent, are exposed to the challenge of new ideas from Greece, where the gods no longer rule, and Kleomenes of Sparta posits a theory of "the good life" based on secular idealism and democracy. Questioning of their beliefs brings inward conflict in both Tarrik and Erif that amounts to psychological disturbance, and which for a time expresses itself in violence and cruelty. Flight to, and eventual escape from, the hierarchical but directionless kingdom of Egypt, where the despot Ptolemy seeks vainly to create his own pantheon of gods, and where the defeated Kleomenes meets his death, brings about their return to Marob. Here the old beliefs are shown to endure in a second generation, albeit infused with the refined version of sacrifice and renewal exemplified by Kleomenes himself. Mitchison enters the hearts and minds of her characters, presenting sensitively and with conviction states of possession and contemplation, the shifting perceptions of the world and each other. Through the precarious equilibrium of human relationships, she investigates the many varieties of love—from platonic friendship to sexual hunger—in a penetrating, clear-sighted manner free from moralistic comment. Her novel explores religion, psychology and art to their roots, indicating through ritual and conversation the potency of the idea whose time has come. In Kleomenes, a well-meaning king who dies for his people, she appears to hint at later Christian beliefs. The story of individuals in a particular place and time, *The Corn King and the Spring Queen* examines a multiplicity of themes, and rewards successive readings with deeper layers of meaning. It is without doubt one of the most significant historical novels.

Later works which might be classed as historical tend to reveal an overt religious belief, and while often excellent, lack the complexity and depth of the earlier novels. *Blood of the Martyrs*, which describes the persecution of Christians in Nero's Rome, and *Behold Your King*, an account of the Crucifixion, are both skilfully constructed, with events viewed by several different characters to give varying perspectives on the action. Once more Mitchison uses a no-nonsense modern style, and effectively presents the thoughts and feelings of her creations, but the specific religious theme robs these books of the multi-faceted power of *The Corn King and the Spring Queen*, or even *Cloud Cuckoo Land*.

A powerful, seminal writer and an innovative stylist, Mitchison remains a major influence on the modern historical novel. Her use of contemporary speech patterns and expressions in historic contexts suggests similarities with Alfred Duggan, while her exploration of inner thoughts and feelings and the visual force of her scenes recall Henry Treece. In her ability to convey deep psychological and religious perceptions, and to show them at work in the minds of her characters, Mitchison has few rivals. On the basis of her early writings, she is unquestionably one of the great historical novelists.

—Geoffrey Sadler

MONTGOMERY, L(ucy) M(aud). Canadian. Born in Clifton (now New London), Prince Edward Island, 30 November 1874. Educated at schools in Cavendish, Prince Edward Island, and Prince Albert, Saskatchewan; Prince of Wales College, Charlottetown, Prince Edward Island, teacher's certificate 1894, teacher's license 1895; Dalhousie College, Halifax, Nova Scotia, 1895–96. Married Ewan Macdonald in 1911; two sons. Schoolteacher, Bideford, 1894–95, 1896–97, and Lower Bedeque, 1897–98, both in Prince Edward Island; assistant postmistress, Cavendish, 1898–1911; staff member, Halifax *Echo*, 1901–02. Fellow, Royal Society of Arts, 1923. O.B.E. (Officer, Order of the British Empire), 1935. *Died 24 April 1942.*

ROMANCE AND HISTORICAL PUBLICATIONS

Novels (series: Anne; Emily; Pat)

Anne of Green Gables. Boston, Page, and London, Pitman, 1908.
Anne of Avonlea. Boston, Page, and London, Pitman, 1909.
Kilmeny of the Orchard. Boston, Page, and London, Pitman, 1910.
The Story Girl. Boston, Page, and London, Pitman, 1911.
The Golden Road. Boston, Page, 1913; London, Cassell, 1914.
Anne of the Island. Boston, Page, and London, Pitman, 1915.
Anne's House of Dreams. New York, Stokes, and London, Constable, 1917.
Rainbow Valley (Anne). Toronto, McClelland and Stewart, and New York, Stokes, 1919; London, Constable, 1920.
Rilla of Ingleside (Anne). Toronto, McClelland and Stewart, New York, Stokes, and London, Hodder and Stoughton, 1921.
Emily of New Moon. New York, Stokes, and London, Hodder and Stoughton, 1923.
Emily Climbs. New York, Stokes, and London, Hodder and Stoughton, 1925.
The Blue Castle. Toronto, McClelland and Stewart, New York, Stokes, and London, Hodder and Stoughton, 1926.
Emily's Quest. New York, Stokes, and London, Hodder and Stoughton, 1927.
Magic for Marigold. Toronto, McClelland and Stewart, New York, Stokes, and London, Hodder and Stoughton, 1929.
A Tangled Web. New York, Stokes, 1931; as *Aunt Becky Began It*, London, Hodder and Stoughton, 1931.
Pat of Silver Bush. New York, Stokes, and London, Hodder and Stoughton, 1933.
Mistress Pat: A Novel of Silver Bush. New York, Stokes, and London, Harrap, 1935.
Anne of Windy Poplars. New York, Stokes, 1936; as *Anne of Windy Willows*, London, Harrap, 1936.
Jane of Lantern Hill. Toronto, McClelland and Stewart, New York, Stokes, and London, Harrap, 1937.
Anne of Ingleside. New York, Stokes, and London, Harrap, 1939.

Short Stories

Chronicles of Avonlea. Boston, Page, and London, Sampson Low, 1912.
Further Chronicles of Avonlea. Boston, Page, 1920; London, Harrap, 1953.
The Road to Yesterday. Toronto, McGraw Hill Ryerson, 1974; London, Angus and Robertson, 1975.
The Doctor's Sweetheart and Other Stories, edited by Catherine McLay. Toronto, McGraw Hill Ryerson, and London, Harrap, 1979.

Akin to Anne: Tales of Other Orphans, edited by Rea Wilmshurst. Toronto, McClelland and Stewart, 1988.

OTHER PUBLICATIONS

Verse

The Watchman and Other Poems. Toronto, McClelland and Stewart, 1916; New York, Stokes, 1917; London, Constable, 1920.
The Poetry of Lucy Maud Montgomery, edited by Kevin McCabe and John Ferns. Markham, Ontario, Fitzhenry and Whiteside, 1987.

Other

Courageous Women, with Marian Keith and Mabel Burns McKinley. Toronto, McClelland and Stewart, 1934.
The Green Gables Letters to Ephraim Weber 1905–1909, edited by Wilfrid Eggleston. Toronto, Ryerson Press, 1960.
The Alpine Path: The Story of My Career. Don Mills, Ontario, Fitzhenry and Whiteside, 1974.
My Dear Mr. M.: Letters to G. B. MacMillan, edited by Francis W. P. Bolger and Elizabeth R. Epperly. Toronto, McGraw Hill Ryerson, 1980.
Spirit of Place: L. M. Montgomery and Prince Edward Island, edited by Francis W. P. Bolger. Toronto, Oxford University Press, 1982.
The Selected Journals 1: 1889–1910 [*2: 1910–1921*], edited by Mary Rubio and Elizabeth Waterston. Toronto, Oxford University Press, 2 vols., 1985–87.

*

Critical Studies: *The Years Before "Anne"* by Francis W. P. Bolger, Charlottetown, Prince Edward Island Heritage Foundation, 1975; *The Wheel of Things: A Biography of L. M. Montgomery* by Mollie Gillen, Don Mills, Ontario, Fitzhenry and Whiteside, 1975, London, Harrap, 1976; *L. M. Montgomery: An Assessment* edited by John Robert Sorfleet, Guelph, Ontario, Canadian Children's Press, 1976; *L. M. Montgomery: A Preliminary Biography* by Ruth Weber Russell, Waterloo, Ontario, University of Waterloo Library, 1986.

*   *   *

L. M. Montgomery is of course rightly celebrated for novels like *Anne of Green Gables* and *Emily of New Moon* which have become classics of children's literature on both sides of the Atlantic. These are also, however, avidly read by grownups as well as children, and indeed their sequels, in which the young and rapturous heroines mature, have a distinctly adult appeal. The author's short stories (collected in *Chronicles of Avonlea, Further Chronicles of Avonlea, The Road to Yesterday*, and *The Doctor's Sweetheart*), though sometimes tenuously linked to the Green Gables characters, are set in a firmly adult world and contain little with which child readers would identify.

But to whatever age group her fiction is addressed, it always includes strong elements of romance. This is at one extreme cosily domestic and at the other ecstatically spiritual. Physical intensity plays little part in the books. It is significant that whenever a young man snatches his first kiss, the typical Montgomery heroine is likely to slap his face in fury. Despite the vividness of the girls' emotional response to life, they actually inhabit a well ordered housewifely world of newpin neatness where, one feels (to use one of Montgomery's own expressions) it must be a heinous sin to allow fluff-rolls to build up on one's linoleum. And so bodily sex, being a disorderly experience, is not allowed to disrupt the social tidiness of the stories. There is plenty of passion; it is sometimes folksy, sometimes fey—but never physical.

Anne, Emily, and other leading ladies have high flown flights of fantasy which spring from their passion for natural beauty. Emily, for example, has an extremely mobile soul which, we are told, slips easily away from mundane matters into "eternity" so that she can say with conviction: "I washed my soul free from dust in the aerial bath of a spring twilight." Similarly Susette in *The Road to Yesterday* refreshes her inner being by "bathing her soul in dawn."

Montgomery's pattern of young love is predictable. After the heroine's initial and dramatic renunciation of romance ("I will not love—to love is to be a slave"), it creeps up from behind like a game of Grandma's Footsteps, catches her unawares, and explodes in a burst of ecstasy that is eventually consummated in happily married fecundity.

Fortunately, however, Anne, for example, never allows the claims of her many offspring and a very busy doctor-husband completely to eclipse her joy in her Lake of Shining Waters or the White Way of Delight. And Emily—who is on the threshold of marriage at the end of the trilogy that features her—will, one feels certain, not let domesticity radically dim her mystical "flashes," or her enjoyment of the sun-steeped ferns in her Land of Uprightness.

It must be said that Montgomery handles these tricky transitions from nature-waif to great-earth-mother far more skilfully than many authors who allow their juvenile heroines to mature in the course of a series. She is not only adept at tackling the theme of young love, but of middle-aged romance. (Significantly, perhaps, she did not marry until she was 36, as she devoted many years of her life to looking after an elderly relative, and the rival claims of love and duty are often featured in her books.) Later flowering love is a recurring theme in her story collections (particularly *The Road to Yesterday* and *The Doctor's Sweetheart*). These are full of misunderstandings, jiltings, estrangements, and nostalgia for what might have been; but also there are reconciliations and endeavours to resurrect romance in relationships that are—at least ostensibly—no longer touched by passion. There are also touches of ironic realism when, for example, Montgomery writes of fine but fading ladies who hold out against the attentions of male admirers for one or even two decades, until they find their own "air of distinction getting a little shopworn."

The complex processes of courtship and consummation in Montgomery's fiction are, as she says of the Canadian spring, "long and fickle and reluctant" but full of "unnameable" and haunting—"charm."

—Mary Cadogan

MOORE, Doris (Elizabeth) Langley. British. Born in Liverpool, Lancashire, in 1903. Educated at convent schools in South Africa, and privately. Married Robin Sugden Moore in 1926 (divorced 1942); one daughter. Author and specialist in costume: founder and adviser, Museum of Costume, Bath, 1955–74; designer of costumes for films. Recipient: British Academy Crawshay prize, for non-fiction, 1975. Fellow, Royal Society of Literature, 1973. O.B.E. (Officer, Order of the British Empire), 1971. *Died 24 February 1989.*

ROMANCE AND HISTORICAL PUBLICATIONS

Novels

A Winter's Passion. London, Heinemann, 1932.
The Unknown Eros. London, Secker, 1935.
They Knew Her When: A Game of Snakes and Ladders. London, Rich and Cowan, 1938; as *A Game of Snakes and Ladders*, London, Cassell, 1955.
Not at Home. London, Cassell, 1948.
All Done by Kindness. London, Cassell, 1951; Philadelphia, Lippincott, 1952.
My Caravaggio Style. London, Cassell, and Philadelphia, Lippincott, 1959.

OTHER PUBLICATIONS

Verse (for children)

Doris Langley Moore's Book of Scraps. London, Deutsch, 1984.

Other

The Technique of the Love Affair (as A Gentlewoman). London, Howe, and New York, Simon and Schuster, 1928; revised edition, as Doris Langley Moore, London, Rich and Cowan, 1936; New York, Knickerbocker, 1946.
Pandora's Letter Box, Being a Discourse on Fashionable Life. London, Howe, 1929.
The Bride's Book; or, Young Housewife's Compendium (with June Moore, as Two Ladies of England). London, Howe, 1932; revised edition, as *Our Loving Duty*, as Doris Langley Moore and June Moore, London, Rich and Cowan, 1936.
The Pleasure of Your Company: A Text-Book of Hospitality, with June Moore. London, Howe, 1933; revised edition, London, Rich and Cowan, 1936.
E. Nesbit: A Biography. London, Benn, 1933; revised edition, Philadelphia, Chilton, 1966; Benn, 1967.
The Vulgar Heart: An Enquiry into the Sentimental Tendencies of Public Opinion. London, Cassell, 1945.
Gallery of Fashion 1790–1822: From Plates by Heideloff and Ackermann. London, Batsford, 1949.
The Woman in Fashion. London, Batsford, 1949.
Pleasure: A Discursive Guide Book. London, Cassell, 1953.
The Child in Fashion. London, Batsford, 1953.
The Great Byron Adventure. Philadelphia, Lippincott, 1959.
The Late Lord Byron: Posthumous Dramas. London, Murray, and Philadelphia, Lippincott, 1961.
Marie and the Duke of H—: The Daydream Love Affair of Marie Bashkirtseff. London, Cassell, and Philadelphia, Lippincott, 1966.
Fashion Through Fashion Plates 1771–1970. London, Ward Lock, 1971; New York, Potter, 1972.
Lord Byron: Accounts Rendered. London, Murray, and New York, Harper, 1974.
Ada, Countess of Lovelace: Byron's Legitimate Daughter. London, Murray, 1977.

Editor, *Good Fare: A Code of Cookery*, by Édouard de Pomiane, translated by Blanche Bowes. London, Howe, 1932.

Translator, *Anacreon: 29 Odes*. London, Howe, 1926.
Translator, *Carlotta Grisi*, by Serge Lifar. London, Lehmann, 1947.

* * *

Doris Langley Moore's novels celebrate the pleasures of connoisseurship and the satisfactions of art, the collector's world, "the little world where beauty was permanent and craftsmanship worth while" (*They Knew Her When*). Her novels, while not at all conventional romances, are comedies which frequently end in marriage, and which seriously investigate the nature of love, often from a contemporary woman's point of view. They complement her biographical and critical works and are worthy and stylish artifacts from the author of *Pleasure: A Discursive Guide Book*.

The Unknown Eros sets out most schematically Moore's concerns with the nature of love—maternal, erotic, intellectual, religious, aesthetic—and gives primacy to the aesthetic. Her heroine, because she is an honest artist, is granted a vision of Eros when the disparate faces of love merge into one figure, that of a schoolboy singing at a speech day. The aesthetic impulse also redeems the betrayals of the narrator of *A Winter's Passion*, for Caroline's lust for her sister's lover is sparked by her unsatisfied artistic ambitions. These novels are more overtly serious than the dazzlingly plotted comedies that follow.

In these, every turn of the plot, rooted in tics of character, is both surprising and inevitable. *All Done by Kindness* is a merry chase after a recently discovered cache of Renaissance masterpieces. The heroine's disinterested love, her honest connoisseurship, is the force which leads to the defeat of the band of aesthetic pretenders, chief among them a dishonest art critic, and to her own marriage.

The narrator of *My Caravaggio Style* is brought to betray his aesthetic principles and his love for Byron by jealousy of his fiancée's attraction to the poet dead more than a hundred years. Quentin's preparations for his forgery of the lost Byron memoirs have the obsessive, hypnotic quality of preparations for a murder.

As *My Caravaggio Style* reprises the pattern and concerns of *All Done by Kindness*, so *Not at Home* repeats the romance pattern of *They Knew Her When*—the story of an actress stranded in Egypt after World War I who is reduced to the position of box office clerk in a cinema in Alexandria by the disastrous charity of a hypocritical friend. The comic resolution, Lucy's marriage to a duke, is deepened by the precise detailing of her slip from her class and the frightening despair engendered by poverty and exile. A similar confrontation between honesty and hypocrisy is repeated in *Not at Home*. This postwar novel recounts a domestic invasion in which the unlikely heroine, a middle-aged, botanical artist, Miss MacFarren, is rescued from a tendency toward spiritual smugness by her suffering at the hands of a slovenly and self-deluding tenant. Here is the most satisfying of Moore's investigations of beauty, friendship, and love, and the heroine's repossession of her solitary domain has overtones of a civilization restored.

—Karen Robertson

MORESBY, Louis. See **BECK, L. Adams.**

MORGAN, Alice. Address: c/o Dell, 666 Fifth Avenue, New York, New York 10103, U.S.A.

ROMANCE AND HISTORICAL PUBLICATIONS

Novels

Masquerade of Love. New York, Dell, 1982.
The Sands of Malibu. New York, Dell, 1982.
Impetuous Surrogate. New York, Dell, 1982.
Deception for Desire. Toronto, Harlequin, 1983(?)
Branded Heart. Toronto, Harlequin, 1983.
Man in Control. New York, Dell, 1984.
Stolen Idyll. New York, Dell, 1985.
Bedroom Magic. New York, Dell, 1987.

* * *

Alice Morgan's romances have featured some interesting plots, but they often have been marred by stylistic problems. Unlike many other authors of contemporary romances, Morgan does not insist on a woman's independence. Her heroines may be strong and determined, but often that determination is focused on finding a man. Marriage may not be the desired outcome, but a sexual relationship is sought, at least at first.

In some of her first books, published in the early 1980's, Morgan tackled very contemporary themes. In *Masquerade of Love*, Brandy sets out to find and seduce any man with the right genes to father her child. As added complications it is revealed that Brandy, though widowed, is still a virgin since her husband was gay and that she also had recently lost their adopted daughter. In *Impetuous Surrogate*, De-Ann plans to act as a surrogate mother for bachelor Derek, who wants a child but not marriage. Of course, such situations rapidly move into the more normal courtship storyline, but they are unusual in category romances.

In many of Morgan's novels a promising love relationship is threatened by deception on the part of one or more partners; this theme is reflected in many of the book titles. In many ways, her first novel, *Masquerade of Love*, sets the tone for subsequent stories. Brandy disguises herself in order to seduce Brad, while she tries to hide the truth about her dead husband and child from her beloved godfather. Trying to maintain these multiple masquerades is the source of her problems. In the next novel, *The Sands of Malibu*, policewoman Carlyn Thomas almost loses her chance at love and her life when she works undercover as a call girl. She is so good at her job that Nick Sandine rejects her rather violently. Nick and Carlyn later make a brief reappearance in *Impetuous Surrogate* as Derek's friends. Derek spends much of the book incensed at what he views as De-Ann's deceit in manipulating him into marriage. In *Deception for Desire*, Honey Bowman begins a masquerade of an engagement to avoid other entanglements but unknowingly becomes embroiled in her "escort's" own plan. Jaclyn Howard (*Stolen Idyll*) conspires to replace a professional "escort" hired to console temporarily blinded Josh Kingman, whom she has long loved from afar. Here again Brandy and Brad Lucas of *Masquerade of Love* enter as friends. Another friend, Logan West, is the deceiving lover of *Bedroom Magic*. It is to Morgan's credit that she manages to make these deceiving, manipulative characters attractive.

Perhaps a greater problem, at least in the earlier books, is the often stiff and stilted dialogue given to the hero and heroine. Comforting the wounded Carlyn, Nick sounds overly pompous when he says, "The picture of your body burgeoning with my child blows my mind, but I have a deep need within me, darling. An insatiable need for you alone." This is typical of many unrealistic passages that tend to interrupt the flow of the plot.

Happily, however, Morgan in her more recent books has been correcting this tendency to overwrite. Dialogue and characters have become much more realistic and believable. Although Morgan cannot be viewed as a major author of romance fiction, she has developed her talent in a reasonable fashion.

—Barbara E. Kemp

* * *

MORRISON, Roberta. See **WEBB, Jean Francis.**

* * *

MOTLEY, Annette. Address: c/o Macdonald Ltd., 66–73 Shoe Lane, London EC4P 4AP, England.

ROMANCE AND HISTORICAL PUBLICATIONS

Novels

My Lady's Crusade. London, Futura, 1977.
The Sins of the Lion. London, Hutchinson, and New York, Stein and Day, 1979.
The Quickenberry Tree. London, Macdonald, 1983; New York, St. Martin's Press, 1984.
Green Dragon, White Tiger. London, Macdonald, and New York, Macmillan, 1986.
Men on White Horses. London, Macdonald, 1988.

* * *

It is always a pleasure to find an author who can write intelligent historical fiction as well as romantic adventure. Annette Motley is such a writer. Here is an author who has thoroughly researched the widely diverse periods covered in her five published novels, *The Sins of the Lion*, *My Lady's Crusade*, *The Quickenberry Tree*, *Green Dragon, White Tiger*, and *Men on White Horses*. Motley very cleverly weaves history into natural sounding dialogue allowing the flow of words and ideas to explain events to the reader.

As in other tales of romance fiction, war, with all its passions and cruelties, serves as a background for handsome heroes and enticingly beautiful heroines. But in Motley's novels this background takes on an aspect of gritty reality. With clear insight she describes the horrors of war as it is experienced by the participants. For Richard the Lionheart (*My Lady's Crusade*) war becomes a way of life, a way to display his ruthless and bloodthirsty courage. For others, such as his more humanitarian lieutenant, Tristan de Jarnac, engagement in battle is necessary only when the cause is just. Killing then becomes an essential but unpleasant duty. In *The Sins of the Lion* the Renaissance Prince Leone de Montevalenti desperately wishes to keep a hard won peace for his city, but when war with his traitorous brother-in-law becomes inevitable, he reluctantly reverts to his warrior role. Feeling like nothing less than a killing machine, completely devoid of fear for himself or compassion for his adversaries he leads his army to victory. In contrast Tom Herron (*The Quickenberry Tree*) when facing his most loathsome enemy, holds to the highest standards of a Royalist cavalier and refuses to take unfair advantage.

In each novel it is the heroine's story that weaves all other events together. The lovely Lady Eden of Hawkhurst (*My Lady's Crusade*) sets out to find her young husband Stephen who had left England years before to fight the Saracens in the Holy Land. Seen through her eyes the sights and sounds of the exotic and often barbarous Outremer pulsate with life. She suffers much

privation in her lonely quest before aid and love come in the form of the chivalrous Knight Tristan. *The Sins of the Lion* is the story of Tulla an exotically beautiful half-Greek, half-Turkish slave bought for the pleasure of Il Leone. As the aristocratic daughter of a Pasha, she possesses a pride which cannot allow her to become the willing mistress to the golden Prince, but eventually even this strong-minded lady falls under the spell of this complex man. In *The Quickenberry Tree* Oliver Cromwell's army plunges England into years of civil strife, all of which is viewed through the eyes of Lucy Herron and members of her Royalist family. Lucy is a young teenager when the story begins and a mature woman at its close 16 years later. During those years, along with agony and fear engendered by civil war, she knew the love of two men, Irish charmer Cathal O'Connor and worldly wise Will Staunton. 7th-century China forms the setting of *Green Dragon, White Tiger*, based on the life of Empress Wu, the only woman to rule this vast country from the exalted Dragon throne. Known throughout most of her life as Black Jade, this highly intelligent, strong-minded lady began her climb to power as the favorite concubine of Emperor Shin-min. She continued her ascent by marrying his weak-willed son, and ruthlessly eliminating her many powerful enemies until she acquired absolute control. *Men on White Horses* tells the story of Sophie, daughter of the ambitious Princess Joanna of Anhalt-Zerbst. Sophie's dream is to become Empress of Russia, a land she sees as full of romance and adventure. With the help of her mother Sophie initially wins the favor of Empress Elisabeth who arranges a marriage with her heir. The novel traces Sophie's journey through life and the Russian court set against a background of religious and political turbulence.

The characters in Motley's novels have flesh and blood reality. For example Eden's anguish is graphically described when she learns that her husband has been seduced into a homosexual relationship with his Saracen captor. The reader sympathizes with both Lucy and Will over the pain each suffers because of Lucy's brief adulterous liaison with Cathal.

Detailed historical background intertwined with a tale of romance characterizes Motley's fiction.

—Patricia Altner

* * *

MULLINS, Edwin (Brandt). British. Born in London, 14 September 1933. Educated at Midhurst Grammar School; Oxford University, B.A. (honours) in English 1957, M.A. 1958. Served in the British Army, 1952–54. Married 1) Gillian Brydone in 1960 (died 1982), two daughters and one son; 2) Anne Kelleher in 1984. Editorial assistant, Medici Society, 1957–58; London editor, *Two Cities*, London, 1958–60; art correspondent, *Illustrated London News*, 1958–62; sale-room correspondent, *Financial Times*, London, 1962–67; art critic, *Sunday Telegraph*, London, 1962–69; art correspondent and adviser, *Daily Telegraph Magazine*, London, 1964–86. Since 1967 broadcaster and presenter of television documentaries. Agent: Curtis Brown, 162–168 Regent Street, London W1R 5TB. Address: 7 Lower Common South, London SW15 1BP, England.

ROMANCE AND HISTORICAL PUBLICATIONS

Novels

The Golden Bird. London, Collins, 1987.
The Lands of the Sea. London, Collins, 1988; as *The Master Painter*, New York, Doubleday, 1989.

OTHER PUBLICATIONS

Novels

Angels on the Point of a Pin. London, Secker and Warburg, 1979.
Sirens. London, Secker and Warburg, 1983.

Other

F. N. Souza: An Introduction. London, Blond, 1962.
Alfred Wallis: Cornish Primitive Painter. London, Macdonald, 1967.
Josef Herman. London, Evelyn Adams and McKay, 1967.
Braque. London, Thames and Hudson, 1968; as *The Art of Georges Braque*, New York, Abrams, 1968.
The Art of Elisabeth Frink. London, Lund Humphries, 1972.
The Pilgrimage to Santiago. London, Secker and Warburg, and New York, Taplinger, 1974.
A Love Affair with Nature. Oxford, Phaidon Press, 1985.
The Painted Witch: Female Body, Male Art. London, Secker and Warburg, and New York, Carroll and Graf, 1985.

Editor, *Great Paintings*. London, BBC Publications, and New York, St. Martin's Press, 1981.
Editor, *The Arts of Britain*. Oxford, Phaidon Press, 1983.

*

Edwin Mullins comments:
My historical novels have been attempts to bring to life through fiction certain periods of history which have particularly fascinated me as an art historian and as a traveller. Historical fiction as a genre does not interest me at all.

*   *   *

Edwin Mullins has, so far, written only two historical novels, *The Golden Bird* and *The Lands of the Sea*. They are intended as mirrors of one another, the first set at the dawn of the Age of Chivalry, the second set in its dusk. In both life was "so violent and motley that it bore the mixed smell of blood and of roses," but in the first book there are few roses.

In A.D. 996 a Norman Master Mason, Rollo, an orphan brought up in a monastery, is invited by Fulk, the Count of Anjou, to build him a church. On the way from Normandy Rollo is revolted by the devastated lands, the work of Fulk's enemy Odo, smoking houses, bodies hacked to pieces, a small child clutching a wooden toy, lying in a pool of its own blood. At the crowded Castle of Angers ruled by the brilliant and rather monstrous Black Fulk, Rollo is surprised by the sight of a naked woman in a doorway, who is later impaled on hooks from the walls, by the Count's enemies and left for the kites to peck. He is ordered to build not a church but a castle.

Rollo makes a good friend, falls in love with a lovely girl, avoids the ladies of the castle who lurk like amorous spiders, and gets on with his building amid all the lust and intrigue. Fulk survives a fierce battle but succumbs to the lies spread around the castle against his good and beautiful wife. When she produces a deformed son he has her burnt as a witch. In remorse he goes on a pilgrimage to Jerusalem, returns to defeat his enemies and marry his cousin. The Golden Bird of the title is the golden oriole, Fulk's emblem, but it makes only brief appearances in the well described countryside. Mullins has created a powerful story full of surprises and horrors.

The Lands of the Sea has a less crude setting. The man of violence is Philip, Duke of Burgundy, who undertakes everything with courage, conviction, and splendour. He aims to rule from the Alps to the North Sea and found a new order of chivalry—the Golden Fleece. In contrast his peaceful court painter, Jan van Eyck of Bruges quietly reads the minds of everyone he paints. He is ordered to do the portraits of the Duke, of Joan of Arc, and of the beautiful wild Jacqueline, the Black Raven of the Lands of the Sea whom both Jan and Philip love. The intrigues and love affairs of the court and of the people of Bruges where a blaze of "torches lit up the tall wooden gables of the houses and smeared the canals with gold" are much discussed. "I've never known such people as the Flemish for worshipping virginity while seeking to steal it at every opportunity."

While Jan paints an altarpiece for a Ghent church using his friends as models for Adam, Eve, the Virgin Mary, and John the Baptist, Philip goes to war with France as the ally of England. Joan of Arc is captured, the Flemish people are taxed heavily. The burghers of Bruges turn against their Duke and are shot, their heads impaled on the walls of the city. Jacqueline loathes him and rides out to her death in the floods of the polderlands. The monstrous Duke is tarnished, but the gentle Margaret returns to Jan. The book ends with an eloquent tribute to humble people and small things. The whole story gives a splendid picture of the glories alongside the degrading horrors of the 15th century.

—Margaret Campbell

<hr/>

MUNRO, Neil. Also wrote as Hugh Fowlis. British. Born in Inveraray, Argyllshire, 3 June 1864. Married. Reporter, *Scottish News*, 1881–93, Greenock *Advertiser*, 1893, and Glasgow *News*; editor, Glasgow *Evening News*, 1918–27. LL.D.: University of Glasgow, 1908. *Died 22 December 1930.*

ROMANCE AND HISTORICAL PUBLICATIONS

Novels

John Splendid: The Tale of a Poor Gentleman and the Little Wars of Lorns. Edinburgh, Blackwood, and New York, Dodd Mead, 1898.
Gilian the Dreamer. London, Isbister, and New York, Dodd Mead, 1899.
Doom Castle: A Romance. Edinburgh, Blackwood, and New York, Doubleday, 1901.
The Shoes of Fortune. London, Isbister, and New York, Dodd Mead, 1901.
Children of the Tempest: A Tale of the Outer Isles. Edinburgh, Blackwood, 1903.
The New Road. Edinburgh, Blackwood, 1914.

Short Stories

The Lost Pibroch and Other Sheiling Stories. Edinburgh, Blackwood, 1896.
Jaunty Jock and Other Stories. Edinburgh, Blackwood, 1918.

OTHER PUBLICATIONS

Novels

The Daft Days. Edinburgh, Blackwood, 1907; as *Bud*, New York, Harper, 1907.
Fancy Farm. Edinburgh, Blackwood, 1910.
Ayrshire Idylls. London, A. and C. Black, 1912.
Jimmy Swan, The Joy Traveller. Edinburgh, Blackwood, 1917.

Short Stories as Hugh Fowlis

Erchie My Droll Friend. Edinburgh, Blackwood, 1904.
The Vital Spark and Her Queer Crew. Edinburgh, Blackwood, 1906.
In Highland Harbours with Para Handy, S.S. Vital Spark. Edinburgh, Blackwood, 1911.
Hurricane Jack of the Vital Spark. Edinburgh, Blackwood, 1923.
Para Handy and Other Tales. Edinburgh, Blackwood, 1931.

Verse

Bagpipe Ballads and Other Poems. Edinburgh, Blackwood, 1917.
The Poetry of Neil Munro. Edinburgh, Blackwood, 1931.

Other

The Clyde: River and Firth, with M. Y. and J. Y. Hunter. London, A. and C. Black, 1907.
The History of the Royal Bank of Scotland 1727–1927. Privately printed, 1928.
The Brave Days: A Chronicle from the North. Edinburgh, Porpoise Press, 1931.
The Looker-on. Edinburgh, Porpoise Press, 1933.

*   *   *

Neil Munro creates a complete picture of the Scottish Highlands in the past. It is not only the old words, the speech, half Gaelic and half English according to the character, and the tartans that convincingly create a sense of the past but also the way of thinking. The power of the Presbyterian Church in the 17th century is demonstrated in *John Splendid* as kirk and court of law act together excommunicating defaulters for crimes great and small, even forbidding women to keep their plaids over their heads during the sermon as it made it impossible to tell if they were asleep or not. Respect is shown for the minister who follows the Campbells in their fighting and takes water to the wounded.

The story keeps up a good pace in recounting the barbaric warfare between the Campbells and the MacDonalds supported by Montrose, with the fury of vengeance wreaked on young and old alike. The people must endure the looting and burning of their homes, as well as intervals of tense waiting, hiding in the hills. Through it all runs a code of hospitality to any wayfarer and a concern for children. Montrose on hearing a child's cry passes by with a wave of his bonnet without searching the building. Everyone wears easily recognizable tartan kilts; a blind woman claims that she can tell the clan by the feel of the cloth. John Splendid himself, a cousin of the Marquis of Argyll, a fierce fighter just returned from fighting with Gustavus in Germany, gets on well with others by claiming that they do everything better than he does. He says the highlanders keep themselves warm by quarrelling with each other.

"It's a gossiping community this, long lugged and scandal loving" says the villain in *Doom Castle*. The power of rumour and scurrilous songs pervades all the novels. This novel is set in 1755, ten years after the failure of Bonnie Prince Charlie's uprising when the Highlands were a prey to spies. A Frenchman comes to Argyll seeking revenge. Everyone is very free with their swords and daggers. Tartans are forbidden to the Jacobites, so the heroine's father wears his kilt only in secret in the attic of Doom Castle, a sinister building on the edge of the sea. Admiration of Highland scenery is another recurring feature: "To the north brooded enormous hills, seen dimly by the stars, couchant terrors, vague vast shapes of dolours and alarums." This story has comic relief in the form of the garrulous dwarf retainer at the Castle who playacts the soldier he was never able to become.

Exhilarating descriptions of wild weather where "the ford was gulping full," details of the women's talk, and the whole way of life among the Catholics of South Uist 50 years after Bonnie Prince Charlie's departure fill *Children of the Tempest*. Here again gossip is all powerful but only on an island could singing a song taunting Duncan that he was only courting the angelic Ann, the virtuous priest's sister, because of her possible fortune, drive him away to the mainland. His half brother Col has the courage to rescue an old man from the sea but, the sea cheated of its prey, takes the old man in the end. At one point in the story the Sergeant takes to his English, a sign that he saw some need for lying. The heroine Ann, much loved by the people, is nearly lost returning one terrible dark night from a funeral and is later kidnapped.

General Wade's roads built across the Highlands after the 1715 Jacobite uprising were unpopular with the Clans. *The New Road* is full of the intrigues between Inveraray and Inverness, the violence among the cattle stealers and the men who traffic in arms. The Duke of Argyll sends Ninian Campbell to Inverness to check up on Jacobites. With him goes young Aeneas to start up business for his uncle. The mystery of his father's death adds to his problems, marauding gangs steal the pay chest meant for the road builders. The two men are followed by Col who has Virgilian tags engraved on his sword but was a "kite and trembling things went clapping in the heather when he hovered, blackmail he lifted like a rent on quarter day." The road builders found the Highlands "dark and deep and cunning" more loyal to their chiefs who held state "in gaunt old keeps where pipers blew from turrets" than to the crown. Aeneas is finally nearly deported to the West Indies for knowing too much.

Between writing his historical novels Munro (as Hugh Fowlis) wrote a number of short humorous tales about the captain and crew of the *Vital Spark*, a steam puffer on the Clyde before World War I.

—Margaret Campbell

MURRAY, D(avid) L(eslie). Born in 1888. *Died in 1962.*

ROMANCE AND HISTORICAL PUBLICATIONS

Novels

The Bride Adorned. London, Constable, and New York, Harcourt Brace, 1929.
Stardust: A Tale of the Circus. London, Constable, and Boston, Little Brown, 1931.

The English Family Robinson: A Tale for the New Poor. London, Constable, 1933; as *Once They Were Rich*, New York, Dutton, 1933.

Regency: A Quadruple Portrait. London, Hodder and Stoughton, and New York, Knopf, 1936.

Trumpeter, Sound! London, Hodder and Stoughton, 1933; New York, Knopf, 1934.

Commander of the Mists. London, Hodder and Stoughton, and New York, Knopf, 1934.

Tale of Three Cities: A Novel in Baroque. London, Hodder and Stoughton, and New York, Knopf, 1940.

Enter Three Witches. London, Hodder and Stoughton, 1942.

Folly Bridge: A Romantic Tale. London, Hodder and Stoughton, 1945.

Leading Lady. London, Hodder and Stoughton, 1947.

Royal Academy: A Victorian Picture Show. London, Hodder and Stoughton, 1950.

Outrageous Fortune: An Edwardian Adventure. London, Hodder and Stoughton, 1952.

Come Like Shadows: A Romance in Three Ages. London, Hodder and Stoughton, 1955.

Roman Cavalier. London, Hodder and Stoughton, 1958.

Hands of Healing. London, Hodder and Stoughton, 1961.

OTHER PUBLICATIONS

Other

Pragmatism. London, Constable, 1912.

Reservation: Its Purpose and Method. London, Mowbray, and Milwaukee, Morehouse, 1923.

Scenes and Silhouettes. London, Cape, 1926; as *Candles and Crinolines*, 1930.

Benjamin Disraeli. London, Benn, and Boston, Little Brown, 1927.

Fortune's Favourite: The Life and Times of Franz Lehár, with W. Macqueen-Pope. London, Hutchinson, 1953.

*   *   *

D. L. Murray wrote long historical novels after the manner of Walter Scott, packed with social details of clothes, food, houses, and the countryside. He claimed, in the preface to *Enter Three Witches*, that he tried to give them the substance and spirit of history.

Tale of Three Cities has a good plot full of surprises as the fortunes of the hero Deodatus rise and fall. In the dramatic beginning he is a frustrated friar attending an altar in Rome when Ludovica, a beautiful Italian, persuades him to help her brother who has just lost his hand in a bomb attack in Paris. This brother haunts the book, constantly appearing and disappearing. In London Deodatus, poor and with no relations, works for a monumental mason, then with a Punch and Judy show; at one point he helps the future Napoleon III hide in Highgate Cemetery. The Emperor shows his gratitude later in Paris by helping Deodatus find his real, and, of course, aristocratic father. There follow grand descriptions of court life as the hero becomes a courtier, then a soldier. At last at Metz during the Franco-Prussian War he is united to his Italian love Ludovica who "trembled passionately in his embrace." It all ends in the horrors of the 1870 siege on Paris.

Trumpeter, Sound! perhaps the best known of Murray's novels also has a good plot. The story starts in 1844 when 9-year-old Mark, a poor boy from Sussex, arrives in London riding in an open third class railway truck. His adopted parents take him to lodge with an elderly toy maker whose daughter Fancy, has humble dancing roles at the theatre. A poor boy's view of the sights, sounds, and smells of London, follows till Mark, after a brawl, takes the Queen's shilling. The discomforts of army life are increased by one of the officers turning out to be his aristocratic half brother. This Lord is attracted by Fancy, takes her to live in a country cottage, goes through a form of marriage with her, leaving her pregnant when he goes off to the Crimean War. Descriptions of Wellington's funeral in St. Paul's, then the Charge of the Light Brigade in the Crimea bring Mark eventually back to London and Fancy.

Murray uses a variety of backgrounds in his novels. *Enter Three Witches* is set amid cabs and gaslight at the end of the last century. Sam, a small and flamboyant Jewish man from Whitechapel, returns to London after making some money in South Africa. He quickly makes more money on the Stock Exchange, then on horse racing and the theatre. He marries and entertains lavishly till he goes bankrupt. The love affairs of his wife and her two sisters keep the story moving. At the end undefeated, Sam holding onto his small son is left preparing to start again.

Outrageous Fortune: An Edwardian Adventure, also deals with the wealthy but does not have such a full canvas, being confined to race courses, gambling houses, and London clubs. The chief characters, all concerned with acquiring wealth swiftly, are a collection of bounders and rogues from all classes of society. George Masterman, a penniless Cockney orphan returned from the Boer War, leads the way by acquiring expensive horses then an expensive mistress. It ends with the dramatic account of a court case against George interspersed with a race at Newmarket. He becomes bankrupt but will rise again. Several problems involve very early motor cars. One night George is driving with a tipster who calls out "I'm shot, Captain." "I wish you were," snarled Masterman, stopping the car. "It's something much worse than that—a puncture and we're finished."

Most of the settings are 19th-century London or Paris or, as in *The Bride Adorned*, papal Rome. *Commander of the Mists* concerns the Jacobites, *Regency* is set in Brighton, *Folly Bridge* in Oxford. Here there is a crowded canvas with 18th-century conversation added which slows down a fairly complicated plot. A public hanging begins and almost ends in this account of a corrupt Oxford University. All the dons hunt and plot, even doing away with a rival by violent means; they seldom open a book or give a lecture. A rural parson's son becomes embroiled with a woman and gambling and ends up joining a gang to rob coaches in order to pay his debts. Murray believed in variety.

—Margaret Campbell

———————

MURRAY, Frances. Pseudonym for Rosemary Booth, née Sutherland. British. Born in Glasgow, Scotland, 10 February 1928. Educated at the University of Glasgow, 1945–47; University of St. Andrews, Fife, M.A. 1965, diploma in education 1966. Married Robert Edward Booth in 1950; three daughters. History teacher, Perth Academy, Scotland, 1966–72. Since 1972 principal teacher of history, Linlathen High School, Dundee. School scriptwriter for BBC radio. Recipient: Romantic Novelists Association Major award, 1974, and Elgin prize, 1974. Agent: David Higham Associates, 5-8 Lower John Street, London W1R 4HA, England.

ROMANCE AND HISTORICAL PUBLICATIONS

Novels

The Dear Colleague. London, Hodder and Stoughton, and New York, St. Martin's Press, 1972.
The Burning Lamp. London, Hodder and Stoughton, and New York, St. Martin's Press, 1973.
The Heroine's Sister. London, Hodder and Stoughton, and New York, St. Martin's Press, 1975.
Red Rowan Berry. London, Hodder and Stoughton, 1976; New York, St. Martin's Press, 1977.
Castaway. London, Hodder and Stoughton, 1978; New York, St. Martin's Press, 1979.
Payment for the Piper. London, Hodder and Stoughton, 1983.
The Belchamber Scandal. London, Hodder and Stoughton, and New York, St. Martin's Press, 1985.

OTHER PUBLICATIONS

Other (for children)

Ponies on the Heather. London, Collins, 1966; revised edition, 1973.
Ponies and Parachutes. London, Hodder and Stoughton, 1975.
White Hope. London, Hodder and Stoughton, 1978.
Shadow over the Islands. London, Hodder and Stoughton, 1986.

*   *   *

If you like your history lessons presented in an easily comprehended manner aided by lots of romance and adventure, then Frances Murray is a safe bet. Her novels are always enjoyable, briskly paced, and set in unusual and interesting times and places. No matter where or when, her heroines are always spirited, liberated females who take command of their destinies with or without the hero's help.

Her first historical novel, *The Dear Colleague*, involved cloak and dagger politics in the British Foreign Office in Paris during Louis Napoleon's bid for emperor. The hero, Hector, and the heroine, Elizabeth, become husband and wife in an arranged marriage of convenience, naturally falling in love by the story's end. The grand finale includes a shoot-out at the Opera House in Paris where, thanks to Britain's intervention, Louis Napoleon escapes unharmed.

The Burning Lamp, almost more of a young adult title, again involves a liberated woman, Euphemia Witherspoon, who has trained as a nurse with Florence Nightingale and sets out for the Wild West to try to establish a hospital. In spite of Comanches, chauvinist townsmen, and incompetent doctors, Phemie still manages to get the hospital built and find herself a man.

The setting for *The Heroine's Sister*, a well-written romance adventure, is Venice in 1868, when it is still under Austrian rule. Again skullduggery and intrigue are the themes as the heroine, a wonderfully resourceful and courageous Victorian lady, foils the military and saves her tall dark Italian nobleman.

Red Rowan Berry is the least historical of her novels. 19th-century Scotland provides the background for the romantic story of Janet Laidlaw and her quest through many trials and tribulations, including a bigamous marriage, to be reunited with her true love.

Another unusual setting occurs in *Castaway*, the tale of a young girl who is shipwrecked off the coast of Guernsey in 1804 at a time when Napoleon is readying troops to invade England. History takes precedence over romance as she finds it difficult to

recognize friend from foe on an island filled with spies and smugglers. A lieutenant in Her Majesty's Royal Navy provides the brief love interest.

Payment for the Piper begins in 1850 and unfolds into a generational saga centering on Hannah Lindsay. Hannah leaves her home in Scotland against the wishes of her parents who have arranged her marriage with the local minister. Undaunted, Hannah sails, alone, in search of her brother to a remote New Zealand sheep farm. Adventures follow quickly culminating 150 years later in Hannah's great-great grandson's musical triumph at an Edinburgh festival. Through each generation Hannah's spirit is the dominant force carrying her descendants through grief, despair, the misery of war, and finally happiness and success.

Murray fills a much-needed niche in the historical romance category. Being neither straight historical nor a sweet-savage saga that uses historical settings to tell an erotic story of love, she falls comfortably in between, granting readers the best of both worlds by giving them true historical romance.

—Marilyn Lockhart

———————

MUSKETT, Netta (Rachel). British. Born in 1887. Former Vice-president, Romantic Novelists Association.

ROMANCE AND HISTORICAL PUBLICATIONS

Novels

The Jade Spider. London, Hutchinson, 1927.
The Open Window. London, Hutchinson, 1930.
After Rain. London, Hutchinson, 1931.
The Flickering Lamp. London, Hutchinson, 1931.
A Mirror for Dreams. London, Hutchinson, 1931.
Nor Any Dawn. London, Hutchinson, 1932.
The Shallow Cup. London, Hutchinson, 1932.
Wings in the Dust. London, Hutchinson, 1933.
Plaster Cast. London, Hutchinson, 1933.
Painted Heaven. London, Hutchinson, 1934.
Silver-Gilt. London, Hutchinson, 1935; New York, Berkley, 1978.
Tamarisk. London, Hutchinson, 1935.
Winter's Day. London, Hutchinson, 1936.
Misadventure. London, Hutchinson, 1936.
Alley-Cat. London, Hutchinson, 1937.
Middle Mist. London, Hutchinson, 1937.
Happy To-Morrow. London, Hutchinson, 1938.
The Shadow Market. London, Hutchinson, 1938.
Blue Haze. London, Hutchinson, 1939; New York, Berkley, 1978.
To-Day Is Ours. London, Hutchinson, 1939.
Wide and Dark. London, Hutchinson, 1940.
Scarlet Heels. London, Hutchinson, 1940.
Twilight and Dawn. London, Hutchinson, 1941.
The Gilded Hoop. London, Hutchinson, 1941.
Love in Amber. London, Hutchinson, 1942.
Candle in the Sun. New York, Liveright, 1943; London, Hutchinson, 1960.
The Quiet Island. London, Hutchinson, 1943.
Time for Play. London, Hutchinson, 1943.
The Wire Blind. London, Hutchinson, 1944.
Golden Harvest. London, Hutchinson, 1944.

The Patchwork Quilt. London, Hutchinson, 1946.
Fire of Spring. London, Hutchinson, 1946.
The Clency Tradition. London, Hutchinson, 1947.
A Daughter for Julia. London, Hutchinson, 1948.
The Durrants. London, Hutchinson, 1948.
Living with Adam. London, Hutchinson, 1949.
Cast the Spear. London, Hutchinson, 1950; New York, Berkley, 1978.
House of Many Windows. London, Hutchinson, 1950.
No May in October. London, Hutchinson, 1951.
The Long Road. London, Hale, 1951.
Rock Pine. London, Hale, 1952.
Safari for Seven. London, Hale, 1952.
Brocade. London, Hutchinson, 1953.
Red Dust. London, Hutchinson, 1954.
Philippa. London, Hutchinson, 1954.
Give Back Yesterday. London, Hutchinson, 1955.
Flowers from the Rock. London, Hutchinson, 1956.
Light from One Star. London, Hutchinson, 1956.
The Crown of Willow. London, Hutchinson, 1957.
The Fettered Past. London, Hutchinson, 1958.
Flame of the Forest. London, Hutchinson, 1958.
The High Fence. London, Hutchinson, 1959.
Through Many Waters. London, Hutchinson, 1961.
The Touchstone. London, Hutchinson, 1962.
The Weir House. London, Hutchinson, 1962.
Love and Deborah. London, Hutchinson, 1963.
Cloudbreak. London, Hutchinson, 1964.

*   *   *

Blue Haze, After Rain, Happy To-Morrow, Flame of the Forest, Through Many Waters, Painted Heaven—behind a succession of such pretty, light-hearted sounding titles lies the urgent attempt to deal conscientiously with serious human problems. After the 1914–18 war, a number of romantic novelists tackled those ethical problems which war had engendered. Netta Muskett looked, for instance, at the "surplus million" women, left on the shelf because of the huge numbers of young men killed in action. The heroine of *Painted Heaven* has the misfortune to lose fiancé, brothers, parents. The orphaned heroine, utterly alone in the world, is of course a much used device, since pathos can be added to her many other predicaments. Doomed to spinsterhood, with no chance of ever finding a husband, this heroine resolves to find "another kind of happiness" through an illegitimate child, only to discover that this offers false security, a false happiness which is no more than a "painted heaven."

By the mid 1950's, with changing social mores, and increasing sexual freedom, there were new problems to be solved. The dreaded peril of permissiveness was threatening to sweep away all that romantic novelists held to be most noble, dear, and beautiful. The reaction of some writers to the increased liberation going on in real life was to tighten up fictional virtue still more, to place their heroines on still higher pedestals. "The romantic novelist is almost alone in presenting a picture of true love, decent and honourable conduct, and the happiness which is the result of these 'old-fashioned things,' " explained a spokeswoman for the Romantic Novelists Association.

While some ignored the new problems, Muskett seized upon them. Not for her the happy-ever-after ending with marriage at the last chapter. Marital unrest, failed marriage, middle-aged marriages, even unconsummated marriages, could provide daring food for thought, an opportunity for psychological insight into human difficulties. *Light from One Star* concerns the marital problems encountered by the older, thoughtful type of man if he mistakenly marries a younger woman. She is a glamorous,

extroverted, television personality. This gives the clue to her flighty selfish behaviour as a bride. Career women, particularly in glamorous, self-advertising work, are not to be trusted. She accepts her husband's generous presents, and continental holidays, but refuses to sleep with him. Time and again, she "denies him his rights." And when, at long last, she finally resolves to give in/be a good wife/allow him to make love to her, which she does "with a pretty little lift of her head and an inviting look in her eyes," and the crude words, "Well—how, about it?," her husband has lost interest. He sadly, but wisely, tells her, "I'm not blaming you, my dear. I ought to have known. As a doctor, I ought to have realised *before it was too late*." Has the poor chap become impotent? Discretion prevents Muskett delving any further into the problem.

Muskett treats her problem novels to a special style of writing. Verbs are left out, random adverbs stuck in, commas here and there. This can be interpreted either, as one critic suggested, as "sloppy writing and false sentiment," or as a specially constructed, neo-realistic, semi-documentary prose appropriate to the important topic.

—Rachel Anderson

———————

NEAL, Hilary. See **NORWAY, Kate.**

———————

NEELS, Betty. British. Married; one daughter. Has worked as a nurse in the Netherlands and England. Lives in Dorset. Address: c/o Mills and Boon Ltd., 18–24 Paradise Road, Richmond, Surrey TW9 1SR, England.

ROMANCE AND HISTORICAL PUBLICATIONS

Novels

Amazon in an Apron. London, Mills and Boon, 1969.
Blow Hot, Blow Cold. London, Mills and Boon, 1969; as *Surgeon from Holland*, Toronto, Harlequin, 1970.
Sister Peters in Amsterdam. London, Mills and Boon, 1969; Toronto, Harlequin, 1970.
Nurse in Holland. Toronto, Harlequin, 1970.
Fate Is Remarkable. London, Mills and Boon, 1970; Toronto, Harlequin, 1971.
Nurse Harriet Goes to Holland. Toronto, Harlequin, 1970.
Damsel in Green. London, Mills and Boon, 1970; Toronto, Harlequin, 1972.
The Fifth Day of Christmas. London, Mills and Boon, 1971; Toronto, Harlequin, 1972.
Tangled Autumn. London, Mills and Boon, 1971; Toronto, Harlequin, 1972.
Tulips for Augusta. London, Mills and Boon, and Toronto, Harlequin, 1971.
Uncertain Summer. London, Mills and Boon, 1972; Toronto, Harlequin, 1974.
Victory for Victoria. London, Mills and Boon, and Toronto, Harlequin, 1972.
Saturday's Child. London, Mills and Boon, 1972; Toronto, Harlequin, 1973.
Tabitha in Moonlight. London, Mills and Boon, 1972; Toronto, Harlequin, 1975.

Wish with the Candles. London, Mills and Boon, and Toronto, Harlequin, 1972.

Three for a Wedding. London, Mills and Boon, and Toronto, Harlequin, 1973.

Winter of Change. London, Mills and Boon, and Toronto, Harlequin, 1973.

Enchanting Samantha. London, Mills and Boon, 1973; Toronto, Harlequin, 1974.

Cassandra by Chance. London, Mills and Boon, and Toronto, Harlequin, 1973.

Stars Through the Mist. London, Mills and Boon, 1973; Toronto, Harlequin, 1974.

Cruise to a Wedding. London, Mills and Boon, 1974; Toronto, Harlequin, 1975.

The End of the Rainbow. London, Mills and Boon, 1974; Toronto, Harlequin, 1975.

The Gemel Ring. London, Mills and Boon, and Toronto, Harlequin, 1974.

The Magic of Living. London, Mills and Boon, 1974; Toronto, Harlequin, 1975.

Henrietta's Own Castle. London, Mills and Boon, 1975; Toronto, Harlequin, 1976.

A Small Slice of Summer. London, Mills and Boon, 1975; Toronto, Harlequin, 1977.

Heaven Is Gentle. Toronto, Harlequin, 1975.

Tempestuous April. London, Mills and Boon, 1975.

Cobweb Morning. London, Mills and Boon, 1975; Toronto, Harlequin, 1976.

Roses for Christmas. London, Mills and Boon, 1975; Toronto, Harlequin, 1976.

A Star Looks Down. London, Mills and Boon, 1975; Toronto, Harlequin, 1976.

The Edge of Winter. London, Mills and Boon, 1976; Toronto, Harlequin, 1977.

The Moon of Lavinia. Toronto, Harlequin, 1976.

Gem of a Girl. London, Mills and Boon, 1976; Toronto, Harlequin, 1977.

Esmeralda. London, Mills and Boon, and Toronto, Harlequin, 1976.

The Hasty Marriage. London, Mills and Boon, and Toronto, Harlequin, 1977.

A Matter of Chance. London, Mills and Boon, and Toronto, Harlequin, 1977.

Grasp a Nettle. London, Mills and Boon, and Toronto, Harlequin, 1977.

The Little Dragon. London, Mills and Boon, 1977; Toronto, Harlequin, 1978.

Britannia All at Sea. London, Mills and Boon, and Toronto, Harlequin, 1978.

Never While the Grass Grows. London, Mills and Boon, 1978; Toronto, Harlequin, 1979.

Philomela's Miracle. London, Mills and Boon, and Toronto, Harlequin, 1978.

Ring in a Teacup. London, Mills and Boon, 1978.

Pineapple Girl. London, Mills and Boon, and Toronto, Harlequin, 1978.

Midnight Sun's Magic. London, Mills and Boon, 1979; Toronto, Harlequin, n.d.

The Promise of Happiness. London, Mills and Boon, 1979.

Sun and Candlelight. London, Mills and Boon, 1979.

Winter Wedding. London, Mills and Boon, 1979; Toronto, Harlequin, 1980.

Caroline's Waterloo. London, Mills and Boon, 1980; Toronto, Harlequin, 1981.

Hannah. London, Mills and Boon, 1980; Toronto, Harlequin, 1981.

Last April Fair. London, Mills and Boon, 1980.

The Silver Thaw. London, Mills and Boon, 1980; Toronto, Harlequin, 1981.

When May Follows. London, Mills and Boon, 1980; Toronto, Harlequin, 1981.

Not Once but Twice. London, Mills and Boon, and Toronto, Harlequin, 1981.

An Apple from Eve. London, Mills and Boon, 1981; Toronto, Harlequin, 1982.

Heaven round the Corner. London, Mills and Boon, 1981.

Judith. London, Mills and Boon, and Toronto, Harlequin, 1982.

All Else Confusion. London, Mills and Boon, 1982; Toronto, Harlequin, 1983.

A Dream Come True. London, Mills and Boon, 1982; Toronto, Harlequin, 1983.

A Girl to Love. London, Mills and Boon, and Toronto, Harlequin, 1982.

Midsummer Star. London, Mills and Boon, 1983.

Never Say Goodbye. London, Mills and Boon, 1983.

Never Too Late. London, Mills and Boon, 1983.

Roses and Champagne. London, Mills and Boon, 1983; Toronto, Harlequin, 1984.

Once for All Time. London, Mills and Boon, 1984.

A Summer Idyll. London, Mills and Boon, 1984.

Year's Happy Ending. London, Mills and Boon, 1984.

Polly. London, Mills and Boon, 1984; Boston, Hall, 1986.

Magic in Vienna. London, Mills and Boon, 1985.

Never the Time and the Place. London, Mills and Boon, 1985.

The Secret Pool. London, Mills and Boon, 1986.

A Girl Named Rose. London, Mills and Boon, 1986.

Two Weeks to Remember. London, Mills and Boon, 1986.

The Doubtful Marriage. London, Mills and Boon, 1987.

Stormy Springtime. London, Mills and Boon, 1987.

Off with the Old Love. London, Mills and Boon, 1987.

The Gentle Awakening. London, Mills and Boon, 1987.

When Two Paths Meet. London, Mills and Boon, 1988.

The Course of True Love. London, Mills and Boon, 1988.

Paradise for Two. London, Mills and Boon, 1988.

Fateful Bargain. London, Mills and Boon, 1989.

No Need to Say Goodbye. London, Mills and Boon, 1989.

The Chain of Destiny. London, Mills and Boon, 1989.

*   *   *

There is a reassuring sameness in Betty Neels's novels that readers anticipate with pleasure. Her stories mirror her own life to a great extent for, although English, she married a Dutchman and lived and worked in Holland for a number of years before-turning to writing. In fact, she could be one of her own heroines, for she was a registered nurse and worked in Dutch hospitals while living there.

It is impossible not to feel her deep affection for the Netherlands as she brings to life the placid, homely qualities of the people. At the same time, she uses skillful touches of description and scenery to entice her readers into an awareness of postage-stamp size gardens, flowering spring bulbs, and narrow, flowing canals that criss-cross the landscape. She carefully avoids the Dutch shoe and windmill clichés by concentrating on modern sights and events.

Her heroines are usually nurses in English hospitals. Often they are pleasing in appearance rather than beautiful; occasionally they are chubby or amazon-like instead of dainty, cute little things. But basically, all are sweet, loving girls who are dedicated to their profession; still, each hopes to meet and marry the right man for her.

Her heroes, however, are sleepy-eyed giants of lazy movement and calm unflappable manner. They are, in turn, highly respected and wealthy Dutch consultants who happen to be involved in a special medical situation that brings the heroine into a close relationship with them. Story development invariably moves from England to Holland and back again, and, for the most part, all of her novels have the same basic plot situation.

It is within this framework, however, that Neels shows an unusual mastery of technique and emerges as a creative writer of romance fiction. From her earliest works, such as *Sister Peters in Amsterdam* or *Blow Hot, Blow Cold*, she constantly builds a careful picture of likeable characters, believable stories, and happy endings.

Frequently she varies her heroines' backgrounds, but usually they come from families who have reached professional levels either in medicine, the law, or the church. Occasionally, however, we find a drab little thing like Olympia Randle who is caught in a circle of enforced duty to an irascible, scheming aunt (*The End of the Rainbow*). Olympia finds that even duty eventually comes to an end, with the help of a willing outside force by the name of Waldo Van Der Graaf. For all that, however, Olympia yet has the innate manners and outlook of a lady so that she is able to fit into the doctor's home nicely. Often family responsibilities or difficulties may crop up for the heroine, but she is always able to balance these with a sensitive awareness of love or at least an understanding nature.

An added enjoyment in Neels's novels is the frequent reappearance of characters from earlier stories. Happy-ever-after is, indeed, a fact, as the reader is allowed to peek into the lives of people several years later as characters become part of a new story and are met again. Thus, Adelaide Peters meets and marries Coenraad Van Essen in *Sister Peters in Amsterdam*. In *Blow Hot, Blow Cold* Sophia Greenslade is introduced to her by Maximillian Van Oosterwelde. By then Adelaide and Coenraad have had a new little baby boy.

Overall, there is a placid, serene unfolding to Neels's stories that gives the reader a sense of inevitableness. Things just could not end any other way. Perhaps this quality has much to do with her popularity. Certainly her novels are constantly being watched for by her readers, even though we already know it will be about an English nurse and a Dutch doctor.

—Arlene Moore

NEILAN, Sarah. British. Born in Newcastle-upon-Tyne, Northumberland. Educated at Oxford University, M.A. Married; four children. Book editor for 12 years. Recipient: Mary Elgin award, 1976. Agent: Peters Fraser and Dunlop, 5th Floor, The Chambers, Chelsea Harbour, Lots Road, London SW10 0XF, England.

ROMANCE AND HISTORICAL PUBLICATIONS

Novels

The Braganza Pursuit. London, Hodder and Stoughton, and New York, Dutton, 1976.
An Air of Glory. London, Hodder and Stoughton, and New York, Morrow, 1977.
Paradise. London, Hodder and Stoughton, 1981; New York, St. Martin's Press, 1982.

*

Sarah Neilan comments:

I am primarily a storyteller, and try to produce a strong, exciting, fast-moving narrative, full of suspense (two of my three novels have been serialized), set against an authentic, unusual, and carefully researched historical background.

"A cheerful adventure gothic" was how one American reviewer described my first novel, *The Braganza Pursuit*, which was a governess story set in England and Brazil. My second novel, *An Air of Glory*, was about early immigrants to Nova Scotia; the book retraced a real journey (though with fictional characters). *Paradise*, my third novel, is a family saga set among British frontier settlers in what is now southern Ontario, at the time of the war of 1812 between Canada and the U.S.A.

My forthcoming novel *Send My Love to Overriver* follows the fortunes of a group of young people who grow up during World War I.

*   *   *

Sarah Neilan's progress as a novelist from fantasy with a base of history to fiction-based-on-fact has been an interesting one.

She claims to have dreamed the opening chapters of her first novel, *The Braganza Pursuit*, the historical details of which were completely unknown to her at the time; and those opening chapters do have the same highly coloured, highly charged, and crystalline quality of Coleridge's "Kubla Khan"—allegedly also the result of a dream.

The plot is fairly standard—the heroine being an early 19th-century penniless but gently born governess caught up in a sinister situation over which she has very little control—but the setting (the revolt in northern Brazil against the Braganzas) is dramatic, exotic, and unusual. The writing is equal to this bravely chosen background, being vigorous and vivid. The characters are convincing and the whole—often audacious—story roars along at a spanking rate.

In her second novel, *An Air of Glory*, Neilan has moved even nearer to history-as-it-happened. It is set, again, in the 19th century at a time when many Highlanders were being driven from their lands and forced, through sheer starvation, to cross the Atlantic to Canada in search of a new life. The description of the conditions in which these emigrants crossed the ocean is graphic, and in places horrific; but it is chiefly the characters in the story, their courage and resource, which capture the imagination and hold the attention. Neilan is married to a Canadian whose forebears actually did reach Canada in much the same way, and a good deal of her research has been done "on the ground," which explains the assurance with which she deals with the historical, and the personal, aspect of her work in this area. What she can do, and does with increasing skill, is graft on to actuality invention which irradiates the past.

Her third, and most ambitious, novel, *Paradise*, deals not with the journey to, and arrival in, Canada, but with life in the early years of settlement. In 1812, which is when the Clares and O'Maras set out to make a new life, the States had recently won their independence and there was still tension between the new Americans and the new Canadians. In addition to clearing forests and establishing farms the two families, whose new home was just north of the American border, must fight a war—and neither family is constitutionally fitted for either.

We all know in theory that life was precarious for such people. Neilan spells it out not only in dramatic, but in domestic, detail and by choosing Canada, rather than the over-exposed country to its south, she opens fresh doors on the experiences of our transatlantic cousins.

—Elizabeth Grey

NEWMAN, Sharan (née Hill). American. Born in Ann Arbor, Michigan, 15 April 1949. Educated at Antioch College, Yellow Springs, Ohio, B.A. 1971; Michigan State University, East Lansing, 1973–75, M.A. 1973. Married Paul Richard Newman in 1971; one daughter. Instructor in English, Temple University, Philadelphia, 1976, and Oxnard College, California, 1977–79; director and teacher, Asian Refugee Committee, Thousand Oaks, California, 1980. Agent: Don Congdon, Harold Matson Company, 276 Fifth Avenue, New York, New York, 10001, U.S.A.

ROMANCE AND HISTORICAL PUBLICATIONS

Novels (series: Guinevere in all books)

Guinevere. New York, St. Martin's Press, 1981; London, Futura, 1984.
The Chessboard Queen. New York, St. Martin's Press, 1983; London, Futura, 1985.
Guinevere Evermore. New York, St. Martin's Press, 1985; London, Futura, 1986.

OTHER PUBLICATIONS

Fiction (for children)

The Dagda's Harp. New York, St. Martin's Press, 1977.

*   *   *

In her three novels, *Guinevere*, *The Chessboard Queen*, and *Guinevere Evermore*, Sharan Newman has retold the Arthurian legend from the point of view of Arthur's queen. There are in the main two distinct styles of relating the legend—the courtly romances, often following Malory's *Le Morte Darthur* in tradition, and those which portray Arthur as King of the Britons—a tribal chieftain rather than the ruler of a medieval-style court. Newman gives us a third type—the legend told as a fantasy, mystical elements interwoven with the romances between Guinevere and both her lovers, Arthur and Lancelot.

Guinevere's story begins when she is 12 years old: she is brought up in a Romano-British Christian household, and has all the right connections, Merlin being a cousin of her mother. As well as most of the traditional characters and many of the well-known adventures (e.g., the Quest for the Grail, the Legend of the Fisher King), Newman introduces several original personalities, mainly members of Guinevere's household and extended family. For example, her nurse Flora who is a member of a pagan cult; Guinevere, although Christian, is strongly influenced by some of Flora's beliefs, and does indeed narrowly escape being sacrificed to the cult. Another, more unusual, character is St. Geraldus (presumably the chronicler Gerald of Wales), whose attendant company of angels adds a touch of gentle humour to the story. Most striking in the first book, and symbolic of the still-pervasive magic of the older religions, is the presence of the unicorn, who is in some way Guinevere's alter ego. As the uni-

corn can only be tamed by a virgin, he no longer appears to Guinevere once she is married to Arthur, and the fantasy element diminishes in the two subsequent books, just as the pagan religions retreat before Arthur's vision of a united, Christian Britain.

Guinevere, although the heroine, is not particularly sympathetically portrayed. She is rather selfish and can be arrogant ("she smiled at everyone in the certainty that she would be forgiven without explanation"—this, when she has kept the entire court waiting for dinner). Merlin (not without reason, one feels) does not approve of her as a wife for Arthur and, having striven unsuccessfully to prevent first their meeting and then their marriage, continues to deplore both her character and her influence on people and events.

Taken in isolation, these three novels are an interesting variation on the theme, but they do not stand comparison with some of the other versions by such authors as Mary Stewart, Rosemary Sutcliff and Gillian Bradshaw—not to mention T. H. White. In bringing a romantic mysticism and a somewhat ethereal atmosphere to portions of the story, does Newman perhaps rather make light of a great legend? Despite the freshness of the approach, it is hard to see that anything of importance is added to the Arthurian canon and indeed one feels that these books are best enjoyed if not regarded as Arthurian. Interestingly, many of the reviews praise these books as fantasy novels rather than as historical fiction, and to this genre they do indeed add an interesting dimension.

—Judith Rhodes

NICHOLSON, C. R. See **NICOLE, Christopher.**

NICHOLSON, Christina. See **NICOLE, Christopher.**

NICHOLSON, Jane. See **STEEN, Marguerite.**

NICHOLSON, Robin. See **NICOLE, Christopher.**

NICOLE, Christopher (Robin). Also writes as Leslie Arlen; Robin Cade; Peter Grange; Caroline Gray; Mark Logan; Simon McKay; C. R. Nicholson; Christina Nicholson; Robin Nicholson; Alison York; Andrew York. British. Born in Georgetown, British Guiana (now Guyana), 7 December 1930. Educated at Harrison College, Barbados; Queen's College, Guyana. Married 1) Jean Barnett in 1951 (divorced), two sons and two daughters; 2) Diana Bachmann. Clerk, Royal Bank of Canada, in the West Indies, 1947–56. Lived in Guernsey for many years after 1957; now domiciled in Spain. Agent: John Farquharson Ltd., 162–168 Regent Street, London W1R 5TB, England.

ROMANCE AND HISTORICAL PUBLICATIONS

Novels (series: Amyot; Black Majesty; China Trilogy; Haggard; Hilton and Warner Families; Japan Trilogy; The New Americans; United States Navy)

Off White. London, Jarrolds, 1959.
Shadows in the Jungle. London, Jarrolds, 1961.
Ratoon. London, Jarrolds, and New York, St. Martin's Press, 1962.
Dark Noon. London, Jarrolds, 1963.
Amyot's Cay. London, Jarrolds, 1964.
Blood Amyot. London, Jarrolds, 1964.
The Amyot Crime. London, Jarrolds, 1965; New York, Bantam, 1974.
White Boy. London, Hutchinson, 1966.
The Self-Lovers. London, Hutchinson, 1968.
The Thunder and the Shouting. London, Hutchinson, and New York, Doubleday, 1969.
The Longest Pleasure. London, Hutchinson, 1970.
The Face of Evil. London, Hutchinson, 1971.
Lord of the Golden Fan. London, Cassell, 1973.
Heroes. London, Corgi, 1973.
Caribee (Hilton and Warner). London, Cassell, and New York, St. Martin's Press, 1974.
The Devil's Own (Hilton and Warner). London, Cassell, and New York, St. Martin's Press, 1975.
Mistress of Darkness (Hilton and Warner). London, Cassell, and New York, St. Martin's Press, 1976.
Black Dawn (Hilton and Warner). London, Cassell, and New York, St. Martin's Press, 1977.
Sunset (Hilton and Warner). London, Cassell, and New York, St. Martin's Press, 1978.
The Secret Memoirs of Lord Byron. Philadelphia, Lippincott, and London, Joseph, 1978; as *Lord of Sin*, London, Corgi, 1980.
The Fire and the Rope (as Alison York). London, W. H Allen, and New York, Berkley, 1979.
The Scented Sword (as Alison York). London, W. H. Allen, 1980.
Haggard. London, Joseph, and New York, New American Library, 1980.
The Friday Spy (as C. R. Nicholson). London, Corgi, 1980; as *A Passion for Treason* (as Robin Nicholson), New York, Jove, 1981.
Haggard's Inheritance. London, Joseph, 1981; as *The Inheritors*, New York, New American Library, 1981.
The New Americans:
  Brothers and Enemies. New York, Berkley, 1982; London, Corgi, 1983.
  Lovers and Outlaws. New York, Berkley, 1982.
The Young Haggards. London, Joseph, and New York, New American Library, 1982.
China trilogy:
  The Crimson Pagoda. New York, New American Library, 1983; London, Joseph, 1984.
  The Scarlet Princess. New York, New American Library, 1984; London, Joseph, 1985.
  Red Dawn. London, Joseph, 1985.
Japan trilogy:
  The Sun Rises. London, Hamlyn, 1984.
  The Sun and the Dragon. London, Hamlyn, 1985.
  The Sun on Fire. London, Arrow, 1985.
The Seeds of Rebellion (Black Majesty). London, Severn House, 1984.
Wild Harvest (Black Majesty). London, Severn House, 1985; New York, Severn House, 1987.

United States Navy series:
  1. *Old Glory*. London, Severn House, 1986; New York, Severn House, 1988.
  2. *The Sea and the Sand*. London, Severn House, 1986; New York, Severn House, 1988.
  3. *Iron Ships, Iron Men*. London, Severn House, 1987.
  4. *The Wind of Destiny*. London, Severn House, 1987.
  5. *Raging Seas, Seering Skies*. London, Severn House, 1988.
  6. *The Power and the Glory*. London, Severn House, 1988.
The Ship with No Name. London, Severn House, 1987.
The High Country. London, Century, 1988.
The Regiment. London, Century, 1988.
Pearl of the Orient. London, Century, 1988.
The Happy Valley. London, Century, 1989.
The Command. London, Century, 1989.

Novels as Peter Grange

King Creole. London, Jarrolds, 1966.
The Devil's Emissary. London, Jarrolds, 1968.
The Tumult at the Gate. London, Jarrolds, 1970.
The Golden Goddess. London, Jarrolds, 1973.

Novels as Mark Logan

Tricolour. London, Macmillan, and New York, St. Martin's Press, 1976; as *The Captain's Woman*, New York, New American Library, 1977.
Guillotine. London, Macmillan, and New York, St. Martin's Press, 1976; as *French Kiss*, New York, New American Library, 1978.
Brumaire. London, Wingate, and New York, St. Martin's Press, 1978; as *December Passion*, New York, New American Library, 1979.

Novels as Christina Nicholson

The Power and the Passion. London, Corgi, and New York, Coward McCann, 1977.
The Savage Sands. London, Corgi, and New York, Coward McCann, 1978.
The Queen of Paris. London, Corgi, 1979.

Novels as Leslie Arlen (series: Borodins)

The Borodins:
  Love and Honor. New York, Berkley, and London, Futura, 1980.
  War and Passion. New York, Berkley, and London, Futura, 1981.
  Fate and Dreams. New York, Berkley, and London, Futura, 1981.
  Destiny and Desire. New York, Berkley, 1982.
  Rage and Desire. New York, Berkley, 1982.
  Hope and Glory. New York, Berkley, 1984.

Novels as Caroline Gray

First Class. London, Joseph, 1984; as *Treasures*, New York, Fawcett, 1984.
Hotel De Luxe. London, Joseph, 1985; as *So Grand*, New York, Fawcett, 1985.
White Rani. London, Joseph, and New York, Fawcett, 1986.

Victoria's Walk. London, Joseph, 1986; New York, Fawcett, 1988.
The Third Life. London, Joseph, and New York, St. Martin's Press, 1988.

Novels as Simon McKay (series: Anderson Line in both books)

The Seas of Fortune. London, Severn House, 1984.
The Rivals. London, Severn House, 1985.

OTHER PUBLICATIONS

Novels as Andrew York

The Eliminator. London, Hutchinson, 1966; Philadelphia, Lippincott, 1967.
The Co-Ordinator. London, Hutchinson, and Philadelphia, Lippincott, 1967.
The Predator. London, Hutchinson, and Philadelphia, Lippincott, 1968.
The Deviator. London, Hutchinson, and Philadelphia, Lippincott, 1969.
The Dominator. London, Hutchinson, 1969.
The Infiltrator. London, Hutchinson, and New York, Doubleday, 1971.
The Expurgator. London, Hutchinson, 1972; New York, Doubleday, 1973.
The Captivator. London, Hutchinson, 1973; New York, Doubleday, 1974.
The Fear Dealers (as Robin Cade). London, Cassell, and New York, Simon and Schuster, 1974.
The Fascinator. London, Hutchinson, and New York, Doubleday, 1975.
Dark Passage. New York, Doubleday, 1975; London, Hutchinson, 1976.
Tallant for Trouble. London, Hutchinson, and New York, Doubleday, 1977.
Tallant for Disaster. London, Hutchinson, and New York, Doubleday, 1978.
The Combination. New York, Doubleday, 1983; London, Severn House, 1984.

Other (for children) as Andrew York

The Doom Fishermen. London, Hutchinson, 1969; as *Operation Destruct*, New York, Holt Rinehart, 1969.
Manhunt for a General. London, Hutchinson, 1970; as *Operation Manhunt*, New York, Holt Rinehart, 1970.
Where the Cavern Ends. London, Hutchinson, and New York, Holt Rinehart, 1971.
Appointment in Kiltone. London, Hutchinson, 1972; as *Operation Neptune*, New York, Holt Rinehart, 1972.

Other

West Indian Cricket. London, Phoenix House, 1957.
The West Indies: Their People and History. London, Hutchinson, 1965.
Introduction to Chess. London, Corgi, 1973.

*

Christopher Nicole comments:
I am a romantic or a gothic writer simply because those are names currently in vogue for historical novels. I regard myself as an historical novelist. I also happen to be a romantic by nature and aim to retell history as entertainingly as possible.

*   *   *

Christopher Nicole denies the primacy of the intellect to stress the physical. Natural forces, the promptings of the senses, savage instincts in individuals and societies, are essentials of his work. His upbringing as a white man in the West Indies with their history of slavery, rebellion, and natural disaster is also evident.

Off White, his first novel, revolves around racial tensions and has an earthquake as its climax. *Ratoon* is, if anything, more accomplished. Based upon the Demerara slave insurrection of 1823, the book describes the relationship between a white woman planter and the black rebel who for a time holds her captive. The two share physical passion, and, though in the end they part, both are changed by the experience. The theme is skillfully handled by Nicole, who uses a pared understated style to bring out the nature of his characters. *Ratoon* has a pristine quality, and the strength of the writing is impressive.

Nicole's early work under his own name is concerned mainly with the West Indian islands and their past. Most memorable are his Amyot trilogy—*Amyot's Cay*, *Blood Amyot*, *The Amyot Crime*—a history of the Bahamas as seen by a white family, and a longer five-volume saga depicting the fortunes of the Hiltons and Warners—*Caribee*, *The Devil's Own*, *Mistress of Darkness*, *Black Dawn*, and *Sunset*. Both sequences feature a succession of despots with undisputed power over the subjects of their plantation world. Often such power brings out their worst instincts, but some combine strong desires with equally strong ideals. Some critics have seen the influence of Edgar Mittelholzer in Nicole's work. Certainly some of the dominant matriarchs are reminiscent of the *Kaywana* novels, but the debt is overstressed. Nicole's work displays greater warmth and humanity, and *Ratoon* is more impressive than anything the older man wrote.

Away from the Caribbean scene, Nicole has written effectively. *The Thunder and the Shouting*, the story of a Polish family during the last war, and the political thriller *The Longest Pleasure* are good examples. *The Face of Evil*, though less striking, is a capable story of witchcraft and ritual murder in modern Britain. He also has a variety of pseudonyms, writing spy novels as C. R. Nicholson and Andrew York, and as Christina Nicholson producing tales of searing passion with tempestuous heroines.

Lord of the Golden Fan describes the adventures of Will Adams, the first Englishman to set foot in Japan. Nicole outlines his rise as the friend of Prince Ieyeyasu, and his involvement in the struggle against the ruthless Princess Yodogimi. The story lacks nothing in excitement, with fearsome battle scenes and descriptions of Will's love for the half-caste Pinto Magdalena, consummated after an earthquake destroys Osaka. The differing lifestyles of puritan Europe and Japan are adroitly presented. *Lord of the Golden Fan* is a fine novel, its story compelling and its characters memorable. The vigour of the narrative cannot conceal its subtler insights.

Haggard and *Haggard's Inheritance* further explore the West Indian rulers, this time transplanted to England. Nicole follows two generations from wealth in Barbados to the Derbyshire squirearchy, where their personalities bring them into conflict with the social order. The violence and brutality of the period are superbly portrayed as he traces the Haggard entanglements—sexual, political, and moral—through a network of bribery, rape, incest, and suicide, set against the background of the Napoleonic wars. The complex characters are revealed in a taut restrained style, the nature of Regency England brilliantly evoked. *The Young Haggards* pursues a third generation of the family through the Victorian era, and maintains the standard of the previous works.

The theme of the exile confronted by an alien culture, encountered in *Lord of the Golden Fan* and the Haggard novels, is explored in Nicole's later writings. Perhaps the most substantial of these is the trilogy *The Sun Rises*, *The Sun and the Dragon*, and *The Sun on Fire*, where through the eyes of the American Ralph Freeman and his descendants Nicole views the history of Japan from the 1860's to World War II. His fascination with Japanese culture is evident, and presents the reader with some unexpected revelations. In recent years his imagination has ranged wider yet. *Brothers and Enemies* is set in Brazil, while in *The High Country* Nicole's hero enters Masai territory on the eve of colonial invasion, and *Pearl of the Orient* reveals a growing interest in Imperial China. These later novels contain some of the author's strongest, most assured writing to date.

Nicole's achievement tends to be overlooked. His portrayal of heroic man in the physical world—dominating his fellows, being dominated in turn by his own passions—is striking and individual. In the genre he has chosen, he cannot be bettered.

—Geoffrey Sadler

NIVEN, Frederick (John). British. Born in Valparaiso, Chile, 31 March 1878; moved to Scotland, 1883. Educated at Hutchesons Grammar School, Glasgow; Glasgow School of Art. Served in the Ministry of Food and the Ministry of Information during World War I. Married Pauline Thorne-Quelch in 1911. Worked in the cloth business briefly, then a librarian in Glasgow and Edinburgh; worked in construction camps in western Canada; journalist: worked for the Glasgow *Weekly Herald*, papers in Edinburgh and Dundee, and reviewer for *Observer*, *Pall Mall Gazette*, and *Bookman*, all London; after 1920 lived in Nelson and Vancouver, British Columbia. *Died 30 January 1944.*

ROMANCE AND HISTORICAL PUBLICATIONS

Novels

The Island Providence. London, Lane, 1910.
Dead Men's Bells. London, Secker, 1912.
The Flying Years. London, Collins, 1935.
Mine Inheritance. London, Collins, and New York, Macmillan, 1940.
Brothers in Arms. London, Collins, 1942.
Under Which King. London, Collins, 1943.
The Transplanted. London, Collins, 1944.

OTHER PUBLICATIONS

Novels

The Lost Cabin Mine. London, Lane, 1908; New York, Lane, 1909.
A Wilderness of Monkeys. London, Secker, and New York, Lane, 1911.
Hands Up! London, Secker, and New York, Lane, 1913.
Ellen Adair. London, Nash, 1913; New York, Boni and Liveright, 1925.
The Porcelain Lady. London, Secker, 1913.

Justice of the Peace. London, Nash, 1914; New York, Boni and Liveright, 1923.
The S.S. Glory. London, Heinemann, 1915; New York, Doran, 1916.
Cinderella of Skookum Creek. London, Nash, 1916.
Two Generations. London, Nash, 1916.
Penny Scot's Treasure. London, Collins, 1918.
The Lady of the Crossing: A Novel of the New West. London, Hodder and Stoughton, and New York, Doran, 1919.
A Tale That Is Told. London, Collins, and New York, Doran, 1920.
The Wolfer. New York, Dodd Mead, 1923.
Treasure Trail. New York, Dodd Mead, 1923.
Queer Fellows. London, Lane, 1927; as *Wild Honey*, New York, Dodd Mead, 1927.
The Three Marys. London, Collins, 1930.
The Paisley Shawl. London, Collins, and New York, Dodd Mead, 1931.
The Rich Wife. London, Collins, 1932.
Mrs. Barry. London, Collins, and New York, Dutton, 1933.
Triumph. London, Collins, and New York, Dutton, 1934.
Old Soldier. London, Collins, 1936.
The Staff at Simson's. London, Collins, 1937.
The Story of Their Days. London, Collins, 1939.

Short Stories

Above Your Heads. London, Secker, 1911.
Sage-Brush Stories. London, Nash, 1917.

Verse

Maple-Leaf Songs. London, Sidgwick and Jackson, 1917.
A Lover of the Land and Other Poems. New York, Boni and Liveright, 1925.

Other

Go North, Where the World Is Young (on Alaska and the Yukon). Privately printed, n.d.
The Story of Alexander Selkirk. London, Wells Gardner, 1929.
Canada West. London, Dent, 1930.
Colour in the Canadian Rockies, with Walter J. Phillips. Toronto, Nelson, 1937.
Coloured Spectacles. London, Collins, 1938.

*   *   *

Frederick Niven, a prolific and popular author of his day, was a man whose own background offered him unusual insight into a problem he very often addressed in his writings: that of the dispossessed and heartsick exile.

For Niven, as for others who suffer from a divided heart, the problem was that of a kind of internalized dual citizenship. When he was in Scotland, he pined for Canada's sweeping plains and egalitarian society; but when in Canada, he yearned for his beloved "country of the mind," with its glorious, bloody history and its heather-scented hills. To compound all this, Niven was actually born in Valparaiso, Chile.

Niven's early work, such as *The Porcelain Lady* was that of a minor but promising writer; readable enough, but totally unmemorable. Subsequent books following in rapid succession were, not to put too fine a point on it, potboilers written "To keep the wolf from the wife." Nevertheless, the urge to write drove him on, and with practice came polish. There was *something* there that suggested more than the mere acquisition of a cheque to pay the rent.

He had a decided flair for dialect, a talent more admired at the turn of the century than it is today; and his skillful use of finely differentiated regional accents helped him to flesh out believable characters. He particularly excelled in the portrayal of "ordinary" little lives, unremarkable until subjected to the close scrutiny he afforded them, in stories set in Glasgow such as those of the warehouse workers in *The Staff at Simson's*, of the struggling artist at odds with a narrowly religious family in *Justice of the Peace*, and in *Mrs. Barry*.

His Mrs. Barry exemplifies the understated gallantry Niven most admired; that of a once-prosperous woman now widowed and fallen upon very hard times, who nevertheless makes no concessions to her altered circumstances. She prefers to go down with her poor little flag flying if tattered, rather than to appeal to a cold and uncaring world for sympathy, fearing pity more than she does poverty or even death; genteel privation to subsiding into the working-class milieu in which she now must live.

Niven's best work was transatlantic in its setting. His "Canadian side" if so it may be described, inspired his major historic output, notably the thematically related trilogy consisting of *Mine Inheritance*, *The Flying Years*, and *The Transplanted*.

Mine Inheritance tells of the fierce struggle of the Selkirk settlers to establish their infant colony on the bleak and unwelcoming prairie that was so unlike the Scottish homes they had left behind, against a flaming background of the fur trade wars. *The Flying Years*, the broadly panoramic story of a man's life between the 1850's and the 1920's links the two lands Niven loved, and has been hailed as his greatest achievement. It is a novel of considerable scope and power, and is the only one of his novels currently available in the country of which it is a celebration.

The years that pass so rapidly are those of Angus Munro, the son of Scots crofters driver out of their beloved home of Loch Brendan by the heartless Highland Clearances, in which people were forced out by the great landowners to make way for sheep and deer.

With his father and mother Angus comes to the empty new land; but while at 16 he is young and adaptable enough to transplant, his parents, particularly his mother, are not. Although she tries very hard to make a new home for her family, her yearning heart is broken, and she soon dies. Not long afterward, her husband too is buried in the alien ground.

Alone now, young Angus becomes almost a native; indeed he marries a lovely Cree, Minota; but he too is poisoned by homesickness that gives him no rest; and he leaves his wife to return to Scotland, promising that he will return to her one day.

It is in the passages describing Angus's unhappy sojourn in the land of his fathers that Niven most poignantly reveals the dilemma of the exile. Angus tries to fit in to the old, cap-in-hand life of a shop clerk, the best his old country has to offer him; but he is haunted by memories of a land where "Jack is as good as his master," and where he tugged his forelock to no man. A chance meeting with Indian visitors to Scotland forces his decision; part of his heart will always remain in Scotland, but he knows now that he will live out his life in Canada.

The Transplanted, which closely parallels Niven's own life, portrays the development of a British Colombia settlement from its first beginnings as a lumbering, mining, ranching area to its emergence as a thriving new city; the history of the West encapsulated.

This, Niven's final novel, posthumously published in 1944, sums up his own story. In his lifetime he worked through the trauma of exile, bringing with him to his final home the riches of a British literary tradition, an immigrant rather than a colonial writer, and a significant figure among those who have brought Canada's history to fictional life.

—Joan McGrath

NOLAN, Frederick. Also writes as Frederick H. Christian; Danielle Rockfern; Donald Severn. British. Born in Liverpool, Lancashire, in 1931. Educated at Aberayron County School, Wales; Liverpool Collegiate. Married Heidi Würmli in 1962; two sons. Editor, Corgi Books, London; sales representative, Penguin Books, London; worked in publicity, Fontana Books, and marketing, Granada Publishing, London, and Ballantine Books, New York; publisher, Warner Communications, London. Agent: Arthur Pine Associates, 1780 Broadway, New York, New York 10019, U.S.A.

ROMANCE AND HISTORICAL PUBLICATIONS

Novels (series: A Call to Arms)

Carver's Kingdom. London, Macmillan, 1978; New York, Warner, 1980.
White Nights, Red Dawn. New York, Macmillan, 1980; London, Hutchinson, 1981.
A Promise of Glory (Call to Arms). London, Arrow, 1983; New York, Bantam, 1984.
Blind Duty (Call to Arms). London, Arrow, 1983; New York, Bantam, 1985.
On the Field of Honour (as Danielle Rockfern). London, Hamlyn, 1985.

OTHER PUBLICATIONS

Novels

The Oshawa Project. London, Barker, 1974; as *The Algonquin Project*, New York, Morrow, 1974; as *Brass Target*, New York, Jove, 1979.
NYPD, No Place to Be a Cop. London, Barker, 1974.
The Ritter Double-cross. London, Barker, 1974; New York, Morrow, 1975.
Kill Petrosino! London, Barker, 1975.
The Mittenwald Syndicate. London, Cassell, and New York, Morrow, 1976.
Wolf Trap. London, Piatkus, 1983; New York, St. Martin's Press, 1984.
Red Centre. London, Grafton, and New York, St. Martin's Press, 1987.
Sweet Sister Death (as Donald Severn). London, Arrow, and New York, Lynx, 1989.

Novels as Frederick H. Christian

Sudden Strikes Back. London, Corgi, 1966.
Sudden Troubleshooter. London, Corgi, 1967.
Sudden at Bay. London, Corgi, 1968.
Sudden: Apache Fighter. London, Corgi, 1969.
Sudden: Dead or Alive. London, Corgi, 1970.
Find Angel. London, Sphere, 1973; New York, Pinnacle, 1974.
Send Angel. London, Sphere, 1973; New York, Pinnacle, 1974, as *Ride Clear of Daranga*, New York, Pinnacle, 1979.

Kill Angel. London, Sphere, 1973; New York, Pinnacle, 1974.
Trap Angel. London, Sphere, 1973; New York, Pinnacle, 1974.
Frame Angel. New York, Pinnacle, 1974; London, Sphere, 1975.
Hang Angel. London, Sphere, and New York, Pinnacle, 1975.
Hunt Angel. London, Sphere, and New York, Pinnacle, 1975.
Warn Angel. London, Sphere, and New York, Pinnacle, 1975.
Stop Angel. London, Sphere, and New York, Pinnacle, 1976.

Play

Screenplay: *Brass Target*, 1978.

Other (for children)

Jesse James. London, Macdonald, 1973.
Cowboys. London, Macdonald, 1974.
Lewis and Clark. London, Macdonald, 1974.
The Wagon Train. London, Macdonald, 1974.
Geronimo. London, Macdonald, 1975.
The Pilgrim Fathers. London, Macdonald, 1975.

Other

The Life and Death of John Henry Tunstall. Albuquerque, University of New Mexico Press, 1965.
Jay J. Armes: Detective. New York, Macmillan, 1976; London, Macdonald, 1977.
Rodgers and Hammerstein: The Sound of Their Music. London, Dent, and New York, Walker, 1978.
An Eyewitness History of the Lincoln County War. Norman, University of Oklahoma Press, 1989.

Editor (as Frederick H. Christian), *The Authentic Life of Billy the Kid*, by Pat Garrett. London, Sphere, 1973.

Translator, *Lucky Luke* series (*The Stage Coach, Jesse James, Dalton City, The Tenderfoot, Western Circus*) (for children) by R. Goscinny. Leicester, Brockhampton Press, 5 vols., 1972–74.
Translator, *Gideon* [*And His Friends, On the Riverbank*], *Gideon's House* (for children) by Benjamin Rabier. London, Hodder and Stoughton, 4 vols., 1979.
Translator, *The Black Forest Clinic*, by Peter Heim. London, Sphere, 1987.

*

Frederick Nolan comments:

Historical fiction is one of my favourite disciplines—indeed it might be said that practically everything I have written for adults under my own name falls into that category. Of all that I write I would like to think I take my cue from Trevelyan, who said that "what is important about history is not what happened, but how people felt when it was happening."

*   *   *

A writer whose fame was established with such popular contemporary thrillers as *The Mittenwald Syndicate* and *The Oshawa Project*, Frederick Nolan has begun to earn a second—and equally valid—reputation as a historical novelist. His interest in the events of the previous two centuries, especially those affecting the United States, is always evident—among his nonfiction works is an account of the battle of the Alamo—and the novels he has so far produced testify to his ability as a fictional

chronicler of the American past. As befits the creations of an "action adventure" writer, Nolan's historical books display a terseness of delivery and a brooding atmospheric power, together with scenes of shocking brutality.

The least typical of his novels, *White Nights, Red Dawn*, is set in Tsarist Russia on the eve of its collapse into war and revolution. Against the background of a regime tottering on the verge of destruction, Nolan explores the love-hate relationship of his heroine Tatiana for the playboy Vladimir Smirnoff, and the more unwelcome attentions of the secret policeman Boris Abrikosov. A further strand of sub-plot involves a series of vicious child-murders, and the final unmasking of the killer. The effect of political developments on the lives of the characters is skillfully portrayed, Tsar and peasant alike caught in the gradual, inexorable slide into dissolution and chaos. Nolan recreates the atmosphere of a land in turmoil, fixing in turn on individuals and huddled city crowds, ruthlessly presenting the Tsarist torture-chambers, the intrigues of Lenin and the German High Command, the hypnotic debauchery of Rasputin. In memorable, panoramic scenes he evokes the agony of Russia, the horrifying slaughter of her armies by the Germans, the wholesale butchery of the Bolshevik executions. Thought at times the welter of savagery threatens to overwhelm, the overall vision is sure, and utterly convincing. *White Nights, Red Dawn* is perhaps the most unusual of Nolan's creations; it is also one of the most satisfying.

More typical, and altogether more ambitious, is the Call to Arms series of novels, where the history of the United States from the War of Independence onwards is traced through the lives of the Strong family. At present, the sequence is unfinished, with two novels completed. *A Promise of Glory* follows the adventures of David Strong, an exiled Englishman won over to the American cause, through the campaigns of Washington against British and Indians in the 1770's. Characterisation is thin—there is a touch of pasteboard about the villainous Wellbeloveds, for instance—but Nolan compensates for this with the power of his battle scenes, and his detailed reconstruction of 18th-century life and death. Sensational incidents abound, and the sickening brutality is excessive at times, but the pace of the work is compelling. Although the most flawed of Nolan's historical works, *A Promise of Glory* has considerable merit. More impressive is its sequel, *Blind Duty*, where a later generation of Strongs find themselves involved in the American Civil War, and divided loyalties threaten to break up the family. In this novel Nolan's characters show greater depth and credibility, and his descriptive writing is at its most inspired. His portrayal of the Civil War itself—whether in its broader sweep, or in the snapshot-image recollections of individual battles—is outstanding, and as ever he excels in the action scenes. Imaginary episodes are neatly interwoven with the actual events of the period, with real-life generals and politicians sharing the stage with Nolan's own creations. *Blind Duty* marks a further advance on its predecessor, and bodes well for subsequent works in the series.

Carver's Kingdom ranks highest of all Nolan's historical novels to date. In this account of the financial empire founded by the Carver brothers, and their personal and business lives, the author at the same time presents a capsule history of the United States during the period 1849 to 1873. Ranging from the Californian goldfields to the plantations of Virginia, from the high society of New York and Washington to the western frontier settlements, Nolan conjures up a vivid picture of America's industrial growth, and through the Carver brothers exemplifies the ruthless determination of its pioneers. His compelling narrative involves the fictional characters and their real-life counterparts without undue strain, providing neat vignettes of such worthies as Jim Fisk, J. C. Fremont, James King, and Andrew Carnegie.

Nolan's mastery of detail is always apparent, and there are several epic scenes as he pursues his characters through Gold Rush and Civil War, and the 1871 Chicago fire, to the final shootout and trial in Wichita, Kansas. *Carver's Kingdom* is a major achievement, a significant historical novel which confirms Nolan's reputation in the genre.

—Geoffrey Sadler

NORCROSS, Lisabet. See **SEBASTIAN, Margaret.**

NORDHOFF, Charles and **HALL, James Norman.** Americans. **NORDHOFF, Charles (Bernard):** Born in London, England, 1 February 1887. Educated at Harvard University, Cambridge, Massachusetts, 1906–09, B.A. 1909. Served as an ambulance driver in France, 1916; pilot in United States Air Service: Lieutenant. Married 1) Pepe Teara in 1920 (divorced), four daughters and two sons; 2) Laura Whiley in 1941. Worked on a sugar plantation, Mexico, 1909–11; secretary and treasurer, Tile and Fine Brick Company, California, 1911–16. *Died 11 April 1947.* **HALL, James Norman:** Also wrote as Fern Gravel. Born in Colfax, Iowa, 22 April 1887. Educated at public schools in Colfax; Grinnell College, Iowa, graduated 1910. Served in the 9th Battalion Royal Fusiliers, 1914–16; pilot in the United States Air Service. Married Sarah Winchester in 1925; one son and one daughter. Social worker, Society for the Prevention of Cruelty to Children, Boston, 1910–14. *Died 5 July 1951.*

ROMANCE AND HISTORICAL PUBLICATIONS

Novels (series: Bounty Trilogy)

Bounty Trilogy. Boston, Little Brown, 1936.
  Mutiny on the Bounty. Boston, Little Brown, 1932; as *Mutiny!*, London, Chapman and Hall, 1933.
  Men Against the Sea. Boston, Little Brown, 1933; London, Chapman and Hall, 1934.
  Pitcairn's Island. Boston, Little Brown, 1934; London, Chapman and Hall, 1935.
Botany Bay. Boston, Little Brown, 1941; London, Chapman and Hall, 1942.

OTHER PUBLICATIONS

Novels

Faery Lands of the South Seas. New York, Harper, 1921.
Falcons of France: A Tale of Youth and the Air. Boston, Little Brown, 1929; London, John Hamilton, 1931.
The Hurricane. Boston, Little Brown, 1936.
The Dark River. Boston, Little Brown, 1938.
No More Gas. Boston, Little Brown, 1940.
Men Without Country. Boston, Little Brown, and London, Chapman and Hall, 1942.
The High Barbaree. Boston, Little Brown, 1945; London, Faber, 1946.
The Far Lands. Boston, Little Brown, 1950; London, Faber, 1951.

Other

The Lafayette Flying Corps. Boston, Houghton Mifflin, 1920.

OTHER PUBLICATIONS by Charles Nordhoff

Novels

The Fledgling. Boston, Houghton Mifflin, 1919.
The Pearl Lagoon. Boston, Atlantic Monthly Press, 1924.
Picaró. New York, Harper, 1924.
The Derelict. Boston, Little Brown, 1928.

Other

In Yankee Windjammers. New York, Dodd Mead, 1940; as *I Served in Windjammers*, London, Chapman and Hall, 1941.

OTHER PUBLICATIONS by James Norman Hall

Novels

Kitchener's Mob. Boston, Houghton Mifflin, and London, Constable, 1916.
High Adventure. Boston, Houghton Mifflin, and London, Constable, 1918.
On the Stream of Travel. Boston, Houghton Mifflin, 1926.
Mid-Pacific. Boston, Houghton Mifflin, 1928.
Under the South. London, Chapman and Hall, 1928.
Flying with Chaucer. Boston, Houghton Mifflin, 1930.
Oh Millersville (as Fern Gravel). Muscatine, Iowa, Prairie Press, 1940.
Under a Thatched Roof. Boston, Houghton Mifflin, 1942.
Lost Island. New York, Sundial Press, 1945.

Short Stories

The Forgotten One and Other True Tales of the South Sea. Boston, Little Brown, 1952.

Verse

A Word for His Sponsor. Boston, Little Brown, 1928.

Other

Mother Goose Land (for children). Boston, Houghton Mifflin, 1930.
The Tale of a Shipwreck (for children). Boston, Houghton Mifflin, 1934.
The Friends (for children). Muscatine, Iowa, Prairie Press, 1939.
Dr. Dogbody's Leg (for children). Boston, Little Brown, 1940.
My Island Home (autobiography). Boston, Little Brown, 1952.

*   *   *

The collaborative team of Charles Nordhoff and James Norman Hall exemplifies the working out of that puzzling anomaly, "a whole that is greater than the sum of its parts." Both men had written competent material on various subjects before they came together to work on the history of the World War I Lafayette Flying Corps of which both had been members, and later on a fictional account, *Falcons of France*. Their writing partnership proved so smoothly agreeable, they debated the possibility of finding other work upon which they could profitably pool their efforts; eventually Hall suggested the story of a mutiny aboard a British ship in 1789 as a possible subject for a novel—perhaps even three novels, if the first proved successful.

It was a true story almost forgotten except by those few people who had read the account published in 1831 by John Barrows, Secretary of the British Admiralty, in a work largely unknown to the general public.

The story of the mutiny and its aftermath was so sensational that had it not been demonstrably based upon fact, the events recounted would have seemed incredible. The authors decided to allow the now elderly Captain Roger Byam, once a lowly midshipman under Captain Bligh, to tell his own well-remembered story of *Mutiny on the Bounty*.

In 1787 the *H.M.S. Bounty* proceeded upon orders to collect a cargo of breadfruit trees from Tahiti for an experimental transplantation in the West Indies. The delicate plants depended upon speedy delivery if they were to survive the voyage, and the officer in command, Captain William Bligh, was absolutely determined that the mission should be a notable success that would redound to his credit.

At a time when ordinary seamen expected and received harsh treatment almost as a matter of course, Bligh's inhumanity was so extreme that it was more than his crew were prepared to endure. Most of them, under the charismatic leadership of mate Fletcher Christian, rose in mutiny against Bligh's tyranny. Bligh himself, and those few men aboard who refused to join the mutineers, were set adrift at sea in an open longboat. The chances of their survival, as they well knew, were slim indeed.

Men Against the Sea describes the almost miraculous safe return of the castaways to landfall at Timor in the East Indies, thanks to the navigational skill of Captain Bligh. He was a hard man with an abusive tongue, ambitious and overbearing even by the standards of his day; but he was a masterful seaman by *any* standards.

Meanwhile the mutineers, all too well aware that they were certain to be hanged if captured, provisioned the *Bounty*, and after persuading a handful of friendly Polynesians to accompany them, set sail to find eventual refuge on *Pitcairn's Island*, an uninhabited speck in mid-ocean.

Men outnumbered the women marooned on the island after the deliberate destruction of the *Bounty*, and the sexual tensions and jealousy aroused by this disparity led to a murderous uprising of the outraged Polynesians. Those who survived were finally discovered in 1808, living peacefully on the island still inhabited by their descendants. Of the mutineers who had refused to flee with Christian on the stolen *Bounty*, three were tried and executed in England.

The *Bounty* trilogy surpassed the authors' fondest hopes with its enormous success, which they were never to repeat, although they continued to work together. The trilogy was the result of a coming together of well-matched talents perfectly suited to the subject matter; their bold, distinctly masculine style of prose was exactly right for the story they had to sell. *Mutiny on the Bounty*, which has been filmed repeatedly, is familiar to millions more than ever read the bestselling books, and remains Nordhoff and Hall's joint masterpiece.

It was said of Nordhoff and Hall that "their friendship was the mainspring of their collaboration." Two very different types, Nordhoff ambitious, skeptical, handsome; Hall more of the plain, homespun dependable sort, together created what neither could accomplish alone: a landmark work of fiction in which a sordid mutiny against authority in the person of a petty tyrant

won for both captain and mutineers alike a place in the annals of courage, endurance, and adventure.

—Joan McGrath

NORRIS, Kathleen (Thompson). American. Born in San Francisco, California, 16 July 1880. Educated at home; attended the University of California, Berkeley, 1905. Married the writer Charles Gilman Norris in 1909 (died 1945); one son and two daughters. Worked as a bookkeeper, saleswoman, and teacher; society editor, *Evening Bulletin*, and reporter, *Call*, both San Francisco, 1907–09; freelance writer from 1909. *Died 18 January 1966.*

ROMANCE AND HISTORICAL PUBLICATIONS

Novels

Mother. New York, Macmillan, 1911.
The Rich Mrs. Burgoyne. New York, Macmillan, 1912.
Saturday's Child. New York, Macmillan, and London, Macmillan, 1914.
The Treasure. New York, Macmillan, 1914.
The Story of Julia Page. New York, Doubleday, and London, Murray, 1915.
The Heart of Rachael. New York, Doubleday, and London, Murray, 1916.
Martie, The Unconquered. New York, Doubleday, 1917; London, Murray, 1918.
Undertow. New York, Doubleday, and London, Curtis Brown, 1917.
Josselyn's Wife. New York, Doubleday, 1918; London, Murray, 1919.
Sisters. New York, Doubleday, and London, Murray, 1919.
The Works. New York, Doubleday, 11 vols., 1920.
Harriet and the Piper. New York, Doubleday, and London, Murray, 1920.
The Beloved Woman. New York, Doubleday, and London, Murray, 1921.
Little Ships. New York, Doubleday, 1921; London, Murray, 1925.
Certain People of Importance. New York, Doubleday, and London, Heinemann, 1922.
Lucretia Lombard. New York, Doubleday, and London, Curtis Brown, 1922.
Butterfly. New York, Doubleday, 1923; as *Poor Butterfly*, London, Heinemann, 1923.
Uneducating Mary. New York, Doubleday, 1923.
Rose of the World. New York, Doubleday, and London, Murray, 1924.
The Callahans and the Murphys. New York, Doubleday, and London, Heinemann, 1924.
The Black Flemings. New York, Doubleday, and London, Murray, 1926; as *Gabrielle*, New York, Paperback Library, 1965.
Hildegarde. New York, Doubleday, and London, Murray, 1926.
Barberry Bush. New York, Doubleday, 1927; London, Murray, 1929.
My Best Girl. New York, Burt, and London, Readers Library, 1927.
The Sea Gull. New York, Doubleday, 1927; London, Murray, 1938.

Beauty and the Beast. New York, Doubleday, 1928; as *Outlaw Love*, London, Murray, 1928.

The Foolish Virgin. New York, Doubleday, and London, Murray, 1928.

Storm House. New York, Doubleday, and London, Murray, 1929.

Red Silence. New York, Doubleday, and London, Murray, 1929.

The Lucky Lawrences. New York, Doubleday, and London, Murray, 1930.

Passion Flower. New York, Doubleday, and London, Murray, 1930.

Margaret Yorke. New York, Doubleday, 1930; London, Murray, 1931.

Belle-Mère. New York, Doubleday, 1931; London, Murray, 1932.

The Love of Julie Borel. New York, Doubleday, and London, Murray, 1931.

Treehaven. New York, Doubleday, and London, Murray, 1932.

Younger Sister. New York, Doubleday, 1932; as *Make Believe Wife*, London, Murray, 1947.

Second Hand Wife. New York, Doubleday, 1932; London, Murray, 1933.

Young Mother Hubbard. London, Benn, 1932.

Tangled Love. London, Murray, 1933.

The Angel in the House. New York, Doubleday, 1933.

Walls of Gold. New York, Doubleday, and London, Murray, 1933.

Wife for Sale. New York, Doubleday, 1933; London, Murray, 1934.

False Morning. London, Murray, 1934.

Maiden Voyage. New York, Doubleday, 1934.

Manhattan Love Song. New York, Doubleday, 1934.

Three Men and Diana. New York, Doubleday, and London, Murray, 1934.

Beauty's Daughter. New York, Doubleday, and London, Murray, 1935.

Shining Windows. New York, Doubleday, and London, Murray, 1935.

Woman in Love. New York, Doubleday, 1935; as *Tamara*, London, Murray, 1935.

The Mystery of Pine Point. London, Murray, 1936.

Secret Marriage. New York, Doubleday, and London, Murray, 1936.

The American Flaggs. New York, Doubleday, 1936; as *The Flagg Family*, London, Murray, 1936.

Bread into Roses. New York, Doubleday, and London, Murray, 1937.

You Can't Have Everything. New York, Doubleday, and London, Murray, 1937.

Heartbroken Melody. New York, Doubleday, and London, Murray, 1938.

Mystery House. New York, Doubleday, 1939.

Lost Sunrise. New York, Doubleday, and London, Murray, 1939.

The Runaway. New York, Doubleday, and London, Murray, 1939.

The Secret of the Marshbanks. New York, Doubleday, and London, Murray, 1940.

The World Is Like That. New York, Doubleday, and London, Murray, 1940.

April Escapade. London, Murray, 1941.

The Venables. New York, Doubleday, and London, Murray, 1941.

An Apple for Eve. New York, Doubleday, 1942; London, Murray, 1943.

Come Back to Me, Beloved. New York, Sun Dial Press, 1942; London, Murray, 1953; as *Motionless Shadows*, New York, Bart House, 1945.

Dina Cashman. New York, Doubleday, 1942; London, Murray, 1943.

Corner of Heaven. New York, Doubleday, 1943; London, Murray, 1944.

Love Calls the Tune. New York, Sun Dial Press, 1944; London, Murray, 1945.

Burned Fingers. New York, Doubleday, 1945; London, Murray, 1946.

Mink Coat. New York, Doubleday, and London, Murray, 1946.

The Secrets of Hillyard House. New York, Doubleday, 1947; as *Romance at Hillyard House*, London, Murray, 1948.

Christmas Eve. London, Murray, 1949.

High Holiday. New York, Doubleday, 1949.

Shadow Marriage. New York, Doubleday, and London, Murray, 1952.

Miss Harriet Townshend. New York, Doubleday, and London, Murray, 1955.

The Best of Kathleen Norris. Garden City, New York, Hanover House, 1955.

Through a Glass Darkly. New York, Doubleday, 1957; as *Cherry*, London, Murray, 1958.

Short Stories

Poor, Dear Margaret Kirby and Other Stories. New York, Macmillan, 1913.

Baker's Dozen. New York, Doubleday, 1938; as *Plain People*, London, Murray, 1938.

Star-Spangled Christmas. New York, Doubleday, 1942.

Over at the Crowleys'. New York, Doubleday, 1946.

OTHER PUBLICATIONS

Plays

The Kelly Kid, with Dan Totheroh. Boston, Baker, 1926.
Victoria. New York, Doubleday, 1934.

Screenplay: *Lucretia Lombard* (*Flaming Passion*), with Bertram Millhauser and Sada Cowan, 1923.

Verse

One Nation Indivisible. New York, Doubleday, 1942.

Other

Noon: An Autobiographial Sketch. New York, Doubleday, 1925.
The Fun of Being a Mother. New York, Doubleday, and London, Heinemann, 1927.
Herbert Hoover as Seen by Kathleen Norris. Washington, D.C., Republican National Committee, 1928.
Home. New York, Dutton, 1928.
What Price Peace? A Handbook of Peace for American Women. New York, Doubleday, 1928.
After the Honey Moon What? New York, Paulist Press, n.d.
Mother and Son. New York, Dutton, 1929.
Beauty in Letters. New York, Doubleday, 1930.
Hands Full of Living: Talks with American Women. New York, Doubleday, 1931.
My San Francisco. New York, Doubleday, 1932.
My California. New York, Doubleday, 1933.

Dedications. Privately printed, 1936.
These I Like Best: The Favorite Novels and Stories of Kathleen Norris, Chosen by Herself. New York, Doubleday, 1941.
Companionate Marriage. New York, Paulist Press, n.d.
Morning Light (for children). New York, Doubleday, 1950; as *Mary-Jo,* London, Dent, 1952.
Family Gathering (memoirs). New York, Doubleday, and London, Murray, 1959.

*   *   *

Kathleen Norris has unfortunately been lumped together with the masses of popular magazine writers of the period from 1910 to 1950, and this, while appropriate for much of her work, does a disservice to her best novels. Possibly a bit defensive about her work because of the more "serious" (but utterly forgotten) work of her husband, Charles Norris (brother of Frank), she saw herself as a professional writer, doing two or three serials a year for leading magazines, even cutting back on her fiction when income tax made it appropriate to do so. But she said in her autobiography: "Most of the critics did not take my work seriously, but then neither did I take the critics too seriously. My writing I took with deadly seriousness."

Certainly the critics were just to ignore much of her work. Norris's central mood hovers between the sentimental and the didactic; together they are a dangerous combination. It often leads to works which point a threadbare moral at the expense of much exploration of character. *The Treasure* (1914) is a "modern" story about social insecurity, "domestic science," and progress. The characters are used as counters in the thematic game—and the result is a "hard" story with little life to it. Usually Norris allows herself more space, but even so many of the novels center on obvious conflicts between ordinary folk and smart or rich people, usually with a romantic plot to keep the theme moving. *Rose of the World* contrasts a socially unacceptable girl with a rich snobbish family, but the girl is given the chance to have the last word, and marry the son of the family after all. *Mink Coat* contrasts a playboy New Yorker with an honest westerner by their effect on one woman. And other novels show rich or shiftless men damaging young susceptible girls. Perhaps a sacrifice has to be made to protect a relative or friend (*Lost Sunrise*)—but the long-term effect is usually a triumph for the heroine.

Norris emphasized her interest in "the fearful power of money upon human lives," and her stories are full of spendthrifts, unworkable household budgets, bank loans, wills, and middle-aged women who don't understand the principle of insurance. But another prime interest is the family itself, and her best novels are those which center on the family or clan as a preserver of traditional right action, even as an expression of the healthy melting pot of America itself.

Because Norris was from a prosperous Irish family from San Francisco, many of her works use this background. And she was not afraid to use simple or even slight themes: "I have no knowledge of those dark forces which fascinate modern writers. I write for people with simple needs and motives because I am like that myself." Her very first long story, *Mother,* brought her fame, and it initiates a constant Norris theme by having a strong sense of family—centered on the unassuming Mrs. Paget—act as a stabilizing force against the false values of a "smart" idle life: "the old beauty that had been hers was chiselled to a mere pure outline now, but there was a contagious serenity in Mrs. Paget's smile, a clear steadiness in her calm eyes, and her forehead, beneath an unfashionably plain sweep of hair, was untroubled and smooth." Other volumes also center on strong mothers (*Over at the Crowleys', The Callahans and the Murphys, Little*

Ships), though sometimes the theme is reversed, so that a weak mother yields to a daughter who learns strength elsewhere (*The Venables*).

The two novels which most convincingly posit Norris's fictional values are *Certain People of Importance* and *The Flagg Family,* and the two books neatly represent two consecutive generations. The "certain people of importance" of the first novel are the members of the Crabtree family. The novel traces the Crabtrees in detail from their arrival in San Francisco in 1849 through the 40 or 50 years to the death of Reuben Crabtree. We see a family begun, a group of traditions started, rivalries and intimacies, financial and spiritual losses and gains—and life continues to surprise Reuben's daughters May and Fannie to the very end. The Flaggs represent the next generation, but their novel covers a shorter span of time (about 10 years) and has a firmer plot. The Flaggs are a large rich clan in northern California, the symbol of tradition and aristocracy to outsiders. Norris allows the clan to be penetrated by an outsider, not in order to debunk the Flaggs, but to show the value of the traditions the Flaggs have built up and learned to accept as part of their future, the richness of the strains that have fed them (English, Indian, Jewish, Italian, Dutch), the compromises that keep them afloat. Even the rather melodramatic plot superimposed on the more substantial edifice—should the newcomer Penelope divorce the spoiled Jeff Flagg to marry the more sedate cousin Tom Flagg?—is worked out in terms of the family theme.

Norris in these two books keeps her sentiments and nostalgia uncontaminated with didacticism, and the results are probing. She represents a second-generation American writer with second-generation American themes, and these are interesting yet today (vulgarized into sentimental myths as pervasive as Ozzie and Harriet or the Kennedys)—and presented with directness and precision.

—George Walsh

NORTON, Bess. See **NORWAY, Kate.**

NORWAY, Kate. Pseudonym for Olive Marion Norton, née Claydon; also writes as Hilary Neal; Bess Norton. British. Born 13 January 1913. Educated at King Edward's School, Birmingham; Birmingham Children's Hospital; Manchester Royal Infirmary. Married George Norton in 1938; one son and three daughters. Nurse, 1930–36: in charge of first aid post during World War II; columnist, Birmingham *News,* 1954–59. Counsellor, Citizens Advice Bureau. *Died in 1973.*

ROMANCE AND HISTORICAL PUBLICATIONS

Novels

Sister Brookes of Bynd's. London, Mills and Boon, 1957; as *Nurse Brookes,* Toronto, Harlequin, 1958.
The Morning Star. London, Mills and Boon, and Toronto, Harlequin, 1959.
Junior Pro. London, Mills and Boon, and Toronto, Harlequin, 1959.

Nurse Elliot's Diary. London, Mills and Boon, and Toronto, Harlequin, 1960.
Waterfront Hospital. London, Mills and Boon, 1961.
The White Jacket. London, Mills and Boon, 1961; Toronto, Harlequin, 1962.
Goodbye, Johnny. London, Mills and Boon, 1962.
The Night People. London, Mills and Boon, 1963.
Nurse in Print. London, Mills and Boon, 1963.
The Seven Sleepers. London, Mills and Boon, 1964.
A Professional Secret. London, Mills and Boon, 1964.
The Lambs. London, Mills and Boon, 1965.
The Nightingale Touch. London, Mills and Boon, 1966.
Be My Guest. London, Mills and Boon, 1966; as *Journey in the Dark*, London, Corgi, 1973.
Merlin's Keep. London, Mills and Boon, 1966.
A Nourishing Life. London, Mills and Boon, 1967.
The Faithful Failure. London, Mills and Boon, 1968.
Dedication Jones. London, Mills and Boon, 1969; Toronto, Harlequin, 1970.
To Care Always. London, Mills and Boon, 1970.
Reluctant Nightingale. London, Mills and Boon, 1970.
Paper Halo. London, Mills and Boon, 1970; Toronto, Harlequin, 1971.
The Bedside Manner. London, Mills and Boon, 1971.
Casualty Speaking. London, Mills and Boon, 1971.
The Dutiful Tradition. London, Mills and Boon, 1971.
The Gingham Year. London, Mills and Boon, 1973.
Voices in the Night. London, Mills and Boon, 1973.

Novels as Bess Norton

The Quiet One. London, Mills and Boon, 1959; Toronto, Harlequin, 1960.
Night Duty at Dukes. London, Mills and Boon, 1960.
The Red Chalet. London, Mills and Boon, 1960.
The Summer Change. London, Mills and Boon, 1961.
The Waiting Room. London, Mills and Boon, 1961; Toronto, Harlequin, 1962.
A Nurse Is Born. London, Mills and Boon, 1962; Toronto, Harlequin, 1963.
The Green Light. London, Mills and Boon, 1963.
The Monday Man. London, Mills and Boon, 1963.
St. Luke's Little Summer. London, Mills and Boon, 1964.
A Miracle at Joe's. London, Mills and Boon, 1965.
St. Julian's Day. London, Mills and Boon, 1965.
What We're Here For. London, Mills and Boon, 1966.
Night's Daughters. London, Mills and Boon, 1966.
The Night Is Kind. London, Mills and Boon, 1967.

Novels as Hilary Neal

Factory Nurse. London, Mills and Boon, 1961; Toronto, Harlequin, 1964.
Tread Softly, Nurse. London, Mills and Boon, and Toronto, Harlequin, 1962.
Star Patient. London, Mills and Boon, 1963.
Love Letter. London, Mills and Boon, 1963.
Houseman's Sister. London, Mills and Boon, 1964.
Nurse Off Camera. London, Mills and Boon, 1964.
Mr. Sister. London, Mills and Boon, 1965.
The Team. London, Mills and Boon, 1965.
Charge Nurse. London, Mills and Boon, 1965.
A Simple Duty. London, Mills and Boon, 1966.
Nurse Meg's Decision. London, Mills and Boon, 1966.

OTHER PUBLICATIONS

Novels as Olive Norton

A School of Liars. London, Cassell, 1966.
Now Lying Dead. London, Cassell, 1967.
The Speight Street Angle. London, Corgi, 1968.
Dead on Prediction. London, Cassell, 1970.
The Corpse-Bird Cries. London, Cassell, 1971.

Play

Radio Play: *Rose*, 1962.

Other as Olive Norton

Bob-a-Job Pony (for children). London, Heinemann, 1961.

*   *   *

The hospital romance has become a popular and fertile branch of novel writing. It dates in Britain only from the start of the National Health Service in 1948, but Kate Norway has established herself as the most successful practitioner of this genre as well as being a crime writer.

Material for her many books is based on first-hand experience of hospital nursing in Britain, and on the whole the pictures she provides of hospitals are very truthful and realistic to the point of being workaday. There is, as a result, much technical medical detail, as well as clear examples of administrative systems, and much of the interest for many readers is contained in those two areas. The romance in many of her novels is intimately mixed with the work; it is even possible to see the romance aspect as subsidiary. Thus, a young reader contemplating a nursing career would read her novels for an inside picture of hospital life which will also be entertaining. *The Gingham Year*, in fact, deals with the transition of a girl from school to nursing. *The Lambs* concerns a group of student nurses.

Plots tend to follow a well-established pattern. They usually revolve around a young female nurse (occasionally doctor) who is dedicated, competent, and attractive. The nurse is attracted to several doctors and surgeons in the hospital, and can be warm and loving. Much of the interest in the plots is produced by a complicating of romantic situations involving the heroine. She is often disturbed in an initially inexplicable way by her attraction to a particular male. This attraction is often despite herself, and directed towards an unpromising suitor. At the same time she is involved with an ostensibly better candidate. Generally the least promising situation turns out to bring true love. Romantic plots are thus normally triangular: a little variety is added by including a subsidiary mystery involving crime. In *The White Jacket*, for instance, there is a masquerading murderer working in the hospital.

Another device used by Norway to add variety to plots is the accident which happens to nurse or doctor. In *Reluctant Nightingale* the nurse herself ends up needing nursing by those intruders, male nurses. Male nurses were once a controversial issue, and this remains true for the world in Norway's books, which is primarily a female one.

An interesting device occurs in *Voices in the Night* where the chapters form separate diaries written in a *sotto voce* style belonging to five characters. They are inter-related, and one sees hospital life from the view of the elderly spinster sister as well as the young nurse and young doctor. This device adds poignancy to the fact that one doctor is loved by two nurses.

Minor issues which appear in several books are motor car, and especially motor bike, accidents. Settings are commonly the English Midlands. The style of writing is simple with much lively dialogue but with a good deal of narrative in the first person; descriptive passages are not overlong. Character is not probed too deeply and judgments are often made in a snappy, personnel-management style.

—P. R. Meldrum

NYE, Robert. British. Born in London, 15 March 1939. Educated at Dormans Land, Sussex; Hamlet Court, Westcliff, Essex; Southend High School, Essex. Married 1) Judith Pratt in 1959 (divorced 1967), three sons; 2) Aileen Campbell in 1968, one daughter, one stepdaughter, and one stepson. Since 1961 freelance writer: since 1967 poetry editor, the *Scotsman*; since 1971 poetry critic, *The Times*. Writer-in-residence, University of Edinburgh, 1976–77. Recipient: Eric Gregory award, 1963; Scottish Arts Council bursary, 1970, 1973, and publication award, 1970, 1976; James Kennaway Memorial award, 1970; *Guardian* Fiction prize, 1976; Hawthornden prize, 1977. Fellow, Royal Society of Literature, 1977. Agent: Anthony Sheil Associates, 43 Doughty Street, London WC1N 2LF, England; or, Wallace and Sheil Inc., 177 East 70th Street, New York, New York 10021, U.S.A. Address: 2 Westbury Crescent, Wilton, Cork, Ireland.

ROMANCE AND HISTORICAL PUBLICATIONS

Novels

Falstaff. London, Hamish Hamilton, and Boston, Little Brown, 1976.
Merlin. London, Hamish Hamilton, 1978; New York, Putnam, 1979.
Faust. London, Hamish Hamilton, 1980; New York, Putnam, 1981.
The Voyage of the Destiny. London, Hamish Hamilton, and New York, Putnam, 1982.

OTHER PUBLICATIONS

Novel

Doubtfire. London, Calder and Boyars, and New York, Hill and Wang, 1968.

Short Stories

Tales I Told My Mother. London, Calder and Boyars, 1969; New York, Hill and Wang, 1970.
Penguin Modern Stories 6, with others. London, Penguin, 1970.
The Facts of Life and Other Fictions. London, Hamish Hamilton, 1983.

Plays

Sawney Bean, with Bill Watson (produced Edinburgh, 1969; London, 1972; New York, 1982). London, Calder and Boyars, 1970.

Sisters (broadcast 1969; produced Edinburgh, 1973). Included in *Penthesilea, Fugue, and Sisters*, 1975.
Penthesilea, adaptation of the play by Heinrich von Kleist (broadcast 1971; produced London, 1983). Included in *Penthesilea, Fugue, and Sisters*, 1975.
The Seven Deadly Sins: A Mask, music by James Douglas (produced Stirling, 1973). Rushden, Northamptonshire, Omphalos Press, 1974.
Mr. Poe (produced Edinburgh and London, 1974).
Penthesilea, Fugue, and Sisters. London, Calder and Boyars, 1975.

Radio Plays: *Sisters*, 1969; *A Bloody Stupit Hole*, 1970; *Reynolds, Reynolds*, 1971; *Penthesilea*, 1971; *The Devil's Jig*, with Humphrey Searle, from a work by Thomas Mann, 1980.

Verse

Juvenilia 1. Northwood, Middlesex, Scorpion Press, 1961.
Juvenilia 2. Lowestoft, Suffolk, Scorpion Press, 1963.
Darker Ends. London, Calder and Boyars, and New York, Hill and Wang, 1969.
Agnus Dei. Rushden, Northamptonshire, Sceptre Press, 1973.
Two Prayers. Richmond, Surrey, Keepsake Press, 1974.
Five Dreams. Rushden, Northamptonshire, Sceptre Press, 1974.
Divisions on a Ground. Manchester, Carcanet, 1976.

Other (for children)

Taliesin. London, Faber, 1966; New York, Hill and Wang, 1967.
March Has Horse's Ears. London, Faber, 1966; New York, Hill and Wang, 1967.
Bee Hunter: Adventures of Beowulf. London, Faber, 1968; as *Beowulf: A New Telling*, New York, Hill and Wang, 1968; as *Beowulf, The Bee Hunter*, Faber, 1972.
Wishing Gold. London, Macmillan, 1970; New York, Hill and Wang, 1971.
Poor Pumpkin. London, Macmillan, 1971; as *The Mathematical Princess and Other Stories*, New York, Hill and Wang, 1972.
Cricket: Three Stories. Indianapolis, Bobbs Merrill, 1975; as *Once upon Three Times*, London, Benn, 1978.
Out of the World and Back Again. London, Collins, 1977; as *Out of This World and Back Again*, Indianapolis, Bobbs Merrill, 1978.
The Bird of the Golden Land. London, Hamish Hamilton, 1980.
Harry Pay the Pirate. London, Hamish Hamilton, 1981.
Three Tales (includes *Beowulf, Wishing Gold, Taliesin*). London, Hamish Hamilton, 1983.

Other

Editor, *A Choice of Sir Walter Ralegh's Verse*. London, Faber, 1972.
Editor, *William Barnes: A Selection of His Poems*. Oxford, Carcanet, 1972.
Editor, *A Choice of Swinburne's Verse*. London, Faber, 1973.
Editor, *The Faber Book of Sonnets*. London, Faber, 1976; as *A Book of Sonnets*, New York, Oxford University Press, 1976.
Editor, *The English Sermon 1750–1850*. Cheadle, Cheshire, Carcanet, 1976.
Editor, *PEN New Poetry*. London, Quartet, 1986.

*

Manuscript Collections: University of Texas, Austin; Colgate University, Hamilton, New York; National Library of Scotland, Edinburgh; University of Edinburgh.

*   *   *

Robert Nye's historical fiction presents a fascinating blend of extensive knowledge, humour, and narrative skill. The most grave and intense of his novels is *The Voyage of the Destiny*, the journal of Sir Walter Raleigh. Raleigh commences his journal when it is apparent that his journey in search of gold has been unsuccessful. He must return to face the displeasure of James I, who had released him from incarceration in the Tower of London to make this expedition. As we read of Raleigh's physical decrepitude and his grief at the death of his son, we are presented with the contrasting reminiscences of his times as a favourite at the court of Elizabeth I and of the intrigues leading to his downfall and imprisonment under sentence of death as a traitor. The descriptions of his relationship with the former Queen and with his wife and sons parallel the development of his relationship with the Indian Christoval who was chosen to return to England with Raleigh after the death of his Spanish master. Raleigh's awareness of the cultural gulf between them echoes the remoteness he feels from his own civilization.

The pervasive sadness of this book contrasts forcefully with the rumbustiousness and vigour of *Falstaff*. Again this novel contains the reminiscences of an elderly man, in this case Shakespeare's Falstaff, but here the narration of fact is of minor importance. Instead we are shown Falstaff in all his self-assured glory, revelling in his achievements, whether actual or imagined, both martial and sexual. The retelling of Shakespeare's plots from the viewpoint of Falstaff himself and his interpretation of his relationship with Prince Hal contribute to the interest of this tale, as does the historical detail of daily life.

Faust is narrated by Christopher Wagner, Faust's student assistant, who accompanies him on a journey to Rome, supposedly in order to murder the Pope, and who attempts to discover how much of Faust's behaviour is attributable to his pact with the devil and how much to drunkenness. The novel again presents a lively background of contemporary life, while concentrating on the relationship between the protagonists. As in *Falstaff*, Nye retells a familiar story from an alternative perspective and challenges the reader by reappraising the commonplace.

Elements of magical and unexplained mystery influence the plot of *Faust* and these become even more evident in *Merlin*, the most fantastic of Nye's novels. This book is Merlin's account of his life, from the time of his conception as "darkling child of virgin and devil." The tale incorporates Merlin's arrival as magician and seer at the court of Uther Pendragon, the legends of the Round Table and the quest for the Holy Grail and Merlin's nurturing of the future King Arthur until his eventual downfall. It is interspersed with commentaries from Merlin's father, the devil, and his associates, Beelzebub and Astarot, who add a timeless quality to the narrative with references to Freud's interpretation of events.

Merlin, *Faust*, and *Falstaff*, all include crude and even obscene episodes, together with scholarly references and slapstick humour. It is this blend of seemingly disparate elements which captures and sustains the reader's interest in Nye's novels.

—Hilary Buswell

OATES, Joyce Carol. American. Born in Millersport, New York, 16 June 1938. Educated at Syracuse University, New York, 1956–60, B.A. in English 1960 (Phi Beta Kappa); University of Wisconsin, Madison, M.A. in English 1961; Rice University, Houston, 1961. Married Raymond J. Smith in 1961. Instructor, 1961–65, and Assistant Professor of English, 1965–67, University of Detroit; member of the Department of English, University of Windsor, Ontario, 1967–78. Since 1978 writer-in-residence, Princeton University, New Jersey. Since 1974 publisher, with Raymond J. Smith, *Ontario Review*, Windsor, later Princeton. Recipient: National Endowment for the Arts grant, 1966, 1968; Guggenheim fellowship, 1967; O. Henry award, 1967, and Special Award for Continuing Achievement, 1970; Rosenthal award, 1968; National Book award, 1970. Member, American Academy, 1978. Address: c/o Dutton Inc., 2 Park Avenue, New York, New York 10016, U.S.A.

ROMANCE AND HISTORICAL PUBLICATIONS

Novels

Bellefleur. New York, Dutton, 1980; London, Cape, 1981.
A Bloodsmoor Romance. New York, Dutton, 1982; London, Cape, 1983.
Mysteries of Winterthurn. New York, Dutton, and London, Cape, 1984.

OTHER PUBLICATIONS

Novels

With Shuddering Fall. New York, Vanguard Press, 1964; London, Cape, 1965.
A Garden of Earthly Delights. New York, Vanguard Press, 1967; London, Gollancz, 1970.
Expensive People. New York, Vanguard Press, 1968; London, Gollancz, 1969.
Them. New York, Vanguard Press, 1969; London, Gollancz, 1971.
Wonderland. New York, Vanguard Press, 1971; London, Gollancz, 1972.
Do with Me What You Will. New York, Vanguard Press, 1973; London, Gollancz, 1974.
The Assassins: A Book of Hours. New York, Vanguard Press, 1975.
Childwold. New York, Vanguard Press, 1976; London, Gollancz, 1977.
Son of the Morning. New York, Vanguard Press, 1978; London, Gollancz, 1979.
Unholy Loves. New York, Vanguard Press, 1979; London, Gollancz, 1980.
Cybele. Santa Barbara, California, Black Sparrow Press, 1979.
Angel of Light. New York, Dutton, and London, Cape, 1981.
Solstice. New York, Dutton, and London, Cape, 1985.
Marya: A Life. New York, Dutton, 1986; London, Cape, 1987.
You Must Remember This. New York, Dutton, 1987; London, Macmillan, 1988.
American Appetites. New York, Dutton, 1989.

Short Stories

By the North Gate. New York, Vanguard Press, 1963.
Upon the Sweeping Flood and Other Stories. New York, Vanguard Press, 1966; London, Gollancz, 1973.

The Wheel of Love. New York, Vanguard Press, 1970; London, Gollancz, 1971.

Cupid and Psyche. New York, Albondocani Press, 1970.

Marriages and Infidelities. New York, Vanguard Press, 1972; London, Gollancz, 1974.

A Posthumous Sketch. Los Angeles, Black Sparrow Press, 1973.

The Girl. Cambridge, Massachusetts, Pomegranate Press, 1974.

Plagiarized Material (as Fernandes/Oates). Los Angeles, Black Sparrow Press, 1974.

The Goddess and Other Women. New York, Vanguard Press, 1974; London, Gollancz, 1975.

Where Are You Going, Where Have You Been? Stories of Young America. Greenwich, Connecticut, Fawcett, 1974.

The Hungry Ghosts: Seven Allusive Comedies. Los Angeles, Black Sparrow Press, 1974; Solihull, Warwickshire, Aquila, 1975.

The Seduction and Other Stories. Los Angeles, Black Sparrow Press, 1975.

The Poisoned Kiss and Other Stories from the Portuguese (as Fernandes/Oates). New York, Vanguard Press, 1975; London, Gollancz, 1976.

The Triumph of the Spider Monkey. Santa Barbara, California, Black Sparrow Press, 1976.

Crossing the Border. New York, Vanguard Press, 1976; London, Gollancz, 1978.

Night-Side. New York, Vanguard Press, 1977; London, Gollancz, 1979.

A Sentimental Education (single story). Los Angeles, Sylvester and Orphanos, 1978.

The Step-Father. Northridge, California, Lord John Press, 1978.

All the Good People I've Left Behind. Santa Barbara, California, Black Sparrow Press, 1979.

Queen of the Night. Northridge, California, Lord John Press, 1979.

The Lamb of Abyssalia. Cambridge, Massachusetts, Pomegranate Press, 1979.

A Middle-Class Education. New York, Albondocani Press, 1980.

A Sentimental Education (collection). New York, Dutton, 1980; London, Cape, 1981.

Last Days. New York, Dutton, 1984; London, Cape, 1985.

Wild Saturday and Other Stories. London, Dent, 1984.

Wild Nights. Athens, Ohio, Croissant, 1985.

Raven's Wing. New York, Dutton, 1986; London, Cape, 1987.

The Assignation. New York, Ecco Press, 1988.

Plays

The Sweet Enemy (produced New York, 1965).

Sunday Dinner (produced New York, 1970).

Ontological Proof of My Existence, music by George Prideaux (produced New York, 1972). Included in *Three Plays*, 1980.

Miracle Play (produced New York, 1979). Los Angeles, Black Sparrow Press, 1974.

Daisy (produced New York, 1980).

Three Plays (includes *Ontological Proof of My Existence*, *Miracle Play*, *The Triumph of the Spider Monkey*). Windsor, Ontario Review Press, 1980.

Presque Isle, music by Paul Shapiro (produced New York, 1982).

Lechery, in *Faustus in Hell* (produced Princeton, New Jersey, 1985).

Verse

Women in Love and Other Poems. New York, Albondocani Press, 1968.

Anonymous Sins and Other Poems. Baton Rouge, Louisiana State University Press, 1969.

Love and Its Derangements. Baton Rouge, Louisiana State University Press, 1970.

Wooded Forms. New York, Albondocani Press, 1972.

Angel Fire. Baton Rouge, Louisiana State University Press, 1973.

Dreaming America and Other Poems. New York, Aloe Editions, 1973.

The Fabulous Beasts. Baton Rouge, Louisiana State University Press, 1975.

Women Whose Lives Are Food, Men Whose Lives Are Money. Baton Rouge, Louisiana State University Press, 1978.

Celestial Timepiece. Dallas, Pressworks, 1980.

Nightless Nights: Nine Poems. Concord, New Hampshire, Ewert, 1981.

Invisible Woman: New and Selected Poems 1970–1982. Princeton, New Jersey, Ontario Review Press, 1982.

The Time Traveller: Poems 1983–1989. New York, Dutton, 1989.

Other

The Edge of Impossibility: Tragic Forms in Literature. New York, Vanguard Press, 1972; London, Gollancz, 1976.

The Hostile Sun: The Poetry of D. H. Lawrence. Los Angeles, Black Sparrow Press, 1973; Solihull, Warwickshire, Aquila, 1975.

New Heaven, New Earth: The Visionary Experience in Literature. New York, Vanguard Press, 1974; London, Gollancz, 1976.

Season of Peril. Santa Barbara, California, Black Sparrow Press, 1977.

The Stone Orchard. Northridge, California, Lord John Press, 1980.

Contraries: Essays. New York, Oxford University Press, 1981.

The Profane Art: Essays and Reviews. New York, Dutton, 1983.

Funland. Concord, New Hampshire, Ewert, 1983.

Luxury of Sin. Northridge, California, Lord John Press, 1984.

On Boxing, photographs by John Ranard. New York, Doubleday, and London, Bloomsbury, 1987.

(Woman) Writer: Occasions and Opportunities. New York, Dutton, 1988.

Editor, *Scenes from American Life: Contemporary Short Fiction*. New York, Vanguard Press, 1973.

Editor, with Shannon Ravenel, *The Best American Short Stories 1979*. Boston, Houghton Mifflin, 1979.

Editor, *Night Walks: A Bedside Companion*. Princeton, New Jersey, Ontario Review Press, 1982.

Editor, *First Person Singular: Writers on Their Craft*. Princeton, New Jersey, Ontario Review Press, 1983.

Editor, with Boyd Litzinger, *Story: Fictions Past and Present*. Lexington, Massachusetts, Heath, 1985.

Editor, with Daniel Halpern, *Reading the Fights* (on boxing). New York, Holt, 1988.

*

Bibliography: *Joyce Carol Oates: An Annotated Bibliography* by Francine Lercangée, New York, Garland, 1986.

Critical Studies: *The Tragic Vision of Joyce Carol Oates* by Mary Kathryn Grant, Durham, North Carolina, Duke University Press, 1978; *Joyce Carol Oates* by Joanne V. Creighton, Boston, Twayne, 1979; *Critical Essays on Joyce Carol Oates* edited by Linda W. Wagner, Boston, Hall, 1979; *Dreaming America: Obsession and Transcendence in the Fiction of Joyce Carol Oates* by G. F. Waller, Baton Rouge, Louisiana State University Press, 1979; *Joyce Carol Oates* by Ellen G. Friedman, New York, Ungar, 1980; *Joyce Carol Oates's Short Stories: Between Tradition and Innovation* by Katherine Bastian, Bern, Switzerland, Lang, 1983; *Isolation and Contact: A Study of Character Relationships in Joyce Carol Oates's Short Stories 1963–1980* by Torborg Norman, Gothenburg, Studies in English, 1984; *Joyce Carol Oates: Artist in Residence* by Eileen Teper Bender, Bloomington, Indiana University Press, 1987; *Understanding Joyce Carol Oates* by Greg Johnson, Columbia, University of South Carolina Press, 1987.

*   *   *

Joyce Carol Oates has said that every third or fourth story she writes is in the mode of Hawthrone, i.e., realism fading into allegory. While this seems a valid statement about most of her fiction, in the romance and historical narratives this modal shift is reversed. The majority of Oates's 19 novels and numerous volumes of short stories have been conceived and executed in a manner so reflective of life in the 20th-century United States that their psychohistorical focus is obscured and they are often wrongly categorized as realism or even naturalism. In contrast to this larger body of work, the three volumes which constitute Oates's romantic and historical fiction begin in the phantasmagoria of romance and mystery only to display in closure the realism of a significant part of American life, long ignored or denied by historiographers.

The historical works at present form a trilogy: *Bellefleur*, *A Bloodsmoor Romance*, and *Mysteries of Winterthurn*. A fourth novel, *The Crosswicks Horror* is forthcoming. *Bellefleur* utilizes epic conventions to present the history of a fantastic and yet paradigmatic family from the arrival of scion Jean Paul Bellefleur (a refugee from France) in the early days of the nation until the destruction of the castle-like Bellefleur manor and the dispersal of his descendants into mid-20th-century America. A genealogy provides dates for the three initial generations; then only blood relationships are indicated, time becoming vague and fluid although the present tense of the work begins with the conception of Germaine Bellefleur and ends on her fourth birthday. The setting is the Chautauqua region of south-western New York, the narrator a third person, omniscient and detached, moves freely between far past, near past, and present. Narrational method evokes in the reader a sense of the moral consequences of past evil, strongly suggestive of Faulkner's technique. Where epic conventions in *Bellefleur* include a beginning *in medias res*, catalogues (of the horses and cars the Bellefleur men have loved), and the descent of the Gods (in a 24-hour bout of diarrhea), their use points to the psychohistorical within the phantastic. Gothic conventions are equally significant to the narrative—a sinister cat, Mahalaleel, who fructifies Leah and Gideon Bellefleur's marriage; a spider who was Leah's familiar and had to be slain by Gideon before he could claim her; a colony of dwarfs; characters who can become animals; a lake beneath whose frozen surface humans are locked in mirror images of their lived lives; even the marriage of a servant girl to an English nobleman in a perfect Barbara Cartland-style wedding. But the bizarre mixture of conventions in this family history is best understood in the context of a metaphor created by the quilt,   "Celestial   Time-

piece," which Mathilde Bellefleur is making: her brother says that it is too complicated for the design to be seen unless one stands far back.

The generations of Bellefleurs are both representative of and products of their times and the novel is clearly a critical commentary on American history in the same mode as those of Oates's more immediately recognizable works of realism and psychohistory (*A Garden of Earthly Delights* and *Wonderland*). The great robber barons and monoplists of the 19th century are identifiable. Slavery, Indian policy, and expansionism are judged unrelentingly. But the final vision in *Bellefleur* is one consistent with the American character: the destruction of Bellefleur Manor with its suggestion of transplanting an European aristocracy ends the captivity of the children to patriarchal structures, freeing them to create a future for themselves in the American tradition of individualism.

A Bloodsmoor Romance traces the Kiddemaster and the Zinn families through the final 20 years of the 19th century in Pennsylvania, New York City, and the west, using the formal and stilted voice and the archaic diction of a maiden woman whose professed innocence of all things sexual is often at wonderful odds with the details she presents. The Fielding-like narrator gives warnings of dire consequences whenever one of the five young daughters of John Quincy and Prudence Kiddemaster Zinn contemplates unbecoming conduct—such as moving or crying out while her husband performs the "unitary" act; and she speculates that the Orlando-like sex exchange of the oldest Zinn daughter may have resulted from her riding split saddle and wearing trousers.

Employing the conventions of the conduct book as well as romance, Oates creates her first comic novel. Through it pass historical personages (Madame Blavatsky, Mark Twain, and others) exposed in all their human foolishness much as E. L. Doctorow had exposed them in *Ragtime*, a novel to which *Bloodsmoor* is related. Although replete with the trappings of romance—lost heirs, secret marriages, sinister noblemen, even a black balloon which spirits one of the Zinn sisters away—*Bloodsmoor*, like *Bellefleur*, is intent upon history. Here it is primarily the history of childhood in an upper-class family of excruciating propriety where everything physical is subordinated to the spiritual and everything childlike to the parental. The elder Zinns evoke memories of the Pontifax family in Butler's *The Way of All Flesh* although the altar upon which childish happiness is sacrificed is science rather than religion: John Quincy Zinn is the inventor of unworkable machines and of processes which he never bothers to patent until the government recognizes him as a national treasure and commissions his greatest invention, the electric chair.

Bloodsmoor is an intricate web of literary allusions, from Fanny Burney to Charlotte Bronte and beyond, including excerpts from a number of alleged women's magazines of the day. But invoking of literary tradition remains as ironic here as the generational structure was in *Bellefleur* for eventually all the Zinn daughters escape the rack of tradition symbolized by their tightly-laced corsets. Even their mother, who had willingly laid aside a career to become the angel in the house, leaves home to live with a college friend in a Manhattan women's hotel and march in the cause of Dress Reform.

The Mysteries of Winterthurn is a trilogy of novellas which use detective story conventions and gothic romance settings to reveal social and family structures similar to those laid bare in *Bellefleur* and *Bloodsmoor*. Set in the Chautauqua region during the end of the 19th and the beginning of the 20th centuries, the tales are unified by Detective Xavier Kilgarvan, an innocent descended from Twain's Pudd'nhead Wilson with touches of Poe's Dupin and the great figures of English and Continental detective fiction. The narrator is a first-person, detached figure who on one occasion refers to herself as the author, but on many others protests that as editor and collector only, her knowledge is limited. Like the two previous volumes, *Winterthurn* uses its conventions ironically, for the tales, like the novels, are about crimes against women, children, and the poor and the trilogy ends with the solution to the crime ignoring evidence quite clear to the careful reader.

Class is a major issue in *Winterthurn* and the first tale, "The Virgin in the Rose Bower," uses a *trompe l'oeil* wall scene as the metaphor for a horrifying incest pattern reminiscent of Faulkner's "A Rose for Emily." In the second tale, "Devil's Half Acre," the narrational voice becomes sharply sardonic, describing the lynching of a Jewish textile mill manager accused of ritual murder and the subsequent acquital of the confessed murderer because of his family connections. "The Bloodstained Bridal Gown" concerns Xavier Kilgarvan in the solving of a crime against the woman he has wanted since the first tale some 20 years earlier. It is Kilgarvan's last case since at its dubious conclusion, one in which the attentive reader fears that Xavier may be taking the real murderer home with him, Xavier turns from the ratiocinative approach to the mysteries of human personality which has isolated him from all humanity and resolves to cultivate his emotions. In his retreat from 20 years of dedication to achieving fame and fortune through discovery of a universal order, Kilgarvan reveals the ineffectuality of much 19th-century thought; thus once again, the conventions of a very narrow genre embrace the themes of mainstream realism.

—Rose Marie Burwell

* * *

O'BRIAN, Patrick. Address: c/o Collins, 8 Grafton Street, London W1X 3LA, England.

ROMANCE AND HISTORICAL PUBLICATIONS

Novels (series: Jack Aubrey and Stephen Maturin)

Three Bear Witness. London, Secker and Warburg, 1952; as *Testimonies*, New York, Harcourt Brace, 1952.
The Catalans. New York, Harcourt Brace, 1953; as *The Frozen Flame*, London, Hart Davis, 1953.
The Road to Samarcand. London, Hart Davis, 1954.
The Golden Ocean. London, Hart Davis, 1956; New York, Day, 1957; revised edition, London, Macmillan, 1970.
The Unknown Shore. London, Hart Davis, 1959.
Richard Temple. London, Macmillan, 1962.
Aubrey and Maturin series
  1. *Master and Commander.* Philadelphia, Lippincott, 1969; London, Collins, 1970.
  2. *Post Captain.* London, Collins, 1972.
  3. *H.M.S. Surprise.* London, Collins, and Philadelphia, Lippincott, 1973.
  4. *The Mauritius Command.* London, Collins, 1977; New York, Stein and Day, 1978.
  5. *Desolation Island.* London, Collins, 1978; New York, Stein and Day, 1979.
  6. *The Fortune of War.* London, Collins, 1979.
  7. *The Surgeon's Mate.* London, Collins, 1980.
  8. *The Ionian Mission.* London, Collins, 1981.
  9. *Treason's Harbour.* London, Collins, 1983.
 10. *The Far Side of the World.* London, Collins, 1984.

 11. *The Reverse of the Medal.* London, Collins, 1986.
 12. *The Letters of Marque.* London, Collins, 1988.

Short Stories

The Last Pool and Other Stories. London, Secker and Warburg, 1950.
The Walker and Other Stories. New York, Harcourt Brace, 1955; as *Lying in the Sun and Other Stories*, London, Hart Davis, 1956.
The Chian Wine and Other Stories. London, Collins, 1974.

OTHER PUBLICATIONS

Other

Men-of-War. London, Collins, 1974.
Pablo Ruiz Picasso: A Biography. London, Collins, 1976; as *Picasso: A Biography*, New York, Putnam, 1976.
Joseph Banks: A Life. London, Collins, 1987.

Editor, *A Book of Voyages.* London, Home and Van Thal, 1947.

Translator, *The Daily Life of the Aztecs on the Eve of the Spanish Conquest*, by Jacques Soustelle. London, Weidenfeld and Nicolson, 1961.
Translator, *Daily Life in Palestine at the Time of Christ*, by Daniel-Rops. London, Weidenfeld and Nicolson, 1962; as *Daily Life in the Time of Jesus*, New York, Hawthorn, 1962.
Translator, *St. Bartholemew's Night: The Massacre of Saint Bartholemew*, by Philippe Erlanger. London, Weidenfeld and Nicolson, and New York, Pantheon, 1962.
Translator, *The Wreathed Head*, by Christine de Rivoyre. London, Hart Davis, 1962.
Translator, *From the New Freedom to the New Frontier: A History of the United States from 1912 to the Present*, by André Maurois. New York, McKay; as *A History of the U.S.A.: From Wilson to Kennedy*, London, Weidenfeld and Nicolson, 1964.
Translator, *A History of the USSR: From Lenin to Kruschchev*, by Louis Aragon. London, Weidenfeld and Nicolson, and New York, McKay, 1964.
Translator, *A Letter to Myself*, by Françoise Mallet-Joris. London, W. H. Allen, and New York, Farrar Straus, 1964.
Translator, *When the Earth Trembles*, by Haroun Tazieff. London, Hart Davis, and New York, Harcourt Brace, 1964.
Translator, *Munich; or, The Phoney Peace*, by Henri Noguères. London, Weidenfeld and Nicolson, 1965; as *Munich: Peace in Our Time*, New York, McGraw Hill, 1965.
Translator, *The Uncompromising Heart: A Life of Marie Mancini, Louis XIV's First Love*, by Françoise Mallet-Joris. London, W. H. Allen, and New York, Farrar Straus, 1966.
Translator, *A Very Easy Death*, by Simone de Beauvoir. London, Deutsch-Weidenfeld and Nicolson, and New York, Putnam, 1966.
Translator, *The Delights of Growing Old*, by Maurice Goudeket. New York, Farrar Straus, 1966; London, Joseph, 1967.
Translator, *The Italian Campaign*, by Michel Mohrt. London, Weidenfeld and Nicolson, and New York, Viking Press, 1967.
Translator, *Memoirs*, by Clara Malraux. London, Bodley Head, and New York, Farrar Straus, 1967.
Translator, *The Quicksand War: Prelude to Vietnam*, by Lucien Bodard. Boston, Little Brown, and London, Faber, 1967.
Translator, *The Horsemen*, by Joseph Kessel. London, Barker, and New York, Farrar Straus, 1968.

Translator, *Les Belles Images*, by Simone de Beauvoir. London, Collins, and New York, Putnam, 1968.

Translator, *Louis XVI; or, The End of a World*, by Bernard Faÿ. London, W. H. Allen, and Chicago, Regnery, 1968.

Translator, *The Woman Destroyed*, by Simone de Beauvoir. London, Collins, and New York, Putnam, 1969.

Translator, *The Japanese Challenge*, by Robert Guillian. Philadelphia, Lippincott, and London, Hamish Hamilton, 1970.

Translator, *A Life's Full Summer*, by André Martinerie. London, Collins, and New York, Harcourt Brace, 1970.

Translator, *Papillon*, by Henri Charrière. London, Hart Davis, 1970.

Translator, *Old Age*, by Simone de Beauvoir. London, Deutsch-Weidenfeld and Nicolson, 1972; as *The Coming of Age*, New York, Putnam, 1972.

Translator, *The Assassination of Heydrich: 27 May 1942*, by Miroslav Ivanov. London, Hart Davis, 1973.

Translator, *Banco: Further Adventures of Papillon*, by Henri Charrière. London, Hart Davis, and New York, Morrow, 1973.

Translator, *All Said and Done*, by Simone de Beauvoir. London, Deutsch-Weidenfeld and Nicolson, and New York, Putnam, 1974.

Translator, *The Paths of the Sea*, by Pierre Schoendoerffer. London, Collins, 1977.

Translator, *Obsession: An American Love Story*, by Yves Berger. New York, Putnam, 1978.

Translator, *When Things of the Spirit Come First: Five Early Tales*, by Simone de Beauvoir. London, Deutsch-Weidenfeld and Nicolson, and New York, Pantheon, 1982.

Translator, *Adieux: A Farewell to Sartre*, by Simone de Beauvoir. London, Deutsch-Weidenfeld and Nicolson, and New York, Pantheon, 1984.

*

Bibliography: *Patrick O'Brian: A Bibliography of First Printings and First British Printings* by A. E. Cunningham, York, Thrommett, 1986.

*   *   *

There are many writers who have chosen as their period the 18th and early 19th centuries, and the naval wars with France resulting from the Revolution and the imperial ambitions of Napoleon Bonaparte. It was an age full of event, and gives writers scope for plenty of action. Of all the writers who have worked in this field, perhaps the most outstanding is Patrick O'Brian.

O'Brian's early stories, *The Golden Ocean* and *The Unknown Shore*, although originally written for children, are long, full-fledged novels which can be enjoyed without a qualm by adults. They are both about the voyage Anson made round the world beginning in 1740—*The Golden Ocean*, set aboard the *Centurion*, has as a background the taking of Spanish treasure fleet in the Pacific and Anson's successful circumnavigation. *The Unknown Shore*, set aboard the *Wager*, is a darker book altogether, dealing as it does with the *Wager*'s shipwreck and the fearful problems of survival on the bleak and inhospitable coast of southern Chile.

The Unknown Shore is of particular interest, because the two chief characters are a prototype for another pair of friends. Jack Byron and Tobias Barrow, midshipman and surgeon's mate, might be in embryo the more developed and more colourful friends Jack Aubrey and Stephen Maturin from the long series of novels set during the Napoleonic wars.

One can begin to see in *The Unknown Shore* some of the problems facing any historical novelist. If one writes of a real historical character, how far can one mould history to make the story acceptable in fictional terms? And if one writes of an invented character, how far can that character intrude upon recorded history? The midshipman Jack Byron falls into the first category. "Foulweather" Jack Byron ended up as an admiral, and was the poet Byron's grandfather. His early adventures make thrilling reading, but clearly there was not enough latitude in his later career to write in a fictionalized form about him—and O'Brian is too honest a writer to invent adventures for an historical personage.

O'Brian faces the opposite problem with Jack Aubrey. Jack's exploits bear more than a passing resemblance to the real-life actions of Lord Cochrane (later Earl of Dundonald). For example, in the first book, *Master and Commander*, Jack takes his 14-gun *Sophie* into action against the 32-gun Spanish xebec-frigate *Cacafuego* and wins—just as Cochrane captured the *Gamo* with his *Speedy*. However, with a fictitious character there is plenty of opportunity for plots and situations that never came the way of Cochrane, as Jack Aubrey's unfolding story discloses. There remain other problems, for example promotion. Can the author promote his hero to high rank, when it is perfectly well-known to any student of the period that no naval officer of Aubrey's name achieved flag rank? O'Brian has in fact solved this by a very neat device in his two latest novels, *The Reverse of the Medal* and *The Letters of Marque*. Jack, ejected from the navy through no fault of his own, can be brought back into the fold (and his many admirers profoundly hope he will be) but will have to face considerable loss of seniority. This is a much more sensitive approach to a perennial problem than simply allowing him to be promoted to the highest rank, as has happened to some other fictional naval heroes.

Stephen Maturin, Jack's close friend, is a remarkable creation. He may have his antecedents in Tobias Barrow, a dedicated natural philosopher brought up on a unique educational principle, but he far surpasses Tobias. Stephen is a physician (rare enough by land, exceptional at sea), a man of wide interests, well-read, cultured, and highly intelligent. His work as a naval surgeon is fascinating, his work as an intelligence agent adds an extra dimension to the plots, for we see not only the tension and danger of that important, lonely profession, but also the political in-fighting and bungling of the vying intelligence services in Whitehall and overseas. Stephen is, however, an outsider in naval matters—at least insofar as they involve actually sailing ships. His attempts to enlighten himself allow us, the readers, to discover what is going on—a simple but effective way of explaining some notoriously obscure activities!

Stephen is at home on land as Jack is not, and one of the most interesting features of the books is the changing balance of the relationship between the two men from sea to shore. At sea Jack is in his element: he is knowledgable, competent, and absolutely to be trusted. On land he is gullible and vulnerable, and it is usually Stephen who rescues him from his troubles, whether emotional entanglement, debt, projectors, or political manoeuvrings.

The friendship between the two is a fascinating relationship between complete opposites: it is made the more believable because it is often strained. This is most clearly seen when they both contend for Diana Villiers in *Post Captain*. Jack draws off and finally marries his first love, Diana Villiers's cousin Sophie Williams, but Diana remains as a sensitive area between them, for Stephen remains devoted to her. Diana Villiers's tendency to bolt to different parts of the world with rich young men is perhaps one of the weaknesses of the books. One can sympathize with her actions to a degree, but she is presented as being a rather more intelligent woman than her actions suggest. The reader becomes aware of a certain tedium when she disappears for the third time.

There is also a slowing of pace in two of the later novels, *The Far Side of the World* and *The Reverse of the Medal*. This may be partly explained by the fact that O'Brian has had a problem with historical chronology. All the stories to this point have fitted into a timescale that accords with actual history. With a series that started in 1801, how can the stories be continued when the Napoleonic war is drawing to a close? Some writers would ignore the problem (some might not even realize that it was a problem!). After what was obviously a considerable internal debate, O'Brian has given us a resolution—a delightful note to explain that extra time will be introduced in the form of hypothetical years "an 1812(a) as it were or even an 1812(b)."

The Reverse of the Medal is the saddest of the novels, ending in pain and disgrace for Jack which are almost tangible. The continuing pain is apparent in *The Letters of Marque*, but Jack's low tide has obviously passed, and the whole tone of the book is much more cheerful and forward-looking.

O'Brian is an extremely intelligent and well-informed writer, who expects his readers to be intelligent in return. His stories embrace broad sweeps of canvas, very richly detailed. One incident from him might form the entire plot of another author's book. Even his minor characters come over as full personalities. His understanding of 18th-century speech is another factor in his ability to bring this period so vividly to life. He is familiar with the smallest details of the construction and sailing methods of ships of the period, but is also at home in many other areas, including literature, natural history, medicine, philosophy, politics, law, and the classics. To this erudition he adds considerable humour, which adds a witty sprightliness and charm to his writing that makes it extremely attractive.

For the best possible picture of Nelson's navy, and of the world of the early 19th century, one would unhestitatingly recommend O'Brian's books; they can, of course, be read individually, but to start with the first (*Master and Commander*) and to read through the sequence is a superb and unforgettable experience.

—Felicity Trotman

OGILVIE, Elisabeth (May). American. Born 20 May 1917. Educated at North Quincy High School, Massachusetts. Lives in Cushing, Maine. Agent: Watkins/Loomis Agency, 150 East 35th Street, New York, New York 10016. Address: c/o McGraw-Hill Book Company, 1221 Avenue of the Americas, New York, New York 10020, U.S.A.

ROMANCE AND HISTORICAL PUBLICATIONS

Novels (series: Jennie)

High Tide at Noon. New York, Crowell, 1944; London, Harrap, 1945.
Storm Tide. New York, McGraw Hill, 1945; London, Harrap, 1947.
Honeymoon (novelization of screenplay). New York, Bartholomew House, 1947.
The Ebbing Tide. New York, Crowell, 1947; London, Harrap, 1948.

Rowan Head. New York, McGraw Hill, 1949; London, Harrap, 1950.
The Dawning of the Day. New York, McGraw Hill, 1954.
No Evil Angel. New York, McGraw Hill, 1956; London, Harrap, 1957.
The Witch Door. New York, McGraw Hill, 1959; London, W. H. Allen, 1961.
Call Home the Heart. New York, McGraw Hill, 1962.
There May Be Heaven. New York, McGraw Hill, 1966.
The Seasons Hereafter. New York, McGraw Hill, 1966.
Waters on a Starry Night. New York, McGraw Hill, 1968.
Bellwood. New York, McGraw Hill, 1969.
The Face of Innocence. New York, McGraw Hill, 1970.
A Theme for Reason. New York, McGraw Hill, 1970.
Weep and Know Why. New York, McGraw Hill, 1972.
Strawberries in the Sea. New York, McGraw Hill, 1973.
Image of a Lover. New York, McGraw Hill, 1974.
Where the Lost Aprils Are. New York, McGraw Hill, 1975.
The Dreaming Swimmer. New York, McGraw Hill, 1976.
An Answer in the Tide. New York, McGraw Hill, 1978.
A Dancer in Yellow. New York, McGraw Hill, 1979.
The Devil in Tartan. New York, McGraw Hill, 1980.
The Silent Ones. New York, McGraw Hill, 1981; Bath, Chivers, 1983.
The Road to Nowhere. New York, McGraw Hill, 1983.
Jennie about to Be. New York, McGraw Hill, 1984.
The World of Jennie G. New York, McGraw Hill, 1986.
The Summer of the Osprey. New York, McGraw Hill, 1987.
When the Music Stopped. New York, McGraw Hill, 1989.

OTHER PUBLICATIONS

Other (for children)

My World Is an Island (for adults; reminiscences). New York, McGraw Hill, 1950; London, Harrap, 1951.
Whistle for a Wind: Maine 1820. New York, Scribner, 1954.
Blueberry Summer. New York, McGraw Hill, 1956.
The Fabulous Year. New York, McGraw Hill, 1958.
How Wide the Heart. New York, McGraw Hill, 1959.
The Young Islanders. New York, McGraw Hill, 1960.
Becky's Island. New York, McGraw Hill, 1961.
Turn Around Twice. New York, McGraw Hill, 1962; as *Mystery on Hopkins Island*, 1966.
Ceiling of Amber. New York, McGraw Hill, 1964.
Masquerade at Sea House. New York, McGraw Hill, 1965.
The Pigeon Pair. New York, McGraw Hill, 1967.
Come Aboard and Bring Your Dory. New York, McGraw Hill, 1969; as *Nobody's Knows about Tomorrow*, London, Heinemann, 1971.
Too Young to Know. London, Hippo, 1983.

* * *

Elisabeth Ogilvie is a writer in love with landscape. Her passion has been primarily directed toward the coastal islands of Maine, although she has extended it to England and to her ancestral home of Scotland in her recent works. Her descriptions of the physical surroundings of her novels are so detailed and portrait-like that the setting almost becomes another character. By the final chapter of each of her books one is so minutely acquainted with every mood and view of the environment that one could be transported to that place and never feel lost. This sensitivity to scene gives these novels an immediacy and reality not often found in romantic novels today.

It is easy to call Ogilvie's works romantic novels; it is not easy to characterize them more specifically as each of her many works is different. Some, like *The Devil in Tartan*, could be classified as gothics, while others, like *A Dancer in Yellow*, are nearly pure suspense. Many of her books are not classifiable beyond the feeling that a thread of romance binds the plot together. Her plots are rich and complex but at the same time easy for the reader to follow. The characters are as vivid as the settings. One feels that these people have lives apart from the span of time covered in the book, that the novel is merely a fascinating slice of a larger life. This feeling is reinforced by the author's ability to use the same characters in a later work as is the case with *Weep and Know Why*, *The Dreaming Swimmer*, and *Summer of the Osprey*. She repeats this success with her historical novels *Jennie About to Be* and *The World of Jennie G*. The successive works might be called sequels, but they are stronger than mere sequels with none of the flavor of afterthought. Ogilvie is an author who observes and notices; her eye for detail is unerring. For this reason, she is skilled at evoking sudden menace in everyday situations. In such works as *Summer of the Osprey* and *The Road to Nowhere* the secrets that people try to keep and the failure of communication between even the closest people show how life can suddenly change for worse as well as for better.

Even Ogilvie's use of the elements of romance cannot be described in general terms. Often her books conclude at a point that may be the germination of a romantic relationship rather than its culmination. She has also chosen, in the series beginning with *Weep and Know Why*, to follow a romance from earliest courtship through comfortable married life. Yet there is no emphasis here on happy endings, nor does culmination automatically bring happiness. Her characters must work hard to make their relationships work; sometimes the relationships are not of their own choosing (as in the Jennie books) but are expedient for one reason or another.

If there is an area of consistency in these novels it is in the characters of the heroes. Ogilvie seems to admire the taciturn, unemotional male who is deeply sensitive beneath a terse exterior. This is not to say that these men lack individuality or realism. Rather it seems that the writer began with a general type and fleshed him out to meet the demands of the story. These men are consistent with their stations in life. Ogilvie does not focus on people of glamour, so sophistication and wit would be jarring characteristics to find in her heroes. Instead, they are workers and survivors, men to lean on. If the heroines do not lean on them very often it is because they are formed by the same forces that shaped their men. They must be strong rather than clinging to survive.

Perhaps the strongest appeal to the reader in Ogilvie's work is the ordinariness of her characters. Even the pseudo-Egyptian princess of *The Face of Innocence* is a normal girl grown into an unremarkable wife and mother. It is the sudden twistings and rearranging of the common events of life that give rise to the plots. One can identify with these everyday people as they deal with upheavals that may be frightening but are also somehow familiar.

—Susan Quinn Berneis

O'GRADY, Rohan. Pseudonym for June O'Grady Skinner; also writes as A. Carleon. Canadian. Born in Vancouver, British Columbia, 23 July 1922. Married Frederick Snowden Skinner in 1948; three children. Newspaper librarian, then freelance writer. Agent: Fox Chase Agency, The Public Ledger Building, Room 930, Independence Square, Philadelphia, Pennsylvania 19016, U.S.A. Address: 2373 Marine Drive, West Vancouver, British Columbia, V7V 1K9, Canada.

ROMANCE AND HISTORICAL PUBLICATIONS

Novels

O'Houlihan's Jest: A Lament for the Irish. New York, Macmillan, and London, Gollancz, 1961.
Pippin's Journal: or, Rosemary for Remembrance. New York, Macmillan, 1962; London, Gollancz, 1963; as *Master of Montrolfe Hall*, New York, Ace, 1965; as *The Curse of the Montrolfes*, Sag Harbor, New York, Second Chance Press, 1983.
Let's Kill Uncle. New York, Macmillan, 1963; London, Longman, 1964.
Bleak November. New York, Dial Press, 1970; London, Joseph, 1971.
The May Spoon (as A. Carleon). New York, Beaufort, 1981.

*

Rohan O'Grady comments:

Each of my books is entirely different. I cannot write to a formula. When an idea comes to me, I am caught up in its web, and am captive of my characters until the last thread is unwound.

*　　*　　*

Rohan O'Grady is never predictable and is always intriguing. Each of her books is unique in its depiction of external horrors with internal manifestations.

Her first novel *O'Houlihan's Jest*, is an Irish historical fantasy, out of time and out of reality, a myth of the collision of an Irish hero and rebel leader, descended from pagan kings, and a Cromwellian-type Englishman, "The Man." The tale waxes poetic eulogizing the virtues of the Irish, despite their squalid daily lives, and denigrating the English as barbaric butchers who set men afire with caps of pitch, gang rape idiot maidens, and hang women and children from trees by their hair. The final encounter between the murdered Irish hero and his vicious opponent is steeped in Irish magic and the horrid power of ancient gods that transform the quick and the dead with chilling effect.

Pippin's Journal, her most popular work, recently reissued as *The Curse of the Montrolfes*, spans several generations, with the sins of the great-grandfather inflicted upon the sons in greater and greater degree. It begins with the first-person narrative of the modern, reclusive Montrolfe, a nuclear scientist, who is strangely cursed with club feet and a hunched back, and who inherits a chiding ancient housekeeper, a decaying ancestral manor, and a vengeful, ghostly enchantress. Then it switches to the diary of the once beautiful, innocent girl who now tempts, beguiles, and destroys the descendants of the cynical, enigmatic Montrolfe who won her love and took her life. This section is a psychological study of a devious womanizer and murderer through the eyes of the young girl he beguiled. Next follows the diary of her guilt-ridden father, a minister seeking to atone for his sexual lapse, then the transcript of the trial of a falsely condemned yeoman, and finally the report of the modern confrontation of the ancestors of the past triangle: murderer, victim, and falsely accused. The main part of the book is the story of the strange relationship between victim and victimizer, her beguiling tricks to keep his favor, and the miscarriage of justice in punishing her supposed murderer. This book is the modern Montrolfe's atonement for his ancestor's crimes. It involves buried treasure, a riddle, a ghostly gothic house, direct and indirect murder, revenge, reincarnation, a curse fulfilled in physical deformity and madness, second sight, and expiation.

The May Spoon is another study of a precocious adolescent, young Isabel McMurry, alias Anna Carleon, who, in a manner reminiscent of J. D. Salinger's Holden Caulfield, recounts her coming of age. An eccentric and caustic father, a reclusive mother, who has never recovered from her son dying in Vietnam, fighting for the Viet Cong, and an all too intelligent older sister make life difficult for Isabel as she seeks a personal identity and an understanding of adulthood, with its love and its human obligations.

Let's Kill Uncle is an exciting story of two children who plot the murder of an ex-Commando "Uncle," a cold-blooded killer whose favorite author is the Marquis de Sade and whose past acts have been to eliminate the heirs to the family fortune—ten million dollars. Using hypnotic suggestion, the "uncle" has turned the young boy into a compulsive hooligan and liar to reduce his credibility and to make him more vulnerable to a future "accident." Nonetheless, friendly islanders, a tough but kindly Canadian Mountie, and an aging cougar the children befriend give them the courage to anticipate and thwart his acts of terror and death.

Bleak November seems to be the story of a splendid mansion, intentionally aged to hide its chilling past—the scene of multiple murders, a berserk father slaughtering his children. The house itself takes on an aura of horror, frightening and changing its tenants, who gradually glimpse its secrets and learn their previously unrealized ties to its past. There is a demon dog, a failed séance to exorcise ghosts, and psychic manifestations of dead children who fill the days and afflict the nights. Finally reality becomes confused and, in an effective twist, the book becomes less a study of a haunted house than of a neurotic, possibly psychotic, narrator.

It is their close characterization and their unexpected final twists that make O'Grady's works memorable.

—Gina Macdonald

OLDFIELD, Pamela. Born in London, in 1931. Has one son and one daughter. Has worked as a teacher and secretary. Lives in Kent. Address: c/o Century Hutchinson, 62–65 Chandos Place, London WC2N 4NW, England.

ROMANCE AND HISTORICAL PUBLICATIONS

Novels (series: Heron Saga; Kent trilogy)

Heron Saga
  The Rich Earth. London, Futura, 1980.
  This Ravished Land. London, Futura, 1980.
  After the Storm. London, Futura, 1981.
  White Water. London, Futura, 1982.
Kent trilogy
  Green Harvest. London, Century Hutchinson, 1983.
  Summer Song. London, Century Hutchinson, 1984.
  Golden Tally. London, Century Hutchinson, 1985.
The Gooding Girl. London, Century Hutchinson, 1985.
The Stationmaster's Daughter. London, Century Hutchinson, 1986.
Lily Golightly. London, Century Hutchinson, 1987.

Turn of the Tide. London, Century Hutchinson, 1988.
A Dutiful Wife. London, Joseph, 1989.

OTHER PUBLICATIONS (for children)

Other

Melanie Brown Goes to School. London, Faber, 1970.
Melanie Brown Climbs a Tree. London, Faber, 1972.
Melanie Brown and the Jar of Sweets. London, Faber, 1974.
The Halloween Pumpkin. London, Hodder and Stoughton, 1974; Chicago, Children's Press, 1976.
The Adventures of Sarah and Theodore Bodgitt. Leicester, Brockhampton Press, 1974.
Simon's Extra Gran. London, Knight, 1974; Chicago, Children's Press, 1976.
A Witch in the Summer House. London, Hodder and Stoughton, 1976.
The Terribly Plain Princess and Other Stories. London, Hodder and Stoughton, 1977.
The Adventures of the Gumby Gang. London, Blackie, 1978.
The Gumby Gang Again. London, Blackie, 1978.
Katy and Dom. Brighton, Angus and Robertson, 1978.
Children of the Plague. London, Hamish Hamilton, 1979.
More About the Gumby Gang. London, Blackie, 1979.
The Princess May-I-Well. London, Hodder and Stoughton, 1979.
The Gumby Gang Strikes Again. London, Blackie, 1980.
The Rising of the Wain. London, Abelard, 1980.
The Riverside Cat. London, Hamish Hamilton, 1980.
Cloppity. London, Hamish Hamilton, 1981.
The Willerbys and the Burglar [*Haunted Mill, Old Castle, Sad Clown, Bank Robbers, Mystery Man*]. London, Blackie, 6 vols., 1981–84.
Parkin's Storm. London, Abelard, 1982.
The Gumby Gang on Holiday. London, Blackie, 1983.
Tommy Dobbie and the Witch-Next-Door. London, Hodder and Stoughton, 1983.
Ghost Stories. London, Blackie, 1984.
Barnaby Bell and the Lost Button. London, Piccadilly, 1985.
Barnaby Bell and the Birthday Cake. London, Piccadilly, 1985.
The Christmas Ghost. London, Blackie, 1985.
Ginger's Nine Lives. London, Blackie, 1986.
The Return of the Gumby Gang. London, Blackie, 1986.
Toby and the Donkey. London, Methuen, 1986.
The Ghosts of Bellering Oast. London, Blackie, 1987.
Spine Chillers. London, Blackie, 1987.
Stories from Ancient Greece. London, Kingfisher, 1988.
Sam, Sue and Cinderella. London, Methuen, 1989.
Bomb Alert. London, Armada, 1989.
Secret Persuader. London, Armada, 1989.

Editor, *Helter Skelter: Stories for Six-Year-Olds.* London, Blackie, 1983.
Editor, *Hurdy Gurdy.* London, Blackie, 1984; as *Merry-Go-Round: Stories for Seven-Year-Olds*, Sevenoaks, Kent, Knight, 1985.
Editor, *Roller Coaster.* London, Blackie, 1986.

*   *   *

The novels of Pamela Oldfield inhabit a world midway between historical fiction and family saga. In most of her works, the Tudor or Edwardian setting and the often precise chronology are far outweighed by such gothic elements as inheritance and scandal, illicit passion, and violent death. Oldfield fixes on individual lives, sketching in the movement of history behind them. Her first important novel-sequence—*The Rich Earth*, *This Ravished Land*, *After the Storm*, and *White Water*—has been collectively titled The Heron Saga. Although these novels cover the period from Henry VII's accession to Elizabeth I's war with Spain, the Heron Saga is far from being a portrayal of the Tudor age; rather, it chronicles four successive generations of the Kendal family, owners of the Heron estate and its tin-mining concerns in Devonshire, recounting their lives, their loves and deaths. Drama and tragedy stalk through the work, with the various protagonists dogged by witchcraft, madness, murder, and guilt. Historic events—the Dissolution of the Monasteries, the sinking of the *Mary Rose*—impinge fleetingly on the story, but are secondary to the fortunes of the Kendals throughout. The Heron Saga is a fast-moving, exciting sequence of novels which are best judged not as historical works, but as excellent examples of their own particular hybrid genre.

The trilogy of novels set in the hopfields of turn-of-the-century Kent—*Green Harvest*, *Summer Song*, and *Golden Tally*—marks a substantial advance on the Heron Saga in every respect. Charting the rise of her heroine, Vinnie Harris, from a childhood in the Whitechapel slums to wealth and happiness as mistress of the Foxearth estate, Oldfield achieves greater depth of characterization and captures the sense of the period more effectively than in previous works. Personalities rather than events remain in the foreground, but the social atmosphere of the 1890's and 1900's is presented with conviction, and there are some fine descriptive scenes. Though melodramatic incidents occur, their frequency is less than in the Heron Saga, and is more than balanced by the periods of domestic routine. While there are a number of fortuitous deaths, and at times an overabundance of minor characters and subplots, the Kent trilogy brings the people and their age memorably to life, and must be counted as one of Oldfield's finest achievements.

The Stationmaster's Daughter and *The Gooding Girl*, set in Kent in the early part of the 20th century, once more combine an authentic recreation of their period with the gothic drama of scandal and inheritance. The former describes the emergence of Amy Turner, daughter of the stationmaster in remote country district, as a fulfilled individual and a successful writer, and incorporates the customary lust, suicide, and violent death. *The Gooding Girl*, the most modern of Oldfield's novels in that it covers the first three decades of this century, is the story of Julia Coulsden, heiress of a fishing business, and evokes a picture of life in the Kentish fishing towns of the period. Though perhaps overlong, both novels succeed on their own terms, and manage an effective blend of drama and domesticity.

Lily Golightly tells the story of a parson's daughter who follows her husband to the goldfields of California in 1849. The rigours of her journey with a wagon train across the wilds of America is ably described by the author, who creates a strong, interesting narrative and a group of living characters with whom the reader identifies at once. *Lily Golightly* is perhaps the most impressive of Oldfield's works to date, and once more emphasizes the ironic fact that her sense of history is most convincing in those works nearest to our own time.

—Geoffrey Sadler

OMAN, Carola (Mary Anima). British. Born in Oxford, 11 May 1897; daughter of the historian Sir Charles Oman. Educated at Wychwood School, Oxford. Served in the British Red

Cross Service, 1916–19 and 1938–58 (President, Hertfordshire Branch, 1947–58). Married Sir Gerald Lenanton in 1922 (died 1952). Recipient (for biography): *Sunday Times* prize, 1947; James Tait Black Memorial prize, 1954. Fellow, Royal Historical Society, Society of Antiquaries, and Royal Society of Literature. C.B.E. (Commander, Order of the British Empire), 1957. *Died 11 June 1978.*

ROMANCE AND HISTORICAL PUBLICATIONS

Novels

Princess Amelia. London, Unwin, and New York, Duffield, 1924.
The Road Royal. London, Unwin, and New York, Duffield, 1924.
King Heart. London, Unwin, 1926.
Mrs. Newdigate's Window (as C. Lenanton). London, Unwin, and New York, Appleton, 1927.
The Holiday (as C. Lenanton). London, Unwin, and New York, Appleton, 1928.
Crouchback. London, Hodder and Stoughton, and New York, Holt, 1929.
Miss Barrett's Elopement (as C. Lenanton). London, Hodder and Stoughton, 1929; New York, Holt, 1930.
Fair Stood the Wind . . . (as C. Lenanton). London, Hodder and Stoughton, 1930.
Major Grant. London, Hodder and Stoughton, 1931; New York, Holt, 1932.
The Empress. London, Hodder and Stoughton, and New York, Holt, 1932.
The Best of His Family. London, Hodder and Stoughton, 1933.
Over the Water. London, Hodder and Stoughton, 1935.
Nothing to Report. London, Hodder and Stoughton, 1940.

OTHER PUBLICATIONS

Verse

The Menin Road and Other Poems. London, Hodder and Stoughton, 1919.

Other

Prince Charles Edward. London, Duckworth, 1935.
Henrietta Maria. London, Hodder and Stoughton, and New York, Macmillan, 1936.
Elizabeth of Bohemia. London, Hodder and Stoughton, 1938; revised edition, 1964.
Britain Against Napoleon. London, Faber, 1942; as *Napoleon at the Channel*, New York, Doubleday, 1942.
Somewhere in England. London, Hodder and Stoughton, 1943.
Nelson. New York, Doubleday, 1946; London, Hodder and Stoughton, 1947.
Sir John Moore. London, Hodder and Stoughton, 1953.
Lord Nelson. London, Collins, 1954; Hamden, Connecticut, Archon, 1968.
David Garrick. London, Hodder and Stoughton, 1958.
Mary of Modena. London, Hodder and Stoughton, 1962.
Ayot Rectory (biography of Mary Sneade Brown). London, Hodder and Stoughton, 1965.
Napoleon's Viceroy: Eugéne de Beauharnais. London, Hodder and Stoughton, 1966; New York, Funk and Wagnalls, 1968.

The Gascoyne Heiress: The Life and Diaries of Frances Mary Gascoyne-Cecil 1802–1839. London, Hodder and Stoughton, 1968.
The Wizard of the North: The Life of Sir Walter Scott. London, Hodder and Stoughton, 1973.
An Oxford Childhood (autobiography). London, Hodder and Stoughton, 1976.

Other (for children)

Ferry the Fearless. London, Pitman, 1936.
Johel. London, Pitman, 1937.
Robin Hood, The Prince of Outlaws: A Tale of the Fourteenth Century from the Lytell Geste. London, Dent, and New York, Dutton, 1937.
Alfred, King of the English. London, Dent, 1939; New York, Dutton, 1940.
Baltic Spy. London, Pitman, 1940.

*   *   *

Carola Oman was a distinguished historian and writer of children's books. Her historical novels are intelligent and meticulously researched as one would expect from an emminent biographer. Although Oman wrote mainly in the 1920's and 1930's, her style is nevertheless contemporary and her novels stand out as classic examples of the genre.

Oman's scholarly approach and fastidious research of historical fact gives her work weight and import without ever becoming patronising or didactic. Her knowledge of history is widespread and her description of all aspects of life, from books to weapons, food and clothes coupled with an acute geographical awareness of the constantly shifting territorial balance inherent in the past, serves to create a cohesive view of life in other countries. Indeed this authenticity underlines the substance of Oman's novels.

Oman does not however allow her books to slip into mere reportage of past events, despite the wealth of detail contained in her novels. She brings colour to her books through her vivid characters. These characters, many of whom are famous historical figures, are given life and vitality—they were after all only human. Thus she endows her protagonists with emotional qualities that are both recognisable and credible. Oman's lively approach sustains interest and adds drama to what are, generally, well known historical events.

The Best of His Family deals with the life of William Shakespeare in a scholarly, yet palatable manner. Shakespeare's early life, as a boy in Stratford is portrayed vividly. Shakespeare watches as his father turns from a fairly successful tradesman into an impoverished debtor, and his mother a gentlewoman of good birth transforms into a hard working shrew. Oman's treatment of Anne, Shakespeare's wife, is unusually down to earth and honest. Forced into an early marriage, for having got Anne (10 years his senior) with child, William is saddled with a wife who is "beautiful lank and mawkish." She is shown as a woman who neglects both the household and their three children, and is ultimately unfaithful to her husband. The portrayal of Shakespeare is equally direct. In his late teens he is a broken man: he drinks too much, poaches, and earns little as a shopkeeper. Oman tells the story of his transformation from a man with little talent except a small skill for mimicry, into England's most revered playwright, with such poignancy. Other well known historical personages do not receive so much compassion; Queen Elizabeth is depicted as a mean, jealous woman with a maniacal temper, and Sir Walter Raleigh is shown as an egotistical ill-mannered adventurer. The novel is liberally sprinkled with references and often direct quotes from Shakespeare's plays. Occasionally this is a little heavy-handed, especially in the case of Jugge's wife's nurse, who has the same character as the nurse in *Romeo and Juliet* and recites lines from the play with her own dialogue.

Crouchback is set in the 15th century and traces the story of Richard III, from long before his accession to the throne to after his death. The main protagonist is Anne, Richard's cousin. As a child Anne is frightened by the rumours of her cousin's strange deformity, and is surprised to discover that he is a wise young man with whom she has a great affinity. The dramatic struggle for the English throne is described in detail throughout the novel and the continual battle scenes are vividly and accurately portrayed yet it is the story of Anne that takes precedence. Anne's fascination for her odd cousin is forcibly curtailled when she is married to the Prince of Wales. After his death in battle, Anne is forced into hiding and works as a kitchen maid for two years until Richard eventually finds and marries her. Oman's treatment of this story is again a reminder that at the centre of great historical events lie individuals with the same emotions and moods that we ourselves possess.

Oman's novels are informative and immensely readable—a balance which some authors find hard to maintain.

—Jane K. Thompson

ONIONS, (George) Oliver. British. Born in Bradford, Yorkshire, in 1873. Educated at National Art Training School (now Royal College of Art), London, 1894–97. Married Berta Ruck, *q.v.,* in 1909; two sons. Editor, *Le Quartier Latin,* Paris, 1897; had various jobs including book illustrator, poster designer, draughtsman and war artist during the Boer War. Recipient: James Tait Black Memorial prize, 1947. *Died 9 April 1961.*

ROMANCE AND HISTORICAL PUBLICATIONS

Novels

The Story of Ragged Robyn. London, Joseph, 1945.
Poor Man's Tapestry. London, Joseph, 1946.
Arras of Youth. London, Joseph, 1949.
A Penny for the Harp. London, Joseph, 1952.

OTHER PUBLICATIONS

Novels

The Compleat Bachelor. London, Murray, 1900; New York, Stokes, 1901.
The Odd-Job Man. London, Murray, 1903.
The Drakestone. London, Hurst and Blackett, 1906.
Pedlar's Pack. London, Nash, 1908.
Little Devil Doubt. London, Murray, 1909.
The Exception. London, Methuen, 1910; New York, Lane, 1911.
Good Boy Seldom: A Romance of Advertisement. London, Methuen, 1911.
In Accordance with the Evidence. London, Secker, 1912; New York, Doran, 1913.
The Debit Account. London, Secker, 1912; New York, Doran, 1913.

The Story of Louie. London, Secker, 1913; New York, Doran, 1914.

The Two Kisses: A Tale of a Very Modern Courtship. London, Methuen, and New York, Doran, 1913.

A Crooked Mile. London, Methuen, and New York, Doran, 1914.

Gray Youth: The Story of a Very Modern Courtship and a Very Modern Marriage (includes *The Two Kisses* and *A Crooked Mile*). New York, Doran, 1914.

Mushroom Town. London, Hodder and Stoughton, and New York, Doran, 1914.

The New Moon: A Romance of Reconstruction. London, Hodder, and Stoughton, 1918.

A Case in Camera. Bristol, Arrowsmith, 1920; New York, Macmillan, 1921.

The Tower of Oblivion. London, Hodder and Stoughton, and New York, Macmillan, 1921.

Peace in Our Time. London, Chapman and Hall, 1923.

The Spite of Heaven. London, Chapman and Hall, 1925; New York, Doran, 1926.

Whom God Hath Sundered (includes *In Accordance with the Evidence*, *The Debit Account*, *The Story of Louie*). London, Secker, 1925; New York, Doran, 1926.

Cut Flowers. London, Chapman and Hall, 1927.

The Open Secret. London, Heinemann, and Boston, Houghton Mifflin, 1930.

A Certain Man. London, Heinemann, 1931.

Catalan Circus. London, Nicholson and Watson, 1934.

The Hand of Kornelius Voyt. London, Hamish Hamilton, 1939.

Cockcrow; or, Anybody's England. London, Hamish Hamilton, 1940.

The Blood Eagle. London, Staples Press, 1941.

A Shilling to Spend. London, Joseph, 1965.

Short Stories

Tales from a Far Riding. London, Murray, 1902.

Back o' the Moon and Other Stories. London, Hurst and Blackett, 1906.

Admiral Eddy and Other Tales. London, Murray, 1907.

Draw in Your Stool. London, Mills and Boon, 1909.

Widdershins. London, Secker, 1911.

Ghosts in Daylight. London, Chapman and Hall, 1924.

The Painted Face. London, Heinemann, 1929.

The Collected Ghost Stories of Oliver Onions. London, Nicholson and Watson, 1935.

The Italian Chest and Other Stories. London, Secker, 1939.

Bells Rung Backwards. London, Staples Press, 1953.

*   *   *

If Oliver Onions is remembered today, it is for the novella, "The Beckoning Fair One," a masterpiece of supernatural terror. A versatile and prolific writer, Onions published his first novel, *The Compleat Bachelor*, in 1900 and his last, *A Shilling to Spend*, in 1961, the year of his death. Though he wrote spy fiction, naturalistic regional stories, and novels exploring social issues, Onions's ghost stories and a historical novel, *The Story of Ragged Robyn*, best stand the test of time. A commercial artist before turning to fiction, Onions is most compelling when he explores the dilemmas facing artists and writers. Onions depicts characters in the grip of sexual obsessions, usually poor young men whose passion for upper-class females is rooted in their desire for wealth and power. Unfortunately, Onions's most provocative work is flawed by his virulent misogyny.

Onions's fiction is dominated by a sense of the past. Comparatively late in his career, he wrote four historical novels: *The Story of Ragged Robyn*, *Poor Man's Tapestry*, *Arras of Youth*, and *A Penny for the Harp*. Enthusiastically received by critics, *The Story of Ragged Robyn* vividly depicts the daily life of farmers and artisans in 17th-century England. As a child, young Robyn is threatened by robbers, led by the Queen of Holderness, a grotesquely deformed dwarf who weirdly affects the manners and dress of royalty. Subsequently, Robyn is apprenticed to Hendryk, a master stonemason. At the estate of Maske Parke, Robyn meets Miss Betty, a golden-haired child, whom he has loved since he caught a glimpse of her in church seven years before. His passion for her causes him to neglect his craft, though he has extraordinary skill in sculpting animals. Expelled from the estate when Miss Betty's father discovers their nightly meetings, Robyn falls into the hands of the robbers who had terrified him as a child. During a mock trial, Robyn kills himself to escape torture. The trial scene has a nightmarish power, as Robyn's almost forgotten childhood fears become reality. The unhappy ending, however, is an odd reversal of the reader's expectation that this talented young man will overcome youthful folly. That the novel is a misogynistic cautionary tale becomes explicit when the implied author addresses Robyn directly: having learned that "women are more dangerous than men," Robyn should have realized that he is at risk equally from the "young and yielding" (Miss Betty) and the "treacherous and pitiless" (Queen of Holderness). The novel reflects another characteristic Onions concern: had Robyn devoted himself singlemindedly to his art, he would have sublimated mischievous impulses.

Much of Onions's fiction explores the moral implications of choices made by writers and artists. In the ghost stories "The Beckoning Fair One," "Benlion," "Resurrection in Bronze," and "The Real People" Onions treats the consequences of an artist's choice either to pursue a sublime vision that the majority of the public will never comprehend or to opt for the financial security of formula fiction or commercial art. To Onions's credit, the consequences of these choices are neither consistent nor simple. In "Resurrection in Bronze," an artist is so obsessed with completing a statue that, when his wife falls to her death into the crucible, he insists that the casting proceed. In one of Onions's most thought-provoking novels, *A Certain Man*, Christopher Darley nearly loses his humanity by making an opposite choice: advertising petroleum rather than fulfilling his artistic promise.

In Onions's ghost stories, works of art or architecture, surviving in a decadent present, embody powerful spiritual forces. In "The Beckoning Fair One" an evil female presence becomes progressively stronger as a young novelist labors obsessively to restore a dilapidated mansion to its former elegance. In "The Rope in the Rafters" a wounded World War I veteran, recuperating in a Henri Quatre chateau, experiences intense cold, a foul smell, and the sound of labored breathing—sensations that duplicate his own wounding and subsequent living burial. The veteran's traumatic experiences have coincided with the circumstances of the death, three hundred years before, of Jean the Smuggler and have brought his ghost to malignant life.

Why would a writer with Onions's elegant style, Jamesian fascination with psychological nuance, sense of the past, and provocative treatment of art and artists be virtually unknown today? Repeatedly, Onions's most promising fictions are ruined because female characters are treated either with cloying sentimentality or with a loathing altogether disproportionate to their actions. Depicting female sexual indiscretion as the blackest possible crime, Onions deplored the "new woman," who had entered the work force after World War I and insisted on sexual gratification. "The Beckoning Fair One" is Onions's sole masterpiece, not because it is less misogynistic than his other fiction, but because feminine evil is shrouded in ambiguity: the murderous ghost may be the figment of a madman's imagination.

—Wendy Bousfield

ONSTOTT, Kyle. See HORNER, Lance.

ORCZY, Baroness (Emma Magdalena Rosalia Maria Josefa Barbara Orczy). British. Born in Tarna-Ors, Hungary, 23 September 1865. Educated in Brussels and Paris; West London School of Art; Heatherley School of Art, London. Married Montagu Barstow in 1894 (died 1943); one son. Artist: exhibited work at the Royal Academy, London. *Died 12 November 1947.*

ROMANCE AND HISTORICAL PUBLICATIONS

Novels (series: Sir Percy Blakeney, The Scarlet Pimpernel)

The Emperor's Candlesticks. London, Pearson, 1899; New York, Doscher, 1908.
The Scarlet Pimpernel. London, Greening, and New York, Putnam, 1905.
By the Gods Beloved. London, Greening, 1905; as *Beloved of the Gods,* New York, Knickerbocker Press, 1905; as *The Gates of Kamt,* New York, Dodd Mead, 1907.
A Son of the People. London, Greening, and New York, Putnam, 1906.
I Will Repay (Pimpernel). London, Greening, and Philadelphia, Lippincott, 1906.
In Mary's Reign. New York, Cupples and Leon, 1907.
The Tangled Skein. London, Greening, 1907.
Beau Brocade. Philadelphia, Lippincott, 1907; London, Greening, 1908.
The Elusive Pimpernel. London, Hutchinson, and New York, Dodd Mead, 1908.
The Nest of the Sparrowhawk. London, Greening, and New York, Stokes, 1909.
Petticoat Government. London, Hutchinson, 1910; as *Petticoat Rule,* New York, Doran, 1910.
A True Woman. London, Hutchinson, 1911; as *The Heart of a Woman,* New York, Doran, 1911.
Meadowsweet. London, Hutchinson, and New York, Doran, 1912.
Fire in the Stubble. London, Methuen, 1912; as *The Noble Rogue,* New York, Doran, 1912.
Eldorado: A Story of the Scarlet Pimpernel. London, Hodder and Stoughton, and New York, Doran, 1913.
Unto Caesar. London, Hodder and Stoughton, and New York, Doran, 1914.
The Laughing Cavalier. London, Hodder and Stoughton, and New York, Doran, 1914.
A Bride of the Plains. London, Hutchinson, and New York, Doran, 1915.
The Bronze Eagle. London, Hodder and Stoughton, and New York, Doran, 1915.
Leatherface: A Tale of Old Flanders. London, Hodder and Stoughton, and New York, Doran, 1916.

A Sheaf of Bluebells. London, Hutchinson, and New York, Doran, 1917.
Lord Tony's Wife: An Adventure of the Scarlet Pimpernel. London, Hodder and Stoughton, and New York, Doran, 1917.
Flower o' the Lily. London, Hodder and Stoughton, 1918; New York, Doran, 1919.
The League of the Scarlet Pimpernel. London, Cassell, and New York, Doran, 1919.
His Majesty's Well-Beloved. London, Hodder and Stoughton, and New York, Doran, 1919.
The First Sir Percy: An Adventure of the Laughing Cavalier. London, Hodder and Stoughton, 1920; New York, Doran, 1921.
Nicolette. London, Hodder and Stoughton, and New York, Doran, 1922.
The Triumph of the Scarlet Pimpernel. London, Hodder and Stoughton, and New York, Doran, 1922.
The Honourable Jim. London, Hodder and Stoughton, and New York, Doran, 1924.
Pimpernel and Rosemary. London, Cassell, 1924; New York, Doran, 1925.
The Celestial City. London, Hodder and Stoughton, and New York, Doran, 1926.
Sir Percy Hits Back: An Adventure of the Scarlet Pimpernel. London, Hodder and Stoughton, and New York, Doran, 1927.
Blue Eyes and Grey. London, Hodder and Stoughton, 1928; New York, Doubleday, 1929.
Marivosa. London, Cassell, 1930; New York, Doubleday, 1931.
A Child of the Revolution. London, Cassell, and New York, Doubleday, 1932.
A Joyous Adventure. London, Hodder and Stoughton, and New York, Doubleday, 1932.
The Way of the Scarlet Pimpernel. London, Hodder and Stoughton, 1933; New York, Putnam, 1934.
A Spy of Napoleon. London, Hodder and Stoughton, and New York, Putnam, 1934.
The Uncrowned King. London, Hodder and Stoughton, and New York, Putnam, 1935.
Sir Percy Leads the Band. London, Hodder and Stoughton, 1936.
The Divine Folly. London, Hodder and Stoughton, 1937.
No Greater Love. London, Hodder and Stoughton, 1938.
Mam'zelle Guillotine: An Adventure of the Scarlet Pimpernel. London, Hodder and Stoughton, 1940.
Price of Race. London, Hodder and Stoughton, 1942.
Will-o'-the-Wisp. London, Hutchinson, 1947.

Short Stories

The Traitor. New York, Paget, 1912.
Two Good Patriots. New York, Paget, 1912.
The Old Scarecrow. New York, Paget, 1916.
A Question of Temptation. New York, Doran, 1925.
Adventures of the Scarlet Pimpernel. London, Hutchinson, and New York, Doubleday, 1929.
In the Rue Monge. New York, Doubleday, 1931.

OTHER PUBLICATIONS

Short Stories

The Case of Miss Elliott. London, Unwin, 1905.
The Old Man in the Corner. London, Greening, 1909; as *The Man in the Corner,* New York, Dodd Mead, 1909; edited by E. F. Bleiler, New York, Dover, 1980.

Lady Molly of Scotland Yard. London, Cassell, 1910; New York, Arno, 1976.

The Man in Grey, Being Episodes of the Chouan Conspiracies in Normandy During the First Empire. London, Cassell, and New York, Doran, 1918.

Castles in the Air. London, Cassell, 1921; New York, Doran, 1922.

The Old Man in the Corner Unravels the Mystery of the Khaki Tunic. New York, Doran, 1923.

The Old Man in the Corner Unravels the Mystery of the Pearl Necklace, and The Tragedy in Bishop's Road. New York, Doran, 1924.

The Old Man in the Corner Unravels the Mystery of the Russian Prince and of Dog's Tooth Cliff. New York, Doran, 1924.

The Old Man in the Corner Unravels the Mystery of the White Carnation, and The Montmartre Hat. New York, Doran, 1925.

The Old Man in the Corner Unravels the Mystery of the Fulton Gardens Mystery, and The Moorland Tragedy. New York, Doran, 1925.

The Miser of Maida Vale. New York, Doran, 1925.

Unravelled Knots. London, Hutchinson, 1925; New York, Doran, 1926.

Skin o' My Tooth. London, Hodder and Stoughton, and New York, Doubleday, 1928.

Plays

The Scarlet Pimpernel, with Montagu Barstow (produced Nottingham, 1903; London, 1905; New York, 1910).

The Sin of William Jackson, with Montagu Barstow (produced London, 1906).

Beau Brocade, with Montagu Barstow, adaptation of the novel by Orczy (produced Eastbourne, Sussex, and London, 1908).

The Duke's Wager (produced Manchester, 1911).

The Legion of Honour, adaptation of her novel *A Sheaf of Bluebells* (produced Bradford, 1918; London, 1921).

Leatherface, with Caryl Fiennes, adaptation of the novel by Orczy (produced Portsmouth and London, 1922).

Other

Les Beaux et les Dandys des Grands Siècles en Angleterre. Monaco, Société des Conférences, 1924.

The Scarlet Pimpernel Looks at the World (essays). London, John Heritage, 1933.

The Turbulent Duchess: H. R. H. Madame le Duchesse de Berri. London, Hodder and Stoughton, 1935; New York, Putnam, 1936.

Links in the Chain of Life (autobiography). London, Hutchinson, 1947.

Editor and Translator, with Montagu Barstow, *Old Hungarian Fairy Tales.* London, Dean, and Philadelphia, Wolf, 1895.

Editor and Translator, *The Enchanted Cat* (fairy tales). London, Dean, 1895.

Editor and Translator, *Fairyland's Beauty* (*The Suitors of Princess Fire-fly*). London, Dean, 1895.

Editor and Translator, *Uletka and the White Lizard* (fairy tales). London, Dean, 1895.

*   *   *

Romance in Baroness Orczy's stories is at more than one level, for she tackles with panache the romanticism of historical and improbably heroic adventures as well as sexual love. The

shadow of the guillotine seems an unlikely breeding ground for the tender passion, but this is most potently conveyed in *The Scarlet Pimpernel* and its sequels which had as their background the French Revolution. Orczy's books are highly wrought and intensely atmospheric. There are vivid contrasts between the rabble-ridden, blood-running, and squalid streets of revolutionary Paris and the glittering splendour of the court of King George III in England.

Sir Percy Blakeney seems to have been equally at home in both, ringing the changes from appearing at London balls and supper-parties as one of the Prince of Wales's favourite associates, to disguising himself as a "loathsome" looking old "jew trader," or some smelly market-hag or fisherman in order to whisk innocent potential victims away from the fury of the French mob, and the ever-devouring "Mam'zelle Guillotine." Those whom he rescued were more often than not aristocratic, and he drew his band of helpers—"The League of the Scarlet Pimpernel"—from the same class (Sir Andrew Ffoulkes, Lord Antony Dewhurst, Lord Hastings, etc.).

Generally speaking, artisans and even middle-class people did not show up too well in Orczy's stories. In spite of her attraction to strongly chivalric ideas, she writes about the "lower orders" with a distinct air of patronage and condescension, especially if they step out of line and fail to respect their "betters." (And, of course, nothing could be more disrespectful than putting the heads of these betters under the guillotine!)

Sir Percy, however, falls heavily in love with someone from a different class *and* a foreigner to boot—Marguerite St. Just, a French actress of considerable beauty and accomplishment who, until she recognizes the ruthless nature of the Revolution, is a republican. Naturally their married relationship is at first fraught with misunderstandings, and to conceal from Marguerite—as well as the rest of the world—that he is the Scarlet Pimpernel, Sir Percy assumes the role of inept but fashionable fop. Readers, of course, suspect his secret from the early stages of the first book, mainly because the foppish exterior never quite conceals his inner reserves of strength, humour, and compassion, or his romantic but slightly sardonic sense of chivalry: "The commands of a beautiful woman are binding on all mankind, even Cabinet Ministers. . . . "

The action of the plot demands that the identity of the Scarlet Pimpernel, intrepid arch-enemy of the French Revolutionary government, *has* to be revealed to his friends and enemies at the end of the first book. Those that followed never quite achieved the same sense of drama or splendid style—but they were always rich in romantic interest. In different books from those in the Scarlet Pimpernel series, Orczy created other gallant and upright English aristocrats but they lacked the charisma of Sir Percy and his associates.

Strangely enough, everything that worked so well in Orczy's creation of Sir Percy seems to have misfired when a little later on she produced a female righter-of-wrongs. In *Lady Molly of Scotland Yard*, the heroine from whom the book derives its name is, like Sir Percy, aristocratic, enigmatic, plucky, and adept at assuming disguises. But whereas Sir Percy remains a complex and endearing character, Lady Molly comes across as an arch and self-indulgent poseuse. However, although her place in literature is in the detective genre rather than the love-story, she is as much a romantic as Sir Percy. Unlike him, she never actually has to rescue her spouse from the threat of the guillotine—but she *does* vindicate his honour and secures his release from unjust imprisonment.

Orczy was adept not only in different literary genres but with different literary forms. *The Scarlet Pimpernel* was originally a successful play co-authored by Orczy and her husband Montagu Barstow. It was then re-written by the Baroness as a beautifully balanced and, of course, bestselling novel. All the other novels in the series are entertaining and dramatic, especially *The Elusive Pimpernel* and *I Will Repay*. In *Adventures of the Scarlet Pimpernel* she skillfully manipulates the romantic/suspense short story.

—Mary Cadogan

ØVSTEDAL, Barbara. See **LAKER, Rosalind.**

PALMER, Diana. Pseudonym for Susan (Eloise Spaeth) Kyle; also writes as Diana Blayne; Katy Currie. American. Born in Cuthbert, Georgia, 12 December 1946. Educated at Chamblee High School, Georgia, 1964; Famous Writers School, Westport, Connecticut, graduated 1968. Married James Edward Kyle in 1972; one son. Legal secretary, Oliver and Oliver, Clarkesville, Georgia, 1965–66, and Crawford and Crawford, Cornelia, Georgia, 1966; clerk, Carwood Manufacturing Company, 1971–72; reporter, *Tri-County Advertiser*, Clarkesville, 1972–82, and Gainesville *Times*, Georgia, 1969–85; freelance journalist, 1986. Agent: Maureen Walters, Curtis Brown, 10 Astor Place, New York, New York 10003. Address: P.O. Box 844, Cornelia, Georgia 30531, U.S.A.

Romance and Historical Publications

Novels (series: Long Tall Texan; Mercenary)

Now and Forever. New York, Macfadden, 1979.
Storm over the Lake. New York, Macfadden, 1979.
To Have and to Hold. New York, Macfadden, 1979.
Sweet Enemy. New York, Macfadden, 1979.
Bound by a Promise. New York, Macfadden, 1979.
To Love and to Cherish. New York, Macfadden, 1979.
Dream's End. New York, Macfadden, 1979.
If Winter Comes. New York, Macfadden, 1979.
At Winter's End. New York, Macfadden, 1979.
The Cowboy and the Lady. New York, Silhouette, 1982.
September Morning. New York, Silhouette, 1982.
Heather's Song. New York, Silhouette, 1982.
Darling Enemy. New York, Silhouette, 1983.
Friends and Lovers. New York, Silhouette, 1983.
Fire and Ice. New York, Silhouette, 1983.
Snow Kisses. New York, Silhouette, 1983.
Diamond Girl. New York, Silhouette, 1984.
Lady Love. New York, Silhouette, 1984.
Roomful of Roses. New York, Silhouette, 1984.
Heart of Ice. New York, Silhouette, 1984.
Passion Flower. New York, Silhouette, 1984.
The Rawhide Man. New York, Silhouette, 1984.
Blind Promises (as Katy Currie). New York, Silhouette, 1984.
The Cattleman's Choice. New York, Silhouette, 1985.
Love by Proxy. New York, Silhouette, 1985.
Soldier of Fortune (Mercenary). New York, Silhouette, 1985.
The Tender Stranger (Mercenary). New York, Silhouette, 1985.
The Australian. New York, Silhouette, 1985.
Loveplay. New York, Silhouette, 1986.
Eye of the Tiger. New York, Silhouette, 1986.
After the Music. New York, Silhouette, 1986.

Champagne Girl. New York, Silhouette, 1986.
Unlikely Lover. New York, Silhouette, 1986.
Betrayed by Love. New York, Silhouette, 1987.
Rage of Passion. New York, Silhouette, 1987.
Rawhide and Lace. New York, Silhouette, 1987.
Fit for a King. New York, Silhouette, 1987.
Enamored (Mercenary). New York, Silhouette, 1988.
Calhoun (Texan). New York, Silhouette, 1988.
Justin (Texan). New York, Silhouette, 1988.
Tyler (Texan). New York, Silhouette, 1988.
The Diamond Spur (as Susan Kyle). New York, Warner, 1988.
Hoodwinked. New York, Silhouette, 1989.
Fire Brand (as Susan Kyle). New York, Warner, 1989.
Reluctant Father. New York, Silhouette, 1989.
Woman Hater. New York, Silhouette, 1989.

Novels as Diana Blayne

A Waiting Game. New York, Dell, 1982.
A Loving Arrangement. New York, Dell, 1983.
White Sand, Wild Sea. New York, Dell, 1983.
Dark Surrender. New York, Dell, 1983.
Color Love Blue. New York, Dell, 1984.
Tangled Destinies. New York, Dell, 1986.

Other Publications

Novel (as Susan S. Kyle)

The Morcai Battalion. New York, Manor, 1980.

*

Diana Palmer comments:
    I draw heavily from my background as a journalist when researching my books. Even though they deal, for the most part, with romance, the factual portions require every bit as much detail as non-fiction works. My books are hallmarked by their regional settings, old-fasioned morality and virtues, spirited heroines, and rugged, uncompromising heroes. I prefer to write books set in the American west and have become known primarily for such books. I have a diverse and loyal reading audience, some of whom have been with me since the very start of my career. I owe everything I am to those wonderful readers and booksellers. I never forget their part in my success. I was orphaned last year, and my readers have become my family-at-large. I am the luckiest lady in the world to have received so much love and loyalty.

*   *   *

    One of the most prolific authors of contemporary romances, Diana Palmer has a special talent for developing disagreeable heroes, then letting them be changed by love. Although her novels are short, she manages to make such a reversal of character believable.
    The men usually are cold, distant and sarcastic. Lonely, they seem bent on maintaining self-isolation rather than risking any emotional trauma. A typical Palmer hero has insulated himself against the pain of loving, pain which he has felt first hand. Often he has had the misfortune of being a mature adult attracted to a much younger girl. In fighting this attraction, he appears to have brutally rejected her when he has really rejected himself. Since the girl is not yet sophisticated or worldly enough

to understand the difference she runs from him. Palmer usually picks up their story when the girl has grown to womanhood and is ready to accept a man's love, although she might still be frightened of the past. This scenario or a variation of it is featured in such works as *Heather's Song*, *Calhoun*, *September Morning*, *The Cowboy and the Lady*, *Eye of the Tiger*, and *Betrayed by Love*.

Another common reason for the hero's coldness is a previous lack of love. Betrayal and abandonment by a mother, wife, or fiancée leads to a condemnation of all women, which is then focused on the heroine. In *After the Music*, Thorn almost destroys Sabina because of his biased view of women. In the appropriately named *Woman Hater*, Nicole must contend with the ghost of Winthrop's former love, who had walked out on him. Blake Donavan in *Reluctant Father* was hit doubly hard by not knowing his mother and by marrying the wrong woman, who eventually walked out on him.

Like many romance authors, Palmer sometimes uses characters from one book in another. One of her most intriguing creations along this line links the stories of several mercenaries. The leader of the group, now a criminal lawyer, is introduced in *Soldier of Fortune*. He comes out of retirement to rescue his sister from terrorists, taking his secretary Gabby along with him. In *The Tender Stranger*, the enigmatic mercenary Eric meets and marries Dani St. Clair but leaves her to fend for herself for a long time. A third "team" member, Diego Laremos, suddenly finds his former wife in dire straits and in need of his help (*Enamored*). Although these three men are in different stages of male-female relationships, it is apparent that all must cope with their own basic impulse to stay separated from emotion. It is not surprising, however, that they eventually, and happily, succumb to love and learn to trust and to accept love.

Palmer is one of the few romance novelists who places a sharper focus on the hero than on the heroine. The stories are not told from the male point of view, but as a general rule, her male characters are more interestingly developed.

—Barbara E. Kemp

PARADISE, Mary. See **EDEN, Dorothy.**

PARGETER, Edith (Mary). Also writes as Ellis Peters. British. Born in Horsehay, Shropshire, 28 September 1913. Educated at Dawley Church of England Elementary School, Shropshire; Coalbrookdale High School for Girls, Oxford School Certificate. Served in the Women's Royal Navy Service, 1940–45: British Empire Medal, 1944. Chemist's assistant, Dawley, 1933–40. Recipient: Mystery Writers of America Edgar Allan Poe award, 1963; Czechoslovak Society for International Relations Gold Medal, 1968; Crime Writers Association Silver Dagger, 1981. Fellow, International Institute of Arts and Letters, 1961. Agent: Deborah Owen, 78 Narrow Street, London E14 8BP. Address: Parkville, Park Lane, Madeley, Telford, Shropshire TF7 5HE, England.

ROMANCE AND HISTORICAL PUBLICATIONS

Novels (series: The Brothers and Gwynedd)

Hortensius, Friend of Nero. London, Lovat Dickson, 1936; New York, Greystone Press, 1937.
Iron-Bound. London, Lovat Dickson, 1936.
The City Lies Foursquare. London, Heinemann, and New York, Reynal, 1939.
Ordinary People. London, Heinemann, 1941; as *People of My Own*, New York, Reynal, 1942.
She Goes to War. London, Heinemann, 1942.
The Eighth Champion of Christendom. London, Heinemann, 1945.
Reluctant Odyssey. London, Heinemann, 1946.
Warfare Accomplished. London, Heinemann, 1947.
The Fair Young Phoenix. London, Heinemann, 1948.
By Firelight. London, Heinemann, 1948; as *By This Strange Fire*, New York, Reynal, 1948.
Lost Children. London, Heinemann, 1951.
Holiday with Violence. London, Heinemann, 1952.
This Rough Magic. London, Heinemann, 1953.
Most Loving Mere Folly. London, Heinemann, 1953.
The Soldier at the Door. London, Heinemann, 1954.
A Means of Grace. London, Heinemann, 1956.
The Heaven Tree. London, Heinemann, and New York, Doubleday, 1960.
The Green Branch. London, Heinemann, 1962.
The Scarlet Seed. London, Heinemann, 1963.
A Bloody Field of Shrewsbury. London, Macmillan, 1972; New York, Viking Press, 1973.
The Brothers of Gwynedd:
  1. *Sunrise in the West*. London, Macmillan, 1974.
  2. *The Dragon at Noonday*. London, Macmillan, 1975.
  3. *The Hounds of Sunset*. London, Macmillan, 1976.
  4. *Afterglow and Nightfall*. London, Macmillan, 1977.
The Marriage of Meggotta. London, Macmillan, and New York, Viking Press, 1979.

Short Stories

The Lily Hand and Other Stories. London, Heinemann, 1965.

OTHER PUBLICATIONS

Novels as Ellis Peters

Fallen into the Pit (as Edith Pargeter). London, Heinemann, 1951.
Death Mask. London, Collins, 1959; New York, Doubleday, 1960.
The Will and the Deed. London, Collins, 1960; as *Where There's a Will*, New York, Doubleday, 1960; as *The Will and the Deed*, New York, Avon, 1966.
Death and the Joyful Woman. London, Collins, 1961; New York, Doubleday, 1962.
Funeral of Figaro. London, Collins, 1962; New York, Morrow, 1964.
Flight of Witch. London, Collins, 1964.
A Nice Derangement of Epitaphs. London, Collins, 1965; as *Who Lies Here?*, New York, Morrow, 1965.
The Piper on the Mountain. London, Collins, and New York, Morrow, 1966.
Black Is the Colour of My True-Love's Heart. London, Collins, and New York, Morrow, 1967.

The Grass-Widow's Tale. London, Collins, and New York, Doubleday, 1968.

The House of Green Turf. London, Collins, and New York, Morrow, 1969.

Mourning Raga. London, Macmillan, 1969; New York, Morrow, 1970.

The Knocker on Death's Door. London, Macmillan, 1970; New York, Morrow, 1971.

Death to the Landlords! London, Macmillan, and New York, Morrow, 1972.

City of Gold and Shadows. London, Macmillan, 1973; New York, Morrow, 1974.

The Horn of Roland. London, Macmillan, and New York, Morrow, 1974.

Never Pick Up Hitch-Hikers! London, Macmillan, and New York, Morrow, 1976.

A Morbid Taste for Bones: A Mediaeval Whodunnit. London, Macmillan, 1977; New York, Morrow, 1978.

Rainbow's End. London, Macmillan, 1978; New York, Morrow, 1979.

One Corpse Too Many. London, Macmillan, 1979; New York, Morrow, 1980.

Monk's-Hood. London, Macmillan, 1980; New York, Morrow, 1981.

Saint Peter's Fair. London, Macmillan, and New York, Morrow, 1981.

The Leper of Saint Giles. London, Macmillan, 1981; New York, Morrow, 1982.

The Virgin in the Ice. London, Macmillan, 1982; New York, Morrow, 1983.

The Sanctuary Sparrow. London, Macmillan, and New York, Morrow, 1983.

The Devil's Novice. London, Macmillan, 1983; New York, Morrow, 1984.

Dead Man's Ransom. London, Macmillan, 1984; New York, Morrow, 1985.

The Pilgrim of Hate. London, Macmillan, 1984.

An Excellent Mystery. London, Macmillan, 1985; New York, Morrow, 1986.

The Raven in the Foregate. London, Macmillan, and New York, Morrow, 1986.

The Rose Rent. London, Macmillan, and New York, Morrow, 1986.

The Hermit of Eyton Forest. London, Headline, 1987; New York, Mysterious Press, 1988.

The Confession of Brother Haluin. London, Headline, 1988; New York, Mysterious Press, 1989.

A Rare Benedictine. London, Headline, 1988.

The Heretic's Apprentice. London, Headline, 1989.

Short Stories

The Assize of the Dying. London, Heinemann, and New York, Doubleday, 1958.

Play

Radio Play: *The Heaven Tree*, 1975.

Other

The Coast of Bohemia. London, Heinemann, 1950.

Translator, *Tales of the Little Quarter: Stories*, by Jan Neruda. London, Heinemann, 1957; New York, Greenwood Press, 1976.

Translator, *The Sorrowful and Heroic Life of John Amos Comenius*, by Frantisek Kosík. Prague, State Educational Publishing House, 1958.

Translator, *A Handful of Linden Leaves: An Anthology of Czech Poetry*. Prague, Artia, 1958.

Translator, *Don Juan*, by Josef Toman. London, Heinemann, and New York, Knopf, 1958.

Translator, *The Abortionists*, by Valja Stýblová. London, Secker and Warburg, 1961.

Translator, *Granny*, by Bozena Nemcová. Prague, Artia, 1962; New York, Greenwood Press, 1976.

Translator, with others, *The Linden Tree* (anthology). Prague, Artia, 1962.

Translator, *The Terezin Requiem*, by Josef Bor. London, Heinemann, and New York, Knopf, 1963.

Translator, *Legends of Old Bohemia*, by Alois Jirásek. London, Hamlyn, 1963.

Translator, *May*, by Karel Hynek Mácha. Prague, Artia, 1965.

Translator, *The End of the Old Times*, by Vladislav Vancura. Prague, Artia, 1965.

Translator, *A Close Watch on the Trains*, by Bohumil Hrabal. London, Cape, 1968.

Translator, *Report on My Husband*, by Josefa Slánská. London, Macmillan, 1969.

Translator, *A Ship Named Hope*, by Ivan Klíma. London, Gollancz, 1970.

Translator, *Mozart in Prague*, by Jaroslav Seifert. Prague, Orbis, 1970.

*   *   *

A writer of many historical novels and mysteries, Edith Pargeter has special appeal for the romance/gothic reader through the medieval setting of so many of her works. Mystery fans have long been fascinated by her stories under the pseudonym Ellis Peters, which, along with many of her other novels, are often set in England's Middle Ages.

After publishing *The Marriage of Megotta*, Pargeter revealed that in writing historical novels she seems "to have retreated into the thirteenth century for keeps." This statement has a ring of truth since so many of her tales take place in that turbulent milieu. Her realistic depiction of daily hardships suffered by the common people, as well as of political intrigues among the nobility speaks clearly of thorough research. As examples, the wars and border skirmishes between England and Wales which dominated that era get close but fair scrutiny, and the often terrifying, quixotic behavior of the English monarchs is intelligently analyzed. She writes in the stylized prose generally associated with medieval historical fiction and carries it off well, managing to create in each character a distinct personality and a unique voice.

Her stoires are not those of knights in shining armour riding out to rescue fair maidens but of real people caught in tragic events often not of their doing. In *The Heaven Tree* Harry Talvace discovers the cruelty of King John's character when the monarch orders the death of a young boy, Owen, foster son of the Welsh Prince Llewellyn. Harry's intense sense of justice will not allow him to stand by while this sentence is carried out. At the risk of his own life he engineers Owen's safe return to Wales. Later Llewellyn shows his gratitude by offering sanctuary to Harry's wife and infant son. *The Marriage of Megotta*, one of Pargeter's more recent novels, offers the poignant tale of two young people, Megotta and Richard, whose love has the purity and innocence reminiscent of Romeo and Juliet. But the scheming world of Henry III's court tears them apart and eventually causes the death of Megotta.

Pargeter's novels evoke the harsh realism of medieval life without dwelling on the brutality. This glossing over of unpleasantries sometimes leads to scenes and dialog that seem melodramatic, but the author's storytelling ability keeps the action moving and does not allow this to become a distraction.

—Patricia Altner

PARGETER, Margaret. British. Born in Northumberland. Married (husband deceased); two sons. Address: c/o Mills and Boon Ltd., 18–24 Paradise Road, Richmond, Surrey TW9 1SR, England.

ROMANCE AND HISTORICAL PUBLICATIONS

Novels

Winds from the Sea. London, Mills and Boon, and Toronto, Harlequin, 1975.
The Kilted Stranger. London, Mills and Boon, 1975; Toronto, Harlequin, 1976.
Ride a Black Horse. London, Mills and Boon, 1975; Toronto, Harlequin, 1976.
Stormy Rapture. London, Mills and Boon, and Toronto, Harlequin, 1976.
Hold Me Captive. London, Mills and Boon, and Toronto, Harlequin, 1976.
Blue Skies, Dark Waters. London, Mills and Boon, 1976; Toronto, Harlequin, 1977.
Better to Forget. London, Mills and Boon, 1977; Toronto, Harlequin, 1978.
Never Go Back. Toronto, Harlequin, 1977.
Flamingo Moon. London, Mills and Boon, 1977; Toronto, Harlequin, 1978.
Wild Inheritance. London, Mills and Boon, 1977; Toronto, Harlequin, 1978.
The Jewelled Caftan. London, Mills and Boon, and Toronto, Harlequin, 1978.
A Man Called Cameron. London, Mills and Boon, 1978.
Marriage Impossible. London, Mills and Boon, 1978.
Midnight Magic. London, Mills and Boon, and Toronto, Harlequin, 1978.
The Wild Rowan. London, Mills and Boon, 1978; Toronto, Harlequin, 1979.
Autumn Song. London, Mills and Boon, 1979.
Boomerang Bride. London, Mills and Boon, 1979; Toronto, Harlequin, 1981.
The Devil's Bride. London, Mills and Boon, 1979.
Only You. London, Mills and Boon, 1979.
Savage Possession. London, Mills and Boon, 1979; Toronto, Harlequin, 1980.
Kiss of a Tyrant. London, Mills and Boon, and Toronto, Harlequin, 1980.
Deception. London, Mills and Boon, 1980; Toronto, Harlequin, 1981.
Dark Surrender. London, Mills and Boon, 1980; Toronto, Harlequin, 1981.
The Dark Oasis. London, Mills and Boon, 1980; Toronto, Harlequin, 1981.
The Loving Slave. London, Mills and Boon, 1981; Toronto, Harlequin, 1982.
Captivity. London, Mills and Boon, and Toronto, Harlequin, 1981.
Collision. London, Mills and Boon, 1981.
At First Glance. London, Mills and Boon, 1981.
Substitute Bride. London, Mills and Boon, 1981; Toronto, Harlequin, 1983.
Man from the Kimberleys. London, Mills and Boon, 1982; Toronto, Harlequin, 1983.
Not Far Enough. London, Mills and Boon, and Toronto, Harlequin, 1982.
Prelude to a Song. London, Mills and Boon, 1982; Toronto, Harlequin, 1983.
Storm Cycle. London, Mills and Boon, 1982.
Storm in the Night. London, Mills and Boon, 1983; Toronto, Harlequin, 1984.
Clouded Rapture. London, Mills and Boon, 1983.
Chains of Regret. London, Mills and Boon, 1983.
Caribbean Gold. London, Mills and Boon, and Toronto, Harlequin, 1983.
The Demitrious Line. London, Mills and Boon, and Toronto, Harlequin, 1983.
The Silver Flame. London, Mills and Boon, 1983.
Born of the Wind. London, Mills and Boon, 1984.
The Odds Against. London, Mills and Boon, 1984.
Captive of Fate. London, Mills and Boon, 1985.
Impasse. London, Mills and Boon, 1985.
Total Surrender. London, Mills and Boon, 1985.
Lost Enchantment. London, Mills and Boon, 1985.
Model of Deception. London, Mills and Boon, 1985.
The Other Side of Paradise. London, Mills and Boon, 1985.
Beyond Reach. London, Mills and Boon, 1986.
A Scarlet Woman. London, Mills and Boon, 1986.

*   *   *

Margaret Pargeter is a relatively new British romance writer. She began being published in the mid-1970's and has continued since then to develop her own style of writing. It is a style that has instantly made her one of the more popular romance writers in years.

She is also one of the "new" romance writers who aims for realism by drawing on modern "literary" techniques of writing. Her plots are generally complicated as are her characters. Inner turmoil plays a constant counter-point as the heroine reacts to events in the novel and her own hopeless love for her hero. Tension, pathos, and despair provide constant reaction for her readers as she maintains near melodramatic levels of stress.

Her early novels do not have this heightened emotionalism, although they do have refreshing plots and well-balanced characters. *Better to Forget* and *Ride a Black Horse* are both in this traditional vein. Liza Dean in *Better to Forget* helps to prevent a fire in the large department store she works in. The shock of the accident and her own emotional problems cause Liza to lose her memory. She is taken care of by Grant Latham, the wealthy owner of the store. Jane Brown in *Ride a Black Horse* applies for a job in an exclusive stables and riding school at High Linton. She gets the job by falsifying her background. She eventually runs away after falling in love with the owner, Karl Grierson. Both of these novels depend on standard reactions and conflicts within the story.

Her later novels have more complicated dimensions that quickly illustrate the complex development of character and Pargeter's development as a writer. In *The Devil's Bride* Sandra is forced by her cousin Alexandra into taking her place after her fiancée, Stein Freeman, is blinded in an accident. He is a well-known writer who spends much of his time in Greece. He discovers the deception and forces Sandra to marry him and return to Greece with him. His treatment of her is cruel and vindictive as he takes out his frustrations and anger on her. There is a constant pressure on Sandra as she grows to love him in spite of his action. Conflict is intense, and reader reaction is just as intense, for emotional buildup is continued and heightened until the very end of the novel.

Even more intense is *Boomerang Bride*. The character development is extremely complex and shows a wealth of complicated emotional reactions. In fact, it comes close to being a psychological study rather than a romance. The central thrust of the plot centers on the McLeods, an "Outback" station family. Only Wade McLeod and his grandfather are left, and their relationship is one of extreme dislike that borders on hate. The grandfather almost fanatically wants an heir for the station. In revenge, and hoping to prevent his grandfather's wishes from coming true, Wade marries Vicki. She is a temporary home-help and he considers her very ineligible. He presents his proposition as a business arrangement and Vicki agrees. He is determined not to have children! His passion and Vicki's unconscious provocation end that, however, and she becomes pregnant. Furious, Wade orders her to leave the station and she does—only to be brought back four years later with their son, Graham. The course of the story picks up their relationship and the final outcome centers on the people as they face the changes that have taken place over these years.

In assessing Pargeter as a writer, one must keep in mind the tremendous changes that have taken place in romance writing over the past few years. Many of these novels are filled with modern writing techniques and have a slightly different frame of reference than just romance. Stream of consciousness plays a much greater part in the novels, as does a more sophisticated outlook. Because of these elements, Pargeter probably appeals to a somewhat different audience from the traditional romance readers. She is also one of the Harlequin Presents writers. These writers tend to show modern love against more complicated and emotional backgrounds.

—Arlene Moore

PARKINSON, C(yril) Northcote. British. Born in Barnard Castle, County Durham, 30 July 1909. Educated at St. Peter's School, York; Emmanuel College, Cambridge (Corbett prize), B.A. 1932, M.A., Ph.D. 1935. Served in the British Army, Queen's Royal Regiment, 1940–45: Major. Married 1) Ethelwyn Graves in 1942 (divorced 1949), one son and one daughter; 2) Ann Fry in 1951 (died 1983), two sons and one daughter; 3) Iris Waters in 1985. Master, Blundell's School, Tiverton, Devon, 1938–39, and Royal Naval College, Dartmouth, Devon, 1939–40; Lecturer in History, University of Liverpool, 1946–50; Raffles Professor of History, University of Malaya, Singapore, 1950–58. Visiting Professor, Harvard University, Cambridge, Massachusetts, 1958, and University of Illinois, Urbana, and University of California, Berkeley, 1959–60. Visiting Professor, 1961–62, and since 1970 Professor Emeritus and Honorary President, Troy State University, Troy, Alabama. LL.D.: University of Maryland, College Park, 1974; D.Litt.: Troy State University, 1976. Fellow, Royal Historical Society. Agent: Curtis Brown, 162–168 Regent Street, London W1R 5TB. Address: 36 Harkness Drive, Canterbury, Kent CT2 7RW, England.

ROMANCE AND HISTORICAL PUBLICATIONS

Novels (series: Richard Delancey in all books except *The Life and Times of Horatio Hornblower*)

The Life and Times of Horatio Hornblower. London, Joseph, and Boston, Little Brown, 1970.
Devil to Pay. London, Murray, and Boston, Houghton Mifflin, 1973.
The Fireship. London, Murray, and Boston, Houghton Mifflin, 1975.
Touch and Go. London, Murray, and Boston, Houghton Mifflin, 1977.
Dead Reckoning. London, Murray, and Boston, Houghton Mifflin, 1978.
So Near so Far. London, Murray, and Boston, Houghton Mifflin, 1981.
The Guernsey Man. London, Murray, and Boston, Houghton Mifflin, 1982.

OTHER PUBLICATIONS

Novel

Jeeves. London, Macdonald and Jane's, and New York, St. Martin's Press, 1979.

Plays

Helier Bonamy (produced Guernsey, 1967).
The Royalist (produced Guernsey, 1969).

Radio Play: *The China Fleet*, 1952 (Singapore).

Other

Edward Pellew, Viscount Exmouth. London, Methuen, 1934.
Trade in the Eastern Seas 1793–1813. London, Cambridge University Press, 1937.
Always a Fusilier: The War History of the Royal Fusiliers. London, Sampson Low, 1949.
The Rise of the Port of Liverpool. Liverpool, University of Liverpool Press, 1952.
War in the Eastern Seas 1793–1815. London, Allen and Unwin, 1954.
Templer in Malaya. Singapore, Moore, 1954.
A Short History of Malaya. Singapore, Moore, 1954; revised edition, 1956.
Britain in the Far East. Singapore, Moore, 1955.
Marxism for Malayans. Singapore, Moore, 1956.
Heroes of Malaya, with Ann Parkinson. Singapore, Moore, 1956.
Parkinson's Law. Boston, Houghton Mifflin, 1957; London, Murray, 1958.
The Evolution of Political Thought. London, University of London Press, and Boston, Houghton Mifflin, 1958.
British Intervention in Malaya. Singapore, University of Malaya Press, 1960.
The Law and the Profits. London, Murray, and Boston, Houghton Mifflin, 1960.
In-Laws and Outlaws. London, Murray, and Boston, Houghton Mifflin, 1962.
East and West. London, Murray, and Boston, Houghton Mifflin, 1963.

Ponies Plot (for children). London, Murray, and Boston, Houghton Mifflin, 1965.

A Law unto Themselves. London, Murray, and Boston, Houghton Mifflin, 1966.

Left Luggage. London, Murray, and Boston, Houghton Mifflin, 1967.

Mrs. Parkinson's Law and Other Stories in Domestic Science. London, Murray, and Boston, Houghton Mifflin, 1968.

The Law of Delay: Interviews and Outerviews. London, Murray, 1970; Boston, Houghton Mifflin, 1971.

The Essential Parkinson: Six Lectures in India. New Delhi, Economic and Scientific Research Foundation, 1970.

Incentives and Penalties. Bombay, Shah, 1973.

Big Business. London, Weidenfeld and Nicolson, and Boston, Little Brown, 1974.

How to Get to the Top Without Ulcers, Tranquillisers, or Heart Attacks, with M. K. Rustomji. New Delhi, Macmillan, 1974.

Watch Your Fingers, with M. K. Rustomji. New Delhi, Macmillan, 1976.

Gunpowder, Treason and Plot. London, Weidenfeld and Nicolson, 1976; New York, St. Martin's Press, 1977.

Britannia Rules: The Classic Age of Naval History 1793–1815. London, Weidenfeld and Nicolson, 1977.

Communicate: Parkinson's Formula for Business Survival, with Nigel Rowe. Englewood Cliffs, New Jersey, Prentice Hall, 1977.

The Rise of Big Business. London, Weidenfeld and Nicolson, 1977.

The Law; or, Still in Pursuit. London, Murray, 1979; Boston, Houghton Mifflin, 1980.

The Law of Longer Life, with Herman Le Compte. Troy, Alabama, Troy State University Press, 1980.

Realities in Management, with M. K. Rustomji. Bombay, IBH, 1981.

The Fur-Lined Mousetrap. Bolton, Lancashire, Anderson, 1983.

The Management Jungle. New Delhi, Tarang, 1984.

Editor, *The Trade Winds.* London, Allen and Unwin, 1948.

Editor, *Portsmouth Point: The Navy in Fiction 1793–1815.* Liverpool, University of Liverpool Press, 1948; Cambridge, Massachusetts, Harvard University Press, 1949.

Editor, *Samuel Walters, Lieutenant R.N.* Liverpool, University of Liverpool Press, 1949.

Editor, *Industrial Disruption.* Epsom, Surrey, Leviathan House, 1973.

Editor and Translator, *The Journal of a Frenchman in Malayan Waters.* Singapore, Royal Asiatic Society, 1952.

*

C. Northcote Parkinson comments:

My works of historical fiction relate to a period known to me as an historian. Characters and events are close to reality. I did not write these novels until C. S. Foster had died.

*   *   *

C. Northcote Parkinson, famous for his Parkinson's Law, has lived in Guernsey since 1960, when not travelling, and has studied among other things naval warfare in Napoleonic times. The result has been six novels devoted to the adventures of Richard Delancey born in Guernsey in 1760.

Delancey goes to sea at 16 as a volunteer to avoid arrest during the Merseyside riots, takes part in the defence of Jersey and Gibraltar in *The Guernseyman*, combats the smugglers of Poole, joins the Guernsey privateers and fights on land in Spain in *Devil to Pay*, and commands a sloop to protect Malta which ends in the sea battles at Algeciras and off Cadiz in *Touch and Go*. In 1803 his French enables him to disguise himself as a Frenchman and sail into Boulogne harbour to lay explosives thus preventing the invasion of England and possibly the kidnapping of the Prime Minister in *So Near so Far*. In *The Fireship* he distinguishes himself at the Battle of Campendern then prevents an attempted invasion by the French off Ireland. Finally in *Dead Reckoning* Delancey is posted to the Far East, captures two French frigates and is knighted in 1811.

The way sailing ships were manned, the preparations for battle, the fights themselves, the allotting of prize money, the appointment of officers, all the technical details are presented unobtrusively in these novels. The fictitious hero himself has dark hair, dark blue eyes, a sturdy figure, a confident and direct manner. "I shouldn't call you exactly handsome but you look interesting" said Fiona. Delancey's position in society was "only marginal"; being the son of a corn chandler he was regarded as a gentleman of sorts so had to make his way without family help. He was a steady fellow who never gambled and bought Anneville, his house on Guernsey, with prize money.

Throughout the series of novels Delancey learns to be a good leader, encouraging the young boys before battle, training them all in gun practice. Only once is he described as going berserk—when boarding a French ship during a battle in *Dead Reckoning*. Here he becomes possessed by the devil, running at the enemy screaming with fury: "Kill the French bastards," raging as he kills a private soldier but failing to extract his sword. Grabbing a fallen boarding pike, he storms on, hurling it at another soldier and then grabbing the man's musket. At the break of the quarterdeck he breaks in a door and wounds a mess servant with the bayonet.

As a young Captain, Delancey makes mistakes but these decrease as his character develops and his quick thinking enables him to foresee what the enemy would do and forestall their action. He enjoys being on land where he is equally good at outwitting the French. In the Far East after losing men he replaces them with mutineers from another ship by pretending to be French, thus risking a court martial.

Only when he considers that he can afford to marry does he pay attention to an influential widow but changes his mind when he meets redheaded Fiona, an illegitimate actress, so his friends help him to leave the lady without ruining his career. Fiona settles down as an exemplary naval wife, spending six years improving their Guernsey house without complaint in spite of their lack of children. Her husband's long devoted letters help the story along in *Dead Reckoning*. This seems, given her background, rather unlikely behaviour, but she manages to act the ladylike wife of a naval officer in a convincing manner.

The Life and Times of Horatio Hornblower, which poses as a serious biography of C. S. Forester's hero, goes with less of a swing. The first chapters question the available information on Hornblower's childhood in the manner of a serious historian but the book becomes easier reading as it progresses. There is much real history to be learnt along with the fiction. The hero has a complete private life with two marriages, the second to the Duke of Wellington's sister, a son and many descendants as he lives to be 80. The illustrations appear wonderfully authentic, and appendices place Forester's books in their historical context.

—Margaret Campbell

PATERSON, Isabel M. (Bowler). Canadian. Born in Manitoulin Island, Alberta, in 1885. Educated at public schools in Mountain View and Cardston, Alberta. Married Kenneth Birrell Paterson. Clerk, Canadian Pacific Railroad, Calgary; journalist, *American* and *Hearst's Magazine*, both New York; columnist, New York *Herald Tribune*. Died in 1961.

ROMANCE AND HISTORICAL PUBLICATIONS

Novels

The Singing Season. New York, Boni and Liveright, 1924; London, Parsons, 1925.
The Fourth Queen. New York, Boni and Liveright, and London, Parsons, 1926.
The Road of the Gods. New York, Liveright, 1930.

OTHER PUBLICATIONS

Novels

The Shadow Riders. London, Lane, 1916.
The Magpie's Nest. London, Lane, 1917.
Never Ask the End. New York, Morrow, 1933.
The Golden Vanity. New York, Morrow, 1934.
If It Prove Fair Weather. New York, Putnam, 1940.

Other

The God of the Machine. New York, Putnam, 1943.

Editor, *A High Wind in Jamaica*, by Richard Hughes. New York, Modern Library, 1932.

*   *   *

Isabel M. Paterson's historical novels form less than half of her fiction titles. Contemporary novels dealing with the romantic adventures of young, urban American men and women between the world wars constitute the larger share of her work. However, romance and youth structure the plots of Paterson's historical novels as well and her style is consistent between her historical and non-historical novels. In Paterson's writing, plot and characterization are not complex nor are they developed in any depth of detail or sophistication. Her novels were well-received in the reviews of the day and their popularity should be acknowledged.

In *The Singing Season* Paterson presents the court and church intrigue in Spain at the time of King Henry and his brother King Pedro. This novel is Paterson's most historically detailed. The plot focuses on the romance between Isabella and Roderigo who become caught up in the larger political forces of the times. Its plot is chronological and the outcome of the romance is predictable, yet Paterson uses historical detail skillfully and rewards the reader's close attention with a fine sense of period and locale. An interesting aspect of her historical novels generally is that archaisms conventionally restricted in the genre to dialogue are carried over into scene description and narrative commentary.

The Fourth Queen is set near the end of the reign of Elizabeth I. The central romance is between Jack, John Philip Sidney Montagu, and Kate, granddaughter of Sir Thomas More. Other major figures presented are Essex and Francis Drake. Again, Paterson's concern is to evoke a sense of court life and the complex web of intrigue and power which ultimately determines the future of nations.

The Road of the Gods is the least conventional of Paterson's three historical novels. It is set in northeastern Europe during the reign of Octavian. She skillfully develops a detailed picture of pre-Christian culture not yet thoroughly penetrated by Roman influence. The novel closes with an impending invasion of the area by Roman forces and the sense that an ancient world is about to give way before the expansion of the Roman empire and the influence of classical civilisation. Paterson carefully undermines the conventional view of life in Europe, before Roman military and cultural advancement, as mindless barbarism. Instead she uses plot, the romance between Hoath and Greda, to explore the possible complexity and richness of a culture and society which had evolved over centuries.

While Paterson's historical novels make pleasant, even provocative, reading, they are not her best work. Perhaps the best is her first novel, *The Shadow Riders*, which examines political and social life in a rapidly growing town in pre-World War I Alberta, Canada. The richness of the characters and the complexity of the plot, which follows two intersecting lines, are developed within a sophisticated narrative to an extent that Paterson does not manage to achieve in any of her later work.

—Heather Iris Jones

———

PAUL, Barbara. See **LAKER, Rosalind.**

———

PAULEY, Barbara Anne (née Cotton). American. Born in Nashville, Tennessee, 12 January 1925. Educated at Wellesley College, Cambridge, Massachusetts, 1942. Married Robert Reinhold Pauley in 1946; one daughter and three sons. Editorial assistant, Ideal Publishing Corporation, then freelance writer. Agent: Blassingame McCauley and Wood, 432 Park Avenue South, Suite 1205, New York, New York 10016. Address: c/o Doubleday, 666 Fifth Avenue, New York, New York 10103, U.S.A.

ROMANCE AND HISTORICAL PUBLICATIONS

Novels

Blood Kin. New York, Doubleday, 1972.
Voices Long Hushed. New York, Doubleday, 1976.

*   *   *

To capture the passions, conflicts, and terrors of the Civil War, Barbara Anne Pauley focuses on a microcosm, an individual and familial situation, that reflects the broader problems of the times. *Blood Kin* focuses on a young Southern miss whose disillusionment and longing for lost relationships and the pleasures of a lost youth lead her to visit neighboring cousins, Union sympathizers firmly entrenched in a symbol of the dying South—a stately family plantation house. In *Voices Long Hushed* a young New England girl seeks her dubious heritage on a Southern plantation, ravaged by war, yet kept operative by poor, dependent Southern relations. In both, the conflicts, like those of the war itself, are family conflicts in which distant relatives conspire against the central characters—to acquire land or wealth or love, to hide sins, to work out personal hatreds.

In *Blood Kin* Leslie Hallam, deprived of family, land, and childhood by war, seeks to recreate her lost world of aristocratic and social comforts at Sycamore Knob, a magnificent Nashville plantation. She arrives amid stormy weather, only to find a more terrifying storm within, a frightening psychological turbulence beneath surface calm: a child terrorized by a nameless "bad thing" that haunts her nights and leaves her clothing bloodied; a fat, pasty-faced woman, once beautiful, whose greed and passions make her strike out in jealousy; her arrogant brother, a model of decadent aristocratic weakness; a dashing, self-possessed confederate soldier, the family black sheep, seemingly crushed by his own spirited steed; a mysteriously wounded head of house whose wit, spirit, and sexuality capture the heart of a vulnerable cousin; a kindly Union officer who suspects but cannot prove fearful undercurrents and dangerous conspiracies. Nightmarish sequences follow: a deadly game of hide and seek, an attic excursion that nearly ends in death by fire, a mad dash in a swift carriage—fleeing madness only to find secret madness inescapable. Amid such gothic horrors, romance blossoms, first in the sudden, physical passion that draws together an experienced man-of-the-world and an innocent girl, and then a gentler, self-giving love that grows with time and proximity.

In *Voices Long Hushed* an uncle's will shatters a young orphan's tranquility. The loss of a lover and the discovery of a live mother, possibly a murderess and a madwoman, compel her to seek the truth of her inheritance at St. Cloud, her mother's plantation. There Stacy begins to untangle the web of deceit spun by an odd assortment of distant, conniving relatives. Her realization that her mother's innocence means another's guilt awakens the conflicts that produced the first murder 25 years before, and once again murder stalks the balconies and shadowy galleries of the old manor. A chain of gothic horrors ensues: an elevator shaft left open in the dark, a poisonous snake left in a bedroom, a slave dead in a trunk, a locked-room murder, a deadly drug that simulates insanity. As three men try to impose their will on pliable Stacy, relationships prove skewed; family hatreds and pre-war wounds are exposed. Destroying the evil depends on a cryptic journal hidden in a slave cabin and restoration of an amnesiac's memory by recreating childhood terror. Ultimately, the young Northern heiress finds her place in the South, and chooses a relationship tangled forever in the tight emotional knots of love and murder, of father killing father.

Together these novels seek to expose and exorcise the terrors and evils that separate brother from brother—the essence, for Pauley, of Civil War conflict—while suggesting the strength that allows one to build from ties on the shaky ground of old horrors, atrocities, and passions.

—Gina Macdonald

PAYE, Robert. See **BOWEN, Marjorie.**

PEAKE, Lilian (Margaret). British. Born in London, 25 May 1924. Married; has children. Has worked as secretary, typist, and journalist: reporter in High Wycombe, fashion writer in London, and writer for *Daily Herald* and *Woman* magazine. Lives in Oxford. Address: c/o Mills and Boon Ltd., 18–24 Paradise Road, Richmond, Surrey TW9 1SR, England.

ROMANCE AND HISTORICAL PUBLICATIONS

Novels

Man of Granite. London, Mills and Boon, 1971; Toronto, Harlequin, 1975.
This Moment in Time. London, Mills and Boon, 1971; Toronto, Harlequin, 1972.
The Library Tree. London, Mills and Boon, and Toronto, Harlequin, 1972.
Man Out of Reach. London, Mills and Boon, 1972; Toronto, Harlequin, 1973.
The Real Thing. London, Mills and Boon, 1972; Toronto, Harlequin, 1973.
A Girl Alone. London, Mills and Boon, 1972; Toronto, Harlequin, 1978.
Mist Across the Moors. London, Mills and Boon, and Toronto, Harlequin, 1972.
No Friend of Mine. London, Mills and Boon, 1972; Toronto, Harlequin, 1977.
Gone Before Morning. London, Mills and Boon, and Toronto, Harlequin, 1973.
Man in Charge. London, Mills and Boon, and Toronto, Harlequin, 1973.
Familiar Stranger. London, Mills and Boon, 1973; Toronto, Harlequin, 1976.
Till the End of Time. London, Mills and Boon, 1973; Toronto, Harlequin, 1975.
The Dream on the Hill. London, Mills and Boon, 1974; Toronto, Harlequin, 1975.
A Sense of Belonging. London, Mills and Boon, and Toronto, Harlequin, 1974.
Master of the House. London, Mills and Boon, and Toronto, Harlequin, 1974.
The Impossible Marriage. London, Mills and Boon, 1974; Toronto, Harlequin, 1975.
Moonrise over the Mountains. London, Mills and Boon, 1975; Toronto, Harlequin, 1976.
Heart in the Sunlight. London, Mills and Boon, 1975; Toronto, Harlequin, 1976.
The Tender Night. London, Mills and Boon, 1975; Toronto, Harlequin, 1976.
The Sun of Summer. London, Mills and Boon, 1975; Toronto, Harlequin, 1976.
A Bitter Loving. London, Mills and Boon, 1976; Toronto, Harlequin, 1977.
The Distant Dream. London, Mills and Boon, and Toronto, Harlequin, 1976.
The Little Impostor. London, Mills and Boon, 1976; Toronto, Harlequin, 1977.
This Man Her Enemy. London, Mills and Boon, 1976; Toronto, Harlequin, 1977.
Somewhere to Lay My Head. London, Mills and Boon, and Toronto, Harlequin, 1977.
Passionate Involvement. London, Mills and Boon, 1977; Toronto, Harlequin, 1978.
No Second Parting. London, Mills and Boon, 1977; Toronto, Harlequin, 1979.
Across a Crowded Room. London, Mills and Boon, 1977; Toronto, Harlequin, 1981.
Day of Possession. London, Mills and Boon, 1978.
Rebel in Love. London, Mills and Boon, and Toronto, Harlequin, 1978.
Run for Your Love. London, Mills and Boon, 1978; Toronto, Harlequin, 1980.

Dangerous Deception. London, Mills and Boon, 1979; Toronto, Harlequin, 1980.

Enemy from the Past. London, Mills and Boon, and Toronto, Harlequin, 1979.

Stranger on the Beach. London, Mills and Boon, and Toronto, Harlequin, 1979.

Promise at Midnight. London, Mills and Boon, 1980; Toronto, Harlequin, 1981.

A Ring for a Fortune. London, Mills and Boon, and Toronto, Harlequin, 1980.

A Secret Affair. London, Mills and Boon, 1980; Toronto, Harlequin, 1981.

Strangers into Lovers. London, Mills and Boon, and Toronto, Harlequin, 1981.

Gregg Barratt's Woman. London, Mills and Boon, and Toronto, Harlequin, 1981.

Capture a Stranger. London, Mills and Boon, 1981.

Stay Till Morning. London, Mills and Boon, 1982.

Bitter Revenge. London, Mills and Boon, 1982.

No Other Man. London, Mills and Boon, 1982.

Passionate Intruder. London, Mills and Boon, 1982.

Come Love Me. London, Mills and Boon, 1983.

Night of Possession. London, Mills and Boon, 1983.

A Woman in Love. London, Mills and Boon, and Toronto, Harlequin 1984.

Elusive Paradise. London, Mills and Boon, 1985; Toronto, Harlequin 1987.

Ice into Fire. London, Mills and Boon, 1985; Toronto, Harlequin 1986.

Never in a Lifetime. London, Mills and Boon, 1985.

Love in the Moonlight. London, Mills and Boon, 1986; Toronto, Harlequin 1987.

The Bitter Taste of Love. London, Mills and Boon, 1988; Toronto, Harlequin 1989.

Take This Woman. London, Mills and Boon, and Toronto, Harlequin 1988.

Dance to My Tune. London, Mills and Boon, 1989.

Climb Every Mountain. London, Mills and Boon, 1989.

*   *   *

Lillian Peake, a Mills and Boon/Harlequin Books author, has written several romances a year for over a decade without writing herself out, without overly-much repetition (except for the basic theme) from book to book, and without deterioration in quality. Her readability is high, and, surprisingly, the 21st book one reads is as entertaining as the first. She is a good, even superior, stylist, and her background enables her to give an accurate, fine-tuned picture of contemporary English domestic and working life. Her limitation, if it is one in this genre, is that she writes the same story over each time, like variations on a musical theme. Her heroines are teachers, secretaries, department store buyers, laboratory assistants, or housekeepers. They are always in a subordinate position to some arrogant, overbearing, sardonic, but attractive man, with whom they have a running battle, interspersed with numerous romantic encounters, until the last pages of the story when the barriers are finally swept away. The novels are set in various parts of England, with the Yorkshire moors figuring several times (*Run for Your Love*, *The Tender Night*, and *Mist Across the Moors*). *The Sun of Summer* takes place on a Rhine cruise, and *Passionate Involvement* is set in Switzerland. The settings in the every-day English world serve to lend a patina of realism to balance the really heady romance in the novels. Events somehow always transpire to throw hero and heroine together in provocative situations. There are trips to conventions and scientific meetings, shared hotel rooms,

school excursions and camping trips with shared sleeping bags. Sometimes there is a marriage of convenience, as in *Somewhere to Lay My Head* and *No Second Parting*, or a pretend engagement as in *Master of the House*. Whatever the circumstances the battle of the sexes goes on to the last. *Gone Before Morning* and *The Tender Night* are two of Peake's best stories. In the former a misogynist determined not to be trapped into marriage by his housekeeper finds himself succumbing, and in the latter a woman jilted by her fiancé is resolved not to fall in love again, but of course finds the one man who overcomes her resistance. Although Peake's novels are essentially backdrops in which she can place the many love scenes which are the purpose for the stories, it is remarkable how good style and well-fleshed-out plots, with lots of detail of every-day life, can produce such enjoyable results.

—Necia A. Musser

PEARL, Jack. See **BLAKE, Stephanie.**

PEDLER, Margaret (Bass). British. Married.

ROMANCE AND HISTORICAL PUBLICATIONS

Novels

This Splendid Folly. London, Mills and Boon, 1918; New York, Doran, 1921.

The House of Dreams-Come-True. London, Hodder and Stoughton, and New York, Doran, 1919.

The Hermit of Far End. London, Hodder and Stoughton, 1919; New York, Doran, 1920.

The Lamp of Fate. London, Hodder and Stoughton, 1920; New York, Doran, 1921.

The Moon Out of Reach. London, Hodder and Stoughton, and New York, Doran, 1921.

The Vision of Desire. London, Hodder and Stoughton, and New York, Doran, 1922.

The Barbarian Lover. London, Hodder and Stoughton, and New York, Doran, 1923.

Red Ashes. London, Hodder and Stoughton, 1924; New York, Doran, 1925.

The Better Love. New York, Doran, 1924.

Her Brother's Keeper. New York, Doran, 1924.

Mrs. Daventry's Reputation. New York, Doran, 1924.

To-morrow's Tangle. London, Hodder and Stoughton, 1925; New York, Doran, 1926.

Yesterday's Harvest. London, Hodder and Stoughton, and New York, Doran, 1926.

Bitter Heritage. London, Hodder and Stoughton, and New York, Doubleday, 1928.

The Guarded Halo. London, Hodder and Stoughton, and New York, Doubleday, 1929.

Fire of Youth. London, Hodder and Stoughton, and New York, Doubleday, 1930.

Many Ways. London, Hodder and Stoughton, 1931.

Kindled Flame. London, Hodder and Stoughton, and New York, Doubleday, 1931.

Desert Sand. London, Hodder and Stoughton, and New York, Doubleday, 1932.
Pitiless Choice. London, Hodder and Stoughton, 1933.
The Greater Courage. New York, Doubleday, 1933.
Green Judgment. London, Hodder and Stoughton, 1934; as *Distant Dawn*, New York, Doubleday, 1934.
The Shining Cloud. London, Hodder and Stoughton, 1935; New York, Doubleday, 1936.
Flame in the Wind. London, Hodder and Stoughton, and New York, Doubleday, 1937.
No Armour Against Fate. London, Hodder and Stoughton, and New York, Doubleday, 1938.
Blind Loyalty. London, Hodder and Stoughton, and New York, Doubleday, 1940.
Not Heaven Itself. London, Hodder and Stoughton, 1940; New York, Doubleday, 1941.
Then Came the Test. London, Hodder and Stoughton, and New York, Doubleday, 1942.
No Gifts from Chance. London, Hodder and Stoughton, and New York, McBride, 1944.
Unless Two Be Agreed. London, Hodder and Stoughton, and New York, McBride, 1947.

Short Stories

Waves of Destiny. London, Hodder and Stoughton, and New York, Doran, 1924.
Checkered Paths. London, Hodder and Stoughton, 1935.

* * *

The stereotyped heroine of the 1930's was uncertain whether she wished to be liberated from man or dominated by him. It is indicative of this confusion (which was replacing the spiritual confusion on matters of the soul, of earlier heroines) that she often seeks out a lover who is paradoxically both fierce yet gentle, who can kiss with stormy, sudden passion, while simultaneously maintaining a "strange and lingering gentleness." This quality of kissing, difficult thought it may be to achieve, is clearly seen as an attractive characteristic, for it has been adopted by a number of present-day heroes, who manage to kiss with "fierce yet tender passion."

Pedler went even further than just fierce tenderness, and invented in *The Barbarian Lover*, a strong, hard, arrogant man with sun-burned hatchet face, and obstinate straight-lipped mouth. He strides about the wide open spaces of the earth in travel-stained riding-kit, always on hand to rescue the heroine from whatever dangerous and unlikely situation she has got herself into. His first act of bravery and chivalry is to save her from a man-eating tiger seconds before it gobbles her up. Later, he rescues her when she is struck by lightening in a forest. He saves her from her bolting horse. He finally concludes that she is over-civilised and if only she would go camping with him, this would make a real woman of her.

"Or a savage," retorted Patricia.
"I suppose that's what you set me down for, isn't it?"
"I certainly think you're—primitive," she returned.
"So is God; so is nature. I don't want to be anything else. After all, it's the big primitive things that count."

The big primitive things in his life are birth, death, and the urgent desire to kiss her. Being a barbarian, he takes what he wants in every fibre of his being: "There was a fire in his eyes—a flaming light of passion barely held in leash that terrified her. He caught her roughly in his arms. His mouth sought

hers, straining against it in fierce, possessive kisses. The love and passion which his iron will had thwarted and held back for months surged over her now in a resistless torrent. The gates had been opened. They could never again be closed."

Though to some extent afraid of this man's unleashed instincts, the girl ultimately gives in to her growing love for him, and learns to lie back and enjoy that fierce, barbarian, yet strangely gentle kissing, to yield tremulously to the imperious passion.

The Barbarian Lover was sold, in its first, 1923, version as one of "Hodders Ninepenny Series" in a jaunty jacket showing the barbarian lover himself, clutched at by the girl behind both superimposed over a crossword puzzle. "First Read the Book," the jacket commands. "Then do the crossword." When re-issued in 1938; it was abridged.

Pedler's other 30-odd titles share similar tangled emotions, and unleashed passion.

—Rachel Anderson

PEMBERTON, Nan. See **PYKARE, Nina.**

PENMAN, Sharon K(ay). American. Address c/o Henry Holt Inc., 115 West 18th Street, New York, New York 10011, U.S.A.

ROMANCE AND HISTORICAL PUBLICATIONS

Novels

The Sunne in Splendour. New York, Holt Rinehart, 1982; London, Macmillan, 1983.
Here Be Dragons. New York, Holt Rinehart, 1985; London, Collins, 1986.
Falls the Shadow. New York, Holt, and London, Joseph, 1988.

* * *

Sharon K. Penman's *The Sunne in Splendour* is a most impressive undertaking for a first work. Exceedingly readable, obviously well researched, this major novel of the life of Richard III brings the 15th century vividly to life. The adjective "panoramic" springs to mind, but with its implication of a fairly shallow treatment of a broad subject this does the book less than justice.

Many writers of Ricardian novels give the impression of being more than a little in love with the protagonist, so that this work is by no means unique in being unashamedly pro-Richard. He is portrayed as a man with a conscience, swept partly against his will into the political machinations rife in the 15th century; this is not a fresh interpretation of Richard's participation in historical events, but what makes it particularly credible is the way in which all the characters are brought alive, making this complex period in history more readily understandable.

Well written, interesting, and even gripping, *The Sunne in Splendour* is in many ways an exceedingly scholarly work. Penman recognises that "While imagination is the heart of any novel, historical fiction needs a strong factual foundation, especially a novel revolving around a man as controversial as Rich ard III.'' She says that she finds herself ''torn between two faiths. The novelist's need for an untrammelled, freeflowing imagination is always at war with the historian's pure passion for verity. I do try to keep fact-tampering to a minimum, but it occasionally is necessary in order to advance the storyline.'' *The Sunne in Splendour* and her other novels do indeed follow the known facts very closely, with embellishments to fill in the blanks. Obviously much must be speculation, but with such integrity does Penman tackle her subjects that these embellishments always have the ring of authenticity. For example, the romance between Anne Neville and Richard is often said to have dated from childhood; this is very handy for the historical novelist, but is it true? Romance and history are in this novel integrated in such a way as to make it plausible, and Penman's technique of weaving known details with the projection of possibilities also sows the seeds of Anne's eventual consumption in the period she spent in hiding disguised as a kitchen maid.

As with any retelling of Ricardian history, *The Sunne in Splendour* is overlaid with a sense of doom, as we not only know the end of the story but are also aware of history's verdict. This in no way diminishes the grip which this novel has upon the reader, but instead seems to increase the power that this tragic period in history still exercises.

The hero of Penman's next book, *Here Be Dragons*, is Llewelyn ab Iowerth, Prince of Gwynedd. This novel makes nowhere near the impact of *The Sunne in Splendour*, perhaps because the author's heart was not given to her subject in quite the same way. The telling is not as detailed or realistic and undoubtedly not as committed; however, in being more dispassionate could it perhaps be considered a better novel? There is certainly more of a sense of pure fiction, perhaps because the historical period dealt with is not so well known or so well documented. Penman herself admits ''it was necessary to rely upon imagination to a greater extent than in my earlier novel of 15th-century England, for Llewelyn's world was not as well chronicled as that of the Yorkist kings. But the structure of *Here Be Dragons* is grounded in fact; even the more unlikely occurrences are validated by medieval chroniclers.'' Thus we are given more detail of personal and romantic interludes, and rather less insight into the broader sweep of history.

The portrayals of major historical characters in this novel and its sequel, *Falls the Shadow*, seem to be borne out by the verdict of history. Henry III was indeed a rather weak, naive and vascillating king; King John (given a surprisingly sympathetic personality) did in fact have rather more winning ways than many historical novelists would have us believe. *Here Be Dragons*, in dealing with both Simon de Montfort and Llewelyn ab Iowerth and his descendants, seeks to portray a very confusing period of history. The narrative flow is not made any clearer by a veritable plethora of Nells, Eleanors, Ellens, and Henrys, Harrys or Hals; it is often rather difficult to distinguish the identity of an individual character. *Falls the Shadow* does not seem to work quite as well as *Here Be Dragons*, being more episodic, and fictionalising more complex situations. Penman, while managing to portray Simon de Montfort sympathetically, makes no bones about his ruthlessness and arrogance; and indeed historians remain divided in their options as to both his character and his motivations.

A third novel involving the Welsh Princes of Gwynedd is planned, as Penman came early to the conclusion that the two characters of de Montfort and Llewelyn ab Gruffydd were too much for one book. Indeed, one flaw in the structure of *Falls the Shadow* is the imbalance between the early part of the book, where the fortunes of de Montfort and the Princes of Gwynedd alternate, and the latter part where the author concentrates primarily on de Montfort.

One of the strengths of all Penman's novels is the way in which she avoids the common pitfall (that Waterloo of so many historical novelists) of language. The speech of Penman's characters is informal (but not too colloquial) 20th century, with an occasional slight stiffness which conveys to us that we are in fact in the 13th or the 15th century.

—Judith Rhodes

* * *

PETER, Elizabeth O.

<small>ROMANCE AND HISTORICAL PUBLICATIONS</small>

Novels

Confident Tomorrows. London, Hurst and Blackett, 1931.
The Third Miss Chance. London, Hurst and Blackett, 1933.
Familiar Treatment. London, Hurst and Blackett, 1940.
At Professor Chummy's. London, Sampson Low, 1946.
Compromise with Yesterday. London, Sampson Low, 1946.

*   *   *

Elizabeth O. Peter wrote only a few novels in the 1930's and early 1940's. There is, however, considerable development in style and mood between the first (*Confident Tomorrows*, 1931) and the last (*Compromise with Yesterday*, 1946). Both deal with the effects of war on romance. The melodrama and set-piece stiff-upper-lip situations of *Confident Tomorrows* fail to convince, but the unashamedly romantic plot of *Compromise with Yesterday* is skilfully and touchingly manipulated.

The first book was probably partly inspired by R. C. Sherriff's *Journey's End*. Jerry Mainwaring is, like Stanhope in Sherriff's play, only able to see the war through by taking to drink. He survives the first world war, but is by then an incurable alcoholic. Thelma (''Tim''), the wife who has adored him ever since they both were children, remains loyal—in spite of Jerry's drunkenness, debts, and degradation. But gradually she and Jerry's friend Michael fall in love, though they nobly damp down their feelings until almost the end of the book. Jerry's increasing depravity through drink, and his repeated reconciliations with Thelma lack conviction, mainly because the book's language is so often stilted: ''Timmy . . . take me back. Let me be your husband again, and your lover, and your pal.'' But the romantic triangle is ultimately resolved successfully when, after Jerry strikes Thelma, Michael declares his love, and Jerry—as usual the worse for drink—gets killed in an accident.

By contrast, *Compromise with Yesterday* is vivid and compulsive from the beginning. David Allen, a first world war pilot who has become an Air Commodore in the RAF by the time of Hitler's war, represents not only the vulnerability of youthful romance but the potency of remembered love affairs. These are, of course, as Peter writes, ''more powerful, more relentless than the living presence, which might disappoint or cease to enchant.'' The author uses the clichés of wartime romantic fiction with aplomb. Her descriptions of snatched meetings between lovers on leave and the fear of sudden death that formed the background of so many people's lives make haunting and memorable reading.

This novel gets as deeply under the emotional skin as, for example, Noël Coward's celebrated drama *Cavalcade*, which was also, like *Compromise with Yesterday*, a family saga of two wars and the years between. Peter uses the sweet-savage images of romance with such impact and intensity that it is surprising she did not follow up her last novel with further love stories.

—Mary Cadogan

PETERS, Elizabeth. See **MICHAELS, Barbara.**

PETERS, Ellis. See **PARGETER, Edith.**

PETERS, Maureen. Also writes as Veronica Black; Catherine Darby; Belinda Grey; Elizabeth Law; Levanah Lloyd; Judith Rothman; Sharon Whitby. British. Born in Caernarvon, Wales, 3 March 1935. Educated at Caernarvon Grammar School, 1945–52; University College, Bangor, 1952–56, B.A. 1956, Dip.Ed. Married and divorced twice; two sons and two daughters. Address: c/o Robert Hale Ltd., 45–47 Clerkenwell Green, London EC1R 0HT, England.

ROMANCE AND HISTORICAL PUBLICATIONS

Novels (series: Greys; Vinegar)

Elizabeth the Beloved. London, Hale, 1965; New York, Beagle, 1972.
Katheryn, The Wanton Queen. London, Hale, 1967; New York, Beagle, 1971.
Mary, The Infamous Queen. London, Hale, 1968; New York, Beagle, 1971.
Bride for King James. London, Hale, 1968.
Joan of the Lilies. London, Hale, 1969.
The Rose of Hever. London, Hale, 1969; as *Anne, The Rose of Hever*, New York, Beagle, 1971.
Flower of the Greys. London, Hale, 1969.
Princess of Desire. London, Hale, 1970; New York, Pinnacle, 1973.
Struggle for a Crown. London, Hale, 1970.
Shadow of a Tudor. London, Hale, 1971.
Seven for St. Crispin's Day. London, Hale, 1971.
The Cloistered Flame. London, Hale, 1971.
Jewel of the Greys. London, Hale, 1972.
The Woodville Wench. London, Hale, 1972.
Henry VIII and His Six Wives (novelization of screenplay). London, Fontana, and New York, St. Martin's Press, 1972.
The Peacock Queen. London, Hale, 1972.
The Virgin Queen. New York, Pinnacle, 1972.
The Queen Who Never Was. New York, Pinnacle, 1972.
Royal Escape. Boston, Lincolnshire, Jones Blakey, 1972.
Destiny's Lady. New York, Pinnacle, 1973.
The Gallows Herd. London, Hale, 1973.
The Maid of Judah. London, Hale, 1973.
Flawed Enchantress. London, Hale, 1974.
So Fair and Foul a Queen. London, Hale, 1974.
The Willow Maid. London, Hale, 1974.
The Curse of the Greys. London, Hale, 1974.
The Queenmaker. London, Hale, 1975.

Tansy. London, Hale, 1975.
Kate Alanna. London, Hale, 1975.
A Child Called Freedom. London, Hale, 1976.
The Crystal and the Cloud. London, Hale, 1977.
Beggar Maid, Queen. London, Hale, 1980.
I, The Maid. London, Hale, 1980.
The Snow Blossom. London, Hale, 1980.
Night of the Willow. London, Hale, 1981; New York, St. Martin's Press, 1982.
Ravenscar. London, Hale, 1981.
Song for a Strolling Player. London, Hale, 1981.
Red Queen, White Queen. London, Hale, 1982.
The Dragon and the Rose. London, Hale, 1982.
Frost on the Rose. London, Hale, 1982.
Imperial Harlot. London, Hale, 1983.
My Lady Troubadour. London, Hale, 1983.
Lackland's Bride. London, Hale, 1983.
Alianor. London, Hale, 1984.
A Song for Marguerite. London, Hale, 1984.
My Philippa. London, Hale, 1984.
Fair Maid of Kent. London, Hale, 1985.
Isabella, The She-Wolf. London, Hale, 1985.
The Vinegar Seed. London, Hale, 1986.
The Vinegar Blossom. London, Hale, 1986.
The Luck-Bride. London, Hale, 1987.
The Vinegar Tree. London, Hale, 1987.
Lady for a Chevalier. London, Hale, 1987.
My Catalina. London, Hale, 1988.
The Noonday Queen. London, Hale, 1988.
Incredible, Fierce Desire. London, Hale, 1988.
Wife in Waiting. London, Hale, 1988.
Patchwork. London, Hale, 1989.

Novels as Veronica Black

Dangerous Inheritance. London, Hale, 1969; New York, Paperback Library, 1970.
Portrait of Sarah. London, Hale, 1969; New York, Berkley, 1973.
The Wayward Madonna. London, Hale, and New York, Lenox Hill Press, 1970.
A Footfall in the Mist. London, Hale, and New York, Lenox Hill Press, 1971.
Master of Malcarew. London, Hale, and New York, Lenox Hill Press, 1971.
Enchanted Grotto. London, Hale, 1972; New York, Lenox Hill Press, 1973.
Moonflete. London, Hale, 1972; New York, Lenox Hill Press, 1973.
Fair Kilmeny. London, Hale, and New York, Berkley, 1972.
Minstrel's Leap. London, Hale, 1973.
Spin Me a Shadow. London, Hale, 1974.
The House That Hated People. London, Hale, 1974.
Echo of Margaret. London, Hale, 1978.
Greengirl. London, Hale, 1979.
Pilgrim of Desire. London, Hale, 1979.
Flame in the Snow. London, Hale, 1980.
My Pilgrim Love. London, Hale, 1982.
Bond Wife. London, Hale, 1983.
Lover Dark, Lady Fair. London, Hale, 1983.
Hoodman Blind. London, Hale, 1984.

Novels as Judith Rothman

With Murder in Mind. London, Hale, 1975.
Dark Gemini. London, Fontana, 1983.

Novels as Sharon Whitby

The Last of the Greenwood. London, Hale, 1975; New York, Pyramid, 1976.
The Unforgotten Face. London, Hale, 1975.
Here Be Dragons. London, Hale, 1980.
The Silky. London, Hale, 1980.
The Houseless One. London, Hale, 1981.
No Song at Morningside. London, Hale, 1981.
The Savage Web. London, Hale, 1982.
Shiver Me a Story. London, Hale, 1982.
Nine Days a-Dying. London, Hale, 1982.
Children of the Rainbow. London, Hale, 1982.

Novels as Catherine Darby (series: Falcon; Moon; Rowan Family; Sabre Family)

Falcon Series:
1. *A Falcon for a Witch*. New York, Popular Library, and London, Hale, 1975.
2. *The King's Falcon*. New York, Popular Library, 1975; as *A Game of Falcons*, London, Hale, 1976.
3. *Fortune for a Falcon*. New York, Popular Library, 1975; London, Hale, 1976.
4. *Season of the Falcon*. New York, Popular Library, and London, Hale, 1976.
5. *Falcon Royal*. New York, Popular Library, 1976; as *A Pride of Falcons*, London, Hale, 1977.
6. *Falcon Tree*. New York, Popular Library, 1976; London, Hale, 1977.
7. *The Falcon and the Moon*. New York, Popular Library, 1976; London, Hale, 1977.
8. *Falcon Rising*. New York, Popular Library, 1976; London, Hale, 1978.
9. *Falcon Sunset*. New York, Popular Library, 1976; London, Hale, 1978.
10. *Seed of the Falcon*. New York, Popular Library, 1978; London, Hale, 1981.
11. *Falcon's Claw*. New York, Popular Library, 1978; London, Hale, 1981.
12. *Falcon to the Lure*. New York, Popular Library, 1978; London, Hale, 1981.
Moon Series:
1. *Whisper Down the Moon*. New York, Popular Library, 1977; London, Hale, 1978.
2. *Frost on the Moon*. New York, Popular Library, 1977; London, Hale, 1979.
3. *The Flaunting Moon*. New York, Popular Library, 1977; London, Hale, 1979.
4. *Sing Me a Moon*. New York, Popular Library, 1977; London, Hale, 1980.
5. *Cobweb Across the Moon*. New York, Popular Library, 1978; London, Hale, 1980.
6. *Moon in Pisces*. New York, Popular Library, 1978; London, Hale, 1980.
A Dream of Fair Serpents. London, Hale, and New York, Popular Library, 1979.
Child of the Flesh. London, Hale, 1982.
Lass of Silver, Lad of Gold. London, Hale, 1982.
Rowan Family:
1. *Rowan Garth*. London, Hale, 1982.
2. *Rowan for a Queen*. London, Hale, 1983.
3. *A Scent of Rowan*. London, Hale, 1983.
4. *A Circle of Rowan*. London, Hale, 1983.
5. *The Rowan Maid*. London, Hale, 1984.
6. *Song of a Rowan*. London, Hale, 1984.

Sangreal. London, Hale, 1984.
Sabre Family:
1. *Sabre*. London, Hale, 1985.
2. *Sabre's Child*. London, Hale, 1985.
3. *The Silken Sabre*. London, Hale, 1985.
4. *House of Sabre*. London, Hale, 1986.
5. *A Breed of Sabre*. London, Hale, 1987.
6. *Morning of a Sabre*. London, Hale, 1987.
7. *Fruit of the Sabre*. London, Hale, 1987.
8. *Gentle Sabre*. London, Hale, 1988.
Heart of Flame. London, Hale, 1986.
Pilgrim in the Wind. London, Hale, 1988.
The Love Knot. London, Hale, 1989.

Novels as Belinda Grey

The Passionate Puritan. London, Mills and Boon, 1978; Toronto, Harlequin, 1979.
Loom of Love. London, Mills and Boon, 1979; Toronto, Harlequin, 1980.
Sweet Wind of Morning. London, Mills and Boon, 1979; Toronto, Harlequin, 1980.
Moon of Laughing Flame. London, Mills and Boon, and Toronto, Harlequin, 1980.
Daughter of Isis. London, Mills and Boon, and Toronto, Harlequin, 1981.
Glen of Frost. London, Mills and Boon, and Toronto, Harlequin, 1981.
Proxy Wedding. London, Mills and Boon, 1982.
Saraband for Sara. London, Mills and Boon, 1984.

Novels as Levanah Lloyd

A Maid Called Wanton. London, Futura, 1981.
Mail Order Bride. London, Futura, 1981.
Cauldron of Desire. London, Futura, 1981.
Dark Surrender. London, Futura, 1981.

Novels as Elizabeth Law

Double Deception. New York, Walker, 1987.
A Scent of Lilac. New York, Walker, 1988.
Regency Morning. New York, Walker, 1988.

OTHER PUBLICATIONS

Other

Jean Ingelow, Victorian Poetess. Ipswich, Boydell Press, and Totowa, New Jersey, Rowman and Littlefield, 1972.
An Enigma of Brontës. London, Hale, and New York, St. Martin's Press, 1974.

*

Maureen Peters comments:
A prolific writer. Writes easily, perhaps too easily, one idea succeeding another. Tries to keep up with but not give in to current trends and make each book the best of its kind. Enjoys using a variety of themes with a particular fondness for inducing a pleasurable terror in the reader. Enjoys Tudor and Plantagenet settings and the 19th century in the USA, also Red Indians and gypsies. Writes in longhand so greatest problem is keeping pace with flow of ideas.

*   *   *

Maureen Peters has written many excellent historical biographies beginning with those of royal personages, *Elizabeth the Beloved* blazing the trail. Following the undoubted success of this book, the author went on to write of Katheryn Howard, Mary, Lady Jane Grey and other Tudors, including the luckless Anne Boleyn in the moving *The Rose of Hever*. Obviously happy with the Tudors of whose period she exactly captured the romance, cruelty, and excitement, Peters continued her series with yet further stories of Henry VIII and his wives, seen through the eyes of the dying king—an unusual touch. This version of the great king's story is engrossing reading, and Peters was clever enough to convey the differences between the six queens, from the cloying Katherine of Aragon to the fascinating Anne Boleyn, the impish childishness of Katherine Howard to the final contentment he found with his last wife, who outlived him. Though stories of the Tudor period are legion, Peters's writing manages to instill a freshness and a reality of period that make one travel back in time.

So on through other novels still nudging history but with an occasional change of period, keeping the same ease of style and readability. *The Maid of Judah* provided a jump forward to Victorian days. This tale of a Jewish orphan's struggle against life in a brothel, with help from an old Jewish artist, and her love for a dancer, is dramatically set against an East End background. The heroine, Michal, is startlingly graphical, and the reader shares her loves and her miseries with pleasure. Peters has a simple style, but she manages to convey a word picture with consummate skill, choosing every one with care; even her choice of adjectives is just right for the mood of the time and place. The theme may seem sad but the telling of it skilfully removes any misery.

Tansy, *Kate Alanna*, and *A Child Called Freedom* constitute a family trilogy, each one complete in itself, yet making up a wonderful whole. The tale begins in Ireland with the young Tansy, whose dreams and passions puzzle her family. The sequel, *Kate Alanna*, reveals how she plans a new life in America with the dangers and excitement ahead, all faced with courage. The final book, *A Child Called Freedom*, is compelling reading, showing Tansy in America, and her love for Tom Wolf, a half Indian, which takes her to the Sacramento Trail. Here Peters has shown her versatility in writing authentically, with a caressing descriptive flair, of the tribal customs of the Indian and life in those pioneering days.

Peters is a prolific author showing her real ability and versatility, and the promise of more such novels is rich indeed. Her first novels set a high standard which has been maintained, even surpassed, with each new book.

—Lornie Leete-Hodge

PETERS, Natasha. Pseudonym for Anastasia N. Cleaver. Address c/o Fawcett, 210 East 50th Street, New York, New York 10022, U.S.A.

ROMANCE AND HISTORICAL PUBLICATIONS

Novels

Savage Surrender. New York, Ace, 1977; London, Arrow, 1978.

Dangerous Obsession. New York, Ace, 1978; London, Arrow, 1979.
The Masquers. New York, Ace, 1979; London, Arrow, 1980.
The Enticers. New York, Fawcett, 1981; London, New English Library, 1983.
The Immortals. New York, Fawcett, 1983.
Darkness into Light. New York, Fawcett, 1984; London, New English Library, 1985.
Wild Nights. New York, Fawcett, 1986.

*   *   *

Historical settings vividly detailed, incredible characters in even more incredible plots, rude talk and sexual encounters provocatively if not pornographically described—these form the basis of the historical romances of Natasha Peters.

Savage Surrender opens in a French château in the 19th century, where the reader meets the novel's heroine, Elise Lesconflair, the spoiled and headstrong niece of Count Lesconflair and the goddaughter of Napoleon. Elise grows up quickly when she is betrothed to Baron Friederich Rolland von Meier, whom the willful Elise detests: '' . . . so terribly dull . . . and so ugly. . . . Grotesquely ugly! That fat belly and those thin blond wisps of baby hair—yes, he looks just like a gigantic baby! And his breath stinks, too.'' In a fit of defiance, Elise runs out into the forest, sheds her clothing, and jumps into a swimming pond, where the villainous Garth McClelland stares at her boldly through pale ice-blue eyes and then proceeds to take advantage of her. Elise's indignant brothers force her to marry McClelland (posing as ''Lord Armand Charles Alexandre Valadon, Marquis de Pellissier'') despite her betrothal to the repugnant Baron. McClelland, alternately a ''beast'' and a gentle lover, takes his ''hell-cat'' Elise off to Nantes, where both board a slave ship headed for Africa and the West Indies. Elise is rescued from cruel Garth by pirate Jean Lafitte, who takes her to his home in Louisiana and installs her as his mistress. Amazingly, Elise and Garth McClelland find each other, villain and hell-cat are reunited, they start a family and eventually go ''out of the gathering gloom of the forest into the brightness of the afternoon sun.''

The Masquers is set in 18th-century Venice—''the beautiful, the sensual city of Venice'' where ''gondolas glide soundlessly through narrow canals, carrying masked lovers to secret trysts, while *cicisbei* (18th century gallants) play court to bored noblewomen.'' Fosca Loredan is the beautiful and bored noblewoman heroine. Her husband is the aristocratic Alessandro; her lover, the bold revolutionary Rafaello Leopardi. The rest you know.

Pre-Communist Shanghai in the 1930's is the setting for *The Enticers*, a story of two sisters—Anne Fox, the ''sensitive, passionate woman whose secret past bound her to this enigmatic land and stood between her and love forever,'' and Kit, Anne's gorgeous sister, ''the queen of a razzle-dazzle social set, who ran from bed to bed savagely trying to fill an empty life''—and the two men they marry—Gilbert Lawrence, Anne's husband, ''a doctor whose lust for his own wife's sister finally drove him to the sweet release of the East—opium,'' and James Innes, Kit's husband, a rich empire-builder ''whose money bought his fashionable wife but could never pave his way into the high society he pretended to scorn.''

The Immortals returns to Shanghai—and to Anne Fox, who has since married Innes after her husband Lawrence (conveniently) killed her sister Kit and then himself. Anne Innes, who runs the institution for orphans and abandoned children that she founded (her office there, in fact, is in the very room where the murder-suicide took place), is now confronted by her long-lost daughter Amalie, the product of her teenage romance with a Chinese Communist student, Chen. ''Clothed in stunning silk and white-hot hate,'' the bitter Amalie Berenger (the name of her adoptive parents) has come to Shanghai to seek revenge from the former Nazi soldier who had brutally assaulted her during the war, but she ends up not only meeting her mother (now dying of cancer) but seducing her mother's good friend, a Roman Catholic priest, Father Michael Cassaday.

Wild Nights begins with a postcard from Emma Louise Vaughan, dated September 8, 1952:

Dear Mom and Aunt Louise,
   WOW! I finally made it to Cambodia! Trip up the Mekong River was beautiful but scary—boats travel in convoys as protection against pirates on water and guerrillas on land. After I explore Phnom Penh, I'm going to find a way to get to Angkor Wat. This has already been the most fantastic experience of my entire life! Can't wait to see what happens next!
                                                                     Love, Emma

Emma has left her life as a Nebraska beauty queen to be a foreign correspondent covering the escalating French military presence in Southeast Asia. Alan Hazan, the first man she meets there, falls in love with her (''Beautiful Emma. Emma of the golden hair and the flashing green eyes''). But it is Captain Robert Janvier of the French Foreign Legion who captures Emma's heart and introduces her to the pleasures of opium as well as ''the sensuality of her young body.'' (Yes, the title is from the Emily Dickinson poem, recited to Emma by Alan, who perseveres: ''Wild Nights—Wild Nights!/Were I with thee/Wild Nights should be/Our luxury!'').

Like the author's pseudonym, each ''Natasha'' novel dazzles with exoticism, then ''Peters'' out in incredulity.

—Marcia G. Fuchs

PIANKA, Phyllis Taylor.

ROMANCE AND HISTORICAL PUBLICATIONS

Novels

Nurse of the Island. New York, Bouregy, 1976.
The Paisley Butterfly. New York, Dell, 1980.
Sleeping Heiress. New York, Dell, 1980.
Heather Wild. New York, Dell, 1982.

OTHER PUBLICATIONS

Other

How to Write Romances. Cincinnati, Writer's Digest, 1988.

*   *   *

Phyllis Taylor Pianka became well-known as one of the Candlelight Romance series writers specializing in Regency period novels. She has continued in this genre by writing for the new Harlequin Regency series although she did venture into the ''Intrigue'' line with one novel.

While Pianka uses the time and setting of the Regency period, she concentrates on plot and character development to provide the necessary conflict. Her novels do not usually depend on historical events or persons to move the story along. Instead, the Regency framework acts as a comfortable background that readers can easily identify with. The setting that is used is typical Regency, the Opera house, Kensington Gardens, and drives in Hyde Park. One has the ''feel'' of the period without the clutter of names, dress descriptions, and extended chatter that is often used to produce that effect.

Because she concentrates on plot, character and conflict, her novels tend to be rapid-paced, entertaining stories that hold her readers' attention effortlessly. Her plots are creatively developed and offer more than the standard sorts of conflict.

For instance, in *Heather Wild*, the heroine is kidnapped from a dressmaker's shop where she had been standing in for a fitting for her niece. The culprit is Arthur Clendennon, the younger brother of Marcus, the Duke of Heatherford. Once delivered to the Duke, Elizabeth learns that her niece was supposedly betrothed to the Duke years ago. He was determined to settle the question of marriage once and for all. But not this way! Arthur stepped in to ''help'' and events immediately become entangled. Elizabeth finds that she doesn't want to return to London to her sister's home where she had been nothing but an unpaid servant. Arthur is home, wounded in a naval battle, and the Duke suddenly finds himself unbelievably jealous of him. The Duke's mind is certainly not on a marriage with Elizabeth's niece. The rest of the novel follows typical romance lines, but provides an extra dab of humor as Elizabeth's maid sets her cap for the new Curate of the Parish. The ending is a satisfactory sigh as all involved get their just deserts, especially Elizabeth.

Pianka's more recent novels are exceptionally well executed. Plotting is more involved, characterization is more complex and events are less predictable.

In *Dame Fortune's Fancy* the hero and heroine meet when she finds him lying in the road. She is Judith Penridge, recent widow who has been cheated out of her home and property by a ruthless gambler. He is in reality the Marquis of Grantsby or as he introduces himself to Judith, Miles Harcourt. Miles had been stranded by the way side not far from a house and Judith manages to get him there. Miles's recovery from being struck by robbers is slow and it takes a day or so for him to recover. Judith is scrupulous about using food and supplies in the house and leaves a note for the owners. As Miles recovers, he is not so bothered. Unknown to Judith, he is the owner. After three or four days there, he makes arrangements for them to go to London. She goes with the idea of earning her living but he is determined to keep her in his own home. The usual conflicts of personalities take place with Judith frequently trying to find a job and Miles's mother finding ways to prevent her. The ending of the story finds Judith's possessions restored to her, the villain caught and Miles desperately trying to convince her that they love each other. Unable to stay with his family since she loves him, she is offered the house in the country until she decides what she should do in the future. There is no doubt as the Marquis arrives as plain Mr. Miles Harcourt, the man she fell in love with.

In all, Pianka has her own individual touch that makes her novels enjoyable and vastly re-readable. Readers of Regency novels tend to collect the better ones and Pianka's are no doubt in this category.

—Arlene Moore

PILCHER, Rosamunde (neé Scott). Has also written as Jane Fraser. British. Born in Lelant, Cornwall, 22 September 1924. Educated at St. Clares, Polwithen, Cornwall; Howell's School, Llandaff; Miss Kerr-Sanders' Secretarial College. Served in the Women's Royal Naval Service, 1943–46. Married Graham Hope Pilcher in 1946; two daughters and two sons. Lives in Invergowrie, Scotland. Agent: Felicity Bryan, 2-A North Parade, Banbury Road, Oxford, England.

ROMANCE AND HISTORICAL PUBLICATIONS

Novels

A Secret to Tell. London, Collins, 1955.
April. London, Collins, 1957.
On My Own. London, Collins, 1965.
Sleeping Tiger. London, Collins, 1967; New York, St. Martin's Press, 1974.
Another View. London, Collins, 1969; New York, St. Martin's Press, 1974.
The End of the Summer. London, Collins, 1971; New York, St. Martin's Press, 1975.
Snow in April. London, Collins, 1972; New York, St. Martin's Press, 1975.
The Empty House. London, Collins, 1973; New York, St. Martin's Press, 1975.
The Day of the Storm. London, Collins, and New York, St. Martin's Press, 1975.
Under Gemini. New York, St. Martin's Press, 1976; London, Collins, 1977.
Wild Mountain Thyme. New York, St. Martin's Press, 1978; London, New English Library, 1980.
The Carousel. New York, St. Martin's Press, 1982; London, Severn House, 1983.
Voices in Summer. New York, St. Martin's Press, 1984; London, Severn House, 1985.
The Shell Seekers. New York, St. Martin's Press, 1987.

Novels as Jane Fraser

Half-way to the Moon. London, Mills and Boon, 1949.
The Brown Fields. London, Mills and Boon, 1951.
Dangerous Intruder. London, Mills and Boon, 1951.
Young Bar. London, Mills and Boon, 1952; Toronto, Harlequin, 1965.
A Day Like Spring. London, Mills and Boon, 1953; Toronto, Harlequin, 1968.
Dear Tom. London, Mills and Boon, 1954.
Bridge of Corvie. London, Mills and Boon, 1956; New York, Fawcett, 1975.
A Family Affair. London, Mills and Boon, 1958.
A Long Way from Home. London, Mills and Boon, 1963; Toronto, Harlequin, 1964.
The Keeper's House. London, Mills and Boon, 1963; Toronto, Harlequin, 1964.

Short Stories

The Blue Bedroom and Other Stories. New York, St. Martin's Press, 1985.

OTHER PUBLICATIONS

Plays

The Dashing White Sergeant, with Charles C. Gairdner (produced London, 1955). London, Evans, 1955.
The Piper of Orde, with Charles C. Gairdner. London, Evans, n.d.
The Tulip Major (produced Dundee, 1957).

*

Rosamunde Pilcher comments:

I try in my work to strike a balance between the out-and-out romantic and the serious woman's writing of today. There is a huge market of intelligent women who sometimes wish to read a light novel without necessarily reading a load of out-dated rubbish. Over the 40 years I have been writing and selling, social conditions, behaviour, and expectations have changed drastically, and I have endeavoured always to keep a fresh and modern outlook, accepting the inevitable permissiveness, and incorporating it into my work, without necessarily condoning it nor encouraging the sort of loveless amorality which was prevalent in the 1960's. My short stories are not so much love stories, but more about human relations, i.e., the love which can exist, not simply between two young people, but also between mothers and children, brothers and sisters, old people and young people.

If the stories do not have a happy ending, then they always have a hopeful ending. Life is a succession of problems and decisions, and sometimes the best we can do is simply to come to terms with them.

*   *   *

Rosamunde Pilcher got her earlier practice writing romance for the ever popular British publisher Mills and Boon. When her apprenticeship had been served, she emerged to write some of the best plotted, well-characterized enchanting romances to be found anywhere. There is a magical, timeless quality to her stories that charms even the most hard-hearted reader. Somehow they are always just perfect—in length, in dialogue, in everything that matters. Each one is a small gem and all are highly recommended to those who scoff at the genre. Pilcher provides a classy read that is positively addicting.

Sleeping Tiger is one of the best. Selina Bruce, a quiet sensible woman, is engaged to marry a quiet sensible man. Everything is quite proper—until one day she decides, on a sudden impulse, to take off for a Spanish island to search for her father and becomes entangled in a delightful love affair with a writer. The tone is wryly gentle with lots of sparkling dialogue that is a true pleasure to read.

Often the stories involve the replacing of a slightly tarnished old love with a new, forever-after love. This is the case in *The End of the Summer* where the heroine finally relinquishes her infatuation with her recklessly handsome cousin in exchange for the steady stable love of a lawyer from Scotland. In *The Empty House* the heroine, Virginia Keile, rediscovers an old flame who had broken her heart ten years ago and falls in love with him all over again, proving that he was worthy of her love in the first place. *Wild Mountain Thyme*'s plot revolves on the same basis, with Victoria Bradshaw renewing her broken affair with Oliver Dobbs only to realize, almost against her will, that she is in love with another, more worthy man.

Under Gemini concerns, naturally, a pair of identical twins. Flora, the good twin, is our heroine, and Rose is the bad one who wants Flora to impersonate her in the sticky situation into which she has landed herself. Lots of complications arise but all is settled quite to the reader's immense satisfaction.

With Pilcher's novels, the enjoyment is in the journey. Every step of the way is paved with all the hallmarks of quality one expects in a good writer, no matter what the scope of the work. Pilcher steadfastly provides it.

—Marilyn Lockhart

* * *

PLAIDY, Jean. See **HOLT, Victoria.**

* * *

PLUMMER, Clare. See **EMSLEY, Clare.**

* * *

POLLAND, Madeleine A(ngela, née Cahill). Also writes as Frances Adrian. British. Born in Kinsale, County Cork, Ireland, 31 May 1918. Educated at Hitchin Girls' Grammar School, Hertfordshire, 1929–37. Served in the Women's Auxiliary Air Force, 1942–45. Married Arthur Joseph Polland in 1946; one daughter and one son. Assistant librarian, Letchworth Public Library, Hertfordshire, 1939–42 and 1945–46. Agent: Hilary Rubinstein, A. P. Watt Ltd., 20 John Street, London WC1N 2DL, England. Address: Edificio Hercules 406, Avenida Gamonal, Arroyo de la Miel, Malaga, Spain.

ROMANCE AND HISTORICAL PUBLICATIONS

Novels

Thicker than Water. New York, Holt Rinehart, 1965; London, Hutchinson, 1967.
The Little Spot of Bother. London, Hutchinson, 1967; as *Minutes of a Murder*, New York, Holt Rinehart, 1967.
Random Army. London, Hutchinson, 1969; as *Shattered Summer*, New York, Doubleday, 1970.
Package to Spain. London, Hutchinson, and New York, Walker, 1971.
Double Shadow (as Frances Adrian). New York, Fawcett, and London, Macdonald and Jane's, 1977.
Sabrina. New York, Delacorte Press, and London, Collins, 1979.
All Their Kingdoms. New York, Delacorte Press, and London, Collins, 1981.
Their Heart Speaks in Many Ways. New York, Delacorte Press, and London, Collins, 1982.
No Price Too High. New York, Delacorte Press, 1984; London, Piatkus, 1985.
As It Was in the Beginning. London, Piatkus, 1987.

OTHER PUBLICATIONS

Fiction (for children)

Children of the Red King. London, Constable, 1960; New York, Holt Rinehart, 1961.

The Town Across the Water. London, Constable, 1961; New York, Holt Rinehart, 1963.
Beorn the Proud. London, Constable, 1961; New York, Holt Rinehart, 1962.
Fingal's Quest. New York, Doubleday, and London, Burns Oates, 1961.
The White Twilight. London, Constable, 1962; New York, Holt Rinehart, 1965.
Chuiraquimba and the Black Robes. New York, Doubleday, and London, Burns Oates, 1962.
City of the Golden House. New York, New York, Doubleday, 1963; Kingswood, Surrey, World's Work, 1964.
The Queen's Blessing. London, Constable, 1963; New York, Holt Rinehart, 1964.
Flame over Tara. New York, Doubleday, 1964; Kingswood, Surrey, World's Work, 1965.
Mission to Cathay. New York, Doubleday, 1965; Kingswood, Surrey, World's Work, 1966.
Queen Without Crown. London, Constable, 1965; New York, Holt Rinehart, 1966.
Deirdre. New York, Doubleday, and Kingswood, Surrey, World's Work, 1967.
To Tell My People. London, Hutchinson, and New York, Holt Rinehart, 1968.
Stranger in the Hills. New York, Doubleday, 1968; London, Hutchinson, 1969.
To Kill a King. London, Hutchinson, 1970; New York, Holt Rinehart, 1971.
Alhambra. New York, Doubleday, 1970; London, Hutchinson, 1971.
A Family Affair. London, Hutchinson, 1971.
Daughter to Poseidon. London, Hutchinson, 1972; as *Daughter of the Sea*, New York, Doubleday, 1972.
Prince of the Double Axe. London, Abelard Schuman, 1976.

*

Manuscript Collection: Mugar Memorial Library, Boston University.

* * *

Madeleine A. Polland has written some very fine historical novels for children set in distant times and far-off places, but for her adult books, she uses settings she knows well and times not too far distant from our own.

She was born in Ireland, grew up in England, and now lives in Spain. All these settings are used in her books. Her love for Ireland is very strong and her sympathy for its tribulations shows in books like *As It Was in the Beginning*, *Thicker Than Water*, and *The Little Spot of Bother*. Her best, most lyrical descriptions, too, are of the Irish countryside. As she says in one of her books, "with Irish exiles, Ireland sort of goes thick in them like condensed milk and they're twice as passionate as the people who stay."

Her beautiful heroines have many difficulties to overcome before they gain the romantic happiness they crave. The heroine of *No Price Too High* suffers a similar fate to Frances Hodgson Burnett's Little Princess; in the 1920's her wealthy father disappears, leaving her school fees unpaid and she is ill-used by a mercenary headmistress. But she is old enough to go out to work although totally unfitted for it by her upbringing. She suffers dreadfully from horrible employers, is tricked into a loveless marriage, and has a crippled child whom her husband will not even look at before her resurrected father arrives to save her, fortuitously bringing an Irish doctor with him with whom she falls in love.

Another high-born heroine who suffers is Irish Emily who is being "finished" in Spain at the time of the Civil War. Emily is swept off her feet by aristocratic Alejandro who leaves her literally at the altar. She returns desolate to Ireland, recovers and is about to marry Dermot (a Viscount) when he is whisked off to war and is posted missing. Grieving Emily joins the WAAF (as did the author) and falls improbably for Sam, a humble mechanic with a chip on his shoulder. She keeps enough distance between them so that at the war's end, when Dermot reappears they can marry but she realises she has ruined Sam's life. Dermot's money has gone so they set out for a new life in Spain.

No aristocrat but a simple Irish girl is orphaned Kate Mary Pearse in *As It Was in the Beginning*, set at the time of the Irish troubles in the 1920's. She suffers the anguish of divided loyalty for her beloved is a Sergeant in the Royal Ulster Constabulary whose mission is to capture Kate's cousin, the local Sinn Fein leader. Her dilemma is impossible—"to pray for victory for one meant praying for the almost certain death of the other." Finally, Kate marries her Sergeant after her cousin's execution, but they have to live exiled from their beloved Ireland.

Polland uses conflict of war (especially civil war in both Spain and Ireland), conflict of class, and conflict of cultures in her plotting. Her characters, especially her Irish people are realistic, and she is adept at portraying atmosphere such as the claustrophobic closeness of Irish village life. Her descriptions are evocative and beautiful; her love for the places she describes shines through. Her stories, however, are very slow moving with more emphasis on emotion than action and they are often sad, with more agony than ecstasy. Indeed, a book like *The Little Spot of Bother* could easily be condensed into a short story as far as the action is concerned. However, Polland's romances are truly romantic and although the reader is battered by the stormy seas of emotion during the books, she reaches the safe harbour of the happy ending eventually.

—Pamela Cleaver

PONSONBY, D(oris) A(lmon). Also writes as Doris Rybot; Sarah Tempest. British. Born in Devonport, Devon, 23 March 1907. Educated at Shrewsbury High School for Girls; Villabelle, Neuchâtel, Switzerland. Married John Rybot in 1933 (died 1979). Sub-editor, Oxford *Times*, reporter, Aldershot *Gazette*, and freelance writer for *South China Morning Post* and Hong Kong *Herald*, 1928–37. Agent: Curtis Brown, 162–168 Regent Street, London, W1R 5TB, England.

ROMANCE AND HISTORICAL PUBLICATIONS

Novels (series: Jaspard Family Chronicle)

The Gazebo. London, Hutchinson, 1945; as *If My Arms Could Hold* (as Doris Ponsonby), New York, Liveright, 1947.
Sophy Valentine. London, Hutchinson, 1946.
Merry Meeting. London, Hutchinson, 1948.
Strangers in My House. London, Hutchinson, 1948.
Bow Window in Green Street. London, Hutchinson, 1949.
Family of Jaspard. London, Hutchinson, and New York, Crowell, 1950; as *The General* and *The Fortunate Adventure*, London, White Lion, 2 vols., 1971.

The Bristol Cousins (Jaspard). London, Hutchinson, 1951.
The Foolish Marriage. London, Hutchinson, 1952.
The Widow's Daughters. London, Hutchinson, 1953.
Royal Purple. London, Hutchinson, 1954.
Dogs in Clover. London, Hutchinson, 1954.
Conquesta's Caravan. London, Hutchinson, 1955.
Unhallowed House. London, Hutchinson, 1956.
So Bold a Choice. London, Hurst and Blackett, 1960.
Romany Sister (as Doris Rybot). London, Hale, 1960.
A Japanese Doll (as Doris Rybot). London, Hale, 1961.
A Living to Earn. London, Hurst and Blackett, 1961.
The Orphans. London, Hurst and Blackett, 1962.
Bells along the Neva. London, Hurst and Blackett, 1964.
The Jade Horse of Merle. London, Hurst and Blackett, 1966.
An Unusual Tutor. London, Hurst and Blackett, 1967.
A Winter of Fear (as Sarah Tempest). London, Hurst and Blackett, 1967; New York, Pyramid, 1968.
The Forgotten Heir. London, Hurst and Blackett, 1969.
The Heart in the Sand. London, Hurst and Blackett, 1970.
Mr. Florian's Fortune. London, Hurst and Blackett, 1971.
Flight from Hanover Square. London, Hurst and Blackett, 1972.
The Gamester's Daughter. London, Hurst and Blackett, 1974.
The Heir to Holtwood. London, Hurst and Blackett, 1975.
An Unnamed Gentlewoman. London, Hurst and Blackett, 1976.
Kaye's Walk. London, Hurst and Blackett, 1977.
Sir William. London, Hurst and Blackett, 1978.
Exhibition Summer. London, Hale, 1982.
A Woman Despised. London, Hale, 1988.

OTHER PUBLICATIONS

Other

Call a Dog Hervey. London, Hutchinson, 1949.
The Lost Duchess: The Story of the Prince Consort's Mother. London, Chapman and Hall, 1958.
A Prisoner in Regent's Park. London, Chapman and Hall, 1961.

Other as Doris Rybot

The Popular Chow Chow, with Lydia Ingleton. London, Popular Dogs, 1954.
My Kingdom for a Donkey. London, Hutchinson, 1963.
A Donkey and a Dandelion. London, Hutchinson, 1966.
It Began Before Noah (on zoos). London, Joseph, 1972.

*

D. A. Ponsonby comments:

In all my historical stories and romances my main aim (apart from telling a good story) is to be as historically accurate as possible, not only in facts, but concerning manners, dress, social attitudes, and everything else.

*   *   *

It is more than 40 years since D. A. Ponsonby's historical novels were first published, yet there is a freshness about them that makes them hold their attraction today.

Her sense of period is accurate and her shrewd knowledge of people splendidly evokes the time in which the tales are set. *The Gazebo*, her first novel, is a gripping family story revealing a young girl's awakening to love, her marriage and its problems. Much of her fiction is told by means of excellent descriptive passages with the conversations slipping into place effortlessly, avoiding the all-too-common failure of so many of today's writers of using mainly jerky conversations for narration.

The novel *Merry Meeting*, about the love of two orphans, begins in a foundling home in the cruel days of the 18th century.Their future lives are mingled, and the boy's eventual sacrifice fits exactly into the story. The author's ability to bring life to her characters ensures a convincing tale.

Bow Window in Green Street is set in 18th-century Bath, and all the hopes and excitement of Regency living are wonderfully captured. One feels one could again knock on the door of the very house in which they all lived. The Regency, in fact, was a favourite period for Ponsonby who vividly recreated its days in her novels. *The Widow's Daughters* is a more light-hearted story of a silly, scheming widow using her wiles to marry off her four daughters who had their own surprising ideas.

The well-worn themes of regency novels take on a new meaning under this writer's narrative skill; the timelessness of her writing is its strong quality. Her sense of period and the fact that her stories can be read and re-read with ease makes them stand out in the morass of historical fiction. My regret is there are not more of them, though their exclusivity is another charm, making them novels to be treasured.

—Lornie Leete-Hodge

POPE, Dudley (Bernard Egerton). British. Born in Ashford, Kent, 29 December 1925. Educated at Ashford Grammar School, 1934–42. Served in the Merchant Navy, 1941–43. Married Kathleen Patricia Hall in 1954; one daughter. Sub-editor and deputy foreign editor, London *Evening News*, 1944–59. Agent: John McLaughlin, Campbell Thomson and McLaughlin Ltd., 31 Newington Green, London N16 9PU, England. Address: Le Pirate 379, B.P. 677, 97150 Marigot, St. Martin, French West Indies.

ROMANCE AND HISTORICAL PUBLICATIONS

Novels (series: Lord Nicholas Ramage; Yorke)

Ramage. London, Weidenfeld and Nicolson, and Philadelphia, Lippincott, 1965.
Ramage and the Drum Beat. London, Weidenfeld and Nicolson, 1967; as *Drumbeat*, New York, Doubleday, 1968.
Ramage and the Freebooters. London, Weidenfeld and Nicolson, 1969; as *Triton Brig*, New York, Doubleday, 1969.
Governor Ramage R.N. London, Secker and Warburg, and New York, Simon and Schuster, 1973.
Ramage's Prize. London, Secker and Warburg, 1974; New York, Simon and Schuster, 1975.
Ramage and the Guillotine. London, Secker and Warburg, and New York, Simon and Schuster, 1975.
Ramage's Diamond. London, Secker and Warburg, 1976.
Ramage's Mutiny. London, Secker and Warburg, 1977.
Ramage and the Rebels. London, Secker and Warburg, 1978; New York, Walker, 1985.
The Ramage Touch. London, Secker and Warburg, 1979; New York, Walker, 1984.
Convoy (Yorke). London, Secker and Warburg, 1979; New York, Walker, 1987.
Ramage's Signal. London, Secker and Warburg, 1980; New York, Walker, 1984.

Buccaneer (Yorke). London, Secker and Warburg, 1981; New York, Walker, 1984.
Ramage and the Renegades. London, Secker and Warburg, 1981.
Admiral (Yorke). London, Secker and Warburg, 1982.
Ramage's Devil. London, Secker and Warburg, 1982.
Decoy (Yorke). London, Secker and Warburg, 1983; New York, Walker, 1984.
Ramage's Trial. London, Secker and Warburg, 1984.
Ramage's Challenge. London, Secker and Warburg, 1985.
Galleon (Yorke). London, Secker and Warburg, 1986; New York, Walker, 1987.
Ramage at Trafalgar. London, Secker and Warburg, 1986.
Corsair (Yorke). London, Secker and Warburg, 1987.
Ramage and the Saracens. London, Secker and Warburg, 1988.
Ramage and the Dido. London, Secker and Warburg, 1989.

OTHER PUBLICATIONS

Other

Flag 4: The Battle of Coastal Forces in the Mediterranean. London, Kimber, 1954.
The Battle of the River Plate. London, Kimber, 1956; as *Graf Spee*, Philadelphia, Lippincott, 1957.
73 North: The Battle of the Barents Sea. London, Weidenfeld and Nicolson, and Philadelphia, Lippincott, 1958.
England Expects. London, Weidenfeld and Nicolson; as *Decision at Trafalgar*, Philadelphia, Lippincott, 1959.
At 12 Mr. Byng Was Shot. London, Weidenfeld and Nicolson, and Philadelphia, Lippincott, 1962.
The Black Ship: Mutiny on the H.M.S. Hermion 1797. London, Weidenfeld and Nicolson, 1963; Philadelphia, Lippincott, 1964.
Guns. London, Weidenfeld and Nicolson, and New York, Delacorte Press, 1965.
The Great Gamble. London, Weidenfeld and Nicolson, and New York, Simon and Schuster, 1972.
Harry Morgan's Way (biography). London, Secker and Warburg, 1977; as *The Buccaneer King*, New York, Dodd Mead, 1978.
Life in Nelson's Navy. London, Allen and Unwin, and Annapolis, Maryland, Naval Institute Press, 1981.
The Devil Himself: The Mutiny of 1800. London, Secker and Warburg, 1987.

*

Manuscript Collection: Reading University, Berkshire.

Dudley Pope comments:
I have specialised in the history of the Navy in Nelson's time, and realised that the best way of describing it was in fictional form, so I created Nicholas Ramage as a young officer in Nelson's day and wrote the Ramage series.

*   *   *

Dudley Pope is an internationally known writer of British naval history. Besides writing numerous non-fiction works about the Royal Navy, he is also the creator of a series of novels about Lord Nicholas Ramage, a lowly Lieutenant in His Majesty's Navy during the Napoleonic period.

Before commenting on Pope's fiction, one must acknowledge his vast store of historical information about the Royal Navy and its history. It is not the kind of knowledge that is found on tediously compiled note-cards. Pope has internalized so much of what he has learned that readers would find it difficult, if not impossible, to detect a false note within his writing. There is no awkward stretch for words, no laborious description, no cut and paste line to show where historical fact blends with narrative need.

Not only does Pope avoid the normal pitfalls inherent in historical writing, he seems effortlessly to weave fact and fiction together. His writing is taut, compelling, and deceptively simple. His characters are works of art, especially Nicholas Ramage.

Ramage is not a super-hero. He doubts, he ponders his decisions. He questions his perceptions and tries to be fair in a world that functioned on patronage, rank, and bribery. He is not a stoic, for he worries. Like other men, he fears the unknowable and the uncontrollable.

The supporting characters in the Ramage series are just as well drawn and uniquely representative of the historical figures Pope brings to life. Finally, one cannot forget the other main character in the Ramage series . . . the Royal Navy. The ships, the daily tasks of living, the seaman's life of storms and wind, the noise of battles; all carry out their part in making Ramage and his adventures the best historical novels in years.

A look at two of the novels that were written sequentially might help illustrate just how readers become addicted to Lieutenant Ramage and his escapades. In *Governor Ramage, R.N.*, the Lieutenant and his crew face daunting odds. They are assigned convoy duty to help escort a fleet of merchant ships to Jamaica. Before they finally reach their destination, Ramage must cope with the following. His ship, the *Triton*, attacks and defeats a French privateer that had slipped into the convoy. He is then caught in a hurricane and eventually lands near a small Spanish island along with the ship owned by Mr. Yorke. The *Triton* is lost as is Mr. Yorke's ship, which carried passengers. The crews of both ships accept Ramage as their natural leader and between them, they capture the island. While waiting to capture the Spanish supply ship that is expected, Ramage and his men find buried treasure. They easily capture the ship when it does arrive and eventually reach Jamaica. Ramage's arrival, however, is less than joyous for he is immediately arrested and charged with cowardliness in battle. At the end of the book Ramage confronts his accusers. Tension and suspense do not resolve themselves until the last two or three pages, keeping the reader gripped by the story.

Ramage's Prize is the sequel to *Governor Ramage R.N.* In it, Ramage is offered further adventures. He and some of his men are still waiting to be posted on another ship in Jamaica, when he is offered an unusual assignment. What he gets is not another brig, but a mail packet! His charge . . . to find out how mail packets from England to Jamaica and back are being intercepted and taken. Whatever the answer, events are creating critical problems for government officials as well as military personnel. There is literally no direct communication with the government in Jamaica either to the different military or diplomatic posts or with London. Ramage does, indeed, face a very puzzling mystery when he sets out to learn exactly what is happening to the mail packets.

Readers have a delightful time keeping up with Ramage's razor-sharp mind as he unravels the tangled knot of deception and traitorous guile. Pope's earlier career as a newspaper writer definitely helped him to learn the value of economic writing where one word did the work of three or four. Certainly the recognition of his scholarly publications helped as well. These two

aspects of his writing life somehow blended to produce a style of fiction that is uniquely his own. If his style is unique, so are his novels.

—Arlene Moore

PORTER, Eleanor H(odgman). Also wrote as Eleanor Stuart. American. Born in Littleton, New Hampshire, 19 December 1868. Educated at the New England Conservatory of Music, Boston. Married John L. Porter in 1892. Choir and concert singer, then teacher; full-time writer from 1901. *Died 21 May 1920.*

ROMANCE AND HISTORICAL PUBLICATIONS

Novels (series: Margaret; Miss Billy; Pollyanna)

Cross Currents: The Story of Margaret. Boston, Wilde, 1907; London, Harrap, 1928.
The Turn of the Tide: The Story of How Margaret Solved Her Problem. Boston, Wilde, 1908; London, Harrap, 1928.
The Story of Marco. Cincinnati, Jennings and Graham, 1911; London, Stanley Paul, 1920.
Miss Billy. Boston, Page, 1911; London, Stanley Paul, 1914.
Miss Billy's Decision. Boston, Page, 1912; London, Stanley Paul, 1915.
Pollyanna. Boston, Page, and London, Pitman, 1913.
Miss Billy—Married. Boston, Page, 1914; London, Stanley Paul, 1915.
Pollyanna Grows Up. Boston, Page, and London, Pitman, 1915.
Just David. Boston, Houghton Mifflin, and London, Constable, 1916.
The Road to Understanding. Boston, Houghton Mifflin, and London, Constable, 1917.
Oh, Money! Money! Boston, Houghton Mifflin, and London, Constable, 1918.
Dawn. Boston, Houghton Mifflin, 1919; as *Keith's Dark Tower*, London, Constable, 1919.
Mary Marie. Boston, Houghton Mifflin, and London, Constable, 1920.
Sister Sue. Boston, Houghton Mifflin, and London, Constable, 1921.

Short Stories

The Tangled Threads. Boston, Houghton Mifflin, 1919.
Across the Years. Boston, Houghton Mifflin, 1919.
The Tie That Binds. Boston, Houghton Mifflin, 1919.
Money, Love, and Kate, Together with The Story of a Nickel. New York, Doran, 1923; London, Hodder and Stoughton, 1924.
Hustler Joe and Other Stories. New York, Doran, 1924.
Little Pardner and Other Stories. New York, Doran, 1926; London, Hodder and Stoughton, 1927.
Just Mother and Other Stories. New York, Doran, 1927.
The Fortunate Mary. New York, Doubleday, 1928.

OTHER PUBLICATIONS

Other (for children)

The Sunbridge Girls at Six Star Ranch (as Eleanor Stuart).
Boston, Page, 1913; as *Six Star Ranch*, London, Stanley Paul,
1916.

*   *   *

When Eleanor H. Porter died in her early fifties, having given
up a singing career for writing only 20 years before, she left
behind her over 20 volumes of fiction. From this prolific output,
posterity has selected a single novel, *Pollyanna*, and given its
name not to one who sees the best side of a bad situation, but to
one who embraces blind and foolish optimism. As with Harriet
Beecher Stowe's Black Christ, so with Porter's little "glad" girl
who brought happiness into lives as afflicted as her own—for
who today would want to be called an Uncle Tom or a Pollyanna?

As a writer of children's stories—for and about children—
Porter belongs in that very American line which runs from Mark
Twain to Booth Tarkington. The boys are mischievous, the girls
responsible; the boys disrupt the social order, though they (even
Huck) ultimately conform to it, the girls work on it from within,
and restore it with certain improvements. The boys foment misunderstandings between unconsenting adults, the girls resolve
them. Tom Sawyer is constantly evading *his* Aunt Polly, Pollyanna nudges *hers* to the altar. Yet the status quo is not quite safe
from either boys or girls: Porter's social blueprint, happily based
upon feminine values, may be as subversive as Twain's "boy's"
books, though repressed by the adult reader. For as a perceptive
reviewer of 1913 noted, *Pollyanna* is "a book for grown-up people who will understand the criticism of convention; it would be
a disaster if many little girls should undertake to imitate the heroine."

It is this "criticism of convention," however defused, which
may give Porter some claim to our continuing attention. There is
a genuine social conscience in her work which distinguished her
from the Alice Hegan Rices and the Gene Stratton Porters, and
brings her closer to the best of all these "cheerful" (if not always quite "glad") writers, Jean Webster. Porter's first novel,
Cross Currents, sets the tone: a poor little rich girl is lost, and
grows up in the slums, amid the sweatshops. The novel vigorously attacks the child labour of its day, and several of Porter's
works at least touch upon social questions. *Pollyanna* certainly
criticizes the same over-zealous do-gooders who will be the villains of Griffith's film *Intolerance* three years later; *Mary
Marie*, in which the character's odd name is a compromise
agreed upon by warring parents, seriously discusses divorce; and
Pollyanna Grows Up accuses the slum landlord.

Though the Six Star Ranch stories deal with a moderately
mischievous group of six girls—"the happy hexagons"—
Porter's typical heroine, as well as being a marital fixer, is, like
Anne of Green Gables or Rebecca of Sunnybrook Farm, an orphan reaching for a family; and her arrangements are not always
selfless, especially since she is so often poor. The formula
works well enough with the girl at its centre, but two of Porter's
more egregiously sentimental works fail by attempting to force
the boy into this stereotyped role. *Dawn* finds a 15-year-old
youth suddenly stricken with blindness; he turns away from human contact, but is won back by the love of the great eye surgeon's stepdaughter, who adopts a false identity to woo him (one
wonders if Lloyd C. Douglas read this novel). And the hero of
Just David, as *The Times* not unjustly remarked, "combines in
his pathetic person the shortcomings of Lord Fauntleroy, Eric,

and Humphrey in *Misunderstood*." Girls could still be prigs, but
boys, after Tom, Huck, and Penrod, could not.

One (or three) of Porter's most effective works is the group of
novels made up of *Miss Billy* (her first major success), *Miss
Billy's Decision*, and *Miss Billy—Married*. Three settled bachelors receive a letter announcing the arrival of the forgotten god-
child of the eldest. Because of her androgynous name, they
assume that *she* is *he,* but their settled existence is in for a much
greater discombobulation. Each falls in love with her, each proposes, and after several misunderstandings she marries the
youngest. By June 1921, these three novels had sold 93, 78, and
86 thousand copies (*Pollyanna* at the same time had sold half a
million, and, as James D. Hart has noted, Porter's publishers
after her death commissioned five further writers of "their" Pollyanna series, which over 40 years sold two million copies).

Porter had a considerable talent for the short story—her novels tend to be episodic—and her best stories are collected in
three volumes published the year before her death: *The Tangled
Threads*, *The Tie That Binds*, and *Across the Years*, dealing with
the three ages of love. The last collection especially shows her
as a benign Mary Wilkins Freeman—the Yankee spareness and
satiric bite of Freeman's famous "The Revolt of Mother" provides a point of comparison, one of many, with Porter's charming but sentimentally lenient "When Mother and Father
Rebelled."

It is easy to sneer at Porter. A reviewer of 1917, condemning
one of her novels, predicts a large sale for it notwithstanding
("take it from a pessimist"). We do better to use as her epitaph
the phrase of a reviewer of her second Pollyanna book: "after
all, she has the right idea."

—Barrie Hayne

PORTER, Gene Stratton (Geneva Grace Stratton Porter).
American. Born in Wabash County, Indiana, 17 August 1863.
Attended public schools. Married Charles Darwin Porter in
1886; one daughter. Regular contributor, *McCall's Magazine*;
photographic editor, *Recreation* magazine; member of the natural
history department, *Outing* magazine; natural history photography specialist, *Photographic Times Annual Almanac*, four years.
Founded Gene Stratton Porter Productions film company, 1922.
Died 6 December 1924.

ROMANCE AND HISTORICAL PUBLICATIONS

Novels

The Song of the Cardinal: A Love Story. Indianapolis, Bobbs
Merrill, 1903; London, Hodder and Stoughton, 1913.
Freckles. New York, Doubleday, 1904; London, Murray, 1905.
At the Foot of the Rainbow. New York, Outing Publishing Com-
pany, 1907; London, Hodder and Stoughton, 1913.
A Girl of the Limberlost. New York, Doubleday, 1909; London,
Hodder and Stoughton, 1911.
The Harvester. New York, Doubleday, and London, Hodder
and Stoughton, 1911.
Laddie: A True-Blue Story. New York, Doubleday, and London,
Murray, 1913.
Michael O'Halloran. New York, Doubleday, and London, Mur-
ray, 1915.
A Daughter of the Land. New York, Doubleday, and London,
Murray, 1918.

Her Father's Daughter. New York, Doubleday, and London, Murray, 1921.

The White Flag. New York, Doubleday, and London, Murray, 1923.

The Keeper of the Bees. New York, Doubleday, and London, Hutchinson, 1925.

The Magic Garden. New York, Doubleday, and London, Hutchinson, 1927.

OTHER PUBLICATIONS

Play

Screenplay: *A Girl of the Limberlost*, 1924.

Verse

Morning Face, illustrated by the author. New York, Doubleday, and London, Murray, 1916.

The Fire Bird. New York, Doubleday, and London, Murray, 1922.

Jesus of the Emerald. New York, Doubleday, and London, Murray, 1923.

Other

What I Have Done with Birds: Character Studies of Native American Birds. Indianapolis, Bobbs Merrill, 1907; revised edition, New York, Doubleday, 1917; as *Friends in Feathers*, London, Curtis Brown, 1917.

Birds of the Bible. Cincinnati, Jennings and Graham, 1909; London, Hodder and Stoughton, 1910.

Music of the Wild, illustrated by the author. Cincinnati, Jennings and Graham, and London, Hodder and Stoughton, 1910.

Moths of the Limberlost, illustrated by the author. New York, Doubleday, 1912; London, Hodder and Stoughton, 1913.

After the Flood. Indianapolis, Bobbs Merrill, 1912.

Birds of the Limberlost. New York, Doubleday, 1914.

Homing with the Birds. New York, Doubleday, and London, Murray, 1919.

Wings. New York, Doubleday, 1923.

Tales You Won't Believe (natural history). New York, Doubleday, and London, Heinemann, 1925.

Let Us Highly Resolve (essays). New York, Doubleday, and London, Heinemann, 1927.

*

Critical Studies: *The Lady of the Limberlost: The Life and Letters of Gene Stratton Porter* by Jeanette Porter Meehan, New York, Doubleday, 1928, as *Life and Letters of Gene Stratton Porter*, London, Hutchinson, 1928; *Gene Stratton Porter* by Bernard F. Richards, Boston, Twayne, 1980.

*   *   *

It seems incredible today that Gene Stratton Porter's books were once among the most popular all over the world, both in English and in translation; that they sold out edition after edition; and that several of them were the subjects of motion pictures. Surely never before or since did such cardboard creations capture and hold a more enthusiastic audience. A good many of her major characters were never even named; they were designated and remain The Swamp Angel, The Man of Affairs, The

Bird Woman, and so on. Stereotypical characterization surely never has been carried to greater length. Her dialogue is a curious combination of simon-pure, frightfully long-winded passion and quirky lectures on diet and nature study, perpetrated by a writer totally deaf to the cadence of natural, colloquial speech; her code of values defies comprehension, muddling as it does fundamental issues of moral integrity and personal worth with trivial concerns of good form and etiquette relevant only to the turn of the century.

Still, when one has laughed at the quaint set speeches, purer-than-life heroes and positively incandescent heroines, and outmoded, bombastic philosophy, a glimmer of the charm that caught and held Porter's millions of readers remains. She created a world of good, honest (if pompous) people who offered one another whole hearts and an enviable confidence in a wholesome, unspoiled world full of the bounty of nature that was to be theirs and their childrens'. "Homely" was to her a word of highest praise. A more cynical generation cannot share this perhaps blinkered simplicity—but it is surely to her credit that it is difficult to believe in the existence of a nuclear arms race while in imagination patrolling the Limberlost woodland trail with Freckles, or keeping bees in the beautiful blue garden with Jamie MacFarlane and his little Scout.

—Joan McGrath

———

PORTER, Hal. Australian. Born in Albert Park, Melbourne, Victoria, 16 February 1911. Educated at Kensington State School, 1917; Bairnsdale State School, Victoria, 1918–21; Bairnsdale High School, 1922–26. Married Olivia Parnham in 1939 (divorced 1943). Cadet reporter, Bairnsdale *Advertiser*, 1927; schoolmaster, Victorian Education Department, 1927–37 and 1940, Queen's College, Adelaide, 1941–42, Prince Alfred College, Kent Town, South Australia, 1943–46, Hutchins School, Hobart, Tasmania, 1946–47, Knox Grammar School, Sydney, 1947, Ballarat College, Victoria, 1948–49, and Nijimura School, Kure, Japan (Australian Army Education), 1949–50; manager, George Hotel, St. Kilda, Victoria, 1949; director, National Theatre, Hobart, 1951–53; municipal librarian, 1953–57, and regional librarian, 1958–61, Bairnsdale and Shepparton, Victoria; from 1961 full-time writer. Australian writers representative, Edinburgh Festival, 1962; Australian Department of External Affairs lecturer, Japan, 1967. Recipient: Sydney Sesquicentenary prize, 1938; Commonwealth Literary Fund fellowship, 1956, 1960, 1964, 1968, 1972, 1974, 1977, 1980, and subsidy, 1957, 1962, 1967; Sydney *Morning Herald* prize, 1958; Sydney Journalists' Club prize, for fiction, 1959, for drama, 1961; Adelaide *Advertiser* prize, for fiction, 1964, 1970, for non-fiction, 1968; Encyclopaedia Brittanica award, 1967; Captain Cook Bi-Centenary prize, 1970; Australia and New Zealand Bank award, for local history, 1977. Member, Order of Australia, 1982. *Died 29 September 1984.*

ROMANCE AND HISTORICAL PUBLICATIONS

Novel

The Tilted Cross. London, Faber, 1961.

OTHER PUBLICATIONS

Novels

A Handful of Pennies. Sydney, Angus and Robertson, 1958;
London, Angus and Robertson, 1959; revised edition in *Hal
Porter*, 1980.
The Right Thing. Adelaide, Rigby, and London, Hale, 1971.

Short Stories

Short Stories. Adelaide, Advertiser Press, 1942.
A Bachelor's Children. Sydney and London, Angus and Robert-
son, 1962.
The Cats of Venice. Sydney, Angus and Robertson, 1965.
Mr. Butterfry and Other Tales of New Japan. Sydney, Angus
and Robertson, 1970.
Selected Stories, edited by Leonie Kramer. Sydney and London,
Angus and Robertson, 1971.
Fredo Fuss Love Life. Sydney, Angus and Robertson, 1974.
An Australian Selection, edited by John Barnes. Sydney, Angus
and Robertson, 1974.
The Clairvoyant Goat and Other Stories. Melbourne, Nelson,
1981.

Plays

The Tower (produced London, 1964). Published in *Three Aus-
tralian Plays*, Melbourne and London, Penguin, 1963.
The Professor (as *Toda-San*, produced Adelaide, 1965; as *The
Professor*, produced London, 1965). London, Faber, 1966.
Eden House (produced Melbourne, 1969; as *Home on a Pig's
Back*, produced Richmond, Surrey, 1972). Sydney, Angus
and Robertson, 1969.
Parker (produced Ballarat, Victoria, 1972). Melbourne, Ar-
nold, 1979.

Screenplay: *The Child* (episode in *Libido*), 1973.

Television Play: *The Forger*, 1967.

Verse

The Hexagon. Sydney, Angus and Robertson, 1956.
Elijah's Ravens. Sydney, Angus and Robertson, 1968.
In an Australian Country Graveyard. Sydney, Angus and Rob-
ertson, 1975.

Other

The Watcher on the Cast-Iron Balcony (autobiography).
London, Faber, 1963.
Australian Stars of Stage and Screen. Adelaide, Rigby, 1965.
The Paper Chase (autobiography). Sydney, Angus and Robert-
son, 1966.
The Actors: An Image of the New Japan. Sydney, Angus and
Robertson, 1968.
The Extra (autobiography). Melbourne, Nelson, 1975.
Bairnsdale: Portrait of an Australian Country Town.
Melbourne, Ferguson, 1977.
Seven Cities of Australia. Sydney, Ferguson, 1978.
Hal Porter (selection), edited by Mary Lord. St. Lucia, Univer-
sity of Queensland Press, 1980.

Editor, *Australian Poetry 1957*. Sydney, Angus and Robertson,
1957.

Editor, *Coast to Coast 1961–1962*. Sydney, Angus and Robertson, 1963.
Editor, *It Could Be You*. Adelaide, Rigby, 1972; London, Hale,
1973.

*

Bibliography: *A Bibliography of Hal Porter* by Janette Finch,
Adelaide, Libraries Board of South Australia, 1966; "A Contribution to the Bibliography of Hal Porter" by Mary Lord, in *Australian Literary Studies* (Hobart, Tasmania), October 1970;
Papers of Hal Porter 1924–1975, Sydney, Mitchell Library, n.d.

Manuscript Collection: Mitchell Library, Sydney.

Critical Studies: *Hal Porter* by Mary Lord, Melbourne, Oxford
University Press, 1974; *Speaking of Writing* edited by R. D.
Walshe and Leonie Kramer, Sydney, Reed, 1975; *Australian
Writers* by Graeme Kinross Smith, Melbourne, Nelson, 1980.

*   *   *

Hal Porter had been writing for many years before he gained
critical recognition and popular acceptance. By the dominant
standards of the Australian literary scene in the 1930's and
1940's his work appeared precious, even wilfully perverse. But a
change of literary fashion brought him a change of literary fortune, and by the 1960's he was counted with the best Australian
authors, his candle dimmed only by Patrick White's.

Short stories dominated his early output and were the basis of
his reputation, but later he assayed many forms. His autobiographical classic *The Watcher on the Cast-Iron Balcony* seems
likely to remain his best-known book. Porter's writing is distinguished by an arresting and very personal style, intricately decorated, sharp-edged, self-conscious, and archly exact. At its
worst this manner can degenerate into an affected sneer, but at
its best it does what Porter admired in Katherine Mansfield, representing a "breathtaking surface texture and, simultaneously,
what the x-ray showed."

Although his play *The Tower* is also set in mid-19th-century
Hobart, *The Tilted Cross* is Porter's only extended piece of historical fiction. It is his second novel, and critical consensus
ranks it his best because of its narrative tightness, carefully researched historical detailing, and metaphysical import. Though
the novel itself consciously parades a Christian analogy, it is perhaps better understood, in common with much of Porter's work,
as swinging on a Rousseauistic axis: untutored goodness versus
civilized corruption. On the one hand there is the hypocritical
world of the mansion of Cindermead, inhabited by the discreetly
promiscuous Lady Rose Knight and her husband's cousin Asnetha Sleep, who is rich, malformed, epileptic, and lonely. On
the other hand is the crude, passionate underworld of a raw penal colony.

The link between these worlds is the cold, arid figure of Judas
Griffin Vaneleigh, at home in both worlds and despising both
equally. Vaneleigh is based closely on the real-life Thomas Grif-
fiths Wainwright, a notorious art forger and suspected murderer
transported to Van Diemen's Land, who found his way into the
pages of Dickens, Hazlitt, Wilde, and many other writers.
Vaneleigh, who has been engaged as a portrait painter at Cindermead, is taken up by the simplehearted (and somewhat simple-
minded) Queely Sheill, who drops his aitches and never tires of
proclaiming his belief in human goodness. Pitying Vaneleigh for
his despairing cynicism, Sheill ends up becoming his attendant
and proceeds to get into a liaison with Asnetha Sleep. Crushed

between Rose Knight's malice and Vaneleigh's moral dissociation, he finally dies a horrible death.

The characters are memorable but lack depth, and the author evidently intends this to be so, for he surrounds them—especially the two central men—with an array of alienation effects (artificial dialogue, ironic authorial comment, dislocated point of view). The aim appears to be a moral parable of universal import. But in this respect Queely Sheill in particular is problematic. While a caricature may effectively represent moral failure, a caricatured impression of goodness tends to undermine the basis of a moral parable.

The morbid action and grotesque characters of *The Tilted Cross* produce a structure of feeling which is piquant or bitter, according to taste: rather more melodramatic than tragic, and rather more sardonic than earnest. The abiding interest of the book will remain the author's extravagantly mannered prose, with its remarkable capacity for disconcerting precision, complexity, and irony.

—Paul Gillen

POWERS, Nora. See **PYKARE, Nina.**

POWYS, John Cowper. British. Born in Shirley, Derbyshire, 8 October 1872; brother of the writers T. F. and Llewelyn Powys. Educated at Sherborne School, Dorset; Corpus Christi College, Cambridge, M.A. 1894. Married Margaret Alice Lyon in 1896 (died 1947); one son. Teacher at a girls school in England, 1894; lecturer on English literature in the United States, 1904–34: returned to England each summer, 1910–28; lived in New York and California, 1928–34; returned to Britain in 1934 and settled in North Wales. Recipient: Foreign Book prize (France), 1966. D. Litt.: University of Wales, Cardiff, 1962. *Died 17 June 1963.*

ROMANCE AND HISTORICAL PUBLICATIONS

Novels

A Glastonbury Romance. New York, Simon and Schuster, 1932; London, Lane, 1933.
Maiden Castle. New York, Simon and Schuster, 1936; London, Cassell, 1937.
Owen Glendower. New York, Simon and Schuster, 2 vols., 1940; London, Lane, 1941.
Porius: A Romance of the Dark Ages. London, Macdonald, 1951; New York, Philosophical Library, 1952.
The Brazen Head. London, Macdonald, and Hamilton, New York, Colgate University Press, 1956.

OTHER PUBLICATIONS

Novels

Wood and Stone: A Romance. New York, Shaw, 1915; London, Heinemann, 1917.
Rodmoor: A Romance. New York, Shaw, 1916; London, Macdonald, 1973.

Ducdame. New York, Doubleday, and London, Richards, 1925.
Wolf Solent. New York, Simon and Schuster, 2 vols., 1929; London, Cape, 1 vol., 1929.
Weymouth Sands. New York, Simon and Schuster, 1934; altered version, as *Jobber Skald*, London, Lane, 1935; original version, as *Weymouth Sands*, London, Macdonald, 1963.
Morwyn; or, The Vengeance of God. London, Cassell, 1937; New York, Arno Press, 1976.
The Inmates. London, Macdonald, and New York, Philosophical Library, 1952.
Atlantis. London, Macdonald, 1954.
All or Nothing. London, Macdonald, 1960.
After My Fashion. London, Pan, 1980.

Short Stories

The Owl, The Duck, and—Miss Rowe! Miss Rowe! Chicago, Black Archer Press, 1930.
Up and Out. London, Macdonald, 1957.
Romer Mowl and Other Stories, edited by Bernard Jones. St. Peter Port, Guernsey, Toucan Press, 1974.
Real Wraiths. London, Village Press, 1974.
Two and Two. London, Village Press, 1974.
You and Me. London, Village Press, 1975.
Three Fantasies. Manchester, Carcanet, 1985.

Plays

The Idiot, with Reginald Pole, adaptation of a novel by Dostoevsky (produced New York, 1922).
Paddock Calls. London, Greymitre, 1984.

Verse

Odes and Other Poems. London, Rider, 1896.
Poems. London, Rider, 1899.
Wolf's Bane: Rhymes. New York, Shaw, and London, Rider, 1916.
Mandragora. New York, Shaw, 1917.
Samphire. New York, Seltzer, 1922.
Lucifer: A Poem. London, Macdonald, 1956.
John Cowper Powys: A Selection from His Poems, edited by Kenneth Hopkins. London, Macdonald, 1964; Hamilton, New York, Colgate University Press, 1965.
Horned Poppies: New Poems. North Walsham, Norfolk, Warren House, 1983.
Verses on the Sad Occasion of the Death of Tippoo Tib. N.p., Marks, 1988.

Other

The War and Culture: A Reply to Professor Münsterberg. New York, Shaw, 1914; as *The Menace of German Culture*, London, Rider, 1915.
Visions and Revisions: A Book of Literary Devotions. New York, Shaw, and London, Rider, 1915.
Confessions of Two Brothers, with Llewelyn Powys. Rochester, New York, Manas Press, 1916; London, Sinclair Browne, 1982.
One Hundred Best Books. New York, Shaw, 1916.
Suspended Judgments: Essays on Books and Sensations. New York, Shaw, 1916; London, Village Press, 1975.
The Complex Vision. New York, Dodd Mead, 1920.
The Art of Happiness. Girard, Kansas, Haldeman Julius, 1923.
Psychoanalysis and Morality. San Francisco, Colbert, 1923.

The Religion of a Sceptic. New York, Dodd Mead, 1925; London, Village Press, 1975.

The Secret of Self Development. Girard, Kansas, Haldeman Julius, 1926; London, Village Press, 1974.

The Art of Forgetting the Unpleasant. Girard, Kansas, Haldeman Julius, 1928.

The Meaning of Culture. New York, Norton, 1929; London, Cape, 1930; revised edition, Norton, 1939; Cape, 1940.

Debate: Is Modern Marriage a Failure?, with Bertrand Russell. New York, Discussion Guild, 1930; edited by Margaret Moran, North Walsham, Norfolk, Warren House, 1983.

In Defence of Sensuality. New York, Simon and Schuster, and London, Gollancz, 1930.

Dorothy M. Richardson. London, Joiner and Steele, 1931.

A Philosophy of Solitude. New York, Simon and Schuster, and London, Cape, 1933.

Autobiography. New York, Simon and Schuster, and London, Lane, 1934.

The Art of Happiness (not same as 1923 book). New York, Simon and Schuster, and London, Lane, 1935.

The Enjoyment of Literature. New York, Simon and Schuster, 1938; revised edition, as *The Pleasures of Literature*, London, Cassell, 1938.

Mortal Strife. London, Cape, 1942.

The Art of Growing Old. London, Cape, 1944.

Pair Dadeni; or, The Cauldron of Rebirth. Carmarthen, Wales, Druid Press, 1946.

Dostoievsky. London, Lane, 1946.

Obstinate Cymric: Essays 1935–1947. Carmarthen, Wales, Druid Press, 1947.

Rabelais. London, Lane, 1948; New York, Philosophical Library, 1951.

In Spite Of: A Philosophy for Everyman. London, Macdonald, and New York, Philosophical Library, 1953.

Letters to Louis Wilkinson 1935–1956. London, Macdonald, and Hamilton, New York, Colgate University Press, 1958.

Homer and the Aether. London, Macdonald, 1959.

Letters to Glyn Hughes, edited by Bernard Jones. Stevenage, Hertfordshire, Ore, 1971.

Letters to Nicholas Ross, edited by Arthur Uphill. London, Rota, 1971.

Letters 1937–1954, edited by Iorweth C. Peate. Cardiff, University of Wales Press, 1974.

An Englishman Upstate. London, Village Press, 1974.

Letters to His Brother Llewelyn 1902–1925, edited by Malcolm Elwin. London, Village Press, 1975.

Letters to Henry Miller. London, Village Press, 1975.

Letters to C. Benson Roberts. London, Village Press, 1975.

Letters to Clifford Tolchard. London, Village Press, 1975.

Letters to G. R. Wilson Knight, edited by Robert Blackmore. London, Cecil Woolf, 1983.

Letters to Sven-Erik Tackmark, edited by Cedric Hentschel. London, Cecil Woolf, 1983.

The Diary 1930, edited by Frederick Davies. London, Greymitre, 1987.

*

Bibliography: *A Bibliography of the Writings of John Cowper Powys* by Thomas Dante, Mamaroneck, New York, Appel, 1975.

Manuscript Collections: Churchill College, Cambridge; Colgate University, Hamilton, New York; Humanities Research Center, University of Texas, Austin.

Critical Studies: *Welsh Ambassadors: Powys Lives and Letters* by Louis Marlow, London, Chapman and Hall, 1936, revised edition, Hamilton, New York, Colgate University Press, 1971; *The Powys Brothers* by R. C. Churchill, London, Longman, 1962; *The Saturnian Quest: A Chart of the Prose Works of John Cowper Powys* by G. Wilson Knight, London, Methuen, and New York, Barnes and Noble, 1964; *John Cowper Powys: Old Earth-Man* by H. P. Collins, London, Barrie and Rockliff, 1966; *The Powys Brothers: A Biographical Appreciation* by Kenneth Hopkins, London, Phoenix House, and Rutherford, New Jersey, Fairleigh Dickinson University Press, 1967; *Essays on John Cowper Powys* edited by Belinda Humfrey, Cardiff, University of Wales Press, 1972; *John Cowper Powys, Novelist* by Glen Cavaliero, Oxford, Clarendon Press, 1973; *The Demon Within: A Study of John Cowper Powys's Novels* by John A. Brebner, London, Macdonald, 1973; *John Cowper Powys* by Jeremy Hooker, Cardiff, University of Wales Press, 1973; *The Immortal Bard* by Henry Miller, London, Village Press, 1973; *John Cowper Powys and the Magical Quest* by Morine Krissdottir, London, Macdonald and Jane's, 1980; *John Cowper Powys: In Search of a Landscape* by C. A. Coates, London, Macmillan, 1982; *The Brothers Powys* by Richard Perceval Graves, London, Routledge, 1983; *The Ecstatic World of John Cowper Powys* by H. W. Fawkner, Rutherford, New Jersey, Fairleigh Dickinson University Press, 1986.

*   *   *

John Cowper Powys once referred in a letter to Louis Wilkinson to "that authentic Brontë touch of old traditional romance so hard to reproduce these days" and to Tom Hart he commented: "I suppose like any other romanticist and semi-historian, my interest is only really and completely stirred by the past." Powys uses the form of romance and history in innovative ways, creating a unique blend of fantasy, psychological exploration, and earthy realism. This combination makes Powys prophetic of the magic realist school of fiction.

Powys began writing romances with regional settings in Somerset and Dorset in late maturity. *Ducdame*, the last and most rewarding novel in this series, links romance to history. The hero, Rook Ashover, before a tragic death, is granted two extraordinary visions: an image of his own son before he is born and, at the time of his son's actual birth, an apparition of his son as an adult. Rook thus compensates for a doubt about the possibility of personal survival after death by an inner conviction of the continuity of experience in future generations.

Wolf Solent begins the major phase of Powys's fiction. This romantic novel, set in Dorset, is dominated by the consciousness of its protagonist, significantly a teacher of history who embarks upon the writing of an historical chronicle. Wolf is able to perceive the seamy history of Dorset as potentially a new genre of history meant to incorporate the succession of human impressions which gather around a place.

This definition of historical fiction is developed in Powys's central masterpiece *A Glastonbury Romance* in which he explores the impact of the historical traditions of the Grail upon the present day inhabitants of this ancient Somerset town. Powys described the novel as "a jumbled up and squeezed together epitome of life's various dimensions" and also once described the concept of the Grail in the novel as "a nucleus of creation and destruction": it can be either creative or destructive according to the nature of the individual affected by it. The original fusion of mythical and historical perspectives is developed in Powys's overtly historical novels. Since each character reacts to the Grail in a different way, each one subtly changes the nature of its influence. The Grail is thus synonymous with history itself for it is reincarnated in the modern world in a way distinct from the medieval past.

Owen Glendower is Powys's first novel set in a distinct historical period. It is substantial, pageant-like, full of colour, atmosphere, and imaginative recreation of place and landscape. It was written just before World War II when Powys had retired from North America to live in North Wales at Bleinau Ffestiniog and later Corwen near such sites as Valle Crucis Abbey and Dinas Bran which are settings for memorable scenes in the novel. These ancient historical sites have an impact on the lives of the 15th-century characters as Glastonbury had on the lives of its modern inhabitants. The past in *Owen Glendower* includes the aboriginal past of Britain and prophetic figures link the past to the reader's present at a time of war.

Owen is a powerful hero who becomes caught up in the inevitable consequences of power at the expense of human values. His political success ceases after the French betray him and he withdraws proudly in his defeat, disappearing into the Welsh fastnesses and rejecting the offer of pardon from the king. Powys suggests that Owen wins greater spiritual victory for the Welsh nation in defeat than he would have from conquest. Powys's most original contribution to the novel is the character Rhisiart, Owen's secretary, whom Powys developed from the barest hint in his sources. He functions as an alter ego for Owen, rational and legalistic rather than passionate and mystical.

Porius takes the reader back to a misty historical period with, nevertheless, a very precise time reference; 499 A.D., a period, again of crisis and transition. The Romanised and aboriginal inhabitants of Britain are on the verge of a Germanic invasion led by the Saxon Colgrim. The relevance to the experience of World War II is clear; the foster-brothers Porius and Rhun, and Porius's affianced bride Morfydd, the daughter of Brochvael, a classical scholar, rise to the challenge of this period of cultural crisis. The marriage of Porius and Morfydd is meant to cement together the two warring Celtic tribes and secure the allegiance of the "Derwydd" or Druid, the most ancient of the aboriginal characters.

Other actors in the novel include an unusual version of Merlin (Myrddin Wyllt), part pastoral nature god and part magician, who is in the thrall of Nineue; the "Amherawdr" or Emperor Arthur is a Romanised character. Powys also includes mythological characters such as Blodeuwedd, based upon the owl-maiden of *The Mabinogion*, whose transformation from maiden to owl the reader witnesses in a powerfully evocative scene. And there is also the Creiddylad, a giantess of the ancient race of the Cewri, whom Porius pursues and ravishes. Later he becomes unwittingly the cause of her death when her father attacks him. Powys, inspired by the location of Corwen, reproduces the landscape and atmosphere of ancient locations from Cader Idris, shrouded in mists, to the underground lair of the Druids. Women oppose the tyranny of men: Morfydd is an important representative of a feminine desire for freedom and independence. The reader is reminded by other feminine characters such as the affectionately named "Three Aunties" or ancient princesses called the "Modrybedd" and the Druid woman Sibylla that "in man and woman two kinds of history fight for power."

In *The Brazen Head*, set in the year 1272, Powys returns to the Dorset setting with an added strain of Welsh fantasy and magic. Roger Bacon, St. Bonaventure, and the rebellious barons who troubled the reign of Henry II are combined with the romantic relationship of Peleg, a Tartar giant and Ghosta, a Jewess. Powys's interest is in the intellectual crisis of the period, for Bacon is persecuted by fanatical and authoritarian representatives of orthodox religion. The novel is largely an apology for Roger Bacon, the representative of enlightened rationalism against the forces of spiritual tyranny. Nevertheless, Bacon's exploration of natural processes unleashes creative and destructive

energies which move the narrative towards an apocalypse. The intellectual struggles of the 13th century are once again reflective of those which are freshly incarnated in the 20th.

—Michael Ballin

POZZESSERE, Heather Graham. Also writes as Shannon Drake. American. Married Dennis Pozzessere; three sons and one daughter. Address: c/o Silhouette Books, 300 East 42nd Street, New York, New York 10017, U.S.A.

ROMANCE AND HISTORICAL PUBLICATIONS

Novels

Night Moves. New York, Silhouette, 1985.
Double Entendre. New York, Silhouette, 1986.
The DiMedici Bride. New York, Silhouette, 1986.
The Game of Love. New York, Silhouette, 1986.
A Matter of Circumstance. New York, Silhouette, 1987.
All in the Family. New York, Silhouette, 1987.
Bride of the Tiger. New York, Silhouette, 1987.
King of the Castle. New York, Silhouette, 1987.
Strangers in Paradise. New York, Silhouette, 1988.
Angel of Mercy. New York, Silhouette, 1988.
Dark Stranger. Toronto, Harlequin, 1988.
Lucia in Love. New York, Silhouette, 1988.
This Rough Magic. New York, Silhouette, 1988.

Novels as Heather Graham (series: Donna Miro and Lorna Doria)

A Season for Love. New York, Dell, 1983.
Forbidden Fruit. New York, Dell, 1983.
Quiet Walks the Tiger. New York, Dell, 1983.
Tempestuous Eden. New York, Dell, 1983.
Tender Taming. New York, Dell, 1983.
When Next We Love. New York, Dell, 1983.
Night, Sea and Stars. New York, Dell, 1983.
Arabian Nights. New York, Dell, 1984.
Hours to Cherish. New York, Dell, 1984.
Red Midnight. New York, Dell, 1984.
Serena's Magic. New York, Dell, 1984.
Tender Deception. New York, Dell, 1984.
Hold Close the Memory. New York, Dell, 1985.
Sensuous Angel (Miro and Doria). New York, Dell, 1985.
An Angel's Share (Miro and Doria). New York, Dell, 1985.
Queen of Hearts. New York, Dell, 1985.
Golden Surrender. New York, Dell, 1985.
Dante's Daughter. New York, Dell, 1986.
Devil's Mistress. New York, Dell, 1986.
Eden's Spell. New York, Dell, 1986.
Handful of Dreams. New York, Dell, 1986.
The Maverick and the Lady. New York, Dell, 1986.
Every Time I Love You. New York, Dell, 1987.
Liar's Moon. New York, Dell, 1987.
Siren from the Sea. New York, Dell, 1987.
Sweet Savage Eden. New York, Dell, 1989.
Rides a Hero. New York, Silhouette, 1989.

Novels as Shannon Drake

Tomorrow the Glory. New York, Pinnacle, 1985.
Blue Heaven, Black Night. New York, Berkley, 1986.
Lie Down in Roses. New York, Charter, 1988.
Ondine. New York, Charter, 1988.
Princess of Fire. New York, Charter, 1989.

*   *   *

Heather Graham Pozzessere is fun to read. Her novels are filled with suspense, excitement, danger, and love. In fact, they belong in that coveted place, the "read again" shelf, because many have that touch of being a favorite friend. They cheer you, they relax you and best of all, they entertain you.

Pozzessere's readers certainly would agree with this opinion, given the awards she has won or has been nominated for. In 1987, her novel, *The Maverick and the Lady* was nominated for the best Ecstasy award of the year. This was published under her pseudonym, Heather Graham. At the same time, *A Matter of Circumstance* was also nominated for the best Silhouette Intimate Moments novel. In 1988, Pozzessere won the award for the best Sensual Romance set during the American Civil War. The book, *Dark Stranger*, is one of the Harlequin historical romances. Her novel *King of the Castle*, also was nominated for the best Silhouette Intimate Moments. She, herself, was nominated for best All-Around Series author. This recognition is not a case of luck. As usual, hard work, constant re-writing and a polishing of skills over the years, has made such recognition possible.

Pozzessere creates wonderfully real people with just the right blend of independence, assertiveness, and sensitivity. Her heroes are masculine, even macho, at times, but in a caring, protective way. Typically, the "hero in love" is vastly different from the actual hero. Self confidence, gives way to uncertainty, tyrants become pussy cats, and smooth talkers become incoherent, at least temporarily.

Her heroines are just as delightful. They are spicy, often mouthy, and inevitably, cuddly as they react to the hero without regard for life or limb. Fortunately, the hero is fascinated by her limbs and rabidly determined to make her life, his—for life.

While Pozzessere is best known for her Silhouette romances, she is also becoming well known as an historical romance writer. Besides the Civil War novel, she has also written *Golden Surrender*, a Viking story set in Ireland during the time of the Danish invasions.

However, her suspense/intrigue novels are among her best work. *Angel of Mercy* pits a DEA enforcer, Brad McKenna, against the Florida swamps, snakes and alligators, as well as human predators who are determined to kill him. On his side is Wendy Hawk, a widow and her in-laws who are Seminole indians. Love flares instantly and explosively between Brad and Wendy with both praying to emerge from that love unscathed and uncommitted. Naturally, compromise seems impossible, especially as danger swirls around them.

Action is fast-paced. Characterization shows all of the ambivalence and heartache that each experiences. Both learn that love can overcome tremendous odds, even in impossible situations. The tension between the two as well as the tension of police action makes the novel more than suspenseful.

Two other novels by Pozzessere must be taken together, although they do present an interesting puzzle in publishing decision-making. *Sensuous Angel*, an Ecstasy romance was published in August 1985. In October 1985 *An Angel's Share* came out as an Ecstasy Supreme. Both novels deal with the same characters and the same suspense plot. The two novels trace the heroines Donna Miro and Lorna Doria who were friends since childhood. In *Sensuous Angel*, Donna goes to New York City to find Lorna, who has mysteriously disappeared. Her initial search lands her in the arms of Father Luke Trudeau, an Episcopalian priest. Father Luke tries to keep her out of trouble and in his arms as they unexpectedly fall in love. Finally he is able to give Donna information about Lorna. She learns that Lorna is being held in protective custody after witnessing a murder.

In the second novel, Lorna's story is told. Events in *An Angel's Share* finally let Lorna return to her home in Massachusetts. Not too far behind her is Andrew Trudeau, Luke's brother who is a New York City detective. Unfortunately, Andrew and Lorna had developed a relationship while she had been held in custody. Both seemed to regret it, so Lorna is less than pleased to see him arrive as her bodyguard again. The actual criminal is a powerful, wealthy man who is determined to eliminate both Lorna and Donna. The ending finds both couples ready for a lifetime of love and marriage. Father Luke and Donna are already married and see nothing wrong in finishing the job they started. Naturally, by the end of the second novel, Andrew and Lorna are more than willing to co-operate. The interplay of police action, suspense, and the two conflicting love stories all act as counterpoints in each novel.

Readers will have a hard time finding novels that match these for enjoyment, good love stories, and pure excitement.

—Arlene Moore

PREEDY, George. See **BOWEN, Marjorie.**

PRESCOTT, H(ilda) F(rances) M(argaret). British. Born in Latchford, Cheshire, 22 February 1896. Educated at Wallasey High School, Cheshire; Lady Margaret Hall, Oxford (Jephson scholar), B.A., M.A.; Manchester University, M.A. Jubilee Research Fellow, Royal Holloway College, Surrey, 1958–60. Recipient: James Tait Black Memorial prize, for non-fiction, 1941; Christopher Medal, 1953. D.Litt.: Durham University, 1957. Fellow, Royal Society of Literature, 1953. *Died 5 May 1972.*

ROMANCE AND HISTORICAL PUBLICATIONS

Novels

The Unhurrying Chase. London, Constable, and New York, Dodd Mead, 1925.
The Lost Fight. London, Constable, and New York, Dodd Mead, 1928.
Son of Dust. London, Constable, 1932; New York, Macmillan, 1956.
The Man on a Donkey: A Chronicle. London, Eyre and Spottiswoode, 2 vols., 1952; New York, Macmillan, 1952.

OTHER PUBLICATIONS

Novel

Dead and Not Buried. London, Constable, and New York, Macmillan, 1938.

Other

Spanish Tudor: The Life of Bloody Mary. London, Constable, and New York, Columbia University Press, 1940; revised edition, London, Eyre and Spottiswoode, and New York, Macmillan, 1953.

Friar Felix at Large: A Fifteenth-Century Pilgrimage to the Holy Land. New Haven, Connecticut, Yale University Press, 1950; as *Jerusalem Journey: Pilgrimage to the Holy Land*, London, Eyre and Spottiswoode, 1954.

Once to Sinai: The Further Pilgrimage of Friar Felix Fabri. London, Eyre and Spottiswoode, 1957; New York, Macmillan, 1958.

Translator, *Flamenca*, by Bernardet the Troubadour. London, Constable, 1933.

*   *   *

As an historical novelist H. F. M. Prescott is noteworthy for her adroit use of scholarly material, her concern with hardship, pain, and self-denial, and for her Christian outlook. Her first three novels are set in France during the Middle Ages. The action of *The Unhurrying Chase* takes place in the late 12th century. The main character is Yves de Rifaucon, dispossessed of his fief and bitterly resentful of his feudal overlords, in particular the future Richard I of England. The book traces his misfortunes and ultimate degradation, together with the love for him of a girl whose loyalty he fails to comprehend, and is to some extent the study of an obsession; at a religious level it recalls Francis Thompson's poem "The Hound of Heaven." The background detail is skilfully incorporated into the story; Prescott also makes powerful use of the devastation of southwestern France by the mercenary armies of the time. Like its two successors, *The Lost Fight* (set in Lorraine and Cyprus during the 13th century) and *Son of Dust* (11th-century Normandy), *The Unhurrying Chase* combines a swiftly-paced narrative with a meticulous use of detail. Prescott lays great stress on knightly codes of honour and of duty to overlords; but the feudal world she depicts is harsh and frequently brutal, and there is nothing superficially picturesque about it. *Son of Dust*, indeed, is based on actual events recorded in the *Historia Ecclesiastica* of Orderic Vitalis, and is, possibly as a result, more broadly focussed than are its predecessors.

All three novels are primarily love stories written from an overtly Christian point of view, their theme being the conflict between the strict rules of chastity imposed by the Church and the importunate needs and desires of the flesh: in *The Lost Fight* and *Son of Dust* the lovers are separated by the laws of both God and man, and pay the price of defying them. (At the same time, lovingly detailed evocations of landscape and of animal and bird life serve as relief from the unflagging intensities of the human relationships.) Both *The Unhurrying Chase* and *The Lost Fight* uphold the values of courtly love celebrated by the Provençal troubadours. The leading male characters in all three novels are stubborn, confused personalities, while the women they love are heroically passive and long-suffering: the sexual sensibility is as much of the late 19th century as medieval, and is presented with great emotional intensity. The historical settings, skilfully handled though they are, thus seem to be occasions for the narration of stories whose ideology would be more difficult to present in a contemporary setting. Both in their themes and in their resolutions these first three novels by Prescott anticipate the early and specifically Catholic fiction of Graham Greene.

Her masterpiece, however, is *The Man on a Donkey*. It was long in preparation, and can fairly claim to be among the most ambitious and persuasive English historical novels to be written in the 20th century. The action covers 30 years, between 1509 and 1539, and reaches its climax with the Pilgrimage of Grace, the rebellion of the North Country Catholics against the dissolution of the monasteries. The book consists of a number of parallel stories centering on five principal characters, whose fortunes are gradually drawn together as the narrative proceeds. They are Christabel Cowper, the Prioress of Marrick Abbey, near Richmond in Swaledale; the elderly Lord Darcy, one of the loyal Catholic nobility; Gilbert Dawe, a Protestant malcontent whose religious intransigence resembles that of the protagonists of *The Unhurrying Chase* and *Son of Dust*; Robert Aske, the Yorkshire squire who becomes the leader of the rebellion; and Julian Savage, a young married woman who loves him. Many historical characters of the period are depicted, including King Henry VIII, Katherine of Aragon, the Princess Mary and Anne Boleyn; Thomas Cromwell and Archbishop Cranmer; Cardinal Wolsey and Sir Thomas More. But their roles are secondary in dramatic terms to those of the Aske family, of the nuns of Marrick, of Julian's devoted husband, and of her sister Margaret, who takes a leading part in the insurrection: this is a novel primarily about people in ordinary walks of life.

The book is written in the form of a discontinuous chronicle, which allows the author to shift her scene with ease between Yorkshire and London, and between character and character. The result is to do away with the artificial and thus distracting element of formal plot, and to secure a close involvement in events as they build up, item by item, full of small, unobtrusive details that serve to heighten the reader's feeling of participation in the life of Tudor England. Both in style and technique this aspect of the novel resembles Rose Macaulay's portrait of Caroline England in *They Were Defeated*.

The Man on a Donkey is also impressive for its breadth of outlook and its humanity. The brooding menace of the rise of a totalitarian state is contrasted with the many descriptions of domestic life, with the placid rigours of the monastic round, and with the beauties of the Yorkshire landscape, all of which lend an element of timelessness to the story. The account of life in Marrick Priory is especially memorable. Although she portrays the nuns' rivalries and limitations with a good deal of not unkindly satirical humour, Prescott is sympathetic to the monastic ideal and to its theological premises. Her Christian outlook encompasses party divisions and religious controversies alike in a vision of transcendent divine love—one that is painfully tested, however, in the account of Aske's death by hanging in chains from York castle keep, a piece of descriptive writing of haunting power. The medium used to convey this impression of a supernatural order is the character of a simple-minded serving woman, a visionary whose words both echo and interpret those of the 14th-century mystic, Julian of Norwich. Thanks to the unstrained and persuasive use of its religious theme, *The Man on a Donkey* is one historical novel which effortlessly achieves a timeless relevance. But for all its emotional and poetic qualities it is naturalistic and based on solid scholarship, also evident in Prescott's biography of Mary Tudor and in her two accounts of 15th-century pilgrims, *Jerusalem Journey* and *Once to Sinai*.

—Glen Cavaliero

———————

PRESTON, Fayrene. Also writes as Jaelyn Conlee. American. Address: c/o Bantam, 666 Fifth Avenue, New York, New York 10103, U.S.A.

ROMANCE AND HISTORICAL PUBLICATIONS

Novels (series: Delaneys; Pearls of Sharah; Shamrock)

Satin and Steele (as Jaelyn Conlee). New York, Berkley, 1982.
Silver Miracles. New York, Bantam, 1983.
That Old Feeling. New York, Bantam, 1983.
The Seduction of Jason. New York, Bantam, 1983.
For the Love of Sami. New York, Bantam, 1984.
Mississippi Blues. New York, Bantam, 1985.
Rachel's Confession. New York, Bantam, 1985.
Fire in the Rain. New York, Bantam, 1986.
Burke, The Kingpin (Shamrock). New York, Bantam, 1986.
Mysterious. New York, Bantam, 1986.
Allure. New York, Bantam, 1987.
Sydney, The Temptress (Delaneys). New York, Bantam, 1987.
Robin and Her Merry People. New York, Bantam, 1987.
Copper Fire (Delaneys). New York, Bantam, 1988.
Silken Thunder (Delaneys). New York, Bantam, 1988.
Emerald Sunshine. New York, Bantam, 1988.
Sapphire Lightning. New York, Bantam, 1988.
Leah's Story (Sharah). New York, Doubleday, 1989.
Alexandra's Story (Sharah). New York, Doubleday, 1989.
Raine's Story (Sharah). New York, Doubleday, 1989.

*   *   *

Fayrene Preston is one of the leading authors in the Loveswept romance line. Chosen to help launch the line in 1983, she has not become one of the most prolific romance writers, at least in comparison to several other writers in the same line, but she has an excellent reputation for providing an entertaining story peopled with believable, likable characters.

Preston combines a deep sensuality with subtle humor. In *The Seduction of Jason*, Jason, the hero, has a somewhat peculiar compliment for Morgan Saunders, the heroine. He tells her she is interesting because, among other things, "you have a name that could belong to a linebacker—yet you're deliciously feminine." Anyone who has wondered at the often bizarre or exotic names given to romance characters has to appreciate such a statement. Preston also reverses the traditional roles in a seduction when Jason and Morgan are torn apart by a misunderstanding. Morgan very openly and aggressively pursues Jason, loading him down with flowers and even declaring her love for him on a billboard.

The story of Morgan and Jason also introduced Morgan's eccentric friend, Samuelina (Sami) Adkinson, who gets her own story in *For the Love of Sami*. An abused child, the adult Sami is a free-spirited, generous woman with some deep-rooted psychological problems. Her romance with Daniel Parker-St. James, a powerful attorney, is a gentler story, again told with humor. It shows another facet of Preston's talent since it is written with great poignancy.

In 1989 Preston introduced a new trilogy. The stories are woven around a fabled necklace of perfectly matched pearls. Each title in the Pearls of Sharah series begins with the same prologue set in ancient Persia, which explains the origin and legend of the necklace. In *Alexandra's Story*, *Raine's Story*, and *Leah's Story* the necklace is used much as a continuing prop. It brings the hero and heroine together and is the source of tension between them. In the end, however, the necklace keeps them together and then passes on to another since it can never truly be possessed.

Preston also has collaborated with two other Loveswept authors, Iris Johansen and Kay Hooper in writing a series of trilogies which chronicle the Delaney family. For the first trilogy, The Shamrock Trinity, which focuses on the contemporary American Delaney brothers, Preston wrote *Burke, The Kingpin*. The second trilogy, The Delaneys of Killaroo, to which Preston contributed *Sydney, The Temptress*, shifted focus to the Australian Delaney sisters. After the success of these trilogies, Preston, Johansen, and Hooper created two "prequel" trilogies, The Delaneys, The Untamed Years and The Delaneys, The Untamed Years II. In *Copper Fire* Preston tells the story of Brianne Delaney and Sloan Lassiter. In *Silken Thunder* their story continues, but the main focus shifts to another couple, Anna Nilsen and Wes McCord, Sloan's enemy.

Working well within the standard romance formula, Preston is not as innovative as Johansen and Hooper, but she is extremely popular. Her novels too are "keepers," destined to be read and re-read.

—Barbara E. Kemp

———

PRESTON, Ivy (Alice, née Kinross). New Zealander. Born in Timaru, 13 November 1913. Educated at Southburn Primary School, 1919–25; Timaru Technical College, 1925–26. Married Percival Edward James Preston in 1937 (died 1956); two sons and two daughters. Address: 95 Church Street, Timaru, New Zealand.

ROMANCE AND HISTORICAL PUBLICATIONS

Novels

Where Ratas Twine. London, Wright and Brown, 1960.
None So Blind. London, Wright and Brown, 1961.
Magic in Maoriland. London, Wright and Brown, 1962.
Rosemary for Remembrance. London, Hale, 1962.
Island of Enchantment. London, Hale, 1963.
Tamarisk in Bloom. London, Hale, 1963.
Hearts Do Not Break. London, Hale, 1964.
The Blue Remembered Hills. London, Hale, 1965.
Secret Love of Nurse Wilson. London, Hale, 1966.
Enchanted Evening. London, Hale, 1966.
Hospital on the Hill. London, Hale, 1967.
Nicolette. London, Hale, 1967.
Red Roses for a Nurse. London, Hale, 1968.
Ticket of Destiny. London, Hale, 1969.
April in Westland. London, Hale, 1969.
A Fleeting Breath. London, Hale, 1970; New York, Beagle, 1971.
Interrupted Journey. London, Hale, 1970; New York, Beagle, 1971.
Portrait of Pierre. London, Hale, 1971.
Petals in the Wind. London, Hale, 1972.
Release the Past. London, Hale, 1973.
Romance in Glenmore Street. London, Hale, 1974; New York, Ace, 1978.
Voyage of Destiny. London, Hale, 1974.
Moonlight on the Lake. London, Hale, 1976.
The House above the Bay. London, Hale, 1976.
Sunlit Seas. London, Hale, 1977.
Where Stars May Lead. London, Hale, 1978.
One Broken Dream. London, Hale, 1979.
Mountain Magic. London, Hale, 1979.
Summer at Willowbank. London, Hale, 1980.
Interlude in Greece. London, Hale, 1982.
Nurse in Confusion. London, Hale, 1983.

Enchantment at Hillcrest. London, Hale, 1984.
Fair Accuser. London, Hale, 1985.
To Dream Again. London, Hale, 1985.
Flight from Heartbreak. London, Hale, 1986.
Threads of Destiny. London, Hale, 1986.
Stranger from the Sea. London, Hale, 1987.
Tumult of the Heart. London, Hale, 1988.
Spring of Granite Peaks. London, Hale, 1988.

OTHER PUBLICATIONS

Other

The Silver Stream (autobiography). Christchurch, Pegasus Press, 1959.

Editor, with Margaret Smith, *Springbook: Seventy-Five Years of Progress* (on Springbook school). Privately printed, 1970.

*

Ivy Preston comments:

I had always intended to be a writer of romance novels for as long as I can remember but, in the event, I began my writing career the wrong way round with an autobiography. Most people wait until they are successful before venturing to write the story of their life. I wrote mine as an ordinary housewife whom nobody except family, friends and neighbours had ever heard of. Oddly enough it was reasonably successful. It was written as a tribute to my late husband who had died suddenly in 1956 leaving me with four young children to bring up alone. Writing that book helped rid me of the mental block I had suffered since his death and I was able to return to the romance novels I had been trying unsuccessfully to write for several years, this time with success. I now average one every nine months . . . like having a baby. Most have a New Zealand setting but now that my family have grown up I am able to travel to other countries and occasionally make use of these experiences for a change of background. I write romance stories because I enjoyed a very happy marriage relationship and believe strongly in love and romance.

*   *   *

Ivy Preston has produced a steady flow of novels since the 1960's. The majority of her novels are set in her native New Zealand; this serves to give the books an exotic quality even though the life-styles of her characters are not unusual. Their lives, homes, and jobs are quite readily identifiable, and their social lives recognisable. The exotic timbre is partly due to descriptive passages of places, such as mountains and bays which are beautiful and deserted and give us a taste of the real New Zealand.

This setting is also enhanced by the suggestion that there may be elements of magic, working with the natives, to produce conclusions, or "happy endings." This "magic" has its roots in Maori folklore and customs, and although not dominant in all her works, is to some degree always present. Preston's love and respect for her country is obvious and this helps make her novels interesting reading.

Preston's characters are all of a similar type: mostly working independent New Zealanders. Many of her heroines are nurses (*Secret Love of Nurse Wilson*, *Nurse in Confusion*, *Hospital on the Hill*) and Preston seems particularly comfortable when writing about medical matters. A Preston heroine is not glamorous or sophisticated, but down-to-earth and "ordinary," and easy for

readers to identify with. The heroes tend to be more sophisticated and worldly, a contrast that heightens the impact of the denouement when the two finally come together.

Preston emphasises the romance at the expense of other elements—the dialogue, for example, can occasionally be clumsy and contrived. However, Preston's novels are well-written and she avoids the trap of dull formula writing by creating interesting characters and well-balanced plots. In the novels romance is always pure and chaste, and despite any problems between the hero and the heroine love finally triumphs and they can live happily-ever-after.

—Jane K. Thompson

———————

PRESTON, Richard. See **LINDSAY, Jack.**

———————

PRICE, Evadne. Also wrote as Helen Zenna Smith. British. Born at sea, in 1896. Educated in West Maitland, New South Wales, and in Belgium. Worked for the Air Ministry during World War I. Married 1) C. A. Fletcher (died); 2) Kenneth A. Attiwill in 1929. Actress from 1906. Columnist, *Sunday Chronicle* and *Sunday Graphic*; feature writer, *Daily Sketch*; war correspondent, the *People*, 1943–45; astrology columnist, *She* magazine, and *Vogue Australia*, Sydney. Recipient: Severigne prize (France). *Died 17 April 1985.*

ROMANCE AND HISTORICAL PUBLICATIONS

Novels

Diary of a Red-Haired Girl. London, Long, 1932.
The Haunted Light. London, Long, 1933.
Strip Girl. London, Hurst and Blackett, 1934.
Probationer! London, Hurst and Blackett, 1934.
Society Girl. London, Harrap, 1935.
Red for Danger! London, Long, 1936.
Glamour Girl. London, Harrap, 1937.
The Dishonoured Wife. London, Jenkins, 1951.
Escape to Marriage. London, Jenkins, 1952.
My Pretty Sister. London, Jenkins, 1952.
Her Stolen Life. London, Milestone, 1954.
What the Heart Says. London, Hale, 1956.
The Love Trap. London, Hale, 1958.
Air Hostess in Love. London, Gresham, 1962.

Novels as Helen Zenna Smith

Not So Quiet . . . : Stepdaughters of War. London, Marriott, 1930; as *Stepdaughters of War*, New York, Dutton, 1930.
Women of the Aftermath. London, Long, 1931; as *One Woman's Freedom*, New York, Longman, 1932.
Shadow Women. London, Long, 1932.
Luxury Ladies. London, Long, 1933.
They Lived with Me. London, Long, 1934.

OTHER PUBLICATIONS

Plays

The Phantom Light, with Joan Roy-Byford (as *The Haunted Light*, produced London, 1928; as *The Phantom Light*, produced London, 1937). London, French, 1949.
Red for Danger (produced Richmond, Surrey, 1938).
Big Ben, with Ruby Miller (produced Malvern, Worcestershire, 1939).
Once a Crook, with Kenneth Attiwill (produced London, 1940). London, French, 1943.
Who Killed My Sister?, with Kenneth Attiwill (produced London, 1942).
Three Wives Called Roland, with Kenneth Attiwill (produced London, 1943).
Through the Door (also director: produced London, 1946).
What Lies Beyond (also director: produced Margate, Kent, 1948).
Cabin for Three, with Kenneth Attiwill (produced Southsea, Hampshire, 1949).
Blonde for Danger (produced London, 1949).
Wanted on Voyage, with Kenneth Attiwill (produced Wimbledon, 1949).

Screenplays: *Wolf's Clothing*, with Brock Williams, 1936; *When the Poppies Bloom Again*, with Herbert Ayres, 1937; *Merry Comes to Town*, with Brock Williams, 1937; *Silver Top*, with Gerald Elliott and Dorothy Greenhill, 1938; *Lightning Conductor*, with J. Jefferson Farjeon and Ivor McLaren, 1938; *Not Wanted on Voyage*, with others, 1957.

Other (for children)

Just Jane. London, John Hamilton, 1928.
Meet Jane. London, Marriott, 1930.
Enter—Jane. London, Newnes, 1932.
Jane the Fourth [*the Sleuth, the Unlucky, the Popular, the Patient, Gets Busy, at War*]. London, Hale, 7 vols., 1937–47.
She Stargazes (for adults; on astrology). London, Ebury Press, 1965.
Jane and Co. (omnibus), edited by Mary Cadogan. London, Macmillan, 1985.

*

Theatrical Activities:
Director: **Plays**—*Through the Door*, London, 1946; *What Lies Beyond*, Margate, Kent, 1948.
Actress: **Plays**—in *Peter Pan* by J. M. Barrie, Sydney, 1906; Nang Ping in *Mr. Wu* by H. M. Vernon and Harold Owen, tour, 1914; toured in South Africa, and in *Oh, I Say* and *Within the Law*, 1915; Suzee in *Five Nights*, tour, 1919; Liliha in *The Bird of Paradise*, London, 1919, 1922; Sua-See in *The Dragon*, London, 1920; Tessie Kearns in *Merton of the Movies* by George S. Kaufman and Marc Connelly, London, 1923; Princess Angelica in *The Rose and the Ring*, London, 1923.

*   *   *

In Evadne Price's lighter books there is often a distinctly drawing-room comedy flavour. (This applies to her "Jane" books for children.) The heroines of her romantic novels often have theatrical careers or other glamorous jobs. These give Price ample opportunity to exploit her flair for lively, dramatic, or "bitchy" situations and relationships. The larger and more colourful than life quality of her love stories is enhanced by flashes of wit, and an overall feeling of exuberance.

Glamour Girl is one of her most incisive theatrical novels in which the temperamental "Glama Gaye"—"Britain's Premier Box-Office Attraction"—rides roughshod over everyone in her orbit—fellow performers, stage hands, dressers, and, most of all, her husband and secretary, who are eventually driven into each other's arms as a result of the star's ruthlessness. Theirs is, however, a triumph of true love—and Glama gets her just deserts in an uneasy relationship with a male "limelight idol" who is as fatally attractive and faithless as herself. The story has a slightly bizarre touch that is characteristic of Price's books; Glama, the striking beauty, and Elna, her rather drab secretary, are actually twin sisters, though the relationship is never publicly acknowledged. But Elna can overcome her mousiness sufficiently to disguise herself as Glama and "double" for her on assignments that Glama finds too dangerous—or too dull—to undertake.

Price uses this twin theme again with dramatic effect in *Air Hostess in Love*. Again, the quieter of the sisters, Judy, is a secretary, while the flashier one, Stella, has the glossy job of air hostess. And as in *Glamour Girl* the sedate young woman has sometimes to substitute for her sister in hazardous situations before her romantic difficulties with the man she loves can be resolved. Although Price skilfully enlists her readers' sympathies for conformist and "ordinary" heroines like these sisters of the high-powered actress or air hostess, she is at her best with more vivid characters, for example, the dancer Carole Iden in *The Love Trap*, who has "a flame of red hair" and "the permanent challenge" of "provocative green eyes." Carole in fact needs all the help that her startling good looks can bring her—because, at the beginning of the story, she has been made pregnant by a dashing test pilot who gets killed before he can marry her. She attracts an older and more stable man who offers her one of those marriages in-name-only that, in the romantic novel genre, always end happily with hero and heroine falling blissfully in love with each other. In some of her other books, Price persuasively exploits several inventive variations on the type of situation used in *The Love Trap*, *Glamour Girl*, and *Air Hostess in Love*.

—Mary Cadogan

PROLE, Lozania. See **BLOOM, Ursula.**

PRYOR, Vanessa. See **YARBRO, Chelsea Quinn.**

PYKARE, Nina. Also writes as Ann Coombs; Nina Coombs; Nan Pemberton; Nora Powers; Regina Towers. American. Address: c/o Silhouette Books, 300 East 42nd Street, New York, New York 10017, U.S.A.

ROMANCE AND HISTORICAL PUBLICATIONS

Novels

The Fire Within (as Ann Coombs). New York, Silhouette, 1978.
Love's Promise. New York, Dell, 1979.
The Scandalous Season. New York, Dell, 1979.
Lady Incognita. New York, Dell, 1980.
Love's Delusion (as Nan Pemberton). New York, Pocket Books, 1980.
The Rake's Companion (as Regina Towers). New York, Dell, 1980.
Love's Folly. New York, Dell, 1980.
Love in Disguise. New York, Dell, 1980.
The Dazzled Heart. New York, Dell, 1980.
Man of Her Choosing. New York, Dell, 1980.
Love Plays a Part. New York, Dell, 1981.
The Innocent Heart. New York, Dell, 1981.
A Matter of Honor. New York, Dell, 1982.
Heritage of the Heart. New York, Dell, 1982.

Novels as Nora Powers

Affairs of the Heart. New York, Silhouette, 1980.
Design for Love. New York, Silhouette, 1980.
Promise Me Tomorrow. New York, Silhouette, 1982.
Dream of the West. New York, Silhouette, 1983.
In a Moment's Time. New York, Silhouette, 1983.
Time Stands Still. New York, Silhouette, 1983.
In a Stranger's Arms. New York, Silhouette, 1984.
This Brief Interlude. New York, Silhouette, 1984.
A Different Reality. New York, Silhouette, 1985.
A Woman's Wiles. New York, Silhouette, 1985.
No Man's Kisses. New York, Silhouette, 1986.
Woman of the West. New York, Silhouette, 1989.

Novels as Nina Coombs

Love So Fearful. New York, New American Library, 1983.
Forbidden Joy. New York, New American Library, 1983.
Passion's Domain. New York, New American Library, 1983.
Sun Spark. New York, New American Library, 1984.
Before It's Too Late. New York, New American Library, 1986.

*   *   *

During the early 1980's Nina Pykare wrote a series of novels for the Silhouette Desire line under the name Nora Powers. As Nina Coombs she wrote *Love so Fearful* for Rapture Romances. Ann Coombs, Nan Pemberton, and Regina Towers are also pseudonyms that she has used.

If one had to pick out some of her most enjoyable novels, however, the choice might be surprising. Writing under her own name, Pykare wrote numerous Regency novels in the early Candlelight Regency Specials. These were delightfully done! They were skillfully plotted and missed the typical pitfalls of many other such novels. Rather than stressing the London Season, she set her hero and heroine in other parts of the country. She also concentrated on plot developments and a strong narrative line. Her characters were believable, if somewhat stereotypical of such stories. To a certain extent, these novels also had definite elements of the gothic interwoven in the rest of the plot. Hidden passages, mysterious noises, flitting ghosts, and dark and mysterious shadows all reinforce the gothic feel in some of her stories. It is difficult to really pin down their appeal because no single element stands out, but a Regency written by Pykare has all the conflict, mystery, and love that a reader could want.

Two novels, *The Rake's Companion* by Regina Towers and *The Dazzled Heart* by Pykare, are good examples of her writing in this genre. *The Rake's Companion* has a tantalizing Cinderella plot. Faith Duncan applies for a position as a nurse-companion to the Countess of Moorshead Castle in Yorkshire. Once she is offered the position and arrives from London, she eventually learns that the Countess is matchmaking, with Faith's hand as the prize as well as the Countess's fortune. The competitors are Felix Kingston and his brother, the Earl of Moorshead, who are both nephews of the Countess. Falling rocks, mysterious intruders, a kidnapping that leaves Faith stranded near deadly bogs all add to the heightened tension. The hero, the Earl, is appropriately cynical and suspicious, while Faith is innocence personified, but thankfully bright enough to help find the real culprit. In spite of rigid determination on the parts of the hero and heroine, they fall madly in love which naturally finds them facing a happy-ever-after ending.

The Dazzled Heart is equally enjoyable. Jennifer Whitcomb is hired as a governess by a family living near Dover. The mother is a confirmed hypochondriac, the father is a bluff retired businessman who patiently copes with his wife and their three spoiled children. The plot centers on the hero, Viscount Haverford's search for spies in the area and on a Monsieur Dupen who is both an hypnotist and the spy being sought. Jennifer's unwitting discovery of the plotters puts her right in the center of things. Only the quick-thinking actions of the hero and the occasional kiss indicate his surrender to love and to Jennifer.

For those readers interested in her contemporary romances, *Time Stands Still* by Nora Powers is a typical example of her work. Libby Collins is a geologist specializing in oil discovery. She works for World Wide Exploration, feeling that this sort of company is just the kind for her. Actually, she is interested in oil discovery, but also in Jared Harper, her ex-husband, who is also part of the company. They eventually meet again on an exploration expedition in Indonesia. Throughout the trip, Libby strives to show Jared that she has grown up, that she is no longer the flighty, immature girl she'd been. Conflicts in the story naturally center on their relationship. Both are very much in love with each other, but both are afraid of being hurt again.

This novel has certain ambiguities that cause some confusion in characterization. Libby is determined to show how mature and independent she has become. Yet, she says, "I'm going to follow you. Everywhere. Until you take me back." Or, "Please say we can try again. Anyway you want it." Somehow, this reaction is contradictory. The heroine is determined to be a "new" women, yet she ends up acting very "old" women and definitely a clinging vine. Perhaps it is this ambivalence that creates a sense of contradiction in the novel. This may have been intentional on Pykare's part to show that a woman need not give up certain traits and characteristics in the modern world. There is enough uncertainty in this particular story to leave readers with mixed messages. In her Regency romances, her heroines fill "traditional" roles and Pykare seems comfortable in portraying them so. Certainly in these types of novels, her creativity, enthusiasm, and abilities as a writer are well evident to all her readers. In any future contemporary romances, she may need to resolve her heroine's basic character and stick with it.

—Arlene Moore

***

QUEST, Erica. See **BUCKINGHAM, Nancy.**

RADCLIFFE, Janette. See **ROBERTS, Janet Louise.**

RADDALL, Thomas Head. Canadian. Born in Hythe, Kent, England, 13 November 1903; emigrated to Canada, 1913. Educated at St. Leonard's School, Hythe; Chebucto School, Halifax, Nova Scotia; Halifax Academy. Wireless operator, Canadian Merchant Marine, 1918–22; served in the 2nd (Reserve) Battalion, West Nova Scotia Regiment, 1942–43: Lieutenant. Married Edith Margaret Freeman in 1927 (died); two children. Accountant in the wood pulp and paper industries in Nova Scotia, 1923–38. Full-time writer since 1938. Recipient: Governor-General's award, 1944, for non-fiction, 1949, 1958; Lorne Pierce Medal, 1956; University of Alberta medal, 1977. LL.D.: Dalhousie University, Halifax, 1949; St. Francis Xavier University, Antigonish, Nova Scotia, 1973; D.Litt.: St. Mary's University, Halifax, 1969; D.C.L.: King's College, Halifax, 1972. Fellow, Royal Society of Canada, 1953. Officer, Order of Canada, 1970. Address: 44 Park Street, Liverpool, Nova Scotia, B0T 1K0, Canada.

ROMANCE AND HISTORICAL PUBLICATIONS

Novels

His Majesty's Yankees. Toronto, McClelland and Stewart, and New York, Doubleday, 1942; Edinburgh, Blackwood, 1944.
Roger Sudden. Toronto, McClelland and Stewart, and New York, Doubleday, 1944; London, Hurst and Blackett, 1946.
Pride's Fancy. Toronto, McClelland and Stewart, and New York, Doubleday, 1946; London, Hurst and Blackett, 1948.
The Governor's Lady. New York, Doubleday, 1960; London, Collins, 1961.
Hangman's Beach. New York, Doubleday, 1966.

OTHER PUBLICATIONS

Novels

Saga of the Rover, with C. H. L. Jones. Halifax, Nova Scotia, Royal, 1931.
The Nymph and the Lamp. Toronto, McClelland and Stewart, and Boston, Little Brown, 1950; London, Hutchinson, 1951.
Son of the Hawk. Philadelphia, Winston, 1950.
Tidefall. Toronto, McClelland and Stewart, and Boston, Little Brown, 1953; London, Hutchinson, 1954; as *Give and Take*, New York, Popular Library, 1954.
The Wings of Night. New York, Doubleday, 1956; London, Macmillan, 1957.

Short Stories

Pied Piper of Dipper Creek and Other Tales. Edinburgh, Blackwood, 1939.
Tambour and Other Stories. Toronto, McClelland and Stewart, 1945.
The Wedding Gift and Other Stories. Toronto, McClelland and Stewart, 1947.
A Muster of Arms and Other Stories. Toronto, McClelland and Stewart, 1954.

At the Tide's Turn and Other Stories. Toronto, McClelland and Stewart, 1959.
The Dreamers. Porters Lake, Nova Scotia, Pottersfield Press, 1986.

Other

A Souvenir from the Land of Maple. Liverpool, Nova Scotia, Mersey Paper Company, n.d.
The Markland Sagas, with C. H. L. Jones. Montreal, Gazette Printing, 1934.
Ogomkegea: The Story of Liverpool, Nova Scotia. Liverpool, Nova Scotia, Liverpool Advance, 1934.
Canada's Deep Sea Fighters. Halifax, Government of Nova Scotia, 1936; revised edition, 1937.
West Novas: A History of the West Nova Scotia Regiment. Montreal, Provincial, 1948.
Halifax, Warden of the North. Toronto, McClelland and Stewart, 1948; London, Dent, 1950; revised edition, New York, Doubleday, 1965; McClelland and Stewart, 1971.
The Path of Destiny: Canada from the British Conquest to Home Rule 1763–1850. New York, Doubleday, 1957.
The Rover: The Story of a Canadian Privateer (for children). London, Macmillan, 1958; New York, St. Martin's Press, 1959.
Halifax and the World in 1809 and 1959. Halifax, Nova Scotia, Halifax Insurance Company, 1959.
Footsteps on Old Floors: True Tales of Mystery. New York, Doubleday, 1968.
This Is Nova Scotia, Canada's Ocean Playground. Halifax, Nova Scotia, Book Room, 1970.
In My Time: A Memoir. Toronto, McClelland and Stewart, 1976.
The Mersey Story. Liverpool, Nova Scotia, Bowater-Mersey Paper Company, 1979.

*

Bibliography: *Thomas Head Raddall: A Bibliography* by Alan R. Young, Kingston, Ontario, Loyal Colonies Press, 1982.

Manuscript Collection: Killam Memorial Library, Dalhousie University, Halifax.

Critical Studies: "Thomas H. Raddall: The Man and His Work" by W. J. Hawkins, in *Queen's Quarterly* (Kingston, Ontario), Spring 1968; "Thomas Raddall: The Art of Historical Fiction" by Donald Cameron, in *Dalhousie Review* (Halifax), Winter 1970; *Thomas Head Raddall* by Alan R. Young, Boston, Twayne, 1983.

*   *   *

Thomas Head Raddall's early historical romances in the 1940's and 1960's, and the three romances with modern settings that he published in the 1950's initially earned him great critical acclaim in Canada. Changing critical tastes have temporarily dimmed his reputation, but a large public in Canada and elsewhere continues to read his work.

From his earliest full-length work, *Saga of the Rover* (1931), Raddall exploited a key formula of historical fiction—the placing of narrative within a historical context that demonstrated the impact of world events upon ordinary people. Raddall's most subtle exploration of this pattern occurs in his historical romance *His Majesty's Yankees*, which depicts the situation of Nova Scotians during the American Revolution. The entire Strang family becomes involved in the conflict when their elected representative in the capital, Halifax, tells the citizens that he has been stripped of his public offices. In a manner typical of historical fiction the Strang family's responses are divided. Matthew, the head of the family, urges non-involvement, but one of his sons joins the rebel cause while another joins the King's forces. David, another son and the hero of the novel, at first has no political position. However, after seeing some of the evils of colonialism and after rescuing a woman from an assault by a British seaman, he takes up with the rebels. The novel then delineates David's growth towards adulthood and political maturity. Eventually, he returns home to embrace a code of domestic values that takes precedence over political causes. Historically, David's point of view is also adopted by Nova Scotia, so that David is to be taken as representative of a people.

Equally typical of historical fiction is Raddall's portrait in this novel of momentous historical transition, in this instance the birth of the American republic and the dissociation of Nova Scotia from its ties with New England, and its shift from neutrality towards loyalty to the crown. Typical too is the manner in which such transitions occasion dramatic conflicts between family members, generations, and societies, the middle way (represented by the hero) ultimately triumphing. As often in historical romance, the political and moral quest of the hero becomes inseparable from the working out of a love plot. David Strang's love is Fear Bingay, daughter of a prominent Tory who marries a British officer. The gulf between David and Fear appears uncrossable, but when her husband dies, the way is open for a marriage that as the novel concludes becomes symbolic of the new social and political balance established between the citizens and the crown. The marriage also symbolizes the triumph of the domestic ideals of peace, marital love, and (typical of Raddall) love for the land that will provide the new family with its livelihood.

To some extent Raddall's subsequent historical romances make use of similar patterns. *Roger Sudden* explores the demise of French imperial power in North America and the simultaneous growth of the British. *Pride's Fancy* explores the conflicts among the traditional planter elite of the West Indies, the supposedly egalitarian society of post-revolution Haiti, the aggressive commercialism of the merchant barons of Nova Scotia, and the different way of life and values espoused by Nathan Cain. The hero of the novel, Cain, ultimately opts for the creative craft of ship-building, domesticity, and love for his native Nova Scotia. *Hangman's Beach* depicts the conflicting forces that transformed the war between Britain and France into something else—the 1812 conflict between Britain and the United States— and *The Governor's Lady* depicts, though far less effectively than *His Majesty's Yankees*, the American Revolution and the demise of British rule in the rebellious North American colonies. The protagonists of these works are, like David Strang, reluctant participants in these conflicts, and only in *The Governor's Lady*, in which Raddall's protagonists (John and Fannie Wentworth) are real historical personages, does Raddall radically (and not very successfully) veer from the pattern that has served him and other historical fiction writers so well.

Generally, Raddall is highly effective at working within the classic framework of the historical novel. He can also brilliantly create a vivid and colourful sense of place and time, and he is a gifted story-teller with a fine sense of drama. Some of these qualities are carried over into the three romances set in his own time—*The Nymph and the Lamp*, *Tidefall*, and *The Wings of Night*. *Tidefall* and *The Wings of Night*, set in pre- and post-World War II Nova Scotia respectively, are only partial successes, but *The Nymph and the Lamp* is arguably Raddall's finest literary achievement. For this work Raddall chose the remote

setting of Marina (Raddall's fictional name for Sable Island, the notorious "Graveyard of the Atlantic"). The plot concerns a radio operator (Matthew Carney), the woman (Isabel Jardine) he "marries" while on shore leave from Marina, and her affair with another radio operator (Greg Skane). This triangular love plot is fairly conventional, but Raddall's handling of it is far from ordinary.

As in a number of his historical romances, Raddall presents his protagonist undergoing a long and painful process of self-discovery, culminating in a crucial choice between opposing sets of values. As in the case of David Strang, Roger Sudden, and Nathan Cain, the fulfillment of this quest is achieved simultaneously with the union between hero and heroine. *The Nymph and the Lamp* is, however, far more complex, chiefly because of Raddall's presentation of Isabel Jardine. Once Raddall has delineated the existential state of Carney's psyche and his retreat to the symbolic isolation of Marina, he focuses his attention almost exclusively on Isabel. At first we see her suffering the indefinable malaise of unfulfilled sexuality. We see her inability to throw off her inherited Puritan conscience once on the island, the paradoxical but temporary release she finds with Skane, and then her return to her rural roots in Nova Scotia's Annapolis Valley, a rich and golden land of orchards, blossoms, and fruit, with all of which Isabel becomes symbolically associated. When Skane arrives to claim the "harvest", however, Isabel rejects his egocentricity and sensuality and chooses the way of loving self-sacrifice (she will be a "lamp" for Carney who is going blind), leaving behind both the world of her birthplace and the materialistic "scrabble for cash" that characterizes city life in Halifax.

Raddall's historical fiction and romances are very much part of the literary tradition in which he was nurtured. They look back to a pre-World War I context in which Scott, Cooper, Kipling, Stevenson, Conan Doyle, and Conrad served as pre-eminent influences. Indeed, all were acknowledged favourites of Raddall in his youth, though he never consciously imitated any of them. Nor does he seem to have imitated any Canadian writer, though he clearly belongs to the same tradition within Canadian literature as John Richardson, Rosanna Mullins, William Kirby, Gilbert Parker, Charles and Theodore Roberts. This is an important (though of late neglected) segment of the Canadian literary heritage, and Raddall is one of its finest representatives.

—Alan R. Young

RAE, Hugh C. See **STIRLING, Jessica.**

RANDALL, Florence Engel. American. Born in Brooklyn, New York, 18 October 1917. Attended Pratt Institute, New York, 1938; New York University, 1939. Married Murray C. Randall in 1939; three children. Agent: Raines and Raines, 71 Park Avenue, New York, New York 10016. Address: 88 Oxford Boulevard, Great Neck, New York 11023, U.S.A.

ROMANCE AND HISTORICAL PUBLICATIONS

Novels

Hedgerow. New York, Harcourt Brace, and London, Heinemann, 1967.

The Place of Sapphires. New York, Harcourt Brace, 1969; London, Millington, 1974.
Haldane Station. New York, Harcourt Brace, 1973; London, Millington, 1975.

OTHER PUBLICATIONS

Other (for children)

The Almost Year. New York, Atheneum, 1971.
A Watcher in the Woods. New York, Atheneum, 1976; London, New English Library, n.d.
All the Sky Together. New York, Atheneum, 1983.

*

Manuscript Collection: Mugar Memorial Library, Boston University.

Florence Engel Randall comments:

Even though all of my adult novels could be classified as gothic, since they contain the necessary ingredients of atmosphere, mystery, and romance, it seems to me they are gothic with a difference. These are modern novels, set in the present time and they vary, one from the other. *Hedgerow* takes place on a farm and is a straight mystery romance, but *The Place of Sapphires* is a romance set within the confines of a ghost story, and *Haldane Station*, since it deals with a form of time travel, could almost be called science fiction.

My "young adult" books are different as well. *The Almost Year* deals with a poltergeist and the race question. *A Watcher in the Woods* is science fiction that has its focus not only in the imagination but reality as well. It has been made into a movie by Walt Disney Productions.

*   *   *

While she was writing romantic short stories in the early 1960's, Florence Engel Randall dreamed of producing a novel. She writes each chapter as she would a short story, yet leaves each incomplete in itself, linked to the others. She allows her characters and her unconscious mind to determine the flow of the story rather than planning the plot in advance.

The heroine of *Hedgerow* is a young ballet student who takes a summer babysitting job as a change from her grueling practice schedule after an illness forces her to rest. She becomes curious about the strange suicide of a member of the Hedge family and is determined to discover its cause. She pries into the family secrets until she deserves the results of the fury she induces. But love conquers all and this novel has more pure romance than the ones that follow.

The Place of Sapphires deals with a ghost and possession. After an accident in which their parents are killed, two sisters take a house which is reputed to be haunted. The injured girl occupies the room of Alarice, the deceased younger sister of the owner, and begins to reflect the behavior of the dead woman. The story is told from the points of view of the two sisters and the ghost in separate sections which relate the same events from three different perspectives. The contrast is striking and well done.

The Almost Year derived from research undertaken for the previous work. The idea of a poltergeist developed into a 15-year-old black girl sent from the ghetto to live with a middle-class white family for nine months. Resentment, anger, and suspicion spark the poltergeist which symbolizes the girl's misery and

frustration. An American Library Association Notable Book, this novel for young adults handles the racial problem with skill, but the poltergeist received mixed reviews.

Haldane Station reveals the author's fascination with time. She uses time measured inwardly or subjectively in a series of flash-forwards as Rachel "remembers" things that have not happened yet and then finds herself in the future remembering much of the past. But the future is not as she recalls it. The complex plot is intriguing, but not every reader will enjoy it.

A Watcher in the Woods also has a time theme. Jan begins to feel the emotions of a girl who seems to be trying to lead her to the resolution of the unsolved disappearance of a child almost 50 years before. When other members of the family are also contacted by the watcher, the child's mother is invited to visit in an attempt to reunite them. The first-person narrative is filled with a 15-year-old's preoccupations, but curiosity is very strong, both in the characters and in the reader.

Randall has developed from a writer of sweet romance short stories into the successful author of occult-like novels and has carved a small niche for herself in the annals of gothic romance literature.

—Andrea Lee Shuey

———

RANDALL, Rona. British. Born in Birkenhead, Cheshire. Educated at Birkenhead High School; Pitman's College, London. Married Frederick Walter Shambrook; one son. Worked in theatre repertory companies, three years, then a journalist. Chairwoman, Women's Press Club of London, 1962–63; founder member, Society of Sussex Authors, 1969. Recipient: Romantic Novelists Association Major award, 1969. Agent: Curtis Brown, 162–168 Regent Street, London W1R 5TB. Address: Conifers, Pembury Road, Tunbridge Wells, Kent TN2 4ND, England.

ROMANCE AND HISTORICAL PUBLICATIONS

Novels (series: Drayton)

The Moon Returns. London, Collins, 1942.
Doctor Havelock's Wife. London, Collins, 1943.
Rebel Wife. London, Collins, 1944.
The Late Mrs. Lane. London, Collins, 1945; New York, Arcadia House, 1946.
The Howards of Saxondale. London, Collins, 1946.
That Girl, Jennifer! New York, Arcadia House, 1946.
The Fleeting Hour. London, Collins, 1947.
I Married a Doctor. London, Collins, 1947; as *The Doctor Takes a Wife*, New York, Arcadia House, 1947.
The Street of the Singing Fountain. London, Collins, 1948.
Shadows on the Sand. London, Collins, 1949; New York, Ace, 1973.
Delayed Harvest. London, Collins, 1950.
Young Doctor Kenway. London, Collins, 1950.
The Island Doctor. London, Collins, 1951.
Bright Morning. London, Collins, 1952.
Girls in White. London, Collins, and New York, Arcadia House, 1952.
Young Sir Galahad. London, Collins, 1953.
Journey to Love. London, Collins, 1953; New York, Ace, 1972.
Faith, Hope, and Charity. London, Collins, 1954.
The Merry Andrews. London, Collins, 1954.

Desert Flower. London, Collins, 1955.
Journey to Arcady. New York, Arcadia House, 1955.
Leap in the Dark. London, Collins, 1956; New York, Ace, 1967.
A Girl Called Ann. London, Collins, 1956; New York, Ace, 1973.
Runaway from Love. London, Collins, 1956.
The Cedar Tree. London, Collins, 1957.
The Doctor Falls in Love. London, Collins, 1958.
Nurse Stacey Comes Aboard. London, Collins, 1958; New York, Ace, 1968.
Love and Dr. Maynard. London, Collins, 1959.
Enchanted Eden. London, Collins, 1960.
Sister at Sea. London, Collins, 1960.
Hotel De Luxe. London, Collins, 1961; New York, Ace, 1967.
Girl in Love. London, Collins, 1961.
House Surgeon at Luke's. London, Collins, 1962.
Walk into My Parlour. London, Collins, 1962; New York, Ace, 1967; revised edition, as *Lyonhurst*, London, Fontana, and New York, Ballantine, 1977.
Lab Nurse. New York, Berkley, 1962.
The Silver Cord. London, Collins, 1963; New York, Ace, 1968.
The Willow Herb. London, Collins, 1965; New York, Ace, 1967.
Seven Days from Midnight. London, Collins, 1965; New York, Ace, 1967.
Arrogant Duke. London, Collins, 1966; New York, Ace, 1972.
Knight's Keep. London, Collins, and New York, Ace, 1967.
Broken Tapestry. London, Hurst and Blackett, 1969; New York, Ace, 1973.
The Witching Hour. London, Hurst and Blackett, and New York, Ace, 1970.
Silent Thunder. London, Hurst and Blackett, 1971.
Mountain of Fear. New York, Ace, 1972; London, Severn House, 1989.
Time Remembered, Time Lost. New York, Ace, 1973.
Glenrannoch. London, Collins, 1973; as *The Midnight Walker*, New York, Ace, 1973.
Dragonmede. London, Collins, and New York, Simon and Schuster, 1974.
Watchman's Stone. London, Collins, and New York, Simon and Schuster, 1975.
The Eagle at the Gate. New York, Coward McCann, 1977; London, Hamish Hamilton, 1978.
The Mating Dance. London, Hamish Hamilton, and New York, Coward McCann, 1979.
The Ladies of Hanover Square. London, Hamish Hamilton, and New York, Coward McCann, 1981.
Curtain Call. London, Hamish Hamilton, 1983.
The Drayton Legacy. London, Hamish Hamilton, 1985.
The Potter's Niece (Drayton). London, Hamish Hamilton, 1987.

OTHER PUBLICATIONS

Other

Jordan and the Holy Land. London, Muller, 1968.
The Model Wife. London, Herbert Press, 1989.

*

Rona Randall comments:

I devote myself to writing historical novels now because they seem to come instinctively; I lose myself in them completely. Because the present day seems to be becoming more distasteful?

Perhaps. I don't know. But it seems significant that my historical novels bring me more appreciative letters from readers of all ages than my "modern" ones. I am particularly attracted to the potteries in the 18th and 19th centuries. The reason for this is quoted on the jackets of my Drayton books: "Rona Randall has herself progressed, through pottery, to become an accomplished modeller in ceramics, and the unusual background for the Drayton novels is one she knows well."

*   *   *

A common theme found in Rona Randall's novels concerns a young woman who becomes involved with a handsome man unworthy of her love. Often the heroine actually marries this man and shares with him a passionate relationship, all the time believing that they will live happily ever after. At first all goes well, but slowly sinister aspects of his personality emerge. Fortunately there is usually another man around willing to offer the kind of love she deserves. Though not necessarily handsome, he is a robust individual who impresses the heroine with a powerful masculine presence. In what has become standard romantic form, the hero and heroine are initially incompatible, often because of his overbearing personality or sarcastic wit. Typically, he is a medical doctor and, through the tender caring of his patients, Randall shows the reader and the heroine his intrinsic goodness.

This format is ideal for the gothic novel of which Randall has written several. Probably one of her best known in *Dragonmede*. In this Victorian tale Eustacia Rochdale falls in love with the aristocratic Julian Kershaw. Although Eustacia is well educated, her family background (a mother who runs an illegal gambling establishment) leaves much to be desired. However, the young man seems genuinely to love her and eventually proposes marriage. She is ecstatic until she first glimpses the ancestral home, Dragonmede, whereupon a feeling of foreboding engulfs her. Her fears are not unfounded for, although Julian proves to be a passionate husband, he has a brooding, sadistic side that eventually destroys Eustacia's love for him. Other sinister characters abound, and with Julian's murder she finds herself in mortal danger. In the end it is the love of a virile young doctor that saves her life and gives her the happy marriage she has always wanted.

An earlier work with a similar plot but fewer of the gothic trappings is *Shadows on the Sand*. Sorrel Dean, a young architect, journeys to Beirut in order to join her fiancé Richard Baily, an archeologist working at a desert site. Soon she finds that he is involved in the theft of valuable relics uncovered by the expedition. Although Sorrel is never directly in danger, her innocent association with this dark character causes her a great deal of emotional stress. Again it is a taciturn but basically compassionate medical doctor who proves to be her true love.

Variations on the eternal triangle theme also run through many of Randall's stories. In *Dragonmede* Julian, although married to Eustacia, still keeps the wickedly beautiful Victoria on the side. In *Watchman's Stone* the lovely Elizabeth marries Calum only to discover his affair with her younger sister. In *The Mating Dance* pretty blonde Lucinda finds her worthless husband in bed with her older sister Clemetine, an irrepressible lady whose obvious enjoyment of sex is in sharp contrast to Lucy's more conventional attitude. Things are even worse for Dulcima Howard one of *The Ladies of Hanover Square*. First she loves Sir Charles Ashleigh then later falls for his evil son, Justin who spurns her even while knowing she carries his child. Her niece Deborah fairs better. Although loved by two men she has eyes for only one, but not until he divorces his wife (she is no good) can Deborah marry him.

Randall's fiction contains equal elements of drama and excitement. Her excellent portrayal of the various characters, especially the heroines, makes the reader care what happens to them. With a fluid writing style this author weaves engaging tales of women in love.

—Patricia Altner

RAYNER, Claire (Berenice). Also writes as Sheila Brandon; Ann Lynton; Ruth Martin. British. Born 22 January 1931. Married Desmond Rayner in 1957; one daughter and two sons. Nurse in the pediatric department, Whittington Hospital, London, until 1960; television presenter, *Pebble Mill* program; columnist, as Ruth Martin, 1966–75, and as Claire Rayner, 1975–88, *Woman's Own*, London; columnist, the *Sun*, 1973–80, the *Sunday Mirror*, 1980–88, and since 1988, *Today*, all London; since 1985 features presenter, TV-AM, London. Agent: Desmond Rayner, Holly Wood House, Roxborough Avenue, Harrow-on-the-Hill, Middlesex, England; or, Aaron M. Priest, Aaron Priest Literary Agency Inc., 565 Fifth Avenue, New York, New York 10017, U.S.A.

ROMANCE AND HISTORICAL PUBLICATIONS

Novels (series: The Performers; The Poppy Chronicles)

The Performers

1. *Gower Street*. London, Cassell, and New York, Simon and Schuster, 1973.
2. *The Haymarket*. London, Cassell, and New York, Simon and Schuster, 1974.
3. *Paddington Green*. London, Cassell, and New York, Simon and Schuster, 1975.
4. *Soho Square*. London, Cassell, and New York, Putnam, 1976.
5. *Bedford Row*. London, Cassell, and New York, Putnam, 1977.
6. *Long Acre*. London, Cassell, 1978; as *Covent Garden*, New York, Putnam, 1978.
7. *Charing Cross*. London, Cassell, and New York, Putnam, 1979.
8. *The Strand*. London, Cassell, and New York, Putnam, 1980.
9. *Chelsea Reach*. London, Weidenfeld and Nicolson, 1982.
10. *Shaftesbury Avenue*. London, Weidenfeld and Nicolson, 1983.
11. *Piccadilly*. London, Weidenfeld and Nicolson, 1985.
12. *Seven Dials*. London, Weidenfeld and Nicolson, 1987.

Family Chorus. London, Hutchinson, 1984.

The Poppy Chronicles

1. *Jubilee*. London, Weidenfeld and Nicolson, 1987.
2. *Flanders*. London, Weidenfeld and Nicolson, 1988.

Novels as Sheila Brandon

The Final Year. London, Corgi, 1962.
Cottage Hospital. London, Corgi, 1963.
Children's Ward. London, Corgi, 1964.
The Lonely One. London, Corgi, 1965.
The Doctors of Downlands. London, Corgi, 1968.
The Private Wing. London, Corgi, 1971.

Nurse in the Sun. London, Corgi, 1972.

OTHER PUBLICATIONS

Novels

Shilling a Pound Pears. London, Hart Davis, 1964.
The House on the Fen. London, Corgi, and New York, Bantam, 1967.
Starch of Aprons. London, Hale, 1967; as *The Hive*, London, Corgi, 1968.
Lady Mislaid. London, Corgi, 1968.
Death on the Table. London, Corgi, 1969.
The Meddlers. London, Cassell, and New York, Simon and Schuster, 1970.
A Time to Heal. London, Cassell, and New York, Simon and Schuster, 1972.
The Burning Summer. London, Allison and Busby, 1972.
Sisters. London, Hutchinson, 1978.
Reprise. London, Hutchinson, 1980.
The Running Years. London, Hutchinson, 1981; as *The Enduring Years*, New York, Delacorte Press, 1982.
The Virus Man. London, Hutchinson, 1985.
Lunching at Laura's. London, Hutchinson, 1986.
Maddie. London, Joseph, 1988.
Clinical Judgements. London, Joseph, 1989.

Other

Mothers and Midwives. London, Allen and Unwin, 1962.
What Happens in the Hospital. London, Hart Davis, 1963.
The Calendar of Childhood: A Guide for All Mothers. London, Ebury Press, 1964.
Your Baby. London, Hamlyn, 1965.
Careers with Children. London, Hale, 1966.
Housework—The Easy Way. London, Corgi, 1967.
Mothercraft (as Ann Lynton). London, Corgi, 1967.
Shall I Be a Nurse? Exeter, Wheaton, 1967.
Home Nursing and Family Health. London, Corgi, 1967.
101 Facts an Expectant Mother Should Know. London, Dickens Press, 1967.
For Children: Equipping a Home for a Growing Family. London, Macdonald, 1967.
Essentials of Out-patient Nursing. London, Arlington, 1967.
101 Key Facts of Practical Baby Care. London, Dickens Press, 1967.
A Parent's Guide to Sex Education. London, Corgi, 1968; Garden City, New York, Dolphin, 1969.
People in Love: A Modern Guide to Sex in Marriage. London, Hamlyn, 1968; revised edition, as *About Sex*, London, Fontana, 1972.
Woman's Medical Dictionary. London, Corgi, 1971.
When to Call the Doctor—What to Do Whilst Waiting. London, Corgi, 1972.
The Shy Person's Book. London, Wolfe, 1973; New York, McKay, 1974.
Childcare Made Simple. London, W. H. Allen, 1973.
Where Do I Come From? Answers to a Child's Questions about Sex. London, Arlington, 1974.
You Know More Than You Think You Do. London, MIND Council, 1975.
Kitchen Garden, with Keith Fordyce. London, Independent Television Publications, 1976.
More Kitchen Garden, with Keith Fordyce. London, Independent Television Publications, 1977.

Family Feelings: Understanding Your Child from 0 to Five.
London, Arrow, 1977.
Claire Rayner Answers Your 100 Questions on Pregnancy.
London, BBC Publications, 1977.
The Body Book (for children). London, G. Whizzard, 1978;
Woodbury, New York, Barron's, 1980.
Related to Sex. New York and London, Paddington Press, 1979.
Everything Your Doctor Would Tell You If He Had the Time.
London, Cassell, and New York, Putnam, 1980.
*Claire Rayner's Lifeguide: A Commonsense Approach to Modern
Living.* London, New English Library, 1980.
*Baby and Young Child Care: A Practical Guide for Parents of
Children Aged 0–5 Years.* Maidenhead, Berkshire, Purnell,
1981.
Growing Pains: And How to Avoid Them. London, Heinemann,
1984.
Claire Rayner's Marriage Guide: How to Make Yours Work.
London, Macmillan, 1984.
The Getting Better Book (for children). London, Deutsch, 1985.
Woman. London, Hamlyn, 1986.
Safe Sex. London, Sphere, 1987.
The Don't Spoil Your Body Book (for children). London, Bod-
ley Head, 1989.

Editor (as Ruth Martin), *Before the Baby—and After.* London,
Hurst and Blackett, 1958.
Editor, *The Mitchell Beazley Atlas of the Body and Mind.*
London, Mitchell Beazley, 1976; as *Rand McNally Atlas of
the Body and Mind*, Chicago, Rand McNally, 1976.
Editor, *When I Grow Up: Children's Views on Adulthood.*
London, Virgin, 1986.

*   *   *

The operating theater and the legitimate (and not-
so-legitimate) theater share the spotlight in the novels of Claire
Rayner. Her Performers series focuses on the Lucas and Lackland families, starting with Lilith Lucas and Abel Lackland.
Lilith and Abel start powerful family traditions of theatrical and
medical success that continue down through their great-
grandchildren. At the same time, the two families are intertwined beginning with the doomed relationship between Lilith
and Abel and continuing through the various successful and unsuccessful alliances between their descendants.

Rayner has chosen a particularly fascinating period of history
to cover. The Victorian age in England saw amazing advances in
medicine, and she toys with this historical truth to arrange matters so that the doctors Lackland are participants in most of
these notable changes. Abel is far ahead of his time in terms of
attitudes toward sanitation, surgery and the obligation of the
physician to care for all, regardless of status or wealth. The
Lacklands are not necessarily innovators, but are supporters and
advancers of the cause of modern medicine in the face of strong
opposition and even ridicule. Rayner has a strong sense of what
it was like to be a maverick in a period of great exploration and
of stubborn superstition in medical practice. She also conveys
the sense of the times in the great disparities between people of
the highest and lowest classes. Only rarely does the "upper
crust" make an appearance in these novels. The emphasis instead is on the very bottom level of society and the middle levels
to which some of the outcasts can aspire. Medicine and theater
represent two ways out of the static social order of the times.
Neither is perfectly respectable in the upper-class mind, but each
is an area of opportunity for ambitious and hard-working people
to escape the unchanging despair of their backgrounds.

The relationships between characters in Rayner's work are often grim, and a reader looking for consistently happy endings
will be disappointed. Like life, the novels sometimes have equivocal endings; happiness is most often a matter of chance. One
recurring theme in these family sagas is the lack of communication between people and the destruction wrought by the inability
to compromise. Especially in Lilith and Abel, but also again in
many of their descendents, Rayner has created some memorably,
even awesomely selfish people. They are people with a great
sense of the rightness of their own desires and choices and a
correspondingly weak sense of the entitlements of others. At the
same time, even while they are destroying their bonds with one
another unnecessarily, they are people of great charm with great
strengths allied to their great weaknesses. The desire for revenge, for the accumulation of wealth and power, or to dominate
one's children may not be attractive emotions, but they are human and recognizable. When they are offset by love, altruism
and the desire to succeed they help to create fully-rounded characters.

Rayner has done her homework in regard to all the details that
flesh out her stories. Her knowledge of and feeling for Victorian
London is immense. Her portrayal of the theater of the time,
from the high-flown productions to the mean little working-class
entertainments, is alternately attractive and repellent. She never
steps out of period, even when her characters are advancing
medical practice toward the 20th century. She also deals with
medical matters unflinchingly, describing such sensitive topics
as illegal abortion or the slide of Celia Lackland into madness
uncompromisingly and accurately. Yet she has a delicacy of
touch that permits her to treat the most unpleasant medical conditions or surroundings with compassion that does not degenerate into sentimentality.

—Susan Quinn Berneis

REID, Henrietta. Address: c/o Mills and Boon Ltd., 18–24
Paradise Road, Richmond, Surrey TW9 1SR, England.

ROMANCE AND HISTORICAL PUBLICATIONS

Novels

Island of Secrets. London, Mills and Boon, 1965.
Return to Candelriggs. London, Mills and Boon, 1966.
Daughter of Lir. London, Mills and Boon, 1966.
Man of the Islands. London, Mills and Boon, 1966; Toronto,
Harlequin, 1967.
My Dark Rapparee. London, Mills and Boon, 1966; Toronto,
Harlequin, 1967.
Substitute for Love. London, Mills and Boon, 1967; Toronto,
Harlequin, 1968.
Bridal Tapestry. London, Mills and Boon, 1967.
Falcon's Keep. London, Mills and Boon, 1968; Toronto, Harle-
quin, 1969.
Beloved Sparrow. London, Mills and Boon, 1968; Toronto,
Harlequin, 1969.
Laird of Storr. London, Mills and Boon, and Toronto, Harle-
quin, 1968.
Reluctant Masquerade. London, Mills and Boon, 1969; Tor-
onto, Harlequin, 1970.
The Thorn Tree. London, Mills and Boon, 1969.

The Black Delaney. London, Mills and Boon, 1970; Toronto, Harlequin, 1971.

Hunter's Moon. London, Mills and Boon, and Toronto, Harlequin, 1970.

Rival Sisters. London, Mills and Boon, 1970; Toronto, Harlequin, 1971.

The Made Marriage. London, Mills and Boon, and Toronto, Harlequin, 1971.

Sister of the Bride. London, Mills and Boon, 1971; Toronto, Harlequin, 1972.

Garth of Tregillis. London, Mills and Boon, and Toronto, Harlequin, 1972.

The Torrent. London, Mills and Boon, 1972.

Bride of Ravenscourt. London, Mills and Boon, 1972.

Dark Usurper. London, Mills and Boon, 1972.

Bird of Prey. London, Mills and Boon, 1973; Toronto, Harlequin, 1974.

Intruder at Windgates. London, Mills and Boon, and Toronto, Harlequin, 1973.

Dragon Island. London, Mills and Boon, 1974; Toronto, Harlequin, 1975.

The Man at the Helm. London, Mills and Boon, and Toronto, Harlequin, 1975.

The Tartan Ribbon. London, Mills and Boon, 1976; Toronto, Harlequin, 1977.

Love's Puppet. Toronto, Harlequin, 1976.

Greek Bridal. London, Mills and Boon, and Toronto, Harlequin, 1976.

Push the Past Behind. Toronto, Harlequin, 1977.

Dear Tyrant. London, Mills and Boon, 1977.

Tomorrow Brings Enchantment. London, Mills and Boon, 1978.

Paradise Plantation. London, Mills and Boon, and Toronto, Harlequin, 1979.

Lord of the Isles. London, Mills and Boon, and Toronto, Harlequin, 1981.

New Boss at Birchfields. London, Mills and Boon, 1982.

*   *   *

Henrietta Reid's novels may read like modern versions of Cinderella, but in reality they are delightful examples of "happy ever after" love stories. She is another writer who finds young innocence full of enchanting possibilities as she sets the stage for her heroines.

Although she does vary the approaches in her novels, she has, perhaps, unconsciously developed a certain kind of pattern that lets her make the fullest use of her gift in creating heartwarming stories. In at least three novels, she portrays a sensitive girl/child heroine who has suddenly been pushed out of her secure nest into the world of strangers. In *Hunter's Moon* Gillian Blake's Aunt Fisher has had to sell her home and move in with a friend her own age. To make it possible for her to do so, Gillian sets out to find a job on her own, by hitch-hiking. Although she has never held a job, she is sure she can get one because she is "good with her hands."

Just as precipitous is Nicola Fletcher in *The Black Delaney* as she is suddenly pitch-forked into the household of Rowan Delaney. Her Aunt Doris decides she has no further need of her now that her own daughter is marrying. Finally, Mandy in *Laird of Storr* is suddenly offered a home by an unknown aunt after spending her life in an orphanage. Mandy, of course, is not aware that her aunt really wants an unpaid servant for the moment.

This tendency to throw her heroine into the deep end naturally gives Reid a wide range of plot complications and offers numer-

ous chances for character development. Her heroines are ingenuous and they are guileless. It makes a touching story for her readers as she is able to show them winning the hero's love without losing that inner radiance of goodness that characterizes them. This is not to imply that they do not grow and mature. Experience must add to a person's knowledge, but their experiences merely re-inforce their own standards of behavior and beliefs. In this sense, their innocence is their protection and one of the strongest impulses of attraction for the heroes.

Reid is able to maintain a strong balance in developing the characters of her heroes. While successful, forceful, and confident, they are yet gentlemen in the true sense of the word. Steven Charlton in *Hunter's Moon* is a business man who maintains a home in the country. His mother and the daughter of an old family friend live there also. He is somewhat cynical, an eligible bachelor, and at heart a "softy." Alisdair Storr in *Laird of Storr* is quite similar in character and outlook. He is just as forceful and holds a place of respect in the community because of his position but also because of his own personality. Rowan Delaney's careless acceptance of Nicola in *The Black Delaney* is typical of a strong man who might befriend a stray kitten, and this is his attitude towards her. He is careless and absent-minded, if impatient, as he tries to fit her into his life and home.

For the most part, Reid's backgrounds are sketched with a minimum of detail and only as it helps to move the story along. She does use the natural world, however, to help establish the heroine's sensitivity and gentleness as she frequently reacts to the beauty around her. Neither does she restrict herself to English scenes, for several of her novels are placed in other parts of the world.

In summarizing Reid as a romance writer, one must acknowledge her talent for portraying her heroines so charmingly. What makes them so nice is the fact that she makes them believable, in spite of modern standards and ideas. In a way, her readers may see her heroines as personifications of modern girls in spite of changing mores. They seem to enjoy the idealistic outlook for it offers endless possibilities for freshness and hope to them.

—Arlene Moore

———

REINER, Max. See **CALDWELL, Taylor.**

———

RENAULT, Mary. Pseudonym for Eileen Mary Challans. British. Born in London, 4 September 1905. Educated at Clifton High School, Bristol, 1921–24; St. Hugh's College, Oxford, 1924–27, B.A. (honours) in English 1928, M.A.; Radcliffe Infirmary, Oxford, S.R.N. (State Registered Nurse) 1937. Nurse in brain surgery ward, Radcliffe Infirmary, 1938–45. Moved to South Africa, 1948: lived in Cape Town. National President, PEN Club of South Africa, 1961. Recipient: M.G.M. award, 1946; National Association of Independent Schools award (U.S.A.), 1963; Silver Pen award, 1971. Fellow, Royal Society of Literature, 1959; Honorary Fellow, St. Hugh's College, 1982. *Died 13 December 1983.*

ROMANCE AND HISTORICAL PUBLICATIONS

Novels (series: Alexander trilogy; Theseus)

The Last of the Wine. London, Longman, and New York, Pantheon, 1956.
The King Must Die (Theseus). London, Longman, and New York, Pantheon, 1958.
The Bull from the Sea (Theseus). London, Longman, and New York, Pantheon, 1962.
The Mask of Apollo. London, Longman, and New York, Pantheon, 1966.
The Alexander Trilogy. London, Penguin, 1984.
  Fire from Heaven. New York, Pantheon, 1969; London, Longman, 1970.
  The Persian Boy. London, Longman, and New York, Pantheon, 1972.
  Funeral Games. London, Murray, and New York, Pantheon, 1981.
The Praise Singer. New York, Pantheon, 1978; London, Murray, 1979.

OTHER PUBLICATIONS

Novels

Purposes of Love. London, Longman, 1939; as *Promise of Love*, New York, Morrow, 1939.
Kind Are Her Answers. London, Longman, and New York, Morrow, 1940.
The Friendly Young Ladies. London, Longman, 1944; as *The Middle Mist*, New York, Morrow, 1945.
Return to Night. London, Longman, and New York, Morrow, 1947.
North Face. New York, Morrow, 1948; London, Longman, 1949.
The Charioteer. London, Longman, 1953; New York, Pantheon, 1959.

Other

The Lion in the Gateway: The Heroic Battles of the Greeks and Persians at Marathon, Salamis, and Thermopylae (for children). London, Longman, and New York, Harper, 1964.
The Nature of Alexander. London, Allen Lane, and New York, Pantheon, 1975.

*

Critical Studies: *Mary Renault* by Peter Wolfe, New York, Twayne, 1969; *The Hellenism of Mary Renault* by Bernard F. Dick, Carbondale, Southern Illinois University Press, 1972.

*   *   *

Mary Renault's training as a nurse shaped her early work, much of it set in and around hospitals. *Purposes of Love* and *The Friendly Young Ladies* however, bear no resemblance to ordinary "nurse" romances; rather, they plumb the intricacies of complex, often murky and unorthodox relationships, a theme the author was to explore throughout her distinguished career. *Return to Night*, the story of a forbidden love affair between a female doctor and her much younger male patient, won the 1946

M.G.M. award of $150,000, and although it was never in fact filmed (indeed, it is difficult to imagine the product if it *had* been), this resounding success brought Renault's work to the world's attention.

Renault came into her own as a star of the first magnitude when she turned from her accomplished novels of contemporary lives and loves to the stunning recreation of a classic Hellenistic world compounded of legendary, shadowy and contradictory history, and the patent Renault enchantment.

The twin Theseus novels, *The King Must Die* and *Bull from the Sea*, had the impact of a thunderbolt. They were unique; never before had the time-honoured tale of the hero Theseus, Ariadne his forsaken love, the Amazon Queen Hippolyta, the dreaded man-eating Minotaur and all the rest been presented as more than highly-coloured fairytale figures, half-remembered from stories told by innumerable firesides.

Now Renault breathed new life into these stock figures. The familiar lumbering, herculean figure of a giant Theseus became an undersized, quicksilver daredevil of uncertain birth, seizing control of his own destiny rather than tamely submitting to the apparent will of the Olympians until, at last in *The Bull from the Sea*, the aging king tries the patience of the unrelenting gods too far and suffers the terrible punishment he has brought upon himself and his house.

The Theseus stories have a pagan majesty of the Bronze Age, yet the cast of finely-detailed characters, whose names are so familiar in song and legend, have a life and vigour that is entirely Renault's contribution. No reader of her work can ever again imagine the world of the Hellenes except as touched by her triumphant imagination.

Farther from legend, closer to history, but still magically transmuted from the chilly recital of battles and conquests, *Fire from Heaven* recreates the formative years of Alexander the Great, from childhood in his father's turbulent court to young manhood at the threshhold of mastery of the known world.

Alexander is a complex figure, shaped by the bitterness of the mother he both loves and hates, and by the barbarian King Philip of Macedon, the father he half-unwillingly admires.

Even as a child, Alexander was not as others; focussed always to luminescence, and possessed of an uncanny ability to bind others to him in lifelong loyalty. In the years in which lesser children play and daydream, young Alexander planned and trained, under the cruel tutor who kept the boy ill-fed and shivering with the cold. By cruel necessity he learned early to disregard physical comfort, as he was to do throughout his short, meteoric life. Renault skillfully weaves a tapestry of known fact, educated surmise, and a generous measure of her own unmatched storytelling magic, to achieve a masterpiece of historical fiction.

Magnificent as it was, *Fire from Heaven* was to be followed by a still more triumphant creation. Acclaimed by many critics as Renault's masterpiece is the sequel in which the second half of Alexander's story is related by Bagoas, *The Persian Boy*. The court eunuch was castrated by slavers to preserve his youthful beauty from coarsening into manhood, and to make him an attractive, saleable sexual toy for the Persian King, Darius. The despairing lad sees a life of futile emptiness and degradation stretching endlessly before him. All too clearly he realizes that he will be used and discarded like any other frivolous, outworn plaything.

Then the might of Darius, the Great King, is utterly, humiliatingly defeated by the strong young warrior king out of the despised, half-civilized West, Alexander of Macedon. Bagoas is offered to the new barbarian king as a part of the conqueror's tribute. Surely now, he fears, he is worse off than before; the only eunuch among a fierce, wild people who scarcely know what a eunuch *is,* and are therefore contemptuously curious, supposing that "one had been cut down to the shape of a woman."

Amazingly, beyond his expectation, beyond even his hope, Bagoas has found the one with whom he can be whole again, if only Alexander can be made to love him: but Alexander has, and has always had, Hephaistion, his boyhood lover, almost his other self.

The tug-of-war, never openly acknowledged, but fierce and determined, between Alexander's lifelong lover and the Persian boy who is "Alexander's dog" is amazingly vivid. A situation utterly alien to Western readers, and repugnant in some of its aspects to the unaccustomed, is rendered most affectingly and effortlessly believable; an enduring love story. *The Persian Boy* transcends time and mores to bring to life not merely a romance, but a true love story that takes its inspiration from the fateful beauty that is both Bagoas's undoing and his salvation.

Another astonishing work, *The Last of the Wine,* is a story of the waning years of the long-drawn-out Peloponnesian War, as told by Alexias son of Myron, a young Athenian of good family, who is the lover of Lysis, a member of Socrates's circle.

The responsibility for one another that commitment entailed has a great deal to do with the nature of their passionate relationship. Theirs was not an adventure to be taken lightly, nor their love an empty affair. The love pledged between Alexias and Lysis was as meaningful and as binding as a marriage vow.

Alexias and his family, Lysis and the girl would one day become his wife, their fellow Athenians, are well-rounded and wholly believable characters. Again it is amazing how through the persuasive conviction of the author, the reader comes readily to accept without shock or question the correctness, in the circumstances, of practices abhorrent to modern thought, such as the father's right of life or death over his children. One even understands Alexias's pangs of conscience in failing to obey his father's instructions that his newborn sibling be exposed on the hillside, should it prove to be a daughter.

The characters of Alexias and Lysis have been compared with those of Andrew and Laurie, heroes of *The Charioteer,* a tale of contemporary Britain; or rather, of Britain only yesterday.

Laurie is convalescing from wounds suffered at Dunkirk; Andrew is a "Conchie", a conscientious objector doing orderly duty in the service hospital. Laurie is finally, unwillingly, forced to face the fact of his homosexuality by his love for Andrew, who sees Laurie only as a valued friend. A rakish figure from Laurie's schooldays, Ralph, brings brisk pragmatism to bear upon the increasingly difficult situation. Ralph has come to terms with his own homosexuality, is perfectly content to be what he is, and has made a satisfactory life for himself. He is more than willing to do the same for Laurie, if and when he can abandon his dream of ideal love with the unconscious object of his devotion.

It is an unusual "triangle," but one in which each of the three men involved is a sympathetic, indeed an admirable character. A work of this nature was a breakthrough at the time of its publication: portraying a forbidden love as simply that, a love, even a selfless love, was a bold step.

In all of Renault's work, so much of which is concerned with various configurations of homosexuality or bisexuality, there is absolutely nothing to shock even the prudish; nothing to suggest a plea for pity or indulgence as for an aberrant condition; merely an understanding and heartfelt portrayal of people acting and being acted upon, with whose problems the reader cannot but be deeply, personally involved.

Other titles, such as *The Mask of Apollo,* the story of Nikeratos, actor and servant of the god, *The Praise Singer,* Simonides the bard, even *Funeral Games,* the third book in *The Alexander Trilogy,* the confused and confusing account of the chaotic years following the untimely death in Babylon, lack the fire and impact of earlier work; all are cooler, sombre, and autumnal in tone. But it is not on these lesser, though quite readable works, that her enduring reputation will be founded. Her accomplishment in bringing new life to a glorious age of hot-blooded men and women to replace the impression of broken statuary and crumbling temples that had for many been all that was known of Ancient Greece, should be saluted as long as readers dare to be swept out of the known and ordinary into the land of enchantment.

—Joan McGrath

RENIER, Elizabeth. Pseudonym for Betty Doreen Baker, née Flook. British. Born in Bristol, 22 November 1916. Educated at the Collegiate School, and Merchant Venturers College, both Bristol. Served in the Voluntary Aid Detachment, attached to the Royal Army Medical Corps, 1940–42. Married Frank Edward Baker (died). Has worked as a doctor's secretary; volunteer, Family Planning Association, 1958–62. Recipient: Romantic Novelists Association Warwick award, 1962. Address: 4 Cranford Close, Exmouth, Devon EX8 2EY, England.

ROMANCE AND HISTORICAL PUBLICATIONS

Novels

The Generous Vine. London, Hurst and Blackett, 1962; New York, Ace, 1972.

The House of Water. London, Hurst and Blackett, 1963; New York, Ace, 1972.

Blade of Justice. London, Hurst and Blackett, 1965; New York, Ace, 1972.

If This Be Treason. London, Hurst and Blackett, 1965; as *If This Be Love,* New York, Ace, 1971.

Valley of Nightingales. London, Hurst and Blackett, 1966.

A Singing in the Woods. London, Hurst and Blackett, 1966; New York, Ace, 1972.

Prelude to Freedom. London, Hurst and Blackett, 1967; as *Prelude to Love,* New York, Ace, 1972.

The House of Granite. London, Hurst and Blackett, 1968; New York, Ace, 1972.

By Sun and Candlelight. London, Hurst and Blackett, 1968; New York, Ace, 1973.

Tomorrow Comes the Sun. London, Hurst and Blackett, 1969; New York, Ace, 1971.

The Spanish Doll. London, Hurst and Blackett, 1970; New York, Ace, 1972.

Valley of Secrets. London, Hurst and Blackett, 1970; New York, Ace, 1972.

Woman from the Sea. London, Hurst and Blackett, 1971; New York, Ace, n.d.

The Renshawe Inheritance. London, Hurst and Blackett, 1972; New York, Ace, 1973.

A Time for Rejoicing. London, Hurst and Blackett, and New York, Ace, 1973.

Ravenstor. London, Hurst and Blackett, 1974.

Yesterday's Mischief. London, Hurst and Blackett, 1975.

The Moving Dream. London, Hurst and Blackett, 1977; New York, Fawcett, 1978.

Landscape of the Heart. London, Hurst and Blackett, 1978; New York, Fawcett, 1979.

OTHER PUBLICATIONS

Other (for children)

The Lightkeepers. London, Hamish Hamilton, 1977.
The Stone People. London, Hamish Hamilton, 1978.
The Dangerous Journey. London, Hamish Hamilton, 1979.
The Post-rider. London, Hamish Hamilton, 1980.
The Mail-Coach Drivers. London, Hamish Hamilton, 1985.
The Night of the Storm. London, Hamish Hamilton, 1986.
The Hiding Place. London, Hamish Hamilton, 1987.
The Secret Valley. London, Hamish Hamilton, 1988.

*   *   *

"Do not hit those children like that as if you were herding cattle." "Cattle'd fetch a better price, m'lady." These lines from Elizabeth Renier's *A Singing in the Woods* typify a dominant theme in her works, that of the wealthy heroine dedicating herself to improving conditions among the less fortunate. This egalitarian theme echoes her own avocational interest in working with deprived children. What is particularly impressive about Renier's novels, however, is a second theme, that of a young heiress pitted against the male dominance which surrounds her in the Devonshire area during the Georgian period. She masterfully creates the spirited innocence of the wealthy heroine of the time, allowing her lady to become a formidable challenge for the male counterpart. She effortlessly depicts the prosaic figure of a lovely woman amidst the splendor of her affluence but at the same time provides her with more than a superficial personality. Renier's heroine is eager to know about the world which surrounds her; she is an amalgam of feistiness, tenaciousness, and strength. Renier captures the rebellious nature of a woman with power during this period without losing the harmony of the poignantly described period setting. The lady always possesses a strong feeling for the grandeur of her homeland, whether it be Stant Lydeard of *A Singing in the Woods*, Merriott of *The Renshawe Inheritance*, or similar settings. The reader can trust the character to be true to her ideals throughout the novel.

Renier's writing is refreshingly free from affectation, simply paced. The plot usually presents an energetic promenade of adventures which entangle the heroine and the hero (frequently land disputes create the dilemmas); but the potentially intolerable wooing scenes are pruned to crisp-in-form but tender-in-content meetings, punctuated with convincing descriptions of historical and graphical details. The heroes range from engaging swashbucklers to the more diffident gentlemen whose psychological strength outperforms their physical strength. Even Renier's minor characters are effective and memorable sketches.

Renier is an equal master in creating the ambiance of the period, providing the reader with an almost illustrated tour, a topocosmography of the Devonshire area with detailed descriptions that almost allow the reader to scent the aroma of the salt air.

Using these themes and style, Renier consistently writes well. With efficacy she creates a stimulating romance novel.

—W. M. von Zharen

REVERE, M. P. See **WILLIAMSON, C. N. and A. M.**

RHYS, Jean. British. Born Ella Gwendolyn Rees Williams in Roseau, Dominica, West Indies, 24 August 1890. Educated at The Convent, Roseau; Perse School, Cambridge, England, 1907–08; Academy (now Royal Academy) of Dramatic Art, London, 1909. Married 1) Jean Lenglet in 1919 (divorced 1932), one son and one daughter; 2) Leslie Tilden Smith in 1934 (died 1945); 3) Max Hamer in 1947 (died 1966). Toured England in chorus of *Our Miss Gibbs*, 1909–10; volunteer worker in soldiers canteen, 1914–17, and worked in a pension office, 1918, both London; lived in Paris, 1919 and 1923–27, and Vienna and Budapest, 1920–22; lived mainly in England after 1927: in Maidstone, Kent, 1950–52, London, 1952–56, Bude and Perranporth, Cornwall, 1956–60, and Cheriton Fitzpaine, Devon, from 1960. Recipient: Arts Council bursary, 1967; W. H. Smith award, 1967; Royal Society of Literature Heinemann award, 1967; Séguier prize, 1979. C.B.E. (Commander, Order of the British Empire), 1978. *Died 14 May 1979.*

ROMANCE AND HISTORICAL PUBLICATIONS

Novel

Wide Sargasso Sea. London, Deutsch, 1966; New York, Norton, 1967.

OTHER PUBLICATIONS

Novels

Postures. London, Chatto and Windus, 1928; as *Quartet*, New York, Simon and Schuster, 1929.
After Leaving Mr. Mackenzie. London, Cape, and New York, Knopf, 1931.
Voyage in the Dark. London, Constable, 1934; New York, Morrow, 1935.
Good Morning, Midnight. London, Constable, 1939; New York, Harper, 1970.

Short Stories

The Left Bank and Other Stories. London, Cape, and New York, Harper, 1927.
Tigers Are Better-Looking, with a Selection from The Left Bank. London, Deutsch, 1968; New York, Harper, 1974.
Penguin Modern Stories 1, with others. London, Penguin, 1969.
Sleep It Off Lady. London, Deutsch, and New York, Harper, 1976.
Tales of the Wide Caribbean, edited by Kenneth Ramchand. London, Heinemann, 1985.
The Collected Short Stories. New York, Norton, 1987.

Other

My Day (essays). New York, Hallman, 1975.
Smile Please: An Unfinished Autobiography. London, Deutsch, 1979; New York, Harper, 1980.
Jean Rhys Letters 1931–1966, edited by Francis Wyndham and Diana Melly. London, Deutsch, and New York, Viking, 1984.

Translator, *Perversity*, by Francis Carco. Chicago, Covici, 1928 (translation attributed to Ford Madox Ford).

Translator, *Barred*, by Edward de Nève. London, Harmsworth, 1932.

*

Bibliography: *Jean Rhys: A Descriptive and Annotated Bibliography of Works and Criticism* by Elgin W. Mellown, New York, Garland, 1984.

Manuscript Collection: University of Tulsa, Oklahoma.

Critical Studies: *Jean Rhys* by Louis James, London, Longman, 1978; *Jean Rhys: A Critical Study* by Thomas F. Staley, London, Macmillan, and Austin, University of Texas Press, 1979; *Jean Rhys* by Peter Wolfe, Boston, Twayne, 1980; *Jean Rhys, Woman in Passage: A Critical Study of the Novels* by Helen E. Nebeker, Montreal, Eden Press, 1981; *Difficult Women: A Memoir of Three* by David Plante, London, Gollancz, and New York, Atheneum, 1983; *Jean Rhys* by Arnold E. Davidson, New York, Ungar, 1985; *Jean Rhys* by Carole Angier, London, Viking, 1985; *Jean Rhys: The West Indian Novels* by Teresa F. O'Connor, New York, New York University Press, 1986; *Jean Rhys and the Novel as Women's Text* by Nancy R. Harrison, Chapel Hill, University of North Carolina Press, 1988.

*   *   *

Critics often view Jean Rhys's fiction as a chronology of the writer's own decline into despair, a biographical focus that relegates the texts to the margins of the literary canon. Yet Rhys insistently transformed biography into metaphor, the personal into the political. Beyond her central figures of women rendered passive by men resonate metonymic images of familial, racial, economic, and linguistic oppression. Thus turning to historical fiction in her last novel represents, not a departure from earlier themes, but a foregrounding of Rhys's lifelong obsession with the collusion in Western culture of imperialism, capitalism, religion, racism, classism, and sexism.

Since *Wide Sargasso Sea* precipitated the "resurrection" of Rhys, it has received more critical attention than her other four novels combined. A prologue to *Jane Eyre* which centers the character of Rochester's mad West Indian wife, Rhys's last novel obviously reflects the author's racial and sexual identification with Charlotte Brontë's minor character. Angry at the silencing of Brontë's Bertha, Rhys sought to give voice to the madwoman in the attic. *Wide Sargasso Sea* creates for Bertha a past in the West Indies of the early 19th century when emancipation disrupted the colonial plantation life. Drawing on family history and her own childhood memories of Dominica, Rhys fictionalizes the untenable Creole position of belonging neither to the British colonial regime nor to the black ex-slave majority.

Called by her French first name, Antoinette Bertha Cosway (later Mason) suffers from childhood an awareness of the fragility of her identity. Rhys expands Rochester's cursory allusion in *Jane Eyre* to Bertha's genetic insanity by portraying Antoinette as witness as well as heir to her mother Annette's disintegration. Widow of a slave-owner, Annette is not only despised by the blacks but scorned by the white Jamaicans for her Martinique background. Her marriage to the British Mr. Mason only exacerbates her decline as his refusal to recognize racial hostility results in the burning by blacks of the Coulibri estate and the consequent death of the favored child Pierre. The first part of the novel traces from Antoinette's retrospective viewpoint, her early rejection by Annette and by her black friend Tia; her terror at Annette's mad degradation; her illicit passion for her black cousin Saudi; and her reluctant, arranged marriage to the British Edward Rochester. Antoinette's foreboding dreams parallel those of Brontë's Jane, suggesting Rhys's view of Bertha Antoinette as a double rather than a nemesis of Jane.

The second part shifts the narrating voice to Rochester, whom Rhys strove to portray not as malicious but as tormented. Like Brontë's character, Rhys's Edward is constrained, as a younger son, to marry Antoinette for her inheritance, which he soon appropriates as he does her voice in the novel. Rhys's portrayal thus does not reflect a mono-dimensional victimization, for Edward, too, suffers familial and national displacement. His fevered disorientation peaks on their Dominican honeymoon in his lust/love for Antoinette; however, a letter from a black, who claims to be Antoinette's illegitimate half-brother, revives Edward's British censorious reserve. The desperate Antoinette, whose voice periodically interrupts her husband's, obtains an *obeah* love potion from her black surrogate mother Christophine; but she cannot be saved by the black culture and, in fact, is finally driven mad when Edward begins to flaunt his relationship with a black servant. Yet, though Edward's imperialistic/male script has objectified his wife into the grey ghost he insists on calling Bertha, Rhys's narrative technique elaborates Edward's agonizing recognition that her madness stems from her desire to convey to him "the secret: . . . she belonged to the magic and the loveliness. She had left me thirsty and all my life would be thirst and longing for what I had lost before I had found it."

Antoinette's narration is retrieved in the third part of the novel only after opening with a passage narrated by Grace Poole, Antoinette's money-counting, drunken warden in the English tower. Such a device further evinces Rhys's determination to preclude a dualistic male/female, white/black, rich/poor, British/Caribbean portrayal of oppression. Antoinette's dream of setting fire to the house and jumping to her death at Tia's beckoning coalesces the foreshadowed destruction of Thornfield with the remembered destruction of Coulibri by the blacks. Yet the victimized blacks had victimized her, offering no more place to the Creole Antoinette than does the white culture; nor does the Caribbean (contrary to critical consensus) represent to Antoinette (or to Rhys) an antidotal opposite to England.

Rhys's one historical novel, then, broadens paradigmatically a recurrent Rhys theme. *Wide Sargasso Sea* enunciates the wideness of the gap between Rhys and Brontë, but Rhys had repeatedly subverted the romance plot in her first four novels. Like Antoinette, the early protagonists also fail to navigate the gap in a civilization that posits them as other, their passivity the byproduct of a thwarted active desire. The historical context of Rhys's last novel reveals that the Sargasso seaweed which entangles the characters is a multi-layered morass inexorably reproduced. Antoinette's envisioned apocalypse images Rhys's vision of all sexes, all classes, all races as entrapped and self-immolating in civilization's dualistic structures.

—Janet Haedicke

———

RICHARD, Susan. See **ELLIS, Julie.**

———

RICHMOND, Grace. See **WOODWARD, Lilian.**

RIEFE, Barbara. Pseudonym for Alan Riefe; also writes as J. D. Hardin; Zachary Hawkes; Jake Logan; Pierce MacKenzie; E. B. Majors; A. R. Riefe. American. Born in Waterbury, Connecticut, 18 May 1925. Educated at Colby College, Waterville, Maine, B.A. 1950. Served in the United States Army during World War II. Married 1) Martha Daggett in 1948 (died 1949); 2) Barbara Dube in 1955; four children. Freelance writer. Agent: Knox Burger Associates, 39½ Washington Square South, New York, New York 10012, U.S.A.

ROMANCE AND HISTORICAL PUBLICATIONS

Novels (series: Dandridge Trilogy)

Barringer House. New York, Popular Library, 1976.
Rowleston. New York, Popular Library, 1976.
Auldearn House. New York, Popular Library, 1976.
Dandridge Trilogy
  This Ravaged Heart. Chicago, Playboy Press, 1977; London, Sphere, 1979.
  Far Beyond Desire. Chicago, Playboy Press, 1978; London, Sphere, 1980.
  Fire and Flesh. Chicago, Playboy Press, 1978; London, Sphere, 1980.
Tempt Not This Flesh. Chicago, Playboy Press, 1979; London, Sphere, 1981.
Black Fire. Chicago, Playboy Press, 1980; London, Sphere, 1982.
So Wicked the Heart. Chicago, Playboy Press, 1980; London, Sphere, 1982.
Olivia. Chicago, Playboy Press, 1981.
Wild Fire. Chicago, Playboy Press, 1981; London, Sphere, 1983.
Julia. Chicago, Playboy Press, 1982.
Lucretia. Chicago, Playboy Press, 1982.
Wicked Fire. New York, Berkley, 1983; London, Sphere, 1985.
This Proud Love. New York, Berkley, 1985.
A Woman of Dreams. New York, Berkley, 1986.

OTHER PUBLICATIONS

Novels as Alan Riefe

The Lady Killers. New York, Popular Library, 1975; London, New English Library, 1976.
The Conspirators. New York, Popular Library, 1975; London, New English Library, 1977.
The Black Widower. New York, Popular Library, 1975.
The Silver Puma. New York, Popular Library, 1975.
The Bullet-Proof Man. New York, Popular Library, 1975.
The Killer with the Golden Touch. New York, Popular Library, 1975.
Tyger at Bay. New York, Popular Library, 1976.
Tyger by the Tail. New York, Popular Library, 1976.
The Smile on the Face of the Tyger. New York, Popular Library, 1976.
Tyger and the Lady. New York, Popular Library, 1976.
Hold That Tyger. New York, Popular Library, 1976.
Tyger, Tyger, Burning Out. New York, Popular Library, 1976.

Novels as Jake Logan

Bloody Trail to Texas. Chicago, Playboy Press, 1976.
White Hell. Chicago, Playboy Press, 1977.
Iron Mustang. Chicago, Playboy Press, 1978.
Montana Showdown. Chicago, Playboy Press, 1978.
See Texas and Die. Chicago, Playboy Press, 1979.

Novels as J. D. Hardin

The Slick and the Dead. Chicago, Playboy Press, 1979.
Blood, Sweat, and Gold. Chicago, Playboy Press, 1979.
The Good, The Bad and the Deadly. Chicago, Playboy Press, 1979.
Bullets, Buzzards, Boxes of Pine. Chicago, Playboy Press, 1980.
Face Down in a Coffin. Chicago, Playboy Press, 1980.
The Man Who Bit Snakes. Chicago, Playboy Press, 1980.
Bloody Time in the Blacktower. New York, Berkley, 1983.
The Man with No Face. New York, Berkley, 1983.
Queens over Deuces. New York, Berkley, 1984.
Carnival of Death. New York, Berkley, 1984.
Tombstone in Deadwood. New York, Berkley, 1984.
The Great Jewel Robbery. New York, Berkley, 1985.
Apache Trail. New York, Berkley, 1985.
Hell's Belle. New York, Berkley, 1985.
The Swindler's Trail. New York, Berkley, 1987.
Thunder Mountain Massacre. New York, Berkley, 1987.
Raider. New York, Berkley, 1987.
The Yuma Roundup. New York, Berkley, 1987.
The Cheyenne Fraud. New York, Berkley, 1988.
Silver City Ambush. New York, Berkley, 1988.

Novels as Zachary Hawkes

Fancy Hatch. New York, Pinnacle, 1984.
The Case Deuce. New York, Pinnacle, 1984.
Solomon King's Mine. New York, Pinnacle, 1984.
The Odds Against Sundown. New York, Pinnacle, 1985.

Novels as E. B. Majors

Slaughter and Son. New York, Warner, 1985.
Nightmare Trail. New York, Warner, 1986.
Hair Trigger and Kill. New York, Warner, 1986.
Death in Durango. New York, Warner, 1986.

Novels as Pierce MacKenzie

The Stolen White Eagle. New York, New American Library, 1987.
The Fleecing of Fodder City. New York, New American Library, 1987.
Winner Take Nothing. New York, New American Library, 1987.
The Spanish Monte Fiasco. New York, New American Library, 1987.
Double Trouble in Skagway. New York, New American Library, 1987.
The Cockeyed Coyote. New York, New American Library, 1987.

Novels as A. R. Riefe

Tucson. New York, New American Library, 1988.
Cheyenne. New York, New American Library, 1989.
San Francisco. New York, New American Library, 1989.

Short Stories

Tales of Horror (as Alan Riefe). New York, Pocket Books, 1965.

Plays (as Alan Riefe)

Television Writing: *Masquerade Party* series, 8 years; *Keep Talking* series, 2 years; and scripts for *Pulitzer Prize Playhouse* and *Studio One* series.

Other

Vip's Illustrated Woman Driver's Manual. New York, Fawcett, 1966.

*   *   *

Since 1976, Alan Riefe, writing under the pseudonym of Barbara Riefe, has turned his writing skills to the genre of historical romance with varying success. Riefe has a solid understanding of those elements which are of interest to the romance reader—true love, adventure in foreign lands, fast-paced action, and a sprinkling of spicy sex, all set in a time period gone by, and eventually leading to the beloved "happy ending."

Riefe's plots are often based on the separation of loved ones by unfortunate circumstances and the ensuing struggle by the loved ones against nearly impossible odds to become reunited. Riefe is at his best when he sends his characters on adventures, most often by sea. His sense of geographical detail—ranging from the United States to Capri to Tasmania to the Far East—and his knowledge of the sea and seafaring vessels add much in the way of credibility to his stories. In addition, fast-paced action, detailed description, and crisp dialogue serve to keep the reader actively interested in what is going to happen next. It is, after all, a good story that the reader of popular fiction is looking for; the main failure of books in the genre of popular fiction comes from the reader's fading desire to want to know what happens next, for there is generally insufficient character development, or logical cause and effect plot—which causes character development and growth—on which to rely in the event of lapses in the story.

When Riefe finds himself in danger of being uninteresting because the reader has become confident of the story's outcome, he uses coincidences and surprises—i.e., information which is known only to him—to cause a reversal or modification in the situation which heightens the reader's interest. Riefe also uses several subplots which are related to, and ultimately merge with, the main plot. These subplots are usually the various adventures of the separated loved ones. Rapid alternations between one plot and another (usually occurring in different geographical locations) serve to maintain and rekindle the reader's interest. (In one instance—in *This Ravaged Heart*—because of the use of witchcraft, the separation is made not only geographical but also temporal.) Should either of these methods fail, there are often graphic sexual interludes to add excitement.

Characterization and character development in these novels are often weak, as is generally the case in popular fiction, and many of the characters remain flat and undeveloped since they are, after all, merely vehicles for the action. Understandably, the character of the heroine is most clearly defined (although it doesn't often develop further in the course of the novel). The heroine exhibits "true, undying love" and the expected moral character necessary to being a good wife. In addition to female beauty and alluring female charms, the traits of solid judgement, intelligence, great mental and emotional strength, and superhuman stamina reveal themselves when she is separated from her husband and allow her to outwit her adversaries and overcome apparently insurmountable situations, ultimately resulting in the rescue of the loved one. These heroines do not bear up under close scrutiny, for they are almost superhuman figures, the good aspects of several men and women rolled into one, but their dialogue when well contrived convinces the reader—momentarily, at least—that it is otherwise. The reader is quite willing to overlook the flaw in the interest of entertainment. Riefe departs from the typical damsel-in-distress romance heroine, and makes his heroines much more products of his century, than of the previous century where he places them in time.

All in all, when Riefe balances the elements which he uses in his novels, he is capable of producing a well-wrought, gripping bit of entertainment that rivals that of many of his competitors. This is especially evident in the first volume of the Dandridge Trilogy, *This Ravaged Heart*, perhaps the best of his romance novels. The second book, *Far Beyond Desire*, is also quite solid entertainment, although there is a prevalence of sexual interludes. The last book, *Fire and Flesh*, becomes a bit tedious because the reader must wade through a great deal of predictable exposition before arriving at the expected ending.

—Michael Held

———

RINEHART, Mary Roberts. American. Born in Pittsburgh, Pennsylvania, 12 August 1876. Educated at elementary and high schools in Pittsburgh; Pittsburgh Training School for Nurses, graduated 1896. Married Stanley Marshall Rinehart in 1896 (died 1932); three sons. Full-time writer from 1903. Correspondent, *Saturday Evening Post*, Philadelphia, during World War I; reported Presidential nominating conventions. Lived in Pittsburgh until 1920, in Washington, D.C., 1920–32, and in New York from 1932. Recipient: Mystery Writers of America Special award, 1953. Litt.D.: George Washington University, Washington, D.C., 1923. *Died 22 September 1958.*

ROMANCE AND HISTORICAL PUBLICATIONS

Novels (series: Nurse Hilda Adams, "Miss Pinkerton")

The Circular Staircase. Indianapolis, Bobbs Merrill, 1908; London, Cassell, 1909.
When a Man Marries. Indianapolis, Bobbs Merrill, 1909; London, Hodder and Stoughton, 1920.
The Man in Lower Ten. Indianapolis, Bobbs Merrill, and London, Cassell, 1909.
The Window at the White Cat. Indianapolis, Bobbs Merrill, 1910; London, Nash, 1911.
Where There's a Will. Indianapolis, Bobbs Merrill, 1912.
The Case of Jennie Brice. Indianapolis, Bobbs Merrill, 1913; London, Hodder and Stoughton, 1919.
The After House. Boston, Houghton Mifflin, 1914; London, Simpkin Marshall, 1915.
The Street of Seven Stars. Boston, Houghton Mifflin, 1914; London, Cassell, 1915.
K. Boston, Houghton Mifflin, and London, Smith Elder, 1915.
Bab, A Sub-Deb. New York, Doran, 1917; London, Hodder and Stoughton, 1920.
Long Live the King! Boston, Houghton Mifflin, and London, Murray, 1917.

Twenty-Three and a Half Hours' Leave. New York, Doran, 1918.

The Amazing Interlude. New York, Doran, and London, Murray, 1918.

Dangerous Days. New York, Doran, and London, Hodder and Stoughton, 1919.

The Truce of God. New York, Doran, 1920.

A Poor Wise Man. New York, Doran, and London, Hodder and Stoughton, 1920.

Sight Unseen, and The Confession. New York, Doran, and London, Hodder and Stoughton, 1921.

The Breaking Point. New York, Doran, and London, Hodder and Stoughton, 1922.

The Out Trail. New York, Doran, 1923.

The Red Lamp. New York, Doran, 1925; as *The Mystery Lamp*, London, Hodder and Stoughton, 1925.

The Bat (novelization of play), with Avery Hopwood. New York, Doran, and London, Cassell, 1926.

Lost Ecstasy. New York, Doran, and London, Hodder and Stoughton, 1927; as *I Take This Woman*, New York, Grosset and Dunlap, 1927.

Two Flights Up. New York, Doubleday, and London, Hodder and Stoughton, 1928.

This Strange Adventure. New York, Doubleday, and London, Hodder and Stoughton, 1929.

The Door. New York, Farrar and Rinehart, and London, Hodder and Stoughton, 1930.

Miss Pinkerton. New York, Farrar and Rinehart, 1932; as *The Double Alibi*, London, Cassell, 1932.

Mary Roberts Rinehart's Crime Book (Adams; 2 novelets). New York, Farrar and Rinehart, 1933; London, Cassell, 1958.

The Album. New York, Farrar and Rinehart, and London, Cassell, 1933.

The State Versus Elinor Norton. New York, Farrar and Rinehart, 1934; as *The Case of Elinor Norton*, London, Cassell, 1934.

Mr. Cohen Takes a Walk. New York, Farrar and Rinehart, 1934.

The Doctor. New York, Farrar and Rinehart, and London, Cassell, 1936.

The Wall. New York, Farrar and Rinehart, and London, Cassell, 1938.

The Great Mistake. New York, Farrar and Rinehart, 1940; London, Cassell, 1941.

Haunted Lady (Adams). New York, Farrar and Rinehart, and London, Cassell, 1942.

The Yellow Room. New York, Farrar and Rinehart, 1945; London, Cassell, 1949.

The Curve of the Catenary. New York, Royce, 1945.

A Light in the Window. New York, Rinehart, and London, Cassell, 1948.

Episode of the Wandering Knife: Three Mystery Tales. New York, Rinehart, 1950; as *The Wandering Knife*, London, Cassell, 1952.

The Swimming Pool. New York, Rinehart, 1952; as *The Pool*, London, Cassell, 1952.

Short Stories (series: Letitia "Tish" Carberry)

The Amazing Adventures of Letitia Carberry. Indianapolis, Bobbs Merrill, 1911; London, Hodder and Stoughton, 1919.

Tish. Boston, Houghton Mifflin, 1916; London, Hodder and Stoughton, 1917.

Love Stories. New York, Doran, 1920.

Affinities and Other Stories. New York, Doran, and London, Hodder and Stoughton, 1920.

More Tish. New York, Doran, and London, Hodder and Stoughton, 1921.

Temperamental People. New York, Doran, and London, Hodder and Stoughton, 1924.

Tish Plays the Game. New York, Doran, 1926; London, Hodder and Stoughton, 1927.

Nomad's Land. New York, Doran, 1926.

The Romantics. New York, Farrar and Rinehart, 1929; London, Hodder and Stoughton, 1930.

Married People. New York, Farrar and Rinehart, and London, Cassell, 1937.

Tish Marches On. New York, Farrar and Rinehart, 1937; London, Cassell, 1938.

Familiar Faces: Stories of People You Know. New York, Farrar and Rinehart, 1941; London, Cassell, 1943.

Alibi for Isabel and Other Stories. New York, Farrar and Rinehart, 1944; London, Cassell, 1946.

The Frightened Wife and Other Murder Stories. New York, Rinehart, 1953; London, Cassell, 1954.

The Best of Tish. New York, Rinehart, 1955; London, Cassell, 1956.

OTHER PUBLICATIONS

Plays

Seven Days, with Avery Hopwood (produced Trenton and New York, 1909; Harrogate, 1913; London, 1915). New York, French, 1931.

Cheer Up (produced New York, 1912).

Spanish Love, with Avery Hopwood (produced New York, 1920).

The Bat, with Avery Hopwood, adaptation of the novel *The Circular Staircase* by Rinehart (produced New York, 1920; London, 1922). New York, French, 1931.

The Breaking Point (produced New York, 1923).

Screenplay: *Aflame in the Sky*, with Ewart Anderson, 1927.

Other

Kings, Queens, and Pawns: An American Woman at the Front. New York, Doran, 1915.

Through Glacier Park: Seeing America First with Howard Eaton. Boston, Houghton Mifflin, 1916.

The Altar of Freedom. Boston, Houghton Mifflin, 1917.

Tenting Tonight: A Chronicle of Sport and Adventure in Glacier Park and the Cascade Mountains. Boston, Houghton Mifflin, 1918.

Isn't That Just Like a Man! New York, Doran, 1920.

My Story (autobiography). New York, Farrar and Rinehart, 1931; London, Cassell, 1932; revised edition, New York, Rinehart, 1948.

Writing Is Work. Boston, The Writer, 1939.

*

Manuscript Collection: University of Pittsburgh Library.

Critical Study: *Improbable Fiction: The Life of Mary Roberts Rinehart* by Jan Cohn, Pittsburgh, University of Pittsburgh Press, 1980.

*   *   *

When Mary Roberts Rinehart turned her pen from mystery with romance to romance by itself, her "world" was still dominated by large houses with servants. This versatile craftsman produced novels and stories of sentiment, humor, and happy endings. Taken together, they offer a limited social history of the U.S.A. from the late 19th century to the late 1940's.

Early romances foreshadow. *When a Man Marries* is farce; its complications include a two-hour substitute "wife" for the visit of an aunt who doles an allowance, an ex-wife, and a butler with small pox. Vienna is the setting for *The Street of Seven Stars*, the romance of young Americans, the girl studying music, the man, medicine. They take care of a dying young boy. In *K*, "K", a surgeon, is a steadying influence on an idealist nurse.

World War I is a backdrop for several works. *The Amazing Interlude* concerns an American girl who dispensed soup, cigarettes, and pure love to wounded soldiers behind the front lines and returned to wait for Henri, her Belgian true-love. *Dangerous Days* centers on a wealthy and patriotic munitions manufacturer, his plant, and his stale marriage. Only the Armistice finally offers a bright future. Hilarity in *Twenty-Three and a Half Hours' Leave* results from a quartermaster's attempt to deal with the problem of no uniforms for a troop about to sail. *Bab, a Sub-Deb* is also very amusing as 17-year-old Barbara Putnam Thatcher records her Experiences, some "sickning." "For is not Romanse itself but breif, the thing of an hour, at least to the Other Sex?" During World War I, she helps to capture a spy.

The war is part of the ambitious scope of *This Strange Adventure* (life), a narrative of the Colfax family, mainly of the enduring Missy, from the 1880's to the war, and of *The Doctor* which chronicles the overlapping professional and love lives of Dr. Arden from 1910 to 1927. In *A Light in the Window* the light is placed by the mother of Ricky for a son off to World War I and by Ricky herself for her son and daughter off to World War II. Lives and loves of two generations of a family unfold.

Other romances vary. *Long Live the King!* has a charming ten-year-old hero, European Prince Otto. *A Poor Wise Man* is an ill-advised attempt to delve into labor problems after World War I, and *The Truce of God* documents a change of heart on Christmas day in medieval times. Through the marriage of a cowboy and an Eastern girl, *Lost Ecstasy* contrasts the hardships of life in the West and the easy, sometimes superficial, life in the affluent East. Slight is the parable of *Mr. Cohen Takes a Walk*; wealthy and elderly, he returns refreshed by good deeds.

Titles of the collections of short stories, except those of Tish, reveal diversified love stories. For 30 years, Tish (Letitia Carberry) led Lizzie, the narrator, and Aggie, the long-suffering, into the wild and woolly adventures of the M.A.T. (Middle-Aged Trio). Laugh-provoking, the stories are full of spirit, including that of Charlie Sand, nephew, and of the medicinal blackberry cordial.

In a long career, Rinehart proved an able storyteller, her plots more complex than can be noted here. For readers of the 1980's, a weakness is the assumption that the best place for women, in spite of talent or intelligence, is in the home. Her humor cannot be faulted.

—Jane Gottschalk

RIPLEY, Alexandra. American. Born in Charleston, South Carolina, 8 January 1934. Educated at Vassar College, Poughkeepsie, New York, A.B. 1955. Has two daughters. Lives in Charlottesville, Virginia. Agent: William Morris Agency, 1350 Avenue of the Americas, New York 10019, U.S.A.

ROMANCE AND HISTORICAL PUBLICATIONS

Novels (series: Tradd Family)

Charleston (Tradd Family). New York, Doubleday, 1981.
On Leaving Charleston (Tradd Family). New York, Doubleday, 1984.
The Time Returns. New York, Doubleday, 1985.
New Orleans Legacy. New York, Macmillan, 1987.

OTHER PUBLICATIONS

Novel

Who's That Sleeping in the President's Bed? New York, Dodd Mead, 1972.

* * *

Alexandra Ripley has been chosen by the William Morris Agency to write what has been called "the long-awaited sequel" to Margaret Mitchell's *Gone with the Wind*. (As of this writing, no publisher has won the rights to this as-yet-unwritten work.) Since the appearance of *Charleston* the name of Mitchell's classic Civil War novel has been invoked in Ripley's reviews. It would do Ripley a disservice, however, to assume that she is merely following in the footsteps of Margaret Mitchell or that she is simply a "moonlight and magnolias" sort of writer.

Ripley's work is indeed steeped in the southern traditions that were presumed to have died with the Union victory, but her novels go far beyond the Civil War. The cities that form the settings are of paramount importance in her tales of Charleston and New Orleans and in her novel of the Florence of Lorenzo de' Medici, *The Time Returns*. The strong social organization of these cities forms the framework that forces the characters to act in certain ways. Ripley understands that a lady of Charleston or a gentleman of Florence is both a citizen of and a creation of that society with its unwritten codes. The continuity of rigid standards of behavior might force a character into decisions that make his life difficult; but at the same time, he has a sense of belonging to his city that affords him support and protection. This theme of belonging to a society surfaces repeatedly in Ripley's books. Similarly, the attraction of the city to outsiders lies both in the city's unchanging, secure social patterns and its closed nature. Those who do not belong to the city sometimes try to force their way into the old order, and sometimes try to destroy it. It is the nature of these self-sufficient societies that outsiders can neither enter nor destroy, but merely intensify the social order as it exists.

The most interesting characters in all of Ripley's books are not the most beautiful, in defiance of the conventions of historical romances. Instead, the eccentric and the outcast come to life most vividly. In fact, the author's sure touch is at its weakest when creating "beautiful people," as in *On Leaving Charleston*. When Garden Tradd is outside her natural milieu the book becomes mere romance. It is only upon her return to her heritage and her acceptance of her place within its structure that she becomes three-dimensional again. This is, of course, in keeping with the theme of belonging, but there are none of the surprises in Garden's "outside" life that otherwise distinguish the plot. It is a tribute to Ripley's skill in creating characters for whom the reader cares deeply that she can carry over leading characters from one book to the next without diluting their personalities. Even in the most thoroughgoing villain there is a naturalness. A character's behavior may be exaggerated, but emotion never is.

The books cover long periods of time without flagging in place. Obviously Ripley is a keen student of history for her fictional events are firmly rooted in historical fact. Her southern novels are perhaps more accessible to the reader than her Florentine novel, but there seems to be a dual reason for that; first, the 15th century has fewer points of familiarity for the modern audience and second, the author actually has experience of the world that she covers in the southern works. Throughout most of her work, the history seems an integral part of the story. Occasionally, however, historical events take such a secondary place to plot that they seem like points on a time line inserted merely to give the reader a sense of the passage of years. The gratuitous inclusion of the death of Isadora Duncan in *On Leaving Charleston* typifies this shift in emphasis. Such jarring notes are minor, however, and Ripley easily slips back into her easy balance of history and storytelling.

—Susan Quinn Berneis

RITCHIE, Claire. Also wrote as Sharon Heath. *Died in 1979.*

ROMANCE AND HISTORICAL PUBLICATIONS

Novels

The Sheltered Flame. London, Hodder and Stoughton, 1949.
Love Builds a House. London, Hodder and Stoughton, 1950.
Bright Meadows. London, Hodder and Stoughton, 1951.
Durable Fire. London, Hodder and Stoughton, 1951.
Lighted Windows. London, Hodder and Stoughton, 1952.
The Green Bough. London, Hodder and Stoughton, 1953.
The Heart Turns Homeward. London, Hodder and Stoughton, 1953.
The Gentle Wind. London, Hodder and Stoughton, 1954.
Sun on the Sea. London, Hodder and Stoughton, 1954.
Gift of the Heart. London, Hale, 1955.
Mending Flower. London, Hale, 1955.
The White Violet. London, Hale, 1956.
Dreaming River. London, Hale, 1957.
Love Will Lend Wings. London, Hale, 1957.
Date with an Angel. London, Hale, 1958.
The Sunflower's Look. London, Hale, 1958.
The Tempest and the Song. London, Hale, 1959.
Vagrant Dream. London, Hale, 1959.
Hatful of Cowslips. London, Hale, 1960.
Shadowed Paradise. London, Hale, 1960.
Sweet Bloom. London, Hale, 1961.
The Fair Adventure. London, Hale, 1961.
Doctor's Joy. London, Hale, 1962.
Heartsease Grows Here. London, Hale, 1962.
Summer at Silverwood. London, Hale, 1962.
You'll Love Me Yet. London, Hale, 1963.
Circle of Gold. London, Hale, 1964.
Ride on Singing. London, Hale, 1964.
For a Dream's Sake. London, Hale, 1965.
The Love That Follows. London, Hale, 1966.
To Greet the Morning. London, Hale, 1966.
Hope Is My Pillow. London, Hale, 1967.
As Waits the Sky. London, Hale, 1969.
This Summer's Rose. London, Hale, 1970.
Give All to Love. London, Hale, 1971.
Dream in the Heart. London, Hale, 1972.

Rainbow Romance. London, Hale, 1974.
Castle Perilous. London, Hale, 1979.
Season for Singing. London, Hale, 1979.
Lodestone for Love. London, Hale, 1980.

Novels as Sharon Heath

A Vacation for Nurse Dean. New York, Ace, 1966.
Nurse at Moorcroft Manor. New York, Ace, 1967.
Nurse on Castle Island. New York, Ace, 1968; as *Master of Trelona* (as Claire Ritchie), London, Hale, 1977.
Nurse at Shadow Manor. New York, Ace, 1973.
Nurse Elaine and the Sapphire Star. New York, Ace, 1973; as *Starshine for Sweethearts* (as Claire Ritchie), London, Hale, 1976.

OTHER PUBLICATIONS

Verse

The White Garden and Other Poems. Crayke, Yorkshire, Guild Press, 1957.
The Mirror and Other Poems. Walton on Thames, Surrey, Outposts, 1970.

Other

Writing the Romantic Novel. London, Bond Street, 1962.

* * *

Claire Ritchie wrote romantic novels in the modern idiom: novels which are light and readable by young but mature adults.

The heroines in Ritchie's novels are up-to-date young ladies of their respective generations, as in *Bright Meadows* (1951) or *Castle Perilous* (1979). The girls are not beautiful but pretty and attractive. They are generally rather ordinary, and, though somewhat experienced in love, still at a formative age. The experiences in the novels help them to mature, to develop a competence in life through a testing experience. Ritchie sets her later novels in holiday or seaside locations with some added glamour; the plots become more complex and action-filled, with an element of mystery and skulduggery which sometimes appears contrived and unrealistic, as in *Castle Perilous*.

These are moral lessons, but Ritchie learned to put them across in a more subtle way than the "Loyalty is a rare quality nowadays" type of remark in *Bright Meadows*. The experiences of the main characters instill in them a wisdom.

The incidental detail such as descriptions of women and the men who love them and the minor aspects of relationships are well handled. The novels are easy to read, having comparatively little dialogue and simple sentences. The main criticism that can be made is that the books are too chaste by modern standards. There is little passion in, for instance, *This Summer's Rose* (1970) where the hero makes do with confessing to himself that he is in love. The romantic climax of this novel is, in fact, an offer to share the middle years.

—P. R. Meldrum

RIVERS, Francine. American. Born in Berkeley, California, 12 May 1947. Educated at the University of Nevada, Reno,

B.A.; California State University, Hayward. Married Richard Rivers in 1969; two sons and one daughter. Former airline stewardess; teacher, Oakland, California. Recipient: Romance Writers of America Golden Medallion, 1985; Silver Pen award, 1986, 1987. Agent: Jane Jordan Browne, Multimedia Product Development Inc., 410 South Michigan Avenue, Suite 724, Chicago, Illinois 60605–1465. Address: 8029 Washington Avenue, Sebastopol, California 95472, U.S.A.

ROMANCE AND HISTORICAL PUBLICATIONS

Novels

Kathleen. New York, Berkley, 1979.
Sycamore Hill. New York, Pinnacle, 1981.
Rebel in His Arms. New York, Ace, 1981.
This Golden Valley. New York, Berkley, 1983.
Sarina. New York, Berkley, 1983.
Hearts Divided. New York, Berkley, 1983.
Heart in Hiding. New York, Berkley, 1984.
Not So Wild a Dream. New York, Berkley, 1984.
Pagan Heart. New York, Berkley, 1985.
Outlaw's Embrace. New York, Berkley, 1986.
A Fire in the Heart. New York, Berkley, 1987.

*

Francine Rivers comments:
I write for the simple joy of creating and entertaining.

*   *   *

Setting most of her novels in 19th-century California, Francine Rivers shows real talent in her descriptions of time and place. The reader feels the heat and dust of a California summer, sees the Sierras, and experiences some of the hardships of frontier life. *Kathleen*, *Sycamore Hill*, and *Rebel in His Arms* all are written in the first person, which lends a certain immediacy to the narrative, but her other novels also are fast-paced, with well-developed characters.

Frequently Rivers's heroines are young Eastern girls compelled by circumstances to try their fortunes in a land alien to their experiences. Kathleen O'Reilly (*Kathleen*), raised as an orphan, discovers she is really the illegitimate child of an actress and a wealthy, married man. Her past shattered, she takes a job as governess to a rancher's niece and nephew. In *Sycamore Hill* Abby McFarland learns she has been cheated of her inheritance by her greedy guardians and must take a job as a schoolteacher in a small western town. Moira Cavendish in *This Golden Valley*, follows her brothers, the last of her family, to California, where they are caught by "gold fever." Amnesty Brown (*A Fire in the Heart*) is exiled after scandalizing Boston society with her radical views. Rivers's other heroines are born westerners but of widely varying classes. Kathryn Durham's family in *Rebel in His Arms* are homesteaders, while Sarina Azevedo Cahill's ancestors were among the first Spanish settlers (*Sarina*). Tempest McClaren, heroine of *Not So Wild a Dream*, is the daughter of an Indian and a trapper, and Beth Tyrell in *Outlaw's Embrace* is a small town sheriff's daughter. No matter their background, however, all of these women demonstrate courage and fortitude when tested.

The men who match these women run the gamut of western heroes and include ranchers, sailors, a gunslinger, and a gambler. All are hard, tough men, who are changed by the gentling influence of a woman.

As might be expected, the characters face many dangers. Rivers manages to inject some new twists to these plots, although some might stretch the reader's credulity. Both Kathleen and Kathryn Durham are pursued by deranged killers from the past, who use such methods as shooting, poison, and rattlesnakes in their efforts to kill the heroines. Moira and her lover, Random Hawthorne, are almost killed by claim jumpers before they are "rescued" by an enormous grizzly bear, the almost supernatural guardian of a huge gold deposit. Sarina, drugged with an hallucinogen, almost dies in childbirth and with her husband, Lang, survives a violent earthquake. Rivers even hints at the truly supernatural in *Sycamore Hill*. Someone terrorizes Abby McFarland by "haunting" the schoolhouse where she lives. The ghost is supposed to be that of the previous teacher who committed suicide. After several minor accidents, Abby confronts the real villain, who confesses killing the teacher and tries to kill Abby. She is saved when the ghost attacks the killer. As a plot device, this is somewhat jarring, but a doubt remains as to whether there really was a ghost or if it is all in the heroine's imagination.

Rivers has proven herself adept at creating interesting characters, intriguing stories with more than a hint of mystery to keep the reader guessing, and spicing it all with a satisfying romance. She has not been a prolific author, but her books are all solid offerings.

—Barbara E. Kemp

ROBBINS, Kay. See **HOOPER, Kay.**

ROBERTS, I. M. See **ROBERTS, Irene.**

ROBERTS, Irene (née Williamson). Also writes as Roberta Carr; Elizabeth Harle; I. M. Roberts; Ivor Roberts; Iris Rowland; Irene Shaw. British. Born in London, 27 September 1925. Left school at age 13. Served in the Women's Land Army during World War II. Married Terence Granville Leonard Roberts in 1947; two sons and one daughter. Worked as shop assistant, typist, and saleswoman, then journalist and writer; woman's page editor, *South Hams Review*, 1977–79, and weekly book reviewer in provincial newspapers. Since 1978 Tutor in Creative Writing, Kingsbridge Community College, Devon. Address: Alpha House, Higher Town, Marlborough, Kingsbridge, South Devon TQ7 3RL, England.

ROMANCE AND HISTORICAL PUBLICATIONS

Novels (series: Ancient Egypt)

Love Song of the Sea. London, Fleetway, 1960.
Squirrel Walk. London, Gresham, 1961.
Only to Part. London, Fleetway, 1961.
Wind of Fate. London, Gresham, 1961.
Beloved Rascals. London, Gresham, 1962.
The Shrine of Marigolds. London, Gresham, 1962.
Come Back Beloved. London, Gresham, 1962.
The Dark Night. London, Fleetway, 1962.

Sweet Sorrel. London, Gresham, 1963.
Tangle of Gold Lace. London, Gresham, 1963.
Cry of the Gulls. London, Fleetway, 1963.
The Whisper of Sea-Bells. London, Hale, 1964.
Echo of Flutes. London, Hale, 1965.
The Mountain Sang. London, Hale, 1965.
Where Flamingoes Fly. London, Hale, 1966.
A Handful of Stars. London, Hale, 1967.
Shadows on the Moon. London, Hale, 1968.
Jungle Nurse. London, Hale, 1968.
Love Comes to Larkswood. London, Hale, 1968.
Alpine Nurse. London, Hale, 1968.
Nurse in the Hills. London, Hale, 1969.
The Lion and the Sun. London, Hale, 1969.
Thunder Heights. London, Hale, 1969.
Surgeon in Tibet. London, Hale, 1970.
Birds Without Bars. London, Hale, 1970.
The Shrine of Fire. London, Hale, 1970.
Gull Haven. London, Hale, 1971.
Sister at Sea. London, Hale, 1971.
Moon over the Temple. London, Hale, 1972.
The Golden Pagoda. London, Hale, 1972.
Desert Nurse. London, Hale, 1976.
Nurse in Nepal. London, Hale, 1976.
Stars above Raffael. London, Hale, 1977.
Hawks Barton. London, Hale, 1979.
Symphony of Bells. London, Hale, 1980.
Nurse Moonlight. London, Hale, 1980.
Weave Me a Moonbeam. London, Hale, 1982.
Jasmine for a Nurse. London, Hale, 1982.
Sister on Leave. London, Hale, 1982.
Nurse in the Wilderness. London, Hale, 1983.
Kingdom of the Sun (Ancient Egypt). London, Mills and Boon, 1987.
Sea Jade. London, Mills and Boon, 1987.
Song of the Nile (Ancient Egypt). London, Mills and Boon, 1987.

Novels as Iris Rowland

The Tangled Web. London, Gresham, 1962.
Island in the Mist. London, Gresham, 1962.
The Morning Star. London, Gresham, 1963.
With Fire and Flowers. London, Gresham, 1963.
Golden Flower! London, Gresham, 1964.
A Fountain of Roses. London, Gresham, 1966.
Valley of Bells. London, Gresham, 1967.
Blue Feathers. London, Gresham, 1967.
A Veil of Rushes. London, Gresham, 1967.
To Be Beloved. London, Gresham, 1968.
Rose Island. London, Gresham, 1969.
Cherries and Candlelight. London, Gresham, 1969.
Nurse at Kama Hall. London, Gresham, 1969.
Moon over Moncrieff. London, Gresham, 1969; New York, Lenox Hill Press, 1974.
The Knave of Hearts. London, Hale, 1970.
Star-Drift. London, Gresham, 1970.
Rainbow River. London, Gresham, 1970.
The Wild Summer. London, Gresham, 1970.
Orange Blossom for Tara. London, Gresham, 1971.
Blossoms in the Snow. London, Gresham, 1971.
Sister Julia. London, Hale, 1972.
To Lisa with Love. London, Hale, 1975.
Golden Bubbles. London, Hale, 1976.
Hunter's Dawn. London, Hale, 1977.
Forgotten Dreams. London, Hale, 1978.

Golden Triangle. London, Hale, 1978.
Dance Ballerina Dance. London, Hale, 1980.
The Romantic Lady. London, Hale, 1981.
Moonlight and Roses. London, Hale, 1981.
Weave Me a Moonbeam. London, Hale, 1982.
Temptation. London, Hale, 1983.
Theresa. London, Hale, 1985.

Novels as Roberta Carr

Red Runs the Sunset. London, Gresham, 1963.
Sea Maiden. London, Gresham, 1965.
Fire Dragon. London, Gresham, 1967.
Golden Interlude. London, Gresham, 1970.

Novels as Elizabeth Harle

Golden Rain. London, Gresham, 1964; as Irene Roberts, New York, Belmont, 1966.
Gay Rowan. London, Gresham, 1965.
Sandy. London, Gresham, 1967.
Spray of Red Roses. London, Gresham, 1971.
The Silver Summer. London, Hale, 1971.
Buy Me a Dream. London, Hale, 1972.
The Burning Flame. London, Hale, 1979.
Come to Me Darling. London, Hale, 1983.
Amber in Love. London, Hale, 1984.

Novels as Irene Shaw

The House of Lydia. London, Wright and Brown, 1967.
Moonstone Manor. London, Wright and Brown, 1968; as *Murder's Mansion*, New York, Doubleday, 1976.
The Olive Branch. London, Wright and Brown, 1968.

Novels as I. M. Roberts (series: Ancient Egypt; China)

The Throne Pharaohs (Ancient Egypt). London, Hale, 1974.
Hatshepsut, Queen of the Nile (Ancient Egypt). London, Hale, 1976.
Monsoon. London, Hale, 1983.
Moonpearl (China). London, Hale, 1983; revised edition, as Irene Roberts, London, Mills and Boon, 1986.
Time of the Seventh Moon (China). London, Hale, 1984.
Hour of the Tiger (China). London, Hale, 1985.

OTHER PUBLICATIONS

Novels as Ivor Roberts

Jump into Hell! London, Brown Watson, 1960.
Trial by Water. London, Micron, 1961.
Green Hell. London, Micron, 1961.

Other (for children)

Laughing Is Fun. London, Micron, 1963.
Holidays for Hanbury. London, Micron, 1964.

*

Irene Roberts comments:

To me writing is as natural as breathing. It is something that I had to do. To this end it was necessary to educate myself and learn to type and spell. Writing is, I find, as exciting as the first real Spring day after a bad Winter. I chose my characters and their situations from a great imaginary mixing-bowl of words that I keep in my head. I knead and shape these words into colourful beads that I love to string together in an interesting, meaningful way. While I am writing I am at one with my characters. I laugh with them and I feel their pain—that is why nine out of ten times I give them happy endings. My great interests are Ancient Egypt and China from the Opium War, Taiping and Boxer Rebellions.

*   *   *

Irene Roberts is a prolific novelist writing under a number of different pseudonyms to denote her diverse styles within the romance genre. Robert's novels are well-written and she uses a stable formula. She raises these stories from mere mundane formula romance, however, by adding elements of mystery, such as in *Theresa*, where the heroine, suffering from amnesia, finds herself ultimately at the centre of a drug smuggling ring. Conversely, Roberts uses well-drawn often eccentric characters, like Del Sharron in *Moonlight and Roses*, and well-researched backgrounds to sustain interest.

Roberts's heroines possess similar qualities throughout her books. They are usually alone in the world, often orphans, and are weak and vulnerable, despite surface elements of independence. The main dynamic of the novels is their struggle between two men generally characterised as the somewhat domineering "father-figure" who offers stability (Chris Chapman in *Theresa*) or the happy-go-lucky glamorous figure who offers excitement (Michael Lawrence in *Theresa*). The heroine usually ends the novel with the former and "comes home" to his arms.

Roberts has a sense of humour, and she is not averse to making light of the romance novelist, and explains her own role as a novelist of this genre within her books. In *Moonlight and Roses* Del Sharron defines the romance fiction genre: "It is my pleasure to dwell on that one, very precious moment in life, when everything gleams under the golden glow of love." Roberts uses the ideal of the "precious moment in life" with her heroes and heroines expressing their passion through kisses while remaining quite chaste.

In the field of historical romance, Roberts chooses settings in exotic locations and although reasonably researched, she makes no excuse for highlighting romance at the expense of often violent action such as the Boxer rebellion. Unlike her contemporary romances, sex is alluded to far more graphically—although, again the heroine is vulnerable and caught between two men. Somewhat disturbing elements creep into Robert's historical romances, especially those set in China. In *Moonpearl* and *Sea Jade*, the heroines are frequently beaten, deprived, and made vassals. Married against their will they are subjected to "wifely duties" which are thinly-disguised rapes, "a fluid very sensuous over-riding of her will." The tenor of these novels suggests that "husbands are heaven and we all know that heaven must be obeyed." This often violent male behaviour is not criticised and the heroines finally come to see things from the male point of view. Elements of wilfulness and independence therefore are soon stamped out of the female protagonists as they soon recognise their place and fulfill their unspoken desire to be dominated.

—Jane K. Thompson

ROBERTS, Janet Louise.** Also writes as Louisa Bronte; Rebecca Danton; Janette Radcliffe. American. Born in New Britain, Connecticut, 20 January 1925. Educated at Fairview High School, Dayton, Ohio; Otterbein College, Westerville, Ohio, B. A. 1946; Columbia University School of Library Science, New York, M. S. 1966. Clerk typist; reference librarian, Dayton and Montgomery County Public Library, Dayton, 1966–78; then full-time writer. Recipient: Porgie award (*West Coast Review of Books*), 1980. H.H.D.: Otterbein College, 1979. *Died in 1984.*

ROMANCE AND HISTORICAL PUBLICATIONS

Novels

The Jewels of Terror. New York, Lancer, 1970; London, Severn House, 1988.
Love Song. New York, Pinnacle, 1970.
The Weeping Lady. New York, Lancer, 1971.
Ravenswood. New York, Avon, 1971.
Dark Rose. New York, Lancer, 1971.
The Devil's Own. New York, Avon, 1972.
The Curse of Kenton. New York, Avon, 1972.
A Marriage of Inconvenience. New York, Dell, 1972.
Rivertown. New York, Avon, 1972.
My Lady Mischief. New York, Dell, 1973.
The Dancing Doll. New York, Dell, 1973.
The Dornstein Icon. New York, Avon, 1973.
The Golden Thistle. New York, Dell, 1973.
Isle of the Dolphins. New York, Dell, 1973.
La Casa Dorada. New York, Dell, 1973.
The Cardross Luck. New York, Dell, 1974.
The First Waltz. New York, Dell, 1974.
Castlereagh. New York, Pocket Books, 1975.
Jade Vendetta. New York, Pocket Books, 1976.
Wilderness Inn. New York, Pocket Books, 1976.
Island of Desire. New York, Ballantine, and London, Sphere, 1977.
Black Pearls. New York, Ballantine, 1979; London, Sphere, 1980.
Golden Lotus. New York, Warner, 1979; London, Sphere, 1981.
Silver Jasmine. New York, Warner, 1980; London, Sphere, 1982.
Flamenco Rose. New York, Warner, 1981; London, Sphere, 1983.
Forget Me Not. New York, Warner, 1982; London, Sphere, 1984.
Scarlet Poppies. New York, Warner, 1983.
Flower of Love. New York, Ballantine, 1983; London, Sphere, 1985.
This Shining Splendor. New York, Berkley, 1984; London, Sphere, 1986.

Novels as Rebecca Danton

Sign of the Golden Goose. New York, Popular Library, 1972.
Black Horse Tavern. New York, Popular Library, 1972.
Amethyst Love. New York, Fawcett, 1977.
Fire Opals. New York, Fawcett, 1977.
Ship of Hate. New York, Dell, 1977.
Star Sapphire. New York, Fawcett, 1979.
The Highland Brooch. New York, Fawcett, 1980.
Ruby Heart. New York, Fawcett, 1980.

Novels as Louisa Bronte (series: American Dynasty; Greystone)

Lord Satan. New York, Avon, 1972.
Her Demon Lover. New York, Avon, 1973.
Greystone Tavern. New York, Ballantine, 1975.
Gathering at Greystone. New York, Ballantine, 1976.
Greystone Heritage. New York, Ballantine, 1976.
Casino Greystone. New York, Ballantine, 1976.
Moonlight at Greystone. New York, Ballantine, 1976.
Freedom Trail to Greystone. New York, Ballantine, 1976.
The Vallette Heritage (American Dynasty). New York, Berkley, 1978; London, Fontana, 1979.
The Van Rhyne Heritage (American Dynasty). New York, Berkley, 1979; London, Fontana, 1980.
The Gunther Heritage (American Dynasty). New York, Berkley, 1981.

Novels as Janette Radcliffe

The Blue-Eyed Gypsy. New York, Dell, 1974.
The Moonlight Gondola. New York, Dell, 1975.
The Gentleman Pirate. New York, Dell, 1975.
White Jasmine. New York, Dell, 1976.
Lord Stephen's Lady. New York, Dell, 1976.
The Azure Castle. New York, Dell, 1976.
The Topaz Charm. New York, Dell, 1976.
A Gift of Violets. New York, Dell, 1977.
The Heart Awakens. New York, Dell, 1977.
Scarlet Secrets. New York, Dell, 1977.
Stormy Surrender. New York, Dell, 1978; London, Sphere, 1979.
Hidden Fires. New York, Dell, 1978.
American Baroness. New York, Dell, 1980.
The Court of the Flowering Peach. New York, Dell, 1981; as Janet Louise Roberts, London, Sphere, 1983.
Vienna Dreams. New York, Dell, 1982.

*

Janet Louise Roberts commented:

(1982) I have always loved to write, since childhood. There is a deep pleasure in working with words, and making them say just what I feel. I find the world unsatisfactory, and in my fiction I try to make things come out the way I want them to, and I love happy endings. My writing is romantic, not realistic. Writing is a profession requiring long study and much dedicated work. There is a tremendous satisfaction in conquering difficulties. It is no fun to do something simple—anybody can. I like to set myself hard problems, because when one gets to the top of the mountain one feels tremendous pride and joy in the conquering of the struggle to get there.

*   *   *

Writing under her own name and three pseudonyms (Janette Radcliffe, Rebecca Danton and Louise Bronte), Jane Louis Roberts was one of the most prolific romance novelists. She wrote modern, gothic, and historical romances and even produced a few "occult romances," in which the devil or a demon takes the place of the traditional hero (*The Devil's Own, Isle of the Dolphins, Lord Satan, Her Demon Lover*).

Although Roberts's books show some variety in plot, setting, and time period, they remain basically the same. Her work is one of the easiest to spot regardless of the pseudonym used. One of the most constant aspects to be found in her stories is her treatment of women. Even in a genre under fire for being sexist,

Roberts's heroines have much to endure. Whether the hero is an arrogant aristocrat (*The Dornstein Icon, A Marriage of Inconvenience, Star Sapphire*) or a captain of industry (*Golden Lotus, Flamenco Rose*), he is rough and overbearing. The woman may put up some token resistance, but she remains totally ineffectual in the face of male domination. It is not uncommon for the heroine to be raped by the hero at least once in the story. Sexual details are not very explicit, but the lack of tenderness and the idea of sex as punishment are apparent. Often the woman is held captive (*The Dornstein Icon, The Court of the Flowering Peach*) until she learns to love her captor. This may or may not be within the marriage bond, and the captivity may be emotional or financial rather than strictly physical, but it is clear that the woman is unable to act in her own interests or do anything but submit to the all-conquering male.

Roberts's books are frequently marred by idiosyncracies. One is her seeming obsession with food. A review of one of her novels once said that reading a Janet Louise Roberts book is like reading a cookbook, and that is not far from the truth. Elaborate descriptions of food and its preparation abound, usually with little or no relation to the story. Another fetish is what only can be termed as "wonder salve." No matter the injury—gunshot wound, concussion, sprain—it can be cured by applying a salve. One cannot help but think that a description of a realistic treatment would not be difficult to write. Roberts also leaps into ridiculous, if not insulting, attempts at conveying ethnic accents. In *Wilderness Inn* two Indians sum up their rescue of the heroine from an unknown attacker by saying, "He grab you, try to carry you away. We watch, we see. We run like hell!" In *Casino Greystone* Fran's Italian accent is implied by dialogue like this: "Won't-a never find Enid there . . . She'll-a be swept out-a to sea."

Such patently silly descriptions and dialogue make her stories less believable, but Roberts's fans are forgiving. In spite of her failings, she remains one of the most popular of the romance novelists. Her view of women as pretty dolls to be used and manipulated by men certainly must cause feminists to gnash their teeth, but she obviously strikes a responsive chord among her readers.

—Barbara E. Kemp

ROBERTS, Kenneth (Lewis). American. Born in Kennebunk, Maine, 8 December 1885. Educated at schools in Malden, Massachusetts; Stone's School, Boston; Cornell University, Ithaca, New York (editor, *Cornell Widow*), 1904–08, A.B. 1908. Served in the United States Army, in the intelligence section of the Siberian Expeditionary Force, 1918–19: Captain. Married Anna Seiberling Mosser in 1911. Worked in leather business in Boston, 1908–09; reporter and columnist, Boston *Post*, 1909–18, and editor of *Sunday Post* humor page, 1915–18; editorial staff member, *Life* magazine, New York, 1915–18; correspondent, in Washington, D.C., and Europe, *Saturday Evening Post*, Philadelphia, 1919–28; thereafter a full-time writer; lived in Italy, 1928–37, then in Kennebunkport, Maine. Recipient: special Pulitzer prize, 1957. Litt.D.: Dartmouth College, Hanover, New Hampshire, 1934; Colby College, Waterville, Maine, 1935; Bowdoin College, Brunswick, Maine, 1937; Middlebury College, Vermont, 1938; Northwestern University, Evanston, Illinois, 1945. Member, American Academy. *Died 21 July 1957.*

ROMANCE AND HISTORICAL PUBLICATIONS

Novels (series: Arundel)

Arundel. New York, Doubleday, 1930; London, Lane, 1936.
The Lively Lady (Arundel). New York, Doubleday, 1931; London, Lane, 1935.
Rabble in Arms (Arundel). New York, Doubleday, 1933; London, Collins, 1939.
Captain Caution: A Chronicle of Arundel. New York, Doubleday, 1934; London, Collins, 1949.
Northwest Passage. New York, Doubleday, 1937; London, Collins, 1938.
Oliver Wiswell. New York, Doubleday, 1940; London, Collins, 1943.
Lydia Bailey. New York, Doubleday, and London, Collins, 1947.
Boon Island. New York, Doubleday, and London, Collins, 1956.

OTHER PUBLICATIONS

Plays

Panatela: A Political Comic Opera, with Romeyn Berry, music by T. J. Lindorff, H. C. Schuyler, and H. E. Childs (produced Ithaca, New York, 1907). Ithaca, New York, Cornell Masque, 1907.
The Brotherhood of Man, with Robert Garland. New York, French, 1934.

Other

Europe's Morning After. New York, Harper, 1921.
Sun Hunting: Adventures and Observations among the Native and Migratory Tribes of Florida. Indianapolis, Bobbs Merrill, 1922.
Why Europe Leaves Home. Indianapolis, Bobbs Merrill, and London, Fisher Unwin, 1922.
The Collector's Whatnot, with Booth Tarkington and Hugh Kahler. Boston, Houghton Mifflin, 1923.
Black Magic. Indianapolis, Bobbs Merrill, 1924.
Concentrated New England: A Sketch of Calvin Coolidge. Indianapolis, Bobbs Merrill, 1924.
Florida Loafing. Indianapolis, Bobbs Merrill, 1925.
Florida. New York, Harper, 1926.
Antiquamania. New York, Doubleday, 1928.
For Authors Only and Other Gloomy Essays. New York, Doubleday, 1935.
It Must Be Your Tonsils. New York, Doubleday, 1936.
Trending into Maine. Boston, Little Brown, 1938; revised edition, New York, Doubleday, 1944.
The Kenneth Roberts Reader. New York, Doubleday, 1945.
I Wanted to Write. New York, Doubleday, 1949.
Don't Say That about Maine! Waterville, Maine, Colby College Press, 1951.
Henry Gross and His Dowsing Rod. New York, Doubleday, 1951.
The Seventh Sense. New York, Doubleday, 1953.
Cowpens: The Great Morale-Builder. N.p., Westholm, 1957; as *The Battle of Cowpens*, New York, Doubleday, 1958.
Water Unlimited. New York, Doubleday, 1957.

Editor, *March to Quebec: Journals of Members of Arnold's Expedition*. New York, Doubleday, 1938; revised edition, 1940, 1953.
Editor and Translator, with Anna M. Roberts, *Moreau de St. Méry's American Journey (1793–1798)*. New York, Doubleday, 1947.

*

Bibliography: *Kenneth Roberts: A Bibliography* by P. Murphy, privately printed, 1975.

Critical Study: *A Century of American History in Fiction: Kenneth Roberts' Novels* by Janet Harris, New York, Gordon Press, 1976.

*   *   *

A prolific verse, short story and editorial writer during the early years of his career, Kenneth Roberts's most memorable and lasting works of literature are found in the historical fiction created in the latter years of his life. Few authors of historical fiction can be as closely identified with the military side of the American Revolution and the early national period. A meticulous researcher, Roberts went to contemporary accounts of the events of which he wrote. He even edited the journal of John Pierce, a member of the Benedict Arnold expedition and translated a Frenchman's account of a journey to the United States. Possessing a conservative philosophy, Roberts's works reflected that perspective of people and events.

With a single exception, all of Roberts's historical fiction have a first-person narrator. His earliest historical novel, *Arundel*, is a tale of Benedict Arnold's expedition throughout the wilderness of present day Maine in an attempt to attack the British stronghold at Quebec. Steven Nason, his narrator, vividly documents the hardships of the march, the intrigues, the heroism and the cowardly actions. In a sense, Roberts tries to rehabilitate the public image of Benedict Arnold whose military reputation had been marred by his later treason. *Rabble in Arms*, continued the story of Arnold and his army from 1776 through 1777 and kept up the support of Arnold's military and naval acumen. Another narrator, Peter Merrill, appears and we see Phoebe Nason's instrumental involvement in the construction of the Colonial fleet on Lake Champlain. Unlike the earlier *Arundel*, the novel was a commercial success and set Roberts on the road to popular acceptance. Both of these novels led the way to *Northwest Passage*, a biography of Major Robert Rogers and his struggles in the French and Indian War and the quest for a northwest passage. In addition, he vividly portrayed the bureaucratic bungling associated with the quest along with the heroics of Rogers and his men. The book became an immediate bestseller and marked the peak of his writing career. Reprinted 15 times in the first year of issue, the book also found a following in Western and Central Europe.

In keeping with his interest in the least popular images of the American Revolutionary era, Roberts next wrote *Oliver Wiswell*, a tale of that time from the perspective of a loyalist. While sympathetic to the American Revolution, Roberts's narrative spoke of the shortcomings of General Washington and the meanspirited conduct of the rebels. He did not fail, however, to point out the errors in judgement by the British general staff.

Lydia Bailey, his penultimate historical novel, quit the North American continent and covered not only Toussaint L'Ouverture's uprising in Haiti but the fledgling United States war with Tripoli at the beginning of the 19th century. Though the novel met with popular acceptance, its plot ranged over half the globe, its heroine appeared weak, and its adventures seemed too unbelievable. *Cowpens: The Great Morale-Builder* came to be published post-humously and told the story of the January 1781 Revolutionary War battle and its critical importance to the colonists' cause. The American leader, Daniel Morgan, comes in for praise by Roberts, when it is remembered that Morgan accompanied Benedict Arnold on his Quebec expedition.

To many European readers, it is Roberts's perception of the American Revolutionary era experience which captures the imagination. While the recipient of a special Pulitzer prize for his contribution to an interest in American history, Roberts longest lasting contribution may be in the journals he edited, the court-martial he discovered and the translation of *Moreau de St. Méry's American Journey 1793–1798*.

—Frank R. Levstick

ROBERTS, Nora (a pseudonym). American. Born in Washington, D.C. Educated at Montgomery Blair High School, Silver Spring, Maryland. Married Ronald Aufdem-Brinke in 1968; 2) Bruce Wilder in 1985; two sons. Secretary, Wheeler and Jarpeck, 1968–70, and R & R Lighting, 1970–75, both Maryland. Agent: Amy Berpower, Writers House, 21 West 26th Street, New York, New York 10010, U.S.A.

ROMANCE AND HISTORICAL PUBLICATIONS

Novels (series: Cordina; Magregor; O'Hurley)

Irish Thoroughbred. New York, Silhouette, and London, Hodder and Stoughton, 1981.
Blithe Images. New York, Silhouette, 1982.
Song of the West. New York, Silhouette, 1982.
Search for Love. New York, Silhouette, 1982.
Island of Flowers. New York, Silhouette, 1982.
The Heart's Victory. New York, Silhouette, 1982.
From This Day. New York, Silhouette, and London, Hodder and Stoughton, 1983.
Her Mother's Keeper. New York, Silhouette, 1983.
Reflections. New York, Silhouette, 1983.
Once More with Feeling. New York, Silhouette, 1983.
Untamed. New York, Silhouette, 1983; London, Hodder and Stoughton, 1984.
Dance of Dreams. New York, Silhouette, 1983.
Tonight and Always. New York, Silhouette, 1983.
This Magic Moment. New York, Silhouette, 1983.
Endings and Beginnings. New York, Silhouette, 1984.
Storm Warning. New York, Silhouette, 1984.
Sullivan's Woman. New York, Silhouette, 1984.
Rules of the Game. New York, Silhouette, 1984.
Less of a Stranger. New York, Silhouette, 1984.
A Matter of Choice. New York, Silhouette, 1984.
The Law Is a Lady. New York, Silhouette, 1984.
First Impressions. New York, Silhouette, 1984.
Opposites Attract. New York, Silhouette, 1984.
Promise Me Tomorrow. New York, Silhouette, and London, Severn House, 1984.
Playing the Odds (Magregor). New York, Silhouette, 1985.
Partners. New York, Silhouette, 1985.
The Right Path. New York, Silhouette, 1985.
Tempting Fate (Magregor). New York, Silhouette, 1985.
Boundary Lines. New York, Silhouette, 1985.

All the Possibilities (Magregor). New York, Silhouette, 1985.
One Man's Art (Magregor). New York, Silhouette, 1985.
Summer Desserts. New York, Silhouette, 1985.
Night Moves. Toronto, Harlequin, 1985.
Dual Image. New York, Silhouette, 1985.
The Art of Deception. New York, Silhouette, 1986.
Affaire Royale (Cordina). New York, Silhouette, 1986.
One Summer. New York, Silhouette, 1986.
Treasures Lost, Treasures Found. New York, Silhouette, 1986.
Risky Business. New York, Silhouette, 1986.
Lessons Learned. New York, Silhouette, 1986.
Second Nature. New York, Silhouette, 1986.
A Will and a Way. New York, Silhouette, 1986.
Home for Christmas. New York, Silhouette, 1986.
For Now, Forever (Magregor). New York, Silhouette, 1987.
Mind Over Matter. New York, Silhouette, 1987.
Command Performance (Cordina). New York, Silhouette, 1987.
Hot Ice. New York, Bantam, 1987.
Temptation. New York, Silhouette, 1987.
The Playboy Prince (Cordina). New York, Silhouette, 1987.
Sacred Sins. New York, Bantam, 1987.
Local Hero. New York, Silhouette, 1988.
Irish Rose. New York, Silhouette, 1988.
Brazen Virtue. New York, Bantam, 1988.
The Last Honest Woman (O'Hurley). New York, Silhouette, 1988.
Dance to the Piper (O'Hurley). New York, Silhouette, 1988.
Rebellion. Toronto, Harlequin, 1988.
Skin Deep (O'Hurley). New York, Silhouette, 1988.
Name of the Game. New York, Silhouette, 1988.
Sweet Revenge. New York, Bantam, 1989.
Loving Jack. New York, Silhouette, 1989.
Best Laid Plans. New York, Silhouette, 1989.

*

Nora Roberts comments:
Over the past 10 years, I have specialized in writing romance novels. I write relationship works because I'm fascinated by relationships and why certain men and women are drawn together. In writing, my first goal is to entertain the reader. I like to think it's the finest goal any novelist can strive for.

*   *   *

Nora Roberts has written more than 40 category romances for Silhouette and has recently entered the mainstream fiction market with tales of romantic adventure and suspense.

Roberts has been one of Silhouette's most popular writers since publication of her first work *Irish Thoroughbred*, the story of Adelia Cunnane, a young woman who comes from the Emerald Isle to make her home with her only living relative, Uncle Paddy, a trainer at one of Maryland's better horse farms. Adelia is typical of Roberts's heroines—independent, feisty, and unaware of her loveliness and charm. The hero who eventually wins her love is Travis Grant. Handsome, articulate, and wealthy, he could have any woman he wants but it is the fiery spirit of Adelea that attracts and holds him.

Because of restrictions placed on writers of category romances the love scenes of Roberts's Silhouette romance novels never go beyond passionate kissing, but that changes when she writes for Silhouette Intimate Moments and Silhouette Special Editions. In these books the stolen kisses—a favorite ploy of the Roberts hero—are much more bruising and passionate, as is the heroine's response.

Roberts's work distinguishes itself from that of many category writers by the well defined characters in her novels. The heroine of one book is not interchangeable with another. Diane Blade of *Tempting Fate* is a Harvard trained lawyer whose unhappy childhood makes it difficult for her to reach out to the love and happiness offered to her by Caine MacGregor. A very different lady is Gwen Lacrosse (*Her Mother's Keeper*), a New York fashion editor who hurries back to Louisiana, ready to do battle in order to protect her sweetly naïve and still beautiful mother from the seductive charms of the handsome Luke Powers. Even minor characters are deftly realized, such as Miri the down-to-earth Hawaiian housekeeper in *Island of Flowers* who doesn't hesitate to give advice or a piece of her mind.

All Roberts's books are well researched, so that the readers have a true sense of what it's like to be in Hawaii or Atlantic City, or Boston, or the Maryland countryside. She also realistically describes the nuances of different professions of her characters such as lawyer (*Tempting Fate*), horse trainer (*Irish Thoroughbred*), magician (*This Magic Moment*), or more recently, jewel thief (*Hot Ice* and *Sweet Revenge*). Added to all this is a keen ear for dialogue and accents so it's little wonder that Roberts enjoys such great popularity.

Until recently most of Roberts's fans had been confined to devotees of category romances, but with recent publication of her novels by Bantam, she has entered the world of mainstream fiction. Although these stories may have more complex plots than the romances, the female protagonists still retain their gritty independence, and the men find this a most enchanting and seductive attribute.

Adventure and suspense are the main ingredients in these stories. In *Sacred Sins* psychiatrist Theresa Court becomes involved in the investigation of a psychopathic killer known as "The Priest." Almost 30 years old, Theresa still hasn't met a man worth emotional involvement until police sergeant Ben Paris enters the picture. Socialite Phoebe Spring of *Sweet Revenge* is an international jewel thief in her spare time and is set on reclaiming two fabulous gems from the despicable father whom she blames for her mother's illness and death. Complications arise when her path crosses that of Phil Chamberlain, himself a reformed jewel thief.

Roberts attracts readers because her stories blend idealized romance with interesting plots and believable characters. This prolific author certainly deserves her wide readership.

Patricia Altner

ROBERTS, Paula. See **LORIN, Amii.**

ROBERTS, Willo Davis. American. Born in Grand Rapids, Michigan, 29 May 1928. Educated at a high school in Pontiac, Michigan, graduated 1946. Married David W. Roberts in 1949; two daughters and two sons. Worked in hospitals and doctors offices, 1964–72; currently conducts a writers workshop in Granite Falls, Washington. Agent: Curtis Brown, 10 Astor Place, New York, New York 10019. Address: 12020 Engebretson Road, Granite Falls, Washington 98252, U.S.A.

ROMANCE AND HISTORICAL PUBLICATIONS

Novels (series: The Black Pearl)

Murder at Grand Bay. New York, Arcadia House, 1955.
The Girl Who Wasn't There. New York, Arcadia House, 1957.
Murder Is So Easy. Fresno, California, Vega, 1961.
The Suspected Four. Fresno, California, Vega, 1962.
Nurse Kay's Conquest. New York, Ace, 1966.
Once a Nurse. New York, Ace, 1966.
Nurse at Mystery Villa. New York, Ace, 1967.
Return to Darkness. New York, Lancer, 1969.
Shroud of Fog. New York, Ace, 1970.
Devil Boy. New York, New American Library, 1970; London, New English Library, 1971.
The Waiting Darkness. New York, Lancer, 1970.
Shadow of a Past Love. New York, Lancer, 1970.
The House at Fern Canyon. New York, Lancer, 1970.
The Tarot Spell. New York, Lancer, 1970.
Invitation to Evil. New York, Lancer, 1970.
The Terror Trap. New York, Lancer, 1971.
King's Pawn. New York, Lancer, 1971.
The Gates of Montrain. New York, Lancer, 1971.
The Watchers. New York, Lancer, 1971.
The Ghosts of Harrel. New York, Lancer, 1971.
Inherit the Darkness. New York, Lancer, 1972.
Nurse in Danger. New York, Ace, 1972.
Becca's Child. New York, Lancer, 1972.
Sing a Dark Song. New York, Lancer, 1972.
The Nurses. New York, Ace, 1972; as *The Secret Lives of the Nurses*, London, Pan, 1975.
The Face of Danger. New York, Lancer, 1972.
Dangerous Legacy. New York, Lancer, 1972.
Sinister Gardens. New York, Lancer, 1972.
The M.D. New York, Lancer, 1972.
The Evil Children. New York, Lancer, 1973.
The Gods in Green. New York, Lancer, 1973.
Nurse Robin. New York, Lenox Hill Press, 1973.
Didn't Anybody Know My Wife? New York, Putnam, 1974; London, Hale, 1978.
White Jade. New York, Doubleday, 1975.
Key Witness. New York, Putnam, 1975; London, Hale, 1978.
Expendable. New York, Doubleday, 1976; London, Hale, 1979.
The Jaubert Ring. New York, Doubleday, 1976.
The House of Imposters. New York, Popular Library, 1977.
Cape of Black Sands. New York, Popular Library, 1977.
Act of Fear. New York, Doubleday, 1977; London, Hale, 1978.
The Black Pearl series:
  The Dark Dowry. New York, Popular Library, 1978.
  The Cade Curse. New York, Popular Library, 1978.
  The Stuart Stain. New York, Popular Library, 1978.
  The Devil's Double. New York, Popular Library, 1979.
  The Radkin Revenge. New York, Popular Library, 1979.
  The Hellfire Heritage. New York, Popular Library, 1979.
  The Macomber Menace. New York, Popular Library, 1979.
  The Gresham Ghost. New York, Popular Library, 1980.
The Search for Willie. New York, Popular Library, 1980.
Destiny's Woman. New York, Popular Library, 1980.
The Face at the Window. Toronto, Harlequin, and New York, Raven Press, 1981; London, Hale, 1983.
A Long Time to Hate. New York, Avon, 1982.
The Gallant Spirit. New York, Popular Library, 1982.
Days of Valor. New York, Warner, 1983.
The Sniper. New York, Doubleday, 1984.
Keating's Landing. New York, Warner, 1984.
The Annalise Experiment. New York, Doubleday, 1985.

My Rebel, My Love. New York, Pocket Books, 1986.
To Share a Dream. Toronto, Worldwide, 1986.
Madawaska. Toronto, Worldwide, 1988.

OTHER PUBLICATIONS

Other (for children)

The View from the Cherry Tree. New York, Atheneum, 1975.
Don't Hurt Laurie! New York, Atheneum, 1977.
The Minden Curse. New York, Atheneum, 1978.
More Minden Curses. New York, Atheneum, 1980.
The Girl with the Silver Eyes. New York, Atheneum, 1980.
House of Fear. New York, Scholastic, 1983.
The Pet-Sitting Peril. New York, Atheneum, 1983.
No Monsters in the Closet. New York, Atheneum, 1983.
Eddie and the Fairy Godpuppy. New York, Atheneum, 1984.
Elizabeth. New York, Scholastic, 1984.
Caroline. New York Scholastic, 1984.
Baby Sitting Is a Dangerous Job. New York, Atheneum, 1985.
Victoria. New York, Scholastic, 1985.
The Magic Book. New York, Atheneum, 1986.
Sugar Isn't Everything. New York, Atheneum, 1987.
Megan's Island. New York, Atheneum, 1988.
What Could Go Wrong? New York, Atheneum, 1989.
Nightmare. New York, Atheneum, 1989.

*

Manuscript Collection: Bowling Green University, Ohio.

Willo Davis Roberts comments:

My latest historical novel is *Madawaska*, a novel detailing the devastating experience of the Acadians, of French descent, the original settlers of Nova Scotia, when their families were split up and they were deported to distant parts of the world, many of them never to meet up again. The historicals *Elizabeth*, *Caroline*, and *Victoria*, though written for young girls, are read by many adults as they are written in the same style as my adult fiction.

*   *   *

The first quality which one recognizes in Willo Davis Roberts's work is her inclusion and perceptive descriptions of accident "victims" and/or health problems. The penchant and thoroughness of her depiction may be the result of her medical training. In any event this accuracy lends credibility to her facile, trim plots. The majority of her novels emphasize mystery-romance more than gothic. *Invitation to Evil*, *King's Pawn*, and *Shroud of Fog*, all deal with deadly danger, catenulate episodes leading up to the answer to "who did it." Many of her novels have New England settings, and Roberts appears well-versed in this topography, placing the novels in remote areas. The elements of mystery are straightforward and unruffled: a concubitant heroine meets a hero with more than an abundance of panache, usually a man of almost superhuman indestructibility. Physical suffering in proportions excelling what mere mortals could endure occurs during the plot development. Events that at first seem tangentially related become part of the not-too-complicated interplay.

The heroine in *King's Pawn* continually and desperately needs to be reassured, assuming a volitionless capacity and eagerness to believe in the hero after the crises she endures; kidnapping, a fall from the tower into the ocean, etc. This is a plausible re-

sponse, therefore, and she never becomes the awe-inspiring blank found in the heroines of many other romance novelists' pages. Indeed, the pain which the heroine suffers is vividly described, forcing the reader to explore and experience the discomfort with the victim. The graphic detail enables the reader to excuse the air of the miraculous which surrounds her survival.

A problem encountered frequently in her novels is her too hastily drawn conclusions in which all the sources of tension are conveniently reconciled. The abrupt endings are particularly disturbing in light of the otherwise well-constructed exposition.

Although her conclusions are often a disappointment, the reader can nonetheless be caught up in Roberts's love of the mystery.

—W. M. von Zharen

ROBINS, Denise (Naomi, née Klein). Also writes as Denise Chesterton; Ashley French; Harriet Gray; Hervey Hamilton; Julia Kane; Francesca Wright. British. Born in London, 1 February 1897. Educated at schools in Staten Island, New York, and San Diego, and at The Convent, Upper Norwood, London. Married 1) Arthur Robins in 1918 (divorced 1938), three daughters, including Claire Lorrimer, *q.v.*; 2) R. O'Neill Pearson in 1939. Journalist, Dundee *Courier*, Scotland, 1914–15, then freelance writer, broadcaster, and journalist. After 1945 editor of the advice column, *She* magazine, London. Founding member, 1960, and President, 1960–66, Romantic Novelists Association. *Died 1 May 1985*.

ROMANCE AND HISTORICAL PUBLICATIONS

Novels

The Marriage Bond. London, Hodder and Stoughton, 1924.
Sealed Lips. London, Hodder and Stoughton, 1924.
The Forbidden Bride. London, Newnes, 1926.
The Man Between. London, Newnes, 1926.
The Passionate Awakening. London, Newnes, 1926.
Forbidden Love. London, Newnes, 1927.
The Inevitable End. London, Mills and Boon, 1927.
Jonquil. London, Mills and Boon, 1927.
The Triumph of the Rat. London, Philip Allan, 1927.
Desire Is Blind. London, Mills and Boon, 1928.
The Passionate Flame. London, Mills and Boon, 1928.
White Jade. London, Mills and Boon, 1928.
Women Who Seek. London, Mills and Boon, 1928.
The Dark Death. London, Mills and Boon, 1929.
The Enduring Flame. London, Mills and Boon, 1929; New York, Ballantine, 1975.
Heavy Clay. London, Mills and Boon, 1929.
Love Was a Jest. London, Mills and Boon, 1929.
And All Because. . . . London, Mills and Boon, 1930; as *Love's Victory*, New York, Watt, 1933.
It Wasn't Love. London, Mills and Boon, 1930.
Swing of Youth. London, Mills and Boon, 1930.
Heat Wave: The Story of the Play by Roland Pertwee. London, Mills and Boon, 1930.
Crowns, Pounds, and Guineas. London, Mills and Boon, 1931; as *The Wild Bird*, New York, Watt, 1932.
Fever of Love. London, Mills and Boon, 1931.
Lovers of Janine. London, Mills and Boon, 1931.

Second Best. London, Mills and Boon, 1931; New York, Watt, 1933.

Blaze of Love. London, Mills and Boon, 1932.

The Boundary Line. London, Mills and Boon, and New York, Watt, 1932.

The Secret Hour. London, Mills and Boon, 1932.

There Are Limits. London, Mills and Boon, 1932; as *No Sacrifice*, New York, Watt, 1934.

Gay Defeat. London, Mills and Boon, 1933.

Life's a Game. London, Mills and Boon, 1933.

Men Are Only Human. London, Mills and Boon, and New York, Macaulay, 1933.

Shatter the Sky. London, Mills and Boon, 1933.

Strange Rapture. London, Mills and Boon, 1933.

Brief Ecstasy. London, Mills and Boon, 1934; New York, Ballantine, 1976.

Never Give All. London, Mills and Boon, and New York, Macaulay, 1934.

Slave-Woman. London, Mills and Boon, 1934; New York, Macaulay, 1935.

Sweet Love. London, Mills and Boon, 1934.

All This for Love. London, Mills and Boon, 1935.

Climb to the Stars. London, Nicholson and Watson, 1935.

How Great the Price. London, Mills and Boon, 1935.

Life and Love. London, Nicholson and Watson, 1935; New York, Avon, 1978.

Murder in Mayfair (novelization of play). London, Mills and Boon, 1935.

Love Game. London, Nicholson and Watson, 1936.

Those Who Love. London, Nicholson and Watson, 1936.

Were I Thy Bride. London, Nicholson and Watson, 1936; New York, Pyramid, 1966; as *Betrayal*, London, Hodder and Stoughton, 1976.

Kiss of Youth. London, Nicholson and Watson, 1937; New York, Avon, 1975.

Set Me Free. London, Nicholson and Watson, 1937.

The Tiger in Men. London, Nicholson and Watson, 1937; New York, Avon, 1979.

The Woman's Side of It. London, Nicholson and Watson, 1937.

Family Holiday (as Hervey Hamilton). London, Nicholson and Watson, 1937.

Restless Heart. London, Nicholson and Watson, 1938; New York, Arcadia House, 1940.

Since We Love. London, Nicholson and Watson, 1938; New York, Arcadia House, 1941.

You Have Chosen. London, Nicholson and Watson, 1938; New York, Ballantine, 1975.

Dear Loyalty. London, Nicholson and Watson, 1939.

Gypsy Lover. London, Nicholson and Watson, 1939.

I, Too, Have Loved. London, Nicholson and Watson, 1939; New York, Avon, 1979.

Officer's Wife. London, Nicholson and Watson, 1939.

Island of Flowers. London, Nicholson and Watson, 1940; New York, Avon, 1977.

Little We Know. London, Hutchinson, 1940.

Sweet Sorrow. London, Nicholson and Watson, 1940; as *Forget That I Remember*, New York, Arcadia House, 1940.

To Love Is to Live. London, Hutchinson, 1940.

If This Be Destiny. London, Hutchinson, 1941.

Set the Stars Alight. London, Hutchinson, 1941; New York, Avon, 1979.

Winged Love. London, Hutchinson, 1941; New York, Avon, 1978.

Love Is Enough. London, Hutchinson, 1941; New York, Avon, 1975.

This One Night. London, Hutchinson, 1942; New York, Avon, 1975.

War Marriage. London, Hutchinson, 1942; as *Let Me Love*, London, Hodder and Stoughton, 1979.

What Matters Most. London, Hutchinson, 1942.

The Changing Years. London, Hutchinson, 1943; New York, Beagle, 1974.

Daughter Knows Best. London, Hutchinson, 1943.

Dust of Dreams. London, Hutchinson, 1943; New York, Avon, 1976.

Escape to Love. London, Hutchinson, 1943; New York, Avon, 1976.

This Spring of Love. London, Hutchinson, 1943.

War Changes Everything. London, Todd, 1943.

Give Me Back My Heart. London, Hutchinson, 1944; New York, Avon, 1976.

How to Forget. London, Hutchinson, 1944.

Never Look Back. London, Hutchinson, 1944.

Desert Rapture. London, Hutchinson, 1945; New York, Avon, 1979.

Love So Young. London, Hutchinson, 1945.

All for You. London, Hutchinson, 1946; New York, Ballantine, 1975.

Heart's Desire. London, Foster, 1946.

Greater Than All. London, Hutchinson, 1946.

Separation. London, Foster, 1946.

The Story of Veronica. London, Hutchinson, 1946.

Figs in Frost (as Hervey Hamilton). London, Macdonald, 1946.

Forgive Me, My Love. Hanley, Staffordshire, Docker, 1947.

More Than Love. London, Hutchinson, 1947.

Could I Forget. London, Hutchinson, 1948; New York, Avon, 1976.

Khamsin. London, Hutchinson, 1948; New York, Avon, 1978.

Love Me No More! London, Hutchinson, 1948.

The Hard Way. London, Hutchinson, 1949.

To Love Again. London, Hutchinson, 1949; Toronto, Harlequin, 1961.

The Uncertain Heart. London, Hutchinson, 1949; New York, Avon, 1977.

The Feast Is Finished. London, Hutchinson, 1950; New York, Avon, 1979.

Love Hath an Island. London, Hutchinson, 1950.

Heart of Paris. London, Hutchinson, 1951.

Infatuation. London, Hutchinson, 1951.

Only My Dreams. London, Hutchinson, 1951; New York, Avon, 1976.

Second Marriage. London, Hutchinson, 1951; New York, Avon, 1979.

Something to Love. London, Hutchinson, 1951.

The Other Love. London, Hutchinson, 1952.

Strange Meeting. London, Hutchinson, 1952.

The First Long Kiss. London, Hutchinson, 1953; New York, Avon, 1976.

My True Love. London, Hutchinson, 1953; New York, Avon, 1977.

The Loves of Lucrezia (as Francesca Wright). London, Rich and Cowan, 1953; New York, Popular Library, 1954.

The Long Shadow. London, Hutchinson, 1954; New York, Avon, 1979.

Venetian Rhapsody. London, Hutchinson, 1954; New York, Avon, 1979.

Bitter-Sweet. London, Hutchinson, 1955.

The Unshaken Loyalty. London, Hutchinson, 1955.

All That Matters. London, Hutchinson, 1956.

The Enchanted Island. London, Hutchinson, 1956; New York, Avon, 1974.

The Seagull's Cry. London, Hutchinson, 1957; New York, Avon, 1979.

The Noble One. London, Hodder and Stoughton, 1957.

Chateau of Flowers. London, Hodder and Stoughton, 1958.

Do Not Go, My Love. London, Hodder and Stoughton, 1959; New York, Ballantine, 1974.

We Two Together. London, Hodder and Stoughton, 1959.

The Unlit Fire. London, Hodder and Stoughton, 1960.

Arrow in the Heart. London, Hodder and Stoughton, 1960.

I Should Have Known. London, Hodder and Stoughton, 1961.

A Promise for Ever. London, Hodder and Stoughton, 1961.

Put Back the Clock. London, Hodder and Stoughton, 1962; New York, Pyramid, 1967.

Mad Is the Heart. London, Hodder and Stoughton, 1963.

Nightingale's Song. London, Hodder and Stoughton, 1963; New York, Pyramid, 1966.

Reputation. London, Hodder and Stoughton, 1963.

Meet Me in Monte Carlo. London, Arrow, 1964; New York, Avon, 1979.

Moment of Love. London, Hodder and Stoughton, 1964; New York, Pyramid, 1966.

Loving and Giving. London, Hodder and Stoughton, 1965; New York, Ballantine, 1975.

The Strong Heart. London, Hodder and Stoughton, 1965.

O Love! O Fire! London, Panther, 1966.

Lightning Strikes Twice. London, Hodder and Stoughton, 1966.

The Crash. London, Hodder and Stoughton, 1966.

Wait for Tomorrow. London, Hodder and Stoughton, 1967.

House of the Seventh Cross. London, Hodder and Stoughton, 1967; as *House by the Watch Tower*, New York, Arcadia House, 1968.

Laurence, My Love. London, Hodder and Stoughton, 1968.

Love and Desire and Hate. London, Hodder and Stoughton, 1969.

A Love Like Ours. London, Hodder and Stoughton, 1969; New York, Ballantine, 1976.

She-Devil: The Story of Jezebel (as Francesca Wright). London, Corgi, 1970; revised edition, as *Jezebel* (as Denise Robins), London, Hodder and Stoughton, 1977.

Sweet Cassandra. London, Hodder and Stoughton, 1970.

Forbidden. London, Hodder and Stoughton, 1971.

The Snow Must Return. London, Hodder and Stoughton, 1971.

The Other Side of Love. London, Hodder and Stoughton, 1973; New York, Ballantine, 1975.

Twice Have I Loved. London, Hodder and Stoughton, 1973; New York, Ballantine, 1975.

Dark Corridor. London, Hodder and Stoughton, 1974.

Come Back Yesterday. London, Hodder and Stoughton, 1976.

Fauna (omnibus). New York, Avon, 1978.

Novels as Ashley French

Once Is Enough. London, Hutchinson, 1953.

The Bitter Core. London, Hutchinson, 1954.

Breaking Point. London, Hutchinson, 1956; as Denise Robins, New York, Bantam, 1975.

Novels as Harriet Gray

Gold for the Gay Masters. London, Rich and Cowan, 1954; New York, Avon, 1956.

Bride of Doom. London, Rich and Cowan, 1956; as *Bride of Violence*, New York, Avon, 1957.

The Flame and the Frost. London, Rich and Cowan, 1957; in *Fauna* (as Denise Robins), 1978.

Dance in the Dust. London, Hale, 1959; as Denise Robins, New York, Avon, 1978.

My Lady Destiny. London, Hale, 1961; as Denise Robins, New York, Avon, 1978.

Novels as Denise Chesterton

Two Loves. London, Merit, 1955; as Denise Robins, New York, Bantam, 1975.

The Price of Folly. London, Merit, 1955.

When a Woman Loves. London, Merit, 1955.

Novels as Julia Kane

Dark Secret Love. London, Hodder and Stoughton, 1962.

The Sin Was Mine. London, Hodder and Stoughton, 1964.

Time Runs Out. London, Hodder and Stoughton, 1965.

Short Stories

One Night in Ceylon and Others. London, Mills and Boon, 1931.

Light the Candles. London, Hurst and Blackett, 1959.

OTHER PUBLICATIONS

Play

Light the Candles, with Michael Pertwee, adaptation of the story by Robins. London, English Theatre Guild, 1957.

Verse

Love Poems and Others. London, Mills and Boon, 1930.

Other

Stranger Than Fiction: Denise Robins Tells Her Life Story. London, Hodder and Stoughton, 1965.

Editor, *The World of Romance* (anthology). London, New English Library, 1964.

*   *   *

Denise Robins is worth noting not just for her prolificity in writing around 170 novels in over 50 years, but for the variety of subject and character treatment she has produced within this genre. Most of her books concentrate on the contemporary love story, and she has exploited nearly every conceivable situation both inside and outside marriage. Even in her early works, the often taboo subjects of divorce and extra-marital relationships are handled with care and sensitivity, as in the poignant *More Than Love*, in which a young girl tells of her affair with a married man, and all the problems such a relationship incurs. Both *Put Back the Clock* and *The Crash* concern marriage on the rebound; *The Bitter Core* deals with the marriage of a woman in her forties to a much younger man; *Give Me Back My Heart* is about an arranged marriage and the girl's struggle to marry the man of her choice; while *O Love! O Fire!* introduces the moral dilemma facing Candy, who, after much heart-searching, sleeps with her boyfriend, only to become pregnant and bear his child while realizing gradually that her love was mere infatuation. Another controversial topic, even today, that of a mother leaving her children with their father, is the theme of both *Figs in Frost* and *Once Is Enough*. The latter tells of a mother's attempts to see her daughter against her estranged husband's will; her mental anguish, the child's bewilderment at being the centre of the struggle, and the subsequent, inevitable tragedy are all movingly described. Occasionally the fast-moving plots sport equal measures of suspense and romance, as in the strong and passionate drama *Heat Wave*, set in Malaya.

The characters and settings are equally as varied as the themes. The central protagonists range in age from 18 to the mid-forties, and vary considerably in temperament and social background; they are treated in reasonable depth, changed for good or bad by the physical and emotional experiences they undergo. The settings of the novels embrace the streets of London, fashionable Paris, the Swiss mountains, and more exotic places such as Egypt, Ceylon, and Morocco, described with just enough authenticity to imbue the story with their particular flavour; sometimes a place is set more firmly in the memory, like the Chateau de Lurmines in *The Snow Must Return*. The character of each decade of the 20th century can also be seen over the range of her novels, especially in fashion details, the intrusion of World War II, the slowly changing attitudes towards divorce and infidelity, and the freedom of women in particular regarding careers and financial and moral independence, and the author keeps up-to-date with both social and political scenes in order to give each novel a realistic touch.

Denise Robins has also produced five historical romances under the pseudonym Harriet Gray. *Gold for the Gay Master*, *Bride of Doom*, and *The Flame and the Frost* make up a trilogy set in the late Georgian and early Victorian periods, tracing the history of a beautiful quadroon slave and her descendants. The stories are well punctuated with dramatic climaxes, moving fast and furiously against a rich backcloth of elaborately painted characters and settings. The two fictional biographies about Lucrezia Borgia and Jezebel, written under the name Francesca Wright, are highly embellished accounts, but equally well filled with drama, romance, and excitement. Of her two collections of short stories, *One Night in Ceylon and Others* is by far the stronger work, with each tale a swift, vigorous slice of life, often with a neat, unexpected twist at the end, as in "Perfectly Acted," "This Is Marriage," and the title story.

Although with such a vast output some of her work is bound to be slighter in form, lacking pace, less well worked-out, and with weaker characterization, Robins writes with a smooth, firm confidence gained from years of consistent popularity; plot and sub-plot move rapidly in a polished flow across the page, the various entanglements neatly resolving to a happy climax, with the passions of both young and old relayed with a sympathy born of experience and observation.

—Tessa Rose Chester

ROBINS, Patricia. See **LORRIMER, Claire.**

ROBY, Mary Linn. Also writes as Pamela D'Arcy; Georgina Grey; Elizabeth Welles; Mary Wilson. American. Born in Bangor, Maine, 31 March 1930. Educated at the University of Maine, Orono, B.A. 1951 (Phi Beta Kappa). Married Kinley E. Roby in 1951; two children. History teacher at State College High School, Pennsylvania, and Orono High School. Since 1972

English teacher, Concord/Carlisle High School, Massachusetts. Address: c/o Dell, 666 Fifth Avenue, New York, New York 10103, U.S.A.

ROMANCE AND HISTORICAL PUBLICATIONS

Novels

Still as the Grave. New York, Dodd Mead, 1964; London, Collins, 1965.
Afraid of the Dark. New York, Dodd Mead, 1965.
Before I Die. London, Hale, 1966.
Cat and Mouse. London, Hale, 1967.
In the Dead of the Night. New York, New American Library, 1969.
Pennies on Her Eyes. New York, New American Library, 1969.
All Your Lovely Words Are Spoken. New York, Ace, 1970.
Some Die in Their Beds. New York, New American Library, 1970.
If She Should Die. New York, New American Library, 1970.
Lie Quiet in Your Grave. New York, New American Library, 1970.
That Fatal Touch. New York, New American Library, 1970.
Dig a Narrow Grave. New York, New American Library, 1971.
This Land Turns Evil Slowly. New York, New American Library, 1971.
Reap the Whirlwind. New York, New American Library, 1972.
And Die Remembering. New York, New American Library, 1972.
When the Witch Is Dead. New York, New American Library, 1972.
The White Peacock. New York, Hawthorn, 1972; as *The Cry of the Peacock*, Aylesbury, Buckinghamshire, Milton House, 1974.
Shadow over Grove House. New York, New American Library, 1973.
Speak No Evil of the Dead. New York, New American Library, 1973.
The House at Kilgallen. New York, New American Library, 1973.
The Broken Key. New York, Hawthorn, 1973; Aylesbury, Buckinghamshire, Milton House, 1974.
Marsh House. New York, Hawthorn, 1974; London, Milton House, 1975.
The Tower Room. New York, Hawthorn, 1974; London, Milton House, 1975.
The Silent Walls. New York, New American Library, 1974.
Christobel. New York, Berkley, 1976.
The Treasure Chest. New York, Berkley, 1976.
Seagull Crag (as Elizabeth Welles). New York, Pocket Books, 1977.
The Hidden Book. New York, Berkley, 1977.
Trapped. New York, Dell, 1977.
A Heritage of Strangers. New York, Dell, 1978.
Fortune's Smile. New York, Warner, 1979.
My Lady's Mask. New York, Warner, 1979.
Passing Fancy. New York, Dell, 1980.
Love's Wilful Call. New York, Warner, 1981.

Novels as Mary Wilson

The Changeling. New York, Dell, 1975.
Wind of Death. New York, Dell, 1976.

Novels as Georgina Grey

The Hesitant Heir. New York, Fawcett, 1978.
Turn of the Cards. New York, Fawcett, 1979.
Both Sides of the Coin. New York, Fawcett, 1980.
Fashion's Frown. New York, Fawcett, 1980.
Franklin's Folly. New York, Fawcett, 1980.
The Last Cotillion. New York, Fawcett, 1980.
The Bartered Bridegroom. New York, Fawcett, 1981.
The Queen's Quadrille. New York, Fawcett, 1981.
The Reluctant Rivals. New York, Fawcett, 1981.

Novels as Pamela D'Arcy

Angel in the House. New York, Berkley, 1980.
Heritage of the Heart. New York, Berkley, 1980.
Magic Moment. New York, Berkley, 1980.

                    *   *   *

Whether she is writing a contemporary gothic of a historical romance, Mary Linn Roby manages to produce a competent, if not exceptional, novel.

Her gothics have all the required ingredients: brooding manors, danger and murder, complicated personal relationships (at least one of which will obviously lead to love), and last minute denouements. *The Tower Room* is a good example of Roby's gothic formula. Family and acquaintances gather in an isolated cliffside castle. An autocratic old woman manipulates those around her, reviving old memories and reopening old wounds. Several murders take place and the young heroine finds herself in danger. Everyone is under suspicion, although the reader obviously knows that the hero and heroine are innocent. The tangled plot is gradually unraveled, the true villain revealed, and justice quickly and efficiently served.

Like her gothics, Roby's Regency romances can be viewed as good representatives of the prevailing formula for the genre. Bright, independent heroines and steadfast heroes overcome numerous obstacles to find true love and happiness. Roby does show one common theme or motif in these romances: the stage or the roles and impersonations carried out by the characters. A major stumbling block to Jennifer's happiness in *Passing Fancy* is the deception practiced by the Earl of Watching when he poses as the less important Sir John Evans. In *Love's Wilful Call* Hannah struggles to follow her father's footsteps in the theatre, yet when she reaches her goal she realizes that she really yearns more for the love of Lord Derwent. Roby brings both themes together in *My Lady's Mask.* Caroline plays the role of a great society lady and becomes involved with several theatre people, most notably the playwright, Lord Troyan, to whom she loses her heart. In spite of many difficulties encountered by the characters, Roby manages to end all of these novels in a happy spate of engagements and weddings. In the category of happy endings, however, few novels can beat *Fortune's Smile*, in which Roby provides at least four engagements and hints at two more to come, all in the final two chapters. Everyone is provided with a satisfactory partner.

As an author of both gothic novels and historical romances, Roby knows the conventions. She includes all the right elements, and the results are enjoyable but lack that extra spark that puts an author's work in the first rank.

—Barbara E. Kemp

ROCKFERN, Danielle. See **NOLAN, Frederick.**

                    _____

ROGERS, Rosemary (née Jansz). American. Born in Panadura, Ceylon, 7 December 1932. Educated at the University of Ceylon, Colombo, B.A. Married 1) Summa Navaratnam (divorced), two daughters; 2) Leroy Rogers (divorced), two sons. Feature writer and information officer, Associated Newspapers of Ceylon, Colombo, 1959–62; secretary, Travis Air Force Base, California, 1964–69, and Solano County Parks Department, Fairfield, California, 1969–74. Formerly reporter, Fairfield *Daily Republic.* Address: c/o Ballantine Books Inc., 201 East 50th Street, New York, New York 10022, U.S.A.

ROMANCE AND HISTORICAL PUBLICATIONS

Novels (series: Ginny Brandon and Steve Morgan)

Sweet Savage Love (Brandon and Morgan). New York, Avon, 1974; London, Futura, 1977.
The Wildest Heart. New York, Avon, 1974; London, Futura, 1978.
Dark Fires (Brandon and Morgan). New York, Avon, 1975; London, Futura, 1977.
Wicked Loving Lies. New York, Avon, 1976; London, Futura, 1977.
The Crowd Pleasers. New York, Avon, 1978; revised edition, 1980.
The Insiders. New York, Avon, and London, Futura, 1979.
Lost Love, Last Love (Brandon and Morgan). New York, Avon, 1980.
Love Play. New York, Avon, 1981; London, Sphere, 1982.
Surrender to Love. New York, Avon, 1982; London, Corgi, 1985.
The Wanton. New York, Avon, 1983; London, Corgi, 1985.
Bound by Desire (Brandon and Morgan). New York, Avon, and London, Century, 1988.

                    *

Rosemary Rogers comments.

I write the kind of books I would like to read, both historical and contemporary.

                    *   *   *

In 1974 Avon published Rosemary Rogers's first swashbuckling tale of passion, *Sweet Savage Love*, an historical novel whose title gave a name to an entire genre. In this novel and those that followed, the respective heroines are ravished by an assortment of men, and suffer slavery, torture (but nothing that mars their breathtaking beauty), and a host of other horrors that would devastate the normal human female. These ladies, however, always emerge triumphant with the man they have loved and hated for approximately 600 pages. The typical Rogers heroine is lovely and ardently desired by every man who meets her. She thinks of herself as willful and independent but then develops a spine of jelly when forced into the arms of the hero.

The male protagonist in hot pursuit of the maiden (which she usually is for the first few pages) must be virile, handsome, well educated or at least highly intelligent, but most of all must have a certain savagery in his lovemaking. Inevitably the heroine's innocence is taken from her by this male animal, who releases in her body an unimaginable passion. Heights of fulfillment the average person may never experience are reached again and again whenever the sweet/savage lovers copulate. The passages depicting this sexual ecstasy leave little to the imagination, but the language, however explicit, is rarely coarse.

Rogers's early works, such as *Sweet Savage Love*, *The Wildest Heart* and *Wicked Loving Lies*, are typical of the novels known in the publishing trade as "bodice busters." Set in the 19th century, the hero and heroine fight and bed their way across Europe and the American West. From the descriptions of the countryside and its inhabitants, it is apparent that Rogers knows this era of European and American history. All this is convincing background to what one book jacket described as "a tale of unquenched desire . . . united in a blaze of undying passion and infinite love." This quite accurately captures the essence of a Rogers novel. In *Sweet Savage Love* Ginny Brandon and Steve Morgan, traveling through Texas and Mexico, leave a fiery trail of passion, hate, lust, and ultimately love. But this is only the beginning of their story. They must pursue and torment each other through two more novels—*Dark Fires* and *Lost Love, Last Love*. In all of these stories Ginny and Steve separate (because of some absurd misunderstanding) and again and again go through the hate-lust-love routine. Meanwhile, each has tried to find consolation in the arms of different lovers, but their desire for one another cannot be quenched.

Rogers has also written novels with contemporary settings, although the basic sweet/savage theme remains. In *The Crowd Pleasers* a young and aristocratic actress/model becomes reluctantly involved with Webb Carnahan, an earthy, dominant male with a hint of cruelty. *Love Play* has the virginal and very uptight British Sara agreeing to impersonate her younger, outrageously liberated American half-sister, Delight. This permits Sara to elope with her rich boyfriend and to escape the evil clutches of his older brother, Marco. Sara and Marco quickly become antagonists, although their mutual lust often infringes upon their interminable arguing.

Though the novels with modern day settings sold well, it is Rogers's historical novels that have proven to be the more popular. *The Wanton* is the story of Trista, a young woman who disguises herself as a man in order to become a doctor, lives through the horrors of the Civil War, and is alternately loved and hated by the handsome Blaze Davenan. *Surrender To Love*, which begins in the exotic locale of Ceylon, tells the passionate adventures of Alexa and Nicolas. And recently, *Bound by Desire* continues the saga of Ginny and Steve through the adventures of their daughter, the ravishingly beautiful Laura, who finds fulfillment, sexual and otherwise, in the strong arms of Trent Challenger.

It is true that all of these novels follow a predictable pattern yet, the plots are often intricate and imaginative, and are built on a foundation of vivid, often witty dialogue. Intrigue of some sort usually surrounds the protagonists, throwing them together, then flinging them apart. But incredible good fortune always brings the lovers together for a passionate and searing conclusion. Love stories with a sado-masochistic touch have made Rogers one of today's most popular romance writers.

—Patricia Altner

ROME, Margaret. British. Married; one son. Address: c/o Mills and Boon Ltd., 18–24 Paradise Road, Richmond, Surrey TW9 1SR, England.

ROMANCE AND HISTORICAL PUBLICATIONS

Novels

The Lottery for Matthew Devlin. London, Mills and Boon, 1968.

The Marriage of Caroline Lindsay. London, Mills and Boon, 1968; Toronto, Harlequin, 1974.

A Chance to Win. Toronto, Harlequin, 1969.

Flower of the Marsh. London, Mills and Boon, 1969.

Man of Fire. London, Mills and Boon, 1970; Toronto, Harlequin, 1974.

Bird of Paradise. London, Mills and Boon, 1970; Toronto, Harlequin, 1973.

Chateau of Flowers. London, Mills and Boon, 1971; Toronto, Harlequin, 1972.

The Girl at Eagles' Mount. London, Mills and Boon, 1971; Toronto, Harlequin, 1973.

Bride of the Rif. London, Mills and Boon, and Toronto, Harlequin, 1972.

Island of Pearls. London, Mills and Boon, 1973; Toronto, Harlequin, 1974.

The Bartered Bride. London, Mills and Boon, 1973; Toronto, Harlequin, 1975.

Palace of the Hawk. London, Mills and Boon, 1974; Toronto, Harlequin, 1975.

Valley of Paradise. Toronto, Harlequin, 1975.

Cove of Promises. London, Mills and Boon, 1975; Toronto, Harlequin, 1976.

The Girl at Dane's Dyke. London, Mills and Boon, and Toronto, Harlequin, 1975.

Adam's Rib. London, Mills and Boon, and Toronto, Harlequin, 1976.

Bride of Zarco. London, Mills and Boon, 1976; Toronto, Harlequin, 1977.

Lion of Venice. London, Mills and Boon, 1977; Toronto, Harlequin, 1978.

The Thistle and the Rose. London, Mills and Boon, and Toronto, Harlequin, 1977.

Son of Adam. London, Mills and Boon, 1978.

Castle of the Fountains. London, Mills and Boon, 1979; Toronto, Harlequin, 1982.

Champagne Spring. London, Mills and Boon, 1979; Toronto, Harlequin, 1980.

Isle of Calypso. London, Mills and Boon, 1979.

Marriage by Capture. London, Mills and Boon, 1980.

Miss High and Mighty. London, Mills and Boon, 1980; Toronto, Harlequin, 1981.

The Wild Man. London, Mills and Boon, 1980; Toronto, Harlequin, 1981.

Second-Best Bride. London, Mills and Boon, and Toronto, Harlequin, 1981.

Castle in Spain. London, Mills and Boon, 1981; Toronto, Harlequin, 1982.

King Kielder. London, Mills and Boon, 1981; Toronto, Harlequin, 1982.

Rapture of the Deep. London, Mills and Boon, 1982; Toronto, Harlequin, 1983.

Valley of Gentians. London, Mills and Boon, and Toronto, Harlequin, 1982.

Lord of the Land. London, Mills and Boon, and Toronto, Harlequin, 1983.

Castle of the Lion. London, Mills and Boon, 1983.

*   *   *

Margaret Rome is an English writer of romance fiction who has been widely published for a number of years. Apparently her own restlessness and curiosity led her in search of change and new experience. She often held jobs such as waitress, theatre usher, office and shop assistant, but all became such humdrum day-in-and-day-out events that eventually she turned to writing to express herself fully. Whatever the cause, however, Rome has her own way of creating enjoyable stories, She is able to develop well-rounded, believable characters that go beyond the stereotype "romance" image. Her female characters reflect their background, and they grow from their past and their own inner beliefs.

Fleur, in *Chateau of Flowers*, is the only child of an elderly couple, her father being a minister. She is a gentle, giving child who marries a blind man because he needs her, aware even as she does so that he does not love her. She travels to his home in the south of France where perfume is made and faces constant inner turmoil because of Alain's inability to accept his blindness.

Tina Donnelly (*Man of Fire*) joins a botanical expedition into the unexplored parts of the Amazon basin in search of rare plant specimens. She does this in spite of the fact that she is deathly afraid of the jungle; to make the situation worse, she must substitute for her aunt who has injured herself.

Finally, there is Sara Battle (*Bride of the Rif*) who swears revenge against Señor Felipe de Panza who has accused her grandfather of cheating at cards. She pretends to be in love with his nephew, Alvarso de Leon, and is presented to the family as his "close friend." In order to prevent any closer ties between the nephew and Sara, Felipe kidnaps Sara, takes her to the area of Morocco where the Rifs live, and goes through a marriage ceremony with her.

Dominating characteristics of sensitivity, courage and, most of all, true femininity are illustrated in all of her female characters. She portrays her heroines especially well in situations where modern concepts of morals or social standards are being advocated or substituted for older ideals, so that the heroine faces more than the usual obstacles before she discovers her heart. Often she is placed in a position of accepting, or seeming to accept, the current "social standard"; yet, she herself clings to a firm belief in older, virtuous ideals. Frequently she is misunderstood by the man she falls in love with because of her seemingly modern outlook and not until nearly the end of the story does it become evident that, for all of her surface sophistication, she is still a naive and virtuous girl. In fact, her sometimes prickly attitudes and flippant manners are her form of self-protection in a world she can't feel comfortable in, but must deal with.

Rome's male characters stand out equally well as they display masculine qualities that balance and temper those of her heroines. All are just enough older to insure a greater degree of sophistication. Their experience helps in letting them understand the real persons the heroines try to hide, and makes it possible for them to see beneath the surface. While most are wealthy, they yet are people of authority who work. Arrogant maleness is tempered with flashes of gentleness and tenderness that show a balanced, assured man of the world. They usually possess all the traits that women instinctively seek—that is, strength, decisiveness, and most of all, a belief in their own abilities to guide their own lives and those of their loved ones.

If Rome's characters are well presented, her plots and settings are equally interesting, since she lets her stories unfold against the background of the Amazon jungle, the exotic islands of Tahiti, or the canals of Venice. Detail of locale is skillfully woven throughout the stories and lends an added touch of realism. In fact, it is this variation of background that permits some of her plots to work. In both *Man of Fire* and *Bride of the Rif* the heroines must fight against physical difficulties as well as mental ones. Physical danger alone forces the heroine to cope with new emotions and experiences at a time when she has little reserves to call upon. Yet in each of her stories the heroine displays unexpected qualities of courage and determination to achieve her happiness.

Basically, Rome is a storyteller. She combines intriguing characters with very strong plots that keep her readers involved. She draws heavily on male/female encounters in such a way that conflict is immediate and sustaining. Finally, she brings those same qualities of curiosity and love of new experiences and adventures to her novels as she has to her own life.

—Arlene Moore

ROSS, Catherine. See **BEATY, Betty.**

ROSS, Helaine. See **DANIELS, Dorothy.**

ROTHMAN, Judith. See **PETERS, Maureen.**

ROWLAND, Iris. See **ROBERTS, Irene.**

ROWLANDS, Effie. See **ALBANESI, Madame.**

ROY, Brandon. See **BARCLAY, Florence L.**

ROYAL, Rosamund. See **SHERWOOD, Valerie.**

RUCK, Berta (Amy Roberta Ruck). British. Born in Murree, India, 2 August 1878. Educated at St. Winifred's School, Bangor, Wales; Lambeth School of Art, and Slade School of Art, both London; Calorossi's, Paris. Married Oliver Onions, *q.v.*, in 1909 (died 1961); two sons. *Died 11 August 1978.*

ROMANCE AND HISTORICAL PUBLICATIONS

Novels

His Official Fiancée. London, Hutchinson, and New York, Dodd Mead, 1914.

The Courtship of Rosamond Fayre. London, Hutchinson, 1915; as *The Wooing of Rosamond Fayre*, New York, Dodd Mead, 1915.

The Lad with Wings. London, Hutchinson, 1915; as *The Boy with Wings*, New York, Dodd Mead, 1915.

Miss Million's Maid. New York, Dodd Mead, 1915; London, Hutchinson, 1916.

The Girls at His Billet. London, Hutchinson, and New York, Dodd Mead, 1916.

In Another Girl's Shoes. New York, Dodd Mead, 1916; London, Hodder and Stoughton, 1917.

The Bridge of Kisses. London, Hutchinson, 1917; New York, Dodd Mead, 1920.

Three of Hearts. New York, Dodd Mead, 1917; London, Hodder and Stoughton, 1918.

The Girl Who Proposed! London, Hodder and Stoughton, 1918.

The Years for Rachel. London, Hodder and Stoughton, and New York, Dodd Mead, 1918.

Arabella the Awful. London, Hodder and Stoughton, 1918.

The Disturbing Charm. London, Hodder and Stoughton, and New York, Dodd Mead, 1919.

The Land-Girl's Love Story. London, Hodder and Stoughton, and New York, Dodd Mead, 1919.

The Wrong Mr. Right. London, Hodder and Stoughton, 1919; New York, Dodd Mead, 1922.

Sweethearts Unmet. New York, Dodd Mead, 1919; London, Hodder and Stoughton, 1922.

Sweet Stranger. London, Hodder and Stoughton, and New York, Dodd Mead, 1921.

The Arrant Rover. London, Hodder and Stoughton, and New York, Dodd Mead, 1921.

Under False Pretences. London, Hodder and Stoughton, 1922.

The Subconscious Courtship. London, Hodder and Stoughton, and New York, Dodd Mead, 1922.

The Bride Who Ran Away—Nurse Henderson. London, Hodder and Stoughton, 1922.

The Elopement of Eve and Prince Playfellow. London, Hodder and Stoughton, 1922.

Sir or Madam? London, Hutchinson, and New York, Dodd Mead, 1923.

The Dancing Star. London, Hodder and Stoughton, and New York, Dodd Mead, 1923.

The Clouded Pearl. London, Hodder and Stoughton, and New York, Dodd Mead, 1924.

The Leap Year Girl. New York, Dodd Mead, 1924.

Lucky in Love. London, Hodder and Stoughton, and New York, Dodd Mead, 1924.

Kneel to the Prettiest. London, Hodder and Stoughton, and New York, Dodd Mead, 1925.

The Immortal Girl. London, Hodder and Stoughton, and New York, Dodd Mead, 1925.

Her Pirate Partner. London, Hodder and Stoughton, 1926; New York, Dodd Mead, 1927.

The Pearl Thief. London, Hodder and Stoughton, and New York, Dodd Mead, 1926.

The Mind of a Minx. London, Hodder and Stoughton, and New York, Dodd Mead, 1927.

Money for One. London, Hodder and Stoughton, 1927; New York, Dodd Mead, 1928.

One of the Chorus. London, Hodder and Stoughton, 1928; as *Joy-Ride*, New York, Dodd Mead, 1929.

The Youngest Venus; or, The Love Story of a Plain Girl. London, Hodder and Stoughton, and New York, Dodd Mead, 1928.

The Unkissed Bride. London, Hodder and Stoughton, and New York, Dodd Mead, 1929.

To-day's Daughter. London, Hodder and Stoughton, 1929; New York, Dodd Mead, 1930.

Post-War Girl. London, Hutchinson, 1930.

Missing Girl. London, Cassell, 1930; as *The Love-Hater*, New York, Dodd Mead, 1930.

Offer of Marriage. London, Cassell, 1930; New York, Dodd Mead, 1931.

Forced Landing. London, Cassell, 1931.

Dance Partner. New York, Dodd Mead, 1931.

The Lap of Luxury. London, Cassell, 1931; New York, Dodd Mead, 1932.

This Year, Next Year, Sometime—. London, Cassell, and New York, Dodd Mead, 1932.

Sudden Sweetheart. London, Cassell, 1932; New York, Dodd Mead, 1933.

Understudy. London, Hodder and Stoughton, and New York, Dodd Mead, 1933.

Eleventh Hour Lover. London, Hutchinson, 1933.

Change Here for Happiness, Written Especially for Those Who Want Some Happy Hours—and a Change! London, Hodder and Stoughton, and New York, Dodd Mead, 1933.

The Best Time Ever. London, Hodder and Stoughton, and New York, Dodd Mead, 1934.

Sunburst. London, Hodder and Stoughton, and New York, Dodd Mead, 1934.

Sunshine-Stealer: The Story of a Cruise. London, Hodder and Stoughton, and New York, Dodd Mead, 1935.

A Star in Love. London, Hodder and Stoughton, and New York, Dodd Mead, 1935.

Spring Comes to Miss Lonely Heart. London, Hodder and Stoughton, 1936; as *Spring Comes*, New York, Dodd Mead, 1936.

Half-Past Kissing Time. London, Hodder and Stoughton, 1936; as *Sleeping Beauty*, New York, Dodd Mead, 1936.

Love on Second Thoughts. London, Hodder and Stoughton, 1936; New York, Dodd Mead, 1937.

Romance Royal. London, Hodder and Stoughton, and New York, Dodd Mead, 1937.

Love Comes Again Later. London, Hodder and Stoughton, and New York, Dodd Mead, 1938.

Handmaid to Fame. London, Hodder and Stoughton, 1938; New York, Dodd Mead, 1939.

Wedding March. London, Hodder and Stoughton, and New York, Dodd Mead, 1938.

Mock-Honeymoon. London, Mills and Boon, and New York, Dodd Mead, 1939.

Arabella Arrives. New York, Dodd Mead, 1939.

Out to Marry Money. London, Mills and Boon, 1940; as *It Was Left to Peter*, New York, Dodd Mead, 1940.

He Learnt about Women. London, Mills and Boon, 1940; as *He Learned about Women*, New York, Dodd Mead, 1940.

Pennies from Heaven. London, Mills and Boon, 1940; as *Money Isn't Everything*, New York, Dodd Mead, 1940; revised edition, as *Third Love Lucky*, London, Hurst and Blackett, 1958; as *Third Time Lucky*, Dodd Mead, 1958.

Fiancées Count as Relatives. London, Mills and Boon, 1941; as *Fiancées Are Relatives*, New York, Dodd Mead, 1941.

Jade Earrings. New York, Dodd Mead, 1941.

Waltz-Contest. London, Mills and Boon, and New York, Dodd Mead, 1941.

Spinster's Progress. London, Mills and Boon, and New York, Dodd Mead, 1942.

Quarrel and Kiss. London, Mills and Boon, 1942.

Footlight Fever. New York, Dodd Mead, 1942.

Bread-and-Grease-Paint. London, Hutchinson, 1943.

Shining Chance. London, Hutchinson, and New York, Dodd Mead, 1944.

Intruder Marriage. New York, Dodd Mead, 1944, and London, Hutchinson, 1945.

You Are the One. New York, Dodd Mead, 1945; London, Hutchinson, 1946.

Surprise Engagement. New York, Dodd Mead, 1946; London, Hutchinson, 1947.

Throw Away Yesterday. London, Hutchinson, and New York, Dodd Mead, 1946.

Tomboy in Lace. London, Hutchinson, and New York, Dodd Mead, 1947.

She Danced in the Ballet. New York, Dodd Mead, 1948; London, Hutchinson, 1949.

Love and Apron-Strings. London, Hutchinson, 1949; as *Gentle Tyrant*, New York, Dodd Mead, 1949.

Hopeful Journey. London, Hutchinson, 1950; as *Joyful Journey*, New York, Dodd Mead, 1950.

Love at a Festival. London, Hutchinson, and New York, Dodd Mead, 1951.

Song of the Lark. London, Hutchinson, 1951; as *The Rising of the Lark*, New York, Dodd Mead, 1951.

Spice of Life. London, Hutchinson, and New York, Dodd Mead, 1952.

Fantastic Holiday. London, Hutchinson, and New York, Dodd Mead, 1953.

Marriage Is a Blind Date. London, Hutchinson, 1953; as *Blind Date*, New York, Dodd Mead, 1953.

The Men in Her Life. London, Hutchinson, and New York, Dodd Mead, 1954.

We All Have Our Secrets. London, Hutchinson, and New York, Dodd Mead, 1955.

Romance in Two Keys. New York, Dodd Mead, 1955; as *Romance of a Film Star*, London, Hutchinson, 1956.

A Wish a Day. London, Hutchinson, and New York, Dodd Mead, 1956.

Admirer Unknown. New York, Dodd Mead, 1957.

Leap Year Love. London, Hurst and Blackett, 1957; as *Leap Year Romance*, New York, Dodd Mead, 1957.

Mystery Boy-Friend. London, Hutchinson, 1957.

Romantic Afterthought. London, Hurst and Blackett, and New York, Dodd Mead, 1959.

Love and a Rich Girl. London, Hurst and Blackett, and New York, Dodd Mead, 1960.

Sherry and the Ghosts. London, Hurst and Blackett, 1961; New York, Dodd Mead, 1962.

Diamond Engagement Ring. London, Hurst and Blackett, 1962.

Runaway Lovers. London, Hurst and Blackett, 1963.

Rendevous in Zagarella. London, Hurst and Blackett, 1964.

Shopping for a Husband. London, Hurst and Blackett, 1967.

Short Stories

Khaki and Kisses. London, Hutchinson, 1915.

The Great Unmet. New York, Harper's Bazaar, 1918.

Rufus on the Rebound. New York, Harper's Bazaar, 1918.

The Dream Domesticated. New York, Harper's Bazaar, 1918.

The Girl Who Was Too Good-Looking. London, Hodder and Stoughton, 1920.

The Post-War Girl and Other Stories. London, Hutchinson, 1922.

Wanted on the Voyage. London, Cassell, 1930.

OTHER PUBLICATIONS

Other

American Snap-Shots. New York, Dodd Mead, 1920.

The Berta Ruck Birthday Book, with Quotations. London, Hodder and Stoughton, and New York, Dodd Mead, 1920.

A Story-Teller Tells the Truth: Reminiscences and Notes. London, Hutchinson, 1935.

A Smile for the Past (autobiography). London, Hutchinson, 1959.

A Trickle of Welsh Blood. London, Hutchinson, 1967.

An Asset to Wales. London, Hutchinson, 1970.

Ancestral Voices. London, Hutchinson, 1972.

*   *   *

The Edwardian era is seen by many as a Golden Age of Romance, a time of gaiety, extravagance, luxury, and flamboyant wealth. Berta Ruck, who published the first of her many novels in 1914, used this background for a number of her stories. "The Edwardian dinner parties," she said recalling that time in a radio interview: "I've been to those . . . when I was very young and I don't think such things again exist . . . those long tables full of guests, and being 'taken in' to dinner. And the long skirts—skirt after skirt after skirt with perhaps a champagne cork caught in the flounce, you'd occasionally see. Masses of flowers—an absolute jungle of pink sweet peas and white gypsophila."

Ruck proved to be an adaptable writer, changing her background, and style according to the times in which she lived. *Arabella the Awful* (1918) is a simple, cheery little tale with some light-hearted satire on the aristocracy thrown in, and jokey references to the German's silliness, and the Englishman's bravery, and was clearly intended as a morale-raiser in time of war. In 1922 appeared a story with a nursing background, *The Bride Who Ran Away*. And, like so many romantic novelists, she too was lured by the desert: "That was, of course, one of those never-to-be-forgotten nights. The moon, instead of being silver, made everything amber and gold—the sands of the desert, I suppose—and the camels. Everything was so ageless." In the 1960's, she was up on the times as shown by *Shopping for a Husband*, a novel dedicated to Heather Jenner, a principal and founder of one of the country's largest marriage bureaux, and written about the seemingly unromantic topic of marriage bureau matches. Kate, on the shelf in her late twenties, and desperate for a marriage, is finally driven, as the title suggests, to go shopping for a husband. After working through numerous men on the bureau's books, she falls for a staggeringly rich north-country steel magnate, and proves that the services of a bureau can be as legitimate and wonderful a way of discovering true love as any more chancey, flash-in-the-pan meeting. As Heather Jenner, the bureau principal, explained in a book about modern marriage: "The whole social concept of marriage has changed, but a man still seeks a wife who fits in with his background and who comes of wholesome stock."

After 50 years of writing, the rather cloying, sickly-sweet, flavour of the earliest stories had given way to a quasi-stream of consciousness style, jerky and chatty, which leaves out finite verbs, definite articles and pronouns, while making the fullest possible use of upper case letters, unorthodox punctuation, and italics, sometimes entire paragraphs being italicised.

Her attitude to her work was optimistic. When accused of leaving out the "unpleasant realities" of life, she justified it like this:

> I belong to the School of Thought (the Non-Thinking School, if you like) that considers "compensating dream fiction," not as opiate, but as tonic, and prefers to leave the tale on a note definitely gay and hopeful. People condemn the story-teller's cheerfully tidied-up last chapters as the flight from reality. Personally I regard it as the entrance into the original real world.
>
> To the people who ask me why I can't face facts, I would suggest that it takes all kinds of facts to make a world; why should I not describe those I prefer? Why, people ask, do I falsify Life? Why, I ask, do they? I think it is very wrong to give Youth the impression that it is unalterably doomed to disappointment. *"C'est en croyant aux roses,"* says a French proverb, *"qu'on les fait éclore."* It is by believing in roses that one brings them into bloom . . .
>
> It is my creed that the world was created to go merry as a marriage-bell and for the whole human race to be healthy, wealthy and wise enough to be happy on all cylinders.

—Rachel Anderson

RUNDLE, Anne. See **MANNERS, Alexandra.**

RYAN, Rachel. See **BROWN, Sandra.**

RYBOT, Doris. See **PONSONBY, D.A.**

SABATINI, Rafael. British. Born in Jesi, Italy, 29 April 1875. Educated at Ecole Cantonale, Zoug, Switzerland, and in Oporto, Portugal. Served in the War Office Intelligence Department during World War I. Married 1) Ruth Goad Dixon in 1905 (divorced); 2) Christine Dixon in 1935. Lived in Clifford, Herefordshire. *Died 13 February 1950.*

ROMANCE AND HISTORICAL PUBLICATIONS

Novels (series: Captain Blood)

The Lovers of Yvonne. London, Pearson, 1902; as *The Suitors of Yvonne*, New York, Putnam, 1902.
The Tavern Knight. London, Richards, 1904; Boston, Houghton Mifflin, 1927.
Bardelys the Magnificent. London, Nash, 1906; Boston, Houghton Mifflin, 1923.
The Trampling of the Lilies. London, Hutchinson, 1906; Boston, Houghton Mifflin, 1924.

Love-at-Arms. London, Hutchinson, 1907; Boston, Houghton Mifflin, 1924.
The Shame of Molly. London, Hutchinson, 1908; Boston, Houghton Mifflin, 1924.
St. Martin's Summer. London, Hutchinson, 1909; Boston, Houghton Mifflin, 1924.
Anthony Wilding. London, Hutchinson, 1910; as *Arms and the Maid; or, Anthony Wilding*, New York, Putnam, 1910.
The Lion's Skin. London, Stanley Paul, and Boston, Houghton Mifflin, 1911.
The Justice of the Duke. London, Stanley Paul, 1912.
The Strolling Saint. London, Stanley Paul, 1913; Boston, Houghton Mifflin, 1924.
The Gates of Doom. London, Stanley Paul, 1914; Boston, Houghton Mifflin, 1926.
The Sea-Hawk. London, Secker, and Philadelphia, Lippincott, 1915.
The Banner of the Bull: Three Episodes in the Career of Cesare Borgia. London, Secker, and Philadelphia, Lippincott, 1915; first episode published as *The Urbinian*, Boston, Houghton Mifflin, 1924.
The Snare. London, Secker, and Philadelphia, Lippincott, 1915.
Scaramouche: A Romance of the French Revolution. London, Hutchinson, and Boston, Houghton Mifflin, 1921.
Captain Blood, His Odyssey. London, Hutchinson, and Boston, Houghton Mifflin, 1922.
Fortune's Fool. London, Hutchinson, and Boston, Houghton Mifflin, 1923.
Mistress Wilding. Boston, Houghton Mifflin, 1924.
The Carolinian. London, Hutchinson, and Boston, Houghton Mifflin, 1925.
Bellarion the Fortunate. London, Hutchinson, and Boston, Houghton Mifflin, 1926.
The Nuptials of Corbal. London, Hutchinson, and Boston, Houghton Mifflin, 1927.
The Hounds of God. London, Hutchinson, and Boston, Houghton Mifflin, 1928.
The Romantic Prince. London, Hutchinson, and Boston, Houghton Mifflin, 1929.
The Reaping. London, Readers Library, 1929.
The Minion. London, Hutchinson, 1930; as *The King's Minion*, Boston, Houghton Mifflin, 1930.
Captain Blood Returns. Boston, Houghton Mifflin, 1931; as *The Chronicles of Captain Blood*, London, Hutchinson, 1932.
The Black Swan. London, Hutchinson, and Boston, Houghton Mifflin, 1932.
The Stalking Horse. London, Hutchinson, and Boston, Houghton Mifflin, 1933.
Venetian Masque. London, Hutchinson, and Boston, Houghton Mifflin, 1934.
Chivalry. London, Hutchinson, and Boston, Houghton Mifflin, 1935.
The Fortunes of Captain Blood. London, Hutchinson, and Boston, Houghton Mifflin, 1936.
The Lost King. London, Hutchinson, and Boston, Houghton Mifflin, 1937.
The Sword of Islam. London, Hutchinson, and Boston, Houghton Mifflin, 1939.
The Marquis of Carabas. London, Hutchinson, 1940; as *Master-at-Arms,* Boston, Houghton Mifflin, 1940.
Columbus. London, Hutchinson, and Boston, Houghton Mifflin, 1942.
King in Prussia. London, Hutchinson, 1944; as *The Birth of Mischief*, Boston, Houghton Mifflin, 1945.
The Gamester. London, Hutchinson, and Boston, Houghton Mifflin, 1949.

Saga of the Sea (omnibus). London, Hutchinson, 1953.
Sinner, Saint, and Jester (omnibus). London, Hutchinson, 1954.
In the Shadow of the Guillotine (omnibus). London, Hutchinson, 1955; Boston, Houghton Mifflin, 1956.

Short Stories

The Historical Nights' Entertainment, 1st–3rd series. Boston, Houghton Mifflin, 3 vols., 1917–38; London, Secker, 1 vol., 1918; London, Hutchinson, 2 vols., 1919–37.
Stories of Love, Intrigue, and Battle, Being Selected Works of Rafael Sabatini. Boston, Houghton Mifflin, 1931.
Turbulent Tales. London, Hutchinson, 1946.

OTHER PUBLICATIONS

Plays

Kuomi, The Jester, with Stephanie Baring (produced Luton, Bedfordshire, 1903).
Bardelys the Magnificent, with Henry Hamilton, adaptation of the novel by Sabatini (produced Birmingham, 1910; London, 1911).
Fugitives (produced London, 1911).
The Rattlesnake, with J. E. Harold Terry (produced New York, 1921; London, 1922).
Scaramouche, adaptation of his own novel (produced New York, 1923; Glasgow and London, 1927).
In the Snare, with Leon M. Lion, adaptation of the novel *The Snare* by Sabatini (produced London, 1924).
The Carolinian, with J. E. Harold Terry (produced Detroit and New York, 1925).
The Tyrant: An Episode in the Life of Cesare Borgia (produced Birmingham and London, 1925; New York, 1930). London, Hutchinson, 1925.

Screenplays: *Bluff*, 1921; *The Recoil*, 1922; *The Scourge (Fortune's Fool)*, 1922.

Other

The Life of Cesare Borgia of Grance. London, Stanley Paul, 1911; New York, Brentano's, 1912.
Torquemada and the Spanish Inquisition. London, Stanley Paul, and New York, Brentano's, 1913; revised edition, Stanley Paul, and Boston, Houghton Mifflin, 1924.
Heroic Lives. London, Hutchinson, and Boston, Houghton Mifflin, 1934.

Editor, *A Century of Sea Stories*. London, Hutchinson, 1934.
Editor, *A Century of Historical Stories*. London, Hutchinson, 1936.
Editor, *The Book of the Sea Trout*, by Hamish Stuart. London, Cape, 1952.

*   *   *

Rafael Sabatini was called the "new Dumas" by his admirers and a sleight-of-hand artist with a "bag of tricks" by skeptics, but his narratives are well crafted and often sparkle with crisp dialogue and rousing adventure. The settings of what he called his period novels ranged over several centuries in England, France, Italy, and in the Caribbean during the heyday of piracy, with a few more scattered around America, Spain, Venice, and elsewhere. In addition to his romantic novels Sabatini wrote fic-

tion and accounts of historical incidents for his three volumes of *Historical Nights' Entertainment*, recreated episodes from the Spanish Inquisition, and wrote novelizations and sketches of the lives of such cultural heroes as Columbus, Saint Francis of Assisi, Joan of Arc, Lord Nelson, and Florence Nightingale. He seems to have read history with great voracity, but he had no more respect for historians than many of them had for his own versions of past events.

Sabatini had been writing historical fiction, biography, and romance for over 30 years when he summarized his views on the writer's responsibilities to his art. Historians, Sabatini argued, are not necessarily more faithful to their material than are period novelists, and they seldom write as well. Citing the accounts of William Tell, the Man in the Iron Mask, and incestual relations among the Borgias as legends which had crept into histories of Europe, Sabatini finds that historical "facts" are all too often based on repeated errors, sensationalism, and the biased reports of dubious witnesses. He says of one of his characters in *Captain Blood* who has just carried off a successful lie that "there was a great historian lost in Wolverstone. He had the right imagination that knows just how far to colour it so as to change its shape for his own purposes." Good period fiction, on the other hand, requires equally serious research, a faithfulness to historical personages and events, and shrewd analysis of the available evidence. According to Sabatini there are basically three kinds of period novels: those which are concerned entirely with historical characters and happenings, those involving imaginary characters set "against a real background to which story and characters must bear some real and true relationship," and those which blend "events that are reasonably and logically imagined, and characters that lived with characters that the author has invented."

Sabatini's *The Minion* (U.S. title: *The King's Minion*) for which he "scarcely invented even a minor character," is an example of the first type. The novel is concerned with intrigues leading to the murder of Sir Thomas Overbury in the court of James I, and Sabatini finds "as a result of close study and close reasoning" that there were initially two conspiracies which later became entangled. *Scaramouche*, which is subtitled "A Romance," is the second type: the title character is imaginary, but the setting is faithful to the milieu of revolutionary France. The hero is "the natural offspring of the circumstances and habits of mind of the time," which molded his character and shaped his fortunes. *Scaramouche* is aptly titled a romance. After being banished from the estate of his foster father, André-Louis Moreau takes the name Scaramouche and joins a traveling band of players. The death of a friend at the hands of a vicious aristocrat leads Scaramouche to seek revenge, and in turn become a notorious polemicist, a fencing master, and a Revolutionary hero. In seeking revenge, André clashes with the aristocrat over an actress he thinks he loves and the lady he has always loved. At the culmination of the Revolution André learns that the aristocrat is his father. This physiological drama is woven interestingly into the players' story where the troup moves from hard times under feudal leadership to great success through André's skills as an early capitalist; he collects personnel, organizes bookings, writes advertising, composes plays based on the classics, and stars in performances.

Sabatini's third kind of novel, a combination of the period novel and the historical romance, is found in *Captain Blood*. Peter Blood is based on Henry Pitman, an English surgeon who was sold into slavery at Barbados after being sentenced to death by Jeffreys at the Bloody Assize for ministering to wounded rebels during Monmouth's Rebellion. Sabatini follows Pitman's biography up to the point of his escape, then follows John [or A. O.] Exquemelin's *History of the Bucaniers of America* and other accounts, including that of Henry Morgan, for models of buccaneer adventures and characters. The success of *Captain Blood* led to *The Chronicles of Captain Blood* (U.S. title: *Captain Blood Returns*) in 1931 and *The Fortunes of Captain Blood* in 1936. The sea is an ideal setting and piracy a useful mode for portraying the struggle for reasonable loyalties in a world of shifting alliances. Like those in *The Sea-Hawk* and *The Black Swan*, Captain Blood's adventures allows Sabatini to play on those gray areas surrounding allegiance to particular nations, religions, and ideals of personal integrity.

In *The Sea-Hawk* Sir Oliver Tressilan loses his estate and is enslaved by Moslems after his brother accuses him of a murder he himself had committed, but Tressilan makes himself invaluable to his master and becomes Sakr-el-Bahr the pirate. *The Black Swan* finds French ex-buccaneer Charles de Bernis drawn into alliance with the last of the renegade pirates, Tom Leach, in order to save his own life.

Sabatini's fiction is effective to the extent that he creates an opposition between the picaresque milieu in which action takes place and the chivalric idealism of the protagonists. In a world of court intrigues, war, and such outlawry as piracy the hero's position is associated with or appears to be compromised by shadowy motives and actions. Despite his protestations, in the lady's eyes the gentleman is compromised, because his chivalrous manner is at odds with what she sees of his actions in the world. Since the hero's immersion in the picaresque life has usually resulted from a betrayal of some sort, he must extract himself by avenging wrongs while he attempts to gain or regain his fortune. While he is away the lady should have the "womanliness to be guided by natural instincts in the selection of her mate," but an admirable woman is courted by many men and since she distrusts him she might, "for position, riches, and a great title barter herself in marriage," or be less cautious with another suitor. The reader identifies the love match early and much of the tension of the novels results from suspension of the courtship during periods of vigorous action. Because the potential lovers are ignorant or distrustful of one another's feelings yet drawn together by an instinctively powerful attraction, meetings between them crackle with misunderstandings and disdainful wit.

Sabatini's period novels and romances have not lost their charm over time for those readers willing to suspend disbelief in their romantic premises. His most popular works inspired motion pictures and he turned some of them into successful stage productions. His popularity weathered the abuse of critics who would have had more realism and historians who demanded more footnotes. His bag of tricks, which included stock characters, a liberal use of "Chance," predictably honorable heroes and heroines, unlikely misunderstandings and so on, seldom intrude into the magical moments of high action and grand verbal exchanges. Readers who made *Scaramouche*, *The Sea-Hawk*, *Mistress Wilding*, *The Carolinian*, and *Captain Blood* best sellers were responding not merely to the lure of romantic fiction, but to energy and courage inspired by one of its most capable spokesmen.

—Larry N. Landrum

ST. CLAIR, Erin. See **BROWN, Sandra.**

ST. JOHN, Mabel. Pseudonym for Henry St. John Cooper.

ROMANCE AND HISTORICAL PUBLICATIONS

Novels (series: Polly Green)

Most Cruelly Wronged. London, Amalgamated Press, 1907.
Only a Singing Girl. London, Amalgamated Press, 1907.
Rival Beauties. London, Amalgamated Press, 1907.
Under a Ban. London, Amalgamated Press, 1907.
Her Father's Sin. London, Amalgamated Press, 1908.
Polly Green: A School Story [*and Coosha, at Cambridge,—Engaged, in Society, at Twenty-One*]. London, Amalgamated Press, 6 vols., 1909–11.
Romany Ruth: A Gipsy Love Story. London, Amalgamated Press, 1909.
Just a Barmaid. London, Amalgamated Press, 1909.
A Daughter Scorned. London, Amalgamated Press, 1911.
Jane Em'ly. London, Amalgamated Press, 1911.
The Twins of Twineham. London, Amalgamated Press, 1911.
The Dear Old Home. London, Amalgamated Press, 1912.
The Best Woman in the World. London, Fleetway House, 1913.
Nell of the Camp; or, The Pride of the Prairie. London, Fleetway House, 1913.
The Outcasts of Crowthorpe College. London, Fleetway House, 1913.
The Schoolgirl Bride. London, Fleetway House, 1913.
Faults on Both Sides. London, Fleetway House, 1914.
Fine Feathers! or, The Wife Who Would Be Smart. London, Fleetway House, 1914.
From Mill to Mansion. London, Fleetway House, 1914.
Kiddy, The Coffee-Stall Girl. London, Fleetway House, 1914.
Little Miss Millions. London, Fleetway House, 1914.
Married to Her Master. London, Fleetway House, 1914.
My Lancashire Queen. London, Fleetway House, 1914.
Sally in Our Alley. London, Fleetway House, 1914.
The Ticket-of-Leave Girl. London, Fleetway House, 1914.
When a Girl's Pretty. London, Fleetway House, 1914.
John Jordan, Slave-Driver. London, Fleetway House, 1915.
Just Jane Ann. London, Fleetway House, 1915.
The Lass That Loved a Sailor. London, Fleetway House, 1915.
Maggie Darling. London, Fleetway House, 1915.
My Girl, Regan. London, Fleetway House, 1915.
The Post Office Girl. London, Fleetway House, 1915.
Shielded from the World. London, Fleetway House, 1915.
Too Wilful for Words! London, Fleetway House, 1915.
The Worst Wife in the World. London, Fleetway House, 1915.
Born in Prison: The Story of a Mill-Girl's Sacrifice. London, Fleetway House, 1916.
Cook at School. London, Fleetway House, 1916.
How the Money Goes! London, Fleetway House, 1916.
In Mother's Place. London, Fleetway House, 1916.
The Mistress of the Fifth Standard. London, Fleetway House, 1916.
The Soul of the Mill. London, Fleetway House, 1916.
The Best Girls Are Here. London, Fleetway House, 1917.
Daisy Earns Her Living. London, Fleetway House, 1917.
Daisy Peach Abroad. London, Fleetway House, 1917.
Liz o' Loomland. London, Fleetway House, 1917.
Married at School. London, Fleetway House, 1917.
Our Nell. London, Fleetway House, 1917.
The "Sixpenny Ha'penny" Duchess. London, Fleetway House, 1917.
What a Woman Can Do! London, Fleetway House, 1917.
The Autograph Hunters. London, Fleetway House, 1918.

Dolly Daydreams! London, Fleetway House, 1918.

For Her Lover's Sake. London, Fleetway House, 1918.

His Sealed Lips! or, The Tale He Would Not Tell! London, Fleetway House, 1918.

Little and Good. London, Fleetway House, 1918.

Little Miss Innocence. London, Fleetway House, 1918.

Millgirl and Dreamer. London, Fleetway House, 1918.

Old Smith's Nurse. London, Fleetway House, 1918.

Pearl of the West. London, Fleetway House, 1918.

Her Stolen Baby. London, Fleetway House, 1919.

Apronstrings. London, Amalgamated Press, 1919.

Ashamed of the Shop; or, Miss High-and-Mighty. London, Amalgamated Press, 1919.

The Belle of the Works. London, Amalgamated Press, 1919.

The Favourite Wins! or, The Bookmaker's Bride. London, Amalgamated Press, 1919.

Good Gracious, Marian! London, Amalgamated Press, 1919.

The Little "Gutter Girl." London, Amalgamated Press, 1919.

Betty on the Stage. London, Amalgamated Press, 1920.

The Wife Who Dragged Him Down! London, Amalgamated Press, 1920.

A Boxer's Sweetheart. London, Amalgamated Press, 1920.

The Wife Who Would Be "Master"! London, Amalgamated Press, 1920.

The Cinderella Girl. London, Amalgamated Press, 1920.

In the Shadows! London, Amalgamated Press, 1920.

Mary Ellen—Mill-Lass. London, Amalgamated Press, 1920.

Mill-Lass o' Mine! London, Amalgamated Press, 1920.

Wedded But Not Wooed; or, Marry Me—Or Go to Prison! London, Amalgamated Press, 1920.

From Pillar to Post; or, No Home of Her Own. London, Amalgamated Press, 1921.

Wife—or Housekeeper? London, Amalgamated Press, 1921.

A House, But Not a Home. London, Amalgamated Press, 1921.

The Husband, The Wife, and the Friend. London, Amalgamated Press, 1921.

A Jealous Wife's Revenge! London, Amalgamated Press, 1921.

Just Jane Em'ly. London, Amalgamated Press, 1921.

Little Miss Lancashire; or, Moll o' the Mill. London, Amalgamated Press, 1921.

Lonely Little Lucy. London, Amalgamated Press, 1921.

Mad for Dress! London, Amalgamated Press, 1921.

Sally All-Smiles. London, Amalgamated Press, 1921.

The School Against Her! London, Amalgamated Press, 1921.

Scorned by "His" Mother. London, Amalgamated Press, 1921.

Ann All-Alone: The Story of a Girl's Great Self-Sacrifice. London, Amalgamated Press, 1922.

Wife or Maid? or, Scorned by Her Workmates. London, Amalgamated Press, 1922.

The Brute! London, Amalgamated Press, 1922.

We Want Our Mummy! London, Amalgamated Press, 1922.

Gipsy Born! London, Amalgamated Press, 1922.

Tattling Tongues. London, Amalgamated Press, 1922.

The Gipsy Schoolgirl. London, Amalgamated Press, 1922.

Girl of the Prairie. London, Amalgamated Press, 1922.

The Home Without a Father! London, Amalgamated Press, 1922.

Mother Knows Best! or, Uttered in Anger! London, Amalgamated Press, 1922.

Mr. Leslie's School for Girls. London, Amalgamated Press, 1922.

Nobody's Girl. London, Amalgamated Press, 1922.

Rich Girl—Charity Girl! London, Amalgamated Press, 1922.

Blood Money! London, Amalgamated Press, 1923.

The Disappearance of Barbara. London, Amalgamated Press, 1923.

Such a Fine Fellow! London, Amalgamated Press, 1923.

The Gipsy Actress. London, Amalgamated Press, 1923.

The Girl Who Married the Wrong Man! London, Amalgamated Press, 1923.

He Couldn't Take Money! or, The "Old Fool" of the Family! London, Amalgamated Press, 1923.

His Wife—or His Mother? or, No Home of Her Own. London, Amalgamated Press, 1923.

I'm Not a Common Girl! London, Amalgamated Press, 1923.

Jenny Luck of Brendon's Mills. London, Amalgamated Press, 1923.

The New Girl at Bellforth. London, Amalgamated Press, 1923.

The Second Husband. London, Amalgamated Press, 1923.

Secrets of the Shop! London, Amalgamated Press, 1923.

Too Old for Her Husband! London, Amalgamated Press, 1924.

Bringing Up Becky! London, Amalgamated Press, 1924.

She Was an Actress. London, Amalgamated Press, 1924.

Go Borrowing—Go Sorrowing. London, Amalgamated Press, 1924.

A Son to Be Proud Of! London, Amalgamated Press, 1924.

He Married a Mill-Lass. London, Amalgamated Press, 1924.

The Island Girl. London, Amalgamated Press, 1924.

Married to His Wife's Family. London, Amalgamated Press, 1924.

She Wrecked Their Home! or, A Son's a Son till He Takes Him a Wife. London, Amalgamated Press, 1924.

Midsummer Madness! London, Amalgamated Press, 1924.

The Mill-Girl's Bargain! London, Amalgamated Press, 1924.

My Man of the Mill! London, Amalgamated Press, 1924.

Poisoned Lives! London, Amalgamated Press, 1924.

The "Sports" of Lyndale. London, Amalgamated Press, 1925.

As the World Judged. London, Amalgamated Press, 1925.

When There's Love at Home. London, Amalgamated Press, 1925.

A Girl's Good Name. London, Amalgamated Press, 1925.

Where Is My Child To-night? London, Amalgamated Press, 1925.

Just 'Liz-beth Ann. London, Amalgamated Press, 1925.

Longing for Love. London, Amalgamated Press, 1925.

Pride Parted Them! London, Amalgamated Press, 1925.

Shamed by Her Husband! London, Amalgamated Press, 1925.

She Posed as Their Friend! London, Amalgamated Press, 1925.

She Shall Never Call You Mother! London, Amalgamated Press, 1925.

And Still She Loved Him. London, Amalgamated Press, 1926.

The Daughter He Didn't Want! London, Amalgamated Press, 1926.

Some Mother's Child! London, Amalgamated Press, 1926.

It Is My Duty! London, Amalgamated Press, 1926.

The Life He Led Her! London, Amalgamated Press, 1926.

Love Needs Telling. London, Amalgamated Press, 1926.

Maggie of Marley's Mill. London, Amalgamated Press, 1926.

The Man Who Married Again. London, Amalgamated Press, 1926.

Rivals at School—Rivals Through Life! London, Amalgamated Press, 1926.

She Sold Her Child! London, Amalgamated Press, 1927.

He'll Never Marry You! London, Amalgamated Press, 1927.

Thou Shalt Love Thy Neighbour—. London, Amalgamated Press, 1927.

Lizbeth Rose. London, Amalgamated Press, 1927.

Tied to Her Apron Strings! London, Amalgamated Press, 1927.

The Long, Long Wooing. London, Amalgamated Press, 1927.

Loved for Her Money. London, Amalgamated Press, 1927.

The New Girl. London, Amalgamated Press, 1927.

She'll Never Marry My Son! London, Amalgamated Press, 1927.

Some Mother's Son! London, Amalgamated Press, 1928.

A Beggar at Her Husband's Door! London, Amalgamated Press, 1928.

Utterly Alone! London, Amalgamated Press, 1928.

His Wife or His Work? London, Amalgamated Press, 1928.

His Wife's Secret! London, Amalgamated Press, 1928.

Nobody Wants You! London, Amalgamated Press, 1928.

He Shall Not Marry a Mill-Lass! London, Amalgamated Press, 1929.

The Husband She Wanted. London, Amalgamated Press, 1930.

Jess o' Jordan's. London, Amalgamated Press, 1930.

Wedded—But Alone! London, Amalgamated Press, 1930.

Another Girl Won Him. London, Amalgamated Press, 1935.

Novels as Henry St. John Cooper

The Master of the Mill. London, Amalgamated Press, 1910.

A Shop-Girl's Revenge. London, Fleetway House, 1914.

The Cotton King. London, Fleetway House, 1915.

The Lass He Left Behind Him! London, Fleetway House, 1915.

The Black Sheep; or, Who Is My Brother? London, Fleetway House, 1916.

Ready—Aye Ready! A Story of the Bull-Dogs of the Ocean. London, Fleetway House, 1916.

The Man with the Money. London, Fleetway House, 1917.

Hero or Scamp? London, Fleetway House, 1918.

Miss Bolo; or, A Spy in the Home. London, Fleetway House, 1918.

The Man of Her Dreams. London, Amalgamated Press, 1919.

The Mill Queen. London, Fleetway House, 1919.

Sunny Ducrow. London, Sampson Low, 1919.

There's Just One Girl. London, Amalgamated Press, 1919.

Vagabond Jess. London, Amalgamated Press, 1919.

"Wild-Fire" Nan. London, Amalgamated Press, 1919.

Fair and False; or, A Whited Sepulchre. London, Amalgamated Press, 1920.

Her Mother-in-Law. London, Amalgamated Press, 1920.

James Bevanwood, Baronet. London, Sampson Low, 1920.

Just a Cottage Maid. London, Amalgamated Press, 1920.

A Lodger in His Own Home. London, Amalgamated Press, 1920.

Married to a Miser. London, Amalgamated Press, 1920.

Men Were Deceivers Ever. London, Amalgamated Press, 1920.

Mountain Lovers. London, Amalgamated Press, 1920.

Two Men and a Maid. London, Amalgamated Press, 1920.

Elizabeth in Dreamland. London, Amalgamated Press, 1921.

The Garden of Memories. London, Sampson Low, 1921.

The Island of Eve. London, Amalgamated Press, 1921.

Love's Waif. London, Amalgamated Press, 1921.

Mabel St. John's Schooldays. London, Amalgamated Press, 1921.

Madge o' the Mill. London, Amalgamated Press, 1921.

Prison-Stained! London, Amalgamated Press, 1921.

We're Not Wanted Now! London, Amalgamated Press, 1921.

Carniss and Company. London, Sampson Low, 1922.

Above Her Station. London, Amalgamated Press, 1922.

A Daughter of the Loom; or, Go and Marry Your Mill-Girl! London, Amalgamated Press, 1922.

Fairweather Friends! or, Fleeced by His Family! London, Amalgamated Press, 1922.

The Imaginary Marriage. London, Sampson Low, 1922.

Poverty's Daughter. London, Amalgamated Press, 1922.

A Snake in the Grass. London, Amalgamated Press, 1922.

The Vagabond's Daughter. London, Amalgamated Press, 1922.

Could She Forgive? London, Amalgamated Press, 1923.

Gipsy Love. London, Amalgamated Press, 1923.

The "Head" of the Family; or, Despised by Them All! London, Amalgamated Press, 1923.

Hidden Hearts. London, Amalgamated Press, 1923.

Kidnapped. London, Amalgamated Press, 1923.

Mary Faithful. London, Amalgamated Press, 1923.

Son o' Mine! London, Amalgamated Press, 1923.

Too Common for Him! London, Amalgamated Press, 1923.

Two's Company . . . ; or, Young Folks Are Best Alone. London, Amalgamated Press, 1923.

Yield Not to Temptation! London, Amalgamated Press, 1923.

The Broken Barrier. London, Amalgamated Press, 1924.

His Wife from the Kitchen! London, Amalgamated Press, 1924.

Just Plain Jim! or, One of the Rank and File. London, Amalgamated Press, 1924.

A Lover in Rags. London, Amalgamated Press, 1924.

Redway Street. London, Amalgamated Press, 1924.

The Unwanted Heiress. London, Amalgamated Press, 1924.

The Fortunes of Sally Luck. London, Sampson Low, 1925.

Lose Money—Lose Friends! London, Amalgamated Press, 1925.

Nan of No Man's Land. London, Amalgamated Press, 1925.

The Cottar's Daughter. London, Amalgamated Press, 1926.

The Gallant Lover: A Queen Anne Story. London, Sampson Low, 1926.

The Golconda Necklace. London, Amalgamated Press, 1926.

Whoso Diggeth a Pit—. London, Amalgamated Press, 1926.

The Woman Who Parted Them! London, Amalgamated Press, 1926.

The Amazing Tramp. London, Amalgamated Press, 1927.

Morning Glory. London, Sampson Low, 1927.

Golden Bait. London, Sampson Low, 1928.

The Red Veil. London, Sampson Low, 1928.

As Fate Decrees. London, Sampson Low, 1929.

Compromise. London, Sampson Low, 1929.

Retribution. London, Sampson Low, 1930.

The Millionaire Tramp. London, Sampson Low, 1930.

When a Man Loves. London, Sampson Low, 1931.

The Forbidden Road. London, Sampson Low, 1931.

Love That Divided. London, Sampson Low, 1932.

The Splendid Love. London, Sampson Low, 1932.

When Love Compels. London, Sampson Low, 1933.

Dangerous Paths. London, Sampson Low, 1933.

As a Woman Wills. London, Sampson Low, 1934.

The Hush Marriage. London, Sampson Low, 1934.

Toils of Silence. London, Sampson Low, 1935.

A Woman's Way. London, Sampson Low, 1935.

At Grips with Fate. London, Sampson Low, 1936.

The Call of Love. London, Sampson Low, 1936.

OTHER PUBLICATIONS

Other

Bull-Dogs and Bull-Dog Breeding. London, Jarrolds, 1905.

Bulldogs and Bulldog Men. London, Jarrolds, 1908.

Bulldogs and All about Them. London, Jarrolds, 1914.

*   *   *

Henry St. John Cooper was a prolific and wide-ranging author. He not only churned out thousands of words of women's fiction every week, but regularly wrote stories of tough, Borstal-like boarding-schools for several boys' papers.

As Mabel St. John he was one of the most popular writers of Lord Northcliffe's *Girls' Friend*, *Girls' Reader*, and *Girls' Home*. Before World War I, these periodicals catered for hard-working and frequently exploited working-girl readers, whose education had begun and ended at elementary schools. St. John's championship of the underdog and the sheer gusto of the stories combined to create an instant recipe for success. (A large number of these magazine serial romances were subsequently re-issued in the form of inexpensive paperback books.) Millgirl and maid-of-all-work readers could easily identify with St. John's heroines, who often occupied similar positions to their own (*Just a Barmaid*, *Liz o' Loomland*, etc.) The fictional "slaveys" and factory workers, however, had the advantage of stumbling more easily on redemptive romance with the bosses' sons than their real-life counterparts were likely to do in the rigid class divisions of Edwardian society.

St. John, who was half-brother to Gladys Cooper, the celebrated actress, used theatrical settings for many of his stories. *Sunny Ducrow* is an attractive account of stage ambitions in a working-class girl. However, his theatre novels owed more to the rumbustious good humour of the music-hall than to the serious drama at which his sister excelled. Until "Mr. Right" came along to provide a permanent escape from their poorly paid drudgery, several St. John heroines abandoned "skivvying" for a career "on the halls," where they would achieve success through unusual enterprise and endeavour. (Em Hammond, for example, despite her much vaunted "yellow hair," manages convincingly to play the part of an Arab girl and also—no mean achievement this—to whistle "The Man Who Broke the Bank at Monte Carlo" through her yashmak!)

The apotheosis of romantic madcap appeal was achieved in Polly Green, whom St. John starred in six of his books. Rather surprisingly, Polly is not a working-class girl but a college student at Cambridge, where she inspires wholesale adulation from male undergraduates. Later she had London society at her feet, and enters into a forced engagement with a horribly ruthless member of the ruling class, whom she sensibly throws over as soon as circumstances permit. Happily he then not only commits suicide but obligingly leaves Polly his fortune, thus smoothing her way to marriage with her besotted but impecunious true love (St. John championing the underdog again!). A notable feature of the Polly Green stories is that Polly had a very long-standing friendship, on equal terms, with Coocha, an outspoken and extremely lively natured black girl. This was for its time a progressive step, but one that seemed immensely popular with Edwardian readers.

With their melodramatic plots and flashes of iconoclastic humour, the St. John romantic novels are certainly not in the classic mould. Their earthy acuteness, however, makes them more memorable than many mainstream love stories.

—Mary Cadogan

ST. JOHN, Nicole. Pseudonym for Norma Johnston. American. Born in Ridgewood, New Jersey. Educated at public schools, in Ramsey, New Jersey; Montclair State College, New Jersey, B.A.; studied acting at American Theatre Wing, New York. Has worked as actress, editor, teacher, and business-woman; founder, president, and director, Geneva Players Inc. Agent: McIntosh and Otis Inc., 310 Madison Avenue, New York, New York 10017; or 79 St. Martin's Lane, London WC2N 4AA, England. Address: Dryden Harris St. John Inc., 103 Godwin Avenue, Midland Park, New Jersey 07432, U.S.A.

ROMANCE AND HISTORICAL PUBLICATIONS

Novels

The Medici Ring. New York, Random House, 1975; London, Collins, 1976.
Wychwood. New York, Random House, 1976; London, Heinemann, 1978.
Guinever's Gift. New York, Random House, 1977; London, Heinemann, 1979.

OTHER PUBLICATIONS

Fiction (for children) as Norma Johnston

The Wishing Star. New York, Funk and Wagnalls, 1963.
The Wider Heart. New York, Funk and Wagnalls, 1964.
Ready or Not. New York, Funk and Wagnalls, 1965.
The Bridge Between. New York, Funk and Wagnalls, 1966.
The Keeping Days. New York, Atheneum, 1973.
Glory in the Flower. New York, Atheneum, 1974.
Of Time and of Seasons. New York, Atheneum, 1975.
Strangers Dark and Gold. New York, Atheneum, 1975.
A Striving after Wind. New York, Atheneum, 1976.
The Sanctuary Tree. New York, Atheneum, 1977.
A Mustard Seed of Magic. New York, Atheneum, 1977.
If You Love Me, Let Me Go. New York, Atheneum, 1978.
The Swallow's Song. New York, Atheneum, 1978.
Both Sides Now. New York, Atheneum, 1978.
The Crucible Year. New York, Atheneum, 1979.
Pride of Lions. New York, Atheneum, 1979.
A Nice Girl Like You. New York, Atheneum, 1980.
Myself and I. New York, Atheneum, 1981.
The Days of the Dragon's Seed. New York, Atheneum, 1982.
Timewarp Summer. New York, Atheneum, 1982.

*

Manuscript Collection: Rutgers University Library, New Brunswick, New Jersey.

*   *   *

"I draw my strength from England," says the American novelist Nicole St. John. Indeed, English history is the underlying theme—the *bas-relief*, if you will—of two of St. John's novels. Hidden within *Wychwood* is the story of Catherine Parr, widow of Henry VIII, and her lover Thomas Seymour, as well as ancient Anglo-Saxon occult rituals. *Guinever's Gift* is a re-enactment of the Arthurian legend, as the central characters investigate its historical validity. *The Medici Ring*, the author's first novel, reveals her appreciation of fine art and antiques. Further, St. John's love of English literature is reflected in her frequent references to Sir Thomas Malory, Shakespeare, Tennyson.

These are novels in the classic gothic tradition. Heroines (who tell their own stories) are always young and pretty, bright, curious, spunky, and alone in the world (typically, Lavinia Stanton, of *The Medici Ring*, is a "young, impecunious, overeducated orphan"). All heroes in St. John's novels are older and wiser, dark and mysterious, with flashing eyes (in short, *Jane Eyre*'s Rochester). The standard settings are: a mansion—the Culhaine mansion, on Marlborough Street in Boston, in *The Medici Ring*; Avalon, an Arthurian-type country house, in *Guinever's Gift*; an English cottage (*Wychwood*); each with many rooms, staircases, and hallways, some of them, of course, secret. The time: the Victorian Age. The plots that unfold are captivating and suspenseful.

Impelled by instinct, interest, and her newly orphaned status, the heroine is directed to the mansion (or country home or cottage), and there meets the dark stranger who, when his veil of mystery drops, will be revealed as her hero. In *The Medici Ring* the orphan Lavinia Stanton suffers another loss when her guardian, "Uncle" Eustace Robinson, dies, leaving her with only a 15th-century ruby ring and a knowledge of art and antiques. Lavinia is invited by Damaris Culhaine, an old school friend, to help catalogue the family's collection of Renaissance art. The Culhaine mansion contains not only paintings and sculpture and jewels, but many mysteries: the possible poisoning of Damaris; the Marchesa Marina Orsini, Damaris's aunt; the theft and forgery of some of the Culhaine's valuable art works; the untimely death (some years before) of Damaris's mother, Isabel; and Damaris's father, the "emerald-eyed" Ross Culhaine. The figures in a hidden Renaissance tapestry unravel these mysteries for Lavinia.

Wychwood, named for the English country cottage to which the orphan sisters Camilla and Nell Jardin move when Nell is paralyzed by an accident at boarding school, likewise abounds in mysteries and apparitions, particularly the "ghost of the Copper Maid." Camilla risks her life and sanity to discover the riddle of her inheritance and the secrets behind the frightening events that occur at Wychwood. Aided by a mysterious neighbor, Jeremy Bushell, she uncovers the secret story of Catherine Parr and Thomas Seymour, and gains her own rightful inheritance.

In *Guinever's Gift* Lydian Wentworth, after the death of her father, travels to Avalon at the invitation of Lord Charles Ransome, a scholar of the Arthurian legend. Although paralyzed, Charles further invites Lydian to marry him. She accepts. Lydian, Charles, and Lawrence Stearns, Charles' young research assistant, seem fated to re-enact the lives of Guinever, Arthur, and Lancelot, until Lydian's courage, determination, and her own knowledge of Arthurian lore save them from the tragic triangle.

St. John writes with an easy elegance and literary *connaissance* that make her a worthy successor to the Brontës.

—Marcia G. Fuchs

SALISBURY, Carola. Pseudonym for Michael Butterworth; also writes as Sarah Kemp. British. Born 10 January 1924. Served in the Royal Naval Volunteer Reserve: Lieutenant. Married Jenny Spalding in 1957; one son and four daughters, and one daughter by previous marriage. Tutor in drawing, Nottingham College of Art, 1950–51; editor, art director, and managing editor, Fleetway Publications, London, 1952–63. Agent: Georges Borchardt, 136 East 57th Street, New York, New York 10022, U.S.A. Address: 13 Lansdown Crescent, Bath, Avon, England.

ROMANCE AND HISTORICAL PUBLICATIONS

Novels

Mallion's Pride. London, Collins, 1975; as *The Pride of the Trevallions*, New York, Doubleday, 1975.
Dark Inheritance. New York, Doubleday, 1975; London, Collins, 1976.

The "Dolphin" Summer. New York, Doubleday, 1976; London, Collins, 1977.
The Winter Bride. London, Collins, and New York, Doubleday, 1978.
The Shadowed Spring. London, Collins, and New York, Doubleday, 1980.
Count Vronsky's Daughter. London, Collins, and New York, Doubleday, 1981.
An Autumn in Araby. London, Century, and New York, Doubleday, 1983.
Daisy Friday. London, Century, 1984.
A Certain Splendour. London, Century, 1985.
The Woman in Grey. London, Century, 1987.

OTHER PUBLICATIONS

Novels as Michael Butterworth

The Soundless Scream. London, Long, and New York, Doubleday, 1967.
Walk Softly, In Fear. London, Long, 1968.
Vanishing Act. London, Collins, 1970; as *The Uneasy Sun*, New York, Doubleday, 1970.
Flowers for a Dead Witch. London, Collins, and New York, Doubleday, 1971.
The Black Look. London, Collins, and New York, Doubleday, 1972.
Villa on the Shore. London, Collins, 1973; New York, Doubleday, 1974.
The Man in the Sopwith Camel. London, Collins, 1974; New York, Doubleday, 1975.
Mind-Breaks of Space, with J. Jeff Jones. New York, Pocket Books, 1975; London, Wingate, 1978.
Remains to Be Seen. London, Collins, and New York, Doubleday, 1976.
Festival! London, Collins, 1976.
The Time of the Hawklords. Henley-on-Thames, Ellis, 1976.
Queens of Deliria. London, W. H. Allen, 1977.
Planets of Peril. New York, Warner, 1977.
X Marks the Spot. London, Collins, and New York, Doubleday, 1978.
The Man Who Broke the Bank at Monte Carlo. London, Collins, and New York, Doubleday, 1983.
A Virgin on the Rocks. London, Collins, and New York, Doubleday, 1985.
The Five Million Dollar Prince. London, Collins, and New York, Doubleday, 1986.

Novels as Sarah Kemp

Goodbye, Pussy. London, Collins, 1979; as *Over the Edge*, New York, Doubleday, 1979.
No Escape. New York, Doubleday, 1984; London, Century, 1985.
The Lure of Sweet Death. London, Century, and New York, Doubleday, 1986.
What Dread Hand? London, Century, and New York, Doubleday, 1987.

*   *   *

Michael Butterworth, writing as Carola Salisbury, is an accomplished author of gothic romances. His experience as a mystery writer clearly shows as he develops the tension of a story, releasing it in exciting, unexpected endings. The sudden realization that Piers Trevallion is still alive (*Mallion's Pride*), the discovery that Melloney has faked her invalid state (*The "Dolphin" Summer*), the final revelation that an entire diplomatic mission has been a red herring to protect the real emissary (*The Shadowed Spring*), and the unmasking of a murderer (*An Autumn in Araby*) all show Butterworth's ability to develop and sustain a feeling of true suspense.

While Butterworth carefully develops his plots, he pays equal attention to the development of his characters. He is particularly adept at the first-person narrative of the heroines. Feminine thoughts and feelings are expressed so naturally that it is difficult to remember that the author is in reality a man. Seen through a woman's eyes, the action is described with just the right mixture of curiosity and fear, without lapsing into the hysteria which sometimes passes for sensitivity in depictions of a gently bred woman confronted by the violence, mystery, and terror in a gothic novel. Butterworth also handles the Victorian-accented dialogue well, which adds to the atmosphere.

The theme of the past affecting the present and the future is prevalent in the Salisbury novels. Previous events and actions taken by others weave a complex web which draws the current characters into a situation that explodes into a resolution of the mystery. Often the secret lies buried in a great family's history, as described in *Mallion's Pride* and *Dark Inheritance*. Old crimes, real or perceived, are resurrected to haunt the present in *The "Dolphin" Summer*, *The Winter Bride*, and *An Autumn in Araby*. Even a classic is used to provide a past for *Count Vronsky's Daughter*, in which Anna Karenina's daughter is the heroine.

The Salisbury novels are carefully plotted to provide above average suspense and intrigue, with many twists to the plots which keep the reader guessing to the very end. Insanity, or at the very least instability, lurks in the minds of the least likely characters. The stories are peopled by colorful, complex characters who engage a reader's imagination and interest. Distinguished by action, adventure, and excitement, these novels must rank high on any list of period gothics. As one critic remarked "you don't have to believe it to enjoy it." It is a mark of Butterworth's talent, however, that you do believe while you are reading.

—Barbara E. Kemp

SALLIS, Susan. Also writes as Susan Meadmore. British. Born in Gloucester, 7 November 1929. Educated at Girls' High School, Gloucester; St. Matthias College of Education, Bristol. Married Brian Sallis in 1951 (died 1983); one daughter and two sons. Teacher, Department of Education and Science, Backwell, Somerset. Agent: Mary Irvine, 11 Upland Park Road, Oxford OX2 7RU. Address: 21 Kingston Avenue, Clevedon, Somerset BS21 6DS, England.

ROMANCE AND HISTORICAL PUBLICATIONS

Novels (series: Rising Family)

Return to Listowel. London, Hale, 1975.
Troubled Waters. London, Hale, 1975.
Richmond Heritage. London, Corgi, 1977.
Four Weeks in Venice. London, Corgi, 1978.

Rising Family:
   A Scattering of Daisies. London, Corgi, 1984; as *April Rising*, New York, St. Martin's Press, 1984.
   The Daffodils of Newent. London, Corgi, 1985.
   Bluebell Windows. London, Corgi, 1987.
   Rosemary for Remembrance. London, Corgi, 1987.
Summer Visitors. London, Corgi, 1988; New York, St. Martin's Press, 1989.
By Sun and Candlelight. London, Corgi, 1989.

Novels as Susan Meadmore

Behind the Mask. London, Hale, 1980.
Mary, Mary. London, Hale, 1982.

OTHER PUBLICATIONS

Fiction (for children)

An Open Mind. New York, Harper, 1978; London, Penguin, 1985.
A Time for Everything. New York, Harper, 1979; as *Thunder in the Hills*, London, Hale, 1981.
Only Love. New York, Harper, 1980; as *Sweet Frannie*, London, Heinemann, 1981.
Secret Places of the Stairs. New York, Harper, 1984.

*

Manuscript Collection: de Grummond Collection, University of Southern Mississippi, Hattiesburg.

Susan Sallis comments:

My books can be divided into three categories: contemporary romance, teenage fiction, and family sagas. They all deal with love: married love, family love, and friendship. The teenage fiction deals with young people coming to terms with the adult world and coping with mental and physical handicaps.

*   *   *

The sure basis of Susan Sallis's fiction is a warm sense of the value and importance of everyday life and quite ordinary emotions. She writes of life not perhaps as most of her readers have experienced it, but the gap between reality and romance is generally not one that demands too great an effort of the imagination, though there is, of course, some heightening of everyday situations and of the characters' responses to them.

Sallis's most ambitious work is the saga of the Rising family which is told in four volumes. Against a background of the great events of the first half of the 20th century, including the two World Wars, Sallis traces the lives of the three daughters—March, May, and April—of Florence Rising, the wife of a struggling tailor in Gloucester. Every detail of the setting is described carefully, whether it is a matter of costume, living conditions or manners generally, and Sallis has an acute sense of the way in which social class conditioned ordinary people's everyday lives at the time. The consequence of all this is that the characters acquire a solidity which is generally convincing. Despite the rather coyly pretty titles of the four novels and the obvious contrivance of the girls' names, the stories are quite tough and explicit. Love is one spur to action, and the desire to escape from a vicious circle of poverty is another. The ambition is entirely understandable, but the price is often high in terms of betrayal by men who take advantage of the girls' desires to break out in a period when, for the first time, women were beginning to have more freedom.

A Scattering of Daisies introduces the characters, showing the clash between economic realities and dreams for self-fulfilment which shape these people's lives. *The Daffodils of Newent* is set in the 1920's, a time when gay young things sometimes seemed to find everything going their way but when the war still cast its long shadow and the economic crisis was just around the corner. The personal problems resulting from unstable sexual relationships are further explored in *Bluebell Windows*. It is set during the 1930's, and that troubled decade is reflected in the turmoil in the lives of the three sisters. They have grown older, of course, and become mothers, but problems remain, especially with regard to illegitimacy. The horrors of the air raids of World War II add to the strains on the three sisters in *Rosemary for Remembrance*. There is a touch of melodrama in some of the responses to family secrets, but it was a time when the improbable was often possible and danger readily brought hidden emotions to the surface with unusual force.

The Rising series is essentially a family saga narrated from a female point of view, but the historical framework serves to bring out the personal dilemmas of the three sisters while creating a persuasive period atmosphere which has an interest of its own.

—Christopher Smith

SALVERSON, Laura Goodman. Canadian. Born in Winnipeg, Manitoba, 9 December 1890. Educated in the United States. Married George Salverson in 1913; one son. Recipient: Governor-General's award, 1937, 1939. *Died in 1970.*

Romance and Historical Publications

Novels

The Viking Heart. New York, Doran, 1923; London, Bretano, 1926.
When Sparrows Fall. Toronto, T. Allen, 1925.
Lord of the Silver Dragon: A Romance of Leif the Lucky. Toronto, McClelland, 1927.
Johan Lind. Toronto, McClelland, 1928.
The Dove of El-Djezaire. Toronto, Ryerson Press, 1933; as *The Dove*, London, Skeffington, 1933.
The Dark Weaver. Toronto, Ryerson Press, and London, Sampson Low, 1937.
Black Lace. Toronto, Ryerson Press, and London, Hutchinson, 1938.
Immortal Rock: The Saga of the Kensington Stone. Toronto, Ryerson Press, 1954; London, Angus and Robertson, 1955.

Other Publications

Verse

Wayside Gleams. Toronto, McClelland, 1925.

Other

Confessions of an Immigrant's Daughter (autobiography). Toronto, Ryerson Press, and London, Faber, 1939.

*   *   *

Laura Goodman Salverson's historical novels make extensive use of her family's background as Icelandic immigrants to North America. Her own part of this experience is recorded in her autobiography, *Confessions of an Immigrant's Daughter*. Although Salverson greatly admired the treatment of the immigrant experience in Frederick Philip Grove's novels, a closer model for the approach she took to her subject may be found in the work of the early Canadian feminist, Nellie McClung, whose novels specifically deal with women's experiences during the settlement of the Canadian west.

In *The Viking Heart*, her first novel, Salverson documents immigrants' lives and times which are closest to those related in her autobiography. This is a compelling novel of the Icelandic settlement near Winnipeg, Manitoba and documents the hardships, despair, and endurance of a family's three generations. In its use of graphic historical detail, this novel is less concerned with the smoothly dramatic plotting characteristic of the realism of historical romance, than with the episodic non-closure of a stark, overarching Darwinian naturalism. Grove's influence can be felt in this aspect of Salverson's writing, but ultimately it is mitigated by a sense of the optimism and strength associated with women in the work of McClung.

While poverty and struggle with the land are at the core of *The Viking Heart*, in a later novel, *The Dark Weaver*, the early prosperity of merchant settlers is presented in a narrative style more consistent with the realism of historical romance. Dealing with two generations of two families, *The Dark Weaver* explores various aspects of women's experience including old world arranged marriage, the victimization of native women by male settlers, the tension between the old and new world mores of the generations, and the potential for larger lives for women in the New World. Developing the naturalism of *The Viking Heart*, the later novel denies the reader a happy ending and tension built by the narrative is left tantalizingly unresolved.

Salverson refers to a more ancient, Viking, past in *Lord of the Silver Dragon* and *Immortal Rock*. The former novel deals with the voyages and reign of Leif the Lucky and explores the fictional possibilities of historical evidence of early Norse settlements along the Atlantic shores of North America. *Immortal Rock* assumes the authenticity of the Kensington Stone, which seems to prove that Norsemen, having penetrated Hudson's Bay and its river system, may have reached the Canadian prairies. The novel depicts the last 24 hours in the lives of the doomed explorers to whose presence the Stone's runes seem to attest. Tension in *Lord of the Silver Dragon* is developed through the constant deferral of Leif's final voyage to Vineland. In *Immortal Rock* tension is built to an excruciating pitch while the doomed men prepare for a final battle against the surrounding Indians. Both novels explore documented ancient connections between North America and Iceland skilfully and imaginatively.

Salverson leaves the Norse world behind altogether in *Black Lace*, a historical romance set early in the reign of Louis XIV of France. Taking Colbert's anti-piracy policies as a point of departure, Salverson evokes a sense of this period as a time of change between a generation which could still recall the days before the Fronde and one which moved toward the French Revolution and the emergence of modern France. Salverson weaves into the romantic plot a sense of the distance between rich and poor which keeps the reader from escapist nostalgia even as the plot reaches its long-anticipated conclusion.

A lesser known aspect of Icelandic history forms the basis of *The Dove*, which recounts the story of a woman, Steffania, captured in a raid on her village and sold into slavery in Algiers. She became known as the "Dove of El-Djezair." This novel is Salverson's most conventional historical romance and succeeds in evoking its exotic setting especially through sense imagery. The forceful characterization of the female Icelandic slaves establishes a link with Salverson's other work and here increases the novel's dramatic effect.

All of Salverson's novels reward the reader with strong plots and characterization as well as the keen sense of time and place necessary to historical fiction. Arguably, however, the novels dealing with the connection between Iceland and North America are her best work. *The Viking Heart* and *The Dark Weaver* in particular provide a valuable alternative point of view, the point of view of women immigrants, to the presentation of men's experience accepted as representative in canonised novels of the Canadian west.

—Heather Iris Jones

SANDERS, Dorothy Lucy. See **WALKER, Lucy.**

SANDYS, Oliver. See **BARCYNSKA, Countess (Hélène).**

SANTMYER, Helen Hooven. American. Born in Cincinnati, Ohio, 25 November 1895. Educated at Wellesley College, Massachusetts, B.A. 1918; Oxford University, B. Litt. 1927. Secretary, *Scribners* magazine, New York, 1919–21; English teacher, Xenia High School, Ohio, 1921–22; Chair of the English Department and Dean of Women, Cedarville College, Ohio, 1936–53; library assistant, Dayton and Montgomery County Public Library, Dayton, Ohio, 1953–60. D. Hum.: Wright State University, Fairborn, Ohio, 1984. *Died 21 February 1986.*

ROMANCE AND HISTORICAL PUBLICATIONS

Novels

Herbs and Apples. Boston, Houghton Mifflin, 1925.
The Fierce Dispute. Boston, Houghton Mifflin, 1929.
. . . and Ladies of the Club. Columbus, Ohio State University Press, 1982; London, Pan, 1985.
Farewell Summer. New York, Harper, 1988.

OTHER PUBLICATIONS

Other

The Spirit of Sisterhood. New York, Young Women's Christian Association, 1915.

Ohio Town: A Portrait of Xenia. Columbus, Ohio State University Press, 1963.

*   *   *

Helen Hooven Santmyer was "discovered" in 1984 when her long novel *. . . and Ladies of the Club* was reissued soon after its original publication and became, on its second appearance, a bestseller. The immense volume was the product of 20 years of work by the 88-year-old author, but it was by no means her first publication. Her first novel, a much shorter work called *Herbs and Apples*, first appeared in 1925. This volume and her other fiction were reprinted following the success of her final work, as was her collection of non-fiction essays called *Ohio Town*.

It is not hard to see why Santmyer's novels struck a chord with the readers of the 1980's. The entire body of her work deals with the period between the Civil War and the New Deal, with the greatest concentration upon the years surrounding the turn of the century. This was a period of tremendous change for women, especially the educated middle-class women who people *. . . and Ladies of the Club* and the shorter novels. Santmyer treats the fears and hopes of young women who are facing life choices that their mothers could hardly have imagined; in *Herbs and Apples*, for example, the college-educated heroine Derrick and her friends leave their Ohio homes to live and work in New York at the beginning of World War I. As the first generation of American middle-class women to choose between marriage and career, these young women face dangers and opportunities like explorers, with no examples but their own from which to learn. There is a theme of conflict between love and freedom and between marriage and self-realization that runs through all the books. Some of the heroines embrace love as the best means of seeking happiness, as does Hilary in *The Fierce Dispute*; some find their happiness in careers. But most of the women created by Santmyer, like the women of the 1980's, find the focus of their needs shifting back and forth from one sphere to another. These are not novels in which every detail winds down to a happy ending. Like life, they are more equivocal.

The realism of the characters is one facet of Santmyer's writing style. She is an observer of the minutest detail, and she captures the essence of the period with wonderful faithfulness. By focusing on the Ohio town that she knew and loved and on a period that was natural to her, she is able to give a fluid reality to her descriptions that research alone could hardly have produced. It is in her descriptive passages that she is most successful. When the narrative gives way to long conversations or speeches, the sure touch falters somewhat. The sharp focus of her narrative also makes the shorter novels and the novella *Farewell Summer* a bit more appealing than the popular *. . . and Ladies of the Club*. The sheer number of characters and preponderance of detail in this novel are reminiscent of Russian novels in length and complexity.

The brilliance of Santmyer's work really lies in her understanding of small-town life, based upon a long lifetime of observation. The reader is permitted to enter the lives of people who know all there is to see of their neighborhoods, and to share the sense of relatedness experienced by lifelong neighbors. Particularly striking is the sense of toleration, if not of tolerance, of the eccentric; odd and sad people like Cousin Bias in *Farewell Summer* and Kate Gordon in *. . . and Ladies of the Club* are beautifully realized characters and also symbols of the small town's treatment of those who are different. Santmyer also has an understanding of isolation, particularly evident in *The Fierce Dispute*, as a function of characters' over-involvement in each other's lives.

Santmyer chronicles a "vanished era" that has not vanished at all, but exists as a metaphor for life today. She represents the storyteller as historian, the keeper of the country's traditions.

—Susan Quinn Berneis

SAUNDERS, Diana. See **COFFMAN, Virginia.**

SAUNDERS, Jean. Also writes as Sally Blake; Jean Innes; Rowena Summers. British. Born in London, 8 February 1932. Educated in Weston-super-Mare, Avon. Married Geoffrey Saunders in 1952; one son and two daughters. Address: 23 Hobbiton Road, Weston-super-Mare, Avon BS22 0HP, England.

ROMANCE AND HISTORICAL PUBLICATIONS

Novels

The Tender Trap. London, Woman's Weekly, 1978.
Lady of the Manor. London, Woman's Weekly, 1978.
Rainbow's End. London, Woman's Weekly, 1978.
Enchantment of Merrowporth. New York, Cameo, 1980.
The Kissing Time. New York, Silhouette, 1982.
Love's Sweet Music. New York, Silhouette, 1983.
The Language of Love. New York, Silhouette, 1983.
Taste the Wine. New York, Silhouette, 1983.
Partners in Love. New York, Silhouette, 1984.
Scarlet Rebel. New York, Ballantine, 1985.
Golden Destiny. New York, Pocket Books, 1986.
All in the April Morning. London, W. H. Allen, 1989.

Novels as Jean Innes

Ashton's Folly. London, Hale, 1975.
Sands of Lamanna. London, Hale, 1975.
The Golden God. London, Hale, 1975.
The Whispering Dark. London, Hale, 1976.
Boskelly's Bride. London, Hale, 1976.
White Blooms of Yarrow. London, Hale, 1976.
The Wishing Stone. London, Hale, 1976.
Cobden's Cottage. London, Hale, 1978.
The Dark Stranger. London, Hale, 1979.
Silver Lady. London, Hale, 1981.
Legacy of Love. London, Hale, 1982.
Scent of Jasmine. New York, Bantam, 1982; London, Century Hutchinson, 1983.
Enchanted Island. New York, Bantam, 1982.
Seeker of Dreams. London, Hale, 1983.
Buccaneer's Bride. New York, Zebra, 1989.

Novels as Sally Blake

The Devil's Kiss. London, Macdonald Futura, 1981.
Moonlight Mirage. London, Macdonald Futura, 1982.
Outback Woman. London, Mills and Boon, 1989.

Novels as Rowena Summers (series: Cornish Trilogy)

Blackmaddie. London, Hamlyn, 1980.

The Savage Moon. London, Severn House, 1982.
The Sweet Red Earth. London, Severn House, 1983.
Willow Harvest. London, Severn House, 1985.
Cornish Trilogy:
   Killigrew Clay. London, Severn House, 1986.
   Clay Country. London, Severn House, 1987.
   Family Ties. London, Severn House, 1988.

OTHER PUBLICATIONS

Fiction (for children)

The Fugitives. London, Heinemann, 1974.
Only Yesterday. London, Heinemann, 1975.
Nightmare. London, Heinemann, 1977.
Roses All the Way. London, Heinemann, 1978.
Anchor Man. London, Heinemann, 1980.

Other

The Craft of Writing Romance. London, Allison and Busby, 1986.
Writing Step By Step. London, Allison and Busby, 1988.

*

Jean Saunders comments:
The term compulsive writer is perhaps a euphemistic one, yet it describes precisely how I regard myself. I am never happier than when I am writing, and the urge to do so has never diminished. My first aim is to entertain my readers, while producing novels of depth and insight into character. I am very conscious of the way that circumstances can change and mould people, and I apply this maxim to my fictional characters by giving them an emotive background in which to grow and develop, such as my current novels involving two World Wars, *All In The April Morning*, and the forthcoming *The Bannister Girls*. Research plays a very large part in my life, whether for contemporary locations and occupations or historical facts that must always be accurate. My writing is sometimes described as earthy. I prefer to call it realistic. I pull no punches in writing about birth and death and everything between. My heroines are always strong, feminine, and survivors against all the odds. I defend romance fiction wholeheartedly. I believe that any novel in any genre is enhanced by a love relationship between the main characters, and I take pride in making my characters and plots as visually believable to the reader as possible.

*   *   *

As well as neatly weaving historical events into her novels, Jean Saunders has the ability to absorb the atmosphere of a period and the attitudes of the people living at that time, then transpose them into her fictional works.
Scarlet Rebel, set in Scotland at the time of the Jacobite rebellion involved considerable research and Saunders admits that she found discrepancies in her sources. When it was not possible to verify facts she had to choose what seemed the most likely occurrences. In this novel particularly, she succeeds in conveying the feel of the period while continually progressing the gripping story of an intensely emotional romance between the

fictional couple who are supporting the Young Pretender in his bid for the English throne. The graphic battle scenes add an extra dimension to the romantic storyline.

Katrina, the coppery-haired beauty from *Scarlet Rebel* makes a fleeting appearance in a later novel, *Golden Destiny*, but only as part of a family legend. *Golden Destiny* takes place more than 100 years later, when a 17-year-old girl sails to India to join her diplomat father. She becomes involved with a dashing male descendant of Katrina's, and faces danger with him by her side during a native uprising.

The author's gothic novels, written as Jean Innes, owe much of their atmosphere to their settings. *Sands of Lamanna* takes place in 19th-century Cornwall and exploits the rugged countryside and the mysterious grey stone houses as well as the folklore and superstitions which were rife in that part of the country at the time. The characters are clear and distinct. An unforgettable gypsy girl named Wenna plays a leading part in this novel. Her father lays a curse on her and her lover, the main male character, who then considers himself doomed. Other characters are involved in the notorious Cornish shipwrecking activities. There are murder, a trial, imprisonment, but in true gothic tradition good prevails and evil gets its just reward.

The novels written as Rowena Summers have a more lusty flavour and take their inspiration from both historical events and locations. Particularly strong in its atmosphere, *The Savage Moon* begins its story in the bleak English Fen country and features two brothers who have fled from the Irish potato famine. They are not welcome in their new surroundings and come into strong conflict with a local family. The attraction between the two Irish boys and the two girls in the family make the male members more determined than ever to chase them off. The story moves on to North America and the Civil War, but desire, rivalry, and love still contrive to tear the two families apart.

Willow Harvest is set in the Somerset Levels with a background of willow harvesting and basket weaving. The father of the heroine takes his baskets to show at the Great Exhibition of 1851, and the heroine becomes involved with a class of people she has not known before. Anyone who reads this novel will find it hard to forget the revolting and libidinous Cyrus Hale's lecherous pursuit of the luckless heroine.

The Devil's Kiss by Sally Blake takes its title from the name of a mysterious Siamese ruby with alleged magical powers. The story, which begins on a tea plantation in Ceylon, moves to the misty Yorkshire moorlands, peopled with traditionally morose and single-minded Yorkshire characters. The gem plays a major role in the story by its influence on the characters.

Saunders's most recent novel, *All in the April Morning*, begins in San Francisco on the day of the 1906 earthquake which orphans two Irish immigrant girls. Bridget, the older girl, becomes obsessed with a desire to return to Ireland but is unable to do so. Her younger sister dies and she is trapped into an unhappy marriage. Eventually, widowed but with a daughter and pregnant with a son, Bridget realises her dream and goes back to Ireland where she is befriended by a wealthy Englishman. There is constant and painful conflict between Bridget and her daughter as the story progresses to World War II. Then the daughter falls in love with an airman whose home is in San Francisco, a place Bridget never wants to see again. Involvement in an air raid shocks Bridget's mind with memories of the earthquake but brings mother and daughter closer together than ever. After the war, Bridget goes back to San Francisco with a new husband, to see her grandson.

This novel which among other things explores with convincing authority and particular sensitivity the complex and moving relationship between the heroine and her daughter, demonstrates how Saunders has gradually expanded and developed her talent and ability to deal successfully with stronger themes and more complex relationships.

—W.H. Bradley

SAUNDERS, Jeanne. See **MANNERS, Alexandra.**

SAVAGE, Elizabeth (neé Fitzgerald). American. Born in Hingham, Massachusetts, in 1918. Educated at Colby College, Waterville, Maine, B.A. 1940. Married Thomas Savage in 1939; two sons and one daughter. Address: c/o Little Brown, 34 Beacon Street, Boston, Massachusetts 02108, U.S.A.

ROMANCE AND HISTORICAL PUBLICATIONS

Novels

Summer of Pride. Boston, Little Brown, 1961; London, Hodder and Stoughton, 1962.
But Not for Love. Boston, Little Brown, 1970.
A Fall of Angels. Boston, Little Brown, 1971.
Happy Ending. Boston, Little Brown, 1972.
The Last Night at the Ritz. Boston, Little Brown, 1973.
A Good Confession. Boston, Little Brown, 1975.
The Girls from the Five Great Valleys. Boston, Little Brown, and London, Prior, 1977.
Willowwood. Boston, Little Brown, 1978; London, Prior, 1979.
Toward the End. Boston, Little Brown, 1980.

*   *   *

Adept at characterization, Elizabeth Savage also evokes place with great skill: the American far west or New England (settings most frequently used in her novels), the Jamaica of *A Fall of Angels*, or Dante Gabriel Rossetti's 19th-century London. Almost always, the weather and seasonal changes are key symbols, humor an enlivening device.

Reflecting Savage's life-long interest, *Willowwood* blends fact and fiction in the story of Rossetti and his talented, capricious circle. In its deft portrayal of intricate relationships among complex characters, *Willowwood*, an atypical Savage novel, is nevertheless linked closely with others among her works.

Less singular but no less intriguing than the pre-Raphaelites are the extended families Savage examines. The organizing event of *Summer of Pride* is the Oliver family's annual picnic which memorializes their history and accomplishments. Matt Oliver, a naively autocratic Idaho rancher, oversees his family's interests despite their best efforts to prevent his interference, even to planning his younger brother's career; but Paul, a poet, intends to marry a stranger whom the family distrusts, move east, and teach. Meanwhile the survival of Matt's own marriage depends largely upon his wife's self-redefinition. Under the eye of Emily, the matriarch, the brothers sort out their obligations, each learning to compromise.

Though their relationships are marred by confusion, misjudgment, and deceit, the clannish Hollister family of *But Not for Love* maintains a haughty facade, but ultimately, Winifred Hollister, the self-abasing wife of Peter, begins to see her in-laws and even her husband as "only people. Very like herself." Like several other female characters, Winifred also discovers her own unsuspected strength. The irony of its title informs almost every relationship and situation of the plot which leaves a dozen questions unanswered but all central problems confronted, its relatively open ending being both satisfying and appropriate.

A Fall of Angels examines a crucial period in the lives of Helena St. John and Luke Strider, thus addressing one of Savage's most frequent topics: a marriage threatened with redefinition or dissolution just when outsiders (and even, perhaps, one of the partners) might pronounce it secure, even enviable. Less successful than other works in the canon, this novel, like *Willowood*, is nonetheless a solid achievement.

Two of Savage's New England novels also depict marriages in crisis. However, neither protagonist wastes much time pitying herself; both immediately confront other important challenges. During the deathbed vigil which bounds the action of *A Good Confession*, Meg Atherton sorts out her reactions to her husband's extra-marital affair, comes to terms with her reckless uncle, and learns important lessons about her attractive, available first love. In *Toward the End* an arduous winter is the central symbol for Jessie Thorne's development after separating from her husband. Happily devoid of pat phrases and cant diagnoses, each plot depicts its protagonist's increasing self-confidence and her growing awareness of the choice most suitable to her needs, her wishes, and her responsibilities. Incorporating a telling portrait of life during the Depression, *Happy Ending* compares love stories, one old, one new. During a long, idyllic Montana winter, the elderly Russells celebrate the joys of family life and watch the developing love between their very young housekeeper, Maryalyse Tyler, an unwed mother, and Bud Perrault, their cowhand. The bonds of affection among this created family are strong and true. Here, Savage's title is quietly, firmly realistic but not ironic; her protagonists learn to change what they can, to accept what they must, and to cherish the good moments. Like all Savage novels, these are love stories informed by honest sentiment and brought to just conclusions. Savage's romances are unfailingly realistic, astringent but never acerbic.

One of the strongest qualities of *Happy Ending* is its adroitly managed, shifting point of view which prompts the reader to identify with several characters. The first-person point of view in *The Last Night at the Ritz*, perhaps Savage's best novel, is equally persuasive. Here, the unnamed narrator, believing herself to be fatally ill, reviews her life—marked by excitement, extravagance, and lost loves—by comparing it with that of her closest friend, Gay, who has led a settled, family-centered existence until her husband's infidelity and her son's rebellion call all their values into question. Able to laugh at herself, markedly sensitive to the needs of others, the narrator persuades readers of her reliability despite her own disclaimers, no mean authorial feat. The women's abiding friendship (one bond is their shared passion for reading, an especially nice touch) and the protagonist's profound affection for her friend's child are beautifully rendered.

The narrator of *The Girls from the Five Great Valleys* conceals her identity until the last sentence; yet her revelation prompts one to realize that Savage has so accurately evoked her character's buoyant, affirming tone that one should have known her all along. Vigorous (but not enduring) early friendship is the motif unifying this examination of three families whose teenage daughters are friends. Comparing and contrasting various parents' capacity for nurture and love, Savage comments tellingly upon child abuse, notes that occasionally youngsters flourish despite neglect, and firmly reminds readers that some families nurture very effectively. Powerful portraits of a wide array of characters of varying ages inform this excellent novel.

An acute observer of American life, Savage consistently demonstrates her understanding of human strengths and weaknesses as well as her technical skill; she is a very good writer.

—Jane S. Bakerman

SAWLEY, Petra. See **WOODWARD, Lilian.**

SAWYER, John. See **BUCKINGHAM, Nancy.**

SAWYER, Nancy. See **BUCKINGHAM, Nancy.**

SAXTON, Judith. Also writes as Judy Turner. British. Born in Norwich, Norfolk, 5 March 1936. Married; four children. Agent: Murray Pollinger, 4 Garrick Street, London WC2E 9HB. Address: 110 Park Avenue, Wrexham, Denbighshire, Wales.

ROMANCE AND HISTORICAL PUBLICATIONS

Novels

The Bright Day Is Done. London, Constable, 1974.
Princess in Waiting. London, Constable, 1976.
Winter Queen. London, Constable, 1977.
The Pride. London, Hamlyn, 1981.
The Glory. London, Hamlyn, 1982.
The Splendour. London, Hamlyn, 1983.
Full Circle. London, Hamlyn, 1984.
Sophie. London, Century, 1985.
Family Feeling. London, Century, 1986; New York, St. Martin's Press, 1987.
All My Fortunes. London, Century, 1987; New York, St. Martin's Press, 1988.
Chasing Rainbows. London, Joseph, 1988.
A Family Affair. London, Grafton, 1989.

Novels as Judy Turner

Cousin to the Queen. London, Constable, 1972; New York, St. Martin's Press, 1974.
Raleigh's Fair Bess. London, Hale, 1972; New York, St. Martin's Press, 1974.
Diamond Bright, Feather Light. London, Hale, 1974.
My Master Mariner. London, Hale, 1974.
The Queen's Corsair. London, Hale, 1976.
Child of Passion. London, Hale, 1978.
The Merry Jade. London, Hale, 1978.
A Gift for Pamela. London, Mills and Boon, 1981.
Triple Tangle. London, Mills and Boon, 1981.
Sherida. London, Mills and Boon, 1981.
Follow the Drum. London, Mills and Boon, 1982.

OTHER PUBLICATIONS

Novel

Jenny Alone. London, Joseph, 1987.

*   *   *

The core of Judith Saxton's novels is a concept of the family as the essential social unit. Far-flung it may be, and not every member sees eye to eye with every other one, but across time as well as across the world the bonds of kinship remain, exerting a force that remains powerful through every trial. As if to demonstrate the strengths of the family unit Saxton sometimes likes to disconcert her readers by sudden leaps in her narrative, from one situation to another, with hardly a word of explanation; but her readers are only puzzled for a moment and then they can pick up the threads again, just as happens in many a home when old relationships are renewed after a lapse of time when an uncle or grandson returns unexpectedly.

The novels range widely in location, from New Zealand to the United States, over a period of three quarters of a century, but they are anchored firmly in the place that Saxton knows best, the delightful and lively cathedral city of Norwich where she grew up. What she chronicles is essentially the history of her own forebears from the late Victorian period to the time of World War II. Her prefaces are testimony to the research she has undertaken, and there can be no doubt that her portrayal of characters owes some of its solidity to the care she has taken to model them on real life. They live and move, moreover, against a closely observed background, which, once again, makes for plausibility and vitality. Public events, such as the Norwich celebrations of Queen Victoria's Diamond Jubilee, mark epochs in the on-going life of the family, and the two World Wars leave a deep imprint on it in ways that parallel the experiences that many have shared. But smaller things are accorded their rightful importance too, and a future social historian may well be interested to see how the development of transport, for instance, is seen to play its part in the way ordinary people lived as the horse gave way to the early motor car and the aeroplane replaced the ship as the normal means of long-distance travel.

The portrayal of the domestic sphere is even more interesting, and Saxton is particularly skilled in showing the everyday life of middle-class people. A quite prosperous Jewish family settled in East Anglia is the foundation of the story, and though they mix freely with those around them its members always possess not only a strong sense of mutual loyalty, which always reasserts itself even if it is strained at times, but also a sense of otherness, which makes them confident of their own worth. Sometimes made to feel strangers even in their own home town, they are more welcoming to foreigners than the common run of Norwich people are generally reckoned to be. The Jewish element is brought out too not in orthodox religious observance, which is shown as gradually slipping away, but in the keeping of family festivals and a partiality for certain creature comforts that recall an earlier period, before the immigration into England. There also seems to be something very characteristic in the way in which the males assume airs of superiority and demand care and attention when it is soon made clear enough that the dominating and most forceful personalities are female.

As Saxton develops the ramifications of her family saga far from its beginnings with a Jewish household in a provincial city in the east of England, there are many surprises and violent changes of fortune. Some might think there are even rather too many, for there are times when it is tempting to think these characters are disaster-prone. Perhaps it is a matter of truth being a little too strange for fiction. This is, however, only a minor criticism to make of a saga with a strong sense of period in which vivid, convincing and highly-sexed characters capture the imagination in a great human web of connections which finally come full circle.

—Christopher Smith

SCOTLAND, Jay. See **JAKES, John.**

SCOTT, Evelyn. Also wrote as Ernest Souza. American. Born Elsie Dunn in Clarksville, Tennessee, 17 January 1893. Educated privately; at Newcomb Preparatory School, Sophie Newcomb College, and Newcomb School of Art, all New Orleans. Married 1) the painter and writer Frederick Creighton Wellman (pseudonym: Cyril Kay Scott) in 1913 (divorced 1928), one son; 2) the writer John Metcalfe in 1930. Freelance writer. Lived in Brazil; travelled in Bermuda, France, North Africa, and England. Recipient: Guggenheim fellowship, 1932. *Died 3 August 1963.*

ROMANCE AND HISTORICAL PUBLICATIONS

Novels

The Narrow House. New York, Boni and Liveright, and London, Duckworth, 1921.
Narcissus. New York, Harcourt, 1922; as *Bewilderment,* London, Duckworth, 1922.
The Golden Door. New York, Seltzer, 1925.
Migrations: An Arabesque in Histories. New York, Boni and Liveright, and London, Duckworth, 1927.
The Wave. New York, Cape and Smith, and London, Cape, 1929.
A Calendar of Sin: American Melodramas. New York, Cape and Smith, 2 vols., 1931.
Eva Gay. New York, Smith and Haas, 1933; London, Lovat Dickson, 1934.
Breathe Upon These Slain. New York, Smith and Haas, and London, Lovat Dickson, 1934.
Bread and a Sword. New York, Scribner, 1937.
The Shadow of the Hawk. New York, Scribner, 1941.

Short Stories

Ideals: A Book of Farce and Comedy. New York, Boni, 1927.

OTHER PUBLICATIONS

Play

Love (produced New York, 1921).

Verse

Precipitations. New York, Brown, 1920.
The Winter Alone. New York, Cape and Smith, 1930.

Other

Escapade (autobiography). New York, Seltzer, 1923; London, Cape, 1930.
In the Endless Sands (for children), with Cyril Kay Scott. New York, Holt, 1925.
Witch Perkins: A Story of the Kentucky Hills (for children). New York, Holt, 1929.
On William Faulkner's The Sound and the Fury. New York, Cape and Smith, 1929.
Blue Rum (for children; as Ernest Souza). New York, Cape and Smith, and London, Cape, 1930.
Billy, The Maverick (for children). New York, Holt, 1934.
Background in Tennessee (autobiography). New York, McBride, 1937.

*

Manuscript Collection: Humanities Research Center, University of Texas, Austin.

Critical Studies: *Pretty Good for a Woman: The Enigmas of Evelyn Scott* by D. A. Callard, London, Cape, 1985; New York, Norton, 1986.

*   *   *

Evelyn Scott's reputation has waned sadly since the time between the two World Wars when she was hailed as one of America's most significant novelists and her historical fiction was praised for its evocative powers, its psychological insight, and its technical daring. Much of her work is a reflection of the tensions and pressures of her own experience as a woman emerging from a restrictive environment, and she added an important extra dimension with three major novels which, though they may be read as if independent of one another, constitute a panorama of America history across a period of nearly three quarters of a century.

Migrations is set in the time of the 1849 Gold Rush; *The Wave* takes the titanic upheaval of the Civil War as its background and is said to have revealed the vast potential of that period as a resource for subsequent American fiction and the films that were based on it; and *A Calendar of Sin: American Melodramas*, in two volumes, takes the form of a superior family chronicle, covering the years from 1867 to 1914.

In general scope and in the abundant detail, the historical basis of Scott's fiction is sound. Though Scott was quite open in admitting that she invented a great deal in her historical novels she also pointed out that where she added to or departed from acknowledged fact, she did so only after informing herself fully about reality as it is recorded, and critics have generally agreed that she did not abuse the freedom she allowed herself. Her object, in any case, is not to provide in her fiction substitutes for history books. Rather she creates a pervasive and persuasive sense of period by the juxtaposition of events, scenes, and characters in order to convey impressions of the experiences which people underwent at the time in question. Characters teem, emotions crowd in, as they do in real life during troubled times, and the richness of an epoch in American history is evoked in all its limitless variety.

For Scott the past, however, was not a time when people were essentially different, and she developed her historical fiction as a means of exploring the fundamental dilemmas that haunted her personally and are also expressed in her novels of contemporary life. In her presentation of the problems of two families as they respond to changing situations and unresolved strains in Ameri-

can life there is much that corresponds to her efforts to make sense of what she perceived as conflicting tendencies in her own heredity. *Migrations* plays upon the paradox that the American dream of "going west to fashion a new life" is, sadly, only a dream, because wherever we may go we remain ourselves. *The Wave* shows how in the Civil War individuals are swept along by the tide of events which they cannot control and which soon cease to be in any way the expression of human will. *A Calendar of Sin* takes as its theme the problems that American women have had in achieving balanced attitudes towards the physical and emotional aspects of love. It is a telling indictment of attitudes that in the title "sin" stands for "sex," and the word "calendar" spotlights not just the idea that this is a narrative of events lived day by day but also has the connotations of a record of crime. By the same token, there is bruising irony in the subtitle "American melodramas," and Scott is not afraid to invent a series of distressingly violent incidents to illustrate her theme in exemplary fashion.

Scott's trilogy of historical novels has great power, and, especially in the context of the current interest in women's writing, it is surprising it has not attracted more interest of late. Perhaps the explanation lies in the substantial length of the books and the deliberate fragmentation of the narrative manner which might be seen as demanding rather too much of her readers.

—Christopher Smith

* * *

SCOTT, Jane. See **McELFRESH, Adeline.**

* * *

SCOTT, Janey. See **LINDSAY, Rachel.**

* * *

SEALE, Sara. Pseudonym for A. D. L. MacPherson. *Died 24 December 1978.*

ROMANCE AND HISTORICAL PUBLICATIONS

Novels

Beggars May Sing. London, Mills and Boon, 1932; Toronto, Harlequin, 1968.
Chase the Moon. London, Mills and Boon, 1933.
Summer Spell. London, Mills and Boon, 1937.
Grace Before Meat. London, Mills and Boon, 1938.
This Merry Bond. London, Mills and Boon, 1938; Toronto, Harlequin, 1961.
Spread Your Wings. London, Mills and Boon, 1939.
Green Grass Growing. London, Mills and Boon, 1940.
Stormy Petrel. London, Mills and Boon, 1941.
Barn Dance. London, Mills and Boon, 1941.
The Silver Sty. London, Mills and Boon, 1941; Toronto, Harlequin, 1976.
House of Glass. London, Mills and Boon, 1944; as *Maggy*, Toronto, Harlequin, 1959.

Folly to Be Wise. London, Mills and Boon, 1946; Toronto, Harlequin, 1966.

The Reluctant Orphan. London, Mills and Boon, 1947; as *Orphan Bride*, Toronto, Harlequin, 1962.

The English Tutor. London, Mills and Boon, 1948; Toronto, Harlequin, 1968.

The Gentle Prisoner. London, Mills and Boon, 1949; Toronto, Harlequin, 1962.

These Delights. London, Mills and Boon, 1949; Toronto, Harlequin, 1965.

Then She Fled Me. London, Mills and Boon, 1950; Toronto, Harlequin, 1963.

The Young Amanda. London, Mills and Boon, 1950; Toronto, Harlequin, 1966.

The Dark Stranger. London, Mills and Boon, 1951; Toronto, Harlequin, 1964.

Wintersbride. London, Mills and Boon, 1951; Toronto, Harlequin, 1960.

The Lordly One. London, Mills and Boon, 1952; Toronto, Harlequin, 1968.

The Forbidden Island. London, Mills and Boon, 1953; Toronto, Harlequin, 1963.

Turn to the West. London, Mills and Boon, 1953.

The Truant Spirit. London, Mills and Boon, 1954; Toronto, Harlequin, 1969.

Time of Grace. London, Mills and Boon, 1955; Toronto, Harlequin, 1965.

Child Friday. London, Mills and Boon, 1956; Toronto, Harlequin, 1965.

Sister to Cinderella. London, Mills and Boon, 1956.

I Know My Love. London, Mills and Boon, 1957; Toronto, Harlequin, 1969.

Trevallion. London, Mills and Boon, 1957; Toronto, Harlequin, 1967.

Lucy Lamb. London, Mills and Boon, 1958; Toronto, Harlequin, 1963.

Charity Child. London, Mills and Boon, 1959; Toronto, Harlequin, 1966.

Dear Dragon. London, Mills and Boon, 1959; Toronto, Harlequin, 1964.

Cloud Castle. London, Mills and Boon, 1960; Toronto, Harlequin, 1967.

The Only Charity. London, Mills and Boon, 1961; Toronto, Harlequin, 1962.

Valentine's Day. London, Mills and Boon, 1962.

The Reluctant Landlord. London, Mills and Boon, 1962.

Doctor's Ward. London, Mills and Boon, and Toronto, Harlequin, 1962.

By Candlelight. London, Mills and Boon, 1963.

The Youngest Bridesmaid. London, Mills and Boon, 1963; Toronto, Harlequin, 1964.

The Third Uncle. London, Mills and Boon, 1964; Toronto, Harlequin, 1965.

To Catch a Unicorn. London, Mills and Boon, 1964; Toronto, Harlequin, 1975.

Green Girl. London, Mills and Boon, 1965; Toronto, Harlequin, 1966.

The Truant Bride. London, Mills and Boon, 1966; Toronto, Harlequin, 1967.

Penny Plain. London, Mills and Boon, 1967; Toronto, Harlequin, 1968.

That Young Person. London, Mills and Boon, 1969; Toronto, Harlequin, 1970.

The Queen of Hearts. Toronto, Harlequin, 1969.

Dear Professor. London, Mills and Boon, 1970; Toronto, Harlequin, 1971.

Mr. Brown. London, Mills and Boon, 1971; as *The Unknown Mr. Brown*, Toronto, Harlequin, 1972.

My Heart's Desire. Toronto, Harlequin, 1976.

*　　　*　　　*

Sara Seale is the pen name of Mrs. A. D. L. MacPherson, a romance writer who wrote from the 1930's to the 1970's. Her first book, *Beggars May Sing* (1932), was the first of almost 50 romances. She often used Irish backgrounds in her novels as well as settings in England and Cornwall.

Her romances have an unusual simplicity and innocence in them that make them strongly evocative and almost timeless in their enjoyment. They are deceptively simple, however, in the sense that Seale brings a highly developed writing skill to them so that their simplicity actually hides a subtle sense of sophistication and complexity.

Her heroines are typically sweet and awakened, often lacking in the usual standards of beauty and attractiveness. They are child-like, fey little creatures who drift somewhere between earth and heaven in a hazy cocoon of rose-tinted dreams, except when age-old wisdom of woman-kind unexpectedly emerges to confound the hero's more earthy beliefs and attitudes about women and love. Their fragile sweetness and charm prevent their naive provocations from becoming blatant efforts to captivate. The fact that these qualities are, in fact, captivating is usually accidental and quite beyond the heroines' intent.

Worldly-wise and world-weary heroes offer instant resistance to the heroines. Experience, knowledge, and often their own unhappiness prove too strong and effective a teacher to let them believe their instinctive reactions. Only gradually do they acknowledge the fact that the heroine holds the key to their ultimate happiness.

In a sense, Seale's novels have an individuality about them that make them remembered and enjoyed over and over again. Her heroines are not goody-goody, trite little charmers who will quickly take on the tired sophistication of older women. Their beliefs and goodness come from within and show Seale's creative ability to an outstanding degree. Goodness, naturalness, and true sensitivity combine in the heroines to make them feminine and womanly in the best sense of the words. They find happiness in little things; they give happiness by practicing constant instinctive virtues that are neatly balanced by quick repartee, occasional glimpses of temper, and natural sweetness of thought.

In at least three of her novels, Seale uses the same type of opening and it proves to be very effective. Basically the story begins with the arrival of the heroine in a strange and usually unwelcoming household. In *Dear Dragon*, a novel set in Cornwall, Alice Brown in thrust rather crudely into the Pendragon house to take care of a child. Bride Aherne in *That Young Person* arrives at Queen's Acre from Ireland to visit her intended's family. She is also to win approval for their marriage from Simon Spender, the estate's trustee. Finally, *My Heart's Desire* moves Gael Cassella from the rural beauty of Ireland's Galway to the fascinating delights and difficulties of "swinging" London.

In each novel the arrival of the heroine acts as a catalyst as she unconsciously draws attention to attitudes and actions of the people living there. False ideals, sophisticated deception, and weakness of character suddenly stand out for what they really are as the heroine reacts to them. In *The Young Person* Simon Spender sheds his cold, monkish outlook and succumbs to warm childish pleasures such as a snow-ball fight with Bride. Alice's rather naive and child-like habit of truthfulness forces the members of the Pendragon family to take stock of themselves. She does it, however, in a way that helps each to discover his own hopes and wishes in life. Gael's fey-like characteristic of seeing good in everyone at first repels the sophisticated members of Richard Saracen's family. His aunt and his cousin as well as their friends find her odd ways embarrassing and often dreadful. At the end, however, they all discover that her qualities and outlook on life are all that really matter, regardless of financial position.

Perhaps the best illustration of Seale's heroines is in the following: "He looked into her strange eyes and saw there something infinitely older, infinitely wiser than himself. 'You are my conscience, my friend, and my true love,' he said simply."

Somehow Seale's readers understood the difference between her heroines and those of other writers. Naivety and the lack of sophisitication are usual traits of heroines, but hers are drawn with an inner strength of knowledge and an ability to hold with solid truths of principle. In her novels, light romance takes on an added dimension. They offer pictures of the best qualities in life that women and girls hope to find in their own lives.

—Arlene Moore

* * *

SEBASTIAN, Margaret. Pseudonym for Arthur M. Gladstone; also writes as Maggie Gladstone; Lisabet Norcross; Cilla Whitmore. American. Born in Brooklyn, New York, 22 September 1921. Educated at New York University, B.A. (cum laude) 1942, M.S. 1947. Served in the United States Army Air Force, 1942–46. Married 1) Margaret Sebastian in 1949 (died 1973); 2) Helen Worth in 1980. Chemist, Pittsburg Coke and Chemical Company, 1948–53; chief chemist and product manager, Nopco Chemical Company, Newark, New Jersey, 1953–59; administrative assistant to the president, Anchor Serum Company, St. Joseph, Missouri, 1959–61; proposals director, Hercules Inc., Cumberland, Maryland, 1961–67; financial planner, Affiliated Business Machines, Brooklyn, 1967–68; supervising chemist, Chemical Insecticide Corporation, Edison, New Jersey, 1967–69; bench chemist, Hartz Mountain Pet Foods, Harrison, New Jersey, 1969–74. Since 1974 full-time writer. Address: c/o Fawcett, 201 East 50th Street, New York, New York 10022, U.S.A.

ROMANCE AND HISTORICAL PUBLICATIONS

Novels (series: Bow Street)

The Honorable Miss Clarendon. New York, Pyramid, 1973.
Meg Miller. New York, Berkley, 1976.
Bow Street Brangle. New York, Popular Library, 1977.
Bow Street Gentleman. New York, Popular Library, 1977.
Lord Orlando's Protegee. New York, Berkley, 1977.
Miss Letty. New York, Popular Library, 1977.
My Lord Rakehell. New York, Popular Library, 1977.
The Young Lady from Alton-St. Pancras. New York, Popular Library, 1977.
The Courtship of Colonel Crowne. New York, Popular Library, 1978.
The Poor Relation. New York, Popular Library, 1978.
That Savage Yankee Squire! New York, Popular Library, 1978.
Lord Dedringham's Divorce. New York, Popular Library, 1978.
Dilemma in Duet. New York, Fawcett, 1979.
Her Knight on a Barge. New York, Popular Library, 1979.
The Awakening of Lord Dalby. New York, Popular Library, 1979.
The Plight of Pamela Pollworth. New York, Fawcett, 1980.

Byway to Love. New York, Fawcett, 1980.
Miss Keating's Temptation. New York, Fawcett, 1981.

Novels as Maggie Gladstone (series: Ballerina; Lacebridge Ladies)

Lacebridge Ladies:
The Fortunate Belle. New York, Playboy Press, 1978.
The Love Duel. New York, Playboy Press, 1978.
The Scandalous Lady. New York, Playboy Press, 1978.
The Impudent Widow. New York, Playboy Press, 1979.
The Love Tangle. New York, Playboy Press, 1979.
The Reluctant Debutante (Ballerina). New York, Playboy Press, 1979.
The Lady's Masquerade. New York, Playboy Press, 1980.
The Reluctant Protegee (Ballerina). New York, Playboy Press, 1980.
A Lesson in Love. New York, Playboy Press, 1981.

Novels as Lisabet Norcross

Masquerade of Love. New York, Berkley, 1978.
Reluctant Heiress. New York, Berkley, 1978.
The Lady and the Rogue. New York, Berkley, 1978.
My Lady Scapegrace. New York, Berkley, 1979.

Novels as Cilla Whitmore

His Lordship's Landlady. New York, Dell, 1979.
Manner of a Lady. New York, Dell, 1979.
Mansion for a Lady. New York, Dell, 1980.

* * *

Arthur M. Gladstone, who writes as Margaret Sebastian, Maggie Gladstone, Cilla Whitmore, and Lisabett Norcross is something of an enigma. He either has an extremely cynical attitude about romance or he is totally amused with the genre and is determined to have as much fun out of writing his novels as his readers have in reading them.

Readers know exactly what to expect in each of Gladstone's modern comedies of manners. Stock characters abound. Befuddled heroes, shrewish heroines, and villainous villains spice his pages as characters tumble from one farcical event to the next. Gladstone also makes full use of the Regency period as a background for his novels. It is such a nice, tidy little world he manipulates so deftly. A handful of well-known lords and ladies, a social outlook rigidly enforced on all who matter, and a brief historical time that bridged the 18th and 19th centuries make up this world. In some cases the setting is immaterial because any relationship between Gladstone's Regency days and the real historical period are completely accidental. Indeed, one senses that some of Gladstone's novels should have started with "once upon a time. . . ." The purist reader of Regency novels may not enjoy Gladstone's irreverent attitude, but others will sit cozily back and enjoy the frothy light-heartedness in his novels.

Novels written under the name Margaret Sebastian have at least one series which include *Dilemma in Duet* and *Byway to Love.* The central characters are a pair of female twins who delight in confusing everyone, including their boyfriends. The fast-paced dialogue is kept alive by constant misunderstandings, irrelevant asides, and character obtuseness. In *The Honorable Miss Clarendon* one finds a more skillful blend of plot and characters. It is only midway through the story that one begins to catch the unique element that makes up Gladstone's style. In this novel, Lady Cynthia Clarendon, now a penniless orphan, sets out by public coach to take a position as a companion. The wreck of the coach, a meeting with the Duke of Somervale (mistaken for a servant), and an eventual misunderstanding between Cynthia and the Duke, leads to a merry chase of a hero in love and a heroine too proud to accept it.

Writing as Maggie Gladstone, he launched two series of heroines. The Ballerina stories and the Lacebridge ladies. The ballerinas are individual members of the Royal Italian Opera House's ballet corps. In *The Reluctant Protegee* Nancy Faulconer the heroine, becomes a member of the corps and is one of the few to achieve "enpointe" dancing. This is toe dancing, and a new and untried method of ballet dance. Surprisingly, Nancy and Lord Anthony Faile, the hero, do not resolve their love in a happy-ever-after ending. She refuses to become his mistress, preferring to "remain her own mistress." This is certainly an unexpected ending to a romance.

The Lacebridge Ladies series involves the stories of five sisters and how each one is launched into society and eventually into matrimony. Plotting naturally involves husbands, friends, and other relatives. In a way, the series is one grand plot with subplots for each sister. Characters from one novel reappear in the next.

As Cilla Whitmore, Gladstone still maintains his own individual sense of the ridiculous. In *Manner of a Lady*, the heroine, Miranda Thorpe takes on the task of helping her uncle in his architectural firm. Her help, however, centers on wanting to be an architect. The unsuspecting hero, Viscount Anthony Farnsworth, commissions her uncle to design a fitting place for his future intended. Miranda, cunningly corrupts the building workers, re-draws her uncle's plans, and ultimately constructs her own dream house. Fortunately, by the end of the story, Miranda also finds her perfect love in the form of Sir Anthony.

In all, Gladstone has produced numerous romances that are light, fluffy bits of confection that require little effort to understand. Period details are kept to a minimum, characters are rounded enough to be characters, but barely, and plot lines teasing enough to keep the reader going. The bottom line, however, is that they are enjoyable silly little things that one keeps coming back to when needing that extra spice of lightness.

—Arlene Moore

SEGER, Maura. Also writes as Jenny Bates; Sara Jennings; Anne MacNeill; Laurel Winslow. American. Born in New York City, 16 September 1951. Attended university; degree in history and economics. Married Michael Seger in 1975. Worked in the advertising department, McGraw-Hill, publishers, New York. Address: c/o Silhouette Books, 300 East 42nd Street, New York, New York 10017, U.S.A.

ROMANCE AND HISTORICAL PUBLICATIONS

Novels (series: Calvert)

Legacy. New York, Silhouette, 1981.
Sea Gate. New York, Silhouette, 1981.
Defiant Love. New York, Pocket Books, 1982; London, Coronet, 1983.
Flame on the Sun. New York, Pocket Books, 1983; London, Coronet, 1984.
Forbidden Love. New York, Pocket Books, 1983; London, Coronet, 1984.

Rebellious Love. New York, Pocket Books, and London, Coronet, 1983.
A Mind of Her Own (as Anne MacNeill). New York, New American Library, 1983.
Gilded Spring (as Jenny Bates). New York, Berkley, 1983.
Gift Beyond Price. New York, Silhouette, 1983.
Empire of the Heart. New York, Pocket Books, 1984.
Shadows of the Heart. New York, Silhouette, 1984.
Silver Zephyr. New York, Silhouette, 1984.
Dazzled (as Jenny Bates). New York, Berkley, 1984.
Heartsongs (as Laurel Winslow). New York, Avon, 1984.
Captured Images (as Laurel Winslow). New York, Avon, 1984.
Eye of the Storm. Toronto, Worldwide, 1985.
Echo of Thunder. Toronto, Worldwide, 1985.
Spring Frost, Summer Fire. Toronto, Harlequin, 1985.
Golden Chimera. New York, Silhouette, 1985.
Comes a Stranger. New York, Silhouette, 1985.
Cajun Summer. New York, Silhouette, 1986.
Edge of Dawn. New York, Silhouette, 1986.
Undercover. London, Mills and Boon, 1986.
Treasure Hunt. New York, Silhouette, 1986.
Quest of the Eagle. New York, Silhouette, 1986.
Dark of the Moon. New York, Silhouette, 1986.
Happily Ever After. New York, Silhouette, 1987.
Sarah (Calvert). Toronto, Worldwide, 1987.
Elizabeth (Calvert). Toronto, Worldwide, 1987.
Catherine (Calvert). Toronto, Worldwide, 1988.
Conflict of Interest. New York, Silhouette, 1988.
Day and Night. New York, Silhouette, 1988.
Summer Heat. New York, Crown, 1988.
Unforgettable. New York, Silhouette, 1988.
Change of Plans. New York, Silhouette, 1989.

Novels as Sara Jennings

Game Plan. New York, Dell, 1984.
Love Not the Enemy. New York, Dell, 1984.
Reach for the Stars. New York, Dell, 1984.
Star-Crossed. New York, Dell, 1985.

*   *   *

Maura Seger has compiled an impressive record for writing outstanding romance novels. In 1986–87, Seger was recognized in *Romantic Times*'s annual Reviewer's Choice awards. She was selected as one of the best all-around series authors and *Legacy* was nominated as the best Silhouette Intimate Moments novel of the year. In 1987–88, *Sea Gate* was nominated as one of the best novels in the same series. Writing awards do not come easily, especially when there are so many outstanding romance writers being published. The fact the Seger has been recognized for her creativity and originality certainly indicates that her place in romance writing is extremely well deserved.

Readers familiar with Seger's novels know that she is published consistently in the various Silhouette lines as well as in the Harlequin Super-romances and Temptations. They may not know that she has published under several pseudonyms. As Jenny Bates, she wrote *Dazzled*, a Regency novel for the Second Chance at Love series. She has also used Sara Jennings, Anne MacNeill, and Laurel Winslow as pen names. The MacNeill novel appeared as a Signet Regency romance, *A Mind of Her Own*. Her Winslow novels includes a Velvet Glove mystery, *Captured Images* and an Avon novel, *Heartsongs*.

It is easy to compile lists of titles and plots. It is much more difficult to choose those novels that best represent Seger as a writer, for she is an eclectic person who is genuinely creative in several different areas. Seger slips deftly from contemporary adventure/mystery to historical or fantasy novels. All her books contain well-rounded characters, complex and exciting plots, as well as that elusive thing called style.

In *A Mind of Her Own* young Courtney Marlowe marries Lord Nigel Davies. Both are typical products of their times, the Regency period. Events within the story awaken Courtney's awareness to contemporary social problems. She stumbles on the fact that very young girls are being kidnapped for the brothels of London. She sets out to publicize their existence and also becomes involved with a children's shelter in East London. Her fight against child kidnapping eventually results in her own kidnapping and auction in a brothel. Lord Nigel arrives just in time to save her. Slowly, he begins to give fuller support to his wife's efforts. Courtney and Lord Nigel later travel to Manchester. During their visit, Courtney is trapped in the crowd that has come to hear a famous speaker. The meeting culminates in the notorious Peterloo Massacre of 1819. The reform movement emerges from the ranks of the working class and idealistic reformers and into the hands of powerful Lords who are able to help bring about the changes so desperately needed.

From the opening scene of marital seduction to the final, moving speech that Nigel makes in the House of Lords, the reader is caught in the furious pace of events. Seger's characters grow from the light, narcissistic images that people most Regency novels into complex, caring individuals who are not afraid to take a stand. This is more than the typical Regency novel and shows Seger at her best.

Seger's contemporary novels are just as exciting. Certainly *Sea Gate* illustrates her originality and her very definite ability as a writer. *Sea Gate* is not a fantasy; it is not science fiction, it is more—What if? What is so delightful, is the fact that she makes us believe that "what if" is possible. Andrew Paxton is a scientist working on classified government research. He and his three-year-old son, Billy, live on a secluded island home in the Caribbean. One night, Billy finds a beautiful woman washed ashore. According to Federal agents, beautiful women don't accidentally arrive at security cleared islands. The woman's name is Marina and in spite of all efforts by the Federal agents to identify her, they simply cannot do so. As Andrew becomes more involved with Marina and more curious about her, he realizes that the limits of scientific knowledge are about to be pushed another step further. No! Marina is not a space alien, nor is she from a country with recognized diplomatic ties. This is one of Seger's most intriguing novels.

There is no easy way to summarize Seger's writing. She is good! Her characters are solidly developed. Her plots are more than imaginative and she captures her reader's attention so completely that few manage to put a book aside without finishing it. With her skills so finely developed, she can only continue to write even better novels.

—Arlene Moore

SEIDEL, Kathleen Gilles. American. Born in Lawrence, Kansas. Educated at the University of Chicago; Johns Hopkins University, Baltimore, Maryland, M.A., Ph.D. in English. Married; two children. Lives in Arlington, Virginia. Address: c/o Adele Leone Agency, 26 Nantucket Place, Scarsdale, New York 10583, U.S.A.

ROMANCE AND HISTORICAL PUBLICATIONS

Novels

The Same Last Name. Toronto, Harlequin, 1983.
A Risk Worth Taking. Toronto, Harlequin, 1983.
Mirrors and Mistakes. Toronto, Harlequin, 1984.
When Love Isn't Enough. Toronto, Harlequin, 1984.
After All These Years. Toronto, Harlequin, 1984.
Don't Forget to Smile. Toronto, Worldwide, 1986.

*   *   *

Kathleen Gilles Seidel began writing and publishing fiction in the early 1980's, which was a period of intense competition in the market for romance fiction. Harlequin, the North American distributor for Mills and Boon, had been challenged successfully by American romance publishers, including Simon and Shuster's Silhouette and Dell's Candlelight series, which had attracted some Harlequin authors and a percentage of Harlequin's readers. To win back portions of its American audience, Harlequin inaugurated a new series, Harlequin American Romances, featuring books with American settings, more modern situations, and longer and more complex plots. To support the new series, the company also actively sought out and encouraged new American authors. Seidel was one of the new line's earliest and best writers, and her work exemplifies several important aspects of the mid-1980's series romance. Her first four books were published in the Harlequin American Romance series. Her fifth and sixth were longer books, one in the Harlequin American Romance Premier Edition series and the other published by Harlequin's affiliate, Worldwide.

Seidel's academic background and her doctorate in English literature contribute to her work, from the playful inversion of two characters partially modeled on Tom Sawyer and Huck Finn in *After All These Years* to the sophisticated and multi-faceted plot of *Don't Forget to Smile*. As a specialist in the British novel, she brings to her books an ability to adapt formal literary structures to traditional romance conventions such as the marriage of convenience plot. More than many of her contemporaries, whose work is frequently loose and episodic, Seidel structures plot built on complex models of development. Extended flashbacks, for example, are rare in series romances, since some editors believe they slow the action; but in *A Risk Worth Taking*, Seidel wrote a fully dramatized 45-page flashback explaining the hero and heroine's relationship in rural Georgia long before the novel opened. The characters had married as teenagers to protect the heroine from sexual abuse by her stepfather; the flashback added important development to the characters and their motivations while also updating the marriage of convenience plot device.

Seidel's plots and characters grow out of clearly defined American settings that are integral to each novel. No matter where they live, her characters always carry with them the traits and values of their pasts; and those regional factors contribute to an understanding of their motivations and actions. Although the hero of *The Same Last Name* is a successful New York lawyer, he can only be understood in the context of his childhood among the Virginia gentry. The heroine of *A Risk Worth Taking* remembers the traditional values of her Georgia upbringing through years as a star of the seductive world of country music. The main characters in *Mirrors and Mistakes* are undemonstrative New Englanders whose sense of propriety inhibits their emotional maturity. The hero of *After All These Years* has fled the painful memories of his past, while the heroine remained in rural South Dakota where they had grown up together. In *Don't Forget to Smile*, the heroine has escaped her southern past as a semi-professional entrant in beauty pageants by opening a bar in a working-class logging town in rural Oregon, where the hero is a union representative. The conflict between the main characters grows from the vast cultural gulf in their backgrounds. In several of her books—*A Risk Worth Taking*, *When Love Isn't Enough*, *Mirrors and Mistakes*, *The Same Last Name*—Seidel skillfully delineates the conflicts of urban professionals whose careers seem to require a sacrifice of home and family values. Several of these characters come from more traditional areas of the country. Although they are ambitious for professional success, like the heroine of *When Love Isn't Enough*, they frequently yearn for a more settled, rooted way of life.

Seidel's prose is spare and ironic, especially in comparison to the sometimes lush and descriptive styles of her contemporaries. She describes her characters in apt, understated phrases. Even in moments of extreme emotion, her characters are rarely effusive; nor do they withdraw in the sort of injured silence that implausibly extends some romance plots. Instead, they often express themselves bluntly so that the grounds of disagreement are open and clear. Because her characters are articulate and honest with themselves and each other, stock romance misunderstandings are absent from her books. Conflicts are far more likely to derive from psychological factors or sincere differences in values than from shallow misunderstandings, accidents, or misinterpretations.

Seidel's novels were published in a period when editors and readers expected writers to include details of sexual relationships and when the old strictures against premarital sexual activity in romances had virtually disappeared. Although her characters are contemporary in their sexual behavior—in *The Same Last Name* and *Mirrors and Mistakes* the characters marry because the heroine is pregnant—the portrayals of sexuality in her books serve to advance the plot and are frequently understated rather than emphasized.

Seidel was one of several talented romance writers who emerged in the early 1980's to redefine the traditional formula. Her particular contributions to the genre derived from a sure sense of the American landscape as an appropriate place for romance and in her high standards of plot construction and prose style. She continues to write, but she has now shifted her focus from series romances to longer novels with romance elements.

—Kay Mussell

SEIFERT, Elizabeth. Also wrote as Ellen Ashley. American. Born in Washington, Missouri, 19 June 1897. Educated at Washington University, St. Louis, A.B. 1918. Married John J. Gasparotti in 1920; three sons and one daughter. Recipient: *Redbook*-Dodd Mead award, 1938. *Died 17 June 1983.*

ROMANCE AND HISTORICAL PUBLICATIONS

Novels

Young Doctor Galahad. New York, Dodd Mead, 1938; as *Young Doctor*, London, Collins, 1939.
A Great Day. New York, Dodd Mead, 1939; London, Collins, 1940.
Thus Doctor Mallory. New York, Dodd Mead, 1940; as *Doctor Mallory*, London, Collins, 1941.
Hillbilly Doctor. New York, Dodd Mead, 1940; as *Doctor Bill*, London, Collins, 1941.

Bright Scalpel. New York, Dodd Mead, 1941; as *Healing Hands*, London, Collins, 1942; as *The Doctor's Healing Hands*, London, Severn House, 1982.
Army Doctor. New York, Dodd Mead, 1942; London, Collins, 1943.
Surgeon in Charge. New York, Dodd Mead, 1942; London, Collins, 1945.
A Certain Doctor French. New York, Dodd Mead, 1943; London, Collins, 1944.
Bright Banners. New York, Dodd Mead, 1943.
Girl in Overalls: A Novel of Women in Defense Today (as Ellen Ashley). New York, Dodd Mead, 1943.
Girl Intern. New York, Dodd Mead, 1944; as *Doctor Chris*, London, Collins, 1946.
Dr. Ellison's Ambition. New York, Dodd Mead, 1944.
Dr. Woodward's Ambition. New York, Dodd Mead, 1945; London, Collins, 1946.
Orchard Hill. New York, Dodd Mead, 1945; London, Collins, 1947.
Old Doc. New York, Dodd Mead, 1946; London, Collins, 1948.
Dusty Spring. New York, Dodd Mead, 1946.
Take Three Doctors. New York, Dodd Mead, 1947; London, Collins, 1949.
So Young, So Fair. New York, Dodd Mead, 1947; London, Collins, 1948.
The Glass and the Trumpet. New York, Dodd Mead, 1948.
Hospital Zone. New York, Dodd Mead, 1948.
The Bright Coin. New York, Dodd Mead, 1949; as *The Doctor Dares*, London, Collins, 1950.
Homecoming. New York, Dodd Mead, 1950.
Pride of the South. London, Collins, 1950.
The Story of Andrea Fields. New York, Dodd Mead, 1950.
Miss Doctor. New York, Dodd Mead, 1951; as *Woman Doctor*, London, Collins, 1951.
Doctor of Mercy. New York, Dodd Mead, 1951; London, Collins, 1953.
The Strange Loyalty of Dr. Carlisle. New York, Dodd Mead, 1952; as *The Case of Dr. Carlisle*, London, Collins, 1953.
The Doctor Takes a Wife. New York, Dodd Mead, 1952; London, Collins, 1954.
Doctor Mollie. London, Collins, 1952.
The Doctor Disagrees. New York, Dodd Mead, 1953; London, Collins, 1954.
Lucinda Marries the Doctor. New York, Dodd Mead, 1953; London, Collins, 1955.
Doctor at the Crossroads. New York, Dodd Mead, 1954; London, Collins, 1955.
Marriage for Three. New York, Dodd Mead, 1954; London, Collins 1956.
A Doctor in the Family. New York, Dodd Mead, 1955; London, Collins, 1956.
Challenge for Doctor Mays. New York, Dodd Mead, 1955; as *Doctor Mays*, London, Collins, 1957.
A Doctor for Blue Jay Cove. New York, Dodd Mead, 1956; as *Doctor's Orders*, London, Collins, 1958.
A Call for Doctor Barton. New York, Dodd Mead, 1956; London, Collins, 1957.
Substitute Doctor. New York, Dodd Mead, 1957; London, Collins, 1958.
The Doctor's Husband. New York, Dodd Mead, 1957; London, Collins, 1959.
The New Doctor. New York, Dodd Mead, 1958; as *Doctor Jamie*, London, Collins, 1959.
Love Calls the Doctor. New York, Dodd Mead, 1958; London, Collins, 1960.

Home-Town Doctor. New York, Dodd Mead, 1959; London, Collins, 1960.

Doctor on Trial. London, Dodd Mead, 1959; London, Collins, 1961.

When Doctors Marry. New York, Dodd Mead, 1960; London, Collins, 1961.

Doctors on Parade (omnibus). New York, Dodd Mead, 1960.

The Doctor's Bride. New York, Dodd Mead, 1960; London, Collins, 1962.

The Doctor Makes a Choice. New York, Dodd Mead, 1961; London, Collins, 1962.

Dr. Jeremy's Wife. New York, Dodd Mead, 1961; London, Collins, 1963.

The Honor of Dr. Shelton. New York, Dodd Mead, 1962; London, Collins, 1963.

The Doctor's Strange Secret. New York, Dodd Mead, 1962; London, Collins, 1964.

Dr. Scott, Surgeon on Call. New York, Dodd Mead, 1963; as *Surgeon on Call*, London, Collins, 1965.

Legacy for a Doctor. New York, Dodd Mead, 1963; London, Collins, 1964.

Katie's Young Doctor. New York, Dodd Mead, 1964; London, Collins, 1965.

A Doctor Comes to Bayard. New York, Dodd Mead, 1964; London, Collins, 1966.

Doctor Samaritan. New York, Dodd Mead, 1965; London, Collins, 1966.

Ordeal of Three Doctors. New York, Dodd Mead, 1965; London, Collins, 1967.

Hegerty, M.D. New York, Dodd Mead, 1966; London, Collins, 1967.

Pay the Doctor. New York, Dodd Mead, 1966; London, Collins, 1968.

Doctor with a Mission. New York, Dodd Mead, 1967; London, Collins, 1969.

The Rival Doctors. New York, Dodd Mead, 1967; London, Collins, 1969.

The Doctor's Confession. New York, Dodd Mead, 1968; London, Collins, 1971.

To Wed a Doctor. New York, Dodd Mead, 1968; London, Collins, 1970.

Bachelor Doctor. New York, Dodd Mead, 1969; London, Collins, 1971.

For Love of a Doctor. New York, Dodd Mead, 1969; London, Collins, 1970.

Doctor's Kingdom. New York, Dodd Mead, 1970.

The Doctor's Two Lives. New York, Dodd Mead, 1970; London, Collins, 1972.

Doctor in Judgment. New York, Dodd Mead, 1971; London, Collins, 1972.

The Doctor's Second Love. New York, Dodd Mead, 1971; London, Collins, 1973.

Doctor's Destiny. New York, Dodd Mead, and London, Collins, 1972.

The Doctor's Reputation. New York, Dodd Mead, 1972; London, Collins, 1974.

The Doctor's Private Life. New York, Dodd Mead, and London, Collins, 1973.

The Two Faces of Dr. Collier. New York, Dodd Mead, 1973; London, Collins, 1974.

The Doctor and Mathilda. New York, Dodd Mead, 1974; London, Collins, 1976.

Doctor in Love. New York, Dodd Mead, 1974; London, Collins, 1976.

The Doctor's Daughter. New York, Dodd Mead, 1974; London, Collins, 1975.

Four Doctors, Four Wives. New York, Dodd Mead, 1975; London, Collins, 1976.

The Doctor's Affair. New York, Dodd Mead, 1975; London, Collins, 1977.

Two Doctors and a Girl. New York, Dodd Mead, 1976; London, Collins, 1978.

The Doctor's Desperate Hour. New York, Dodd Mead, 1976; London, Collins, 1977.

Doctor Tuck. New York, Dodd Mead, 1977; London, Collins, 1979.

The Doctors of Eden Place. New York, Dodd Mead, 1977; London, Collins, 1978.

The Doctors Were Brothers. New York, Dodd Mead, 1978; London, Collins, 1980.

Rebel Doctor. New York, Dodd Mead, 1978; London, Collins, 1980.

The Doctor's Promise. New York, Dodd Mead, 1979; London, Collins, 1981.

The Problems of Doctor A. New York, Dodd Mead, 1979; London, Collins, 1981.

Two Doctors, Two Loves. New York, Dodd Mead, 1982; London, Collins, 1983.

*

Manuscript Collection: Boston University.

Elizabeth Seifert commented:
(1982) I have written novels of current life, often in small towns of America, and with only a few exceptions the subject matter has been medical.

*   *   *

One is not likely to find Elizabeth Seifert citations on academic reading lists, nor mention of her in college library catalogues or critical reference works; but go to almost any public library in the country and you will find book after book, or you would if so many weren't in circulation, of this prolific writer—who produced one or two novels a year from 1938 to 1979. Her popularity has surely stood the test of time, since most of her early work has been reprinted. Nearly all Seifert's books have also been published in England, and many have been published in 14 other countries as well. How can this phenomenon be explained? Is the general reading public so intrigued by the mystique of the medical profession that any title with "doctor" in it, as nearly all Seifert's titles have, will be avidly sought after? There's much more to it than this.

Though Seifert's books have medical backgrounds and center primarily on the professional, social, and ethical problems of doctors and their families, usually in an American midwestern setting, they cannot be defined as medical fiction. Her stories are about people who happen to be doctors. Her books are easy to read and consist almost entirely of brief descriptions and dialogue. The reader is not subjected to long paragraphs of exposition. We learn about the characters by how they look, what they wear, what they say, and the plots unfold through their words and actions. We know what their homes look like, how they are furnished, how they are landscaped. And we know these people—for they exist in every neighborhood in the Western world. Though her characters belong to a glamorous profession, they do the same things readers do—bake pies, tell each other how to raise their children, help each other look for lost dogs, plan programs for cub scouts, grapple with problems of middle age. Seifert's male characters are apt to be heroic and larger than life, but she is right on target with women, their strengths and weaknesses, their hopes and fears. She generally closes with happy endings; but often they are bittersweet, as with her first book, the $10,000 prize novel—*Young Doctor Galahad*, whose protagonist won a professional battle but slid gallantly into marriage with a woman he didn't love.

Though her first novel dealt well with a post-depression town and proselytized in favor of clinics and socialized medicine, much to the chagrin of many doctors then as now—indeed, though the theme of public health is prevalent in many of her novels—her stories do not reflect the changing influences and current events of half a century, nor do they keep up with the many technological advances. But human nature does not change with the times, so her early novels are as valid in their characterizations as the later ones. Many of them form the Bayard Books, named for a Missouri town, featuring the same characters, one time in major roles, and the next only incidentally. The Bayard Folk become our own families, and it's no wonder that we eagerly wish to learn what happens to them. Seifert was successful because she was plain, direct, and recognizable; and because she liked people.

—Marion Hanscom

SELLERS, Alexandra. Canadian and British. Educated at the Royal Academy of Dramatic Art, London, 1969–71; University of British Columbia, Vancouver, 1986–87. Has two stepsons and one stepdaughter. Lives in London. Agent: P. Tornetta, Box 423, Croton-on-Hudson, New York 10521, U.S.A.

ROMANCE AND HISTORICAL PUBLICATIONS

Novels

The Indifferent Heart. New York, Dell, 1980; London, Hale, 1981.
Captive of Desire. Toronto, Harlequin, 1981.
Fire in the Wind. Toronto, Harlequin, 1982.
Season of Storm. Toronto, Harlequin, 1983.
The Forever Kind. Toronto, Harlequin, 1984.
The Real Man. New York, Silhouette, 1984.
The Male Chauvinist. New York, Silhouette, 1985.
The Old Flame. New York, Silhouette, 1986.

*   *   *

Both the challenge and the fun of writing fiction lies in the search for metaphors to carry the message the author wants to convey to readers. The more subtle and complex the message, the more difficult it is to find the right characters and action that will at the same time entertain and excite the imagination of readers. That Alexandra Sellers succeeds in doing just that within the confines of the category (series) romance is a commentary on both the ability of this exceptional writer and also the sociopolitical climate of the time in which she is writing. There is no better illustration of the changing and evolving sensibilities of the time, in fact, than the three novels Sellers wrote for the Silhouette Intimate Moments line—*The Real Man*, *The Male Chauvinist*, and *The Old Flame*—which stand as a trilogy of sorts, with each one describing a different kind of man.

What Sellers is really writing about, however, are the socially constructed perceptions of sexuality and gender that serve to make men the enemies of women (and sometimes the reverse),

and which often hide our real values, motives, and feelings even from ourselves. Seller's metaphors become more forceful and her ideas more clearly defined as the trilogy progresses. Sellers's love scenes are both sexually explicit and powerful (at times even shockingly unexpected, as is the scene on the boat dock early in *The Old Flame*). They are also among her best metaphors, conveying as they do the capacity of her characters to feel deeply and passionately, especially about some of the injustices and misunderstandings that have plagued relations between males and females through most of human history.

The Male Chauvinist opens with the heroine swimming topless at a beach in Greece, which occasions some reflexive (internal) dialogue on the subject of the arbitrary social constrictions her own society places on women. "No inner voice had ever told her that certain parts of her body were shameful. . . . So, if [covering those parts of her body] was not instinctive in women, what had caused the taboo in the first place? Or who? Well, monotheistic religion, for a start. Judaism, Christianity and Islam all seemed to have gone a little rabid on the subject of female modesty. But of course all the great monotheistic religions had more in common than the One God: they were all also fiercely male-supremacist." While researching an article she's writing about the hero's archeological dig, the heroine comes to the full realization that "most of the Western world's art, literature and artifacts reflected the masculine. And nearly anything in the modern world that reflected the feminine reflected it from the masculine point of view, and a degrading point of view at that; a point of view that allowed women to be nothing much more than sex objects." This hero is anything but a chauvinist, as it turns out. He is, in fact, searching for new evidence of an ancient matriarchal society, a place and time when women were central to society and its symbols, and is even able to articulate his empathy for her personal struggle. "It must be very difficult to live in a world where the battle for a sense of self-worth is so arduous . . . so much of women's imagination is being diverted to that battle, it is no wonder they no longer rule the world."

The lawyer heroine in *The Old Flame* runs up against "the male club" in both her professional and personal life, a social phenomenon so slippery that most reporters of the social scene and even feminists find it difficult to identify in terms of specific behavior or events. "This was something no woman could explain to any man—or none that she had ever known. Men were a club when the chips were down. A club where each member defended the other against outside attack without question." Sellers uses the trial of a man charged with rape and a defense lawyer who attacks the victim as her metaphor, and makes her point when the hero, also a lawyer, excuses it as "Just legal tactics. Everybody does it." She accuses, he excuses. A male may not like what he sees or hears in other males, he explains, but "suddenly the choices yawn in front of him: he can be true to himself and be ostracized, or he can shut up and be part of the male club. And once you make the choice, it just gest easier and easier to block [what you don't like] out, to stick a grin on your face and let it all go by." But because he loves her he tries harder to see his own behavior (and that of her other male colleagues as well) from her point of view, and in the process comes to know himself as he never has before. It is Sellers's hero who learns, as philosopher Robert Solomon has point out, that "loving another is essential to discovering one's own identity."

—Carol Thurston

SETON, Anya. British. Born in New York City; daughter of the writer Ernest Thompson Seton. Educated privately in England; at Oxford University. Married twice; three children. Former member of the Editorial Board, *Writers Magazine*. Address: Binney Lane, Old Greenwich, Connecticut 06870, U.S.A.

ROMANCE AND HISTORICAL PUBLICATIONS

Novels

My Theodosia. Boston, Houghton Mifflin, 1941; London, Hodder and Stoughton, 1945.
Dragonwyck. Boston, Houghton Mifflin, 1944; London, Hodder and Stoughton, 1945.
The Turquoise. Boston, Houghton Mifflin, and London, Hodder and Stoughton, 1946.
The Hearth and the Eagle. Boston, Houghton Mifflin, and London, Hodder and Stoughton, 1948.
Foxfire. Boston, Houghton Mifflin, and London, Hodder and Stoughton, 1951.
Katherine. Boston, Houghton Mifflin, and London, Hodder and Stoughton, 1954.
The Winthrop Woman. Boston, Houghton Mifflin, and London, Hodder and Stoughton, 1958.
Devil Water. Boston, Houghton Mifflin, and London, Hodder and Stoughton, 1962.
Avalon. Boston, Houghton Mifflin, 1965; London, Hodder and Stoughton, 1966.
Green Darkness. Boston, Houghton Mifflin, and London, Hodder and Stoughton, 1972.

OTHER PUBLICATIONS

Other (for children)

The Mistletoe and Sword: A Story of Roman Britain. New York, Doubleday, 1955; Leicester, Brockhampton Press, 1956.
Washington Irving. Boston, Houghton Mifflin, 1960.
Smouldering Fires. New York, Doubleday, 1975; London, Hodder and Stoughton, 1976.

*   *   *

As a writer of long, meticulously researched historical romances, Anya Seton may be the best of her generation. Her output is relatively small for a romance writer, but the quality is uniformly high. Unlike some of her contemporaries who choose a historical period and stay with it for book after book, Seton selects a different time and place for each novel. She often uses actual men and women in history as the basis for her plots, and she makes their stories both interesting and compelling.

Seton's early novel *Dragonwyck* is a straight gothic romance set along the Hudson River among the descendants of Dutch settlers. *The Hearth and Eagle* is a romance set in Marblehead, Massachusetts. Both these novels had interest, but it was in *My Theodosia* that Seton displayed what would become the hallmark of her work: fictional recreations of the lives of actual historical women. *My Theodosia* is the story of Theodosia Burr, the daughter of the American scapegrace politician Aaron Burr. Seton considered historical controversies about the Burrs as well as the legends that grew up around the romantic Theodosia, including stories about her early romance with Meriwether Lewis and about her mysterious death.

Seton's classic novel is probably *Katherine*, a fictional treatment of the life of Katherine Swynford, mistress and later wife of John of Gaunt, Duke of Lancaster, in the 14th century. Katherine is significant to history because of a fluke—her descendants (born bastards but legitimized by Parliament) won the War of the Roses, making her a direct ancestress of the British Royal Family. Seton's research for *Katherine* was extensive and meticulous. She used original documents in Middle French and Middle English to supplement her Latin, and she addressed historical controversies about the character of John of Gaunt, a difficult task considering the nature of the sources for the period. She also created an engaging fictional portrait of Katherine's brother-in-law, Geoffrey Chaucer. The "Author's Note" delineates her research methods and the way she approached her subjects before she began to write.

In *Katherine* and later novels—*Devil Water*, *Avalon*, *The Winthrop Woman*—Seton blends historical accuracy (insofar as she can) with legend to produce love stories appealing to modern sensibilities. She portrays women who rise above historical limitations and who exemplify contemporary values about love, marriage, and family. Although Katherine Swynford lived in an age that valued women for their family connections more than personal qualities and in which marriage was often more political alliance than love match, Seton's Katherine is a woman who transcends her time. She is portrayed as an excellent wife and mother, even in an early marriage of convenience. After her long illicit liaison with John of Gaunt she deserves her elevation to Duchess of Lancaster because she remained faithful to him and genuinely repented for her sins against morality. The political realities of 14th-century England may have denied her a place as his wife until late in their lives, but because her situation was not "her fault," she could be redeemed from disgrace.

The Winthrop Woman, one of the all-time American bestsellers, is about Elizabeth Winthrop, the scandalous niece of John Winthrop who was the first governor of the Massachusetts Bay Colony. Again, Seton plays out the love story against a background of historical limits on women's lives. Elizabeth's desire for true love was thwarted by a repressive Puritan society. *Devil Water*, set in 18th-century England and America, is about the life of a woman who may exist only in a family legend. Most of the characters, however, are real; and Seton mixes fact and legend convincingly. *Avalon*, set in 10th-century England, Cornwall, and Iceland, takes her even farther away from the known and factual as she delineates the Age of Faith against a background of vicious Viking raids. *Green Darkness* is about the Protestant Reformation, although in this book Seton dabbles in reincarnation and sets short sections in the modern world. Other books, including *The Turquoise* and *Foxfire*, are not based on fact.

In many of her books, Seton uses an author's note to inform readers of both her research methods and her formulations about historical truth. She acknowledges that the lives of women in history were of only passing interest to the historical record and that it is extraordinarily difficult to recreate personal lives and motivations after many centuries. She describes how she determines the most likely version of the truth. In her books, fact and fiction often work together effectively to produce lengthy and fascinating portraits of her characters. Unlike some other authors in her subfield of romance, she does not take shortcuts or distort the historical record; instead, she spins her tale within the limits of the known.

Seton has the ability to use history as the vehicle for a compelling love story. Her books move quickly, building a record of historical detail without letting research dominate her characters. Her descriptions of places are both evocative and accurate, so that even today many of the locations about which she writes can be found without recourse to a map.

Seton's historical romances have remained in print over many years; it is her ability to make history accessible to modern readers that makes her stand out among her competitors.

—Kay Mussell

———————

SHAW, Irene. See **ROBERTS, Irene.**

———————

SHEARD, Virna (née Stanton). Canadian. Born in Cobourg, Ontario, in 1865. Married Charles Sheard in 1885 (died 1929). *Died 22 February 1943.*

ROMANCE AND HISTORICAL PUBLICATIONS

Novels

Trevelyan's Little Daughter. Toronto, Briggs, 1898.
A Maid of Many Moods. Toronto, Copp Clark, New York, Potts, and London, Bagster, 1902.
By the Queen's Grace. New York, Stokes, 1904; revised edition, as *Fortune Turns Her Wheel*, Toronto, McClelland and Stewart, 1929.
Below the Salt. Toronto, Ryerson Press, 1936; London, Sampson Low, 1937.
Leaves in the Wind. Toronto, Ryerson Press, 1938.

Short Stories

The Golden Apple Tree. Toronto, McClelland and Stewart, and New York, Coward McCann, 1920.

OTHER PUBLICATIONS

Novel

The Man at Lone Lake. London, Cassell, 1912.

Verse

The Miracle and Other Poems. Toronto, Dent, 1913.
Carry On! Toronto, Warwick and Rutter, 1917.
Candle Flame and Other Poems. Toronto, McClelland and Stewart, 1926.
Fairy Dors. Toronto, McClelland and Stewart, 1926.

Other

The Ballad of the Quest. Toronto, McClelland and Stewart, and New York, McCann, 1922.

*   *   *

In her historical fiction Virna Sheard specialized in novels set in 16th-century London. To evoke a sense of period she uses archaic language and careful descriptions of cultural and social practices and locale. While Sheard's characters and ro-

mantic scenarios are strictly conventional, her plots tend to be surprising.

In *The Golden Apple Tree* Sheard updates the fairytale. Indeed the King, Queen, Prince, and Princess scenario is undermined consistently by Sheard's 20th-century democratic sensibilities even while she adeptly weaves her seven enchanting stories. Although not conventional historical fiction, these stories merit mention because they demonstrate a sense of the history of ideas about women and the central place of these ideas in the fairy tale genre.

Using a contemporary Canadian setting, *The Man at Lone Lake* presents the Canadian north as populated by Cree Indians, Métis, a young English Lord, a woodswoman, nuns, and the Royal Canadian Mounted Police. At the end of this pastiche of clichés, the heroine, Nance McCullough, and the hero, soon to be Sir Richard Wynn and the man of the title, leave for Scotland and civlization as if life in the Canadian north were nothing but a bad dream. Canadian readers will note with interest the nostalgic treatment of the British connection which reverses the trend of emigration as the Canadian, Nance, returns to the land from which her grandfather came.

In quite a different vein, *A Maid of Many Moods* involves a player in Shakespeare's the King's Men, Darby Thornbury, who has been assigned the role of Juliet in the new play being rehearsed. Sheard uses Darby's profession as an opportunity to address the issue of the ban on women stage players and skillfully develops her plot to include a triumphant performance in *Romeo and Juliet* by her heroine, Darby's look-alike sister, Deborah. This issue provides the cornerstone of provocative interest in what is otherwise a brief novel with a conventional romantic plot.

By the Queen's Grace is one of Sheard's more complex novels in which the heroine, Joyce Davenport, pits her personal integrity and need for love against her father's mercenary motives and an arranged marriage. Set in 1580's and 1590's London, the two different worlds of London Bridge and the Elizabethan Court at Somerset Palace are evoked with skill, imagination, and a convincing attention to details of convention, character, and locale. This novel was republished in a lengthened version in 1929 as *Fortune Turns Her Wheel*.

Sheard's other Canadian novel, *Below the Salt*, is set in Ontario just prior to her own time and follows the complex plot lines formed by an Irish patriarch farmer's attempt to control the lives of his family. Sheard's novels are balanced between the subjects of the Canadian present and the English past. The historical novels are more detailed narratives, yet they share the smooth prose style which characterizes all of her work.

—Heather Iris Jones

———————

SHEARING, Joseph. See **BOWEN, Marjorie.**

———————

SHELBOURNE, Cecily. See **EBEL, Suzanne.**

———————

SHELLABARGER, Samuel. Also wrote as John Esteven; Peter Loring. American. Born in Washington, D.C., 18 May 1888. Educated at private schools; Princeton University, New

Jersey, 1905–09, A.B. 1909; studied in Munich, 1910–11; Harvard University, Cambridge, Massachusetts, 1911–14, Ph.D. 1917. Served in Ordnance and Military Intelligence, and as assistant military attaché, U.S. Legation, Stockholm, 1918–19: Captain. Married Vivan Borg in 1915; two sons and two daughters. Instructor, 1914–16, and Assistant Professor of English, 1919–23, Princeton University; lived in Europe, 1923–31; headmaster, Columbus School for Girls, Ohio, 1938–46; then full-time writer. *Died 20 March 1954.*

ROMANCE AND HISTORICAL PUBLICATIONS

Novels

The Black Gale. New York, Century, 1929.
Grief Before Night (as Peter Loring). Philadelphia, Macrae Smith, 1938; London, Hodder and Stoughton, 1939.
Miss Rolling Stone (as Peter Loring). Philadelphia, Macrae Smith, 1939; as *He Travels Alone*, London, Hodder and Stoughton, 1939.
Captain from Castile. Boston, Little Brown, 1945; London, Macmillan, 1947.
Prince of Foxes. Boston, Little Brown, 1947; London, Hamish Hamilton, 1948.
The King's Cavalier. Boston, Little Brown, 1950; as *Blaise of France*, London, Hamish Hamilton, 1950.
Lord Vanity. Boston, Little Brown, 1953; London, Collins, 1954.
Tolbecken. Boston, Little Brown, 1956; London, Bles, 1957.

Novels as John Esteven

The Door of Death. New York, Century, 1928; London, Methuen, 1929.
Voodoo. New York, Doubleday, and London, Hutchinson, 1930.
By Night at Dinsmore. New York, Doubleday, and London, Harrap, 1935.
While Murder Waits. London, Harrap, 1936; New York, Doubleday, 1937.
Graveyard Watch. New York, Modern Age, 1938.
Blind Man's Night. London, Hodder and Stoughton, 1938.
Assurance Double Sure. London, Hodder and Stoughton, 1939.

OTHER PUBLICATIONS

Other

The Chevalier Bayard: A Study in Fading Chivalry. New York, Century, 1928.
Lord Chesterfield. New York and London, Macmillan, 1935.
Lord Chesterfield and Manners (lecture). Claremont, California, Pomona College, 1938.
Lord Chesterfield and His World. Boston, Little Brown, 1951.
The Token (for children). Boston, Little Brown, 1955.

*   *   *

Samuel Shellabarger is one of those rare authors who made a financially successful transition from academic life to fiction. Though his most famous novels are rousing adventures, he will be best remembered for his meticulous attention to historical detail, particularly of 16th century Spain, Italy, and France. In his major novels, *Captain from Castile*, *Prince of Foxes*, *The King's Cavalier*, and *Lord Vanity*, his mastery of genealogy, battles,

customs, manners, and folklore is impressive. His backgrounds create an authentic surface realism that survives the sometimes overly melodramatic plots and superficial characterization often found in the historical romance. It is tempting to dismiss the literary aspects of Shellabarger's fiction, which critics who have underestimated the difficulty of the genre have sometimes done, yet moments of art are found throughout his work.

Shellabarger's early Rae Norse mysteries carried the pen name John Esteven. As Peter Loring he wrote *Miss Rolling Stone*, a romance set in Baghdad, and *Grief Before Night*, a light novel of tangled love which drew its background from Shellabarger's residence in Sweden prior to and during World War I. It was not until the publication of *Captain from Castile* in 1945, however, that Shellabarger achieved widespread popular success. After the publication of this book several of his novels would be adapted to the motion pictures and for more than a decade he could be assured of a receptive audience.

Since *Captain from Castile* represents the pinnacle of Shellabarger's success, it is useful to delineate several of its major themes. The story follows the youthful son of a Spanish Don, Pedro de Vargas, from his infatuation with the aristocrat Duena Luisa through his adventures with Cortes in Mexico and back to Spain. Woven into the plot is the conflict in Pedro's mind between the traditional match with Luisa, representing the now decadent chivalric ideal, and Pedro's "natural" attraction to the tavern dancer, Catana, who follows him from Spain to Mexico and back. The episodic adventures of the novel are provided by the conquest of Mexico and the machinations of the arch villain de Silva, who betrays the innocent de Vargas family to the Inquisition, casually marries Luisa in Pedro's absence, allows Pedro and several comrades to be captured for humiliation and sacrifice by the Aztecs, and tries to have Pedro executed for betraying the king. Shellabarger neatly parallels the Spanish Inquisition with Aztec sacrificial rites and has a corrupt Inquisitor burned by the Aztecs. Underlying the surface of the novel are characteristic American ambivalences of the time toward success and race. In order to avoid having Pedro directly profit from the slaughter of the Aztecs, Shellabarger has Pedro's own treasure given to him by an Indian whom he had helped escape from brutal servitude in Spain. The Aztecs and Indians are nevertheless inferior; Montezuma's "stone-age self could not cope with the thrust of Cortes's personality," and though the Indians side with the Spanish against the Aztecs, "it was the white force that counted."

Pedro is not the clever hero of picaresque Romance, he is more akin to those of Horatio Alger, and the Aztecs might as well have been lifted from a western. Pedro does change from a spirited youth dominated by his father to a man tempered by his experiences, but as a character he remains undistinguished. Shellabarger further mined the 16th-century in *Prince of Foxes*, set in the court of the Borgias in Italy, and in *The King's Cavalier*, set in France during the reign of Francis I, while he moved the action of *Lord Vanity* to 18th-century England, Italy, and France. In these novels Shellabarger continued his struggle to create believable characters and eliminate cumbersome plots while developing competent and sometimes brilliant settings and backgrounds.

—Larry N. Landrum

————————

SHERWOOD, Valerie. Also writes as Rosamund Royal. American. Address: c/o New American Library, 1633 Broadway, New York, New York 10019, U.S.A.

ROMANCE AND HISTORICAL PUBLICATIONS

Novels (series: Imogene and Georgiana; Carolina Lightfoot)

This Loving Torment. New York, Warner, 1977.
These Golden Pleasures. New York, Warner, 1977.
This Towering Passion. New York, Warner, 1978.
Rapture (as Rosamund Royal). New York, Popular Library, 1979.
Her Shining Splendor. New York, Warner, 1980.
Bold Breathless Love (Imogene and Georgiana). New York, Warner, 1981; London, Macdonald, 1985.
Rash Reckless Love (Imogene and Georgiana). New York, Warner, 1981; London, Macdonald, 1985.
Wild Willful Love (Imogene and Georgiana). New York, Warner, 1982; London, Macdonald, 1985.
Rich Radiant Love (Imogene and Georgiana). New York, Warner, 1983; London, Macdonald, 1985.
Lovely Lying Lips. New York, Warner, 1983.
Born to Love. New York, Warner, 1984; London, Macdonald, 1985.
Lovesong (Lightfoot). New York, Pocket Books, 1985; London, Grafton, 1986.
Windsong (Lightfoot). New York, Pocket Books, 1986; London, Grafton, 1987.
Nightsong (Lightfoot). New York, Pocket Books, 1986; London, Grafton, 1988.
To Love a Rogue. New York, New American Library, 1987.
Lisbon. New York, New American Library, 1988.

* * *

In the author's note to her novel *Nightsong* Valerie Sherwood extolls the virtues of the buccaneers who sailed the seas of the 17th century, preying upon the ships of Spain and disposing of their booty in England and its colonies. It is in this swashbuckling era that she sets many of her tales—an era that brings to mind the elegantly handsome Errol Flynn on the foredeck of a tall-masted schooner, sword in hand, fighting and conquering an evil foe. For readers who are enraptured by such scenes Sherwood's books will satisfy any craving for stories of this glorified past. There are beautiful, enticing heroines in distress, and more than one strong, virile man willing to extricate them from their plight.

The Sherwood heroine, usually a blonde, has the kind of irresistible beauty expected in a romantic tale. The hero is typically tall, dark, handsome, and completely captivated by the heroine's stunning good looks. The attraction between the two is immediate, and within a very short space of time they consummate their love. "Fueled by bursts of passion, they spun together toward the farther stars, whirled as one toward infinity. Locked together, panting in soul shattering ecstasy, they went over the brink together" (*Lovely Lying Lips*). There will be several times throughout the novel when the lovers will share such bliss. Do not expect scenes of rape or graphic violence. At times the heroine may be reluctant and need to be coaxed by the hero, but always there exists an element of tenderness between them.

Most Sherwood plots have a young beauty who finds her true love in the handsome hero only to lose him for a time. Often she thinks he has abandoned her for another woman, but this of course is a misunderstanding on the heroine's part, and a series of improbable coincidences brings them back together for a satisfying conclusion. For example, Carolina Lightfoot, the silver-haired heroine of a trilogy (*Lovesong*, *Windsong*, and *Nightsong*) thought she had found everlasting love in the arms of Irish buccaneer Rye Evistock, known on the high seas as Captain Kells.

Yet in *Nightsong* she is convinced he has left her for a Spanish beauty and briefly seeks consolation in the arms of another man.

Sometimes the innocent young lady gives herself first to someone undeserving as does Lorraine London with the cad Philip in *To Love a Rogue*. Soon enough, however, she finds a worthy man in the renegade gunrunner Raile Cameron. Another example is Imogene who conceives a daughter, Georgiana, by Steve, a charmer with two wives. But it is in the strong arms of buccaneer van Ryker that she finds true happiness. The love stories of this mother and daughter pair are told in a series of four novels: *Bold Breathless Love*, *Rash Reckless Love*, *Wild Willful Love*, and *Rich Radiant Love*.

There are romance, adventure, and sumptuous living aplenty in all of Sherwood's books. Although the historical data seems accurate enough, its main purpose is to serve as background for a sensuous love story. Readers who understand this can sit back, relax, and enjoy a few hours of romantic fantasy.

—Patricia Altner

SHOESMITH, Kathleen A(nne). British. Born in Keighley, Yorkshire, 17 July 1938. Educated at Avery Hill Teachers' Training College, London, diploma 1956. Since 1958 teacher in Keighley: since 1973 at Lees County Primary School. Address: 351 Fell Lane, Keighley, Yorkshire BD22 6DB, England.

ROMANCE AND HISTORICAL PUBLICATIONS

Novels

Cloud over Calderwood. London, Hale, 1969; New York, Ace, 1973.
Jack O'Lantern. London, Hale, 1969; New York, Ace, 1973.
The Tides of Tremannion. London, Hale, 1970; New York, Ace, 1973.
Mallory's Luck. London, Hale, 1971; New York, Ace, 1974.
Return of the Royalist. London, Hale, 1971.
The Reluctant Puritan. London, Hale, 1972; New York, Ace, 1973.
Belltower. London, Hale, 1973; New York, Ace, 1974.
The Highwayman's Daughter. London, Hale, 1973; New York, Ace, 1974.
The Black Domino. London, Hale, 1975.
Elusive Legacy. London, Hale, 1976.
The Miser's Ward. London, Hale, 1977.
Smuggler's Haunt. London, Hale, 1978.
Guardian at the Gate. London, Hale, 1979.
Brackenthorpe. London, Hale, 1980.
Autumn Escapade. London, Hale, 1981.
Rustic Vineyard. London, Hale, 1982.
A Minor Bequest. London, Hale, 1984.

OTHER PUBLICATIONS (for children)

Easy to Read (*Helen and Her Hamster, Karen and Her Kitten, Ruth and Her Rabbit, Gordon and His Goldfish, Tony and His Tortoise, Barry and His Budgerigar*). London, Charles, 6 vols., 1967.
The Judy Stories (*Judy in the Garden* [*in the Wind, in the Snow, on the Sand*]). London, Charles, 4 vols., 1967.

Playtime Stories (The Birthday Kitten, Jack and the Robin, The Bird and the Milk, John's Ship, The Lost Ball, The Christmas Tree). Leeds, E. J. Arnold, 6 vols., 1967.
How do They Grow? (Apples, Butterflies and Moths, Daffodils, Frogs). London, Charles, 4 vols., 1967.
Do You Know About Claws? [Feathers?, Tails?, Wings?, Ears?, Hair?, Shells?, Teeth?, Clocks?, Steps?, Wheels?, Windows?, Bridges?, Feet?, Mirrors?, Skin?]. London, Burke, 16 vols., 1970–75.
Use Your Senses (Listen and Hear, Look and See, Scent and Smell, Taste and Flavour, Touch and Feel). London, Burke, 5 vols., 1973.

*   *   *

Romance is the primary element in the novels of Kathleen A. Shoesmith. Love of the spirited heroine for the aloof, yet attractive hero is at the core of all her works, whose precise historical settings are an integral, yet secondary part of the novels as a whole. More than most, Shoesmith's works fit neatly into the category of historical romance, and her books display the skills of one of the most competent exponents of the form. Her style is already well established in early novels such as *Jack o'Lantern* and *The Tides of Tremannion*, where the familiar gothic and romantic themes serve as a background plot to the central love story. Its continuation, virtually unaltered, in subsequent works, together with the remarkably consistent level of her writing, has ensured that Shoesmith's novels achieve a fairly standard relation one to another, with none of the peaks and troughs associated with the work of other writers. Her vision appears to fix itself on a few, selected periods of history notably the English Civil War (*The Reluctant Puritan, Return of the Royalist*), the 18th century (*The Highwayman's Daughter, Smuggler's Haunt, Guardian at the Gate*), the Napoleonic era (*Elusive Legacy, The Black Domino*), and the early Victorian period of the 1840's and 1850's (*Belltower, The Miser's Ward, A Minor Bequest*). Shoesmith's novels invariably have English locations, with Yorkshire and Sussex the favoured counties, although the early part of *A Minor Bequest* is set in Venice. Into these accurate, precisely noted times and places—Shoesmith usually gives a specific year to each novel—the author plunges hero and heroine together, enmeshing both in the drama and violence of the adventure. Her writing ransacks the gothic novel for themes, which recur continually. Shoesmith's heroines, through whose eyes the action is presented, are invariably daughters of gentry fallen on hard times, poverty-stricken and sometimes orphaned, yet proud and self-reliant. Employed as governesses or tutors in ancestral homes, they encounter ghostly apparitions, learn dark family secrets, and explore underground passages in search of hidden treasure. Inheritances figure largely in Shoesmith's novels—*Elusive Legacy* and *A Minor Bequest* are typical examples—and not infrequently the heroine is transformed from rags to riches by the end. Heroes tend to be stern and remote, forbidding almost, their severe personalities thawed at last by love. Villains are sinister, and often foreign—Marie-Elizabeth Delon in *The Black Domino* and Andre Durand of *Elusive Legacy* are two who spring immediately to mind. Smugglers and spies abound, with the occasional miser or highwayman, and generally much violence ensues before their dastardly plans are thwarted. Deaths occur in most of Shoesmith's novels, but these are rarely depicted in a sensational manner—the brutal murder of Matthew Herald in *The Miser's Ward* takes place "offstage," for example, and in most other cases the violent scenes are presented swiftly and with understatement. For instance, the fall of the villainous Crosbie from the Sussex cliffs in *Smuggler's Haunt* and the flurry of demises at the end of *The Black Domino* are noted rather than dwelt upon, meriting the slightest of pauses before the action continues. Love, rather than violence, remains the centre of Shoesmith's fiction, and in spite of the threats and horrors of her villains, the author's vision is one of hope. Shoesmith's ghosts are mostly benevolent, her formidable heroes are warmed to humanity by the fires of passion, and good overcomes evil in the end. The sense of kinship one feels for her courageous heroines—heightened by the immediacy of a first-person narrative in many cases—combines well with the compelling atmosphere, lively dialogue, and exciting plot to engage the interest of the reader. Some of Shoesmith's novels show more invention in their themes than others; *Guardian at the Gate*, which describes young Marcus Grant's appointment as legal guardian to a proud gentry family reduced to poverty, and the problems he encounters, is perhaps one of the most imaginative. Similarly, *A Minor Bequest* has a deft story-line where the tutor heroine inherits money only on condition that she brings up an orphan child. Adoption is a theme which occurs again in *The Black Domino*, which also features a restless ghost, smugglers, and spies.

Whether unusual or familiar in their choice of themes, Shoesmith's books are never less than interesting. Her writing uses gothic conventions and elements in an individual manner, matching them neatly with precise chronology and the perennial pain and fulfilment of love.

—Geoffrey Sadler

SHUTE, Nevil (Nevil Shute Norway). British. Born in Ealing, London, 17 January 1899. Educated at Dragon School, Oxford; Shrewsbury School, Oxford; Royal Military Academy, Woolwich, London; Balliol College, Oxford, 1919–22, E. A. in engineering 1922. Served as a private in the Suffolk Regiment, British Army, 1918; commissioned in the Royal Naval Volunteer Reserve, 1940: Lieutenant Commander; retired 1945. Married Frances Mary Heaton in 1931; two daughters. Calculator, de Havilland Aircraft Company, 1923–24; chief calculator, 1924–28, and deputy chief engineer, 1928–30, on the construction of Rigid Airship R. 100 for the Airship Guarantee Company: twice flew Atlantic in R. 100, 1930; managing director, Yorkshire Aeroplane Club Ltd., 1927–30; founder and joint managing director, Airspeed Ltd., airplane constructors, 1931–38. Lived in Australia after 1950. Fellow, Royal Aeronautical Society, 1934. *Died 12 January 1960.*

ROMANCE AND HISTORICAL PUBLICATIONS

Novels

Marazan. London, Cassell, 1926.
Landfall: A Channel Story. London, Heinemann, and New York, Morrow, 1940.
An Old Captivity. London, Heinemann, and New York, Morrow, 1940.
Pastoral. London, Heinemann, and New York, Morrow, 1944.
A Town Like Alice. London, Heinemann, 1950; as *The Legacy*, New York, Morrow, 1950.
The Far Country. London, Heinemann, and New York, Morrow, 1952.
Requiem for a Wren. London, Heinemann, 1955; as *The Breaking Wave*, New York, Morrow, 1955.

Stephen Morris. London, Heinemann, and New York, Morrow, 1961.

OTHER PUBLICATIONS

Novels

So Disdained. London, Cassell, 1928; as *Mysterious Aviator*, Boston, Houghton Mifflin, 1928.
Lonely Road. London, Cassell, and New York, Morrow, 1932.
Ruined City. London, Cassell, 1938; as *Kindling*, New York, Morrow, 1938.
What Happened to the Corbetts. London, Heinemann, 1939; as *Ordeal*, New York, Morrow, 1939.
Pied Piper. New York, Morrow, 1941; London, Heinemann, 1942.
Most Secret. London, Heinemann, and New York, Morrow, 1945.
The Chequer Board. London, Heinemann, and New York, Morrow, 1947.
No Highway. London, Heinemann, and New York, Morrow, 1948.
Round the Bend. London, Heinemann, and New York, Morrow, 1951.
In the Wet. London, Heinemann, and New York, Morrow, 1953.
Beyond the Black Stump. London, Heinemann, and New York, Morrow, 1956.
On the Beach. London, Heinemann, and New York, Morrow, 1957.
Trustee from the Toolroom. London, Heinemann, and New York, Morrow, 1960.

Play

Vinland the Good (screenplay). London, Heinemann, and New York, Morrow, 1946.

Other

Slide Rule: The Autobiography of an Engineer. London, Heinemann, and New York, Morrow, 1954.

*

Manuscript Collection: National Library of Australia, Canberra.

Critical Study: *Nevil Shute (Nevil Shute Norway)* by Julian Smith, Boston, Twayne, 1976.

*   *   *

Nevil Shute, a popular novelist of the 1940's and 1950's best known for his futuristic novel *On the Beach*, based the majority of his 22 novels on his experiences as an aeronautical engineer and aviator in both world wars, and set many in Australia, where he finally settled. A good storyteller, with a quiet, understated style, superb technical details, and highly plausible personalities, Shute always includes a romance, though one unconventional or subordinated to his fascination with machinery, entrepreneurship, and exploration.

An Old Captivity focuses on an archeological aerial survey in Greenland. Oxford professor Lockwood and his daughter Alix engage Donald Ross, a seaplane pilot experienced in far north flying, to help photograph Viking ruins. The hazardous environ-

ment of ice floes and fog strains Ross's nerves, which, already weakened by an addiction to sleeping pills, begin to fray as he dreams of Erik the Red, Leif Erikson, and the latter's fabled trip to Cape Cod, the Norsemen's "Vinland the Good." Once recovered from his drifting dream state, Ross still feels his fantasies are more real than his present life, and that Alix is in fact a reincarnation of Hekja, a Celtic slave girl that Ross, named Haki a thousand years earlier, loved and settled down with in the New World. Physical proof of Haki and Hekja's existence found by Ross and the Lockwood's trip to the Massachusetts coast lends substance to these incredible illusions.

The dream vision technique allows Shute to build the novel on his strengths, his precise knowledge of aviation and his sensitivity to a modern love story, while indulging his taste for far-distant history. The modern characters and the Viking vision combine neatly and credibly in the eerie empty setting of Greenland, a place of stark landscapes where normality seems suspended. A flashback technique used in other Shute works here ameliorates the fantastic with a realistic frame: a much older Ross recounting his dream experience to a psychiatrist on a stalled train.

Vinland the Good expands the story of Leif Erikson and his two Scottish slaves, Haki and Haekia, in a film script format. Beginning with a schoolteacher newly returned from World War II, lecturing a history class about the discovery of America, the action cuts back and forth from class to story, with the teacher's lecture as voiceover. Like his professorial hero, Shute is taken by the lack of "grandiose . . . pomp and dignity" in this "journey by the common man, a farmer, seeking to get a load of lumber to build cowhouses and discovering America on the side." Using the academic lecture as a frame allows Shute to stress the historical truth of his story, while fleshing out the characters with romantic dialogue to appeal to the schoolboy "audience." For example, Erik the Red's banishment from Norway to Iceland and then to Greenland is ascribed to his violence but also to his weakness for other men's wives; his son Leif the Lucky's affair with a Hebridean princess is set up as a bittersweet idyll replete with "beautiful" scenes. Shute thus has the best of both worlds: a scholarly historian narrator gives his tale credibility while his rhetorical need to captivate his youthful listeners justifies Shute's popularizing. Besides working out his historical interests, the frame allows Shute slyly to satirize the teaching of history in British schools, as his teacher hero, after a brilliant but unconventional lecture which has clearly engaged his pupils, is advised by his stuffy headmaster to pursue a job selling electric razors.

Shute's romances include more details about aviation and business than about the emotional states of the amorous couple and, in the early works, the love interest seems secondary, though it becomes more organic in the later works. Basically they suggest domesticity as a powerful civilizing force, one that might well spur men to dreams and action. Shute's men are industrious, competent, and driven, while his women are supportive, and ultimately save men from shortsightedness or from personal limitations. In *Stephen Morris*, a young engineer's work for a struggling aircraft builder takes precedence over his proposing to the girl of his dreams, while in *Marazan* Shute's adventurous heroine mainly provides a motive for the protagonist's economic success. In *Landfall*, when everyone rejects a Navy pilot who destroyed a British submarine, thinking it German, the barmaid he strove to seduce pieces together clues indicating two subs sunk in the same area; she thereby saves the pilot's reputation and his conscience, and wins his love and his hand, despite their class differences. *Pastoral*, in turn, is an ironic idyll of a soldier on leave who strikes up a romance by offering to share a huge pike with a young woman. *The Far*

Country tells of an English girl, who, while visiting on a sheep station in Australia, meets and falls in love with a Czech refugee, helps him amputate the leg of a man trapped under a bulldozer and operate on the crushed skull of another, and goes on to find with him a vitality undreamed of back home in England. *A Town Like Alice* is in part a contrived romance, an English woman's romantic search for the Australian lorry-driver who stood up for her and others against the Japanese occupation forces in Malaya, and her finding a new life in rural Australia.

Requiem for a Wren is typical of Shute's major love stories. Spanning the better part of a decade and two continents, it tells how Alan Duncan, the son of a wealthy Australian sheep farmer, returns to the family station in 1953 to discover that his parents' parlourmaid had committed suicide just before he arrived. Alan learns that, unknown to his family, she was Janet Prentice, the English Wren once engaged to his brother Bill. After Bill was killed just before the invasion of Normandy, Alan, having fallen in love with Janet, had searched unsuccessfully for her. The bulk of the text is a series of flashbacks as Alan reads Janet's diaries and recalls his obsessive search. As in *A Town Like Alice*, an Australian seeks in England an English girl who in turn seeks him in Australia, but in this case with less happy results.

This sadly ironic love story with its finely drawn characters is set against detailed description of navy life near the Isle of Wight just prior to D-Day, with specifics of the physical landscape, words from contemporary navy slang, and much recounting of everyday occurrences painting an utterly convincing picture of period and place. The nervous preparations and rehearsals for the "day the balloon goes up" are, ironically, the high point in the young lives of the protagonists, who will never again feel as useful nor as fulfilled by their later civilian lives. The war years liberate young women and mix the British classes, yet the sad survivors of this tumultuous period find themselves going back to conventional and banal lives. Thus Shute writes a classic World War II love story, but reverses the usual emphasis: these were the best of times far more than the worst of times.

Shute's forte is to reduce the historical and the romantic to life-sized dimensions, to capture the excitement of the humdrum and the ordinariness of the historic, to pursue the effects of change on the common man—all in an artfully casual style. His works reflect an old-fashioned sense of goodness; they involve characters with a strong sense of purpose, of decency, of right, characters who enjoy being caught up in the unfolding of great enterprises. Major Callender sums up Shute's view of history when he tells his class in *Vinland the Good*: "History is made by plain and simple people like ourselves, doing the best we can with each job as it comes along." Shute himself sums up his reason for including romance: "people in love are normally clean and brave and self-sacrificing, at their best."

—Gina and Andrew Macdonald

SINCLAIR, Olga (Ellen, née Waters). Also writes as Ellen Clare; Olga Daniels. British. Born in Watton, Norfolk, 23 January 1923. Educated at Convent of the Sacred Heart, Swaffham, Norfolk. Married Stanley G. Sinclair in 1945; three sons. Since 1966 Justice of the Peace for Norfolk. Recipient: Society of Authors Margaret Rhondda award, 1972. Address: Dove House Farm, Potter Heigham, Norfolk NR29 5LJ, England.

ROMANCE AND HISTORICAL PUBLICATIONS

Novels

Man at the Manor. London, Gresham, 1967; New York, Dell, 1972.
Man of the River. London, Hale, 1968.
Hearts by the Tower. London, Hale, 1968; as *Night of the Black Tower*, New York, Lancer, 1968.
Bitter Sweet Summer. London, Hale, 1970; New York, Simon and Schuster, 1972.
Wild Dream. London, Hale, 1973.
Tenant of Binningham Hall. London, Woman's Weekly Library, 1975.
Where the Cigale Sings. London, Woman's Weekly Library, 1976.
My Dear Fugitive. London, Hale, 1976.
Never Fall in Love. London, Hale, 1977.
Master of Melthorpe. London, Hale, 1979.
Gypsy Julie. London, Woman's Weekly Library, 1979.
Ripening Vine (as Ellen Clare). London, Mills and Boon, 1981.
Orchids from the Orient. London, Hale, 1986.

Novels as Olga Daniels

Lord of Leet Castle. London, Mills and Boon, 1984.
The Gretna Bride. London, Mills and Boon, 1986.
The Bride from Faraway. London, Mills and Boon, 1987.
The Untamed Bride. London, Mills and Boon, 1988.

OTHER PUBLICATIONS

Other (for children)

Gypsies. Oxford, Blackwell, 1967.
Dancing in Britain. Oxford, Blackwell, 1970.
Children's Games. Oxford, Blackwell, 1972.
Toys and Toymaking. Oxford, Blackwell, 1975.
Gypsy Girl. London, Collins, 1981.

Other

When Wherries Sailed By. North Walsham, Norfolk, Poppyland, 1987.
Gretna Green: A Romantic History. London, Unwin Hyman, 1989.

*

Olga Sinclair comments:

I enjoy writing historical romance and take great care to incorporate realistic background details into my novels. For this reason *The Bride from Faraway* is very special to me because I drew on the personal reminiscences of Lithuanian immigrants to Scotland in the early years of this century, among whom were my husband's ancestors.

My latest book, *The Untamed Bride*, was inspired by a visit to my youngest son and his family, who were then living in Sarawak, Malaysia, the land of the headhunters. He took me on an expedition into the jungle to see the Niah caves, where the local men climb hazardously long poles to reach the birds' nests craved by gourmets to make soup. We also visited a longhouse, where we were most hospitably received and had tea in the headman's *bilek*, surrounded by black-haired village children, spotlessly clean and with impeccable manners. These scenes, combined with the dry words of old books I came across in my research, worked a magic in my imagination and the idea for my book became vividly alive to me.

Gretna Green: A Romantic History is non-fiction but carries the same theme. For nearly 250 years this small village, just over the border that separates Scotland from England, has captured the attention and imagination of journalists and romantics everywhere. It calls itself "the village of runaway marriages" and abounds with stories of young couples racing to marry there, with an irate and outraged father in hot pursuit, while the world holds its breath. The eloping lovers come from all walks of life, and from all parts of Britain, Europe, and indeed the world. The "marriage trade" produced outlandish local characters, charlatans, scoundrels, and bigamists, but nothing can obscure the true spirit of love and romance which has highlighted the village right through time and is still there in the present day.

*   *   *

Olga Sinclair has written romantic and historical fiction with fairly plain plots and characters. Her romantic fiction normally has a Norfolk setting and she writes with familiarity of the attractive English countryside. She has, however, used other settings such as a seaside town in *Hearts by the Tower* or Czechoslovakia, Austria, and Germany in *Bitter Sweet Summer*. The background adds a lot to Sinclair's novels, the Czechoslovakia of 1968 adding topical excitement to the rather pedestrian story line and a contrast to the tranquility of the Austrian countryside.

Sinclair is, however, at home setting her books in Norfolk. The loneliness of the Norfolk broads in winter features in *Wild Dream*, and the broads also feature in *Master of Melthorpe* and *Man of the River*. Sinclair's world is the world of village life rather than town life, although her heroines have often lived some time in London.

The novels revolve around young women as heroines, and generally concern triangles of attraction towards two lovers, one of whom is much less charming and worthy of her love than the other. Her first feelings towards a fiancé she comes to question, as in *Man of the River*, and is gradually attracted towards another suitor. In *Master of Melthorpe* the heroine at first finds the Lord of the Manor too dominating and arrogant, but ends up realizing his real nature and consenting to marry him.

Suspense features strongly, and the heroine is often surprised by the sudden unravelling of an enigmatic young man (*Bitter Sweet Summer*). Other novels employ strange plots with interesting twists. The heroine in *Wild Dream* is in peril in a black magic context; her father has a mystery past and she an unknown half-sister in *Man of the River*. Mysterious circumstances surround the heroine's predecessor, as wife in *Hearts by the Tower*, or as fiancée in *Master of Melthorpe*. Plots can be rather contrived and depend heavily on the "mystery" as a central feature.

Characters are sometimes rather shallow, as the father in *Never Fall in Love*, although the women are developed a good deal more particularly as regards their romantic feelings. Love is, however, very chaste, and a kiss or an offer of marriage can be the climax of a book.

—P. R. Meldrum

SISSON, Rosemary Anne. British. Born in London, 13 October 1923. Educated at Cheltenham Ladies' College; University College, London, B.A. (honours) in English 1946; Newnham College, Cambridge, M. Lit. 1948. Served in the Royal Observer Corps, 1943–45. Lecturer in English, University of Wisconsin, Madison, 1949–50, University College, London, 1950–53, and University of Birmingham, 1954–57; drama critic, Stratford-on-Avon *Herald*, 1954–57. Co-chairperson, Writers Guild of Great Britain, 1979–80. Agent: Andrew Mann Ltd., 1 Old Compton Street, London W1V 5PH. Address: 167 New King's Road, London SW6 4SN, England.

ROMANCE AND HISTORICAL PUBLICATIONS

Novels

The Exciseman. London, Mayflower, 1972.
The Stratford Story. London, W. H. Allen, 1975; as *Will in Love*, New York, Morrow, 1976.
The Queen and the Welshman. London, W. H. Allen, 1979.
Bury Love Deep. London, Love Stories, 1985; New York, Medallion, 1986.
Beneath the Visiting Moon. London, Love Stories, 1986.

OTHER PUBLICATIONS

Novels

The Killer on Horseman's Flats. London, Hale, and New York, Doubleday, 1973.
The Manions of America (novelization of television series). New York, Dell, 1981; London, Penguin, 1982.
The Bretts (novelization of television series). London, Penguin, 1987.

Plays

The Queen and the Welshman (produced London, 1957). London, French, 1958.
Fear Came to Supper (produced Birmingham, 1958). London, French, 1959.
The Splendid Outcasts (produced Pitlochry, Perth, 1959; London, 1960). Published in *Plays of the Year 19*, edited by J. C. Trewin, London Elek, 1959.
The Royal Captivity (produced London, 1960).
Home and the Heart (produced Lincoln, 1961).
Bitter Sanctuary (produced Salisbury, 1963). London, French, 1964.
The Acrobats (produced Coventry, 1965). London, French, 1965.
The Man in the Case (for children), in *Eight Plays 2*, edited by Malcolm Stuart Fellows. London, Cassell, 1965.
I Married a Clever Girl (produced Windsor, 1967).
Catherine of Aragon (televised 1970). Published in *The Six Wives of Henry VIII*, edited by J. C. Trewin, London, Elek, 1972.
The Marriage Game (televised 1971). Published in *Elizabeth R*, edited by J. C. Trewin, London, Elek, 1972.
For Love of Love (televised 1972; produced Leamington, Warwickshire, 1975).
A Ghost on Tiptoe, with Robert Morley (produced Birmingham and London, 1974). London, French, 1975.
The Dark Horse (produced Guildford and London, 1978). London, French, 1979.

Screenplays: *Ride a Wild Pony*, 1976; *Escape from the Dark* (*The Littlest Horse Thieves*), with Burt Kennedy, 1976; *Candleshoe*, with David Swift, 1978; *The Watcher in the Woods*, with Brian Clemens and Harry Spalding, 1982; *The Wind in the Willows*, 1983.

Radio Plays: *Trapped*, 1968; *Dear Aunt Jane*, 1972.

Television Plays: *The Vagrant Heart*, 1959; *The Man from Brooklyn*, 1960; *The Ordeal of Richard Feverel*, from the novel by George Meredith, 1964; *The Rescue of Pluffles*, from story by Kipling, 1964; *The Mill on the Floss*, from the novel by George Eliot, 1965; *Catherine of Aragon* (*The Six Wives of Henry VIII* series), 1970; *The Expert Witness*, 1970; *The Marriage Game* (*Elizabeth R* series), 1971; *For Love of Love*, 1972; *Finders Keepers*, 1973; *Beyond Our Means*, 1973; *Upstairs, Downstairs* series (12 episodes), 1973–84; *Failing to Report*, 1974; *Let's Marry Liz* (*Seven Faces of Woman* series), 1974; *A Patriotic Offering*, 1974; *The Hero's Farewell*, 1974; *Laugh a Little Louder Please*, 1975; *Will Ye No' Come Back Again*, 1975; *Joke Over*, 1975; *The Truth Game*, 1975; *The New Man*, 1976; *Horse in the House*, from story by William Corbin, 1977; *Tug of War*, 1977; *Together*, 1980; *A Town Like Alice*, with Tom Hegarty, from the novel by Nevil Shute, 1981; *The Manions of America* series, 1981; *The Irish R. M.* series, with others, from stories by Edith Somerville and Martin Ross, 1983–85; *The Wind in the Willows*, from the story by Kenneth Grahame, 1984; *Mistral's Daughter*, with Terence Feely, from the novel by Judith Krantz, 1984; *Seal Morning*, from the book by Rowena Farr, 1986; *The Bretts* series, with others, 1987.

Other Scripts: *Heart of a Nation* (son et lumière script), London, 1983; *Dawn to Dusk* (Royal Tournament script), London, 1984.

Other (for children)

The Adventures of Ambrose. London, Harrap, 1951; New York, Dutton, 1952.
The Impractical Chimney Sweep. London, Macmillan, and New York, Watts, 1956.
Mr. Nobody. London, Macmillan, 1957.
The Young Shakespeare. London, Parrish, and New York, Roy, 1959.
The Isle of Dogs. London, Macmillan, and New York, St. Martin's Press, 1959.
The Young Jane Austen. London, Parrish, 1962; New York, Roy, 1963.
The Young Shaftesbury. London, Parrish, 1964.
Escape from the Dark (novelization of screenplay). London, W. H. Allen, 1976; as *The Littlest Horse Thieves*, New York, Pocket Books, 1977.

*

Rosemary Anne Sisson comments:
I have written many stage plays, television plays and series, and novels, equally divided between the historical and the contemporary—but then I have never really made the distinction between the two. The truth is that I try to write interesting stories about people we can care about, either on the stage or on television or, in the case of a novel, acted out in the mind and imagination of the reader.

*   *   *

Rosemary Anne Sisson writes short readable novels with lively characters, but in spite of correct references to contemporary events they seem, as do those in her television plays in *The Six Wives of Henry VIII* and *Elizabeth R* series, rather like modern people dressed up. Some pages of *The Stratford Story* read very like pages of her *Bury Love Deep*, a modern love story which begins at the end of the last war.

William Shakespeare is 18 at the beginning of *The Stratford Story*, an amiable youth, quiet and considerate, very aware of the feelings of others. The small town of Stratford seems like a prison to him as he writes poetry in secret on scraps of paper stolen from his father's account books. Taking his young brother to market he meets Anne Hathaway from Shottery. She is an unhappy girl living with a stepmother she hates. William's perky sister Joanne is the most entertaining person in the story. Once married to Anne, William is determined to escape from her to the theatre and London; he ages quickly as he achieves this. He remains absorbed with people but no longer considers his family. Only the death of his son at the age of 11 brings him back to Stratford.

But at the end of the story—as William refuses to lie to his mother by saying that her beloved son Edmund has sent her a message as he was dying, when he actually died in the arms of a prostitute—does the picture of the writer come nearer to the author of the plays. "William knew now that this was his ultimate faith which he must stand to, that it was not in false prettiness, but in the very bitter truth of human nature and human life that hope and beauty lay, miraculously light in all the darkness."

The exact period in which *The Exciseman* is set is vague, as smuggling went on in the 18th and early 19th centuries until Free Trade legislation. Raphael Blunt makes a likeable hero. He leaves Oxford and applies for work as an exciseman in order to pay off his father's debts and release him from a debtors' prison. While staying at a pub in Sussex he poses as an artist. He soon realises that the building is the centre of the local smuggling, and his life further complicated by falling in love with Rebecca, the pub-keeper's daughter. There is a grand finale when, acting on Raphael's information, the Dragoons charge in and he is nearly killed. All the problems are solved in a hasty ending and Raphael marries Rebecca. The book has all the ingredients of a light historical romance and is typical of Sisson's work.

Sisson has a fresh pleasant style but lacks depth. It is hard to take seriously any account of Shakespeare which makes too little reference to his plays. Similarly some solid information about smuggling would have helped *The Exciseman*.

—Margaret Campbell

SLAUGHTER Frank G(ill). Has also written as G. Arnold Haygood; C. V. Terry. American. Born in Washington, D.C., 25 February 1908. Educated at Oxford High School, North Carolina; Duke University, Durham, North Carolina, A.B. (magna cum laude) 1926; Johns Hopkins Medical School, Baltimore, M.D. 1930. Served in the United States Army Medical Corps, 1942–46: Lieutenant Colonel. Married Jane Mundy in 1933; two sons. Intern and resident surgeon, Jefferson Hospital, Roanoke, Virginia, 1930–34; resident in thoracic surgery, Herman Kiefer Hospital, Detroit, 1934; staff surgeon, Riverside Hospital, Jacksonville, Florida, 1934–42; then full-time writer. Fellow, American College of Surgeons. D.H.L.: Jacksonville University, Florida. Agent: Brandt and Brandt, 1501 Broadway, New York, New York 10036. Address: Box 14, Ortega Station, Jacksonville, Florida 32210, U.S.A.

ROMANCE AND HISTORICAL PUBLICATIONS

Novels

That None Should Die. New York, Doubleday, 1941; London, Jarrolds, 1942.

Spencer Brade, M.D. New York, Doubleday, 1942; London, Jarrolds, 1943.

Air Surgeon. New York, Doubleday, 1943; London, Jarrolds, 1944.

Battle Surgeon. New York, Doubleday, 1944.

A Touch of Glory. New York, Doubleday, 1945; London, Jarrolds, 1946.

In a Dark Garden. New York, Doubleday, 1946; London, Jarrolds, 1952.

The Golden Isle. New York, Doubleday, 1947; London, Jarrolds, 1950.

Sangaree. New York, Doubleday, 1948; London, Jarrolds, 1950.

Divine Mistress. New York, Doubleday, 1949; London, Jarrolds, 1951.

The Stubborn Heart. New York, Doubleday, 1950; London, Jarrolds, 1953.

Fort Everglades. New York, Doubleday, and London, Jarrolds, 1951.

The Road to Bithynia: A Novel of Luke, The Beloved Physician. New York, Doubleday, 1951; London, Jarrolds, 1952.

East Side General. New York, Doubleday, 1952; London, Jarrolds, 1953.

Storm Haven. New York, Doubleday, 1953; London, Jarrolds, 1954.

The Galileans: A Novel of Mary Magdalene. New York, Doubleday, 1953; London, Jarrolds, 1954.

The Song of Ruth. New York, Doubleday, 1954; London, Jarrolds, 1955.

The Healer. New York, Doubleday, and London, Jarrolds, 1955.

Flight from Natchez. New York, Doubleday, 1955; London, Jarrolds, 1956.

The Scarlet Cord: A Novel of the Woman of Jericho. New York, Doubleday, and London, Jarrolds, 1956.

The Warrior. New York, Doubleday, 1956; as The Flaming Frontier, London, Jarrolds, 1957.

The Mapmaker: A Novel of the Days of Prince Henry, The Navigator. New York, Doubleday, 1957; London, Jarrolds, 1958.

Sword and Scalpel. New York, Doubleday, and London, Jarrolds, 1957.

Daybreak. New York, Doubleday, and London, Jarrolds, 1958.

Deep Is the Shadow (as G. Arnold Haygood). New York, Doubleday, 1959; London, Hutchinson, 1975; as Shadow of Evil (as Frank G. Slaughter), New York, Pocket Books, 1975.

The Crown and the Cross: The Life of Christ. Cleveland, World, and London, Jarrolds, 1959.

The Thorn of Arimathea. New York, Doubleday, and London, Jarrolds, 1959.

Lorena. New York, Doubleday, 1959; London, Hutchinson, 1960.

Pilgrims in Paradise. New York, Doubleday, 1960; as Puritans in Paradise, London, Hutchinson, 1960.

Epidemic! New York, Doubleday, and London, Hutchinson, 1961.

The Curse of Jezebel: A Novel of the Biblical Queen of Evil. New York, Doubleday, 1961; as Queen of Evil, London, Hutchinson, 1962.

Tomorrow's Miracle. New York, Doubleday, and London, Hutchinson, 1962.

Devil's Harvest. New York, Doubleday, and London, Hutchinson, 1963.

Upon This Rock: A Novel of Simon Peter, Prince of the Apostles. New York, Coward McCann, 1963; London, Hutchinson, 1964.

A Savage Place. New York, Doubleday, and London, Hutchinson, 1964.

Constantine: The Miracle of the Flaming Cross. New York, Doubleday, 1965; London, Hutchinson, 1966.

The Purple Quest: A Novel of Seafaring Adventure in the Ancient World. New York, Doubleday, and London, Hutchinson, 1965.

Surgeon, U.S.A. New York, Doubleday, 1966; as War Surgeon, London, Hutchinson, 1967.

Doctors' Wives. New York, Doubleday, 1967; London, Hutchinson, 1971.

God's Warrior. New York, Doubleday, and London, Hutchinson, 1967.

The Sins of Herod: A Novel of Rome and the Early Church. New York, Doubleday, 1968; London, Hutchinson, 1969.

Surgeon's Choice: A Novel of Medicine Tomorrow. New York, Doubleday, and London, Hutchinson, 1969.

Countdown. New York, Doubleday, and London, Hutchinson, 1970.

Code Five. New York, Doubleday, 1971; London, Hutchinson, 1972.

Convention, M.D.: A Novel of Medical In-Fighting. New York, Doubleday, 1972; London, Hutchinson, 1973.

Women in White. New York, Doubleday, 1974; as Lifeblood, London, Hutchinson, 1974.

Stonewall Brigade. New York, Doubleday, 1975; London, Hutchinson, 1976.

Plague Ship. New York, Doubleday, 1976; London, Hutchinson, 1977.

Devil's Gamble. New York, Doubleday, 1977; London, Hutchinson, 1978.

The Passionate Rebel. New York, Doubleday, and London, Hutchinson, 1979.

Gospel Fever: A Novel about America's Most Beloved TV Evangelist. New York, Doubleday, 1980.

Doctor's Daughters. New York, Doubleday, 1981; London, Hutchinson, 1982.

Doctors at Risk. New York, Doubleday, and London, Hutchinson, 1983.

No Greater Love. New York, Doubleday, and London, Hutchinson, 1985.

Transplant. London, Hutchinson, 1987.

Novels as C. V. Terry

Buccaneer Surgeon. New York, Hanover House, 1954; as Buccaneer Doctor, London, Jarrolds, 1955.

Darien Venture. New York, Hanover House, and London, Jarrolds, 1955.

The Golden Ones. New York, Hanover House, 1955; London, Jarrolds, 1958.

The Deadly Lady of Madagascar. New York, Doubleday, and London, Jarrolds, 1959.

OTHER PUBLICATIONS

Play

Screenplay: *Naked in the Sun*, with John Hugh, 1957.

Other

The New Science of Surgery. New York, Messner, 1946; London, Sampson Low, 1948; revised edition, as *Science and Surgery*, New York, Permabooks, 1956.
Medicine for Moderns: The New Science of Psychosomatic Medicine. New York, Messner, 1947; London, Jarrolds, 1953; as *The New Way to Mental and Physical Health*, New York, Grosset and Dunlap, 1949; as *Your Body and Your Mind*, New York, New American Library, 1953.
Immortal Magyar: Semmelweis, Conqueror of Childbed Fever. New York, Schuman, 1950; as *Semmelweis, Conqueror of Childbed Fever*, New York, Collier, 1961.
Apalachee Gold: The Fabulous Adventures of Cabeza de Vaca (for children). New York, Doubleday, 1954; London, Hutchinson, 1955.
The Land and the Promise: The Greatest Stories from the Bible. Cleveland, World, 1960; London, Hutchinson, 1961.
David, Warrior and King: A Biblical Biography. Cleveland, World, 1962; London, Hutchinson, 1963.

*

Manuscript Collections: Mugar Memorial Library, Boston University; Duke University, Durham, North Carolina.

Frank G. Slaughter comments:

I am primarily a storytellerwho writes to entertain and also inform. As such, I am meticulous in my research and polish my writings through an average of ten revisions. Critics have dubbed me "the undisputed master of medical fiction," an accolade I prize very much.

*   *   *

Though Frank G. Slaughter has been turning out novels at the rate of about one every ten months for more than 40 years, he received very little critical comment in the 1970's. He doesn't need it. His books will sell anyway. He is still a master craftsman, a professional who is expert at moving a story along from one climax to the next. Novice writers need only study a few of Slaughter's novels to learn about structure and style. Slaughter must be a happy millionaire by now. Over 60 million copies of his books have been sold, in 21 countries.

Though his talent is clearly evident in his depiction of action, background, color, and plot, Slaughter lacks the touch of genius that would make him a great writer. His characterizations fall short. His people are just not believable. They talk in long, long sentences, especially in the medical novels which comprise the largest segment of his work. On the positive side, the medical novels surely do keep up with the time as far as medical technology and current events are concerned—from exposing to the public eye the none too admirable practices of many physicians in *That None Should Die*, to big city summer gang wars and public housing development problems in *Epidemic!*, to the energy shortage, Haitian refugees, and Florida condominiums in *Doctor's Daughters*; from his physician protagonists in all kinds of situations and through all the wars this nation has suffered to the very recent controversy surrounding the inordinate number of coronary by-pass operations being done that might better be treated medically. His empathy with people, however, fails to keep pace, especially his women who do not even begin to reflect the very real changes that women have undergone in the last half of the 20th century. In my review of *Women in White* (1974), I wrote, "Lest anyone think this new medical novel promotes the women's cause, forget it. The nurses are fine women; the female doctors have reached their high standing through judicious use of their lovely bodies, not their intellect." In *Doctor's Daughters* (1981) he made a stab at rectifying this by featuring three sisters, all of them successful doctors in their own right who earned their caducei by study and hard work. But the denouement of the tale is finding of a true love for each one, all in one short week. Slaughter's women are glossy counterfeits. A pattern has emerged in most of his novels, even some of the biblical ones. There is usually a crusading hero, most often a physician with a cause, and two women, one of them naughty; the other, good, wholesome, and eminently marriageable. When the subject of demonic possession was in vogue, Slaughter brought these two women together in one body in *Devil's Gamble*—a neat trick.

Slaughter's novels are of three types: historical, biblical, and medical, or frequently a combination of these. His historical novels are least pedantic. They neither preach nor present long treatises on surgical procedures. When he writes under the name of C. V. Terry he seems to have more fun. His language is expansive and adventuresome. He tends more to the ribald and is freer in this portrays of sexual encounters. In all his work, the historical research is accurate if lacking depth. His descriptions of places and events are marvelous—there is an especially graphic scene of a sea battle in *The Purple Quest*—but the significance of the event is not his primary concern. In both the historical and biblical novels, Slaughter has commandeered excessive dramatic licence when dealing with those famed personages who actually walked this earth by putting his words into their mouths and by ascribing his feelings to their hearts and minds.

Readers of gothic and romance literature have much to thank Slaughter for. He has lifted them out of their armchairs to many lands in many times, and perhaps sent some scurrying to their encyclopedias to learn more about the Phoenicians, the Spanish Inquisition, the Civil War. Many have turned to their bibles to read what the scriptures have to say about Ruth, Jezebel, and Christ. What's more, his fascinating descriptions of dazzling new medical equipment and sophisticated technology have reassured his fans that they can enjoy long and healthy lives. With all this magic, who really cares that his characters lack vitality!

—Marion Hanscom

SLOANE, Sara. See **BLOOM, Ursula.**

SMALL, Bertrice. American. Born in New York City, 9 December 1937. Educated at St. Mary's School, Peekskill, New York, 1950–55; Western College for Women, Oxford, Ohio, 1955–58; Katherine Gibbs Secretarial School, New York, 1959. Married George Sumner Small IV in 1963; one son. Secretary, Young and Rubicam Advertising, New York, 1959–60; sales assistant, Weed Radio and Television Representatives, 1960–61, and Edward J. Petrie and Co., 1961–63, both New York; owner,

Fat Cat gift shop, Southold, New York, 1976–81. Agent: Edward J. Acton, Acton Agency, 928 Broadway, New York, New York 10010. Address: P.O. Box 765, Southold, New York, 11971, U.S.A.

ROMANCE AND HISTORICAL PUBLICATIONS

Novels (series: O'Malley Saga)

The Kadin. New York, Avon, 1978.
Love Wild and Fair. New York, Avon, 1978; London, Fontana, 1979.
Adora. New York, Ballantine, and London, Fontana, 1980.
Skye O'Malley. New York, Ballantine, 1980.
Unconquered. New York, Ballantine, 1982.
Beloved. New York, Ballantine, 1983.
All the Sweet Tomorrows (O'Malley). New York, Ballantine, 1984.
This Heart of Mine (O'Malley). New York, Ballantine, 1985.
A Love for All Time (O'Malley). New York, New American Library, 1986.
Enchantress Mine. New York, New American Library, 1987.
Blaze Wyndham. New York, New American Library, 1988.
Lost Love Found (O'Malley). New York, Ballantine, 1989.

*

Bertrice Small comments:

I write commercial fiction in the historical romance genre. I think of myself as an author turned out from the same mold that cast authors like Taylor Caldwell, Jan Westcott, Jean Plaidy, Sergeanne Golon, and my personal favorite, Anya Seton. I plot my fiction around historical events, in past eras, bringing to life actual historical personages who co-habit quite comfortably on the pages of my books with my own fictitious characters. It's fun for me, and both entertaining and informative for the readers, many of whom have not been taught history, but find themselves fascinated by it. Unlike straight historical fiction I give just enough of the flavor of a period to make that period come to life, although I never alter historical events to fit my plot. Rather, I plot to fit historical event. I may, however, disagree with certain historical interpretations. Historians are, after all, only human and as subject to their own prejudices and opinions as other mortals. It is particularly difficult to research famous women of distant eras because women are usually identified as someone's daughter, wife, or mistress, and had to be considered either saints or sinners to get mentioned for anything other than their reproductive abilities, or dynastic pretentions. It didn't help either to have the historians of past eras men, and in the A.D. eras, usually churchmen. I am particularly fond of British history, and early to mid-Ottoman history.

*   *   *

Bertrice Small's historical romance novels fall in direct line of descent from Sergeanne Golon's nine-volume saga (the first of which was published in the United States in 1960) about a heroine named Angelique who, buffeted by the winds of political change after being separated from her newly-wed husband, sets out on a long and arduous trek across the world. Along the way she encounters one lover (subhero) after another, some of whom are antiheroes, until she is at last reunited with her first and only true love. Though many variations on the theme have appeared since, Bertrice Small's *Skye O'Malley* is easily the best of them and remains unsurpassed today, even by Small herself. One

reader described *Skye O'Malley* as "the romance that has everything"—incest, rape, the *droit du seigneur*, a woman of independent means, and true love repeated again and again, not to mention a political tug-of-war with the queen of England. It was Angelique and Skye, along with hundreds of their sisters who came in between, who ripped the fabric of the conventional wisdom that romance is virtually the only adventure literature allows females. In the process, they stirred the embers of a revolution in romance (the heat of which is still being felt around the world) that within the space of one decade wrought dramatic changes in both the character and conventions of the genre.

In *The Kadin* Small transports her heroine to the Middle East, where she paints a breathtaking picture of the intimate and sensual fantasies we associate with life in a harem while involving her heroine in a political power play in which the stakes are life or death for both herself and her son (a flight of fancy reminiscent of what is presumed to have happened to Aimée Dubucq de Rivery, cousin to Napoleon's Josephine, who was captured while on her way to Martinique and given to the Sultan of Turkey). It is this interweaving of political intrigue with explicitly described sexual adventures that has become a Small trademark, with her heroines operating at two levels, both personal and societal, in their struggle for power and autonomy.

Skye O'Malley has several sexual partners during the course of her story and truly loves four different men—alliances that depict the love of one woman for more than one kind of man, and four different kinds of relationships. No one male is fully developed as *the* hero, however, until near the end of the sequel, though each one plays that role for a limited time. All but the last of her liaisons, which the reader is brought to realize is the mature relationship she has been moving toward the entire time, exit via a coffin, allowing the indomitable Skye to move on to the next installment of her life with vigor and enthusiasm—in full control of herself, her children, and the family shipping business that has given her economic independence from the beginning. Niall Burke is Skye's first love and we assume, in what appears to be the closing of a circle at the end of *Skye O'Malley*, her last. But as *All the Sweet Tomorrows* opens we discover that he, too, has gone the way of all the others (*Lost Love Found* is the fifth title in the O'Malley family saga). "Niall Burke was essentially a weak man," Small explains. "He couldn't have held a woman like Skye for any length of time (so) I had to get rid of him." In spite of a plethora of subheroes and "lusty" sex scenes, however, weak men are also a Small trademark. Though her subsequent novels lack the originality (she even returns one heroine to the harems of the Middle East) and verve of her earlier work, Small's strength continues to be her strong, independent-minded women—"It's extremely pleasant being your mistress, but 'tis even more pleasant being my own mistress"—who are always in the thick of the action and political intrigue, whether behind the scenes as in *The Kadin* or center stage as in *Skye O'Malley*, on the land and on the sea, in 14th century Byzantium or 16th-century Ireland.

—Carol Thurston

SMITH, Doris E(dna Elliott). Irish. Born in Dublin, 12 August 1919. Educated at Alexandra College, Dublin. From 1938 worked for an insurance group, Dublin. Recipient: Romantic Novelists Association Major award, 1969. *Died*.

ROMANCE AND HISTORICAL PUBLICATIONS

Novels

Star to My Barque. London, Ward Lock, 1964.
The Thornwood. London, Ward Lock, 1966.
Song from a Lemon Tree. London, Ward Lock, 1966.
The Deep Are Dumb. London, Ward Lock, 1967.
Comfort and Keep. London, Ward Lock, 1968.
Fire Is for Sharing. London, Mills and Boon, 1968; Toronto, Harlequin, 1969.
To Sing Me Home. London, Mills and Boon, 1969; Toronto, Harlequin, 1970.
Seven of Magpies. London, Mills and Boon, and Toronto, Harlequin, 1970.
Cup of Kindness. London, Mills and Boon, 1971.
The Young Green Corn. London, Mills and Boon, 1971.
Dear Deceiver. London, Mills and Boon, and Toronto, Harlequin, 1972.
The One and Only. London, Mills and Boon, and Toronto, Harlequin, 1973.
The Marrying Kind. London, Mills and Boon, 1974.
Green Apple Love. London, Mills and Boon, 1974.
Haste to the Wedding. London, Mills and Boon, 1974.
Cotswold Honey. Toronto, Harlequin, 1975; London, Mills and Boon, 1976.
Smuggled Love. London, Mills and Boon, and Toronto, Harlequin, 1976.
Wild Heart. London, Mills and Boon, 1976; Toronto, Harlequin, 1977.
My Love Came Back. London, Mills and Boon, 1978.
Mix Me a Man. London, Mills and Boon, 1978.
Back o' the Moon. London, Mills and Boon, 1981.
Catch a Kingfisher. London, Hale, 1981.
Marmalade Witch. London, Mills and Boon, 1982.
Noah's Daughter. London, Hale, 1982.

*   *   *

Doris E. Smith was born in Ireland and grew up near Dublin. Her childhood years were spent there just before World War II and were quite happy ones. They opened her mind and imagination to all sorts of influences which later emerged in her writing. Her natural facility with words edged her towards writing, but she was over 40 before she was published. Although not a prolific writer, she is yet a good one. Recognition for her ability came in 1969 when the Romantic Novelists Association awarded her their prize for the best romance of that year.

Her novels combine a very slight hint of Irish charm, and an obvious love of words and descriptions. She is, in fact, one of the "happy" writers who love a good romance and who can't refrain from producing one every so often.

Predictably she uses an Irish background in some of her novels, *Smuggled Love*, for instance, or *Dear Deceiver*. In the latter, she uses that part of Ireland she is most familiar with, the Wicklow area near Dublin. She has not limited herself to this background, however, for several of her novels take place against the physical beauty of the Cotswolds and the low rolling hills of the border country between Scotland and England. Smith has a slow, yet captivating way of letting her stories unfold, for she blends dialogue, description, and action in just the right amount to entice her readers on.

Wild Heart, is perhaps one of the best examples of her work and illustrates the care and planning that goes into her work. Victoria Elliott inherits a cottage in the Selkirk area of Scotland from her Great-Aunt Elizabeth and she goes there planning to sell it. Her sister, Lorraine, also goes with her. She has just experienced a shock as her fiancé has had second thoughts about marriage just days before their wedding. During the novel, Lorraine grows up and realizes that she herself contributed to this decision by her weaknesses and immaturity. Victoria, on the other hand, is one of the "fighters" of the world who tries to stand on her own feet just as her great-aunt had. The owner of the near-by castle is Dugald Douglas and, from their first meeting, Victoria is intrigued by him. Her efforts to redevelop her aunt's animal shelter and later to deny her growing love for Dugald are the major focus points in the novel. The counterpoint of Lorraine's problems play a motivating force in the plot. Smith has her character's personality well in hand during the novel. She is able to show the underlying facets of their personality in such a way that one is instantly sympathetic towards them. For all of Victoria's considerable success in her own field, she is still the sensitive child that her great-aunt had befriended with the words "welcome to my world"—a world of stray dogs and abandoned kittens.

Smith's obvious love of animals emerges frequently as she uses settings that incorporate them. Charlotte Lavender in *Cotswold Honey* is a veterinary nurse who leaves a practice to go into a rural one. Dugald Douglas in *Wild Heart* has a famous kennel and raises and trains hunting dogs.

Smith's novels are quiet ones in a way; emotional yes, even unhappy at times, but the reader is allowed to peek behind the scenes and understands that everything will right itself before the ending. Misunderstandings and mis-read hints or words are clarified so that the reader leaves her novels with a sense of happy completion.

—Arlene Moore

SMITH, Lady Eleanor (Furneaux). British. Born in Birkenhead, Cheshire, in 1902. Educated at Miss Douglas's School, London, and at a boarding school. Columnist and film critic for London *Dispatch*, *Sphere*, and *Bystander*. *Died 20 October 1945.*

ROMANCE AND HISTORICAL PUBLICATIONS

Novels

Red Wagon: A Study of the Tober. London, Gollancz, and Indianapolis, Bobbs Merrill, 1930.
Flamenco. London, Gollancz, and Indianapolis, Bobbs Merrill, 1931.
Ballerina. London, Gollancz, and Indianapolis, Bobbs Merrill, 1932.
Tzigane. London, Hutchinson, 1935; as *Romany*, Indianapolis, Bobbs Merrill, 1935.
Portrait of a Lady. London, Hutchinson, 1936; New York, Doubleday, 1937.
The Spanish House. London, Hutchinson, and New York, Doubleday, 1938.
Lovers' Meeting. London, Hutchinson, and New York, Doubleday, 1940.
The Man in Grey: A Regency Romance. London, Hutchinson, 1941; New York, Doubleday, 1942.
A Dark and Splendid Passion. New York, Ace, 1941.
Caravan. London, Hutchinson, and New York, Doubleday, 1943.

Magic Lantern. London, Hutchinson, 1944; New York, Doubleday, 1945.

Short Stories

Satan's Circus and Other Stories. London, Gollancz, 1932; Indianapolis, Bobbs Merrill, 1934.
Christmas Tree. London, Gollancz, and Indianapolis, Bobbs Merrill, 1933; as *Seven Trees*, Bobbs Merrill, 1935 (?).

OTHER PUBLICATIONS

Other

Life's a Circus (autobiography). London, Longman, 1939; New York, Doubleday, 1940.
British Circus Life, edited by W. J. Turner. London, Harrap, 1948.
The Etiquette of Letter Writing. Hemel Hempstead, Hertfordshire, John Dickinson, 1950 (?).

*

Critical Study: *Lady Eleanor Smith: A Memoir* by Lord Birkenhead, London, Hutchinson, 1953.

*   *   *

Lady Eleanor Smith claimed that she was partly of gypsy ancestry. It is not known whether this is true, but gypsies certainly play a large part in her fiction, both realistically and symbolically. In one aspect the gypsy displays a mode of life around carnivals or on the drom (road); in the other, the gypsy is a dark, brooding lover, a symbol of a highly felt sexuality that is both free and tragic.

Smith's first novel, *Red Wagon*, was based on her travels, in the 1920's, as a sort of publicity agent with a circus. Set in the 19th century, it describes the life history of Joe Prince, one-time roustabout, who marries a gypsy and eventually acquires his own circus. It is noteworthy for a wealth of realistic detail about circus life. Similarly pseudo-biographical is *Ballerina*, the tragic story of a Victorian dancing girl who becomes a prima ballerina, but suffers a sad decline and death.

Gypsies are central to six of Smith's novels. *Flamenco* and *The Spanish House* echo *Wuthering Heights*, with gypsies as sex symbols and with alienation plots. *Flamenco* describes the life of a gypsy dancing girl closely, while *The Spanish House* has excellent pictures of carnival life, together, with episodes set in Hollywood that are almost prophetic of the career of Marilyn Monroe. In *Tzigane* (U.S. title *Romany*) a gypsy dancing girl, madly in love with Brazil, a gypsy animal trainer, marries a gorgio (non-gypsy) when she thinks Brazil is dead. Years later, happily married, she must decide what to do when Brazil turns up. *Portrait of a Lady*, Victorian in setting, depicts a married woman who has the strength of character to resist the remarkable charms of a young gypsy. *Magic Lantern* describes the marriage of a Devon squire to a gypsy girl, and the life of their son. *Caravan*, however, is concerned more with adventure and political intrigue than with heightened emotional situations, and is perhaps ultimately grounded upon George Borrow's adventures among the gypsies of Spain.

In addition to her gypsy gothic fiction, Smith wrote a historical romance, *The Man in Grey*, which is similar to *Vanity Fair* in basic situation, and several supernatural stories. *Lovers' Meeting*, which invokes love, magic, and time travel to the past, is

well done, and is unusual (for this type of story) in not having a happy ending. *Satan's Circus and Other Stories* contains several supernatural stories that used to be anthologized frequently in the 1930's and 1940's.

Smith's fiction usually displays an odd contrast between, on the one hand, highly romantic themes, florid sexuality, and exaggerated emotion, and, on the other hand, many realistic characterizations and detailed, almost ethnographic accounts of subculture life. Her work is primarily fiction of event, told in a clear, detached manner, without analysis, but nicely paced and often fascinating in its detail.

—E. F. Bleiler

SMITH, Joan. American. Born in 1938. Address: c/o Fawcett, 201 East 50th Street, New York, New York 10022, U.S.A.

ROMANCE AND HISTORICAL PUBLICATIONS

Novels

An Affair of the Heart. New York, Fawcett, 1977.
Escapade. New York, Fawcett, 1977.
La Comtesse. New York, Fawcett, 1978.
Imprudent Lady. New York, Walker, 1978.
Dame Durden's Daughter. New York, Walker, 1978.
Aunt Sophie's Diamonds. New York, Fawcett, 1979.
Flowers of Eden. New York, Fawcett, 1979.
Sweet and Twenty. New York, Fawcett, 1979.
Talk of the Town. New York, Walker, 1979.
Aurora. New York, Walker, 1980.
Babe. New York, Fawcett, 1980.
Endure My Heart. New York, Fawcett, 1980.
Lace for Milady. New York, Walker, 1980.
Delsie. New York, Fawcett, 1981.
Lover's Vows. New York, Fawcett, 1981.
The Blue Diamond. New York, Fawcett, 1981.
Perdita. New York, Fawcett, 1981.
Valerie. New York, Fawcett, 1981.
Love's Way. New York, Fawcett, 1982.
Reluctant Bride. New York, Fawcett, 1982.
Reprise. New York, Fawcett, 1982.
Wiles of a Stranger. New York, Fawcett, 1982.
Prelude to Love. New York, Fawcett, 1983.
Chance of a Lifetime. New York, Silhouette, 1984.
Royal Revels. New York, Fawcett, 1985.
The Devious Duchess. New York, Fawcett, 1985.
Midnight Masquerade. New York, Fawcett, 1985.
Bath Belles. New York, Fawcett, 1986.
Strange Capers. New York, Fawcett, 1986.
True Lady. New York, Fawcett, 1986.
Country Flirt. New York, Fawcett, 1987.
A Country Wooing. New York, Fawcett, 1987.
Love's Harbinger. New York, Fawcett, 1987.
Larcenous Lady. New York, Fawcett, 1988.

*   *   *

Of all the Georgette Heyer imitators, Joan Smith has been the most successful in duplicating Heyer's wit. Her heroines and heroes are always intelligent, and their conversations always amusing. She also has Heyer's gift for depicting various kinds of entertaining fools and dolts as minor characters. As comedies of character, these romances have much more substance that most in the genre. Unfortunately, her best books are her earliest, and her more recent works are in some cases somewhat dull.

An Affair of the Heart is her first book, and one of her wittiest. A girl who lacks beauty, in a family of beauties, wins the heart of a lord, but can't believe it, especially when this lord's foolish best friend keeps telling her about her predecessor, complicating both the relationship and the plot. In *Escapade* (modeled on Heyer's *Sylvester?*) a young woman who writes a gossip column falls in love with the chief target of her column. Among the minor characters, the three young ladies competing for the attentions of the hero are outstandingly absurd and amusing. In *Aunt Sophie's Diamonds*, the diamonds, which are supposed to be buried with her, touch off an inspired comedy, resembling Heyer's *The Talisman Ring* (in situation, rather than plot). The heroine is a 24-year-old woman, deprived all her life of adventure, romance, and even friendship, who enters wholeheartedly into the young people's plans to dig up the corpse; the happy result for her is adventure, friendship, and romance. *La Comtesse* is a conventional good-bad girl story, in which Lord Dashford investigates the possibility that "la Comtesse" is a Napoleonic spy, and falls in love with her despite himself. The story is not up to Smith's usual standard. *Imprudent Lady* is akin to Heyer's *Venetia* and *Black Sheep* in that an unworldly maiden lady receives the confidences of a confirmed rake, who falls in love with her. As the hero and heroine are writers, we are given a glimpse of the Regency's literary figures as well. The hero and heroine are among Smith's wittiest, and the heroine's uncle is a memorable ass. *Aurora* is about a missing heir, an heiress who wants him to stay that way, and a girl who falls in love with the soi-disant heir. This is unusual among Smith's works in the presence of downright villainy. *Endure My Heart* and *Lace for Milady* are both about smuggling. The heroine of *Endure My Heart* falls into the leadership of a band of smugglers, but falls in love with the man assigned to catch them. Smith actually makes this sound plausible, and it is one of her entertaining books. *Lace for Milady* doesn't work anywhere near so well. *Delsie* resembles *The Reluctant Widow* in every way except that it is not interesting. *Lover's Vows* again deals with a woman in her mid-twenties, surrounded by fools, and unappreciated except by the hero. It is not prime Smith, but even at that, it is well-written.

Despite the derivative nature of her work, Smith is capable of considerable originality and imagination. Her attention to period detail is excellent, though she occasionally jars the reader with a glaring anachronism. Even though her later works are not up to the standard she herself set, there is always a good chance that her books will provide entertainment and pleasure.

—Marylaine Block

SNOW, Lyndon. See **ELSNA, Hebe.**

SOMERS, Suzanne. See **DANIELS, Dorothy.**

SPELLMAN, Cathy Cash. American. Born in New Jersey. Educated at Vassar College, Poughkeepsie, New York. Married Joseph X. Spellman in 1975; two daughters. Creative director, J. P. Stevens, 1965–69, and Revlon, 1969–74, vice-president, Bloomingdale's, 1974–76, and president, Cathy Cash Spellman Inc., 1976–83, all New York. Lives in Westport, Connecticut. Agent: Morton L. Janklow, 598 Fifth Avenue, New York, New York 10022, U.S.A.

ROMANCE AND HISTORICAL PUBLICATIONS

Novels

So Many Partings. New York, Delacorte Press, and London, Heinemann, 1983.
An Excess of Love. New York, Delacorte Press, and London, Collins, 1985.

OTHER PUBLICATIONS

Other

Notes to My Daughter. New York, Crown, 1981.

*　　*　　*

Cathy Cash Spellman's family sagas deal with the lives of the Irish on both sides of the Atlantic during the late 19th and early 20th centuries. Her first novel, *So Many Partings*, concentrates on Tom Dalton, the illegitimate son of an Anglo-Irish nobleman, Michael Harrington, and an Irish servant, Mary Dalton. Although Michael remains true to Mary and treats his son kindly, the rest of his family despises the pair. After Michael's untimely death, Mary and Tom are forced from the estate, she to the United States and he to a Roman Catholic boarding school. In America Mary remarries to escape her life as a servant, but she conceals her past from her husband. Tom's arrival in the United States after he reaches adulthood compromises her respectable life. After participating in the union battles of the longshoremen of New York City, Tom eventually amasses a fortune through a combination of luck and hard work. In his personal relationships, however, he remains decidedly unlucky. His wife is murdered; his children turn against him. Only in his granddaughter, Megan, does he find a kindred spirit. At the novel's end, she journeys to Ireland to claim the family legacy.

Spellman's other novel, *An Excess of Love*, concerns the events before, during, and after the Easter Uprising of 1916. The three children of an Irish Protestant lord, Con, Beth, and Des FitzGibbon, all aid the Republican cause to some degree. Family and political struggles continue into the next generation as Ireland plunges into civil war.

Although Spellman includes lengthy digressions on Irish myth and history in both books, the only non-fictional character in *So Many Partings* is union organizer Andrew Furuseth. Tom Dalton's experiences are based to some degree on those of Spellman's own maternal grandfather.

An Excess of Love contains many historical figures from Ireland's struggle for independence, including W. B. Yeats, Maud Gonne, Padraic Pearse, Eamon de Valera, and Michael Collins. In fact, the strain of integrating the historical events of the Irish uprising bogs down the narrative, especially after the deaths of Con FitzGibbon and her poet husband Tierney O'Connor, the two most compelling characters in the novel. Their romantic devotion to Ireland's struggle for liberty and their consuming love for each other make the civil war and selfish manuevering of the lackluster generation after them seem petty in comparison. In short, Spellman is a more compelling author of romance than history.

Spellman portrays most rich people in her novels as uncaring and unemotional oppressors of the lower class. Those who sympathize with the poor usually must embrace poverty themselves to find true love. For example, Con exchanges her family estate for a Dublin tenement to share her life with Tierney. Her sister Beth leaves a loveless marriage to an Irish nobleman to find happiness with a revolutionary leader. Dierdre Mulvaney gives up her chance to marry into New York society to join Tom Dalton's life of poverty.

Such matches are marked by passionate and enduring sexual relationships. Indeed, in Spellman's fictional worlds sexual satisfaction is an automatic byproduct of true love. As Tom tells Deirdre in *So Many Partings*, "This gift of the love between a man and woman makes us able to bear with all the rest of it." Nothing else is as important to an individual as such a relationship.

Ironically, Spellman's main characters usually end up rich themselves. Tom Dalton accumulates enough wealth to buy the Harrington family estate from which he and his mother had been evicted. Tahg O'Connor inherits the FitzGibbon lands and fortune from his childless uncle.

Spellman excels in creating interesting characters with whom readers can empathize. Although her style is straightforward narrative in *So Many Partings*, in *An Excess of Love* she experiments a bit by juxtaposing third-person perspective with Beth FitzGibbon's first-person reminiscences.

—Kathy Piehl

SPENCER, LaVyrle. American. Born in Browerville, Minnesota. Married Dan Spencer in 1962; two daughters. Lives in Stillwater, Minnesota. Address: c/o Berkley, 200 Madison Avenue, New York, New York 10016, U.S.A.

ROMANCE AND HISTORICAL PUBLICATIONS

Novels

The Fulfillment. New York, Avon, 1979.
The Endearment. New York, Dell, 1982.
A Promise to Cherish. New York, Berkley, 1983.
Hummingbird. New York, Berkley, 1983.
Sweet Memories. Toronto, Harlequin, 1984; London, Severn House, 1989.
Twice Loved. New York, Berkley, 1984.
The Hellion. Toronto, Harlequin, 1984; New York, Berkley, 1989.
Spring Fancy. London, Mills and Boon, 1984.
Separate Beds. New York, Berkley, 1985; London, Macdonald, 1986.
A Heart Speaks (includes *A Promise to Cherish* and *Forsaking All Others*). New York, Berkley, 1986.
Years. New York, Berkley, 1986; London, Macdonald, 1987.
The Gamble. New York, Berkley, 1987.

Vows. New York, Berkley, 1988.
Morning Glory. New York, Berkley, 1989.

* * *

Following in the tradition of Anya Seton rather than Sergeanne Golon, LaVyrle Spencer's novels focus on the inner life of her characters, and on their personal rather than worldly concerns. In choosing to explore the turf of ordinary people with real human problems, she has succeeded in creating warm and vulnerable characters (male as well as female) with whom the female reader can experience a sense of intimacy. What she is writing about, in fact, are the many faces love can wear; that she does so with a delightful touch of humor is an indication of the understanding and compassion that marks this author's writing as unique in the genre. Though Spencer has moved away from the romance label in her recent titles, she continues to write love stories. They are not one-dimensional romances, however, perhaps because she writes out of the conviction that "When you depict love only, without developing the characters as people who live and interact with other people, it's shallow (and) the characters are self-centered."

Spencer started out determined to do "something different" from the bodice rippers that were so popular at the time she began her writing career, and indeed *The Fulfillment* was that. Set on a Minnesota farm in the late 1800's, this is the story of a three-way relationship that develops between a sterile man, his childless wife, and his brother, who the husband asks to serve in his stead to give him a son. Though the plot line itself is neither original nor unique, Spencer's sensitively developed characters are. In *Hummingbird* the author sets up a confrontation between contrasting types, a straight-laced Victorian virgin and a mustachioed lothario she believes to be a train robber. Rejected by one publisher (Avon) as too humorous and "too narrow in scope"— almost every scene takes place inside one house—and because the first love (sex) scene was a failure for her heroine, *Hummingbird* eventually became Spencer's most popular book and is still in print.

The Endearment is a historical romance with a difference as well, since the hero who orders a bride by mail is clearly the protagonist; he is also a virgin, while the heroine is not. In *Twice Loved* Spencer sets up another triangle, with the heroine married first to a Nantucket sailor who is presumed dead when his whaler is lost at sea, and then to a childhood friend. When her first husband reappears, she is torn between two men, both of whom she loves but in different ways and for different reasons. Each has a history with her from which she cannot escape, bringing home to the reader the agony of a dilemma in which there is no single good or right answer.

In *Sweet Memories*, Spencer's talent for plumbing the internal life of her characters clearly pushes her work beyond the genre. Here the protagonist is a young woman with unusually large breasts, a condition that has had a withering effect on both her self-image and her social development. Spencer details the developing relationship between her heroine and the first man who even tries to see the woman behind the breasts, so to speak—a friend of her brother's who ultimately is able to breach the emotional barriers she has erected to protect herself from the responses she has learned to expect from males. Eventually this young woman makes a decision that is entirely her own, to risk the loss of both sensitivity and function in exchange for physical and emotional health by having the surgery that will correct what is more than simply a cosmetic problem (despite opposition from her insensitive mother). Spencer has written other contemporary romance novels (*Separate Beds*, *The Hellion*) but seems more at home in her historical settings.

—Carol Thurston

* * *

SPRIGGE, Elizabeth (Miriam Squire). British. Born in London, 10 June 1900; daughter of the writer and editor Sir Squire Sprigg. Educated at St. Paul's Girls' School, London; Havergal College, Toronto; Bedford College, London University. Married Mark Napier in 1921 (divorced 1946); two daughters. Swedish specialist, British Ministry for Information, London, 1941–44; co-founder and director, Watergate Theatre Club, 1949–52; lecturer and broadcaster on literature and theatre. Lived in Sweden, 1923–25. *Died 9 December 1974.*

ROMANCE AND HISTORICAL PUBLICATIONS

Novels

Home Is the Hunter, with H. T. Munn. New York, Knopf, 1930.
Castle in Andalusia. New York, Macmillan, and London, Heinemann, 1935.
The Raven's Wing. London, Macmillan, 1940.

OTHER PUBLICATIONS

Novels

A Shadowy Third. New York, Knopf, 1927.
Faint Amorist. New York, Knopf, 1927.
The Old Man Dies. New York, Macmillan, and London, Heinemann, 1935.
The Son of the House. London, Collins, 1937.

Plays

Elizabeth of Austria, with Katriona Sprigge (produced London, 1938).
Mary Stuart in Scotland, adaptation of a play by Bjørnstjerne Bjørnson (produced Edinburgh, 1960).

Other

Children Alone (for children). London, Eyre and Spottiswoode, 1935.
Pony Tracks (for children). London, Eyre and Spottiswoode, and New York, Scribner, 1936.
Two Lost on Dartmoor (for children). London, Eyre and Spottiswoode, 1940.
The Strange Life of August Strindberg. London, Hamish Hamilton, and New York, Macmillan, 1949.
Gertrude Stein: Her Life and Work. London, Hamish Hamilton, and New York, Harper, 1957.
The Dolphin Bottle (for children), with Elizabeth Müntz. London, Gollancz, 1965.
Jean Cocteau: The Man and the Mirror, with Jean Jacques Kihm. London, Gollancz, and New York, Coward McCann, 1968.
Sybil Thorndike Casson (biography). London, Gollancz, 1971.
The Life of Ivy Compton-Burnett. London, Gollancz, 1973.

Translator, with Claude Napier, *Kings, Churchills and Statesmen: A Foreigner's View*, by Knut Hjalmar Hagberg. London, Lane, and New York, Dodd Mead, 1929.
Translator, with Claude Napier, *Personalities and Power*, by Knut Hjalmar Hagberg. London, Lane, 1930.
Translator, with Claude Napier, *Sinners in Summertime*, by Sigurd Hoel. New York, Coward McCann, 1930.
Translator, with Claude Napier, *Economic Progress and Economic Crisis*, by Johan Henrik Akerman. London, Macmillan, 1932.
Translator, with Claude Napier, *Impressions of England 1809–1810*, by Erik Gustaf Geijer. London, Anglo-Swedish Literary Foundation, 1932.
Translator, with Claude Napier, *An Eyewitness in Germany*, by Martin Fredrik Christofferson Böök. London, Lovat Dickson, 1933.
Translator, with Claude Napier, *The Marriage of Ebba Garland*, by Dagmar Edqvist. London, Lovat Dickson, 1933.
Translator, with Claude Napier, *Riddles of the Gobi Desert*, by Sven Anders Hedin. London, Routledge, and New York, Dutton, 1933.
Translator, with Claude Napier, *The Street of the Sandalmakers*, by Nis Johan Petersen. London, Lovat Dickson, and New York, Macmillan, 1933.
Translator, with Claude Napier, *The Eaglet*, by Harald Victorin. London, Lovat Dickson, 1933.
Translator, with Claude Napier, *Tents in Mongolia—Yabonak: Adventures and Experiences among the Nomads of Central Asia*, by Henning Haslund-Christensen. London, Kegan Paul, and New York, Dutton, 1934.
Translator, with Claude Napier, *Men and Gods in Mongolia—Zayagan*, by Henning Haslund-Christensen. London, Kegan Paul, and New York, Dutton, 1935.
Translator, with Claude Napier, *The Head of the Firm*, by Hjalmar Fredrik Elgerus Bergman. London, Allen and Unwin, 1936.
Translator, with Claude Napier, *The Morning of Life*, by Kristmann Gudmundsson. London, Heinemann, 1936.
Translator, with Anna Sturge, *The Brig Three Lilies*, by Olle Mattson. London, University of London Press, 1960.
Translator, with Anna Sturge, *Michel Seafarer*, by Olle Mattson. London, University of London Press, 1961.
Translator, *Twelve Plays of Strindberg*. London, Constable, 1963.
Translator, *The Difficulty of Being*, by Jean Cocteau. London, Owen, 1966.
Translator, *The Red Room: Scenes of Artistic and Literary Life*, by August Strindberg. London, Dent, and New York, Dutton, 1967.

* * *

Elizabeth Sprigge's writings mainly consist of novels of American urban middle-class life between the two world wars. She also wrote two mildly adventurous novels for children, *Pony Tracks* and *Two Lost on Dartmoor*, dealing with young adult protagonists and their ponies. Sprigge's interest in examining the disintegration of traditional values and ways of living caused by World War I is reflected, however, in her historical novels *The Raven's Wing*, *Home Is the Hunter*, and *Castle in Andalusia*.

The Raven's Wing follows the life of Elizabeth of Austria from her young girlhood, her marriage to Franz Joseph, to her approaching death. Sprigge develops a detailed picture of the waning years of European royalty at a time when the conventional conflict between personal happiness and monarchical duty gains a special poignancy due to the increasing social and cultural obsolescence of the imperial position in the modern world. Sprigge's novel presents a nostalgic atmosphere in its admiration of the power and tradition behind the arranged marriages and royal court intrigue. Yet its modern context is revealed in Elizabeth's recognition of the inevitable disintegration of her world.

Home Is the Hunter develops Sprigge's interest in naturalism. The novel is set in the mid-19th century and opens in the whaling town of Dundee, Scotland. Sprigge uses dialect and description skilfully but the main interest in the novel is the theme of heredity which was central to the literary expression of naturalism. A whaler, Alan Cameron, has fathered a child who is described as half-Eskimo. The plot follows his son, Alan, as his hereditary destiny works itself out. A brilliant engineer, he "often felt vaguely discontented and had an inexplicable longing for some wider, wilder life in which he could come more directly to grips with the terrible, fascinating forces of nature." Alan travels to New York where he meets a "half-breed" couple, who speak a French-Canadian dialect, and goes with them to the Canadian northwest, to Fort Garry near present-day Winnipeg. Moving still further north, Alan marries an "Eskimo" wife and, eventually, meets his natural mother. Sprigge's argument blends nicely with the period and the Darwinism that dominated ideas of heredity and natural selection at this time. She maintains a breath-taking pace of plot throughout the novel and skilfully weaves two major story lines into a satisfying conclusion.

In *Castle in Andalusia* Sprigge writes of her own times. Nevertheless, the novel has historical interest because, as in *The Raven's Wing*, she uses the opening of the Spanish Civil War to examine the passing of the era of the Dons and royal court life. One reviewer remarked that "her story has pace and colour, and a passionate humanity." She writes with fairness and candour, if with a touch of the old English prejudice against the Catholicism of Spain." The same reviewer regrets that Sprigge is so obviously on the side of the Republicans. Her English heroine, Catharine, has married a Don but, ultimately, loves the rebel Pedro. Sprigge's politics are written into the dynamics of this three-sided relationship.

Sprigge's interest in her later writing turned to biographical research which focused on major figures of her own time. Her interest in the modernist work of many of these people is reflected in *The Old Man Dies*, which was hailed as a "brilliant performance" by J. E. S. Arrowsmith in a review in the *London Mercury*. Here Sprigge concentrates on the evocation of character psychology and leaves behind the intricate and finely-wrought plots of her earlier, historical novels.

—Heather Iris Jones

STANFIELD, Anne. See **COFFMAN, Virginia.**

STANFORD, Sondra. American. Born in Texas. Educated at the University of Southwestern Louisiana, Lafayette. Married Huey Stanford in 1961; two daughters. Founding member, Romance Writers of America, Houston, Texas, 1980. Agent: Anita Diamant, 310 Madison Avenue, New York, New York 10017. Address: 4117 Birchwood Drive, Corpus Christi, Texas 78412, U.S.A.

ROMANCE AND HISTORICAL PUBLICATIONS

Novels

A Stranger's Kiss. London, Mills and Boon, and Toronto, Harlequin, 1978.
Bellefleur. London, Mills and Boon, and Toronto, Harlequin, 1980.
Golden Tide. New York, Silhouette, 1980.
Shadow of Love. New York, Silhouette, 1980.
No Trespassing. New York, Silhouette, 1980.
Storm's End. New York, Silhouette, 1980.
Long Winter's Night. New York, Silhouette, 1981.
And Then Came Dawn. New York, Silhouette, 1981.
Whisper Wind. New York, Silhouette, 1981.
Yesterday's Shadow. New York, Silhouette, 1981.
Tarnished Vows. New York, Silhouette, 1982.
Silver Mist. New York, Silhouette, 1982.
Magnolia Moon. New York, Silhouette, 1982.
Sun Lover. New York, Silhouette, 1982.
Love's Gentle Chains. New York, Silhouette, 1983.
The Heart Knows Best. New York, Silhouette, 1984.
For All Time. New York, Silhouette, 1984.
A Corner of Heaven. New York, Silhouette, 1984.
Cupid's Task. New York, Silhouette, 1985.
Bird in Flight. New York, Silhouette, 1986.
Equal Shares. New York, Silhouette, 1986.
Stolen Trust. New York, Silhouette, 1987.
Heart of Gold. New York, Silhouette, 1988.
Through All Eternity. New York, Silhouette, 1988.
Proud Beloved. New York, Silhouette, 1989.

*   *   *

A prolific author of series romances, Sondra Stanford has focused many of her efforts on stories about relationships which have been damaged or destroyed. Her couples are given a rare second chance to correct old mistakes and rebuild on a solid foundation.

The lovers, who may have been married, have been separated by circumstances that caused one partner to lose trust in the other. In the appropriately titled *Stolen Trust* Alan Daniels gains a second chance with Rose Bennington seven years after jilting her only days before their wedding. Rose still loves him but says, "I'm terrified he'll leave me again someday no matter how many times he promises he won't." Unless she understands his reasons for leaving the first time, she cannot trust him not to hurt her again. Sometimes trust is destroyed by unreasoning jealousy or unfounded belief that a betrayal has occurred. Both men and women can be guilty of destroying trust. Tony Nugent drives Lisa Knight (*For All Time*) away by accusing her of betraying him. As she says to a friend, "Of course I can forgive him. And I do love him . . . But I can't endure his constant assumptions that I'm some sort of horrible monster out to stab him in the back!" Jana Parrish twice assumes her husband Miles is unfaithful (*Tarnished Vows*). The second time he tells her they are through because "Love involves trust, and that's something you never could give me." In *Bird in Flight*, Bill Sheridan is reluctant to remarry Andrea because she had rejected his love once and he cannot help being afraid she would do it again. Many times this loss of trust is related to pride and an inability or unwillingness to communicate. Rather than discussing the original problem, the partner who feels betrayed opts out of the relationship by pushing the other away or by leaving herself/himself.

Stanford's novels involve more bitterness than is usual in most series romances. She is skillful enough that this tone does not overwhelm the characters yet it is clearly apparent. She draws the reader into a world of pain in which it is easy to understand how one can love another, yet still distrust that person. She conveys the inner turmoil such an emotional division causes. This is not an easy task when working within the confines of series romance formulas, but Stanford succeeds remarkably well.

—Barbara E. Kemp

STARR, Kate. See **DINGWELL, Joyce.**

STEEL, Danielle. American. Born in New York City, 14 August 1947. Educated at schools in Europe; New York University, 1963–67; Parsons School of Art, New York. Married four times; 1) in 1964 (divorced 1973), two children; 4) John Traina in 1981, five children and two stepchildren. Copywriter, San Francisco, 1973–74; journalist; helped start a public relations firm in New York. Agent: Morton Janklow, 598 Madison Avenue, New York, New York 10022. Address: c/o Delacorte Press, 1 Dag Hammarskjold Plaza, 245 East 47th Street, New York, New York 10017, U.S.A.

ROMANCE AND HISTORICAL PUBLICATIONS

Novels

Going Home. New York, Pocket Books, 1973; London, Sphere, 1980.
Passion's Promise. New York, Dell, 1977; as *Golden Moments,* London, Sphere, 1980.
Now and Forever. New York, Dell, 1978; London, Sphere, 1979.
The Promise (novelization of screenplay). New York, Dell, and London, Sphere, 1978.
Season of Passion. New York, Dell, and London, Sphere, 1979.
The Ring. New York, Delacorte Press, 1980; London, Sphere, 1982.
Loving. New York, Dell, 1980; Loughton, Essex, Piatkus, 1981.
To Love Again. New York, Dell, 1980.
Remembrance. New York, Delacorte Press, 1981; London, Hodder and Stoughton, 1982.
Palomino. New York, Dell, 1981; Loughton, Essex, Piatkus, 1982.
Summer's End. New York, Dell, 1981.
A Perfect Stranger. New York, Dell, and Loughton, Essex, Piatkus, 1982.
Once in a Lifetime. New York, Dell, 1982; Loughton, Essex, Piatkus, 1983.
Crossings. New York, Delacorte Press, 1982; London, Hodder and Stoughton, 1983.
Thurston House. New York, Dell, and London, Sphere, 1983.
Changes. New York, Delacorte Press, and London, Hodder and Stoughton, 1983.
Full Circle. New York, Delacorte Press, and London, Hodder and Stoughton, 1984.
Family Album. New York, Delacorte Press, and London, Joseph, 1985.

Secrets. New York, Delacorte Press, and London, Joseph, 1985.
Wanderlust. New York, Delacorte Press, and London, Joseph, 1986.
Fine Things. New York, Delacorte Press, and London, Joseph, 1987.
Kaleidoscope. New York, Delacorte Press, and London, Joseph, 1987.
Zoya. New York, Delacorte Press, and London, Joseph, 1988.
Star. New York, Delacorte Press, and London, Joseph, 1989.

OTHER PUBLICATIONS

Verse

Love: Poems. New York, Dell, 1981; revised edition, New York, Delacorte Press, 1984.

Other (for children)

Martha's Best Friend [*New Daddy, New School*]. New York, Delacorte Press, 3 vols., 1989.
Max's Daddy Goes to Hospital. New York, Delacorte Press, 1989.
Max and the Baby Sitter. New York, Delacorte Press, 1989.
Max's New Baby. New York, Delacorte Press, 1989.

*   *   *

Danielle Steel writes about the women who inhabit the upper echelon of society. She presents no serious psychological portraits of her characters, but the trappings of the good life—the best and most expensive restaurants, designer dresses, Gucci shoes and bags, posh parties—are described in loving detail by a lady who knows whereof she speaks. Steel has mastered the art of creating sumptuous scenes of life at the top. Her heroines all have good breeding and class made obvious by the way they walk, talk, or toss an always luxurious mane of hair. They have the kind of looks and style that make others envious, yet each one suffers some terrible romantic tragedy that in the end makes her a stronger, freer person.

These heroines, brimming with brains and talent, must overcome many obstacles to find happiness and fulfillment. Some find a way to accomplish this through love, such as Kezia Saint Martin (*Passion's Promise*) whose lover convinces her that she can break out of her gilded cage to become a serious writer. Deanna Durcas in *Summer's End* has an affair with a handsome art dealer, freeing her to defy a husband who consistently ridicules her efforts at painting. She goes on to establish herself as a successful artist. Others have an even more difficult time. In *Now and Forever* Jessica Clarke lives through the nightmare of her innocent husband's trial for rape and his year-long imprisonment. The aforementioned Kezia shares an all-consuming love with Lucas only to lose him first to jail and then death. In *Kaleidoscope* a brutal crime of passion separates three sisters, Hilary, Alexandra, and Megan, while they are children. Not until many years later when a dying millionaire seeks to appease his conscience are they reunited. A slight twist to the normal Steel tale is found in *Fine Things* because here the protagonist is a man. Bernie Fine, the smart, handsome vice president of an upscale department store faces a host of disasters—the cancer of his young wife and subsequent widowerhood, and a distressing custody battle for his young stepdaughter.

Exotic locales and newsmaking history form the backdrop to many of Steel's novels. In *The Ring* Kassandra von Gotthard and her daughter Ariana both love and lose their men in the horror that engulfed Nazi Germany. The very wealthy Audry Driscoll (*Wanderlust*) travels to the Orient and finds herself stranded in Japanese-occupied Manchuria of 1934. Many pages and many trials later she is reunited with Charles, the love of her life. *Zoya*, a distant cousin of Tsar Nicolas II flees the Russian revolution, and suffers a harsh Parisian winter before meeting a handsome American captain and moving to the United States where even more troubles await.

There is an element of soap-opera inherent in all of Steel's tales, but her characters, despite some physical and social similarities, are distinctive and appealing. Her ear for dialogue is excellent, which helps make some farfetched situations almost believable. Bittersweet love in a world of glitz and glamour are the hallmarks of Steel's novels.

—Patricia Altner

STEEN, Marguerite. Also wrote as Lennox Dryden; Jane Nicholson. British. Born Marguerite Elena May Benson in Liverpool, Lancashire, 12 May 1894; took surname of foster parents. Educated privately, and at Moorhurst School, Lancashire, 5 years; Kendal High School; Froebel School, Sheffield, 3 years. Kindergarten teacher in Hertfordshire, 1914–18; taught dance and eurythmics, Halifax, 1919–22; toured with the Fred Terry-Julia Neilson theatrical company, 1923–26; teacher and writer after 1926; columnist, *Sunday Graphic*, London, 1940's. Fellow, Royal Society of Literature. *Died 4 August 1975.*

ROMANCE AND HISTORICAL PUBLICATIONS

Novels (series: Flood Trilogy)

The Gilt Cage. London, Bles, 1926; New York, Doran, 1927.
Duel in the Dark. London, Bles, 1928; as *Dark Duel*, New York, Stokes, 1929.
The Reluctant Madonna. London, Cassell, 1929; New York, Stokes, 1930.
They That Go Down. London, Cassell, 1930; as *They That Go Down in Ships*, New York, Cosmopolitan, 1931.
Ancestors (as Lennox Dryden). London, Cassell, 1930.
When the Wind Blows. London, Cassell, 1931.
Unicorn. London, Gollancz, 1931; New York, Century, 1932.
The Wise and the Foolish Virgins. London, Gollancz, and Boston, Little Brown, 1932.
Spider. London, Gollancz, and Boston, Little Brown, 1933.
Stallion. London, Gollancz, and Boston, Little Brown, 1933.
Matador. London, Gollancz, and Boston, Little Brown, 1934.
The One-Eyed Moon. London, Gollancz, and Boston, Little Brown, 1935.
The Tavern. London, Gollancz, 1935; Indianapolis, Bobbs Merrill, 1936.
Return of a Heroine. London, Gollancz, and Indianapolis, Bobbs Merrill, 1936.
Who Would Have Daughters? London, Collins, 1937.
The Marriage Will Not Take Place. London, Collins, 1938.
Family Ties. London, Collins, 1939.
Flood Trilogy:
  The Sun Is My Undoing. London, Collins, and New York, Viking Press, 1941.
  Twilight on the Floods. London, Collins, and New York, Doubleday, 1949.

Phoenix Rising. London, Collins, 1952; as *Jehovah Blues*, New York, Doubleday, 1952.
Shelter (as Jane Nicholson). London, Harrap, and New York, Viking Press, 1941.
Rose Timson. London, Collins, 1946; as *Bell Timson*, New York, Doubleday, 1946.
Granada Window. London, Falcon Press, 1949.
The Swan. London, Hart Davis, 1951; Boston, Houghton Mifflin, 1953.
Anna Fitzalan. London, Collins, and New York, Doubleday, 1953.
Bulls of Parral. London, Collins, and New York, Doubleday, 1954.
The Unquiet Spirit. London, Collins, 1955; New York, Doubleday, 1956.
The Tower. London, Collins, 1959; New York, Doubleday, 1960.
The Woman in the Back Seat. London, Collins, and New York, Doubleday, 1959.
A Candle in the Sun. London, Longman, and New York, Doubleday, 1964.

Short Stories

A Kind of Insolence and Other Stories. London, Collins, 1940.

OTHER PUBLICATIONS

Plays

Oakfields Plays, Including the Inglemere Christmas Play (for children). London, Nicholson and Watson, 1932.
Peepshow (for children). London, Nicholson and Watson, 1933.
Matador, with Matheson Lang, adaptation of the novel by Steen (produced Edinburgh, 1937).
French for Love, with Derek Patmore (produced London, 1939). London, Collins, 1940.
The Grand Manner (produced Manchester, 1942).

Screenplays: *The Man from Morocco*, with others, 1945; *Beware of Pity*, with W. P. Lipscomb and Elizabeth Baron, 1946.

Other

Hugh Walpole: A Study. London, Nicholson and Watson, and New York, Doubleday, 1933.
The Lost One: A Biography of Mary—Perdita—Robinson. London, Methuen, 1933.
William Nicholson. London, Collins, 1943.
Little White King (on cats). London, Joseph, and Cleveland, World, 1956.
A Pride of Terrys: A Family Saga. London, Longman, 1962; Westport, Connecticut, Greenwood Press, 1978.
Looking Glass: An Autobiography. London, Longman, 1966.
Pier Glass: More Autobiography. London, Longman, 1968.

*   *   *

Born in Liverpool in 1894, Marguerite Steen was persuaded to take up writing by her friends, among them the author Hugh Walpole and the famous actress Ellen Terry. Her novels reflect her extensive travelling, with Bristol, Spain, and the American deep south providing a focus for some of her finest work. Bristol is the setting of her first significant book, *They That Go Down*, which describes the adventures of the lively Jane Carradus and her press-ganged lover during the period of Trafalgar. The style is strong—if elaborate in description—and characters and period strikingly portrayed. Steen's early work tends to the gothic, fixing on fierce extremes of human nature in remote situations. The headstrong Sanchia Mullyon of *When the Wind Blows* is a typical example. So too is Jim Devoke, the womanizing "hero" of *Stallion*, a more impressive novel where a sensual violence pervades the pages. Jim's infidelities—a parallel to the stud services of the prize shire stallion he leads from one farm to the next—lead him to the satanic Tamar, whose love takes a savage toll when he rejects her at last. The quiet rural setting and stable family background serve to throw the characters into sharper relief.

Steen's mature fiction shows a change of emphasis, as well as a heightening of perception. The style is more direct and forceful, shorn of the earlier description. There is too a greater reliance on contemporary themes. Without a doubt her most important work is to be found in the "Spanish" novels and the trilogy based on the fortunes of the Flood family of Bristol. In the former, her knowledge of Spain and identification with its tradition—embodied in the ritual of the bullfight—are used to great effect. *Matador*, with its story of the retired torero living vicariously through his sons, is memorable as a study of the Spanish character in action. The theme of the bullfight was subsequently pursued, with success, in *Bulls of Parral*. The Flood trilogy follows the family of Bristol slavers to success and opulence as legitimate traders and squires, and examines the conflict of ideals raised by their inextricable involvement with Africa and the blacks. *The Sun Is My Undoing*, a bestseller and Book Society Choice, remains the best known, but its sequel, *Twilight on the Floods*, is equally good, switching adroitly from Victorian Bristol to West Africa at the time of the Ashantie war. *Phoenix Rising*, the final volume of the trilogy, is less satisfying, perhaps due to its being heavily cut prior to publication. Nevertheless, the trilogy as a whole deserves to be ranked with Steen's finest achievements.

Though less significant than the Spanish and Flood trilogies, a number of the contemporary novels are well worth consideration. *Family Ties* is an excellent study of personal lives in crisis in the publishing world, and both *Anna Fitzalan* and *Rose Timson*—the latter of a story of a mother's obsessive love for her daughters—are outstanding analyses of female character. Though not highly regarded by the author, Steen's last novel, *A Candle in the Sun*, is a clear and effective presentation of marital breakdown and its effects on a growing child.

—Geoffrey Sadler

STEINBECK, John (Ernst). American. Born in Salinas, California, 27 February 1902. Educated at Salinas High School, graduated 1919; Stanford University, California, intermittently 1919–25. Married 1) Carol Henning in 1930 (divorced 1942); 2) Gwyn Conger (i.e., the actress Gwen Verdon) in 1943 (divorced 1948), two sons; 3) Elaine Scott in 1950. Worked at various jobs, including reporter for New York *American*, apprentice hodcarrier, apprentice painter, chemist, caretaker of an estate at Lake Tahoe, California, surveyor, and fruit picker, 1925–35; full-time writer from 1935; settled in Monterey, California, then New York City; special writer for the United States Army Air Force during World War II; correspondent in Europe, New York *Herald Tribune*, 1943. Recipient: New York Drama Critics Circle award, 1938; Pulitzer prize, 1940; King Haakon Liberty Cross (Norway), 1946; O. Henry award, 1956; Nobel Prize for Literature, 1962; Presidential Medal of Freedom, 1964; United States Medal of Freedom, 1964. Member, American Academy, 1939. *Died 20 December 1968.*

ROMANCE AND HISTORICAL PUBLICATIONS

Novels

Cup of Gold: A Life of Henry Morgan, Buccaneer, with Occasional Reference to History. New York, McBride, 1929; London, Heinemann, 1937.
The Acts of King Arthur and His Noble Knights, From the Winchester Manuscripts of Malory and Other Sources, edited by Chase Horton. New York, Farrar Straus, and London, Heinemann, 1976.

OTHER PUBLICATIONS

Novels

The Pastures of Heaven. New York, Brewer Warren and Putnam, 1932; London, Philip Allan, 1933.
To a God Unknown. New York, Ballou, 1933; London, Heinemann, 1935.
Tortilla Flat. New York, Corvici Friede, and London, Heinemann, 1935.
In Dubious Battle. New York, Covici Friede, and London, Heinemann, 1936.
Of Mice and Men. New York, Covici Friede, and London, Heinemann, 1937.
The Grapes of Wrath. New York, Viking Press, and London, Heinemann, 1939; edited by Peter Lisca, New York, Viking Press, 1972.
The Moon Is Down. New York, Viking Press, and London, Heinemann, 1942.
Cannery Row. New York, Viking Press, and London, Heinemann, 1945.
The Wayward Bus. New York, Viking Press, and London, Heinemann, 1947.
The Pearl. New York, Viking Press, 1947; London, Heinemann, 1948.
Burning Bright: A Play in Story Form. New York, Viking Press, 1950; London, Heinemann, 1951.
East of Eden. New York, Viking Press, and London, Heinemann, 1952.
Sweet Thursday. New York, Viking Press, and London, Heinemann, 1954.
The Short Reign of Pippin IV: A Fabrication. New York, Viking Press, and London, Heinemann, 1957.
The Winter of Our Discontent. New York, Viking Press, and London, Heinemann, 1961.

Short Stories

Saint Katy the Virgin. New York, Covici Friede, 1936.
The Red Pony. New York, Covici Friede, 1937; London, Heinemann, 1949.
The Long Valley. New York, Viking Press, 1938; London, Heinemann, 1939.
The Short Novels. New York, Viking Press, 1953; London, Heinemann, 1954.

Plays

Of Mice and Men, adaptation of his own novel (produced San Francisco and New York, 1937). New York, Covici Friede, 1937.
The Forgotten Village (screenplay). New York, Viking Press, 1941.
The Moon Is Down, adaptation of his own novel (produced New York, 1942; London, 1943). New York, Dramatists Play Service, 1942; London, English Theatre Guild, 1943.
A Medal for Benny, with Jack Wagner and Frank Butler, in *Best Film Plays 1945*, edited by John Gassner and Dudley Nichols. New York, Crown, 1946.
Burning Bright, adaptation of his own novel (produced New York, 1950). New York, Dramatists Play Service, 1951.
Viva Zapata! The Original Screenplay, edited by Robert E. Morsberger. New York, Viking Press, 1975.

Screenplays: *The Forgotten Village* (documentary), 1941; *Lifeboat*, with Jo Swerling, 1944; *A Medal for Benny*, with Jack Wagner and Frank Butler, 1945; *La perla* (*The Pearl*), with Jack Wagner and Emilio Fernandez, 1946; *The Red Pony*, 1949; *Viva Zapata!*, 1952.

Other

Their Blood Is Strong. San Francisco, Lubin Society of California, 1938.
John Steinbeck Replies (letter). New York, Friends of Democracy, 1940.
Sea of Cortez: A Leisurely Journal of Travel and Research, with Edward F. Ricketts. New York, Viking Press, 1941.
Bombs Away: The Story of a Bomber Team. New York, Viking Press, 1942.
The Viking Portable Library Steinbeck, edited by Pascal Covici. New York, Viking Press, 1943; abridged edition, as *The Steinbeck Pocket Book*, New York, Pocket Books, 1943; revised edition, as *The Portable Steinbeck*, Viking Press, 1946, 1958; revised edition, edited by Pascal Covici, Jr., Viking Press, 1971; London, Penguin, 1976; 1946 edition published as *The Indispensable Steinbeck*, New York, Book Society, 1950, and as *The Steinbeck Omnibus*, London, Heinemann, 1951.
The First Watch (letter). Los Angeles, Ward Ritchie Press, 1947.
Vanderbilt Clinic. New York, Presbyterian Hospital, 1947.
A Russian Journal, photographs by Robert Capa. New York, Viking Press, 1948; London, Heinemann, 1949.
The Log from the Sea of Cortez. New York, Viking Press, 1951; London, Heinemann, 1958.
Once There Was a War. New York, Viking Press, 1958; London, Heinemann, 1959.
Travels wtih Charley in Search of America. New York, Viking Press, and London, Heinemann, 1962.
Speech Accepting the Nobel Prize for Literature . . . New York, Viking Press, 1962(?).
America and Americans. New York, Viking Press, and London, Heinemann, 1966.
Journal of a Novel: The East of Eden Letters. New York, Viking Press, 1969; London, Heinemann, 1970.
Steinbeck: A Life in Letters, edited by Elaine Steinbeck and Robert Wallsten. New York, Viking Press, and London, Heinemann, 1975.
Letters to Elizabeth: A Selection of Letters from John Steinbeck to Elizabeth Otis, edited by Florian J. Shasky and Susan F. Riggs. San Fransisco, Book Club of California, 1978.

Conversations with John Steinbeck, edited by Thomas Fensch. Jackson, University Press of Mississippi, 1988.
Working Days: The Journals of The Grapes of Wrath, edited by Robert DeMott. New York, Viking, 1989.

*

Bibliography: *A New Steinbeck Bibliography 1929–1971* and *1971–1981* by Tetsumaro Hayashi, Metuchen, New Jersey, Scarecrow Press, 2 vols., 1973–83; *John Steinbeck: A Bibliographical Catalogue of the Adrian H. Goldstone Collection* by Adrian H. Goldstone and John R. Payne, Austin, University of Texas Humanities Research Center, 1974; *Steinbeck Bibliographies: An Annotated Guide* by Robert B. Harmon, Metuchen, New Jersey, Scarecrow Press, 1987.

Critical Studies (selection): *The Novels of John Steinbeck: A First Critical Study* by Harry T. Moore, Chicago, Normandie House, 1939, as *John Steinbeck and His Novels*, London, Heinemann, 1939; *Steinbeck and His Critics: A Record of Twenty-Five Years* edited by E. W. Tedlock, Jr., and C. V. Wicker, Albuquerque, University of New Mexico Press, 1957; *The Wide World of John Steinbeck*, New Brunswick, New Jersey, Rutgers University Press, 1958, and *Steinbeck, Nature, and Myth*, New York, Crowell, 1978, both by Peter Lisca; *John Steinbeck* by Warren French, New York, Twayne, 1961, revised edition, 1975; *John Steinbeck* by F. W. Watt, New York, Grove Press, and Edinburgh, Oliver and Boyd, 1962; *John Steinbeck: An Introduction and Interpretation* by Joseph Fontenrose, New York, Barnes and Noble, 1964; Steinbeck Monograph series, Muncie, Indiana, Ball State University English Department, from 1972, and *A Study Guide to John Steinbeck: A Handbook to His Major Works*, Metuchen, New Jersey, Scarecrow Press, 2 vols., 1974–79, both edited by Tetsumaro Hayashi; *Steinbeck: A Collection of Critical Essays* edited by Robert Murray Davis, Englewood Cliffs, New Jersey, Prentice Hall, 1972; *John Steinbeck and Edward F. Ricketts: The Shaping of a Novelist* by Richard Astro, Minneapolis, University of Minnesota Press, 1973; *The Novels of John Steinbeck: A Critical Study* by Howard Levant, Columbia, University of Missouri Press, 1974; *John Steinbeck: The Errant Knight: An Intimate Biography of His California Years* by Nelson Valjean, San Francisco, Chronicle Books, 1975; *The Intricate Music: A Biography of John Steinbeck* by Thomas Kiernan, Boston, Little Brown, 1979; *John Steinbeck* by Paul McCarthy, New York, Ungar, 1980; *The True Adventures of John Steinbeck, Writer: A Biography* by Jackson J. Benson, New York, Viking, and London, Heinemann, 1984; *John Steinbeck: The California Years* by Brian St. Pierre, San Francisco, Chronicle Books, 1984; *John Steinbeck's Re-vision of America* by Louis Owens, Athens, University of Georgia Press, 1985; *John Steinbeck's Fiction: The Aesthetics of the Road Taken* by John H. Timmerman, Norman, University of Oklahoma Press, 1986.

*   *   *

John Steinbeck's chief claim to fame is as a writer of the realist school, and as a chronicler of the contemporary American scene of the 1920's and 1930's. He did, however, write two historical novels. These two works stand at the beginning and the end of a distinguished literary career: *Cup of Gold*, loosely based on the life of the 17th-century buccaneer Henry Morgan, was published in 1929, and *The Acts of King Arthur and His Noble Knights*, a modern version of Malory's *Le Morte Darthur*, was published posthumously in an unfinished state in 1976.

Cup of Gold is very much an apprentice work. Sub-titled *A Life of Henry Morgan, Buccaneer, with Occasional Reference to*

History, it is a hybrid production which arguably not only fails in many respects as fictionalized history, but also fails as an excursion into the fabular genre. Steinbeck's lifelong fascination with Arthurian legend is early established in the book with the introduction of the old Welsh seer, Merlin, to whom the young Henry goes to seek advice before embarking on his adventures in the West Indies. The Arthurian theme is perpetuated when Morgan's unformulated longings finally channel themselves into a search for his own version of the Holy Grail. This takes the form of an obsessive ambition to capture the fabulous city of Panama (the "Cup of Gold" of the book's title), and to possess the legendary beauty, La Santa Roja. Once having achieved his goal, the city of Panama conquered and pillaged, Morgan experiences the inevitable destruction of his dreams. He is coldly rejected and humiliated by La Santa Roja, and, although he is subsequently knighted by his King and created Governor of Jamaica, he lives out his last days a broken and disillusioned man. On his deathbed, he inquires after Merlin, and, as if in confirmation of the ethereal quality of his past ambitions and desires, he is told that the old seer is "herding dreams" in Avalon. Despite its shortcomings—its structural imbalance and its somewhat cardboard characters—*Cup of Gold* contains some vivid writing, heavily influenced by Donn Byrne and James Branch Cabell, and some moments of pleasing dry humour. As a first novel, it is certainly better than most. Many of the themes which were to be developed in Steinbeck's later and more accomplished fiction are already evident here.

Although uncompleted at the time of his death, *The Acts of King Arthur and His Noble Knights* was not, in fact, the last piece of writing Steinbeck worked on. He began his translation of Malory's masterpiece in New York during the summer of 1958, after having devoted several years of research to the subject, and continued to work on it through most of the following year while living in a cottage in Bruton, Somerset, close by Cadbury Hill, Glastonbury and the Vale of Avalon. He abandoned the work when he returned home to New York at the end of 1959. By then, he had translated only three of the first four of Malory's romances, having omitted the third romance, "The Tale of the Noble King Arthur That Was Emperor Himself Through Dignity of His Hands," from his manuscript. He had a typescript of something over 500 pages, but he had still four more of Malory's romances, comprising something like two-thirds of the total work, to translate. Although to the end of his life he continued to plan to finish the book, he was clearly and understandably deterred by the enormity of the task and by the pressing need to produce books of a more commercial nature. The first five sections of *The Acts of King Arthur* are written in a beautifully controlled, economic style which closely follows Malory's text. Beginning with the story of the Triple Quest, however, Steinbeck's imagination takes wing, and he proceeds to open up the sparse narrative to create a detailed and living tapestry of those ancient days. In the Sir Lancelot story, Steinbeck's creativity soars to even greater heights, and he introduces into the narrative the sights and the sounds of the West Country he had explored and come so much to love while living in Bruton. *The Acts of King Arthur* could surely have been Steinbeck's *magnum opus*, and even in its unfinished state (the published text is further truncated by the omission of Steinbeck's version of the fourth of Malory's romances, "The Tale of Sir Gareth of Orkney") it is impressive in its impeccable fusion of prose style, narrative, and scholarship. It is a literary tragedy of major proportions that Steinbeck never did complete the project.

—Roy S. Simmonds

STERN, G(ladys) B(ronwyn). British. Born 17 June 1890. Educated at Notting Hill High School, London. Married Geoffrey Lisle Holdsworth in 1919 (divorced). *Died 19 September 1973.*

ROMANCE AND HISTORICAL PUBLICATIONS

Novels

See-Saw. London, Hutchinson, 1914.
Two and Threes. London, Nisbet, 1916.
Grand-Chain. London, Nisbet, 1917.
A Marrying Man. London, Nisbet, 1918.
Children of No Man's Land. London, Duckworth, 1919; as *Debatable Ground*, New York, Knopf, 1921.
Larry Munro. London, Chapman and Hall, 1920; as *The China Shop*, New York, Knopf, 1921.
The Room. London, Chapman and Hall, and New York, Knopf, 1922.
The Back Seat. London, Chapman and Hall, and New York, Knopf, 1923.
Tents of Israel. London, Chapman and Hall, 1924; as *The Matriarch: A Chronicle*, New York, Knopf, 1925; revised edition, Knopf, 1936; London, Virago Press, 1987.
Thunderstorm. London, Chapman and Hall, and New York, Knopf, 1925.
A Deputy Was King. London, Chapman and Hall, and New York, Knopf, 1926.
The Dark Gentleman. London, Chapman and Hall, and New York, Knopf, 1927.
Debonair: The Story of Peresphone. London, Chapman and Hall, and New York, Knopf, 1928.
Modesta. New York, Knopf, 1929.
Petruchia. London, Chapman and Hall, 1929.
Mosaic. London, Chapman and Hall, and New York, Knopf, 1930.
Pantomime. London, Hutchinson, 1931.
The Shortest Night. London, Heinemann, and New York, Knopf, 1931.
Long-Lost Father. London, Benn, 1932; New York, Knopf, 1933.
The Rakonitz Chronicles. London, Chapman and Hall, 1932.
Little Red Horses. London, Heinemann, 1932; as *The Rueful Mating*, New York, Knopf, 1933.
The Augs. London, Heinemann, 1933; as *Summer's Play: An Exaggeration*, New York, Knopf, 1934.
Shining and Free: A Day in the Life of a Matriarch. London, Heinemann, and New York, Knopf, 1935.
Oleander River. London, Cassell, and New York, Macmillan, 1937.
The Ugly Dachshund. London, Cassell, and New York, Macmillan, 1938.
The Woman in the Hall. London, Cassell, and New York, Macmillan, 1939.
A Lion in the Garden. London, Cassell, and New York, Knopf, 1940.
The Young Matriarch. London, Cassell, and New York, Macmillan, 1942.
Trumpet Voluntary. London, Cassell, and New York, Macmillan, 1944.
The Reasonable Shores. London, Cassell, and New York, Macmillan, 1946.
No Son of Mine. London, Cassell, and New York, Macmillan, 1948.

A Duck to Water. London, Cassell, and New York, Macmillan, 1949.

Ten Days of Christmas. London, Collins, 1950.

The Donkey Shoe. London, Collins, and New York, Macmillan, 1952.

Johnny Forsaken. London, Collins, and New York, Macmillan, 1954.

For All We Know. London, Collins, and New York, Macmillan, 1956.

Seventy Times Seven. London, Collins, and New York, Macmillan, 1957.

Unless I Marry. London, Collins, and New York, Macmillan, 1959.

Bernadette. Edinburgh, Nelson, 1960.

One Is Only Human. Chicago, Regnery, 1960.

Credit Title. Edinburgh, Nelson, 1961.

Dolphin Cottage. London, Collins, 1962.

Promise Not to Tell. London, Collins, 1964.

Short Stories

Smoke Rings. London, Chapman and Hall, 1923; New York, Knopf, 1924.

Jack O'Manory. London, Chapman and Hall, 1927.

The Slower Judas. New York, Knopf, 1929.

Pelican Walking. London, Heinemann, 1934.

Long Short Story. London, Cassell, 1939.

Dogs in an Omnibus. London, Cassell, 1942.

OTHER PUBLICATIONS

Plays

A Dance at Dawn (produced London, 1909).

For One Night Only (produced London, 1911).

For Husbands Only, with Mrs. D. F. C. Harding (produced London, 1920).

The Happy Medler, with Geoffrey Holdsworth. London, Ward Lock, 1926.

The Matriarch, adaptation of her novel *Tents of Israel* (produced London, 1929; New York, 1930). London, French, 1931.

Debonair, with Frank Vosper, adaptation of the novel by Stern (produced London, 1930).

Gala Night at The Willows, with Rupert Croft-Cooke. London, Deane, 1950.

Raffle for a Bedspread. London, Methuen, 1953.

Other

Bouquet: Travels in the Wine-Producing Regions. London, Chapman and Hall, and New York, Knopf, 1927.

Monogram (memoirs). London, Chapman and Hall, and New York, Knopf, 1936.

Another Part of the Forest (autobiography). London, Cassell, and New York, Macmillan, 1941.

Talking of Jane Austen, with Sheila Kaye Smith. London, Cassell, 1943; as *Speaking of Jane Austen*, New York, Harper, 1944.

Benefits Forgot (memoirs). London, Cassell, and New York, Macmillan, 1949.

More about Jane Austen, with Sheila Kaye Smith. New York, Harper, 1949; as *More Talk of Jane Austen*, London, Cassell, 1950.

Robert Louis Stevenson (biography). London, Longman, 1952.

A Name to Conjure With (autobiography). London, Collins, and New York, Macmillan, 1953.

All in Good Time (autobiography). New York, Sheed and Ward, 1954.

He Wrote Treasure Island: The Story of Robert Louis Stevenson. London, Heinemann, 1954; as *Robert Louis Stevenson: The Man Who Wrote Treasure Island*, New York, Macmillan, 1954.

The Way it Worked Out (autobiography). New York, Sheed and Ward, 1956.

And Did He Stop to Speak to You? London, Coram, 1957; Chicago, Regnery, 1958.

The Patience of a Saint; or, Example Is Better than Precept. London, Coram, 1958.

The Personality of Jesus (for children). New York, Doubleday, 1961.

*   *   *

G. B. Stern used her own family as inspiration for her five novels about the Rakonitz tribe. *Tents of Israel*, published in the United States as *The Matriarch*, is based on true characters. This story of a wealthy Jewish family concentrates on developing some of the leading characters.

The Chronicle begins in 1805 with 15-year-old Babette, the daughter of a wine merchant, walking demurely with two of Napoleon's officers on her right and three on her left, through Pressburg acting as an interpreter. Her mother is a large hospitable figure "carelessly spilling a glassful of wine in a red stain across the cloth, so that her peasant guests may not feel uncomfortable if they should clumsily stain the cloth afterwards." Babette's granddaughter Anastasia, the extravagant Matriarch of the title, controls a large household from a big house in Holland Square, London. Here she cooks much of the Sunday lunch herself from family recipes which are savoured and discussed. Anastasia's brother Maximilian has laid down a good cellar, added to whenever he secures a big deal in rubies. After the meal he often shakes some of these out of a little packet onto the brilliant white tablecloth, saying "Choose."

There are any number of personalities seen in London, Paris, and Vienna, most of them with blue eyes and long noses, all interfering and advising each other over everything from houses and occupations to hair styles. In 1919 the matriarch's grandchildren rebel, but one of them, Toni, a successful businesswoman, becomes another matriarch. Her story continues in *A Deputy was King*. The family saga is continued in *Mosaic* with some minor alterations in the family tree. This story starts in 1870 when Anastasia and her husband flee from the siege of Paris.

In contrast to the Rakonitz family novels Stern writes a different style of novel with fewer characters. *Little Red Horses* starts at the beginning of this century when 11-year-old Halcyon Day meets 12-year-old Eden in the grounds of Beaulieu Abbey. Halcyon's father, a breezy naval officer, has just brought her over from America where, since her mother's death, her relations have made her into a famous child poet. Life is very different in England and Halcyon cannot understand why she is regarded as a little horror. Eden, a cockney child actor who has supported his large family since he was eight years old, is considered no fit friend for Halcyon, but the two children persist in their friendship, eventually marrying at the age of 17 and 18, in spite of everyone's strong disapproval. They prove to be a splendidly resilient couple. "You belong to a decent family. I'm not going to have you mixed up with a lot of mummers" bellows Captain Day. Halcyon is sent to a variety of schools where she feels like an outcast. The little red horses of the title are a picture Eden gives her, taking it from his own home. Halcyon clings to it, in a convent in Suffolk, in the New Forest House, in hotels, and in her boarding school in Munich. Halcyon reads a lot; Eden reads nothing and complains "You know all about it, don't you. Now do you mind not telling me any more." There are many different characters and incidents among the feather boas, horse-drawn cabs and early motor cars.

No Son of Mine is very different. A tramp, Robert Black, who knows nothing about his real parents, having been brought up in a charity home, cashes in on his likeness to Robert Louis Stevenson by pretending to be his son. In 1911 Miss Gibson, a spinster who keeps an Edinburgh bookshop takes him into her home and teaches him about the writer. He stays with her on and off for four months. Then with money he has begged he goes off to London, calls on J. M. Barrie who does not believe his tale, then idles his way to the south of France to haunt the district where Stevenson lived. Here a bored wealthy bachelor, although he knows Robert is a phony, keeps him until his death in a crash. Then an American offers him a programme in the States, but Robert turns it down to return to a hard life on a west highland sheep farm. Stern claimed this book was neither fiction nor biography. Robert Black is wholly imagined; all the information about Robert Louis Stevenson is authentic.

Stern's original and cosmopolitan historical fiction increased the scope and variety of the genre.

—Margaret Campbell

STEVENSON, Anne. Pseudonym for Felicity Avery. American. Address: c/o Harold Ober Associates Ltd., 40 East 49th Street, New York, New York 10017, U.S.A.

ROMANCE AND HISTORICAL PUBLICATIONS

Novels

Ralph Dacre. New York, Walker, and London, Collins, 1967.
Flash of Splendour. London, Collins, 1968.
A Relative Stranger. New York, Putnam, and London, Collins, 1970.
A Game of Statues. New York, Putnam, and London, Collins, 1972.
The French Inheritance. New York, Putnam, and London, Collins, 1974.
Coil of Serpents. New York, Putnam, and London, Collins, 1977.
Mask of Treason. New York, Putnam, 1979; Loughton, Essex, Piatkus, 1981.
Turkish Rondo. New York, Morrow, and Loughton, Essex, Piatkus, 1981.

*   *   *

Anne Stevenson's special gift as a writer of romantic suspense is her ability to place ordinary people in extraordinary, even im-

probable situations and yet to retain a strong sense of reality. The heroines of her novels are neither so glamorous and sophisticated nor so young and beautiful that the average reader cannot sympathize or identify with them. At the same time these women, from shop assistant to operatic costume designer, are not insipid marionettes wandering heedlessly into dangerous situations. Instead each deals competently with the challenges that she faces without relinquishing control of her life to the men who appear to offer protection and love. In fact, the crises weathered by these women serve to strengthen them.

It is notable that one of Stevenson's novels, *The French Inheritance*, features a hero rather than a heroine, with two female characters competing for his affections. This is a very neat reversal of the usual gothic pattern. The hero is as believable and as deftly drawn as all of Stevenson's creations. If a weakness can be found in any of these works it might be the occasionally jarring note in characterization. As an example, Ben, the child in *A Game of Statues*, seems at times both younger and older than his stated age of eight. Some of the other less-central characters, like Mr. Rizzio in *Coil of Serpents*, lean close to caricature. These faintly false notes are only jarring in retrospect, however, since all the characters in the novels are woven so firmly into compelling plots that the reader is carried along.

Stevenson has a brisk and straightforward prose style which avoids the florid descriptive passages that often mark this genre. She also has a remarkably accurate ear for dialogue that renders such description unnecessary.

The plots of these relatively long novels are reminiscent of the work of both Mary Stewart and Helen MacInnes, although they are in no way derivative. The resolutions of the plots are neither obvious nor entirely unexpected, although several of the books feature a clever last-minute twist at the moment that a less confident writer might conclude the tale. No loose end ever remains dangling; often a minor character or scene from an early chapter is pivotal.

The romance element is invariably handled with delicacy and restraint. Romance is, of course, integral to novels of this kind, but these stories stand on their own as adventures. As well-crafted contemporary works on suspense these books are likely to appeal to readers of gothics and to those ordinarily put off by the gothic approach.

—Susan Quinn Berneis

STEVENSON, D(orothy) E(mily). British. Born in Edinburgh, Scotland, in 1892. Educated privately in England and France. Married James Reid Peploe in 1916; two sons and one daughter. *Died 30 December 1973.*

ROMANCE AND HISTORICAL PUBLICATIONS

Novels (series: Mrs. Tim; Miss Buncle)

Peter West. London, Chambers, 1923.
Mrs. Tim of the Regiment (published anonymously). London, Cape, 1932; as *Mrs. Tim Christie*, New York, Holt Rinehart, 1973.

Miss Buncle's Book. London, Jenkins, 1934; New York, Farrar and Rinehart, 1937.

Golden Days. London, Jenkins, 1934.

Divorced from Reality. London, Jenkins, 1935; as *Miss Dean's Dilemma*, New York, Farrar and Rinehart, 1938; as *The Young Clementina*, London, Collins, and New York, Holt Rinehart, 1970.

Miss Buncle, Married. London, Jenkins, 1936; New York, Farrar and Rinehart, 1937.

Smouldering Fire. London, Jenkins, 1936; New York, Farrar and Rinehart, 1938.

The Empty World: A Romance of the Future. London, Jenkins, 1936; as *A World in Spell*, New York, Farrar and Rinehart, 1939.

The Story of Rosabelle Shaw. London, Chambers, 1937; New York, Farrar and Rinehart, 1939; as *Rosabelle Shaw*, London, Collins, 1967.

Miss Bun, The Baker's Daughter. London, Collins, 1938; as *The Baker's Daughter*, New York, Farrar and Rinehart, 1938.

Green Money. London, Collins, and New York, Farrar and Rinehart, 1939.

The English Air. London, Collins, and New York, Farrar and Rinehart, 1940.

Rochester's Wife. London, Collins, and New York, Farrar and Rinehart, 1940.

Spring Magic. New York, Farrar and Rinehart, 1941; London, Collins, 1942.

Mrs. Tim Carries On. London, Collins, and New York, Farrar and Rinehart, 1941.

Mrs. Tim (omnibus). London, Collins, 1941.

Crooked Adam. New York, Farrar and Rinehart, 1942; London, Collins, 1969.

Celia's House. London, Collins, and New York, Farrar and Rinehart, 1943.

The Two Mrs. Abbotts. London, Collins, and New York, Farrar and Rinehart, 1943.

Listening Valley. London, Collins, and New York, Farrar and Rinehart, 1944.

The Four Graces. London, Collins, and New York, Rinehart, 1946.

Kate Hardy. London, Collins, and New York, Rinehart, 1947.

Mrs. Tim Gets a Job. London, Collins, and New York, Rinehart, 1947.

Young Mrs. Savage. London, Collins, 1948; New York, Rinehart, 1949.

Trilogy:
> *Vittoria Cottage.* London, Collins, and New York, Rinehart, 1949.
> *Music in the Hills.* London, Collins, and New York, Rinehart, 1950.
> *Winter and Rough Weather.* London, Collins, 1951; as *Shoulder the Sky*, New York, Rinehart, 1951.

Mrs. Tim Flies Home. London, Collins, and New York, Rinehart, 1952.

Five Windows. London, Collins, and New York, Rinehart, 1953.

Charlotte Fairlie. London, Collins, 1954; as *Blow the Wind Southerly*, New York, Rinehart, 1954.

Amberwell. London, Collins, and New York, Rinehart, 1955.

Summerhills. London, Collins, and New York, Rinehart, 1956.

The Tall Stranger. London, Collins, and New York, Rinehart, 1957.

Anna and Her Daughters. London, Collins, and New York, Rinehart, 1958.

Still Glides the Stream. London, Collins, and New York, Rinehart, 1959.

The Musgraves. London, Collins, and New York, Holt Rinehart, 1960.

Bel Lamington. London, Collins, and New York, Holt Rinehart, 1961.

Fletchers End. London, Collins, and New York, Holt Rinehart, 1962.

The Blue Sapphire. London, Collins, and New York, Holt Rinehart, 1963.

Miss Buncle (omnibus). New York, Holt Rinehart, 1964.

Katherine Wentworth. London, Collins, and New York, Holt Rinehart, 1964.

Katherine's Marriage. London, Collins, 1965; as *The Marriage of Katherine*, New York, Holt Rinehart, 1965.

The House on the Cliff. London, Collins, and New York, Holt Rinehart, 1966.

Sarah Morris Remembers. London, Collins, and New York, Holt Rinehart, 1967.

Sarah's Cottage. London, Collins, and New York, Holt Rinehart, 1968.

Gerald and Elizabeth. London, Collins, and New York, Holt Rinehart, 1969.

The House of the Deer. London, Collins, 1970; New York, Holt Rinehart, 1971.

OTHER PUBLICATIONS

Verse

Meadow-Flowers. London, Macdonald, 1915.
The Starry Mantle: Poems. London, Stockwell, 1926.

Other (for children)

Alister and Co.: Poems. New York, Farrar and Rinehart, 1940.
It's Nice to Be Me (verse). London, Methuen, 1943.

*   *   *

The author of innumerable romances and family chronicles, as well as the popular "Mrs. Tim" books, D. E. Stevenson is an excellent example of a romance writer who expands the possibilities of the genre while recognizing its limitations.

Her novels might best be classified as novels of manners, in the same way as Dorothy L. Sayers's works are so described in the detective genre. The interest lies always in the development and exploration of character, in both the individual and collective sense. Thus, the Mrs. Tim novels, written in the epistolary mode, reveal not only Mrs. Tim's own psychological development, but also the changing nature of English wartime society. Her other novels, while they can be read on their own, often allude to characters and locations in previous works. What emerges is a kind of *roman fleuve* of English life and culture of a particular kind, at a particular time. This effect strikes one as being essentially unselfconscious, though it is obviously the result of considerable skill.

There is very little element of the gothic in Stevenson's work; what there is exists mainly in an atmosphere which is always essential to plot or theme: Celia's ghost in *Celia's House* is not so much an agent of the supernatural as of the house itself (the real "hero" of the novel). The house, Dunnian, goes through various changes during the novel, over the period of the two world wars, and thus is both a device for revealing social change and a symbol of continuity.

While primarily novels of character, Stevenson's works are noteworthy also for their effective realization of locale. The

Scottish setting of *Sarah's Cottage* is vividly described, as are the English locations in the same book. Setting is effectively related to character, and vice-versa; indeed, the interconnection of character and setting might be said to be a recurring theme in the novels, particularly in those with an Anglo-Germanic interest (*Sarah's Cottage, The English Air*).

Though skillfully plotted, the novels lack a major element of mystery or suspense of a conventional kind. Even when a mystery precipitates the plot, as in *Green Money*, it is ultimately a mystery of character, a why-dunnit rather than a who-dunnit. In *The English Air* the wartime exploits of the hero, Franz, are presented not as elements of an espionage thriller, but in relation to the character and his romance with his English cousin. Nevertheless, the novels are utterly engrossing, and probably represent the pure English modern romance at its very best.

—Joanne Harack Hayne

STEVENSON, Florence. Also writes as Zandra Colt; Lucia Curzon; Zabrina Faire; Ellen Fitzgerald. American. Born in Los Angeles, California. Educated at Yale University, New Haven, Connecticut; University of Southern California, Los Angeles, B.A., M.A. Drama columnist, Los Angeles *Mirror*, 1949–50; editorial assistant, *Mademoiselle*, New York, 1956–57; press assistant, James D. Proctor, 1957–58; assistant editor, 1959–60, and contributing editor, 1960–70, *Opera News*, New York; columnist ("Opera Boutique"), *Metropolitan Opera Program*, New York, for 10 years; columnist ("Things of Beauty"), *Lincoln Center Program*, New York, for 10 years; associate editor, *FM Guide*, New York, 1964–65; contributing editor, *Weight Watchers*, 1968–75, and *New Ingenue*, 1974–75, both New York. Agent: Phyllis Westberg, Harold Ober Associates, 40 East 49th Street, New York, New York 10017. Address: 227 East 57th Street, New York, New York 10022, U.S.A.

ROMANCE AND HISTORICAL PUBLICATIONS

Novels (series: Kitty Telefair)

Ophelia. New York, New American Library, 1968.
Feast of Eggshells. New York, New American Library, 1970.
The Curse of the Concullens. New York, World, 1970.
The Witching Hour (Telefair). New York, Award, 1971.
Where Satan Dwells (Telefair). New York, Award, 1971.
Bianca, with Patricia Hagan Murray. New York, New American Library, 1973.
Kilmeny in the Dark Wood. New York, New American Library, 1973.
Altar of Evil (Telefair). New York, Award, 1973.
The Mistress of Devil's Manor (Telefair). New York, Award, 1973.
The Sorcerer of the Castle (Telefair). New York, Award, 1974.
Dark Odyssey. New York, New American Library, 1974.
The Ides of November. New York, New American Library, 1975.
A Shadow on the House. New York, New American Library, 1975.
Witch's Crossing. New York, New American Library, 1975.
The Silent Watcher (Telefair). New York, Award, 1975.
A Darkness on the Stairs. New York, New American Library, 1976.
The House at Luxor. New York, New American Library, 1976.

Dark Encounter. New York, New American Library, 1977.
The Horror from the Tombs. New York, Award, 1977.
Julie. New York, New American Library, 1978.
The Golden Galatea. New York, Berkley, 1979.
The Moonlight Variations. New York, Berkley, 1981.
The Cactus Rose (as Zandra Colt). New York, Berkley, 1982.
Splendid Savage (as Zandra Colt). New York, Berkley, 1983.

Novels as Zabrina Faire

Lady Blue. New York, Warner, 1979.
The Midnight Match. New York, Warner, 1979.
The Romany Rebel. New York, Warner, 1979.
Enchanting Jenny. New York, Warner, 1979.
Wicked Cousin. New York, Warner, 1980.
Athena's Airs. New York, Warner, 1980.
Bold Pursuit. New York, Warner, 1980.
Pretender to Love. New York, Warner, 1981.
Pretty Kitty. New York, Warner, 1981.
Tiffany's True Love. New York, Warner, 1981.

Novels as Lucia Curzon

The Chadbourne Luck. New York, Berkley, 1981.
Adverse Alliance. New York, Berkley, 1981.
The Mourning Bride. New York, Berkley, 1982.
Queen of Hearts. New York, Berkley, 1982.
The Dashing Guardian. New York, Berkley, 1983.

Novels as Ellen Fitzgerald

A Novel Alliance. New York, New American Library, 1984.
Lord Caliban. New York, New American Library, 1985.
The Irish Heiress. New York, New American Library, 1985.

OTHER PUBLICATIONS

Other

The Story of Aida, Based on the Opera by Giuseppe Verdi (for children). New York, Putnam, 1965.
Call Me Counselor, with Sara Halbert. Philadelphia, Lippincott, 1977.

*   *   *

It is hard not to like an author who can inject as much humor in her books as can Florence Stevenson. Lucinda Ayers, a governess in *The Curse of the Concullens*, must be one of the most indomitable gothic heroines ever created. A mere slip of a girl, she encounters and copes with just about every occult manifestation possible. She befriends both the local banshee and the family vampire and deals calmly with the fact that her two young charges are werewolves. Even an encounter with the Devil himself does not shake her. Dimitri O'Hagan is an appropriately mysterious and brooding hero, given to clandestine activities. In fact he is an Irish patriot working against the hated British. The intrepid Lucy solves all the mysteries and manages to bring a degree of happiness to a remarkably unfortunate family, at the same time finding true love for herself.

Stevenson's selection of a pseudonym for most of her Regency novels, Zabrina Faire, again reflects a sense of humor and mischief. *Lady Blue*, one of Zabrina Faire's early novels, has a predictably happy ending after a somewhat rocky romance, but Stevenson develops the plot along some rather unusual lines.

Meriel, also a governess, is the victim of a malicious prank played by her young charge. He spills ink on her hair, turning it blue. Dismissed for slapping him, Meriel is hired by Lord Farr to impersonate a ghostly blue lady. Later she is kidnapped and forced to perform in a circus sideshow as a blue mermaid. Lord Farr, who luckily is a proficient magician, uses his skills to rescue her and foil the villains.

Unfortunately for those who appreciate such humor, Stevenson's later Regencies, both by Faire and a later pseudonym, Lucia Curzon, are standard formula novels. All the conventions are followed quite competently. The results are enjoyable to read but not readily distinguishable from most similar books. It is Stevenson's occasional humorous novel, gently spoofing the genre, which sets her apart, adding real sparkle to her work and keeping readers hoping for more.

—Barbara E. Kemp

STEWART, Mary (Florence Elinor, née Rainbow). British. Born in Sunderland, County Durham, 17 September 1916. Educated at Eden Hall, Penrith, Cumberland; Skellfield School, Ripon, Yorkshire; St. Hild's College, University of Durham, B.A. (honours) 1938, M.A. 1941. Served in the Royal Observer Corps during World War II. Married Sir Frederick Henry Stewart in 1945. Lecturer in English, Durham University, 1941–45. Recipient: Crime Writers Association Silver Dagger, 1961; Frederick Niven award, 1971; Scottish Arts Council award, 1975. Fellow, Royal Society of Arts, 1968; Fellow, Newnham College, Cambridge, 1986. Lives in Edinburgh. Address: c/o Hodder and Stoughton Ltd., Mill Road, Dunton Green, Sevenoaks, Kent TN13 2YA, England.

ROMANCE AND HISTORICAL PUBLICATIONS

Novels (series: Merlin Trilogy)

Madam, Will You Talk? London, Hodder and Stoughton, 1955; New York, Mill, 1956.
Wildfire at Midnight. London, Hodder and Stoughton, and New York, Appleton Century Crofts, 1956.
Thunder on the Right. London, Hodder and Stoughton, 1957; New York, Mill, 1958.
Nine Coaches Waiting. London, Hodder and Stoughton, 1958; New York, Mill, 1959.
My Brother Michael. London, Hodder and Stoughton, and New York, Mill, 1960.
The Ivy Tree. London, Hodder and Stoughton, 1961; New York, Mill, 1962.
The Moon Spinners. London, Hodder and Stoughton, 1962; New York, Mill, 1963.
This Rough Magic. London, Hodder and Stoughton, and New York, Mill, 1964.
Airs above the Ground. London, Hodder and Stoughton, and New York, Mill, 1965.
The Gabriel Hounds. London, Hodder and Stoughton, and New York, Mill, 1967.
The Wind Off the Small Isles. London, Hodder and Stoughton, 1968.
Merlin Trilogy. New York, Morrow, 1980.
    The Crystal Cave. London, Hodder and Stoughton, and New York, Morrow, 1970.

The Hollow Hills. London, Hodder and Stoughton, and New York, Morrow, 1973.
The Last Enchantment. London, Hodder and Stoughton, and New York, Morrow, 1979.
Touch Not the Cat. London, Hodder and Stoughton, and New York, Morrow, 1976.
The Wicked Day. London, Hodder and Stoughton, and New York, Morrow, 1983.
Thornyhold. London, Hodder and Stoughton, and New York, Morrow, 1988.

OTHER PUBLICATIONS

Plays

Radio Plays: *Lift from a Stranger, Call Me at Ten-Thirty, The Crime of Mr. Merry,* and *The Lord of Langdale,* 1957–58.

Other (for children)

The Little Broomstick. Leicester, Brockhampton Press, 1971; New York, Morrow, 1972.
Ludo and the Star Horse. Leicester, Brockhampton Press, 1974; New York, Morrow, 1975.
A Walk in Wolf Wood. London, Hodder and Stoughton, and New York, Morrow, 1980.

*

Manuscript Collection: National Library of Scotland, Edinburgh.

*   *   *

Although Mary Stewart's novels are usually categorized as contemporary or gothic romances because of their subject matter and plot lines, it may be unfair to label her a genre writer. From 1955 through 1967, Stewart wrote a highly popular set of novels of romantic suspense that, for convenience, were often reviewed as gothics. But, although her novels had similarities to those of Victoria Holt and Phyllis Whitney (her two most popular contemporaries), Stewart transcended their work and the formula romance of which these were the three most significant writers. After *The Gabriel Hounds* Stewart turned to historical romance, writing a trilogy (*The Crystal Cave, The Hollow Hills,* and *The Last Enchantment*) about Merlin and Arthur, a series that differed from her other books. In the mid-1970's she published *Touch Not the Cat,* a return to her earlier work but with a plot that depended upon telepathy, a new ingredient for her fiction. She has also written fantasies for children.

Of her romance writings, Stewart's most important work came during her earlier period, although the Merlin trilogy may be her most enduring literary contribution. From *Madam, Will You Talk?* to *The Gabriel Hounds,* her books were excellent and original romances that relied heavily upon her ability to evoke a place, to create complex characters, and to weave sophisticated and compelling stories.

Her two best contemporary romances are *Nine Coaches Waiting* and *My Brother Michael,* set respectively in France and Greece. *Nine Coaches Waiting* is her only "governess gothic," a novel about an orphaned heroine who is employed to teach the heir to a vast French estate. When she discovers the child's life is in danger, the heroine protects him and earns the love of the boy's older cousin, who has not been—despite appearances—a part of the conspiracy. Stewart's academic background in literature informs this novel as it does each of her others. The heroine consciously recalls her literary predecessors (especially Cinderella and Jane Eyre) as Stewart plays off the resonance of the literary history of romance against the modern heroine's sensibility and experience.

My Brother Michael employs a background of ancient and recent Greek history, myth, and legend with thematic elements from John Donne. The heroine joins the hero's search for the truth about the fate of his brother, who died during World War II near Delphi. In addition to learning what had happened, the characters also find a buried ancient Greek statue.

Wildfire at Midnight, set on the Isle of Skye, works against a background of ancient Celtic myth. *This Rough Magic*, on Corfu, finds its inspiration in Shakespeare's *The Tempest*. *The Gabriel Hounds* derives from the story of Lady Hester Stanhope. Other novels are set in the south of France, in Northumbria, and in Austria. In each, Stewart evokes the place in a rich and compelling manner.

The originality of her literary sensibility is most fully realized in the nature of her characters. Stewart's heroes and heroines are people of commitment, not just to each other as in many other romances but especially to others and to abstract concepts of truth and justice. Their values may seem archaic in the modern world, but Stewart portrays them so sensitively that they remain believable. Without preaching or moralizing, she places her characters in situations of extreme danger where it would be acceptable for them to walk away from someone else's trouble. They do not, and her delineation of their motivation and personal growth is always crucial to understanding their stories.

Although each of Stewart's contemporary romances contains a love story as an integral part of the plot, she does not allow the vicissitudes of the lovers to dominate. Her characters are selfless, sometimes (as the heroine of *Nine Coaches Waiting*) making decisions that require the apparent sacrifice of the love affair in the cause of justice. But despite their "stiff upper lip" morality, the heroines are attractive, lively, and admirable without being either stuffy or priggish. She portrays the success of the love relationship as a product of the heroine's maturity rather than as an end in itself.

In addition, Stewart is a fine stylist. Reviewers consistently praise the quality of her prose, especially her descriptions of food and place as well as the charm and good humor with which her heroines tell their tales. Without padding her stories with extraneous details, she describes her scenes vividly, offering not a travelogue but a concrete sense of what it must be like to experience an exotic place fraught with dramatic and emotional events. Stewart defies categorization because, although her books may resemble those of other writers, she remains, even in her weaker books, a writer of uncommon originality and grace. She may work within a formula, but her scene is the larger setting of romance through centuries of literature, making her novels both rewarding and inimitable.

—Kay Mussell

STIRLING, Jessica. British. Originally pseudonym for Peggie Coghlan and Hugh C. Rae; since 1984 for Hugh C. Rae alone. British. **COGHLAN, Peggie:** Born in Glasgow, Scotland, 26 January 1920. Educated at Notre Dame High School. Married Eugene O. Coghlan; two daughters. Address: 249 Morningside Street, Edinburgh, Scotland. **RAE, Hugh C(rauford):** Also writes as James Albany; Robert Crawford; R. B. Houston; Stuart Stern. Born in Glasgow, Scotland, 22 November

1935. Educated at Knightswood School, Glasgow. Served in the Royal Air Force, 1954–56. Married Elizabeth Dunn in 1960; one daughter. Assistant, John Smith and Son, antiquarian bookseller, Glasgow, 1952–65; then full-time writer. Lecturer in creative writing, University of Glasgow. Founding member, Association of Scottish Writers; president, Romantic Novelists Association, Scotland. Address: Drumore Farm Cottage, Balfron Station, Stirlingshire, Scotland.

ROMANCE AND HISTORICAL PUBLICATIONS

Novels (series: Beckman Trilogy; Patterson Trilogy; Stalker Trilogy)

The Spoiled Earth (Stalker). London, Hodder and Stoughton, 1974; as *Strathmore*, New York, Delacorte Press, 1975.
The Hiring Fair (Stalker). London, Hodder and Stoughton, 1976; as *Call Home the Heart*, New York, St. Martin's Press, 1977.
The Dresden Finch. New York, Delacorte Press, 1976; as *Beloved Sinner*, London, Pan, 1980.
The Dark Pasture (Stalker). London, Hodder and Stoughton, 1977; New York, St. Martin's Press, 1978.
The Deep Well at Noon (Beckman). London, Hodder and Stoughton, 1979; as *The Drums of Time*, New York, St. Martin's Press, 1980.
The Blue Evening Gone (Beckman). London, Hodder and Stoughton, and New York, St. Martin's Press, 1981.
The Gates of Midnight (Beckman). London, Hodder and Stoughton, and New York, St. Martin's Press, 1983.
Treasures on Earth (Patterson). London, Hodder and Stoughton, and New York, St. Martin's Press, 1985.
Creature Comforts (Patterson). London, Hodder and Stoughton, and New York, St. Martin's Press, 1986.
Hearts of Gold (Patterson). London, Hodder and Stoughton, and New York, St. Martin's Press, 1987.
The Good Provider. London, Hodder and Stoughton, 1988; New York, St. Martin's Press. 1989.
The Asking Price. London, Hodder and Stoughton, 1989.

OTHER PUBLICATIONS by Hugh C. Rae

Novels

Skinner. London, Blond, and New York, Viking Press, 1965.
Night Pillow. London, Blond, and New York, Viking Press, 1967.
A Few Small Bones. London, Blond, 1968; as *The House at Balnesmoor*, New York, Coward McCann, 1969.
The Interview. London, Blond, and New York, Coward McCann, 1969.
The Saturday Epic. London, Blond, and New York, Coward McCann, 1970.
The Marksman. London, Constable, and New York, Coward McCann, 1971.
The Shooting Gallery. London, Constable, and New York, Coward McCann, 1972.
Two for the Grave (as R. B. Houston). London, Hale, 1972.
The Rock Harvest. London, Constable, 1973.
The Rookery. London, Constable, 1974; New York, St. Martin's Press, 1975.
Harkfast: The Making of a King. London, Constable, and New York, St. Martin's Press, 1976.

The Minotaur Factor (as Stuart Stern). London, Futura, 1977; Chicago, Playboy Press, 1978.
The Poison Tree (as Stuart Stern). London, Futura, and Chicago, Playboy Press, 1978.
Sullivan. London, Constable, and Chicago, Playboy Press, 1978.
The Travelling Soul. New York, Avon, 1978.
The Haunting at Waverley Falls. London, Constable, 1980.
Privileged Strangers. London, Hodder and Stoughton, 1982.

Novels as Robert Crawford

The Shroud Society. London, Constable, and New York, Putnam, 1969.
Cockleburr. London, Constable, 1969; New York, Putnam, 1970; as *Pay as You Die*, New York, Berkley, 1971.
Kiss the Boss Goodbye. London, Constable, 1970; New York, Putnam, 1971.
The Badger's Daughter. London, Constable, 1971.
Whip Hand. London, Constable, 1972.

Novels as James Albany

Warrior Caste. London, Pan, 1982.
Mailed Fist. London, Pan, 1982.
Deacon's Dagger. London, Pan, 1982.
Close Combat. London, Pan, 1983.
Marching Fire. London, Pan, 1983.
Last Bastion. London, Pan, 1984.
Borneo Story. London, Pan, 1984.

Plays

The Freezer (broadcast 1972; produced Leicester, 1973).

Radio Play: *The Freezer*, 1972.

Television Plays: *The Dear Ones*, 1966; *Swallowtale*, 1969.

Other

Editor, with Philip Ziegler and James Allen Ford, *Scottish Short Stories 1977*. London, Collins, 1977.
Editor, *Scottish Short Stories 1978*. London, Collins, 1978.

*

Peggie Coghlan comments:
(1982) For many years my writing was slanted exclusively in the direction of the magazine field. It was my friend and mentor Hugh C. Rae who suggested that I change direction and write a novel. The help and guidance I received from Mr. Rae cannot be estimated, and it is no exaggeration to say that without him the books would not have been written.

Contemplating the first book, and being a member of a fairly large family, I suppose it was natural that I should decide to write a family story. For me, the work of a book is divided into two parts. First, the research, which I enjoy very much and tend to spin out far beyond what is required, and the actual writing which is hard and demanding work but is at the same time deeply satisfying when what appears on the printed page nearly approximated what, at the beginning, I planned in my head and felt in my heart.

A picture, it is said, is worth more than a thousand words, so equally, too, will not a thousand words evoke a memorable picture? That, to me, is what novel writing is all about.

Hugh C. Rae comments:
In 1984 my co-author, Peggie Coghlan, elected to retire from writing and generously suggested that I might care to tackle future Jessica Stirling novels on my own. Peggie Coghlan's contribution had always been considerable, but, with trepidation and not a few teething troubles, I assumed the female persona. To judge by Jessica's continued popularity I learned my lessons well from Mrs. Coghlan in the area of plotting and characterisation, and will always be grateful for her generosity.

*   *   *

The strong female protagonists of Jessica Stirling's novels are believable, attractive, and beleaguered by difficulties. They "carry on" and show their mettle while remaining stable and appealingly feminine. Careful character development and settings which powerfully complement and justify these characters are distinctive features of Stirling's fiction.

The search for dignity, independence, and love by Mirrin Stalker of the Stalker trilogy is played out against the background of a coal-mining village in 19th-century Scotland. The feudal system in which she and her family seem trapped begins to show some cracks, and Mirrin is among the first to realize that coalmaster Houston Lamont is as human and touchable as she, and therefore as vulnerable. Mirrin and her proud family get caught up in the changes taking place. The proprieties and bleakness of this narrow society are intricately presented with the powerful characters gaining advantages only to lose them again.

Holly Beckman, in the Beckman trilogy, must also contend with disadvantage while trying to find her place in the world. Her disreputable father and evil brother pose continuous threats to the position she works so hard to maintain. In the first novel Holly finds her niche in the antiques trade in London just after World War I. Her employer, a kindly mentor, provides her with a share of the business after his death, giving her the chance to make something of herself. The antiques business adds interest and validity to the novels and allows Holly to obtain respectability and eventual affluence. Her personal life is often in turmoil, however. In *The Blue Evening Gone* Holly's mid-thirties "crisis" is portrayed beautifully in counterpoint to the turmoil in Europe in the years prior to World War II. Holly's life circles around in *The Gates of Midnight* set during the London Blitz after she has been widowed and her son has joined the RAF. David Aspinall, Chris's real father, returns from the Orient and with sensitivity and style becomes a part of Holly's life again, this time on her terms.

The Patterson trilogy is set in 19th-century Scotland. It is the story of Elspeth Patterson from her start as a foundling pried from the arms of her dead mother to her rightful place as mistress of Balnesmoor and owner of a prosperous weaving empire. *Treasures on Earth* is largely the story of Gaddy Patterson, the drover's woman whose life is changed when she finds a baby who desperately needs her care. She scratches out a living in a community where she is not welcome. She prevails, marries a farmer, and has another daughter, Anna. In *Creature Comforts* and *Hearts of Gold*, Elspeth comes of age, and the melodrama continues as her sister steals her beau, and a flood ruins the homestead, all but killing Gaddy. These events lead Elspeth to the practical solution of marrying James Moodie, the older, ruthless, weaver. She had been troubled by their strange platonic relationship and sought comfort with a romantic young man she met on the moors, bearing his child. As a result, Moodie's terrible secret comes out: Moodie was Elspeth's father, wracked by guilt over his abandonment of her mother. Elspeth, in horror, runs away, taking her daughter with her, ending up with a coalminer's family. Elspeth prevails in spite of the horrors of this life. It takes tragedy in the mine to reveal the knowledge to her that Moodie has committed suicide in order for her to inherit his estate and regain her rightful home.

These trilogies are written with style and passion, and the characters tie in with one another in astounding yet believable ways, often reappearing to change the course of events. After being asked by a father where his lost son was now, Elspeth replies, "I don't know. I doubt if we—any of us—will hear of him again, though it's odd how things come round sometimes." Stirling is masterful at making "things come round" in her novels for her admirable women characters.

Stirling has also created intriguing male characters. One doesn't easily forget the brilliant and haughty Drew Stalker who, in *The Dark Pasture*, mellows only enough to seem human at last. Nor does one pass lightly over the men in Holly Beckman's life, from the caddish David Aspinall, her first lover, to highly sensitive Christopher Deems, the husband who perishes; as well as steadfast Kennedy King, her second husband and business partner, and attractive, but callow Peter Freeman, the American dancer who almost spoils it all. The Patterson trilogy has many interesting men who help or hinder Elspeth's desire to make a decent life for herself and her daughter. The evil but troubled James Moodie and the single-minded Jock Bennet, the coalman who never gives in, are powerful forces with whom she has to come to terms. Misguided Matt Sinclair weaves in and out of her life causing unexpected difficulties for Elspeth and her sister and the other fascinating families whose lives are linked in this rich tale.

All of Stirling's stories are well crafted, believably plotted, with intriguing characters seemingly constructed around the belief that Drew Stalker expressed in an off-guard moment, "You are, you can be, what you choose to be."

—Allayne C. Heyduk

STONE, Irving. American. Born Irving Tannenbaum in San Francisco, California, 14 July 1903; adopted in 1912. Educated at Lowell High School, San Francisco; Manual Arts High School, Los Angeles; University of California, Berkeley, A.B. 1923, graduate study, 1924–26; University of Southern California, Los Angeles, M.A. 1924. Married Jean Factor in 1934; one daughter and one son. Teaching Fellow in Economics, University of Southern California, 1923–24, and University of California, Berkeley, 1924–26. Visiting Lecturer in Creative Writing, University of Indiana, Bloomington, 1948, and University of Washington, Seattle, 1961; lecturer on the writing of biography and the biographical novel, University of Southern California, 1966; lecturer, California State Colleges, 1966, and New York University and Johns Hopkins University, Baltimore, 1985. From 1984 Regents Professor, University of California, Los Angeles. Art critic, Los Angeles *Mirror-News*, 1959–60. United States Department of State Cultural Exchange Specialist, in the Soviet Union, Poland, and Yugoslavia, 1962. President, California Writers Guild, 1960–61; founder, Academy of American Poets, 1962; founder, California State Colleges Committee for the Arts, 1967; trustee, Douglass House Foundation, Watts, Los Angeles, 1967–74; president, Dante Alighieri Society, Los Angeles, 1968–69. From 1955 founder and president, Fellows for

Schweitzer, Southern California; from 1963 vice president, Eugene V. Debs Foundation, Terre Haute, Indiana, and member, Advisory Board, University of California Institute for the Creative Arts; from 1969 president, Affiliates of the Department of English, University of California, Los Angeles. "Irving Stone Day" observed in Los Angeles, 1983. Recipient: Christopher award, 1957; Western Writers of America Spur award, 1957; McGovern award, 1988. D.L.: University of Southern California, 1965; D.Litt.: Coe College, Cedar Rapids, Iowa, 1967; California State Colleges, 1971; LL.D.: University of California, Berkeley, 1968; D.H.L.: Hebrew Union College, Cincinnati, 1978. Commendatore (Knight Commander), Republic of Italy, 1962; Grande Ufficiale (Italy), 1982; Commandant, Order of Arts and Letters (France), 1984. *Died 26 August 1989.*

ROMANCE AND HISTORICAL PUBLICATIONS

Novels

Lust for Life. New York, Longman, and London, Lane, 1934.
Sailor on Horseback. Boston, Houghton Mifflin, and London, Collins, 1939; as *Jack London, Sailor on Horseback*, New York, Doubleday, 1947.
Immortal Wife. New York, Doubleday, 1944; London, Falcon Press, 1950.
Adversary in the House. New York, Doubleday; 1947; London, Falcon Press, 1950.
The Passionate Journey. New York, Doubleday, 1949; London, Falcon Press, 1950.
The President's Lady. New York, Doubleday, 1951; London, Lane, 1952.
Love Is Eternal. New York, Doubleday, 1954; London, Collins, 1955.
The Agony and the Ecstasy. New York, Doubleday, and London, Collins, 1961.
Those Who Love. New York, Doubleday, 1965; London, Cassell, 1966.
The Passions of the Mind. New York, Doubleday, and London, Cassell, 1971.
The Greek Treasure. New York, Doubleday, and London, Cassell, 1975.
The Origin. New York, Doubleday, 1980; London, Cassell, 1981.
Depths of Glory. New York, Doubleday, and London, Bodley Head, 1985.

OTHER PUBLICATIONS

Novels

Pageant of Youth. New York, King, 1933.
False Witness. New York, Doubleday, 1940.

Plays

The Dark Mirror (produced New York, 1928).
The White Life: A Play Based on the Life of Baruch Spinoza (produced Jersey City, New Jersey, 1929). New York, League of Jewish Community Associations, 1932.
Truly Valiant (produced New York, 1936).

Screenplay: *The Magnificent Doll*, 1946.

Other

Clarence Darrow for the Defense. New York, Doubleday, 1941;
as *Darrow for the Defence*, London, Lane, 1950.
*They Also Ran: The Story of the Men Who Were Defeated for the
Presidency.* New York, Doubleday, 1943; revised edition,
1945.
The Evolution of an Idea. Privately printed, 1945.
Earl Warren. New York, Prentice Hall, 1948.
*Men to Match My Mountains: The Opening of the Far West
1840–1900.* New York, Doubleday, 1956; London, Cassell,
1967.
Three Views of the Novel, with John O'Hara and MacKinlay
Kantor. Washington, D.C., Library of Congress, 1957.
The Irving Stone Reader. New York, Doubleday, 1963.
The Story of Michelangelo's Pietà. New York, Doubleday,
1964.
The Great Adventure of Michelangelo (for children). New York,
Doubleday, 1965.
*There Was Light: Autobiography of a University, Berkeley 1868–
1968.* New York, Doubleday, 1970.
Mary Todd Lincoln: A Final Judgement? Springfield, Illinois,
Abraham Lincoln Association, 1973.

Editor, *Dear Theo: The Autobiography of Vincent van Gogh.*
Boston, Houghton Mifflin, and London, Constable, 1937.
Editor, with Richard Kennedy, *We Speak for Ourselves: Self Por-
trait of America.* New York, Doubleday, 1950.
Editor, with Allan Nevins, *Lincoln: A Contemporary Portrait.*
New York, Doubleday, 1962.
Editor, with Jean Stone, *I, Michelangelo, Sculptor: An Autobiog-
raphy Through Letters.* New York, Doubleday, 1962; Lon-
don, Collins, 1963.
Editor, *Irving Stone's Jack London.* New York, Doubleday,
1977.

*

Bibliography: *Irving Stone: A Bibliography* by Lewis F. Stieg,
Los Angeles, Friends of the Libraries of the University of Southern California, 1973.

Manuscript Collection: Special Collections, University of California Library, Los Angeles.

Irving Stone comments:
The biographical novel is a true and documented story of one
human being's journey across the face of the years, transmuted
from the raw material into the delight and purity of an authentic
art form. The research must be honest and far reaching, but the
result must stand as a compelling novel.

*   *   *

The historian in Irving Stone has cohabited with the artist
through a dozen or so novels now, and although the public sanctions the arrangement by purchasing and reading the offspring
books, the union is neither literarily nor historically holy. The
novels that come of it suffer congenital defects; for all their
broad appeal, there are problems with historical novels that are
inescapable. Stone is an astute novelist, insofar as he recognizes
a compelling story and can control the reader's attention for the
most part, and he is a willing historian who researches his ma-

terial copiously. But in the novels the historian tends to inhibit
the inventive imagination, embalming the dialogue and losing
the plot for long periods in thickets of detail, while the artist
always opens the history to a doubt that the most impressive bibliographical lists cannot still. This is, of course, true of all historical novelists, to an extent, but paradoxically, the generic
difficulty is more acute in the case of more serious ones, such as
Stone, than in the case of slighter ones, such as Frank G.
Slaughter, whose concern is entertainment and not authenticity,
and whose works may be consumed like popcorn.

The point may be illustrated by any of Stone's novels. *Love Is
Eternal*, for example, which treats the relationship between
Mary Todd and Abraham Lincoln to the time of Lincoln's assassination, demonstrates Stone's characteristic use of the most
minute details to evoke a sense of historical place. But while the
setting and circumstances in which the main characters play are
without doubt essentially correct, there remains the question of
whether or not the conception of the characters is accurate as
well. Stone is unconvincing in his attempt to restore the reputation of Mary Todd Lincoln, who has been excoriated by history.
He may be right in his judgment of her, or his vindication of her
may be simply an act of sentimental gallantry. There is no way
to be certain; if the novel is an unfounded interpretation of her,
Stone has misrepresented, and if there is historical evidence for
his view, she would have been far better served by a documented
history.

Stone is apparently aware, consciously or unconsciously, of
the dilemma created by writing fiction that purports to echo
fact, for, as in *The Passionate Journey* a fictional biography of
the American painter John Noble, he is usually better when his
characters act and react with each other according to the scenario provided by historical fact than when he seeks to interpret
motivation. Perhaps the use of detail to the point of tediousness
is an attempt to bring the problem that is imposed by the genre
under control—an attempt to overwhelm it. *Those Who Love*, for
instance, a treatment of the life and times of John and Abigail
Adams, is not only lumbered with wooden dialogue, but overburdened with historical minutiae. The Michelangelo study, *The
Agony and the Ecstasy*, as if to counter the effect of a great deal
of love interest that smacks of modern interpolation, contains
endless description of stone cutting and of anatomy, in a way
that is reminiscent of Melville's whaling chapters but is less easily justifiable.

But the biographical novel does exist, of course, and Stone is
undeniably one of its ablest practitioners. The history he spoon-
feeds is far more palatable and interesting than popcorn, and it is
no wonder that an enormous public should devour it.

—Alan R. Shucard

STORM, Virginia. See **CHARLES, Theresa.**

STORY, Josephine. See **LORING, Emilie.**

STRATTON, Rebecca. Also wrote as Lucy Gillen. British.
Served in the Women's Auxiliary Air Force and the Fire Service
during World War II. Worked at many jobs before becoming a

civil servant for the Coventry County Court, 1957–67; then a full-time writer. *Died 5 January 1982*.

ROMANCE AND HISTORICAL PUBLICATIONS

Novels

The Golden Madonna. London, Mills and Boon, 1973; Toronto, Harlequin, 1974.
The Bride of Romano. London, Mills and Boon, 1973; Toronto, Harlequin, 1974.
Castles in Spain. London, Mills and Boon, 1973; Toronto, Harlequin, 1974.
The Yellow Moon. London, Mills and Boon, 1974; Toronto, Harlequin, 1975.
Island of Darkness. London, Mills and Boon, 1974; Toronto, Harlequin, 1975.
Autumn Concerto. London, Mills and Boon, 1974; Toronto, Harlequin, 1975.
The Flight of the Hawk. London, Mills and Boon, 1974; Toronto, Harlequin, 1975.
Run from the Wind. London, Mills and Boon, and Toronto, Harlequin, 1974.
Fairwinds. London, Mills and Boon, and Toronto, Harlequin, 1974.
The Warm Wind of Farik. London, Mills and Boon, and Toronto, Harlequin, 1975.
Firebird. London, Mills and Boon, and Toronto, Harlequin, 1975.
The Fire and the Fury. London, Mills and Boon, 1975; Toronto, Harlequin, 1976.
The Goddess of Mavisu. London, Mills and Boon, 1975; Toronto, Harlequin, 1976.
Isle of the Golden Drum. London, Mills and Boon, 1975; Toronto, Harlequin, 1976.
Moon Tide. London, Mills and Boon, 1975; Toronto, Harlequin, 1976.
The White Dolphin. London, Mills and Boon, 1976.
Proud Stranger. London, Mills and Boon, and Toronto, Harlequin, 1976.
The Road to Gafsa. London, Mills and Boon, 1976; Toronto, Harlequin, 1977.
Gemini Child. London, Mills and Boon, 1976; Toronto, Harlequin, 1977.
Chateau d'Armor. London, Mills and Boon, and Toronto, Harlequin, 1976.
Dream of Winter. London, Mills and Boon, 1977; Toronto, Harlequin, 1978.
Girl in a White Hat. London, Mills and Boon, and Toronto, Harlequin, 1977.
More Than a Dream. London, Mills and Boon, and Toronto, Harlequin, 1977.
Spindrift. London, Mills and Boon, 1977; Toronto, Harlequin, 1978.
Inherit the Sun. London, Mills and Boon, 1977; Toronto, Harlequin, 1978.
The Sign of the Ram. London, Mills and Boon, 1977; Toronto, Harlequin, 1978.
The Velvet Glove. London, Mills and Boon, 1977; Toronto, Harlequin, 1978.
Lost Heritage. London, Mills and Boon, 1978.
Image of Love. London, Mills and Boon, and Toronto, Harlequin, 1978.
Bargain for Paradise. London, Mills and Boon, and Toronto, Harlequin, 1978.

The Corsican Bandit. London, Mills and Boon, and Toronto, Harlequin, 1978.
The Eagle of the Vincella. London, Mills and Boon, 1978.
Close to the Heart. London, Mills and Boon, and Toronto, Harlequin, 1979.
Lark in an Alien Sky. London, Mills and Boon, and Toronto, Harlequin, 1979.
The Tears of Venus. London, Mills and Boon, 1979; Toronto, Harlequin, 1980.
Trader's Cay. London, Mills and Boon, 1980.
The Leo Man. London, Mills and Boon, 1980.
The Inherited Bride. London, Mills and Boon, 1980.
Apollo's Daughter. London, Mills and Boon, 1980.
The Black Invader. London, Mills and Boon, 1981.
Dark Enigma. London, Mills and Boon, 1981.
The Silken Cage. London, Mills and Boon, 1981.
Charade. London, Mills and Boon, and Toronto, Harlequin, 1982.
The Golden Spaniard. London, Mills and Boon, and Toronto, Harlequin, 1982.
The Man from Nowhere. London, Mills and Boon, 1982; Toronto, Harlequin, 1983.

Novels as Lucy Gillen

The Ross Inheritance. London, Mills and Boon, 1969.
Good Morning, Doctor Houston. London, Mills and Boon, 1969; Toronto, Harlequin, 1970.
The Silver Fishes. London, Mills and Boon, 1969; Toronto, Harlequin, 1970.
A Wife for Andrew. London, Mills and Boon, 1969; Toronto, Harlequin, 1970.
Heir to Glen Ghyll. London, Mills and Boon, and Toronto, Harlequin, 1970.
Nurse Helen. London, Mills and Boon, 1970; Toronto, Harlequin, 1971.
Doctor Toby. London, Mills and Boon, 1970; Toronto, Harlequin, 1972.
The Girl at Smuggler's Rest. London, Mills and Boon, 1970; Toronto, Harlequin, 1971.
My Beautiful Heathen. London, Mills and Boon, 1970; Toronto, Harlequin, 1972.
The Whispering Sea. London, Mills and Boon, 1971.
Winter at Cray. London, Mills and Boon, 1971; Toronto, Harlequin, 1972.
Dance of Fire. London, Mills and Boon, 1971.
Marriage by Request. London, Mills and Boon, and Toronto, Harlequin, 1971.
Summer Season. London, Mills and Boon, 1971; Toronto, Harlequin, 1973.
The Enchanted Ring. London, Mills and Boon, 1971; Toronto, Harlequin, 1973.
Sweet Kate. London, Mills and Boon, 1971; Toronto, Harlequin, 1973.
That Man Next Door. London, Mills and Boon, 1971; Toronto, Harlequin, 1972.
A Time Remembered. London, Mills and Boon, 1971; Toronto, Harlequin, 1973.
The Pretty Witch. London, Mills and Boon, 1971; Toronto, Harlequin, 1974.
Dangerous Stranger. London, Mills and Boon, 1972; Toronto, Harlequin, 1973.
Glen of Sighs. London, Mills and Boon, 1972; Toronto, Harlequin, 1975.
Means to an End. London, Mills and Boon, 1972; Toronto, Harlequin, 1975.

The Changing Years. London, Mills and Boon, 1972; Toronto, Harlequin, 1975.

Painted Wings. London, Mills and Boon, 1972; Toronto, Harlequin, 1974.

The Pengelly Jade. London, Mills and Boon, 1972; Toronto, Harlequin, 1974.

The Runaway Bride. London, Mills and Boon, 1972; Toronto, Harlequin, 1974.

An Echo of Spring. London, Mills and Boon, 1973.

Moment of Truth. London, Mills and Boon, 1973.

A Touch of Honey. London, Mills and Boon, 1973; Toronto, Harlequin, 1975.

Gentle Tyrant. London, Mills and Boon, 1973; Toronto, Harlequin, 1975.

A Handful of Stars. London, Mills and Boon, 1973; Toronto, Harlequin, 1976.

The Stairway to Enchantment. London, Mills and Boon, 1973; Toronto, Harlequin, 1975.

Come, Walk with Me. London, Mills and Boon, 1974.

Web of Silver. London, Mills and Boon, 1974; Toronto, Harlequin, 1975.

All the Summer Long. London, Mills and Boon, 1975; Toronto, Harlequin, 1976.

Return to Deepwater. London, Mills and Boon, 1975; Toronto, Harlequin, 1976.

The Hungry Tide. London, Mills and Boon, 1975; Toronto, Harlequin, 1976.

The House of Kingdom. London, Mills and Boon, and Toronto, Harlequin, 1976.

Mark of Tregarron. London, Mills and Boon, 1976.

Master of Ben Ross. London, Mills and Boon, and Toronto, Harlequin, 1977.

Heron's Point. London, Mills and Boon, 1977; Toronto, Harlequin, 1978.

Back of Beyond. London, Mills and Boon, and Toronto, Harlequin, 1978.

Hepburn's Quay. London, Mills and Boon, 1979.

The Storm Eagle. London, Mills and Boon, 1980.

*   *   *

Rebecca Stratton was an unexpected mixture of late blooming talent, a checkered working career, and an unusual ability to write romances. In all, she produced more than 80 novels since 1969, with roughly half of them published under her pseudonym, Lucy Gillen. There is a progressive development evident in her work as she moves from sweet simplicity to the more sophisticated involvement that modern readers are looking for. In fact, two of her later novels appeared in the Harlequin Presents series. Because of this development, her readers sometimes find it difficult to decide which type of romance they prefer.

Writing as Lucy Gillen, her novels are more traditional with the plot kept fairly simple. Conflict actually depends on the heroine's gradual awakening love, but in a slow, puzzled way that finds her wondering what is happening even as the hero declares himself. That is the situation that Kim Anders is in in the novel *That Man Next Door*. Kim has come to stay with an aunt and uncle and hopes to get a job as a secretary to a writer that lives near them. She also meets James Fleming and the three small relatives whom he is temporarily caring for. Since he lives right next door, their continued meeting can't be avoided, much as she would like to, considering his dislike of and cruelty to the children. Because of his attitude, Kim finds herself becoming more and more involved with them and in spite of childish remarks soon learns that the children have exaggerated his attitude. Her job as secretary, the return of James's former girlfriend, and constant upsets with the children offer numerous chances for misunderstandings and reactions. Through the whole story, Kim's emotional reactions swing constantly from gradual liking to renewed dislike. Finally, when she hears that he is going to marry, she forces herself to accept the fact that she had mistaken her feelings and his seeming encouragement. "You *will* marry me, won't you?" forces her to revise her thoughts as the final misunderstanding is reconciled. Generally, the tone is light, although Kim is aware of unfamiliar emotional turmoil. The subplots and minor incidents offer humor and at times satisfaction as Kim feels that she has managed to score a point against James's rather autocratic disregard of the children.

Lost Heritage (Rebecca Stratton) offers a different kind of romance, for ultimate happiness seems very dim to Charlotte Kennedy as she encounters Raoul Menais. Suspense is much more heightened, character conflict more frequent and more damaging as Charlotte takes a job as a secretary/companion to Lizette Menais. Charlotte learns that she was adopted as a baby and was given a bracelet with the name "Menais" on it. With her adoptive parents dead, Charlotte sets out to learn about her real parents. As she travels to France to live with the family, she gradually learns the hidden secrets of the Menais family. Confrontation with Raoul Menais occurs as he becomes suspicious of her when she is slowly drawn into the family conflicts. Tension is high as 20-year-old events surface and Charlotte learns the truth about her family. Charlotte's constant need to remain in the background, yet her equally compelling need to protect her employer, Lizette, forces her to face repeated difficulties with Raoul and others in the family. The fact that she falls in love with Raoul is an added burden to her heart for she feels that nothing can ever come of it, especially if her birth is questionable. The end, of course, gives her her answers and her heart's desire.

Readers instantly react to the different styles that Stratton uses in her novels and certainly there are many readers who prefer her Lucy Gillen stories. However, since 1974 she gradually chose to write under her own name and in the more sophisticated style that is becoming more acceptable to modern readers. Perhaps young love and tender naivety are becoming less realistic, even unbelievable, in today's world. Certainly Stratton's novels tend to be more complex with hidden psychological situations and sharper character delineations.

—Arlene Moore

—————

STUART, Alex. See **STUART, Vivian.**

—————

STUART, Vivian. Pseudonym for Violet Vivian Mann, née Finlay; also wrote as Barbara Allen; Fiona Finlay; William Stuart Long; Alex Stuart; V. A. Stuart. British. Born in Rangoon, Burma, 2 January 1914. Educated at the University of London; Balogh Institute of Pathology, Hungary, pathology qualification, 1938; Technical Institute, Newcastle, New South Wales, Australia, diploma in industrial chemistry and laboratory technique 1942. Served in the British Army, non-combatant duty with Australian forces, 1942–43; Women's Auxiliary Service in Burma, Sumatra, Java, Singapore, and Malaya, 1944–45: Lieutenant Colonel. Married Cyril William Mann in 1958 (second marriage); five children. Co-founder and chairwoman, Romantic Novelists Association, 1960–63; chairwoman, Writers Summer School, London, 1964–67, 1969–71. *Died in August 1986.*

ROMANCE AND HISTORICAL PUBLICATIONS

Novels

Proud Heart. London, Jenkins, 1953.
Along Came Ann. London, Jenkins, 1953.
Eyes of the Night. London, Jenkins, 1954.
The Unlit Heart. London, Jenkins, 1954.
Pilgrim Heart. London, Jenkins, 1955.
Lover Betrayed. London, Jenkins, 1955.
No Single Star. London, Hale, 1956.
Moon over Madrid (as Fiona Finlay). London, Mills and Boon, 1957; Toronto, Harlequin, 1968.
Life Is the Destiny. London, Hale, 1958.
The Summer's Flower. London, Hale, 1961.
Like Victors and Lords. London, Hale, 1964; as *Victors and Lords* (as V. A. Stuart), New York, Pinnacle, 1972.
The Valiant Sailors. London, Hale, 1964; as V. A. Stuart, New York, Pinnacle, 1972.
Black Sea Frigate. London, Hale, 1971; as *Hazard's Command* (as V. A. Stuart), New York, Pinnacle, 1972.

Novels as Alex Stuart

The Captain's Table. London, Mills and Boon, 1953.
Ship's Nurse. London, Mills and Boon, 1954.
Soldier's Daughter. London, Mills and Boon, 1954.
Island for Sale. London, Mills and Boon, 1955.
Gay Cavalier. London, Mills and Boon, 1955.
Huntsman's Folly. London, Mills and Boon, 1956.
A Cruise for Cinderella. London, Mills and Boon, 1956.
Bachelor of Medicine. London, Mills and Boon, 1956.
The Last of the Logans. London, Mills and Boon, 1957.
Queen's Counsel. London, Mills and Boon, 1957.
Master of Guise. London, Mills and Boon, 1957.
Garrison Hospital. London, Mills and Boon, 1957.
Arcadia House. London, Mills and Boon, 1958.
Daughters of the Governor. London, Mills and Boon, 1958.
Master of Surgery. London, Mills and Boon, 1958.
Castle in the Mist. London, Mills and Boon, 1959.
The Peacock Pagoda. London, Mills and Boon, 1959.
Star of Oudh. London, Mills and Boon, 1960; as *On Her Majesty's Orders*, Mills and Boon, 1977.
Spencer's Hospital. London, Mills and Boon, 1961.
Sister Margarita. London, Mills and Boon, 1961.
Doctor Mary Courage. London, Mills and Boon, 1961.
Doctor on Horseback. London, Mills and Boon, 1962.
The Dedicated. London, Mills and Boon, 1962.
The Piper of Laide. London, Mills and Boon, 1963.
Maiden Voyage. London, Mills and Boon, 1964.
Samaritan's Hospital. London, Mills and Boon, 1965.
There But for Fortune. London, Mills and Boon, 1966.
Strangers When We Meet. London, Mills and Boon, 1968.
Random Island. London, Mills and Boon, 1968.
Young Doctor Mason. London, Mills and Boon, 1970.
Research Fellow. London, Mills and Boon, 1971.
The Bikers. London, New English Library, 1971.
A Sunset Touch. London, Mills and Boon, 1972.
The Last Trip. London, New English Library, 1972.

Novels as Barbara Allen

Serenade on a Spanish Guitar. London, Mills and Boon, 1956.
Doctor Lucy. London, Mills and Boon, 1956.
Someone Else's Heart. London, Mills and Boon, 1958.
The Gay Gordons. London, Mills and Boon, 1961.
The Scottish Soldier. London, Mills and Boon, 1965.

Novels as V. A. Stuart (series: Philip Hazard; Alexander Sheridan)

Brave Captains (Sheridan). New York, Pinnacle, 1972.
Hazard of Huntress. New York, Pinnacle, and London, Hale, 1973.
Hazard in Circassia. New York, Pinnacle, and London, Hale, 1973.
Massacre at Cawnpore (Hazard). New York, Pinnacle, 1973; London, Hale, 1974.
Victory at Sebastopol (Hazard). New York, Pinnacle, and London, Hale, 1973.
The Sepoy Mutiny (Sheridan). New York, Pinnacle, 1973; as *Mutiny in Meerat*, London, Hale, 1973; as *Mutiny at Dawn*, London, Tandem, 1975.
Cannons of Lucknow (Sheridan). New York, Pinnacle, 1974.
Hazard to the Rescue. New York, Pinnacle, 1974.
The Heroic Garrison (Sheridan). New York, Pinnacle, and London, Hale, 1975.
Guns to the Far East (Hazard). New York, Pinnacle, 1975; as *Shannon's Brigade*, London, Hale, 1976.
Battle for Lucknow (Sheridan). London, Hale, 1975.

Novels as William Stuart Long (series: The Australians in all books)

The Exiles. New York, Dell, 1979; Henley-on-Thames, Oxfordshire, Ellis, 1980.
The Settlers. New York, Dell, 1980; London, Futura, 1981.
The Traitors. New York, Dell, 1981; London, Futura, 1982.
The Explorers. New York, Dell, and Henley-on-Thames, Oxfordshire, Ellis, 1983.
The Adventurers. New York, Dell, and Henley-on-Thames, Oxfordshire, Ellis, 1983.
The Colonists. New York, Dell, and Henley-on-Thames, Oxfordshire, Ellis, 1984.
The Gold Seekers. New York, Dell, and Henley-on-Thames, Oxfordshire, Ellis, 1985.
The Gallant. New York, Dell, 1986; as *The Patriots*, Henley-on-Thames, Oxfordshire, Ellis, 1986.
The Empire Builders. Henley-on-Thames, Oxfordshire, Ellis, 1987.

OTHER PUBLICATIONS

Other

The Beloved Little Admiral: The Life and Times of Admiral of the Fleet, The Honourable Sir Henry Keppel 1809–1904. London, Hale, 1967; New York, Pinnacle, 1968.
His Majesty's Sloop-of-War Diamond Rock, with George T. Eggleston. London, Hale, 1978.

*   *   *

Vivian Stuart was a surprisingly creative writer. She was also one who saw opportunities to develop her craft. Instead of resting on past successes, she accepted a challenge so unique that few writers could dare face it and hope to achieve the worldwide recognition that she did. This opportunity was the chance to write a fictionalized historical account of the settlement of Australia.

Stuart began her writing career in the romance and gothic fields. Some of her earlier novels could be described as typical Mills and Boon or Harlequin romances. She wrote as Alex Stuart, Fiona Finlay, Barbara Allen, V. A. Stuart, and, finally, William Stuart Long. These early stories depended on sensitive characterization more than typical plot complications, although these played an important part in her novels as well. *Queen's Counsel* is representative of the early part of Stuart's writing career. Normal misunderstandings, overheard conversations, deathly illness, and critical operations all weave a suspenseful story of love and devotion. While slightly melodramatic, Stuart still managed to carry off such tales with believability and finesse.

In the 1960's and 1970's Stuart turned her attention to historical novels. During this time, she wrote two major series that explored the history of the British Empire on the seas and in India. In fact, it was many years before V. A. Stuart, the author of the Philip Hazard series, was revealed as a woman. Her expertise in naval history made her such an authority on the subject that novels dealing with this period were frequently referred to her, to be checked for historical accuracy.

Two of her novels of this period reflect her writing ability and hint at her future directions. *On Her Majesty's Orders* was originally published in 1960 as *Star of Oudh* (written by Alex Stuart). For this novel she received recognition from the Romantic Novelists Association for one of the best romances of that year. This novel traces the inevitable breakdown of British rule in India by the East India Company. Caught in the very early days just before the impending massacres are Emma Lindsay and Captain Hugh Richmond. Emma believes, as do most of the other British residents, that it is inconceivable for the Indian regiments to revolt, in spite of growing evidence to the contrary. Captain Richmond knows better, but he is hampered by the division of authority between military leaders and civilian commissioners. Both Emma and Captain Richmond face death and danger during the critical months of summer 1857 and only his courage and resourcefulness ensure that he and Emma are among the few who reach safety.

Stuart's research of the Indian Mutiny of the 1850's later reappeared in her Sheridan series. What also emerged was her keen knowledge of British military thought and character. In *On Her Majesty's Orders*, she uses the anticipated anniversary of the Siege of Jawan as a point of illustration. The British officers saw no contradiction in celebrating a major defeat of Indian forces by using Indian Sepoy regiments as part of that celebration. Stuart shows the appalling lack of sensitivity on the part of many of the British as well as their deliberate blindness to events occurring all around them during this period.

Guns to the Far East gives another viewpoint of the mutiny in 1857. In this novel, Commander Philip Hazard leaves China on sick leave after sustaining wounds during the capture of the Canton River. He sails on a ship bound for Calcutta with relief forces for the British garrisons in India. Philip's two sisters, Harriet and Lavinia, are in the midst of the mutiny. Lavinia, caught at Cawnpore, is lost during the massacre, while Harriet is able to find refuge at Lucknow until the relief forces free them. The Hazard novels trace the career of Philip Hazard from his early days at sea through each promotion as a naval officer. Newer and swifter steamships change the old navy of Nelson into a modern force, capable of vast destruction of enemy forces. At the same time, it could and did ensure numerous victories for the British forces. In all, Stuart wrote seven novels of the Hazard series in which she traced the British fleet in the Crimean War and five novels covering the Indian Mutiny with Alexander Sheridan as the hero. Her style of writing is swift-moving, concentrating on tightly developed action. Her characters avoid the "larger than life" image, instead, being humanly blessed with normal virtues and vices. Her work during these years earned her the reputation of being an outstandingly creative writer.

Stuart not only looked at individual events and people, but also at the broader view, illustrating quite graphically, at times, the consequences of past actions and beliefs. It is in this context that one must view her final series, *The Australians*. This series is composed of nine novels by Stuart (*The Empire Builders* was completed after her death), with subsequent volumes by other authors using her name; it traces the early days of Australia as a penal colony through to the mid-19th century. Each volume covers a significant group of people as they make their impact on the isolated settlements in New South Wales.

This is not a series one would normally sit down to enjoy, in the purest sense of the word. Some readers might be repulsed by the cruelty and insensitivity of those early settlers and jailers. Others will look for hope and optimism and find very little. Nor will readers be able to draw a parallel between the settlement of the American colonies and Australia. In reality, Australia proved to be a vastly different sort of colony. Settlement was kept under rigid control by the military and civilian authorities and remained that way for many years. Once a convict, always a convict was a firmly held belief. As a consequence social classes split between the Exclusives and the Emancipists. For a brief time the country faced a real threat of internal rebellion and unrest.

This series was a complete departure from Stuart's previous works. The conciseness of her earlier writing is lost as she writes with an eye for minute detail and effect. Characters appear in several novels and their earlier importance is lost as events are forgotten. Family relationships become confused as readers seek to relate events from one story to the next. In fact, if one does not start with the first volume and read onward, much remains somewhat confused and contradictory. Given the complex history of Australia's early years, and the nearly impossible task of condensing it into readable novels, Stuart's achievement is impressive. At this time it is too soon to judge whether or not these novels will be her most remembered works.

—Arlene Moore

STUBBS, Jean. British. Born in Denton, Lancashire, 23 October 1926. Educated at Manchester High School for Girls, 1938–44; Manchester School of Art, 1944–47. Married; one daughter and one son. Reviewer, *Books and Bookmen*, London, 1966–80. Recipient: Tom-Gallon Trust award, for short story, 1965. Agent: Macmillan London Ltd., 4 Little Essex Street, London WC2R 3LF. Address: Trewin, Nancegollan, near Helston, Cornwall TR13 0AJ, England.

ROMANCE AND HISTORICAL PUBLICATIONS

Novels (series: Howarth Chronicles; Inspector John Joseph Lintott)

The Rose-Grower. London, Macmillan, 1962; New York, St. Martin's Press, 1963.

The Travellers. London, Macmillan, and New York, St. Martin's Press, 1963.
Hanrahan's Colony. London, Macmillan, 1964.
The Straw Crown. London, Macmillan, 1966.
My Grand Enemy. London, Macmillan, 1967; New York, Stein and Day, 1968.
The Passing Star. London, Macmillan, 1970; as *Eleanora Duse*, New York, Stein and Day, 1970.
The Case of Kitty Ogilvie. London, Macmillan, 1970; New York, Walker, 1971.
An Unknown Welshman. London, Macmillan, and New York, Stein and Day, 1972.
Dear Laura (Lintott). London, Macmillan, and New York, Stein and Day, 1973.
The Painted Face: An Edwardian Mystery (Lintott). London, Macmillan, and New York, Stein and Day, 1974.
The Golden Crucible (Lintott). New York, Stein and Day, 1976; London, Macmillan, 1977.
A Timeless Place. London, Macmillan, 1978.
Kit's Hill (Howarth). London, Macmillan, 1978; as *By Our Beginnings*, New York, St. Martin's Press, 1979.
The Ironmaster (Howarth). London, Macmillan, 1981; as *An Imperfect Joy*, New York St. Martin's Press, 1981.
The Vivian Inheritance (Howarth). London, Macmillan, and New York, St. Martin's Press, 1982.
The Northern Correspondent (Howarth). London, Macmillan, and New York, St. Martin's Press, 1984.
A Long Way to Go. London, Macmillan, 1987.
A Lasting Spring. London, Macmillan, and New York, St. Martin's Press, 1987.
Like We Used to Be. London, Macmillan, 1989.

OTHER PUBLICATIONS

Play

Television Play: *Family Christmas*, 1965.

Other

100 Years Around the Lizard. Bodmin, Cornwall, Bossiney, 1985.
Great Houses of Cornwall. Bodmin, Cornwall, Bossiney, 1987.

*   *   *

The author of many novels, short stories, and a television play, Jean Stubbs is a writer whose works defy easy classification. She has described her crime novels as "why-done-its and not who-done-its"; yet this distinction fails to capture the unique qualities of meticulous historical detail and compelling characterization which the works embody. An intriguing paradox is that, while two of these novels are re-constructions of actual crimes (*My Grand Enemy*, *The Case of Kitty Ogilvie*), they are presented in a thoroughly imaginative way; conversely, the Inspector Lintott novels (*Dear Laura*, *The Painted Face*, *The Golden Crucible*), which are wholly fictional, give the impression of being part fact. These novels are mysteries in the most general sense, presenting a series of contrasts between fact and fantasy, reality and dream—between, in short, life and art.

Such dichotomies appear as recurring motifs in the other novels as well. In *The Rose-Grower*, for example, we are presented with the history of a man's life from his own point of view, from the point of view of other characters, and from an objective narrative viewpoint; these views ebb and flow, advance and recede

as the man himself grapples with a personification of death. The degree to which this "history" is a creation of the rose-grower as thwarted artist, or is merely the reconstruction of a sick man, is never absolutely clear. Hence, if the plot takes an occasionally fanciful turn, this seems appropriate to the dream logic of the narrative, with its blending of past and present.

Characterization is clearly more important to Stubbs than plot. On the other hand, her use of historical setting is never as a mere backdrop for the characters. Rather, characters are shown in the act of defining themselves, and this can only be accomplished in a social context. In *The Straw Crown* Stubbs presents a mythical island colony, steeped in archaic and exclusive tradition, faced with the necessity of disbanding because their island is to be used for nuclear tests. The confrontation between the old and the new values, occasionally comic and invariably touching, is embodied in the character of a female archaeologist who comes to study the tribe. Indubitably a woman of the present, she is also compellingly linked to the past. Her struggles to save the island, and to sort out her own relationships and values, are presented with sympathy. What might be regarded as fantastic plots become, in the author's intelligent hands, means of examining, through the eyes of her characters, our own assumptions about the nature of reality.

—Joanne Harack Hayne

STUYVESANT, Alice. See WILLIAMSON, C. N. and A. M.

STYRON, William. American. Born in Newport News, Virginia, 11 June 1925. Educated at Christchurch School, Virginia; Davidson College, North Carolina, 1942–43; Duke University, Durham, North Carolina, 1943–44, 1946–47, B.A. 1947 (Phi Beta Kappa). Served in the United States Marine Corps, 1944–45, 1951: 1st Lieutenant. Married Rose Burgunder in 1953; three daughters and one son. Associate editor, McGraw Hill, publishers, New York, 1947. Since 1952 advisory editor, *Paris Review*, Paris and New York; member of the editorial board, *American Scholar*, Washington, D.C., 1970–76. Since 1964 Fellow, Silliman College, Yale University, New Haven, Connecticut; Honorary Consultant in American Letters, Library of Congress, Washington, D.C. Recipient: American Academy Rome prize, 1952, and Howells Medal, 1970; Pulitzer prize, 1968; American Book award, 1980; Connecticut Arts award, 1984; Cino del Duca prize, 1985. Litt.D.: Duke University 1968. Member, American Academy, and American Academy of Arts and Sciences; Commander, Order of Arts and Letters (France). Address: R.F.D., Roxbury, Connecticut 06783, U.S.A.

ROMANCE AND HISTORICAL PUBLICATIONS

Novel

The Confessions of Nat Turner. New York, Random House, 1967; London, Cape, 1968.

OTHER PUBLICATIONS

Novels

Lie Down in Darkness. Indianapolis, Bobbs Merrill, 1951; London, Hamish Hamilton, 1952.
The Long March. New York, Random House, 1956; London, Hamish Hamilton, 1962.
Set This House on Fire. New York, Random House, 1960; London, Hamish Hamilton, 1961.
Sophie's Choice. New York, Random House, and London, Cape, 1979.

Short Story

Shadrach. Los Angeles, Sylvester and Orphanos, 1979.

Play

In the Clap Shack (produced New Haven, Connecticut, 1972). New York, Random House, 1973.

Other

The Four Seasons, illustrated by Harold Altman. University Park, Pennsylvania State University Press, 1965.
Admiral Robert Penn Warren and the Snows of Winter: A Tribute. Winston-Salem, North Carolina, Palaemon Press, 1978.
The Message of Auschwitz. Blacksburg, Virginia, Press de la Warr, 1979.
Against Fear. Winston-Salem, North Carolina, Palaemon Press, 1981.
As He Lay Dead, a Bitter Grief (on William Faulkner). New York, Albondocani Press, 1981.
This Quiet Dust and Other Writings. New York, Random House, 1982; London, Cape, 1983.
Conversations with William Styron (interviews), edited by James L. W. West III. Jackson, University Press of Mississippi, 1985.

Editor, *Best Short Stories from the Paris Review*. New York, Dutton, 1959.

*

Bibliography: *William Styron: A Descriptive Bibliography* by James L. W. West III, Boston, Hall, 1977; *William Styron: A Reference Guide* by Jackson R. Bryer and Mary B. Hatem, Boston, Hall, 1978; *William Styron: An Annotated Bibliography of Criticism* by Philip W. Leon, Westport, Connecticut, Greenwood Press, 1978.

Manuscript Collections: Library of Congress, Washington, D.C.; Duke University, Durham, North Carolina.

Critical Studies: *William Styron* by Robert H. Fossum, Grand Rapids, Michigan, Eerdmans, 1968; *William Styron* by Cooper R. Mackin, Austin, Texas, Steck Vaughn, 1969; *William Styron* by Richard Pearce, Minneapolis, University of Minnesota Press, 1971; *William Styron* by Marc L. Ratner, New York, Twayne, 1972; *William Styron* by Melvin J. Friedman, Bowling Green, Ohio, Popular Press, 1974; *The Achievement of William Styron* edited by Irving Malin and Robert K. Morris, Athens, University of Georgia Press, 1975, revised edition, 1981; *Critical Essays on William Styron* edited by Arthur D. Casciato and James L. W. West III, Boston, Hall, 1982; *The Root of All Evil: The Thematic Unity of William Styron's Fiction* by John K. Crane, Columbia, University of South Carolina Press, 1985.

*   *   *

"Less an 'historical novel' in conventional terms than a meditation on history." This is how William Styron described his only piece of historical fiction, *The Confessions of Nat Turner*. Whether or not this rather nebulous statement hints at contemporary parallels, the novel was immediately absorbed into the high-temperature political debate surrounding racial unrest in the late 1960's. It describes, through the first-person vantage of its protagonist, the inspiration, preparation, and execution of the only substantial black slave revolt in United States history.

In August 1831 a slave called Nat Turner, self-created preacher and prophet, led a bloody uprising in rural Virginia. Around 50 people were killed, and the hundred or so slaves he commanded came very close to overrunning the county seat, capturing weapons, and thus being in a position to inspire a wider insurrection. Those, at least, are the bare "historical facts" of the matter. Naturally, in the year of the novel's publication (the year of the Watts riots and widespread black unrest) it excited much comment from all sides. White reactionary opinion predictably branded the author a liberal, and left the label at that. More surprisingly, perhaps, black writers also condemned the book, saying that Styron had adjusted the historical facts to suit his own purpose. They pointed out that his main historical source, a pamphlet that claimed to be a verbatim confession by Nat Turner, was a discredited piece of slave-owning propaganda aimed at the suspiciously abolitionist north by the southern oligarchy. The fact that the earlier source served as the inspiration to a wealth of southern racist fantasies (among them Poe's *Arthur Gordon Pym*) merely added to their alarm. Vilified by both extremes, Styron's novel was nonetheless awarded the respectability of a Pulitzer prize that same year.

In many respects the political objections are grounded on an almost wilful neglect of the book's ironic complexity. Styron's black slaves are presented as Uncle Tom caricatures; but the point is made that only as such caricatures could slaves survive the bizarre society of the pre-Civil War south. More seriously, it has been alleged, the rebel group contains sociopathic monsters who delight in the atrocities they commit. If this is so, it reflects the thoughts of Frederick Douglass, who as an ex-slave saw that the inherent cruelty of the system produced nothing but brutality from master downwards: "Everybody, in the South, wants the privilege of whipping everybody else." It is this closed, claustrophobic world of reciprocal injustice that Styron's blood-frenzied slaves represent.

The only "liberal" in the novel is Nat's first master, and namesake, Samuel Turner. Like Jefferson, this man aspires to a vague scheme of ultimate liberation for the slaves; but it is his inability to accept the continuing, current obscenity of slavery that causes him to lose all his slaves to shrewder and more realistic men. Naturally, the sold slaves all are destined for the *ne plus ultra* of slave society, the nightmarish territory of the deep south. Revealed to be weak and ineffectual, his slaves all sold down the river, it is Samuel Turner's failure that inspires in Nat the rage he needs to plan and execute comprehensive revenge on the white race. Again, Douglass's words on the matter seem prescient: "Give a slave a *bad* master, and he aspires to a *good* master; give him a good master and he wishes to be his *own* master." Nat achieves mastery not only over himself, but over a gathering conspiracy to which only his fervour can give direction.

It is in the character of Nat himself that Styron's narrative powers are revealed. Despite the fact that the whole narrative is related in the first person, the reader is still left in some doubt as to the protagonist's underlying sanity. The prophetic visions which visit him are credible both as the products of famine and of fevered imagination, or as extensions of the surreal society; in this light it is all too easy to believe he has indeed received divine sanction for his programme of righteous revenge. One scene could serve as a model for this. Immediately following Nat's central vision or hallucination (in which he sees black and white angels fighting in the sky) he encounters, in the company of his master, a starving "free" black man. The starving man reacts not with the usual deference, but with a string of obscene abuse; in response, the white man is rendered impotent. The horror of this scene is exact and everyday, and rendered more powerful than the apocalyptic visions of Nat Turner.

If *The Confessions of Nat Turner* disappointed both white and black extremes, it is perhaps because it suggests no programmatic response to the undeniable ugliness of the racial injustice it portrays in the past and reflects in the present. It is an uneasy book, filled with unpleasantly hard facts; but the apocalypse it portrays attains somehow, almost despite the reader's revulsion, an undeniably tragic scale.

—Alan Murphy

SUMMERS, Essie (Ethel Snelson Summers). New Zealander. Born in Christchurch, 24 July 1912. Educated at North Linwood Primary School; Christchurch Technical College. Married William N. Flett in 1940 (died 1984); one son and one daughter. Prior to World War II, worked for Londontown Drapers, Christchurch, 7 years, at Millers Ltd., 4 years, and as a costing clerk. Columnist ("Parish Meditations," as Tamsin), Timaru *Herald*, 6 years; freelance journalist. Address: 32-A Tom Parker Avenue, Napier, New Zealand.

ROMANCE AND HISTORICAL PUBLICATIONS

Novels

New Zealand Inheritance. London, Mills and Boon, 1957; as *Heatherleigh*, Toronto, Harlequin, 1963.
The Time and the Place. London, Mills and Boon, 1958; Toronto, Harlequin, 1964.
Bachelors Galore. London, Mills and Boon, 1958; Toronto, Harlequin, 1965.
The Lark in the Meadow. London, Mills and Boon, 1959; as *Nurse Abroad*, Toronto, Harlequin, 1961.
The Master of Tawhai. London, Mills and Boon, 1959; Toronto, Harlequin, 1965.
Moon over the Alps. London, Mills and Boon, 1960; Toronto, Harlequin, 1964.
Come Blossom-Time, My Love. London, Mills and Boon, 1961; Toronto, Harlequin, 1963.
No Roses in June. London, Mills and Boon, 1961; Toronto, Harlequin, 1962.
The House of the Shining Tide. London, Mills and Boon, 1962; Toronto, Harlequin, 1963.
South to Forget. London, Mills and Boon, 1963; as *Nurse Mary's Engagement*, Toronto, Harlequin, 1964.
Where No Roads Go. London, Mills and Boon, and Toronto, Harlequin, 1963.

Bride in Flight. London, Mills and Boon, 1964; Toronto, Harlequin, 1965.
The Smoke and the Fire. London, Mills and Boon, and Toronto, Harlequin, 1964.
No Legacy for Lindsay. London, Mills and Boon, and Toronto, Harlequin, 1965.
No Orchids by Request. London, Mills and Boon, 1965; Toronto, Harlequin, 1966.
Sweet Are the Ways. London, Mills and Boon, 1965; Toronto, Harlequin, 1966.
Heir to Windrush Hill. London, Mills and Boon, and Toronto, Harlequin, 1966.
His Serene Miss Smith. London, Mills and Boon, 1966; Toronto, Harlequin, 1967.
Postscript to Yesterday. London, Mills and Boon, 1966; Toronto, Harlequin, 1967.
A Place Called Paradise. London, Mills and Boon, and Toronto, Harlequin, 1967.
Rosalind Comes Home. London, Mills and Boon, 1968; Toronto, Harlequin, 1969.
Meet on My Ground. London, Mills and Boon, 1968; Toronto, Harlequin, 1969.
The Kindled Fire. London, Mills and Boon, 1969; Toronto, Harlequin, 1970.
Revolt—and Virginia. London, Mills and Boon, and Toronto, Harlequin, 1969.
The Bay of the Nightingales. London, Mills and Boon, and Toronto, Harlequin, 1970.
Summer in December. London, Mills and Boon, and Toronto, Harlequin, 1970.
Return to Dragonshill. London, Mills and Boon, and Toronto, Harlequin, 1971.
The House on Gregor's Brae. London, Mills and Boon, and Toronto, Harlequin, 1971.
South Island Stowaway. London, Mills and Boon, 1971; Toronto, Harlequin, 1972.
The Forbidden Valley. London, Mills and Boon, and Toronto, Harlequin, 1973.
A Touch of Magic. London, Mills and Boon, and Toronto, Harlequin, 1973.
Through All the Years. London, Mills and Boon, 1974; Toronto, Harlequin, 1975.
The Gold of Noon. London, Mills and Boon, 1974; Toronto, Harlequin, 1975.
Anne of Strathallan. London, Mills and Boon, and Toronto, Harlequin, 1975.
Beyond the Foothills. London, Mills and Boon, and Toronto, Harlequin, 1976.
Not by Appointment. London, Mills and Boon, and Toronto, Harlequin, 1976.
Adair of Starlight Peaks. London, Mills and Boon, 1977; Toronto, Harlequin, 1978.
Goblin Hill. London, Mills and Boon, and Toronto, Harlequin, 1977.
The Lake of the Kingfisher. London, Mills and Boon, 1978; Toronto, Harlequin, 1979.
Spring in September. London, Mills and Boon, and Toronto, Harlequin, 1978.
My Lady of the Fuchsias. London, Mills and Boon, and Toronto, Harlequin, 1979.
One More River to Cross. London, Mills and Boon, 1979; Toronto, Harlequin, 1980.
The Tender Leaves. London, Mills and Boon, and Toronto, Harlequin, 1980.
Autumn in April. London, Mills and Boon, 1981; Toronto, Harlequin, 1986.

Daughter of the Misty Gorges. London, Mills and Boon, 1981; Toronto, Harlequin, 1983.
A Lamp for Jonathan. London, Mills and Boon, 1982; Toronto, Harlequin, 1984.
A Mountain for Luenda. London, Mills and Boon, and Toronto, Harlequin, 1983.
Season of Forgetfulness. London, Mills and Boon, 1983; Toronto, Harlequin, 1984.
MacBride of Tordarroch. London, Mills and Boon, 1984.
Winter in July. London, Mills and Boon, 1984; Toronto, Harlequin, 1985.
To Bring You Joy. London, Mills and Boon, 1985; Toronto, Harlequin, 1986.
High Country Governess. London, Mills and Boon, 1987; Toronto, Harlequin, 1988.

OTHER PUBLICATIONS

Other

The Essie Summers Story. London, Mills and Boon, 1974.

*   *   *

Essie Summers, a New Zealand writer with a strong English background, grew up with traditions that honor the poet and storyteller. Perhaps this background accounts for her unique qualities as a writer of romance fiction. One does not sit down to read a novel by her with the intent of passing a brief hour or so. Her books have to be approached with plenty of time on one's hands and they have to be saved for that special time when one needs a real sense of recreation. For that is what Summers does: she recreates whole families, generations even, that fill her novels with deep vibrant love, both for each other and for their country, New Zealand.

Pace in her novels lends a slow unfolding of the story and characters so that one is able to grasp the subtle elements of conflict and tension between the main characters of the story. While most of her novels show initial antagonism between the lead characters, Summers will occasionally have a situation where another character deliberately causes trouble for those in love. For the most part, however, Summers depends on her characters to move the story along and to show the developing plot to her readers.

Usually her novels take place in remote farming areas of the country, and this in itself gives an added dimension to her works, for action, motivation, and resolution take place against an almost panoramic background of harsh, rugged country and hard-working people. It is impossible not to gain an understanding of the earlier settlers of the country and those who still hold the land as she incorporates these struggles in her stories.

For instance, in *Return to Dragonshill*, the heroine, Henrietta, agrees to return to the high-country sheep ranch to act as governess to the children there. She also meets the man she had loved (and she thought lost) several years ago for he has returned as well. His reason for returning is to build a bridge over an impassable river, an undertaking that is going to open that part of the country up to all-weather travel for the first time. Within her cast of characters, Summers takes special pains to create the character of Madame. She is 100 years old; she and her husband were the very first settlers in that part of the country. Reminiscences of early tragedies, of stark, primitive living conditions, are woven into the narrative in such a way that one feels and sees the hardships of these early settlers.

Touches of homey, sentimental events instill a mood of serenity as Madame brings out scrap books of those early days containing touches of poetry, mention of short stories and essays, as well as newspaper clippings that tell of those early years. There is a sense of timelessness and security that touches the lives of the characters in the stories, but also the lives of her readers, for much of the faith and belief that shines through these little scraps reach out to them as well.

Over and over again Summers draws vivid pictures of their way of life. Her ability to recreate the mood and life of her country and to people it with strong, sensitive characters shows remarkable creativity. The slow unfolding of her stories draws her readers toward the characters and makes them want to know that they do find a much deserved happiness. In a way, her readers feel that they have sat down with a long cozy letter from home that tells the joys and sorrows of well-loved friends and relatives. Of all modern romance writers, Summers has taken this unique way of telling her stories and has made it her own.

—Arlene Moore

———————

SUMMERS, Rowena. See **SAUNDERS, Jean.**

———————

SUMMERTON, Margaret. Also wrote as Jan Roffman. British. Born in Birmingham, Warwickshire. Educated at a convent school and schools in Derbyshire and London. Worked for a publishing house in Paris; reporter, London *Daily Mail* in the Netherlands and Germany during and immediately after World War II; after the war worked on several magazines in London. *Died.*

ROMANCE AND HISTORICAL PUBLICATIONS

Novels

The Sunset Hour. London, Hodder and Stoughton, 1957.
The Red Pavilion. London, Hodder and Stoughton, 1958.
A Small Wilderness. London, Hodder and Stoughton, 1959.
The Sea House. London, Hodder and Stoughton, and New York, Holt Rinehart, 1961.
Theft in Kind. London, Hodder and Stoughton, 1962.
Nightingale at Noon. London, Hodder and Stoughton, and New York, Dutton, 1963.
Quin's Hide. London, Hodder and Stoughton, 1964; New York, Dutton, 1965.
Ring of Mischief. London, Hodder and Stoughton, and New York, Dutton, 1965.
A Memory of Darkness. London, Hodder and Stoughton, and New York, Dutton, 1967.
The Sand Rose. London, Collins, and New York, Doubleday, 1969.
Sweetcrab. London, Collins, and New York, Doubleday, 1971.
The Ghost Flowers. London, Collins, and New York, Doubleday, 1973.
The Saffron Summer. London, Collins, 1974; New York, Doubleday, 1975.
A Dark and Secret Place. London, Collins, and New York, Doubleday, 1977.

Novels as Jan Roffman

With Murder in Mind. New York, Doubleday, 1963.
Likely to Die. London, Bles, 1964.
Winter of the Fox. London, Bles, 1964; as *Death of a Fox*, New York, Doubleday, 1964; as *Reflection of Evil*, New York, Ace, 1967.
A Penny for the Guy. London, Bles, and New York, Doubleday, 1965; as *Mask of Words*, New York, Ace, 1973.
The Hanging Woman. London, Bles, 1965.
Ashes in an Urn. New York, Doubleday, 1966.
A Daze of Fears. New York, Doubleday, 1968.
Grave of Green Water. London, Long, and New York, Doubleday, 1968.
Seeds of Suspicion. London, Long, 1968.
A Walk in the Dark. London, Long, 1969; New York, Doubleday, 1970.
A Bad Conscience. New York, Doubleday, 1972.
A Dying in the Night. New York, Doubleday, 1974; London, Macdonald and Jane's, 1975.
Why Someone Had to Die. London, Macdonald and Jane's, and New York, Doubleday, 1976.
One Wreath with Love. New York, Doubleday, 1978; London, Hale, 1979.

*   *   *

Conflicts of interest, clashes of loyalties, the quest for a loving family . . . these are the characteristics of Margaret Summerton's novels of romantic suspense. While the settings may vary from well-described remote estates in England to exotic locales abroad (*The Sand Rose* in Tunisia, *The Ghost Flowers* in Cyprus, for instance) the novels typically focus on a competent woman with career interests who is in love with a man who seems to be unavailable, or who is surprised by love when she least expects it. Sometimes nursing memories of a dead or lost lover, she may be wooed by another man as well as the romantic hero. While the heroine wins her true love in the end, what usually escapes her is the comfort of a secure family.

Typically, Lucy in *Quin's Hide* suspects her half-brother, her employer, and Hamer, the man she has always loved, of being involved in a sinister scheme that starts with theft and fraud and develops into murder. Although Hamer is cleared and finally declares his long-hidden love for Lucy, she loses forever the love of her foster mother and half-sister when the brother is killed escaping from the police. The sudden malice of a supposedly kind-hearted woman toward a girl who had lived with her since childhood is apparently all that can be expected in this hard life. The feeling, so pervasive in this novel, that one cannot know where to place one's trust, that one is ultimately alone in an unsafe world, is typical of Summerton's books.

In *The Sand Rose* Rachel's sister-in-law, a beautiful but arid woman who is the sole focus of her husband's devotion, attempts to locate her brother, politically at odds with the Tunisian government. Her actions thrust Rachel and the filmmaker she comes to love into a swirl of intrigue in a colorful background; but the pivotal moment comes when Rachel's brother reveals that she is completely unimportant to him in balance with his wife's happiness.

Even Elizabeth in *A Dark and Secret Place*, lucky in having a loving mother of her own, realizes that her father had cared more for her adoptive sister Olivia. It is Elizabeth who must rescue the rich Olivia from her evil husband and his sinister cohorts in Italy, with the help of Olivia's first love, who becomes Elizabeth's wooer. Just as Elizabeth becomes aware of the true affection she feels for Olivia, buried as it has been under years of resentment and jealousy, she must estrange her by taking away from her the love Olivia perceives as hers.

As stories told from a woman's point of view, Summerton's novels tend to concentrate on intangibles of mood and character. The heroes combine conventional romantic features—good looks, interesting jobs, kind natures—and are differentiated more by the interests of the different heroines than by anything intrinsic to themselves. The hero of *The Ghost Flowers* is as well realized as most, although he is physically absent for much of the book.

A stronger portrayal of a male character is found in *Why Someone Had to Die*, more strictly speaking a crime novel. It is also distinguished for the portrait of Georgina Latham, a good woman—wife and mother—but as committed as any other Summerton heroine to a relationship with a man she cannot trust even after many years of marriage. Georgina, trying to respond to the need she senses in her young lodger, risks her own life when the young woman mysteriously disappears. But her other motive, which she tries to hide even from herself, is the fear that her hot-tempered, unfaithful husband has done something to the mysterious "Helen Jones." Georgina is willing to make any sacrifice to conceal from her husband her fears for, and about, him.

Despite a strong initial situation and the usual effective depiction of place and atmosphere, *Sweetcrab* is not as well plotted as Summerton's other novels. Christina returns to the village where her aunt raised her and encounters again the family of her fiancé Cary who had fled after killing his father. In *Sweetcrab*, as in *The Saffron Summer*, there is no villainous criminal genius, just a number of people caught by events circumstances, and making decisions that turn out badly. When Claudine comes as an orphan to her grandmother's estate in *The Saffron Summer*, she is looking for memories of her long-dead father; she is horrified to find her relatives, including her bastard half-brother, convinced that she is after a share of the old woman's fortune. Also in a false position is Maggie in *Ring of Mischief*, whose imperious godmother hinted to her victims that Maggie is helping her in her blackmail plot.

When Summerton does include a villain, his evil tends to be so excessive that one wonders why the other characters do not recognize it sooner. Heller, the smuggler, and Kim, his weak accomplice, fool Maria in her quest for her vanished employer in *The Ghost Flowers* for longer than is quite credible. The television star who attacks Maggie in *Ring of Mischief* has fooled all those who know him, but he reveals his evil to her as soon as they meet.

Along with the fear of betrayal and the impossibility of happy families, Summerton's books are recognizable by their evocative atmosphere, combining weather, place, and a pervasive sense of encroachment from hard-to-understand human emotions.

—Susan Branch

———————

SWAN, Annie S. Also wrote as David Lyall. British. Born in Mountskip, Gorebridge, Scotland. Educated at the Queen Street Ladies' College, Edinburgh; and privately. Married James Burnett Smith in 1883 (died 1927); one daughter and one son. Writer and journalist from the 1870's; editor, *Woman at Home* magazine, London, 1893–1917, the *Annie S. Swan Penny Stories*, later *Penny Weekly*, 1898–99, and the *Annie S. Swan Annual* from 1924. *Died 17 June 1943.*

ROMANCE AND HISTORICAL PUBLICATIONS

Novels (series: Elizabeth Glen)

Ups and Downs: A Family Chronicle. London, Charing Cross, 1878.
Shadowed Lives. Glasgow, Marr, 1880.
Bess: The Story of a Waif. Glasgow, Marr, 1880.
Grandmother's Child. London, Partridge, 1882; as *Grannie's Little Girl*, 1925.
Inside the Haven. London, Blackie, 1882.
Aldersyde: A Border Tale of Seventy Years Ago. Edinburgh, Oliphant, and New York, Carter, 1883.
The Better Part. London, Partridge, 1884.
Carlowrie; or, Among Lothian Folks. Edinburgh, Oliphant, 1884; Cincinnati, Jennings and Pye, n.d.
Dorothea Kirke; or, Free to Serve. Edinburgh, Oliphant, and Cincinnati, Cranston and Stowe, 1884.
Mark Desborough's Vow. London, Partridge, 1884.
Ursula Vivian, The Sister-Mother. Edinburgh, Oliphant, 1884; Cincinnati, Cranston and Stowe, 1890.
Warner's Chase; or, The Gentle Heart. London, Blackie, 1884.
Adam Hepburn's Vow: A Tale of Kirk and Covenant. London, Cassell, 1885; New York, Cassell, 1888.
A Divided House: A Study from Life. Edinburgh, Oliphant, 1885.
Thankful Rest. London, Nelson, 1885.
Freedom's Sword: A Tale of the Days of Wallace and Bruce. London, Cassell, 1886.
The Gates of Eden: A Story of Endeavour. Edinburgh, Oliphant, 1886; Cincinnati, Cranston and Stowe, 1890.
Robert Martin's Lesson. Edinburgh, Oliphant, 1886; Cincinnati, Cranston and Stowe, 1890.
Sundered Hearts. Edinburgh, Oliphant, 1886.
Thomas Dryburgh's Dream: A Story of the Sick Children's Hospital. Edinburgh, Oliphant, 1886.
Briar and Palm: A Study of Circumstance and Influence. Edinburgh, Oliphant, 1887; Cincinnati, Cranston and Stowe, 1890.
Jack's Year of Trial. London, Nelson, 1887.
The Strait Gate. London, Partridge, 1887.
Doris Cheyne: The Study of a Noble Life. Edinburgh, Oliphant, 1888; Cincinnati, Cranston and Stowe, 1890.
Hazell & Sons, Brewers. Edinburgh, Oliphant, 1888; Cincinnati, Cranston and Stowe, 1891.
The Secret Panel. Edinburgh, Oliphant, 1888.
St. Veda's; or, The Pearl of Orr's Haven. Edinburgh, Oliphant, 1889; Cincinnati, Cranston and Stowe, n.d.
Sheila. Edinburgh, Anderson and Ferrier, 1890; Cincinnati, Cranston and Stowe, 1891.
Across Her Path. Cincinnati, Cranston and Stowe, 1890; London, Leng, 1925.
Maitland of Laurieston: A Family History. Edinburgh, Oliphant, 1890; Cincinnati, Jennings and Pye, n.d.
A Vexed Inheritance. Edinburgh, Oliphant, 1890; Cincinnati, Cranston and Stowe, 1893.
The Ayres of Studleigh. Edinburgh, Oliphant, and New York, Hunt and Eaton, 1891.
Who Shall Serve? A Story for the Times. Edinburgh, Oliphant, 1891.
The Guinea Stamp: A Story of Modern Glasgow. Edinburgh, Oliphant, and Cincinnati, Cranston and Stowe, 1892.
A Bitter Debt: A Tale of the Black Country. London, Hutchinson, 1893.
Homespun: A Study of Simple Folk. London, Hutchinson, 1893; New York, Dutton, n.d.

The Answer to a Christmas Prayer. New York, Collier, 1894.
A Foolish Marriage: An Edinburgh Story of Student Life. London, Hutchinson, 1894.
A Lost Ideal. Edinburgh, Oliphant, 1894.
A Victory Won. London, Hutchinson, 1895.
Fettered Yet Free: A Study in Heredity. New York, Dodd Mead, 1895.
Elizabeth Glen, M.B.: The Experience of a Lady Doctor. London, Hutchinson, 1895.
Kinsfolk. London, Hutchinson, 1896.
A Stormy Voyager. London, Hutchinson, 1896.
The Curse of Cowden. London, Hutchinson, 1897.
Mrs. Keith Hamilton, M.B.: More Experiences of Elizabeth Glen. London, Hutchinson, 1897.
The Ne'er-Do-Weel. London, Hutchinson, 1897.
Conscience Money (as David Lyall). London, Hodder and Stoughton, 1898.
Greater Love (as David Lyall). London, Hodder and Stoughton, 1898.
Not Yet: A Page from a Noble Life. London, Hutchinson, 1898.
Wyndham's Daughter: A Story of To-day. London, Hutchinson, 1898.
A Son of Erin. London, Hutchinson, 1899.
Twice Tried. Cincinnati, Cranston and Stowe, n.d.; London, Leng, 1928.
An American Wife. London, Hutchinson, 1900; as *An American Woman*, New York, Dutton, n.d.
The Burden-Bearers. London, Hutchinson, 1900.
Love Grown Cold. London, Methuen, 1902.
Mary Garth: A Clydeside Romance. London, Hodder and Stoughton, 1904.
Christian's Cross; or, Tested and True. London, Hodder and Stoughton, 1905.
Love, The Master Key. London, Hodder and Stoughton, 1905.
A Mask of Gold: The Mystery of the Meadows. London, Hodder and Stoughton, 1906.
Nancy Nicholson; or, Who Shall Be Heir? London, Hodder and Stoughton, 1906.
Love Unlocks the Door. London, Hodder and Stoughton, 1907.
Anne Hyde, Travelling Companion. London, Hodder and Stoughton, 1908.
The Broad Road. London, Hurst and Blackett, 1908.
Hester Lane. London, Hodder and Stoughton, 1908.
The Inheritance. London, Hodder and Stoughton, 1909.
The Old Moorings: A Story of Modern Life. London, Hodder and Stoughton, 1909.
Love's Barrier. London, Cassell, 1910.
Love's Miracle. London, Hodder and Stoughton, 1910.
Margaret Holroyd; or, The Pioneers. London, Hodder and Stoughton, 1910.
The Mystery of Barry Ingram. London, Cassell, 1910.
Rhona Keith. London, Hodder and Stoughton, 1910.
What Shall It Profit? or, Roden's Choice. London, Partridge, 1910.
The Last of Their Race. London, Hodder and Stoughton, 1911.
To Follow the Lead. London, Kelly, 1911.
The Bondage of Riches. London, Partridge, 1912.
A Favourite of Fortune. London, Cassell, 1912.
Woven of the Wind. London, Hodder and Stoughton, 1912.
The Bridge Builders. London, Hodder and Stoughton, 1913.
The Farrants: A Story of Struggle and Victory. London, Kelly, 1913.
The Fairweathers: A Story of the Old World and the New. London, Hodder and Stoughton, 1913.
Prairie Fires. London, Cassell, 1913.
Corroding Gold. London, Cassell, 1914.

Meg Hamilton: An Ayrshire Romance. London, Hodder and Stoughton, 1914.

Love Gives Itself: The Story of a Blood Feud. London, Hodder and Stoughton, 1915.

The Step-Mother. London, Hodder and Stoughton, 1915.

The Woman's Part. London, Hodder and Stoughton, 1916.

Young Blood. London, Hodder and Stoughton, 1917.

Hands Across the Sea. London, Oliphant, 1919.

The Ruling Passion. London, Leng, 1920.

The Ivory God. London, Hodder and Stoughton, 1923.

Macleod's Wife: A Highland Romance. London, Hodder and Stoughton, 1924.

A Maid of the Isles: A Romance of Skye. London, Hodder and Stoughton, 1924.

Wrongs Righted. London, Leng, 1924.

Elsie Thorburn. London, Leng, 1926; as *The World Well Lost*, 1935.

Closed Doors. London, Leng, 1926.

The Pendulum. London, Hodder and Stoughton, 1926; New York, Doran, 1927.

For Love of Betty. London, Leng, 1928.

Love the Prodigal. London, Leng, 1929.

Fiona Macrae. London, Leng, 1929; as *The Pride of Fiona Macrae*, 1934.

A Wild Harvest. London, Leng, 1929.

The Forerunners. London, Hodder and Stoughton, 1930.

The House on the Rock. London, Leng, 1930.

The Marching Feet. London, Hodder and Stoughton, 1931.

The Luck of the Livingstones. London, Leng, 1932.

The Maclure Mystery. London, Leng, 1932.

The Shore Beyond. London, Hodder and Stoughton, 1932.

Christine Against the World. London, Leng, 1933.

The Last of the Laidlaws: A Romance of the Border. London, Leng, 1933.

The Little Stranger. London, Leng, 1933.

A Winsome Witch. London, Leng, 1933.

The Purchase Price. London, Leng, 1934.

Between the Tides. London, Hodder and Stoughton, 1935.

A Homing Bird. London, Leng, 1935.

The Way of Escape. London, Leng, 1935.

A Breaker of Hearts. London, Leng, 1937.

A Portrait of Destiny. London, Leng, 1937.

The Road to Damascus. London, Hodder and Stoughton, 1937.

The Family Secret. London, Leng, 1938.

The Greater Freedom. London, Leng, 1938.

The Head of the House. London, Leng, 1938.

The White House of Marisaig; or, The Interloper. London, Leng, 1938.

The Witch in Pink. London, Leng, 1938.

Double Lives. London, Leng, 1939.

These Are Our Masters. London, Hodder and Stoughton, 1939.

A Trust Betrayed. London, Leng, 1939.

The Uninvited Guest. London, Leng, 1939.

Peggy Fordyce. London, Leng, 1940.

Proud Patricia. London, Leng, 1940.

Rebel Hearts. London, Leng, 1940.

The Secret of Skye. London, Leng, 1940.

The Third Generation. London, Leng, 1940.

Dreams Come True. London, Leng, 1941.

The Mischief-Makers. London, Leng, 1941.

The Younger Brother. London, Leng, 1941.

The Dark House. London, Leng, 1941.

The Family Name. London, Leng, 1942.

Who Are the Heathen? London, Hodder and Stoughton, 1942.

Short Stories

Climbing the Hill. London, Blackie, 1883.

For Lucy's Sake: A Homely Story. London, Partridge, 1883.

Katie's Christmas Lesson. Edinburgh, Oliphant, 1883.

Marion Forsyth; or, Unspotted from the World. Edinburgh, Oliphant, 1883; with *Mistaken*, Cincinnati, Cranston and Stowe, 1892.

Mistaken. Edinburgh, Oliphant, 1883; with *Marion Forsyth*, Cincinnati, Cranston and Stowe, 1892.

Tony's Memorable Christmas. Edinburgh, Oliphant, 1883.

A Year at Coverley. London, Blackie, 1883.

The Bonnie Jean. Glasgow, Scottish Temperance Society, 1884.

Holidays at Sunnycroft. London, Blackie, 1885.

Wilful Winnie. London, Nelson, 1886.

Miss Baxter's Bequest. Edinburgh, Oliphant, 1888.

Climbing the Hill and Other Stories. London, Blackie, 1891.

A Bachelor in Search of a Wife, and Roger Marcham's Ward. Edinburgh, Oliphant, 1892.

The Bonnie Jean and Other Stories. Edinburgh, Oliphant, 1895.

The Secret of Dunston Mere. London, Hodder and Stoughton, 1898.

For the Sake of the Family. London, Hodder and Stoughton, 1898.

An Elder Brother. London, Hodder and Stoughton, 1898.

A Runaway Daughter. London, Hodder and Stoughton, 1898.

The Lady Housekeeper. London, Hodder and Stoughton, 1898.

A Blessing in Disguise. London, Hodder and Stoughton, 1898.

Alone in Paris. London, Hodder and Stoughton, 1898.

The Wedding of Kitty Barton. London, Hodder and Stoughton, 1898.

In Haste to Be Rich. London, Hodder and Stoughton, 1898.

The Dream of Mary Muldoon. London, Hodder and Stoughton, 1898.

Jasper Dennison's Christmas. London, Hodder and Stoughton, 1898.

Seth Newcome's Wife. London, Hodder and Stoughton, 1898.

The False and the True. London, Hodder and Stoughton, 1898.

Stephen Glyn. London, Hodder and Stoughton, 1898.

Married in Haste. London, Hodder and Stoughton, 1898.

What She Could. London, Hodder and Stoughton, 1898.

Sir Roderick's Will: A Love Story. London, Hodder and Stoughton, 1898.

Two Friends. London, Hodder and Stoughton, 1898.

A Married Man. London, Hodder and Stoughton, 1898.

An Only Son. London, Hodder and Stoughton, 1898.

A New Woman. London, Hodder and Stoughton, 1898.

Aunt Anne's Money. London, Hodder and Stoughton, 1898.

After Many Years. London, Hodder and Stoughton, 1899.

A Truant Wife. London, Hodder and Stoughton, 1899.

Good Out of Evil. London, Hodder and Stoughton, 1899.

Gable Farm. London, Hodder and Stoughton, 1899.

A Blessing in Disguise and Other Stories. London, Hodder and Stoughton, 1902.

The False and the True and Other Stories. London, Hodder and Stoughton, 1902.

Good Out of Evil and Other Stories. London, Hodder and Stoughton, 1902.

An Only Son and Other Stories. London, Hodder and Stoughton, 1902.

The Secret of Dunston Mere and Other Stories. London, Hodder and Stoughton, 1902.

Stephen Glyn and Other Stories. London, Hodder and Stoughton, 1902.

The Homecoming of the Boys. Edinburgh, Clark, 1916.

For Lucy's Sake and Other Stories. London, Wright and Brown, 1935.
The Collected Stories of Annie S. Swan. London, Clarke, 1942.

OTHER PUBLICATIONS

Verse

Songs of Memory and Hope. Edinburgh, Nimmo, and New York, Caldwell, 1911; as *Love's Crown*, Nimmo, 1913.

Other

Courtship and Marriage, and the Gentle Art of Home-Making. London, Hutchinson, 1893.
Memories of Margaret Grainger, Schoolmistress. London, Hutchinson, 1896.
From a Turret Window. London, Hodder and Stoughton, 1902.
The Outsiders, Being a Sketch of the Social Work of the Salvation Army. London, Salvation Army, 1905.
Letters to a War Bride. London, Hodder and Stoughton, 1915.
An Englishwoman's Home. New York, Doran, 1918.
As Others See Her. Boston, Houghton Mifflin, 1919; as *America at Home: Impressions of a Visit in War Time*, London, Oliphant, 1920.
My Life: An Autobiography. London, Nicholson and Watson, 1934.
We Travel Alone. London, Nicholson and Watson, 1935.
The Land I Love. London, Nicholson and Watson, 1936.
Seed Time and Harvest: The Story of the Hundred Years' Work of the Women's Foreign Mission of the Church of Scotland. London, Nelson, 1937.
The Enchanted Door: A Fireside Philosophy. London, Nicholson and Watson, 1938.
The Letters of Annie S. Swan, edited by Mildred Robertson Nicoll. London, Hodder and Stoughton, 1945.

*   *   *

Annie S. Swan was, in her day, in the league of superwriters of romance fiction, and is said to have written over 250 novels and stories. Her advice was even marketed in non-fiction form. Her works were reprinted as late as the 1950's but today are largely of antiquarian interest, being unreadable by modern standards.

Settings of some of her novels are firmly of their period, such as the family-run department store in *Love, The Master Key* (1905) or the suffragette movement in *Margaret Holroyd* (1910). Some of the backgrounds are historical settings: *A Mask of Gold* (1906), *The Forerunners* (1930), and *Woven of the Wind* (1912) all have early 19th-century Scottish settings. It is not the historical novels which appear so dated, however, but the turn-of-the-century life which is often effectively portrayed, such as the hard-heartedness of City of London financiers in *What Shall It Profit?* (1910), or the penny trams so many of her heroines take and the toques that so many of them wear.

The world that Swan sees is essentially the world seen through women's eyes. This world is often hard ("It's a hard thing to be a woman") on the unemancipated women who live and sometimes work in it. Downtrodden shop assistants and servants get much less out of life than the upper-class ladies who also populate this world, and live by a hard, but also a Christian, fatalism. Pride is fierce and reputation important, even among those who suffer a genteel poverty, as in *Love Unlocks the Door* (1907); this novel also stresses the tight bonds of 19th-century social order. There is much thwarted ambition, thwarted nature, and stifled love in Swan's novels.

Some of the webs of relationships rival in complexity those of the novels of George Eliot but do not contain her intellectual depth. Many of the plots are very contrived, containing secret marriages and runaway sons and daughters. There are sometimes, as in *Love Unlocks the Door* and *For Lucy's Sake* (1883), violent confrontations between two principal male characters over the love of a girl. As well as some melodrama, there is also plenty of maudlin sentimentality, as in the death of Lucy, the climax of *For Lucy's Sake*, and the use of her gravestone inscription as the last few lines of the story.

The location of many of her books is Scotland and northeast England and sometimes serves to add an element of caricature to character portrayal of oppressed women. The picture of Edinburgh in which she portrays the carefully graded strata of Scottish society is particularly authentic. But the use of the dialect "Scotch" language by many characters (sometimes only at unguarded moments) lessens their credibility and also makes the books difficult for the modern reader; the Geordie dialect transliteration is almost incomprehensible. In her later novels, Swan uses less dialogue (*The Pendulum*, 1926), but uses a rather more exaggerated style of description.

Swan had a keen ear for the social groundswell of the period she lived in, and keeps this sense of period updated in her later novels. The characters in the later books tend to be better dressed, higher in the social scale, and English. Swan's characterisation is much improved in her later novels, but this is offset by open invocation of the Christian religion and almost mystical tendencies. Her love scenes are always very chaste.

—P. R. Meldrum

SWANSON, Neil H(arman). American. Born in Minneapolis, Minnesota, 30 June 1896. Educated at the University of Minnesota, Minneapolis. Served in the United States Army in France, 1914–18. Editorial assistant and managing editor, Minneapolis *Journal*; managing editor, Pittsburgh *Press*, 1930–32; assistant editor, Baltimore *Evening Sun*, 1932–39. *Died 5 February 1983.*

ROMANCE AND HISTORICAL PUBLICATIONS

Novels

The Judas Tree. New York, Putnam, 1933.
The Flag Is Still There. New York, Putnam, 1933.
The Phantom Emperor. New York, Putnam, 1934.
The First Rebel. New York, Farrar and Rinehart, 1937.
The Forbidden Ground. New York, Farrar and Rinehart, 1938.
The Silent Drum. New York, Farrar and Rinehart, 1940.
The Unconquered: A Novel of the Pontiac Conspiracy. New York, Doubleday, 1947.
The Star-Spangled Banner, with Anne S. Swanson. Philadelphia, Winston, 1958.

OTHER PUBLICATIONS

Other

The Perilous Flight. New York, Farrar and Rinehart, 1945.

*   *   *

Neil H. Swanson began his writing career as a newspaper writer and editor. He held positions on several newspapers, including the Baltimore *Evening Sun*. He was also the author of several non-fiction books dealing with the American colonial period and became well-known for his expertise on the War of 1812.

Swanson's fiction evolved from a writing plan to recreate the life and history of four colonies, Maryland, Virginia, Delaware, and Pennsylvania, as well as the Ohio territory. His goal was to complete 30 novels, each an independent work, that built on characters and events in the others. He hoped that this series would give a continuous narrative of the American frontier and its settling as far west as the Mississippi.

This grand design began in 1933 with the publication of *The Judas Tree*. As intended, some of the characters later appeared in *The Silent Drum* and in *The Unconquered*. Swanson apparently had several volumes planned for he indicated their titles in the preface of *The Unconquered*, but he never completed them. He did complete *The Silent Drum, The Forbidden Ground*, and *The First Rebel*.

Swanson explored two major beliefs about the early colonial period. First, he sought to identify the nebulous concept of the "American character." He felt that by 1763 the elements that made the American character were well ingrained in the minds and thoughts of the colonists. These beliefs were not limited to people born there; new arrivals seemed instinctively to accept the concepts. He noted, "They were not always pleasant people. . . . They weren't easy to conquer—they believed too deeply that whatever they wanted was right and was theirs by right." Hardships were forgotten or ignored, distance meant nothing to these early settlers and they were bound by no limits, few laws, and almost no social barriers.

The second element Swanson noted was the refusal of the colonists to remain "Tide-water" bound. Until the French and Indian wars, colonial settlements remained on the eastern sea coast and extended only to the eastern slope of the Alleghenys. Settlements were limited by British military forces and colonial land grants. Explorers, trappers, and traders were all aware of the western slopes and beyond, but it was the war itself that eventually provided the impetus and chances for the western movement.

Swanson found that the continued battle for the Fort Pitt area was the key to making the expansion possible. Time and again he returned to this theme when he used Fort Pitt and the Ohio territory as the battleground between colonists and Indians. He held a firm belief that "men create their own disasters." The resulting bloody battles fought over the Ohio valley more than illustrate his opinion.

The Unconquered is more than a fast-paced exciting tale of Indian attacks and atrocities. It is more than a love story between a condemned felon, Abigail Martha Hale, and Christopher Holden, surveyor and colonist. It is also the story of treachery, cunning, and deliberate murder that Martin Garth resorts to as he sets out to control the vast territory of the Ohio Valley. The plot is actually straightforward. Chris returns from London where he traced Garth's activities in buying guns and other weapons to trade to the Indians. Garth is also the husband of Guyasuta's daughter, Hannah. Guyasuta, himself, is one of the foremost Seneca chiefs and close to Chief Pontiac. By allying himself to these Indians, Garth hopes to obtain absolute title to the lands of the Ohio Valley once the settlers have been driven out. Abigail is basically a pawn between Chris and Garth. Generally she reacts to situations with courage and strength, if not a great deal of understanding. Abby grows to love Chris after he manages to save her from Garth and the Indians.

The major action of the novel centers on Chris's attempts to warn the settlers of a massive Indian uprising, an event known as Pontiac's conspiracy. Its uniqueness centers on the fact that numerous Indian tribes, even those who were enemies, banded together to defeat the white invasion. The method used by the Indians is to encourage the forts to surrender with the promise of safe conduct under a flag of truce. The Indians, instead, massacre the settlers after their surrender. However, many settlers manage to flee to Fort Pitt and they are eventually relieved by a British military force.

Characterization is well done. Although some of the characters tend to be stereotypical, they are believable. Swanson had a definite feel for the British character, showing their gallantry and military stubbornness during this period with fascinating results. For instance, Chris is sent with peace belts to various Indian villages. He is gone for two weeks and covers several hundred miles. Yet, when he returns to Fort Pitt, he is arrested for dereliction of duty. Swanson's writing is tight, compelling, stark at times, forcing his readers to feel the emotions of his characters. His novels are exciting, action packed, vivid with detail, and entertaining.

Swanson is one of the few writers who sought to tell the story of this early period of American history. His work is meticulous and his obvious commitment to truth adds an unsurpassed dimension to his writing. He was truly an outstanding writer of historical fiction.

—Arlene Moore

SWINDELLS, Madge. Address: c/o Macdonald and Company Ltd., 66–73 Shoe Lane, London EC4P 4AP, England.

ROMANCE AND HISTORICAL PUBLICATIONS

Novels

Summer Harvest. London, Macdonald, 1983; New York, Doubleday, 1984.
Song of the Wind. London, Macdonald, and New York, Doubleday, 1985.
Shadows on the Snow. London, Macdonald, 1987.
The Corsican Woman. London, Macdonald, and New York, Warner, 1988.

*   *   *

Madge Swindells's first novel, *Summer Harvest*, appeared in 1983. Set in South Africa and spanning 30 years, 1938 to 1968, it follows the fortunes of Anna van Achtenburgh. Born the daughter of a wealthy landowner, she marries impoverished Simon Smit. She is disinherited and works to create her own fortune—only to face ruin through scandal before she can achieve true happiness. Compared critically with Colleen McCullough's *The Thornbirds*, it joined the ranks of *Dallas*-style sagas exemplified by such writers as Judith Krantz and Jackie Collins, and sets the pattern for Swindells's subsequent novels.

Swindells's world is that of the wealthy and powerful. Her novels deal almost exclusively with characters who move in such circles whether in London or a Corsican village. Wealth and power are the most important criteria for success. When, as often happens, one of the protagonists falls on hard times, the poverty is usually extreme but allows the business acumen of those involved to be exercised, leading to success. Wealth is rarely inherited—rather it is the reward for hard work (and frequently cunning manoeuvring) and therefore deserved. However without love it is seen as a barren reward.

The background to the books is international—often cosmopolitan—South Africa, the fashion world of London, Yugoslavia, Corsica. However it rarely intrudes upon the action. Place is not important in terms of adding depth to the novels; it adds local colour to a certain extent—the descriptions of the Namib Desert and the coast of South Africa, the Corsican landscape as a background to resistance against the Nazis. But not even in *Summer Harvest*, set in the farming community of the Cape of Good Hope country, nor in *The Corsican Woman*, where the action is completely localised, is there any specific atmosphere of place. The events might be occurring anywhere.

Of far more importance to Swindells are the characters whose careers are followed over several years often by means of a flashback technique. She employs a large cast. Characterisation is therefore not deep, but her protagonists are dramatic. Nor are there clear-cut distinctions between heroes (or heroines) and villains. Rather the chief characters, for all their good points, are seen as having some fatal obsession which almost destroys them, while many of the apparent villains are redeemed in the end.

The women, especially the female protagonists, are self-willed, independent, intelligent, assertive, and beautiful, and are seen as succeeding in male-dominated areas of endeavour. Often presented as hard and calculating (Anna in *Summer Harvest*, Marika in *Song of the Wind*, Eleanor in *Shadows on the Snow*) they are really totally feminine underneath: "tough outside, a stern unbending virago to strangers but warm and compassionate to those she knew and trusted." It is usually the absence or failure of love that has caused this facade and it is not until the denouement that it can be broken by the rediscovery of love so long denied or rejected. Their beauty is almost always dramatic and is constantly emphasised in fulsome terms, like Sybilia in *The Corsican Woman*: "but even then she was lovely with a bruised sensuous beauty that incited male aggression and the rancour of unfulfilled desires." Marika in *Song of the Wind* is "a woman of incredible loveliness. Her skin was porcelain white and quite flawless, her unusual golden hair hung around her shoulders, her features were perfect, her figure tempting and voluptuous, her face was dominated by her enormous slanting amber-brown eyes."

The men likewise are unfailingly good looking and usually "arrogantly male." This, however, is tempered in the heroes by an innate sensitivity and kindness, while the villains display harshness, even cruelty. This is particularly apparent in the scenes of sexual passion which are an important and recurring feature of all of the novels. Rape has its place as an ingredient in the crowded plots, as does loss of virginity. Love is seen very much in terms of its physical expression.

But almost more important than sex, which is obligatory in novels of this type, is the revenge motif. It is desire for revenge that directs Swindells's characters and determines their actions and reactions. It is the implacable and unrelenting pursuit of revenge that leads to the near downfall of these characters. So Anna achieves success to gain revenge on her husband only to have it all snatched from her; Marika pursues a vendetta against the Nazi she blames for her parent's death—again to her detriment; Sybilia shoots her father-in-law as an act of revenge. Finally, dramatic revelation, frequently in court, is used to restore equilibrium and allow the action to reach a traditional happy ending.

—Ferelith Hordon

TATE, Ellalice. See **HOLT, Victoria.**

TATTERSALL, (Honor) Jill (neé Blunt). British. Born in Tintagel, Cornwall, 18 December 1931. Educated privately in England and Switzerland. Married Robin Erskine Tattersall in 1953 (divorced 1982); four sons. Has worked as gift wrapper, typist, model, actress, receptionist, horse trainer, and nursery school teacher. Agent: Lisa Eveleigh, A.P. Watt Ltd., 20 John Street, London WC1N 2DL. Address: 26 East Street, Alresford, Hampshire, England.

ROMANCE AND HISTORICAL PUBLICATIONS

Novels

A Summer's Cloud. London, Collins, 1965.
Enchanter's Castle. London, Collins, 1966.
The Midnight Oak. London, Collins, 1967.
Lyonesse Abbey. London, Collins, and New York, Morrow, 1968.
A Time at Tarragon. London, Collins, 1969.
Lady Ingram's Retreat. London, Collins, 1970; as *Lady Ingram's Room*, New York, Morrow, 1981.
Midsummer Masque. London, Collins, and New York, Morrow, 1972.
The Wild Hunt. London, Hodder and Stoughton, and New York, Morrow, 1974.
The Witches of All Saints. London, Hodder and Stoughton, and New York, Morrow, 1975.
The Shadows of Castle Fosse. New York, Morrow, and London, Hodder and Stoughton, 1976.
Chanters Chase. New York, Morrow, and London, Hodder and Stoughton, 1978.
Dark at Noon. New York, Morrow, and London, Hodder and Stoughton, 1979.
Damnation Reef. New York, Morrow, 1979; London, Hodder and Stoughton, 1980.

*

Jill Tattersall comments:
Mystery and romance in period settings, with detailed backgrounds.

*   *   *

Jill Tattersall's novels present the reader with a complete catalogue of the most tried and true gothic literary devices. She skillfully manipulates forbidding castles, malevolent happenings, plucky heroines, and tormented heroes. With these familiar strands she weaves complicated stories, building and sustaining suspense until the very end.

Not unexpectedly, the heroines are beautiful, virtuous young women, who are appealingly feisty. Orphaned or lacking adequate familial protection, they must make their ways in an indifferent or hostile world. Each has a combination of curiosity and courage which enables her to solve the mystery facing her and, in the process, intrigue and attract the brooding, enigmatic hero. It is through the efforts of these inquisitive females that strong men, who are otherwise quite capable, are saved from sinister, ensnaring pasts and bleak futures. In *Lyonesse Abbey* it is Tessa who not only uncovers the secret of Damon's brother, but probes until she learns the truth of his brother's madness. Knowing that it is the result of an accident rather than an inherited flaw frees Damon to lead a normal life as husband and father. Perdita, in *Enchanter's Castle*, is used as the key to unlock the puzzles of the disappearance of Sir Owen and the death of his son, Sir Irwyn. Again, the truth frees her love, Sir Gareth, by cleaning the stains of patricide and suicide from the family honor.

Madness, witchcraft, the supernatural, and legends all play large parts in creating the suspense in Tattersall's books. Sometimes, as in *Chanters Chase*, it is all taken quite seriously, with no "logical" explanations given to dilute the tale involving witchcraft and a sibyl with her crystal ball. In other cases, rational causes for seemingly unexplainable happenings are offered. *Enchanter's Castle* is full of the presence of Arthur, Merlin, and other characters of Welsh legend. While it is the pervasive sense of these mythical and supernatural personages that ultimately is the source of the family tragedy, the actual deaths are the result of direct human action. On occasion, however, Tattersall seems almost to parody these suspenseful devices. The ghoulish band of body snatchers in *The Midnight Oak* becomes much less sinister when revealed to be a group of common smugglers, and Damon's unusual father (*Lyonesse Abbey*) seems to mock the idea of madness when he arrives in full regalia as a Muslim.

Like most authors of gothic tales, Tattersall varies little from the approved formula in terms of actual plots. The similarity in story lines can usually be discerned, but it is very apparent in *A Summer's Cloud* and *The Midnight Oak*. Only the hero and heroine are different in each, and even their problems are basically the same. In *A Summer's Cloud* Henrietta is torn between her love for Lord St. Ives and her patriotic duty to stop his nefarious, possibly traitorous activities. Her cousin, Sophia, faces the same dilemma in *The Midnight Oak* when she falls in love with Guy Carleton whom she believes to be the leader of the resurrectionists. Most of the other characters, all residents of West Mead, Essex, appear in both books, although their roles vary in importance. Perhaps the most surprising thing is that Tattersall chose Sophia as the heroine of the second novel after portraying her as such a spoiled, petulant child in the first.

Tattersall's work must be classified with the gothic genre, but within this formula she has developed a distinct style. While her stories are not strikingly original, they are suspenseful, well-written, and highly entertaining. The willing suspension of disbelief, necessary in reading a gothic novel, is easy to achieve when reading a Tattersall book.

—Barbara E. Kemp

TAYLOR, Janelle (Diane Williams). American. Born in Athens, Georgia, 28 June 1944. Educated at Athens High School, 1958–62; Augusta College, Georgia, 1980–81. Married Michael Howard Taylor in 1965; two daughters. Orthodontic nurse, Athens, 1962–65, and Augusta, 1967–68 and 1973–74; research technologist, Medical College of Georgia, Augusta, 1975–77; lecturer in writing, 1982–85. Agent: Adele Leone Agency, 26

Nantucket Place, Scarsdale, New York 10583. Address: 4366 Deerwood Lane, Evans, Georgia 30809, U.S.A.

Romance and Historical Publications

Novels (series: Princess Alysa; Sioux Saga)

Savage Ecstasy (Sioux). New York, Zebra, 1981.
Defiant Ecstasy (Sioux). New York, Zebra, 1982.
Forbidden Ecstasy (Sioux). New York, Zebra, 1982.
Brazen Ecstasy (Sioux). New York, Zebra, 1983.
Love Me with Fury. New York, Zebra, 1983.
Tender Ecstasy (Sioux). New York, Zebra, 1983.
First Love, Wild Love. New York, Zebra, 1984; London, Sphere, 1986.
Golden Torment. New York, Zebra, 1984.
Valley of Fire. New York, Silhouette, 1984.
Savage Conquest (Sioux). New York, Zebra, 1985.
Stolen Ecstasy (Sioux). New York, Zebra, 1985.
Destiny's Temptress. New York, Zebra, 1986.
Moondust and Madness. New York, Bantam, 1986; London, Sphere, 1988.
Sweet, Savage Heart. New York, Zebra, 1986.
Bittersweet Ecstasy (Sioux). New York, Zebra, 1987.
Wild Is My Love (Alysa). New York, Bantam, 1987.
Fortune's Flames. New York, Zebra, 1988.
Passions Wild and Free. New York, Zebra, 1988.
Wild Sweet Promise (Alysa). New York, Bantam, 1989.
Kiss of the Night Wind. New York, Zebra, 1989.

*

Manuscript Collection: University of Georgia Library, Athens.

Janelle Taylor comments:

Most of my works are authentic, adventurous, romantic historical fiction. To catch and retain a reader's interest, I make every attempt to be fast-paced, suspenseful, and original. My characters are created with love and great care to be realistic, memorable, and admirable. I write about strong, passionate, courageous characters who are a blend of real and fictional people. I weave tales around factual events, difficult and heroic times, and fascinating periods to reveal the traits, dreams, turmoils, and tests of people who made—or could have made—America great. I have used the settling of the old west, the Alaska Gold Rush, the Civil War, Texas ranger exploits, the War of 1812, and the Indian conflicts as backdrops for my novels. Although my main love and interest lie in the rip-roaring west, I've written about England, Vikings, pirates, and British East Africa. I usually prefer to remain in America, between 1700 and 1900. I try to find a unique angle and fresh approach to plots used many times. Determined to be authentic and detailed, I am very careful with research, to the point of checking out the smallest fact. It is my aim to enlighten and enrich while entertaining. I want my readers to enjoy learning about olden days and people, so I strive to bring history to life in a stimulating way. My books touch their emotions; help them through bad times; and teach them about the many facets of life, love, and commitment. When people read my works, I want them to finish feeling happy and satisfied with a well-told tale. My dream is that more women and men will look beyond the often stigmatized genre of romance to discover what well-crafted novels these are so they, too, can enjoy them.

*   *   *

Janelle Taylor has made her reputation in the romance field by writing passionate sagas set in the old American west. Her Sioux saga about American Indian lovers has proven especially popular. Four of these novels center on the love story of the beautiful white woman Alisha and the handsome Sioux warrior Gray Eagle. In the muscular arms of this handsome brave she finds a fulfillment she never believed possible. There are problems and resentments caused by this mixed marriage but by the end of the fourth novel in this series, *Brazen Ecstasy*, most of those barriers have been destroyed. Their decendants pursue similar lives of romance and adventure such as can be found in *Stolen Ecstasy* and *Savage Conquest*. In the first book, *Savage Ecstasy*, heroine Rebecca Kinny thinks back to the days of misery when she lived among her own white people. It was her capture by Bright Arrow, son of Gray Eagle and Alisha, that gave her a chance at true happiness. But now that happiness is in jeopardy because Bright Arrow's tribe has banished him for marrying a white woman instead of having her live with him as his slave. *Savage Conquest* has a slightly different twist since the female protagonist has an Indian mother and a pride in her Indian heritage. While walking along a river bank she meets Blazing Star (a descendant of Gray Eagle). The attraction between them is instantaneous.

Lots of adventure awaits the characters in Taylor's work but, when not dodging bandits or other assorted outlaws, the hero and heroine spend a great deal of time making love and then discussing where their relationship is leading them. The old west in its most romanticized form provides the background to Taylor's best novels, since the author has an obvious love for that time and has researched thoroughly to give the books a tone of authenticity. Her depiction of Indian life although glamorized still includes enough accurate detail to portray the dignity of this often maligned people.

Many of her stories center on the interaction of the white and Indian cultures. Rana Michaels of *Sweet, Savage Heart* was captured by the Sioux as a child. Now her grandfather, a wealthy rancher, has found out that she is still alive and so, with the help of the hero, Travis, he sets out to find her. Travis, himself knows the problems of mixed cultures. He grew up among the Sioux (his mother's people), but as a young man was forced to leave that life and make his way among whites.

Taylor also writes more traditional western romances such as *Passions Wild and Free*, in which heroine Randee Hollis seeks a gunman to help her avenge the murder of her uncle's family by the notorious Epson gang. The handsome stranger whom she hires is Marsh Logan, a special government agent, who has his own reasons for wanting to capture these outlaws. In *First Love, Wild Love*, Calinda Braxton is in Texas looking for a father she hasn't seen since she was a child. His last known location was the Cardone ranch where she meets and soon falls under the spell of the virile, secretive Lynx.

Taylor has broken out of the western mode with such novels as *Destiny's Temptress*, set during the Civil War, *Wild Is My Love*, which takes place in 5th-century Britain, and *Moondust and Madness*, a pseudo science fiction romance that works as neither. The plot of this latter book is so silly and the science so ludicrous that even the soaring passion of the hero and heroine (''the most beautiful woman in the universe'') cannot bring it off.

Taylor does best when she follows the advice most often given to writers—"write what you know." Her western sagas are competently written and will appeal to readers who like blazing romance with a touch of history.

—Patricia Altner

TAYLOR, Jayne. See **KRENTZ, Jayne Ann.**

TEMPEST, Jan. See **CHARLES, Theresa.**

TEMPEST, Sarah. See **PONSONBY, D. A.**

TERRY, C. V. See **SLAUGHTER, Frank G.**

THANE, Elswyth. American. Born in Burlington, Iowa, 16 May 1900. Married the naturalist William Beebe in 1927 (died 1962). Journalist and film writer. *Died.*

ROMANCE AND HISTORICAL PUBLICATIONS

Novels (series: Williamsburg)

Riders of the Wind. New York, Stokes, 1926; London, Murray, 1928.
Echo Answers. New York, Stokes, and London, Murray, 1927.
His Elizabeth. New York, Stokes, and London, Murray, 1928.
Cloth of Gold. New York, Stokes, and London, Murray, 1929.
Bound to Happen. New York and London, Putnam, 1930.
Queen's Folly. New York, Harcourt Brace, and London, Constable, 1937.
Tryst. New York, Harcourt Brace, and London, Constable, 1939.
Remember Today: Leaves from a Guardian Angel's Notebook. New York, Duell, 1941; London, Hale, 1948.
From This Day Forward. New York, Duell, 1941; London, Hale, 1947.
Williamsburg series:
  Dawn's Early Light. New York, Duell, 1943; London, Hale, 1945.
  Yankee Stranger. New York, Duell, 1944; London, Hale, 1947.
  Ever After. New York, Duell, 1945; London, Hale, 1948.
  The Light Heart. New York, Duell, 1947; London, Hale, 1950.
  Kissing Kin. New York, Duell, 1948; London, Hale, 1951.
  This Was Tomorrow. New York, Duell, 1951; London, Hale, 1952.
  Homing. New York, Duell, 1957; London, Hale, 1958.
Melody. New York, Duell, 1950; London, Hale, 1952.
The Lost General. New York, Duell, 1953; London, Hale, 1954.

Letter to a Stranger. New York, Duell, 1954; London, Hale, 1955.

OTHER PUBLICATIONS

Plays

The Tudor Wench (produced London, 1933). London, French, 1933.
Young Mr. Disraeli (produced London, 1934; New York, 1937). London, French, 1935.
Bound to Happen (produced New York, 1939).

Other

The Tudor Wench. New York, Brewer Warren and Putnam, 1932; London, Hurst and Blackett, 1933.
Young Mr. Disraeli. New York, Harcourt Brace, and London, Constable, 1936.
England Was an Island Once. New York, Harcourt Brace, 1940; London, Constable, 1941.
The Bird Who Made Good. New York, Duell, 1947.
Reluctant Farmer. New York, Duell, 1950; as *The Strength of the Hills*, New York, Christian Herald House, 1976.
The Family Quarrel: A Journey Through the Years of the Revolution. New York, Duell, 1959; London, Hale, 1960.
Washington's Lady. New York, Duell, 1960.
Potomac Squire. New York, Duell, 1963.
Mount Vernon Is Ours: The Story of Its Preservation. New York, Duell, 1966.
Mount Vernon Family (for children). New York, Macmillan, 1968.
The Virginia Colony (for children). New York, Macmillan, 1969.
Dolley Madison: Her Life and Times. New York, Macmillan, 1970.
The Fighting Quaker: Nathanael Greene. New York, Hawthorn, 1972.

*   *   *

Elswyth Thane was a prolific writer notable for the variety of her work. She wrote a number of contemporary romantic novels in addition to her well-known biographies, yet she achieved greatest success with her historical romances, especially the popular Williamsburg novels. Her early works, all set in England, are improbable romantic adventures, in which briefly sketched characters move through confusing plots. *Queen's Folly* was the first work to break out of this mold with some success, and also introduced a supernatural theme which was to recur in Thane's later work. The characters in *Queen's Folly* are rather less fanciful than their predecessors, but Thane's major breakthrough is in her use of historical settings. Her most successful and most popular works combine her love of England and her ability convincingly to depict the past in love stories which still charm modern readers.

The Williamsburg novels follow the fortunes of the intertwined Day-Sprague-Campion families from just before the American Revolution to the London blitz in World War II. Her characters experience the Revolutionary War (*Dawn's Early Light*), the Civil War (*Yankee Stranger*), the Spanish-American War (*Ever After*), World War I (*The Light Heart*), the rise of the Nazis (*Kissing Kin* and *This Was Tomorrow*), and the early stages of World War II (*Homing*). The plots are organized around historical events which Thane takes pains to describe ac-

curately. Her descriptions of Williamsburg, New York in the 1890's, and the Cotswolds are quite detailed, and provide depth to the novels. While there are no real villains (Prince Conrad in the *The Light Heart* and his son, Victor, in *This Was Tomorrow* come close, but are tragically flawed rather than utterly wicked), war and totalitarianism are the serious threats to her lovers' happiness. The Williamsburg novels should be read as part of a series, although the first three can stand on their own.

For all Thane's characters, family is tremendously important, and her few orphans (Julian in *Dawn's Early Light*, Gwen and Dinah in *Ever After*) find not just mates, but roots and well-branched family trees. The men are brave in battle and crisis, and they are portrayed as level-headed fellows used to taking charge and coping with major and minor tragedies. Many are journalists (Julian Day is a writer, Cabot and Bracken Murray and Jeff Day are newsmen), a device which allows them to observe and comment on the historical events of their periods. Thane's women are occasionally independent (Phoebe Sprague in *The Light Heart* is a writer) but are happy to settle down in blissful domesticity after their romantic adventures. From that secure position they can occasionally aid the next generation in its respective romantic involvements. Thane's heroines are frequently in need of rescue—from a drunken father, Yankee soldiers, the wreck of the Lusitania, even the snares of a Nazi spy—by her capable and experienced heroes. The lovers feel passion, but consummate their love discreetly within marriage—these novels are not "bodice-rippers." In *Homing* the hero and heroine are reincarnations of Julian and Tibby, the main characters of the first Williamsburg novel (*Dawn's Early Light*), and the rescue is mutual. Mab/Tibby saves Jeff/Julian from his depression while he in turn rescues her from her own fears.

Thane used her own experiences and her careful historical research to enrich her work, so that her historical novels are somewhat denser and more compelling than others of the genre. Her attractive and likeable characters are easy to care for, and Thane's readers are carried into a happy world where men are true and women are gentle, and where true love triumphs, despite the adversities of war and revolution. The modern reader may be occasionally jarred to encounter stereotypes like the happy loyal slaves of the Williamsburg novels, but Thane's intent is to entertain, not to expose the less attractive aspects of the past.

—Mary C. Lynn

THAYER, Geraldine. See **DANIELS, Dorothy.**

THOMAS, Rosie. Recipient: Romantic Novelists Association Major award, 1985. Address: c/o Bantam, 666 Fifth Avenue, New York, New York 10103, U.S.A.

ROMANCE AND HISTORICAL PUBLICATIONS

Novels

Love's Choice. New York, Avon, 1982.
Celebration. Loughton, Essex, Piatkus, 1982.
Follies. Loughton, Essex, Piatkus, 1983.
Sunrise. London, Piatkus, 1984.

The White Dove. London, Collins, and New York, Viking, 1986.
Strangers. London, Collins, and New York, Simon and Schuster, 1987.
Bad Girls, Good Women. London, Joseph, 1988; New York, Bantam, 1989.

*   *   *

Although it was with one of Rosie Thomas's earlier novels (*Sunrise*) that she won the Romantic Novelists Association Major award, it is with her more recent books that she has shown herself to be a writer of some stature.

The White Dove is a gripping portrayal of a relationship which transcends the barriers of class and social standing. The honourable Amy Lovell, born in 1912, is the daughter of Lord Lovell and Adeline, his second wife, a rich American heiress. Brought up to a life of luxury and privilege, Amy acquires a social conscience and starts to associate with communist sympathisers, then takes up nursing and eventually goes to Spain to nurse in the Civil War. The chief character in the other thread to the story is Nick Penry, a fiery Welsh miner and political activist; married with a handicapped son, Nick is forced to compromise his principles in order to support his family. The scenes involving the mining industry and those set at political meetings or rallies are convincing in their portrayal of the tensions of the time; these scenes lend interest and depth to what might otherwise be a formulaic romance novel. By the end of the novel, a year before the outbreak of World War II, the relationship between Amy and Nick has, after an exceedingly rocky start (but what else do you expect in a self-respecting romance novel?), taken root, flourished, and come to its inevitable end. The widely differing settings range from the Hotel du Palais, Biarritz to a poverty-stricken miner's cottage in South Wales; from a political meeting in East London to a psychiatric nursing home in Chertsey. Both Amy and Nick are completely credible characters; she with her doubts and self-doubts, trying to reconcile her lifestyle with her newly awakened beliefs, he with his unshakeable convictions. Their love is inevitable and so is its conclusion.

In *Strangers* Thomas again brings two characters together in a situation in which a love affair is the only possible outcome, and the termination of this affair is the only possible conclusion. In contrast to *The White Dove*, however, it is with some relief that one realises that the lovers are not going to stroll happily into the sunset, as the hero is one of the less sympathetic creations of romance fiction—in fact he is totally selfish, and far from heroic. The novel starts promisingly: Annie, a rather bored suburban housewife, and Steve, a successful advertising executive, are both trapped in the rubble when a bomb destroys a crowded department store just before Christmas. In the terrifying hours before they are rescued each lends strength to the other, and the seeds of a relationship are sown. Unfortunately for the balance of the plot, Thomas heightens the tension to such a degree that there is an unavoidable anticlimax, and the story never quite recovers its momentum. It is inevitable that the relationship will continue, and because of Steve's serious flaws, the fact that the love affair ends and Annie goes back to her husband is in fact a happy ending. Had Steve been a totally sympathetic character, and given the fact that Martin (Annie's husband) is pleasant but unexceptional, either of the possible resolutions would have been in some part unsatisfactory.

It is one of Thomas's strengths as a writer that she can take a similar combination of relationships and give them a totally dissimilar yet equally satisfactory ending. In *Sunrise* Angharad, the heroine, ultimately rejects Jamie, the kind, loving, and totally sympathetic man who has cared for her and her child, and resumes her relationship with the father of the child. The latter man is a complex character who develops (although we do not see this development as it takes place outside the pages of the novel) from a spoilt arrogant adolescent to a mature man willing to sacrifice his own and the heroine's happiness to protect his unbalanced and too-loving sister. Although the reader feels that the resolution of the problems (i.e., the heroine will obviously live her life with the father of her child) is the correct one romantically, we have a real and abiding sympathy for Jamie—yet this in no way detracts from the feeling that the conclusion is satisfactory. It is a measure of Thomas's confidence in her own capabilities that she obviously felt able to reject all the clichés with which she could have ended the story.

In *Celebration* Thomas writes in lighter vein, this time using the basic format of a traditional romance novel; she adds a touch of humour, an interesting and well researched background, and the two heroes whom we are now beginning to see as obligatory. The story sets traditional against modern values and, as in the previous two novels, we are for a while kept guessing as to which will triumph. The emancipated heroine, Bel, is forced to choose between a rich count who is cool and reserved, with an underlying smouldering passion (unfortunately he is also married, and even more unfortunately a devout Roman Catholic), and a lively, amusing, philandering American millionaire. The plot is lightly controlled and builds well towards the climax, which is an unusual duel to the death on motorbikes. The style is lighter than in most of her other works, but this by no means detracts from an entertainingly romantic novel.

By far Thomas's best book to date is *Bad Girls, Good Women*. This is the story of two independent and strong-willed women, from their rebellious girlhood to their respective successful careers—Mattie as an actress, Julia as a fashionable businesswoman. Each has had a disturbed childhood (Mattie was abused by her father while Julia, brought up in a repressive home, was adopted, although she does not find this out until later), each encounters setbacks and even tragedy in her adult life. The first part of the novel is set in the 1960's, a period now much written about, and here rather glamorised. Thomas, despite incorporating a large cast of lesser personalities, manages to avoid stereotypes—yet all the characters are believable, albeit a little larger than life. Each has an individuality which holds the reader's attention throughout this densely packed novel.

The White Dove and *Bad Girls, Good Women* contrast strongly with *Follies*, one of her earliest novels. Littered with stereotyped characters—the poor but studious heroine, the rich doomed aristocrat (very reminiscent of Evelyn Waugh's Sebastian Flyte), the solid dependable type (so low key that you just know he will marry the heroine), this novel contains such convoluted relationships and such a welter of partner-swapping that one really needs to construct a chart in order to keep track of the plot. Even though the novel itself does develop some pace and engages the reader's interest to some extent, the characters themselves never develop to the level of those in Thomas's later novels.

—Judith Rhodes

————————

THOMPSON, E(rnest) V(ictor). British. Born in London in 1931. Served in the Royal Navy, nine years. Founder member of the Bristol Police Force vice squad; investigator, British Overseas Airways Corporation; worked with the Hong Kong Police Narcotics Bureau; chief security officer, Rhodesia Department of Civil Aviation. Also factory worker, hotel detective, and civil servant, Plymouth dockyard. Since 1977 full-time writer. Address: c/o Macmillan Publishers Ltd., 4 Little Essex Street, London WC2R 3LF, England.

ROMANCE AND HISTORICAL PUBLICATIONS

Novels (series: Nathan Jago; Retallick)

Chase the Wind (Retallick). London, Macmillan, 1977.
Harvest of the Sun (Retallick). London, Macmillan, 1978; New York, Coward McCann, 1979.
The Music Makers. London, Macmillan, 1979.
Ben Retallick. London, Macmillan, 1980; New York, St. Martin's Press, 1981.
The Dream Traders. London, Macmillan, 1981.
Singing Spears (Retallick). London, Macmillan, 1982.
The Restless Sea (Jago). London, Macmillan, 1983.
Cry Once Alone. London, Macmillan, 1984; as *Republic*, New York, Watts, 1985.
Polrudden (Jago). London, Macmillan, 1985.
The Stricken Land (Retallick). London, Macmillan, 1986.
Becky. London, Macmillan, 1988.
God's Highlander. London, Macmillan, 1989.

OTHER PUBLICATIONS

Other

Discovering Bodmin Moor. Bodmin, Cornwall, Bossiney, 1980.
Discovering Cornwall's South Coast. Bodmin, Cornwall, Bossiney, 1982.
Sea Stories of Devon. Bodmin, Cornwall, Bossiney, 1984.
E. V. Thompson's West Country. Bodmin, Cornwall, Bossiney, 1986.

*   *   *

Adventure is a central element in the novels of E. V. Thompson, whose writing matches a powerful story-telling style with the use of varied and exotic locations. Thompson's Retallick series follows several generations of his characters from their native Cornwall to Southern Africa, spanning a period between the Napoleonic era and the latter stages of the Boer War, while other novels explore events in China, Texas, and the famine-stricken Ireland of the 1840's. At their best, his books manage to accommodate a strong humanitarian message while losing none of their pace and impact on the reader. Thompson's anger at past injustices is evident, and his sympathies are made plain by his heroes and their actions. At the same time his writing suggests a distrust of official solutions and a dislike of revolutionary violence. There is a constant sense of man's helplessness in the face of history, of the inevitability of tragedy and loss. The humane act of a Thompson character is seen to be hedged with limitations; there is no way his heroes can turn back the relentless tide of events.

These themes are recurrent threads in the five Retallick novels, the largest single sequence of works that Thompson has yet produced. *Chase the Wind* concerns the adventures of the mining engineer Josh Retallick in the Bodmin region of Cornwall, and his sentencing to transportation after his unwitting involvement in a riot of his fellow-miners. *Harvest of the Sun* continues the story with the shipwreck of Josh, his mistress, and his son Daniel in Southern Africa, and their new life as neighbours of the powerful Matabele nation. In *Singing Spears* Daniel grows to manhood, fathers sons of his own, and eventually meets his death at the hands of the Matabele, who are themselves destroyed by the new imperialism of Cecil Rhodes. *The Stricken Land*, which concludes the sequence of novels, gives a hard-hitting account of the Boer War, in which Daniel's sons find themselves fighting on opposite sides. Each novel is fraught with tragedy and violence, whether it be the rapes committed on several Retallick heroines, or the downfall of entire nations.

Thompson depicts the extermination of the Bushmen, the defeat of the Matabele, with a resigned sympathy, presenting them as doomed figures in the path of progress. *Ben Retallick* does not follow the main chronology, going back to early 19th-century Cornwall with the story of a mining community and its struggle against the parliamentary corruption and privilege that bind its people to the will of the landed Vincent family. In a series of dramatic scenes Thompson recounts the tale of Ben Retallick's love for Jesse Henna, his unwilling involvement in the reform movement, and his eventual overthrow of Colman Vincent. Here, more than in any of the Retallick novels, the detailed research of the author is made evident. Thompson's vision of the prison hulks, the public hanging of Judy Lean, the horrors of Newgate prison, weds descriptive power to authenticity of detail. *Ben Retallick* is a strongly written adventure novel which attacks injustice through living characters, in a credibly recreated historical setting. To a lesser extent, the same is true of the entire Retallick series.

For all the obvious virtues of the Retallick novels, it could be argued that Thompson's finest work has been produced outside the major sequence. Of the non-Retallick novels, *The Restless Sea* and *Polrudden* are perhaps the weakest. A kind of "mini-saga" featuring the prize-fighter and fisherman Nathan Jago, these books contain plenty in the way of action, but there is about them a lack of that depth and coherence one associates with Thompson's other works. More impressive are *Cry Once Alone* and *The Music Makers*, where strength of narrative is combined with a forceful presentation of historical events, the former set in pioneer Texas, the latter in the Ireland of the Great Famine.

Arguably Thompson's finest novel is *The Dream Traders*, whose action takes place in China at the time of the Opium War. Viewing developments through the eyes of his trader hero Luke Trewarne, Thompson explores the economics of the opium business, the political intrigues of East and West, and the nature of love and friendship between individuals of different races. Once again, his well-meaning characters are thwarted by the overwhelming force of history, lives lost and an evil trade reintroduced at gunpoint in order to secure British economic interests. In *The Dream Traders* Thompson contains history and adventure in perfect balance throughout, the message ably presented while at no time impeding the momentum of the story. His recent work *Becky* describes the love of an artist for a girl from the slums of Bristol, and again combines an interesting narrative with an authentic portrayal of the social background.

—Geoffrey Sadler

THORNE, Nicola. See **ELLERBECK, Rosemary.**

THORPE, Kay. British. Married; one son. Address: c/o Mills and Boon Ltd., 18–24 Paradise Road, Richmond, Surrey TW9 1SR, England.

ROMANCE AND HISTORICAL PUBLICATIONS

Novels

Devon Interlude. London, Mills and Boon, 1968; Toronto, Harlequin, 1969.
The Last of the Mallorys. London, Mills and Boon, and Toronto, Harlequin, 1968.
Opportune Marriage. London, Mills and Boon, 1968; Toronto, Harlequin, 1975.
Rising Star. London, Mills and Boon, and Toronto, Harlequin, 1969.
Curtain Call. London, Mills and Boon, and Toronto, Harlequin, 1971.
Not Wanted on Voyage. London, Mills and Boon, and Toronto, Harlequin, 1972.
Olive Island. London, Mills and Boon, 1972; Toronto, Harlequin, 1973.
Sawdust Season. London, Mills and Boon, and Toronto, Harlequin, 1972.
Man in a Box. London, Mills and Boon, 1972.
An Apple in Eden. London, Mills and Boon, 1973; Toronto, Harlequin, 1974.
The Man at Kambala. London, Mills and Boon, 1973; Toronto, Harlequin, 1974.
Remember This Stranger. London, Mills and Boon, 1974.
The Iron Man. London, Mills and Boon, 1974; Toronto, Harlequin, 1975.
The Shifting Sands. London, Mills and Boon, and Toronto, Harlequin, 1975.
Sugar Cane Harvest. London, Mills and Boon, 1975; Toronto, Harlequin, 1976.
The Royal Affair. London, Mills and Boon, and Toronto, Harlequin, 1976.
Safari South. London, Mills and Boon, 1976; Toronto, Harlequin, 1977.
Caribbean Encounter. London, Mills and Boon, 1976; Toronto, Harlequin, 1978.
The River Lord. London, Mills and Boon, and Toronto, Harlequin, 1977.
Storm Passage. London, Mills and Boon, and Toronto, Harlequin, 1977.
Lord of La Pampa. London, Mills and Boon, 1977; Toronto, Harlequin, 1978.
Bitter Alliance. London, Mills and Boon, 1978.
Full Circle. London, Mills and Boon, 1978.
Timber Boss. London, Mills and Boon, and Toronto, Harlequin, 1978.
The Wilderness Trail. London, Mills and Boon, 1978; Toronto, Harlequin, 1979.
The Dividing Line. London, Mills and Boon, 1979; Toronto, Harlequin, 1980.
The Man from Tripoli. London, Mills and Boon, and Toronto, Harlequin, 1979.
This Side of Paradise. London, Mills and Boon, 1979; Toronto, Harlequin, 1980.
Chance Meeting. London, Mills and Boon, and Toronto, Harlequin, 1980.
No Passing Fancy. London, Mills and Boon, 1980.
Copper Lake. London, Mills and Boon, and Toronto, Harlequin, 1981.

Floodtide. London, Mills and Boon, and Toronto, Harlequin, 1981.
Temporary Marriage. London, Mills and Boon, 1981.
The New Owner. London, Mills and Boon, and Toronto, Harlequin, 1982.
A Man of Means. London, Mills and Boon, 1982; Toronto, Harlequin, 1983.
The Land of the Incas. London, Mills and Boon, and Toronto, Harlequin, 1983.
Master of Morley. London, Mills and Boon, and Toronto, Harlequin, 1983.
Never Trust a Stranger. London, Mills and Boon, 1983.
The Inheritance. London, Mills and Boon, 1984.
Dangerous Moonlight. London, Mills and Boon, 1985.
Double Deception. London, Mills and Boon, 1985.
South Seas Affair. London, Mills and Boon, 1985.
Jungle Island. London, Mills and Boon, 1986.
Win or Lose. London, Mills and Boon, 1986.
Time Out of Mind. London, Mills and Boon, 1987.
Land of Illusion. London, Mills and Boon, 1988.
Tokyo Tryst. London, Mills and Boon, 1988.
Skin Deep. London, Mills and Boon, 1989.

*   *   *

Kay Thorpe's slow but steady output of series romances since 1968 includes a number of carefully crafted formula stories. She is particularly adept at portraying heroines in interesting professions and at writing novels that hinge upon successive misunderstandings and misinterpretations between potential lovers. Her books move swiftly and maintain their suspense.

In some books, her heroines are "spoiled brats," too immature to sustain adult relationships. Inevitably, they behave badly and alienate their lovers or husbands. In others, she portrays women who are misinterpreted as "gold diggers," who must somehow convince the heroes to trust them. She sets her novels in exciting and interesting places: the theatre, the circus, a cruise ship, a department store, or a newspaper office. Her women are usually competent in their fields, even though they must be instructed in love by the heroes.

An unusual feature of Thorpe's romances is that she sometimes leaves the relationship with room to grow at the end of the book. Most other series romance writers describe a complete reconciliation by the final page, but Thorpe does not always wrap up the ends so neatly. In *Bitter Alliance* and *Floodtide* her heroes at the end have not learned the difference between "wanting" and "loving," a critical issue in most series romances, for without an acknowledgement of that distinction, no self-respecting heroine can submit sexually to the hero. Thorpe's heroines remain confident that the hero will change in time and so they agree to be patient.

Because Thorpe is less prolific than many of her colleagues, her novels are sometimes more complex than theirs. She has been prominent as a series writer because of the care with which she constructs her plots.

—Kay Mussell

THORPE, Sylvia. Pseudonym for June Sylvia Thimblethorpe. British. Born in London in 1926. Educated at a school in Brondesbury, Kilburn High School for Girls, Slade School of Fine Arts, and University College, all London. Secretary, 1949–

52; school teacher, 1952–53. Recipient: Romantic Novelists Association Historical award, 1971. Address: c/o Century Hutchinson Ltd., 62–65 Chandos Place, London WC2N 4NW, England.

ROMANCE AND HISTORICAL PUBLICATIONS

Novels

The Scandalous Lady Robin. London, Hutchinson, 1950; New York, Fawcett, 1975.

The Sword and the Shadow. London, Hutchinson, 1951; New York, Fawcett, 1976.

Beggar on Horseback. London, Hutchinson, 1953; New York, Fawcett, 1977.

Smugglers' Moon. London, Rich and Cowan, 1955; as *Strangers on the Moor*, New York, Pyramid, 1966.

The Golden Panther. London, Rich and Cowan, 1956; New York, Fawcett, 1976.

Sword of Vengeance. London, Rich and Cowan, 1957; New York, Fawcett, 1977.

Rogues' Covenant. London, Hurst and Blackett, 1957; New York, Fawcett, 1976.

Captain Gallant. London, Hurst and Blackett, 1958; New York, Fawcett, 1978.

Beloved Rebel. London, Hurst and Blackett, 1959; New York, Fawcett, 1978.

Romantic Lady. London, Hurst and Blackett, 1960; New York, Fawcett, 1976.

The Devil's Bondsman. London, Hurst and Blackett, 1961; New York, Fawcett, 1980.

The Highwayman. London, Hurst and Blackett, 1962; New York, Fawcett, 1979.

The House at Bell Orchard. London, Hurst and Blackett, 1962; New York, Fawcett, 1979.

The Reluctant Adventuress. London, Hurst and Blackett, 1963; New York, Fawcett, 1974.

Fair Shine the Day. London, Hurst and Blackett, 1964; New York, Fawcett, 1977.

Spring Will Come Again. London, Hurst and Blackett, 1965; New York, Fawcett, 1974.

The Changing Tide. London, Hurst and Blackett, 1967; New York, Fawcett, 1978.

Dark Heritage. London, Hurst and Blackett, 1968; as *Tarrington Chase*, London, Corgi, 1977.

No More A-Roving. London, Hurst and Blackett, 1970; New York, Fawcett, 1979.

The Scarlet Domino. London, Hurst and Blackett, 1970; New York, Fawcett, 1975.

The Scapegrace. London, Hurst and Blackett, 1971; New York, Fawcett, 1978.

Dark Enchantress. London, Hurst and Blackett, 1973; New York, Fawcett, 1980.

The Silver Nightingale. London, Hurst and Blackett, and New York, Fawcett, 1974.

The Witches of Conyngton. London, Hurst and Blackett, 1976.

A Flash of Scarlet. New York, Fawcett, 1978.

The Varleigh Medallion. London, Hurst and Blackett, and New York, Fawcett, 1979.

The Avenhurst Inheritance. London, Hutchinson, 1981.

Mistress of Astington. London, Hutchinson, 1983.

*   *   *

June Sylvia Thimblethorpe, better known as Sylvia Thorpe, is a very prolific historical novelist. Her stories are marked by careful attention to historical detail and extremely well-drawn characters.

Her Regency romances are among the best written. Combining romance with adventure and intrigue, they are filled with believable, sympathetic people. *The Silver Nightingale* is both a mystery and a love story in which snowbound travelers are threatened by a killer. Justin, Lord Chayle, must flush out the murderer in order to protect his fiancée, Sarah. In *Romantic Lady* Caroline's impetuousness leads her into danger and involves Guy Ravenshaw in several rescues in spite of himself. Thorpe's ladies are spirited and courageous, and are suitable mates for their dashing partners.

Similar in nature to the Regencies are Thorpe's Georgian romances. The same mixture of romance and adventure is present, with slightly more emphasis on forceful action as befits an earlier age. The heroes tend to be more roguish in these novels. The hero of *Captain Gallant* is a daring highwayman. Geraint St. Arvan (*The Scarlet Domino*) is taken from the Common Debtors' Ward in Newgate to marry Antonia. Philip Digby in *Rogues' Covenant* has a mysterious past that leads to violence. In spite of these flaws (which really make the characters more interesting), these men are reformed, or at least captured, by the love of their heroines.

Many of Thorpe's historical romances are set in even earlier times. The Commonwealth under Cromwell is not one of the most popular eras for historical novelists to use, but it provides extremely fertile ground for Thorpe's imagination. The exiles and wanderers created by the English Civil War provide excellent material for action-packed tales of rogues and pirates. Set against the lush tropical background of the Caribbean, bold love stories come alive in the true swashbuckling tradition. Using a place and time of violent men, Thorpe wisely puts more focus on the men in these stories, but does so without slighting the women or diluting the romance. Thorpe's talent can be seen in the fact that women can read these novels for the romance, while men can enjoy an escape to high adventure. *The Golden Panther, No More A-Roving, The Devil's Bondsman*, and *The Sword and the Shadow* are all examples of Thorpe's ability to portray some rousing action.

Thorpe is a consummate storyteller. Her craftsmanship is evident in each of her novels, raising them above standard formula stories. Many authors could learn a great deal about writing historical romances by reading her books.

—Barbara E. Kemp

THUM, Marcella. American. Born in St. Louis, Missouri. Educated at Washington University, St. Louis, 1948; University of California, Berkeley, M.L.S. 1954; Webster University, St. Louis, M.A. 1977. Divorced. Civilian librarian and historical writer, United States Army bases in Okinawa, Germany, Korea, and Hawaii, 1949–61; high school librarian, Affton, Missouri, 1962–67; librarian, St. Louis Community College, 1968–78, and Air Transport School, Scott Air Force Base, Illinois, 1979–85. Recipient: Mystery Writers of America Edgar Allan Poe award, for children's book, 1965. Agent: Eleanor Wood, 432 Park Avenue South, New York, New York 10016. Address: 6507 Gramond Drive, St. Louis, Missouri 63123, U.S.A.

ROMANCE AND HISTORICAL PUBLICATIONS

Novels

Fernwood. New York, Doubleday, 1973; as *The Haunting Cavalier*, Aylesbury, Buckinghamshire, Milton House, 1974.
Abbey Court. New York, Doubleday, 1976.
The White Rose. New York, Fawcett, 1980.
Blazing Star. New York, Fawcett, 1983.
Jasmine. New York, Fawcett, 1984.
Wild Laurel. New York, Fawcett, 1987.
Margarite. New York, Fawcett, 1987.
Mistress of Paradise. New York, Fawcett, 1988.

OTHER PUBLICATIONS

Novels

Mystery at Crane's Landing. New York, Dodd Mead, 1964.
Treasure of Crazy Quilt Farm. New York, Watts, 1966.
Librarian with Wings. New York, Dodd Mead, 1967.
Secret of the Sunken Treasure. New York, Dodd Mead, 1969.

Other

Anne of the Sandwich Islands (for children). New York, Dodd Mead, 1967.
The Persuaders: Propaganda in War and Peace, with Gladys Thum. New York, Atheneum, 1972.
Exploring Black America. New York, Atheneum, 1975.
Exploring Literary America. New York, Atheneum, 1979.
Exploring Military America. New York, Atheneum, 1982.
Airlift: Story of the Military Airlift Command, with Gladys Thum. New York, Dodd Mead, 1986.

*

Marcella Thum comments:

Almost all my books, both historical novels and non-fiction, have required a lot of historical research. The writing is hard work; the research is fun. Of course, having been a reference librarian helps! To me, plot and characterization in a novel are important but they are only two dimensional without a well-researched, interesting background against which to place them.

*   *   *

Marcella Thum's clutch of popular, super-sized romances are "bodice rippers" of the first rank. That is to say, they promise—and deliver—steamy adventures starring a bevy of unbelievably beautiful and spirited young women whose various tangled romances with a matching number of handsome, muscular, adventurous men may never run smoothly, but do run with predictable regularity, toward the triumphant nuptials.

These young women, Star, Jasmine, Lucinda, and the rest, always eager virgins as the stories begin, and never as they end, quite frequently suffer the sort of sexual violence and indignity never visited upon the governesses and ladies' companions of milder popular romances. In *Wild Laurel*, for example, the heroine, in flight from an unjust accusation of the murder of her wealthy cousin Sophia, is hunted down and raped by a bounty-hunting, sadistic murderer.

It is indicative of Thum's ambivalent treatment of her heroines that Laurel responds physically, though entirely unwillingly, to the practiced, cruel assailant, exactly as he intends she should,

even though she fears and loathes him. The rape, a sickening and unpleasant event, is, however, not allowed to affect her later, happier relationship with the man she will one day marry, and with whom she will leave the ugly memories behind to make a new life in California.

Thum's historical settings are widely varied and quite unusual, including Hawaii in the great days of the whaling ships, and later during the disturbance and political unrest of the reign of Queen Liliuokalani, in *Jasmine*, and again in the story of Lani, Jasmine's granddaughter, the *Mistress of Paradise*.

The flight of the starving Irish peasantry from their hungry land to the promise of a new life in America, is the starting point for *Wild Laurel*, a romance-murder mystery. *The White Rose*, set in the days of the American Civil War, is a story of espionage, in which the heroine, actress Lucinda Appleton, is a Union spy, who successfully disguises herself as a black maid-servant, Sukey, to gain access to Confederate secrets. She, like Laurel, suffers a forced sexual encounter; and there is a most disagreeable implication that the rape means less than it might have done, because Lucinda/Sukey is apparently black.

The same deplorable double standard is evident in the course of events of *Jasmine*, in which the hero, whaling captain Morgan Tucker, overcomes the resistance of a young women he presumes to be a "wahine," and therefore fair game in spite of all protests, and discovers to his (somewhat) dismayed surprise that the girl had been until that moment a virgin. He does, however, "do the right thing" when the girl's angry (and influential) father confronts him. It was all a mistake, and she is, after all, a *lady*.

Mistress of Paradise follows the adventures of Jasmine's and Morgan's granddaughter, Lani Tucker, who believes herself to be sole mistress of the great Hawaiian ranch "Palekaiko" or Paradise, blissfully unaware that her guardian has lost the title to her beloved home in a card game. The new owner, Adam, is the brother of the villainous object of Lani's girlish infatuation. In the depths of a black night, foolish Lani steals into the wrong bedroom, to encounter, again all unknowingly, *good* brother Adam who will become her husband. Will she continue to moon over the phantom lover with whom she believes she shared her first experience of passion?

Blazing Star, and later the story of Star's adopted stepson Patrick and his love, *Margarite*, are set in Mexico and Austria. The more interesting of the two has as its background the story of the ill-fated Maximilian, Emperor of Mexico, and his sad, neglected Empress Carlota, who sat so briefly upon the Cactus Throne. Margarite is sent to her unknown uncle in Mexico to serve the caprice of her stepmother in Austria. When Uncle Don Manuel's party is attacked and savaged by fierce guerrillas, a blow on the head leaves the young Austrian countess, sole survivor of the outrage, amnesiac. Rescued by half-Mexican adventurer Patrick O'Malley, she rides with him and his men dressed as a boy: and since her name is unknown even to herself, she becomes la Niña. Slowly memory returns; and mistakenly she comes to fear that Patrick, her rescuer, was a party to the murder of her uncle. And you know where *that* will lead. . . .

It's all rich, ripe, sensual stuff, soft, sweet, and fuzzy as peach flesh. The heroines tend to merge into one: the colour of hair and eyes may vary, but the reader well knows that under the multicoloured icing the cake will be sugar and spice.

Thum's works do not greatly resemble life as it is really lived: but, as her popularity demonstrates, they *do* portray life, steamy, searing life, as a good many people love to imagine it.

—Joan McGrath

TORDAY, Ursula. See **BLACKSTOCK, Charity.**

TOWERS, Regina. See **PYKARE, Nina.**

TRANTER, Nigel (Godwin). Has also written as Nye Tredgold. British. Born in Glasgow, Scotland, 23 November 1909. Educated at St. James's Episcopal School, Edinburgh, 3 years; George Heriot's School, Edinburgh, 9 years. Served in the Royal Artillery during World War II: Lieutenant. Married May Jean Campbell Grieve in 1933 (died 1979); one daughter, and one son (deceased). Accountant and inspector in family insurance company, Edinburgh, 1929–39. Since 1946 full-time writer, broadcaster, and lecturer. Chairman, Scottish Convention, Edinburgh, 1948–51; Scottish President, PEN, 1962–66; Scottish Chairman, Society of Authors, 1966–72, and National Book League, 1973–78. M.A.: Edinburgh University, 1971. Knight Commander, Order of St. Lazarus of Jerusalem, 1961; O.B.E. (Officer, Order of the British Empire), 1983. Address: Quarry House, Aberlady, East Lothian EH32 0QB, Scotland.

ROMANCE AND HISTORICAL PUBLICATIONS

Novels (series: Montrose; Robert the Bruce Trilogy; Stuart Trilogy)

Trespass. Edinburgh, Moray Press, 1937.
Mammon's Daughter. London, Ward Lock, 1939.
Harsh Heritage. London, Ward Lock, 1939.
Eagles Feathers. London, Ward Lock, 1941.
Watershed. London, Ward Lock, 1941.
The Gilded Fleece. London, Ward Lock, 1942.
Delayed Action. London, Ward Lock, 1944.
Tinker's Pride. London, Ward Lock, 1945.
Man's Estate. London, Ward Lock, 1946.
Flight of Dutchmen. London, Ward Lock, 1947.
Island Twilight. London, Ward Lock, 1947.
Root and Branch. London, Ward Lock, 1948.
Colours Flying. London, Ward Lock, 1948.
The Chosen Course. London, Ward Lock, 1949.
Fair Game. London, Ward Lock, 1950.
High Spirits. London, Collins, 1950.
The Freebooters. London, Ward Lock, 1950.
Tidewrack. London, Ward Lock, 1951.
Fast and Loose. London, Ward Lock, 1951.
Bridal Path. London, Ward Lock, 1952.
Cheviot Chase. London, Ward Lock, 1952.
Ducks and Drakes. London, Ward Lock, 1953.
The Queen's Grace. London, Ward Lock, 1953.
Rum Week. London, Ward Lock, 1954.
The Night Riders. London, Ward Lock, 1954.
There Are Worse Jungles. London, Ward Lock, 1955.
Rio d'Oro. London, Ward Lock, 1955.
The Long Coffin. London, Ward Lock, 1956.
MacGregor's Gathering. London, Hodder and Stoughton, 1957.
The Enduring Flame. London, Hodder and Stoughton, 1957.
Balefire. London, Hodder and Stoughton, 1958.
The Stone. London, Hodder and Stoughton, 1958; New York, Putnam, 1959.

The Man Behind the Curtain. London, Hodder and Stoughton, 1959.
The Clansman. London, Hodder and Stoughton, 1959.
Spanish Galleon. London, Hodder and Stoughton, 1960.
The Flockmasters. London, Hodder and Stoughton, 1960.
Kettle of Fish. London, Hodder and Stoughton, 1961.
The Master of Gray. London, Hodder and Stoughton, 1961.
Drug on the Market. London, Hodder and Stoughton, 1962.
Gold for Prince Charlie. London, Hodder and Stoughton, 1962.
The Courtesan. London, Hodder and Stoughton, 1963.
Chain of Destiny. London, Hodder and Stoughton, 1964.
Past Master. London, Hodder and Stoughton, 1965.
A Stake in the Kingdom. London, Hodder and Stoughton, 1966.
Lion Let Loose. London, Hodder and Stoughton, 1967.
Cable from Kabul. London, Hodder and Stoughton, 1968.
Black Douglas. London, Hodder and Stoughton, 1968.
Robert the Bruce Trilogy. London, Hodder and Stoughton, 1985.
 The Steps to the Empty Throne. London, Hodder and Stoughton, 1969; New York, St. Martin's Press, 1971.
 The Path of the Hero King. London, Hodder and Stoughton, 1970; New York, St. Martin's Press, 1973.
 The Price of the King's Peace. London, Hodder and Stoughton, 1971; New York, St. Martin's Press, 1973.
The Young Montrose. London, Hodder and Stoughton, 1972.
Montrose, The Captain-General. London, Hodder and Stoughton, 1973.
The Wisest Fool. London, Hodder and Stoughton, 1974.
The Wallace. London, Hodder and Stoughton, 1975.
Stuart Trilogy:
 Lords of Misrule. London, Hodder and Stoughton, 1976.
 A Folly of Princes. London, Hodder and Stoughton, 1977.
 The Captive Crown. London, Hodder and Stoughton, 1977.
Macbeth the King. London, Hodder and Stoughton, 1978.
Margaret the Queen. London, Hodder and Stoughton, 1979.
David the Prince. London, Hodder and Stoughton, 1980.
True Thomas. London, Hodder and Stoughton, 1981.
The Patriot. London, Hodder and Stoughton, 1982.
Lord of the Isles. London, Hodder and Stoughton, 1983.
Unicorn Rampant. London, Hodder and Stoughton, and New York, Beaufort, 1984.
The Riven Realm. London, Hodder and Stoughton, 1984; New York, Beaufort, 1985.
James, By the Grace of God. London, Hodder and Stoughton, 1985; New York, Beaufort, 1986.
Rough Wooing. London, Hodder and Stoughton, 1986; New York, Beaufort, 1987.
Columba. London, Hodder and Stoughton, 1987.
Cache Down. London, Hodder and Stoughton, 1987.
Flowers of Chivalry. London, Hodder and Stoughton, 1988.
Mail Royal. London, Hodder and Stoughton, 1989.

OTHER PUBLICATIONS

Novels as Nye Tredgold

Thirsty Range. London, Ward Lock, 1949.
Heartbreak Valley. London, Ward Lock, 1950.
The Big Corral. London, Ward Lock, 1952.
Trail Herd. London, Ward Lock, 1952.
Desert Doublecross. London, Ward Lock, 1953.
Cloven Hooves. London, Ward Lock, 1954.
Dynamite Trail. London, Ward Lock, 1955.
Rancher Renegade. London, Ward Lock, 1956.
Trailing Trouble. London, Ward Lock, 1957.

Dead Reckoning. London, Ward Lock, 1957.
Bloodstone Trail. London, Ward Lock, 1958.

Other (for children)

Spaniards' Isle. Leicester, Brockhampton Press, 1958.
Border Rising. Leicester, Brockhampton Press, 1959.
Nestor the Monster. Leicester, Brockhampton Press, 1960.
Birds of a Feather. Leicester, Brockhampton Press, 1961.
The Deer Poachers. London, Blackie, 1961.
Something Very Fishy. London, Collins, 1962.
Give a Dog a Bad Name. London, Collins, 1963; New York,
    Platt and Munk, 1964.
Silver Island. London, Nelson, 1964.
Smoke Across the Highlands. New York, Platt and Munk, 1964.
Pursuit. London, Collins, 1965.
Fire and High Water. London, Collins, 1967.
Tinker Tess. London, Dobson, 1967.
To the Rescue. London, Dobson, 1968.

Other

The Fortalices and Early Mansions of Southern Scotland 1400–
    1650. Edinburgh, Moray Press, 1935.
The Fortified House in Scotland. Edinburgh, Oliver and Boyd,
    4 vols., 1962–66; London, Chambers, 1 vol., 1970.
The Pegasus Book of Scotland. London, Dobson, 1964.
Outlaw of the Highlands: Rob Roy. London, Dobson, 1965.
Land of the Scots. London, Hodder and Stoughton, and New
    York, Weybright and Talley, 1968.
The Queen's Scotland. London, Hodder and Stoughton, 4 vols.,
    1971–77.
Portrait of the Border Country. London, Hale, 1972.
Portrait of the Lothians. London, Hale, 1979; revised edition,
    as *The Illustrated Portrait of the Border Country*, London,
    Hale, 1987.
Nigel Tranter's Scotland: A Very Personal View. Glasgow,
    Drew, 1981.
Scottish Castles: Tales and Traditions. London, Macdonald,
    1982.
The Travellers Guide to the Scotland of Robert the Bruce, with
    Michael Cyprien. London, Routledge, 1985.
The Story of Scotland. London, Routledge, 1987.

Editor, *No Tigers in the Hindu Kush*, by Philip Tranter. London,
    Hodder and Stoughton, 1968.

*

Manuscript Collection: National Library of Scotland, Edinburgh.

Nigel Tranter comments:
    Wrote ordinary novels of adventure and romance, usually set
in Scotland, from 1938 onwards, including four written in army
during active service. In 1961 wrote *The Master of Gray*, first of
long and carefully researched historical novels, since when have
concentrated on these, in an attempt to cover most of the spectrum of Scotland's colourful and dramatic story, in a way which
would make it palatable for the ordinary reader who would seldom open a "straight" history book. Have endeavoured to stick
closely to fact as far as possible with the very minimum of invented characters.

*   *   *

Nigel Tranter is a prolific writer of historical novels dealing
with almost every aspect and every period of Scottish history—
indeed to read his books is to take a painless course in that subject. He is obviously a scrupulous and indefatigable researcher,
setting great store by accuracy, and he turns history into novels
by adding romantic fiction to historical fact. For instance, in
Gold for Prince Charlie the historical fact that the French gold
which was sent to Scotland in 1745 arrived too late to be of use
in the Jacobite rebellion is used to make an exciting adventure
for Duncan McGregor and Caroline Cameron. In *MacGregor's
Gathering* he uses the facts that Rob Roy strove to get the pro-
scription of the clan lifted and that he was against the Act of
Union, but adds to that the love story of Rob Roy's nephew. *The
Clansman* is Tranter's interpretation of Rob Roy's behaviour at
Sherrifmuir when he did not fight but held the MacGregors im-
mobile in the midst of battle.

But Tranter's real forte is the fictional biography. He has covered practically the whole conspectus of Scottish history in a
series of biographical novels, beginning in the Celtic twilight
with *Macbeth the King*, in which he gives us something different
from the dramatic but inaccurate picture drawn by Shakespeare
and puts Macbeth where he belongs in Scottish history. In *Margaret the Queen* he draws a portrait of the Saxon princess who
married Malcolm Canmore and civilised the Scottish court.
Margaret was made a saint but she emerges from the book as a
warm human being. *David the Prince* tells of Scotland in the
12th century, and the 13th century is covered by *True Thomas*, a
book which puts at the centre the legendary Thomas the
Rhymer, poet and prophet, rather than Alexander III, although
we learn his story too. *The Wallace* continues the account of that
bleak, cruel era when England and Scotland were perpetually at
war. Wallace is, of course, one of Scotland's great heroes and is
so portrayed by Tranter, and Edward I (known to English history
as Longshanks and Lawgiver and above all Hammer of the
Scots) emerges as a double-dyed villain. All these books lead up
to Robert the Bruce, the most famous Scottish king who is
known even to English children because of the spider—Tranter
takes three books to tell his story, *The Steps to the Empty
Throne*, *The Path of the Hero King*, and *The Price of the King's
Peace*.

There are many more historical novels: the rise of the house of
Stuart is covered in *Lords of Misrule*, *A Folly of Princes*, and
The Captive Crown, and so it goes on through the years. *Lion
Let Loose* tells of James I, *Chain of Destiny* James IV, and his
series featuring the Master of Grey contrasts the Tudor court of
Elizabeth with the Scottish court. All these books are craftsmanlike works with accurate history, but alas with no great sense of
period. You do not get the feeling which some novelists convey
that through the eyes of the main character you are looking at a
very different scene, living at a different period, assessing things
differently because the values of that character are different from
your own. You never seem to get inside the skins of the people
of earlier times. The dialogue is stilted and often very strangely
punctuated. Although I admire his industry and his accuracy,
Tranter's books do not come alive for me.

—Pamela Cleaver

TRASK, Betty (Margaret Elizabeth Trask). British. Born in
1895. Lived in Frome, Somerset. *Died in January 1983*.

ROMANCE AND HISTORICAL PUBLICATIONS

Novels

Cotton Glove Country. London, Hodder and Stoughton, 1928.
Flute, Far and Near. London, Hodder and Stoughton, 1929.
Beauty, Retire. London, Hutchinson, 1932.
How Change the Moons. London, Hutchinson, 1932.
Mannequin. London, Collins, 1933.
A Bus at the Ritz. London, Collins, 1935.
Only the Best. London, Collins, 1935.
Desire Me Not. London, Collins, 1935.
Rustle of Spring. London, Collins, 1936.
Enticement. London, Collins, 1936.
She Shall Be Queen. London, Collins, 1936.
I Tell My Heart. London, Collins, 1937.
Love with a Song. London, Collins, 1937.
Feather Your Nest. London, Collins, 1938.
Give Me My Youth. London, Collins, 1938.
Love Locked Out. London, Collins, 1938.
Love Has No Limits. London, Collins, 1939.
Love Has Wings. London, Collins, 1939.
The Sun Fades the Stars. London, Collins, 1940.
Ring of Roses. London, Collins, 1940.
From Here to a Star. London, Collins, 1941.
Change for a Farthing. London, Collins, 1942.
Promise. London, Collins, 1944.
Pride to the Winds. London, Hale, 1946.
I Will Be True. London, Hale, 1948.
Evergold. London, Hale, 1950.
Grand. London, Hale, 1951.
Thunder Rose. London, Hale, 1952.
And Confidential. London, Hale, 1953.
Just a Song at Sunrise. London, Hale, 1954.
Bitter Sweetbriar. London, Hale, 1955.
Irresistible. London, Hale, 1955.
The Merry Belles of Bath. London, Hale, 1957.

*   *   *

The works of Betty Trask had virtually been forgotten when in 1983 her estate bequeathed £400,000 to the Society of Authors to fund the Betty Trask award, then Britain's richest literary prize. Surprisingly, for a woman whose generous bequest continues to sponsor new writing in the romance genre, in most of her own work Trask merely flirts with the theme of romance. The eventual outcome of her novels is of love won at last—or tainted forever, yet the path to one or other ending is indistinct, a side issue almost. It is an expression, perhaps, of the virtuous posture of postwar little England in which couples met and married, apparently having the decency to know little about one another as they tied the knot. Trask's would-be lovers admire from a distance or have brief, rather meaningless encounters during which the flames of passion are somehow fanned.

Towards the end of *Irresistible*, Dr. Meynell, "the most handsome young man in Vidcomb," meets his love, Terry Roper, in a tea shop. Until this point, they have met infrequently and only in the early stages of the novel is there any mention of an attraction between them. At first sight there is a deep sensuality when they are together, heightened by the fact that Terry Roper is married to the parson and therefore forbidden territory, but this tails off disappointingly. Between these points however, Trask weaves a complex tale around an indomitable European dancer who takes over the doctor's house. So powerful is this subplot that it eclipses the relationship between Terry Roper and Dr. Meynell. When they eventually meet in the tea shop (Terry Roper now released from her husband by his sudden death) they converse drably and there seems little reason for the doctor's anger at her apparent indifference to him—he has been sidetracked too long, and so have we. Oddly enough, the European dancer then fades from the scene and another strong subplot is killed off by a falling statue. Red herrings disposed of, the Roper/Meynell story is revealed as the novel's raison d'être and Meynell decides suddenly to marry his love.

And Confidential has as its central character a middle-aged estate agent who, twice widowed, is now beyond any desire for romantic liaison. He is an observer and it is through his eyes that we experience the love affairs of the young. These involve a quartet of characters: his youngest daughter; a disinherited poetess; a moody eccentric poet; and an unspecified young man named Tony Hertford. Yet here again Trask creates an intricate story which is eventually left hanging. The only resolution is of who ends up with whom out of the four. However, this is the sole clue for love interest being the novel's main subject. Unfortunately, the middle-aged observer is kept out of the picture, the affairs of the young being no business of his. As he then has only few occasions to exercise his intuition and as this is largely unreliable, we are left rather confused as to how, or if, the lovers have been loving at all.

Trask's problem in these books is that they revolve around decent, middle-class characters who live in small, nosey communities. They are hidebound by etiquette and a tendency to bury their emotions from the gaze of the outside world. Trask sometimes manages to release her characters and her writing from these narrow constraints, by the introduction of less conventional characters. These are frequently the personalities who form the subplots and are largely responsible for the loss of interest in the duller lovers at the centre of the action. Mme. Doré, for instance, is the dancer in *Irresistible*. She explodes onto the scene, invites herself into Dr. Meynell's house, and makes an excellent job of running his life. She struts and orders in the truly irresistible style of a European matriarch with just a trace of broken English. She has a startling intuitive skill too. When walking into a deserted house with Dr. Meynell, she says: "I will tell you the trouble which I sense as if I smelt it. Wicked persons, and worse, weak ones, have had power here. And foolish ones plan to come but perhaps they will learn wisdom." Mme. Doré is such a tour de force that both Dr. Meynell and the reader believe she will be proved right. All the more anticlimactic when Trask fails to investigate Mme. Doré's suspicions further. The house stands empty and as the novel progresses, Mme. Doré becomes increasingly, and inexplicably, "cool, detached and monstrously polite." Trask's story and writing miss her badly.

Other such characters appear in the novels, all notably irrelevant to the love interest. Malevolent servants abound. There is a Dickensian pair in *And Confidential*; one a "round-shouldered gnome," the other sporting "truncheon elbows" and a "nasty mouth." Meanwhile, poor Dr. Meynell lives under the shadow of his Irish housekeeper who entered his service "with the intention of doing exactly as she pleased, which was very little when it was a question of keeping the place tidy, but far too much when it came to interfering." In *The Merry Belles of Bath*, a simplified *Pride and Prejudice*, a fantastic opera singer is introduced. He makes his entrance, "a vast pink carnation topping the profile of a huge masculine chest" and converses with an intermittent exclamation of "do-do-mi-rée-boum!" Eventually, he bursts into song in the middle of a chintzed drawing room. Sadly, he like the others makes a token appearance only, though one feels that were he to stay longer, the demands of sustaining such a strong character would eventually fail Trask, as happens with Mme. Doré.

There is an exception in the novel *Just a Song at Sunrise*. Here, the central character, Fairlight Vivian, is not accepted by small-town society. She is one of the "less conventional" characters usually reserved for a bit-part. Described as "outlandish" by the local matron, she is free to display real passion and so is released from the everydayness of the other lovers. She shivers with delight when invited into "the set," yet recognises how "stony and unforgiving" it can be. And, being "x-ho-tick," she may kiss her lover before the end of the novel, waylaying him half way through. She is the one who "presses her cheek against his breast" and whose "lips start questing." Fairlight Vivian is black and although the setting is not dissimilar from that in *Irresistible* or *And Confidential,* she is not bound by the etiquette of the other leading characters, even though she does strive to acquire it. The love interest here shares its motive with the rest of the novel. Fairlight at first assumes rejection, then challenges indifference and eventually knows that she will rise above it to become not just accepted, but a leader. The strength of this character is demonstrated by the fact that Trask does not entirely resolve the story. It has become unnecessary because the character has grown through the novel. In the weaker novels, all the nothingness must be explained, for without real motive having been established, it would be impossible to predict an outcome.

Just a Song at Sunrise is problematic in a modern context. In its attempt to accommodate and understand immigrant feeling in 1950's Britain it is naive and its liberal views mildly racist. Fairlight Vivian is a sympathetic character because she assimilates into an English country lifestyle. Her flamboyant mother and brother by comparison are endearing figures of fun, though Trask does seem to admire and perhaps even envy them. Some of her most sensuous writing pictures a scene in which the whole Vivian family breaks into song over dinner:

> Mom started to croon, little Robbitt scrambled into her lap and blew into her breast as into a great grand trombone. Victor got up and turned on the wireless and whistled to it . . . from the vast rosette of his pursed lips came long, irresistible mating calls . . . Then Fairlight began to sing against, with and glorying over the whistling, the wireless, the crooning and Robbitt's musical bubble in and out of the maternal trombone.

Scenes like this recur throughout the book and it is a relief to discover that the flashes of inventive description and well-observed characterisation seen in other Trask novels can permeate an entire story and create a satisfying whole. The romance is more exciting for being tinged with a little seediness as well as spice, while both main and subplots maintain their direction. They are drawn together by the actions and feelings of Fairlight Vivian.

If Trask's plots generally suffer from coyness and inconsistency, she was a writer who could be sensitive, amusing, and sensual when non-conformity burst into her books. It is a pity that *Just a Song at Sunrise* is one of the few examples which display Trask's real ability and which show her to be a more imaginative and truly romantic writer than she perhaps allowed.

—Pat Gordon-Smith

* * *

TREECE, Henry. British. Born in Wednesbury, Staffordshire, 22 December 1911. Educated at Wednesbury High School for Boys; Birmingham University, B.A. 1933, Dip. Ed. 1934. Served in the Royal Air Force, 1941–46: Flight Lieutenant. Married Mary Woodman in 1939; two sons and one daughter. Teacher, Leicestershire Home Office School, Shustoke, 1934; English master, The College, Cleobury Mortimer, Shropshire, 1934–35, and Tynemouth School for Boys, Northumberland, 1935–38; English master, 1938–41, and senior English master, 1946–59, Barton on Humber Grammar School, Lincolnshire. Recipient: Arts Council prize, for play, 1955. *Died 10 June 1966.*

ROMANCE AND HISTORICAL PUBLICATIONS

Novels

The Dark Island. London, Gollancz, and New York, Random House, 1952; as *The Savage Warriors*, New York, Avon, 1959.
The Rebels. London, Gollancz, 1953.
The Golden Strangers. London, Lane, 1956; New York, Random House, 1957; as *The Invaders*, New York, Avon, 1960.
The Great Captains. London, Lane, and New York, Random House, 1956.
Red Queen, White Queen. London, Bodley Head, and New York, Random House, 1958; as *The Pagan Queen*, New York, Avon, 1959.
The Master of Badger's Hall. New York, Random House, 1959; as *A Fighting Man*, London, Bodley Head, 1960.
Jason. London, Bodley Head, and New York, Random House, 1961.
The Amber Princess. New York, Random House, 1962; as *Electra*, London, Bodley Head, 1963.
Oedipus. London, Bodley Head, 1964; as *The Eagle King*, New York, Random House, 1965.
The Green Man. London, Bodley Head, and New York, Putnam, 1966.

Short Stories

I Cannot Go Hunting Tomorrow. London, Grey Walls Press, 1946.

OTHER PUBLICATIONS

Plays

Carnival King (produced Nottingham, 1954). London, Faber, 1955.
Footsteps in the Sea (produced Nottingham, 1955).
Hounds of the King, with Two Radio Plays (for children; includes *Harold Godwinson* and *William, Duke of Normandy*). London, Longman, 1965.

Radio Plays: *Harold Godwinson*, 1954; *William, Duke of Normandy*, 1954.

Verse

38 Poems. London, Fortune Press, 1940.
Towards a Personal Armageddon. Prairie City, Illinois, Press of James A. Decker, 1941.
Invitation and Warning. London, Faber, 1942.
The Black Seasons. London, Faber, 1945.
Collected Poems. New York, Knopf, 1946.
The Haunted Garden. London, Faber, 1947.
The Exiles. London, Faber, 1952.

Other (for children)

Legions of the Eagle. London, Lane, 1954.
The Eagles Have Flown. London, Lane, 1954.
Desperate Journey. London, Faber, 1954.
Ask for King Billy. London, Faber, 1955.
Viking's Dawn. London, Lane, 1955; New York, Criterion, 1956.
Hounds of the King. London, Lane, 1955.
Men of the Hills. London, Lane, 1957; New York, Criterion, 1958.
The Road to Miklagard. London, Lane, and New York, Criterion, 1957.
Hunter Hunted. London, Faber, 1957.
Don't Expect Any Mercy! London, Faber, 1958.
The Children's Crusade. London, Bodley Head, 1958; as *Perilous Pilgrimage*, New York, Criterion, 1959.
The Return of Robinson Crusoe. London, Hulton Press, 1958; as *The Further Adventures of Robinson Crusoe*, New York, Criterion, 1958.
The Bombard. London, Bodley Head, 1959; as *Ride to Danger*, New York, Criterion, 1959.
Wickham and the Armada. London, Hulton Press, 1959.
Castles and Kings. London, Batsford, 1959; New York, Criterion, 1960.
The True Book about Castles. London, Muller, 1960.
Viking's Sunset. London, Bodley Head, 1960; New York, Criterion, 1961.
Red Settlement. London, Bodley Head, 1960.
The Jet Beads. Leicester, Brockhampton Press, 1961.
The Golden One. London, Bodley Head, 1961; New York, Criterion, 1962.
Man with a Sword. London, Bodley Head, 1962; New York, Pantheon, 1964.
War Dog. Leicester, Brockhampton Press, 1962; New York, Criterion, 1963.
Horned Helmet. Leicester, Brockhampton Press, and New York, Criterion, 1963.
Know about the Crusades. London, Blackie, 1963; as *About the Crusades*, Chester Springs, Pennsylvania, Dufour, 1966.
Fighting Men: How Men Have Fought Through the Ages, with Ewart Oakeshott. Leicester, Brockhampton Press, 1963.
The Burning of Njal. London, Bodley Head, and New York, Criterion, 1964.
The Last of the Vikings. Leicester, Brockhampton Press, 1964; as *The Last Viking*, New York, Pantheon, 1966.
The Bronze Sword. London, Hamish Hamilton, 1965; augmented edition, as *The Centurian*, New York, Meredith Press, 1967.
Splintered Sword. Leicester, Brockhampton Press, 1965; New York, Duell, 1966.
Killer in Dark Glasses. London, Faber, 1965.
Bang, You're Dead! London, Faber, 1966.
The Queen's Brooch. London, Hamish Hamilton, 1966; New York, Putnam, 1967.
Swords from the North. London, Faber, and New York, Pantheon, 1967.
The Windswept City. London, Hamish Hamilton, 1967; New York, Meredith Press, 1968.
Vinland the Good. London, Bodley Head, 1967; as *Westward to Vinland*, New York, Phillips, 1967.
The Dream-Time. Leicester, Brockhampton Press, 1967; New York, Meredith Press, 1968.
The Invaders: Three Stories. Leicester, Brockhampton Press, and New York, Crowell, 1972.

Other

How I See Apocalypse. London, Drummond, 1946.
Dylan Thomas: "Dog among the Fairies." London, Drummond, 1949; New York, de Graff, 1954; revised edition, London, Benn, and New York, de Graff, 1956.
The Crusades. London, Bodley Head, and New York, Random House, 1962.

Editor, with J. F. Hendry, *The New Apocalypse.* London, Fortune Press, 1939.
Editor, with J. F. Hendry, *The White Horseman: Prose and Verse of the New Apocalypse.* London, Routledge, 1941.
Editor, with Stefan Schimanski, *Wartime Harvest.* London, Bale and Staples, 1943.
Editor, with Stefan Schimanski, *Transformation.* London, Gollancz, 1943.
Editor, with Stefan Schimanski, *Transformation 2–4.* London, Drummond, 3 vols., 1944–47.
Editor, *Herbert Read: An Introduction.* London, Faber, 1944; Port Washington, New York, Kennikat Press, 1969.
Editor, with John Pudney, *Air Force Poetry.* London, Lane, 1944.
Editor, with Stefan Schimanski, *A Map of Hearts: A Collection of Short Stories.* London, Drummond, 1944.
Editor, with J. F. Hendry, *The Crown and the Sickle: An Anthology.* London, King and Staples, 1945.
Editor, with Stefan Schimanski, *Leaves in the Storm: A Book of Diaries.* London, Drummond, 1947.
Editor, *Selected Poems*, by Algernon Charles Swinburne. London, Grey Walls Press, 1948.
Editor, with Stefan Schimanski, *New Romantic Anthology.* London, Grey Walls Press, 1949.

*

Critical Study: *Henry Treece* by Margery Fisher (includes bibliography by Antony Kamm), in *Three Bodley Head Monographs*, London, Bodley Head, 1969.

*   *   *

Henry Treece depicts a universe in the throes of violent change. His characters move through overturning worlds, proud but lonely figures in the eye of the storm. Delving back through history for the roots of primal myth, Treece explores the nature of kingship, its attributes of godhead and sacrifice, presenting individuals in situations of fearful choice. At once heroic and tragic, his re-creation of past ages and leaders celebrates while at the same time foretelling the inevitable catastrophe. A chronicler of violence, he is also an advocate of peace, stressing the need for reconciliation between victor and vanquished.

A late convert to literature, Treece came to the novel last of all, following recognition as a poet and radio dramatist. The apprenticeship proved useful, adding to the broader view of the novelist a poetic concentration of utterance and a feeling for dramatic construction and dialogue. The New Apocalypse poetic movement of which he was a founding member championed individual expression and the need for a unifying myth representative of the age, both vital aspects of Treece's personal vision. His athletic abilities provided a further dimension, lending his novels a unique animal vigour. Treece's writings share a striking visual power, long-vanished cultures presented with a force so breath-taking they seem to be less read than encountered intuitively through the senses. Yet closer analysis reveals the strong, controlling intelligence behind them.

The early stories in *I Cannot Go Hunting Tomorrow* show a writer still seeking an individual voice, and are competent but derivative. An exception is "The Visitor," in which a tense account of a youth held at knifepoint by a psychopathic killer convinces utterly, and prefigures later use of the life-and-death situation in Treece's fiction. The title story, set in Roman Britain, is less powerful, but its concept and characters foreshadow his first novel, *The Dark Island*. This novel marks the emergence of Treece as a mature stylist. In it he describes the overthrow of the Catuvellauni, the destruction of the fixed order of their world by the Roman legions, and the downfall of their leader Caradoc. In a charged poetic prose, Treece traces the inexorable decline, revealing the flaws in the nature of the Celts that render them vulnerable to defeat. A grim, mysterious, smoky work of fiction, *Dark Island* impresses by its visual and narrative force, bringing to life a hostile world and its lurking tribal magic. Although it is Treece's earliest novel, it is one of his best.

The Rebels, set in Victorian Staffordshire, explores the same theme in personal terms, showing the secure, privileged world of the Fisher family at the moment of disintegration. Unusually ambitious, it moves backward through chronological time, the opening scene gradually explained by various family members. The book is not completely successful—there are imbalances between individual sections, and too much secondary detail—but is nevertheless a powerful, compelling work. *The Great Captains* and *The Golden Strangers* complete the early phase of Treece's writing and constitute an advance on previous work. The former, an inspired, realistic portrayal of Arthurian legend, is a tour de force. Artos, the Celtic chieftain, is presented as a complex figure, half-savage yet a champion of Romano-British civilization against the invading Saxons. His doomed, heroic stand against the inevitable barbarian triumph is superbly evoked, Treece's vision of a desolate, ruined Britain living on in the mind. *The Golden Strangers*, one of his finest novels, records the collapse of the Neolithic culture at the hands of the Celts. Both peoples are brilliantly brought alive on the page, Treece seeming instinctively to enter the minds of his creations and their binding laws of ritual and taboo. Garroch, tribal chief and sacrificial god-king, is portrayed as the archetype of all mythic heroes. Following him through the ritual dances, hunts, and battles, Treece blasts the consciousness of the reader with the sight, sound and scent of a vanished age. His grasp of the preliterate sensibility, the complexity of a supposedly "primitive" culture, is stunning in its conviction. A milestone of achievement, *Golden Strangers* succeeds totally and remains unique. Later works equal, but do not surpass it.

Red Queen, White Queen and *A Fighting Man* are lesser novels, but possess virtues of their own. The first, set at the time of Boudicca's rebellion, is the nearest thing to an "entertainment" its author ever wrote. Fast-paced and enjoyable, its tragic theme is offset by bawdy humour and a final, moving reconciliation. *A Fighting Man* pictures the downfall of a Regency prize-fighter, who as an aged pauper recounts this days of glory from the workhouse in the manner of Oedipus at Colonus. It suffers from an over-elaborate plot whose loose ends are abruptly tied, but remains an effective portrayal of an elegant but vicious age.

With his trilogy of Greek novels Treece embarked on the final phase of his search, pursuing classical myth to its prehistoric origins, his individual tragedies cast against the background of worlds in turmoil. In *Jason*, where themes of identity, godhead, and quest pulse behind the narrative, the Minoan-Hellene conflict endures in a struggle between kings and priestesses, typified by Jason's lover and nemesis, the sinister Medea. A dark, terrifying work, *Jason* is overlong and lacks the coherence of *Electra*, where related themes are explored more narrowly but with greater intensity. The most perfectly balanced of the trilogy, *Electra* has a tighter construction that lends its message an added force. Here, as in *Jason*, Treece tears aside the veneer of civilisation to reveal the grim, bestial urges beneath. Both novels reek with darkness and corruption, their revelations increasingly repellent. Each is a tribute to the author who brings them so horribly to life. *Oedipus*, last of the sequence, breaks fresh ground, Treece attempting a synthesis of myths as he follows the club-foot hero—a child-man seeking father and mother—through the murky, violent world of prehistoric Greece. God-king and sacrificial scapegoat, Oedipus serves as a focus for the flux of migrating nations that merges Aryans and Nilotic African herders, and battles for supremacy with the priestess-queen Jocasta. Less overtly violent than its predecessors, *Oedipus* exudes a sense of looming horror, and in two extended dream-sequences interweaves myths and gods alike as Oedipus metamorphoses into Christ, Krishna, Arthur, and Hamlet. Using a hard, pared style Treece explores the fascinating blend of cultures that constitutes the ancient Mediterranean. An accomplished work, *Oedipus* with its attempted intermeshing of myths looks forward to *The Green Man* and the culmination of Treece's achievement.

In *The Green Man*, exploring the Hamlet legend to its Dark Age origins, Treece recreates a brutal age whose archetypal hero-figures embody basic animal urges, and whose underlying theme is the continual cyclic process of growth and decay. The intricate plot takes in murder, incest, madness and parricide, and accommodates several distinct mythic heroes. In a honed, bardic style reminiscent of Scandinavian saga, Treece brings each man powerfully to life—Amleth, the murderous innocent and potent fertility symbol, reincarnated as the Green Man; Beowulf, vainglorious and cunning, a formidable warrior terrified at the thought of his own mortality; and Arthur, the bitter, crippled veteran to whom Amleth appears as son and rival. These and others follow the story to its fearsome conclusion. Treece's poetic and intuitive qualities are at their most inspired, his pared style complementing a stunning visual sense. *The Green Man* completes the author's search, the unifying myth superbly achieved in a narrative which blends separate mythic strands into a single impressive work of art.

Treece's writing for younger readers parallels his adult novels, advancing from simple adventure stories like *Desperate Journey* and *Ask for King Billy* to a more mature form of expression. His Romano-British novels, *Legions of the Eagle* and *The Eagles Have Flown*, combine exciting action with deeper portrayals of the nature of friendship and betrayal against the background of war. The same is true of his magnificent Viking trilogy—*Viking's Dawn, The Road to Miklagard, Viking's Sunset*—which memorably evokes that restless, violent age. Treece returned to the same era with retellings of saga (*The Burning of Njal*) and the lives of such heroes as Hereward and Harald Hardrada, gradually adopting a terse, laconic style shorn of nonessential elements. As adventure gave way to deeper perceptions, he re-emphasized the necessity for peace and co-operation, a message enshrined in his final masterpiece, *The Dream-Time*. Set in the prehistoric past, and spanning several evolutionary periods, *The Dream-Time* presents the creative power of art as a positive force against the negatives of war, distrust, and separation. Twilight, the craftsman hero, in his search for new artistic forms, his hatred of taboos, wars, and secret languages, strongly expresses the author's beliefs. Treece ends by affirming the strength of dreams in this last and most appealing of his works.

—Geoffrey Sadler

TREMAINE, Jennie. See **CHESNEY, Marion.**

TRESILLIAN, Richard. Also writes as Richard Devine. Address: c/o Century Hutchinson Ltd., 62–65 Chandos Place, London WC2N 4NW, England.

ROMANCE AND HISTORICAL PUBLICATIONS

Novels (series: Bloodheart; Bondmaster)

The Bondmaster. London, Arlington, 1977.
Blood of the Bondmaster. New York, Warner, 1977; London, Arlington, 1978.
The Bondmaster Breed. London, Arlington, 1979.
Fleur. London, Arlington, 1979.
Bondmaster Fury. London, Arlington, 1982.
Bondmaster's Revenge. London, Arlington, 1983.
Bondmaster Buck. London, Arlington, 1984.
Bloodheart. London, Century, 1985.
Bloodheart Royal. London, Century, 1986.
Bloodheart Feud. London, Sphere, 1988.
Giselle. London, Century, 1988.

Novels as Raynard Devine (series: The Flesh Traders, in all books)

Master of Black River. London, Futura, 1984.
Black River Affair. London, Futura, 1985.
Black River Breed. London, Futura, 1985.
Revenge at Black River. London, Futura, 1985.

*   *   *

There is always tension in the sultry, enervating air in Richard Tresillian's *Bondmaster* saga, and lust, fear, and violence make an explosive mixture. The setting of the novels is the remote Roxborough Estate on the West Indian island of Dominica, a British colony then, and the period is the early decades of the 19th century when increasingly effective regulation of the slave trade made it essential to replace traditional methods of supplementing the workforce by importing fresh slaves with a programme of making the best use of existing resources by breeding from existing stock. All thought of humanity is forgotten; the black slaves are treated like animals, and the terminology employed—bucks, fillies, whelps and so on—is borrowed flagrantly from the stock yard. The only concern shown for the individuals lies in their masters' desire to control mating so that the young men shall not become exhausted by over-exertion and so that the characteristics of the various African tribes are blended to produce offspring particularly suited to the various tasks to which they will be put later on in life, when they are sold on to new owners.

The Todds, the masters of Roxborough, live far from other Europeans, though they visit them from time to time, even crossing the Atlantic on occasion. Most of the time, however, they spend alone on the estate, quaffing rum, though sugar production has ceased to be the major business that once it was, keeping up some pretence of genteel manners, trying to preserve some heritage for the next generation, and finding sexual gratification with the privileged slaves who tend them in their home. For the men—the gentlemen, as they prefer to regard themselves—there are satisfactions in maintaining grim discipline among the slaves, and when they are bored they will go to the town for a break. The white women have a harder lot; when, to relieve the tedium and enjoy some tenderness, they turn to the more handsome of the slaves, a harsh double standard operates. What is acceptable in their husbands—even commendable, since light-skinned slaves command high prices—is regarded as abhorrent in their womenfolk, and savage retribution swiftly follows. Roxborough represents a society in decline, with poverty always a prospect and with rebellion, either by the slaves on the estate or by others who have run away earlier and formed desperate bands up in the hills, a menace which can never be entirely ignored. As tensions mount, the novels present a steady escalation of horror until it seems that there is no imaginable inhumanity left to inflict. There is, it is plain, some historical warrant for the picture presented here, but the piling up of atrocities eventually becomes hard to swallow and some readers will judge that the novels are too sensational to be genuinely sensuous.

The narrative moves rapidly, and the saga is so constructed that any individual novel can be read separately, though it is best to master the family tree before beginning the text as it contains facts of which even those characters most concerned are sometimes unaware until it is too late. Tresillian uses a sober style for the white masters of Roxborough with just the occasional turn of phrase that reminds us of the period of the novels. What mainly characterises their speech is an unremitting directness in their references to the bodies and breeding of the slaves; as Carlton Todd puts it in *The Bondmaster's Revenge*, "false modesty don't belong in a slave breeder." Into the mouths of the slaves Tressillian puts a creole dialect, a form of English with a much simplified grammar, which serves as a constant indicator of their inferior status, just as the occasional unfamiliar noun, derived from French or local patois, helps create the West Indian scene.

The geographical location is different in the two volumes of *The Fleshtraders*, set in Mauritius, and in the *Bloodheart* novels—which relate the introduction of West Indian slavers methods in Ceylon at the beginning of the 19th century—and in *Fleur*—which sees things rather more from a female viewpoint in the American south just before the Civil War. The major theme of different races in close proximity remains, however, much the same, as does its underpinning with historical fact and, equally important, a sense of period.

—Christopher Smith

TROLLOPE, Joanna. Also writes as Caroline Harvey. British. Born in Gloucestershire, 9 December 1943. Educated at St. Hugh's College, Oxford (Gamble scholar), 1962–65, M.A. in English 1972. Married 1) David Potter in 1966, two daughters; 2) the playwright Ian Curteis in 1985. Research assistant, Foreign Office, London, 1965–67; teacher in preparatory schools and adult foreign student classes, 1968–78. Recipient: Romantic Novelists Association Major award, 1980. Agent: A. D. Peters, Fifth Floor, The Chambers, Chelsea Harbour, Lots

Road, London SW10 0XF. Address: The Mill House, Coln St. Aldwyns, Cirencester, Gloucestershire, England.

ROMANCE AND HISTORICAL PUBLICATIONS

Novels

Eliza Stanhope. London, Hutchinson, 1978; New York, Dutton, 1979.
Parson Harding's Daughter. London, Hutchinson, 1979; as *Mistaken Virtues*, New York, Dutton, 1980.
Leaves from the Valley. London, Hutchinson, 1980; New York, St. Martin's Press, 1984.
The City of Gems. London, Hutchinson, 1981.
The Steps of the Sun. London, Hutchinson, 1983; New York, St. Martin's Press, 1984.
The Taverners' Place. London, Hutchinson, 1986; New York, St. Martin's Press, 1987.

Novels as Caroline Harvey (series: Legacy of Love)

Legacy of Love. London, Octopus, 1983.
  Charlotte. London, Sundial, 1980.
  Alexandra. London, Sundial, 1980.
  Cara. London, Octopus, 1983.

OTHER PUBLICATIONS

Novels

The Choir. London, Hutchinson, 1988.
A Village Affair. London, Bloomsbury, 1989.

Other

Britannia's Daughters: Women of the British Empire. London, Hutchinson, 1983.

*

Joanna Trollope comments:

There are, certainly, love stories in my books, but they are only a part of the whole. The whole is my desire to bring history to life, not just to superimpose a 20th-century story on to a historical background. I want to give a sense of life as it was lived in the past, and to that end I do more than twice as much research as I need for each book so that I am, myself, thoroughly familiar with each period.

*   *   *

Joanna Trollope, who also writes as Caroline Harvey, writes excellent historical novels. In order to explore events of the past, she puts her fictional characters into real situations, but what makes her books unusual is that she gives her heroines serious flaws in their character (often due to youth, inexperience, or a misguided upbringing) which they have to overcome before the happy ending. Eliza Stanhope, the eponymous heroine of Trollope's first novel is described as "not being like other women and she did like doing what was forbidden," and this could apply to nearly all Trollope's heroines.

Eliza goes to Brussels and the battlefield of Waterloo following her husband. She is willful and arrogant but learns humility and gains maturity through assisting a surgeon on the battlefield and nursing her wounded husband. Caroline, in *Parson Harding's Daughter*, lacks self-confidence and finds it hard to accept gracefully what is offered her out of kindness or love. She has a very hard time in 18th-century India. Trapped in a loveless marriage, she finds true love with another but cannot for some time accept the happiness she is offered. This book deservedly won the Romantic Novelists Association Major award.

Maria in *The City of Gems* is a maddening character—the sort of person with whom it is difficult to empathise. She is arrogant, selfish, and imperious. Against the background of the barbaric splendor of Mandalay in the 1880's, she finally learns a little graciousness, but almost too late. Other characters are more interesting—pale Grace Prior, the missionary's daughter, and Archie Tennant, the only man who understands Maria although the reader is tempted to wonder why such an attractive person should bother with her.

In *The Steps of the Sun* there is no obvious hero or heroine and all the main characters have faults to overcome. The Boer War is seen through the eyes of several people. There is scapegrace Matthew Paget who falls in love with the country and a Boer girl; his cousin Will, a regular soldier who finds war less to his taste than he expected and comes home to face a court martial; Adelaide Munro, a supporter of women's suffrage who goes to South Africa to nurse; and Frances Paget, torn between Will and a peace-supporting journalist Oliver, who stays in England and is a "new woman"—one of the first to study at Oxford.

Legacy of Love, written as Caroline Harvey, is an omnibus containing three stories in a family saga, written in a lighter vein. *Charlotte*, a vivid adventurous girl, marries Hugh to get away from her claustrophobic life in Richmond and to follow him to India, dragging her timid sister Emily (the narrator) in her wake. Charlotte falls in love with India and when they are in Kabul finds her true love too late. They are all caught up in the doomed retreat and after much adventure, find their way to a happy ending. *Alexandra* is Charlotte's granddaughter. Her life in Edwardian Scotland is dull and empty until great-aunt Emily invites her to Cornwall where she makes mistakes, learns many lessons, finds contentment in farming, and knows love at last. *Cara* is Alexandra's daughter. She is spoiled, selfish, and overconfident. At the outbreak of World War I she is longing to leave Cornwall and go into the services. But Alexandra has an accident and Cara has to stay at home as a land girl which she loathes and which makes her sulky. She, too, has many painful lessons to learn before she finally finds love and fulfillment.

Writing under either name Trollope excels in description. She is equally good describing colourful bazaars in India, the beauties of the English countryside, the steamy splendour and squalor of Mandalay, or the bare beauty of the African veldt. Her interiors are meticulously observed and graphically rendered. " . . . pictures hung as closely together as if they were stamps in a stamp collection" is an image she obviously likes as she uses it in two of her books.

Each one of Trollope's books tells a good story and stands the acid test of the historical novel—that the same story could not have been set in another era; the events of the time shape the action and the thinking. The love stories contained in the books, however, are romantic and universal.

—Pamela Cleaver

TROY, Katherine. See MAYBURY, Anne.

TURNER, Judy. See **SAXTON, Judith.**

VAIZEY, Mrs. George de Horne. (Jessie Bell Vaizey, née Mansergh). British. Born in 1857.

ROMANCE AND HISTORICAL PUBLICATIONS

Novels (series: Pixie O'Shaughnessy; Peggy Saville)

A Rose-Coloured Thread. London, Bowden, 1898.
About Peggy Saville. London, Religious Tract Society, 1900; New York, Putnam, 1917.
Sisters Three. London and New York, Cassell, 1900.
Tom and Some Other Girls: A Public School Story. London and New York, Cassell, 1901.
More about Peggy. London, Religious Tract Society, 1901.
A Houseful of Girls. London, Religious Tract Society, 1902.
Pixie O'Shaughnessy. London, Religious Tract Society, 1903; Philadelphia, Jacobs, 1907.
More about Pixie. London, Religious Tract Society, 1903.
The Daughters of a Genius: Story of a Brave Endeavour. London, Chambers, and Philadelphia, Lippincott, 1903.
How Like the King. London, Bousfield, 1905.
The Heart of Una Sackville. London, Partridge, 1907.
The Fortunes of the Farrells. London, Religious Tract Society, 1907; Philadelphia, Jacobs, 1908.
Betty Trevor. London, Religious Tract Society, 1907; New York, Putnam, 1917.
Big Game: A Story for Girls. London, Religious Tract Society, 1908.
Flaming June. London, Cassell, 1908.
The Conquest of Chrystabel. London, Cassell, 1909.
A Question of Marriage. London, Hodder and Stoughton, 1910; New York, Putnam, 1911.
Etheldreda the Ready: A School Story. London and New York, Cassell, 1910.
Cynthia Charrington. London and New York, Cassell, 1911.
A Honeymoon in Hiding. London and New York, Cassell, 1911.
The Adventures of Billie Belshaw. London, Mills and Boon, 1912.
A College Girl. London, Religious Tract Society, 1913; New York, Putnam, 1916.
An Unknown Lover. London, Mills and Boon, and New York, Putnam, 1913.
Grizel Married. London, Mills and Boon, 1914; as *Lady Cassandra*, New York, Putnam, 1914.
The Love Affairs of Pixie. London, Religious Tract Society, 1914.
Salt of Life. London, Mills and Boon, 1915.
The Independence of Claire. London, Religious Tract Society, 1915.
The Lady of the Basement Flat. London, Religious Tract Society, 1917.
Harriet Mannering's Paying Guests. London, Mills and Boon, 1917.

Short Stories

Old Friends and New. London, Hodder and Stoughton, 1909.
What a Man Wills. London, Cassell, and New York, Putnam, 1915.

The Right Arm and Other Stories. London, Mills and Boon, 1918.

*   *   *

Most of Mrs. de Horne Vaizey's novels dealt with "the essence of femininity in the springtide of life," and several were originally serialized in the *Girl's Own Paper*. They cannot, however, be classified as children's fiction but are essentially light Edwardian romances designed to appeal both to teenage girls and adult women.

For their time, the stories were refreshingly vigorous. Vaizey sent a string of heroines to college or to embark upon careers, although she actually disapproved of women's suffrage, and considered that men should manage the country and the business world. Even the most lively of her girls would eventually be forced into the realization that a woman's place was firmly in "the shelter of her lover's arms" and subsequently, of course, in acquiescent domesticity.

Her most perceptive and rewarding book is *The Independence of Claire*, which vividly highlights a 19-year-old high-school teacher's struggles against poverty and prejudice, from which romance happily provides the ultimate escape. However, her most loved character is without doubt Pixie O'Shaughnessy, "the wild Irish tornado." Pixie must have been one of the first of the irrepressible Irish heroines who were eventually to become stock figures in the English light fiction genre. She progresses from exuberant schoolgirl—"the joy and terror of the school," in fact—to elegant adult in the course of the three books that describe her exploits.

These and the Peggy Saville stories were the most popular of Vaizey's works, but the author preferred *Salt of Life*, which was based on the experiences of her own family and friends. This is a perceptive and witty story about two families of girls on the threshold of adult life and romance. The romantic threads in her family sagas are low key rather than lush, but nevertheless effective. And at least the male characters for whom her heroines abdicate all their career ambitions are three-dimensional people, and not simply the cyphers of simplistic (and boring) masculinity that are featured in more run-of-the-mill romantic novels.

—Mary Cadogan

VALENTINE, Jo. See **ARMSTRONG, Charlotte.**

---

van der ZEE, Karen (a pseudonym). Also writes as Mona van Wieren. Dutch. Born in Sneek, Friesland, Netherlands, 26 May 1947. Educated in the Netherlands. Married in 1969; three children. Has lived in Kenya, Ghana, and Indonesia. Address: c/o Mills and Boon Ltd., 18–24 Paradise Road, Richmond, Surrey TW9 1SR, England.

ROMANCE AND HISTORICAL PUBLICATIONS

Novels

Sweet Not Always. London, Mills and Boon, 1979.

Love Beyond Reason. London, Mills and Boon, 1980.
A Secret Sorrow. London, Mills and Boon, 1981.
Going Underground. London, Mills and Boon, 1982.
Waiting. London, Mills and Boon, 1982.
One More Time. London, Mills and Boon, 1983.
Soul Ties. London, Mills and Boon, 1984.
Staying Close. London, Mills and Boon, 1984.
Pelangi Haven. London, Mills and Boon, 1985.
Fancy Free. London, Mills and Boon, 1986.
Time for Another Dream. London, Mills and Boon, 1986.
Shadows on Bali. London, Mills and Boon, 1988.
Hot Pursuit. London, Mills and Boon, 1988.
Rhapsody in Bloom (as Mona van Wieren). London, Mills and Boon, 1989.
Brazilian Fire. London, Mills and Boon, 1989.

*

Karen van der Zee comments:

I love writing because I am free to use my imagination, to draw word pictures, to create people and feelings—to make something that other people can enjoy. I'd like to think that I can bring to my readers worlds they may have no chance to explore themselves, and show them something new and exciting. This is the reason I like to read myself—entertainment and discovery.

I started writing my first romance in Ghana. I had struggled for years trying to perfect *my* English, as it made no sense to keep writing in Dutch. I'd had a couple of small successes in Holland, and I knew that writing was what I really wanted to do. Needless to say, I was ecstatic when I sold my first novel.

I have written more than 16 romances to date and I still love what I'm doing. I like being my own boss and having the freedom to decide my own work schedule. I think I'll just keep on writing.

*   *   *

Karen van der Zee's romances usually start with an explosive piece of information which the heroine discovers either about herself of someone close to her. This news, usually tragic in nature, becomes the focus around which the rest of the novel evolves and develops. Often the heroine's inability to come to terms with or express the problem she is faced with prevents the otherwise seemingly perfect love relationship. Van der Zee's romances are different from the conventional ones in their characterization. Her heroes are not always inscrutable, mysterious, and hard; rather they are virile and competent, yet tolerant and sensitive. They frequently declare their love or attraction for the heroine early on in the story. It is the woman who is usually burdened with a secret or difficulty which creates a psychological and emotional barrier between the lovers.

Normally the settings for van der Zee's novels are in the United States and the heroines are American girls. However, some heroines travel to distant lands, to Sydney, Bali, or Kenya. While they tend to be young, in their early to mid-twenties, they are educated and have interesting careers or goals. Faye Sherwood in *A Secret Sorrow* is a technical writer and translates French and Spanish, while Kristin in *Staying Close* is working towards a masters degree in Library Science. Beth Anderson in *Going Underground* was one of the top art directors in a big Washington advertising agency by the age of 26. All insist on their independence and would rather not rely on the strong man in their lives to rescue them from their predicament.

The fatal plights that van der Zee's heroines fall into sometimes verge on the melodramatic; nevertheless, they are realistically explained. The author seems to be able to pick out and make use of some of the most common fears women have as the basis for the heroine's quandary in her romances. Two interesting plots involving pregnancy and childbirth occur in *A Secret Sorrow* and *Staying Close*. In *A Secret Sorrow*, Faye finds out that she will be unable to bear children because of abdominal injuries sustained in a serious car accident. While recovering from the shock of the discovery at her brother's home, she meets and slowly falls in love with the handsome and gentle Kai Ellington. He dreams of marrying her and raising their numerous blond, freckled-faced children in a low ranch house in Texas. Much of the novel's emotional power comes from the sensitive psychological exploration of the heroine's source of depression. With insight van der Zee describes the heroine's pain: "She wanted to scream. Children. I'll never have children . . . I'll never waddle around with a big belly worrying if I'll ever get my shape back. I'll never be a mother, never nurse a baby." With Kai's help, Faye learns to accept the inevitable and eventually stops looking at herself as a "machine with a defect."

In *Staying Close* Kristen inadvertently loses her virginity to a close friend who leaves for Tunisia and is subsequently killed. Not realizing that her friend has impregnated her, she goes to spend her Christmas break with her mother and meets her mom's talented step-son Paul who shows her some of the most enchanting sights of Australia. Feeling more than a passing fancy for her Paul comes to visit Kristen four or five months later in the States and discovers that she is very pregnant with someone else's child. Van der Zee's skill shows through when she is able to blend passion with some of the harsher realities of being unwedded at the last trimester of maternity.

Not all her novels are related to pregnancy and babies, however. *Going Underground* deals with a very current and real concern for working women today: the pressures resulting from fulfilling one's ambition in a career and the desire to succeed in an ideal love relationship at the same time. In one of her most sensuous and sexually explicit romances, *Shadows on Bali*, van der Zee resorts to a more conventional plot of the reunion of past and thwarted lovers. This small sample of the ever-increasing work of van der Zee illustrates her dexterity in writing romances which creatively handle some pertinent issues facing women of the 1980's and the 1990's.

—Eleanor Ty

———

VANSITTART, Peter. British. Born in Bedford, 27 August 1920. Educated at Marlborough House School; Haileybury College, Hertford; Worcester College, Oxford (major scholar in modern history). Director, Burgess School, London, 1947–59; formerly, publisher, Park Editions, London. Recipient: Society of Authors travelling scholarship, 1969; Arts Council bursary, 1981, 1984. Fellow, Royal Society of Literature, 1986. Agent: Anthony Sheil Associates Ltd., 43 Doughty Street, London WC1N 2LF. Address: 9 Upper Park Road, London, N.W.3; or, Little Manor, Kersey, Ipswich, Suffolk, England.

ROMANCE AND HISTORICAL PUBLICATIONS

Novels

Lancelot. London, Owen, 1978.
The Death of Robin Hood. London, Owen, 1981.
Harry. London, Park, 1981.
Three Six Seven. London, Owen, 1983.

Parsifal. London, Owen, 1988; Chester Springs, Pennsylvania, Dufour, 1989.

OTHER PUBLICATIONS

Novels

I Am the World. London, Chatto and Windus, 1942.
Enemies. London, Chapman and Hall, 1947.
The Overseer. London, Chapman and Hall, 1949.
Broken Canes. London, Lane, 1950.
A Verdict of Treason. London, Lane, 1952.
A Little Madness. London, Lane, 1953.
The Game and the Ground. London, Reinhardt, 1956; New York, Abelard Schuman, 1957.
Orders of Chivalry. London, Bodley Head, 1958; New York, Abelard Schuman, 1959.
The Tournament. London, Bodley Head, 1959; New York, Walker, 1961.
A Sort of Forgetting. London, Bodley Head, 1960.
Carolina. London, New English Library, 1961.
Sources of Unrest. London, Bodley Head, 1962.
The Friends of God. London, Macmillan, 1963; as *The Siege*, New York, Walker, 1963.
The Lost Lands. London, Macmillan, and New York, Walker, 1964.
The Story Teller. London, Owen, 1968.
Pastimes of a Red Summer. London, Owen, 1969.
Landlord. London, Owen, 1970.
Quintet. London, Owen, 1976.
Aspects of Feeling. London, Owen, 1986.

Other

The Dark Tower: Tales from the Past (for children). London, Macdonald, 1965; New York, Crowell, 1969.
The Shadow Land: More Stories from the Past (for children). London, Macdonald, 1967.
Green Knights, Black Angels: The Mosaic of History (for children). London, Macmillan, 1969.
Vladivostok (essay). London, Covent Garden Press, 1972.
Dictators. London, Studio Vista, 1973.
Worlds and Underworlds: Anglo-European History Through the Centuries. London, Owen, 1974.
Flakes of History. London, Park, 1978.
The Ancient Mariner and the Old Sailor: Delights and Uses of Words. London, Centre for Policy Studies, 1985.
Paths from a White Horse: A Writer's Memoir. London, Quartet, 1985.

Editor, *Voices from the Great War*. London, Cape, 1981; New York, Watts, 1984.
Editor, *Voices: 1870–1914*. London, Cape, 1984; New York, Watts, 1985.
Editor, *John Masefield's Letters from the Front 1915–1917*. London, Constable, 1984; New York, Watts, 1985.
Editor, *Happy and Glorious: An Anthology of Royalty*. London, Collins, 1988.
Editor, *Voices of the French Revolution*. London, Collins, 1989.

*

Peter Vansittart comments:

Though I have published non-fiction, novels alone excite my ambitions; not plays, short stories, poems, manifestos, sermons.

My novels have been appreciated, if not always enjoyed, more by critics than the reading public, which shows no sign of enjoying them at all. This must be partly due to my obsession with language and speculation at the expense of narrative, however much I relish narrative in others. Today I take narrative more seriously, though still relying, perhaps over-relying, on descriptive colour, unexpected imagery, the bizarre and curious—no formula for popular success. *The Game and the Ground, The Tournament, Lancelot*, and *Quintet*, have succeeded the most in expressing initial vision and valid situation in fairly accessible terms. Others—*A Verdict of Treason, A Sort of Forgetting*—had interesting and provocative material, clumsily handled. *The Story Teller*, my own favourite, failed through excess of ambition. *A Little Madness* and *Sources of Unrest*, through too little.

My novels range in time from the 2nd millennium BC, to AD 1986. They share the effect of time, and the apparently forgotten or exterminated on the present, time transmuting, distorting, travestying, ridiculing facts and ideas, loves and hates, generous institutions and renowned reputations. I was long impressed by the woeful distinction between the historical Macbeth and Shakespeare's: by the swift transformation of E. M. Forster's very English Mrs. Moore into an Indian goddess. Such phenomena relate very immediately to my own work, in which myth can be all too real, and the real degenerate into fantasy.

*   *   *

There is nothing cosy about Peter Vansittart's historical novels. In prose that is spare and chaste, using words with rare respect to create vivid and compelling images of the past with no blurring from fustian archaism, he looks hard at a panorama of crumbling civilisations and finds little to cheer him. The precise relevance to our present age is not pointed out, yet the reader can scarcely ignore the implications.

Three Six Seven, for instance, portrays the period of the decline of Roman power in Britain through the eyes of Drusus who is presented as "a very important person" and who would never for a moment imagine there was the slightest tinge of irony in that characterisation. To convey the sense of the crumbling of authority and the decline of civilisation into hideous barbarism Vansittart deploys both historical documentation and novelistic imagination, for disaster in public affairs is reflected in the distorting mirror of personality. Drusus is experienced, cool-headed and able, as he imagines, to appraise situations and even to profit from them; in fact he cannot remain alien from the climate of his age, and we realise that he is a victim of the values he has inherited from a Rome which can itself no longer uphold them.

A similar pessimism pervades *Lancelot*. From before Malory until after Byrne-Jones its hero has been swathed in romanticism, but Vansittart will have none of it. Instead he employs the familiar figure for an exploration of the final phase of the decline of Roman Britain and the confusion that accompanied the Saxon invasions. There are violence and atrocity at every turn, weird rites are practised, and sexuality, far from being etherealised, is brutish and strange. *The Death of Robin Hood* is more demanding on the reader than the earlier novels, for it is not a life-history or a fragment of one, but rather an evocation of a myth of liberation which is embodied in the freedom supposed to be located in the greenwood of Nottinghamshire. The first section describes the forest; the second is set in the time of John's attempt to usurp the throne of Richard I; the third transports us to the Luddite revolts of 1812; and in the fourth Vansittart comes up to the 1930's. Recurrent figures, as well as repeated themes, link the sections, each of which are introduced by a series of epigraphs borrowed from a wide variety of sources which start chains of thought and suggestions which readers must control as best they can.

Parsifal is no less ambitious, taking Richard Wagner for the starting point of an adventure in scholarship and imagination back into the past and forward into the 20th century. The effect is kaleidoscopic and always potentially chaotic, as fact and fiction are fused to form myth which at times is only fleetingly conveyed. Yet it is hard to reject these odd creations. An historian by training, Vansittart possesses real and unusual erudition; his evocations of the past, even when they are deliberately fragmented, carry conviction, and his characters, however remote, have psychological traits which ring true, so that we follow their fortunes with attention and listen to their opinions with more than usual interest, especially as they always seem to know more than they reveal. Sinister forces always seem to pose real threats, which creates tension, and Vansittart constantly juxtaposes rationality to powers which may prove stronger still. The mind is always alert, seeing and sensing, but whether it is in command is another question.

Vansittart's historical novels have received a mixed reception, some reviewers blaming him for obscurity and others disliking his prose which is sometimes clipped almost to the point of breathlessness. There are, however, a number of critics who find Vansittart one of the most exciting historical novelists of the present generation with a style which is very much his own.

—Christopher Smith

VAN SLYKE, Helen (Lenore, née Vogt). Also wrote as Sharon Ashton. American. Born in Washington, D.C., 9 July 1919. Married William Woodward Van Slyke in 1946 (divorced 1952). Fashion editor, Washington *Evening Star*, 1938–43; beauty editor, 1945–55, and promotion director, 1955–60, *Glamour* magazine, New York; promotion and advertising director, Henri Bendel, New York, 1960–61; vice-president and creative director, Norman Craig and Kummel, advertising agency, New York, 1961–63; president, House of Fragrance (Genesco), New York, 1963–68; vice-president for Creative Activities, Helena Rubinstein, New York, 1968–72; then full-time writer and lecturer. *Died in 1979.*

ROMANCE AND HISTORICAL PUBLICATIONS

Novels

The Rich and the Righteous. New York, Doubleday, 1971; London, Cassell, 1972.
All Visitors Must Be Announced. New York, Doubleday, 1972; London, Cassell, 1973; as *The Best People,* New York, Popular Library, 1976.
The Heart Listens. New York, Doubleday, 1973; London, New English Library, 1974.
The Santa Ana Wind (as Sharon Ashton). New York, Doubleday, 1974; London, New English Library, 1975.
The Mixed Blessing. New York, Doubleday, 1975; London, New English Library, 1976.
The Best Place to Be. New York, Doubleday, and London, New English Library, 1976.
Always Is Not Forever. New York, Doubleday, 1977; London, New English Library, 1978.

Sisters and Strangers. New York, Doubleday, 1978; London, Heinemann, 1979.
A Necessary Woman. New York, Doubleday, and London, Heinemann, 1979.
No Love Lost. Philadelphia, Lippincott, and London, Heinemann, 1980.
Public Smiles, Private Tears, completed by James Elward. New York, Harper, and London, Heinemann, 1982.

*   *   *

Helen Van Slyke viewed her books pragmatically: "perhaps what I write is romantic sentimental nonsense, but if two million or more people want to read it, that's important. If you're in a business, you should act as if you're in a business, with something to sell, and every now and then you must forget about artistic merit. I know I don't write literature, for heaven's sake . . . ''

What she did write and promote are phenomenally successful "women's novels," which she referred to as "soap operas between covers." Only the first book has a man as its central character. In the rest, the main characters are women who are usually affluent and often middle-aged. They confront problems familiar to the contemporary reader. Sheila Callahan in *The Best Place to Be* faces widowhood. Alice Winters (*Sister and Strangers*) is married to a wife beater. Charlene Jenkins (*The Heart Listens*) is married to a black man, and her daughter Toni (*The Mixed Blessing*) must resolve identity problems resulting from her inter-racial heritage. Mary Morgan in *A Necessary Woman* has to deal with her successful career and a weak husband.

Like Mary, Van Slyke's women are generally stronger than their male counterparts. Some of them use their strength to help others. Elizabeth Quigly (*The Heart Listens* and *The Mixed Blessing*) works indefatigably for her family and friends. Others use their power to destroy people's lives. Mary Morgan's sister Pat seduces Mary's husband to hurt her sister.

Although Van Slyke's women enjoy sex, they are more likely to remain faithful to their marriage commitments than are their husbands, many of whom assume that extramarital liaisons are a male prerogative. In *No Love Lost* that attitude eventually drives Pauline Thresher to leave her husband—with her mother-in-law's support.

Van Slyke's women need and like men, but they also have strong relationships with other women. A letter from her daughter helps Sheila Callahan resolve a long-standing conflict with her own mother. Relationships between sisters are explored in *A Necessary Woman* and *Sisters and Strangers*. The importance of friendship between women is evident in *Always Is Not Forever*. Susan Langdon's former boss is honest enough to help Susan confront her drinking problem, marital difficulties, and need for an identity apart from her husband.

But the exploration of character never dominates Van Slyke's action-filled stories. Like the soap operas to which she compared her books, her plots include one crisis after another. Van Slyke believed in "the power of storytelling" to reach her readers with a tale "that is comprehensible within the realm of their own experience." The popularity of her books bears witness to her success in meeting her goal.

—Kathy Piehl

---

van WIEREN, Mona. See **van der ZEE, Karen.**

VERYAN, Patricia. Pseudonym for Patricia V. Bannister. British/American (dual citizenship). Born in London, England, 21 November 1923. Educated at Mitcham Central Girls School, Surrey, 1934–37; Miss Lodge Secretarial School, London, 1937–38. Married Allan Louis Berg in 1946 (died 1980); one daughter and one son. Secretary, Navy, Army, and Air Force Institutes, London, 1938–40, Columbia Pictures, London, 1940–42, United States Army, London, Paris, and Frankfurt, 1942–46, Pacific Telephone, Sacramento, California, 1949, National Cash Register Company, Los Angeles, 1950, Southern Counties Gas Company, Los Angeles, 1951–52, and Humble Oil and Refining Company, Los Angeles, 1952–55; Secretary for Graduate Affairs, University of California, Riverside, 1971–85. Agent: Florence Feiler Literary Agency, 1524 Sunset Plaza Drive, Los Angeles, California 90069. Address: 10129 Main Street, Apartment 204, Bellevue, Washington 98004, U.S.A.

ROMANCE AND HISTORICAL PUBLICATIONS

Novels (series: Golden Chronicles; Sanguinet Saga)

The Lord and the Gypsy. New York, Walker, 1978; as *Debt of Honour*, London, Souvenir Press, 1980.
Love's Duet. New York, Walker, 1979; as *A Perfect Match*, London, Souvenir Press, 1981.
Mistress of Willowvale. New York, Walker, 1980.
Sanguinet Saga:
  1. *Nanette.* New York, Walker, 1981.
  2. *Feather Castles.* New York, St. Martin's Press, 1982.
  3. *Married Past Redemption.* New York, St. Martin's Press, 1983.
  4. *The Noblest Frailty.* New York, St. Martin's Press, 1983.
  5. *Sanguinet's Crown.* New York, St. Martin's Press, 1985.
  6. *Give All to Love.* New York, St. Martin's Press, 1987.
Some Brief Folly. New York, St. Martin's Press, 1981.
The Wagered Widow. New York, St. Martin's Press, 1984.
Golden Chronicles:
  1. *Practice to Deceive.* New York, St. Martin's Press, 1985.
  2. *Journey to Enchantment.* New York, St. Martin's Press, 1986.
  3. *The Tyrant.* New York, St. Martin's Press, 1987.
  4. *Love Alters Not.* New York, St. Martin's Press, 1987.
  5. *Cherished Enemy.* New York, St. Martin's Press, 1987.
  6. *The Dedicated Villain.* New York, St. Martin's Press, 1989.

*

Patricia Veryan comments:

Almost every period of history has its highlights, its subtle nuances of life at every level that would warrant much happy digging and delving into, so as to gain a fairly well-rounded picture of the time. Of them all, however, I am most fascinated by Britain's crowded past: the perilous days of the Stuarts, the Jacobite uprisings, and the Regency (1811–20). This latter time I find especially intriguing, for it was surely, as Sir Arthur Bryant dubbed it, "The Age of Elegance." Were one to cover the era fully, and from every side, there must be some very dark pages, of course; and some, perhaps darkest of all, shadowed by the shape of things to come. I am not a historian, however, although I attempt to hold true to historical detail. I do not write to moralise, or educate, but to entertain, and if I may thereby leave my reader with a little deeper appreciation of the period, why, so much the better.

And what a period it was! The Napoleonic Wars, and the incredible heroism of the men who fought them on land and sea, whether French, English, or their Allies. The many-faceted Regent himself, later to become George IV, who, despite his numerous failings, encouraged a deeper interest in art, music, and architecture, and left us so rich a heritage of beauty. The preoccupation with manners, the niceties of fashion, and that rare and wonderful intangible, the Code of Honour. Regency gentlemen lived, and sometimes died, by this same Code that valued honour above all things, and next to honour, courage, loyalty, and gentleness. By its unwritten yet inviolate precepts, parents must be respected and obeyed; women revered; children, the weak, and the helpless protected. A man's character was judged by his adherence to his given word, and the crime unforgivable was cowardice. A religion rather? Perhaps. A religion seldom spoken of, but quietly lived. It was a time of contrasts we now find astounding; of sordid poverty and squalor, and great wealth; medical horrors, and the emergence of self-cleanliness; exquisitely gowned ladies instructed from the cradle in the graces and attributes necessary to becoming a good wife, gallant gentlemen, and the savageries of child labour; oppression and tyranny, and yet withal a prosperity unrivalled in the Europe of that day, and a nationwide and innate courtesy and chivalry.

Against this rich canvas, my books are set. They may differ slightly from others of the genre, in that I perhaps insert a trifle more of action and adventure than is the usual fashion, for it was so much a period of action.

If I have, to any extent, achieved success, much of the credit must go to my superb teachers. These have been many, for from every author one gleans something. In my own field however, two were outstanding: the first of these was Jeffrey Farnol, who wrote with such gentleness, warmth, and charm, in the early years of this century; the second, Georgette Heyer, whose wit, masterful style, rich humour, and knowledge of her period, were so incomparable. Without these two great friends, whom I dearly loved, and from whom I learned so much, countless happy hours would have been lost to me. For this, besides what they taught me, I do most humbly, if posthumously, thank them.

To others I leave the task of painting the harsh realities of life; the bewilderments of today's world; the savageries of drugs and the pity of lost morality. Life is difficult enough to live, I do not choose to carry such harshness into my writing. I fashion my tales lightly, in the hope that my readers—especially those who may be wearied of the daily grind, or ill, or discouraged, or lonely (surely the cruellest of sorrows)—may perhaps find a smile, or a tug at the heartstrings, or a tingle of excitement within the pages of my books, and thus escape to the thunderous elegance of not so long ago.

*   *   *

Patricia Veryan has developed into one of the most outstanding authors of historical romances writing today. She is adept at creating some of the most interesting characters and intriguing stories to be found in the genre. She has researched her periods (usually Georgian or Regency England) well and writes convincingly of the manners of the time.

A basic theme in her work is the preservation of honor and integrity in the face of betrayal and suffering. Both men and women must bear the burden, sometimes with great loneliness. In *Mistress of Willowvale* Leonie braves public disgrace and the contempt of the man she loves to protect her nephew and the memory of her sister. The Marquis of Damon, hero of *Love's Duet*, endures his father's scorn and the shame of a dishonorable reputation in order to bring the true villains to justice. Lucian St. Clair in *The Lord and the Gypsy* endures great emotional and physical suffering as the ultimate atonement for past wrongs committed. Similarly, Anthony Farrar, branded a coward and a murderer in *Love Alters Not*, undergoes great hardship before his name is cleared.

Veryan's books are distinguished by well-developed central characters and many interesting minor personages. Often the primary focus is on the male characters and their friendships, although the female characters are not slighted. There is great romantic involvement, but no explicit sexual details. In fact, Veryan reserves some of her longest, most detailed passages for carefully orchestrated mayhem, which forms an integral part of the suffering to be borne by the hero. Lucian St. Clair participates in, and almost loses, a brutal sword fight; Harry Redmond (*Nanette*) becomes a fugitive hunted throughout England and eventually is thrown into Newgate Prison; Mitchel Redmond, Harry's brother, battles his way across England to save the Prince Regent (*Sanguinet's Crown*); and Christopher Thorndyke (*Mistress of Willowvale*) is branded a traitor and narrowly avoids death in an all-out battle which takes place in a kitchen. Detailed as the descriptions of the action become, there is no gratuitous violence, and Veryan tempers all the serious themes and action with a very satisfying love story.

An unusual aspect of Veryan's work has been the gradual forging of complete social worlds for her characters. Where other authors often rely heavily on real historical figures, such as the Prince Regent, to create the sense of aristocratic society in which their characters move, Veryan introduces her readers to new members of that society in each book. Often the protagonist in one book played a minor role in an earlier work or appears in a later work. This sense of society is, perhaps, strongest in the Regency novels, which evolved into the story of the "Nine Knights" and their struggles to combat the evil Sanguinet brothers, but it also is apparent in the novels which make up the Golden Chronicles series. While *Practice to Deceive* is the first volume named in the series, several characters (the Duke of Marbury, his rogue of a grandson, Roland Otton/Mathieson, and Trevelyan de Villars) appear in the earlier *Mistress of Willowvale* and *The Wagered Widow*. Even the two series are linked through families and estates. Marbury's estate, Dominer, returns as the location of *Some Brief Folly*, in which Garret Hawkhurst is descended from the Thorndykes.

This intertwining of stories, even across time, creates a real sense of continuity. The appearances of recurring characters never seem contrived but are worked into the narrative quite naturally. Soon it is like receiving news of an old and dear friend.

—Barbara E. Kemp

VIDAL, Gore (Eugene Luther Vidal, Jr.). Has also written as Edgar Box. American. Born in West Point, New York, 3 October 1925. Educated at Los Alamos School, New Mexico, 1939–40; Phillips Exeter Academy, Exeter, New Hampshire, 1940–43. Served in the United States Army, 1943–46: Warrant Officer. Editor, E. P. Dutton, publishers, New York, 1946. Lived in Antigua, Guatemala, 1947–49, and Italy, from 1967. Member, Advisory Board, *Partisan Review*, New Brunswick, New Jersey, 1960–71; Democratic-Liberal candidate for Congress, New York, 1960; member, President's Advisory Committee on the Arts, 1961–63; co-chairman, New Party, 1968–71. Recipient: Mystery Writers of America Edgar Allan Poe award, for television play, 1954; National Book Critics Circle award, for

criticism, 1983. Address: La Rondinaia, Ravello, 84010 Salerno, Italy; or c/o Random House Inc., 201 East 50th Street, New York, New York 10022, U.S.A.

ROMANCE AND HISTORICAL PUBLICATIONS

Novels

A Search for the King: A Twelfth Century Legend. New York, Dutton, 1950; London, New English Library, 1967.
Messiah. New York, Dutton, 1954; London, Heinemann, 1955; revised edition, Boston, Little Brown, 1965; Heinemann, 1966.
Julian. Boston, Little Brown, and London, Heinemann, 1964.
Washington, D.C. Boston, Little Brown, and London, Heinemann, 1967.
Burr. New York, Random House, 1973; London, Heinemann, 1974.
1876. New York, Random House, and London, Heinemann, 1976.
Creation. New York, Random House, and London, Heinemann, 1981.
Lincoln. New York, Random House, and London, Heinemann, 1984.
Empire. New York, Random House, and London, Deutsch, 1987.

OTHER PUBLICATIONS

Novels

Williwaw. New York, Dutton, 1946; London, Panther, 1965.
In a Yellow Wood. New York, Dutton, 1947; London, New English Library, 1967.
The City and the Pillar. New York, Dutton, 1948; London, Lehmann, 1949; revised edition, Dutton, and London, Heinemann, 1965.
The Season of Comfort. New York, Dutton, 1949.
Dark Green, Bright Red. New York, Dutton, and London, Lehmann, 1950.
The Judgment of Paris. New York, Dutton, 1952; London, Heinemann, 1953; revised edition, Boston, Little Brown, 1965; Heinemann, 1966.
Three: Williwaw, A Thirsty Evil, Julian the Apostate. New York, New American Library, 1962.
Myra Breckinridge. Boston, Little Brown, and London, Blond, 1968.
Two Sisters: A Memoir in the Form of a Novel. Boston, Little Brown, and London, Heinemann, 1970.
Myron. New York, Random House, 1974; London, Heinemann, 1975.
Kalki. New York, Random House, and London, Heinemann, 1978.
Duluth. New York, Random House, and London, Heinemann, 1983.
Hollywood. New York, Random House, 1990.

Novels as Edgar Box

Death in the Fifth Position. New York, Dutton, 1952; London, Heinemann, 1954.
Death Before Bedtime. New York, Dutton, 1953; London, Heinemann, 1954.

Death Likes It Hot. New York, Dutton, 1954; London, Heinemann, 1955.

Short Stories

A Thirsty Evil: Seven Short Stories. New York, Zero Press, 1956; London, Heinemann, 1958.

Plays

Visit to a Small Planet (televised 1955). Included in *Visit to a Small Planet and Other Television Plays*, 1956; revised version (produced New York, 1957; London, 1960), Boston, Little Brown, 1957; in *Three Plays*, 1962.
Honor (televised 1956). Published in *Television Plays for Writers: Eight Television Plays*, edited by A. S. Burack, Boston, The Writer, 1957; revised version, as *On the March to the Sea: A Southron Comedy* (produced Bonn, Germany, 1961), in *Three Plays*, 1962.
Visit to a Small Planet and Other Television Plays (includes *Barn Burning, Dark Possession, The Death of Billy the Kid, A Sense of Justice, Smoke, Summer Pavilion, The Turn of the Screw*). Boston, Little Brown, 1956.
The Best Man: A Play about Politics (produced New York, 1960). Boston, Little Brown, 1960; in *Three Plays*, 1962.
Three Plays. London, Heinemann, 1962.
Romulus: A New Comedy, adaptation of a play by Friedrich Dürrenmatt (produced New York, 1962). New York, Dramatists Play Service, 1962.
Weekend (produced New York, 1968). New York, Dramatists Play Service, 1968.
An Evening with Richard Nixon and . . . (produced New York, 1972). New York, Random House, 1972.

Screenplays: *The Catered Affair*, 1956; *I Accuse*, 1958; *The Scapegoat*, with Robert Hamer, 1959; *Suddenly, Last Summer*, with Tennessee Williams, 1959; *The Best Man*, 1964; *Is Paris Burning?*, with Francis Ford Coppola, 1966; *Last of the Mobile Hot-Shots*, 1970; *The Sicilian*, 1987.

Television Plays: *Barn Burning*, from the story by Faulkner, 1954; *Dark Possession*, 1954; *Smoke*, from the story by Faulkner, 1954; *Visit to a Small Planet*, 1955; *The Death of Billy the Kid*, 1955; *A Sense of Justice,* 1955; *Summer Pavilion*, 1955; *The Turn of the Screw*, from the story by Henry James, 1955; *Honor*, 1956; *The Indestructible Mr. Gore*, 1960; *Vidal in Venice* (documentary), 1985; *Dress Gray*, from the novel by Lucian K. Truscott IV, 1986.

Other

Rocking the Boat (essays). Boston, Little Brown, 1962; London, Heinemann, 1963.
Sex, Death, and Money (essays). New York, Bantam, 1968.
Reflections upon a Sinking Ship (essays). Boston, Little Brown, and London, Heinemann, 1969.
Homage to Daniel Shays: Collected Essays 1952–1972. New York, Random House, 1972; as *Collected Essays 1952–1972*, London, Heinemann, 1974.
Matters of Fact and of Fiction: Essays 1973–1976. New York, Random House, and London, Heinemann, 1977.
Sex Is Politics and Vice Versa (essay). Los Angeles, Sylvester and Orphanos, 1979.
Views from a Window: Conversations with Gore Vidal, with Robert J. Stanton. Secaucus, New Jersey, Lyle Stuart, 1980.

The Second American Revolution and Other Essays 1976–1982. New York, Random House, 1982; as *Pink Triangle and Yellow Star and Other Essays*, London, Heinemann, 1982.
Vidal in Venice, edited by George Armstrong, photographs by Tore Gill. New York, Summit, and London, Weidenfeld and Nicolson, 1985.
Armageddon? Essays 1983–1987. London, Deutsch, 1987; as *Time for a Change*, New York, Random House, 1988.

Editor, *Best Television Plays.* New York, Ballantine, 1956.

*

Bibliography: *Gore Vidal: A Primary and Secondary Bibliography* by Robert J. Stanton, Boston, Hall, and London, Prior, 1978.

Manuscript Collection: University of Wisconsin, Madison.

Critical Studies: *Gore Vidal* by Ray Lewis White, New York, Twayne, 1968; *The Apostate Angel: A Critical Study of Gore Vidal* by Bernard F. Dick, New York, Random House, 1974; *Gore Vidal* by Robert F. Kiernan, New York, Ungar, 1982.

Theatrical Activities:
Actor: **Film**—*Roma* (*Fellini Roma*), 1972.

*   *   *

Gore Vidal has written five novels about United States history, which, taken together, provide a panorama of the growth of empire, an idea apparent in the title of his recent work, *Empire.* Even before the design of Vidal's fictional history was apparent, however, he revealed his intent in *Washington, D.C.*, the first of his ventures into the American past. "Overnight," Vidal wrote in reference to the impact of World War II, "everyone took it for granted that without design and by God's election, the American Empire existed to rule the world." While the birth of empire may appear to have arrived unannounced, history, as Vidal shows in his novels, indicates otherwise.

In *Burr* Vidal covers the period from the American Revolution to the 1830's in which great and small minds fought for power. He looks in particular at Jeffersonian expansionism as it affected the Presidency, the growth of Continental America, and the transformation of political attitudes from Jefferson to Jacksonian Democracy. In *Lincoln* and *1876* he describes America's great internal crises (the Civil War and Reconstruction), the consolidation of power, the emergence of the mercantile mind, and the subsequent alterations in culture and the body politic. *Empire* deals with the Spanish-American war years, expansionist America, and the internationalization of political perspectives in the United States; and *Washington, D.C.*, focuses on the 20-year period from the late 1930's to the early 1950's—the zenith, as Vidal cynically remarks, of America's empire. From Jefferson and Burr in *Burr* to James Burden Day and Clay Overbury, the political leaders in *Washington, D.C.* the growth of empire contrasts sharply with a decline in political character, almost as if world domination were predicated on a corresponding decline in vision, integrity, and depth of character. Vidal's usual pattern, in fact, is to contrast men of integrity with those who seek merely power. Aaron Burr and Martin Van Buren, heroes in Vidal's eyes, give way to the power-seekers, Jefferson and Jackson; Lincoln and Tilden are replaced by Grant and Hayes; McKinley and Franklin D. Roosevelt are succeeded by Teddy Roosevelt and Clay Overbury, Vidal's version of the media personalities who typify contemporary politics. From this point of view, Vidal's historical novels are a public record of the rise and fall of political giants and the private observation on the whole of the American experience. The path that leads from the 18th to the 20th century, from *Burr* to *Washington, D.C.*, from Thomas Jefferson to Clay Overbury is clear and tragic to Vidal. This path, moreover, is one not necessarily marked in textbooks or in the minds of American citizenry.

In this sense Vidal belongs to the new school of American historical novelists—the revisionists and debunkers of mythic history such as Thomas Berger, Thomas Flanagan, John Barth, and Robert Coover—all of whom question history as generally presented and who blur distinction between fact and fiction since history is itself nothing more than a fictive version of the past. In his gossipy novels, Vidal attempts to reconstruct the missing pages of history by enlarging the personal lives of public figures whose historical reputations are themselves a blend of history and fiction.

In addition, Vidal ties his novels together (and makes history credible) through the presence of an "historical" family—the descendants of Aaron Burr, father to a nation. The protagonist and narrator of *Burr* is Charlie Schuyler, Burr's illegitimate son who, disenchanted with the course of the American experiment, leaves for an extended stay in Europe with his daughter. For much of his background information, Vidal turned to documents of the period including an 1861 novel, *Margaret Moncrieff: The First Love of Aaron Burr* by Charles Burdett, the actual illegitimate son of Burr and the model for Schuyler. Vidal's interest in Burdett provided him with a plot within a plot featuring the quasi-historical Schuylers who appear in subsequent novels.

Lincoln, for example, closes with a scene at the palace of the Tuileries where a reception is being held for the diplomatic corps. At the reception, John Hay, Lincoln's former secretary, meets "the American historian" Charles Schermerhorn Schuyler and his daughter Emma, the princess d'Agrigente. Schuyler left New York in "thirty-six, to be, like you," he tells Hay, "a diplomat. Only I went to Italy, and never returned home." In this scene, Charlie's role as an American expatriate, curious about his changing homeland, is clear enough. His questions about Lincoln, the Presidency, and politics allow Vidal one last chance for a melancholy glance at the Lincoln years. Schuyler hints that it might be time for him to return to America "which plainly bears no resemblances to the one I left." In *1876* Schuyler and his daughter have indeed returned home where he is hired to write a campaign tract for Tilden, a work which turns out to be the manuscript of *1876*, a cynical comment on a country which has lost its tradition and direction.

A generation later in *Empire*, Charlie and Emma are distant but still powerful shadows. Emma is mysteriously remembered as the "darkly beautiful Princess d'Agrigente" and Charlie is described by Henry James as one who "believed in the necessity of living on this side of the Atlantic, some distance from our newspapered democracy." The Schuyler connection is extended to the protagonists, Caroline, the daughter of Emma and her second husband, Colonel Sanford, and her stepbrother Blaise, both of whom own newspapers in a country seemingly run by William Randolph Hearst who claims, "I just made up this country pretty much as it happens to be at the moment." Vidal's disdain for Hearst's America (and for history) is illustrated late in the novel in a conversation between Hearst and Teddy Roosevelt. "History invented me, not you!" Roosevelt claims, to which Hearst replies, "I am history—or at least the creator of the record."

Vidal ends his historical cycle where he began it—in *Washington, D.C.* with Peter Sanford, son of Blaise. At various times the novel calls upon the ghosts of the past. A portrait of Aaron Burr hangs in the Sanford house, and Lincoln's name is invoked

as a standard which America has never quite met. Vidal's real interest, however, is in the new phase of empire. Franklin D. Roosevelt, we are told, has reassembled the fragments of broken empires into a new pattern. What is more, he is the "proud creator of the new imperium." Vidal, through his spokesman, Senator James Burden Day, says that the United States has abandoned the design of the Republic and that elections are now only periodic referendums to change the dictator. History is in the hands of the Clay Overburys and a new set of values and system far removed from the times and the likes of Aaron Burr, a man who made history. In fact, Hearst's and Roosevelt's debate about history becomes a mocking comment on history in the novel. "Must we have history?," Peter Sanford is asked at the end of it all. Sanford's reply serves as an epitaph for all the novels and, sadly, as a comment on the American empire. "It passes the time," Sanford responds.

In his five novels about the American past, Vidal is irreverent, witty, daring, and incisive. His historical landscape is charged with satirical energy while his narrative strategy, especially his on-going affair with the mysteries of Aaron Burr, reveals the mind of the leading historical novelist of the day. Over the last 20 years he has turned most often to history for his satire and, in the process, has produced the most noteworthy sequence of historical novels of any 20th-century American writer.

—Thomas S. Gladsky

VINCENT, Claire. See **ALLEN, Charlotte Vale.**

VITEK, Donna (Kinel). Also writes as Donna Alexander. Address: c/o Dell, 666 Fifth Avenue, New York, New York 10103, U.S.A.

ROMANCE AND HISTORICAL PUBLICATIONS

Novels

Red Roses, White Lilies (as Donna Alexander). New York, Macfadden, 1979.
No Turning Back (as Donna Alexander). New York, Macfadden, 1979.
In from the Storm (as Donna Alexander). New York, Macfadden, 1979.
A Different Dream. New York, Silhouette, 1980.
Promises from the Past. New York, Silhouette, 1981.
Showers of Sunlight. New York, Silhouette, 1981.
Veil of Gold. New York, Silhouette, 1981.
Where the Heart Is. New York, Silhouette, 1981.
Valaquez Bride. New York, Silhouette, and London, Hodder and Stoughton, 1982.
A Game of Chance. New York, Silhouette, 1982; London, Hodder and Stoughton, 1983.
Garden of the Moongate. New York, Silhouette, 1982.
Sweet Surrender. New York, Silhouette, 1982.
Morning Always Comes. New York, Silhouette, 1982.
Passion's Price. New York, Silhouette, 1983.
Blue Mist of Morning. New York, Dell, 1983.
Dangerous Embrace. New York, Dell, 1983.

No Promise Given. New York, Dell, 1983.
Warmed by the Fire. New York, Dell, 1983.
Never Look Back. New York, Dell, 1983.
An Unforgettable Caress. New York, Dell, 1984.
Breaking the Rules. New York, Dell, 1984.
Asking for Trouble. New York, Dell, 1984.
Thrill of the Chase. New York, Dell, 1985.
Deep in the Heart. New York, Dell, 1985.
Players in the Shadows. New York, Dell, 1985.
One Step Ahead. New York, Dell, 1985.
Best-Kept Secret. New York, Dell, 1985.
Dream Maker. New York, Dell, 1986.
Playing with Fire. New York, Dell, 1986.
Morning Glory. New York, Dell, 1986.
Laying Down the Law. New York, Dell, 1986.
First-Class Male. New York, Dell, 1987.
Adventure with a Stranger. New York, Dell, 1987.

*   *   *

Donna Vitek has written a number of consistently good novels. She develops solid characters that reflect all of the contradictions and ambiguities of real people. Her heroines are women, not young girls. They cope quite well with their lives and are self-confident enough to take on anything that comes their way.

Vitek's heroes are equally individualistic. Usually they are professional men or they hold some sort of job that reflects a broad education. They are often in dangerous situations but are usually well trained to handle such occurrences. On the other hand, some of her heroes are hesitant about establishing permanent relations with a woman or they are unconsciously afraid of long-term commitments. Their ambivalence frequently causes misunderstandings, but these are finally resolved in the arms of the heroine. Both the hero and the heroine realize that the thought of the future without each other is more terrifying than making the initial commitment.

Vitek's plots are also an added element in her favor. Despite following the standard romance/intrigue/suspense formula, they are skillfully developed. Events and scenes keep the pages turning as crises are piled one on top of the other. She balances the various elements of her plots adding enough complication to round the novels out, yet not enough to detract from the essential conflict. She is just as careful to show the romantic relationships evolving in a believable way, weaving love and danger into a satisfying conclusion. Finally, she has such a readable style that it is very difficult to put one of her novels down.

One Step Ahead is a case in point. Callie Simpson is on vacation at St. Croix in the Bahamas. Her rental boat is suddenly commandeered by Jonathan Harper, a magazine reporter. To suggest that his story is bizarre would be an understatement. It is also one that the heroine has difficulty in believing. Jonathan has been researching a far-right political group in the United States who plan to take control of the government by supposedly legal means (plus a few terror tactics). He has uncovered the group, knows someone with written evidence, and is in pursuit of it while fleeing the group's own hit men. The chase goes from the Caribbean, to Houston, to Mexico, to Europe, and back to the States with Callie keeping step right along with Jonathan. In fact, her fast thinking and courage save the day and their lives several times. Callie is the one who actually secures the evidence and gives it to Jonathan. In all, the title is very appropriate. They are just one step ahead of danger throughout the novel.

First-Class Male is another good example of Vitek's style. In this novel, her writing is balanced between the conflict of the plot and the development of believable characters and their per-

sonal conflicts. Michelle Vance is a psychologist specializing in battered women. She is approached by Jon Wyatt to testify as an expert witness in his defense of Doris Keaton. Doris has been accused of the attempted murder of her husband, Vincent Keaton. The conflict in the novel centers on the wife and on Jon's preparation for the trial. Related to this is the fact that Michelle begins to receive threats, has her home vandalized, and eventually has to have Jon move in with her for protection.

Michelle and Jon are two settled professionals who have their own life style. They find that they have many things in common and as the novel progresses, they fall in love, but not without the usual spate of misunderstandings. In this novel Vitek concentrates on showing the motivation and growth of her central characters. Michelle is reserved and rather defensive around men. Jon is not exactly looking for a permanent relationship, but will not avoid one should it evolve. The art of compromise is a lesson well learned by each of them before the end of the novel.

Altogether, Vitek is well on her way to becoming a major romance writer.

—Arlene Moore

WADDELL, Helen (Jane). Irish. Born in Tokyo, Japan, 31 May 1889. Educated at Victoria College; Queen's University, Belfast, B.A. (honours) in English 1911, M.A. 1912. Freelance writer, 1912–19; lecturer in Latin, Somerville College, Oxford 1920–22; Cassell lecturer, St. Hilda's College, Oxford, 1921; lecturer, Bedford College, University of London, 1922–23; literary adviser and reader, Constable, publishers, London; assistant editor, the *Nineteenth Century*, London, 1938–45. Recipient: Susette Taylor travelling fellowship, 1923; A. C. Benson Silver Medal, 1927. D. Litt.: University of Durham, 1932; Columbia University, New York, 1934; Queen's University, 1934. Fellow, Royal Society of Literature, 1927; member, Irish Academy of Letters, 1932. *Died 5 March 1965.*

ROMANCE AND HISTORICAL PUBLICATIONS

Novel

Peter Abelard. London, Constable, and New York, Holt, 1933.

OTHER PUBLICATIONS

Plays

The Spoiled Buddha (produced Dublin, 1919). Dublin, Talbot, and London, Unwin, 1919.
The Abbé Prévost (produced Croydon, Surrey, 1935). Privately printed, 1931.

Verse

Lyrics from the Chinese (from J. Legge's prose translation of the Shih Ching). London, Constable, and Boston, Houghton Mifflin, 1913.

Other

The Wandering Scholars. London, Constable, and Boston, Houghton Mifflin, 1927; revised edition, Constable, 1932.

New York City. Newtown, Montgomeryshire, Gregynog Press, 1935.
Poetry in the Dark Ages (lecture). Glasgow, Barnes and Noble, 1948.
Stories from Holy Writ (for children). London, Constable, 1949; New York, Macmillan, 1950.
The Fairy Ring (for children). Leeds, E. J. Arnold, 1921; as *The Princess Splendour and Other Stories*, London, Longman, 1969.

Editor, *A Book of Medieval Latin for Schools*. London, Constable, 1931.

Translator, *Mediaeval Latin Lyrics*. London, Constable, 1929; New York, Smith, 1930; revised edition, Constable, 1933.
Translator, *The History of the Chevalier Des Grieux and of Manon Lescaut*, by Abbé Prévost. London, Constable, 1931.
Translator, *The Hollow Field*, by Marcel Aymé. London, Constable, 1933.
Translator, *Beasts and Saints* (saints' lives). London, Constable, and New York, Holt, 1934.
Translator, *The Desert Fathers*. London, Constable, 1936; New York, Sheed and Ward, 1942.
Translator, *A French Soldier Speaks*, by Jacques (i.e., Guy Robin). London, Constable, 1941.
Translator, *Lament for Damon*, by John Milton. London, Constable, 1943.
Translator, *More Latin Lyrics: From Virgil to Milton*, edited by Felicitus Corrigan. London, Gollancz, 1976.

*

Manuscript Collections: Queen's University Library, Belfast; Stanbrook Abbey, Worcester.

Critical Studies: *The Mark of the Maker* by Monica Blackett, London, Constable, 1973; *Helen Waddell: A Biography* by Felicitus Corrigan, London, Gollancz, 1986.

*   *   *

Helen Waddell's historical novel *Peter Abelard* presents the reader with a timeless romance of star-crossed lovers set against a vividly detailed background of early 12th-century French life. Peter Abelard is a gifted religious scholar and teacher. He makes the acquaintance of Heloise, an educated girl who is half his age, through her protective uncle, Fulbert. Against all expectations, both their own and their society's, they fall in love, their relationship embodying "the absolute of human passion."

Their liaison and the birth of their son are successfully concealed, but Abelard secretly marries Heloise to appease her uncle, although public knowledge of this marriage would end Abelard's chances of preferment. Fulbert, however, suspects that Abelard has rejected Heloise because she takes refuge in a nunnery, although she has in fact retired there because she fears her uncle's deranged fury. Heloise does avoid his anger, but Abelard is betrayed by his servant and suffers Fulbert's violent physical vengeance, which tragically ends their relationship. Both retire to pursue religious lives and achieve a degree of resignation to their fates and an ability to recognise "God in suffering."

The poignancy of this tale, based on individuals who actually lived and whose correspondence survives, is increased by the sensitivity with which Waddell, herself a medieval scholar, portrays the philosophical and religious context within which the characters existed. Conversations between Abelard and his colleagues and former teachers illuminate the dilemma which he

has to confront by admitting his human desires when he has previously lived the life of a pious cleric, by strict religious principle. There is a conflict between his scholarly pursuit of learning and knowledge and the human passion for Heloise which he attempts to resist.

Heloise is not merely Abelard's foil but is also a carefully drawn character with an independent will and determined spirit. She is prepared to forfeit her reputation rather than jeopardize Abelard's career by their marriage. Her commitment to Abelard is unquestioning and her greatest fear is that "the day will come when I am no longer Heloise but just a woman."

Waddell includes much contemporary writing, particularly verse, both in Latin and in translation, which demonstrates the social and religious mores which contribute to make the characters' situation insoluble, and which also adds to the sympathetic style of narration. The conflict of duties and the moral dilemma, together with a beautifully portrayed love story are the elements of this tale which endure in the reader's memory.

—Hilary Buswell

———

WALKER, Lucy. Pseudonym for Dorothy Lucy Sanders, née McClemans; also writes as Shelley Dean. Australian. Born in Boulder Gold Fields, Western Australia, 4 May 1907. Educated at Perth College, Western Australia, 10 years; University of Western Australia, Nedlands, part-time study, 4 years; Claremont Teachers College, teachers certificate 1938. Married Colsell S. Sanders in 1936; two sons and one daughter. Teacher in Western Australia, 1928–36, and in London, 1936–38. Former member of the State Advisory Board to the Australian Broadcasting Commission, and member of the State Library Board, Western Australia. Address: 20 Jukes Way, Wembley Gardens, Western Australia 6016, Australia.

ROMANCE AND HISTORICAL PUBLICATIONS

Novels

The One Who Kisses. London, Collins, 1954.
Sweet and Faraway. London, Collins, 1955; New York, Arcadia House, 1957.
Come Home, Dear! London, Collins, 1956; New York, Ballantine, 1975.
Heaven Is Here. London, Collins, and New York, Arcadia House, 1957.
Master of Ransome. London, Collins, and New York, Arcadia House, 1958.
Orchard Hill. New York, Arcadia House, 1958.
The Stranger from the North. London, Collins, 1959; New York, Ballantine, 1976.
Kingdom of the Heart. London, Collins, 1959; New York, Ballantine, 1971.
Love in a Cloud. London, Collins, 1960.
The Loving Heart. London, Collins, 1960.
The Moonshiner. London, Collins, 1961; as *Cupboard Love*, New York, Arcadia House, 1963.
Wife to Order. London, Collins, 1961; New York, Arcadia House, 1962.
The Distant Hills. London, Collins, 1962.
Down in the Forest. London, Collins, 1962.
The Call of the Pines. London, Collins, 1963; New York, Arcadia House, 1966.

Follow Your Star. London, Collins, 1963; New York, Ballantine, 1976.

The Man from Outback. London, Collins, 1964; New York, Ballantine, 1974.

A Man Called Masters. London, Collins, 1965; New York, Ballantine, 1976.

The Other Girl. London, Collins, 1965; New York, Arcadia House, 1967.

Reaching for the Stars. London, Collins, 1966; New York, Ballantine, 1976.

The Ranger in the Hills. London, Collins, 1966.

South Sea Island (as Shelley Dean). London, Mills and Boon, 1966.

Island in the South (as Shelley Dean). London, Mills and Boon, 1967.

The River Is Down. London, Collins, 1967; New York, Ballantine, 1972.

Home at Sundown. London, Collins, 1968; New York, Ballantine, 1976.

The Gone-Away Man. London, Collins, 1969; New York, Ballantine, 1974.

Joyday for Jodi. London, Collins, 1971; New York, Ballantine, 1976.

The Mountain That Went to the Sea. London, Collins, 1971; New York, Beagle, 1973.

Girl Alone. London, Collins, 1973; New York, Ballantine, 1976.

The Runaway Girl. London, Collins, and New York, Ballantine, 1975.

Gamma's Girl. London, Collins, 1977.

So Much Love. New York, Ballantine, 1977.

Novels as Dorothy Lucie Sanders (series: Pepper Tree)

Fairies on the Doorstep. Sydney, Australasian, 1948; as *Pool of Dreams* (as Lucy Walker), New York, Ballantine, 1973.

The Randy. Sydney, Australasian, 1948.

Pepper Tree series:

Six for Heaven. London, Hodder and Stoughton, 1952.

Shining River. London, Hodder and Stoughton, 1954.

Waterfall. London, Hodder and Stoughton, 1956; as *The Bell Branch* (as Lucy Walker), London, Collins, 1971; New York, Ballantine, 1972.

Ribbons in Her Hair. London, Hodder and Stoughton, 1957.

Pepper Tree Bay. London, Hodder and Stoughton, 1959.

Monday in Summer. London, Hodder and Stoughton, 1961.

*   *   *

Within recent years, Australia has produced several outstanding romance writers. Few, however, achieve quite the same originality as Lucy Walker for she does more than use Australia as a background for her books.

Woven intricately through her novels and adding in some cases a tremendous emotional quality are the nearly mystical elements of aboriginal beliefs and customs. These touches lend support to the romantic involvement and seem to heighten the sense of inevitability as two people find each other. Not only does she use these native elements in her writing, but she also uses situations and events that may be unique to Australia, given their land tenure and mining policies. Thus we find Katie James in *The Ranger in the Hills* involved with mining surveys and the race to see that a mining right is recognized first.

In *So Much Love* Nairee has such close empathy with the aboriginal people that she unconsciously carries out a simple, primitive ritual of creating her own "spirit land" by making a circle of pretty stones and dotting larger ones in its middle. Symbolically the circle is the home of a person's spirit. Nairee is a young girl, brought up in the outback by an old woman. She is an orphan who yet has people interested in her future. Her return to The Patch in the Outback is the beginning of the story as she finally learns who she is and to whom she really belongs.

Lucy Walker's heroines are typically nice girls, a little strong minded, often naive and groping into adulthood. They are not aggressively women's lib candidates; however, they don't mind trying something new and illustrate a determined sense of independence in their actions and outlook. *Kingdom of the Heart*, for instance, is about a girl who inherits half a cattle farm in the Australian outback and proceeds to go to live there. Kimberly Wentworth in *Home at Sundown* joins a botanical expedition into the outback to find samples of rare plants for medical studies.

Typically Walker's heroes are older, more experienced men. Often they are wealthy "station" owners who have developed a sixth sense in avoiding the matrimonial trap. They flirt, and they draw women to them unwittingly and unintentionally at times by their masculinity and their habit of superiority. Frequently they personify their surroundings as they take on the bleak harshness of their land.

Walker balances the force of her characters against the force of the physical background where the story takes place. Constantly the tremendous isolation of the people living in the outback shapes and moves her characters. This isolation of station life in turn brings out qualities in character that she skillfully exploits to the fullest. In *Down in the Forest* Kim Baxter is more than a station manager; he is also appointed to turn his part of the country, the Darjalup district, into an international show case for foreign visitors. A bush fire neatly sets him back to the beginning and the story progresses from the arrival of Jill Dawson to become his right-hand man in this gigantic undertaking.

In *The Call of the Pines* a plane crash leaves four people stranded in the dense outback jungle. Cherry Landin is a young girl hired to help with the children of the station and she is one of those in the plane. Stephen Denton, the owner of the station, has to call on all his ability to lead them out of the jungle and along a cattle trail until they are rescued, all the while watching out for poisonous plants, dangerous animals, and still finding them food and water for the journey.

In all, Walker gives her readers an unusual glimpse into another world entirely. Given the nature of her country, she could not create her novels without building on its uniqueness, and over and over again this special feeling for Australia comes through. In a sense, one could not justifiably say she uses Australia as a background; it is too much a part of the story, too much of a character within it, to be merely considered background.

—Arlene Moore

WALKER, Margaret (Abigail). American. Born in Birmingham, Alabama, 7 July 1915. Educated at Northwestern University, Evanston, Illinois, B.A. 1935; University of Iowa, Iowa City, M.A. 1940, Ph.D. 1965; Yale University, New Haven, Connecticut (Ford fellow), 1954. Married Firnist James Alexander in 1943; two sons and two daughters. Has worked as social worker, reporter, and magazine editor; teacher at Livingstone College, Salisbury, North Carolina, 1941–42, 1945–46, and West Virginia State College, Institute, 1942–43. Since 1949 Professor of English, and since 1968, director of the Institute for the Study of the History, Life and Culture of Black Peoples,

Jackson State College, Mississippi. Recipient: Yale Series of Younger Poets award, 1942; Rosenwald fellowship, 1944; Houghton Mifflin fellowship, 1966; Fulbright fellowship, 1971; National Endowment for the Arts grant, 1972. D.Litt.: Northwestern University, 1974; Rust College, Holly Springs, Mississippi, 1974; D.F.A.: Denison University, Granville, Ohio, 1974; D.H.L.: Morgan State University, Baltimore, 1976. Address: 2205 Guynes Street, Jackson, Mississippi 39213, U.S.A.

ROMANCE AND HISTORICAL PUBLICATIONS

Novel

Jubilee. Boston, Houghton Mifflin, 1966.

OTHER PUBLICATIONS

Novel

Come Down from Yonder Mountain. Toronto, Longman, 1962.

Verse

For My People. New Haven, Connecticut, Yale University Press, 1942.
Ballad of the Free. Detroit, Broadside Press, 1966.
Prophets for a New Day. Detroit, Broadside Press, 1970.
October Journey. Detroit, Broadside Press, 1973.

Recording: *The Poetry of Margaret Walker*, Folkways, 1975.

Other

How I Wrote Jubilee. Chicago, Third World Press, 1972.
A Poetic Equation: Conversations Between Margaret Walker and Nikki Giovanni. Washington, D.C., Howard University Press, 1974.
Black Women and Liberation Movements. Washington, D.C., Howard University Press, 1981.
The Daemonic Genius of Richard Wright. Washington, D.C., Howard University Press, 1982.

*   *   *

Margaret Walker's literary reputation rests primarily on *For My People*, her award-winning first volume of poetry. However, in addition to writing poetry she also wrote the historical novel *Jubilee*, an antecedent text for the numerous historical novels since written by African-Americans.

During college creative writing class, Walker began reformulating and writing the slavery story of her great-grandmother that her grandmother had told her when Walker was a youngster. Since she was experiencing success with writing poetry, however, she put fiction aside. Walker's determination to write the Civil War story of her great-grandmother occupied many years of her life. Researching the historical background and writing and revising the text eventually stretched from 1942 to 1965.

Jubilee merits considerable attention as a forerunner in black historical fiction where Walker's goals and design were unprecedented. Arna Bontemps's historical novel *Black Thunder* (1936), though well written and incorporating folk elements,

was predicated on a limited historical perspective with slave insurrectionist Gabriel Prosser at its core. Walker's vision, in contrast, encompasses a broad canvas on which she paints boldly but perceptively. *Jubilee* is realistic historical fiction in which slaves and slave culture are the focus, rather than the lives of their white owners. At the center of *Jubilee* is Vyry Dutton, a slave on John Dutton's plantation in Georgia, whose life is set against the panoramic history of the antebellum, Civil War, and Reconstruction years. Vyry's growth from child to adult constitutes an engaging narrative of survival against adverse circumstances, including Mistress Dutton's overt hatred for her, Vyry's legal inability to acquire freedom to marry her free black lover, and a flogging for attempted escape. Having survived the destitution of the war years and the destruction and death of most of the Dutton family members, Vyry, her children, and a second husband are displaced among hundreds of others who begin another struggle to survive, now as freed people. She and her family find acceptance in a community where she becomes a midwife. Remarkably, she survives slavery and its aftermath without rancor against her oppressors.

Walker's depiction of the historic periods, the political interests of the Dutton family, and slavery as an economic institution offer a realistic context for Vyry's story and the stories of other characters. In addition to Vyry, Randall Ware, her first lover, the father of her two children, and a free blacksmith, is an anomaly in the antebellum south. Nevertheless, his nationalistic ideas are representative of black intellectuals and abolitionists of the period. Similarly, the depiction of Missy Dutton as plantation mistress is representative of prevailing, predictable attitudes, but Walker resists stereotyping her characters. Rather, she infuses them with originality as she does in the depiction of Ed Grimes, the plantation overseer.

Walker's novel was widely praised for its authenticity in reconstructing a black folk environment. Most of her black characters, though enslaved, perceive themselves independently of the images of their owners. In their slave community they create and perpetuate folklore—secular songs, spirituals, dances, children's rhymes, stories, creative prayers, sick remedies using herbs, and protective devices using conjure. Folk sayings preface each of the 58 chapters in order to reinforce the folkloric context. The folklore is central to the lives of the characters and to the well being of the slave community, emerging as a natural characteristic. Some of the resources of folklore work as equalizers in distributing justice, others in insuring the health of the community's inhabitants.

Moreover, Walker's transcription of spoken black English is primary to an essential representation of the folk environment and of black southern culture. The language is rich in imaginative metaphor and subtlety of meaning.

Although the idea for *Jubilee* originated in the history of Walker's great-grandmother, Walker researched and documented the oral tradition that was transmitted to her. She subordinates fidelity in the oral account to the demands of novelistic form and artistic integrity. Within its conventional, chronological narrative form, the action is carefully structured and ordered within the three historical periods and provides a memorable and rich evocation of the difficult existence African-Americans endured during those years.

Walker has not chosen to follow *Jubilee* with other historical fiction, although her poetry consistently indicates a perspective enhanced by history. The importance of *Jubilee* as a model historical text cannot be overestimated. Its setting, strong narrative, and emphasis on character—the ordinary female slave rather than the historic heroine—signals an important example to future writers: slavery and the years of its aftermath as a complex and viable setting for the exploration in fiction of African-

American men and women has been ignored for too long. Many stories are waiting to be written.

—Joyce Pettis

———————

WALPOLE, (Sir) Hugh (Seymour). British. Born in Auckland, New Zealand, 13 March 1884, of English parents. Educated at King's School, Canterbury, Kent, and Durham School; Emmanuel College, Cambridge, 1903–06, B.A. (honours) in history 1906. Served with the Russian Red Cross in Galicia, 1914–16; director, Anglo-Russian Propaganda Bureau, Petrograd, 1916–17. Lay minister, Mersey Mission to Seamen, 1906; travelled in France and Germany, 1907; assistant master, Epsom College, Surrey, 1908; full-time writer, in London, from 1909; became a friend of Henry James and Arnold Bennett; gave lecture tours in the United States, from 1919; Rede Lecturer, Cambridge University, 1925. First Chairman of the Selection Committee, Book Society, London, from 1929; first Chairman, Society of Bookmen (now National Book League). Recipient: James Tait Black Memorial prize, 1919, 1920. Fellow, Royal Society of Literature. C.B.E. (Commander, Order of the British Empire), 1918. Knighted, 1937. *Died 1 June 1941.*

Romance and Historical Publications

Novels (series: Herries)

The Dark Forest. London, Secker, and New York, Doran, 1916.
The Secret City. London, Macmillan, and New York, Doran, 1919.
The Cathedral. London, Macmillan, and New York, Doran, 1922.
The Herries Chronicle:
   Rogue Herries. London, Macmillan, and New York, Doubleday, 1930.
   Judith Paris. London, Macmillan, and New York, Doubleday, 1931.
   The Fortress. London, Macmillan, and New York, Doubleday, 1932.
   Vanessa. London, Macmillan, and New York, Doubleday, 1933.
   The Bright Pavilions. London, Macmillan, and New York, Doubleday, 1940.
   Katherine Christian (unfinished). New York, Doubleday, 1943; London, Macmillan, 1944.

Other Publications

Novels

The Wooden Horse. London, Smith Elder, 1909; New York, Doran, 1915.
Maradick at Forty: A Transition. London, Smith Elder, 1910; New York, Duffield, 1911.
Mr. Perrin and Mr. Traill: A Tragi-Comedy. London, Mills and Boon, 1911; as *The Gods and Mr. Perrin*, New York, Century, 1911.
The Prelude to Adventure. London, Mills and Boon, and New York, Century, 1912.

Fortitude, Being the True and Faithful Account of the Education of an Explorer. London, Secker, and New York, Doran, 1913.
The Duchess of Wrexe, Her Decline and Death: A Romantic Commentary. London, Secker, and New York, Doran, 1914.
The Green Mirror: A Quiet Story. New York, Doran, 1917; London, Macmillan, 1918.
Jeremy. London, Cassell, and New York, Doran, 1919.
The Captives. London, Macmillan, and New York, Doran, 1920.
The Young Enchanted: A Romantic Story. London, Macmillan, and New York, Doran, 1921.
Jeremy and Hamlet. London, Cassell, and New York, Doran, 1923.
The Old Ladies. London, Macmillan, and New York, Doran, 1924.
Portrait of a Man with Red Hair: A Romantic Macabre. London, Macmillan, and New York, Doran, 1925.
Harmer John: An Unworldly Story. London, Macmillan, and New York, Doran, 1926.
Jeremy at Crale. London, Cassell, and New York, Doran, 1927.
Wintersmoon. London, Macmillan, and New York, Doubleday, 1928.
Farthing Hall, with J. B. Priestley. London, Macmillan, and New York, Doubleday, 1929.
Hans Frost. London, Macmillan, and New York, Doubleday, 1929.
Above the Dark Circus. London, Macmillan, 1931, as *Above the Dark Tumult*, New York, Doubleday, 1931.
Captain Nicholas. London, Macmillan, and New York, Doubleday, 1934.
The Inquisitor. London, Macmillan, and New York, Doubleday, 1935.
A Prayer for My Son. London, Macmillan, and New York, Doubleday, 1936.
John Cornelius. London, Macmillan, and New York, Doubleday, 1937.
The Joyful Delaneys. London, Macmillan, and New York, Doubleday, 1938.
The Sea Tower: A Love Story. London, Macmillan, and New York, Doubleday, 1939.
The Blind Man's House. London, Macmillan, and New York, Doubleday, 1941.
The Killer and the Slain. London, Macmillan, and New York, Doubleday, 1942.

Short Stories

The Golden Scarecrow. London, Cassell, and New York, Doran, 1915.
The Thirteen Travellers. London, Hutchinson, and New York, Doran, 1921.
The Silver Thorn. London, Macmillan, and New York, Doubleday, 1928.
All Souls' Night. London, Macmillan, and New York, Doubleday, 1933.
Cathedral Carol Service. London, Faber, 1934.
Head in Green Bronze and Other Stories. London, Macmillan, and New York, Doubleday, 1938.
Mr. Huffam and Other Stories. London, Macmillan, 1948.

Plays

Robin's Father, with Rudolf Besier (produced Liverpool, 1918).

The Cathedral, adaptation of his own novel (produced London, 1932). London, Macmillan, 1937.
The Young Huntress (produced London, 1933).
The Haxtons (produced Liverpool, 1939). London, Deane, and Boston, Baker, 1939.

Screenplays: *David Copperfield*, with Howard Estabrook, 1934; *Vanessa: Her Love Story*, 1935; *Little Lord Fauntleroy*, 1936.

Radio Serial: *Behind the Screen*, with others, 1930.

Other

Joseph Conrad. London, Nisbet, and New York, Holt, 1916; revised edition, Nisbet, 1924.
The Art of James Branch Cabell. New York, McBride, 1920.
A Hugh Walpole Anthology. London, Dent, and New York, Dutton, 1921.
The Crystal Box. Privately printed, 1924.
The English Novel: Some Notes on Its Evolution (lecture). Cambridge, University Press, 1925.
Reading: An Essay. London, Jarrolds, and New York, Harper, 1926.
A Stranger (for children), with *Red Pepper*, by Thomas Quayle. Oxford, Blackwell, 1926.
Anthony Trollope. London and New York, Macmillan, 1928.
My Religious Experience. London, Benn, 1928.
The Apple Trees: Four Reminiscences. Waltham St. Lawrence, Berkshire, Golden Cockerell Press, 1932.
A Letter to a Modern Novelist. London, Hogarth Press, 1932.
Extracts from a Diary. Privately printed, 1934.
Works (Cumberland Edition). London, Macmillan, 30 vols., 1934–40.
Claude Houghton: Appreciations, with Clemence Dane. London, Heinemann, 1935.
Roman Fountain (travel). London, Macmillan, and New York, Doubleday, 1940.
A Note . . . on the Origins of the Herries Chronicle. New York, Doubleday, 1940.
The Freedom of Books. London, National Book Council, 1940.
Open Letter of an Optimist. London, Macmillan, 1941.
Women Are Motherly. London, Todd, 1943.

Editor, *The Waverley Pageant: The Best Passages from the Novels of Sir Walter Scott*. London, Eyre and Spottiswoode, 1932.
Editor, *Essays and Studies 18*. London, English Association, 1933.
Editor, with Wilfred Partington, *Famous Stories of Five Centuries*. New York, Farrar and Rinehart, 1934.
Editor, with others, *The Nonesuch Dickens*. London, Nonesuch Press, 23 vols., 1937–38.
Editor, *A Second Century of Creepy Stories*. London, Hutchinson, 1937.

*

Manuscript Collections: Fitz Park Museum, Keswick, Cumberland; King's School, Canterbury, Kent; British Library, London; Berg Collection, New York Public Library; Library of Congress, Washington, D.C.

Critical Studies: *Hugh Walpole: A Study* by Marguerite Steen, London, Nicholson and Watson, and New York, Doubleday, 1933; *Hugh Walpole: A Biography* by Rupert Hart-Davis, London and New York, Macmillan, 1952; *Hugh Walpole* by Elizabeth Steel, New York, Twayne, 1972.

*　　*　　*

Some 40 green chunky novels, gold-lettered and dignified, by Hugh Walpole, made a familiar clutch on pre-war shelves. On both sides of the Atlantic they sold in their thousands, several being made into films. His children's books popularised the name Jeremy. Today, perhaps a dozen books survive in print, and the young may know nothing of him. Students may still notice F. R. Leavis's dismissal of an "utterly untalented manufacturer of Book Society Classics." Of one section of his most ambitious work, The Herries Chronicle, his friend Virginia Woolf, whose admiration he craved and never received, wrote, "True, it's competent enough, spare in the wording—but words without roots, yes, that's it, all a trivial litter of bright objects to be swept up."

Readers thought otherwise, and the main volumes of the Herries saga, spanning 1730 to 1932, *Rogue Herries, Judith Paris, The Fortress*, and *Vanessa*, can be found in public libraries and in paperbacks, all much read, though perhaps by veterans from a pre-television era, which cherished leisurely, sprawling plots and a teeming variety of interrelated characters, breeding sequels that ended only with their author's life. Enriched by historical facts, sentimental, lush, occasionally tragic, the Herries clan rivalled the Forsytes. They are, however, more vigorously committed to heroic adventure, villainous intrigue and betrayal, griefs, loves and domestic tyranny, set against national conflict and social change, public triumphs and disasters, ancient houses, London, alternately tempestuous and grave, and, where Walpole was most at home, the English countryside, particularly Cumberland, always changing, now sullen and mysterious, now open and radiant.

Walpole himself judged this "lakeland epic" his masterpiece. "My view of the Herries is frankly a romantic one . . . not realistic, comic, scientific, but a piece of gaily-tinted tapestry worked in English colours."

Walpole wanted to be ranked among the best, but at no time has his formula been a guarantee of critical acclaim, and in a literature dominated by Joyce and Lawrence, Woolf and Huxley, Hemingway and Fitzgerald, the dons scorned Walpole and the public that cherished him. His most high-flying work, the Herries books and the Polchester novels, were dismissed as facile, careless, sententious, and academic. This last is true enough, meaning not that the work lacked life or talent, but that it conformed too closely to that of his beloved predecessors: Scott, Trollope, James. Here he took the novel as he found it, rejoiced in it, cheerfully worked within its limitations. The truth is, however, that only when he trusted his own experiences, in the wartime Russian Red Cross and in the hell-pit of a minor public school common room, did he achieve a success that may better endure.

Scott is the prevailing genius behind the Herries books, though Walpole's lively invention is all his own. He was a natural storyteller, sometimes grotesque, sometimes lyrical, but always in love with his subject. In these books, as in his short psychological thrillers, he was skilled in depicting cruelty. A notoriously vulnerable man, he had early realised the perils lurking outside a bright nursery, within a quiet cathedral town, a school playground, a Cumberland landscape of daffodils and blue water. Written with no great subtlety, in broad, uninhibited, sometimes melodramatic strokes, the "grand impetuosity" praised by J. B. Priestley, the historical romances do fail at the highest level. But they can still offer pleasures to those who seek highly-charged narrative from a writer not much perturbed by literary and psychological schools, and anything that seemed to question individual reality. He believed in his heroes and heroines, writing for those to whom "well-made" was not a term of abuse.

—Peter Vansittart

WALSH, Sheila. Also writes as Sophie Leyton. British. Born in Birmingham, Warwickshire, 10 October 1928. Educated at Notre Dame Convent, Birkdale, Lancashire; Southport College of Art, Lancashire, 1945–48. Married Desmond Walsh in 1950; two daughters. Secretary, 1983, and chairwoman, 1985–87, Romantic Novelists Association. Recipient: Romantic Novelists Association Netta Muskett award, 1973, and Major award, 1984. Agent: Mary Irvine, 11 Upland Park Road, Oxford OX2 7RU. Address: 35 Coudray Road, Southport, Merseyside PR9 9NL, England.

ROMANCE AND HISTORICAL PUBLICATIONS

Novels

The Golden Songbird. London, Hurst and Blackett, and New York, New American Library, 1975.
Madalena. London, Hurst and Blackett, 1976; New York, New American Library, 1977.
The Sergeant Major's Daughter. London, Hurst and Blackett, 1977; New York, New American Library, 1978.
A Fine Silk Purse. London, Hurst and Blackett, 1978; as *Lord Gilmore's Bride*, New York, New American Library, 1979.
The Incomparable Miss Brady. London, Hutchinson, and New York, New American Library, 1980.
Lady Cecily's Dilemma (as Sophie Leyton). London, Octopus, 1980; as *The Pink Parasol* (as Sheila Walsh), New York, New American Library, 1985.
The Rose Domino. New York, New American Library, 1981; London, Hutchinson, 1982.
A Highly Respectable Marriage. London, Hutchinson, 1983.
The Runaway Bride. London, Hutchinson, 1984.
Cousins of a Kind. London, Mills and Boon, 1985; as *The Diamond Waterfall*, New York, New American Library, 1985.
Improper Aquaintances. London, Mills and Boon, 1985; as *The Incorrigible Rake*, New York, New American Library, 1985.
The Wary Widow. New York, New American Library, 1985; as *An Insubstantial Pageant*, London, Century, 1986.
Bath Intrigue. New York, New American Library, 1986; London, Century, 1987.
Lady Aurelia's Bequest. New York, New American Library, 1987; London, Century, 1989.
Minerva's Marquis. London, Mills and Boon, and New York, New American Library, 1988.
The Nabob. London, Mills and Boon, and New York, New American Library, 1989.

*

Sheila Walsh comments:

All my books to date have been set in or around the Regency period, and are essentially light-hearted amusing stories in the Georgette Heyer tradition—an entertaining "read," I hope, for anyone wanting to forget their problems for a little while.

*   *   *

One of the best and most prolific of the current Regency novelists, Sheila Walsh writes in the classic style and tradition of Georgette Heyer. Her novels are marked by well-developed, sympathetic characters and intriguing, if predictable, plots. She is skillful in following the conventions of the genre, combining dangerous situations for her heroines with appealing love stories.

The focal point of Walsh's stories is obviously the heroine. Each of these women is proud, fiercely independent, and seeks her own solutions to her problems. Felicity (*The Sergeant Major's Daughter*) is severely beaten by the villain but continues to operate a village school, even at the risk of her own life. Clementina (*The Incomparable Miss Brady*) is abducted by an unprincipled rake, but when the hero arrives to save her, he finds her tending her wounded abductor. Pilar (*A Fine Silk Purse*) saves her husband and father by killing her wicked uncle. Perdita (*Bath Intrigue*) also is abducted but befriends the poor family charged with holding her for her evil cousin. Although their efforts may be thwarted by superior strength or numbers, these intrepid women think and act courageously.

Walsh also is successful in creating some interesting perils, which allow a great deal of action to develop. Incarceration in a brothel (*The Golden Songbird*), blackmail (*The Rose Domino*), and fire (*The Sergeant Major's Daughter*) are only a few of the dangers which threaten the lives and honor of the heroines, but abduction and attempted murder by a scheming relative or rival play a part in several stories (*Bath Intrigue*, *Minerva's Marquess*, *A Highly Respectable Marriage*, *Cousins of a Kind*).

The male counterparts of these resourceful women are cast in the common mold of the handsome, somewhat dictatorial aristocrat, who is often a rake about to be reformed. Frequently the heroine is pursued by two seemingly eligible men, but usually it is soon obvious which is to be her love. It is equally obvious that the two temperaments will lead to a clash of wills. That, after all, is a major source of interest in the Regency novel. Walsh, however, manages to keep the antagonistic aspects of such relationships within bounds and develop her characters so that the reader can believe in the development of mutual respect and affection and the inevitable happy ending. Overall Walsh is one of the most reliable of traditional Regency novelists.

—Barbara E. Kemp

WARE, Monica. See **WOODWARD, Lilian.**

WARNER, Rex (Ernest). British. Born in Birmingham, Warwickshire, 9 March 1905. Educated at St. George's School, Harpenden, Hertfordshire; Wadham College, Oxford (open classical scholar), B.A. (honours) in classics and English literature 1928. Served in the Home Guard, London, 1942–45. Married 1) Frances Chamier Grove in 1929, two sons and one daughter; 2) Barbara, Lady Rothschild in 1949, one daughter; 3) remarried Frances Chamier Grove in 1966. Schoolmaster in Egypt and England, 1928–45; worked for the Control Commission in Berlin, 1945, 1947; director, British Institute, Athens, 1945–47; Tallman Professor, Bowdoin College, Brunswick, Maine, 1962–63; Professor of English, University of Connecticut, Storrs, 1964–74. Recipient: James Tait Black Memorial prize, 1961. D.Litt.:

Rider College, Trenton, New Jersey, 1968. Honorary Fellow, Wadham College, 1973. Commander, Royal Order of the Phoenix, Greece, 1963. *Died 24 June 1986.*

ROMANCE AND HISTORICAL PUBLICATIONS

Novels

The Young Caesar. London, Collins, and Boston, Little Brown, 1958.
Imperial Caesar. London, Collins, and Boston, Little Brown, 1960.
Pericles the Athenian. London, Collins, and Boston, Little Brown, 1963.
The Converts. London, Bodley Head, and Boston, Little Brown, 1967.

OTHER PUBLICATIONS

Novels

The Wild Goose Chase. London, Boriswood, and New York, Knopf, 1937.
The Professor. London, Boriswood, 1938; New York, Knopf, 1939.
The Aerodrome. London, Lane, 1941; Philadelphia, Lippincott, 1946.
Why Was I Killed? A Dramatic Dialogue. London, Lane, 1943; as *Return of the Traveller*, Philadelphia, Lippincott, 1944.
Men of Stones: A Melodrama. London, Lane, 1949; Philadelphia, Lippincott, 1950.
Escapade: A Tale of Average. London, Lane, 1953.

Plays

Screenplays (documentaries): *World with End*, 1953; *The Immortal Land*, 1958.

Verse

Poems. London, Boriswood, 1937; New York, Knopf, 1938; revised edition, as *Poems and Contradictions*, London, Lane, 1945.

Other

The Kite (for children). Oxford, Blackwell, 1936; revised edition, London, Hamish Hamilton, 1963.
English Public Schools. London, Collins, 1945.
The Cult of Power: Essays. London, Lane, 1946; Philadelphia, Lippincott, 1947.
John Milton. London, Parrish, 1949; New York, Chanticleer Press, 1950.
Views of Attica and Its Surroundings. London, Lehmann, 1950.
E. M. Forster. London, Longman, 1950.
Men and Gods. London, MacGibbon and Kee, 1950; New York, Farrar Straus, 1951.
Ashes to Ashes: A Post-Mortem on the 1950–51 Tests, with Lyle Blair. London, MacGibbon and Kee, 1951.
Greeks and Trojans. London, MacGibbon and Kee, 1951.
Eternal Greece, photographs by Martin Hurlimann. London, Thames and Hudson, and New York, Viking Press, 1953.
The Vengeance of the Gods. London, MacGibbon and Kee, 1954.

Athens. London, Thames and Hudson, and New York, Studio, 1956.
The Greek Philosophers. New York, New American Library, 1958.
Look at Birds (for children). London, Hamish Hamilton, 1962.
The Stories of the Greeks. New York, Farrar Straus, 1967; London, Granada, 1979.
Athens at War: Retold from the History of the Peloponnesian War of Thucydides. London, Bodley Head, 1970; New York, Dutton, 1971.
Men of Athens: The Story of Fifth Century Athens. London, Bodley Head, and New York, Viking Press, 1972.

Editor, with Laurie Lee and Christopher Hassall, *New Poems 1954*. London, Joseph, 1954.
Editor, *Look Up at the Skies! Poems and Prose*, by Gerard Manley Hopkins. London, Bodley Head, 1972.

Translator, *The Medea of Euripides.* London, Lane, 1944; New York, Chanticleer Press, 1949.
Translator, *Prometheus Bound*, by Aeschylus. London, Lane, 1947; New York, Chanticleer Press, 1949.
Translator, *The Persian Expedition*, by Xenophon. London, Penguin, 1949.
Translator, *Hippolytus*, by Euripides. London, Lane, 1949; New York, Chanticleer Press, 1950.
Translator, *Helen*, by Euripides. London, Lane, 1951.
Translator, *The Peloponnesian War*, by Thucydides. London, Penguin, 1954.
Translator, *The Fall of the Roman Republic: Marius, Sulla, Crassus, Pompey, Caesar, Cicero: Six Lives*, by Plutarch. London, Penguin, 1958; revised edition, 1972.
Translator, *Poems of George Seferis.* London, Bodley Head, 1960; Boston, Godine, 1979.
Translator, *War Commentaries of Caesar.* New York, New American Library, 1960.
Translator, *Confessions of St. Augustine.* New York, New American Library, 1963.
Translator, with Th. D. Frangopoulos, *On the Greek Style: Selected Essays in Poetry and Hellenism*, by George Seferis. Boston, Little Brown, 1966; London, Bodley Head, 1967.
Translator, *A History of My Times*, by Xenophon. London, Penguin, 1966.
Translator, *Moral Essays*, by Plutarch. London, Penguin, 1971.

*

Manuscript Collection: University of Connecticut, Storrs.

Critical Studies: *Rex Warner, Writer* by A. L. McLeod, Sydney, Wentworth Press, 1960, and *The Achievement of Rex Warner* (includes bibliography) edited by McLeod, Wentworth Press, 1965.

*   *   *

Rex Warner, classical scholar, poet, essayist, novelist, won a pre-war reputation primarily for three novels, allegorical, at times surrealistic, sometimes glibly compared to Kafka with their experiments in grotesquely heightened vision of contemporary life and objects. Actually, however, their fantasy, imagery, and humour, were very English, almost Dickensian, with strong anti-totalitarian insights. Thenceforward, feeling perhaps that he was at a dead end, he made a severe change of course with his fiction, notably his historical novels set in the classical world.

Warner's historical novels are conventional, in a form popularised by Robert Graves, Naomi Mitchison, and Peter Green;

they are written in a style clear, precise, vivid, with the poet's feeling for words. Each centres on a celebrated historical figure: Julius Caesar, Pericles, Augustine of Hippo. The dangers of this are obvious, but on a level serious, though without genius, they succeed admirably. Warner had always been profoundly engrossed with power, its responsibilities and pitfalls, its opportunities for human betterment and for frantic self-indulgence, its philosophical implications in the realm of good and evil. This theme pervades the historical novels, where he is thoroughly at home in the intricacies of Roman and Athenian politics, the tortuous debates of early Christians and North African Manichees.

In *The Young Caesar* Warner speaks through Julius, elegant, sophisticated, and intelligent, the paradoxical saviour of society who, disdainful of violence, nevertheless storms 800 cities and subdues 300 peoples. A realist, Caesar is shocked by stupidity, conceit, inefficiency, and greed for its own sake, so conspicuous among the power-politicians crowding around him, and the corrupt and unproductive Roman populace so easily fooled by doles and operatics. He shows magnanimity, both civilised and calculating in his own pursuit of power, first for personal, then for national survival. His self-belief grows with disappointments at the follies of others, and his disillusion with Republican traditions and institutions.

In this and the later novels Warner writes as if from the hero's hindsight, coolly, smooth as a lawyer's brief, without much tension or unusual factual or stylistic invention; here is Caesar:

It is, as experience will show, not at all uncommon for middle-aged men to fall passionately in love, and Pompey now fell in love with my daughter Julia. Nothing, of course, could suit my interests better than to have Pompey as my son-in-law: moreover, I was beginning to like him and could see that he would almost certainly make my daughter happy; Julia too was attracted both by him personally and not unreasonably, by the prospect of becoming the wife of one who was still known as the greatest man in the world. Then I had the somewhat embarrassing task of persuading my old friend Servilia that it was necessary to break off what had amounted to an engagement between Julia and her own son, young Brutus. Here, as so often, Servilia showed herself extremely sensible. It was about this time, I think, that I bought for her a pearl, for which I paid more money than had ever been paid before in Rome for a single piece of jewellery.

For some of Warner's original admirers, this passage may represent a failure of nerve. The whole enterprise could be dismissed as pastiche, cut-price scholarship, the successful product of an ageing, very literate scholar, of substance but without verve, certainly not quaint or antiquarian, but following trails long charted by others. There is certainly no more experiment. But the four novels, *The Young Caesar, Imperial Caesar, Pericles the Athenian*, and *The Converts*, are not escapist romances. They aim to put flesh on events and people fairly familiar but always engrossing, facing problems of power, belief, and self-mastery that remain topical. None is a great novel with complexities elevated to myth or epic, but each provides glosses on tales over which intelligent people have absorbed themselves for nearly two millennia.

—Peter Vansittart

WARNER, Sylvia Townsend. British. Born in Harrow, Middlesex, 6 December 1893. Educated privately. Worked in a munitions factory, 1916; member of the editorial board, *Tudor Church Music*, Oxford University Press, London, 1917–26; lived with the writer Valentine Ackland, 1930–69; joined Communist Party, 1935; Red Cross volunteer, Barcelona, 1935; contributor to the *New Yorker* from 1936. Recipient: Katherine Mansfield-Menton prize, 1968. Fellow, Royal Society of Literature, 1967; honorary member, American Academy, 1972. *Died 1 May 1978.*

ROMANCE AND HISTORICAL PUBLICATIONS

Novels

Summer Will Show. London, Chatto and Windus, and New York, Viking Press, 1936.
After the Death of Don Juan. London, Chatto and Windus, 1938; New York, Viking Press, 1939.
The Corner That Held Them. London, Chatto and Windus, and New York, Viking Press, 1948.
The Flint Anchor. London, Chatto and Windus, and New York, Viking Press, 1954; as *The Barnards of Loseby*, New York, Popular Library, 1974.

OTHER PUBLICATIONS

Novels

Lolly Willowes; or, The Loving Huntsman. London, Chatto and Windus, and New York, Viking Press, 1926.
Mr. Fortune's Maggot. London, Chatto and Windus, and New York, Viking Press, 1927.
The True Heart. London, Chatto and Windus, and New York, Viking Press, 1929.

Short Stories

The Maze: A Story to Be Read Aloud. London, The Fleuron, 1928.
Some World Far from Ours; and Stay, Corydon, Thou Swain. London, Mathews and Marrot, 1929.
Elinor Barley. London, Cresset Press, and Chicago, Argus, 1930.
A Moral Ending and Other Stories. London, Joiner and Steele, 1931.
The Salutation. London, Chatto and Windus, and New York, Viking Press, 1932.
More Joy in Heaven and Other Stories. London, Cresset Press, 1935.
24 Short Stories, with Graham Greene and James Laver. London, Cresset Press, 1939.
The Cat's Cradle-Book. New York, Viking Press, 1940; London, Chatto and Windus, 1960.
A Garland of Straw and Other Stories. London, Chatto and Windus, and New York, Viking Press, 1943.
The Museum of Cheats. London, Chatto and Windus, and New York, Viking Press, 1947.
Winter in the Air and Other Stories. London, Chatto and Windus, 1955; New York, Viking Press, 1956.
A Spirit Rises. London, Chatto and Windus, and New York, Viking Press, 1962.
A Stranger with a Bag and Other Stories. London, Chatto and Windus, 1966; as *Swans on an Autumn River*, New York, Viking Press, 1966.

The Innocent and the Guilty. London, Chatto and Windus, and New York, Viking Press, 1971.

Kingdoms of Elfin. London, Chatto and Windus, and New York, Viking Press, 1977.

Scenes of Childhood. London, Chatto and Windus, 1981; New York, Viking Press, 1982.

One Thing Leading to Another and Other Stories, edited by Susanna Pinney. London, Chatto and Windus, and New York, Viking, 1984.

Selected Stories, edited by Susanna Pinney and William Maxwell. London, Chatto and Windus, 1988.

Verse

The Espalier. London, Chatto and Windus, and New York, Dial Press, 1925.

Time Importuned. London, Chatto and Windus, and New York, Viking Press, 1928.

Opus 7: A Poem. London, Chatto and Windus, and New York, Viking Press, 1931.

Rainbow. New York, Knopf, 1932.

Whether a Dove or a Seagull, with Valentine Ackland. New York, Viking Press, 1933; London, Chatto and Windus, 1934.

Two Poems. Privately printed, 1945.

Twenty-eight Poems, with Valentine Ackland. Privately printed, 1957.

Boxwood: Sixteen Engravings by Reynolds Stone Illustrated in Verse. Privately printed, 1957; revised edition, as *Boxwood: Twenty-one Engravings*, London, Chatto and Windus-Cape, 1960.

King Duffus and Other Poems. Privately printed, 1968.

Azrael and Other Poems. Privately printed, 1978; as *Twelve Poems*, London, Chatto and Windus, 1980.

Collected Poems, edited by Claire Harman. Manchester, Carcanet, and New York, Viking Press, 1982.

Selected Poems. Manchester, Carcanet, and New York, Viking, 1985.

Other

Somerset. London, Elek, 1949.

Jane Austen 1775–1817. London, Longman, 1951; revised edition, 1957.

Sketches from Nature (reminiscences). Privately printed, 1963.

T. H. White: A Biography. London, Cape-Chatto and Windus, 1967; New York, Viking Press, 1968.

Letters, edited by William Maxwell. London, Chatto and Windus, 1982; New York, Viking Press, 1983.

Editor, *The Week-end Dickens*. London, Maclehose, 1932; New York, Loring and Mussey, 1932(?).

Editor, *The Portrait of a Tortoise: Extracted from the Journals and Letters of Gilbert White*. London, Chatto and Windus, 1946.

Translator, *By Way of Saint-Beuve*, by Marcel Proust. London, Chatto and Windus, 1958; as *On Art and Literature 1896–1917*, New York, Meridian, 1958.

Translator, *A Place of Shipwreck*, by Jean René Huguenin. London, Chatto and Windus, 1963.

Published Music: *Alleluia: Anthem for Five Voices*, London, Oxford University Press, 1925.

*

Critical Studies: *This Narrow Place: Sylvia Townsend Warner and Valentine Ackland: Life, Letters and Politics 1930–1951* by Wendy Mulford, London, Pandora Press, 1988; *Sylvia Townsend Warner: A Biography* by Claire Harman, London, Chatto and Windus, 1989.

*   *   *

In her historical novels Sylvia Townsend Warner provides a hint of what Jane Austen might have accomplished, had she chosen to step outside her private, middle-class world, and treat the world at large. Warner shares Austen's middle-class origins as well as her predilection for irony; but, in *Summer Will Show* and *After the Death of Don Juan*, she leaves the comfortable world of *Lolly Willowes* to follow the path of revolution into France and Spain.

Jack Lindsay, of Fanfrolico Press fame, had great faith in the historical novel "as a fighting weapon and a cultural instrument"; and, for a time, at least, Warner seems to have shared that faith. Her first unequivocally historical novel, *Summer Will Show*, takes us back to 1848, the Year of Revolution, but at least one perceptive reviewer in the *Literary Digest* realised that it was also "in a sense a parable of our own troubled time." Sophia Willoughby, an upper-middle-class wife and mother, had often dreamed of "leading a wild romantic life," but it takes the death of her children from smallpox to get her out of Blandamer House, Dorset. No revolutionary at first, she journeys to Paris in the hope that her errant husband, Frederick, will take time off from his Bohemian mistress, Minna Lemuel, to father another child. Once in Paris, however, Sophia is inexorably drawn into the revolution by the woman who is ostensibly her rival; for Minna has already achieved a personal freedom of which Sophia has only dreamed. We are obviously intended to draw the parallel between the revolution in progress on the barricades and that being stirred within Sophia herself. In particular, we are meant to recognise the shared economic roots of both. When Frederick freezes her assets and cuts off her income, Ingelbrecht, the revolutionary theorist, characterises Sophia as the victim of a lockout. And Martin, the communist leader, chides her for her political naivety: "Really Madame, for an Englishwoman, reared at the very hearth of political economy, you have been a little dense." By the end of the novel Sophia is ready to die for the revolution she had once disdained. Ironically, she is spared because the officer in charge of the firing squad exclaims: "I cannot consent to the death of a *lady*." The novel ends with Sophia reading—"obdurately attentive and by degrees absorbed"—a tract which calls for a Communist Manifesto.

In spite of being frankly political, *Summer Will Show* succeeds as a novel because it harmonises the external struggle with the internal so well, and effects a triumphant integration of the individual into revolutionary society. As important as Sophia's political radicalisation is her sexual reorientation. Sophia Willoughby is, to some extent, of course, a projection of Sylvia Warner (and Willoughby is not far from Willowes). Liberated from marriage, Sophia is drawn to a movement in which the key figure, Minna, is a woman and a storyteller. Soon enough, Sophia has stolen the affections of her estranged husband's mistress. The moment when their love crystallises is over four lines of a poem by Andrew Marvell discovered by the two women at a secondhand bookstall:

> My love is of a birth as rare
> As 'tis of object strange and high
> It was begotten by despair
> Upon impossibility

Warner's own long-time relationship with Valentine Ackland, recently made public, in fact began in 1930; so the novel can now be read as doubly revolutionary, and as rather more than a political statement.

Warner's growing political commitment in the 1930's (she joined the Communist Party) led her to make two long trips to Spain during the Spanish Civil War—first to Barcelona in 1935, and then to Madrid and Valencia for the Writers Congress in 1937. On her return, she dedicated herself, with characteristic energy, to writing about the Republican cause—poems, reviews, and essays, many of which appeared in *Left Review*. Inevitably this commitment extended to her fiction, now to be written beneath the banner of "Art for Man's Sake." So although *After the Death of Don Juan* is set in late 18th-century Spain, it is properly regarded as Warner's contribution to the literature of the Spanish Civil War. For in the novel she attempts, with commendable restraint, to weigh the future of Spain in terms of its past. In a letter to Nancy Cunard, she later called it "a parable [that word again], if you like the word, or an allegory . . . of the political chemistry of the Spanish War, with the Don Juan . . . developing as the Fascist of the piece." The action is centred in Tenorio Viejo, a village too small even to be marked on the maps. Into this "array of lime-washed hovels," comes a society group from Seville, led by Dona Ana and Don Ottavio, to inform Don Saturno of the terrible fate of his son, Don Juan, reportedly dragged down to Hell by devils. Don Saturno, owner of the estate within which the village lies, has brought education to his people, though well aware of the possible cost: "All progress . . . must rebound upon the bestower. In times to come, no doubt, my simple village will be a hive of revolutionaries." The unexpected reappearance of Don Juan, whose past extravagance has frustrated all hopes of a long-promised and much-needed irrigation system, leads to open conflict between the peasants and the nobility in the castle. Without his father's consent, Don Juan sends for troops who begin, reluctantly but bloodily, to put down the rebellion. In the final scene, two of the ringleaders, Diego and Ramon Perez, the village "man of reason," are trapped in the schoolhouse, and face imminent death: "They looked at each other long and intently, as though they were pledged to meet again and would ensure a recognition."

In her two postwar novels Warner continues her preoccupation with society rather than with the individual. But where the two novels of the 1930's address, at least in part, the very nature of society itself, the later novels retreat to a world every bit as circumscribed as that of Jane Austen, and, in some ways, far more claustrophobic. The settings are now both English and resolutely domestic. In *The Corner That Held Them* the focus is upon a 14th-century Benedictine convent. The nuns of Oby have consciously cut themselves off from the world, hoping to keep at bay both the Black Death and the not-so-distant rumblings of social unrest. Yet they prove to be no less subject to sin than outsiders, and they must still grapple with such calamities as the collapse of the convent spire and the defection of one of their members. Moreover, they are demonstrably "prisoners of darkness, and fettered with the bonds of a long night," to quote the *Wisdom of Solomon*, source of the novel's title. Significantly too, their patron is St. Leonard, "patron of the convent and of all prisoners."

The Flint Anchor is a 19th-century family chronicle with the same pervasive claustrophobic atmosphere as *The Corner That Held Them*. At the centre of the novel is the stern patriarch John Barnard, who, for all his righteousness, "had spread around him a desert of mendacity and discomfort." Some members of the Barnard family actually escape from behind the 12-foot flint walls of Anchor House; but for Euphemia it is a dubious escape

to a Moravian religious community, while Ellen's dreams merely hover round a cloister.

—J. Lawrence Mitchell

WARREN, Mary Douglas. See **GREIG, Maysie.**

WARREN, Robert Penn. American. Born in Guthrie, Kentucky, 24 April 1905. Educated at Guthrie High School; Vanderbilt University, Nashville, Tennessee, 1921–25, B.A. (summa cum laude) 1925; University of California, Berkeley, M.A. 1927; Yale University, New Haven, Connecticut, 1927–28; Oxford University (Rhodes scholar), B. Litt. 1930. Married 1) Emma Brescia in 1930 (divorced 1950); 2) the writer Eleanor Clark in 1952, one son and one daughter. Assistant Professor, Southwestern College, Memphis, Tennessee, 1930–31, and Vanderbilt University, 1931–34; Assistant and Associate Professor, Louisiana State University, Baton Rouge, 1934–42; Professor of English, University of Minnesota, Minneapolis, 1942–50. Professor of Playwriting, 1950–56, Professor of English, 1962–73, and from 1973 Professor Emeritus, Yale University. Member of the Fugitive Group of poets: co-founding editor, the *Fugitive*, Nashville, 1923–25; founding editor, *Southern Review*, Baton Rouge, Louisiana, 1935–42; advisory editor, *Kenyon Review*, Gambier, Ohio, 1942–63. Consultant in Poetry, Library of Congress, Washington, D.C., 1944–45; Jefferson Lecturer, National Endowment for the Humanities, 1974. Recipient: Caroline Sinkler award, 1936, 1937, 1938; Levinson prize, 1936, Union League Civic and Arts Foundation prize, 1953, and Harriet Monroe prize, 1976 (*Poetry*, Chicago); Houghton Mifflin fellowship, 1939; Guggenheim fellowship, 1939, 1947; Shelley Memorial award, 1943; Pulitzer prize, for fiction, 1947, for poetry, 1958, 1979; Screenwriters Guild Meltzer award, 1949; Foreign Book prize (France), 1950; Sidney Hillman prize, 1957; Edna St. Vincent Millay Memorial prize, 1958; National Book award, for poetry, 1958; New York *Herald-Tribune* Van Doren award, 1965; Bollingen prize, for poetry, 1967; National Endowment for the Arts grant, 1968, and lectureship, 1974; Henry A. Bellaman prize, 1970; Van Wyck Brooks award, for poetry, 1970; National Medal for Literature, 1970; Emerson-Thoreau Medal, 1975; Copernicus award, 1976; Presidential Medal of Freedom, 1980; Common Wealth award, 1981; MacArthur fellowship, 1981; Brandeis University Creative Arts award, 1983. D.Litt.: University of Louisville, Kentucky, 1949; Kenyon College, Gambier, Ohio, 1952; Colby College, Waterville, Maine, 1956; University of Kentucky, Lexington, 1957; Swarthmore College, Pennsylvania, 1959; Yale University, 1960; Fairfield University, Connecticut, 1969; Wesleyan University, Middletown, Connecticut, 1970; Harvard University, Cambridge, Massachusetts, 1973; Southwestern College, 1974; University of the South, Sewanee, Tennessee, 1974; Monmouth College, Illinois, 1979; New York University, 1983; Oxford University, 1983; LL.D.: Bridgeport University, Connecticut, 1965; University of New Haven, Connecticut, 1974; Johns Hopkins University, Baltimore, 1977. Member, American Academy, and American Academy of Arts and Sciences; Chancellor, Academy of American Poets, 1972. Poet Laureate, 1986. *Died 15 September 1989.*

ROMANCE AND HISTORICAL PUBLICATIONS

Novels

World Enough and Time: A Romantic Novel. New York, Random House, 1950; London, Eyre and Spottiswoode, 1951.
Band of Angels. New York, Random House, 1955; London, Eyre and Spottiswoode, 1956.
Wilderness: A Tale of the Civil War. New York, Random House, 1961; London, Eyre and Spottiswoode, 1962.

OTHER PUBLICATIONS

Novels

Night Rider. Boston, Houghton Mifflin, 1939; London, Eyre and Spottiswoode, 1940.
At Heaven's Gate. New York, Harcourt Brace, 1943; London, Eyre and Spottiswoode, 1946.
All the King's Men. New York, Harcourt Brace, 1946; London, Eyre and Spottiswoode, 1948.
The Cave. New York, Random House, and London, Eyre and Spottiswoode, 1959.
Flood: A Romance of Our Time. New York, Random House, and London, Collins, 1964.
Meet Me in the Green Glen. New York, Random House, 1971; London, Secker and Warburg, 1972.
A Place to Come To. New York, Random House, and London, Secker and Warburg, 1977.

Short Stories

Blackberry Winter. Cummington, Massachusetts, Cummington Press, 1946.
The Circus in the Attic and Other Stories. New York, Harcourt Brace, 1948; London, Eyre and Spottiswoode, 1952.

Plays

Proud Flesh (in verse, produced Minneapolis, 1947; revised [prose] version, produced New York, 1947).
All the King's Men, adaptation of his own novel (as *Willie Stark: His Rise and Fall*, produced Dallas, 1958; as *All the King's Men*, produced New York, 1959). New York, Random House, 1960.

Verse

Thirty-Six Poems. New York, Alcestis Press, 1936.
Eleven Poems on the Same Theme. New York, New Directions, 1942.
Selected Poems 1923–1943. New York, Harcourt Brace, 1944; London, Fortune Press, 1952.
Brother to Dragons: A Tale in Verse and Voices. New York, Random House, 1953; London, Eyre and Spottiswoode, 1954; revised edition, Random House, 1979.
To a Little Girl, One Year Old, in a Ruined Fortress. Privately printed, 1956.
Promises: Poems 1954–1956. New York, Random House, 1957; London, Eyre and Spottiswoode, 1959.
You, Emperors, and Others: Poems 1957–1960. New York, Random House, 1960.
Selected Poems: New and Old 1923–1966. New York, Random House, 1966.

Incarnations: Poems 1966–1968. New York, Random House, 1968; London, W. H. Allen, 1970.
Audubon: A Vision. New York, Random House, 1969.
Or Else: Poem/Poems 1968–1974. New York, Random House, 1974.
Selected Poems 1923–1975. New York, Random House, and London, Secker and Warburg, 1977.
Now and Then: Poems 1976–1978. New York, Random House, 1978.
Two Poems. Winston-Salem, North Carolina, Palaemon Press, 1979.
Being Here: Poetry 1977–1980. New York, Random House, and London, Secker and Warburg, 1980.
Love. Winston-Salem, North Carolina, Palaemon Press, 1981.
Rumor Verified: Poems 1979–1980. New York, Random House, and London, Secker and Warburg, 1981.
Chief Joseph of the Nez Perce. New York, Random House, and London, Secker and Warburg, 1983.
New and Selected Poems 1923–1985. New York, Random House, 1985.

Recordings: *Robert Penn Warren Reads from His Own Works*, CMS, 1975; *Robert Penn Warren Reads Selected Poems*, Caedmon, 1980.

Other

John Brown: The Making of a Martyr. New York, Payson and Clarke, 1929.
I'll Take My Stand: The South and the Agrarian Tradition, with others. New York, Harper, 1930.
Understanding Poetry: An Anthology for College Students, with Cleanth Brooks. New York, Holt, 1938; revised edition, 1950, Holt Rinehart, 1960, 1976.
Understanding Fiction, with Cleanth Brooks. New York, Crofts, 1943; revised edition, Appleton Century Crofts, 1959; Englewood Cliffs, New Jersey, Prentice Hall, 1979; abridged edition, as *The Scope of Fiction*, 1960.
A Poem of Pure Imagination: An Experiment in Reading, in *The Rime of the Ancient Mariner*, by Samuel Taylor Coleridge. New York, Reynal, 1946.
Modern Rhetoric: With Readings, with Cleanth Brooks. New York, Harcourt Brace, 1949; revised edition, 1958, 1970, 1979.
Fundamentals of Good Writing: A Handbook of Modern Rhetoric, with Cleanth Brooks. New York, Harcourt Brace, 1950; London, Dobson, 1952.
Segregation: The Inner Conflict in the South. New York, Random House, 1956; London, Eyre and Spottiswoode, 1957.
Selected Essays. New York, Random House, 1958; London, Eyre and Spottiswoode, 1964.
Remember the Alamo! (for children). New York, Random House, 1958; as *How Texas Won Her Freedom*, San Jacinto, Texas, San Jacinto Museum of History, 1959.
The Gods of Mount Olympus (for children). New York, Random House, 1959; London, Muller, 1962.
The Legacy of the Civil War: Meditations on the Centennial. New York, Random House, 1961.
Who Speaks for the Negro? New York, Random House, 1965.
A Plea in Mitigation: Modern Poetry and the End of an Era (lecture). Macon, Georgia, Wesleyan College, 1966.
Homage to Theodore Dreiser. New York, Random House, 1971.
John Greenleaf Whittier's Poetry: An Appraisal and a Selection. Minneapolis, University of Minnesota Press, 1971.

A Conversation with Robert Penn Warren, edited by Frank Gado. Schenectady, New York, The Idol, 1972.

Democracy and Poetry (lecture). Cambridge, Massachusetts, Harvard University Press, 1975.

Robert Penn Warren Talking: Interviews 1950–1978, edited by Floyd C. Watkins and John T. Hiers. New York, Random House, 1980.

Jefferson Davis Gets His Citizenship Back. Lexington, University Press of Kentucky, 1980.

A Robert Penn Warren Reader. New York, Random House, 1987.

Portrait of a Father. Lexington, University Press of Kentucky, 1988.

New and Selected Essays. New York, Random House, 1989.

Editor, with Cleanth Brooks and John Thibaut Purser, *An Approach to Literature: A Collection of Prose and Verse with Analyses and Discussions*. Baton Rouge, Louisiana State University Press, 1936; revised edition, New York, Crofts, 1939, Appleton Century Crofts, 1952; Englewood Cliffs, New Jersey, Prentice Hall, 1975.

Editor, *A Southern Harvest: Short Stories by Southern Writers*. Boston, Houghton Mifflin, 1937.

Editor, with Cleanth Brooks, *An Anthology of Stories from the Southern Review*. Baton Rouge, Louisiana State University Press, 1953.

Editor, with Albert Erskine, *Short Story Masterpieces*. New York, Dell, 1954.

Editor, with Albert Erskine, *Six Centuries of Great Poetry*. New York, Dell, 1955.

Editor, with Albert Erskine, *A New Southern Harvest*. New York, Bantam, 1957.

Editor, with Allen Tate, *Selected Poems*, by Denis Devlin. New York, Holt Rinehart, 1963.

Editor, *Faulkner: A Collection of Critical Essays*. Englewood Cliffs, New Jersey, Prentice Hall, 1966.

Editor, with Robert Lowell and Peter Taylor, *Randall Jarrell 1914–1965*. New York, Farrar Straus, 1967.

Editor, *Selected Poems of Herman Melville*. New York, Random House, 1970.

Editor and part author, with Cleanth Brooks and R. W. B. Lewis, *American Literature: The Makers and the Making*. New York, St. Martin's Press, 2 vols., 1973.

Editor, *Katherine Anne Porter: A Collection of Critical Essays*. Englewood Cliffs, New Jersey, Prentice Hall, 1979.

Editor, *The Essential Melville*. New York, Ecco Press, 1987.

*

Bibliography: *Robert Penn Warren: A Reference Guide* by Neil Nakadate, Boston, Hall, 1977; *Robert Penn Warren: A Descriptive Bibliography 1922–79* by James A. Grimshaw, Jr., Charlottesville, University Press of Virginia, 1981.

Manuscript Collection: Beinecke Library, Yale University, New Haven, Connecticut.

Critical Studies (selection): *Robert Penn Warren* (in German) by Klaus Poenicke, Heidelberg, Winter, 1959; *Robert Penn Warren: The Dark and Bloody Ground* by Leonard Casper, Seattle, University of Washington Press, 1960; *The Faraway Country* by Louis D. Rubin, Jr., Seattle, University of Washington Press, 1963; *The Hidden God* by Cleanth Brooks, New Haven, Connecticut, Yale University Press, 1963; *Robert Penn Warren* by Charles H. Bohner, New York, Twayne, 1964, revised edition, 1981; *Robert Penn Warren* by Paul West, Minneapolis, University of Minnesota Press, 1964, London, Oxford University Press, 1965; *Robert Penn Warren: A Collection of Critical Essays* edited by John Lewis Longley, Jr., New York, New York University Press, 1965; *The Burden of Time* by John Lincoln Stewart, Princeton, New Jersey, Princeton University Press, 1965; *Web of Being: The Novels of Robert Penn Warren* by Barnett Guttenberg, Nashville, Vanderbilt University Press, 1975; *Robert Penn Warren: A Vision Earned* by Marshall Walker, Edinburgh, Harris, and New York, Barnes and Noble, 1979; *Robert Penn Warren: A Collection of Critical Essays* edited by Richard Gray, Englewood Cliffs, New Jersey, Prentice Hall, 1980; *Critical Essays on Robert Penn Warren* edited by William B. Clark, Boston, Twayne, 1981; *Robert Penn Warren: Critical Perspectives* edited by Neil Nakadate, Lexington, University Press of Kentucky, 1981; *The Achievement of Robert Penn Warren* by James H. Justus, Baton Rouge, Louisiana State University Press, 1981; *Homage to Robert Penn Warren* edited by Frank Graziano, Durango, Colorado, Logbridge Rhodes, 1982; *Robert Penn Warren* by Katherine Snipes, New York, Ungar, 1983; *A Southern Renascence Man: Views of Robert Penn Warren* edited by Walter B. Edgar, Baton Rouge, Louisiana State University Press, 1984; *Robert Penn Warren and American Idealism* by John Burt, New Haven, Connecticut, Yale University Press, 1988.

*   *   *

Honored as a major American poet and novelist, Robert Penn Warren is a most versatile man of letters whose awards include two Pulitzer prizes for poetry and fiction respectively. The subject of his novels, and much of his poetry, is life in the south. A native Kentuckian, Warren displays a rootedness in his subject and its values, a concern with moral issues, and a gift for dialogue and detailed historical background that lend distinctiveness to his three novels classifiable as historical romance: *World Enough and Time*, *Band of Angels*, and *Wilderness: A Tale of the Civil War*. As a writer of historical fiction Warren is not constricted by allegiance to verifiable fact but uses history as a backdrop for illuminating characters and thematic issues that speak to contemporary time.

"The story of every soul," Warren once commented, "is the story of its self-definition for good or evil, salvation or damnation." This statement highlights a major theme in Warren's fiction: the search for self-knowledge. This theme is often intertwined with corollary themes of alienation, regeneration, the acceptance or rejection of a father figure, and the complexities of guilt and love and evil. A characteristic plot pattern focuses on a protagonist's search for self-definition and concludes either with a violent destiny when self-realization is defeated, or with regeneration when it succeeds. During the quest a father figure is confronted who is accepted or repulsed. This overall pattern is evident in Warren's historical fiction.

World Enough and Time imaginatively recreates a Kentucky murder case of the early 19th century. A narrator recounts the journal of Jeremiah Beaumont, a young attorney who becomes enamored of a woman of quality whom he comes to learn has been seduced and betrayed by a prominent politician, his fatherly benefactor in the past. Beaumont's marriage proposal wins acceptance with the obligation to kill the seducer. Driven to forge his identity in the frontier world around him, the romantically idealistic hero pursues his chivalrous revenge like a knight in search of the Grail even as his wife Rachel urgently retracts his obligation. Beaumont basely murders the politician-seducer and is arrested, convicted, and sentenced to hang. Helped to escape, he and Rachel are taken to an outlaw settlement where his remorseful wife kills herself and he, drained of pretension, is murdered for bounty. Although the narrative is overlong and its arrogant hero unsympathetic, the novel is handsomely filled with detailed historical background, exciting melodrama, rich language, and a perceptive examination of evil wrought by the pursuit of false values.

Demonstrating a penetrating historical imagination, Warren creates in *Band of Angels* a panoramic tapestry of the American Civil War and the Reconstruction era in which to weave his characters and issues. A submissive victim of dependency all her life, the novel's mulatto heroine Amantha Starr (''Manty'') chronicles her life beginning as a Kentucky plantation owner's motherless daughter who discovers upon her debt-ridden father's death that she is legally a slave and must be sold as property. She describes her ownership by a caring slavemaster; her freedom after the fall and occupation of New Orleans; her encounters with abolitionist men, including one she marries, and a self-freed black demanding her allegiance to her race. The kindly white men in Manty's life intensify her tensions as they reveal themselves unable to consider her as an equal. She ultimately discovers that true freedom of soul can only be gained by liberating herself and discarding the trap of dependence. While the heroine seems overly slow in achieving self-knowledge, the novel is effective in its lively epic plot, environmental detail, and diversely interesting characters.

Differing in form from its predecessors in the simplicity of its direct narrative, *Wilderness* tells the story of Adam Rosenzweig, a revolutionary's son and Bavarian Jew who journeys to America to fight for freedom in its Civil War. In New York Adam is shocked to confront the savagely anti-black draft riots. A deformed foot precluding army recruitment, he reaches Union lines as a sutler. There he witnesses the callous prejudice of Yankee soldiers undedicated to black freedom, and finally, upon shooting a Confederate, Adam realizes he is no better than other men. Warren uses his ability with words and ideas to compose an affecting portrait of an idealist who is forced to test his vision of reality against the real world, and who, when he discovers the deficiencies in that world and in himself, gains self-knowledge without abandoning his idealism.

Warren's rich re-imagining of the past with meanings for the present enhances the fiction of historical romance. Both craftsman and thinker, Warren stands as a genuine and powerful American voice dedicated to observing and questioning the American experience.

—Christian H. Moe

WATSON, Julia. See **FITZGERALD, Julia.**

WAY, Margaret. Address: c/o Mills and Boon Ltd., 18–24 Paradise Road, Richmond, Surrey TW9 1SR, England.

ROMANCE AND HISTORICAL PUBLICATIONS

Novels

Blaze of Silk. London, Mills and Boon, 1970; Toronto, Harlequin, 1971.
King Country. London, Mills and Boon, 1970; Toronto, Harlequin, 1971.

The Time of the Jacaranda. London, Mills and Boon, and Toronto, Harlequin, 1970.
Return to Belle Amber. London, Mills and Boon, 1971; Toronto, Harlequin 1974.
Summer Magic. London, Mills and Boon, 1971; Toronto, Harlequin, 1972.
Bauhinia Junction. London, Mills and Boon, 1971; Toronto, Harlequin, 1975.
The Man from Bahl Bahla. London, Mills and Boon, and Toronto, Harlequin, 1971.
Noonfire. London, Mills and Boon, 1972; Toronto, Harlequin, 1973.
Ring of Jade. London, Mills and Boon, and Toronto, Harlequin, 1972.
A Man Like Daintree. London, Mills and Boon, 1972; Toronto, Harlequin, 1975.
Copper Moon. London, Mills and Boon, 1972; Toronto, Harlequin, 1975.
The Rainbow Bird. London, Mills and Boon, 1972; Toronto, Harlequin, 1975.
Storm over Mandargi. London, Mills and Boon, 1973; Toronto, Harlequin, 1974.
Wind River. London, Mills and Boon, 1973; Toronto, Harlequin, 1974.
Sweet Sundown. London, Mills and Boon, 1974; Toronto, Harlequin, 1975.
The Love Theme. London, Mills and Boon, and Toronto, Harlequin, 1974.
McCabe's Kingdom. London, Mills and Boon, 1974; Toronto, Harlequin, 1975.
Reeds of Honey. London, Mills and Boon, and Toronto, Harlequin, 1975.
Storm Flower. London, Mills and Boon, 1975; Toronto, Harlequin, 1976.
A Lesson in Loving. London, Mills and Boon, 1975; Toronto, Harlequin, 1976.
Flight into Yesterday. London, Mills and Boon, and Toronto, Harlequin, 1976.
The Man on Half-Moon. London, Mills and Boon, 1976; Toronto, Harlequin, 1977.
Red Cliffs of Malpara. London, Mills and Boon, and Toronto, Harlequin, 1976.
Swans' Reach. London, Mills and Boon, 1976; Toronto, Harlequin, 1977.
One Way Ticket. London, Mills and Boon, and Toronto, Harlequin, 1977.
Portrait of Jaime. London, Mills and Boon, 1977; Toronto, Harlequin, 1978.
Mutiny in Paradise. London, Mills and Boon, 1977; Toronto, Harlequin, 1978.
Black Ingo. London, Mills and Boon, 1977; Toronto, Harlequin, 1978.
The Awakening Flame. London, Mills and Boon, and Toronto, Harlequin, 1978.
Wake the Sleeping Tiger. London, Mills and Boon, 1978.
The Wild Swan. London, Mills and Boon, and Toronto, Harlequin, 1978.
Ring of Fire. London, Mills and Boon, 1978; Toronto, Harlequin, 1979.
Blue Lotus. London, Mills and Boon, 1979; Toronto, Harlequin, 1980.
The Butterfly and the Baron. London, Mills and Boon, 1979; Toronto, Harlequin, 1980.
Valley of the Moon. London, Mills and Boon, 1979.
White Magnolia. London, Mills and Boon, 1979.
The Winds of Heaven. London, Mills and Boon, 1979.

The Golden Puma. London, Mills and Boon, 1980.
Flamingo Park. London, Mills and Boon, 1980; Toronto, Harlequin, 1981.
Lord of the High Valley. London, Mills and Boon, 1980; Toronto, Harlequin, 1981.
Temple of Fire. London, Mills and Boon, 1980; Toronto, Harlequin, 1981.
Shadow Dance. London, Mills and Boon, and Toronto, Harlequin, 1981.
A Season for Change. London, Mills and Boon, and Toronto, Harlequin, 1981.
Home to Morning Star. London, Mills and Boon, 1981; Toronto, Harlequin, 1982.
The McIvor Affair. London, Mills and Boon, 1981; Toronto, Harlequin, 1982.
North of Capricorn. London, Mills and Boon, 1981.
Broken Rhapsody. London, Mills and Boon, and Toronto, Harlequin, 1982.
Hunter's Moon. London, Mills and Boon, 1982; Toronto, Harlequin, 1983.
The Silver Veil. London, Mills and Boon, 1982; Toronto, Harlequin, 1984.
Spellbound. London, Mills and Boon, 1982; Toronto, Harlequin, 1983.
The Girl at Cobalt Creek. London, Mills and Boon, and Toronto, Harlequin, 1983.
House of Memories. London, Mills and Boon, 1983.
No Alternative. London, Mills and Boon, 1983.
A Place Called Rambula. London, Mills and Boon, 1984.
Almost a Stranger. London, Mills and Boon, 1984.
Fallen Idol. London, Mills and Boon, 1984.
Eagle's Ridge. London, Mills and Boon, 1985.
Diamond Valley. London, Mills and Boon, 1986.
Innocent in Eden. London, Mills and Boon, 1986.
Tiger's Cage. London, Mills and Boon, 1986.
Devil Moon. London, Mills and Boon, 1988.
Mowana Magic. London, Mills and Boon, 1988.
Rise of an Eagle. London, Mills and Boon, 1988.
Hungry Heart. London, Mills and Boon, 1988.

*   *   *

Margaret Way began writing for Mills and Boon and Harlequin in 1970. Since then, she has had more than 60 novels published. The backgrounds that she uses in her novels indicate that she is an Australian romance writer who is especially familiar with that country. Queensland and the "Outback" figure frequently as physical locations where her characters meet and fall in love. While she does make use of the physical background, and her descriptions are both enjoyable and informative, this is not the element that stands out in her writing. Rather, Way has a unique and highly creative method of developing elliptical dialogue that moves her novels along as she shows her characters meeting and instinctively fighting one another. This ability to develop tense, lightning-struck scenes between her heroines and heroes is uniquely her own.

Her heroines are generally young, innocent things who often have known the hero as a child. Genny in *Black Ingo* is typical of the sort of female lead characters that she develops. Earlier events cause antagonism as she goes to visit her cousin, Ingo Faulkner, on the outback station of Tandarro. The reader has an immediate awareness of the instant male/female confrontation that occurs when they meet again after several years.

Both Genny and Ingo have had traumatic childhoods that have left marks on their characters. Genny's mother is a child-like scatty female who indulges in numerous love affairs which usu-

ally end in marriage. The effect of her mother's affairs, however, influences Genny and her ideals of love and marriage. Her exposure to this sort of background through her formative teenage years makes it especially hard for her to see that love and marriage can be the natural outcome of a relationship. Ingo has had a similar background, for his mother deserted him and left him with his father and a straitlaced aunt with little feminine gentleness. Their childhood influences naturally make both extremely suspicious of the opposite sex and far harder to understand in their reactions.

The principal characters in *Return to Belle Amber* have similar kinds of problems to overcome. Karen Hartmann has been taught by her mother from her early teen years to hate her father's family and all members of it. Her mother's death leaves her to bring up her 10-year-old brother. The death, however, brings Guy Amber back into her life as he persuades her to make Belle Amber her home again. Karen must fight to overcome her mother's spiteful reactions to the Amber family and she must learn to tolerate and later love Guy Amber, first as the head of the family and then as the man who breached her defenses and won her heart.

It is not until well into the novels that the subtle shift of emphasis takes place and the girl is able to realize that her apparent antagonism really is a dawning physical awareness of the hero as a man. The earlier overtones of hostility may have started from her misunderstanding of a situation, but slowly the heroine realizes that her reaction is all wrong and for all the wrong reasons. Generally, the hero is aware of her reactions and feelings and is aware of the actual causes, so that his cryptic retorts and subtle hints seem to be more than merely taunting insults at times. It is as if he promises and warns her all at the same time. Few writers have her talent for saying so little and hinting at so much.

Way's skill in creating fascinating characters is reinforced by her ability to develop tight emotional scenes between her leading characters. Her readers are kept constantly involved with the movement of the story and the slow unfolding of the contest between the girl and the man. Way has a truly individualized style of writing that her readers look forward to with each new novel. They know that they will be entertained by fast-paced, elusive dialogue, and characters that are enjoyable to know.

—Arlene Moore

WEALE, Anne. Also writes as Andrea Blake. British. Married to Malcolm Blakeney; one son. Formerly, staff reporter, *Eastern Evening News*, Norwich, *Western Daily Press*, Bristol, and *Yorkshire Evening Press*, York. Address: Apartado 150, San Carlos de la Rápita, Tarragona, Spain.

ROMANCE AND HISTORICAL PUBLICATIONS

Novels

Winter Is Past. London, Mills and Boon, 1955; Toronto, Harlequin, 1961.
The Lonely Shore. London, Mills and Boon, 1956; Toronto, Harlequin, 1966.
The House of Seven Fountains. London, Mills and Boon, 1957; Toronto, Harlequin, 1960.
Never to Love. London, Mills and Boon, 1958; Toronto, Harlequin, 1962.

Sweet to Remember. London, Mills and Boon, 1958; Toronto, Harlequin, 1964.
Castle in Corsica. London, Mills and Boon, 1959; Toronto, Harlequin, 1960.
Hope for Tomorrow. London, Mills and Boon, 1959; Toronto, Harlequin, 1965.
A Call for Nurse Templar. London, Mills and Boon, 1960; as *Nurse Templar*, Toronto, Harlequin, 1961.
Until We Met. London, Mills and Boon, 1961; Toronto, Harlequin, 1964.
The Doctor's Daughters. London, Mills and Boon, 1962; Toronto, Harlequin, 1963.
The House on Flamingo Cay. London, Mills and Boon, 1962; Toronto, Harlequin, 1963.
If This Is Love. London, Mills and Boon, 1963; Toronto, Harlequin, 1964.
The Silver Dolphin. London, Mills and Boon, and Toronto, Harlequin, 1963.
All I Ask. London, Mills and Boon, and Toronto, Harlequin, 1964.
Islands of Summer. London, Mills and Boon, 1964; Toronto, Harlequin, 1965.
Three Weeks in Eden. London, Mills and Boon, 1964.
Doctor in Malaya. London, Mills and Boon, and Toronto, Harlequin, 1965.
Girl about Town. London, Mills and Boon, 1965.
The Feast of Sara. London, Mills and Boon, 1965; Toronto, Harlequin, 1966.
Christina Comes to Town. London, Mills and Boon, and Toronto, Harlequin, 1966.
Terrace in the Sun. London, Mills and Boon, and Toronto, Harlequin, 1966.
The Sea Waif. London, Mills and Boon, and Toronto, Harlequin, 1967.
South from Sounion. London, Mills and Boon, and Toronto, Harlequin, 1968.
The Man in Command. London, Mills and Boon, and Toronto, Harlequin, 1969.
Sullivan's Reef. London, Mills and Boon, and Toronto, Harlequin, 1970.
That Man Simon. London, Mills and Boon, and Toronto, Harlequin, 1971.
A Treasure for Life. London, Mills and Boon, and Toronto, Harlequin, 1972.
The Fields of Heaven. London, Mills and Boon, and Toronto, Harlequin, 1974.
Lord of the Sierras. London, Mills and Boon, and Toronto, Harlequin, 1975.
The Sun in Splendour. London, Mills and Boon, 1975.
Now or Never. London, Mills and Boon, and Toronto, Harlequin, 1978.
The River Room. London, Mills and Boon, 1978.
Separate Bedrooms. London, Mills and Boon, 1979.
Stowaway. London, Mills and Boon, 1979; Toronto, Harlequin, 1983.
The Girl from the Sea. London, Mills and Boon, 1979.
The First Officer. London, Mills and Boon, 1980.
The Last Night at Paradise. London, Mills and Boon, 1980.
Touch of the Devil. London, Mills and Boon, 1980; Toronto, Harlequin, 1982.
Blue Days at Sea. London, Mills and Boon, 1981.
Passage to Paxos. London, Mills and Boon, 1981.
Rain of Diamonds. London, Mills and Boon, 1981.
Bed of Roses. London, Mills and Boon, 1981; Toronto, Harlequin, 1982.
Antigua Kiss. Toronto, Worldwide, 1982.

Portrait of Bethany. London, Mills and Boon, and Toronto, Harlequin, 1982.
Wedding of the Year. London, Mills and Boon, 1982.
All That Heaven Allows. London, Century, and Toronto, Harlequin, 1983.
Ecstasy. London, Mills and Boon, 1983; Toronto, Harlequin, 1984.
Flora. Toronto, Worldwide, 1983.
Yesterday's Island. London, Mills and Boon, and Toronto, Harlequin, 1983.
Summer's Awakening. London, Mills and Boon, 1984.
Frangipani. London, Mills and Boon, 1985.
Girl in a Golden Bed. London, Mills and Boon, 1986.
All My Worldly Goods. London, Century, 1987.
Lost Lagoon. London, Century, 1987.
Night Train. London, Mills and Boon, 1987.
Neptune's Daughter. London, Mills and Boon, 1987.
Catalan Christmas. London, Mills and Boon, 1988.
Do You Remember Babylon? London, Mills and Boon, 1989.
Time and Chance. London, Century, 1989.

Novels as Andrea Blake

September in Paris. London, Mills and Boon, and Toronto, Harlequin, 1963.
Now and Always. London, Mills and Boon, and Toronto, Harlequin, 1964.
Whisper of Doubt. London, Mills and Boon, and Toronto, Harlequin, 1965.
Night of the Hurricane. London, Mills and Boon, and Toronto, Harlequin, 1965.

*   *   *

With more than 60 novels published in the last three decades, Anne Weale is one of the most prolific romance writers currently working. Having travelled extensively, she often makes use of exotic and historically-rich landscapes as background in her novels. These settings, ranging from Hawaii to Fiji, Italy, Spain, Corsica, New England, as well as the English countryside, are described in great detail in her books. In *Yesterday's Island* we are given an elaborate and concise tour of Nantucket island, along with a history of its whaling and fishing industry. Weale attempts to capture not only the geography but also the local customs and manners of the inhabitants. Her affinity for water, the sea, and ships is evident as many of her romances take place either in a coastal town or on a boat itself, as in *Frangipani*. Some of her most attractive heroes are rugged, tanned captains whose dexterity in maneuvering and commanding ships is matched by their skill in handling women and their expertise in lovemaking.

Weale's heroines are most often, though not exclusively, young and inexperienced virgins in their early twenties who come to discover love, and later, are initiated into the pleasures of sex by their older, worldly-wise, and, inevitably, rich and handsome heroes. While the author does follow this basic pattern, she is careful to change the locale, the occupation or hobby of the main characters, the circumstances of their meeting, and the eventual admission of their love for each other so that each romance is surprisingly fresh and different. While they are sexually naïve, her heroines are usually sensible, intelligent, and well-read. In *Yesterday's Island*, for example, Caroline Murray reads *Moby-Dick* and cites Emerson as one of her favourite authors. In *All That Heaven Allows* the heroine, who has had no formal education, quotes Cardinal Newman and enjoys reading informative travel books. In *Frangipani* Cassandra Vernon reunites with the aloof Nick Carroll at the opera *Lucia di Lammer-moor* in a park in Sydney.

An illustration of Weale's effort to keep up with and perhaps also capitalize on current events can be found in *All That Heaven Allows*. The novel, published shortly after the royal wedding, has a heroine called Diana who chooses an embroidery design from the Royal Wedding sampler commemorating the wedding of the Prince and Princess of Wales. Later she shops for her wedding dress at Caroline Charles, and goes to the Princess of Wales's milliner, John Boyd, for a hat. These contemporary references, however, do not distract from the main interest of the story which revolves around Diana's marriage of convenience to the wealthy and tough Reid Lockwood. 20-year-old Diana reluctantly weds Reid in order to save her ailing mother's 16th-century ancestral home, Mirefleur Abbey, and the baronial title of the family. Because of one initial bad experience at 18, Diana believes she is sexually frigid and has to be slowly coaxed out of this erroneous idea by Reid, who turns out to be passionate and tender, craving not just her body but her love as well.

In her romances published in the 1980's Weale seems to want to acknowledge the relevance of the feminist movement. Her efforts, however, seem to be mere tokenism. Usually near the beginning of her novels, the hero and the heroine briefly discuss their views on the role of women in society. Hawkesworth Cabot Lowell of *Yesterday's Island* typifies the attitude of her heroes: "In general, like you, I'm in favour of both sexes doing whatever they want. I even go along with the idea of the woman being the breadwinner and the man the housekeeper if that's the logical arrangement. However on a personal level, if I ever marry my wife will have to make most of the concessions. I couldn't give up my way of life, and I shouldn't be prepared to see her as infrequently as the whalers saw their wives. She would have to live on my ship with me." Independent and spirited as they may be at the start, Weale's heroines usually end up giving up their jobs or their goals entirely to be the devoted wife of the already prosperous man. Despite the variety of occupations available to and held by women today, Weale tends to cling to the stereotypical image of the female as the angel of the house.

Possibly signalling a new direction in Weale's writing is the recent novel *Girl in a Golden Bed*. This romance features an older heroine—Liz Redwood is 28—who has had two lovers in the past, and who has a flourishing career as a painter of miniatures and a writer and illustrator of children's books. Liz stays at Sir David Castle's villa in Portofino and falls in love with the owner, who is also an artist. The two become sexually involved early on in the novel and share an idyllic summer vacationing in the sun, trying Italian cuisine, as well as painting. Presumably Liz, unlike other Weale heroines, can continue to work even after her marriage. One wonders if this more contemporary type of heroine and attitude will feature in the next romances created by this already highly imaginative and successful writer.

—Eleanor Ty

WEAVER, Ward. See **MASON, F. Van Wyck.**

WEBB, Jean Francis. Also writes as Ethel Hamill; Ian Kavanaugh; Roberta Morrison; Lee Davis Willoughby. American. Born in White Plains, New York, 1 October 1910. Educated at Amherst College, Massachusetts, 1927–31, B.A. 1931. Married Nancy Bukeley in 1936; four sons. Actor in repertory, 1932-33; worked at Bergdorf-Goodman, New York, 1933; then full-time writer. Taught writing courses at the University of Hawaii, Honolulu, 1958. Member of the Board of Directors, Mystery Writers of America, 1975–79, and since 1981. Agent: McIntosh and Otis, 475 Fifth Avenue, New York, New York 10017. Address: 242 East 72nd Street, New York, New York 10021, U.S.A.

ROMANCE AND HISTORICAL PUBLICATIONS

Novels

Love They Must. New York, Washburn, 1933.
Tree of Evil (as Roberta Morrison). New York, Paperback Library, 1966.
The Craigshaw Curse. New York, Meredith Press, 1968.
Carnavaron's Castle. New York, Meredith Press, 1969.
Roses from a Haunted Garden. New York, McKay, 1971.
Somewhere Within This House. New York, McKay, 1973.
The Bride of Cairngore. New York, McKay, 1974.

Novels as Ethel Hamill

Reveille for Romance. New York, Arcadia House, 1946.
Challenge to Love. New York, Arcadia House, 1946.
Honeymoon in Honolulu. New York, Avalon, 1950; London, Foulsham, 1952.
Tower in the Forest. New York, Avalon, 1951; as *Tower of Dreams*, London, Ward Lock, 1961.
Nurse on Horseback. New York, Avalon, 1952; London, Ward Lock, 1960.
The Dancing Mermaid. New York, Avalon, 1952; as *All for Love*, New York, Paperback Library, 1965.
Bluegrass Doctor. New York, Avalon, 1953.
The Minister's Daughter. New York, Avalon, 1953.
Gloria and the Bullfighter. New York, Avalon, 1954.
A Nurse Comes Home. New York, Avalon, 1954; as *Nurse Elizabeth Comes Home*, London, Foulsham, 1955.
Runaway Nurse. New York, Avalon, 1955; London, Ward Lock, 1959.
A Nurse for Galleon Key. New York, Avalon, 1957.
The Golden Image. New York, Avalon, 1959.
Aloha Nurse. New York, Avalon, 1961.
Sudden Love. New York, Avalon, 1962.
The Nurse from Hawaii. New York, Avalon, 1964.

Short Stories

Forty Brothers. Menasha, Wisconsin, Collegiate Press, 1934.

OTHER PUBLICATIONS

Novels

No Match for Murder. New York, Macmillan, 1942.
Little Women (novelization of screenplay). New York, Dell, 1949.
Anna Lucasta (novelization of screenplay). New York, Dell, 1949.
King Solomon's Mines (novelization of screenplay). New York, Dell, 1950.
Is This Coffin Taken? New York, Zebra, 1978.
The Cajuns (as Lee Davis Willoughby). New York, Dell, 1981.

A Waltz on the Wind (as Ian Kavanaugh). New York, Dell, 1983.
The Empty Attic. New York, Scholastic, 1983.

Plays

Cabaña (produced White Plains, New York, 1933).
The Fate That Is Worse Than Death (produced White Plains, New York, 1933).

Radio Plays: *Chick Carter, Boy Detective* series, with Nancy Webb, 1943–45.

Other

Golden Feathers (for children), with Nancy Webb. New York, Avalon, 1954.
The Hawaiian Islands from Monarchy to Democracy, with Nancy Webb. New York, Viking Press, 1956; revised edition, 1963.
Kaiulani, Crown Princess of Hawaii, with Nancy Webb. New York, Viking Press, 1962.
Will Shakespeare and His America, with Nancy Webb. New York, Viking Press, 1964.

*

Jean Francis Webb comments:

My writing over the years has been so diverse that any description of it would be difficult. During the 1930's, 1940's, and 1950's, when magazine fiction was still in demand, my work encompassed romance, western, detective, and adventure stories for a wide variety of slick and pulp publications. As Ethel Hamill (my mother's name) I have since done many career-girl novels, and under my own name a string of gothics and mysteries. In recent years, believing soft-cover novels to be the probable future of popular fiction, I have been turning more and more in that direction. I have few illusions as to the rare literary quality of my work; but I try to write each "entertainment" to the best of my ability.

* * *

Jean Francis Webb has been writing professionally since 1931. He has written a great deal of formula fiction in which the "new" girl falls in love. But the course of true love is not always smooth and misunderstandings occur before romance wins out. This is the theme of his many novels written under the pseudonym Ethel Hamill. They are light and typical of the paperback romance variety.

Webb's last five novels are of the gothic genre. The first of these, *The Craigshaw Curse*, has been compared to Hawthorne's *The House of the Seven Gables*. Beautiful Constance Craigshaw is called home suddenly to contend with a ghost walking the family mansion in swampy Florida. Her timorous secretary accompanies her and does some investigating on her own. Jill's life is endangered after she is shadowed by a newspaperman and a stranger. The description of the estate is detailed and fascinating, and the characters are well drawn.

The building in *Carnavaron's Castle* would make a fabulous movie set. A modern castle of medieval design complete with ruins is the home of the widow of the romantic actor, Charles Carnavaron. Jennifer is the first to visit the remote island off the coast of Maine. She revels in the famous man's relics but finds much more than a museum. She is attacked by a ghost and

haunted by a younger copy of the actor. Webb weaves a complicated plot into a thrilling maze of history and romance.

The last three novels are set in Hawaii and give a good picture of the island's history. Legend and description combined with interesting stories make all three worth reading. In *Roses from a Haunted Garden* Bethany is terrified that her husband intends to kill her. Not enough clues are given for the villain's actions, and the reader is left with the feeling that something has been omitted. Although Bethany is incredibly naive, her terror is realistic and the reader is compelled to keep turning pages all the way to the end. In *Somewhere Within This House* Ellen arrives in Hawaii in 1886 to find the true cause of her fiancé's death and is caught up in the missionary versus royalist struggle of pre-annexation. She is employed to care for the blind daughter of a dead Hawaiian princess, and finds the answers to several mysteries. Here, too, is painful yet glorious love in an exciting gothic. Jessica *(The Bride of Cairngore)* is hired to convert a long-deserted mansion into a small hotel. Her client is the duplicate of his great-grandfather who supposedly murdered his wife, the reputed ghost of this house. Jessica is drawn to three men and finds she does not trust any of them when she is stranded after dark and chased through the deserted unlighted building by a tangible human being. This is a real "haunting," all tightly told and neatly explained.

Webb is a careful writer with well-thought-out plots, believable characters, and superb descriptive ability. He offers his readers many hours of enjoyment.

—Andrea Lee Shuey

WEBSTER Jean (Alice Jane Chandler Webster). American. Born in Fredonia, New York, 24 July 1876; grandniece of the writer Mark Twain. Educated at schools in Fredonia; Lady Jane Grey School, Binghamton, New York, graduated 1896; Vassar College, Poughkeepsie, New York, B.A. in English and economics 1901. Married Glenn Ford McKinney in 1915; one daughter. *Died 11 June 1916.*

ROMANCE AND HISTORICAL PUBLICATIONS

Novels

The Wheat Princess. New York, Century, 1905; London, Hodder and Stoughton, 1916.
Jerry, Junior. New York, Century, and London, Gay and Bird, 1907; as *Jerry*, London, Hodder and Stoughton, 1916.
The Four-Pools Mystery (published anonymously). New York, Century, 1908; as Jean Webster, London, Hodder and Stoughton, 1916.
Much Ado about Peter. New York, Doubleday, 1909; London, Hodder and Stoughton, 1916.
Daddy-Long-Legs. New York, Century, 1912; London, Hodder and Stoughton, 1913.
Dear Enemy. New York, Century, and London, Hodder and Stoughton, 1915.

Short Stories (series: Patty)

When Patty Went to College. New York, Century, 1903; as *Patty and Priscilla*, London, Hodder and Stoughton, 1915.
Just Patty. New York, Century, 1911; London, Hodder and Stoughton, 1915.

OTHER PUBLICATIONS

Play

Daddy Long-Legs, adaptation of her own novel (produced New York, 1914; London, 1916). New York, French, 1922; London, French, 1927.

Verse

Vitriol and Lilacs. Cleveland, Press of Flozari, 1943.

*   *   *

Mark Twain was Jean Webster's "Uncle Sam": her maternal grandmother was Jane Clemens, Twain's elder sister, and her father was Charles Webster, Twain's publisher and partner, whose imprint appears on both *Huckleberry Finn* and General Grant's memoirs. After the failure of Twain's finances with the Paige typesetter in the late 1890's, Twain used Charley Webster as his scapegoat ("not a man, but a hog," as he wrote to W. D. Howells). That Webster at Vassar did not admit to the relationship with Twain may partly be traced to family animosities; her brother, 50 years later in *Mark Twain, Businessman*, noted that their great-uncle "never forgave anyone he had injured," and that though "a joy to live with," he was "a devil to do business with." But Twain privately praised Webster's first book (the only one he lived to read): "it is limpid, bright, sometimes brilliant; it is easy, flowing, effortless, & brimming with girlish spirits. . . . Its humor is genuine, & not often overstrained."

With her Southern mother and Northern father, there is in Webster something of the same division that one sees in her great-uncle. She wrote one mystery novel, *The Four-Pools Mystery*, the only work she published anonymously, in which a postwar plantation system is seen approvingly, and comic darkies abound, but in which the lordly temper of the master is seen as more responsible for his murder than the black who actually kills him—whom he has beaten, and who is allowed to escape the penalty of the law.

Of all her sentimental contemporaries—Mrs. Rice, Mrs. Wiggin, Mrs. Montgomery, the two Mrs. Porters—she comes closest to combining romance effectively with realism—surely Twain's great strength, though with her the realism most often takes the form of social concern. Implicitly, her most famous work, *Daddy-Long-Legs*, is a criticism of the contemporary treatment of the orphan; it is no fortuity that it produced, at Vassar and elsewhere, a system of sponsorship of parentless children by wealthy undergraduates. Her own favorite of her novels, *The Wheat Princess*, has elements of a Jamesian international novel—set in Italy and peopled largely by Americans—but it is more informed by a sense of the wrong done by the heroine's father, a tycoon who has cornered the wheat market. His action produces a famine amongst the Italian peasantry, who in revenge besiege the villa occupied by his brother, a philanthropist; and the heroine too is endangered. "Some day," the hero says at the end of the book, "I will tell you that I'm proud to be an American. Don't ask me just yet." Which sounds more like Pudd'nhead Wilson than Pollyanna.

It is this "combination of serious social modernity with the other modernity of gayety and humor" (as the *New York Times* saw it in 1915) which marks Webster's best work, *Daddy-Long-Legs* and its sequel *Dear Enemy*. The heroines of both novels, especially Judy of the first, are resourceful, much less accepting of their lots than Rebecca, Anne, or even (a special case) Pollyanna. Judy has been played by Ruth Chatterton in Webster's own stage adaptation, and by Mary Pickford on the screen; and these

are happier visual equivalents than her later impersonators. Judy fits Pickford's image of contemporary American girlhood better than the more conventionally girlish Rebecca or Pollyanna do—Shirley Temple, who repeated these last two roles, would be impossible as Judy. Even Janet Gaynor and Leslie Caron, however, are sentimentalized versions of the original—further stages in the normal evolution of a bestselling character, blurring and domesticating what may be threatening or anti-social.

Judy is generally thought to be based on Webster's college mate and fellow writer Adelaide Crapsey; so too is her next most attractive character, the Patty of her first book, as well as of *Just Patty*. The stories in *When Patty Went to College*, published in the Vassar newspaper, find the enterprising girl in a variety of scrapes, from which she almost always emerges triumphant—whether applying her Social Studies to her Latin class and leading a "Virgil strike," or enrolling a fictitious student in the German club; her specialty is "local color" ("Baron Münchhausen himself would have blushed at her creations"). Patty is a more elegant Judy, equipped with wealthy parents; and in her private schools she is free of the restrictions of the orphanage.

But all of these "juvenile" works create enclosed women's worlds into which men intrude as schoolmasters, janitors, brothers, fathers, occasionally suitors. That in her most popular work the suitor is also the father, the "daddy" long legs, may say something about Webster's own urge to tame and even rival the highly undomesticated, dominating father of the Clemens family (Charley Webster had died when Jean was 15). But it no doubt says a great deal more about the continued appeal of her books to adolescent girls—if there are still such—who want the marital palm without the dust.

—Barrie Hayne

———————

WELLES, Elizabeth. See **ROBY, Mary Linn.**

———————

WESLEY, Elizabeth. See **McELFRESH, Adeline.**

———————

WEST, (Mary) Jessamyn. American. Born in North Vernon, Indiana, 18 July 1902. Educated at Union High School, Fullerton, California, graduated 1919; Whittier College, California, 1919, 1921–23, A.B. in English 1923; Fullerton Junior College, 1920–21; University of California, Berkeley, 1929–31. Married Harry Maxwell McPherson in 1923; two foster daughters. Teacher and secretary, Hemet, California, 1924–29; taught at Bread Loaf Writers Conference, Vermont, Indiana University, Bloomington, University of Notre Dame, Indiana, University of Utah, Salt Lake City, University of Washington, Seattle, Stanford University, California, and Wellesley College, Cambridge, Massachusetts. Recipient: Monsen award, 1958; Janet Kafka prize, 1976. Honorary degrees: Whittier College; Mills College, Oakland, California; Swarthmore College, Pennsylvania; Indiana University; Western College for Women, Oxford, Ohio. *Died 23 February 1984.*

ROMANCE AND HISTORICAL PUBLICATIONS

Novel

The Massacre at Fall Creek. New York, Harcourt Brace, and
London, Macmillan, 1975.

Short Stories

The Friendly Persuasion. New York, Harcourt Brace, 1945;
London, Hodder and Stoughton, 1946.
*Except for Me and Thee: A Companion to The Friendly Persua-
sion*. New York, Harcourt Brace, and London, Macmillan,
1969.

OTHER PUBLICATIONS

Novels

The Witch Diggers. New York, Harcourt Brace, 1951; London,
Heinemann, 1952.
Little Men, in *Star Short Novels*, edited by Frederik Pohl. New
York, Ballantine, 1954; published separately, as *The Chile-
kings*, 1967.
South of the Angels. New York, Harcourt Brace, 1960; London,
Hodder and Stoughton, 1961.
A Matter of Time. New York, Harcourt Brace, 1966; London,
Macmillan, 1967.
Leafy Rivers. New York, Harcourt Brace, 1967; London, Mac-
millan, 1968.
The Life I Really Lived. New York, Harcourt Brace, 1979.
The State of Stony Lonesome. New York, Harcourt Brace, 1984.

Short Stories

Cress Delahanty. New York, Harcourt Brace, 1953; London,
Hodder and Stoughton, 1954.
Love, Death, and the Ladies' Drill Team. New York, Harcourt
Brace, 1955; as *Learn to Say Goodbye*, London, Hodder and
Stoughton, 1957.
Crimson Ramblers of the World, Farewell. New York, Harcourt
Brace, 1970; London, Macmillan, 1971.
The Story of a Story and Three Stories. Berkeley, University of
California, 1982.
Collected Stories of Jessamyn West. San Diego, Harcourt
Brace, 1986.

Plays

A Mirror for the Sky, music by Gail Kubik (produced Eugene,
Oregon, 1958). New York, Harcourt Brace, 1948.

Screenplays: *Friendly Persuasion* (uncredited), with Michael
Wilson, 1956; *The Big Country*, with others, 1958; *The Stolen
Hours*, 1963.

Verse

The Secret Look. New York, Harcourt Brace, 1974.

Other

The Reading Public (address). New York, Harcourt Brace,
1952.

Friends and Violence. Philadelphia, Friends General Confer-
ence, n.d.
To See the Dream. New York, Harcourt Brace, 1957; London,
Hodder and Stoughton, 1958.
Love Is Not What You Think. New York, Harcourt Brace, 1959;
as *A Woman's Love*, London, Hodder and Stoughton, 1960.
Hide and Seek: A Continuing Journey. New York, Harcourt
Brace, and London, Macmillan, 1973.
The Woman Said Yes: Encounters with Life and Death: Memoirs.
New York, Harcourt Brace, 1976; as *Encounters with Death
and Life*, London, Gollancz, 1977.
Double Discovery: A Journey. New York, Harcourt Brace,
1980.

Editor, *The Quaker Reader*. New York, Viking Press, 1962.

*

Manuscript Collection: Whittier College, California.

Critical Studies: *Jessamyn West* by Alfred S. Shivers, New York,
Twayne, 1972; *Jessamyn West* by Ann Dahlstrom Farmer, Boise,
Idaho, Boise State University, 1982.

*   *   *

Jessamyn West's credentials for admission into the ranks of
historical writers rest primarily on her two collections of related
short stories on Indiana Quaker life, *The Friendly Persuasion*
and *Except for Me and Thee*. She is, however, a writer who resists any narrow classification. Her work ranges from vivid fiction created out of fragments of history (*The Massacre at Fall
Creek*) to tender and perceptive stories of coming of age (*Cress
Delahanty, The State of Stony Lonesome*). Some of her best work
takes the form of short stories or vignettes that meld together
into a sort of novel-without-plot but with a strong central theme.
Romance is hardly a feature of West's work, because romance is
rooted in unreality. What distinguishes all of her work, short
stories or novels, is their clear, unflinching reality.

Character is obviously what interests West the most. All of
her work revolves around the ways that people's lives and personalities are shaped, how they respond to tragedy and what
makes them laugh. Like life, West's tales swing back and forth
from tragedy through serenity to real comedy. Her Quaker characters Jess and Eliza, for example, in the course of two books
face the loss of a child, the testing of their peaceful principles by
the Civil War, and the trials of a hard life on the frontier. At the
same time, they find beauty in their surroundings, Jess in his
orderly outdoor world and Eliza in her faith and her family.
Their flaws are as realistically and compassionately drawn as
their strengths, which makes them real people to the reader.
None of these people is faced with larger-than-life situations, yet
the books are replete with drama. The most narrow, bigoted,
and wrong-headed of West's creations, like George Benson in
The Massacre at Fall Creek, is still so human that the reader can
feel sympathy for his bewilderment in the face of change. History has moved along faster than George can cope with it.

Love, not romance, is a continuing theme in West's work;
sometimes it is the love between man and woman, or between
parent and child, or between people and their community. West
recognizes that love is rarely free from conflict, that people
make unfounded assumptions about each other and have expectations and beliefs that are unreasonable. These problems and
the inability or unwillingness of people to communicate with one
another are what drive the plots along. "Fitting in" is another
motif that interconnects with love; these are people who crave

belonging, who wish to have a place for themselves among people who love them. The realization that belonging comes from acceptance of difference as much or more than from recognition of sameness marks maturation and real participation in the community. West's characters are most content when they can maintain their individuality successfully in the framework of their larger society.

The land plays a large role in West's novels and short stories. Sometimes the love for the land is a rejoicing in its beauty and plenty; sometimes it is merely greed for possession. Whatever the feelings of the characters toward the landscape, West never fails to notice and record the details of the terrain, the effects of the changing seasons, the play of light at different times of day. Often, indeed, the episodic elements of a book are divided by seasons, as in *Cress Delahanty*. There is a strong feel for setting here, whether the land is Indiana or California, that acquaints the reader with the moods and disguises of the countryside. The features of the scenery might change with the passage of time and with the efforts of the people, but the land itself is unchanging, a symbol of stability even when the fabric of society is threatened by war or crime or intolerance. There is a feeling in West's writing that much of the emotional development in it comes directly from West's own experiences. The repetitive themes of maturation and change have about them an honesty and an immediacy that makes the reader know that they come from the heart.

—Susan Quinn Berneis

* * *

WESTCOTT, Jan (née Vlachos). American. Born in Philadelphia, Pennsylvania, 23 February 1912. Educated at Swarthmore College, Pennsylvania, 1929–30. Married Robert P. Barden in 1954; two sons. Agent: Harold Matson Company, 276 Fifth Avenue, New York, New York 10001, U.S.A.

ROMANCE AND HISTORICAL PUBLICATIONS

Novels

The Border Lord. New York, Crown, 1946; London, Sampson Low, 1948.
Captain for Elizabeth. New York, Crown, 1948.
The Hepburn. New York, Crown, 1950; London, Hodder and Stoughton, 1951.
Captain Barney. New York, Crown, 1951.
The Walsingham Woman. New York, Crown, 1953; London, Hodder and Stoughton, 1954.
The Queen's Grace. New York, Crown, 1959.
Condottiere. New York, Random House, 1962; as *The Mercenary*, London, Redman, 1963.
The White Rose. New York, Putnam, 1969; as *The Lion's Share*, London, Hale, 1972.
Set Her on a Throne. Boston, Little Brown, 1972.
The Tower and the Dream. New York, Putnam, 1974.
A Woman of Quality. New York, Putnam, 1978; London, Hale, 1980.

* * *

Jan Westcott holds an unassailable position in the ranks of historical fiction writers. While she has written of other periods, Westcott is best noted for her outstanding novels about the Tudor-Stuart period of English history.

Her novels offer depth and breadth in characterization, setting, and plot development. Most important, however, is her ability to weave factual information and historical personalities into her stories. In fact, several could almost be considered biographical in nature, except for the fact that she creates a fictional setting for everyday events. The immediacy of the events, personal conflicts, and her ability to make the actions of her characters seem inevitable adds to the enjoyment of her writing.

Westcott's earlier novels showed promise of her later abilities. In *Captain Barney*, she uses the American Revolution as the background for the novel. Events take place in the Caribbean and along the eastern sea coast of the colonies. The hero is a fictional presentation of a real person, Captain Joshua Barney of the American Navy. The fictional character is Captain Benjamin Barney, a naval captain who makes a policy of capturing British ships. One such capture results in him obtaining the Royal Navy's code books which he later uses to defeat a British naval force. Lady Douglass Harris, a widow, is an unlikely heroine who takes up residence in the colonies. She is a titled lady without money, rigidly opposed to the war and to the American cause. She also presents a definite problem for the hero.

The action centers on sea encounters and Dutch held islands in the Caribbean which are used as ''neutral'' trading areas by all countries. The British later attack the islands and seize all goods. Events culminate with the French intervention in the war which results in the surrender of General Cornwallis. Characterization and plotting make this an extremely readable novel, but there are flaws. Motivation is contradictory and even lacking at times. The historical details are interesting but too sketchy to give the larger events their proper significance within the story. Reviews of this early work rated it as ''good adventure, good historical romance.''

It is within the Tudor-Stuart period that Westcott really makes herself at home. Several of her novels deal with historical people and are fictionalized accounts of their lives. The *Border Lord* is about the 5th Earl of Bothwell. *The White Rose* deals with Elizabeth Woodville, Edward IV, and their children. The children are those who were killed later by their uncle Richard III.

The Queen's Grace covers the life of Katherine Parr, the last wife of Henry VIII. As noted earlier, characterization in many of Westcott's novels borders on the biographical, and *The Queen's Grace* illustrates this point. Beginning with Katherine's meeting with Thomas Seymour in 1529, the novel follows her life through four marriages. The first to Lord Borough, then to Lord Latimer, then Henry VIII, and finally to Thomas Seymour. She died at the age of 35 after giving birth to a little girl. The novel traces the most intimate details of her life. The information about daily life in the period is exceptionally well done, as is the book's analysis of women's place in the scheme of things. Katherine accurately reflects the realities of life in the 1500's. Her rise to being Queen of England is dramatically detailed and makes this novel a rich tapestry of intrigue, power, and love.

A word of caution is in order, however. It is obvious that Westcott carries out extensive research for her novels. It is also obvious that her skill in weaving history and fiction together might create difficulties for some readers: how to separate the fact from the fiction? For instance, did Thomas Seymour arrive in time to free Katherine from her son-in-law immediately after Lord Borough's death? Did Lady Katherine really kill her stepson, Thomas Borough? He apparently came searching for her husband, Lord Latimer, who was suspected of being involved in the rebellion that preceded the Pilgrimage of Grace.

Unless one is a serious student of this period, one simply cannot sort out all of the actual facts. Readers should only assume that names and general characteristics of historical persons, dates, and major historical events are true. Detailed characterization, subplots, settings, and motivation are pure Westcott. With this in mind readers can sit back and enjoy another world and another time presented by an unusually perceptive and creative writer.

—Arlene Moore

WESTMACOTT, Mary. Pseudonym for Agatha Mary Clarissa Christie, née Miller. British. Born in Torquay, Devon, 15 September 1890. Educated privately at home; studied singing and piano in Paris. Married 1) Colonel Archibald Christie in 1914 (divorced 1928), one daughter; 2) the archaeologist Max Mallowan in 1930. Served as a Voluntary Aid Detachment nurse in a Red Cross Hospital in Torquay during World War I, and worked in the dispensary of University College Hospital, London, during World War II; assisted Mallowan on excavations in Iraq and Syria and on Assyrian cities. President, Detection Club. Recipient: Mystery Writers of America Grand Master award, 1954; New York Drama Critics Circle award, 1955. D.Litt.: University of Exeter, Devon, 1961. Fellow, Royal Society of Literature, 1950. C.B.E. (Commander, Order of the British Empire), 1956; D.B.E. (Dame Commander, Order of the British Empire), 1971. *Died 12 January 1976.*

ROMANCE AND HISTORICAL PUBLICATIONS

Novels

Giants' Bread. London, Collins, and New York, Doubleday, 1930.
Unfinished Portrait. London, Collins, and New York, Doubleday, 1934.
Absent in the Spring. London, Collins, and New York, Farrar and Rinehart, 1944.
The Rose and the Yew Tree. London, Heinemann, and New York, Rinehart, 1948.
A Daughter's a Daughter. London, Heinemann, 1952; New York, Dell, 1963.
The Burden. London, Heinemann, 1956; New York, Dell, 1963.

OTHER PUBLICATIONS as Agatha Christie

Novels

The Mysterious Affair at Styles. London, Lane, 1920; New York, Dodd Mead, 1927.
The Secret Adversary. London, Lane, and New York, Dodd Mead, 1922.
The Murder on the Links. London, Lane, and New York, Dodd Mead, 1923.
The Man in the Brown Suit. London, Lane, and New York, Dodd Mead, 1924.
The Secret of Chimneys. London, Lane, and New York, Dodd Mead, 1925.
The Murder of Roger Ackroyd. London, Collins, and New York, Dodd Mead, 1926.
The Big Four. London, Collins, and New York, Dodd Mead, 1927.
The Mystery of the Blue Train. London, Collins, and New York, Dodd Mead, 1928.

The Seven Dials Mystery. London, Collins, and New York, Dodd Mead, 1929.
The Murder at the Vicarage. London, Collins, and New York, Dodd Mead, 1930.
The Floating Admiral, with others. London, Hodder and Stoughton, 1931; New York, Doubleday, 1932.
The Sittaford Mystery. London, Collins, 1931; as *The Murder at Hazelmoor*, New York, Dodd Mead, 1931.
Peril at End House. London, Collins, and New York, Dodd Mead, 1932.
Lord Edgware Dies. London, Collins, 1933; as *Thirteen at Dinner*, New York, Dodd Mead, 1933.
Why Didn't They Ask Evans? London, Collins, 1934; as *The Boomerang Clue*, New York, Dodd Mead, 1935.
Murder on the Orient Express. London, Collins, 1934; as *Murder in the Calais Coach*, New York, Dodd Mead, 1934.
Murder in Three Acts. New York, Dodd Mead, 1934; as *Three Act Tragedy*, London, Collins, 1935.
Death in the Clouds. London, Collins, 1935; as *Death in the Air*, New York, Dodd Mead, 1935.
The A.B.C. Murders. London, Collins, and New York, Dodd Mead, 1936; as *The Alphabet Murders*, New York, Pocket Books, 1966.
Cards on the Table. London, Collins, 1936; New York, Dodd Mead, 1937.
Murder in Mesopotamia. London, Collins, and New York, Dodd Mead, 1936.
Death on the Nile. London, Collins, 1937; New York, Dodd Mead, 1938.
Dumb Witness. London, Collins, 1937; as *Poirot Loses a Client*, New York, Dodd Mead, 1937.
Appointment with Death. London, Collins, and New York, Dodd Mead, 1938.
Hercule Poirot's Christmas. London, Collins, 1938; as *Murder for Christmas*, New York, Dodd Mead, 1939; as *A Holiday for Murder*, New York, Avon, 1947.
Murder Is Easy. London, Collins, 1939; as *Easy to Kill*, New York, Dodd Mead, 1939.
Ten Little Niggers. London, Collins, 1939; as *And Then There Were None*, New York, Dodd Mead, 1940; as *Ten Little Indians*, New York, Pocket Books, 1965.
One, Two, Buckle My Shoe. London, Collins, 1940; as *The Patriotic Murders*, New York, Dodd Mead, 1941; as *An Overdose of Death*, New York, Dell, 1953.
Sad Cypress. London, Collins, and New York, Dodd Mead, 1940.
Evil under the Sun. London, Collins, and New York, Dodd Mead, 1941.
N or M? London, Collins, and New York, Dodd Mead, 1941.
The Body in the Library. London, Collins, and New York, Dodd Mead, 1942.
The Moving Finger. New York, Dodd Mead, 1942; London, Collins, 1943.
Five Little Pigs. London, Collins, 1942; as *Murder in Retrospect*, New York, Dodd Mead, 1942.
Death Comes as the End. New York, Dodd Mead, 1944; London, Collins, 1945.
Towards Zero. London, Collins, and New York, Dodd Mead, 1944.
Sparkling Cyanide. London, Collins, 1945; as *Remembered Death*, New York, Dodd Mead, 1945.
The Hollow. London, Collins, and New York, Dodd Mead, 1946; as *Murder after Hours*, New York, Dell, 1954.
Taken at the Flood. London, Collins, 1948; as *There Is a Tide . . .*, New York, Dodd Mead, 1948.

Crooked House. London, Collins, and New York, Dodd Mead, 1949.

A Murder Is Announced. London, Collins, and New York, Dodd Mead, 1950.

They Came to Baghdad. London, Collins, and New York, Dodd Mead, 1951.

They Do It with Mirrors. London, Collins, 1952; as *Murder with Mirrors*, New York, Dodd Mead, 1952.

Mrs. McGinty's Dead. London, Collins, and New York, Dodd Mead, 1952; as *Blood Will Tell*, New York, Detective Book Club, 1952.

After the Funeral. London, Collins, 1953; as *Funerals Are Fatal*, New York, Dodd Mead, 1953; as *Murder at the Gallop*, London, Fontana, 1963.

A Pocket Full of Rye. London, Collins, 1953; New York, Dodd Mead, 1954.

Destination Unknown. London, Collins, 1954; as *So Many Steps to Death*, New York, Dodd Mead, 1955.

Hickory, Dickory, Dock. London, Collins, 1955; as *Hickory, Dickory, Death*, New York, Dodd Mead, 1955.

Dead Man's Folly. London, Collins, and New York, Dodd Mead, 1956.

4:50 from Paddington. London, Collins, 1957; as *What Mrs. McGillicuddy Saw!*, New York, Dodd Mead, 1957; as *Murder She Said*, New York, Pocket Books, 1961.

Ordeal by Innocence. London, Collins, 1958; New York, Dodd Mead, 1959.

Cat among the Pigeons. London, Collins, 1959; New York, Dodd Mead, 1960.

The Pale Horse. London, Collins, 1961; New York, Dodd Mead, 1962.

The Mirror Crack'd from Side to Side. London, Collins, 1962; as *The Mirror Crack'd*, New York, Dodd Mead, 1963.

The Clocks. London, Collins, 1963; New York, Dodd Mead, 1964.

A Caribbean Mystery. London, Collins, 1964; New York, Dodd Mead, 1965.

At Bertram's Hotel. London, Collins, 1965; New York, Dodd Mead, 1966.

Third Girl. London, Collins, 1966; New York, Dodd Mead, 1967.

Endless Night. London, Collins, 1967; New York, Dodd Mead, 1968.

By the Pricking of My Thumbs. London, Collins, and New York, Dodd Mead, 1968.

Hallowe'en Party. London, Collins, and New York, Dodd Mead, 1969.

Passenger to Frankfurt. London, Collins, and New York, Dodd Mead, 1970.

Nemesis. London, Collins, and New York, Dodd Mead, 1971.

Elephants Can Remember. London, Collins, and New York, Dodd Mead, 1972.

Postern of Fate. London, Collins, and New York, Dodd Mead, 1973.

Curtain: Hercule Poirot's Last Case. London, Collins, and New York, Dodd Mead, 1975.

Sleeping Murder. London, Collins, and New York, Dodd Mead, 1976.

The Scoop, and Behind the Scenes, with others. London, Gollancz, 1983.

Short Stories

Poirot Investigates. London, Lane, 1924; New York, Dodd Mead, 1925.

Partners in Crime. London, Collins, and New York, Dodd Mead, 1929; reprinted in part as *The Sunningdale Mystery*, Collins 1933.

The Under Dog. London, Readers Library, 1929.

The Mysterious Mr. Quin. London, Collins, and New York, Dodd Mead, 1930.

The Thirteen Problems. London, Collins, 1932; as *The Tuesday Club Murders*, New York, Dodd Mead, 1933; selection, as *The Mystery of the Blue Geranium and Other Tuesday Club Murders*, New York, Bantam, 1940.

The Hound of Death and Other Stories. London, Collins, 1933.

Parker Pyne Investigates. London, Collins, 1934; as *Mr. Parker Pyne, Detective*, New York, Dodd Mead, 1934.

The Listerdale Mystery and Other Stories. London, Collins, 1934.

Murder in the Mews and Three Other Poirot Cases. London, Collins, 1937; as *Dead Man's Mirror and Other Stories*, New York, Dodd Mead, 1937.

The Regatta Mystery and Other Stories. New York, Dodd Mead, 1939.

The Mystery of the Baghdad Chest. Los Angeles, Bantam, 1943.

The Mystery of the Crime in Cabin 66. Los Angeles, Bantam, 1943.

Poirot and the Regatta Mystery. Los Angeles, Bantam, 1943.

Poirot on Holiday. London, Todd, 1943.

Problem at Pollensa Bay, and Christmas Adventure. London, Todd, 1943.

The Veiled Lady, and The Mystery of the Baghdad Chest. London, Todd, 1944.

Poirot Knows the Murderer. London, Todd, 1946.

Poirot Lends a Hand. London, Todd, 1946.

The Labours of Hercules. London, Collins, and New York, Dodd Mead, 1947.

The Witness for the Prosecution and Other Stories. New York, Dodd Mead, 1948.

The Mousetrap and Other Stories. New York, Dell, 1949; as *Three Blind Mice and Other Stories*, New York, Dodd Mead, 1950.

The Under Dog and Other Stories. New York, Dodd Mead, 1951.

The Adventure of the Christmas Pudding, and Selection of Entrées. London, Collins, 1960.

Double Sin and Other Stories. New York, Dodd Mead, 1961.

13 for Luck! A Selection of Mystery Stories for Young Readers. New York, Dodd Mead, 1961; London, Collins, 1966.

Surprise! Surprise! A Collection of Mystery Stories with Unexpected Endings, edited by Raymond T. Bond. New York, Dodd Mead, 1965.

Star over Bethlehem and Other Stories (as Agatha Christie Mallowan). London, Collins, and New York, Dodd Mead, 1965.

13 Clues for Miss Marple. New York, Dodd Mead, 1966.

The Golden Ball and Other Stories. New York, Dodd Mead, 1971.

Poirot's Early Cases. London, Collins, 1974; as *Hercule Poirot's Early Cases*, New York, Dodd Mead, 1974.

Miss Marple's Final Cases and Two Other Stories. London, Collins, 1979.

The Agatha Christie Hour. London, Collins, 1982.

Hercule Poirot's Casebook: Fifty Stories. New York, Dodd Mead, 1984.

Miss Marple: Complete Short Stories. New York, Dodd Mead, 1985.

Plays

Black Coffee (produced London, 1930). London, Ashley, and Boston, Baker, 1934.

Ten Little Niggers, adaptation of her own novel (produced Wimbledon and London, 1943). London, French, 1944; as *Ten Little Indians* (produced New York, 1944), New York, French, 1946.

Appointment with Death, adaptation of her own novel (produced Glasgow and London, 1945). London, French, 1956; in *The Mousetrap and Other Plays*, 1978.

Murder on the Nile, adaptation of her novel *Death on the Nile* (as *Little Horizon*, produced Wimbledon, 1945; as *Murder on the Nile* produced London and New York, 1946). London and New York, French, 1948.

The Hollow, adaptation of her own novel (produced Cambridge and London, 1951; Princeton, New Jersey, 1952; New York, 1978). London and New York, French, 1952.

The Mousetrap, adaptation of her story "Three Blind Mice" (broadcast 1952; produced Nottingham and London, 1952; New York, 1960). London and New York, French, 1954.

Witness for the Prosecution, adaptation of her own story (produced Nottingham and London, 1953; New York, 1954). London and New York, French, 1954.

Spider's Web (produced Nottingham and London, 1954; New York, 1974). London and New York, French, 1957.

Towards Zero, with Gerald Verner, adaptation of the novel by Christie (produced Nottingham and London, 1956). New York, Dramatists Play Service, 1957; London, French, 1958.

Verdict (produced Wolverhampton and London, 1958). London, French, 1958; in *The Mousetrap and Other Plays*, 1978.

The Unexpected Guest (produced Bristol and London, 1958). London, French, 1958; in *The Mousetrap and Other Plays*, 1978.

Go Back for Murder, adaptation of her novel *Five Little Pigs* (produced Edinburgh and London, 1960). London, French, 1960; in *The Mousetrap and Other Plays*, 1978.

Rule of Three: Afternoon at the Seaside, The Patient, The Rats (produced Aberdeen and London, 1962; *The Rats* produced New York, 1974; *The Patient* produced New York, 1978). London, French, 3 vols., 1963.

Fiddlers Three (produced Southsea, 1971; London, 1972).

Akhnaton (as *Akhnaton and Nefertiti*, produced New York, 1979; as *Akhnaton*, produced London, 1980). London, Collins, and New York, Dodd Mead, 1973.

The Mousetrap and Other Plays (includes *Witness for the Prosecution, Ten Little Indians, Appointment with Death, The Hollow, Towards Zero, Verdict, Go Back for Murder*). New York, Dodd Mead, 1978.

Radio Plays: *The Mousetrap*, 1952; *Personal Call*, 1960.

Verse

The Road of Dreams. London, Bles, 1925.
Poems. London, Collins, and New York, Dodd Mead, 1973.

Other

Come, Tell Me How You Live (travel). London, Collins, and New York, Dodd Mead, 1946; revised edition, 1976.
An Autobiography. London, Collins, and New York, Dodd Mead, 1977.

*

Bibliography: by Louise Barnard, in *A Talent to Deceive: An Appreciation of Agatha Christie* by Robert Barnard, London, Collins, and New York, Dodd Mead, 1980.

Critical Studies: *The Life and Crimes of Agatha Christie* by Charles Osborne, London, Collins, 1982, New York, Holt Rinehart, 1983; *The Agatha Christie Companion* by Dennis Sanders and Len Lovallo, New York, Delacorte Press, 1984, London, W. H. Allen, 1985; *Agatha Christie: A Biography* by Janet Morgan, London, Cape, 1984, New York, Knopf, 1985.

*   *   *

Agatha Christie was a product of the English upper middle class. That society with which she was so familiar became the setting for her plots during the more than 56 years of her writing life. Her dozens of mystery novels are known to readers around the world. Since her death in 1976, many writers of the genre have been billed as Christie's successors. And Christie fans are frustrated that the annual Christie mystery is no longer the event they eagerly awaited each year.

There was another side to Christie the writer. Even staunch Christie fans may be unaware that she wrote six romances under a pseudonym. Writing as Mary Westmacott was Agatha Christie's alternative to plotting mysteries as well as her escape from being First Lady or Queen of Mysteries. While she was a best seller in the mystery field, her six "straight" novels never enjoyed the same success.

Christie was ingenious in outlining mysteries, and when she wrote her romance novels she put them together like detective novels with an element of mystery introduced into each. The Westmacott mystery factor, however, revolved around people's character or relationships among individuals. Christie was better able to introduce psychological elements into her Westmacott books than in her mysteries. Some read like psychological studies of the characters.

However, Christie was never able to become a great success as a romance or gothic writer. Indeed, if she had not also been Agatha Christie, Mary Westmacott might have disappeared from the literary world forever.

The Westmacott novels are simple in style. The plots are uncomplicated. They are all about women and their problems or their life style. If one reads any of the Christie biographies or even her autobiography, another common trait becomes apparent: much that transpires in the novels resembles events in Christie's life.

In *Giants' Bread*, the first of the Westmacott romances, Christie utilized her love for music in the plot and emphasized making choices based on personal preference as well as society's expectations. This book appeared about the time of her remarriage, two years after her divorce from Archibald Christie. There is a typical Christie country house setting. Tragic deaths in the Boer War and World War I create twists in the plots and force the characters into unfamiliar life styles. It was while her first husband was serving in World War I that Christie began writing; her first mystery was finally accepted for publication in 1920. After her husband's return from the war, the marriage began to founder. Thus, while planning and writing *Giants' Bread*, Christie herself was undergoing drastic changes in her life.

Christie's own childhood had been fairly quiet. She had been tutored by her mother and then had studied music in Paris. In both *Giants' Bread* and *Unfinished Portrait* the nursery motif, complete with mauve iris wallpaper, is repeated. In both these novels there is a tragedy leading to reduced family circumstances. Divorce from a husband depicted as a philanderer is another parallel to Christie's own life. Some biographers have felt Miriam in *Unfinished Portrait* is based on Christie's mother.

It was 10 years before *Absent in the Spring* was published. The chief character, a woman en route back to England after visiting one daughter, spends several days in an isolated desert region, and begins thinking how she has controlled her husband's life to meet her desires in life rather than his, and how she has stage managed both daughters' lives. The isolation of the area and the lack of companionship force her into long periods of reflection. She must face the knowledge that she hasn't been the perfect wife and mother. Whether this is a parallel to Christie's life we don't know, but she incorporated her Middle East experiences with her second husband in to the plot. Christie, writing from first hand experience, effectively depicts the isolation of the desert.

One of the talents of Christie the mystery writer was her use of narrators to tell the story. In *The Rose and the Yew Tree* an invalid becomes the very observant narrator of village life. Making unpopular life choices is the theme; characters with questionable backgrounds are the participants.

The last two Westmacott novels were written in the 1950's. *A Daughter's a Daughter* reverses the theme of *Absent in the Spring* with the daughter trying to manage her mother's romantic life. The two women almost reach the destructive point in their relationship before they realize what is happening. In *The Burden* a sister is guilt ridden by her brother's death and her wish for her sister's death. She seeks refuge in working for good causes.

Characteristic of the Westmacott books are several factors: deaths, usually in a war, causing reduced financial circumstances; choices made that are based on what society expects; the difficulty of making decisions that will change one's life; punishment of self for misdeeds imagined or real. Several settings or parts of stories are carried from book to book.

Because of her use of events from her own life, the reader may wonder if the plotting and writing of these romance novels was a form of catharsis for her. Was Mary Westmacott the depicter of what Christie envisioned happening or wanted to happen? The Westmacott novels often end unresolved or with endings unsatisfactory to the characters. Is this how Christie expected life to be? These novels lack the spark and plotting of the Christie mysteries, but offer a glimpse into how Agatha Christie viewed life.

—Jennifer Cargill

WESTON, Helen Gray. See **DANIELS, Dorothy.**

WESTWOOD, Gwen (née Knox). British. Born in Warrington, Lancashire, 27 June 1915. Educated at the University of Birmingham, B.A. 1936. Married Gladwin Westwood in 1938; one daughter and one son. Former teacher. Address: c/o Mills and Boon Ltd., 18–24 Paradise Road, Richmond, Surrey TW9 1SR, England.

ROMANCE AND HISTORICAL PUBLICATIONS

Novels

Keeper of the Heart. London, Mills and Boon, and Toronto, Harlequin, 1969.

Bright Wilderness. London, Mills and Boon, 1969; Toronto, Harlequin, 1970.
The Emerald Cuckoo. London, Mills and Boon, 1970; Toronto, Harlequin, 1971.
Castle of the Unicorn. London, Mills and Boon, and Toronto, Harlequin, 1971.
Pirate of the Sun. London, Mills and Boon, and Toronto, Harlequin, 1972.
Citadel of Swallows. London, Mills and Boon, and Toronto, Harlequin, 1973.
Sweet Roots and Honey. London, Mills and Boon, 1974; Toronto, Harlequin, 1975.
Ross of Silver Ridge. London, Mills and Boon, 1975; Toronto, Harlequin, 1976.
Blossoming Gold. London, Mills and Boon, and Toronto, Harlequin, 1976.
Bride of Bonamour. London, Mills and Boon, and Toronto, Harlequin, 1977.
A Place for Lovers. London, Mills and Boon, 1978.
Forgotten Bride. London, Mills and Boon, 1980.
Zulu Moon. London, Mills and Boon, 1980; Toronto, Harlequin, 1981.
Dangerous to Love. London, Mills and Boon, 1981; Toronto, Harlequin, 1982.
Secondhand Bride. London, Mills and Boon, 1983.
Bitter Deception. London, Mills and Boon, 1987.

OTHER PUBLICATIONS

Other (for children)

Monkey Business. London, Hamish Hamilton, 1965.
The Gentle Dolphin. London, Hamish Hamilton, 1965.
The Red Elephant Blanket. London, Hamish Hamilton, 1966.
The Pumpkin Year. London, Hamish Hamilton, 1966.
Narni of the Desert. London, Hamish Hamilton, 1967; Chicago, Rand McNally, 1968.
A Home for Digby. London, Hamish Hamilton, 1968.

*   *   *

Gwen Westwood's love affair with South Africa began the day she left England to join her future husband in South Africa. There her husband's career took them to various parts of that country and they lived in several places before settling in Durban. Two factors have made her a talented romance writer; the first is, of course, her wide knowledge of South Africa and her obvious love of the country with all of its colorful history. The second factor is her own life, for she seems to draw upon her own years of love and happiness as she writes her romances. Although she favors her own country in many of her novels, she does write of other countries.

Citadel of Swallows takes place in Greece. In this novel Stacey Grant and a friend, Lauren, go to the Greek islands, Lauren for a modeling assignment and Stacey merely to see Lauren's brother again. It is Stacey's belief that she and Lauren's brother have an "understanding." In fact, she had given him most of her savings so he would have time to write an anticipated best seller. Her encounter with Stavros Demetrios, however, changes everything as she falls in love with him. In this novel, Stacey is the traditional romance heroine as she makes bumbling mistakes and says things that instantly tell of her naivety. Stavros is also a traditional romance character and has all the sophisticated élan that any good hero should have.

In *Ross of Silver Ridge* Taryn Bartlett is hired to accompany three children from London to South Africa and to stay with them as their housekeeper. Taryn is 20 an orphan now that her grandparents have died, and is totally unsuited for most kinds of work since she has had no formal training. She finds her own age and inexperience a definite problem as Ross Trent, the children's uncle, finds her far too young for the job. Her efforts to control the children and to fit into his home prove unusually difficult for her, and additionally she quickly succumbs to Ross's undeniable attraction. The fact that another woman, Coral Swann, is the most likely woman to be his wife complicates Taryn's emotions, and much of the story centers on her efforts to deny or suppress her love for Ross. After all, he is wealthy, important, and extremely eligible, what could she offer him that he would want!

In another novel, we find Perry Vaughan returning to South Africa to see Tarquin Winslow, her husband. The title, of course, gives the clue—*Forgotten Bride*. She returns after five years to find that an accident the day after their secret marriage has caused him to lose any memory of her. The illness of her aunt, the death of her grandparents, and the spite of a jealous woman all brought about the circumstances that Perry faces as she first tries to deny her love, and then slowly gives in to it, only to have him reject her completely until surgery restores his memory and his love.

These three novels illustrate the transitional stages of Westwood as a writer. Her heroines begin in the traditional manner, but slowly she emphasizes more complexity of character, more inner strength and sureness in her heroines. The innocence of Stacey gives way to the gradual maturing of Taryn and then to the more adult character of Perry as she faces the crumbling of carefully built defenses after long lonely years. Her gradual shift from young, unawakened love to rejected love is more than simple plot complication, for it shows a more experienced hand at developing her female characters.

—Arlene Moore

WEYMAN, Stanley (John). British. Born in Ludlow, Shropshire, 7 August 1855. Educated at Shrewsbury School; Christ Church College, Oxford, B.A. in modern history. History master, King's School, Chester, one year. Called to the Bar, Inner Temple, London, 1881; lawyer for six years. Imprisoned in France for suspected espionage, 1886. Lived in Plas Llanrhyd, Denbighshire. *Died 10 April 1928.*

ROMANCE AND HISTORICAL PUBLICATIONS

Novels

The House of the Wolf. London, Longman, 1890.
The New Rector. London, Smith Elder, 2 vols., 1891.
The Story of Francis Cludde. London, Cassell, 1891; New York, Longman, 1898.
A Gentleman of France, Being the Memoirs of Gaston de Bonne, Sieur de Marsac. London, Longman, 3 vols., 1893.

The Man in Black. London, Cassell, and New York, Longman, 1894.
My Lady Rotha. London, Cassell, and New York, Longman, 1894.
Under the Red Robe. London, Methuen, 2 vols., and New York, Longman, 2 vols., 1894.
From the Memoirs of a Minister of France. London, Cassell, and New York, Longman, 1895.
The Red Cockade. London, Longman, 1895; New York, Harper, 1896.
The Castle Inn. London, Smith Elder, and New York, Longman, 1898.
Shrewsbury: A Romance. London, Longman, 1898.
Sophia. London, Longman, 1900.
Count Hannibal. London, Smith Elder, and New York, Longman, 1901.
The Long Night. London, Longman, and New York, McClure Phillips, 1903.
The Abbess of Vlaye. London, Longman, 1904.
Starvecrow Farm. London, Hutchinson, and New York, Longman, 1905.
Chippinge. London, Smith Elder, 1906; as *Chippinge Borough*, New York, McClure Phillips, 1906.
The Great House. London, Murray, and New York, Longman, 1919.
Ovington's Bank. London, Murray, and New York, Longman, 1922.
The Traveller in the Fur Coat. London, Hutchinson, and New York, Longman, 1924.
Queen's Folly. London, Murray, and New York, Longman, 1925.

Short Stories

The King's Stratagem and Other Stories. New York, Caldwell, 1891.
For the Cause. Chicago, Sergel, 1897.
In King's Byways. London, Smith Elder, and New York, Longman, 1902.
Laid Up in Lavender. London, Smith Elder, and New York, Longman, 1907.

OTHER PUBLICATIONS

Novels

A Little Wizard. New York, Fenno, 1895.
The Wild Geese. London, Hodder and Stoughton, 1908; New York, Doubleday, 1909.
The Lively Peggy. London, Murray, and New York, Longman, 1928.

*   *   *

Stanley Weyman's novels present a colourful panorama of different periods in English, German, Swiss, and French history, from the middle of the 16th century to the end of the 18th, with an occasional look at 19th-century England in such tales as *Ovington's Bank.* Despite this range, Weyman was most famous in his day and is best remembered now for his swashbuckling romances of France in the stirring times of the last of the Valois kings and the first of the Bourbons.

The general influence of the swash-buckling tradition begun with such engaging vigour during the Romantic period by Alexandre Dumas *père*, the author of *The Three Musketeers* and a

host of similar romances, certainly should not be discounted
The more direct source of inspiration when Weyman turned to
writing historical fiction was, however, the six-volume *History
of the Huguenots*, published between 1879 and 1895, in which
the eminent American scholar H. M. Baird explored sympathetically the long struggle of the French Protestants from the time
of the Reformation, through the grim period of the Wars of Religion which culminated in the triumph of the charismatic Henri
of Navarre, who became king of France in 1589, and on to the
reassertion of Catholic supremacy under Richelieu and the final
rejection of compromise between warring religious faction with
the revocation of the Edict of Nantes in 1688. In these well-
documented accounts of troubled times when passions ran high
and great personalities emerged and asserted their individuality
Weyman did not only find exciting tales of derring-do, with gentlemen of high principle galloping across hostile country to save
their masters from treachery and generally being rewarded for
their breath-taking, hair's-breadth escapes with the love of some
innocent maiden whose loveliness they had once glimpsed from
afar. He also discovered characters and attitudes that appealed
directly to his rather narrow preferences, which were, it must be
added, those of many of his readers. He was not enough of an
historian to think that more sympathy for Catholicism would
have been fitting when treating French history. He was less concerned with being dispassionate than in finding vivid characters
in strong situations.

Historical events, such as the massacre of St. Batholomew's
Eve in 1572 or the assassination of the Duke de Guise 16 years
later, are the foundations of Weyman's romances, and he takes
some care over accuracy both in events and background. Though
historical characters, also introduced with some scruple for fact,
determine the general pattern of the action and cross the scene
from time to time, the main focus of attention is on heroes who
are Weyman's invention, albeit that imagination is tempered
with some concern for truth to type. They are witnesses to the
affairs of state with whom the reader can readily identify, rather
than the personages who determine the outcome of history. It
has to be admitted that their psychology is generally only fairly
rudimentary, even in *A Gentleman of France*, the novel that really made Weyman's reputation in 1893 and is couched in the
form of a first-person memoir. Gaston de Bonne, Sieur de Marsac, tells a rattling good yarn, but most of the time he has little
idea of what is actually going on and his reflections on his predicament, even with the benefits of hindsight, are generally superficial, not to say puerile. There is some love interest too, but
it is handled in a gingerly fashion, with females making only
brief appearances. Weyman's narrative manner is leisurely and
well-ordered, and his language, in dialogue as well as descriptions, tends to be staid, with a certain amount of archaism and,
worse still, some display of erudition.

Weyman's romances still possess a certain boyish charm, and
as well as *A Gentleman of France*, *Under the Red Robe* (in the
France of Richelieu), *The Long Night* (featuring the famous
"night escalade" of Geneva in 1602), and *The Red Cockade* (a
tale of Royalists during the French Revolution) are all worth the
effort they demand of the reader. The stories in the collection
called *In King's Byways* will provide a somewhat less strenuous
introduction to Weyman's style of historical fiction.

—Christopher Smith

WHITBY, Sharon. See **PETERS, Maureen.**

WHITE, Patrick (Victor Martindale). Australian. Born in
London, England, 28 May 1912. Educated at Tudor House,
Moss Vale, and other schools in Australia, 1919–25; Cheltenham
College, England, 1925–29; King's College, Cambridge, 1932–
35, B.A. in modern languages 1935. Served in the Royal Air
Force, in the Middle East, 1941–45: Intelligence Officer. Trav-
elled in Europe and the United States, and lived in London, be-
fore World War II; returned to Australia in 1948. Recipient:
Australian Literature Society Gold Medal, for fiction, 1939;
Miles Franklin award, 1958, 1962; W. H. Smith Literary award,
1959; National Conference of Christians and Jews Brotherhood
award, 1962; Nobel Prize for Literature, 1973. A.C. (Companion, Order of Australia), 1975 (returned 1976). Lives in Sydney.
Agent: Barbara Mobbs, 73/35-A Sutherland Crescent, Darling
Point, New South Wales 2027, Australia.

ROMANCE AND HISTORICAL PUBLICATIONS

Novels

The Tree of Man. New York, Viking Press, 1955; London, Eyre
and Spottiswoode, 1956.
Voss. New York, Viking Press, and London, Eyre and Spottis-
woode, 1957.
A Fringe of Leaves. London, Cape, 1976; New York, Viking
Press, 1977.

OTHER PUBLICATIONS

Novels

Happy Valley. London, Harrap, 1939; New York, Viking Press,
1940.
The Living and the Dead. London, Routledge, and New York,
Viking Press, 1941.
The Aunt's Story. London, Routledge, and New York, Viking
Press, 1948.
Riders in the Chariot. New York, Viking Press, and London,
Eyre and Spottiswoode, 1961.
The Solid Mandala. New York, Viking Press, and London,
Eyre and Spottiswoode, 1966.
The Vivisector. New York, Viking Press, and London, Cape,
1970.
The Eye of the Storm. London, Cape, 1973; New York, Viking
Press, 1974.
The Twyborn Affair. London, Cape, 1979; New York, Viking
Press, 1980.
Memoirs of Many in One. London, Cape, and New York, Vi-
king Press, 1986.

Short Stories

The Burnt Ones. New York, Viking Press, and London, Eyre
and Spottiswoode, 1964.
The Cockatoos: Shorter Novels and Stories. London, Cape,
1974; New York, Viking Press, 1975.
A Cheery Soul and Other Stories. Tokyo, Kenkyusha, 1983.
Three Uneasy Pieces. London, Cape, 1988.

Plays

Bread and Butter Women (produced Sydney, 1935).
The School for Friends (produced Sydney, 1935).

Return to Abyssinia (produced London, 1947).

The Ham Funeral (produced Adelaide, 1961; Crewe, Cheshire, 1969). Included in *Four Plays*, 1965.

The Season at Sarsaparilla (produced Adelaide, 1962). Included in *Four Plays*, 1965.

A Cheery Soul, adaptation of his own story (produced Melbourne, 1963). Included in *Four Plays*, 1965.

Night on Bald Mountain (produced Adelaide, 1964). Included in *Four Plays*, 1965.

Four Plays. London, Eyre and Spottiswoode, 1965; New York, Viking Press, 1966; as *Collected Plays 1*, Sydney, Currency Press, 1985.

Big Toys (produced Sydney, 1977). Sydney, Currency Press, 1978.

The Night the Prowler (screenplay). Melbourne, Penguin, 1977.

Signal Driver: A Morality Play for the Times (produced Adelaide, 1982). Sydney, Currency Press, 1983.

Netherwood (produced Adelaide, 1983). Sydney, Currency Press, 1983.

Shepherd on the Rocks (produced Adelaide, 1983).

Screenplay: *The Night the Prowler*, 1979.

Verse

Thirteen Poems. Privately printed, 1930(?).

The Ploughman and Other Poems. Sydney, Beacon Press, 1935.

Habitable Places: Poems New and Selected. Dunvegan, Ontario, Cormorant, 1988.

Other

Flaws in the Glass: A Self-Portrait. London, Cape, 1981; New York, Viking Press, 1982.

*

Bibliography: *A Bibliography of Patrick White* by Janette Finch, Adelaide, Libraries Board of South Australia, 1966.

Critical Studies (selection): *Patrick White* by Geoffrey Dutton, Melbourne, Lansdowne Press, 1961, revised edition, Melbourne, London, and New York, Oxford University Press, 1971; *Patrick White* by Robert F. Brissenden, London, Longman, 1966; *Patrick White* by Barry Argyle, Edinburgh, Oliver and Boyd, 1967; *Ten Essays on Patrick White Selected from Southerly* edited by G. A. Wilkes, Sydney and London, Angus and Robertson, 1970; *The Mystery of Unity: Theme and Technique in the Novels of Patrick White* by Patricia A. Morley, Montreal, McGill-Queen's University Press, 1972; *Fossil and Psyche* by Wilson Harris, Austin, University of Texas, 1974; *Patrick White* by Alan Lawson, Melbourne and New York, Oxford University Press, 1974, London, Oxford University Press, 1975; *The Eye in the Mandala: Patrick White: A Vision of Man and God* by Peter Beatson, London, Elek, and New York, Barnes and Noble, 1976; *Patrick White: A General Introduction* by Ingmar Bjorksten, translated by Stanley Gerson, St. Lucia, University of Queensland Press, and Atlantic Highlands, New Jersey, Humanities Press, 1976; *Patrick White's Fiction* by William Walsh, London, Allen and Unwin, and Totowa, New Jersey, Rowman and Littlefield, 1977; *Patrick White: A Critical Symposium* edited by Ron E. Shepherd and Kirpal Singh, Bedford Park, South

Australia, Flinders University Centre for Research, and Washington, D.C., Three Continents, 1978; *Patrick White* by Manly Johnson, New York, Ungar, 1980; *Patrick White* by Brian Kiernan, London, Macmillan, and New York, St. Martin's Press, 1980; *A Tragic Vision: The Novels of Patrick White* by A. M. McCulloch, St. Lucia, University of Queensland Press, 1983; *Aspects of Time, Ageing and Old Age in the Novels of Patrick White 1939–1979* by Mari-Ann Berg, Gothenburg, Gothenburg Studies in English, 1983; *Laden Choirs: The Fiction of Patrick White* by Peter Wolfe, Lexington, University Press of Kentucky, 1983; *Patrick White* by John Colmer, London, Methuen, 1984; *Patrick White* by John A. Weigel, Boston, Twayne, 1984; *Patrick White's Fiction: The Paradox of Fortunate Failure* by Carolyn Bliss, London, Macmillan, 1986; *Patrick White: Fiction and the Unconscious* by David J. Tacey, Oxford, Oxford University Press, 1988; *Vision and Style in Patrick White: A Study of Five Novels* by Rodney Stenning Edgecombe, University, University of Alabama Press, 1989.

*   *   *

Patrick White, the 1973 Nobel Laureate and the current grand old man of Australian letters, spearheaded the astonishing Antipodean literary flowering which has developed since the end of World War II. Although a third-generation Australian, White was born in England, and spent the majority of his formative years from the age of 13 onwards in both England and Europe. This distancing from his true native roots at such a time has enabled him, in many of the novels and short stories he has written since his permanent return to Australia in 1947, to contrast with a detached, quasi-European eye and sensibility the vast emptiness of the Australian interior with the crowded and swiftly expanding middle-class urban communities on the coast.

The fundamental conflict between nature and civilization is one of the principal themes inherent in each of his three historical novels, *The Tree of Man*, *Voss*, and *A Fringe of Leaves*. *The Tree of Man*, the first book White published (perhaps significantly following a seven-year silence) after returning to Australia, can be viewed in retrospect as possibly the book he felt the need to write to dispel the vestigial influences of what he had come to regard as the sterile intellectualism of postwar England, and thus establish a fresh, uncluttered base on which to build his future work. In many respects, *The Tree of Man* is the most purely indigenous of all White's major novels. While White does not entirely succeed in making the lives of his ordinary and mainly inarticulate main characters consistently interesting, this long, dense narrative certainly never becomes turgid in the telling. It follows the fortunes of Stan and Amy Parker and their neighbours as they struggle against drought, fire, and flood to bring up their families, and attempt to tame and cultivate the wilderness around the tiny community they have founded a few miles from turn-of-the-century Sydney. The uneasy Eden these simple folk have created is, however, under constant threat, not only from the elements but from civilization itself. The city limits encroach nearer and nearer, until eventually the tiny community is overrun and becomes absorbed into the suburbs.

There is, on the other hand, nothing intrinsically "ordinary" about the characters in *Voss*, considered by many to be White's masterpiece. Loosely based on historical fact—Ludwig Leichhardt's ill-fated expedition of 1848 to cross the Australian continent from east to west—*Voss* tells the saga of a similar fictional expedition in the 1840's, led by the German, Johann Ulrich Voss. A supreme egoist and a precursor of the Nietzsche superman figure, Voss is financed by a prosperous Sydney draper, Edmund Bonner, and embarks with six disparate companions on his ill-conceived and ill-prepared journey, unshakeably confident of ultimate success. Voss's ruthless egoism and manic obsession inevitably spark off a mutiny, instigated by the ex-convict, Judd. Judd deserts, taking two others of the party with him. The remaining four men, accompanied by an aborigine guide, Jackie, whom they acquired en route, press on into the unknown. One of the four meets his death at the hands of the tribe of aborigines which has been shadowing the little band; another commits suicide; another dies of hunger and exhaustion. Finally, Voss, ill and in a delirium, alone in the terrible landscape of the outback and surrounded by the hostile aborigines, is put to death by Jackie, who stabs him and then messily decapitates him. In the true-life Leichhardt expedition, there were no survivors and no trace was ever found of the remains of its members. In *Voss*, however, the mutineer Judd does survive, and returns to civilization 20 years later to tell his distorted version of events. Superimposed upon the story of the expedition is the strange love of Voss and Bonner's niece, Laura Trevelyan. Their love for each other is born during the few occasions on which they meet prior to Voss's departure into the interior, and then is subsequently perpetuated not only by correspondence, most of which is, of course, never delivered, but more potently by a powerful telepathic contact. Laura suffers Voss's vicissitudes by proxy. When he is killed, she is smitten by a mysterious illness, and almost succumbs. This mystical unity between Voss and Laura gives a tremendous, unforgettable depth to the novel, and is, moreover, perhaps the most convincing depiction of pure love between a man and a woman in the whole of White's fiction.

A *Fringe of Leaves* is also based on historical fact. Set in the 1830's, it follows fairly closely the story of Mrs. Elizabeth Fraser (see, for example, Michael Alexander's 1971 account, *Mrs. Fraser on the Fatal Shore*). The novel relates how Ellen Roxburgh, a respectable member of Moreton Bay society, returning with her husband by sea from a visit to her brother-in-law in Van Diemen's Land, is shipwrecked off the coast of Queensland. Passengers and crew take to the longboat, and after several weeks—during which Ellen, the only female among the survivors, gives birth to a still-born child—they land on an inhospitable shore. They are captured by aborigines, and all the men are killed. Ellen is taken into captivity, stripped of her clothes, and treated as a slave. She is able to survive all these ordeals by drawing on the resilience acquired from her lower-class origins in Cornwall. Eventually, she is rescued by an escaped convict, Jack Chance, and returned to civilization, but back in Moreton Bay experiences some difficulty in accepting again the mantle of middle-class respectability her marriage had given her. In *A Fringe of Leaves*, the conflict between nature (in this case, the uninhibited, ritual society of the aborigines) and civilization (the artificial elegance and etiquette of 19th-century colonial society) is portrayed in consummate fashion in its most basic terms.

White writes in a highly individual and mannered prose style, a style that vividly conveys the vast emptiness and awful grandeur of the Australian landscape, and provides what is at times an almost unbearable insight into the human psyche. White is one of the most carnal of modern intellectual writers; his obvious distaste for the frailties (in all aspects) of human flesh has become more pronounced in his later work, as has the bitter and savage satirical posture he so often adopts when describing the mores of middle-class society. White is a writer of genius, and indisputably the most considerable literary figure to have emerged from the Antipodes since World War II.

—Roy S. Simmonds

WHITE, T(erence) H(anbury). Also wrote as James Aston. British. Born in Bombay, India, 29 May 1906; brought to England, 1911. Educated at Cheltenham College, 1920–24; Queens' College, Cambridge (exhibitioner), 1925–27, 1928–29, B.A. 1929. Taught at a preparatory school, 1930–32; head of the English department, Stowe School, Buckinghamshire, 1932–36; lived in Ireland, 1939–46, and in Jersey, 1946–47, and Alderney, 1947–64, Channel Islands. *Died 17 January 1964.*

ROMANCE AND HISTORICAL PUBLICATIONS

Novels (series: The Once and Future King)

Farewell Victoria. London, Collins, 1933; New York, Smith and Haas, 1934.
The Sword in the Stone. London, Collins, 1938; New York, Putnam, 1939; revised edition in *The Once and Future King*, 1958.
The Witch in the Wood. New York, Putnam, 1939; London, Collins, 1940; revised edition, as *The Queen of Air and Darkness*, in *The Once and Future King*, 1958.
The Ill-Made Knight. New York, Putnam, 1940; London, Collins, 1941; revised edition in *The Once and Future King*, 1958.
Mistress Masham's Repose. New York, Putnam, 1946; London, Cape, 1947.
The Once and Future King. London, Collins, and New York, Putnam, 1958.
The Book of Merlyn: The Unpublished Conclusion to The Once and Future King. Austin, University of Texas Press, 1977; London, Collins, 1978.

Short Stories

The Maharajah and Other Stories, edited by Kurth Sprague. London, Macdonald, and New York, Putnam, 1981.

OTHER PUBLICATIONS

Novels

Dead Mr. Nixon, with R. McNair Scott. London, Cassell, 1931.
Darkness at Pemberley. London, Gollancz, 1932; New York, Century, 1933.
They Winter Abroad (as James Aston). London, Chatto and Windus, and New York, Viking Press, 1932.
First Lesson (as James Aston). London, Chatto and Windus, 1932; New York, Knopf, 1933.
Earth Stopped; or, Mr. Marx's Sporting Tour. London, Collins, 1934; New York, Putnam, 1935.
Gone to Ground. London, Collins, and New York, Putnam, 1935.
The Elephant and the Kangaroo. New York, Putnam, 1947; London, Cape, 1948.

Verse

Loved Helen and Other Poems. London, Chatto and Windus, and New York, Viking Press, 1929.
The Green Bay Tree; or, The Wicked Man Touches Wood. Cambridge, Heffer, 1929.
Verses. Privately printed, 1962.
A Joy Proposed. London, Rota, 1980; Athens, University of Georgia Press, 1983.

Other

England Have My Bones. London, Collins, and New York, Macmillan, 1936.

Burke's Steerage; or, The Amateur Gentleman's Introduction to Noble Sports and Pastimes. London, Collins, 1938; New York, Putnam, 1939.

The Age of Scandal: An Excursion Through a Minor Period. London, Cape, and New York, Putnam, 1950.

The Goshawk (on falconry). London, Cape, 1951; New York, Putnam, 1952.

The Scandalmonger (on English scandals). London, Cape, and New York, Putnam, 1952.

The Master: An Adventure Story (for children). London, Cape, and New York, Putnam, 1958.

The Godstone and the Blackymor (on Ireland). London, Cape, and New York, Putnam, 1959.

America at Last: The American Journal of T. H. White. New York, Putnam, 1965.

The White/Garnett Letters, edited by David Garnett. London, Cape, and New York, Viking Press, 1968.

Letters to a Friend: The Correspondence Between T. H. White and L. J. Potts, edited by François Gallix. New York, Putnam, 1982; Gloucester, Sutton, 1984.

Editor and Translator, *The Book of Beasts, Being a Translation from a Latin Bestiary of the Twelfth Century.* London, Cape, 1954; New York, Putnam, 1955.

*

Bibliography: *T. H. White: An Annotated Bibliography* by François Gallix, New York, Garland, 1986.

Critical Studies: *T. H. White: A Biography* by Sylvia Townsend Warner, London, Cape-Chatto and Windus, 1967, New York, Viking Press, 1968; *T. H. White* by John K. Crane, New York, Twayne, 1974.

*   *   *

Like Tolkien, T. H. White has devoted readers in both Britain and the United States where many of his books are either constantly reprinted or can be found in most public libraries. Although he published more than 25 volumes, White is mostly remembered as the author of *The Once and Future King*, his modern retelling of Malory's *Le Morte Darthur*. Walt Disney made a feature cartoon out of the first part, *Merlyn the Enchanter* (1963); *Camelot* (1961) was a Broadway musical by Lerner and Loewe based on White's adaptation of the Arthurian legends and the book was finally made into a film directed by Joshua Logan in 1967.

White felt more at ease in the company of Malory, Swift, Walpole, and Cobbett than with his own contemporaries with very few exceptions such as David Garnett or L. J. Potts. He sought a refuge in the past and especially in the second part of the 18th century: *The Age of Scandal* and *The Scandalmonger* are lively chronicles of historical characters and British eccentrics of that period. *Farewell Victoria* is an original piece of historical fiction; it is the nostalgic evocation of Victorian England and its difficult transition into the 20th century, as seen through the eyes of a stable groom.

Mistress Masham's Repose is also a return to the historical past since the moral lesson given to the 10-year-old heroine of this sequel to *Gulliver's Travels* is to imitate the wise descendants of Swift's Lilliputians who managed to preserve their ancestors' traditions throughout the 20th century.

But it was above all about the mythical early Middle Ages of the Arthurian legends that White dreamed. His interest in Malory started early in his youth and his Cambridge dissertation in 1927 was on the *Morte Darthur*; he was to spend the next 30 years working on the Matter of Britain. While following his model closely, White also left his personal mark, particularly by giving a new psychological depth to the main characters: Arthur, Lancelot, Guenever, and Morgause.

In the first book, *The Sword in the Stone*, which owes very little to Malory, White, disguised under the mask of Merlyn, invented the youth of the future King Arthur and gave him the sort of practical and moral education he himself would have loved to have received by transforming Arthur into various animals. The book was well received by the critics and was selected by the American Book of the Month Club in August 1938.

The second volume, *The Witch in the Wood*, proved much more difficult to write and several different versions were produced. White finally realized that he could not come to terms with the character of Morgause in which he had tried to put all the hatred he felt for his mother. He heaped all the blame on the Queen for the incest committed with King Arthur that would lead to his doom and to the failure of the Round Table. The third book focuses on Lancelot and White chose to interpret "Le chevalier mal fêt" as "The Ill-Made Knight."

During the war, White's life and Arthurian work seemed to get inextricably mixed up together. Since he was unable to decide whether or not he should take part in the conflict, he decided to add a new fifth volume and rewrite the whole series as a satirical pamphlet against modern barbarism. His idea was to make Merlyn into a pacifist philosopher who would be his mouthpiece in trying to create a war-free world. The fifth book was finally abandoned. (Published posthumously in 1977 as *The Book of Merlyn*, it remained on the New York *Times* bestseller list for 24 weeks.)

In the first part of the tetralogy that came out in 1958, White included two very crucial chapters from the discarded book in which the future King visits the totalitarian society of the warfaring ants inspired by *Brave New World* and prefiguring *Nineteen Eighty-Four*, and the peace-loving wild geese.

White managed to preserve all the magic of the eternal dream-world of Arthur and his knights of the Round Table while adding a very personal touch that was praised by most critics. As a talented story-teller like Kipling, White was particularly successful in communicating his enthusiasm and his never-ending curiosity for every aspect of learning. *The Once and Future King* has not aged and has now become a necessary reference when writing about the modern adaptations of the Arthurian myths.

—François Gallix

WHITMORE, Cilla. See **SEBASTIAN, Margaret.**

WHITNEY, Phyllis A(yame). American. Born in Yokohama, Japan, 9 September 1903. Educated at schools in Japan, China, the Philippines, California, and Texas; McKinley High School, Chicago, graduated 1924. Married 1) George A. Garner in 1925 (divorced 1945), one daughter; 2) Lovell F. Jahnke in 1950 (died

1973). Dance instructor, San Antonio, Texas, one year; children's books editor, Chicago *Sun*, 1942–46, and Philadelphia *Inquirer*, 1947–48; instructor in children's fiction writing, Northwestern University, Evanston, Illinois, 1945, and New York University, 1947–58. Member, Board of Directors, 1959–62, and president, 1975, Mystery Writers of America. Recipient: Mystery Writers of America Edgar Allan Poe award, for children's book, 1961, 1964, and Grand Master award, 1984. Lives in Virginia. Agent: c/o McIntosh and Otis Inc., 310 Madison Avenue, New York, New York 10017, U.S.A.

ROMANCE AND HISTORICAL PUBLICATIONS

Novels

Red Is for Murder. Chicago, Ziff Davis, 1943; as *Red Carnelian*, New York, Paperback Library, 1968; London, Coronet, 1976.

The Quicksilver Pool. New York, Appleton Century Crofts, 1955; London, Coronet, 1973.

The Trembling Hills. New York, Appleton Century Crofts, 1956; London, Coronet, 1974.

Skye Cameron. New York, Appleton Century Crofts, 1957; London, Hurst and Blackett, 1959.

The Moonflower. New York, Appleton Century Crofts, 1958; as *The Mask and the Moonflower*, London, Hurst and Blackett, 1960.

Thunder Heights. New York, Appleton Century Crofts, 1960; London, Coronet, 1973.

Blue Fire. New York, Appleton Century Crofts, 1961; London, Hodder and Stoughton, 1962.

Window on the Square. New York, Appleton Century Crofts, 1962; London, Coronet, 1969.

Seven Tears for Apollo. New York, Appleton Century Crofts, 1963; London, Coronet, 1969.

Black Amber. New York, Appleton Century Crofts, 1964; London, Hale, 1965.

Sea Jade. New York, Appleton Century Crofts, 1965; London, Hale, 1966.

Columbella. New York, Doubleday, 1966; London, Hale, 1967.

Silverhill. New York, Doubleday, 1967; London, Heinemann, 1968.

Hunter's Green. New York, Doubleday, 1968; London, Heinemann, 1969.

The Winter People. New York, Doubleday, 1969; London, Heinemann, 1970.

Lost Island. New York, Doubleday, 1970; London, Heinemann, 1971.

Listen for the Whisperer. New York, Doubleday, and London, Heinemann, 1972.

Snowfire. New York, Doubleday, and London, Heinemann, 1973.

The Turquoise Mask. New York, Doubleday, 1974; London, Heinemann, 1975.

Spindrift. New York, Doubleday, and London, Heinemann, 1975.

The Golden Unicorn. New York, Doubleday, 1976; London, Heinemann, 1977.

The Stone Bull. New York, Doubleday, and London, Heinemann, 1977.

The Glass Flame. New York, Doubleday, 1978; London, Heinemann, 1979.

Domino. New York, Doubleday, 1979; London, Heinemann, 1980.

Poinciana. New York, Doubleday, 1980; London, Heinemann, 1981.

Vermilion. New York, Doubleday, 1981; London, Heinemann, 1982.

Emerald. New York, Doubleday, and London, Heinemann, 1983.

Rainsong. New York, Doubleday, and London, Heinemann, 1984.

Dream of Orchids. New York, Doubleday, and London, Hodder and Stoughton, 1985.

The Flaming Tree. New York, Doubleday, and London, Hodder and Stoughton, 1986.

Silversword. New York, Doubleday, and London, Hodder and Stoughton, 1987.

Feather on the Moon. New York, Doubleday, and London, Hodder and Stoughton, 1988.

Rainbow in the Mist. New York, Doubleday, 1989.

OTHER PUBLICATIONS

Fiction (for children)

A Place for Ann. Boston, Houghton Mifflin, 1941.

A Star for Ginny. Boston, Houghton Mifflin, 1942.

A Window for Julie. Boston, Houghton Mifflin, 1943.

The Silver Inkwell. Boston, Houghton Mifflin, 1945.

Window Hill. New York, Reynal, 1947.

Ever After. Boston, Houghton Mifflin, 1948.

Mystery of the Gulls. Philadelphia, Westminster Press, 1949.

Linda's Homecoming. Philadelphia, McKay, 1950.

The Island of Dark Woods. Philadelphia, Westminster Press, 1951; as *Mystery of the Strange Traveler*, 1967.

Love Me, Love Me Not. Boston, Houghton Mifflin, 1952.

Step to the Music. New York, Crowell, 1953.

Mystery of the Black Diamonds. Philadelphia, Westminster Press, 1954; as *Black Diamonds*, Leicester, Brockhampton Press, 1957.

A Long Time Coming. Philadelphia, McKay, 1954.

Mystery on the Isle of Skye. Philadelphia, Westminster Press, 1955.

The Fire and the Gold. New York, Crowell, 1956.

The Highest Dream. Philadelphia, McKay, 1956.

Mystery of the Green Cat. Philadelphia, Westminster Press, 1957.

Secret of the Samurai Sword. Philadelphia, Westminster Press, 1958.

Creole Holiday. Philadelphia, Westminster Press, 1959.

Mystery of the Haunted Pool. Philadelphia, Westminster Press, 1960.

Secret of the Tiger's Eye. Philadelphia, Westminster Press, 1961.

Mystery of the Golden Horn. Philadelphia, Westminster Press, 1962.

Mystery of the Hidden Hand. Philadelphia, Westminster Press, 1963.

Secret of the Emerald Star. Philadelphia, Westminster Press, 1964.

Mystery of the Angry Idol. Philadelphia, Westminster Press, 1965.

Secret of the Spotted Shell. Philadelphia, Westminster Press, 1967.

Secret of Goblin Glen. Philadelphia, Westminster Press, 1968.

The Mystery of the Crimson Ghost. Philadelphia, Westminster Press, 1969.

Secret of the Missing Footprint. Philadelphia, Westminster Press, 1969.

The Vanishing Scarecrow. Philadelphia, Westminster Press, 1971.

Nobody Likes Trina. Philadelphia, Westminster Press, 1972.

Mystery of the Scowling Boy. Philadelphia, Westminster Press, 1973.

Secret of Haunted Mesa. Philadelphia, Westminster Press, 1975.

Secret of the Stone Face. Philadelphia, Westminster Press, 1977.

Other

Writing Juvenile Fiction. Boston, The Writer, 1947; revised edition, 1960.

Writing Juvenile Stories and Novels: How to Write and Sell Fiction for Young People. Boston, The Writer, 1976.

Guide to Fiction Writing. Boston, The Writer, 1982; London, Poplar Press, 1984.

*

Manuscript Collection: Mugar Memorial Library, Boston University.

Phyllis A. Whitney comments:

Since I have lived in many different places, I have no "roots." Thus I must look for a fresh setting for each suspense novel I write. Once I have chosen my setting, I visit it to collect impressions and information firsthand. Then I do a great deal of research at home. Eventually, I develop a young woman character with a serious problem facing her, and in my imagination I set her down in the background I mean to use. Around her I place other characters who will bring conflict and further problems into her life. As these characters grow, both in my mind and on paper, my story begins to emerge a bit at a time, until the whole thing is clear before I write. The setting itself often becomes an important character in my novels.

*   *   *

When I was growing up, my mother and those friends of hers who were avid readers were discriminating in their addictions: not just any romance would do. It ought to be historical, spirited, suspenseful, and if it had a bit of literary merit that didn't hurt at all. Any new Victoria Holt sufficed, as did the latest by Mary Stewart or Daphne du Maurier. What these writers offered my mother and her friends was not simply romantic intrigue, but rather romance with a decidedly British accent. All the more surprising then that in the mid-1960's those ladies added to their brief, cherished list of favorites the books of Phyllis A. Whitney—an American, and one, moreover, who set her romances mainly in America and almost exclusively in modern dress. Place and time, those two staples of gothic fiction, had been transformed, at least for my mother's circle, from "an old house in England a long time ago" to "here and now."

Not exactly down the street, of course. Whitney chooses her settings for their romantic possibilities. Yet she avoids the predictably romantic American locations, those places which resonate loudest in the American psyche: the South, Los Angeles, New York. The latter she uses only historically (*Window on the Square*), or as a point of departure from which the heroines of *Vermilion*, *The Winter People*, *Sea Jade*, *Domino* and several other books flee, seeking sanctuary or confronting the past in ancestral homes elsewhere. Remarkable in Whitney is where

"elsewhere" is. She has a proclivity for sustaining romantic suspense in what could easily be prosaic locations—the Poconos and Catskills, the Hamptons, New Hampshire, even northern New Jersey, all resort areas for the middle class. Whitney achieves this transformation of these otherwise hum-drum locales by means of some standard gothic devices: the heroine's seeming isolation amid a hostile household whose shifting moods she only dimly understands; the gothic house itself, be it old hotel or mansion; the careful removal of dailiness. In a Whitney novel, as in other gothics, characters gather for meals less to eat than to confront each other, dress not to keep warm but to show off the latest fashions, and go to bed mostly to be disturbed by ominous noises, bad dreams, and an occasional murderer. Furthermore, while virtually all of Whitney's heroines are "career-girls," hardly a one continues to work during the course of the novel, except at a new job, often of near-servant status: a governess, companion, or hostess.

This displacement from accustomed work, and usually from what had been home, is all the more appropriate since Whitney has created a species of romance fiction which might be called Tourist Gothic. She writes well and lovingly of the various places in which her books are set, but always with the enthusiasm of a visitor, not with an inhabitant's long knowledge of place. Thus Whitney provides her readers with a kind of exciting vacation, replete with interesting locations, confusing romances, and outright danger. Book after book is set in or near a resort: in the Tennessee or New Hampshire mountains, at a reconstructed Colorado mining town, near Santa Fe or Tlaquepaque, in a Newport mansion or a palatial hotel in the shadowy Catskills. What reader wouldn't love to spend a week in one of these places, under the spell of an older man by whom she will feel, as does Megan Kincaid of *Window on the Square*, "unaccountably drawn and yet a little repelled?"

If these resort locations are chosen for romance and heightened by contrived isolation, they also serve for Whitney an educative function. As others have noted, Americans like a little learning with their light reading; in so pragmatic a culture nothing should be just for pleasure and even on vacation one should learn. A Whitney heroine learns about her own resourcefulness and the true feelings of those around her, especially those of that attractive but disconcerting older man. But she, and consequently the reader, learns more as well. Each of Whitney's romances instructs us in some facet of local color or history: Caribbean seashells and hurricanes in *Columbella*, Turkish mosaics in *Black Amber*, Japanese netsuke in *Poinciana*, herbalism in *Thunder Heights*, Hopi Indian culture in *Vermilion*, topiary in *Hunter's Green*, South African diamonds and apartheid in *Blue Fire*. The list is as long as Whitney's publication history, for each novel supplies a new location and with it a new factual knowledge.

Constant in Whitney's work, however, is her preoccupation with art and her passion for environmentally sound architecture and land development. That art would figure prominently is not surprising, the unstable artist being a common enough romantic device. And Whitney does use artists conventionally, creating in *The Winter People*, *The Golden Unicorn*, *Thunder Heights*, and *Window on the Square* tortured, often deranged, painters and sculptors. Occasionally she goes against type, presenting in *The Stone Bull* a sculptor whose work is expressive of the dark side of his nature but whose actions are good, and in *Vermilion*, the Indian paintings of Alice Spencer whose art is angry but whose personality is deeply calm. The artistic process itself holds a fascination for Whitney beyond romantic convention; her characters seem constantly perplexed by its moral and emotional valence, as if the author herself were ambivalent about the worth of an art deeper than that which she practices.

The value of an architecture mindful of its surroundings Whitney easily recognizes, however. Her passion for beautiful building and sound development drives the plots of several novels. In *Thunder Heights*, set in the 19th-century Hudson Valley, the engineer hero dreams of bridging the river in a careful, environmentally sound manner; in *The Trembling Hills*, which takes place in San Francisco during the year of the great earthquake, a young architect enthuses about the new Chicago School which has been "preaching that form should follow function" and predicts great things from "a young fellow named Wright. . . . " The contemporary issue of land use comes up in *The Glass Flame* where the love interest is an architect and planner who is building a lake community in the Tennessee hills, even as in the earlier book, *The Winter People*, the main conflict centers on the potential development of a wilderness area. Whitney's devotion to this topic is peculiar to her romances, even as her knowledge of architecture extends beyond the traditional Gothic devices of towers and secret passageways. From the Norwegian kirks in *Listen for the Whisperer* to the reconstructed mining town in *Domino*, Whitney uses architecture for its tangible as well as symbolic value.

A tourist's enthusiasm, some local learning, a passion for good houses on well-used land: these hardly seem the stuff of which romantic dreams are woven. But such is Whitney's gift that she can make the prosaic mysterious and transform business and environmental issues into the source of romantic conflicts. This is her distinct contribution, I think, for in other ways her novels are unfailingly conventional. I can pick any book at random from my stack of Whitney novels and know as well before as after I open it that her heroine will be alone, will have recently lost one or both parents, will have been devoted to her father and at odds with her mother, and—most importantly—will be about to investigate the past, usually her own familial past, to confront some long repressed, traumatic event. Romance readers want certain constants, of course, what Whitney herself has referred to as "the dear familiar landscape" of romance: the lone woman, the troubling man, the mysterious danger. She provides all these, but happily is an inventive enough writer to twist her own devices when they become tired, as in the recent *Vermilion* where the familiar Whitney convention of giving her heroine a vague, partial, terrifying memory of a violent or criminal act witnessed in childhood is transformed into the haunting of the narrator's adult self by a spirited imaginary playmate, a doppelganger who expresses the heroine's more violent emotions. If Whitney's psychology is not deep here, it is convincing, for as she has done now in more than 30 romance novels she assures her readers that even a young woman haunted by a repressed memory of violence or by an imaginary friend unwilling to be banished may be resourceful enough to undo wrongs, save herself from danger, and win the love of a strong, mysterious man. It's not so unlikely, really. Not when we have been made to believe that gothic romance may exist in prosaic north Jersey and that anything at all may happen on the resort vacations that are Whitney's books.

—Nancy Regan

WIAT, Philippa. Pseudonym for Philippa Ferridge (née Wyatt). British. Born in London. Educated at Wimbledon County School, London. Married Dennis Ferridge; three daughters. Address: 19 Normandale, Bexhill-on-Sea, East Sussex TN39 3LU England.

ROMANCE AND HISTORICAL PUBLICATIONS

Novels (series: Black Boar; Charlton Mead; Edward III; Howard; Wilmington; Wyatt)

Like as the Roaring Waves (Howard). London, Hale, 1972.
The Heir of Allington (Wyatt). London, Hale, 1973.
The Master of Blandeston Hall (Wyatt). London, Hale, 1973.
The Knight of Allington (Wyatt). London, Hale, 1974.
The Rebel of Allington (Wyatt). London, Hale, 1974.
Lord of the Black Boar. London, Hale, 1975.
Sword of Woden (Black Boar). London, Hale, 1975.
Lion Without Claws (Howard). London, Hale, 1976; New York, St. Martin's Press, 1977.
The Queen's Fourth Husband (Howard). London, Hale, 1976.
Tree of Vortigern (Black Boar). London, Hale, 1976.
My Lute Be Still (Wyatt). London, Hale, 1977.
Sound Now the Passing-Bell (Wyatt). London, Hale, 1977.
The Atheling (Black Boar). London, Hale, 1977.
Maid of Gold (Howard). London, Hale, 1978.
Raven in the Wind (Black Boar). London, Hale, 1978.
Yet a Lion (Howard). London, Hale, 1978.
The Four-Poster (Wilmington). London, Hale, 1979.
The Golden Chariot. London, Hale, 1979.
Westerfalca (Black Boar). London, Hale, 1979.
Lord of the Wolf (Black Boar). London, Hale, 1980.
Shadow of Samain (Wilmington). London, Hale, 1980.
The King's Vengeance. London, Hale, 1981.
The Mistletoe Bough (Charlton Mead). London, Hale, 1981.
Bride in Darkness (Charlton Mead). London, Hale, 1982.
Wychwood (Charlton Mead). London, Hale, 1982.
Children of the Spring. London, Hale, 1983.
Five Gold Rings. London, Hale, 1983.
Cartismandua. London, Hale, 1984.
Prince of the White Rose. London, Hale, 1984.
Queen-Gold (Edward III). London, Hale, 1985.
Fair Rosamond. London, Hale, 1985.
The Grey Goose Wing (Edward III). London, Hale, 1986.
The Whyte Swan (Edward III). London, Hale, 1986.
Wear a Green Kirtle (Howard). London, Hale, 1987.
The Cloister and the Flame. London, Hale, 1988.
Phantasmagoria. London, Hale, 1988.

*

Philippa Wiat comments:

As an historical novelist, I write first and foremost about people. History as one learns it at school—or as I myself learned it at school—can be pretty daunting. It is not so much the monarchs, battles, and treaties that make the past such fascinating reading, as the people who lived in those times—those who were part and parcel of the Magna Carta and the Battle of Crécy; those who experienced the Black Death or saw Richard III and Wat Tyler.

To bring such people to life, to make history live and work for us, to heed its warnings and take part in its debates, is the task of the historical novelist. The secret? One must see into the minds of one's characters; be on the inside looking out, sharing their thoughts, beliefs, fears, and aspirations. One must subjugate one's identity to theirs.

*   *   *

In less than 20 years Philippa Wiat has written nearly 40 historical novels, prompted initially to do so by her researches into her own family, that of the poet and courtier Sir Thomas Wyatt. Her novels cover a wide range of periods—from the 1st century A.D. to the 16th century—with varying degrees of success. There is no doubt that Wiat is happiest when writing of the 16th century, and it is in this era that the bulk of her novels are set. Her approach varies—in some novels actual historical personages form the pivot of the story, in others the characters are wholly fictional, and one trilogy, the Charlton Mead novels, is based on an old Oxfordshire legend.

Every historical novelist has a decision to make about the use of spoken language within the framework of the narrative—should it be readable (and this usually means modern and colloquial) or should it be faithful to the period? Choosing the latter often results in stilted and unnatural phraseology, and unfortunately in some of Wiat's books this is indeed what the reader gets. Ironically the language is least ornate in those of her novels in which courtly language would not be out of place (i.e., those of the 16th century), and it is in those set in the 1st century that the speech reaches the ultimate in improbability. Would Prasatagus (*The Golden Chariot*) really have said "Boadicea, for all your dignity and queenliness, you are at heart a primitive person, although perchance only I, your lover, recognise it"—or even words to that effect? The few modern idioms which do creep in jar all the more, given the over-formality of the rest of the speech.

Characterisation is often the factor upon which the success of an historical novel can depend. The individuals need to be believable not only in the context of the setting but also in their actions and decisions. Wiat imputes to particular individuals decisions and actions which are known to have happened, but often without giving us any more than very shallow character sketches. However, where she does allow the personalities to develop, the novels at once become more interesting and more believable—notably in *The Whyte Swan*, the third part of a trilogy about Edward III. This is certainly one of her better novels, perhaps because the characters have had time to evolve over the length of the trilogy and the author may thus have a greater sense of involvement. One particular scene in this book, between Edward and his mother Isabella the She-Wolf of France, is especially successful because the strength of the personalities, and the interplay between them, are allowed full rein.

It is all too easy for an historical novel to be merely a romance, adventure, or mystery which happens to be set in historical times, and with those of Wiat's novels not involving actual people this is indeed the case, as she often fails to paint a realistic background. On the other hand, she is not afraid to tackle controversial subjects and place them in an historical setting. For example in *Five Gold Rings* and again in *Lord of the Wolf* the subject of incest is introduced as an integral part of the plot. In *The Cloister and the Flame* a young girl who is forced against her will to become a nun has an affair with an equally reluctant priest and becomes pregnant. Although the plot develops into a phenomenally improbable tangle of relationships and identities, the basic scenario is unusual and interesting, and a few touches of humour are provided in some of the convent scenes.

The painting in of background facts is always a problem for the novelist. The device of exposition through thought or conversation (i.e., one character thinking the plot aloud or telling another character what he or she must obviously already know) is often used successfully in drama (Shakespeare did it all the time!) but needs to be handled carefully in the context of a novel. If skilfully done this technique can be very effective, but unfortunately in many of Wiat's novels it is rather less than successful.

In her better novels Wiat shows that she is capable of strong characterisation, unusual plots, and interesting exposition of historical facts. It is a shame that not all her novels demonstrate these strengths.

—Judith Rhodes

WIEBE, Rudy (Henry). Canadian. Born in Fairholme, Saskatchewan, 4 October 1934. Educated at Alberta Mennonite High School; University of Alberta, Edmonton, 1953–56, 1958–60 (International Nickel graduate fellow, 1958–59; Queen Elizabeth graduate fellow, 1959–60), B.A. 1956, M.A. 1960; University of Tübingen, Germany (Rotary fellow), 1957–58; University of Manitoba, Winnipeg, 1961; University of Iowa, Iowa City, 1964. Married Tena F. Isaak in 1958; one daughter and two sons. Research officer, Glenbow Foundation, Calgary, 1956; foreign service officer, Ottawa, 1960; high school teacher, Selkirk, Manitoba, 1961; editor, Mennonite Brethren *Herald*, Winnipeg, 1962–63; Assistant Professor of English, Goshen College, Indiana, 1963–67. Assistant Professor, 1967–70, Associate Professor, 1970–77, and since 1977 Professor of English, University of Alberta. Recipient: Canada Council arts scholarship, 1964, award, 1971, grant, 1977; Lorne Pierce Medal, 1987. D.Litt.: University of Winnipeg, Manitoba, 1986. Member, Royal Society of Canada, 1987. Address: 5315 143rd Street, Edmonton, Alberta T6H 4E3, Canada.

ROMANCE AND HISTORICAL PUBLICATIONS

Novels

Peace Shall Destroy Many. Toronto, McClelland and Stewart, 1962; Grand Rapids, Michigan, Eerdmans, 1964.
The Blue Mountains of China. Toronto, McClelland and Stewart, and Grand Rapids, Michigan, Eerdmans, 1970.
The Temptations of Big Bear. Toronto, McClelland and Stewart, 1973.
The Scorched-Wood People. Toronto, McClelland and Stewart, 1977.
The Mad Trapper. Toronto, McClelland and Stewart, 1980.

Short Stories

Where Is the Voice Coming From? Toronto, McClelland and Stewart, 1974.
Personal Fictions, with others, edited by Michael Ondaatje. Toronto, Oxford University Press, 1977.
Alberta: A Celebration, edited by Tom Radford. Edmonton, Alberta, Hurtig, 1979.
The Angel of the Tar Sands and Other Stories. Toronto, McClelland and Stewart, 1982.

OTHER PUBLICATIONS

Novels

First and Vital Candle. Toronto, McClelland and Stewart, and Grand Rapids, Michigan, Eerdmans, 1966.
My Lovely Enemy. Toronto, McClelland and Stewart, 1983.
War in the West. Toronto, McClelland and Stewart, 1985.

Play

Far as the Eye Can See, with Theatre Passe Muraille. Edmonton, Alberta, NeWest Press, 1977.

Other

A Voice in the Land: Essays by and about Rudy Wiebe, edited by W. J. Keith. Edmonton, Alberta, NeWest Press, 1981.

Editor, *The Story-Makers: A Selection of Modern Short Stories*. Toronto, Macmillan, 1970.
Editor, *Stories from Western Canada: A Selection*. Toronto, Macmillan, 1972.
Editor, with Andreas Schroeder, *Stories from Pacific and Arctic Canada: A Selection*. Toronto, Macmillan, 1974.
Editor, *Double Vision: An Anthology of Twentieth-Century Stories in English*. Toronto, Macmillan, 1976.
Editor, *Getting Here: Stories*. Edmonton, Alberta, NeWest Press, 1977.
Editor, with Aritha van Herk, *More Stories from Western Canada*. Toronto, Macmillan, 1980.
Editor, with Aritha van Herk and Leah Flater, *West of Fiction*. Edmonton, Alberta, NeWest Press, 1982.

*

Manuscript Collection: University of Calgary Library, Alberta.

Critical Studies: *The Comedians: Hugh Hood and Rudy Wiebe* by Patricia A. Morley, Toronto, Clarke Irwin, 1977; *Epic Fiction: The Art of Rudy Wiebe* by W. J. Keith, Edmonton, University of Alberta Press, 1981; articles in *A Voice in the Land*, 1981, and *Journal of Commonwealth Literature* (Edinburgh), vol. 19, no. 1, 1984.

*   *   *

The vastness of the Canadian North; a native population beset by ruthless adversaries, hunger and diminishing numbers, scattered over several thousand miles; a gentle people devoted to utopian principles, driven throughout four continents, faced with hostile environments and cruel governments. The scope and themes of Rudy Wiebe's fiction surpass, in area and agony at least, the combined exploits and wanderings of Odysseus and Aeneas. But the epic magnitude notwithstanding, Wiebe has no intention of embarking on any heroic saga. Instead he chooses a mode one might term contemplative, or simply poetic. The approach yields some intriguing patterns as well some uncanny personal reflections generated by those who are experiencing soul-searing moments.

Though circumstances are frequently harsh and unrelenting, and the prognosis far from promising, Wiebe's method rarely yields a tragic perspective. In *The Blue Mountains of China* a young Mennonite girl shows not only resilience in the face of a ceaseless succession of plague, poverty, and enforced migration, but she develops a self-contained comic outlook that is unself-conscious and remarkably sane. In reference to the onslaught of funerals (some of which are for her own siblings), she discovers in the mannerisms of the minister a fascination which yields an amusement that is in fact deep enjoyment rather than an escape from the intolerable. The somber setting, the earth-deriding hymns, and the solemn faces provide for her a spectacle well worth repeating. This response is tendered in a manner that is by no means ghoulish, not even irreverent or rebellious. It is, however, intensely personal and, more important, self sustaining.

More significantly, it contains an awareness of her own unique place in happenings which might ordinarily prompt the self to surrender to futility. The horror and magnitude of the situation remains, but the human spirit emerges as an artist who finds intense satisfaction in crafting perspectives and in giving even the inexorable the stamp of individuality.

Liesel the Mennonite lass, crammed among the afflicted nomads in the ship's steerage, bravely fixes her skirt the best she can in order to promenade undetected by effecting the habit of the fine ladies in First Class. She successfully makes her way to the upper deck, notices in full detail a couple making love, and is amazed not at what to her group would be sinful conduct, but at the awkwardness of the woman. Even with an intensely religious upbringing she can withhold judgement while relishing in an opportunity to weave the actions and postures of others into a fabric that is her own. Such an authorlike stance is common among Wiebe's characters, even the lesser ones. The ship ceases for a while to be a vehicle of exile and becomes an instrument which allows the willing to mingle freely among humanity's infinite variety and to focus eyes and thoughts upon the intriguing patterns produced by their conduct. Liesel does not abandon her faith. She does not have to. She is in her own way an artist and as such has the leverage of perspective with her at all times.

There is much historical matter in this book on the problems and peregrinations of the Mennonites, just as there is ample detail in *The Temptations of Big Bear*, where divisions between the Indian leaders and the insidious conduct of the government provide the setting for much of the reflective meditation that is Wiebe's forte. The treachery and hardships cannot eclipse the ultimate human challenge, to arrive at a resolution of approach to crisis while remaining faithful both to the self and the cause. The much-told tale of Louis Riel benefits from this multiperspective in *The Scorched-Wood People*. Even more striking than Wiebe's grasp of historic fact is the manner in which he parcels out the insights through those who view the scene firsthand.

Even in his most straightforward narrative, *The Mad Trapper*, Wiebe's subject, the forever enigmatic and largely unknown Albert Johnson, is created principally out of the theories and partial glimpses of journalists, law enforcement agents and other coinhabitants of the north. Johnson did in fact exist, although he is tailor-made for Wiebe's artistic profile. The real Johnson remains largely unknown, even to the readers of Wiebe's novel. When shot to death in 1932, who and what he was were transferred from journalists and mounties to poets and novelists. Wiebe finds in him a figure fit for the immense and imponderable landscape where inhabitants do considerably more than survive. Johnson, this dot upon the frozen tundra who weaves deftly in and out of herds of caribou, and who can thrive in a tent through Arctic winters, is the stuff of legends, a narrative of a landscape that triggers the most distinctively human of all acts—contemplation. It is not surprising that Wiebe's forthcoming book on the Arctic is entitled *Playing Dead*, and subtitled *A Contemplation on the Arctic*. Like Liesel, seemingly a faceless figure among the similarly attired Mennonites and Johnson the man of unknown dimensions, the Arctic might appear dead and unvaried. In fact it is the moulding mind of observation and thought, which inevitably leads on to the telling of tales. Wiebe is among those ready to embrace this energy in all its fullness.

—Leonard R. Mendelsohn

WILDER, Thornton (Niven). American. Born in Madison, Wisconsin, 17 April 1897. Educated at Thacher School, Ojai, California, 1912–13; Berkeley High School, California, graduated 1915; Oberlin College, Ohio, 1915–17; Yale University, New Haven, Connecticut, 1917, 1919–20, A.B. 1920; American Academy in Rome, 1920–21; Princeton University, New Jersey, 1925–26, A.M. 1926. Served in the United States Coast Artillery Corps, 1918; in the United States Army Air Intelligence, rising to the rank of Lieutenant-Colonel, 1942–45: honorary M.B.E. (Member, Order of the British Empire), 1945. French teacher, 1921–25, and house master, 1927–28, Lawrenceville School, New Jersey. Full-time writer from 1928. Part-time Lecturer in Comparative Literature, University of Chicago, 1930–36; Visiting Professor, University of Hawaii, Honolulu, 1935; Charles Eliot Norton Professor of Poetry, Harvard University, Cambridge, Massachusetts, 1950–51. United States Delegate: Institut de Cooperation Intellectuelle, Paris, 1937; International PEN Club Congress, England, 1941; Unesco Conference of the Arts, Venice, 1952. Recipient: Pulitzer prize, for fiction, 1928, for drama, 1938, 1943; American Academy Gold Medal, 1952; Freedom prize (Frankfurt), 1957; Brandeis University Creative Arts award, 1959; MacDowell Medal, 1960; Presidential Medal of Freedom, 1963; National Medal for Literature, 1965; National Book award, for fiction, 1968. D.Litt.: New York University, 1930; Yale University, 1947; Kenyon College, Gambier, Ohio, 1948; College of Wooster, Ohio, 1950; Northeastern University, Boston, 1951; Oberlin College, 1952; University of New Hampshire, Durham, 1953; Goethe University, Frankfurt, 1957; University of Zurich, 1961; LL.D.: Harvard University, 1951. Chevalier, Legion of Honor (France), 1951; member, Order of Merit (Peru); Order of Merit (Germany), 1957; honorary member, Bavarian Academy of Fine Arts; Mainz Academy of Science and Literature; member, American Academy. *Died 7 December 1975.*

ROMANCE AND HISTORICAL PUBLICATIONS

Novels

The Bridge of San Luis Rey. New York, Boni, and London, Longman, 1927.
The Woman of Andros. New York, Boni, and London, Longman, 1930.
Heaven's My Destination. London, Longman, 1934; New York, Harper, 1935.
The Ides of March. New York, Harper, and London, Longman, 1948.
The Eighth Day. New York, Harper, and London, Longman, 1967.

OTHER PUBLICATIONS

Novels

The Cabala. New York, Boni, and London, Longman, 1926.
Theophilus North. New York, Harper, 1973; London, Allen Lane, 1974.

Plays

St. Francis Lake, in *Oberlin Literary Magazine* (Oberlin, Ohio), December 1915.
Flamingo Red, in *Oberlin Literary Magazine* (Oberlin, Ohio), January 1916.
Brother Fire, in *Oberlin Literary Magazine* (Oberlin, Ohio), May 1916.

A Christmas Interlude, in *Oberlin Literary Magazine* (Oberlin, Ohio), December 1916.
The Walled City, in *Yale Literary Magazine* (New Haven, Connecticut), April 1918.
In Praise of Guynemer, in *Yale Literary Magazine* (New Haven, Connecticut), December 1918.
The Trumpet Shall Sound (produced New York, 1926). Published in *Yale Literary Magazine* (New Haven, Connecticut), October-December 1919, January 1920.
The Angel That Troubled the Waters and Other Plays (includes *Nascuntur Poetae, Proserpina and the Devil, Fanny Otcott, Brother Fire, The Penny That Beauty Spent, The Angel on the Ship, The Message and Jehanne, Childe Roland to the Dark Tower Came, Centaurs, Leviathan, And the Sea Shall Give Up Its Dead, Now Thy Servant's Name Was Malchus, Mozart and the Gray Steward, Hast Thou Considered My Servant Job?, The Flight into Egypt*). New York, Coward McCann, and London, Longman, 1928.
The Long Christmas Dinner (produced New Haven, Connecticut, 1931; Liverpool, 1932). Included in *The Long Christmas Dinner and Other Plays*, 1931; libretto for opera version, as *Das Lange Weihnachtsmal*, music by Paul Hindemith (produced Mannheim, Germany, 1961; New York, 1963), Mainz and New York, Schott, 1961.
The Happy Journey to Trenton and Camden (produced New Haven, Connecticut, 1931). Included in *The Long Christmas Dinner and Other Plays*, 1931; revised version, as *The Happy Journey* (produced New York, 1939), New York, French, 1934; London, French, 1947.
Such Things Only Happen in Books (produced New Haven, Connecticut, 1931). Included in *The Long Christmas Dinner and Other Plays*, 1931.
Love and How to Cure It (produced New Haven, Connecticut, 1931; Liverpool, 1932). Included in *The Long Christmas Dinner and Other Plays*, 1931.
The Long Christmas Dinner and Other Plays in One Act. New York and New Haven, Connecticut, Coward McCann-Yale University Press, and London, Longman, 1931.
Queens of France (produced Chicago, 1932; New York, 1949). Included in *The Long Christmas Dinner and Other Plays*, 1931.
Pullman Car Hiawatha (produced New York, 1962). Included in *The Long Christmas Dinner and Other Plays*, 1931.
Lucrèce, adaptation of a play by André Obey (produced New York, 1932). Boston, Houghton Mifflin, and London, Longman, 1933.
A Doll's House, adaptation of a play by Ibsen (produced Central City, Colorado, 1937).
Our Town (produced Princeton, New Jersey, and New York, 1938; London, 1946). New York, Coward McCann, 1938; London, Longman, 1956.
The Merchant of Yonkers, adaptation of a play by Johann Nostroy, based on *A Well-Spent Day* by John Oxenford (produced Boston and New York, 1938; London, 1951). New York, Harper, 1939; revised version, as *The Matchmaker* (produced Edinburgh and London, 1954; Philadelphia and New York, 1955), in *Three Plays*, 1957; published separately, London, Longman, 1958.
The Skin of Our Teeth (produced New Haven, Connecticut, and New York, 1942; London, 1945). New York, Harper, 1942.
Our Century (produced New York, 1947). New York, Century Association, 1947.
The Victors, adaptation of a play by Sartre (produced New York, 1949).
Die Alkestiade (as *A Life in the Sun*, produced Edinburgh, 1955; as *Die Alkestiade*, music by Louise Talma, produced Frank-

furt, Germany, 1962). Frankfurt, Fischer, 1960; as *The Alcestiad; or, A Life in the Sun*, with *The Drunken Sisters: A Satyr Play*, New York, Harper, 1977.
Bernice, and The Wreck of the 5:25 (produced Berlin, 1957).
The Drunken Sisters (produced New York, 1970). New York, French, 1957.
Three Plays (includes *Our Town, The Skin of Our Teeth, The Matchmaker*). New York, Harper, 1957; London, Longman, 1958.
Plays for Bleecker Street (includes *Infancy, Childhood, Someone from Assisi*) (produced New York, 1962; *Infancy* and *Childhood* produced London, 1972). *Childhood* and *Infancy* published New York, French, 2 vols., 1960–61.

Screenplays: *We Live Again*, with others, 1934; *Our Town*, with Frank Craven and Harry Chandlee, 1940; *Shadow of a Doubt*, with others, 1943.

Other

The Intent of the Artist, with others. Princeton, New Jersey, Princeton University Press, 1941.
James Joyce 1882–1941. Aurora, New York, Wells College Press, 1944.
Kultur in einer Demokratie. Frankfurt, Fischer, 1957.
American Characteristics and Other Essays, edited by Donald Gallup. New York, Harper, 1979.
The Journals of Thornton Wilder 1939–1961 (includes unfinished play *The Emporium*), edited by Donald Gallup. New Haven, Connecticut, Yale University Press, 1985.

*

Bibliography: *Thornton Wilder: An Annotated Bibliography of Works by and about Thornton Wilder* by Richard H. Goldstone and Gary Anderson, New York, AMS Press, 1982.

Manuscript Collection: Beinecke Library, Yale University, New Haven, Connecticut.

Critical Studies: *Thornton Wilder* by Rex Burbank, New York, Twayne, 1961, revised edition, 1978; *Thornton Wilder* by Bernard Grebanier, Minneapolis, University of Minnesota Press, 1964; *The Art of Thornton Wilder* by Malcolm Goldstein, Lincoln, University of Nebraska Press, 1965; *Thornton Wilder* by Helmut Papajewski, New York, Ungar, 1968; *Thornton Wilder* by Hermann Stresau, New York, Ungar, 1971; *Thornton Wilder: The Bright and the Dark* by Mildred Christophe Kuner, New York, Crowell, 1972; *Thornton Wilder: An Intimate Portrait* by Richard H. Goldstone, New York, Saturday Review Press, 1975; *Thornton Wilder: His World* by Linda Simon, New York, Doubleday, 1979; *A Vast Landscape: Time in the Novels of Thornton Wilder* by Mary Ellen Williams, Pocatello, Idaho State University Press, 1979; *Thornton Wilder and His Public* by Amos Wilder, Philadelphia, Fortress Press, 1980; *The Enthusiast: A Life of Thornton Wilder* by Gilbert A. Harrison, New Haven, Connecticut, Ticknor and Fields, 1983; *Thornton Wilder* by David Castronovo, New York, Ungar, 1986.

Theatrical Activities:
Actor **Plays**—Stage Manager in *Our Town*, New York, 1938, and on other occasions; Mr. Antrobus in *The Skin of Our Teeth*, Cohasset, Massachusetts, 1946, and on other occasions.

*   *   *

The historical romances of Thornton Wilder cannot be compared with those of any other American writer except Eudora Welty, and his work in this myth-making vein is more extensive. Almost all of his novels are historical, yet they are likely to puzzle or annoy readers who seek adventurous escape into the past or carefully researched reconstructions of other eras (like those of James A. Michener). Wilder, who wrote in his most ambitious work, *The Eighth Day*, that all history is one "enormous tapestry," is not interested in detailed re-creations of great events, but in making broad statements about the significance of the past. He believes that "there are no Golden Ages and no Dark Ages," but only "the ocean like monotony of the generations of men under the alterations of fair and foul weather" (*The Eighth Day*). All times and places, he feels, are much alike, usually tragically self-destructive, but occasionally magically rewarding.

Wilder's first novel, *The Cabala*, published in 1926 at the peak of the Age of Ballyhoo, introduces some historical figures like the poet John Keats, but the lack of a chronological time scheme frustrates readers seeking historical information from this obscurist fantasy about American expatriates being the heirs to the triumphs and undoings of the pagan gods of classical Rome.

However, only a year later Wilder scored his greatest success with this next novel, *The Bridge of San Luis Rey*, a stylized fable set in colonial Peru, where a famous rope bridge over a deep chasm collapses while five travelers, all of whom just seemed to be starting to make new lives for themselves after wasted years, fall to their deaths. A scholarly monk piously sets out to learn all he can of their histories in an effort to determine whether the fall can be attributed to divine design or accident, but for his trouble both he and his work are burned by the Inquisition.

Wilder's third novel, *The Woman of Andros*, provoked an uproar in New York literary circles. It was attacked by Michael Gold, proletarian author of the novel *Jews Without Money*, as the work of a "Christian gentleman" that was irrelevant to the sufferings of the poor during the Depression. Genteel critics rushed to the defense of the world-weary work that portrayed through the circumspect tale of a wise courtesan and her ambitious young lover how the ancient Greek world had given way to a Christian society that 2000 years later seemed about to share the fate of its predecessor.

Although Wilder ignored the controversy, he was obviously affected by it for his next novel was a folksy account of the contemporary American midwest; and he devoted most of the 1930's to theatrical works. It is impossible to discuss his historical fictions, however, without mentioning his highly successful play *The Skin of Our Teeth* (1942), a fantasy that traced the history of the human race from the ice age to World War II.

After army service Wilder returned to the ancient Rome conjured up in his first novel for the seeming start of a new career with *The Ides of March*. This bewilderingly complex work presents four tellings of the same basic tale about the profanation of an ancient ritual, each longer and encompassing more events than the preceding one. Wilder's leisurely paced cautionary tale about ominous parallels between the days of Julius Caesar's triumphs and those following the American victory in World War II was too subtle and dependent upon classical allusion to appeal to restless modern readers.

Readers' indifference led Wilder to abandon fiction for theatrical work; but 20 years later in 1967 at the age of 70 he surprised the literary world with his most ambitious novel, *The Eighth Day*, another extremely complicated narrative that moves back and forth through the 20th century to recount the fate of a talented inventor and potential human benefactor accused of murder in a small Illinois town early in the century and hounded by human piranhas most of his life until his ironic, accidental death after his vindication. The cleverly contrived mystery story is only, however, the backdrop for Wilder's observation that "The human race gets no better. Mankind is vicious, slothful, quarrelsome, and self-centered," except for those rare individuals who transcend themselves through creative work.

This hard-hitting statement of fashionable alienation was not, however, Wilder's last word. He ended a career full of surprises with another when his final novel, *Theophilus North*, proved a mellow account of a seeming history of nine stages in the growth of the fashionable resort of Newport, Rhode Island. Again, however, the setting serves only as a backdrop for the story of a sensitive young man's exploration of nine possible careers before he discovers that he can encompass all of them by becoming a writer.

One learns little textbook history from Wilder's romances, but one may learn much of how a sense of history's ironic repetitions can liberate the imaginative individual from their "ocean-like monotony."

—Warren French

WILLIAMS, Bronwyn. See **BROWNING, Dixie.**

WILLIAMS, Claudette. Address: c/o Fawcett, 210 East 50th Street, New York, New York 10022, U.S.A.

ROMANCE AND HISTORICAL PUBLICATIONS

Novels

Spring Gambit. New York, Fawcett, 1976.
Sassy. New York, Fawcett, 1977.
Sunday's Child. New York, Fawcett, 1977.
After the Storm. New York, Fawcett, 1977.
Blades of Passion. New York, Fawcett, 1978; London, Arrow, 1979.
Cotillion for Mandy. New York, Fawcett, 1978.
Myriah. New York, Fawcett, 1978.
Cassandra. New York, Fawcett, and London, Arrow, 1979.
Jewelene. New York, Fawcett, 1979.
Lacey. New York, Fawcett, 1979.
Mary, Sweet Mary. New York, Fawcett, 1980.
Naughty Lady Ness. New York, Fawcett, 1980.
Passion's Pride. New York, Fawcett, 1980.
Desert Rose, English Moon. New York, Fawcett, 1981.
Sweet Disorder. New York, Fawcett, 1981.
Lady Magic. New York, Fawcett, 1983.
Song of Silkie. New York, Fawcett, 1984.
Fire and Desire. New York, Fawcett, 1985.
Regency Star. New York, Fawcett, 1985.
Wild Dawn Fever. New York, Fawcett, 1986.
Lady Bell. New York, Fawcett, 1986.
Lady Madcap. New York, Fawcett, 1987.

*   *   *

Claudette Williams seems to be an author with a split personality. Where most writers of historical romances stick with one style or formula, at least for each pseudonym, Williams produces two distinct types of books under one name.

Her largest output has been in the familiar Regency formula novel. *Spring Gambit*, *Sassy*, *Jewelene*, *Lacey* are only some examples of her work in this genre. Her virginal heroines and handsome, rakish heroes fit the common mold but are elevated by some engaging dialogue. The earlier novels in this vein (*After the Storm*, *Sassy*, *Sunday's Child*) allowed for more development of character and plot, but the more recent titles seem to be hurried and place greater reliance on the formula: a little bit of danger to the heroine, but rescue always in time. Rarely is there a hint of more than a kiss or, perhaps, a discreetly passionate embrace.

Readers accustomed to this fare were in for a shock when *Blades of Passion* appeared. Suddenly Williams joined the ranks of those authors producing steamy, explicit sex scenes. The rules of the game change in this formula. Here the heroine loses her virginity before marriage but remains true to the hero throughout. Rape becomes seduction as lust turns into tenderness. The books are longer and so there are more dangerous situations to encounter, but most of the plot revolves around the antagonism which exists between hero and heroine, and how long it will take them to recognize it as love. *Passion's Pride* and, to a lesser extent, *Cassandra*, follow this formula too. *Passion's Pride* is less successful than *Blades of Passion* because of an awkward attempt to develop two parallel stories which only occasionally touch on one another. *Desert Rose, English Moon* is Williams's only novel in a modern setting, but all the elements of *Blades of Passion* are present.

Williams is a good romantic novelist. She has the ability to create likeable characters, and while her stories may stretch the reader's credulity, they are no more far-fetched than many other historical romances.

—Barbara E. Kemp

WILLIAMSON, C. N. and A. M. Also wrote as Charles de Crespigny; M. P. Revere; Dona Teresa de Savallo; Alice Stuyvesant; Mrs. Harcourt Williamson. **WILLIAMSON, C(harles) N(orris)**: British. Born in Exeter, Devon, in 1859. Educated at University College, London. Married Alice Livingston in 1895. Journalist, *Graphic*, 1882–90; founding editor, *Black and White* magazine, 1891. *Died 3 October 1920*. **WILLIAMSON, A(lice) M(uriel, née Livingston)**: American. Born near Poughkeepsie, New York, in 1869. Educated privately. Lived in England after 1893. *Died 24 September 1933*.

ROMANCE AND HISTORICAL PUBLICATIONS

Novels (series: Loveland)

The Lightning Conductor: The Strange Adventures of a Motor-Car. London, Methuen, 1902; New York, Holt, 1903.
The Princess Passes: A Romance of a Motor Car. London, Methuen, 1904; New York, Holt, 1905.
My Friend the Chauffeur. London, Methuen, and New York, McClure, 1905.

The Car of Destiny and Its Errand to Spain. London, Methuen, 1906; as *The Car of Destiny*, New York, McClure, 1906.

Lady Betty Across the Water. London, Methuen, and New York, McClure, 1906.

Rosemary in Search of a Father. London, Hodder and Stoughton, and New York, McClure, 1906; as *Rosemary: A Christmas Story*, New York, Burt, 1909.

The Botor Chaperon. London, Methuen, 1907; as *The Chauffeur and the Chaperon*, New York, McClure, 1908; as *The Chaperon*, New York, Burt, 1912.

The Powers and Maxine. New York, Empire, 1907.

The Marquis of Loveland. New York, McClure, 1908.

Love and the Spy. London, Leng, 1908.

The Motor Maid. London, Hodder and Stoughton, 1909; New York, Doubleday, 1910.

Set in Silver. London, Methuen, and New York, Doubleday, 1909.

The Golden Silence. London, Methuen, and New York, Doubleday, 1910.

Lord Loveland Discovers America. London, Methuen, and New York, Doubleday, 1910.

The Demon. London, Methuen, 1912.

The Heather Moon. London, Methuen, and New York, Doubleday, 1912.

The Guests of Hercules. London, Methuen, and New York, Doubleday, 1912; as *Mary at Monte Carlo*, Methuen, 1920.

Champion: The Story of a Motor Car. London, Cassell, 1913.

The Love Pirate. London, Methuen, 1913; as *The Port of Adventure*, New York, Doubleday, 1913.

The Wedding Day. London, Methuen, 1914.

A Soldier of the Legion. London, Methuen, and New York, Doubleday, 1914.

It Happened in Egypt. London, Methuen, and New York, Doubleday, 1914.

Secret History. London, Methuen, 1915; as *Secret History Revealed by Lady Peggy O'Malley*, New York, Doubleday, 1915.

The Shop-Girl. London, Methuen, and New York, Grosset and Dunlap, 1916; as *Winnie Childs, The Shop Girl*, Grosset and Dunlap, 1926.

The War Wedding. London, Methuen, 1916; as *Where the Path Breaks* (as Captain Charles de Crespigny), New York, Century, 1916.

The Lightning Conductress. London, Methuen, 1916; as *The Lightning Conductress Discovers America*, New York, Doubleday, 1916.

Angel Unawares: A Story of Christmas Eve. New York, Harper, 1916.

This Woman to This Man. London, Methuen, 1917.

The Cowboy Countess. London, Methuen, 1917.

Tiger Lily. London, Mills and Boon, 1917.

Lord John in New York. London, Methuen, 1918.

Crucifix Corner: A Story of Everyman's Land. London, Methuen, 1918; as *Everyman's Land*, New York, Doubleday, 1918.

Briar Rose. London, Odhams, 1919.

The Lion's Mouse. London, Methuen, and New York, Doubleday, 1919.

The Second Latchkey. New York, Doubleday, 1920.

The Dummy Hand. London, Hutchinson, 1920.

Alias Richard Power. London, Hodder and Stoughton, 1921.

The Great Pearl Secret. London, Methuen, and New York, Doubleday, 1921.

The House of Silence. London, Hodder and Stoughton, 1921.

The Night of the Wedding. London, Hodder and Stoughton, 1921; New York, Doran, 1923.

Vision House. New York, Doubleday, 1921.

The Brightener. New York, Doubleday, 1921; London, Hutchinson, 1922.

The Lady from the Air. London, Hodder and Stoughton, 1922; New York, Doubleday, 1923.

Novels by A. M. Williamson

The Barn Stormers, Being the Tragical Side of a Comedy. London, Hutchinson, 1897; as Mrs. Harcourt Williamson, New York, Stokes, 1897.

Fortune's Sport. London, Pearson, 1898.

A Woman in Grey. London and New York, Routledge, 1898.

Lady Mary of the Dark House. London, Bowden, 1898.

The House by the Lock. London, Bowden, 1899; New York, Dodge, 1906.

The Newspaper Girl. London, Pearson, 1899.

My Lady Cinderella. London, Routledge, 1900; New York, Dodge, 1906.

Ordered South. London, Routledge, 1900.

The Adventure of Princess Sylvie. London, Methuen, 1900; as *The Princess Virginia*, New York, McClure, 1909.

Queen Sweetheart. London, White, 1901.

A Bid for a Coronet. London, Routledge, 1901.

'Twixt Devil and Deep Sea. London, Pearson, 1901.

Papa. London, Methuen, 1902.

The Silent Battle. London, Hurst and Blackett, 1902; New York, Doubleday, 1909.

The Woman Who Dared. London, Methuen, 1903.

The Little White Nun. London, White, 1903.

The Sea Could Tell. London, Methuen, 1904.

The Turnstile of Night. London, Hurst and Blackett, 1904.

The Castle of Shadows. London, Methuen, 1905; New York, Hudson Press, 1909.

The Girl Who Had Nothing. London, Ward Lock, 1905.

The House of the Lost Court (as Dona Teresa de Savallo). New York, McClure, 1908.

The Underground Syndicate. London, Hodder and Stoughton, 1910.

The Vanity Box (as Alice Stuyvesant). New York, Doubleday, 1911; as A. M. Williamson, London, Hodder and Stoughton, 1913.

The Flower Forbidden. London, Hodder and Stoughton, 1911.

The Girl of the Passion Play. London, Hodder and Stoughton, 1911.

The Bride's Hero (as M. P. Revere). New York, Stokes, 1912.

To M. L. G.; or, He Who Passes. New York, Stokes, 1912.

The Life Mask. New York, Stokes, 1913.

What I Found Out in the House of a German Prince, by an English Governess. London, Chapman and Hall, and New York, Stokes, 1915.

Name the Woman. London, Methuen, 1924.

The Million Dollar Doll. New York, Doran, 1924.

The Man Himself. London, Philpot, 1925.

Secret Gold. London, Methuen, and New York, Doubleday, 1925.

Publicity for Anne. London, Mills and Boon, 1926.

Cancelled Love. London, Methuen, 1926; as *Golden Butterfly*, New York, Doran, 1926.

Sheikh Bill. London, Mills and Boon, 1927; as *Bill—The Sheik*, New York, Doran, 1927.

Hollywood Love. London, Chapman and Hall, 1928.

Black Sleeves: It Happened in Hollywood. London, Chapman and Hall, 1928.

Children of the Zodiac. London, Chapman and Hall, 1929.

Frozen Slippers. London, Chapman and Hall, 1930.

The Golden Carpet. London, Chapman and Hall, 1931.

Honeymoon Hate. London, Chapman and Hall, 1931.
Bewitched. London, Chapman and Hall, and New York, Kinsey, 1932.
Last Year's Wife. London, Benn, 1932.
Keep This Door Shut. London, Benn, 1933.
The Lightning Conductor Comes Back. London, Chapman and Hall, 1933.
The Girl in the Secret. London, Wright and Brown, 1934.

Short Stories

Scarlet Runner. London, Methuen, 1908.
The Minx Goes to the Front. London, Mills and Boon, 1919.
Berry Goes to Monte Carlo. London, Mills and Boon, 1921.
The Fortune Hunters and Others. London, Mills and Boon, 1923.
The Indian Princess (by A. M. Williamson). London, Mills and Boon, 1924.
Told at Monte Carlo (by A. M. Williamson). London, Mills and Boon, 1926; as *Black Incense: Tales of Monte Carlo*, New York, Doran, 1926.

OTHER PUBLICATIONS by A. M. Williamson

Other

Memoirs of the Life and Writings of Thomas Carlyle, by C. N. Williamson and Richard Herne Shepherd. London, W. H. Allen, 1881.
Queen Alexandra, The Nation's Pride. London, Partridge, 1902.
Princess Mary's Locked Book (published anonymously). London, Cassell, 1912; New York, Cassell, 1913.
The Bride's Breviary (published anonymously). London, Hodder and Stoughton, 1912.
The Lure of Monte Carlo. London, Mills and Boon, 1924; New York, Doubleday, 1926.
Alice in Movieland. London, Philpot, 1927; New York, Appleton, 1928.
The Inky Way (autobiography). London, Chapman and Hall, and New York, Putnam, 1931.

*   *   *

Charles Norris Williamson of Exeter, England, had co-authored a book on Thomas Carlyle before he met Alice Muriel Livingston of Poughkeepsie, New York, and after their marriage (in 1895) they combined their literary talents to write books of a very different nature. These were mostly romantic novels with motoring and travel backgrounds. Charles's informed interest in science and engineering gave the stories a sense of technical modernity, while Alice seems to have injected them with robust romanticism.

There is an Edwardian charm even in the novels that appeared during the 1920's, and much of the Williamsons' best work was published between 1900 and 1910. The couple made their home at Cap Martin and gave many of their books a continental setting, though the main characters, expectedly, were often British or American. *The Lightning Conductor*, *The Princess Passes*, *The Car of Destiny*, and *My Friend the Chauffeur* are notable examples of the Williamsons' roaming-European-romances, which convey motoring and sight-seeing adventures with wit and whimsy. The stories are, for their time, fast moving, and only romantic clinches are allowed sometimes to slow down the crackling pace.

In *The Botor Chaperon* three pairs of lovers—assortedly Dutch, English, and American—take to the canals and waterways of Holland. Anglo-American themes are expectedly prominent in the novels. The hero is frequently an impeccable English milord whose opinions (at first) seem to the more questioning American heroine to have survived "crusted and spider-webbed from the cellars of the Stone Age" (*Lord John in New York* and *Lord Loveland Discovers America*). Nevertheless the Williamsons appear to have a very soft spot for upper-crust Englishmen (though less for their female counterparts). Their aristocratic male arrogance could of course eventually be loosened by American honesty and liveliness, as embodied by a string of attractive heroines.

Many of these leading girl characters pursue careers, though romance generally marks the end of job ambitions. *The Newspaper Girl*, which Mrs. Williamson wrote on her own, is a briskly perceptive account of an American incognito-heiress trying to scrape a living in London as a "penny-a-liner journalist," but ending up, with relief, as an English Lady-by-marriage. The Williamsons apparently relished the creation of witty vignettes of exotic continental or American women trying to make advances to restrained Englishmen, and nobody does this better in their novels than Maxine de Renzie, the Polish actress/spy operating in Paris in *Love and the Spy*. She is beautiful, cultivated, quick-witted, and far-seeing in the plots and counterplots of espionage—and, of course, of romance.

—Mary Cadogan

————

WILLIAMSON, Harcourt. See **WILLIAMSON, C. N. and A. M.**

————

WILSON, Mary. See **ROBY, Mary Linn.**

————

WINCH, John. See **BOWEN, Marjorie.**

————

WINSLOW, Laurel. See **SEGER, Maura.**

————

WINSOR, Kathleen. American. Born in Olivia, Minnesota, 16 October 1919. Educated at the University of California, Berkeley, A.B. 1938. Married 1) Robert Herwig in 1936 (divorced 1946); 2) the musician Artie Shaw in 1946; 3) Arnold Robert Krakower in 1949 (divorced 1953); 4) Paul A. Porter in 1956 (died 1975). Address: c/o Roslyn Targ Literary Agency Inc., 105 West 13th Street, New York, New York 10011, U.S.A.

ROMANCE AND HISTORICAL PUBLICATIONS

Novels

Forever Amber. New York, Macmillan, 1944; London, Macdonald, 1945.
Star Money. New York, Appleton Century Crofts, and London, Macdonald, 1950.
The Lovers. New York, Appleton Century Crofts, and London, Macdonald, 1952.
America, With Love. New York, Putnam, 1957; London, Davies, 1958.
Wanderers Eastward, Wanderers West. New York, Random House, and London, Davies, 1965.
Calais. New York, Doubleday, 1979; London, Sidgwick and Jackson, 1980.
Jacintha. New York, Crown, 1983; London, Inner Circle, 1985.
Robert and Arabella. New York, Crown, 1986; London, Severn House, 1987.

*   *   *

Kathleen Winsor writes serious novels. To say this is at once to acknowledge Winsor's ambitions and to lament her humorlessness. Romance fiction is not known for its wittiness, to be sure, but it is light reading. Winsor has something else in mind than providing escapist fantasies for her audience; in fact, for all the love affairs in her books, she does not really write romances. Rather, she writes leisurely, languid, temporizing stories of driven, obsessive women. If Winsor books are a species of romance then it is the romance of ambition she details. Her women are in love neither with love itself nor with a strong, rescuing man, but instead with their own achievements, having wrested from life what they most needed.

Baldly stated, what Winsor's women need from life is success: to be a star, to be loved, to have money. Not the swooning passive ladies of light romance, Winsor's heroines typically achieve fame, adoration, and wealth through their own dogged efforts. "I've worked hard for what I have," choruses Shireen Delaney throughout *Star Money*, reminding the reader again and again of the four and a half years she spent writing the bestseller which has made her rich and famous. Such effort apparently excuses all manner of unscrupulous behavior, both in Shireen and in Winsor's other heroines. Ambitious and sensual, greedy, uncaring and often fickle, Amber St. Clare sets the pattern for these heroines, for she is above all determined. At first Amber seems determined to find love with Bruce Carlton, to take life on his terms. But as the novel unfolds at its languid pace it becomes clear that so romantic a goal is unfit for a Winsor heroine. Like her later incarnations, Shireen and Lily Malone, Amber is an opportunist; her unscrupulous will to prosper lifts her from the placid village of Marygreen to the London stage and ultimately to Charles II's court and bedroom. That she steals and whores and murders along the way is inconsequential to heroine and author alike. Arguably, the scandalous Amber is bested—if not punished—at the end of the novel, chasing off to America after Bruce because she has been deceived. Yet because so many previous times in *Forever Amber* events that have looked bad for her have turned out well, it is hard to believe she won't land on her feet. This lack of punishment is a refreshing change from romance fictions generic insistence on the goodliness of its heroines. Amber is a rogue, even as Shireen Delaney in *Star Money* is a feckless ravener and Lily Malone of *Calais* is a vengeful tyrant. Moreover, all these women are sensualists, women who, unlike the typical romance heroines, do not deny or misidentify their sexual longings. Again, this is a refreshing change from the enforced and often hypocritical chastity present in most romances.

Given these driven, sensual, unscrupulous central characters, it is surprising that Winsor's books are strangely uncompelling. With the partial exception of *Calais*, none builds to a climax; most end arbitrarily. Amber could as easily continue her adventures in Virginia; Shireen might as well have another affair, since having seen her devour most of the men in *Star Money* without so much as a hiccough, we've no reason to suppose that the wreck of her marriage is going to give her dyspepsia. Winsor's novels don't end so much as they stop, and prior to stopping they have wandered (as in the aptly named *Wanderers Eastward, Wanderers West*) and gone on nearly "forever." The dilatory pace of her narratives is all the more surprising considering Winsor's obvious love of drama. Her major heroines are all connected with the theater; in fact, Winsor's most convincing and memorable character is Lily Malone/Arlette Morgan of *Calais*, her most rounded novel. Unlike Winsor's earlier works, *Calais* moves toward a necessary, not arbitrary resolution. When Lily Malone drops into the sea, she has been doomed by—though not punished for—her intractable remembrance of things, sadness, and loss—her tenacious vengeance on the past.

"Everything seems pretty grim with you," Shireen Delaney's secretary tells her toward the end of *Star Money* (a title expressive of Winsor's preoccupations), and to an extent this judgment applies to Winsor's works as a whole. Was there ever a bawdy romp less joyful than *Forever Amber* or a success story more cheerless than *Star Money*? Like her heroines, Winsor commands our respect with her thoroughness, her concentration, her diligent effort, but her novels, which mix strangely langorous prose with obsessive subjects, fail finally to engage our full attention and sympathy.

—Nancy Regan

WINSPEAR, Violet. British. Born in London, 28 April 1928. Factory worker in London, 1942–63. *Died in January 1989.*

ROMANCE AND HISTORICAL PUBLICATIONS

Novels

Lucifer's Angel. London, Mills and Boon, and Toronto, Harlequin, 1961.
Wife Without Kisses. London, Mills and Boon, 1961; Toronto, Harlequin, 1973.
The Strange Waif. London, Mills and Boon, 1962; Toronto, Harlequin, 1974.
House of Strangers. London, Mills and Boon, 1963; Toronto, Harlequin, 1973.
Beloved Tyrant. London, Mills and Boon, 1964; Toronto, Harlequin, 1966.
Cap Flamingo. London, Mills and Boon, 1964; as *Nurse at Cap Flamingo*, Toronto, Harlequin, 1965.
Love's Prisoner. London, Mills and Boon, 1964; Toronto, Harlequin, 1974.
Bride's Dilemma. London, Mills and Boon, 1965; Toronto, Harlequin, 1966.
Desert Doctor. London, Mills and Boon, and Toronto, Harlequin, 1965.
The Tower of the Captive. London, Mills and Boon, 1966; Toronto, Harlequin, 1967.

The Viking Stranger. London, Mills and Boon, 1966; Toronto, Harlequin, 1967.

Tender Is the Tyrant. London, Mills and Boon, 1967; Toronto, Harlequin, 1968.

The Honey Is Bitter. London, Mills and Boon, 1967; Toronto, Harlequin, 1973.

Beloved Castaway. London, Mills and Boon, 1968; Toronto, Harlequin, 1971.

Court of the Veils. London, Mills and Boon, 1968; Toronto, Harlequin, 1969.

The Dangerous Delight. London, Mills and Boon, 1968; Toronto, Harlequin, 1969.

Pilgrim's Castle. London, Mills and Boon, 1969; Toronto, Harlequin, 1973.

The Unwilling Bride. London, Mills and Boon, 1969; Toronto, Harlequin, 1973.

Blue Jasmine. London, Mills and Boon, 1969; Toronto, Harlequin, 1970.

Dragon Bay. London, Mills and Boon, 1969; Toronto, Harlequin, 1973.

Palace of the Peacocks. London, Mills and Boon, and Toronto, Harlequin, 1969.

The Chateau of St. Avrell. London, Mills and Boon, 1970; Toronto, Harlequin, 1974.

The Cazalet Bride. London, Mills and Boon, and Toronto, Harlequin, 1970.

Tawny Sands. London, Mills and Boon, 1970; Toronto, Harlequin, 1974.

Black Douglas. London, Mills and Boon, 1971; Toronto, Harlequin, 1972.

Dear Puritan. London, Mills and Boon, 1971; Toronto, Harlequin, 1973.

Bride to Lucifer. London, Mills and Boon, 1971; Toronto, Harlequin, 1973.

The Castle of the Seven Lilacs. London, Mills and Boon, and Toronto, Harlequin, 1971.

Raintree Valley. London, Mills and Boon, 1971; Toronto, Harlequin, 1972.

The Little Nobody. London, Mills and Boon, 1972; Toronto, Harlequin, 1973.

The Pagan Island. London, Mills and Boon, and Toronto, Harlequin, 1972.

Rapture of the Desert. London, Mills and Boon, 1972; Toronto, Harlequin, 1973.

The Silver Slave. London, Mills and Boon, and Toronto, Harlequin, 1972.

The Glass Castle. London, Mills and Boon, 1973; Toronto, Harlequin, 1974.

Devil in a Silver Room. London, Mills and Boon, and Toronto, Harlequin, 1973.

Forbidden Rapture. London, Mills and Boon, 1973; Toronto, Harlequin, 1974.

The Kisses and the Wine. London, Mills and Boon, and Toronto, Harlequin, 1973.

Palace of the Pomegranate. London, Mills and Boon, 1974; Toronto, Harlequin, 1975.

The Girl at Golden Hawk. London, Mills and Boon, 1974; Toronto, Harlequin, 1975.

The Noble Savage. London, Mills and Boon, 1974; Toronto, Harlequin, 1975.

Satan Took a Bride. London, Mills and Boon, 1975; Toronto, Harlequin, 1976.

Dearest Demon. London, Mills and Boon, 1975; Toronto, Harlequin, 1976.

The Devil's Darling. London, Mills and Boon, and Toronto, Harlequin, 1975.

Darling Infidel. London, Mills and Boon, and Toronto, Harlequin, 1976.

The Burning Sands. London, Mills and Boon, 1976; Toronto, Harlequin, 1977.

The Child of Judas. London, Mills and Boon, and Toronto, Harlequin, 1976.

The Sun Tower. London, Mills and Boon, 1976; Toronto, Harlequin, 1977.

The Sin of Cynara. London, Mills and Boon, and Toronto, Harlequin, 1976.

The Loved and the Feared. London, Mills and Boon, 1977; Toronto, Harlequin, 1978.

Love Battle. London, Mills and Boon, 1977; Toronto, Harlequin, 1978.

Love in a Stranger's Arms. London, Mills and Boon, and Toronto, Harlequin, 1977.

Passionate Sinner. London, Mills and Boon, 1977; Toronto, Harlequin, 1978.

Time of the Temptress. London, Mills and Boon, 1977; Toronto, Harlequin, 1978.

The Valdez Marriage. London, Mills and Boon, 1978; Toronto, Harlequin, 1979.

The Awakening of Alice. London, Mills and Boon, and Toronto, Harlequin, 1978.

Desire Has No Mercy. London, Mills and Boon, 1979.

The Sheik's Captive. London, Mills and Boon, 1979.

Love Is the Honey. London, Mills and Boon, and Toronto, Harlequin, 1980.

A Girl Possessed. London, Mills and Boon, 1980; Toronto, Harlequin, 1981.

Love's Agony. London, Mills and Boon, and Toronto, Harlequin, 1981.

No Man of Her Own. London, Mills and Boon, 1981.

The Man She Married. London, Mills and Boon, 1982; Toronto, Harlequin, 1983.

Bride's Lace. London, Mills and Boon, 1984.

By Love Bewitched. London, Mills and Boon, 1984.

Secret Fire. London, Mills and Boon, 1984.

Sun Lord's Woman. London, Mills and Boon, 1985.

House of Storms. Toronto, Worldwide, and London, Mills and Boon, 1985.

The Honeymoon. Toronto, Worldwide, and London, Mills and Boon, 1986.

A Silken Barbarity. London, Mills and Boon, 1988.

*   *   *

Violet Winspear has said: "I am a true spinster of romances, for in the old days the word spinster meant a woman who spun, and in the writing of a story one spins and weaves and forms a pattern that is hoped will prove pleasant and satisfactory" (*Thirty Years of Harlequin*, 1979). In fact, a distinctive pattern has been woven into Winspear's storytelling, a pattern that has fulfilled the hopes of readers for over 20 years. Realizing people's need for escape, Winspear creates fast-paced, dramatic romances set in exotic lands inhabited by strange and wonderful peoples.

Winspear's romances feature immediate, intense conflict between the hero and the heroine which gives way to passionate unification by the end of the novel. As early as page 10, the hero and heroine are engaged in open warfare. Often their first words to each other are hostile; their first encounter may lead to physical violence between them. They are attracted to each other, but are initially repulsed by the strength of their feelings. Winspear uses extreme contrasts and emphasizes the attraction of opposites to build the tension between the hero and heroine:

heaven and hell, pleasure and pain, devil and angel, love and hate, saint and sinner, fire and ice, hard and soft, dark and fair.

The hero in Winspear's novels is an impossibly strong, dominant man who is smoothly cultured but who, at the slightest provocation from the heroine, reverts to the type of his primitive ancestors. Be he Danish, Greek, Spanish, or Arabic, the hero is a pagan and a pirate. Book titles like *Bride to Lucifer*, *Dearest Demon*, and *Satan Took a Bride* make reference to the demonic qualities of the hero. The hero is the most compelling character in a Winspear romance because he is a man with a secret. Neither the heroine nor the reader initially knows why the hero is attractively scarred, why he is so bitter about women, why he is temporarily estranged from his family, or why he is evasive about his past. Gradually, the hero's misleading devilish reputation is stripped away to reveal the saint within. He is a man who puts others before himself and his business, who is capable of making noble sacrifices without any acknowledgement, and who is capable of controlling his powerful sexuality even when incredibly aroused.

The typical Winspear heroine undergoes the reverse process. In the beginning, she is the ice-cool angel with the modesty of a Madonna. She is like an "ice bombe, bursting with chilled cream and the tang of bitter cherry." However, contact with the hero melts that icy exterior and reveals the temperamental sensualist within. Thus, the conflict and its resolution not only lead to a marriage of opposites, but also allow both characters to express previously hidden aspects of their selves. The reader is willing to allow Winspear her excesses and exaggerations of character traits because this is such a satisfying conclusion.

Winspear's flamboyancy is also apparent in her writing style. She has a stock of romantic words which inevitably surface in her descriptions of characters, objects, or scenery. These are words like tawny, creamy, smoky, silken, taut, honey, and savage, the latter because " . . . there is generally a touch of savagery in anything truly romantic, as if it has to be tested by steel or fire." Winspear is willing to invent new forms of words if they are evocative, for example, " . . . he brought her tigerishly close to him. . . . " She frequently hyphenates words for romantic effect as well (the hero's "iron-hard jaw" or "sun-dark skin," the "honey-warm air").

Another characteristic of Winspear's writing is that she liberally sprinkles foreign names and expressions, particularly endearments, throughout the novel. She does not concentrate on any one country or locale. Rather she varies her settings by writing about the Caribbean, South America, the Middle East, Europe, and the United States. Interestingly, in a genre that has usually been purged of any overt political references, Winspear does mention the political turmoil found in some of the countries she writes about, and she occasionally uses it as part of the plot, although such references are generally kept vague. Winspear's heroes are always citizens of these exciting lands but the heroines are invariably English.

The sense of worldly sophistication created in the novels by the multi-lingualism is further heightened by Winspear's literary references to Dante, Byron, Chekov, Balzac, Browning, etc. The hero and heroine are likely to recite bits of poetry and prose during the course of the story. Winspear also likes to use mythology as a motif in her romances. Thus the hero and heroine will be compared to mythological characters such as Apollo and Daphne or Proserpina and Aidoneus, or "romantic" historical figures like the Sabine women and their captors. Winspear also borrows from other popular fiction. For instance, *Blue Jasmine* is very closely modeled after E. M. Hull's *The Sheik*.

When asked why she does not write about an ordinary Englishman, a "Herbert Smith," or her childhood home in London's East End, Winspear replied: "Quite frankly I do often write about Herbert Smith but I give him a more romantic name and disguise him in a tailored suit." She added: "I often write about the East End, for my Eastern bazaars are straight out of Petticoat Lane. My Greeks and Italians reside there, the aroma of exotic food has been breathed there . . . I have often plucked strands for my stories from that rich tapestry." The results show that Winspear has the ability to transform her observations of everyday people, places, and events into glamorous romances.

—Margaret Jensen

WINSTON, Daoma. American. Born in Washington, D.C., 3 November 1922. Educated at George Washington University, Washington, D.C., A.B. 1946 (Phi Beta Kappa). Married Murray Strasberg in 1944. Lives in Washington, D.C. Agent: Jay Garon-Brooke Associates, 415 Central Park West, New York, New York 10025, U.S.A.

ROMANCE AND HISTORICAL PUBLICATIONS

Novels

The Secrets of Cromwell Crossing. New York, Lancer, 1965; London, Piatkus, 1984.
Sinister Stone. New York, Paperback Library, 1966; London, Piatkus, 1985.
The Mansion of Smiling Masks. New York, New American Library, 1967.
Shadow of an Unknown Woman. New York, Lancer, 1967; Loughton, Essex, Piatkus, 1979.
The Castle of Closing Doors. New York, Belmont, 1967.
The Carnaby Curse. New York, Belmont, 1967.
Shadow on Mercer Mountain. New York, Lancer, 1967; London, Piatkus, 1988.
Pity My Love. New York, Belmont, 1967.
The Trificante Treasure. New York, Lancer, 1968.
The Long and Living Shadow. New York, Belmont, 1968.
Dennison Hill. New York, Paperback Library, 1970.
House of Mirror Images. New York, Lancer, 1970; Loughton, Essex, Piatkus, 1981.
The Love of Lucifer. New York, Lancer, 1970; London, Piatkus, 1986.
The Vampire Curse. New York, Paperback Library, 1971.
Flight of a Fallen Angel. New York, Lancer, 1971; Loughton, Essex, Piatkus, 1982.
The Devil's Daughter. New York, Lancer, 1971.
The Devil's Princess. New York, Lancer, 1971; Loughton, Essex, Piatkus, 1980.
Seminar in Evil. New York, Lancer, 1972.
The Victim. New York, Popular Library, 1972; London, Piatkus, 1985.
The Return. New York, Avon, 1972.
The Inheritance. New York, Avon, 1972; London, Piatkus, 1987.
Kingdom's Castle. New York, Berkley, 1972; Loughton, Essex, Piatkus, 1981.
Skeleton Key. New York, Avon, 1972; Loughton, Essex, Piatkus, 1980; as *The Mayeroni Myth*, New York, Lancer, 1972.
Moorhaven. New York, Avon, 1973; London, Futura, 1976.
The Trap. New York, Popular Library, 1973; London, Piatkus, 1989.
The Unforgotten. New York, Berkley, 1973.

The Haversham Legacy. New York, Simon and Schuster, 1974; London, Futura, 1977.
Mills of the Gods. New York, Avon, 1974; London, Macdonald and Jane's, 1980.
Emerald Station. New York, Avon, 1974; London, Futura, 1977.
The Golden Valley. New York, Simon and Schuster, 1975; London, Futura, 1978.
Gallows Way. New York, Simon and Schuster, 1976; London, Macdonald and Jane's, 1978.
The Adventuress. New York, Simon and Schuster, 1978; London, Macdonald and Jane's, 1979.
The Hands of Death. Loughton, Essex, Piatkus, 1982.
Family of Strangers. Loughton, Essex, Piatkus, 1983.
The Fall River Line. New York, Marek, 1983; London, Century, 1984.

OTHER PUBLICATIONS

Novels

Tormented Lovers. Derby, Connecticut, Monarch, 1962.
Love Her, She's Yours. Derby, Connecticut, Monarch, 1963.
The Wakefield Witches. New York, Award, 1966; London, Piatkus, 1987.
The Moderns. New York, Pyramid, 1968; London, Severn House, 1988.
Bracken's World. New York, Paperback Library, 1969.
Mrs. Berrigan's Dirty Book. New York, Lancer, 1970.
Beach Generation. New York, Lancer, 1970.
Wild Country. New York, Paperback Library, 1970.
Sound Stage. New York, Paperback Library, 1970.
Death Watch. New York, Ace, 1975; London, Piatkus, 1986.
A Visit After Dark. New York, Ace, 1975; Loughton, Essex, Piatkus, 1983.
Walk Around the Square. New York, Ace, 1975; London, Piatkus, 1984.
The Dream Killers. New York, Ace, 1976; London, Severn House, 1987.
The Lotteries. New York, Morrow, and London, Macdonald, 1980.
A Sweet Familiarity. New York, Arbor House, 1981; London, Macdonald, 1983.
Mira. New York, Arbor House, and London, Macdonald, 1982.
Maybe This Time. London, Century, 1988.

*   *   *

The novels of Daoma Winston contain much romance but also complex stories and psychology. They centre around women rather than men and involve a fairly deep level of characterisation. They seem to be divisible into two types: long historical novels and shorter works that, but for the added romantic element, could fall into the category of mystery novels. These latter are very exciting and contain a well-developed crescendo of suspense, to which the romantic element is subordinate.

The heroines are strong, complex, and exceedingly logical, and have to deal with serious family problems as well as very masculine but wayward men. Usually one or more of the minor characters poses a mortal threat to the heroine, either because of greed, jealousy, envy, or desire for revenge. In fact, apart from a difference in setting and background detail, her shorter novels are really explorations of one theme: strong emotions becoming twisted and serving as motives for destruction. The heroines find themselves in ever-increasing danger as a series of mysterious deaths occur, each death coming closer to the heroine herself. It is the heroine who ultimately uncovers the killer and his motive; the heroine to whom the killer reveals all in an exciting but contrived denouement.

The bizarre features prominently, as in, for example, the spiritualist cult in *The Devil's Princess* or the curse of the Mayeroni in *Skeleton Key*. Except in her historical novels, the plots and backgrounds appear contrived and far-fetched.

Winston's historical novels such as *Moorhaven*, *The Golden Valley* and *Gallows Way* are more powerful and substantial and have met with greater popularity in Britain than her other works. Unfortunately she does not exploit her skill in recreating historical events, instead using the setting primarily as a vehicle for her exploration of the emotions and motive already mentioned. This leads to a weakening of the romantic thriller element, since romance is often delayed until the very end of the novel when the heroine is finally moved by the hero's love for her. The historical element is often overpowered by a strong, all-pervading sense of doom. The action is sometimes spread over several generations, as in *Moorhaven*, and this compounds the doom which afflicts the inhabitants of the Golden Valley and the family mansion Moorhaven.

An interesting feature of character drawing is the way that twins are used as main characters (*House of Mirror Images*, *Skeleton Key*, *Kingdom's Castle*, *The Golden Valley*): considerable attention is devoted to their psychological (and sometimes pathological) interdependence. Winston likes to explore situations in which grown-up children are brought to a state where they cause violence because of their parents keeping them as children beyond childhood. Their settings are, however, stylised and they often appear mannequin-like.

Winston has latterly developed a sure touch and mastered the craft of romantic novel writing. In her latest novels, her work has matured, and she now develops stronger plots and story lines as well as a faster pace of action. In *Mills of the Gods* these features are combined with an accurate and minutely researched historical setting at the turn of the century. The vivid descriptions of clothes and facial appearances provide a comprehensive catalogue of the minutiae of romantic attraction. Personal attraction grows and wanes against a strong background of family and social disturbance, but people are perhaps more forward sexually than might be expected for the time. In *The Lotteries* the setting again includes New England but is largely a rather grimy and greasy contemporary America. A favourite theme of fortune and its twists reappears, as does the theme of the disadvantages of wealth. The emotions and behaviour shown are, however, very up-to-date as are the sexual mores of the characters.

Winston provides, in addition to romantic escape, useful insights into some bogeys of the American psyche.

—P. R. Meldrum

WOOD, Barbara (née Lewandowski). Also writes as Kathryn Harvey. American. Born in England, 30 January 1947. Educated at the University of California, Santa Barbara, 1964–66. Married George Wood in 1966. Surgical technician, Santa Monica Hospital, California, 1973–77; instructor, University of California, Riverside. Address: c/o Random House, 210 East 50th Street, New York, New York 10022, U.S.A.

Novels

The Magdalene Scrolls. New York, Doubleday, and London, Methuen, 1978.
Hounds and Jackals. New York, Doubleday, 1978; London, Eyre Methuen, 1979.
Curse This House. New York, Dell, 1978; London, Magnum, 1979.
Night Trains, with Gareth Wootton. New York, Morrow, and London, Eyre Methuen, 1979.
Yesterday's Child. New York, Doubleday, 1979; London, Hamlyn, 1981.
The Watchgods. New York, Dell, 1980; London, New English Library, 1981.
Childsong. New York, Doubleday, 1981; Loughton, Essex, Piatkus, 1982.
Domina. New York, Doubleday, and Loughton, Essex, Piatkus, 1983.
Vital Signs. New York, Doubleday, and London, Piatkus, 1985.
Soul Flame. New York, Random House, and London, Piatkus, 1987.
Green City in the Sun. New York, Random House, and London, Macmillan, 1988.
Butterfly (as Kathryn Harvey). New York, Villard, 1988; London, Headline, 1989.

*   *   *

Barbara Wood uses her medical training to good advantage in her novels. She varies the periods and the locations, but almost every work deals with medicine in some way.

The Magdalene Scrolls is a thriller of possession and is the only book without the medical motif. *Night Trains* is based on a true event in World War II Poland, when a faked typhus epidemic kept the Nazis at bay. *Childsong* deals with parthenogenesis and a virgin birth in 1963. Wood's other novels fit neatly into the romance genre.

In *Hounds and Jackals* surgical nurse Lydia Harris receives an urgent telephone call from her estranged sister. After a package arrives which contains a carved jackal, one piece of an ancient Egyptian game set, Lydia flies to Rome to answer the summons. Another message sends her to Cairo where a man is murdered, and Lydia is taken from the scene by an Arab who will tell her nothing. Several adventures later, Lydia and Ahmed travel to the Valley of the Kings where Lydia almost loses her life again before being rescued, finding her sister, and falling in love. Easy reading and good characterization make this a lightweight romance, flawed but fun.

In *Curse This House* a young woman returns to the house she left as an infant, only to learn that she has inherited a medical condition which turns those afflicted into killers. Her suspicion of the truth of this situation and her love for her "cousin" are important factors in solving all the mysteries in an interesting gothic.

Yesterday's Child also features a young woman who returns to her place of birth. Andrea goes to England to take her mother's place at her grandfather's deathbed. Staying in the house her family has owned for 62 years, she is subjected to episodes from the past in a time slip in which she learns the truth about her great-grandfather's actions. (He was a doctor.) She also learns about herself and comes to care for others so deeply that she is able to ease her grandfather's death with the truth she has learned. This is a different romantic ghost story which keeps the pages turning.

Domina tells of the struggle Samantha has to raise herself from the London slums to an American medical school in the late 19th century when women were not allowed to become doctors. Along the way she is helped by a number of medical practitioners and falls in love with a man she cannot have. After graduation she keeps fighting: to be accepted as an intern, to cure her patients, and to protect women from patent medicines which kill. She falls in love again and enlists her suitor in her battles. This is a good romance with a thorough background in the medical practices of that era.

In *Vital Signs* three women meet in medical school. They stick together to help each other throughout the rest of their lives. They prove able to have careers and love at the same time, but each sacrifices something in the effort. There are no surprises, but the story is gripping. The *Soul Flame* is the way Selene aids healing in a tale of medicine in the 1st century A.D. Separated from her parents at birth and her betrothed before marriage, Selene wanders the known world helping others and searching for her identity and her man. She has many adventures which keep the reader entranced. The book is full of ancient folklore and the nostrums of the age. *Green City in the Sun* is the saga of two families who fight over the same patch of land in Kenya. When the bwana cuts down a sacred tree, the native medicine woman curses his entire family, including his sister, the missionary Doctor Grace, whose journal tells the story. History is neatly interwoven with romance and intrigue in Wood's best novel to date.

Wood uses too many medical terms for the average reader without in-text explanation. The finicky reader might keep a medical dictionary at hand, but most will skip over the terms and read her books for the sheer pleasure of a well-told story.

—Andrea Lee Shuey

WOODIWISS, Kathleen E(rin, née Hogg). American. Born in Alexandria, Louisiana, 3 June 1939. Educated at schools in Alexandria. Married Ross Woodiwiss in 1956; three sons. Address: c/o Avon Books, 105 Madison Avenue, New York, New York 10016, U.S.A.

Novels

The Flame and the Flower. New York, Avon, 1972; London, Futura, 1975.
The Wolf and the Dove. New York, Avon, 1974; London, Piatkus, 1986.
Shanna. New York, Avon, and London, Futura, 1977.
Ashes in the Wind. New York, Avon, 1979; London, Macdonald Futura, 1980.
A Rose in Winter. New York, Avon, and Loughton, Essex, Piatkus, 1983.
Come Love a Stranger. New York, Avon, 1984; London, Piatkus, 1985.

*   *   *

Kathleen E. Woodiwiss's impact on the genre, especially in the United States, has been substantial, if not revolutionary.

When *The Flame and the Flower*, her first novel, arrived at Avon Books in 1972, the field of romance publishing was still dominated by the contemporary "gothics" of writers such as Mary Stewart, Victoria Holt, and Phyllis Whitney. A good 300 pages longer than the gothics, *The Flame and the Flower* differed from them further in that it contained long, erotic passages describing the sexual encounters of heroine and hero in surprising detail. When Woodiwiss's novel met with immediate success, her publishers followed it with Rosemary Rogers's similar *Sweet Savage Love* and then created a new romantic subgenre that has since been dubbed "the erotic historical" or, less reverently, "the bodice-ripper."

Woodiwiss's novels, which include, in addition to *The Flame and the Flower*, *The Wolf and the Dove*, *Shanna*, *Ashes in the Wind*, *A Rose in Winter*, and *Come Love a Stranger*, do not deserve the latter epithet, as do those of some of her imitators. Although her heroines encounter male violence as Heather does in *The Flame and the Flower* when she is raped by her future husband because he thinks her a prostitute, Woodiwiss never multiplies such scenes or dwells on their brutal details simply to titillate her readers. Not only are such events rare in her books but they are also carefully integrated into complex plots which all focus on the *gradual* development of love between the two principal characters. Unlike many of the writers of this subgenre who keep the heroine and hero apart until the final pages of the novel, Woodiwiss brings them into contact early in the tale. Having established their initial attraction for each other, she then shows how love develops between two extraordinary individuals, emphasizes that the relationship must be cultivated carefully, and demonstrates that compromise, tenderness, and generosity are necessary to maintain it. The erotic scenes in all of Woodiwiss's novels are presented as integral parts of this deepening relationship and, as a consequence, she places most of her emphasis on the increasing tenderness with which the hero treats the heroine.

Woodiwiss's stories are further distinguished from those of her imitators by the fact that her characters exhibit somewhat more androgynous personalities than do those that typically populate the genre. Although all her heroines are unusually beautiful, sensitive, and particularly adept at nursing or caring for others, they are also asserted to be willful, forceful, intelligent, and capable of initiating action on their own. Interestingly enough, each Woodiwiss heroine is more independent and active than was her predecessor. Aislinn (*The Wolf and the Dove*) and Shanna (*Shanna*) both challenge their heroes in ways Heather (*The Flame and the Flower*) does not, just as they are portrayed as the intellectual equals of their men. This apparent emphasis on equality is carried even further in *Ashes in the Wind* when Alaina masquerades as a boy throughout the entire first half of the novel, saves the hero's life, and generally proves herself capable of fending for herself. The heroes, on the other hand, though typically Byronic, commanding, and spectacularly male, are also capable of reflection, sympathy, and tenderness. By the end of her novels, each Woodiwiss hero, like Brandon in *The Flame and the Flower*, confesses openly his dependence on the heroine and his love for her special qualities. It seems possible, then, that although she does not challenge the validity of the romance's essential message that female happiness can be secured most successfuly in the arms of a protective male, Woodiwiss has been influenced by the feminism of the 1970's to the extent that she unfailingly asserts verbally that her heroines are not mere children whose every whim and desire must be gratified by a man. Rather, she insists, they are independent women who desire a loving relationship that is also an equal partnership. Her extraordinary and sudden popularity may well have been a function of this ability to embody some of the ideas of the feminist movement in changed character types without also upsetting the traditional structural relationship between the sexes.

—Janice Radway

WOODWARD, Lilian. Pseudonym for John Marsh; also writes as Julia Davis; John Elton; John Harley; Harrington Hastings; Irene Lawrence; Joan Marsh; Grace Richmond; Petra Sawley; Monica Ware. British. Born in 1907. Address: Chalfont, Rawson Avenue, Halifax HX3 0LN, Yorkshire, England.

ROMANCE AND HISTORICAL PUBLICATIONS

Novels

Nursing Assignment. London, Hale, 1959.
Cruise to Romance. London, Hale, 1960.
Nurse Frayne's Strange Quest. London, Hale, 1960.
The Hidden Past. London, Hale, 1961.
Nurse to the Maharajah. London, Hale, 1961.
Appointment with Love. London, Hale, 1962.
The Wrong Love. London, Hale, 1962.
Love Me—Love Me Not. London, Hale, 1966.
The House on the Moor. London, Hale, 1967.
Flight to Romance. London, Hale, 1969.
Prisoner of Love. London, Hale, 1971.
The Tuscan Chalice. London, Hale, 1972.
So Dear to Their Hearts. London, Hale, 1974.
North Sea Nurse. London, Hale, 1975.
Mill Town Nurse. London, Hale, 1976.
A Very Special Love. London, Hale, 1976.
That Man in Her Life. London, Hale, 1977.
Dangerous Secret. London, Hale, 1978.
The Doctors of Doncastle. London, Hale, 1978.
Flying Nurse. London, Hale, 1979.
Folly of Love. London, Hale, 1979.
Nurse to Princess Jasmine. London, Hale, 1979.
Agency Nurse. London, Hale, 1980.
The Barrier Between Them. London, Hale, 1980.
Design for Loving. London, Hale, 1980.
Flight to Sandaha. London, Hale, 1981.
Love's a Magician. London, Hale, 1981.
Give All to Love. London, Hale, 1982.
Out of the Past. London, Hale, 1982.
Reflections of Love. London, Hale, 1983.
Lover from Yesterday. London, Hale, 1984.
Mystery Lover. London, Hale, 1985.

Novels as Grace Richmond

She Followed Her Heart. London, Fiction House, 1944.
June Fairley—Air Hostess. London, Hale, 1959.
When There's Love at Home. London, Hale, 1959.
Too Young to Wed. London, Hale, 1960.
The Touch of Your Hand. London, Hale, 1960.
Marriage Is Like That. London, Hale, 1961.
The Greater Love. London, Hale, 1961.
The Doctor's Secret. London, Hale, 1962.
The Love Race. London, Hale, 1967.
Island of Secrets. London, Hale, 1968.
Waters of Conflict. London, Hale, 1969.

Passport to Romance. London, Hale, 1969.
Yesterday's Love. London, Hale, 1972.
Run Away from Love. London, Hale, 1974.
Legacy Without Love. London, Hale, 1976.
Nurse to Doctor James. London, Hale, 1976.
Testament of Love. London, Hale, 1977.
Two Doctor Greys. London, Hale, 1977.
Don't Cling to the Past. London, Hale, 1978.
At the Villa Mimosa. London, Hale, 1978.
Believe the Heart. London, Hale, 1979.
Fugitive from Love. London, Hale, 1980.
Haunted Love. London, Hale, 1980.
Vision of Love. London, Hale, 1980.
Air Ambulance Nurse. London, Hale, 1981.
Nurse Hanson's Strange Case. London, Hale, 1981.
That Villa in Spain. London, Hale, 1981.
Guardian of the Trees. London, Hale, 1982.
The Cottage in the Wood. London, Hale, 1983.
House of Strangers. London, Hale, 1983.
No Place for Lovers. London, Hale, 1983.
Reach Out for Happiness. London, Hale, 1984.

Novels as John Harley

The Four Doctors. London, Hale, 1960.
Doctor with Four Hands. London, Hale, 1962.
Doctor to the House of Jasmine. London, Gifford, 1967.
Doctor in Spain. London, Hale, 1968.
Doctor in Danger. London, Hale, 1970.

Novels as Petra Sawley

No Time for Love. London, Gresham, 1967.
No Place for Love. London, Gresham, 1967.
Love on Ice. London, Gresham, 1967.
Their Mysterious Patient. London, Gresham, 1970.
Love's Dark Shadow. London, Gresham, 1970.
That Strange Holiday. London, Hale, 1972.
Doctor with a Past. London, Hale, 1973.
Dream of Past Loves. London, Hale, 1975.

Novels as Joan Marsh

Love in Peril. London, Gresham, 1967.
Love Spins the Wheel. London, Gresham, 1967.
Love Takes the Helm. London, Gresham, 1967.
The Bride's House. London, Gresham, 1968.
Prince of Hearts. London, Gresham, 1970.
Conflict of the Heart. London, Gresham, 1971.
The Truth about Janice Henderson. London, Hale, 1972.
Victim of Love. London, Hale, 1973.
Lord of Imchay. London, Hale, 1975.

Novels as Irene Lawrence

World Without Love. London, Gresham, 1967.
Love Is Like That. London, Gresham, 1967.
Switch on to Love. London, Gresham, 1967.
Love Rides the Skies. London, Gresham, 1968.
Love Came Unaware. London, Gresham, 1970.
Love's Last Barrier. London, Gresham, 1971.
Nurse Farnley's Secret. London, Hale, 1972.
Hostage of Love. London, Hale, 1973.
No Escape from Love. London, Hale, 1974.

Novels as Monica Ware

Au Pair Girl. London, Gresham, 1967.
Make Way for Love. London, Gresham, 1967.
Stranger to Love. London, Gresham, 1967.
The Ties of Love. London, Gresham, 1968.
Love Knows No Frontier. London, Gresham, 1970.
The Love She Hid. London, Gresham, 1970.
Her Mystery Man. London, Gresham, 1971.
Love in Danger. London, Hale, 1972.
Disco in Spain. London, Hale, 1976.

Novels as Julia Davis

Love in the Lead. London, Gresham, 1967.
Holiday for Lovers. London, Gresham, 1967.
Her Unexpected Summer. London, Gresham, 1967.
That Affair in Spain. London, Gresham, 1969.
Sands of Desire. London, Gresham, 1970.
The Doctor's Favourite Nurse. London, Gresham, 1971.
Nurse in Arabia. London, Hale, 1972.
Fly High, My Heart. London, Hale, 1972.
Love's Treasure Trove. London, Hale, 1973.
Magic of the Desert. London, Hale, 1976.
African Interlude. Aylesbury, Buckinghamshire, Hunt Barnard, 1982.

OTHER PUBLICATIONS as John Marsh

Novels

Criminal Square (with Florence Shepherd, as Harrington Hastings). London, Hutchinson, 1929.
The War Dog Stirs (with Florence Shepherd, as Harrington Hastings). London, Hutchinson, 1930.
Maiden Armour. London, Stanley Paul, 1932.
Lonely Pathway. London, Stanley Paul, 1933.
Return They Must. London, Stanley Paul, 1933.
The Wrong That Was Done. London, Leng, 1935.
Body Made Alive. London, Stanley Smith, 1936.
A Glimpse of Paradise. London, Boardman, 1944.
Many Parts. London, Swan, 1946.
Two Mrs. Farrells. London, Boardman, 1946.
Shipwrecked Schoolship. London, Swan, 1949.
By the World Condemned. London, Amalgamated Press, 1949.
The Secret of the Seven Sisters. London, Ward, 1950.
The Brain of Paul Menoloff. London, Robertson, 1953.
The Cruise of the Carefree. London, Ward, 1955.
The Green Plantations (as John Elton). London, Ward Lock, 1955.
House of Echoes. London, Gifford, 1956.
The Hidden Answer. London, Gifford, 1956.
Murderer's Maze. London, Gifford, 1957.
Operation Snatch. London, Gifford, 1958.
City of Fear. London, Gifford, 1958.
The Reluctant Executioner. London, Hale, 1959.
Small and Deadly. London, Hale, 1960.
Girl in a Net. London, Hale, 1962.
The Golden Teddybear. London, Boardman, 1965.
Not My Murder. London, Gifford, 1967.
Monk's Hollow. London, Gifford, 1968; New York, Ace, 1969.
Hate Thy Neighbour. London, Hale, 1969.
Master of High Beck. London, Hale, 1969.

Other

The Young Winston Churchill. London, Evans, 1955.
Clip a Bright Guinea: The Yorkshire Coiners of the Eighteenth Century. London, Hale, 1971.

*   *   *

There is a skill to writing love stories. The mere existence of the formula (man, woman, attraction, problems, reconciliation, and rosy sunset) does not guarantee automatic success in practice. No matter how many incompetent hands it passes through, however, the principle remains. Modifications are made to keep up with the times of course, for sex precedes marriage and men now know where the tea towels are kept and how to use them, but generally there are few real differences. Men are men; women are women, and thus the twain shall meet.

Because John Marsh has written over such a long time-span, under the names of Julia Davis, John Harley, Irene Lawrence, Joan Marsh, Grace Richmond, Petra Sawley, and Lilian Woodward, the inevitable shifts in attitude can easily be traced between his earlier and later work. In *She Followed Her Heart* (1944, as Grace Richmond) Eve, who is kind to little old ladies and compassionate to RAF widows and orphans, falls instantly in love with a blue uniform and a pair of silver wings. She is the stereotypical dress shop assistant heroine. By *Waters of Conflict* (1969) however, the same figure has evolved into a woman of the world caught in the middle of a dispute between Welsh nationalists and the British government.

Marsh's greatest skill lies in his ability to recognise and respond to the new demands of his audience. We would not be satisfied with a figure like the protagonist of *June Fairley—Air Hostess* (1959) who is hysterical, weepy, and easily duped, but we do feel somewhat closer to the capable and resourceful Janet of *Passport to Romance* (1969). Marsh's more recent heroines resemble the earlier models by working in the caring roles of nannies and nurses (*Nurse to Princess Jasmine*, *Agency Nurse*).

These figures are now acceptable to today's readership because the setting has kept apace with the changing times. Maggie and Jill in *Air Ambulance Nurse* are in a traditional female profession, but Jill becomes a jet-setting career woman—something unthinkable for her counterpart in a romantic novel 20 years ago. Marsh's constant use of a medical background is arguably repetitive and unimaginative, but within it he works hard to reflect social changes. It serves as a constant base from which he can explore new perceptions.

The heroes are rarely the classic specimens of rough manhood tameable in the right hands, nor are they the seductive charmers favoured by other writers. Instead of condescending to awaken adult feelings in the neurotic female with a kiss, they are warm and caring, the epitome of the boy next door. Occasionally the rugged persona does appear, for example Ralph in *Master of High Beck* or Ben in *No Place for Lovers*, but since this is a facade on the part of the proud and vulnerable male ego, they remain in line with their counterparts in Marsh's other books—sensitive and human.

Marsh does not usually rely on fantasy and escapism for appeal, but on accessibility and identification. Domestic affairs are central to his plots, with such marital problems as suspected infidelity frequently the focus (this happens on a grand scale in *When There's Love at Home*). In these situations the woman is usually the figure of power with the final say, and Marsh carries off this reversal with conviction. The later novels may be more fanciful and exotic, but at heart they too support these values.

Marsh stands above the normal run of romance fiction writers mainly because he turns the established format in a new direction, and yet retains enough of the essentials to be considered a writer of traditional romances. He takes risks with a popular genre, making him unusual in a field that relies heavily on the familiar.

—L. M. Quinn

WOOLF, Victoria. See **LAMB, Charlotte.**

WORBOYS, Anne (Annette Isobel Worboys, née Eyre). Also writes as Annette Eyre; Vicky Maxwell; Anne Eyre Worboys. British. Born in Auckland, New Zealand. Served in the Royal New Zealand Air Force, 1942–45. Married Walter Worboys in 1946; two daughters. Recipient: Mary Elgin award, 1975; Romantic Novelists Association Major award, 1977. Agent: David Higham Associates Ltd., 5–8 Lower John Street, London W1R 4HA. Address: The White House, Leigh, near Tonbridge, Kent, England.

ROMANCE AND HISTORICAL PUBLICATIONS

Novels

The Lion of Delos. New York, Delacorte Press, 1974; London, Hodder and Stoughton, 1975.
Every Man a King. London, Hodder and Stoughton, 1975; New York, Scribner, 1976; as *Rendezvous with Fear*, New York, Ace, 1977.
The Barrancourt Destiny. London, Hodder and Stoughton, 1977; New York, Scribner, 1978.
The Bhunda Jewels. London, Severn House, 1980; New York, Ace, 1981.
Run, Sara, Run. New York, Scribner, 1981; London, Severn House, 1982.
A Kingdom for the Bold. London, Century, 1986.
Aurora Rose. New York, Dutton, 1988.

Novels as Anne Eyre Worboys

Dream of Petals Whim. London, Ward Lock, 1961.
Palm Rock and Paradise. London, Ward Lock, 1961.
Call for a Stranger. London, Ward Lock, 1962.

Novels as Annette Eyre

Three Strings to a Fortune. London, Hurst and Blackett, 1962.
Visit to Rata Creek. London, Hurst and Blackett, 1964.
The Valley of Yesterday. London, Hurst and Blackett, 1965.
A Net to Catch the Wind. London, Hurst and Blackett, 1966.
Return to Bellbird Country. London, Hurst and Blackett, 1966.
The House of Five Pines. London, Hurst and Blackett, 1967.
The River and Wilderness. London, Hurst and Blackett, 1967; as *Give Me Your Love*, New York, New American Library, 1975.
A Wind from the Hill. London, Hurst and Blackett, 1968.
Thorn-Apple. London, Hurst and Blackett, 1968.
Tread Softly in the Sun. London, Hurst and Blackett, 1969.
The Little Millstones. London, Hurst and Blackett, 1970.

Dolphin Bay. London, Hurst and Blackett, 1970. *Rainbow Child.* London, Hurst and Blackett, 1971.
The Magnolia Room. London, Hurst and Blackett, 1972; New York, New American Library, 1975.
Venetian Inheritance. London, Hurst and Blackett, 1973; New York, New American Library, 1975.

Novels as Vicky Maxwell

Chosen Child. London, Collins, 1973; New York, Ace, 1980.
Flight to the Villa Mistra. London, Collins, 1973; New York, Ace, 1981.
The Way of the Tamarisk. London, Collins, 1974; as Anne Worboys, New York, Delacorte Press, 1975.
High Hostage. London, Collins, 1976.
The Other Side of Summer. London, Collins, 1977; New York, Ace, 1979.

*   *   *

Anne Worboys is a prolific writer of romance and romantic suspense novels who always turns out a readable, well-paced story. As Annette Eyre, she writes romance novels in the standard format. Under the pseudonym Vicky Maxwell, she writes novels of suspense. Similar in construction and content to the Vicky Maxwell titles are the novels issued under the name Anne Worboys. With one exception, these are the most well-written and interesting fiction of this enjoyable author.

The Lion of Delos, her first, combines a setting on the sunny Greek island of Mykonos with the slightly confusing plot of a missing twin sister. Well-wrought dialog and flashes of real excellence in the storyline provide a preview of her later works.

Every Man a King proves to be one of her best books, an intriguing story set in Spain with its roots in the Spanish Civil War over 30 years ago. Suzanne Cole comes to discover the mystery surrounding her stepmother's involvement with the wealthy de Merito family. The scenery is spectacular and a ride on horses through the Sierra Nevadas provides a thrilling finale.

The Barrancourt Destiny is a fitting followup to *Every Man a King.* Again family problems and mysteries dominate as Victoria Brown comes to England to solve the riddle of her family background and her possible connection to the Barrancourts of Alconleigh. She is lucky enough to find a job there, meeting first the heir (who is having an affair with his father's young wife) and then cousin Louis, enigmatic and handsome, who takes care of the riding stables. The mystery aspect is quite well-handled, and the romance is a charmer complete with a tension-filled midnight tour by candlelight of the estate.

Unfortunately, Worboys's novel, *Run, Sara, Run,* more of a mystery than her usual romantic suspense, is an annoying, unsatisfying tale of an actress, Sara Tindale, who along with her baby is being stalked by a vengeful killer. Part of the disappointment derives from the fact that the reader expects another *Barrancourt Destiny.*

—Marilyn Lockhart

WREN, P(ercival) C(hristopher). British. Born in Devon in 1885. Educated at Oxford University, M.A. Married; one son. Worked as schoolmaster, journalist, farm hand, explorer, hunter, soldier: trooper in a British cavalry regiment, and served in the French Foreign Legion; lived in India: Assistant Director of Education, Bombay, 10 years, and Justice of the Peace; Major in the Indian Forces in East Africa during World War I: invalided home. *Died 22 November 1941.*

ROMANCE AND HISTORICAL PUBLICATIONS

Novels (series: Geste Family; Sinbad Dysart)

Father Gregory; or, Lures and Failures: A Tale of Hindostan. London, Longman, 1913; New York, Stokes, 1926.
Snake and Sword. London, Longman, 1914; as *The Snake and the Sword,* New York, Stokes, 1923.
The Wages of Virtue. London, Murray, 1916; New York, Stokes, 1917.
Driftwood Spars. London, Longman, 1916; New York, Stokes, 1927.
Cupid in Africa; or, The Baking of Bertram in Love and War—A Character Study. London, Cranton, 1920.
Beau Geste. London, Murray, 1924; New York, Stokes, 1925.
Beau Sabreur (Geste). London, Murray, and New York, Stokes, 1926.
Beau Ideal (Geste). London, Murray, and New York, Stokes, 1928.
Soldiers of Misfortune: The Story of Otho Belleme. London, Murray, and New York, Stokes, 1929.
Mysterious Waye: The Story of "The Unsetting Sun." London, Murray, and New York, Stokes, 1930.
The Mammon of Righteousness: The Story of Coxe and the Box. London, Murray, 1930; as *Mammon,* New York, Stokes, 1930.
Sowing Glory: The Memoirs of "Mary Ambree," The English Woman—Legionary. London, Murray, and New York, Stokes, 1931.
Valiant Dust. London, Murray, and New York, Stokes, 1932.
Action and Passion (Sinbad). London, Murray, and New York, Stokes, 1933.
Beggars' Horses. London, Murray, 1934; as *The Dark Woman,* Philadelphia, Macrae Smith, 1943.
Sinbad the Soldier. London, Murray, and Boston, Houghton Mifflin, 1935.
Explosion. London, Murray, 1935.
Spanish Maine. London, Murray, 1935; as *The Desert Heritage,* Boston, Houghton Mifflin, 1935.
Fort in the Jungle: The Extraordinary Adventures of Sinbad Dysart in Tonkin. London, Murray, and Boston, Houghton Mifflin, 1936.
Bubble Reputation. London, Murray, 1936; as *The Courtenay Treasure,* Boston, Houghton Mifflin, 1936.
The Man of a Ghost. London, Murray, 1937; as *The Spur of Pride,* Boston, Houghton Mifflin, 1937.
Worth Wile. London, Murray, 1937; as *To the Hilt,* Boston, Houghton Mifflin, 1937.
Cardboard Castle. London, Murray, and Boston, Houghton Mifflin, 1938.
Paper Prison. London, Murray, 1939; as *The Man the Devil Didn't Want,* Philadelphia, Macrae Smith, 1940.
The Disappearance of General Jason. London, Murray, 1940.
Two Feet from Heaven. London, Murray, 1940; Philadelphia, Macrae Smith, 1941.
Stories of the Foreign Legion (omnibus). London, Murray, 1947.

Short Stories

Dew and Mildew: Semi-Detached Stories from Karabad, India.
London, Longman, 1912; as *Dew and Mildew: A Loose-Knit Tale of Hindustan*, New York, Stokes, 1927.
Stepsons of France. London, Murray, and New York, Stokes, 1917.
The Young Stagers, Being Further Faites and Gestes of the Junior Curlton Club of Karabad, India. . . . London, Longman, 1917; New York, Stokes, 1926.
Good Gestes: Stories of Beau Geste, His Brothers, and Certain of Their Comrades in the French Foreign Legion. London, Murray, and New York, Stokes, 1929.
Flawed Blades: Tales from the Foreign Legion. London, Murray, and New York, Stokes, 1933.
Port o' Missing Men: Strange Tale of the Stranger Regiment. London, Murray, 1934; Philadelphia, Macrae Smith, 1943.
Rough Shooting: True Tales and Strange Stories. London, Murray, 1938; Philadelphia, Macrae Smith, 1944.
Odd—But Even So: Stories Stranger Than Fiction. London, Murray, 1941; Philadelphia, Macrae Smith, 1942.
The Hunting of Henri. London, Vallancey Press, 1944.
Dead Men's Boot and Other Tales from the Foreign Legion. London, Gryphon, 1949.

OTHER PUBLICATIONS

Other

The Indian Teacher's Guide to the Theory and Practice of Mental, Moral, and Physical Education. Bombay, Longman, 1910.
Indian School Organization, Management, Discipline, Tone, and Equipment, Being the Indian Headmaster's Guide. Bombay, Longman, 1911.
The "Direct" Teaching of English in Indian Schools. Bombay, Longman, 1911.
Chemistry and First Aid for Standard VII, with H. E. H. Pratt. Bombay, Longman, 1913.
Physics and Mechanics, with N. B. Macmillan. Bombay, Longman, 1914.
With the Prince Through Canada, New Zealand, and Australia. Bombay, Athenaeum Press, 1922.
Work, Wealth, and Wages (for children), revision of a work by Ernest F. Row. Bombay, Cooper, 1950.
First Lessons in English Grammar. Bombay, Cooper, 1961.

Editor, *The World and India, Adapted for Use in Indian Schools.* Calcutta, Oxford University Press, 1905.
Editor, *Ivanhoe* (simplified), by Scott. London, Frowde, 1912.
Editor, *Longmans' Science Series for Indian High Schools.* Bombay, Longman, 11 vols., 1913–14.
Editor, *Gulliver's Travels* (simplified), by Swift. Calcutta, Oxford University Press, 1963.

*   *   *

P. C. Wren's works range from potboilers indistinguishable from the fulminations of pulp writers to novels that presented an integrated world-view and fully developed characters; these latter efforts were recognizable bids for recognition as a serious artist—a recognition that his popularity seemed to preclude. Wren mixed melodrama with the lightest comic banter, exotic settings with the most brutal realism, and romantic idealism with an almost overwhelmingly cynical fatalism.

The melodrama in Wren most often grows out of basic conflicts; circumstances demand the characters choose a course of action that frustrates personal needs but satisfies the character's sense of honor. Wren was also not afraid of employing outdated superstitions—e.g., prenatal conditioning (*Snake and Sword*) or yogic telepathy (*Beggars' Horses*)—in order to underscore his basic interest in fiction: men in a state of struggle, in which the external conflict only works as a metaphor for the internal conflict. Wren's melodramatic (Dickensian?) use of coincidence also serves a purpose apparently unnoticed by his contemporaries: it represents an attachment to Oriental fatalism that is deeply rooted in his own Anglo-Saxon origins—the warrior in conflict with Wyrd, with only individual courage and the aid of kinsmen to stave off an inevitable death.

Beneath the melodrama is the humorous banter of English boys that changes little as the public-school heroes grow into men. In Wren, the inevitable and thankless manifest destiny of the British Empire to shape the remote corners of the world is often set forth in schoolboy exchanges that counterpoint a complex emotional and psychological framework reminiscent of Conrad, though without his allusive obscurity. His characters are usually joined in a metaphorical or actual fraternity, most commonly in a military unit in which family relationships are disguised (*Beau Geste*) or unknown (*Wages of Virtue*). This ironic, half-humorous approach shows events in multiple focus: the stiff-upper-lip narration often reveals, beneath the total belief in Great Britain, a tottering personal emotional security pivoting on a conflict of honor against survival. Though the values of British upbringing appear never to be questioned, circumstances ironically point to an emotionally empty or fateful universe that overwhelms the values of the individual. The bland assurances of organized religion ring hollow for Wren's characters. Only in death does the sense of purpose or significance of individual life seem vindicated.

The most successful of Wren's books was *Beau Geste*, which incorporates the most characteristic themes and values of Wren's world-view. This story of three brothers who join the Foreign Legion in order to preserve the family honor and fulfill their own boyhood military fantasies becomes an elaborately realized celebration of the theme of human brotherhood. The Gestes (the Anglo-French pun, as always in Wren, is intended) are orphans whose real family is unknown to us. Their rootlessness is paralleled by the international and anonymous make-up of the French Foreign Legion whose brotherhood the Gestes soon join. The existential overtones of the defense of Fort Zinderneuf are obvious today through hindsight, but it may be doubted that many of Wren's original readers caught the philosophical significance of the repeated ascents of the watchtower by men marked for death or the dead soldiers standing watch at the machicolations while Digby prepares Beau's "Viking's funeral." Death with honor is the ultimate seal of human commitments. These themes of the commitment to brotherhood and of disguised relationships recur in the two sequels to *Beau Geste: Beau Sabreur* and *Beau Ideal.* (*Good Gestes*, Wren's farewell to the characters that made him famous, is a set of excellent stories that add nothing to our knowledge of the Gestes and could have been about anybody. And an indirectly connected work, *Spanish Maine*, appeared in 1935.)

Other series characters appear in later works, though none so fully or satisfactorily drawn as the Gestes. Sinclair Noel Brody Dysart ("Sinbad") appears in *Action and Passion*, *Sinbad the Soldier*, and *The Fort in the Jungle*. Several figures involved in British intelligence in India recur in novels the most interesting of which is *Beggars' Horses*, an ironic *tour de force*. This novel examines the disastrous effects on a handful of skeptical inquirers into the alleged prophecies of a famous yogi when the angry yogi *grants* each of them their dearest wish. Another outstanding departure is the neglected masterpiece of psychological disintegration and sexual captivity, *Mammon of Righteousness*, in which Wren's insights into the effects of repression result in one of his most agonizing and involving stories.

In the face of all this sardonic irony, with characters moving under the shadow of immanent death, there is still in Wren's best work the clear affirmation that life has meaning, despite the efforts of a universe apparently antipathetic to human hopes and wishes. That meaning lies in commitment to our essential brotherhood and to the values and traditions of the British Empire.

—Thomas R. Tietze

WRIGHT, Francesca. See **ROBINS, Denise.**

WYLIE, Laura. See **MATTHEWS, Patricia.**

WYNDHAM, Esther. Pseudonym for Mary Lutyens. British. Born in London, 31 July 1908; daughter of the architect Edwin Lutyens; sister of the composer Elisabeth Lutyens. Educated at home; Queen's College, London, 1919–23. Married 1) Anthony Sewell in 1930, one daughter; 2) Joseph G. Links in 1945. Writer from 1930: columnist ("Mrs. Marriott"), *Woman's Weekly*, for a few months during World War II and for *Woman and Home* for several years after World War II. Fellow, Royal Society of Literature, 1976. Agent: Jane Turnbull, 13 Wendell Road, London W12 9RS. Address: 8 Elisabeth Close, London W9 1BN, England.

ROMANCE AND HISTORICAL PUBLICATIONS

Novels

Come Back, Elizabeth. London, Nimmo Hay and Mitchell, 1948.
Black Charles. London, Mills and Boon, 1952; Toronto, Harlequin, 1962.
Man of Steel. London, Mills and Boon, 1952.
Mistress of Merryweather. London, Mills and Boon, 1953.
Master of the Manor. London, Mills and Boon, 1953.
Above the Clouds. London, Mills and Boon, 1954; Toronto, Harlequin, 1964.
Tiger Hall. London, Mills and Boon, 1954; Toronto, Harlequin, 1965.
Once You Have Found Him. London, Mills and Boon, 1954; Toronto, Harlequin, 1964.
The House of Discontent. London, Mills and Boon, 1955; Toronto, Harlequin, 1966.

The Blue Rose. London, Mills and Boon, 1957; Toronto, Harlequin, 1967.

OTHER PUBLICATIONS as Mary Lutyens

Novels

Perchance to Dream. London, Murray, 1935.
Rose and Thorn. London, Murray, 1936.
Spider's Silk. London, Joseph, 1939.
Family Colouring. London, Joseph, 1940.
A Path of Gold. London, Joseph, 1941.
Together and Alone. London, Joseph, 1942.
So Near to Heaven. London, Joseph, 1943.
And Now There Is You. London, Hale, 1953.
Week-End at Hurtmore. London, Hutchinson, 1954.
The Lucian Legend. London, Hutchinson, 1955.
Meeting in Venice. London, Hutchinson, 1956.
Cleo. London, Joseph, 1973; New York, Stein and Day, 1974.

Short Stories

Forthcoming Marriages. London, Murray, and New York, Dutton, 1933.

Other

Julie and the Narrow Valley (for children). London, Guildford Press, 1947.
To Be Young: Some Chapters of Autobiography. London, Hart Davis, 1959.
Millais and the Ruskins. London, Murray, 1967; New York, Vanguard Press, 1968.
The Ruskins and the Grays. London, Murray, 1972.
Krishnamurti: The Years of Awakening. London, Murray, and New York, Farrar Straus, 1975.
The Lyttons in India: An Account of Lord Lytton's Viceroyalty 1876–1880. London, Murray, 1979.
Edwin Lutyens. London, Murray, 1980.
Krishnamurti: The Years of Fulfilment. London, Murray, and New York, Farrar Straus, 1983.
Krishnamurti: The Open Door. London, Murray, and New York, Farrar Straus, 1988.

Editor, *Lady Lytton's Court Diary*. London, Hart Davis, 1960.
Editor, *Effie in Venice*. London, Murray, 1965; as *Young Mrs. Ruskin in Venice: Her Picture of Society and Life with John Ruskin 1849–1852*, New York, Vanguard Press, 1966.
Editor, *Freedom from the Known*, by Krishnamurti. London, Gollancz, 1968; New York, Harper, 1969.
Editor, *The Only Revolution*, by Krishnamurti. London, Gollancz, and New York, Harper, 1970.
Editor, *The Penguin Krishnamurti Reader* [and second reader]. London, Penguin, 2 vols., 1970–73.
Editor, *The Urgency of Change*, by Krishnamurti. London, Gollancz, 1971.
Editor, *Krishnamurti's Notebook*. London, Gollancz, and New York, Harper, 1976.
Editor, *Rainy Days at Brig O'Turk: The Highland Sketch Book of John Everett Millais*, with Malcolm Warner. Westerham, Kent, Dalrymple, 1983.

*

Manuscript Collection: Mugar Memorial Library, Boston University.

Esther Wyndham comments:

I first started writing romantic serials in the late 1930's under the pseudonym of Esther Wyndham to supplement the inadequate income I was making from the novels I *wanted* to write. Since the fees were high and the stories were afterwards published as books, this work was very rewarding financially. The 10 serials I wrote came out either in *Woman's Weekly* or *Woman and Home*. I had a wonderful editor at the Amalgamated Press, Winifred Johnson, who had first approached me and who taught me this difficult craft which should never be underrated. For 10 instalments the hero and heroine had to meet constantly, yet could not be brought together until the last instalment, and each instalment had to end with an emotional cliff-hanger.

The hero and heroine had to conform to Miss Johnson's romantic formula. Lady Diana Spencer would never have qualified as a Johnson Heroine, except that she was a virgin and loved children, for she was far too beautiful, too rich, and had had too easy a life. The Prince of Wales might just have squeezed through as a Johnson hero, for in spite of being a prince he worked hard, had had rumoured involvements with other girls, and had not declared himself until the last instalment; however, there was a quality of mystery lacking in him.

One never penetrated the hero's mind until the end of the story, whereas every nuance of the heroine's feelings was revealed. In some stories she started by hating the hero because of his supposed arrogance until about instalment three when she began to feel drawn to him in spite of her better judgement. His behaviour was always a mystery to her. Disappointment and chagrin quickly followed those rare occasions when she felt he *cared*. There must invariably be another girl or older woman to make mischief out of jealousy, for it was only through misunderstandings on both sides that the couple could be kept apart for 70,000 words. A foreign setting was always a help.

The hero had to be brave, strong, rich, and frantically busy. It was best if he was self-made; if an aristocrat with inherited wealth he must be a model landlord who laboured to improve his estate for the sake of his tenants. The spirited heroine must not only have a wonderful way with children and old people but some previous tragedy or hardship in her life. And, of course, she had to work hard for her living. It was her character rather than her looks that attracted; she became beautiful only at rare moments, preferably when the hero was looking at her without her knowing it. Naturally, she became permanently beautiful at the end when irradiated with requited love.

Miss Johnson would give me guide-lines: "We want a heroine this time of about 28 who feels that life has passed her by," or, "Let's have a young girl in your next who has never been in love before." When writing in the war years it was easier to have a hero in a reserved occupation, hence Miss Johnson's plea to her authors after the war, "*Please*, no more farmers or doctors." When once the characters and story-line were more or less settled one wrote from the heart. To write down would have been fatal and I never felt any temptation to do so.

Miss J. only started publishing a serial when she had the complete story. This had not been the rule when she first entered the office as a junior. The great Ethel M. Dell had then been writing serials for the Amalgamated Press, and in a late instalment of one story it transpired to the horror of the editor that the unwed heroine was going to have a baby. She searched frantically through previous instalments to see when this could have happened and found that the heroine had come back one day from a walk with the hero with harebells in her hair. Thereafter the injunction ran through the office, "No more harebells."

I would write an instalment in three or four days and post it to Miss J. Next day her assistant would ring up either to say, "Go ahead," or "Miss Johnson would like to see you." Dread words,

for I knew that somehow I had gone off the rails and would have to re-write the instalment. There was no arguing with Miss J. because she was quite deaf. Since her magazines sold widely in Ireland there must not be the slightest hint of impropriety, let alone "harebells." In one story when my hero was in Washington with the heroine, his secretary, and I had allowed her to sleep in the sitting-room of his hotel suite because all the hotels were full (a situation helpful to romance), Miss J. sent me a telegram, for I had gone abroad between instalments: "Please make another effort to find Elizabeth a room of her own." And when I was writing my first story, almost every instalment of which had to be re-written, and I had made the hero say that he was feeling ill in order to get away from a party, she wrote indignantly, "Who can have respect for a man who feels ill at a party?" A great editor, but one who could hardly have functioned successfully today.

* * *

It was one of Mary Lutyens's stories in *Forthcoming Marriages* that led to her being invited by Winifred Johnson to contribute romantic serials to the Amalgamated Press's women's papers. The first half of this story ("Mr. Raymond Skedley and Miss Katherine N. Robinson") conveyed the current of the heroine's thoughts on her wedding morning; the second half was concerned with emotional incidents leading up to and surrounding the ceremony later that day. Without perhaps realizing it, Lutyens had already arrived at a satisfying and atmospheric balance of inner and outer mood that was exactly appropriate to the romantic story, and, as "Esther Wyndham," in her subsequent serial/novels she explored and exploited this to the full.

In the tradition of the genre, her heroines suffer the usual tremulous feelings of inadequacy that are sparked off by the challenge of relating to handsome but arrogant and enigmatic heroes. Wyndham's leading ladies, however, are spirited, capable of decisive action, and, occasionally, of going against the tide of public opinion. (Generally they are working girls who take their careers quite seriously—an advanced shorthand-typist in *Come Back, Elizabeth*, a dedicated bookseller's assistant in *Above the Clouds*, an antique dealer in *Black Charles*.)

Even when overwhelmed by masculine magnetism and the intensity of their own sexual/romantic feelings, these heroines resolutely cling to a few robust strands of inner resource and intellectual independence. Their honest and slightly rueful self-awareness makes them interesting and extremely sympathetic to read about, and marks them as forerunners of the intelligent and highly individualised heroines who were two or three decades later to be at the centre of thriller romances by Mary Stewart in England, and Barbara Michaels in the USA.

The stories are tightly structured, and punctuated with humorous incident to counterbalance strong suspense. There is plenty of the latter, because the novels were originally written as serials with cliff hanger endings to each episode.

The author's vivid feeling for place gives the books a special intensity, but, though adept at evoking exotic foreign and romantic settings (Venice, for example, in *Above the Clouds*), Wyndham is at her best with the traditional English country house background (as in *Black Charles*). This is, expectedly, not gruesomely Gothic but graciously Lutyens-esque!

—Mary Cadogan

———

WYNNE, May. Pseudonym for Mabel Winifred Knowles; also wrote as Lester Lurgan. British. Born in Streatham, London, in January 1875. Educated at home. Worked in an East End Church of England mission. *Died 29 November 1949.*

ROMANCE AND HISTORICAL PUBLICATIONS

Novels

For Faith and Navarre. London, Long, 1904.
Ronald Lindsay. London, Long, 1904.
A King's Tragedy. London, Digby Long, 1905.
The Temptation of Philip Carr. London, Sonnenschein, 1905.
Maid of Brittany. London, Greening, 1906.
The Goal. London, Digby Long, 1907.
When Terror Ruled. London, Greening, 1907.
Henry of Navarre: A Romance of August, 1572 (as Mabel W. Knowles). New York, Putnam, 1908; as May Wynne, London, Greening, 1909.
Let Erin Remember. London, Greening, 1908.
The Tailor of Vitré. London, Gay and Hancock, 1908.
For Church and Chieftain. London, Mills and Boon, 1909.
For Charles the Rover. London, Greening, 1909; New York, Fenno, 1910.
The Gipsy Count. New York, McBride, 1909.
A Blot on the Scutcheon. London, Mills and Boon, 1910; New York, Fenno, 1912.
A King's Masquerade. London, Greening, 1910.
Mistress Cynthia. London, Greening, 1910.
The Gallant Graham. London, Greening, 1911.
Honour's Fetters. London, Stanley Paul, 1911.
The Master Wit. London, Greening, 1911.
The Claim That Won. London, Everett, 1912.
Hey for Cavaliers! London, Greening, 1912.
The Red Fleur-de-Lys. London, Stanley Paul, 1912.
The Brave Brigands. London, Stanley Paul, 1913.
The Destiny of Claude. London, Stanley Paul, 1913.
The Secret of the Zenana. London, Greening, 1913.
A Run for His Money. London, Aldine, 1913.
The Curse of Gold. London, Aldine, 1914.
Goring's Girl. London, Mascot, 1914.
The Hero of Urbino. London, Stanley Paul, 1914.
The Silent Captain. London, Stanley Paul, 1914.
The Regent's Gift. London, Chapman and Hall, 1915.
Foes of Freedom. London, Chapman and Hall, 1916.
Marcel of the "Zephyrs." London, Jarrolds, 1916.
The Gipsy King. London, Chapman and Hall, 1917.
The Lyons Mail. London, Jarrolds, 1917.
Penance. London, Mascot, 1917.
A Spy for Napoleon. London, Jarrolds, 1917.
The Taint of Tragedy. London, Mascot, 1917.
The "Veiled Lady," with Draycot M. Dell. London, Jarrolds, 1918.
The King of a Day. London, Jarrolds, 1918.
Queen Jennie. London, Chapman and Hall, 1918.
The Red Whirlwind, with Draycot M. Dell. London, Jarrolds, 1919.
Robin the Prodigal. London, Jarrolds, 1919.
Love Finds a Way. London, Greening, 1920.
A Prince of Intrigue: A Romance of Mazeppa. London, Jarrolds, 1920.
A Gallant of Spain. London, Stanley Paul, 1920.
Janie's Great Mistake. London, Odhams Press, 1920.
The Spendthrift Duke. London, Holden and Hardingham, 1920.
The Ambitions of Jill. London, Long, 1920.
Mog Megone. London, Jarrolds, 1921.
My Lady's Honour. London, Lloyds, 1921.

The Red Rose of Lancaster. London, Holden and Hardingham, 1921.
A Trap for Navarre. London, Holden, 1922.
A King in the Lists. London, Stanley Paul, 1922.
The Witch-Finder. London, Jarrolds, 1923.
Jill the Hostage. London, Pearson, 1925.
Rachel Lee. London, Leng, 1925.
Theodore. London, Rivers, 1926.
Gwennola. London, Rivers, 1926.
The Fires of Youth. London, Rivers, 1927.
Plotted in Darkness. London, Stanley Paul, 1927.
King Mandrin's Challenge. London, Stanley Paul, 1927.
A Royal Traitor. London, Stanley Paul, 1927.
Love's Penalty. London, Stanley Paul, 1927.
The Terror of the Moor. London, Rivers, 1928.
Gipsy-Spelled. London, Rivers, 1929.
Red Fruit. London, Rivers, 1929.
Hamlet: A Romance from Shakespeare's Play. London, Rivers, 1930.
The Girl Upstairs. London, Thomson, 1932.
The Unseen Witness. London, Leng, 1932.
Stella Maris. London, Leng, 1932.
The Tempter's Power. London, Leng, 1932.
Tangled Fates. London, Mellifont Press, 1935.
Flower o' the Moor. London, Houghton and Scott-Snell, 1935.
The Choice of Mavis. London, Mellifont Press, 1935.
Temptation. London, Mellifont Press, 1937.
Whither? London, Heath Cranton, 1938.
Love Dismayed. London, Mellifont Press, 1942.
Echoed from the Past. London, Mellifont Press, 1944.
The Pursuing Shadow. London, Mellifont Press, 1944.
The Unsuspected Witness. London, Mellifont Press, 1945.
The Secret of the Caves. London, Mellifont Press, 1945.

Novels as Lester Lurgan

Bohemian Blood. London, Greening, 1910.
The Mill-Owner. London, Greening, 1910.
The League of the Triangle. London, Greening, 1911.
A Message from Mars. London, Greening, 1912.
The Ban. London, Stanley Paul, 1912.
The Wrestler on the Shore. London, Everett, 1913.

OTHER PUBLICATIONS

Fiction (for children)

Mollie's Adventures. London, Russell, 1903.
Jimmy: The Tales of a Little Black Bear. London, Partridge, 1910.
Phil's Cousins. London, Blackie, 1911.
Crackers: The Tale of a Mischievous Monkey. London, Partridge, 1911.
The Story of Heather. London, Nelson, 1912; New York, Sully, 1913.
Tony's Chums. London, Blackie, 1914.
Murray Finds a Chum. London, Stanley Paul, 1914.
When Auntie Lil Took Charge. London, Blackie, 1915.
An English Girl in Serbia. London, Collins, 1916.
Three's Company. London, Blackie, 1917.
Stranded in Belgium. London, Blackie, 1918.
A Cousin from Canada. London, Blackie, 1918.
The Honour of the School. London, Nisbet, 1918.

Dick. London, Religious Tract Society, 1919.

Phyllis in France. London, Blackie, 1919. The Little Girl Beautiful. London, Religious Tract Society, 1919.

Nan and Ken. London, Nelson, 1919.

Nipper & Co. London, Stanley Paul, 1919.

Scouts for Serbia. London, Nelson, 1919.

Comrades from Canada. London, Blackie, 1919.

The Adventures of Dolly Dingle: A Fairy Story. London, Jarrolds, 1920.

Adventures of Two. London, Blackie, 1920.

The Heroine of Chelton School. London, Stanley Paul, 1920.

The Girls of Beechcroft School. London, Religious Tract Society, 1920.

Roseleen at School. London, Cassell, 1920.

Three Bears and Gwen. London, Blackie, 1920.

Little Ladyship. London, Religious Tract Society, 1921.

Lost in the Jungle. London, Stanley Paul, 1921.

Mervyn, Jock, or Joe. London, Blackie, 1921.

Peggy's First Term. London, Ward Lock, 1922.

Angela Goes to School. London, Jarrolds, 1922; Cleveland, World, 1929.

The Girls of the Veldt Farm. London, Pearson, 1922.

The Red Boy's Gratitude. Exeter, Wheaton, 1922.

Christmas at Holford. London, Blackie, 1922.

Two Girls in the Wild. London, Blackie, 1923; abridged edition, as *Sisters Out West*, 1930.

The Best of Chums. London, Ward Lock, 1923.

A Heather Holiday. London, Blackie, 1923; as *Wendy's Adventure in Scotland*, 1933; as *An Adventurous Holiday* (reader), 1933.

Blundering Bettina. London, Religious Tract Society, 1924.

The Girl Who Played the Game. London, Ward Lock, 1924.

Bertie, Bobby, and Belle. London, Blackie, 1924.

The Girls of Clanways Farm. London, Cassell, 1924.

Kits at Clynton Court School. London, Warne, 1924.

The Sunshine Children. London, Nelson, 1924.

Three and One Over. London, Cassell, 1924.

A Rebel at School. London, Jarrolds, 1924.

Two and a Chum. London, Pearson, 1924.

Hootie Toots of Hollow Tree. Philadelphia, Altemus, 1925.

The Girls of Old Grange School. London, Ward Lock, 1925.

Over the Hills and Far Away. London, Religious Tract Society, 1925.

Dare-All Jack and the Cousins. London, Religious Tract Society, 1925.

Hazel Asks Why. London, Ward Lock, 1926.

Carol of Hollydene School. London, Sampson Low, 1926.

The Secret of Carrock School. London, Jarrolds, 1926.

Diccon the Impossible. London, Religious Tract Society, 1926.

The Girl over the Wall. London, Religious Tract Society, 1926.

Jean Plays Her Part. London, Religious Tract Society, 1926.

Dinah's Secret. London, Religious Tract Society, 1927.

Jean of the Lumber Camp. London, Ward Lock, 1927.

Robin Hood to the Rescue. Exeter, Wheaton, 1927.

Terry the Black Sheep. London, Pearson, 1928.

The Girls of Mackland Court. London, Ward Lock, 1928.

Little Sally Mandy's Christmas Present. Philadelphia, Altemus, 1929.

The House of Whispers. London, Ward Lock, 1929.

The Guide's Honour. London, Warne, 1929.

A Term to Remember. London, Aldine, 1930.

Two Girls in the Hawk's Den. London, Pearson, 1930.

Bobbety the Brownie. London, Warne, 1930.

The Masked Rider. Chicago, Laidlaw, 1931.

Patient Pat Joins the Circus. Philadelphia, Altemus, 1931.

Peter Rabbit and the Big Black Crows. Philadelphia, Altemus, 1931.

Juliet of the Mill. London, Ward Lock, 1931.

Girls of the Pansy Patrol. London, Aldine, 1931.

Patsy from the Wilds. London, Warne, 1931.

Belle and Her Dragons. London, Jarrolds, 1931.

The Secret of Marigold Marnell. London, Religious Tract Society, 1931.

The Old Brigade. London, Religious Tract Society, 1932.

Who Was Wendy? London, Newnes, 1932.

The Heart of Glenayrt. London, Nelson, 1932.

The School Mystery. London, Readers' Library, 1933.

The Camping of the Marigolds. London, Marshall Morgan and Scott, 1933.

The Greater Covenant. London, Marshall Morgan and Scott, 1933.

Pixie's Mysterious Mission. London, Newnes, 1933.

Enter Jenny Wren. London, Ward Lock, 1933.

Comrades to Robin Hood. London, Religious Tract Society, 1934.

Malys Rockell. London, Ward Lock, 1934.

The Smugglers of Penreen. London, Religious Tract Society, 1934.

The Mysterious Island. London, Mellifont Press, 1935.

Their Girl Chum. London, Religious Tract Society, 1935.

Under Cap'n Drake. London, Religious Tract Society, 1935.

Up to Val. London, Newnes, 1935.

"Peter," The New Girl. London, Queensway Press, 1936.

The Daring of Star. London, Religious Tract Society, 1936.

Bunny and the Aunt. London, Religious Tract Society, 1936.

The Haunted Ranch. London, Dean, 1936.

Thirteen for Luck. London, Ward Lock, 1936.

Vivette on Trial. London, Queensway Press, 1936.

The Secret of Brick House. London, Ward Lock, 1937.

Two Maids of Rosemarkie. London, Epworth Press, 1937.

The Luck of Penrayne. London, Religious Tract Society, 1937.

Audrey on Approval. London, Ward Lock, 1937.

The Girl Sandy. London, Ward Lock, 1938.

The Lend-a-Hand Holiday. London, Epworth Press, 1938.

Heather the Second. London, Nelson, 1938.

The Term of Many Adventures. London, Nelson, 1939.

The Unexpected Adventure. London, Ward Lock, 1939.

The Coming of Verity. London, Ward Lock, 1940.

Sadie Comes to School. London, Epworth Press, 1942; as *Sally Comes to School*, London, Ward Lock, 1949.

Little Brown Tala. London, Mellifont Press, 1944.

Brown Tala Finds Little Tulsi. London, Mellifont Press, 1945.

Little Brown Tala Stories. London, Harrap, 1947.

Patch the Piebald. Croydon, Surrey, Blue Book, 1947.

Playing the Game. Croydon, Surrey, Blue Book, 1947.

Snow Fairies. London, Mellifont Press, 1947.

Ginger Ellen. London, Nelson, 1947.

The Great Adventure. London, Ward Lock, 1948.

The Furry Fairies. London, Mellifont Press, 1949.

Merion Plays the Game. London, Readers' Library, 1951.

Secrets of the Rockies. London, Ward Lock, 1954.

Other

Life's Object; or, Some Thoughts for Young Girls. London, Nisbet, 1899.

In the Shadows; or, Thoughts for Mourners. London, Marshall, 1900.

Sympathy. London, Skeffington, 1901.

The Life and Reign of Victoria the Good. London, Stanley Paul, 1913.

The Seven Champions of Christendom: A Legendary Chronicle (for children). London, Jarrolds, 1919.

* * *

May Wynne infused romantic elements into the children's stories at which she excelled in the form of exotic locations and charismatic personalities. Her love stories for adults also exploit glamorously foreign settings and colourful people like gipsies or intrepid adventurer-explorers. *The Gipsy King* (1917) includes characters of both these types. Bampfylde Carew, who starts off as something of a wastrel, leaves his vicarage home, attracted by "the merry fiddling of the gipsies . . . and the crackling of their wood fires," sounds that, apparently, "echo louder, more enticing, more alluring than the sonorous music of his father's preaching. . . . " Wynne thus sets the scene for a much-used theme in her romances: the conflict between duty, which she sees as synonymous with the acceptance of orthodox Christianity, and the attractions of the "free" and socially untrammelled life. Generally she includes the finding of true love and its attendant pattern of committal to married domesticity as part and parcel of the hero or heroine's redemptive adoption of a religious faith. However, Bampfylde Carew has a long way to go (roaming with the gipsies, having lusty adventures on the high seas and in the Indian territories of America) before he is eventually brought back to the path of Christian virtue by loyal and loving Letty Gray, from his own village.

The Fires of Youth (1927) is concerned with similar issues, and particularly with the return to rustic roots (also equatable in Wynne's stories with the romantic and religious experience). For Tom Tarrock, illusions of freedom take the shape of making money in a big way—but like Bampfylde in *The Gipsy King*, and many other of this author's heroes, he has an innocent village girl (in this case Jessamy Windell, who becomes a Church Army Sister), waiting patiently to feel—eventually—his passionate but purified kiss on her "firm, sweet lips."

With her insistent linking of romantic and domestic love to Christian conversion, Wynne is harking back to the mood of many Victorian "tales of home life." Her love stories, however, have less of the retributive tone of their 19th-century forerunners, though they never achieve the liveliness of her children's stories.

—Mary Cadogan

YARBRO, Chelsea Quinn. Also writes as Terry Nelson Bonner; Vanessa Pryor. American. Born in Berkeley, California, 15 September 1942. Attended San Francisco State College, 1960–63. Married Donald P. Simpson in 1969 (divorced 1982). Theatre manager and playwright, Mirthmakers Children's Theatre, San Francisco, 1961–64; children's counsellor, 1963; cartographer, C. E. Erickson and Associates, Oakland, California, 1963–70; composer; card and palm reader, 1974–78. Secretary, Science Fiction Writers of America, 1970–72; president, Horror Writers of America, 1988–89. Lives in Berkeley. Agent: Ellen Levine Literary Agency, 432 Park Avenue South, Suite 1205, New York, New York 10016, U.S.A.

ROMANCE AND HISTORICAL PUBLICATIONS

Novels (series: Charlie Moon; Olivia; Count Ragoczy Saint-Germain)

Ogilvie, Tallant, and Moon. New York, Putnam, 1976.

Hôtel Transylvania: A Novel of Forbidden Love (Saint-Germain). New York, St. Martin's Press, 1978; London, New English Library, 1981.
Music When Sweet Voices Die (Moon). New York, Putnam, 1979.
The Palace (Saint-Germain). New York, St. Martin's Press, 1979; London, New English Library, 1981.
Blood Games (Saint-Germain). New York, St. Martin's Press, 1980.
Ariosto. New York, Pocket Books, 1980.
Path of the Eclipse (Saint-Germain). New York, St. Martin's Press, 1981.
Tempting Fate (Saint-Germain). New York, St. Martin's Press, 1982.
A Taste of Wine (as Vanessa Pryor). New York, Pocket Books, 1982.
The Godforsaken. New York, Warner, 1983.
The Making of Australia 5: The Outback (as Terry Nelson Bonner). New York, Dell, 1983.
A Mortal Glamour. New York, Bantam, 1985.
To the High Redoubt. New York, Warner, 1985.
A Flame in Byzantium (Olivia). New York, Tor, 1987.
Crusader's Torch (Olivia). New York, Tor, 1988.
Candles for D'Artagnan (Olivia). New York, Tor, 1989.

Short Stories

Cautionary Tales. New York, Doubleday, 1978; expanded edition, New York, Warner, and London, Sidgwick and Jackson, 1980.
On Saint Hubert's Thing. New Castle, Virginia, Cheap Street, 1982.
The Saint-Germain Chronicles. New York, Pocket Books, 1983.
Signs and Portents. Santa Cruz, California, Dream Press, 1984.

OTHER PUBLICATIONS

Novels

Time of the Fourth Horseman. New York, Doubleday, 1976; London, Sidgwick and Jackson, 1980.
False Dawn. New York, Doubleday, 1978; London, Sidgwick and Jackson, 1979.
Dead and Buried (novelization of screenplay). New York, Warner, and London, Star, 1980.
Sins of Omission. New York, New American Library, 1980.
Hyacinths. New York, Doubleday, 1983.
Nomads (novelization of screenplay). New York, Bantam, 1984.
A Baroque Fable. New York, Berkley, 1986.
Firecode. New York, Popular Library, 1987.
Taji's Syndrome. New York, Popular Library, 1988.
Beastnights. New York, Popular Library, 1989.
The Law in Charity. New York, Doubleday, 1989.

Other

Messages from Michael on the Nature of the Evolution of the Human Soul. Chicago, Playboy Press, 1979.
Locadio's Apprentice (for children). New York, Harper, 1984.
Four Horses for Tishtry (for children). New York, Harper, 1985.
Floating Illusions (for children). New York, Harper, 1986.
More Messages from Michael. New York, Berkley, 1986.
Michael's People. New York, Berkley, 1988.

Editor, with Thomas N. Scortia, *Two Views of Wonder*. New York, Ballantine, 1973.

*   *   *

Known to science fiction and fantasy readers, Chelsea Quinn Yarbro attracted a new audience with the 1978 publication of *Hôtel Transylvania*. Here she introduced gothic and historical romance readers to the vampire Count Ragoczy Saint-Germain. Compassionate, even humane, this immortal searches throughout the world for love and understanding.

Yarbro is a master at interweaving history and fiction in novels of historical horror with the horror coming not from the supernatural but from actual events in our past. The Saint-Germain series exemplifies this. The setting for *Hôtel Transylvania* is mid-18th-century Paris, where the exquisite Madelaine De Montalia becomes the victim of a satanic cult. In *The Palace* the incredibly beautiful Demitrice, former mistress of Lorenzo the Magnificent, is arrested and tortured by the followers of Savonarola. Olivia, a character whose letters of love and friendship appear in *The Palace* and *Path of the Eclipse*, meets Saint-Germain for the first time in *Blood Games*, a tale of debauchery set in the Rome of Nero. The last of the series, *The Saint-Germain Chronicles*, contains a collection of short stories as well as an essay on the historical Count Saint-Germain, a mysterious man who hobnobbed with 18th-century nobles and kings. Although he led a very public life, he remained an enigma even to those who thought they knew him best. He delighted in throwing out tantalizing clues about his background, yet, to this day little about him has been discovered.

In more recent works Olivia, herself now a vampire, has held center stage as the heroine of *A Flame in Byzantium*, a novel set at a time when the center of civilization was shifting from Rome to Constantinople, and in *Crusader's Torch* which finds her in 12th-century Tyre trying to return to her beloved Rome. In each story Olivia's despair and loneliness are no less heartfelt than Saint-Germain's and are actually compounded by the fact that as a woman her life and thus her options are more severely restricted.

The plight of women is a theme often found in Yarbro's work. Perhaps the best example of this can be found in her more mainstream historical novel, *A Mortal Glamour*. Here a group of nuns living in the 14th century, a time when Avignon fought Rome for the papacy, is held hostage by a malevolent force that seems to have penetrated the convent walls. In the end the women are as much victimized by the male dominated church as by any evil, real or imagined.

Scenes of violence are graphically depicted in Yarbro's novels while scenes of love have a more elusive, highly erotic quality. A practiced writer and storyteller, Yarbro immerses her readers in historical times, displaying a rhythmic, flowing style to conjure up the mood of the period. Her work will appeal to those who enjoy either romance or historical fiction.

—Patricia Altner

YATES, Dornford. Pseudonym for Cecil William Mercer. British. Born in Upper Walmer, Kent, 7 August 1885. Educated at St. Clare, Walmer, 1894–99; Harrow School, 1899–1904; University College, Oxford (President, Dramatic Society, 1907), B.A. in jurisprudence 1907; Inner Temple, London: called to the Bar 1909. Served in the 3rd County of London Yeomanry in Egypt and Salonika during World War I: Captain; with the East Africa Command, 1942–43, then in Southern Rhodesia forces: Major. Married 1) Bettine Stokes Edwards in 1919 (marriage dissolved 1933), one son; 2) Elizabeth Lucy Bowie in 1934. Practicing solicitor from 1909: worked on the Crippen case, 1910; lived in France after World War I, and in Southern Rhodesia after World War II. *Died 5 March 1960.*

ROMANCE AND HISTORICAL PUBLICATIONS

Novels

Anthony Lyveden. London, Ward Lock, 1921.
Valerie French. London, Ward Lock, 1923.
The Stolen March. London, Ward Lock, 1926; New York, Minton Balch, 1933.
Blind Corner. London, Hodder and Stoughton, and New York, Minton Balch, 1927.
Perishable Goods. London, Hodder and Stoughton, and New York, Minton Balch, 1928.
Blood Royal. London, Hodder and Stoughton, 1929; New York, Minton Balch, 1930.
Summer Fruit. New York, Minton Balch, 1929.
Fire Below. London, Hodder and Stoughton, 1930; as *By Royal Command*, New York, Minton Balch, 1931.
Adele & Co. New York, Minton Balch, 1931; London, Hodder and Stoughton, 1932.
Safe Custody. London, Hodder and Stoughton, and New York, Minton Balch, 1932.
Storm Music. London, Hodder and Stoughton, and New York, Minton Balch, 1934.
She Fell among Thieves. London, Hodder and Stoughton, and New York, Minton Balch, 1935.
She Painted Her Face. London, Ward Lock, and New York, Putnam, 1937.
This Publican. London, Ward Lock, 1938; as *The Devil in Satin*, New York, Doubleday, 1938.
Gale Warning. London, Ward Lock, 1939; New York, Putnam, 1940.
Shoal Water. London, Ward Lock, 1940; New York, Putnam, 1941.
An Eye for a Tooth. London, Ward Lock, 1943; New York, Putnam, 1944.
The House That Berry Built. London, Ward Lock, and New York, Putnam, 1945.
Red in the Morning. London, Ward Lock, 1946; as *Were Death Denied*, New York, Putnam, 1946.
Cost Price. London, Ward Lock, 1949; as *The Laughing Bacchante*, New York, Putnam, 1949.
Lower Than Vermin. London, Ward Lock, 1950.
Ne'er-Do-Well. London, Ward Lock, 1954.
Wife Apparent. London, Ward Lock, 1956.

Short Stories (series: Berry)

The Brother of Daphne. London, Ward Lock, 1914.
The Courts of Idleness. London, Ward Lock, 1920.
Berry and Co. London, Ward Lock, 1921; New York, Minton Balch, 1928.
Jonah and Co. London, Ward Lock, 1922; New York, Minton Balch, 1927.
And Five Were Foolish. London, Ward Lock, 1924.
As Other Men Are. London, Ward Lock, 1925.
Maiden Stakes. London, Ward Lock, 1929.
And Berry Came Too. London, Ward Lock, and New York, Minton Balch, 1936.

Period Stuff. London, Ward Lock, 1942.
The Berry Scene. London, Ward Lock, and New York, Minton Balch, 1947.

OTHER PUBLICATIONS

Play

Eastward Ho!, with Oscar Asche, music by Grace Torrens and John Ansell (produced London, 1919).

Other

As Berry and I Were Saying. London, Ward Lock, 1952.
B-Berry and I Look Back. London, Ward Lock, 1958.

*

Critical Study: *Dornford Yates: A Biography* by A. J. Smithers, London, Hodder and Stoughton, 1982.

*   *   *

Dornford Yates reflected the modes and manners of certain sections of English society with an accuracy derived from personal acquaintance. With little fear of contradiction, one may describe him as a romantic. His books can certainly be placed in that category, but it is necessary to use the dictionary definition of the term. With Yates a love affair is not the be-all and end-all of romance, and his books encompass chivalry, imagination, fantasy, and passion in its widest sense. He is in the romantic tradition of John Buchan, Anthony Hope, Conan Doyle and "Sapper."

Yates is a good example of a writer whose books mirror his own experience and social scene, if only as a starting point from which he develops plots and characters somewhat larger than life. His education at Harrow and Oxford, his profession as a barrister, his war service as an officer, his extensive travelling and love of elegant cars, his residence in the South of France and the colonies are all reflected in the sort of fiction he wrote and the characters he created. His books were once described by *The Times* as affording the maximum of entertainment with the minimum of likelihood, and they found in their heyday countless readers who were clearly eager to lose themselves in his world, perhaps attracted by the snob appeal of the Yates milieu and certainly enthralled by what Milton Crane called "the verve and excitement by which the puppets are manipulated."

His early stories, collected in such volumes as *The Brother of Daphne*, *The Courts of Idleness*, and *Berry and Co.*, secured for Yates a reputation as an accomplished spinner of light-hearted yarns. His fictional family, the Pleydells and the Mansels, became over many years a very real institution to the reading public. Although their social position and their houses, White Ladies and Gracedieu, were beyond the personal experience of the average reader, even in those more affluent years of the British Empire, they must have held for many the fascination and curiosity value of their present-day equivalents in mass-media soap opera. Yates gave his faithful readers what they clearly enjoyed; not always to be taken too seriously, he projected in his stories a certain boyishness and irresponsibility together with an element of Victorian romance. Although he wrote exclusively of the leisured classes, he did so with authority; the world of White Ladies had social stability as its essence, of which Yates heartily approved and of which he was part. Indeed, the stories were an expression of Yates himself in the person of the witty and amorous Boy Pleydell.

Such social stability can be threatened, however, and this is where Yates can be related to such writers as Buchan and "Sapper," and contributed his influence to a whole school of gentlemen-adventurers which endured well into the second half of the 20th century. Leslie Charteris owes something to Yates, and it would not be fanciful to suggest that even the more explicit and brutal Ian Fleming carried on the Yates tradition. The basic thesis, as seen in Yates and his contemporaries and developed by later writers, is that any threat to the British way of life (and particularly to the security of the upper classes) must be resisted with vigour until the status quo is restored. Where other writers tended to see violence as the only way to meet villainy and aggression, Yates had the more British approach and depicted violence less gratuitously.

From the cloistered atmosphere of the gentlemen's clubs, Yates heroes set forth to engage the enemy. A spin-off from the Berry Pleydell books, cousin Jonah Mansel is the principal heroic figure in such works as *Blind Corner*, *She Fell among Thieves*, *An Eye for a Tooth*, and *Cost Price*. A much-travelled bachelor, with distinguished service in World War I (including counter-espionage), Jonah spends the inter-war years as a freelance crime-fighter and returns to the Secret Service in 1939. His partner in adventure, William Chandos, is also the narrator of their exploits in what are called the "Chandos Books" in Yates's bibliography, which distinguishes them, from the family-related but lighter Berry books. Jonah and Chandos complement each other, with qualities and abilities that make for a first-class team equipped for adventure and romance. Well-heeled Jonah, with combat skills and friends in high places, is the manly hero with the stiff upper lip, whereas Chandos is equally tough in a tight corner but supplies most of the romantic interest with the devastatingly beautiful women who populate their escapades. They take readers into a world of unreality, where the economic need to earn one's daily bread is absent and there is unlimited time to indulge in the pursuit of those described by someone (was it Charteris?) as the ungodly.

Yates was, above all, a highly competent storyteller. In spite of his often quaint use of language, the readability of his books is not in question. His motivation has sometimes been criticised—was he fascist in his depiction of the lower orders, and in his use and treatment of obviously Jewish villains, or was he merely in keeping with the popular literature of his time? He was, of course, a great lover of England and a protector of the traditions of his class, and in many respects his books are a yearning for the England of yesteryear. Although time has not stood still, his books can be read and enjoyed today because they can be placed in the context of their time and Yates's own world. His snob appeal has disintegrated, but perhaps we still need a dream world, especially when presented to us with what Cyril Connolly described in 1935 as "a wit that is ageless united to a courtesy that is extinct."

—Melvyn Barnes

YERBY, Frank (Garvin). American. Born in Augusta, Georgia, 5 September 1916. Educated at Paine College, Augusta, A.B. 1937; Fisk University, Nashville, Tennessee, M.A. 1938; University of Chicago, 1939. Married 1) Flora Helen Claire Williams in 1941 (divorced), two sons and two daughters; 2) Blanca Calle Pérez in 1956. Instructor, Florida Agricultural and Mechanical College, Tallahassee, 1938–39, and Southern University and A. and M. College, Baton Rouge, Louisiana, 1939–41; laboratory technician, Ford Motor Company, Dearborn, Michigan, 1941–44; Magnaflux inspector, Ranger (Fairchild) Aircraft, Jamaica, New York, 1944–45; full-time writer from 1945; settled in Madrid, 1954. Recipient: O. Henry award, 1944. D.Litt.: Fisk University, 1976. Agent: Owen Laster, William Morris Agency, 1350 Avenue of the Americas, New York, New York 10019, U.S.A. Address: Edificio Torres Blancas, Apartamento 710, Avenida de America 37, 28002 Madrid, Spain.

ROMANCE AND HISTORICAL PUBLICATIONS

Novels

The Foxes of Harrow. New York, Dial Press, 1946; London, Heinemann, 1947.

The Vixens. New York, Dial Press, 1947; London, Heinemann, 1948.

The Golden Hawk. New York, Dial Press, 1948; London, Heinemann, 1949.

Pride's Castle. New York, Dial Press, 1949; London, Heinemann, 1950.

Floodtide. New York, Dial Press, 1950; London, Heinemann, 1951.

A Woman Called Fancy. New York, Dial Press, 1951; London, Heinemann, 1952.

The Saracen Blade. New York, Dial Press, 1952; London, Heinemann, 1953.

The Devil's Laughter. New York, Dial Press, 1953; London, Heinemann, 1954.

Benton's Row. New York, Dial Press, 1954; London, Heinemann, 1955.

Bride of Liberty. New York, Dial Press, 1954; London, Heinemann, 1955.

The Treasure of Pleasant Valley. New York, Dial Press, 1955; London, Heinemann, 1956.

Captain Rebel. New York, Dial Press, 1956; London, Heinemann, 1957.

Fairoaks. New York, Dial Press, 1957; London, Heinemann, 1958.

The Serpent and the Staff. New York, Dial Press, 1958; London, Heinemann, 1959.

Jarrett's Jade. New York, Dial Press, 1959; London, Heinemann, 1960.

Gillian. New York, Dial Press, 1960; London, Heinemann, 1961.

The Garfield Honor. New York, Dial Press, 1961; London, Heinemann, 1962.

Griffin's Way. New York, Dial Press, 1962; London, Heinemann, 1963.

The Old Gods Laugh: A Modern Romance. New York, Dial Press, and London, Heinemann, 1964.

An Odor of Sanctity. New York, Dial Press, 1965; London, Heinemann, 1966.

Goat Song: A Novel of Ancient Greece. New York, Dial Press, 1967; London, Heinemann, 1968.

Judas, My Brother: The Story of the Thirteenth Disciple. New York, Dial Press, and London, Heinemann, 1969.

Speak Now. New York, Dial Press, 1969; London, Heinemann, 1970.

The Dahomean. New York, Dial Press, 1971; as *The Man from Dahomey*, London, Heinemann, 1971.

The Girl from Storyville: A Victorian Novel. New York, Dial Press, and London, Heinemann, 1972.

The Voyage Unplanned. New York, Dial Press, and London, Heinemann, 1974.

Tobias and the Angel. New York, Dial Press, and London, Heinemann, 1975.

A Rose for Ana Maria. New York, Dial Press, and London, Heinemann, 1976.

Hail the Conquering Hero. New York, Dial Press, 1977; London, Heinemann, 1978.

A Darkness at Ingraham's Crest. New York, Dial Press, 1979; London, Granada, 1981.

Western: A Saga of the Great Plains. New York, Dial Press, 1982; London, Granada, 1983.

Devilseed. New York, Doubleday, and London, Granada, 1984.

McKenzie's Hundred. New York, Doubleday, 1985; London, Grafton, 1986.

*

Manuscript Collection: Mugar Memorial Library, Boston University.

Critical Studies: *Behind the Magnolia Mask: Frank Yerby as Critic of the South* by William Werdna Hill, Jr., unpublished thesis, Auburn University, Alabama, 1968; "The Guilt of the Victim: Racial Themes in Some Frank Yerby Novels" by Jack B. Moore, in *Journal of Popular Culture* (Bowling Green, Ohio), Spring 1975; *Anti-Heroic Perspectives in the Life and Works of Frank Yerby* by James Lee Hill, unpublished thesis, University of Iowa, 1976.

Frank Yerby comments:

It seemed a rather pleasant way to make a living. And for a while, it *was*. Now I wish I'd taken up plumbing!

*   *   *

In writing more than 30 novels, most of which are historical, Frank Yerby has become the most popularly successful black novelist yet to appear in the United States. His novels have made him rich but have brought him little critical acclaim; rather, his works sell in the millions while being dismissed by most critics as melodramatic potboilers aimed solely at the cash register. He has also been consistently attacked for betraying his race by not continuing to write the social protest fiction, such as the often anthologized "Health Card," with which he began his career. Over the years, in facing this charge, Yerby has repeatedly used some variation of a single defence: "The novelist hasn't any right to inflict on the public his private ideas on politics, religion or race." This attitude is directly related to his view of the novel itself: "a novel is not life, but a deliberate distortion of it, solely designed to give pleasure to a reader"; that is, Yerby considers his fiction romance and its purpose "entertainment," his own word. Nevertheless, in such works as *Speak Now*, a modern novel of inter-racial love, and *The Dahomean*, as much treatise on African culture as novel, Yerby has written seriously, if not always with full control, on racial injustice and the black heritage.

His longest statement on his fiction appears in "How and Why I Write the Costume Novel" (*Harper's Magazine*, October 1959). Though he states that he does extensive research, the notes always bulking larger than the finished novel, and though there are often notes and references (*The Saracen Blade* has 17 pages of notes as an appendix), as well as historical digressions, even lectures, Yerby prefers "costume novel" to historical novel, for he says that his publishers rightly remove "ninety-nine and ninety-nine one-hundredths" of the history so that the novels will entertain. Aside from the history, his principal elements are a picaresque protagonist, who must be a dominant male, emotionally immature, which Yerby defines as "romantic," in his relationships with women; an even more emotionally immature beautiful heroine; understated sex; "a strong, exteriorized conflict, personified in a continuing, antagonist or antagonists," and presented dramatically; and as a theme, "something ennobling to life." He states that he has been most successful with the theme of "the eternal warfare of the sexes," but the true underlying theme of most of his fiction, and frequently expressed by his protagonists, is one that he says he has held since the late 1930's: "many, if not most, of life's problems cannot be solved at all."

Yerby's usually long novels have complex, if episodic, plot lines, providing for the introduction (and then elimination) of numerous minor characters, as well as historical color, whether sordid, exotic, or idyllic. In some ways Yerby is a direct descendant of Sir Walter Scott: in his use of a clash of cultures—masters and slaves, aristocrats and plebeians, Saracens or Moors and Christians, Guelfs and Ghibellines, etc.—as a plot-unifying principle, and in the young hero, always more modern in thought and feeling than his adversaries, thrown into a world different from what he has previously known to make his way amidst brutality and treachery. In a sense, though the romance plot (most often of lovers separated by social circumstances) plays a much larger part in Yerby's novels than in Scott's, it still serves as a thread upon which to hang the historical events and local color and to demonstrate that clash of cultures.

Except for the few early short stories and the two novels *The Old Gods Laugh* and *Speak Now*, Yerby's work ranges widely in history. His first novel, *The Foxes of Harrow*, which is set in Louisiana, was a gigantic success, and it has been followed by a number of antebellum, Civil War, and Reconstruction novels, including, among others, *The Vixens*, *Floodtide*, *A Woman Called Fancy*, *Benton's Row*, *Griffin's Way*, and *A Darkness at Ingraham's Crest*. As a result, Yerby is associated in most readers' minds with the romance of the old south, but it is hardly a "moonlight and magnolias" south, though all of the paraphernalia of that tradition is present—white-columned mansions on huge plantations, crinolined ladies, extensive description of food, manners, etc. Instead, it is a world of parvenues, greedy entrepreneurs, racists, and blind chauvinists, where wealth and position are more important than humanity. When not writing about his native south, Yerby has moved back in time from the French and American Revolutions (*The Devil's Laughter* and *Bride of Liberty*), through the 17th century (*The Golden Hawk*), the Middle Ages (*An Odor of Sanctity* and *The Saracen Blade*), the time of Christ (*Judas, My Brother*) to ancient Greece (*Goat Song*). Such works are written to the same formulas as those of the old south, being, however, usually more episodic and covering more territory through the hero's travels. Their antagonists are similar, if more powerful, and identical motives—greed, lust for power, rivalry in love—generate the conflict.

To explain the enormous popularity of Yerby's novels is ultimately impossible, for other writers have used the same plot formulas, the same perfervid prose, the same aura of eroticism, and the same strongly typed and contrasted characters, without coming near his sales or public fame. Perhaps the principal reason, despite his critical reputation, is that readers can sense an ethical underpinning to the exciting action and sexy romance. His heroes are nearly always idealists or sceptics, and often the idealists become sceptics, if not stoics, thus fulfilling the theme that most of man's problems have no solutions. This existential view, however bleak, pervades the novels and accounts for the frequent less-than-happy endings. Yerby has yet to be taken as seriously as he deserves by either literary or sociological critics, the fate of most extremely popular writers. Yet his historical fiction is firmly based upon mid-20th-century *angst*, and in the interplay between historical action and contemporary sensibility lies the nexus of his achievement.

—Earl F. Bargainnier

YORK, Alison. See **NICOLE, Christopher.**

YORKE, Katherine. See **ELLERBECK, Rosemary.**

YOUNG, Stark. American. Born in Como, Mississippi, 11 October 1881. Educated at the University of Mississippi, Oxford, 1897–1901, B.A. in English 1901 (Phi Beta Kappa); Columbia University, New York, M.A. 1902. Assistant in English, University of Mississippi, 1904–07; Instructor, 1907–10, and Professor of English, 1910–15, University of Texas, Austin; Professor of English, Amherst College, Massachusetts, 1915–21; drama critic, *New Republic*, Washington, D.C., 1922–47; associate editor, *Theatre Arts* magazine, New York, 1922–48; drama critic, *New York Times*, 1924–25. Artist: paintings exhibited in New York, 1943–46. *Died 6 January 1963.*

ROMANCE AND HISTORICAL PUBLICATIONS

Novels

Heaven Trees. New York, Scribner, 1926.
So Red the Rose. New York, Scribner, 1934; London, Cassell, 1935.

OTHER PUBLICATIONS

Novels

The Torches Flare. New York, Scribner, 1928.
River House. New York, Scribner, 1929.

Short Stories

The Street of the Islands. New York, Scribner, 1930.
Feliciana. New York, Scribner, 1935.

Plays

Guenevere. New York, Grafton Press, 1906.
Addio, Madretta and Other Plays (includes *The Star in the Trees*, *The Twilight Saint*, *The Dead Poet*, *The Seven Kings and the Wind*, *The Queen of Sheba*). Chicago, Sergel, 1912.
At the Shrine. New York, Theatre Arts, 1919.
The Colonnade (produced London, 1920). New York, Theatre Arts, and London, Benn, 1924.

Three One-Act Plays: Madretta, At the Shrine, Addio. Cincinnati, Kidd, 1921.
The Queen of Sheba. New York, Theatre Arts, 1922.
The Saint (produced London, 1924). New York, Boni and Liveright, 1925.
The Twilight Saint. New York, French, 1925.
Sweet Times and the Blue Policeman (for children). New York, Holt, 1925.
The Sea Gull, adaptation of a play by Chekhov (produced New York, 1928). New York, Scribner, 1929.
Artemise. Privately printed, 1942.

Verse

The Blind Man at the Window and Other Poems. New York, Grafton Press, 1906.

Other

The Flower in Drama. New York, Scribner, 1923.
The Three Fountains (travel). New York, Scribner, 1924.
Glamour: Essays on the Art of the Theatre. New York, Scribner, 1925.
Encaustics. New York, New Republic, 1926.
Theatre Practice. New York, Scribner, 1926.
The Theatre. New York, Doran, 1927.
Maurice Sterne: A Retrospective Exhibition. New York, New Republic, 1933.
Immortal Shadows: A Book on Dramatic Criticism. New York, Scribner, 1948.
The Pavilion: Of People and Times Remembered, of Stories and Places (autobiography). New York, Scribner, 1951.
The Flower in Drama and Glamour: Theatre Essays and Criticism. New York, Scribner, 1955; revised edition, New York, Octagon, 1973.
Stark Young: A Life in the Arts: Letters 1900–1962, edited by John Pilkington. Baton Rouge, Louisiana State University Press, 2 vols., 1975.

Editor, with others, *The English Humorists of the Eighteenth Century.* Boston, Ginn, 1911.
Editor, *A Southern Treasury of Life and Literature.* New York, Scribner, 1937.

Translator, *The Sole Heir*, by Jean François Regnard. Austin, University of Texas Press, 1912.
Translator, *George Dandin*, by Molière. New York, Theatre Arts, 1925.
Translator, *Mandragola*, by Machiavelli. New York, Macaulay, 1927.
Translator, *The Three Sisters*, by Chekhov. New York, French, 1941.
Translator, *The Cherry Orchard*, by Chekhov. New York, French, 1947.
Translator, *Uncle Vanya*, by Chekhov. New York, French, 1956.

*

Critical Studies: *New York Jew* by Alfred Kazin, New York, Knopf, and London, Secker and Warburg, 1978; *Stark Young* by John Pilkington, Boston, Twayne, 1985.

*   *   *

Inveterate southerner Stark Young takes an agrarian stand throughout his best work: an intense love of his native land, tremendous emphasis upon the family as a nourishing and culturally cohesive structure, and a political and social contempt for new south capitalism and industry. Like his intellectual forebear Thomas Jefferson, Young seems to posit that those close to the earth are enriched and made noble by it.

A seldom read novel, or, as some see it, a set of loosely connected stories, *Heaven Trees* suggests the philosophical attitude which gave birth to Young's masterpiece *So Red the Rose*. *Heaven Trees* focuses on Mississippi life in the 1850's, the golden era of southern plantation life. Lacking the realism of his better work, *Heaven Trees* idealizes the family home, a symbol for a way of life now lost. Using the history of his birthplace, Como, Mississippi, Young creates Panola, Mississippi, without commerce or trade—a pristine, agrarian ideal. The Hugh Stark McGehee family in the novel becomes the paradigm of the southern family.

In one month alone *So Red the Rose* sold in excess of 400,000 copies, making it the most popular and best known of all southern historical novels before Margaret Mitchell's *Gone with the Wind* (1936). As John Pilkington observed, it became a "commentary on a civilization rather than a history." Historically oriented, this quintessential Civil War novel contains three movements: "the prelude to the war, the war, and its aftermath" from November 1860 to November 1865.

Characteristic of Young's agrarianism, the novel centers on family, chronicling in near epic fashion the relationship of the McGehees and Bedfords of Portobello and Montrose plantations. The family drama was, in large part, drawn by the novelist from his own personal history. The most dramatic scene in the novel, the burning of Montrose, for example, was inspired by the burning of Bowling Green in Young's own family.

Donald Davidson, himself a leading agrarian, early recognized the theme of the novel when he noted that it "draws into focus the battle between tradition and anti-tradition that has been waged since the Renaissance." Deceptively set in the past, the novel nonetheless spoke directly to issues of the 1920's and 1930's. The McGehees and the Bedfords become repositories of traditional southern virtue, exponents of agrarianism. Their unification as a family suggests the cultural cohesion of the south. General Sherman, on the other hand, is the enemy of cultural cohesion: he is industrial sterility, a divided personality. Sam Shaw, is a personification for the new south, a sorry replacement for the planter aristocracy.

So Red the Rose takes its place alongside many novels on the same subject by later writers like Clifford Dowdey, William Faulkner, Caroline Gordon, Andrew Lytle, and Allen Tate. It was, however, the most realistic at its time of publication, establishing, as one critic noted, in "critical grace the Civil War genre which had for so long been bogged in the 'treacly sentimentality' of crinolines and trailing banners . . . "

—George C. Longest

TITLE
INDEX

The following list includes the titles of all novels and short stories (designated "s") cited as romance and historical publications. The name in parenthesis is meant to direct the reader to the appropriate entry where fuller information is given.

Abandoned for Love (Courtney), 1982
Abba Abba (Burgess), 1977
Abbess of Vlaye (Weyman), 1904
Abbey Court (Thum), 1976
Abbeygate (Crowe), 1977
Abbie in Love (Corcoran), 1981
Abbot's House (Elsna), 1969
Abduction (Lamb), 1981
Abiding City (Bloom), 1958
Abigail (Corcoran), 1981
Abode of Love (Bowen, as Shearing), 1945
About Mrs. Leslie (Delmar), 1950
Above All Things (Albanesi, as Rowlands), 1915
Above and Beyond (Brown, as St. Claire), 1986
Above Her Station (M. St. John, as H. Cooper), 1922
Above Rubies (Hampson), 1978
Above the Clouds (Wyndham), 1954
Above the Lattice (J. MacLeod), 1949
Abraham, Prince of Ur (Hardy), 1935
Absent in the Spring (Westmacott), 1944
Acapulco Moonlight (Lewty), 1985
Accident Call (E. Harrison), 1971
Accidental Bride (Barrie), 1967
Accompanied by His Wife (Burchell), 1941
According to the Pattern (G. Hill), 1903
Ace of Cads (s Arlen), 1927
Aces High (Hooper), 1989
Achilles His Armour (Green), 1955
Acquittal (Elsna, as Conway), 1973
Across a Crowded Room (Peake), 1977
Across a Starlit Sea (Brandewyne), 1989
Across Her Path (Swan), 1890
Across the Counter (Burchell),1960
Across the Lagoon (R. Lane), 1974
Across the River of Yesterday (Johansen), 1987
Across the Years (Loring), 1939
Across the Years (s E. Porter), 1919
Act of Betrayal (Craven), 1985
Act of Darkness (P. Hastings), 1969
Act of Fear (W. Roberts), 1977
Act of God (Kennedy), 1955
Act of Love (B. Hastings), 1983
Act of Possession (Mather), 1985
Act of Will (Bradford), 1986
Acting Sister (Bloom, as Burns), 1968
Action and Passion (Wren), 1933
Action at Aquila (H. Allen), 1938
Activities of Lavie Jutt (Barcynska, as Barclay), 1911
Acts of Kindness (C. Allen), 1979
Acts of King Arthur and His Noble Knights (Steinbeck), 1976
Adair of Starlight Peaks (Summers), 1977
Adam and Eve (Erskine), 1927
Adam and Evelina (Blackstock, as Allardyce), 1956
Adam Hepburn's Vow (Swan), 1885
Adam of a New World (J. Lindsay), 1936
Adam Penfeather, Buccaneer (Farnol), 1940
Adams, Nurse Hilda series (Rinehart), from 1932
Adam's Daughters (Bloom), 1947
Adam's Eden (Baldwin), 1977
Adam's Fall (Brown), 1988
Adam's Rib (Blackstock, as Allardyce), 1963
Adam's Rib (Rome), 1976

Adam's Wife (J. MacLeod), 1972
Adelaide the Enchantress (Hooper), 1987
Adele & Co. (Yates), 1931
Admiral (Pope), 1982
Admiral of the Ocean-Sea (M. Johnston), 1923
Admiral's House (Asquith), 1969
Admiral's Lady (Gibbs), 1975
Admirer Unknown (Ruck), 1957
Adora (Small), 1980
Adorable Doctor (Bloom, as Essex), 1968
Adrien Leroy (Garvice), 1912
Adultress (Holt, as Carr), 1982
Advantageous Marriage (Ley), 1977
Adventure in Romance (Bloom, as Burns), 1955
Adventure of Princess Sylvie (A. Williamson), 1900
Adventure with a Stranger (Vitek), 1987
Adventurer (Cartland), 1977
Adventurers (Hodge), 1965
Adventurers (Stuart, as Long), 1983
Adventures of Billie Belshaw (Vaizey), 1912
Adventures of Gerard (s Doyle), 1903
Adventuress (Chesney), 1987
Adventuress (Winston), 1978
Adventurous Heart (Bloom, as Burns), 1940
Adversaries (Bennetts), 1969
Adversary in the House (Stone), 1947
Adverse Alliance (Stevenson, as Curzon), 1981
Aegean Quest (Ashton), 1977
Affair at Alkali (Coffman), 1960
Affair at Marrakesh (Daniels), 1968
Affair in Hong Kong (Daniels, 1969
Affair in Tangier (Blair), 1962
Affair in Venice (R. Lindsay), 1975
Affair of Honor (Krentz, as James), 1983
Affair of Risk (Krentz, as Castle), 1982
Affair of the Heart (J. Smith), 1977
Affair to Forget (R. Lindsay), 1978
Affaire Royale (N. Roberts), 1986
Affairs of Love (Ellerbeck, as Thorne), 1983
Affairs of Love (Finley), 1980
Affairs of Men (Bowen), 1922
Affairs of the Heart (Pykare, as Powers), 1980
Affinities (s Rinehart), 1920
Afraid (Cartland), 1981
Afraid of the Dark (Roby), 1965
African Dream (Hoy), 1971
African Interlude (Woodward, as Davis), 1982
African Mountain (Hunter, as Chace), 1960
After a Famous Victory (Andrews), 1984
After All (Elsna, as Snow), 1961
After All These Years (Seidel), 1984
After House (Rinehart), 1914
After Long Journeying (J. MacLeod),1955
After Many Days (Albanesi, as Rowlands), 1910
After Many Years (s Swan), 1899
After Office Hours (Burchell), 1939
After Rain (Muskett), 1931
After Sundown (Hampson), 1974
After the Death of Don Juan (S. Warner), 1938
After the Hurricane (J. MacLeod), 1987
After the Lady (Blackstock, as Allardyce), 1954
After the Music (Palmer), 1986

After the Night (Cartland), 1944
After the Storm (Dailey), 1975
After the Storm (Oldfield), 1981
After the Storm (Williams), 1977
After the Verdict (Hichens), 1924
After Tomorrow (Greig, as Ames), 1951
After Tomorrow (Hichens), 1895
After-Glow (Ayres), 1936
Afterglow (Burghley), 1966
Afterglow (s Hichens), 1935
Afterglow and Nightfall (E. Pargeter), 1977
Afternoon for Lizards (Eden), 1962
Afternoon of an Autocrat (Lofts), 1956
Afternoon Walk (Eden), 1971
Afterwards (Lowndes), 1925
Again the Bugle (s Kantor), 1958
Again This Rapture (Cartland), 1947
Against the Rules (L. Howard), 1983
Against the Stream (Cartland), 1946
Against the World (Albanesi, as Rowlands), 1923
Age Cannot Wither (Bloom), 1942
Agency Nurse (Woodward), 1980
Agony and the Ecstasy (Stone), 1961
Agrippa's Daughter (Fast), 1964
Ailsa Page (Chambers), 1910
Air Ambulance (J. MacLeod), 1959
Air Ambulance Nurse (Woodward, as Richmond), 1981
Air Hostess in Love (Price), 1962
Air Liner (Bloom, as Burns), 1948
Air Ministry, Room 28 (Frankau), 1942
Air of Glory (Neilan), 1977
Air Surgeon (Slaughter), 1943
Air That Kills (Millar), 1957
Air Ticket (Barrie), 1957
Airing in a Closed Carriage (Bowen, as Shearing), 1943
Airport Nurse (Beaty), 1986
Airs above the Ground (Stewart), 1965
Akin to Anne (s Montgomery), 1988
Alaska (Michener), 1988
Alathea (Belle), 1985
Albany (Black), 1984
Albatross (Anthony), 1982
Albatross (s Armstrong), 1957
Albert the Beloved (Bloom, as Prole), 1974
Alberta (s Wiebe), 1979
Albion Walk (Butler), 1982
Album (Rinehart), 1933
Album Leaf (Bowen, as Shearing), 1933
Alchemy (s Lytle), 1979
Aldersyde (Swan), 1882
Aleta's Terrible Secret (Libbey), n.d.
Alex and the Raynhams (Bromige), 1961
Alex Rayner, Dental Nurse (Lewty), 1965
Alexa (Melville), 1979
Alexa (Holt, as Burford), 1948
Alexander series (Renault), from 1969
Alexandra (Trollope, as Harvey), 1980
Alexandra, The Ambivalent (Kimbrough), 1981
Alexandra's Story (F. Preston), 1989
Alexandrovitch Is Missing! (Edwards), 1970
Alianor (M. Peters), 1984
Alias Richard Power (C. N. and A. M. Williamson), 1921
Alibi for Isabel (s Rinehart), 1944
Alibi for Murder (Armstrong), 1956
Alice, Where Are You? (Charles, as Lance), 1940
Alice, Where Art Thou? (Cadell), 1959

Alicia series (Brown), from 1983
Alien Corn (Bloom), 1947
Alien Corn (R. Lindsay), 1954
Alien Vengence (Craven), 1985
Alien Wife (Mather), 1977
Alimony (Baldwin), 1929
Alinor (Gellis), 1978
All Consuming Passion (Mather), 1985
All Done by Kindness (Moore), 1951
All Earth to Love (P. Hastings), 1968
All Else Confusion (Neels), 1982
All Else Is Folly (Gaskin), 1951
All Enchantment Die (Maybury), 1941
All for Love (Gallagher), 1981
All for Love (Webb, as Hamill), 1965
All for the Love of a Fair Face (Libbey), 1889
All for You (Robins), 1946
All I Ask (Charles, as Chandos), 1939
All I Ask (Weale), 1964
All in the April Morning (Saunders), 1989
All in the Day's Work (Elsna, as Snow), 1950
All in the Family (Pozzessere), 1987
All Is Not Fair in Love (s Garvice), 1913
All Made of Wishes (Lewty), 1974
All Men Are Murderers (Blackstock), 1958
All My Enemies (R. Harris), 1967
All My Fortunes (Saxton), 1987
All My Worldly Goods (Weale), 1987
All Our Tomorrows (Elsna, as Lancaster), 1958
All Over Again (Ayres), 1934
All over the Town (Delderfield), 1947
All Passion Spent (Chard), 1979
All Past Years (Elsna, as Lancaster), 1949
All She Can Be (F. Michaels), 1983
All Swans (Elsna), 1932
All That Glitters (L. Howard), 1982
All That Glitters (Keyes), 1941
All That Heaven Allows (Weale), 1983
All That Matters (Robins), 1956
All the Days of Summer (Dingwell), 1978
All the Fire (Mather), 1971
All the King's Sons (Clarke, as Honeyman), 1976
All the Possibilities (N. Roberts), 1985
All the Queen's Men (Anthony), 1960
All the Rivers Run (Cato), 1958
All the Summer Long (Stratton, as Gillen), 1975
All the Sweet Tomorrows (Small), 1984
All the Trumpets Sounded (Hardy), 1942
All Their Kingdoms (Polland), 1981
All Things Come Round (Burgin), 1929
All This and Heaven Too (Field), 1938
All This for Love (Robins), 1935
All This I Gave (Charles, as Tempest), 1937
All Through the Day (Clarke), 1983
All Through the Night (G. Hill), 1945
All under Heaven (Buck), 1973
All Visitors Ashore (Elsna), 1938
All Visitors Must Be Announced (Van Slyke), 1972
All Your Lovely Word Are Spoken (Roby), 1970
Allandale's Daughters (Burgin), 1928
Allan's Wife (s Haggard), 1889
Allegra (Darcy), 1975
Alley of Flashing Spears (s Byrne), 1933
Alley-Cat (Muskett), 1937
All's Well with the World (Albanesi), 1932
All-the-Way Man (Dingwell), 1980

Allure (F. Preston),1987
Almond, Wild Almond (Broster), 1933
Almost a Stranger (Way), 1984
Almost Forever (L. Howard), 1986
Alms for Oblivion (Bigland), 1937
Aloha Means Goodbye (Hintze),1972
Aloha Nurse (Webb, as Hamill), 1961
Alone and Afraid (Cartland), 1985
Alone in Paris (Cartland), 1978
Alone in Paris (s Swan), 1898
Alone with Me (Elsna, as Snow), 1955
Along a Dark Path (V. Johnston), 1967
Along Came Ann (Stuart), 1953
Along Came Jones (Browning), 1988
Alphabet of Love (Libbey), 1892
Alpine Coach (Coffman), 1976
Alpine Condo Cross Fire (Eberhart), 1984
Alpine Doctor (Burghley), 1970
Alpine Nurse (I. Roberts), 1968
Alpine Rhapsody (Ashton), 1973
Also the Hills (Keyes), 1943
Altar of Evil (F. Stevenson), 1973
Altar of Honour (Dell), 1929
Alternative (McCutcheon), 1909
Always (Johansen), 1986
Always a Rainbow (Bevan), 1975
Always Another Man (Charles, as Tempest), 1941
Always Is Not Forever (Van Slyke), 1977
Always Remember (Elsna, as Snow), 1954
Always Tomorrow (Ayers), 1933
Always Yours (Burchell), 1941
Alyx (Burford), 1977
Amaranth Flower (Farnes), 1979
Amateur Gentleman (Farnol), 1913
Amateur Governess (Gibbs, 1964
Amazing Interlude (Rinehart), 1918
Amazing Marriage (Elsna, as Lancaster), 1958
Amazing Tramp (M. St. John, as H. Cooper), 1927
Amazon in an Apron (Neels), 1969
Ambassador's Women (Gaskin), 1985
Ambassadress (Keyes), 1938
Amber Cat (Gibbs, as Ford), 1976
Amber Enchantment (Delinsky, as Drake), 1982
Amber Five (Beaty), 1958
Amber Princess (Treece), 1962
Amberstone (Bennetts), 1980
Amberwell (D. Stevenson), 1955
Amberwood (Manners, as Rundle), 1972
Ambitions of Jill (Wynne), 1920
Ambulance Call (E. Harrison), 1972
America (Chambers), 1924
America, with Love (Winsor), 1957
American (Fast), 1946
American Baroness (J. Roberts, as Radcliffe), 1980
American Beauty (Ferber), 1931
American Bred (Franken, as Meloney), 1941
American Captain (E. Marshall), 1954
American Dynasty series (J. Roberts), from 1978
American Eden (M. Harris), 1987
American Family (Baldwin), 1935
American Flaggs (Norris), 1936
American Heiress (Eden), 1980
American Wife (Swan), 1900
American Woman (Swan)
Americans (Jakes), 1980
Ames, Verity series (Krentz), from 1988

Amethyst Love (J. Roberts, as Danton), 1977
Amethyst Meadows (Danbury), 1974
Ammie, Come Home (B. Michaels), 1968
Among the Wolves (s Case), 1982
Among Those Present (s Ferber), 1923
Amorelle (G. Hill), 1934
Amorous Bicycle (Bloom, as Essex), 1944
Amyot series (Nicole), from 1964
Ancestors (Steen, as Dryden), 1930
Ancient Egypt series (I. Roberts and I. M. Roberts), from 1974
Ancient Sin (s Arlen), 1930
And All Because . . . (Robins), 1930
And Be Thy Love (Burghley), 1958
And Call It Accident (Lowndes), 1936
And Confidential (Trask), 1953
And Die Remembering (Roby), 1972
And Falsely Pledge My Love (Burchell), 1957
And Five Were Foolish (s Yates), 1924
And Gold Was Ours (Brandewyne), 1984
And in the Morning (Darrell), 1986
. . . and Ladies of the Club (Santmyer), 1982
And New Stars Burn (Baldwin), 1941
And No Regrets (Blair, as Brett), 1948
And Now the Screaming Starts (s Case), 1973
And Now Tomorrow (Field), 1942
And Sometimes Death (Armstrong, as Valentine), 1954
And Still She Loved Him (M. St. John), 1926
And Still They Dream (Ayres), 1938
And the Desert Blooms (Johansen), 1986
And Then Came Dawn (Stanford), 1981
And Then Came Love (R. Lindsay, as Leigh), 1954
And Then Face to Face (s Ertz), 1927
And Then There Was Georgia (Blackmore), 1975
And Then You Came (Bridge), 1948
And We in Dreams (J. MacLeod), 1947
Anderson Line series (Nicole, as McKay), from 1984
Andersonville (Kantor), 1955
Andrew Leicester's Wife (Albanesi, as Rowlands)
Angel in Hell (Cartland), 1976
Angel in the House (Norris), 1933
Angel in the House (Roby, as D'Arcy), 1980
Angel of Evil (Albanesi, as Rowlands), 1905
Angel of His Presence (G. Hill), 1902
Angel of Mercy (Pozzessere), 1988
Angel of the Tar Sands (s Wiebe), 1982
Angel Runs Away (Cartland), 1986
Angel Unawares (C. and A. Williamson), 1916
Angel Who Couldn't Sing (Cleugh), 1935
Angela's Lover (Garvice, as Hart)
Angel's Eyes (Barcynska), 1957
Angel's Kiss (Barcynska, as Sandys), 1937
Angel's Share (Possezzere, as Graham), 1985
Angel's Tear (Blackmore), 1974
Angel's Wickedness (Corelli), 1900
Anger in the Sky (Ertz), 1943
Angevin King (Bennetts), 1972
Angry Man (Dingwell), 1979
Angry Tide (Graham), 1977
Angry Wife (Buck, as Sedges), 1947
Anitra's Dance (Hurst), 1934
Ann All-Alone (M. St. John), 1921
Ann and the Hoosier Doctor (McElfresh), 1955
Ann Foster, Lab Technician (McElfresh, as Wesley), 1956
Ann Kenyon, Surgeon (McElfresh), 1960
Ann, The Gentle (Kimbrough), 1978
Anna and Her Daughters (D. Stevenson), 1958

Anna Fitzalan (Steen), 1953
Anna Heritage (M. Howard), 1944
Annabelle (Chesney, as Fairfax), 1980
Annalise Experiment (W. Roberts), 1985
Anne series (Montgomery), from 1908
Anne Boleyn (Anthony), 1957
Anne Boleyn (Beck, as Barrington), 1932
Anne Hyde, Travelling Companion (Swan), 1908
Anne Marguerite (Cleugh), 1932
Anne of Austria (Anthony), 1968
Anne of Cleves (J. Fitzgerald, as Hamilton), 1972
Anne of Green Gables series (Montgomery)
Anne of Strathallan (Summers), 1975
Anne, The Rose of Hever (M. Peters), 1971
Another Cynthia (Leslie), 1939
Another Dawn (Brown), 1985
Another Eden (Hampson), 1982
Another Girl Won Him (M. St. John), 1935
Another Kind of Magic (C. Allen), 1977
Another Man's Murder (Eberhart), 1957
Another Man's Wife (Lowndes), 1934
Another View (Pilcher), 1969
Another Time, Another Place (Britt), 1981
Another Woman's House (Eberhart), 1947
Another Woman's Shoes (Charles, as Chandos), 1939
Answer as a Man (Caldwell), 1981
Answer in the Tide (Ogilvie), 1978
Answer to a Christmas Prayer (Swan), 1894
Answer to Heaven (Gallagher), 1964
Antagonists (Gann), 1970
Anthea series (Ley), from 1984
Anthony Adverse (H. Allen), 1933
Anthony Lyveden (Yates), 1921
Anthony Wilding (Sabatini), 1910
Antic Years (Franken),1958
Antichrist (C. Holland), 1970
Antigua Kiss (Weale), 1982
Antonia (Jacob), 1954
Antonia (Jagger), 1978
Any Old Iron (Burgess), 1989
Any Two Can Play (Cadell), 1981
Any Village (Baldwin), 1971
Anything But Love (Greig, as Ames), 1933
Anything Can Happen (Elsna, as Snow), 1962
Anywoman (Hurst), 1950
Anzac's Bride, (MacGill), 1917
Apollo Fountain (Daniels), 1974
Apollo Man (J. MacLeod), 1986
Apollo's Daughter (Stratton), 1980
Apollo's Seed (Mather), 1979
Apothecary's Daughter (Gibbs), 1962
Appassionata (Hurst), 1926
Apple for Eve (Norris), 1943
Aple from Eve (Neels), 1981
Apple in Eden (K. Thorpe), 1973
Apples of Gold (Deeping), 1923
Apple Tree (s du Maurier), 1952
Appointment with Love (Woodward), 1962
April (Pilcher), 1957
April After (Bloom), 1928
April Escapade (Norris), 1941
Apple for the Doctor (Bloom, as Essex), 1950
April Girl (Bromige), 1967
April Gold (G. Hill), 1936
April in Westland (I. Preston), 1969
April Lady (Heyer), 1957
April Morning (Fast), 1961

April Rising (Sallis), 1984
April Wooing (Bromige), 1951
April's Day (Ayres), 1945
April's Grave (Howatch), 1969
Apron-Strings (Mackinlay), 1937
Apronstrings (M. St. John), 1919
Arabella (Heyer), 1949
Arabella Arrives (Ruck), 1939
Arabella the Awful (Ruck), 1918
Arabian Nights (Pozzessere, as Graham), 1984
Araby (Hutten), 1904
Aragon, Tom series (Millar), from 1976
Arcadia House (Stuart, as A. Stuart), 1958
Arcadian series (Eaton), from 1940
Ardath (Corelli), 1889
Ardent Protector (Delinsky, as Drake), 1982
Arena (Jakes, as Scotland), 1963
Ariel Custer (G. Hill), 1925
Ariosto (Yarbro), 1980
Arise, Oh Sun! (Maybury), 1942
Arizona Star (Baldwin), 1945
Arkady (Duffield), 1948
Arm and the Darkness (Caldwell), 1943
Armored Giants (F. Mason), 1980
Armour Against Love (Cartland), 1945
Arms and the Maid (Sabatini), 1910
Army Doctor (Seifert), 1942
Around the Rugged Rock (Cadell), 1954
Arouse and Beware (Kantor), 1936
Arousing Touch (Dingwell), 1983
Arranged Marriage (Kidd), 1980
Arrant Rover (Ruck), 1921
Arras of Youth (Onions), 1949
Arrogance of Love (Mather), 1968
Arrogant Duke (Mather), 1970
Arrogant Duke (Randall), 1966
Arrogant Lover (Kidd), 1986
Arrow in My Heart (Elsna, as Snow), 1972
Arrow in the Heart (Robins), 1960
Arrow of Love (Cartland), 1975
Art of Deception (N. Roberts), 1986
Artemia (P. Hill), 1989
Arthur Rex (T. Berger), 1978
Arundel series (K. Roberts), from 1930
As a Man Loves (Albanesi), 1936
As a Woman Wills (M. St. John, as Cooper), 1934
As Bends the Bough (Bloom), 1952
As Eagles Fly (Cartland), 1975
As Fate Decreases (M. St. John, as Cooper), 1929
As It Was in the Beginning (Polland), 1987
As Long as I Live (Loring), 1937
As Long as You Live (P. Hastings), 1951
As Other Men Are (s Yates), 1925
As the Tree Falls (Leslie), 1958
As the World Judged (M. St. John), 1925
As Time Goes By (B. Hastings), 1986
As Waits the Sky (Ritchie), 1969
Ashamed of the Shop (M. St. John), 1919
Ashes in an Urn (Summerton, as Roffman), 1966
Ashes in the Wind (Woodiwiss), 1979
Ashes of Empire (Chambers), 1898
Ashes of Falconwyck (Daniels, as Gray), 1973
Ashes of Love (Garvice), 1910
Ashley Hall (Ellis, as Richard), 1967
Ashton's Folly (Saunders, as Innes), 1975
Ask for Me Tomorrow (Millar), 1976
Ask Me Again (Charles, as Tempest), 1955

Ballad-Maker of Paris (Blackstock, as Torday), 1935
Ballerina series (Sebastian, as Gladstone), from 1979
Ballerina (E. Smith), 1932
Balloon Man (Armstrong), 1968
Bamboo Wedding (R. Lane), 1977
Ban (Wynne, as Lurgan), 1912
Band of Angels (Warren), 1955
Bandersnatch (Hardwick), 1989
Bandit and the Priest (Erskine-Lindop), 1953
Bannaman Legacy (Cookson), 1985
Banner of the Bull (Sabatini), 1915
Banners series (Carnegie), from 1968
Banners of Silk (Laker), 1981
Banshee (Millar), 1983
Banshee Tide (Dwyer-Joyce), 1977
Barabbas (Corelli), 1893
Barbara Owen, Girl Reporter (McElfresh, as Scott), 1956
Barbara Rebell (Lowndes), 1905
Barbara, The Valiant (Kimbrough), 1977
Barbara's Love Story (Albanesi, as Rowlands), 1911
Barbarian (Mitchison), 1961
Barbarian Lover (Pedler), 1924
Barbarian Stories (s Mitchison), 1929
Barbarians (Chambers), 1917
Barbarians (F. Mason), 1954
Barbary Moon (Blair), 1954
Barbary Sheep (Hichens), 1907
Barberry Bush (Norris), 1927
Barbours and Bouchards series (Caldwell), from 1938
Bard (Llywelyn), 1984
Bardelys the Magnificent (Sabatini), 1906
Barden, Julie series (Manley-Tucker), from 1968
Barefoot Saint (s Benét), 1929
Barforth series (Jagger), from 1980
Bargain Bride (Kidd), 1976
Bargain for Paradise (Stratton), 1978
Bargain in Love (Elsna, as Conway), 1960
Bargain with the Devil (Krentz, as Castle), 1981
Barn Dance (Seale), 1941
Barn Stormers (A. Williamson), 1897
Barnards of Loseby (S. Warner), 1974
Barons of Runnymede (Bennetts), 1974
Barrancourt Destiny (Worboys), 1977
Barren Corn (Heyer), 1930
Barren Harvest (M. Lewis), 1981
Barren Metal (Jacob), 1936
Barrier Between Them (Woodward), 1980
Barrier Between Us (Maybury), 1940
Barriers Between (Garvice), 1910
Barringer House (Riefe), 1976
Barrow Sinister (Lee), 1969
Barry Leroy (Bailey), 1919
Bars of Iron (Dell), 1915
Bartered Bride (MacGill), 1920
Bartered Bride (Rome), 1973
Bartered Bridegroom (Roby, as Grey), 1981
Bartholomew Fair (P. Hastings), 1974
Base Metal (Bloom), 1928
Basilissa (Masefield), 1940
Bastard (Jakes), 1974
Bastard King (Holt, as Plaidy), 1974
Bat (Rinehart), 1926
Bath Belles (J. Smith), 1986
Bath Intrigue (Walsh), 1986
Bath Tangle (Heyer), 1955
Battle Dress (Beaty, as Ross), 1979

Battle for Lucknow (Stuart, as V. A. Stuart), 1975
Battle of Love (Blair), 1961
Battle of the Queens (Holt, as Plaidy), 1978
Battle of the Villa Fiorita (Godden), 1963
Battle Prize (Krentz, as James), 1983
Battle Surgeon (Slaughter), 1944
Bauhinia Junction (Way), 1971
Bay of Moonlight (Burghley), 1968
Bay of the Nightingales (Summers), 1970
Bayou Road (Eberhart), 1979
Bazalgettes (Delafield), 1935
Be All and End All (Berckman), 1976
Be Buried in the Rain (B. Michaels), 1985
Be More Than Dreams (Hoy), 1968
Be My Guest (Cadell), 1964
Be My Guest (Norway), 1966
Be Still, My Heart (Charles, as Tempest), 1936
Be True to Me (Elsna, as Conway), 1957
Be Valiant Still (J. Lane), 1935
Beach House (Coffman), 1970
Beach of Sweet Returns (Hilton), 1975
Beacon at Alexandria (Brandshaw), 1986
Beads of Nemesis (Hunter), 1974
Bearkeeper's Daughter (Bradshaw), 1987
Beast in View (Millar), 1955
Beat to Quarters (Forester), 1937
Beatrice (Haggard), 1890
Beau and the Bluestocking (Ley), 1975
Beau Barron's Lady (Bennetts), 1981
Beau Brocade (Orczy), 1907
Beau Geste (Wren), 1924
Beau Ideal (Wren), 1928
Beau Sabreur (Wren), 1926
Beau Wyndham (Heyer), 1941
Beaujeu (Bailey), 1905
Beaumaroy Home from the Wars (Hope), 1919
Beaumont Tradition (Daniels), 1971
Beautiful Coquette (Libbey), 1892
Beautiful Ione's Lover (Libbey), 1892
Beautiful Is Vanished (Caldwell), 1951
Beauty (Baldwin), 1933
Beauty and the Beast (Norris), 1928
Beauty Beast (Kantor), 1968
Beauty for Ashes (G. Hill), 1935
Beauty of the Devil (J. Fitzgerald), 1988
Beauty of the Season (Garvice), 1910
Beauty, Retire (Trask), 1932
Beauty Surgeon (Bloom, as Burns), 1967
Beauty's Daughter (Hardwick), 1976
Beauty's Daughter (Norris), 1935
Beauty's Tears (Mackinlay), 1961
Beauvallet (Heyer), 1929
Because I Love You (Inglis), 1940
Because I Wear Your Ring (Charles, as Chandos), 1947
Because My Love Is Come (Charles, as Tempest), 1938
Because My Love Is Coming (Charles, as Tempest), 1958
Because of Doctor Danville (Hoy), 1956
Because of Stephen (G. Hill), 1904
Because of These Things . . . (Bowen), 1915
Because There Is Hope (Charles, as Tempest), 1958
Because You're Mine (Grimstead, as Manning), 1960
Becca's Child (W. Roberts), 1972
Beckman series (Stirling), from 1979
Beckoning (Coffman), 1965
Beckoning Dream (Berckman), 1955
Beckoning from Moura (Coffman), 1977

Beckoning Trails (Loring), 1947
Becky (Thompson), 1988
Becoming (C. Allen), 1977
Bed Disturbed (Holt, as Ford), 1952
Bed of Grass (Dailey), 1979
Bed of Roses (Weale), 1981
Bedford Row (Rayner), 1977
Bedford Village (H. Allen), 1944
Bedroom Magic (Morgan), 1987
Beds in the East (Burgess), 1959
Bedside Manner (Norway), 1971
Beechy (Hutten), 1909
Beetle's Career (R. Fraser), 1951
Before I Die (Roby), 1966
Before I Kissed (M. Howard), 1955
Before I Make You Mine (Charles, as Chandos), 1938
Before It's Too Late (Pykare, as Coombs), 1986
Before the Storm (Lowndes), 1941
Beggar at Her Husband's Door (M. St. John), 1928
Beggar Girl's Gift (Elsna, as Lancaster), 1943
Beggar Maid, Queen (M. Peters), 1980
Beggar Man (Ayres), 1920
Beggar on Horseback (S. Thorpe), 1953
Beggar Wished . . . (Cartland), 1934
Beggarman (s G. Hill), 1932
Beggars' Horses (Wren), 1934
Beggars May Sing (Seale), 1932
Begin to Live (Holt, as Burford), 1956
Behind a Closed Door (Donnelly), 1979
Behind the Cloud (Loring), 1958
Behind the Mask (Sallis, as Meadmore), 1980
Behold, Here's Poison! (Heyer), 1936
Behold the Brown-Faced Man (Kantor), 1952
Behold Your King (Mitchison), 1957
Belchamber Scandal (F. Murray), 1985
Believe in To-morrow (Asquith), 1955
Believe Me, Beloved—(Charles, as Tempest), 1936
Believe the Heart (Holt, as Burford), 1950
Believe the Heart (Woodward, as Richmond), 1979
Believers (Giles), 1957
Believing in Giants (C. Allen, as Vincent), 1978
Bel Lamington (D. Stevenson), 1961
Bell (Daniels), 1971
Bell Branch (L. Walker), 1971
Bell from a Distant Temple (R. Fraser), 1954
Bell Timson (Steen), 1946
Bella (J. Cooper), 1976
Bella (Eden), 1964
Bella Donna (Hichens), 1909
Bellarion the Fortunate (Sabatini), 1926
Belle of Santiago (Burgin), 1911
Belle of the Works (M. St. John), 1919
Bellefleur (Oates), 1980
Bellefleur (Stanford), 1980
Belle-Mère (Norris), 1931
Bellerose Bargain (Carr), 1982
Belles of Vaudroy (Burgin), 1906
Bells along the Neva (Ponsonby), 1964
Bells in the Wind (Dingwell, as Starr), 1967
Bells of Bruges (Ashton), 1973
Bells of St. Martin (Beaty, as Campbell), 1979
Bells of the City (Lamb, as Coates), 1975
Bells Still Ring (Bloom, as Burns), 1976
Belltower (Shoesmith), 1973
Bellwood (Ogilvie), 1969
Belonging (Browning), 1987

Belonging to Taylor (Hooper, as Robbins), 1986
Beloved (Delmar), 1956
Beloved (Small), 1983
Beloved and Unforgettable (Bloom, as Burns), 1953
Beloved Ballerina (R. Lindsay, as Leigh), 1953
Beloved Burden (Barcynska), 1954
Beloved Captive (Gower), 1981
Beloved Castaway (Winspear), 1968
Beloved Creditor (Bloom), 1939
Beloved Deceiver (Kidd), 1987
Beloved Diana (Ley), 1977
Beloved Enemies (Barrie, as Kent), 1967
Beloved Enemy (Albanesi), 1913
Beloved Enemy (Corcoran), 1981
Beloved Enemy (Duffield), 1950
Beloved Enemy (Maybury), 1957
Beloved Knight (Greig, as Ames), 1959
Beloved Man (Bloom, as Burns), 1957
Beloved of the Gods (Orczy), 1905
Beloved Physician (Jacob), 1930
Beloved Rake (Hampson), 1972
Beloved Rascals (I. Roberts), 1962
Beloved Rebel (S. Thorpe), 1959
Beloved Sinner (Stirling), 1980
Beloved Sparrow (Reid), 1968
Beloved Stranger (Blackmore), 1953
Beloved Stranger (Mather), 1966
Beloved Stranger (G. Hill), 1933
Beloved Traitor (Gower), 1981
Beloved Tyrant (Winspear), 1964
Beloved Vagabond (Hampson), 1981
Beloved Woman (Norris), 1921
Below the Salt (Costain), 1957
Below the Salt (Sheard), 1936
Belshazzar (Haggard), 1930
Belt of Gold (C. Holland), 1984
Beltane the Smith (Farnol), 1915
Belvedere (Gibbs, as Ford), 1973
Ben Retallick (Thompson), 1980
Bend in the River (Bromige), 1975
Bend Sinister (Dymoke), 1962
Bendish (Hewlett), 1913
Beneath a Spell (Albanesi, as Rowlands), 1900
Beneath the Magic (Hichens), 1950
Beneath the Moon (Lorrimer, as Robins), 1951
Beneath the Passion Flower (Bowen, as Preedy), 1932
Beneath the Visiting Moon (Sisson), 1986
Benefactress (Elizabeth), 1901
Benevolent Despot (Ashton), 1970
Bengal Tiger (E. Marshall, as Hunter), 1962
Benita (Haggard), 1906
Benjamin Blake (E. Marshall), 1941
Bennett's Welcome (Fletcher), 1950
Benton's Row (Yerby), 1954
Bermuda Grapevine (s Eberhart), 1949
Bernadette (Stern), 1960
Berry series (s Yates), from 1921
Berry Goes to Monte Carlo (s C. and A. Williamson), 1921
Bertrand of Brittany (Deeping), 1908
Beside a Norman Tower (de la Roche), 1934
Besieger of Cities (Duggan), 1963
Bess (Swan), 1880
Bess of the Woods (Deeping), 1906
Best Girls Are Here (M. St. John), 1917
Best Kept Secrets (Brown), 1989
Best Laid Plans (Chase), 1984

Best Laid Plans (N. Roberts), 1989
Best Love of All (Maybury), 1932
Best Loved Person (Elsna, as Snow), 1976
Best Man (G. Hill), 1914
Best of His Family (Oman), 1933
Best People (Van Slyke), 1976
Best Place to Be (Van Slyke), 1976
Best Time Ever (Ruck), 1934
Best Way to Lose (Dailey), 1983
Best Woman in the World (M. St. John), 1913
Best-Kept Secret (Vitek), 1985
Beth Mason (Albanesi, as Rowlands), 1913
Betrayal (Lamb), 1983
Betrayal (Robins), 1976
Betrayed by Love (Palmer), 1987
Better Love (Pedler), 1924
Better Man (s Chambers), 1916
Better Part (Swan), 1884
Better Than Life (Garvice), 1910
Better to Eat You (Armstrong), 1954
Better to Forget (M. Pargeter), 1977
Better to Marry (Bloom), 1933
Betty (Baldwin), 1928
Betty on the Stage (M. St. John), 1920
Betty Trevor (Vaizey), 1907
Between Pride and Passion (Kidd), 1982
Between the Lines (Krentz), 1986
Between the Rides (Swan), 1935
Between You and Me (Ayres), 1935
Bevy of Maids (Duffield), 1941
Beware, Beware the Bight of Benin (McCutchan), 1974
Beware My Heart (Finley), 1978
Beware of the Banquet (Aiken), 1966
Beware of the Stranger (Dailey), 1978
Beware the Heart (Mather), 1976
Beware the Night (Blackmore), 1958
Bewildered Heart (Blair), 1950
Bewilderment (Scott), 1922
Bewitched (Cartland), 1975
Bewitched (A. Williamson), 1932
Beyond All Frontiers (Darrell, as Drummond), 1983
Beyond Control (Kidd), 1981
Beyond Ecstasy (J. Fitzgerald), 1985
Beyond Fantasy (Delinsky, as Douglass), 1983
Beyond Life (Cabell), 1919
Beyond Reach (M. Pargeter), 1986
Beyond Reasonable Doubt (Elsna), 1962
Beyond the Blue Mountains (Holt, as Plaidy), 1947
Beyond the City (Doyle), 1893
Beyond the Foothills (Summers), 1976
Beyond the Lagoon (Lewty), 1981
Beyond the Mountain (Asquith), 1970
Beyond the Ranges (Bevan), 1970
Beyond the Reef (J. MacLeod), 1984
Beyond the Rocks (Glyn), 1906
Beyond the Sound of Guns (Loring), 1945
Beyond the Sunset (Kidd), 1973
Beyond the Sweet Waters (Hampson), 1970
Beyond This Limit (s Mitchison), 1986
Beyond This Point Are Monsters (Millar), 1970
Beyond Tomorrow (F. Michaels), 1981
Bhowani Junction (Masters), 1954
Bhunda Jewels (Worboys), 1980
Bianca (F. Stevenson), 1973
Bid for a Coronet (A. Williamson), 1901
Bid Me Love (Chappell), 1967

Bid Time Return (Elsna), 1979
Big Barn (Edmonds), 1930
Big Ben (Ayres), 1939
Big Blue Soldier (G. Hill), 1923
Big Family (Delmar), 1961
Big Fellah (Ayres), 1931
Big Fisherman (Douglas), 1948
Big Frogs and Little Frogs (s Ertz), 1938
Big Game (Vaizey), 1908
Big Man (M. Howard), 1965
Big Sky Country (Dailey), 1978
Bikers (Stuart, as A. Stuart), 1971
Bilbao Looking Glass (C. MacLeod), 1983
Bill—The Sheik (A. Williamson), 1927
Biography of the Life of Manuel (Cabell)
Bird in a Storm (Albanesi), 1924
Bird in Flight (Stanford), 1986
Bird in Hand (Browning), 1985
Bird in the Chimney (Eden), 1963
Bird of Dawning (Masefield), 1933
Bird of Paradise (Rome), 1970
Bird of Prey (Reid), 1973
Bird under Glass (R. Fraser), 1938
Birds (s du Maurier), 1968
Birds' Fountain (Hutten), 1915
Birds in a Gilded Cage (Glover), 1988
Birds in the Tree (Goudge), 1940
Bird's Nest (Jackson), 1955
Birds of Mingalay (J. MacLeod), 1967
Birds of Silence (Mackinlay), 1974
Birds Without Bars (I. Roberts), 1970
Birdwatcher (Gordon), 1974
Birth of Mischief (Sabatini), 1945
Birth of Roland (s Hewlett), 1911
Bishop of Hell (s Bowen), 1949
Bit of a Bounder (Gibbs), 1952
Bitter Alliance (K. Thorpe), 1978
Bitter Bride-Bed (Manners, as Lamont), 1971
Bitter Conquest (Blackstock), 1959
Bitter Core (Robins, as French), 1954
Bitter Creek (Boyd), 1939
Bitter Debt (Swan), 1893
Bitter Deception (Westwood), 1987
Bitter Harvest (Hampson), 1982
Bitter Heritage (Pedler), 1928
Bitter Honey (Blackmore), 1960
Bitter Lotus (s Bromfield), 1944
Bitter Loving (Peake), 1976
Bitter Love (Blackmore), 1956
Bitter Masquerade (Hilton), 1970
Bitter Rapture (Duffield), 1937
Bitter Reason (Cowen), 1966
Bitter Revenge (Peake), 1982
Bitter Sweet (Albanesi, as Rowlands), 1910
Bitter Sweet Summer (Sinclair), 1970
Bitter Sweetbriar (Trask), 1955
Bitter Taste of Love (Peake), 1988
Bitter Winds (Cartland), 1938
Bitter Winds of Love (Cartland), 1976
Bittersweet (Bloom), 1978
Bitter-Sweet (Robins), 1955
Bittersweet Ecstasy (Taylor), 1987
Bittersweet Rain (Brown, as St. Claire), 1984
Bixby Girls (R. Marshall), 1957
Black Amber (Whitney), 1964
Black Bartlemy's Treasure (Farnol), 1920

Black Benedicts (Barrie, as Charles), 1956
Black Bethlehem (L. Cooper), 1947
Black Boar series (Wiat), from 1975
Black Cameron (J. MacLeod), 1964
Black Charles (Wyndham), 1952
Black Dawn (Nicole), 1977
Black Delaney (Reid), 1970
Black Domino (Shoesmith), 1975
Black Douglas (Tranter), 1968
Black Douglas (Winspear), 1971
"Black Duchess" (Knight), 1980
Black Eagle (Hampson), 1973
Black Fire (Riefe), 1980
Black Flemings (Norris), 1926
Black Gale (Shellabarger), 1929
Black Gold (Gower), 1988
Black Harvest (Barcynska), 1960
Black Heart and White Heart (s Haggard), 1900
Black Heather (Coffman), 1966
Black Horse Tavern (J. Roberts, as Danton), 1972
Black Hunter (Donnelly), 1978
Black Incense (s A. Williamson), 1926
Black Ingo (Way), 1977
Black Invaders (Stratton), 1981
Black Is White (McCutcheon), 1915
Black Knight (Dell), 1926
Black Knight (Kidd), 1976
Black Lace (Salverson), 1938
Black Lyon (Deveraux), 1980
Black Magic (Bowen), 1909
Black Majesty series (Nicole), from 1984
Black Man—White Maiden (Bowen, as Preedy), 1941
Black Milestone (Gavin), 1941
Black Moon (Graham), 1973
Black Moth (Heyer), 1921
Black Narcissus (Godden), 1939
Black Panther (Cartland), 1939
Black Pearl (Harrod-Eagles), 1982
Black Pearl (McEvoy), 1988
Black Pearl series (W. Roberts), from 1978
Black Pearls (J. Roberts), 1979
Black Plantagenet (Bennetts), 1969
Black Rainbow (B. Michaels), 1982
Black River series (Tresillian), from 1984
Black Rose (Costain), 1945
Black Sand, White Sand (J. MacLeod), 1981
Black Sea Frigate (Stuart), 1971
Black Sheep (Ayres), 1917
Black Sheep (Heyer), 1966
Black Sheep (M. St. John, as Cooper), 1916
Black Sheep, White Lamb (Davis), 1965
Black Sleeves (A. Williamson), 1928
Black Spaniel (s Hichens), 1905
Black Sparta (s Mitchison), 1928
Black Sun (Horner), 1967
Black Swan (Sabatini), 1932
Black Velvet Gown (Cookson), 1984
Black Venus (s Carter), 1985
Black Venus's Tale (s Carter), 1980
Black Virgin of the Gold Mountain (P. Hastings), 1956
Blackberry Summer (P. Hastings), 1982
Black-Eyed Stranger (Armstrong), 1951
Blackground (Aiken), 1989
Blackmaddie (Saunders, as Summers), 1980
Black-Out Symphony (Barcynska), 1942
Blackthorn (Daniels), 1975

Blackwell's Ghost (Daniels, as Gray), 1972
Blade of Justice (Renier), 1965
Blades (McCutcheon), 1928
Blades of Passion (Williams), 1978
Bladon's Rock (Barrie, as Kent), 1963
Blaise of France (Shellabarger), 1950
Blaize (Melville), 1981
Blakeney, Sir Percy series (Orczy), from 1905
Blakeney Papers series (Clayton), from 1984
Blake's Reach (Gaskin), 1958
Blanche Fury (Bowen, as Shearing), 1939
Blanket of the Dark (Buchan), 1931
Blaze (S. Johnson), 1986
Blaze of Love (Robins), 1932
Blaze of Noon (Holt, as Burford), 1958
Blaze of Passion (Blake), 1978
Blaze of Silk (Way), 1970
Blaze of Sunlight (Baldwin), 1959
Blaze Wyndham (Small), 1988
Blazing Star (Thum), 1983
Bleak Heritage (J. MacLeod), 1942
Bleak November (O'Grady), 1970
Bledding Sorrow (M. Harris), 1976
Bless This House (Lofts), 1954
Blessed Plot (Berckman), 1976
Blessing in Disguise (Farnes), 1958
Blessing in Disguise (s Swan), 1898
Blind Corner (Yates), 1927
Blind Date (Ruck), 1953
Blind Duty (Nolan), 1983
Blind Journey (J. MacLeod), 1942
Blind Loyalty (Pedler), 1940
Blind Man's Night (Shellabarger, as Esteven), 1939
Blind Man's Year (Deeping), 1937
Blind Miller (Cookson), 1963
Blind Mother (s Caine), 1892
Blind Promises (Palmer, as Currie), 1984
Blind Raftery and His Wife Hilaria (Byrne), 1924
Blind Villain (Berckman), 1957
Blind-Girl's-Buff (Berckman), 1962
Blinkeyes (Barcynska, as Sandys), 1925
Bliss, Vicky series (B. Michaels, as Peters), from 1973
Blithe Images (N. Roberts), 1982
Blood Games (Yarbro), 1980
Blood Kin (Pauley), 1972
Blood Line (Knight), 1989
Blood Money! (M. St. John), 1923
Blood of the Martyrs (Mitchison), 1939
Blood Red Oscar (Lee), 1962
Blood Red, Sister Rose (Keneally), 1974
Blood Royal (Hardwick), 1988
Blood Royal (Yates), 1929
Blood Sport (Coffman, as Cross), 1966
Bloodheart series (Tresillian), from 1985
Bloodied Toga (Hardy), 1979
Bloodrose House (Crowe), 1985
Bloodsmoor Romance (Oates), 1982
Bloodstock (s Irwin), 1953
Bloody Field by Shrewsbury (E. Pargeter), 1972
Bloom on the Gorse (Farnes), 1941
Blossom Like the Rose (Lofts), 1939
Blossoming Gold (Westwood), 1976
Blossoms in the Snow (I. Roberts, as Rowland), 1971
Blot on the Scutcheon (Wynne), 1910
Blow Hot, Blow Cold (Neels), 1969
Blow the Wind Southerly (D. Stevenson), 1954

Brazilian Stardust (McEvoy), 1967
Bread and a Sword (Scott) 1937
Bread into Roses (Norris), 1937
Bread of Deceit (s Lowndes), 1925
Bread of Tears (Burgin), 1899
Bread-and-Grease-Paint (Ruck), 1943
Breadwinners (Bloom), 1932
Breaker of Hearts (Swan), 1937
Breakfast in Bed (Brown), 1983
Breakfast with the Nikolides (Godden), 1942
Breaking Point (s du Maurier), 1959
Breaking Point (Rinehart), 1922
Breaking Point (Robins, as French), 1956
Breaking the Rules (Vitek), 1984
Breaking Wave (Shute), 1955
Breath of Air (Godden), 1950
Breath of Life (Baldwin), 1942
Breathe Upon These Slain (Scott), 1934
Breathless Summer (Hooper), 1982
Breathless Surrender (Hooper), 1982
Breeze from Camelot (Delmar), 1959
Breeze from the Bosphorus (Ashton), 1978
Breeze off the Ocean (Lorin), 1980
Brentwood (G. Hill), 1937
Breta's Double (Garvice), 1911
Brethren (Haggard), 1904
Brewster's Millions (McCutcheon, as Greaves),
    1903
Briar and Palm (Swan), 1887
Briar Patch (Blackstock), 1960
Briar Rose (C. N. and A. M. Williamson), 1919
Bridal Affair (Finley), 1972
Bridal Array (Caudell), 1957
Bridal Black (Daniels), 1980
Bridal Lamp (Ainsworth), 1975
Bridal Path (Tranter), 1952
Bridal Sweet (Bloom, as Burns), 1942
Bridal Tapestry (Reid), 1967
Bridal Wreath (Mackinlay), 1971
Bride (Irwin), 1939
Bride Adorned (D. Murray), 1929
Bride Alone (Bloom, as Burns), 1943
Bride by Arrangement (Burghley), 1960
Bride by Candlelight (Eden), 1954
Bride for a Captain (Kidd), 1981
Bride for a Day (Libbey), n.d.
Bride for a Night (Hampson), 1979
Bride for King James (M. Peters), 1968
Bride from Faraway (Sinclair, as Daniels), 1987
Bride in Darkness (Wiat), 1982
Bride in Flight (Summers), 1964
Bride in Waiting (Barrie), 1961
Bride—Maybe (Bloom, as Burns), l946
Bride of Ae (P. Hill), 1983
Bride of Alaine (Burghley), 1966
Bride of Bonamour (Westwood), 1977
Bride of Caringore (Webb), 1974
Bride of Doom (Robins, as Gray), 1956
Bride of Emersham (Charles, as Lance), 1967
Bride of Kylsaig (Danbury), 1963
Bride of Lenore (Daniels, as Kavanaugh), 1966
Bride of Liberty (Yerby), 1954
Bride of Moat House (Lofts, as Curtis), 1969
Bride of Pendorric (Holt), 1963
Bride of Ravenscourt (Reid), 1972
Bride of Romano (Stratton), 1973
Bride of the Delta Queen (Dailey), 1978

Bride of the Plains (Orczy), 1915
Bride of the Rif (Rome), 1972
Bride of the Sun (Hunter), 1980
Bride of the Tiger (Pozzessere), 1987
Bride of the Wind (Blake), 1984
Bride of Violence (Robins, as Gray), 1975
Bride of Zarco (Rome), 1976
Bride on Approval (Ashton), 1986
Bride Price (Hunter), 1974
Bride Said No (Lamb), 1985
Bride to a Brigand (Cartland), 1984
Bride to Lucifer (Winspear), 1971
Bride to the King (Cartland), 1980
Bride Who Ran Away—Nurse Henderson (Ruck), 1922
Bride's Dilemma (Winspear), 1965
Bride's Hero (A. Williamson, as Revere), 1912
Bride's House (Woodward, as Marsh), 1968
Bride's Lace (Winspear), 1984
Brides of Bellenmore (Maybury), 1964
Brides of Friedberg (Butler), 1977
Bridge Builders (Swan), 1913
Bridge of a Hundred Dragons (Darrell, as Drummond), 1986
Bridge of Corvie (Pilcher, as Fraser), 1956
Bridge of Desire (Deeping), 1916
Bridge of Fear (Eden), 1966
Bridge of Kisses (Ruck), 1917
Bridge of Rainbows (J. Fitzgerald), 1989
Bridge of San Luis Rey (Wilder), 1927
Bridge of Sighs (J. Lane), 1973
Bridge of Strange Music (Blackmore), 1952
Bridge of Years (J. MacLeod), 1945
Bridge to the Moon (Maybury), 1960
Bridge to Yesterday (Gluyas), 1981
Bridie Climbing (Ellerbeck, as Thorne), 1969
Brief Ecstasy (Robins), 1934
Brief Enchantment (J. MacLeod), 1979
Brief Excursion (Farnes), 1944
Brief Fulfillment (J. MacLeod), 1945
Brief Heroine (Elsna), 1937
Brief Hour of François Villon (Erskine), 1937
Brief Is the Glory (Gluyas), 1975
Brief Light (J. Lindsay), 1939
Brief Rapture (Duffield), 1938
Brief Return (Eberhart), 1939
Brief Springtime (Bloom), 1957
Brigadier Gerard series (s Doyle), from 1896
Bright Arrows (G. Hill), 1946
Bright Banners (Seifert), 1943
Bright Cantonese (Cordell), 1967
Bright Coin (Seifert), 1949
Bright Day Is Done (Saxton), 1974
Bright Destiny (Ayres), 1952
Bright Face of Honour (Elsna, as Snow), 1965
Bright Flows the River (Caldwell), 1978
Bright Journey (Derleth), 1940
Bright Meadows (Ritchie), 1951
Bright Morning (Ellerbeck, as Thorne), 1986
Bright Morning (R. Randall), 1952
Bright Pavilions (Walpole), 1940
Bright Promise (Chappell), 1960
Bright Scalpel (Seifert), 1941
Bright Skies (Loring), 1946
Bright Son of York (Bennetts), 1971
Bright Tomorrow (Holt, as Burford), 1952
Bright Wilderness (Westwood), 1969
Bright Winter (Charles, as Lance), 1965
Bright Young Things (M. Howard, as Edgar), 1986

Brightener (C. and A. Williamson), 1921
Brightest Star (R. Lane), 1978
Brimming Cup (Elsna), 1965
Brimstone Club (F. Mason), 1971
Brimstone in the Garden (Cadell),1950
Bring Larks and Heroes (Keneally), 1967
Bringing Up Becky! (M. St. John), 1924
Bristol Cousins (Ponsonby), 1951
Britannia All at Sea (Neels), 1978
Brittany Blue (Hunter, as Chace), 1967
Brittle Bondage (Blair, as Brett), 1951
Brittle Glass (Lofts), 1942
Brittle Shadow (Bloom), 1938
Broad Acres series (Jacob), from 1931
Broad Highway (Farnol), 1910
Broad Road (Swan), 1908
Broadway Interlude (Baldwin), 1929
Brocade (Muskett), 1953
Broken Armour (Mackinlay), 1963
Broken Barrier (M. St. John, as Cooper), 1924
Broken Barriers (Cartland), 1938
Broken Bough (Bromige), 1973
Broken Gate (Charles, as Tempest), 1940
Broken Halo (Barclay), 1913
Broken Key (Roby), 1973
Broken Rhapsody (Way), 1982
Broken Sphinx (Kimbrough), 1972
Broken Tapestry (R. Randall), 1967
Broken Wing (Burchell), 1966
Bronze Eagle (Orczy), 1915
Bronze Mystique (Delinsky), 1984
Bronzed Hawk (Johansen), 1983
Brooding Lake (Eden), 1966
Broome Stages (Dane), 1931
Broomsticks in the Hall (Blackmore), 1970
Brother Bedford (Clarke, as Honeyman), 1972
Brother of Daphne (s Yates), 1914
Brother Saul (Byrne), 1927
Brother Sinister (Kimbrough, as Bramwell), 1973
Brother Wolf (Dingwell), 1983
Brothers and Enemies (Nicole), 1982
Brothers in Arms (Niven), 1942
Brothers of Gwynedd series (E. Pargeter), from 1974
Brown Eyes of Mary (Albanesi), 1905
Brown Fields (Pilcher, as Fraser), 1951
Brown Sugar (Ayres), 1921
Brown Sugar (Cato), 1974
Brumaire (Nicole, as Logan), 1978
Brute! (M. St. John), 1922
Bubble over Thorn (Barcynska), 1951
Bubble Reputation (Wren), 1936
Bubbling Springs (Duffield), 1940
Buccaneer (Pope), 1981
Buccaneer Doctor (Slaughter, as Terry), 1955
Buccaneer Surgeon (Slaughter, as Terry), 1954
Buccaneer's Bride (Saunders, as Innes), 1989
Bull from the Sea (Renault), 1962
Bulls of Parral (Steen), 1954
Bump in the Night (I. Holland), 1988
Bunch of Blue Ribbons (Albanesi, as Rowlands), 1926
Burden (Westmacott), 1956
Burden-Bearers (Swan), 1900
Burke, The Kingpin (F. Preston), 1986
Burn All Your Bridges (Darrell, as Drew), 1976
Burned Fingers (Norris), 1945
Burning Beacon (Charles), 1956

Burning Flame (Grimstead), 1956
Burning Flame (I. Roberts as Harle), 1979
Burning Glass (Bowen), 1918
Burning Inheritance (Mather), 1987
Burning Is a Substitute for Loving (Butler, as Melville),1963
Burning Lamp (F. Murray), 1973
Burning Land (Darrell, as Drummond), 1979
Burning Memories (Lamb, as Hardy), 1981
Burning Sands (Winspear), 1976
Burr (Vidal), 1973
Bury Love Deep (Sisson), 1985
Bury the Past (Greig, as Ames), 1938
Bus at the Ritz (Trask), 1935
Business Affair (Finley), 1983
Business Affair (R. Lindsay), 1960
But Joy Kissed Me (Elsna, as Snow), 1942
But Never Free (Cartland), 1937
But Not for Love (Savage), 1970
But Not for Me (Burchell), 1938
But Still the Stream (Cato), 1962
But Yesterday—(Diver), 1927
Butter Market House (Gibbs, as Ford), 1958
Buttercup Joe (P. Hastings), 1980
Buttered Side Down (s Ferber), 1912
Butterflies (Barcynska, as Sandys), 1932
Butterflies in the Rain (Barcynska, as Sandys), 1958
Butterfly (Norris), 1923
Butterfly (Wood, as Harvey), 1988
Butterfly and the Baron (Way), 1979
Butterfly Man (McCutcheon), 1910
Butterfly Picnic (Aiken), 1972
Butterfly Plague (Findley), 1969
Butterfly's Hour (Elsna, as Conway), 1964
Butternut Tree (Beaty), 1958
Buy Me a Dream (I. Roberts, as Harle), 1972
By Any Other Name (Browning), 1985
By Candlelight (Seale), 1963
By Command of the Viceroy (McCutchan, as MacNeil), 1975
By Dangerous Ways (Garvice), 1909
By Firelight (E. Pargeter), 1948
By Fountains Wild (Hampson), 1970
By Love Bewitched (Winspear), 1984
By Love Transformed (Elsna, as Conway), 1959
By Night at Dinsmore (Shellabarger, as Esteven), 1935
By Order of the Company (M. Johnston), 1900
By Our Beginnings (Stubbs), 1979
By Request (Dell), 1927
By Right of Arms (Carr), 1986
By Royal Command (Yates), 1931
By Sun and Candlelight (Renier), 1968
By Sun and Candlelight (Sallis), 1989
By the Gate of Pity (Ayres), 1927
By the Gods Beloved (Orczy), 1905
By the Green of the Spring (Masters), 1981
By the Light of the Moon (Heaven, as Fecher), 1985
By the Queen's Grace (Sheard), 1904
By the Silvery Moon (Corcoran), 1981
By the Sword Divided (Hardwick), 1983
By the World Forgot (Ayres), 1932
By This Strange Fire (E. Pargeter), 1948
By Way of the Silverthorns (G. Hill), 1941
By Yet Another Door (Arbor), 1950
Byeways (s Hichens), 1897
Byway to Love (Sebastian), 1980

C. J.'s Fate (Hooper), 1984

Captive Daughter (Farnes), 1950
Captive Destiny (Mather), 1978
Captive Freedom (Darrell, as Drummond), 1987
Captive Heart (Cartland), 1956
Captive Herd (Atkin), 1922
Captive of Desire (Sellers), 1981
Captive of Fate (M. Pargeter), 1985
Captive of Kensington Palace (Holt, as Plaidy), 1972
Captive of Sahara (Hull), 1931
Captive Queen of Scots (Holt, as Plaidy), 1962
Captive Wife (Deeping), 1933
Captive Woman (Edmonds), 1962
Captivity (M. Pargeter), 1981
Capture a Stranger (Peake), 1981
Capture the Rainbow (Johansen), 1984
Captured Heart (Finley), 1975
Captured Heart (Grimstead), 1952
Captured Images (Seger, as Winslow), 1984
Car of Destiny and Its Errand to Spain (C. N. and A. M.
    Williamson), 1905
Cara (Trollope, as Harvey), 1983
Caravan (E. Smith), 1943
Caravan of Chance (Bloom), 1971
Caravan to Xanadu (E. Marshall), 1954
Caravaners (Elizabeth), 1909
Carberry, Letitia series (s Rinehart), from 1911
Cardboard Castle (Wren), 1938
Cardigan (Chambers), 1901
Cardigan Square (Manners), 1977
Cardinal and the Queen (Anthony), 1968
Cardinal Rules (Delinsky), 1987
Cardross Luck (J. Roberts), 1974
Careen (Coffman), 1977
Career by Proxy (Baldwin), 1939
Career of David Noble (Keyes), 1921
Career of Katherine Bush (Glyn), 1916
Career of Stella Merlin (Elsna, as Lancaster), 1972
Career Wife (Finley), 1964
Caretaker Within (Mackinlay), 1938
Carey, Come Back! (Charles, as Tempest), 1937
Caribbean (Michener), 1989
Caribbean Encounter (K. Thorpe), 1976
Caribbean Gold (M. Pargeter), 1983
Caribee (Nicole), 1974
Caring Kind (Lamb, as Holland), 1976
Carla (Albanesi, as Rowlands)
Carlowrie (Swan), 1884
Carlton's Wife (Albanesi, as Rowlands), 1911
Carnaby Curse (Winston), 1967
Carnavaron's Castle (Webb), 1969
Carniss and Company (M. St. John, as Cooper),
    1922
Carnival at San Cristobal (Asquith), 1971
Carnival Coast (Lamb), 1973
Carnival of Florence (Bowen), 1915
Carol, The Pursued (Kimbrough), 1979
Carolina series (Fletcher), from 1940
Carolina and Julia (Darcy), 1982
Caroline (Chappell), 1962
Caroline (Mather), 1965
Caroline Terrace (Deeping), 1955
Caroline, The Queen (Holt, as Plaidy), 1968
Caroline's Waterloo (Neels), 1980
Carolinian (Sabatini), 1925
Carousel (Pilcher), 1982
Carpenter's Lady (Delinsky, as Douglass), 1983
Carpet of Dreams (Barrie), 1955

Carr (Bentley), 1929
Carradine Affair (Blackstock, as Allardyce), 1976
Carson Inheritance (Daniels), 1969
Cartismandua (Wiat), 1984
Carver's Kingdom (Nolan), 1978
Casa Dorada (J. Roberts), 1973
Casa Grande (Deveraux), 1982
Casa Madrone (Eberhart), 1980
Casanova's Women (Erskine), 1941
Case in Nullity (Berckman), 1967
Case Is Closed (Elsna, as Conway), 1980
Case of Dr. Carlisle (Siefert), 1953
Case of Elinor Norton (Rinehart), 1934
Case of Heart Trouble (Barrie), 1963
Case of Jennie Brice (Rinehart), 1913
Case of Kitty Ogilvie (Stubbs), 1970
Case of the Weird Sisters (Armstrong), 1932
Cases of Susan Dare (s Eberhart), 1934
Cashelmara (Howatch), 1974
Cashmere (Ellerbeck, as Thorne), 1982
Cassandra (Williams), 1979
Cassandra by Chance (Neels), 1973
Cast a Long Shadow (Elsna), 1976
Cast the Spear (Muskett), 1950
Castaway (F. Murray), 1978
Castle at Witches' Coven (Coffman), 1966
Castle Barebane (Aiken), 1976
Castle Barra (Coffman), 1966
Castle Clodha (Knight), 1972
Castle Craneycrow (McCutcheon), 1902
Castle Doom (McEvoy), 1970
Castle Dor (du Maurier), 1962
Castle in Andalusia (Sprigge), 1935
Castle in Corsica (Weale), 1959
Castle in Spain (Duffield), 1958
Castle in Spain (Farnes), 1971
Castle in Spain (Rome), 1981
Castle in the Air (Greig), 1947
Castle in the Mist (Stuart, as A. Stuart), 1959
Castle in the Swamp (E. Marshall), 1948
Castle in the Trees (R. Lindsay), 1958
Castle Inn (Weyman), 1898
Castle Kelpiesloch (Charles), 1973
Castle Made for Love (Cartland), 1978
Castle Man (Burgin), 1898
Castle Morvant (Daniels), 1972
Castle of Closing Doors (Winston), 1967
Castle of Doves (Heaven), 1984
Castle of Eagles (Heaven), 1974
Castle of Fear (Cartland), 1974
Castle of Foxes (Knight), 1981
Castle of Shadows (A. Williamson), 1905
Castle of Temptation (Kidd), 1978
Castle of the Enchantress (J. Fitzgerald), 1987
Castle of the Fountains (Rome), 1979
Castle of the Lion (Rome), 1983
Castle of the Seven Lilacs (Winspear), 1971
Castle of the Unicorn (Westwood), 1971
Castle on the Hill (Goudge), 1941
Castle Perilous (V. Johnston), 1971
Castle Perilous (Ritchie), 1979
Castle Raven (Black), 1978
Castle Thunderbird (Barrie), 1965
Castlereagh (J. Roberts), 1975
Castles in Spain (Holt, as Burford), 1954
Castles in Spain (Stratton), 1973
Castles in the Air (Gallagher), 1976

Castles of Sand (Mather), 1981
Castile for Isabella (Holt, as Plaidy), 1960
Casualty Speaking (Norway), 1971
Casualty Ward (Bloom, as Burns), 1968
Cat among the Pigeons (J. Lane), 1959
Cat and Mouse (Roby), 1967
Cat on a Broomstick (Manners, as Marshall), 1969
¡Catacrok! (s Graves), 1956
Catalan Christmas (Weale), 1988
Catalans (O'Brian), 1953
Catch a Falling Star (B. Hastings), 1988
Catch a Kingfisher (D. Smith), 1981
Catch at a Rainbow (Maybury), 1935
Catch the Gentle Dawn (Freeman), 1983
Catch Up to Love (Greig), 1960
Catch-as-Catch-Can (Armstrong), 1952
Cathedral (Walpole), 1922
Catherine (Seger), 1988
Catherine de'Medici series (Holt, as Plaidy), from 1951
Cat-in-the-Manger (Bentley), 1923
Cat's Prey (Eden), 1952
Cattleman (Dingwell), 1974
Cattleman's Choice (Palmer), 1985
Caught by Love (Cartland), 1982
Cauldron of Desire (M. Peters, as Lloyd), 1981
Cautionary Tales (s Yarbro), 1978
Cautious Lover (Krentz, as James), 1985
Cavalcade (Butler), 1984
Cavalcade series (Coffman), from 1981
Cave of the White Rose (Kidd), 1972
Cazalet Bride (Winspear), 1970
Cease Firing (M. Johnston), 1912
Cecily (Darcy), 1972
Cedar Tree (R. Randall), 1957
Celebration (Thomas), 1982
Celeste (R. Marshall), 1949
Celestial City (Orczy), 1926
Celia Garth (Bristow), 1959
Celia's House (D. Stevenson), 1943
Cell (s Case), 1969
Centennial (Michener), 1974
Central Line (s Binchy), 1978
Ceremony of the Innocent (Caldwell), 1976
Certain Compass (L. Cooper), 1960
Certain Crossroad (Loring), 1925
Certain Doctor French (Seifert), 1943
Certain Hour (s Cabell), 1916
Certain People of Importance (Norris), 1922
Certain Smile (Lewty), 1979
Certain Splendour (Salisbury), 1985
Certain Spring (Asquith), 1956
Certified Bride (Barcynska), 1928
Chad Hanna (Edmonds), 1940
Chadbourne Luck (F. Stevenson, as Curzon), 1981
Chain Lighting (Lowell), 1988
Chain of Destiny (Neels), 1989
Chain of Destiny (Tranter), 1964
Chained Eagle (Maybury), 1939
Chains of Fate (Belle), 1984
Chains of Love (Melville, as Betteridge), 1965
Chains of Regret (M. Pargeter), 1983
Chalet Diabolique (Coffman), 1971
Chalet in the Sun (J. MacLeod), 1948
Challenge for Doctor Mays (Seifert), 1955
Challenge of Love (Deeping), 1932
Challenge of Spring (Bromige), 1965
Challenge to Clarissa (Delafield), 1931

Challenge to Happiness (Greig), 1936
Challenge to Love (Webb, as Hamill), 1946
Challengers (G. Hill), 1932
Challoner Bride (Krentz, as James), 1987
Champagne (Ellerbeck, as Thorne), 1989
Champagne Girl (Manley-Tucker), 1967
Champagne Girl (Palmer), 1986
Champagne Kiss (Barcynska, as Sandys), 1929
Champagne Nights (Buckingham, as John), 1984
Champagne Spring (Rome), 1979
Champion (C. N. and A. M. Williamson), 1913
Chance Encounter (Grimstead, as Manning), 1975
Chance for Love (Bromige), 1975
Chance Meeting (K. Thorpe), 1980
Chance of a Lifetime (G. Hill), 1931
Chance of a Lifetime (Krentz), 1987
Chance of a Lifetime (J. Smith), 1984
Chance Romance (Bloom, as Burns), 1948
Chance the Winds of Fortune (McBain), 1980
Chance to Win (Rome), 1969
Chance Tomorrow (Browning), 1981
Chances Are (Delinsky), 1985
Chance for a Farthing (Trask), 1942
Change Here for Happiness (Ruck), 1933
Change of Air (Hope), 1983
Change of Heart (Albanesi, as Rowlands)
Change of Heart (Baldwin), 1944
Change of Heart (Bloom), 1979
Change of Heart (Farnes), 1963
Change of Plans (Seger), 1989
Changeling (s Byrne), 1924
Changeling (Holt, as Carr), 1989
Changeling (Roby, as Wilson), 1975
Changeling Queen (J. Fitzgerald, as Hamilton), 1977
Changes (Steel), 1983
Changing Pilots (Ayres), 1932
Changing Tide (Bromige), 1987
Changing Tide (S. Thorpe), 1967
Changing Years (Robins), 1943
Changing Years (Stratton, as Gillen), 1972
Chant of Jimmie Blacksmith (Keneally), 1972
Chantal (Lorrimer), 1980
Chantemerle (Broster), 1911
Chanters Chase (Tattersall), 1978
Chaperon (C. N. and A. M. Williamson), 1912
Chaperone (Gordon), 1973
Chappy—That's All (Barcynska, as Sandys), 1922
Charade (Stratton), 1982
Charge It (Bacheller), 1912
Charge Nurse (Norway, as Neal), 1965
Charge of Cowardice (McCutchan, as MacNeil), 1978
Charing Cross (Rayner), 1979
Charity Child (Seale), 1959
Charity Girl (Albanesi, as Rowlands), 1900
Charity Girl (Heyer), 1970
Charity's Chosen (Ayres), 1926
Charles Rex (Dell), 1922
Charles II series (Holt, as Plaidy), from 1956
Charles the King (Anthony), 1961
Charleston (Ripley), 1981
Charlie Come Home (Delderfield), 1976
Charlie Is My Darling (Hardwick), 1977
Charlotte (Lofts), 1972
Charlotte (Trollope, as Harvey), 1980
Charlotte Fairlie (D. Stevenson), 1954
Charlotte Wade (McElfresh), 1952
Charlotte's Hurricane (Mather), 1970

Charlton Mead series (Wiat), from 1981
Charmed Circle (Ertz), 1956
Charmed Circle (Gaskin), 1988
Charmian, Lady Vibart (Farnol), 1932
Charming Couple (Gibbs, as Ford), 1975
Chase a Green Shadow (Mather), 1973
Chase a Rainbow (Grimstead), 1968
Chase the Moon (Seale), 1933
Chase the Wind (Thompson), 1977
Chasing Rainbows (Saxton), 1988
Chaste Diana (Beck, as Barrington), 1923
Chautauqua Idyl (G. Hill), 1887
Chateau Bougy-Villars (Ellis, as Marvin), 1975
Chateau d'Armor (Stratton), 1976
Chateau in Provence (R. Lindsay, as Lake), 1975
Chateau in the Palms (Hampson), 1979
Chateau in the Shadows (Ellis, as Marvin), 1969
Chateau of Fire (Barrie, as Kent), 1961
Chateau of Flowers (Robins), 1958
Chateau of Flowers (Rome), 1971
Chateau of Pines (Danbury), 1969
Chateau of St. Avrell (Winspear), 1970
Chateau Saxony (Ellis, as Richard), 1970
Chatelaine (Lorrimer), 1981
Chauffeur and the Chaperon (C. N. and A. M. Williamson),
   1908
Cheap Day Return (Delderfield), 1967
Cheats (Bowen), 1920
Checkered Paths (s Pedler), 1935
Checkmate (Dunnett), 1975
Checkmate (Lofts), 1975
Checquered Pattern (Bromige), 1947
Cheerful, by Request (s Ferber), 1918
Chelsea Reach (Rayner), 1982
Chelynne (Carr), 1980
Cherished Enemy (Veryan), 1987
Cherished One (Elsna), 1974
Cherries and Candlelight (I. Roberts, as Rowland), 1969
Cherry (Barcynska, as Sandys), 1929
Cherry (Norris), 1958
Cherry Blossom Love (Greig), 1961
Cherry Hat (s Bloom), 1904
Cherry-Blossom Clinic (Hunter), 1961
Cherrystones (Barcynska, as Sandys), 1959
Chesapeake (Michener), 1978
Chess Players (Keyes), 1960
Chessboard Queen (Newman), 1983
Cheval Glass (Bloom), 1973
Chevalier (Harrod-Eagles), 1984
Cheviot Chase (Tranter), 1952
Chian Wine (s O'Brian), 1974
Chianti Flask (Lowndes), 1934
Chicagoans (Craig, as M. S. Craig), 1981
Chicane (Barcynska, as Sandys), 1912
Chieftain (Dwyer-Joyce), 1980
Chieftain Without a Heart (Cartland), 1978
Chiffon Scarf (Eberhart), 1939
Child Called Freedom (M. Peters), 1976
Child Friday (Seale), 1956
Child from the Sea (Goudge), 1970
Child of Darkness (Daniels), 1974
Child of Judas (Winspear), 1976
Child of Music (Burchell), 1970
Child of Night (Edwards), 1975
Child of Passion (Elsna), 1928
Child of Passion (Saxton, as Turner), 1978

Child of Storm (Haggard), 1913
Child of the Flesh (M. Peters, as Darby), 1982
Child of the Revolution (Orczy), 1932
Child of the Sun (Horner), 1966
Child Royal (Broster), 1937
Children of Houndstooth (Kimbrough), 1972
Children of Lucifer (P. Hill), 1984
Children of No Man's Land (Stern), 1919
Children of the Rainbow (M. Peters, as Whitby), 1982
Children of the Spring (Wiat), 1983
Children of the Tempest (Munro), 1903
Children of the Wolf (Duggan), 1959
Children of the Zodiac (A. M. Williamson), 1929
Children's Nurse (Blair), 1961
Children's Ward (Rayner, as Brandon), 1964
Childsong (Wood), 1981
Chilling Deception (Krentz, as Castle), 1986
China series (Nicole), from 1983
China series (I. Roberts, as I. M. Roberts), from 1983
China Court (Godden), 1961
China Flight (Buck), 1945
China Princess (Elsna), 1965
China Shop (Stern), 1921
China Sky (Buck), 1942
Chinese Alice (Barr), 1981
Chinese Box (McEvoy), 1973
Chinese Door (Coffman), 1967
Chinese Puzzle (Godden), 1936
Chink in the Armour (Lowndes), 1912
Chip and the Block (Delafield), 1925
Chippinge (Weyman), 1906
Chippinge Borough (Weyman), 1906
Chivalry (s Cabell), 1909
Chivalry (Sabatini), 1935
Chocolate Cobweb (Armstrong), 1948
Choice of Mavis (Wynne), 1935
Choose the One You'll Marry (Burchell), 1960
Choose Which You Will (Burchell), 1949
Chosen Child (Worboys, as Maxwell), 1973
Chosen Course (Tranter), 1949
Christening Party (Elsna, as Snow), 1945
Christian (Caine), 1897
Christian Marlowe's Daughter (Keyes), 1934
Christian's Cross (Swan), 1905
Christina (Eliot, as Arnett), 1980
Christina Comes to Town (Weale), 1966
Christine (Elizabeth, as Cholmondeley), 1917
Christine Against the World (Swan), 1933
Christine Diamond (Lowndes), 1940
Christmas Bride (G. Hill), 1934
Christmas Eve (Norris), 1949
Christmas in London (s Field), 1946
Christmas Tree (s E. Smith), 1933
Christobel (Roby), 1976
Christopher and Columbus (Elizabeth), 1919
Christopher Strong (Frankau), 1932
Chronicles of Avonlea (Montgomery), 1912
Chronicles of Count Antonio (Hope), 1895
Chronicles of the Imp (Farnol), 1915
Cimarron (Ferber), 1930
Cinder Path (Cookson), 1978
Cinderella after Midnight (Burchell), 1945
Cinderella Girl (M. St. John), 1920
Cinderella Had Two Sisters (Charles, as Tempest), 1948
Cinderella in Mink (R. Lindsay, as Leigh), 1973
Cinders to Satin (F. Michaels), 1984

Cinnabar House (Lorrimer, as Robins), 1970
Circle in the Water (Bowen), 1939
Circle of Doubt (J. MacLeod), 1943
Circle of Dreams (Grimstead, as Manning), 1962
Circle of Evil (V. Johnston), 1972
Circle of Fate (Lamb), 1987
Circle of Gold (Ritchie), 1964
Circle of Guilt (Daniels), 1976
Circular Staircase (Rinehart), 1908
Circular Tour (R. Fraser), 1946
Circus for Love (Cartland), 1987
Cissy (Albanesi), 1913
Citadel of Swallows (Westwood), 1973
Citizen Tom Paine (Fast), 1943
City in the Dawn (H. Allen), 1950
City Lies Foursquare (E. Pargeter), 1939
City Nurse (Arbor), 1956
City of Bells (Goudge), 1936
City of Dreams (Hoy), 1959
City of Fire (G. Hill), 1922
City of Gems (Trollope), 1981
City of God (C. Holland), 1979
City of Libertines (Hardy), 1957
City of Masks (McCutcheon), 1918
City of Palms (Barrie, as Kent), 1957
City of the Sun (R. Fraser), 1961
Civil Contract (Heyer), 1961
Civil War series (Kantor), from 1935
Claim That Won (Wynne), 1912
Claire (Garvice), 1899
Claire and Circumstances (Albanesi), 1928
Clan (Knight), 1985
Clan of the Cave Bear (Auel), 1980
Clandara (Anthony), 1963
Clandestine Betrothal (Ley), 1967
Clandestine Queen (Harwood), 1979
Clansman (Tranter), 1959
Clarissa (Eliot, as Arnett), 1976
Clarkton (Fast), 1947
Claudia (Eliot, as Arnett), 1978
Claudia series (Franken), from 1939
Claudine's Daughter (Laker), 1979
Claudius series (Graves), from 1934
Claw (Lofts), 1981
Clay Country (Saunders, as Summers), 1987
Clay Hand (Davis), 1950
Clear Stream (Albanesi), 1930
Clemency Page (Elsna), 1947
Clementina (A. Mason), 1901
Clency Tradition (Muskett), 1947
Cleopatra (Beck, as Barrington), 1934
Cleopatra (Haggard), 1889
Cleopatra Boy (Malpass), 1974
Cleric's Secret (Deeping), 1944
Cliffs of Dread (Coffman), 1972
Cliffside Castle (Daniels), 1965
Climb Every Mountain (Peake), 1989
Climb to the Stars (Robins), 1935
Climbing the Hill (s Swan), 1883
Cloak and Dagger Lover (Greig), 1955
Cloister and the Flame (Wiat), 1988
Cloistered Flame (M. Peters), 1971
Cloisterman (Dymoke), 1969
Close Quarters (Golding), 1987
Close to the Heart (Stratton), 1979
Close Your Eyes (Charles, as Tempest), 1947

Closed Doors (Swan), 1926
Closing Door (Blackmore), 1955
Closing Web (McEvoy, as Harte), 1973
Cloth of Gold (Thane), 1929
Cloud Castle (Seale), 1960
Cloud Cuckoo Land (Mitchison), 1925
Cloud over Calderwood (Shoesmith), 1969
Cloud over Malverton (Buckingham), 1967
Cloudbreak (Muskett), 1964
Clouded Hills (Jagger), 1980
Clouded Moon, (M. Howard), 1948
Clouded Pearl (Ruck), 1924
Clouded Rapture (M. Pargeter), 1983
Clouded Veil (Hunter, as Chace), 1976
Clouds over Vellanti (Lee), 1965
Cloudy Jewel (G. Hill), 1920
Clove Orange (Dingwell), 1967
Clover Field (Ebel), 1987
Clown Without Background (Bigland), 1950
Cluster of Palms (May), 1967
Cluster of Separate Sparks (Aiken), 1972
Clutch of the Marriage Tie (Libbey), 1920
Clyde Valley (Gavin), 1938
Cobden's Cottage (Saunders, as Innes), 1978
Cobweb Mist (Elsna, as Lancaster), 1961
Cobweb Morning (Neels), 1975
Code Five (Slaughter), 1971
Coffee at Dobree's (E. Harrison), 1965
Coffin, Inspector John series (Butler), from 1957
Coil of Serpents (A. Stevenson), 1977
Coin of Carthage (Bryher), 1963
Coin of Love (Cartland), 1956
Coleman and Langston series (Brown), from 1984
Colin Lowrie (Lofts), 1939
Colla's Children (Knight), 1982
College Girl (Vaizey), 1913
Collision (M. Pargeter), 1981
Collision Course (Donnelly), 1975
Colonel (Carnegie), 1979
Colonel Greatheart (Bailey), 1908
Colonel Quaritch, V. C. (Haggard), 1888
Colonel Stow (Bailey), 1908
Colonists (Stuart, as Long), 1984
Color Love Blue (Palmer, as Blayne), 1984
Colorado (Bromfield), 1947
Colors of Vaud (Bryher), 1969
Colour Blind (Cookson), 1953
Colour of Power (Bradshaw), 1989
Coloured Lights (Albanesi), 1931
Colours Flying (Tranter), 1948
Colours of the Night (Beaty, as Ross), 1962
Columba (Tranter), 1987
Columbella (Whitney), 1966
Columbus (Sabatini), 1942
Come and Get It (Ferber), 1935
Come Autumn—Come Winter (Maybury), 1935
Come Back Beloved (I. Roberts), 1962
Come Back, Elizabeth (Wyndham), 1948
Come Back, Miranda (Duffield), 1955
Come Back My Dream (Hoy), 1942
Come Back to Love (Dingwell), 1980
Come Back to Me, Beloved (Norris), 1942
Come Back Yesterday (Robins), 1976
Come Be My Guest (Cadell), 1964
Come Blossom-Time, My Love (Summers), 1961
Come by Chance (Chappell), 1963

Come Home and Be Killed (Butler, as Melville), 1962
Come Home at Last (s J. Lindsay), 1936
Come Home Charlie and Face Them (Delderfield), 1969
Come Home, Dear! (L. Walker), 1956
Come Home to Love (Lorin, as Roberts), 1980
Come Lasses and Lads (Maddocks), 1944
Come Lie with Me (L. Howard), 1984
Come Like Shadows (D. Murray), 1955
Come Love a Stranger (Woodiwiss), 1984
Come Love, Come Hope (Bromige), 1962
Come Love Me (Peake), 1983
Come, My Beloved (Buck), 1953
Come On, Fortune! (Loring), 1933
Come Out to Play (Irwin), 1914
Come Pour the Wine (Freeman), 1981
Come Running (Mather), 1976
Come the Vintage (Mather), 1975
Come to My Wedding (Ayres), 1933
Come to My Wedding (Elsna, as Snow), 1949
Come to the March (J. Lane), 1937
Come, Walk with Me (Stratton, as Gillen), 1974
Come Wind, Come Weather (s du Maurier), 1940
Comedies of Courtship (s Hope), 1896
Comedy of Terrors (Lee), 1964
Comes a Stranger (Seger), 1985
Comfort and Keep (D. Smith), 1968
Coming Through the Rye (G. Hill), 1926
Command (Nicole), 1989
Command Performance (J. Lane), 1957
Command Performance (N. Roberts), 1987
Commander of the Mists (D. Murray), 1934
Commitments (Delinsky), 1988
Commodore (Forester), 1945
Common Cheat (Cleugh), 1928
Company of Saints (Anthony), 1983
Company of Swans (Ibbotson), 1985
Complacent Wife (Cartland), 1972
Compromise (Ayres), 1935
Compromise (M. St. John, as Cooper), 1929
Compromise with Yesterday (Peter), 1946
Compulsion (Lamb), 1980
Comtesse, La (J. Smith), 1978
Conceived in Liberty (Fast), 1939
Concerning Peter Jackson (s Frankau), 1931
Concession (Kimbrough, as Ashton), 1981
Concord in Jeopardy (Leslie), 1938
Concubine (Lofts), 1963
Condottiere (Westcott), 1962
Confederates (Keneally), 1979
Confessions of Nat Turner (Styron), 1967
Confident Tomorrows (Peter), 1931
Confirmed Bachelor (R. Lindsay, as Leigh), 1981
Conflict (Baldwin), 1935
Conflict of Interest (Krentz, as Castle), 1983
Conflict of Interest (Seger), 1988
Conflict of Love (Britt), 1981
Conflict of the Heart (Woodward, as Marsh), 1971
Conflict with a God (Bigland), 1938
Conformable Wife (Ley), 1981
Conies in the Hay (J. Lane), 1957
Conjurer's Daughter (Elsna, as Snow), 1979
Conjuror (Barcynska), 1950
Connelly's Castle (Bevan), 1974
Conover's Folly (Daniels), 1972
Conquer (Masefield), 1941
Conquered (Mitchison), 1923

Conquered by Love (Cartland), 1977
Conqueror (Heyer), 1931
Conqueror (E. Marshall), 1962
Conquest of Chrystabel (Vaizey), 1909
Conquesta's Caravan (Ponsonby), 1955
Conscience Money (Swan, as Lyall), 1898
Conscience of the King (Duggan), 1951
Consequences (Delafield), 1919
Conservatory (P. Hastings), 1973
Consider the Lilies (Cadell, as Ainsworth), 1956
Consider the Lilies (s du Maurier), 1944
Consider These Women (Elsna), 1954
Consort to the Queen (Bloom, as Prole), 1959
Conspiracy of Kisses (Courtney), 1986
Conspirators (Chambers), 1899
Constant Companion (Chesney), 1980
Constant Heart (Ayres), 1941
Constant Heart (Farnes), 1956
Constant Heart (Lorrimer, as Robins), 1964
Constant Image (Davenport), 1960
Constant Nymph (Kennedy), 1924
Constant Rabbit (Barcynska, as Sandys), 1949
Constantine (Slaughter), 1965
Consulting Surgeon (Arbor), 1959
Contract (s Glyn), 1913
Contrary Mary (Albanesi, as Rowlands), 1910
Convenient Marriage (Heyer), 1934
Convention, M.D. (Slaughter), 1972
Convert (Elsna), 1952
Converts (R. Warner), 1967
Convivial Codfish (C. MacLeod), 1984
Convoy (Pope), 1979
Conway Touch (Bromige), 1958
Cook at School (M. St. John), 1916
Coolibah Creek (Hampson), 1979
Coombe St. Mary's (Diver), 1925
Copenhagen Connection (B. Michaels, as Peters), 1982
Copper Cloud (Gower), 1976
Copper Fire (F. Preston), 1988
Copper Kingdom (Gower), 1983
Copper Lake (K. Thorpe), 1981
Copper Moon (Way), 1972
Copper-Haired Marshal (P. Hill), 1983
Copsi Castle (Lofts, as Astley), 1978
Cora, The Pet of the Regiment (Libbey), n.d.
Coral Kiss (Krentz), 1987
Coral Tree (Dingwell), 1958
Cordelia (Graham), 1949
Cordina series (N. Roberts), from 1986
Cords of Vanity (Cabell), 1909
Corinthian (Heyer), 1940
Cormac Legend (Daniels), 1979
Cormorant's Breed (Fletcher), 1959
Corn in Egypt (Deeping), 1941
Corn King and the Spring Queen (Mitchison), 1931
Cornelian Strand (Dwyer-Joyce), 1982
Corner House (Burchell), 1959
Corner of Eden (M. Lewis), 1970
Corner of Heaven (Norris), 1944
Corner of Heaven (Stanford), 1984
Corner Shop (Cadell), 1966
Corner That Held Them (S. Warner), 1948
Cornish series (Saunders, as Summers), from 1986
Cornish Farm (s Graham), 1982
Cornish Hearth (Hunter, as Chace), 1975
Cornish Heiress (Gellis), 1981

Cornish Rhapsody (Bloom, as Burns), 1972
Coromandel (Barr), 1988
Coromandel! (Masters), 1955
Coronet of Shame (Garvice), 1900
Corporate Affair (Krentz, as James), 1982
Corporation Boss (Dingwell), 1975
Corporation Wife (Gaskin), 1960
Corpse in Oozak's Pond (C. MacLeod), 1986
Corroding Gold (Swan), 1914
Corsair (Pope), 1987
Corsican Bandit (Stratton), 1978
Corsican Woman (Swindells), 1988
Cortez and Marina (E. Marshall), 1963
Cost Price (Yates), 1949
Cotillion (Heyer), 1953
Cotillion for Mandy (Williams), 1978
Cotswold Honey (D. Smith), 1975
Cottage at Drimble (Gibbs, as Ford), 1958
Cottage Hospital (Rayner, as Brandon), 1963
Cottage in Spain (Blair, as Brett), 1955
Cottage in the Wood (Woodward, as Richmond), 1983
Cottager's Daughter (M. Howard), 1972
Cottar's Daughter (M. St. John, as Cooper), 1926
Cotton Glove Country (Trask), 1928
Cotton King (M. St. John, as Cooper), 1915
Couching at the Door (s Broster), 1942
Could I Forget (Robins), 1948
Could She Forgive? (M. St. John, as Cooper), 1923
Coulton's Wife (Albanesi, as Rowlands), 1930
Count Belisarius (Graves), 1938
Count Bohemond (Duggan), 1964
Count Hannibal (Weyman), 1901
Count the Stars (Cartland), 1981
Count Vronsky's Daughter (Salisbury), 1981
Countdown (Slaughter), 1970
Counterfeit Bride (Craven), 1982
Counterfeit Lady (Deveraux), 1984
Counterpoint (I. Holland), 1980
Countess (M. Howard, as Edgar), 1978
Countess at War (J. Lane), 1974
Countess Below Stairs (Ibbotson), 1981
Countess Fanny (Bowen), 1928
Countess Glika (s Deeping), 1919
Country Air (Chappell), 1977
Country Flirt (J. Smith), 1987
Country Holiday (Gibbs, as Ford), 1966
Country Love (Garvice), 1912
Country Nurse (Daniels), 1963
Country of the Falcon (Mather), 1975
Country of the Heart (J. MacLeod, as Airlie), 1961
Country Wooing (J. Smith), 1987
Courage of Love (Albanesi), 1930
Courier of Love (Courtney), 1984
Course of True Love (Neels), 1988
Court of New York (McCutcheon), 1919
Court of the Flowering Peach (J. Roberts, as Radcliffe), 1981
Court of the Veils (Winspear), 1968
Courtenay Treasure (Wren), 1936
Courtesan (Tranter), 1963
Courting of Joanna (Ley), 1976
Courts of Idleness (s Yates), 1920
Courts of Illusion (Jarman), 1983
Courts of Love (Holt, as Plaidy), 1987
Courtship of Colonel Crowne (Sebastian), 1978
Courtship of Morrice Buckler (A. Mason), 1896
Courtship of Rosamond Fayre (Ruck), 1915

Cousin Amelia (Chappell), 1982
Cousin Kate (Heyer), 1968
Cousin Mark (Ashton), 1971
Cousin to Terror (Kimbrough, as Bramwell), 1972
Cousin to the Queen (Saxton, as Turner), 1972
Cousins (Ebel, as Goodwin), 1985
Cousins by Courtesy (Charles, as Lance), 1977
Cousins May Kiss (Charles, as Chandos), 1948
Cousins of a Kind (Walsh), 1985
Cove of Promises (Rome), 1975
Covenant (Michener), 1980
Cover Girl (McEvoy, as Harte), 1968
Cove's End (Hufford), 1977
Cowardice Court (McCutcheon), 1906
Cowardly Custard (Hutten), 1936
Cowboy and the Lady (Palmer), 1982
Cowboy Countess (C. N. and A. M. Williamson), 1917
Craddock's Kingdom (Charles, as Tempest), 1957
Craigshaw Curse (Webb), 1968
Crane Castle (J. MacLeod), 1965
Crash (Robins), 1966
Craven Legacy (Heaven), 1986
Crazy Quilt (s Bloom), 1933
Cream of the Jest (Cabell), 1917
Creation (Vidal), 1981
Creature Comforts (Stirling), 1986
Creature of the Twilight (Kirk), 1966
Creatures of Destiny (Garvice)
Credit Title (Stern), 1961
Crescendo (Bellamann), 1928
Crescendo (Bentley), 1958
Crescendo (Lamb), 1980
Crescent Carnival (Keyes), 1942
Crescent Moon (Hunter), 1973
Cresselly Inheritance (Blackmore), 1973
Cressida (Darcy), 1977
Cressida (Lowndes), 1928
Cressida's First Lover (J. Lindsay), 1931
Cressy (Chappell), 1973
Cricket Heron (Bacheller), 1909
Crime at Honotassa (Eberhart), 1962
Crime of Hallo-e'en (Libbey), 1891
Crime of Laura Sarelle (Bowen, as Shearing), 1941
Crimes of Old London (s Bowen), 1919
Crimson Mountain (G. Hill), 1942
Crimson Pagoda (Nicole), 1983
Crimson Paw (s Eberhart), 1958
Crimson Ramblers (Barcynska, as Sandys), 1927
Crimson Roses (G. Hill), 1928
Crimson Tapestry (Lorrimer, as Robins), 1971
Crinklenose (Barcynska, as Sandys), 1938
Crisis (Churchill), 1901
Crisis at St. Chad's (Charles), 1977
Crisis at Valcour (Daniels), 1985
Crista Moon (Elsna), 1936
Croatan (M. Johnston), 1923
Crocodile on the Sandbank (B. Michaels, as Peters), 1975
Crooked Adam (D. Stevenson), 1942
Crooked Coronet (s Arlen), 1937
Crooked Furrow (Farnol), 1937
Cross Currents (E. Porter), 1907
Crossing (Churchill), 1904
Crossing (Fast), 1971
Crossings (Steel), 1982
Crouchback (Oman), 1929
Crow Hollow (Eden), 1950

Crowd Pleasers (Rogers), 1978
Crown and the Cross (Slaughter), 1959
Crown and the Shadow (P. Hill), 1955
Crown Estate (Berckman), 1976
Crown for a Lady (Hoy), 1937
Crown for a Lie (J. Lane), 1962
Crown for Normandy (Bennetts), 1971
Crown in Candlelight (Jarman), 1978
Crown of Aloes (Lofts), 1974
Crown of Flowers (Dingwell), 1969
Crown of Glory (Jarman), 1987
Crown of Thorns (Leslie), 1979
Crown of Willow (Ashton), 1975
Crown of Willow (Muskett), 1957
Crown Usurped (Lamb, as Coates), 1972
Crowned Lovers (Beck, as Barrington), 1935
Crowned with Love (Cartland), 1985
Crowning Glory (P. Hastings), 1952
Crowns, Pounds, and Guineas (Robins), 1931
Crucifix Corner (C. N. and A. M. Williamson),
    1918
Cruel Count (Cartland), 1974
Cruel Deception (J. MacLeod), 1981
Cruel Flame (Lamb), 1978
Cruise (Grieg, as Ames), 1934
Cruise for Cinderella (Stuart, as A. Stuart), 1956
Cruise Ship Nurse (Daniels), 1963
Cruise to a Wedding (Neels), 1974
Cruise to Romance (Woodward), 1960
Cruiser in the Bay (Britt), 1975
Crusade (Byrne), 1928
Crusader's Torch (Yarbro), 1988
Cry of Morning (Cleeve), 1971
Cry of the Gulls (I. Roberts), 1963
Cry of the Peacock (Roby), 1974
Cry Once Alone (Thompson), 1984
Cry the Soft Rain (Dwyer-Joyce), 1972
Cry Witch (Hintze), 1975
Crying Child (B. Michaels), 1973
Crystal (Bennetts), 1987
Crystal and the Cloud (M. Peters), 1977
Crystal Cat (V. Johnston), 1985
Crystal Cave (Stewart), 1970
Crystal Clear (Cadell), 1953
Crystal Crow (Aiken), 1968
Crystal Crown (Harrod-Eagles), 1982
Crystal Flame (Krentz), 1986
Crystal Gull (Andrews), 1978
Crystal Spring (Farnes), 1940
Crystal Villa (M. Howard), 1970
Crystal Window (Matthews, as Brisco), 1973
Cuba Libre (Kantor), 1940
Cuckoo at Candlemas (Manners, as Marshall), 1968
Cuckoo Cottage (Mackinlay), 1953
Cuckoo in Spring (Cadell), 1954
Cuckoo in the Night (Barrie, as Kent), 1966
Cuckoo Never Weds (Bloom, as Burns), 1950
Cultured Handmaiden (Cookson), 1988
Cunning of the Dove (Duggan), 1960
Cunningham's Revenge (McCutchan, as MacNeil), 1980
Cup of Gold (Steinbeck), 1929
Cup of Kindness (D. Smith), 1971
Cup, The Blade, or the Gun (Eberhart), 1961
Cupboard Love (R. Lindsay, as Leigh), 1976
Cupboard Love (L. Walker), 1963
Cupid in Africa (Wren), 1920
Cupid Rides Pillion (Cartland), 1952

Cupid's Task (Stanford), 1985
Curate's Egg (s Hutten), 1930
Cure for Dying (Butler, as Melville), 1989
Curious Happenings (s Bowen), 1917
Curled Hands (Barcynska, as Sandys), 1926
Curse Not the King (Anthony), 1954
Curse of Carranca (Lee), 1966
Curse of Cowden (Swan), 1897
Curse of Gold (Wynne), 1914
Curse of Halewood (Laker, as Paul), 1976
Curse of Jezebel (Slaughter), 1961
Curse of Kenton (J. Roberts), 1972
Curse of Mallory Hall (Daniels), 1970
Curse of the Clan (Cartland), 1977
Curse of the Clodaghs (Cowen), 1974
Curse of the Concullens (F. Stevenson), 1970
Curse of the Giant Hogweed (C. MacLeod), 1985
Curse of the Greys (M. Peters), 1974
Curse of the Kings (Holt), 1973
Curse of the Montrolfes (O'Grady), 1983
Curse of the Pharaohs, (B. Michaels, as Peters), 1981
Curse on the Island Pool (Coffman), 1965
Curse This House (Wood), 1978
Curtain Call (R. Randall), 1983
Curtain Call (K. Thorpe), 1971
Curtain Rises (Burchell), 1969
Curtain Will Go Up (Barcynska, as Sandys),
    1936
Curve of the Cantenary (Rinehart), 1945
Cut and a Kiss (s Hope), 1899
Cutlass Empire (F. Mason), 1949
Cutting Edge (L. Howard), 1985
Cynthia Charrington (Vaizey), 1911
Cypress Garden (Arbor), 1969
Cypresses Grow Dark (Bloom), 1932
Cyrilla Seeks Herself (Burgin), 1922

Daddy-Long-Legs (Webster), 1912
Daffodils of Newent (Sallis), 1985
Dahomean (Yerby), 1971
Daily Rate (G. Hill), 1900
Daisy Boy (Cleugh), 1931
Daisy Brooks (Libbey), 1889
Daisy Earns Her Living (M. St. John), 1917
Daisy Friday (Salisbury), 1984
Daisy Gordon's Folly (Libbey), 1892
Daisy Peach Abroad (M. St. John), 1917
Dakota Dreamin' (Dailey), 1981
Dale of Dreams (Burgin), 1927
Dalton's Daughter (Dingwell, as Starr), 1967
Damaged Angel (Burchell), 1967
Damask Rose (Hunter, as Chace), 1968
Dame Durden's Daughter (J. Smith), 1978
Damnation Reef (Tattersall), 1980
Damsel and the Sage (Glyn), 1903
Damsel in Green (Neels), 1970
Dance at the Four Corners (Burgin), 1894
Dance Ballerina Dance (I. Roberts, as Rowland), 1980
Dance Barefoot (Maddocks), 1966
Dance in Darkness (Daniels), 1965
Dance in the Dust (Robins, as Gray), 1959
Dance, Little Gentleman! (Frankau), 1929
Dance of Courtship (Kidd), 1976
Dance of Dreams (N. Roberts), 1983
Dance of Fire (Stratton, as Gillen), 1971
Dance of Summer (Grimstead, as Manning), 1974
Dance on a Hornet's Nest (Blackmore), 1970

Dance on My Heart (Cartland), 1977
Dance Partner (Ruck), 1931
Dance to My Tune (Peake), 1989
Dance to the Piper (N. Roberts), 1988
Dancer in Yellow (Ogilvie), 1979
Dancer of Dreams (Matthews), 1984
Dancer's Daughter (M. Howard, as Edgar), 1968
Dancers in the Dark (MacGill), 1929
Dancing Doll (J. Roberts), 1973
Dancing Hill (Lamb, as Holland), 1978
Dancing Master (Ayres), 1920
Dancing Mermaid (Webb, as Hamill), 1952
Dancing Star (Ruck), 1923
Dandelion Clock (Bloom), 1966
Dandridge series (Riefe), from 1977
Daneclere (P. Hill), 1978
Danger by the Nile (Cartland, as McCorquodale), 1964
Danger in Eden (Greig, as Ames), 1950
Danger in the Dark (Eberhart), 1937
Danger Mansion (Daniels), n.d.
Danger Money (Eberhart), 1975
Danger Wakes My Heart (Greig, as Ames), 1949
Dangerous (Lamb), 1981
Dangerous Call (E. Harrison), 1976
Dangerous Child, (Cowen), 1975
Dangerous Dandy (Cartland), 1974
Dangerous Days (Rinehart), 1919
Dangerous Deception (Peake), 1979
Dangerous Delight (Winspear), 1968
Dangerous Doctor (Bloom, as Essex), 1970
Dangerous Embrace (Vitek), 1983
Dangerous Encounter (Kidd), 1983
Dangerous Engagement (Courtney), 1979
Dangerous Experiment (Cartland), 1936
Dangerous Flirtation (Libbey), n.d.
Dangerous Friendship (Hampson), 1976
Dangerous Holiday (Gibbs, as Ford), 1967
Dangerous Holiday (Greig, as Ames), 1939
Dangerous Husband, (Bloom, as Prole), 1966
Dangerous Inheritance (M. Peters, as Black), 1969
Dangerous Intruder (Pilcher, as Fraser), 1951
Dangerous Islands (Bridge), 1963
Dangerous Kind of Love (Blair), 1964
Dangerous Legacy (W. Roberts), 1972
Dangerous Living (Maybury), 1941
Dangerous Love (Blackmore), 1958
Dangerous Loving (Burchell), 1963
Dangerous Magic (Krentz, as James), 1982
Dangerous Male (Lewty), 1983
Dangerous Masquerade (Dailey), 1976
Dangerous Moonlight (K. Thorpe), 1985
Dangerous Obsession (J. MacLeod), 1938
Dangerous Obsession (N. Peters), 1978
Dangerous Paths (M. St. John, as Cooper), 1933
Dangerous Places (Chase), 1987
Dangerous Pretence (Kidd), 1977
Dangerous Rhapsody (Mather), 1969
Dangerous Secret (Woodward), 1978
Dangerous Stranger (Stratton, as Gillen), 1972
Dangerous to Know (Ashton), 1974
Dangerous to Love (Westwood), 1981
Dangerous Waters (Blair, as Brett), 1960
Dangerous Winter (Ebel), 1965
Dangerous Woman (Albanesi, as Rowlands), 1910
Dangerous Years (Frankau), 1937
Dangerous Yesterday (Asquith), 1967
Daniel Airlie (Hichens), 1937

Danielle, My Darling (Bloom, as Essex), 1954
Daniels, Charmian series (Butler, as Melville), from 1962
Danny Boy (Dwyer-Joyce), 1979
Danse Macabre (Holt, as Kellow), 1952
Dante's Daughter (Pozzessere, as Graham), 1986
Danvers Touch (Lowell), 1983
Daphne (Chesney), 1984
Daphne Deane (G. Hill), 1937
Darcourt (I. Holland), 1976
Dare and Do (Albanesi, as Rowlands), 1911
Dare I Be Happy? (Burchell), 1943
Dare the Devil (Chase), 1987
Dare to Love (Finley), 1977
Dare to Marry (Maybury), 1940
Dare-Devil Doctor (Bloom, as Essex), 1965
Darien Venture (Slaughter, as Terry), 1955
Daring Deception (Cartland), 1973
Daring Deception (Farnes), 1965
Daring Heart (Courtney), 1983
Dark and Secret Place (Summerton), 1977
Dark and Splendid Passion (E. Smith), 1941
Dark Angel (Ashton), 1974
Dark Ann (s Bowen), 1927
Dark at Noon (Tattersall), 1979
Dark Avenger (Hampson), 1972
Dark Before the Rising Sun (McBain), 1982
Dark Beneath the Pines (Eliot), 1974
Dark Between the Stars (Blackmore), 1961
Dark Beyond Moura (Coffman), 1977
Dark Bondage (Manley-Tucker), 1961
Dark Carnival (Greig), 1950
Dark Castle (Mather), 1975
Dark Changeling (Manners, as Lamont), 1970
Dark Conspiracy (J. Lane), 1952
Dark Corners (Chase), 1988
Dark Corridor (Robins), 1974
Dark Death (Robins), 1929
Dark Desire (Coffman), 1987
Dark Dominion (Lamb), 1979
Dark Dowry (W. Roberts), 1978
Dark Dream (Elsna, as Conway), 1976
Dark Dream (Miles), 1929
Dark Duel (Steen), 1929
Dark Duet (B. Michaels), 1983
Dark Eden (Kevern), 1973
Dark Enchantment (Macardle), 1953
Dark Enchantress (S. Thorpe), 1973
Dark Enemy (Mather), 1971
Dark Enigma (Stratton), 1981
Dark Fantasy (Lamb, as Hardy), 1983
Dark Farm (Bloom, as Essex), 1974
Dark Fire (Lowell), 1988
Dark Fires (Rogers), 1975
Dark Forest (Walpole), 1916
Dark Fortune (J. MacLeod), 1962
Dark Garden (Eberhart), 1933
Dark Gemini (M. Peters, as Rothman), 1983
Dark Gentleman (Ayres), 1953
Dark Gentleman (Stern), 1927
Dark Gentleman, Fair Lady (Bloom, as Essex), 1951
Dark Heritage (Daniels), 1976
Dark Heritage (S. Thorpe), 1968
Dark Hills Shine (Hampson), 1971
Dark Horse (Godden), 1981
Dark Horse, Dark Rider (Hoy), 1960
Dark House (Deeping), 1942
Dark House (Swan), 1941

Dawning Splendour (Barrie, as Kent), 1963
Dawn's Early Light (Thane), 1943
Day and Night (Seger), 1988
Day Comes Round (Ayres), 1949
Day Like Spring (Pilcher, as Fraser), 1953
Day of Grace (Elsna), 1952
Day of Possession (Peake), 1978
Day of Roses (Grimstead, as Manning), 1976
Day of the Butterfly (Lofts), 1979
Day of the Dancing Sun (P. Hastings), 1971
Day of the Dog (McCutcheon), 1904
Day of the Storm (Gibbs, as Ford), 1971
Day of the Storm (Pilcher), 1975
Day That the Rain Came Down (Hunter, as Chace), 1970
Daybreak (Slaughter), 1958
Daylight Fear (Cowen), 1969
Days of Grace (Jagger), 1983
Days of Valor (W. Roberts), 1983
Days of Winter (Freeman), 1978
Daze of Fears (Summerton, as Roffman), 1968
Dazzle on the Sea (Kidd), 1971
Dazzled (Seger, as Bates), 1984
Dazzled Heart (Pykare), 1980
Dead in a Row (Butler), 1957
Dead March in Three Keys (Lofts, as Curtis), 1940
Dead Men's Bells (Niven), 1912
Dead Men's Boot (s Wren), 1949
Dead Men's Plans (Eberhart), 1952
Dead Ned (Masefield), 1938
Dead Reckoning (Parkinson), 1978
Dead Sea Cipher (B. Michaels, as Peters), 1970
Deadfall (Harrod-Eagles), 1982
Deadly Eurasian (Cordell), 1968
Deadly Is the Diamond (s Eberhart), 1949
Deadly Lady of Madagascar (Slaughter, as Terry), 1959
Deadly Travellers (Eden), 1959
Dealings of Captain Sharkey (s Doyle), 1925
Dean's Watch (Goudge), 1960
Dear Adversary (Blair), 1953
Dear and Glorious Physician (Caldwell), 1959
Dear Benefactor (Hampson), 1976
Dear Brute (R. Lane), 1984
Dear Caliban (Donnelly), 1977
Dear Chance (Holt, as Burford), 1947
Dear Colleague (F. Murray), 1972
Dear Conquistador (Hilton), 1972
Dear Deceiver (D. Smith), 1972
Dear Delusion (Holt, as Burford), 1952
Dear Doctor Everett (J. MacLeod), 1954
Dear Dragon (Seale), 1959
Dear Enemy (Webster), 1915
Dear Fugitive (Hoy), 1960
Dear Intruder (Arbor), 1955
Dear Kate (Ebel), 1972
Dear Laura (Stubbs), 1973
Dear Lost Love (Maybury), 1957
Dear Loyalty (Robins), 1939
Dear Mr. Dean (Barcynska, as Sandys), 1957
Dear Old Home (M. St. John), 1912
Dear Patience (Charles, as Lance), 1983
Dear Plutocrat (Hampson), 1973
Dear Professor (Seale), 1970
Dear Puritan (Winspear), 1971
Dear Sir (Burchell), 1958
Dear Stranger (Hampson), 1973
Dear Stranger (Hoy), 1946

Dear Tiberius (Barrie), 1956
Dear Tom (Pilcher, as Fraser), 1954
Dear Trustee (Burchell), 1958
Dear Tyrant (Reid), 1977
Dear Yesterday (Elsna, as Snow), 1946
Dearest Demon (Winspear), 1975
Dearest Doctor (Bloom, as Harvey), 1968
Dearest Enemy (Elsna, as Snow), 1953
Dearest Enemy (Blair), 1951
Dearest Mamma (Elsna, as Conway), 1969
Dearest Neighbor (Chapell), 1981
Dearest Tiger (Darrell, as Dawes), 1975
Dearly Beloved (Burchell), 1944
Dearly Beloved of Benjamin Cobb (Dane), 1927
Death among Friends (Cadell, as Ainsworth), 1964
Death at St. Anselm's (I. Holland), 1984
Death Descending (Beaty, as Campbell), 1976
Death Filled the Glass (Armstrong), 1945
Death in the Castle (Buck), 1965
Death in the Fog (Eberhart), 1934
Death in the Garden (Butler, as Melville), 1987
Death in the Life (Davis), 1976
Death in the Stocks (Heyer), 1935
Death Is a Red Rose (Eden), 1956
Death Lives Next Door (Butler), 1960
Death My Lover (Blackstock, as Allardyce), 1959
Death of a Fox (Summerton, as Roffman), 1964
Death of a Spartan King (s J. Lindsay), 1974
Death of an Old Sinner (Davis), 1957
Death of Attila (C. Holland), 1973
Death of Robin Hood (Vansittart), 1981
Death of the Red King (Bennetts), 1976
Death Strikes Out (Finley), 1957
Death to the French (Forester), 1932
Death Walk (Buckingham, as Quest)
Death-Scented Flower (P. Hastings), 1977
Deb and Destiny (Inglis), 1950
Debatable Ground (Stern), 1921
Debonair (Stern), 1928
Debt of Honor (Cartland), 1970
Debt of Honour (Veryan), 1980
Debutante in Uniform (Greig), 1938
Decameron Cocktails (Barcynska), 1926
Deceivers (Masters), 1952
December Love (Hichens), 1922
December Passion (Nicole, as Logan), 1979
Deception (Aiken), 1987
Deception (Daniels, as Kavanaugh), 1966
Deception (M. Pargeter), 1980
Deception for Desire (Morgan), 1983(?)
Deck with Flowers (Cadell), 1973
Decoy (Pope), 1983
Dedicated (Stuart, as A. Stuart), 1962
Dedicated Villain (Veryan), 1989
Dedication Jones (Norway), 1969
Deed of Innocence (Blackmore), 1969
Deedee (Ellis, as Lord), 1969
Deeds of the Disturber (B. Michaels, as Peters), 1988
Deemster (Caine), 1887
Deep Are Dumb (D. Smith), 1967
Deep in the Forest (Dingwell), 1976
Deep in the Heart (Vitek), 1985
Deep Is the Shadow (Slaughter, as Haygood), 1959
Deep Pool (Blackmore), 1972
Deep Summer (Bristow), 1937
Deep Well at Noon (Stirling), 1979

Devil's Desire (McBain), 1975
Devil's Double (W. Roberts), 1979
Devil's Due (Burgin), 1905
Devil's Emissary (Nicole, as Grange), 1968
Devil's Fire, Love's Revenge (Laker, as Paul), 1976
Devil's Gamble (Slaughter), 1977
Devil's Harvest (Slaughter), 1963
Devil's Hole (Ainsworth), 1971
Devil's Innocent (M. Howard, as Edgar), 1972
Devil's Jig (Bowen, as Paye), 1930
Devil's Kiss (Saunders, as Blake), 1981
Devil's Laughter (Yerby), 1953
Devil's Mistress (Coffman), 1969
Devil's Mistress (Pozzessere, as Graham), 1986
Devil's Motor (Corelli), 1910
Devil's Mount (Mather), 1976
Devil's Own (Brown, as St. Claire), 1987
Devil's Own (Lofts, as Curtis), 1960
Devil's Own (Nicole), 1975
Devil's Own (J. Roberts), 1972
Devil's Own Dear Son (Cabell), 1949
Devil's Princess (Winston), 1971
Devil's Sonata (Hufford), 1976
Devil's Vineyard (Kevern), 1975
Devil's Virgin (Coffman), 1970
Devilseed (Yerby), 1984
Devious Duchess (J. Smith), 1985
Devon Interlude (K. Thorpe), 1968
Devotion (Hampson), 1983
Dew and Mildew (s Wren), 1912
Dewdrops (s Kennedy), 1928
Dewey Death (Blackstock), 1956
Diablo Manor (Daniels), 1971
Diamond Bay (L. Howard), 1987
Diamond Bright, Feather Light (Saxton, as Turner), 1974
Diamond Cage (Dwyer-Joyce), 1976
Diamond Cut Diamond (Donnelly), 1982
Diamond Engagement Ring (Ruck), 1962
Diamond Girl (Palmer), 1984
Diamond Spur (Palmer, as Kyle), 1988
Diamond Valley (Way), 1986
Diamond Waterfall (Haines), 1984
Diamond Waterfall (Walsh), 1985
Diamonds and Daisies (May), 1989
Diamonds for My Love (Finley), 1986
Diana (Delderfield), 1960
Diana and Destiny (Garvice), 1906
Diana Comes Home (Bromige), 1955
Diana Falls in Love (Albanesi), 1919
Diana Goes to Tokyo (Greig, as Ames), 1961
Diana of Dreams (Burgin), 1910
Diana the Huntress (Chesney), 1985
Diana's Destiny (Garvice)
Diary of a Provincial Lady (Delafield), 1930
Diary of a Red-Haired Girl (Price), 1932
Dick Heriot's Wife (Inglis), 1947
Dickie Dilver (Burgin), 1912
Dickon (Bowen), 1929
Did She? (Glyn), 1934
Didn't Anybody Know My Wife? (W. Roberts), 1974
Die for Love (B. Michaels, as Peters), 1984
Die She Must (Hutten), 1934
Died on a Rainy Sunday (Aiken), 1972
Different Dream (Vitek), 1980
Different Kind of Summer (Butler, as Melville), 1967
Different Reality (Pykare, as Powers), 1985

Difficult Decision (Dailey), 1980
Difficult to Love (Elsna, as Snow), 1963
Dig a Narrow Grave (Roby), 1971
Digby (P. Hill), 1987
Dilemma in Duet (Sebastian), 1979
Dimbie and I—and Amelia (Grundy), 1907
DiMedici Bride (Pozzessere), 1986
Dina Cashman (Norris), 1942
Dinah (Gibbs), 1981
Dinah Faire (Coffman), 1979
Dinah's Husband (Bloom), 1941
Dine and Be Dead (Butler), 1960
Dinner Along the Amazon (s Findley), 1984
Dinner at Antoine's (Keyes), 1948
Dinner of Herbs (Cookson), 1985
Diona and a Dalmation (Cartland), 1983
Diplomatic Honeymoon (Greig, as Ames), 1942
Diplomatic Lover (Lee), 1971
D'Iri and I (Bacheller), 1901
Disappearance of Barbara (M. St. John), 1923
Disappearance of General Jason (Wren), 1940
Disco in Spain (Woodward, as Ware), 1976
Disgraceful Duke (Cartland), 1976
Disheartened Doctor (Bloom, as Burns), 1961
Dishonoured Wife (Price), 1951
Dismal Thing to Do (C. MacLeod, as Craig), 1986
Disorderly Knights (Dunnett), 1966
Disputed Passage (Douglas), 1939
Distant Choices (Jagger), 1986
Distant Dawn (Pedler), 1934
Distant Dream (Peake), 1976
Distant Drum (Charles), 1940
Distant Hills (L. Walker), 1962
Distant Island (Cato), 1988
Distant Landscape (Elsna), 1975
Distant Paradise (J. MacLeod), 1984
Distant Song (Bromige), 1977
Distant Sound of Thunder (Mather), 1972
Distant Trap (Bevan), 1969
Distant Voices (Corelli), 1896
Distant Wood (Harrod-Eagles), 1981
District Nurse (Baldwin), 1932
Disturbing Charm (Ruck), 1918
Disturbing Stranger (Lamb), 1978
Divided Battle (G. Hill), 1938
Divided Duty (Mackinlay), 1957
Divided Heart (Marsh), 1983
Divided House (Swan), 1885
Dividing Line (K. Thorpe), 1979
Divine Folly (Orczy), 1937
Divine Lady (Beck, as Barrington), 1924
Divine Mistress (Slaughter), 1949
Diviner (M. Harris), 1983
Divorce? Of Course (Bloom, as Essex), 1945
Divorced from Reality (D. Stevenson), 1935
Do Evil in Return (Millar), 1950
Do Not Forget Me (Elsna, as Snow), 1954
Do Not Go, My Love (Burchell), 1964
Do Not Go, My Love (Robins), 1959
Do Something Dangerous (Hoy), 1958
Do You Know This Voice? (Berckman), 1960
Do You Remember Babylon? (Weale), 1989
Doctor (Rinehart), 1936
Doctor and Lover (Bloom, as Essex), 1964
Doctor and Mathilda (Seifert), 1974
Doctor and the Dancer (Greig), 1965

Dr. Artz (Hichens), 1929
Doctor at Drumlochan (Danbury), 1966
Doctor at the Crossroads (Seifert), 1954
Doctor Barbara (McElfresh, as Wesley), 1958
Doctor Benedict (Dingwell), 1962
Doctor Bill (Seifert), 1941
Doctor Brad's Nurse (Greig), 1966
Doctor Called Caroline (E. Harrison), 1979
Doctor Called David (Bloom, as Burns), 1966
Doctor Called Harry (Bloom, as Harvey), 1971
Dr. Chaos (Bowen, as Preedy), 1933
Doctor Chris (Seifert), 1946
Doctor Comes to Bayard (Seifert), 1964
Doctor Dares (Seifert), 1950
Doctor Decides (Greig, as Warren), 1963
Dr. Dee series (McElfresh, as Wesley), from 1960
Doctor Delightful (Bloom, as Burns), 1964
Doctor Disagrees (Seifert), 1953
Doctor Divine (Bloom, as Burns), 1966
Dr. Dorothy's Choice (McElfresh, as Wesley), 1963
Dr. Ellison's Decision (Seifert), 1944
Doctor Falls in Love (R. Randall), 1958
Doctor for Blue Jay Cove (Seifert), 1956
Doctor Gregory's Partner (Bloom, as Burns), 1960
Dr. Guardian of the Gate (Bloom, as Essex), 1962
Doctor Havelock's Wife (R. Randall), 1943
Dr. Hudson's Secret Journal (Douglas), 1939
Doctor in Danger (Woodward, as Harley), 1970
Doctor in Exile (Greig), 1960
Doctor in Judgment (Seifert), 1971
Doctor in Love (Seifert), 1974
Doctor in Malaya (Weale), 1965
Doctor in Spain (Woodward, as Harley), 1968
Doctor in Suspense (Elsna, as Lancaster), 1962
Doctor in the Family (Seifert), 1955
Doctor in the Snow (Charles, as Lance), 1980
Dr. Irresistible, M.D. (Bloom, as Burns), 1962
Doctor Is a Lady (Greig), 1962
Doctor Is Engaged (Asquith), 1962
Doctor Jamie (Seifert), 1959
Dr. Jane series (McElfresh), from 1954
Dr. Jeremy's Wife (Seifert), 1961
Doctor Lucy (Stuart, as Allen), 1956
Doctor Makes a Choice (Seifert), 1961
Doctor Mallory (Seifert), 1941
Doctor Mary Courage (Stuart, as A. Stuart), 1961
Doctor Max (Farnes), 1963
Doctor Mays (Seifert), 1957
Doctor Mollie (Seifert), 1952
Doctor Mysterious (McEvoy, as Harte), 1965
Doctor of Mercy (Seifert), 1951
Doctor on Call (Bloom, as Essex), 1961
Doctor on Duty Bound (Bloom, as Essex), 1969
Doctor on Horseback (Stuart, as A. Stuart), 1962
Doctor on Trial (Seifert), 1959
Doctor on Wings (Greig), 1966
Doctor Overboard (J. MacLeod, as Airlie), 1966
Doctor Robert Comes Around (Asquith), 1965
Dr. Ross series (Dwyer-Joyce)
Doctor Samaritan (Seifert), 1965
Dr. Scott, Surgeon on Call (Seifert), 1963
Doctor Takes a Holiday (Greig, as Ames), 1969
Doctor Takes a Wife (R. Randall), 1947
Doctor Takes a Wife (Seifert), 1952
Doctor Ted's Clinic (Greig, as Ames), 1967
Doctor Therne (Haggard), 1898

Doctor to the House of Jasmine (Woodward, as Harley), 1967
Doctor to the Rescue (Bloom, as Burns), 1961
Doctor Toby (Stratton, as Gillen), 1970
Doctor Tuck (Seifert), 1977
Doctor Westland (Blair), 1965
Doctor Who Fell in Love (Bloom, as Harvey), 1974
Doctor with a Mission (Seifert), 1967
Doctor with a Past (Woodward, as Sawley), 1973
Doctor with Four Hands (Woodward, as Harley), 1962
Dr. Woodward's Ambition (Seifert), 1945
Doctor's Affair (Seifert), 1975
Doctors are Different (Charles, as Chandos), 1954
Doctor's Assistant (Blair, as Conway), 1964
Doctors at Risk (Slaughter), 1983
Doctor's Bride (Seifert), 1960
Doctor's Child (Bigland), 1934
Doctor's Circle (Farnes), 1970
Doctor's Confession (Seifert), 1968
Doctor's Daughter (Blackstock, as Allardyce), 1955
Doctor's Daughter (J. MacLeod), 1965
Doctor's Daughter (Seifert), 1974
Doctor's Daughters (Slaughter), 1981
Doctor's Daughters (Weale), 1962
Doctor's Delusion (Collin), 1967
Doctor's Desperate Hour (Seifert), 1976
Doctor's Destiny (Seifert), 1972
Doctor's Distress (Bloom, as Burns), 1964
Doctor's Favourite Nurse (Woodward, as Davis), 1971
Doctor's Healing Hands (Seifert), 1982
Doctor's Husband (Seifert), 1957
Doctors in Conflict (McEvoy, as Harte), 1963
Doctor's Joy (Ritchie), 1962
Doctor's Kingdom (Seifert), 1970
Doctor's Love (Bloom, as Essex), 1974
Doctor's Nurse (Greig, as Ames), 1959
Doctors of Doncastle (Woodward), 1978
Doctors of Downlands (Rayner, as Brandon), 1968
Doctors of Eden Place (Seifert), 1977
Doctor's Office (Lee), 1968
Doctors on Parade (Seifert), 1960
Doctor's Orders (Farnes), 1963
Doctor's Orders (Seifert), 1958
Doctor's Private Life (Seifert), 1973
Doctor's Promise (Seifert), 1979
Doctor's Reputation (Seifert), 1972
Doctor's Second Love (Seifert), 1971
Doctor's Secret (Woodward, as Richmond), 1962
Doctor's Strange Secret (Seifert), 1962
Doctor's Sweetheart (s Montgomery), 1979
Doctors Three (Collin), 1964
Doctor's Two Lives (Seifert), 1970
Doctor's Ward (Seale), 1962
Doctors Were Brothers (Seifert), 1978
Doctor's Wife (Farnes), 1943
Doctor's Wife (Greig), 1937
Doctors' Wives (Slaughter), 1967
Dogs in an Omnibus (s Stern), 1942
Dogs in Clover (Ponsonby), 1954
Dolan of Sugar Hills (Dingwell, as Starr), 1967
Dollars for the Duke (Cartland), 1981
Dollmaster (R. Marshall), 1955
Dolly series (Dunnett), from 1968
Dolly Daydreams! (M. St. John), 1918
Dolly Dialogues (Hope), 1894
Dolphin Bay (Bevan), 1976
Dolphin Bay (Worboys, as Eyre), 1970
Dolphin Cottage (Stern), 1962

Dolphin Summer (Salisbury), 1976
Domestic Blister (Bloom, as Essex), 1948
Domina (Wood), 1983
Domino (Whitney), 1979
Domnei (Cabell), 1920
Don Pedro's Captain (Bennetts), 1978
Dona Celestis (Dell), 1933
Donkey Shoe (Stern), 1952
Don't Cage Me Wild (Dwyer-Joyce), 1970
Don't Cling to the Past (Woodward, as Richmond), 1978
Don't Forget to Smile (Seidel), 1986
Don't Give Your Heart Away (Charles, as Chandos), 1966
Don't Look Now (s du Maurier), 1971
Don't Shut Me Out (Elsna, as Snow), 1974
Don't Walk Alone (Donnelly), 1969
Doom Castle (Munro), 1901
Doomsday (Deeping), 1927
Door (Rinehart), 1930
Door Between (Elsna), 1950
Door into Terror (Coulson), 1972
Door into the Rose Garden (Hoy), 1961
Door of Death (Shellabarger, as Esteven), 1928
Door of the Heart (Grimstead), 1965
Door Without a Key (Manley-Tucker), 1967
Dora Miller (Libbey), 1892
Doria, Lorna series (Pozzessere, as Graham), from 1985
Dorinda's Lovers (Albanesi, as Rowlands), 1930
Doris (Garvice), 1911
Doris Cheyne (Swan), 1888
Dornstein Icon (J. Roberts), 1973
Dorothea Kirke (Swan), 1884
Dorothy, The Terrified (Kimbrough), 1977
Dot on the Spot (Barcynska, as Sandys), 1949
Double Alibi (Rinehart), 1932
Double Dallilay (Bowen, as Preedy), 1933
Double Dealing (Krentz, as Castle), 1984
Double Deception (M. Peters, as Law), 1987
Double Deception (K. Thorpe), 1985
Double Entendre (Pozzessere), 1986
Double Harness (Hope), 1904
Double Heart (L. Cooper), 1962
Double Jeopardy (B. Hastings), 1986
Double Lives (Swan), 1939
Double Occupancy (Chase), 1982
Double Rainbow (Ebel), 1977
Double Shadow (Polland, as Adrian), 1977
Double Snare (R. Harris), 1974
Double Standards (McNaught), 1984
Doubtful Marriage (Neels), 1987
Doubting Heart (Mackinlay), 1937
Dove (Salverson), 1933
Dove in the Mulberry Tree (Bowen, as Preedy), 1939
Dove of El-Djezaire (Salverson), 1933
Dove's Nest (Hardwick), 1980
Down in the Forest (L. Walker), 1962
Down the Long Wind (Bradshaw), 1984
Doxy Masque (Coffman, as Stanfield), 1986
Dragon and the Pearl (Cartland), 1977
Dragon and the Rose (M. Peters), 1982
Dragon at Noonday (E. Pargeter), 1975
Dragon Bay (Winspear), 1969
Dragon for Edward (Bennetts), 1975
Dragon Island (Reid), 1974
Dragonfly (Bloom), 1968
Dragonmede (R. Randall), 1974
Dragon's Cave (Hunter, as Chace), 1972

Dragon's Eye (Butler, as Melville), 1976
Dragon's Lair (Craven), 1978
Dragon's Tail (Duffield), 1939
Dragon-Slayer (Loring), 1924
Dragonwyck (Seton), 1944
Dram of Poison (Armstrong), 1956
Drawback the Curtain (Elsna, as Lancaster), 1950
Drayton series (R. Randall), from 1985
Dream and the Dancer (Farnes), 1951
Dream and the Destiny (Cordell), 1975
Dream and the Glory (Cartland), 1977
Dream and the World (Elsna), 1947
Dream Awhile (Bloom, as Burns), 1937
Dream Come True (Chase), 1982
Dream Come True (Neels), 1982
Dream Daughter (Elsna, as Snow), 1944
Dream Domesticated (s Ruck), 1918
Dream from the Night (Cartland), 1976
Dream in Spain (Cartland), 1986
Dream in the Heart (Ritchie), 1972
Dream Island (R. Lane), 1981
Dream Maker (Vitek), 1986
Dream Master (Lamb, as Hardy), 1982
Dream of Fair Serpents (M. Peters, as Darby), 1979
Dream of Fair Woman (Armstrong), 1966
Dream of Mary Muldoon (s Swan), 1898
Dream of Orchids (Whitney), 1985
Dream of Past Loves (Woodward, as Sawley), 1975
Dream of Petals Whim (Worboys, as A. E. Worboys), 1961
Dream of the West (Pykare, as Powers), 1983
Dream of Winter (Stratton), 1977
Dream of Yesterday (Buckingham, as John), 1984
Dream on the Hill (Peake), 1974
Dream Prevails (Diver), 1938
Dream Street (Grimstead), 1959
Dream Tea (s Beck), 1934
Dream Towers (Blackstock), 1981
Dream Traders (Thompson), 1981
Dream Train (C. Allen), 1988
Dream Walker (Armstrong), 1955
Dream Within (Cartland), 1947
Dreamer Wakes (Ayres), 1945
Dreaming River (Ritchie), 1957
Dreaming Suburb (Delderfield), 1958
Dreaming Swimmer (Ogilvie), 1976
Dreaming Tower (Manners, as Marshall), 1969
Dreaming Tree (Matthews), 1989
Dreams (Krentz), 1988
Dreams and Delights (s Beck), 1926
Dreams Come True (Swan), 1941
Dreams Do Come True (Cartland), 1981
Dream's End (Palmer), 1979
Dreams Get You Nowhere (Greig), 1937
Dreams in the Sun (Grimstead, as Manning), 1967
Dreamtime (Hampson), 1983
Dresden Finch (Stirling), 1976
Drift of Jasmine (Dingwell), 1977
Drifting Sands (Lee), 1966
Driftwood Spars (Wren), 1916
Drink (Caine), 1906
Drink for the Bridge (Knight), 1976
Driving of Desire (Bloom), 1925
Drop of the Dice (Holt, as Carr), 1981
Drug on the Market (Tranter), 1962
Drum (Horner), 1962
Drummer and the Song (Dingwell), 1969

Drummer of Corrae (J. MacLeod), 1966
Drums (Boyd), 1925
Drums along the Khyber (McCutchan, as MacNeil), 1969
Drums along the Mohawk (Edmonds), 1936
Drums of Aulone (Chambers), 1927
Drums of Love (Cartland), 1979
Drums of Mer (Idriess), 1933
Drums of Time (Stirling), 1980
Drury Randall (M. Johnston), 1934
Drusilla's Point of View (Albanesi), 1908
Dual Enchantment (Courtney), 1985
Dual Image (N. Roberts), 1985
Dublin 4 (s Binchy), 1982
Duchess (M. Howard, as Edgar), 1976
Duchess Caine (P. Hill), 1983
Duchess Disappeared (Cartland), 1979
Duchess Hotspur (R. Marshall), 1946
Duchess in Disguise (Courtney), 1979
Duchess Intervenes (Lowndes), 1933
Duchess Laura series (Lowndes), from 1929
Duchess of Duke Street series (Hardwick), from 1976
Duck to Water (Stern), 1949
Ducks and Drakes (Tranter), 1953
Duel in the Dark (Steen), 1928
Duel of Desire (Lamb), 1978
Duel of Hearts (Cartland), 1949
Duel of Queens (Beck, as Barrington), 1930
Duel with Destiny (Cartland), 1977
Dueling Oaks (Daniels, as Dorsett), 1972
Duelling Fire (Mather), 1981
Duet (Daniels), 1968
Duff, MacDougal series (Armstrong), from 1942
Duke and the Preacher's Daughter (Cartland), 1979
Duke Comes Home (Cartland), 1984
Duke in Danger (Cartland), 1983
Duke's Diamonds (Chesney), 1983
Duke's Stratagem (Burgin), 1931
Duke's Twins (Burgin), 1914
Dulcie (Garvice), 1910
Dull Dead (Butler), 1958
Dummy Hand (C. N. and A. M. Williamson), 1920
Duncan Dynasty (Daniels), 1973
Duplicate Death (Heyer), 1951
Durable Fire (Ritchie), 1951
Durrants (Muskett), 1948
Duskin (G. Hill), 1929
Dusky Cactus (McEvoy), 1968
Dust in the Sunlight (Gaskin), 1950
Dust Is My Pillow (P. Hastings), 1955
Dust of Dreams (Robins), 1943
Dusty Dawn (Duffield), 1949
Dusty Spring (Seifert), 1946
Dutch Uncle (Hilton), 1966
Dutiful Tradition (Norway), 1971
Dutiful Wife (Oldfield), 1989
Dweller on the Threshold (Hichens), 1911
Dwelling (G. Hill), 1938
Dwelling Place (Cookson), 1971
Dying in the Night (Summerton, as Roffman), 1974
Dynasty series (Harrod-Eagles), from 1980
Dynasty of Death (Caldwell), 1938
Dysart, Sinbad series (Wren), from 1935

Each Hour a Peril (MacGill), 1921

Each Song Twice Over (Arbor), 1948
Eager Search (Ayres), 1923
Eagle at the Gate (R. Randall), 1977
Eagle in the Sky (F. Mason), 1948
Eagle King (Treece), 1965
Eagle of Degarra (Danbury), 1966
Eagle of the Vincella (Stratton), 1978
Eagle Swooped (Hampson), 1970
Eagle's Feathers (Tranter), 1941
Eagles Gather (Caldwell), 1940
Eagle's Nest (Daniels), 1967
Eagle's Ridge (Way), 1985
Eagle's Shadow (Cabell), 1904
Eaglescliffe (McEvoy), 1971
Earl (C. Holland), 1971
Earl's Daughter (Garvice), 1910
Earl's Heir (Garvice)
Early Autumn (Bromfield), 1926
Early Blossom (Elsna, as Snow), 1946
Earth Giant (E. Marshall), 1960
Earth Queen, Sky King (J. Fitzgerald), 1989
Earth-Bound (s Macardle), 1924
Earth's Children series (Auel), from 1980
East and West (s Buck), 1975
East of the Setting Sun (McCutcheon), 1924
East of Today (Browning), 1981
East Side General (Slaughter), 1952
East Side, West Side (Davenport), 1947
East Wind (Ellis), 1983
East Wind: West Wind (Buck), 1930
Ebbing Tide (Ogilvie), 1947
Eben Holden series (Bacheller), from 1900
Echo Answers (Thane), 1927
Echo from Afar (Elsna), 1945
Echo of Applause (Mackinlay), 1948
Echo of Flutes (I. Roberts), 1965
Echo of Margaret (M. Peters, as Black), 1978
Echo of Passion (Lamb), 1988
Echo of Spring (Stratton, as Gillen), 1973
Echo of Thunder (Seger), 1985
Echoed from the Past (Wynne), 1944
Echoes (Binchy), 1985
Echoes and Embers (Gallagher), 1983
Echoes from the Hills (B. Johnson), 1983
Echoes from the Macabre (s du Maurier), 1976
Echoes from the Past (McEvoy), 1979
Echoes of Another Spring (Baldwin), 1965
Echoes of Love (Beresford), 1979
Echoing Green (Leslie), 1929
Echoing Yesterday (Manners), 1981
Ecstasy series (Taylor), from 1981
Ecstasy (Weale), 1983
Eddy and Edouard (Hutten), 1928
Eden (Ellis), 1975
Eden series (M. Harris), from 1977
Eden's Spell (Pozzessere, as Graham), 1986
Edge of Beyond (Hunter, as Chace), 1973
Edge of Dawn (Seger), 1986
Edge of Glass (Gaskin), 1967
Edge of Temptation (Mather), 1982
Edge of Terror (Cowen), 1970
Edge of Winter (Neels), 1976
Edinburgh Excursion (Andrews), 1970
Edna's Secret Marriage (Garvice), 1905
Education of Miss Paterson (Chesney), 1985
Edward, Edward (Burford), 1973

Edward Longshanks (Holt, as Plaidy), 1979
Edward III series (Wiat), from 1985
Edward the Warrior (Clarke, as Honeyman), 1975
Edwardian Day-Dream (Bloom), 1972
Egyptian Honeymoon (Ashton), 1981
1876 (Vidal), 1976
Eighth Champion of Christendom (E. Pargeter), 1945
Eighth Day (Wilder), 1967
Elaine (Garvice), 1911
Elder Brother (s Swan), 1898
Elder Sister (Greig, as Ames), 1938
Eldest Daughter (Elsna), 1974
Eldorado (Orczy), 1913
Eleanor Jowitt, Antiques (Bloom), 1950
Eleanor of Aquitaine (Lamb, as Holland), 1978
Eleanor the Queen (Lofts), 1955
Eleanora Duse (Stubbs), 1970
Electra (Treece), 1963
Electric Torch (Dell), 1934
Elephants and Castles (Duggan), 1963
Eleventh Hour Lover (Ruck), 1933
Elgin Marble (Hutten), 1937
Eligible Connection (Lee), 1974
Elissa (s Haggard), 1900
Eliza (Blackstock, as Allardyce), 1975
Eliza Stanhope (Trollope), 1978
Elizabeth (Anthony), 1960
Elizabeth series (Glyn), from 1900
Elizabeth (Seger), 1987
Elizabeth and the Prince of Spain (Irwin), 1953
Elizabeth Browne, Children's Nurse (Blair, as Brett), 1965
Elizabeth, Captive Princess (Irwin), 1948
Elizabeth Glen, M.B. (Swan), 1895
Elizabeth in Dreamland (M. St. John, as Cooper), 1921
Elizabeth the Beloved (M. Peters), 1965
Elizabeth Visits America (Glyn), 1909
Elizabethan Lover (Cartland), 1953
Elopement of Eve and Prince Playfellow (Ruck), 1922
Eloquent Silence (Brown, as Ryan), 1982
Elsie Brant's Romance (Albanesi, as Rowlands), 1913
Elsie Thorburn (Swan), 1926
Elusive Crown (Elsna), 1973
Elusive Dawn (Hooper, as Robbins), 1983
Elusive Desire (Mather), 1983
Elusive Earl (Cartland), 1976
Elusive Harmony (Burchell), 1976
Elusive Legacy (Shoesmith), 1976
Elusive Lover (Cowen), 1981
Elusive Paradise (Peake), 1985
Elusive Quest (Cowen), 1965
Elyza (Darcy), 1976
Ember in the Ashes (J. Lane), 1960
Embers of Dawn (Matthews), 1982
Embroidered Sunset (Aiken), 1970
Emerald (Bennetts), 1983
Emerald (Ebel, as Goodwin), 1980
Emerald (Whitney), 1983
Emerald Cave (Bevan), 1981
Emerald Cuckoo (Westwood), 1970
Emerald Garden (Britt), 1976
Emerald Hill (Daniels), 1970
Emerald Station (Winston), 1974
Emerald Sunshine (F. Preston), 1988
Emergency Call (E. Harrison), 1970
Emergency in the Pyrenees (Bridge), 1965
Emily (Blackstock, as Allardyce), 1976

Emily (J. Cooper), 1975
Emily series (Montgomery), from 1923
Emma Hart (Bloom, as Prole), 1951
Emma McChesney & Co. (s Ferber), 1915
Emma the Queen (Clarke, as Honeyman), 1978
Emperor (Harrod-Eagles), 1988
Emperor's Candlesticks (Orczy), 1899
Emperor's Daughter (J. Fitzgerald, as Hamilton), 1978
Empire (Matthews), 1982
Empire (Vidal), 1987
Empire Builders (Stuart, as Long), 1987
Empire of the Heart (Seger), 1984
Empress (Oman), 1932
Empress of Hearts (Beck, as Barrington), 1928
Empty Heart (Gibbs, as Ford), 1957
Empty House (Pilcher), 1973
Empty Nest (Cadell), 1986
Empty World (D. Stevenson), 1936
Enamored (Palmer), 1988
Enchanted (Delmar), 1965
Enchanted (Hoy), 1952
Enchanted (Matthews), 1987
Enchanted April (Elizabeth), 1922
Enchanted August (Grimstead), 1955
Enchanted Barn (G. Hill), 1918
Enchanted Cup (Ainsworth), 1980
Enchanted Dawn (Hampson), 1972
Enchanted Eden (R. Randall), 1960
Enchanted Evening (I. Preston), 1966
Enchanted Garden (Bromige), 1956
Enchanted Grotto (M. Peters, as Black), 1972
Enchanted Island (Farnes), 1970
Enchanted Island (Mather), 1969
Enchanted Island (Robins), 1956
Enchanted Island (Saunders, as Innes), 1982
Enchanted Journey (Bloom), 1933
Enchanted Kingdom (Maybury), 1932
Enchanted Land (Deveraux), 1978
Enchanted Moment (Cartland), 1949
Enchanted Oasis (Baldwin), 1938
Enchanted Ring (Stratton, as Gillen), 1971
Enchanted Trap (Dingwell, as Starr), 1965
Enchanted Valley (Charles, as Tempest), 1954
Enchanted Waltz (Cartland), 1955
Enchanted Wilderness (Hoy), 1940
Enchanted Wood (Ashton), 1971
Enchanted Woods (Britt), 1978
Enchanter's Castle (Tattersall), 1966
Enchanter's Nightshade (Bridge), 1937
Enchanter's Nightshade (Maybury, as Troy), 1963
Enchanting Clementina (Cleugh), 1930
Enchanting Courtesan (Bloom, as Prole), 1955
Enchanting Evil (Cartland), 1968
Enchanting Island (Blair), 1952
Enchanting Jenny (F. Stevenson, as Faire), 1979
Enchanting Princess (Bloom, as Prole), 1970
Enchanting Samantha (Neels), 1973
Enchantment (Chard), 1989
Enchantment (Duffield), 1937
Enchantment (Elsna, as Conway), 1956
Enchantment (Gibbs), 1952
Enchantment (Hampson), 1982
Enchantment at Hillcrest (I. Preston), 1984
Enchantment in Blue (Kidd), 1975
Enchantment of Merrowporth (Saunders), 1980
Enchantress series (Ellerbeck, as Yorke), from 1979

Enchantress Mine (Small), 1987
Encounter (Blackstock), 1971
Encounter at Alpenrose (Bromige), 1970
Encounter in Berlin (Chard), 1976
End Crowns All (Albanesi, as Rowlands), 1906
End of Cornwall (J. Lindsay, as Preston), 1937
End of Her Honeymoon (Lowndes), 1913
End of the Rainbow (Neels), 1974
End of the Summer (Pilcher), 1971
End of the World (Delmar), 1934
End of the World News (Burgess), 1982
End of Track (F. Mason, as Weaver), 1943
Endearing Young Charms (Chappell), 1957
Endearment (Spencer), 1982
Endings and Beginnings (N. Roberts), 1984
Endure My Heart (J. Smith), 1980
Enduring Flame (Robins), 1929
Enduring Flame (Tranter), 1957
Enduring Hills (Giles), 1950
Enemy and Brother (Davis), 1966
Enemy from the Past (Peake), 1979
Enemy in Camp (Dailey), 1980
Enemy in the Blanket (Burgess), 1958
Enemy in the House (Eberhart), 1962
Enemy Lover (Barrie, as Kent), 1964
Enemy of Love (Coffman), 1977
Enemy Within (Cordell), 1974
England for Sale (J. Lane), 1943
English Air (D. Stevenson), 1940
English Boss (Dingwell), 1964
English Daughter (Hunter, as Chace), 1972
English Family Robinson (D. Murray), 1933
English Heiress (Gellis), 1980
English Paragon (Bowen), 1930
English Rose (Gibbs, as Ford), 1953
English Tutor (Seale), 1948
English Wife (Blackstock), 1964
Entanglement (Fellows), 1979
Enter Mrs. Belchamber (Cadell), 1951
Enter Second Murderer (Knight), 1988
Enter Three Witches (D. Murray), 1942
Entertainment (s Delafield), 1927
Enticement (Trask), 1936
Enticers (N. Peters), 1981
Envious Casca (Heyer), 1941
Envious Eliza (Albanesi), 1909
Environment (Bentley), 1922
Envoy from Elizabeth (Bennett), 1970
Epidemic! (Slaughter), 1961
Episode at Toledo (Bridge), 1966
Episode of Sparrows (Godden), 1955
Episode of the Wandering Knife (Rinehart), 1950
Epitaph for Three Women (Holt, as Plaidy), 1981
Equal Chance (Clarke), 1989
Equal Shares (Stanford), 1986
Eric Brighteyes (Haggard), 1891
Erie Water (Edmonds), 1933
Ernestine Sophie (Cleugh), 1925
Errant Bride (Ashton), 1973
Escapade (J. Smith), 1977
Escape (Cartland), 1985
Escape from Passion (Cartland), 1945
Escape Me Never (Craven), 1985
Escape the Night (Eberhart), 1944
Escape to Happiness (Beresford), 1964
Escape to Love (Robins), 1943

Escape to Marriage (Price), 1952
Escape to Paradise (Grimstead), 1956
Escape to Yesterday (s Frankau), 1942
Escort (s du Maurier), 1943
Esmerelda (Neels), 1976
Establishment (Fast), 1979
Estella (Knight), 1986
Esther (Lofts), 1950
Eternal Circle (Arbor), 1952
Eternal City (Caine), 1901
Eternal Justice (Burgin), 1932
Eternal Summer (Hampson), 1969
Eternal Tomorrow (Bloom), 1929
Etheldreda the Ready (Vaizey), 1910
Etruscan Smile (V. Johnston), 1977
Eugenia (Darcy), 1977
Eugénie (Bowen), 1971
Eugenie (Chapman), 1961
Eulalie (Ellis), 1976
Eva Gay (Scott), 1933
Eve and I (Charles, as Chandos), 1943
Eve Didn't Care (Bloom, as Essex), 1941
Eve Originals (Daniels), 1962
Evelyn, The Ambitious (Kimbrough), 1978
Even Chance (Harrod-Eagles, as Bennett), 1984
Evening in the Spring (Derleth), 1941
Evening Star (Baldwin), 1966
Ever After (Thane), 1945
Ever Thine (Chapman), 1951
Evergold (Trask), 1950
Evergreen Gallant (Holt, as Plaidy), 1965
Everlasting (Johansen), 1986
Everlasting Covenant (Carr), 1987
Every Goose a Swan (Manley-Tucker), 1972
Every Man a King (Worboys), 1975
Every Other Gift (Jacob), 1950
Every Soul Hath Its Song (s Hurst), 1914
Every Time I Love You (Pozzessere, as Graham), 1987
Every Woman's Doctor (Greig), 1964
Every Woman's Man (Greig), 1961
Everyman's Land (C. N. and A. M. Williamson), 1918
Everyone Loves Lorraine (Elsna), 1941
Everywoman (Frankau), 1933
Evil at Hillcrest (Ellis), 1971
Evil at Queens Priory (Coffman), 1973
Evil at Roger's Cross (Cookson, as Marchant), 1966
Evil Children (W. Roberts), 1973
Evil in the House (Holt, as Ford), 1954
Evil of Time (Berckman), 1954
Except for Me and Thee (s West), 1969
Except My Love (Burchell), 1937
Excess of Love (Spellman), 1985
Exchange of Hearts (Beaty), 1980
Exchange Royal (Bowen), 1940
Exciseman (Sisson), 1972
Exhibition Summer (Ponsonby), 1982
Exile (Deeping), 1930
Exile (M. Johnston), 1927
Exiles (Deeping), 1930
Exiles (Stuart, as Long), 1980
Exit Betty (G. Hill), 1920
Exit Renee (Barcynska), 1934
Exorcism (Blackstock), 1961
Exorcism of Jenny Slade (Daniels), 1974
Exotic Young Lady (Mackinlay), 1932
Expendable (W. Roberts), 1976

Experiment in Springtime (Millar), 1947
Experiments in Crime (s Frankau), 1937
Expiation (Elizabeth), 1929
Exploits of Brigadier Gerard (s Doyle), 1896
Explorer (Keyes), 1964
Explorers (Stuart, as Long), 1983
Explorers of the Dawn (s de la Roche), 1922
Explosion (Wren), 1935
Explosion of Love (Cartland), 1980
Explosive Meeting (Lamb), 1985
Express to Danger (s Eberhart), 1949
Exquisite Perdita (Beck, as Barrington), 1926
Extraordinary Engagement (Lewty), 1972
Eye for a Tooth (Yates), 1943
Eye of the Beholder (Hooper, as Robbins), 1985
Eye of the Storm (Seger), 1985
Eye of the Tiger (Palmer), 1986
Eyes of Doctor Karl (Bloom, as Burns), 1962
Eyes of Horus (Grant), 1942
Eyes of Love (Deeping), 1933
Eyes of Love (Garvice), n.d.
Eyes of the Night (Stuart), 1954

Fabric of Dreams (J. MacLeod, as Airlie), 1951
Fabulous Beast (Krentz, as James), 1984
Fabulous Island (Britt), 1970
Fabulous Marriage (Elsna, as Snow), 1961
Fabulous Nell Gwynne (Bloom, as Prole), 1954
Facade (Bloom), 1948
Face at the Window (W. Roberts), 1981
Face in the Shadows (V. Johnston), 1971
Face of an Angel (Eden, as Paradise), 1961
Face of Danger (W. Roberts), 1972
Face of Evil (Nicole), 1971
Face of Innocence (Ogilvie), 1970
Face the Music—for Love (Charles, as Tempest), 1938
Face the Tiger (Donnelly), 1983
Factor's Wife (Blackstock), 1964
Factory Nurse (Norway, as Neal), 1961
Facts of Love (R. Lindsay, as Leigh), 1978
Fade Out (Jacob), 1937
Faint Heart (Ayres), 1926
Faint Heart, Fair Lady (Greig), 1932
Faint with Pursuit (Bloom, as Burns), 1949
Fair Accuser (I. Preston), 1985
Fair Adventure (Ritchie), 1961
Fair and False (M. St. John, as Cooper), 1920
Fair Company (Leslie), 1936
Fair Deal (Lorrimer, as Robins), 1952
Fair Game (Tranter), 1950
Fair Horizon (Blair, as Brett), 1952
Fair Imposter (Garvice), 1909
Fair Invader (Blair), 1952
Fair Island (Hampson), 1972
Fair Kilmeny (M. Peters, as Black), 1972
Fair Maid of Kent (M. Peters), 1985
Fair Margaret (Haggard), 1907
Fair Prisoner (Bromige), 1960
Fair Rosamond (Wiat), 1985
Fair Shine the Day (S. Thorpe), 1964
Fair Shines the Day (Maddocks), 1952
Fair Stood the Wind. . . . (Oman, as Lenanton), 1930
Fair Tomorrow (Loring), 1931
Fair Warning (Eberhart), 1936
Fair Wind of Love (Laker), 1974
Fair Young Phoenix (E. Pargeter), 1948

Fair Young Widow (Bowen, as Preedy), 1939
Fairer Than She (Charles), 1953
Fairest of All (P. Hill), 1982
Fairies' Baby (s Goudge), 1919
Fairies on the Doorstep (L. Walker, as Sanders), 1948
Fairoaks (Yerby), 1957
Fairweather Friends! (M. St. John, as Cooper), 1922
Fairweathers (Swan), 1913
Fairwinds (Stratton), 1974
Fairytales (Freeman), 1977
Faith, Hope, and Charity (R. Randall), 1954
Faithful Failure (Norway), 1968
Faithful Fool (Burgin), 1921
Faithful Heart (Brett), 1977
Faithful Traitor (Albanesi, as Rowlands), 1896
Faithless Dove (Bloom), 1945
Faithless Friend (Farnes), 1949
Faithless One (Hoy), 1966
Falcon series (M. Peters, as Darby), from 1975
Falcon for a Queen (Gaskin), 1972
Falcon Gold (Ellerbeck, as Yorke), 1980
Falcon on the Hill (Lamb, as Holland), 1974
Falconhurst series (Horner and Onstott), from 1957
Falcon's Flight (Lorin, as Hohl), 1987
Falcon's Keep (Reid), 1968
Falcon's Shadow (Maybury, as Troy), 1966
Fall of Angels (Savage), 1971
Fall of Lucas Kendrick (Hooper), 1988
Fall of Midas (Lofts, as Astley), 1975
Fall River Line (Winston), 1984
Fallen Angel (Mather), 1978
Fallen Idol (Way), 1984
Fallen Woman (J. Fitzgerald), 1981
Falling in Love Again (Lewty), 1988
Falling Stream (Chapman), 1954
Falls of Gard (Black), 1986
Falls the Shadow (Penman), 1988
False and the True (s Swan), 1898
False and True (Albanesi, as Rowlands)
False Colours (Heyer), 1963
False Faith (Albanesi, as Rowlands), 1911
False Morning (Norris), 1934
False Relations (Mackinlay), 1963
False Star (Duffield), 1939
Falstaff (Nye), 1976
Fame's Fetters (Mackinlay), 1931
Familiar Faces (s Rinehart), 1941
Familiar Stranger (Peake), 1973
Familiar Treatment (Peter), 1940
Families Are Such Fun (Charles, as Chandos), 1952
Family (Ayres), 1928
Family (Glyn), 1919
Family! (Hurst), 1960
Family Affair (Eberhart), 1981
Family Affair (Lamb), 1974
Family Affair (Pilcher, as Fraser), 1958
Family Affair (Saxton), 1989
Family Affairs (Gaskin), 1980
Family Album (Steel), 1985
Family at Castle Trevissa (Marsh), 1979
Family at Redburn (Chappell), 1985
Family at the Farm (Charles, as Lance), 1978
Family Chorus (Rayner), 1984
Family Favourites (s Duggan), 1960
Family Feeling (Saxton), 1986
Family Fortune (Eberhart), 1976

Family Fortunes (Melville), 1984
Family Feeling (Ebel), 1973
Family Gathering (Cadell), 1979
Family Holiday (Robins, as Hamilton), 1937
Family Likeness (Gilbert), 1977
Family Name (Swan), 1942
Family of Jaspard (Ponsonby), 1950
Family of Strangers (Winston), 1983
Family Orchestra (M. Howard), 1945
Family Portraits (Chappell), 1973
Family Secret (Swan), 1938
Family Ties (Saunders, as Summers), 1989
Family Ties (Steen), 1939
Family Way (Krentz), 1987
Family Web (Bromige), 1963
Famous Island (Britt), 1973
Famous Last Words (Findley), 1981
Fanatic (Miles), 1924
Fancy Free (van der Zee), 1986
Fanfare for Lovers (Hoy), 1953
Fanny Herself (Ferber), 1917
Fanny McBride (Cookson), 1959
Fanta C (Brown), 1987
Fantasia (Deeping), 1939
Fantastic Holiday (Ruck), 1953
Fantastic Summer (Macardle), 1946
Fantoccini (Barcynska), 1930
Fanuela (Burgin), 1907
Far and Near (s Buck), 1947
Far Beyond Desire (Riefe), 1978
Far Blue Horizons (M. Howard), 1940
Far Country (Shute), 1952
Far, Far the Mountain Peak (Masters), 1957
Far Flies the Eagle (Anthony), 1955
Far from Jupiter (P. Hastings), 1952
Far Morning (Clarke), 1982
Far Pavilions (Kaye), 1978
Far Sanctuary (Arbor), 1958
Far Seeks the Heart (Laker), 1970
Far Side of the World (O'Brian), 1984
Far to Seek (Diver), 1921
Farewell Romance (Frankau), 1936
Farewell Summer (Santmyer), 1988
Farewell the Tranquil Mind (Delderfield), 1950
Farewell to Dreams (Maybury), 1934
Farewell to Sadness (Mackinlay), 1970
Farewell to the White Cockade (J. Lane), 1961
Farewell to Veronica (Elsna, as Lancaster), 1940
Farewell to Winter (Bromige), 1986
Farewell Victoria (T. White), 1933
Farm (Bromfield), 1933
Farm by the Sea (Charles, as Chandos), 1967
Farmer Holy's Daughter (Garvice), 1908
Faro, Inspector series (Knight), from 1988
Faro's Daughter (Heyer), 1941
Farramonde (Maybury, as Troy), 1968
Farrants (Swan), 1913
Fascinating Doctor (Bloom, as Essex), 1972
Fascination (Hampson), 1981
Fashion's Frown (Roby, as Grey), 1980
Fast and Loose (Tranter), 1951
Fast Courting (Delinsky, as Douglass), 1983
Faster! Faster! (Delafield), 1936
Fatal Affair (V. Johnston), 1986
Fatal Assignation (Ley), 1987
Fatal Elopement (Libbey), n.d.

Fatal Fortune (Krentz, as Castle), 1986
Fatal Ruby (Garvice), 1909
Fatal Wooing (Libbey), 1888
Fate (Garvice), 1912
Fate and Dreams (Nicole, as Arlen), 1981
Fate Cries Out (s Dane), 1935
Fate Is Remarkable (Neels), 1970
Fate Takes a Holiday (Browning), 1988
Fateful Bargain (Neels), 1989
Fateful Fraud (Burgin), 1934
Fateful Promise (Albanesi, as Rowlands)
Fateful Summer (V. Johnston), 1981
Father (Elizabeth), 1931
Father Abraham (Bacheller), 1925
Father Abraham (Hardy), 1935
Father Gregory (Wren), 1913
Father Stafford (Hope), 1891
Fault of One (Albanesi, as Rowlands), 1897
Faults on Both Sides (M. St. John), 1914
Fauna (Robins), 1978
Faust (Nye), 1980
Favourite of Fortune (Swan), 1912
Favourite Wins! (M. St. John), 1919
Fear Kissed My Lips (Greig, as Ames), 1947
Fear No More (Chapman), 1968
Fear of Heights (Coffman), 1973
Fear Stalks the Bayou (Coulson), 1976
Fearful Paradise (Greig, as Ames), 1953
Feast (Kennedy), 1950
Feast Is Finished (Robins), 1950
Feast of Eggshells (F. Stevenson), 1970
Feast of Sara (Weale), 1965
Feast of the Candles (Danbury), 1968
Feast of the Peacock (P. Hastings), 1978
Feather (Ayres), 1935
Feather Castles (Veryan), 1982
Feather in the Wind (Danbury), 1959
Feather on the Moon (Whitney), 1988
Feather Your Nest (Trask), 1938
Feathered Shaft (Arbor), 1970
Feathers in the Fire (Cookson), 1971
Feel of Silk (Dingwell), 1967
Felix (Hichens), 1904
Female Editor (Garvice), 1908
Fen Tiger (Cookson, as Marchant), 1963
Fenfallow (P. Hill), 1987
Fengriffen (s Case), 1970
Fenny (L. Cooper), 1953
Fenwick Houses (Cookson), 1960
Fernwood (Thum), 1973
Festival Summer (Lamb), 1977
Fetch (Bowen, as Shearing), 1942
Fettered Past (Muskett), 1958
Fettered Yet Free (Swan), 1895
Fetters of Gold (Donnelly), 1988
Fetters of Hate (Hampson), 1974
Fever (Lamb), 1979
Fever (Lowell), 1988
Fever in the Blood (Mather), 1989
Fever of Love (Robins), 1931
Few Days in Endel (Andrews, as Gordon), 1968
Few Fiends to Tea (Coffman), 1967
Fiametta (Duffield), 1956
Fiancees Are Relatives (Ruck), 1941
Fiancées Count as Relatives (Ruck), 1941
Fickle Fortune (Garvice), 1912

Fiddler's Ferry (Gower), 1987
Fiddler's Green (Mackinlay), 1954
Field of Honor (Byrne), 1929
Field of Roses (P. Hastings), 1955
Field of the Forty Footsteps (Hastings), 1978
Fielding's Folly (Keyes), 1940
Fields of Heaven (Weale), 1974
Fiend (Millar), 1964
Fierce Dispute (Santmyer), 1929
Fierce Encounter (Donnelly), 1983
Fiery Gate (R. Fraser), 1943
Fiesta San Antonio (Dailey), 1977
Fifteen Streets (Cookson), 1952
Fifth Day of Christmas (Neels), 1971
Fifth Queen series (Ford), from 1906
Fighting Chance (Eberhart), 1986
Fighting Man (Treece), 1960
Fighting Spirit (Albanesi, as Rowlands), 1930
Figs in Frost (Robins, as Hamilton), 1946
Figures of Earth (Cabell), 1921
File on Devlin (Gaskin), 1965
Final Hour (Caldwell), 1944
Final Test (Burgin), 1928
Final Year (Rayner, as Brandon), 1962
Financial Times (R. Fraser), 1942
Finch's Fortune (de la Roche), 1931
Find Another Eden (Charles, as Chandos), 1953
Find Me a River (Giles), 1964
Find Out the Way (Burchell), 1946
Findernes' Flowers (Bowen, as Preedy), 1941
Finders Keepers (Browning), 1982
Finding of Jasper Holt (G. Hill), 1916
Fine Feathers (Albanesi, as Rowlands), 1928
Fine Feathers! (M. St. John), 1914
Fine Romance (Britt), 1969
Fine Silk Purse (Walsh), 1978
Fine Things (Steel), 1987
Finger Prints (Delinsky), 1984
Finger to Her Lips (Berckman), 1971
Finished (Haggard), 1917
Fiona (Gaskin), 1970
Fiona Macrae (Swan), 1929
Fire and Desire (Williams), 1985
Fire and Flesh (Riefe), 1978
Fire and Ice (Dailey), 1975
Fire and Ice (Palmer), 1983
Fire and the Fury (Stratton), 1975
Fire and the Rope (Nicole, as York), 1979
Fire and the Rose (Bloom), 1977
Fire Below (Yates), 1930
Fire Brand (Palmer, as Kyle), 1989
Fire Dawn (Coffman), 1978
Fire Down Below (Golding), 1989
Fire Down Below (Irwin), 1928
Fire Dragon (I. Roberts, as Carr), 1967
Fire from Heaven (Renault), 1969
Fire in the Ash (May), 1984
Fire in the Blood (Cartland), 1983
Fire in the Diamond (Lewty), 1976
Fire in the Heart (Rivers), 1987
Fire in the Rain (F. Preston), 1986
Fire in the Wind (Sellers), 1982
Fire Is for Sharing (D. Smith), 1968
Fire Meets Fire (Hampson), 1976
Fire of Driftwood (s Broster), 1932
Fire of Love (Cartland), 1964

Fire of Spring (Lowell), 1986
Fire of Spring (Muskett), 1946
Fire of the Andes (Coulson), 1979
Fire of Youth (Pedler), 1930
Fire on the Snow (Cartland), 1975
Fire Opal (P. Hill), 1980
Fire Opals (J. Roberts, as Danton), 1977
Fire over England (A. Mason), 1936
Fire People (Cordell), 1972
Fire Song (Gellis), 1984
Fire Still Burns (Heaven), 1989
Fire Will Freeze (Millar), 1944
Fire Within (Pykare, as A. Coombs), 1978
Firebird (J. Fitzgerald), 1983
Firebird (Stratton), 1975
Firebrand (Bradley), 1987
Firedrake (C. Holland), 1966
Firefly Summer (Binchy), 1987
Fires in Smithfield (J. Lindsay), 1950
Fires of Brimstone (Gallagher), 1966
Fires of Eden (Lowell), 1986
Fires of Glenlochy (Heaven), 1976
Fires of Heaven (R. Lane), 1983
Fires of Spring (Grimstead), 1973
Fires of the Heart (Blake), 1983
Fires of Torretta (Danbury), 1974
Fires of Winter (Gellis), 1987
Fires of Winter (Lindsey), 1980
Fires of Youth (Wynne), 1927
Fireship (Parkinson), 1975
First American Gentleman (Cabell), 1942
First and Favourite Wife (Charles, as Chandos), 1952
First and Last (Garvice), 1908
First, Best and Only (Delinsky), 1986
First Class (Nicole, as Gray), 1984
First Class, Lady? (Cartland), 1935
First Elizabeth (Bloom), 1953
First Gentleman of America (Cabell), 1942
First I Must Forget (Charles, as Storm), 1951
First Impressions (N. Roberts), 1984
First Lady Brendon (Hichens), 1931
First Long Kiss (Robins), 1953
First Love (Delafield), 1929
First Love—Last Love (Burchell), 1946
First Love, Wild Love (Taylor), 1984
First Night (Hodge), 1989
First Officer (Weale), 1980
First Rebel (Swanson), 1937
First the Blade (Dane), 1918
First, the Dream (Maybury), 1951
First Things First (Delinsky), 1985
First Things Last (Browning), 1984
First Waltz (J. Roberts), 1974
First Week in September (Elsna), 1940
First Wife (s Buck), 1933
First Year (Andrews), 1957
First-Class Male (Vitek), 1987
First-Time of Asking (Charles, as Tempest), 1954
Fishy, Said the Admiral (Cadell), 1948
Fit for a King (Palmer), 1987
Five and Ten (Hurst), 1929
Five Farthings (Chappel), 1974
Five for Sorrow, Ten for Joy (Godden), 1979
Five Gold Rings (Wiat), 1983
Five Houses (Mackinlay), 1952
Five Mrs. Lorrimers (Elsna, as Conway), 1966

Five Passengers from Lisbon (Eberhart), 1946
Five People (Bowen), 1925
Five Windows (D. Stevenson), 1953
Five Winds (Bowen), 1927
Five Women (s Baldwin), 1942
Five-Hooded Cobra (Barcynska, as Sandys), 1932
Five-Minute Marriage (Aiken), 1977
Fixed as the Stars (Elsna, as Lancaster), 1946
Flag Is Still There (Swanson), 1933
Flagg Family (Norris), 1936
Flamboyant Tree (Hunter, as Chace), 1972
Flame and the Flower (Woodiwiss), 1972
Flame and the Frost (Robins, as Gray), 1957
Flame in Byzantium (Yarbro), 1987
Flame in Fiji (Bevan), 1973
Flame in the Snow (M. Peters, as Black), 1980
Flame Is Love (Cartland), 1975
Flame of Diablo (Craven), 1979
Flame of Fate (Hampson), 1975
Flame of Life (MacGill), 1921
Flame of Love (Albanesi, as Rowlands), 1923
Flame of the East (J. Fitzgerald), 1986
Flame of the Forest (Muskett), 1958
Flame of the South (Gluyas), 1979
Flame on the Sun (Seger), 1983
Flamenco (E. Smith), 1931
Flamenco Rose (J. Roberts), 1981
Flames (Hichens), 1897
Flames in the Wind (Pedler), 1937
Flames of Glory (Matthews), 1983
Flames of Love (Blackmore), 1981
Flaming Felicia (Duffield), 1934
Flaming Frontier (Slaughter), 1957
Flaming Janet (P. Hill), 1954
Flaming June (Vaizey), 1908
Flaming Tree (Whitney), 1986
Flamingo Flying South (Dingwell), 1974
Flamingo Moon (M. Pargeter), 1977
Flamingo Park (Way), 1980
Flamingoes on the Lake (Hunter, as Chace), 1961
Flanders (Rayner), 1988
Flash for Freedom! (G. Fraser), 1971
Flash of Emerald (Arbor), 1977
Flash of Scarlet (S. Thorpe), 1978
Flash of Splendour (A. Stevenson), 1968
Flash Point (Donnelly), 1981
Flashman series (G. Fraser), from 1969
Flaunting Cactus (May), 1986
Flaunting Extravagant Queen (Holt, as Plaidy),
  1957
Flavia (Jacob), 1965
Flawed Blades (s Wren), 1933
Flawed Enchantress (M. Peters), 1974
Flawless (Craven), 1989
Fledgling (Cadell), 1975
Fleeing Shadows (Duffield), 1934
Fleeting Breath (Preston), 1970
Fleeting Hour (R. Randall), 1947
Flesh and the Devil (Holt, as Ford), 1950
Fletchers End (D. Stevenson), 1962
Fleur (Tresillian), 1979
Fleurette of Four Corners (Burgin), 1925
Flickering Candle (Ainsworth), 1968
Flickering Lamp (Muskett), 1931
Flies (s Hutten), 1927
Flight (Eaton), 1954
Flight from Hanover Square (Ponsonby), 1972

Flight from Heartbreak (I. Preston), 1986
Flight from Natchez (Slaughter), 1955
Flight into Fear (Greig, as Ames), 1954
Flight into Love (Blackmore), 1964
Flight into Yesterday (Way), 1976
Flight of a Fallen Angel (Winston), 1971
Flight of Dutchmen (Tranter), 1947
Flight of the Archangel (I. Holland), 1985
Flight of the Falcon (Bloom), 1969
Flight of the Falcon (du Maurier), 1965
Flight of the Flamingo (Darrell), 1989
Flight of the Hawk (Stratton), 1974
Flight of the Heron (Broster), 1925
Flight of the Swan (Farnes), 1959
Flight of the Swan (Lamb, as Coates), 1973
Flight of Wild Geese (R. Fraser), 1955
Flight to Happiness (Beresford), 1983
Flight to Happiness (Greig, as Ames), 1950
Flight to Romance (Woodward), 1969
Flight to Sandaha (Woodward), 1981
Flight to the Stars (Barrie, as Kent), 1959
Flight to the Villa Mistra (Worboys, as Maxwell), 1973
Flint Anchor (S. Warner), 1954
Flints and Roses (Jagger), 1981
Flip Side of Yesterday (Delinsky, as Douglass), 1983
Flirt (Chesney), 1985
Flirt and the Flapper (Glyn), 1930
Flirtations of a Beauty (Libbey), 1890
Flockmasters (Tranter), 1960
Flood series (Steen), from 1941
Flood of Passion (Bloom), 1932
Floods of Spring (Bellamann), 1942
Floodtide (Ebel, as Goodwin), 1983
Flood-Tide (Harrod-Eagles), 1986
Floodtide (K. Thorpe), 1981
Floodtide (Yerby), 1950
Flora (Weale), 1983
Flora Garland's Courtship (Libbey), n.d.
Flora Temple (Libbey), n.d.
Florabel's Lover (Libbey), 1892
Florentine Spring (Lamb), 1977
Floris (Garvice), 1910
Flower and the Fruit (Charles, as Tempest), 1964
Flower and the Nettle (Charles), 1975
Flower Forbidden (Williamson), 1911
Flower Girls (Dane), 1954
Flower of Eternity (Hilton), 1970
Flower of Ethiopia (Hunter, as Chace), 1969
Flower of Love (J. Roberts), 1983
Flower of Silence (Manners, as Marshall), 1970
Flower o' the Broom (J. MacLeod), 1943
Flower of the Desert (R. Lindsay, as Leigh), 1979
Flower of the Greys (M. Peters), 1969
Flower of the Heart (Grimstead, as Manning),
  1963
Flower o' the Lily (Orczy), 1918
Flower o' the Moor (Wynne), 1935
Flower of the Morning (Blair, as Conway), 1960
Flower of the Nettle (Arbor), 1953
Flower on the Rock (Arbor), 1972
Flower Phantoms (R. Fraser), 1926
Flower That's Free (S. Harrison), 1984
Flower Without Root (Bigland), 1952
Flowering Cactus (Hunter, as Chace), 1970
Flowering Desert (Hoy), 1965
Flowering Wilderness (Blair), 1951
Flowering Year (Bromige), 1959

Flowers for Lilian (Gilbert), 1980
Flowers for My Love (Britt), 1979
Flowers for the Doctor (Andrews), 1963
Flowers for the God of Love (Cartland), 1978
Flowers from the Rock (Muskett), 1956
Flowers in Stony Places (Lewty), 1975
Flowers in the Grass (Hewlett), 1920
Flowers in the Wind (Blair, as Conway), 1954
Flowers of Chivalry (Tranter), 1988
Flowers of Eden (J. Smith), 1979
Flowers of Fire (Blake), 1977
Flowers of Fire (Burgin), 1908
Flowers of the Field (S. Harrison), 1980
Flowers of the Marsh (Rome), 1969
Flute, Far and Near (Trask), 1929
Flutter of White Wings (Ashton), 1972
Fly Away, Love (Beaty), 1975
Fly Beyond the Sunset (Hampson), 1978
Fly High, My Heart (Woodward, as Davis), 1972
Fly with My Love (Darrell, as Dawes), 1978
Flyers (McCutcheon), 1907
Flying Colours (Forester), 1938
Flying Draper (R. Fraser), 1924
Flying Dutchman (Arlen), 1939
Flying Nurse (Bloom, as Burns), 1967
Flying Nurse (Woodward), 1979
Flying Swans (Bloom), 1940
Flying Years (Niven), 1935
Flynn of the Inland (Idriess), 1932
Foes (M. Johnston), 1918
Foes of Freedom (Wynne), 1916
Fog (Gibbs, as Ford), 1933
Foggy, Foggy Dew (Blackstock), 1958
Follies (Thomas), 1983
Follies of the King (Holt, as Plaidy), 1980
Follow a Shadow (Hampson), 1971
Follow a Shadow (Manners, as Marshall), 1974
Follow a Stranger (Lamb), 1973
Follow Me Down (Foote), 1950
Follow the Drum (Saxton, as Turner), 1982
Follow the Shadow (Ayres), 1936
Follow Your Dream (Greig, as Ames), 1957
Follow Your Heart (Loring), 1963
Follow Your Hearts (Maybury), 1955
Follow Your Love (Greig), 1959
Follow Your Star (Elsna, as Snow), 1941
Follow Your Star (L. Walker), 1963
Following of the Star (Barclay), 1911
Folly Bridge (D. Murray), 1945
Folly by Candlelight (Lamb, as Holland), 1978
Folly Island (Deeping), 1939
Folly of Eustace (s Hichens), 1896
Folly of Love (Woodward), 1979
Folly of Princes (Tranter), 1977
Folly of the Heart (Arbor), 1955
Folly of the Heart (Burghley), 1967
Folly to Be Wise (Seale), 1946
Folly's End (Leslie), 1944
Fond Adventures (s Hewlett), 1905
Fond Fancy (s Bowen), 1932
Food for Love (Cartland), 1975
Food for Love (R. Lindsay), 1974
Food of Love (Mackinlay), 1960
Fool (Bailey), 1921
Fool and His Money (McCutcheon), 1913
Fool—Be Still (Hurst), 1964
Fool Beloved (Farnol), 1949

Fool Errant (Hewlett), 1905
Fool of the Family (Kennedy), 1930
Fool of Virtue (Mackinlay), 1964
Foolish Heart (Lorrimer, as Robins), 1956
Foolish Marriage (Ponsonby), 1952
Foolish Marriage (Swan), 1894
Foolish Virgin (Norris), 1929
Fool's Enchantment (Maddocks), 1969
Fool's Haven (M. Howard), 1954
Fools in Mortar (Leslie), 1928
Footfall in the Mist (M. Peters, as Black), 1971
Footlight Fever (Ruck), 1942
Footsteps in the Dark (Heyer), 1932
Footsteps in the Fog (Bennetts), 1979
For a Dream's Sake (Charles, as Chandos), 1949
For a Dream's Sake (Elsna, as Conway), 1967
For a Dream's Sake (Ritchie), 1965
For Adults Only (Lamb), 1984
For All Eternity (Cartland), 1981
For All Time (Stanford), 1984
For All We Know (Stern), 1956
For All Your Life (Loring), 1952
For an Earldom (Garvice)
For Bitter or Worse (Dailey), 1978
For Charles the Rover (Wynne), 1909
For Church and Chieftain (Wynne), 1909
For Ever and a Day (Albanesi, as Rowlands), 1911
For Ever and Ever (Burchell), 1956
For Ever True (Albanesi, as Rowlands), 1904
For Faith and Navarre (Wynne), 1904
For Her Lover's Sake (M. St. John), 1918
For Her Only (Garvice), 1902
For Her to See (Bowen, as Shearing), 1947
For I Have Lived Today (Dwyer-Joyce), 1971
For Love (Ayres), 1918
For Love Alone (Elsna, as Snow), 1957
For Love and Honor (Albanesi, as Rowlands)
For Love and Valcour (Daniels), 1983
For Love of a Doctor (Seifert), 1969
For Love of a Pagan (Hampson), 1978
For Love of Anne Lambert (Albanesi), 1910
For Love of Betty (Swan), 1928
For Love of Sigrid (Albanesi, as Rowlands), 1906
For Love of Speranza (Albanesi, as Rowlands),
   1910
For Love of the King (Bloom, as Prole), 1960
For Love or Honor (Garvice, as Hart)
For Love's Sake Only (Chard), 1988
For Love's Sake Only (Hoy), 1951
For Lucy's Sake (s Swan), 1883
For Mike's Sake (Dailey), 1979
For My Great Folly (Costain), 1942
For My Sins (Blair, as Brett), 1966
For Now, Forever (N. Roberts), 1987
For the Cause (s Weyman), 1897
For the Love of God (Dailey), 1981
For the Love of Sami (F. Preston), 1984
For the Love of Sara (Mather), 1975
For the Sake of the Family (s Swan), 1898
For Those in Love (Charles, as Tempest), 1956
For What? (Cartland), 1930
Forbidden (Lorrimer, as Robins), 1967
Forbidden (Mather), 1976
Forbidden (Maybury), 1956
Forbidden (Robins), 1971
Forbidden Bride (Robins), 1926
Forbidden Ecstasy (Taylor), 1982

Forbidden Fiancé (Bloom, as Essex), 1957
Forbidden Fire (Lamb), 1979
Forbidden Flame (Mather), 1981
Forbidden Fruit (B. Hastings), 1987
Forbidden Fruit (Pozzessere, as Graham), 1983
Forbidden Ground (Swanson), 1938
Forbidden Island (Seale), 1953
Forbidden Joy (Pykare, as Coombs), 1983
Forbidden Love (Courtney), 1980
Forbidden Love (R. Lindsay), 1977
Forbidden Love (Robins), 1927
Forbidden Love (Seger), 1983
Forbidden Marriage (Libbey), 1888
Forbidden Rapture (J. MacLeod), 1941
Forbidden Rapture (Winspear), 1973
Forbidden Road (Albanesi), 1908
Forbidden Road (M. St. John, as Cooper), 1931
Forbidden Valley (Summers), 1973
Force Field (Donnelly), 1987
Forced Landing (Ruck), 1931
Forefathers (Cato), 1982
Foreign Girl (Melville, as Betteridge), 1960
Forerunners (Swan), 1930
Forest and the Fort (H. Allen), 1943
Forest Lovers (Hewlett), 1898
Forest Lure (Burgin), 1926
Forest of Fear (Manners, as Rundle), 1969
Forest of Stone (P. Hastings, as Mayfield), 1957
Forest of Terrible Things (Hull), 1939
Forest of the Night (Donnelly), 1978
Forever Amber (Winsor), 1944
Forever and a Day (Loring), 1965
Forever Autumn (Bloom), 1979
Forever Dream (Johansen), 1985
Forever Faithful (McEvoy), 1962
Forever Instinct (Delinsky), 1985
Forever Kind (Sellers), 1984
Forever My Love (Brandewyne), 1982
Forever Spring (Lorin, as Hohl), 1988
Forever To-morrow (Duffield), 1946
Forget Me Not (Lowell), 1984
Forget Me Not (J. Roberts), 1982
Forget Not Ariadne (P. Hill), 1965
Forget That I Remember (Robins), 1940
Forget the Glory (Darrell, as Drummond), 1985
Forget-Me-Not (Bowen, as Shearing), 1932
Forgive Me, My Love (Robins), 1947
Forgive Us Our Trespasses (Douglas), 1932
Forgotten Bride (Westwood), 1980
Forgotten City (Cartland), 1936
Forgotten Dreams (I. Roberts, as Rowland), 1978
Forgotten Heir (Ponsonby), 1969
Forgotten Marriage (R. Lindsay), 1978
Forgotten Smile (Kennedy), 1961
Forgotten Story (Graham), 1945
Forsaking All Others (Loring), 1971
Forsaking All Others (Spencer), n.d.
Fort Everglades (Slaughter), 1951
Fort in the Jungle (Wren), 1936
Fortress (Gavin), 1964
Fortress (J. MacLeod), 1970
Fortress (Walpole), 1932
Fortress in the Forth (J. Lane), 1950
Fortunate (Ponsonby), 1971
Fortunate Belle (Sebastian, as Gladstone), 1978
Fortunate Mary (s E. Porter), 1928

Fortune Hunter (Ayres), 1921
Fortune Hunters (Aiken), 1965
Fortune Hunters (s C. and A. Williamson), 1923
Fortune in Romance (Greig), 1940
Fortune My Foe (Erskine-Lindop), 1947
Fortune of War (O'Brian), 1979
Fortune Turns Her Wheel (Sheard), 1929
Fortune's Bride (Gellis), 1983
Fortune's Flames (Taylor), 1988
Fortune's Fool (Sabatini), 1923
Fortune's Footballs (Burgin), 1897
Fortunes of Bridget Malone (Lowndes), 1937
Fortunes of Garin (M. Johnston), 1915
Fortunes of Love (Courtney), 1980
Fortunes of Sally Luck (M. St. John, as Cooper), 1925
Fortunes of Springfield (Farnes), 1955
Fortunes of the Farrells (Vaizey), 1907
Fortune's Slave (Mackinlay), 1975
Fortune's Smile (Roby), 1979
Fortune's Sport (A. Williamson), 1898
Fortune's Whirlwind (Jakes), 1975
40 Acres and No Mule (Giles), 1952
Forty Brothers (s Webb), 1934
Forty Is Beginning (Bloom, as Essex), 1952
Forward Pass (B. Hastings), 1986
Foul Matter (Aiken), 1983
Found Treasure (G. Hill, as Macdonald), 1928
Founder of the House (Jacob), 1935
Founding (Harrod-Eagles), 1980
Founding Fathers (Duggan), 1959
Foundling (Heyer), 1948
Fountain of Roses (I. Roberts, as Rowland), 1966
Fountain of Youth (P. Hastings), 1959
Fountains of Paradise (Hunter), 1983
Four Days in June (Gibbs, as Ford), 1951
Four Doctors (Woodward, as Harley), 1960
Four Doctors, Four Wives (Seifert), 1975
Four Generations (Jacob), 1934
Four Graces (D. Stevenson), 1946
Four of Hearts (Grimstead, as Manning), 1967
Four Roads to Windrush (Barrie), 1957
Four Swans (Graham), 1976
Four Weeks in Venice (Sallis), 1978
Four Weeks in Winter (Donnelly), 1977
Four-Part Setting (Bridge), 1939
Four-Poster (Wiat), 1979
Four-Pools Mystery (Webster), 1908
1492 (M. Johnston), 1922
Fourteenth of October (Bryher), 1952
Fourth Cedar (Bloom), 1944
Fourth Chamber (Bowen, as Preedy), 1944
Fourth Man on the Rope (Berckman), 1972
Fourth Mary (Cleeve), 1982
Fourth Queen (Paterson), 1924
Fox from His Lair (Cadell), 1965
Fox Farm (Deeping), 1911
Foxes of Harrow (Yerby), 1946
Foxfire (Seton), 1951
Foxfire Light (Dailey), 1982
Fractured Silence (Cowen), 1969
Fragile Years (Franken), 1952
Fragrant Flower (Cartland), 1976
Frail Sanctuary (Hilton), 1970
Frame of Dreams (Cartland), 1975
Frances Fights for Herself (Albanesi, as Rowlands), 1934

Francesca (Elsna, as Snow), 1970
Francis Cludde, The Story of (Weyman), 1891
Franco-Prussian War series (Chambers), from 1895
Frangipani (Weale), 1985
Franklin's Folly (Roby, as Grey), 1980
Fräulein Schmidt and Mr. Anstruther (Elizabeth), 1907
Freckles (G. Porter), 1904
Freddy for Fun (Bloom, as Essex), 1943
Frederica (Heyer), 1965
Frederica in Fashion (Chesney), 1985
Free Fishers (Buchan), 1934
Free from Fear (Cartland), 1980
Free Spirit (F. Michaels), 1983
Free Traders (P. Hastings), 1984
Freebody Heiress (Gordon), 1974
Freebooters (Tranter), 1950
Freedom Farewell! (Bentley), 1936
Freedom Road (Fast), 1944
Freedom Trail to Greystone (J. Roberts, as Bronte), 1976
Freedom's Sword (Swan), 1886
Freer's Cove (Gordon), 1972
Freeways (Delmar), 1971
French Affair (Chesney), 1984
French Bride (Anthony), 1964
French Girl in Love (Greig), 1963
French Husband (Gordon), 1977
French Inheritance (A. Stevenson), 1974
French Kiss (Nicole, as Logan), 1978
French Lieutenant's Woman (Fowles), 1969
Frenchman (V. Johnston), 1976
Frenchman and the Lady (Cadell), 1952
Frenchman's Creek (du Maurier), 1941
Frenchwoman (Laker, as Paul), 1977
Frey and His Wife (Hewlett), 1916
Friday Spy (Nicole, as Nicholson), 1980
Friday's Child (Heyer), 1944
Friday's Laughter (Dingwell), 1972
Friend of the Bride (Grimstead, as Manning), 1968
Friendly Air (Cadell), 1970
Friendly Persuasion (s West), 1945
Friends and Lovers (Palmer), 1983
Friend's Counsel (s Hope), 1894
Frightened Bride (Cartland), 1975
Frightened Heart (Greig, as Ames), 1952
Frightened Wife (s Rinehart), 1953
Fringe of Heaven (Bevan), 1978
Fringe of Leaves (P. White), 1976
Frivolous Cupid (s Hope), 1895
From Fairest Flower (Charles), 1969
From Hate to Love (Cartland), 1983
From Hell to Heaven (Cartland), 1981
From Here to a Star (Trask), 1941
From Mill to Mansion (M. St. John), 1914
From Out the Vasty Deep (Lowndes), 1921
From Pillar to Post (M. St. John), 1921
From Satan, With Love (Coffman), 1972
From Such a Seed (J. MacLeod, as Airlie), 1949
From the Housetops (McCutcheon), 1916
From the Memoirs of a Minister of France (Weyman), 1895
From the Snare of the Hunter (J. Lane), 1968
From the Vasty Deep (Lowndes), 1920
From This Dark Stairway (Eberhart), 1931
From This Day (N. Roberts), 1983
From This Day Forward (Ayres), 1934
From This Day Forward (Beaty, as Ross), 1959
From This Day Forward (Thane), 1941

From Want to Wealth (Garvice, as Hart)
From Worse Than Death (Garvice, as Hart), n.d.
Frontier (s Kantor), 1959
Frontier Passage (Bridge), 1942
Frost and the Fire (Bevan), 1973
Frost at Dawn (Mackinlay), 1968
Frost in the Sun (Lorrimer), 1986
Frost on the Rose (M. Peters), 1982
Frozen Fire (Lamb), 1980
Frozen Flame (O'Brian), 1953
Frozen Fountain (Maddocks), 1959
Frozen Heart (Donnelly), 1988
Frozen Jungle (Donnelly), 1981
Frozen Slippers (A. M. Williamson), 1930
Fruit on the Bough (Bloom), 1931
Fruitful Vine (Hichens), 1911
Fruits of the Year (Farnes), 1942
Frustration (Lamb), 1979
Fugitive from Love (Cartland), 1978
Fugitive from Love (Charles, as Chandos), 1950
Fugitive from Love (Woodward, as Richmond), 1980
Fugitive Romantic (Bloom, as Essex), 1960
Fugitive Wife (Craven), 1980
Fugue in Time (Godden), 1945
Fulfillment (Delinsky), 1988
Fulfillment (Lee), 1969
Fulfillment (Spencer), 1979
Full Bloom (Krentz), 1988
Full Circle (Saxton), 1984
Full Circle (Steel), 1984
Full Circle (K. Thorpe), 1978
Full Flavour (Leslie), 1934
Full Fruit Flavour (Bloom, as Essex), 1949
Full Meridian (Jacob), 1939
Full Summer's Kiss (Grimstead, as Manning), 1966
Full Tide (Blair, as Conway), 1954
Funeral Games (Renault), 1981
Furies (Jakes), 1976
Future Is Forever (M. Lewis), 1967

G (J. Berger), 1972
Gable Farm (s Swan), 1899
Gabriel Hounds (Stewart), 1967
Gabriella (Maybury), 1979
Gabrielle (Norris), 1965
Gad's Hall (Lofts), 1977
Gail Talbot (Elsna), 1953
Galahad (Erskine), 1926
Galahad's Garden (Burgin), 1908
Galaxy (Ertz), 1929
Gale Warning (Yates), 1939
Galileans (Slaughter), 1953
Gallant (Blackstock), 1962
Gallant (Stuart, as Long), 1986
Gallant Graham (Wynne), 1911
Gallant Lover (M. St. John, as Cooper), 1926
Gallant of Spain (Wynne), 1920
Gallant Spirit (W. Roberts), 1982
Gallantry (s Cabell), 1907
Gallants (Beck, as Barrington), 1924
Gallant's Fancy (Kidd), 1974
Galleon (Pope), 1986
Gallows Herd (M. Peters), 1973
Gallows Way (Winston), 1976
Gallows Wedding (Martin), 1978
Gamble (Spencer), 1987

Gamble with Hearts (Cartland), 1975
Gamble with Love (Ayres), 1922
Gambler in Love (Matthews), 1985
Gambler's Love (Lorin), 1982
Gambler's Woman (Krentz, as James), 1984
Gambling Man (Cookson), 1975
Game and the Candle (s Kennedy), 1928
Game in Diamonds (Cadell), 1976
Game Is Played (Lorin), 1981
Game of Hazard (Blackstock, as Allardyce), 1955
Game of Hearts (Burgin), 1915
Game of Kings (Dunnett), 1961
Game of Life (Albanesi, as Rowlands), 1910
Game of Love (Garvice, as Hart), n.d.
Game of Love (Pozzessere), 1986
Game of Statues (A. Stevenson), 1972
Game Plan (Seger, as Jennings), 1984
Gamesmaster (Krentz, as James), 1983
Gamester (Sabatini), 1949
Gamesters (Bailey), 1916
Gamester's Daughter (Ponsonby), 1974
Gaming House (Manners), 1984
Gamma's Girl (L. Walker), 1977
Garden for My Child (Bloom), 1946
Garden Oats (Baldwin), 1929
Garden of Allah (Hichens), 1904
Garden of Don José (Burghley), 1964
Garden of Dreams (Craven), 1975
Garden of Memories (M. St. John, as Cooper), 1921
Garden of Persephone (Asquith), 1967
Garden of Shadows (Coffman), 1973
Garden of the Gods (Ashton), 1978
Garden of the Moongate (Vitek), 1982
Garden of Vision (Beck), 1929
Garden of Wishes (Maybury), 1935
Garden Room (Chappell), 1964
Gardenia (s Hichens), 1934
Gardenia Tree (Barrie, as Kent), 1965
Garfield Honor (Yerby), 1961
Garland of Marigolds (Hunter, as Chace), 1967
Garland of Youth (Albanesi, as Rowlands), 1923
Garment (Cookson), 1962
Garment of Gold (Barcynska, as Sandys), 1921
Garnet (Bennetts), 1985
Garnetta (Libbey), 1897
Garrison Hospital (Stuart, as A. Stuart), 1957
Garth of Tregillis (Reid), 1972
Gascoigne's Ghost (Burgin), 1896
Gaslight Sonatas (s Hurst), 1918
Gate Leads Nowhere (M. Howard), 1953
Gate Marked "Private" (Dell), 1928
Gate to the Sea (Bryher), 1958
Gated Road (Bloom), 1963
Gated Road (J. MacLeod), 1959
Gates of Dawn (Barrie), 1954
Gates of Doom (Sabatini), 1914
Gates of Eden (Swan), 1886
Gates of Happiness (Albanesi, as Rowlands), 1927
Gates of Kami (Orczy), 1907
Gates of Kunarja (McCutchan, as MacNeil), 1972
Gates of Midnight (Stirling), 1983
Gates of Montrain (W. Roberts), 1971
Gates of Morning (P. Hastings), 1973
Gates of Paradise (s Hichens), 1930
Gates of Steel (Hampson), 1970
Gateway to Nowhere (Cowen), 1978

Gather Up the Years (Maybury), 1939
Gathering Wolves (Darrell), 1980
Gay Cavalier (Stuart, as A. Stuart), 1955
Gay Courage (Loring), 1928
Gay Defeat (Robins), 1933
Gay Fiesta (Duffield), 1938
Gay Galliard (Irwin), 1941
Gay Gordons (Stuart, as Allen), 1961
Gay Intruder (Bromige), 1954
Gay Is Life (M. Howard), 1943
Gay Knight I Love (Charles, as Chandos), 1938
Gay Life (Delafield), 1933
Gay Lord Robert (Holt, as Plaidy), 1955
Gay of Heart (Maybury), 1959
Gay Pursuit (Cadell), 1948
Gay Rowan (I. Roberts, as Harle), 1965
Gay Unfortunate (Elsna), 1958
Gaynor Women (Coffman), 1978
Gazebo (Ponsonby), 1945
Geisha in the House (Greig, as Ames), 1963
Gem of a Girl (Neels), 1976
Gemel Ring (Neels), 1974
Gemini Child (Stratton), 1976
Gemstone (Delinsky, as Drake), 1983
Gene (Godden), 1968
General (Ponsonby), 1971
General Crack (Bowen, as Preedy), 1928
General Danced at Dawn (s G. Fraser), 1970
General's Lady (Forbes), 1938
General's Wench (R. Marshall), 1954
Generous Vine (Renier), 1962
Gentian series (J. Fitzgerald, as Watson), from 1969
Gentian Hill (Goudge), 1949
Gentle Annie (Kantor), 1942
Gentle Awakening (Neels), 1987
Gentle Despot (Burgin), 1919
Gentle Feuding (Lindsey), 1984
Gentle Flame (Britt), 1971
Gentle Highwayman (Blackstock as Allardyce), 1961
Gentle Invader (Danbury), 1957
Gentle Murderer, (Davis), 1951
Gentle Obsession (Cowen), 1968
Gentle Pirates (Krentz, as Castle), 1980
Gentle Prisoner (Seale), 1949
Gentle Sex (Blackstock, as Allardyce), 1974
Gentle Stranger (C. Allen), 1977
Gentle Tyrant (Ruck), 1949
Gentle Tyrant (Stratton, as Gillen), 1973
Gentle Wind (Ritchie), 1954
Gentleman (E. Marshall), 1956
Gentleman Adventurer (Bailey), 1914
Gentleman Anonymous (Lowndes), 1934
Gentleman Called (Davis), 1958
Gentleman Called James (Bloom, as Essex), 1951
Gentleman in Love (Cartland), 1980
Gentleman Insists (Lorin, as Hohl), 1989
Gentleman of Fortune (Bailey), 1907
Gentleman of France (Weyman), 1893
Gentleman Pirate (J. Roberts, as Radcliffe), 1975
Gentleman Rogue (Blackstock, as Allardyce), 1975
Gentlemen Go By, (Cadell), 1954
Gentlemen's Agreement (Hutten), 1936
Georgian series (Holt, as Plaidy), from 1967
Georgian Rake (Ley), 1960
Georgina (Darcy), 1971
Gerald and Elizabeth (D. Stevenson), 1969

Gerald Cranston's Lady (Frankau), 1924
Geste Family series (Wren), from 1924
Geste of Duke Jocelyn (Farnol), 1919
Ghost Child (Hintze), 1983
Ghost Dancers (Daniels, as Gray), 1971
Ghost Flowers (Summerton), 1973
Ghost in Green Velvet (B. Michaels), 1977
Ghost in Monte Carlo (Cartland), 1951
Ghost Kings (Haggard), 1908
Ghost of a Chance (Krentz), 1984
Ghost of Archie Gilroy (Blackstock, as Allardyce), 1970
Ghost of Fiddler's Hill (Bloom, as Essex), 1968
Ghost of June (Charles, as Tempest), 1942
Ghost of Monsieur Scarron (J. Lewis), 1959
Ghost Song (Daniels), 1974
Ghost Stories (s Arlen), 1927
Ghost That Haunted a King (Bloom, as Prole), 1963
Ghost Town (Blackstock), 1976
Ghost Who Fell in Love (Cartland), 1978
Ghosts of Fontenoy (Blackstock, as Keppel), 1981
Ghosts of Harrel (W. Roberts), 1971
Giant (Ferber), 1952
Giant in Chains (Bowen), 1938
Giant of Medabi (Dailey), 1978
Giants' Bread (Westmacott), 1930
Gibbet Fen (Dwyer-Joyce), 1984
Gideon Faber's Choice (Barrie, as Kent), 1965
Gift Beyond Price (Seger), 1983
Gift for a Lion (Craven), 1977
Gift for Pamela (Saxton, as Turner), 1981
Gift of Fire (Krentz), 1989
Gift of Gold (Krentz), 1988
Gift of My Heart (Elsna, as Snow), 1949
Gift of the Gods (Cartland), 1981
Gift of the Heart (Ritchie), 1955
Gift of Violets (J. Roberts, as Radcliffe), 1977
Gift Shop (Armstrong), 1967
Gifted Friend (Elsna, as Conway), 1965
Gifts of Love (C. Allen), 1978
Gigolo (s. Ferber), 1920
Gilded Fleece (Tranter), 1942
Gilded Hoop (Muskett), 1941
Gilded Ladder (Elsna), 1945
Gilded Splendour (Laker), 1982
Gilded Spring (Seger, as Bates), 1983
Gilian the Dreamer (Munro), 1899
Gillian (Yerby), 1960
Giliane (Gellis), 1979
Gilt Cage (Steen), 1926
Gin and Bitters (J. Lane), 1945
Ginger Griffin (Bridge), 1934
Gingerbread House (Bigland), 1934
Gingerbread House (Dwyer-Joyce), 1977
Ginger-Jar (Barcynska, as Sandys), 1926
Gingham Year (Norway), 1973
Ginny (Chesney, as Tremaine), 1980
Gipsy Actress (M. St. John), 1923
Gipsy Born! (M. St. John), 1922
Gipsy Count (Wynne), 1909
Gipsy Flower (Bloom), 1949
Gipsy King (Wynne), 1917
Gipsy Love (M. St. John, as Cooper), 1923
Gipsy Lover (Bloom, as Harvey), 1973
Gipsy Schoolgirl (M. St. John), 1922
Gipsy Vans Come Through (Bloom), 1936
Gipsy-Spelled (Wynne), 1929

Girl (Cookson), 1977
Girl about Town (Weale), 1965
Girl Alone (Blackmore), 1964
Girl Alone (Peake), 1972
Girl Alone (Walker), 1973
Girl and Her Money (Greig), 1971
Girl at Cobalt Creek (Way), 1983
Girl at Dane's Dyke (Rome), 1975
Girl at Eagles' Mount (Rome), 1971
Girl at Golden Hawk (Winspear), 1974
Girl at Smuggler's Rest (Stratton, as Gillen), 1970
Girl at Snowy River (Dingwell), 1959
Girl at White Draft (Blair, as Brett), 1962
Girl Bewitched (Lewty), 1981
Girl by the Sea (Ebel), 1974
Girl Called Ann (R. Randall), 1956
Girl Called Evelyn (Charles), 1959
Girl Called Tegi (Britt), 1980
Girl Crusoe (Hilton), 1969
Girl Disappears (Elsna), 1953
Girl for a Millionaire (R. Lindsay, as Leigh), 1977
Girl for Sale (Grundy), 1920
Girl from Montana (G. Hill), 1908
Girl from Nowhere (Greig), 1936
Girl from Nowhere (Lamb), 1981
Girl from Paris (Aiken), 1982
Girl from Rome (Asquith), 1973
Girl from Storyville (Yerby), 1972
Girl from the Sea (Weale), 1979
Girl from the South (Garvice), 1910
Girl He Forsook (Libbey), n.d.
Girl in a Golden Bed (Weale), 1986
Girl in a White Hat (Stratton), 1977
Girl in Blue (Britt), 1976
Girl in Jeopardy (Greig), 1967
Girl in Love (Garvice), 1919
Girl in Love (R. Randall), 1961
Girl in Overalls (Seifert, as Ashley), 1943
Girl in the 'bacca Shop (s Garvice), 1920
Girl in the Blue Dress (Burchell), 1958
Girl in the Green Valley (Hoy), 1973
Girl in the Mauve Mini (Charles, as Lance), 1979
Girl in the Secret (A. M. Williamson), 1934
Girl in White (Ellis), 1976
Girl Intern (Seifert), 1944
Girl Men Talked About (Greig), 1938
Girl Must Marry (Greig), 1931
Girl Named Rose (Neels), 1986
Girl Named Smith (Arbor), 1960
Girl Next Door (Ayres), 1919
Girl of His Choice (Mackinlay, as Grey), 1965
Girl of Spirit (Garvice), 1906
Girl of the Limberlost (G. Porter), 1909
Girl of the Passion Play (A. Williamson), 1911
Girl of the Prairie (M. St. John), 1922
Girl of the Woods (G. Hill), 1942
Girl on His Hands (Greig), 1939
Girl on the Beach (V. Johnston), 1987
Girl on the Make (Baldwin), 1932
Girl Outside (Melville, as Betteridge), 1971
Girl Possessed (Winspear), 1980
Girl to Come Home To (G. Hill), 1945
Girl to Love (Neels), 1982
Girl Upstairs (Wynne), 1932
Girl Who Got Out (Burgin), 1916
Girl Who Had Nothing (A. M. Williamson), 1905

Girl Who Loved Crippen (Bloom), 1955
Girl Who Married the Wrong Man! (M. St. John), 1923
Girl Who Proposed! (Ruck), 1918
Girl Who Was Brave (Albanesi, as Rowlands), 1916
Girl Who Was Too Good-Looking (s Ruck), 1920
Girl Who Wasn't There (W. Roberts), 1957
Girl Who Wasn't Welcome (Greig), 1969
Girl with a Challenge (Burchell), 1965
Girl with a Heart (Albanesi, as Rowlands), 1911
Girl with a Million (Greig), 1945
Girl with a Secret (Armstrong), 1959
Girl with the Crystal Dove (Hardwick), 1985
Girl Without a Heart (s Garvice), 1912
Girl Without Credit (Greig), 1941
Girl Without Money (Greig), 1957
Girlie (s Bloom), 1904
Girls (Ellerbeck, as Thorne), 1967
Girls (Ferber), 1921
Girls at His Billet (Ruck), 1916
Girls from the Five Great Valleys (Savage), 1977
Girl's Good Name (M. St. John), 1925
Girls in White (R. Randall), 1952
Girl's Kingdom (Albanesi, as Rowlands)
Giselle (Tresillian), 1988
Gitana (Chambers), 1931
Giuliano the Magnificent (J. Lindsay), 1940
Give All to Love (Lorrimer, as Robins), 1956
Give All to Love (Ritchie), 1971
Give All to Love (Veryan), 1987
Give All to Love (Woodward), 1982
Give Back Yesterday (Muskett), 1955
Give Her Gardenias (Charles, as Tempest), 1953
Give Love the Air (Baldwin), 1947
Give Me Back My Dreams (Maybury), 1936
Give Me Back My Heart (Robins), 1944
Give Me Liberty (Erskine), 1940
Give Me My Youth (Trask), 1938
Give Me New Wings (Hoy), 1944
Give Me One Summer (Loring), 1936
Give Me the Daggers (Gavin), 1972
Give Me This Day (M. Lewis), 1964
Give Me Your Golden Hand (Eaton), 1951
Give Me Your Love (Worboys, as Eyre), 1975
Give Us This Day (Delderfield), 1973
Giving Him Up (Ayres), 1930
Glad Heart (Albanesi), 1910
Glad Summer (Farnol), 1951
Glade of Jewels (J. Fitzgerald), 1989
Gladiators (Koestler), 1939
Gladiola's Two Lovers (Libbey), n.d.
Glamour Girl (Price), 1937
Glamorous Powers (Howatch), 1988
Glass and the Trumpet (Seifert), 1948
Glass Castle (Winspear), 1973
Glass Flame (Whitney), 1978
Glass Heiress (Dwyer-Joyce), 1981
Glass Island (Clarke), 1978
Glass Palace (Gibbs), 1973
Glass Slipper (Eberhart), 1938
Glass Virgin (Cookson), 1969
Glass-Blowers (du Maurier), 1963
Glastonbury Romance (Powys), 1932
Gleam in the North (Broster), 1927
Glen, Elizabeth series (Swan), from 1895
Glen of Frost (M. Peters, as Grey), 1981
Glen of Sighs (Stratton, as Gillen), 1972

Glen o'Weeping (Bowen), 1907
Glendraco (Black), 1977
Glenrannoch (R. Randall), 1973
Glimpses of the Sun (R. Fraser), 1952
Glittering Heights (Duffield), 1936
Glittering Images (Howatch), 1987
Glittering Lights (Cartland), 1974
Glitter-Dust (Dwyer-Joyce), 1978
Gloria and the Bullfighter (Webb, as Hammill), 1954
Glorious Angel (Lindsey), 1982
Glorious Apollo (Beck, as Barrington), 1925
Glorious Flames (Glyn), 1932
Glorious Morning (Ellis), 1982
Glory (Saxton), 1982
Glory and the Lightning (Caldwell), 1974
Glory Game (Dailey), 1985
Glory of Egypt (Beck, as Moresby), 1926
Glory Road (Gavin), 1987
Glove Shop in Vienna (s Ibbotson), 1984
Go Ask the River (Eaton), 1969
Go Borrowing—Go Sorrowing! (M. St. John), 1924
Goal (Wynne), 1907
Goat Song (Yerby), 1967
Goblin Hill (Summers), 1977
God and Mr. Aaronson (Barcynska), 1937
God and My Right (Duggan), 1955
God and the King (Bowen), 1911
God and the Wedding Dress (Bowen), 1938
God in the Car (Hope), 1894
God Is an Englishman (Delderfield), 1970
God Must Be Sad (Hurst), 1961
God of Clay (Bailey), 1908
God Speed the Night (Davis), 1968
God Within Him (Hichens), 1926
Goddess Abides (Buck), 1972
Goddess and the Gaiety Girl (Cartland), 1980
Goddess of Gray's Inn (Burgin), 1901
Goddess of Love (Cartland), 1987
Goddess of Mavisu (Stratton), 1975
Goddess of the Green Room (Holt, as Plaidy), 1971
Godforsaken (Yarbro), 1983
Gods Forget (Cartland), 1939
God's Good Man (Corelli), 1904
God's Highlander (Thompson), 1989
Gods in Green (W. Roberts), 1973
God's Men (Buck), 1951
God's Playthings (s Bowen), 1912
God's Warrior (Slaughter), 1967
Godson (Dane), 1964
Going All the Way (Hufford), 1980
Going Home (Steel), 1973
Going Underground (van der Zee), 1982
Golconda Necklace (M. St. John, as Cooper), 1926
Gold for Gay Masters (Robins, as Gray), 1954
Gold for My Girl (Blackmore), 1967
Gold for Prince Charlie (Tranter), 1962
Gold from Crete (s Forester), 1970
Gold in the Dust (Albanesi), 1929
Gold in the Gutter (Garvice), 1907
Gold Is the Sunrise (Hampson), 1971
Gold of Apollo (Lamb, as Holland), 1976
Gold of Noon (Summers), 1974
Gold Pennies (Franken), 1938
Gold Seekers (Stuart, as Long), 1985
Gold Shoe (G. Hill), 1930
Gold Slippers (Keyes), 1958

Golden series (Veryan), from 1985
Golden Admiral (F. Mason), 1953
Golden Apollo (P. Hastings), 1958
Golden Apple Island (Arbor), 1967
Golden Apple Tree (s Sheard), 1920
Golden Bait (M. St. John, as Cooper), 1928
Golden Bay (Bevan), 1987
Golden Bird (Mullins), 1987
Golden Bubbles (I. Roberts, as Rowland), 1976
Golden Butterfly (A. M. Williamson), 1926
Golden Cage (Bromige), 1950
Golden Carpet (A. M. Williamson), 1931
Golden Chariot (Wiat), 1979
Golden Chimera (Seger), 1985
Golden Chronicles series (Veryan), from 1985
Golden Collar (Cadell), 1969
Golden Cord (Deeping), 1935
Golden Crucible (Stubbs), 1976
Golden Dawn (Albanesi, as Rowlands), 1912
Golden Days (D. Stevenson), 1934
Golden Destiny (Saunders), 1986
Golden Door (Scott), 1925
Golden Empire (Lowell, as Maxwell), 1979
Golden Flame (Bloom), 1941
Golden Flames (Hooper), 1988
Golden Fleece (Bailey), 1925
Golden Fleece (Graves), 1944
Golden Fleece (Lofts), 1944
Golden Flower (I. Roberts, as Rowland), 1964
Golden Future (Elsna, as Snow), 1950
Golden Galatea (F. Stevenson), 1979
Golden Garden (Greig), 1968
Golden Girl (Ashton), 1978
Golden Goat (Byrne), 1930
Golden God (Saunders, as Innes), 1975
Golden Goddess (Krentz, as James), 1985
Golden Goddess (Nicole, as Grange), 1973
Golden Gondola (Cartland), 1958
Golden Griffin (Clarke, as Honeyman), 1976
Golden Harvest (Muskett), 1944
Golden Hawk (Yerby), 1948
Golden Horizons (Duffield), 1935
Golden Illusion (Cartland), 1976
Golden Image (Webb, as Hamill), 1959
Golden Interlude (I. Roberts, as Carr), 1970
Golden Isle (Slaughter), 1947
Golden Lasso (F. Michaels), 1980
Golden Lion (Haines), 1986
Golden Lotus (J. Roberts), 1979
Golden Madonna (Stratton), 1973
Golden Marguerite (Coffman, as Stanfield), 1981
Golden Moment (Grimstead), 1962
Golden Moments (Steel), 1980
Golden Ocean (O'Brian), 1956
Golden Ones (Slaughter, as Terry), 1958
Golden Packet (Daniels, as Gray), 1971
Golden Pagoda (I. Roberts), 1972
Golden Panther (S. Thorpe), 1956
Golden Parakeet (Marsh), 1986
Golden Peaks (Farnes), 1951
Golden Penny (Burgin), 1937
Golden Puma (Way), 1980
Golden Rain (I. Roberts as Harle), 1964
Golden Road (Montgomery), 1913
Golden Roof (Bowen), 1928
Golden Rose (Blair), 1959

Golden Silence (C. and A. Williamson), 1910
Golden Shoestring (Baldwin), 1949
Golden Skylark (s Godden), 1941
Golden Snail (s Barcynska), 1927
Golden Songbird (Walsh), 1975
Golden Spaniard (Stratton), 1982
Golden Strangers (Treece), 1956
Golden Stud (Horner), 1975
Golden Summer (Bromige), 1972
Golden Summer (Duffield), 1954
Golden Surrender (Pozzessere, as Graham), 1985
Golden Tally (Oldfield), 1985
Golden Thistle (J. Roberts), 1973
Golden Tide (Stanford), 1980
Golden Torment (Taylor), 1984
Golden Touch (London, as James), 1982
Golden Triangle (I. Roberts, as Rowland), 1978
Golden Unicorn (Whitney), 1976
Golden Urchin (Brent), 1986
Golden Valkyrie (Johansen), 1984
Golden Valley (Winston), 1975
Golden Venture (Bloom), 1938
Golden Violet (Bowen, as Shearing), 1936
Golden Years (Hardwick), 1976
Goldsmith's Wife (Holt, as Plaidy), 1950
Gollantz Saga (Jacob), from 1935
Gone (s Godden), 1968
Gone Before Morning (Peake), 1973
Gone with the Wind (Mitchell), 1936
Gone-Away Man (L. Walker), 1969
God Gestes (s Wren), 1929
Good Confession (Savage), 1975
Good Deed (s Buck), 1969
Good Duke Humphrey (Clarke, as Honeyman), 1973
Good Earth (Buck), 1931
Good Gracious, Marian! (M. St. John), 1919
Good Man's Love (Delafield), 1932
Good Morning, Doctor Houston (Stratton, as Gillen), 1969
Good Old Anna (Lowndes), 1915
Good Out of Evil (s Swan), 1899
Good Provider (Stirling), 1988
Good Sport (Greig), 1934
Good Venture (L. Cooper), 1928
Good Woman (Bromfield), 1927
Goodbye, Doctor Galahad (McEvoy, as Harte), 1962
Goodbye Hamilton (Cookson), 1984
Goodbye, Johnny (Norway), 1962
Goodbye, My Love (Maybury), 1952
Gooding Girl (Oldfield), 1985
Gorgeous Brute (Barcynska), 1949
Gorgeous Lover (s Bowen), 1929
Goring's Girl (Wynne), 1914
Gospel Fever (Slaughter), 1980
Goss Boys (Kantor), 1958
Gossamer Dream (Bloom), 1931
Gossip (Duffield), 1938
Gossip from the Forest (Keneally), 1975
Governess (P. Hill), 1985
Governess (Lee, as Cromwell), 1969
Governor of England (Bowen), 1913
Governor's Lady (Raddall), 1960
Gower Street (Rayner), 1973
Grace Before Meat (Seale), 1938
Grace Latouche and the Warringtons (s Bowen), 1931
Graces (Beck, as Barrington), 1934
Gracious Lady (Bloom), 1955

Grafton Girls (M. Howard), 1956
Graham, Davina series (Anthony), from 1980
Grain of Gold (May), 1971
Granada Window (Steen), 1949
Grand (Trask), 1951
Grand Duchess (Duffield), 1954
Grand Man (Cookson), 1954
Grand Relations (Greig), 1940
Grand Sophy (Heyer), 1950
Grand-Chain (Stern), 1917
Grandmère (Delmar), 1967
Grandmother and the Priests (Caldwell), 1963
Grandmother's Child (Swan), 1882
Grania (Llywelyn), 1986
Grasp a Nettle (Neels), 1977
Graustark series (McCutcheon), from 1901
Grave of Green Water (Summerton, as Roffman), 1968
Grave of Truth (Anthony), 1979
Graveyard Watch (Shellabarger, as Estevan), 1938
Great Adventure (Giles), 1966
Great Alone (Dailey), 1986
Great Amulet (Diver), 1908
Great Beginning (Bloom), 1924
Great Black Oxen (Jacob), 1962
Great Boomerang (Idriess), 1941
Great Captains (Treece), 1956
Great Day (Seifert), 1939
Great Fright (Macbeth), 1929
Great House (Weyman), 1919
Great Husband Hunt (Grundy), 1922
Great Laughter (Hurst), 1936
Great Lion of God (Caldwell), 1970
Great Maria (C. Holland), 1974
Great Miss Driver (Hope), 1908
Great Mistake (Rinehart), 1940
Great Moment (Glyn), 1923
Great Oak (J. Lindsay), 1957
Great Pearl Secret (C. and A. Williamson), 1921
Great Romantic (Beck, as Barrington), 1933
Great Roxhythe (Heyer), 1922
Great Shadow (Doyle), 1892
Great Smith (E. Marshall), 1943
Great Son (Ferber), 1945
Great Tradition (Keyes), 1939
Great Unmet (s Ruck), 1918
Great Valley (M. Johnston), 1926
Greater Courage (Pedler), 1933
Greater Freedom (Swan), 1938
Greater Gain (Burgin), 1917
Greater Happiness (Britt), 1974
Greater Love (Swan, as Lyall), 1898
Greater Love (Woodward, as Richmond), 1961
Greater Than All (Robins), 1946
Greatest Nurse of Them All (Bloom, as Prole), 1968
Greatheart (Dell), 1918
Grecian Rhapsody (Duffield), 1938
Greek Bridal (Reid), 1976
Greek Island Magic (Bevan), 1983
Greek Treasure (Stone), 1975
Greek Wedding (Hodge), 1970
Green, Polly series (M. St. John), from 1909
Green Apple Love (D. Smith), 1974
Green Bay Tree (Bromfield), 1924
Green Beetle (Gibbs, as Ford), 1972
Green Bough (Ritchie), 1953
Green Branch (E. Pargeter), 1962
Green Caravan (Barcynska, as Sandys), 1922

Green Carnation (Hichens), 1894
Green City in the Sun (Wood), 1988
Green Country (Albanesi), 1927
Green Darkness (Seton), 1972
Green Dolphin Country (Goudge), 1944
Green Dolphin Street (Goudge), 1944
Green Dragon, White Tiger (Motley), 1986
Green Empress (Cadell), 1958
Green Fancy (McCutcheon), 1917
Green Fire (Krentz, as James), 1986
Green Fire (Maybury), 1963
Green Gauntlet (Delderfield), 1968
Green Girl (Seale), 1965
Green Glass Moon (Manners, as Lamont), 1970
Green Grass (Maddocks), 1963
Green Grass Growing (Seale), 1940
Green Grows the Vine (Cato), 1960
Green Harvest (Ashton), 1977
Green Harvest (Oldfield), 1983
Green Hat (Arlen), 1924
Green Judgment (Pedler), 1934
Green Lacquer Pavilion (Beauclerk), 1926
Green Leaves (Blair, as Brett), 1947
Green Light (Douglas), 1935
Green Light (Norway, as Norton), 1963
Green Lightning (Mather), 1983
Green Limelight (Mackinlay), 1943
Green Man (Treece), 1966
Green Memory (Eldershaw), 1931
Green Money (D. Stevenson), 1939
Green Mountain Man (Dailey), 1978
Green Patch (Hutten), 1910
Green Rushes (J. MacLeod, as Airlie), 1953
Green Salamander (P. Hill), 1977
Green Valleys (Albanesi, as Rowlands), 1932
Greenfingers Farm (Dingwell), 1955
Greengage Summer (Godden), 1958
Greengirl (M. Peters, as Black), 1979
Greenwood Shady (Cadell), 1951
Gregg Barratt's Woman (Peake), 1981
Grenelle (I. Holland), 1976
Grenfell Legacy (McEvoy), 1968
Gresham Ghost (W. Roberts), 1980
Gretna Bride (Sinclair, as Daniels), 1986
Grey Beginning (Michaels), 1984
Grey Ghyll (Manners, as Rundle), 1978
Grey Goose Wing (Wiat), 1986
Greygallows (B. Michaels), 1972
Greys series (M. Peters), from 1969
Greystone series (J. Roberts), from 1975
Grief Before Night (Shellabarger, as Loring), 1938
Griffin's Way (Yerby), 1962
Grizel Married (Vaizey), 1914
Groping (Jacob), 1933
Grotto of Jade (Hilton), 1967
Grove of Eagles (Graham), 1963
Grove of Olives (Ebel), 1976
Grow Up, Little Lady! (Charles, as Tempest), 1937
Growing Moon (Arbor), 1977
Growing Season (Lamb, as Holland), 1975
Growth of a Man (de la Roche), 1938
Grub-and-Stakers series (C. MacLeod, as Craig), from 1981
Guarded Gates (Britt), 1973
Guarded Halo (Pedler), 1929
Guardian (Carnegie), 1966
Guardian (Gibbs), 1958
Guardian at the Gate (Shoesmith), 1979

Hard to Win (Elsna, as Conway), 1956
Hard Way (Robins), 1949
Hard-Hearted Doctor (Bloom, as Essex), 1964
Hardie series (Melville), from 1987
Hark to Rover! (L. Cooper), 1933
Harlot's Daughter (Hastings), 1967
Harness the Winds (Maybury), 1934
Harold (Cookson), 1985
Harold of the English (Clarke, as Honeyman), 1979
Harpoon in Eden (F. Mason), 1969
Harps in the Wind (Hichens), 1945
Harriet (J. Cooper), 1976
Harriet and the Piper (Norris), 1920
Harriet Mannering's Paying Guests (Vaizey), 1917
Harriet, The Haunted (Kimbrough), 1976
Harrogate Secret (Cookson), 1988
Harry (Vansittart), 1981
Harry the King (Clarke, as Honeyman), 1971
Harry's Last Love (Bloom, as Prole), 1958
Harsh Heritage (Tranter), 1939
Harte Family series (Bradford), from 1979
Harvest of a House (Bloom), 1935
Harvest of Hope (Baldwin), 1962
Harvest of the Sun (Thompson), 1978
Harvester (G. Porter), 1911
Harvest-Home Come Sunday (Bloom), 1962
Harvesting (Bacheller), 1934
Haste to the Wedding (D. Smith), 1974
Hasting Day (Chappell), 1970
Hasty Marriage (Neels), 1977
Hasty Wedding (Eberhart), 1938
Hate Begins at Home (Aiken), 1967
Hate That Lasts (Burgin), 1925
Hatful of Cowslips (Ritchie), 1960
Haunted (Cartland), 1986
Haunted (Lamb), 1983
Haunted by the Past (Chard), 1982
Haunted Castle (Lofts), 1978
Haunted Headsman, (Bloom, as Prole), 1965
Haunted Lady (Rinehart), 1942
Haunted Landscape (Bromige), 1976
Haunted Life (Garvice, as Hart)
Haunted Light (Price), 1933
Haunted Love (Woodward, as Richmond), 1980
Haunted Place (Coffman), 1966
Haunted Portrait (Kimbrough, as Ashton), 1976
Haunted Sisters (Holt, as Plaidy), 1966
Haunted Summer (Edwards), 1972
Haunted Vintage (Bowen), 1921
Haunting Cavalier (Thum), 1974
Haunting Compulsion (Mather), 1981
Haunting Me (Blackstock, as Allardyce), 1978
Haunting of Gas's Hall (Lofts), 1979
Haunting of Helen Farley (Cowen), 1976
Haunting of Hill House (Jackson), 1959
Haunting of Sara Lessingham (Bennetts, as James), 1978
Hauntings (s Lofts), 1975
Haunts of Men (s Chambers), 1899
Have Courage, My Heart (M. Howard), 1943
Haversham Legacy (Winston), 1974
Hawaii (Michener), 1959
Hawaii for Danger (Hintze), 1973
Hawk and the Dove (Hampson), 1970
Hawk and the Honey (Browning), 1984
Hawk in a Blue Sky (Lamb), 1977
Hawk of May (Bradshaw), 1980

Hawk O'Toole's Hostage (Brown), 1988
Hawkridge (Blackmore), 1976
Hawks Barton (I. Roberts), 1979
Hawk's Head (Charles, as Lance), 1981
Hayes, Julie series (Davis), from 1976
Haymaker (Cadell), 1972
Haymarket (Rayner), 1974
Hazard, Philip series (Stuart, as V. Stuart), from 1973
Hazard of Hearts (Cartland), 1949
Hazards of Belinda (Cleugh), 1933
Hazel of Heatherland (Grundy), 1906
Hazell & Sons, Brewers (Swan), 1888
He and Hecuba (Hutton), 1905
He Brings Great News (Dane), 1944
He Couldn't Take Money! (M. St. John), 1923
He Is Mine (Lorrimer, as Robins), 1957
He Learnt about Women (Ruck), 1940
He Loved but Was Lured Away (Libbey), 1891
He Loves Me, He Loves Me Not (Garvice), 1911
He Married a Doctor (Baldwin), 1944
He Married a Mill-Lass (M. St. John), 1924
He Married His Parlourmaid (Barcynska), 1929
He Shall Not Marry a Mill-Lass! (M. St. John), 1929
He Stooped to Conquer (J. Lane), 1943
He Travels Alone (Shellabarger, as Loring), 1939
He'll Never Marry You! (M. St. John), 1927
Head of Chancery (Beaty), 1972
Head of the Family (M. St. John, as Cooper), 1923
Head of the House (Elsna, as Snow), 1967
Head of the House (G. Hill), 1940
Head of the House (Swan), 1938
Headhunters of the Coral Sea (Idriess), 1941
Healer (Slaughter), 1955
Healer of Hearts (Britt), 1969
Healing Hands (R. Lindsay), 1955
Healing Hands (Seifert), 1942
Healing Time (Andrews), 1969
Health unto His Majesty (Holt, as Plaidy), 1956
Heart Alone (Grimstead, as Manning), 1959
Heart Appeal (Greig), 1934
Heart Awakens (J. Roberts, as Radcliffe), 1977
Heart Cannot Forget (Burchell), 1953
Heart Expects Adventure (Arbor), 1951
Heart for Heart (Garvice)
Heart for Sale (Albanesi), 1929
Heart Has Wings (Baldwin), 1937
Heart, Have You No Wisdom? (Hoy), 1962
Heart in Darkness (Greig, as Ames), 1947
Heart in Hiding (Rivers), 1984
Heart in Pilgrimage (Eaton), 1948
Heart in the Sand (Ponsonby), 1970
Heart in the Sunlight (Peake), 1975
Heart Is Broken (Cartland), 1972
Heart Is Never Fair (Maybury), 1954
Heart Is Stolen (Cartland), 1980
Heart Knows Best (Stanford), 1984
Heart Line (Albanesi, as Rowlands), 1936
Heart Listens (Van Slyke), 1973
Heart Must Choose (Burchell), 1953
Heart of a Maid (Garvice), 1910
Heart of a Rose (Lindsay), 1961
Heart of a Woman (Albanesi, as Rowlands), 1913
Heart of a Woman (Orczy), 1911
Heart of Angela Brent (Albanesi, as Rowlands), 1917
Heart of Flame (M. Peters, as Darby), 1986
Heart of Gold (Stanford), 1988

Her Heart's Desire (Garvice), 1900
Her Heart's Desire (Greig, as Ames), 1961
Her Heart's Longing (Albanesi, as Rowlands), 1910
Her Humble Lover (Garvice), 1904
Her Husband (Albanesi, as Rowlands), 1914
Her Husband and Her Love (Albanesi, as Rowlands), 1905
Her Kingdom (Albanesi, as Rowlands), 1910
Her Knight on a Barge (Sebastian), 1979
Her Love So True (Garvice)
Her Mad Month (Grundy), 1917
Her Mistake (Albanesi, as Rowlands), 1911
Her Mother-in-Law (M. St. John, as Cooper), 1920
Her Mother's Keeper (N. Roberts), 1983
Her Mystery Man (Woodward, as Ware), 1971
Her Name Was Eve (Maybury), 1953
Her Pirate Partner (Ruck), 1926
Her Punishment (Albanesi, as Rowlands), 1910
Her Ransom (Garvice), 1903
Her Right to Love (Garvice, as Hart)
Her Shining Splendor (Sherwood), 1980
Her Sister's Children (Burchell), 1965
Her Stolen Baby (M. St. John), 1919
Her Stolen Life (Price), 1954
Her Undying Past (MacGill), 1924
Her Unexpected Summer (Woodward, as Davis), 1967
Her Way and His (Ayres), 1921
Her Wedding Garment (s G. Hill), 1932
Her Weight in Gold (s McCutcheon), 1911
Her Wild Voice Singing (Hoy), 1963
Her World of Men (Greig, as Ames), 1937
Herb for Happiness (Cartland), 1987
Herb of Grace (Goudge), 1948
Herb of Healing (Burgin), 1915
Herbs and Apples (Santmyer), 1925
Hercules, My Shipmate (Graves), 1945
Here Be Dragons (Penman), 1985
Here Be Dragons (M. Peters, as Whitby), 1980
Here Comes a Candle (Hodge), 1967
Here Comes the Sun! (Loring), 1924
Here I Belong (Burchell), 1951
Here I Stay (Michaels), 1983
Here Lies Margot (P. Hill), 1957
Here Lies Our Soveriegn Lord (Holt, as Plaidy), 1957
Here Today and Gone Tomorrow (s Bromfield), 1934
Here Was a Man (Lofts), 1936
Heritage (Keyes), 1968
Heritage of Folly (Cookson, as Merchant), 1962
Heritage of Hate (Garvice), 1909
Heritage of Shadows (Brent), 1983
Heritage of Strangers (Roby), 1978
Heritage of the Heart (Pykare), 1982
Heritage of the House (Roby, as D'Arcy), 1980
Heritage Perilous (Farnol), 1946
Hermit of Bonneville (Burgin), 1904
Hermit of Far End (Pedler) 1919
Hermitage Bell (McEvoy), 1971
Hermitage Hill (Daniels), 1978
Hermits of Gray's Inn (Burgin), 1899
Hero for Love's Sake (Albanesi, as Rowlands)
Hero of Herat (Diver), 1912
Hero of Urbino (Wynne), 1914
Hero or Scamp? (M. St. John, as Cooper), 1918
Heroes (Nicole), 1973
Heroes of Clone (Kennedy), 1957
Heroic Garrison (Stuart, as V. A. Stuart), 1975
Heroine's Sister (Murray), 1975

Heron series (Oldfield), from 1980
Heron Family series (Belle), from 1983
Heronbrook (Manners), 1974
Heron's Nest (Gibbs, as Ford), 1960
Heron's Point (Stratton, as Gillen), 1977
Herries series (Walpole), from 1930
Herring's Nest (Bloom, as Essex), 1949
Hesitant Heart (Edwards), 1974
Hesitant Heir (Roby, as Grey), 1978
Hesitation Waltz (Farnes), 1939
Hessian (Fast), 1972
Hester (Cleeve), 1979
Hester Lane (Swan), 1908
Hester Roon (Lofts), 1940
Hester Trefusis (Albanesi, as Rowlands), 1912
Heu-Heu (Haggard), 1924
Hey for Cavaliers! (Wynne), 1912
Heywood Inheritance (Fellows), 1975
Hibiscus House (Charles, as Chandos), 1955
Hidden Book (Roby), 1977
Hidden Evil (Cartland), 1963
Hidden Fires (Brown, as Jordan), 1982
Hidden Fires (McGill), 1921
Hidden Fires (J. Roberts, as Radcliffe), 1978
Hidden Flower (Buck), 1952
Hidden Gift (Albanesi), 1936
Hidden Heart (Cartland), 1946
Hidden Heart of Fire (Darrell, as Dawes), 1976
Hidden Hearts (M. St. John, as Cooper), 1923
Hidden in the Flame (Mather), 1985
Hidden in the Wind (J. MacLeod, as Airlie), 1953
Hidden Malice (Berckman), n.d.
Hidden Meanings (C. Allen), 1976
Hidden Past (Woodward), 1961
Hidden Rapture (R. Lane), 1978
Hidden Terror (Garvice, as Hart), 1910
Hide and Seek (Lamb), 1987
Hideaway Heart (R. Lane), 1967
High Adventure (Farnol), 1926
High Country (Nicole), 1988
High Country Governess (Summers), 1987
High Fence (Muskett), 1959
High Heaven (Duffield), 1939
High Holiday (Norris), 1949
High Hostage (Worboys, as Maxwell), 1976
High Master of Clere (Arbor), 1966
High of Heart (Loring), 1938
High Noon (Ayres), 1936
High Place (Cabell), 1923
High Price to Pay (Craven), 1986
High Road (Baldwin), 1939
High Road (Greig, as Warren), 1954
High Spirits (Tranter), 1950
High Terrace (Coffman), 1966
High Tide at Midnight (Craven), 1978
High Tide at Noon (Ogilvie), 1944
High Towers (Costain), 1949
High Valley (Mather), 1971
Highclyffe Hall series (Brandewyne), from 1988
High-Country Wife (Bevan), 1974
Highest Bidder (Ayres), 1921
Highest Bidder (MacGill), 1921
Highest Peak (May), 1967
Highland Brooch (J. Roberts, as Danton), 1980
Highland Countess (Chesney), 1983
Highland Holiday (Inglis), 1952

Highland Interlude (Andrews), 1968
Highland Masquerade (Elgin), 1966
Highland Mist (Burghley), 1962
Highland Velvet (Deveraux), 1982
Highly Respectable Marriage (Walsh), 1983
Highwayman (Bailey), 1915
Highwayman (S. Thorpe), 1962
Highwayman's Daughter (Shoesmith), 1973
Hilary in His Heart (Charles, as Tempest), 1938
Hilary on Her Own (Grundy), 1908
Hildegarde (Norris), 1927
Hill Country Nurse (McElfresh), 1959
Hillbilly Doctor (Seifert), 1940
Hills Beyond (Britt), 1978
Hills of Fire (Daniels), 1973
Hills of Kalamata (Hampson), 1976
Hills of Maketu (Bevan), 1969
Hills Stand Watch (Derleth), 1960
Hilltops Clear (Loring), 1933
Hilton and Warner Families series (Nicole), from 1974
Himalayan Moonlight (R. Lane), 1977
Hindu (s Hichens), 1917
Hired Baby (s Corelli), 1891
Hiring Fair (Stirling), 1976
His Dupe (MacGill), 1922
His Elizabeth (Thane), 1928
His Fight Is Ours (J. Lane), 1946
His Guardian Angel (Garvice), 1911
His Hour (Glyn), 1910
His Lordship (s Burgin), 1893
His Lordship's Landlady (Sebastian, as Whitmore), 1979
His Love So True (s Garvice), 1896
His Majesty's Well-Beloved (Orczy), 1919
His Majesty's Yankees (Raddall), 1942
His Official Fiancee (Ruck), 1914
His One Love (Albanesi, as Rowlands), 1912
His Perfect Trust (Garvice), n.d.
His Sealed Lips! (M. St. John), 1918
His Serene Highness (Bailey), 1920
His Serene Miss Smith (Summers), 1966
His Shadow on the Wall (Elsna, as Snow), 1965
His Ukelele Girl (MacGill), 1927
His Wife—or His Mother? (M. St. John), 1923
His Wife or His Work? (M. St. John), 1928
His Wife's Secret (M. St. John), 1928
His Word of Honour (Ayres), 1921
Historical Nights' Entertainment (s Sabatini)
Hold Back the Heart (Bloom, as Burns), 1951
Hold Close the Memory (Pozzessere, as Graham), 1985
Hold Hard, My Heart (Bloom, as Burns), 1946
Hold Me Captive (M. Pargeter), 1976
Hold Me in Your Heart (Chard), 1983
Hold On to Your Heart (Baldwin), 1976
Hold the Dream (Bradford), 1985
Holden, Eben series (Bacheller), from 1900
Holden, Nikki series (Chase), from 1987
Holiday (Oman, as Lenanton), 1928
Holiday Affair (Grimstead, as Manning), 1969
Holiday Engagement (Gibbs, as Ford), 1963
Holiday for Love (Finley), 1976
Holiday for Lovers (Woodward, as Davis), 1967
Holiday with Violence (E. Pargeter), 1953
Holidays at Sunnycroft (s Swan), 1885
Hollow Hills (Stewart), 1973
Hollow Night (Harrod-Eagles), 1980
Hollow of Her Hand (McCutcheon), 1912

Hollywood Honeymoon (Barcynska, as Sandys), 1939
Hollywood Love (A. M. Williamson), 1928
Hollywood Madness (MacGill), 1936
Hollywood Star Dust (MacGill), 1936
Holy Flower (Haggard), 1915
Holy Orders (Corelli), 1910
Homage to a Rose (Hill), 1979
Home Again My Love (Browning, as Dozier), 1977
Home at Sundown (L. Walker), 1968
Home for Christmas (Douglas), 1937
Home for Christmas (N. Roberts), 1986
Home for Jocelyn (Farnes), 1953
Home for Joy (Burchell), 1968
Home for the Wedding (Cadell), 1971
Home from the Sky (Danbury), 1964
Home Is Goodbye (Hunter, as Chace), 1971
Home Is the Hero (Charles, as Chandos), 1946
Home Is the Hunter (Sprigge), 1930
Home to Morning Star (Way), 1981
Home to My Country (M. Howard), 1971
Home Without a Father (M. St. John), 1922
Homecoming (Elsna, as Lancaster), 1951
Homecoming (Lofts), 1975
Homecoming (McElfresh), 1953
Homecoming (Seifert), 1950
Homecoming of the Boys (s Swan), 1916
Homeplace (Dailey), 1976
Homer's Daughter (Graves), 1955
Homesick for a Dream (Mackinlay), 1968
Homespun (Swan), 1893
Home-Town Doctor (Seifert), 1959
Homeward Bound (Farnes), 1975
Homeward the Heart (Hoy), 1964
Homeward Winds the River (B. Johnson), 1979
Homing (G. Hill), 1938
Homing (Thane), 1957
Homing Bird (Swan), 1935
Honey (Burchell), 1959
Honey for Tea (Cadell), 1961
Honey Is Bitter (Winspear), 1967
Honey Island (Asquith), 1957
Honey Pot series (Barcynska), from 1916
Honeyball Farm (Dell), 1937
Honeymoon (Ogilvie), 1947
Honeymoon (Winspear), 1986
Honeymoon Alone (Greig, as Ames), 1940
Honeymoon for One (Greig), 1971
Honeymood Hate (Williamson), 1931
Honeymoon Holiday (Hoy), 1967
Honeymoon in Hiding (Vaizey), 1911
Honeymoon in Honolulu (Webb, as Hamill), 1950
Honeymoon in Manila (Greig, as Ames), 1962
Honeymoon Island (Bloom), 1938
Honeymoon Island (Lewty), 1987
Honeymoons Arranged (Greig), 1938
Honor Bound (Baldwin), 1934
Honor Bound (Brown, as St. Claire), 1986
Honor Bright (Keyes), 1936
Honor Girl (Hill, as Macdonald), 1927
Honor of Dr. Shelton (Seifert), 1962
Honorable Miss Clarendon (Sebastian), 1973
Honor's Price (Bloom), 1979
Honour Comes Back—(Jacob), 1935
Honour of Four Corners (Burgin), 1934
Honourable Jim (Orczy), 1924
Honourable Mr. Twanish (Farnol), 1913

Honoured Guest (Elsna, as Snow), 1952
Honour's a Mistress (Jacob), 1947
Honour's Fetters (Wynne), 1911
Hoodman Blind (M. Peters, as Black), 1984
Hoodwinked (Palmer), 1989
Hope and Glory (Nicole, as Arlen), 1984
Hope for Tomorrow (Weale), 1959
Hope Is My Pillow (Ritchie), 1967
Hopeful Journey (Ruck), 1950
Horatia (Gibbs), 1961
Horizons of Love (Cartland), 1980
Hornblower, Horatio series (Forester), from 1937
Horns of the Moon (Manners, as Lamont), 1979
Horror at Gull House (Matthews, as Brisco), 1970
Horror from the Tomb (F. Stevenson), 1977
Horse Goddess (Llywelyn), 1982
Horseman Riding By (Delderfield), 1966
Hortensius, Friend of Nero (E. Pargeter), 1936
Hospital Call (E. Harrison), 1975
Hospital Circles (Andrews), 1967
Hospital Corridors (Burchell), 1955
Hospital Hill (McElfresh), 1961
Hospital of Fatima (Hunter, as Chace), 1963
Hospital of the Heart (Bloom, as Essex), 1966
Hospital on the Hill (I. Preston), 1967
Hospital Summer (Andrews), 1958
Hospital Zone (Seifert), 1948
Hostage Bride (Dailey), 1981
Hostage Most Royal (Knight, as Hope), 1979
Hostage of Love (Woodward, as Lawrence), 1973
Hostile Shore (Gavin), 1940
Hosts of Rebecca (Cordell), 1960
Hot Breath (S. Harrison), 1985
Hot Day in High Summer (P. Hastings), 1962
Hot Ice (N. Roberts), 1987
Hot Pursuit (van der Zee), 1988
Hotel at Treloan (Barrie), 1964
Hotel Belvedere (Danbury), 1961
Hotel by the Loch (Danbury), 1968
Hotel De Luxe (Nicole, as Gray), 1985
Hotel De Luxe (R. Randall), 1961
Hotel Hostess (Baldwin), 1938
Hotel Jacarandas (Britt), 1980
Hotel Mirador (Blair, as Brett), 1959
Hotel Southerly (Dingwell), 1968
Hotel Stardust (Barrie), 1955
Hôtel Transylvania (Yarbro), 1978
Hound of Ireland (s Byrne), 1934
Hounds and Jackals (Wood), 1978
Hounds of Carvello (Cowen), 1970
Hounds of God (Sabatini), 1928
Hounds of Hell (Coffman), 1967
Hounds of Sunset (E. Pargeter), 1976
Hour Before Midnight (V. Johnston), 1978
Hour Before Moonrise (Buckingham), 1967
Hour of the Siesta (M. Lewis), 1982
Hour of the Tiger (I. Roberts, as I. M. Roberts), 1985
Hours of Iris (Eaton), 1928
Hours to Cherish (Pozzessere, as Graham), 1984
House above Hollywood (V. Johnston), 1968
House above the Bay (I. Preston), 1976
House Across the Hedge (s G. Hill), 1932
House at Bell Orchard (S. Thorpe), 1962
House at Cupid's Cross (Holt, as Burford), 1949
House at Fern Canyon (W. Roberts), 1970
House at Kilgallen (Roby), 1973

House at Luxor (F. Stevenson), 1976
House at Old Vine (Lofts), 1961
House at Sandalwood (Coffman), 1974
House at Sunset (Lofts), 1962
House at Tegwani (Blair), 1950
House Behind the Judas Tree (s Frankau), 1929
House, But Not a Home (M. St. John), 1921
House by the Lake (Farnes), 1952
House by the Lock (A. Williamson), 1899
House by the Sea (Lowndes), 1937
House by the Sea (Eberhart), 1972
House by the Watch Tower (Robins), 1968
House Called Edenhythe (Buckingham), 1970
House Called Pleasance (Elsna), 1963
House Called Sakura (Britt), 1974
House Divided (Buck), 1935
House for Sharing (Hunter, as Chace), 1964
House for Sister Mary (Andrews), 1966
House for the Season series (Chesney), from 1984
House in Candle Square (Bennetts), 1977
House in the Dust (Leslie), 1942
House in the Park (R. Fraser), 1937
House in the Timberwoods (Dingwell), 1959
House in the Woods (Charles, as Lance), 1980
House Is Built (Eldershaw), 1929
House of a Thousand Lanterns (Holt), 1974
House of Adventure (Deeping), 1921
House of Broken Dolls (Daniels), 1972
House of Conflict (Bromige), 1953
House of Conflict (Burchell), 1962
House of Candles (Matthews, as Brisco), 1973
House of Cray (P. Hill), 1982
House of Discontent (Wyndham), 1955
House of Discord (Arbor), 1983
House of Dreams (Collin), 1971
House of Dreams-Come-True (Pedler), 1919
House of Earth (Buck), 1935
House of Eve (Daniels, as Somers), 1962
House of False Faces (Daniels, as Weston), 1967
House of Fand (Maybury, as Troy), 1966
House of Fiske (Burgin), 1927
House of Five Pines (Worboys, as Byre), 1967
House of Fulfillment (Beck), 1927
House of Glass (Seale), 1944
House of Granite (Renier), 1968
House of Happiness (s Dell), 1927
House of Imposters (W. Roberts), 1977
House of Jackdaws (Dwyer-Joyce), 1980
House of Kingdom (Stratton, as Gillen), 1976
House of Kuragin (Heaven), 1972
House of Larne (Cowen), 1980
House of Lies, M. Howard, 1960
House of Lorraine (R. Lindsay), 1959
House of Lydia, (I. Roberts as Shaw), 1967
House of Many Doors (Daniels), 1971
House of Many Shadows (B. Michaels), 1974
House of Many Windows (Muskett), 1950
House of Memories (Way), 1983
House of Men (Cookson, as Marchant), 1963
House of Mirror Images (Winston), 1970
House of Moreys (Bentley), 1953
House of Niccolò series (Dunnett), from 1986
House of Nightingales (Ebel), 1985
House of Oliver (J. MacLeod), 1947
House of Peril (Lowndes), 1912
House of Pines (Charles, as Tempest), 1975

House of Ravensbourne (Gibbs), 1965
House of Scissors (Hunter, as Chace), 1972
House of Seven Courts (Daniels), 1967
House of Seven Fountains (Weale), 1957
House of Silence (Daniels), 1980
House of Silence (C. N. and A. M. Williamson), 1921
House of Spies (Deeping), 1913
House of Stolen Memories (Daniels), 1967
House of Storm (Eberhart), 1949
House of Storms (Winspear), 1985
House of Strange Music (Hilton), 1976
House of Strangers (Winspear), 1963
House of Strangers (Woodward, as Richmond), 1983
House of Sunshine (Albanesi, as Rowlands), 1912
House of Terror (Berckman), 1960
House of the Amulet (Hilton), 1970
House of the Deer (D. Stevenson), 1970
House of the Eagles (Ashton), 1974
House of the Laird (Barrie), 1956
House of the Lost Court (A. M. Williamson, as de Savallo),
    1908
House of the Pines (Charles, as Tempest), 1946
House of the Seventh Cross (Robins), 1967
House of the Shining Tide (Summers), 1962
House of the Three Ganders (Bacheller), 1928
House of the Twelve Caesars (P. Hastings), 1975
House of the Winds (R. Lane), 1968
House of the Wolf (Weyman), 1890
House of Vandekar (Anthony), 1988
House of War (Gavin), 1970
House of Water (Renier), 1963
House of Women (Malpass), 1975
House on Bostwick Square (V. Johnston), 1987
House on Brinden Water (Asquith), 1958
House on Circus Hill (Daniels), 1972
House on Flamingo Cay (Weale), 1962
House on Gregor's Brae (Summers), 1971
House on Hay Hill (s Eden), 1976
House on Malador Street (P. Hastings), 1970
House on Octavia Street (La Tourrette), 1984
House on the Cliff (D. Stevenson), 1966
House on the Fens (Cookson, as Marchant), 1965
House on the Hill (Bloom), 1977
House on the Left Bank (V. Johnston), 1975
House on the Moat (Coffman), 1972
House on the Moor (Woodward), 1967
House on the Mound (Derleth), 1958
House on the Nile (Duffield), 1937
House on the Rock (Cleeve), 1980
House on the Rock (Swan), 1930
House on the Rocks (Charles), 1962
House on the Roof (Eberhart), 1935
House on the Strand (du Maurier), 1969
House on Thunder Hill (Daniels, as Somers), 1973
House on Twyford Street (Gluyas), 1976
House on Windswept Ridge (Kimbrough), 1971
House Party (Delafield), 1931
House Possessed (Blackstock), 1962
House Surgeon at Luke's (R. Randall), 1962
House That Berry Built (Yates), 1945
House That Died Alone (Bloom) 1964
House That Hated People (M. Peters, as Black), 1974
House That Jane Built (Albanesi), 1921
House with the Myrtle (Gibbs, as Ford), 1942
House with the Watching (Hintze), 1970
House Without a Heart (Cowen), 1978

House Without Love (Bromige), 1964
Houseful of Girls (Vaizey), 1902
Houseless One (M. Peters, as Whitby), 1981
Houseman's Sister (Norway, as Neal), 1964
Hovering Darkness (Berckman), 1957
How Can I Forget? (Charles, as Tempest), 1948
How Change the Moons (Trask), 1932
How Dark, My Lady! (Bloom), 1951
How Dear Is My Delight! (Bloom, as Burns), 1955
How Far to Bethlehem? (Lofts), 1965
How Great the Price (Robins), 1935
How High the Moon (Mackinlay, as Grey), 1966
How Like an Angel (Millar), 1962
How Like the King (Vaizey), 1905
How Many Miles to Babylon? (Irwin), 1913
How Much You Mean to Me (Charles), 1966
How Rich Is Love? (Bloom, as Burns), 1957
How Sleep the Brave (Gavin), 1980
How the Money Goes! (M. St. John), 1916
How to Forget (Robins), 1944
Howard series (Wiat), from 1972
Howards of Saxondale (R. Randall), 1946
Howarth series (Stubbs), from 1978
Howling in the Woods (V. Johnston), 1968
Human Symphony (J. MacLeod), 1937
Humbug (Delafield), 1922
Hummingbird (Spencer), 1983
Humoresque (s Hurst), 1919
Hundredth Chance (Dell), 1917
Hundredth Man (Burgin), 1927
Hungry for Love (Cartland), 1976
Hungry Heart (Way), 1988
Hungry Hill (du Maurier), 1943
Hungry Tide (Stratton, as Gillen), 1975
Hunt with the Hounds (Eberhart), 1950
Hunter in the Shadows (Butler, as Melville), 1969
Hunter of the East (Hampson), 1973
Hunter's Dawn (I. Roberts, as Rowland), 1977
Hunter's Green (Whitney), 1968
Hunter's Mate (Blackmore), 1971
Hunter's Moon (Bloom), 1969
Hunter's Moon (Reid), 1970
Hunter's Moon (Way), 1982
Hunting of Henri (s Wren), 1944
Hunting Shirt (M. Johnston), 1931
Huntsman's Folly (Stuart, as A. Stuart), 1956
Husband (Cookson), 1976
Husband and Foe (Albanesi, as Rowlands), 1900
Husband for Gail (Corcoran), 1981
Husband for Hire (Charles, as Chandos), 1940
Husband Hunters (Cartland), 1976
Husband in Name (Mackinlay, as Grey), 1972
Husband She Wanted (M. St. John), 1930
Husband, The Wife, and the Friend (M. St. John), 1921
Husbands at Home (Charles, as Chandos), 1955
Husbands of Edith (McCutcheon), 1908
Hush Marriage (M. St. John, as Cooper), 1934
Hustler Joe (s E. Porter) 1924
Hut by the River (Burgin), 1916
Hyde Place (Coffman), 1974

I Am Gabriella! (Maybury), 1962
I and My Heart (Dingwell), 1967
I Bequeath (Elsna), 1955
I Came to the Castle (V. Johnston), 1969
I Came to the Highlands (V. Johnston), 1975

I Cannot Go Hunting Tomorrow (s Treece), 1946
I, Claudius (Graves), 1934
I Could Be Good to You (Blackstock, as Keppel), 1980
I Dare Not Dream (Maybury), 1937
I Dwelt in High Places (Bowen), 1933
I Have Lived Today (Elsna), 1944
I Hear Adventure Calling (Loring), 1948
I, Judas (Caldwell), 1977
I Know a Maiden (Albanesi), 1906
I Know My Life (Gaskin), 1962
I Know My Love (Seale), 1957
I Know Not Whither (Elsna, as Conway), 1979
I Live Again (Deeping), 1942
I Lost My Heart (Greig), 1935
I Love a Lass (Cadell), 1956
I Loved a Fairy (Barcynska), 1933
I Loved Her Yesterday (Greig), 1945
I Married a Doctor (R. Randall), 1947
I Married Mr. Richardson (Greig, as Ames), 1945
I Met a Gypsy (s Lofts), 1935
I Met Him Again (Greig), 1948
I Met Murder on the Way (Blackstock), 1977
I Remember Love (Hardwick), 1982
I Return (Leslie), 1962
I Saw My Mortal Sight (Eaton), 1959
I See You (s Armstrong), 1966
I Seek My Love (Greig, as Ames), 1936
I Should Have Known (Robins), 1961
I Start Counting (Erskine-Lindop), 1966
I Take This Man (Loring), 1954
I Take This Woman (Rinehart), 1927
I Tell My Heart (Trask), 1937
I Thank a Fool (Erskine-Lindop), 1958
I, The King (Keyes), 1966
I, The Maid (M. Peters), 1980
I, Too, Have Loved (Robins), 1939
I Walk the Mountain Tops (Farnes), 1940
I Was Shown Heaven (Barcynska), 1962
I Will Be Good (Chapman), 1945
I Will Be True (Trask), 1948
I Will Love You Still (Burchell), 1949
I Will Maintain (Bowen), 1910
I Will Repay (Orczy), 1906
Ice Forest (Coffman), 1975
Ice Girl (Inglis), 1938
Ice into Fire (Peake), 1985
Ice Palace (Ferber), 1958
Iceberg in the Tropics (May), 1983
Ideals (s Scott), 1927
Ides of March (Wilder), 1948
Ides of November (F. Stevenson), 1975
Idlers' Gate (Bowen, as Winch), 1932
If Dreams Came True (R. Lindsay, as Leigh), 1974
If Ever I Cease to Love (Keyes), 1943
If I Love Again (Charles, as Tempest), 1937
If I Were You (Aiken), 1987
If Love Be Love (Kidd), 1972
If Love Comes (Kimbrough as Ashton), 1987
If Love Were Wise (Hoy), 1954
If Love You Hold (Dingwell), 1958
If My Arms Could Hold (D. A. Ponsonby, as Doris Ponsonby),
   1947
If She Should Die (Roby), 1970
If the South Had Won the Civil War (Kantor), 1961
If the Tree Is Saved (Cartland), 1929
If There Be Dragons (Hooper), 1984

If This Be Destiny (Robins), 1941
If This Be Love (Renier), 1971
If This Be Sin (Elsna, as Conway), 1975
If This Be Treason (Renier), 1965
If This Is Love (Weale), 1963
If This Were All (Burchell), 1949
If Today Be Sweet (Britt), 1976
If We Will (Cartland), 1947
If Winter Comes (Palmer), 1979
If Wishes Were Horses (Barcynska), 1917
If You Believe the Soldiers (Cordell), 1973
If You Care (Burchell), 1948
If You'll Marry Me (Charles, as Tempest), 1942
Ikon on the Wall (s Goudge), 1943
Ilene, The Superstitious (Kimbrough), 1977
I'll Find You Again (Hoy), 1941
I'll Get over It (Greig, as Ames), 1935
I'll Go with You (Burchell), 1940
I'll Never Be Young Again (du Maurier), 1932
I'll Ride Beside You (Charles, as Lance), 1965
I'll Try Anything Once (Charles, as Tempest), 1939
I'll Walk with My Love (Maybury), 1940
Illegal Possession (Hooper), 1985
Ill-Made Knight (T. White), 1940
Ills Men Do (Burgin), 1937
Illusion (Lamb), 1981
Illusion at Haven's Edge (Daniels), 1975
Illusions (C. Allen), 1987
Illusions of Love (Freeman), 1984
Illyrian Spring (Bridge), 1935
Illyrian Summer (Danbury), 1965
I'm Not a Common Girl! (M. St. John), 1923
Image of a Ghost (Daniels), 1973
Image of a Lover (Ogilvie), 1974
Image of Love (Browning), 1984
Image of Love (Stratton), 1978
Image of Truth (Daniels, as Somers), 1963
Image-Maker (P. Hastings), 1976
Images of Love (Mather), 1980
Images of Rose (Gilbert), 1974
Imagination of the Heart (Glover), 1989
Imaginary Marriage (M. St. John, as Cooper), 1922
Imaginative Man (Hichens), 1895
Imitation of Life (Hurst), 1933
Immigrants series (Fast), from 1977
Immortal Flower (Hoy), 1972
Immortal Girl (Ruck), 1925
Immortal Morning (Hoy), 1949
Immortal Rock (Salverson), 1954
Immortal Wife (Stone), 1944
Immortals (N. Peters), 1983
Imogen (J. Cooper), 1978
Imogene (Garvice)
Impasse (M. Pargeter), 1985
Imperfect Joy (Stubbs), 1981
Imperfect Lady (S. Harrison), 1988
Imperfect Secretary (Lewty), 1959
Imperial Caesar (R. Warner), 1960
Imperial Harlot (M. Peters), 1983
Imperial Highness (Anthony), 1953
Imperial Purple (Bradshaw), 1989
Imperial Splendour (Cartland), 1979
Imperial Woman (Buck), 1956
Impetuous Duchess (Cartland), 1975
Impetuous Masquerade (Mather), 1982
Impetuous Surrogate (Morgan), 1982

Important Family (Eden), 1982
Impossible Man to Love (R. Lindsay, as Leigh), 1987
Impossible Marriage (Greig, as Ames), 1943
Impossible Marriage (Peake), 1975
Improper Acquaintances (Walsh), 1985
Imprudent Lady (J. Smith), 1978
Impudence of Youth (Deeping), 1946
Impudent Widow (Sebastian, as Gladstone), 1979
In a Class by Itself (Brown), 1984
In a Dark Garden (Slaughter), 1946
In a Glass Darkly (Caird), 1966
In a Moment's Time (Pykare, as Powers), 1983
In a Stranger's Arms (Pykare, as Powers), 1984
In an Edinburgh Drawing Room (Andrews), 1983
In Another Girl's Shoes (Ruck), 1916
In Cupid's Chains (Garvice), 1902
In Daffodil Time (Albanesi, as Rowlands), 1913
In Exchange for Love (Garvice), 1914
In Fine Feathers (Garvice), 1912
In from the Storm (Vitek, as Alexander), 1979
In Haste to Be Rich (s Swan), 1898
In King's Byways (s Weyman), 1902
In Love (Ellerbeck, as Thorne), 1974
In Love with Claire (Albanesi), 1932
In Love with the Man (Lewty), 1986
In Love's Land (Albanesi, as Rowlands), 1912
In Mary's Reign (Orczy), 1907
In Me My Enemy (Erskine-Lindop), 1948
In Mother's Place (M. St. John), 1916
In Name Only (R. Lindsay, as Leigh), 1951
In Search of Love (Elsna, as Lancaster), 1955
In Search of Mr. Rochester (Chappell), 1976
In Serena's Web (Hooper), 1987
In Storm and in Calm (Andrews), 1975
In the Arms of Love (Cartland), 1981
In the Cool of the Day (Ertz), 1961
In the Day's March (Ayres), 1930
In the Days of Poor Richard (Bacheller), 1922
In the Dead of the Night (Roby), 1969
In the Hands of the Senecas (Edmonds), 1947
In the Heart of Love (Chard), 1978
In the Matter of a Letter (Garvice), 1908
In the Mountains (Elizabeth), 1920
In the Palm of Her Hand (Browning), 1986
In the Portico (s Hutten), 1931
In the Quarter (Chambers), 1894
In the Rue Monge (s Orczy), 1931
In the Shade of the Palms (R. Lane), 1972
In the Shadow of the Crown (Holt, as Plaidy), 1988
In the Shadow of the Guillotine (Sabatini), 1956
In the Shadows (Daniels), 1978
In the Shadows (M. St. John), 1920
In the Way (G. Hill), 1897
In the Wilderness (Hichens), 1917
In This House of Brede (Godden), 1969
In Times Like These (Loring), 1968
In Tune with Wedding Bells (G. Hill), 1941
In What Torn Ship (Eaton), 1944
In Winter's Shadow (Bradshaw), 1982
In Wolf's Clothing (Garvice), 1908
Incense Tree (La Tourrette), 1986
Incident at a Corner (Armstrong), 1959
Incident at Villa Rahmana (Eliot), 1972
Inclination to Murder (Ellerbeck), 1965
Incognito (Hichens), 1947
Incomparable Miss Brady (Walsh), 1980

Incorrigible Rake (Walsh), 1985
Incredible Duchess (Leslie), 1974
Incredible, Fierce Desire (M. Peters), 1988
Incredible Honeymoon (Cartland), 1976
Incredible Year (Baldwin), 1929
Incumbent (P. Hill), 1974
Indecent Exposure (Berckman), 1975
Indecent Obsession (McCullough), 1981
Independence of Claire (Vaizey), 1915
Independent Wife (L. Howard), 1982
Independent Woman (Jagger), 1983
India Fan (Holt), 1988
Indian series (Masters), 1978
Indian Princess (s A. Williamson), 1924
Indian Silk (Dingwell), 1986
Indifferent Heart (Sellers), 1980
Indiscretion of the Duchess (Hope), 1894
Indiscretions of the Queen (Holt, as Plaidy), 1970
Indy Man (Dailey), 1978
Inevitable End (Robins), 1927
Inevitable Hour (E. Marshall), 1957
Infamous Army (Heyer), 1937
Infatuation (Lamb), 1984
Infatuation (Robins), 1951
Infinite Woman (E. Marshall), 1950
Informed Risk (Carr), 1989
Inherit My Heart (Burchell), 1962
Inherit the Darkness (W. Roberts), 1972
Inherit the Sun (Stratton), 1977
Inheritance (Bentley), 1932
Inheritance (Swan), 1909
Inheritance (K. Thorpe), 1984
Inheritance (Winston), 1972
Inherited Bride (Stratton), 1980
Inheritors (Golding), 1955
Injured Lover (Lowndes), 1939
Inland Paradise (Dingwell), 1976
Inn of the Hawk and Raven (McCutcheon), 1926
Innocent (Corelli), 1914
Innocent and the Wicked (P. Hastings), 1956
Innocent Bystander (Baldwin), 1934
Innocent Deception (R. Lindsay), 1975
Innocent Enchantress (Elsna, as Conway), 1953
Innocent Fire (B. Hastings), 1980
Innocent Flower (Armstrong), 1945
Innocent Girl (Garvice), 1898
Innocent Heart (Pykare), 1981
Innocent Heiress (Cartland), 1970
Innocent in Eden (Way), 1986
Innocent in Paris (Cartland), 1971
Innocent in Russia (Cartland), 1981
Innocent Obsession (Mather), 1981
Inscrutable Nymph (Duffield), 1942
Inshine Girl (Hilton), 1970
Inside the Haven (Swan), 1882
Insiders (Rogers), 1979
Instead of the Thorn (Heyer), 1923
Insubstantial Pageant (Walsh), 1986
Interested Parties (B. Hastings), 1984
Interloper (Albanesi, as Rowlands)
Interloper (Butler), 1959
Interloper (Howard), 1967
Interlude for Love (Barrie, as Charles), 1958
Interlude in Arcady (Hilton), 1969
Interlude in Greece (I. Preston), 1982
Interrupted Journey (I. Preston), 1970

Intimate Friends (C. Allen), 1983
Intimate Story (Franken), 1955
Intimate Strangers (B. Hastings), 1982
Into a Golden Land (Hoy), 1971
Into the Net (Mackinlay), 1935
Intrepid Miss Hayden (Ley), 1983
Introduction to Sally (Elizabeth), 1926
Intruder (Donnelly), 1977
Intruder (M. Howard), 1959
Intruder at Maison Benedict (Ellis, as Richard), 1967
Intruder at Windgates (Reid), 1973
Intruder Marriage (Ruck), 1944
Intrusions of Peggy (Hope), 1902
Invaders (Treece), 1960
Invalided Out (Ayres), 1918
Invasion (J. Lewis), 1932
Invincible Amelia (Albanesi), 1909
Invisible Cord (Cookson), 1975
Invisible Wife (Arbor), 1981
Invisible Worm (Millar), 1941
Invitation (Cookson), 1970
Invitation to Alannah (Maybury), 1983
Invitation to Evil (W. Roberts), 1970
Invitation to Folly (Ertz), 1953
Invitation to Live (Douglas), 1940
Ione (Libbey), 1890
Ionian Mission (O'Brian), 1981
Iris (Garvice), 1914
Iris in Winter (Cadell), 1949
Iris, The Bewitched (Kimbrough), 1982
Irish Beauties (Beck, as Barrington), 1931
Irish Boy (Jacob), 1955
Irish Heiress (F. Stevenson, as Fitzgerald), 1985
Irish Lover (Albanesi, as Rowlands), 1914
Irish Rose (N. Roberts), 1988
Irish Thoroughbred (N. Roberts), 1981
Iron Facade (Cookson, as Marchant), 1976
Iron Gates (Millar), 1945
Iron Man (K. Thorpe), 1974
Iron Ships, Iron Men (Nichole), 1987
Iron-Bound (E. Pargeter), 1936
Ironmaster (Stubbs), 1981
Ironwood (Butler, as Melville), 1972
Irresistible (Trask), 1955
Irresistible Buck (Cartland), 1972
Irresistible Force (Cartland), 1978
Irresistible Impulse (Delinsky, as Douglass), 1983
Irresponsibles (Gibbs, as Ford), 1946
Is Anybody There? (s Lofts), 1974
Isabella and Ferdinand series (Holt, as Plaidy), from 1960
Isabella, The She-Wolf (M. Peters), 1985
Isabelle, The Frantic (Kimbrough), 1978
Island series (Manners), from 1981
Island Affair (Grimstead), 1971
Island Conquest (B. Hastings), 1981
Island Doctor (R. Randall), 1951
Island for Doctor Phillipa (Emsley, as Plummer), 1969
Island for Dreams (Britt), 1980
Island for Sale (Stuart, as A. Stuart), 1955
Island Girl (M. St. John), 1924
Island House (Charles, as Lance), 1976
Island in the Mist (I. Roberts, as Rowland), 1962
Island in the South (L. Walker, as Dean), 1967
Island Magic (Goudge), 1934
Island Nurse (Daniels), 1964
Island of Bitter Memories (Daniels), 1974

Island of Cyclones (May), 1979
Island of Darkness (Stratton), 1974
Island of Desire (J. Roberts), 1977
Island of Dreams (Marsh), 1987
Island of Enchantment (I. Preston), 1963
Island of Eve (M. St. John, as Cooper), 1921
Island of Evil (Daniels), 1970
Island of Flowers (N. Roberts), 1982
Island of Flowers (Robins), 1940
Island of Love (Cartland), 1984
Island of Mermaids (Danbury), 1970
Island of Pearls (Rome), 1973
Island of Secrets (Reid), 1965
Island of Secrets (Woodward, as Richmond), 1968
Island of Shadows (Beresford), 1966
Island of Youth (s Byrne), 1932
Island on the Hill (Browning), 1982
Island Providence (Niven), 1910
Island Stranger (J. MacLeod), 1977
Island Twilight (Tranter), 1947
Islands of Summer (Weale), 1964
Islands of Unwisdom (Graves), 1949
Isle at the Rainbow's End (Hampson), 1976
Isle of Calypso (Rome), 1979
Isle of Desire (Hampson), 1978
Isle of Pomegranates (Danbury), 1969
Isle of the Dolphins (J. Roberts) 1973
Isle of the Golden Drum (Stratton), 1975
Isle of the Rainbow (Hampson), 1970
Isle of the Undead (Coffman), 1969
Isles of Despair (Idriess), 1947
Isles of the Blest (Llywelyn), 1989
Isles of Unwisdom (Graves), 1950
It (s Glyn), 1927
It Began in Te Rangi (Bevan), 1971
It Began in Vauxhall Gardens (Holt, as Kellow), 1955
It Couldn't Happen to Me (Blackmore), 1962
It Had to Be You (Hoy), 1940
It Had to Happen (Bromfield), 1936
It Happened in Egypt (C. N. and A. M. Williamson), 1914
It Happened in Paris (Hoy), 1970
It Happened One Flight (Greig), 1951
It Is My Duty! (M. St. John), 1926
It Started in Hongkong (Greig, as Ames), 1961
It Takes a Thief (Hooper), 1989
It Takes All Kinds (s Bromfield), 1939
It Was Left to Peter (Ruck), 1940
It Was Like This (s H. Allen), 1940
It Was Romance (M. Howard), 1939
It Wasn't Love (Robins), 1930
Italian Woman (Holt, as Plaidy), 1952
It's A Great World (Loring), 1935
It's All in the Family (Millar), 1948
It's Lonely Without You (Elsna, as Conway), 1962
It's Rumoured in the Village (Burchell), 1946
It's Spring, My Heart! (Bloom, as Essex), 1958
It's Wise to Forget (Hoy), 1945
I've Always Loved You (Greig), 1943
Ivorstone Manor (Lee, as Cromwell), 1970
Ivory Cane (Dailey), 1977
Ivory Child (Haggard), 1916
Ivory God (Swan), 1920
Ivy Tree (Stewart), 1961

Jacaranda Island (Danbury), 1972
Jacintha (Winsor), 1983

Jack Be Nimble (Barcynska, as Sandys), 1941
Jack London, Sailor on Horseback (Stone), 1947
Jack O'Lantern (Shoesmith), 1969
Jack O'Manory (s Stern), 1927
Jackal's Head (B. Michaels, as Peters), 1968
Jackie (Barcynska), 1921
Jackpot (Barcynska), 1957
Jack's Year of Trial (Swan), 1887
Jacob Ussher (Jacob), 1925
Jacobite series (Broster), from 1925
Jade (Barr), 1982
Jade Alliance (Darrell), 1979
Jade Dragon (Buckingham), 1974
Jade Earrings (Ruck), 1941
Jade Green (Daniels), 1973
Jade Horse of Merle (Ponsonby), 1966
Jade Moon (J. Fitzgerald), 1988
Jade of Destiny (Farnol), 1931
Jade Spider (Muskett), 1927
Jade Vendetta (J. Roberts), 1976
Jago, Nathan series (Thompson), from 1983
Jake Howard's Wife (Mather), 1973
Jalna series (de la Roche), from 1927
Jamaica Inn (du Maurier), 1936
James Bevanwood, Baronet (M. St. John, as Cooper), 1920
James, By the Grace of God (Tranter), 1985
James River series (Deveraux), from 1984
James Shore's Daughter (Benét), 1934
Jane (Corelli), 1897
Jane Cable (McCutcheon), 1906
Jane Em'ly (M. St. John), 1911
Jane Hadden (R. Marshall), 1952
Jane of Lantern Hill (Montgomery), 1937
Jane Oglander (Lowndes), 1911
Jane Ryan, Dietician (McElfresh, as Wesley), 1959
Jane, The Courageous (Kimbrough), 1975
Janice (Greig), 1947
Janie's Great Mistake (Wynne), 1920
Janus Imperative (Anthony), 1980
Japan series (Nicole), from 1984
Japanese Doll (Ponsonby, as Rybot), 1961
Japanese Girl (s Graham), 1971
Japanese Lantern (Hunter, as Chace), 1960
Japanese Screen (Mather), 1974
Jarrett's Jade (Yerby), 1959
Jasmine (Thum), 1984
Jasmine Farm (Elizabeth), 1934
Jasmine for a Nurse (I. Roberts), 1982
Jasmine Harvest (Arbor), 1963
Jasmine Sorcery (Delinsky), 1986
Jasmine—Take Care! (Greig), 1930
Jason (Treece), 1961
Jaspard Family series (Ponsonby), from 1950
Jasper Dennison's Christmas (s Swan), 1898
Jassy (Lofts), 1944
Jaubert Ring (W. Roberts), 1976
Jaunty Jock (s Munro), 1918
Jealous Wife's Revenge! (M. St. John), 1921
Jean Huguenot (Benét), 1923
Jeanne (Garvice), 1902
Jeanne Margot (Cleugh), 1927
Jeannie Urquhart (P. Hill), 1988
Jeb (Ellis, as Lord), 1970
Jeff Benton, M.D. (McElfresh), 1962
Jehovah Blues (Steen), 1952
Jennie series (Ogilvie), from 1984

Jennie about to Be (Ogilvie), 1984
Jennifer and Cage series (Brown, as St. Claire), from 1985
Jennifer James, R.N. (Daniels), 1962
Jenny Luck of Brendon's Mills (M. St. John), 1923
Jenny Newstead (Lowndes), 1932
Jenny W.R.E.N. (Bloom, as Burns), 1945
Jerry (Webster), 1916
Jerry, Junior (Webster), 1907
Jess (Haggard), 1887
Jess Mawney, Queen's Nurse (Arbor), 1954
Jess o'Jordan's (M. St. John), 1930
Jessamy Court (Maybury), 1974
Jessica (Maybury), 1965
Jest (Bowen), 1922
Jest of Fate (Garvice), 1904
Jewel of Death (Berckman), 1968
Jewel of the Greys (M. Peters), 1972
Jeweled Dagger (Ellis), 1973
Jewelene (Williams), 1979
Jewelled Caftan (M. Pargeter), 1978
Jewelled Darkness (Coffman), 1989
Jewelled Daughter (Maybury), 1976
Jewelled Path (Laker), 1983
Jewelled Serpent (J. Fitzgerald), 1984
Jewelled Snuff Box (Ley), 1959
Jewels of Terror (J. Roberts), 1970
Jezebel (Robins), 1977
Jig-Saw (Cartland), 1925
Jill (Delafield), 1926
Jill Nolan series (McElfresh)
Jill Takes a Chance (Inglis), 1949
Jill the Hostage (Wynne), 1925
Jinks (Barcynska, as Sandys), 1930
Joan Haste (Haggard), 1895
Joan of the Lilies (M. Peters), 1969
Joan of the Tower (Deeping), 1911
Joanna (Blackmore), 1963
Joanna (Gellis), 1978
Joanna at the Grange (Burchell), 1957
Joanne, The Unpredictable (Kimbrough), 1976
Job for Jenny (Baldwin), 1945
Job's Niece (G. Hill), 1927
Johan Lind (Salverson), 1928
John Burnet of Barns (Buchan), 1898
John Galbraith's Wife (Albanesi, as Rowlands), 1910
John Helsby's Wife (Albanesi, as Rowlands), 1920
John Jordan, Slave-Driver (M. St. John), 1915
John o' the Green (Farnol), 1935
John Splendid (Munro), 1898
Johnny Danger (Blackstock, as Allardyce), 1960
Johnny Forsaken (Stern), 1954
Johnny Osage (Giles), 1960
Johnny Pye and the Fool-Killer (s Benét) 1938
Johnson Family series (Chambers), from 1901
Jolly Sally Pendleton (Libbey), n.d.
Jonah and Co. (s Yates), 1922
Jones, Guinevere series (Krentz, as Castle), from 1986
Jonquil (Robins), 1927
Jordan County (Foote), 1954
Joshua Tree (J. MacLeod), 1970
Jonty in Love (Hampson), 1975
Joseph Stone (La Tourrette), 1971
Josselyn's Wife (Norris), 1918
Journey (Michener), 1989
Journey for Two Travellers (Farnes), 1946
Journey from a Foreign Land (Melville, as Betteridge), 1972

Journey from Yesterday (Ebel), 1963
Journey Home (Elsna, as Conway), 1978
Journey Home (Grimstead), 1950
Journey in the Dark (Barrie, as Kent), 1962
Journey in the Dark (Greig, as Ames), 1945
Journey in the Dark (Norway), 1973
Journey in the Sun (J. MacLeod), 1957
Journey into Morning (Maybury), 1944
Journey into Spring (J. MacLeod), 1976
Journey into Stone (Erskine-Lindop), 1972
Journey into Terror (Daniels), 1971
Journey to a Star (Cartland), 1984
Journey to Arcady (R. Randall), 1955
Journey to Enchantment (Veryan), 1986
Journey to Love (Finley), 1970
Journey to Love (R. Randall), 1953
Journey to Paradise (Cartland), 1974
Journey to Quiet Waters (Browning), 1984
Journey Up (Hichens), 1938
Journeyer (Jennings), 1984
Journey's End (Berckman), 1977
Journey's Eve (Cadell), 1953
Joy (Krentz), 1988
Joy Comes After (Barcynska), 1943
Joy of Life (Albanesi, as Rowlands), 1913
Joy Shop (Barcynska), 1931
Joy Street (Keyes), 1950
Joyce, The Beloved (Kimbrough), 1979
Joyday for Jodi (L. Walker), 1971
Joyful Journey (Ruck), 1950
Joyous Adventure (Ashton), 1979
Joyous Adventure (Barcynska), 1932
Joyous Story of Astrid (Beck), 1931
Joy-Ride (Ruck), 1929
Jubilee (Rayner), 1987
Jubilee (M. Walker), 1966
Jubilee Hospital (Charles, as Tempest), 1966
Jubilee Trail (Bristow), 1950
Judas Cat (Davis), 1949
Judas Figure (Erskine-Lindop), 1956
Judas Flowering (Hodge), 1976
Judas Iscariot—Traitor! (Bloom, as Prole), 1971
Judas Kiss (Holt), 1981
Judas, My Brother (Yerby), 1969
Judas Trap (Mather), 1979
Judas Tree (Swanson), 1933
Judge of Jerusalem (Bloom), 1926
Judge of the Four Corners (Burgin), 1896
Judged by Fate (Albanesi, as Rowlands), 1913
Judgement of Love (Cartland), 1978
Judgement of the Sword (Diver), 1913
Judith (Cleeve), 1978
Judith (Neels), 1982
Judith Lammeter (Manners, as Rundle), 1976
Judith Paris (Walpole), 1931
Judy Bovenden (Bailey), 1928
Juice of the Pomegranate (Dell), 1938
Julia (P. Hill), 1967
Julia (Hutten), 1924
Julia (Riefe), 1982
Julia Ballantyne (Bowen, as Preedy), 1952
Julia in Ireland (Bridge), 1973
Julia Involved (Bridge), 1962
Julia Roseingrave (Bowen, as Paye), 1933
Julian (Vidal), 1964
Julian Maze (P. Hastings), 1986

Julian Probert (Ertz), 1931
Julia's Sister (C. Allen), 1978
Julia's Sister (Ebel), 1982
Julie (F. Stevenson), 1978
June Fairley—Air Hostess (Woodward, as Richmond), 1959
June for Enchantment (Hoy), 1949
June in Her Eyes (Charles, as Chandos), 1949
Jungle (Blackstock), 1972
Jungle Captive (Hull), 1939
Jungle Island (K. Thorpe), 1986
Jungle Nurse (I. Roberts), 1968
Jungle of Desire (Kidd), 1977
Junie's Love Test (Libbey), 1886
Junior Pro (Norway), 1959
Juniper Tree (Baldwin), 1952
Juniper Hill (Daniels), 1976
Jupiter in the Chair (R. Fraser), 1958
Jurgen (Cabell), 1919
Jury of One (Eberhart), 1961
Just a Barmaid (M. St. John), 1909
Just a Cottage Maid (M. St. John, as Cooper), 1920
Just a Girl (Garvice), 1898
Just a Little Longer (Charles, as Chandos), 1944
Just a Nice Girl (Burchell), 1941
Just a Song at Sunrise (Trask), 1954
Just Around the Corner (Gibbs, as Ford), 1952
Just Around the Corner (s Hurst), 1914
Just Before the Wedding (Charles, as Chandos), 1954
Just David (E. Porter), 1916
Just Desserts (Browning), 1984
Just for One Weekend (Charles), 1978
Just Jane Ann (M. St. John), 1915
Just Jane Em'ly (M. St. John), 1921
Just Lil (Barcynska, as Sandys), 1933
Just 'Liz-beth Ann (M. St. John), 1925
Just Mother (s E. Porter), 1927
Just Off Piccadilly (Cartland), 1933
Just Plain Jim! (M. St. John, as Cooper), 1924
Just You Wait (Berckman), 1973
Justice by Midnight (Farnol), 1956
Justice of the Duke (Sabatini), 1912
Justin (Palmer), 1988

K (Rinehart), 1915
Kadin (Small), 1978
Kaleidoscope (Steel), 1987
Kara (Ellis), 1974
Karen's Memory (Duffield), 1939
Karl of Erbach (Bailey), 1902
Karma of Love (Cartland), 1974
Karran Kinrade (Manners), 1982
Kasia and the Empress (Carnegie), 1973
Kate (Cleeve), 1977
Kate Alanna (M. Peters), 1975
Kate Hardy (D. Stevenson), 1947
Kate Hannigan (Cookson), 1950
Kate, The Curious (Kimbrough), 1976
Katharine of Aragon series (Holt, as Plaidy), from 1961
Katharine, The Virgin Widow (Holt, as Plaidy), 1961
Katharine's Yesterday (s G. Hill), 1895
Katherine (J. MacLeod), 1950
Katherine (Seton), 1954
Katherine of Aragon (J. Fitzgerald, as Hamilton), 1972
Katherine Christian (Walpole), 1943
Katherine, The Returned (Kimbrough), 1980
Katherine the Tragic Tudor (J. Fitzgerald, as Hamilton), 1974

Katherine Wentworth (D. Stevenson), 1964
Katherine's Marriage (D. Stevenson), 1965
Katheryn, The Wanton Queen (M. Peters), 1967
Kathleen (Rivers), 1979
Katie Mulholland (Cookson), 1967
Katie's Christmas Lesson (s Swan), 1883
Katie's Young Doctor (Seifert), 1964
Kay Manion, M.D. (McElfresh), 1959
Kay Rogers, Copy Writer (McElfresh, as Scott), 1956
Kaye's Walk (Ponsonby), 1977
Keate, Sarah series (Eberhart), from 1929
Keating's Landing (W. Roberts), 1984
Kecksies (s Bowen), 1976
Keep Cheery (Barcynska), 1937
Keep This Door Shut (A. M. Williamson), 1933
Keeper of the Bees (G. Porter), 1925
Keeper of the Door (Dell), 1915
Keeper of the Heart (Westwood), 1969
Keeper's House (Pilcher, as Fraser), 1963
Keepers of the Faith (Loring), 1944
Keeping Up with Lizzy (Bacheller), 1911
Keeping Up with William (Bacheller), 1918
Keith's Dark Tower (E. Porter), 1919
Kelling, Sarah series (C. MacLeod), from 1979
Kenjiro (Barr), 1985
Kenny (s Bromfield), 1947
Kent series (Oldfield), from 1983
Kent Family series (Jakes), from 1974
Kent Heiress (Gellis), 1982
Kentuckians (Giles), 1953
Kentucky Trace (Arnow), 1974
Kept Woman (Delmar), 1929
Kerry (G. Hill), 1931
Kettle of Fish (Tranter), 1961
Key (Kevern), 1974
Key Diablo (Daniels), 1971
Key of Dreams (Beck), 1922
Key to Many Doors (Loring), 1967
Key Witness (W. Roberts), 1975
Keys from a Window (Berckman), 1965
Khaki and Kisses (s Ruck), 1915
Khamsin (Robins), 1948
Kiddy, The Coffee-Stall Girl (M. St. John), 1914
Kidnapped (M. St. John, as Cooper), 1923
Kilgaren (I. Holland), 1974
Killigrew Clay (Saunders, as Summers), 1986
Kilmeny in the Dark Wood (F. Stevenson), 1973
Kilmeny of the Orchard (Montgomery), 1910
Kilted Stranger (M. Pargeter), 1975
Kind of Insolence (s Steen), 1940
Kind of War (Haines), 1976
Kind of Warfare (Dymoke), 1981
Kinder Bees (Macbeth, as Knox), 1935
Kinder Love (Charles), 1955
Kindled Fire (Summers), 1969
Kindled Flame (Pedler), 1931
Kindling and Ashes (McCutcheon), 1926
Kindly Giant (Dingwell), 1964
King and a Coward (Albanesi, as Rowlands), 1899
King and a Few Dukes (Chambers), 1896
King Behind the King (Deeping), 1914
King Country (Way), 1970
King Creole (Nicole, as Grange), 1966
King Heart (Oman), 1926
King Henry's Sweetheart (Bloom, as Prole), 1967
King Hereafter (Dunnett), 1982

King in Love (Cartland), 1982
King in Prussia (Sabatini), 1944
King in the Lists (Wynne), 1922
King in Yellow (s Chambers), 1895
King Is a Witch (Eaton), 1965
King Jesus (Graves), 1946
King Kielder (Rome), 1981
King Liveth (Farnol), 1943
King Mandrin's Challenge (Wynne), 1927
King Must Die (Renault), 1958
King of a Day (Wynne), 1918
King of Athelrey (Duggan), 1961
King of Four Corners (Burgin), 1910
King of Spades (Britt), 1974
King of the Castle (Barrie, as Charles), 1963
King of the Castle (Holt), 1967
King of the Castle (Pozzessere), 1987
King Solomon's Mines (Haggard), 1885
King Waits (s Dane), 1929
King Was in His Counting House (Cabell), 1938
Kingdom for the Bold (Worboys), 1986
Kingdom of a Heart (Albanesi, as Rowlands), 1899
Kingdom of Dreams (McNaught), 1989
Kingdom of Summer (Bradshaw), 1981
Kingdom of the Heart (L. Walker), 1959
Kingdom of the Sun (I. Roberts), 1987
Kingdom of the Wicked (Burgess), 1985
Kingdom's Castle (Winston), 1972
Kingfisher Morning (Lamb), 1977
Kingfisher Tide (Arbor), 1965
Kingfishers Catch Fire (Godden), 1953
Kingmaker (Clarke, as Honeyman), 1969
King's Bastard (Elsna), 1971
King's Brat (Gluyas), 1972
King's Cavalier (Shellabarger), 1950
King's Critic (J. Lane), 1936
King's Crusader (Jakes, as Scotland), 1977
King's Daughter (Bloom, as Prole), 1975
King's Favourite (Bowen), 1971
King's General (du Maurier), 1946
King's Grey Mare (Jarman), 1973
Kings in Winter (C. Holland), 1968
King's Legacy (Heaven, as Fecher), 1967
King's Masquerade (Wynne), 1910
King's Minion (Sabatini), 1930
King's Minions (Clarke, as Honeyman), 1974
King's Mirror (Hope), 1899
King's Mistress (J. Fitzgerald, as Watson), 1970
King's Mistress (Holt, as Plaidy), 1952
King's Pawn (W. Roberts), 1971
King's Plaything (Bloom, as Prole), 1962
King's Pleasure (Bloom, as Prole), 1954
King's Pleasure (Holt, as Plaidy), 1949
King's Pleasure (Lofts), 1969
King's Rhapsody (Chapman), 1950
Kings Row (Bellamann), 1940
King's Secret Matter (Holt, as Plaidy), 1962
King's Stratagem (s Weyman), 1891
King's Tale (Clarke, as Honeyman), 1977
King's Tragedy (Wynne), 1905
King's Traitor (Leslie), 1973
King's Vengeance (Wiat), 1981
King's Vixen (P. Hill), 1954
King's Wife (Bloom), 1950
Kings-at-Arms (Bowen), 1918
Kingsmead (Hutten), 1909

Kinsfolk (Swan), 1896
Kinsman's Sin (Albanesi, as Rowlands)
Kirby, Jacqueline series (B. Michaels, as Peters), from 1972
Kirkby's Changeling (Brent), 1975
Kirkland Revels (Holt), 1962
Kiss (Burgin), 1924
Kiss a Stranger (Finley), 1972
Kiss and a Promise (Hampson), 1982
Kiss—and Forget (Charles, as Tempest), 1936
Kiss for the King (Cartland), 1975
Kiss from Aphrodite (J. Fitzgerald), 1987
Kiss from Satan (Hampson), 1973
Kiss in a Gondola (Britt), 1968
Kiss in Sunlight (Greig), 1956
Kiss in the Sun (Grimstead), 1959
Kiss Me Again, Stranger (s du Maurier), 1953
Kiss of a Tyrant (M. Pargeter), 1980
Kiss of Fire (Lamb), 1987
Kiss of Hot Sun (Buckingham), 1969
Kiss of Life (Cartland), 1981
Kiss of Paris (Cartland, as McCorquodale), 1956
Kiss of Promise (Greig), 1960
Kiss of Silk (Cartland, as McCorquodale), 1959
Kiss of the Devil (Cartland), 1955
Kiss of the Night Wind (Taylor), 1989
Kiss of Youth (Robins), 1937
Kiss Remembered (Brown, as St. Claire), 1983
Kiss the Moon (Barcynska, as Sandys), 1951
Kiss the Moonlight (Cartland), 1977
Kissed by Magic (Hooper, as Robbins), 1983
Kisses and the Wine (Winspear), 1973
Kisses for Three (Grimstead, as Manning), 1958
Kissing Gate (Dingwell), 1975
Kissing Gate (Haines), 1981
Kissing Kin (Thane), 1948
Kissing Time (Saunders), 1982
Kith and Kin (s Bentley), 1960
Kit's Hill (Stubbs), 1978
Kitty (Chesney, as Tremaine), 1980
Kitty (Deeping), 1927
Kitty (R. Marshall), 1943
Kleath (Macbeth), 1917
Knave of Diamonds (Dell), 1913
Knave of Hearts (Cartland), 1950
Knave of Hearts (Holt, as Carr), 1983
Knave of Hearts (I. Roberts, as Rowland), 1970
Kneel for Mercy (Cartland), 1982
Kneel to the Prettiest (Ruck), 1925
Knight at Arms (Bailey), 1924
Knight in Red Armor (Daniels), 1966
Knight in Shining Armor (Deveraux), 1989
Knight of Allington (Wiat), 1974
Knight of Spain (Bowen), 1913
Knight with Armour (Duggan), 1950
Knightly Love (Delinsky, as Douglass), 1982
Knight's Acre (Lofts), 1975
Knight's Honor (Gellis), 1964
Knight's Keep (R. Randall), 1967
Knock at a Star (P. Hill), 1981
Knock at Midnight (Blackstock), 1966
Knock Four Times (Irwin), 1927
Knock on the Door (Hichens), 1909
Knot Garden (s Bowen, as Preedy), 1933
Kona Winds (Dailey), 1979
Königsmark (A. Mason), 1938
Kowhai Country (Bevan), 1979

Kuragin series (Heaven), from 1972
Kuzan series (S. Johnson), from 1979
Kyra's Fate (Garvice), 1908

Lab Nurse (R. Randall), 1962
Labour of Hercules (s Lowndes), 1943
Lace for Milady (J. Smith), 1980
Lacebridge Ladies series (Sebastian, as Gladstone), from 1978
Lacey (Williams), 1979
Lachlan's Woman (Dwyer-Joyce), 1979
Lackland's Bride (M. Peters), 1983
Lacquer Couch (Duffield), 1928
Lad with Wings (Ruck), 1915
Ladder of Understanding (Arbor), 1949
Laddie (G. Porter), 1913
Ladies (s Beck, as Barrington), 1922
Ladies of Hanover Square (R. Randall), 1981
Ladies of Lark (Chappell), 1965
Ladies of Lyndon (Kennedy), 1923
Ladies of Missalonghi (McCullough), 1987
Ladies of the Manor (Burgin), 1903
Ladies Whose Bright Eyes (Ford), 1911
Lady and the Pirate (Blackstock, as Allardyce), 1957
Lady and the Rogue (Sebastian, as Norcross), 1978
Lady and the Unicorn (Godden), 1937
Lady and the Unicorn (Johansen), 1984
Lady Anne's Deception (Chesney, as Tremaine), 1986
Lady Aurelia's Bequest (Walsh), 1987
Lady Be Bad (Chase), 1984
Lady Bell (Williams), 1986
Lady Betty Across the Water (C. and A. Williamson), 1906
Lady Blanche Farm (Keyes), 1931
Lady Blue (F. Stevenson, as Faire), 1979
Lady Cassandra (Vaizey), 1914
Lady Cecily's Dilemma (Walsh, as Leyton), 1980
Lady Chatterley's Daughter (Lorrimer, as Robins), 1961
Lady Fell in Love (M. Howard), 1956
Lady Fell in Love (Maybury), 1943
Lady Feo's Daughter (Albanesi, as Rowlands), 1926
Lady for a Chevalier (M. Peters), 1987
Lady for Ransom (Duggan), 1953
Lady from London (Ayres), 1944
Lady from the Air (C. and A. Williamson), 1922
Lady Housekeeper (s Swan), 1898
Lady Ice (Lorin, as Hohl), 1987
Lady in a Veil (Bowen, as Preedy), 1943
Lady in Berkshire (Gibbs), 1970
Lady in the Limelight (Ashton), 1976
Lady in the Mist (Charles), 1966
Lady in the Tower (Holt, as Plaidy), 1986
Lady Incognita (Pykare), 1980
Lady Ingram's Retreat (Tattersall), 1970
Lady Ingram's Room (Tattersall), 1981
Lady into Fox (Garnett), 1922
Lady, It Is Spring! (Maybury), 1938
Lady Living Alone (Lofts, as Curtis), 1945
Lady—Look Ahead (Elsna, as Lancaster), 1944
Lady Lost in Time (Cato), 1985
Lady Love (Palmer), 1984
Lady Madcap (Williams), 1987
Lady Magic (Williams), 1983
Lady Margery's Intrigues (Chesney), 1980
Lady Mary of the Dark House (A. Williamson), 1898
Lady Mary's Money (Burgin), 1918
Lady Misjudged (Elsna), 1941
Lady of Blossholme (Haggard), 1909

Lady of Darracourt (Garvice), 1902
Lady of Mallow (Eden), 1962
Lady of Quality (Heyer), 1972
Lady of Spain (Burgin), 1911
Lady of the Basement Flat (Vaizey), 1917
Lady of the Garter (Dymoke), 1979
Lady of the Heavens (Haggard), 1908
Lady of the House (J. Lane), 1953
Lady of the Lakes (Ellerbeck, as Yorke), 1981
Lady of the Manor (Saunders), 1978
Lady of the Masque (Bennetts), 1982
Lady of the Pool (Hope), 1894
Lady of the Shadows (Daniels), 1968
Lady of the Torch (Mackinlay), 1944
Lady of Wildersley (M. Howard, as Edgar), 1975
Lady on the Coin (Elsna), 1963
Lady Pamela (Darcy), 1975
Lady Patricia's Faith (Albanesi, as Rowlands), 1913
Lady Serena (Coffman, as Duval), 1979
Lady Thief (Hooper), 1981
Lady! This Is Love! (Bloom, as Burns), 1938
Ladybird (G. Hill), 1930
Lady's Choice (Krentz), 1989
Lady's Masquerade (Sebastian, as Gladstone), 1980
Laid Up in Lavender (s Weyman), 1907
Laird and the Lady (Grant), 1949
Laird of Glenfernie (M. Johnston), 1919
Laird of Locharrun (Hampson), 1980
Laird of Storr (Reid), 1968
Laird's Choice (R. Marshall), 1951
Lake in Kyoto (Lewty), 1985
Lake of Darkness (Cowen), 1971
Lake of Gold (Buchan), 1941
Lake of Shadows (Arbor), 1964
Lake of the Kingfisher (Summers), 1978
Lamb, Sergeant series (Graves), from 1940
Lamb to the Slaughter (Eden), 1953
Lambs (Norway), 1965
Lame Daddy (Barcynska, as Sandys), 1942
Lame Englishman (Deeping), 1910
Lament for a Lost Lover (Holt, as Carr), 1977
Lament for a Lover (J. MacLeod), 1967
Lament for Four Brides (Berckman), 1959
Lament for Lost Lovers (Knight), 1972
Lamont of Ardgoyne (J. MacLeod), 1944
Lamp for Jonathan (Summers), 1982
Lamp in the Desert (Dell), 1919
Lamp of Fate (Pedler), 1920
Lamp of Friendship (Albanesi, as Rowlands), 1936
Lamplight and the Stars (Malpass), 1985
Lancaster Men (Dailey), 1981
Lancelot (Vansittart), 1978
Land Beyond the Mountains (Giles), 1958
Land Called Deseret (Dailey), 1979
Land of Afternoon (Macbeth, as Knox), 1925
Land of Enchantment (Dailey), 1975
Land of Heart's Desire (J. MacLeod, as Airlie), 1957
Land of Illusion (K. Thorpe), 1988
Land of My Fathers (Cordell), 1983
Land of Silence (Burgin), 1904
Land of the Far Island (Holt), 1975
Land of the Incas (K. Thorpe), 1983
Land of the Lotus-Eaters (Hunter, as Chace), 1966
Landfall (Shute), 1940
Land-Girl's Love Story (Ruck), 1919
Landowner Legacy (Holt), 1984

Lands of the Sea (Mullins), 1988
Landscape of the Heart (Renier), 1978
Landscape with Figures (R. Fraser), 1925
Language of Love (Saunders), 1983
Language of the Heart (Cadell), 1962
Lanier Riddle (Daniels), 1972
Lantern in the Night (Lamb, as Holland), 1973
Lantern Lane (Deeping), 1921
Lantern-Light (Duffield), 1933
Lap of Luxury (Ruck), 1931
Larcenous Lady (J. Smith), 1988
Larger than Life (Hooper), 1986
Lark Ascending (de la Roche), 1932
Lark in an Alien Sky (Stratton), 1979
Lark in the Meadow (Summers), 1959
Lark Shall Sing (Cadell), 1955
Larksbrook (Maddocks), 1962
Larksghyll (Heaven), 1986
Larrabee Heiress (Daniels), 1972
Larry Munro (Stern), 1920
Larry Vincent (Keyes), 1953
Lass a King Loved (Bloom, as Prole), 1975
Lass He Left Behind Him! (M. St. John, as Cooper), 1915
Lass of Silver, Lad of Gold (M. Peters, as Darby), 1982
Lass That Loved a Sailor (M. St. John), 1915
Lassetter's Last Ride (Idriess), 1931
Last Act (Hodge), 1979
Last April Fair (Neels), 1980
Last Bouquet (s Bowen), 1932
Last Bridge Home (Johansen), 1987
Last Chance (Lorrimer, as Robins), 1961
Last Confession (s Caine), 1892
Last Cotillion (Roby, as Grey), 1981
Last Days with Cleopatra (J. Lindsay), 1935
Last Enchantment (Stewart), 1979
Last Frontier (Fast), 1941
Last Galley (s Doyle), 1911
Last Gamble (Graham), 1955
Last Great Love (M. Harris), 1981
Last Honest Woman (N. Roberts), 1988
Last Love (Costain), 1963
Last Love of a King (Bloom, as Prole), 1974
Last Movement (Aiken), 1977
Last Night at Paradise (Weale), 1980
Last Night at the Ritz (Savage), 1973
Last of the Greenwood (M. Peters, as Whitby), 1975
Last of the Kintyres (J. MacLeod, as Airlie), 1959
Last of the Laidlaws (Swan), 1933
Last of the Legions (s Doyle), 1925
Last of the Logans (Stuart, as A. Stuart), 1957
Last of the Mallorys (K. Thorpe), 1968
Last of the Mansions (Daniels), 1966
Last of the Stuarts (Holt, as Plaidy), 1977
Last of the Tudors (J. Fitzgerald, as Hamilton), 1971
Last of the Wine (Renault), 1956
Last of Their Race (Swan), 1911
Last Pool (s O'Brian), 1950
Last Princess (Freeman), 1988
Last Run (Harrod-Eagles, as Bennett), 1984
Last Straw for Harriet (Cadell), 1947
Last Supper (s Fast), 1955
Last Time (s Hichens), 1923
Last Trip (Stuart, as A. Stuart), 1972
Last Tsarina (Bloom, as Prole), 1970
Last Year's Nightingale (Lorrimer), 1984
Last Year's Roses (Charles, as Chandos), 1945

Letty (Darcy), 1980
Letty (Lofts), 1968
Letty and the Law (Baldwin), 1940
Letty Lynton (Lowndes), 1931
Lewis Rand (M. Johnston), 1908
Liar's Moon (Pozzessere, as Graham), 1987
Libertine in Love (Courtney), 1982
Library Tree (Peake), 1972
Lie Down in Roses (Pozzessere, as Drake), 1988
Lie Quiet in Your Grave (Roby), 1970
Lies for Love (Cartland), 1983
Lieutenant of the Line (McCutchan, as MacNeil), 1970
Life and Death of Richard Yeah-and-Nay (Hewlett), 1900
Life—and Erica (Frankau), 1924
Life and Love (Robins), 1935
Life and Mary Ann (Cookson), 1962
Life and Times of Horatio Hornblower (Parkinson), 1970
Life as Carola (Grant), 1939
Life Begins Tomorrow (Manley-Tucker), 1975
Life Everlasting (Corelli), 1911
Life for Two (J. MacLeod), 1936
Life He Led Her! (M. St. John), 1926
Life Is the Destiny (Stuart), 1958
Life Line (Albanesi, as Rowlands), 1924
Life Mask (A. M. Williamson), 1913
Life Steps in (Ayres), 1928
Life Story (Bentley), 1948
Lifeblood (Slaughter), 1974
Life's a Game (Robins), 1933
Life's Love (Albanesi, as Rowlands), 1911
Light a Penny Candle (Binchy), 1982
Light from One Star (Muskett), 1956
Light Heart (Hewlett), 1920
Light Heart (Thane), 1947
Light in Italy (J. Lindsay), 1941
Light in the Clearing (Bacheller), 1917
Light in the Swamp (V. Johnston), 1970
Light in the Tower (J. MacLeod), 1971
Light in the Ward (Andrews), 1965
Light in the Window (Lynn), 1967
Light in the Window (Rinehart), 1948
Light of Love (Cartland), 1981
Light of the Gods (Cartland), 1984
Light of the Moon (Cartland), 1979
Light on Lucrezia (Holt, as Plaidy), 1959
Light That Lies (McCutcheon), 1916
Light the Candles (s Robins), 1959
Light to the Heart (Cartland, as McCorquodale), 1962
Light Woman (Gavin), 1986
Lighted Room (L. Cooper), 1925
Lighted Windows (Loring), 1930
Lighted Windows (Ritchie), 1952
Lighthearted Quest (Bridge), 1956
Lightning Conductor series (C. N. and A. M. Williamson)
Lightning Strikes Twice (Robins), 1966
Lightning Tree (Aiken), 1980
Lights and Shadows (Albanesi, as Rowlands), 1929
Lights, Laughter and a Lady (Cartland), 1983
Lights of London (Andrews), 1985
Lights of Love (Cartland, as McCorquodale), 1958
Like as the Roaring Waves (Wiat), 1972
Like Summer Brave (Elsna), 1938
Like Victors and Lords (Stuart), 1964
Like We Used to Be (Stubbs), 1989
Likely to Die (Summerton, as Roffman), 1964
Likewise the Lyon (L. Cooper), 1928

Lil, The Dancing Girl (Garvice, as Hart)
Lilac Awakening (Delinsky, as Drake), 1982
Lilac Bus (s Binchy), 1984
Lilac Is for Sharing (Blackmore), 1969
Lilamani (Diver), 1911
Lilith (Holt, as Kellow), 1954
Lilla (Lowndes), 1916
Lilli Barr (Bromfield), 1926
Lillian Harley (Cockrell), 1943
Lillian's Vow (Garvice, as Hart)
Lily and the Leopards (Harwood), 1949
Lily Christine (Arlen), 1928
Lily Golightly (Oldfield), 1987
Lily Hand (s Pargeter), 1965
Lily Pond (Daniels), 1965
Lily-of-the-Valley (Bloom), 1938
Limelight for Jane (Gibbs, as Ford), 1970
Limmerston Hall (Chapman), 1972
Lincoln (Vidal), 1984
Linden Leaf (Arbor), 1971
Lindy Lou (Cleugh), 1934
Line of Love (s Cabell), 1905
Link in the Chain (Elsna), 1975
Linked by Fate (Garvice), 1905
Linnet Singing (Eden), 1972
Linnie (Garvice), 1908
Lintott, Inspector John Joseph series (Stubbs), from 1973
Lion and Francis Conway (Carnegie), 1958
Lion and the Sun (I. Roberts), 1960
Lion at the Door (P. Hastings), 1983
Lion by the Mane (Darrell, as Dane), 1975
Lion in the Garden (Stern), 1940
Lion in the Valley (B. Michaels, as Peters), 1986
Lion Let Loose (Tranter), 1967
Lion of Delos (Worboys), 1974
Lion of Ireland (Llywelyn), 1979
Lion of Justice (Holt, as Plaidy), 1975
Lion of Mortimer (Dymoke), 1979
Lion of Trevarrock (Heaven, as Fecher), 1969
Lion of Venice (Rome), 1977
Lion Triumphant (Holt, as Carr), 1974
Lion Without Claws (Wiat), 1976
Lioness and the Lily (Cartland), 1981
Lionors (B. Johnson), 1975
Lion's Legacy (Dymoke), 1974
Lion's Mouse (C. N. and A. M. Williamson), 1919
Lion's Shadow (Hunter), 1980
Lion's Share (Westcott), 1972
Lion's Skin (Sabatini), 1911
Lion-Tamer (Hull), 1928
Lips for a Stranger (Greig, as Ames), 1949
Lisbon (Sherwood), 1988
Listen for the Whisperer (Whitney), 1970
Listen, Please Listen (Hintze), 1972
Listen to Danger (Eden), 1959
Listen to the Children (Butler, as Melville), 1986
Listener (Caldwell), 1960
Listening Valley (D. Stevenson), 1944
Listening Walls (Millar), 1959
Litter of Rose Leaves (s Benét), 1930
Little Adventure (Cartland), 1973
Little and Good (Ayres), 1940
Little and Good (M. St. John), 1918
Little Big Man (T. Berger), 1964
Little Bit of Luck (Melville, as Betteridge), 1967
Little Brothers (Davis), 1973

Little Brown Girl (Charles, as Tempest), 1940
Little Brown Mouse (Albanesi), 1906
Little Doctor (J. MacLeod), 1960
Little Dragon (Neels), 1977
Little Emperors (Duggan), 1951
Little Goddess (Elsna), 1961
Little ''Gutter Girl,'' (M. St. John), 1919
Little Heiress (Cowen), 1961
Little Iliad (Hewlett), 1915
Little Imposter (Peake), 1976
Little Kit (Albanesi, as Rowlands), 1895
Little Lady (Albanesi), 1937
Little Lady Charles (Albanesi, as Rowlands), 1899
Little Lady in Lodgings (Ayres), 1922
Little Leafy (Libbey), 1891
Little Less Than Gods (Ford), 1928
Little Less Than Kind (Armstrong), 1963
Little Man (Ayres), 1931
Little Matron of the Cottage Hospital (Bloom, as Harvey),
    1969
Little Millstones (Worboys, as Eyre), 1970
Little Miss Innocence (M. St. John), 1918
Little Miss Lancashire (M. St. John), 1921
Little Miss Millions (M. St. John), 1914
Little Mountebank (Mackinlay), 1930
Little Nobody (Winspear), 1972
Little Novels of Italy (s Hewlett), 1899
Little Nurse (Bloom, as Essex), 1967
Little Pardner (s E. Porter), 1926
Little Pretender (Cartland), 1951
Little Princess (Garvice, as Hart)
Little Red Foot (Chambers), 1921
Little Red Horses (Stern), 1932
Little Romp Edda (Libbey), n.d.
Little Rosebud's Lovers (Libbey), 1888
Little Ships (Norris), 1921
Little Sinner (Ayres), 1940
Little Sister (Burchell), 1939
Little Sisters Don't Count (Greig), 1932
Little Spot of Bother (Polland), 1967
Little Stranger (Swan), 1933
Little Tiger (Hope), 1925
Little Victoria (Bloom, as Prole), 1957
Little Wax Doll (Lofts, as Curtis), 1970
Little We Know (Robins), 1940
Little White Doves of Love (Cartland), 1980
Little White Nun (A. Williamson), 1903
Little Wig-Maker of Bread Street (Bloom, as Prole), 1959
Littl'st Lover (Ayres), 1917
Live and Kicking Ned (Masefield), 1939
Live Bait (s Dell), 1932
Live Happily—Love Song (Bloom, as Burns), 1952
Lively Corpse (Millar), 1956
Lively Lady (K. Roberts), 1931
Lives of a Woman (Hutten), 1935
Living Apart (Ayres), 1937
Living Phantom (Harwood), 1973
Living Reed (Buck), 1963
Living to Earn (Ponsonby), 1961
Living with Adam (Mather), 1972
Living with Adam (Muskett), 1949
Living with Paula (Elsna, as Conway), 1972
Liz o' Loomland (M. St. John), 1917
Lizbeth Rose (M. St. John), 1927
Lizzie (Jackson), 1957
Lizzie Borden (Lowndes), 1939

Lo, Michael! (G. Hill), 1913
Loaded Stick (Jacob), 1934
Loan of a Lover (Libbey), n.d.
Lobelia Falls series (C. MacLeod, as Craig), from 1981
Local Hero (N. Roberts), 1988
Loch (Caird), 1968
Lodestar (Belle), 1987
Lodestone for Love (Ritchie), 1980
Lodger (Lowndes), 1913
Lodger in His Own Home (M. St. John, as Cooper), 1920
Lofty Banners (Clarke), 1979
Log of a Naval Officer's Wife (Bloom), 1932
Logic of the Heart (Browning), 1982
Lombard Cavalcade (Coffman), 1982
Lombard Heiress (Coffman), 1983
London and Paris (s du Maurier), 1945
London Goes to Heaven (J. Lane), 1947
London, Here I Come (Greig), 1951
London Pride (Hunter), 1983
London Transports (s Binchy), 1983
London Venture (Arlen), 1920
Londoners (Hichens), 1898
Lone Point (G. Hill), 1898
Lonely Bride (Duffield), 1947
Lonely Doctor (Baldwin), 1964
Lonely Dreamer (Elsna), 1961
Lonely Farrow (J. MacLeod), 1940
Lonely Furrow (Diver), 1923
Lonely Furrow (Lofts), 1976
Lonely House (Blackmore), 1957
Lonely House (Lowndes), 1920
Lonely Little Lucy (M. St. John), 1921
Lonely Man (Baldwin), 1964
Lonely Man (Frankau), 1932
Lonely Night (Blackmore), 1969
Lonely One (Rayner, as Brandon), 1965
Lonely Parade (Hurst), 1942
Lonely Place (Daniels), 1978
Lonely Queen (Bailey), 1911
Lonely Quest (Lorrimer, as Robins), 1959
Lonely Road (Farnol), 1938
Lonely Road (Manley-Tucker), 1983
Lonely Shadow (Bloom), 1942
Lonely Shore (Weale), 1956
Lonely Strangers (Blackstock), 1972
Lonesome Road (Charles, as Tempest), 1966
Long Acre (Rayner), 1978
Long and Living Shadow (Winston), 1968
Long Arm of the Prince (Berckman), 1968
Long Barnaby (P. Hastings), 1961
Long Coffin (Tranter), 1956
Long Corridor (Cookson), 1965
Long Dance of Love (Melville, as Betteridge), 1963
Long Dark Night of the Soul (Ellis), 1978
Long Division (Chapman), 1943
Long, Hot Days (M. Lewis), 1966
Long Hunt (Boyd), 1930
Long Lane to Happiness (Ayres), 1915
Long Live the King! (Rinehart), 1918
Long, Long Wooing (M. St. John), 1927
Long Masquerade (Brent), 1981
Long Night (Lytle), 1936
Long Night (Weyman), 1903
Long Remember (Kantor), 1934
Long Road (Muskett), 1951
Long Roll (M. Johnston), 1911

Long Shadow (Donnelly), 1973
Long Shadow (Gilbert), 1983
Long Shadow (Harrod-Eagles), 1983
Long Shadow (Robins), 1954
Long Shadows (Jacob), 1964
Long Short Story (s Stern), 1939
Long Summer Days (Delderfield), 1974
Long Surrender (Lamb), 1978
Long Tall Texan series (Palmer), from 1988
Long Time Ago (Kennedy), 1932
Long Time Coming (Brown), 1989
Long Time to Hate (W. Roberts), 1982
Long Traverse (Buchan), 1941
Long Wait (Lorrimer, as Robins), 1962
Long Way from Home (Pilcher, as Fraser), 1963
Long Way Home (Charles, as Tempest), 1943
Long Way to Go (Stubbs), 1987
Long Week-End (s Kennedy), 1927
Long Winter's Night (Stanford), 1981
Longest Pleasure (Mather), 1986
Longest Pleasure (Nicole), 1970
Longing for Love (M. St. John), 1925
Long-Lost Father (Stern), 1932
Look, Listen, and Love (Cartland), 1977
Look of Innocence (Gilbert), 1975
Look Out for Liza (Baldwin), 1950
Look to the Spring (Ayres), 1932
Look to the Stars (Loring), 1957
Look with Love (Cartland), 1985
Lookalike Love (Buckingham, as John), 1986
Looking for Love (Cartland), 1982
Looking-Glass (Coffman), 1979
Loom of Fate (Garvice), 1913
Loom of Love (M. Peters, as Grey), 1979
Loose Ladies (s Delmar), 1929
Lord and Mary Ann (Cookson), 1956
Lord and the Gypsy (Veryan), 1978
Lord Caliban (F. Stevenson, as Fitzgerald), 1985
Lord Dedringham's Divorce (Sebastian), 1978
Lord Geoffrey's Fancy (Duggan), 1962
Lord Gilmore's Bride (Walsh), 1979
Lord John in New York (C. and A. Williamson), 1918
Lord Loveland Discovers America (C. and A. Williamson),
    1910
Lord of Greenwich (Dymoke), 1980
Lord of Himself (Garvice), 1911
Lord of Imchay (Woodward, as Marsh), 1975
Lord of La Pampa (K. Thorpe), 1977
Lord of Leet Castle (Sinclair, as Daniels), 1984
Lord of Little Langton (Burgin), 1924
Lord of Ravensley (Heaven), 1978
Lord of Sin (Nicole), 1980
Lord of the Black Boar (Wiat), 1975
Lord of the East (R. Fraser), 1956
Lord of the Golden Fan (Nicole), 1973
Lord of the High Lonesome (Dailey), 1980
Lord of the High Valley (Way), 1980
Lord of the Hollow Dark (Kirk), 1979
Lord of the Horizon (Grant), 1943
Lord of the Isles (Reid), 1981
Lord of the Isles (Tranter), 1983
Lord of the Land (Rome), 1983
Lord of the Manor (Blackmore), 1975
Lord of the Sierras (Weale), 1975
Lord of the Silver Dragon (Salverson), 1927
Lord of the Wolf (Wiat), 1980

Lord of Zaracus (Mather), 1970
Lord Orlando's Protegee (Sebastian), 1977
Lord Ravenscar's Revenge (Cartland), 1978
Lord Satan (J. Roberts, as Bronte), 1972
Lord Sin (Gluyas), 1980
Lord Stephen's Lady (J. Roberts, as Radcliffe), 1976
Lord Tony's Wife (Orczy), 1917
Lord Vanity (Shellabarger), 1953
Lordly One (Seale), 1952
Lords of Lancaster (Bennetts), 1973
Lords of Misrule (Tranter), 1976
Lords of Vaumartin (C. Holland), 1988
Lordship of Love (Hutten), 1909
Lorena (Slaughter), 1959
Loren's Baby (Mather), 1978
Lorimer series (Melville), from 1977
Loring, Sir Nigel series (Doyle), from 1891
Loring Mystery (Farnol), 1925
Lorna Neale (Miles), 1932
Lorraine (Chambers), 1897
Lorrie (Garvice), 1899
Lose Money—Lose Friends! (M. St. John, as Cooper), 1925
Loss of Eden series (Masters), from 1979
Lost (Macbeth), 1948
Lost Angel (s Goudge), 1971
Lost Birthright (J. Lindsay), 1939
Lost Children (E. Pargeter), 1951
Lost Colony (E. Marshall), 1964
Lost Ecstasy (Rinehart), 1927
Lost Enchantment (Cartland), 1972
Lost Enchantment (M. Pargeter), 1985
Lost Fight (Prescott), 1928
Lost Garden (Hodge), 1982
Lost General (Thane), 1953
Lost Heritage (Stratton), 1978
Lost Ideal (Swan), 1894
Lost Island (Whitney), 1970
Lost King (Sabatini), 1937
Lost Lady (Deveraux), 1985
Lost Lady of Old Years (Buchan), 1899
Lost Lagoon (Weale), 1987
Lost Lake (s Kirk), 1966
Lost Laughter (Cartland), 1980
Lost Lotus (Manners, as Rundle), 1972
Lost Love (Cartland), 1970
Lost Love Found (Small), 1989
Lost Love, Last Love (Rogers), 1980
Lost Madonna (I. Holland), 1981
Lost Melody (Manley-Tucker), 1959
Lost Message (G. Hill), 1938
Lost One (Cowen), 1977
Lost Ones (Lofts), 1969
Lost Pibroch (s Munro), 1896
Lost Property (Ayres), 1943
Lost Queen (Lofts), 1969
Lost Summer (Charles, as Chandos), 1948
Lost Sunrise (Norris), 1939
Lost Yesterday (Arbor), 1984
Lottery (s Jackson), 1949
Lottery for Matthew Devlin (Rome), 1968
Lotus and the Wind (Masters), 1953
Louis, The Well-Beloved (Holt, as Plaidy), 1959
Louise, The Restless (Kimbrough), 1978
Lovable Stranger (Duffield), 1949
Love (Elizabeth), 1925
Love Almost Lost (Albanesi, as Rowlands), 1905

Love Alters Not (Kidd), 1967
Love Alters Not (Veryan), 1987
Love among the Ruins (Deeping), 1904
Love and a Lie (Ayres), 1923
Love and a Lie (Garvice)
Love and a Rich Girl (Ruck), 1960
Love and Apron-Strings (Ruck), 1949
Love—and Carol (MacGill), 1925
Love and Deborah (Muskett), 1963
Love and Desire and Hate (Robins), 1969
Love and Doctor Benedict (Dingwell), 1978
Love and Dr. Forrest (R. Lindsay), 1971
Love and Dr. Maynard (R. Randall), 1959
Love and Hatred (Lowndes), 1917
Love and Honor (Nicole, as Arlen), 1980
Love and Lady Lovelace (Chesney), 1982
Love and Let Me Go (Greig), 1935
Love and Linda (Cartland), 1976
Love and Louisa (Albanesi), 1902
Love and Lucia (Cartland), 1983
Love and Lucy (Hewlett), 1916
Love and Lucy Brown (Dingwell), 1975
Love and Lucy Granger (R. Lindsay), 1967
Love and Mary Ann (Cookson), 1962
Love and Money (s Bentley), 1957
Love and No Marriage (R. Lindsay, as Leigh), 1980
Love and the Kentish Maid (Beaty), 1971
Love and the Loathsome Leopard (Cartland), 1977
Love and the Locusts (Burgin), 1922
Love and the Marquis (Cartland), 1982
Love—and the Philosopher (Corelli), 1923
Love and the S.S. Beatrice (Beresford), 1972
Love and the Spy (C. N. and A. M. Williamson), 1908
Love and War (Jakes), 1984
Love at a Festival (Ruck), 1951
Love at Forty (Cartland), 1977
Love Battle (Winspear), 1977
Love Beyond Reason (Brown, as Ryan), 1981
Love Beyond Reason (van der Zee), 1980
Love Builds a House (Ritchie), 1950
Love by Proxy (Palmer), 1985
Love Calls Me Home (Elsna, as Conway), 1952
Love Calls the Doctor (Seifert), 1958
Love Calls the Tune (Norris), 1944
Love Came Laughing (Loring), 1949
Love Came Unaware (Woodward, as Lawrence), 1970
Love Campaign (Ebel), 1965
Love Cannot Die (Lorrimer, as Robins), 1955
Love Casts out Fears (Cartland), 1986
Love, Cherish Me (Brandewyne), 1983
Love Child (Holt, as Burford), 1950
Love Climbs In (Cartland), 1979
Love Comedy (Garvice), 1908
Love Comes Again Later (Ruck), 1938
Love Comes to Larkswood (I. Roberts), 1968
Love Comes to Mary (Ayres), 1932
Love Comes Unseen (Ayres), 1943
Love Comes West (Cartland), 1984
Love Decided (Garvice), 1904
Love Deferred (Duffield), 1951
Love Dismayed (Wynne), 1942
Love Duel (Sebastian, as Gladstone), 1978
Love Eternal (Haggard), 1918
Love Finds a Way (Wynne), 1920
Love for a Rogue (Finley), 1976
Love for a Stranger (Donnelly), 1978

Love for All Time (Small), 1986
Love for Love (Albanesi, as Rowlands), 1910
Love for Sale (Cartland), 1980
Love Forbidden (Blackmore), 1974
Love Forbidden (Cartland, as McCorquodale), 1957
Love, Forever More (Matthews), 1977
Love Game (Robins), 1936
Love Games (Lamb), 1984
Love Gives Itself (Swan), 1915
Love Goes South (Mackinlay), 1935
Love Grown Cold (Swan), 1902
Love Has His Way (Cartland), 1980
Love Has No Limits (Trask), 1939
Love Has No Resurrection (s Delafield), 1939
Love Has No Secrets (Bloom, as Harvey), 1972
Love Has Two Faces (Grimstead), 1962
Love Has Two Faces (M. Lewis), 1981
Love Has Wings (Trask), 1939
Love Hath an Island (Hampson), 1970
Love Hath an Island (Robins), 1950
Love Him or Leave Him (Burchell), 1950
Love Holds the Cards (Cartland), 1965
Love, Honour, and Obey (Greig), 1933
Love in a Cloud (L. Walker), 1960
Love in a Dry Season (Foote), 1951
Love in a Far Country (Greig, as Ames), 1960
Love in a Mist (Lamb, as Holland), 1971
Love in a Rainy Country (Melville, as Betteridge), 1969
Love in a Snare (Garvice), 1912
Love in a Stranger's Arms (Winspear), 1977
Love in Amber (Muskett), 1942
Love in Apron Strings (Hoy), 1933
Love in Danger (Finley), 1973
Love in Danger (Woodward, as Ware), 1972
Love in Disguise (R. Lindsay), 1975
Love in Disguise (Pykare), 1980
Love in Hazard (Marsh), 1989
Love in Hiding (Cartland), 1959
Love in Peril (Woodward, as Marsh), 1967
Love in Pity (Cartland), 1977
Love in Store (R. Lindsay, as Leigh), 1978
Love in the Afternoon (Burghley), 1959
Love in the Clouds (Cartland), 1979
Love in the Dark (Cartland), 1979
Love in the Dark (Lamb), 1986
Love in the East (Greig, as Ames), 1960
Love in the Lead (Woodward, as Davis), 1967
Love in the Moon (Cartland), 1980
Love in the Moonlight (Peake), 1986
Love in Waiting (Courtney), 1984
Love Is a Dangerous Game (Lewty), 1980
Love Is a Flame (Lowndes), 1932
Love Is a Flower (Barcynska, as Sandys), 1938
Love Is a Frenzy (Lamb), 1979
Love Is a Gamble (Cartland), 1985
Love Is a Gamble (Greig, as Ames), 1954
Love Is a Gambler (Greig), 1958
Love Is a Lady (Barcynska), 1945
Love Is a Thief (Greig), 1959
Love Is an Eagle (Cartland), 1951
Love Is Contraband (Cartland), 1968
Love Is Dangerous (Cartland, as McCorquodale), 1963
Love Is Enough (Robins), 1941
Love Is Eternal (Stone), 1954
Love Is Everything (Bloom), 1933
Love Is Fire (Kidd), 1971

Love Is Heaven (Cartland), 1984
Love Is Innocent (Cartland), 1975
Love Is Like That (Woodward, as Lawrence), 1967
Love Is Mine (Cartland, as McCorquodale), 1952
Love Is My Reason (Burchell), 1957
Love Is Not Enough (Corcoran), 1981
Love Is So Blind (Ayres), 1933
Love Is the Enemy (Cartland), 1952
Love Is the Honey (Winspear), 1980
Love Itself (Glyn), 1924?
Love Joins the Clan (Cartland), 1986
Love Knot (M. Peters, as Darby), 1989
Love Knows No Frontier (Woodward, as Ware), 1970
Love Leaves at Midnight (Cartland), 1978
Love Letter (Norway, as Neal), 1963
Love Lies North (Finley), 1972
Love Life (C. Allen), 1976
Love Like Ours (Robins), 1969
Love Locked In (Cartland), 1977
Love Locked Out (Trask), 1938
Love, Lords, and Lady-Birds (Cartland), 1978
Love—Love Me Not (Woodward), 1966
Love Made the Choice (Burchell), 1942
Love Maggy (Barcynska), 1918
Love Match (Albanesi, as Rowlands), 1912
Love Match (Elsna), 1956
Love Match (Fellows), 1977
Love Match (R. Lindsay, as Leigh), 1980
Love Me (Greig), 1971
Love Me for Ever (Cartland), 1953
Love Me for Ever (Elsna, as Snow), 1955
Love Me Forever (Matthews), 1977
Love Me No More! (Robins), 1948
Love Me To-morrow (Bloom, as Burns), 1952
Love Me Tomorrow (Lorrimer, as Robins), 1966
Love Me with Fury (Taylor), 1983
Love Must Wait (Lorrimer, as Robins), 1958
Love Needs Telling (M. St. John), 1926
Love Never Dies (Barcynska), 1943
Love Not the Enemy (Seger, as Jennings), 1984
Love of a Life Time (Garvice)
Love of His Life (Albanesi, as Rowlands), 1912
Love of Julie Borel (Norris), 1931
Love of Long Ago (s Corelli), 1920
Love of Lucifer (Winston), 1970
Love of My Life (Courtney), 1981
Love of Robert Dennison (Ayres), 1921
Love of the Foolish Angel (Beauclerk), 1929
Love of the Lion (Daniels, as Gray), 1980
Love, Old and New (Bloom), 1933
Love on a Shoestring (Mackinlay), 1958
Love on Dark Wings (Greig, as Ames), 1957
Love on Ice (Woodward, as Sawley), 1967
Love on Second Thoughts (Ruck), 1936
Love on the Run (Cartland, as McCorquodale), 1965
Love on the Wind (Cartland), 1983
Love Only Once (Lindsey), 1985
Love Pirate (Cartland), 1977
Love Pirate (C. and A. Williamson), 1913
Love Play (Rogers), 1981
Love Plays a Part (Pykare), 1981
Love Race (Woodward, as Richmond), 1967
Love Remembered (Beresford), 1970
Love Rides the Skies (Woodward, as Lawrence), 1968
Love Rules (Cartland), 1982
Love She Hid (Woodward, as Ware), 1970

Love So Fearful (Pykare, as Coombs), 1983
Love So Rare (Hampson), 1983
Love So Young (Robins), 1945
Love Song (J. Fitzgerald, as Watson), 1981
Love Song (J. Roberts), 1970
Love Song for a Raven (Lowell), 1987
Love Song in Springtime (Manley-Tucker), 1960
Love Song of the Sea (I. Roberts), 1960
Love Spins the Wheel (Woodward, as Marsh), 1967
Love, Spread Your Wings (Manley-Tucker), 1967
Love Springs Eternal (Gallagher), 1985
Love Stories (s Rinehart), 1920
Love Stories of India (s E. Marshall), 1950
Love Storm (S. Johnson), 1981
Love Story of Dr. Duke (Bloom, as Essex), 1960
Love Story of Nurse Julie (Bloom, as Harvey), 1975
Love Takes the Helm (Woodward, as Marsh), 1967
Love Talker (B. Michaels, as Peters), 1980
Love Tangle (Sebastian, as Gladstone), 1979
Love That Divided (M. St. John, as Cooper), 1932
Love That Follows (Ritchie), 1966
Love That Is Stronger Than Life (Maybury), 1932
Love That Lasts (Burgin), 1913
Love That Lasts (Charles, as Lance), 1974
Love That Lives (Albanesi), 1937
Love, The Adventurous (Garvice), 1917
Love, The Magician (Ebel), 1956
Love, The Master Key (Swan), 1905
Love the Prodigal (Swan), 1929
Love, The Tyrant (Garvice), 1905
Love Theme (Way), 1974
Love They Must (Webb), 1933
Love Thing (Browning), 1984
Love This Enemy (Blair), 1958
Love This Stranger (Blair, as Brett), 1951
Love to the Rescue (Cartland), 1967
Love Token (Gellis, as Hamilton), 1979
Love Trap (Cartland), 1986
Love Trap (Delmar), 1949
Love Trap (Price), 1958
Love Triumphant (Courtney), 1980
Love Triumphant (Maybury), 1932
Love under Fire (Cartland), 1960
Love Unlocks the Door (Swan), 1907
Love Unmasked (Courtney), 1979
Love Was a Jest (Robins), 1929
Love While You Wait (Charles, as Tempest), 1944
Love Wild and Fair (Small), 1978
Love Will Lend Wings (Ritchie), 1957
Love Will Win (Greig), 1969
Love Wins (Albanesi, as Rowlands), 1912
Love Wins (Cartland), 1981
Love with a Song (Trask), 1937
Love with Honor (Loring), 1969
Love Without Wings (Ayres), 1953
Love-at-Arms (Sabatini), 1907
Lovechild (J. Fitzgerald, as Watson), 1967
Love-Child (Holt, as Carr), 1978
Loved and the Cherished (Manley-Tucker), 1964
Loved and the Feared (Winspear), 1977
Loved for Her Money (M. St. John), 1927
Love-Hater (Ruck), 1907
Love-in-a-Mist (Albanesi), 1907
Loveland series (C. and A. Williamson), from 1908
Loveless Marriage (Ayres), 1921
Lovely and the Lonely (Kimbrough), 1984

Lovely Clay (Greig), 1930
Lovely Day (Grimstead), 1970
Lovely Destiny (Maybury), 1936
Lovely Lying Lips (Sherwood), 1983
Lovely, Though Late (Charles, as Tempest), 1946
Lovely Wanton (Heaven, as Fecher), 1977
Loveplay (Palmer), 1986
Lover (Dane), 1924
Lover (s du Maurier), 1961
Lover Betrayed (Stuart), 1955
Lover Come Lonely (Grimstead, as Manning), 1965
Lover Dark, Lady Fair (M. Peters, as Black), 1983
Lover from the Sea (Delinksy, as Drake), 1983
Lover from Yesterday (Woodward), 1984
Lover in Pursuit (Krentz, as James), 1982
Lover in Rags (M. St. John, as Cooper), 1924
Lover in the Rough (Lowell), 1984
Lover on Loan (MacGill), 1923
Lover Scorned (I. Holland), 1986
Lover Who Died (Ayres), 1922
Lovers (Ayres), 1929
Lovers (s Buck), 1977
Lovers (Ebel, as Goodwin), 1988
Lovers (Winsor), 1952
Lovers All Untrue (Lofts), 1970
Lovers and Outlaws (Nicole), 1982
Lover's Fate (s Hope), 1894
Lovers in Darkness (Elsna, as Lancaster), 1955
Lovers in Lisbon (Cartland), 1987
Lovers in Paradise (Cartland), 1978
Lovers in the Dark (Greig, as Ames), 1946
Lovers in Waiting (Elsna, as Conway), 1962
Lovers' Knots (Bowen), 1912
Lovers' Meeting (Farnes), 1962
Lovers Meeting (Hardwick), 1979
Lovers' Meeting (E. Smith), 1940
Lovers of Janine (Robins), 1931
Lovers of Yvonne (Sabatini), 1902
Lover's Staff (Elsna, as Lancaster), 1954
Lovers' Tale (Hewlett), 1915
Lovers under the Sun (Greig), 1954
Lover's Victory (Courtney), 1984
Lover's Vows (J. Smith), 1981
Love's a Magician (Woodward), 1981
Love's a Puzzle (Baldwin), 1933
Love's a Stage (London), 1981
Love's Agony (Winspear), 1981
Love's Avenging Heart (Matthews), 1977
Love's Barrier (Swan), 1910
Love's Blindness (Glyn), 1926
Love's Bold Journey (Matthews), 1980
Love's Bright Flame (Lamb, as Holland), 1978
Love's Choice (Thomas), 1982
Love's Cousin (Miles), 1927
Love's Cruel Whim (Albanesi, as Rowlands)
Love's Daring Dream (Matthews), 1978
Love's Dark Shadow (Woodward, as Sawley), 1970
Love's Defiance (MacGill), 1926
Love's Delusion (Pykare, as Pemberton), 1980
Love's Dilemma (Garvice), 1902
Love's Duet (Veryan), 1979
Love's Encore (Brown, as Ryan), 1981
Love's Fire (Albanesi, as Rowlands), 1911
Love's Folly (Pykare), 1980
Love's Gentle Chains (Stanford), 1983
Love's Golden Destiny (Matthews), 1979

Love's Greatest Gift (Albanesi, as Rowlands), 1906
Love's Harbinger (J. Smith), 1987
Love's Harvest (Albanesi, as Rowlands), 1911
Love's Hidden Fire (Finley), 1971
Love's Hour (Glyn), 1932
Love's Last Barrier (Woodward, as Lawrence), 1971
Love's Last Reward (Barcynska), 1920
Love's Logic (s Hope), 1908
Love's Magic Moment (Matthews), 1979
Love's Magic Spell (Finley), 1974
Love's Mask (Albanesi, as Rowlands), 1913
Love's Masquerade (Courtney), 1981
Love's Memory (Duffield), 1936
Love's Miracle (Swan), 1910
Loves of a Virgin Princess (Bloom, as Prole), 1968
Loves of an Actress (Hutten), 1929
Loves of Lucrezia (Robins, as Wright), 1953
Love's Pagan Heart (Matthews), 1978
Love's Penalty (Wynne), 1927
Love's Perilous Passage (Harrod-Eagles, as Woodhouse), 1978
Love's Playthings (Bloom), 1932
Love's Prisoner (Elsna, as Conway), 1954
Love's Prisoner (Winspear), 1964
Love's Promise (Pykare), 1979
Love's Puppet (Reid), 1976
Love's Raging Tide (Matthews), 1980
Love's Revenge (Lowndes), 1929
Love's Rugged Path (Garvice, as Hart)
Love's Second Chance (Elsna, as Lancaster), 1962
Love's Sweet Agony (Matthews), 1980
Love's Sweet Music (Saunders), 1983
Love's Temptation (Finley), 1979
Love's Treasure Trove (Woodward, as Davis), 1973
Love's Victory (Robins), 1933
Love's Waif (M. St. John, as Cooper), 1921
Love's Waiting Game (Finley), 1985
Love's Way (J. Smith), 1982
Love's Wildest Promise (Matthews), 1977
Love's Wilful Call (Roby), 1981
Love's Young Dream (Albanesi, as Rowlands), 1914
Lovesong (Sherwood), 1985
Love-Story of Aliette Brunton (Frankau), 1922
Loving (Steel), 1980
Loving and Giving (Farnes), 1968
Loving and Giving (Robins), 1965
Loving Arrangement (Palmer, as Blayne), 1983
Loving Cup (Graham), 1984
Loving Gamble (Kidd), 1988
Loving Heart (Chappell), 1977
Loving Heart (Inglis), 1954
Loving Heart (L. Walker), 1960
Loving Heritage (Marsh), 1987
Loving Highwayman (Bennetts), 1983
Loving Is Different (Elsna, as Conway), 1964
Loving Is Giving (Burchell), 1956
Loving Jack (N. Roberts), 1989
Loving Meddler (R. Marshall), 1954
Loving Partnership (Marsh), 1978
Loving Rescue (Browning), 1982
Loving Sands, Deadly Sands (Blackstock, as Keppel), 1975
Loving Slave (M. Pargeter), 1981
Loving Spirit (du Maurier), 1931
Loving You Always (Elsna, as Conway), 1953
Low Country Liar (Dailey), 1979
Lower Than Vermin (Yates), 1950
Loyal Defence (Albanesi, as Rowlands), 1932

Loyal in All (Burchell), 1957
Loyal Lady (Cleugh), 1932
Loyal Man's Love (Albanesi, as Rowlands), 1910
Loyalty (Albanesi), 1930
Lucia in Love (Pozzessere), 1988
Lucifer and the Angel (Cartland), 1980
Lucifer Cove series (Coffman), from 1969
Lucifer's Angel (Winspear), 1961
Lucile Cléry (Bowen, as Shearing), 1932
Lucille (Garvice), n.d.
Lucinda (Hope), 1920
Lucinda Marries the Doctor (Seifert), 1953
Luck of the Livingstones (Swan), 1932
Luck-Bride (M. Peters), 1987
Luckiest Lady (Ayres), 1927
Lucky in Love (Cartland), 1982
Lucky in Love (Ruck), 1924
Lucky Lawrences (Norris), 1930
Lucky Number (Dell), 1920
Lucky One (Lewty), 1961
Lucretia (Riefe), 1982
Lucretia Lombard (Norris), 1922
Lucrezia Borgia series (Holt, as Plaidy), from 1958
Lucy (Chapman), 1965
Lucy (Chesney, as Tremaine), 1980
Lucy Carmichael (Kennedy), 1951
Lucy in London (Grimstead, as Manning), 1964
Lucy Lamb (Seale), 1958
Lucy's Cottage (Bennetts), 1981
Lullaby of Murder (Davis), 1984
Lummox (Hurst), 1923
Lupin Valley (R. Lane), 1982
Lure of Eagles (Mather), 1979
Lust for Life (Stone), 1934
Lusty Wind for Carolina (Fletcher), 1944
Lute Player (Lofts), 1951
Luxury Husband (Greig), 1928
Lydia (Darcy), 1973
Lydia Bailey (K. Roberts), 1947
Lydian Inheritance (Bromige), 1966
Lying in the Sun (s O'Brian), 1956
Lymond series (Dunnett), from 1961
Lyndall's Temptation (Libbey), 1892
Lyndley Waters (Bowen, as Preedy), 1942
Lynmara Legacy (Gaskin), 1975
Lyonesse Abbey (Tattersall), 1968
Lyonhurst (R. Randall), 1977
Lyons Mail (Wynne), 1917
Lyon's Share (Dailey), 1977
Lyra, My Love (Charles, as Tempest), 1969
Lysander (F. Mason), 1956
Lysbeth (Haggard), 1901

M.D. (W. Roberts), 1972
MF (Burgess), 1971
Mabel St. John's Schooldays (M. St. John, as Cooper), 1921
Macbeth, King of Scots (Clarke, as Honeyman), 1977
Macbeth the King (Tranter), 1978
MacBride of Tordarroch (Summers), 1984
MacGregor's Gathering (Tranter), 1957
MacKenzie's Mountain (L. Howard), 1989
Macleod's Wife (Swan), 1924
Maclure Mystery (Swan), 1932
MacLyon (Burford), 1974
Macomber Menace (W. Roberts), 1979
Mad Barbara (Deeping), 1908

Mad Betrothal (Libbey), 1890
Mad for Dress! (M. St. John), 1921
Mad Is the Heart (Robins), 1963
Mad Trapper (Wiebe), 1980
Madalena (Walsh), 1976
Madam Claire (Ertz), 1923
Madam, Will You Talk? (Stewart), 1955
Madam, You Must Die (Blackstock, as Keppel), 1974
Madame Adastra (Barcynska, as Sandys), 1964
Madame Castel's Lodger (Keyes), 1962
Madame du Barry (Holt, as Tate), 1959
Madame Fears the Dark (s Irwin), 1935
Madame Geneva (J. Lane), 1946
Madame Juno (Mackinlay), 1931
Madame Serpent (Holt, as Plaidy), 1951
Madame Tudor (Gluyas), 1979
Madawaska (W. Roberts), 1988
Maddalena (P. Hill), 1963
Madderleys Married (Charles, as Tempest), 1963
Made in Heaven (Elsna, as Snow), 1952
Made Marriage (Reid), 1971
Made to Marry (Charles, as Chandos), 1944
Madeleine (Gavin), 1957
Madensky Square (Ibbotson), 1988
Madge o' the Mill (M. St. John, as Cooper), 1921
Madness of Love (Albanesi, as Rowlands), 1911
Madness of Love (Garvice, as Hart)
Madolin Rivers (Libbey), 1885
Madonna Creek Witch (La Tourrette), 1973
Madonna of the Seven Hills (Holt, as Plaidy), 1958
Madselin (Lofts), 1969
Mag Pye (Hutten), 1917
Magdalene Scrolls (Wood), 1978
Maggie (Chesney, as Tremaine), 1984
Maggie Darling (M. St. John), 1915
Maggie, Her Marriage (Caldwell), 1953
Maggie of Marley's Mill (M. St. John), 1926
Maggie Rowan (Cookson), 1954
Maggot (Fowles), 1985
Maggy (Seale), 1959
Magic and Mary Rose (Baldwin), 1924
Magic City (Grimstead, as Manning), 1973
Magic Flutes (Ibbotson), 1982
Magic for Marigold (Montgomery), 1929
Magic Garden (G. Porter), 1927
Magic in Maoriland (I. Preston), 1962
Magic in Vienna (Neels), 1985
Magic Lantern (E. Smith), 1944
Magic Moment (Roby, as D'Arcy), 1980
Magic of Living (Neels), 1974
Magic of Love (Cartland), 1977
Magic of the Desert (Woodward, as Davis), 1976
Magic of the Moon (Grimstead, as Manning), 1961
Magic or Mirage? (Cartland), 1978
Magic Place (Bromige), 1971
Magic Ring (Daniels), 1978
Magic Scalpel of Dr. Farrer (McElfresh), 1965
Magic Symphony (Farnes), 1952
Magnificent Courtesan (Bloom, as Prole), 1950
Magnificent Folly (Johansen), 1987
Magnificent Marriage (Cartland), 1974
Magnificent Obsession (Douglas), 1929
Magnolia Moon (Stanford), 1982
Magnolia Room (Worboys, as Eyre), 1972
Magnolias (Ellis), 1976
Magregor series (N. Roberts), from 1985

Maharajah (s T. White), 1981
Mahatma and the Hare (Haggard), 1911
Mahdi (Caine), 1894
Mahound (Horner), 1969
Maia (R. Fraser), 1948
Maid Called Wanton (M. Peters, as Lloyd), 1981
Maid of Brittany (Wynne), 1906
Maid of Gold (Wiat), 1978
Maid of Judah (M. Peters), 1973
Maid of Many Moods (Sheard), 1902
Maid of Stonystream (Baldwin), 1924
Maid of the Isles (Swan), 1924
Maida (Garvice), 1901
Maid-at-Arms (Chambers), 1902
Maiden (Deveraux), 1988
Maiden (Harrod-Eagles), 1985
Maiden Castle (Lamb, as Holland), 1978
Maiden Castle (Powys), 1936
Maiden Flight (Beaty), 1956
Maiden of the Morning (Krentz, as Bentley), 1979
Maiden Stakes (s Yates), 1929
Maiden Voyage (Norris), 1934
Maiden Voyage (Stuart, as A. Stuart), 1964
Maids of Paradise (Chambers), 1902
Mail Order Bride (M. Peters, as Lloyd), 1981
Mail Royal (Tranter), 1989
Main Attraction (Krentz), 1987
Mainwaring (Hewlett), 1920
Maisie's Romance (Albanesi), 1910
Maison Jennie (Ellis), 1984
Maitland of Laurieston (Swan), 1890
Maiwa's Revenge (Haggard), 1888
Major Grant (Oman), 1931
Make Believe Wife (Norris), 1947
Make Me a Murderer (Butler), 1961
Make the Man Notice You (Greig, as Ames), 1940
Make Way for Love (Woodward, as Ware), 1967
Make Way for Tomorrow (Bevan), 1971
Make Way for Tomorrow (M. Lewis), 1966
Make-Believe (Baldwin), 1930
Make-Believe Bride (Buckingham, as John), 1982
Makebelieve Marriage (Kidd), 1982
Maker of Moons (s Chambers), 1896
Makeshift Marriage (Lewty), 1982
Making of a Lover (Ayres), 1921
Making of a Man (Ayres), 1915
Malady in Madeira (Bridge), 1969
Malaspiga Exit (Anthony), 1974
Male Chauvinist (Sellers), 1985
Malice Domestic (Hardwick), 1986
Malice of Men (Deeping), 1939
Mallen series (Cookson), from 1973
Mallion's Pride (Salisbury), 1975
Mallory's Luck (Shoesmith), 1971
Malvie Inheritance (P. Hill), 1973
Mammon (Wren), 1930
Mammon of Righteousness (Wren), 1930
Mammon's Daughter (Tranter), 1939
Mammoth Hunters (Auel), 1985
Mam'zelle Guillotine (Orczy), 1940
Man Always Pays (Mackinlay), 1940
Man and His Model (s Hope), n.d.
Man and Maid (Glyn), 1922
Man and the Moment (Glyn), 1914
Man—and Waif (Charles, as Tempest), 1938
Man Apart (Donnelly), 1968

Man at Kambala (K. Thorpe), 1973
Man at Key West (Britt), 1982
Man at Mulera (Blair), 1959
Man at the Gate (Albanesi, as Rowlands), 1911
Man at the Helm (Reid), 1975
Man at the Manor (Sinclair), 1967
Man at Windmere (V. Johnston), 1988
Man Behind (Burgin), 1923
Man Behind the Curtain (Tranter), 1959
Man Behind the Mask (Lorrimer, as Robins), 1967
Man Between (Robins), 1926
Man Called Cameron (A. Pargeter), 1978
Man Called Mallory (Donnelly), 1974
Man Called Masters (L. Walker), 1965
Man for Always (Buckingham, as John), 1981
Man for Margaret (Charles, as Chandos), 1945
Man for Me (Charles), 1965
Man for the Ages (Bacheller), 1919
Man Friday (Ayres), 1943
Man from Bahl Bahla (Way), 1971
Man from Brodney's (McCutcheon), 1908
Man from Cannae (Jakes, as Scotland), 1977
Man from Ceylon (Ayres), 1950
Man from Dahomey (Yerby), 1971
Man from Half Moon Bay (Johansen), 1988
Man from Nowhere (Stratton), 1982
Man from Outback (L. Walker), 1964
Man from Singapore (M. Howard), 1946
Man from the Kimberleys (M. Pargeter), 1982
Man from the Mists (Elgin), 1965
Man from the Sea (Barrie, as Kent), 1968
Man from the Valley (Dingwell), 1966
Man from the West (Albanesi, as Rowlands), 1927
Man from Tripoli (K. Thorpe), 1979
Man from Turkey (Burgin), 1921
Man from Yesterday (Daniels), 1970
Man Himself (A. Williamson), 1925
Man Hunt (Lamb), 1985
Man in a Box (K. Thorpe), 1972
Man in a Million (R. Lindsay, as Leigh), 1975
Man in Authority (J. MacLeod), 1954
Man in Black (Weyman), 1894
Man in Chains (Deeping), 1953
Man in Charge (Peake), 1973
Man in Command (Weale), 1969
Man in Control (Morgan), 1984
Man in Grey (E. Smith), 1941
Man in Her Life (Ayres), 1935
Man in Lower Ten (Rinehart), 1909
Man in the Corner (Burgin), 1939
Man in the Mirror (s Hichens), 1950
Man in the Next Room (Donnelly), 1971
Man in the Yellow Raft (s Forester), 1969
Man in the Zoo (Garnett), 1924
Man Is Always Right (Greig), 1940
Man Like Brady (Dingwell), 1981
Man Like Daintree (Way), 1972
Man Missing (Eberhart), 1954
Man Next Door (Eberhart), 1943
Man of a Ghost (Wren), 1937
Man of Destiny (Burghley), 1965
Man of Fire (Rome), 1970
Man of Granite (Peake), 1971
Man of Her Choosing (Pykare), 1980
Man of Her Dreams (M. St. John, as Cooper), 1919
Man of His Time (Bentley), 1966

Man of His Word (Ayres), 1916
Man of Ice (R. Lindsay), 1980
Man of Kent (Hunter, as Chace), 1973
Man of Mark (Hope), 1890
Man of Means (K. Thorpe), 1982
Man of My Dreams (Charles, as Chandos), 1937
Man of Nazareth (Burgess), 1979
Man of Power (Blackmore), 1966
Man of Steel (Wyndham), 1952
Man of Stone (M. Howard), 1958
Man of the Desert (G. Hill), 1914
Man of the Family (Charles, as Lance), 1952
Man of the Islands (Reid), 1966
Man of the Moment (Mackinlay), 1956
Man of the Outback (Hampson), 1980
Man of the River (Sinclair), 1968
Man of Wrath (Blackstock, as Allardyce), 1956
Man on a Donkey (Prescott), 1952
Man on Half-Moon (Way), 1976
Man on the Island (Collin), 1968
Man on the Peak (Britt), 1979
Man on the White Horse (Deeping), 1934
Man Outside (Donnelly), 1975
Man She Bought (Greig), 1930
Man She Loved (Albanesi, as Rowlands), 1900
Man She Married (Albanesi, as Rowlands), 1910
Man She Married (Winspear), 1982
Man the Devil Didn't Want (Wren), 1940
Man the Women Loved (Ayres), 1925
Man to Be Feared (Hampson), 1976
Man to Follow (Charles, as Chandos), 1943
Man to Protect You (Greig), 1939
Man to Tame (R. Lindsay), 1976
Man to Watch (Donnelly), 1979
Man Under Authority (Dell), 1925
Man Who Came Back (Barrie, as Kent), 1967
Man Who Cried (Cookson), 1979
Man Who Died (Burgin), 1903
Man Who Found Himself (Jacob), 1929
Man Who Had Everything (Bromfield), 1935
Man Who Listens (Caldwell), 1961
Man Who Lived Alone (Ayres), 1950
Man Who Married Again (M. St. John), 1926
Man Who Wasn't Mac (Charles, as Chandos), 1939
Man Who Went Back (Deeping), 1940
Man With a Past (Krentz), 1985
Man with One Hand (Hurst), 1953
Man with the Broken Nose (s Arlen), 1927
Man with the Money (M. St. John, as Cooper), 1917
Man with the Scales (Bowen), 1954
Man Without a Heart (Ayres), 1923
Man Without a Heart (Hampson), 1981
Man Without a Heart (R. Lindsay, as Leigh), 1976
Man Without Honour (Hampson), 1982
Man Without Mercy (Hilton), 1971
Mandala (Buck), 1970
Mandingo (Horner), 1957
Mandolins of Mantori (Danbury), 1973
Manetta's Marriage (Burgin), 1922
Mango Walk (Martin), 1981
Manhattan Love Song (Norris), 1934
Manhattan Nights (Baldwin), 1937
Manhold (Bentley), 1941
Manila Galleon (F. Mason), 1961
Man-Made Miracle (Charles), 1948
Mannequin (Hurst), 1928

Mannequin (Trask), 1933
Manner of a Lady (Sebastian, as Whitmore), 1979
Manor Farm (Greig, as Warren), 1951
Man's Estate (Tranter), 1946
Man's Protection (Krentz, as Castle), 1982
Man's Way (Ayres), 1921
Man's World (Lamb), 1980
Mansell, Edward series (Masefield), from 1938
Mansfield Revisited (Aiken), 1984
Mansion for a Lady (Sebastian, as Whitmore), 1980
Mansion of Lost Memories (Daniels), 1969
Mansion of Smiling Masks (Winston), 1967
Mansion of the Golden Windows (Lee), 1966
Mantle of Innocence (Mackinlay), 1957
Manxman (Caine), 1894
Many a Human Heart (Elsna, as Lancaster), 1954
Many Ways (Margaret Pedler), 1931
Maplechester series (Gibbs, as Ford), from 1963
Mapmaker (Slaughter), 1957
Marazan (Shute), 1926
Marble Angel (Daniels), 1970
Marble City (Burgin), 1905
Marble Hills (Daniels), 1975
Marble Leaf (Daniels), 1966
Marble Mountain (Danbury), 1964
Marcaboth Women (Delmar), 1951
Marcel of the "Zephyrs" (Wynne), 1916
March to Corunna (Dymoke), 1985
Marching Feet (Swan), 1931
Marching On (Boyd), 1927
Marchington Inheritance (I. Holland), 1979
Marchwood (Bromige), 1949
Marcia (G. Hill), 1921
Marcia Drayton (Garvice), 1908
Marcia Schuyler (G. Hill), 1908
  arcia, The Innocent (Kimbrough), 1976
Margaret (Haggard), 1907
Margaret series (E. Porter), from 1907
Margaret Dent (Albanesi, as Rowlands), 1913
Margaret Normanby (M. Howard, as Edgar), 1982
Margaret, The Faithful (Kimbrough), 1975
Margaret the Queen (Tranter), 1979
Margaret Yorke (Norris), 1930
Margarite (Thum), 1987
Margery Daw (Albanesi), 1886
Marguerite's Wonderful Year (Grundy), 1906
Maria (Hutten), 1914
Marian Sax (Albanesi), 1905
Marianna (Buckingham), 1981
Marie (Haggard), 1912
Marie Powell, The Story of (Graves), 1943
Mariette's Lovers (Burgin), 1925
Marigold (G. Hill), 1938
Marion Forsyth (s Swan), 1883
Marionette (Bennetts), 1979
Maris (G. Hill), 1938
Marivosa (Orczy), 1930
Marjorie of Scotland (P. Hill), 1956
Mark Desborough's Vow (Swan), 1884
Mark of the Hand (Armstrong), 1963
Mark of Tregarron (Stratton, as Gillen), 1976
Marks upon the Snow (Elsna), 1960
Marlborough's Unfair Lady (Bloom, as Prole), 1965
Marmalade Man (C. Allen), 1981
Marmalade Witch (D. Smith), 1982
Marquess (Gibbs), 1982

Marquis (Garvice), 1896
Marquis and Miss Jones (Bennetts), 1981
Marquis of Carabas (Sabatini), 1940
Marquis of Loveland (C. and A. Williamson), 1908
Marquis Takes a Bride (Chesney, as Crampton), 1982
Marquis Takes a Wife (R. Lindsay), 1976
Marquis Who Hated Women (Cartland), 1977
Marr'd in Making (Hutten), 1901
Marriage and Mary Ann (Cookson), 1964
Marriage Bond (Robins), 1924
Marriage by Capture (Rome), 1980
Marriage by Conquest (Deeping), 1915
Marriage by Request (Stratton, as Gillen), 1971
Marriage Chest (Eden), 1965
Marriage Deal (Craven), 1986
Marriage for Three (Seifert), 1954
Marriage Handicap (Ayres), 1925
Marriage Has Been Arranged (Blackstock, as Allardyce), 1959
Marriage Impossible (M. Pargeter), 1978
Marriage in Heaven (Bloom), 1943
Marriage in Heaven (R. Fraser), 1932
Marriage in Mexico (Kidd), 1978
Marriage Is a Blind Date (Ruck), 1953
Marriage Is Like That (Woodward, as Richmond), 1961
Marriage Made in Heaven (Cartland), 1983
Marriage Masque (Fellows), 1974
Marriage Merger (Finley), 1978
Marriage of Barry Wicklow (Ayres), 1920
Marriage of Caroline Lindsay (Rome), 1968
Marriage of Inconvenience (J. Roberts), 1972
Marriage of Katherine (D. Stevenson), 1965
Marriage of Leonora (Bloom), 1953
Marriage of Margaret (Albanesi), 1909
Marriage of Martha Todd (Leslie), 1968
Marriage of Mary Chard (Inglis), 1935
Marriage of Meggotta (E. Pargeter), 1979
Marriage of Pierrot (Bloom), 1936
Marriage Racket (Delmar), 1933
Marriage Wheel (Barrie), 1968
Marriage Will Not Take Place (Steen), 1938
Marriage Without a Ring (Greig), 1972
Marriage-Broker (Lowndes), 1937
Married at School (M. St. John), 1917
Married at Sight (Garvice), 1894
Married in Haste (Holt, as Burford), 1956
Married in Haste (s Swan), 1898
Married Lover (Holt, as Burford), 1942
Married Lovers (Kidd), 1987
Married Man (s Swan), 1898
Married Man's Girl (Inglis), 1934
Married or Unmarried (Hichens), 1941
Married Past Redemption (Veryan), 1983
Married People (s Rinehart), 1937
Married Quarters (Greig), 1964
Married to a Miser (M. St. John, as Cooper), 1920
Married to Her Master (M. St. John), 1914
Married to His Wife's Family (M. St. John), 1924
Marriott Hall (Daniels), 1965
Marry a Stranger (Barrie), 1954
Marry for Money (Baldwin), 1948
Marry in Haste (Greig), 1935
Marry in Haste (Hodge), 1969
Marry to Taste (Bloom, as Essex), 1942
Marryers (Bacheller), 1914
Marrying a Doctor (E. Harrison), 1984
Marrying Kind (Cadell), 1980

Marrying Kind (Elsna), 1957
Marrying Kind (D. Smith), 1974
Marrying Man (Stern), 1918
Marsanne (Coffman), 1976
Marsh Blood (Andrews, as Marcus), 1980
Marsh House (Roby), 1974
Marshall Family (Burchell), 1967
Martie, The Unconquered (Norris), 1917
Martin Conisby's Vengeance (Farnol), 1921
Martin Make-Believe (Frankau), 1930
Martin Valiant (Deeping), 1917
Martyrdom (s Deeping), 1929
Martyred Love (Garvice), 1902
Mary Ann series (Cookson), from 1956
Mary Ann and Jane (Grundy), 1944
Mary Anne (du Maurier), 1954
Mary Ann's Angels (Cookson), 1965
Mary Arden (G. Hill), 1948
Mary at Monte Carlo (C. N. and A. M. Williamson), 1920
Mary Dunbar's Love (Albanesi, as Rowlands), 1921
Mary Ellen—Mill-Lass (M. St. John), 1920
Mary Faithful (M. St. John, as Cooper), 1923
Mary Garth (Swan), 1904
Mary Hallam (Ertz), 1947
Mary Marie (E. Porter), 1920
Mary, Mary (Sallis, as Meadmore), 1982
Mary Midthorne (McCutcheon), 1911
Mary of Delight (Jacob), 1949
Mary of Marion Isle (Haggard), 1929
Mary Olivane (Elsna), 1973
Mary Pechell (Lowndes), 1912
Mary, Queen of France (Holt, as Plaidy), 1964
Mary, Sweet Mary (Williams), 1980
Mary, The Infamous Queen (M. Peters), 1968
Mary Wakefield (de la Roche), 1949
Masculine Touch (Britt), 1970
Mask (s Chambers), 1929
Mask (Hichens), 1951
Mask and the Moonflower (Whitney), 1960
Mask of Apollo (Renault), 1966
Mask of Comedy (Elsna), 1970
Mask of Evil (Armstrong), 1958
Mask of Gold (R. Lindsay), 1956
Mask of Gold (Swan), 1906
Mask of Love (Cartland), 1975
Mask of Passion (Hooper), 1982
Mask of Scars (Mather), 1973
Mask of the Enchantress (Holt), 1980
Mask of Treason (A. Stevenson), 1979
Mask of Words (Summerton, as Roffman), 1973
Masque (Lamb, as Holland), 1979
Masque by Gaslight (Coffman), 1970
Masque of Satan (Coffman), 1971
Masque of the Red Death (Lee), 1964
Masquerade (Mather), 1966
Masquerade for a Nurse (McEvoy, as Harte), 1964
Masquerade for Love (Elsna, as Lancaster), 1938
Masquerade in Venice (V. Johnston), 1973
Masquerade Marriage (Kidd), 1987
Masquerade of Love (Morgan), 1982
Masquerade of Love (Sebastian, as Norcross), 1978
Masquerade of Vengeance (Ley), 1989
Masquerade with Music (Burchell), 1982
Masqueraders (Heyer), 1928
Masquerading Heart (Courtney), 1984
Masquers (N. Peters), 1979

Masques of Gold (Gellis), 1988
Massacre at Cawnpore (Stuart, as V. A. Stuart), 1973
Massacre at Fall Creek (West), 1975
Master (Bacheller), 1909
Master and Commander (O'Brian), 1969
Master and the Maiden (Ley), 1977
Master at Arms (Beaty), 1973
Master Fiddler (Dailey), 1977
Master Man (Ayres), 1920
Master of Badger's Hall (Treece), 1959
Master of Ben Ross (Stratton, as Gillen), 1977
Master of Blacktower (B. Michaels), 1966
Master of Blandeston Hall (Wiat), 1973
Master of Blue Mire (Coffman), 1971
Master of Chaos (Bacheller), 1932
Master of Comus (Lamb), 1977
Master of Falcon's Head (Mather), 1970
Master of Forrestmead (Hampson), 1978
Master of Glenkeith (J. MacLeod), 1955
Master of Gray (Bailey), 1903
Master of Gray (Tranter), 1961
Master of Guise (Stuart, as A. Stuart), 1957
Master of Her Fate (R. Lane), 1986
Master of Heronsbridge (Bromige), 1969
Master of Jethart (Dwyer-Joyce), 1976
Master of Keills (J. MacLeod), 1967
Master of Liversedge (Ley), 1966
Master of Love (Finley), 1978
Master of Lynch Towers (Albanesi, as Rowlands),
    1910
Master of Mahia (Bevan), 1981
Master of Malcarew (M. Peters, as Black), 1971
Master of Man (Caine), 1921
Master of Melincourt (Barrie), 1966
Master of Melthorpe (Sinclair), 1979
Master of Montrolfe Hall (O'Grady), 1965
Master of Moonrock (Hampson), 1973
Master of Morley (K. Thorpe), 1983
Master of Penrose (Hodge), 1968
Master of Ransome (L. Walker), 1958
Master of Silence (Bacheller), 1892
Master of Stair (Bowen), 1907
Master of Surgery (Stuart, as A. Stuart), 1958
Master of the House (Peake), 1974
Master of the Manor (Wyndham), 1953
Master of the Mill (M. St. John, as Cooper), 1910
Master of the Tawhai (Summers), 1959
Master of Trelona (Ritchie), 1977
Master Painter (Mullins), 1989
Master Wit (Wynne), 1911
Master Workman's Oath (Libbey), 1892
Master-at-Arms (Sabatini), 1940
Master-Christian (Corelli), 1902
Masterson (Frankau), 1926
Matador (Steen), 1934
Match for a Murderer (Dunnett), 1971
Match Is Made (Charles, as Tempest), 1950
Matched Pearls (G. Hill), 1933
Matchmaker Nurse (Beaty), 1984
Matchmakers (Dailey), 1978
Matchmaker's Moon (Browning), 1985
Matherson Marriage (Ayres), 1922
Matilda, Governess of the English (Cleugh), 1924
Matilda the Adventuress (Johansen), 1987
Mating Dance (R. Randall), 1979
Mating of Marcus (Grundy), 1923

Mating Season (Dailey), 1980
Matriarch (Stern), 1925
Matter for the Regiment (McCutchan, as MacNeil), 1982
Matter of Business (s Farnol), 1940
Matter of Chance (Neels), 1977
Matter of Choice (N. Roberts), 1984
Matter of Circumstance (Pozzessere), 1987
Matter of Honor (Pykare), 1982
Matter of Sixpence (La Tourrette), 1972
Matter of Time (B. Hastings), 1982
Matter of Timing (Browning), 1987
Matters of the Heart (C. Allen), 1985
Matthew, Mark, Luke, and John (Bloom), 1954
Maturin, Stephen series (O'Brian), from 1969
Maulever Hall (Hodge), 1964
Maurice Durant (Garvice), 1875
Mauritius Command (O'Brian), 1977
Maverick and the Lady (Pozzessere, as Graham), 1986
Maverton Heiress (Charles, as Lance), 1975
Mavis of Green Hill (Baldwin), 1921
Mavreen (Lorrimer), 1976
May Fair (s Arlen), 1925
May Spoon (O'Grady, as Carleon), 1981
Maya Temple (Daniels), 1972
Mayenga Farm (Blair), 1951
Mayeroni Myth (Winston), 1972
McAuslan in the Rough (s G. Fraser), 1974
McCabe's Kingdom (Way), 1974
McIvor Affair (Walsh), 1981
McKeever (Delmar), 1976
McKenzie's Hundred (Yerby), 1985
McLeod's Folly (s Bromfield), 1948
Meadowsweet (Barcynska, as Sandys), 1942
Meadowsweet (Orczy), 1912
Meaning of a Kiss (McEvoy), 1961
Means of Grace (E. Pargeter), 1956
Means to an End (Stratton, as Gillen), 1972
Meant for Each Other (Burchell), 1945
Meant to Meet (Charles, as Tempest), 1967
Measure of Love (Chappell), 1961
Medical Center (Baldwin), 1940
Medici Lover (Mather), 1977
Medici Mistress (J. Fitzgerald, as Watson), 1968
Medici Ring (N. St. John), 1975
Mediterranean Madness (Bloom), 1934
Medusa Connection (Cowen), 1976
Meet Love on Holiday (Bloom, as Burns), 1940
Meet Me Again (Burchell), 1954
Meet Me by Moonlight (Charles, as Tempest), 1953
Meet Me in Istanbul (Barrie, as Kent), 1958
Meet Me in Monte Carlo (Robins), 1964
Meet Me in Time (C. Allen), 1978
Meet on My Ground (Summers), 1968
Meet the Sun Halfway (Arbor), 1974
Meeting at Midnight (Kidd), 1981
Meeting in Madrid (J. MacLeod), 1979
Meeting in the Spring (Gibbs, as Ford), 1954
Meg (Daniels), 1979
Meg Hamilton (Swan), 1914
Meg Miller (Sebastian), 1976
Melbury Square (Eden), 1970
Melinda (Eliot, as Arnett), 1975
Melissa (Caldwell), 1948
Melody (Thane), 1950
Melody of Love (R. Lindsay, as Scott), 1960
Melody of Malice (Hufford), 1979

Melon in the Cornfield (Blackstock), 1969
Melora (Eberhart), 1959
Melting Fire (Mather), 1979
Mem (Hutten), 1934
Memories (C. Allen), 1983
Memory of Darkness (Summerton), 1967
Memory of Love (R. Lindsay, as Scott), 1959
Memory of Summer (Manley-Tucker),1961
Memory Serves My Love (Arbor), 1952
Men Act That Way (Greig), 1933
Men Against the Sea (Nordhoff and Hall), 1933
Men and Angels (Cadell), 1952
Men Are Dangerous (Lamb, as Hardy), 1984
Men Are Only Human (Robins), 1933
Men Are So Strange (Elsna, as Lancaster), 1937
Men Are Such Fools! (Baldwin), 1936
Men as Her Stepping Stones (Greig, as Barclay), 1937
Men Dislike Women (Arlen), 1931
Men in Her Life (Ruck), 1954
Men Made the Town (Ayres), 1931
Men, Maids, and Mustard-Pot (s Frankau), 1924
Men of Albemarle (Fletcher), 1942
Men of Forty-Eight (J. Lindsay), 1948
Men of the Frontier Force (Diver), 1930
Men on White Horses (Haines), 1978
Men on White Horses (Motley), 1988
Men Out of Reach (Peake), 1972
Men They Hanged (Chambers), 1926
Men Were Deceivers Ever (M. St. John, as Cooper), 1920
Menagerie (Cookson), 1958
Mending Flower (Ritchie), 1955
Menfreya (Holt), 1966
Menfreya in the Morning (Holt), 1966
Mercenary series (Palmer), from 1985
Mercenary (Westcott), 1963
Merchant of the Ruby (Harwood), 1951
Merchant Prince (Bailey), 1926
Merchant's Daughter (Lamb, as Holland), 1980
Merely Murder (Heyer), 1935
Merivales (McCutcheon), 1929
Merlin (Nye), 1978
Merlin series (Stewart), from 1970
Merlin's Keep (Brent), 1977
Merlin's Keep (Norway), 1966
Mermaid (Millar), 1982
Merrily All the Way (Barcynska, as Sandys), 1943
Merry Andrews (R. Randall), 1954
Merry Belles of Bath (Trask), 1957
Merry Goes the Time (Farnes), 1935
Merry Jade (Saxton, as Turner), 1978
Merry Maid (Hardwick), 1984
Merry Meeting (Ponsonby), 1948
Message from Hong Kong (Eberhart), 1969
Message from Mars (Wynne, as Lurgan), 1912
Messalina of the Suburbs (Delafield), 1924
Messenger of Love (Cartland), 1961
Messer Marco Polo (Byrne), 1921
Messiah (Vidal), 1954
Micah Clarke (Doyle), 1889
Mice for Amusement (Hutten), 1933
Michael and All the Angels (Lofts), 1943
Michael Forth (M. Johnston), 1919
Michael O'Halloran (G. Porter), 1915
Michaelmas Tree (Bennetts), 1982
Michael's Wife (Frankau), 1948
Michael's Wife (Millhiser), 1972

Midas Touch (Kennedy), 1938
Midday Moon (Daniels), 1966
Middle Mist (Muskett), 1937
Middle Window (Goudge), 1935
Midnight Dancers (Maybury), 1973
Midnight Encounter (Finley), 1981
Midnight Is Mine (Mackinlay), 1954
Midnight Jewels (Krentz), 1987
Midnight Lavender (Matthews), 1985
Midnight Lover (Lamb), 1982
Midnight Masquerade (J. Smith), 1985
Midnight Match (F. Stevenson, as Faire), 1979
Midnight Matinee (Elsna), 1949
Midnight Music (M. Pargeter), 1978
Midnight Oak (Tattersall), 1967
Midnight Rainbow series (L. Howard), from 1986
Midnight Sailing (Hufford), 1975
Midnight Sun (Britt), 1979
Midnight Sun's Magic (Neels), 1979
Midnight Walker (R. Randall), 1973
Midnight Whispers (Matthews), 1981
Midsummer Madness! (M. St. John), 1924
Midsummer Masque (Tattersall), 1972
Midsummer Morning (Bennetts), 1984
Midsummer Star (Neels), 1983
Midsummer's Eve (Holt, as Carr), 1986
Midwinter (Buchan), 1923
Mighty Atom (Corelli), 1896
Mignonette (Bowen, as Shearing), 1948
Migrations (Scott), 1927
Miklos Alexandrovitch Is Missing (Edwards), 1970
Milady Charlotte (Holt, as Kellow), 1959
Milady in Love (Chesney), 1987
Mill in the Meadow (Donnelly), 1972
Mill Queen (M. St. John, as Cooper), 1919
Mill Town Nurse (Woodward), 1976
Miller's Dance (Graham), 1982
Millgirl and Dreamer (M. St. John), 1918
Mill-Girl's Bargain! (M. St. John), 1924
Millijoy, The Determined (Kimbrough), 1977
Milliner's Shop (Gibbs), 1981
Million (Hichens), 1940
Million Dollar Doll (A. M. Williamson), 1924
Million Stars (Lewty), 1959
Millionaire Tramp (M. St. John, as Cooper), 1930
Millionaire's Daughter (Eden), 1973
Mill-Lass o' Mine! (M. St. John), 1920
Mill-Owner (Wynne, as Lurgan), 1910
Mills of the Gods (Winston), 1974
Milly Comes to Town (Barcynska), 1928
Mind of a Minx (Ruck), 1927
Mind of Her Own (Seger, as MacNeill), 1983
Mind Over Matter (N. Roberts), 1987
Mine for a Day (Burchell), 1951
Mine Inheritance (Niven), 1940
Minerva (Chesney), 1982
Minerva Stone (Maybury), 1968
Minerva's Marquis (Walsh), 1988
Minion (Sabatini), 1930
Ministering Angel (Albanesi, as Rowlands), 1933
Minister's Daughter (Webb, as Hamilton), 1953
Minister's Son (G. Hill), 1938
Mink Coat (Norris), 1946
Minor Bequest (Shoesmith), 1984
Minstrel's Court (Elsna), 1963
Minstrel's Leap (M. Peters, as Black), 1973

Mint Walk (Barcynska), 1927
Minutes of a Murder (Polland), 1967
Minx Goes to the Front (s C. and A. Williamson), 1919
Miracle at Joe's (Norway, as Norton), 1965
Miracle at St. Burno's (Holt, as Carr), 1972
Miracle for a Madonna (Cartland), 1984
Miracle in Music (Cartland), 1982
Miracle of Lac Blanche (M. Lewis), 1973
Miracle Stone of Wales (Barcynska, as Barclay), 1957
Mirage for Love (Hoy), 1939
Mirage of Love (Bloom), 1978
Mirage on the Horizon (Bloom), 1974
Miranda (Bigland), 1947
Miranda (Blackmore), 1966
Miranda (G. Hill), 1914
Miranda's Marriage (Hilton), 1973
Miro, Donna series (Pozzessere, as Graham), from 1985
Mirror (Millhiser), 1978
Mirror for Dreams (Muskett), 1931
Mirror of the Sun (Blackstock, as Torday), 1938
Mirrors (Matthews), 1988
Mirrors and Mistakes (Seidel), 1984
Misadventure (Muskett), 1936
Misadventures of Bethany Price (Cockrell), 1979
Mischief (Armstrong), 1950
Mischief-Makers (Swan), 1941
Miser of Mayfair (Chesney), 1986
Miser's Ward (Shoesmith), 1977
Miss Barrett's Elopement (Oman, as Lenanton), 1929
Miss Baxter's Bequest (s Swan), 1888
Miss Bede Is Staying (Gilbert), 1982
Miss Billy series (E. Porter), from 1911
Miss Bolo (M. St. John, as Cooper), 1918
Miss Bun, The Baxter's Daughter (D. Stevenson), 1938
Miss Buncle series (D. Stevenson), from 1934
Miss Charley (Blackstock), 1979
Miss Charlotte's Fancy (Lamb, as Holland), 1980
Miss Carmichael's Conscience (Hutten), 1900
Miss Columbine and Harley Quinn (Hilton), 1970
Miss Dean's Dilemma (D. Stevenson), 1938
Miss Delicia Allen (M. Johnston), 1933
Miss Doctor (Seifert), 1951
Miss Estcourt (Garvice), 1911
Miss Fenny (Blackstock), 1957
Miss Fiona's Fancy (Chesney), 1987
Miss Harriet Townshend (Norris), 1955
Miss High and Mighty (Rome), 1980
Miss Jonas's Boy (Blackstock, as Allardyce), 1972
Miss Keating's Temptation (Sebastian), 1981
Miss Lavinia's Call (s G. Hill), 1949
Miss Letty (Sebastian), 1977
Miss Lucifer (R. Fraser), 1939
Miss Martha Mary Crawford (Cookson, as Marchant), 1975
Miss Marvel (Forbes), 1935
Miss Mayhew and Ming Yun (Duffield), 1928
Miss Middleton's Lover (Libbey), 1888
Miss Miranda's Walk (Beaty), 1967
Miss Mission's Maid (Ruck), 1915
Miss Nobody from Nowhere (Ashton), 1975
Miss Paraffin (Barcynska, as Sandys), 1944
Miss Philadelphia Smith (Blackstock, as Allardyce), 1977
Miss Pinkerton series (Rinehart), from 1932
Miss Rolling Stone (Shellabarger, as Loring), 1939
Miss Smith's Fortune (s Garvice), 1920
Miss Spring (Crowe), 1953
Miss Venus of Aberdovey (Barcynska), 1956

Miss Willie (Giles), 1951
Missing from Home (Burchell), 1968
Missing Girl (Ruck), 1930
Missing Hour (Blackmore), 1959
Missing the Tide (Ayres), 1948
Mission to Argana (Marsh), 1988
Mission to Malaspiga (Anthony), 1974
Mission to Monte Carlo (Cartland), 1983
Missionary's Daughter (Beaty), 1983
Mississippi Blues (F. Preston), 1985
Missouri Moon (Kantor), 1952
Mist Across the Hills (J. MacLeod), 1938
Mist Across the Moors (Peake), 1972
Mist at Darkness (Coffman), 1968
Mist of Evil (Matthews, as Brisco), 1976
Mist of Morning (Farnes), 1955
Mist on the Hills (M. Howard), 1950
Mist over Talla (Erskine-Lindop), 1957
Mistaken (s Swan), 1883
Mistaken Virtues (Trollope), 1980
Mr. American (G. Fraser), 1980
Mr. Anthony (Barcynska, as Sandys), 1925
Mr. Bingle (McCutcheon), 1915
Mr. Brown (Seale), 1971
Mr. Cardonnel (Bailey), 1931
Mr. Christopoulos (Blackstock), 1963
Mr. Cohen Takes a Walk (Rinehart), 1934
Mr. Florian's Fortune (Ponsonby), 1971
Mr. Gurney and Mr. Slade (Deeping), 1944
Mr. Leslie's School for Girls (M. St. John), 1922
Mr. Meeson's Will (Haggard), 1888
Mr. Misfortunate (Bowen), 1919
Mr. Rodriguez (M. Howard), 1979
Mr. Rowl (Broster), 1924
Mr. Scribbles (Barcynska, as Sandys), 1930
Mr. Sermon (Delderfield), 1970
Mr. Sister (Norway, as Neal), 1965
Mr. Skeffington (Elizabeth), 1940
Mr. Smith (Bromfield), 1951
Mr. Tyler's Saints (Bowen), 1939
Mr. Victoria (Dingwell), 1970
Mister Washington (Bowen), 1915
Mr. Witt's Widow (Hope), 1892
Mistletoe and Holly (Dailey), 1982
Mistletoe Bough (Wiat), 1981
Mrs. Bridges' Story (Hardwick), 1975
Mistress Cynthia (Wynne), 1910
Mrs. Daventry's Reputation (Pedler), 1924
Mistress Devon (Coffman), 1972
Mrs. Drummond's Vocation (Hutten), 1913
Mistress for the Valois (J. Fitzgerald, as Watson), 1969
Mrs. Harter (Delafield), 1925
Mrs. Keith Hamilton, M. B. (Swan), 1897
Mrs. Lancelot (Hewlett), 1912
Mrs. Maitland's Affair (Lynn), 1963
Mrs. Marden (Hichens), 1919
Mistress Masham's Repose (T. White), 1946
Mrs. Maxon Protests (Hope), 1911
Mrs. Melbourne (Elsna), 1958
Mistress Nell Gwyn (Bowen), 1926
Mrs. Newdigate's Window (Oman, as Lenanton), 1927
Mistress of Astington (S. Thorpe), 1983
Mistress of Brown Furrows (Barrie), 1952
Mistress of Castlemount (Charles, as Tempest), 1961
Mistress of Court Regina (Garvice), 1909
Mistress of Darkness (Nicole), 1976

Mistress of Devil's Manor (F. Stevenson), 1973
Mistress of Falcon Hill (Daniels), 1965
Mistress of Fortune (Lamb, as Lancaster), 1982
Mistress of Mellyn (Holt), 1960
Mistress of Merryweather (Wyndham), 1953
Mistress of Mount Fair (Lee), 1977
Mistress of Paradise (Thum), 1988
Mistress of Rogues (R. Marshall), 1956
Mistress of Shenstone (Barclay), 1910
Mistress of Tanglewood (Marsh), 1981
Mistress of the Farm (Albanesi, as Rowlands), 1910
Mistress of the Fifth Standard (M. St. John), 1916
Mistress of the House (Farnes), 1946
Mistress of Willowdale (Veryan), 1980
Mrs. Oliver Cromwell (s Irwin), 1935
Mrs. Parkington (Bromfield), 1943
Mistress Pat (Montgomery), 1935
Mrs. Tim series (D. Stevenson), from 1932
Mrs. Westerby Changes Course (Cadell), 1968
Mistress Wilding (Sabatini), 1924
Mists of Avalon (Bradley), 1982
Mists of Memory (Cookson, as Marchant), 1965
Mists of Mourning (Daniels, as Somers), 1966
Mists of the Moor (Mackinlay), 1967
Misty Angel (Barcynska, as Sandys), 1931
Mix Me a Man (D. Smith), 1978
Mixed Blessing (Van Slyke), 1975
Mixed Blessings (Cockrell), 1978
Mixed Company (Cockrell), 1979
Mixed Emotions (C. Allen), 1977
Mixed Marriage (Cadell), 1963
Mixed Singles (Mackinlay, as Grey), 1971
Mock-Honeymoon (Ruck), 1939
Model Girl's Farm (Charles, as Chandos), 1958
Model of Deception (M. Pargeter), 1985
Modern Hero (Bromfield), 1932
Modern Juliet (Garvice), 1900
Modern Micawbers (Mackinlay, as Grey), 1933
Modern Tragedy (Bentley), 1934
Modern Witch (Albanesi, as Rowlands), 1912
Modesta (Stern), 1929
Mog Megone (Wynne), 1921
Moll Walbee (Cordell), 1989
Molly (Chesney, as Tremaine), 1980
Molly of the Lone Pine (MacGill), 1922
Moment I Saw You (Charles, as Tempest), 1941
Moment in Paris (Burghley), 1961
Moment of Decision (J. MacLeod), 1972
Moment of Love (Robins), 1964
Moment of Truth (Elsna, as Snow), 1968
Moment of Truth (Stratton, as Gillen), 1973
Moment Past Midnight (Krentz, as Bentley), 1979
Moment to Moment (Delinsky, as Drake), 1984
Moments Harsh, Moments Gentle (Lorin, as Hohl), 1984
Moments of Love (Cartland), 1982
Moments of Meaning (C. Allen), 1979
Moncrieff (I. Holland), 1975
Monday in Summer (L. Walker, as Sanders), 1961
Monday Man (Norway, as Norton), 1963
Monday's Child (Hardwick), 1981
Money for One (Ruck), 1927
Money Isn't Everything (Ruck), 1940
Money, Love, and Kate (s E. Porter), 1923
Money, Magic, and Marrige (Cartland), 1980
Money Moon (Farnol), 1911
Money or Wife? (Albanesi, as Rowlands), 1914

Moneyman (Costain), 1947
Monkey on a Chain (Blackstock), 1965
Monkey Tree in a Flower Pot (Bloom), 1958
Monkey-Puzzle (Hutten), 1932
Monkshood (Mather), 1972
Monsoon (I. Roberts, as I. M. Roberts), 1983
Monte Carlo (Daniels), 1981
Montezuma's Daughter (Haggard), 1893
Montgomery series (Deveraux), from 1981
Montrose series (Tranter), from 1972
Mooltiki (s Godden), 1957
Moon series (M. Peters, as Darby), from 1977
Moon, Charlie series (Yarbro), from 1976
Moon and Bride's Hill (Barrie, as Charles), 1958
Moon at the Full (Barrie), 1961
Moon Dragon (Hampson), 1978
Moon Endureth (s Buchan), 1912
Moon for Lavinia (Neels), 1976
Moon in a Bucket (Gibbs), 1972
Moon in the Water (Ayres), 1939
Moon in the Water (Belle), 1983
Moon into Blood (Gavin), 1966
Moon Is Feminine (Dane), 1938
Moon Is Square (Maddocks), 1975
Moon Lady (Donnelly), 1984
Moon Marriage (Manners, as Rundle), 1967
Moon of Aphrodite (Craven), 1980
Moon of Israel (Haggard), 1918
Moon of Laughing Flame (M. Peters, as Grey), 1980
Moon of Romance (Albanesi), 1932
Moon Out of Reach (Pedler), 1921
Moon over Africa (Barrie, as Kent), 1955
Moon over Eden (Cartland), 1976
Moon over Madrid (Stuart, as Finlay), 1957
Moon over Moncrieff (I. Roberts, as Rowland), 1969
Moon over Stamboul (Duffield), 1936
Moon over the Alps (Summers), 1960
Moon over the Danube (McEvoy), 1966
Moon over the Temple (I. Roberts), 1972
Moon over the Water (Greig, as Warren), 1956
Moon Returns (R. Randall), 1942
Moon Shadow (Kimbrough, as Allyson), 1976
Moon Song (Bloom), 1953
Moon Through Glass (Albanesi), 1928
Moon Tide (Stratton), 1975
Moon Witch (Mather), 1970
Moon Without Stars (Hampson), 1974
Moonbranches (Manners, as Rundle), 1986
Moondrift (Mather), 1984
Moondust and Madness (Taylor), 1986
Moonflete (M. Peters, as Black), 1972
Moonflower (J. MacLeod), 1967
Moonflower (Whitney), 1958
Moongate Wish (Buckingham, as John), 1985
Moonlight and Magic (R. Lindsay), 1962
Moonlight and Roses (I. Roberts, as Rowland), 1981
Moonlight Gondola (J. Roberts, as Radcliffe), 1975
Moonlight Mirage (Saunders, as Blake), 1982
Moonlight Mist (London), 1979
Moonlight on the Lake (I. Preston), 1976
Moonlight on the Nile (Ashton), 1979
Moonlight on the Sphinx (Cartland), 1984
Moonlight Rhapsody (Hooper, as Robbins), 1984
Moonlight Variations (F. Stevenson), 1981
Moonlight Witchery (Elsna, as Snow), 1959
Moonlighters (Blackstock, as Allardyce), 1966

Moonlit Door (Maybury), 1967
Moonlit Way (Dwyer-Joyce), 1974
Moonpearl (I. Roberts, as I. M. Roberts), 1983
Moonraker's Bride (Brent), 1973
Moonrise over the Mountains (Peake), 1975
Moon's Our Home (Baldwin), 1936
Moonshiner (L. Walker), 1961
Moon-Spinners (Stewart), 1962
Moonstone Manor (I. Roberts, as Shaw), 1968
Moonstruck Madness (McBain), 1977
Moorhaven (Winston), 1973
Moorland Magic (Ashton), 1973
Mops (Barcynska, as Sandys), 1928
More Than a Dream (Stratton), 1977
More Than Conqueror (G. Hill), 1944
More Than Friendship (M. Howard), 1960
More Than Love (Robins), 1947
Moreton's Kingdom (J. MacLeod), 1981
Morgan, Steve series (Rogers), from 1974
Morgan Wade's Woman (Lorin), 1981
Morgan's Woman (Gower), 1986
Morning Always Comes (Vitek), 1982
Morning Glory (M. St. John, as Cooper), 1927
Morning Glory (Spencer), 1989
Morning Glory (Vitek), 1986
Morning Rose (Lorin), 1982
Morning Rose, Evening Savage (Lorin), 1980
Morning Star (Haggard), 1910
Morning Star (Norway), 1959
Morning Star (I. Roberts, as Rowland), 1963
Morning Will Come (Jacob), 1953
Mortal Glamour (Yarbro), 1985
Mortimer Brice (Hichens), 1932
Mosaic (Stern), 1930
Moses, Prince of Egypt (Fast), 1958
Moses the Lawgiver (Keneally), 1975
Moss Rose (Bowen, as Shearing), 1934
Most Auspicious Star (Ebel), 1968
Most Cruelly Wronged (M. St. John), 1907
Most Loving Mere Folly (E. Pargeter), 1953
Most Romantic City (Gibbs), 1976
Most Sacred of All (Farnol), 1948
Mostly by Moonlight (Daniels), 1968
Mostly Canallers (s Edmonds), 1934
Moth (Cookson), 1986
Moth to the Flame (Craven), 1979
Mother (Buck), 1934
Mother (Norris), 1911
Mother Knows Best (s Ferber), 1927
Mother Knows Best! (M. St. John), 1922
Mother-in-Law (Hutten), 1922
Motionless Shadows (Norris), 1945
Motive (Lowndes), 1938
Motor Maid (C. N. and A. M. Williamson), 1909
Mountain and the Tree (Beauclerk), 1935
Mountain Clinic (J. MacLeod), 1962
Mountain for Luenda (Summers), 1983
Mountain Heritage (Ashton), 1976
Mountain Lovers (M. St. John, as Cooper), 1920
Mountain Magic (Barrie), 1964
Mountain Magic (I. Preston), 1979
Mountain of Fear (R. Randall), 1972
Mountain of Light (Gavin), 1944
Mountain of Stars (J. MacLeod, as Airlie), 1956
Mountain Sang (I. Roberts), 1965
Mountain That Went to the Sea (L. Walker), 1971

Mountford Show (Gibbs, as Ford), 1948
Moura series (Coffman), from 1959
Mourning Bride (F. Stevenson, as Curzon), 1982
Mourning Trees (V. Johnston), 1972
Mouth of Truth (Hunter, as Chace), 1977
Moving Dream (Renier), 1977
Mowana Magic (Way), 1988
Much Ado about Peter (Webster), 1909
Much Needed Holiday (Lorin, as Hohl), 1986
Much-Loved (Ayres), 1934
Mud on My Stockings (Barcynska, as Sandys), 1938
Mullah from Kashmir (McCutchan, as MacNeil), 1976
Mummy Case (B. Michaels, as Peters), 1985
Murder at Grand Bay (W. Roberts), 1955
Murder by an Aristocrat (Eberhart), 1932
Murder by Nail (Farnol), 1942
Murder Goes to Market (s Eberhart), 1949
Murder Has a Pretty Face (Butler, as Melville), 1981
Murder in Focus (Dunnett), 1973
Murder in Mayfair (Robins), 1935
Murder in the Round (Dunnett), 1970
Murder in the Tower (Holt, as Plaidy), 1964
Murder in Waiting (Eberhart), 1973
Murder in Waltz Time (s Eberhart), 1958
Murder Is So Easy (W. Roberts), 1961
Murder Most Royal (Holt, as Plaidy), 1949
Murder of Delicia (Corelli), 1896
Murder of Miranda (Millar), 1979
Murder of My Patient (Eberhart), 1934
Murder Reflected (Caird), 1965
Murder Remote (Caird), 1973
Murder Scholastic (Caird), 1967
Murderers' Houses (Butler, as Melville), 1964
Murdering Kind (Butler), 1958
Murder's Mansion (I. Roberts, as Shaw), 1976
Murder's Nest (Armstrong), 1954
Murders of Richard III (B. Michaels, as Peters), 1974
Murray River series (Cato), from 1958
Muscle Beach (Lee), 1964
Musgraves (D. Stevenson), 1960
Music at Midnight (J. MacLeod), 1952
Music from Behind the Moon (s Cabell), 1926
Music from the Heart (Cartland), 1982
Music I Heard with You (Hoy), 1969
Music in the Hills (D. Stevenson), 1950
Music in Winter (Ebel), 1975
Music Makers (Thompson), 1979
Music of Our House (Maybury), 1952
Music of the Heart (Burchell), 1972
Music When Sweet Voices Die (Yarbro), 1979
Musk and Amber (A. Mason), 1942
Must the Dream End (Elsna, as Lancaster), 1941
Mustee (Horner), 1967
Mutiny! (Nordhoff and Hall), 1933
Mutiny at Dawn (Stuart, as V. A. Stuart), 1975
Mutiny in Meerat (Stuart, as V. A. Stuart), 1973
Mutiny in Paradise (Way), 1977
Mutiny on the Bounty (Nordhoff and Hall), 1932
Mutual Look (Dingwell), 1973
My Beautiful Heathen (Stratton, as Gillen), 1970
My Best Girl (Norris), 1927
My Brother Michael (Stewart), 1960
My Brother's Keeper (Davenport), 1954
My Brother's Wife (Elsna, as Snow), 1964
My Caravaggio Style (Moore), 1959
My Catalina (M. Peters), 1988

My Cousin Lola (Elsna, as Snow), 1966
My Cousin Rachel (du Maurier), 1951
My Dark Rapparee (Reid), 1966
My Dear Aunt Flora (Cadell), 1946
My Dear Cousin (Blair, as Conway), 1959
My Dear Duchess (Chesney, as Fairfax), 1979
My Dear Fugitive (Sinclair), 1976
My Dear Lady (Elsna), 1957
My Dear Lover England (Bennets), 1975
My Dear Miss Emma (Blackstock, as Allardyce), 1958
My Dearest Elizabeth (Maybury), 1964
My Dearest Love (Loring), 1954
My Desert Friend (s Hichens), 1931
My Dream Fulfilled (Elsna, as Snow), 1962
My Dream Is Yours (Asquith), 1954
My Enemy and I (Charles), 1941
My Enemy the Queen (Holt), 1978
My Fellow Laborer (Haggard), 1888
My Four Uncles (P. Hastings), 1984
My Friend the Chauffeur (C. N. and A. M. Williamson), 1905
My Friend the Professor (Andrews), 1960
My Girl, Regan (M. St. John), 1915
My Glorious Brothers (Fast), 1948
My Grand Enemy (Stubbs), 1967
My Head ! My Head ! (Graves), 1925
My Heart a Traitor (Danbury), 1958
My Heart at Your Feet (Barrie, as Charles), 1957
My Heart Has Wings (Hoy), 1957
My Heart Remembers (Kidd), 1971
My Heart's a Dancer (R. Lindsay, as Leigh), 1970
My Heart's Desire (Seale), 1976
My Heart's Down Under (Greig), 1951
My Heart's in the Highlands (J. MacLeod), 1956
My Heart's Right There (Barclay), 1914
My Lady Benbrook (Gluyas), 1975
My Lady Caprice (Farnol), 1907
My Lady Cinderella (A. M. Williamson), 1900
My Lady Destiny (Robins, as Gray), 1961
My Lady Disdain (Ashton), 1976
My Lady Glamis (P. Hill), 1985
My Lady Mischief (J. Roberts), 1973
My Lady of Dreadwood (Albanesi, as Rowlands), 1906
My Lady of Orange (Bailey), 1901
My Lady of Snow (Garvice), 1908
My Lady of the Fuchsias (Summers), 1979
My Lady Pride (Garvice), 1902
My Lady Rotha (Weyman), 1894
My Lady Scapegrace (Sebastian, as Norcross), 1979
My Lady Troubadour (M. Peters), 1983
My Lady's Crusade (Motley), 1977
My Lady's Honour (Wynne), 1921
My Lady's Mask (Roby), 1979
My Lancashire Queen (M. St. John), 1914
My Life for My Sheep (Duggan), 1955
My Little Bit (Corelli), 1919
My Lord Foxe (Gluyas), 1976
My Lord John (Heyer), 1975
My Lord of Wrybourne (Farnol), 1948
My Lord Rakehell (Sebastian), 1977
My Lords, Ladies, and Marjorie (Chesney), 1981
My Love (Loring), 1955
My Love Came Back (D. Smith), 1978
My Love Has a Secret (Maybury), 1958
My Love Johnny (McEvoy), 1971
My Love Kitty (Garvice), 1911
My Love! My Little Queen! (Bloom, as Prole), 1961

My Lute Be Still (Wiat), 1977
My Man of the Mill! (M. St. John), 1924
My Master Mariner (Saxton, as Turner), 1974
My Name Is Clary Brown (Blackstock, as Keppel), 1976
My Old Love Came (Ayres), 1930
My Old Love Came (Burchell), 1943
My Only Love (Charles, as Tempest), 1939
My Philippa (M. Peters), 1984
My Pilgrim Love (M. Peters, as Black), 1982
My Pretty Sister (Price), 1954
My Rebel, My Love (W. Roberts), 1986
My Secret Love (Hoy), 1967
My Self, My Enemy (Holt, as Plaidy), 1983
My Sister Celia (Burchell), 1961
My Sister Erica (Blackmore), 1973
My Sister Sophie (M. Howard, as Edgar), 1964
My Sister's Keeper (R. Lindsay), 1979
My Surgeon Neighbour (Arbor)
My Sweetheart Idabell (Libbey), 1890
My Tattered Loving (Bowen, as Preedy), 1937
My Theodosia (Seton), 1941
My True Love (Charles), 1971
My True Love (Robins), 1953
My Wanton Tudor Rose (Bloom, as Prole), 1956
My Wonderful Wife (Corelli), 1889
Myriah (Williams), 1978
Mysteries of Winterthurn (Oates), 1984
Mysterious (F. Preston), 1986
Mysterious Maid-Servant (Cartland), 1977
Mysterious Waye (Wren), 1930
Mystery at Little Heaven (Delmar), 1933
Mystery Boy-Friend (Ruck), 1957
Mystery Castle (Lee), 1973
Mystery Flowers (G. Hill), 1936
Mystery House (Norris), 1939
Mystery Lamp (Rinehart), 1925
Mystery Lover (Woodward), 1985
Mystery of Barry Ingram (Swan), 1910
Mystery of Choice (s Chambers), 1897
Mystery of Hunting's End (Eberhart), 1930
Mystery of Mary (G. Hill), 1912
Mystery of Pine Point (Norris), 1936
Mystic Manor (Daniels, as Weston), 1966
Mystic Rose (Gallagher), 1977

Nabob (Walsh), 1989
Nabob's Widow (Lee), 1976
Nada the Lily (Haggard), 1892
Naked Battle (Cartland), 1977
Naked Flame (Lamb), 1984
Naked Once More (B. Michaels, as Peters), 1989
Naked Runner (P. Hastings), 1987
Name for Evil (Lytle), 1947
Name in Lights (Ebel), 1968
Name Is Mary (Hurst), 1951
Name of the Game (N. Roberts), 1988
Name the Woman (A. M. Williamson), 1924
Nameless Bess (Garvice, as Hart)
Nameless Coffin (Butler), 1966
Nan—and the New Owner (Charles as Chandos), 1959
Nan of No Man's Land (M. St. John, as Cooper),
   1925
Nance (Garvice), 1900
Nancy Nicholson (Swan), 1906
Nancy, The Daring (Kimbrough), 1976
Nanette (Veryan), 1981

Napoleon series (Coffman), from 1975
Napoleon Symphony (Burgess), 1974
Narcissus (Scott), 1922
Narrow House (Scott), 1921
National Provincial (L. Cooper), 1938
Naughty Lady Ness (Williams), 1980
Navy Blue Lady (Grimstead), 1951
Necessary Woman (Van Slyke), 1979
Ned series (Masefield), from 1938
Nedra (McCutcheon), 1905
Ne'er-Do-Well (Swan), 1897
Ne'er-Do-Well (Yates), 1954
Negotiated Surrender (Krentz, as Castle), 1982
Nell Alone (Butler, as Melville), 1966
Nell Gwyn (Bowen), 1926
Nell of Shorne Mills (Garvice), 1900
Nell of the Camp (M. St. John), 1913
Nellie (Garvice), 1913
Nellie, The Obvious (Kimbrough), 1978
Nelson's Love (Bloom, as Prole), 1966
Neptune's Daughter (Weale), 1987
Nest of the Sparrowhawk (Orczy), 1909
Nesting Cats (Bloom, as Essex), 1941
Net to Catch the Wind (Worboys, as Eyre), 1966
Nethergate (Lofts), 1973
Nevada Gunslinger (Coffman), 1962
Nevada Silver (Lorin, as Hohl), 1987
''Never Again!'' Said Nicola (Charles, as Tempest), 1944
Never Another Love (Charles, as Tempest), 1949
Never Call It Loving (Eden), 1966
Never Call It Loving (Lewty), 1958
Never Fall in Love (Sinclair), 1977
Never Forget Love (Cartland), 1986
Never Give All (Robins), 1934
Never Go Back (M. Pargeter), 1977
Never in a Lifetime (Peake), 1985
Never Laugh at Love (Cartland), 1976
Never Look Back (Eberhart), 1951
Never Look Back (Robins), 1944
Never Look Back (Vitek), 1983
Never Love a Stranger (Harrod-Eagles, as Woodhouse), 1978
Never Say Goodbye (Neels), 1983
Never Such Innocence (Ellerbeck, as Thorne), 1985
Never the Same (Greig), 1970
Never the Time and the Place (Neels), 1985
Never to Love (Weale), 1958
Never Too Late (Buckingham, as John), 1983
Never Too Late (Neels), 1983
Never Trust a Stranger (K. Thorpe), 1983
Never Turn Back (Donnelly), 1971
Never Victorious, Never Defeated (Caldwell), 1954
Never While the Grass Grows (Neels), 1978
New Americans series (Nicole), from 1982
New Boss at Birchfields (Reid), 1982
New Broom (Dingwell), 1974
New Canterbury Tales (s Hewlett), 1901
New Day (Barcynska, as Sandys), 1957
New Doctor (Seifert), 1958
New Girl (M. St. John), 1927
New Girl at Bellforth (M. St. John), 1923
New Girl in Town (Baldwin), 1975
New House (L. Cooper), 1936
New Kind of Killer, An Old Kind of Death (Butler, as Melville), 1970
New Life for Joanna (Bromige), 1958
New Lord Whinbridge (Charles, as Lance), 1973

New Love (Hichens), 1895
New Love for Cynthia (McElfresh, as Scott), 1958
New Moon Through a Window (Greig), 1937
New Name (G. Hill), 1926
New Orleans Lady (Delmar), 1949
New Orleans Legacy (Ripley), 1987
New Owner (Bromige), 1956
New Owner (K. Thorpe), 1982
New Rector (Weyman), 1891
New Road (Munro), 1914
New Sister Theater (Andrews), 1964
New Way of Life (Hichens), 1942
New Woman (s Swan), 1898
New World (Atkin), 1921
New Year (Buck), 1968
New Zealand Inheritance (Summers), 1957
New Zealander (Dingwell), 1963
Newspaper Girl (A. Williamson), 1899
Next of Kin (Eberhart), 1982
Next Tuesday (Bloom), 1949
Niccolò series (Dunnett), from 1986
Nice Bloke (Cookson), 1969
Nice Girl Comes to Town (Greig), 1930
Nice Girl's Story (R. Harris), 1968
Nickel Nurse (Dingwell), 1970
Nicola (Daniels), 1980
Nicola (Erskine-Lindop), 1959
Nicolette (Orczy), 1922
Nicolette (I. Preston), 1967
Night at Sea Abbey (Coffman), 1972
Night Bell (Mackinlay), 1936
Night Call (McElfresh), 1961
Night Child (De Blasis), 1975
Night Duty at Duke's (Norway, as Norton), 1960
Night Games (M. Harris), 1987
Night Heat (Mather), 1987
Night in Bombay (Bromfield), 1940
Night in Cold Harbour (Kennedy), 1960
Night Is Kind (Norway, as Norton),1967
Night Is Thine (Lorrimer, as Robins), 1964
Night Magic (C. Allen), 1989
Night Moves (Pozzessere), 1985
Night Moves (N. Roberts), 1985
Night Music (Lamb), 1980
Night My Enemy (Maybury), 1962
Night of Carnival (Greig, as Ames), 1956
Night of Four Hundred Rabbits (B. Michaels, as Peters), 1971
Night of Gaiety (Cartland), 1981
Night of Love (R. Lindsay, as Leigh), 1978
Night of Possession (Peake), 1983
Night of Stars (Holt, as Burford), 1960
Night of Tears (Kimbrough, as Kimbro), 1976
Night of the Beguine (R. Lane), 1985
Night of the Black Tower (Sinclair), 1968
Night of the Bonfire (Blackmore), 1974
Night of the Bulls (Mather), 1972
Night of the Condor (Craven), 1987
Night of the Cotillion (Dailey), 1976
Night of the Enchantress (Maybury, as Troy), 1967
Night of the Hurricane (Weale, as Blake), 1965
Night of the Letter (Eden), 1967
Night of the Magician (Krentz, as James), 1984
Night of the Party (Bromige), 1974
Night of the Party (Elsna, as Conway), 1969
Night of the Singing Birds (Barrie), 1970
Night of the Stranger (Blackmore), 1961

Night of the Wedding (C. N. and A. M. Williamson), 1921
Night of the Willow (M. Peters), 1981
Night of the Wolf (Heaven, as Fecher), 1972
Night of the Yellow Moon (Kidd), 1977
Night on the Mountain (Kidd), 1973
Night People (Norway), 1963
Night Riders (Tranter), 1954
Night, Sea and Stars (Pozzessere, as Graham), 1983
Night Shade (Daniels), 1976
Night Striker (Lorin), 1985
Night the Roof Blew Off (P. Hastings), 1962
Night Train (Weale), 1987
Night Trains (Wood), 1979
Night Visitor (Matthews, as Wylie), 1979
Night Way (Dailey), 1981
Night with a Stranger (Buckingham, as John), 1984
Nightbound (Hichens), 1951
Nightcap and Plume (Bowen, as Preedy), 1945
Nightfall (Daniels), 1977
Nightingale at Noon (Summerton), 1963
Nightingale Once Sang (Bloom, as Essex), 1958
Nightingale Sang (Cartland), 1979
Nightingale Touch (Norway), 1966
Nightingales (Burchell), 1980
Nightingale's Song (Robins), 1963
Nightmare (s Forester), 1954
Nightmare at Riverview (Daniels, as Gray), 1973
Nightmare Chase (Berckman), 1975
Nightmare Country (Millhiser), 1981
Nightmare Ends (Cowen), 1970
Nightrunners of Bengal (Masters), 1951
Nights at the Circus (Carter), 1984
Night's Dark Secret (Bowen, as Campbell), 1975
Night's Daughters (Norway, as Norton), 1966
Nightshade at Morning (Bloom), 1944
Nightsong (Sherwood), 1988
Nightstar (F. Michaels), 1982
Nightwalker (Krentz, as James), 1984
Nile Dusk (Barrie, as Kent), 1972
Nina (Ertz), 1924
Nine Coaches Waiting (Stewart), 1958
Nine Days a-Dying (M. Peters, as Whitby), 1982
Nine Lives (Bloom), 1951
Nine Moons Wasted (Manners, as Lamont), 1977
Nine O'Clock Tide (Eberhart), 1978
Ninth Earl (Farnol), 1950
Ninth of July (R. Fraser), 1934
Ninth Vibration (s Beck), 1922
Nitana (Burgin), 1928
No Adam in Eden (Metalious), 1963
No Alternative (Way), 1983
No Armour Against Fate (Pedler), 1938
No Barrier (Dark), 1953
No Bed of Roses (Baldwin), 1973
No Business to Love (R. Lindsay), 1966
No Castle of Dreams (McEvoy), 1960
No Darkness for Love (Cartland), 1974
No Dowry for Jennifer (Greig), 1957
No Easy Way (Jacob), 1938
No Easy Way Out (Chase), 1983
No Eden for a Nurse (McEvoy, as Harte), 1971
No Enemy But Time (Anthony), 1987
No Escape from Love (Cartland), 1977
No Escape from Love (Charles, as Chandos), 1937
No Escape from Love (Woodward, as Lawrence), 1974
No Evil Angel (Ogilvie), 1956

No Faint Heart (Barcynska, as Sandys), 1943
No Females Wanted (Dingwell), 1970
No Fields of Amaranth (Elsna), 1943
No Friend of Mine (Peake), 1972
No Gentle Love (Brandewyne), 1980
No Gentle Possession (Mather), 1975
No Gifts from Chance (Pedler), 1944
No Good as a Nurse (Elsna, as Lancaster), 1962
No Greater Love (Gallagher), 1979
No Greater Love (Orczy), 1938
No Greater Love (Slaughter), 1985
No Heart Is Free (Cartland), 1948
No Hearts to Break (Ertz), 1937
No Hero—This (Deeping), 1936
No Just Cause (Barrie), 1965
No Known Grave (Berckman), 1958
No Lady Buys a Cot (Bloom), 1943
No Lady in Bed (Bloom), 1944
No Lady in the Cart (Bloom), 1949
No Lady with a Pen (Bloom), 1947
No Laggard in Love (Charles, as Lance), 1971
No Lease for Love (Arbor), 1950
No Legacy for Lindsay (Summers), 1965
No Limit to Love (Charles, as Chandos), 1937
No Love Lost (Van Slyke), 1980
No Man of Her Own (Winspear), 1981
No Man's Kisses (Pykare, as Powers), 1986
No Man's Mistress (R. Lindsay, as Leigh), 1989
No May in October (Muskett), 1951
No More A-Roving (S. Thorpe), 1970
No More Lonely Nights (Lamb), 1988
No More Loving (Lorrimer, as Robins), 1965
No Need to Say Goodbye (Neels), 1989
No One Hears But Him (Caldwell), 1966
No One Will Know (Delafield), 1941
No Orchids by Request (Summers), 1965
No Orchids for a Nurse (McEvoy, as Harte), 1964
No Other Haven (Blair), 1950
No Other Man—(Charles, as Tempest), 1937
No Other Man (Peake), 1982
No Passing Fancy (K. Thorpe), 1980
No Peace for the Wicked (Blackstock, as Torday), 1937
No Place for Love (M. Lewis), 1963
No Place for Love (Woodward, as Sawley), 1967
No Place for Lovers (Woodward, as Richmond), 1983
No Place to Run (Donnelly), 1988
No Price Too High (Polland), 1984
No Private Heaven (Baldwin), 1946
No Promise Given (Vitek), 1983
No Quarter Asked (Dailey), 1974
No Question of Murder (Lofts, as Curtis), 1959
No Real Relation (Burchell), 1953
No Red Roses (Johansen), 1984
No Retreat from Love (Greig), 1942
No Regrets (Elsna, as Conway), 1958
No Room at the Inn (s Ferber), 1941
No Room for Joanna (Gibbs, as Ford), 1964
No Room for Loneliness (Mackinlay), 1965
No Roses in June (Summers), 1961
No Sacrifice (Robins), 1934
No Second Parting (Peake), 1977
No Shallow Stream (Elsna), 1950
No Silver Spoon (Arbor), 1959
No Single Star (Stuart), 1956
No Smoke Without Fire (Harwood), 1964
No Son of Mine (Stern), 1948

No Song at Morningside (M. Peters, as Whitby), 1981
No Sooner Met (Hunter), 1965
No Stone Unturned (Lorrimer, as Robins), 1969
No Summer Beauty (Charles, as Lance), 1967
No Tears Tomorrow (Daniels, as Ross), 1962
No Through Road (Charles), 1960
No Time for a Man (Charles, as Tempest), 1942
No Time for Love (Cartland), 1976
No Time for Love (Loring), 1970
No Time for Love (Woodward, as Sawley), 1967
No Time for Marriage (R. Lindsay, as Leigh), 1985
No Time for Tears (Freeman), 1981
No Trespassers in Love (Bloom, as Burns), 1949
No Trespassing (Stanford), 1980
No Turning Back (Vitek, as Alexander), 1979
No Way Home (Bowen, as Preedy), 1947
No Way Out (Donnelly), 1980
No Wind of Blame (Heyer), 1939
Noah's Daughter (D. Smith), 1982
Noble House (Clavell), 1981
Noble in Reason (Bentley), 1955
Noble One (Robins), 1957
Noble Purpose (Carnegie), 1954
Noble Rogue (Orczy), 1912
Noble Savage (Winspear), 1974
Noblest Frailty (Veryan), 1983
Nobody Asked Me (Burchell), 1937
Nobody Else—Ever (Charles, as Tempest), 1950
Nobody Wants You! (M. St. John), 1928
Nobody's Child (J. MacLeod, as Airlie), 1954
Nobody's Girl (M. St. John), 1922
Nobody's in Town (Ferber), 1938
Nobody's Lovers (Ayres), 1921
Nobody's Wife (Garvice, as Hart)
Nolan, Jill series (McElfresh), from 1962
Nomad's Land (s Rinehart), 1926
None Better Loved (Mackinlay), 1941
None But He (Lorrimer, as Robins), 1973
None Dare Call It Treason (Gavin), 1978
None So Blind (I. Preston), 1961
None So Pretty (Irwin), 1930
Nonesuch (Heyer), 1962
Noonday Queen (M. Peters), 1988
Noonfire (Way), 1972
Nor Any Dawn (Muskett), 1932
Nor Evil Dreams (R. Harris), 1974
Nora Meade, M.D. (McElfresh, as Wesley), 1955
Norah (P. Hill), 1976
Norah Stroyan (P. Hill), 1976
Norman series (Holt, as Plaidy), from 1974
Norris, Mrs. series (Davis), from 1957
North and South series (Jakes), from 1982
North of Capricorn (Way), 1981
North Sea Nurse (Woodward), 1975
Northern Correspondent (Stubbs), 1984
Northern Magic (Dailey), 1982
Northwater (Crowe), 1968
North-West by South (Cato), 1965
Northwest Passage (K. Roberts), 1937
Not a Marrying Man (R. Lindsay, as Leigh), 1978
Not after Midnight (s du Maurier), 1971
Not at Home (Moore), 1948
Not by Appointment (Summers), 1976
Not Even for Love (Brown, as St. Claire), 1982
Not Far Enough (M. Pargeter), 1982
Not Far from Heaven (Hampson), 1974

Not for This Alone (Charles, as Tempest), 1945
Not Free to Love (Bloom, as Burns), 1950
Not Heaven Itself (Pedler), 1940
Not in Our Stars (Holt, as Burford), 1945
Not in the Calendar (Kennedy), 1964
Not Love Alone (Cartland), 1933
Not Once but Twice (Neels), 1981
Not One of Us (Greig, as Ames), 1939
Not So Quiet (Price, as Smith), 1930
Not So Wild a Dream (Rivers), 1984
Not Under the Law (G. Hill), 1925
Not Wanted on the Voyage (Findley), 1984
Not Wanted on Voyage (K. Thorpe), 1972
Not Without Love (R. Lindsay, as Leigh), 1989
Not Without You (Burchell), 1947
Not Yet (Swan), 1898
Notable Princess (Barclay), 1905
Nothing Hurts for Long (s du Maurier), 1943
Nothing Is Safe (Delafield), 1937
Nothing Like the Sun (Burgess), 1964
Nothing Lovelier (Ayres), 1942
Nothing to Report (Oman), 1940
Notorious Gentleman (Lamb, as Holland), 1980
Notorious Lady (Leslie), 1976
Notorious Mrs. Gatacre (s Hutten), 1933
Nourishing Life (Norway), 1967
Novel Alliance (F. Stevenson, as Fitzgerald), 1984
November Tree (Maddocks), 1964
Now and Always (Charles, as Tempest), 1950
Now and Always (Weale, as Blake), 1964
Now and Forever (Palmer), 1979
Now and Forever (Steel), 1978
Now Barabbas Was a Robber (Bloom, as Mann), 1968
Now East, Now West (Ertz), 1927
Now, God Be Thanked (Masters), 1979
Now I Can Forget (Charles, as Lance), 1973
Now or Never (Weale), 1978
Now Rough—Now Smooth (Cartland), 1941
Now That April's Gone (Holt, as Burford), 1961
Now We Set Out (Ertz), 1934
Numbered Account (Bridge), 1960
Nun's Castle (Butler, as Melville), 1973
Nuptials of Corbal (Sabatini), 1927
Nurse Abroad (Summers), 1961
Nurse Alice in Love (Charles), 1964
Nurse Alison's Trust (Burchell), 1964
Nurse at Barbazon (Blair), 1964
Nurse at Cap Flamingo (Winspear), 1965
Nurse at Danger Mansion (Daniels), 1966
Nurse at Kama Hall (I. Roberts, as Rowland), 1969
Nurse at Moorcroft Manor (Ritchie, as Heath), 1967
Nurse at Mystery Villa (W. Roberts), 1967
Nurse at Noongwalla (R. Lane), 1973
Nurse at Rowanbank (Kidd), 1966
Nurse at St. Catherine's (Greig), 1963
Nurse at Shadow Manor (Ritchie, as Heath), 1973
Nurse at the Top (Collin), 1964
Nurse Atholl Returns (Arbor), n.d.
Nurse Brookes (Norway), 1958
Nurse by Accident (Charles), 1974
Nurse Called Liza (Bloom, as Essex), 1973
Nurse Comes Home (Webb, as Hamill), 1954
Nurse Elaine and the Sapphire Star (Ritchie, as Heath), 1973
Nurse Elizabeth Comes Home (Webb, as Hamill), 1955
Nurse Elliot's Diary (Norway), 1960
Nurse Errant (Andrews), 1961

Nurse Farnley's Secret (Woodward, as Lawrence), 1972
Nurse for Doctor Keith (Daniels), 1962
Nurse for Galleon Key (Webb, as Hamill), 1957
Nurse for Mercy's Mission (McElfresh), 1976
Nurse for Rebel's Run (McElfresh, as Scott), 1960
Nurse Frayne's Strange Quest (Woodward), 1960
Nurse from Hawaii (Webb, as Hamill), 1964
Nurse from Killarney (Bloom, as Essex), 1963
Nurse Greve (Arbor), n.d.
Nurse Hanson's Strange Case (Woodward, as Richmond), 1981
Nurse Harriet Goes to Holland (Neels), 1970
Nurse Helen (Stratton, as Gillen), 1970
Nurse in Arabia (Woodward, as Davis), 1972
Nurse in Confusion (I. Preston), 1983
Nurse in Danger (Greig), 1964
Nurse in Danger (W. Roberts), 1972
Nurse in Holland (Neels), 1970
Nurse in Nepal (I. Roberts), 1976
Nurse in Print (Norway), 1963
Nurse in the Dark (Collin), 1965
Nurse in the Hills (I. Roberts), 1969
Nurse in the Orient (McEvoy, as Harte), 1962
Nurse in the Sun (Rayner, as Brandon), 1972
Nurse in the Wilderness (I. Roberts), 1983
Nurse in the Woods (Charles, as Lance), 1969
Nurse in Waiting (Arbor), 1962
Nurse Is Born (Norway, as Norton), 1962
Nurse Jane in Teneriffe (J. MacLeod, as Airlie), 1967
Nurse Jess (Dingwell), 1959
Nurse Judy (McElfresh, as Wesley), 1958
Nurse Kathy (McElfresh), 1957
Nurse Kay's Conquest (W. Roberts), 1966
Nurse Lang (J. MacLeod), 1960
Nurse Laurie (Blair), 1962
Nurse Maria (Collin), 1963
Nurse Marika (Burchell), 1963
Nurse Marlowe (Arbor), 1959
Nurse Mary's Engagement (Summers), 1964
Nurse Meg's Decision (Norway, as Neal), 1966
Nurse Moonlight (I. Roberts), 1980
Nurse Most Likely (Dingwell, as Starr), 1962
Nurse Nancy (McElfresh, as Scott), 1959
Nurse Nolan (Barrie), 1961
Nurse of All Work (Arbor), 1962
Nurse of the Island (Pianka), 1976
Nurse Off Camera (Norway, as Neal), 1964
Nurse on an Island (Collin), 1970
Nurse on Bodmin Moor (Bloom, as Harvey), 1970
Nurse on Castle Island (Ritchie, as Heath), 1968
Nurse on Holiday (Blair, as Brett), 1963
Nurse on Horseback (Webb, as Hamill), 1952
Nurse Pro Tem (Finley), 1967
Nurse Robin (W. Roberts), 1973
Nurse Smith, Cook (Dingwell), 1968
Nurse Stacey Comes Abroad (R. Randall), 1958
Nurse Templar (Weale), 1961
Nurse to Doctor James (Woodward, as Richmond), 1976
Nurse to Princess Jasmine (Woodward), 1979
Nurse to the Maharajah (Woodward), 1961
Nurse Trent's Children (Dingwell), 1961
Nurse Verena in Weirwater (Charles, as Lance), 1970
Nurse Who Fell in Love (Bloom, as Essex), 1972
Nurse Who Shocked the Matron (Bloom, as Burns), 1970
Nurse Willow's Ward (Charles, as Tempest), 1965
Nursery Maid (Gibbs), 1975
Nurses (W. Roberts), 1972

Nurse's Holiday (Greig, as Ames), 1965
Nurses in the House (Collin), 1989
Nurse's Story (Greig, as Ames), 1965
Nursing Assignment (Woodward), 1959

O Genteel Lady! (Forbes), 1926
O Love! O Fire! (Robins), 1966
Oak Apple (Harrod-Eagles), 1982
Oasis (Matthews), 1988
Oath of Silence (Bentley), 1967
Obsession (Lamb), 1980
Obsession of Victoria Gracen (G. Hill), 1915
Obstacle Race (Dell), 1921
Occupying Power (Anthony), 1973
Octavia (Blackstock, as Allardyce), 1965
Octavia (J. Cooper), 1977
October Cabaret (Buckingham, as Quest), 1979
October Witch (Knight), 1971
Odd—But Even So (s Wren), 1941
Odds (s Dell), 1925
Odds Against (M. Pargeter), 1984
Odds on Love (Greig), 1936
Odious Duke (Cartland), 1973
Odor of Sanctity (Yerby), 1965
Odtaa (Masefield), 1926
Oedipus (Treece), 1964
Of Great Riches (Franken), 1937
Of Human Frailty (Malpass), 1987
Of Lena Geyer (Davenport), 1936
Of Love and Intrigue (Coffman), 1969
Of No Fixed Abode (M. Lewis), 1968
Of the Ring of Earls (Dymoke), 1970
Of Time and the Seasons (N. St. John), 1975
Of Wind and Fire (Blackmore), 1980
Off White (Nicole), 1959
Off with the Old Love (Neels), 1987
Offer of Marriage (Ruck), 1930
Office Wife (Baldwin), 1930
Officer's Wife (Robins), 1939
Ogilvie, James series (McCutchan, as MacNeil), from 1969
Ogilvie, Tallant, and Moon (Yarbro), 1976
Oh, Darling Joy! (Maybury), 1937
Oh, Money! Money! (E. Porter), 1918
O'Halloran's Luck (s Benét), 1944
O'Houlihan's Jest (O'Grady), 1961
O'Hurley series (N. Roberts), from 1988
Ola and the Sea Wolf (Cartland), 1980
Old Adam (Bloom), 1967
Old Baxter Place (McElfresh), 1954
Old Captivity (Shute), 1940
Old Doc (Seifert), 1946
Old Dominion (M. Johnston), 1899
Old Elm Tree (Bloom), 1974
Old Flame (Sellers), 1986
Old Fox (L. Cooper), 1927
Old Friends and New (s Vaizey), 1909
Old Glory (Duffield), 1942
Old Glory (Nicole), 1986
Old Gods Laugh (Yerby), 1964
Old Gray Homestead (Keyes), 1919
Old Hat (Barcynska, as Sandys), 1939
Old House of Fear (Kirk), 1961
Old Hunting Lodge (Inglis), 1961
Old Love's Domain (Bromige), 1982
Old Man's Marriage (Burgin), 1897
Old Mischief (Deeping), 1950

Old Moorings (Swan), 1909
Old Patch's Medley (s Bowen), 1930
Old Pines (s Boyd), 1952
Old Priory (Lofts), 1981
Old Pybus (Deeping), 1928
Old Rectory (Bloom), 1973
Old Roses (Barcynska, as Sandys), 1923
Old Scarecrow (s Orczy), 1916
Old Sinners Never Die (Davis), 1959
Old Smith's Nurse (M. St. John), 1918
Old Wine and New (Deeping), 1932
Old World Dies (Deeping), 1954
Old-Fashioned Heart (Ayres), 1953
Oleander River (Stern), 1937
O'Leary, Lance series (Eberhart), from 1929
Olive Branch (I. Roberts, as Shaw), 1968
Olive Grove (J. MacLeod), 1986
Olive Island (K. Thorpe), 1973
Oliver October (McCutcheon), 1923
Oliver Trenton (Frankau), 1951
Oliver Wiswell (K. Roberts), 1940
Olive's Courtship (Libbey), 1892
Olivia (Garvice), 1902
Olivia (Riefe), 1981
Olivia series (Yarbro), from 1987
Olivia and Others (Garvice), 1908
Olivia Mary (Albanesi), 1912
Olivia, The Tormented (Kimbrough), 1976
O'Malley series (Small), from 1980
O'Malley of Shanganagh (Byrne), 1925
On Call (E. Harrison), 1974
On Her Doorstep (Hooper, as Robbins), 1986
On Her Majesty's Orders (Stuart, as A. Stuart), 1977
On Leaving Charleston (Ripley), 1984
On Love's Altar (Garvice), 1892
On My Own (Pilcher), 1965
On Saint Hubert's Thing (s Yarbro), 1982
On the Air (Burchell), 1956
On the Field of Honour (Nolan, as Rockfern), 1985
On the High Road (Albanesi, as Rowlands), 1914
On the Night of the Seventh Moon (Holt), 1972
On the Screen (Hichens), 1929
On the Wings of Love (Albanesi, as Rowlands)
On the Wings of Magic (Hooper), 1983
On the Wings of Dreams (Gallagher), 1985
On Wings of Love (Harrod-Eagles, as Woodhouse), 1978
On Wings of Song (Burchell), 1985
Once a Nurse (W. Roberts), 1966
Once and Always (McNaught), 1987
Once and Future King series (T. White), from 1938
Once for All Time (Neels), 1984
Once in a Life (Garvice), 1910
Once in a Lifetime (Steel), 1982
Once Is Enough (Robins, as French), 1953
Once More with Feeling (N. Roberts), 1983
Once to Every Heart (J. MacLeod), 1951
Once They Were Rich (D. Murray), 1933
Once upon a Christmas (s Buck), 1972
Once upon a Kiss (Grimstead), 1965
Once You Have Found Him (Wyndham), 1954
Ondine (Pozzessere, as Drake), 1988
One and Only (D. Smith), 1973
One Basket (s Ferber), 1947
One Between (Cowen), 1967
One Brief Sweet Hour (Arbor), 1980
One Broken Dream (Preston), 1979

One Coin in the Fountain (Barrie, as Charles), 1957
One Dark Night (Bennetts), 1978
One Day, My Love (Bromige), 1980
One Enchanted Summer (Danbury), 1958
One Fight More (Ertz), 1939
One Fine Day (Gibbs, as Ford), 1954
One Girl in the World (Garvice), 1915
One Is Only Human (Stern), 1960
One Little Room (Chappell), 1960
One Love (J. MacLeod), 1945
One Man Too Many (Coffman), 1968
One Man's Art (N. Roberts), 1985
One Man's Evil (Albanesi, as Rowlands), 1900
One Man's Heart (Burchell), 1940
One Month at Sea (Ayres), 1929
One More River to Cross (Summers), 1979
One More Time (Baldwin), 1972
One More Time (Hunter), 1982
One More Time (van der Zee), 1983
One Night in Ceylon (s Robins), 1931
One Night in London (Andrews), 1979
One of the Boys (Dailey), 1980
One of the Chorus (Ruck), 1928
One of the Crowd (Albanesi), 1913
One of the Family (Burchell), 1939
One of Those Ways (Lowndes), 1929
One Room for His Highness (Greig), 1944
One Sees Stars (Ayres), 1952
One Step Ahead (Vitek), 1985
One Step from Heaven (Hoy), 1943
One String for Her Bow (Dingwell), 1970
One String for Nurse Bow (Dingwell), 1969
One Summer (Ayres), 1930
One Summer (N. Roberts), 1986
One Summer's Day (J. MacLeod, as Airlie), 1961
One Thing I Wanted (Charles, as Tempest), 1944
One to Live With (Ayres), 1938
One Touch of Topaz (Johansen), 1988
One Tough Hombre (Lorin, as Hohl), 1987
One Traveller Returns (Burgin), 1931
One Unwanted (Ayres), 1921
One Way Out (Hutten), 1906
One Way Out (J. MacLeod), 1941
One Way Ticket (Way), 1977
One Way to Venice (Hodge), 1974
One Who Cares (Lorrimer, as Robins), 1954
One Who Counted (Albanesi), 1937
One Who Forgot (Ayres), 1919
One Who Kisses (Lewty), 1983
One Who Kisses (L. Walker), 1954
One Who Looked On (Elsna, as Snow), 1965
One Who Paid (Albanesi, as Rowlands), 1935
One Who Remembers (Charles), 1976
One Who Stood By (Ayres), 1923
One Woman (Albanesi, as Rowlands), 1911
One Woman Too Many (Ayres), 1952
One Woman's Freedom (Price, as Smith), 1932
One Wreath with Love (Summerton, as Roffman), 1978
One-Eyed Moon (Steen), 1935
One-Faced Girl (Armstrong), 1963
One-Man Girl (Greig), 1931
Onesiphore, Our Neighbor (Macbeth), 1929
Only a Girl's Love (Garvice), 1901
Only a Mechanic's Daughter (Libbey), 1892
Only a Singing Girl (M. St. John), 1907
Only a Touch (Charles, as Chandos), 1941

Only Charity (Seale), 1961
Only Her Husband (Mackinlay), 1939
Only Love (Cartland), 1980
Only Love's Cross for Her (Libbey), 1908
Only My Dreams (Robins), 1951
Only My Heart to Give (Asquith), 1955
Only One Love (Garvice), 1910
Only Our Love (Bromige), 1968
Only Sin (Ellis), 1986
Only Son (s Swan), 1898
Only the Best (Trask), 1935
Only to Part (I. Roberts), 1961
Only World (Burgin), 1906
Only You (M. Pargeter), 1979
Opal (Bennetts), 1986
Open Country (Hewlett), 1909
Open Day at the Manor (Gibbs, as Ford), 1977
Open Door (Maddocks), 1980
Open Marriage (Kidd), 1984
Open Not the Door (Britt), 1978
Open the Door to Love (Charles, as Tempest), 1952
Open Window (Muskett), 1930
Open Wings (Cartland), 1942
Openers of the Gate (s Beck), 1930
Opening Flower (Farnes), 1948
Ophelia (F. Stevenson), 1968
Ophelia, The Anxious (Kimbrough), 1977
Opportune Marriage (K. Thorpe), 1968
Opposites Attract (N. Roberts), 1984
Optimist (Delafield), 1922
Oracles (Kennedy), 1955
Orange Blossom for Sandra (Bloom), 1951
Orange Blossom for Tara (I. Roberts, as Rowland), 1971
Orange Blossom Shop (Charles, as Tempest), 1946
Orange Blossoms (s Bowen, as Shearing), 1938
Orange Girl (Bloom, as Prole), 1972
Orange Sash (Dymoke), 1958
Oranges and Lemons (Hunter, as Chace), 1967
Orchard Hill (Seifert), 1945
Orchard Hill (L. Walker), 1958
Orchards (Deeping), 1922
Orchid Girl (Charles, as Lance), 1978
Orchid Tree (Coffman), 1984
Orchids for the Bride (Grimstead), 1967
Orchids from the Orient (Sinclair), 1986
Ordeal of Elizabeth (Elizabeth), 1901
Ordeal of Three Doctors (Seifert), 1965
Ordered South (A. M. Williamson), 1900
Ordinary People (E. Pargeter), 1941
Origin (Stone), 1980
Original Miss Honeyford (Chesney), 1985
Orphan Bride (Seale), 1962
Orphans (Ponsonby), 1962
O'Shaughnessy, Pixie series (Vaizey), from 1903
Other Cathy (Buckingham), 1978
Other Girl (Garvice), 1911
Other Juliet (Maybury), 1955
Other Karen (V. Johnston), 1983
Other Linding Girl (Burchell), 1966
Other Lips Have Loved You (Burchell), 1938
Other Love (Robins), 1952
Other Men's Arms (Greig, as Barclay), 1936
Other Miss Donne (Arbor), 1971
Other One (Charles, as Chandos), 1953
Other People's Fires (Elsna), 1931
Other Room (Blackmore), 1968

Other Side of Love (Robins), 1973
Other Side of Paradise (M. Lewis), 1975
Other Side of Paradise (M. Pargeter), 1985
Other Side of Sorrow (Chard), 1977
Other Side of Summer (Worboys, as Maxwell), 1977
Other Side of the Street (Jackson), 1956
Other Woman (Delmar), 1930
Other Woman (Garvice), 1905
Other Women's Beauty (Greig), 1938
Oubliette (Farnol), 1912
Our Admirable Betty (Farnol), 1918
Our Avenue (s Ayres), 1922
Our Dearest Emma (Bloom, as Prole), 1949
Our Lady of Marble (Bloom), 1926
Our Lady of the Beeches (Hutten), 1902
Our Little Life (Elsna), 1942
Our Living Stone Age (Idriess), 1963
Our Miss Penny (Grimstead, as Manning), 1964
Our Nell (M. St. John), 1917
Our Valiant Few (F. Mason), 1956
Out of a Clear Sky (Albanesi, as Rowlands), 1925
Out of Control (Lamb), 1988
Out of Reach (Cartland), 1945
Out of the Dark (Asquith), 1972
Out of the Dark (Lofts), 1972
Out of the House (Irwin), 1916
Out of the Nest (Cadell), 1987
Out of the Past (Garvice), n.d.
Out of the Past (Woodward), 1982
Out of the Shadows (Chard), 1978
Out of the Shadows (Duffield), 1944
Out of the Storm (G. Hill, as Macdonald), 1929
Out of the Swim (Burgin), 1930
Out of the War? (Lowndes), 1918
Out of the Whirlwind (Erskine-Lindop), 1951
Out of This Nettle (Lofts), 1938
Out to Marry Money (Ruck), 1940
Out Trail (Rinehart), 1923
Outback (Yarbro, as Bonner), 1983
Outback Summer (Buckingham, as John), 1981
Outback Woman (Saunders, as Blake), 1989
Outcast of the Family (Garvice), 1900
Outcasts of Crowthorpe College (M. St. John), 1913
Outer Ring (Erskine-Lindop), 1955
Outlaw (Hewlett), 1919
Outlaw Derek (Hooper), 1988
Outlaw Hearts (Brandewyne), 1986
Outlaw Love (Norris), 1928
Outlaw's Embrace (Rivers), 1986
Outrageous Fortune (Gibbs, as Ford), 1955
Outrageous Fortune (D. Murray), 1952
Outrageous Lady (Cartland), 1977
Outside Chance (Mackinlay), 1966
Outsider (Craven), 1987
Over at the Crowleys' (s Norris), 1946
Over the Blue Mountains (Burchell), 1952
Over the Castle Wall (J. MacLeod), 1974
Over the Hills (Farnol), 1930
Over the Water (Oman), 1935
Overheard (Ayres), 1925
Overlooker (P. Hastings), 1982
Overseas Nurse (Greig, as Ames), 1961
Ovington's Bank (Weyman), 1922
Owen Glendower (Powys), 1940
Owner Gone Abroad (Ayres), 1937
Oxen of the Sun (Bacheller), 1935

Passionate Springtime (Bloom, as Essex), 1956
Passionate Stranger (Kidd), 1981
Passionate Summer (Grimstead), 1953
Passionate Touch (Delinsky, as Drake), 1981
Passionate Witness (Holt, as Burford), 1941
Passion's Domain (Pykare, as Coombs), 1983
Passions in the Sand (Cartland), 1976
Passions of Medora Graeme (Lee), 1972
Passions of the Mind (Stone), 1971
Passion's Price (Vitek), 1983
Passion's Pride (Williams), 1980
Passion's Promise (Steel), 1977
Passions Wild and Free (Taylor), 1988
Passport to Happiness (Greig), 1955
Passport to Love (Grimstead, as Manning), 1958
Passport to Romance (Woodward, as Richmond), 1969
Past All Forgetting (Craven), 1978
Past Master (Tranter), 1965
Past Must Die (Elsna, as Lancaster), 1959
Past Tense of Love (Cadell), 1970
Pastel (Heyer), 1929
Pastoral (Bloom), 1934
Pastoral (Shute), 1944
Pastor's Wife (Elizabeth), 1914
Pat series (Montgomery), from 1933
Patarran (La Tourrette), 1983
Patch of Blue (G. Hill), 1932
Patchwork (M. Peters), 1989
Patchwork Quilt (Muskett), 1946
Path of the Eclipse (Yarbro), 1981
Path of the Hero King (Tranter), 1970
Path of the King (s Buchan), 1921
Path of the Moonfish (Beaty), 1964
Path to Love (Grimstead), 1960
Paths of Summer (Bromige), 1979
Pathway to Paradise (Greig), 1942
Patient in Cabin C (Eberhart), 1983
Patient in Love (Charles), 1963
Patient in Room 18 (Eberhart), 1929
Patricia (G. Hill), 1939
Patricia and Life (Albanesi), 1920
Patricia Plays a Part (Grundy), 1913
Patricia, The Beautiful (Kimbrough), 1975
Patrick Henry and the Frigate's Keel (s Fast), 1945
Patriot (Tranter), 1982
Patriots (Stuart, as Long), 1986
Patriot's Dream (B. Michaels), 1976
Pattern (Eberhart), 1937
Pattern (Franken), 1925
Pattern of Murder (Eberhart), 1948
Patterson series (Stirling), from 1985
Patterson Limit (Macbeth), 1923
Patty series (Webster), from 1903
Paul in Possession (Ayres), 1924
Pavement of Pearl (Danbury), 1975
Pavilion (Bloom), 1951
Pavilion at Monkswood (Maybury), 1965
Pavilion of Honour (Bowen, as Preedy), 1932
Pavilion of Women (Buck), 1946
Pawn in Frankincense (Dunnett), 1969
Pay Me Tomorrow (Burchell), 1940
Pay the Doctor (Seifert), 1966
Paying Pests (Grundy), 1941
Payment for the Piper (F. Murray), 1983
Payment in Full (Hampson), 1980
Peabody, Amelia series (B. Michaels, as Peters), from 1975

Peace Shall Destroy Many (Wiebe), 1962
Peacock Bed (Manners, as Marshall), 1978
Peacock Hill (Mackinlay), 1948
Peacock in the Jungle (May), 1982
Peacock Pagoda (Stuart, as A. Stuart), 1959
Peacock Queen (M. Peters), 1972
Peacock Spring (Godden), 1975
Peak of the Furnace (May), 1986
Pearl (Bennetts), 1984
Pearl of the Habsburgs (J. Fitzgerald, as Hamilton), 1978
Pearl of the Orient (Nicole), 1988
Pearl of the West (M. St. John), 1918
Pearl Thief (Ruck), 1926
Pearl-Maiden (Haggard), 1903
Pearls of Sharah series (F. Preston), from 1989
Pedlar's Pack (s Goudge), 1937
Peerless Jim (Cordell), 1984
Peggy series (Vaizey)
Peggy by Request (Dell), 1928
Peggy Fordyce (Swan), 1940
Peggy of Beacon Hill (Greig), 1924
Peggy, The Concerned (Kimbrough), 1981
Peggy the Pilgrim (Burgin), 1907
Peking Picnic (Bridge), 1932
Pelangi Haven (van der Zee), 1985
Pelican Walking (s Stern), 1934
Pelicans (Delafield), 1918
Penalty for Living (J. MacLeod), 1942
Penance (Wynne), 1917
Pendulum (Swan), 1926
Penelope (Chesney, as Fairfax), 1982
Penelope's Man (Erskine), 1928
Pengelly Jade (Stratton, as Gillen), 1972
Penhallow (Heyer), 1942
Penmarris (Howatch), 1971
Pennies from Heaven (Ruck), 1940
Pennies on Her Eyes (Roby), 1969
Penniless Heir (Cartland), 1974
Penniless Heiress (Gibbs), 1975
Penny Box (Dywer-Joyce), 1981
Penny for the Guy (Summerton, as Roffman), 1965
Penny for the Harp (Onions), 1952
Penny Plain (Seale), 1967
Peony (Buck), 1948
People Are So Respectable (Elsna), 1937
People from the Sea (V. Johnston), 1979
People in Glass House (Blackstock), 1975
People of My Own (E. Pargeter), 1942
People of the Mist (Haggard), 1894
People on the Hill (V. Johnston), 1971
Pepper Tree series (Walker, as Sanders), from 1952
Pepper's Way (Hooper), 1984
Perchance to Dream (Bloom), 1971
Perchance to Marry (Blair, as Conway), 1961
Perdita (J. Smith), 1981
Perdita's Prince (Holt, as Plaidy), 1969
Peregrine's Progress (Farnol), 1922
Perfect Fools (C. Allen), 1981
Perfect Gentleman (Chesney), 1988
Perfect Love (Gallagher), 1987
Perfect Marriage (Elsna, as Lancaster), 1949
Perfect Match (Veryan), 1981
Perfect Stranger (Ebel), 1966
Perfect Stranger (Steel), 1982
Perfect Wife (Leslie), 1960
Perfect Wife and Mother (Ellerbeck, as Thorne), 1980

Perfection of Love (Cartland), 1980
Performers series (Rayner), from 1973
Perfume of the Gods (Cartland), 1987
Perfume of the Rainbow (s Beck), 1923
Pericles the Athenian (R. Warner), 1963
Peridot Flight (Leslie), 1956
Peril and the Princess (Cartland), 1984
Peril at Polvellyn (McEvoy), 1973
Perilous Quest (Greig, as Ames), 1960
Perilous Voyage (Night, as Hope), 1983
Perilous Waters (Blackmore), 1954
Period Stuff (s Yates), 1942
Perishable Goods (Yates), 1928
Perrine (Daniels), 1978
Persian Boy (Renault), 1972
Persian Price (Anthony), 1975
Persian Ransom (Anthony), 1975
Persistent Lover (Farnes), 1958
Person in the House (Burgin), 1900
Person Unknown (Chard), 1988
Personal Affair (Kidd), 1981
Personality Plus (s Ferber), 1914
Perturbing Spirit (Caird), 1966
Petals Drifting (Hampson), 1971
Petals in the Wind (I. Preston), 1972
Petenera's Daughter (Bellamann), 1926
Peter, A Parasite (Albanesi), 1901
Peter Abelard (Waddell), 1933
Peter Day-by-Day (Barcynska, as Barclay), 1916
Peter Jackson, Cigar Merchant (Frankau), 1920
Peter Jameson (Frankau), 1920
Peter West (D. Stevenson), 1923
Petruchia (Stern), 1929
Petticoat Government (Orczy), 1910
Petticoat Rule (Orczy), 1910
Peverills (Leslie), 1946
Peyton Place series (Metalious), from 1956
Phantasmagoria (Wiat), 1988
Phantasy (Duffield), 1932
Phantom Cottage (V. Johnston), 1970
Phantom Emperor (Swanson), 1934
Phantom Flame of Wind House (Kimbrough), 1973
Phantom Lover (Ayres), 1919
Phantom Pipes (J. MacLeod), 1975
Phantom Reflection (Kimbrough, as Ashton), 1978
Phenwick Women series (Kimbrough), from 1975
Philippa (Muskett), 1954
Phillippa (Garvice), n.d.
Philomela's Miracle (Neels), 1978
Philosopher and the Sentimentalist (Corelli), 1911
Philosopher's Daughter (Ertz), 1976
Phoebe Dean (G. Hill), 1909
Phoenix and the Laurel (J. Lane), 1954
Phoenix Rising (Steen), 1952
Phoenix Syndrome (Andrews), 1987
Photogenic Soprano (Dunnett), 1968
Phroso (Hope), 1897
Physicians (E. Harrison), 1966
Piccadilly (Rayner), 1985
Piccadilly Inn (Mackinlay), 1946
Pick Up and Smile (Barcynska), 1936
Pieces of Dreams (C. Allen), 1984
Pied Tulip (Ashton), 1969
Pierrepont's Daughter (Burgin), 1935
Pilate's Wife (Bloom, as Mann), 1976
Pilgrim Heart (Stuart), 1955

Pilgrim in the Wind (M. Peters, as Darby), 1988
Pilgrim of Desire (M. Peters, as Black), 1979
Pilgrim Soul (Bloom), 1932
Pilgrim's Castle (Winspear), 1969
Pilgrims in Paradise (Slaughter), 1960
Pilgrim's Inn (Goudge), 1948
Pilgrims of Circumstance (Burgin), 1920
Pillar of Fire (Bailey), 1918
Pillar of Iron (Caldwell), 1965
Pillar of the Sky (C. Holland), 1985
Pilot's Point (Mackinlay), 1949
Pineapple Girl (Neels), 1978
Pink Parasol (Walsh), 1985
Pink Sands (May), 1974
Pink Snow (Darrell, as Dawes), 1975
Pious Fraud (Burgin), 1938
Pious Pilgrimage (s Elizabeth), 1901
Piper in the Hills (Manley-Tucker), 1974
Piper of Laide (Stuart, as A. Stuart), 1963
Piper's Gate (Manley-Tucker), 1960
Piper's Pool (Mackinlay), 1946
Piper's Tune (Maddocks), 1954
"Piping Times" (Farnol), 1945
Pippa (Grundy), 1932
Pippin's Journal (O'Grady), 1962
Piracy (Arlen), 1922
Pirate of the Sun (Westwood), 1972
Pirate's Love (Lindsey), 1978
Pistols for Two (s Heyer), 1960
Pitcairn's Island (Nordhoff and Hall), 1934
Pitiless Choice (Pedler), 1933
Pity My Love (Winston), 1967
Pixie series (Vaizey)
Place Called Paradise (Summers), 1967
Place Called Rambula (Way), 1984
Place for Everyone (s Mellville, as Betteridge), 1977
Place in the Sun (Ellerbeck, as Thorne), 1987
Place for Lovers (Westwood), 1978
Place of Ravens (P. Hill), 1980
Place of Sapphires (F. Randall), 1969
Place of Stones (Heaven), 1975
Place of Storms (Craven), 1977
Place to Hide (Anthony), 1987
Place to Stand (Bridge), 1953
Plague Ship (Slaughter), 1976
Plain Jane (Chesney), 1986
Plain Old Man (C. MacLeod), 1985
Plain People (Norris), 1938
Plantagenet series (Holt, as Plaidy), from 1976
Plantagenets series (Dymoke), from 1978
Plantation series (Bristow), from 1937
Plantation Boss (Hampson), 1972
Plantation Doctor (Blair), 1962
Plantation Moon (Bevan), 1978
Plantation of Vines (May), 1977
Planter and the Tree (Ayres), 1926
Plaster Cast (Muskett), 1933
Play (S. Johnson), 1987
Play Fair with Love (Lorrimer, as Robins), 1972
Playboy (Deeping), 1948
Playboy Prince (N. Roberts), 1987
Player King (Ashton), 1975
Player Queen (Heaven, as Fecher), 1968
Players (J. Cooper), 1989
Player's Boy (Bryher), 1953
Players in the Shadows (Vitek), 1985

Playing for Keeps (B. Hastings), 1980
Playing the Odds (N. Roberts), 1985
Playing with Fire (Lamb, as Hardy), 1981
Playing with Fire (Vitek), 1986
Playmaker (Keneally), 1987
Pleasant Husband (s Bowen), 1921
Please Burn after Reading (Bloom, as Burns), 1954
Pleasure and the Pain (Mather), 1971
Pleasure Garden (Barcynska, as Sandys), 1923
Pleasure Seekers (M. Howard), 1970
Plight of Pamela Pollworth (Sebastian), 1980
Plot (Bailey), 1922
Plotted in Darkness (Wynne), 1927
Plough (Jacob), 1928
Plum Thicket (Giles), 1954
Plume of Dust (May), 1975
Pocahontas (Garnett), 1933
Poellenberg Inheritance (Anthony), 1972
Poinciana (Whitney), 1980
Point of View (s Glyn), 1913
Poison Flower (Daniels), 1977
Poison in Pimlico (Holt, as Ford), 1950
Poisoned Lives! (M. St. John), 1924
Poisoners (Bowen, as Preedy), 1936
Point of View (Glyn), 1913
Poland (Michener), 1983
Poldark, Ross series (Graham), from 1945
Polly (Chesney, as Tremaine), 1980
Polly (Neels), 1984
Polly Kettle (Gibbs), 1963
Polly, The Worried (Kimbrough), 1978
Pollyanna series (E. Porter), from 1913
Polly's Summer Stock (McElfresh, as Wesley), 1957
Polonaise (Hodge), 1987
Polonaise (Leslie), 1943
Polrudden (Thompson), 1985
Pompeii Scroll (La Tourrette), 1975
Pool (Rinehart), 1952
Pool of Dreams (L. Walker), 1971
Pool of Pink Lilies (Dingwell), 1970
Pool of St. Branok (Holt, as Carr), 1987
Poor Butterfly (Elsna, as Snow), 1951
Poor, Dear Margaret Kirby (s Norris), 1913
Poor Governess (Cartland), 1982
Poor Man's Tapestry (Onions), 1946
Poor Millionaire (Burgin), 1933
Poor Relation (Chesney), 1984
Poor Relation (Elsna, as Snow), 1968
Poor Relation (Sebastian), 1978
Poor Straws! (Jacob), 1933
Poor Wise Man (Rinehart), 1920
Poppett & Co. (Barcynska, as Sandys), 1944
Poppies in the Corn (Albanesi), 1911
Poppy (Chesney, as Tremaine), 1982
Poppy series (Rayner), from 1987
Poppy and the Rose (Barcynska, as Sandys), 1962
Porius (Powys), 1951
Port of Adventure (C. and A. Williamson), 1913
Port o' Missing Men (s Wren), 1934
Portent (M. Harris), 1980
Portrait (Ford), 1910
Portrait in Gold (Ainsworth), 1971
Portrait of a Gentleman in Colours (Farnol), 1935
Portrait of a Lady (E. Smith), 1936
Portrait of a Marriage (Buck), 1945
Portrait of a Playboy (Deeping), 1947
Portrait of a Witch (Daniels), 1976

Portrait of Bethany (Weale), 1982
Portrait of Destiny (Swan), 1937
Portrait of Jaime (Way), 1977
Portrait of Jill (Ebel), 1972
Portrait of Lorraine (Elsna, as Conway), 1971
Portrait of Love (Cartland), 1982
Portrait of Paula (Grimstead), 1968
Portrait of Pierre (Preston), 1971
Portrait of Sarah (M. Peters, as Black), 1969
Portrait of Susan (Blair, as Brett), 1956
Portraits (Freeman), 1979
Portuguese Affair (Melville, as Betteridge), 1966
Portuguese Escape (Bridge), 1958
Possessed (Daniels), 1975
Possession (Bromfield), 1925
Possession (de la Roche), 1923
Possession (Lamb), 1979
Possession of Tracy Corbin (Daniels), 1973
Post Captain (O'Brian), 1972
Post of Honor (Delderfield), 1974
Post Office Girl (M. St. John), 1915
Postmark Murder (Eberhart), 1956
Postscript to Yesterday (Summers), 1966
Post-War Girl (s Ruck), 1930
Potter's Niece (R. Randall), 1987
Poverty's Daughter (M. St. John, as Cooper), 1922
Powder and Patch (Heyer), 1930
Power (Jacob), 1927
Power and Seduction (Lorin), 1985
Power and the Glory (Bentley), 1940
Power and the Glory (Nicole), 1988
Power and the Passion (Nicole, as Nicholson), 1977
Power and the Prince (Cartland), 1980
Power of Love (Albanesi, as Rowlands), 1911
Power of the Dog (Byrne), 1929
Power Play (Krentz, as Castle), 1982
Power to Kill (Hichens), 1934
Powers and Maxine (C. N. and A. M. Williamson),
    1907
Practical Dreamer (Browning), 1983
Practice for Sale (Mackinlay), 1964
Practice to Deceive (Veryan), 1985
Prairie Fires (Swan), 1913
Praise Singer (Renault), 1978
Pray to the Earth (Eaton), 1938
Precious Jeopardy (Douglas), 1933
Precious Waif (Hampson), 1969
Predestined (Duffield), 1929
Prelude for Two Queens (Elsna), 1972
Prelude to a Song (M. Pargeter), 1982
Prelude to Enchantment (Mather), 1972
Prelude to Freedom (Renier), 1967
Prelude to Kingship (J. Lane), 1936
Prelude to Louise (Maybury) 1954
Prelude to Love (Renier), 1972
Prelude to Love (J. Smith), 1983
Prelude to Yesterday (Bloom), 1961
Prescription for Love (R. Lindsay), 1977
Prescription for Melissa (Dwyer-Joyce), 1974
Presence and the Power (Bowen), 1924
Presence in an Empty Room (V. Johnston), 1980
President Is Born (Hurst), 1928
President's Lady (Stone), 1951
Pretence (R. Lindsay, as Leigh), 1956
Pretender to Love (F. Stevenson, as Faire), 1981
Pretenders (M. Howard), 1962
Prettiest Girl (Burchell), 1955

Promise of Glory (Nolan), 1983
Promise of Happiness (Neels), 1979
Promise of Morning (Manley-Tucker), 1962
Promise of Murder (Eberhart), 1961
Promise of Paradise (Charles, as Tempest), 1949
Promise of the Unicorn (Craven), 1985
Promise to Cherish (Spencer), 1983
Promises (C. Allen), 1980
Promises (Gaskin), 1982
Promises from the Past (Vitek), 1981
Promising Affair (Finley), 1974
Property of a Gentleman (Gaskin), 1974
Prophet of Berkeley Square (Hichens), 1901
Prophetic Marriage (Deeping), 1920
Props (Jacob), 1932
Pro's Daughter (Mackinlay), 1934
Proselyte (Ertz), 1933
Protégé (Armstrong), 1970
Proud and the Free (Fast), 1950
Proud Beloved (Stanford), 1989
Proud Breed (De Blasis), 1978
Proud Citadel (Charles), 1967
Proud Citadel (Hoy), 1942
Proud Harvest (Mather), 1978
Proud Heart (Stuart), 1953
Proud Lover (Grimstead, as Manning), 1966
Proud Mary (Gower), 1984
Proud New Flags (F. Mason), 1951
Proud Patricia (Swan), 1940
Proud Princess (Cartland), 1976
Proud Servant (Irwin), 1934
Proud Stranger (Stratton), 1976
Provincial Lady series (Delafield), from 1930
Proxy Wedding (M. Peters, as Grey), 1982
Prude and the Prodigal (Cartland), 1980
Prudence (J. Cooper), 1978
Prudence Langford's Ordeal (Albanesi, as Rowlands),
    1914
Prye, Dr. Paul series (Millar), from 1941
Psychiatrist's Wife (Gellis, as Jacobs), 1966
Public Smiles, Private Tears (Van Slyke), 1982
Publicity Baby (Barcynska), 1935
Publicity for Anne (A. M. Williamson), 1926
Puller of Strings (Burgin), 1917
Pullman (Dell), 1930
Pulse of Life (Lowndes), 1908
Punch and Judy (Albanesi), 1919
Punished with Love (Cartland), 1980
Punishment of a Vixen (Cartland), 1977
Puppets Parade (Leslie), 1932
Purchase Price (Swan), 1934
Pure and Untouched (Cartland), 1981
Pure as the Lily (Cookson), 1972
Puritan Strain (Baldwin), 1935
Puritans in Paradise (Slaughter), 1960
Purple and the Gold (Daniels), 1980
Purple Parasol (McCutcheon), 1905
Purple Quest (Slaughter), 1965
Pursuing Shadow (Wynne), 1944
Pursuit and the Capture (Farnes), 1966
Pursuit of Pleasure (Elsna), 1969
Push the Past Behind (Reid), 1977
Put Back the Clock (Robins), 1962
Put Love Aside (Inglis), 1939
Pyramid (Hichens), 1936
Pyrates (G. Fraser), 1983

Quadrille (Chesney), 1981
Quaint Place (Barcynska, as Sandys), 1952
Quality of Music (Burghley), 1966
Quarrel, Jonas series (Krentz), from 1988
Quarrel and Kiss (Ruck), 1942
Quatermain, Allan series (Haggard), from 1885
Queen and Lord M (Holt, as Plaidy), 1973
Queen and Mortimer (Clarke, as Honeyman), 1974
Queen and the Gypsy (Heaven), 1977
Queen and the Welshman (Sisson), 1979
Queen Anne's Lace (Keyes), 1930
Queen for England (Bloom, as Prole), 1957
Queen for the Regent (Bloom, as Prole), 1971
Queen from Provence (Holt, as Plaidy), 1979
Queen Guillotine (Bloom, as Prole), 1962
Queen in Waiting (Holt, as Plaidy), 1967
Queen in Waiting (Lofts), 1955
Queen Jennie (Wynne), 1918
Queen Jezebel (Holt, as Plaidy), 1953
Queen Kate (Garvice), 1909
Queen of Air and Darkness (T. White), 1958
Queen of Diamonds (Holt, as Tate), 1958
Queen of Evil (Slaughter), 1962
Queen of Hearts (Krentz, as Castle), 1979
Queen of Hearts (Pozzessere, as Graham), 1985
Queen of Hearts (Seale), 1969
Queen of Hearts (F. Stevenson, as Curzon), 1982
Queen of Paris (Nicole, as Nicholson), 1979
Queen of Spades (McEvoy), 1975
Queen of the Castle (J. Lane), 1958
Queen of the Dawn (Haggard), 1925
Queen of the Realm (Holt, as Plaidy), 1984
Queen Sheba's Ring (Haggard), 1910
Queen Sweetheart (A. M. Williamson), 1901
Queen Truganini (Cato), 1976
Queen Who Never Was (M. Peters), 1972
Queen Who Was a Nun (Bloom, as Prole), 1967
Queen-Gold (Wiat), 1985
Queenmaker (M. Peters), 1975
Queen's Affair (Bloom), 1979
Queen's Caprice (Bowen, as Preedy), 1934
Queen's Captain (Knight, as Hope), 1978
Queen's Confession (Holt), 1968
Queen's Corsair (Saxton, as Turner), 1976
Queen's Counsel (Stuart, as A. Stuart), 1957
Queen's Daughters (Bloom, as Prole), 1973
Queen's Delight (Heaven, as Fecher), 1966
Queen's Diamond (Dymoke), 1983
Queen's Favorite (Heaven, as Fecher), 1974
Queen's Favourites (Holt, as Plaidy), 1966
Queen's Folly (Thane), 1937
Queen's Folly (Weyman), 1925
Queen's Fourth Husband (Wiat), 1976
Queen's Gift (Fletcher), 1952
Queen's Grace (Tranter), 1953
Queen's Grace (Westcott), 1959
Queen's Harbour (Gibbs, as Ford), 1944
Queen's Husband (Holt, as Plaidy), 1973
Queen's Letter (Lamb, as Coates), 1973
Queen's Messenger (Cartland), 1971
Queen's Midwife (Bloom, as Prole), 1961
Queen's Nurse (Arbor), 1960
Queens of England series (Holt, as Plaidy), from 1983
Queens' Play (Dunnett), 1964
Queen's Quadrille (Roby, as Grey), 1981
Queen's Quair (Hewlett), 1904

Queen's Ward (Elsna), 1966
Quest (Asquith), 1964
Quest for Alexis (Buckingham), 1973
Quest for Love (Marsh), 1984
Quest of Glory (Bowen), 1912
Quest of the Eagle (Seger), 1986
Quest of Youth (Farnol), 1927
Questing Beast (J. Lane), 1970
Questing Heart (Ashton), 1978
Questing Trout (Bloom), 1934
Question of Marriage (R. Lindsay), 1972
Question of Marriage (Vaizey), 1910
Question of Quality (Albanesi), 1909
Question of Temptation (s Orczy), 1925
Quick and the Dead (Bennetts), 1980
Quickenberry Tree (Motley), 1983
Quicksilver Pool (Whitney), 1955
Quiet Gentleman (Heyer), 1951
Quiet Heart (Barrie), 1966
Quiet Heart (Franken), 1954
Quiet Hills (Bromige), 1967
Quiet Holiday (Blair, as Brett), 1957
Quiet House (Maddocks), 1947
Quiet Island (Muskett), 1943
Quiet One (Norway, as Norton), 1959
Quiet Valley (Farnes), 1944
Quiet Village (Bloom), 1965
Quiet Walks the Tiger (Pozzessere, as Graham), 1983
Quiet Wards (Andrews), 1956
Quietly My Captain Waits (Eaton), 1940
Quill's Window (McCutcheon), 1921
Quin's Hide (Summerton), 1964
Quisanté (Hope), 1900
Quorum (Bentley), 1950

R.S.V.P. Murder (Eberhart), 1965
Rabbits in the Hay (J. Lane), 1958
Rabble in Arms (K. Roberts), 1933
Race for Love (Cartland), 1978
Race of the Tiger (Cordell), 1963
Rachel Lee (Wynne), 1925
Rachel, The Possessed (Kimbrough), 1975
Rachel Trevellyan (Mather), 1974
Rachel's Confession (F. Preston), 1985
Radiance (Maybury), 1979
Radkin Revenge (W.Roberts), 1979
Rafe the Maverick (Hooper), 1986
Rafferty's Wife (Hooper), 1987
Ragamuffin (Greig), 1929
Rage and Desire (Nicole, as Arlen), 1982
Rage of Passion (Palmer), 1987
Ragged Robyn, Story of (Onions), 1945
Raging Fire (Heaven), 1987
Raging Seas, Searing Skies (Nicole), 1988
Raging Waters (Daniels), 1970
Raider (Deveraux), 1987
Rain of Diamonds (Weale), 1981
Rain on the Wind (Hunter), 1984
Rainbird's Revenge (Chesney), 1988
Rainbow (Buck), 1974
Rainbow after Rain (Charles), 1977
Rainbow at Dusk (Loring), 1942
Rainbow Bird (Way), 1972
Rainbow Child (Worboys, as Eyre), 1971
Rainbow Cottage (G. Hill), 1934
Rainbow Days (J. MacLeod), 1973

Rainbow Glass (Dwyer-Joyce), 1973
Rainbow in My Hand (Manley-Tucker),1965
Rainbow in the Mist (Whitney), 1989
Rainbow Isle (J. MacLeod), 1939
Rainbow on the Road (Forbes), 1954
Rainbow River (I. Roberts, as Rowland), 1970
Rainbow Romance (Ritchie), 1974
Rainbow Shell (Danbury), 1960
Rainbow Summer (Harrod-Eagles, as Woodhouse), 1976
Rainbow to Heaven (Cartland), 1976
Rainbow Valley (Montgomery), 1919
Rainbow's End (Saunders), 1978
Raine's Story (F. Preston), 1989
Rains Came (Bromfield), 1937
Rainsong (Whitney), 1984
Raintree County (Lockridge), 1948
Raintree Valley (Winspear), 1971
Rainwood series (Bromige), from 1966
Rake and the Hussy (Chambers), 1930
Rakehell (Manners, as Rundle), 1970
Rake's Companion (Pykare, as Towers), 1980
Rake's Progress (Bowen), 1912
Rake's Progress (Chesney), 1984
Rakonitz Chronicles (Stern), 1932
Rakóssy (C. Holland), 1967
Raleigh's Eden (Fletcher), 1940
Raleigh's Fair Bess (Saxton, as Turner), 1972
Ralph Carey (Miles), 1922
Ralph Dacre (A.Stevenson), 1967
Ramage, Lord Nicholas series (Pope), from 1965
Rana Look (Brown), 1986
Rancher Needs a Wife (Blair, as Conway), 1962
Rancho Rio, El (Eberhart), 1970
Random Army (Polland), 1969
Random Island (Stuart, as A. Stuart), 1968
Randy (L. Walker, as Sanders), 1948
Ranger in the Hills (L. Walker), 1966
Ransom (G. Hill), 1933
Raoul (Bailey), 1907
Rape of the Fair Country (Cordell), 1959
Rapture (P. Hastings), 1966
Rapture (Sherwood, as Royal), 1979
Rapture in My Rags (P. Hastings), 1954
Rapture of the Deep (Rome), 1982
Rapture of the Desert (Winspear), 1972
Rascals' Heaven (F. Mason), 1965
Rash Reckless Love (Sherwood), 1981
Ratoon (Nicole), 1962
Ravelston Affair (E. Harrison), 1967
Raven in the Wind (Wiat), 1978
Raven on the Wing (Hooper), 1987
Raven Wings (Edwards), 1977
Ravenburn (Black), 1978
Ravenden (Blackmore), 1976
Raven's Forge (Butler, as Melville), 1975
Raven's Prey (Krentz, as James), 1984
Raven's Wing (Sprigge), 1940
Ravenscar (M. Peters), 1981
Ravenscrag (J. MacLeod), 1948
Ravenscroft (Eden), 1965
Ravensley series (Heaven), from 1978
Ravensmount (McEvoy), 1974
Ravenstor (Renier), 1974
Ravenswood (J. Roberts), 1971
Ravenswood Hall (Daniels, as Gray), 1973
Ravishers (Coffman, as Duval), 1980

Raw Summer (Blackmore), 1967
Rawhide and Lace (Palmer), 1987
Rawhide Man (Palmer), 1984
Raxl, Voodoo Princess (Daniels), 1970
Reach for the Shadows (Dwyer-Joyce), 1972
Reach for the Stars (Seger, as Jennings), 1984
Reach Out for Happiness (Woodward, as Richmond),
  1984
Reach Out to Cherish (Browning), 1983
Reaching for the Stars (L. Walker), 1966
Ready—Aye Ready! (M. St. John, as Cooper), 1916
Real David Copperfield (Graves), 1925
Real Gold (Albanesi, as Rowlands), 1924
Real Man (Sellers), 1984
Real Thing (Delinsky), 1987
Real Thing (Peake), 1972
Realm of the Pagans (Hampson), 1982
Realms of Gold (Hunter), 1976
Reap the Whirlwind (Hampson), 1975
Reap the Whirlwind (Roby), 1972
Reaping (Sabatini), 1929
Reason Why (Glyn), 1911
Reason Why (Lowndes), 1932
Reasonable Doubts (B. Hastings), 1984
Reasonable Shores (Stern), 1946
Rebecca (du Maurier), 1938
Rebecca, The Mysterious (Kimbrough), 1975
Rebel (Bailey), 1923
Rebel Against Love (Ashton), 1981
Rebel Bride (Hampson), 1971
Rebel Doctor (Seifert), 1978
Rebel Heart (Maybury), 1959
Rebel Hearts (Swan), 1940
Rebel Heiress (Hodge), 1975
Rebel in His Arms (Rivers), 1981
Rebel in Love (Peake), 1978
Rebel Lover (Blackstock, as Allardyce), 1979
Rebel of Allington (Wiat), 1974
Rebel Princess (Anthony), 1953
Rebel Princess (Cartland), 1985
Rebel Princess (Leslie), 1970
Rebel Waltz (Hooper), 1986
Rebel Wife (R. Randall), 1944
Rebellion (N. Roberts), 1988
Rebellious Love (Seger), 1983
Rebels (Jakes), 1975
Rebels (Treece), 1953
Receipt for Hardness (Elsna), 1935
Receipt for Murder (Butler), 1956
Reckless Adventure (Farnes), 1942
Reckless Angel (Lowndes), 1939
Reckless Love (Lowell), 1989
Reckless Passion (Krentz, as James), 1982
Reckless Pilgrim (J. MacLeod), 1941
Reckoning (Chambers), 1905
Re-Creations (G. Hill), 1924
Recycled Citizen (C. MacLeod), 1987
Red Ashes (Pedler), 1924
Red Bird (Manners), 1984
Red Branch (Llywelyn), 1989
Red Carnelian (Whitney), 1968
Red Chalet (Norway, as Norton), 1960
Red Cherry Summer (Laker, as Øvstedal), 1973
Red Chief (Idriess), 1953
Red Cliffs (Farnes), 1961
Red Cliffs of Malpara (Way), 1976
Red Cockade (Weyman), 1895

Red Cross Barge (Lowndes), 1916
Red Daniel (McCutchan, as MacNeil), 1973
Red Dawn (Nicole), 1985
Red Dust (Muskett), 1954
Red Eve (Haggard), 1912
Red Flame (Miles), 1921
Red Fleur-de-Lys (Wynne), 1912
Red for Danger! (Price), 1936
Red Fruit (Wynne), 1929
Red Ginger Blossom (Dingwell), 1972
Red Hair (Glyn), n.d.
Red in the Morning (Yates), 1946
Red Is for Murder (Whitney), 1943
Red Lamp (Rinehart), 1925
Red Lotus (J. MacLeod, as Airlie), 1958
Red Midnight (Pozzessere, as Graham), 1984
Red Pavilion (Summerton), 1958
Red Queen, White Queen (M. Peters), 1982
Red Queen, White Queen (Treece), 1958
Red, Red Rose (McEvoy), 1960
Red Republic (Chambers), 1895
Red Rose of Anjou (Holt, as Plaidy), 1982
Red Rose of Lancaster (Wynne), 1921
Red Roses for a Nurse (I. Preston), 1968
Red Roses, White Lilies (Vitek, as Alexander),
  1979
Red Rowan Berry (F. Murray), 1976
Red Runs the Sunset (I. Roberts, as Carr), 1963
Red Saint (Deeping), 1909
Red Signal (G. Hill), 1919
Red Silence (Norris), 1929
Red Sky at Morning (Kennedy), 1927
Red Sky at Night (Holt, as Burford), 1959
Red Sky at Night: Lovers' Delight? (Hodge), 1977
Red Staircase (Butler), 1979
Red Veil (M. St. John, as Cooper), 1928
Red Wagon (E. Smith), 1930
Red Whirlwind (Wynne), 1919
Red, White, and Grey (Miles), 1921
Redcoat (Cornwell), 1987
Redeemed by Love (Garvice, as Hart)
Red-Headed Bastard (Elsna), 1981
Redway Street (M. St. John, as Cooper), 1924
Redwood Empire (Lowell, as Maxwell), 1987
Reeds of Honey (Way), 1975
Reef of Dreams (M. Howard), 1942
Refining Felicity (Chesney), 1988
Reflection (Kimbrough, as Ashton), 1979
Reflection of Evil (Summerton, as Roffman), 1967
Reflections (Hufford), 1981
Reflections (N. Roberts), 1983
Reflections in a Lake (Ebel), 1988
Reflections of Ambrosine (Glyn), 1902
Reflections of Love (Woodward), 1983
Refugees (Doyle), 1893
Regency (D. Murray), 1936
Regency Buck (Heyer), 1935
Regency Gold (Chesney), 1980
Regency Morning (M. Peters, as Law), 1988
Regency Rogue (Bennetts), 1982
Regency Scandal (Ley), 1979
Regency Star (Williams), 1985
Regent's Daughter (Holt, as Plaidy), 1971
Regent's Gift (Wynne), 1915
Regiment (Nicole), 1988
Regiment of Women (Dane), 1917
Regina (Darcy), 1976

Rehearsal for Love (Baldwin), 1940
Reilly's Woman (Dailey), 1978
Rekindled Flame (Ashton), 1980
Rekindled Flame (Marsh), 1982
Relative Stranger (A. Stevenson), 1970
Release the Past (I. Preston), 1973
Relenting Fate (s Garvice), 1912
Relentless Adversary (Krentz, as Castle), 1982
Relentless Desire (Brown), 1983
Relentless Storm (Lorrimer), 1975
Reluctant Adventuress (S. Thorpe), 1963
Reluctant Bride (Cartland), 1970
Reluctant Bride (Grimstead), 1957
Reluctant Bride (Mackinlay), 1939
Reluctant Bride (J. Smith), 1982
Reluctant Cinderella (Greig, as Ames), 1952
Reluctant Debutante (Sebastian, as Gladstone),
    1979
Reluctant Dreamer (Browning), 1986
Reluctant Father (Palmer), 1989
Reluctant Folly (J. MacLeod), 1942
Reluctant Governess (Mather), 1971
Reluctant Guest (Blair, as Brett), 1959
Reluctant Heiress (Sebastian, as Norcross), 1978
Reluctant Landlord (Seale), 1962
Reluctant Lark (Johansen), 1983
Reluctant Madonna (Steen), 1929
Reluctant Maiden (Finley), 1975
Reluctant Masquerade (Reid), 1969
Reluctant Millionaire (Greig), 1944
Reluctant Nightingale (Norway), 1970
Reluctant Odyssey (E. Pargeter), 1947
Reluctant Orphan (Seale) 1947
Reluctant Partnership (Ashton), 1979
Reluctant Protegee (Sebastian, as Gladstone), 1980
Reluctant Puritan (Shoesmith), 1972
Reluctant Relation (Burchell), 1961
Reluctant Rivals (Roby, as Grey), 1981
Reluctant Voyager (Britt), 1973
Reluctant Widow (Heyer), 1946
Remains to Be Seen (Cadell), 1983
Remedy for Love (Kidd), 1972
Remember September (Dingwell), 1978
Remember This Stranger (K. Thorpe), 1974
Remember Today (Thane), 1941
Remembered Kiss (Ayres), 1918
Remembered Serenade (Burchell), 1975
Remembered Spring (Maddocks), 1949
Remembering Louise (Gilbert), 1978
Remembrance (Steel), 1981
Renaissance series (Bowen), from 1928
Renaissance Man (Krentz, as James), 1982
Rendezvous (Anthony), 1967
Rendezvous (Buckingham, as John), 1985
Rendezvous (s du Maurier), 1980
Rendezvous (Franken), 1954
Rendezvous in Lisbon (Danbury), 1967
Rendezvous in Venice (Ashton), 1978
Rendezvous in Vienna (Ellis), 1976
Rendezvous in Zagarella (Ruck), 1964
Rendezvous with Fear (Worboys), 1977
Rendezvous with Love (Chard), 1983
Renegade (Graham), 1951
Renegade Girl (Gibbs), 1981
Renegade Player (Browning), 1982
Renny's Daughter (de la Roche), 1951
Renshawe Inheritance (Renier), 1972

Rent a Wife (Lindsay, as Leigh), 1980
Repeating Pattern (M. Howard), 1968
Repent at Leisure (Duffield), 1945
Reprieve (Deeping), 1945
Reprise (J. Smith), 1982
Republic (Thompson), 1985
Reputation (Robins), 1963
Reputation Dies (Ley), 1984
Requiem for a Patriot (Cordell), 1988
Requiem for a Wren (Shute), 1955
Requiem for Idols (Lofts), 1938
Research Fellow (Stuart, as A. Stuart), 1971
Respectable Miss Parkington-Smith (Blackstock, as Allardyce),
    1964
Rest Harrow (Hewlett), 1910
Rest Is Magic (Lewty), 1973
Rest Is Silence (Coffman), 1967
Rest of My Life with You (Baldwin), 1942
Restless Are the Sails (Eaton), 1941
Restless Beauty (Greig, as Ames), 1944
Restless Dream (Mackinlay), 1949
Restless Frontier (McCutchan, as MacNeil), 1979
Restless Heart (Beresford), 1982
Restless Heart (Robins), 1938
Restless Is the River (Derleth), 1939
Restless Lady (s Keyes), 1963
Restless Passion (Delmar), 1947
Restless Sea (Thompson), 1983
Restless Years (J. MacLeod, as Airlie), 1950
Retallick series (Thompson), from 1977
Retreat from Love (Greig), 1937
Retribution (Lamb), 1981
Retribution (M. St. John, as Cooper), 1930
Return (Anthony), 1978
Return (Winston), 1972
Return Engagement (Finley), 1981
Return Engagement (Hooper, as Robbins), 1982
Return I Dare Not (Kennedy), 1931
Return Journey (Ayres), 1938
Return Journey (Delderfield), 1974
Return Match (Cadell), 1979
Return of a Heroine (Steen), 1936
Return of Simon (Blair, as Conway), 1953
Return of the Cuckoo (Charles, as Lance), 1976
Return of the Eagles (F. Mason), 1959
Return of the Gypsy (Holt, as Carr), 1985
Return of the Petticoat (Deeping), 1909
Return of the Royalist (Shoesmith), 1971
Return to Aylforth (Eliot), 1967
Return to Bellbird Country (Worboys, as Eyre), 1966
Return to Belle Amber (Way), 1971
Return to Candelriggs (Reid), 1966
Return to Darkness (W. Roberts), 1969
Return to Deepwater (Stratton, as Gillen), 1975
Return to Delphi (Melville, as Betteridge), 1964
Return to Dragonshill (Summers), 1971
Return to Elysium (Grant), 1947
Return to Glenshael (Elgin), 1965
Return to King's Mere (Charles, as Lance), 1967
Return to Listowel (Sallis), 1975
Return to Love (Blackmore), 1964
Return to Love (M. Howard), 1946
Return to Love (Lorrimer, as Robins), 1968
Return to Love (Maybury), 1939
Return to Santa Flores (Johansen), 1984
Return to Sender (Manley-Tucker), 1968
Return to Silbersee (Arbor), 1978

Return to Spring (J. MacLeod), 1939
Return to Terror (Charles), 1966
Return to Tip Row (Gower), 1977
Return to Tremarth (Barrie), 1969
Return to Tremarth (Burghley), 1969
Return to Vienna (Buckingham), 1971
Return to Wuthering Heights (Ellerbeck, as L'Estrange), 1977
Returned Empty (Barclay), 1920
Reuben (Garvice), 1912
Reunion in Reno (Greig, as Warren), 1941
Reveille for Romance (Webb, as Hamill), 1946
Revenge of the Heart (Cartland), 1984
Reverse of the Medal (O'Brian), 1986
Reversion to Type (Delafield), 1923
Revolt—and Virginia (Summers), 1969
Revolt of Sarah Perkins (Cockrell), 1965
Revolt of the Eaglets (Holt, as Plaidy), 1977
Revolution of Love (Cartland), 1987
Reward of Faith (s Goudge), 1950
Rhapsody in Bloom (van der Zee, as van Wieren), 1989
Rhapsody of Love (Cartland), 1977
Rhiannon (Gellis), 1982
Rhona Keith (Swan), 1910
Rhys, Madoc series (C. MacLeod, as Craig), from 1980
Rhythm of Flamenco (Hunter, as Chace), 1966
Rib of the Hawk (R. Marshall), 1956
Ribbons and Laces (Ayres), 1924
Ribbons in Her Hair (L. Walker, as Sanders), 1957
Ribs of Death (Aiken), 1967
Rice Dragon (Darrell, as Drummond), 1980
Rich and the Righteous (Van Slyke), 1971
Rich are Different (Howatch), 1977
Rich Are Not Proud (Greig, as Warren), 1942
Rich Earth (Oldfield), 1980
Rich Girl—Charity Girl (M. St. John), 1922
Rich Girl, Poor Girl (Baldwin), 1938
Rich Is Best (Ellis), 1985
Rich Man, Poor Girl (Greig), 1935
Rich Mrs. Burgoyne (Norris), 1912
Rich Radiant Love (Sherwood), 1983
Rich Twin, Poor Twin (Greig), 1940
Richard and the Knights of God (Bennetts), 1970
Richard by Grace of God (Clarke, as Honeyman), 1968
Richard Carvel (Churchill), 1899
Richard Chatterton, V.C. (Ayres), 1915
Richard Temple (O'Brian), 1962
Richest Girl in the World (Coffman), 1967
Richest Woman in Town (Bellamann), 1932
Richmond and Elizabeth (Clarke, as Honeyman), 1970
Richmond Heritage (Sallis), 1977
Riddle of a Lady (Mackinlay), 1955
Ride a Black Horse (M. Pargeter), 1975
Ride a White Dolphin (Maybury), 1971
Ride on Singing (Ritchie), 1964
Ride Out the Storm (Donnelly), 1975
Ride the Blue Riband (Laker), 1977
Ride the Thunder (Dailey), 1981
Ride with Me (Costain), 1944
Riders (J. Cooper), 1985
Riders of the Wind (Thane), 1926
Rides a Hero (Pozzessere, as Graham), 1989
Ridin' High (Mackinlay), 1941
Riding to the Moon (Cartland), 1982
Rifleman Dodd (Forester), 1943
Right Arm (s Vaizey), 1918
Right Grand Girl (M. Howard), 1972

Right Line of Cedric (Duggan), 1961
Right of Possession (Krentz, as Castle), 1981
Right Path (N. Roberts), 1985
Right Time to Love (Kimbrough, as Ashton), 1986
Riley in the Morning (Brown), 1985
Rilla of Ingleside (Montgomery), 1921
Rio d'Oro (Tranter), 1955
Ring (Steel), 1980
Ring for a Fortune (Peake), 1980
Ring for Nurse Raine (Charles), 1962
Ring in a Teacup (Neels), 1978
Ring in the New (Bentley), 1969
Ring o' Roses (Andrews), 1972
Ring of Crystal (Donnelly), 1985
Ring of Fire (Way), 1978
Ring of Hope (Mackinlay), 1965
Ring of Jade (Way), 1972
Ring of Mischief (Summerton), 1965
Ring of Roses (Trask), 1940
Ring on Her Finger (Burchell), 1953
Ring the Bell Softly (Bennetts), 1978
Ring Tree (Bloom), 1964
Ring Without Romance (Greig, as Ames), 1940
Ringed Castle (Dunnett), 1971
Ripening Vine (Sinclair, as Clare), 1982
Rise of an Eagle (Way), 1988
Rise of Henry Morcar (Bentley), 1946
Rising Family series (Sallis), from 1984
Rising of the Lark (Ruck), 1951
Rising Star (K. Thorpe), 1969
Risk Worth Taking (Seidel), 1983
Risky Business (N. Roberts), 1986
Rites of Passage (Golding), 1980
Rival Beauties (M. St. John), 1907
Rival Doctors (Seifert), 1967
Rival Heiresses (Garvice, as Hart)
Rival Sisters (Reid), 1970
Rivals (J. Cooper), 1988
Rivals (Dailey), 1989
Rivals (Nicole, as McKay), 1985
Rivals at School—Rivals Through Life! (M. St. John), 1926
Riven Realm (Tranter), 1984
River (Godden), 1946
River and Wilderness (Worboys, as Eyre), 1967
River Is Down (L. Walker), 1967
River Lady (Deveraux), 1985
River Lodge (Cadell), 1949
River Lord, (K. Thorpe), 1977
River Nurse (Dingwell), 1962
River of Love (Cartland), 1981
River Road (Keyes), 1945
River Room (Weale), 1978
River Voices (Ebel), 1976
Rivers of Damascus (s Byrne), 1931
Rivers of Glory (F. Mason), 1942
Rivertown (J. Roberts), 1972
Rivet in Grandfather's Neck (Cabell), 1915
Riviera Romance (Lewty), 1984
Road (Deeping), 1931
Road Boss (Dingwell), 1976
Road of the Gods (Paterson), 1930
Road Royal (Oman), 1924
Road That Bends (Ayres), 1916
Road Through the Wall (Jackson), 1948
Road to Bithynia (Slaughter), 1951
Road to Damascus (Swan), 1937

Road to Gafsa (Stratton), 1976
Road to Nowhere (Ogilvie), 1983
Road to Paradise Island (Holt), 1985
Road to Revelation (Lofts), 1941
Road to Samarcand (O'Brian), 1954
Road to the Border (Ashton), 1974
Road to Understanding (E. Porter), 1917
Road to Yesterday (s Montgomery), 1974
Roads to Liberty (F. Mason), 1972
Roadway to the Past (J. MacLeod), 1951
Roanoke Hundred (Fletcher), 1948
Roast Beef, Medium (s Ferber), 1913
Robe (Douglas), 1942
Robe of Honor (Cordell), 1960
Robert and Arabella (Winsor), 1986
Robert Martin's Lesson (Swan), 1886
Robert the Bruce series (Tranter), from 1969
Robin and Her Merry People (F. Preston), 1987
Robin in a Cage (Bloom), 1943
Robin the Prodigal (Wynne), 1919
Rochester, The Mad Earl (Holt, as Kellow), 1957
Rochester's Wife (D. Stevenson), 1940
Rochford series (Lorrimer), from 1981
Rock (Masters), 1970
Rock and Sand (Jacob), 1926
Rock Pine (Muskett), 1952
Rocklitz (Bowen, as Preedy), 1930
Rocks of Arachenza (Ashton), 1973
Rocks of Valpré (Dell), 1913
Rocks under Shining Water (Donnelly), 1973
Rococo (Bowen), 1921
Rodney Stone (Doyle), 1896
Roger Marcham's Ward (s Swan), 1892
Roger Sudden (Raddall), 1944
Rogue (Dailey), 1980
Rogue Cavalier (R. Marshall), 1955
Rogue Gentleman (E. Marshall), 1963
Rogue Herries (Walpole), 1930
Rogue Roman (Horner), 1965
Rogue's Covenant (S. Thorpe), 1957
Rogue's Harbor (Fletcher), 1964
Rogue's Lady (Blackstock, as Allardyce), 1979
Rogue's March (Cordell), 1981
Rogue's Mistress (Gluyas), 1977
Rolande (Darcy), 1978
Roll River (Boyd), 1935
Roman series (Hardy), from 1957
Roman Affair (R. Lindsay), 1976
Roman Cavalier (D. Murray), 1958
Roman Summer (Arbor), 1973
Roman Wall (Bryher), 1954
Romance (Ford), 1903
Romance and Nurse Margaret (Bloom, as Burns), 1972
Romance at Hillyard House (Norris), 1948
Romance at Wrecker's End (Charles, as Lance), 1976
Romance for Rose (Charles, as Tempest), 1959
Romance for Sale (Greig, as Ames), 1934
Romance in Glenmore Street (I. Preston), 1974
Romance in Two Keys (Ruck), 1955
Romance Is Always Young (Elsna, as Snow), 1957
Romance Is Mine (Bloom, as Burns), 1941
Romance of a Film Star (Ruck), 1956
Romance of a Rogue (Ayres), 1923
Romance of Atlantic (Caldwell), 1976
Romance of Charles Dickens (Bloom), 1960
Romance of Dr. Dinah (Bloom, as Essex), 1967

Romance of Enola (Libbey), 1893
Romance of Jenny W.R.E.N. (Bloom, as Burns), 1944
Romance of Rosy Ridge (Kantor), 1937
Romance of Summer (Bloom, as Essex), 1959
Romance of Two Worlds (Corelli), 1886
Romance on a Cruise (Greig), 1935
Romance on Ice (Charles, as Tempest), 1942
Romance on the Rhine (Lee), 1974
Romance Royal (Ruck), 1937
Romantic Afterthought (Ruck), 1959
Romantic Assignment (Lee), 1974
Romantic Assignment (McElfresh), 1961
Romantic Cottage Hospital (Bloom, as Burns), 1967
Romantic Frenchman (Gibbs), 1967
Romantic Fugitive (Bloom, as Burns), 1943
Romantic Intruder (Bloom, as Burns), 1952
Romantic Journey (Buckingham), 1968
Romantic Lady (s Arlen), 1921
Romantic Lady (I. Roberts, as Rowland), 1981
Romantic Lady (S. Thorpe), 1960
Romantic Melody (Farnes), 1938
Romantic Prince (Sabatini), 1929
Romantic Rivals (Courtney), 1980
Romantic Spirit (Finley), 1973
Romantic Summer Sea (Bloom, as Burns), 1956
Romantic Theatre Sister (Bloom, as Essex), 1965
Romantic Touch (Charles, as Chandos), 1957
Romantic Widow (Chappell), 1978
Romantics (s Rinehart), 1929
Romany (E. Smoth), 1935
Romany Curse (Daniels, as Somers), 1971
Romany Magic (Harrod-Eagles, as Woodhouse), 1977
Romany Rebel (F. Stevenson, as Faire), 1979
Romany Sister (Ponsonby, as Rybot), 1960
Rome for Sale (J. Lindsay), 1934
Rome Haul (Edmonds), 1929
Romeo in Moon Village (McCutcheon), 1925
Romula, The Dedicated (Kimbrough), 1981
Ronald Lindsay (Wynne), 1904
Room (Stern), 1922
Room in the Tower (Blackmore), 1972
Room with Dark Mirrors (V. Johnston), 1975
Room Without a Door (Manley-Tucker), 1970
Roomates (Lee), 1976
Roomful of Roses (Palmer), 1984
Rooms at Mrs. Oliver's (Holt, as Kellow), 1953
Rooney (Cookson), 1957
Root and Branch (Tranter), 1948
Rooted in Dishonour (Mather), 1978
Roots (Jacob), 1931
Rope Dancer (Gellis), 1986
Roper's Row (Deeping), 1929
Rosa Mundi (s Dell), 1921
Rosabelle Shaw (D. Stevenson), 1967
Rosalie's Career (Baldwin), 1928
Rosalind Comes Home (Summers), 1968
Rosary (Barclay), 1909
Rose and the Thorn (Farnes), 1968
Rose and the Yew Tree (Westmacott), 1948
Rose Anstey (R. Fraser), 1930
Rose Domino (Walsh), 1981
Rose for Ana Maria (Yerby), 1976
Rose for Virtue (Lofts), 1971
Rose from Lucifer (Hampson), 1979
Rose Galbraith (G. Hill), 1940
Rose in Heather (Ebel), 1978

Rose in May (Clarke), 1984
Rose in the Bud (Barrie), 1966
Rose in the Rind (McCutcheon), 1910
Rose in Winter (Woodiwiss), 1983
Rose Island (I. Roberts, as Rowland), 1969
Rose of Rapture (Brandewyne), 1984
Rose o' the Sea (Barcynska), 1920
Rose of the Dawn (Dell), 1917
Rose of Glenconnel (MacGill), 1916
Rose of Hever (M. Peters), 1969
Rose of Life (Albanesi, as Rowlands), 1912
Rose of the Desert (R. Lane), 1967
Rose of the World (Norris), 1924
Rose of Yesterday (Albanesi), 1908
Rose Princess (Charles, as Lance), 1979
Rose, Rose, Where Are You? (Ellerbeck), 1978
Rose Sweetman (Bloom), 1933
Rose Timson (Steen), 1946
Roseanne (Albanesi), 1922
Rosebud and Stardust (Bloom, as Burns), 1951
Rose-Coloured Thread (Vaizey), 1898
Rose-Grower (Stubbs), 1962
Roseheath (Maybury, as Troy), 1969
Roselynde series (Gellis), from 1978
Rosemary (C.N. and A.M. Williamson),1909
Rosemary—For Forgetting (Ayres), 1941
Rosemary for Remembrance (I. Preston), 1962
Rosemary for Remembrance (Sallis), 1987
Rosemary in Search of a Father (C.N. and A.M. Williamson), 1906
Rosemary Tree (Goudge), 1956
Roses and Champagne (Neels), 1983
Roses for Breakfast (Grimstead), 1970
Roses for Christmas (Neels), 1975
Roses for the Bride (Grimstead, as Manning), 1962
Roses from a Haunted Garden (Webb), 1971
Roses in the Snow (Hoy), 1936
Rose's Last Summer (Millar), 1952
Roses round the Door (Beresford), 1965
Rosevean (Bromige), 1962
Rose-Walled Castle (Danbury), 1959
Rosewood Box (Burchell), 1970
Ross, Dr. Esmond series (Dwyer-Joyce), from 1966
Ross Inheritance (Stratton, as Gillen), 1969
Ross of Silver Ridge (Westwood), 1975
Rough Diamond (B.Hastings), 1982
Rough Diamond Lover (R. Lindsay), 1978
Rough Seas to Sunrise (Greig, as Ames), 1956
Rough Shooting (s Wren), 1938
Rough Weather (Bromige), 1972
Rough Wooing (Tranter), 1986
Round Dozen (Cadell), 1978
Round Tower (Cookson), 1968
Rouseabout Girl (Bevan), 1983
Rowan Family series (M. Peters, as Darby), 1982
Rowan Head (Ogilvie), 1949
Rowan Tree (J. MacLeod), 1943
Rowleston (Riefe), 1976
Royal Academy (D. Murray), 1950
Royal Affair (K. Thorpe), 1976
Royal Box (Keyes), 1954
Royal Deputy (Elsna, as Lancaster), 1957
Royal Dynasty series (Gellis), from 1981
Royal Escape (Heyer), 1938
Royal Escape (M. Peters), 1972
Royal Flash (G. Fraser), 1970

Royal Flush (Irwin), 1932
Royal Griffin (Dymoke), 1978
Royal Intrigue (Anthony), 1954
Royal Pledge (Cartland), 1970
Royal Punishment (Cartland), 1984
Royal Purple (Barrie), 1962
Royal Purple (Ponsonby), 1954
Royal Regiment (Frankau), 1938
Royal Revels (J. Smith), 1985
Royal Road to Fotheringay (Holt, as Plaidy), 1955
Royal Signet (Garvice)
Royal Slave (J. Fitzgerald), 1978
Royal Summer (Coffman, as Stanfield), 1986
Royal Summons (Cadell), 1973
Royal Swords at Agincourt (Bennetts), 1971
Royal Traitor (Wynne), 1927
Royal William (Leslie), 1940
Ruaig Inheritance (J. MacLeod), 1978
Ruan (Bryher), 1960
Rubber Princess (Burgin), 1919
Rubies (Beck, as Moresby), 1927
Rubies for My Love (Farnes), 1969
Ruby (Bennetts), 1984
Ruby (Delmar), 1956
Ruby Heart (J. Roberts, as Danton), 1980
Rueful Mating (Stern), 1933
Rufus on the Rebound (s Ruck), 1918
Rugged Path (Garvice), 1908
Ruinous Face (s Hewlett), 1909
Rule Britannia (du Maurier), 1972
Rules of the Game (Chase), 1980
Rules of the Game (N. Roberts), 1984
Ruling Passion (Swan), 1920
Rum Week (Tranter), 1954
Run a Wild Horse (Donnelly), 1987
Run Away from Love (J. MacLeod), 1939
Run Away from Love (Woodward, as Richmond), 1974
Run for His Money (Wynne), 1913
Run for Your Love (Peake), 1978
Run from the Wind (Stratton), 1974
Run, Sara, Run (Worboys), 1981
Run Scared (Eberhart), 1963
Runaway (Norris), 1939
Runaway Bride (Hodge), 1975
Runaway Bride (Hoy), 1939
Runaway Bride (Stratton, as Gillen), 1972
Runaway Bride (Walsh), 1984
Runaway Daughter (s Swan), 1898
Runaway from Love (R. Randall), 1956
Runaway Girl (L. Walker), 1975
Runaway Heart (Cartland, as McCorquodale), 1961
Runaway Lovers (Ruck), 1963
Runaway Nurse (Webb, as Hamill), 1955
Runaway Star (Cartland), 1978
Runaway Visitors (Farnes), 1973
Runaways (Lorrimer, as Robins), 1962
Running Away (C. Allen), 1977
Running Free (s Barcynska), 1929
Running of the Tide (Forbes), 1948
Running Thursday (P. Hastings), 1980
Rupert of Hentzau (Hope), 1898
Russet Jacket (Barcynska), 1924
Rust of Rome (Deeping), 1910
Rustic Vineyard (Shoesmith), 1982
Rustle of Bamboo (Blair, as Conway), 1957
Rustle of Spring (Trask), 1936
Ruth, The Unsuspecting (Kimbrough), 1977

Rutherford, Justin series (Ley), from 1984
Ruthless Rake (Cartland), 1974
Ruth's Romance (Albanesi, as Rowlands), 1913

S.O.S. Queenie (s Barcynska, as Sandys), 1928
Sable for the Count (P. Hill), 1985
Sable Hunter (Manners), 1977
Sabre Family series (M. Peters, as Darby), from 1985
Sabrina (Polland), 1979
Sac Prairie series (Derleth), from 1937
Sackcloth into Silk (Deeping), 1935
Sacked City (Bowen, as Preedy), 1949
Sacred Bullock (s de la Roche), 1939
Sacred Sins (N. Roberts), 1987
Sacrifice (Melville, as Betteridge), 1973
Sacrifice to Art (Garvice), 1908
Sadhu on the Mountain Peak (McCutchan, as MacNeil), 1971
Safari for Seven (Muskett), 1952
Safari South (K. Thorpe), 1976
Safe at Last (Cartland), 1985
Safe Bridge (Keyes), 1934
Safe Custody (Yates), 1932
Safety for My Love (Elsna, as Conway), 1963
Safety-Curtain (s Dell), 1917
Saffron (Fitzgerald, as Watson), 1972
Saffron Sky (Hunter, as Chace), 1968
Saffron Summer (Summerton), 1974
Saffroned Bridesails (Jacob, as Gray), 1928
Saga at Forty (Cartland), 1937
Saga of the Sea (Sabatini), 1953
Sail a Jeweled Ship (Laker), 1971
Sailor on Horseback (Stone), 1939
Sailor's Love (Bloom, as Essex), 1961
Sailor's Return (Garnett), 1925
Saint and the Sinner (Cartland), 1977
St. Julian's Day (Norway, as Norton), 1965
St. Luke's Little Summer (Norway, as Norton), 1964
St. Martha's Hospital series (Andrews), from 1979
St. Martin's Summer (Rafael Sabatini), 1909
Saint or Satyr? (s Glyn), 1933
Saint or Sinner? (Holt, as Burford), 1951
St. Thomas's Eve (Holt, as Plaidy), 1954
St. Veda's (Swan), 1889
Saint-Germain, Count Ragoczy series (Yarbro), from 1978
Saints and Strangers (s Carter), 1986
Salamanca Drum (Eden), 1977
Salamander (J. Fitzgerald), 1981
Sally (Chesney, as Tremaine), 1982
Sally All-Smiles (M. St. John), 1921
Sally Gets Married (Albanesi), 1927
Sally in a Service Flat (Grundy), 1934
Sally in Her Alley (Albanesi), 1925
Sally in Our Alley (M. St. John), 1914
Sally in the Sunshine (Hoy), 1937
Sally of Sloper's (Barcynska, as Sandys), 1930
Sally Scarth (Jacob), 1940
Sally Serene (Barcynska, as Sandys), 1924
Sally's Sweetheart (Burgin), 1923
Salt Harbor (Greig, as Warren), 1953
Salt of Life (Vaizey), 1915
Salt of the Earth (Ayres), 1946
Salute Me Darling (Greig), 1942
Salute to Adventurers (Buchan), 1915
Sam Benedict (Lee), 1963
Samantha (Eden), 1960
Samaritan's Hospital (Stuart, as A. Stuart), 1965

Same Last Name (Seidel), 1983
Sample of Prejudice (Garvice), 1908
Sanchez Tradition (Mather), 1971
Sanctuary for Louise (Marsh), 1983
Sanctuary in the Desert (Ashton), 1976
Sand Against the Wind (Marsh), 1973
Sand Rose (Summerton), 1969
Sandals for My Feet (P. Hastings), 1960
Sandflower (Arbor), 1959
Sands, Inspector series (Millar), from 1942
Sands of Desire (Woodward, as Davis), 1970
Sands of Lamanna (Saunders, as Innes), 1975
Sands of Malibu (Morgan), 1982
Sandstorm (Mather), 1980
Sandy (I. Roberts, as Harle), 1967
Sangaree (Slaughter), 1948
Sangor Hospital Story (Bloom, as Essex), 1963
Sangreal (M. Peters, as Darby), 1984
Sanguinet series (Veryan), from 1981
Sanity Jane (Barcynska), 1919
Santa Ana Wind (Van Slyke, as Ashton), 1974
Santa Barbara series (Masefield), from 1924
Santiago Road (Horner), 1967
Sapphire (Bennetts), 1985
Sapphire in the Sand (Lorrimer, as Robins), 1968
Sapphire Lightning (F. Preston), 1988
Sapphires in Siam (Cartland), 1987
Sara (Cleeve), 1976
Sara Dane (Gaskin), 1955
Sara Gay series (R. Lindsay, as Scott)
Sara Steps In (Inglis), 1947
Saraband for Sara (M. Peters, as Grey), 1984
Saraband for Two Sisters (Holt, as Carr), 1976
Saracen Blade (Yerby), 1952
Sarah (Seger), 1987
Sarah Morris Remembers (D. Stevenson), 1967
Sarah's Child series (L. Howard), from 1985
Sarah's Cottage (D. Stevenson), 1968
Sarah's Story (Hardwick), 1973
Saratoga (Daniels), 1981
Saratoga Trunk (Ferber), 1941
Sard Harker (Masefield), 1924
Sargasso Sea (s Byrne), 1932
Sarina (Rivers), 1983
Sassy (Williams), 1977
Satan and the Nymph (Hampson), 1976
Satan Never Sleeps (Buck), 1952
Satan Took a Bride (Winspear), 1975
Satan's Circus (s E. Smith), 1932
Satan's Coast (Lee), 1969
Satan's Sunset (Hufford), 1977
Satin and Steele (F. Preston, as Conlee), 1982
Satin for the Bride (Dingwell, as Starr), 1968
Satin Ice (Johansen), 1988
Satin Straps (Greig), 1929
Saturday's Child (Beresford), 1968
Saturday's Child (Neels), 1972
Saturday's Child (Norris), 1914
Savage Aristocrat (R. Lindsay, as Leigh), 1978
Savage Beauty (Mather), 1973
Savage Conquest (Taylor), 1985
Savage Ecstasy (Taylor), 1981
Savage Eden (Gluyas), 1976
Savage Family series (Masters), from 1951
Savage Land (Dailey), 1974
Savage Marquess (Chesney), 1988

Savage Moon (Saunders, as Summers), 1982
Savage Oaks (Ellis), 1977
Savage Place (Slaughter), 1964
Savage Possession (M. Pargeter), 1979
Savage Sanctuary (Donnelly), 1979
Savage Sands (Nicole, as Nicholson), 1978
Savage Surrender (Lamb), 1980
Savage Surrender (N. Peters), 1977
Savage Warriors (Treece), 1959
Savage Web (M. Peters, as Whitby), 1982
Savanna (Giles), 1961
Savannah Purchase (Hodge), 1971
Saved by Love (Cartland), 1987
Saville, Peggy series (Vaizey), from 1900
Saving Face (s Lofts), 1983
Sawdust (Cartland), 1926
Sawdust and Dreams (Marsh), 1980
Sawdust and Spangles (Collin), 1972
Sawdust Season (K. Thorpe), 1972
Saxon's Folly (Elsna), 1966
Saxon's Lady (Krentz, as James), 1987
Say Yes, Samantha (Cartland), 1975
Say You're Sorry (Charles, as Tempest), 1939
Scales of Love (Grimstead), 1957
Scandalous (Lamb), 1984
Scandalous Lady (Sebastian, as Gladstone), 1978
Scandalous Lady Robin (S. Thorpe), 1950
Scandalous Season (Pykare), 1979
Scapegoat (Caine), 1891
Scapegoat (du Maurier), 1957
Scapegrace (S. Thorpe), 1971
Scar (Ayres), 1920
Scaramouche (Sabatini), 1921
Scarecrow Lover (P. Hastings), 1960
Scarf of Flame (May), 1979
Scarlet Banners of Love (Carnegie), 1968
Scarlet Cloak (Holt, as Tate), 1957
Scarlet Cord (Slaughter), 1956
Scarlet Domino (S. Thorpe), 1970
Scarlet Feather (Grant), 1945
Scarlet Heels (Muskett), 1940
Scarlet Kisses (Blake), 1981
Scarlet Mantle (Hardy), 1978
Scarlet Night (Davis), 1980
Scarlet Pimpernel series (Orczy), from 1905
Scarlet Poppies (J. Roberts), 1983
Scarlet Princess (Nicole), 1984
Scarlet Rebel (Saunders), 1985
Scarlet Runner (s C. and M. Williamson), 1908
Scarlet Secrets (J. Roberts, as Radcliffe), 1977
Scarlet Seed (E. Pargeter), 1963
Scarlet Shadows (Darrell, as Drummond), 1978
Scarlet Woman (J. Fitzgerald), 1979
Scarlet Woman (M. Pargeter), 1986
Scarlet Women (J. Fitzgerald, as de Vere), 1969
Scattering of Daisies (Sallis), 1984
Scent of Cloves (Lofts), 1957
Scent of Jasmine (Saunders, as Innes), 1982
Scent of Juniper (J. MacLeod), 1971
Scent of Lilac (M. Peters, as Law), 1988
Scent of Lilacs (Lorin, as Hohl), 1986
Scent of Sandalwood (Ashton), 1974
Scent of Water (Goudge), 1963
Scented Danger (Cowen), 1966
Scented Hills (R. Lane), 1970
Scented Island (Danbury), 1976

Scented Sword (Nicole, as York), 1980
Sceptre and the Rose (Leslie), 1967
School Against Her! (M. St. John), 1921
School for Hearts (Albanesi, as Rowlands), 1934
Schoolgirl Bride (M. St. John), 1913
Schoolmaster's Daughters (Eden), 1948
Scorched Wings (Ashton), 1972
Scorched-Wood People (Wiebe), 1977
Scorned by "His" Mother (M. St. John) 1921
Scorpion God (s Golding), 1971
Scorpion's Dance (Mather), 1978
Scots Never Forget (Cartland), 1984
Scotswoman (Fletcher), 1955
Scott Pelham's Princess (Loring), 1958
Scottish Soldier (Stuart, as Allen), 1965
Screen Lover (Greig), 1969
Screen Test for Laurel (Daniels), 1967
Scribblers' Club (Garvice), 1909
Scudders (Bacheller), 1923
Sculptor's Wooing (Garvice)
Sea series (Golding), from 1980
Sea and the Sand (Nicole), 1986
Sea Ants (s Cato), 1964
Sea Beggars (C. Holland), 1982
Sea Captain (Bailey), 1913
Sea Change (J. MacLeod, as Airlie), 1965
Sea Could Tell (A. Williamson), 1904
Sea Fret (Bloom), 1953
Sea Gate (Seger), 1981
Sea Gull (Norris), 1927
Sea Gypsy (F. Michaels), 1980
Sea House (Summerton), 1961
Sea Is So Wide (Eaton), 1943
Sea Jade (I. Roberts), 1987
Sea Jade (Whitney), 1964
Sea King's Daughter (B. Michaels), 1975
Sea Maiden (I. Roberts, as Carr), 1965
Sea of Zanj (R. Lane), 1969
Sea Urchins (Gibbs), 1968
Sea 'venture (F. Mason), 1961
Sea Waif (Weale), 1967
Sea Without a Haven (Broster), 1941
Seacage (Burford), 1979
Seagull Crag (Roby, as Welles), 1977
Seagull's Cry (Robins), 1957
Sea-Hawk (Sabatini), 1915
Sealed Knot (J. Lane), 1952
Sealed Lips (Robins), 1924
Search (G. Hill), 1919
Search at Brighton (Ley), 1971
Search for a Background (Jacob), 1960
Search for a New Dawn (Delinsky, as Douglass), 1982
Search for Love (Cartland), 1937
Search for Love (N. Roberts), 1982
Search for the King (Vidal), 1950
Search for the Shadows (B. Michaels), 1987
Search for Willie (W. Roberts), 1980
Search for Yesterday (J. MacLeod), 1978
Search the Shadows (B. Michaels), 1988
Seas of Fortune (Nicole, as McKay), 1984
Season for Change (Way), 1981
Season for Love (Pozzessere, as Graham), 1983
Season for Singing (Ritchie), 1979
Season of Enchantment (Farnes), 1956
Season of Evil (Lee), 1965
Season of Forgetfulness (Summers), 1983

Season of Mist (Mather), 1982
Season of Passion (Steel), 1979
Season of Storm (Sellers), 1983
Season of Swans (De Blasis), 1989
Sea-Song (Manners, as Marshall), 1973
Season's Greetings (Elsna), 1954
Seasons Hereafter (Ogilvie), 1966
Seasons of the Heart (Freeman), 1986
Seats of the Mighty (Harwood), 1956
Second Best (Robins), 1931
Second Best Wife (Hunter, as Chace), 1978
Second Chance (Dingwell), 1956
Second Empire series (Gavin), from 1957
Second Generation (Fast), 1978
Second Hand Wife (Norris), 1932
Second Harvest (Jacob), 1954
Second Honeymoon (Ayres), 1918
Second Honeymoon (Charles), 1970
Second Husband (M. St. John), 1923
Second Key (Lowndes), 1936
Second Latchkey (C. and A. Williamson), 1920
Second Lesson (Lady Miles), 1936
Second Love (Lorrimer, as Robins), 1964
Second Marriage (Burchell), 1971
Second Marriage (Robins), 1951
Second Mrs. Rivers (Bromige), 1960
Second Nature (N. Roberts), 1986
Second Romance (Lee), 1974
Second Season (Lee), 1973
Second Sighter's Daughter (Burgin), 1913
Second Spring (R. Lane), 1980
Second String (Hope), 1910
Second Thoughts (Elsna, as Snow), 1941
Second Time (Dailey), 1982
Second Tomorrow (Hampson), 1980
Second Wife (Krentz, as James), 1986
Second Winning (Maybury), 1933
Second World War series (Gavin), from 1976
Second Youth (Deeping), 1919
Second-Best Bride (Rome), 1981
Secondhand Bride (Westwood), 1983
Secret Affair (Peake), 1980
Secret Armour (Andrews), 1955
Secret Chronicle (J. Lane), 1977
Secret City (Walpole), 1919
Secret Fear (Cartland), 1970
Secret Fire (Lindsey), 1987
Secret Fire (Winspear), 1984
Secret for a Nightingale (Holt), 1986
Secret Gold (A. Williamson), 1925
Secret Harbour (Cartland), 1982
Secret Heart (Cartland), 1970
Secret Heart (Inglis), 1959
Secret Heiress (Farnes), 1956
Secret History (C. and A. Williamson), 1915
Secret Hour (Robins), 1932
Secret in Her Life (Mackinlay), 1958
Secret Information (Hichens), 1938
Secret Intimacy (Lamb), 1983
Secret Island (Hodge), 1985
Secret Lives (Elsna, as Lancaster), 1960
Secret Lives of the Nurses (W. Roberts), 1975
Secret Love (Buckingham, as John), 1986
Secret Love of Nurse Wilson (I. Preston), 1966
Secret Lover (Bloom), 1930
Secret Marriage (Blair, as Brett), 1947

Secret Marriage (Hunter, as Chace), 1966
Secret Marriage (Norris), 1936
Secret Memoirs of Lord Byron (Nicole), 1978
Secret of Chateau Kendall (Ellis, as Richard), 1967
Secret of Chateau Laval (Ellis, as Marvin), 1973
Secret of Dunston Mere (s Swan), 1898
Secret of Love (Finley), 1987
Secret of Quarry House (Lorrimer), 1976
Secret of Seven Oaks (Coulson), 1972
Secret of Shower Tree (Coffman), 1966
Secret of Skye (Swan), 1940
Secret of the Caves (Wynne), 1945
Secret of the Ghostly Shroud (Buckingham), 1969
Secret of the Glen (Cartland), 1976
Secret of the Mosque (Cartland), 1986
Secret of the Rose (Maybury), 1941
Secret of the Stone (Delinsky), 1985
Secret of the Tower (Hope), 1919
Secret of the Villa Como (Ellis, as Marvin), 1966
Secret of the Zenana (Wynne), 1913
Secret of Weir House (Cowen), 1975
Secret Panel (Swan), 1888
Secret Pleasure (Kidd), 1985
Secret Pool (Neels), 1986
Secret Power (Corelli), 1921
Secret Sanctuary (Deeping), 1923
Secret Services (s Frankau), 1934
Secret Sins (Blake), 1980
Secret Sorrow (van der Zee), 1981
Secret Splendor (Brown, as St. Claire), 1983
Secret to Tell (Pilcher), 1955
Secret Valentine (Browning), 1983
Secret Woman (Holt), 1970
Secretary Wife (R. Lindsay), 1976
Secrets (Cartland), 1985
Secrets (Lamb, as Holland), 1983
Secrets (Steel), 1985
Secrets of Cromwell Crossing (Winston), 1965
Secrets of Hillyard House (Norris), 1947
Secrets of the Heart (s Buck), 1976
Secrets of the Marshbanks (Norris), 1940
Secrets of the Shop! (M. St. John), 1923
Secrets to Keep (Lamb, as Holland), 1980
Secret-Service Operator (Chambers), 1934
Security Man (Browning), 1986
Seduction (Lamb), 1980
Seduction by Design (Brown, as St. Claire), 1983
Seduction of Jason (F. Preston), 1983
Seductive Stranger (Lamb), 1989
See My Shining Palace (Elsna), 1942
See No Evil (Lorrimer, as Robins), 1945
See the Bright Morning (M. Lewis), 1965
Seed Was Kind (Macardle), 1944
Seeds of Enchantment (Frankau), 1921
Seeds of Rebellion (Nicole), 1984
Seeds of Suspicion (Summerton, as Roffman), 1968
Seeing Life! (s Bowen), 1923
Seeker of Dreams (Saunders, as Innes), 1983
Seekers (Jakes), 1975
Seen by Candlelight (Mather), 1974
Seen Unknown . . . (Jacob), 1931
See-Saw (Stern), 1914
Seized by Love (S. Johnson), 1979
Self-Appointed Saint (Erskine-Lindop), 1975
Self-Lovers (Nicole), 1968
Self-Made Woman (Baldwin), 1932

Selina's Love Story (Albanesi, as Rowlands), n.d.
Seminar in Evil (Winston), 1972
Senator Marlowe's Daughter (Keyes), 1933
Send for Miss Marshall (Greig), 1959
Send No Flowers (Brown), 1984
Senhouse, John Maxwell series (Hewlett), from 1908
Sensation (Lamb), 1979
Sense of Belonging (Peake), 1974
Sensuous Angel (Possezzere, as Graham), 1985
Sensuous Burgundy (Delinsky, as Drake), 1981
Sentimental Family (Bloom), 1951
Sentimental Journey (Dailey), 1979
Sentimental Spy (Ley), 1977
Separate Bedrooms (Weale), 1979
Separate Beds (Spencer), 1985
Separate Cabins (Dailey), 1983
Separation (Robins), 1946
Sepoy Mutiny (Stuart, as V. A. Stuart), 1973
September in Paris (Weale, as Blake), 1963
September Morning (Palmer), 1982
September September (Foote), 1978
September Street (Dingwell), 1969
September's Girl (Grimstead), 1969
Sequel (Lowell), 1986
Sequel to Youth (J. MacLeod), 1938
Sequence 1905–1912 (Glyn), 1913
Serena (Chappell), 1980
Serenade of Santa Rose (Danbury), 1970
Serenade on a Spanish Guitar (Stuart, as Allen),
    1956
Serena's Magic (Pozzessere, as Graham), 1984
Sergeant Lamb of the Ninth (Graves), 1940
Sergeant Lamb's America (Graves), 1940
Sergeant Major's Daughter (Walsh), 1977
Serpent and the Staff (Yerby), 1958
Serpent in Eden (Dymoke), 1973
Serpent in Eden (Farnes), 1971
Serpent in Paradise (Krentz, as James), 1983
Serpent in the Garden (Dell), 1938
Serpent of Satan (Cartland), 1979
Serpent's Tooth (Deeping), 1956
Serpent's Tooth (Manners, as Lamont), 1983
Servant of the Public (Hope), 1905
Set Her on a Throne (Westcott), 1972
Set in Silver (C. N. and A. M. Williamson), 1909
Set Me Free (Robins), 1937
Set the Stars Alight (Robins), 1941
Set with Green Herbs (Bowen), 1933
Seth Newcome's Wife (s Swan), 1898
Seton's Wife (Chappell), 1975
Settled Out of Court (Burgin), 1898
Settlers (Stuart, as Long), 1980
Seven Days from Midnight (R. Randall), 1965
Seven Days in New Crete (Graves), 1949
Seven Deadly Sins (s Bowen), 1926
Seven Dials (Rayner), 1987
Seven for St. Crispin's Day (M. Peters), 1971
Seven Lonely Years (Chard), 1980
Seven Loves (Lorrimer, as Robins), 1962
Seven Mansions (Cleeve), 1980
Seven Men Came Back (Deeping), 1934
Seven Men of Gascony (Delderfield), 1949
Seven of Magpies (D. Smith), 1970
Seven Red Roses (Mackinlay), 1959
Seven Seats to the Moon (Armstrong), 1969
Seven Sleepers (Norway), 1964
Seven Streams (Deeping), 1905

Seven Tears for Apollo (Whitney), 1963
Seven Trees (s E. Smith)
Seventeen Widows of Sans Souce (Armstrong), 1959
Seventeenth Stair (Laker, as Paul), 1975
Seventh Commandment (Glyn)
Seventh Hour (G. Hill), 1939
Seventh Sinner (B. Michaels, as Peters), 1972
Seventy Times Seven (Stern), 1957
Severed Crown (J. Lane), 1972
Sevier Secret (Daniels), 1967
Sew a Fine Seam (M. Howard), 1954
Sex War (Lamb), 1983
Shabby Summer (Deeping), 1939
Shackles (Macbeth), 1926
Shade of Darkness (Elsna), 1954
Shade of the Palms (R. Lindsay, as Leigh), 1974
Shades of Gray (Hooper), 1988
Shadow (s Farnol), 1929
Shadow Across My Heart (Greig, as Ames), 1948
Shadow and Flame (J. Lindsay, as Preston), 1936
Shadow Behind the Curtain (V. Johnston), 1985
Shadow Between (Hampson), 1977
Shadow Box (Coffman), 1966
Shadow Dance (Way), 1981
Shadow Falls (Atkin), 1954
Shadow Falls (Lorrimer), 1974
Shadow Flies (Macaulay), 1932
Shadow Glen (Daniels), 1965
Shadow in the Glass (Derleth), 1963
Shadow Lawn (Mackinlay), 1934
Shadow Man (s Ayres), 1919
Shadow Market (Muskett), 1938
Shadow Marriage (Elsna, as Conway), 1961
Shadow Marriage (Norris), 1952
Shadow of a Crime (Caine), 1885
Shadow of a Lady (Hodge), 1973
Shadow of a Lion (Edwards), 1972
Shadow of a Man (Daniels), 1975
Shadow of a Past Love (W. Roberts), 1970
Shadow of a Smile (Mackinlay, as Grey), 1968
Shadow of a Stranger (Maybury), 1960
Shadow of a Tudor (M. Peters), 1971
Shadow of a Vow (J. MacLeod), 1941
Shadow of a Witch (Eden, as Paradise), 1962
Shadow of an Unknown Woman (Winston), 1967
Shadow of Apollo (Hampson), 1981
Shadow of Desire (Craven), 1980
Shadow of Evil (Slaughter), 1975
Shadow of Her Life (Garvice), n.d.
Shadow of Love (Stanford), 1980
Shadow of Murder (Blackstock), 1959
Shadow of My Loving (Maybury), 1938
Shadow of Night (Derleth), 1943
Shadow of Palaces (P. Hill), 1955
Shadow of Polperro (Cowen), 1969
Shadow of Samain (Wiat), 1980
Shadow of Sin (Cartland), 1975
Shadow of Suspicion (Farnes), 1972
Shadow of Suspicion (Loring), 1955
Shadow of the Court (Collin), 1967
Shadow of the East (Hull), 1921
Shadow of the Hawk (Forester), 1928
Shadow of the Hawk (Scott), 1941
Shadow of the Hills (Hoy), 1938
Shadow of the Lynx (Holt), 1971
Shadow of the Moon (Kaye), 1957
Shadow of the Peak (Beaty, as Ross), 1985

Shining River (L. Walker, as Sanders), 1954
Shining Windows (Norris), 1935
Shining Years (Loring), 1972
Ship in a Bottle (Bloom), 1962
Ship of Hate (J. Roberts, as Danton), 1977
Ship of the Line (Forester), 1938
Ship of Truth (L. Cooper), 1930
Ship with No Name (Nicole), 1987
Ships Come Home (Barcynska), 1922
Ship's Doctor (Dingwell, as Starr), 1964
Ship's Doctor (Greig), 1966
Ships in the Bay! (Broster), 1931
Ship's Nurse (Stuart, as A. Stuart), 1954
Ships of Youth (Diver), 1931
Ship's Surgeon (Blair, as Conway), 1962
Shirt Front (Blackstock), 1977
Shiver Me a Story (M. Peters, as Whitby), 1982
Shivering Sands (Holt), 1969
Shoal Water (Yates), 1940
Shock Wave (Davis), 1972
Shoes of Fortune (Munro), 1901
Shōgun (Clavell), 1975
Shooting Star (Melville, as Betteridge), 1968
Shop-Girl (C. N. and A. M. Williamson), 1916
Shop-Girl's Revenge (M. St. John, as Cooper), 1914
Shopping for a Husband (Ruck), 1967
Shore Beyond (Swan), 1932
Short Engagement (Lewty), 1978
Short Lease (Elsna, as Lancaster), 1950
Short-Cut to the Stars (Charles, as Tempest), 1949
Shortest Night (Stern), 1931
Shot with Crimson (McCutcheon), 1918
Shoulder the Sky (D. Stevenson), 1951
Shout (s Graves), 1978
Show Boat (Ferber), 1926
Show Me (Dailey), 1976
Show Must Go On (Barcynska, as Sandys), 1936
Showers of Sunlight (Vitek), 1981
Shreds of Circumstances (Macbeth), 1947
Shrewsbury (Weyman), 1898
Shriek in the Midnight Tower (Kimbrough), 1975
Shrine of Fire (I. Roberts), 1970
Shrine of Marigolds (I. Roberts), 1962
Shripney Lady (Laker), 1972
Shroud of Fog (W. Roberts), 1970
Shroud of Silence (Buckingham), 1970
Shrouded Tower (Charles), 1966
Shrouded Walls (Howatch), 1968
Shrouded Way (Caird), 1973
Shrouded Web (Mather), 1973
Sicilian Summer (Ashton), 1980
Siege in the Sun (Eden), 1967
Siege of Krishnapur (Farrell), 1973
Siege Perilous (s Diver), 1924
Sigh No More (Ashton), 1973
Sight Unseen (Erskine-Lindop), 1969
Sight Unseen (Rinehart), 1921
Sign of Love (Cartland), 1977
Sign of the Golden Goose (J. Roberts, as Danton), 1972
Sign of the Ram (Stratton), 1977
Signa's Sweetheart (Garvice), 1910
Signpost Has Four Arms (P. Hastings), 1957
Signpost to Love (Cartland), 1980
Signs and Portents (s Yarbro), 1984
Silas Strong (Bacheller), 1906
Silence Is Golden (Elsna, as Snow), 1958

Silence Is Golden (Lee), 1971
Silence of Herondale (Aiken), 1964
Silence of the Maharajah (Corelli), 1895
Silent Battle (A. Williamson), 1902
Silent Bondage (J. MacLeod), 1940
Silent Captain (Wynne), 1914
Silent Drum (Swanson), 1940
Silent Grow the Guns (s Kantor), 1958
Silent Halls of Ashenden (Daniels), 1973
Silent Lady (Dwyer-Joyce), 1964
Silent Nightingale (Danbury), 1961
Silent Ones (Ogilvie), 1981
Silent Pool (Cowen), 1977
Silent Song (Andrews), 1973
Silent Thunder (R. Randall), 1971
Silent Valley (J. MacLeod), 1953
Silent Walls (Roby), 1974
Silent Watcher (F. Stevenson), 1975
Silhouette in Scarlet (Michaels, as Peters), 1983
Silk Vendetta (Holt), 1987
Silken Barbarity (Winspear), 1988
Silken Bond (Kidd), 1980
Silken Cage (Stratton), 1981
Silken Captive (J. Fitzgerald), 1986
Silken Purse (Mackinlay), 1970
Silken Thunder (F. Preston), 1988
Silken Trap (Lamb), 1979
Silken Web (Brown, as Jordan), 1982
Silky (M. Peters, as Whitby), 1980
Silver Angel (Lindsey), 1988
Silver Answer (Maddocks), 1965
Silver Arrow (Ashton), 1980
Silver Boy (s Elsna), 1936
Silver Bride (Dell), 1932
Silver Cage (Donnelly), 1976
Silver Castle (Buckingham, as Quest), 1978
Silver Chain (Beresford), 1980
Silver Chalice (Costain), 1952
Silver Cord (R. Randall), 1963
Silver Cross (M. Johnston), 1922
Silver Dolphin (V. Johnston), 1979
Silver Dolphin (Weale), 1963
Silver Dragon (J. MacLeod), 1961
Silver Falcon (Anthony), 1977
Silver Fishes (Stratton, as Gillen), 1969
Silver Flame (S. Johnson), 1988
Silver Flame (M. Pargeter), 1983
Silver Fox (Delinsky, as Drake), 1983
Silver Fruit upon Silver Trees (Mather), 1974
Silver Ghost (C. MacLeod), 1987
Silver Jasmine (J. Roberts), 1980
Silver Lady (Saunders, as Innes), 1981
Silver Leopard (F. Mason), 1955
Silver Maiden (Hoy), 1951
Silver Miracles (F. Preston), 1983
Silver Mirror (Gellis), 1989
Silver Mist (Stanford), 1982
Silver Nightingale (S. Thorpe), 1974
Silver Nutmeg (Hunter), 1982
Silver Nutmeg (Lofts), 1947
Silver Orchids (Bloom), 1941
Silver Peaks (Duffield), 1935
Silver Ring (Bloom), 1955
Silver Slave (Winspear), 1972
Silver Snare (Krentz, as James), 1983
Silver Stallion (Cabell), 1926

Silver Stallion (Danbury), 1973
Silver Sty (Seale), 1941
Silver Summer (I. Roberts, as Harle), 1971
Silver Thaw (Neels), 1980
Silver Touch (Laker), 1987
Silver Tree (Britt), 1977
Silver Unicorn (Blackmore), 1977
Silver Veil (Way), 1982
Silver Wedding (Ayres), 1937
Silver Wedding (s Binchy), 1988
Silver Wedding (Dell), 1932
Silver Wings (G. Hill), 1931
Silver Wings, Santiago Blue (Dailey), 1984
Silver Zephyr (Seger), 1984
Silver-Gilt (Muskett), 1935
Silverhill (Whitney), 1967
Silversword (Whitney), 1987
Simon Dale (Hope), 1898
Simon the Coldheart (Heyer), 1925
Simple Case of Ill-Will (Berckman), 1964
Simple Duty (Norway, as Neal), 1966
Simple Savage (Burgin), 1909
Simple Simon (Albanesi), 1907
Sin of Cynara (Winspear), 1976
Sin Was Mine (D. Roberts, as Kane), 1964
Sinbad the Soldier (Wren), 1935
Since First We Met (Charles, as Chandos), 1948
Since Summer (Chappell), 1967
Since We Love (Robins), 1938
Sincerity (Deeping), 1912
Sinews of Love (Cordell), 1965
Sing a Dark Song (W. Roberts), 1972
Sing for Your Supper (Elsna), 1970
Sing Witch, Sing Death (Gellis), 1975
Singapore Grip (Farrell), 1978
Singer Not the Song (Erskine-Lindop), 1953
Singer Passes (Diver), 1934
Singing Heart (Cadell), 1959
Singing in the Wilderness (Hunter, as Chace), 1976
Singing in the Woods (Renier), 1966
Singing Season (Paterson), 1924
Singing Shadows (Eden), 1940
Singing Spears (Thompson), 1982
Singing Swans (Manners), 1975
Singing Uphill (Barcynska, as Sandys), 1940
Singing Waters (Bridge), 1946
Single Rose (Delinsky), 1987
Single to New York (Melville, as Betteridge), 1965
Sinister Abbey (Lee), 1967
Sinister Gardens (W. Roberts), 1972
Sinister Island (Greig, as Ames), 1968
Sinister Melody (Cowen), 1976
Sinister Stone (Winston), 1966
Sinister Touch (Krentz, as Castle), 1986
Sinner, Saint, and Jester (Sabatini), 1954
Sinners in Paradise (Greig, as Ames), 1963
Sins of Herod (Slaughter), 1968
Sins of the Fathers (Howatch), 1980
Sins of the Lion (Motley), 1979
Sioux series (Taylor), from 1981
Sir Boxer (Barcynska, as Sandys), 1934
Sir Devil-May-Care (J. Lane), 1937
Sir Isumbras at the Ford (Broster), 1918
Sir John Dering (Farnol), 1923
Sir Mortimer (M. Johnston), 1904
Sir Nigel (Doyle), 1906

Sir or Madam? (Ruck), 1923
Sir Percy series (Orczy)
Sir Quixote of the Moors (Buchan), 1895
Sir Roderick's Will (s Swan), 1898
Sir Scoundrel (Jakes, as Scotland), 1962
Sir William (Ponsonby), 1978
Siren from the Sea (Pozzessere, as Graham), 1987
Siren Song (Gellis), 1981
Siren's Heart (Albanesi, as Rowlands)
Sirocco (Melville, as Betteridge), 1970
Sirocco (Mather), 1983
Sister Anne (Albanesi), 1908
Sister at Sea (R. Randall), 1960
Sister at Sea (I. Roberts), 1971
Sister Brookes of Bynd's (Norway), 1957
Sister Christine (Inglis), 1953
Sister Julia (I. Roberts, as Rowland), 1972
Sister Loving Heart (Bloom, as Burns), 1971
Sister Margarita (Stuart, as A. Stuart), 1961
Sister Marion's Summer (Grimstead, as Manning), 1965
Sister of the Bride (Reid), 1971
Sister of the Housemaster (Farnes), 1954
Sister on Leave (I. Roberts), 1982
Sister Peters in Amsterdam (Neels), 1969
Sister Pussycat (Dingwell), 1971
Sister Rose's Holiday (Grimstead), 1975
Sister Sue (E. Porter), 1921
Sister Sylvan (Charles, as Chandos), 1962
Sister to a Stranger (Bloom, as Harvey), 1971
Sister to Cinderella (Seale), 1956
Sisters (Ebel, as Goodwin), 1984
Sisters (Elsna, as Conway), 1971
Sisters (P. Hill), 1986
Sisters (Norris), 1919
Sisters and Brothers (Glover), 1984
Sisters and Strangers (Van Slyke), 1978
Sisters in Love (Charles, as Lance), 1960
Sisters in Love (Hardwick), 1979
Sisters of Valcour (Daniels), 1981
Sisters Three (Vaizey), 1900
Six Days (Glyn), 1924
Six Fools and a Fairy (Bloom, as Essex), 1948
Six for Heaven (L. Walker, as Sanders), 1952
Six Impossible Things (Cadell), 1961
Six Passengers for the "Sweet Bird" (Blackstock, as
   Allardyce), 1967
Six Sisters series (Chesney), from 1982
Six Wax Candles (Mackinlay), 1950
Six White Horses (Dailey), 1977
Six-Fingered Stud (Horner), 1975
Six-Horse Hitch (Giles), 1969
Sixpence in Her Shoe (M. Howard), 1950
Sixpenny Ha'penny Duchess (M. St. John), 1917
1649 (J. Lindsay), 1938
Sixth of October (Hichens), 1936
Sixth Wife (Holt, as Plaidy), 1953
Skeleton Key (Winston), 1972
Skin Deep (Hufford), 1978
Skin Deep (N. Roberts), 1989
Skin Deep (K. Thorpe), 1989
Skye Cameron (Whitney), 1957
Skye O'Malley (Small), 1980
Skyscraper (Baldwin), 1931
Skyscraper Hotel (Grimstead, as Manning), 1959
Skyscraper Souls (Baldwin), 1931
Slade (Deeping), 1943

Slanderers (Deeping), 1905
Slave (Hichens), 1899
Slave Lady (J. Fitzgerald, 1980
Slave Masters (Bennetts), 1983
Slave of the Lake (Garvice), 1908
Slave of the Wind (J. MacLeod), 1962
Slave Ship (M. Johnston), 1924
Slaves of Allah (Burgin), 1909
Slaves of Love (Cartland), 1976
Slaves of the Ring (Burgin), 1936
Slave-Woman (Robins), 1934
Sleep in Peace (Bentley), 1938
Sleep in the Woods (Eden), 1960
Sleeping Beauty (Baldwin), 1947
Sleeping Beauty (Ruck), 1936
Sleeping Bride (Eden), 1959
Sleeping Desire (Lamb), 1985
Sleeping Dogs (Grundy), 1924
Sleeping Heiress (Pianka), 1980
Sleeping Sword (Jagger), 1982
Sleeping Tiger (McEvoy), 1983
Sleeping Tiger (Pilcher), 1967
Sleeping Swords (Cartland, as McCorquodale),
   1942
Slender Thread (Bromige), 1985
Slinky Jane (Cookson), 1959
Slither of Silk (May), 1972
Slow Awakening (Cookson, as Marchant), 1976
Slow Heat in Heaven (Brown), 1988
Slower Judas (s Stern), 1929
Small Slice of Summer (Neels), 1975
Small Tawny Cat (Coffman), 1967
Small Wilderness (Summerton), 1959
Smile in the Mirror (Barcynska), 1963
Smile of the Stranger (Aiken), 1978
Smire (Cabell), 1937
Smirt (Cabell), 1934
Smith (Cabell), 1935
Smith (Deeping), 1932
Smith and the Pharaohs (s Haggard), 1920
Smoke and Mirrors (B. Michaels), 1989
Smoke and the Fire (Summers), 1964
Smoke into Flame (Arbor), 1976
Smoke Rings (s Stern), 1923
Smokescreen (Mather), 1982
Smouldering Fire (D. Stevenson), 1936
Smouldering Flame (Mather), 1976
Smuggled Heart (Cartland), 1959
Smuggled Love (D. Smith), 1976
Smuggler's Bride (Laker), 1975
Smuggler's Haunt (Shoesmith), 1978
Smugglers' Moon (S. Thorpe), 1955
Snake and Sword (Wren), 1914
Snake and the Sword (Wren), 1923
Snake in the Grass (Elsna, as Lancaster), 1961
Snake in the Grass (M. St. John, as Cooper), 1922
Snake-Bite (s Hichens), 1919
Snare (Sabatini), 1915
Snare the Wild Heart (Hoy), 1955
Sniper (W. Roberts), 1984
Snow and Roses (L. Cooper), 1976
Snow Blossom, (M. Peters), 1980
Snow Bride (Hilton), 1979
Snow in April (Pilcher), 1972
Snow in Summer (Albanesi), 1932
Snow Kisses (Palmer), 1983
Snow Mountain (Gavin), 1973

Snow Must Return (Robins), 1971
Snow Queen (J. Fitzgerald, as Hamilton), 1978
Snowbound Weekend (Lorin), 1982
Snowfire (Whitney), 1973
So Big (Ferber), 1924
So Bold a Choice (Ponsonby), 1960
So Dear to My Heart (Barrie), 1956
So Dear to Their Hearts (Woodward), 1974
So Deep Suspicion (Gibbs, as Ford), 1950
So Evil My Love (Bowen, as Shearing), 1947
So Fair and Foul a Queen (M. Peters), 1974
So Fair My Love (Elsna, as Snow), 1956
So Fair, So False (Garvice), 1902
So Frail a Thing (Beauclerk), 1940
So Grand (Nicole, as Gray), 1985
So Like a Man (Albanesi, as Rowlands), 1905
So Long a Winter (Donnelly), 1981
So Loved and So Far (Hoy), 1954
So Many Miles (Ayres), 1932
So Many Partings (Spellman), 1983
So Many Tomorrows (Buckingham, as John), 1982
So Many Worlds (Elsna, as Lancaster), 1948
So Merciful a Queen, So Cruel a Woman (Harwood), 1939
So Moses Was Born (Grant), 1952
So Much Good (Frankau), 1928
So Much Love (L. Walker), 1977
So Near so Far (Parkinson), 1981
So Nearly Lost (Garvice), 1902
So Nearly Married (Charles, as Chandos), 1956
So New to Love (Elsna, as Conway), 1955
So Red the Rose (Young), 1934
So Speaks the Heart (Lindsey), 1983
So Sweet a Sin (B. Hastings), 1989
So the Dreams Depart (Holt, as Burford), 1944
So This Is Love (Lorrimer, as Robins), 1954
So Wicked My Desire (Blake), 1979
So Wicked the Heart (Riefe), 1980
So Wild a Heart (V. Johnston, as Jason), 1981
So Young, So Fair (Seifert), 1947
Society Girl (Price), 1935
Soft Talkers (Millar), 1957
Soft Velvet Night (Hampson), 1983
Softly Treads Danger (McEvoy), 1963
Soho Square (Rayner), 1976
Soldier at the Door (E. Pargeter), 1954
Soldier from Virginia (Bowen), 1912
Soldier of Fortune (Palmer), 1985
Soldier of the Legion (C. and A. Williamson), 1914
Soldiers and Lovers (M. Howard), 1973
Soldier's Daughter (Stuart, as A. Stuart), 1954
Soldiers' Daughters Never Cry (Erskine-Lindop), 1948
Soldiers of Misfortune (Wren), 1929
Solitaire (Craven), 1979
Solitary Horseman (Loring), 1927
Solomon, My Son! (Erskine), 1935
Some Brief Folly (Veryan), 1981
Some Day (Ayres), 1935
Some Day My Love (Grimstead, as Manning), 1968
Some Day You'll Love Me (Elsna, as Snow), 1960
Some Die in Their Beds (Roby), 1970
Some Far Elusive Dawn (Darrell, as Drummond), 1988
Some Men and Women (s Lowndes), 1925
Some Mother's Child (M. St. John), 1926
Some Mother's Son! (M. St. John), 1928
Somebody Else (Ayres), 1936
Someone Else's Heart (Stuart, as Allen), 1958
Someone in the House (B. Michaels), 1981

Someone New to Love (Charles, as Tempest), 1936
Someone Waiting (Lorin, as Hohl), 1986
Someone Waiting (Maybury, as Troy), 1961
Someone Who Cares (Charles, as Lance), 1982
Somersault (Ebel), 1971
Something about Eve (Cabell), 1927
Something Between (Cockrell), 1946
Something Blue (Armstrong), 1962
Something Different (Hooper), 1984
Something Extra (Dailey), 1975
Something for Herself (Browning), 1985
Something Special (Baldwin), 1940
Something the Cat Dragged In (C. MacLeod), 1983
Something to Love (Robins), 1951
Something Wonderful (McNaught), 1988
Sometimes Spring Is Late (Ayres), 1941
Sometimes Spring Returns (Elsna, as Lancaster),
    1940
Somewhere to Lay My Head (Peake), 1977
Somewhere Within This House (Webb), 1973
Son of a Hundred Kings (Costain), 1950
Son of Adam (Rome), 1978
Son of Erin (Swan), 1899
Son of Hagar (Caine), 1887
Son of Mammon (Burgin), 1901
Son o'Mine! (M. St. John, as Cooper), 1923
Son of Summer (Mackinlay, as Grey), 1970
Son of the Morning (Frankau), 1949
Son of the People (Orczy), 1906
Son of York (J. Fitzgerald, as Hamilton), 1973
Son to Be Proud Of! (M. St. John), 1924
Song and the Sea (Hunter, as Chace), 1962
Song Begins (Burchell), 1965
Song Bird (Cleugh), 1930
Song Cycle (Burchell), 1974
Song for a Strolling Player (M. Peters), 1981
Song for Marguerite (M. Peters), 1984
Song for Two Voices (Corcoran), 1981
Song from a Lemon Tree (D. Smith), 1966
Song in My Heart (R. Lindsay), 1961
Song in the House (s Bridge), 1936
Song of Dust (Prescott), 1932
Song of Life (s Hurst), 1927
Song of Love (Cartland), 1980
Song of Miriam (s Corelli), 1898
Song of Philomel (Bloom), 1950
Song of Promise (Deveraux), 1983
Song of Renny (Hewlett), 1911
Song of Ruth (Slaughter), 1954
Song of Salome (Bloom, as Mann), 1969
Song of Silkie (Williams), 1984
Song of Summer (Farnes), 1954
Song of Surrender (Grimstead), 1953
Song of the Cardinal (G. Porter), 1903
Song of the Earth (Cordell), 1969
Song of the Lark (Ruck), 1951
Song of the Mockingbird (Duffield), 1946
Song of the Nile (I. Roberts), 1987
Song of the Siren (Holt, as Carr), 1980
Song of the Waves (Hampson), 1976
Song of the West (N. Roberts), 1982
Song of the Wind (Swindells), 1985
Song Twice Over (Jagger), 1985
Songless Wood, (Elsna, as Snow), 1979
Sonora Sundown (Dailey), 1978
Sons (Buck), 1932
Sons and the Daughters (Gallagher), 1961

Sons of the Falcon (Garnett), 1972
Sons of the Sheik (Hull), 1925
Sons of the Wolf (B. Michaels), 1967
Sooner or Later (Glyn), 1933
Sophia (Lamb, as Holland), 1979
Sophia (Weyman), 1900
Sophie (Saxton), 1985
Sophy of Kravonia (Hope), 1906
Sophy Valentine (Ponsonby), 1946
Sorcerer of the Castle (F. Stevenson), 1974
Sorcerers (Barcynska, as Sandys), 1927
Sorrell and Son (Deeping), 1925
Sorrows of Satan (Corelli), 1895
Sot-Weed Factor (Barth), 1960
Soul Flame (Wood), 1987
Soul of Lilith, (Corelli), 1892
Soul of Mary Olivane (Elsna), 1949
Soul of Melicent (Cabell), 1913
Soul of the Mill (M. St. John), 1916
Soul Ties (van der Zee), 1984
Sound Now the Passing-Bell (Wiat), 1977
Sound of the Trumpet (G. Hill), 1943
Sound of Thunder (Caldwell), 1957
Source (Michener), 1965
South African Quirt (Edmonds), 1985
South from Sounion (Weale), 1968
South Island Stowaway (Summers), 1971
South of Capricorn (Hampson), 1975
South of Mandraki (Hampson), 1971
South of the Moon (Hampson), 1979
South Sea Island (L. Walker, as Dean), 1966
South Seas Affair (K. Thorpe), 1985
South to Forget (Summers), 1963
South to the Sun (Beaty), 1956
Southarn Folly (Blackstock, as Allardyce), 1958
Southern Nights (Dailey), 1980
Southern Star (Greig, as Warren), 1950
Southern Sunshine (Bevan), 1985
Souvenir from Sweden (Laker, as Øvstedal),
    1974
Sovereign's Key (Laker), 1969
Sow the Seeds of Hemp (Jennings), 1976
Sow the Tempest (J. Lane), 1960
Sowing Glory (Wren), 1931
Sown among Thorns (Dell), 1939
Sown in the Wind (J. MacLeod), 1946
Spain for the Sovereigns (Holt, as Plaidy), 1960
Spangle (Jennings), 1987
Spangles (Barcynska, as Sandys), 1934
Spanish Bayonet (Benét), 1926
Spanish Bride (Heyer), 1940
Spanish Bridegroom (Holt, as Plaidy), 1954
Spanish Chapel (Daniels), 1972
Spanish Doll (Renier), 1970
Spanish Galleon (Tranter), 1960
Spanish Grandee (Britt), 1975
Spanish House (Buckingham, as John), 1981
Spanish House (E. Smith), 1938
Spanish Inheritance (Hunter), 1975
Spanish Jade (Hewlett), 1908
Spanish Lace (Dingwell), 1969
Spanish Maine (Wren), 1935
Spanish Summer (M. Howard), 1977
Spartacus (Fast), 1951
Speak No Evil (Eberhart), 1941
Speak No Evil of the Dead (Roby), 1973
Speak Now (Yerby), 1969

Speak to Me of Love (Eden), 1972
Special Breed (Giles), 1966
Special Delivery (Chase), 1984
Special Messenger (Chambers), 1909
Special Something (Delinsky), 1984
Specter of Dolphin Cove (Kimbrough), 1973
Spectral Bride (Bowen, as Shearing), 1942
Spell of the Enchanter (Hilton), 1972
Spell of the Island (Hampson), 1983
Spell of the Seven Stones (Donnelly), 1978
Spell of Ursula (Albanesi, as Rowlands), 1894
Spellbinder (Johansen), 1987
Spellbound (Krentz, as Castle), 1982
Spellbound (Way), 1982
Spencer Brade, M.D. (Slaughter), 1942
Spencer's Hospital (Stuart, as A. Stuart), 1961
Spending of the Pile (Burgin), 1924
Spendthrift Duke (Wynne), 1920
Spice Box (G. Hill), 1943
Spice of Life (Ruck), 1952
Spiced with Cloves (Hunter), 1962
Spider (Steen), 1933
Spider and the Fly (Garvice)
Spider Dance (Mackinlay), 1950
Spider in the Cup (Bowen, as Shearing), 1934
Spider Webs (Millar), 1986
Spider's Web (Hunter, as Chace), 1966
Spilled Salt (Bloom), 1927
Spin Me a Shadow (M. Peters, as Black), 1974
Spindrift (Manners, as Sanders), 1974
Spindrift (Stratton), 1977
Spindrift (Whitney), 1975
Spinner of the Years (Bentley), 1928
Spinner's Wharf (Gower), 1985
Spinster of This Parish (Elsna, as Snow), 1966
Spinster's Progress (Ruck), 1942
Spire (Golding), 1964
Spirit in Prison (Hichens), 1908
Spirit Lake (Kantor), 1961
Spirit of Atlantis (Mather), 1980
Spirit of Bambatse, (Haggard), 1906
Spirit of the Time (Hichens), 1921
Splendid Destiny (Albanesi, as Rowlands), 1910
Splendid Friend (Albanesi, as Rowlands), 1917
Splendid Legacy (Farnes), 1973
Splendid Love (Albanesi, as Rowlands), 1911
Splendid Love (M. St. John, as Cooper), 1932
Splendid Man (Albanesi, as Rowlands), 1905
Splendid Savage (F. Stevenson, as Colt), 1983
Splendour (Saxton), 1983
Spoiled Earth (Stirling), 1974
Spoilt Music (Ayres), 1926
Sport Royal (s Hope), 1893
''Sports'' of Lyndale (M. St. John), 1925
Spotlight on Susan (Mackinlay), 1960
Spray of Edelweiss (Britt), 1972
Spray of Red Roses (I. Roberts, as Harle), 1971
Spread Wings (Bloom), 1933
Spread Your Wings (Seale), 1939
Spreading Sails (Charles, as Lance), 1963
Sprig Muslin (Heyer), 1956
Spring (Cleugh), 1929
Spring Always Comes (Loring), 1966
Spring at the Villa (Blair, as Brett), 1961
Spring Comes (Ruck), 1936
Spring Comes to Miss Lonely Heart (Ruck), 1936

Spring Comes to the Crescent (Gibbs, as Ford), 1949
Spring Fancy (Spencer), 1984
Spring Frost, Summer Fire (Seger), 1985
Spring Gambit (Williams), 1976
Spring Green (Cadell), 1953
Spring in Morocco (Melville, as Betteridge), 1962
Spring in September (Bloom), 1941
Spring in September (Summers), 1978
Spring in the Heart (Albanesi, as Rowlands), 1929
Spring Madness of Mr. Sermon (Delderfield), 1963
Spring Magic (D. Stevenson), 1941
Spring of a Lion (Haggard), 1899
Spring of Granite Peaks (I. Preston), 1988
Spring of the Ram (Dunnett), 1987
Spring of the Tiger (Holt), 1979
Spring Picture (s du Maurier), 1945
Spring Rainbow (Mackinlay), 1961
Spring Will Come Again (S. Thorpe), 1965
Springtime (Bailey), 1907
Springtime for Sally (Charles, as Lance), 1962
Springtime for Sophie (Chappell), 1983
Spring-Time of Love (Garvice), 1910
Spun by the Moon (Charles, as Lance), 1960
Spur of Pride (Wren), 1937
Spurned Proposal (Albanesi, as Rowlands)
Spy at the Villa Miranda (Lee), 1967
Spy Concerto (Heaven, as Merlin), 1980
Spy for Napoleon (Wynne), 1917
Spy Number 13 (Chambers), 1935
Spy of Napoleon (Orczy), 1934
Squire (Barcynska, as Sandys), 1932
Squirrel Walk (I. Roberts), 1961
Stacy (R. Lindsay, as Leigh), 1958
Stage of Love (Ebel, as Shelbourne), 1978
Stairway to Enchantment (Stratton, as Gillen), 1973
Stake in the Game (Berckman), 1971
Stake in the Kingdom (Tranter), 1966
Stalemate (Berckman), 1966
Stalker series (Stirling), from 1974
Stalking Horse, (Sabatini), 1933
Stalking Terror (Coffman), 1977
Stallion (Steen), 1933
Stallion Man (Glover), 1982
Stamboul Love (Duffield), 1934
Standish Place (I. Holland), 1976
Stands a Calder Man (Dailey), 1982
Star (Steel), 1989
Star Creek (Barrie, as Kent), 1965
Star Eyes (Kimbrough, as Ashton), 1983
Star in Love (Ruck), 1935
Star in the Dark (Albanesi), 1933
Star Light, Star Bright (Johansen), 1988
Star Looks Down (Neels), 1975
Star Money (Winsor), 1950
Star of Danger (Lee), 1971
Star of Desire (Grimstead, as Manning), 1961
Star of Lancaster (Holt, as Plaidy), 1981
Star of Oudh (Stuart, as A. Stuart), 1960
Star of Rendevi (McEvoy), 1984
Star of the Greys (Harwood), 1939
Star on Her Shoulder (s Baldwin), 1942
Star Patient (Norway, as Neal), 1963
Star Quality (Burchell), 1959
Star Sapphire (J. Roberts, as Danton), 1979
Star to My Barque (D. Smith), 1964
Star-Crossed (M. Howard), 1949

Star-Crossed (Lamb), 1976
Star-Crossed (Seger, as Jennings), 1985
Star-Drift (I. Roberts, as Rowland), 1970
Stardust (Hampson), 1982
Star-Dust (Hurst), 1921
Stardust (D. Murray), 1931
Stardust in Her Eyes (Mackinlay, as Grey), 1964
Starless Night (Ayres), 1943
Starling (Leslie), 1927
Starry Wood (Maybury), 1935
Stars above Raffael (I. Roberts), 1977
Stars Are My Children (P. Hastings), 1970
Stars Cannot Tell (Maybury), 1958
Stars Grow Pale (Maybury), 1936
Stars in Her Eyes (Cartland), 1971
Stars in My Heart (Cartland), 1957
Stars in Your Eyes (Loring), 1941
Stars of San Cecilio (Barrie), 1958
Stars of Spring (Hampson), 1971
Stars on the Sea (F. Mason), 1940
Stars over Egypt (Hoy), 1938
Stars over Sarawak (Hampson), 1974
Stars Through the Mist (Neels), 1973
Starshine for Sweethearts (Ritchie), 1976
Star-Spangled Banner (Swanson), 1958
Star-Spangled Christmas (s Norris), 1942
Starvecrow Farm (Weyman), 1905
State of Mind (J. Lane), 1964
State Versus Elinor Norton (Rinehart), 1934
Stateroom for Two (Finley), 1980
Station Wagon in Spain (Keyes), 1959
Station Wagon Set (Baldwin), 1939
Stationmaster's Daughter (Oldfield), 1986
Statues of Snow (Lorrimer, as Robins), 1947
Staunch as a Woman (Garvice), 1903
Staunch of the Heart (Garvice), 1903
Stay But till Tomorrow (Bromige), 1946
Stay Through the Night (Kidd), 1979
Stay Till Morning (Peake), 1982
Stay Until Tomorrow (Maybury), 1961
Staying Close (van der Zee), 1984
Steadfast Lover (Beresford), 1980
Steady Burns the Candle (Ainsworth), 1970
Stealer of Hearts (Elsna, as Snow), 1959
Steamboat Gothic (Keyes), 1952
Steering by a Star (Ayres), 1949
Stella Fregelius (Haggard), 1904
Stella Maris (Wynne), 1932
Stella's Fortune (Garvice), 1912
Step in the Dark (Cowen), 1962
Stepdaughter (Bromige), 1966
Stepdaughters of War (Price, as Smith), 1930
Stephanie (Blackmore), 1972
Stephanie (Eliot, as Arnett), 1979
Stephen and the Sleeping Saints (Bennetts), 1977
Stephen Glyn (s Swan), 1898
Stephen Morris (Shute), 1961
Step-Mother (Swan), 1915
Stepmother of Five (Charles, as Tempest), 1936
Stepmother's House (Kimbrough, as Bramwell), 1972
Stepping Stones (Chappell), 1985
Stepping under Ladders (Greig), 1938
Steps of the Sun (Trollope), 1983
Steps to the Empty Throne (Tranter), 1969
Stepsons of France (s Wren), 1917
Steven's Wife (Inglis), 1958

Still as the Grave (Roby), 1964
Still Blooms the Rose (P. Hill), 1984
Still Glides the Stream (D. Stevenson), 1959
Still House of O'Darrow (Bacheller), 1894
Still Is the Summer Night (Derleth), 1937
Still She Wishes for Company (Irwin), 1924
Still Waters (Ayres), 1941
Stinging Nettles (Bowen), 1923
Stolen Bride (Bowen), 1933
Stolen Ecstasy (Taylor), 1985
Stolen Halo (Cartland), 1940
Stolen Heart (Burchell), 1952
Stolen Idyll (Morgan), 1985
Stolen March (Yates), 1926
Stolen Summer (Mather), 1985
Stolen Trust (Stanford), 1987
Stone (Tranter), 1958
Stone Bull (Whitney), 1977
Stone Carnation (Hintze), 1971
Stone House (Daniels), 1973
Stone Lily (Chapman), 1957
Stone Maiden (V. Johnston), 1980
Stone Maiden (Manners), 1973
Stone of Blood (Coulson), 1975
Stonewall Brigade (Slaughter), 1975
Stony Ground (Miles), 1923
Stooping Lady (Hewlett), 1907
Stop at a Winner (Delderfield), 1961
Stopover in Paradise (Greig), 1938
Stories of China (s Buck), 1964
Stories Without Women (s Byrne), 1915
Storm and Treasure (Bailey), 1910
Storm at Sea (J. Lindsay), 1935
Storm Bird (Bloom, as Burns), 1959
Storm Centre (Lamb) 1980
Storm Cycle (M. Pargeter), 1982
Storm Drift (Dell), 1930
Storm Eagle (Stratton, as Gillen), 1980
Storm Flower (Way), 1975
Storm Haven (Slaughter), 1953
Storm Heaven (Maybury), 1949
Storm House (Norris), 1929
Storm in a Rain Barrel (Mather), 1971
Storm in the Family (Blackmore), 1956
Storm in the Mountains (Buckingham), 1967
Storm in the Night (M. Pargeter), 1983
Storm Music (Yates), 1934
Storm of Desire (Finley), 1977
Storm of Time (Dark), 1945
Storm of Wrath (Dwyer-Joyce), 1977
Storm over Mandargi (Way), 1973
Storm over Roseheath (Maybury, as Troy), 1969
Storm over the Lake (Palmer), 1979
Storm Passage (K. Thorpe), 1977
Storm Tide (Ogilvie), 1945
Storm Warning (N. Roberts), 1984
Stormcloud and Sunrise (Farnes), 1945
Storm's End (Stanford), 1980
Storms of Love (Cartland), 1985
Stormspell (Mather), 1982
Stormswift (Brent), 1984
Stormwatch (Browning), 1984
Stormy Challenge (Krentz, as James), 1982
Stormy Encounter (R. Lane), 1974
Stormy Haven (Blair, as Brett), 1952
Stormy Masquerade (Hampson), 1980

Stormy Petrel (Seale), 1941
Stormy Rapture (M. Pargeter), 1976
Stormy Springtime (Neels), 1987
Stormy Surrender (J. Roberts, as Radcliffe), 1978
Stormy Vows (Johansen), 1983
Stormy Voyager (Swan), 1896
Stormy the Way (Hampson), 1973
Storrington Papers (Eden), 1978
Story de Luxe (Danbury), 1963
Story Girl (Montgomery), 1911
Story of a Passion (Bacheller), 1899
Story of a Passion (Garvice), 1908
Story of a Whim (G. Hill), 1903
Story of Andrea Fields (Seifert), 1950
Story of Fish and Chips (Ayres), 1951
Story of Ivy (Lowndes), 1927
Story of John Willie (Ayres), 1948
Story of Julia Page (Norris), 1915
Story of Julian (Ertz), 1931
Story of Marco (E. Porter), 1911
Story of Rosabelle Shaw (D. Stevenson), 1937
Story of the Lost Star (G. Hill), 1932
Story of Veronica (Robins), 1946
Story Teller (s Kantor), 1967
Stowaway (Weale), 1979
Straight from the Heart (Delinsky), 1986
Strait Gate (Swan), 1887
Strait-Jacket (Elsna), 1930
Strand (Rayner), 1980
Strange Adventure (Craven), 1977
Strange as a Dream (Kidd), 1968
Strange Beauty (Greig), 1938
Strange Bedfellow (Berckman), 1956
Strange Bedfellow (Dailey), 1979
Strange Beginning (Jacob), 1961
Strange Bewilderment (Britt), 1973
Strange Capers (J. Smith), 1986
Strange Case of Lucile Cléry (Bowen, as Shearing), 1941
Strange Case of Miss Annie Spragg (Bromfield), 1928
Strange Involvement (Mackinlay), 1972
Strange Journey (McEvoy, as Harte)
Strange Lady (Hichens), 1950
Strange Love Story (Albanesi, as Rowlands), 1919
Strange Loyalties (Arbor), 1949
Strange Loyalty of Dr. Carlisle (Seifert), 1952
Strange Marriage (Garvice, as Hart)
Strange Meeting (Robins), 1952
Strange Paradise (Daniels), 1969
Strange Paths (M. Howard), 1948
Strange Patient for Sister Smith (Bloom, as Essex), 1963
Strange Prodigal (G. Hill), 1935
Strange Quest of Anne Weston (Burchell), 1964
Strange Quest of Nurse Anne (Burchell), 1965
Strange Rapture (Robins), 1933
Strange Recompense (J. MacLeod, as Airlie), 1952
Strange Roads (Diver), 1918
Strange Secrets (Coffman), 1976
Strange Victory (Franken, as Meloney), 1939
Strange Visitation of Josiah McNason (Corelli), 1904
Strange Visitor (Elsna), 1956
Strange Waif (Winspear), 1962
Strange Yesterday (Fast), 1934
Strangeling (Harwood), 1954
Stranger at Pembroke (Eliot), 1971
Stranger at the Gate (M. Howard, as Edgar), 1973
Stranger at the Gates (Anthony), 1973

Stranger at Wildings (Brent), 1976
Stranger by Night (Lynn), 1963
Stanger Came (Donnelly), 1972
Stranger Came By (Knight), 1974
Stranger from the North (L. Walker), 1959
Stranger from the Sea (Graham), 1981
Stranger from the Sea (I. Preston), 1987
Stranger in Love (Charles, as Chandos), 1966
Stranger in My Grave (Millar), 1960
Stranger in the Glen (Kidd), 1975
Stranger in the Night (Lamb), 1980
Stranger in Their Midst (J. MacLeod), 1953
Stranger on the Beach (Melville, as Betteridge), 1974
Stranger on the Beach (Peake), 1979
Stranger Prince (Irwin), 1937
Stranger Sweetheart (Greig, as Ames), 1938
Stranger Than Truth (Albanesi, as Rowlands), 1913
Stranger to Love (Charles, as Tempest), 1960
Stranger to Love (Woodward, as Ware), 1967
Stranger Within the Gates (G. Hill), 1939
Strangers (Thomas), 1987
Strangers' Forest (P. Hill), 1978
Strangers in Company (Hodge), 1971
Strangers in Flight (Eberhart), 1941
Strangers in Love (Delmar), 1951
Strangers in Love (M. Howard), 1939
Strangers in My House (Ponsonby), 1948
Strangers in Paradise (Pozzessere), 1988
Strangers into Lovers (Peake), 1981
Stranger's Kiss (Stanford), 1978
Strangers May Kiss (Grimstead), 1952
Strangers May Marry (Burchell), 1941
Strangers May Marry (Hampson), 1982
Strangers on the Moor (S. Thorpe), 1966
Stranger's Trespass (Arbor), 1968
Strangers When We Meet (Stuart, as A. Stuart), 1968
Strategy of Suzanne (Grundy), 1929
Stratford Affair (P. Hastings), 1978
Stratford Story (Sisson), 1975
Strathgallant (Black), 1981
Strathmore (Stirling), 1975
Stratton Story, (Cadell), 1967
Straw Crown (Stubbs), 1966
Strawberries in the Sea (Ogilvie), 1973
Straws in Amber (Jacob), 1938
Street Below (Ayres), 1922
Street of Seven Stars (Rinehart), 1914
Street of the City (G. Hill), 1942
Street of the Five Moons (B. Michaels, as Peters), 1978
Street of the Singing Fountain (R. Randall), 1948
Street of the Sun (Horner), 1956
Streets (s Hichens), 1928
Stricken Land (Thompson), 1986
Strike the Black Flag (Jakes, as Scotland), 1961
String of Silver Beads (Ainsworth), 1972
Strip (Ellis, as Lord), 1970
Strip Girl (Price), 1934
Strolling Players (Dwyer-Joyce), 1975
Strolling Saint (Sabatini), 1913
Strong City (Caldwell), 1942
Strong Hand (Deeping), 1912
Strong Heart (Robins), 1965
Strong, Hot Winds (Johansen), 1988
Strong Hours (Diver), 1919
Stronger Passion (Bloom, as Burns), 1941
Stronger Spell (Farnes), 1959

Strongest of All Things (Albanesi), 1907
Struggle for a Crown (M. Peters), 1970
Struggle for a Heart (Libbey), 1889
Stuart series (Tranter), from 1976
Stuart Sisters (Bloom, as Prole), 1958
Stuart Stain (W. Roberts), 1978
Stuarts series (Holt, as Plaidy), from 1965
Stubborn Heart (Slaughter), 1950
Studies in Love and Terror (s Lowndes), 1913
Studies in Wives (s Lowndes), 1909
Study of Sara (Elsna), 1930
Subaltern's Choice (McCutchan, as MacNeil), 1974
Subconscious Courtship (Ruck) 1922
Substitute Bride (M. Pargeter), 1981
Substitute Doctor (Seifert), 1957
Substitute for Love (Reid), 1967
Substitute for Sherry (Charles, as Chandos), 1940
Substitute Guest (G. Hill), 1936
Suburban Young Man (Delafield), 1928
Success Story (M. Howard), 1984
Such a Fine Fellow! (M. St. John), 1923
Such a Mighty Race (Clayton), 1985
Such Bitter Business (Holt, as Ford), 1953
Such Frail Armour (Arbor), 1953
Such Is Love (Burchell), 1939
Such Men Are Dangerous (s Glyn), 1933
Sudden Love (Webb, as Hamill), 1962
Sudden Sweetheart (Ruck), 1932
Suddenly, In the Air (Beaty, as Campbell), 1969
Sue Verney (J. Lindsay), 1937
Suffer a Sea Change (De Blasis), 1976
Suffer to Sing (Barcynska, as Sandys), 1955
Suffolk series (Lofts), from 1959
Sugar Candy Cottage (Cadell), 1958
Sugar Cane Harvest (K. Thorpe), 1975
Sugar in the Morning (Hunter, as Chace), 1969
Sugar Island (Duffield), 1951
Sugar Island (J. MacLeod), 1964
Sugar Mouse (Gibbs), 1965
Suitors of Yvonne (Sabatini), 1902
Sullivan's Reef (Weale), 1970
Sullivan's Woman (N. Roberts), 1984
Summer at Barbazon (Blair), 1960
Summer at San Milo (Asquith), 1965
Summer at Silverwood (Ritchie), 1962
Summer at Willowbank (I. Preston), 1980
Summer Change (Norway, as Norton), 1961
Summer Comes to Albarosa (Danbury), 1971
Summer Cypress (P. Hill, as Fiske), 1981
Summer Desserts (N. Roberts), 1985
Summer Dust (Eaton), 1936
Summer Every Day (Arbor), 1966
Summer Fruit (Yates), 1929
Summer Games (Lowell), 1984
Summer Gone (Maddocks), 1957
Summer Harvest (Swindells), 1983
Summer Heat (Seger), 1988
Summer House (Daniels), 1976
Summer Idyll (Neels), 1984
Summer in December (Summers), 1970
Summer Island (J. MacLeod), 1968
Summer Magic (Way), 1971
Summer Mahogany (Dailey), 1978
Summer Motley (Farnes), 1944
Summer of Confict (R. Lane), 1984
Summer of Fear (Ellis, as Marvin), 1971

Summer of Pride (Savage), 1961
Summer of Sighs (Gallagher), 1971
Summer of the Dragon (B. Michaels, as Peters), 1979
Summer of the Osprey (Ogilvie), 1987
Summer of the Raven (Craven), 1981
Summer of the Spanish Woman (Gaskin), 1977
Summer of the Unicorn (Hooper), 1988
Summer People (Charles, as Lance), 1969
Summer Rain (J. MacLeod), 1938
Summer Rhapsody (Buckingham, as John), 1983
Summer Season (Stratton, as Gillen), 1971
Summer Smile (Johansen), 1985
Summer Song (Grimstead, as Manning), 1972
Summer Song (Oldfield), 1984
Summer Spell (Seale), 1937
Summer Stock Romance (McElresh, as Wesley), 1961
Summer Storm (Last), 1976
Summer Story (Chappell), 1972
Summer Sunday (Eden), 1946
Summer Thunder (Lowell), 1983
Summer to Love (R. Lane), 1968
Summer Visitors (Sallis), 1988
Summer Wife (Kidd), 1976
Summer Will Show (S. Warner), 1936
Summerhills (D. Stevenson), 1956
Summer-House (R. Harris), 1956
Summer's Awakening (Weale), 1984
Summer's Cloud (Tattersall), 1965
Summer's End (Steel), 1981
Summer's Flower (Stuart), 1961
Summer's Grace (Charles, as Lance), 1961
Summer's Play (Stern), 1934
Sun and Candlelight (Neels), 1979
Sun and the Dragon (Nicole), 1985
Sun and the Sea (Ayres), 1935
Sun Fades the Stars (Trask), 1940
Sun Hawk (Chambers), 1929
Sun in Scorpio (R. Fraser), 1949
Sun in Splendour (Dymoke), 1980
Sun in Splendour (Holt, as Plaidy), 1982
Sun in Splendour (Weale), 1975
Sun in the Morning (Asquith), 1974
Sun Is My Undoing (Steen), 1941
Sun Lord's Woman (Winspear), 1985
Sun Lover (Stanford), 1982
Sun of Summer (Peake), 1975
Sun on Fire (Nicole), 1985
Sun on the Mountain (Collin), 1969
Sun on the Sea (Ritchie), 1954
Sun Rises (Nicole), 1984
Sun, Sea and Sand (May), 1970
Sun Spark (Pykare, as Coombs), 1984
Sun Still Shines (Elsna, as Conway), 1959
Sun Tower (Winspear), 1976
Sunburst (Ruck), 1934
Sunday Evening (Lynn), 1969
Sunday Love (Bloom), 1978
Sunday's Child (Williams), 1977
Sundered Hearts (Swan), 1886
Sundial (Jackson), 1958
Sunflower's Look (Ritchie), 1958
Sunia (s Diver), 1913
Sunlight Beyond (Albanesi, as Rowlands), 1930
Sunlit Hills (Albanesi), 1914
Sunlit Seas (I. Preston), 1977
Sunne in Splendour (Penman), 1982

Sunny Chandler's Return (Brown), 1987
Sunny Ducrow (M. St. John, as Cooper), 1919
Sunny Island (Greig, as Warren), 1952
Sunrise (Duffield), 1944
Sunrise (G. Hill), 1937
Sunrise (Thomas), 1984
Sunrise at Even (Cowen), 1982
Sunrise for Georgie (Ayres), 1941
Sunrise in the West (E. Pargeter), 1974
Sunset (Nicole), 1978
Sunset and Dawn (Albanesi, as Rowlands), 1915
Sunset Cloud (Hampson), 1976
Sunset Dream (Gavin), 1983
Sunset Embrace (Brown), 1984
Sunset Hour (Elsna, as Lancaster), 1946
Sunset Hour (Summerton), 1957
Sunset in the East (Carnegie), 1955
Sunset Is Dawn (Barcynska, as Barclay), 1953
Sunset Touch (Stuart, as A. Stuart), 1972
Sunshine-Stealer (Ruck), 1935
Sup with the Devil (Craven), 1983
Surest Bond (Albanesi, as Rowlands), 1913
Surgeon at St. Mark's (E. Harrison), 1986
Surgeon at Sea (Bloom, as Burns), 1969
Surgeon Called Amanda (E. Harrison), 1982
Surgeon from Holland (Neels), 1970
Surgeon in Charge (Seifert), 1942
Surgeon in Tibet (I. Roberts), 1970
Surgeon of Distinction (Burchell), 1959
Surgeon on Call (Seifert), 1965
Surgeon She Married (E. Harrison), 1988
Surgeon, U.S.A. (Slaughter), 1966
Surgeon's Affair (E. Harrison), 1985
Surgeon's Call (E. Harrison), 1973
Surgeon's Choice (Slaughter), 1969
Surgeon's Dilemma (M. Howard), 1961
Surgeon's Life (E. Harrison), 1983
Surgeon's Marriage (Blair), 1963
Surgeon's Mate (O'Brien), 1980
Surgeon's Reputation (Charles), 1979
Surgeon's Sweetheart (Bloom, as Burns), 1966
Surgeon's Sweetheart (Charles), 1982
Surly Sullen Bell (s Kirk), 1962
Surprise Engagement (Ruck), 1946
Surprising Results (R. Fraser), 1935
Surrender by Moonlight (Delinsky, as Drake), 1981
Surrender, My Love (Finley), 1974
Surrender to Love (Rogers), 1982
Survivor of Darkness (Coffman), 1973
Survivors (Edwards), 1968
Survivors of Darkness (Daniels), 1969
Susan Crowther (Jacob), 1945
Susannah and One Elder (Albanesi), 1903
Susannah, The Righteous (Kimbrough), 1975
Susie (Chesney, as Tremaine), 1981
Susie's Career (Hichens), 1935
Suspected Four (W. Roberts), 1962
Suspicion (Elsna, as Lancaster), 1955
Sussex series (Glover), from 1982
Sussex series (P. Hastings), from 1968
Sutburys (P. Hill), 1988
Suvla John (Deeping), 1924
Suzerain (Bennetts), 1968
Swallow (Haggard), 1899
Swallows of San Fedora (Beaty), 1970
Swan series (De Blasis), from 1984

Swan (Steen), 1951
Swan House (Hutten), 1930
Swan River Story (P. Hastings), 1968
Swans and Turtles (s Godden), 1968
Swans' Reach (Way), 1976
Sweeping Tide (Duffield), 1940
Sweet Adventure (Burchell), 1952
Sweet Adventure (Cartland), 1957
Sweet and Faraway (L. Walker), 1955
Sweet and Lovely (Albanesi), 1933
Sweet and Twenty (J. Smith), 1979
Sweet Anger (Brown, as St. Claire), 1985
Sweet Are the Ways (Summers), 1965
Sweet as a Rose (Garvice), 1910
Sweet Barbary (Barrie, as Kent), 1957
Sweet Bloom (Ritchie), 1961
Sweet Cassandra (Robins), 1970
Sweet Compulsion (Lamb, as Woolf), 1979
Sweet Cymbeline (Garvice), 1911
Sweet Danger (Greig), 1935
Sweet Deceiver (Blair), 1955
Sweet Disorder (Williams), 1981
Sweet Ember (Delinsky, as Drake), 1981
Sweet Enchantress (Cartland, as McCorquodale), 1958
Sweet Enemy (Palmer), 1979
Sweet Epitaph (Lynn), 1971
Sweet Fellows (Barcynska, as Sandys), 1942
Sweet Friday (Grimstead, as Manning), 1972
Sweet Genevieve (Derleth), 1942
Sweet Impulse (Bloom, as Burns), 1956
Sweet Is the Web (Hampson), 1977
Sweet Kate (Stratton, as Gillen), 1971
Sweet Kitty Clover (Libbey), 1898
Sweet Lass of Richmond Hill (Holt, as Plaidy), 1970
Sweet Lost Years (Elsna), 1955
Sweet Love (Robins), 1934
Sweet Love Remembered (Chard), 1982
Sweet Love, Survive (S. Johnson), 1985
Sweet Marie-Antoinette (Bloom, as Prole), 1969
Sweet Masquerade (Chesney), 1984
Sweet Meadows (Burchell), 1963
Sweet Memories (Spencer), 1984
Sweet Nell (Bloom, as Prole), 1965
Sweet Not Always (van der Zee), 1979
Sweet Peril (Greig, as Ames), 1935
Sweet Prisoner (Grimstead), 1961
Sweet Promise (Dailey), 1976
Sweet Punishment (Cartland), 1931
Sweet Red Earth (Saunders, as Summers), 1983
Sweet Revenge (Mather), 1970
Sweet Revenge (N. Roberts), 1989
Sweet Rocket (M. Johnston), 1920
Sweet Roots and Honey (Westwood), 1974
Sweet Rosemary (Charles, as Chandos), 1972
Sweet Sanctuary (Lamb), 1976
Sweet Savage Eden (Pozzessere, as Graham), 1989
Sweet, Savage Heart (Taylor), 1986
Sweet Savage Love (Rogers), 1974
Sweet Second Love (Hampson), 1984
Sweet Serenity (Delinsky, as Douglass), 1983
Sweet Shipwreck (Elsna, as Lancaster), 1942
Sweet Simplicity (Ashton), 1971
Sweet Sorrel (I. Roberts), 1963
Sweet Sorrow (Robins), 1940
Sweet Spring of April (Bloom), 1979
Sweet Starfire (Krent), 1986

Sweet Stranger (Ruck), 1921
Sweet Sundown (Way), 1974
Sweet Surrender (Burghley), 1959
Sweet Surrender (Vitek), 1982
Sweet to Remember (Weale), 1958
Sweet Torment (Kidd), 1978
Sweet Waters (Blair, as Brett), 1955
Sweet Will (Malpass), 1973
Sweet William (Albanesi), 1906
Sweet Wind of Morning (M. Peters, as Grey), 1979
Sweet Wind, Wild Wind (Lowell), 1987
Sweet Wine of Youth (Elsna, as Lancaster), 1960
Sweetbriar (Deveraux), 1983
Sweetbriar Lane (Barcynska), 1938
Sweetcrab (Summerton), 1971
Sweeter Music (C. Allen), 1976
Sweeter Unpossessed (Elsna), 1929
Sweetheart Tree (Grimstead), 1966
Sweetheart Will You Be True? (Libbey), 1901
Sweethearts Unmet (Ruck), 1919
Sweyn's Eye series (Gower), from 1983
Swift Flows the River (Ellerbeck, as Yorke), 1988
Swift Water (Loring), 1929
Swiftest Eagle (Dwyer-Joyce), 1979
Swimming Pool (Rinehart), 1952
Swindler (s Dell), 1914
Swing High, Swing Low (Greig, as Barclay), 1936
Swing of Youth (Robins), 1930
Switch on to Love (Woodward, as Lawrence), 1967
Sword and Scalpel (Slaughter), 1957
Sword and the Cross (Deeping), 1957
Sword and the Shadow (S. Thorpe), 1951
Sword and the Swan (Gellis), 1977
Sword Decides! (Bowen), 1908
Sword in the Stone (T. White), 1938
Sword in the Sun (Hoy), 1946
Sword of Islam (Sabatini), 1939
Sword of Mithras (Heaven, as Merlin), 1982
Sword of Pleasure (Green), 1957
Sword of Vengeance (S. Thorpe), 1957
Sword of Woden (Wiat), 1975
Sword to the Heart (Cartland), 1974
Swordlight (Manners, as Rundle), 1968
Sybelle (Gellis), 1983
Sycamore Hill (Rivers), 1981
Sycamore Song (Hunter), 1975
Sydney (Garvice), n.d.
Sydney (F. Preston), 1987
Sylvester (Heyer), 1957
Sylvia Cary (Keyes), 1962
Sylvia Lyndon (Diver), 1940
Sylvia Sorelle (Hoy), 1944
Sympathetic Surgeon (Bloom, as Essex), 1968
Symphony for Two Players (M. Lewis), 1969
Symphony of Bells (I. Roberts), 1980

TLC (Delinsky), 1988
Tabitha in Moonlight (Neels), 1972
Table for Two (Greig), 1946
Tabloid News (s Bromfield), 1930
Taboo (J. Fitzgerald), 1985
Taffy Came to Cairo (Duffield), 1944
Tailor of Vitré (Wynne), 1908
Taint of Tragedy (Wynne), 1917
Tai-Pan (Clavell), 1966
Taj Mahal, Shrine of Desire (Bloom as Prole), 1972

Take a Chance (Bloom, as Burns), 1937
Take a Chance (Charles, as Lance), 1940
Take Back Your Love (Britt), 1975
Take Courage (Bentley), 1940
Take Heed of Loving Me (Elsna), 1970
Take Love Easy (Hoy), 1941
Take Me with You (Burchell), 1944
Take Pity upon Youth (Elsna), 1962
Take the Far Dream (Donnelly), 1970
Take This Man (Greig), 1947
Take This Woman (Peake), 1988
Take Three Tenses (Godden), 1945
Take What You Want (Baldwin), 1970
Take What You Want (Mather), 1975
Take Your Choice, Lady (Greig, as Ames), 1946
Taken by Storm (Finley), 1982
Taken by Storm (Hooper, as Robbins), 1983
Taking of the Cry (Masefield), 1934
Tale of Three Cities (D. Murray), 1940
Tale of Three Lions (Haggard), 1887
Tales Before Midnight (s Benét), 1939
Tales for a Stormy Night (s Davis), 1984
Tales from Tiger Bay (s Cordell), 1986
Tales of Grace and Favour (Leslie), 1956
Tales of Long Ago (s Doyle), 1922
Tales of Pirates and Blue Water (s Doyle), 1922
Tales of the Broad Acres (Naomi Jacob), 1955
Tales of Two People (Hope), 1907
Talisman (Crowe), 1979
Talisman Ring (Heyer), 1936
Talk of the Town (J. Smith), 1979
Tall Headlines (Erskine-Lindop), 1950
Tall Hunter (Fast), 1942
Tall Pines (Blair, as Conway), 1956
Tall Stranger (D. Stevenson), 1957
Tamara (Norris), 1935
Tamarind Seed (Anthony), 1971
Tamarisk (Lorrimer), 1978
Tamarisk (Muskett), 1935
Tamarisk Bay (Blair), 1956
Tamarisk in Bloom (I. Preston), 1963
Tamberlyn (Manley-Tucker), 1981
Tamboti Moon (May), 1969
Tame the Restless Heart (Matthews), 1986
Taming (Deveraux), 1989
Taming of Annabelle (Chesney), 1983
Taming of Lady Lorinda (Cartland), 1977
Taming of Laura (R. Lindsay), 1959
Taming of Lisa (Kidd), 1972
Taming of Princess Olga (Garvice), 1908
Tana Maguire (Coffman, as Saunders), 1986
Tangle in Sunshine (Blair, as Brett), 1957
Tangle of Gold Lace (I. Roberts), 1963
Tangled Autumn (Neels), 1972
Tangled Destinies (Palmer, as Blayne), 1986
Tangled Fates (Wynne), 1935
Tangled Harmonies (Farnes), 1936
Tangled Love (Norris), 1933
Tangled Roots (Bromige), 1948
Tangled Shadows (Kidd), 1979
Tangled Skein (Orczy), 1907
Tangled Tapestry (Mather), 1969
Tangled Thread (Harrod-Eagles), 1987
Tangled Threads (s E. Porter), 1919
Tangled Web (Farnes), 1963
Tangled Web (Montgomery), 1931

Tangled Web (I. Roberts, as Rowland), 1962
Tangled Wood (Bromige), 1969
Tansy (M. Peters), 1975
Tapestry of Dreams (Gellis), 1985
Tara (Blackmore), 1985
Tara's Healing (Giles), 1951
Tara's Song (B. Johnson), 1978
Tarnish (Bloom), 1929
Tarnished Vows (Stanford), 1982
Tarot Spell (W. Roberts), 1970
Tarot's Tower (Butler, as Melville), 1978
Tarrington Chase (S. Thorpe), 1977
Tartan Ribbon (Reid), 1976
Tartan Touch (Hunter, as Chace), 1972
Taste for Love (Dingwell), 1967
Taste for Rich Things (Lorin, as Hohl), 1984
Taste of Fears (Millar), 1950
Taste of Wine (Yarbro, as Pryor), 1982
Taste the Wine (Saunders), 1983
Tattling Tongues (M. St. John), 1922
Tattooed Road (Horner), 1960
Tavern (Steen), 1935
Tavern Knight (Sabatini), 1904
Taverners' Place (Trollope), 1986
Tawny Are the Leaves (May), 1968
Tawny Gold Man (Lorin), 1980
Tawny Sands (Winspear), 1970
Tea at Gunter's (Haines), 1974
Tea Is So Intoxicating (Bloom, as Essex), 1950
Tea on Sunday (L. Cooper), 1973
Teach Me to Forget (Elsna, as Conway), 1961
Teach Me to Love (Charles, as Tempest), 1947
Team (Norway, as Neal), 1965
Team-Up for Ann (McElfresh), 1959
Tears and Red Roses (Lamb, as Hardy), 1982
Tears in Paradise (Blackmore), 1959
Tears of Gold (McBain), 1979
Tears of Love (Cartland), 1975
Tears of Peace (Barcynska), 1944
Tears of the Renegade (L. Howard), 1985
Tears of Venus (Stratton), 1979
Telefair, Kitty series (F. Stevenson), from 1971
Tell Me My Fortune (Burchell), 1951
Tell Me My Heart (Baldwin), 1950
Tell Me No Lies (B. Hastings), 1984
Tell Me No Lies (Lowell), 1986
Temp (Melville, as Betteridge), 1976
Temperamental People (s Rinehart), 1924
Temperatures Rising (Brown), 1989
Tempest and the Song, (Ritchie), 1959
Tempest at Sea (Johansen), 1983
Tempest in Eden (Brown), 1983
Tempest in the Tropics (R. Lane), 1986
Tempestuous Affair (Courtney), 1983
Tempestuous April (Neels), 1975
Tempestuous Eden (Pozzessere, as Graham), 1983
Tempestuous Petticoat (Gibbs), 1977
Temple Bells (McEvoy), 1985
Temple of Butterflies (J. Fitzgerald), 1989
Temple of Dawn (Hampson), 1979
Temple of Love (Cartland), 1988
Temple of the Moon (Craven), 1977
Templeton Memoirs (Daniels), 1966
Temporal Power (Corelli), 1902
Temporary Address: Reno (Baldwin), 1941
Temporary Boy (P. Hastings), 1971

Temporary Marriage (K. Thorpe), 1981
Temporary Wife (R. Lindsay as Leigh), 1975
Tempt Not This Flesh (Riefe), 1979
Temptation (Albanesi, as Rowlands), 1912
Temptation (Lamb), 1979
Temptation (I. Roberts, as Rowland), 1983
Temptation (N. Roberts), 1987
Temptation (Wynne), 1937
Temptation for a Teacher (Cartland), 1985
Temptation of Mary Barr (Albanesi, as Rowlands)
Temptation of Philip Carr (Wynne), 1905
Temptation of Torilla (Cartland), 1977
Temptation's Kiss (Brown), 1983
Temptations of Big Bear (Wiebe), 1973
Tempted by Love (Albanesi, as Rowlands)
Tempted to Love (Cartland), 1983
Tempted to Love (Kidd), 1982
Tempter's Power (Wynne), 1932
Tempting Fate (N. Roberts), 1985
Tempting Fate (Yarbro), 1982
Temptress (Deveraux), 1980
Temptress (R. Marshall), 1953
Ten Cent Love (Greig), 1934
Ten Commandments (Deeping), 1931
Ten Days of Christmas (Stern), 1950
Tenant of Binningham Hall (Sinclair), 1970
Tenant of Chesdene Manor (Ley), 1974
Tenant of San Mateo (R. Lane), 1976
Tenants of Time (Flanagan), 1988
Ten-Day Queen (Bloom, as Prole), 1972
Tender Barbarian (Browning), 1985
Tender Chord (Grimstead), 1967
Tender Conquest (Dingwell), 1960
Tender Deception (Pozzessere, as Graham), 1984
Tender Ecstasy (Taylor), 1983
Tender Glory (J. MacLeod), 1965
Tender Is the Storm (Lindsey), 1985
Tender Is the Tyrant (Winspear), 1967
Tender Leaves (Summers), 1980
Tender Night (Peake), 1975
Tender Only to One (Inglis), 1938
Tender Pilgrim (Grimstead), 1955
Tender Rebel (Lindsey), 1988
Tender Stranger (Palmer), 1985
Tender Taming (Pozzessere, as Graham), 1983
Tender Trap (Saunders), 1978
Tender Triumph (McNaught), 1983
Tender Victory (Caldwell), 1956
Tender Vine (Grimstead), 1974
Tender Warrior (F. Michaels), 1983
Tender Winds of Spring (Dingwell), 1978
Tender Yearnings (Chase), 1981
Tender Years (Hampson), 1982
Tension (Delafield), 1920
Tents of Israel (Stern), 1924
Terminus (Leslie), 1931
Terminus Tehran (R. Lane), 1969
Terms of Surrender (Dailey), 1982
Terrace in the Sun (Weale), 1966
Terracotta Palace, (Maybury), 1971
Terrible Tide (C. MacLeod, as Craig), 1983
Terriford Mystery (Lowndes), 1924
Terror at Nelson Woods (Ellis, as Richard), 1973
Terror in the Sun (Cartland), 1979
Terror of the Moor (Wynne), 1928
Terror of the Twin (Daniels), 1976

Terror the Black Sheep (Wynne), 1928
Terror Trap (W. Roberts), 1971
Tesha (Barcynska), 1923
Tessacott Tragedy (s Garvice), 1913
Test of Time (Krentz), 1987
Testament of Love (Woodward, as Richmond), 1977
Testament of Trust (Baldwin), 1960
Testimonies (O'Brian), 1952
Testimony of Two Men (Caldwell), 1968
Tetherstones (Dell), 1923
Texas series (F. Michaels), from 1985
Texas (Michener), 1985
Texas Gold (Lorin, as Hohl), 1986
Thames Camp (Grundy), 1902
Than This World Dreams Of (Ayres), 1934
Thanesworth House (Kimbrough), 1972
Thank Heaven Fasting (Delafield), 1932
Thankful Rest (Swan), 1885
Thanks to Elizabeth (Burchell), 1944
That Affair in Spain (Woodward, as Davis), 1969
That Awful Scar (Garvice, as Hart)
That Boston Man (Dailey), 1979
That Carolina Summer (Dailey), 1981
That Enchantress (Leslie), 1950
That Fatal Touch (Roby), 1970
That Girl in Nice (Greig), 1954
That Girl, Jennifer! (R. Randall), 1946
That Island Summer (Hoy), 1973
That Man in Her Life (Woodward), 1977
That Man Is Mine! (Baldwin), 1936
That Man Next Door (Stratton, as Gillen), 1971
That Man Simon (Weale), 1971
That Nice Nurse Nevin (Charles, as Tempest), 1963
That Night (Blackmore), 1963
That None Should Die (Slaughter), 1941
That Old Feeling (F. Preston, as Conlee), 1983
That Pretty Young Girl (Libbey), 1889
That Savage Yankee Squire! (Sebastian), 1978
That Strange Girl (Garvice), 1911
That Strange Holiday (Woodward, as Sawley), 1972
That Summer at Bacclesea (Gibbs, as Ford), 1956
That Trouble Piece! (Barcynska), 1939
That Villa in Spain (Woodward, as Richmond), 1981
That Which Is Hidden (Hichens), 1939
That Which Is Passed (Atkin), 1923
That Young Person (Seale), 1969
Thawing of Mara (Dailey), 1980
Thea (Maddocks), 1971
Theatre Sister in Love (Bloom, as Burns), 1963
Theft in Kind (Summerton), 1962
Theft of the Heart (Cartland, as McCorquodale), 1966
Their Flowers Were Always Black (P. Hastings), 1967
Their Heart Speaks in Many Ways (Polland), 1982
Their Mysterious Patient (Woodward, as Sawley), 1970
Theirs Was the Kingdom (Delderfield), 1971
Thelma (Corelli), 1887
Theme for Reason (Ogilvie), 1970
Theme Song (Mackinlay), 1938
Then Came the Test (Pedler), 1942
Then Came Two Women (Armstrong), 1962
Then Come Kiss Me (Burchell), 1948
Then She Fled Me (Seale), 1950
Theodora (Eliot, as Arnett), 1977
Theodore (Wynne), 1926
There Are Limits (Robins), 1932
There Are Worse Jungles (Tranter), 1955

There But for Fortune (Stuart, as A. Stuart), 1966
There Came a Tyrant (Hampson), 1972
There Is a Season (Baldwin), 1966
There Is a Tide . . . (Charles, as Chandos), 1950
There Is Always Love (Loring), 1940
There Is But One (Lorrimer, as Robins), 1965
There Lies Your Love (Butler, as Melville), 1965
There May Be Heaven (Ogilvie), 1966
There Must Be Showers (Hampson), 1983
There Once Was a Lover (Browning), 1987
There Was a Fair Maid Dwelling (Delderfield), 1960
There Was a Time (Caldwell), 1947
There Was Another (Ayres), 1938
There Were Nine Castles (Hunter), 1967
There Were Three Men (Beauclerk), 1949
There Were Three Princes (Dingwell), 1972
There Were Two Pirates (Cabell), 1946
Therefore Must Be Loved (Charles), 1972
There's Just One Girl (M. St. John, as Cooper), 1919
Theresa (I. Roberts, as Rowland), 1985
Theresa and a Tiger (Cartland), 1984
These Are Our Masters (Swan), 1939
These Changing Years (Barcynska), 1961
These Charming People (s Arlen), 1923
These Delights (Seale), 1949
These Golden Pleasures (Sherwood), 1977
These Mortals (Irwin), 1925
These My Children (M. Lewis), 1977
These Old Shades (Heyer), 1926
These Roots Go Deep (Bloom), 1939
These White Hands (Deeping), 1937
Theseus series (Renault), from 1958
They Brought Their Women (s Ferber), 1933
They Came to Valeira (Blair, as Brett), 1950
They Dreamed Too Much (Maybury), 1938
They Found Him Dead (Heyer), 1937
They Hanged My Saintly Billy (Graves), 1957
They Knew Her When (Moore), 1938
They Laugh That Win (Albanesi, as Rowlands), 1899
They Left the Land (Jacob), 1940
They Lived with Me (Price, as Smith), 1934
They Loved in Donegal (Elsna, as Lancaster), 1944
They Met in Zanzibar (Blair), 1962
They That Go Down (Steen), 1930
They That Go Down in Ships (Steen), 1931
They Were Defeated (Macaulay), 1932
They Were Not Divided (Elsna, as Lancaster), 1952
They Who Love (s Baldwin), 1948
Thicker than Water (Polland), 1965
Thicket (Gallagher), 1973
Thief of Love (Cartland, as McCorquodale), 1957
Thieving Magpie (Bloom), 1960
Thin Ice (Browning), 1989
Thine Is My Heart (Burchell), 1942
Thing That Happens to You (Berckman), 1964
Third Boat (Mackinlay), 1967
Third Estate (Bowen), 1917
Third Eye (Glyn), 1940
Third Generation (Swan), 1940
Third George (Holt, as Plaidy), 1969
Third Grave (Case), 1981
Third in the House (Dingwell), 1961
Third Life (Nicole, as Gray), 1988
Third Love Lucky (Ruck), 1958
Third Miss Chance (Peter), 1933
Third Miss Wenderby (Grundy), 1911

Third Richard (Bennetts), 1972
Third Time Lucky (Ruck), 1958
Third Uncle (Seale), 1964
Third Wife (Elsna), 1928
Thirteen O'Clock (s Benét), 1937
Thirteenth Girl (Greig), 1947
This Alien Heart (Duffield), 1942
This Ancient Evil (Daniels), 1966
This Brief Interlude (Pykare, as Powers), 1984
This Clay Suburb (Elsna), 1938
This Desirable Bachelor (Greig), 1941
This Dragon of Desire (Bloom, as Burns), 1958
This Errant Heart (Maybury), 1937
This Fearful Paradise (Greig), 1953
This Fierce Splendor (Johansen), 1988
This Flower (Miles), 1933
This Foolish Heart (Inglis), 1940
This Foolish Love (Marsh), 1982
This for Caroline (Leslie), 1964
This Golden Estate (Farnes), 1975
This Golden Valley (Rivers), 1983
This Heart of Mine (Small), 1985
This Is Marriage (Bloom), 1935
This January Tale (Bryher), 1966
This King of Love (Blair), 1964
This Land Turns Evil Slowly (Roby), 1971
This Lovely Hour (Maybury), 1937
This Loving Torment (Sherwood), 1977
This Magic Moment (N. Roberts), 1983
This Man Her Enemy (Peake), 1976
This Man Is Not for Marrying (Bloom, as Essex), 1959
This Merry Bond (Seale), 1938
This Moment in Time (Peake), 1971
This Much to Give (J. MacLeod), 1945
This Must Be for Ever (Lewty), 1962
This Narrow World (Bigland), 1938
This One Night (Robins), 1942
This Other Eden (Gaskin), 1947
This Other Eden (M. Harris), 1977
This Outward Angel (Knight), 1972
This Passion Called Love (Glyn), 1925
This Porcelain Clay (Jacob), 1939
This Proud and Savage Land (Cordell), 1987
This Proud Love (Riefe), 1985
This Publican (Yates), 1938
This Ravaged Heart (Riefe), 1977
This Ravished Land (Oldfield), 1980
This Rough Magic (E. Pargeter), 1953
This Rough Magic (Pozzessere), 1988
This Rough Magic (Stewart), 1964
This Second Spring (Arbor), 1948
This Shining Land (Laker), 1985
This Shining Splendor (J. Roberts), 1984
This Side of Glory (Bristow), 1940
This Side of Innocence (Caldwell), 1946
This Side of Paradise (K. Thorpe), 1979
This Son of Adam (Burgin), 1910
This Splendid Folly (Pedler), 1918
This Spring of Love (Robins), 1943
This Strange Adventure (Rinehart), 1929
This Summer's Rose (Ritchie), 1970
This Sweet and Bitter Earth (Cordell), 1977
This Time It's Love (Cartland), 1977
This Time It's Love (Charles, as Chandos), 1951
This Towering Passion (Sherwood), 1978
This Was a Man (Holt, as Tate), 1961

This Was Tomorrow (Thane), 1951
This Way to Happiness (Greig), 1931
This Wild Enchantment (Elsna, as Lancaster), 1938
This Woman to This Man (C. N. and A. M. Williamson), 1917
This Year, Next Year, Sometime— (Ruck), 1932
Thistle and the Rose (Holt, as Plaidy), 1963
Thistle and the Rose (Rome), 1977
Thomas and Sarah (Hardwick), 1978
Thomas Dryburgh's Dream (Swan), 1886
Thorgils (Hewlett), 1917
Thorgils and Treadholt (Hewlett), 1917
Thorn of Arimathea (Slaughter), 1959
Thorn Tree (Reid), 1969
Thorn-Apple (Worboys, as Eyre), 1968
Thornbirds (McCullough), 1977
Thorne's Way (Lorin, as Hohl), 1982
Thornwood (D. Smith), 1966
Thornyhold (Stewart), 1988
Those Difficult Years (Baldwin), 1925
Those Dominant Hills (Barcynska), 1951
Those Endearing Young Charms (Chesney), 1986
Those Fragile Years (Franken), 1952
Those Who Love (Robins), 1936
Those Who Love (Stone), 1965
Thou Shalt Love Thy Neighbour— (M. St. John), 1927
Thou Shalt Not Kill (Lowndes), 1927
Though I Bid Farewell (Hoy), 1948
Though Worlds Apart (Burchell), 1967
Thought of Honour (Cordell), 1954
Thousand Candles (Dingwell), 1971
Thousand Ways of Loving (Dingwell), 1986
Thousandth Man (Ayres), 1939
Threads of Destiny (I. Preston), 1986
Threats and Promises (Delinsky), 1986
Three Bear Witness (O'Brian), 1952
Three Candles for the Dark (R. Harris), 1976
Three Cedars (Bloom), 1937
Three Cries of Terror (Kimbrough, as Ashton), 1980
Three Crowns (Holt, as Plaidy), 1965
Three Daughters of Madame Liang (Buck), 1969
Three Days for Emeralds (Eberhart), 1988
Three Englishmen (Frankau), 1935
Three Faces of Love (Baldwin), 1957
Three for a Wedding (Neels), 1973
Three Happy Pilgrims (Farnes), 1937
Three Harbours (F. Mason), 1938
Three Latch Keys (Elsna, as Snow), 1943
Three Letters to Pan (Blackmore), 1955
Three Lives (L. Cooper), 1957
Three Loves (Lorrimer, as Robins), 1949
Three Marriages (Delafield), 1939
Three Men and Diana (Norris), 1934
Three Men and Jennie (Jacob), 1960
Three Men in Her Life (Inglis), 1951
Three of Hearts (Ruck), 1917
Three of Us (Charles, as Chandos), 1970
Three Passionate Queens (Bloom, as Prole), 1964
Three People (Grundy), 1924
Three Roads to Heaven (Elsna, as Lancaster), 1939
Three Roads to Romance (Charles, as Chandos), 1945
Three Rooms (Deeping), 1924
Three Sisters of Briarwick (Kimbrough), 1973
Three Six Seven (Vansittart), 1983
Three Sons (Bloom), 1946
Three Strings to a Fortune (Worboys, as Eyre), 1962
Three Weeks (Glyn), 1907

Three Weeks in Eden (Weale), 1964
Three Wise Men of Gotham (s Corelli), 1896
Three Women (Baldwin), 1926
Three Women (Blair, as Conway), 1955
Three Women (Clarke), 1985
Three Years to Play (MacInnes), 1970
Three's Company (Duggan), 1958
Threshold (Millhiser), 1984
Thresholds (Baldwin), 1925
Thrill of the Chase (Vitek), 1985
Thrill of Victory (Brown, as St. Claire), 1989
Through a Glass Darkly (Norris), 1957
Through All Eternity (Stanford), 1988
Through All the Years (Summers), 1974
Through Many Waters (Muskett), 1961
Through My Eyes (Delinsky), 1989
Through the Green Woods (Chard), 1974
Through the Mist (Albanesi), 1934
Through the Postern Gate (Barclay), 1912
Through These Fires (G. Hill), 1943
Through Weal and Through Woe (Albanesi, as Rowlands),
  1913
Throw Away Yesterday (Ruck), 1946
Throw Wide the Door (Loring), 1962
Throw Your Bouquet (Mackinlay, as Grey), 1967
Throw-Back (Burgin), 1918
Thunder and the Shouting (Nicole), 1969
Thunder Heights (I. Roberts), 1969
Thunder Heights (Whitney), 1960
Thunder of Her Heart (Beresford), 1978
Thunder on St. Paul's Day (J. Lane), 1954
Thunder on Sunday (Beaty, as Campbell), 1972
Thunder on the Right (Stewart), 1957
Thunder Rose (Trask), 1952
Thunder Underground (J. Lindsay), 1965
Thunderer (Beck, as Barrington), 1927
Thunderstorm (Stern), 1925
Thursday and the Lady (Matthews), 1987
Thursday's Child (Baldwin), 1976
Thursday's Child (Brown), 1985
Thursday's Children (Godden), 1984
Thurston House (Steel), 1983
Thus Doctor Mallory (Seifert), 1940
Thy Bride Am I (Bloom, as Burns), 1942
Ticket of Destiny (Preston), 1969
Ticket-of-Leave Girl (M. St. John), 1914
Tidal Wave (s Dell), 1919
Tide at Full (May), 1971
Tide Mill (Daniels), 1975
Tide of Life (Cookson), 1976
Tides of Love (Hunter), 1988
Tides of Love (Matthews), 1981
Tides of Spring Flow Fast (Bloom), 1956
Tides of Tremannion (Shoesmith), 1970
Tidewater Lover (Dailey), 1978
Tidewrack (Tranter), 1951
Tidings of Great Joy (Brown), 1987
Tie That Binds (s E. Porter), 1919
Tied to Her Apron Strings! (M. St. John), 1927
Ties of Love (Woodward, as Ware), 1968
Ties That Bind (Krentz), 1986
Tiffany's True Love (F. Stevenson, as Faire), 1981
Tiger (s Bloom), 1903(?)
Tiger and the Goat (Melville, as Betteridge), 1978
Tiger Hall (Wyndham), 1954
Tiger in Men (Robins), 1937

Tiger Lily (C. N. and A. M. Williamson), 1917
Tiger Prince (Brown, as St. Claire), 1985
Tiger's Cage (Way), 1986
Tiger's Claw (Burgin), 1900
Tiger's Heaven (P. Hastings), 1981
Tiger's Woman (De Blasis), 1981
Tight White Collar (Metalious), 1960
Tightening String (Bridge), 1962
Til the End of Time (Johansen), 1987
Till the End of Time (Peake), 1973
Till Then, My Love (M. Lewis), 1968
Tilly (Chesney, as Tremaine), 1981
Tilly series (Cookson), from 1980
Tilly Trotter series (Cookson), from 1980
Tilly-Make-Haste (Barcynska, as Sandys), 1924
Tilsit Inheritance (Gaskin), 1963
Tilted Cross (H. Porter), 1961
Tilthammer (Lamb, as Lancaster), 1980
Timber Boss (K. Thorpe), 1978
Timber Man (Dingwell), 1964
Time after Time (Hooper), 1986
Time and Chance (Weale), 1989
Time and the Hour (Baldwin), 1974
Time and the Loving (Lewty), 1977
Time and the Place (Summers), 1958
Time and Tide (Browning), 1984
Time at Tarragon (Tattersall), 1969
Time, Flow Softly (Cato), 1960
Time for a Tiger (Burgess), 1956
Time for Another Dream (van der Zee), 1986
Time for Happiness (Asquith), 1959
Time for Play (Muskett), 1943
Time for Pleasure (P. Hastings), 1957
Time for Rejoicing (Renier), 1973
Time for Titans (Delmar), 1974
Time Is Noon (Buck), 1967
Time Is—Time Was (Elsna), 1960
Time May Change (Asquith), 1961
Time of Curtain Fall (Hilton), 1976
Time of the Dragon (Eden), 1975
Time of the Hunter's Moon (Holt), 1983
Time of the Jacaranda (Way), 1970
Time of the Seventh Moon (I. Roberts, as I. M. Roberts),
  1984
Time No Longer (Caldwell, as Renier), 1941
Time of Dreaming (M. Howard, as Edgar), 1968
Time of Glory (Giles), 1966
Time of Grace (Seale), 1955
Time of the Singing Birds (G. Hill), 1945
Time of the Temptress (Winspear), 1977
Time of Their Lives (s Melville, as Betteridge), 1974
Time on Her Hands (Mackinlay), 1942
Time Out of Mind (Field), 1935
Time Out of Mind (K. Thorpe), 1987
Time Piece (Jacob), 1936
Time Remembered (Stratton, as Gillen), 1971
Time Remembered, Time Lost (R. Randall), 1973
Time Returns (Ripley), 1985
Time Runs Out (Robins, as Kane), 1965
Time Stands Still (Pykare, as Powers), 1983
Time Suspended (J. MacLeod), 1974
Time to Heal (Deeping), 1952
Time to Love (Chard), 1987
Time to Love (Delinsky, as Douglass), 1982
Time to Love (R. Lindsay, as Scott), 1960
Time to Wed (Hunter), 1984

Timed for Love (Finley), 1979
Timeless Land (Dark), 1941
Timeless Place (Stubbs), 1978
Times of Triumph (C. Allen), 1979
Time/Steps (C. Allen), 1986
Timid Cleopatra (Greig, as Ames), 1962
Tinker's Pride (Tranter), 1945
Tinsel and the Gold (Barcynska, as Sandys), 1959
Tinsel Kisses (Grimstead), 1958
Tinted Dream (Greig, as Ames), 1936
Tiptoes (Barcynska, as Sandys), 1935
Tish series (s Rinehart), from 1911
Titans (Jakes), 1976
Title Role (Harrod-Eagles, as Bennett), 1980
To an Unknown Shore (Jakes), 1975
To Be a Bride (Charles, as Tempest), 1945
To Be a King (Chapman), 1934
To Be Beloved (I. Roberts, as Rowland), 1968
To Be So Loved (Chard), 1988
To Be the Best (Bradford), 1988
To Bed at Noon (Bowen, as Shearing), 1951
To Bring You Joy (Summers), 1985
To Buy a Bride (R. Lindsay, as Leigh), 1976
To Buy a Memory (Hampson), 1983
To Cage a Whirlwind (Donnelly), 1985
To Care Always (Norway), 1970
To Catch a Bride (Finley), 1977
To Catch a Butterfly (Lewty), 1977
To Catch a Dream (Grimstead, as Manning), 1970
To Catch a Unicorn (Seale), 1964
To Dance with Kings (Laker), 1988
To Dream Again (I. Preston), 1985
To Dream of Love (Chesney), 1986
To Each Her Dream (McElfresh), 1961
To Everything a Season (Glover), 1986
To Follow the Lead (Swan), 1911
To Greet the Morning (Ritchie), 1966
To Have and to Hold (M. Johnston), 1900
To Have and to Hold (Palmer), 1979
To Journey Together (Burchell), 1956
To Lisa with Love (I. Roberts, as Rowland), 1975
To Live with Fear (Chard), 1985
To Look and Pass (Caldwell), 1974
To Love a Dark Stranger (Coffman), 1969
To Love a Rogue (Sherwood), 1987
To Love a Stranger (Laker, as Paul), 1978
To Love Again (Robins), 1949
To Love Again (Steel), 1980
To Love and to Cherish (Albanesi, as Rowlands), 1912
To Love and to Cherish (Palmer), 1979
To Love and to Honor (Loring), 1950
To Love Is to Live (Robins), 1940
To M. L. G. (A. M. Williamson), 1912
To Marry a Tiger (Hunter, as Chace), 1971
To Meet a Stranger (Holt, as Burford), 1957
To Mend a Heart (E. Harrison), 1977
To Play with Fire (Kidd), 1977
To Save My Life (Charles), 1946
To See a Fine Lady (Lofts), 1946
To See a Stranger (Lynn), 1961
To See Ourselves (Field), 1937
To See the Glory (Caldwell), 1963
To Seek a Star (Ebel), 1973
To Serve Them All My Days (Delderfield), 1972
To Share a Dream (W. Roberts), 1986

To Sing Me Home (D. Smith), 1969
To Slay the Dreamer (Cordell), 1980
To Tame a Vixen (Hampson), 1978
To Tame the Hunter (Krentz, as James), 1983
To Taste the Wine (F. Michaels), 1987
To Tell the Truth (Dailey), 1977
To the High Redoubt (Yarbro), 1985
To the Hilt (Wren), 1937
To the Stars (Lorrimer, as Robins), 1944
To Trust Tomorrow (John), 1981
To Wear Your Ring (Inglis), 1938
To Wed a Doctor (Seifert), 1968
To Whom Be Glory (F. Mason), 1957
To Win a Paradise (Hoy), 1947
Toast of the Town (Ley), 1969
Toast to Lady Mary (Leslie), 1954
Tobias and the Angel (Yerby), 1975
Today and Forever (s Buck), 1941
Today Is Mine (Bowen), 1941
To-Day Is Ours (Muskett), 1939
Today Is Yours (Loring), 1938
To-Day We Live (Maybury), 1942
To-Day's Daughter (Ruck), 1929
Today's Virtue (Baldwin), 1931
Together (Diver), 1928
Together Again (Kidd), 1979
Together and Apart (Kennedy), 1936
Together They Rode (Holt, as Plaidy), 1945
Toil of the Brave (Fletcher), 1946
Toils of Silence (M. St. John, as Cooper), 1935
Tokyo Tryst (K. Thorpe), 1988
Tolbecken (Shellabarger), 1956
Told at Monte Carlo (s A. Williamson), 1926
Toll-Gate (Heyer), 1954
Tom and Some Other Girls (Vaizey), 1901
Tomalyn's Quest (Burgin), 1896
Tomboy in Lace (Ruck), 1947
Tomorrow about This Time (G. Hill), 1923
Tomorrow Brings Enchantment (Reid), 1978
Tomorrow Comes the Sun (Renier), 1969
To-morrow for Apricots (Bloom), 1929
To-morrow Is Eternal (Bloom, as Burns), 1948
Tomorrow Is Forever (Bristow), 1943
Tomorrow Is Theirs (Duffield), 1952
Tomorrow the Glory (Pozzessere, as Drake), 1985
Tomorrow We Marry (Bloom, as Burns), 1953
To-morrow's Bargain (J. MacLeod), 1949
To-morrow's Hero (M. Howard), 1941
Tomorrow's Miracle (Slaughter), 1962
Tomorrow's Promise (Brown), 1983
To-morrow's Promise (Elsna, as Snow), 1956
Tomorrow's Sun (May), 1989
To-morrow's Tangle (Pedler), 1925
Tongues of Conscience (s Hichens), 1900
Tonight and Always (N. Roberts), 1983
To-night, Josephine! (Bloom, as Prole), 1954
Tontine (Costain), 1955
Tony's Memorable Christmas (s Swan), 1883
Tony's Wife (Albanesi), 1919
Too Bad to Be True (R. Lindsay, as Leigh), 1987
Too Close for Comfort (B. Hastings), 1987
Too Common for Him! (M. St. John, as Cooper), 1923
Too Few for Drums (Delderfield), 1964
Too Hot to Handle (Hampson), 1982
Too Hot to Handle (Lowell), 1986
Too Late for Tears (M. Lewis), 1972

Too Many Men (Inglis), 1939
Too Many Women (Greig, as Ames), 1941
Too Much Alone (Greig, as Ames), 1950
Too Much Love of Living (Hichens), 1947
Too Much Together (Ayres), 1936
Too Old for Her Husband! (M. St. John), 1924
Too Well Beloved (Elsna), 1964
Too Wilful for Words! (M. St. John), 1915
Too Young to Love (R. Lindsay, as Leigh), 1977
Too Young to Marry (Blair, as Brett), 1958
Too Young to Wed (Woodward, as Richmond), 1960
Top of the Beanstalk (Charles, as Tempest), 1940
Top of the Climb (Beaty), 1962
Top of the Tree (Albanesi, as Rowlands), 1937
Top of the World (Dell), 1920
Topaz (Bennetts), 1987
Topaz Charm (J. Roberts, as Radcliffe), 1976
Topaz Island (Lorrimer, as Robins), 1965
Tormented (Daniels), 1969
Tormentil (Chard, as Chase), 1984
Tormenting Flame (Buckingham, as John), 1981
Torquemada (Fast), 1966
Torrent (Reid), 1972
Total Surrender (M. Pargeter), 1985
Touch a Star (Cartland), 1982
Touch and Go (Parkinson), 1977
Touch Me (Daniels, as Somers), 1973
Touch Not the Cat (Stewart), 1976
Touch of Glory (Slaughter), 1945
Touch of Honey (Stratton, as Gillen), 1973
Touch of Love (Cartland), 1977
Touch of Love (Finley), 1985
Touch of Magic (Hunter), 1981
Touch of Magic (Summers), 1973
Touch of the Devil (Weale), 1980
Touch of Your Hand (Woodward, as Richmond), 1960
Touch the Horizon (Johansen), 1984
Touch the Wind (Dailey), 1979
Touched by Fire (Donnelly), 1978
Touching the Clouds (Greig), 1936
Touchstone (Muskett), 1962
Tournament (Foote), 1949
Toward the End (Savage), 1980
Toward the Morning (H. Allen), 1948
Towards the Dawn (Arbor), 1956
Towards the Stars (Cartland), 1971
Towards the Sun (Blair, as Brett), 1953
Tower (Steen), 1959
Tower Abbey (I. Holland), 1978
Tower and the Dream (Westcott), 1974
Tower in the Forest (Webb, as Hamill), 1951
Tower of Dreams (Webb, as Hamill), 1961
Tower of Kilraven (Crowe), 1965
Tower of Strength (Hunter), 1983
Tower of the Captive (Winspear), 1966
Tower of the Winds (Hunter), 1973
Tower Room (Daniels), 1965
Tower Room (Roby), 1974
Towers in the Mist (Goudge), 1938
Town House (Lofts), 1959
Town Like Alice (Shute), 1950
Town Nurse—Country Nurse (Lewty), 1970
Town of Masks (Davis), 1952
Town That Nearly Died (M. Lewis), 1973
Townsman (Buck, as Sedges), 1945
Toy Sword (Cadell), 1962

Traceys (Bromige), 1946
Trackless Way (Bloom), 1931
Tradd Family series (Ripley), from 1981
Trade Wind (Kaye), 1963
Trader's Cay (Stratton), 1980
Trading Secrets (Krentz, as Castle), 1985
Tradition of Pride (Dailey), 1982
Trail of Conflict (Loring), 1922
Trailing Glory (Bloom), 1940
Train at Bundarbar (McCutchan, as MacNeil), 1981
Traitor (s Orczy), 1912
Traitors (Stuart, as Long), 1981
Traitors' Gate (Gavin), 1976
Traitors' Legion (Jakes, as Scotland), 1963
Traitor's Road (Daniels), 1967
Traitor's Son (Heaven, as Fecher), 1967
Trampling of the Lilies (Sabatini), 1906
Tranquil Haven (J. MacLeod), 1946
Transformation of Philip Jettan (Heyer, as Martin), 1923
Transplant (Slaughter), 1987
Transplanted (Niven), 1944
Trap (Winston), 1973
Trap for Lovers (Blackmore), 1960
Trap for Navarre (Wynne), 1922
Trapped (Roby), 1977
Traveling Man (Lowell), 1985
Traveller in the Fur Coat (Weyman), 1924
Travellers (Stubbs), 1963
Travelling Kind (Dailey), 1981
Tread Softly (Miles), 1926
Tread Softly in the Sun (Worboys, as Eyre), 1969
Tread Softly, Nurse (Norway, as Neal), 1962
Tread Softly on Dreams (Mackinlay, as Grey), 1970
Treason in November (Dymoke), 1961
Treason's Harbour (O'Brian), 1983
Treasure (Norris), 1914
Treasure Chest (Roby), 1976
Treasure for Life (Weale), 1972
Treasure Hunt (Seger), 1986
Treasure Is Love (Cartland), 1979
Treasure of Heaven (Corelli), 1906
Treasure of Ho (Beck), 1924
Treasure of Pleasant Valley (Yerby), 1955
Treasure of the Lake (Haggard), 1926
Treasure Worth Seeking (Brown, as Ryan), 1982
Treasures (Nicole, as Gray), 1984
Treasures Lost, Treasures Found (N. Roberts), 1986
Treasures on Earth (Stirling), 1985
Tree Drops a Leaf (Ayres), 1938
Tree of Evil (Webb, as Morrison), 1966
Tree of Gold (Laker), 1986
Tree of Heaven (s Chambers), 1907
Tree of Idleness (Hunter), 1973
Tree of Man (P. White), 1955
Tree of Paradise (Arbor), 1976
Tree of Vortigern (Wiat), 1976
Treehaven (Norris), 1932
Trees Die at the Top (Ferber), 1938
Tregaron's Daughter (Brent), 1971
Trellised Walk (Manners, as Marshall), 1973
Trelawny (I. Holland), 1974
Trelawny's Fell (I. Holland), 1976
Trembling Hills (Whitney), 1956
Trespass (Tranter), 1937
Trevallion (Seale), 1957
Trevelyan's Little Daughter (Sheard), 1898

Trevithick (P. Hill), 1989
Trial and Error (Elsna, as Snow), 1973
Trial Marriage (Mather), 1977
Trial of Innocence (Hufford), 1978
Trial of Sören Qvist (J. Lewis), 1947
Trickster (Burgin), 1909
Tricoleur (Nicole, as Logan), 1976
Trificante Treasure (Winston), 1968
Trio (Bentley), 1930
Triple Tangle (Saxton, as Turner), 1981
Tristam of Blent (Hope), 1901
Tristan and Isolde (Erskine), 1932
Triumph (Gann), 1986
Triumph of Love (Albanesi, as Rowlands), 1911
Triumph of O'Rourke, (Cleeve), 1972
Triumph of the Rat (Robins), 1927
Triumphant Beast (Bowen), 1934
Trojan Gold (B. Michaels, as Peters), 1987
Tropical Affair (Beresford), 1967
Tropical Affairs (Beresford), 1968
Tropical Tempest (Kidd), 1983
Tropical Waters (R. Fraser), 1933
Troubadour's Romance (Carr), 1985
Trouble in Thor (Armstrong, as Valentine), 1953
Trouble with Product X (Aiken), 1966
Troubled Waters (Sallis), 1975
Troubles (Farrell), 1970
Trout's Testament (R. Fraser), 1960
Troy Chimneys (Kennedy), 1952
Truant Bride (Seale), 1966
Truant Happiness (Albanesi), 1918
Truant Spirit (Seale), 1954
Truant Wife (s Swan), 1899
Truce of God (Rinehart), 1920
True Colors (Krentz), 1986
True Lady (J. Smith), 1986
True Love's Reward (Libbey), 1904
True Thomas (Tranter), 1981
True Woman (Orczy), 1911
Trumpet Voluntary (Stern), 1944
Trumpeter, Sound! (D. Murray), 1933
Trumpets at Rome (Bowen), 1936
Trumpets of God (Bacheller), 1927
Trust Betrayed (Swan), 1939
Trust in Tomorrow (Hilton), 1971
Trust Me, My Love (Charles), 1975
Trustworthy Redhead (Johansen), 1984
Truth about Janice Henderson (Woodward, as Marsh),
    1972
Truth Game (Dingwell), 1978
Truth Game (Melville, as Betteridge), 1966
Truth in a Circle (Albanesi), 1922
Truxton King (McCutcheon), 1909
Tryst (G. Hill), 1921
Tryst (Thane), 1939
Trysting Tower (Beaty, as Ross), 1966
Tsar's Woman (P. Hill), 1977
Tudor series (Cowen, as Hyde), from 1972
Tudor series (Heaven, as Fecher), from 1966
Tudor Boy (Bloom, as Prole), 1960
Tudor Ghosts (Bennetts), 1971
Tudor Rose (J. Fitzgerald, as Watson), 1972
Tuesday's Child (Grimstead), 1973
Tulip Tree (Gibbs), 1979
Tulip Tree (Blair), 1958
Tulips for Augusta (Neels), 1971

Tully, Jasper series (Davis), from 1957
Tumbled Wall (Browning), 1980
Tumult at the Gate (Nicole, as Grange), 1970
Tumult in the North (Bowen, as Preedy), 1931
Tumult of the Heart (I. Preston), 1988
Tune of Time (Bloom), 1970
Tunnel Tigers (Cordell), 1986
Turbulent Messiters (Gibbs, as Ford), 1967
Turbulent Tales (s Sabatini), 1946
Turkish Rondo (A. Stevenson), 1981
Turn Back the Leaves (Delafield), 1930
Turn Back the River (Hardy), 1938
Turn of Life's Road (Bloom), 1976
Turn of the Cards (Roby, as Grey), 1979
Turn of the Road (Elsna, as Conway), 1960
Turn of the Tide (Oldfield), 1988
Turn of the Tide (E. Porter), 1908
Turn the Page (Asquith), 1970
Turn to the Sun (Duffield), 1944
Turn to the West (Seale), 1953
Turnbulls (Caldwell), 1943
Turning of Griggsby (Bacheller), 1913
Turning Point (Charles, as Tempest), 1961
Turning Towards Home (Krentz, as Bentley), 1979
Turnstile of Night (A. M. Williamson), 1904
Turquoise (Seton), 1946
Turquoise Mask (Whitney), 1974
Turret Room (Armstrong), 1965
Tuscan Chalice (Woodward), 1972
Tuxter's Little Maid (Burgin), 1895
'Twas Love's Fault (Garvice)
Twelve Across (Delinsky), 1987
Twenty-Four Hours (Bromfield), 1930
Twenty-Four Hours a Day (Baldwin), 1937
Twenty-One (Barcynska), 1924
Twenty-Three and a Half Hours' Leave (Rinehart), 1918
22 Indigo Place (Brown), 1986
Twice a Boy (Ayres), 1951
Twice Born (Franken), 1935
Twice Have I Loved (Robins), 1973
Twice Tried (Swan), n.d.
Twice-Born (Crowe), 1972
Twilight and Dawn (Muskett), 1941
Twilight at the Elms (Daniels), 1976
Twilight Moment (Mackinlay), 1976
Twilight of a Tudor (Bloom), 1952
Twilight on the Floods (Steen), 1949
Twilight Return (Kimbrough), 1976
Twilight Whispers (Delinsky), 1987
Twin series (Deveraux), from 1985
Twins of Twineham (M. St. John), 1911
Twist of Fate (Krentz), 1986
Twist of Fate (Lamb), 1979
Twisted Cameo (Kimbrough), 1971
Twisted Road (Bloom), 1975
Twisted Road (Grimstead), 1951
Twists and Turns of Love (Cartland), 1978
'Twix Smile and Tear (Garvice)
'Twixt Devil and Deep Sea (A. M. Williamson), 1901
Two Alone (Brown, as St. Claire), 1987
Two and Threes (Stern), 1916
Two Black Sheep (Deeping), 1933
Two by Two (Garnett), 1963
Two Carnations (Bowen), 1913
Two Doctor Greys (Woodward, as Richmond), 1977
Two Doctors and a Girl (Seifert), 1976

Two Doctors, Two Loves (Seifert), 1982
Two Faces of Dr. Collier (Seifert), 1974
Two Faces of Love (Barcynska), 1958
Two Fair Daughters (Elsna, as Conway), 1965
Two Feet from Heaven (Wren), 1940
Two Flags for France (Dymoke), 1986
Two Flights Up (Rinehart), 1928
Two for Joy (Manley-Tucker), 1979
Two Friends (s Swan), 1898
Two Girls and a Man (Garvice), 1937
Two Good Patriots (s Orczy), 1912
Two Hearts Apart (Lee, as Gordon), 1973
Two in a Tent—and Jane (Grundy), 1913
Two in a Train (s Deeping), 1935
Two in Shadow (Blackmore), 1962
Two Little Rich Girls (Eberhart), 1972
Two Loves (Robins, as Chesterton), 1955
Two Loves for Tamara (Charles, as Tempest), 1951
Two Loves Have I (Burchell), 1976
Two Loves Have I (M. Howard), 1950
Two Loves in Her Life (Holt, as Burford), 1955
Two Maids and a Man (Garvice), 1912
Two Men and a Maid (M. St. John, as Cooper), 1920
Two Men and Gwenda (Grundy), 1910
Two Miss Speckles (Grundy), 1946
Two Mrs. Abbotts (D. Stevenson), 1943
Two Names under the Shore (Ertz), 1947
Two of a Kind (Hampson), 1974
Two of Us (Greig, as Ames), 1964
Two Other People (Charles, as Chandos), 1964
Two Paths (J. MacLeod), 1944
Two Pins in a Fountain (Arbor), 1977
Two Pools in a Field (Bloom), 1967
Two Queen Annes (Bloom, as Prole), 1971
Two Ravens (C. Holland), 1977
Two Saplings (de la Roche), 1942
Two Valleys (Fast), 1933
Two Waifs (Albanesi, as Rowlands), 1914
Two Walk Apart (Elsna, as Snow), 1948
Two Walk Together (Mackinlay), 1945
Two Weeks to Remember (Neels), 1986
Two Worlds of Peggy Scott (Daniels), 1974
Two-and-Twenty (s Forester), 1931
Two's Company . . . (M. St. John, as Cooper), 1923
Tycoon for Ann (Finley), 1968
Tyler (Palmer), 1988
Tyrant (Veryan), 1987
Tzigane (E. Smith), 1935

Ugly Dachshund (Stern). 1938
Ugly Head (Bloom), 1965
Ugly Prince (Charles, as Storm), 1950
Ukelele Girl (MacGill), 1927
Ultimate Prizes (Howatch), 1989
Ultimate Surrender (Charles), 1958
Umbrella-Maker's Daughter (Caird), 1980
Unbaited Trap (Cookson), 1966
Unbidden Dream (Marsh), 1981
Unbidden Melody (Burchell), 1973
Unborn Tomorrow (Frankau), 1953
Unbreakable Spell (Cartland), 1984
Unbroken Link (Elsna, as Lancaster), 1959
Uncertain Flame (Inglis), 1937
Uncertain Heart (Chard), 1976
Uncertain Heart (Robins), 1949
Uncertain Joy (Lorrimer, as Robins), 1966

Uncertain Lover (Elsna), 1935
Uncertain Summer (Neels), 1972
Uncharted Romance (M. Howard), 1941
Uncharted Seas (Loring), 1932
Uncle Bernac (Doyle), 1897
Uncle Jeremy (Burgin), 1920
Uncle Patterley's Money (Burgin), 1936
Uncle Peel (Bacheller), 1933
Unconquered (Diver), 1917
Unconquered (Small), 1982
Unconquered (Swanson), 1947
Uncrowned King (Orczy), 1935
Uncrowned Queen (Harwood), 1983
Uncut Jade (Barr), 1983
Undarkening Green (Bloom), 1959
Undaunted (J. Lane), 1934
Undefended Gate (Ertz), 1953
Under a Ban (M. St. John), 1907
Under Castle Walls (Bailey), 1906
Under False Pretences (Ruck), 1922
Under Gemini (Pilcher), 1976
Under Heaven (Clarke), 1988
Under Joint Management (Burchell), 1947
Under Moonglow (Hampson), 1978
Under New Management (Jacob), 1941
Under the Big Top (Barcynska), 1933
Under the Red Robe (Weyman), 1894
Under the Sky (Lorrimer, as Robins), 1970
Under the Stars of Paris (Burchell), 1954
Under Which King (Niven), 1943
Undercover (Seger), 1986
Underground Syndicate (A. M. Williamson), 1910
Understudy (Ruck), 1933
Undertow (Norris), 1917
Undressed Heroine (Grundy), 1916
Undying Past (Elsna), 1964
Unearthly (Daniels), 1970
Unearthly (Hichens), 1926
Uneaseful Death (Hardwick), 1988
Uneasy Alliance (Krentz), 1984
Uneasy Conquest (Mackinlay), 1959
Uneasy Freehold (Macardle), 1941
Uneasy Lies the Head (Holt, as Plaidy), 1982
Uneducating Mary (Norris), 1923
Unfinished (Harrod-Eagles, as Bennett), 1983
Unfinished Clue (Heyer), 1934
Unfinished Portrait (Westmacott), 1934
Unforeseen (Macardle), 1946
Unforgettable (Seger), 1988
Unforgettable Caress (Vitek), 1984
Unforgiven (M. Lewis), 1974
Unforgiving Moment (Cowen), 1971
Unforgotten (Elsna, as Conway), 1969
Unforgotten (Winston), 1973
Unforgotten Face (M. Peters, as Whitby), 1975
Unframed Portrait (Albanesi), 1935
Unfulfilled (Hardy), 1951
Unguarded (Daniels), 1965
Unguarded Hour (J. MacLeod, as Airlie), 1956
Unguarded Moment (Craven), 1982
Unhallowed House (Ponsonby), 1956
Unhappy Bargain (Albanesi, as Rowlands)
Unhappy Parting (Lee), 1973
Unholy Desires (Blake), 1981
Unholy Woman (Holt, as Plaidy), 1954
Unhurrying Chase (Prescott), 1925

Unicorn (Sheen), 1931
Unicorn Rampant (Tranter), 1984
Unicorn Summer (Martin), 1984
Unidentified Woman (Eberhart), 1943
Uninvited (Macardle), 1942
Uninvited Guest (Charles, as Tempest), 1939
United States Navy series (Nicole), from 1986
Unjust Skies (Delderfield), 1962
Unkissed Bride (Ruck), 1929
Unknown Ajax (Heyer), 1959
Unknown Eros (Moore), 1935
Unknown Heart (Cartland), 1969
Unknown Heart (Grimstead), 1958
Unknown Joy (Charles, as Tempest), 1941
Unknown Lover (Vaizey), 1913
Unknown Mr. Brown (Seale), 1972
Unknown Quantity (Eberhart), 1953
Unknown Quantity (Dell), 1924
Unknown Quest (Britt), 1971
Unknown Shore (O'Brian), 1959
Unknown Welshman (Stubbs), 1972
Unlamented (Daniels), 1975
Unless I Marry (Stern), 1959
Unless Two Be Agreed (Pedler), 1947
Unlikely Lover (Palmer), 1986
Unlit Fire (Robins), 1960
Unlit Heart (Stuart), 1954
Unlived Year (J. MacLeod, as Airlie), 1962
Unmarried Couple (Greig), 1940
Unmasking Kelsey (Hooper), 1988
Unnamed Gentlewoman (Ponsonby), 1976
Unofficial Wife (Ayres), 1937
Unpredictable Bride (Cartland), 1964
Unquiet Spirit,The (Sheen), 1955
Unreasonable Summer (Browning), 1980
Unrest (Deeping), 1916
Unseen To-morrow (J. MacLeod), 1943
Unseen Torment (Kimbrough), 1974
Unseen Witness (Wynne), 1932
Unshaken Loyalty (Robins), 1955
Unsuspected (Armstrong), 1946
Unsuspected Witness (Wynne), 1945
Untamed (N. Roberts), 1983
Untamed Bride (Sinclair, as Daniels), 1988
Untamed Heart (M. Howard), 1940
Until Death (Daniels, as Somers), 1973
Until I Find Her (Charles, as Tempest), 1950
Until the Day Break (Bromfield), 1942
Until the Sun Falls (C. Holland), 1969
Until We Met (Weale), 1961
Untitled Story (Byrne), 1925
Unto Caesar (Orczy), 1914
Untouched Wife (R. Lindsay), 1981
Untrodden Snow (Robins), 1958
Unusual Behaviour (L. Cooper), 1986
Unusual Tutor (Ponsonby), 1967
Unvanquished (Fast), 1942
Unwanted Bride (Hampson), 1982
Unwanted Heiress (M. St. John, as Cooper), 1924
Unwanted Wedding (Cartland), 1984
Unwanted Wife (R. Lindsay), 1976
Unwary Heart (Hampson), 1969
Unwilling Bride (Winspear), 1969
Unwilling Bridegroom (R. Lindsay, as Leigh),
  1976
Unwilling Guest (G. Hill), 1902
Unwinding Corner (Dwyer-Joyce), 1983

Unwise Wanderer (Mackinlay), 1952
Up She Rises (Garnett), 1977
Upas Tree (Barclay), 1912
Uphill Path (Mackinlay), 1979
Uphill Road (Ayres), 1921
Upon a Moon-Dark Moor (Brandewyne), 1988
Upon This Rock (Slaughter), 1963
Ups and Downs (Swan), 1878
Upstairs, Downstairs series (Hardwick), from 1973
Upstart (E. Marshall), 1945
Upturned Palms (Elsna), 1933
Urbinian (Sabatini), 1924
Ursula Vivian, The Sister-Mother (Swan), 1884
Usurper (Garvice), n.d.
Uther and Igraine (Deeping), 1903
Utility Husband (Charles, as Tempest), 1944
Utterly Alone! (M. St. John), 1928
Uttermost Farthing (Lowndes), 1908

Vaaldorp Diamond (Darrell, as Dane), 1978
Vacation for Nurse Dean (Ritchie, as Heath), 1966
Vacillations of Hazel (Grundy), 1905
Vagabond Daughter (Mackinlay), 1955
Vagabond Harvest (Bloom), 1925
Vagabond Jess (M. St. John, as Cooper), 1919
Vagabond's Daughter (M. St. John, as Cooper), 1922
Vagabond's Way (Leslie), 1962
Vagrant Dream (Ritchie), 1959
Vagrant Lover (Bloom, as Burns), 1945
Vail d'Alvery (Keyes), 1947
Vain Delighted (Mackinlay), 1962
Valaquez Bride (Vitek), 1982
Valcour series (Daniels), from 1981
Valdez Marriage (Winspear), 1978
Valentina (Anthony), 1966
Valentina (F. Michaels), 1978
Valentine's Day (Seale), 1962
Valerie (J. Smith), 1981
Valerie French (Yates), 1923
Valiant Dust (Wren), 1932
Valiant Sailors (Stuart), 1964
Vallette Heritage (Roberts, as Bronte), 1979
Valley Deep, Mountain High (Mather),1976
Valley Forge (Kantor), 1975
Valley Forge (F. Mason), 1950
Valley of Aloes (May), 1967
Valley of Bells (I. Roberts, as Rowland), 1967
Valley of Decision (Davenport), 1942
Valley of Desire (J. MacLeod, as Airlie), 1955
Valley of Fire (Taylor), 1984
Valley of Flowers (Blair), 1957
Valley of Gentians (Rome), 1982
Valley of Horses (Auel), 1982
Valley of Lilacs (Chappell), 1972
Valley of Night (Farnol), 1942
Valley of Nightingales (Renier), 1966
Valley of Palms (J. MacLeod), 1950
Valley of Paradise (Rome), 1975
Valley of Roses (Maybury), 1945
Valley of Secrets (Renier), 1970
Valley of Tall Chimneys (Manners, as Marshall),
  1975
Valley of the Eagles (Farnes), 1972
Valley of the Kings (C. Holland, as Carter), 1977
Valley of the Moon (Way), 1979
Valley of the Ravens (Buckingham), 1973
Valley of the Reindeer (Laker, as Øvstedal), 1973

Valley of the Shadows (Daniels), 1980
Valley of the Snows (J. MacLeod), 1985
Valley of the Sun (Lowell), 1985
Valley of the Vapours (Dailey), 1976
Valley of Yesterday (Worboys, as Eyre), 1965
Valour (Deeping), 1918
Vampire Curse (Winston)j, 1971
Vampyre of Moura (Coffman), 1970
Van Rhyne Heritage (J. Roberts, as Bronte), 1980
Vanderlyn's Adventure (Lowndes), 1931
Vane Pursuit (C. MacLeod), 1989
Vanessa (Fellows), 1978
Vanessa (Walpole), 1933
Vanish in an Instant (Millar), 1952
Vanity Box (A. M. Williamson, as Stuyvesant),
    1911
Vanquished Heart (Hoy), 1949
Variation on a Theme (Delinsky, as Douglass), 1985
Varick's Legacy (Burgin), 1912
Varleigh Medallion (S. Thorpe), 1979
Veil of Gold (Vitek), 1981
Veil of Rushes (I. Roberts, as Rowland), 1967
Veil of Treachery (Daniels), 1979
Veil'd Delight (Bowen), 1933
Veiled Lady (Wynne), 1918
Veils (Hichens), 1943
Veils of Salome (Jakes, as Scotland), 1962
Velvet Angel (Deveraux), 1983
Velvet Glove (Stratton), 1977
Velvet Hammer (Baldwin), 1969
Velvet Horn (Lytle), 1957
Velvet Jungle (Ellis), 1987
Velvet Lightning (Hooper), 1988
Velvet Promise (Deveraux), 1981
Velvet Song (Deveraux), 1983
Velvet Spur (Arbor), 1974
Velvet Touch (Hilton), 1979
Velvet Touch (Krentz, as James), 1982
Velvet Trap (Blackmore), 1969
Venables (P. Hill), 1986
Venables (Norris), 1941
Vendetta (Corelli), 1886
Vendetta Castle (Ellis, as Marino), 1971
Veneer (Bloom), 1929
Venetia (Heyer), 1958
Venetian (Bennetts), 1968
Venetian Inheritance (Worboys, as Eyre), 1973
Venetian Lover (Gordon), 1982
Venetian Masque (Sabatini), 1934
Venetian Rhapsody (Robins), 1954
Vengeance of Love (Garvice, as Hart)
Vengeful Heart (R. Lindsay, as Leigh), 1952
Venice Affair (Dingwell), 1968
Venture Once More (Graham), 1954
Venus of Konpara (Masters), 1960
Venus Rising (J. Fitzgerald), 1982
Venus, The Lonely Goddess (Erskine), 1949
Venus with Sparrows (R. Harris), 1961
Vera (Elizabeth), 1921
Verdict of the Heart (Garvice), 1912
Vergilius (Bacheller), 1904
Verity (Jagger), 1980
Vermilion (Whitney), 1981
Veronica (Beresford), 1967
Veronique (Coffman), 1975
Vertical City (s Hurst), 1922
Very House (de la Roche), 1937

Very Naughty Angel (Cartland), 1975
Very Special Love (Woodward), 1976
Very Special Man (Lewty), 1979
Very Special Person (Mackinlay, as Grey), 1967
Very Unusual Wife (Cartland), 1984
Vesey Inheritance (Butler), 1975
Vexed Inheritance (Swan), 1890
Vibration of Love (Cartland), 1982
Vicar of Moura (Coffman), 1972
Vice Avenged (Burford), 1971
Vicissitudes of Evangeline (Glyn), 1905
Vicky (Elsna), 1961
Victim (Winston), 1972
Victim of Love (Buckingham), 1967
Victim of Love (Woodward, as Marsh), 1973
Victim of the Aurora (Keneally), 1977
Victims (Blake, as Pearl), 1972
Victoire (Darcy), 1974
Victoria (Anthony), 1959
Victoria and Albert (Anthony), 1958
Victoria and the Nightingale (Barrie), 1967
Victoria Grandolet (Bellamann), 1944
Victoria in the Wings (Holt, as Plaidy), 1972
Victoria Line (s Binchy), 1980
Victoria Victorious (Holt, as Plaidy), 1985
Victorian series (Holt, as Plaidy), from 1972
Victorian Album (Berckman), 1973
Victoria's Walk (Nicole, as Gray), 1986
Victorine (Keyes), 1958
Victors and Lords (Stuart, as V. A. Stuart), 1972
Victory (Harrod-Eagles), 1989
Victory at Sebastopol (Stuart, as V. A. Stuart), 1973
Victory for Love (Cartland), 1985
Victory for Victoria (Neels), 1972
Victory Won (Swan), 1895
Video Vixen (Chase), 1983
Vienna Dreams (J. Roberts, as Radcliffe), 1982
Vienna Summer (Buckingham), 1979
View of the Sea (Maddocks), 1973
Viking (E. Marshall), 1951
Viking Heart (Salverson), 1923
Viking Song (J. MacLeod), 1977
Viking Stranger (Winspear), 1966
Villa Faustina (Britt), 1977
Villa Fountains (Coffman), 1968
Villa in the Sun (Lewty), 1986
Village Nurse (Bloom, as Harvey), 1967
Village of Fear (Cowen), 1974
Village of Souls (Child), 1933
Villains (Blackstock, as Keppel), 1980
Vinegar series (M. Peters), from 1986
Vines of Yarrabee (Eden), 1969
Vineyard Chapel (Daniels), 1976
Vineyard in a Valley (Bevan), 1972
Vintage of Surrender (Krentz, as Castle), 1979
Viola Gwyn (McCutcheon), 1922
Violante (Bowen, as Preedy), 1932
Violation (Lamb), 1983
Violet (Garvice), 1911
Violett (Hutten), 1904
Violetta (Duffield), 1960
Viper of Milan (Bowen), 1906
Virgin in Mayfair (Cartland), 1932
Virgin in Paris (Cartland), 1966
Virgin of the Sun (Haggard), 1922
Virgin Queen (M. Peters), 1972
Virgin Thorn (Bloom), 1941

Viscount's Revenge (Chesney), 1983
Visibility Nil (Elgin), 1963
Visible Heart (Browning), 1984
Vision House (C. N. and A. M Williamson), 1921
Vision of Balmaine (Burgin), 1911
Vision of Desire (Pedler), 1922
Vision of Love (Woodward, as Richmond), 1980
Vision of Stephen (Burford), 1972
Vision Splendid (Broster), 1913
Visit from Venus (R. Fraser), 1958
Visit to Rata Creek (Worboys, as Eyre), 1964
Visit to Rowanbank (Kidd), 1966
Visits to Elizabeth (Glyn), 1900
Vista (Barcynska, as Sandys), 1928
Vista (R. Fraser), 1928
Vital Signs (Wood), 1985
Vittoria Cottage (D. Stevenson), 1949
Vivian Inheritance (Stubbs), 1982
Vixen in Velvet (F. Michaels), 1976
Vixens (Yerby), 1947
Vixen's Revenge (Blackstock, as Allardyce), 1980
Voice in the Dark (Lorrimer), 1967
Voice in the Darkness (Bennetts), 1979
Voice in the Night (V. Johnston), 1984
Voice in the Thunder (Hunter), 1975
Voice in the Wilderness (G. Hill), 1916
Voice of Air (Berckman), 1970
Voice of Bugle Ann (Kantor), 1935
Voice of the Dolls (Eden), 1950
Voice of the Heart (Bradford), 1983
Voice on the Wind (Daniels), 1969
Voices from the Dust (s Farnol), 1932
Voices in a Haunted Room (Holt, as Carr), 1984
Voices in an Empty House (Aiken), 1975
Voices in Summer (Pilcher), 1984
Voices in the Night (Norway), 1973
Voices Long Hushed (Pauley), 1976
Voices on the Wind (Anthony), 1985
Volunteer Nurse (Duffield), 1942
Voodoo (Shellabarger, as Esteven), 1930
Voodoo Widow (Coffman), 1970
Voss (P. White), 1957
Vote for Love (Cartland), 1977
Vow on the Heron (Holt, as Plaidy), 1980
Vows (Spencer), 1988
Voyage of Captain Bart (Erskine), 1943
Voyage of Destiny (Preston), 1974
Voyage of Enchantment (Ashton), 1977
Voyage of the Destiny (Nye), 1982
Voyage to Cytherea (R. Harris), 1958
Voyage to Santa Fe (Giles), 1962
Voyage Unplanned (Yerby), 1974

Wager for Love (Courtney), 1979
Wagered Weekend (Krentz, as Castle), 1981
Wagered Widow (Veryan), 1984
Wages of Virtue (Wren), 1916
Wagon to a Star (Greig), 1952
Waif of the River (Farnol), 1952
Waif's Wedding (Ayres), 1921
Wait (Berckman), 1973
Wait for Night (Cowen), 1980
Wait for Tomorrow (Robins), 1967
Wait for What Will Come (B. Michaels), 1978
Waiting (van der Zee), 1982
Waiting at the Church (Blackstock, as Allardyce), 1968

Waiting Darkness (W. Roberts), 1970
Waiting for Willa (Eden), 1970
Waiting Game (Cadell), 1985
Waiting Game (Harrod-Eagles), 1972
Waiting Game (Krentz), 1985
Waiting Game (Palmer, as Blayne), 1982
Waiting Room (Norway, as Norton), 1961
Waiting Sands (Howatch), 1966
Wake the Sleeping Tiger (Way), 1978
Wakefield's Course (de la Roche), 1941
Walk a Tightrope (Ellis), 1975
Walk in the Dark (Summerton, as Roffman), 1969
Walk in the Paradise Garden (Maybury), 1972
Walk in the Wood (Gilbert), 1989
Walk into Darkness (Ellis), 1973
Walk into My Parlour (Eden), 1947
Walk into My Parlour (Lofts), 1975
Walk into My Parlour (R. Randall), 1962
Walk into the Wind (Arbor), 1970
Walk Out on Death (Armstrong), 1954
Walker (s O'Brian), 1955
Walker in Shadows (B. Michaels), 1979
Wall (Rinehart), 1938
Wall of Eyes (Millar), 1943
Wall of Partition (Barclay), 1914
Wallace (Tranter), 1975
Wallflower (Ayres), 1940
Walls of Gold (Norris), 1933
Walsingham Woman (Westcott), 1953
Waltz of Hearts (Cartland), 1980
Waltz-Contest (Ruck), 1941
Wanderers (s M. Johnston), 1917
Wanderers Eastward, Wanderers West (Winsor), 1965
Wanderer's Necklace (Haggard), 1914
Wandering Knife (Rinehart), 1952
Wandering Prince (Holt, as Plaidy), 1956
Wandering Stars (Dane), 1924
Wanderings of Wenamen (J. Lindsay), 1936
Wanderlust (Steel), 1986
Wanted for Love (Finley), 1983
Wanted—Girl Friday (Mackinlay), 1968
Wanted on the Voyage (s Ruck), 1930
Wanton (Rogers), 1983
War and Passion (Nicole, as Arlen), 1981
War Changes Everything (Robins), 1943
War Marriage (Robins), 1942
War Paint and Rouge (Chambers), 1931
War Surgeon (Slaughter), 1967
War to End Wars (Hardwick), 1975
War Wedding (C. N. and A. M. Williamson), 1916
Ward of Lucifer (Burchell), 1947
Warfare Accomplished (E. Pargeter), 1947
Warleggan (Graham), 1953
Warlock's Daughter (Daniels, as Gray), 1973
Warm Side of the Island (Browning, as Dozier), 1977
Warm Wind of Farik (Stratton), 1975
Warmed by the Fire (Vitek), 1983
Warner's Chase (Swan), 1884
Warrick (M. Harris), 1985
Warrior (Slaughter), 1956
Warrior King (Clarke, as Honeyman), 1972
Warrior King (Leslie), 1977
Warriors (Jakes), 1977
Wars (Findley), 1977
Wartime Beauty (s Bloom), 1943
Warwhoop (Kantor), 1952

War-Workers (Delafield), 1918
Warwyck series (Laker), from 1978
Wary Widow (Walsh), 1985
Was She Sweetheart or Wife? (Libbey), n.d.
Washington, D.C. (Vidal), 1967
Washington, U.S.A. (Baldwin), 1943
Wasted Love (Garvice), n.d.
Waster (Garvice), 1918
Watch the North Wind Rise (Graves), 1949
Watch the Wall, My Darling (Hodge), 1966
Watch the Wall My Darling (Hunter), 1963
Watcher in the Dark (Daniels, as Gray), 1973
Watchers (W. Roberts), 1971
Watchers at the Strait Gate (s Kirk), 1984
Watchgods (Wood), 1980
Watchman's Stone (R. Randall), 1975
Waterfall (Walker, as Sanders), 1956
Waterfalls of the Moon (Mather), 1973
Waterfront Hospital (Norway), 1961
Watermen (Michener), 1979
Waters of Conflict (Woodward, as Richmond), 1969
Waters on a Starry Night (Ogilvie), 1968
Watershed (Tranter), 1941
Wave (Scott), 1929
Waves of Destiny (s Pedler), 1924
Waves of Fire (Hampson), 1971
Way Beyond (Farnol), 1933
Way in the Dark (J. MacLeod), 1956
Way Men Love (Charles), 1967
Way of a Man (Elsna, as Lancaster), 1956
Way of a Man (Hilton), 1981
Way of a Tyrant (Hampson), 1974
Way of Ambition (Hichens), 1913
Way of an Eagle (Dell), 1911
Way of Compassion (Maybury), 1933
Way of Ecben (Cabell), 1929
Way of Escape (Swan), 1935
Way of Stars (Beck), 1925
Way of the Spirit (Haggard), 1906
Way of the Tamarisk (Worboys, as Maxwell), 1974
Way of Youth (Albanesi, as Rowlands), 1925
Way Out (Burgin), 1900
Way the Wind Blows (Asquith), 1963
Way Things Are (Delafield), 1927
Way Through the Forest (Farnes), 1957
Way Through the Maze (Elsna, as Conway), 1963
Way Through the Valley (J. MacLeod), 1971
Way to the Lantern (Erskine-Lindop), 1961
Way Up (Hardwick), 1976
Way We Used to Be (Charles, as Tempest), 1965
Ways of Love (J. MacLeod, as Airlie), 1955
Wayside Flower (May), 1982
Wayside Tavern (Lofts), 1980
Wayward as the Swallow (Charles), 1970
Wayward Heart (Marsh), 1989
Wayward Love (Elsna, as Snow), 1953
Wayward Madonna (M. Peters, as Black), 1970
Wayward Stream (Farnes), 1949
We All Have Our Secrets (Ruck), 1955
We Are for the Dark (Eden), 1944
We Are Ten (s Hurst), 1937
We Are the Pilgrims (Elsna), 1931
We Have Always Lived in the Castle (Jackson), 1962
We Have Come to a Country (L. Cooper), 1935
We Lost Our Way (Barcynska), 1948
We Parted at the Altar (Libbey), 1892

We Ride the Gale! (Loring), 1934
We Speak No Treason (Jarman), 1971
We Two Together (Robins), 1959
We Want Our Mummy! (M. St. John), 1922
We Women! (Barcynska), 1923
Weak-Eyed (Millar), 1942
Wealth of the Islands (Hunter, as Chace), 1971
Wear a Green Kirtle (Wiat), 1987
Weathercock (Maddocks), 1971
Weave Me a Moonbeam (I. Roberts, as Rowland), 1982
Weave Me Some Wings (M. Howard), 1947
Web of Love (Hoy), 1952
Web of Passion (Buckingham, as John), 1982
Web of Peril (Daniels), 1974
Web of Silver (Stratton, as Gillen), 1974
Webs (Barcynska), 1922
Wedded—But Alone! (M. St. John), 1930
Wedded But Not Wooed (M. St. John), 1920
Wedding Bells for Willow (Charles, as Tempest), 1956
Wedding Day (C. N. and A. M. Williamson), 1914
Wedding Dress (Burchell), 1962
Wedding for Three (Grimstead), 1963
Wedding Journey (Edmonds), 1947
Wedding March (Ruck), 1938
Wedding of Kitty Barton (s Swan), 1898
Wedding of the Year (Grimstead, as Manning), 1974
Wedding of the Year (Weale), 1982
Wedding Took Place (Elsna), 1939
Wednesday's Children (Dingwell), 1957
Week by the Sea (Gibbs, as Ford), 1962
Week-end Bride (Bloom, as Burns), 1939
Weekend for Love (Finley), 1984
Weekend in the Garden (Andrews), 1981
Week-End Marriage (Baldwin), 1932
Week-End Woman (Ayres), 1939
Weep and Know Why (Ogilvie), 1972
Weep Not for Dreams (Bloom, as Harvey), 1968
Weeping and the Laughter (Chard), 1975
Weeping Ash (Aiken), 1980
Weeping Lady (J. Roberts), 1971
Weight Carriers (Edginton), 1909
Weir House (Muskett), 1962
Wellington Wendy (Barcynska, as Sandys), 1941
Well-Painted Passion (Harrod-Eagles, as Woodhouse), 1976
Wellspring (s Giles), 1975
Were Death Denied (Yates), 1946
Were I Thy Bride (Robins), 1936
We're Not Wanted Now! (M. St. John, as Cooper), 1921
West of the River (Dingwell), 1970
West Riding series (s Bentley), from 1952
West Wind (Baldwin), 1962
West Wind Drift (McCutcheon), 1920
West with the Vikings (E. Marshall), 1961
Westerbury series (Chesney), from 1982
Westerfalca (Wiat), 1979
Western (Yerby), 1982
Western Man (Dailey), 1983
Westward to Laughter (MacInnes), 1969
Westward to My Love (Charles, as Tempest), 1944
Wexford (Ellis), 1976
What a Man Wills (s Vaizey), 1915
What a Woman Can Do! (M. St. John), 1917
What Became of Anna Bolton (Bromfield), 1944
What Happened Is This (Hutten), 1938
What I Found Out in the House of a German Prince (A. M. Williamson), 1915

What Is Love? (Delafield), 1928
What Matters Most (D. Robins), 1942
What of the Night? (s Lowndes), 1943
What Really Happened (Lowndes), 1926
What Shall It Profit? (Swan), 1910
What She Could (s Swan), 1898
What the Heart Keeps (Laker), 1984
What the Heart Says (Price), 1956
What Then Is Love (Loring), 1956
What Timmy Did (Lowndes), 1921
What We're Here For (Norway, as Norton), 1966
What Wild Lie—(Jacob), 1930
Whatagirl (Barcynska, as Sandys), 1939
What's-His-Name (McCutcheon), 1911
Wheat Princess (Webster), 1905
Wheel Fortune (Beaty, as Campbell), 1973
Wheel of Fortune (Howatch), 1984
Wheels of Chance (J. MacLeod, as Airlie), 1964
Wheels of Fate (Burgin), 1933
Wheels of Time (Barclay), 1908
When a Girl's Pretty (M. St. John), 1914
When a Man Loves (M. St. John, as Cooper), 1931
When a Man Marries (Rinehart), 1909
When a Woman Doctor Loves (Bloom, as Essex) 1969
When a Woman Loves (Robins, as Chesterton), 1955
When All the World Is Young (Holt, as Burford), 1943
When April Sings (Grimstead), 1964
When Birds Do Sing (Kidd), 1970
When Clouds Part (Hampson), 1973
When Doctors Disagree (Franken, as Meloney), 1940
When Doctors Love (Bloom, as Burns), 1964
When Doctors Marry (Seifert), 1960
When Dreams Come True (Burgin), 1932
When First I Loved . . . (Charles, as Tempest), 1938
When Four Ways Meet (Charles, as Chandos), 1961
When His Hour Comes (Glyn), 1915
When His Love Grew Cold (Libbey), 1895
When I Say Goodbye, I'm Clary Brown (Blackstock, as Keppel), 1977
When Hearts Are Light Again (Loring), 1943
When Lightning Strikes (Donnelly), 1980
When Love Awaits (Lindsey), 1986
When Love Comes (Hampson), 1983
When Love Compels (M. St. John, as Cooper), 1933
When Love Is Blind (Burchell), 1967
When Love Is Young (Garvice)
When Love Isn't Enough (Seidel), 1984
When Love Meets Love (Garvice), 1906
When Love Speaks (Finley), 1973
When Lovely Maiden Stoops to Folly (Libbey), 1896
When Lovers Meet (Kidd), 1987
When Love's Beginning (Burchell), 1954
When May Follows (Neels), 1980
When Michael Came to Town (Albanesi), 1917
When Next We Love (Pozzessere, as Graham), 1983
When Next We Meet (Elsna, as Conway), 1957
When No Man Pursueth (Lowndes), 1910
When Other Hearts (Holt, as Burford), 1955
When Paris Fell (Bloom, as Prole), 1976
When Sparrows Fall (Salverson), 1925
When Terror Ruled (Wynne), 1907
When the Bough Breaks (Hampson), 1970
When the Bough Breaks (s Mitchison), 1924
When the Dream Fades (Hoy), 1980
When the Gallows Is High (P. Hastings), 1971
When the Journey's Over (Chard), 1981

When the Music Stopped (Ogilvie), 1989
When the Splendor Falls (McBain), 1985
When the Sun Goes Down (Blackstock), 1965
When the Wind Blows (Steen), 1931
When the Witch Is Dead (Roby), 1972
When the World Shook (Haggard), 1919
When There's Love at Home (M. St. John), 1925
When There's Love at Home (Woodward, as Richmond), 1959
When Three Walk Together (Charles, as Chandos), 1939
When Time Stands Still (Charles, as Chandos), 1946
When Two Paths Meet (Neels), 1988
When We Are Married (Holt, as Burford), 1953
When We Two Parted (Charles, as Chandos), 1940
When We're Alone (Donnelly), 1989
When Women Love (s Delafield), 1938
When You Have Found Me (Hoy), 1951
Where Are You Going? (Ayres), 1946
Where Beauty Dwells (Loring), 1941
Where Breezes Falter (May), 1970
Where Duty Lies (Lorrimer, as Robins), 1957
Where Eagles Nest (Hampson), 1980
Where Flamingoes Fly (I. Roberts), 1966
Where Is Holly Carleton? (Ellis, as Marvin), 1974
Where Is Love? (Cartland), 1971
Where Is My Child To-night? (M. St. John), 1925
Where Is the Voice Coming From? (s Wiebe), 1974
Where Love Leads (Garvice), 1907
Where No Roads Go (Summers), 1963
Where Ratas Twine (I. Preston), 1960
Where Satan Dwells (F. Stevenson), 1971
Where Shall I Wander? (Burchell), 1942
Where Stars May Lead (I. Preston), 1978
Where the Cigale Sings (Sinclair), 1976
Where the Dark Streets Go (Davis), 1969
Where the Dream Begins (Chard), 1982
Where the Heart Is (Charles, as Tempest), 1955
Where the Heart Is (Vitek), 1981
Where the Lost Aprils Are (Ogilvie), 1975
Where the Moonflower Weaves (R. Lane), 1974
Where the Path Breaks (C. N. and A. M. Williamson, as de Crespigny), 1916
Where the Rivers Meet (Ellerbeck, as Thorne), 1982
Where the Treasure Is (Beauclerk), 1944
Where the Wolf Leads (Arbor), 1980
Where There Are Women (Barcynska, as Barclay), 1915
Where There's a Will (Rinehart), 1912
Where Three Roads Meet (Dell), 1935
Where Two Ways Met (G. Hill), 1947
Which Woman? (Burgin), 1907
While Faith Endures (Albanesi, as Rowlands), 1929
While Murder Waits (Shellabarger, as Estevan), 1936
While the Fire Rages (Lorin), 1984
While the Patient Slept (Eberhart), 1930
Whim of Fate (J. MacLeod), 1940
Whip (Cookson), 1983
Whirlwind (Clavell), 1986
Whirlwind (Lamb), 1987
Whirlwind Courtship (Krentz, as Taylor), 1979
Whisper in the Dark (Maybury, as Troy), 1961
Whisper My Name (F. Michaels), 1981
Whisper of Darkness (Lynn), 1965
Whisper of Darkness (Mather), 1980
Whisper of Doubt (Weale, as Blake), 1965
Whisper of Sea-Bells, (I. Roberts), 1964
Whisper to the Stars (Grimstead), 1963
Whisper Who Dares (M. Lewis), 1983

Whisper Wind (Stanford), 1981
Whispered Promise (Delinsky, as Drake), 1982
Whispering Dark (Saunders, as Innes), 1976
Whispering Grove (Hilton), 1971
Whispering Palms (Blair, as Brett), 1954
Whispering Sea (Stratton, as Gillen), 1971
Whispers in the Sun (Greig), 1949
Whistle and I'll Come (Kidd), 1966
Whistle for the Crows (Eden), 1962
Whistle in the Wind (Daniels), 1976
Whistling Cat (Chambers), 1932
Whistling Thorn (Hunter, as Chace), 1977
White Abbey (Albanesi, as Rowlands), 1911
White Banners (Douglas), 1936
White Blooms of Yarrow (Saunders, as Innes), 1976
White Boy (Nicole), 1966
White Branches (Albanesi), 1933
White Castello (McEvoy), 1969
White Christmas (Hurst), 1942
White Cockade (Dymoke), 1979
White Cockade (J. MacLeod), 1960
White Cockatoo (Eberhart), 1933
White Company (Doyle), 1891
White Doctor (Blair, as Conway), 1961
White Dolphin (Stratton), 1976
White Dove (Thomas), 1986
White Dress (Eberhart), 1946
White Flag (G. Porter), 1923
White Flame (Albanesi), 1930
White Flower (G. Hill), 1927
White Gate (Deeping), 1913
White Heat (Barrie, as Kent), 1966
White Hell of Pity (Lofts), 1937
White House of Marisaig (Swan), 1938
White Hunter (Hoy), 1951
White in the Black (Albanesi), 1926
White Jacket (Norway), 1961
White Jade (W. Roberts), 1975
White Jade (Robins), 1928
White Jasmine (J. Roberts, as Radcliffe), 1976
White Ladies of Worcester (Barclay), 1917
White Lady (G. Hill, as Macdonald), 1930
White Lies (L. Howard), 1988
White Lilac (Cartland), 1984
White Magic (Baldwin), 1939
White Magnolia (Way), 1979
White Moths (Rundle, as Manners), 1979
White Nights, Red Dawn (Nolan), 1980
White Oleander (Blair), 1953
White Orchids (G. Hill), 1935
White Pavilion (V. Johnston), 1973
White Peacock (Roby), 1972
White Prophet (Caine), 1909
White Rani (Nicole, as Gray), 1986
White Robe (s Cabell), 1928
White Rose (Knight), 1973
White Rose (Thum), 1980
White Rose (Westcott), 1969
White Rose of Love (Barrie, as Charles), 1963
White Rose of Winter (Mather), 1973
White Sand, Wild Sea (Palmer, as Blayne), 1983
White Satin (Johansen), 1985
White Violet (Ritchie), 1956
White Water (Oldfield), 1982
White Wings (s Goudge), 1952
White Witch (Ashton), 1982

White Witch (Browning, as Williams), 1988
White Witch (Goudge), 1958
White Wool (Jacob), 1944
Whiteoak (Jalna) series (de la Roche)
Whither? (Wynne), 1938
Whitney, My Love (McNaught), 1985
Whitton's Folly (P. Hill), 1975
Who Are the Heathen? (Swan), 1942
Who Can Deny Love? (Cartland), 1979
Who Knows Sammy Halliday? (M. Howard), 1974
Who Loses Pays (Burgin), 1935
Who Loves Believes (Hoy), 1955
Who Rides a Tiger (Lowndes), 1935
Who Rides the Tiger (Mather), 1970
Who Shall Serve? (Swan), 1891
Who Walks by Moonlight (McEvoy), 1966
Who Will Remember? (Irwin), 1924
Who Would Have Daughters? (Steen), 1937
Whole Armor (Baldwin), 1951
Whole of the Short (s Bentley), 1935
Whom Love Hath Chosen (MacGill), 1919
Who's Been Sitting in My Chair? (Armstrong), 1962
Who's Been Sleeping in My Bed? (Lamb), 1985
Who's Calling (Holt, as Burford), 1962
Whoso Diggeth a Pit—(M. St. John, as Cooper), 1926
Why It Happened (Lowndes), 1938
Why Shoot a Butler? (Heyer), 1933
Why Someone Had to Die (Summerton, as Roffman), 1976
Why They Married (s Lowndes), 1923
Why Wouldn't He Wait? (Charles, as Tempest), 1940
Whyte Swan (Wiat), 1986
Wicked Angel (Caldwell), 1965
Wicked Cousin (F. Stevenson, as Faire), 1980
Wicked Day (Stewart), 1983
Wicked Fire (Riefe), 1983
Wicked Grandmother (Chesney), 1987
Wicked Is My Flesh (Blake), 1980
Wicked Lady (Fletcher), 1962
Wicked Loving Lies (Rogers), 1976
Wicked Marquis (Cartland), 1973
Wicked Pack of Cards (R. Harris), 1969
Wicked Sir Dare (Garvice), 1938
Wicked Water (Kantor), 1949
Wicked Wynsleys (Knight), 1977
Wide and Dark (Muskett), 1940
Wide House (Caldwell), 1945
Wide Is the Water (Hodge), 1981
Wide Pastures (Blair, as Conway), 1957
Wide Sargasso Sea (Rhys), 1966
Widening Stream (R. Lindsay), 1952
Widow (Blackstock), 1967
Widow and the Wastrel (Dailey), 1977
Widow Jones (Chappell), 1956
Widow of Windsor (Holt, as Plaidy), 1974
Widower's Wife (Charles), 1963
Widow's Daughters (Ponsonby), 1953
Wife after Work (Charles, as Tempest), 1943
Wife Apparent (Yates), 1956
Wife by Arrangement (Burchell), 1946
Wife by Contract (Kidd), 1980
Wife for a Penny (Hampson), 1973
Wife for a Wager (Charles, as Chandos), 1938
Wife for a Year (R. Lindsay, as Leigh), 1980
Wife for Andrew (Stratton, as Gillen), 1969
Wife for Sale (Norris), 1933
Wife for the Admiral (Gibbs), 1974

Winds of Chance (Farnol), 1934
Winds of Desire (Grimstead), 1954
Winds of Enchantment (Blair, as Brett), 1949
Winds of Fear (Greig), 1956
Winds of Fortune (Farnol), 1934
Winds of Heaven (Way), 1979
Winds of Night (Maybury), 1967
Winds of Spring (Maybury), 1948
Winds of the World (Ayres), 1918
Windscreen Weepers (s Aiken), 1969
Windsong (Sherwood), 1986
Windsor Red (Butler, as Melville), 1988
Windward Crest (Hampson), 1973
Wine of Illusion (R. Fraser), 1957
Wine, Women, and Waiters (s Frankau), 1932
Wines of Cyprien (Daniels), 1977
Wingarden (Lee), 1971
Winged Love (Robins), 1941
Winged Magic (Cartland), 1981
Winged Pharaoh (Grant), 1937
Winged Victory (Cartland), 1982
Wings in the Dust (Muskett), 1933
Wings in the West (Macbeth), 1937
Wings for Nurse Bennett (McElfresh), 1960
Wings of Chance (Albanesi, as Rowlands), 1931
Wings of Ecstasy (Cartland), 1981
Wings of Fear (Eberhart), 1945
Wings of Love (Beaty), 1988
Wings of Love (Cartland), 1962
Wings of Memory (Farnes), 1953
Wings of the Falcon (Michaels), 1977
Wings of the Morning (Beaty), 1982
Wings of the Morning (Chard), 1985
Wings of the Night (Hampson), 1971
Wings on My Heart (Cartland, as McCorquodale), 1954
Winifred (s Bloom), 1903
Winner Take All (Ayres), 1937
Winner Take All (B. Hastings), 1981
Winnie Childs, The Shop Girl (C. N. and A. M. Williamson), 1926
Winning Game (Macbeth), 1910
Winsome Witch (Swan), 1933
Winter, William series (Butler), from 1957
Winter and Rough Weather (D. Stevenson), 1951
Winter at Cray (Stratton, as Gillen), 1971
Winter Blossom (Browning), 1981
Winter Bride (Salisbury), 1978
Winter Harvest (Lofts), 1955
Winter in July (Summers), 1984
Winter Is Past (Weale), 1955
Winter Landscape (Clarke), 1986
Winter of Change (Neels), 1973
Winter of Discontents (Frankau), 1941
Winter of Fear (Ponsonby, as Tempest), 1967
Winter of the Fox (Summerton, as Roffman), 1964
Winter of the Witch (J. Fitzgerald, as Watson), 1972
Winter People (Whitney), 1969
Winter Quarters (Duggan), 1956
Winter Queen (Saxton), 1977
Winter Rose (Grimstead), 1972
Winter Sisters (Ebel, as Goodwin), 1980
Winter Song (Gellis), 1982
Winter Spring (Ebel, as Goodwin), 1978
Winter Wedding (Neels), 1979
Winter Woman (Browning), 1986
Wintercombe (Belle), 1988

Winter's Child (Jagger), 1984
Winter's Day (Muskett), 1936
Winter's Passion (Moore), 1932
Wintersbride (Seale), 1951
Wintersweet (Chappell), 1978
Winterwood (Eden), 1967
Winthrop Woman (Seton), 1958
Wire Blind (Muskett), 1944
Wisconsin series (Derleth), from 1940
Wisdom's Daughter (Haggard), 1923
Wise and the Foolish Virgins (Steen), 1932
Wise and the Steadfast (Barcynska, as Sandys), 1961
Wise Forget (M. Howard), 1944
Wise Is the Heart (Duffield), 1947
Wisest Fool (Tranter), 1974
Wish a Day (Ruck), 1956
Wish for Love (Cartland), 1983
Wish on the Moon (Burchell), 1949
Wish upon a Dream (Elsna, as Conway), 1958
Wish with the Candles (Neels), 1972
Wishing Star (Greig), 1942
Wishing Stone (Saunders, as Innes), 1976
Witch (M. Johnston), 1914
Witch (B. Michaels), 1973
Witch Doctor (Ogilvie), 1959
Witch from the Sea (Holt, as Carr), 1975
Witch in Pink (Swan), 1938
Witch in the Wood (T. White), 1939
Witch Wood (Buchan), 1927
Witchcraft (Krentz), 1985
Witches (Lofts, as Curtis), 1966
Witches of All Saints (Tattersall), 1975
Witches of Conyngton (S. Thorpe), 1976
Witches' Sabbath (Blackstock, as Allardyce), 1961
Witch-Finder (Wynne), 1923
Witching Hour (Craven), 1981
Witching Hour (R. Randall), 1970
Witching Hour (F. Stevenson), 1971
Witch's Castle (Daniels), 1971
Witch's Crossing (F. Stevenson), 1975
Witch's Harvest (Craven), 1987
Witch's Head (Haggard), 1884
Witch's House (Armstrong), 1963
Witch's Island (Daniels), 1972
Witch's Spell (Cartland), 1984
Witchstone (Mather), 1974
Witch-Woman (s Cabell), 1948
With a Delicate Air (s Buck), 1962
With a Little Luck (Dailey), 1981
With All Her Heart (Garvice), 1910
With All My Heart (Asquith), 1954
With All My Love (Lorrimer, as Robins), 1963
With All My Worldly Goods (Burchell), 1938
With Banners (Loring), 1935
With Every Year (Gaskin), 1949
With Fire and Flowers (I. Roberts, as Rowland), 1963
With Fondest Thoughts (Blackstock), 1980
With Heart So True (Albanesi, as Rowlands)
With Murder in Mind (M. Peters, as Rothman), 1975
With Murder in Mind (Summerton, as Roffman), 1963
With Somebody Else (Charles), 1981
With This Ring (Eberhart), 1941
With This Ring (Loring), 1960
Withering Fires (Bowen), 1931
Within a Year (Baldwin), 1934
Within Reach (Delinsky), 1986

Within the Bubble (Bowen, as Shearing), 1950
Within the Gates (Burgin), 1914
Without a Honeymoon (Charles, as Tempest), 1952
Without Warning (F. Michaels), 1981
Witness (G. Hill), 1917
Witness at Large (Eberhart), 1966
Wives and Lovers (Millar), 1954
Wizard (Haggard), 1896
Wizard (Krentz, as James), 1985
Wizard's Daughter (B. Michaels), 1980
Wolf and the Dove (Woodiwiss), 1974
Wolf and the Unicorn (J. Fitzgerald, as Watson), 1971
Wolf in Man's Clothing (Eberhart), 1942
Wolf in the Fold (McCutchan, as MacNeil), 1977
Wolf of Heimra (J. MacLeod), 1965
Woman Against Her (Albanesi, as Rowlands)
Woman Alive (Ertz), 1935
Woman at the Door (Deeping), 1937
Woman at the Wheel (Mackinlay), 1940
Woman Called Fancy (Yerby), 1951
Woman Called Mary (Bloom, as Mann), 1960
Woman Decides (Garvice), 1908
Woman Despised (Ponsonby), 1988
Woman Doctor (Bloom), 1978
Woman Doctor (Seifert), 1951
Woman from the Sea (Renier), 1971
Woman Hater (Ayres), 1920
Woman Hater (Palmer), 1989
Woman in Grey (Salisbury), 1987
Woman in Grey (A. Williamson), 1898
Woman in It (Garvice), 1911
Woman in Love (Norris), 1935
Woman in Love (Peake), 1984
Woman in Silk and Shadows (Daniels), 1977
Woman in the Back Seat (Steen), 1959
Woman in the Cloak (P. Hill), 1988
Woman in the Firelight (Barcynska, as Sandys), 1911
Woman in the Hall (Stern), 1939
Woman in the House (Hichens), 1945
Woman in the Woods (C. Blackstock, as L. Blackstock), 1958
Woman Like Us (Ellerbeck, as Thorne), 1979
Woman of Andros (Wilder), 1930
Woman of Dreams (Riefe), 1986
Woman of Experience (Barcynska), 1931
Woman of Fury (Gluyas), 1978
Woman of Iron (Lamb, as Holland), 1985
Woman of Knockaloe (Caine), 1923
Woman of Property (M. Lewis), 1976
Woman of Quality (Westcott), 1978
Woman of Substance (Bradford), 1979
Woman of the Horizon (Frankau), 1917
Woman of the Shee (s Byrne), 1932
Woman of the West (Pykare, as Powers), 1989
Woman on Her Own (Baldwin), 1946
Woman on Her Own (Blackmore), 1957
Woman on the Roof (Eberhart), 1968
Woman Scorned (Albanesi, as Rowlands), 1899
Woman Thou Gavest Me (Caine), 1913
Woman Who Came Between (Albanesi, as Rowlands), 1895
Woman Who Came Between (Garvice, as Hart)
Woman Who Dared (A. Williamson), 1903
Woman Who Parted Them (M. St. John, as Cooper), 1926
Woman Who Was Changed (s Buck), 1979
Woman Who Was Tomorrow (Bloom), 1940
Woman with the Fan (Hichens), 1904
Woman Without a Heart (Burgin), 1930

Woman Without Lies (Lowell), 1985
Woman Worth Winning (Albanesi, as Rowlands), 1911
Woman Wronged (Garvice, as Hart)
Woman's Estate (Gellis), 1984
Woman's Fault (Albanesi, as Rowlands), 1915
Woman's Part (Swan), 1916
Woman's Place (Ellerbeck, as Yorke), 1983
Woman's Side of It (Robins), 1937
Woman's Soul (Garvice), 1902
Woman's Touch (Krentz), 1989
Woman's War (Deeping), 1907
Woman's Way (Burgin), 1908
Woman's Way (Garvice), 1914
Woman's Way (M. St. John, as Cooper), 1935
Woman's Wiles (Pykare, as Powers), 1985
Women Always Forgive (Elsna), 1934
Women Are Like That (s Delafield), 1929
Women Are So Simple (Charles, as Chandos), 1941
Women at Work (s Kennedy), 1966
Women Barbers of Drury Lane (P. Hastings), 1985
Women Have Hearts (Cartland), 1980
Women in Love (Elsna, as Lancaster), 1957
Women in White (Slaughter), 1974
Women Live Too Long (Delmar), 1932
Women Money Buys (Greig), 1931
Women of Eden (M. Harris), 1980
Women of the Aftermath (Price, as Smith), 1931
Women Who Pass By (Delmar), 1929
Women Who Seek (Robins), 1928
Wonder Cruise (Bloom), 1933
Wonder of Love (Albanesi), 1911
Wonder of the World (C. Holland), 1970
Wonder Trip (Bloom, as Burns), 1939
Wondrous To-Morrow (Maybury), 1936
Wood and the Trees (Elgin), 1967
Wood Is My Pulpit (Barcynska), 1942
Wooden Wives (Libbey), 1923
Woodville Wench (M. Peters), 1972
Wooing of Rosamond Fayre (Ruck), 1915
Wooing of Rose (Albanesi, as Rowlands), 1912
Wooing of the Queen (Beck, as Barrington), 1934
Words of Silk (Brown, as St. Claire), 1984
Workaday Lady (Greig), 1936
Working Girl's Honor (Garvice, as Hart)
World Enough and Time (Warren), 1950
World Full of Strangers (Freeman), 1975
World in Spell (D. Stevenson), 1939
World Is Like That (Norris), 1940
World Keeps Turning (Hardwick), 1977
World of Christy Pembroke (Elsna, as Snow), 1978
World of Dreams (Albanesi, as Rowlands), 1935
World of Jennie G. (Ogilvie), 1986
World under Snow (Broster), 1935
World We Live In (s Bromfield), 1944
World Well Lost (Swan), 1935
World Without End (Frankau), 1943
World Without Love (Woodward, as Lawrence), 1967
World's a Stage (Holt, as Kellow), 1960
Worlds Apart (Chapman), 1946
World's Bane (s Bentley), 1918
World's Desire (Haggard), 1890
World's Fair Nurse (Daniels), 1964
Wormwood (Corelli), 1890
Worse Than Murder (Berckman), 1957
Worst Wife in the World (M. St. John), 1915
Worth Wile (Wren), 1937

Wounded Heart (Garvice), 1911
Wounded Name (Broster), 1922
Woven of the Wind (Swan), 1912
Woven on Fate's Loom (Garvice), 1903
Wreath for Arabella (Leslie), 1948
Wreath of Holly (Chappell), 1959
Wreck of the Grey Cat (Graham), 1958
Wren of Paradise (Browning), 1981
Wrestler on the Shore (Wynne, as Lurgan), 1912
Write from the Heart (Greig, as Ames), 1972
Writing Man (Barcynska), 1939
Written in the Stars (Hunter), 1982
Wrong Doctor John (Dingwell, as Starr), 1967
Wrong Love (Woodward), 1962
Wrong Man (Britt), 1980
Wrong Mr. Right (Ruck), 1919
Wrong Woman (Burgin), 1932
Wrongs Righted (Swan), 1924
Wyatt series (Wiat), from 1973
Wych Stone (McEvoy), 1974
Wychwood (N. St. John), 1976
Wychwood (Wiat), 1982
Wyndham's Daughter (Swan), 1898
Wynne of Windwhistle (Ayres), 1926

Yankee Pasha (E. Marshall), 1948
Yankee Stranger (Thane), 1944
Year After (Ayres), 1916
Year at Coverley (s Swan), 1883
Year of Her Life (Elsna, as Snow), 1951
Year of the Dragon (Dingwell), 1978
Year of the French (Flanagan), 1979
Year of the Pageant (Gibbs), 1971
Years (Spencer), 1986
Years for Rachel (Ruck), 1918
Year's Happy Ending (Neels), 1984
Years of Change (Hardwick), 1974
Yellow Brick Road (Cadell), 1960
Yellow God (Haggard), 1908
Yellow Is for Fear (s Eden), 1968
Yellow Joss (s Idriess), 1934
Yellow Moon (Stratton), 1974
Yellow Poppy (Broster), 1920
Yellow Room (Rinehart), 1945
Yellow Straw Hat (Chappell), 1983
Yesterday and Tomorrow (Elsna, as Snow), 1971
Yesterday Came Suddenly (M. Lewis), 1975
Yesterday Is Tomorrow (Barcynska, as Barclay), 1950
Yesterday's Child (Wood), 1979
Yesterday's Evil (Daniels), 1979
Yesterday's Harvest (Pedler), 1926
Yesterday's Island (Weale), 1983
Yesterday's Love (Woodward, as Richmond), 1972
Yesterday's Lover (Grimstead, as Manning), 1969
Yesterday's Madness (Cockrell), 1943
Yesterday's Magic (Arbor), 1957
Yesterday's Mischief (Renier), 1975
Yesterday's Promises (Ellerbeck, as Thorne), 1986
Yesterday's Shadow (Stanford), 1981
Yesterday's Tomorrow (Bloom), 1968
Yet a Lion (Wiat), 1978
Yet Love Remains (Burchell), 1938
Yet She Follows (Cartland), 1944
Yield Not to Temptation! (M. St. John, as Cooper), 1923
Yolanda (Jacob), 1963
Yollop (McCutcheon), 1922

York the Renegade (Johansen), 1986
Yorke series (Pope), from 1979
You Are the One (Berta Ruck), 1945
You Belong to Me (Hoy), 1938
You Can Love a Stranger (Lamb), 1988
You Can Never Look Back (Bigland), 1940
You Can't Escape (Baldwin), 1942
You Can't Have Everything (Norris), 1937
You Can't Live Alone (Hoy), 1944
You Can't Lose Yesterday (Hoy), 1940
You Can't Run Away (J. Lane), 1940
You Get What You Give (s Bromfield), 1951
You Have Chosen (Robins), 1938
You Never Knew (Elsna), 1933
You Should Have Warned Me (Charles, as Chandos), 1940
You Took My Heart (Hoy), 1939
You'll Like My Mother (Hintze), 1960
You'll Love Me Yet (Ritchie), 1963
Young Amanda (Seale), 1950
Young Ames (Edmonds), 1942
Young and Broke (Elsna), 1943
Young and Lonely King (J. Lane), 1969
Young Ann (Gibbs, as Ford), 1973
Young at Heart (Ayres), 1942
Young Bar (Pilcher, as Fraser), 1952
Young Blood (Swan), 1917
Young Caesar (R. Warner), 1958
Young Clementina (D. Stevenson), 1970
Young Commissioner (Fletcher), 1951
Young Curmudgeon (Charles, as Lance), 1964
Young Deloraine (Burgin), 1926
Young Diana (Corelli), 1918
Young Doctor (Seifert), 1939
Young Doctor Galahad (Seifert), 1938
Young Doctor Goddard (E. Harrison), 1978
Young Doctor Kenway (R. Randall), 1950
Young Doctor Kirkdene (Hoy), 1955
Young Doctor Mason (Stuart, as A. Stuart), 1970
Young Doctor Randall (McElfresh), 1957
Young Doctors Downstairs (Andrews), 1963
Young Ellis (Hilton), 1966
Young Emmanuel (Jacob), 1932
Young Green Corn (D. Smith), 1971
Young Hearts (Albanesi, as Rowlands), 1924
Young Intruder (Farnes), 1953
Young Invader (Maybury), 1947
Young Is My Love (Ayres), 1941
Young Jonathan (Cleugh), 1932
Young Kangaroos Prefer Riding (Bloom, as Essex), 1947
Young Labelle (Burgin), 1924
Young Ladies' Room (Gibbs, as Ford), 1945
Young Lady (M. Howard), 1950
Young Lady from Alton-St. Pancras (Sebastian), 1977
Young Lady from Paris (Aiken), 1982
Young Lady of Fashion (Gibbs), 1978
Young Lady with Red Hair (Gibbs), 1959
Young Love Wakes (Elsna, as Snow), 1940
Young Lovell (Ford), 1913
Young Lovers (Bailey), 1917
Young Lucifer (Blackstock), 1960
Young Man Comes to London (s Arlen), 1931
Young Man from the Country (Albanesi), 1906
Young Man in a Hurry (s Chambers), 1904
Young Man with Ideas (Gibbs), 1950
Young Man Without Money (Greig), 1958
Young Man's Slave (Mackinlay), 1936

ADVISERS AND CONTRIBUTORS

ALTNER, Patricia. Librarian, Department of Defense, Washington, D.C. Reviewer of historical fiction for *Library Journal*, and associate editor, *The Year's Scholarship in Science Fiction, Fantasy, and Horror Literature*. **Essays:** Pamela Bennetts; Rebecca Brandewyne; Mary Ann Gibbs; Velda Johnston; Alanna Knight; Marjorie McEvoy; Annette Motley; Edith Pargeter; Rona Randall; Nora Roberts; Rosemary Rogers; Valerie Sherwood; Danielle Steel; Janelle Taylor; Chelsea Quinn Yarbro.

ANDERSON, Rachel. Freelance writer: children's book reviewer for *Good Housekeeping*. Author of *The Purple Heart Throbs: The Sub-Literature of Love*, 1974, *Dream Lovers* (autobiography), 1978, and fiction for adults and children including, most recently, *Little Angel Comes to Stay*, 1984, *The War Orphan*, 1987, and *Little Angel, Bonjour!*, 1988. **Essays:** Madame Albanesi; Ruby M. Ayres; Florence L. Barclay; G. B. Burgin; Hall Caine; Ethel M. Dell; Maud Diver; Maysie Greig; E. M. Hull; Netta Muskett; Margaret Pedler; Berta Ruck.

BAKERMAN, Jane S. Professor of English, Indiana State University, Terre Haute. Author of numerous critical essays, interviews, and reviews; adviser and contributor to *American Women Writers*, 1979 and *Twentieth-Century Crime and Mystery Writers*, 1980, 1985, and contributor to *Armchair Detective*, *American Literature*, *Writer's Yearbook*, and other periodicals. **Essays:** Daphne du Maurier; Edna Ferber; Elizabeth Savage.

BALLIN, Michael. Lecturer in English, Wilfrid Laurier University, Waterloo, Ontario. **Essay:** John Cowper Powys.

BARGAINNIER, Earl F. Formerly Fuller E. Callaway Professor of English Language and Literature, Wesleyan College, Macon, Georgia; editor, *Studies in Popular Culture*. Author of *The Gentle Art of Murder: The Detective Fiction of Agatha Christie*, 1980. Editor of *Ten Women of Mystery*, 1981, and *Twelve Englishmen of Mystery*, 1984. **Essays:** Lance Horner and Kyle Onstott; Edison Marshall; Frank Yerby.

BARNES, Melvyn. Director of Libraries and Art Galleries, City of London. Author of *Best Detective Fiction: A Guide from Godwin to the Present*, 1975, *Youth Library Work*, 1976 (2nd edition), *Dick Francis*, 1986, and *Murder in Print: A Guide to Two Centuries of Crime Fiction*, 1986. Editor of the Remploy Deerstalker crime fiction reprints. Adviser and contributor to *Twentieth-Century Crime and Mystery Writers*, 1980, 1985, and contributor to *Novels and Novelists*, 1980. **Essays:** Evelyn Berckman; Gwendoline Butler; Mignon G. Eberhart; Dornford Yates.

BERGMANN, Linda S. Instructor in English, Columbia College, Chicago. Author of "The Contemporary Letter as Literature" in *Women's Studies Quarterly*, forthcoming. **Essay:** Jean M. Auel.

BERNEIS, Susan Quinn. Freelance writer. Former librarian. **Essays:** Laura Black; Madeleine Brent; Gwen Bristow; Cecily Crowe; Julie Ellis; Inglis Fletcher; Naomi A. Hintze; Marlys Millhiser; Elisabeth Ogilvie; Claire Rayner; Alexandra Ripley; Helen Hooven Santmyer; Anne Stevenson; Jessamyn West.

BLEILER, E. F. Freelance writer. Former executive vice-president, Dover Publications; editorial consultant, Scribner's. Author of *The Checklist of Science-Fiction and Supernatural Fiction*, 1978. Editor of *A Treasury of Victorian Detective Stories*, *A Treasury of Victorian Ghost Stories*, and of works by Ernest Bramah, R. Austin Freeman, Emile Gaboriau, Robert H.

van Gulik, and Roy Vickers, and anthologies of dime novelists and Victorian sensational novelists. **Essays:** L. Adams Beck; D. K. Broster; Robert Hichens; Dorothy Macardle; Lady Eleanor Smith.

BLOCK, Marylaine. Assistant director, McMullen Library, Davenport, Iowa. Book reviewer for *Library Journal*. **Essays:** Janet Caird; Marian Cockrell; Catherine Fellows; Rachel Lindsay; Margaret Lynn; Charlotte MacLeod; Joan Smith.

BOUSFIELD, Wendy. English and linguistics librarian, Syracuse University, Syracuse, New York. Contributor to *Science Fiction, Fantasy, and Weird Fiction Magazines*. **Essays:** Robert W. Chambers; Russell Kirk; Oliver Onions.

BOYLE, Bill. Advisory teacher, Wirral Local Education Authority; deputy editor, *Junior Education*; reviewer for the *Guardian*, *Books for Keeps*, and *School Librarian*. Author of *What's in a Poem?*, *Local Directories*, and *Your Geography*, and "Words Joined Together," a Thames Television poetry documentary. **Essays:** Judy Chard; Rhona Martin.

BRADLEY, W. H. Freelance writer and author of the romance novels, *Savage Desire*, *Heritage of Love*, and *The Yielding Time*. **Essay:** Jean Saunders.

BRANCH, Susan. Librarian, Worthington, Ohio. Reviewer for *Newsletter on Intellectual Freedom*. **Essays:** Joan Aiken; H. C. Bailey; John Buchan; Elizabeth Cadell; Barbara Corcoran; Juanita Coulson; Jeffery Farnol; Margaret Summerton.

BUCHANAN, Jean. Freelance writer. Former lexicographer on *A Supplement to the Oxford English Dictionary* and *The Pocket Oxford Dictionary*, 6th edition. Author of *The History of the English Faculty Library, Oxford*, 1979, a romance novel (*No Remedy for Love*), short stories, and a television play for children (*The Princess and the Lute Player*). **Essays:** Helen Beauclerk; Marion Collin; Mabel Barnes Grundy; Baroness von Hutten; Nora Lofts; Mrs. Patrick MacGill; Lady Miles.

BULL, Angela. Children's writer and critic. Author of several books of children's fiction including, most recently, *A Wish at the Baby's Grave*, 1988, *Up the Attic Stairs*, 1989, and of biographies of Anne Frank, Florence Nightingale, Marie Curie, Elizabeth Fry, and Noel Streatfeild. **Essay:** Phyllis Bentley.

BURWELL, Rose Marie. Professor of English, Northern Illinois University, DeKalb. Author of *A Chronological Catalogue of the Reading of D. H. Lawrence*, 1970 (addenda in *D. H. Lawrence Review*, 1973), and several articles on Joyce Carol Oates; contributor to *A D. H. Lawrence Handbook*, 1982. **Essay:** Joyce Carol Oates.

BUSWELL, Hilary. Lecturer in business communication. **Essays:** Robert Nye; Helen Waddell.

BUTTS, Dennis. Freelance writer and critic; editor, *Henty Society Bulletin*. Formerly principal lecturer in English, Bulmershe College of Higher Education, Reading, Berkshire. Author of *Living Words* (with John Merrick), 1966, and *R. L. Stevenson*, 1966. Editor of *Pergamon Poets 8*, 1970, *Good Writers for Young Readers: Critical Essays*, 1977, and *The Secret Garden*, by Frances Hodgson Burnett, 1987. **Essay:** A. E. W. Mason.

CADOGAN, Mary. Secretary of an educational trust, governor of an international school, and freelance writer. Author of three books on popular literature with Patricia Craig—*You're a Brick, Angela!*, 1976, *Women and Children First*, 1978, *The Lady Investigates*, 1981—three volumes of *The Charles Hamilton Companion* (with John Wernham), 1976–82, *The Morcove Companion* (with Tommy Keen), 1981, *From Wharton Lodge to Linton Hall: The Charles Hamilton Christmas Companion* (with Tommy Keen), 1984, *Richmal Crompton: The Woman Behind William*, 1986, and *Frank Richards: The Chap Behind the Chums*, 1988. **Essays:** Barbara Cartland; Theresa Charles; Jilly Cooper; Frances Cowen; R. F. Delderfield; Valerie Fitzgerald; Cynthia Freeman; Margery Hilton; Patricia Matthews; L. M. Montgomery; Baroness Orczy; Elizabeth O. Peter; Evadne Price; Mabel St. John; Mrs. George de Horne Vaizey; C. N. and A. M. Williamson; Esther Wyndham; May Wynne.

CAMPBELL, Margaret. Freelance writer. Author of *Lend a Hand: Social Work for the Young*, 1966, articles on Oxfordshire personalities for *Limited Edition*, and articles and reviews for *British Book News*, *Countryman*, and other journals. Editor of *The Countryman Book Series*, 3 vols., 1973–75. **Essays:** Donn Byrne; Edwin Mullins; Neil Munro; D. L. Murray; C. Northcote Parkinson; Rosemary Anne Sisson; G. B. Stern.

CARGILL, Jennifer. Associate University Librarian, Rice University, Houston, Texas. **Essay:** Mary Westmacott.

CARTLAND, Barbara. See her own entry.

CAVALIERO, Glen. Member of faculty of English, University of Cambridge. Author of *John Cowper Powys: Novelist*, 1973, *The Rural Tradition in the English Novel 1900–1939*, 1977, *A Reading of E. M. Forster*, 1979, *Charles Williams: Poet of Theology*, 1983. **Essays:** Bryher; William Golding; Rose Macaulay; H. F. M. Prescott.

CHESTER, Tessa Rose. Curator, Renier Collection of Children's Books, Bethnal Green Museum of Childhood, London. **Essays:** Patricia Ainsworth; Elisabeth Beresford; Iris Bromige; Susan Inglis; Denise Robins.

CLARK, Anderson. Associate Professor of English, and Director of the International English Institute, Belmont College, Nashville. **Essay:** Shelby Foote.

CLEAVER, Pamela. Freelance journalist; tutor, London School of Journalism. Author of *The Sparrow Book of Record Breakers* [*Animal Records*], 2 vols., 1981–82. **Essays:** Pamela Belle; Marjorie Bowen; Ann Bridge; Louis Bromfield; Hester W. Chapman; Dorothy Dunnett; Catherine Gavin; Joan Grant; H. Rider Haggard; Rosemary Harris; Margaret Irwin; Jane Lane; Madeleine A. Polland; Nigel Tranter; Joanna Trollope.

COOMBS, Scott. Freelance writer. **Essay:** Harriette Arnow.

DESY, Peter. Member of the English Department, Ohio University, Lancaster. Author of fiction and poetry in many journals and anthologies. **Essay:** Walter D. Edmonds.

DEVANEY, Douglas. Freelance journalist and playwright. **Essay:** M. M. Kaye.

FRENCH, Warren. Professor of English and Director of the Center for American Studies, Indiana University-Purdue University, Indianapolis, retired, 1986; member of the Editorial Board, *American Literature* and *Twentieth-Century Literature*; series ed-

itor for Twayne publishers. Author of *John Steinbeck*, 1961 (revised 1975), *Frank Norris*, 1962, *J. D. Salinger*, 1963 (revised 1976), *A Companion to "The Grapes of Wrath,"* 1963, *The Social Novel at the End of an Era*, 1966, *A Season of Promise*, 1968, *The South in Film*, 1981, and *Jack Kerouac*, 1986. Editor of a series on American literature, *The Thirties*, 1967, *The Forties*, 1968, *The Fifties*, 1971, and *The Twenties*, 1975. **Essays:** Henry Bellamann; Warwick Deeping; Frances Parkinson Keyes; F. Van Wyck Mason; Grace Metalious; Thornton Wilder.

FUCHS, Marcia G. Reference librarian and cataloguer, Guilford Free Library, Connecticut; reviewer for *Library Journal*. **Essays:** Stephanie Blake; Lolah Burford; David Case; Pamela Hill; Natasha Peters; Nicole St. John.

GALLIX, François. Professor of English, the Sorbonne, Paris. Author of *T. H. White: An Annotated Bibliography*, 1986. Editor of *Letters to a Friend: The Correspondence Between T. H. White and L. J. Potts*, 1982, and translator of *Contes Étranges et Histoires Fantastiques* by T. H. White, 1987. **Essay:** T. H. White.

GIFFORD, Judith A. Librarian, Salve Regina College, Newport, Rhode Island. Reviewer for *Library Journal*, and Dow Jones/Salem Press on-line book reviews. **Essays:** Rosalind Laker; Morgan Llywelyn.

GILLEN, Paul. Lecturer, University of Technology, Sydney. **Essays:** Ion L. Idriess; Jack Lindsay; Hal Porter.

GLADSKY, Thomas S. Associate Professor of English, Central Missouri State University, Warrensburg. Author of articles on historical fiction and ethnic literature in *New England Quarterly*, *Studies in the Novel*, *Critique*, *Modern Age*, *Southern Studies*, and other periodicals. **Essay:** Gore Vidal.

GORDON-SMITH, Pat. Editorial secretary. **Essay:** Betty Trask.

GOTTSCHALK, Jane. Professor of English, University of Wisconsin, Oshkosh. Author of articles on Afro-American literature for *Wisconsin Review*, *Phylon*, *Renascence*, and on themes and types of mystery fiction for *Armchair Detective*. Contributor to *Mystery, Detective, and Espionage Magazines*, 1983, and *Twentieth-Century Crime and Mystery Writers*, 1985. **Essays:** Charlotte Armstrong; Mary Roberts Rinehart.

GREY, Elizabeth. Freelance writer and broadcaster. Author of numerous books, including biographies on Edith Clavell and Amy Johnson, *The Story of Journalism*, 1968, and *The Noise of Drums and Trumpets*, 1971. Romantic and historical fiction reviewer for *The Times*, *Good Book Guide*, and *Books and Bookmen*. **Essays:** Lucilla Andrews; Betty Beaty; Suzanne Ebel; Anna Gilbert; Elizabeth Harrison; Mary Howard; Sarah Neilan.

GUERARD, Albert. Professor of English, Stanford University, California. Author of *Robert Bridges*, 1942, *Joseph Conrad*, 1947, *Thomas Hardy*, 1949, *André Gide*, 1951, *Conrad the Novelist*, 1958, *The Triumph of the Novel: Dickens, Dostoevsky, Faulkner*, 1976, *The Touch of Time: Myth, Memory and the Self*, 1980, and seven novels including, most recently, *Christine/Annette*, 1985. Editor of *Mirror and Mirage*, 1980. **Essay:** Janet Lewis.

GUILEY, Rosemary. Author of *Love Lines: The Romance Reader's Guide to Printed Pleasures*, 1983.

HAEDICKE, Janet V. Instructor in English, Northeast Louisiana University, Monroe. **Essay:** Jean Rhys.

HANSCOM, Marion. Assistant Director for Special Collections and Fine Arts, State University of New York, Binghamton. Reviewer for *Library Journal*, and editor of two manuscript collections held at her library. **Essays:** Ernest K. Gann; Cecelia Holland; John Jakes; Elizabeth Seifert; Frank G. Slaughter.

HAYNE, Barrie. Professor of English, St. Michael's College, Toronto. Author of numerous papers for the Popular Culture Association. **Essays:** Eleanor H. Porter; Jean Webster.

HAYNE, Joanne Harack. Teacher of courses on detective literature in continuing studies programs. Author of several papers on crime and detective writing for the Popular Culture Association. **Essays:** Susan Ertz; Barbara Michaels; D. E. Stevenson; Jean Stubbs.

HELD, Michael. Freelance writer. **Essay:** Barbara Riefe.

HEYDUK, Allayne C. School librarian and freelance writer. Reviewer for *Library Journal* and *Magill Book Reviews*. **Essays:** Phyllis Hastings; Jessica Stirling.

HIGDON, David Leon. Paul Whitfield Professor of English, Texas Tech University, Lubbock. Author of *Time and English Fiction*, 1977, and *Shadows of the Past in Contemporary British Fiction*, 1984. General editor, *Conradiana*. **Essays:** John Fowles; George MacDonald Fraser.

HINKEMEYER, Joan. Librarian, Denver Public Library; columnist, *Energy/Environment Newsletter*, Denver. Former English professor, assistant editor, *Colorado Libraries*, and reviewer for *Library Journal* and *Rocky Mountain News*. **Essays:** Sophia Cleugh; Anne Edwards.

HORDON, Ferelith. Freelance writer. **Essays:** Lloyd C. Douglas; Cynthia Harrod-Eagles; Madge Swindells.

JAMES, Louis. Professor of English, University of Kent, Canterbury. Author of *Islands in Between*, 1968, *Fiction for the Working Man 1830–60*, 1974, *Print and the People*, 1976, and *Jean Rhys*, 1978. **Essays:** Marie Corelli; Anthony Hope.

JENSEN, Margaret. Associate Professor of Sociology, Hamline University, St. Paul, Minnesota. Author of *Love's $weet Return: The Harlequin Story*, 1984, and articles in *A Room of One's Own*, *Minnesota Women's Press*, and *St. Paul Pioneer Press*. **Essays:** Mary Burchell; Joyce Dingwell; Anne Hampson; Susan Johnson; Emilie Loring; Violet Winspear.

JONES, Heather Iris. Graduate student; freelance writer. Author of "Laura Secord, History, and Melodrama; or, The Unmaking of a Feminist Nation" in *Canadian Literature*. **Essays:** Grace Murray Atkin; Evelyn Eaton; Madge Macbeth; Isabel M. Paterson; Laura Goodman Salverson; Virna Sheard; Elizabeth Sprigge.

KEMP, Barbara E. Head of the Humanities and Social Sciences Libraries, Washington State University, Pullman. Author of numerous professional articles; reviewer for *Library Journal* and *American Reference Books Annual*. **Essays:** Sandra Brown; Robyn Carr; Elaine Raco Chase; Caroline Courtney; Hebe Elsna; Roberta Gellis; Kay Hooper; Linda Howard; Iris Johansen; Alice Chetwynd Ley; Johanna Lindsey; Laura London; Amii Lorin;

Elizabeth Lowell; Laurie McBain; Judith McNaught; Alice Morgan; Diana Palmer; Fayrene Preston; Francine Rivers; Janet Louise Roberts; Mary Linn Roby; Carola Salisbury; Sondra Stanford; Florence Stevenson; Jill Tattersall; Sylvia Thorpe; Patricia Veryan; Sheila Walsh; Claudette Williams.

LANDRUM, Larry N. Associate Professor of English, Michigan State University, East Lansing. Author of *American Popular Culture*, 1982. Co-editor, *Dimensions of Detective Fiction*, 1976; contributed "Guide to Detective Fiction" to *Handbook of American Popular Culture*, 1978. **Essays:** Rafael Sabatini; Samuel Shellabarger.

LEE, Linda. Freelance writer and writing instructor. Author of *How to Write and Sell Romance Novels*, 1988, and of romance novels (as Hope Goodwin), including, most recently, *Shadows over Paradise*, 1987, and *Yesterday's Promises*, 1987. **Essays:** Dixie Browning; Brooke Hastings.

LEETE-HODGE, Lornie. Freelance writer and editor. Author of many children's books including, most recently, Oscar Wilde's *The Happy Prince*, 1986, and *Sinbad the Sailor*, 1986, and books on Wiltshire and the Royal Family. **Essays:** Ursula Bloom; Maureen Peters; D. A. Ponsonby.

LEVSTICK, Frank R. Archives and regional administrator, Kentucky Department for Libraries and Archives, Frankfort. Author of *A Directory of State Archives in the United States*, 1977, *Kentucky Historical Records Needs Assessment*, 1982, and of numerous articles on United States history; co-author of *Union Bibliography of Ohio Printed State Documents*, 1974. **Essays:** Irving Bacheller; August Derleth; Esther Forbes; Kenneth Roberts.

LOCKHART, Marilyn. Freelance writer; former librarian. Reviewer for *Library Journal*. **Essays:** Anne Eliot; Rosemary Ellerbeck; Jacqueline La Tourrette; Frances Murray; Rosamunde Pilcher; Anne Worboys.

LONGEST, George C. Associate Professor of English, Virginia Commonwealth University, Richmond. Author of *Three Virginia Writers: Mary Johnston, Thomas Nelson Page, and Amélie Rives Troubetzkoy: A Reference Guide*, 1978, and of many articles and reviews. **Essays:** Mary Johnston; Andrew Lytle; Stark Young.

LYNN, Mary C. Member of the American Studies Department, Skidmore College, Saratoga Springs, New York. **Essays:** Clare Darcy; Jane Aiken Hodge; Elswyth Thane.

MACDONALD, Andrew. Member of the English Department, Loyola University, New Orleans. Author of articles on Jonson, Shakespeare, English as a second language, science fiction, and popular culture. **Essays** (with Gina Macdonald): James Clavell; Nevil Shute.

MACDONALD, Gina. Member of the English Department, Tulane University, New Orleans. Author of articles on southwestern writers, Shakespeare, Robert Greene, English as a second language, science fiction, and popular culture. **Essays:** Anthony Burgess; James Clavell (with Andrew Macdonald); Brian Cleeve; Thomas B. Costain; Howard Fast; Winston Graham; Susan Hufford; Shirley Jackson; Barbara Ferry Johnson; Barbara Kevern; Arthur Koestler; Marie Belloc Lowndes; Rohan O'Grady; Barbara Anne Pauley; Nevil Shute (with Andrew Macdonald).

McGRATH, Joan. Library consultant, Toronto Board of Education; book review editor, *Reviewing Librarian*. Columnist for *In Review* and *Emergency Librarian*, and reviewer for Toronto *Star*, *Quill and Quire*, *Canadian Materials*, and *Canadian Book Review Annual*. Contributor to *Twentieth-Century Children's Writers*, *Growing with Books*, and *Writers on Writing*. **Essays:** Charlotte Vale Allen; Hervey Allen; Evelyn Anthony; Michael Arlen; Pearl S. Buck; Marcia Davenport; Mazo de la Roche; Rachel Field; Gilbert Frankau; Rose Franken; Janice Holt Giles; Elizabeth Goudge; W. G. Hardy; Georgette Heyer; Fannie Hurst; Naomi Jacob; Margaret Kennedy; Doris Leslie; Rosamond Marshall; Frederick Niven; Charles Nordhoff and James Norman Hall; Gene Stratton Porter; Mary Renault; Marcella Thum.

McNALL, Sally Allen. Member of the English Department, University of Kansas, Lawrence. Author of *Who Is in the House? A Psychological Study of Two Centuries of Women's Fiction in America, 1795 to the Present*, 1981. **Essay:** Marilyn Harris.

MELDRUM, P. R. Freelance writer. Worked in the Public Record Office, London, 11 years. **Essays:** Mollie Chappell; Anne Duffield; Hettie Grimstead; Leila Mackinlay; Kate Norway; Claire Ritchie; Olga Sinclair; Annie S. Swan; Daoma Winston.

MENDELSOHN, Leonard R. Associate Professor of English, Concordia University, Montreal. Former editor of *Children's Literature*. Author of "The Survival of the Spirit in Holocaust Children's Literature" in *Triumph of the Spirit in Children's Literature* edited by Francelia Butler, 1986, and of articles on Aeschylus, Milton, Kafka, Renaissance drama, speed reading, toys, utopian writing, and other subjects in *Studies in English Literature*, *Comparative Drama*, *Studies in Short Fiction*, *Language Arts*, and other journals. **Essays:** Eileen Bigland; James Boyd; James Branch Cabell; Ronald Fraser; Rudy Wiebe.

MITCHELL, J. Lawrence. Professor of English, University of Minnesota, Minneapolis. Author of many articles in journals including *Powys Review*, *Planet*, *Scriptorium*, and *Canadian Journal of Linguistics*. Editor of *Computers in the Humanities*, 1974, and *Some Modern British Short Stories*, 1985. **Essays:** David Garnett; Sylvia Townsend Warner.

MOE, Christian H. Professor of Theatre, Southern Illinois University, Carbondale; member of the Advisory Board, Institute of Outdoor Drama; director of Playwrights program, Association for Theatre in Higher Education; associate member, Dramatists Guild. Author of *Creating Historical Drama* (with George McCalmon), 1965, an essay on D. H. Lawrence as playwright, and, with Cameron Garbutt, several plays for children. Joint editor of *The William and Mary Theatre : A Chronicle*, 1968, "Bibliography of Theatrical Craftsmanship" (published annually), 1971–80, and *Six New Plays for Children*, 1971. **Essay:** Robert Penn Warren.

MOORE, Arlene. Reference and government documents librarian, Wichita State University, Kansas. Author of articles on popular culture and librarianship, and forthcoming works on anonymous literature of the 19th century, and on the author Bertha M. Clay. Co-editor, *The North American Union List of Victorian Periodicals*. **Essays:** Jane Arbor; Elizabeth Ashton; Nan Asquith; Susan Barrie; Gloria Bevan; Kathryn Blair; Rose Burghley; Marion Chesney; Sara Craven; Barbara Delinsky; Jane Donnelly; Eleanor Farnes; Charles Garvice; Elizabeth Hoy; Elizabeth Hunter; Flora Kidd; Jayne Ann Krentz; Roumelia Lane;

Marjorie Lewty; Laura Jean Libbey; Wynne May; Betty Neels; Margaret Pargeter; Phyllis Taylor Pianka; Dudley Pope; Heather Graham Pozzessere; Nina Pykare; Henrietta Reid; Margaret Rome; Sara Seale; Margaret Sebastian; Maura Seger; Doris E. Smith; Rebecca Stratton; Vivian Stuart; Essie Summers; Neil H. Swanson; Donna Vitek; Lucy Walker; Margaret Way; Jan Westcott; Gwen Westwood.

MORRISEY, Thomas J. Professor and chairperson, English Department, State University of New York, Plattsburgh. Author of "Flanagan's *The Year of the French* and the Language of Multiple Truth" in *Eire-Ireland*, 1984, and of articles on Donne, Synge, T. S. Eliot, and science fiction in journals including *Centennial Review*, *Notre Dame English Journal*, and *Science Fiction Studies*. **Essay:** Thomas Flanagan.

MOTTELER, Marilynn. Part-time lecturer, California Polytechnic State University, San Luis Obispo. **Essays:** Catherine Cookson; Dorothy Eden; Anne Maybury.

MURPHY, Alan. Freelance writer and media monitor for a news agency. **Essays:** John Berger; Thomas Berger; Marion Zimmer Bradley; Robert Graves; Gary Jennings; Thomas Keneally; John Masters; James A. Michener; Willliam Styron.

MUSSELL, Kay. Professor of American Studies and chair of the Department of Literature, American University, Washington, D.C. Author of *Women's Gothic and Romantic Fiction: A Reference Guide*, 1981, *Fantasy and Reconciliation: Contemporary Formulas of Women's Romance Fiction*, 1984. **Essays:** Mary Elgin; Victoria Holt; Charlotte Lamb; Anne Mather; Kathleen Gilles Seidel; Anya Seton; Mary Stewart; Kay Thorpe.

MUSSER, Necia A. Assistant Dean, Western Michigan University Libraries, Kalamazoo. Reviewer for *Library Journal*. **Essays:** Katrina Britt; Iris Danbury; Katheryn Kimbrough; Adeline McElfresh; Lilian Peake.

NEUBURG, Victor. Former member of the School of Librarianship, Polytechnic of North London. Author of *Popular Literature: A History and Guide from the Beginning of Printing to the Year 1897*, 1977, *The Batsford Companion to Popular Literature*, 1982, and *A Guide to the Western Front: A Companion for Travellers*, 1988. Editor of *London Labour and the London Poor* by Henry Mayhew, 1985, and, with Neil Philip, of *A December Vision: His Social Journalism* by Charles Dickens, 1986.

OLPIN, Larry. Professor of English, Central Missouri State University, Warrensburg. Author of *A New Classical Rhetoric* (with R. L. Kendreick and F. M. Paterson), 1980, and "Hyperbole and Abstraction: The Comedy of Emily Dickinson" in *Dickinson Studies*, 1982. **Essays:** Stephen Vincent Benét; Winston Churchill.

PAYNTER, Kim. Freelance writer. **Essays:** Countess Barcynska; Clare Emsley; Jean S. MacLeod.

PETTIS, Joyce. Assistant Professor in English, North Carolina State University, Raleigh. Criticism editor, *Obsidian II: Black Literature in Review*. **Essays:** Ernest J. Gaines; Margaret Walker.

PIEHL, Kathy. Education/Reference librarian, Mankato State University, Minnesota. Author of articles on children's writers, E. L. Doctorow, and John Knowles. **Essays:** Elizabeth Darrell; Judith Glover; Rumer Godden; Iris Gower; Isabelle Holland; Cathy Cash Spellman; Helen Van Slyke.

POGEL, Nancy H. Associate Professor of American Thought and Language, Michigan State University, East Lansing. Author of *Woody Allen*, 1987, an article on Constance Mayfield Rourke in *American Woman Writers*, and sections in *Handbook of American Popular Culture*. **Essay:** George Barr McCutcheon.

QUINN, L. M. Bookseller and freelance writer. **Essays:** C. Guy Clayton; Mollie Hardwick; Alice Harwood; Philip McCutchan; Anne Melville; Lilian Woodward.

RADCLIFFE, Elsa J. Author of *Gothic Novels of the Twentieth Century: An Annotated Bibliography*, 1979.

RADFORD, Jean. Lecturer, Hatfield Polytechnic, Hertfordshire. Editor of *The Progress of Romance: The Politics of Popular Fiction*, 1987.

RADWAY, Janice. Member of the American Civilization Department, University of Pennsylvania, Philadelphia. Author of *Reading the Romance: Women, Patriarchy, and Popular Literature*, 1984. **Essay:** Kathleen E. Woodiwiss.

RAVEN, Simon. Novelist. Author of more than 30 books; his most recent novels include *Before the Cock Crow*, 1986, *New Seed for Old*, 1988, and *Blood of My Bone*, 1989. **Essay:** Peter Green.

REGAN, Nancy. Freelance writer. Author of "A Home of One's Own: Women's Bodies in Recent Women's Fiction" in *Journal of Popular Culture*, 1978, and *The Institute of Chartered Financial Analysts: A Twenty-Five Year History*, 1989. **Essays:** Faith Baldwin; Janet Dailey; Margaret Mitchell; Phyllis A. Whitney; Kathleen Winsor.

RHODES, Judith. Librarian, Leeds City Libraries, Yorkshire. **Essays:** Sacha Carnegie; Nancy Cato; Brenda Clarke; Jude Deveraux; Sarah Harrison; Eva Ibbotson; Brenda Jagger; Sharan Newman; Sharon K. Penman; Rosie Thomas; Philippa Wiat.

ROBERTS, Bette B. Professor of English, Westfield State College, Massachusetts. Author of *The Gothic Romance: Its Appeal to Women Readers and Writers in Late Eighteenth-Century England*, 1980, and articles on gothic writing. **Essays:** Virginia Coffman; Dorothy Daniels.

ROBERTSON, Karen. Visiting Assistant Professor of English, Vassar College, Poughkeepsie, New York. Co-editor of *Sexuality and Renaissance Drama*, and author of a forthcoming novel. **Essays:** Maeve Binchy; Gillian Bradshaw; Doris Langley Moore.

ROGERS, Lucy, and **Peggy YORK.** Lucy Rogers was a teacher and freelance writer. Died. Peggy York has worked in general nursing, then midwifery and district nursing; also a short story writer. **Essay:** Audrie Manley-Tucker.

RUGGIERO, Josephine A., and **Louise C. WESTON.** Josephine Ruggiero is Professor of Sociology, Providence College, Rhode Island. Louise Weston is President, Environmental Strategies Inc., Ridgefield, Connecticut. They have collaborated on several articles on women's issues. **Essays:** Susan Howatch; Elsie Lee.

SADLER, Geoffrey. Assistant librarian, Local Studies, Chesterfield, Derbyshire. Author of 14 western novels (as Jeff Sadler), including, most recently, *Return of Amarillo*, 1986, *Montana Mine*, 1987, *Saltillo Road*, 1987, *Long Gun War*, 1988,

Palamino Stud, 1988, and *Chulo* (as Wes Calhoun), 1988. **Essays:** Pat Barr; Bernard Cornwell; Dorothy Salisbury Davis; E. M. Delafield; Alice Dwyer-Joyce; Catherine Gaskin; Constance Gluyas; Pamela Haines; Constance Heaven; MacKinlay Kantor; Claire Lorrimer; Eric Malpass; Naomi Mitchison; Christopher Nicole; Frederick Nolan; Pamela Oldfield; Kathleen Shoesmith; Marguerite Steen; E. V. Thompson; Henry Treece.

SAUNDERS, Jean. See her own entry.

SHIELDS, Anne M. Specialist social worker (mental health). **Essays:** Charity Blackstock; Juliet Dymoke.

SHUCARD, Alan R. Associate Professor of English, University of Wisconsin-Parkside, Kenosha. Author of three books of poetry, a study of Countée Cullen, and *American Poetry: The Puritans Through Walt Whitman*, 1988. **Essay:** Irving Stone.

SHUEY, Andrea Lee. Branch Manager, Dallas Public Library. Contributor to *Contemporary Literary Criticism*; editor of Dallas County Library *Newsletter*, 1986–89; reviewer for *Library Journal*. **Essays:** Barbara Taylor Bradford; Celeste de Blasis; Viña Delmar; Audrey Erskine-Lindop; Ethel Edison Gordon; Rosemary Hawley Jarman; Alexandra Manners; Florence Engel Randall; Jean Francis Webb; Barbara Wood.

SIMMONDS, Roy. Author of *Steinbeck's Literary Achievement*, 1976, *The Two Worlds of William March*, 1984, *William March: An Annotated Checklist*, 1988, and of articles on Steinbeck, March, Hemingway, and Edward O'Brien. **Essays:** John Steinbeck; Patrick White.

SMITH, Christopher. Senior Lecturer, School of Modern Languages and European History, University of East Anglia, Norwich; editor of *Seventeenth-Century French Studies*. Author of *Alabaster, Bikinis, and Calvados: An A.B.C. of Toponymous Words*, 1985, and *Jean Anouilh: Life, Work and Criticism* (forthcoming). Editor of continental emblem books, and of works by Prévost, Betham-Edwards, and Balzac. **Essays:** Maurice Hewlett; Colin MacInnes; Susan Sallis; Judith Saxton; Evelyn Scott; Richard Tresillian; Peter Vansittart; Stanley Weyman.

SMITHERS, David Waldron. Professor of Radiotherapy, University of London, retired. Author of *Dickens's Doctors*, 1979, *Castles in Kent*, 1980, *Jane Austen in Kent, Therefore Imagine: The Works of Clemence Dane*, 1988, and numerous medical books. **Essays:** Clemence Dane; Arthur Conan Doyle.

STAPLES, Katherine. Head of the Technical Communications Department, Austin Community College, Texas. Contributor to *Twentieth-Century Crime and Mystery Writers*, 1980 (revised 1985), and *American Women Writers*, 1981. Translator of works by Rimbaud, Aragon, and Henri Rousseau. **Essays:** Taylor Caldwell; Elinor Glyn; Margaret Millar.

STERNLICHT, Sanford. Adjunct Professor of English, Syracuse University, New York. Author of *John Webster's Imagery and the Webster Canon*, 1972, *John Masefield*, 1977, *C. S. Forester*, 1981, *Padraic Colum*, 1985, *John Galsworthy*, 1987, and *R. F. Delderfield*, 1988. **Essays:** C. S. Forester; John Masefield.

SUMMERS, Judith. Freelance writer. Author of two novels—*Dear Sister*, 1985, and *I, Gloria Gold*, 1988—and of *Soho: A History of London's Most Colourful Neighborhood*, 1989. **Essays:** Julia Fitzgerald; Maynah Lewis; Margaret Maddocks; Jean Marsh.

THOMPSON, Jane K. Actress and freelance writer. **Essays:** Carola Oman; Ivy Preston; Irene Roberts.

THURSTON, Carol. Writer and market research consultant. Author of *The Romance Revolution: Erotic Novels for Women and the Quest for a New Sexual Identity*, 1987, two novels, and numerous articles in *Journal of Communication, Journal of Popular Culture, Journalism Quarterly*, and other periodicals. Coauthor of *Case Studies in Institutional Licensee Management*, 1980. **Essays:** Fern Michaels; Alexandra Sellers; Bertrice Small; LaVyrle Spencer.

TIETZE, Thomas R. Freelance writer. **Essay:** P. C. Wren.

TROTMAN, Felicity. Co-partner, Signpost Books, London. Formerly with the publishers Collins, Dent, Penguin, and Macmillan. Author of *The Travels of Marco Polo*, 1986, *The Sorcerer's Apprentice*, 1986, *Davy Crockett*, 1986, *William Tell*, 1987. Editor (with Treld Pelkley Bicknell), *How to Write and Illustrate Children's Books and Get Them Published!*, 1988. **Essay:** Patrick O'Brian.

TY, Eleanor. Lecturer in English, Erindale College, University of Toronto. Author of *Romantic Revolutionaries: Women Novelists of the 1790's* (dissertation), and of articles in *Notes and Queries*, and *Tulsa Studies in Women's Literature*. **Essays:** Timothy Findley; Karen van der Zee; Anne Weale.

VANSITTART, Peter. See his own entry. **Essays:** Alfred Duggan; Hugh Walpole; Rex Warner.

von ZHAREN, W. M. Freelance writer. **Essays:** Jane Blackmore; Glenna Finley; Grace Livingston Hill; Elizabeth Renier; Willo Davis Roberts.

WALSH, George. Publisher and freelance writer. **Essays:** Elizabeth; Patricia Gallagher; Kathleen Norris.

WEARING, Catherine S. Freelance writer. Researcher on various projects for Pandora Press; contributor to *Encyclopaedia of British Women Writers*, 1988; co-author of a forthcoming book on women's work in the theatre and on television. **Essays:** Angela Carter; John Erskine; J. G. Farrell; Ford Madox Ford.

WESTON, Louise C. See the entry for Josephine A. Ruggiero above.

WHITE, Kerry. Freelance writer and bibliographer. Formerly, tutor and lecturer in 20th-century women's writing and children's books, University of Wollongong, New South Wales. Author of articles and reviews in *Reading Time, Magpies, Rees Archives Journal, Orana*, and *Australian Feminist Studies*, and a forthcoming bibliography of Australian children's books 1973–88. **Essays:** Eleanor Dark; M. Barnard Eldershaw; Colleen McCullough.

WHITE, Ray Lewis. Professor of English, Illinois State University, Normal. Author of books on Sherwood Anderson, Gore Vidal, Heinrich Böll, Pär Lagerkvist, Günter Grass, and R. K. Narayan; his most recent books are *Gertrude Stein and Alice B. Toklas: A Reference Guide*, 1984, *Arnold Zweig in the USA*, 1986, *Index to Best American Short Stories and O. Henry Prize Stories*, 1988, and *Sherwood Anderson: Early Writings*, 1989. **Essays:** John Barth; Ross Lockridge.

WOOD, Dorothy. Co-partner, Signpost Books, London. Formerly with the publishers Allen and Unwin, Pantheon Books, Puffin Books, and Scholastic Publications. **Essays:** Lettice Cooper; Alexander Cordell.

YARDLEY, M. Jeanne. Lecturer in English, University of Waterloo, Ontario. Author of "The Maple Leaf as Maple Leaf: Facing the Failure of the Search for Emblems in Canadian Literature" in *Studies in Canadian Literature*, 1987. Member of editorial board, *New Quarterly*, 1981–84. **Essay:** Philip Child.

YORK, Peggy. See the entry for Lucy Rogers above.

YOUNG, Alan R. Professor of English and head of department, Acadia University, Wolfville, Nova Scotia. Author of *Ernest Buckler*, 1976, *Henry Peacham*, 1979, *The English Prodigal Son Plays*, 1979, *Thomas Head Raddall: A Bibliography*, 1982, *Thomas Head Raddall*, 1983, *Tudor and Jacobean Tournaments*, 1987, and *The English Tournament Imprese*, 1988. **Essay:** Thomas Head Raddall.

ZIESELMAN, Paula M. Professional assistant to the executive director of the Metropolitan Reference and Research Library Agency, New York. Formerly reference librarian, New Rochelle Public Library, New York. Editor, *Westchester County Union List of Serials*. Reviewer for *Library Journal*. **Essay:** Nancy Buckingham.